Great Britain & Ireland
2007

ontents

Sommaire
Sommario
Inhaltsverzeichnis

How to use this guide

TOURIST INFORMATION

Local tourist attractions, golf courses, means of transport, tourist information offices, distances from main towns...

CAMBERLEY Surrey **504** R29 – pop. 47,123 (inc. Frimley).
London 40 – Reading 13 – Southampton 48.

🏨 **Felix Hall**, Conifer Drive, GU15 2 BG, East:¾ m.
ℰ (0870) 400 8245, salesfelixhall@macdonald-
ℰ, ⬛, ⬛, ▥ – 🔆 & ⬛ – ᐸ 250. ◉◉
Linda : Rest 18.95/28.00 ♀ – ⬛ 12.95 – **92 rm** ✝2
● Ivy-clad Victorian manor. A carved wooden sta
traditional with inlaid mahogany furniture, other
with contemporary furnishings.

CAMBRIDGE Cambs **504** U27 Great Britain G.– pop.
See : Town★★★ – St John's College★★★ ACY – K
Museum★★ ZM1 – Trinity College★★ Y – Kett
Exc. : Audley End★★, S: 13 m. by A 1309 – In
🏨 Cambridgeshire Moat House Hotel, Bar H
🛬 Cambridge Airport : ℰ (01223) 3737
Wheeeler St ℰ (01223
🛈 The Old Library, Wheeler St ℰ (01223
London 55 – Coventry 88 – Ipswich 54 – Lei

🏨 **Hotel Gloria** ⬛, Whitehouse lane,
A1307 ℰ (01223) 277985, help@hotelg
&, ℙ – ᐸ 50. ◉◉ ᴀᴇ ◑ 𝗩𝗜𝗦𝗔
The Melrose : Rest 16.50 (lunch) and
✝✝ 168.00/255.00.
● Built as a private house in 1852, no
rary rooms include state-of-the art

🍴🍴🍴 **Alexander House** (Johns), M
resa@alexanderhouse.co.uk, Fa
closed 2 weeks Christmas, 2 w
Rest (dinner only and lunch Fri
Spec. Salad of smoked eel, pig
tachios and asparagus. Canne
● A river Cam idyll. Chic co
with blissful views over the

🍴🍴 **The Roasted Pepper**, 3
roastedpepper.co.uk, Fax
closed Christmas-New Ye
● Personally run Victoria
dishes with mild Asian i

at Histon North : 3 m. on B 104

🏨 **Blue House Farm**, N
bluehousefarm.uk.co
closed 2 weeks Ch
● Red-brick 18C lis
overlooks meadow
preserves. Immac

🍴 **Phoenix**, 20 T
closed 25-27 T
⬛ 50/43.00 s.

HOTELS

From 🏨🏨🏨🏨 to 🏨, 🏠:
categories of comfort.
The most pleasant: in red.

RESTAURANTS

From 🍴🍴🍴🍴🍴 to 🍴, 🅐:
categories of comfort.
The most pleasant: in red.

STARS

🟢🟢🟢 Worth a special journey.
🟢🟢 Worth a detour.
🟢 A very good restaurant.

GOOD FOOD AND ACCOMMODATION AT MODERATE PRICES

🅐 Bib Gourmand.
🅑 Bib Hotel.

4

LOCATING THE TOWN

Location of the town on the local map: refer to the town printed in blue.

OTHER MICHELIN PUBLICATIONS

References for the Michelin map and Michelin Tourist Guide which cover the area.

LOCATING THE ESTABLISHMENT

Located on the town plan (coordinates and letters giving the location).

DESCRIPTION OF THE ESTABLISHMENT

Atmosphere, style, character and specialities.

QUIET HOTELS

🔊 quiet hotel.
🔊 very quiet hotel.

FACILITIES AND SERVICES

PRICES

---

nouth Rd (A325)
.uk, Fax (0870) 4008246,

210.00.
ds to the bedrooms; some are
nt and modern. 19C restaurant

ge★★ Z The Backs★★ YZ – Fitzwilliam
YM2 – Queen's College★ ACZ.
r Museum★, Duxford, S:9 m. on M11.
54) 249988 X.
on A 1303 X.
tourism@cambridge.gov.uk.
Norwich 61 – Nottingham 88 – Oxford 100.
on Rd, CB3 0LX, Northwest: 1 ½ m. by
x, Fax (01223) 277986, 🍴, 🚗 – 🛏 ⇆ 📶
Z d

25.20/35.50 ♀ – ⇱ 7.50 – **52 rm** ⚹136.00 –

odern and stylish public areas. The contempo-
sleek restaurant overlooks garden and terrace.
Common, CB4 1HA, ℰ (01223) 369 245,
Y a
369246, 🍴 – ⇆ ⇔ 16. 🖭 ⓞ 𝖵𝖨𝖲𝖠
ust, 1 week spring, Sunday and Monday –
ay) 30.00/50.00 ♀ 𝅘.
nd apple purée. Braised turbot with peanuts and pis-
ricot, Strawberry sorbet, fraises des bois and mint.
dining room with smart first floor bar and terrace
Y c

ton Rd, CB4 3AX, ℰ (01223) 351872, seancarter@
351873 – ▤ 🖭 ⓞ 𝖵𝖨𝖲𝖠
nday – **Rest** (booking essential) (dinner only) 24.95.
ouse with smartly clad tables. Classic French and Italian
served at reasonable prices.

Cambridge:
st., 44 High St, CB3 7HV, ℰ (01223) 262164, reservations@
223) 262166, 🚗 🔊 – ⇆ 🅿 ⇌
ew Year – **4 rm** ⇱ ⚹38.00 – ⚹⚹60.00.
ouse on a working farm... with beautiful blue windows; house
garden room for breakfast, including home-made bread and
ms.
CB4 9JA, ℰ (01223) 233756 – ⇆ ▤ 🖭 🖭 ⓞ 𝖵𝖨𝖲𝖠 and a la carte
– **Rest** – Chinese (Peking, Szechuan) - 17.50/29.50 and a la carte
bowties. Spicy highlights from Szechuan; Peking classics.
k pub overlooking village green. Within, Chinese dishes are served by
Mill Rd, CB1 2AS, ℰ (01223) 313704, daniels@btconnect.com,
🖭 🖭 ⓞ 𝖵𝖨𝖲𝖠 ... lunch and Bank Holidays – **Rest** a la carte
... appealing artwork. Enclosed
...ranean base.

5

Commitments

"This volume was created at the turn of the century and will last at least as long".

This foreword to the very first edition of the MICHELIN Guide, written in 1900, has become famous over the years and the Guide has lived up to the prediction. It is read across the world and the key to its popularity is the consistency of its commitment to its readers, which is based on the following promises.

The MICHELIN Guide's commitments :

Anonymous inspections: our inspectors make regular and anonymous visits to hotels and restaurants to gauge the quality of products and services offered to an ordinary customer. They settle their own bill and may then introduce themselves and ask for more information about the establishment. Our readers' comments are also a valuable source of information, which we can then follow up with another visit of our own.

Independence: Our choice of establishments is a completely independent one, made for the benefit of our readers alone. The decisions to be taken are discussed around the table by the inspectors and the editor. The most important awards are decided at a European level. Inclusion in the Guide is completely free of charge.

Selection and choice: The Guide offers a selection of the best hotels and restaurants in every category of comfort and price. This is only possible because all the inspectors rigorously apply the same methods.

Annual updates: All the practical information, the classifications and awards are revised and updated every single year to give the most reliable information possible.

Consistency: The criteria for the classifications are the same in every country covered by the Michelin Guide.

… and our aim: to do everything possible to make travel, holidays and eating out a pleasure, as part of Michelin's ongoing commitment to improving travel and mobility.

Dear reader

Dear reader,

We are delighted to introduce the 34th edition of The Michelin Guide Great Britain & Ireland.

This selection of the best hotels and restaurants in every price category is chosen by a team of full-time inspectors with a professional background in the industry. They cover every corner of the country, visiting new establishments and testing the quality and consistency of the hotels and restaurants already listed in the Guide.

Every year we pick out the best restaurants by awarding them from ✿ to ✿✿✿. Stars are awarded for cuisine of the highest standards and reflect the quality of the ingredients, the skill in their preparation, the combination of flavours, the levels of creativity and value for money, and the ability to combine all these qualities not just once, but time and time again.

This year again, a number of restaurants have been newly awarded stars for the quality of their cuisine. ´N´ highlights the new promotions for this new 2007 edition, announcing their arrival with one, two or three stars.

In addition, we have continued to pick out a selection of « *Rising Stars* ». These establishments, listed in red, are the best in their present category. They have the potential to rise further, and already have an element of superior quality; as soon as they produce this quality consistently, and in all aspects of their cuisine, they will be hot tips for a higher award. We've highlighted these promising restaurants so you can try them for yourselves; we think they offer a foretaste of the gastronomy of the future.

We're very interested to hear what you think of our selection, particularly the " *Rising Stars* ", so please continue to send us your comments. Your opinions and suggestions help to shape your Guide, and help us to keep improving it, year after year. Thank you for your support. We hope you enjoy travelling with the Michelin Guide 2007.

Consult the Michelin Guide at www.ViaMichelin.com
and write to us at:
themichelinguide-gbirl@uk.michelin.com

Classification
& awards

CATEGORIES OF COMFORT

The Michelin Guide selection lists the best hotels and restaurants in each category of comfort and price. The establishments we choose are classified according to their levels of comfort and, within each category, are listed in order of preference.

🏨🏨🏨🏨	XXXXX	Luxury in the traditional style
🏨🏨🏨	XXXX	Top class comfort
🏨🏨	XXX	Very comfortable
🏨	XX	Comfortable
🏨	X	Quite comfortable
🏮		Traditional pubs serving good food
↑		Other recommended accommodation (Guesthouses, farmhouses and private homes)
without rest.		This hotel has no restaurant
with rm		This restaurant also offers accommodation

THE AWARDS

To help you make the best choice, some exceptional establishments have been given an award in this year's Guide. They are marked ✿ or ⊕ and **Rest**.

THE BEST CUISINE

Michelin stars are awarded to establishments serving cuisine, of whatever style, which is of the highest quality. The cuisine is judged on the quality of ingredients, the skill in their preparation, the combination of flavours, the levels of creativity, the value for money and the consistency of culinary standards.

✿✿✿	**Exceptional cuisine, worth a special journey**
	One always eats extremely well here, sometimes superbly.
✿✿	**Excellent cooking, worth a detour**
✿	**Very good cooking in its category**

GOOD FOOD AND ACCOMMODATION AT MODERATE PRICES

⊕	**Bib Gourmand** Establishment offering good quality cuisine for under £28 or €40 in the Republic of Ireland (price of a 3 course meal not including drinks).
⊕	**Bib Hotel** Establishment offering good levels of comfort and service, with most rooms priced at under £75 or under €105 in the Republic of Ireland (price of a room for 2 people, including breakfast).

PLEASANT HOTELS AND RESTAURANTS

Symbols shown in red indicate particularly pleasant or restful establishments: the character of the building, its décor, the setting, the welcome and services offered may all contribute to this special appeal.

⌂, 🏠 to 🏨🏨🏨   **Pleasant hotels**

🍴, ✕ to ✕✕✕✕✕   **Pleasant restaurants**

OTHER SPECIAL FEATURES

As well as the categories and awards given to the establishment, Michelin inspectors also make special note of other criteria which can be important when choosing an establishment.

LOCATION

If you are looking for a particularly restful establishment, or one with a special view, look out for the following symbols:

🖐   **Quiet hotel**

🖐   **Very quiet hotel**

≼   **Interesting view**

≼   **Exceptional view**

WINE LIST

If you are looking for an establishment with a particularly interesting wine list, look out for the following symbol:

🍇   **Particularly interesting wine list**
This symbol might cover the list presented by a sommelier in a luxury restaurant or that of a simple pub or restaurant where the owner has a passion for wine. The two lists will offer something exceptional but very different, so beware of comparing them by each other's standards.

Facilities
& services

30 rm	Number of rooms
	Lift (elevator)
	Air conditioning (in all or part of the establishment)
	Establishment with areas reserved for non-smokers. In Scotland and the Republic of Ireland the law prohibits smoking in all pubs, restaurants and hotel public areas
	Fast Internet access in bedrooms
	Establishment at least partly accessible to those of restricted mobility
	Special facilities for children
	Meals served in garden or on terrace
	Wellness centre: an extensive facility for relaxation and well-being
	Sauna – Exercise room
	Swimming pool: outdoor or indoor
	Garden – Park
	Tennis court – Golf course and number of holes
	Landing stage
	Fishing available to hotel guests. A charge may be made
150	Equipped conference room: maximum capacity
12	Private dining rooms: maximum capacity
	Hotel garage (additional charge in most cases)
P	Car park for customers only
	No dogs allowed (in all or part of the establishment)
	Nearest Underground station (in London)
May-October	Dates when open, as indicated by the hotelier

Prices

Prices quoted in this Guide were supplied in autumn 2006 and apply to low and high seasons. They are subject to alteration if goods and service costs are revised. By supplying the information, hotels and restaurants have undertaken to maintain these rates for our readers.

In some towns, when commercial, cultural or sporting events are taking place the hotel rates are likely to be considerably higher.

Prices are given in £ sterling, except for the Republic of Ireland where € euro are quoted.

All accommodation prices include both service and V.A.T. All restaurant prices include V.A.T. Service is also included when an **s.** appears after the prices.

Where no **s.** is shown, prices may be subject to the addition of a variable service charge which is usually between 10 % - 15 %.

(V.A.T. does not apply in the Channel Islands).

Out of season, certain establishments offer special rates. Ask when booking.

RESERVATION AND DEPOSITS

Some hotels will require a deposit which confirms the commitment of both the customer and the hotelier. Ask the hotelier to provide you with all the terms and conditions applicable to your reservation in their written confirmation.

CREDIT CARDS

Credit cards accepted by the establishment:

AE ⓓ ⓜⓞ VISA American Express – Diners Club – MasterCard – Visa

ROOMS

rm ♦ 50.00/90.00 Lowest price 50.00 and highest price 90.00 for a comfortable single room

rm ♦♦ 70.00/120.00 Lowest price 70.00 and highest price 120.00 for a double or twin room for 2 people

rm ⌷ 55.00/85.00 Full cooked breakfast (whether taken or not) is included in the price of the room

⌷ 6.00 Price of breakfast

SHORT BREAKS

Many hotels offer a special rate for a stay of two or more nights which comprises dinner, room and breakfast usually for a minimum of two people. Please enquire at hotel for rates.

RESTAURANT

Set meals: lowest price £13.00, highest price £28.00, usually for a 3 course meal. The lowest priced set menu is often only available at lunchtimes.

A la carte meals: the prices represent the range of charges from a simple to an elaborate 3 course meal.

s. Service included

😀 Restaurants offering lower priced pre and/or post theatre menus

♀ Wine served by the glass

⌂: Dinner in this category of establishment will generally be offered from a fixed price menu of limited choice, served at a set time to residents only. Lunch is rarely offered. Many will not be licensed to sell alcohol.

Towns

GENERAL INFORMATION

✉ York	Postal address
501 M27, ⑩	Michelin map and co-ordinates or fold
Great Britain G.	See the Michelin Green Guide Great Britain
pop. 1057	Population
	Source: 2001 Census (Key Statistics for Urban Areas)
	Crown copyright 2004
BX **a**	Letters giving the location of a place on a town plan
⌐18	Golf course and number of holes (handicap sometimes required, telephone reservation strongly advised)
☀ ≤	Panoramic view, viewpoint
✈	Airport
⚓	Shipping line (passengers & cars)
⚓	Passenger transport only
🛈	Tourist Information Centre

STANDARD TIME

In winter, standard time throughout the British Isles is Greenwich Mean Time (GMT). In summer, British clocks are advanced by one hour to give British Summer Time (BST). The actual dates are announced annually but always occur over weekends in March and October.

TOURIST INFORMATION

STAR-RATING

★★★	Highly recommended
★★	Recommended
★	Interesting
AC	Admission charge

LOCATION

See	Sights in town
Envir.	On the outskirts
Exc.	In the surrounding area
N, S, E, W	The sight lies north, south, east or west of the town
A 22	Take road A 22, indicated by the same symbol on the Guide map
2m.	Distance in miles (In the Republic of Ireland kilometres are quoted).

Town plans

ⓐ ● a	Hotels – restaurants

SIGHTS

■ ▢	Place of interest
▮ ᴊ	Interesting place of worship

ROADS

M 1	Motorway
➍ ➍	Numbered junctions: complete, limited
	Dual carriageway with motorway characteristics
	Main traffic artery
A 2	Primary route (GB) and National route (IRL)
◄ :::::::	One-way street – Unsuitable for traffic or street subject to restrictions
├──┤ ─── ····	Pedestrian street – Tramway
Piccadilly P R	Shopping street – Car park – Park and Ride
╪ ╪╞ ╪╞╪	Gateway – Street passing under arch – Tunnel
15'5	Low headroom (16'6" max.) on major through routes
▬▬ 🚆	Station and railway
⊙++++⊙ ●▪●▪●	Funicular – Cable-car
⚠ B	Lever bridge – Car ferry

VARIOUS SIGNS

🛈	Tourist Information Centre
♱ ☿ ☒	Church/Place of worship - Mosque – Synagogue
⸙ ⸙	Communications tower or mast – Ruins
▦ ▨	Garden, park, wood – Cemetery
◯ 🏇 🏌	Stadium - Racecourse - Golf course
▶ ⛸	Golf course (with restrictions for visitors) – Skating rink
⚓ ▨	Outdoor or indoor swimming pool
◀ ▧	View – Panorama
■ ◦ ✚ 🏪	Monument – Fountain – Hospital – Covered market
⚓ ⚓	Pleasure boat harbour – Lighthouse
✈ ⊖ ● 🚌	Airport – Underground station – Coach station
⛴	Ferry services: passengers and cars
✉	Main post office
	Public buildings located by letter:
C H J	- County Council Offices – Town Hall – Law Courts
M T U	- Museum – Theatre – University, College
POL.	- Police (in large towns police headquarters)

LONDON

BRENT WEMBLEY	Borough – Area
	Borough boundary
	Congestion Zone – Charge applies Monday-Friday 07.00-18.00
⊖	Nearest Underground station to the hotel or restaurant

13

Local maps

MAY WE SUGGEST
THAT YOU CONSULT THEM

Sould you be looking for a hotel or restaurant not too far from Leeds, for example, you can now consult the map along with the town plan.

The local map (opposite) draws your attention to all places around the town or city selected, provided they are mentioned in the Guide.

Places located within a range of 16 miles/25 km are clearly identified by the use of a different coloured background.

The various facilities recommended near the different regional capitals can be located quickly and easily.

NOTE:

Entries in the Guide provide information on distances to nearby towns.

Whenever a place appears on one of the local maps, the name of the town or city to which it is attached is printed in BLUE.

EXAMPLE:

ILKLEY W. Yorks **502** O 22
– pop. 13 472.
🏠 Myddleton ✆ (01943) 607277
🚉 Station Rd ✆ (01943) 602319
London 210 – Bradford 13 – Harrogate 17 –
Leeds 16 – Preston 46

ILKLEY
is to be found
on the local map
LEEDS.

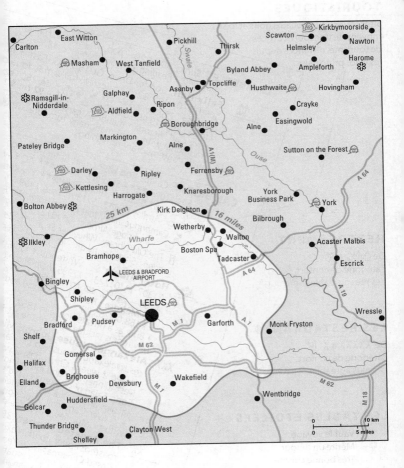

Mode d'emploi

INFORMATIONS TOURISTIQUES

Sites touristiques locaux, golfs et loisirs,
moyens de transports, offices
de tourisme, distances depuis
les villes principales...

HÉBERGEMENT

De 🏨 à 🏠, ↑:
catégorie de confort.
Les plus agréables : en rouge.

LES RESTAURANTS

De XXXXX à X, 🍴:
catégorie de confort.
Les plus agréables : en rouge.

LES TABLES ÉTOILÉES

❀❀❀ Vaut le voyage.
❀❀ Mérite un détour.
❀ Très bonne cuisine.

LES MEILLEURES ADRESSES À PETITS PRIX

🥢 Bib Gourmand.
🏠 Bib Hôtel.

16

CAMBERLEY Surrey 504 R29 – pop. 47 123 (inc. Frimley).
London 40 – Reading 13 – Southampton 48.

🏨 **Felix Hall**, Conifer Drive, GU15 2 BG, East:¾ m.
℘ (0870) 400 8245, salesfelixhall@macdonalc
F₆, ≦s, 🔲, 🌳 – ⇔ 🍽 🔳 ℘ & 🅿 – 🛗 250. ⬭
Linda : Rest 18.95/28.00 ♀ – ♀ 12.95 – **92 rm** ⇄2
• Ivy-clad Victorian manor. A carved wooden st
traditional with inlaid mahogany furniture, othe
with contemporary furnishings.

CAMBRIDGE Cambs 504 U27 Great Britain G. – pop.
See : Town★★★ – StJohn's College★★★ ACY –
Museum★★ ZM1 – Trinity College★★ Y – Ket
Exc. : Audley End★★, S: 13 m. by A 1309 –
🛫 Cambridgeshire Moat House Hotel, Bar H
Cambridge Airport : ℘ (01223) 3737
🛈 The Old Library, Wheeleer St ℘ (01223
London 55 – Coventry 88 – Ipswich 54 – Le

🏨 **Hotel Gloria** ⇄, Whitehouse lane,
A1307 ℘ (01223) 277985, help@hotel
& 🅿 – 🛗 50. 🆗 ⬭ 🆎 ① 𝖵𝖨𝖲𝖠
The Melrose : Rest 16.50 (lunch) and
⭒⭒ 168.00/255.00.
• Built as a private house in 1852, n
rary rooms include state-of-the art

XXX **Alexander House** (Johns), Fa
❀❀ resa@alexanderhouse.co.uk, 2 v
closed 2 weeks Christmas, 2 v
Rest (dinner only and lunch Fri
Spec. Salad of smoked eel, pig
tachios and asparagus. Canne
• A river Cam idyll. Chic co
with blissful views over the

XX **The Roasted Pepper**, 3
roastedpepper.co.uk, Fax
closed Christmas-New Ye
• Personally run Victoria
dishes with mild Asian

at Histon North : 3 m. on B 104°

↑ **Blue House Farm**, ∖
bluehousefarm.uk.cc
closed 2 weeks Ch
• Red-brick 18C lis
overlooks meado
preserves. Immac

XX **Phoenix**, 20 TI
closed 25-27 I
29.50/43.00 s.

LOCALISER LA VILLE
Repérage de la localité sur la carte de voisinage : voir la ville signalée en bleu.

AUTRES PUBLICATIONS MICHELIN
Références de la carte et du Guide Vert Michelin où vous retrouverez la localité.

LES HÔTELS TRANQUILLES
  hôtel tranquille.
  hôtel très tranquille.

LOCALISER L'ÉTABLISSEMENT
Localisation sur le plan de ville (coordonnées et indice).

DESCRIPTION DE L'ÉTABLISSEMENT
Atmosphère, style, caractère et spécialités.

ÉQUIPEMENTS ET SERVICES

PRIX

smouth Rd (A325)
co.uk, Fax (0870) 4008246,

★★210.00.
ads to the bedrooms; some are
ght and modern. 19C restaurant

llege★★ Z The Backs★★ YZ – Fitzwilliam
★ YM2 – Queen's College★ ACZ.
Var Museum★, Duxford, S:9 m. on M11.
1954) 249988 X.
m. on A 1303 X.
1, tourism@cambridge.gov.uk
– Norwich 61 – Nottingham 88 – Oxford 100.

gton Rd, CB3 0LX, Northwest: 1 ½ m. by
o.uk, Fax (01223) 277986, — **52 rm** ★136.00 –

te 25.20/35.50 – 7.50 – **52 rm** ★136.00 –
modern and stylish public areas. The contempo-
s. Sleek restaurant overlooks garden and terrace.
ner Common, CB4 1HA, (01223) 369 245,
23) 369246, – 16. Y a
August, 1 week spring, Sunday and Monday –
urday) 30.00/50.00 .
r and apple purée. Braised turbot with peanuts and pis-
apricot, Strawberry sorbet, fraises des bois and mint.
ory dining room with smart first floor bar and terrace

sterton Rd, CB4 3AX, (01223) 351872, seancarter@
3) 351873 – Y c
Sunday – **Rest** (booking essential) (dinner only) 24.95.
house with smartly clad tables. Classic French and Italian
ces, served at reasonable prices.

Cambridge:
t rest., 44 High St, CB3 7HV, (01223) 262164, reservations@
(01223) 262166, – ★★60.00.
s-New Year – **4 rm** ★38.00 – with beautiful blue windows; house
rmhouse on a working farm... including home-made bread and
ny garden room for breakfast,
rooms.

en, CB4 9JA, (01223) 233756 – 17.50/29.50 and a la carte
– **Rest** – Chinese (Peking, Szechuan) – 17.50/29.50 and a la carte
ber – **Rest** – Chinese (Peking, Szechuan). Within, Chinese dishes are served by
Spicy highlights from Szechuan; Peking classics.
brick pub overlooking village green. Within, Chinese dishes are served by
and bowties. Spicy highlights from Szechuan; Peking classics.
Mill Rd, CB1 2AS, (01223) 313704, daniels@btconnect.com,
day lunch and Bank Holidays – **Rest** a la carte
and appealing artwork. Enclosed
diterranean base.

17

Engagements

« Ce guide est né avec le siècle et il durera autant que lui. »

Cet avant-propos de la première édition du Guide MICHELIN 1900 est devenu célèbre au fil des années et s'est révélé prémonitoire. Si le Guide est aujourd'hui autant lu à travers le monde, c'est notamment grâce à la constance de son engagement vis-à-vis de ses lecteurs.

Nous voulons ici le réaffirmer.

Les engagements du Guide Michelin :

La visite anonyme : les inspecteurs testent de façon anonyme et régulière les tables et les chambres afin d'apprécier le niveau des prestations offertes à tout client. Ils paient leurs additions et peuvent se présenter pour obtenir des renseignements supplémentaires sur les établissements. Le courrier des lecteurs nous fournit par ailleurs une information précieuse pour orienter nos visites.

L'indépendance : la sélection des établissements s'effectue en toute indépendance, dans le seul intérêt du lecteur. Les décisions sont discutées collégialement par les inspecteurs et le rédacteur en chef. Les plus hautes distinctions sont décidées à un niveau européen. L'inscription des établissements dans le guide est totalement gratuite.

La sélection : le Guide offre une sélection des meilleurs hôtels et restaurants dans toutes les catégories de confort et de prix. Celle-ci résulte de l'application rigoureuse d'une même méthode par tous les inspecteurs.

La mise à jour annuelle : chaque année toutes les informations pratiques, les classements et les distinctions sont revus et mis à jour afin d'offrir l'information la plus fiable.

L'homogénéité de la sélection : les critères de classification sont identiques pour tous les pays couverts par le Guide Michelin.

… et un seul objectif : tout mettre en œuvre pour aider le lecteur à faire de chaque sortie un moment de plaisir, conformément à la mission que s'est donnée Michelin : contribuer à une meilleure mobilité.

Cher lecteur,

Nous avons le plaisir de vous proposer notre 34e édition du Guide Michelin Great Britain & Ireland. Cette sélection des meilleurs hôtels et restaurants dans chaque catégorie de prix est effectuée par une équipe d'inspecteurs professionnels, de formation hôtelière. Tous les ans, ils sillonnent le pays pour visiter de nouveaux établissements et vérifier le niveau des prestations de ceux déjà cités dans le Guide.

Au sein de la sélection, nous reconnaissons également chaque année les meilleures tables en leur décernant de ۞ a ۞ ۞ ۞. Les étoiles distinguent les établissements qui proposent la meilleure qualité de cuisine, dans tous les styles, en tenant compte des choix de produits, de la créativité, de la maîtrise des cuissons et des saveurs, du rapport qualité/prix ainsi que de la régularité.

Cette année encore, de nombreuses tables ont été remarquées pour l'évolution de leur cuisine. Un « N » accompagne les nouveaux promus de ce millésime 2007, annonçant leur arrivée parmi les établissements ayant une, deux ou trois étoiles.

De plus, nous souhaitons indiquer les établissements « *espoirs* » pour la catégorie supérieure. Ces établissements, mentionnés en rouge dans notre liste, sont les meilleurs de leur catégorie. Ils pourront accéder à la distinction supérieure dès lors que la régularité de leurs prestations, dans le temps et sur l'ensemble de la carte, aura progressé. Par cette mention spéciale, nous entendons vous faire connaître les tables qui constituent à nos yeux, les espoirs de la gastronomie de demain.

Votre avis nous intéresse, en particulier sur ces « espoirs » ; n'hésitez pas à nous écrire. Votre participation est importante pour orienter nos visites et améliorer sans cesse votre Guide. Merci encore de votre fidélité. Nous vous souhaitons de bons voyages avec le Guide Michelin 2007.

...ssement
& distinctions

LES CATÉGORIES DE CONFORT

Le Guide Michelin retient dans sa sélection les meilleures adresses dans chaque catégorie de confort et de prix. Les établissements sélectionnés sont classés selon leur confort et cités par ordre de préférence dans chaque catégorie.

⛨	XXXXX	Grand luxe et tradition
⛨	XXXX	Grand confort
⛨	XXX	Très confortable
⛨	XX	De bon confort
⛨	X	Assez confortable
	🍺	Pub traditionnel servant des repas
⛫		Autres formes d'hébergement conseillées (b&b, logis à la ferme et cottages)
without rest.		L'hôtel n'a pas de restaurant
with rm		Le restaurant possède des chambres

LES DISTINCTIONS

Pour vous aider à faire le meilleur choix, certaines adresses particulièrement remarquables ont reçu une distinction : étoiles ou Bib Gourmand. Elles sont repérables dans la marge par ✿ ou ⊛ et dans le texte par **Rest**.

LES ÉTOILES : LES MEILLEURES TABLES

Les étoiles distinguent les établissements, tous les styles de cuisine confondus, qui proposent la meilleure qualité de cuisine. Les critères retenus sont : le choix des produits, la créativité, la maîtrise des cuissons et des saveurs, le rapport qualité/prix ainsi que la régularité.

✿✿✿	**Cuisine remarquable, cette table vaut le voyage** On y mange toujours très bien, parfois merveilleusement.
✿✿	**Cuisine excellente, cette table mérite un détour**
✿	**Une très bonne cuisine dans sa catégorie**

LES BIB : LES MEILLEURES ADRESSES À PETIT PRIX

⊛	**Bib Gourmand** Établissement proposant une cuisine de qualité à moins de £28 ou €40 en République d'Irlande (repas composé de 3 plats, hors boisson).
⊛	**Bib Hôtel** Établissement offrant une prestation de qualité avec une majorité des chambres à moins de £75 ou moins de €105 en République d'Irlande (prix d'une chambre double, petit-déjeuner compris).

LES ADRESSES LES PLUS AGRÉABLES

Le rouge signale les établissements particulièrement agréables. Cela peut tenir au caractère de l'édifice, à l'originalité du décor, au site, à l'accueil ou aux services proposés.

🏠, 🏫 to 🏨🏨🏨🏨🏨   **Hôtels agréables**

🍴, 🍽 to 🍽🍽🍽🍽🍽   **Restaurants agréables**

LES MENTIONS PARTICULIÈRES

En dehors des distinctions décernées aux établissements, les inspecteurs Michelin apprécient d'autres critères souvent importants dans le choix d'un établissement.

SITUATION

Vous cherchez un établissement tranquille ou offrant une vue attractive ?
Suivez les symboles suivants :

      🔖   **Hôtel tranquille**

      🔖   **Hôtel très tranquille**

      ≼   **Vue intéressante**

      ≼   **Vue exceptionnelle**

CARTE DES VINS

Vous cherchez un restaurant dont la carte des vins offre un choix particulièrement intéressant ? Suivez le symbole suivant :

            Carte des vins particulièrement attractive

                      Toutefois, ne comparez pas la carte présentée par le sommelier d'un grand restaurant avec celle d'un pub ou d'un restaurant beaucoup plus simple. Les deux cartes vous offriront de l'exceptionnel, mais de niveau très différent.

Équipements & services

30 rm	Nombre de chambres
	Ascenseur
	Air conditionné (dans tout ou partie de l'établissement)
	Établissement possédant des zones réservées aux non-fumeurs. En Écosse et République d'Irlande, il est formellement interdit de fumer dans les pubs, restaurants et hôtels.
	Connexion Internet à Haut débit dans la chambre
	Établissement en partie accessible aux personnes à mobilité réduite.
	Équipements d'acceuil pour les enfants
	Repas servi au jardin ou en terrasse
	Wellness centre : bel espace de bien-être et de relaxation
	Sauna - Salle de remise en forme
	Piscine : de plein air ou couverte
	Jardin – Parc
	Court de tennis, golf et nombre de trous
	Ponton d'amarrage
	Pêche ouverte aux clients de l'hôtel (éventuellement payant)
150	Salles de conférences : capacité maximum
12	Salon privé : capacité maximum
	Garage dans l'hôtel (généralement payant)
P	Parking réservé à la clientèle
	Accès interdit au chiens (dans tout ou partie de l'établissement)
	Station de métro à proximité (Londres)
May-October	Période d'ouverture (ou fermeture), communiquée par l'hôtelier

Prix

Les prix indiqués dans ce guide ont été établis à l'automne 2006 et s'appliquent en basse et haute saisons. Ils sont susceptibles de modifications, notamment en cas de variation des prix des biens et des services. Les hôteliers et restaurateurs se sont engagés, sous leur propre responsabilité, à appliquer ces prix aux clients. Dans certaines villes, à l'occasion de manifestations commerciales ou touristiques, les prix demandés par les hôteliers risquent d'être considérablement majorés. Les prix sont indiqués en livres sterling sauf en République d'Irlande où ils sont donnés en euros. Les tarifs de l'hébergement comprennent le service et la T.V.A. La T.V.A. est également incluse dans les prix des repas. Toutefois, le service est uniquement compris dans les repas si la mention « s. » apparaît après le prix. Dans le cas contraire, une charge supplémentaire variant de 10 à 15 % du montant de l'addition est demandée. (La T.V.A. n'est pas appliquée dans les Channel Islands). Hors saison, certains établissements proposent des conditions avantageuses, renseignez-vous dès votre réservation.

LES ARRHES

Certains hôteliers demandent le versement d'arrhes. Il s'agit d'un dépôt-garantie qui engage l'hôtelier comme le client. Bien demander à l'hôtelier de vous fournir dans sa lettre d'accord toutes les précisions utiles sur la réservation et les conditions de séjour.

CARTES DE PAIEMENT

Carte de paiement acceptées :

AE ① ⑩ⓢ VISA   American Express – Diners Club – Mastercard – Visa.

CHAMBRES

rm † 50.00/90.00	Prix minimum/maximum pour une chambre confortable d'une personne
rm †† 70.00/120.00	Prix minimum/maximum pour une chambre de deux personnes
rm ⊆ 55.00/85.00	Prix de la chambre petit-déjeuner compris
⊆ 6.00	Prix du petit-déjeuner si non inclus

SHORT BREAKS

Certains hôtels proposent des conditions avantageuses pour un séjour de deux ou trois nuits. Ce forfait, calculé par personne pour 2 personnes au minimum, comprend le dîner, la chambre et le petit-déjeuner. Se renseigner auprès de l'hôtelier.

RESTAURANT

Menu à prix fixe : minimum £13, maximum £28 comprenant généralement 3 plats. Le prix minimum correspond souvent à celui d'un déjeuner.

Repas à la carte : le 1er prix correspond à un repas simple comprenant une entrée, un plat du jour et un dessert. Le 2e prix concerne un repas plus complet (avec spécialité) comprenant un hors d'œuvre, un plat principal, fromage ou dessert

s.	Service compris
🎭	Restaurants proposant des menus à prix attractifs servis avant ou après le théâtre
⍾	Vin servi au verre

⋏ : Dans les établissements de cette catégorie, le dîner est servi à heure fixe exclusivement aux personnes résidentes. Le menu à prix unique offre un choix limité de plats. Le déjeuner est rarement proposé. Beaucoup de ces établissements ne sont pas autorisés à vendre des boissons alcoolisées.

Villes

GÉNÉRALITÉS

✉ York	Numéro de code postal et nom du bureau distributeur du courrier
501 M27, ⑩	Numéro des cartes Michelin et carroyage ou numéro du pli
Great Britain G.	Voir le Guide Vert Michelin Grande-Bretagne
pop. 1057	Population (d'après le recensement de 2001)
BX **a**	Lettre repérant un emplacement sur le plan
⌐18	Golf et nombre de trous (handicap parfois demandé, réservation par téléphone vivement recommandée)
☼ ≤	Panorama, point de vue
✈	Aéroport
⛴	Transports maritimes
⛵	Transports maritimes (pour passagers seulement)
🛈	Information touristique

HEURE LÉGALE

Les visiteurs devront tenir compte de l'heure officielle en Grande-Bretagne : une heure de retard sur l'heure française.

INFORMATIONS TOURISTIQUES

INTÉRÊT TOURISTIQUE

★★★	Vaut le voyage
★★	Mérite un détour
★	Intéressant
AC	Entrée payante

SITUATION

See	Dans la ville
Envir.	Aux environs de la ville
Exc.	Excursions dans la région
N, S, E, W	La curiosité est située : au Nord, au Sud, à l'Est, à l'Ouest
A 22	On s'y rend par la route A 22, repérée par le même signe que sur le plan du Guide
2m.	Distance en miles (calculée en kilomètre pour la République d'Irlande)

Plans

⊚ ● a	Hôtels – Restaurants

CURIOSITÉS

	Bâtiment intéressant
	Édifice religieux intéressant

VOIRIE

M 1	Autoroute
④ ④	Numéro d'échangeur : complet, partiel
	Route à chaussée séparées de type autoroutier
	Grande voie de circulation
A 2	Itinéraire principal (GB) - Route nationale (IRL)
◀ ⋯⋯⋯	Sens unique – Rue impraticable, réglementée
Piccadilly P R	Rue piétonne – Tramway
	Rue commerçante – Parking – Parking Relais
÷ ╪╞ ╪╞	Porte – Passage sous voûte – Tunnel
15'5	Passage bas (inférieur à 16'6'') sur les grandes voies de circulation
	Gare et voie ferrée
▷+++++◁ ●━●━●	Funiculaire – Téléphérique, télécabine
△ B	Pont mobile – Bac pour autos

SIGNES DIVERS

🛈	Information touristique
♦ ჯ ⊠	Église/édifice religieux – Mosquée – Synagogue
⚊ ⁖	Tour ou pylône de télécommunication – Ruines
⬚ ⠿	Jardin, parc, bois – Cimetière
◯ ⚞ ₉	Stade – Hippodrome – Golf
�️	Golf (réservé) – Patinoire
⚌ ⛰	Piscine de plein air, couverte
⤙ ⚜	Vue – Panorama
■ ◉ ⊞ ⊠	Monument – Fontaine – Hôpital – Marché couvert
⚓ ⚐	Port de plaisance – Phare
✈ ⊖ ● 🚒	Aéroport – Station de métro – Gare routière
⛴	Transport par bateau :
	– passagers et voitures
⊗	Bureau principal
	Bâtiment public repéré par une lettre :
C H	- Bureau de l'Administration du comté – Hôtel de ville
J	Palais de justice
M T U	- Musée - Théâtre - Université, grande école
POL.	- Police (Commissariat central)

LONDRES

BRENT WEMBLEY	Nom d'arrondissement (borough) - de quartier (area)
	Limite de « borough »
	Zone à péage du centre-ville lundi-vendredi 7h-18h
⊖	Station de métro à proximité de l'hôtel ou du restaurant

Cartes de voisinage

AVEZ-VOUS PENSÉ À LES CONSULTER ?

Vous souhaitez trouver une bonne adresse, par exemple, aux environs de Leeds ?
Consultez la carte qui accompagne le plan de la ville.

La "carte de voisinage" (ci-contre) attire votre attention sur toutes les localités citées au Guide autour de la ville choisie, et particulièrement celles situées dans un rayon de 16 miles/25 km (limite de couleur).

Les "cartes de voisinage" vous permettent ainsi le repérage rapide de toutes les ressources proposées par le Guide autour des métropoles régionales.

NOTA :

Lorsqu'une localité est présente sur une "carte de voisinage", sa métropole de rattachement est imprimée en BLEU sur la ligne des distances de ville à ville.

EXEMPLE :

ILKLEY W. Yorks **502** O 22
– *pop. 13 472.*

ILKLEY
is to be found
on the local map
LEEDS.

⊞ *Myddleton* 🖉 *(01943) 607277*
🚉 *Station Rd* 🖉 *(01943) 602319*
London 210 – Bradford 13 – Harrogate 17 –
Leeds 16 – Preston 46

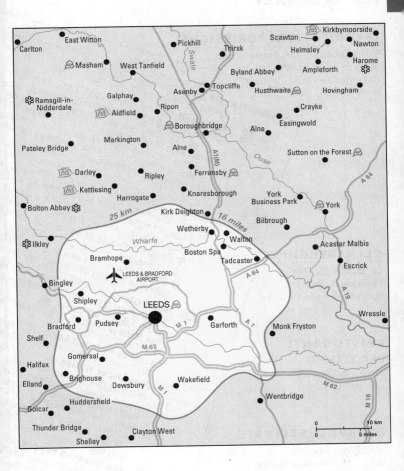

Carlton • East Witton • Pickhill • Thirsk • Scawton • Kirkbymoorside
🏛 Masham • West Tanfield • Helmsley • Nawton • Harome ❄
Byland Abbey • Ampleforth •
🌸 Ramsgill-in-Nidderdale • Galphay • Asenby • Topcliffe • Husthwaite 🏛 • Hovingham
🏛 Aldfield • Ripon • Crayke •
🏛 Boroughbridge • Alne • Easingwold •
Pateley Bridge • Markington • Alne • Ouse • Sutton on the Forest 🏛
Ferrensby 🏛
🏛 Darley • Ripley • A1(M) •
🏛 Kettlesing • Knaresborough • York Business Park • 🏛 York
Bolton Abbey ❄ • Harrogate • Kirk Deighton • 16 miles • Bilbrough
❄ Ilkley • Wharfe • Wetherby • Walton • Acaster Malbis
25 km • Boston Spa • Escrick
Bramhope • Tadcaster • A 64
✈ LEEDS & BRADFORD AIRPORT
Bingley • Wressle
Shipley • LEEDS 🏛 • M 1 • Garforth • A 1 • Monk Fryston • A 19
Bradford • Pudsey •
Shelf • M 62 • M 62 • M 18
Halifax • Gomersal •
Elland • Brighouse • Dewsbury • Wakefield • Wentbridge
Golcar • Huddersfield • M 1
Thunder Bridge • Clayton West
Shelley •

Swale
Ouse
Wharfe

| 0 | | 10 km |
| 0 | | 5 miles |

Come leggere la guida

INFORMAZIONI TURISTICHE

Siti turistici locali, golfs e tempo libero, mezzi di trasporto, uffici turismo, distanza dalle città di riferimento...

GLI ALBERGHI

Da 🏨🏨🏨🏨 a 🏠, ↑:
categorie di confort.
I più ameni: in rosso.

I RISTORANTI

Da XXXXX a X, 🍴:
categorie di confort.
I più ameni: in rosso.

LE TAVOLE STELLATE

😊😊😊 Vale il viaggio.
😊😊 Merita una deviazione.
😊 Ottima cucina.

I MIGLIORI ESERCIZI A PREZZI CONTENUTI

😊 Bib Gourmand.
😊 Bib Hotel.

28

CAMBERLEY Surrey **504** R29 – pop. 47 123 (inc. Frimley).
London 40 – Reading 13 – Southampton 48.

🏨 **Felix Hall**, Conifer Drive, GU15 2 BG, East:¾ m.
ℰ (0870) 400 8245, salesfelixhall@macdonald-
ℰ, 🔲, 🛏 – 🕸 🗖 🚗 – 🕰 250. ⊙⊙ 🖭21
Ɛ, 🚭, ☎ – 🏌 🛏 🖭 12.95 – **92 rm** ✝21
Linda : Rest 18.95/28.00 ☑ – ☑ 12.95 – **92 rm** ✝21
♦ Ivy-clad Victorian manor. A carved wooden sta
traditional with inlaid mahogany furniture, other
with contemporary furnishings.

CAMBRIDGE Cambs **504** U27 Great Britain G.– pop.
See : Town★★★ – St John's College★★★ AC Y – K
Museum★★ ZM1 – Trinity College★★ Y – Kettl
Exc. : Audley End★★, S: 13 m. by A 1309 – In
🛫 Cambridgeshire Moat House Hotel, Bar H
✈ Cambridge Airport : ℰ (01223) 37373
🚉 The Old Library, Wheeleer St ℰ (01223)
London 55 – Coventry 88 – Ipswich 54 – Leic

🏨 **Hotel Gloria** ⬆, Whitehouse lane, t
A1307 ℰ (01223) 277985, help@hotelg
&, 🅿 – 🕰 50. ⊙⊙ 🖭 ⊙ 🖭
The Melrose : Rest 16.50 (lunch) and
✝✝168.00/255.00.
♦ Built as a private house in 1852, no
rary rooms include state-of-the art f

XXXX **Alexander House** (Johns), Mi
😊😊 resa@alexanderhouse.co.uk, Fax
closed 2 weeks Christmas, 2 w
Rest (dinner only and lunch Frid
Spec. Salad of smoked eel, pig's
tachios and asparagus. Cannel
♦ A river Cam idyll. Chic con
with blissful views over the ri

XX **The Roasted Pepper**, 3
😊 roastedpepper.co.uk, Fax
closed Christmas-New Yea
♦ Personally run Victoriar
dishes with mild Asian in

at Histon North : 3 m. on B 1049

↑ **Blue House Farm**, v
😊 bluehousefarm.uk.co.
closed 2 weeks Chr
♦ Red-brick 18C list
overlooks meadow
preserves. Immac

XX **Phoenix**, 20 Th
closed 25-27 D
00 **s**

ALTRE PUBBLICAZIONI MICHELIN

Riferimento alla carta ed alla Guida Verde Michelin in cui figura la località.

GLI ALBERGHI TRANQUILLI

⟡ Albergo tranquillo.
⟡ Albergo molto tranquillo.

LOCALIZZARE L'ESERCIZIO

Localizzazione sulla pianta di città (coordinate ed indice).

DESCRIZIONE DELL'ESERCIZIO

Atmosfera, stile, carattere e spécialità.

INSTALLAZIONI E SERVIZI

PREZZI

mouth Rd (A325)
o.uk, Fax (0870) 4008246,

VISA
★210.00.
ads to the bedrooms; some are
ght and modern. 19C restaurant

ege★★ Z The Backs★★ YZ – Fitzwilliam
★ YM2 – Queen's College★ ACZ.
ar Museum★, Duxford, S:9 m. on M11.
954) 249988 X.
m. on A 1303 X.
tourism@cambridge.gov.uk.
– Norwich 61 – Nottingham 88 – Oxford 100.
ton Rd, CB3 OLX, Northwest: 1 ½ m. by
uk, Fax (01223) 277986, 😊, 🌳 – 📶 🐾 🐾   Z d
e 25.20/35.50 ⚍ – ⚍ 7.50 – **52 rm** ★136.00 –

modern and stylish public areas. The contempo-
. Sleek restaurant overlooks garden and terrace.   Y a
er Common, CB4 1HA, 𝒫 (01223) 369 245,
3) 369246, 😊 – 🏵 ❁ 16. 🝙 ① *VISA*
ugust, 1 week spring, Sunday and Monday –
rday) 30.00/50.00 ⚍ 🍴.
and apple purée. Braised turbot with peanuts and pis-
apricot, Strawberry sorbet, fraises des bois and mint.
ory dining room with smart first floor bar and terrace

terton Rd,CB4 3AX, 𝒫 (01223) 351872, seancarter@   Y c
3) 351873 – 📧 🝙 🝙 *VISA*
Sunday – **Rest** (booking essential) (dinner only) 24.95.
house with smartly clad tables. Classic French and Italian
es, served at reasonable prices.

🌳 Cambridge:
rest., 44 High St, CB3 7HV, 𝒫 (01223) 262164, reservations@
01223) 262166, 🌳 🅿 🝙 – ❁ 🝙 ★38.00 – ★★60.00.
-New Year – **4 rm** ⚍ ★38.00 – ★★60.00.
mhouse on a working farm... with beautiful blue windows; house
ny garden room for breakfast, including home-made bread and
ooms.
en, CB4 9JA, 𝒫 (01223) 233756 – ❁ 🝙 🝙 🝙 ① *VISA*
per – **Rest** – Chinese (Peking, Szechuan) - 17.50/29.50 and a la carte
brick pub overlooking village green. Within, Chinese dishes are served by
howties. Spicy highlights from Szechuan, Peking classics.
CB1 2AS, 𝒫 (01223) 313704, daniels@btconnect.com,
🝙 ① *VISA*   h and Bank Holidays – **Rest** a la carte
n base.   ealing artwork. Enclosed

29

Principi

« Quest'opera nasce col secolo e durerà quanto esso. »

La prefazione della prima Edizione della Guida MICHELIN 1900, divenuta famosa nel corso degli anni, si è rivelata profetica. Se la Guida viene oggi consultata in tutto il mondo è grazie al suo costante impegno nei confronti dei lettori.

Desideriamo qui ribadirlo.

I principi della Guida Michelin:

La visita anonima: per poter apprezzare il livello delle prestazioni offerte ad ogni cliente, gli ispettori verificano regolarmente ristoranti ed alberghi mantenendo l'anonimato. Questi pagano il conto e possono presentarsi per ottenere ulteriori informazioni sugli esercizi. La posta dei lettori fornisce peraltro preziosi suggerimenti che permettono di orientare le nostre visite.

L'indipendenza: la selezione degli esercizi viene effettuata in totale indipendenza, nel solo interesse del lettore. Gli ispettori e il caporedattore discutono collegialmente le scelte. Le massime decisioni vengono prese a livello europeo. La segnalazione degli esercizi all'interno della Guida è interamente gratuita.

La selezione: la Guida offre una selezione dei migliori alberghi e ristoranti per ogni categoria di confort e di prezzo. Tale selezione è il frutto di uno stesso metodo, applicato con rigorosità da tutti gli ispettori.

L'aggiornamento annuale: ogni anno viene riveduto e aggiornato l'insieme dei consigli pratici, delle classifiche e della simbologia al fine di garantire le informazioni più attendibili.

L'omogeneità della selezione: i criteri di valutazione sono gli stessi per tutti i paesi presi in considerazione dalla Guida Michelin.

... e un unico obiettivo: prodigarsi per aiutare il lettore a fare di ogni spostamento e di ogni uscita un momento di piacere, conformemente alla missione che la Michelin si è prefissata: contribuire ad una miglior mobilità.

Editoriale

Caro lettore,

Abbiamo il piacere di presentarle la nostra 34a edizione della Guida Michelin Gran Bretagna & Irlanda.

Questa selezione, che comprende i migliori alberghi e ristoranti per ogni categoria di prezzo, viene effettuata da un'équipe di ispettori professionisti di formazione alberghiera. Ogni anno, percorrono l'intero paese per visitare nuovi esercizi e verificare il livello delle prestazioni di quelli già inseriti nella Guida.

All'interno della selezione, vengono inoltre assegnate ogni anno da ✿ a ✿✿✿ alle migliori tavole. Le stelle contraddistinguono gli esercizi che propongono la miglior cucina, in tutti gli stili, tenendo conto della scelta dei prodotti, della creatività, dell'abilità nel raggiungimento della giusta cottura e nell'abbinamento dei sapori, del rapporto qualità/prezzo, nonché della costanza.

Anche quest'anno diversi ristoranti hanno ricevuto la stella per la qualità della loro cucina. Una « N » evidenzia le nuove promozioni per questa edizione del 2007 annunicicandone il loro inserimento con una, due o tre stelle.

Abbiano inoltre continuato a selezionare le « *promesse* » per la categoria superiore. Questi esercizi, evidenziati in rosso nella nostra lista, sono i migliori della loro categoria e potranno accedere alla categoria superiore non appena le loro prestazioni avranno raggiunto un livello costante nel tempo, e nelle proposte della carta. Con questa segnalazione speciale, è nostra intenzione farvi conoscere le tavole che costituiscono, dal nostro punto di vista, le principali promesse della gastronomia di domani.

Il vostro parere ci interessa, specialmente riguardo a queste « *promesse* ». Non esitate quindi a scriverci, la vostra partecipazione è importante per orientare le nostre visite e migliorare costantemente la vostra Guida. Grazie ancora per la vostra fedeltà e vi auguriamo buon viaggio con la Guida Michelin 2007.

Consultate la Guida Michelin su
www.ViaMichelin.com
e scriveteci a:
themichelinguide-gbirl@uk.michelin.com

Categorie
& simboli distintivi

LE CATEGORIE DI CONFORT

Nella selezione della Guida Michelin vengono segnalati i migliori indirizzi per ogni categoria di confort e di prezzo.Gli esercizi selezionati sono classificati in base al confort che offrono e vengono citati in ordine di preferenza per ogni categoria.

🏨🏨🏨🏨	XXXXX	Gran lusso e tradizione
🏨🏨🏨	XXXX	Gran confort
🏨🏨	XXX	Molto confortevole
🏨	XX	Di buon confort
🏨	X	Abbastanza confortevole
	🍴	Pub tradizionali con cucina
↑		Pensione, fattorie, case private (forme alternative di ospitalità)
without rest.		L'albergo non ha ristorante
with rm		Il ristorante dispone di camere

I SIMBOLI DISTINTIVI

Per aiutarvi ad effettuare la scelta migliore, segnaliamo gli esercizi che si distinguono in modo particolare. Questi ristoranti sono evidenziati nel testo con ✿ o 🍃 e **Rest.**

LE MIGLIORI TAVOLE

Le stelle distinguono gli esercizi che propongono la miglior qualità in campo gastronomico, indipendentemente dagli stili di cucina. I criteri presi in considerazione sono: la scelta dei prodotti, l'abilità nel raggiungimento della giusta cottura e nell'abbinamento dei sapori, il rapporto qualità/prezzo nonché la costanza.

✿✿✿	**Una delle migliori cucine, questa tavola vale il viaggio**
	Vi si mangia sempre molto bene, a volte meravigliosamente.
✿✿	**Cucina eccellente, questa tavola merita una deviazione**
✿	**Un'ottima cucina nella sua categoria**

I MIGLIORI ESERCIZI A PREZZI CONTENUTI

🍃	**Bib Gourmand**
	Esercizio che offre una cucina di qualità a meno di £28 (€40 per l'Irlanda). Prezzo di un pasto, bevanda esclusa.
🏠	**Bib Hotel**
	Esercizio che offre un soggiorno di qualità a meno di £75 (€105 per l'Irlanda) per la maggior parte delle camere. Prezzi per 2 persone, prima colazione esclusa.

GLI ESERCIZI AMENI

Il rosso indica gli esercizi particolarmente ameni. Questo per le caratteristiche dell'edificio, le decorazioni non comuni, la sua posizione ed il servizio offerto.

⌂, 🏠 to 🏠🏠🏠🏠   **Alberghi ameni**

🏠, ✗ to ✗✗✗✗✗   **Ristoranti ameni**

LE SEGNALAZIONI PARTICOLARI

Oltre alle distinzioni conferite agli esercizi, gli ispettori Michelin apprezzano altri criteri spesso importanti nella scelta di un esercizio.

POSIZIONE

Cercate un esercizio tranquillo o che offre una vista piacevole ? Seguite i simboli seguenti:

       🖐   **Albergo tranquillo**

       🖐   **Albergo molto tranquillo**

       ⋞   **Vista interessante**

       ⋞   **Vista eccezionale**

CARTA DEI VINI

Cercate un ristorante la cui carta dei vini offre una scelta particolarmente interessante ? Seguite il simbolo seguente:

       🍇   **Carta dei vini particolarmente interessante**

              Attenzione a non confrontare la carta presentata da un somme-lier in un grande ristorante con quella di un pub o di un ristorante più semplice. Le due carte vi offriranno degli ottimi vini di diverso livello.

Installazioni & servizi

30 rm	Numero di camere
	Ascensore
	Aria condizionata (in tutto o in parte dell'esercizio)
	Esercizio riservato in parte ai non fumatori. In Scozia e Irlanda la legge vieta il fumo in tutti i pub, ristoranti e le zone comuni degli alberghi.
	Connessione Internet ad alta velocità in camera
	Esercizio accessibile in parte alle persone con difficoltà motorie
	Attrezzatura per accoglienza e ricreazione dei bambini
	Pasti serviti in giardino o in terrazza
	Wellness centre: centro attrezzato per il benessere ed il relax
	Sauna - Palestra
	Piscina: all'aperto, coperta
	Giardino – Parco
18	Campo di tennis – Golf e numero di buche
	Pontile d'ormeggio
	Pesca aperta ai clienti dell'albergo (eventualmente a pagamento)
150	Sale per conferenze: capienza massima
120	Saloni particolari: capienza massima
	Garage nell'albergo (generalmente a pagamento)
P	Parcheggio riservato alla clientela
	Accesso vietato ai cani (in tutto o in parte dell'esercizio)
	Stazione della metropolitana più vicina (a Londra)
May-October	Periodo di apertura, comunicato dall'albergatore

I prezzi riportati nella guida ci sono stati forniti nell'autunno del 2006 e si applicano alla bassa e all'alta stagione. Potranno subire delle variazioni in relazione ai cambiamenti dei prezzi di beni e servizi. Gli albergatori e i ristoratori si sono impegnati, sotto la propria responsabilità, a praticare questi prezzi ai clienti. In occasione di alcune manifestazioni commerciali o turistiche i prezzi richiesti dagli albergatori potrebbero subire un sensibile aumento nelle località interessate e nei loro dintorni. I prezzi sono indicati in lire sterline (1 £ = 100 pence) ad eccezione per la Repubblica d'Irlanda dove sono indicati in euro. Tutte le tariffe per il soggiorno includono sia servizio che I.V.A. Tutti i prezzi dei ristoranti includono l'I.V.A., il servizio è incluso quando dopo il prezzo appare « s. ». Quando non compare « s. », il prezzo può essere soggetto ad un aumento per il servizio solitamente compreso tra il 10 % e il 15 %. In bassa stagione, alcuni esercizi applicano condizioni più vantaggiose, informatevi al momento della prenotazione. Entrate nell'albergo o nel ristorante con la guida in mano, dismostrando in tal modo la fiducia in chi vi ha indirizzato.

LA CAPARRA

Alcuni albergatori chiedono il versamento di una caparra. Si tratta di un deposito-garanzia che impegna sia l'albergatore che il cliente. Vi consigliamo di farvi precisare le norme riguardanti la reciproca garanzia di tale caparra.

CARTE DI CREDITO

Carte di credito accettate:

AE ⓘ ⓜ **VISA** American Express – Diners Club – MasterCard – Visa

CAMERE

rm ♦ 50.00/90.00 Prezzo minimo e massimo per una camera singola di buon confort
rm ♦♦ 70.00/120.00 Prezzo minimo e massimo per una camera doppia per due persone
rm ⌷ 55.00/85.00 Prezzo della camera compresa la prima colazione
⌷ 6.00 Prezzo della prima colazione

SHORT BREAKS

Alcuni alberghi propongono delle condizioni particolarmente vantaggiose o short break per un soggiorno minimo di due notti. Questo prezzo, calcolato per persona e per un minimo di due persone, comprende: camera, cena e prima colazione. Informarsi presso l'albergatore.

RISTORANTE

Menu a prezzo fisso: prezzo minimo £13 e massimo £28 comprendente generalmente 3 piatti. Il menu a prezzo minimo è spesso disponibile solo a pranzo.
Pasto alla carta: il primo prezzo corrisponde ad un pasto semplice comprendente: primo, piatto del giorno e dessert. Il secondo prezzo corrisponde ad un pasto più completo (con specialità) comprendente: due piatti e dessert.

s. Servizio compreso
🎭 Ristoranti che offrono menu a prezzi ridotti prima e/o dopo gli spettacoli teatrali
♀ Vino servito al bicchiere

⌂ : Negli alberghi di questa categoria, la cena viene servita, ad un'ora stabilita, esclusivamente a chi vi alloggia. Il menu, a prezzo fisso, offre una scelta limitata di piatti. Raramente viene servito anche il pranzo. Molti di questi esercizi non hanno l'autorizzazione a vendere alcolici.

Città

GENERALITÀ

⊠ York	Codice di avviamento postale
501 M27, ⑩	Numero della carta Michelin e del riquadro
Great Britain G.	Vedere la Guida Verde Michelin Gran Bretagna
pop. 1057	Popolazione residente
BX a	Lettere indicanti l'ubicazione sulla pianta
┡18	Golf e numero di buche (handicap generalmente richiesto, prenotazione telefonica vivamente consigliata)
⁎ ≼	Panorama, vista
✈	Aeroporto
⛴	Trasporti marittimi
⛵	Trasporti marittimi (solo passeggeri)
🛈	Ufficio informazioni turistiche

ORA LEGALE

I visitatori dovranno tenere in considerazione l'ora ufficiale nelle Isole Britanniche: un'ora di ritardo sull'ora italiana.

INFORMAZIONI TURISTICHE

INTERESSE TURISTICO

★★★	Vale il viaggio
★★	Merita una deviazione
★	Interessante
AC	Entrata a pagamento

UBICAZIONE

See	Nella città
Envir.	Nei dintorni della città
Exc.	Nella regione
N, S, E, W	Il luogo si trova a Nord, a Sud, a Est, a Ovest della località
A 22	Ci si va per la strada A 22 indicata con lo stesso segno sulla pianta
2 m.	Distanza in miglia (solo per la Gran Bretagna)

Piante

⊘ ● a   Alberghi – Ristoranti

CURIOSITÀ

Edificio interessante
Costruzione religiosa interessante

VIABILITÀ

Autostrada
numero dello svincolo: completo, parziale
Strada a carreggiate separate
Grande via di circolazione
Itinerario principale: Primary route (GB) o National route (IRL)
Senso unico – Via impraticabile, a circolazione regolamentata
Via pedonale – Tranvia
Piccadilly Via commerciale – Parcheggio – Parcheggio Ristoro
Porta – Sottopassaggio – Galleria
Sottopassaggio (altezza inferiore a 15'5) sulle grandi vie di circolazione
Stazione e ferrovia
Funicolare – Funivia, cabinovia
Ponte mobile – Traghetto per auto

SIMBOLI VARI

Ufficio informazioni turistiche
Chiesa – Moschea – Sinagoga
Torre o pilone per telecomunicazioni – Ruderi
Giardino, parco, bosco – Cimitero
Stadio – Ippodromo – Golf
Golf riservato – Pattinaggio
Piscina: all'aperto, coperta
Vista – Panorama
Monumento – Fontana – Ospedale – Mercato coperto
Porto turistico – Faro
Aeroporto – Stazione della metropolitana – Autostazione
Trasporto con traghetto: passeggeri ed autovetture
Ufficio postale centrale
Edificio pubblico indicato con lettera:
C H J   Sede dell'Amministrazione di Contea – Municipio – Palazzo di Giustizia
M T U   Museo – Teatro – Università, Scuola superiore
POL.   Polizia (Questura, nelle grandi città)

LONDRA

BRENT WEMBLEY Distretto amministrativo (Borough) – Quartiere (Area)
Limite del Borough
Area con circolazione a pagamento Lunedì-Venerdì 07.00-18.00
Stazione della metropolitana più vicina all'albergo o al ristorante

Carte dei dintorni

SAPETE COME USARLE?

Se desiderate, per esempio, trovare un buon indirizzo nei dintorni di Leeds, la "carta dei dintorni" (qui accanto) richiama la vostra attenzione su tutte le località citate nella Guida che si trovino nei dintorni della città prescelta, e in particolare su quelle raggiungibili nel raggio di 16 miles/25 km (limite di colore).

Le "carte dei dintorni" coprono l'intero territorio e permettono la localizzazione rapida di tutte le risorse proposte dalla Guida nei dintorni delle metropoli regionali.

NOTA:

Quando una località è presente su una "carta dei dintorni", la città a cui ci si riferisce è scritta in BLU nella linea delle distanze da città a città.

ESEMPIO:

ILKLEY W. Yorks **502** O 22
– pop. 13 472.

ILKLEY is to be found on the local map LEEDS.

🛏 *Myddleton* 🕿 *(01943) 607277*
🔋 *Station Rd* 🕿 *(01943) 602319*
London 210 – Bradford 13 – Harrogate 17 – Leeds 16 – Preston 46

38

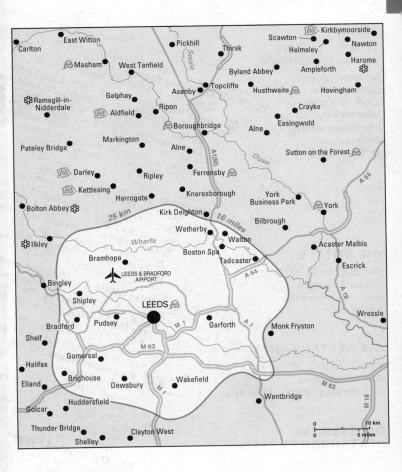

Hinweise zur Benutzung

TOURISTISCHE INFORMATIONEN

Sehenswürdigkeiten, Golfplätze und lokale Veranstaltungen, Verkehrsmittel, Informationsstellen, Entfernungen zu größeren Städten, ...

DIE HOTELS

Von 🏨🏨🏨 bis 🏠, ⚲:
Komfortkategorien.
Besonders angenehme Häuser: in rot.

DIE RESTAURANTS

Von XXXXX bis X, ᵀᴰ:
Komfortkategorien.
Besonders angenehme Häuser: in rot.

DIE STERNE-RESTAURANTS

❀❀❀ Eine Reise wert.
❀❀ Verdient einen Umweg.
❀ Eine sehr gute Küche.

DIE BESTEN PREISWERTEN ADRESSEN

🅐 Bib Gourmand.
🅑 Bib Hotel.

CAMBERLEY Surrey **504** R29 – pop. 47,123 (inc. Frimley).
London 40 – Reading 13 – Southampton 48.

🏨 **Felix Hall**, Conifer Drive, GU15 2 BG, East:¾
 𝒫 (0870) 400 8245, salesfelixhall@macdon
 ⅛, ⥱ˢ, ◨ ⍰ ⟜ 🅿 – 🔥 250.
 ⍰ ⥱ˢ, ◨ ⍰ ⟜ 🅿 – 🔥 250.
 Linda : Rest 18.95/28.00 ♀ – ⬜ 12.95 – **92 rm**
 • Ivy-clad Victorian manor. A carved wooden
 traditional with inlaid mahogany furniture, ot
 with contemporary furnishings.

CAMBRIDGE Cambs **504** U27 Great Britain G. – po
 See : Town★★★ – St John's College★★★ ACY
 Museum★★ ZM1 – Trinity College★★ Y – K
 Exc. : Audley End★★, S: 13 m. by A 1309 –
 ⅛ Cambridgeshire Moat House Hotel, Ba
 ⅛ Cambridge Airport : 𝒫 (01223) 37
 🛈 The Old Library, Wheeleer St 𝒫 (012
 London 55 – Coventry 88 – Ipswich 54 –

🏨 **Hotel Gloria** ♐, Whitehouse lan
 A1307 𝒫 (01223) 277985, help@ho
 ⅙ 🅿 – 🔥 50. ⍰ AE ⍰ VISA
 The Melrose : Rest 16.50 (lunch) a
 ✝✝168.00/255.00.
 • Built as a private house in 1852
 rary rooms include state-of-the a

XXX **Alexander House** (Johns),
❀❀ resa@alexanderhouse.co.uk, 2
 closed 2 weeks Christmas, 2
 Rest (dinner only and lunch F
 Spec. Salad of smoked eel, p
 tachios and asparagus. Can
 • A river Cam idyll. Chic
 with blissful views over th

XX **The Roasted Pepper**
🅐 roastedpepper.co.uk, F
 closed Christmas-New
 • Personally run Victo
 dishes with mild Asia

at Histon North : 3 m. on B 1

⚲ **Blue House Farm**
🅑 bluehousefarm.uk
 closed 2 weeks
 • Red-brick 18C
 overlooks mea
 preserves. Imm

XX **Phoenix**, 20
 closed 25-27
 29.50/43.00

LAGE DER STADT

Markierung des Ortes auf der Umgebungskarte der blau gekennzeichneten Stadt.

ANDERE MICHELIN-PUBLIKATIONEN

Angabe der Michelin-Karte und des Grünen Michelin-Reiseführers, wo der Ort zu finden ist.

LAGE DES HAUSES

Markierung auf dem Stadtplan (Planquadrat und Koordinate).

BESCHREIBUNG DES HAUSES

Atmosphäre, Stil, Charakter und Spezialitäten.

RUHIGE HOTELS

⟨⟩ ruhiges Hotel.
⟨⟩ sehr ruhiges Hotel.

EINRICHTUNG UND SERVICE

PREISE

rtsmouth Rd (A325)
s.co.uk, Fax (0870) 4008246,
– 🅥🅘🅢🅐 210.00.
leads to the bedrooms; some are
bright and modern. 19C restaurant

17.
College★★ Z The Backs★★ YZ – Fitzwilliam
ard★ YM2 – Queen's College★ AC Z.
al War Museum★, Duxford, S:9 m. on M11.
(01954) 249988 X.
2 m. on A 1303 X.
581, tourism@cambridge.gov.uk.
74 – Norwich 61 – Nottingham 88 – Oxford 100.
ngton Rd, CB3 OLX, Northwest: 1 ½ m. by   Z d
.co.uk, Fax (01223) 277986, 🍴, ⬛, – 🔁 🔄 🅦
carte 25.20/35.50 ♀ – ♀ 7.50 – **52 rm** ♦ 136.00 –

with modern and stylish public areas. The contempo-
ties. Sleek restaurant overlooks garden and terrace.
nmer Common, CB4 1HA, ℰ (01223) 369 245,   Y a
223) 369246, 🍴, – 🔄 ✿ 16. 🅰🅴 🅞 🅥🅘🅢🅐 –
s August, 1 week spring, Sunday and Monday –
aturday) 30.00/50.00 ♀ ☐.
ter and apple purée. Braised turbot with peanuts and pis-
of apricot, Strawberry sorbet, fraises des bois and mint.
vatory dining room with smart first floor bar and terrace
.   Y c

hesterton Rd,CB4 3AX, ℰ (01223) 351872, seancarter@
223) 351873 – 🞐 🅰🅴 🅞 🅥🅘🅢🅐
nd Sunday – **Rest** (booking essential) (dinner only) 24.95.
wn house with smartly clad tables. Classic French and Italian
ences, served at reasonable prices.

– ✉ Cambridge:
out rest., 44 High St, CB3 7HV, 🍴 🔂 – 🔄 📞 🔄
x (01223) 262166, 🍴 ☐ ♦ 38.00 – ♦♦ 60.00.
nas–New Year – **4 rm** ☐ ♦ 38.00 – ♦♦ 60.00.
farmhouse on a working farm... with beautiful blue windows; house
sunny garden room for breakfast, including home-made bread and
le rooms.
green, CB4 9JA, ℰ (01223) 233756 – 🔄 🞐 🅰🅴 🅞 🅥🅘🅢🅐
ember – **Rest** – Chinese (Peking, Szechuan) - 17.50/29.50 and a la carte
                    Within, Chinese dishes are served by
                    highlights from Szechuan; Peking classics.
edbrick pub overlooking village green. Within, daniels@btconnect.com,
s and bowties. Spicy highlights from Szechuan, ℰ (01223) 313704,
Mill Rd, CB1 2AS, 🞐 🅰🅴 🅞 🅥🅘🅢🅐 – **Rest** a la carte
              day lunch and Bank Holidays and appealing artwork. Enclosed
                                        diterranean base.

41

Grundsätze

„Dieses Werk hat zugleich mit dem Jahrhundert das Licht der Welt erblickt, und es wird ihm ein ebenso langes Leben beschieden sein."

Das Vorwort der ersten Ausgabe des MICHELIN-Führers von 1900 wurde im Laufe der Jahre berühmt und hat sich inzwischen durch den Erfolg dieses Ratgebers bestätigt. Der MICHELIN-Führer wird heute auf der ganzen Welt gelesen. Den Erfolg verdankt er seiner konstanten Qualität, die einzig den Lesern verpflichtet ist und auf festen Grundsätzen beruht.

Die Grundsätze des Michelin-Führers:

Anonymer Besuch: Die Inspektoren testen regelmäßig und anonym die Restaurants und Hotels, um deren Leistungsniveau zu beurteilen. Sie bezahlen alle in Anspruch genommenen Leistungen und geben sich nur zu erkennen, um ergänzende Auskünfte zu den Häusern zu erhalten. Für die Reiseplanung der Inspektoren sind die Briefe der Leser im Übrigen eine wertvolle Hilfe.

Unabhängigkeit: Die Auswahl der Häuser erfolgt völlig unabhängig und ist einzig am Nutzen für den Leser orientiert. Die Entscheidungen werden von den Inspektoren und dem Chefredakteur gemeinsam getroffen. Über die höchsten Auszeichnungen wird sogar auf europäischer Ebene entschieden. Die Empfehlung der Häuser im Michelin-Führer ist völlig kostenlos.

Objektivität der Auswahl: Der Michelin-Führer bietet eine Auswahl der besten Hotels und Restaurants in allen Komfort- und Preiskategorien. Diese Auswahl erfolgt unter strikter Anwendung eines an objektiven Maßstäben ausgerichteten Bewertungssystems durch alle Inspektoren.

Einheitlichkeit der Auswahl: Die Klassifizierungskriterien sind für alle vom Michelin-Führer abgedeckten Länder identisch.

Jährliche Aktualisierung: Jedes Jahr werden alle praktischen Hinweise, Klassifizierungen und Auszeichnungen überprüft und aktualisiert, um ein Höchstmaß an Zuverlässigkeit zu gewährleisten.

... und sein einziges Ziel – dem Leser bestmöglich behilflich zu sein, damit jede Reise und jeder Restaurantbesuch zu einem Vergnügen werden, entsprechend der Aufgabe, die sich Michelin gesetzt hat: die Mobilität in den Vordergrund zu stellen.

Lieber Leser,

Wir freuen uns, Ihnen die 34. Ausgabe des Michelin-Führers Great Britain & Ireland vorstellen zu dürfen. Diese Auswahl der besten Hotels und Restaurants in allen Preiskategorien wird von einem Team von Inspektoren mit Ausbildung in der Hotellerie erstellt. Sie bereisen das ganze Jahr hindurch das Land. Ihre Aufgabe ist es, die Qualität und Leistung der bereits empfohlenen und der neu hinzu kommenden Hotels und Restaurants kritisch zu prüfen. In unserer Auswahl weisen wir jedes Jahr auf die besten Restaurants hin, die wir mit ✿ bis ✿✿✿ kennzeichnen. Die Sterne zeichnen die Häuser mit der besten Küche aus, wobei untersc-hiedliche Küchenstilrichtungen vertreten sind. Als Kriterien dienen die Wahl der Produkte, die fachgerechte Zubereitung, der Geschmack der Gerichte, die Kreativität und das Preis-Leistungs-Verhältnis, sowie die Beständigkeit der Küchenleistung. Auch in diesem Jahr werden einige Restaurants erstmals für die Qualität ihrer Küche ausgezeichnet. Um diese neuen Ein-, Zwei- oder Drei-Sterne-Häuser zu präsentieren, haben wir sie in der Sterneliste mit einem "**N**" gekennzeichnet.

Außerdem haben wir wieder eine Auswahl an "*Hoffnungsträger*" für die nächsthöheren Kategorien getroffen. Diese Häuser, die in der Liste in Rot aufgeführt sind, sind die besten ihrer Kategorie und könnten in Zukunft aufsteigen, wenn sich die Qualität ihrer Leistungen dauerhaft und auf die gesamte Karte bezogen bestätigt hat. Mit dieser besonderen Kennzeichnung möchten wir Ihnen die Restaurants aufzeigen, die in unseren Augen die Hoffnung für die Gastronomie von morgen sind. Ihre Meinung interessiert uns! Bitte teilen Sie uns diese mit, insbesondere hinsichtlich dieser "*Hoffnungsträger*". Ihre Mitarbeit ist für die Planung unserer Besuche und für die ständige Verbesserung des Michelin-Führers von großer Bedeutung.

Wir danken Ihnen für Ihre Treue und wünschen Ihnen angenehme Reisen mit dem Michelin-Führer 2007.

Den Michelin-Führer finden Sie auch im Internet unter
www.ViaMichelin.com
oder schreiben Sie uns eine E-Mail:
themichelinguide-gbirl@uk.michelin.com

Kategorien
& Auszeichnungen

KOMFORTKATEGORIEN

Der Michelin-Führer bietet in seiner Auswahl die besten Adressen jeder Komfort-
und Preiskategorie. Die ausgewählten Häuser sind nach dem gebotenen Komfort
geordnet; die Reihenfolge innerhalb jeder Kategorie drückt eine weitere
Rangordnung aus.

🏰	XXXXX	Großer Luxus und Tradition
🏯	XXXX	Großer Komfort
🏛	XXX	Sehr komfortabel
🏠	XX	Mit gutem Komfort
🏚	X	Mit Standard-Komfort
🍺		Traditionelle Pubs, die Speisen anbieten
↑		Andere empfohlene Übernachtungsmöglichkeiten (Gästehäuser, Bauernhäuser und private Übernachtungsmöglichkeiten)
without rest.		Hotel ohne Restaurant
with rm		Restaurant vermietet auch Zimmer

AUSZEICHNUNGEN

Um ihnen behilflich zu sein, die bestmögliche Wahl zu treffen, haben einige besonders bemerkenswerte Adressen dieses Jahr eine Auszeichnung erhalten. Die Sterne
bzw. „Bib Gourmand" sind durch das entsprechende Symbol bzw. und **Rest**
gekennzeichnet.

DIE BESTEN RESTAURANTS

Die Häuser, die eine überdurchschnittlich gute Küche bieten, wobei alle Stilrichtungen
vertreten sind, wurden mit einem Stern ausgezeichnet. Die Kriterien sind: die Wahl
der Produkte, die Kreativität, die fachgerechte Zubereitung und der Geschmack,
sowie das Preis-Leistungs-Verhältnis und die immer gleich bleibende Qualität.

✿✿✿	**Eine der besten Küchen: eine Reise wert**
	Man isst hier immer sehr gut, öfters auch exzellent.
✿✿	**Eine hervorragende Küche: verdient einen Umweg**
✿	**Ein sehr gutes Restaurant in seiner Kategorie**

DIE BESTEN PREISWERTEN HÄUSER

	Bib Gourmand
	Häuser, die eine gute Küche für weniger als £28 (GB) bzw. €40 (IRE) bieten (Preis für eine dreigängige Mahlzeit ohne Getränke).
	Bib Hotel
	Häuser, die eine Mehrzahl ihrer komfortablen Zimmer für weni- ger als £75 (GB) bzw. €105 (IRE) anbieten (Preis für 2 Personen inkl. Frühstück).

DIE ANGENEHMSTEN ADRESSEN

Die rote Kennzeichnung weist auf besonders angenehme Häuser hin. Dies kann sich auf den besonderen Charakter des Gebäudes, die nicht alltägliche Einrichtung, die Lage, den Empfang oder den gebotenen Service beziehen.

🏠, 🏨 to 🏨🏨🏨🏨 **Angenehme Hotels**

🍴, ✕ to ✕✕✕✕✕ **Angenehme Restaurants**

BESONDERE ANGABEN

Neben den Auszeichnungen, die den Häusern verliehen werden, legen die Michelin-Inspektoren auch Wert auf andere Kriterien, die bei der Wahl einer Adresse oft von Bedeutung sind.

LAGE

Wenn Sie eine ruhige Adresse oder ein Haus mit einer schönen Aussicht suchen, achten Sie auf diese Symbole:

    🕊 Ruhiges Hotel

    🕊 Sehr ruhiges Hotel

    ≼ Interessante Sicht

    ≼ Besonders schöne Aussicht

WEINKARTE

Wenn Sie ein Restaurant mit einer besonders interessanten Weinauswahl suchen, achten Sie auf dieses Symbol:

    🍇 Weinkarte mit besonders attraktivem Angebot

        Aber vergleichen Sie bitte nicht die Weinkarte, die Ihnen vom Sommelier eines großen Hauses präsentiert wird, mit der Auswahl eines Gasthauses, dessen Besitzer die Weine der Region mit Sorgfalt zusammenstellt.

Einrichtung & Service

30 rm	Anzahl der Zimmer
🛗	Fahrstuhl
☷	Klimaanlage (im ganzen Haus bzw. in den Zimmern oder im Restaurant)
🚭	Nichtraucherzimmer vorhanden. In Schottland und der Republik Irland ist Rauchen per Gesetz verboten: in allen Pubs, Restaurants und in den öffentlichen Bereichen der Hotels.
📞	High-Speed Internetzugang in den Zimmern möglich
♿	Für Körperbehinderte leicht zugängliches Haus
🧒	Spezielle Angebote für Kinder
☂	Terrasse mit Speisenservice
🅦	Wellnessbereich
⊆s ⅃	Sauna - Fitnessraum
🏊 🐬	Freibad oder Hallenbad
🛋 🌳	Liegewiese, Garten – Park
🎾 ⛳18	Tennisplatz – Golfplatz und Lochzahl
⚓	Bootssteg
🎣	Angelmöglichkeit für Hotelgäste, evtl. gegen Gebühr
🏛 150	Konferenzraum mit Kapazität
🖵 120	Veranstaltungsraum mit Kapazität
🚗	Hotelgarage (wird gewöhnlich berechnet)
P	Parkplatz reserviert für Gäste
🐕	Hunde sind unerwünscht (im ganzen Haus bzw. in den Zimmern oder im Restaurant)
⊖	Nächstgelegene U-Bahnstation (in London)
May-October	Öffnungszeit, vom Hotelier mitgeteilt

Preise

Die in diesem Führer genannten Preise wurden uns im Herbst 2006. Der erste Preis ist der Mindestpreis in der Nebensaison, der zweite Preis der Höchstpreis in der Hauptsaison. Sie können sich mit den Preisen von Waren und Dienstleistungen ändern. Die Häuser haben sich verpflichtet, die von den Hoteliers selbst angegebenen Preise den Kunden zu berechnen. Anlässlich größerer Veranstaltungen, Messen und Ausstellungen werden von den Hotels in manchen Städten und deren Umgebung erhöhte Preise verlangt. Die Preise sind in Pfund Sterling angegeben (1 £ = 100 pence) mit Ausnahme der Republik Irland, wo sie in Euro angegeben sind. Alle Übernachtungspreise enthalten Bedienung und MWSt. Die Restaurantpreise enthalten die MWSt., Bedienung ist enthalten, wenn ein **s.** nach dem Preis steht. Wo kein **s.** angegeben ist, können unterschiedliche Zuschläge erhoben wer-den, normalerweise zwischen 10%-15% (keine MWSt. auf den Kanalinseln). Erkundigen Sie sich bei den Hoteliers nach eventuellen Sonderbedingungen.

RESERVIERUNG UND ANZAHLUNG

Einige Hoteliers verlangen zur Bestätigung der Reservierung eine Anzahlung. Dies ist als Garantie sowohl für den Hotelier als auch für den Gast anzusehen. Bitten Sie den Hotelier, dass er Ihnen in seinem Bestätigungsschreiben alle seine Bedingungen mitteilt.

KREDITKARTEN

	Akzeptierte Kreditkarten:
AE ⊙ MC VISA	American Express – Diners Club – Mastercard – Visa

ZIMMER

rm 🚹 50.00/90.00	Mindestpreis 50.00 und Höchstpreis 90.00 für ein Einzelzimmer
rm 🚹🚹 70.00/120.00	Mindestpreis 70.00 und Höchstpreis 120.00 für ein Doppelzimmer
rm ☕ 55.00/85.00	Zimmerpreis inkl. Frühstück (selbst wenn dieses nicht eingenommen wird)
☕ 6.00	Preis des Frühstücks

SHORT BREAKS

Einige Hotels bieten Vorzugskonditionen für einen Mindestaufenthalt von zwei Nächten oder mehr (Short break). Der Preis ist pro Person kalkuliert, bei einer Mindestbeteiligung von zwei Personen und schließt das Zimmer, Abendessen und Frühstück ein. Bitte fragen Sie im Hotel nach dieser Rate.

RESTAURANT

Menupreise: mindestens £13.00, höchstens £28.00 für eine dreigängige Mahlzeit. Das Menu mit dem niedrigen Preis ist oft nur mittags erhältlich.

Mahlzeiten „à la carte“: Die Preise entsprechen einer dreigängigen Mahlzeit.

s.	Bedienung inkl.
🎭	Restaurants mit preiswerten Menus vor oder nach dem Theaterbesuch
🍷	Wein wird glasweise ausgeschenkt

⌂ : In dieser Hotelkategorie wird ein Abendessen normalerweise nur zu bestimmten Zeiten für Hotelgäste angeboten. Es besteht aus einem Menu mit begrenzter Auswahl zu festgesetztem Preis. Mittagessen wird selten angeboten. Viele dieser Hotels sind nicht berechtigt, alkoholische Getränke auszuschenken.

Städte

ALLGEMEINES

✉ *York*	Postadresse
501 M27, ⑩	Nummer der Michelin-Karte mit Koordinaten
Great Britain G.	Siehe Grünen Michelin-Reiseführer Großbritannien
pop. 1057	Einwohnerzahl
BX **a**	Markierung auf dem Stadtplan
⊺18	Golfplatz mit Lochzahl (Handicap manchmal erforderlich, telefonische Reservierung empfehlenswert)
☀ ≼	Rundblick, Aussichtspunkt
✈	Flughafen
⛴	Autofähre
⛴	Personenfähre
🛈	Informationsstelle

UHRZEIT

In Großbritannien ist eine Zeitverschiebung zu beachten und die Uhr gegen-über der deutschen Zeit um 1 Stunde zurückzustellen.

SEHENSWÜRDIGKEITEN

BEWERTUNG

★★★	Eine Reise wert
★★	Verdient einen Umweg
★	Sehenswert
AC	Eintrittspreis

LAGE

See	In der Stadt
Envir.	In der Umgebung der Stadt
Exc.	Ausflugsziele
N, S, E, W	Im Norden, Süden, Osten, Westen der Stadt
A 22	Zu erreichen über die Straße A 22
2m.	Entfernung in Meilen (in der Republik Irland in Kilometern)

Stadtpläne

● ● a   Hotels – Restaurants

SEHENSWÜRDIGKEITEN

Sehenswertes Gebäude
Sehenswerte Kirche

STRASSEN

 Autobahn
④ ④   Nummern der Anschlussstellen: Autobahnein - und/oder - ausfahrt
Schnellstraße
Hauptverkehrsstraße
A 2   Fernverkehrsstraße (Primary route: GB – National route: IRL))
◄ :::::::   Einbahnstraße – Gesperrte Straße, mit Verkehrsbeschränkungen
Fußgängerzone – Straßenbahn
Piccadilly P R   Einkaufsstraße – Parkplatz, Parkhaus – Park-and-Ride-Plätze
✚ ⁼⊦⊧ ⊣⊢   Tor – Passage – Tunnel
16'6"   Unterführung (Höhe bis 16'6'') auf Hauptverkehrsstraßen
🚆   Bahnhof und Bahnlinie
Standseilbahn – Cable Car
⚠ B   Bewegliche Brücke – Autofähre

SONSTIGE ZEICHEN

🛈   Informationsstelle
☦ ☖ ⊠   Kirche/Gebetshaus – Moschee – Synagoge
📡 ♣   Funk-, Fernsehturm – Ruine
🌳 🗒   Garten, Park, Wäldchen – Friedhof
◯ 🏇 ⛳   Stadion – Pferderennbahn – Golfplatz
⛳ ⛸   Golfplatz (Zutritt bedingt erlaubt) – Eisbahn
🏊 🏊   Freibad – Hallenbad
≼ ⟱   Aussicht – Rundblick
▪ ⊞ ⌂   Denkmal – Brunnen – Krankenhaus – Markthalle
⚓ 🗼   Jachthafen – Leuchtturm
✈ ⊖ ● 🚌   Flughafen – U-Bahnstation – Autobusbahnhof
🛥   Schiffsverbindungen: Autofähre – Personenfähre
⊗   Hauptpostamt
▢   Öffentliches Gebäude, durch einen Buchstaben gekennzeichnet:
C H J   – Sitz der Grafschaftsverwaltung – Rathaus-Gerichtsgebäude
M T U   – Museum – Theater – Universität, Hochschule
POL.   – Polizei (in größeren Städten Polizeipräsidium)

LONDON

BRENT WEMBLEY – Name des Stadtteils (borough) – Name des Viertels (area)
– Grenze des «borough»
– Gebührenpflichtiger Innenstadtbereich (Mo-Fr 7-18 Uhr)
⊖   – Dem Hotel oder Restaurant nächstgelegene U-Bahnstation

49

Umgebungskarten

Die Umgebungskarten sollen Ihnen die Suche eines Hotels oder Restaurants in der Nähe der größeren Städte erleichtern.

Wenn Sie beispielsweise eine gute Adresse in der Nähe von Leeds brauchen, gibt Ihnen die Karte schnell einen Überblick über alle Orte, die in diesem Michelin-Führer erwähnt sind.

Innerhalb der in Kontrastfarbe gedruckten Grenze liegen Gemeinden, die im Umkreis von 16 miles/25 km zu erreichen sind.

ANMERKUNG:

Auf der Linie der Entfernungen zu anderen Orten erscheint im Ortstext die jeweils nächste Stadt mit Umgebungskarte in „BLAU".

BEISPIEL:

ILKLEY W. Yorks **502** O 22
– *pop. 13 472.*

ILKLEY
is to be found
on the local map
LEEDS.

🚏 *Myddleton* ℘ *(01943) 607277*
🅑 *Station Rd* ℘ *(01943) 602319*
London 210 – Bradford 13 – Harrogate 17 –
Leeds 16 – Preston 46

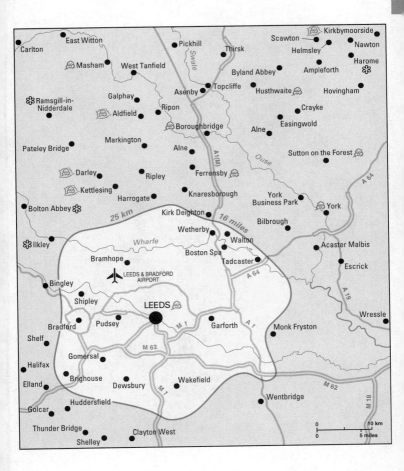

Carlton
East Witton
Pickhill
Thirsk
Scawton
Kirkbymoorside
Helmsley
Nawton
Masham
West Tanfield
Byland Abbey
Ampleforth
Harome
Ramsgill-in-Nidderdale
Galphay
Asenby
Topcliffe
Husthwaite
Hovingham
Aldfield
Ripon
Crayke
Easingwold
Boroughbridge
Alne
Pateley Bridge
Markington
Alne
Sutton on the Forest
Darley
Ripley
Ferrensby
Kettlesing
Knaresborough
Harrogate
York Business Park
York
Bolton Abbey
Kirk Deighton
Wetherby
Bilbrough
Ilkley
Walton
Acaster Malbis
Bramhope
Boston Spa
Tadcaster
Escrick
LEEDS & BRADFORD AIRPORT
Bingley
Shipley
LEEDS
Wressle
Bradford
Pudsey
Garforth
Monk Fryston
Shelf
Halifax
Gomersal
Elland
Brighouse
Dewsbury
Wakefield
Wentbridge
Golcar
Huddersfield
Thunder Bridge
Clayton West
Shelley

Swale
Ouse
A1(M)
A64
A19
Wharfe
16 miles
25 km
A64
A1
M1
M62
M18

0   10 km
0   5 miles

Awards 2007

Distinctions 2007
Le distinzioni 2007
Auszeichnungen 2007

Starred establishments

Les tables étoilées
Esercizi con stelle
Sterne-Restaurants

❀ ❀ ❀

ENGLAND		London	Gordon Ramsay
Bray-on-Thames	Fat Duck		
–	The Waterside Inn		

❀ ❀

ENGLAND		Newbury	Vineyard N
Cambridge	Midsummer House	**Oxford**	Le Manoir aux Quat' Saisons
Chagford	Gidleigh Park		
Cheltenham	Le Champignon Sauvage	**SCOTLAND**	
London	The Capital Restaurant	**Auchterarder**	Andrew Fairlie at Gleneagles
–	Le Gavroche		
–	Pétrus N	**IRELAND**	
–	Pied à Terre	Republic of Ireland	
–	The Square	**Dublin**	Patrick Guilbaud
Ludlow	Hibiscus		

❀

In red, the 2007 Rising Stars for ❀ ❀
→ En rouge, les espoirs 2007 pour ❀ ❀
→ In rosso, le promesse 2007 per ❀ ❀
→ In roter Schrift, die Hoffnungsträger 2007 für ❀ ❀

ENGLAND			
Abinger Hammer	Drakes on the Pond	**Biddenden**	The West House
Altrincham	Juniper	**Birmingham**	Jessica's
Baslow	Fischer's at Baslow Hall	–	Simpsons
		Blackburn	Northcote Manor
Bath	Bath Priory	**Blakeney**	Morston Hall
–	Lucknam Park	**Bolton Abbey**	The Devonshire Arms Country House
		Brockenhurst	Le Poussin at Whitley Ridge
		Chester	Arkle
		Cuckfield	Ockenden Manor
		Dartmouth	The New Angel
		East Grinstead	Graveteye Manor
		Emsworth	36 on the Quay

N New ❀, ❀ ❀
→ Nouveau ❀, ❀ ❀   → Nuovo ❀, ❀ ❀   → Neu ❀, ❀ ❀

55

Bib Gourmand

Good food at moderate prices

Repas soignés à prix modérés

Pasti accurati a prezzi contenuti

Sorgfältig zubereitete, preiswerte Mahlzeiten

⊛

ENGLAND			
Aldeburgh	The Lighthouse	**Jersey**	Green Island
Alderley Edge	The Wizard	–	Village Bistro
Blackpool	Twelve	**Kenilworth**	Simply Simpsons
Boroughbridge	thediningroom	**Knaresborough**	The General
Bray-on-Thames	Hinds Head	–	Tarleton Inn
Brighton and Hove	The Real Eating Company	**Leeds**	Anthony's at Flannels N
		–	Brasserie Forty Four
–	Terre à Terre	**Liverpool**	Simply Heathcotes
Bromsgrove	Epic	**London**	L'Accento
Budleigh Salterton	Gardiners N	–	Agni
Burnham Market	The Restaurant (at The Hoste Arms)	–	Al Duca
		–	Anchor & Hope
Bury	The Waggon N	–	Brasserie Roux
Cambridge	22 Chesterton Road	–	Brula Bistrot
–	The Hole in the Wall N	–	The Butcher & Grill N
Canterbury	The Granville	–	Café Spice Namaste
Castle Cary	The Camelot	–	Chapter Two
Chipping Campden	Churchill Arms	–	Comptoir Gascon
Cranbrook	Apicius	–	The Havelock Tavern N
Danehill	Coach & Horses	–	Ma Cuisine (Kew)
Durham	Bistro 21	–	Ma Cuisine (Twickenham)
Exeter	Jack in the Green Inn	–	Malabar
Faversham	The Dove	–	Mello
Guernsey	The Pavilion	–	Metrogusto
Haddenham	Green Dragon	–	The Parsee
Hurley	Black Boys Inn	–	Racine
Husthwaite	The Roasted Pepper	–	Salt Yard
Hutton Magna	Oak Tree Inn N	–	Sarkhel's
Itteringham	Walpole Arms	–	Tangawizi N
		–	Via Condotti N
		Loughborough	Lang's

N New ⊛

→ Nouveau ⊛   → Nuovo ⊛   → Neu ⊛

Lowick	*Snooty Fox*
Manchester	*Café Jem&I*
–	*Palmiro* N
Masham	*Vennell's*
Melton Mowbray	*Red Lion Inn*
Mistley	*The Mistley Thorn*
Newcastle upon Tyne	*Amer's* N
Norwich	*1 Up at The Mad Moose Arms*
–	*Wildebeest Arms*
Oldham	*The White Hart Inn*
Orford	*The Trinity (at Crown and Castle H.)*
Oxford	*Mole Inn*
Padstow	*Rick Stein's Café*
Preston	*Inside Out*
–	*Winckley Square Chop House*
Ross-on-Wye	*The Lough Pool Inn*
Royal Tunbridge Wells	*George and Dragon*
Rushlake Green	*Stone House*
St Albans	*Sukiyaki*
Saxmundham	*The Bell*
Sheffield	*Artisan*
Skipton	*Angel Inn*
Southport	*Warehouse Brasserie*
Sowerby Bridge	*The Millbank*
Stamford	*The Jackson Stops Inn*
–	*Jim's Yard* N
Stow-on-the-Wold	*The Old Butchers*
Summercourt	*Viners*
Sutton-on-the-Forest	*Rose & Crown*
Tetbury	*The Gumstool Inn (at Calcot Manor H.)* N
Tynemouth	*Sidney's*
Ullingswick	*Three Crowns Inn*
Wells	*The Old Spot* N
Westfield	*The Wild Mushroom*
West Malling	*The Swan*

Whitstable	*The Sportsman*
Witney	*The Navy Oak*
Woodbridge	*The Captain's Table*
York	*J. Baker's* N

SCOTLAND

Crieff	*The Bank*
Edinburgh	*Atrium*
Kintyre (Peninsula)	
Kilberry	*Kilberry Inn*
Perth	*63 Tay Street* N
Sorn	*Sorn Inn*
Strathyre	*Creagan House*

WALES

Abergavenny	*The Hardwick* N
Newport	*The Chandlery*

IRELAND

Northern Ireland

Belfast	*Cayenne*
–	*Deanes Brasserie*
Holywood	*Fontana*

Republic of Ireland

Baltimore	*Customs House*
Cashel	*Cafe Hans*
Dingle	*The Chart House*
Dublin	*Bang Café*
–	*La Maison des Gourmets*
Duncannon	*Aldridge Lodge* N
Durrus	*Good Things Cafe*
Kenmare	*The Lime Tree*
Kilbrittain	*Casino House*
Kinsale	*Fishy Fishy Cafe*

Bib Hotel

Good accommodation at moderate prices
Bonnes nuits à petits prix
Buona sistemazione a prezzo contenuto
Hier übernachten Sie gut und preiswert

ENGLAND

Alderney	Maison Bourgage	
Armscote	Willow Corner	
Askrigg	The Apothecary's House	
Barnard Castle	Greta House	
Battle	Fox Hole Farm	
Belford	Market Cross	N
Biddenden	Barclay Farmhouse	
Bishop's Stortford	Chimneys	
Bodmin	Bokiddick Farm	
Bovey Tracey	Brookfield House	N
Bury St Edmunds	Manorhouse	
Carlisle	Aldingham House	
Cheddleton	Choir Cottage	
Corbridge	Town Barns	N
Darley	Cold Cotes	
Dawlish	Lammas Park House	N
Devizes	Blounts Court Farm	
Dunster	Exmoor House	
Eastbourne	Brayscroft	
East Mersea	Mersea Vineyard	
Ely	Springfields	
Haltwhistle	Ashcroft	N
Harrogate	Knabbs House	
Hartland	Golden Park	N
Hastings	Tower House	
Helston	Cobblers Cottage	
Henfield	Frylands	
Hexham	West Close House	
Hungerford	Fishers Farm	N
Ironbridge	Bridge House	
Kirkby Lonsdale	Pickle Farm	
Kirkbymoorside	Brickfields Farm	
Littlehampton	Amberley Court	
Longtown	Bessiestown Farm	
Morpeth	Thistleyhaugh Farm	N
Nantwich	The Limes	
North Bovey	The Gate House	
Norwich	Beaufort Lodge	
Oxhill	Oxbourne House	
Penrith	The Old School	
Pickering	Bramwood	
Ripon	Bay Tree Farm	
–	Sharow Cross House	
Rochdale	Hindle Pastures	
Ross-on-Wye	Lumleys	
Rothbury	Farm Cottage	N
–	Thropton Demesne Farmhouse	N
Saffron Walden	Chaff House	
Saxmundham	The Bell	N
St Just	Boscean Country	
South Molton	Kerscott Farm	N
Stow-on-the-Wold	Number Nine	N
Taunton	Tilbury Farm	
Telford	Dovecote Grange	
Torquay	Colindale	N
Upton-on-Severn	Yew Tree House	
Wareham	Gold Court House	
Wells	Beaconsfield Farm	
Whitby	The Lawns	
Winchelsea	Strand House	
Woodstock	The Laurels	

N New
→ Nouveau   → Nuovo   → Neu

SCOTLAND

Aberdeen	Penny Meadow N
Anstruther	The Spindrift
Auchencairn	Balcary Mews N
Aviemore	The Old Minster's
–	Guest House
Ayr	No. 26 The Crescent
Ballater	Moorside House N
Banchory	The Old West Manse
Blairgowrie	Gilmore House
Brora	Glenaveron
Carnoustie	The Old Manor
Crieff	Merlindale
Dumfries	Redbank House
Dunkeld	Letter Farm
Duror	Bealach House N
Edinburgh	The Beverley
Forres	The Old Kirk N
Killin	Breadalbane House
Kingussie	Hermitage N
Linlithgow	Arden House
Lochearnhead	Mansewood
–	Country House
Nairn	Bracadale House N
North Berwick	Beach Lodge
Oban	The Barriemore
Perth	Taythorpe
Skye *(Isle of)*	Tigh an Dochais N
Stonehaven	Arduthie Guest House N
Strathpeffer	Craigvar
Thornhill	Gillbank House
Ullapool	Point Cottage

WALES

Betws Garmon	Betws Inn N
Betws-Y-Coed	Bryn Bella N
Brecon	Canal Bank N
Dolgellau	Tyddyn Mawr
Llandrindod Wells	Guidfa House
Llangrannog	The Grange N
Llanuwchllyn	Eifionydd N
Ruthin	Firgrove
St Clears	Coedllys Country House N

NORTHERN IRELAND

Bangor	Cairn Bay Lodge
–	Hebron House N
Belfast	Ravenhill House
Crumlin	Caldhame Lodge
Downpatrick	Pheasants' Hill Farm
Dundrum	The Carriage House N

REPUBLIC OF IRELAND

Ballyvaughan	Drumcreehy House
Carlingford	Beaufort House
Carlow	Barrowville Town House
Cashel	Aulber House
Castlegregory	The Shores Country House
Donegal	Ardeevin N
Drogheda	Boyne Haven House
Dungarvan	An Bohreen
Ennis	Fountain Court
Killarney	Kingfisher Lodge
Listowel	Allo's
New Ross	Riversdale House
Oughterard	Waterfall Lodge
Schull	Corthna Lodge
Toormore	Fortview House
Tramore	Glenorney

Particularly pleasant hotels

Hôtels agréables
Alberghi ameni
Angenehme Hotels

🏨🏨🏨🏨

ENGLAND

London	The Berkeley
–	Claridge's
–	Dorchester
–	Mandarin Oriental Hyde Park
–	The Ritz
–	Savoy
New Milton	Chewton Glen
Taplow	Cliveden

IRELAND *Republic of Ireland*

Straffan	The K Club

🏨🏨🏨

ENGLAND

Aylesbury	Hartwell House
Bath	Lucknam Park
–	The Royal Crescent
Daventry	Fawsley Hall
Ipswich	Hintlesham Hall
London	The Bentley Kempinski
–	Connaught
–	The Goring
–	The Soho
Malmesbury	Whatley Manor
Newbury	Vineyard
Oxford	Le Manoir aux Quat' Saisons
St Saviour (Jersey)	Longueville Manor

SCOTLAND

Ballantrae	Glenapp Castle
Bishopton	Mar Hall
Dunkeld	Kinnaird
Eriska (Isle of)	Isle of Eriska
Fort William	Inverlochy Castle

IRELAND
Republic of Ireland

Dublin	The Merrion
Kenmare	Park
–	Sheen Falls Lodge
Killarney	Killarney Park

🏨🏨🏨

ENGLAND

Amberley	Amberley Castle
Bath	Bath Priory
Bolton Abbey	The Devonshire Arms Country House
Bourton-on-the-Water	Lower Slaughter Manor
Broadway	Buckland Manor
Castle Combe	Manor House
Chagford	Gidleigh Park
Chipping Campden	Cotswold House
Dedham	Maison Talbooth
East Grinstead	Gravetye Manor
Evershot	Summer Lodge
Gillingham	Stock Hill Country House
La Pulente (Jersey)	Atlantic

Littlehampton	Bailiffscourt
London	Blakes
–	Capital
–	Charlotte Street
–	Covent Garden
–	Draycott
–	The Halkin
–	The Milestone
–	One Aldwych
–	The Pelham
Oakham	Hambleton Hall
Reading	The Forbury
Royal Leamington Spa	Mallory Court
Sandiway	Nunsmere Hall
Scilly (Isles of)	
St Martin's	St Martin's on the Isle
Tresco	The Island
Seaham	Seaham Hall
Taunton	The Castle
Tetbury	Calcot Manor
Ullswater	Sharrow Bay Country House
Windermere	Gilpin Lodge
York	Middlethorpe Hall

SCOTLAND

Blairgowrie	Kinloch House
Edinburgh	The Howard
–	Prestonfield
Inverness	Culloden House
Peebles	Cringletie House
Torridon	Loch Torridon

WALES

| Llandudno | Bodysgallen Hall |
| Llangammarch Wells | Lake Country House & Spa |

IRELAND

Republic of Ireland

Galway	The G
Gorey	Marlfield House
Mallow	Longueville House

ENGLAND

Ambleside	The Samling
Bath	Queensberry
Brampton	Farlam Hall
Burnham Market	The Hoste Arms
Cheltenham	On the Park
Cirencester	Barnsley House
Cuckfield	Ockenden Manor
Frome	Babington House
Helmsley	Feversham Arms
Hereford	Castle House
Horley	Langshott Manor
Kingsbridge	Buckland-Tout-Saints
King's Lynn	Congham Hall
Lewdown	Lewtrenchard Manor
London	Knightsbridge
–	Number Sixteen
Milford-on-Sea	Westover Hall
Oxford	Old Parsonage
Purton	Pear Tree at Purton
Rushlake Green	Stone House
St Helier (Jersey)	Eulah Country House
St Mawes	Tresanton
Tavistock	Hotel Endsleigh
Torquay	Orestone Manor
Wareham	Priory
Wellington	Bindon Country House
Windermere	Holbeck Ghyll
Woodstock	Feathers
Yarmouth (I.O.W.)	The George

SCOTLAND

Achiltibuie	Summer Isles
Arran (Isle of)	Kilmichael Country House
Gullane	Greywalls
Port Appin	Airds
Portpatrick	Knockinaam Lodge

WALES

Ll andudno	Osborne House
Machynlleth	Ynyshir Hall
Swansea	Fairyhill
Talsarnau	Maes-y-Neuadd

IRELAND

Republic of Ireland

Arthurstown	*Dunbrody Country House*
Athlone	*Wineport Lodge*
Ballingarry	*Mustard Seed at Echo Lodge*
Castlebaldwin	*Cromleach Lodge*
Craughwell	*St Clerans*
Glin	*Glin Castle*
Kinsale	*Perryville House*
Shanagarry	*Ballymaloe House*

ENGLAND

Ashwater	*Blagdon Manor*
Blakeney	*Morston Hall*
Bourton-on-the-Water	*The Dial House*
Dartmouth	*Nonsuch House*
Dorchester	*Birkin House*
Dulverton	*Ashwick House*
Helmsley	*Cross House Lodge*
	At The Star Inn
Keswick	*Swinside Lodge*
Leominster	*Ford Abbey*
Lynton	*Hewitt's – Villa Spaldi*
North Walsham	*Beechwood*
Porlock	*Oaks*
Portscatho	*Driftwood*
St Ives	*Blue Hayes*
Salisbury	*Howard's House*
Staverton	*Kingston House*
Teignmouth	*Thomas Luny House*
Ullswater	*Old Church*
Wight (Isle of)	
Seaview	*Seaview*

SCOTLAND

Annbank	*Enterkine*
Ballater	*Balgonie Country House*
Kelso	*Edenwater House*
Killin	*Ardeonaig*
Maybole	*Ladyburn*
Muir of Ord	*Dower House*
Nairn	*Boath House*
Tain	*Glenmorangie House*

WALES

Betws-y-Coed	*Tan-y-Foel Country House*
Llansanffraid Glan Conwy	*Old Rectory Country House*

IRELAND

Republic of Ireland

Bagenalstown	*Kilgraney Country House*
Clifden	*Dolphin Beach Country House*
Dingle	*Emlagh House*
Lahinch	*Moy House*
Riverstown	*Coopershill*

ENGLAND

Ash	*Great Weddington*
Askrigg	*Helm*
Bath	*Haydon House*
Billinghurst	*Old Wharf*
Blackpool	*Number One*
Calne	*Chilvester Hill House*
Chipping Campden	*Malt House*
Clun	*Birches Mill*
Crackington Haven	*Manor Farm*
Cranbrook	*Cloth Hall Oast*
East Hoathly	*Old Whyly*
Faversham	*Frith Farm House*
Hawkshead	*West Vale*
Helmsley	*Oldstead Grange*
Honiton	*Cokesputt House*
Ilminster	*The Old Rectory*
Iron Bridge	*Severn Lodge*
Ivychurch	*Olde Moat House*
Kendal	*Beech House*
Lavenham	*Lavenham Priory*
Ledbury	*Hall End*
Lizard	*Landewednack House*
Ludlow	*Bromley Court*
Malpas	*Tilston Lodge*
Man (Isle of)	*Aaron House*
Marazion	*Ednovean Farm*
North Bovey	*The Gate House*
Petworth	*Old Railway Station*
Pickering	*The Moorlands Country House*

Ripon	*Sharow Cross House*
St Austell	*Anchorage House*
St Blazey	*Nanscawen Manor House*
Shrewsbury	*Pinewood House*
Stow-on-the-Wold	*Rectory Farmhouse*
Tavistock	*Quither Mill*
–	*Tor Cottage*
Thursford Green	*Holly Lodge*
Wareham	*Gold Court House*
Wold Newton	*Wold Cottage*
York	*Alexander House*

SCOTLAND

Ballantrae	*Cosses Country House*
Bute (Isle of)	*Balmory Hall*
Connel	*Ards House*
Fort William	*Crolinnhe*
–	*The Grange*
Inverness	*Millwood House*
Islay (Isle of)	*Kilmeny*
Linlithgow	*Arden House*
Mull (Isle of)	*Gruline Home Farm*
–	*Ptarmigan House*

Perth	*Over Kinfauns*
Skirling	*Skirling House*
Stathpeffer	*Craigvar*

WALES

Betws-Y-Coed	*Penmachno Hall*
Colwyn Bay	*Rathlin Country House*
Menai Bridge	*Neuadd Lwyd*
Pwllheli	*The Old Rectory*

IRELAND

Northern Ireland

Dungannon	*Grange Lodge*
Holywood	*Beech Hill*

Republic of Ireland

Castlegregory	*The Shores Country House*
Castlelyons	*Ballyvolane House*
Cong	*Ballywarren House*
Fethard	*Mobarnane House*
Galway	*Killeen House*
Kanturk	*Glenlohane*
Kenmare	*Sallyport House*
Kilkenny	*Blanchville House*
Portlaoise	*Ivyleigh House*

Particularly pleasant restaurants

Restaurants agréables
Ristoranti ameni
Angenehme Restaurants

ХХХХХ

ENGLAND

London	The Restaurant (at Ritz H.)

ХХХХ

ENGLAND

Bray-on-Thames	Waterside Inn (with rm)
London	Angela Hartnett at The Connaught
–	1880 (at The Bentley Kempinski)
–	Pétrus (at The Berkeley H.)
–	The Savoy Grill
Taplow	Waldo's (at Cliveden H.)
Winteringham	Winteringham Fields (with rm)

IRELAND

Republic of Ireland

Dublin	Patrick Guilbaud

ХХХ

ENGLAND

Baslow	Fischer's at Baslow Hall (with rm)
Birmingham	Simpsons (with rm)
Cambridge	Midsummer House
Dedham	Le Talbooth
Emsworth	36 on the Quay (with rm)

Grange-over-Sands	L'Enclume (with rm)
London	Bibendum
–	The Capital Restaurant (at Capital H.)
–	Orrery
–	Oxo Tower
–	Le Pont de la Tour
–	The Wolseley
Newcastle upon Tyne	Fisherman's Lodge
Skipton	Angel Inn & Barn Lodgings (with rm)
Welwyn Garden City	Auberge du Lac

WALES

Llandrillo	Tyddyn Llan (with rm)

ХХ

ENGLAND

Derby	Darleys
Goring	Leatherne Bottel
Grantham	Harry's Place
Jersey	Jersey Pottery (Garden Rest)
–	Suma's
Kirkby Lonsdale	HippingHall (with rm)
London	Le Caprice
–	J. Sheekey
–	Mon Plaisir
–	Rules
Ludlow	Mr Underhill's at Dinham Weir (with rm)
Malmesbury	Le Mazot (at Whatley Manor)
Medbourne	Horse & Trumpet (with rm)

Nayland	*White Hart Inn (with rm)*
Padstow	*The Seafood (with rm)*
Pateley Bridge	*Yorke Arms (with rm)*
Windermere	*Miller Howe (with rm)*
Yeovil	*Little Barwick House (with rm)*

SCOTLAND

Kingussie	*The Cross (with rm)*
Lochinver	*The Albannach (with rm)*
Skye (Isle of)	*Three Chimneys*
	& The House Over-By (with rm)

WALES

Builth Wells	*The Drawing Room (with rm)*
Pwllheli	*Plas Bodegroes (with rm)*

IRELAND

Republic of Ireland

Dunfanaghy	*The Mill (with rm)*
Kenmare	*The Lime Tree*
Kilbrittain	*Casino House*
Tramore	*Coast (with rm)*

ENGLAND

Burnham Market	*The Restaurant*
	(at The Hoste Arms)
High Ongar	*The Wheatsheaf Brasserie*
London	*L'Atelier de Joël Robuchon*
–	*Blueprint Café*
–	*Oxo Tower Brasserie*
Millbrook	*The View*
Mousehole	*Cornish Range (with rm)*
Stanton	*Leaping Hare*
Studland	*Shell Bay*

WALES

Aberaeron	*Harbourmaster (with rm)*

IRELAND

Republic of Ireland

Dingle	*The Chart House*

ENGLAND

Ambleside	*Drunken Duck Inn (with rm)*
Barnard Castle	*Rose & Crown (with rm)*
Biggleswade	*The Hare & Hounds*
Bildeston	*The BildestonCrown (with rm)*
Broadhembury	*Drewe Arms*
Chichester	*The Royal Oak Inn (with rm)*
Cirencester	*The Bell*
Corscombe	*The Fox Inn (with rm)*
Evershot	*Acorn Inn (with rm)*
Helmsley	*The Star Inn*
Henley-in-Arden	*Crabmill*
Ilmington	*The Howard Arms (with rm)*
Kendal	*The Punch Bowl Inn (with rm)*
Keyston	*Pheasant Inn*
Lydford	*Dartmoor Inn*
Melksham	*Pear Tree Inn (with rm)*
Milton Keynes	*Crooked Billet*
Oundle	*The Falcon Inn*
Royston	*The Cabinet at Reed*
Shefford	*The Black Horse (with rm)*
Skipton	*Angel Inn*
South Molton	*The Masons Arms*
Stadhampton	*Crazy Bear (with rm)*
Stow-on-the-Wold	*Fox Inn (with rm)*
Sutton-on-the-Forest	*Rose & Crown*
Tarr Steps	*Tarr Farm Inn (with rm)*
Taunton	*Blue Ball Inn (with rm)*
Winchester	*Wykeham Arms (with rm)*
Woburn	*The Birch*

WALES

Brecon	*Felin Fach Griffin (with rm)*
Caersws	*Talkhouse (with rm)*
Newport	*The Newbridge (with rm)*
Skenfrith	*The Bell at Skenfrith (with rm)*

IRELAND

Northern Ireland

Donaghadee	*Grace Neills*

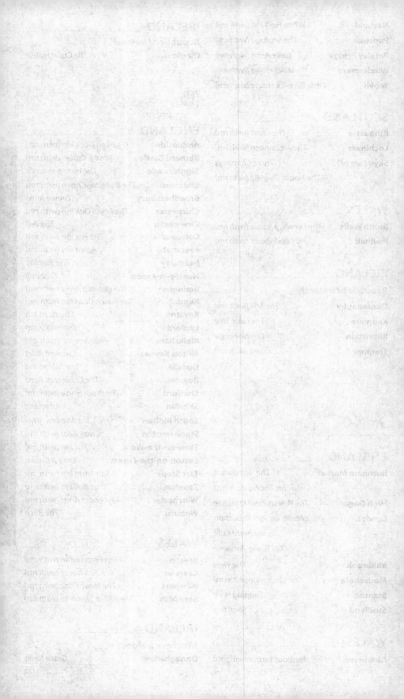

Further information

Pour en savoir plus
Per saperne di piú
Gut zu wissen

Beer

Beer is one of the oldest and most popular alcoholic drinks in the world. Traditional draught beer is made by grinding malted barley, heating it with water and adding hops which add the familiar aroma and bitterness. Beers in Britain can be divided into 2 principal types: Ales and Lagers which differ principally in their respective warm and cool fermentations. In terms of sales the split between the two is approximately equal. Beer can also be divided into keg or cask.

Keg beer – is filtered, pasteurised and chilled and then packed into pressurised containers from which it gets its name.

Cask beer – or `Real Ale' as it is often referred to, is not filtered, pasteurised or chilled and is served from casks using simple pumps. It is considered by some to be a more characterful, flavoursome and natural beer.

There are several different beer styles in Britain and Ireland:

Bitter – whilst it is the most popular traditional beer in England and Wales it is now outsold by lager. Although no precise definition exists it is usually paler and dryer than Mild with a high hop content and slightly bitter taste.

Mild – is largely found in Wales, the West Midlands and the North West of England. The name refers to the hop character as it is gentle, sweetish and full flavoured beer. It is generally lower in alcohol and sometimes darker in colour, caused by the addition of caramel or by using dark malt.

Stout – the great dry stouts are brewed in Ireland and are instantly recognisable by their black colour and creamy head. They have a pronounced roast flavour with plenty of hop bitterness.

In Scotland the beers produced are full bodied and malty and are often known simply as Light, Heavy, or Export which refers to the body and strength of the beer.

Although Ireland is most famous for its stouts, it also makes a range of beers which have variously been described as malty, buttery, rounded and fruity with a reddish tinge.

Whisky

The term whisky is derived from the Scottish Gaelic *uisage beatha* and the Irish Gaelic *uisce beathadh*, both meaning "water of life". When spelt without an e it usually refers to Scotch Whisky which can only be produced in Scotland by the distillation of malted and unmalted barley, maize, rye, and mixtures of two or more of these. Often simply referred to as Scotch it can be divided into 2 basic types: malt whisky and grain whisky.

Malt whisky – is made only from malted barley which is traditionally dried over peat fires. The malt is then milled and mixed with hot water before mashing turns the starches into sugars and the resulting liquid, called wort, is filtered out. Yeast is added and fermentation takes place followed by two distilling processes using a pot still. The whisky is matured in oak, ideally sherry casks, for at least three years which affects both its colour and flavour. All malts have a more distinctive smell and intense flavour than grain whiskies and each distillery will produce a completely individual whisky of great complexity. A single malt is the product of an individual distillery. There are approximately 100 malt whisky distilleries in Scotland.

Grain whisky – is made from a mixture of any malted or unmalted cereal such as maize or wheat and is distilled in the Coffey, or patent still, by a continuous process. Very little grain whisky is ever drunk unblended.

Blended whisky – is a mix of more than one malt whisky or a mix of malt and grain whiskies to produce a soft, smooth and consistent drink. There are over 2,000 such blends which form the vast majority of Scottish whisky production.

Irish Whiskey – differs from Scotch whisky both in its spelling and method of production. It is traditionally made from cereals, distilled three times and matured for at least 7 years. The different brands are as individual as straight malt and considered by some to be gentler in character.

La bière

La bière est l'une des plus anciennes et populaires boissons alcoolisées dans le monde. Pour produire la bière pression traditionnelle, on écrase l'orge maltée que l'on chauffe ensuite avec de l'eau à laquelle on ajoute le houblon. C'est ce qui lui donne son arôme et son goût amer bien connus. Deux types de bières sont principalement vendues en Grande-Bretagne : les Ales fermentées à chaud et les Lagers fermentées à froid. Elles se divisent en « keg beer » et en « cask beer ».

Bière en keg : elle est filtrée, pasteurisée et refroidie, puis versée dans des tonnelets pressurisés appelés kegs.

Bière en cask ou « Real Ale » : elle n'est ni filtrée, ni pasteurisée, ni refroidie mais tirée directement du tonneau à l'aide d'une simple pompe. Selon certains, cette bière, de qualité bien distincte, a plus de saveur et est plus naturelle.

Types de bières vendues au Royaume-Uni et en Irlande :

Bitter – C'est la bière traditionnelle la plus populaire en Angleterre et au pays de Galles mais ses ventes diminuent au profit des lagers. La Bitter est généralement plus pâle et son goût plus sec que la Mild. Son contenu en houblon est élevé et elle a un goût légèrement amer.

La Mild se consomme surtout au pays de Galles, dans le Midlands de l'Ouest et dans le Nord-Ouest de l'Angleterre. On l'appelle ainsi en raison de son goût moelleux légèrement douceâtre conféré par le houblon. Cette bière, généralement moins alcoolisée, est plus foncée par le caramel qui lui est ajouté ou par l'utilisation de malt plus brun.

Stout – les grandes marques de bières brunes sont brassées en Irlande et sont reconnaissables par leur couleur noire rehaussée de mousse crémeuse. Elles ont un goût prononcé de houblon grillé et une saveur amère.

Celles produites en Écosse sont maltées ; elles ont du corps et se dénomment le plus souvent Light, Heavy ou Export en référence au corps et à leur teneur en alcool.

Whisky

Le mot whisky est un dérivé du gaélique écossais *uisage beatha e*t du gaélique irlandais *uisce beathadh* signifiant tous deux « eau de vie ». Quand il est écrit sans e, il se réfère au whisky écossais qui ne peut être produit qu'en Écosse par la distillation de céréales maltées ou non comme l'orge, le maïs, le seigle ou d'un mélange de deux ou plus de ces céréales. Souvent appelé tout simplement Scotch il se réfère à deux types de whiskies : whisky pur malt ou whisky de grain.

Le whisky pur malt est fait seulement à partir d'orge maltée qui est traditionnellement séchée au-dessus de feux de tourbe. Le malt est moulu et mélangé avec de l'eau chaude, puis le brassage transforme l'amidon en sucre ; le moût est ensuite filtré. On y ajoute de la levure et après la fermentation on fait distiller deux fois dans un alambic. Le whisky est alors vieilli pendant au moins trois ans dans des fûts de chêne, ayant contenu de préférence du sherry, ce qui transforme son goût et sa couleur. Tous les whiskies pur malt ont un arôme particulier et une saveur plus intense que les whiskies de grain et chaque distillerie produit son propre whisky avec des qualités bien distinctes. Il y a environ une centaine de distilleries de whiskies pur malt en Écosse.

Le whisky de grain est fait d'un mélange de céréales, maltées ou non, comme le maïs ou le froment et est distillé dans un alambic de type Coffey suivant un procédé continu. Très peu de whiskies de grain sont consommés à l'état pur. On procède à des mélanges pour la consommation.

Blended whisky est le mélange d'un ou plusieurs whiskies pur malt et de whiskies de grain afin de produire un alcool léger, moelleux et de qualité. Il existe plus de 2 000 marques de blended whiskies qui forment la majeure partie de la production écossaise.

Le whisky irlandais, différent du whisky écossais par sa fabrication, est traditionnellement produit à partir de céréales ; il est ensuite distillé trois fois et vieilli pendant au moins sept ans. Certains le trouvent plus moelleux.

La Birra

La birra è una delle bevande alcoliche più antiche e popolari. La tradizionale birra alla spina si ottiene macinando l'orzo, riscaldandolo con l'acqua e aggiungendo il luppolo, che le conferiscono l'aroma e il tipico sapore amaro.

Le birre britanniche si dividono in due tipi principali: Ales e Lagers, che differiscono essenzialmente per la fermentazione, rispettivamente calda e fredda. In termini di vendita, i due tipi approssimativamente si equivalgono. La birra può anche dividersi in keg (lett, barilotto), e cask (lett botte).

La keg beer è filtrata, pastorizzata e raffreddata, e poi messa in contenitori pressurizzati, da cui deriva il nome.

La cask beer, o Real Ale, come viene comunemente indicata, non è filtrata, pastorizzata o raffeddata, ed è servita dalle botti, usando semplici pompe. Alcuni la considerano una birra più ricca di carattere e di gusto e più naturale.

In Gran Bretagna e Irlanda, le birre si caratterizzano anche in base a « stili » diversi.

Le bitter costituisce la birra tradizionalmente più popolare in Inghilterra e nel Galles, ma è ora « superata » dalla lager. Non esiste definizione specifica per la birra bitter, ma si può dire che si tratta in genere di una birra più pallida e secca della mild, dall'alto contenuto di luppolo e dal gusto leggermente amaro.

La mild è diffusa in Galles, West Midlands e Inghilterra nord-occidentale. Il nome richiama il carattere del luppolo, essendo delicata, dolce e dal gusto pieno. Contiene solitamente una limitata quantità di alcol ed è talvolta scura per l'aggiunta di caramello e per l'impiego di malto scuro.

La secche stouts vengono prodotte in Irlanda e sono immediatamente riconoscibili dal colore nero e dalla schiuma cremosa. Hanno una decisa fragranza di tostatura e un gusto amaro di luppolo.

Whisky

Il termine whisky deriva dal gealico scozzese *uisage beatha* e dal gaelico irlandese *uisce beathadh*, che significano « acqua di vita ». Se scritto senza la e, indica di solito lo Scotch Whisky, che può essere unicamente prodotto in Scozia dalla distillazione di malto e orzo, granturco e segale, e dall'unione di due o più di questi ingredienti. Spesso chiamato semplicemente Scoveri, si divide in due tipi: malt whisky e grain whisky.

Il malt whisky viene prodotto unicamente con malto, tradizionalmente seccato su fuochi alimentati con torba. Il malto viene poi macinato e gli viene aggiunta acqua bollente prima che l'impasto muti gli amidi in zuccheri e il liquido che ne deriva, chiamato wort (mosto di malto), venga filtrato. Si amalgama poi il lievito e avviene la fermentazione, seguita da due processi di distillazione nell'alambicco. Il whisky è lasciato invecchiare in legno di quercia, idealmente in botti di sherry, per almeno tre anni, perchè acquisti colore e sapore. Ogni tipo di malt whisky ha un profumo più distintivo e un gusto più intenso del grain whisky. Ogni distilleria produce un whisky dal carattere individuale, che richiede un processo di grande complessità. Un solo malt whisky è il prodotto di una specifica distilleria. In Scozia, esistono circa 100 distillerie di malt whisky.

Il grain whisky è il risultato della fusione di qualsiasi cereale con o senza malto, come il granturco o il frumento, es viene distillato nel Coffey, o alambicco brevettato, grazie ad un processo continuo. È molto scarsa la quantità di grain whisky che si beve puro.

Il blended whisky nasce dalla fusione di più di un malt whisky, o da quella di malt e grain whiskies. Il risultato è una bevanda dal gusto delicato, dolce e pieno. Esistono più di 2000 whisky di questo tipo, che costituiscono la parte più consistente della produzione scozzese.

Bier

Bier ist eines der ältesten und beliebtesten alkoholischen Getränke der Welt. Das traditionelle Fassbier wird aus gemahlener und gemalzter Gerste hergestellt, die in Wasser erhitzt wird. Durch Beigabe von Hopfen werden das bekannte Aroma und der typische bittere Geschmack erzeugt.

Die Biersorten in Großbritannien unterteilen sich in zwei Hauptgruppen: Ales und Lagers, wobei die Art der Gärung – im einen Fall warm, im anderen kalt – ausschlaggebend für das Endresultat ist. Beide Sorten haben hierzulande einen ungefähr gleichen Marktanteil. Da sich die meisten Brauvorgänge anfangs gleichen, entscheiden erst die Endphasen des Brauens, welche der verschiedenen Biersorten entsteht.

Darüber hinaus kann das englische Bier auch nach der Art seiner Abfüllung in Keg- bzw. Cask-Bier unterschieden werden:

Keg beer wird gefiltert, pasteurisiert, abgekühlt und anschließend in luftdichte, unter Druck gesetzte Metallbehälter gefüllt, von denen das Bier auch seinen Namen erhält.

Cask beer, gewöhnlich Real Ale genannt, wird weder gefiltert, noch pasteurisiert oder gekühlt, sondern mit einfachen (zumeist Hand-) Pumpen vom Faß gezapft.

Es gibt folgende Biersorten in Großbritannien und Irland: Bitter ist das meistbekannte traditionelle Bier in England und Wales. Eine genaue Definition, was ein Bitter ausmacht, sucht man vergeblich; es ist gewöhnlich heller und trockener als das Mild, hat einen hohen Hopfenanteil und einen leicht bitteren Geschmack. In den letzten Jahren hat das – meist importierte oder in Lizenz gebraute – Lager ihm jedoch den Rang abgelaufen.

Mild ist übergewiegend in Wales, in den westlichen Midlands und Nordwestengland zu finden. Der Name bezieht sich auf den Hopfenanteil, der es zu einem milden, etwas süßlichen und vollmundigen Bier macht. Es hat einen geringeren Alkoholgehalt und besitzt wegen der Zugabe von Karamel oder dunklem Malz bisweilen eine dunklere Farbe.

Stouts von hervorragendem trockenem Geschmack werden in Irland gebraut und sind unmittelbar an ihrer schwarzen Farbe und der cremigen Blume erkennbar. Sie haben einen ausgesprochen starken Geschmack nach bitterem Hopfen.

In Schottland hergestellte Biere sind alkoholstark und malzig; sie sind oft einfach bekannt als: Light, Heavy oder Export – Bezeichnungen, die auf Körper und Stärke des Bieres hinweisen.

Whisky

Die Bezeichnung Whisky entstammt dem Gälischen, wo im Schottischen der Ausdruck *uisage beatha*, im Irischen des Ausdruck *uisce beathadh* jeweils « Wasser des Lebens » bedeuten. Wird Whisky ohne ein e am Ende geschrieben, ist Scotch Whisky gemeint, der nur in Schottland aus gemalzter und ungemalzter Gerste, Mais, Roggen oder aus Mischungen zweier oder mehrerer dieser Zutaten gebrannt werden darf. Oft auch nur als Scotch bezeichnet, kann dieser in zwei Grundarten unterschieden werden: malt whisky und grain whisky.

Malt (Malz) whisky wird nur aus gemalzter Gerste hergestellt, die traditionell über Torffeuern getrocknet wird. Danach wird das Malz gemahlen und mit heißem Wasser vermischt, wonach in der Maische die Stärke in Zucker umgewandelt wird. Die dadurch entstandene Flüssigkeit, « wort » genannt, wird gefiltert und mit Hefe versetzt, was den Gärungsprozess einleitet. Anschließend folgen zwei Destillierungen im herkömmlichen Topf über offenem Feuer. Der Whisky reift danach mindestens drei Jahre lang in Eichenholz, idealerweise in Sherry-Fässern, was sich sowohl auf Farbe wie auf Geschmack des Whiskys auswirkt. Alle malts haben einen ausgeprägteren Geruch und intensiveren Geschmack als die grain-Whiskies; und jede Destillerie erzeugt einen völlig eigenen Whisky mit individueller Geschmacksnote und großer Komplexität. Ein sogenannter single malt entstammt aus einer einzigen Destillerie. Es gibt ungefähr 100 Malt Whisky-Destillerien in Schottland.

Grain (Korn) whisky wird aus Mischungen von gemalzten und ungemalzten Getreidesorten, wie Mais oder Weizen, hergestellt und wird in einem kontinuierlichen Prozeß in dem sogenannten « Coffey » destilliert. Nur sehr wenige Kornwhisky-Sorten sind nicht das Ergebnis von blending, dem Abstimmen des Geschmacks durch Mischung.

Blended whisky wird aus mehr als einer Sorte Malt Whisky oder aus Malt und Grain Whiskies gemischt, um ein weiches, geschmacklich harmonisches Getränk von beständiger Güte zu garantieren. Die über 2000 im Handel zu findenden blends stellen den Großteil der schottischen Whiskyerzeugung dar.

Irish Whiskey unterscheidet sich vom Scotch Whisky sowohl in der Schreibweise wie auch dem Herstellungsverfahren. Er wird traditionell aus Getreide hergestellt, wird dreifach destilliert und reift mindestens sieben Jahre lang. Die verschiedenen Sorten sind so individuell ausgeprägt wie reine Malt Whiskies und werden oft als weicher und gefälliger empfunden.

B. Pérousse/MICHELIN

Tower Bridge

Towns
from A to Z

Villes
de A à Z

Città
de A a Z

Städte
von A bis Z

England
Channel Islands
Isle of Man

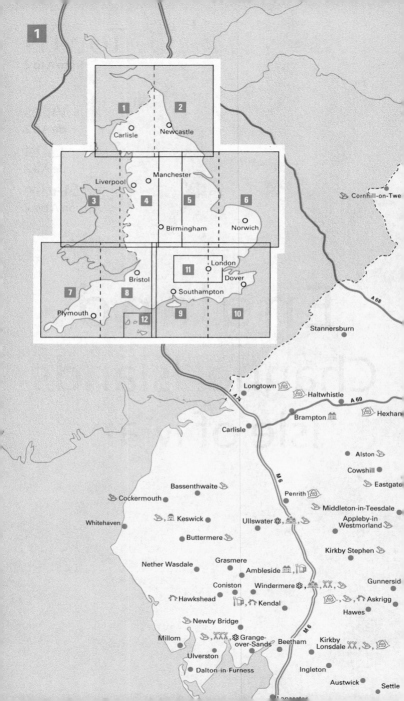

1

Carlisle · Newcastle

1 **2**

Liverpool · Manchester

3 **4** **5** **6**

Birmingham · Norwich

Bristol · London · Dover

11

Southampton

7 **8** **9** **10**

Plymouth

12

Cornhill-on-Twe

Stannersburn

Longtown · Haltwhistle

Brampton · Hexham

Carlisle

Alston

Cowshill

Eastgate

Bassenthwaite

Cockermouth · Penrith

Middleton-in-Teesdale

Keswick · Ullswater

Appleby-in-Westmorland

Whitehaven · Buttermere

Kirkby Stephen

Nether Wasdale · Grasmere

Ambleside

Coniston · Windermere

Gunnersid

Hawkshead · Kendal

Askrigg

Newby Bridge

Hawes

Millom · Grange-over-Sands · Beetham

Kirkby Lonsdale

Ulverston

Dalton-in-Furness

Ingleton

Austwick · Settle

Lancaster

Place with at least _____

a hotel or restaurant	● Ripon
a pleasant hotel or restaurant	🏨, ↑, X, 🍴
Good accommodation at moderate prices	🏠
a quiet, secluded hotel	🦢
a restaurant with	❀, ❀❀, ❀❀❀, 🚗 Rest
Town with a local map	●

Localité offrant au moins _____

une ressource hôtelière	● Ripon
un hôtel ou restaurant agréable	🏨, ↑, X, 🍴
Bonnes nuits à petits prix	🏠
un hôtel très tranquille, isolé	🦢
une bonne table à	❀, ❀❀, ❀❀❀, 🚗 Rest
Carte de voisinage : voir à la ville choisie	●

La località possiede come minimo _____

una risorsa alberghiera	● Ripon
Albergo o ristorante ameno	🏨, ↑, X, 🍴
Buona sistemazione a prezzi contenuti	🏠
un albergo molto tranquillo, isolato	🦢
un'ottima tavola con	❀, ❀❀, ❀❀❀, 🚗 Rest
Città con carta dei dintorni	●

Ort mit mindestens _____

einem Hotel oder Restaurant	● Ripon
einem angenehmen Hotel oder Restaurant	🏨, ↑, X, 🍴
Hier übernachten Sie gut und preiswert	🏠
einem sehr ruhigen und abgelegenen Hotel	🦢
einem Restaurant mit	❀, ❀❀, ❀❀❀, 🚗 Rest
Stadt mit Umgebungskarte	●

Berwick-upon-Tweed

Swinton

Belford • Bamburgh
• Seahouses
Beadnell

Wooler

Alnwick

Warkworth

Rothbury

Kirkwhelpington

Morpeth

A 696 Tynemouth

Matfen

Corbridge Heddon- Newcastle-Upon-Tyne, XXX
on-the-Wall Gateshead Sunderland
Washington
Carterway Heads Seaham
Chester-le-Street

Durham

Spennymoor

A 1

Stockton-on-Tees

Barnard Castle Staithes
Middlesbrough Runswick Bay
Yarm
Hutton Magna Darlington Guisborough Whitby
Stokesley
Reeth Moulton Great Broughton Goathland
Richmond Osmotherley
Leyburn Patrick Northallerton Rosedale Abbey
Aysgarth Brompton Hutton-le-Hole Lastingham Scarborough
Middleham Carthorpe Kirkbymoorside
W. Witton E. Witton Pickhill Hawnby Pickering
W. Burton Masham Thirsk Helmsley Snainton
Kettlewell W. Tanfield Husthwaite Hovingham
Kilnsey Ripon Wold Newton
Grassington Pateley Bridge, XX Easingwold Whitwell-on-the-Hill
Darley Boroughbridge Westow Thwing

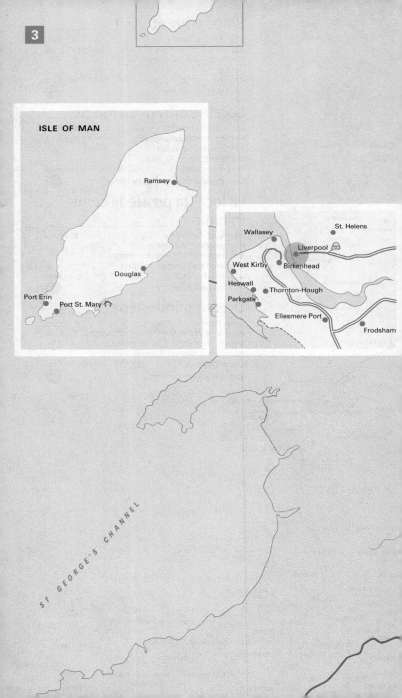

ISLE OF MAN

Ramsey

Douglas

Port Erin
Port St. Mary

Wallasey
West Kirby
Heswall
Parkgate

St. Helens
Liverpool
Birkenhead
Thornton-Hough
Ellesmere Port
Frodsham

ST GEORGE'S CHANNEL

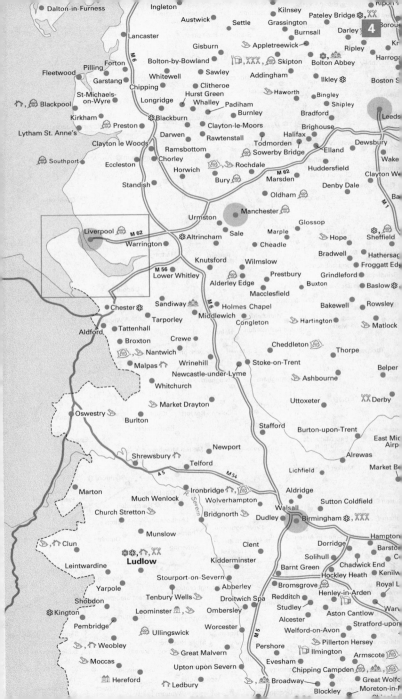

BRISTOL CHANNEL

ISLE
OF LUNDY

Ilfracombe
Woolacombe
Croyde
Saunton
Barnsta
Appledore
Bideford
Clovelly
Umberlei
Hartland
Horn's
Cross
Parkham
Bude
Crackington Haven
Boscastle
Virginstow
Ashwater
Lewdown
Lifton
Lydfo
Rock
Tavistock
Padstow
Bodmin
Liskeard
Callington
St. Mawgan
A 30
Newquay
St. Blazey
Plymouth
Summercourt
St. Austell
Fowey
Looe
Yealmpton
St. Agnes
Ladock
Grampound
Polperro
Millbrook
Illogan
Truro
Veryan
Mevagissey
Noss Mayo
St. Ives
Phillegh
Portloe
Zennor
Portscatho
Penzance
Marazion
Falmouth
St. Mawes
St. Just
Mousehole
Helston
Constantine
Porthleven
St. Keverne
Mullion
Coverack
Lizard

ISLES OF SCILLY
Bryher
St. Martin's
Tresco
St. Mary's
St.Agnes

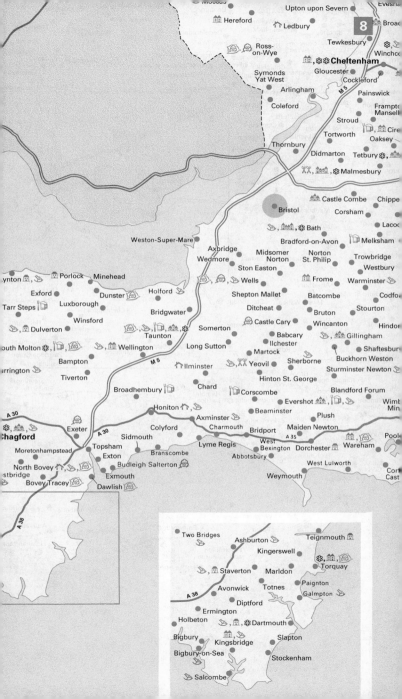

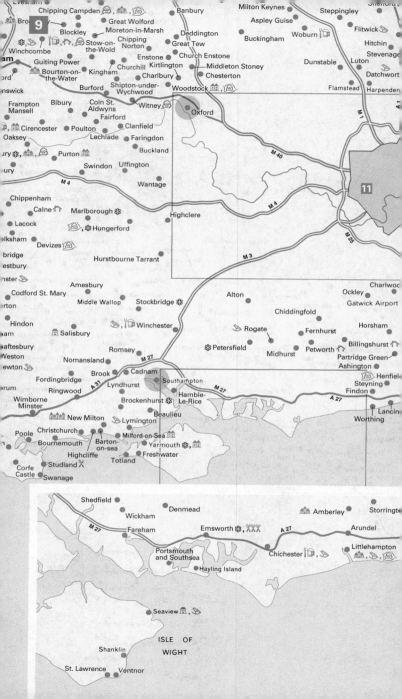

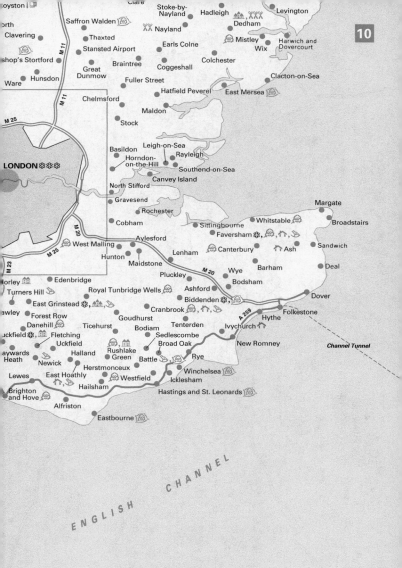

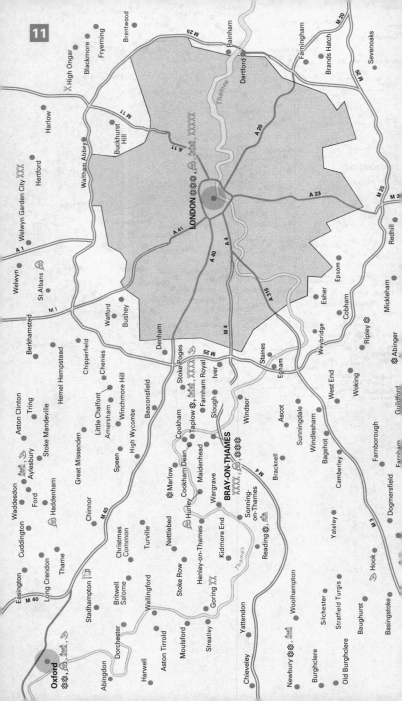

Channels Islands

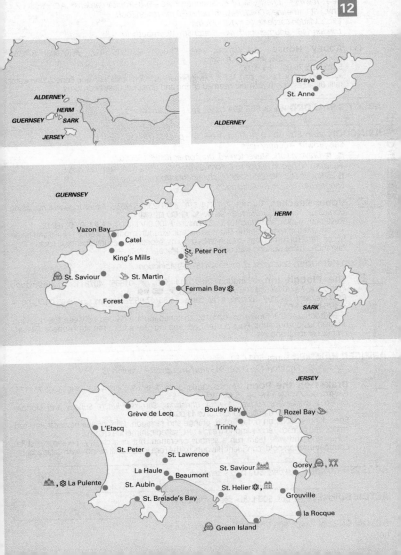

ALDERNEY
HERM
GUERNSEY • SARK
JERSEY

ALDERNEY

Braye
St. Anne

GUERNSEY

Vazon Bay
Catel
King's Mills
St. Peter Port
St. Saviour • St. Martin
Fermain Bay ❄
Forest

HERM

SARK

JERSEY

Grève de Lecq
L'Etacq
Bouley Bay
Trinity
Rozel Bay
St. Peter
St. Lawrence
La Haule • Beaumont
St. Saviour
Gorey
La Pulente
St. Aubin
St. Helier ❄,
St. Brelade's Bay
Grouville
la Rocque
Green Island

ABBERLEY *Worcs.* 503 504 M 27 – *pop. 654* – ⊠ *Worcester.*
London 137 – Birmingham 27 – Worcester 13.

🏠 **The Elms**, WR6 6AT, West : 2 m. on A 443 *ℰ* (01299) 896666, *info@theelmshotel.co.uk*, Fax (01299) 896804, ≤, 🐎, 🏊, 🛝 – ⇆ rest, **P.** – 🔏 50. **ⓄⓄ** 🄰🄴 *VISA*. 🛠
Rest 17.50/35.00 and a la carte approx 41.00 ♀ – **22 rm** ⊡ ✦70.00/80.00 – ✦✦200.00/250.00.
* Queen Anne mansion with sweeping gardens and croquet lawn. Period details include carved wooden fireplace and ornate plasterwork. Antique furnishings and spacious bedrooms. Restaurant makes good use of fresh herbs from kitchen garden.

ABBOTSBURY *Dorset* 503 504 M 32 *The West Country G.* – *pop. 422.*
See : *Town*★★ - *Chesil Beach*★★ - *Swannery*★ *AC* – *Sub-Tropical Gardens*★ *AC.*
Env. : *St Catherine's Chapel*★ , ½ m. uphill (30 mn rtn on foot).
Exc. : *Maiden Castle*★★ (≤★) *NE* : 7½ m.
London 146 – Bournemouth 44 – Exeter 50 – Weymouth 10.

🏠 **Abbey House** 🌿 without rest., Church St, DT3 4JJ, *ℰ* (01305) 871330, Fax (01305) 871088, 🐎 – ⇆ **P.** 🛠
5 rm ⊡ ✦75.00 – ✦✦80.00.
* Historic stone house, part 15C abbey infirmary. Garden holds a unique Benedictine water mill. Breakfast room with low beamed ceiling and fireplace. Cosy bedrooms.

ABBOT'S SALFORD *Warks.* 503 504 O 27 – *see Evesham (Worcs.).*

ABINGDON *Oxon.* 503 504 Q 28 *Great Britain G.* – *pop. 36 010.*
See : *Town*★ – *County Hall*★.
🏌, 🏌 *Drayton Park, Steventon Rd, Drayton* *ℰ* (01235) 550607.
⛴ *from Abingdon Bridge to Oxford (Salter Bros. Ltd) 2 daily (summer only).*
🛈 *25 Bridge St* *ℰ* (01235) 522711, *abingdontic@btconnect.com.*
London 64 – Oxford 6 – Reading 25.

🏨 **Upper Reaches**, Thames St, OX14 3JA, *ℰ* (01235) 522536, *info@upperreaches-abing* *don.co.uk*, Fax (01235) 555182 – 🄻 ⇆ 📞 **P.** **ⓄⓄ** 🄰🄴 *VISA*
Rest 14.95 (lunch) and a la carte ♀ – **31 rm** ⊡ ✦100.00/120.00 – ✦✦120.00/180.00.
* Converted corn mill on the Thames. Historic exterior, modern interior - greys and beige décor. Tasteful furnishings extend to bedrooms, especially executive heritage rooms. Restaurant features working water wheel and millrace.

at Clifton Hampden *Southeast : 3 m. on A 415* – ⊠ *Abingdon.*

🏠 **The Plough Inn**, Abingdon Rd, OX14 3EG, *ℰ* (01865) 407811, *admin@plough* *inns.co.uk*, Fax (01865) 407136, 🐎 – ⇆ 📞 ₺ **P.** **ⓄⓄ** *VISA*
Rest *(closed Sunday dinner)* a la carte 14.85/47.85 ♀ – **8 rm** ⊡ ✦65.00/75.00 – ✦✦75.00/150.00.
* Bedrooms at this family-run part 16C thatched inn are divided between the main inn and various outbuildings. Four poster beds and log fires add to the atmosphere. Restaurant or bar meal options.

ABINGER HAMMER *Surrey* 504 S 30.
London 35 – Brighton 40 – Dover 91 – Portsmouth 50 – Reading 33.

XX **Drakes on the Pond** (Morris), Dorking Rd, RH5 6SA, on A 25 *ℰ* (01306) 731174, 🕸 Fax (01306) 731174 – ⇆ 🍴 **P.** **ⓄⓄ** *VISA*
closed 2 weeks late August, 1 week Christmas, Saturday lunch, Sunday and Monday – **Rest** 23.50 (lunch) dinner and a la carte 41.00/51.00 ♀.
Spec. King scallops on potato rösti, orange and tarragon. Fillet of sea bass, caramelised shallot and tomato Tatin. Almond treacle tart, salted caramel ice cream.
* Husband and wife team run a serious operation, but in a cheery, personable style. Cottagey interior; bold, confident flavours to the fore in seasonal menus with Gallic accent.

ACASTER MALBIS *N. Yorks.* 502 Q 22 – *see York.*

ACTON BURNELL *Shrops.* 503 L 26 – *see Shrewsbury.*

ACTON GREEN *Worcs.* 503 504 M 27 – *see Great Malvern.*

ADDINGHAM *W. Yorks.* **502** O 22 *Great Britain G.* – *pop. 3 215.*
Env. : *Bolton Priory***AC**, N : *3.5 m. on B 6160.*
London 225 – Bradford 16 – Ilkley 4.

🍴 **The Fleece,** 154 Main St, LS29 0LY, ℰ (01943) 830491, *chris@monkmansbistro.fsbusiness.co.uk* – 🅿. **🆆🅾 VISA**
Rest a la carte 15.00/25.00 ☼.
 ◆ Personally run pub on village main street. Open fires, solid stone floor, rustic walls filled with country prints. Wide ranging menu with good use of seasonal ingredients.

ALBRIGHTON *Shrops.* **502 503** L 25 – *see Shrewsbury.*

ALCESTER *Warks.* **503 504** O 27 – *pop. 7 068.*
London 104 – Birmingham 20 – Cheltenham 27 – Stratford-upon-Avon 8.

🏨 **Kings Court,** Kings Coughton, B49 5QQ, North : 1 ½ m. on A 435 ℰ (01789) 763111, *info@kingscourthotel.co.uk*, Fax (01789) 400242, 🐾 – 🕭 🅿 – 🔬 130. **🆆🅾 AE VISA**
closed 24-30 December – **Rest** 13.00 (lunch) and a la carte 17.45/25.70 ☼ – **41 rm** ☞ ✚42.00/73.00 – ✚✚76.00/90.00.
 ◆ Refurbished hotel popular for weddings and conferences. Some bedrooms in original Tudor part of building retain oak beams lending them a certain rustic charm. Welcoming dining room with courtyard garden; log fire in bar.

ALDEBURGH *Suffolk* **504** Y 27 – *pop. 2 654.*
🏌 *Thorpeness Golf Hotel, Thorpeness* ℰ *(01728) 452176.*
🛈 *152 High St* ℰ *(01728) 453637, atic@suffolkcoastal.gov.uk.*
London 97 – Ipswich 24 – Norwich 41.

🏰 **Wentworth,** Wentworth Rd, IP15 5BD, ℰ (01728) 452312, *stay@wentworth-aldeburgh.co.uk*, Fax (01728) 454343, ≤, 🍴, 🐾 – 🔆 🅿. **🆆🅾 AE ⓞ VISA**
Rest 21.50 ☼ – **35 rm** ☞ ✚75.00/85.00 – ✚✚93.00/100.00.
 ◆ Carefully furnished, traditional seaside hotel; coast view bedrooms are equipped with binoculars and all have a copy of "Orlando the Marmalade Cat", a story set in the area. Formal dining room offers mix of brasserie and classic dishes.

🏨 **Brudenell,** The Parade, IP15 5BU, ℰ (01728) 452071, *info@brudenellhotel.co.uk*, Fax (01728) 454082, ≤, 🍴 – 📶 🔆 📺 🕭 🅿. **🆆🅾 AE ⓞ VISA**
Rest 26.50 (dinner) and a la carte 17.40/45.45 ☼ – **41 rm** ☞ ✚68.00/102.00 – ✚✚103.00/144.00, 1 suite.
 ◆ Seaside hotel facing pebble beach and sea. Contemporary décor in pastel shades. Good rooms with modern amenities; most with view. Bright and modern dining room with terrace. Light informal menus offering modern dishes and British classics, using local produce.

🍴 **The Lighthouse,** 77 High St, IP15 5AU, ℰ (01728) 453377, *sarafox@diron.co.uk*, Fax (01728) 4543831, 🍴 – 🔆 🍽. **🆆🅾 AE VISA**
closed 3-11 January and 1 week November – **Rest** (booking essential) a la carte 17.45/32.50 ☼.
 ◆ Busy, unpretentious bistro boasts a wealth of Suffolk produce from local meats to Aldeburgh cod and potted shrimps. Good choice of wines; amiable service.

🍴 **152,** 152 High St, IP15 5AX, ℰ (01728) 454594, *info@152aldeburgh.co.uk*, Fax (01728) 454618, 🍴 – **🆆🅾 AE VISA**
Rest 18.85 and dinner a la carte 28.00 approx ☼.
 ◆ Choose between the bright, informal restaurant or the courtyard terrace on summer days to enjoy the keenly priced menu that features a wide variety of local produce.

🍴 **Regatta,** 171-173 High St, IP15 5AN, ℰ (01728) 452011, Fax (01728) 453324 – 🍽. **🆆🅾 AE VISA**
– **Rest** - Seafood specialities - a la carte 15.50/26.50 **s.**
 ◆ Maritime murals on the walls and cheerful décor make this fish-inspired eatery a good catch. Local seafood's a speciality: it's good quality and prepared in a sure-footed way.

at Friston *Northwest : 4 m. by A 1094 on B 1121* – ✉ *Aldeburgh.*

🏠 **The Old School** *without rest.*, IP17 1NP, ℰ (01728) 688173, *fristonoldschool@btinternet.com*, 🐾 – 🔆 📺 🅿. 🛇
3 rm ☞ ✚50.00 – ✚✚60.00.
 ◆ Redbrick former school house in pleasant garden. Good breakfast served family style in spacious room. Comfortable modern rooms with good amenities in the house or annexe.

ALDERLEY EDGE Ches. 502 503 504 N 24 – pop. 5 280.

🏌 Wilmslow, Great Warford, Mobberley ℰ (01565) 872148.

London 187 – Chester 34 – Manchester 14 – Stoke-on-Trent 25.

🏨 **Alderley Edge,** Macclesfield Rd, SK9 7BJ, ℰ (01625) 583033, sales@alderleyedgehotel.com, Fax (01625) 586343, ☞ – ▐ **P.** – 🏛 90. 🆗 🆎 ⑩ 𝘝𝘐𝘚𝘈. ⊛
Rest – (see **The Alderley** below) – ⌖ 12.50 – **51 rm** ✦125.00 – ✦✦140.00, 1 suite.
♦ A substantial late Victorian house with an easy-going style. Relaxing lounges furnished with cushion-clad easy chairs. Well-furnished, comfortable bedrooms, some with views.

XXX **The Alderley** (at Alderley Edge H.), Macclesfield Rd, SK9 7BJ, ℰ (01625) 583033, sales@alderleyedgehotel.com, Fax (01625) 586343, ☞ – ⊱ ▤ **P.** 🆗 🆎 ⑩ 𝘝𝘐𝘚𝘈
Rest 17.95 (lunch) and a la carte 25.95/31.95 ⌖.
♦ Conservatory dining room; comfortably spaced tables. The cuisine, served by dinner-suited staff, is modern British. Particularly proud of 500 wine list and 100 Champagnes.

X **The Alderley Bar & Grill,** 50 London Rd, SK9 7DZ, ℰ (01625) 599999, Fax (01625) 599913, ☞ – ▤. 🆗 🆎 𝘝𝘐𝘚𝘈
Rest a la carte 17.95/29.95 ⌖.
♦ High street restaurant with wood-decked pavement terrace. Stylish interior on two floors with old slapstick movies projected onto walls. Modern menus, world-wide influences.

X **The Wizard,** Macclesfield Rd, SK10 4UB, Southeast : 1¼ m. on B 5087 ℰ (01625) 584000, Fax (01625) 585105, ☞, ☞ – ⊱ **P.** 𝘝𝘐𝘚𝘈. ⊛
Rest (closed Sunday dinner and Monday) a la carte 20.00/40.00 ⌖.
♦ Located in a National Trust area, this 200-year old pub restaurant serves up-to-date dishes at reasonable prices. Sticky puddings of chocolate, toffee or caramel feature.

ALDERNEY C.I. 503 Q 33 and 517 ⑨ – see Channel Islands.

ALDFIELD N. Yorks. – see Ripon.

ALDFORD Ches. 502 L 24.
London 189 – Chester 6 – Liverpool 25.

🍴 **The Grosvenor Arms,** Chester Rd, CH3 6HJ, ℰ (01244) 620228, grosvenorarms@brunningandprice.co.uk, Fax (01244) 620247, ☞, ☞ – **P.** 🆗 🆎 𝘝𝘐𝘚𝘈
closed dinner 25-26 December and 1 January – Rest a la carte 14.40/29.45 ⌖.
♦ Large, red-brick 19C pub in rural village with sprawling summer terrace and conservatory. Equally spacious, bustling interior. Daily changing menus offer modern/rustic dishes.

ALDRIDGE W. Mids. 502 503 504 O 26 – pop. 15 659 – ✉ Walsall.
London 130 – Birmingham 12 – Derby 32 – Leicester 40 – Stoke-on-Trent 38.

Plan : see Birmingham p. 5

🏨 **Fairlawns,** 178 Little Aston Rd, WS9 0NU, East : 1 m. on A 454 ℰ (01922) 455122, welcome@fairlawns.co.uk, Fax (01922) 743210, 🛁, ≦s, 🔲, ☞, ※ – ⊱, ▤ rest, 🍷 🐧 **P.** – 🏛 60. 🆗 🆎 ⑩ 𝘝𝘐𝘚𝘈
CT n
restricted opening 24 December- 2 January – Rest (closed Saturday lunch and Bank Holidays) 22.50/32.50 ⌖ – **44 rm** ⌖ ✦79.50/165.00 – ✦✦89.50/180.00, 6 suites.
♦ Privately owned hotel with well-equipped leisure facility. A choice range of rooms from budget to superior, all comfy and spacious, some with good views over open countryside. Restaurant gains from its rural ambience.

ALFRISTON E. Sussex 504 U 31 – pop. 1 721 – ✉ Polegate.
London 66 – Eastbourne 9 – Lewes 10 – Newhaven 8.

🏨 **Star Inn,** High St, BN26 5TA, ℰ (01323) 870495, bookings@star-inn-alfriston.com, Fax (01323) 870922 - ⊱ **P.** – 🏛 30. 🆗 🆎 𝘝𝘐𝘚𝘈
Rest (bar lunch Monday-Saturday)/dinner 26.00 ⌖ – **37 rm** ⌖ ✦44.00/89.00 – ✦✦88.00/138.00.
♦ 14C coaching inn with original half-timbered façade where smugglers once met. Décor includes flagstone floor and beamed ceilings; bar serves real ale. Well-kept bedrooms. Atmospheric Tudor style restaurant.

🍴 **The George Inn** with rm, High St, BN26 5SY, ℰ (01323) 870319, info@thegeorge-alfriston.com, ☞, ☞ – ⊱ rm, ▤ rm. 🆗 𝘝𝘐𝘚𝘈
closed 25-26 December – Rest a la carte 19.00/27.00 ⌖ – **6 rm** ⌖ ✦50.00/60.00 – ✦✦100.00/120.00.
♦ Revered 15C timbered pub with dried hops, open fire, original floor boards. Popular with walkers. Local suppliers provide backbone to eclectic menus. Carefully restored rooms.

ALNE N. Yorks. 502 Q 21 – see Easingwold.

ALNWICK Northd. 501 502 O 17 Great Britain G. – pop. 7 767.

See : Town ★ – Castle★★ AC.
Exc. : Dunstanburgh Castle★ AC, NE : 8 m. by B 1340 and Dunstan rd (last 2½ m. on foot).
🏐 Swansfield Park ℰ (01665) 602632.
🛈 2 The Shambles ℰ (01665) 510665, alnwicktic@alnwick.gov.uk.
London 320 – Edinburgh 86 – Newcastle upon Tyne 34.

⌂ **Aln House** without rest., South Rd, NE66 2NZ, Southeast : ¾ m. by B 6346 on Newcastle
rd ℰ (01665) 602265, enquiries@alnhouse.co.uk, 🚗 – ⬥✕ 🅿. 🐾 VISA. ✺
6 rm 🖭 ✚30.00/60.00 – ✚✚60.00/70.00.
 ◆ Semi detached Edwardian house with mature front and rear gardens, an easy walk from
castle. Homely lounge enhanced by personal touches. Individually appointed rooms.

⌂ **Charlton House** without rest., 2 Aydon Gdns, South Rd, NE66 2NT, Southeast : ½ m. on
B 6346 ℰ (01665) 605185 – ⬥✕ 🅿. ✺
closed 10 November - 20 February – **5 rm** 🖭 ✚30.00 – ✚✚60.00.
 ◆ Victorian terraced house, the first to be lit by hydro-electricity. Breakfast in colourful
front room where local produce is proudly served. Bright and breezy bedrooms.

at North Charlton North : 6¾ m. by A 1 – ✉ Alnwick.

⌂ **North Charlton Farm** 🐾 without rest., NE67 5HP, ℰ (01665) 579443, stay@north
charltonfarm.co.uk, Fax (01665) 579407, ≤, 🚗, 🐴 – ⬥✕ 🅿. ✺
April-October – **3 rm** 🖭 ✚40.00/45.00 – ✚✚60.00/70.00.
 ◆ Attractive house on working farm with agricultural museum. Offers traditional accommodation. Each bedroom is individually decorated and has countryside views.

at Newton on the Moor South : 5½ m. by A 1 – ✉ Alnwick.

🍴 **The Cook and Barker Inn** with rm, NE65 9JY, ℰ (01665) 575234, Fax (01665) 575234,
🍴, ♬ – ⬥✕ 🅿. 🐾 🅐🅔 VISA. ✺
Rest 25.00 (dinner) and a la carte 25.00/32.00 ✿ – **19 rm** 🖭 ✚47.00 – ✚✚70.00/75.00.
 ◆ Attractive stone-faced inn with traditional décor and linen-clad dining room.
Extensive menu - classic pub food and more adventurous dishes. Smart modern en suite
bedrooms.

Your opinions are important to us:
please write and let us know about your discoveries and experiences –
good and bad!

ALREWAS Staffs. 502 503 504 O 25.
London 128.5 – Burton-upon-Trent 10 – Derby 20.

🍴 **The Old Boat,** Kings Bromley Rd, DE13 7DB, ℰ (01283) 791468, mikegething@hot
mail.com, 🍴, 🚗 – ⬥✕ 🅿. VISA. ✺
Rest a la carte 20.00/30.00 ✿.
 ◆ Tucked away in corner of village, with regular canal boat clientele. An informal
pub/restaurant, it boasts a strong range of dishes from bangers and mash to modern
creations.

ALSTON Cumbria 501 502 M 19 – pop. 2 218.
🏐 Alston Moor, The Hermitage ℰ (01434) 381675.
🛈 The Alstonmorry Information Centre, Town Hall ℰ (01434) 382244.
London 309 – Carlisle 28 – Newcastle upon Tyne 45.

🏠 **Lovelady Shield Country House** 🐾, Nenthead Rd, CA9 3LF, East : 2½ m. on A 689
ℰ (01434) 381203, enquiries@lovelady.co.uk, Fax (01434) 381515, ≤, 🚗 – ⬥✕ 🅿. 🐾 🅐🅔
VISA
weekends only in January – Rest (closed Sunday lunch) (booking essential for non-residents) (dinner only and Sunday lunch)) 38.50 ✿ – **12 rm** (dinner included) 🖭 ✚110.00 –
✚✚310.00.
 ◆ Stately, personally run 18C Georgian house in very quiet position by River Nent. Open
fires and restful atmosphere throughout. Bedrooms boast a quality, up-to-date feel.
Peaceful dining room with modern English cooking.

ALTON Hants. 504 R 30 – pop. 16 005.

  🏌 Old Odiham Rd 𝒫 (01420) 82042.

  🛈 7 Cross and Pillory Lane 𝒫 (01420) 88448, altoninfo@btconnect.com.

  London 53 – Reading 24 – Southampton 29 – Winchester 18.

🏨 **Alton Grange,** London Rd, GU34 4EG, Northeast : 1 m. on A 3004 𝒫 (01420) 86565, info@altongrange.co.uk, Fax (01420) 541346, ☞ – ⇔ ✆ 🄿 – 🏛 100. ◍ 🄰🄴 ◍ 𝘝𝘐𝘚𝘈 ⋘
closed 24-31 December – **Truffles :** Rest 28.50 ♀ – 30 rm ☲ ✿90.00/100.00 –
✿✿110.00/160.00.
  • Hotel set in well-kept, oriental inspired gardens. The bar serves bistro-style snacks. Bed-rooms are individually decorated, particularly junior suites and Saxon room. Dining room boasts myriad of Tiffany lamps and fusion cuisine.

ALTRINCHAM Gtr Manchester 502 503 504 N 23 – pop. 40 695.

  🏌 Altrincham Municipal, Stockport Rd, Timperley 𝒫 (0161) 928 0761 – 🏌 Dunham Forest, Oldfield Lane 𝒫 (0161) 928 2605 – 🏌 Ringway, Hale Mount, Hale Barns 𝒫 (0161) 980 2630.

  🛈 20 Stamford New Rd 𝒫 (0161) 912 5931, tourist.information@trafford.gov.uk.

  London 191 – Chester 30 – Liverpool 30 – Manchester 8.

🍴🍴🍴 **Juniper** (Kitching), 21 The Downs, WA14 2QD, 𝒫 (0161) 929 4008, reservations@juniper-restaurant.co.uk, Fax (0161) 929 4009 – ⇔ ▤. ◍ 🄰🄴 𝘝𝘐𝘚𝘈
❄ restricted opening Christmas and closed 1 week February, 2 weeks August, Sunday, Mon-day and lunch Tuesday-Thursday. – Rest (Tuesday dinner set menu only) 20.00/60.00 and lunch a la carte 25.00/38.00.
Spec. Carrot and cardamom soup, Granny Smith pureé. Baked turbot, beetroot and brown rice. Ginger cake soufflé, sea salt ice cream.
  • Simple appearance; pre-prandials in basement bar/lounge. Richly opulent first-floor res-taurant. Highly innovative alchemy of ingredients used to create very original dishes.

🍴🍴 **Dilli,** 60 Stamford New Rd, WA14 1EE, 𝒫 (0161) 929 7484, info@dilli.co.uk, Fax (0161) 929 1213 – ⇔ ✿ 40. ◍ 🄰🄴 𝘝𝘐𝘚𝘈
closed 25 December – Rest - Indian - 14.95 (lunch) a la carte 18.70/33.40.
  • Intriguing interior: the décor is a mix of Indian wooden fretwork and minimalism. Totally authentic Indian dishes use quality ingredients. Lunches are particularly good value.

at Little Bollington Southwest : 3¼ m. on A 56 – ⊠ Altrincham.

🏠 **Ash Farm** ☜, Park Lane, WA14 4TJ, 𝒫 (0161) 929 9290, jan@ashfarm97.fsnet.co.uk, Fax (0161) 928 5002, ☞ – ⇔ 🄿. ◍ 🄰🄴 𝘝𝘐𝘚𝘈 ⋘
closed 20 December - 18 January – Rest 20.00 4 rm ✿49.00/57.00 – ✿✿72.00/79.00.
  • Attractive, creeper-clad 18C former farmhouse in quiet location, a short walk from Dunham Deer Park. Pretty stone-flagged breakfast room; cosy, individually styled bed-rooms. Home-cooked dinners proudly served.

If breakfast is included the ☲ symbol appears after the number of rooms.

ALVELEY Shrops. – see Bridgnorth.

ALVESTON Warks. – see Stratford-upon-Avon.

ALWALTON Cambs. 502 504 T 26 – see Peterborough.

ALWESTON Dorset 503 504 M 31 – see Sherborne.

AMBERLEY W. Sussex 504 S 31 Great Britain G. – pop. 525 – ⊠ Arundel.

  Env. : Bignor Roman Villa (mosaics★) AC, NW : 3½ m. by B 2139 via Bury.

  London 56 – Brighton 24 – Portsmouth 31.

🏨 **Amberley Castle** ☜, BN18 9LT, Southwest : ½ m. on B 2139 𝒫 (01798) 831992, info@amberleycastle.co.uk, Fax (01798) 831998, ☞, 🏊, ⋇ – ⇔ 🄿 – 🏛 40. ◍ 🄰🄴 ◍ 𝘝𝘐𝘚𝘈 ⋘
Queen's Room : Rest (booking essential) 30.00/55.00 – ☲ 16.50 – 13 rm ✿155.00/175.00 – ✿✿310.00/345.00, 6 suites.
  • Historic yet intimate, a 14C castle in the South Downs - majestic battlements and lux-urious rooms with jacuzzis. White peacocks and black swans inhabit the serene gardens. Barrel-vaulted dining room with graceful lancet windows and mural.

AMBLESIDE *Cumbria 502* L 20 *Great Britain G.* – pop. 3 064.

Env. : Lake Windermere★★ – Dove Cottage, Grasmere★ *AC* AY A – Brockhole National Park
Centre★ *AC*, SE : 3 m. by A 591 AZ.

Exc. : Wrynose Pass★★, W : 7½ m. by A 593 AY – Hard Knott Pass★★, W : 10 m. by A 593
AY.

🖪 Central Buildings, Market Cross ℰ (015394) 32582 AZ, amblesidetic@southlake
land.gov.uk – Main Car Park, Waterhead ℰ (015394) 32729 (summer only) BY.

London 278 – Carlisle 47 – Kendal 14.

Plan on next page

🏠 **The Samling** ⤬, Ambleside Rd, LA23 1LR, South : 1½ m. on A 591 ℰ (015394) 31922,
info@thesamling.com, Fax (015394) 30400, ≤ Lake Windermere and mountains, ⌖, ⌖ –
⤬ ⅌. ⬛ ⯑ ⬤ **VISA**. ⬞
Rest (booking essential for non-residents) 38.00/48.00 s. ⯑ – **9 rm** ⥿ ⭑195.00 –
⭑⭑485.00, 2 suites.
♦ Late 18C Lakeland house with superb views of Lake Windermere and surrounding moun-
tains. Stylishly relaxing and informal environment. Elegant, individually decorated rooms.
Imaginative, modern cuisine in smart dining room.

🏠 **The Waterhead,** Lake Rd, LA22 0ER, ℰ (015394) 32566, waterhead@elhmail.co.uk,
Fax (015394) 31255, ≤, ⌖, ⌖ – ⤬ ⅌ ⅌. – ⯑ 40. ⬛ ⯑ ⬤ **VISA**   BY x
The Bay : Rest (light lunch Monday-Saturday)/dinner a la carte 23.95/30.55 s. ⯑ – **41 rm** ⥿
⭑95.00/120.00 – ⭑⭑230.00/250.00.
♦ Set close to Lake Windermere; modernised in 2004, resulting in a stylish, airy, open plan
feel. Bedrooms, in modish creams and browns, have flat screen TVs and DVDs. Restaurant
boasts original cooking, sleek décor and lovely terrace views to lake.

🏠 **Rothay Manor,** Rothay Bridge, LA22 0EH, South : ½ m. on A 593 ℰ (015394) 33605,
hotel@rothaymanor.co.uk, Fax (015394) 33607, ⌖ – ⤬ ⅌. ⬛ ⯑ ⬤ **VISA**. ⬞   BY r
closed 3 January - 26 February – **Rest** a la carte 12.00/18.50 – **16 rm** ⥿ ⭑85.00/135.00 –
⭑⭑135.00/180.00, 3 suites.
♦ Elegant Regency country house in landscaped gardens. Family run with long traditions:
many regulars. Bedrooms furnished in modern tones. Free use of nearby leisure club.
Gardens can be admired from dining room windows.

🏠 **Brathay Lodge** without rest., Rothay Rd, LA22 0EE, ℰ (01539) 432000, brathay@glob
alnet.co.uk – ⤬ ⅌ ⅌. ⬛ **VISA**   AZ e
21 rm ⭑50.00/84.00 – ⭑⭑60.00/140.00.
♦ Stylish accommodation in the heart of Ambleside. Unfussy, bright and warm décor.
Continental breakfast only. All bedrooms have spa baths and some boast four posters.

🏠 **Lakes Lodge** without rest., Lake Rd, LA22 0DB, ℰ (015394) 33240, u@lakeslodge.co.uk,
Fax (015394) 33240 – ⤬ ⅌. ⬛ ⯑ **VISA**   AZ s
12 rm ⭑49.00/79.00 – ⭑⭑79.00/99.00.
♦ Characterful house with traditional exterior but modern facilities and relaxed atmosphere. Good size bedrooms with contemporary style. Buffet style Continental breakfast.

🏠 **Elder Grove** without rest., Lake Rd, LA22 0DB, ℰ (015394) 32504, info@elder
grove.co.uk, Fax (015394) 32251 – ⤬ ⅌ ⅌. ⬛ **VISA**   AZ a
restricted opening December and January – **10 rm** ⥿ ⭑28.00/40.00 – ⭑⭑56.00/84.00.
♦ Homely establishment with warm, family run appeal. Distinctive cosy bar has firemen's
memorabilia. Traditionally furnished throughout, including bedrooms. Cumbrian breakfasts.

🏠 **Red Bank** without rest., Wansfell Rd, LA22 0EG, ℰ (015394) 34637, info@redbank.co.uk,
⌖ – ⤬ ⅌. **VISA**. ⬞   AZ r
3 rm ⥿ ⭑60.00/80.00 – ⭑⭑86.00.
♦ Edwardian house, well sited a minute's walk from town. Cosy central lounge and pleasant breakfast room overlooking garden. Attractively furnished rooms with wrought iron
beds.

🏠 **Riverside** ⤬ without rest., Under Loughrigg, LA22 9LJ, ℰ (015394) 32395, info@river
side-ambleside.co.uk, Fax (015394) 32240, ⌖ – ⅌. ⬤ **VISA**. ⬞   BY s
closed Christmas-New Year – **6 rm** ⥿ ⭑40.00/60.00 – ⭑⭑72.00/96.00.
♦ 19C country house with river Rothay on the doorstep and access to Loughrigg Fell.
Lovely rear fellside garden. Nicely decorated bedrooms commanding admirable views.

🍴🍴 **The Log House** with rm, Lake Rd, LA22 0DN, ℰ (015394) 31077, nicola@loghouse.co.uk,
⌖ – ⤬ ⅌. ⬤ **VISA**   BY v
closed Monday and Tuesday-Thursday lunch in winter – **Rest** a la carte 22.70/31.40 ⯑ – **3 rm**
⥿ ⭑65.00 – ⭑⭑75.00.
♦ Artist Alfred Heaton Cooper imported this house from Norway for use as a studio. It's
now a polished restaurant serving tasty cooking with imaginative touches. Comfy bedrooms.

ENGLAND

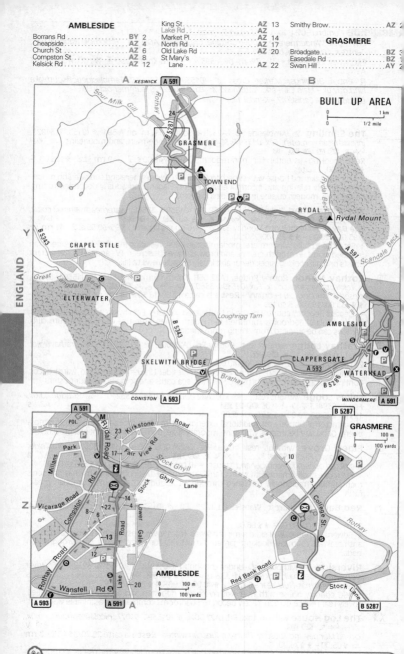

Look out for red symbols, indicating particularly pleasant establishments.

92

X **Glass House,** Rydal Rd, LA22 9AN, ℰ (015394) 32137, *info@theglasshouserestaur
ant.co.uk, Fax (015394) 33384,* 🍴 – 🗱 🐼 *VISA*
AZ **v**
closed 24-26 December and Tuesday – **Rest** (booking essential) a la carte 20.85/30.75 ♀.
• Chic, split-level, converted 15C mill with water wheel next to glass making studio; maker
of dining room light fittings. Sophisticated, well-executed dishes; classy snacks.

🍴 **Drunken Duck Inn** with rm, Barngates, LA22 0NG, Southwest : 3 m. by A 593 and B
5286 on Tarn Hows rd ℰ (015394) 36347, *info@drunkenduckinn.co.uk, Fax (015394) 36781,*
≼, 🌿, ♨ – 🗱 rest, 🅿, 🐼 🖭 *VISA*
closed 25 December – **Rest** – **Rest** a la carte 26.00/32.00 ♀ – **16 rm** ⇌ ✸165.70 – ✸✸220.00.
• Named after a 19C landlady who found her ducks drunk, this part 16C inn boasts an
on-site brewery, cosy bar with oak settles and restaurant serving modern fare. Smart
rooms.

at Skelwith Bridge West : 2½ m. on A 593 – ⊠ Ambleside.

🏨 **Skelwith Bridge,** LA22 9NJ, ℰ (015394) 32115, *skelwithbr@aol.com,
Fax (015394) 34254* – 🗱 🐼 *VISA*
AY **v**
The Bridge : **Rest** (dinner only and Sunday lunch)/dinner 28.50 **s.** ♀ – **28 rm** ⇌
✸45.00/90.00 – ✸✸76.00/116.00.
• 17C Lakeland inn at entrance to the stunningly picturesque Langdale Valley. Traditional,
simple bedrooms; panelled, clubby bar; busy Badgers Bar for walkers. Popular restaurant
has large windows overlooking fells.

at Elterwater West : 4½ m. by A 593 off B 5343 – ⊠ Ambleside.

🏨 **Langdale H. & Country Club,** Great Langdale, LA22 9JD, Northwest : ½ m. on B 5343
ℰ (015394) 37302, Reservations (Freephone) 0500 051197, *info@langdale.co.uk,
Fax (015394) 37130,* ☎, 🎣, ⥓, 🎳, ♨, ✍, squash – 🗱 rest, ✈ 🅿 – 🔄 60. 🐼 🖭 *VISA*
🍴
AY **c**
Purdeys : **Rest** (dinner only) 25.00 and a la carte 24.85/33.40 ♀ – **The Terrace :** **Rest** a la
carte 14.75/25.15 – **57 rm** ⇌ ✸90.00/110.00 – ✸✸130.00/170.00.
• Family friendly, part-timeshare estate hidden in a forest, on site of former gunpowder
works. Lots of ponds and streams; smart leisure centre. Hotel and lodge rooms available.
Purdeys with local stone and water features. Informal Terrace boasts wi-fi access.

at Little Langdale West : 5 m. by A 593 – ⊠ Langdale.

🏠 **Three Shires Inn** 🦢, LA22 9NZ, ℰ (015394) 37215, *enquiry@threeshiresinn.co.uk,
Fax (015394) 37127,* ≼, 🌿 – 🗱 🅿, 🐼 *VISA*. 🍴
AY **c**
restricted opening December-January – **Rest** (bar lunch)/dinner a la carte 15.75/25.95 –
10 rm ⇌ ✸60.00/80.00 – ✸✸86.00/100.00.
• Traditional slate inn, built 1872; named after meeting point of old counties of Cumber-
land, Westmorland, Lancashire. Neatly turned rooms in quiet colours; some have views.
Dining room boasts hearty, rustic atmosphere.

AMERSHAM (Old Town) Bucks. 504 S 29 – pop. 21 470.

🏌 Little Chalfont, Lodge Lane ℰ (01494) 764877.
London 29 – Aylesbury 16 – Oxford 33.

XX **Artichoke,** 9 Market Sq., HP7 0DF, ℰ (01494) 726611, *info@theartichokerestaur
ant.co.uk* – 🗱 🐼 *VISA*
closed 2 weeks late summer, 1 week spring, 1 week Christmas, Sunday and Monday – **Rest**
22.50/36.00 and lunch a la carte 32.50/34.50 ♀.
• Charmingly converted from its 16C origins but still retaining much period detail: thick
walls, exposed beams. Distinctive modern cooking using interesting combinations.

X **Gilbey's,** 1 Market Sq, HP7 0DF, ℰ (01494) 727242, *oldamersham@gilbeygroup.com,
Fax (01494) 431243,* 🍴 – 🐼 🖭 ⓞ *VISA*
closed 24-26 December and 1 January – **Rest** (booking essential) a la carte 25.40/29.40 ♀.
• Atmospheric exposed brick dining room. The bold menu includes inventive accompani-
ments such as bacon and cabbage hash, black bean salsa and grain mustard creamed
potatoes.

AMESBURY Wilts. 503 504 O 30 The West Country G. – pop. 8 312.

Env. : Stonehenge★★★ AC, W : 2 m. by A 303.
Exc. : Wilton Village★ (Wilton House★★ AC, Wilton Carpet Factory★ AC), SW : 13 m. by A
303, B 3083 and A 36.
🛈 Amesbury Library, Smithfield St ℰ (01980) 622833, amesburytic@salisbury.gov.uk.
London 87 – Bristol 52 – Southampton 32 – Taunton 66.

🏠 **Mandalay** without rest., 15 Stonehenge Rd, SP4 7BA, via Church St ℰ (01980) 623733,
Fax (01980) 626642, 🌿 – 🗱 🅿, 🐼 🖭 ⓞ *VISA*. 🍴
5 rm ⇌ ✸40.00/55.00 – ✸✸65.00/75.00.
• Only two minutes' drive from Stonehenge, this brick-built house boasts a bygone style
and pleasant garden. Varied breakfasts. Individual rooms, named after famous authors.

AMPLEFORTH N. Yorks. 502 Q 21 – see Helmsley.

ANSTY W. Mids. – see Coventry.

APPLEBY-IN-WESTMORLAND Cumbria 502 M 20 – pop. 2 570 (inc. Bongate).
  ⓕ Appleby, Brackenber Moor ℘ (017683) 51432.
  ⓘ Moot Hall, Boroughgate ℘ (017683) 51177, tic@applebytown.org.uk.
  London 285 – Carlisle 33 – Kendal 24 – Middlesbrough 58.

  🏛 **Appleby Manor Country House** ⑤, Roman Rd, CA16 6JB, East : 1 m. by B 6542
  and Station Rd ℘ (017683) 51571, reception@applebymanor.co.uk, Fax (017683) 52888, ≤,
  ⊑s, 🐾 – ⇆ 🅿 – 🔏 40. 🐵 🖭 ⑩ 𝘝𝘐𝘚𝘈. ✆
  closed 24-26 December – **Rest** a la carte 24.40/34.00 s. ♀ – 30 rm ⊑ ✝82.00/97.00 –
  ✝✝130.00/140.00.
  ◆ Wooded grounds and good views of Appleby Castle at this elevated 19C pink sandstone
  country manor. Main house bedrooms have most character; coach house annex welcomes
  dogs. Dining options: oak ceilinged restaurant or lighter, chandelier equipped room.

  🏛 **Tufton Arms**, Market Sq, CA16 6XA, ℘ (017683) 51593, info@tuftonarmshotel.co.uk,
  Fax (017683) 52761, 🐾 – 🅿 – 🔏 100. 🐵 🖭 ⑩ 𝘝𝘐𝘚𝘈
  closed 25-26 December – **Rest** 28.50 (dinner) and a la carte 18.20/28.50 – 22 rm ⊑
  ✝67.00/77.00 – ✝✝110.00/165.00.
  ◆ 19C coaching inn; quaint, atmospheric interiors. Homely, country rooms and bar
  adorned with sepia photographs. Inn runs a sporting agency; fly fishing can be arranged.
  Charming conservatory restaurant overlooking cobbled mews courtyard.

at Maulds Meaburn Southwest: 5¾ m. by B 6260 – ✉ Appleby-in-Westmorland.

  ⌂ **Crake Trees Manor** ⑤, CA10 3JG, South : ½ m. on Crosby Ravensworth rd ℘ (01931)
  715205, ruth@craketreesmanor.co.uk, ≤ The Pennine Hills, 🐾, ⚘ – ⇆ 🅿 🐵 🖭 𝘝𝘐𝘚𝘈
  closed January and February – **Rest** (by arrangement) (communal dining) 25.00 – 5 rm ⊑
  ✝50.00 – ✝✝90.00/100.00.
  ◆ Superbly located modern barn conversion built of stone, slate, ash and oak. Splendid
  Pennine views; guests encouraged to walk the paths. Comfy public areas and tasteful
  rooms. Dining room where good home cooking is a mainstay.

APPLEDORE Devon 503 H 30 The West Country G. – pop. 2 114.
  See : Town★.
  London 228 – Barnstaple 12 – Exeter 46 – Plymouth 61 – Taunton 63.

  ⌂ **West Farm** without rest., Irsha St, EX39 1RY, West : ¼ m. ℘ (01237) 425269, west
  farm@appledore-devon.co.uk, ⚘ – ⇆. ✆
  closed Christmas and New Year – 3 rm ⊑ ✝60.00 – ✝✝94.00.
  ◆ 17C house, boasting particularly pleasant garden at the back, in a charming little coastal
  village. Delightfully appointed sitting room. Bedrooms feel comfortable and homely.

APPLETREEWICK N. Yorks. 502 O 21.
  London 236 – Harrogate 25 – Skipton 11.

  ⌂ **Knowles Lodge** ⑤ without rest., BD23 6DQ, South : 1 m. on Bolton Abbey rd
  ℘ (01756) 720228, pam@knowleslodge.com, Fax (01756) 720381, 🐾, ⚘, ⚘ – ⇆ 🅿. 🐵
  𝘝𝘐𝘚𝘈
  3 rm ⊑ ✝50.00 – ✝✝80.00.
  ◆ Unusual Canadian ranch-house style guesthouse, clad in timber and sited in quiet dales
  location. Large sitting room with fine outlook. Cosy bedrooms have garden views.

ARDENS GRAFTON Warks. – see Stratford-upon-Avon.

ARLINGHAM Glos. 503 504 M 28 – pop. 377 – ✉ Gloucester.
  London 120 – Birmingham 69 – Bristol 34 – Gloucester 16.

  ✕ **The Old Passage Inn** ⑤ with rm, Passage Rd, GL2 7JR, West : ¾ m ℘ (01452) 740547,
  oldpassageinn@ukonline.co.uk, Fax (01452) 741871, ≤, 🐾 – ⇆ 🅿. 🐵 🖭 𝘝𝘐𝘚𝘈. ✆
  closed 24-30 December – **Rest** - Seafood - (closed Sunday dinner and Monday) a la carte
  23.50/33.50 ♀ 🖐 – 3 rm ⊑ ✝55.00/60.00 – ✝✝95.00.
  ◆ Former inn with simple style and bright ambience, attractively set on banks of Severn.
  Friendly, relaxed dining. Seafood based menu. Modern, funky bedrooms in a vivid palette.

ARMSCOTE Warks. **504** P 27.

London 91 – Birmingham 36 – Oxford 38.

⌂ **Willow Corner** without rest., CV37 8DE, ℰ (01608) 682391, *trishandalan@willow corner.co.uk*, ☞ – ⇔ **P**. ⅍
closed Christmas-New Year – 3 rm ⌷ ✝50.00 – ✝✝70.00.
♦ Cosy 18C cottage at village periphery, personally run by dedicated owner. Thatched roof; snug interiors plus a vast inglenook. Well-kept rooms with host of thoughtful extras.

🍴 **The Fox & Goose Inn** with rm, Front St, CV37 8DD, ℰ (01608) 682293, *mail@foxandg oose.co.uk*, Fax (01608) 682292, ☞ – **P**. **⬤⬤** **VISA**
Rest a la carte 20.00/30.00 ⅄ – 4 rm ⌷ ✝50.00/70.00 – ✝✝90.00/120.00.
♦ Rustic inn with stone floor, wattle walls and warming log fires. Traditional country cooking in "olde worlde" setting with cask ales from bar. Eccentrically styled bedrooms.

ARUNDEL W. Sussex **504** S 31 Great Britain G. – pop. 3 297.

See : Castle★★ AC.
🛈 61 High St ℰ (01903) 882268, *tourism@arun.gov.uk*.
London 58 – Brighton 21 – Southampton 41 – Worthing 9.

at Burpham Northeast : 3 m. by A 27 – ✉ Arundel.

🏠 **Old Parsonage** ॐ without rest., BN18 9RJ, ℰ (01903) 882160, *info@oldparson age.co.uk*, Fax (01903) 884627, ≤, ☞ – ⇔ **P**. ⅍
closed Christmas-New Year – 10 rm ⌷ ✝40.00/65.00 – ✝✝110.00/120.00.
♦ Reputedly a hunting lodge for the Duke of Norfolk, this quiet hotel constitutes the ideal "stress remedy break". Calm, pastel coloured bedrooms overlook exquisite gardens.

🍴 **George and Dragon,** Main St, BN18 9RR, ℰ (01903) 883131, Fax (01903) 883341 – ⇔ **P**. **⬤⬤** **VISA**. ⅍
closed 25 December – Rest (closed Sunday dinner) a la carte 22.00/29.00.
♦ Pleasant, characterful pub in pretty village. Bar and more formal restaurant both serve robust British menus, prepared with care and attention, employing seasonal produce.

at Walberton West : 3 m. by A 27 off B 2132 – ✉ Arundel.

🏨 **Hilton Avisford Park,** Yapton Lane, BN18 0LS, on B 2132 ℰ (01243) 551215, *gen eral.manager@hilton.com*, Fax (01243) 552485, ≤, **I₆**, ≋, ⅊ heated, ☒, ⬛, ☞, ♘, ⅍, squash – ⇔ **⬤** & **P** – 🔏 500. **⬤⬤** **AE** **⬤** **VISA**. ⅍
closed 24-26 December – Rest (bar lunch Monday-Saturday)/dinner 25.95 s. ⅄ – ⌷ 15.95 – 134 rm ✝99.00/250.00 – ✝✝109.00/260.00, 5 suites.
♦ Former school and one-time home of Baronet Montagu, Nelson's admiral; retains a stately air with grand façade and 62-acre grounds. Generous drapes and furnishings in rooms. Dining room features honours board listing prefects of yesteryear.

ASCOT Windsor & Maidenhead **504** R 29 – pop. 17 509 (inc. Sunningdale).

🏌 Mill Ride, Ascot ℰ (01344) 886777.
London 36 – Reading 15.

🏨 **Berystede,** Bagshot Rd, Sunninghill, SL5 9JH, South : 1½ m. on A 330 ℰ (0870) 4008111, *general.berystede@macdonald-hotels.co.uk*, Fax (01344) 873061, ⅊ heated, ☞ – 🖗 ⇔, 🍽 rest, **P** – 🔏 120. **⬤⬤** **AE** **⬤** **VISA**. ⅍
Hyperion : Rest (closed Saturday lunch) 19.50/32.00 and dinner a la carte 32.00/42.50 ⅄ – 118 rm ⌷ ✝211.00/250.00 – ✝✝221.00/260.00, 7 suites.
♦ Popular with the sporting fraternity, this turreted, ivy clad hotel includes a bar styled on a gentleman's smoking room, a panelled library lounge and immaculate bedrooms. Restaurant overlooks the open air swimming pool.

🏨 **Royal Berkshire Ramada Plaza** ॐ, London Rd, Sunninghill, SL5 0PP, East : 2 m. on A 329 ℰ (01344) 623322, *sales.royalberkshire@ramadajarvis.co.uk*, Fax (01344) 874240, ☞, ≋, ☒, ☞, ♘, ⅍ – ⇔ **⬤** & **P** – 🔏 100. **⬤⬤** **AE** **⬤** **VISA**
Rest (closed Saturday lunch) a la carte 22.50/45.00 s. – ⌷ 15.50 – 60 rm ✝120.00/225.00 – ✝✝120.00/650.00, 3 suites.
♦ Former home to the Churchill family, this Queen Anne mansion welcomes with tasteful, elegant furnishings and lounge bar with private library. Light, spacious bedrooms. Sedate restaurant overlooks gardens: all-day menu.

XX **Ascot Oriental,** SL5 0PU, East : 2 ¼ m. on A 329 ℰ (01344) 621877, *info@ascotorien tal.com*, Fax (01344) 621885, ☞ – 🍽 **P** ✿ 20. **⬤⬤** **AE** **VISA**
closed 25-26 December – Rest - Chinese - 25.00/26.00 and a la carte 23.40/38.00 ⅄.
♦ Stylish modern restaurant with a vibrantly hued interior. Private dining in attractive conservatory. An interesting menu of Chinese dishes prepared with originality and verve.

at Sunninghill *South : 1½ m. by A 329 on B 3020 –* ✉ *Ascot.*

XX **Jade Fountain**, 38 High St, SL5 9NE, ℘ (01344) 627070, *jadefountain328@aol.com,* Fax (01344) 627070 – 🔳 🐼 🌐 💳 *VISA*
Rest - Chinese - 21.00/27.00 and a la carte 20.00/26.00.
♦ Chinese restaurant specialising in sizzling dishes from Szechuan and Beijing - Peking duck, spring rolls and noodles amongst them. Also some Thai specialities.

ASENBY *N. Yorks. – see Thirsk.*

ASH *Kent 504 X 30.*
London 70 – Canterbury 9.5 – Dover 15.5.

⌂ **Great Weddington**, CT3 2AR, Northeast : ½ m. by A 257 on Weddington rd ℘ (01304) 813407, *traveltale@aol.com,* Fax (01304) 812531, ☞, ⚘ – 🔌 **P**. 🐼 🌐 *VISA*. ⚘
closed Christmas and New Year – **Rest** (by arrangement) (communal dining) 30.00 – **3 rm**
⊐ ✦65.00/68.00 – ✦✦96.00/102.00.
♦ Charming Regency country house, ideally located for Canterbury and Dover. Well appointed drawing room and terrace. Thoughtfully furnished, carefully co-ordinated rooms. Communal dining room; owner an avid cook.

The ✿ award is the crème de la crème.
This is awarded to restaurants
which are really worth travelling miles for!

ENGLAND

ASHBOURNE *Derbs. 502 503 504 O 24 Great Britain G. – pop. 5 020.*
Env. : Dovedale★★ (Ilam Rock★) NW : 6 m. by A 515.
🅱 *13 Market Pl ℘ (01335) 343666, ashbourneinfo@derbyshiredales.gov.uk.*
London 146 – Birmingham 47 – Manchester 48 – Nottingham 33 – Sheffield 44.

🏨 **Callow Hall** ♨, Mappleton Rd, DE6 2AA, West : ¾ m. by Union St (off Market Pl)
℘ (01335) 300900, *reservations@callowhall.co.uk,* Fax (01335) 300512, ≤, ⚘, ☞, ♨ – ⚑ ⚙
P. 🐼 🌐 ① *VISA*
closed 25-26 December – **Rest** – (see *The Restaurant* below) – **17 rm** ⊐ ✦95.00/120.00 –
✦✦140.00/190.00, 1 suite.
♦ Owned originally by a corset manufacturer earning it the nickname of "Corset Castle", this Victorian country house overlooks the River Dove valley. Some rooms with views.

XX **The Restaurant** (at Callow Hall), Mappleton Rd, DE6 2AA, West : ¾ m. by Union St (off Market Pl) ℘ (01335) 300900, *Fax (01335) 300512 –* ⚑ **P**. 🐼 🌐 ① *VISA*
closed Sunday dinner to non-residents, and 25-26 December – **Rest** (dinner only and Sunday lunch)/dinner 42.00 and a la carte 32.50/39.25 ⚒.
♦ Proud of its culinary traditions which include homebaking, smoking and curing, crafts that have been passed down through the generations. Local game and range of fine wines.

XX **the dining room**, 33 St Johns St, DE6 1GP, ℘ (01335) 300666 – ⚑. 🐼 *VISA*
closed 26 December-9 January, 1 week March, 1 week September, Sunday and Monday –
Rest 22.00 (lunch) and a la carte 36.00/40.00.
♦ 17C building in central location. Huge display of orchids as part of contemporary décor. Wooden tables and wine display case. Wide ranging menu of modern dishes.

🍴 **Bramhall's** with rm, 6 Buxton Rd, DE6 1EX, ℘ (01335) 346158, *info@bramhalls.co.uk,*
☞, ☞ – ⚑. 🐼 *VISA*. ⚘
closed 25-26 December and 2 weeks from 1 January – **Rest** (closed Sunday dinner November-Easter) 13.95 (lunch) and a la carte 18.65/28.15 – **10 rm** ⊐ ✦30.00 – ✦✦75.00.
♦ An unassuming inn just off the Market Square with dining terrace and stepped garden. Modern style cooking with daily blackboard specials. Contemporary bedrooms.

at Marston Montgomery *Southeast : 7½ m. by A 515 –* ✉ *Ashbourne.*

🍴 **Bramhall's at The Crown Inn** with rm, Riggs Lane, DE6 2FF, ℘ (01889) 590541, *info@bramhalls.co.uk,* Fax (01889) 591576, ☞ – ⚑. 🐼 🌐 *VISA*. ⚘
closed 25 December and 1 January – **Rest** (closed Sunday dinner) 14.95 (lunch) and a la carte approx 30.00 ⚒ – **7 rm** ⊐ ✦50.00 – ✦✦65.00/75.00.
♦ Relaxed and welcoming pub with exposed beams and open fire. Daily blackboard menu of good simple dishes. Cosy but modern bedrooms.

ASHBURTON *Devon 503* I *32 The West Country G.* – *pop. 3 309.*
Env. : *Dartmoor National Park*★★.
London 220 – Exeter 20 – Plymouth 25.

🏛 **Holne Chase** ⌂, TQ13 7NS, West : 3 m. on Two Bridges rd ✆ (01364) 631471,
info@holne-chase.co.uk, Fax (01364) 631453, <, 🌭, 🐾, 🐕 – 🔆 🅿 ⓂⓄ 𝘝𝘐𝘚𝘈
Rest (light lunch Monday) 25.00/35.50 – **8 rm** 🖙 ✚130.00 – ✚✚215.00, **9 suites** 🖙
200.00/215.00.
◆ Former hunting lodge to Buckfast Abbey, with country house ambience, in 70 acres of
Dartmoor woodland. This is walking country - dogs welcome. Rooms in main house or
stables. Country style dining room utilising local produce.

✗ **Agaric** with rm, 30 and 36 North St, TQ13 7QD, ✆ (01364) 654478, *eat@agaricrestaur*
ant.co.uk, 🏤 – 🔆✗ ⓂⓄ 𝘝𝘐𝘚𝘈
closed last 2 weeks August, 2 weeks Christmas, Sunday-Tuesday and Saturday lunch – **Rest**
(booking essential) a la carte 23.85/36.90 – **5 rm** 🖙 ✚50.00/60.00 – ✚✚120.00.
◆ 200 year-old house, selling home-made jams, fudge and olives. Relaxed neighbourhood
restaurant using a blend of cooking styles. Very stylish, individually themed bedrooms.

ASHFORD *Kent 504* W *30.*
Channel Tunnel : *Eurostar information and reservations* ✆ (08705) 186186.
🚹 18 The Churchyard ✆ (01233) 629165, *tourism@ashford.gov.uk.*
London 56 – Canterbury 14 – Dover 24 – Hastings 30 – Maidstone 19.

🏰 **Eastwell Manor** ⌂, Eastwell Park, Boughton Lees, TN25 4HR, North : 3 m. by A 28 on
A 251 ✆ (01233) 213000, *enquiries@eastwellmanor.co.uk, Fax (01233) 635530*, <, Ⓠ, 𝑭᷅,
🛋, ⌧ heated, 🔲, 🞉, 🏐, ✗ – 📶, 🔆✗ rest, ☎ 🅿 – 🛎 250. ⓂⓄ ⒶⒺ 𝘝𝘐𝘚𝘈
Manor : **Rest** 15.00/37.50 and a la carte 32.95/92.00 ♀ – *Brasserie :* **Rest** 15.00/50.00 and
a la carte 21.10/37.50 – **20 rm** 🖙 ✚160.00 – ✚✚415.00, 3 suites.
◆ Mansion house in formal gardens, replete with interesting detail including carved panel-
led rooms and stone fireplaces. Smart individual bedrooms. Manor offers seasonal menus.
Swish brasserie in luxury spa with marbled entrance hall.

🏨 **Ashford International**, Simone Weil Ave, TN24 8UX, North : 1½ m. by A 20 ✆ (01233)
219988, *sales@ashfordinthotel.com, Fax (01233) 647743*, 𝑭᷅, 🏐, 🔲 – 📶 🔆✗ 🕭 🅿 –
🛎 400. ⓂⓄ ⒶⒺ Ⓓ 𝘝𝘐𝘚𝘈
Alhambra : **Rest** *(closed Sunday dinner and Bank Holidays)* 15.95/30.00 ♀ – *Mistral Bras-*
serie : **Rest** (carvery) (dinner only and Sunday lunch)/dinner 21.00 ♀ – 🖙 10.95 – **177 rm**
✚110.00 – ✚✚145.00.
◆ Enormous corporate oriented hotel with large central atrium containing shops and
coffee bars to relax in. Modern, comfortable bedrooms. Alhambra noted for range of
modern dishes. Informal, relaxed Mistral.

ASHFORD-IN-THE-WATER *Derbs. 502 503 504* O *24* – *see Bakewell.*

ASHINGTON *W. Sussex 504* S *31* – *pop. 2 351* – ✉ *Pulborough.*
London 50 – Brighton 20 – Worthing 9.

🏠 **Mill House**, Mill Lane, RH20 3BZ, ✆ (01903) 892426, *info@millhousesussex.co.uk,*
Fax (01903) 893846, 🞉 – 🅿 – 🛎 30. ⓂⓄ ⒶⒺ Ⓓ 𝘝𝘐𝘚𝘈
Rest 14.50/25.95 ♀ – **9 rm** 🖙 ✚59.00 – ✚✚89.00/110.00.
◆ Once the home of the owners of Ashington Water and Wind Mills, this 17C cottage with
conservatory, inglenook fireplace and pastel painted rooms makes a quiet retreat. Restau-
rant with tranquil blue décor and watercolours on the walls.

ASHURST *W. Sussex 504* T *31* – *see Steyning.*

ASHWATER *Devon.*
London 218 – Bude 16.5 – Virginstow 3.

🏠 **Blagdon Manor** ⌂, Beaworthy, EX21 5DF, Northwest : 2 m. by Holsworthy rd on
Blagdon rd ✆ (01409) 211224, *stay@blagdon.com, Fax (01409) 211634*, <, 🞉, 🐾 – 🔆✗ 🅿.
ⓂⓄ 𝘝𝘐𝘚𝘈
closed 2 weeks January and 1 week autumn and 3 days New Year – **Rest** *(closed lunch*
Monday and Tuesday) (booking essential) (residents only Monday and Sunday dinner)
20.00/35.00 – **7 rm** 🖙 ✚85.00 – ✚✚120.00.
◆ Idyllic rural setting, with splendid views to match. Charming breakfast conservatory;
characterful bar has original flag floors. Carefully styled rooms designed by owners. Characterfully rustic dining room: classic dishes with modern touch.

ASKRIGG *N. Yorks.* **502** N 21 – *pop. 1 002* – ✉ *Leyburn.*
London 251 – Kendal 32 – Leeds 70 – Newcastle upon Tyne 70 – York 63.

Helm without rest., Helm, DL8 3JF, West : 1½ m., turning right at Helm rd after 1 m.
☎ (01969) 650443, *holiday@helmyorkshire.com, Fax (01969) 650443,* ≤ Wensleydale – P. MC VISA.
closed November and December – **3 rm** ☐ ✝60.00 – ✝✝85.00.
• A steep lane winds up to this 17C stone farmhouse still in possession of an underground dairy with cheese press used in making Wensleydale cheese. Compact, homely bedrooms.

The Apothecary's House without rest., Market Pl, DL8 3HT, ☎ (01969) 650626, *bookings@apothecaryhouse.co.uk* – P.
closed 25-26 December, 31 December and 1 January – 3 rm ☐ ✝37.50 – ✝✝65.00.
• Built in 1756 by the local apothecary in centre of village; overlooks church. Combined lounge and breakfast room has fresh, modern feel. Rear bedroom boasts exposed timbers.

ASPLEY GUISE *Beds.* **504** S 27 – *pop. 2 236.*
18 Woburn Sands, West Hill ☎ (01908) 583596 – 18 Lyshott Heath, Ampthill ☎ (01525) 840252.
London 52 – Bedford 13 – Luton 16 – Northampton 22 – Oxford 46.

Moore Place, The Square, MK17 8DW, ☎ (01908) 282000, *business@mooreplace.com, Fax (01908) 281888,* – P. – 40. MC AE VISA
Rest *(closed Saturday lunch and Bank Holidays* 16.50/26.00 and a la carte 26.00/28.50 ♀ –
62 rm ☐ ✝114.00/124.00 – ✝✝134.00/145.00, 1 suite.
• Elegant Georgian mansion house with waterfall in garden, lobby lounge and bar. Bedrooms each have bowls of fruit and two small "welcome" drinks decanters. Restaurant with tried-and-tested menu and lighter options.

The red symbol?
This denotes the very essence of peace
– only the sound of birdsong first thing in the morning ...

ASTON CANTLOW *Warks.* **503 504** O 27 *Great Britain G.*
Env. : *Mary Arden's House★ AC, SE : 2 m. by Wilmcote Lane and Aston Cantlow Rd.*
London 106 – Birmingham 20 – Stratford-upon-Avon 5.

The King's Head, 21 Bearley Rd, B95 6HY, ☎ (01789) 488242, *info@thekh.co.uk, Fax (01789) 488137,* – P. MC VISA
closed 25 December and 1 January – **Rest** a la carte 18.00/27.00 ♀.
• Charming, cottagey 15C pub with timbers. Pleasant terrace and garden; real fire and polished flag flooring. Hearty, eclectic range of dishes with a real gastro feel.

ASTON CLINTON *Bucks.* **504** R 28 – *pop. 3 467* – ✉ *Aylesbury.*
London 42 – Aylesbury 4 – Oxford 26.

West Lodge without rest., 45 London Rd, HP22 5HL, ☎ (01296) 630362, *jibwl@westlodge.co.uk, Fax (01296) 630151,* – P.
10 rm ☐ ✝58.00/64.00 – ✝✝79.00.
• 19C former lodge house and part of the Rothschild estate, boasting a beautiful garden with tranquil fish pond. Elegant public areas and cosy, well-kept bedrooms. Montgolfier Room enlivened by hot-air balloon décor.

ASTON TIRROLD *Oxon..*
London 58 – Reading 16 – Streatley 4.5.

The Sweet Olive at The Chequers Inn, Baker St, OX11 9DD, ☎ (01235) 851272, – P. MC AE VISA
closed February – **Rest** *(closed Wednesday and Sunday dinner in winter)* (booking essential) a la carte 10.00/25.00.
• Redbrick Victorian pub in pleasant Oxfordshire countryside. Large bar and snug dining room. "Bonjours" and "bon appetits" aplenty to accompany hearty Gallic based cuisine.

ATCHAM *Shrops.* **503 504** L 25 – *see Shrewsbury.*

AUSTWICK N. Yorks. 502 M 21 – pop. 467 – ⊠ Lancaster (Lancs.).
London 259 – Kendal 28 – Lancaster 20 – Leeds 46.

🏨 **Austwick Traddock** ≫, LA2 8BY, ℰ (015242) 51224, info@austwicktraddock.co.uk,
Fax (015242) 51796, � – 🖐 **P**, **Ⓞ** **Æ** **VISA**
Rest (booking essential for non-residents) (dinner only and Saturday and Sunday
lunch)/dinner 30.00 and a la carte 27.50/35.00 ⅋ – **10 rm** ⊑ **†**80.00/110.00 –
††140.00/180.00.
   ◆ A Georgian country house decorated with both English and Asian antiques. Bedrooms
are individually styled to a high standard and overlook the secluded gardens. Dining room
split into two rooms and lit by candlelight.

⌂ **Wood View** without rest., The Green, LA2 8BB, ℰ (015242) 51190, stay@woodview
bandb.com, Fax (015242) 51190, 🌫 – 🖐 **P**, **ⓄⓄ** **VISA**
closed 24-26 December – **6 rm** ⊑ **†**40.00 – **††**56.00/70.00.
   ◆ In a charming spot on the village green, the cottage dates back to 17C with many of the
original features still in place including exposed rafters in several bedrooms.

AVONWICK Devon.
London 202 – Plymouth 17.5 – Totnes 8.

🍴 **The Turtley Corn Mill,** TQ10 9ES, Northwest : 1 m. on Plymouth rd ℰ (01364) 646100,
mill@avonwick.net, Fax (01364) 646101, 🌇, 🌫 – 🖐 **P**, **ⓄⓄ** **VISA**
closed dinner 25 December – **Rest** a la carte 18.50/25.00 ⅋.
   ◆ Refurbished 18C mill in six acres, with original beams and pillars in situ. A clean, light and
airy feel helps enhance the enjoyment of dishes ranging from classics to modern.

🍴 **The Avon Inn,** TQ10 9NB, ℰ (01364) 73475, rosec@beeb.net, 🌇, 🌫 – 🖐 **P**, **ⓄⓄ** **VISA**
⅋
closed Monday lunch – **Rest** (closed Sunday dinner) a la carte 18.00/26.75.
   ◆ Homely pub with an interior of beams and hop bines. French owner/chef serves accomplished dishes with classic Gallic base and plenty of local seafood and fish.

AXBRIDGE Somerset 503 L 30 – pop. 2 025.
London 142 – Bristol 17 – Taunton 27 – Weston-Super-Mare 11.

⌂ **The Parsonage** without rest., Parsonage Lane, Cheddar Rd, BS26 2DN, East : ¾ m. on A
371 ℰ (01934) 733078, Fax (01934) 733078, ≼, 🌫 – 🖐 **P**, ⅋
3 rm ⊑ **†**45.00 – **††**52.00.
   ◆ Former Victorian parsonage nestling in the southern slopes of the Mendip Hills overlooking the Somerset Levels. The comfortable bedrooms are tastefully furnished.

AXMINSTER Devon 503 L 31 The West Country G. – pop. 4 952.
Env. : Lyme Regis★ - The Cobb★, SE : 5½ m. by A 35 and A 3070.
🔟 The Old Courthouse, Church St ℰ (01297) 34386, axminster@btopenworld.com.
London 156 – Exeter 27 – Lyme Regis 5.5 – Taunton 22 – Yeovil 24.

🏨 **Fairwater Head Country House** ≫, Hawkchurch, EX13 5TX, Northeast : 5 ¼ m.
by B 3261 and A 35 off B 3165 ℰ (01297) 678349, info@fairwaterheadhotel.co.uk,
Fax (01297) 678459, ≼ Axe Vale, 🌇, 🌫 – 🖐 **P**, **ⓄⓄ** **Æ** **VISA**
closed 27 December- January – **Rest** (bar lunch Monday-Saturday)/dinner 27.50 ⅋ – **20 rm**
⊑ **†**80.00/105.00 – **††**180.00/190.00.
   ◆ Edwardian hotel in flower-filled gardens. Tea and fresh cakes served in the afternoon.
Many rooms have Axe Valley views. Attractive outlook over garden and countryside accompanies diners enjoying locally sourced cooking.

🏠 **Kerrington House** without rest., Musbury Rd, EX13 5JR, Southwest : ½ m. ℰ (01297)
35333, enquiries@kerringtonhouse.com, 🌫 – 🖐 **ⓥ** **P**, **ⓄⓄ** **VISA**, ⅋
6 rm ⊑ **†**75.00 – **††**110.00.
   ◆ Pleasantly converted Victorian house with original tiles and homely character; close to
town centre. Warm, welcoming owners. Spacious sitting room. Large, comfy bedrooms.

AYCLIFFE Darlington – see Darlington.

Good food and accommodation at moderate prices?
Look for the Bib symbols:
red Bib Gourmand for food, blue Bib Hotel ⌂ for hotels

AYLESBURY *Bucks.* 504 R 28 *Great Britain G.* – *pop. 69 021.*

Env. : *Waddesdon Manor*★★, NW : 5½ m. by A 41 – *Chiltern Hills*★.

 Weston Turville, New Rd ☎ (01296) 424084 – *Hulcott Lane, Bierton* ☎ (01296) 393644.
🛈 *The Kings Head Passage off Market St* ☎ (01296) 330559, *info@aylesbury-tourist.org.uk.*
London 46 – Birmingham 72 – Northampton 37 – Oxford 22.

Hartwell House ⌖, Oxford Rd, HP17 8NL, Southwest : 2 m. on A 418 ☎ (01296)
747444, *info@hartwell-house.com*, Fax (01296) 747450, ≤, ☺, ℡, ≦s, ◰, ⇗, 🖈, ₰, ⚘ –
▮ ⅙ ⚓ **P** – 🔏 80. **◐◐** ⬛ ⬛
Rest 22.00/38.00 a la carte 37.75/50.00 ⚎ – ⚌ 6.50 – **33 rm** ✷155.00/220.00 – ✷✷280.00,
13 suites 380.00/800.00.
◆ Magnificent stately home rich in history; Louis XVIII was exiled here in 1809. Gothic hall
and carved stairway lead to superb heritage bedrooms. Many have four-poster beds. Fine
dining in peacefully located restaurant with garden aspect.

AYLESFORD *Kent* 504 V 30.

London 37 – Maidstone 3.5 – Rochester 8.

XXX **Hengist**, 7-9 High St, ME20 7AX, ☎ (01622) 719273, *the.hengist@btconnect.com*,
Fax (01622) 715077 – ⅙ ▤ ⇄ 14. **◐◐** ⬛ ⬛
closed 26 December, 1 January, Sunday dinner and Monday – **Rest** 18.95/25.50 and a la
carte 27.65/36.65 ⚎.
◆ Converted 16C town house, elegantly appointed throughout, with bonus of exposed
rafters and smart private dining room upstairs. Accomplished modern cooking with seasonal base.

AYSGARTH *N. Yorks.* 502 O 21.

London 249 – Ripon 28 – York 56.5.

ᴵ◲ **George and Dragon Inn** with rm, DL8 3AD, ☎ (01969) 663358, *info@georgeanddra
gonaysgarth.co.uk*, Fax (01969) 663773, ⇗ – **P**. **◐◐** ⬛
closed 2 weeks January – **Rest** 25.00 (dinner) and a la carte 15.00/25.00 – **7 rm** ⚌
✷36.00/40.00 – ✷✷72.00/79.00.
◆ Traditional pub near Aysgarth falls. Smart terrace with thatched umbrellas. Local ales
dominate welcoming bar. Wide range of fresh fare: local produce to fore. Comfy rooms.

BABCARY *Somerset* 403 M 30.

London 128.5 – Glastonbury 12 – Yeovil 12.

ᴵ◲ **The Red Lion Inn**, TA11 7ED, ☎ (01458) 223230, Fax (01458) 224510, ⇗, 🖈 – ⅙ **P**.
◐◐ ⬛ ⬛ ⌖
closed 25 December – **Rest** *(closed Sunday dinner)* a la carte 21.75/27.50.
◆ Attractive thatched pub in cosy village. Tasteful interior that's full of squashy sofas and
dining pub style. Accomplished menus, modern in substance, suit the surroundings.

BAGSHOT *Surrey* 504 R 29 – *pop. 5 247.*

⛳ *Windlesham, Grove End* ☎ (01276) 452220.
London 37 – Reading 17 – Southampton 49.

Pennyhill Park ⌖, London Rd, GU19 5EU, Southwest : 1 m. on A 30 ☎ (01276) 471774,
enquiries@pennyhillpark.co.uk, Fax (01276) 473217, ≤, ☺, ℡, ⬛ heated, ◰, ⬛, ⇗, 🖈,
₰, ⚘ – ⅙ rest, ₰, **P** – 🔏 150. **◐◐** ⬛ ⬛ **◐** ⬛
Brasserie and Oyster bar : **Rest** (buffet lunch) a la carte 32.50/41.50 ⚎ – (see also **The
Latymer** below) – ⚌ 17.50 – **113 rm** ✷258.50 – ✷✷258.50, 10 suites.
◆ Sympathetically extended ivy-clad 19C manor house in wooded parkland. Intimate
lounges. Outstanding spa. Rooms with fine antique furniture share a relaxing period elegance. Marble and stained glass enhanced restaurant overlooks garden.

XXX **The Latymer** (at Pennyhill Park H.), London Rd, GU19 5EU, Southwest : 1 m. on A 30
☎ (01276) 471774, *pennyhillpark@msn.com*, Fax (01276) 473217, 🖈 – ⅙ ▤ **P**. **◐◐** ⬛ **◐**
⬛
closed 26-30 December, 1-15 January, and Saturday-Monday lunch – **Rest** (booking essential) 25.00/75.00 ⚎.
◆ Robust flavours in an ambitious, elaborately presented modern British menu. Oak
panels, oil lamps and attentive service uphold Victorian country house tradition.

BAKEWELL Derbs. 502 503 504 O 24 Great Britain G. – pop. 3 676.

Env. : Chatsworth★★★ (Park and Garden★★★) AC, NE : 2½ m. by A 619 – Haddon Hall★★ AC, SE : 2 m. by A 6.

🛈 Old Market Hall, Bridge St ℰ (01629) 816558, bakewell@peakdistrict-mpa.gov.uk.

London 160 – Derby 26 – Manchester 37 – Nottingham 33 – Sheffield 17.

↑ **Haddon House Farm** without rest., Haddon Rd, DE45 1BN, South : ½ m. on A 6 ℰ (01629) 814024, m@great-place.co.uk – ⤾⤳ 🅿. ✼

4 rm ⌚ ✝45.00/50.00 – ✝✝85.00/95.00.

♦ Friendly guesthouse, just out of town. Cottagey breakfast room with Aga. Individual rooms: ask for the Monet, painted to make you feel you're in the middle of a waterfall.

at Ashford-in-the-Water Northwest : 1¾ m. by A 6 and A 6020 – ✉ Bakewell.

🏨 **Riverside House,** Fennel St, DE45 1QF, ℰ (01629) 814275, riversidehouse@enta.net, Fax (01629) 812873, 🌿 – ⤾⤳ 🅿. 🆎 🆎 🛈 𝘝𝘐𝘚𝘈. ✼

Rest – (see **The Riverside Room** below) – 14 rm ⌚ ✝110.00 – ✝✝170.00.

♦ Extended 18C country house on the banks of the Wye; immaculate, tastefully appointed and individually furnished bedrooms, comfortable drawing room and modern conservatory.

✕✕ **The Riverside Room** (at Riverside House), Fennel St, DE45 1QE, ℰ (01629) 814275, Fax (01629) 812875 – ⤾⤳ 🅿. 🆎 🆎 🛈 𝘝𝘐𝘚𝘈

Rest 44.95 (dinner) and lunch a la carte 24.50/29.40.

♦ Panelled bar adjoins two intimate dining rooms, one centred around a gleaming Victorian range. Seasonal modern cuisine, flavourful and well-prepared. Welcoming service.

BALSALL COMMON W. Mids. – see Coventry.

BAMBURGH Northd. 501 502 O 17 Great Britain G.

See : Castle★ AC.

London 337 – Edinburgh 77 – Newcastle upon Tyne 51.

🏨 **Lord Crewe,** Front St, NE69 7BL, ℰ (01668) 214243, lordcrewebamburgh@tiscali.co.uk, Fax (01668) 214273 – ⤾⤳ 🅿. 🆎 𝘝𝘐𝘚𝘈

February-November – Rest (bar lunch)/dinner a la carte 22.00/27.00 – 18 rm ⌚ ✝47.00/74.00 – ✝✝88.00/126.00.

♦ In the shadow of the Norman castle, a neat and traditional market town hotel, still in private hands. Smartly fitted bedrooms; spacious, comfy lounge. Characterful beamed bar. Alluring timber and stone retaurant.

at Waren Mill West : 2¾ m. on B 1342 – ✉ Belford.

🏨 **Waren House** ⤻, NE70 7EE, ℰ (01668) 214581, enquiries@warenhousehotel.co.uk, Fax (01668) 214484, ≤, 🌿 – ⤾⤳ 🅿. – 🏧 30. 🆎 🆎 🛈 𝘝𝘐𝘚𝘈

Rest (dinner only) 29.50 ⌚ – 11 rm ⌚ ✝85.00/110.00 – ✝✝124.00/165.00, 2 suites.

♦ A Georgian country house in attractive grounds and formal gardens, with views to Lindisfarne. Individually decorated bedrooms with themes ranging from Oriental to Edwardian. Classical dining room overlooking gardens.

BAMPTON Devon 503 J 31 – pop. 1 617.

London 189 – Exeter 18 – Minehead 21 – Taunton 15.

🏨 **Bark House,** Oakfordbridge, EX16 9HZ, West : 3 m. by B 3227 on A 396 ℰ (01398) 351236, bark.house.hotel@btinternet.com, 🌿 – ⤾⤳ 🅿.

Rest (booking essential for non-residents) (dinner only) (set menu only) 29.50 s. – 5 rm ⌚ ✝50.00/89.00 – ✝✝89.00/119.00.

♦ Neat, personally run stone cottages which once stored wood from Exmoor forest. Bright bedrooms of different sizes are decorated in pretty floral fabrics. Terraced rear garden. Home-cooking proudly served in neat dining room.

Your opinions are important to us:
please write and let us know about your discoveries and experiences – good and bad!

BANBURY Oxon. 503 504 P 27 *Great Britain G. – pop. 43 867.*

Exc. : *Upton House* ★ *AC, NW : 7 m. by A 422.*

ᵗₛ *Cherwell Edge, Chacombe* ℰ *(01295) 711591.*

🖪 *Spiceball Park Rd* ℰ *(01295) 259855.*

London 76 – Birmingham 40 – Coventry 25 – Oxford 23.

🏛️ **Whately Hall,** Horsefair, by Banbury Cross, OX16 0AN, ℰ (0870) 4008104, *sales.what elyhall@macdonald-hotels.co.uk,* Fax (01295) 271736, 🐎 – ⭐ ℃ 🖻 – 🔏 80. 🕮 🖭 ⓪ **VISA**

Rest (bar lunch Monday-Saturday)/dinner 27.00 ♀ – ➴ 13.95 – **67 rm** ♀125.00/135.00 – ✚✚135.00, 6 suites.
♦ Renowned for hidden staircases, priest holes and a resident ghost, this part 17C inn has an eccentric floor plan of well-appointed rooms and panelled, black-beamed corridors. Dining room of local stone and leaded windows overlooks croquet lawn.

🏛️ **Banbury House,** Oxford Rd, OX16 9AH, ℰ (01295) 259361, *sales@banburyhouse.co.uk,* Fax (01295) 270954 – ⭐ rm, 🖻 – 🔏 70. 🕮 🖭 ⓪ **VISA**. 🛇
closed 24 December-2 January – **Rest** (bar lunch)/dinner 21.00 ♀ – ➴ 15.00 – **64 rm** ♀50.00/150.00 – ✚✚100.00/205.00.
♦ Handsome, extensive Georgian house, smartly and enthusiastically managed. Rear facing rooms are quieter, but all are spacious and well kept, modernised with taste and care. Subdued dining room with potted palms and botanical prints.

at North Newington *West : 2¼ m. by B 4035 –* ⊠ *Banbury.*

🏠 **The Mill House** 🌢 *without rest.,* OX15 6AA, ℰ (01295) 730212, *lamadonett@aol.com,* Fax (01295) 730363, 🐎 – ⭐ 🖻. 🕮 **VISA**. 🛇
closed Christmas and New Year – **7 rm** ➴ ♀59.00/80.00 – ✚✚80.00/110.00.
♦ Friendly, personally run guesthouse in 17C paper mill, set in peaceful gardens beside a stream. Comfortable bedrooms, prettily decorated with individual touches.

at Sibford Gower *West : 8 m. by B 4035 –* ⊠ *Banbury.*

🍴 **The Wykham Arms,** Temple Mill Rd, OX15 5RX, ℰ (01295) 788808, *info@wykha marms.co.uk,* Fax (01295) 788806, 🏡, 🐎 – ⭐ 🖻. 🕮 **VISA**. 🛇
closed 25-26 December – **Rest** *(closed Sunday dinner and Monday)* a la carte 21.90/35.00 ♀.
♦ Former 17C farmhouse, now a pretty thatched pub with spacious terrace. Bright interior with original inglenook and low beams. Local ingredients to fore on modern menus.

at Hanwell *Northwest : 3½ m. by A 422 and B 4100 –* ⊠ *Oxon.*

🍴 **Moon & Sixpence,** Main St, OX17 1HW, ℰ (01295) 730544, *moonand.sixpence@vir gin.net,* Fax (01295) 730147, 🏡 – ⭐ 🖻. 🕮 **VISA**
Rest *(closed Monday lunch)* 7.50 and a la carte 20.00/35.00.
♦ Personally run by two brothers who've re-established the community pub. Spacious interior exudes warm traditionality. Appealing menus offer an eclectic range of styles.

> Look out for red symbols, indicating particularly pleasant establishments.

BARFORD *Warks. 503 504 P 27 – see Warwick.*

BARHAM *Kent 504 X 30.*

London 66 – Canterbury 7 – Dover 11.

🏠 **Elmstone Court,** Out Elmstead Lane, CT4 6PH, *North : ¾ m.* ℰ (01227) 830433, *info@elmstonecourt.com,* Fax (01227) 832403, 🐎 – 🖻. 🛇
closed 25-26 December **Rest** *(by arrangement)* *(communal dining)* 25.00 – **4 rm** ➴ ✚60.00/70.00 – ✚✚90.00/110.00.
♦ Georgian house with earlier origins on cusp of village; striking gardens. Modern artwork in all areas; period style drawing room with open fire. All rooms individually themed. Communal dining room; local organic produce to the fore.

BAR HILL *Cambs. 504 U 27 – see Cambridge.*

BARNARD CASTLE *Durham 502 O 20 Great Britain G. – pop. 6 714.*

See : *Bowes Museum* ★ *AC.*

Exc. : *Raby Castle* ★ *AC, NE : 6½ m. by A 688.*

ᵗₛ *Harmire Rd* ℰ *(01833) 638355.*

🖪 *Woodleigh, Flatts Rd* ℰ *(01833) 690909.*

London 258 – Carlisle 63 – Leeds 68 – Middlesbrough 31 – Newcastle upon Tyne 39.

↑ **Greta House** without rest., 89 Galgate, DL12 8ES, ✆ (01833) 631193, *kathches man@btinternet.com, Fax (01833) 631193,* 🐴 – ✗. 🏠
3 rm 🖨 ✝40.00/45.00 – ✝✝65.00.
♦ Part of a Victorian terrace with leafy garden. Bedrooms are spacious and individually decorated. Evening snacks may be taken in your room; plenty of books to browse through.

↑ **Demesnes Mill** 🌿 without rest., DL12 8PE, Southeast : ½ m. by The Bank and Gray Lane, through the playing field ✆ (01833) 637929, *themillbarnardcastle@btopen world.com,* ⬳, 🐴 – ✗ ⬳.
March-October – 3 rm 🖨 ✝40.00 – ✝✝55.00/75.00.
♦ Set just out of town centre, a sensitively restored 15C mill abounding in period character. Large rooms, including one with an open fire. Conservatory with views of the Tees.

↑ **Homelands** without rest., 85 Galgate, DL12 8ES, ✆ (01833) 638757, *enquiries@home landsguesthouse.co.uk,* 🐴 – ✗. 🅼🅾 💳. 🏠
closed 23 December-2 January – 5 rm 🖨 ✝36.00/50.00 – ✝✝60.00/70.00.
♦ Immaculately maintained 19C terraced house on main road. Cosy lounge and compact but pleasantly furnished, well-priced rooms, some overlooking the long mature rear garden.

at Greta Bridge Southeast : 4½ m. off A 66 – ✉ Barnard Castle.

🏨 **Morritt Arms,** DL12 9SE, ✆ (01833) 627232, *relax@themorritt.co.uk, Fax (01833) 627392,* ⬳, 🐴 – ✗ 🅿 – 🔬 250. 🅼🅾 💳
The Morritt : Rest a la carte 19.00/30.00 🍷 – *Bistro/Bar :* Rest a la carte 16.00/31.00 🍷 –
27 rm 🖨 ✝85.00/105.00 – ✝✝105.00/150.00.
♦ 19C coaching inn where Charles Dickens stayed in 1839. The Dickens bar has murals by John Gilroy, historian of the Guinness firm. All rooms individually designed. The Morritt is oak panelled restaurant. Informal warmth at Bistro/Bar.

at Romaldkirk Northwest : 6 m. by A 67 on B 6277 – ✉ Barnard Castle.

🏠 **Rose and Crown** with rm, DL12 9EB, ✆ (01833) 650213, *hotel@rose-and-crown.co.uk, Fax (01833) 650828,* 🌿 – ✗ 🅿. 🅼🅾 💳
closed 24-26 December – **The Restaurant :** Rest (dinner only and Sunday lunch) 26.00 🍷
⬳ – 12 rm 🖨 ✝75.00 – ✝✝126.00/140.00.
♦ Fine 1733 coaching inn set back from the green. Characterful, well thought-out rooms. Firelit lounge and bar; beams and rough stone walls hung with brasses and etchings. Dining room decorated with curios and antique china.

BARNARD GATE Oxon. 503 504 P 28 – see Witney.

BARNSLEY Glos. 503 504 O 28 – see Cirencester.

BARNSLEY S. Yorks. 502 504 P 23 – pop. 71 599.
🏌 Wakefield Rd, Staincross ✆ (01226) 382856 – 🏌 Silkstone, Field Head, Elmhirst Lane ✆ (01226) 790328 – 🏌 Wombwell Hillies, Wentworth View, Wombwell ✆ (01226) 754433.
🛈 Central Library, Shambles St ✆ (01226) 206757.
London 177 – Leeds 21 – Manchester 36 – Sheffield 15.

🏨 **Tankersley Manor,** Church Lane, S75 3DQ, South : 6 ¼ m. on A 61 ✆ (01226) 744700, *adminbm@marstonhotels.com, Fax (01226) 74242,* 🎗, 🏋, 🏊, 🐴 – 🔲 ✗, 🍽 rest, ✆ 🔬
🅿 – 🔬 400. 🅼🅾 🆎 ① 💳. 🏠
Rest (closed Saturday lunch) 17.95 (lunch) and dinner a la carte 26.50/31.50 🍷 – 🖨 14.95 –
98 rm ✝139.00 – ✝✝177.50, 2 suites.
♦ Part 17C house, sympathetically enlarged to cater for corporate functions and weddings. Low-beamed lounge and bar with Regency-style furniture. Rooms have useful mod cons. Formal or informal option: characterful pub or stone-walled dining room.

BARNSTAPLE Devon 503 H 30 The West Country G. – pop. 30 765.
See : Town★ - Long Bridge★.
Env. : Arlington Court★★ (Carriage Collection★) AC, NE : 6 m. by A 39.
🏌, 🏌 Chulmleigh, Leigh Rd ✆ (01769) 580519.
🛈 Museum of North Devon, The Square ✆ (01271) 375000.
London 222 – Exeter 40 – Taunton 51.

🏨 **Imperial,** Taw Vale Parade, EX32 8NB, ✆ (01271) 345861, *info@brend-imperial.co.uk, Fax (01271) 324448* – 🔲, ✗ rest, 🍽 rest, 🅿 – 🔬 60. 🅼🅾 🆎 ① 💳. 🏠
Rest 15.00/25.00 s. – 🖨 12.50 – 63 rm ✝85.00/95.00 – ✝✝140.00/160.00.
♦ Attractive riverside hotel dating from the turn of 20C. Convivial bar and smart accommodation: deluxe front bedrooms have balconies overlooking the Taw. Grand, bay-windowed dining room.

at Bishop's Tawton South : 2¾ m. by A 39 on A 377 – ⊠ Barnstaple.

🏛 **Halmpstone Manor** 🦢, EX32 0EA, Southeast : 3 m. by Chittlehampton rd ℰ (01271) 830321, charles@halmpstonemanor.co.uk, Fax (01271) 830826, ≤, ☞, ♨ – **P**. **@⊙** **VISA** closed Christmas and New Year – **Rest** (dinner only) (residents only) (communal dining) (set menu) 35.00 – **4 rm** ☑ ✦70.00 – ✦✦140.00.
♦ A 400 year old manor set in charming Devon countryside. Log fires, deep sofas, sherry decanters, four poster and brass coronet beds; peace and relaxation assured.

BARNT GREEN Birmingham.
London 114.5 – Birmingham 11 – Bromsgrove 9.5.

✕ **The Barnt Green Inn**, 22 Kendal End Rd, B45 8PZ, on B 4120 ℰ (0121) 445 4949, Fax (0121) 447 9912, 佘, ☞ – ✦✦ ▤ **P**. **@⊙** **VISA**
– **Rest** a la carte 16.00/32.00 ♀.
♦ Huge mock Tudor establishment in the Birmingham hinterland. Smoochy lounge area and bar; separate restaurant with an informal air: modern international menus predominate.

BARROWDEN Rutland.
London 94 – Peterborough 17.5 – Stamford 8.5.

🍴 **Exeter Arms** with rm, 28 Main St, LE15 8EQ, ℰ (01572) 747247, joeallsopp@aol.com, Fax (01572) 747247, 佘, ☞ – ✦✦ **P**. **@⊙** **VISA**. ⋇
Rest (closed Sunday dinner and Monday) a la carte 20.65/32.85 ♀ – **3 rm** ☑ ✦37.50 – ✦✦75.00.
♦ Stone-built, family owned 17C inn overlooking green and duck pond. Ales from pub's own micro brewery. Accomplished cuisine proffers modernity with Asian undercurrent.

If breakfast is included the ☑ symbol appears after the number of rooms.

BARSTON W. Mids. 504 O 26.
London 110 – Birmingham 17 – Coventry 11.

🍴 **The Malt Shovel**, Barston Lane, B92 0JP, West : ¾ m ℰ (01675) 443223, Fax (01675) 443223, 佘, ☞ – **P**. **@⊙** **VISA**. ⋇
closed 25 December and 1 January – **Rest** (closed Sunday dinner) (lunch bookings not accepted) 25.00 (dinner) and a la carte 18.85/30.85 ♀.
♦ Modern dining pub, an oasis in a rustic hideaway, with large garden and patio. Good sized menus: noteworthy seafood specials. Busy at lunchtimes - you can't book so go early!

BARTON-ON-SEA Hants. 503 504 P 31.
London 108 – Bournemouth 11 – Southampton 24 – Winchester 35.

⌂ **Tower House** without rest., Christchurch Rd, BH25 6QQ, West : 1 m. on A 337 ℰ (01425) 629508, bandb@towerhouse-newforest.co.uk, Fax (01425) 629508, ☞ – ✦✦ **P**. closed Christmas - New Year – **3 rm** ☑ ✦60.00/70.00 – ✦✦70.00.
♦ Proudly run Edwardian guesthouse close to main road. Particularly good breakfasts, with ingredients sourced from local farm shop. Bright, cheery and very comfortable bedrooms.

✕ **Pebble Beach** with rm, Marine Drive, BH25 7DZ, ℰ (01425) 627777, email@pebble beach-uk.com, Fax (01425) 610689, ≤, 佘 – ✦✦ **P**. **@⊙** **VISA**
Rest - Seafood specialities - (closed dinner 25 December and 1 January) a la carte 18.90/49.50 ♀ – ☑ 5.00 – **3 rm** ✦49.95 – ✦✦69.95.
♦ Cliff-top position: striking terrace views over Solent and The Needles. Bright, modish interior with large windows. Wide range of choice on modern menus. Well-equipped rooms.

BARWICK Somerset 503 504 M 31 – see Yeovil.

BASILDON Essex 504 V 29 – pop. 102 913 (inc. North Benfleet).
🏌 Clayhill Lane, Sparrow's Hearne ℰ (01268) 533297 – 🏌 Langdon Hills, Lower Dunton Rd, Bulphan ℰ (01268) 548444.
London 30 – Chelmsford 17 – Southend-on-Sea 13.

at Wickford North : 5¼ m. by A 132 – ✉ Basildon.

🏠 **Chichester,** Old London Rd, Rawreth, SS11 8UE, East : 2 ¾ m. by A 129 ☎ (01268) 560555, *reception@chichester-hotel.com*, Fax (01268) 560580, ☞ – ✗ rest, 🛏 rest, ✆ ₺.
🅿 📶 🆎 ① 💳 ✗
Rest (dinner only and Sunday lunch)/dinner a la carte 15.15/23.45 – ☑ 9.95 – **35 rm**
♦61.75 – ♦♦69.75.
◆ Surrounded by open farmland, a traditional hotel with a relaxing open-plan bar and lounge and well-proportioned rooms around a central courtyard. Restaurant has tried-and-tested dishes.

BASINGSTOKE Hants. 503 504 Q 30 – pop. 90 171.
🏌 Test Valley, Micheldever Rd, Overton ☎ (08707) 459020 – 🏌 Weybrook Park, Rooksdown Lane, Basingstoke ☎ (01256) 320347.
🛈 Willis Museum, Old Town Hall, Market Pl ☎ (01256) 817618.
London 55 – Reading 17 – Southampton 31 – Winchester 18.

BASINGSTOKE

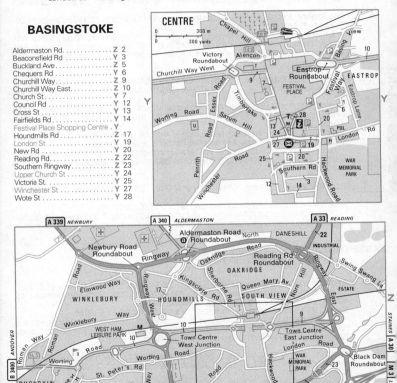

Apollo, Aldermaston Roundabout, RG24 9NU, North : 1 m. on A 340 ℘ (01256) 796700, *admin@apollohotels.com, Fax* (01256) 796794, ₤₅, ₷, 🖥 – 🔌, ↹ rm, 🍽 rest, ✆ 🅿 – ♨ 250. 🆗 🆎 ① 🆅🅸🆂🅰. 🛇

Z A

Vespers : Rest (dinner only) a la carte approx 32.45 ♀ – **Brasserie :** Rest (buffet) 19.00/22.00 and a la carte approx 18.95 ♀ – ⌸ 15.00 – **122 rm** ✚155.00/170.00 – ✚✚170.00, 3 suites.

◆ Smart, modern hotel aimed at business clients; well situated on Basingstoke ring road. Extensive conference and leisure facilities. Modern, well equipped rooms. Vespers is an intimate fine dining room. Large, modern Brasserie with centre servery.

BASLOW *Derbs.* **502 503 504** P 24 *Great Britain G.* – ✉ Bakewell.
See : Chatsworth★★★ *(Park and Garden★★★) AC.*
London 161 – Derby 27 – Manchester 35 – Sheffield 13.

Cavendish, Church Lane, DE45 1SP, on A 619 ℘ (01246) 582311, *info@cavendish-ho tel.net, Fax* (01246) 582312, ≼ Chatsworth Park, 🦢, 🌳 – ↹ ✆ 🅿 – ♨ 25. 🆗 🆎 ① 🆅🅸🆂🅰. 🛇

The Gallery : Rest 29.50/51.50 – **Garden Room :** Rest a la carte 23.90/35.20 – ⌸ 14.90 – **23 rm** ✚113.00/118.00 – ✚✚165.00/170.00, 1 suite.

◆ Antiques and fine art complement an elegant, welcoming, country house interior. Well-proportioned rooms, handsomely decorated in the 18C wing, overlook Chatsworth Park. The Gallery includes one table in the kitchen. Conservatory Garden Room has rural views.

Fischer's at Baslow Hall with rm, Calver Rd, DE45 1RR, on A 623 ℘ (01246) 583259, *m.s@fischers-baslowhall.co.uk, Fax* (01246) 583818, 🌳 – ↹ ✆ 🅿. 🆗 🆎 🆅🅸🆂🅰.

closed 25-26 and 31 December – Rest *(closed Sunday dinner to non-residents and Monday lunch)* (booking essential) 35.00/65.00 ♀ 🍷 – ⌸ 9.50 – **10 rm** ✚100.00/130.00 – ✚✚180.00, 1 suite.

Spec. Roast scallops, artichoke purée, honey and soy dressing. Roast rack and braised shoulder of Derbyshire lamb, pea tortellini. Fischer's dessert assiette.
◆ Edwardian manor with formal yet relaxed ambience: smooth service and elegant settings. Balanced modern British menu uses local produce to imaginative effect. Smart rooms.

Rowley's, Church Lane, DE45 1RY, ℘ (01246) 583880, 🍴 – ↹ 🅿. 🆗 🆎 ① 🆅🅸🆂🅰

Rest *(closed Monday and Sunday dinner)* a la carte 23.00/35.00.
◆ Owners of Fischer's run this stone-built pub enclosed by church and graveyard! Modern range of colours enhance sharp, smart interior. Matured steaks the star of modish menus.

BASSENTHWAITE *Cumbria* **501 502** K 19.
London 300 – Carlisle 24 – Keswick 7.

Armathwaite Hall 🦢, CA12 4RE, West : 1 ½ m. on B 5291, ✉ Keswick ℘ (017687) 76551, *reservations@armathwaite-hall.com, Fax* (017687) 76220, ≼ Bassenthwaite Lake, ₤₅, ₷, 🖥, 🦢, 🌳, ⚘, 🎾 – 🔌 ↹🅿 – ♨ 80. 🆗 🆎 ① 🆅🅸🆂🅰
Rest 21.95/41.95 **42 rm** (dinner included) ☐ ✚166.00/196.00 – ✚✚400.00.
◆ Lakeside mansion dominates tranquil 400-acre woods and deer park. Rooms, some in rebuilt stables, vary in size and, like the panelled hall, marry modern and period fittings. 'Old-World' restaurant with carved oak ceiling and fireplace.

The Pheasant, CA13 9YE, Southwest : 3 ¼ m. by B 5291 on Wythop Mill rd, ✉ Cockermouth ℘ (017687) 76234, *info@the-pheasant.co.uk, Fax* (017687) 76002, 🌳, ⚘ – ↹ rest, ✆ 🅿. 🆗 🆅🅸🆂🅰. 🛇
closed 25 December – Rest *(closed Monday lunch)* 27.50/33.95 ♀ – **15 rm** ☐ ✚80.00/105.00 – ✚✚135.00/180.00.
◆ Bright bedrooms, sensitively and individually updated, in a rural 16C coaching inn. Firelit bar with oak settles, local prints and game fish trophies serves regional ales. Charmingly simple restaurant decorated with chinaware.

Ravenstone, CA12 4QG, South : 1 ½ m. on A 591 ℘ (017687) 76240, *info@ravenstone-hotel.co.uk, Fax* (017687) 76733, ≼, 🌳 – ↹ rest, 🅿. 🆗 🆎 🆅🅸🆂🅰. 🛇
Rest (dinner only) 20.00/30.00 – **20 rm** (dinner included) ✚65.00 – ✚✚140.00.
◆ Once home to Baron of Penrith's mother, now a well-kept hotel. Boasts large games room with snooker table, piano. Bedrooms in soft floral fabrics harmonise with outside views. Fine vistas of lake from restaurant.

🏠 **Ravenstone Lodge,** CA12 4QG, South : 1 ½ m. on A 591 *β* (017687) 76629, *raven stone.lodge@talk21.com, Fax (017687) 76629*, ≤, 🌳 – **P**, **QO** **AE** **VISA**
Rest (residents only) (dinner only) 18.50 ♀ – **10 rm** ☞ **⋆**38.00 – **⋆⋆**84.00.
  ◆ Converted 19C stables with conservatory at the base of Ullock Pike. Sympathetically modernised rooms, most west-facing with views over walled gardens to Bassenthwaite Lake. Homely meals utilising local produce.

BATCOMBE *Somerset* 503 504 M 30 – ⊠ *Shepton Mallet.*
  London 130 – Bristol 24 – Bournemouth 50 – Salisbury 40 – Taunton 40.

🍴 **The Three Horseshoes Inn** with rm, BA4 6HE, *β* (01749) 850359, *shirley@threehor seshoesinn.co.uk, Fax (01749) 850615*, 🍽 , 🌳 – ⊱ **P**, **QO** **VISA**
  closed Monday – **Rest** a la carte 20.00/30.00 ♀ – **3 rm** ☞ **⋆**50.00 – **⋆⋆**70.00.
  ◆ By the parish church, a rustic bar in exposed stone and timber with a stove and in-glenook fireplace. Varied menus are imaginative and well prepared. Smart, refurbished rooms.

ENGLAND

Bath, Royal Crescent

BATH

Bath & North East Somerset **503 504** M 29 *Great Britain G.* – *pop. 90 144.*

London 119 – Bristol 13 – Southampton 63 – Taunton 49.

TOURIST INFORMATION

🏛 *Abbey Chambers, Abbey Church Yard ☎ (0906) 711 2000; tourism@bathnes.gov.uk.*

PRACTICAL INFORMATION

🏌, 🏌, 🏌 , *Tracy Park, Bath Rd, Wick ☎ (0871) 663 0566.*
🏌 *Lansdown ☎ (01225) 422138.*
🏌 *Entry Hill ☎ (01225) 834248.*

SIGHTS

See: *City*★★★ – *Royal Crescent*★★★ AV *(No. 1 Royal Crescent*★★ *AC* AV **A)** – *The Circus*★★★ AV – *Museum of Costume*★★★ *AC* AV **M7** – *Roman Baths*★★ *AC* BX **D** – *Holburne Museum and Crafts Study Centre*★★ *AC* Y **M5** – *Pump Room*★ BX **B** - *Assembly Rooms*★ AV – *Bath Abbey*★ BX – *Pulteney Bridge*★ BV – *Bath Industrial Heritage Centre*★ *AC* AV **M1** – *Lansdown Crescent*★★ *(Somerset Place*★ *)* Y – *Camden Crescent*★ Y – *Beckford Tower and Museum AC (prospect*★ *)* Y **M6** – *Museum of East Asian Art*★ AV **M9** – *Orange Grove*★ BX.

Env.: *Claverton (American Museum)*★★ *AC*, *Claverton Pumping Station*★ *AC) E : 3 m. by A 36* Y.

Exc.: *Corsham Court*★★ *AC*, *NE : 8½ m. by A 4* – *Dyrham Park*★ *AC*, *N : 6½ m. by A 4 and A 46.*

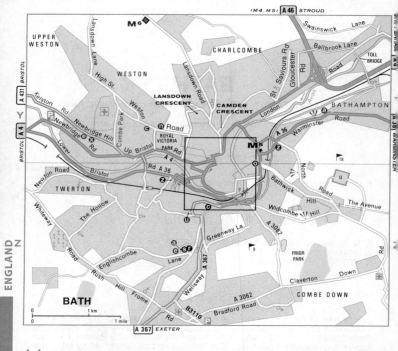

BATH

ENGLAND

The Royal Crescent, 16 Royal Crescent, BA1 2LS, ℰ (01225) 823333, *info@royalcrescent.co.uk*, Fax (01225) 339401, ≤, 斎, ②, I♨, ⇌s, 🔲, 澤 – 🛊 ﬁ ☰ ⟷ – 🛦 40. 🐵🅒 🅐🅔
🅞 VISA

AV a

Pimpernels : Rest 25.00/55.00 ♀ – **35 rm** ☲ ✚252.00/865.00 – ✚✚252.00/865.00, 10 suites ☲520.00/840.00.

◆ Meticulously restored town house in sweeping Georgian crescent. Service, like the superbly appointed rooms and lounges, is flawless in every charming detail. Dower house restaurant with French windows opening onto beautiful lawned garden.

Bath Spa, Sydney Rd, BA2 6JF, ℰ (0870) 4008222, *sales.bathspa@macdonald-hotels.co.uk*, Fax (01225) 444006, 斎, ②, I♨, ⇌s, 🔲 – 🛊 ﬁ ☚ & 🅟 – 🛦 120. 🐵🅒 🅐🅔 🅞
VISA

Y z

Vellore : Rest (dinner only and Sunday lunch) 39.50 and a la carte 44.95/48.95 ♀ –
Alfresco : Rest - Mediterranean - *(closed Sunday lunch)* 17.95 (lunch) and a la carte 22.40/49.45 ♀ – ☲ 17.95 – **118 rm** ✚170.00/205.00 – ✚✚280.00/350.00, 11 suites.

◆ Part 19C mansion in formal gardens: from the classical lobby to luxuriously appointed, high ceilinged rooms, all is space, elegance and English refinement. Alfresco features murals and exotic palms. Vellore for formal dining beneath a grand domed ceiling.

Bath Priory, Weston Rd, BA1 2XT, ℰ (01225) 331922, *mail@thebathpriory.co.uk*, Fax (01225) 448276, ②, I♨, ⇌s, 🔟 heated, 🔲, 澤 – ﬁ ☚ & 🅟 ⟷ 18 – 🛦 30. 🐵🅒 🅐🅔 🅞
VISA. ✗

Y c

Rest 25.00/49.50 ♀ 🍴 – **27 rm** ☲ ✚200.00 – ✚✚245.00/360.00, 4 suites.

Spec. Summer vegetables with asparagus. Red mullet, avocado purée. Olive brittle with wild strawberries and berry juice.

◆ Set in beautiful gardens, a stunning 19C series of houses in Bath stone. Charmingly appointed rooms, varying in style, and comfy firelit lounges with vivid artwork on walls. Showpiece cuisine in formal yet intimate environment of burgundy and gold.

Homewood Park, Hinton Charterhouse, BA2 7TB, Southeast : 6 ½ m. on A 36 ℰ (01225) 723731, *info@homewoodpark.co.uk*, Fax (01225) 723820, 🔟 heated, 澤, 🚲 – ﬁ rest, ☚ 🅟. 🐵🅒 🅐🅔 🅞 VISA

Rest 22.00/44.00 ♀ – **19 rm** ☲ ✚120.00/195.00 – ✚✚160.00/280.00.

◆ Well-proportioned bedrooms, with views of the idyllic wooded gardens and croquet lawn, and cosy country house drawing rooms retain strong elements of the Georgian interior. Ask for dining room window table when garden is in full bloom.

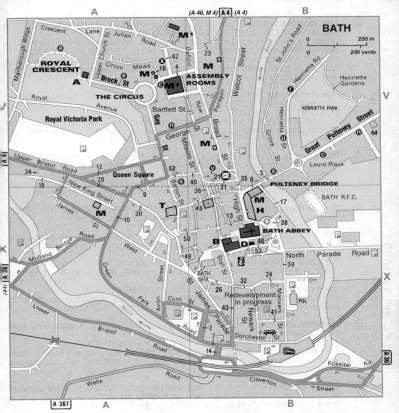

BATH

🏛 **Queensberry,** Russell St, BA1 2QF, ☎ (01225) 447928, *reservations@thequeens berry.co.uk, Fax (01225) 446065*, ☞ – 🔊 🅿. 🐾🅾 🅰🅴 𝘝𝘐𝘚𝘈. ✂
AV x
Rest – (see *Olive Tree* below) – ☱ 14.50 – **29 rm** ✸95.00/300.00 – ✸✸95.00/300.00.
◆ Classy boutique merger of Georgian town house décor with contemporary furnishing, understated style and well-chosen detail. Ample, unfussy rooms; pretty courtyard garden.

🏛 **Dukes,** Great Pulteney St, BA2 4DN, ☎ (01225) 787960, *info@dukesbath.co.uk, Fax (01225) 787961*, ☞ – ✂✕. 🐾🅾 🅰🅴 🅾 𝘝𝘐𝘚𝘈. ✂
BV n
Cavendish: Rest 15.95 (lunch) and dinner a la carte 15.95/36.40 – ☱ 7.95 – **13 rm** ✸100.00/115.00 – ✸✸135.00/155.00, 4 suites.
◆ Attractive townhouse in fine Georgian street. Paved terrace with parasols. Spacious, autumnally coloured bar with leather sofas. Classically styled rooms with rich décor. Lower ground floor restaurant for modern British cuisine.

ENGLAND

The Windsor, 69 Great Pulteney St, BA2 4DL, ✆ (01225) 422100, *sales@bathwindsorhotel.com*, Fax (01225) 422550 – ✦✦ ✆ ⬅ **P**, **◖◗** **AE** **①** **VISA**. ✦✦   BV c
closed 1 week Christmas – **Sakura :** Rest - Japanese - *(closed Sunday-Monday)* (booking essential) (dinner only) 25.00/28.00 **s.** – **14 rm** ⌷ **†**65.00/125.00 – **††**145.00/250.00.
◆ Grade I listed building in Georgian boulevard. Fine furniture and tastefully co-ordinated floral fabrics in individually styled rooms, some overlooking a Japanese garden. Small Japanese restaurant specialising in teppan- yaki and shabu-shabu.

The Residence without rest., Weston Rd, BA1 2XZ, ✆ (01225) 750180, *info@theresidencebath.com*, Fax (01225) 750181, ⬅, ✦✦ – ✦✦ **TV** ✆ **P**.   Y n
6 rm ⌷ **†**150.00 – **††**300.00.
◆ Unobtrusive service underpins this beautifully restored Grade I Georgian house boasting secluded garden, summer house and terrace, sleek breakfast room and stunning bedrooms.

The County without rest., 18-19 Pulteney Rd, BA2 4EZ, ✆ (01225) 425003, *reservations@county-hotel.co.uk*, Fax (01225) 466493 – ✦✦ ✆ **P**, **◖◗** **AE** **VISA**. ✦✦   Z o
closed 21 December-12 January – **22 rm** ⌷ **†**75.00/95.00 – **††**112.00/115.00.
◆ Well-maintained Edwardian house in sight of the Abbey and rugby ground. Comprehensively but sensitively updated rooms, larger on first floor, and comfortable Reading Room.

The Ayrlington without rest., 24-25 Pulteney Rd, BA2 4EZ, ✆ (01225) 425495, *mail@ayrlington.com*, Fax (01225) 469029, ✦✦ – ✦✦ ♿ **P**, **◖◗** **AE** **VISA**. ✦✦   Z o
closed 23 December-2 January – **14 rm** ⌷ **†**75.00/125.00 – **††**175.00.
◆ An interesting blend of Georgian styling and Asian artefacts develops through twelve spacious, subtly themed rooms. Charming cherry tree garden overlooks croquet club.

Paradise House without rest., 86-88 Holloway, BA2 4PX, ✆ (01225) 317723, *info@paradise-house.co.uk*, Fax (01225) 482005, ⬅, ✦✦ – ✦✦ ⬅ **P**, **◖◗** **AE** **①** **VISA**. ✦✦   Z c
closed 4 days Christmas – **11 rm** ⌷ **†**69.00/170.00 – **††**65.00/165.00.
◆ Elegant yet homely hotel on Beechen Cliff. Most rear-facing rooms have exceptional city views; all reflect 18C origins in their décor and boast Jacuzzis. Beautiful gardens.

Oldfields without rest., 102 Wells Rd, BA2 3AL, ✆ (01225) 317984, *info@oldfields.co.uk*, Fax (01225) 444471, ✦✦ – ✦✦ **P**, **◖◗** **VISA**. ✦✦   Z u
closed 24-26 December – **16 rm** ⌷ **†**49.00/95.00 – **††**75.00/150.00.
◆ Spaciously elegant Victorian house with comfy, well-furnished drawing room, breakfast room boasting 'Bath rooftops' view and bedrooms that exude a high standard of comfort.

Apsley House without rest., 141 Newbridge Hill, BA1 3PT, ✆ (01225) 336966, *info@apsley-house.co.uk*, Fax (01225) 425462, ✦✦ – ✦✦ **P**, **◖◗** **AE** **VISA**. ✦✦   Y x
closed 22-27 December – **11 rm** ⌷ **†**55.00/75.00 – **††**85.00/155.00.
◆ Built for the Duke of Wellington and staffed with the unobtrusive calm of an English private house. Spacious individual rooms; two open on to a peaceful, mature rear garden.

Kennard without rest., 11 Henrietta St, BA2 6LL, ✆ (01225) 310472, *reception@kennard.co.uk*, Fax (01225) 460054 – ✦✦ **P**, **◖◗** **AE** **①** **VISA**. ✦✦   BV u
12 rm ⌷ **†**54.00/79.00 – **††**85.00/128.00.
◆ Beautifully furnished townhouse from Bath's golden age; each bedroom individually appointed in classic or contemporary style to very high standard. Charming breakfast room.

Cheriton House without rest., 9 Upper Oldfield Park, BA2 3JX, ✆ (01225) 429862, *info@cheritonhouse.co.uk*, Fax (01225) 428403, ✦✦ – ✦✦ ✆ **P**, **◖◗** **VISA**. ✦✦   Z u
12 rm ⌷ **†**60.00/90.00 – **††**80.00/160.00.
◆ Comfortable, sizeable rooms and lounge, refurbished in keeping with the house's 19C origins, with some fine tiled fireplaces. Conservatory breakfast room. Charming hosts.

Dorian House without rest., 1 Upper Oldfield Park, BA2 3JX, ✆ (01225) 426336, *info@dorianhouse.co.uk*, Fax (01225) 444699, ⬅, ✦✦ – ✦✦ **P**, **◖◗** **AE** **VISA**. ✦✦   Z u
11 rm ⌷ **†**55.00/180.00 – **††**75.00/180.00.
◆ Charming 19C house preserves original tiling and stained glass; attic rooms are refreshingly modern, others Victorian. Breakfast to recordings of owner's cello performances.

Bloomfield House without rest., 146 Bloomfield Rd, BA2 2AS, ✆ (01225) 420105, *info@ecobloomfield.com*, ⬅, ✦✦ – ✦✦ **P**, **◖◗** **AE** **VISA**. ✦✦   Z r
6 rm ⌷ **†**65.00 – **††**100.00/140.00.
◆ Bath's first eco-hotel is in this Grade II listed Georgian building. Breakfast produce is organic, fair trade or, whenever possible, locally sourced. Tastefully elegant rooms.

Tasburgh House without rest., Warminster Rd, BA2 6SH, East : 1 m. on A 36   *℘* (01225) 425096, *hotel@bathtasburgh.co.uk*, Fax (01225) 463842, ≤, 🐾 – ✗ ⌒ 🅿 📧 *VISA*. ✗   Y a

closed Christmas – **12 rm** ⌒ 60.00/75.00 – ✦✦130.00.
* Personally run by charming owner. Rear bedrooms, decorated with original artwork and named after British authors, overlook Avon Valley. Walk along the canal into Bath.

Villa Magdala without rest., Henrietta Rd, BA2 6LX,   *℘* (01225) 466329, *office@villamag dala.co.uk*, Fax (01225) 483207, 🐾 – ✗ 🅿 📧 *VISA*. ✗   BV r

closed 25-26, 31 December, and 1 January – **18 rm** ✦75.00/85.00 – ✦✦98.00/150.00.
* Named after Napier's 1868 victory. Well-equipped rooms, floral furnishings; carefully preserved ornate balustrade and showpiece bedroom with four-poster and chaise longue.

Harington's, 8-10 Queen St, BA1 1HE,   *℘* (01225) 461728, *post@haringtonshotel.co.uk*, Fax (01225) 444804 – ✗ ⌒ 🅿 📧 *AE* *VISA*. ✗   AV s

closed 1-12 January – **Rest** a la carte 17.00/23.00 s. ⌒ – **13 rm** ⌒ ✦68.00/118.00 – ✦✦88.00/148.00.
* 18C houses on a cobbled street in the heart of the city and perfectly located for the shops. Simply styled but diligently maintained accommodation on offer. Bar in hot ochre and yellow adjoins restaurant.

Express by Holiday Inn without rest., Lower Bristol Rd, Brougham Hayes, BA2 3QU,   *℘* (0870) 4442792, *bath@expressholidayinn.co.uk*, Fax (0870) 4442793 – 📶 ✗ ♿ 🅿 – 🔬 30. 📧 *AE* ⓞ *VISA*   Z z

126 rm ✦69.00/99.00 – ✦✦69.00/99.00.
* Lodge style accommodation close to main railway station: the city centre is just five minutes' walk away. Modern bedrooms with power showers. Breakfast area near foyer.

Haydon House without rest., 9 Bloomfield Park, off Bloomfield Rd, BA2 2BY,   *℘* (01225) 444919, *stay@haydonhouse.co.uk*, Fax (01225) 427351, 🐾 – ✗ 🅿 📧 *VISA*. ✗   Z a

5 rm ⌒ 55.00/85.00 – ✦✦75.00/130.00.
* Pristine bedrooms and lounge in calm pastels, full of the charming, thoughtful details of a family home. Leafy bowers and trellises. Friendly hosts serve delicious breakfasts.

The Town House without rest., 7 Bennett St, BA1 2QJ,   *℘* (01225) 422505, *stay@the townhousebath.co.uk*, Fax (01225) 422505 – ✗. 📧 *AE* *VISA*   AV c

closed January – **3 rm** ⌒ ✦75.00/80.00 – ✦✦88.00/95.00.
* Welcoming 18C house in excellent location, designed by John Wood and rebuilt after war damage. Spacious bedrooms with South African wildlife décor. Communal breakfast.

Lavender House without rest., 17 Bloomfield Park, off Bloomfield Rd, BA2 2BY,   *℘* (01225) 314500, *lavenderhouse@btinternet.com*, Fax (01225) 448564, 🐾 – ✗. ✗   Z s

5 rm ⌒ ✦48.00/75.00 – ✦✦90.00/98.00.
* Edwardian house run with confidence and brio. Comfortable, smartly refurbished rooms in rose, blue, gold, terracotta and lavender. Guesthouse cats patrol a pleasant garden. Smart dining room overlooks garden.

Meadowland without rest., 36 Bloomfield Park, off Bloomfield Rd, BA2 2BX,   *℘* (01225) 311079, *stay@meadowlandbath.co.uk*, Fax (01225) 311079, 🐾 – ✗ 🅿 📧 *VISA*. ✗   Z e

3 rm ⌒ 55.00/65.00 – ✦✦85.00/95.00.
* Small suburban guesthouse with a welcoming ambience; comfortably furnished and immaculately maintained accommodation. A neat breakfast room gives onto a lawned garden.

Brocks without rest., 32 Brock St, BA1 2LN,   *℘* (01225) 338374, *brocks@brocksguest house.co.uk* – ✗. 📧 *VISA*. ✗   AV e

closed Christmas and New Year – **6 rm** ⌒ 63.00/70.00 – ✦✦85.00/99.00.
* Between the Circus and the Royal Crescent, a 1765 terraced house, welcoming and well run, offering homely, comfortable en suite rooms. Well-priced for its excellent location.

Athole without rest., 33 Upper Oldfield Park, BA2 3JX,   *℘* (01225) 334307, *info@athole house.co.uk*, Fax (01225) 320009, 🐾 – ✗ ⌒ 🅿 📧 *VISA*. ✗   Z i

4 rm ⌒ ✦52.00/62.00 – ✦✦82.00.
* Spacious, bay windowed Victorian guesthouse with large garden, away from city centre. Bright breakfast room; conservatory lounge. Light, airy, contemporary bedrooms.

Cranleigh without rest., 159 Newbridge Hill, BA1 3PX,   *℘* (01225) 310197, *cran leigh@btinternet.com*, Fax (01225) 423143, 🐾 – ✗ 🅿 📧 *VISA*. ✗   Y e

closed 25-26 December – **9 rm** ⌒ ✦45.00/65.00 – ✦✦60.00/95.00.
* Airy, high-ceilinged bedrooms, the largest ideal for families, with brightly patterned fabrics. Pleasant south-facing garden. Smoked salmon and eggs a breakfast speciality.

XX   **Olive Tree** (at Queensberry H.), Russell St, BA1 2QF,   *℘* (01225) 447928, *reserva tions@thequeensberry.co.uk*, Fax (01225) 446065 – ✗ 📧 *AE* *VISA*   AV x

closed Monday lunch – **Rest** 16.50 (lunch) and a la carte 30.95/40.95 ⌒ ⌒.
* Up-to-date restaurant with a classy, stylish and contemporary ambience. Modern artworks adorn the split-level basement. Modern British cooking. Helpful staff.

ENGLAND

X **Hole in the Wall**, 16 George St, BA1 2EH, ℰ (01225) 425242, info@theholeinthe
wall.co.uk, Fax (01225) 425242 – ✦✦ ✧ 10. ◍◉ 𝗩𝗜𝗦𝗔
AV r
closed 25-26 December and Sunday lunch – **Rest** 13.95 (lunch) and a la carte 13.95/27.65 ♀
♦ Once a starting point of British culinary renaissance; former coal hole mixes whitewashed walls, antique chairs and a relaxed mood. Slightly eclectic cuisine.

X **No.5**, 5 Argyle St, BA2 4BA, ℰ (01225) 444499, Fax (01225) 444499 – ✦✦. ◍◉ 𝗔𝗘
𝗩𝗜𝗦𝗔
BV s
closed 25-26 December and 1-3 January – **Rest** a la carte 23.95/31.40 𝒸🍴 ♀.
♦ Unfussy bistro with a distinctly buzzy feel. Personally run by cheery French owner. Fish
night on Wednesday a speciality. Menus offer ample variety; some are good value, too.

X **Fishworks**, 6 Green St, BA1 2JY, ℰ (01225) 448707, bath@fishworks.co.uk, 🍴 – ✦✦
◍◉ 𝗔𝗘 𝗩𝗜𝗦𝗔
BV a
closed 25-26 December, 1 January, Sunday, Monday and Bank Holidays – **Rest** – Seafood -
(booking essential) a la carte 20.00/40.00 ♀.
♦ Behind a quality fish shop, whose produce appears on menus. Bustling ambience. Extensive, daily changing blackboard specials; the cooking is straightforward and unfussy.

at Box *Northeast : 4¾ m. on A 4 –* Y *– ✉ Bath.*

🍴 **The Northey**, Bath Rd, SN13 8AE, ℰ (01225) 742333, ohhcompany@aol.com,
Fax (01225) 742333, 🍴, 🌲 – ✦✦ 🅿. ◍◉ 𝗩𝗜𝗦𝗔. 🦆
closed 25, 26 and dinner 31 December and dinner 1 January – **Rest** a la carte 20.00/30.00 ♀.
♦ Spacious roadside pub with pleasant rear terrace. Modern interior dominated by
chunky wooden tables and rattan chairs. Serious modern cooking lays claim to restaurant
style.

at Colerne *(Wilts.) Northeast : 6½ m. by A 4 –* Y *– , Batheaston rd and Bannerdown Rd – ✉ Chippenham.*

🏨 **Lucknam Park** 🌿, SN14 8AZ, North : ½ m. on Marshfield rd ℰ (01225) 742777, reserva
✿ tions@lucknampark.co.uk, Fax (01225) 743536, ≼, ⌖, Ⅰₛ, ≅ₛ, 🔲, 🌲, 🦆 – ✦✦ rest, ✆ 🅿 –
🖘 40. ◍◉ 𝗔𝗘 ◍ 𝗩𝗜𝗦𝗔. 🦆
Rest (booking essential) 30.00/55.00 s. ♀ – 🖙 18.50 – **37 rm** ✸245.00 – ✸✸635.00, 4 suites.
Spec. Devon duck three ways. Pork belly with foie gras and caramelised apples. Vanilla
cream, feuillantine of raspberries.
♦ Luxurious Palladian mansion set in 500 acres of listed parkland and superb gardens.
Drawing rooms, panelled library and spacious bedrooms, all in delightful period style.
Chandeliered restaurant where accomplished cuisine matches the style of the surround-
ings.

Do not confuse X with ✿!
X defines comfort, while stars are awarded for the best cuisine,
across all categories of comfort.

BATTLE *E. Sussex 504 V 31 Great Britain G. – pop. 5 190.*
See : *Town★ – Abbey and Site of the Battle of Hastings★ AC.*
🛈 *Battle Abbey, High St ℰ (01424) 773721, battletic@rother.gov.uk.*
London 55 – Brighton 34 – Folkestone 43 – Maidstone 30.

🏛 **PowderMills** 🌿, Powdermill Lane, TN33 0SP, South : 1½ m. by A 2100 on Catsfield rd
ℰ (01424) 775511, powdc@aol.com, Fax (01424) 774540, ≼, 🍴, ⌧, 🦢, 🌲, 🛥 – ✦✦ rest,
✆ 🅿 – 🖘 250. ◍◉ 𝗔𝗘 ◍ 𝗩𝗜𝗦𝗔. 🦆
Orangery : Rest 18.75/29.50 and dinner a la carte 35.00/40.00 – **40 rm** 🖙 ✸99.00 –
✸✸130.00/195.00.
♦ Part Georgian gunpowder mill in 150 acres of woods and lakes. Individually decorated
rooms - more sizable in annex and with better views - combine antiques and modern
pieces. Dining room terrace overlooks pool.

⌂ **Fox Hole Farm** 🌿 without rest., Kane Hythe Rd, TN33 9QU, Northwest : 2½ m. by A
🏚 2100 and A 271 on B 2096 (Netherfield rd) ℰ (01424) 772053, foxholefarm@amserve.com,
Fax (01424) 772053, 🌲, 🛥 – ✦✦ 🅿. ◍◉ 𝗩𝗜𝗦𝗔
closed Christmas and January – 3 rm 🖙 ✸40.00/49.00 – ✸✸58.00/63.00.
♦ Peaceful 18C woodcutters cottage by 1000 acres of protected forest. Simple pine
furnished bedrooms with sea-grass matting. Timbered lounge centred around a log
stove.

BAUGHURST Hants..
London 61 – Camberley 28 – Farnborough 27.

 The Wellington Arms, Baughurst Rd, RG26 5LP, Southwest : ¾ m. ✆ (0118) 982 0110, *simon@thewellingtonarms.com,* 斎, 辭 – ✕ 🄿 🆖 *VISA*
Rest *(closed Monday, Tuesday lunch and Sunday dinner)* (booking essential) 15.00 (lunch) and a la carte 22.00/35.00 ♀.
♦ 16C former hunting lodge: characterful interior includes books, ornaments and original terracotta tiles. Worldwide influences smoothly underpin modern British cooking.

BAWBURGH Norfolk **504** X 26 – *see Norwich.*

BEACONSFIELD Bucks. **504** S 29 – *pop. 12 292.*
🄸 *Beaconsfield Seer Green* ✆ (01494) 676545.
London 26 – Aylesbury 19 – Oxford 32.

🏨 **Bellhouse,** Oxford Rd, HP9 2XE, East : 1 ¾ m. on A 40 ✆ (01753) 893891, *info@bellhousehotel.co.uk,* Fax (01753) 888231, 🛵, 🚅, 🔲, 辭 – 🛗 ✕ 🄿 – 🔬 400. 🆖 🄰🄴 *VISA*
Archways : Rest *(closed lunch Saturday and Bank Holidays)* (buffet lunch)/dinner 17.00/24.75 – **Aquarium :** Rest *(closed lunch Saturday and Bank Holidays)* 17.00 (lunch) and a la carte 24.75/35.00 **s.** – **145 rm** ♀ 🛏160.00/180.00 – 🛏🛏200.00, 1 suites.
♦ A splendid level of modern facilities, particularly in the more boldly decorated executive rooms. Smartly run and commercially driven, with extensive conference suites. Archways is centred round a gleaming grand piano. Aquarium tables overlook pool.

at Wooburn Common Southwest : 3½ m. by A 40 – ⊠ Beaconsfield.

🏠 **Chequers Inn** 🍽, Kiln Lane, HP10 0JQ, Southwest : 1 m. on Bourne End rd ✆ (01628) 529575, *info@chequers-inn.com,* Fax (01628) 850124, 斎, 辭 – 🄿, 🔬 45. 🆖 🄰🄴 🄾 *VISA*. 🍽
closed dinner 25 December and dinner 1 January – **Rest** 19.95 (lunch) and a la carte 30.00/45.00 ♀ – **17 rm** ♀ 🛏99.50 – 🛏🛏107.50.
♦ Coaching inn dating from 18C. Good-sized bedrooms with leaded lattice windows and something of a country cottage feel. Popular with business travellers. Restaurant boasts exposed beams and brickwork.

BEADNELL Northd. **501 502** P 17.
London 341 – Edinburgh 81 – Newcastle upon Tyne 47.

🏠 **Beach Court** without rest., Harbour Rd, NE67 5BJ, ✆ (01665) 720225, *info@beachcourt.com,* Fax (01665) 721499, ≤ Beadnell Bay – ✕ 🄿, 🆖 🄰🄴 *VISA*
closed Christmas - New Year – ♀ 4.95 – **3 rm** 🛏64.50 – 🛏🛏99.00/119.00 139.00.
♦ Turreted house enjoys fine views of Beadnell Bay. Simple, traditional en suite rooms; leafy little conservatory. Hospitable owners with a real enthusiasm for entertaining.

BEAMHURST Staffs. – *see Uttoxeter.*

BEAMINSTER Dorset **503** L 31 – *pop. 2 791.*
🄸 *Chedington Court, South Perrott* ✆ (01935) 891413.
London 154 – Exeter 45 – Taunton 30 – Weymouth 29.

🏨 **Bridge House,** 3 Prout Bridge, DT8 3AY, ✆ (01308) 862200, *enquiries@bridgehouse.co.uk,* Fax (01308) 863700, 辭 – ✕ 🌜 🄿, 🆖 🄰🄴 *VISA*
– **Rest** *(closed Monday-Tuesday November-April)* (residents only Sunday and Monday dinner) 36.50 (dinner) and a la carte 35.00/45.50 ♀ – **14 rm** ♀ 🛏50.00/106.00 – 🛏🛏140.00/150.00.
♦ Priest's house reputed to date back to the 1200s. Large bedrooms, in the new block, with cheerful floral fabrics. Firelit lounge, charming walled garden, informal, rural feel. Oak beamed restaurant with conservatory.

We try to be as accurate as possible when giving room rates.
But prices are susceptible to change,
so please check rates when booking.

BEARSTED Kent 504 V 30 – see Maidstone.

BEAULIEU Hants. 503 504 P 31 Great Britain G. – ⊠ Brockenhurst.
See : Town★★ - National Motor Museum★★ AC.
Env. : Buckler's Hard★ (Maritime Museum★ AC) SE : 2 m.
London 102 – Bournemouth 24 – Southampton 13 – Winchester 23.

🏨🏨 **Montagu Arms,** Palace Lane, SO42 7ZL, ℰ (01590) 612324, reservations@montaguarm
shotel.co.uk, Fax (01590) 612188, 🛱, 🖛 – 📞 ℙ – 🕍 40. 🐠 ẞ 🖐 🗺. 🛠
Terrace : Rest 39.00 s. – **Monty's Brasserie :** Rest a la carte 18.95/34.00 s. ⌾ – 21 rm ⌷
⭑125.00/135.00 – ⭑⭑180.00, 2 suites.
♦ Ivy-covered 18C inn. Bedrooms, in various shapes and sizes, can't quite match the
warmth of the inviting panelled lounge with log fires, but are tidy with useful mod cons. A
pretty garden adjoins panelled Terrace. Monty's is bright, warm brasserie.

at Bucklers Hard South : 2½ m. – ⊠ Brockenhurst.

🏨 **Master Builder's House** 🦢, SO42 7XB, ℰ (01590) 616253, res@themasterbuild
ers.co.uk, Fax (01590) 616297, ≼, 🛱, 🖛 –⬜, ✎ rm, ℙ– 🕍 40. 🐠 🖐 🗺. 🛠
Riverview : Rest 19.50/25.95 and a la carte 21.95/35.00 ⌾ – 23 rm ⌷ ⭑75.00/139.00 –
⭑⭑99.00/190.00, 2 suites.
♦ In 18C village, once home to the master shipwright. Lounge boasts inglenook, restored
with easy country house style. Rooms in the old house have naval prints and sea chests.
Riverview is smartly set by Beaulieu River.

Red = Pleasant. Look for the red 🋲 and 🏠 symbols.

ENGLAND

BEAUMONT Channel Islands – see Jersey.

BEDFORD Beds. 504 S 27 – pop. 82 488.
🏌 Bedfordshire, Bromham Rd, Biddenham ℰ (01234) 261669 Y – 🏌 Mowsbury, Kimbolton
Rd ℰ (01234) 771041.
🅱 The Old Town Hall, St Paul's Sq ℰ (01234) 215226, tourisminfo@bedford.gov.uk.
London 59 – Cambridge 31 – Colchester 70 – Leicester 51 – Lincoln 95 – Luton 20 – Oxford
52 – Southend-on-Sea 85.

Plan opposite

🏨🏨 **The Barns,** Cardington Rd, MK44 3SA, East : 2 m. on A 603 ℰ (0870) 6096108, bed
ford@corushotels.com, Fax (01234) 273102, 🖛 – ✎ 🕭 ℙ – 🕍 120. 🐠 ẞ 🖐 🗺 Y n
Rest (closed Saturday lunch) 18.50 and a la carte 21.50/32.50 ⌾ – ⌷ 10.50 – 48 rm ⭑99.00
– ⭑⭑99.00/149.00.
♦ In 3 acres of gardens on the banks of the Great Ouse. Spacious, well equipped rooms.
Fine 13C tithe barn, now a function room: lofty timbered ceiling, agricultural curios. Adjoining cocktail bar and riverside brasserie.

🏨🏨 **Bedford Swan,** The Embankment, MK40 1RW, ℰ (01234) 346565, info@bedfordswan
hotel.co.uk, Fax (01234) 212009, 🛱, 🖳 – 🛗 ✎, 🍴 rest, ℙ – 🕍 250. 🐠 ẞ 🖐 🗺
🛠   X a
Rest 16.00/22.50 and a la carte 23.85/32.65 s. – ⌷ 11.95 – 113 rm ⭑130.00 – ⭑⭑135.00
140.00.
♦ Impressive Georgian house, built in 1794 for the Duke of Bedford. The more modern
bedrooms have ample work space, and a grandiose indoor pool has ancient Roman style.
Restaurant on the banks of the Great Ouse.

at Elstow South : 2 m. by A 6 – ⊠ Bedford.

🍴🍴 **St Helena,** High St, MK42 9XP, ℰ (01234) 344848, 🖛 – ✎ ℙ. 🐠 ẞ 🖐 🗺   Y r
closed Christmas-New Year, Saturday lunch, Sunday and Monday – **Rest** 21.00/35.00 and a
la carte 29.75/46.50.
♦ Part light, modern conservatory, part antique-furnished dining room of 16C origin.
Personally run. Creative, seasonal menus and appetising daily specials. Attentive service.

at Houghton Conquest South : 6½ m. by A 6 – Y – ⊠ Bedford.

🏠 **Knife and Cleaver,** The Grove, MK45 3LA, ℰ (01234) 740387, info@knifeandclea
ver.com, Fax (01234) 740900, 🛱, 🖛 – ✎ rest, 🛗 ℙ. 🐠 ẞ 🖐 🗺
closed 27-30 December – **Rest** (closed Sunday dinner) 15.95/22.50 and a la carte
22.00/34.00 ⌾ – 9 rm ⌷ ⭑59.00 – ⭑⭑59.00/84.00.
♦ An intimate bar, panelled in Jacobean oak and serving real ales and ciders, plus traditionally styled bedrooms in a redbrick village pub opposite All Saints church. Leafy conservatory
restaurant spread with rugs.

BEDFORD

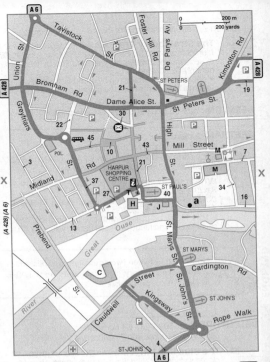

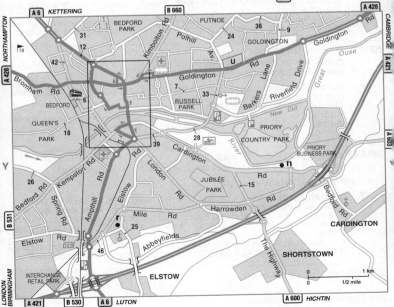

117

at Milton Ernest Northwest : 5 m. on A 6 – Y – ⊠ Bedford.

XX **The Strawberry Tree**, Radwell Rd, MK44 1RY, ☎ (01234) 823633, strawberrytree–res taurant@yahoo.co.uk, Fax (01234) 823633, 🌧 – ⇆ **P**. **MO** **OD** **VISA**
closed January, 2 weeks summer, and Sunday-Wednesday – **Rest** (booking essential) (dinner only) 32.50/45.00.
• 18C thatched cottage run by enthusiastic family team. Market-fresh produce and some seasonal ingredients from the garden combine to create a confident, well-balanced menu.

BEESTON Notts. 502 503 504 Q 25 – see Nottingham.

BEETHAM Cumbria Great Britain G.
Env. : Levens Hall★, N : 2 m. by A 6.
Exc. : Cartmel Priory★, W : 10 m. by A 6, A 590 and B 5277.
London 263 – Carnforth 8 – Milnthorpe 1.

🍴 **Wheatsheaf Inn** with rm, LA7 7AL, ☎ (015395) 62123, wheatbeeth@aol.com, Fax (015395) 64840 – ⇆ **P**. **MO** **VISA**. 🍽
closed 8-18 January and 25 December – **Rest** a la carte 17.50/28.00 ⌿ – **6 rm** ⊇ ✱55.00/65.00 – ✱✱75.00/95.00.
• Part 16C stone built inn with two dining areas, one bustling, the other relaxed. Menus cover interesting range of British dishes: watch for Charlie the parrot! Homely rooms.

Undecided between two equivalent establishments?
Within each category, establishments are classified
in our order of preference.

ENGLAND

BELCHFORD Lincs. 502 T 24 – ⊠ Horncastle.
London 169 – Horncastle 5 – Lincoln 28.

🍴 **The Blue Bell Inn**, 1 Main Rd, LN9 6LQ, ☎ (01507) 533602 – ⇆ **P**. **MO** **VISA**
closed second and third week January – **Rest** (closed Sunday dinner and Monday) a la carte 14.45/24.40 ⌿.
• Yes, a huge blue bell hangs outside (provenance unclear). Cosy pub, personally run, with beams and exposed brick. Comfy armchairs at bar. Adventurous dishes and pub classics.

BELFORD Northd. 501 502 O 17.
🛈 Belford, South Rd ☎ (01668) 213323.
London 335 – Edinburgh 71 – Newcastle upon Tyne 49.

⌂ **Market Cross** without rest., 1 Church St, NE70 7LS, ☎ (01668) 213013, details@market cross.net, 🌧 – ⇆ **MO** **VISA**
4 rm ⊇ ✱45.00/65.00 – ✱✱65.00/75.00.
• 200 year-old stone house in rural town centre. Warmly decorated lounge, homely touches in tasteful bedrooms. Wide, locally inspired breakfast choice in cosy pine surroundings.

BELPER Derbs. 502 503 504 P 24 – pop. 21 938.
London 141 – Birmingham 59 – Leicester 40 – Manchester 55 – Nottingham 17.

at Shottle Northwest : 4 m. by A 517 – ⊠ Belper.

🏠 **Dannah Farm** 🌆, Bowmans Lane, DE56 2DR, North : ¼ m. by Alport rd ☎ (01773) 550273, reservations@dannah.co.uk, Fax (01773) 550590, 🌧, 🖫 – ⇆ 🛎 **P**. **MO** **VISA**. 🍽
closed 24-26 December – **Rest** closed Sunday-Monday (booking essential) (residents only) (dinner only) (set menu only) 24.50 **s**. – **8 rm** ⊇ ✱65.00/85.00 – ✱✱100.00/160.00, 2 suites.
• Ivy-clad house, well run by a husband and wife team, in over 100 acres of working farmland. Two inviting, thoughtfully furnished lounges; cosy bedrooms in old-English style.

BELTON Leics. – see Loughborough.

BEPTON W. Sussex – see Midhurst.

BERKHAMSTED *Herts.* **504** S 28 *Great Britain G.* – *pop. 18 800.*

> Exc. : *Whipsnade Wild Animal Park*★ *AC,* N : 9½ m. on A 4251, B 4506 and B 4540.
> *London 34 – Aylesbury 14 – St Albans 11.*

XX **The Pink Orchid,** 333-337 High St, HP4 1AL, *℘* (01442) 878799 – ▤. **⬤❸ VISA**
closed 25-26 December and Thai New Year – **Rest** - Thai - *(closed Monday)* 9.95/29.95 and a
la carte 18.95/30.10.
◆ Airy, comfortable interior with pink cloth-clad tables, Thai statues; hand-made wooden
menu covers. Carefully selected Thai menus: attention paid to authentic ingredients.

BERWICK-UPON-TWEED *Northd.* **501 502** O 16 *Great Britain and Scotland G.* – *pop. 12 870.*

> See : *Town*★ - *Walls*★.
> Env. : *Foulden*★, NW : 5 m. – *Paxton House (Chippendale furniture*★*) AC,* W : 5 m. by A
> 6105, A 1 and B 6461.
> Exc. : *St Abb's Head*★★ (≤★), NW : 12 m. by A 1, A 1107 and B 6438 – SW : *Tweed Valley*★★
> – *Eyemouth Museum*★ *AC,* N : 7½ m. by A 1 and A 1107 – *Holy Island*★ *(Priory ruins*★ *AC,*
> *Lindisfarne Castle*★ *AC),* SE : 9 m. by A 1167 and A 1 – *Manderston*★ *(stables*★*),* W : 13 m. by
> A 6105 – *Ladykirk (Kirk o'Steil*★*),* SW : 8½ m. by A 698 and B 6470.
> ▸ᴵ₈ *Goswick ℘* (01289) 387256 – ▸ᴵ₈ *Magdalene Fields ℘* (01289) 306130.
> 🛈 *106 Marygate ℘* (01289) 330733, *tourism@berwick-upon-tweed.gov.uk.*
> *London 349 – Edinburgh 57 – Newcastle upon Tyne 63.*

🏠🏠 **Marshall Meadows Country House** ⟋, TD15 1UT, North : 2 ¾ m. by A 1
℘ (01289) 331133, *stay@marshallmeadows.co.uk,* Fax (01289) 331438, ≤, ≋, 🐾 – ↹↤ 🅿. –
🄰 180. **⬤❸ AE VISA**
closed 18 December - 2 January – **Rest** *(bar lunch)/dinner* 26.00 – **18 rm** ⊇ ✸85.00/95.00
– ✸✸115.00/150.00, 1 suite.
◆ Privately owned Georgian country house with sympathetic extension, neat lawned gardens, woodland walks. Co-ordinated country house style rooms; larger in original building.
Two traditional, formal dining rooms.

🏠 **Sallyport,** 1 Sallyport, TD15 1EZ, off Bridge St *℘* (01289) 308827, *info@sallyport.co.uk* –
↹↤. **⬤❸ VISA**
Rest *(communal dining)* 35.00 – **5 rm** ⊇ ✸90.00 – ✸✸90.00/150.00.
◆ 17C Grade II listed house on cobbled alley. The bedrooms are a strong point: they boast
a boutique style, with a high standard of facilities, and lots of homely extra touches.
Characterful farmhouse kitchen style dining room.

🏠 **West Coates,** 30 Castle Terrace, TD15 1NZ, North : ¾ m. by Castlegate on Kelso rd
℘ (01289) 309666, *karenbrownwestcoates@yahoo.com,* Fax (01289) 309666, ▨, ≋ – ↹↤
🅿. **⬤❸ VISA**
closed Christmas-New Year – **Rest** *dinner only* (by arrangement) *(communal dining)* 35.00
– **3 rm** ✸60.00/70.00 – ✸✸100.00.
◆ Step off the train and you're practically at the front door of this personally run 19C
house set in mature garden and grounds. Welcoming lounge; annex boasts pool and hot
tub. Communal dining table; fine border ingredients are sourced.

BEVERLEY *East Riding* **502** S 22 *Great Britain G.* – *pop. 29 110* – ✉ *Kingston-upon-Hull.*

> See : *Town*★ - *Minster*★★ - *St Mary's Church*★.
> ▸ᴵ₈ *The Westwood ℘* (01482) 868757.
> 🛈 *34 Butcher Row ℘* (01482) 867430, *beverley.tic@eastriding.gov.uk.*
> *London 188 – Kingston-upon-Hull 8 – Leeds 52 – York 29.*

🏠🏠 **Tickton Grange,** Tickton, HU17 9SH, Northeast : 3 ¾ m. on A 1035 *℘* (01964) 543666,
info@ticktongrange.co.uk, Fax (01964) 542556, ≋ – ↹↤ 🅿. – 🄰 200. **⬤❸ AE ⬤ VISA**. ⁑
Squires Dining Room : **Rest** 21.00/36.50 and dinner a la carte 29.20/35.20 ⁑ – **17 rm** ⊇
✸90.00 – ✸✸140.00/140.00.
◆ Carefully renovated bedrooms blend Georgian and contemporary architecture, antique
and period-inspired furniture. Richly swagged fabrics and open fires in an inviting lounge.
Dine in the Georgian style; large bay windows look out onto the lawn.

at South Dalton *Northwest : 5 m. by A 164 and B 1248* – ✉ *Beverley.*

🍴 **The Pipe and Glass Inn,** West End, HU17 7PN, *℘* (01430) 810246, ≋ – ↹↤ 🅿. **⬤❸**
VISA. ⁑
closed 2 weeks January and 25 December – **Rest** *(closed Sunday dinner and Monday)* a la
carte 20.00/30.00.
◆ Resurrected 18C inn benefitting from injection of money, time and effort. Snug bar,
stylish sitting area, and restaurant serving tasty, seasonal food with East Riding accent.

BEYTON *Suffolk* **504** W 27 – *see Bury St Edmunds.*

BIBURY *Glos.* **503 504** O 28 *Great Britain G.* – ⊠ *Cirencester.*

See : *Village★.*

London 86 – Gloucester 26 – Oxford 30.

🏨 **The Swan,** GL7 5NW, ℰ (01285) 740695, info@swanhotel.co.uk, Fax (01285) 740473, ㊟, 🍸, 🐎 – 🛗 ⅙★ 🅿 – 🔏 140. 🕮 🗛 ⓪ 𝐕𝐈𝐒𝐀. ⅍

Gallery : Rest (dinner only) 29.95 – **Café Swan :** Rest a la carte 17.35/26.65 – **18 rm** ⊡ ✱99.00/180.00 – ✱✱220.00/260.00.

♦ Ivy-clad 17C coaching inn with private gardens; idyllic location by a trout stream. Comfortable rooms in pretty country style, some with canopied beds. Gallery is formally stylish and spacious. Café Swan is a brasserie with stone-flagged courtyard.

⌂ **Cotteswold House** without rest., Arlington, GL7 5ND, on B 4425 ℰ (01285) 740609, enquiries@cotteswoldhouse.org.uk, Fax (01285) 740609 – ⅙★ 🅿. 🕮 𝐕𝐈𝐒𝐀. ⅍

3 rm ⊡ ✱45.00 – ✱✱65.00.

♦ Set in a manicured garden outside the picturesque village. Simple, spotless and modestly priced bedrooms, comprehensively remodelled behind a Victorian façade. Non smoking.

BIDDENDEN *Kent* **504** V 30 *Great Britain G.* – pop. 2 205.

Exc. : *Bodiam Castle★★, S : 10 m. by A 262, A 229 and B 2244 – Sissinghurst Garden★, W : 3 m. by A 262 – Battle Abbey★, S : 20 m. by A 262, A 229, A 21 and A 2100.*

London 52 – Ashford 13 – Maidstone 16.

⌂ **Barclay Farmhouse** without rest., Woolpack Corner, TN27 8BQ, South : ½ m. by A 262 on Benenden rd ℰ (01580) 292626, info@barclayfarmhouse.co.uk, Fax (01580) 292288, 🐎 – ⅙★ 📞 🅿. 🕮 𝐕𝐈𝐒𝐀. ⅍

3 rm ⊡ ✱55.00/60.00 – ✱✱70.00/85.00.

♦ Set in an acre of pleasant garden: well-priced, very comfortable accommodation with fine French oak flooring and furniture. Inventive breakfasts in granary or barn conversion.

⌂ **Bishopsdale Oast** 🐎, TN27 8DR, South : 3 m. by A 262 and Benenden rd on Tenterden rd ℰ (01580) 291027, drysdale@bishopsdaleoast.co.uk, ㊟, 🐎 – ⅙★ 🅿. 🕮 𝐕𝐈𝐒𝐀. ⅍

closed Christmas Day – **Rest** (by arrangement) (communal dining) 28.20 – **5 rm** ⊡ ✱46.00/56.40 – ✱✱62.00/82.50.

♦ Extended oast house in four acres of mature grounds with wild flower garden. Comfy lounge with log fire; plenty of trinkets and books in bright, clean, good sized rooms. Family size dining table; interesting meals employ home-grown, organic produce.

✗ **The West House** (Garrett), 28 High St, TN27 8AH, ℰ (01580) 291341, thewest house@btconnect.com, Fax (01580) 291341 – 🅿. 🕮 𝐕𝐈𝐒𝐀.

❀ closed Christmas-New Year, 2 weeks August, Saturday lunch, Sunday dinner and Monday – Rest 24.00/29.50 ⚍.

Spec. Pea soup with foie gras and truffle cream. Fillet of John Dory, samphire and crab tortellini. Chocolate caramel tart, salted peanut ice cream.

♦ Characterful timbered cottages - with wood-burner and golden beams - on pretty street. Dine on refined, original dishes making good use of carefully sourced ingredients.

🍽 **The Three Chimneys,** Hareplain Rd, TN27 8LW, West : 1 ½ m. off A 262 ℰ (01580) 291472, ㊟, 🐎 – 🅿. 🕮 🗛 𝐕𝐈𝐒𝐀

closed 25 and 31 December – **Rest** (booking essential) a la carte 20.00/31.00.

♦ 15C pub with coir mat, yellow walls, dried hops, characterful original beams. Smart rear restaurant facing garden. Tasty, regularly changing menus: home-made puds of renown.

BIDEFORD *Devon* **503** H 30 *The West Country G.* – pop. 16 262.

See : *Bridge★★ – Burton Art Gallery★ AC.*

Env. : *Appledore★, N : 2 m.*

Exc. : *Clovelly★★, W : 11 m. by A 39 and B 3237 – Lundy Island★★, NW : by ferry – Rosemoor★ – Great Torrington (Dartington Crystal★ AC) SE : 7½ m. by A 386.*

🏌 *Royal North Devon, Golf Links Rd, Westward Ho* ℰ (01237) 473824 – 🏌 *Torrington, Weare Trees* ℰ (01805) 622229.

⚓ *to Lundy Island (Lundy Co. Ltd) (1 h 45 mn).*

🛈 *Victoria Park, The Quay* ℰ (01237) 477676, bidefordtic@torridge.gov.uk.

London 231 – Exeter 43 – Plymouth 58 – Taunton 60.

🏛 **Yeoldon House** 🐎, Durrant Lane, Northam, EX39 2RL, North : 1 ½ m. by B 3235 off A 386 ℰ (01237) 474400, yeoldonhouse@aol.com, Fax (01237) 476618, ≤, 🐎 – ⅙★ 🅿. 🕮 🗛 𝐕𝐈𝐒𝐀

closed 1 week Christmas – **Rest** (closed Sunday) (booking essential for non-residents) (dinner only) 30.00 ⚍ – **10 rm** ⊡ ✱70.00/120.00.

♦ Privately run 19C house with lovely gardens overlooking the Torridge. Comfortable lounge bar with books, dried flowers and curios. Period-style rooms, some with balconies. Smart restaurant overlooking river.

Memories
XX **Memories,** 8 Fore St, Northam, EX39 1AW, North : 2 m. by B 3235 off A 386 ℰ (01237) 473419, Fax (01237) 473419 – ⚒ 🔲 🆖 🆔 *VISA*
closed 1 week September, 25-26 December, 1 January, Sunday-Monday and Tuesday evening – **Rest** (dinner only) 18.00 (mid week) and a la carte at weekends 19.50/26.40.
✦ Simple, blue and white painted restaurant with vibrant local ambience. Enthusiastic owners serve well-prepared, traditional menus at a reasonable price.

at Instow *North : 3 m. by A 386 on B 3233* – ✉ *Bideford.*

🏨 **Commodore,** Marine Parade, EX39 4JN, ℰ (01271) 860347, admin@commodore-in stow.co.uk, Fax (01271) 861233, ≤ Appledore and Torridge estuary, 🌤, 🌲 – ⚒ 🅿 🆖
VISA. ⚘
Rest (bar lunch Monday-Saturday)/dinner 20.00/40.00 – **25 rm** (dinner included) ⊆
✝70.00/120.00 – ✝✝120.00/200.00.
✦ Extended former gentleman's residence, family run in a friendly spirit for over 30 years. Trim, comfy accommodation: front-facing balcony rooms overlook the estuary. Immaculate, classically styled dining room.

XX **Decks,** Marine Parade, EX39 4JJ, ℰ (01271) 860671, decks@instow.net, Fax (01271) 860820, ≤ Appledore and Torridge estuary, 🌤 – ⚒ 🔲, 🆖 🆎 *VISA*
closed 25-26 December and Sunday-Monday – **Rest** 21.45/24.50 and a la carte approx 32.15.
✦ Sit on the outside deck and watch the sun go down over Appledore. Enjoy accomplished modern dishes while contemplating the wacky murals. Superb views from all vantage points.

at Monkleigh *South : 4 m. by A 386 on A 388* – ✉ *Bideford.*

⌂ **Monkleigh House** without rest., EX39 5JR, ℰ (01805) 625453, info@monkleigh house.co.uk, 🌲 – ⚒ 🅿. ⚘
closed 3-11 February, 23 February-8 March, 24 March-1 April and 24-26 December – **3 rm**
⊆ ✝65.00/90.00 – ✝✝80.00/100.00.
✦ Attractive Georgian house set in mature gardens. Much original character remains: staircase, pelmet boards, Regency breakfast room. Stylish bedrooms with luxurious feel.

ENGLAND

Your opinions are important to us:
please write and let us know about your discoveries and experiences – good and bad!

BIGBURY
BIGBURY Devon 503 I 33 *The West Country G.*
Exc. : Kingsbridge★, E : 13 m. by B 3392 and A 379.
London 195 – Exeter 41 – Plymouth 22.

X **The Oyster Shack,** Milburn Orchard Farm, Stakes Hill, TQ7 4BE, East : 1 m. on Easton rd ℰ (01548) 810876, bigbury@oystershack.co.uk, 🌤 – ⚒ 🅿. 🆖 *VISA*
Rest - Seafood *(closed Monday October-May)* (booking essential) a la carte 17.40/34.75.
✦ Eccentric venue, half a lovely covered terrace, decorated with fishing nets. Seafood, particularly local oyster dishes; classic and modern dishes using the freshest produce.

BIGBURY-ON-SEA
BIGBURY-ON-SEA Devon 503 I 33 – ✉ Kingsbridge.
London 196 – Exeter 42 – Plymouth 23.

🏨 **Burgh Island** ⚘, TQ7 4BG, South : ½ m. by sea tractor ℰ (01548) 810514, recep tion@burghisland.com, Fax (01548) 810243, ≤ Bigbury Bay, 🌤, ⚐, 🌲, ⚲, 🎾 – 📶 ⚒ 🅿.
🆖 *VISA*. ⚘
closed 2-26 January – **Rest** (booking essential for non-residents) (dancing Wednesday and Saturday evening) 30.00 – **13 rm** (dinner included) ⊆ ✝285.00 – ✝✝340.00, 10 suites 340.00/500.00.
✦ Unique Grade II listed 1930s country house in private island setting: stylishly romantic Art Deco interior. Charmingly individual rooms with views: some have fantastic style. Ballroom dining: dress in black tie. Owners pride themselves on accomplished cooking.

🏨 **Henley** ⚘, Folly Hill, TQ7 4AR, ℰ (01548) 810240, enquiries@thehenleyhotel.co.uk, Fax (01548) 810240, ≤ Bigbury Bay and Bolt Tail, 🌲 – ⚒ 🅿. 🆖 *VISA*
March-October – **Rest** (booking essential for non-residents) (dinner only) 29.00 – **6 rm** ⊆
✝55.00/64.00 – ✝✝90.00/110.00.
✦ Personally run cottage of 16C origin. Stunning views of the bay and Bolt Tail from modern conservatory with deep wicker chairs and pleasant, individual rooms in pastel tones. Homely dining room with magnificent sea views.

BIGGLESWADE *Beds.* **504** T 27 – *pop. 15 383.*
London 46 – Bedford 12 – Luton 24.

at Old Warden *West : 3½ m. by A 6001 off B 658 – ✉ Biggleswade.*

Hare & Hounds, The Village, SG18 9HQ, ☎ (01767) 627225, *Fax (01767) 627588,* – P. MC VISA.
closed Monday except lunch Bank Holiday Monday – **Rest** *(closed Sunday dinner)* a la carte 20.00/25.00 ♀.
◆ Stylish dining pub with lawn and terrace. Very pleasant restaurant section boasts autumnal shades and tweeds. Winning mix of modern or classic dishes; locally sourced produce.

BILBROUGH *N. Yorks* **502** Q 22.

The Three Hares, Main St, YO23 3PH, ☎ (01937) 832128, *threehares@ukf.net, Fax (01937) 834626,* – P. MC VISA.
Rest *(closed Sunday dinner and Monday)* a la carte 16.00/26.00 ♀.
◆ Immaculately extended inn with 18C origins. There are four different rooms in which to dine: menus, featuring much that is local, mix Yorkshire staples and modish invention.

BILDESTON *Suffolk* **504** W 27.
London 85.5 – Bury St Edmunds 18.5 – Ipswich 15.

The Bildeston Crown with rm, 104 High St, IP7 7EB, ☎ (01449) 740510, *hayley@thebildestoncrown.co.uk, Fax (01449) 741843,* – P. MC AE VISA
Rest a la carte 28.00/50.00 – **10 rm** ☐ ★55.00/70.00 – ★★100.00/150.00.
◆ Stylishly modernised pub with 15C roots, typified by beamed bar and inglenook. Dining room merges period and modern decor. Elaborate or classic dishes. Delightful bedrooms.

ENGLAND

BILLESLEY *Warks. – see Stratford-upon-Avon.*

BILLINGSHURST *W. Sussex* **504** S 30 – *pop. 5 465.*
London 44 – Brighton 24 – Guildford 25 – Portsmouth 40.

Old Wharf without rest., Wharf Farm, Newbridge, RH14 0JG, West : 1 ¾ m. on A 272 ☎ (01403) 784096, *david.mitchell@farming.co.uk, Fax (01403) 784096,* – P.
closed 2 weeks Christmas, New Year and restricted opening in winter – **3 rm** ☐ ★50.00 – ★★85.00/100.00.
◆ Charming touches to former 19C canalside warehouse: antiques, dried flowers and brimming bookshelves. Breakfast in farmhouse kitchen; cosy country house rooms overlook water.

BILSBORROW *Lancs. – see Garstang.*

BINFIELD HEATH *Oxon. – see Henley-on-Thames.*

BINGHAM *Notts.* **502 504** R 25 – *pop. 8 658.*
London 125 – Leicester 26 – Lincoln 28 – Nottingham 11 – Sheffield 35.

XX **Yeung Sing** with rm, Market St, NG13 8AB, ☎ (01949) 831222, *manager@yeung-sing.co.uk, Fax (01949) 838833* – P. MC AE VISA
closed 25-26 December – **Rest** - Chinese (Canton) - *(closed lunch Monday-Wednesday)* a la carte 18.50/40.00 – **16 rm** ☐ ★47.00/67.00 – ★★67.00/90.00.
◆ Carefully prepared, authentic Cantonese and regional Chinese cuisine served amid Oriental prints and wall-hangings. Smartly attired staff in discreet, friendly attendance.

The ✿ award is the crème de la crème.
This is awarded to restaurants
which are really worth travelling miles for!

BINGLEY _W. Yorks._ **502** O 22 – _pop. 19 884_ – ⊠ _Bradford._

  ⓖ _St Ives Est._ _ℰ_ _(01274) 562436._
  London 204 – Bradford 6 – Leeds 15 – Skipton 13.

  ⌂ **Five Rise Locks,** Beck Lane, BD16 4DD, via Park Rd _ℰ_ (01274) 565296, _info@five-rise-locks.co.uk, Fax (01274) 568828,_ 🍴 , 🌭 – ↦ 🅿. 🆖 _VISA_
      Rest _(closed Sunday dinner)_ (dinner only and lunch Sunday)/dinner a la carte 15.00/26.00 –
      9 rm ⚏ ✦50.00/60.00 – ✦✦72.00.
      ✦ Neat mid-Victorian house named after the locks on the nearby Leeds-Liverpool canal.
      Cheerful, modern, individuallly styled rooms, some with views of the distant dales. Well-
      kept dining room employs local produce on menus.

BINLEY _W. Mids._ – _see Coventry._

BIRCHOVER _Derbs._ – _see Matlock._

BIRKENHEAD _Mersey._ **502 503** K 23 – _pop. 83 729._

  ⓖ _Arrowe Park, Woodchurch_ _ℰ_ _(0151) 677 1527_ – ⓖ _Prenton, Golf Links Rd, Prenton_
  _ℰ_ _(0151) 609 3426._
  Mersey Tunnels (toll).
  ⛴ _to Liverpool and Wallasey (Mersey Ferries) frequent services daily._
  🖪 _Woodside Ferry Booking Hall_ _ℰ_ _(0151) 647 6780, touristinfo@wirral.gov.uk._
  London 222 – Liverpool 2.

Plan : see Liverpool p. 3

  ⌂ **River Hill,** Talbot Rd, Oxton, CH43 2HJ, Southwest : 2 ¼ m. by A 552 on B 5151 _ℰ_ (0151)
      653 3773, _reception@theriverhill.co.uk, Fax (0151) 653 7162,_ 🌭 – ↦ rest, 🅿. 🆖 🆎 ⓪
      VISA
      Rest (dinner only and Sunday lunch)/dinner 18.95 and a la carte 22.20/28.20 ♀ – ⚏ 7.95 –
      15 rm ✦69.75/79.75 – ✦✦79.75 129.00/159.00.
      ✦ Imposing redbrick Victorian house with purpose-built extension. Sizeable lounge and
      bar. Spacious, characterful rooms with chintz décor and fabrics. Carefully tended garden
      adjoins restaurant.

  XXX **Fraiche,** 11 Rosemount, Oxton, CH43 5SG, Southwest : 2 ¼ m. by A 552 and B 5151
      _ℰ_ (0151) 652 2914, _contact@restaurantfraiche.com_ – ↦. 🆖 _VISA_
      closed Sunday-Monday – **Rest** (booking essential) (dinner only and lunch Friday and Satur-
      day) 35.00/45.00.
      ✦ Immaculately appointed neighbourhood restaurant, enhanced by vivid pieces of mod-
      ern glassware. Gourmet and tasting menus a highlight of the inspired, original cooking.

ENGLAND

Birmingham, the Bullring

BIRMINGHAM

W. Mids. **503 504** O 26 *Great Britain G. – pop. 970 892.*

London 122 – Bristol 91 – Liverpool 103 – Manchester 86 – Nottingham 50.

TOURIST INFORMATION

🛈 *The Rotunda, 150 New St ✆ (0870) 225 0127, Fax (0121) 616 1038.*
🛈 *Tourism Centre, National Exhibition Centre ✆ (0121) 202 5099.*

PRACTICAL INFORMATION

🛈 *Edgbaston, Church Road ✆ (0121) 454 1736,* FX.
🛈 *Hilltop, Park Lane, Handsworth ✆ (0121) 554 4463,* CU.
🛈 *Hatchford Brook, Coventry Road, Sheldon ✆ (0121) 743 9821.*
🛈 *Brandhall, Heron Road, Oldbury, Warley ✆ (0121) 552 7475,* BU.
🛈 *Harborne Church Farm, Vicarage Road, Harborne ✆ (0121) 427 1204,* EX
✈ *Birmingham International Airport : ✆ (08707) 335511, E : 6½ m. by A 45* DU.

SIGHTS

See : *City★ – Museum and Art Gallery★★* LY **M2** *– Barber Institute of Fine Arts★★ (at Birmingham University)* EX **U** *– Cathedral of St Philip (stained glass portrayals★)* LMY *– Thinktank★, Millennium Point* FV.

Env. : *Aston Hall★★* FV **M.**

Exc. : *Black Country Museum★, Dudley, NW : 10 m. by A 456 and A 4123* AU *– Bournville★, SW : 4 m. on A 38 and A 441.*

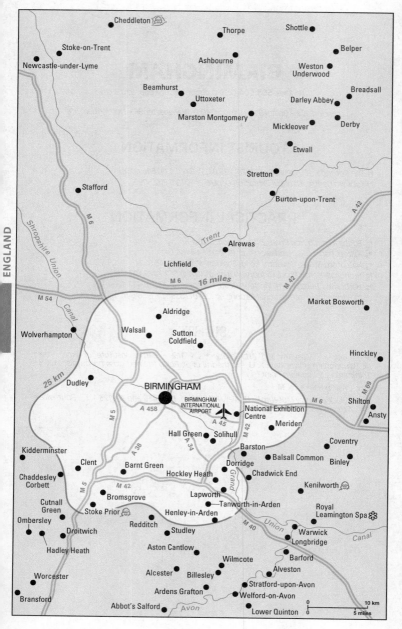

INDEX OF STREET NAMES IN BIRMINGHAM

ENGLAND

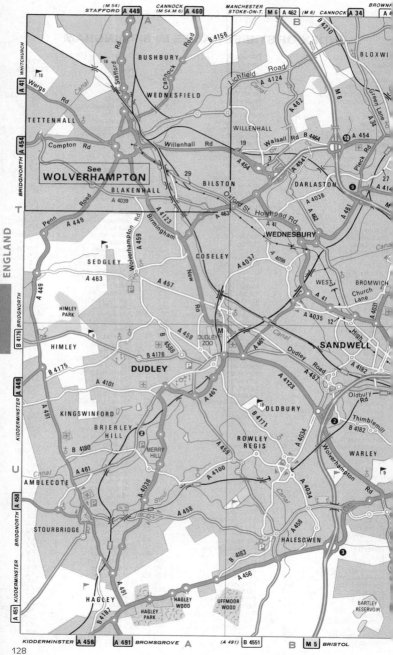

BIRMINGHAM AND WOLVERHAMPTON

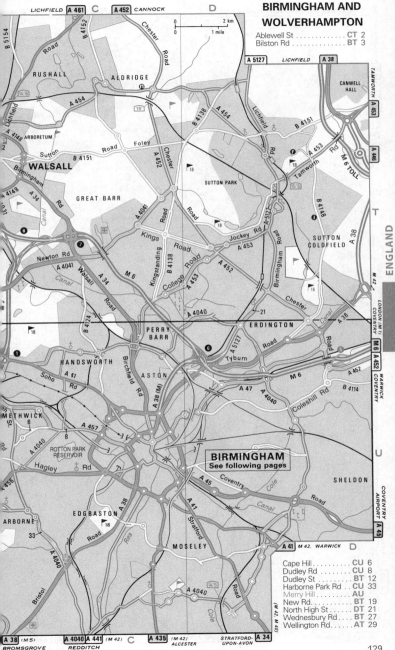

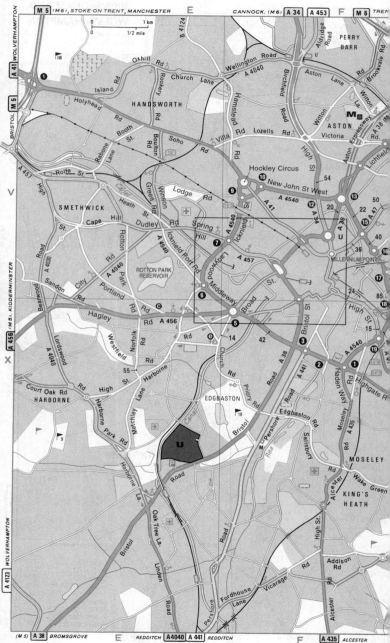

BIRMINGHAM

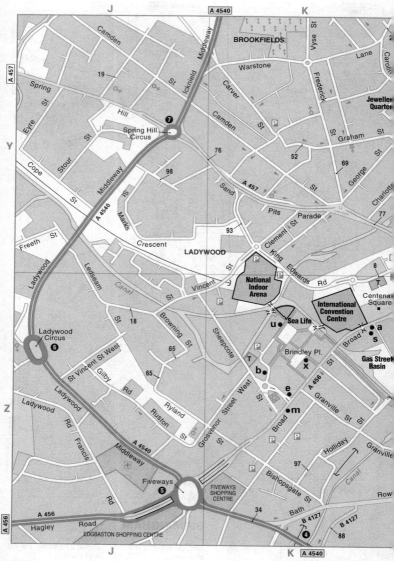

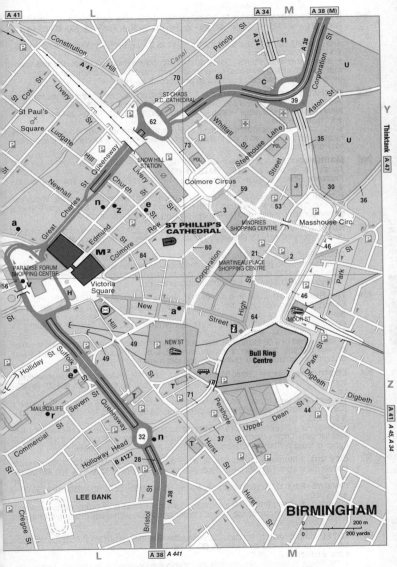

Town plans: Birmingham pp. 3-9

Hyatt Regency, 2 Bridge St, B1 2JZ, *(0121) 643 1234, birmingham@hyattintl.com, Fax (0121) 616 2323,* ≤, ⊘, 16, ≋, ⊠ – ⎸, ✼ rm, ▤ ❦ ❧ ➾ – 🏛 200. **⍾ ◉ ⦵ VISA** ⚬
KZ a
Aria : Rest 13.50/16.75 and a la carte 28.75/34.45 ♀ – ⊑ 15.25 – **315 rm** ✲99.00/199.00 – ✲✲99.00/199.00, 4 suites.
• Striking mirrored exterior. Glass enclosed lifts offer panoramic views. Sizeable rooms with floor to ceiling windows. Covered link with International Convention Centre. Contemporary style restaurant in central atrium; modish cooking.

Radisson SAS, 12 Holloway Circus, B1 1BT, *(0121) 654 6000, info.birmingham@radissonsas.com, Fax (0161) 654 6001,* ≤ – ⎸ ▤ ❦ ❧ – 🏛 130. **⍾ ◉ ⦵ VISA**
LZ n
Filini : Rest *(closed Sunday)* - Italian - a la carte 18.50/34.50 – ⊑ 14.50 – **204 rm** ✲135.00 – ✲✲135.00, 7 suites.
• Occupies 18 uber-modern floors of a city centre skyscraper. Well-equipped business facilities; ultra stylish bedrooms in three distinctly slinky themes. Modern bar leads to airy, easy-going Italian restaurant.

Malmaison, Mailbox, 1 Wharfside St, B1 1RD, *(0121) 246 5000, Fax (0121) 246 5002,* 16, ≋ – ⎸ ✼ rm ▤ ❦ ❧ – 🏛 45. **⍾ ◉ ⦵ VISA** ⚬
LZ e
Brasserie : Rest 14.50 (lunch) and a la carte 24.90/43.50 ♀ – ⊑ 12.75 – **184 rm** ✲140.00 – ✲✲140.00, 5 suites.
• Stylish, modern boutique hotel, forms centrepiece of Mailbox development. Stylish bar. Spacious contemporary bedrooms with every modern facility; superb petit spa. Brasserie serving contemporary French influenced cooking at reasonable prices.

Hotel Du Vin, 25 Church St, B3 2NR, *(0121) 200 0600, info@birmingham.hotelduvin.com, Fax (0121) 236 0889,* ❁, 16, ≋ – ⎸, ✼ rest, ▤ rm, ❦ ❧ – 🏛 85. **⍾ ◉ ⦵ VISA** ⚬
LY e
Bistro : Rest a la carte 28.00/31.45 ❁ – ⊑ 13.50 – **66 rm** ✲140.00 – ✲✲140.00.
• Former 19C eye hospital in heart of shopping centre; has relaxed, individual, boutique style. Low lighting in rooms of muted tones: Egyptian cotton and superb bathrooms. Champagne in "bubble lounge"; Parisian style brasserie.

The Burlington, Burlington Arcade, 126 New St, B2 4JQ, *(0121) 643 9191, mail@burlingtonhotel.com, Fax (0121) 643 5075,* 16, ≋ – ⎸ ✼ ▤ ❦ ❧ – 🏛 400. **⍾ ◉ ⦵ VISA**
LZ a
closed 25-26 December – **Berlioz :** Rest (dinner only) 27.00 and a la carte 27.25/42.20 – **110 rm** ⊑ ✲165.00 – ✲✲175.00, 2 suites.
• Approached by a period arcade. Restored Victorian former railway hotel retains much of its original charm. Period décor to bedrooms yet with fax, modem and voice mail. Elegant dining room: ornate ceiling, chandeliers and vast mirrors.

Copthorne, Paradise Circus, B3 3HJ, *(0121) 200 2727, reservations.birmingham@millcop.com, Fax (0121) 200 1197,* 16, ≋ – ⎸ ✼, ▤ rest, ❧ P – 🏛 250. **⍾ ◉ ⦵ VISA** ⚬
LZ v
Turners Grill : Rest *(closed Saturday lunch and Sunday)* a la carte 23.45/28.85 ♀ – **Goldie's Brasserie :** Rest 10.95/19.00 and a la carte 20.95/33.95 ♀ – ⊑ 15.75 – **209 rm** ✲155.00 – ✲✲175.00, 3 suites.
• Overlooking Centenary Square. Corporate hotel with extensive leisure club and cardio-vascular gym. Cricket themed bar. Connoisseur rooms offer additional comforts. Flambé dishes offered in intimate Turner's Grill. Goldies is all-day relaxed brasserie.

City Inn, 1 Brunswick Sq, Brindley Pl, B1 2HW, *(0121) 643 1003, birmingham.reservations@cityinn.com, Fax (0121) 643 1005,* ❁, 16, – ⎸, ✼ rm, ▤ ❦ ❧ – 🏛 100. **⍾ ◉ ⦵ VISA** ⚬
KZ b
City Café : Rest 12.50/16.50 and a la carte 16.50/40.00 ♀ – ⊑ 12.50 – **238 rm** ✲159.00 – ✲✲159.00.
• In heart of vibrant Brindley Place; the spacious atrium with bright rugs and blond wood sets the tone for equally stylish rooms. Corporate friendly with many meeting rooms. Eat in restaurant, terrace or bar.

TOTEL without rest., 19 Portland Rd, Edgbaston, B16 9HN, *(0121) 454 5282, info@toteluk.com, Fax (0121) 456 4668* – ✼ P, **⍾ ◉ VISA**
EX c
1 rm, **9 suites** 75.00/105.00.
• 19C house converted into comfortable, spacious fully-serviced apartments, individually styled with modern facilities. Friendly service. Continental breakfast served in room.

Novotel, 70 Broad St, B1 2HT, *(0121) 643 2000, h1077@accor.com, Fax (0121) 643 9786,* 16, ≋ – ⎸ ✼ rm ▤ ❦ ❧ – 🏛 300. **⍾ ◉ ⦵ VISA**
KZ e
Rest a la carte 19.95/32.00 s. ♀ – **148 rm** ⊑ ✲65.00/145.00 – ✲✲95.00/155.00.
• Well located for the increasingly popular Brindleyplace development. Underground parking. Modern, well-kept, branded bedrooms suitable for families. Modern, open-plan restaurant.

Express by Holiday Inn without rest., 65 Lionel St, B3 1JE, ℘ (0121) 200 1900, ebhi-bhamcity@btconnect.com, Fax (0121) 200 1910 – 🛗 ❄✦ 🗐 ✆ ⅙ 🚗 – 🏛 30. 🐠 🗚 ① 𝗩𝗜𝗦𝗔. ⅙
LY a

120 rm ✦55.00/95.00 – ✦✦55.00/95.00.

❖ Well-kept, well-managed hotel situated in a handy location for visitors to the city centre. Tidy, comfortable accommodation to suit tourists or business travellers alike.

Simpsons (Antona) with rm, 20 Highfield Rd, Edgbaston, B15 3DU, ℘ (0121) 454 3434, info@simpsonsrestaurant.co.uk, Fax (0121) 454 3399, ㋛, ☞ – ❄✦, 🗐 rest, 🅿 ⇆ 18. 🗚 𝗩𝗜𝗦𝗔
EX e

closed 24-27 December and 31 December-3 January – Rest (closed Sunday dinner) 27.50/30.00 and a la carte 41.45/46.95 ⅒ – **4 rm** ✦95.00/125.00 – ✦✦160.00/225.00.

Spec. Crab cocktail, Granny Smith jelly, crab spring roll. Roast loin of venison, butternut squash, cabbage, truffle sauce. Chocolate délice, salted pine nuts.

❖ Restored Georgian residence; its interior a careful blend of Victorian features and contemporary style. Refined, classically based cooking. Elegant bedrooms.

Jessica's (Purnell), 1 Montague Rd, B16 9HN, ℘ (0121) 455 0999 – ❄✦ 🗐. 🐠 𝗩𝗜𝗦𝗔
EX c

closed last 2 weeks July, 1 week Easter, 1 week Christmas, Saturday lunch, Sunday and Monday – Rest 24.95/36.95 ⅒.

Spec. Ham hock with salad of cockles, gooseberries and pickle. Poached cod, vanilla and lettuce. Ravioli of lavender and strawberry.

❖ Georgian 'outbuilding' and conservatory offering excellently presented, highly original French influenced modern British cooking sourced from quality Midland suppliers.

Opus, 54 Cornwall St, B3 2DE, ℘ (0121) 200 2323, restaurant@opusrestaurant.co.uk, Fax (0121) 200 2090 – ❄✦ 🗐 ⇆ 64. 🐠 🗚 𝗩𝗜𝗦𝗔
LY z

closed 25 December- 1 January, Saturday lunch, Sunday and Bank Holidays – Rest 15.00/17.50 and a la carte 24.50/34.75 ⅒.

❖ Restaurant of floor-to-ceiling glass in evolving area of city. Seafood and shellfish bar for diners on the move. Assured cooking underpins modern menus with traditional base.

Lasan, 3-4 Dakota Buildings, James St, B3 1SD, ℘ (0121) 212 3664, info@lasan.co.uk, Fax (0121) 212 3665 – ❄✦. 🐠 🗚 𝗩𝗜𝗦𝗔
KY a

closed 25-27 December and Saturday lunch – Rest - Indian - a la carte 17.85/21.20.

❖ Jewellery quarter restaurant of sophistication and style; good quality ingredients allow the clarity of the spices to shine through in this well-run Indian establishment.

Bank, 4 Brindleyplace, B1 2JB, ℘ (0121) 633 4466, birmres@bankrestaurants.com, Fax (0121) 633 4465, ㋛ – 🗐 ⇆ 100. 🐠 🗚 ① 𝗩𝗜𝗦𝗔
KZ u

closed 26 December and 1 January – Rest 15.00 (lunch) and a la carte 23.90/36.45 ⅏ ⅒.

❖ Capacious, modern and busy bar-restaurant where chefs can be watched through a glass wall preparing the tasty modern dishes. Pleasant terrace area.

Metro Bar and Grill, 73 Cornwall St, B3 2DF, ℘ (0121) 200 1911, Fax (0121) 200 1611 – 🗐. 🐠 🗚 𝗩𝗜𝗦𝗔
LY n

closed 25 December-1 January, Sunday and Bank Holidays – Rest (booking essential) a la carte 22.15/29.85 ⅒.

❖ Gleaming chrome and mirrors in a bright, contemporary basement restaurant. Modern cooking with rotisserie specialities. Spacious, ever-lively bar serves lighter meals.

Shimla Pinks, 214 Broad St, B15 1AY, ℘ (0121) 633 0366, info@shimlapinks.com, Fax (0121) 643 3325 – 🗐. 🐠 🗚 𝗩𝗜𝗦𝗔
KZ m

closed lunch Saturday and Sunday – Rest - Indian - a la carte 17.40/28.40.

❖ A vast establishment in a street full of restaurants. Buzzy ambience prevails: open-plan kitchen adds to atmosphere. Authentic, modern Indian cuisine; impressive set menus.

Zinc Bar and Grill, Regency Wharf, Broad St, B1 2DS, ℘ (0121) 200 0620, Fax (0121) 200 0630, ㋛ – 🗐 ⇆ 40. 🐠 🗚 ① 𝗩𝗜𝗦𝗔
KZ s

closed 25-26 December and Sunday – Rest 11.50/14.50 and a la carte 17.00/35.00 ⅏ ⅒.

❖ Purpose-built restaurant in lively pub and club area of city. Spiral staircase leads to dining area, including terrace overlooking canal. Modern, classically toned, dishes.

Brasserie Blanc, 9 Brindleyplace, B1 2HS, ℘ (0121) 633 7333, birmingham@lepetit blanc.co.uk, Fax (0121) 633 7444, ㋛ – ❄✦ 🗐. 🐠 🗚 𝗩𝗜𝗦𝗔
KZ x

closed 25 December – Rest 12.50 (lunch) and a la carte 23.45/30.45 ⅏ ⅒.

❖ Outside, a central square and offices. Within, an atmospheric brasserie in relaxed, contemporary environment serving predominantly French classics. Special menu for children.

Lazeez Signature, 116 Wharfside St, The Mailbox, B1 1RF, ℘ (0121) 643 7979, Fax (0121) 643 4546, ㋛ – 🗐. 🐠 🗚 𝗩𝗜𝗦𝗔
LZ r

– Rest - Indian - a la carte 15.85/21.85 ⅒.

❖ Located in fashionable Mailbox. Large, open plan establishment, kitchen included. Polite, friendly service. Authentic accurate Indian cooking with quality ingredients.

ENGLAND

at Hall Green Southeast : 5¾ m. by A 41 on A 34 – ⊠ Birmingham.

XX **Liaison,** 1558 Stratford Rd, B28 9HA, ✆ (0121) 733 7336, Fax (0121) 733 1677 – ✦✗, ◉◎
◉ VISA
GX i
closed 2 weeks Christmas-New Year, 1 week September, Saturday lunch, Sunday and Monday – **Rest** 16.95/28.95 ♀.
♦ Pleasant restaurant with understated décor in residential location. Linen table cloths and friendly service. Classically based modern eclectic cooking.

at Birmingham Airport Southeast : 9 m. by A 45 – DU – ⊠ Birmingham.

🏨 **Novotel Birmingham Airport,** Passenger Terminal, B26 3QL, ✆ (0121) 782 7000,
h1158@accor.com, Fax (0121) 782 0445 – 📳 ✦✗ ✆ ♿ – 🛦 35. ◎◎ 🖭 ⓪ VISA
Rest (bar lunch Saturday, Sunday and Bank Holidays) 17.95/24.95 and a la carte
18.00/32.95 ♀ – ☲ 12.95 – **195 rm** ✦129.00 – ✦✦129.00.
♦ Opposite main terminal building: modern hotel benefits from sound proofed doors and double glazing. Mini bars and power showers provided in spacious rooms with sofa beds. Open-plan garden brasserie.

at National Exhibition Centre Southeast : 9½ m. on A 45 – DU – ⊠ Birmingham.

🏨 **Crowne Plaza,** Pendigo Way, B40 1PS, ✆ (0870) 400 9160, necroomsales@icho
telsgroup.com, Fax (0121) 781 4321, ▮♖, ☎ – 📳 ✦✗ ▤ ✆ ♿ 🅿 – 🛦 200. ◎◎ 🖭 VISA, ✵
Rest (closed Saturday lunch) a la carte 28.50/31.75 – ☲ 15.95 – **242 rm** ✦195.00/240.00 –
✦✦195.00/240.00.
♦ Modern hotel adjacent to NEC. Small terrace area overlooks lake. Extensive conference facilities. State-of-the-art bedrooms with a host of extras. Basement dining room: food with a Yorkshire twist.

🏨 **Express by Holiday Inn** without rest., Bickenhill Parkway, Bickenhill, B40 1QA,
✆ (0870) 720 2297, exhi-nec@foremosthotels.co.uk, Fax (0870) 720 2298 – 📳 ✦✗ ♿ 🅿 –
🛦 100. ◎◎ 🖭 ⓪ VISA
179 rm ✦115.00 – ✦✦115.00.
♦ Handy for the NEC and airport. Modern budget hotel ideal for the corporate traveller. Extensive cold buffet breakfast included.

BIRMINGHAM AIRPORT W. Mids. 503 504 O 26 – see Birmingham.

BISHOP'S STORTFORD Herts. 504 U 28 Great Britain G. – pop. 35 325.
Env. : Audley End★★ AC, N : 11 m. by B 1383.
✈ Stansted Airport : ✆ (0870) 0000303, NE : 3½ m.
🅱 The Old Monastery, Windhill ✆ (01279) 655831, tic@bishopsstortford.org.
London 34 – Cambridge 27 – Chelmsford 19 – Colchester 33.

🏠 **The Cottage** ⌂ without rest., 71 Birchanger Lane, CM23 5QA, Northeast : 2¼ m. by B
1383 on Birchanger rd ✆ (01279) 812349, bookings@thecottagebirchanger.co.uk,
Fax (01279) 815045, ☞ – ✦✗ 🅿, ◎◎ 🖭 ⓪ VISA, ✵
closed Christmas and New Year – **15 rm** ☲ ✦50.00/60.00 – ✦✦75.00/80.00.
♦ Part 17C and 18C cottages in 2-acre garden. Conservatory breakfast room and comfortable panelled lounge. Bedrooms are simple but pristine and spacious. Convenient for airport.

X **The Lemon Tree,** 14-16 Water Lane, CM23 2LB, ✆ (01279) 757788, mail@lemon
tree.co.uk, Fax (01279) 757766 – ✦✗ ▤. ◎◎ 🖭 ⓪ VISA
Y s
closed 25-26 December, 1 January, Sunday dinner and Monday – **Rest** 18.00/20.00 and a la carte 19.75/29.75 ♀.
♦ Indebted to the London scene in concept and cooking. A bright, informal, smartly run restaurant; its Mediterranean accented dishes are satisfying and modestly priced.

X **Host,** 4 The Corn Exchange, Market Sq, CM23 3UU, ✆ (01279) 657000, Fax (01279) 655566,
🍴 – ✦✗ ▤. ◎◎ 🖭 ⓪ VISA
closed Sunday dinner – **Rest** 12.50 (lunch) and dinner a la carte 15.00/25.00 ♀.
♦ Grade I listed building, situated in former Corn Exchange. Airy, modern restaurant with unique rooftop terrace and relaxed atmosphere. Eclectic, well priced brasserie menus.

at Stansted Mountfitchet Northeast : 3½ m. by B 1383 on B 1051 – ⊠ Bishop's Stortford.

⌂ **Chimneys** without rest., 44 Lower St, CM24 8LR, on B 1351 ✆ (01279) 813388,
info@chimneysguesthouse.co.uk – ✦✗ ✆ 🅿. ◎◎ VISA
4 rm ☲ ✦47.00/55.00 – ✦✦72.00.
♦ 17C Grade II listed house boasts immaculate interior: lounge with log fire, cloth-clad breakfast room with fresh flowers. Personally decorated, thoughtfully designed bedrooms.

ENGLAND

at Hatfield Heath *(Essex) Southeast : 6 m. on A 1060 –* ⊠ *Bishop's Stortford.*

Down Hall Country House ⌂, CM22 7AS, South : 1 ½ m. by Matching Lane
🖉 (01279) 731441, *reservations@downhall.co.uk, Fax* (01279) 730416, ≤, ⊜, ⬚, ☀, ♨,
⚒ – 🕸 ☆, ▦ rest, 🕻 📞 – 🛦 200. ⬤ ⟐ ⓪ 𝘝𝘐𝘚𝘈
Ibbetsons : Rest *(closed Saturday lunch)* 20.00/30.00 (lunch) and a la carte 26.00/38.00 ♀ –
The Grill Room : Rest *(closed Saturday lunch)* (booking essential for non-residents) a la
carte 18.50/28.10 ♀ – ☷ 15.95 – **99 rm** ✶89.00/99.00 – ✶✶99.00/129.00.
♦ In expansively landscaped grounds, a 19C Italianate mansion touching on the palatial.
Period-style bedrooms in mahogany, brass and swagged fabrics, half in the new wing.
Ibbetsons exudes contemporary elegance. The Grill Room has light, formal feel.

BISHOP'S TAWTON *Devon 503 H 30 – see Barnstaple.*

BLABY *Leics. 502 503 504 Q 26 – see Leicester.*

BLACKBURN *Blackburn 502 M 22 – pop. 105 085.*
🗔 *Pleasington* 🖉 (01254) 202177 – 🗔 *Wilpshire, 72 Whalley Rd* 🖉 (01254) 248260 – 🗔 *Great
Harwood, Harwood Bar* 🖉 (01254) 884391.
🈐 *50-54 Church St* 🖉 (01254) 53277, *askus@blackburn.gov.uk.*
London 228 – Leeds 47 – Liverpool 39 – Manchester 24 – Preston 11.

at Langho *North : 4½ m. on A 666 –* ⊠ *Whalley.*

The Avenue, Brockhall Village, Old Lango, BB6 8AY, North : 1 ¼ m. by A 666 and A 59 on
Northcote rd 🖉 (01254) 244811, *bookingenquiries@theavenuehotel.co.uk,
Fax* (01254) 244812 – ☆ rm, ▦ rest, 🕻 📞 – 🛦 40. ⬤ ⟐ ⓪ 𝘝𝘐𝘚𝘈 ⚒
closed 24-25 December – **Rest** *(closed Sunday)* (bar lunch)/dinner a la carte 14.95/20.00 –
19 rm ☷ ✶55.00/65.00 – ✶✶60.00/70.00, 2 suites.
♦ Modern hotel located within a new village near old Langho, and ideal for football fans as
it overlooks Blackburn Rovers' training ground. Stylish, contemporary bedrooms. Modern,
informal café/bar restaurant.

Northcote Manor (Haworth) with rm, Northcote Rd, BB6 8BE, North : ½ m. on A 59 at
junction with A 666 🖉 (01254) 240555, *sales@northcotemanor.com, Fax* (01254) 246568,
☀ – ☆ rest, 🕻 📞 ⇄ – 🛦 26 – 🛦 40. ⬤ ⟐ 𝘝𝘐𝘚𝘈 ⚒
❄️ *closed 25 December and 1 January –* Rest *(closed Bank Holiday Mondays)* 20.00 (lunch) and
a la carte 36.90/53.00 ♀ ⅏ – **14 rm** ☷ ✶120.00/155.00 – ✶✶155.00/190.00.
Spec. Black pudding and trout with mustard and nettle sauce. British white beef with
smoked foie gras and crispy blackpudding. Chocolate sphere, sheep's milk ice cream.
♦ Seriously run, stylish, contemporary - yet classic - restaurant in keeping with stately
manor. Highly original, locally imbued, carefully considered menus. Smart rooms.

at Mellor *Northwest : 3¼ m. by A 677 –* ⊠ *Blackburn.*

Stanley House, BB2 7NP, Southwest : ¾ m. by A 677 and Further Lane 🖉 (01254)
769200, *info@stanleyhouse.co.uk, Fax* (01254) 769206, ≤, ☀, ♨ – 🕸 ☆ ▦ 🕻 📞 – 🛦 250.
⬤ ⟐ 𝘝𝘐𝘚𝘈 ⚒
Rest –(see **Cassis** below) – **12 rm** ☷ ✶150.00 – ✶✶200.00.
♦ 17C manor with superb rural views. Relaxing, tastefully toned bar. Strong emphasis on
conference facilities. Elegantly proportioned rooms defined by wonderfully rich colours.

Millstone, Church Lane, BB2 7JR, 🖉 (01254) 813333, *info@millstonehotel.co.uk,
Fax* (01254) 812628 – ☆ 🕻 📞 – 🛦 20. ⬤ ⟐ ⓪ 𝘝𝘐𝘚𝘈 ⚒
Rest (bar lunch)/dinner 27.95 and a la carte 26.50/32.85 ♀ – **22 rm** ☷ ✶109.00 –
✶✶130.00/130.00, 1 suite.
♦ Attractive little sandstone former coaching inn in quiet village. Lounge bar with log fire
and comfy sofas. Cosy bedrooms: matching floral patterns, botanical prints. Elegant wood
panelled dining room warmed by fire.

Cassis (at Stanley House), BB2 7NP, Southwest : ¾ m. by A 677 and Further Lane
🖉 (01254) 769220, *Fax* (01254) 769206 – ☆ ▦ 📞 ⬤ ⟐ 𝘝𝘐𝘚𝘈
closed lunch Monday, Tuesday and Saturday – Rest 18.95 (lunch) and a la carte
34.00/44.00 ♀.
♦ Independent from main hotel. Name derives from rich blackcurrant theme throughout!
Vast raised mezzanine for apéritifs. Weekly evolving menus with vibrant Lancashire accent.

The red ⌂ symbol?
This denotes the very essence of peace
– only the sound of birdsong first thing in the morning …

ENGLAND

BLACKMORE Essex.

London 26 – Brentwood 7 – Chelmsford 8.

🍴 **Leather Bottle**, The Green, CM4 0RL, ℰ (01277) 823538, *leatherbottle@tiscali.co.uk*, 🚗 – 💳 VISA, ✄

Rest *(closed Sunday dinner)* a la carte 17.50/30.00.
♦ Characterful black-and-white pub on the green. Real fire in a wood burner; conservatory room and paved terrace. Satisfying modern menus with an evolving, eclectic influence.

BLACKPOOL Blackpool 502 K 22 Great Britain G. – pop. 142 283.

See : Tower★ AC AY A.

🇮🇸 Blackpool Park, North Park Drive ℰ (01253) 397916 BY – 🇮🇸 Poulton-le-Fylde, Myrtle Farm, Breck Rd ℰ (01253) 892444.

✈ Blackpool Airport : ℰ (08700) 273777, S : 3 m. by A 584.

🇮🇸 1 Clifton St ℰ (01253) 478222.

London 246 – Leeds 88 – Liverpool 56 – Manchester 51 – Middlesbrough 123.

Plan opposite

🏨 **Imperial**, North Promenade, FY1 2HB, ℰ (01253) 623971, *imperialblackpool@paramount-hotels.co.uk*, Fax (01253) 751784, <, ⅙, ≘, ⬛ – 📶 ❋ ✆ ☏ – ⚒ 500. 💳 🅰 ⑩ VISA
Palm Court : Rest (carvery lunch)/dinner 22.50 and a la carte approx 33.40 ☕ – ⛔ 13.50 – 173 rm ⛔ ✱69.00/175.00 – ✱✱79.00/185.00, 7 suites.
AY c
♦ Imposing, classic 19C promenade hotel. Grand columned lobby, well-appointed rooms, many with views. Photos in the convivial No.10 bar recall PMs and past party conferences. Elegant restaurant with smartly liveried staff.

🏨 **Hilton Blackpool**, North Promenade, FY1 2JQ, ℰ (01253) 623434, *reservations.blackpool@hilton.com*, Fax (01253) 294371, <, ⅙, ≘, ⬛ – 📶 ❋, ▤ rest, ₺ ☏ – ⚒ 700. 💳 🅰 ⑩ VISA, ✄
AY x
The Promenade : Rest (bar lunch Monday-Saturday)/dinner 21.95 and a la carte 20.00/40.00 s. ☕ – ⛔ 14.50 – 268 rm ✱75.00/235.00 – ✱✱85.00/245.00, 6 suites.
♦ Open-plan, marble-floored lobby and smartly equipped rooms in contemporary style, almost all with views over the sea-front. Cabaret shows on most Fridays and Saturdays. Informal dining after cocktail lounge aperitifs.

🏨 **De Vere Herons' Reach**, East Park Drive, FY3 8LL, ℰ (01253) 838866, Fax (01253) 798800, ☕, ⅙, ≘, ⬛, 🇮🇸, ✕, squash – 📶 ❋, ▤ rest, ₺ ☏ – ⚒ 600. 💳 🅰 ⑩ VISA, ✄
BZ a
Brasserie : Rest (bar lunch Monday-Saturday)/dinner 24.50 ☕ – 170 rm ✱91.00/137.00 – ✱✱91.00/137.00, 2 suites.
♦ Purpose-built hotel: state-of-the-art leisure club and floodlit driving range. Comfortable, well-equipped bedrooms; some, like the clubby bar, overlook the golf course. Extensive modern restaurant.

🏠 **Number One** without rest., 1 St Lukes Rd, FY4 2EL, ℰ (01253) 343901, *info@numberoneblackpool.com*, Fax (01253) 343901, 🚗 – ❋ ✆ ☏. 💳 VISA, ✄
AZ a
3 rm ⛔ ✱75.00/120.00 – ✱✱120.00/150.00.
♦ Engagingly run, enticingly stylish guesthouse. The good value nature of the establishment is enhanced by an elegant breakfast room and luxuriously appointed bedrooms.

at Thornton Northeast : 5½ m. by A 584 – BY – on B 5412 – ✉ Blackpool.

✕✕ **Twelve**, Marsh Mill, Fleetwood Rd South, FY5 4JZ, North : ½ m. on A 585 ℰ (01253) 821212, *info@twelve-restaurant.co.uk*, Fax (01253) 821212 – 💳 🅰 ⑩ VISA
closed first 2 weeks January and Monday – **Rest** (dinner only and lunch Thursday and December) 15.50/17.95 and dinner a la carte 29.15/37.95.
♦ Converted dance studio attractively located in the shadow of famous restored windmill. Interesting, original dishes with a modern flair, employing abundance of local produce.

at Singleton Northeast : 7 m. by A 586 – BY – on B 5260 – ✉ Blackpool.

🏨 **Singleton Lodge** ✦, Lodge Lane, FY6 8LT, North : ¼ m. on B 5260 ℰ (01253) 883854, *enquiries@singletonlodgehotel.co.uk*, Fax (01253) 894432, 🚗 – ❋ rest, ☏ – ⚒ 60. 💳 🅰 VISA
closed 25-31 December – **Rest** *(closed Sunday dinner)* (dinner only and Sunday lunch)/dinner 16.50 – 12 rm ⛔ ✱55.00 – ✱✱85.00.
♦ Family owned Georgian former rectory with traditional country house décor. Firelit lounges and spacious, individual rooms, some front-facing with views of the long drive. Dining room overlooks the rolling lawned grounds.

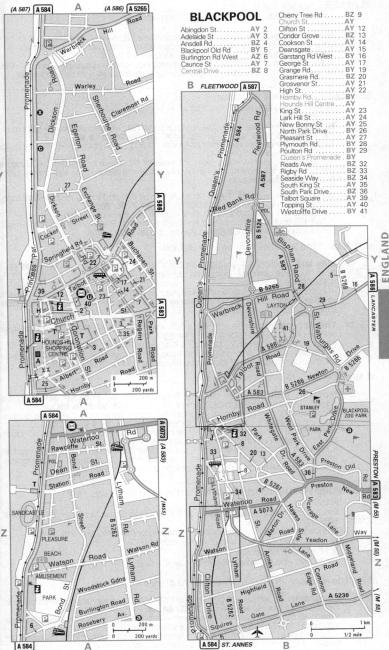

BLACKPOOL

139

BLAKENEY Glos. 503 504 M 28.

London 134 – Bristol 31 – Gloucester 16 – Newport 31.

⚐ **Viney Hill Country Guesthouse** without rest., Viney Hill, GL15 4LT, West : ¾ m. by A 48 ℘ (01594) 516000, info@vineyhill.com, Fax (01594) 516018, ✿ – ⅍ ₺ ᵽ. ⓪ ᵛⁱˢᵃ. ॐ
Rest (by arrangement only) 19.50 **7 rm** ☞ ✷66.00 – ✷✷76.00.
    ♦ Part 18C former farmhouse with sympathetic extensions and gardens on a quiet road. Simple, pine furnished bedrooms. Ideal base for Forest of Dean, right on its doorstep.

BLAKENEY Norfolk 504 X 25 – ⊠ Holt.

London 127 – King's Lynn 37 – Norwich 28.

🏨 **Blakeney,** The Quay, NR25 7NE, ℘ (01263) 740797, reception@blakeney-hotel.co.uk, Fax (01263) 740795, ≤, ☎, 🖃, ✿ – 🛗 ⅍ ᵽ. – 🔬 150. ⓪ ᴬᴱ ⓪ ᵛⁱˢᵃ
Rest (light lunch Monday-Saturday)/dinner 22.50 ♀ – **60 rm** (dinner included) ☞ ✷84.00/158.00 – ✷✷168.00/196.00.
    ♦ Traditional hotel on the quayside with views of estuary and a big sky! Sun lounge a delightful spot for the vista. Bedrooms vary in size and décor, some with private patio. Armchair dining with estuary views.

🍴 **White Horse** with rm, 4 High St, NR25 7AL, ℘ (01263) 740574, enquiries@blakeney whitehorse.co.uk, Fax (01263) 741339, ☎ – ⅍ rest, ᵽ. ⓪ ᵛⁱˢᵃ. ॐ
Rest a la carte 15.00/25.00 ♀ – **9 rm** ☞ ✷40.00/60.00 – ✷✷65.00/130.00.
    ♦ Part 17C brick-and-flint coaching inn near the harbour. Friendly, real ale bar and rustic restaurant in the old stables offering seafood specials. Cosy rooms.

at Cley next the Sea East : 1½ m. on A 149 – ⊠ Holt.

⚐ **Cley Mill** ॐ, NR25 7RP, ℘ (01263) 740209, Fax (01263) 751324, ≤, ✿ – ⅍ ᵽ. ⓪ ᵛⁱˢᵃ
Rest (by arrangement) (communal dining) 18.50 – **8 rm** ☞ ✷40.00/90.00 – ✷✷88.00/126.00.
    ♦ Restored 18C redbrick windmill in salt marshes with a viewing gallery: a birdwatcher's paradise. Neatly kept rooms, full of character, in the mill, stable and boatshed. Flagstoned dining room; communal table.

🍴 **The George** with rm, High St, NR25 7BY, ℘ (01263) 740652, thegeorge@cleynextthe sea.com, Fax (01263) 741275, ☎, ✿ – ⅍ 📺 ᵽ. ⓪ ᵛⁱˢᵃ
Rest a la carte 20.50/27.00 ♀ – **12 rm** ☞ ✷70.00/80.00 – ✷✷120.00/140.00, 1 suite.
    ♦ Imposing, stalwart Victorian/Edwardian pub. Warmly hued bar and restaurant. Rustic British cuisine to fore; lots of local seafood. Book top floor bedrooms for best views.

at Morston West : 1½ m. on A 149 – ⊠ Holt.

🏛 **Morston Hall** (Blackiston) ॐ, The Street, NR25 7AA, ℘ (01263) 741041, recep ₷ tion@morstonhall.com, Fax (01263) 740419, ✿ – ⅍ rest, ᵽ. ⓪ ᴬᴱ ⓪ ᵛⁱˢᵃ
closed January – Rest (booking essential) (set menu only) (dinner only and Sunday lunch)/dinner 44.00 ♀ – **7 rm** (dinner included) ✷130.00/145.00 – ✷✷260.00/280.00.
Spec. Velouté of sweetcorn with poached lobster. Fillet of local pork "en croute", sauce Albuféra. Raspberry soufflé, raspberry ripple ice cream and custard.
    ♦ Attractive country house in pristine gardens. Attentive service. Charming flagged hall with log fire. Airy, stylish rooms boast thoughtful extras. TV in two of the bathrooms. Accomplished seasonal no-choice menu, classic and modern in inspiration.

BLANDFORD FORUM Dorset 503 504 N 31 The West Country G. – pop. 9 854.

See : Town★.
Env. : Kingston Lacy★★ AC, SE : 5½ m. by B 3082 – Royal Signals Museum★, NE : 2 m. by B 3082.
Exc. : Milton Abbas★, SW : 8 m. by A 354 – Sturminster Newton★, NW : 8 m. by A 357.
🖟 Ashley Wood, Wimborne Rd ℘ (01258) 452253.
🚩 1 Greyhound Yard ℘ (01258) 454770.
London 124 – Bournemouth 17 – Dorchester 17 – Salisbury 24.

at Chettle Northeast : 7¼ m. by A 354 – ⊠ Blandford Forum.

🍴🍴 **Castleman** ॐ with rm, DT11 8DB, ℘ (01258) 830096, enquiry@castlemanhotel.co.uk, ₷ Fax (01258) 830051, ≤, ✿ – ⅍ rest, ᵽ. ⓪ ᵛⁱˢᵃ. ॐ
closed February and 25-26 and 31 December – Rest (dinner only and Sunday lunch)/dinner a la carte 16.50/27.50 – **8 rm** ☞ ✷50.00 – ✷✷90.00.
    ♦ Attractive part 16C dower house with Victorian extensions. Ingredients sourced from small local producers: game from their own estate. Classic cooking with a French base.

at Farnham *Northeast : 7½ m. by A 354 – ⊠ Blandford Forum.*

The Museum Inn with rm, DT11 8DE, *℘ (01725) 516261, enquiries@museuminn.co.uk,*
Fax (01725) 516988, 🍴 – **P. MO VISA**
closed 25 December and dinner 1 January – **Rest** (bookings not accepted) a la carte
25.50/31.00 ♀ – **8 rm** ☞ ✦85.00/110.00 – ✦✦95.00/150.00.
♦ Part thatched 17C inn offering locally produced and carefully prepared modern British
cooking. Dine in the bar or more formal Shed restaurant. Comfortable bedrooms.

BLEDINGTON *Oxon.* 503 504 P 28 *– see Stow-on-the-Wold.*

BLOCKLEY *Glos.* 503 504 O 27 *– ⊠ Moreton-in-Marsh.*
London 91 – Birmingham 39 – Oxford 34.

Lower Brook House, Lower St, GL56 9DS, *℘ (01386) 700286, info@lowerbrook*
house.com, Fax (01386) 701400, 🌳 – 🍴 **P. MO AE VISA**
closed Christmas – **Rest** *(closed Sunday)* (booking essential for non-residents) (dinner only)
25.00 – **6 rm** ☞ ✦80.00/95.00 – ✦✦165.00.
♦ Personally run, adjoining 17C Cotswold stone cottages with huge inglenooks, beams and
flagged floors. Characterful and stylish from every aspect. Individually appointed rooms.
Imaginative evening menus of local Cotswold produce.

BLUNDELLSANDS *Mersey.* 502 503 L 23 *– see Liverpool.*

BLUNSDON *Wilts.* 503 504 O 29 *– see Swindon.*

BLYTH *Notts.* 502 503 504 Q 23 *– ⊠ Worksop.*
London 166 – Doncaster 13 – Lincoln 30 – Nottingham 32 – Sheffield 20.

Charnwood, Sheffield Rd, S81 8HF, West : ¾ m. on A 634 *℘ (01909) 591610, charn*
wood@bestwestern.co.uk, Fax (01909) 591427, **ᒭ,** 🌳 – 🍴 rest, **P. – 🔬 120. MO AE ⓪**
VISA.
The Lantern : **Rest** a la carte 23.70/40.90 **s.** ♀ – **45 rm** ☞ ✦65.00/100.00 –
✦✦100.00/160.00.
♦ Privately owned hotel designed largely with the business traveller in mind. Practically
appointed bedrooms are consistently well kept; some overlook the landscaped gardens.
Restaurant with hanging lanterns and exposed beams.

BODIAM *E. Sussex* 504 V 30 *Great Britain G.*
See : Castle★★.
Exc. : Battle Abbey★, S : 10 m. by B 2244, B 2089, A 21 and minor rd – Rye★★, SW : 13 m. by
A 268.
London 58 – Cranbrook 7 – Hastings 13.

The Curlew, Junction Rd, TN32 5UY, Northwest : 1 ½ m. at junction with B 2244
℘ (01580) 861394, enquiries@thecurlewatbodiam.co.uk, 🌳 – 🍴 **P. MO VISA**
Rest *(closed Sunday and Monday dinner)* 21.95 and a la carte 24.00/33.00 ♀ ☞.
♦ Smart, serious dining pub in deep burgundy with beams, dried hops and elegant tableware. Simple or elaborate traditional menus with French base; notable fine wine list.

BODMIN *Cornwall* 503 F 32 *The West Country G. – pop. 12 778.*
See : St Petroc Church★.
Env. : Bodmin Moor★★ – Lanhydrock★★, S : 3 m. by B 3269 – Blisland★ (Church★), N : 5½
m. by A 30 and minor roads – Pencarrow★, NW : 4 m. by A 389 and minor roads – Cardin-
ham (Church★), NE : 4 m. by A 30 and minor rd – St Mabyn (Church★), N : 5½ m. by A 389,
B 3266 and minor rd.
Exc. : St Tudy★, N : 7 m. by A 389, B 3266 and minor rd.
🗗 *Shire Hall, Mount Folly Sq ℘ (01208) 76616.*
London 270 – Newquay 18 – Plymouth 32 – Truro 23.

Trehellas House, Washaway, PL30 3AD, Northwest: 3 m. on A 389 *℘ (01208) 72700,*
trehellashouse@btconnect.com, Fax (01208) 73336, ☑ heated, 🌳 – 🍴 **P. MO AE VISA**
closed Christmas and New Year – **Rest** *(closed Sunday)* (dinner only) a la carte 17.70/32.45 –
11 rm ☞ ✦62.50/77.50 – ✦✦100.00/180.00.
♦ Relaxed, personally run country house with a cottage facade. Owners' original Cornish
art on show in listed room. Cosy lounges with flag floors. Airy, pastel painted bedrooms.
Characterful restaurant; owners take pride in local, fresh, seasonal produce.

Bokiddick Farm ⚘ without rest., Lanivet, PL30 5HP, South : 5 m. by A 30 following signs for Lanhydrock and Bokiddick ℘ (01208) 831521, *gillhugo@bokiddickfarm.co.uk*, Fax (01208) 831481, ☞, ₤ – ✝✕ **P**, **◐◉** **VISA**, ✻
closed Christmas and New Year – 5 rm ☑ ✝45.00/55.00 – ✝✝70.00/75.00.
• Sizeable house on dairy farm: do take a quick tour. Warm welcome assured. Neat, well priced rooms with added amenities in old house; smart stable conversion for more rooms.

at Helland *Northeast : 4½ m. by A 389 off B 3266* – ☒ *Bodmin.*

Tredethy Country House ⚘ without rest., Helland Bridge, PL30 4QS, ℘ (01208) 841262, *tredethyhouse@aol.com*, Fax (01208) 841707, ≤, ⌇ heated, ☞, ₤ – ✝✕ **P**, **◐◉** **AE** **◐** **VISA**
– **11 rm** ☑ ✝85.00 – ✝✝118.00/165.00.
• Victorian house overlooking the Camel Valley. Books and family photos of former resident, Prince Chula of Thailand, in the reading room. Spacious well appointed bedrooms. Ornate dining room with fareaching views.

BODSHAM *Kent.*
London 65 – Ashford 10 – Canterbury 10.

Froggies at the Timber Batts, School Lane, TN25 5JQ, ℘ (01233) 750237, *joel@thetimberbatts.co.uk*, Fax (01233) 750176, ☞ – **P**, **◐◉** **AE** **VISA**
closed first 2 weeks March, 25 December and 1 January – **Rest** - French - *(closed Monday and Tuesday after Bank Holidays)* a la carte 25.00/32.00.
• Creeper-clad, 15C pub with welcoming Gallic owner. Large dining area has menus in French: staff readily translate. Fine local produce in unfussy, French country style dishes.

ENGLAND

BOLNHURST *Beds.*
London 64.5 – Bedford 8 – St Neots 7.

The Plough at Bolnhurst, Kimbolton Rd, MK44 2EX, South : ½ m. on B 660 ℘ (01234) 376274, *theplough@bolnhurst.com*, ㎡, ☞ – ✝✕ **P**, **◐◉** **VISA**, ✻
closed from 29 December for 2 weeks – **Rest** *(closed Sunday dinner and Monday)* 15.00 (lunch) and a la carte 20.00/35.00 ☑.
• Sympathetically refurbished 15C pub with terraces boasting charmingly rustic interior inducing pronounced feel of relaxation. Local produce a speciality in seasonal dishes.

BOLTON ABBEY *N. Yorks.* 502 O 22 *Great Britain G.* – ☒ *Skipton.*
See : *Bolton Priory★ AC.*
London 216 – Harrogate 18 – Leeds 23 – Skipton 6.

The Devonshire Arms Country House ⚘, BD23 6AJ, ℘ (01756) 710441, *res@devonshirehotels.co.uk760*, Fax (01756) 710564, ≤, ⊚, ₤₅, ≋, ⌇, ⌇, ☞, ₤, ✼ – ✝✕ ✆ **P** – ⚿ 90. **◐◉** **AE** **◐** **VISA**
The Burlington : **Rest** *(closed Monday)* (dinner only and Sunday lunch) 58.00 ☑ ⌂ – ☑ 16.50 – **38 rm** ✝160.00 – ✝✝195.00/340.00, 2 suites.
Spec. Poached saddle of rabbit, carpaccio of langoustine and crab. New season lamb with braised shoulder, anchovy beignets and rosemary foam. Iced praline parfait, honey glazed apricot and Earl Grey tea.
• Extended part 17C coaching inn owned by Duke and Duchess of Devonshire: elegant country house rooms with art and antiques. Close to spectacular ruins of 12C Bolton Priory. Candlelit refined dining with views of Italian Garden.

BOLTON-BY-BOWLAND *Lancs.* 502 M/N 22 *Great Britain G.*
Exc. : *Skipton - Castle★ , E : 12 m. by A 59 – Bolton Priory★, E : 17 m. by A 59.*
London 246 – Blackburn 17 – Skipton 15.

Middle Flass Lodge ⚘, Settle Rd, BB7 4NY, North : 2½ m. by Clitheroe rd on Settle rd ℘ (01200) 447259, *info@middleflasslodge.fsnet.co.uk*, Fax (01200) 447300, ≤, ☞ – ✝✕ **P**, **◐◉** **VISA**, ✻
Rest (by arrangement) 28.00 – **7 rm** ☑ ✝36.00/45.00 – ✝✝56.00/65.00.
• Friendly, welcoming owners in a delightfully located barn conversion. Plenty of beams add to rustic effect. Pleasantly decorated, comfy rooms with countryside outlook. Blackboard's eclectic menu boasts local, seasonal backbone.

BOROUGHBRIDGE *N.Yorks.* **502** P 21 – *pop. 3 311.*

🚹 *Fishergate* ℘ *(01423) 323373 (summer only).*
London 215 – Leeds 19 – Middlesbrough 36 – York 16.

XX 🍴 **thedingroom,** 20 St James's Sq, YO51 9AR, ℘ *(01423) 326426, Fax (01423) 326426 –*
⤶ **⓪** **VISA**
closed June, 25 December, 1 January, Sunday dinner and Monday – Rest *(booking essen-tial) (dinner only and Sunday lunch)* 25.00 ♀.
◆ Characterful cottage with beamed dining room. Vivid fireside sofas and Impressionist oils, as modern as the well-prepared dishes: duck on rocket and pesto features.

BORROWDALE *Cumbria* **502** K 20 – *see Keswick.*

BOSCASTLE *Cornwall* **503** F 31 *The West Country G.*

See : *Village*★.
Env. : *Poundstock Church*★ – *Tintagel Old Post Office*★.
London 260 – Bude 14 – Exeter 59 – Plymouth 43.

🏨 **The Bottreaux,** PL35 0BG, South : ¾ m. by B 3263 on B 3266 ℘ *(01840) 250231,*
info@boscastlecornwall.co.uk, Fax (01840) 250170 – ⤶ **P**, **⓪** **AE** **VISA**. ⌘
Rest *(closed Sunday-Monday) (booking essential in winter) (dinner only)* 28.00 ♀ – **7 rm** �
★60.00/75.00 – ★★75.00/90.00.
◆ On a hill outside the village, a privately owned, well-run hotel. The rooms, some with king-size beds, and the public areas have a sleek, stylish ambience. Dining room offers well-sourced, local, modern dishes.

⌂ **Trerosewill Farm** ⌘ without rest., Paradise, PL35 0BL, South : 1 m. off B 3263
℘ *(01840) 250545, cheryl@trerosewill.co.uk, Fax (01840) 250727,* ≤, ⌗, ⚑ – ⤶ **⛟** **P**, **⓪**
VISA. ⌘
closed mid December - mid January – **6 rm** � ★50.00/65.00 – ★★80.00/85.00.
◆ Modern house on 50-acre working farm: fine views of the coast and good clifftop walks. Lovely conservatory breakfast room. Bedrooms in matching patterns, some with Jacuzzis.

BOSHAM *W. Sussex* **504** R 31 – *see Chichester.*

BOSTON SPA *W. Yorks.* **502** P 22 – *pop. 5 952.*
London 127 – Harrogate 12 – Leeds 12 – York 16.

⌂ **Four Gables** ⌘ without rest., Oaks Lane, LS23 6DS, West : ¼ m. by A 659 ℘ *(01937)*
845592, info@fourgables.co.uk, Fax (01937) 849031, ⌗ – ⤶ **⛟** **P**
closed Christmas and New Year – **4 rm** � ★46.00/75.00 – ★★65.00/90.00.
◆ Down a quiet private road, a 1900 house, after Lutyens: period fireplaces, stripped oak and terracotta tile floors. Traditional, individually decorated rooms. Croquet lawn.

XX **Spice Box,** 152 High St, LS23 6BW, ℘ *(01937) 842558, info@thespicebox.com,*
Fax (01937) 849955 – ⤶ **⓪** **⓪** **VISA**
closed 26 December, 1 January, Sunday dinner and Monday – Rest 14.50 *(lunch)* and a la carte approx 19.00/34.00.
◆ Former chemist shop, evidenced by display of original artefacts. Smart, modern, two-roomed restaurant with warm burgundy décor. Carefully prepared modern British cook-ing.

BOULEY BAY *Jersey (Channel Islands)* **503** L 33 – *see Channel Islands.*

BOURNEMOUTH *Bournemouth* **503** **504** O 31 *The West Country G. – pop. 167 527.*

See : *Compton Acres*★★ *(English Garden* ≤★★★*) AC* **AX** – *Russell-Cotes Art Gallery and Museum*★★ *AC* **DZ** **M1** - *Shelley Rooms AC* **EX** **M2**.
Env. : *Poole*★, W : 4 m. by A 338 – *Brownsea Island*★ *(Baden-Powell Stone* ≤★★*) AC, by boat from Sandbanks* **BX** *or Poole Quay* – *Christchurch*★ *(Priory Church*★*) E : 4 ½ m. on A 35.*
Exc. : *Corfe Castle*★, SW : 18 m. by A 35 and A 351 – *Lulworth Cove*★ *(Blue Pool*★*) W : 8 m. of Corfe Castle by B 3070 – Swanage*★, E : 5 m. of Corfe Castle by A 351.
🏌 *Queens Park, Queens Park West Drive* ℘ *(01202) 302611,* **DV** – 🏌 *Bournemouth and Meyrick Park, Central Drive* ℘ *(01202) 786000,* **CY**.
✈ *Bournemouth (Hurn) Airport* : ℘ *(01202) 364000, N : 5 m. by Hurn -* **DV**.
🚹 *Westover Rd* ℘ *(01202) 451700.*
London 114 – Bristol 76 – Southampton 34.

Plans on following pages

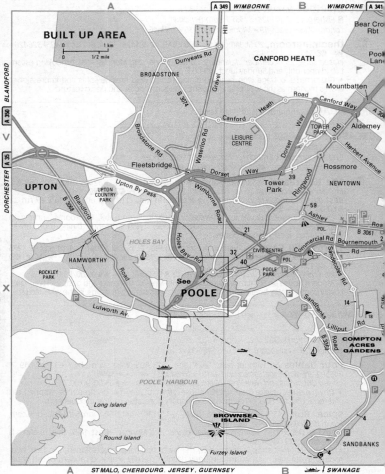

ST MALO, CHERBOURG, JERSEY, GUERNSEY — SWANAGE

BOURNEMOUTH
AND POOLE

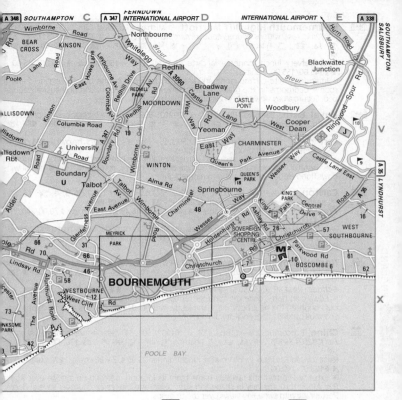

Wimborne Road
BEAR CROSS
KINSON
Northbourne
Whitelegg Way
Redhill A 3060
Broadway Lane
CASTLE POINT
Woodbury
Blackwater Junction
Stour
Poole Lane
East Howe Lane
Coombe Av
Leybourne Av
Redhill Drive
REDHILL PARK
Castle Lane
MOORDOWN
West Way
Yeoman Rd
Cooper Dean
Ringwood Spur Rd
18

ALLISDOWN
Kinson Road
Columbia Road
Boundary Rd
A 347
19
East Way
Queen's Park
CHARMINSTER
West
Avenue
Wessex Way
Castle Lane East
18
9

Ilsdown
University Road
WINTON
Wimborne Road
QUEEN'S PARK
18
KING'S PARK
Central Drive
A 35 LYNDHURST
16

Alisdown Rbt
Boundary U
Talbot
Alma Rd
Springbourne
King's Park
Ashley Rd
SOVEREIGN SHOPPING CENTRE
26
57
WEST SOUTHBOURNE

Alder Road
Glenferness Avenue
Talbot Av
East Avenue
Wimborne Road
Charminster Rd
Wessex Rd
48
Holdenhurst
Way
Rd
Christchurch
Parkwood Rd
M 2
10
61
62

66
31
66
MEYRICK PARK
46
58
BOURNEMOUTH
Christchurch
7
e
BOSCOMBE 6

Rd 70
Lindsay Rd
WESTBOURNE
West Cliff Rd
12
73
The Avenue
Alumhurst Road
42
PINKSOME PARK

POOLE BAY

X

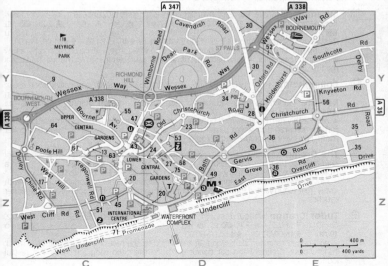

Cavendish Road
30
Wessex Rd
BOURNEMOUTH
A 338

MEYRICK PARK
18
Wimborne Road
Dean Park Rd
ST PAULS
Way
30
52
Southcote Rd
Derby Rd

9
Wessex Way
A 338
RICHMOND HILL
Way
Wessex
34 POL
Oxford Rd
Holdenhurst
Knyveton Rd
56
A 35

BOURNEMOUTH WEST
A 338
UPPER CENTRAL GARDENS
Bourne Av
55
47
H
Old Christchurch Road
J
28
Christchurch
Rd

64
Poole Hill
67
13
63
43
53
23
24
36
Road

Durley
West Hill
Tregonwell Rd
LOWER CENTRAL GARDENS
27
68
75
Bath Rd
Gervis
49
East Grove
36
Overcliff Drive
35
35

17
Chine Rd
20
20
T
M 1
a
Rd
a

West Cliff Rd
51
45
INTERNATIONAL CENTRE
2
WATERFRONT COMPLEX
Undercliff Drive

West Undercliff Promenade
71
r

0   400 m
0   400 yards

C   D   E

145

ENGLAND

Bournemouth Highcliff Marriott, St Michael's Rd, West Cliff, BH2 5DU, ℰ (0870) 4007211, reservations.bournemouth@marriotthotels.co.uk, Fax (0870) 4007311, ≼, ㍿, ℻, Ⓕ, ⓢ, ⏌ heated, ▨, ✿, ✗ – ▮ ✼ ▤ & P – ▵ 350. ⑩ ◯ ◯ VISA
CZ z
Rest (carvery lunch)/dinner a la carte 26.35/42.35 ♀ – **158 rm** ☷ ✱115.00/145.00 – ✱✱145.00/155.00, 2 suites.
♦ Imposing white clifftop landmark, linked by funicular to the beach. Elegant drawing rooms; bedrooms, in the grand tradition, and leisure centre are comprehensively equipped. Secure a bay view table in elegant formal restaurant.

Royal Bath, Bath Rd, BH1 2EW, ℰ (01202) 555555, royal.bath@devere-hotels.com, Fax (01202) 554158, ≼, Ⓕ, ⓢ, ▨, ✿ – ▮, ✼ rest, ⇄ – ▵ 400. ⑩ VISA.
DZ a
Rest (dinner only) a la carte 25.45/42.50 s. ♀ – (see also *Oscars* below) – **133 rm** ☷ ✱95.00/195.00 – ✱✱135.00/210.00, 7 suites.
♦ Classic Victorian hotel in secluded gardens retains the conscientious service of another age. Tastefully co-ordinated, generously appointed rooms, some with sea views. Tall windows flood elegant restaurant with natural light.

Carlton, East Overcliff, BH1 3DN, ℰ (01202) 552011, Fax (01202) 299573, ≼, ㍿, Ⓕ, ⓢ, ⏌ heated, ▨, ✿ – ▮ ✼ ▤ rest, ✆ ⇄ P – ▵ 160. ⑩ ◯ VISA
EZ a
Frederick's : Rest 14.95/29.95 and a la carte 29.00/46.45 ♀ – **71 rm** ☷ ✱70.00/240.00 – ✱✱140.00/240.00, 5 suites.
♦ Behind a 30s-styled façade, spacious, updated accommodation in matching colours, amply provided with mod cons. Relax in richly decorated lounges or by a palm-lined pool. Restaurant with views of the garden.

Norfolk Royale, Richmond Hill, BH2 6EN, ℰ (01202) 551521, sales@englishroseho tels.co.uk, Fax (01202) 294031, ⓢ, ▨ – ▮ ✼ ▤ rest, ✆ & ⇄ – ▵ 90. ⑩ ◯ ◯ VISA.
CY u
Echoes : Rest 19.50/37.50 s. – **91 rm** ☷ ✱75.00/130.00 – ✱✱125.00/180.00, 4 suites.
♦ Edwardian hotel, once the summer retreat of the Duke of Norfolk. Bold, modern colours brighten the neat bedrooms; the lobby, with its deep sofas, has a more clubby feel. Spacious candlelit conservatory dining room.

Chine, Boscombe Spa Rd, BH5 1AX, ℰ (01202) 396234, reservations@chinehotel.co.uk, Fax (01202) 391737, ≼, Ⓕ, ⓢ, ⏌ heated, ▨, ✿ – ▮ ✼ P – ▵ 120. ⑩ ◯ ◯ VISA
DX e
Rest (closed Saturday lunch) (buffet lunch)/dinner 25.95 s. ♀ – **88 rm** ☷ ✱70.00/105.00 – ✱✱120.00/140.00.
♦ Extended former spa takes its name from its location, perched on a ridge over Poole Bay. Modern rooms vary in shape and size; conference suites extend over several floors. Restaurant with sweeping views over the treetops.

Miramar, 19 Grove Rd, East Overcliff, BH1 3AL, ℰ (01202) 556581, sales@miramar-bournemouth.com, Fax (01202) 291242, ≼, ✿ – ▮ ✼ & P – ▵ 200. ⑩ ◯ VISA
DZ u
Rest (closed Saturday lunch) 13.95/25.00 ♀ – **43 rm** ☷ ✱40.95/84.95 – ✱✱81.90/119.90.
♦ Along the handsome lines of a grand Edwardian villa. Large, well cared for rooms, a few with curved balconies, in floral patterns. Library and a sun terrace facing the sea. Traditional menu.

Collingwood, 11 Priory Rd, BH2 5DF, ℰ (01202) 557575, info@hotel-collingwood.co.uk, Fax (01202) 293219, ⓢ, ▨ – ▮ ✼ rest, P. ⑩ ◯ VISA
CZ n
Rest (bar lunch Monday-Saturday)/dinner 16.95 – **53 rm** (dinner included) ☷ ✱64.00/146.00 – ✱✱128.00/146.00.
♦ A smoothly run, family owned hotel of long standing, its modern accommodation comfortably decorated in warm pastel shades. Bar terrace and reverently hushed snooker room. Effusively decorative dining room.

The Orchid without rest., 34 Gervis Rd, BH1 3DH, ℰ (01202) 551600, reservations@or chid-hotel.co.uk, Fax (01202) 553737 – ▮ ✼ & P – ▵ 100. ⑩ ◯ VISA
DY a
closed 24 December-2 January – **33 rm** ☷ ✱30.00/75.00 – ✱✱60.00/140.00.
♦ As you might expect, images of the orchid abound in this personally run hotel with lovely rear courtyard. Modern, minimalist style prevails. Comfy rooms with designer touches.

Tudor Grange without rest., 31 Gervis Rd, East Cliff, BH1 3EE, ℰ (01202) 291472, Fax (01202) 311503, ✿ – P. ⑩ ◯ ◯ VISA
EY o
10 rm ☷ ✱45.00/60.00 – ✱✱60.00/80.00.
♦ Well-priced rooms in dark wood, in keeping with the rest of the half-timbered mock Tudor house. Greenery and oak panels surround the deep wing armchairs in a restful lounge.

XXX **Oscars** (at Royal Bath H.), Bath Rd, BH1 2EW, $\mathscr{C}$ (01202) 555555, Fax (01202) 554158 – ✁
▤ ⬅, ⓜⓞ *VISA*
DZ **a**
– Rest a la carte 25.45/42.50 ♈.
♦ Pristine settings and discreet, impeccable service distinguish this elegant restaurant, serving modern British dishes, many infused with flavours of French country cooking.

XX **Noble House,** 3-5 Lansdowne Rd, BH1 1RZ, $\mathscr{C}$ (01202) 291277, Fax (01202) 291312 – ▤.
ⓜⓞ ⒶⒺ ⓞ *VISA*
DEY **i**
Rest - Chinese - 6.00/28.00 and a la carte 12.40/28.65.
♦ A hospitable family team are behind a comprehensive menu of authentic Chinese cuisine, carefully prepared from fresh ingredients. Smoothly run; handy town centre location.

BOURTON-ON-THE-HILL *Glos. – see Moreton-in-Marsh.*

BOURTON-ON-THE-WATER *Glos. 503 504 O 28 Great Britain G. – pop. 3 093.*

See : *Town★.*
Env. : *Northleach (Church of SS. Peter and Paul★, Wool Merchants' Brasses★), SW : 5 m. by A 429.*
London 91 – Birmingham 47 – Gloucester 24 – Oxford 36.

🏠 **The Dial House,** The Chestnuts, High St, GL54 2AN, $\mathscr{C}$ (01451) 822244, *info@dialhouse hotel.com, Fax (01451) 810126,* ☕, 🌳 – ✁ ℙ. ⓜⓞ ⒶⒺ *VISA* . ⅍
Rest (booking essential for non-residents) 15.00 (lunch) and a la carte approx 34.50 ♈ –
13 rm ⇌ ✦55.00/110.00 – ✦✦110.00/180.00.
♦ Charming and personally run, this is the oldest Cotswold stone property in the village. Delightful, individually styled rooms: four in 18C former dairy are most characterful. Two intimate dining rooms with original fireplaces.

🏠 **Coombe House** without rest., Rissington Rd, GL54 2DT, $\mathscr{C}$ (01451) 821966, *info@coombehouse.net, Fax (01451) 810477,* 🌳 – ✁ ℙ. ⅍
restricted opening in winter – 6 rm ⇌ ✦50.00/60.00 – ✦✦70.00/80.00.
♦ Creeper-clad 1920s house on the quiet outskirts of the village, near the local bird sanctuary. Homely lounge and spotless, comfortable, cottage style bedrooms in soft chintz.

🏠 **Alderley** without rest., Rissington Rd, GL54 2DX, $\mathscr{C}$ (01451) 822788, *alderleyguest house@hotmail.com, Fax (01451) 822788* – ✁ ℙ. ⅍
3 rm ⇌ ✦50.00/60.00 – ✦✦65.00/70.00.
♦ Short walk from town centre on main road. Combined lounge and eating room; terrace for summer breakfasts; good quality local produce used. Bright, homely, floral bedrooms.

🏠 **Manor Close** without rest., High St, GL54 2AP, $\mathscr{C}$ (01451) 820339, *davanzo@aol.com,* 🌳 – ✁ ℙ. ⅍
closed 25 December – 3 rm ⇌ ✦55.00/55.00 – ✦✦60.00/65.00.
♦ Superb central but quiet location. Lounge and breakfast room in Cotswold stone house; comfortable floral rooms in purpose-built garden annexe, one on ground floor.

at Lower Slaughter *Northwest : 1¾ m. by A 429 – ✉ Cheltenham.*

🏰 **Lower Slaughter Manor** ⌂, GL54 2HP, $\mathscr{C}$ (01451) 820456, *info@lowerslaugh ter.co.uk, Fax (01451) 822150,* ☕, 🌳, ⚘ – ✁ ℙ. ⓜⓞ ⒶⒺ
Rest a la carte 28.00/45.00 ♈ – 18 rm ⇌ ✦185.00 – ✦✦225.00, 1 suite.
♦ Beautiful listed part 17C manor in warm Cotswold stone. A wealth of objets d'art, fine oils and sense of enveloping period comfort extends from firelit hall to airy bedrooms. Ornate dining room with lithographs and Wedgewood.

🏰 **Washbourne Court,** GL54 2HS, $\mathscr{C}$ (01451) 822143, *info@washbournecourt.co.uk, Fax (01451) 821045,* ☕, 🌳 – ✁ ℙ. – ⚐ 30. ⓜⓞ ⒶⒺ ⓞ *VISA*
Rest (bar lunch Monday-Saturday)/dinner 40.00/50.00 ♈ – 23 rm ⇌ ✦90.00/110.00 –
✦✦120.00/140.00, 8 suites.
♦ Extended part 1800s manor house by the Eyre. Spacious rooms in floral fabrics at their traditional best in the old building. Flag-floored, timbered bar with terrace. Restaurant offers views of tree-lined lawns.

at Upper Slaughter *Northwest : 2½ m. by A 429 – ✉ Bourton-on-the-Water.*

🏰 **Lords of the Manor** ⌂, GL54 2JD, $\mathscr{C}$ (01451) 820243, *enquiries@lordsofthema nor.com, Fax (01451) 820696,* ☕, 🐟, 🌳 – ✁ ℙ. – ⚐ 30. ⓜⓞ ⒶⒺ ⓞ *VISA*
Rest (light lunch) 21.50/49.00 – 26 rm ✦110.00 – ✦✦250.00, 1 suite.
♦ Former 17C Cotswold stone rectory with mature gardens and parterre. Country house style typified by antique strewn drawing rooms and bedrooms boasting beams and four posters. Modern, original cuisine prepared in a skilled and accomplished manner.

ENGLAND

BOVEY TRACEY *Devon 503 I 32 The West Country G. –* ⊠ *Newton Abbot.*

See : *St Peter, St Paul and St Thomas of Canterbury Church*★.
Env. : *Dartmoor National Park*★★.

🏌 *Newton Abbot* ℘ *(01626) 52460.*
London 214 – Exeter 14 – Plymouth 32.

🏛 **Edgemoor**, Haytor Rd, TQ13 9LE, West : 1 m. on B 3387 ℘ (01626) 832466, *reservations@edgemoor.co.uk, Fax (01626) 834760,* 🌲 – 🍴 🄿 – 🏌 50. ◍◍ 𝘝𝘐𝘚𝘈
closed 27 December- 13 January – **Rest** (bar lunch)/dinner 35.50 **s.** 🍷 – **16 rm** � **★**85.00/120.00 – **★★**130.00/140.00.
♦ Country style, creeper-clad former school house. Lofty beamed, firelit lounge has deep chintz armchairs. Smart rooms - in main house or ex-schoolrooms - in floral prints. Elegantly proportioned dining room.

⌂ **Brookfield House** 🌾 without rest., Challabrook Lane, TQ13 9DF, Southwest : ¾ m. by Brimley rd ℘ (01626) 836181, *brookfieldH@tinyworld.co.uk, Fax (01626) 836182,* 🌲 – 🍴 🄿. ◍◍ 𝘝𝘐𝘚𝘈. 🌾
closed December-January – 3 rm ⊡ **★**45.00/52.00 – **★★**60.00/74.00.
♦ Well-kept early Edwardian house in two acres of attractive gardens surrounded by Dartmoor. The three large bedrooms have expansive windows and are immaculately appointed.

at Haytor Vale *West : 3½ m. by B 3387 –* ⊠ *Newton Abbot.*

🍴 **The Rock Inn** with rm, TQ13 9XP, ℘ (01364) 661305, *inn@rock-inn.co.uk, Fax (01364) 661242,* 🍽, 🌲 – 🍴 📞 🄿. ◍◍ ◑ 𝘝𝘐𝘚𝘈. 🌾
closed 25-26 December – **Rest** 19.95 and a la carte 23.95/27.95 🍷 – **9 rm** ⊡ **★**65.95 – **★★**96.95/106.95.
♦ Steadfastly traditional 18C inn; relaxed, firelit bar in polished oak and brass. En suite rooms, named after Grand National winners, are true to the old-world style.

BOWNESS-ON-WINDERMERE *Cumbria 502 L 20 – see Windermere.*

BOX *Bath & North East Somerset 503 504 N 29 – see Bath.*

BRACKNELL *Bracknell Forest 504 R 29 – pop. 70 795.*

🏌 *Downshire, Easthampstead Park, Wokingham* ℘ *(01344) 302030.*
🅱 *The Look Out, Discovery Park, Nine Mile Ride* ℘ *(01344) 354409.*
London 35 – Reading 11 – Southampton 51.

🏨 **Coppid Beech**, John Nike Way, RG12 8TF, West : 3 m. on B 3408 ℘ (01344) 303333, *sales@coppid-beech-hotel.co.uk, Fax (01344) 301200,* ⒣, 🛋, 🈺, 🔲 – 📶 🍴, 🍽 rest, 📞 🕭 🄿 – 🏌 350. ◍◍ 🄰🄴 ◑ 𝘝𝘐𝘚𝘈
Rowans : **Rest** 18.00 and a la carte 30.00/40.00 🍷 – **Brasserie in the Keller :** **Rest** (closed Sunday) (dinner only) a la carte approx 15.00 **s.** 🍷 – **205 rm** ⊡ **★**185.00 – **★★**205.00/255.00.
♦ Striking, alpine style hotel offering modern rooms; meticulously kept throughout, with a full range of mod cons. Large open-plan lounge bar and a discreetly located nightclub. Rowans is formal with a sage-green palette. German themed Brasserie in the Keller.

BRADFORD *W. Yorks. 502 O 22 Great Britain G. – pop. 293 717.*

See : *City*★ – *National Museum of Photography, Film and Television*★ *AZ* **M**.

🏌 *West Bowling, Newall Hall, Rooley Lane* ℘ *(01274) 724449 BY* – 🏌 *Woodhall Hills, Woodhall Rd, Calverley, Pudsley* ℘ *(0113) 256 4771,* – 🏌 *Bradford Moor, Scarr Hill, Pollard Lane* ℘ *(01274) 771716 BX* – 🏌 *East Brierley, South View Rd* ℘ *(01274) 681023 BX* – 🏌 *Queensbury, Brighouse Rd, Queensbury* ℘ *(01274) 882155 AY.*
✈ *Leeds and Bradford Airport :* ℘ *(0113) 250 9696, NE : 6 m. by A 658 BX.*
🅱 *City Hall* ℘ *(01274) 433678.*
London 212 – Leeds 9 – Manchester 39 – Middlesbrough 75 – Sheffield 45.

Plan of Enlarged Area : see Leeds

🏨 **Hilton Bradford**, Hall Ings, BD1 5SH, ℘ (01274) 734734, Fax (01274) 306146 – 📶 🍴, 🍽 rest, 📞 🕭 – 🏌 700. ◍◍ 🄰🄴 ◑ 𝘝𝘐𝘚𝘈
BZ e
City 3 : Rest a la carte 10.00/20.00 **s.** 🍷 – ⊡ 15.95 – **116 rm ★**65.00/120.00 – **★★**75.00/130.00, 4 suites.
♦ City centre hotel, convenient for rail travellers. Don't be put off by dated 60s exterior. Neatly equipped modern accommodation; smart and comfortable cocktail lounge. Easy informality is the by-word in restaurant.

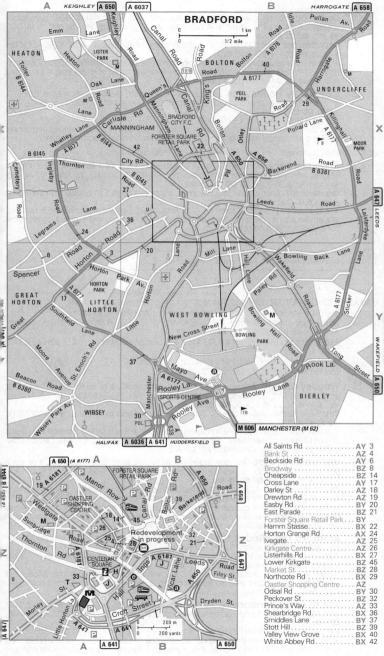

BRADFORD

🏨 Cedar Court, Mayo Ave, off Rooley Lane, BD5 8HZ, ℰ (01274) 406606, *sales@cedar courtbradford.co.uk*, Fax (01274) 406600, ⅙, ⅀, 🖾, ☞ – ⅋ ⅍, ▤ rest, ℃, 🖃 – ⅍ 800. ⅏ AE VISA. ⅍
BY a
Four Seasons : Rest 21.95/35.00 and a la carte 24.95/42.00 s. – ⅀ 12.95 – **130 rm** ✦49.00/130.00 – ✦✦65.00/130.00.
◆ Subtly co-ordinated décor and mod cons make this a popular business option. Comfortable modern lounge by a long mahogany bar. Near the home of rugby league's Bradford Bulls. Restaurant exudes relaxing informality.

🏨 Express By Holiday Inn without rest., The Leisure Exchange, Vicar Lane, BD1 5LD, ℰ (0870) 7872064, *bradford@morethanhotels.com*, Fax (0870) 7872066 – ⅋ ⅍ & 🖃 – ⅍ 40. ⅏ AE ⅈ VISA. ⅍
BZ a
120 rm ✦59.00/69.00 – ✦✦59.00/69.00.
◆ Located above a large entertainment centre in the heart of the city. Aimed at business travellers with ample desk space and meeting rooms. Good value accommodation.

at Gomersal *Southeast : 7 m. by A 650 on A 651 – ⊠ Bradford.*

🏨 Gomersal Park, Moor Lane, BD19 4LJ, Northeast : 1½ m. by A 651 off A 652 ℰ (01274) 869386, *reservations@gomersalparkhotel.com*, Fax (01274) 861042, ⅙, ⅀, 🖾, ☞ – ⅋ ⅍, ▤ rest, & 🖃 – ⅍ 200. ⅏ AE ⅈ VISA
BU u
Brasserie 101 : Rest *(closed Saturday lunch)* a la carte 21.00/28.50 s. – **100 rm** ⅀ ✦105.00 – ✦✦105.00/240.00.
◆ Well-equipped corporate hotel on greenfield site; comprehensive conference facilities. Modern bedrooms: the executive style provides more comfort. Well-stocked, comfortable bar is ideal stopping point before dining.

ENGLAND

BRADFORD-ON-AVON Wilts. 503 504 N 29 *The West Country G. – pop. 9 072.*
See : *Town★★ - Saxon Church of St Lawrence★★ - Tithe Barn★ – Bridge★.*
Env. : *Great Chalfield Manor★ (All Saints★) AC, NE : 3 m. by B 3109 – Westwood Manor★ AC, S : 1½ m. by B 3109 – Top Rank Tory (≼★).*
Exc. : *Bath★★★, NW : 7½ m. by A 363 and A 4 – Corsham Court★★ AC, NE : 6½ m. by B 3109 and A 4.*
🛈 *The Greenhouse, 50 Margaret's Street ℰ (01225) 865797.*
London 118 – Bristol 24 – Salisbury 35 – Swindon 33.

🏨 Woolley Grange, Woolley Green, BA15 1TX, Northeast : ¾ m. by B 3107 on Woolley St ℰ (01225) 864705, *info@woolleygrangehotel.co.uk*, Fax (01225) 864059, ☞, ⅃ heated, ☞, 🖳 – ⅍ ℃ ₊₊ 🖃 – ⅍ 30. ⅏ AE
✦✦290.00/350.00, 7 suites.
Rest 37.50 (dinner) and a la carte 22.50/36.50 – **19 rm** (dinner included) ⅀ ✦140.00/270.00
◆ Modern art, period furniture: innumerable charming details spread through the rooms of a beautiful Jacobean manor. This is an hotel very much geared to families. Classic British cooking in restaurant, conservatory or terrace.

🏨 Widbrook Grange ⅍, Trowbridge Rd, Widbrook, BA15 1UH, Southeast : 1 m. on A 363 ℰ (01225) 864750, *stay@widbrookgrange.com*, Fax (01225) 862890, ⅙, 🖾, ☞, 🖳 – ⅍ ℃ & 🖃 – ⅍ 25. ⅏ AE ⅈ VISA. ⅍
closed 24 December-1 January – **The Medlar Tree :** Rest *(closed Sunday)* (dinner only) a la carte 23.50/31.50 – **20 rm** ⅀ ✦95.00/95.00 – ✦✦120.00/120.00.
◆ Georgian house and outbuildings, once the centre of an 11-acre model farm; cosy bedrooms, subtly reflecting the past, overlook peaceful fields and a pleasant mature garden. Pre-prandial relaxation in comfy drawing rooms.

⌂ Bradford Old Windmill, 4 Masons Lane, BA15 1QN, on A 363 ℰ (01225) 866842, Fax (01225) 866648, ≼, ☞ – ⅍ 🖃. ⅏ VISA
3 March-October – Rest - Vegetarian - (by arrangement) (communal dining) 25.00 – **3 rm** ⅀ ✦69.00/99.00 – ✦✦79.00/109.00.
◆ 1807 windmill in redressed local stone; Gothic windows and restored bridge. Rooms and circular lounge, stacked with books and curios, share a homely, unaffected quirkiness. Flavourful vegetarian menus.

⌂ The Beeches Farmhouse without rest., Holt Rd, BA15 1TS, East : 1¼ m. on B 3107 ℰ (01225) 865170, *beeches-farmhouse@netgates.co.uk*, Fax (01225) 865170, ☞ – ⅍ 🖃. ⅏ VISA. ⅍
4 rm ⅀ ✦45.00 – ✦✦80.00/90.00.
◆ 18C farmhouse where sheep and ducks roam. Charming main bedroom boasts Victorian bath; log stove heats a cosy lounge. Pine furnished bedrooms in converted outbuildings.

at Holt East : 2 m. on B 3107 – ✉ Bradford-on-Avon.

🛏 **The Tollgate Inn** with rm, Ham Green, BA14 6PX, ℘ (01225) 782326, alison@tollgate
holt.co.uk, Fax (01225) 782805, 🍴, 🌳 – ✦ **P. ₵❹ VISA**
closed 25-26 December and 1 January – **Rest** (closed Sunday dinner and Monday) (booking
essential) 12.95 (lunch) and a la carte 22.00/32.00 ♀ – **4 rm** �), ✦50.00 – ✦✦95.00.
♦ Friendly, log-fired pub built of Bath stone. Twin dining areas with simple wooden tables
and chairs. Interesting à la carte menu serves food with international elements.

BRADWELL Derbs. **502 503 504** O 24 – pop. 1 728 – ✉ Sheffield.
London 181 – Derby 51 – Manchester 32 – Sheffield 16 – Stoke-on-Trent 41.

🏠 **Stoney Ridge** ⌘ without rest., Granby Rd, S33 9HU, West : ¾ m. via Town Lane
℘ (01433) 620538, toneyridge@aol.com, ◅, 🔲, 🌳 – **P. ₵❹ VISA**
4 rm �) ✦40.00 – ✦✦52.00/67.00.
♦ Extensive, modern hilltop bungalow with views of the village and distant moors. Cosy
lounge with open fire and family ornaments. Homely bedrooms in individual floral fabrics.

BRAINTREE Essex **504** V 28 – pop. 42 393.
🔸 Kings Lane, Stisted ℘ (01376) 346079 – 🔸 Towerlands, Panfield Rd ℘ (01376) 326802.
🏛 Town Hall Centre, Market Pl ℘ (01376) 550066.
London 45 – Cambridge 38 – Chelmsford 12 – Colchester 15.

🏨 **Express by Holiday Inn** without rest., Galley's Corner, Cressing Rd, CM77 8DJ, Southeast : 2 ¼ m. on B 1018 ℘ (01376) 551141, Fax (01376) 551142 – ✦ ♿ **P** – ♿ 30. **₵❹ AE**
① VISA. 🍴
47 rm ✦59.95 – ✦✦59.95.
♦ Purpose-built hotel offering smart, contemporary rooms, well lit with ample work
space, on the outskirts of the town. Take-away breakfast option for travellers in a hurry.

BRAITHWAITE Cumbria **502** K 20 – see Keswick.

BRAMFIELD Suffolk **504** Y 27 – pop. 1 778 (inc. Cratfield) – ✉ Ipswich.
London 215 – Ipswich 27 – Norwich 28.

🛏 **Queen's Head,** The Street, IP19 9HT, ℘ (01986) 784214, qhbfield@aol.com,
Fax (01986) 784797, 🍴 – ✦ **P. ₵❹ AE VISA**
closed 26 December – **Rest** a la carte 16.85/23.95 ♀.
♦ Village pub with real rustic character draws on local, organic farm produce, including
rare-breed meats, for an eclectic menu. Roaring log fires in winter.

BRAMHOPE W. Yorks. **502** P 22 – see Leeds.

BRAMPTON Cambs. **504** T 27 – pop. 5 030 – see Huntingdon.

BRAMPTON Cumbria **501 502** L 19 Great Britain G. – pop. 3 965.
Env. : Hadrian's Wall★★, NW : by A 6077.
🔸 Talkin Tarn ℘ (016977) 2255 – 🔸 Brampton Park, Huntingdon ℘ (01480) 434700.
🏛 Moot Hall, Market Pl ℘ (016977) 3433.
London 317 – Carlisle 9 – Newcastle upon Tyne 49.

🏛 **Farlam Hall** ⌘, CA8 2NG, Southeast : 2 ¾ m. on A 689 ℘ (016977) 46234,
Fax (016977) 46683, ◅, 🌳 – ✦ ℂ **P. ₵❹ AE VISA**
closed 26-30 December – **Rest** (booking essential for non-residents) (dinner only) 38.00 🍴
– **12 rm** (dinner included) �) ✦150.00/180.00 – ✦✦330.00.
♦ Family run 19C coal baron's country seat in fine established gardens with an ornamental
lake. Luxuriously furnished drawing rooms, comfortable bedrooms in bold floral décor.
Period styled dining room with staff in eveningwear.

at Kirkcambeck North : 7¾ m. by A 6071 and Walton rd – ✉ Brampton.

🏠 **Cracrop Farm** ⌘ without rest., CA8 2BW, West : 1 m. by B 6318 on Stapleton rd
℘ (016977) 48245, cracrop@aol.com, Fax (016977) 48333, ◅, ⛲, 🌳, ⬜ – ✦ **P. VISA**. 🍴
– **3 rm** �) ✦35.00 – ✦✦80.00.
♦ Run with real friendliness, a spotlessly kept house on a working farm. Comfy rooms
furnished in solid pine overlook rolling fields. Breakfasts at antique dining table.

at **Castle Carrock** *South : 4 m. on B 6413* – ⊠ *Brampton.*

 The Weary at Castle Carrock with rm, CA8 9LU, ✆ (01228) 670230,
Fax (01228) 670089, ☞ – ✺ **P**. **⑩** **AE** **VISA**, ✀
Rest a la carte 14.50/35.00 – **5 rm** ☑ ✦65.00/85.00 – ✦✦95.00/105.00.
♦ Based in a small village near the Talkin Tarn beauty spot. Bold, stylish interior. Dine
on sofas, in the conservatory or on the terrace. Tasty modern dishes. Modish
bedrooms.

BRANDESBURTON *East Riding 502* T 22 – *pop. 1 835* – ⊠ *Great Driffield.*
London 197 – Kingston-upon-Hull 16 – York 37.

 Burton Lodge, YO25 8RU, Southwest : ½ m. on Leven rd ✆ (01964) 542847, enqui
ries@burton-lodge.co.uk, Fax (01964) 544771, 🏌, ☞, ✾ – ✺ **P**. **⑩** **AE** **VISA**
closed 25-26 December – **Rest** (residents only) (dinner only) 17.00 s. ♀ – **9 rm** ☑
✦40.00/50.00 – ✦✦59.00/62.00.
♦ Personally run, extended 1930s house. Neat, modern bedrooms in soft pastels, some
overlooking the golf course - perfect for an early round. A short drive to Beverley Minster.

BRANDS HATCH *Kent 504* U 29 – ⊠ *Dartford.*
🏌 *Corinthian, Gay Dawn Farm, Fawkham, Dartford ✆ (01474) 707144.*
London 22 – Maidstone 18.

at **Fawkham Green** *East : 1½ m. by A 20* – ⊠ *Ash Green.*

 Brands Hatch Place, DA3 8NQ, ✆ (01474) 875000, brandshatchplace@hand
picked.co.uk, Fax (01474) 879652, ⑰, 🏌, ✺, 🔲, ☞, 🐾, ✾, squash – ✺, ▤ rest, ✆ &
✦✦ **P** – 🏛 120. **⑩** **AE** **⑩** **VISA**
Rest (closed Saturday lunch) 28.50 s. – ☑ 12.95 – **38 rm** ✦155.00 – ✦✦155.00.
♦ Sensitively extended Georgian house in 12 acres offering smart bedrooms, some in the
annexe, with hi-tech facilities. Also, a range of conference and entertainment packages.
Smart, contemporary restaurant.

> **Good food and accommodation at moderate prices?**
> **Look for the Bib symbols:**
> **red Bib Gourmand 🅑 for food, blue Bib Hotel 🅑 for hotels**

BRANSCOMBE *Devon 503* K 31 *The West Country G.* – ⊠ *Seaton.*
See : *Village★.*
Env. : *Seaton (≤★★), NW : 3 m – Colyton★.*
London 167 – Exeter 20 – Lyme Regis 11.

 Masons Arms, EX12 3DJ, ✆ (01297) 680300, reception@masonsarms.co.uk,
Fax (01297) 680500, ☞ – ✺ ✆ **P**. **⑩** **VISA**
Rest (bar lunch)/dinner 25.00 and a la carte 15.20/27.50 ♀ – **19 rm** ☑ ✦40.00 – ✦✦160.00.
♦ Family run 14C inn; cosy, unspoilt bar with slate floors and ships' timbers, popular with
locals. Bedrooms in the inn have more character; those in the annex are much larger. Dine
in the populous bar with its dressed stone interior and huge open fire.

BRANSFORD *Worcs.* – see Worcester.

BRANSTON *Lincs. 502* S 24 – see Lincoln.

BRATTON *Wrekin* – see Telford.

BRAYE *Alderney (Channel Islands) 503* Q 33 and *517* A 34 – see Channel Islands.

BRAY MARINA *Windsor & Maidenhead* – see Bray-on-Thames.

BRAY-ON-THAMES *Windsor & Maidenhead* **504** R 29 – ✉ *Maidenhead.*
London 34 – Reading 13.

Plan : see Maidenhead

XXXXX ✿✿✿ **The Waterside Inn** (Roux) with rm, Ferry Rd, SL6 2AT, ☎ (01628) 620691, *reservations@waterside-inn.co.uk, Fax (01628) 784710,* ≤ Thames-side setting – ⚓ ⇔ ▤ P ⇔ 14. MC AE D VISA. ✈ X s
closed 26 December-1 February and 11-12 April – **Rest** - French - *(closed Tuesday except dinner June-August and Monday)* (booking essential) 42.00/91.00 and a la carte 78.50/120.70 – **8 rm** ☕ ✝180.00/260.00 – ✝✝180.00/260.00, 3 suites.
Spec. Tronçonnettes de homard poêlées minute au Porto blanc. Filets de lapereau grillés aux marrons glacés. Péché Gourmand.
◆ Ever delightful Thames idyll: drinks in summer house or on terrace, exquisite French cuisine and matchless service. Luxurious bedrooms are restful and classically chic.

XX ✿✿✿ **Fat Duck** (Blumenthal), High St, SL6 2AQ, ☎ (01628) 580333, *Fax (01628) 776188* – ⇔. MC AE VISA X e
closed 25-26 December, Sunday dinner and Monday – **Rest** (booking essential) 80.00/97.75 ♀.
Spec. Roast foie gras, almond fluid gel, cherry and chamomile. Best end of lamb, purée of onion and thyme, hot pot of shoulder. "Nitrogen" scrambled egg and bacon ice cream, tea jelly, parsnip cereal.
◆ History and science combine in an innovative alchemy of contrasting flavours and textures. Modern art, stylish, relaxing milieu, confident service.

The Hinds Head, High St, SL6 2AB, ☎ (01628) 626151, *info@hindsheadhotel.co.uk, Fax (01628) 623394* – ⇔ P ⇔ 26. MC AE D VISA. ✈ X e
closed 25-26 December – **Rest** - British - *(closed Sunday dinner)* (booking essential) a la carte 25.00/45.00 ♀.
◆ Characterful 17C village pub; inside a wealth of panelling and charm. Enjoy a sip of mead or a glass of perry with tasty and heart-warming classic British cooking.

The Royal Oak, Paley St, SL6 3JN, Southwest : 3 ½ m. by A 308, A 330 on B 3024 ☎ (01628) 620541, ☂ – ⇔ P. MC AE VISA. ✈
closed 27 December-2 January – **Rest** *(closed Sunday dinner)* 19.50 (lunch) and a la carte 20.00/30.00.
◆ Welcoming traditional pub adorned by beams, wattle walls and photos of celebs who've impacted on owner Michael Parkinson's career. Simple pub style menus; warm service.

at Bray Marina *Southeast : 2 m. by B 3208, A 308 – X – on Monkey Island Lane – ✉ Bray-on-Thames.*

X **Riverside Brasserie**, SL6 2EB, (follow road through the marina) ☎ (01628) 780553, *Fax (01628) 674312,* ☂ – ⚓ ⇔ P. MC AE D VISA
January - September – **Rest** a la carte 22.00/36.00 ♀.
◆ Marina boathouse, idylically set on the banks of the Thames. Very simply appointed interior and decked terrace. Inventive cooking in informal, busy and buzzy surroundings.

BREADSALL *Derby – see Derby.*

BREEDON ON THE HILL *Leics. – see Castle Donington.*

BRENTWOOD *Essex* **504** V 29 – *pop. 47 593.*
18 Bentley G. & C.C., Ongar Rd ☎ (01277) 373179 – 18, 9 Warley Park, Magpie Lane, Little Warley ☎ (01277) 224891.
Pepperell House, 44 High St ☎ (01277) 200300.
London 22 – Chelmsford 11 – Southend-on-Sea 21.

Marygreen Manor, London Rd, CM14 4NR, Southwest : 1 ¼ m. on A 1023 ☎ (01277) 225252, *info@marygreenmanor.co.uk, Fax (01277) 262809,* – ⇔ ▤ ♿ P – 🎪 50. MC AE D VISA. ✈
Rest *(closed Sunday dinner)* 25.50/55.00 and a la carte 46.50/54.50 **s.** ♀ – ☕ 15.00 – **55 rm** ✝135.00 – ✝✝150.00, 1 suite.
◆ Half timbered 16C house. Some rooms, named after Henry VIII's wives, with carved oak beds, others off a courtyard garden: all well-equipped. Cosy lounge with ornate ceiling. Dining hall with spiral oak pillars, criss-crossing beams.

Look out for red symbols, indicating particularly pleasant establishments.

ENGLAND

BRIDGNORTH Shrops. 502 503 504 M 26 *Great Britain G.* – pop. 11 891.

Exc. : Ironbridge Gorge Museum★★ AC (The Iron Bridge★★ - Coalport China Museum★★ - Blists Hill Open Air Museum★★ - Museum of the Gorge and Visitor Centre★) NW : 8 m. by B 4373.

⛳ Stanley Lane ℘ (01746) 763315.

🛈 The Library, Listley St ℘ (01746) 763257.

London 146 – Birmingham 26 – Shrewsbury 20 – Worcester 29.

at Worfield Northeast : 4 m. by A 454 – ⊠ Bridgnorth.

🏨 **The Old Vicarage** ⌂, WV15 5JZ, ℘ (01746) 716497, admin@the-old-vicarage.demon.co.uk, Fax (01746) 716552, 🍴, � – 🔆 ⅙ 🅿 ⑩ VISA
Rest (booking essential) 23.50 and dinner a la carte 32.00/45.65 ♀ – **13 rm** ⊆ ♣65.00/85.00 – ♣♣99.50, 1 suite.
♦ Antiques, rare prints and rustic pottery: a personally run Edwardian parsonage in a rural setting with thoughtfully appointed bedrooms, some in the coach house. Delightful orangery dining room overlooking garden; modern British cooking.

at Alveley Southeast : 7 m. by A 442 – ⊠ Bridgnorth.

🏨 **Mill,** Birdsgreen, WV15 6HL, Northeast : ¾ m. ℘ (01746) 780437, info@themill-hotel.co.uk, Fax (01746) 780850, 🌾 – 📶 🔆 ℄ 🅿 – 🔬 250. ⑩ ᴁᴇ ⓞ VISA 🌾
Waterside : Rest 14.50/26.00 and a la carte 22.30/40.95 ♀ – ⊆ 15.00 – **41 rm** ♣90.00/125.00. – ♣♣180.00/200.00.
♦ Hugely extended water mill. Below traditionally styled rooms in flowery patterns, ducks paddle around the pond and fountain. Popular wedding venue. Capacious restaurant, busy at weekends, overlooks garden and duck pond.

BRIDGWATER Somerset 503 L 30 *The West Country G.* – pop. 35 563.

See : Town★ – Castle Street★ – St Mary's★ – Admiral Blake Museum★ AC.

Env. : Westonzoyland (St Mary's Church★★) SE : 4 m. by A 372 – North Petherton (Church Tower★★) S : 3½ m. by A 38.

Exc. : Stogursey Priory Church★★, NW : 14 m. by A 39.

⛳ Enmore Park, Enmore ℘ (01278) 671103.

🛈 King Sq ℘ (01278) 436438.

London 160 – Bristol 39 – Taunton 11.

at Woolavington Northeast : 5 m. by A 39 on B 3141 – ⊠ Bridgwater.

🏠 **Chestnut House Village H.,** Hectors Stones Lower Road, TA7 8EF, ℘ (01278) 683658, paul@chestnuthousehotel.com, Fax (01278) 684333, 🌾 – 🔆 🅿 ⑩ VISA 🌾
closed February and Christmas – Rest (residents only) (dinner only) 25.00 – **7 rm** ⊆ ♣67.50 – ♣♣88.00.
♦ Converted farmhouse, spotless and personally run, the exposed stone and beams in the homely lounge testify to its 16C origins. Rooms are neat, comfortable; and all en suite. Dining room with comfy wicker chairs and garden views.

at Cannington Northwest : 3½ m. by A 39 – ⊠ Bridgwater.

🏠 **Blackmore Farm** without rest., TA5 2NE, Southwest : 1½ m. by A 39 on Bradley Green rd ℘ (01278) 653442, dyerfarm@aol.com, Fax (01278) 653427, 🌾, 🐾 – 🔆 ⅙ 🅿 ⑩ ᴁᴇ ⓞ VISA 🌾
5 rm ⊆ ♣40.00/55.00 – ♣♣65.00/85.00.
♦ Part 15C manor, now a working dairy farm, with great hall and chapel, set against a backdrop of the Quantocks. Huge, well-priced bedrooms brimming with character.

BRIDPORT Dorset 503 L 31 *The West Country G.* – pop. 12 977.

Env. : – Mapperton Gardens★, N : 4 m. by A 3066 and minor rd.

Exc. : Lyme Regis★ – The Cobb★, W : 11 m. by A 35 and A 3052.

⛳ Bridport and West Dorset, East Cliff, West Bay ℘ (01308) 422597.

🛈 47 South St ℘ (01308) 424901.

London 150 – Exeter 38 – Taunton 33 – Weymouth 19.

🏨 **Roundham House** without rest., Roundham Gdns, West Bay Rd, DT6 4BD, South : 1 m. by B 3157 ℘ (01308) 422753, cyprencom@compuserve.com, Fax (01308) 421500, ≤, 🌾 – 🔆 🅿 ⑩ VISA
March-October – **8 rm** ⊆ ♣50.00/80.00 – ♣♣84.00/96.00.
♦ Elegant 1903 house with trim, spacious bedrooms, their broad windows overlooking woods, fields and a lawned garden. Coffee in the smart lounge with its marble fireplace. Breakfast room has pleasant views of the countryside.

⋔ **Britmead House** without rest., West Bay Rd, DT6 4EG, South : 1 m. on B 3157 *℘* (01308) 422941, *britmead@talk21.com*, Fax (01308) 422516, ☞ – ⅍ ℗, ⓪ 𝑽𝑰𝑺𝑨
8 rm ☑ ✭38.00/50.00 – ✭✭56.00/70.00.
  ♦ On the road to West Bay and the Dorset Coast Path, a neat, redbrick Edwardian house with well-proportioned rooms and a comfortable lounge leading out to the garden.

✕ **Riverside**, West Bay, DT6 4EZ, South : 1 ¾ m. by B 3157 *℘* (01308) 422011, Fax (01308) 458808, ⩽, 🏠 – ⓪ 𝑽𝑰𝑺𝑨
14 February-25 November – **Rest** - Seafood - *(closed Sunday dinner and Monday except Bank Holidays) (booking essential) (restricted opening February-March and October-November)* a la carte 24.00/41.00 ☑.
  ♦ Follow the footbridge across the river to this popular seafood café overlooking the harbour, renowned for its extensive choice of specials and its friendly service.

✕ **Chez Cuddy**, 47 East St, DT6 3JX, *℘* (01308) 458770 – ⅍, ⓪ 𝑽𝑰𝑺𝑨
closed 2 weeks Summer and Sunday – **Rest** *(lunch only)* a la carte 13.75/17.50.
  ♦ Inviting, personably run, centrally located, café style eatery. Simple décor enhanced by vivid artwork. Interesting seasonal menus: accomplished execution of modern dishes.

at Shipton Gorge *Southeast : 3 m. by A 35 –* ⊠ *Bridport.*

⋔ **Innsacre Farmhouse** ⌂, Shipton Lane, DT6 4LJ, North : 1 m. *℘* (01308) 456137, *innsacre.farmhouse@btinternet.com*, Fax (01308) 421187, ☞, ⅏, – ⅍ ℗, ⓪ 𝑽𝑰𝑺𝑨
closed mid September- end October, 1 week Christmas and New Year – **Rest** *(by arrangement)* 21.50 – **4 rm** ☑ ✭95.00 – ✭✭105.00.
  ♦ 17C farmhouse in acres of lawns and orchards. Simple comfortable lounge centred on old fireplace. Sizeable rooms in bold colours. Intimate dining room using carefully sourced ingredients.

BRIGGSWATH *N. Yorks.* **502** S 20 *– see Whitby.*

BRIGHOUSE *W. Yorks.* **502** O 22 *– pop. 32 360.*
  ◪ *Crow Nest Park, Coach Rd, Hove Edge* *℘* (01484) 401121.
  London 213 – Bradford 12 – Burnley 28 – Leeds 15 – Manchester 35 – Sheffield 39.

🏨 **Waterfront Lodge**, Huddersfield Rd, HD6 1JZ, *℘* (01484) 715566, *info@waterfrontlodge.co.uk*, Fax (01484) 715588 – |🛗|, ⅍ rm, ▤ rest, &, – 🕭 90. ⓪ ⒶⒺ ⓪ 𝑽𝑰𝑺𝑨. ⅍
closed 25 December and 1 January – **Prego** : **Rest** - Italian - *(closed Saturday lunch)* a la carte 12.70/29.95 – ☑ 6.95 – **58 rm** ✭44.00/49.95 – ✭✭49.95 90.00.
  ♦ A privately owned converted flour mill on the canal in the centre of town. Lodge-style accommodation with uniform décor of colourful fabrics and good bedroom facilities. Ask for a window table to enjoy restaurant's canal views.

✕✕ **Brook's**, 6 Bradford Rd, HD6 1RW, *℘* (01484) 715284, *info@brooks-restaurant.co.uk*, Fax (01484) 712641 – ⅍ ⇄ 20. ⓪ ⒶⒺ 𝑽𝑰𝑺𝑨
closed 2 weeks January, 1 week July and Sunday – **Rest** *(dinner only and lunch in December)/dinner 26.00.*
  ♦ Eclectic art collection fills the walls of this informal restaurant and wine bar with its vaguely Edwardian upstairs lounge. Robust, tasty cooking with 'Spam' on the menu!

BRIGHSTONE *Isle of Wight* **504** P 32 *– see Wight (Isle of).*

BRIGHTON AND HOVE *Brighton and Hove* **504** T 31 *Great Britain G. – pop. 206 628.*
  See : *Town★★ - Royal Pavilion★★★ AC CZ – Seafront★★ – The Lanes★ BCZ – St Bartholomew's★ AC CX B.*
  Env. : *Devil's Dyke (⩽★) NW : 5 m. by Dyke Rd (B 2121) BY.*
  ◪ *East Brighton, Roedean Rd* *℘* (01273) 604838 CV – ◪ *The Dyke, Devil's Dyke, Dyke Rd* *℘* (01273) 857296, BV – ◪ *Hollingbury Park, Ditchling Rd* *℘* (01273) 552010, CV – ◪ *Waterhall, Waterhall Rd* *℘* (01273) 508658, AV.
  ✈ *Shoreham Airport :* *℘* (01273) 296900, W : 8 m. by A 27 AV.
  🚩 *10 Bartholomew Sq* *℘* (0906) 711 2255.
  London 53 – Portsmouth 48 – Southampton 61.

Plans on following pages

🏰 **Grand**, Kings Rd, BN1 2FW, *℘* (01273) 224300, *general@grandbrighton.co.uk*, Fax (01273) 720613, ⩽, ⅊, 🏠, ◩ – |🛗| ⅍ ℂ &, ⇦ – 🕭 800. ⓪ ⒶⒺ ⓪ 𝑽𝑰𝑺𝑨 BZ V
Kings : **Rest** a la carte 35.00/50.00 s. ☑ – **196 rm** ☑ ✭120.00/275.00 – ✭✭120.00/275.00, 4 suites.
  ♦ Imposing, white Victorian edifice with a prime place in the sun. Ornate marble, striking staircase, elegant rooms, indulgent cream teas in a quintessentially English lounge. Discreet, traditional grandeur distinguishes restaurant.

BRIGHTON AND HOVE

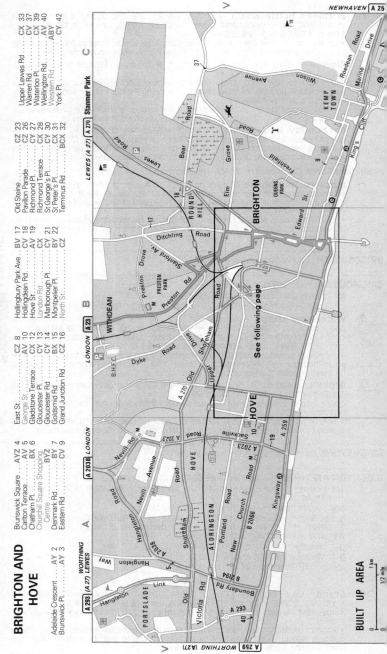

BUILT UP AREA

CENTRE

0   300 m
0   300 yards

157

Hilton Brighton Metropole, Kings Rd, BN1 2FU, ℘ (01273) 775432, *reserva tions.brightonmet@hilton.com*, Fax (01273) 207764, ≤, ⍥, ℔, ⇌, ◻ – ▯ ⤆, ▤ rest, ♿ – ▨ 1300. ⬛⬤ ⒶⒺ ⓪ 𝘝𝘐𝘚𝘈. ⌘
BZ s
Rest *(closed Saturday lunch)* (buffet lunch) 22.95 – ⌸ 15.50 – **327 rm** ⚦220.00 – ⚦⚦220.00, 7 suites.
♦ Impressive late 19C hotel, thoroughly updated: vast conference centres; leisure and beauty suites in the west wing. Spacious, well-kept, modern rooms, some with sea views. Strong traditionality underpins restaurant.

Hotel du Vin, Ship St, BN1 1AD, ℘ (01273) 718588, *reception@brighton.hotelduvin.com*, Fax (01273) 718599 – ⤆ ▤ ⚓ ⌂ – ▨ 30. ⬛⬤ ⒶⒺ 𝘝𝘐𝘚𝘈
CZ a
Bistro : **Rest** *(booking essential)* a la carte 28.00/30.70 ⚥ ⍖ – ⌸ 13.50 – **37 rm** ⚦140.00/180.00 – ⚦⚦140.00/280.00.
♦ 19C part Gothic building. Style is the keyword here: lounge bar full of wine books; mezzanine cigar gallery has billiard table. Striking, minimalist rooms, some with terraces. Bistro with bohemian slant: cellar stocks predictably huge wine selection.

drakes, 43-44 Marine Parade, BN2 1PE, ℘ (01273) 696934, *info@drakesofbrighton.com*, Fax (01273) 684805, ≤ – ⤆ ⌂ ⬛⬤ ⒶⒺ 𝘝𝘐𝘚𝘈. ⌘
CZ u
Rest – (see **The Gingerman** below) – ⌸ 12.50 – **20 rm** ⚦95.00/120.00 – ⚦⚦195.00/250.00.
♦ Refurbished seaside hotel, now with Asian ambience, including Thai artwork. Informal lounge/reception. Stylish rooms with plasma TVs: choose between sea or city views.

Seattle, Brighton Marina, BN2 5WA, ℘ (01273) 679799, *seattle@aliashotels.com*, Fax (01273) 679899, ≤, ⊞ – ▯, ⤆ rest, ▤ rest, ⌂ ♿ 🄿 – ▨ 120. ⬛⬤ ⒶⒺ ⓪ 𝘝𝘐𝘚𝘈 CV c
Café Paradiso : **Rest** a la carte 20.00/27.50 ⚥ – ⌸ 10.00 – **71 rm** ⚦145.00 – ⚦⚦145.00.
♦ Striking marina setting: exploits its position with delightful "Saloon" lounge and decked terrace. Cocktail bar with Beatles portraits. Light, airy rooms in modish palette. Informal restaurant with totally relaxed feel; absorbing marina views.

Blanch House, 17 Atlingworth St, BN2 1PL, ℘ (01273) 603504, *info@blanchhouse.co.uk*, Fax (01273) 689813 – ⤆ rest, ⌂ ⬛⬤ ⒶⒺ 𝘝𝘐𝘚𝘈
CZ o
closed 25-26 December, minimum stay 2 nights at weekends – **Rest** *(closed Sunday dinner and Monday)* 16.00/30.00 ⚥ – **12 rm** ⌸ ⚦80.00/100.00 – ⚦⚦160.00/230.00.
♦ For something different, this is the place to be. Individually themed bedrooms, all with CDs and videos. Red roses are pinned up in one room; another is full of snow shakers. Stark, minimalist restaurant beyond famed cocktail bar.

Nineteen without rest., 19 Broad St, BN2 1TJ, ℘ (01273) 675529, *info@hotelnineteen.co.uk*, Fax (01273) 675531 – ⌂ ⬛⬤ 𝘝𝘐𝘚𝘈
CZ z
minimum 2 night stay at weekends. – **8 rm** ⚦70.00/90.00 – ⚦⚦130.00/180.00.
♦ Sleek white bedrooms, some have beds with glass base of panels illuminated by blue lighting. Other attractive features include complimentary Champagne with Sunday breakfast.

Adelaide without rest., 51 Regency Sq, BN1 2FF, ℘ (01273) 205286, *info@adelaidehotel.co.uk*, Fax (01273) 220904 – ⬛⬤ 𝘝𝘐𝘚𝘈. ⌘
BZ z
closed 25 December and 5-15 January – **12 rm** ⌸ ⚦39.00/65.00 – ⚦⚦75.00/95.00.
♦ Listed Regency town house run by friendly owners. Pretty, period-inspired rooms in floral patterns, some with coronet draped bed heads, and a spacious bow fronted lounge.

Brighton Pavilions without rest., 7 Charlotte St, BN2 1AG, ℘ (01273) 621750, *brightonpavilions@tiscali.co.uk*, Fax (01273) 622477 – ⤆. ⬛⬤ ⒶⒺ 𝘝𝘐𝘚𝘈
CV e
10 rm ⌸ ⚦40.00/65.00 – ⚦⚦144.00/160.00.
♦ Terraced house yards from seafront with something a little different - bedrooms all have individual themes: for example, Titanic Room has clock set at time it hit iceberg!

Brighton House without rest., 52 Regency Sq, BN1 2FF, ℘ (01273) 323282, *info@brighton-house.co.uk*, Fax (01273) 773307 – ⤆ ⌂. ⬛⬤ ⓪ 𝘝𝘐𝘚𝘈. ⌘
BZ c
14 rm ⌸ ⚦40.00/85.00 – ⚦⚦80.00/125.00.
♦ Beautiful Regency house on four floors in charming square. Clean, classic décor throughout. Rooms benefit from period detail such as high ceilings and plenty of space.

Esteban without rest., 35 Upper Rock Gdns, BN2 1QF, ℘ (01273) 681161, *reservations@estebanhotel.co.uk*, Fax (01273) 676945 – ⤆ ⌂. ⌘
CZ s
– **12 rm** ⌸ ⚦30.00/65.00 – ⚦⚦65.00/80.00.
♦ To the east of the centre, a smartly kept, personally run, 19C hotel. Compact, affordable, co-ordinated rooms with modern bathrooms.

ENGLAND

XX **One Paston Place**, 1 Paston Pl, Kemp Town, BN2 1HA, ✆ (01273) 606933, *info@one pastonplace.co.uk, Fax (01273) 675686* – ✦✦ ■. 🆖 🅰🅴 *VISA*   CV a
closed Sunday-Monday – Rest 19.00/29.00 and a la carte 36.50/46.00.
  ◆ Elegant framed mirrors run the length of this stylish, personally run restaurant, a busy local favourite. Appealing menu; assured, balanced and carefully sourced.

XX **The Gingerman at drakes**, 44 Marine Parade, BN2 1PE, ✆ (01273) 696934, *info@gingermanrestaurants.com, Fax (01273) 684805* – ■ ✦ 10. 🆖 🅰🅴 *VISA*   CZ u
Rest 18.00/35.00 ☻.
  ◆ Set in hotel basement, this cool, contemporary eatery conveys a soft, moody atmosphere. The menus present a good balanced choice of modern British dishes with Gallic twists.

XX **The Gingerman**, 21A Norfolk Sq, BN1 2PD, ✆ (01273) 326688, *info@gingermanrestaurants.com, Fax (01273) 326688* – ✦✦ ■. 🆖 🅰🅴 *VISA*   BZ i
closed 1 week Christmas-New Year and Monday – Rest (booking essential) 27.00.
  ◆ Tucked away off the promenade; French and Mediterranean flavours to the fore in a confident, affordable, modern repertoire: genuine neighbourhood feel.

X **Sevendials**, 1 Buckingham Pl, BN1 3TD, ✆ (01273) 885555, *sam@sevendialsrestaurant.co.uk, Fax (01273) 888911*, 🍴 – ✦ 20. 🆖 🅰🅴 ⓞ *VISA*   BX a
closed 25-29 December – Rest 15.00/20.00 (lunch) and a la carte 20.00/40.00 ☻.
  ◆ Former bank on street corner: the vault now acts as function room. Light, airy feel with high ceiling. Modern menus with local ingredients admirably to fore. Good value lunch.

X **Terre à Terre**, 71 East St, BN1 1HQ, ✆ (01273) 729051, *mail@terreaterre.co.uk, Fax (01273) 327561*, 🍴 – ■. 🆖 🅰🅴 ⓞ *VISA*   CZ e
closed 24-26 December, 1 January, Monday and lunch Tuesday – Rest - Vegetarian - a la carte 24.85/29.55 ☻.
  ◆ Hearty helpings of bold, original vegetarian cuisine lyrically evoked on an eclectic menu. Despite its popularity, still friendly, hip and suitably down-to-earth.

X **Havana**, 32 Duke St, BN1 1AG, ✆ (01273) 773388, *Fax (01273) 748923* – 🆖 🅰🅴 *VISA* CZ c
Rest 20.00/32.95 and a la carte 26.60/50.80.
  ◆ 1790s theatre, now a busy, spacious, two-tiered restaurant, its pediments and balustrades combined with mock-colonial styling. International dishes and exotic combinations.

X **The Real Eating Company**, 86-87 Western Rd, BN3 1JB, ✆ (01273) 221444, *Fax (01273) 221442* – ✦✦ 🆖 🅰🅴 *VISA*   AY x
closed Christmas, 1 January and Sunday (except at Bank Holidays)-Tuesday – Rest (booking essential at dinner) a la carte 15.00/24.00 ☻.
  ◆ Unique food store, bursting with speciality foods and 'food to go'. Ground floor dining area exudes buzzy ambience: superb in-house cooking using produce sold in the shop.

X **Due South**, 139 King's Rd Arches, BN1 2FN, ✆ (01273) 821218, *info@duesouth.co.uk,* 🍴 – ✦✦ 🆖 🅰🅴 *VISA*   BZ x
closed 25 December - 3 January – Rest a la carte 17.95/32.95 ☻.
  ◆ Beside the beach, with lovely arch interior: best tables upstairs facing half-moon window overlooking sea. Organic prominence in modern menus using distinctly local produce.

at Hove.

🏠 **Claremont House** without rest., Second Ave, BN3 2LL, ✆ (01273) 735161, *info@claremonthousehotel.co.uk, Fax (01273) 735161*, 🌱 – ✦✦. 🆖 🅰🅴 *VISA*. ✂   AY c
11 rm ☞ ✸60.00/80.00 – ✸✸180.00.
  ◆ Personally run Victorian town house with a neat garden; its tall windows and high ceilings lend a sense of space to the spotlessly kept, traditionally decorated bedrooms. Straightforward home cooking.

BRIMFIELD *Herefordshire* 503 504 L 27 *– see Ludlow.*

BRIMSCOMBE *Glos.* 503 504 N 28 *– see Stroud.*

Do not confuse X with ✿!
X defines comfort, while stars are awarded for the best cuisine,
across all categories of comfort.

ENGLAND

Bristol, the Clifton Suspension Bridge

BRISTOL

503 504 M 29 *Great Britain G. – pop. 420 556.*

London 121 – Birmingham 91.

TOURIST INFORMATION

🄱 *The Annexe, Wildscreen Walk, Harbourside* ℘ *(0906) 711 2191; bristol@tourism.bristol.gov.uk*

PRACTICAL INFORMATION

🏌 *Mangotsfield, Carsons Rd* ℘ *(0117) 956 5501,* BV.
🏌 *Beggar Bush Lane, Failand, Clifton* ℘ *(01275) 393117,* AX.
🏌 *Knowle, Fairway, West Town Lane, Brislington* ℘ *(0117) 977 0660,* BX.
🏌 *Long Ashton, Clarken Coombe* ℘ *(01275) 392229,* AX.
🏌 *Stockwood Vale, Stockwood Lane, Keynsham* ℘ *(0117) 986 6505,* BX.
Severn Bridge (toll).
✈ *Bristol Airport :* ℘ *(0870) 1212747, SW : 7 m. by A 38* AX.

SIGHTS

See : City★★ – St Mary Redcliffe★★ DZ – At-Bristol★★ CZ – Brandon Hill★★ AX – Georgian House★★ AX K – Harbourside Industrial Museum★★ CZ M3 – SS Great Britain and Maritime Heritage Centre★★ AC AX S2 – The Old City★ CYZ : Theatre Royal★★ CZ T – Merchant Seamen's Almshouses★ CZ Q – St Stephen's City★ CY S1 – St John the Baptist★ CY – College Green★ CYZ (Bristol Cathedral★, Lord Mayor's Chapel★) – City Museum and Art Gallery★ AX M1.

Env. : Clifton★★ AX (Suspension Bridge★★ (toll), RC Cathedral of St Peter and St Paul★★ F1, Bristol Zoological Gardens★★ AC, Village★) – Blaise Hamlet★★ – Blaise Castle House Museum★, NW : 5 m. by A 4018 and B 4057 AV.

Exc. : Bath★★★, SE : 13 m. by A 4 BX – Chew Magna★ (Stanton Drew Stone Circles★ AC) S : 8 m. by A 37 – BX – and B 3130 – Clevedon★ (Clevedon Court★ AC, ⩽★) W : 11½ m. by A 370, B 3128 – AX – and B 3130.

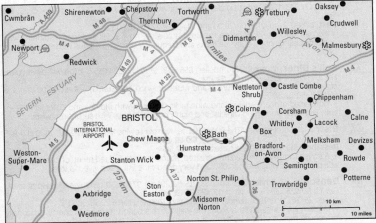

Bristol Marriott Royal, College Green, BS1 5TA, ℰ (0117) 9255100, Fax (0117) 251515, ℚ, ℔, ⇌, 🖂, – 🖽 ✦ 🐾 & ⟲ – 🛦 250. ◍◍ 🆑 ⑩ 𝘃𝘪𝘴𝘢. ℅ CZ a
Terrace : Rest 18.95 (lunch) and a la carte 37.00/38.00 ♀ – ⇌ 16.95 – **230 rm**
★149.00/165.00 – ★★149.00/165.00, 12 suites.
♦ Striking Victorian building next to the cathedral and facing College Green. Bedrooms, classic and individual, combine period styling and an array of modern facilities. Classic style at Terrace: wide variety of dishes to suit all tastes.

Bristol Marriott City Centre, 2 Lower Castle St, Old Market, BS1 3AD, ℰ (0117) 929 4281, events.bristolcity@marriotthotels.co.uk, Fax (0117) 927 6377, ≤, ℚ, ℔, ⇌, 🖂, – 🖽
✦ ✆ & 🅿 – 🛦 600. ◍◍ 🆑 ⑩ 𝘃𝘪𝘴𝘢. ℅ DY s
Mediterrano : Rest (bar lunch) a la carte 21.15/36.40 s. ♀ – ⇌ 14.95 – **301 rm**
★135.00/155.00 – ★★135.00/190.00.
♦ Stalwart, purpose-built block with smart, well-proportioned rooms, aimed at the business market, and providing many mod cons. Spacious modern lounges and coffee shop. Light, modern Mediterranean cooking.

Hotel du Vin, The Sugar House, Narrow Lewins Mead, BS1 2NU, ℰ (0117) 925 5577, info@bristol.hotelduvin.com, Fax (0117) 925 1199 – 🖽 ✦, ☰ rm, ✆ ⟲ 🅿 – 🛦 65. ◍◍ 🆑
⑩ 𝘃𝘪𝘴𝘢 CY e
Rest – (see **Bistro** below) – ⇌ 12.95 – **40 rm** ★140.00 – ★★360.00.
♦ A massive chimney towers over the 18C sugar refinery; stylish loft rooms in minimalist tones: dark leather and wood, low-slung beds, Egyptian linen and subtle wine curios.

The Brigstow, 5-7 Welsh Back, BS1 4SP, ℰ (0117) 929 1030, brigstow@fullers.co.uk, Fax (0117) 929 2030, ✦, ☰ rm, 🖽 & – 🛦 60. ◍◍ 🆑 ⑩ 𝘃𝘪𝘴𝘢. ℅ CY n
Ellipse : Rest (closed Christmas to New Year) a la carte 17.00/34.00 ♀ – ⇌ 13.00 – **115 rm**
★100.00/145.00 – ★★100.00/145.00, 1 suite.
♦ Smart city centre hotel with charming riverside position. Stylish public areas typified by lounges and mezzanine. 21C rooms, full of curves, bright colours and plasma TVs. Modern brasserie and bar overlooking river.

City Inn, Temple Way, BS1 6BF, ℰ (0117) 925 1001, bristol.reservations@cityinn.com, Fax (0117) 910 2727, ℔ – 🖽 ✦ ☰ & 🅿 – 🛦 45. ◍◍ 🆑 ⑩ 𝘃𝘪𝘴𝘢. ℅ DZ e
closed 26-28 December – **City Café :** Rest 14.95/16.50 (lunch) and a la carte 19.70/33.45 ♀
– ⇌ 12.50 – **167 rm** ★149.00 – ★★149.00.
♦ An affordable, central hotel. Airy, well-insulated rooms in intelligent contemporary designs and usefully supplied with mod cons. Sharp brasserie; terrace overlooks Temple Gardens.

Novotel, Victoria St, BS1 6HY, ℰ (0117) 976 9988, h5622@accor.com, Fax (0117) 925 5040, ℔ – 🖽 ✦ ☰ ✆ & ⟲ – 🛦 150. ◍◍ 🆑 ⑩ 𝘃𝘪𝘴𝘢 DZ n
Rest a la carte 17.20/28.40 – ⇌ 12.00 – **130 rm** ★104.00 – ★★134.00, 1 suite.
♦ Purpose-built hotel in heart of business district, close to Temple Meads station. Ample conference facilities. Bedrooms are spacious and up-to-date. Open-plan lounge bar and restaurant catering for many tastes.

XX **Bordeaux Quay (The Restaurant)**, First Floor, V-Shed, Canons Way, BS1 5UH, ℰ (0117) 943 1200, info@bordeaux-quay.co.uk, Fax (0117) 906 5567 – 🖽 ✦ ⟲ 25. ◍◍
𝘃𝘪𝘴𝘢 CZ e
Rest (closed Sunday) 25.00/28.00 and a la carte 22.00/40.00 ♀.
♦ Former dockside warehouse for Bordeaux wine, now a deli and vast restaurant with concrete ceiling, good quayside views and frequently changing menus with strong ethical base.

XX **Bell's Diner**, 1 York Rd, Montpelier, BS6 5QB, ℰ (0117) 924 0357, info@bellsdiner.co.uk, Fax (0117) 924 4280 – ✦. ◍◍ 🆑 𝘃𝘪𝘴𝘢 AX s
closed 24-30 December, Saturday and Monday lunch and Sunday – Rest 45.00 and a la carte 25.50/32.50 ♀.
♦ Converted grocery; shelves and wine racks cluttered with old tins and Kilner jars. Pleasantly laid-back. Very good wine list and highly original menus with surprising twists.

XX **Bistro** (at Hotel du Vin), The Sugar House, Narrow Lewins Mead, BS1 2NU, ℰ (0117) 925 5577, Fax (0117) 925 1199 – ✦ ⟲ 12. ◍◍ 🆑 ⑩ 𝘃𝘪𝘴𝘢 CY e
Rest (booking essential) a la carte approx 27.50 ✦.
♦ A stylish candlelit milieu artfully created; flavourful, well-judged menu of classics, alongside plethora of wine memorabilia and very good wine list: a bon viveur's treat.

XX **Deason's**, 43 Whiteladies Rd, BS8 2LS, ℰ (0117) 973 6230, enquiries@deasons.co.uk, Fax (0117) 923 7394 – ✦ ☰ ⟲ 12. ◍◍ 🆑 ⑩ 𝘃𝘪𝘴𝘢 AX e
closed 25-26 December, Sunday and Monday – Rest a la carte 22.50/30.75 ♀.
♦ Modern art hangs stylishly from the walls of this period terraced property. Seasonally influenced menus offer a bold mix of modern, classic and traditional dishes.

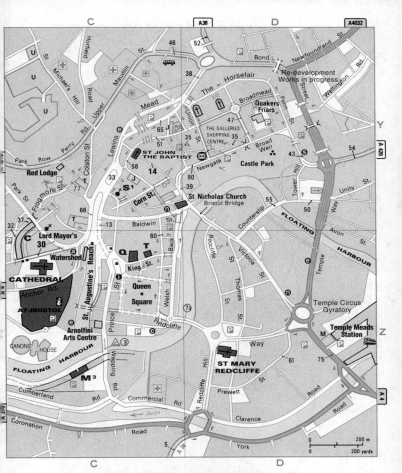

INDEX OF STREET NAMES IN BRISTOL

163

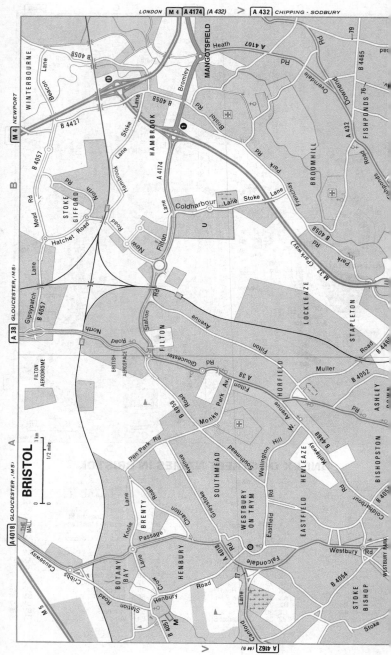

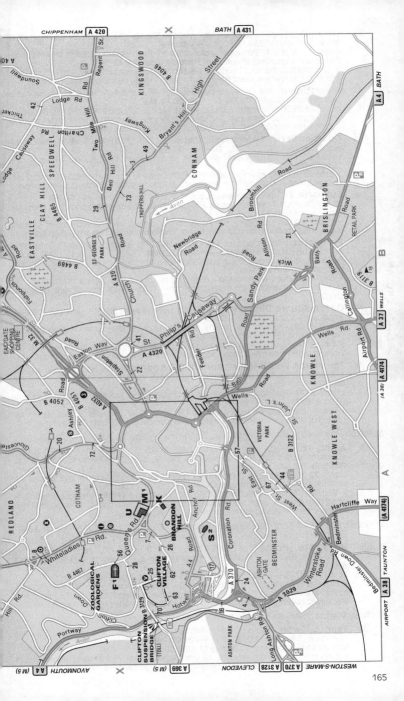

XX **Casamia**, 38 High St, Westbury-on-Trym, BS9 3DZ, Northwest : 2 m. by A 4018 *ℰ* (0117) 959 2884, Fax (0117) 959 3658, 🍴 – ✖. **🏧🅾 VISA**   AV e
closed 25-26 and 31 December and 1 January – **Rest** - Italian - *(closed Saturday lunch, Sunday and Monday)* 13.95 (lunch) and a la carte 20.40/38.35.
• Seek and find this neighbourhood restaurant hidden in a pleasant village suburb. Sip an aperitif in cosy bar and select from a wide-ranging menu with strong Italian roots.

X **Riverstation**, The Grove, Harbourside, BS1 4RB, *ℰ* (0117) 914 4434, *relax@riversta tion.co.uk, Fax (0117) 934 9990*, 🍴 – ✖. **🏧🅾 ① VISA**   CZ c
closed 24-26 December and 1 January – **Rest** 14.50 (lunch) and a la carte 27.50/34.00 ☘.
• Striking first floor restaurant, and ground floor café, with great views of harbour activity. Open plan with lots of glass. Full-flavoured mains; good value lunches, too.

X **Quartier Vert**, 85 Whiteladies Rd, Clifton, BS8 2NT, *ℰ* (0117) 973 4482, *info@quartier vert.co.uk, Fax (0117) 904 8617*, 🍴 – ✖. **🏧 VISA**   AX i
closed Christmas and Sunday dinner in winter – **Rest** 19.50 (lunch) and a la carte 25.50/38.00 ☘.
• Modern, bustling eatery at forefront of city's organic movement. Med influenced daily changing menus, tapas bar, coffees on terrace. Good organic ingredients always to fore.

X **Culinaria**, 1 Chandos Rd, Redland, BS6 6PG, *ℰ* (0117) 973 7999 – ✖. **🏧🅾 VISA**   AX x
closed Christmas, New Year, Sunday and Tuesday – **Rest** (dinner only and lunch Friday and Saturday) a la carte 22.20/28.75.
• Combined deli and eatery; the personally run diner is informal with lots of light and space. Sound cooking behind a collection of Mediterranean, English and French dishes.

X **Fishworks**, 128 Whiteladies Rd, Clifton, BS8 2RS, *ℰ* (0117) 974 4433, *bristol@fish works.co.uk, Fax (0117) 974 4933* – ✖. ▤. **🏧🅾 ① VISA**   AX o
closed 25-26 December, 1 January, Sunday and Monday – **Rest** - Seafood - (booking essential) a la carte 24.35/44.00 ☘.
• Bustling seafood restaurant in a fishmongers: choose your ingredients from the fish counter. Menus created from whatever arrives fresh on the day. Vibrant blackboard choice.

🍴 **Queen Square Dining Room & Bar**, Queen Square, BS1 4JL, *ℰ* (0117) 929 0700, *info@queen-square.com*, 🍴 – **🏧🅾 ⒶⒺ VISA**   CZ i
closed 25-30 December, 1-6 January, Saturday lunch, Sunday dinner, Monday and Bank Holidays – **Rest** 21.00 (lunch) and dinner a la carte 20.50/30.00.
• Close to delightful Queen Square, a smart pub with leather sofas in bar and linen-clad tables in dining room. Well-priced, accomplished range of dishes to please all tastes.

🍴 **The Albion Public House and Dining Rooms**, Boyces Ave, Clifton Village, BS8 4AA, *ℰ* (0117) 973 3522, *info@thealbionclifton.co.uk, Fax (0117) 973 9768*, 🍴 – ✖ ◇ 12. **🏧🅾 VISA**   AX v
closed 25-26 December, 1 January and Monday – **Rest** (booking essential) a la carte 30.00/40.00 ☘.
• Grade II listed 17C inn hidden away in Clifton. Loads of character: settles, beams and roaring fire lend a suitably rustic feel for the enjoyment of tasty West Country fare.

at Patchway *(South Gloucestershire)* North : 6½ m. on A 38 – BV – ✉ Bristol.

🏨 **Aztec**, Aztec West Business Park, BS32 4TS, North : 1 m. by A 38 *ℰ* (01454) 201090, *aztec@shirehotels.com, Fax (01454) 201593*, 🍴, 🛁, ⒮, 🔲 – 🕸 ✖ ▤ & 🅿 – 🔬 200. **🏧 ⒶⒺ ① VISA**. 🍽
closed 22-28 December – **Quarterjacks :** Rest *(closed lunch Saturday and Sunday)* a la carte 27.00/35.40 ☘ – **125 rm** ⚏ ✱174.00 – ✱✱229.00/269.00, 3 suites.
• Reclaimed beams and Cotswold stone add warmth to a smartly run group hotel. State of art gym facilities. Large, well-appointed rooms; some, with patios, overlook small lake. Restaurant has sheltered terrace for alfresco dinners.

at Hunstrete *(Bath & North East Somerset)* Southeast : 10 m. by A 4 and A 37 – BX – off A 368 – ✉ Bristol.

🏨 **Hunstrete House** 🌿, BS39 4NS, *ℰ* (01761) 490490, *reception@hunstrete house.co.uk, Fax (01761) 490732*, <, 🔲 heated, 🌱, ⚘, ※ – ✖ 🅿 – 🔬 40. **🏧 ⒶⒺ ① VISA**
Rest 25.00/47.75 s. ☘ – **22 rm** ⚏ ✱135.00 – ✱✱215.00/170.00, 3 suites.
• Fine late 17C manor and deer park near the Mendips. Drawing room, library and bed-rooms with antiques, period style furniture and the idiosyncratic charm of a family seat. Restaurant, overlooking courtyard, uses produce from its walled kitchen garden.

at Chew Magna South : 8¼ m. by A 37 – BX – on B 3130 – ✉ Bristol.

🍴 **Bear & Swan**, South Parade, BS40 8SL, *ℰ* (01275) 331100, *enquiries@bearand swan.co.uk, Fax (01275) 332187*, 🍴 – ✖ 🅿. **🏧 VISA**
Rest *(closed Sunday dinner)* a la carte 17.00/30.00 ☘.
• Food is very much the emphasis of this 19C stone pub. At a pleasant dining area of reclaimed floorboards and antique tables and chairs, you can enjoy modern eclectic dishes.

at Stanton Wick (Bath & North East Somerset) South : 9 m. by A 37 – **BX** – and A 368 on Stanton Wick rd – ⊠ Bristol.

🏠 **Carpenters Arms** with rm, BS39 4BX, 𝒫 (01761) 490202, carpenters@bucca neer.co.uk, Fax (01761) 490763, 😤 – ⭐ **P**. **MO** **AE** **①** **VISA**. 𝒮
closed dinner 25 and 26 December – **Rest** a la carte 19.00/27.00 🏵 – **12 rm** 🛏 **†**67.00 – **††**95.00.
♦ A row of converted miners' cottages in a rural village: cosy, firelit real ale bar with exposed stone walls and good-sized, pine furnished rooms in subtle floral patterns. Popular beamed "parlour" for meals.

BRITWELL SALOME Oxon.
London 75 – Oxford 21 – Reading 19.

🏠 **The Goose,** OX49 5LG, 𝒫 (01491) 612304, thegooseatbritwellsalome@fsmail.net, Fax (01491) 613945, 😤 – ⭐ **P**. **MO** **AE** **VISA**
closed 1 January, 26 December and Sunday dinner – **Rest** 19.00 and a la carte 22.50/49.50 🏵.
♦ Smart yet snug hostelry with a cosy bar and intimate sage green dining room: modern dishes are cooked with an assured, knowledgable touch and well-sourced local ingredients.

BROAD CAMPDEN Glos. – see Chipping Campden.

BROADHEMBURY Devon 503 K 31 – ⊠ Honiton.
London 191 – Exeter 17 – Honiton 5 – Taunton 23.

🏠 **The Drewe Arms,** EX14 3NF, 𝒫 (01404) 841267, Fax (01404) 841267, 😤, 🌳 – ⭐ **P**. **MO** **AE** **VISA**
closed 25 December – **Rest** - Seafood - (closed Sunday dinner) (booking essential) a la carte 12.00/40.00 🏵 📖.
♦ Intimate and instantly likeable medieval thatched pub with flagged floor and log fire. Robust chalkboard menu, featuring prime local seafood; simple and flavourful. Local ale.

BROAD OAK E. Sussex.
London 62.5 – Hastings 8 – Rye 7.

🏠 **Fairacres** without rest., Udimore Rd, TN31 6DG, on B 2089 𝒫 (01424) 883236, john-shelagh@fairacres.fsworld.co.uk, Fax (01424) 883236, 🌳 – ⭐ **P**
closed Christmas and New Year – **3 rm** 🛏 **†**60.00 – **††**90.00.
♦ Listed 17C cottage in picture-postcard pink. Big breakfasts under low beams. Individual rooms: one overlooks superb magnolia tree in garden. All have many thoughtful extras.

BROADSTAIRS Kent 504 Y 29.
London 77.5 – Canterbury 18.5 – Ramsgate 2.

🏠 **The Victoria** without rest., 23 Victoria Parade, CT10 1QL, 𝒫 (01843) 871010, mul lin@thevictoriabroadstairs.co.uk, Fax (01843) 860888, ≤, 🌳 – ⭐ 📞 **P**. **MO** **VISA**. 𝒮
6 rm 🛏 **†**35.00/70.00 – **††**129.00.
♦ Large 19C house with views to Viking Bay, harbour and gardens. Proud use of Kentish produce at breakfast. Spotless rooms: The Balcony, in prime position, overlooks the front.

BROADWAY Worcs. 503 504 O 27 Great Britain G. – pop. 2 496.
See : Town★.
Env. : Country Park (Broadway Tower ☀★★★), SE : 2 m. by A 44 – Snowshill Manor★ (Terrace Garden★) AC, S : 2½ m.
🄱 1 Cotswold Court 𝒫 (01386) 852937.
London 93 – Birmingham 36 – Cheltenham 15 – Oxford 38 – Worcester 22.

🏛 **The Lygon Arms,** High St, WR12 7DU, 𝒫 (01386) 852255, info@thelygonarms.co.uk, Fax (01386) 854470, 🐾, ┣♨, ≘s, 🏊, 🌳, 𝒮ℰ – 🔟 rest, **P** – 🔬 80. **MO** **AE** **①** **VISA**
The Great Hall : Rest a la carte 41.00/60.00 s. 🏵 – (see also **Goblets** below) – **66 rm** 🛏 **†**249.00 – **††**249.00, 3 suites.
♦ Superbly enticing, quintessentially English coaching inn with many 16C architectural details in its panelled, beamed interiors and rooms Charles I and Cromwell once stayed in. Refined dining and baronial splendours: heraldic friezes and minstrels' gallery.

ENGLAND

Dormy House, Willersey Hill, WR12 7LF, East : 3 ¼ m. by A 44 and Broadway Golf Club rd *&* (01386) 852711, *reservations@dormyhouse.co.uk*, Fax (01386) 858636, ♖, ♖, ♖, ♖ – ♖ ♖ ♖ – ♖ 170. ♖ ♖ ♖ ♖
closed 24-27 December – **The Dining Room :** Rest (dinner only and Sunday lunch)/dinner 35.00 and a la carte 35.95/47.95 ♖ – **Barn Owl :** Rest a la carte approx 18.90 ♖ – **42 rm** ♖ ♖120.00 – ♖ ♖220.00, 3 suites.
• Creeper-clad 17C farmhouse and outbuildings. Sizeable rooms and comfortable lounge: open fires, wing armchairs and a warm country house palette. Dine in cosy, rustic rooms or conservatory. Barn Owl is an A-framed hall with flagged floors.

The Broadway, The Green, WR12 7AA, *&* (01386) 852401, *info@broadwayhotel.info*, Fax (01386) 853879, ♖, ♖ – ♖ ♖ ♖ ♖ ♖
The Courtyard : Rest 14.95/25.00 ♖ – **19 rm** ♖ ♖135.00/155.00 – ♖ ♖135.00/175.00.
• A 16C inn on the green, built as an abbot's retreat; sympathetically updated rooms in a pretty mix of rural patterns with an atmospheric, horse racing themed, timbered bar. Half-timbered restaurant with leaded windows.

The Olive Branch without rest., 78 High St, WR12 7AJ, *&* (01386) 853440, *david pam@theolivebranch-broadway.fsnet.co.uk*, Fax (01386) 859070 – ♖ ♖ ♖ ♖
8 rm ♖ ♖45.00/60.00 – ♖ ♖78.00/90.00.
• A 1590s former staging post on the high street run by a friendly husband and wife team. Flagged floors, sandstone walls and compact bedrooms with a few charming touches.

Windrush House without rest., Station Rd, WR12 7DE, *&* (01386) 853577, *evan@broadway-windrush.co.uk*, ♖ – ♖ ♖ ♖ ♖ ♖
5 rm ♖ ♖65.00/70.00 – ♖ ♖75.00/80.00.
• Personally run guesthouse and landscaped garden with an updated Edwardian elegance and subtle period style. Tastefully individual rooms; pleasant views to front and rear.

Whiteacres without rest., Station Rd, WR12 7DE, *&* (01386) 852320, *whiteacres@btin ternet.com*, ♖ – ♖ ♖ ♖
5 rm ♖ ♖45.00/50.00 – ♖ ♖65.00/70.00.
• Spacious accommodation - homely, pleasantly updated and modestly priced - in a personally owned Victorian house, a short walk from the village centre.

Russell's with rm, 20 High St, WR12 7DT, *&* (01386) 853555, *info@russellsofbroad way.com*, ♖ – ♖ ♖ ♖ ♖ ♖
Rest (closed Sunday dinner) 19.95 (lunch) and a la carte 26.25/40.65 ♖ – **7 rm** ♖ ♖70.00/115.00 – ♖ ♖115.00/350.00.
• Behind the splendid Cotswold stone façade lies a stylish modern restaurant with terrace front and rear. Seasonally influenced, regularly changing menus. Smart, comfy bedrooms.

Goblets, High St, WR12 7DU, *&* (01386) 854418, Fax (01386) 858611 – ♖ ♖ ♖ ♖ ♖ ♖
Rest (booking essential) a la carte 44.00/60.00 ♖.
• Characterfully firelit in rustic dark oak. Modern dining room at front more atmospheric than one to rear. Menus of light, tasty, seasonal dishes offered.

at Buckland (Glos.) Southwest : 2¼ m. by B 4632 – ✉ Broadway.

Buckland Manor ♖, WR12 7LY, *&* (01386) 852626, *info@bucklandmanor.co.uk*, Fax (01386) 853557, ♖, ♖, ♖ – ♖ ♖ ♖ ♖ ♖
Rest (booking essential for non-residents) 25.50 (lunch) and dinner a la carte 39.70/52.50 ♖ ♖ – **14 rm** ♖ ♖225.00 – ♖ ♖420.00.
• Secluded part 13C country house with beautiful gardens. Individually furnished bedrooms boast high degree of luxury. Fine service throughout as old-world serenity prevails. Restaurant boasts elegant crystal, fine china and smooth service.

BROCKDISH Norfolk 504 X 26 – see Diss.

BROCKENHURST Hants. 503 504 P 31 Great Britain G. – pop. 2 865.
Env. : New Forest★★ (Rhinefield Ornamental Drive★★, Bolderwood Ornamental Drive★★).
♖ Brockenhurst Manor, Sway Rd *&* (01590) 623332.
London 99 – Bournemouth 17 – Southampton 14 – Winchester 27.

Rhinefield House ♖, Rhinefield Rd, SO42 7QB, Northwest : 3 m. *&* (01590) 622922, *rhinefieldhouse@handpicked.co.uk*, Fax (01590) 622800, ♖, ♖, ♖, ♖, ♖ – ♖ ♖ ♖ – ♖ 120. ♖ ♖ ♖ ♖ ♖. ♖
Armada : Rest 19.95/34.95 ♖ – **34 rm** ♖ ♖230.00 – ♖ ♖230.00/330.00.
• A long ornamental pond reflects this imposing 19C New Forest mansion, surveying parterres and a yew maze. Panelled drawing room. Handsomely appointed bedrooms in 21C wing. Dining room in gleaming oak with forest views.

Careys Manor, Lyndhurst Rd, SO42 7RH, on A 337 🖉 (08707) 512305, *stay@careysma nor.com*, Fax (08707) 512306, 🍴, ₤, ⇆, 🌂, 🍴 – ⇆ ⊟ 🅿 – 🔥 150. 🆗 🆎 ① 𝘝𝘐𝘚𝘈, 🍴
Rest (dinner only) 29.50 – *Blaireau's* (🖉 (01590) 623032) : Rest - French - a la carte
20.40/29.95 – *The Zen Garden* : Rest - Thai - *(closed dinner Sunday and Monday)* a la carte
20.40/29.95 – **78 rm** ⇆ ✦139.00 – ✦✦178.00, 1 suite.
◆ Smartly run, substantial 19C house with modern additions, near the main road. Some
bedrooms have balcony overlooking gardens; the manor house rooms are the best. Fine
dining in smart restaurant. Blaireau's is informal bistro with hints of French styling.

New Park Manor 🦢, Lyndhurst Rd, SO42 7QH, North : 1 ½ m. on A 337 🖉 (01590)
623467, *info@newparkmanorhotel.co.uk*, Fax (01590) 622268, ⇆, 🍷, ₤, ⇆, 🏊 heated,
🍴, 🍴, 🐎, 🍴 – ⇆ 🅿 – 🔥 120. 🆗 🆎 𝘝𝘐𝘚𝘈
Stag : Rest 32.50/38.00 – **24 rm** ⇆ ✦117.50/127.50 – ✦✦205.00/245.00.
◆ Extended, elegantly proportioned hunting lodge with equestrian centre for guided forest treks. Rooms, some in former servants' quarters, have four posters and parkland views.
Candlelit fine dining.

Cloud, Meerut Rd, SO42 7TD, 🖉 (01590) 622165, *enquiries@cloudhotel.co.uk*,
Fax (01590) 622818, 🌲 – ⇆ 🅿. 🆗 𝘝𝘐𝘚𝘈
closed 27 December-1 January – Rest 14.75/30.00 – **17 rm** ⇆ ✦70.00/160.00 –
✦✦220.00/240.00.
◆ Well-kept, comfortable and personally owned, with something of a country cottage
character. Simple, pine furnished accommodation; views over the wooded countryside.
Intimate little restaurant with pleasant covered terrace.

The Cottage without rest., Sway Rd, SO42 7SH, 🖉 (01590) 622296, *chris@cottageho tel.org*, Fax (01590) 623014, – ⇆ 🅿. 𝘝𝘐𝘚𝘈 ①
closed Christmas and restricted opening in winter – **9 rm** ⇆ ✦50.00/100.00 –
✦✦50.00/140.00.
◆ 300-year old former forester's cottage in the heart of the village: family run and faultlessly kept. Low oak beamed ceiling, cosy snug bar and large, neatly appointed rooms.

Le Poussin at Whitley Ridge (Aitken) 🦢 with rm, Beaulieu Rd, SO42 7QL, East : 1
m. on B 3055 🖉 (01590) 622354, *sales@lepoussin.co.uk*, Fax (01590) 622856, ⇆, 🌲, 🍴, ₤, 🍴 – ⇆ 🅿. 🆎 𝘝𝘐𝘚𝘈
Rest 25.00/45.00 and a la carte 44.50/59.50 – ⇆ 5.00 – **22 rm** ✦100.00/150.00 –
✦✦130.00/220.00, 1 suite.
Spec. Lobster poached in butter, pearl barley and saffron risotto. Veal cutlet with wild
mushrooms. Caramelised apple tart, rosemary custard, truffle ice cream.
◆ Secluded Georgian house, surrounded by acres of parkland. Two period style dining
rooms serving accomplished, classically based menus. Individual rooms, some with steam
cabin.

Simply Poussin, The Courtyard, rear of 49-51 Brookley Rd, SO42 7FZ, 🖉 (01590)
623063, *simply@lepoussin.co.uk*, Fax (01590) 623144 – ⇆. 🆗 🆎 𝘝𝘐𝘚𝘈
closed Sunday-Monday – Rest (booking essential) 15.50 (lunch) and a la carte 19.25/29.70 ⇆.
◆ Intimate little mews restaurant, tucked away off the village centre, with well-spaced,
subtly spotlit tables. Capable, flavourful modern British menu; unobtrusive service.

Thatched Cottage with rm, 16 Brookley Rd, SO42 7RR, 🖉 (01590) 623090,
sales@thatchedcottage.co.uk, Fax (01590) 623479 – ⇆ rest, 🅿. 🆗 🆎 𝘝𝘐𝘚𝘈
closed 3 January-10 February – Rest *(closed Sunday dinner, Tuesday lunch and Monday)*
(booking essential) (light lunch)/dinner 45.00 – **5 rm** ⇆ ✦70.00/90.00 – ✦✦130.00/160.00.
◆ 17C farmhouse and one-off rooms with a touch of eccentricity to their blend of curios,
pictures and bright flowers. Open kitchen; elaborate, locally sourced menu.

at Sway Southwest : 3 m. by B 3055 – ✉ Lymington.

The Nurse's Cottage with rm, Station Rd, SO41 6BA, 🖉 (01590) 683402, *nurses.cot tage@lineone.net*, Fax (01590) 683402, 🍴 – ⇆ 🅿. 🆗 🆎 𝘝𝘐𝘚𝘈
closed 3 weeks November – Rest (booking essential) (dinner only) 23.00 ⇆ – **5 rm** (dinner
included) ⇆ ✦80.00/90.00 – ✦✦160.00.
◆ Personally run, welcoming conservatory restaurant with an intimate charm. Traditional
menus make good use of Hampshire's larder. Pristine, comfy rooms with pretty details.

BROCKTON *Shrops. – see Much Wenlock.*

BROCKWORTH *Glos. 504 N 28 – see Cheltenham.*

BROME *Suffolk 504 X 26 – see Diss (Norfolk).*

BROMFIELD *Shrops. 503 L 26 – see Ludlow.*

BROMSGROVE Worcs. 503 504 N 26 – pop. 29 237.

🏛 Bromsgrove Museum, 26 Birmingham Rd ℘ (01527) 831809.
London 117 – Birmingham 14 – Bristol 71 – Worcester 13.

⌂ **Bromsgrove Country House** without rest., 249 Worcester Rd, Stoke Heath, B61
7JA, Southwest : 2 m. on B 4091 ℘ (01527) 835522, Fax (01527) 871257, 🚗 – ⇔ P. 🐵
VISA. ⅙
closed 2 weeks Christmas-New Year – ⊊ 4.90 – **8 rm** ✦55.00 – ✦✦66.00.
♦ Personally run, redbrick Victorian house, on a main road, converted but with original
tiling and other period features intact. Sizeable rooms are homely and well kept.

at Stoke Prior Southwest : 2¼ m. by A 38 on B 4091 – ⊠ Bromsgrove.

XXX **Epicurean**, 68 Hanbury Rd, B60 4DN, ℘ (01527) 871929, epic.bromsgrove@virgin.net,
Fax (01527) 575647 – ⇔ P. 🐵 🔤 VISA
closed Sunday-Monday – **Rest** 17.95/43.00 a la carte 35.00/43.00.
♦ In Epic's former lounge, where stylish and comfortable surroundings are accentuated
by silken drapes. Experienced chef creates skilfully accomplished modern European
dishes.

X **Epic**, 68 Hanbury Rd, B60 4DN, ℘ (01527) 871929, epic.bromsgrove@virgin.net,
🍴 Fax (01527) 575647, 🌣 , 🚗 – ⇔ P. ⇆ 12. 🐵 🔤 ① VISA. ⅙
closed Sunday-Monday – **Rest** 12.95 (lunch) and a la carte 19.00/29.00 �.
♦ Heavily extended former roadside pub: tiled floor and some beams remain. Vast bar;
brick and wood cleverly worked into open-plan dining area. Large menus of modern classics.

> If breakfast is included the ⊊ symbol appears after the number of rooms.

ENGLAND

BROOK Hants. 503 504 P 31 – ⊠ Lyndhurst.
London 92 – Bournemouth 24 – Southampton 14.

🏨 **Bell Inn**, SO43 7HE, ℘ (023) 8081 2214, bell@bramshaw.co.uk, Fax (023) 8081 3958, ⛳,
🚗 – ⇔ P. – ♨ 40. 🐵 🔤 ① VISA
Rest (bar lunch Monday-Saturday)/dinner 28.00 and a la carte 20.95/29.95 – **25 rm** ⊊
✦65.00/140.00 – ✦✦140.00/170.00.
♦ Family owned for over 200 years, an extended inn with golf course and clubhouse. Cosy,
clubby bar with an open fire and tasty light menu; neat, modern, pine fitted rooms.

BROUGHTON Cambs. – see Huntingdon.

BROUGHTON Lancs. 502 L 22 – see Preston.

BROXTON Ches. 502 503 L 24.
London 197 – Birmingham 68 – Chester 12 – Manchester 44 – Stoke-on-Trent 29.

🏨 **De Vere Carden Park**, CH3 9DQ, West : 1 ½ m. on A 534 ℘ (01829) 731000, reserva
tions.carden@devere-hotels.co.uk, Fax (01829) 731032, 🌣 , 🎬, ⛳, ⇆, 🖳, ⛳, 🎣, 🚗, ♨,
🎾 – ⛐ ⇔, ≡ rest, 🕭 ﻦ, ✦✦ P – ♨ 400. 🐵 🔤 ① VISA. ⅙
Garden Restaurant : **Rest** (dinner only and Sunday lunch)/dinner 27.50 and a la carte
27.95/31.95 **s.** � – **The Brasserie** : **Rest** 16.95/27.50 **189 rm** ⊊ ✦80.00/210.00 –
✦✦90.00/220.00, 7 suites.
♦ Very well equipped and up-to-date leisure hotel with extensive grounds in a rural location. Golf breaks a speciality. Main house or courtyard rooms are equally comfortable.
Formal Garden Restaurant with Carden estate wines. Smart Brasserie.

BRUNDALL Norfolk 504 Y 26.
London 118.5 – Great Yarmouth 15 – Norwich 8.

XX **The Lavender House**, 39 The Street, NR13 5AA, ℘ (01603) 712215 – ⇔ P. 🐵
VISA
closed 24-31 December, Sunday and Monday – **Rest** (booking essential) (dinner only)
36.00 **s.** �.
♦ Locally renowned restaurant with pleasant lounge for pre-prandials. Intimate, beamed
dining room. Proudly local menus with the suppliers listed; ingredients are in season.

170

BRUNTINGTHORPE *Leics. Great Britain G.*

> EXC. : *Leicester - Museum and Art Gallery★, Guildhall★ and St Mary de Castro Church★, N :*
> *11 m. by minor rd and A 5199.*
> *London 96 – Leicester 10 – Market Harborough 15.*

🏠 **Joiners Arms,** Church Walk, LE17 5QH, ✆ (0116) 247 8258, *stephenjoiner@btcon*
nect.com, Fax (0116) 247 8258 – **P.** **CO** **VISA**
closed 25 December and Bank Holidays – **Rest** *(closed Sunday dinner and Monday)* (booking
essential) 12.95 (lunch) and a la carte 22.00/29.00 ♀.
   ◆ 18C pub with beams in small rural village; cosy drinking area. The compact menus and
blackboard specials provide well executed, good value dishes with a country flavour.

BRUSHFORD *Somerset* 503 J 30 *– see Dulverton.*

BRUTON *Somerset* 503 504 M 30 *The West Country G. – pop. 2 982.*

> EXC. : *Stourhead★★★ AC, W : 8 m. by B 3081.*
> *London 118 – Bristol 27 – Bournemouth 44 – Salisbury 35 – Taunton 36.*

XX **Bruton House,** 2-4 High St, BA10 0AA, ✆ (01749) 813395, *info@brutonhouse.co.uk –*
✆⊷ **CO** **AE** **VISA**
closed 2 weeks January and 2 weeks August – **Rest** 35.00 and lunch a la carte approx
19.85 **s.**
   ◆ 15C/18C townhouse; beams and fireplace of yore meet interesting contrast in modern
art work on walls. Quality locally sourced produce in imaginative, well-executed dishes.

XX **Truffles,** 95 High St, BA10 0AR, ✆ (01749) 812255, *deborah@trufflesbruton.co.uk –* ✆⊷
▤ **CO** **①** **VISA**
closed Sunday dinner - Wednesday lunch – **Rest** 16.95/28.95 ♀.
   ◆ Cottagey façade; intimate and cosy two-level interior. Personally run, the husband and
wife team take pride in a small, well prepared menu rich in market fresh local produce.

> We try to be as accurate as possible when giving room rates.
> But prices are susceptible to change,
> so please check rates when booking.

BRYHER *Cornwall* 503 ㉚ *– see Scilly (Isles of).*

BUCKDEN *Cambs.* 504 T 27 *– pop. 2 385 – ⊠ Huntingdon.*

> *London 65 – Bedford 15 – Cambridge 20 – Northampton 31.*

🏨 **The George,** High St, PE19 5XA, ✆ (01480) 812300, *manager@thegeorgebuckden.com,*
Fax (01480) 813920, 🌳 – 🚷 ✆⊷ **P.** **CO** **AE** **①** **VISA** 🛏
Rest *– (see* ***Brasserie*** *below) –* **12 rm** ✸80.00/130.00 – ✸✸100.00/130.00.
   ◆ 19C former coaching inn in village centre, now refurbished with individuality and high
quality soft furnishings. Smart, stylish rooms, all named after famous 'Georges'.

🏠 **Lion,** High St, PE19 5XA, ✆ (01480) 810313, *reception.lionhotel@virgin.net,*
Fax (01480) 811070 – ✆⊷ rest, ✆ **P.** **CO** **AE** **①** **VISA** 🛏
Rest 17.50 (lunch) and a la carte 21.30/29.45 – **15 rm** ☐ ✸45.00/73.50 – ✸✸60.00/90.00.
   ◆ 15C Grade II listed with attendant period details: original fireplace with carved Tudor
Rose, five spoke ceiling with Lamb and Papal pennant. Has resident ghost. Cosy rooms.
Silver service in large panelled restaurant.

X **Brasserie** (at The George H.), High St, PE19 5XA, ✆ (01480) 812300, *manager@thegeor*
gebuckden.com, Fax (01480) 813920, 🌳 – ✆⊷ **P.** **CO** **AE** **VISA** 🛏
Rest a la carte 22.50/31.50 ♀.
   ◆ Modish bar leads into brasserie where modern cooking holds plenty of appeal. Outside
is a lovely courtyard terrace with olive trees, whitewashed walls and waxed wood tables.

BUCKHORN WESTON *Dorset.*

🏠 **The Stapleton Arms** with rm, Church Hill, SP8 5HS, ✆ (01963) 370396, *relax@thesta*
pletonarms.com, Fax (01963) 370396, 🌳 , 🌿 – ✆⊷ **P.** **CO** **AE** **①** **VISA**
Rest a la carte 20.00/24.20 ♀ – **4 rm** ☐ ✸80.00/96.00 – ✸✸100.00/120.00.
   ◆ Village centre Georgian pub with a striking, refurbished façade. Eat wide-ranging pub
grub in the stylish flag-floored bar or elegant dining room. Spacious, modern bedrooms.

BUCKHURST HILL *Essex – pop. 11 243.*

London 12 – Brighton 82 – Cambridge 48 – Ipswich 73 – Oxford 68.

Plan : see Greater London (North-East) 4

Express by Holiday Inn, High Rd, IG9 5HT, on A 121 📞 (020) 8504 4450, Fax (020) 8498 0011 – ✦⟵ rm, ⬚ **P** – ⬚ 30. **MO AE ① VISA**
Rest (grill rest.) – **49 rm** ✦69.95 – ✦✦69.95.
HT e
* With Epping Forest on the doorstep, and golfing facilities 3km away, this conveniently positioned lodge offers modern, comfortable accommodation. Toby carvery for meals.

BUCKINGHAM *Bucks. 503 504 Q 27 Great Britain G.*

Env. : *Stowe Gardens★★, NW : 3 m. by minor rd.*
Exc. : *Claydon House★ AC, S : 8 m. by A 413.*
⯅ *Silverstone, Silverstone Rd, Stowe 📞 (01280) 850005 –* ⯅ *Tingewick Rd 📞 (01280) 813282.*

London 64 – Birmingham 61 – Northampton 20 – Oxford 25.

Villiers, 3 Castle St, MK18 1BS, 📞 (01280) 822444, www.oxfordshire-hotels.co.uk, Fax (01280) 822113 – ⧄ ♿ **P** – ⬚ 200. **MO AE ① VISA**. ✦
Villiers : Rest a la carte 19.40/33.15 ♀ – **42 rm** ⊒ ✦135.00/165.00 – ✦✦150.00/175.00, 4 suites.
* Former coaching inn built around a cobbled courtyard; a town centre landmark ever since its Cromwellian heyday, with a characterful beamed bar and modern lounge and bedrooms. Intimate restaurant to rear of hotel.

BUCKLAND *Glos. 503 504 O 27 – see Broadway (Worcs.).*

BUCKLAND *Oxon. 503 504 P 28 –* ✉ *Faringdon.*

London 78 – Oxford 16 – Swindon 15.

The Lamb Inn, Lamb Lane, SN7 8QN, 📞 (01367) 870484, enquiries@thelambatbuckland.co.uk, Fax (01367) 870675, ⌖ – ✦⟵ rest, **P. MO VISA**. ✦
closed 25 December-8 January – **Rest** *(closed Sunday dinner and Monday)* 15.00 and a la carte 20.00/35.00 ♀.
* Sheep motifs appear in paintings, curios and carpet of this 18C real ale pub, well established and family owned. Tasty traditional menu: seafood fricassee, summer pudding.

BUCKLERS HARD *Hants. 503 504 P 31 – see Beaulieu.*

BUCKMINSTER *Leics. 502 504 R 25.*

London 114 – Grantham 11 – Melton Mowbray 10.

Tollemache Arms with rm, 48 Main St, NG33 5SA, 📞 (01476) 860007, enquiries@the tollemachearms.com, ⌖, ⌖ – ✦⟵ rm, **P** ⬚ 16. **MO AE VISA**
Rest *(closed Sunday dinner and Monday)* 14.00 and a la carte 21.50/35.00 ♀ – **5 rm** ⊒ ✦45.00 – ✦✦60.00.
* Late 19C former coaching inn with 21C interior: wood floor, stainless steel bar, huge leather sofas. Modern British à la carte served in evenings. Simple, good value rooms.

BUDE *Cornwall 503 G 31 The West Country G. – pop. 8 071 (inc. Stratton).*

See : *The Breakwater★★ – Compass Point (≤★).*
Env. : *Poughill★ (church★★), N : 2½ m. – E : Tamar River★★ – Kilkhampton (Church★), NE : 5 ½ m. by A 39 – Stratton (Church★), E : 1½ m. – Launcells (Church★), E : 3 m. by A 3072 – Marhamchurch (St Morwenne's Church★), SE : 2½ m. by A 39 – Poundstock★ (≤★★, church★, guildhouse★), S : 4½ m. by A 39.*
Exc. : *Morwenstow (cliffs★★, church★), N : 8½ m. by A 39 and minor roads – Jacobstow (Church★), S : 7 m. by A 39.*
⯅ *Burn View 📞 (01288) 352006.*
🛈 *Bude Visitor Centre, The Crescent 📞 (01288) 354240.*
London 252 – Exeter 51 – Plymouth 50 – Truro 53.

Falcon, Breakwater Rd, EX23 8SD, 📞 (01288) 352005, reception@falconhotel.com, Fax (01288) 356359, ≤, ⌖ – ✦⟵ ✆ **P** – ⬚ 180. **MO AE ① VISA**. ✦
closed 25 December – **Rest** (bar lunch Monday-Saturday)/dinner a la carte 16.00/27.00 s. ♀ – **29 rm** ⊒ ✦55.00/70.00 – ✦✦110.00/140.00.
* An imposing, personally run hotel with the proudly traditional character of a bygone age. Contemporary and classic blend in bedrooms. Separate private garden. Formal dining.

🏨 **Hartland,** Hartland Terrace, EX23 8JY, ℘ (01288) 355661, *hartlandhotel@aol.com*, Fax (01288) 355664, ←, ⌐ heated – ⬚ ⇔ **P**.
closed January-February – **Rest** *(bar lunch)/dinner 24.00/26.00* – **28 rm** ⌐ ✦57.00/70.00 – ✦✦96.00/104.00.
♦ Sizeable seaside hotel, family owned and run for over 30 years. Individually appointed rooms mix modern or period furniture with African, Egyptian and nautical themes. Dine by the dance floor on red leather banquettes.

🏨 **Bude Haven,** Flexbury Ave, EX23 8NS, ℘ (01288) 352305, *enquiries@budehavenhotel.com*, Fax (01288) 352662 – ⇔ **P**. **OO** **VISA**
Rest *(closed Sunday and Wednesday)* *(booking essential for non-residents)* *(dinner only)* a la carte 17.00/21.95 – **10 rm** ⌐ ✦32.50/48.50 – ✦✦65.00/77.00.
♦ Large, privately owned Edwardian house on the quiet outskirts of the town. Comfortable lounge, traditionally styled rooms with hot-tubs; affordable and well kept. Dining room with jazz piano on a Saturday night.

BUDLEIGH SALTERTON *Devon* 503 K 32 *The West Country G.* – pop. 4 801.
Env. : East Budleigh (Church★), N : 2½ m. by A 376 – Bicton★ (Gardens★) AC, N : 3 m. by A 376.
🛆 East Devon, North View Rd ℘ (01395) 443370.
🛈 Fore St ℘ (01395) 445275.
London 182 – Exeter 16 – Plymouth 55.

⌂ **The Long Range,** 5 Vales Rd, EX9 6HS, by Raleigh Rd ℘ (01395) 443321, *info@thelongrangehotel.co.uk*, Fax (01395) 442132, 🌫 – ⇔ **P**. **OO** **VISA**. ✕
Rest *(closed Sunday, Monday and Thursday)* *(dinner only)* 23.75 – **7 rm** ⌐ ✦42.50/68.50 – ✦✦89.50/94.50.
♦ Homely and unassuming guesthouse, personally run in quiet residential street. Sun lounge with bright aspect, overlooking broad lawn and neat borders. Simple, unfussy rooms. Tasty, locally sourced dishes in a comfy dining room.

XX **Gardiners,** 53 High St, EX9 6LE, ℘ (01395) 445829 – ⇔ ▤. **OO** **AE** **VISA**
closed 1-14 January, Sunday dinner and Monday – **Rest** *(dinner only and Sunday lunch)* a la carte 21.95/27.20 ⌐.
♦ Modern frosted glass façade reflected in vivid artwork on interior walls. Clean, unadulterated modern British cooking supported by prominent local produce and keen pricing.

BUDOCK WATER *Cornwall* – see Falmouth.

BUNBURY *Ches.* 502 503 504 M 24 – see Tarporley.

BUNGAY *Suffolk* 504 Y 26 *Great Britain G.* – pop. 4 895.
Exc. : Norwich★★ - Cathedral★★, Castle Museum★, Market Place★, NW : 15 m. by B 1332 and A 146.
London 108 – Beccles 6 – Ipswich 38.

at Earsham (Norfolk) *Southwest : 3 m. by A 144 and A 143* – ✉ Bungay.

⌂ **Earsham Park Farm** ⏳ *without rest.*, Old Railway Rd, NR35 2AQ, on A 143 ℘ (01986) 892180, *bobbie@earsham-parkfarm.co.uk*, Fax (01986) 894796, ←, 🌫, 🐎 – ⇔ **TV** **P**. **OO** **VISA**
3 rm ⌐ ✦43.00/46.00 – ✦✦74.00/88.00.
♦ Isolated red-brick Victorian farmhouse, surrounded by working farm. Admire the view while enjoying local produce for breakfast. Well appointed rooms with rural names.

BURCOMBE *Wilts.* – see Salisbury.

BURFORD *Oxon.* 503 504 P 28.
🛆 ℘ (01993) 822583.
🛈 The Brewery, Sheep St ℘ (01993) 823558.
London 76 – Birmingham 55 – Gloucester 32 – Oxford 20.

🏨 **Bay Tree,** 12-14 Sheep St, OX18 4LW, ℘ (01993) 822791, *info@baytreehotel.info*, Fax (01993) 823008, 🌫 – ⇔ rest, **P**. – �︎ 30. **OO** **AE** **OO** **VISA**
Rest *18.95/29.95 and a la carte 21.85/44.85* ⌐ – **21 rm** ⌐ ✦119.00/165.00 – ✦✦215.00, 3 suites.
♦ Handsome, ivy-clad 16C hotel. Warm, antique furnished library lounge. Hunting trophies over a broad stone fireplace. Thoughtfully appointed rooms in rich chintz and tartans. Flagged country dining room overlooks walled rose and herb garden.

The Lamb Inn, Sheep St, OX18 4LR, ℘ (01993) 823155, *info@lambinn-burford.co.uk,* Fax (01993) 822228, 🌣, ☞ – 🛬 rest. 🏧 VISA
Rest (bar lunch Monday-Saturday)/dinner 32.50 and a la carte �« – **15 rm** ☝ ✦115.00 – ✦✦235.00.
* Relaxing, part 14C inn in weathered local stone. Window seats, broad rugs and age-old wooden armchairs in a charming lounge. Trim cottage rooms: floral fabrics and antiques. Classically formal restaurant reflects inn's age.

Burford House without rest., 99 High St, OX18 4QA, ℘ (01993) 823151, *stay@burford house.co.uk,* Fax (01993) 823240, ☞ – 🛬 🏧 AE VISA. 🛦
8 rm ☝ ✦85.00/95.00 – ✦✦105.00/160.00.
* 17C town house. Paintings, antiques and rich fabrics in welcoming lounges and elegantly composed rooms, some with Victorian baths. Lavish afternoon teas with home-made cakes.

BURGHCLERE *Hants.* 503 504 Q 29.
London 67 – Newbury 4 – Reading 30.

Carnarvon Arms with rm, Winchester Rd, Whitway, RG20 9LE, South : 1½ m. by Highclare Rd on Whitway Rd ℘ (01635) 278222, *info@carnarvonarms.com,* Fax (01635) 278222 – 🛬 ⅙ 🅿 ⇄ 24. 🏧 VISA. 🛦
Rest 14.95 (lunch) and a la carte 18.00/28.00 �« – **12 rm** ☝ ✦79.95 – ✦✦89.95.
* Smartly refurbished 19C pub with contemporary interior: comfy sofas, plenty of newspapers and mags. Interesting modern dishes or timeless Brit classics. Pleasant bedrooms.

BURLEYDAM *Ches. – see Whitchurch (Shrops.).*

BURLTON *Shrops. – ✉ Shrewsbury.*
London 235 – Shrewsbury 10 – Wrexham 20.

The Burlton Inn with rm, SY4 5TB, ℘ (01939) 270284, *bean@burltoninn.co.uk,* Fax (01939) 270204, 🌣 – 🅿, 🏧 VISA
closed 25-26 December, 1 January and lunch Bank Holiday Monday – **Rest** (restricted lunch Monday) a la carte 16.70/29.85 �« – **6 rm** ☝ ✦50.00 – ✦✦90.00.
* Bustling, family run pub with a characterful, wood furnished interior. Extensive menus of traditional fare. Bedrooms in contemporary style. Four Poster bed available.

BURNHAM MARKET *Norfolk* 504 W 25 *Great Britain G..*
Env. : *Holkham Hall✶✶ AC, E : 3 m. by B 1155.*
🇮🇦 *Lambourne, Dropmore Rd ℘ (01628) 666755.*
London 128 – Cambridge 71 – Norwich 36.

The Hoste Arms, The Green, PE31 8HD, ℘ (01328) 738777, *reception@hos tearms.co.uk,* Fax (01328) 730103, ☞ – 🛬 🅿 ⇄ 26 – 🅐 25. 🏧 VISA
Rest – (see *The Restaurant* below) – **36 rm** ☝ ✦88.00/160.00 – ✦✦117.00/260.00, 1 suite.
* Renowned and restored 17C inn in this pretty village. Intriguing wing in Zulu style. Individually designed rooms provide a high level of comfort. Informal ambience.

The Restaurant (at The Hoste Arms), The Green, PE31 8HD, ℘ (01328) 738777, Fax (01328) 730103, 🌣 – 🛬 🍽 🅿 ⇄ 26. 🏧 VISA
Rest (booking essential) a la carte 23.00/42.00 �« 🛦.
* North Sea fish features in an Anglo-European and oriental fusion menu. Delightful terrace with Moroccan theme for summer dining. Invariably friendly staff.

Fishes, Market Pl, PE31 8HE, ℘ (01328) 738588, *ob1@sizzel.net,* Fax (01328) 730534 – 🛬 🍽 🏧 VISA
closed 1 week Christmas, Sunday dinner, Monday except Bank Holidays and high season. –
Rest - Seafood - 19.50/37.00 �«.
* Attractive restaurant with simple bistro feel and local artwork in centre of popular North Norfolk town. Locally caught seafood dishes are well prepared and tasty.

at Burnham Thorpe *Southeast : 1¼ m. by B 1355 – ✉ Burnham Market.*

The Lord Nelson, Walsingham Rd, PE31 8HL, ℘ (01328) 738241, *enquiries@nelsonslo cal.co.uk,* Fax (01328) 738241, 🌣, ☞ – 🛬 🅿, 🏧 VISA
closed Monday October-June except school and Bank Holidays – **Rest** (closed Sunday dinner) a la carte 15.00/28.30 �«.
* Cosy, characterful pub in small village - Nelson was indeed born here: much memorabilia to remind you. Flagged floors, beams and a tiny bar. Good value, tasty dishes.

BURNHAM THORPE *Norfolk* 504 W 25 – *see Burnham Market.*

BURNLEY *Lancs.* 502 N 22 – *pop. 73 021.*

> 🏌 , 🏌 *Towneley, Towneley Park, Todmorden Rd* ℘ *(01282) 451636 –* 🏌 *Glen View* ℘ *(01282) 451281.*
>
> 🚍 *Bus Station, Croft St* ℘ *(01282) 664421.*
>
> *London 236 – Bradford 32 – Leeds 37 – Liverpool 55 – Manchester 25 – Middlesbrough 104 – Preston 22 – Sheffield 68.*

🏨 **Oaks,** Colne Rd, Reedley, BB10 2LF, Northeast : 2 ½ m. on A 56 ℘ (01282) 414141, *oaks@shirehotels.com*, Fax (01282) 433401, ⅃₆, ≘ς, ⬜, 🌳 – ⁕⧟ **P** – 🚗 120. **① Æ ⓪ VISA**. ⁒
Quills : **Rest** *(closed Saturday, Sunday and Bank Holidays)* (dinner only) a la carte 25.45/35.25 ⌾ – *Archives Brasserie :* **Rest** *(closed Saturday-Sunday and Bank Holidays)* (lunch only) (buffet) a la carte 11.95 approx ⌾ – **51 rm** ⊆ ✚104.00 – ✚✚129.00.
✦ Extended 19C house with accent on business traveller. Clubby lounge with leather sofas and mahogany staircase dappled in colour from superb stained glass window. Comfy rooms. Quills boasts views over neat lawns. Archives Brasserie in brick vaulted cellars.

🏨 **Rosehill House,** Rosehill Ave, Manchester Rd, BB11 2PW, South : 1 ¼ m. by A 56 ℘ (01282) 453931, *rhhotel@provider.co.uk*, Fax (01282) 455628, 🌳 – ⁕⧟ rest, ⚫ **P**. **① Æ ⓪ VISA**. ⁒
closed 26 December and 1 January **Dugdales :** **Rest** a la carte 22.40/30.85 ⌾ – *El Nino's :* **Rest** - Tapas - a la carte 16.45/23.45 – **31 rm** ⊆ ✚50.00/60.00 – ✚✚75.00/100.00, 2 suites.
✦ Turreted 19C house in wooded grounds; residentially set. Airy lounge with long leather Chesterfields. Carefully repaired ornate ceilings a particular feature of various rooms. Imposing, elegantly panelled Dugdales evokes period charm. Tapas at El Nino's.

> Red = Pleasant. Look for the red 🌮 and 🏠 symbols.

BURNSALL *N. Yorks.* 502 O 21 – ✉ *Skipton.*
> *London 223 – Bradford 26 – Leeds 29.*

🏠 **The Red Lion,** BD23 6BU, ℘ (01756) 720204, *redlion@daelnet.co.uk*, Fax (01756) 720292, ≤, ⬛, 🌳 – ⁕⧟ **P** – 🚗 90. **① Æ ⓪ VISA**
Rest – (see *The Restaurant* below) – **14 rm** ⊆ ✚60.00/65.00 – ✚✚120.00/150.00, 3 suites.
✦ Part 16C inn on the River Wharfe, ideal for walks, fishing and shooting. Cosy bedrooms, some in adjacent cottage: all have 19C brass beds or overlook the village green.

🏠 **Devonshire Fell,** BD23 6BT, ℘ (01756) 729000, *manager@devonshirefell.co.uk*, Fax (01756) 729009, ≤, 🌳 – ⁕⧟ **P** – 🚗 70. **① Æ ⓪ VISA**
Rest a la carte 20.05/27.95 ⌾ – **10 rm** ⊆ ✚75.00 – ✚✚155.00/195.00, 2 suites.
✦ Once a club for 19C mill owners; strikingly updated by Lady Hartington with vivid colours and Hockney prints. Wide-ranging modern menu. Stylish rooms with Dales views.

🌮🌮 **The Restaurant** (at The Red Lion H.), BD23 6BU, ℘ (01756) 720204, Fax (01756) 720292, 🌳 – ⁕⧟ **P**. **① Æ ⓪ VISA**
Rest (bar lunch Monday-Saturday) 22.95/32.95 and a la carte 25.00/35.00 ⌾.
✦ Dales meat, game and local cheeses in robust, seasonal menu. Eat in the firelit, oak-panelled bar or the dining room with mullioned windows facing the green. Keen staff.

BURPHAM *W. Sussex* 504 S 30 – *see Arundel.*

BURRINGTON *Devon* 503 I 31.
> *London 260 – Barnstaple 14 – Exeter 28 – Taunton 50.*

🏨 **Northcote Manor** ⌘, EX37 9LZ, Northwest : 2 m. on A 377 ℘ (01769) 560501, *rest@northcotemanor.co.uk*, Fax (01769) 560770, ≤, 🌳, ⬜, 🌮 – ⁕⧟ rest, **P** – 🚗 80. **①** **Æ VISA**
Rest (booking essential) (lunch by arrangement)/dinner 25.00/38.00 and a la carte 14.50/38.00 ⌾ – **10 rm** (dinner included) ⊆ ✚135.00 – ✚✚230.00, 1 suite.
✦ Creeper-clad hall above River Tew dating from 1716. Fine fabrics and antiques in elegant, individually styled rooms; attention to well-judged detail lends air of idyllic calm. Country house restaurant features eye-catching murals.

BURTON-ON-THE-WOLDS *Leics.* 502 503 504 Q 25 – *see Loughborough.*

BURTON-UPON-TRENT Staffs. 502 503 504 O 25 – pop. 43 784.

    🏌 Branston G. & C.C., Burton Rd ℰ (01283) 528320 – 🏌 Craythorne, Craythorne Rd, Stretton ℰ (01283) 564329.

    🛈 Coors Visitor Centre, Horninglow St ℰ (01283) 508111.

    London 128 – Birmingham 29 – Leicester 27 – Nottingham 27 – Stafford 27.

🏨 **Express by Holiday Inn** without rest., 2nd Ave, Centrum 100, DE14 2WF, Southwest : 2 m. by A 5121 ℰ (01283) 504300, info@exhiburton.co.uk, Fax (01283) 504301 – 🔄 🛬 ♿ 🗜 – 🔏 60. ♨ 🟥 ① 𝘝𝘐𝘚𝘈.
82 rm ★78.00 – ★★78.00.
    ◆ On the outskirts of the town near a business park, a short drive from the Bass Brewery Museum. Comfortable, carefully designed bedrooms in a modern hotel.

at Stretton North : 3¼ m. by A 5121 (A 38 Derby) – ✉ Burton-upon-Trent.

🏠 **Dovecliff Hall** 🐾, Dovecliff Rd, DE13 0DJ, ℰ (01283) 531818, enquiries@doveclifffhall hotel.co.uk, Fax (01283) 516546, ≤, ⌲, 🐾, ♫ – 🛬, 🖻 rest, 🗜, 🔏 – 🔏 40. 𝘝𝘐𝘚𝘈. ⌘
Rest (closed Sunday dinner) 16.50/28.50 and a la carte 28.00/41.00 – 15 rm ⌂ ★65.00/90.00 – ★★170.00.
    ◆ Imposing, listed 1790s house with lovely gardens and spacious rooms, nestling in an elevated position above the Trent. Airy bedrooms, most boasting garden vistas. Formal dining rooms in restaurant and delightful orangery.

BURY Gtr Manchester 502 N 23 503 ③ 504 N 23 – pop. 60 718.

    🏌 Greenmount ℰ (01204) 883712.

    🛈 The Met Art Centre, Market St ℰ (0161) 253 5111.

    London 211 – Leeds 45 – Liverpool 35 – Manchester 9.

✗ **The Waggon**, 131 Bury and Rochdale Old Rd, Birtle, BL9 6UE, East : 2 m. on B 6222 ℰ (01706) 622955 – 🛬 🗜 ⇄ 16. ♨ 🟥 𝘝𝘐𝘚𝘈
closed 2 weeks August, 1 week January, Saturday lunch, Monday and Tuesday – Rest a la carte 18.65/25.50 ℤ.
    ◆ Unprepossessing façade hides a pleasantly decorated eatery with good value, no-non-sense cooking featuring a decidedly strong Lancashire base and the famous Bury Black Pudding.

BURY ST EDMUNDS Suffolk 504 W 27 Great Britain G. – pop. 36 218.

    See : Town★ – Abbey and Cathedral★.

    Env. : Ickworth House★ AC, SW : 3 m. by A 143.

    🏌 Suffolk G. & C.C., St John's Hill Plantation, The Street, Fornham All Saints ℰ (01284) 706777.

    🛈 6 Angel Hill ℰ (01284) 764667.

    London 79 – Cambridge 27 – Ipswich 26 – Norwich 41.

🏨 **Angel**, 3 Angel Hill, IP33 1LT, ℰ (01284) 714000, reservations@theangel.co.uk, Fax (01284) 714001 – 🔄 🛬 🖻 rm, ♫ – 🔏 90. ♨ 🟥 ① 𝘝𝘐𝘚𝘈
The Vaults : Rest a la carte 23.85/34.85 ℤ – 74 rm ⌂ ★85.00/127.00 – ★★137.00, 2 suites.
    ◆ 15C inn near the Abbey Gardens with a fine Georgian façade. Rooms offer a bright, modern take on classic style; a few, named after famous visitors, have four poster beds. The Vaults are in atmospheric 12C cellars.

🏨 **Priory**, Tollgate, IP32 6EH, North : 1¾ m. on A 1101 ℰ (01284) 766181, reservations@pri oryhotel.co.uk, Fax (01284) 767604, 🌳, ⌲ – 🛬 ♿ 🗜 – 🔏 40. ♨ 🟥 ① 𝘝𝘐𝘚𝘈
closed 27-29 December – **The Garden :** Rest (closed Saturday lunch) 17.00/22.00 – 39 rm ⌂ ★91.00/123.00 – ★★143.00.
    ◆ 13C former Franciscan Priory with a listed Georgian façade. Traditionally styled in the main house with some usefully appointed modern rooms in the later Garden wings. Conservatory restaurant overlooks neatly manicured garden.

🏠 **Ounce House** without rest., Northgate St, IP33 1HP, ℰ (01284) 761779, enqui ries@ouncehouse.co.uk, Fax (01284) 768315, ⌲ – 🛬 ♫ 🗜. ♨ 🟥 ① 𝘝𝘐𝘚𝘈. ⌘
3 rm ⌂ ★65.00/85.00 – ★★90.00/120.00.
    ◆ 1870s redbrick town house; very well furnished with Victorian elegance. Spacious, in-dividually styled bedrooms; well-chosen antiques contribute to a characterful interior.

✗✗ **Maison Bleue**, 30-31 Churchgate St, IP33 1RG, ℰ (01284) 760623, info@maison bleue.co.uk, Fax (01284) 761611 – 🛬. ♨ 𝘝𝘐𝘚𝘈
closed January, 2 weeks Summer, Sunday and Monday – **Rest** - Seafood - 16.95/24.95 and a la carte 20.40/34.85.
    ◆ 17C house with attractive façade and window boxes. Timbered interior with maritime memorabilia. A number of different rooms to eat in; predominantly seafood menu.

at Ixworth *Northeast : 7 m. by A 143 –* ⊠ *Bury St Edmunds.*

XX **Theobalds,** 68 High St, IP31 2HJ, ℘ (01359) 231707, Fax (01359) 231707 – ⇆, **⬤** **VISA**
closed 10 days Spring – **Rest** *(dinner only and lunch Sunday, Wednesday and Friday)/dinner*
26.00 (midweek) and a la carte at weekends 28.95/34.50.
 ◆ Beamed part 16C cottage with a cosy firelit lounge. Friendly service and well-judged
seasonal menus combine heartwarming favourites and contemporary dishes.

at Rougham Green *East : 4 m. by A 14 –* ⊠ *Bury St Edmunds.*

▦ **Ravenwood Hall,** IP30 9JA, ℘ (01359) 270345, enquiries@ravenwood.co.uk,
Fax (01359) 270788, 佘, ⊤ heated, 舞 – ⇆ P. – 益 150. **⬤** **AE** **⑩** **VISA**
Rest 25.75 and a la carte approx 35.95 ♀ – **14 rm** ⊵ ✦87.50 – ✦✦170.00.
 ◆ Tudor dower house set in seven acres of calm lawns and woods. Welcoming lounge and
individually designed bedrooms, more compact in the mews, are furnished with antiques.
Restaurant with old wooden beams and inglenook fireplace.

at Beyton *East : 6 m. by A 14 –* ⊠ *Bury St Edmunds.*

⌂ **Manorhouse** without rest., The Green, IP30 9AF, ℘ (01359) 270960, manorhouse@bey
ton.com, 舞 – ⇆ P. ⋘
closed Christmas and New Year – 4 rm ⊵ ✦58.00 – ✦✦68.00.
 ◆ Part 15C Suffolk longhouse in idyllic spot overlooking village green. Two rooms are in
converted barn; all have a rustic feel to them. Breakfast of eggs from owner's hens.

at Horringer *Southwest : 3 m. on A 143 –* ⊠ *Bury St Edmunds.*

▦▦ **The Ickworth** ≫, IP29 5QE, ℘ (01284) 735350, info@ickworthhotel.com,
Fax (01284) 736300, ≼, ⅋, ⊤ heated, ▨, 舞, ⅋, ⋘ – |≣| ⋐ ⁂ P – 益 30. **⬤** **AE** **⑩** **VISA**
Fredericks : **Rest** *(dinner only)* a la carte 37.50 ♀ – **28 rm** (dinner included) ⊵ ✦180.00 –
✦✦480.00/585.00, 10 suites.
 ◆ Ickworth House's east wing mixes modern and country house styles. Three airy drawing
rooms; conservatory breakfasts. Comfy rooms with views. A favourite with young families.
Fredericks overlooks gardens.

▯ **The Beehive,** The Street, IP29 5SN, ℘ (01284) 735260, Fax (01284) 735532, 佘 – P. **⬤**
VISA. ⋘
closed 25-26 December – **Rest** *(closed Sunday dinner)* a la carte 18.00/25.00 ♀.
 ◆ Rustic, low-ceilinged, brick-and-flint pub near Ickworth House. Tasty daily specials like
scallops in garlic butter affably served at pine tables or on a sheltered terrace.

BUSHEY *Herts.* **504** S 29.

▯₁₈ Bushey Hall, Bushey Hall Drive ℘ (01923) 222253, BT – ▯₅ Bushey G. & C.C., High St
℘ (020) 8950 2283, BT.
London 18 – Luton 21 – Watford 3.

Plan : see Greater London (North-West) 1

XX **st James,** 30 High St, WD23 3HL, ℘ (020) 8950 2480, Fax (020) 8950 4107 – ⇆ ≣. **⬤** **AE**
VISA
closed 25 December, Sunday and Bank Holidays – **Rest** a la carte 26.15/33.95 ♀.
 ◆ Likeable neighbourhood venue - choose the airy, wood floored front room by the wine
bar. Flavourful chalkboard specials from the modern British repertory, helpful service.

BUTTERMERE *Cumbria* **502** K 20 – ⊠ *Cockermouth.*
London 306 – Carlisle 35 – Kendal 43.

▦ **Bridge,** CA13 9UZ, ℘ (017687) 70252, enquiries@bridge-hotel.com, Fax (017687) 70215,
≼ – ⇆ ⋐ P. **⬤** **VISA**
Rest (booking essential) (bar lunch Monday-Saturday)/dinner 25.00 – **21 rm** ⊵
✦45.00/112.50 – ✦✦90.00/190.00.
 ◆ A family-run Lakeland hotel, first licensed as a coaching inn in 1735. After a day's walking
in the Fells relax in front of the log fire. Some bedrooms have four-posters. Warm yellow
dining room is oldest part of house.

⌂ **Wood House** ≫, CA13 9XA, Northwest : ½ m. on B 5289 ℘ (017687) 70208, wood
house.guest@virgin.net, Fax (017687) 70241, ≼ Crummock Water and Melbreak, ⟋, 舞 –
⇆ P. ⋘
March-October – **Rest** (by arrangement) (communal dining) 29.00 – **3 rm** ⊵ ✦55.00 –
✦✦90.00.
 ◆ This period house boasts a stunning lakeside setting, providing views of Crummock
Water and the mountains. Tranquility is assured. Charming sitting room, simple bedrooms.
Dinner is served around a single antique table.

BUXTON Derbs. 502 503 504 O 24 – pop. 20 836.

⌂ Buxton and High Peak, Townend ℘ (01298) 26263.

🖪 The Crescent ℘ (01298) 25106.

London 172 – Derby 38 – Manchester 25 – Stoke-on-Trent 24.

🏨 **Lee Wood**, The Park, SK17 6TQ, on A 5004 ℘ (01298) 23002, *leewoodhotel@btinter
net.com*, Fax (01298) 23228, 斧, 舜 – 劇, ⇔ rm, 🌜 🅿 – 🔏 100. ◍◍ 🖭 ⑪ 🚾
Garden : Rest 25.00 (lunch) and a la carte 21.50/35.00 ♀ – **40 rm** ⊇ ✸70.00/90.00 –
✸✸100.00/145.00.
◆ An extended country house dating back to Buxton's heyday. Front-facing rooms overlook the gardens; others, in the annex, are quieter - all are sizeable and neatly kept.
Spacious conservatory dining room.

🏠 **Buxton's Victorian** without rest., 3A Broad Walk, SK17 6JE, ℘ (01298) 78759, *buxton
victoria@btconnect.com*, Fax (01298) 74732 – ⇔ 🅿, ◍◍ 🖭 🚾. ⅏
closed Christmas-New Year – **8 rm** ⊇ ✸48.00/76.00 – ✸✸74.00/90.00.
◆ Spacious, charming Victorian house overlooking delightful gardens. Oriental themed
breakfast room with wall-mounted kimono. Comfy sitting room. Immaculately kept bedrooms.

↥ **Grendon** without rest., Bishops Lane, SK17 6UN, ℘ (01298) 78831, *grendonguest
house@hotmail.com*, Fax (01298) 79257, 舜 – ⇔ 🅿, ◍◍ 🚾
closed 3-20 January – **5 rm** ⊇ ✸32.00/65.00 – ✸✸70.00/85.00.
◆ A serene Edwardian house down a country lane which leads to a hill, ideal for ramblers.
Comfortable rooms in pastel colours with guide books and armchairs to read them in.

BYFORD Herefordshire 503 L 27 – see Hereford.

BYLAND ABBEY N. Yorks. 502 Q 21 – see Helmsley.

CADNAM Hants. 503 504 P 31 – pop. 1 875.
London 91 – Salisbury 16 – Southampton 8 – Winchester 19.

↥ **Walnut Cottage** without rest., Old Romsey Rd, SO40 2NP, off A 3090 ℘ (023) 8081
2275, 舜 – ⇔ 🅿, ⅏
closed 25-26 December – **3 rm** ⊇ ✸40.00 – ✸✸55.00.
◆ A pretty white Victorian forester's cottage with views over the garden and good for
forays into the New Forest. Charming, simply furnished bedrooms.

CALLINGTON Cornwall 503 H 32.
London 237 – Exeter 53 – Plymouth 15 – Truro 46.

XX **Langmans**, 3 Church St, PL17 7RE, ℘ (01579) 384933, *dine@langmansrestaurant.co.uk*
– ⇔ ◍◍ 🚾
closed Sunday-Wednesday – Rest (booking essential) (dinner only) (set tasting menu only)
31.95.
◆ Truly individual establishment: seven course tasting menus change monthly, employing
skilful cooking with finesse; ingredients from small local suppliers. Booking essential.

at Rilla Mill *Northwest* : 6½ m. by A 388 off B 3257 – ⊠ Callington.

🖻 **The Manor House Inn**, PL17 7NT, ℘ (01579) 362354, 斧 – ⇔ 🅿, ◍◍ 🚾
closed 25-26 December and 1 January – Rest *(closed Monday)* a la carte 20.00/31.50.
◆ 17C inn that's had a total refurbishment: very pleasant bar, perfectly shelved books,
homely touches. Thoughtfully appointed dining areas with local, seasonal menus.

CALNE Wilts. 503 504 O 29 *The West Country G.* – pop. 13 789.
Env. : Bowood House★ *AC*, (Library ⩽★) SW : 2 m. by A 4 – Avebury★★ (The Stones★,
Church★) E : 6 m. by A 4.
London 91 – Bristol 33 – Southampton 63 – Swindon 17.

↥ **Chilvester Hill House**, SN11 OLP, West : ¾ m. by A 4 on Bremhill rd ℘ (01249) 813981,
gill.dilley@talk21.com, Fax (01249) 814217, 舜 – ⇔ rest, 🅿, ◍◍ 🖭 ⑪ 🚾. ⅏
Rest (by arrangement) (communal dining) 20.00/25.00 – **3 rm** ⊇ ✸60.00/70.00 –
✸✸90.00/100.00.
◆ 19C Bath stone house with lots of William Morris wallpapering, Persian carpeted drawing
room, and spacious bedrooms. Charming mature owners are its very heart and soul.

CAMBER E. Sussex 504 W 31 – see Rye.

178

CAMBERLEY *Surrey* **504** R 29 – *pop. 47 123 (inc. Frimley).*

Ⓖ *Camberley Heath, Golf Drive* ℰ *(01276) 23258.*
London 40 – Reading 13 – Southampton 48.

🏨 **Frimley Hall** ≫, Lime Ave via Conifer Drive, GU15 2BG, East : ¾ m. off Portsmouth Rd (A 325) ℰ (0870) 400 8224, *sales.frimleyhall@macdonald-hotels.co.uk*, Fax (01276) 691253, **Ⅰ₅, ≦s, ◻, 屏 – ⅛ ⇔ ⚓ & P – ☖** 250. **⓪⓪ ⅍ ⑩ 𝘝𝘐𝘚𝘈**
Linden : Rest *(closed Saturday lunch)* 21.00/32.50 and dinner a la carte 27.00/42.00 **s.** Ŷ – ⊠ 15.95 – **98 rm** ⋆125.00/155.00 – ⋆⋆148.00/170.00.
♦ Ivy-clad Victorian manor. A carved wooden staircase leads to the bedrooms; some are traditional with inlaid mahogany furniture, others are bright and modern. 19C restaurant with contemporary furnishings.

CAMBOURNE *Cambs. – see Cambridge.*

CAMBRIDGE *Cambs.* **504** U 27 *Great Britain G. – pop. 117 717.*

See : *Town*★★★ – *St John's College*★★★ *AC* Y – *King's College*★★ *(King's College Chapel*★★★*)* Z *The Backs*★★ YZ – *Fitzwilliam Museum*★★ Z **M1** – *Trinity College*★★ Y – *Clare College*★ Z **B** – *Kettle's Yard*★ Y **M2** – *Queen's College*★ *AC* Z.
Exc. : *Audley End*★★, *S : 13 m. on Trumpington Rd, A 1309, A 1301 and B 1383 – Imperial War Museum*★, *Duxford, S : 9 m. on M 11.*
Ⓖ *Cambridgeshire Moat House Hotel, Bar Hill* ℰ *(01954)* 249988 X.
✈ *Cambridge Airport : ℰ (01223) 373765, E : 2 m. on A 1303* X.
🚉 *The Old Library, Wheeler St* ℰ *(0871) 2268006, tourism@cambridge.gov.uk.*
London 55 – Coventry 88 – Ipswich 54 – Kingston-upon-Hull 137 – Leicester 74 – Norwich 61 – Nottingham 88 – Oxford 100.

Plan on next page

🏨 **Hotel Felix** ≫, Whitehouse Lane, Huntingdon Rd, CB3 0LX, Northwest : 1 ½ m. by A 1307 ℰ (01223) 277977, *help@hotelfelix.co.uk*, Fax (01223) 277973, 屏, 舟 – ⅛ ⇔ ⚓ & P – ☖ 50. **⓪⓪ ⅍ ⑩ 𝘝𝘐𝘚𝘈**
Graffiti : Rest 16.50 (lunch) and a la carte 34.20/47.95 Ŷ – ⊠ 7.50 – **52 rm** ⋆140.00 – ⋆⋆285.00.
♦ Built as a private house in 1852, now with modern extensions. Public areas are smart, modern and stylish. The contemporary rooms include state-of-the art facilities. Sleek restaurant overlooks garden and terrace.

🏨 **Crowne Plaza**, Downing St, CB2 3DT, ℰ (0870) 4009180, *reservations-cambridgecp@ichotelsgroup.com*, Fax (01223) 464440, **Ⅰ₅, ≦s – ⅛**, ⇔ rm, ▤ & P – ☖ 250. **⓪⓪ ⅍ ⑩ 𝘝𝘐𝘚𝘈**
Z a
Rest *(closed sunday lunch)* a la carte 18.45/28.25 – ⊠ 15.95 – **198 rm** ⋆160.00 – ⋆⋆160.00/350.00.
♦ Concierge parking to greet you, then unwind in the Bloomsbury bar on the mezzanine level. Modern bedrooms: King Superior and Junior suites offer highest levels of comfort. A la carte restaurant or Irish themed bar.

🏨 **University Arms**, Regent St, CB2 1AD, ℰ (01223) 273000, *dua.sales@devere-hotels.com*, Fax (01223) 273037 – ⅛ ⇔ ▤ & P – ☖ 300. **⓪⓪ ⅍ ⑩ 𝘝𝘐𝘚𝘈**
Z e
Rest (bar lunch)/dinner a la carte 25.00/40.00 **s.** Ŷ – **119 rm** ⊠ ⋆110.00/170.00 – ⋆⋆115.00/175.00, 1 suite.
♦ Extended Victorian hotel overlooking Parker's Piece with grand lounge and bar. Spacious bedrooms, some with balconies and views over the green. Contemporary restaurant with street entrance.

🏨 **Gonville**, Gonville Pl, CB1 1LY, ℰ (01223) 366611, *info@gonvillehotel.co.uk*, Fax (01223) 315470 – ⅛ ⇔, ▤ rest, P – ☖ 200. **⓪⓪ ⅍ ⑩ 𝘝𝘐𝘚𝘈**. ✻
Z r
Rest (bar lunch)/dinner a la carte 16.95/25.15 **s** Ŷ – ⊠ 11.50 – **73 rm** ⋆79.00/139.00 – ⋆⋆99.00/155.00.
♦ Overlooks the green where cricketer Jack Hobbs honed his talents. Caters for corporate visitors and tourists. Bedrooms in newer extension benefit from air conditioning. International menu served in the relaxed atrium.

🏨 **Centennial**, 63-71 Hills Rd, CB2 1PG, ℰ (01223) 314652, *reception@centennialhotel.co.uk*, Fax (01223) 315443 – ⇔ P, **⓪⓪ ⅍ ⑩ 𝘝𝘐𝘚𝘈**. ✻
X x
closed 23 December-2 January – **Rest** *(dinner only)* 15.50 and a la carte 21.50/26.50 – **39 rm** ⊠ ⋆70.00/80.00 – ⋆⋆88.00/96.00.
♦ Converted terraced Victorian houses with chesterfield sofas, chairs and dresser in a smart lounge. Friendly bar. Traditional bedrooms, some with canopied beds. Table flowers prettify the dining room.

CAMBRIDGE

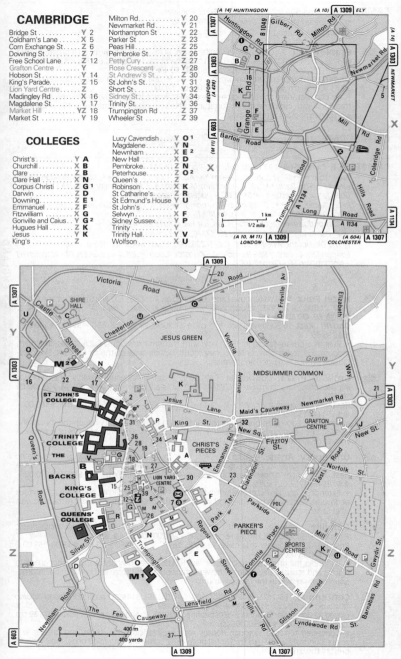

Cambridge Lodge, 139 Huntingdon Rd, CB3 0DQ, ☎ (01223) 352833, *cam bridge.lodge@bt.connect.com*, Fax (01223) 355166, 🛌 – ✝✝ **P**. **MO AE VISA** ✝ X i
closed 24 December - 2 January – **Rest** *(closed Sunday dinner)* (dinner only and Sunday lunch) dinner 27.00 and a la carte 30.75/39.20 ⅞ – **15 rm** ∧∧79.50/100.00 – ✝✝102.00.
◆ Mock Tudor house, privately owned, with genteel ambience, provides a good starting point for a sortie into the city. Oak beamed lounge and neat rooms to touch down in. Intimate restaurant: rich interior, dark beamed.

Express by Holiday Inn without rest., 15-17 Coldhams Park, Norman Way off Coldhams Lane, CB1 3LH, East : 2 m. off A 1303 ☎ (0870) 9904081, *cambridge@expressholi dayinn.co.uk*, Fax (0870) 9904062 – 🛍 ✝✝ ♧ **P**. – ⛊ 50. **MO AE O VISA**
100 rm ✝100.00 – ✝✝100.00.
◆ Set in recent development to city's east, next to David Lloyd Leisure Centre. Airy breakfast room with leather chairs in turquoise and chocolate. Modern, co-ordinated rooms.

Midsummer House (Clifford), Midsummer Common, CB4 1HA, ☎ (01223) 369299, *reservations@midsummerhouse.co.uk*, Fax (01223) 302672, 🛌 – ✝✝ ♧ 16. **MO AE VISA** Y a
closed 21 December-9 January, 2 weeks August - September, 1 week Easter, Sunday and Monday – **Rest** (dinner only and lunch Friday-Saturday) 55.00/75.00 ⅞ ⛆.
Spec. Salad of smoked eel, pig's trotter and apple purée. Braised turbot with peanuts and pistachios, asparagus and squash purée. Tart Tatin, garlic and bay leaf foam, vanilla ice cream.
◆ A river Cam idyll: see it lit up in the evenings over the bridge. Inventive, exciting cooking a perfect partner to original, innovative menus. Pleasantly understated service.

22 Chesterton Road, 22 Chesterton Rd, CB4 3AX, ☎ (01223) 351880, *davidcar ter@restaurant22.co.uk*, Fax (01223) 323814 – ■. **MO AE VISA** Y c
closed Christmas-New Year, Sunday and Monday – **Rest** (booking essential) (dinner only) 24.95.
◆ Personally run Victorian town house with smartly clad tables. Classic French and Italian dishes with mild Asian influences, served at reasonable prices.

Bruno's Brasserie, 52 Mill Rd, CB1 2AS, ☎ (01223) 312702, *bruno5@btconnect.com*, Fax (01223) 312702, 🛌 – ✝✝ ■ **MO AE VISA** Z u
closed 24 December-2 January, Sunday and Monday lunch and Bank Holidays – **Rest** 14.00 (lunch) and a la carte 21.00/34.00.
◆ Converted shop with spacious simply decorated interior and appealing artwork. Enclosed patio garden with arbour. Fresh and zingy menu with a strong Mediterranean base.

at Histon North : 3 m. on B 1049 – X – ✉ Cambridge.

Phoenix, 20 The Green, CB4 9JA, ☎ (01223) 233766 – ■. **MO VISA**
closed 25-28 December – **Rest** - Chinese (Peking, Szechuan) - 17.50/29.00 and a la carte 43.00/93.00 **s**.
◆ A 100-year old redbrick pub overlooking village green. Within, Chinese dishes are served by staff in waistcoats and bowties. Spicy highlights from Szechuan; Peking classics.

at Horningsea Northeast : 4 m. by A 1303 – X – and B 1047 on Horningsea rd – ✉ Cambridge.

Crown & Punchbowl with rm, High St, CB5 9JG, ☎ (01223) 860643, *crown@cambs cuisine.com*, Fax (01223) 441814, 🛌 – ✝✝ **P**. **MO AE VISA**. ⛆
closed 26-28 December – **Rest** *(closed Sunday dinner)* a la carte 20.00/30.00 ⅞ – **5 rm** ∧✝69.95 – ✝✝89.95.
◆ Former 17C village inn with characterful beams. Farmhouse tables and chairs sit cosily by real fire. Blend of tasty dishes amiably served. Clean, modern rooms.

at Little Wilbraham East : 7¼ m. by A 1303 – X – ✉ Cambridge.

The Hole in the Wall, 2 High St, CB1 5JY, ☎ (01223) 812282, *info@the-holeinthe wall.com* – **P**. **MO VISA**
closed 25 December and dinner 26 December – **Rest** *(closed Sunday dinner and Monday except Bank Holiday Monday dinner)* a la carte 20.00/30.00 ⅞.
◆ Pretty little village hostelry. Owners ran popular Lough Pool Inn in Herefordshire. Pub's traditional qualities balanced by new kitchen serving interesting, good value food.

at Little Shelford South : 5½ m. by A 1309 – X – off A 10 – ✉ Cambridge.

Sycamore House, 1 Church St, CB2 5HG, ☎ (01223) 843396 – ✝✝ **P**. **MO VISA**
closed Christmas-New Year and Sunday-Tuesday – **Rest** (booking essential) (dinner only) 25.00.
◆ Restaurant divided by central brick chimney with cast-iron, coal burning stove in centre. Fresh produce, fish and game available on set menu. Simple, honest cooking.

ENGLAND

at Madingley *West : 4½ m. by A 1303 – X –* ⊠ *Cambridge.*

XX **The Three Horseshoes,** High St, CB3 8AB, *℘* (01954) 210221, *3hs@btconnect.com,*
Fax (01954) 212043, 🍽 – ⤫ **P.** ⏀ **AE** ⏀ **VISA** ⌖
closed 1-2 January – **Rest** a la carte 20.00/40.00 ♀ ⌖.
• Thatched yet modern pub. Eat in the bar and sample the bar-grill menu or the conservatory restaurant for innovative cuisine. Excellent range of wine by the glass.

at Hardwick *West : 5 m. by A 1303 – X –* ⊠ *Cambridge.*

⌂ **Wallis Farmhouse** without rest., 98 Main St, CB3 7QU, *℘* (01954) 210347, *enquiries@wallisfarmhouse.co.uk, Fax* (01954) 210988, 🍴, ⅃ – ⤫ **P.** ⏀ **AE** **VISA** ⌖
4 rm ⊡ ✦45.00/50.00 – ✦✦65.00/70.00.
• Spacious, timbered bedrooms, all en suite, in converted stables of a redbrick Georgian farmhouse: Wimpole Way bridle path to the rear. Friendly owner serves hearty breakfasts.

at Cambourne *West : 7 m. by A 428 – X –* ⊠ *Cambridge.*

🏨 **The Cambridge Belfry,** Back Lane, CB3 6BN, *℘* (01954) 714995, *cambridge@marstonhotels.com, Fax* (01954) 714998, ⏀, ⅂₆, ⌾, ⍁, 🍴 – ⷭ ⤫, ▤ rest, **P** – ⌂ 220. ⏀
AE **VISA** ⌖
Bridge : **Rest** *(closed Saturday lunch and Sunday dinner)* 26.50 *(dinner)* and a la carte –
Brookes Brasserie : **Rest** 26.50 and a la carte – **110 rm** ⊡ ✦149.00 – ✦✦179.00, 10 suites.
• Brick-built hotel, constructed around central courtyard and opened in 2004, in modern village. Well-equipped leisure centre. Bedrooms boast a pleasant, contemporary style. Formal, linen-clad Bridge. All-day, informal dining at Brookes Brasserie.

at Bar Hill *Northwest : 5½ m. by A 1307 – X – off A 14 –* ⊠ *Cambridge.*

🏨 **Cambridgeshire Moat House,** CB3 8EU, *℘* (01954) 249988, *cambridge@menzieshotels.co.uk, Fax* (01954) 780010, ⅂₆, ⌾, ⍁, ⍓, 🍴, ⅗ – ⷭ ⤫, ▤ rest, ⅄ **P** – ⌂ 200. ⏀ **AE** ⏀ **VISA**
Rest *(buffet lunch)/dinner* 19.95 and a la carte 21.95/33.40 – **134 rm** ⊡ ✦70.00/135.00 –
✦✦80.00/145.00.
• Distinguished by its golf course. Caters for business visitors as well as sightseers which is reflected in the range of rooms. Executive suites have chestnut veneer décor. Well-run, family-friendly dining room.

Undecided between two equivalent establishments?
Within each category, establishments are classified
in our order of preference.

CANNINGTON *Somerset* **503** K 30 *– see Bridgwater.*

CANTERBURY *Kent* **504** X 30 *Great Britain G. – pop. 43 552.*
See : *City*★★★ - *Cathedral*★★★ Y – *St Augustine's Abbey*★★ *AC* YZ K – *King's School*★ Y –
Mercery Lane★ Y **12** - *Christ Church Gate*★ Y D – *Museum of Canterbury*★ *AC* Y **M1** - *St Martin's Church*★ Y N – *West Gate Towers*★ *AC* Y R.
🚺 *12-13 Sun St, Buttermarket* *℘* (01227) 378100, *canterburyinformation@canterbury.gov.uk.*
London 59 – Brighton 76 – Dover 15 – Maidstone 28 – Margate 17.

Plan opposite

🏨 **Abode Canterbury,** High St, CT1 2RX, *℘* (01227) 826670, *Fax* (01227) 784874 – ⷭ ▤
TV ⌖ ⇦ **P** – ⌂ 110. ⏀ **AE** ⏀ **VISA**
Y a
Rest – (see **Michael Caines** below) – ⊡ 12.95 – **72 rm** ✦125.00 – ✦✦165.00.
• Centrally located, this smart hotel has undergone a vast top-to-toe transformation. A distinctive modern feel pertains, typified by sleek, airy bedrooms.

🏢 **Ebury,** 65-67 New Dover Rd, CT1 3DX, *℘* (01227) 768433, *info@ebury-hotel.co.uk,*
Fax (01227) 459187, ⍁, 🍴 – ⤫ ⅄ **P.** ⏀ **AE** **VISA**
Z r
closed 3 weeks Christmas-New Year – **Rest** *(closed Sunday) (dinner only)* 21.00 – **15 rm** ⊡
✦70.00/95.00 – ✦✦90.00/110.00.
• 1850s redbrick hotel where drinks are served in a lounge holding a collection of Bulls Eye clocks. Bedrooms are all spacious and comfortable. Restaurant ambience reflects age of hotel.

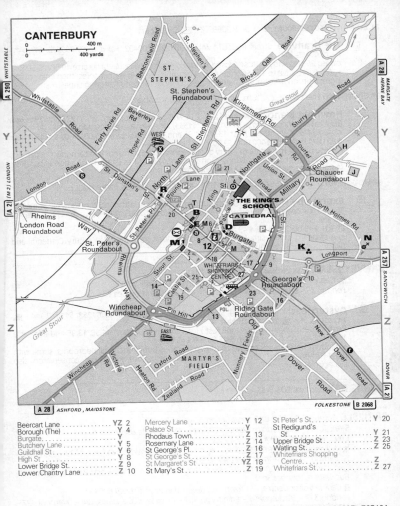

CANTERBURY

0 — 400 m
0 — 400 yards

⌂ **Magnolia House** without rest., 36 St Dunstan's Terr, CT2 8AX, ℘ (01227) 765121, info@magnoliahousecanterbury.co.uk, Fax (01227) 765121, 🌺 – ⇌ 🅿. 🌐 🆎 VISA ⅝
Y s

closed 24-26 December – **7 rm** � ✝55.00/75.00 – ✝✝95.00/135.00.
• Gracious Georgian house with calm, sunny interior and plush bedrooms including four-poster suite. Breakfast room offers good choice, and boasts charming garden outlook.

XX **Michael Caines** (at Abode Canterbury), High St, CT1 2RX, ℘ (01227) 886670, Fax (01227) 784874 – ⇌ rest, ▤. 🌐 🆎 ① VISA
Y a
Rest 17.50/25.00 a la carte 32.50/41.25.
• Enjoy a glass of Champagne in smart bar before repairing to the upmarket restaurant to enjoy modern British cooking utilising a variety of styles and classical techniques.

X **The Goods Shed**, Station Rd West, St Dunstans, CT2 8AN, ℘ (01227) 459153 – ⇌ 🅿. 🌐 🆎 ① VISA
Y x
closed Sunday dinner and Monday – **Rest** a la carte 20.50/29.50.
• Once derelict railway shed, now a farmers' market that's open all day. Its eating area offers superbly fresh produce with no frills and real flavours very much to the fore.

at Lower Hardres South : 3 m. on B 2068 – Z – ⊠ Canterbury.

The Granville, Street End, CT4 7AL, ℘ (01227) 700402, Fax (01227) 700925, 佘 , 帚 –
🖃 🅿, 🝳 🖭 𝘝𝘐𝘚𝘈
closed 25 December – Rest (closed Sunday dinner and Monday) a la carte 19.50/29.50 ♀.
◆ A close relative to The Sportsman in Whitstable. Relax in leather sofas, then enjoy quality ingredients on a well-priced, very interesting modern menu featuring superb fish.

at Chartham Hatch West : 3¼ m. by A 28 – Z – ⊠ Canterbury.

Howfield Manor, Howfield Lane, CT4 7HQ, Southeast : 1 m. ℘ (01227) 738294, how field@swallowhotels.com, Fax (01227) 731535, 帚 – ⚑✖ 🅿 – 🝳 100. 🝳 🖭 𝘝𝘐𝘚𝘈. 🝳
closed 24-31 December – Rest 18.95/21.95 and dinner a la carte 23.00/31.00 s. – 15 rm 🝳
✸80.00/115.00 – ✸✸100.00/130.00.
◆ Once part of the estate of Priory of St Gregory, this 19C manor is set amongst deciduous trees and lawned garden. Sunny rooms; "Manor Suite" has dance floor, cocktail bar. Restaurant takes name from well hole where monks once drew water.

at Upper Harbledown Service Area West : 4 m. on A 2 – Y – ⊠ Canterbury.

Express by Holiday Inn without rest., CT2 9HX, (eastbound carriageway) ℘ (01227) 865000, canterbury@morethanhotels.com, Fax (01227) 865100 – ✖✖ 🝳 🅿 – 🝳 35. 🝳 🖭 🝳 𝘝𝘐𝘚𝘈
89 rm ✸49.00/75.00 – ✸✸49.00/75.00.
◆ A standard lodge; simply furnished rooms. Well placed for Canterbury Cathedral and Canterbury Heritage museum.

CANVEY ISLAND Essex 504 V 29 – pop. 37 479.
🝳 Castle Point, Waterside Farm, Somnes Ave ℘ (01268) 510830.
London 35 – Chelmsford 19 – Maidstone 44 – Southend-on-Sea 13.

Oysterfleet, Knightswick Rd, SS8 7UX, ℘ (01268) 510111, Fax (01268) 511420, 帚 – 🖨, 🖃 rest, 🝳 🅿 – 🝳 200. 🝳 🖭 𝘝𝘐𝘚𝘈. 🝳
Rest (closed Sunday dinner) (grill rest.) (carvery lunch Sunday) 14.50/18.95 and a la carte 15.85/22.40 – 🝳 5.00 – 41 rm ✸45.00 – ✸✸45.00.
◆ Modern hotel stands on site of the eponymous pub. Functional bedrooms, some with floral furnishings and views of the lake. Family restaurant adjoins bar; conservatory also available for dining.

CARBIS BAY Cornwall 503 D 33 – see St Ives.

CARLISLE Cumbria 501 502 L 19 Great Britain G. – pop. 71 773.
See : Town★ – Cathedral★ (Painted Ceiling★) AY E – Tithe Barn★ BY A.
Env. : Hadrian's Wall★★, N : by A 7 AY.
🝳 Aglionby ℘ (01228) 513029 BY – 🝳 Stony Holme, St Aidan's Rd ℘ (01228) 625511 BY – 🝳 Dalston Hall, Dalston ℘ (01228) 710165, AZ.
✈ Carlisle Airport ℘ (01228) 573641, NW : 5½ m. by A 7 – BY – and B 6264 – Terminal : Bus Station, Lowther St.
🝳 Carlisle Visitor Centre, Old Town Hall, Green Market ℘ (01228) 625600.
London 317 – Blackpool 95 – Edinburgh 101 – Glasgow 100 – Leeds 124 – Liverpool 127 – Manchester 122 – Newcastle upon Tyne 59.

Plan opposite

Cumbria Park, 32 Scotland Rd, CA3 9DG, North : 1 m. on A 7 ℘ (01228) 522887, enqui ries@cumbriaparkhotel.co.uk, Fax (01228) 514796, 🝳, 🝳 – 🖨 ✖✖, 🖃 rest, 🅿 – 🝳 120. 🝳 🖭 🝳 𝘝𝘐𝘚𝘈. 🝳
closed 25-26 December – Rest a la carte 14.15/23.80 – 47 rm 🝳 ✸77.00 – ✸✸125.00.
◆ Personally run hotel, tiny piece of Hadrian's Wall visible in car park.Smart gym and sauna. Family curios decorate interiors. Sizeable rooms; some have whirlpool baths. Eat in bar among the fishtanks, or more formal 'Roman' themed restaurant.

Number Thirty One, 31 Howard Pl, CA1 1HR, ℘ (01228) 597080, pruirving@aol.com, Fax (01228) 597080 – ✖✖. 🝳 🖭 𝘝𝘐𝘚𝘈. 🝳
BY a
closed 25 December – Rest (dinner only) (by arrangement) 25.00 ♀ – 3 rm 🝳 ✸60.00/69.00 – ✸✸85.00/100.00.
◆ Classic 19C town house in residential area. Luxuriously and stylishly furnished throughout with many thoughtful extras. Three rooms decorated in either yellow, green or blue.

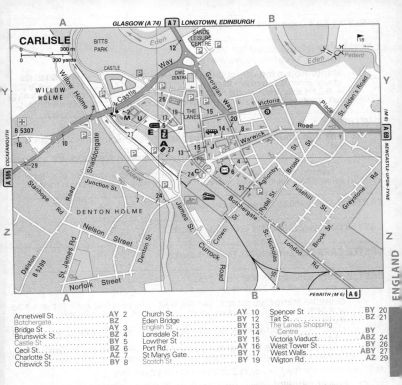

CARLISLE

Annetwell St	AY 2	Church St	AY 10	Spencer St	BY 20
Botchergate	BZ	Eden Bridge	BY 12	Tait St	BZ 21
Bridge St	AY 3	English St	BY 13	The Lanes Shopping
Brunswick St	BY 5	Lonsdale St	BY 14	Centre	BY
Castle St	BZ	Lowther St	BY 15	Victoria Viaduct	ABZ 24
Cecil St	AZ 7	Port Rd	AY 16	West Tower St	BY 26
Charlotte St	BY	St Marys Gate	BY 17	West Walls	ABY 27
Chiswick St	BY 8	Scotch St	BY 19	Wigton Rd	AZ 29

⌂ **Aldingham House** without rest., 1 Eden Mount, Stanwix, CA3 9LZ, North : ¾ m. on A 7 🖉 (01228) 522554, stay@aldinghamhouse.co.uk, Fax (0871) 2771644 – ⇄ 🚻 🅿 ⊕ ⓪ **VISA** 🎵
3 rm ⊴ ✦50.00 – ✦✦75.00.
• Classic 19C townhouse in terrace of matching properties; original features firmly in situ. Delightful drawing room with grand piano. Rooms decorated with considerable style.

XX **Gallo Rosso**, Parkhouse Rd, Kingstown, CA6 4BY, Northwest : 2 ¾ m. by A 7 on Rock-cliffe rd 🖉 (01228) 526037, Fax (01228) 550074 – ⇄ 🗏 🅿 ⊕ **VISA**
closed January to mid February – **Rest** - Italian - a la carte 14.65/28.75.
• City outskirts setting: watch chef at work in central open plan kitchen. Bright, airy surroundings. Soundly prepared Italian dishes, from pasta to meat and fish classics.

at Crosby-on-Eden Northeast : 5 m. by A 7 – BY – and B 6264 off A 689 – ⊠ Carlisle.

🏠 **Crosby Lodge Country House** ⬎, High Crosby, CA6 4QZ, 🖉 (01228) 573618, en quiries@crosbylodge.co.uk, Fax (01228) 573428, ≤, 🌳 – ⇄ rest, 🅿 ⊕ ⓪ **VISA**
closed Christmas-mid January – **Rest** (Sunday dinner residents only) 40.00 (dinner) and a la carte 24.00/44.45 ⊉ – 11 rm ⊴ ✦90.00/100.00 – ✦✦150.00/200.00.
• Secluded castellated 19C country mansion with walled gardens in rural setting. Plenty of period character including antiques and curios. Pets allowed in converted stable rooms. Elegant restaurant boasts silver cutlery and crystal glassware.

at Wetheral East : 6¼ m. by A 69 – BY – ⊠ Carlisle.

🏠 **Crown**, CA4 8ES, 🖉 (01228) 561888, info@crownhotelwetheral.co.uk, Fax (01228) 561637, 🌳, 🎵, ⛲, 🏊, 🌳, squash – ⇄ 🛏 & 🅿 – 🛧 175. ⊕ ⓪ **VISA**
Rest 17.95/23.95 s. ⊉ – 49 rm ⊴ ✦120.00/135.00 – ✦✦135.00, 2 suites.
• Former 18C farmhouse: period character visible in lounges and rustic bar. Clean-cut, unfussy rooms. Executive rooms have balconies and garden views. Good leisure facilities. Main conservatory or bar dining options.

CARLTON-IN-COVERDALE N. Yorks. 502 O 21 – see Middleham.

CARLYON BAY Cornwall 503 F 33 – see St Austell.

CARTERWAY HEADS Northd. 501 502 O 19 – ⊠ Shotley Bridge.
London 272 – Carlisle 59 – Newcastle upon Tyne 21.

   🏠 **Manor House Inn** with rm, DH8 9LX, on A 68 ℘ (01207) 255268 – ⤢ **P**, **⑩** **AE** **VISA**
closed dinner 25 December – **Rest** a la carte 17.00/25.00 ♀ – **4 rm** ⊭ ✱60.00 – ✱✱70.00.
   • 18C inn with views over the moors; whet your whistle in the bar or dine in the smartly refurbished restaurant. Tasty dishes and home-made desserts. Smart rooms with views.

CARTHORPE N. Yorks..

   🏠 **Fox and Hounds**, DL8 2LG, ℘ (01845) 567433, Fax (01845) 567155 – ⤢ rest, **P**, **⑩**
VISA
closed 25-31 December, 1 week January and Monday – **Rest** 14.95 and a la carte 19.35/38.85.
   • Former smithy in rural village close to A1; eye constantly engaged by all sorts of pub paraphernalia. Eat in bar area or dining room: home-made dishes steeped in tradition.

CARTMEL Cumbria 502 L 21 – see Grange-over-Sands.

CASTERTON Cumbria 502 M 21 – see Kirkby Lonsdale.

CASTLE CARROCK Cumbria 502 L 19 – see Brampton.

CASTLE CARY Somerset 503 M 30 – pop. 3 056.
London 127 – Bristol 28 – Wells 13.

   ⌂ **Clanville Manor** without rest., BA7 7PJ, West : 2 m. by B 3152 and A 371 on B 3153
℘ (01963) 350124, info@clanvillemanor.co.uk, Fax (01963) 350719, ⌕ heated, ☞, ♨ – ⤢
P, **⑩** **VISA**. ✑
closed Christmas and New Year and restricted opening in winter – – **4 rm** ⊭ ✱30.00/55.00
– ✱✱60.00/70.00.
   • Comely 18C house full of period style and charm. Heirlooms and antiques abound. Breakfasts served from the Aga. Walled garden boasts heated pool. Individualistic rooms.

at South Cadbury South : 4½ m. by B 3152 off A 359 – ⊠ Castle Cary.

   ⌂ **Lower Camelot** without rest., Church Rd, BA22 7HA, ℘ (01963) 440581, info@south
cadbury.co.uk, ☞ – ⤢ **P**, **⑩** **VISA**. ✑
closed 21 December - 9 March – **3 rm** ⊭ ✱42.50 – ✱✱68.00.
   • Owners go out of their way to make your stay pleasurable in guesthouse named after King Arthur's castle. Lovely garden; good breakfasts in the conservatory. Smart rooms.

   🏠 **The Camelot**, Chapel Rd, BA22 7EX, ℘ (01963) 440448, enquiry@thecamelot.co.uk,
Fax (01963) 441462, ⌖, ☞ – ⤢ **P**, **⑩** **VISA**
Rest a la carte 22.50/35.90 ♀.
   • Owned by award-winning cheese makers who've modernised this old pub, alongside the restored skittle alley. Upstairs restaurant-style dining room serves good value dishes.

at Lovington West : 4 m. by B 3152 and A 371 on B 3153 – ⊠ Castle Cary.

   🏠 **The Pilgrims at Lovington**, BA7 7PT, ℘ (01963) 240600, thejooles@btinternet.com,
⌖ – ⤢ **P**, **⑩** **AE** **VISA**. ✑
closed first 2 weeks October and first week May – **Rest** (closed Monday, Tuesday and dinner Sunday) a la carte 17.00/36.00.
   • Unprepossessing façade disguises lovely olive green rustic interior with watercolours and beams. Interesting, hearty menus include meat, ice cream and beer from the village!

CASTLE COMBE Wilts. 503 504 N 29 The West Country G. – ⊠ Chippenham.
See : Village★★.
London 110 – Bristol 23 – Chippenham 6.

   🏛 **Manor House H. and Golf Club** ⌂, SN14 7HR, ℘ (01249) 782206, enqui
ries@manor-housecc.co.uk, Fax (01249) 783100, ⌖, 🕮, ⌬, ☞, ♨, ✑ – ⤢ **P** –
A 100. **⑩** **AE** **①** **VISA**
The Bybrook : **Rest** 25.00/70.00 and a la carte 49.50/70.00 – **44 rm** ⊭ ✱185.00/235.00 –
✱✱185.00/235.00, 4 suites.
   • Particularly peaceful manor in a sweeping green with trout in the river. Fine fabrics and oak panelling exude history. Luxurious bedrooms in mews cottages or main house. Smart restaurant: English country style menus.

🏛 **Castle Inn**, SN14 7HN, ℰ (01249) 783030, *enquiries@castle-inn.info, Fax (01249) 782315*
– ⇔ ⌘ AE VISA
closed 25 December – **Rest** a la carte 19.00/29.00 ⅌ – **11 rm** (dinner included) ⊇
✿69.50/89.50 – ✿✿100.00/165.00.
◆ A hostelry dating back to the 12C in the middle of a delightful and historic village. Much
character, from the wooden beams in the bedrooms to the rustic bar. Large glass ceiling
creates light-flooded dining room.

at Nettleton Shrub *West : 2 m. by B 4039 on Nettleton rd (Fosse Way)* – ✉ *Chippenham.*

⌂ **Fosse Farmhouse** ⧉, SN14 7NJ, ℰ (01249) 782286, *caroncooper@compuserve.com,*
Fax (01249) 783066, ☞ – ⇔ P. VISA. ⅋
Rest *closed 2 January - 3 February* (by arrangement) 32.00 – **3 rm** ⊇ ✿55.00/65.00 –
✿✿85.00/125.00.
◆ 18C Cotswold Stone farmhouse personally run by enthusiastic owner. Cream teas served
in the garden in summer. Welcoming bedrooms with French artefacts and Gallic style.

CASTLE DONINGTON *Leics.* 502 503 504 P 25 – *pop.* 5 977 – ✉ *Derby.*
✈ *Nottingham East Midlands Airport :* ℰ (0871) 919 9000, *S : by B 6540 and A 453.*
London 123 – Birmingham 38 – Leicester 23 – Nottingham 13.

🏛 **Priest House on the River**, Kings Mills, DE74 2RR, *West : 1 ¾ m. by Park Lane*
ℰ (01332) 810649, *thepriesthouse@handpicked.co.uk, Fax (01332) 811141*, ≤, ⧉, ♨
⇔ rest, ✆ P. – 🅰 130. ⌘ AE ① VISA. ⅋
Rest (dinner only and Sunday lunch)/dinner 32.50 and a la carte 22.85/40.95 ⅌ – ⊇ 14.95 –
39 rm ✿96.00/155.00 – ✿✿96.00/155.00, 3 suites.
◆ Extended mill where modernity holds sway: plasma TVs in the bedrooms, which are
divided between the main house with Trent views, and charming former mill workers'
cottages. Elegantly formal main dining room, or relaxing informal brasserie.

at Breedon on the Hill *Southwest : 4 m. by Breedon rd off A 453* – ✉ *Castle Donington.*

🏠 **The Three Horseshoes**, Main St, DE73 8AN, ℰ (01332) 695129, *ian@thehorse*
shoes.com, Fax (01332) 695128, ☞ – ⇔ P. ⌘ VISA
Rest (closed Sunday) a la carte 15.95/31.00.
◆ 18C pub where locals gather round the bar's open fire. Eat here or in two dining areas:
large blackboard menus offer dishes using carefully sourced and combined ingredients.

Your opinions are important to us:
please write and let us know about your discoveries and experiences –
good and bad!

CATEL *Guernsey (Channel Islands)* 503 P 33 and 517 ⑨ – *see Channel Islands.*

CAUNTON *Notts.* 502 504 R 24 – *see Newark-on-Trent.*

CAVENDISH *Suffolk* 504 V 27.
London 70 – Cambridge 30 – Colchester 20.

⌂ **Embleton House** without rest., Melford Rd, CO10 8AA, ℰ (01787) 280447, *silv*
erned@aol.com, Fax (01787) 282396, ⊿ heated, ☞, ⅋ – ⇔ P.
5 rm ⊇ ✿40.00/50.00 – ✿✿58.00/74.00.
◆ Spacious, comfy Edwardian house in attractive, mature gardens. Breakfast with extensive menu served at large communal table. Well-kept rooms. Holistic therapies available.

CHADDESLEY CORBETT *Worcs.* 503 504 N 26 – *see Kidderminster.*

CHADWICK END *W. Mids.* 503 504 O 26.
London 106 – Birmingham 13 – Leicester 40 – Stratford-upon-Avon 16.

🏠 **The Orange Tree**, Warwick Rd, B93 0BN, on A 4141 ℰ (01564) 785364, *theorange*
tree@lovelypubs.co.uk, Fax (01564) 782988, ☞, ☞ – ⇔ P. ⌘ VISA
Rest (closed Sunday dinner) (booking essential) a la carte 25.00/32.00 ⅌.
◆ Modern roadside dining pub with attractive exterior and stylish interior. The menu of
modish classics is good value and has an appealing, flexible range.

Env. : *Dartmoor National Park★★*.
London 218 – Exeter 17 – Plymouth 27.

🏰 **Gidleigh Park** 🦢, TQ13 8HH, Northwest : 2 m. by Gidleigh Rd ℰ (01647) 432367,
❀❀ *gidleighpark@gidleigh.co.uk*, Fax (01647) 432574, ≼ Teign Valley, woodland and Meldon
Hill, 🦢, 🌳, ₤, 🍽 – ✤ rest, ₠ P. **MO AE OD VISA**
Rest (booking essential) 35.00/75.00 ₽ ♨ – **22 rm** (dinner included) ☞ ✦280.00/365.00 –
✦✦440.00/600.00, 2 suites.
Spec. Tartlet of quail with onion confit, black truffle and smoked bacon. Lobster fricassée
with summer vegetables and herbs. Trio of chocolate.
♦ Stunningly refurbished in 2006 and set in 45 Dartmoor acres; classic country house feel
typified by fine English fabrics and antiques. Sumptuous rooms the epitome of style.
Superb cuisine, prepared with skill and flair, showcases local produce.

XX **22 Mill Street** with rm, 22 Mill St, TQ13 8AW, ℰ (01647) 432244 – ✤ rest. **MO VISA**
closed first 2 weeks January and 1 week June – Rest *(closed Sunday-Monday)*
27.00/39.00 **s.** – ☞ 5.50 – **2 rm** ✦✦75.00.
♦ This keenly run restaurant is based in a very characterful high street cottage. The owner/
chef's accomplished modern cooking is rightfully lauded. Simple bedrooms.

at Easton *Northeast : 1½ m. on A 382 – ⊠ Chagford.*

⌂ **Easton Court** without rest., Easton Cross, TQ13 8JL, ℰ (01647) 433469,
stay@easton.co.uk, Fax (01647) 433654, 🌳 – ✤ P. **MO VISA**
5 rm ☞ ✦45.00/50.00 – ✦✦70.00/75.00.
♦ Well appointed accommodation and a high ceilinged lounge overlooking the immaculate gardens. Home made marmalade a speciality. Friendly atmosphere.

at Sandypark *Northeast : 2¼ m. on A 382 – ⊠ Chagford.*

🏨 **Mill End,** TQ13 8JN, on A 382 ℰ (01647) 432282, *info@millendhotel.com*,
Fax (01647) 433106, 🦢, 🌳 – ✤ P. **MO VISA**
Rest (light lunch)/dinner 38.00 ₽ – **14 rm** ☞ ✦85.00/110.00 – ✦✦110.00/155.00.
♦ Country house with mill wheel; river Teign runs through garden. Framed pictures, curios
grace interiors. Upstairs bedrooms have views; those downstairs have private patios. Pretty
restaurant, bright and comfortable.

⌂ **Parford Well** 🦢 without rest., TQ13 8JW, on Drewsteignton rd ℰ (01647) 433353,
tim@parfordwell.co.uk, 🌳 – ✤. 🍽
closed Christmas and New Year – **3 rm** ☞ ✦40.00/70.00 – ✦✦80.00.
♦ Tastefully maintained with superbly tended gardens. Elegant sitting room has plenty of
books and French windows to garden. Two breakfast rooms. Homely, immaculate rooms.

🍴 **Sandy Park Inn** with rm, TQ13 8JW, ℰ (01647) 433267, *sandyparkinn@aol.com*, 🍴,
🦢, 🌳 – ✤. **MO AE VISA**
Rest a la carte approx 18.50 ₽ – **5 rm** ✦45.00 – ✦✦80.00.
♦ Tiny 17C thatched pub with bags of character. Cram into three snugs with flags, beams
and open fires. Delightful garden on hillside. Locally sourced dishes. Cosy bedrooms.

- → *Discover the best restaurant ?*
- → *Find the nearest hotel ?*
- → *Find your bearings using our maps and guides ?*
- → *Understand the symbols used in the guide...*

Follow the red Bibs !

Advice on restaurants from **Chef Bib**.

Tips and advice from **Clever Bib** on finding your way around the guide and on the road.

Advice on hotels from **Bellboy Bib**.

Gorey: the impressive Mont Orgueil Castle

ALDERNEY

C.I. **503** Q 33 and **517** ⑨ *The West Country G.* – pop. 2 294

See: Braye Bay★ – Mannez Garenne (⩽★ from Quesnard Lighthouse) – Telegraph Bay★ – Vallee des Trois Vaux★ – Clonque Bay★ .

✈ *Aurigny Air Services ℰ (0871) 871 0717.*

🚩 *States Office, Queen Elizabeth II St ℰ (01481) 822994.*

Braye *C.I.*

✗ **First and Last**, GY9 3TH, ℰ (01481) 823162, ⩽ harbour – **AE** **VISA**
Easter-October – **Rest** - Seafood specialities - (dinner only) a la carte 26.15/31.50.
♦ Positioned by the harbour with scenic views. Simple pine furniture, blue gingham table-cloths. Nautical theme prevails. Keen use of island produce with seafood base.

St Anne *C.I.*

⌂ **Farm Court** without rest., Le Petit Val, GY9 3UX, ℰ (01481) 822075, relax@farmcourt-alderney.co.uk, Fax (01481) 822075, � – ⅍⅍. **MO** ⓪ **VISA**. ⅋
closed 1 week Christmas – **9 rm** ⴹ ✸78.00/140.00.
♦ Converted stone farm buildings around cobbled courtyard and garden. Sitting room and breakfast room. Spacious well-appointed bedrooms with contemporary and antique furniture.

⌂ **Maison Bourgage** without rest., 2 Le Bourgage, GY9 3TL, ℰ (01481) 824097, info@maisonbourgage.com, � – ⅍⅍ ✆, **MO** **VISA**. ⅋
closed December-January – **3 rm** ⴹ ✸42.00/62.00 – ✸✸56.00/76.00.
♦ Part Georgian house on quiet, cobbled, town centre street. Neat, enclosed decked patio and garden face south. Leather furnished lounge and breakfast room. Bright, airy rooms.

GUERNSEY

C.I. **503** OP 33 and **517** ⑨ ⑩ *The West Country G.* – pop. 58 867

See: Island★ – Pezeries Point★★ – Icart Point★★ – Côbo Bay★★ – St Martin's Point★★ – St Apolline's Chapel★ – Vale Castle★ – Fort Doyle★ – La Gran'mere du Chimquiere★ – Roc-quaine Bay★ – Jerbourg Point★ .

✈ *Service Air ℰ (01481) 237766, Aurigny Air ℰ (0871) 871 0717.*

🚢 from St Peter Port to France (St Malo) and Jersey (St Helier) (Condor Ferries Ltd) – from St Peter Port to Jersey (St Helier) and Weymouth (Condor Ferries Ltd).

🚢 – from St Peter Port to France (St Malo) and Jersey (St Helier) (Condor Ferries Ltd) 2 weekly – from St Peter Port to France (Dielette) (Emeraude Lines) (summer only) (1 h 15 mn) – from St Peter Port to Herm (Herm Seaway) (25 mn) – from St Peter Port to Sark (Isle of Sark Shipping Co. Ltd) (45 mn) – from St Peter Port to Jersey (St Helier) (Emeraude Lines) (50 mn) – from St Peter Port to Jersey (St Helier) (Condor Ferries Ltd) daily.

🚩 *P.O. Box 23, North Esplanade ℰ (01481) 723552 – Passenger Terminal, New Jetty ℰ (01481) 715885.*

Catel/Castel *C.I.*

🏨 **Hougue du Pommier** ⌕, Hougue du Pommier Rd, GY5 7FQ, ℰ (01481) 256531, hotel@houguedupommier.guernsey.net, Fax (01481) 256260, � , ⅀s , ⬛ heated, 🌸 , ⅌ – ⅍⅍ **P**. **MO** **VISA**
Tudor Bar : **Rest** a la carte 12.20/17.85 – *The Restaurant* : **Rest** (dinner only and Sunday lunch)/dinner 21.95 and a la carte 22.95/34.45 – **43 rm** ⴹ ✸52.50/79.50 – ✸✸85.00/135.00.
♦ A personally run 18C farmhouse with later extensions. Lovely outdoor pool and decking area. Occasional medieval banquets. Comfortable bedrooms, warmly decorated. Restaurant with beams and oak panelling. Tudor Bar for unique Feu du Bois cooking over open flame.

🏨 **Cobo Bay**, Cobo Coast Rd, GY5 7HB, ℰ (01481) 257102, reservations@cobobayho tel.com, Fax (01481) 254542, ⩽, ⅀s – ⅃ ⅍⅍, ▤ rest, **P**. **MO** **AE** **VISA**. ⅋
closed January-February – **Rest** (dinner only and Sunday lunch)/dinner 16.50/22.50 – **36 rm** ⴹ ✸44.00/89.00 – ✸✸68.00/118.00.
♦ Modern hotel on peaceful, sandy Cobo Bay; an ideal location for families. The rooms are pleasant with bright décor and some have the delightful addition of seaview balconies. Romantic dining with views of sunsets.

🏨 **Harton Lodge**, Rue de Galaad, GY5 7FJ, ℰ (01481) 256341, Fax (01481) 255716, 🌸 , ⅀s , ⬛ – ⅍⅍ **P**. **MO** **VISA**
Rest (bar lunch)/dinner 20.00 s. – **20 rm** ⴹ ✸50.00/60.00 – ✸✸60.00/100.00.
♦ Sunny yellow painted house with a neat and tidy appeal; close to beach. Two bars, one with a pool table. Decking to rear with small pool and sauna. Bright bedrooms. Linen-laid dining room: conservatory extension boasts comfy leather sofas.

Fermain Bay *C.I.*

Fermain Valley �, Fort Rd, GY4 6SD, ℰ (01481) 235666, *info@fermainvalley.com*, Fax (01481) 235413, ≤, 佘, ⊜s, ⬚, 〒 – ♦ ♢, ■ rest, 📺 ◩ ℙ ⬚ ㎈ 瓬
Restaurant : Rest (dinner only and Sunday lunch) a la carte 23.75/31.25 ⊻ – **Brasserie :** Rest a la carte 20.50/25.95 ⊻ – **45 rm** ⬚ ✱✱160.00 = ✱✱200.00.
• Fine sea views through the trees. Smart contemporary country house theme prevails: sleek lounges, decked terrace, library, and fresh, carefully appointed rooms with balconies. Fine dining in comfortable Restaurant. Fresh fish and simple grills at the Brasserie

XXX **Christophe** (Vincent), Fort Rd, GY1 1ZP, ℰ (01481) 230725, Fax (01481) 230726, ≤, 佘, ❀ – ♦ ℙ ♢ 12. ㎈ ㎈ 瓬
❀ *closed 2 weeks February, 2 weeks November, Sunday dinner and Monday –* **Rest** 18.50 (lunch) and a la carte 29.00/46.00 ⊻.
Spec. Lobster, crab, truffle and yolk cone on pea purée. Roast veal fillet, lobster ravioli and morel sauce. Banana dessert.
• This seriously comfortable restaurant has fine sea views and serves innovative, tasty dishes with a firmly classic Gallic base: most produce from quality French suppliers.

Forest *C.I. – pop. 1 386.*

⌂ **Maison Bel Air** without rest., Le Chene, GY8 0AL, ℰ (01481) 238503, *juliette@maisonbelair.com*, Fax (01481) 239403, ❀ – ♦ ℙ ㎈ ㎈ 瓬
closed November and December – **6 rm** ⬚ ✱25.00/40.00 – ✱✱46.00/62.00.
• Welcoming peach and white guesthouse, near airport; overlooking Petit Bot Valley with shady, peaceful, south facing garden. Smart breakfast room. Comfortable bedrooms.

Kings Mills *C.I.*

🛏 **Fleur du Jardin** with rm, GY5 7JT, ℰ (01481) 257996, *info@fleurdujardin.com*, Fax (01481) 256874, 佘, ⬚ heated, ❀ – ♦ rest, ℙ ㎈ ㎈ 瓬, ❀
closed dinner 25 and 26 December – **Rest** (bar lunch)/dinner a la carte 20.00/26.00 ⊻ – **17 rm** ⬚ ✱47.50/70.00 – ✱✱78.00/116.00.
• Daily menus of local seafood give this granite 15C inn a standing of quiet renown. Cosy interior: rough hewn walls, alcoves, stone fireplace. Cottagey, traditional rooms.

St Martin *C.I. – pop. 6 082.*
St Peter Port 2.

🏨 **Bon Port** ⚎, Moulin Huet Bay, GY4 6EW, ℰ (01481) 239249, *mail@bonport.com*, Fax (01481) 239596, ≤ Moulin Huet Bay and Jerbourg Point, 佘, ⬚, ❀ – ♦ ℙ ㎈ 瓬
closed January-February – **Rest** (bar lunch Monday-Saturday)/dinner 24.95 and a la carte 25.50/50.50 – **21 rm** ⬚ ✱50.00/105.00 – ✱✱65.00/175.00, 1 suite.
• Perched on the top of the cliff, with a commanding view of the bay, this hotel is very keenly and personally run. Rooms vary in size and style and some have balconies. Large two tier dining room with bay views.

🏨 **Jerbourg** ⚎, Jerbourg Point, GY4 6BJ, ℰ (01481) 238826, *stay@hoteljerbourg.com*, Fax (01481) 238238, ≤ sea and neighbouring Channel Islands, 佘, ⬚, ❀ – ♦, ■ rest, ℙ. ㎈ 瓬 ❀
mid March- October – **Rest** (bar lunch Monday-Saturday)/dinner and a la carte 16.85/28.85 s. ⊻ – **30 rm** ⬚ ✱40.00/85.00 – ✱✱100.00/170.00.
• In a prime position for walks to sandy bays. Popular terrace for afternoon teas. Equipped with solar heated outdoor pool and garden patio. Most rooms have pleasant sea views. Finely presented, fish based cuisine.

🏨 **La Barbarie** ⚎, Saints Bay, GY4 6ES, ℰ (01481) 235217, *reservations@labarbariehotel.com*, Fax (01481) 235208, 佘, ⬚ heated, ❀ – ♦ ℙ ㎈ 瓬 ❀
10 March-October – **Rest** (carvery lunch Sunday) 19.95 (dinner) and a la carte 19.15/27.20 – **22 rm** ⬚ ✱52.00/70.00 – ✱✱64.00/99.00, 1 suite.
• Stone-built former farmhouse with a welcoming, cottagey style. Characterful bar; well-kept pool and terrace. Eclectic range of rooms, including 10 larger annexed apartments. Mediterranean buzz from the restaurant.

🏨 **Saints Bay** ⚎, Icart, GY4 6JG, ℰ (01481) 238888, *info@saintsbayhotel.com*, Fax (01481) 235558, 佘, ⬚ heated, ❀ – rm, ℙ ㎈ ㎈ ⓞ 瓬 ❀
Rest (bar lunch Monday-Saturday)/dinner 18.50 and a la carte 16.50/24.75 – **35 rm** ⬚ ✱34.50/74.50 – ✱✱69.00/128.00.
• Located on Icart Point, overlooking Fisherman's Harbour, the southern tip of the island, perfect for cliff top walks. Multilingual staff; neat bedrooms with all amenities. Broad choice of menus.

🏨 **La Michele** ⚎, Les Hubits, GY4 6NB, ℰ (01481) 238065, *info@lamichelehotel.com*, Fax (01481) 239492, ⬚ heated, ❀ – ♦ ℙ ㎈ 瓬 ❀
Easter-10 October – **Rest** (residents only) (dinner only) 15.50 – **16 rm** (dinner included) ⬚ ✱39.00/56.00 – ✱✱78.00/112.00.
• Painted and canopied façade with conservatory lounge and secluded garden. Lovely seating area around the pool. Fermain bay is nearby; pleasant, unfussy bedrooms.

Sunnydene ⌂, Rue des Marettes, GY4 6JH, ✆ (01481) 236870, *info@sunnydenecoun tryhotel.com, Fax (01481) 237468*, ☒ heated, ☞, ☞ – ☒ ☒ ☒ ☒ ☒ ☒
Easter-early October – **Rest** (dinner only) 15.00 s. **20 rm** ☒ ☒40.00/60.00 –
☒☒66.00/80.00.
◆ Neat and tidy hotel with pitch and putt to rear of garden! Comfortable, homely lounge; linen-laid dining room. Pretty pool and terrace area. Rooms in house or garden.

The Auberge, Jerbourg Rd, GY4 6BH, ✆ (01481) 238485, *theauberge@cwgsy.net, Fax (01481) 238485*, ≤ Sea and neighbouring Channel Islands, ☞, ☞ – ☒ ☒ ☒ ☒ ☒ ☒
VISA
closed 25 December – **Rest** (booking essential) a la carte 24.65/31.70 ☒.
◆ A splendid spot to sample contemporary brasserie-style dishes. Modern informal style, attractive terrace and excellent views of sea and islands.

St Peter Port C.I. *The West Country G.* – pop. 16 648.

See : *Town*★★ – *St Peter's Church*★ Z – *Hauteville House*★ AC Z – *Castle Cornet*★ (≤★) AC Z.
Env. : *Saumarez Park*★ (*Guernsey Folk Museum*★), W : 2 m. by road to Catel Z – *Little Chapel*★, SW : 2¼ m. by Mount Durand road Z.
🖎 Rohais, St Pierre Park ✆ (01481) 727039, Z.

Plan on next page

Old Government House, St Ann's Pl, GY1 2NU, ✆ (01481) 724921, *ogh@theoghho tel.com, Fax (01481) 724429*, ≤, ⓥ, ☒, ☒, ☒ heated, ☞ – ☒ ☒ ☒ ☒ ☒ ☒ 300. ☒☒
☒ ☒ *VISA*. ☞
Governors : **Rest** (booking essential) 13.50/18.50 and a la carte 27.50/32.50 s. ☒ – *The Brasserie :* **Rest** a la carte 24.75/31.75 s. – **63 rm** ☒ ☒105.00/125.00 – ☒☒185.00/245.00.
◆ Refurbished hotel in 18C house, built for island governors. State-of-art leisure facilities. Conservatory is popular for tea. Comfortable rooms, some boasting harbour views. Impressively spacious Governors. Informal Mediterranean favourites at the Brasserie.

Duke of Richmond, Cambridge Park, GY1 1UY, ✆ (01481) 726221, *duke@guern sey.net, Fax (01481) 728945*, ≤, ☞, ☒ heated – ☒ ☒ – ☒ 120. ☒☒ ☒ ☒ *VISA*
Rest (closed lunch Monday-Friday) 13.50/19.95 and a la carte 24.10/28.40 s. – **73 rm** ☒
☒60.00/80.00 – ☒☒120.00/155.00, 1 suite.
◆ Boasts views over Candie Gardens. Equipped with rooms of pine and co-ordinated furnishings. Rear rooms overlook pool and gardens. Resident band plays in the ballroom. Basement dining room.

Les Rocquettes, Les Gravees, GY1 1RN, West : 1 m. by St Julian's Ave and Grange Rd
✆ (01481) 722146, *rocquettes@sarniahotels.com, Fax (01481) 714543*, ☒, ☒, ☒, ☞ –
☒, ☒ rest, ☒ – ☒ 100. ☒☒ ☒ ☒ *VISA*. ☞
Rest (bar lunch Monday-Saturday)/dinner 18.50 and a la carte 19.25/25.00 – **51 rm** ☒
☒47.00/95.00 – ☒☒94.00/132.00.
◆ Stately mansion with impressive health suite. Well-equipped bedrooms of various shapes and sizes. Superior rooms have balconies; others overlook the rear garden. Early suppers for children in dining room.

De Havelet, Havelet, GY1 1BA, ✆ (01481) 722199, *havelet@sarniahotels.com, Fax (01481) 714057*, ☒, ☒, ☞ –☒ ☒, ☒ rest, ☒ ☒ ☒ ☒ ☒ ☒
Wellington Boot : **Rest** (dinner only and Sunday lunch)/dinner 22.00 and a la carte
22.00/33.00 – *Havelet Grill :* **Rest** (closed Sunday lunch and Monday dinner) 22.50 and a la carte 18.50/32.00 s. – **34 rm** ☒ ☒48.00/105.00 – ☒☒82.00/140.00.
◆ Comfortable rooms, fine gardens and a hilltop location are among the many appealing features of this hotel. Elegant indoor pool and a courtesy bus for trips into town. Wellington Boot is in a converted coach house. Informal Havelet Grill.

La Frégate ⌂, Les Cotils, GY1 1UT, ✆ (01481) 724624, *enquiries@lafregatehotel.com, Fax (01481) 720443*, ≤ town harbour and neighbouring Channel Islands, ☞, ☞ – ☒ rest,
☒ rest, ☒ ☒ – ☒ 25. ☒☒ ☒ ☒ *VISA*
The Restaurant : **Rest** 17.95/27.50 and a la carte 18.65/44.00 ☒ – **11 rm** ☒ ☒85.00/170.00
– ☒☒185.00.
◆ Kaleidoscopic views of harbour life and St Peter Port to be savoured from large windows in most bedrooms in this charming hillside hotel. Peaceful location; modern interior. Stylish restaurant with lovely terrace.

L'Escalier, 6 Tower Hill, GY1 1DF, ✆ (01481) 710088, *armelleetdean@hotmail.com, Fax (01481) 710878*, ☞ – ☒ ☒. ☒☒ *VISA*
closed Saturday lunch and Monday – **Rest** a la carte 26.00/37.50 s ☒.
◆ Tucked away in the old quarter of town, a personally run restaurant with a sheltered terrace and attentive service. Complex dishes use both local and French produce.

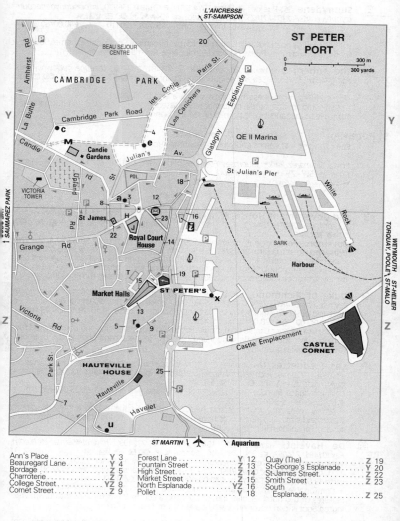

XX **Saltwater**, Albert Pier, GY1 1AD, ℰ (01481) 720823, info@saltwater.gg, Fax (01481) 772702, ≤ – ✳ ☰, ⓜⓒ 🅰🅴 𝑉𝐼𝑆𝐴
Z x
closed 23 December - 7 January, Saturday lunch and Sunday – Rest - Seafood specialities - 15.00 and a la carte approx 34.95.
♦ Warmly run restaurant in impressive location at end of historic pier overlooking harbour near large marina. Modern feel. Extensive menus have a solid seafood slant.

XX **The Absolute End**, Longstore, GY1 2BG, North : ¾ m. by St George's Esplanade ℰ (01481) 723822, Fax (01481) 729129, ㅁ – ✿ 16. ⓜⓒ 𝑉𝐼𝑆𝐴
closed 26 December - 25 January and Sunday – Rest - Seafood specialities - 15.00 (lunch) and a la carte 24.00/43.00.
♦ Distinctive whitewashed house just out of town. Inspired freshly cooked seafood dishes, prepared with flair, served by friendly staff. Lovely enclosed decked terrace to rear.

St Saviour C.I. – pop. 2 419.
St Peter Port 4.

🏨 **Atlantique,** Perelle Bay, GY7 9NA, ✆ (01481) 264056, *enquiries@perellebay.com*, Fax (01481) 263800, ≤, ⚓ heated, 🌳 – ❌, 🍴 rest, 🅿. ⬤⬤ VISA ❄
closed mid December-February – **Atlantique :** Rest (dinner only) 15.95/24.95 and a la carte 17.00/35.95 ♀ – **22 rm** ☸ ✚40.00/90.00 – ✚✚60.00/130.00, 1 suite.
◆ Traditionally styled hotel in a delightful spot on Perelle Bay, only a few metres from the sea: fine views from front-facing rooms. Charmingly formal Atlantique.

✗ **The Pavilion,** Le Gron, GY7 9RN, ✆ (01481) 264165, *lecknleck@cwgsy.net*,
☕ Fax (01481) 267396, ☕, 🌳 – ❌ 🅿. ⬤⬤ VISA
closed Monday in winter, Christmas and January – Rest (lunch only) a la carte 18.85/24.85 ♀.
◆ Located in grounds of jewellers Bruce Russell and Son. Pleasant interior of exposed stone and beams. Excellent value, well executed dishes using good quality local produce.

Vazon Bay C.I. – ✉ Catel.

🏨 **La Grande Mare,** Vazon Coast Rd, GY5 7LL, ✆ (01481) 256576, *hotellagrande mare@cwgsy.net*, Fax (01481) 256532, ≤, ☕, 🎱, ☎, ⚓ heated, 🔲, 🎱, ☏, 🌳, 🍷, ✗ – 🔞 ❌ 🅿 – ⚒ 30. ⬤⬤ ⬤⬤ VISA ❄
Rest 16.95/22.50 and a la carte 24.15/36.45 ♀ – **12 rm** ☸ ✚93.00/119.00 – ✚✚166.00/186.00, **12 suites** ☸ 218.00/250.00.
◆ Resort complex with large bedrooms of magnolia and pine furnishings; some have balconies, some well-equipped small kitchens. Family friendly, with indoor/outdoor activities. Formal dining room overlooks golf course.

😊 Look out for red symbols, indicating particularly pleasant establishments.

HERM
C.I. **503** P 33 and **517** ⑩ The West Country G. – pop. 97

See: Le Grand Monceau★.

🚢 to Guernsey (St Peter Port) (Herm Seaway) (20 mn).

🏨 **White House** 🌿, GY1 3HR, ✆ (01481) 722159, *hotel@herm-island.com*, Fax (01481) 710066, ≤ Belle Greve Bay and Guernsey, ☕, ⚓ heated, 🌳, ☏, ✗ – ❌ rest. ⬤⬤ ☒ VISA ❄
closed 29 March-7 October – **Conservatory :** Rest (booking essential) 24.50 (dinner) and lunch a la carte 21.85/25.90 – **Ship Inn :** Rest (closed Sunday dinner) (bar lunch)/dinner 18.00 – **40 rm** (dinner included) ☸ ✚76.00/130.00 – ✚✚228.00.
◆ Hotel with real country house feel: offset by verdant hills, the beach extends to the door. Guernsey and Jethou can be viewed from the hushed lounge. Attractive rooms. Formal Conservatory with seafood emphasis. Relaxed Ship Inn.

JERSEY
C.I. **503** 0P 33 and **517** ⑩ The West Country G. – pop. 87 500

See: Island★★ – Jersey Zoo★★ AC – Jersey Museum★ – Eric Young Orchid Foundation★ – St Catherine's Bay★ (≤★★) – Grosnez Point★ – Devil's Hole★ – St Matthews Church, Millbrook (glasswork★) – La Hougue Bie★ (Neolithic tomb★ AC) – Waterworks Valley - Hamptonne Country Life Museum★ – St Catherine's Bay★ (≤★★) – Noirmont Point★.

🛬 States of Jersey Airport : ✆ (01534) 492000.

🚢 from St Helier to France (St Malo) and Guernsey (St Peter Port) (Condor Ferries Ltd) – from St Helier to Sark (Condor Ferries Ltd) (50 mn) – from St Helier to Guernsey (St Peter Port) and Weymouth (Condor Ferries Ltd).

🚢 from St Helier to France (St Malo) (Condor Ferries Ltd) (summer only) – from St Helier to France (St Malo) (Condor Ferries Ltd) 3 weekly – from Gorey to France (Carteret) (Emeraude Lines) (summer only) (30-40 mn) – from St Helier to Guernsey (St Peter Port) (Condor Ferries Ltd) (50 mn) – from St Helier to Guernsey (St Peter Port) (Condor Ferries Ltd) daily.

🚺 Liberation Sq, St Helier ✆ (01534) 500777.

Beaumont C.I.

✗ **Bistro Soleil,** La Route de la Haule, JE3 7BA, ✆ (01534) 720249, Fax (01534) 625621, ≤ St Aubins Bay, ☕ – 🅿. ⬤⬤ ☒ VISA
closed 25-26 December, Sunday dinner, Monday and Bank Holidays – Rest 16.85/25.50 and a la carte 22.10/26.45 ♀.
◆ Series of connected rooms with superb views over St Aubins Bay. Minimalist style: just a couple of modern pictures. Freshly prepared, bold menus with Mediterranean accent.

Bouley Bay *C.I..*
St Helier 6.

🏨 **The Water's Edge,** JE3 5AS, 🖉 (01534) 862777, *mail@watersedgehotel.co.je*, ≤ Bouley Bay, ⌥ heated, ☞ – 🛄, ✦ rest, ℙ – 🔒 40. 🐠 🖭 🖭 *VISA*. ✦
early April-mid October – **Waterside :** Rest (dinner only) 23.00 and a la carte 29.95/37.40 – **Black Dog Bar :** Rest a la carte 15.40/21.35 **s.** – **47 rm** ⌥ ✦42.00/93.00 – ✦✦104.00/156.00, 3 suites.
✦ Refurbished, revitalised hotel of long standing that boasts breathtaking bay views. Secluded garden with well-manicured lawns. Comfortable, well-appointed accommodation. Formal Waterside for tables-with-a-view. Black Dog Bar with quarterdeck al fresco area.

Gorey *C.I. The West Country G.* – ✉ St Martin.
See : Mont Orgueil Castle★ (≤★★) AC – Jersey Pottery★.
St Helier 4.

🏨 **Old Court House,** Gorey Village, JE3 9FS, 🖉 (01534) 854444, *ochhotel@itl.net*, Fax (01534) 853587, ⇌, ⌥ heated, ☞ – 🛄 ℙ, 🐠 *VISA*
April-October – **Rest** (residents only) (bar lunch)/dinner 18.00 – **58 rm** ⌥ ✦46.00/63.50 – ✦✦92.00/127.00.
✦ A popular, spacious hotel opposite three miles of sandy beach of the Royal Bay of Grouville. Large balconies in the second and third floor bedrooms. Pleasant gardens. Part 15C dining room: low beamed ceilings, exposed granite walls.

🏠 **Moorings,** Gorey Pier, JE3 6EW, 🖉 (01534) 853633, *reservations@themooringshotel.com*, Fax (01534) 857618 – ▤ rest. 🐠 🖭 *VISA*
Rest 20.50/27.50 and a la carte 28.00/52.50 ♀ – **16 rm** ⌥ ✦47.00/84.00 – ✦✦94.00/118.00.
✦ Located at the base of Gorey Castle, overlooking the waterfront, once the heart of the oyster fishing industry. Well-priced; the first floor bedrooms have terraces. Pleasant decked area at front of restaurant.

XX **Jersey Pottery (Garden Restaurant),** Gorey Village, JE3 9EP, 🖉 (01534) 850850, *enquiries@jerseypottery.com*, Fax (01534) 856403, ㊟, ☞ – ℙ. 🐠 🖭 *VISA*. ✦
closed January-March, and Sunday – **Rest** - Seafood specialities - (lunch only) 19.50 and a la carte 23.50/41.00 **s.** ♀ ㊟.
✦ Unusual restaurant in a working pottery: polished service and an impressive choice of seafood specialities. Dine among rich foliage in the orangery-style covered terrace.

XX **Suma's,** Gorey Hill, JE3 6ET, 🖉 (01534) 853291, Fax (01534) 851913, ≤ Gorey harbour and castle, ㊟ – ▤. 🐠 🖭 🖭 *VISA*
closed Christmas-New Year – **Rest** (booking essential) 15.00 (lunch) and a la carte 25.00/40.00 **s.** ♀ ㊟.
✦ Cheerful and contemporary; fine terrace views of Gorey Castle and harbour. Dishes are carefully prepared and innovatively presented; pleasant service enhances the enjoyment.

X **Village Bistro,** Gorey Village, JE3 9EP, 🖉 (01534) 853429, *thevillagebistro@yahoo.co.uk*, ㊟ Fax (01534) 858730, ㊟ – ✦. 🐠 *VISA*
closed 3 weeks November, Sunday dinner and Monday – **Rest** 14.50/17.50 (lunch) and a la carte 21.65/28.25.
✦ Local produce sourced daily from small suppliers. Unpretentious feel; interesting choices to be made, particularly of seafood dishes.

Green Island *C.I.*

X **Green Island,** St Clement, JE2 6LS, 🖉 (01534) 857787, *greenislandrestaurant@jersey mail.co.uk*, ㊟ – 🐠 *VISA*
closed 20 December-mid March, Sunday dinner and Monday – **Rest** - Seafood specialities - (booking essential) a la carte 23.85/32.90.
✦ Lovely location on the beach; coir carpeted, nautically fitted restaurant with wide ranging, daily changing menu at affordable prices. Welcoming, casual atmosphere.

Grève De Lecq *C.I.* – ✉ St Ouen.

🏠 **Des Pierres** without rest., JE3 2DT, on B 65 🖉 (01534) 481858, *despierres@jersey hols.com*, Fax (01534) 485273 – ℙ. 🐠 *VISA*. ✦
closed mid November-mid February – **16 rm** ⌥ ✦33.50/52.00 – ✦✦58.00/64.00.
✦ A personally run hotel, well situated for exploring the north of the island; close to the old smuggling harbour of Grève de Lecq. Simply furnished rooms; some have views.

Grouville *C.I.*
St Helier 3.

✗ **Cafe Poste**, La Rue de la ville ES Renauds, JE3 9FY, ✆ (01534) 859696, ☂ – ✝✗ **P.** **⬢⬢** **VISA**
closed 2 weeks mid November Monday and Tuesday – **Rest** (booking essential) a la carte 24.15/32.25.
   ◆ Former post office and general store with hidden decked area for outdoor dining. Very much a neighbourhood favourite. Strong use of island produce on eclectic, modish menus.

La Haule *C.I.* – ✉ St Brelade.

🏨 **La Place** ⬡, Route du Coin, JE3 8BT, by B 25 on B 43 ✆ (01534) 744261, *reserva tions@hotellaplacejersey.com*, Fax (01534) 745164, ☂, ⬆s, ⌇ heated, ✿ – ✝✗ ✔ **P.** – **⬢** 100, **⬢⬢** **AE** **①** **VISA**
closed January – **The Retreat** : Rest (dinner only and Sunday lunch) 35.00 and a la carte 24.00/45.00 ⵢ – **42 rm** ⵤ ✦50.00/135.00 – ✦✦125.00/150.00.
   ◆ Built round the remains of a 17C farmhouse; peaceful gardens and pool. Suited to both holiday makers and business clientele; spacious rooms, includes executive study rooms. Medieval inspired restaurant and adjoining conservatory.

🏨 **La Haule Manor** without rest., St Aubin's Bay, JE3 8BS, ✆ (01534) 746013, *lahaulema nor@jerseymail.co.uk*, Fax (01534) 745501, ≤ St Aubin's Fort and Bay, ✿ – ✝✗ **P.** **⬢⬢** **VISA**.
⬡
10 rm ✦65.00/80.00 – ✦✦70.00/100.00.
   ◆ Attractive, extended Georgian house with fine coastal outlook. Period style sitting room; stylish breakfast room; large basement bar. Airy, well-kept bedrooms with good view.

🏠 **Au Caprice**, Route de la Haule, JE3 8BA, on A 1 ✆ (01534) 722083, *aucaprice@jersey mail.co.uk*, Fax (01534) 280058 – ✝✗ **⬢⬢** **VISA** **①**. ⬡
April-October – **Rest** (by arrangement) 9.00 – **12 rm** ⵤ ✦42.00/45.00 – ✦✦43.00/64.00.
   ◆ Clean-lined white guesthouse with French windows; light and airy, providing homely good value rooms; two of them share large balcony at the front. Close to large sandy beach. Each morning, guests told dining room menu.

La Pulente *C.I.* – ✉ St Brelade.
🏌 Les Mielles G. & C.C., St Ouens Bay ✆ (01534) 482787.
St Helier 7.

🏨 **Atlantic** ⬡, Le Mont de la Pulente, JE3 8HE, on B 35 ✆ (01534) 744101, *info@theatlanti chotel.com*, Fax (01534) 744102, ≤, ☂, ⶡⱶ, ⬆s, ⌇ heated, ☒, ✿, ✗ – |⬧|, ✝✗ rest, ✔ **P.**
⬢ – ⬢ 60, **⬢⬢** **AE** **①** **VISA**. ⬡
⬡ closed 2 January-2 February – **Ocean** : Rest (booking essential) 19.50/47.50 – **49 rm** ⵤ ✦145.00/185.00 – ✦✦190.00/550.00, 1 suite.
   Spec. Scallops with a pea purée, sticky oxtail and purple cress. Tranche of turbot with creamed cabbage and sautéed langoustine. New season raspberries with nougatine wafers and pistachio cream.
   ◆ Privately owned luxury hotel fringed by gardens. Stylish, modern rooms in pale, cool colours. Garden suites have own terrace; fine views from upper floors. Cool, clean restaurant; chef an ambassador of Jersey's fine larder; attentive, high calibre service.

La Rocque *C.I.*
St Helier 8.

✗✗ **Borsalino Rocque**, JE3 9FF, ✆ (01534) 852111, *reservations@borsalinorocque.com*, Fax (01534) 856404, ☂ – **P.** **⬢⬢** **AE** **VISA**
closed 25-26 December and Tuesday – **Rest** - Seafood - 23.50 and a la carte 19.25/31.05.
   ◆ Well-spaced tables in large conservatory and dining room filled with curios. A long-established family business, popular with island residents. Wide choice in menus.

Rozel Bay *C.I.* – ✉ St Martin.
St Helier 6.

🏨 **Chateau La Chaire** ⬡, Rozel Valley, JE3 6AJ, ✆ (01534) 863354, *res@chateau-la-chaire.co.uk*, Fax (01534) 865137, ☂, ✿ – ✝✗ ✔ **P.** **⬢⬢** **AE** **①** **VISA**. ⬡
Rest 27.95 (dinner) and a la carte 28.85/39.85 – **12 rm** ⵤ ✦84.50/127.00 –
✦✦191.00/274.00, 2 suites.
   ◆ Imposing chateau dated 1843, rich in paintings and antiques: individually decorated bedrooms overlook the quiet wooded grounds. Ornate sitting room. Conservatory dining room; terrace popular in summer.

197

🏫 **Beau Couperon,** JE3 6AN, ℰ (01534) 865522, *beaucouperon@southernhotels.com,* Fax (01534) 865332, ≤, ⊥ heated – ⇝ rest, 🅿 🕸 🆎 ⓞ 𝑉𝐼𝑆𝐴 . 𝒮𝒺
4 April - 29 October – **Rest** 13.10/15.30 (lunch) and a la carte 24.50/43.30 **s.** ⵏ – **32 rm** ⊂⊃ ✶64.20/120.60 – ✶✶128.40/160.40.
♦ A converted Napoleonic fortress with splendid views of the bay and harbour. The famous zoo and wildlife trust are very close by. Most of the well-sized rooms have balconies. Cool blue dining room with sea views.

XX **Le Frère,** Le Mont de Rozel, JE3 6AN, East : ½ m. on B 38 ℰ (01534) 861000, *lefrere@jer seymail.co.uk,* Fax (01534) 864007, ≤ Sea and French coastline, 🎄, 🌿 – ⇝ 🅿 ⇄ 50. 🕸 🆎 𝑉𝐼𝑆𝐴 . 𝒮𝒺
closed January, Sunday dinner and Monday – **Rest** - Seafood specialities - 15.00 (lunch) and a la carte 18.25/40.00 ⵏ.
♦ Dine alfresco with the sea breeze on your face or inside with views from panoramic windows. Menus with strong fish base. Classic style and service.

St Aubin *C.I. – ⊠ St Brelade.*
St Helier 4.

🏫 **Somerville,** Mont du Boulevard, JE3 8AD, South : ¾ m. via harbour ℰ (01534) 741226, *somerville@dolanhotels.com,* Fax (01534) 746621, ≤ St Aubin's Bay, ⊥ heated, 🌿 – ⒾⓈ, ⇝ rest, ▤ rest, 🅿 🕸 🆎 𝑉𝐼𝑆𝐴 . 𝒮𝒺
Tides : Rest 12.50/25.00 and a la carte 26.40/33.95 **s.** ⵏ – **58 rm** ⊂⊃ ✶124.20/151.20 – ✶✶138.00/168.00.
♦ Delightful views of the harbour, bay and village. Courtesy bus runs from hotel into town. Evening entertainment laid on. Cheerful rooms, some in superior style. Cloth clad, classic dining room.

🏠 **Panorama** without rest., La Rue du Crocquet, JE3 8BZ, ℰ (01534) 742429, *info@panor amajersey.com,* Fax (01534) 745940, ≤ St Aubin's Fort and Bay, 🌿 – ⇝ 🕾, 🕸 🆎 ⓞ 𝑉𝐼𝑆𝐴 . 𝒮𝒺
March - October – **14 rm** ⊂⊃ ✶36.00/76.00 – ✶✶92.00/122.00.
♦ Personally run hotel with conservatory, garden and bay views. Also boasts a teapot collection. The superior style bedrooms are very pleasant. All rooms boast good amenities.

⌂ **Sabots d'or,** High St, JE3 8BZ, ℰ (01534) 43732, *sandralecorre@yahoo.co.uk,* Fax (01534) 490142 – ⇝ rest. 🕸 𝑉𝐼𝑆𝐴
closed 1 week Christmas-New Year, October and February half-terms **Rest** (by arrangement) 12.00 – **12 rm** ⊂⊃ ✶24.00/40.00 – ✶✶52.00/62.00.
♦ Traditional floral furnishings in homely and cosy bedrooms. Well located for shops, watersports; its cobbled high street position not far from picturesque harbour. Homemade desserts a dining room highlight.

⌂ **Porthole Cottage** without rest., La Route au Moestre (Market Hill), JE3 8AE, ℰ (01534) 745007, *portcott@itl.net,* Fax (01534) 490336, ≤, 🌿 – 🅿 🕸 𝑉𝐼𝑆𝐴 . 𝒮𝒺
April-12 October – **11 rm** ⊂⊃ ✶24.00/64.00 – ✶✶48.00/79.00.
♦ Brick and stone guesthouse overlooking St Aubins harbour; shrub-filled, elevated rear garden. Nautically inspired breakfast room with beams and galley window. Cottagey rooms.

🍴 **Old Court House Inn** with rm, St Aubin's Harbour, JE3 8AB, ℰ (01534) 746433, Fax (01534) 745103, ≤, 🎄 – 🕸 🆎 ⓞ 𝑉𝐼𝑆𝐴
Rest 10.00 and a la carte 25.00/50.00 ⵏ – **9 rm** ⊂⊃ ✶40.00/60.00 – ✶✶40.00/120.00.
♦ Atmospheric quayside inn, once a courthouse and merchant's house, dating from 15C. Bar featured in Bergerac TV series. Cosmopolitan menu with seafood emphasis. Neat bedrooms.

St Brelade's Bay *C.I. The West Country G. – pop. 9 560 – ⊠ St Brelade.*
See : Fishermen's Chapel (frescoes★).
St Helier 6.

🏨 **L'Horizon,** JE3 8EF, ℰ (01534) 743101, *lhorizon@handpicked.co.uk,* Fax (01534) 746269, ≤ St Brelade's Bay, 🎄, ⓜ, 🏋, 🕾, 🏊 – ⒾⓈ, ⇝ rm, ▤ rest, ⅻ, ★★ 🅿 – 🔬 300. 🕸 🆎 ⓞ 𝑉𝐼𝑆𝐴 . 𝒮𝒺
Brasserie : Rest 30.00 (dinner) and a la carte 21.20/31.00 ⵏ – (see also **The Grill** below) – **99 rm** ⊂⊃ ✶60.00/175.00 – ✶✶160.00/220.00, 7 suites.
♦ Period hotel right on the beach and consequently popular for its stunning views from the terrace and some of its tastefully decorated front bedrooms. Serene indoor pool. Informal brasserie adjacent to the sea.

ENGLAND

🏨🏨 **St Brelade's Bay,** Rue de la Baie, JE3 8EF, ℰ (01534) 746141, *info@stbreladesbayho tel.com*, Fax (01534) 747278, ≤ St Brelade's Bay, ℐℴ, 🈺, 🔲 heated, 🐾, ※ – |韋| 🛖 P, 🅾🅾 AE VISA ✂
27 April-8 October – **Rest** 25.00/35.00 (dinner) and a la carte 18.00/35.00 – **69 rm** � ✦83.00/157.00 – ✦✦226.00/304.00, 3 suites.
◆ Traditional seafront hotel with mouth-watering views of bay and resplendent gardens with pool. Rattan furnished sitting room and spacious bedrooms. Friendly and family run. Front, sea-facing restaurant.

🏨 **Golden Sands,** La Route de la Baie, JE3 8EF, ℰ (01534) 741241, *goldensands@dolanho tels.com*, Fax (01534) 499366, ≤ – |韋|, 🛇 rest. 🅾🅾 AE VISA ✂
April-September – **Rest** (bar lunch)/dinner 21.00 and a la carte 17.85/23.85 – **62 rm** � ✦44.00/156.60 – ✦✦68.00/174.00.
◆ With adjacent sweep of a sandy bay and many of the bedrooms south-facing with balconies, this hotel is a popular spot. Within easy reach of the airport and St Helier. Seasonal menus.

XXX **The Grill** (at L'Horizon H.), JE3 8EF, ℰ (01534) 490082, Fax (01534) 746269, ≤ St Brelade's Bay, 🍽 – 🛇 ■ P, 🅾🅾 AE ① VISA
closed Sunday and Monday – **Rest** (dinner only) 29.50 ♀.
◆ Intimately styled grill room with tasteful cream and brown banquettes and framed photos of film stars. Seafood stars but faces competition from a strong suit of meat dishes.

St Helier *C.I. The West Country G.* – pop. 27 523.
   See : *Jersey Museum★ AC* Z – *Elizabeth Castle* (≤★) *AC* Z – *Fort Regent* (≤★ *AC*) Z.
   Env. : *St Peter's Valley - German Underground Hospital★ AC*, NW : 4 m. by A 1, A 11 St Peter's Valley rd and C 112.

Plan on next page

🏨🏨 **The Club Hotel & Spa,** Green St, JE2 4UH, ℰ (01534) 876500, *reservations@theclub jersey.com*, Fax (01534) 720371, 🄌, 🈺, 🔲 – |韋| 🛇 🍴 🄑 & P, – 🕰 30. 🅾🅾 AE ① VISA ✂   Z e
closed 24-29 December – **Rest** *(Saturday brunch)* a la carte 20.45/30.45 – (see also **Bohemia** below) – � 7.50 – **42 rm** ✦195.00 – ✦✦195.00, 4 suites.
◆ Above the Bohemia restaurant, a town house hotel of contemporary luxury with particularly pleasant roof terrace; the cosy bedrooms are fitted with many stylish mod cons. Small New York café style restaurant.

🏨🏨 **Hotel de France,** St Saviours Rd, JE1 7XP, ℰ (01534) 614000, *general@defrance.co.uk*, Fax (01534) 614999, 🍽, 🄌, ℐℴ, 🈺, 🔲, 🐾 – |韋| ■ P, – 🕰 800. 🅾🅾 AE ① VISA ✂   Y b
closed Christmas-New Year – **Gallery :** Rest *(closed Sunday)* (dinner only) 35.00 and a la carte 27.85/34.95 s. ♀ – **Café Aroma :** Rest 18.95 (dinner) and a la carte 21.70/28.30 ♀ – **277 rm** � ✦105.00/135.00 – ✦✦160.00/180.00, 8 suites.
◆ A well-located grand hotel with sweeping balustraded staircase leading to neatly furnished rooms. Cinema on complex and extensive range of business facilities. Gallery restaurant boasts intimate, fine dining experience. Informal Cafe Aroma.

🏨🏨 **Grand,** Esplanade, JE4 8WD, ℰ (01534) 722301, *grand.jersey@devere-hotels.com*, Fax (01534) 737815, ≤, ℐℴ, 🈺, 🔲 – |韋| 🛇 rest, 🕹 – 🕰 180. 🅾🅾 AE ① VISA ✂   Y u
The Regency : Rest (dinner only and Sunday lunch)/dinner a la carte approx 27.50 – **113 rm** � ✦90.00/170.00 – ✦✦150.00/200.00, 5 suites.
◆ Impressive Victorian hotel with pitched white façade overlooking St Aubins Bay. Elegant wing armchairs in smart lounge. Strong leisure facilities and comfortable bedrooms. Smart dining room.

🏨 **Eulah Country House** without rest., Mont Cochon, JE2 3JA, Northwest : 2 m. by A 1 on B 27 ℰ (01534) 626626, *eulah@jerseymail.co.uk*, Fax (01534) 626600, ≤ St Aubin's Bay, 🈺, 🔲 heated, 🐾 – 🛇 P, 🅾🅾 AE VISA ✂
11 rm � ✦105.00/125.00 – ✦✦190.00/230.00.
◆ Informally run Edwardian country house proves pleasantly unconventional. Stylish combined lounge and breakfast room, luxurious bedrooms and superb views of St Aubin's Bay.

↑ **La Bonne Vie** without rest., Roseville St, JE2 4PL, ℰ (01534) 735955, *labonnevieguest house@yahoo.com*, Fax (01534) 733357 – 🛇 🍴, 🅾🅾 VISA ✂   Z a
10 rm � ✦25.00/64.00 – ✦✦50.00/64.00.
◆ Floral fabrics and pastel colours enliven interiors in this "home from home" guesthouse. Comfy lounge and breakfast room. All bedrooms have showers; some have four posters.

XXX **Bohemia** (at The Club Hotel & Spa), Green St, JE2 4UH, ℰ (01534) 880588, *bohe mia@huggler.com*, Fax (01534) 875054 – 🛇 ■, 🅾🅾 AE ① VISA   Z e
🌼 *closed Sunday* – **Rest** (Saturday brunch) 19.50/52.00 ♀.
   Spec. Roast foie gras with mango and mint chutney. Lobster tail with macaroni, crab and fennel. Apple and vanilla assiette.
◆ Smart modern restaurant with a touch of West-End style: its bar is very popular at weekends. Original, contemporary cooking and very good service set the tone.

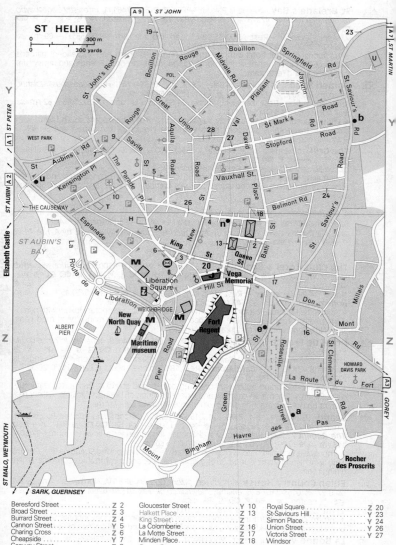

ST HELIER

XX   **La Capannina**, 65-67 Halkett Pl, JE2 4WG, ✆ (01534) 734602, *Fax (01534) 877628* – 🔲
🔄 16. 🅼🅂 🅰🄴 🄾 *VISA*   Z n
closed 10 days Christmas, Sunday and Bank Holidays – **Rest** - Italian - 14.00/22.00 and a la
carte 19.00/34.00.
   ◆ A buffet display of seafood and Parma ham preside over airy dining room with
prints of Venice and Pisa. Choose between Jersey fish and Italian pasta. Dessert from the
trolley.

St Lawrence C.I.

Cristina, Mont Felard, JE3 1JA, ℰ (01534) 758024, *cristina@dolanhotels.com,* Fax (01534) 758028, ≤, ⅃ heated, ⇆ – ⅍ rest, ℙ. ⑩ ㏂ 𝘝𝘐𝘚𝘈. ℅
April-October – *Indigo :* **Rest** (bar lunch)/dinner 23.00 and a la carte 16.65/27.90 ℤ – **63 rm**
⌂ ✸62.10/153.90 – ✸✸69.00/171.00.
◆ Traditional, white painted hotel in elevated position. Well-kept pool and garden terrace area. Spacious bar and wicker furnished lounge. Modern, pristine bedrooms. Tiled floors, suede fabrics add character to restaurant.

St Peter C.I. The West Country G. – pop. 4 228.

See : *Living Legend★*.
St Helier 5.

Greenhill's Country H. ⌂, Mont de l'Ecole, Coin Varin, JE3 7EL, on C 112 ℰ (01534) 481042, *greenhills@messages.co.uk,* Fax (01534) 485322, ⅃ heated, ⇆ – ⅍ rest, ▤ rest, ℙ. ⑩ ㏂ 𝘝𝘐𝘚𝘈. ℅
8 February-15 December – **Rest** 13.50/26.95 and a la carte 23.15/38.65 ℤ – **30 rm** ⌂ ✸51.00/104.00 – ✸✸102.00/148.00, 1 suite.
◆ Very popular with regular guests, this part 17C stone farmhouse is a fine place to settle down in, with flower-filled gardens, country style rooms and wood panelled lounge. Restaurant with plush pink predominating.

St Saviour C.I. – pop. 12 680.

St Helier 1.

Longueville Manor, Longueville Rd, JE2 7WF, on A 3 ℰ (01534) 725501, *longueville manor@relaischateaux.com,* Fax (01534) 731613, ⌨, ⅃ heated, ⇆, ⅄, ℀ – ▯, ⅍ rest, ℂ ℙ. ⑩ ㏂ ⑩ 𝘝𝘐𝘚𝘈
Rest 15.00 (lunch) and a la carte 49.25/55.50 ℤ ℰ – **28 rm** ⌂ ✸175.00/215.00 – ✸✸300.00/400.00, 2 suites.
◆ Exemplary part 14C manor for a special stay; every detail from furnishings to service is considered. Sumptuous rooms, delightful garden, poolside terrace. Panelled restaurant and terrace room overlooking garden; locally-inspired classics with modern twists.

Trinity C.I. – pop. 2 639.

The Highfield Country H., Route d'Ebenezer, JE3 5DT, Northwest : ½ m. on A 8 ℰ (01534) 862194, *reservations@highfieldjersey.com,* Fax (01534) 865342, ⅃₆, ⊜, ⅃, ⇆ – ▯ ⅍ ℂ ℙ. ⑩ ㏂ ⑩ 𝘝𝘐𝘚𝘈. ℅
April-October – **Rest** (bar lunch)/dinner 18.50 and a la carte 20.00/32.50 ℤ – **28 rm** ⌂ ✸65.00 – ✸✸100.00/120.00, 10 suites.
◆ Family oriented hotel, well placed for zoo and coast. Bedrooms are particularly large, some with equally spacious sitting rooms. Equipped with games room and conservatory. Children's options appear on the seafood based menu.

SARK
C.I. **503** P 33 and **517** ⑩ The West Country G. – pop. 550
See: *Island★★ – La Coupée★★★ – Port du Moulin★★ – Creux Harbour★ – La Seigneurie★* AC – *Pilcher Monument★ – Hog's Back★*.
⚓ to Jersey (St Helier) (Condor Ferries Ltd) (50 mn).
⚓ to Guernsey (St Peter Port) (Isle of Sark Shipping Co. Ltd) (summer only) (45 mn).
🛈 Harbour Hill ℰ (01481) 832345.

Aval du Creux ⌂, Harbour Hill, GY9 0SB, ℰ (01481) 832036, *reservations@avaldu creux.co.uk,* Fax (01481) 832368, ⌨, ⅃ – ⅍ rest, ℅
May-September – **The Lobster :** Rest 23.50 (dinner) and a la carte 20.70/33.50 – **20 rm** ⌂ ✸71.50/83.00 – ✸✸103.00/127.00.
◆ Secluded stone built hotel - the closest to the harbour - with 21C extensions. South facing mature gardens. Comfortable modern bedrooms. Dining room and terrace overlook garden and pool.

Stocks Island ⌂, GY9 0SD, ℰ (01481) 832001, *enquiries@stockshotel.com,* Fax (01481) 832130, ⌨, ⅃, ⇆ – ⅍, ⑩ ㏂ ⑩ 𝘝𝘐𝘚𝘈
April-September **Rest** (bar lunch)/dinner 26.00 and a la carte 18.50/29.50 s. ℤ – **18 rm** (dinner included) ⌂ ✸55.00/95.00 – ✸✸150.00/190.00.
◆ A mellow granite former farmhouse built in 1741, family owned and very personally run. Quiet location facing wooded valley. Well-kept bedrooms and period beamed bar. Organic produce to fore in charming restaurant.

ENGLAND

🏠 **Petit Champ** ॐ, GY9 0SF, ℰ (01481) 832046, info@hotelpetitchamp.co.uk, Fax (01481) 832469, ≤ coast, Herm, Jetou and Guernsey, 🍴, 🏊 heated, 🌲 – ⇔ rest. ◍◉ 🅰🄴 ◍ VISA. ✇

Easter - October – **Rest** 20.75 (dinner) and a la carte 14.00/27.75 – **10 rm** (dinner included) ⊑ ✦61.75/71.25 – ✦✦119.50/138.50.

• Ideal for views of neighbouring islands, with three sun lounges to enjoy them from; neat, tidy rooms. Quarry, from which hotel's stone comes, is site of solar heated pool. Dining room features Sark specialities.

%% **La Sablonnerie** ॐ with rm, Little Sark, GY9 0SD, ℰ (01481) 832061, Fax (01481) 832408, 🍴, 🌲 – ◍◉ 🅰🄴 VISA. ✇

Easter-mid October – **Rest** 25.80/28.80 and a la carte 21.60/28.80 – **21 rm** (dinner included) ⊑ ✦59.50/99.75 – ✦✦135.00/169.00, 1 suite.

• Immaculately whitewashed 16C former farmhouse: a long low building. Diners greeted from jetty by Victorian horse and carriage. Home-produced ingredients to fore. Smart rooms.

CHANNEL TUNNEL Kent 504 X 30 – *see Folkestone.*

CHAPELTOWN N. Yorks. 502 503 504 P 23 – *see Sheffield.*

CHARD Somerset 503 L 31 – pop. 12 008.

🛈 The Guildhall, Fore St ℰ (01460) 65710.

London 157 – Exeter 32 – Lyme Regis 12 – Taunton 18 – Yeovil 17.

🏠 **Bellplot House,** High St, TA20 1QB, ℰ (01460) 62600, info@bellplothouse.co.uk, Fax (01460) 62600, 🌲 – ⇔ rest, ☎ 🄿. ◍◉ 🅰🄴 VISA. ✇

Rest *(closed Sunday)* (dinner only and Sunday lunch)/dinner a la carte 21.40/29.50 – ⊑ 9.50 – **7 rm** ✦79.50/89.50 – ✦✦89.50/99.50.

• Impressive mid-Georgian house named after shape of original plot of land. Lounge with plush sofas and fitted bar. Bedrooms stylishly modern with bright yellow décor. Locally renowned restaurant where local, seasonal produce is very much centre stage.

CHARLBURY Oxon. 503 504 P 28 – pop. 2 984.

London 72 – Birmingham 50 – Oxford 15.

🏠 **Bull Inn** with rm, Sheep St, OX7 3RR, ℰ (01608) 810689, info@bullinn-charlbury.com – 🄿. ◍◉ VISA. ✇

closed 25 December – **Rest** *(closed Monday in autumn and winter, Sunday dinner and Monday lunch)* a la carte 17.00/26.00 ♀ – **4 rm** ⊑ ✦65.00 – ✦✦85.00.

• Charming part 17C inn with friendly ambience. Simple bar menu; restaurant dishes are more elaborate without sacrificing personal touch. Neat, well-kept bedrooms.

CHARLESTOWN Cornwall 503 F 32 – *see St Austell.*

CHARLTON W. Sussex 504 R 31 – *see Chichester.*

CHARLWOOD Surrey 504 T 30 – ✉ Horley.

London 30 – Brighton 29 – Royal Tunbridge Wells 28.

🏠 **Stanhill Court** ॐ, Stan Hill, RH6 0EP, Northwest : 1 m. by Norwood Hill Rd ℰ (01293) 862166, enquiries@stanhillcourthotel.co.uk, Fax (01293) 862773, ≤, 🍴, ⚗ – ⇔ 🄿 – ☎ 350. ◍◉ 🅰🄴 ◍ VISA. ✇

Rest (booking essential for non-residents) 19.95/25.95 and a la carte 21.85/42.45 – **34 rm** ⊑ ✦75.00/95.00 – ✦✦95.00/145.00.

• Attractive Victorian country house in 30 acres of parkland. Striking panelled baronial hall with stained glass. Huge conservatory. Bedrooms retain some original features. Pleasant dining room in classic style.

The ✿✿✿ award is the crème de la crème.
This is awarded to restaurants
which are really worth travelling miles for!

CHARMOUTH *Dorset* **503** L 31 – ✉ *Bridport.*
London 157 – Dorchester 22 – Exeter 31 – Taunton 27.

White House, 2 Hillside, The Street, DT6 6PJ, ✆ (01297) 560411 – ⇔ P. MC VISA. ✈
closed January and restricted opening in winter – **Rest** (dinner only) 30.00 – **6 rm** ☕ ✝106.00 – ✝✝143.00.
• Gleaming white Regency hotel a stone's throw from magnificent coastal scenery; popular with fossil hunters. Tasteful rooms, with pretty furnishings and a bold palette. Garden herbs and fruit used in home-cooked meals.

CHARTHAM HATCH *Kent* **504** X 30 – *see Canterbury.*

CHEADLE *Ches.* **502 503** N 23.
London 200 – Manchester 7 – Stoke-on-Trent 33.

Village H. & Leisure Club, Cheadle Rd, SK8 1HW, South : ¾ m. by A 5149 ✆ (0161) 428 0404, *tom.hendry@village-hotels.com, Fax (0161) 428 1191,* ⊚, Ƒ₆, ≘s, ◪, squash – |≑| ⇔, ▤ rest, ♿ P – ⛺ 200. MC AE ⓓ VISA
Rest a la carte 12.00/25.50 ♀ – **117 rm** ☕ ✝65.00/125.00 – ✝✝65.00/125.00.
• Corporate hotel in leafy suburb, convenient for Manchester airport and offering range of rooms; the executive rooms are larger with extra touches. Excellent leisure club. Bustling restaurant with cosmopolitan offerings.

CHEDDLETON *Staffs.* **502 503 504** N 24 – *pop. 2 719* – ✉ *Leek.*
London 125 – Birmingham 48 – Derby 33 – Manchester 42 – Stoke-on-Trent 11.

Choir Cottage without rest., Ostlers Lane, via Hollow Lane (opposite Red Lion on A 520), ST13 7HS, ✆ (01538) 360561, *enquiries@choircottage.co.uk,* ⛱ – ⇔ P. ✈
3 rm ☕ ✝45.00/49.00 – ✝✝65.00/75.00.
• Personally run 17C stone cottage, formerly church owned, and let to the poor, rent used to buy choir gowns. Individually furnished bedrooms with four-posters.

CHELMSFORD *Essex* **504** V 28 – *pop. 99 962.*
ℹ *County Hall, Market Rd ✆ (01245) 283400, tic@cheltenham.gov.uk.*
London 33 – Cambridge 46 – Ipswich 40 – Southend-on-Sea 19.

The Alma, 37 Arbour Lane, CM1 7RG, Northeast : 1 m. by B 1137 (Springfield Rd) ✆ (01245) 256783, *the-alma@hotmail.com, Fax (01245) 256793,* ⛱ – ⇔ ▤ P. MC VISA
closed dinner 25-26 December – **Rest** 14.95/18.50 and a la carte 16.95/24.95 ♀.
• Yellow painted extended pub with crazy paved terrace. Comfy lounge and bar. Loos feature 'piped' comedy classics! Smart restaurant serves modern à la carte with classic base.

at Great Baddow *Southeast : 3 m. by A 1114* – ✉ *Chelmsford.*

Pontlands Park ⛰, West Hanningfield Rd, CM2 8HR, ✆ (01245) 476444, *sales@pontlandsparkhotel.co.uk, Fax (01245) 478393,* ←, Ƒ₆, ≘s, ⛆ heated, ◪, ⛱ – P – ⛺ 100. MC AE ⓓ VISA. ✈
closed 23 December-3 January – **Rest** *(closed Saturday lunch and Sunday dinner)* a la carte 24.50/32.00 – ☕ 12.00 – **32 rm** ✝75.00/140.00 – ✝✝150.00/170.00, 4 suites.
• Family run converted and extended Victorian house with commanding views of countryside. Many rooms share vistas; all are individually furnished, some with brass bedsteads. Formal linen-clad dining in the main house.

CHELTENHAM *Glos.* **503 504** N 28 *Great Britain G.* – *pop. 98 875.*
See : *Town*★.
Exc. : *Sudeley Castle*★ *(Paintings*★*) AC, NE : 7 m. by B 4632* A.
⛳18 *Cleeve Hill ✆ (01242) 672025* A – ⛳18 *Cotswold Hills, Ullenwood ✆ (01242) 515264* A.
ℹ *77 Promenade ✆ (01242) 522878.*
London 99 – Birmingham 48 – Bristol 40 – Gloucester 9 – Oxford 43.

Plan on next page

The Queen's, Promenade, GL50 1NN, ✆ (0870) 4008107, *queens@macdonald-hotels.co.uk, Fax (01242) 224145,* ⛱, ⛱ – |≑| ⇔, ▤ rest, ✆ ♿ P – ⛺ 150. MC AE ⓓ VISA BZ n
Napier : **Rest** 25.00/35.00 and a la carte 22.00/35.00 ♀ – **79 rm** ☕ ✝120.00/170.00 – ✝✝130.00/170.00.
• A white columned neo-classical building with views over Imperial Square and the Ladies College. Grand reception and wood panelled bar. Individually styled bedrooms. Restaurant named after the famous British general.

CHELTENHAM

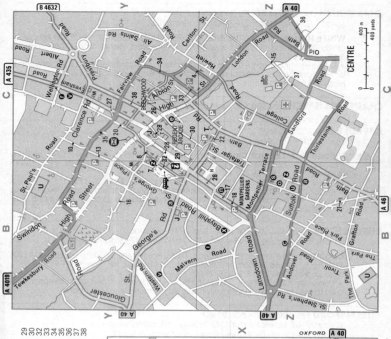

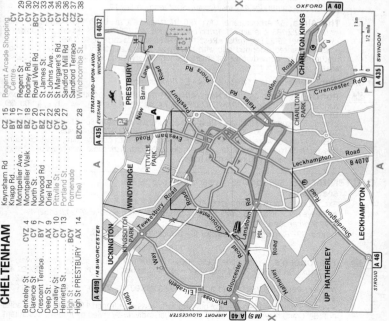

On the Park, 38 Evesham Rd, GL52 2AH, ☏ (01242) 518898, *stay@hotelonthepark.com*, Fax (01242) 511526, ⇔ – ⇔ ↩ **P**. ⍟⊕ **AE** ⍟ **VISA**. ⍟ CY r
Rest – (see *Parkers* below) – ⍿ 10.50 – **12 rm** ✦99.00 – ✦✦126.00/186.00.
♦ Regency town house of distinction. Bedrooms are named after dukes and dignitaries; individually decorated with paintings, antiques, mirrors and lamps. Stately library.

Kandinsky, Bayshill Rd, GL50 3AS, ☏ (01242) 527788, *kandinsky@aliashotels.com*, Fax (01242) 226412, ⇔ – ⊟, ⇔ rest, ↩ **P**. ⍟⊕ **AE** ⍟ **VISA** BZ x
Café Paradiso: Rest 13.95 (lunch) and a la carte 18.95/28.40 ⍿ – **47 rm** ✦75.00/105.00 – ✦✦105.00/130.00, 1 suite.
♦ Bohemian set-up with distressed furniture in minimalist bedrooms; each contains a different Kandinsky print. Sparkle in 1950s style basement club; live jazz some nights. Restaurant boasts long, open-plan kitchen with wood fired pizza oven.

The George, St George's Rd, GL50 3DZ, ☏ (01242) 235751, *hotel@stayatthe george.co.uk*, Fax (01242) 224359 – ⇔, ⊟ rest, ↩ **P**. ⍟⊕ ⚷ 30. ⍟⊕ **AE** ⍟ **VISA**. ⍟ BY a
closed 24-26 December – **Monty's**: Rest a la carte 24.85/38.85 ⍿ – **38 rm** ⍿ ✦60.00/110.00 – ✦✦110.00/125.00.
♦ In a good central location amongst other Regency town houses. Bright, modern, well-equipped bedrooms; larger variety boasts extra facilities. Two rooms called 'Monty's' serve brasserie style food and seafood respectively.

Beaumont House without rest., 56 Shurdington Rd, GL53 0JE, ☏ (01242) 223311, *reservations@bhhotel.co.uk*, Fax (01242) 520044, ⇔ – ⇔ ↩ **P**. ⍟⊕ **AE** ⍟ **VISA**. ⍟ AX u
16 rm ⍿ ✦59.00/74.00 – ✦✦99.00.
♦ Escape the rat race in sleek, bay windowed 19C comfort. Stunningly themed, luxurious bedrooms, some with views of Leckhampton Hill. Neat garden by breakfast room.

Lypiatt House without rest., Lypiatt Rd, GL50 2QW, ☏ (01242) 224994, *stay@ly piatt.co.uk*, Fax (01242) 224996, ⇔ – ⇔ **P**. ⍟⊕ **AE** **VISA**. ⍟ BZ c
10 rm ⍿ ✦70.00/90.00 – ✦✦80.00/110.00.
♦ A privately owned, serene Victorian house with friendly service. Rooms on top floor with dormer roof tend to be smaller than those on the ground floor. Soft, pale colours.

Butlers without rest., Western Rd, GL50 3RN, ☏ (01242) 570771, *info@butlers-ho tel.co.uk*, Fax (01242) 528724, ⇔ – ⇔ ↩ **P**. ⍟⊕ **VISA** BY v
9 rm ⍿ ✦50.00/65.00 – ✦✦85.00/120.00.
♦ Personally managed hotel where bedrooms constitute a peaceful haven with stylish drapes and canopies. Rooms named after famous butlers; some overlook wooded garden to rear.

Charlton Kings, London Rd, Charlton Kings, GL52 6UU, ☏ (01242) 231061, *enqui ries@charltonkingshotel.co.uk*, Fax (01242) 241900, ⇔ – ⇔ **P**. ⍟⊕ **AE** **VISA** AX c
Rest (bar lunch Monday-Saturday)/dinner a la carte 20.50/27.00 – **13 rm** ⍿ ✦65.00/85.00 – ✦✦120.00.
♦ A clean-lined, white purpose-built hotel with unfussy pastel interiors. Pristine, plainly painted bedrooms with light wood furniture. The rural setting bestows tranquillity. Dining room enhanced by a simple, modern design.

Georgian House without rest., 77 Montpellier Terrace, GL50 1XA, ☏ (01242) 515577, *penny@georgianhouse.net*, Fax (01242) 545929 – ⇔ ↩ **P**. ⍟⊕ **AE** ⍟ **VISA**. ⍟ BZ s
closed 2 weeks Christmas-New Year – **3 rm** ⍿ ✦55.00 – ✦✦80.00/90.00.
♦ Smart, terraced Georgian house, hospitably run, in sought-after Montpelier area. Good-sized bedrooms decorated in authentic period style. Comfy, elegant communal rooms.

Hannaford's without rest., 20 Evesham Rd, GL52 2AB, ☏ (01242) 515181, *sue@hanna fords.icom43.net*, Fax (01242) 580102 – ⇔ ↩ **P**. ⍟⊕ **AE** **VISA**. ⍟ CY v
10 rm ⍿ ✦45.00 – ✦✦80.00.
♦ Attractive, family run Georgian terraced townhouse near the centre. Hearty breakfast selection; cosy bar overlooks snug flagstoned terraced area. Ask for a coach-house room.

XXX **Le Champignon Sauvage** (Everitt-Matthias), 24-28 Suffolk Rd, GL50 2AQ, ☏ (01242) 573449, *mail@lechampignonsauvage.com*, Fax (01242) 254365 – ⇔. ⍟⊕ **AE** ⍟
✿✿ **VISA** BZ a
closed 3 weeks June, 10 days Christmas, Sunday and Monday – Rest 28.00/48.00 ⍿.
Spec. Seared scallops, cauliflower purée and cumin froth. Braised veal, roasted sweet-breads, broad beans and morels. Bitter chocolate and salted caramel délice, malted milk ice cream.
♦ Stylish destination restaurant renowned for its colourful artwork and intimate personality. Masterful cooking: ingredients employed with great invention to seduce the palette.

XX **Lumière**, Clarence Parade, GL50 3PA, ☏ (01242) 222200, *dinner@lumiere.cc* – ⇔ ⊟. ⍟⊕ **VISA** BCY z
closed first 2 weeks January, 2 weeks late summer, Sunday and Monday – Rest (dinner only) 41.00.
♦ Personally run, intimate glass fronted restaurant decked out in chic browns and leather. Original colourful artwork. Skilfully concocted cooking covering a modern range.

ENGLAND

205

ENGLAND

XX **Parkers** (at On the Park H.), 38 Evesham Rd, GL52 2AH, ✆ (01242) 227713, Fax (01242) 511526 – ✦✦ **P**. **MC** **AE** **VISA**
CY r
Rest 14.95 (lunch) and dinner a la carte 23.85/34.40 ℤ.
◆ A carefully decorated restaurant with mirrors, high ceilings, hand painted cornices and murals. Modern British cooking with classical undertones and a good range of wine.

XX **The Daffodil**, 18-20 Suffolk Parade, GL50 2AE, ✆ (01242) 700055, mail@thedaffodil.wanadoo.co.uk, Fax (01242) 700088 – ✦✦ ▤. **MC** **AE** **VISA**
BZ u
closed 25-26 December, Sunday and Bank Holidays – **Rest** 14.50 (lunch) and dinner a la carte 28.60/37.15 ℤ.
◆ Move from the art of film to the art of food in this 1920s converted cinema. The open-plan kitchen occupies the original screen area. Modern cooking with generous puddings.

X **Brosh**, 8 Suffolk Parade, Montpellier, GL50 2AB, ✆ (01242) 227277, info@broshrestaurant.co.uk, Fax (01242) 227277 – ✦✦ **VISA**
BZ o
closed 2 weeks January and Sunday-Tuesday – **Rest** - Mediterranean - a la carte 13.00/30.40.
◆ Cosy restaurant with atmospheric Moroccan-styled interior: evening candles and dimmed lights make for a great atmosphere. Specialist 'east' Mediterranean cooking with mezze.

X **Vanilla**, 9-10 Cambray Pl, GL50 1JS, ✆ (01242) 228228, vanillas@btconnect.com, Fax (01242) 228228 – ✦✦. **MC** **VISA**
CY e
closed 24-26 December, 1 January and Sunday – **Rest** a la carte 17.20/28.95.
◆ Centrally located, in Regency house basement; discreet, soft spot lighting, wooden floors, scoopback chairs. Staff serve light, mdern dishes garnished with home-made sauces.

X **Le Petit Blanc**, Promenade, GL50 1NN, ✆ (01242) 266800, cheltenham@lepetitblanc.co.uk, Fax (01242) 266801 – ✦✦ ▤. **MC** **AE** **①** **VISA**
BZ n
closed 25 December – **Rest** - Brasserie - 12.50 (lunch) and a la carte 19.50/30.45 ℤ.
◆ Spacious, invariably busy brasserie from Raymond Blanc stable. Gallic mainstays on the menu are enhanced by wine suggestions. The large bar is a high volume, buzzy area.

⌂ **The Beehive**, 1-3 Montpellier Villas, GL50 2XE, ✆ (01242) 702270, beehive@slak.co.uk, Fax (01242) 269330, ╬ – ✦✦. **MC** **AE** **①** **VISA**
BZ z
closed 25 December – **Rest** (closed Sunday dinner) a la carte 20.00/27.50 ℤ.
◆ Georgian corner pub with original green and frosted glass façade. Based in charming Montpellier area. Genuine, unaffected ambienece. Good, honest cooking in restaurant style.

at Cleeve Hill Northeast : 4 m. on B 4632 – AX – ✉ Cheltenham.

🏠 **Cleeve Hill** without rest., GL52 3PR, ✆ (01242) 672052, info@cleevehill-hotel.co.uk, Fax (01242) 679969, ≤, ╬ – ✦✦ ✆ **P**. **MC** **AE** **VISA**. ✦
10 rm ☞ ✦45.00/55.00 – ✦✦95.00.
◆ Edwardian house in elevated spot; most bedrooms have views across Cleeve Common and the Malvern Hills. Breakfast room is in the conservatory; admire the landscape over coffee.

XX **Hacketts** with rm, GL52 3PR, ✆ (01242) 672017, paul.hackett@btconnect.com, ≤, ╬, ╬ – ✦✦ **P**. **MC** **①** **VISA**
closed first 3 weeks January and last week October – **Rest** (closed Tuesday lunch, Sunday dinner and Monday) 15.95/25.00 and a la carte 29.50/41.25 – **4 rm** ☞ ✦65.00 – ✦✦90.00.
◆ Pleasant, personally run restaurant up a hill with views to distant Malverns. Classically styled lounges; modern British cooking with good value choice. Well-appointed rooms.

at Shurdington Southwest : 3¾ m. on A 46 – AX – ✉ Cheltenham.

🏰 **The Greenway** ◈, GL51 4UG, ✆ (01242) 862352, info@thegreenway.co.uk, Fax (01242) 862780, ╬, ☜ – ✦✦ **P** – ⚒ 40. **MC** **AE** **VISA**
Rest 21.00/45.00 and a la carte 21.00/55.00 ℤ – **20 rm** ☞ ✦90.00/120.00 – ✦✦140.00/240.00, 1 suite.
◆ Part Elizabethen manor house with elegant country house style in mature grounds outside the city. Floral bedrooms with the Cotswold hills providing a pleasnt backdrop. Garden and lily pond on view from restaurant.

at Brockworth Southwest : 5½ m. on A 46 – AX – ✉ Cheltenham.

🏰 **Cheltenham and Gloucester Moat House**, Shurdington Rd, GL3 4PB, on A 46 ✆ (01452) 519988, cheltenhamevents@qhotels.co.uk, Fax (01452) 519977, ✦6, ⚒s, ▤, ╬ – ⌖ ✦✦, ▤ rest, ✆ & **P** – ⚒ 350. **MC** **AE** **①** **VISA**. ✦
Rest (closed Saturday lunch) 15.50 (lunch) and dinner a la carte 21.00/32.50 **s**. – **118 rm** ☞ ✦120.00/150.00 – ✦✦140.00/220.00, 2 suites.
◆ A modern corporate hotel located in landscaped grounds on the edge of the Cotswolds. Good leisure facilities. The "Crown Executive" rooms are particularly well equipped. Formulaic restaurant with lunchtime carvery.

at Witcombe *Southwest : 6 m. by A 46 –* AX *– and Bentham rd –* ⊠ *Cheltenham.*

⌂ **Crickley Court** *without rest., Dog Lane, GL3 4UF,* ℘ *(01452) 863634, lizpilgrimmor ris@yahoo.co.uk, Fax (01452) 863634,* ⊥, ⚘ *–* ⊷ ❋ 𝐏, ⓜⓞ 𝐕𝐈𝐒𝐀. ⅍
3 rm ⊡ ✲35.00 – ✲✲70.00.
◆ Old inn dating from 16C. Lounge provided with an array of books. Family style breakfast. Outdoor pool. Spacious, bright and clean rooms with modern amenities.

CHENIES *Bucks.* 504 S 28 *–* ⊠ *Rickmansworth (Herts.).*
London 30 – Aylesbury 18 – Watford 7.

🏨 **Bedford Arms,** *WD3 6EQ,* ℘ *(01923) 283301, contact@bedfordarms.co.uk, Fax (01923) 284825,* ⚘, ⚘ *–* ⊷ rm, ❋ 𝐏, ⓜⓞ ⒶⒺ ⓞ 𝐕𝐈𝐒𝐀
closed 26 December-3 January **Rest** *(closed Sunday dinner)* 16.95 (lunch) and a la carte 29.25/34.75 ⊡ *–* **18 rm** ⊡ ✲90.00/110.00. – ✲✲120.00.
◆ A homely hotel, pub-like in character. Well proportioned rooms, some with views of a pretty garden. Country house style bars and a meeting room for business guests. Oak panelled dining room; adjacent cocktail bar.

🐦 Red = Pleasant. Look for the red ✕ and 🏨 symbols.

CHESTER *Ches.* 502 503 L 24 *Great Britain G. –* pop. 80 121.
See : City★★ *- The Rows*★★ B *- Cathedral*★ B *- City Walls*★ B.
Env. : Chester Zoo★ *AC,* N *: 3 m. by A 5116.*
🏌 *Upton-by-Chester, Upton Lane* ℘ *(01244) 381183* A *–* 🏌 *Curzon Park* ℘ *(01244) 675130* A.
🛈 *Town Hall, Northgate St* ℘ *(01244) 402111 – Chester Visitor and Craft Centre, Vicars Lane* ℘ *(01244) 402111.*
London 207 – Birkenhead 7 – Birmingham 91 – Liverpool 21 – Manchester 40 – Preston 52 – Sheffield 76 – Stoke-on-Trent 38.

Plans on following pages

🏰🏰🏰 **The Chester Grosvenor and Spa,** *Eastgate, CH1 1LT,* ℘ *(01244) 324024, reserva tions@chestergrosvenor.com, Fax (01244) 313246,* 🌀, ℔, ☎ *–* 📶 ⊷ ▤ ❋ & 𝐏 *–* ⚒ 250.
ⓜⓞ ⒶⒺ ⓞ 𝐕𝐈𝐒𝐀. ⅍   **B a**
closed 24-27 December – **Rest** *– (see* **Arkle** *and* **La Brasserie** *below) –* ⊡ 18.50 *–* **76 rm** ✲229.10 – ✲✲229.10, 4 suites.
◆ 19C coaching inn in heart of city. Lavishly furnished with antiques and oil paintings. Superb spa facilities. Luxuriously appointed, individually styled bedrooms.

🏰🏰🏰 **Crabwall Manor** ⌂, *Parkgate Rd, Mollington, CH1 6NE, Northwest : 2 ¼ m. on A 540* ℘ *(01244) 851666, swallow.crabwell@londoninns.com, Fax (01244) 851400,* 🌀, ℔, ☎, ⊡, ⚘, ⚘ *–* ⊷, ▤ rest, 𝐏 *–* ⚒ 100. ⓜⓞ ⒶⒺ 𝐕𝐈𝐒𝐀. ⅍   **A d**
Conservatory : **Rest** *(light lunch)/dinner a la carte approx 28.00* s. *–* **43 rm** ⊡ ✲85.00/170.00 – ✲✲350.00/189.00, 5 suites.
◆ 17C manor with castellated façade and mature grounds heavily extended into an individually furnished and comfortable business and leisure hotel. Amply proportioned bedrooms. Fine dining at classic conservatory restaurant.

🏨 **Green Bough,** *60 Hoole Rd, CH2 3NL, on A 56* ℘ *(01244) 326241, luxury@green bough.co.uk, Fax (01244) 326265 –* ⊷ ❋ 𝐏 *–* ⚒ 30. ⓜⓞ ⒶⒺ 𝐕𝐈𝐒𝐀. ⅍   **A t**
closed 25 December and 1 January – **Olive Tree :** **Rest** 25.00/45.00 ⊡ *–* **13 rm** ⊡ ✲105.00/150.00 – ✲✲175.00/245.00, 2 suites.
◆ Personally run and very comfortable, boasting high quality decor; owner pays notable attention to detail. Individually styled, generously sized rooms with wrought iron beds. Dine formally in attractive surroundings.

🏨 **Alton Lodge,** *78 Hoole Rd, CH2 3NT,* ℘ *(01244) 310213, reception@altonlodge.co.uk, Fax (01244) 319206 –* ⊷ ❋ 𝐏. ⓜⓞ ⒶⒺ 𝐕𝐈𝐒𝐀. ⅍   **A t**
closed Christmas and New Year – **Rest** *(closed Friday-Sunday)* (residents only) (dinner only) a la carte 21.00/26.00 s. ⊡ *–* **17 rm** ⊡ ✲50.00/98.00 – ✲✲70.00/128.00.
◆ A family run, good value hotel. Pine furnished breakfast room, bar and lounge. Compact, annexed rooms provide a comfy night's accommodation after enjoying the city's sights.

🏨 **Express by Holiday Inn** *without rest., The Racecourse, New Crane St, CH11 2LY,* ℘ *(0870) 9904065, Fax (0870) 9904066,* ← *–* 📶 ⊷ & 𝐏 *–* ⚒ 30. ⓜⓞ ⒶⒺ ⓞ 𝐕𝐈𝐒𝐀   **B c**
97 rm ✲82.50 – ✲✲85.00.
◆ Ultimate race-goers accommodation: by the main stand of Chester race course. Very comfortable, good value, well-equipped rooms: some have great views of final furlong.

(margin) ENGLAND

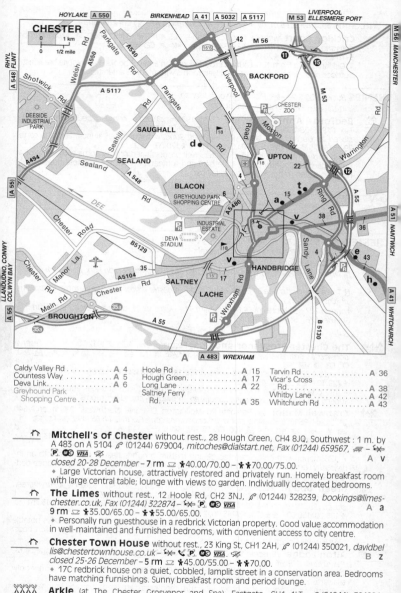

CHESTER

HOYLAKE A 550	A	BIRKENHEAD A 41 A 5032 A 5117
		LIVERPOOL ELLESMERE PORT M 53

0 1 km
0 1/2 mile

BACKFORD

CHESTER ZOO

SAUGHALL

d ●

UPTON

SEALAND

BLACON

GREYHOUND PARK SHOPPING CENTRE

a ●

t ●

15

v ●

INDUSTRIAL ESTATE

DEVA STADIUM

v ●

HANDBRIDGE

SALTNEY

LACHE

e ●

h ●

BROUGHTON

A 483 WREXHAM

⌂ **Mitchell's of Chester** without rest., 28 Hough Green, CH4 8JQ, Southwest : 1 m. by A 483 on A 5104 ✆ (01244) 679004, *mitoches@dialstart.net, Fax (01244) 659567,* 🚗 – ⇌
P. MO VISA. 彩
closed 20-28 December – **7 rm** � ✝40.00/70.00 – ✝✝70.00/75.00.
A v
◆ Large Victorian house, attractively restored and privately run. Homely breakfast room with large central table; lounge with views to garden. Individually decorated bedrooms.

⌂ **The Limes** without rest., 12 Hoole Rd, CH2 3NJ, ✆ (01244) 328239, *bookings@limes-chester.co.uk, Fax (01244) 322874* – ⇌ **P. MO VISA**
A a
9 rm ⊇ ✝35.00/65.00 – ✝✝55.00/65.00.
◆ Personally run guesthouse in a redbrick Victorian property. Good value accommodation in well-maintained and furnished bedrooms, with convenient access to city centre.

⌂ **Chester Town House** without rest., 23 King St, CH1 2AH, ✆ (01244) 350021, *davidbel lis@chestertownhouse.co.uk* – ⇌ 📞 **P. MO VISA**
B z
closed 25-26 December – **5 rm** ⊇ ✝45.00/55.00 – ✝✝70.00.
◆ 17C redbrick house on a quiet, cobbled, lamplit street in a conservation area. Bedrooms have matching furnishings. Sunny breakfast room and period lounge.

XXXX **Arkle** (at The Chester Grosvenor and Spa), Eastgate, CH1 1LT, ✆ (01244) 324024, 🏵 *Fax (01244) 313246* – ⇌ ▤ **P. MO AE ① VISA**
B a
closed 24-27 December,1-22 January, 1 week August, Sunday and Monday – **Rest** (dinner only) 55.00 and a la carte 55.00/65.00 ♀ 🏵.
Spec. Cod with ravioli, crayfish and corn. Grilled squab with mushroom jelly and foie gras. "Tutti frutti".
◆ A distinguished performer, like the eponymous racehorse, renowned for excellent, modern dishes using top quality ingredients and a legendary wine cellar of over 600 bins.

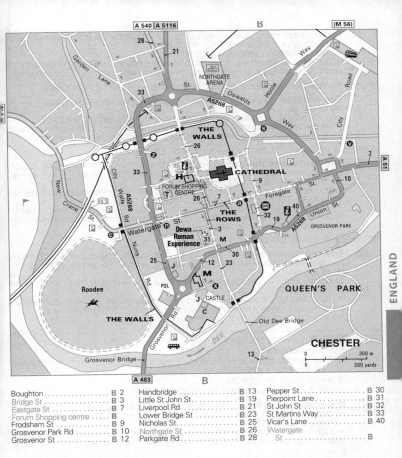

XX **La Brasserie** (at The Chester Grosvenor and Spa), Eastgate, CH1 1LT, ℰ (01244) 324024, *Fax (01244) 313246* – ⅍✕ 🗏 🄿. 🐾 🄰🄴 ⓵ 𝘝𝘐𝘚𝘈
B a
– **Rest** a la carte 21.95/38.65 ♈.
• Burnished interior, Parisian-style eatery with mirrors and glass frontage. Eclectic menu with classic French and Italian staples of pasta and meat dishes. Weekend live music.

XX **Upstairs at the Grill**, 70 Watergate St, CH1 2LA, ℰ (01244) 344883, *katie.hearse@upstairsatthegrill.co.uk, Fax (01244) 329720* – ⅍✕ 🗏. 🐾 🄰🄴 𝘝𝘐𝘚𝘈
B n
closed 25 December – **Rest** - Steak specialities - (dinner only) a la carte 22.85/32.95.
• Door bell entry to 19C building; sumptuous first floor bar has leather sofas and roulette table. Cow theme predominates. Prime quality Welsh steaks chargrilled to perfection.

XX **Locus**, 111 Boughton, CH3 5BH, ℰ (01244) 311112, *Fax (01244) 344860* – ⅍✕ 🄿. 🐾 🄰🄴 ⓵ 𝘝𝘐𝘚𝘈
A v
closed 25-26 December and Monday – **Rest** (dinner only) a la carte 22.20/30.90 ♈.
• Unprepossessing exterior, but this small restaurant has a stylish, modern interior with atmospheric low lighting. Varied, interesting menus using well-sourced ingredients.

XX **Brasserie 10-16**, Brookdale Pl, CH1 3DY, ℰ (01244) 322288, *Fax (01244) 322325* – ⅍✕ 🗏. 🐾 🄰🄴 𝘝𝘐𝘚𝘈
B s
closed 25 and 31 December, 1 January – **Rest** a la carte 15.95/31.50 s. 🏵♈.
• Contemporary brasserie on two levels. Open plan kitchen on ground floor. Large modern British menu with Mediterranean touches, including plenty for the more adventurous.

209

Old Harkers Arms, 1 Russell St, CH3 5AL, *℘* (01244) 344525, *harkers.arms@brunnin gandprice.co.uk*, Fax (01244) 344812 – **❶❸ AE VISA**
B V
closed 25 December – **Rest** a la carte 20.00/28.00 ♀.
♦ Pub set in converted warehouse by canal. Homespun personality in interior décor of prints, bookshelves and wooden flooring. Offers traditional English meals and sandwiches.

at Little Barrow Northeast : 6½ m. by A 56 (Warrington Rd) – A – on B 5132 – ✉ Chester.

The Foxcote, Station Lane, CH3 7JN, *℘* (01244) 301343, Fax (01244) 303287 – **✦ P. ❶❸ AE VISA**. ✦
closed Sunday dinner – **Rest** - Seafood - 10.95 (lunch) and a la carte 23.15/28.95 ♀.
♦ Off the beaten track; traditional inn now given over to dining tables. Vast number of blackboard specials, mostly seafood dishes utilising broad range of fresh ingredients.

at Pulford Southwest : 5 m. by A 483 – A – and B 5445 – ✉ Chester.

The Grosvenor Pulford, Wrexham Rd, CH4 9DG, on B 5445 *℘* (01244) 570560, reservations@grosvenorpulfordhotel.co.uk, Fax (01244) 570809, *Ⅰб, ☎, ▨, ✍, ✗ – ▯*, ✦ rest, *TV* & *P* – *▲* 200. **❶❸ AE ⓿ VISA**
Ciro's : Rest - Brasserie - (closed lunch Saturday and Bank Holiday Mondays) a la carte 24.00/30.95 – **73 rm** ☑ ✸90.00 – ✸✸120.00/150.00.
♦ Family owned hotel 10 minutes' drive from city. Popular business and wedding venue. Pleasant gardens; spacious gym and pool. Diverse range of individualistic rooms. Large brasserie with Mediterranean menus.

at Rowton Southeast : 3 m. on A 41 – ✉ Chester.

Rowton Hall, Whitchurch Rd, CH3 6AD, *℘* (01244) 335262, rowtonhall@rowton hall.co.uk, Fax (01244) 335464, *☂, ◷, Ⅰб, ☎, ▨, ✍, ✗ – ✦, ▤ rest, ✆ P* – *▲* 170. **❶❸ AE VISA**. ✦
A h
Langdale : Rest 16.50/26.50 (dinner) and lunch a la carte 26.50/40.00 ♀ – ☑ 12.50 – **36 rm** ✸135.00 – ✸✸145.00, 2 suites.
♦ Gracious 18C sandstone hotel with many original features: hand-carved staircase, Robert Adam fireplace, range of bedrooms. Business facilities offered. Country house style. Colonial style restaurant with wooden blinds and rattan furniture.

CHESTERFIELD Derbs. 502 503 504 P 24 Great Britain G. – pop. 70 260.
Env. : Bolsover Castle★ AC, E : 5 m. by A 632.
Ⅰь, Ⅰь Chesterfield Municipal, Murray House, Crow Lane *℘* (01246) 273887 – *Ⅰь* Grassmoor, North Wingfield Rd *℘* (01246) 856044.
Ⅰ Rykneld Square *℘* (01246) 345777.
London 152 – Derby 24 – Nottingham 25 – Sheffield 12.

Ibis without rest., Lordsmill St, S41 7RW, at junction of A 619 and A 632 *℘* (01246) 221333, h3160@accor.com, Fax (01246) 221444 – ▯ ✦ & *P* – *▲* 30. **❶❸ AE ⓿ VISA**
– **86 rm** ✸52.00 – ✸✸52.00.
♦ Lodge within walking distance of the town, yet on the main ring road. All mod cons which include in-house movies in up-to-date bedrooms. A Continental buffet for breakfast.

CHESTER-LE-STREET Durham 501 502 P 19.
Ⅰь Lumley Park *℘* (0191) 388 3218 – *Ⅰь* Roseberry Grange, Grange Villa *℘* (0191) 370 0670.
London 275 – Durham 7 – Newcastle upon Tyne 8.

Lumley Castle ♨, DH3 4NX, East : 1 m. on B 1284 *℘* (0191) 389 1111, reserva tions@lumleycastle.com, Fax (0191) 389 1881, *✍ – ✦ P* – *▲* 150. **❶❸ AE ⓿ VISA**. ✦
closed 24-26 December and 1 January – **Black Knight :** Rest (closed Saturday lunch) 32.50 and dinner a la carte 30.50/40.50 s. ♀ – ☑ 14.65 – **73 rm** ✸120.00 – ✸✸185.00, 1 suite.
♦ Norman castle, without additions, underscoring its uniqueness. Rich, gothic interiors of carved wood, chandeliers, statues, tapestries, rugs. Rooms imbued with atmosphere. Restaurant offers classical dishes with an original twist.

CHESTERTON Oxon. 504 Q 28 – ✉ Bicester.
Ⅰь Bicester *℘* (01869) 241204.
London 69 – Birmingham 65 – Northampton 36 – Oxford 15.

Bignell Park, OX26 1UE, on A 4095 *℘* (01869) 326550, enq@bignellparkhotel.co.uk, Fax (01869) 322729, *✍ – & P* – *▲* 25. **❶❸ AE VISA**. ✦
Rest 17.95/22.95 – **22 rm** ☑ ✸100.00/110.00 – ✸✸145.00/155.00.
♦ A traditional Cotswold house built in 1740, sits in lovely gardens. A homely lounge and bar set the tone of a warm, friendly atmosphere. Sizeable, comfy bedrooms. Oak beamed cocktail bar; restaurant with minstrels gallery.

ENGLAND

CHETTLE Dorset – see Blandford Forum.

CHEW MAGNA Somerset 503 504 M 29 – see Bristol.

CHICHESTER W. Sussex 504 R 31 Great Britain G. – pop. 27 477.

See : City★★ – Cathedral★★ BZ A – St Mary's Hospital★ BY D – Pallant House★ AC BZ M.
Env. : Fishbourne Roman Palace★★ (mosaics★) AC AZ R.
Exc. : Weald and Downland Open Air Museum★★ AC, N : 6 m. by A 286 AY.
 Goodwood, Kennel Hill ℘ (01243) 755130, AY – ℔, ℔, ℔ Chichester Golf Centre, Hunston Village ℘ (01243) 533833, AZ.
🛈 29a South St ℘ (01243) 775888.
London 69 – Brighton 31 – Portsmouth 18 – Southampton 30.

CHICHESTER

Birdham Rd.	AZ 2	Kingsham Rd	BZ 13	St Paul's Rd	BY 27
Bognor Rd	BZ 6	Lavant Rd	AY 14	Sherborne Rd.	AZ 28
Chapel St	BY 6	Little London	BY 15	Southgate	BZ 29
Chartres (Av. de)	BZ 7	Market Rd.	BZ 16	South Pallant	BZ 31
Chichester Arundel Rd.	AY 8	Northgate	BY 17	South St	BZ
East Pallant	BZ	North Pallant	BZ 19	Spitalfield Lane	BY 32
East St	BZ	North St	BYZ	Stockbridge Rd.	AZ 33
Florence Rd	AZ 10	Oaklands Way	BY 18	Tower St	BY 35
Hornet (The)	BZ 12	St Jame's	AZ 21	Via Ravenna	AZ 37
		St John's St.	BZ 23	Westhampnett	
		St Martin's Square	BY 24	Rd	AYZ 38
		St Pancras	BY 25	West Pallant	BZ 39

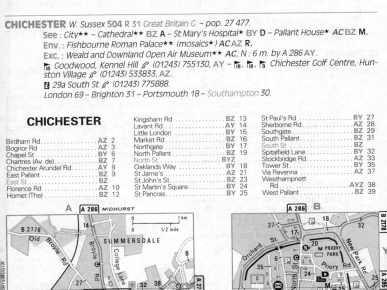

🏠 **Crouchers Country H.,** Birdham Rd, Apuldram, PO20 7EH, Southwest : 2 ½ m. on A 286 ℘ (01243) 784995, info@crouchersbottom.com, Fax (01243) 539797, ☞ – ⇆ ૐ ℙ.
🕮 🖭 ⓞ 𝘝𝘐𝘚𝘈
Rest 12.50/15.50 and a la carte 19.50/27.50 – **18 rm** ☷ ✸65.00/95.00 – ✸✸95.00/130.00.
◆ 1900s farmhouse surrounded by fields. Bedrooms are in a separate coach house, some on ground floor; furnished with matching floral fabrics. Admire waterfowl in nearby pond. Bright, modern dining room.

XX **Comme ça,** 67 Broyle Rd, PO19 6BD, on A 286 ℘ (01243) 788724, comme.ca@commeca.co.uk, Fax (01243) 530052, ☞, ☞ – ⇆ ℙ ⇄ 12. 🕮 ⓞ 𝘝𝘐𝘚𝘈   AY C
closed 2 weeks Christmas, New Year, Monday, Tuesday lunch and Sunday dinner – **Rest** - French - 22.95 (lunch) and a la carte 28.25/31.95 🌿 ℤ.
◆ Strong French cooking ministered by Normand chef; generous à la carte, set menus and French family lunch on Sundays. Festoons of hops on exposed beams complete the décor.

XX **The Dining Room at Purchases,** 31 North St, PO19 1LY, ℘ (01243) 537352, info@thediningroom.biz, Fax (01243) 780773, ☞ – ⇆. 🕮 🖭 ⓞ 𝘝𝘐𝘚𝘈   BY C
closed 25 December, Sunday and Bank Holidays – **Rest** a la carte 23.40/40.90 ℤ.
◆ Charming Georgian house owned by country's oldest wine merchant; garden terrace, new wine bar, deep red hued restaurant serving shellfish and game menus. Great wine selection.

at East Lavant *North : 2½ m. off A 286 –* AY *– ⊠ Chichester.*

🍽️ **The Royal Oak Inn** with rm, Pook Lane, PO18 0AX, 𝒫 (01243) 527434, *ro@thesussex pub.co.uk, Fax* (01243) 775062, 😄 *–* 💶, 🆗 AE VISA. 🍴
closed 25 December and 1 January – **Rest** a la carte 22.00/40.00 ♀ *–* **6 rm** 🛏 ✦60.00/70.00 *–* ✦✦110.00/130.00.
◆ Utterly charming village pub with summer terraces. Modern rustic feel enhanced by leather sofas. All-encompassing restaurant: very well executed cooking. Comfy, modern rooms.

at Charlton *North : 6¼ m. by A 286 –* AY *– ⊠ Chichester.*

🏛️ **Woodstock House** without rest., PO18 0HU, 𝒫 (01243) 811666, *info@woodstockhou sehotel.co.uk, Fax* (01243) 811666, 😄 *–* 💶 P, 🆗 AE VISA
13 rm 🛏 ✦55.00/75.00 *–* ✦✦90.00/112.00.
◆ In a row of flint and whitewashed cottages close to Goodwood Racecourse. Indoors, relax in the mulberry coloured, cottage style lounge or the floral furnished bedrooms. Enjoy the home cooking, undertaken with pride, in mellow restaurant.

🍽️ **The Fox Goes Free** with rm, PO18 0HU, 𝒫 (01243) 811461, *thefoxgoesfree.al ways@virgin.net, Fax* (01243) 811926, 😄 *–* 💶 P, 🆗 VISA
Rest a la carte 18.00/27.50 *–* **5 rm** 🛏 ✦55.00 *–* ✦✦80.00/100.00.
◆ Flint and brick pub, oozing 14C charm, balanced by appealing, modern tones. Antique church furniture, huge fire, cosy snug; hearty, fresh cooking. Welcoming beamed bedrooms.

at Halnaker *Northeast : 3¼ m. on A 285 –* BY *– ⊠ Chichester.*

🏠 **The Old Store** without rest., Stane St, PO18 0QL, on A 285 𝒫 (01243) 531977, *theold store4@aol.com,* 😄 *–* 💶 P, 🆗 VISA. 🍴
7 rm 🛏 ✦40.00/50.00 *–* ✦✦65.00/75.00.
◆ An 18C listed building, originally belonging to the Goodwood Estate and used as a village store and bakery. Floral bedrooms. Well placed for Goodwood events and Chichester.

at Tangmere *East : 2 m. by A 27 –* AY *– ⊠ Chichester.*

XX **Cassons,** Arundel Rd, PO18 0DU, Northwest : ¼ m. off A 27 (westbound) 𝒫 (01243) 773294, *cassonsresto@aol.com,* 😄 *–* 💶 P, 🆗 VISA
closed 2 weeks January, 25-26 December, Sunday dinner, Monday and Tuesday lunch – **Rest** 17.95 (lunch) and a la carte 27.40/39.40.
◆ Eponymous owners run a homely and appealing neighbourhood restaurant where theme evenings (eg, India, New Zealand) gel with the locally renowned classical, seasonal cooking.

at Bosham *West : 4 m. by A 259 –* AZ *– ⊠ Chichester.*

🏛️ **Millstream,** Bosham Lane, PO18 8HL, 𝒫 (01243) 573234, *info@millstream-hotel.co.uk, Fax* (01243) 573459, 😄 *–* 💶, 🍽 rest, 🗸 ♿ 💶, 🆗 AE ① VISA
Rest 28.50 (dinner) and lunch a la carte 20.50/26.40 ♀ *–* **32 rm** 🛏 ✦79.00/109.00 *–* ✦✦138.00/208.00, 3 suites.
◆ Pretty hotel with garden that backs onto stream bobbing with ducks. Cosy bedrooms, individually co-ordinated fabric furnishings, sandwash fitted furniture and large windows. Seasonal, daily changing menus.

🏠 **Charters** without rest., Bosham Lane, PO18 8HG, 𝒫 (01243) 572644, *louise@charters bandb.co.uk, Fax* (01243) 572644, 😄 *–* 💶 P, 🆗 AE VISA. 🍴
restricted opening in winter – **5 rm** 🛏 ✦55.00 *–* ✦✦110.00.
◆ Luxurious appointments knit seamlessly with a contemporaray design, as defined by freshly painted walls, teak and leather furnishings, and smart, swish rooms. Aga breakfasts.

at West Stoke *Northwest : 2¾ m. by B 2178 –* AY *– off B 2146 – ⊠ Chichester.*

XX **West Stoke** 😊 with rm, Downs Rd, PO18 9BN, 𝒫 (01243) 575226, *info@weststoke house.co.uk, Fax* (01243) 574655, ◁, 😄, 🐾 *–* 💶 🗸 💶, 🆗 AE ① VISA
closed 24-26 December – **Rest** *(closed Sunday-Tuesday)* 22.50/35.00 *–* **5 rm** 🛏 ✦85.00 *–* ✦✦150.00.
◆ Charmingly peaceful part 17C manor, set in very pleasant gardens. Reception with log burner seamlessly blends subtle elegance to modern art; strikingly understated rooms. Modish menus at full linen tables.

at Funtington *Northwest : 4¾ m. by B 2178 –* AY *– on B 2146 – ⊠ Chichester.*

XX **Hallidays,** Watery Lane, PO18 9LF, 𝒫 (01243) 575331 *–* 💶 P, 🆗 VISA
closed 2 weeks March, 1 week late August, Monday, Tuesday, Saturday lunch and Sunday dinner – **Rest** 19.50 (lunch) and a la carte 25.25/34.00.
◆ A row of part 13C thatched cottages; confident and keen chef delivers a lively medley of frequently changing set menus and à la carte. Modern meals sit alongside classics.

CHIDDINGFOLD Surrey 504 S 30.
London 47 – Guildford 10 – Haslemere 5.

Ⓘ **The Swan Inn** with rm, Petworth Rd, GU8 4TY, ℰ (01428) 682073, *enquiries@theswa ninn.biz*, Fax (01428) 683259, 佘 – ⁕× ▤ **P**, **⑩⑩** **AE** **VISA**
Rest a la carte 18.00/28.00 – ☑ 5.00 – **11 rm** ✱65.00/120.00 – ✱✱65.00/120.00.
◆ Located on the main road of a leafy, red-brick village; refurbishment has created a pub with a neo-rustic atmosphere. Elaborate menus. Smart, contemporary bedrooms.

CHIEVELEY Berks. 503 504 Q 29.
London 60 – Newbury 5 – Swindon 25.

ⅩⅩ **The Crab at Chieveley** with rm, Wantage Rd, RG20 8UE, West : 2 ½ m. by School Rd on B 4494 ℰ (01635) 247550, *info@crabatchieveley.com*, Fax (01635) 247440, 佘 – ⁕× ✿ **P**, **⑩⑩** **AE** **VISA**
Rest - Seafood - 19.50 and a la carte 19.50/35.00 – **17 rm** ☑ ✱100.00/120.00 – ✱✱120.00/170.00.
◆ Thatched former inn, a lively venue, on a country road with wheat fields. Choice of bistro or restaurant for seafood menu. Highly original bedrooms themed as famous hotels.

CHILLATON Devon 503 H 32 – *see Tavistock.*

CHINNOR Oxon. 504 R 28 *Great Britain G.* – *pop. 5 407.*
Exc. : Ridgeway Path★★.
London 45 – Oxford 19.

at Sprigg's Alley Southeast : 2½ m. by Bledlow Ridge rd – ✉ Chinnor.

ⅩⅩ **Sir Charles Napier**, OX39 4BX, ℰ (01494) 483011, *info@sircharlesnapier.co.uk*, Fax (01494) 485311, 佘 – **P**, **⑩⑩** **VISA**. ✿
closed 3 days Christmas – **Rest** *(closed Sunday dinner and Monday)* a la carte 30.00/38.75 ☑ ℬ.
◆ Off the beaten track for exciting menus where fish features alongside game (mallard, roast partridge) and funghi and berries brought in by locals. Sculptural ornamentation.

at Kingston Blount Southwest : 1¾ m. on B 4009 – ✉ Chinnor.

↑ **Lakeside Town Farm** without rest., Brook St, OX39 4RZ, (off Sydenham rd) ℰ (01844) 352152, *townfarmcottage@oxfree.com*, Fax (01844) 352152, ☞ – ⁕× **P**, **⑩⑩** **⑩** **VISA**. ✿
closed 20 December - 2 January – **3 rm** ☑ ✱50.00 – ✱✱75.00.
◆ Modern building, on a working farm, in a sympathetic style that engenders a traditional, old-fashioned ambience. Charming, Victorian-style bedrooms. Attractive gardens.

CHIPPENHAM Wilts. 503 504 N 29 *The West Country G.* – *pop. 33 189.*
See : Yelde Hall★.
Env. : Corsham Court★★ AC, SW : 4 m. by A 4 – Sheldon Manor★ AC, W : 1½ m. by A 420 – Biddestone★, W : 3½ m. – Bowood House★ AC (Library ⩽★) SE : 5 m. by A 4 and A 342.
Exc. : Castle Combe★★, NW : 6 m. by A 420 and B 4039.
🅑 Monkton Park (Par Three) ℰ (01249) 653928.
🅓 Yelde Hall, Market Place ℰ (01249) 665970.
London 106 – Bristol 27 – Southampton 64 – Swindon 21.

at Stanton Saint Quintin North : 5 m. by A 429 – ✉ Chippenham.

🏛 **Stanton Manor** ⌖, SN14 6DQ, ℰ (0870) 8902880, *reception@stantonmanor.co.uk*, Fax (0870) 8902881, 佘, ☞, 🐾 – ⁕× ✿ **P** – 🔬 100. **⑩⑩** **AE** **⑩** **VISA**
Rest 15.00/27.00 and a la carte 17.00/28.00 ☑ – **23 rm** ☑ ✱120.00 – ✱✱222.00.
◆ Extended 19C manor in formal gardens; popular commercial/wedding venue. There's some noise from adjacent M4, but this is more than made up for by appealing range of bedrooms. Elegant restaurant uses produce from the garden.

The red ⌖ symbol?
This denotes the very essence of peace
– only the sound of birdsong first thing in the morning …

ENGLAND

CHIPPERFIELD Herts. 504 S 28 – ⊠ Kings Langley.
London 27 – Hemel Hempstead 5 – Watford 6.

🏨 **Two Brewers Inn,** The Common, WD4 9BS, ℰ (01923) 265266, two.brew
ers.4086@thespiritgroup.com, Fax (01923) 261884 – 😽 rm, ✆ 🅿. 🐼 🆎 VISA ⚡
Rest a la carte 14.85/26.15 ☍ – ☍ 6.95 – **20 rm** ☆60.00/90.00 – ☆☆60.00/90.00.
♦ A row of pretty white terraced cottages overlooking the common and run by friendly
staff. Rooms are all of a similar standard, comfortable and practically furnished. Open-plan
restaurant with extensive blackboard menus.

CHIPPING Lancs. 502 M 22 – ⊠ Preston.
London 233 – Lancaster 30 – Leeds 54 – Manchester 40 – Preston 12.

🏨 **Gibbon Bridge** ≫, PR3 2TQ, East : 1 m. on Clitheroe rd ℰ (01995) 61456, recep
tion@gibbon-bridge.co.uk, Fax (01995) 61277, ₭₅, ☞, ♨, ⚒ – 🛗, 😽 rest, ✆ ₺ 🅿 –
₰ 120. 🐼 🆎 ① VISA ⚡
Rest 17.00 (lunch) and dinner a la carte 28.00/34.00 ☍ – **11 rm** ☍ ☆80.00 – ☆☆120.00,
18 suites ☍ 150.00/230.00.
♦ Converted stone farm buildings set in the heart of the Trough of Bowland. Bedrooms,
all of which are very comfy and individual, include split-level suites with four-posters. Own
bakery produce in restaurant, which overlooks delightful gardens.

CHIPPING CAMPDEN Glos. 503 504 O 27 Great Britain G. – pop. 1 943.
See : Town★.
Env. : Hidcote Manor Garden★★ AC, NE : 2½ m.
🅱 Old Police Station ℰ (01285) 654180.
London 93 – Cheltenham 21 – Oxford 37 – Stratford-upon-Avon 12.

🏨 **Cotswold House,** The Square, GL55 6AN, ℰ (01386) 840330, reception@cotswold
house.com, Fax (01386) 840310, ㎡, ☞ – 😽, 🍽 rest, ✆ 🅿 – ₰ 60. 🐼 🆎 VISA
Juliana's : Rest (dinner only and Sunday lunch)/dinner 49.50 ☍ – (see also **Hicks'** below) –
27 rm ☍ ☆140.00/285.00 – ☆☆395.00/425.00, 2 suites.
♦ Enviably stylish Regency town house with graceful spiral staircase winding upwards to
luxurious rooms, some very modern, boasting every mod con imaginable. Impressive
service. Formal though stylish Juliana's for accomplished cooking with an original style.

🏨 **Noel Arms,** High St, GL55 6AT, ℰ (01386) 840317, reception@noelarmshotel.com,
Fax (01386) 841136 – 😽 🅿 – ₰ 50. 🐼 🆎 ① VISA
Rest 14.95 (lunch) and a la carte 20.50/26.00 ☍ – **26 rm** ☍ ☆90.00/120.00 –
☆☆130.00/220.00.
♦ A 14C former coaching inn; lounge and reception decked in civil war armoury and
antique furniture. This extends to some heritage style rooms, one has 14C ornate four-
poster. Colourful, intimate dining room with menu of Asian dishes.

🏨 **The Kings,** The Square, GL55 6AW, ℰ (01386) 840256, info@kingscampden.co.uk,
Fax (01386) 841598, ㎡, ☞ – 😽 🅿. 🐼 🆎 VISA
Rest a la carte 20.00/35.00 – **24 rm** ☍ ☆72.50/105.00 – ☆☆85.00/165.00.
♦ 17C inn with archetypal Cotswold stone walls, unmissable on the main street. Characterful interior oozes antique-furnished rustic charm. Impeccably tasteful rooms. Skilfully created, quality dishes.

✗ **Hicks'** (at Cotswold House), The Square, GL55 6AN, ℰ (01386) 840330, Fax (01386) 840310
– 😽 🅿. 🐼 🆎 VISA
Rest (booking essential) a la carte 20.75/31.70 s. ☍.
♦ Named after local benefactor. Booking advised; open all day serving locals and
residents with modern varied menu. Morning coffees, afternoon teas, home-made cake
available.

🏠 **Eight Bells Inn** with rm, Church St, GL55 6JG, ℰ (01386) 840371, neilhargreaves@bel
linn.fsnet.co.uk, Fax (01386) 841669, ㎡ – 😽 🐼 VISA ⚡
closed 25 December – **Rest** a la carte 22.00/28.50 ☍ – **7 rm** ☍ ☆50.00 – ☆☆115.00.
♦ A 14C stone inn, once used by stonemasons working on adjacent church; still exudes
history in wood and stone interior. Traditional robust menu: blackboard specials.

at Mickleton North : 3¼ m. by B 4035 and B 4081 on B 4632 – ⊠ Chipping Campden.

🏨 **Three Ways House,** GL55 6SB, ℰ (01386) 438429, reception@puddingclub.com,
Fax (01386) 438118, ☞ – 🛗 😽, 🍽 rest, ✆ 🅿 – ₰ 80. 🐼 🆎 ① VISA
Rest 38.00 s. ☍ – **48 rm** ☍ ☆79.00/92.00 – ☆☆130.00/165.00.
♦ Built in 1870; renowned as home of the "Pudding Club". Two types of room, in original
house and modern block, all very comfy and modern. Bar with antique tiled floor. Arcaded
dining room; Pudding Club meets here to vote after tastings.

⚐ **Nineveh Farm** without rest., GL55 6PS, West : ½ m. on B 4081 ℰ (01386) 438923, *ninevehfarm@hotmail.com*, 🌲 – ✕ 🄿 🆆🄾 🆅🄸🅂🄰 ✕
5 rm ⌂ ✱55.00 – ✱✱65.00.
♦ Georgian farmhouse in pleasant garden. Warm welcome; local information in resident's lounge. Comfortable rooms with view in house or with French windows in garden house.

⚐ **Myrtle House** without rest., GL55 6SA, ℰ (01386) 430032, *kate@myrtlehouse.co.uk*, 🌲 – ✕ 🄲 🄿 🆆🄾 🆅🄸🅂🄰
5 rm ⌂ ✱45.00 – ✱✱75.00.
♦ Part Georgian house with large lawned garden. Bedrooms named and styled after flowers and plants, those on top floor most characterful.

at Paxford Southeast : 3 m. by B 4035 – ✉ Chipping Campden.

🄳 **Churchill Arms** with rm, GL55 6XH, ℰ (01386) 594000, *mail@thechurchillarms.com*, Fax (01386) 594005, 🌮 – ✕ rm, 🄲 🄿 🆆🄾 🆅🄸🅂🄰 ✕
Rest (bookings not accepted) a la carte 17.50/26.00 ♀ – **4 rm** ⌂ ✱40.00 – ✱✱70.00.
♦ Popular Cotswold stone and brick pub; mellow interior. Good value menus chalked on blackboard. Organic local produce used. Comfortable bedrooms.

at Broad Campden South : 1¼ m. by B 4081 – ✉ Chipping Campden.

⚐ **Malt House** ⌂ without rest., GL55 6UU, ℰ (01386) 840295, *info@themalt-house.free serve.co.uk*, Fax (01386) 841334, 🌲 – ✕ 🄿 🆆🄾 🄰🄴 🆅🄸🅂🄰
closed 1 week Christmas – **7 rm** ⌂ ✱85.00 – ✱✱140.00.
♦ For a rare experience of the countryside idyll, this 16C malting house is a must. Cut flowers from the gardens on view in bedrooms decked out in fabrics to delight the eye.

⚐ **Marnic House** without rest., GL55 6UR, ℰ (01386) 840014, *marnic@zoom.co.uk*, Fax (01386) 840441, 🌲 – ✕ 🄿 ✕
mid March-mid October – **3 rm** ⌂ ✱50.00 – ✱✱80.00.
♦ A stone built cottage with pleasing, well tended back gardens and views over country-side. Rear rooms share vistas and are quieter. Full breakfasts served on large oak table.

CHIPPING NORTON Oxon. 503 504 P 28 – pop. 5 688.
London 77 – Oxford 22 – Stow-on-the-Wold 9.

🄳 **The Masons Arms,** Banbury Rd, Swerford, OX7 4AP, Northeast : 5 m. by A 361 ℰ (01608) 683212, *themasonschef@hotmail.com*, Fax (01608) 683105, 🌮, 🌲 – 🄿 🆆🄾 🄰🄴 🆅🄸🅂🄰 ✕
closed 25-26 December – **Rest** a la carte 18.00/27.00 ♀.
♦ Cotswold stone roadside inn with pleasant terrace, garden and fine views. Bright, con-temporary interior. Appealing menus make use of local, well-chosen ingredients.

CHISELDON Wilts. 503 504 O 29 – see Swindon.

CHORLEY Lancs. 502 504 M 23 – pop. 33 536.
🄸 Duxbury Park, Duxbury Hall Rd ℰ (01257) 265380 – 🄸 Shaw Hill Hotel G. & C.C., Preston Rd, Whittle-le-Woods ℰ (01257) 269221.
London 222 – Blackpool 30 – Liverpool 33 – Manchester 26.

at Whittle-le-Woods North : 2 m. on A 6 – ✉ Chorley.

🏨 **Shaw Hill H. Golf & Country Club,** Preston Rd, PR6 7PP, ℰ (01257) 269221, *info@shaw-hill.co.uk*, Fax (01257) 261223, 🌊, 🖫, 🚣, 🖵, 🄸 – ✕ rest, 🄿 – 🄰 200. 🆆🄾 🄰🄴 🆅🄸🅂🄰 ✕
Vardon : Rest (closed Saturday lunch, Bank Holiday Monday lunch, 1-2 January and 26 December) 14.95/21.95 and a la carte 26.20/39.25 – **30 rm** ⌂ ✱75.00/85.00 – ✱✱95.00/130.00.
♦ Dignified Georgian hotel presides over 18 hole golf course. Golfing memorabilia adorns smart interiors. Variety of rooms, tastefully wallpapered; some overlook course. Classic dining room with golfing views.

🏠 **Parkville Country House,** 174 Preston Rd, PR6 7HE, ℰ (01257) 261881, Fax (01257) 273171, 🌲 – 🄿 🆆🄾 🄰🄴 🆅🄸🅂🄰 ✕
Truffles : Rest (closed Monday) 17.95 and a la carte 17.90/31.40 – ⌂ 5.00 – **5 rm** ✱50.00/70.00 – ✱✱60.00/70.00.
♦ A large converted house with conservatory extension not far from Shaw Hill Golf Club. Tidy bedrooms, all similarly furnished, some with jacuzzis. Well tended lawned gardens. Conservatory restaurant with gourmet club.

CHORLTON-CUM-HARDY Gtr. Manchester 502 503 504 N 23 – see Manchester.

ENGLAND

CHRISTCHURCH *Dorset 503 504* O 31 *The West Country G. – pop. 40 208.*

See : *Town★ – Priory★ – Env. : Hengistbury Head★ (≤★★) SW : 4½ m. by A 35 and B 3059.*

🏌 *Highcliffe Castle, 107 Lymington Rd, Highcliffe-on-Sea* 🎟 *(01425) 272953 –* 🏌 *Riverside Ave* 🎟 *(01202) 436436 –* 🛈 *49 High St* 🎟 *(01202) 471780.*

London 111 – Bournemouth 6 – Salisbury 26 – Southampton 24 – Winchester 39.

⌂ **Druid House** without rest., 26 Sopers Lane, BH23 1JE, 🎟 *(01202) 485615, reservations@druid-house.co.uk, Fax (01202) 473484,* 🌱 – ⊁ rm, 🅿. ⓪⑤ *VISA*. ⅍
8 rm 🖙 ✦30.00/60.00 – ✦✦70.00 88.00.
* 1930s house that appeals with bright, fresh ambience: cottagey breakfast room, light and airy conservatory sitting room, smart bar. Spacious bedrooms, two with balconies.

※※ **Splinters,** 12 Church St, BH23 1BW, 🎟 *(01202) 483454, eating@splinters.uk.com, Fax (01202) 480180 –* ⊁ ⇄ 26. ⓪⑤ *VISA*
closed 1 January, 26 December, Sunday and Monday – **Rest** 12.95/36.50 𝄞.
* Brasserie-like exterior; two dining areas inside: one has intimate pine booths; upstairs more formal with high-backed chairs. French-influenced cuisine.

※ **Fishworks,** 10 Church St, BH23 1BW, 🎟 *(01202) 487000, christchurch@fishworks.co.uk, Fax (01202) 487001 –* ⊁ ▤. ⓪⑤ *AE VISA*
closed 25-26 December, Sunday September-June and Monday – **Rest** - Seafood - (booking essential) a la carte 27.00/43.00 𝄞.
* An informal eatery which has its own well-stocked fish counter: choose your selection with the aid of helpful chefs. Tasty, prime quality produce.

at Mudeford *Southeast : 2 m. –* ✉ *Christchurch.*

🏢 **Avonmouth,** 95 Mudeford, BH23 3NT, 🎟 *(01202) 483434, stay@theavonmouth.co.uk, Fax (01202) 479004,* ≤, 🌱 – ⬇ ⊁ rm 🅿 – 🔏 60. ⓪⑤ *AE* ⓪ *VISA*
Rest a la carte 20.00/32.00 𝄞 – 🖙 15.00 – **39 rm** ✦90.00 – ✦✦130.00/140.00, 3 suites.
* Built in the 1820s, affording splendid views of estuary and Mudeford Quay; sailing craft on hire for the beachcomber. Feature bedrooms particularly good; all are well-kept. Harbour view restaurant.

🏢 **Waterford Lodge,** 87 Bure Lane, Friars Cliff, BH23 4DN, 🎟 *(01425) 272948, waterford@bestwestern.co.uk, Fax (01425) 279130,* 🌱 – ⊁ 🅿 – 🔏 80. ⓪⑤ *AE VISA*
Rest 16.50/27.50 – **18 rm** 🖙 ✦70.00 – ✦✦85.00/120.00.
* Family run hotel. Take a sea stroll with the dog, as they are welcome, or enjoy free swimming at local leisure centre. Rooms overlook rooftops and countryside on top floor. Hand-made truffles round off tasty meals.

CHRISTMAS COMMON *Oxon.*
London 41 – Oxford 18 – Reading 13.

🍴 **The Fox & Hounds,** OX49 5HL, 🎟 *(01491) 612599, kiran.daniels@btconnect.com,* 🍽 – 🅿. ⓪⑤ *VISA* – **Rest** a la carte 23.00/31.00 𝄞.
* Red brick and flint pub with beamed bar, fire and distinctive red and black tiled floor. Eat in barn conversion: carefully chosen local suppliers. Blend of cooking styles.

CHURCH ENSTONE *Oxon. –* ✉ *Chipping Norton.*
London 72 – Banbury 13 – Oxford 38.

🍴 **The Crown Inn,** Mill Lane, OX7 4NN, 🎟 *(01608) 677262, Fax (01608) 677394,* 🍽 – 🅿. ⓪⑤ *VISA*
closed 25-26 December and 1 January – **Rest** *(closed Sunday dinner and Monday lunch)* a la carte 18.00/25.00 𝄞.
* 17C Cotswold stone pub in charming village. Bar with seagrass carpet; bright dining room boasts red-hued walls and conservatory extension. Expansive menus, honest cooking.

CHURCHILL *Oxon. 503 504* P 28 – ✉ *Chipping Norton.*
London 79 – Birmingham 46 – Cheltenham 29 – Oxford 23 – Swindon 31.

⌂ **The Forge** without rest., OX7 6NJ, 🎟 *(01608) 658173, rushbrooke@madasafish.com –* ⊁ 🅿. ⓪⑤ *VISA*. ⅍
5 rm 🖙 ✦52.00/57.00 – ✦✦66.00/81.00.
* Converted smithy run by friendly owners. Limitless hot drinks at breakfast. Thoughtful extras in bedrooms; some have four-posters, two with jacuzzi. Non smoking.

🍴 **The Chequers,** Church Rd, OX7 6NJ, 🎟 *(01608) 659393,* 🍽 – 🅿. ⓪⑤ *VISA*. ⅍
Rest *(closed 25 December)* a la carte 18.50/20.00.
* Recently renovated honeystone Cotswold pub. Spacious contemporary interior with high ceiling and beams; upstairs lounge. Appealing mix of British menus with local ingredients.

Innovation has good prospects whenever it is cleaner, safer and more efficient.

 The MICHELIN Energy green tyre offers
a shorter braking distance and lasts 25% longer*.
It also provides fuel savings of 2 to 3%
while reducing CO_2 emissions.

*on average compared to competing tyres in the same category.

Making tyre performance last from the first to the last mile, another way to ensure a better way forward.

You may not know it, but a Michelin tyre can last a distance of more than once around the Earth. Indeed Michelin's 4000 researchers innovate using all their technological expertise to deliver you optimum performance from the first mile to the last.

www.michelin.co.uk

A better way forward

CHURCH STRETTON *Shrops.* 502 503 L 26 *Great Britain G.* – *pop. 3 941.*

Env. : *Wenlock Edge*★ , *E : by B 4371.*

🏌 *Trevor Hill &* (01694) 722281.

London 166 – Birmingham 46 – Hereford 39 – Shrewsbury 14.

↑ **Jinlye** ⊗ *without rest.,* Castle Hill, All Stretton, SY6 6JP, North : 2¼ m. by B 4370 turning left beside telephone box in All Stretton *&* (01694) 723243, *info@jinlye.co.uk,* Fax (01694) 723243, ≤, 💐, 📖 – ⁝✕⁝ ⚿ 🅿. ⬢⬢ 𝐕𝐈𝐒𝐀. ⚘
7 rm ⊇ ✲45.00/55.00 – ✲✲70.00/85.00.
 ♦ Enjoy wonderful views of Long Mynd from this characterful crofter's cottage high in the hills, run by charming owner and daughter. Grandiose breakfast room. 19C conservatory.

XX **The Studio,** 59 High St, SY6 6BY, *&* (01694) 722672, *info@thestudiorestaurant.net,* ☕, 💐 – ⁝✕⁝. ⬢⬢ 𝐕𝐈𝐒𝐀
closed 8-31 January, 25 December, Sunday and Monday – **Rest** (dinner only) a la carte 23.75/28.75 ♀.
 ♦ Personally run former art studio; walls enhanced by local artwork. Pleasant rear terrace for sunny lunches. Tried-and-tested dishes: much care taken over local produce.

Good food without spending a fortune?
Look out for the Bib Gourmand ☺

CIRENCESTER *Glos.* 503 504 O 28 *Great Britain G.* – *pop. 15 861.*

See : *Town*★ – *Church of St John the Baptist*★ – *Corinium Museum*★ *(Mosaic pavements*★ *)* AC.

Env. : *Fairford : Church of St Mary*★ *(stained glass windows*★★ *) E : 7 m. by A 417.*

🏌 *Cheltenham Rd, Bagendon &* (01285) 652465.

🛈 *Corn Hall, Market Pl &* (01285) 654180.

London 97 – Bristol 37 – Gloucester 19 – Oxford 37.

↑ **No 12** *without rest.,* 12 Park St, GL7 2BW, *&* (01285) 640232, *no12cirencester@ukgate way.net,* 💐 – ⁝✕⁝ ⚿. ⬢⬢ 𝐀𝐄 𝐕𝐈𝐒𝐀. ⚘
4 rm ⊇ ✲60.00 – ✲✲100.00.
 ♦ 16C property with Georgian façade, hidden away in the old alleyways. Delightful rear walled garden. Excellent organic breakfast. Stylish rooms charmingly blend old and new.

↑ **The Old Brewhouse** *without rest.,* 7 London Rd, GL7 2PU, *&* (01285) 656099, *info@theoldbrewhouse.com,* Fax (01285) 656099 – ⁝✕⁝ ⚹ 🅿. ⬢⬢ 𝐀𝐄 𝐕𝐈𝐒𝐀. ⚘
6 rm ⊇ ✲45.00/55.00 – ✲✲65.00.
 ♦ Former 17C brewhouse with a cosy, cottagey ambience. Exposed stone in two breakfast rooms. Cast iron bedsteads adorn some of the rooms, all of which boast period character.

at Barnsley *Northeast : 4 m. by A 429 on B 4425 –* ⊠ *Cirencester.*

🏠🏠 **Barnsley House** ⊗, GL7 5EE, *&* (01285) 740000, *info@barnsleyhouse.com,* Fax (01285) 740925, ≤, ☕, 💐, 📖, ╳ – ⁝✕⁝ 🅿. ⬢⬢ 𝐕𝐈𝐒𝐀. ⚘
Rest 25.50/39.50 – (see also **The Village Pub** below) – ⊇ 16.50 – **5 rm** ✲270.00 – ✲✲385.00, **5 suites** 295.00/475.00.
 ♦ 17C manor house in Cotswold stone with magnificent gardens. Original features retained in contemporary décor. Stunning bedrooms with every modern comfort. Dining room opening on to terrace and gardens. Interesting modern menu using home-grown produce.

🍴 **The Village Pub** *with rm,* GL7 5EF, *&* (01285) 740421, *reservations@thevillage pub.co.uk,* ☕ – ⁝✕⁝ 🅿. ⬢⬢ 𝐕𝐈𝐒𝐀
Rest a la carte 24.50/28.50 ♀ – **6 rm** ⊇ ✲75.00 – ✲✲90.00.
 ♦ 17C pub: flagstone and oak floors, exposed timbers, open fireplaces. Home-made bread, local dishes, organic ingredients allied to modern English cooking. Rustic bedrooms.

at Ewen *Southwest : 3¼ m. by A 429 –* ⊠ *Cirencester.*

🍴 **The Wild Duck Inn** *with rm,* Drake's Island, GL7 6BY, *&* (01285) 770310, *wduck inn@aol.com,* Fax (01285) 770924, ☕ – ⁝✕⁝ rest, ⚹ 🅿. ⬢⬢ 𝐀𝐄 𝐕𝐈𝐒𝐀
closed dinner 25 December – **Rest** a la carte 18.00/26.00 ♀ – **12 rm** ⊇ ✲70.00 – ✲✲95.00/120.00.
 ♦ Cotswold stone Elizabethan inn; rich interiors, beams garlanded with hops. A quirky, eclectic menu to peruse as you take in the delightfully characterful surroundings.

at Sapperton West : 5 m. by A 419 – ✉ Cirencester.

🍴 **The Bell,** GL7 6LE, 𝒸 (01285) 760298, thebell@sapperton66.freeserve.co.uk,
Fax (01285) 760761, 🈺, 🌿 – 🌡️ 🅿 ↻ 10, ⬤⬤ 𝘝𝘐𝘚𝘈
closed 3-10 January and 25 December – **Rest** a la carte 21.00/35.00 ♀ ⌂.
• Charming, personally run pub made up of three cottages. Log fires and beams inside
and a terrace outside. Mix of English and European cooking; superb wine list.

CLACTON-ON-SEA Essex 504 X 28 – pop. 51 284.
  🏉 West Rd 𝒸 (01255) 421919.
  🚩 Town Hall, Station Rd 𝒸 (01255) 423400.
  London 76 – Chelmsford 37 – Colchester 14 – Ipswich 28.

🏠 **Chudleigh** without rest., 13 Agate Rd, Marine Parade West, CO15 1RA, 𝒸 (01255)
425407, reception@chudleighhotel.com, Fax (01255) 470280 – 🌡️ 🅿, ⬤⬤ 𝘝𝘐𝘚𝘈
closed 2 weeks October and 2 weeks Spring – **10 rm** ⌂ ✱41.00/50.00 – ✱✱60.00/65.00.
• Victorian terraced house within easy reach of pier, seafront and the shops. Decorated in
a traditional style with simple, comfortable lounge and floral bedrooms.

Good food and accommodation at moderate prices?
Look for the Bib symbols:
red Bib Gourmand for food, blue Bib Hotel 🏨 for hotels

CLANFIELD Oxon. 503 504 P 28 – pop. 1 709 (inc. Shilton).
  London 75 – Oxford 24 – Swindon 16.

🏨 **Plough at Clanfield,** Bourton Rd, OX18 2RB, on A 4095 𝒸 (01367) 810222, info@the
ploughclanfield.co.uk, Fax (01367) 810596, 🌿 – 🌡️ 🔥 🅿, ⬤⬤ 𝘝𝘐𝘚𝘈 ⌂
Rest a la carte 16.90/32.45 ♀ – **12 rm** ⌂ ✱75.00/105.00 – ✱✱210.00/270.00.
• Restored Elizabethan manor (1560), sitting in pretty gardens. Serene lounge with origi-
nal fireplace; choice of rooms with character in main house and larger, newer rooms.
Intimate restaurant.

CLARE Suffolk 504 V 27 – pop. 1 975 – ✉ Sudbury.
  London 67 – Bury St Edmunds 16 – Cambridge 27 – Colchester 24 – Ipswich 32.

🏠 **Ship Stores** without rest., 22 Callis St, CO10 8PX, 𝒸 (01787) 277834, shipclare@aol.com,
Fax (01787) 277183 – 🌡️ 🔥, ⬤⬤ 𝘝𝘐𝘚𝘈 ⌂
7 rm ⌂ ✱40.00/55.00 – ✱✱60.00/70.00.
• Three converted cottages which once sheltered sheep farmers and now double as the
village shop. Simple, pine furnished rooms, four in the adjacent annex. Breakfast room
with low ceiling, nooks and crannies.

CLAVERING Essex 504 U 28 – pop. 1 663 – ✉ Saffron Walden.
  London 44 – Cambridge 25 – Colchester 44 – Luton 29.

🍴 **Cricketers** with rm, CB11 4QT, 𝒸 (01799) 550442, cricketers@lineone.net,
Fax (01799) 550882, 🈺, 🌿 – 🌡️ 🔥 🅿, ⬤⬤ 𝔸𝔼 𝘝𝘐𝘚𝘈 ⌂
closed 25-26 December – **Rest** 26.00 (dinner) and a la carte 21.00/26.00 ♀ – **14 rm** ⌂
✱70.00 – ✱✱100.00.
• Jamie Oliver grew up in this 16C inn and cooked here; it's still owned by the family.
Exciting dishes with influences old and new. Rooms, too, have modern or traditional feel.

CLAYTON-LE-MOORS Lancs. 502 M 22 – pop. 8 289 – ✉ Accrington.
  London 232 – Blackburn 3.5 – Lancaster 37 – Leeds 44 – Preston 14.

🏨 **Sparth House,** Whalley Rd, BB5 5RP, 𝒸 (01254) 872263, mail.sparth@btinternet.com,
Fax (01254) 872263, 🌿 – 🌡️ rest, 🔥 🅿 – 🔒 100, ⬤⬤ 𝔸𝔼 ⓞ 𝘝𝘐𝘚𝘈 ⌂
Rest a la carte 15.85/30.95 ♀ – **16 rm** ⌂ ✱68.00/78.00 – ✱✱99.00/110.00.
• A Georgian house in wooded grounds with wood panelled interiors. Some rooms are
modern, others traditional; one has antiques from the Titanic's sister liner. Traditional
dining in wood-panelled room with open fire.

CLAYTON-LE-WOODS *Lancs.* 502 M 24 – *pop. 14 173* – ⊠ *Chorley.*
London 220 – Liverpool 34 – Manchester 26 – Preston 5.5.

🏥 **The Pines,** 570 Preston Rd, PR6 7ED, on A 6 at junction with B 5256 *𝒫* (01772) 338551, *mail@thepineshotel.co.uk, Fax* (01772) 629002, 🍴, 🌳 – ⇔ rm, 📞 📶 – 🏃 350. 🌐 ﯼ 🅾
VISA 🍴
closed 24-25 December – **Haworths Bistro :** *Rest* 12.50/16.50 and a la carte 12.50/22.50 ⅞
– **34 rm** ⊑ ✦65.00/85.00 – ✦✦85.00/120.00, 2 suites.
♦ Prospering on a heady round of weddings and cabarets, this redbrick Victorian hotel boasts two fashionable lounges and a smart set of bedrooms, all individually decorated. Restaurant with unique stained glass roof and modern, assured cooking.

CLAYTON WEST *W. Yorks.* 502 504 P 23 – *pop. 7 932 (inc. Skelmanthorpe)* – ⊠ *Huddersfield.*
London 190 – Leeds 19 – Manchester 35 – Sheffield 24.

🏥 **Bagden Hall,** Wakefield Rd, Scissett, HD8 9LE, Southwest : 1 m. on A 636 *𝒫* (01484) 865330, *info@bagdenhallhotel.co.uk, Fax* (01484) 861001, 🍴, 🏌, 🌳, 🅟 – ⇔ rest, ▦ rest, 🔥 📞 – 🏃 220. 🌐 ﯼ 🅾 **VISA**. 🍴
closed 25-26 December and 1 January – **Glendale :** *Rest* 18.95/24.95 and dinner a la carte 18.40/33.85 ⅞ – **Pippins :** *Rest* a la carte 16.50/21.95 – **36 rm** ⊑ ✦70.00/90.00 – ✦✦90.00/130.00.
♦ 19C house in Georgian style with extensive, mature gardens, lake, 16C boathouse and golf course. Suites and bedrooms in country house style. Bar with conservatory extension. Formal dining in Glendale. Pippins brasserie named after racehorse buried in grounds!

CLEARWELL *Glos.* – see Coleford.

CLEETHORPES *N.E. Lincs.* 502 504 U 23 – *pop. 31 853.*
✈ Humberside Airport : *𝒫* (01652) 688456, *W* : 16 m. by A 46 and A 18 Y.
🛈 42-43 Alexandra Rd *𝒫* (01472) 323111.
London 171 – Lincoln 38 – Sheffield 77.

❌❌ **Riverside Bar and Restaurant,** 2 Alexandra Rd, DN35 0SP, *𝒫* (01472) 600515, *info@theriversidebarandrestaurant.com, Fax* (01472) 290270 – ⇔ ▦ ⇕ 20. 🌐 **VISA**
closed 25-26 December, Sunday and Monday – **Rest** 15.95 (lunch) and a la carte 21.85/35.90 ⅞.
♦ Actually looking out to sea, this 19C terraced property has a modern interior with a ground floor bar and smart restaurant upstairs where modern classics take centre stage.

CLEEVE HILL *Glos.* 503 504 N 28 – see Cheltenham.

CLENT *Worcs.* 504 N 26 *Great Britain G.*
EXC. : *Black Country Museum★, N : 7 m. by A 491 and A 4036 – Birmingham★ - Museum and Art Gallery★★, Aston Hall★★, NE : 10 m. by A 491 and A 456.*
London 127 – Birmingham 12 – Hagley 2.

🍴 **Bell & Cross,** Holy Cross, DY9 9QL, West : ½ m. off A 491 (northbound carriageway) (Bromsgrove rd) *𝒫* (01562) 730319, *Fax* (01562) 731733, 🍴, 🌳 – ⇔ 🅟. 🌐 **VISA**. 🍴
closed 25 December – **Rest** a la carte 22.00/25.00.
♦ Early 19C village pub with gardens and dining terrace. Traditional public bar and five intimate dining rooms. Friendly service; blackboard specials and seasonal produce.

CLEY NEXT THE SEA *Norfolk* 504 X 25 – see Blakeney.

CLIFTON HAMPDEN *Devon* 503 504 Q 29 – see Abingdon.

CLIMPING *W. Sussex* 504 S 31 – see Littlehampton.

CLIPSHAM *Rutland* – see Stamford.

CLITHEROE *Lancs.* 502 M 22 – *pop. 14 697.*
🏌 Whalley Rd *𝒫* (01200) 422618.
🛈 12-14 Market Pl *𝒫* (01200) 425566.
London 64 – Blackpool 35 – Manchester 31.

⛫ **Brooklyn** without rest., 32 Pimlico Rd, BB7 2AH, *𝒫* (01200) 428268 – ⇔. 🌐 🅾 **VISA**
🍴
4 rm ⊑ ✦32.00 – ✦✦58.00.
♦ Stone 19C house, two minutes' walk from town, with floral furnished rooms, quieter at the rear. Homely lounge to relax in after a day's exploration of the Trough of Bowland.

CLOVELLY Devon 503 G 31 The West Country G. – pop. 439 – ⊠ Bideford.

See : Village★★.

Env. : SW : Tamar River★★.

Exc. : Hartland : Hartland Church★ – Hartland Quay★ (viewpoint★★) – Hartland Point ≤★★★, W : 6½ m. by B 3237 and B 3248 – Morwenstow (Church★, cliffs★★), SW : 11½ m. by A 39.

London 241 – Barnstaple 18 – Exeter 52 – Penzance 92.

🏠 **Red Lion,** The Quay, EX39 5TF, ℰ (01237) 431237, redlion@clovelly.co.uk, Fax (01237) 431044, ≤ – ⇄ 🅿. 🐵 🖭 VISA. ⋘
Rest (bar lunch)/dinner 25.00 s. – **11 rm** (dinner included) ⊡ ✦77.00/99.50 – ✦✦154.00/169.00.
• Cosy little hotel/inn on the quayside; a superb location. All rooms enjoy sea and harbour views and are dressed in soft, understated colours, providing a smart resting place. Simple dining room looks out to harbour.

CLUN Shrops. 503 K 26.

London 173 – Church Stretton 16 – Ludlow 16.

🏠 **Birches Mill** ⧖ without rest., SY7 8NL, Northwest : 3 m. by A 488, Bicton rd, Mainstone rd and Burlow rd ℰ (01588) 640409, gill@birchesmill.fsnet.co.uk, Fax (01588) 640409, ☞ – ⇄ 🅿. 🐵 VISA. ⋘
April-October – – **3 rm** ⊡ ✦62.00/66.00 – ✦✦76.00/80.00.
• High quality comforts in remote former corn mill: interior has characterful 17C/18C structures. Flagged lounge with lovely inglenook. Simple but tastefully decorated rooms.

> 🐾 Look out for red symbols, indicating particularly pleasant establishments.

COBALT BUSINESS PARK Tyne and Wear – see Newcastle upon Tyne.

COBHAM Surrey 504 S 30 – pop. 16 360 (inc. Oxshott).
London 24 – Guildford 10.

Plan : see Greater London (South-West) 5

🏨 **Hilton Cobham,** Seven Hills Road South, KT11 1EW, West : 1½ m. by A 245 ℰ (01932) 864471, gm-cobham@hilton.com, Fax (01932) 868017, 🏤, 👪, 🚋, 🔲, ☞, ⋘ – 🛗, ⇄ rm, 🍴 rest, 📞 🅿 – 🕍 300. 🐵 🖭 ① VISA
Rest (bar lunch Saturday) a la carte 19.70/25.70 ⅌ – ⊡ 17.95 – **155 rm** ✦205.00 – ✦✦215.00, 3 suites.
• Designed with the corporate traveller in mind, this large hotel set in woodland offers comfortable, well-kept rooms fitted with pine furniture. Mediterranean influenced menus.

at Stoke D'Abernon Southeast : 1½ m. on A 245 – ⊠ Cobham.

🏨 **Woodlands Park,** Woodlands Lane, KT11 3QB, on A 245 ℰ (01372) 843933, woodlandspark@handpicked.co.uk, Fax (01372) 842704, ☞, 🔥, ⋘ – 🛗, ⇄ rm, 🅿 – 🕍 150. 🐵 🖭 ① VISA. ⋘
Oak Room : Rest (closed Sunday dinner and Monday) (dinner only and Sunday lunch)/dinner 39.00 – **Brasserie :** Rest a la carte 17.50/30.45 – ⊡ 12.50 – **57 rm** ✦175.00 – ✦✦325.00.
• Designed in 1885 for son of founder of Bryant and May match company; one of first houses with electricity. Frequented by Prince of Wales and Lillie Langtry. Modish rooms. Appealingly welcoming Oak Room restaurant; also brasserie.

COCKERMOUTH Cumbria 501 502 J 20 – pop. 7 446.

🏌 Embleton ℰ (017687) 76223.

🛈 Town Hall, Market St ℰ (01900) 822634.

London 306 – Carlisle 25 – Keswick 13.

🏨 **Trout,** Crown St, CA13 0EJ, ℰ (01900) 823591, enquiries@trouthotel.co.uk, Fax (01900) 827514, 🏤, 🐟, ☞ – ⇄ 📞 🅿 – 🕍 50. 🐵 🖭 VISA
The Restaurant : Rest (dinner only and Sunday lunch)/dinner 28.50 ⅌ – **The Terrace :** Rest 15.95/28.50 – **43 rm** ⊡ ✦89.95/109.00 – ✦✦109.00/149.00.
• Extended 17C house on the banks of the River Derwent, now a hotel catering for trout and salmon fishing. Rooms in modern wing or stick with rustic style in original house. Two dining options.

at Lorton *Southeast : 4¼ m. by B 5292 –* ⊠ *Cockermouth.*

🏠 **Winder Hall Country House** ⚜, CA13 9UP, on B 5289 ℘ (01900) 85107, *nick@winderhall.co.uk, Fax (01900) 85479,* ≤, *☞* – ⤢ 🅿 ⓪ⓈＡＥ **VISA**. ⚘
closed January–mid February – **Rest** (booking essential for non-residents) (dinner only) 32.00 **s.** – **7 rm** ⊏⊐ ✦70.00/75.00 – ✦✦80.00/100.00.
♦ A mellow manor house by the river Cocker dating from 14C. Stone mullions and leaded windows. Slip into peaceful rooms with flowers and chocolates and views of the fells. Classic white and black dining room with oak panelling.

🏠 **New House Farm,** CA13 9UU, South : 1¼ m. on B 5289 ℘ (01900) 85404, *hazel@new house-farm.co.uk, Fax (01900) 85478,* ≤, *☞*, ⚘ – ⤢ 🅿 ⓪Ⓢ **VISA**
Rest 21.00 **s.** – **5 rm** ⊏⊐ ✦71.00/91.00 – ✦✦142.00.
♦ A converted 17C-19C farmhouse in spectacular countryside of hills and lakes. Fine rambling territory but if wet, sit back and admire the scenery from the bedroom window. Home cooking with local ingredients.

COCKLEFORD *Glos. –* ⊠ *Cheltenham.*
London 95 – Bristol 48 – Cheltenham 7.

🏠 **The Green Dragon Inn** with rm, GL53 9NW, ℘ (01242) 870271, *green-dragon@buc caneer.co.uk, Fax (01242) 870171,* 斉, *☞* – ⤢ 🅿 – ⚖ 40. ⓪Ⓢ ＡＥ **VISA**
Rest (booking essential) a la carte 20.00/35.00 – **9 rm** ⊏⊐ ✦57.00 – ✦✦75.00.
♦ 17C country inn of old Cotswold stone, "in the middle of nowhere", with beams, log fire and large outside terrace. Tasty meals employing good use of local ingredients. Smart rooms.

CODFORD ST MARY *Wilts.* 504 N 30 *Great Britain G.*
EXC. : *Stonehenge★★★ AC, E : 10½ m. by A 36 and A 303.*
London 101 – Bristol 38 – Warminster 8.

🏠 **George** with rm, High St, BA12 0NG, ℘ (01985) 850270, 斉 – ⤢ rm, 🅿 ⓪Ⓢ **VISA**. ⚘
closed Tuesday and dinner Sunday – **Rest** a la carte 18.00/35.00 – **3 rm** ⊏⊐ ✦45.00 – ✦✦70.00.
♦ Whitewashed 18C pub/hotel in pretty village. Large bar with real ales, mix and match furniture. Concise menu, accomplished dishes using fresh produce. Simply appointed rooms.

COGGESHALL *Essex* 504 W 28 – *pop. 3 919 –* ⊠ *Colchester.*
London 49 – Braintree 6 – Chelmsford 16 – Colchester 9.

🏛 **White Hart,** Market End, CO6 1NH, ℘ (01376) 561654, *whitehart.coggeshall@greenek ing.co.uk, Fax (01376) 561789 –* 🅿 ⓪Ⓢ ＡＥ ⓪ **VISA**
Rest (in bar Sunday dinner) 15.00 (lunch) and a la carte 21.90/35.35 ♈ – **18 rm** ⊏⊐ ✦75.00/85.00 – ✦✦115.00.
♦ Part 15C guildhall, a meeting place for merchants (the south road used to pass between entrance hall and reception). Individually furnished rooms have contemporary style. Timbered 'olde worlde' restaurant.

XX **Baumann's Brasserie,** 4-6 Stoneham St, CO6 1TT, ℘ (01376) 561453, *food@bau manns.brasserie.co.uk, Fax (01376) 563762 –* ⓪Ⓢ ＡＥ **VISA**
closed first 2 weeks January, Monday and Tuesday – **Rest** 15.50/21.00 and a la carte 28.00/34.95 ♈.
♦ A local institution. The colourful pictures on the walls help create an agreeably relaxed ambience in which to sample exciting, traditional cuisine in a wide variety of menus.

COLCHESTER *Essex* 504 W 28 *Great Britain G. – pop. 104 390.*
See : *Castle and Museum★ AC* BZ.
🐦 *Birch Grove, Layer Rd* ℘ (01206) 734276.
🏛 *Visitor Information Centre, Trinity St* ℘ (01206) 282920.
London 52 – Cambridge 48 – Ipswich 18 – Luton 76 – Southend-on-Sea 41.

Plan on next page

🏛 **George,** 116 High St, CO1 1TD, ℘ (01206) 578494, *reservations.colchester@swallowho tels.com, Fax (01206) 761732,* 斉 – ⤢ rm, ▦ rest, 🅿 – ⚖ 70. ⓪Ⓢ ＡＥ ⓪ **VISA**   BZ **b**
Rest 12.95 (lunch) and a la carte 20.65/26.95 ♈ – ⊏⊐ 9.95 – **47 rm** ✦95.00 – ✦✦105.00/195.00.
♦ The atmosphere of a 500-year old coaching inn pervades the hotel with its arched and timbered interior, beamed ceilings and wooden floors. Bedrooms have charm of bygone age. Relaxed brasserie and sumptuous lounge.

ENGLAND

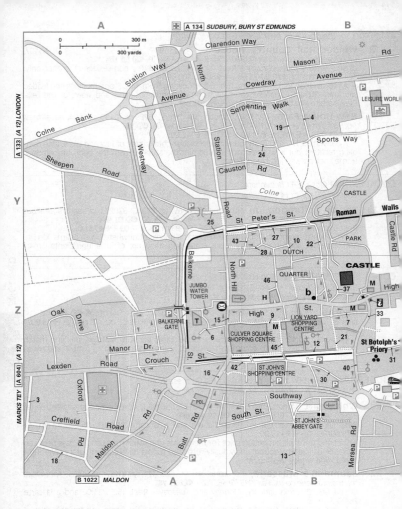

Rose and Crown, East St, Eastgates, CO1 2TZ, *☎* (01206) 866677, *info@rose-and-crown.com, Fax* (01206) 866616 – ≤⇔ & P. – ⚒ 100. 🕮 AE ① VISA. ⚘   **CZ d**
closed 27-29 December **Rest** *(closed Sunday dinner)* a la carte 19.70/29.85 – ⚌ 9.95 – 38 rm ✝80.00/95.00 – ✝✝150.00/155.00.
   • The Tudor bar sits snug in the oldest part of this 14C extended timbered inn where locally brewed beer is served. Beamed bedrooms rub shoulders with those in modern style. Warm, atmospheric dining room; menu of Indian and French fusion cuisine.

Red House without rest., 29 Wimpole Rd, CO1 2DL, *☎* (01206) 509005, *theredhousecol chester@hotmail.com, Fax* (01206) 509005, ≈ – ≤⇔. ⚘   **CZ a**
3 rm ⚌ ✝35.00/40.00 – ✝✝60.00.
   • Red-brick Victorian house within walking distance of the centre. Pleasant period style lounge; ample breakfast choice. Well-appointed rooms with good level of amenities.

If breakfast is included the ⚌ symbol appears after the number of rooms.

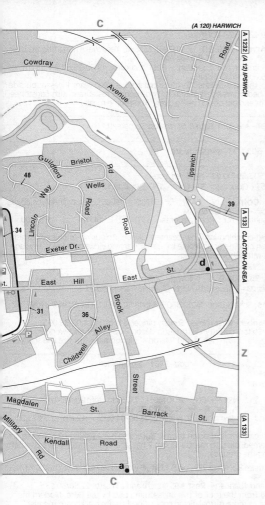

COLCHESTER

ENGLAND

COLEFORD Glos. 503 504 M 28 Great Britain G. – pop. 10 145.

Env. : W : Wye Valley★.

⟨ Forest of Dean, Lords Hills ℘ (01594) 832583 – ⟨ Forest Hills, Mile End Rd ℘ (01594) 810620.

🄱 High St ℘ (01594) 812388.

London 143 – Bristol 28 – Gloucester 19 – Newport 29.

🏨 **Speech House**, Forest of Dean, GL16 7EL, Northeast : 3 m. by B 4028 on B 4226 ℘ (01594) 822607, relax@thespeechhouse.co.uk, Fax (01594) 823658, 🌱 – 쏙, 🍽 rest, 📞 ⅖ 🄿 – 🔬 50. 🅜🅢 🄰🄴 🄾 𝚅𝙸𝚂𝙰
The Verderer's Court : Rest a la carte 21.95/26.70 s. – **31 rm** ⊇ ✦65.00/70.00 – ✦✦98.00/190.00.

◆ Charles II's hunting lodge within the Forest of Dean. Many period featues in situ. Modern rooms in annexe; more characterful in lodge: some of these boast huge four posters. Dining room wooden dais and bench hint at royal history.

at Clearwell South : 2 m. by B 4228 – ⊠ Coleford.

🏠 **The Wyndham Arms**, GL16 8JT, 𝒫 (01594) 833666, res@thewyndhamhotel.co.uk, Fax (01594) 836450, 🍽 – ⇆ rest, 🅿 ⓒⓞ 𝗩𝗜𝗦𝗔 🛇
closed 26 and 31 December and 1 January – **Rest** a la carte 19.50/29.50 ♀ – **18 rm** ☆45.00/60.00 – ☆☆75.00/115.00, 1 suite.
◆ Set in a quiet village, this whitewashed former inn dates back 600 years. Pleasant outside terrace; some of the bedrooms boast antiques. Two-roomed restaurant with flagstones, bare white walls, beams and old bread baking oven; wholesome meals.

COLERNE Wilts. 503 504 M 29 – see Bath (Bath & North East Somerset).

COLLYWESTON Northants. 502 S 26 – see Stamford.

COLN ST ALDWYNS Glos. 503 504 O 28 – ⊠ Cirencester.
London 101 – Bristol 53 – Gloucester 20 – Oxford 28 – Swindon 15.

🏠 **New Inn At Coln**, GL7 5AN, 𝒫 (01285) 750651, stay@new-inn.co.uk, Fax (01285) 750657, 🍽 – ⇆ 🅿 ⓒⓞ 𝗔𝗘 𝗩𝗜𝗦𝗔
Rest (booking essential for non-residents) 38.00 ♀ – **14 rm** ☲ ☆109.00 – ☆☆126.00/163.00.
◆ Pretty 16C Cotswold coaching inn. Low-beamed lounge. Colour co-ordinated furnishings. Bedrooms in main building or dovecote to rear. Rewarding views over fields or village. Intimate dining room with subdued lighting.

COLSTON BASSETT Notts. 502 504 R 25 – ⊠ Nottingham.
London 129 – Leicester 23 – Lincoln 40 – Nottingham 15 – Sheffield 51.

🍽 **The Martins Arms**, School Lane, NG12 3FD, 𝒫 (01949) 81361, Fax (01949) 81039, 🍽, 🍴 – 🅿 ⓒⓞ 𝗔𝗘 𝗩𝗜𝗦𝗔 🛇
closed dinner 25 December – **Rest** (closed Sunday dinner) a la carte 21.00/35.00 ♀.
◆ Charming pub in "Stilton country" with rustic décor - open fire and wooden tables. Makes good use of assets: Stilton rarebit and "Martin's" ploughman's are sizeable snacks.

COLTISHALL Norfolk 504 Y 25 Great Britain G. – pop. 2 161 – ⊠ Norwich.
Env. : Norfolk Broads★.
London 133 – Norwich 8.

🏠🏠 **Norfolk Mead** ﹩, NR12 7DN, 𝒫 (01603) 737531, info@norfolkmead.co.uk, Fax (01603) 737521, ≤, 🌊, 🍲, 🍽, 🍴 – ⇆ ⓒ 🅿 ⓒⓞ 𝗔𝗘 𝗩𝗜𝗦𝗔
Rest (dinner only and Sunday lunch) a la carte 23.50/34.00 ♀ – **12 rm** ☲ ☆75.00 – ☆☆190.00.
◆ Restful 18C manor; gardens lead down to river Bure; also has a fishing lake. Rooms are individually colour themed: blue, terracotta. Room 7 has jacuzzi and lovely views. Candlelit restaurant overlooking the grounds.

🍽 **King's Head**, Wroxham Rd, NR12 7EA, on B 1354 𝒫 (01603) 737426, Fax (01603) 737426 – 🅿 ⟲ 15. ⓒⓞ 𝗔𝗘 𝗩𝗜𝗦𝗔 🛇
closed 26 December and 1 January – **Rest** 9.95 (lunch) and a la carte 22.50/30.95 ♀.
◆ Fishing curios hang from the roof of this unassuming pub by the Bure. Modern menu served in the firelit bar or more formal dining room. Good choice blackboard menus.

COLWALL Herefordshire – see Great Malvern.

COLYFORD Devon 503 K 31 Great Britain G. – ⊠ Colyton.
Env. : Colyton★ (Church★), N : 1 m. on B 3161 – Axmouth (≤★), S : 1 m. by A 3052 and B 3172.
London 168 – Exeter 21 – Taunton 30 – Torquay 46 – Yeovil 32.

🏠 **Swallows Eaves**, EX24 6QJ, 𝒫 (01297) 553184, swallows–eaves@hotmail.com, Fax (01297) 553574, 🍽 – ⇆ 🅿 🛇
Rest (residents only) (dinner only) 27.50 ♀ – **8 rm** ☲ ☆59.00/69.00 – ☆☆118.00.
◆ Pristine 1920s house with bright, spright rooms, some with views over the Axe Valley. Personally run by friendly, experienced couple. Listen out for birdsong on the marshes. Cooking for residents by the owner.

COMPTON ABBAS Dorset – see Shaftesbury.

CONGLETON *Ches.* **502 503 504** N 24 *Great Britain G.* – *pop. 25 400.*

Env. : *Little Moreton Hall★★ AC, SW : 3 m. by A 34.*

Biddulph Rd ☎ (01260) 273540.

Town Hall, High St ☎ (01260) 271095.

London 183 – Liverpool 50 – Manchester 25 – Sheffield 46 – Stoke-on-Trent 13.

Sandhole Farm without rest., Hulme Walfield, CW12 2JH, North : 2 ¼ m. on A 34 ☎ (01260) 224419, *veronica@sandholefarm.co.uk, Fax (01260) 224766,* – P. VISA.

15 rm ✝55.00 – ✝✝65.00.

◆ Former farm with its stable block converted into comfy, well-equipped bedrooms with a rustic feel. Breakfast taken in the farmhouse's conservatory overlooking the countryside.

Pecks, Newcastle Rd, Moreton, CW12 4SB, South : 2 ¾ m. on A 34 ☎ (01260) 275161, *Fax (01260) 299640* – P 25. AE VISA

closed 25-31 December, Sunday dinner and Monday – **Rest** 16.75/36.50 **s.** ♀.

◆ Airy, modish restaurant with jaunty yellow décor: well regarded locally. 5 or 7 course dinners served sharp at 8pm. Dishes are an interesting mix of modern and traditional.

L'Endroit, 70-72 Lawton St, CW12 1RS, ☎ (01260) 299548, *Fax (01260) 299548* – . VISA

closed 2 weeks February, 1 week late June, 1 week late September, Saturday lunch, Sunday dinner and Monday – **Rest** - French - a la carte 18.15/32.95.

◆ Relaxing eatery, away from town centre, boasting the tangible feel of a bistro: vivid walls with foodie prints, chunky wood tables. Tasty French dishes with seasonal specials.

CONISTON *Cumbria* **502** K 20 *Great Britain G.* – *pop. 1 304.*

Env. : *Coniston Water★ – Brantwood★ AC, SE : 2 m. on east side of Coniston Water.*

Exc. : *Hard Knott Pass★★, Wrynose Pass★★, NW : 10 m. by A 593 and minor road.*

Ruskin Ave ☎ (015394) 41533, conistontic@lake-district.gov.uk.

London 285 – Carlisle 55 – Kendal 22 – Lancaster 42.

Coniston Lodge without rest., Station Rd, LA21 8HH, ☎ (015394) 41201, *info@coniston-lodge.com, Fax (015394) 41201* – P. VISA.

6 rm ✝64.00/70.00 – ✝✝99.00/115.00.

◆ Personally run hotel; Donald Campbell's Bluebird memorabilia adorns lounge. Home-made jams for sale - and for breakfast. Rooms named after tarns; some overlook garden.

at Torver *Southwest : 2¼ m. on A 593 – ✉ Coniston.*

Old Rectory, LA21 8AX, Northeast : ¼ m. by A 593 ☎ (015394) 41353, *enquiries@theoldrectoryhotel.com, Fax (015394) 41156,* ←, – P. VISA

Rest (residents only) (dinner only) 23.00 **s.** – **9 rm** ✝48.00 – ✝✝72.00/78.00.

◆ Beneath the Coniston Old Man, close to Coniston Water stands this country house built in 1868 for the Rev Thomas Ellwood. Snug bedrooms afford panoramic views of landscape. Fine meadow vistas from conservatory style dining room.

Wheelgate Country Guest House without rest., Little Arrow, LA21 8AU, Northeast : ¾ m. on A 593 ☎ (015394) 41418, *enquiry@wheelgate.co.uk, Fax (015394) 41114,* – P. VISA.

5 rm ✝42.00/84.00 – ✝✝84.00.

◆ Pretty, wisteria-clad, converted 17C farmhouse in mature gardens. Quaint interiors: oak beams, low ceilings, antique furniture. Cottage-style bedrooms and snug rustic bar.

CONSTABLE BURTON *N. Yorks.* **502** O 21 – *see Leyburn.*

CONSTANTINE *Cornwall* **503** E 33 *The West Country G.* – ✉ *Falmouth.*

Env. : *Mawgan-in-Meneage (Church★), S : 3 m. by minor roads.*

London 303 – Falmouth 15 – Penzance 25 – Truro 24.

Trengilly Wartha Inn with rm, Nancenoy, TR11 5RP, South : 1 ½ m. by Fore St off Port Navas rd ☎ (01326) 340332, *reception@trengilly.co.uk, Fax (01326) 340332,* – P. AE VISA

Rest *(closed 25 December)* 29.00 (dinner) and a la carte 23.00/29.00 ♀ – **8 rm** ✝50.00 – ✝✝80.00/96.00.

◆ Well-established landmark. Name means "settlement above the trees": stands in area of natural beauty. Dishes of local meat, game and fish with rich desserts. Cosy rooms.

CONSTANTINE BAY *Cornwall* **503** E 32 – *see Padstow.*

ENGLAND

COOKHAM Windsor & Maidenhead 504 R 29 Great Britain G. – pop. 5 304 – ⊠ Maidenhead.

See : Stanley Spencer Gallery★ AC.

🚢 to Marlow, Maidenhead and Windsor (Salter Bros. Ltd) (summer only).

London 32 – High Wycombe 7 – Oxford 31 – Reading 16.

XX **Manzano's**, 19-21 Station Hill Parade, SL6 9BR, 𝒫 (01628) 525775 – ⅙⅞. 🕾 ⓞ 𝘝𝘐𝘚𝘈
closed 2 weeks August, 1 week Christmas, Saturday lunch, Sunday and Bank Holidays – Rest
- Spanish specialities - 19.50 (lunch) and a la carte 29.50/42.50.
  ◆ Popular, personally run neighbourhood restaurant on a busy parade. Warm, homely feel
  pervades. Frequently changing seasonal Spanish influenced menus with a classical base.

🛏 **The Ferry**, Sutton Rd, SL6 9SN, 𝒫 (01628) 525123, 😤 – ⏬, ⅙⅞ rest, ▤ 𝗣. 🕾 ₳ⅇ 𝘝𝘐𝘚𝘈.
⅞
Rest a la carte 21.00/30.00.
  ◆ Part 14C riverside inn with its own landing stage. Delightful decked dining terrace. Inside,
  characterful beams and sofas mix the modern and the rustic. Eclectic pub dishes.

COOKHAM DEAN Windsor and Maidenhead Great Britain G.

Env. : Windsor Castle★★★, Eton★★ and Windsor★, S : 5 m. by B 4447, A 4 (westbound) and
A 308.

London 32 – High Wycombe 7 – Oxford 31 – Reading 16.

XX **The Inn on the Green** with rm, The Old Cricket Common, SL6 9NZ, 𝒫 (01628) 482638,
reception@theinnonthegreen.com, Fax (01628) 487474, 😤, 😤 – ⅙⅞ rm, 𝗣. 🕾 ₳ⅇ 𝘝𝘐𝘚𝘈
Rest (closed Monday and Sunday dinner) (booking essential) (dinner only and Sunday
lunch) a la carte 26.70/47.00 ⅞ – 9 rm ⇌ ✦90.00/130.00 – ✦✦100.00/160.00.
  ◆ Part timbered inn with delightful patio terrace. Rustic bar; two dining rooms and conservatory: modern British cooking. Individually furnished rooms in the inn or annex.

COPTHORNE W. Sussex 504 T 30 – see Crawley.

CORBRIDGE Northd. 501 502 N 19 Great Britain G. – pop. 2 800.

Env. : Hadrian's Wall★★, N : 3 m. by A 68 – Corstopitum★ AC, NW : ½ m.

🅱 Hill St 𝒫 (01434) 632815 (Easter-October).

London 300 – Hexham 3 – Newcastle upon Tyne 18.

⌂ **Town Barns** without rest., NE45 5HP, by Middle St and Hexham rd 𝒫 (01434) 633345,
😤 – ⅙⅞ 𝗣. ⅞
late March-September – 3 rm ⇌ ✦45.00 – ✦✦60.00.
  ◆ Modern cottage-style house on edge of town enjoys views of the Tyne Valley. Spacious,
  comfortable guests' sitting room and well-furnished bedrooms.

⌂ **Riggsacre** without rest., Appletree Lane, NE45 5DN, by B 6321 (Aydon rd) 𝒫 (01434)
632617, atclive@supernet.com, 😤 – ⅙⅞ 𝗣.
closed Christmas and New Year – 3 rm ✦48.00 – ✦✦76.00.
  ◆ Charming owners run an immaculate, well-priced guesthouse in a peaceful area. Mature
  gardens; communal breakfast room. Thoughtful extras enhance delightful, good sized
  rooms.

🛏 **The Angel Inn** with rm, Main St, NE45 5LA, 𝒫 (01434) 632119, 😤 – ⅙⅞ 𝗣. 🕾 𝘝𝘐𝘚𝘈
⅞
Rest (closed Sunday dinner) a la carte 16.00/30.00 ⅞ – 5 rm ⇌ ✦60.00 – ✦✦85.00.
  ◆ 18C cream-washed village centre coaching inn. Wood-panelled lounge with leather
  Chesterfield. Tasty, Northumbrian dishes in bar or restaurant. Smart rooms with quality
  decor.

at Great Whittington North : 5½ m. by A 68 off B 6318 – ⊠ Corbridge.

🛏 **Queens Head Inn**, NE19 2HP, 𝒫 (01434) 672267 – ⅙⅞ 𝗣. 🕾 𝘝𝘐𝘚𝘈. ⅞
closed 1 week spring and 1 week autumn – Rest (closed Sunday dinner and Monday) a la
carte 19.50/25.00.
  ◆ Personally run 17C pub in sleepy village. Real ales in pleasant timbered bar. Traditional
  menus employ locally sourced produce - game, cheese and meat all from Northumberland.

CORFE CASTLE Dorset 503 504 N 32 The West Country G. – ⊠ Wareham.

See : Castle★ (≤★★) AC.

London 129 – Bournemouth 18 – Weymouth 23.

🏛 **Mortons House**, 45 East St, BH20 5EE, 𝒫 (01929) 480988, stay@mortonshouse.co.uk,
Fax (01929) 480820, ≤, 😤, 😤 – 👍 𝗣. 🕾 𝘝𝘐𝘚𝘈. ⅞
Rest a la carte 27.00/49.00 – 18 rm ⇌ ✦75.00/152.00 – ✦✦150.00/152.00, 3 suites.
  ◆ Elizabethan manor built in the shape of an "E" in Queen's honour. Wood panelled draw-
  ing room; range of bedrooms, some themed: the Victoria room has original Victorian bath.
  Colourful dining room with views over courtyard.

CORNHILL-ON-TWEED Northd. 501 502 N 17 Scotland G.

Env. : Ladykirk (Kirk o'Steil★), NE : 6 m. by A 698 and B 6470.

London 345 – Edinburgh 49 – Newcastle upon Tyne 59.

Tillmouth Park ♨, TD12 4UU, Northeast : 2 ½ m. on A 698 ℰ (01890) 882255, recep tion@tillmouthpark.f9.co.uk, Fax (01890) 882540, ≼, ☞, 🐾 – ✟✕ rest, **P**. **⨠** **VISA**

Rest 17.50 (lunch) and a la carte 17.90/22.25 – **The Library :** Rest (bar lunch Monday-Saturday)/dinner 32.50 ♀ – **14 rm** ⌷ ✟50.00/90.00 – ✟✟110.00/120.00.

  ◆ In an area renowned for its fishing, a 19C country house in mature grounds and wood-land. Inside one finds stained glass windows, grand staircases and antique furniture. Light meals in bistro. Large, panelled Library restaurant has good views of grounds.

Coach House, Crookham, TD12 4TD, East : 4 m. on A 697 ℰ (01890) 820293, stay@coachhousecrookham.com, Fax (01890) 820284, ☞ – ✟✕ 🔥 **P**. **⨠** **VISA**

closed Christmas **Rest** (booking essential for non-residents) (dinner only) 19.50 ♀ – **10 rm** ⌷ ✟39.00/49.00 – ✟✟45.00.

  ◆ Converted from a collection of farm buildings, including a 1680s dower house, and set around a courtyard. Recently modernised, comfortable rooms with character.

CORSCOMBE Dorset 503 L 31 – ✉ Dorchester.

London 153 – Exeter 47 – Taunton 30 – Weymouth 24.

The Fox Inn with rm, DT2 0NS, Northeast : ¾ m. on Halstock rd ℰ (01935) 891330, Fax (01935) 891330 – ✟✕ rm, **P**. **⨠** **VISA**. ✕

closed 25 December – **Rest** a la carte 19.00/32.00 – **4 rm** ⌷ ✟55.00 – ✟✟100.00.

  ◆ Popular thatched inn with quaint interior: gingham tablecloths, beamed ceiling and conservatory. Light, modern cooking with fine fish dishes. Country-style bedrooms.

CORSE LAWN Worcs. – see Tewkesbury (Glos.).

CORSHAM Wilts. 504 N 29 – pop. 11 318.

London 107 – Bristol 22 – Chippenham 5.

Heatherly Cottage ♨ without rest., Ladbrook Lane, Gastard, SN13 9PE, Southeast : 1 ¼ m. by B 3353 ℰ (01249) 701402, pandj@heatherly.plus.com, Fax (01249) 701412, ☞ – ✟✕ **P**. ✕

March-November – **3 rm** ⌷ ✟45.00/48.00 – ✟✟62.00/66.00.

  ◆ Part 17C stone cottage set down a quiet country road close to small village. Three very good value rooms: spacious, individually furnished and with good facilities.

CORSLEY Wilts. – see Warminster.

CORTON DENHAM Somerset – see Sherborne.

COSHAM Portsmouth 503 504 Q 31 – see Portsmouth and Southsea.

COTEBROOK Ches. – see Tarporley.

COTTINGHAM Kingston-upon-Hull 502 S 22 – see Kingston-upon-Hull.

COVENTRY W. Mids. 503 504 P 26 Great Britain G. – pop. 303 475.

See : City★ - Cathedral★★★ AC AV – Old Cathedral★ AV B – Museum of British Road Transport★ AC AV M2.

🏌 Windmill Village, Birmingham Rd, Allesley ℰ (024) 7640 4041 – 🏌 Sphinx, Sphinx Drive ℰ (024) 7645 1361.

🛈 4 Priory Row ℰ (024) 7622 7264.

London 100 – Birmingham 18 – Bristol 96 – Leicester 24 – Nottingham 52.

Plan on next page

Brooklands Grange, Holyhead Rd, CV5 8HX, Northwest : 2 ½ m. on A 4114 ℰ (024) 7660 1601, info@brooklandsgrange.co.uk, Fax (024) 7660 1277, ☞ – ✟✕ 🍴 🔥 **P**. **⨠** **AE** **VISA**

AY e

closed 26 December - 3 January – **Rest** 25.95 and a la carte 27.90/39.25 ♀ – **31 rm** ⌷ ✟75.00/95.00 – ✟✟95.00/120.00.

  ◆ Part 16C yeoman's farmhouse with comfy, snug bar and neatly kept rooms furnished in dainty prints. Attentive service. On main route into city with good motorway connections. Victorian restaurant and conservatory.

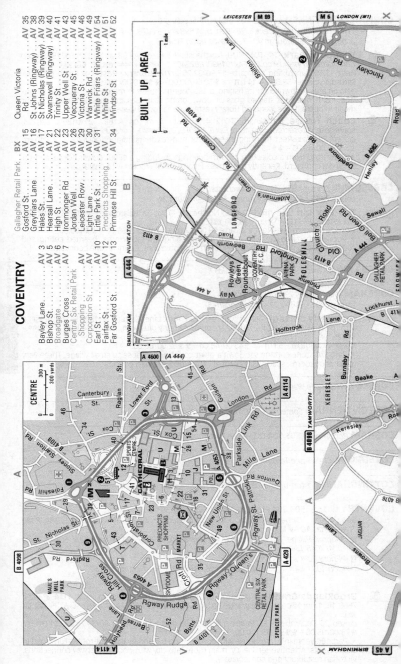

COVENTRY

Bayley Lane	AV 3
Bishop St.	AV 5
Broadgate	AV 6
Burges Cross	AV 7
Central Six Retail Park Shopping	
Corporation St.	AV
Earl St.	AV 10
Fairfax St.	AV 12
Far Gosford St.	AV 13

Gallagher Retail Park	BX
Gosford St.	AV 15
Greyfriars Lane	AV 16
Hales St.	AV 17
Hearsall Lane	AY 21
High St.	AY 22
Ironmonger Rd	AY 23
Jordan Well	AV 26
Leicester Row	AV 29
Light Lane	AV 30
Little Park St.	AV 31
Precincts Shopping	AV
Primrose Hill St.	AV 34

Queen Victoria Rd	AV 35
St Johns (Ringway)	AV 38
St Nicholas (Ringway)	AV 39
Swanswell (Ringway)	AV 40
Trinity St.	AV 41
Upper Well St.	AV 43
Vecqueray St.	AV 45
Victoria St.	AV 46
Warwick Rd	AV 49
White Friars (Ringway)	AV 54
White St.	AV 51
Windsor St.	AV 52

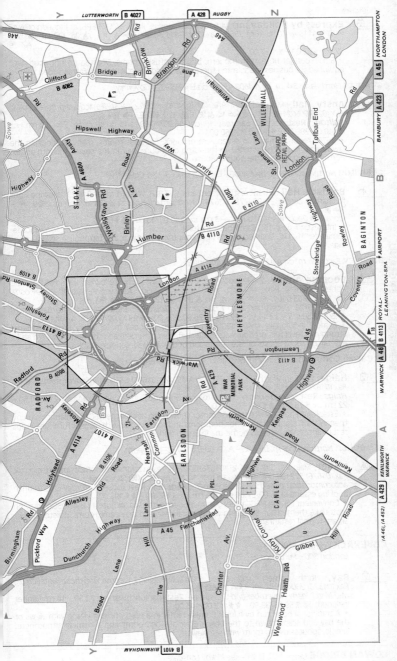

Express by Holiday Inn without rest., Kenpas Highway, CV3 6PB, at junction of A 45 with B 4113 ℘ (024) 7641 7555, Fax (024) 7641 3388 – ✸ & 🅿 – 🚗 25. 🐵 🅰🅴 ⓘ 𝘝𝘐𝘚𝘈. ✸

AZ e

37 rm ✦67.00 – ✦✦67.00.

♦ Small, budget hotel with modern, bright, unfussy rooms. Situated on ring road: well equipped for business people and short stays. Good value, with breakfast included.

at Ansty *Northeast : 5¾ m. by A 4600 – BX – on B 4065 – ✉ Coventry.*

Ansty Hall, Main Rd, CV7 9HZ, ℘ (02476) 612222, ansty@macdonald-hotels.co.uk, Fax (02476) 602155, 🌳 – 📶 ✸ 🐾 🅿 – 🚗 120. 🐵 🅰🅴 ⓘ 𝘝𝘐𝘚𝘈
Shilton : Rest *(closed Saturday lunch)* 16.95/40.00 and a la carte ♀ – **62 rm** ➪ ✦140.00/280.00 – ✦✦200.00/360.00.

♦ 1670s redbrick manor in seven-acre grounds. Spacious rooms, many overlooking the lawns: half, more characterful, in the listed old house, half in the smart, modern annex. Formal dining room in the original house.

at Shilton *Northeast : 6¾ m. by A 4600 – BX – on B 4065 – ✉ Coventry.*

Barnacle Hall without rest., Shilton Lane, CV7 9LH, West : 1 m. by B 4029 following signs for garden centre ℘ (024) 7661 2629, rose@barnaclehall.co.uk, Fax (024) 7661 2629, 🌳 – ✸ 🅿. ✸
closed 24 December - 2 January – **3 rm** ➪ ✦30.00/40.00 – ✦✦65.00.

♦ Interesting part 16C farmhouse in rural location. Westerly facing 18C stone façade; remainder 16/17C. Beamed rooms have countryside outlook and farmhouse style furnishings.

at Binley *East : 3½ m. on A 428 – BY – ✉ Coventry.*

Coombe Abbey ✨, Brinklow Rd, CV3 2AB, East : 2 m. following signs for Coombe Abbey Country Park (A 427) ℘ (024) 7645 0450, reservations@combeabbey.com, Fax (024) 7663 5101, ≤, 🌳 – 📶 ✸ 🅿 – 🚗 120. 🐵 🅰🅴 ⓘ 𝘝𝘐𝘚𝘈. ✸
closed 25-26 December and 1 January – **Cloisters :** Rest *(closed Saturday lunch)* 27.50/32.50 s. ♀ – ➪ 14.50 – **82 rm** ✦175.00/205.00 – ✦✦175.00/420.00, 1 suite.

♦ A most individually styled 12C former Cistercian abbey in Capability Brown gardens. Strong medieval feel predominates: the staff are costumed, and the bedrooms are striking. Dining room boasts ornate ceiling and unusual raised, canopied tables.

at Balsall Common *West : 6¾ m. by B 4101 – AY – ✉ Coventry.*

Haigs, 273 Kenilworth Rd, CV7 7EL, on A 452 ℘ (01676) 533004, info@haigsemail.co.uk, Fax (01676) 535132, 🌳 – ✸ 🐾 🅿. 🐵 🅰🅴 𝘝𝘐𝘚𝘈
Haigs : Rest *(closed Sunday lunch)* (dinner only and Sunday lunch)/dinner 17.95/24.50 – 22 rm ➪ ✦75.00 – ✦✦107.50/120.00.

♦ Established hotel where the first motor show to be held at the NEC was planned; run by friendly staff. Light floral themed bedrooms and spacious bar with elegant furniture. Haigs restaurant serves carefully home-made British dishes.

at Meriden *Northwest : 6 m. by A 45 – AX – on B 4104 – ✉ Coventry.*

Manor, Main Rd, CV7 7NH, ℘ (01676) 522735, reservations@manorhotelmeriden.co.uk, Fax (01676) 522186, 🌳 – 📶 ✸, 🍽 rest, 🐾 🅿 – 🚗 275. 🐵 🅰🅴 ⓘ 𝘝𝘐𝘚𝘈
accommodation closed 24-30 December – **Regency :** Rest *(closed Saturday lunch)* (lunch booking essential) 25.00/27.00 s. – **108 rm** ➪ ✦135.00 – ✦✦195.00, 2 suites.

♦ Convenient for the NEC, a Georgian manor converted to an hotel in the 1950s. Triumph motorbike themed bar. Sweeping wooden staircase leads to sizable rooms, quieter at rear. Smart, formal restaurant.

COVERACK *Cornwall 503 E 33.*
London 300 – Penzance 25 – Truro 27.

Bay, North Corner, TR12 6TF, ℘ (01326) 280464, enquiries@thebayhotel.co.uk, Fax (01326) 280464, ≤, 🌳 – ✸ 🅿. 🐵 𝘝𝘐𝘚𝘈
mid March-early November and Christmas – Rest *(bar lunch)*/dinner 22.50 – **14 rm** (dinner included) ➪ ✦59.95/89.90 – ✦✦119.00/143.00.

♦ A traditional hotel run by a local Cornish family in a pretty fishing village with views of the bay and steps down to the beach. Spacious bedrooms and a homely atmosphere. Simple, spotless dining room with sea views.

COWAN BRIDGE *Lancs. 502 M 21 – see Kirkby Lonsdale.*

ENGLAND

COWHILL Durham 502 N 19.

London 295 – Newcastle upon Tyne 42 – Stanhope 10 – Wolsingham 16.

↑ **Low Comriggs Farm** ॐ, Weardale, DL13 1AQ, Northwest : ¼ m. on A 689 ℘ (01388) 537600, enquiries@lowcomriggsfarm.fsnet.co.uk, Fax (01388) 537777, ≤, 拏, ॰ – ⅙ ℙ. ॐ
closed Christmas – **Rest** (by arrangement) 16.00 – **3 rm** ⚏ ✦34.00 – ✦✦52.00.
◆ Stone-built 300 year-old farmhouse boasting some superb views over Teesdale. Conservatory dining room for summer use. Cosy, pine-furnished bedrooms. Beamed dining room offers hearty, home-cooked, organic dishes.

CRACKINGTON HAVEN Cornwall 503 G 31 The West Country G. – ⊠ Bude.

Env. : *Poundstock★ (≤★★, church★, guildhouse★), NE : 5 ½ m. by A 39 – Jacobstow (Church★), E : 3½ m.*
London 262 – Bude 11 – Plymouth 44 – Truro 42.

↑ **Manor Farm** ॐ without rest., EX23 0JW, Southeast : 1 ¼ m. by Boscastle rd taking left turn onto Church Park Rd after 1.1 m. then taking first right onto unmarked lane ℘ (01840) 230304, ≤, 拏, ॰ – ⅙ ℙ. ॐ
closed 25 December – – **3 rm** ⚏ ✦45.00 – ✦✦80.00.
◆ Appears in the Domesday Book and belonged to William the Conqueror's half brother. A lovely manor in beautifully manicured grounds. Affable owner and comfortable rooms.

CRANBROOK Kent 504 V 30 Great Britain G. – pop. 4 225.

Env. : *Sissinghurst Castle★ AC, NE : 2½ m. by A 229 and A 262.*
🛈 Vestry Hall, Stone St ℘ (01580) 712538 (summer only).
London 53 – Hastings 19 – Maidstone 15.

↑ **Cloth Hall Oast** ॐ, Coursehorn Lane, TN17 3NR, East : 1 m. by Tenterden rd ℘ (01580) 712220, clothhalloast@aol.com, Fax (01580) 712220, ⊠ heated, 拏 – ⅙ rm, ℙ. ॐ
closed Christmas – **Rest** (by arrangement) (communal dining) 24.00 – **3 rm** ⚏ ✦55.00/75.00 – ✦✦90.00/120.00.
◆ Run by former owner of Old Cloth Hall, with well-tended garden, rhododendrons lining the drive. Peaceful spot. Charming sitting room. Immaculate bedrooms exude personal style.

XX **Apicius,** 23 Stone St, TN17 3HE, ℘ (01580) 714666 – ⅙ 🞄 🏵 VISA
closed 2 weeks Christmas-New Year, 2 weeks summer, Sunday dinner, Monday, Tuesday and Saturday lunch – Rest 23.50/28.00 ꭍ.
◆ Stylish restaurant in Grade II listed building; named after Greek author of world's first cookbook. Smartly priced, modern French menus proffer a well-executed originality.

at Sissinghurst Northeast : 1¾ m. by B 2189 on A 262 – ⊠ Cranbrook.

X **Rankins,** The Street, TN17 2JH, on A 262 ℘ (01580) 713964, rankins@btconnect.com – ⅙. 🏵 VISA
closed Sunday dinner, Monday, Tuesday and Bank Holidays – **Rest** (booking essential) (dinner only and Sunday lunch)/dinner 31.50.
◆ A friendly, well-established, family run bistro-style restaurant, not far from Sissinghurst Castle. The set menu has an international focus.

CRANTOCK Cornwall 503 E 32 – see Newquay.

CRAWLEY W. Sussex 504 T 30 – pop. 100 547.

🖈, 🖈 Cottesmore, Buchan Hill, Pease Pottage ℘ (01293) 528256 – 🖈, 🖈 Tilgate Forest, Titmus Drive, Tilgate ℘ (01293) 530103 – 🖈 Gatwick Manor, London Rd, Lowfield Heath ℘ (01293) 538587 – 🖈 Pease Pottage, Horsham Rd ℘ (01293) 521706.
🛈 County Mall Shopping Centre ℘ (01293) 846968, vip@countymall.co.uk.
London 33 – Brighton 21 – Lewes 23 – Royal Tunbridge Wells 23.

Plan of enlarged Area : see Gatwick

🏨 **Arora International,** Southgate Ave, Southgate, RH10 6LW, ℘ (01293) 530000, gat wickreservations@arorainternational.com, Fax (01293) 515515, ᒪᕽ – 🛉, ⅙ rm, 🛏 👤 ᕇ ℙ –
🔏 270. 🏵 ᴀᴇ ① VISA. ॐ   BZ a
mono brasserie : Rest a la carte 17.85/32.85 ꭍ – ⚏ 11.95 – **431 rm** ✦165.00 – ✦✦175.00, 1 suite.
◆ Futuristically designed, business oriented hotel with airport rail access. Calming water features and striking open-plan atrium. Impressive leisure facilities and bedrooms. Easygoing brasserie offers tried-and-tested menus.

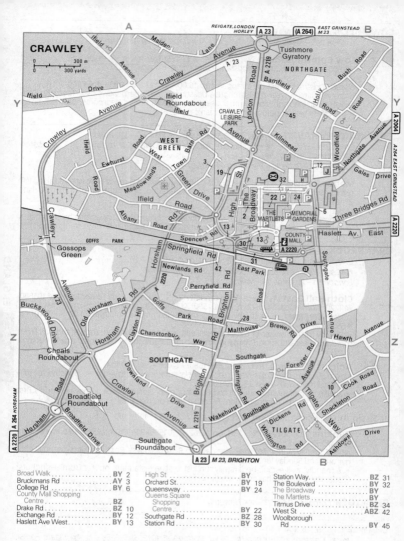

CRAWLEY

REIGATE, LONDON HORLEY **A 23** (A 264) EAST GRINSTEAD M 23

🏨 **Express by Holiday Inn** without rest., The Squareabout, Haslett Ave East, RH10 1UA, ℘ (01293) 525523, Fax (01293) 525529 – |✿| ✛✿ ᴋ ℙ – ₤ 35. ◍❸ ᴀᴇ ⓞ 𝘝𝘐𝘚𝘈. ✸
74 rm ★69.95 – ★★69.95.
on Gatwick town plan **Z a**
 • A bright, modern lodge with tiled and tasteful reception area and fresh, crisp bedrooms. Within easy reach of Crawley town centre and leisure complex. Grill and pub nearby.

at Copthorne Northeast : 4½ m. on A 264 – BY – ✉ Crawley.

🏛 **Copthorne Effingham Park,** West Park Rd, RH10 3EU, on B 2028 ℘ (0870) 8900214, sales.effingham@mill-cop.com, Fax (0870) 8900215, ᴵ₆, ⥱, ☒, 🏌, 🎾, ⚽, ⋇ –
|✿| ✛✿ ᴋ ℙ – ₤ 600. ◍❸ ᴀᴇ 𝘝𝘐𝘚𝘈. ✸
Rest (bar lunch)/dinner a la carte 29.45/64.50 ☿ – **122 rm** ★141.00 – ★★141.00.
 • Modern hotel in 40 acres of grounds with 9 hole golf course, floodlit tennis courts and jogging track. 6 miles to airport. Superior rooms have private balconies with views. Restaurant or bar meal alternatives.

232

CRAYKE N. Yorks. – see Easingwold.

CRAY'S POND Oxon. – see Goring.

CREWE Ches. 502 503 504 M 24 – pop. 67 683.

⌐ Queen's Park, Queen's Park Drive ℘ (01270) 662378 – ⌐ Fields Rd, Haslington ℘ (01270) 584227.

London 174 – Chester 24 – Liverpool 49 – Manchester 36 – Stoke-on-Trent 15.

Crewe Hall, Western Rd, CW1 6UZ, Southeast : 1 ¾ m. on A 5020 ℘ (01270) 253333, crewehall@marstonhotels.com, Fax (01270) 253322, ☞, ℅ – ⌷ ⇥ ☏ ⌂ P – ☝ 230. ◉◉ ᴀᴇ ⓞ VISA ✋

Ranulph Room : Rest *(closed Sunday lunch)* 17.50 s. (lunch) and a la carte 20.00/37.40 – **TIr² Brasserie :** Rest 17.50 (lunch) and la carte 20.00/37.50 s. – **60 rm** ☵ ✦116.00/164.00 – ✦✦141.00/329.00, 5 suites.

◆ Impressive 17C mansion with formal gardens. Victorian décor featuring alabaster, marble and stained glass. Rooms offer luxurious comfort. Formal dining in Ranulph Room with its wood panelling and ornate plaster work. Popular modern menu in the chic Brasserie.

CRICK Northants. 503 504 Q 26 – see Rugby.

CRICKET MALHERBIE Somerset 503 L 31 – see Ilminster.

CROFT-ON-TEES Durham 502 P 20 – see Darlington.

CROMER Norfolk 504 X 25 – pop. 8 836.

⌐ Royal Cromer, Overstrand Rd ℘ (01263) 512884.
🛈 Prince of Wales Rd ℘ (01263) 512497.
London 132 – Norwich 23.

at Overstrand Southeast : 2½ m. by B 1159 – ✉ Cromer.

Sea Marge, 16 High St, NR27 0AB, ℘ (01263) 579579, info@mackenziehotels.com, Fax (01263) 579524, ≤, ☞ – ⌷ ⇥ P. ◉◉ VISA
Rest (bar lunch)/dinner a la carte 18.20/28.70 ♀ – **25 rm** ☵ ✦83.00/126.00 – ✦✦126.00/158.00.

◆ Mock Elizabethan house built in 1908; gardens lead down to beach. Interiors feature Delft tiles alongside panelled bar, minstrel gallery. Most bedrooms have sea views. Restaurant offers views from a large leaded window.

at Northrepps Southeast : 3 m. by A 149 and Northrepps rd – ✉ Cromer.

Shrublands Farm without rest., NR27 0AA, ℘ (01263) 579297, youngman@farming.co.uk, Fax (01263) 579297, ☞ – ⇥ P. ◉◉ VISA. ✋
3 rm ☵ ✦40.00 – ✦✦60.00.
◆ Whitewashed part 18C arable farm in wooded gardens. Conservatory, lounge, neat rooms with cut flowers and garden views. Guests are encouraged to explore the farm.

CROSBY-ON-EDEN Cumbria 501 502 L 19 – see Carlisle.

CROSTHWAITE Cumbria 502 L 21 – see Kendal.

CROYDE Devon 503 H 30 – ✉ Braunton.
London 232 – Barnstaple 10 – Exeter 50 – Taunton 61.

Whiteleaf, Hobbs Hill, EX33 1PN, ℘ (01271) 890266, ☞ – ⇥ P. ◉◉ VISA
closed 24-26 December – Rest (by arrangement) a la carte 19.45/30.60 – **5 rm** ☵ ✦50.00/60.00 – ✦✦70.00/86.00.
◆ Homely guesthouse close to North Devon and Somerset coastal path; views of Baggy Point, Lundy Island. Co-ordinated accommodation with mini-bars: choose the four-poster room. Restaurant looks out onto garden.

CRUDWELL Wilts. 503 504 N 29 – see Malmesbury.

CUCKFIELD W. Sussex 504 T 30 – pop. 2 879.
London 40 – Brighton 15.

Ockenden Manor ⌂, Ockenden Lane, RH17 5LD, ℰ (01444) 416111, *reserva tions@ockenden-manor.com*, Fax (01444) 415549, �_, 🛏 – ⅙ rest, ✆ 🅿 – 🔬 50. 🆎 🆎
① 𝓥𝓘𝓢𝓐 . ⌘
Rest (lunch booking essential) 25.00/49.50 ♀ – **19 rm** ⌂ ✦110.00 – ✦✦298.00, 3 suites.
Spec. Grilled scallops with guacamole, tomato and ginger. Pork with croquette of confit shoulder. Savarin of red cherries with crème fraîche ice cream.
✦ Secluded part 16C manor; heritage is on display in antique furnished bedrooms, many named after previous owners. Ideal for golfers, historians and the romantic. Wood panelled dining room offers some of Sussex's finest cooking.

CUDDINGTON Bucks. 503 504 M 24 Great Britain G.
Env. : Waddesdon Manor★★ AC, NE : 6 m. via Cuddington Hill, Cannon's Hill, Waddesdon Hill and A 41.
London 48 – Aylesbury 6 – Oxford 17.

Crown, Aylesbury Rd, HP18 0BB, ℰ (01844) 292222, *david@anniebaileys.com* – 🅿. 🆎 🆎
𝓥𝓘𝓢𝓐 . ⌘
Rest (closed 25 December) a la carte 17.00/23.00.
✦ Thatched, Grade II listed inn in pretty village: small windows, flag floors and period fireplaces. Tasty food mixing modern British with pub staples and heartwarming puddings.

Do not confuse ✗ with ✿!
✗ defines comfort, while stars are awarded for the best cuisine, across all categories of comfort.

CUTNALL GREEN Worcs. 503 504 N 27 – see Droitwich Spa.

DALTON N. Yorks. 502 O 20 – see Richmond.

DALTON-IN-FURNESS Cumbria 502 K 21 – pop. 8 057.
🏌 The Dunnerholme, Duddon Rd, Askham-in-Furness ℰ (01229) 462675.
London 283 – Barrow-in-Furness 3.5 – Kendal 30 – Lancaster 41.

Clarence House Country, Skelgate, LA15 8BQ, North : ½ m. on Askam rd ℰ (01229) 462508, *clarencehsehotel@aol.com*, Fax (01229) 467177, 🌿 – ⅙ 🅿 – 🔬 100. 🆎 🆎 ①
𝓥𝓘𝓢𝓐
closed 25-26 December – **The Orangery :** Rest (closed Sunday dinner) 15.95 (lunch) and a la carte 23.95/40.00 ♀ – **18 rm** ⌂ ✦85.00 – ✦✦105.00.
✦ Welcoming hotel with spacious, comfortable bedrooms in a distinctive 19C building. Features a conservatory sitting room and fine period tiling in the entrance hall. Dine in a most attractive conservatory overlooking gardens.

Park Cottage ⌂ without rest., Park, LA15 8JZ, North : 1½ m. by Askam rd off Romney Park Rd ℰ (01229) 462850, *joan@parkcottagedalton.co.uk*, 🔧, 🌿 – ⅙ 🅿
closed 29 January- 8 February – – **3 rm** ⌂ ✦48.00 – ✦✦65.00.
✦ Quaint little 18C house hidden away in four wooded acres. Two cosy lounges: from one you can observe garden's many feathered visitors. Pleasant rooms overlook garden and lake.

DANEHILL E. Sussex Great Britain G.
Env. : Sheffield Park Garden★, S : 3 m. on A 275.
London 53 – Brighton 21 – East Grinstead 7.

Coach & Horses, School Lane, RH17 7JF, Northeast : ¾ m. on Chelwood Common rd ℰ (01825) 740369, *coachandhorses@danehill.biz*, 🌿, 🌿 – 🅿. 🆎 𝓥𝓘𝓢𝓐
closed dinner 25-26 December and 1 January – Rest a la carte 24.00/25.00 ♀.
✦ An atmospheric 'locals' bar leads to two separate dining areas: one is a converted beamed stable. Modern menus have a distinctly French base and fine dining style.

DARESBURY Warrington 502 M 23 – see Warrington.

DARGATE Kent – see Faversham.

234

DARLEY N. Yorks..
London 217.5 – Harrogate 8.5 – Ripon 16.5.

Cold Cotes ⌛ without rest., Cold Cotes Rd, Felliscliffe, HG3 2LW, South : 2 m. by Kettlesing rd, going straight over crossroads and on Harrogate rd ℰ (01423) 770937, *cold cotes@btopenworld.com*, Fax (01423) 779284, ⇜ – ✕ ❤ 🅿. 🐧 ᴠɪsᴀ. ⅏
closed January – 5 rm � ✚55.00 – ✚✚65.00/75.00.
* Victorian farmhouse in five acres of lovely gardens. Cosy lounge with open fire. Communal breakfasts overlooking grounds. Extra touches adorn the pleasant, well-priced rooms.

DARLEY ABBEY Derbs. 502 503 504 P 25 – see Derby.

DARLINGTON Darlington 502 P 20 – pop. 86 082.
🔣 Blackwell Grange, Briar Close ℰ (01325) 464458 – 🔣 Stressholme, Snipe Lane ℰ (01325) 461002.
✈ Teesside Airport : ℰ (01325) 332811, E : 6 m. by A 67.
🛈 13 Horsemarket ℰ (01325) 388666.
London 251 – Leeds 61 – Middlesbrough 14 – *Newcastle upon Tyne 35*.

🏨 **Hotel Bannatyne,** Southend Ave, DL3 7HZ, Southwest : ¾ m. by A 167 ℰ (01325) 365859, *enquiries@hotelbannatyne.com*, Fax (01325) 487111, ⇜ – |≢| ✕, 🍴 rest, ⅙ 🅿. – ⨯ 100. 🐧 ᴀᴇ ᴠɪsᴀ
Maxine's : Rest (light lunch)/dinner a la carte 18.85/26.15 s. ♀ – **60 rm** � ✚70.00 – ✚✚90.00.
* In a converted late Georgian villa with recent sympathetic extensions, the hotel has generally modern décor with spacious, stylish rooms. Book a rear one for enhanced peace. Uncluttered dining room with bar.

at Aycliffe North : 5½ m. on A 167 – ⌧ Darlington.

🍴 **The County,** 13 The Green, DL5 6LX, ℰ (01325) 312273 – ✕ 🅿. 🐧 ᴀᴇ ⓞ ᴠɪsᴀ. ⅏
closed 25-26 December – **Rest** *(closed Sunday)* (booking essential) a la carte 17.00/30.00 ♀.
* A village pub, overlooking the green, with minimalist décor and a busy atmosphere. Tasty, balanced modern dishes. Seasonally inspired menus of modern British cooking.

at Croft-on-Tees South : 3½ m. on A 167 – ⌧ Darlington.

🏠 **Clow Beck House** ⌛, Monk End Farm, DL2 2SW, West : ¾ m. by A 167 off Barton rd ℰ (01325) 721075, *heather@clowbeckhouse.co.uk*, Fax (01325) 720419, ≼, ⌇, ⇜, ⅖ – ⅙ 🅿. 🐧 ᴀᴇ ᴠɪsᴀ. ⅏
closed 24 December-2 January – **Rest** (residents only) (dinner only) a la carte 22.00/37.50 s. ♀ – **13 rm** � ✚80.00 – ✚✚120.00.
* Collection of stone houses styled on an old farm building. The residence has a friendly, homely atmosphere. Spacious rooms with individual character. Tasty, home-cooked meals.

at Headlam Northwest : 8 m. by A 67 – ⌧ Gainford.

🏨 **Headlam Hall** ⌛, DL2 3HA, ℰ (01325) 730238, *admin@headlamhall.co.uk*, Fax (01325) 730790, ≼, ⅃₆, ⬄, ⬜, 🏷₉, ⌇, ⇜, ⅖, ✕ – ✕ ❤ ⅙ 🅿. – ⨯ 150. 🐧 ᴀᴇ ⓞ ᴠɪsᴀ
closed 24-26 December and 2-5 January – **Rest** 17.50 (lunch) and a la carte 24.00/32.00 s. – **40 rm** � ✚80.00/90.00 – ✚✚110.00, 1 suite.
* Part Georgian, part Jacobean manor house in delightful, secluded countryside with charming walled gardens. Period interior furnishings and antiques. Good leisure facilities. Country house restaurant in four distinctively decorated rooms.

at Redworth Northwest : 7 m. by A 68 on A 6072 – ⌧ Bishop Auckland.

🏨 **Redworth Hall,** DL5 6NL, ℰ (01388) 770600, *redworthhall@paramount-hotels.co.uk*, Fax (01388) 770654, ⓥ, ⅃₆, ⬄, ⬜, ⇜, ⅖, ✕ – |≢| ✕ ❤ ⅙ 🅿. – ⨯ 250. 🐧 ᴀᴇ ⓞ ᴠɪsᴀ
Conservatory : Rest 25.00 and a la carte 17.50/46.00 s. ♀ – **1744 :** Rest *(closed Sunday-Monday)* (dinner only) – � 13.95 – **96 rm** ✚69.00/150.00 – ✚✚69.00/250.00, 4 suites.
* 17C manor house of Elizabethan origins with a tranquil ambience. Original features include a period banqueting hall. Comfortable, modern bedrooms. Good leisure. Conservatory restaurant has light, open atmosphere. Creative dishes at 1744.

We try to be as accurate as possible when giving room rates.
But prices are susceptible to change,
so please check rates when booking.

DARTFORD Kent 504 U 29 – pop. 56 818.
Dartford Tunnel and Bridge (toll).
London 20 – Hastings 51 – Maidstone 22.

at Wilmington Southwest : 1½ m. A 225 on B 258 – ⊠ Dartford.

🏰 **Rowhill Grange** ॐ, DA2 7QH, Southwest : 2 m. on Hextable rd (B 258) ℘ (01322)
615136, admin@rowhillgrange.com, Fax (01322) 615137, 斺, ⑩, ₤₆, ≘ṣ, ⊠, 斺 – 🛗 ⇔
📞 ৳ 🅿 – 🔬 160. 🆗 🄰🄴 🅾 𝗩𝗜𝗦𝗔. ⋇
Truffles : Rest (closed Saturday lunch) 25.00/44.00 a la carte 35.00/44.00 ♀ – **Brasserie :**
Rest a la carte 19.95/25.25 – **37 rm** ⊑ ৳165.00 – ৳৳190.00, 1 suite.
◆ Extended 19C thatched house set in pretty, nine-acre gardens. Bold-coloured rooms
with teak beds, eight in the converted clockhouse. Smart, up-to-date leisure club. Kentish
ingredients to fore in modern Truffles. Flag-floored Brasserie next to Leisure.

DARTMOUTH Devon 503 J 32 The West Country G. – pop. 5 512.
See : Town★★ (≤★) – Old Town - Butterwalk★ - Dartmouth Castle (≤★★★) AC.
Exc. : Start Point (≤★) S : 13 m. (including 1 m. on foot).
🄱 The Engine House, Mayor's Ave ℘ (01803) 834224, enquire@dartmouth-tourism.org.uk.
London 236 – Exeter 36 – Plymouth 35.

🏰 **Dart Marina,** Sandquay, TQ6 9PH, ℘ (01803) 832580, reservations@dartmarina.com,
Fax (01803) 835040, ≤ Dart Marina, 斺, ₤₆, ⊠ – 🛗 ⇔, 🍽 rest, ৳ 🅿. 🆗 🄰🄴 𝗩𝗜𝗦𝗔
River Restaurant : Rest (dinner only and Sunday lunch)/dinner 35.95 ♀ – **Wildfire :** Rest
a la carte 24.50/48.75 – **49 rm** ⊑ ৳100.00/140.00 – ৳৳139.00/230.00, 12 suites.
◆ Lovely location with excellent views over the Dart Marina. The hotel has smart, comfy
bedrooms, many with balconies. Welcoming, bright, modern public areas. Stylish River
Restaurant; terrace overlooks river. Modern, informal Wildfire offers eclectic menus.

🏛 **Royal Castle,** 11 The Quay, TQ6 9PS, ℘ (01803) 833033, enquiry@royalcastle.co.uk,
Fax (01803) 835445, ≤ – ⇔ 📞 🅿. 🆗 🄰🄴 🅾 𝗩𝗜𝗦𝗔
Rest 16.50 (dinner) and a la carte 22.45/32.95 ♀ – **25 rm** ⊑ ৳85.00/199.00 –
৳৳169.00/199.00.
◆ Harbour views and 18C origins enhance this smart hotel with its cosy bar and open log
fires. Each of the comfortable rooms is individually styled, some boast four-poster beds.
Harbour-facing restaurant particularly proud of sourcing fresh fish.

🏛 **Brown's Hotel,** 27-29 Victoria Rd, TQ6 9RT, ℘ (01803) 832572, enquiries@brownsho
teldartmouth.co.uk – ⇔. 🆗 🄰🄴 𝗩𝗜𝗦𝗔
closed 24-26 December and January-mid February – **Rest** - Tapas - (closed Sunday-Monday) (dinner only) a la carte 17.00/30.50 – **10 rm** ৳60.00/80.00 – ৳৳85.00/170.00.
◆ Georgian charm, in a personally run hotel, close to the harbour, with a chic modern
townhouse style. Bedrooms are individually appointed with clean modern lines. Informal
tapas-style dining; great original art.

⌂ **Barrington House** without rest., Mount Boone, TQ6 9HZ, via A 3122 and Townstall Rd
℘ (01803) 835545, enquiries@barrington-house.com, ≤ Dartmouth and Kingswear, 斺 –
⇔ 🅿 🄰🄴 🅾 𝗩𝗜𝗦𝗔. ⋇
6 rm ⊑ ৳75.00/90.00 – ৳৳100.00/150.00.
◆ Big house with even bigger views! Spacious garden and terrace. Breakfast individually
cooked in front of you! Great views from airy rooms: top floor penthouse is luxurious.

⌂ **Wadstray House** without rest., Blackawton, TQ9 7DE, West : 4 ½ m. on A 3122
℘ (01803) 712539, wadstraym@aol.com, Fax (01803) 712539, ≤, 斺, ♨ – ⇔ 🅿. ⋇
closed 25-26 December – **3 rm** ⊑ ৳60.00 – ৳৳90.00.
◆ An attractive house with beautifully kept gardens, delightful courtyard and verandah.
Highly individual rooms decorated in pretty hues. Library sitting room.

⌂ **Woodside Cottage** ॐ without rest., Blackawton, TQ9 7BL, West : 5½ m. by A 3122 on
Blackawton rd ℘ (01803) 898164, stay@woodsidedartmouth.co.uk, Fax (0870) 686417, 斺
– ⇔ 🅿. ⋇
closed 24-26 December – **3 rm** ⊑ ৳70.00 – ৳৳90.00.
◆ Pleasant former farmhouse/cottage in pretty rural setting. Attractive landscaped gardens lead into well-furnished sitting room and conservatory. Simple, bright and airy
rooms.

⌂ **Westbourne House** without rest., 4 Vicarage Hill, TQ6 9EW, ℘ (01803) 832213, peter
walton@westbourne-house.co.uk, Fax (01803) 839209 – ⇔ 🅿. 🆗 𝗩𝗜𝗦𝗔. ⋇
closed Christmas – **4 rm** ⊑ ৳65.00 – ৳৳85.00.
◆ Imposing 19C house a few minutes' walk from quayside. Lovely Victorian drawing room
ideal for relaxation; doubles as communal breakfast room. Tastefully appointed bedrooms.

⛬ **New Angel Rooms,** 51 Victoria Rd, TQ6 9RT, ℰ (01803) 839425, *reservations@thene wangel.co.uk, Fax (01803) 839567* – ⋇ ⓥ ℙ ⓜⓢ ℡ ⓥⓢⓐ ⅀
closed January – **Rest** – (see **The New Angel** below) – 6 rm ⌷ ♦90.00 – ♦♦140.00.
✦ Townhouse tucked away from quayside towards rear of town. Good quality break-fasts amongst oak wood and rattan. Stylish guests' lounge; rooms a mix of modish and antique.

⛬ **Broome Court** ⦜ without rest., Broomhill, TQ6 0LD, West : 2 m. by A 3122 and Venn Lane ℰ (01803) 834275, *boughtontml@aol.com, Fax (01803) 833260*, ≤, ⋙ – ⋇ ℙ.
3 rm ⌷ ♦50.00/60.00 – ♦♦80.00/120.00.
✦ Pretty house in a stunning, secluded location. Two sitting rooms: one for winter, one for summer. Breakfast "en famille" in huge kitchen, complete with Aga. Cottagey bed-rooms.

XX **The New Angel** (Burton-Race), 2 South Embankment, TQ6 9BH, ℰ (01803) 839425, *reservations@thenewangel.co.uk, Fax (01803) 839567*, ≤ Dart Estuary ⋇ ⟲ 12. ⓜⓢ ℡ ⓥⓢⓐ
closed January, Sunday dinner and Monday except Bank Holidays – **Rest** (booking essential) a la carte 33.00/42.50 ⅀.
Spec. Fillet of sea bass, smoked sausage, new potatoes amd tarragon. Braised Dartmouth lobster, baby carrots, broad beans and peas. Strawberry shortcake with lemon mousse.
✦ The famous "Carved Angel" reborn under TV personality chef John Burton-Race. Modern décor; open-plan kitchen. Refined cooking concentrates on local ingredients.

at Kingswear East : via lower ferry – ⊠ Dartmouth.

🏠 **Nonsuch House,** Church Hill, TQ6 0BX, from lower ferry take first right onto Church Hill before Steam Packet Inn ℰ (01803) 752829, *enquiries@nonsuch-house.co.uk, Fax (01803) 752357*, ≤ Dartmouth Castle and Warfleet, ⋙ – ⋇ ⓜⓢ ⓥⓢⓐ. ⅀
Rest *(closed Tuesday, Wednesday and Saturday)* (residents only) (dinner only) (set menu only) (unlicensed) 27.50 – **3 rm** ⌷ ♦70.00/85.00 – ♦♦100.00/125.00.
✦ Charming, personably run Edwardian house stunningly sited above the river town. Smart conservatory terrace and large, well appointed bedrooms. Good, homely breakfasts.

at Strete Southwest : 4 m. on A 379 – ⊠ Dartmouth.

🏠 **The Kings Arms,** Dartmouth Rd, TQ6 0RW, ℰ (01803) 770377, *kingsarms-devon-fish@hotmail.com, Fax (01803) 771008*, ⛱, ⋙ – ⋇ ℙ. ⓜⓢ ℡ ⓥⓢⓐ
closed Sunday dinner and Monday November-Easter – **Rest** - Seafood - a la carte 20.00/33.00 ⅀.
✦ Mid-18C pub with rear terrace that looks to sea. Smart restaurant is where serious, accomplished cooking takes place: local, seasonal produce well utilised on modern menus.

DARWEN Blackburn 502 504 M 22.
🔟 Winter Hill ℰ (01254) 701287.
London 222 – Blackburn 5 – Blackpool 34 – Leeds 59 – Liverpool 43 – Manchester 24.

🏨 **Astley Bank,** Bolton Rd, BB3 2QB, South : ¾ m. on A 666 ℰ (01254) 777700, *sales@as tleybank.co.uk, Fax (01254) 777707*, ⋙ – ⋇ ⓥ ℙ. – ⛪ 70. ⓜⓢ ℡ ⓥⓢⓐ. ⅀
Rest 17.50/23.50 and a la carte 22.25/34.70 – **37 rm** ⌷ ♦92.00 – ♦♦132.00.
✦ Part Georgian, part Victorian privately owned hotel in elevated position above town. Varied rooms overlook the pleasant gardens. Well-equipped conference rooms. Conserva-tory dining is elegantly semi-split.

DATCHWORTH Herts. 504 T 28.
London 31 – Luton 15 – Stevenage 6.

🏨 **Coltsfoot Country Retreat** ⦜, Coltsfoot Lane, Bulls Green, SG3 6SB, South : ¾ m. by Bramfield Rd ℰ (01438) 212800, *info@coltsfoot.com, Fax (01438) 212840*, ⋙, ⛺ – ⋇ ⓥ ⛪ ℙ. ⓜⓢ ℡ ⓞ ⓥⓢⓐ. ⅀
closed 25 December – **Rest** *(closed Sunday)* (booking essential) (dinner only) a la carte 22.40/32.15 – **15 rm** ⌷ ♦125.00 – ♦♦145.00/155.00.
✦ Stylish hotel, once a working farm, in 40 rural acres. Lounge bar with log-burning stove. Highly individual rooms around courtyard have vaulted ceilings and rich furnishings. Main barn houses restaurant: concise modern menus employ good seasonal produce.

DAVENTRY Northants. 504 Q 27 – pop. 21 731.

 Norton Rd ℰ (01327) 702829 – , Hellidon Lakes H. & C.C., Hellidon ℰ (01327) 62550 – Staverton Park, Staverton ℰ (01327) 302000.

 Moot Hall, Market Sq ℰ (01327) 300277.

London 79 – Coventry 23 – Leicester 31 – Northampton 13 – Oxford 46.

Fawsley Hall , Fawsley, NN11 3BA, South : 6 ½ m. by A 45 off A 361 ℰ (01327) 892000, reservations@fawsleyhall.com, Fax (01327) 892001, ≤, ⌖, Ⅰ⌂, ⌖, ⌖, ⌖, ⌖, ⌖ – ℙ – ⌖ 100. ⓄⓈ ⌖ ⓄⓈ ⌖

The Knightley : Rest (dinner only and Sunday lunch)/dinner 37.50/75.00 and a la carte 45.50/49.00 ⌖ – ⌖ 8.00 – **41 rm** ⌖149.00/159.00 – ⌖⌖305.00/365.00, 2 suites.

◆ Magnificent Tudor manor house with Georgian and Victorian additions in a secluded rural location. Open fires, a great hall and impressive period interiors throughout. Interesting, Italian influenced dishes, in three-roomed restaurant.

The Daventry, Sedgemoor Way, off Ashby Rd, NN11 0SG, North : 2 m. on A 361 ℰ (01327) 307000, daventry@paramount-hotels.co.uk, Fax (01327) 706313, Ⅰ⌂, ⌖, ⌖ – ⌖ ⌖, ⌖ rest, ⌖ ℙ – ⌖ 600. ⓄⓈ ⌖ ⓄⓈ ⌖ ⌖

Rest (closed Saturday lunch) (carvery lunch)/dinner 28.00 and a la carte 24.20/49.65 s. ⌖ – **138 rm** ⌖75.00/275.00 – ⌖⌖95.00/295.00.

◆ A large and spacious modern hotel with comprehensive conference facilities and a well equipped leisure centre. Contemporary, comfy rooms, some with "study areas". Restaurant has pleasant views over Drayton Water.

at Staverton Southwest : 2¾ m. by A 45 off A 425 – ⌖ Daventry.

Colledges House, Oakham Lane, NN11 6JQ, off Glebe Lane ℰ (01327) 702737, lizjarrett@colledgeshouse.co.uk, Fax (01327) 300851, ⌖ – ⌖ rm, ℙ. ⓄⓈ ⌖ ⌖

Rest (by arrangement) (communal dining) 29.50 – **4 rm** ⌖ ⌖62.50 – ⌖⌖98.00.

◆ Part 17C house in a quiet village. Full of charm with antiques, curios, portraits and an inglenook fireplace. Homely rooms are in the main house and an adjacent cottage. Evening meals served at elegant oak table.

> Undecided between two equivalent establishments?
> Within each category, establishments are classified
> in our order of preference.

DAWLISH Devon 503 J 32.

London 184 – Exeter 13 – Teignmouth 3.5.

Lammas Park House, 3 Priory Rd, EX7 9JF, via High St and Strand Hill ℰ (01626) 888064, lammaspark@hotmail.com, Fax (01626) 888064, ≤, ⌖ – ⌖ ℙ. ⓄⓈ ⌖ ⓄⓈ ⌖ ⌖

Rest (by arrangement) (communal dining) 16.95 – **3 rm** ⌖ ⌖65.00 – ⌖⌖85.00.

◆ Lovely early 19C townhouse boasting a superb secluded rear terrace garden and handsome period details in situ. Clean, uncluttered rooms. Sit and admire views from observatory. Dinners served in communal style; owners are experienced restaurateurs.

DEAL Kent 504 Y 30 – pop. 29 248.

 Walmer & Kingsdown, The Leas, Kingsdown ℰ (01304) 373256.

 129 High St ℰ (01304) 369576.

London 78 – Canterbury 19 – Dover 8.5 – Margate 16.

Dunkerley's, 19 Beach St, CT14 7AH, ℰ (01304) 375016, ddunkerley@btconnect.com, Fax (01304) 380187, ≤ – ⌖. ⓄⓈ ⌖ ⓄⓈ ⌖ ⌖

Rest – (see **Restaurant** below) – **16 rm** ⌖ ⌖70.00 – ⌖⌖100.00/130.00.

◆ The hotel faces the beach and the Channel. Bedrooms are comfortably furnished and the principal rooms have jacuzzis. Comfortable bar offers a lighter menu than the restaurant.

Sutherland House, 186 London Rd, CT14 9PT, ℰ (01304) 362853, info@sutherland house.fsnet.co.uk, Fax (01304) 381146, ⌖ – ⌖ ⌖ ℙ. ⓄⓈ ⌖ ⓄⓈ ⌖

Rest (by arrangement) 21.00 – **4 rm** ⌖ ⌖47.00/55.00 – ⌖⌖57.00/65.00.

◆ An Edwardian house with garden in a quiet residential area. Stylish, welcoming bedrooms are individually decorated. Friendly, relaxed atmosphere. Refined dining room with homely ambience.

Restaurant (at Dunkerley's H.), 19 Beach St, CT14 7AH, ℰ (01304) 375016, Fax (01304) 380187 – ⌖ ⌖ ⓄⓈ ⌖ ⓄⓈ ⌖

closed Monday lunch – Rest 14.95/26.50 and a la carte 36.40/43.85 ⌖.

◆ With views of the Channel, the restaurant is best known for preparing locally caught seafood, although non-seafood options are also available. Wide ranging wine list.

DEDDINGTON *Oxon.* 503 504 Q 28 – *pop. 1 595.*
London 72 – Birmingham 46 – Coventry 33 – Oxford 18.

🏠 **Holcombe,** High St, OX15 0SL, ℰ (01869) 338274, *holcombe@oxfordshire-hotels.co.uk,*
Fax (01869) 337010, 🐾 – ❄ 🗗 rest, 🅿. 🆎 🎫 ⓞ 𝗩𝗜𝗦𝗔. ※
Rest a la carte 13.85/27.25 Ⓨ – **14 rm** 🖙 ✱90.00/99.00 – ✱✱99.00/110.00.
♦ A traditional 17C stone house on village main road. Exposed oak beams and tidy public
areas contribute to the relaxed ambience. Each bedroom is individually decorated. Bright,
informal, Mediterranean style dining.

🏠 **Deddington Arms,** Horsefair, OX15 0SH, ℰ (01869) 338364, *deddarms@oxfordshire-*
hotels.co.uk, Fax (01869) 337010 ❄ rm, 🗗 rest, ✆ & 🅿. – 🛜 30. 🆎 🎫 ⓞ 𝗩𝗜𝗦𝗔. ※
Rest a la carte 25.45/31.70 Ⓨ – **27 rm** 🖙 ✱90.00 – ✱✱99.00/130.00.
♦ Traditional coaching inn with a smart, modish ambience, on the market place. Spacious
modern bedrooms in rear extension. Stylish rooms, two four-postered, in the main house.
The restaurant is decorated in a warm and contemporary style.

DEDHAM *Essex* 504 W 28 *Great Britain G.* – ✉ *Colchester.*
Env. : *Stour Valley★ – Flatford Mill★, E : 6 m. by B 1029, A 12 and B 1070.*
London 63 – Chelmsford 30 – Colchester 8 – Ipswich 12.

🏠 **Maison Talbooth** ⑤, Stratford Rd, CO7 6HN, West : ½ m. ℰ (01206) 322367, *mai*
son@milsomhotels.com, Fax (01206) 322752, ≼, 🐾 – 🅿. 🆎 🎫 ⓞ 𝗩𝗜𝗦𝗔. ※
Rest – (see *Le Talbooth* below) – **9 rm** 🖙 ✱120.00 – ✱✱350.00, 1 suite.
♦ Quiet, Victorian country house with intimate atmosphere, lawned gardens and views
over river valley. Some rooms are smart and contemporary, others more traditional in
style.

🏠 **Milsoms,** Stratford Rd, CO7 6HW, West : ¾ m. ℰ (01206) 322795, *milsoms@milsomho*
tels.co.uk, Fax (01206) 323689, 🌫, 🐾 – ❄ rm, 🗗 rest, & 🅿. 🆎 🎫 ⓞ 𝗩𝗜𝗦𝗔.
Rest (bookings not accepted) a la carte 20.25/30.95 Ⓨ – 🖙 15.00 – **15 rm** 🖙 ✱80.00 –
✱✱140.00.
♦ Modern hotel overlooking Constable's Dedham Vale with attractive garden and stylish
lounge. Bright, airy and welcoming rooms feature unfussy décor and modern colours.
Likeably modish, wood-floored bistro.

 XXX **Le Talbooth,** Gun Hill, CO7 6HP, West : 1 m. ℰ (01206) 323150, *talbooth@milsomho*
tels.com, Fax (01206) 322309, 🌫, 🐾 – 🅿. 🆎 🎫 ⓞ 𝗩𝗜𝗦𝗔
closed Sunday dinner September - May – **Rest** 25.00 (lunch) and a la carte 35.20/48.45 Ⓨ ᴥ.
♦ Part Tudor house in attractive riverside setting. Exposed beams and real fires contribute
to the traditional atmosphere matched by a traditional menu. Well chosen wine list.

XX **Fountain House & Dedham Hall** ⑤ with rm, Brook St, CO7 6AD, ℰ (01206)
323027, *sarton@dedhamhall.demon.co.uk, Fax (01206) 323293,* 🐾 – ❄ rest, 🅿. 🆎 𝗩𝗜𝗦𝗔.
※
closed Christmas-New Year – **Rest** *(closed Sunday-Monday)* (booking essential) (dinner
only) 28.50 Ⓨ – **5 rm** 🖙 ✱55.00 – ✱✱95.00.
♦ In a quiet, country house dating back to 15C with traditional, uncluttered ambience.
Weekly changing traditionally based set menu. Comfortable rooms also available.

🛏 **The Sun Inn** with rm, High St, CO7 6DF, ℰ (01206) 323351, *info@thesuninnded*
ham.com, 🐾 – ❄ rm, 🅿. 🆎 𝗩𝗜𝗦𝗔
closed 25-26 December – **Rest** *(closed Sunday dinner)* a la carte 15.00/25.00 Ⓨ – **5 rm** 🖙
✱55.00/105.00 – ✱✱80.00/150.00.
♦ Modernised 15C coaching inn in heart of village. Welcoming sunny yellow façade; spacious interior. Interesting, original Mediterranean style menus. Boutique bedrooms.

DENBY DALE *W. Yorks.* 502 504 P 23.
London 192 – Leeds 22 – Manchester 37.

XX **Aagrah,** 250 Wakefield Rd, HD8 8SU, Northeast : ¾ m. on A 636 ℰ (01484) 866266 – 🅿.
🆎 🎫 𝗩𝗜𝗦𝗔
closed 25 December – **Rest** - Indian (Kashmiri) - (booking essential) (dinner only) 15.00 and
a la carte approx 18.00 **s.**
♦ The Eastern influenced interior décor reflects the authentic feel of the good quality
Indian-Kashmiri dishes on offer. A busy, bustling atmosphere prevails.

> **Your opinions are important to us:**
> please write and let us know about your discoveries and experiences –
> good and bad!

ENGLAND

DENHAM *Bucks. 504* S 29 *Great Britain G. – pop. 2 269.*

Env. : Windsor Castle★★★, Eton★★ and Windsor★, S : 10 m. by A 412.

London 20 – Buckingham 42 – Oxford 41.

🏠 **The Swan Inn,** *Village Rd, UB9 5BH,* ℘ *(01895) 832085, info@swaninndenham.co.uk, Fax (01895) 835516,* 🍴, 🚗 *– P. ⦿⦿ ⧆ VISA*

closed 25-26 December – **Rest** *(booking essential) a la carte 19.00/27.75* ℙ.

♦ Ivy-covered inn; part bar, part restaurant leading through to pleasant terrace and spacious garden. Good modern dishes with blackboard specials changing daily.

DENMEAD *Hants. 503* Q 31 *– pop. 5 788.*

London 70 – Portsmouth 11 – Southampton 27.

✕✕ **Barnard's,** *Hambledon Rd, PO7 6NU,* ℘ *(023) 9225 7788, Fax (023) 9225 7788,* 🚗 – ✦✦. ⦿⦿ ⧆ VISA

closed 1 week Christmas, 1 week May, 1 week August, Saturday lunch, Sunday and Monday – **Rest** *(light lunch)/dinner a la carte 20.15/32.20* ℙ.

♦ Friendly village centre shop conversion; bright and airy with a small bar area. Classic and modern dishes: ricotta and basil gnocchi, chorizo salad or pork in mustard sauce.

DERBY *Derby 502 503 504* P 25 *Great Britain G. – pop. 229 407.*

See : City★ – Museum and Art Gallery★ (Collection of Derby Porcelain★) YZ **M1** *– Royal Crown Derby Museum★ AC Z* **M2.**

Env. : Kedleston Hall★★ AC, NW : 4½ m. by Kedleston Rd X.

📍 *Wilmore Rd, Sinfin* ℘ *(01332) 766323 –* 📍 *Mickleover, Uttoxeter Rd* ℘ *(01332) 513339 –* 📍 *Kedleston Park, Kedlston, Quardon* ℘ *(01332) 840035 –* 📍, 📍 *Marriott Breadsall Priory H. & C.C., Moor Rd, Morley* ℘ *(01332) 832235 –* 📍 *Allestree Park, Allestree Hall, Allestree* ℘ *(01332) 550616.*

✈ *Nottingham East Midlands Airport, Castle Donington :* ℘ *(0871) 919 9000, SE : 12 m. by A 6 X.*

🚹 *Assembly Rooms, Market Pl* ℘ *(01332) 255802.*

London 132 – Birmingham 40 – Coventry 49 – Leicester 29 – Manchester 62 – Nottingham 16 – Sheffield 47 – Stoke-on-Trent 35.

Plan opposite

🏨 **Midland,** *Midland Rd, DE1 2SQ,* ℘ *(01332) 345894, sales@midland-derby.co.uk, Fax (01332) 293522,* – 📶, ✦✦ rm, 📍 – 🔺 150. ⦿⦿ ⧆ VISA ⦿⦿   Z **i**

closed 25-26 December – **Rest** *(closed Saturday lunch) a la carte 21.45/41.00 –* ⊑ *13.95 –* **99 rm** ✶102.00/130.00 – ✶✶140.00, 1 suite.

♦ A pleasant, early-Victorian railway hotel with good sized modern rooms and traditionally decorated public areas. Wide array of conference rooms. Pretty dining room in the Victorian style of the hotel.

at Darley Abbey *North : 2½ m. off A 6 – X – ⊠ Derby.*

✕✕ **Darleys,** *Darley Abbey Mill, DE22 1DZ,* ℘ *(01332) 364987, info@darleys.com, Fax (01332) 364987 –* 📶 📍 ⦿⦿ VISA

closed Sunday dinner – **Rest** *15.95 (lunch) and dinner a la carte 15.95/29.55* ℙ.

♦ A converted cotton mill in an attractive riverside setting. The interior is modern, stylish and comfortable. High quality British cuisine of satisfying, classical character.

at Breadsall *Northeast : 4 m. by A 52 – X – off A 61 – ⊠ Derby.*

🏨 **Marriott Breadsall Priory H. & Country Club** 🏌, *Moor Rd, Morley, DE7 6DL, Northeast : 1¼ m. by Rectory Lane* ℘ *(01332) 832235, Fax (01332) 833509,* ≤, 🍴, 🏊, ✶, ⛳, ⛱, 📶, ⛳, 🚗, ✕ – 📶 ✦✦, ▤ rest, 🕭. 📍 – 🔺 110. ⦿⦿ ⧆ ⦿ VISA

Priory : Rest *(dinner only and Sunday lunch) 38.00* ℙ *– Long Weekend : Rest a la carte 18.50/33.50* ℙ *–* ⊑ *14.95 –* **107 rm** ✶125.00 – ✶✶125.00, 5 suites.

♦ Quiet, characterful hotel with main house of 13C origins retaining original elements. Mixture of modern and period rooms. Good leisure facilities and parkland. Priory restaurant housed within arches of building's old wine cellars. Long Weekend is all day bistro.

at Etwall *Southwest : 5 m. by A 38 – X – and A 516 – ⊠ Derby.*

✕✕ **Blenheim House** *with rm, Main St, DE65 6LP,* ℘ *(01283) 732254, info@theblenheim house.com, Fax (01283) 733860 –* ✦✦ 📍 ⦿⦿ ⧆ VISA

Rest *(closed Sunday dinner) 15.95 (lunch) and a la carte 21.85/31.85* ℙ *–* **10 rm** ⊑ ✶60.00/75.00 – ✶✶85.00/135.00.

♦ Extended red-brick farmhouse. Dining areas enhanced by good-sized, linen-clad tables. Polite service. Well executed, extensive menus. Some bedrooms in the annexe.

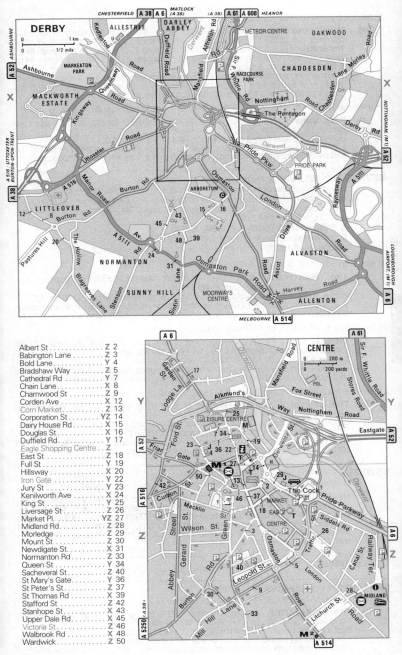

DERBY

CHESTERFIELD A 38 A 6   MATLOCK (A 38)   A 61 A 608   HEANOR

CENTRE

at Mickleover *Southwest : 3 m. by A 38 – X – and A 516 –* ⊠ *Derby.*

 Mickleover Court, Etwall Rd, DE3 0XX, ℰ (01332) 521234, *mickleover@menzies-ho tels.co.uk, Fax (01332) 521238,* ₤₆, ≘s, ⬚ – ⧄ – ₴⇆ rm, ▦ ⅙, **P** – ⚐ 200. ⚫◉ AE ◉ ⱽᴵˢᴬ
The Brasserie : Rest 14.95/27.00 and a la carte 24.40/35.90 – **Stelline Trattoria :** Rest -
Italian - *(closed Sunday-Thursday)* (dinner only) a la carte 17.40/30.40 – ⚌ 14.95 – **91 rm**
★150.00 – ★★150.00, 8 suites.
• A large central atrium with 2 café-bar areas. Rooms are spacious and well equipped, with
good use of natural light. Comprehensive leisure and conference facilities. Vibrant, spacious Brasserie. Stelline Trattoria is authentic Italian restaurant.

at Weston Underwood *Northwest : 5½ m. by A 52 – X – and Kedleston Rd –* ⊠ *Derby.*

⌂ **Park View Farm** without rest., DE6 4PA, ℰ (01335) 360352, *enquiries@parkview farm.co.uk, Fax (01335) 360352,* ≤, ⌧ – ₴⇆ **P**. ⅍
closed 24-26 December – **3 rm** ⚌ ★50.00/60.00 – ★★80.00/85.00.
• Friendly couple run this elegant house on a working farm, in sight of Kedleston Hall.
Antique-filled lounge with oils and a Victorian fireplace. Simple rooms in stripped pine.

DEVIZES *Wilts.* 503 504 O 29 *The West Country G.* – *pop. 14 379.*

See : *St John's Church*★★ – *Market Place*★ – *Wiltshire Heritage Museum*★ *AC.*

Env. : *Potterne (Porch House*★★ *) S : 2½ m. by A 360 – E : Vale of Pewsey*★*.*

Exc. : *Stonehenge*★★★ *AC, SE : 16 m. by A 360 and A 344 – Avebury*★★ *(The Stones*★*, Church*★ *) NE : 7 m. by A 361.*

▮₆ *Erlestoke Sands, Erlestoke* ℰ (01380) 831069.

🅱 *Cromwell House, Market Sq* ℰ (01380) 729408.

London 98 – Bristol 38 – Salisbury 25 – Southampton 50 *– Swindon 19.*

at Marden *Southeast : 6½ m. by A 342 –* ⊠ *Devizes.*

⍾◻ **The Millstream,** SN10 3RH, ℰ (01380) 848308, *mail@the-millstream.co.uk, Fax (01380) 848337,* ⌖, ⌧ – ₴⇆ **P**. ⚫◉ ⱽᴵˢᴬ
closed 25 December and Monday except Bank Holidays – **Rest** a la carte 22.00/28.00 ⅀.
• Lovingly run with smart outside terrace; modern rusticity invoked in stylish interior.
Carefully prepared, tasty, modish menus. Super wine list and Champagne always available!

at Potterne *South : 2¼ m. on A 360 –* ⊠ *Devizes.*

⌂ **Blounts Court Farm** ⍟ without rest., Coxhill Lane, SN10 5PH, ℰ (01380) 727180,
⌂ *caroline@blountscourtfarm.co.uk,* ⌧, ⋤ – ₴⇆ **P**. ⚫◉ ⱽᴵˢᴬ. ⅍
3 rm ⚌ ★36.00/68.00 – ★★60.00/68.00.
• Working farm personally run by charming owner: good value accommodation in blissful
spot. Cosy rooms in converted barn are handsomely furnished with interesting artefacts.

at Rowde *Northwest : 2 m. by A 361 on A 342 –* ⊠ *Devizes.*

⍾◻ **The George & Dragon,** High St, SN10 2PN, ℰ (01380) 723053, *thegandd@tis cali.co.uk,* ⌖, ⌧ – ₴⇆ **P**. ⚫◉ ⱽᴵˢᴬ. ⅍
closed first week January – **Rest** - Seafood specialities - *(closed Sunday dinner and Monday)*
(booking essential) 15.50 (lunch) and a la carte 20.00/33.50 ⅀.
• Characterful little pub with rustic fittings and open fire. Robust modern classics and fish
specials hold sway in a cosy, personally run atmosphere. Real ale.

DEWSBURY *W. Yorks.* 502 P 22 *– pop. 54 341.*

London 205 – Leeds 9 – Manchester 40 – Middlesbrough 76 – Sheffield 31.

🏠 **Heath Cottage,** Wakefield Rd, WF12 8ET, East : ¾ m. on A 638 ℰ (01924) 465399,
bookings@heathcottage.co.uk, Fax (01924) 459405 – ₴⇆, ▦ rest, **P** – ⚐ 70. ⚫◉ ⱽᴵˢᴬ. ⅍
Rest 12.95/15.95 and dinner a la carte 23.00/34.85 **s.** – **27 rm** ⚌ ★49.50 – ★★63.00/74.00.
• Extended Victorian house; former doctors' surgery. Bright décor and furnishings
throughout with rooms of varying shapes and sizes. Cocktail bar in comfortable lounge
area. Tried-and-tested cuisine.

DICKLEBURGH *Norfolk* 504 X 26 *– see Diss.*

DIDMARTON *Glos.* 503 504 N 29 *–* ⊠ *Tetbury.*

London 120 – Bristol 20 *– Gloucester 27 – Swindon 33.*

⍾◻ **The Kings Arms** with rm, The Street, GL9 1DT, on A 433 ℰ (01454) 238245,
Fax (01454) 238249, ⌖, ⌧ – ₴⇆ **P**. ⚐ 24. ⚫◉ ⱽᴵˢᴬ. ⅍
Rest a la carte 17.95/22.95 ⅀ – **4 rm** ⚌ ★55.00 – ★★80.00.
• Busy, bustling former coaching inn with 17C façade, open fires and low beams. Large,
traditional pub menu served in bar or dining area. Comfortable bedrooms. Lawned garden.

DIDSBURY *Gtr Manchester* 502 503 504 N 23 – *see Manchester.*

DIPTFORD *Devon* 503 I 32 – ⊠ *Totnes.*

⌂ **The Old Rectory** ⌖, TQ9 7NY, ℰ (01548) 821575, *kitchens@oldrectorydiptford.co.uk*,
≤, ⋯ – ⊱✕ **P**. **©©** **AE** **VISA**
closed Christmas and New Year, minimum 2 night stay – **Rest** (by arrangement) 25.00 –
3 rm ⌑ ✦60.00 – ✦✦90.00.
 ◆ Classic Georgian house of cavernous proportions with a three-acre garden. The lounge,
though, is small and cosy. Airy rooms benefit from rural views; luxurious bathrooms. Food
taken seriously: fine home-cooked meals served with pride.

DISS *Norfolk* 504 X 26 – *pop. 7 444.*
🄴 *Meres Mouth, Mere St* ℰ (01379) 650523.
London 98 – Ipswich 25 – Norwich 21 – Thetford 17.

at Dickleburgh *Northeast : 4½ m. by A 1066 off A 140 –* ⊠ *Diss.*

⌂ **Dickleburgh Hall Country House** *without rest.*, Semere Green Lane, IP21 4NT,
North : 1 m. ℰ (01379) 741259, *johnandberyl@dickhall.freeserve.co.uk*, ⛾, ⋯ – ⊱✕ **P**.
⊁
March-September – **3 rm** ⌑ ✦45.00 – ✦✦80.00/90.00.
 ◆ 16C house still in private hands. Trim rooms in traditional patterns, beamed lounge with
an inglenook fireplace; snooker room and golf course.

at Brockdish *East : 7 m. by A 1066, A 140 and A 143 –* ⊠ *Diss.*

⌂ **Grove Thorpe** ⌖ *without rest.*, Grove Rd, IP21 4JR, North : ¾ m. ℰ (01379) 668305,
b-b@grovethorpe.co.uk, ⟋, ⋯, ⌖ – ⊱✕ **P**. ⊁
closed Christmas and New Year – **3 rm** ⌑ ✦50.00/55.00 – ✦✦74.00/80.00.
 ◆ Pretty 17C bailiff's house in peaceful pastureland with fishing; very welcoming owners.
Cosy ambience. Characterful interior with oak beams, inglenook and antique furniture.

at Brome *(Suffolk) Southeast : 2¾ m. by A 1066 on B 1077 –* ⊠ *Eye.*

🄱🄰 **The Cornwallis** ⌖, IP23 8AJ, ℰ (01379) 870326, *info@thecornwallis.com*,
Fax (01379) 870051, ⌂, ⋯, ⌖ – ⊱✕ **P**. – **⊠** 30. **©©** **VISA**. ⊁
Rest (booking essential) a la carte 20.00/30.50 ⌑ – **16 rm** ⌑ ✦99.00 – ✦✦120.00/175.00.
 ◆ Part 16C dower house with quiet topiary gardens. Spacious, individually decorated tim-
bered rooms with antique furniture. 60ft well in very characterful bar dating from 1561.
Dining room with delightful conservatory lounge overlooking gardens.

DITCHEAT *Somerset.*
London 124 – Bath 29.

🄸🄳 **Manor House Inn** *with rm*, BA4 6RB, ℰ (01749) 860276, ⌂, ⋯ – ⊱✕ **⋓** **P**. **©©** **VISA**
⊁
Rest *(closed dinner 25 December and Sunday dinner)* a la carte 16.00/30.00 ⌑ – **3 rm** ⌑
✦50.00 – ✦✦80.00.
 ◆ Watch the horses on their way to the gallops from this characterful 17C pub. Drink at
flag-floored or sports bars. Dishes are satisfyingly rustic. Pleasant rooms in annex.

DOGMERSFIELD *Hants..*
London 44.5 – Farnham 6 – Fleet 2.

🄷🄷🄷🄷 **Four Seasons,** Dogmersfield Park, Chalky Lane, RG27 8TD, ℰ (01252) 853000,
Fax (01252) 853010, ⌗, ⊆s, ⬛, ⟋, ⋯, ℒ, ⊁ – ⮁ ⊱✕ ⬛ ⌖ ⌖, ✥✥ **P**. – **⊠** 240. **©©** **AE** **①**
VISA
Seasons : **Rest** *(closed lunch Monday-Friday)* a la carte 39.50/57.50 – ⌑ 24.00 – **111 rm**
✦323.00 – ✦✦323.00, 22 suites.
 ◆ Part Georgian splendour in extensive woodlands; many original features in situ. Superb
spa facilities: vast selection of leisure pursuits. Luxurious, highly equipped bedrooms. Res-
taurant has thoroughly modish, relaxing feel.

> The ❀ award is the crème de la crème.
> This is awarded to restaurants
> which are really worth travelling miles for!

DONCASTER S. Yorks. 502 503 504 Q 23 – pop. 67 977.

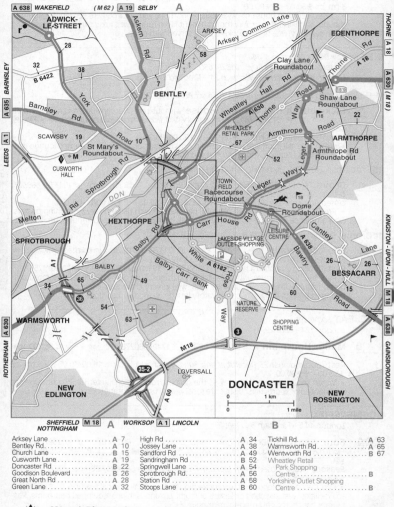

- Doncaster Town Moor, Bawtry Rd, Belle Vue ℘ (01302) 533778, B – Crookhill Park, Conisborough ℘ (01709) 862979 – Wheatley, Amthorpe Rd ℘ (01302) 831655, B – Owston Park, Owston Hall, Owston ℘ (01302) 330821.
- 38-40 High St ℘ (01302) 734309.

London 173 – Kingston-upon-Hull 46 – Leeds 30 – Nottingham 46 – Sheffield 19.

Arksey Lane	A 7	High Rd	A 34	Tickhill Rd	A 63
Bentley Rd	A 10	Jossey Lane	A 38	Warmsworth Rd	A 65
Church Lane	B 15	Sandford Rd	A 49	Wentworth Rd	B 67
Cusworth Lane	A 19	Sandringham Rd	B 52	Wheatley Retail Park Shopping Centre	B
Doncaster Rd	B 22	Springwell Lane	A 54	
Goodison Boulevard	B 26	Sprotbrough Rd	A 56	Yorkshire Outlet Shopping Centre	B
Great North Rd	A 28	Station Rd	A 58	
Green Lane	A 32	Stoops Lane	B 60	

Mount Pleasant, Great North Rd, DN11 0HW, Southeast : 6 m. on A 638 ℘ (01302) 868696, reception@mountpleasant.co.uk, Fax (01302) 865130, ♨, ☞ – ⇔, ☰ rest, ✆ ♿ ℙ – ☒ 200. ◖◗ ﹩ AE ⓪ VISA. ✀

closed 25 December – **Garden** : Rest 14.95 (lunch) and dinner a la carte 28.70/35.70 s. ♀ – 54 rm ☲ ✝79.00 – ✝✝99.00, 2 suites.

♦ Stone-built farmhouse with sympathetic extension. Traditionally styled throughout: wood panelled lounges and a small bar. Well-kept bedrooms, including one with a five-poster! Restaurant with garden views.

DONCASTER

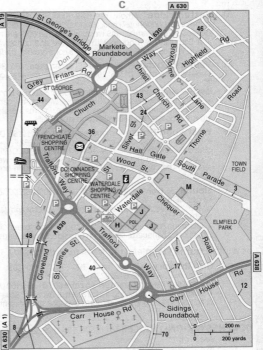

XX **Aagrah**, Great North Rd, Woodlands, DN6 7RA, Northwest : 4 m. on A 638 ℰ (01302)
728888 – 🖃 **P**. **⬤⬤** **AE** **VISA**   A r
closed 25 December – **Rest** - Indian (Kashmiri) - (booking essential) (dinner only) 16.00 and
a la carte 10.60/14.60 **s**.
  ◆ The Eastern influenced interior décor reflects the authentic feel of the good quality
Indian-Kashmiri dishes. Busy, bustling atmosphere.

DONHEAD ST ANDREW *Wilts.* 503 504 N 30 – *see Shaftesbury (Dorset).*

DORCHESTER *Dorset* 503 504 M 31 *The West Country G.* – pop. 16 171.

  See : *Town★ - Dorset County Museum★ AC*.
  Env. : *Maiden Castle★★ (⇐★) SW : 2½ m. – Puddletown Church★, NE : 5½ m. by A 35*.
  Exc. : *Moreton Church★★, E : 7½ m. – Bere Regis★ (St John the Baptist Church★ - Roof★★)
  NE : 11 m. by A 35 – Athelhampton House★ AC, NE : 6½ m. by A 35 - Cerne Abbas★,
  N : 7 m. by A 352 – Milton Abbas★, NE : 12 m. on A 354 and by-road.*
  🛅 *Came Down* ℰ (01305) 813494.
  🛃 *11 Antelope Walk* ℰ (01305) 267992.
  London 135 – Bournemouth 27 – Exeter 53 – Southampton 53.

🏠 **Birkin House** without rest., Stinsford, DT2 8QD, East : 1 ¼ m. by B 3150 ℰ (01305)
260262, *info@birkinhouse.com, Fax* (01305) 259510, 🌳, 🐾 – 🛬 **P**. **⬤⬤** **①** **VISA**
🗭
closed Christmas-New Year – **12 rm** 🖃 ✱60.00 – ✱✱160.00.
  ◆ Greystone Victorian mansion in formal gardens. Brims with antiques and style. Imposing
hallway; elegant lounge; opulent drawing room; cosy bar/library. Well furnished
rooms.

Casterbridge without rest., 49 High East St, DT1 1HU, ☎ (01305) 264043, *reception@casterbridgehotel.co.uk*, Fax (01305) 260884 – 🐾 🏧 *VISA*. ❄
closed 25-26 December – **15 rm** ☑ ✦50.00/80.00 – ✦✦110.00/125.00.
♦ A Georgian town house with courtyard and conservatory at the bottom of the high street. Well decorated throughout in a comfortable, traditional style. Bar and quiet lounge.

Yalbury Cottage ⬧, Lower Bockhampton, DT2 8PZ, East : 2 ¼ m. by B 3150 and Bockhampton rd ☎ (01305) 262382, *yalburyemails@aol.com*, Fax (01305) 266412, ☞ – ✦✕ **P**.
closed 2 weeks January – **Rest** (dinner only) 34.00 – **8 rm** ☑ ✦70.00 – ✦✦112.00.
♦ Characterful converted 17C cottages with pretty garden and quiet country location. Uncluttered lounge with original fireplace. Rooms are simply furnished and spacious. Dining room boasts beamed ceiling and stone walls.

Westwood House without rest., 29 High West St, DT1 1UP, ☎ (01305) 268018, *reservations@westwoodhouse.co.uk*, Fax (01305) 250282 – ✦✕ **P**. ❄
closed 1 week christmas - New Year – **7 rm** ☑ ✦40.00/55.00 – ✦✦60.00/85.00.
♦ Georgian town house on the high street with a welcoming atmosphere. Breakfast served in the conservatory. Rooms are decorated in bold colours and are well kept and spacious.

Sienna, 36 High West St, DT1 1UP, ☎ (01305) 250022, *browns@siennarestaurant.co.uk* – ✦✕ ▤ 🐾 *VISA*
closed 2 weeks Spring, 2 weeks October, Sunday and Monday – **Rest** (booking essential) 18.50/32.00 ♀.
♦ Charming, intimate restaurant at top of high street. Cheerful yellow walls with modern artwork and banquette seating on one side. Modern British dishes using local produce.

at Winterbourne Steepleton West : 4¾ m. by B 3150 and A 35 on B 3159 – ✉ Dorchester.

Old Rectory without rest., DT2 9LG, ☎ (01305) 889468, *caroline@theoldrectorybandb.co.uk*, Fax (01305) 889737, ☞ – ✦✕ **P**. ❄
closed Christmas and New Year – **4 rm** ✦60.00 – ✦✦100.00.
♦ Built in 1850 and having a characterful exterior. Situated in the middle of a charming village. Well kept, good sized rooms overlook the pleasant garden.

DORCHESTER-ON-THAMES Oxon. 503 504 Q 29 Great Britain G. – pop. 2 256.
See : Town★.
Exc. : Ridgeway Path★★.
London 51 – Abingdon 6 – Oxford 8 – Reading 17.

White Hart, 26 High St, OX10 7HN, ☎ (01865) 340074, *whitehart@oxfordshire-hotels.co.uk*, Fax (01865) 341082 – ✦✕ **P**. – 🔥 40. 🐾 🏧 ⑩ *VISA*. ❄
Rest 13.95 (lunch) and a la carte 21.95/36.20 ♀ – **26 rm** ☑ ✦85.00/95.00 – ✦✦95.00/105.00, 2 suites.
♦ 17C coaching inn with charm and character. The comfortable bar has large leather armchairs. Well-kept pretty bedrooms with smart bathrooms. Striking beamed dining room.

DORKING Surrey 504 T 30 – pop. 16 071.
🏌 Betchworth Park, Reigate Rd ☎ (01306) 882052.
London 26 – Brighton 39 – Guildford 12 – Worthing 33.

Burford Bridge, Box Hill, RH5 6BX, North : 1½ m. on A 24 ☎ (0870) 4008283, *burfordbridge@macdonald-hotels.co.uk*, Fax (01306) 880386, 🔥 heated, ☞ – ✦✕ 📞 **P**. – 🔥 300. 🐾 🏧 ⑩ *VISA*
Rest 20.95/29.50 and a la carte 41.35/56.50 ♀ – **57 rm** ☑ ✦135.00/185.00 – ✦✦145.00/195.00.
♦ Wordsworth and Sheridan frequented this part 16C hotel. Well run, high quality feel throughout. Antique paintings in public areas, embossed wallpaper in bedrooms. The dining room has a smart, well kept air.

DORRIDGE W. Mids. 503 504 O 26 – ✉ Birmingham.
London 109 – Birmingham 11 – Warwick 11.

The Forest with rm, 25 Station Approach, B93 8JA, ☎ (01564) 772120, *info@forest-hotel.com*, Fax (01564) 732680, 🍽 – ✦✕, ▤ rest, **P**. – 🔥 100. 🐾 🏧 *VISA*
closed 25 December – **Rest** (closed Sunday dinner) a la carte 19.95/29.00 ♀ – **12 rm** ✦76.00/130.00 – ✦✦110.00/150.00.
♦ Attractive red-brick and timber former pub with a busy ambience. Food is its backbone: modern classics served in stylish bar and restaurant. Cool, modern bedrooms.

DOUGLAS *Isle of Man* 502 G 21 – *see Man (Isle of)*.

DOVER *Kent* 504 Y 30 *Great Britain G.* – pop. 34 087.
See : *Castle*★★ *AC* Y.
Env. : *White Cliffs, Langdon Cliffs, NE : 1 m. on A 2* Z *and A 258.*
↪ to France (Calais) (P & O Stena Line) frequent services daily (1 h 15 mn) – to France (Calais) (SeaFrance S.A.) frequent services daily (1 h 30 mn) – to France (Calais) (Hoverspeed Ltd) frequent services daily (55 mn) – to France (Boulogne) (SpeedFerries) 3-5 daily (50 mn).
🛈 *The Old Town Gaol, Biggin* ✆ (01304) 205108, tic@doveruk.com.
London 76 – Brighton 84.

DOVER

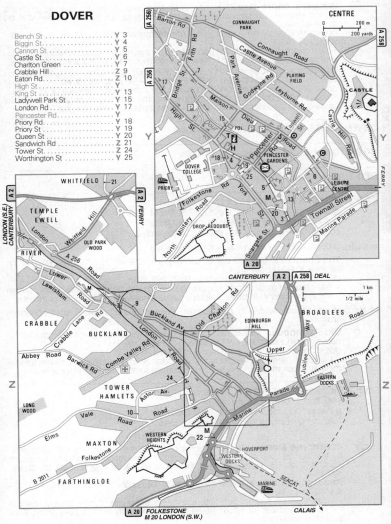

⌂ **East Lee** without rest., 108 Maison Dieu Rd, CT16 1RT, ℰ (01304) 210176, elgh@eclipse.co.uk, Fax (01304) 206705 – ⊁⊱ **P**. **MC** **VISA**. ⊰⊱ Y o
closed 2 weeks October, Christmas and New Year – **4 rm** ⊑ ★38.00/45.00 – ★★50.00/60.00.
♦ Tile hung, mid-terraced Victorian residence. Thoughtfully restored with attractive breakfast room and antique pine furnished bedrooms. A totally non-smoking establishment.

⌂ **Number One** without rest., 1 Castle St, CT16 1QH, ℰ (01304) 202007, res@number1guesthouse.co.uk, Fax (01304) 214078, ⊰⊱ – ⇦⊶ **MC** **VISA**. ⊰⊱ Y c
4 rm ⊑ ★35.00/40.00 – ★★40.00/56.00.
♦ Peach painted Georgian townhouse with traditional guesthouse appeal. Breakfast offered in bedrooms: these are compact, and cosy with a cottagey feel.

at St Margaret's at Cliffe Northeast : 4 m. by A 258 – Z – ⊠ Dover.

🏠🏠 **Wallett's Court**, West Cliffe, CT15 6EW, Northwest : ¾ m. on Dover rd ℰ (01304) 852424, wc@wallettscourt.com, Fax (01304) 853430, ⑰, Ⅰ⑤, ⊑s, ⊡, ⊰⊱, ⊁ – ⊁⊱ **P**. **MC** **AE** **①** **VISA**. ⊰⊱
closed 24-26 December – **Rest** – (see **The Restaurant** below) – **17 rm** ⊑ ★109.00 – ★★129.00/169.00.
♦ With origins dating back to the Doomsday Book, a wealth of Jacobean features remain in this relaxed country house. Most characterful rooms in main house; luxurious spa rooms.

✗✗ **The Restaurant** (at Wallett's Court H.), West Cliffe, CT15 6EW, Northwest : ¾ m. on Dover rd ℰ (01304) 852424, Fax (01304) 853430, ⊰⊱ – ⊁⊱ **P**. **MC** **AE** **①** **VISA**.
closed 24-26 December and lunch Monday and Saturday – **Rest** 19.50/39.00 ⊑ ⊰.
♦ Local produce dominates the imaginative, monthly changing, seasonal menu. Dine by candlelight in the beamed restaurant after drinks are taken by the open fire.

DOWNHOLME N. Yorks. 502 O 20 – see Richmond.

DOWNTON Hants. 503 504 P 31 – see Lymington.

DRIFT Cornwall – see Penzance.

DROITWICH SPA Worcs. 503 504 N 27 – pop. 22 585.
🏌 Droitwich G. & C.C., Ford Lane ℰ (01905) 774344.
🛈 St Richard's House, Victoria Sq ℰ (01905) 774312.
London 129 – Birmingham 20 – Bristol 66 – Worcester 6.

at Cutnall Green North : 3 m. on A 442 – ⊠ Droitwich Spa.

🍴 **The Chequers**, Kidderminster Rd, WR9 0PJ, ℰ (01299) 851292, Fax (01299) 851744, Ⅰ⑤, ⊰⊱ – ⊁⊱ **P**. **MC** **VISA**. ⊰⊱
closed 25 December – **Rest** a la carte 21.50/25.95 ⊑.
♦ Half-timbered roadside pub, comprising main bar with beams and fire or cosy garden room. Impressively wide range of highly interesting dishes, firmly traditional or modern.

at Hadley Heath Southwest : 4 m. by Ombersley Way, A 4133 and Ladywood rd – ⊠ Droitwich Spa.

⌂ **Old Farmhouse** without rest., WR9 0AR, ℰ (01905) 620837, judylambe@theoldfarmhouse.uk.com, Fax (01905) 621722, ⊰⊱, ⊁ – ⊁⊱ **P**. ⊰⊱
closed Christmas-New Year – **5 rm** ⊑ ★40.00 – ★★70.00.
♦ Converted farmhouse in quiet and rural location. Spacious comfortable rooms, three in the main house and two, more private and perhaps suited to families, in the annex.

DUDLEY W. Mids. 502 503 504 N 26 Great Britain G. – pop. 304 615.
See : Black Country Museum★.
🛈 Dudley Library, St James's Rd ℰ (01384) 812830.
London 132 – Birmingham 10 – Wolverhampton 6.

Plan : see Birmingham p. 4

🏨🏨 **Copthorne Merry Hill**, The Waterfront, Level St, Brierley Hill, DY5 1UR, Southwest : 2 ¼ m. by A 461 ℰ (01384) 482882, reservations.merryhill@mill-cop.com, Fax (01384) 482773, Ⅰ⑤, ⊑s, ⊡ – |ἡ|, ⊁⊱ rm, ⊞ rest, ⅙ **P**. – ⊿ 500. **MC** **AE** **①** **VISA**. ⊰⊱
AU z
Faradays : Rest 16.00/21.00 and a la carte 28.50/37.00 s. ⊑ – ⊑ 15.75 – **137 rm** ★150.00 – ★★160.00, 1 suite.
♦ Large, spacious, purpose-built hotel in a busy business park. Variety of room levels, all comfortable and well furnished. Extensive leisure and conference facilities. Smart, brasserie-style dining room.

DULVERTON Somerset 503 J 30 The West Country G.

See : Village★.

Env. : Exmoor National Park★★ – Tarr Steps★★ , NW : 6 m. by B 3223.

London 198 – Barnstaple 27 – Exeter 26 – Minehead 18 – Taunton 27.

🏠 **Ashwick House** ⌘, TA22 9QD, Northwest : 4 ¼ m. by B 3223 turning left after second cattle grid ℰ (01398) 323868, reservations@ashwickhouse.com, Fax (01398) 323868, ≤, 🍴, 🐎 – ⌘ ℙ, ⓂⓈ VISA , ⌘

Rest (booking essential for non-residents) (lunch by arrangement)/dinner 29.95 – **6 rm** ⌂ ✦80.00 – ✦✦120.00.

◆ Delightful, peaceful and secluded Edwardian country house in extensive gardens with pheasants and rabbits. Smartly appointed, airy rooms with thoughtful touches. Classic cuisine with strong local flavour in elegant dining room.

at Brushford South : 1¾ m. on B 3222 – ✉ Dulverton.

🏠 **Three Acres Country House** without rest., TA22 9AR, ℰ (01398) 323730, enquiries@threeacrescountryhouse.co.uk, 🐎 – ⌘ ℃ ℙ, ⓂⓈ VISA , ⌘ Ⓞ VISA

6 rm ⌂ ✦55.00/70.00 – ✦✦110.00.

◆ Keenly run 20C guesthouse that's more impressive in than out: super-comfy bedrooms are the strong point. There's an airy lounge, cosy bar and breakfasts are locally sourced.

The red ⌘ symbol?
This denotes the very essence of peace
– only the sound of birdsong first thing in the morning ...

DUNSLEY N. Yorks. – see Whitby.

DUNSTER Somerset 503 J 30.

See : Town★★ – Castle★★ AC (upper rooms ≤★) – Water Mill★ AC – St George's Church★ – Dovecote★.

London 185 – Minehead 3 – Taunton 23.

🏠 **Exmoor House** without rest., 12 West St, TA24 6SN, ℰ (01643) 821268, stay@exmoorhousehotel.co.uk, Fax (01643) 821268, 🐎 – ⌘ ⓂⓈ VISA , ⌘

early February-early November – 6 rm ⌂ ✦35.00/40.00 – ✦✦55.00/65.00.

◆ Georgian terraced house with pink exterior, enhanced by colourful window boxes. Spacious, comfy lounge and welcoming breakfast room. Chintz rooms with pleasing extra touches.

🏠 **Dollons House** without rest., Church St, TA24 6SH, ℰ (01643) 821880, dollonshouse@btconnect.com – ⌘ ℙ, ⓂⓈ VISA , ⌘

closed Christmas and New Year – 3 rm ⌂ ✦37.50 – ✦✦55.00/58.00.

◆ Grade II listed guesthouse in centre of attractive village. Entrance via busy gift shop to homely lounge cum breakfast room. Cottagey rooms: two have views of Dunster Castle.

DURHAM Durham 501 502 P 19 Great Britain G. – pop. 42 939.

See : City★★★ - Cathedral★★★ (Nave★★★, Chapel of the Nine Altars★★★, Sanctuary Knocker★) B – Oriental Museum★★ AC (at Durham University by A 167) B – City and Riverside (Prebends' Bridge ≤★★★ A , Framwellgate Bridge ≤★★ B) – Monastic Buildings (Cathedral Treasury★ , Central Tower≤★) B – Castle★ (Norman chapel★) AC B.

Exc. : Hartlepool Historic Quay★ , SE : 14 m. by A 181, A 19 and A 179.

🏌 Mount Oswald, South Rd ℰ (0191) 386 7527.

🛈 2 Millennium Pl ℰ (0191) 384 3720.

London 267 – Leeds 77 – Middlesbrough 23 – Newcastle upon Tyne 20 – Sunderland 12.

Plan on next page

🏨 **Durham Marriott H. Royal County,** Old Elvet, DH1 3JN, ℰ (0191) 386 6821, mhrs.vudm.frontdesk@marriott.com, Fax (0191) 386 0704, ⓩ, 🏋, ≋, 🏊 – 🛗, ⌘ rest, & ℙ – 🔏 150. ⓂⓈ AE Ⓞ VISA

B a

County : Rest (dinner only) a la carte 19.15/29.05 ⌂ – **Cruz** : Rest 12.50 (lunch) a la carte 19.15/29.05 s. ⌂ – **147 rm** ⌂ ✦145.00 – ✦✦155.00, 3 suites.

◆ Scene of miners' rallies in the 1950s and 60s. The quality of accommodation at this town centre hotel is of a comfortable, refined, modern standard. Good leisure facilities. County has elegant décor and linen settings. Bright, relaxed Cruz brasserie.

249

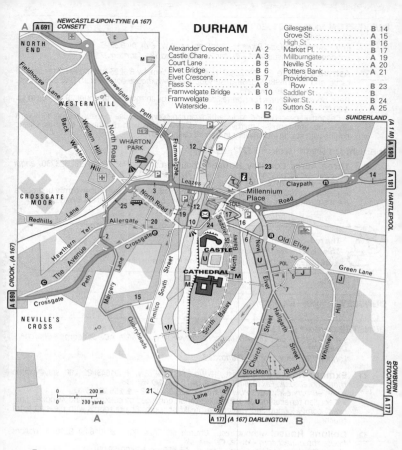

DURHAM

🏛 **Farnley Tower,** The Avenue, DH1 4DX, ℰ (0191) 375 0011, *enquiries@farnley-tower.co.uk, Fax (0191) 383 9694*, 🌳 – ⇆✕ 🅿 🅜🅒 *VISA* **A c**
Rest 15.00/30.00 and a la carte 14.50/23.50 **s.** – **13 rm** 🖙 ✵55.00/80.00 – ✵✵90.00/100.00.
 ♦ Spacious Victorian house in quiet residential area close to city centre. Modern, airy, well-equipped bedrooms with a good degree of comfort. Simple, neat and tidy restaurant; views to cathedral and castle.

🏠 **Cathedral View Town House** without rest., 212 Lower Gilesgate, DH1 1QN, ℰ (0191) 386 9566, *cathedralview@hotmail.com*, 🌳 – ⇆✕ ⚟ 🅜🅒 *VISA*. ✄ **B n**
6 rm 🖙 ✵60.00 – ✵✵80.00.
 ♦ Alluring Georgian townhouse with terraced garden in older part of the city near the centre. Attractive breakfast room with good views. Spacious, individually named rooms.

🏠 **Castle View** without rest., 4 Crossgate, DH1 4PS, ℰ (0191) 386 8852, *castle–view@hot mail.com* – ⇆✕ 🅞 🅓 *VISA*. ✄ **A e**
closed Christmas and New Year – 6 rm 🖙 ✵50.00/75.00 – ✵✵75.00/80.00.
 ♦ Attractive Georgian townhouse off steep cobbled hill, reputedly once the vicarage to adjacent church. Breakfast on terrace in summer. Individually furnished bedrooms.

✕ **Bistro 21,** Aykley Heads House, Aykley Heads, DH1 5TS, Northwest : 1 ½ m. by A 691 and
🍷 B 6532 ℰ (0191) 384 4354, *Fax (0191) 384 1149*, 🌤 – ⇆✕ 🅿 ✍ 30. 🅜🅒 🅐🅔 *VISA*
closed Sunday 25 December and Bank Holidays – Rest 15.50 (lunch) and a la carte 21.50/37.00 🍷.
 ♦ Part 17C villa with an interior modelled on a simple, Mediterranean style. Good modern British food, with some rustic tone, served in a beamed room or an enclosed courtyard.

250

at Shincliffe *Southeast : 2 m. on A 177 (Bowburn rd)* – B – ⊠ *Durham.*

🏠 **Bracken,** Shincliffe, DH1 2PD, on A 177 ℰ (0191) 386 2966, *r.whitley.brackenhol@am serve.com*, Fax (0191) 384 5423, ☜ – ⇌ ₺ **P**. **☎⊚** *VISA*. ⅍
closed Christmas - New Year **Rest** *(closed Sunday)* (residents only) (dinner only) a la carte 26.00/32.45 **s.** ♀ – **13 rm** ⊆ ✦55.00/70.00 – ✦✦90.00/120.00.
◆ Just outside the city and with good access, lying just off busy main road. The family owned hotel is in a much extended building. Compact bedrooms with modern furnishings. Home-cooked meals.

DUXFORD *Cambs.* 504 U 27 – *pop. 1 836* – ⊠ *Cambridge.*
London 50 – Cambridge 11 – Colchester 45 – Peterborough 45.

🏨 **Duxford Lodge,** Ickleton Rd, CB2 4RT, ℰ (01223) 836444, *admin@duxfordlodgeho tel.co.uk*, Fax (01223) 832271, ☜ – ⇌ **P**. – ⅍ 30. **☎⊚** *VISA*
Le Paradis : Rest 16.50/28.00 and a la carte approx 44.90 ♀ – **15 rm** ⊆ ✦76.00/91.00 – ✦✦116.00/126.00.
◆ Large, smart, redbrick building set in an acre of garden in a quiet village. Public areas and bedrooms, which are tidy and well proportioned, have co-ordinated chintz décor. Themed dining room overlooks garden.

Good food and accommodation at moderate prices?
Look for the Bib symbols:
red Bib Gourmand 🍴 for food, blue Bib Hotel 🏠 for hotels

EARLS COLNE *Essex* 504 W 28 *Great Britain G.* – *pop. 3 504* – ⊠ *Colchester.*
Exc. : *Colchester - Castle and Museum★, E : 11 m. by A 1124 and A 12.*
London 53 – Cambridge 37 – Colchester 11.

🏨 **de Vere Arms,** 53 High St, CO6 2PB, ℰ (01787) 223353, *info@deverearms.com*, Fax (01787) 223365 – ⇌ ℂ ₺ **P**. **☎⊚** *VISA*. ⅍
Rest *(closed Saturday lunch)* 17.00/25.00 and a la carte approx 35.00 **s.** – ⊆ 7.50 – **9 rm** ✦80.00/100.00 – ✦✦110.00/220.00.
◆ High Street hotel. Comfortable lounge bar with deep sofas and modern artwork. Well-appointed individually-styled bedrooms, three in annexe. Dining room with slate floor, red walls, beams and elegant tableware. Assured modern British cooking.

EARSHAM *Norfolk* 504 Y 26 – *see Bungay.*

EASINGTON *Bucks.*
London 54 – Aylesbury 13 – *Oxford 18.*

🛏 **Mole & Chicken** with rm, The Terrace, HP18 9EY, ℰ (01844) 208387, *shanepellis@hot mail.com*, Fax (01844) 208250 – ⇌ rm, **P**. **☎⊚** ⁅ *VISA*. ⅍
closed 25 December – **Rest** (booking essential) a la carte 22.00/30.00 ♀ – **5 rm** ⊆ ✦50.00 – ✦✦65.00.
◆ Friendly pub with country style character and décor. Regularly changing menu of inter-national modern dishes. Bedrooms in adjoining cottages have rural feel and good views.

EASINGWOLD *N. Yorks.* 502 Q 21 – *pop. 3 975* – ⊠ *York.*
🏌 Stillington Rd ℰ (01347) 821486.
🛈 Chapel Lane ℰ (01347) 821530.
London 217 – *Leeds 38* – Middlesbrough 37 – York 14.

🏠 **Old Vicarage** without rest., Market Pl, YO61 3AL, ℰ (01347) 821015, *kirman@oldvic-easingwold.freeserve.co.uk*, Fax (01347) 823465, ☜ – ⇌ **P**. ⅍
February-November – **4 rm** ⊆ ✦70.00 – ✦✦90.00.
◆ Spacious, part Georgian country house with walled rose garden and adjacent croquet lawn. Immaculately kept throughout with fine period antiques in the elegant sitting room.

at Crayke *East : 2 m. on Helmsley Rd* – ⊠ *York.*

🛏 **The Durham Ox** with rm, Westway, YO61 4TE, ℰ (01347) 821506, *enquiries@thedurha mox.com*, Fax (01347) 823326, ☞ – ⇌ rest, **P** ⇄ 16. **☎⊚** ⁅ *VISA*. ⅍
Rest *(closed 25 December)* (booking essential) a la carte 20.00/33.00 ♀ – **8 rm** ⊆ ✦60.00 – ✦✦80.00.
◆ Open fires, finest English oak bar panelling and exposed beams create a great country pub atmosphere. Hearty dishes from local ingredients. Well-kept rooms.

at Alne *Southwest : 4½ m. by A 19 –* ⊠ *Easingwold.*

Aldwark Manor, Y061 1UF, Southwest : 3 ½ m. by Aldwark Bridge rd on Aldwark rd
℘ (01347) 838146, *aldwark@marstonhotels.com, Fax (01347) 838867,* ☜, ⅃₆, ⅀s, ⬚, ⅃₈,
☞, ₤ – ▐▌ ﹩ ⅋ P̄ – ⩍ 240. ⓂⓈ ⒜⒠ ⓞ VISA
Rest *(bar lunch Saturday)* 18.95/25.50 ⱅ – **54 rm** ⱅ ✦139.00 – ✦✦177.50, 1 suite.
♦ Part Victorian manor house surrounded by parkland and golf course. Contemporary
styling in some rooms and a country house feel in those in the original house. Classic
formal dining.

EASTBOURNE *E. Sussex* **504** *U 31 Great Britain G. – pop. 106 562.*

See : *Seafront★.*

Env. : *Beachy Head★★★, SW : 3 m. by B 2103 Z.*

⅂₆, ⅂₉ *Royal Eastbourne, Paradise Drive* ℘ *(01323) 729738* Z – ⅂₉ *Eastbourne Downs, East
Dean Rd* ℘ *(01323) 720827* – ⅂₉ *Eastbourne Golfing Park, Lottbridge Drove* ℘ *(01323)
520400.*

🄱 *Cornfield Rd* ℘ *(0906) 7112212, tic@eastbourne.gov.uk.*

London 68 – Brighton 25 – Dover 61 – Maidstone 49.

Plan opposite

Grand, King Edward's Parade, BN21 4EQ, ℘ (01323) 412345, *reservations@grandeast
bourne.co.uk, Fax (01323) 412233,* ≤, ⅃₆, ⅀s, ⬚ heated, ⬚, ☞ – ▐▌ ﹩ rest, ▤ rest, ✆
⅋ ⩲ P̄ – ⩍ 300. ⓂⓈ ⒜⒠ ⓞ VISA   Z X
Garden Restaurant : Rest 18.00/35.00 s. ⱅ – (see also ***Mirabelle*** below) – **128 rm** ⱅ
✦125.00/145.00 – ✦✦155.00/175.00, 24 suites.
♦ Huge, pillared lobby with ornate plasterwork sets the tone of this opulently refurbished,
Victorian hotel in prime seafront location. High levels of comfort throughout. Garden
Restaurant exudes a light, comfy atmosphere.

Lansdowne, King Edward's Parade, BN21 4EE, ℘ (01323) 725174, *reception@lans
downe-hotel.co.uk, Fax (01323) 739721,* ≤ – ▐▌ ﹩ ⅋ ⩲ – ⩍ 80. ⓂⓈ ⒜⒠ ⓞ VISA   Z Z
closed 2-12 January – **Rest** (bar lunch Monday-Saturday)/dinner 21.95 and a la carte
16.85/20.70 ⱅ – **101 rm** ⱅ ✦50.00/116.00 – ✦✦128.00/168.00.
♦ Traditional seaside hotel in the same family since 1912. Bedrooms are a mix of décor,
either traditional or modern, some with sea views. Dining room has classic feel.

Cherry Tree without rest., 15 Silverdale Rd, BN20 7AJ, ℘ (01323) 722406, *lynda@cherry
tree-eastbourne.co.uk –* ﹩ ✆, ⓂⓈ VISA, ✺   Z u
9 rm ⱅ ✦35.00/55.00 – ✦✦70.00/90.00.
♦ Comfy guesthouse in semi-detached redbrick building, in quiet residential area near the
seafront. Interior of traditional standard and spotlessly kept. A non smoking house.

Brayscroft, 13 South Cliff Ave, BN20 7AH, ℘ (01323) 647005, *brayscroft@hotmail.com
–* ﹩ ⓂⓈ VISA, ✺   Z n
Rest (by arrangement) 14.00 – **6 rm** ✦34.00/38.00 – ✦✦66.00/76.00.
♦ Immaculately kept with individual style, antiques, original local art and comfy furnishings
throughout. Well run by charming owners. Dining room overlooks a smart terrace.

Mirabelle (at Grand H.), King Edward's Parade, BN21 4EQ, ℘ (01323) 435066, *reserva
tions@grandeastbourne.co.uk, Fax (01323) 412233 –* ﹩ ▤ P̄. ⓂⓈ ⒜⒠ ⓞ VISA   Z X
closed 1-14 January, Sunday and Monday – **Rest** (booking essential) 19.00/55.00 s. ⱅ ᵃ.
♦ Elegant, comfortable restaurant with a seasonally changing menu of original dishes. A
bar lounge in the basement and wine list of impressive names.

at Jevington *Northwest : 6 m. by A 259 –* Z *– on Jevington Rd –* ⊠ *Polegate.*

Hungry Monk, The Street, BN26 5QF, ℘ (01323) 482178, *Fax (01323) 483989 –* ﹩ ▤
P̄. ⟳ 16. ⓂⓈ ⒜⒠ VISA
– **Rest** (booking essential) (dinner only and Sunday lunch)/dinner 32.95 ⱅ.
♦ Part 17C Elizabethan cottages with garden. Welcoming, relaxed atmosphere; antique
chairs and log fires add to the charm. Menu offers good and hearty, traditional fare.

at Wilmington *Northwest : 6½ m. by A 22 on A 27 –* Y *–* ⊠ *Eastbourne.*

Crossways, Lewes Rd, BN26 5SG, ℘ (01323) 482455, *stay@crosswayshotel.co.uk,
Fax (01323) 487811,* ☞ – ﹩ P̄. ⓂⓈ ⒜⒠ VISA, ✺
closed 24 December-24 January – **Rest** *(closed Sunday-Monday)* (dinner only) 35.95 – **7 rm**
ⱅ ✦64.00 – ✦✦99.00/115.00.
♦ Pretty, detached country house with well tended garden. Linen covered tables in cosy
dining room. Cuisine acknowledges the classics with locally sourced, seasonal dishes.

ENGLAND

EASTBOURNE

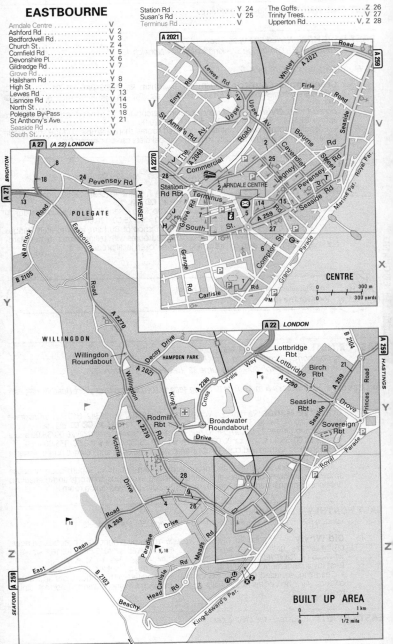

CENTRE

BUILT UP AREA

BEACHY HEAD, SEVEN SISTERS

253

EAST CHILTINGTON *E. Sussex – see Lewes.*

EAST DEREHAM *Norfolk* 504 W 25 – *pop. 17 779.*
London 109 – Cambridge 57 – King's Lynn 27 – Norwich 16.

at Wendling *West : 5½ m. by A 47.*

X **Greenbanks Country H.** with rm, Swaffham Rd, NR19 2AB, ℰ (01362) 687742, *jenny@greenbanks.co.uk*, Fax (01362) 687760, ⌂, ☒, ⬞, ℛ – ⊁ rest, ᵗ, ℙ, ⓪ ⓪ VISA
closed 1 week Christmas – **Rest** (lunch booking essential) 25.00 (dinner) and lunch a la carte approx 21.30 s. – **9 rm** ⌂ ✦70.00 – ✦✦100.00/120.00.
♦ Friendly, informal restaurant and pine fitted rooms share a simple cottage style. Traditional cooking is fresh and locally sourced - special diets can be catered for.

EASTGATE *Durham* 502 N 19.
London 288 – Bishop Auckland 20 – Newcastle upon Tyne 35 – Stanhope 3.

▥ **Horsley Hall** ⬞, DL13 2LJ, Southeast : 1 m. by A 689 ℰ (01388) 517239, *hotel@horsley hall.co.uk*, Fax (01388) 517608, ⬞, ℛ, ℛ, ☒ – ⊁ rest, ℙ, ⓪ VISA. ⬞
– **Rest** *(closed Sunday dinner to non-residents)* (booking essential for non-residents) (lunch by arrangement) 23.00 s. – **7 rm** ⌂ ✦65.00/75.00 – ✦✦75.00/120.00.
♦ Ivy-clad 17C former shooting lodge, built for Bishop of Durham, in exquisitely tranquil setting. Country house style lounge. Spacious bedrooms with telling extra touches. Baronial style dining room with ornate ceiling: homecooked local produce.

For a pleasant stay in a charming hotel,
look for the red ⬆... 🏨🏨 symbols.

EAST GRINSTEAD *W. Sussex* 504 T 30 – *pop. 26 222.*
🖆 Copthorne, Borers Arm Rd ℰ (01342) 712508.
London 48 – Brighton 30 – Eastbourne 32 – Lewes 21 – Maidstone 37.

at Gravetye *Southwest : 4½ m. by B 2110 taking second turn left towards West Hoathly – ✉ East Grinstead.*

🏨 **Gravetye Manor** (Raffan) ⬞, Vowels Lane, RH19 4LJ, ℰ (01342) 810567, *info@grave tyemanor.co.uk*, Fax (01342) 810080, ⬞, ℛ, ℛ, ℛ – ⊁ rest, ᵗ, ℙ, ⓪ ᴬᴱ VISA. ⬞
❀ **Rest** *(closed dinner 25 December to non-residents)* (booking essential) 26.00/38.00 and a la carte 38.00/55.00 s. ℛ – ⌂ 20.00 – **18 rm** ✦110.00/335.00 – ✦✦165.00/335.00.
Spec. Smoked salmon and crab. Fillet of beef with cèpe crust and celeriac purée. Assiette of desserts.
♦ 16C manor house; gardens and grounds by William Robinson. Superb country house ambience: antiques, open fires and wood panelling. Luxurious comforts and meticulous details. Exceptional traditional food in marvellous, oak-panelled dining room.

EAST HOATHLY *E. Sussex* 504 U 31.
London 60 – Brighton 16 – Eastbourne 13 – Hastings 25 – Maidstone 32.

⬆ **Old Whyly** ⬞, London Rd, BN8 6EL, West : ½ m., turning right after post box on right, taking centre gravel drive after approx. 400 metres ℰ (01825) 840216, *stay@old whyly.co.uk*, Fax (01825) 840738, ⬞, ☒ heated, ℛ, ℛ, ℛ – ⊁ rm, ᵗ ℙ. ⬞
Rest (by arrangement) (communal dining) 30.00 – **3 rm** ⌂ – ✦✦100.00/130.00.
♦ Charming, secluded Georgian manor house decorated with antiques, oils and watercolours. Airy bedrooms individually styled. Delightful owner. Warm, informal dining room.

EAST LAVANT *W. Sussex – see Chichester.*

EASTLING *Kent* 504 W 30 – *see Faversham.*

EAST MERSEA *Essex.*

London 72 – Colchester 13 – Ipswich 29.

Mersea Vineyard without rest., Rewsalls Lane, CO5 8SX, ℰ (01206) 385900, *roger.bar ber@merseawine.com*, Fax (01206) 383600, ≤ – ✲ **P**.
closed Christmas – 3 rm ⌂ ✱40.00 – ✱✱60.00.
♦ Serious working vineyard producing about 15,000 bottles a year. Sunny courtyard; family style breakfast room. Well priced. Carefully co-ordinated rooms have vineyard views.

EASTON *Devon* 503 I 31 *– see Chagford.*

EASTON *Hants. – see Winchester.*

EASTON *Somerset – see Wells.*

EAST WITTON *N. Yorks.* 502 O 21 – ⊠ *Leyburn.*

London 238 – Leeds 45 – Middlesbrough 30 – York 39.

The Blue Lion with rm, DL8 4SN, ℰ (01969) 624273, *bluelion@breathemail.net*, Fax (10969) 624189, 綜, 綜 – **P**. **◍⊚** **VISA**
Rest *(closed 25 December and Sunday lunch)* (booking essential) a la carte 19.00/31.00 ♀ – 15 rm ⌂ ✱57.50 – ✱✱79.00/99.00.
♦ Characterful, rustic feel throughout: flagstone floors, log fires, antiques and curios. Good value, traditional bar food. Extensive wine list and hand-pumped ales. Cosy rooms.

ECCLESTON *Lancs.* 502 L 23 – pop. 4 708 (inc. Heskin).

London 219 – Birmingham 103 – Liverpool 29 – Preston 11.

Parr Hall Farm without rest., Parr Lane, PR7 5SL, ℰ (01257) 451917, *par rhall@talk21.com*, Fax (01257) 453749, 綜 – ✲ **P**. **◍⊚** **VISA**. ✼
12 rm ⌂ ✱35.00 – ✱✱60.00.
♦ Part 18C former farmhouse with neat lawned gardens in small, pleasant town. Warmly decorated breakfast room with pine dressers. Cosy bedrooms with flowery fabrics.

EDENBRIDGE *Kent* 504 U 30 *Great Britain G. – pop. 7 196.*

Env. : Hever Castle★ *AC*, E : 2½ m. – Chartwell★ *AC*, N : 3 m. by B 2026.
🏌️, 🏌️, 🏌️ Edenbridge G & C.C., Crouch House Rd ℰ (01732) 867381.
London 35 – Brighton 36 – Maidstone 29.

Haxted Mill, Haxted Rd, TN8 6PU, West : 2 ¼ m. on Haxted Rd ℰ (01732) 862914, *david@haxtedmill.co.uk*, 綜, 綜 – ✲ **P**. **◍⊚** **VISA**
closed 23 December-15 January, Sunday dinner and Monday – **Rest** 21.95/26.95 and a la carte 27.90/43.45 ♀.
♦ Converted 17C clapboard stables located next to the watermill with large terrace overlooking the river Eden. Seasonally changing menu with emphasis on seafood in the summer.

at Four Elms *Northeast : 2½ m. on B 2027 – ⊠ Edenbridge.*

Oak House Barn ⊚ without rest., Mapleton Rd, TN8 6PL, Northwest : 1 m. off B 269 ℰ (01732) 700725, *christinaking01@aol.com*, 綜 – ✲ **P**. ✼
closed 15 December - 1 February – 3 rm ⌂ ✱45.00 – ✱✱60.00.
♦ Converted part 16C barn located close to Chartwell in a quiet setting. Rooms are simply decorated and guest areas include a conservatory lounge next to courtyard garden.

EGHAM *Surrey* 504 S 29 – pop. 27 666.

London 29 – Reading 21.

Runnymede, Windsor Rd, TW20 0AG, on A 308 ℰ (01784) 436171, *info@runnymedeho tel.com*, Fax (01784) 436340, 🄘, ⌁, ≋, ⊡, 綜, ✼ – 🛗 🔄, ✲ rm, ▤ **P** – 🔒 350. **◍⊚** **Æ** **◍** **VISA**. ✼
Left Bank : Rest *(closed Saturday lunch and Sunday dinner)* 22.95 (lunch) and dinner a la carte 29.00/33.50 ♀ – ⌂ 13.95 – **177 rm** ✱211.00/241.00 – ✱✱287.00, 3 suites.
♦ Riverside setting; indeed some of the comfortable, co-ordinated rooms have river views. Well maintained with smart, modern décor throughout. Good leisure and fitness. Bustling, Mediterranean influenced brasserie-style restaurant.

Great Fosters, Stroude Rd, TW20 9UR, South : 1 ¼ m. by B 388 *ρ* (01784) 433822, *enquiries@greatfosters.co.uk, Fax* (01784) 472455, ⫎ heated, ⚘, ✲ – ⭲ rest, ✦ ℙ – ♨ 130. **①③** Æ **①** *VISA*. ✲
Rest *(closed Saturday lunch)* 22.50/32.50 and a la carte 40.00/50.00 ♀ – ⚌ 15.50 – **40 rm** ♦90.00/150.00 – ♦♦150.00/425.00, 3 suites.
♦ Elizabethan mansion with magnificent gardens. Delightfully original interior has tapestries, oak panelling and antiques. Bedrooms in the main house especially notable. Two historic dining rooms: one an ancient tithe barn, the other in 16C French style.

✕✕ **Monsoon,** 20 High St, TW20 9DT, *ρ* (01784) 432141, *Fax* (01784) 432194 – ▤. **①③** Æ *VISA*
closed 25-26 December – **Rest** - Indian - a la carte 11.75/20.20.
♦ Smart, stylish restaurant that prides itself on immaculate upkeep and personable service. Contemporary artwork enlivens the walls. Freshly cooked, authentic Indian dishes.

ELLAND *W. Yorks.* 502 O 22 – *pop.* 14 554 – ✉ *Halifax.*
🎏 *Hammerstones Leach Lane, Hullen Edge ρ* (01422) 372505.
London 204 – Bradford 12 – Burnley 29 – Leeds 17 – Manchester 30.

✕ **La Cachette,** 31 Huddersfield Rd, HX5 9AW, *ρ* (01422) 378833, *Fax* (01422) 327567 – ▤. **①③** *VISA*
closed last 2 weeks August, 26 December-4 January, Sunday and Bank Holidays – **Rest** a la carte 21.50/28.40 s. ♀.
♦ A busy, bustling brasserie-style restaurant with sprinkling of French panache. Menu of eclectically blended interpretations served in the dining room or well-stocked wine bar.

ELLESMERE PORT *Mersey.* 502 503 L 24 – *pop.* 66 265.
London 211 – Birkenhead 9 – Chester 9 – Liverpool 12 – Manchester 44.

🏨 **Holiday Inn Ellesmere Port Cheshire Oaks,** Centre Island, Waterways, Lower Mersey St, CH65 2AL, Northeast : 1 ½ m. by A 5032 (M 53 junction 9) *ρ* (0151) 356 8111, *sales@hiellesmereport.com, Fax* (0151) 356 8444, **I₄**, ⇌s, ◪ – ▯, ⭲ rm, ▤ ✦ & ℙ – ♨ 250. **①③** Æ **①** *VISA*
The Locks : Rest *(closed lunch Saturday and Sunday)* a la carte 17.05/26.45 – ⚌ 11.95 – **83 rm** ♦112.00 – ♦♦112.00/185.00.
♦ Purpose-built hotel on marina beside boat museum. Uniform styling in carefully designed, modern rooms, all with waterway views. Convenient for land and air transport links. Bustling, split-level restaurant.

ELSTED *W. Sussex* 504 R 31 – *see Midhurst.*

ELSTOW *Beds.* 504 S 27 – *see Bedford.*

ELTERWATER *Cumbria* – *see Ambleside.*

ELTON *Cambs.* 504 S 26.

🍴 **The Crown Inn,** 8 Duck St, PE8 6RQ, *ρ* (01832) 280232, ⬸ – ℙ. **①③** Æ *VISA*
Rest *(closed Sunday dinner and Monday)* a la carte 18.00/32.00.
♦ Charming 17C thatched mellow stone inn overlooking the green in pretty village. Beams, log fire and a wide-ranging beer choice. Fresh, tasty dishes, many with seafood slant.

ELY *Cambs.* 504 U 26 *Great Britain G.* – *pop.* 13 954.
See : *Cathedral*★★ *AC.*
Exc. : *Wicken Fen*★, *SE : 9 m. by A 10 and A 1123.*
🎏 *107 Cambridge Rd ρ* (01353) 662751.
🛈 *Oliver Cromwell's House, 29 St Mary's St ρ* (01353) 662062.
London 74 – Cambridge 16 – Norwich 60.

✕ **The Boathouse,** 5-5A Annesdale, CB7 4BN, *ρ* (01353) 664388, *boathouse@cambscuisine.com, Fax* (01353) 666688, ≤, ⬸ – ⭲ ▤. **①③** *VISA*
closed 26-28 December – **Rest** *(booking essential)* a la carte 15.85/26.85 ♀.
♦ A riverside setting makes for a charming ambience: bag a terrace table if you can. Airy, dark wood interior where worldwide menus benefit from numerous creative touches.

at Little Thetford South : 2¾ m. off A 10 – ⊠ Ely.

⌂  **Springfields** without rest., Ely Road, CB6 3HJ, North : ½ m. on A 10 ℰ (01353) 663637, springfields@talk21.com, Fax (01353) 663130, ☞ – ⇐⇒ **P**. ⅍
closed December – **3 rm** ⊑ ✚65.00 – ✚✚65.00.
♦ Spotlessly kept guesthouse and gardens. Breakfast served at communal table. Chintz bedrooms with bric-a-brac and extras such as perfume, fresh flowers and sweets.

at Sutton Gault West : 8 m. by A 142 off B 1381 – ⊠ Ely.

🏠 **The Anchor Inn** with rm, CB6 2BD, ℰ (01353) 778537, anchorinn@popmail.bta.com, Fax (01353) 776180, ☞ – ⇐⇒ **P**. **MO AE VISA** ⅍
closed 26 December – **Rest** a la carte 15.00/35.00 ♀ – **4 rm** ⊑ ✚55.00/95.00 – ✚✚150.00.
♦ Part 17C inn on the western edge of the Isle of Ely, enhanced by open fires. Balanced à la carte menu of traditional British food from the blackboard. Comfortable bedrooms.

EMSWORTH Hants. 504 R 31 – pop. 18 139 (inc. Southbourne).
London 75 – Brighton 37 – Portsmouth 10 – Southampton 22.

XXX **36 on the Quay** (Farthing) with rm, 47 South St, The Quay, PO10 7EG, ℰ (01243)
✿ 375592, Fax (01243) 375593, ≼ – ⇐⇒ **P**. **MO AE VISA**
closed 1-24 January, 1 week late October and Christmas – **Rest** (closed Sunday-Monday) (booking essential) 23.95/45.00 – **4 rm** ✚79.00/90.00 – ✚✚95.00/135.00, 1 suite.
Spec. Sea bass, crab and spring onion beignet and black olive dressing. Lemon sole, langoustine fritters, fennel foam and shellfish stock. Peanut parfait, butterscotch doughnuts.
♦ A delightful quayside restaurant with smart, slinky cream and brown interior and chic, sleek bedrooms. Outstanding, innovative contemporary food with global influences.

X **Spencers**, 36 North St, PO10 7DG, ℰ (01243) 372744, Fax (01243) 372744 – 🖥. **MO AE VISA**
closed 25-26 December and Sunday – **Rest** a la carte 21.45/27.65 ♀.
♦ Ground floor brasserie-style with central bar and wood flooring, first floor more formal with brightly coloured dining-booths. Good variety of modern English dishes.

X **Fat Olives**, 30 South St, PO10 7EH, ℰ (01243) 377914, info@fatolives.co.uk, ☞ – ⇐⇒.
MO VISA
closed 2 weeks June, 2 weeks Christmas - New Year – **Rest** (booking essential) 17.25 (lunch) and a la carte 24.25/33.15.
♦ Small terraced house with a welcoming ambience. Simply decorated with wood floor and rough plaster walls. Tasty modern British menu and, yes, fat olives are available!

ENSTONE Oxon. 503 504 P 28 – ⊠ Chipping Norton.
London 73 – Birmingham 48 – Gloucester 32 – Oxford 18.

⌂ **Swan Lodge** without rest., OX7 4NE, on A 44 ℰ (01608) 678736, Fax (01608) 677963,
☞ – **P**. ⅍
3 rm ⊑ ✚45.00/55.00 – ✚✚65.00/70.00.
♦ 18C former coaching inn ideally situated for the Cotswolds. Well kept and furnished with antiques and log fires. Sizeable, comfy, mahogany furnished bedrooms.

EPSOM Surrey 504 T 30 – pop. 64 493 (inc. Ewell).
⛳ Longdown Lane South, Epsom Downs ℰ (01372) 721666 – ⛳, ⛳ Horton Park C.C., Hook Rd ℰ (020) 8393 8400.
London 17 – Guildford 16.

🏨 **Chalk Lane**, Chalk Lane, KT18 7BB, Southwest : ½ m. by A 24 and Woodcote Rd
ℰ (01372) 721179, smcgregor@chalklanehotel.com, Fax (01372) 727878, ☞, ☞ – ⇐⇒ ⚓
P – 🔌 140. **MO AE VISA**
Rest 22.50 (lunch) and a la carte 25.00/40.00 ♀ – **22 rm** ⊑ ✚95.00/180.00 –
✚✚130.00/180.00.
♦ At the foot of the Epsom Downs and near to the racecourse. Quality furnishings throughout; the neatly kept bedrooms are most comfortable. Smart, modern dining room.

XX **Le Raj**, 211 Fir Tree Rd, Epsom Downs, KT17 3LB, Southeast : 2 ¼ m. by B 289 and B 284
on B 291 ℰ (01737) 371371, bookings@lerajrestaurant.co.uk, Fax (01737) 211903 – 🖥. **MO**
AE ① VISA
closed 25-26 December – **Rest** - Bangladeshi - a la carte 15.20/30.85.
♦ Original, interesting menu makes good use of fresh ingredients and brings a modern style to traditional Bangladeshi cuisine. Smart, vibrant, contemporary interior décor.

ENGLAND

ERMINGTON Devon.

London 216 – Plymouth 11 – Salcombe 15.

XX **Plantation House** with rm, PL21 9NS, Southwest : ½ m. on A 3121 𝒫 (01548) 831100, info@plantationhouseivybridge.co.uk, 🍴, 🚗 – ↩ 🐾 📵 📶 🆎 VISA, 🐾
Rest (booking essential for non-residents) 30.00/45.00 – **9 rm** ⊇ ✦55.00/75.00 – ✦✦89.50/99.50.
♦ Appealing, converted Georgian rectory with smart gardens and terraced seating area. Personally run. Sound cooking of locally sourced ingredients. Individually styled bedrooms.

ERPINGHAM Norfolk 504 X 25.

London 123 – Cromer 8 – King's Lynn 46 – Norwich 16.

🏠 **The Saracen's Head** with rm, Wolterton, NR11 7LX, West : 1 ½ m. on Itteringham rd 𝒫 (01263) 768909, Fax (01263) 768993, 🍴, 🚗 – ↩ rm, 📵 📶 🆎 VISA
closed 25 December and dinner 26 December, minimum 2 night stay at weekends – **Rest** (booking essential) a la carte 20.00/28.50 – **6 rm** ⊇ ✦50.00 – ✦✦85.00.
♦ Personally run 19C coaching inn with courtyard and walled garden. Log fires, stone floors and bright en suite rooms. Blackboard menu of unpretentious, country dishes.

> We try to be as accurate as possible when giving room rates.
> But prices are susceptible to change,
> so please check rates when booking.

ESCRICK N. Yorks. 502 Q 22 – see York.

ESHER Surrey 504 S 29 – pop. 50 344 (inc. Molesey).

🏌 Thames Ditton & Esher, Portsmouth Rd 𝒫 (020) 8398 1551 BZ – 🏌 Moore Place, Portsmouth Rd 𝒫 (01372) 463533 BZ – 🏌, 🏌 Sandown Park, More Lane 𝒫 (01372) 468093 BZ.
London 20 – Portsmouth 58.

Plan : see Greater London (South-West) 5

XXX **George,** 104 High St, KT10 9QJ, 𝒫 (01372) 471500, reservations@george-esher.com, Fax (01372) 471501 – ↩ 🍽 📶 🆎 VISA
closed 1-2 January, 25-26 December, Sunday and lunch Saturday and Monday – **Rest** 25.00/40.00 ⊇.
♦ Elegant and understated restaurant with added refinement of airy cocktail bar. Immaculately laid tables lend a formal air to modern dishes that change with the seasons.

XX **Good Earth,** 14-18 High St, KT10 9RT, 𝒫 (01372) 462489, Fax (01372) 460668 – 🍽 📶 🆎 VISA
BZ **e**
closed 23-30 December – **Rest** - Chinese - 10.00/40.00 and a la carte 14.60/56.60 ⊇.
♦ A large Chinese restaurant with a smart, smooth style in décor and service. Well presented menu with much choice including vegetarian sections.

ESHOTT Northd. – see Morpeth.

ETWALL Derby 502 503 504 P 25 – see Derby.

EVERSHOT Dorset 503 504 M 31 – ✉ Dorchester.

London 149 – Bournemouth 39 – Dorchester 12 – Salisbury 53 – Taunton 30 – Yeovil 10.

🏛 **Summer Lodge** 🍴, 9 Fore St, DT2 0JR, 𝒫 (01935) 482000, summer@relaischateaux.com, Fax (01935) 482040, 🍴, 🧖, 🏊, ≋, 🎾, 🚗, 🐾 – ↩ 🍽 🐾 & 📵 📶 🆎 ⓞ VISA
Rest 25.00/44.50 – **20 rm** ⊇ ✦152.50/195.00 – ✦✦320.00/375.00, 4 suites.
♦ Part Georgian dower house in quiet village, in the best tradition of stylish, English country hotels. Boasts a range of sleek, smart, up-to-date bedrooms. Elegant dining room overlooking walled garden and terrace.

🏠 **Acorn Inn** with rm, 28 Fore St, DT2 0JW, 𝒫 (01935) 83228, stay@acorn-inn.co.uk, Fax (01935) 83707, 🍴 – ↩ rm, 📵 📶 🆎 VISA
Rest a la carte 20.00/32.50 ⊇ – **10 rm** ⊇ ✦75.00 – ✦✦140.00.
♦ 16C inn in idyllically archetypal English setting. Characterful main bar with open fire and beamed ceiling. Hearty British cooking with modern touches. Smart, cottagey rooms.

EVESHAM Worcs. 503 504 O 27 – pop. 22 179.

🛈 The Almonry, Abbey Gate ℰ (01386) 446944.
London 99 – Birmingham 30 – Cheltenham 16 – Coventry 32.

🏨 **Wood Norton Hall,** WR11 4WN, Northwest: 2 ¼ m. on A 4538 ℰ (01386) 425780, info@wnhall.co.uk, Fax (01386) 425781, ⟨symbols⟩.
Le Duc's : Rest (booking essential) a la carte 31.50/39.50 – **44 rm** ⊇ ✦100.00/120.00 – ✦✦150.00/160.00, 1 suite.
♦ Superbly wood-panelled 19C Vale of Evesham country house. Built by a French duke, and once a BBC training centre. Antiques, original fittings and a library. Large, airy rooms. Formal elements define restaurant.

🏨 **Evesham,** Coopers Lane, WR11 1DA, off Waterside ℰ (01386) 765566, Reservations (Freephone) 0800 716969, reception@eveshamhotel.com, Fax (01386) 765443, ⟨symbols⟩.
closed 25-26 December – ☞ **Cedar :** Rest a la carte 21.10/31.20 s. – **40 rm** ⊇ ✦76.00/91.00 – ✦✦124.00/168.00.
♦ Idiosyncratic family run hotel in a quiet location. Guest families well catered for, with jolly japes at every turn. Individual rooms with cottage décor and eclectic themes. Unconventional menus in keeping with hotel style.

at Abbot's Salford (Warks.) Northeast : 5 m. by A 4184 and B 4088 on Bidford rd – ✉ Evesham.

🏨 **Salford Hall,** WR11 8UT, ℰ (01386) 871300, reception@salfordhall.co.uk, Fax (01386) 871301, ⟨symbols⟩.
closed 24-30 December – **Standford Room :** Rest (closed Saturday lunch) 16.25/35.00 ⨍ – **34 rm** ⊇ ✦60.00/90.00 – ✦✦100.00/150.00.
♦ Tudor mansion with early 17C extension and gatehouse. Some very characterful public areas with exposed brickwork conducive to a more formal ambience. Eclectic bedrooms. Oak-panelled, candlelit dining room.

EWEN Glos. 503 504 O 28 – see Cirencester.

EXETER Devon 503 J 31 The West Country G. – pop. 106 772.
See : City★★ - Cathedral★★ Z – Royal Albert Memorial Museum★ Y.
Exc. : Killerton★★ AC, NE : 7 m. by B 3181 V – Ottery St Mary★ (St Mary's★) E : 12 m. by B 3183 – Y – A 30 and B 3174 – Crediton (Holy Cross Church★), NW : 9 m. by A 377.
🏌 Downes Crediton, Hookway ℰ (01363) 773025.
✈ Exeter Airport : ℰ (01392) 367433, E : 5 m. by A 30 V – Terminal : St. David's and Central Stations.
🛈 Civic Centre, Dix's Field ℰ (01392) 265700.
London 201 – Bournemouth 83 – Bristol 83 – Plymouth 46 – Southampton 110.

Plan on next page

🏨 **Abode Exeter,** The Royal Clarence, Cathedral Yard, EX1 1HD, ℰ (01392) 319955, info@abodehotels.co.uk, Fax (01392) 439423, ⟨symbols⟩.
Y Z
Rest – (see **Michael Caines** below) – ⊇ 12.95 – **52 rm** ✦95.00/125.00 – ✦✦145.00/165.00, 1 suite.
♦ Georgian-style frontage; located on the doorstep of the cathedral. Boutique style hotel with a very modern, stylish interior. Understated bedrooms feature good mod cons.

🏨 **Barcelona,** Magdalen St, EX2 4HY, ℰ (01392) 281000, barcelona@aliashotels.com, Fax (01392) 281001, ⟨symbols⟩.
Z s
Café Paradiso : Rest 15.00 (lunch) and a la carte 22.00/32.95 ⨍ – ⊇ 11.50 – **46 rm** ✦95.00/110.00 – ✦✦130.00.
♦ Trendy hotel located in Victorian former infirmary. Informal atmosphere. Two fashionable lounges with contemporary furniture. Autumnal coloured rooms with modern facilities. Informality marks restaurant style and menus.

🏨 **The Queens Court,** Bystock Terrace, EX4 4HY, ℰ (01392) 272709, enquiries@queenscourt-hotel.co.uk, Fax (01392) 491390, ⟨symbols⟩.
Y n
Olive Tree : Rest - Mediterranean - (closed Sunday lunch) 15.00 and a la carte 19.00/29.00 ⨍ – **18 rm** ⊇ ✦85.00 – ✦✦109.00.
♦ A town house hotel located close to Central train station. Bright public areas decorated in a clean, modern style. Well-equipped, tidily furnished and co-ordinated bedrooms. Brightly painted, clean-lined restaurant.

🏨 **The Edwardian** without rest., 30-32 Heavitree Rd, EX1 2LQ, ℰ (01392) 276102, michael@edwardianexeter.co.uk, Fax (01392) 253393 – ⟨symbols⟩.
V a
closed 25-26 December – **12 rm** ⊇ ✦50.00 – ✦✦76.00.
♦ Personally run hotel with a welcoming ambience. Edwardian themed lounge. Rooms vary between the modern and the traditional and some have four-poster beds.

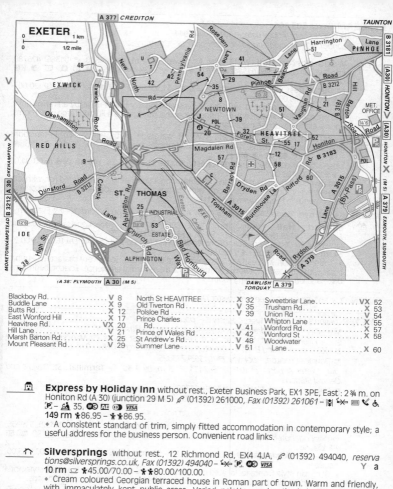

EXETER

1 km
1/2 mile

Express by Holiday Inn without rest., Exeter Business Park, EX1 3PE, East : 2 ¾ m. on Honiton Rd (A 30) (junction 29 M 5) ℰ (01392) 261000, Fax (01392) 261061 – 🛗 ⟨⟩ 📺 ✆ ৬.
📶 – 🏛 35. ⑨🅶 🅰🅴 ① 𝘝𝘐𝘚𝘈
149 rm ✦86.95 – ✦✦86.95.
♦ A consistent standard of trim, simply fitted accommodation in contemporary style; a useful address for the business person. Convenient road links.

Silversprings without rest., 12 Richmond Rd, EX4 4JA, ℰ (01392) 494040, reservations@silversprings.co.uk, Fax (01392) 494040 – ⟨⟩ 📶. ⑨🅶 𝘝𝘐𝘚𝘈   **Y a**
10 rm ⊑ ✦45.00/70.00 – ✦✦80.00/100.00.
♦ Cream coloured Georgian terraced house in Roman part of town. Warm and friendly, with immaculately kept public areas. Varied palettes and cathedral views distinguish rooms.

The Grange ⟩ without rest., Stoke Hill, EX4 7JH, Northeast : 1 ¾ m. by Old Tiverton Rd ℰ (01392) 259723, dudleythegrange@aol.com, ⊒ heated, ⌾ – ⟨⟩ 📶. ⟨⟩
3 rm ✦50.00/55.00 – ✦✦50.00/55.00.
♦ Quiet, detached, 1930s country house set in three acres of woodland yet conveniently located for the city. Accommodation is simple and homely.

Michael Caines (at Abode Exeter), The Royal Clarence, Cathedral Yard, EX1 1HD, ℰ (01392) 223638, tables@michaelcaines.com – ⟨⟩ 📺. ⑨🅶 🅰🅴 ① 𝘝𝘐𝘚𝘈   **Y z**
closed Sunday – **Rest** 17.50 (lunch) and a la carte 37.95/46.45 ⟳.
♦ Comfortable, contemporary stylish restaurant overlooking Cathedral. Menu has good choice of well-balanced and confident modern British cooking. Pleasant, efficient service.

Blue Fish Brasserie, 44-45 Queen St, EX4 3SR, ℰ (01392) 493581, info@bluefishbrasserie.com, Fax (01392) 219019 – ⟨⟩ ⑨🅶 🅰🅴 𝘝𝘐𝘚𝘈   **Y c**
closed 25 December and Sunday lunch – **Rest** - Seafood - a la carte 24.85/38.85.
♦ Tropical fish tank links bar to bright, spacious brasserie in a Grade II listed Georgian building. Well prepared fish dishes sourced from St. Ives. Some meat specials, too.

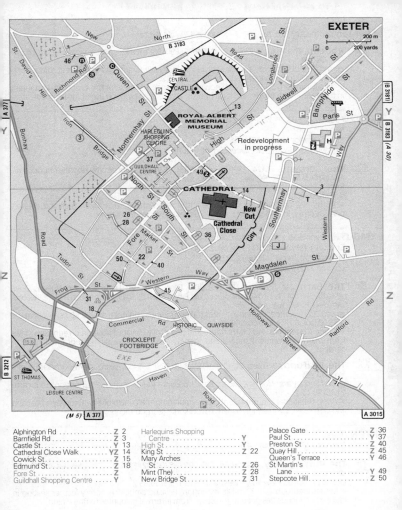

EXETER

at Stoke Canon *North : 5 m. by A 377 on A 396 –* V *– ⊠ Exeter.*

Barton Cross ⊗, Huxham, EX5 4EJ, East : ½ m. on Huxham rd ℰ (01392) 841245, *bartonxhuxham@aol.com, Fax (01392) 841942,* 🍽 *–* ⊱ 🅿, 🄬🄾 🄰🄴 𝗩𝗜𝗦𝗔
Rest *(closed Sunday for non-residents)* (dinner only) 32.50 and a la carte 21.50/32.50 ♀ –
9 rm ⊆ ✦70.00/76.00 – ✦✦98.00/120.00.
• Quietly situated part 17C thatched cottages with a simple, country atmosphere and furnishings. Small, beamed lounge bar. Bedrooms are similarly simple yet spacious. Pretty, timbered dining room.

at Rockbeare *East : 6¼ m. by A 30 –* V *– ⊠ Exeter.*

Jack in the Green Inn, London Rd, EX5 2EE, ℰ (01404) 822210, *info@jackinthe green.uk.com, Fax (01404) 823445,* 🍽 *,* 🍽 *–* ⊱ 🆑 🅿, 🄬🄾 𝗩𝗜𝗦𝗔 ⌘
closed 5-6 January and 25 December – Rest *(closed Sunday)* a la carte 18.00/30.00 ♀.
• Heavily extended pub with traditional carpeted interior. Restaurant spans three rooms: dine on good value dishes, both accomplished and sophisticated, in modern British style.

261

at Kenton Southeast : 7 m. by A 3015 – X – on A 379 – ⊠ Exeter.

XX **Rodean,** The Triangle, EX6 8LS, ℰ (01626) 890195, *excellence@rodeanrestaurant.co.uk* –
✦× ⬛◎ 𝘝𝘐𝘚𝘈
closed 2 weeks August, 1 week February, Sunday dinner and Monday – **Rest** (dinner only
and Sunday lunch)/dinner a la carte 22.75/35.25 ♀.
♦ Family run early 20C butchers shop in pretty spot. Bar area for pre-prandials. Restaurant
in two rooms with beams and local photos. Menus employ good use of local ingredients.

EXFORD Somerset 503 J 30 The West Country G.
See : Church★.
Env. : Exmoor National Park★★.
London 193 – Exeter 41 – Minehead 14 – Taunton 33.

🏠 **The Crown,** TA24 7PP, ℰ (01643) 831554, *info@crownhotelexmoor.co.uk*,
Fax (01643) 831665, �’, ☛ – ✦× P. ◎ 𝘝𝘐𝘚𝘈
Rest (bar lunch)/dinner a la carte 18.50/37.40 – **15 rm** ⊊ ✸55.00/69.50 –
✸✸110.00/130.00.
♦ Pretty 17C coaching inn with a delightful rear water garden. Open fires and country
prints. Comfy, individualistic rooms, some retaining period features.

EXMOUTH Devon 503 J 32 The West Country G. – pop. 32 972.
Env. : A la Ronde★ AC, N : 2 m. by B 3180.
🏢 Alexandra Terr ℰ (01395) 222299.
London 210 – Exeter 11.

🏠 **The Barn** ⬙, Foxholes Hill, EX8 2DF, East : 1 m. via Esplanade and Queens Drive
ℰ (01395) 224411, *info@barnhotel.co.uk*, Fax (01395) 225445, ≤ Exmouth Bay, ⬚ heated,
🐎 – ✦× P. ◎ 𝘝𝘐𝘚𝘈 ⬚
closed 23 December-3 January – **Rest** (closed Sunday) (dinner only) 21.00 **s.** – **11 rm** ⊊
✸35.00/106.00 – ✸✸70.00/106.00.
♦ Grade II listed Arts and Crafts house in a peacefully elevated position offering sea views
from many bedrooms. Personal and friendly service. Simple dining room looks out to
gardens.

XX **The Seafood,** 9 Tower St, EX8 1NT, ℰ (01395) 269459, *seafoodexmouth@aol.com* –
✦× ◎ 𝘝𝘐𝘚𝘈
closed Sunday and Monday, except Bank Holidays – **Rest** - Seafood - (dinner only) a la carte
21.15/28.45.
♦ Cosy, traditional and unpretentious restaurant in the centre of town, run by a husband
and wife team. Interestingly varied, flavoursome seafood menu.

EXTON Devon.
London 176.5 – Exmouth 4.5 – Topsham 3.

🍺 **The Puffing Billy,** Station Rd, EX3 0PR, ℰ (01392) 877888, ☕ – ✦× ▤ P. ◎ 𝘝𝘐𝘚𝘈
⬚
closed Christmas-New Year – **Rest** a la carte 17.65/30.85 ♀.
♦ Modernised pub with barn-like extension. Relaxed ambience: comfy leather seating in
lounge bar. Menus designed to please all, from informal favourites to fine dining.

FADMOOR N. Yorks. – see Kirkbymoorside.

FAIRFORD Glos. 503 504 O 28 Great Britain G. – pop. 2 960.
See : Church of St Mary★ (Stained glass windows★★).
Exc. : Cirencester★ - Church of St John the Baptist★ - Corinium Museum★ (Mosaic Pave-
ments★), W : 9 m. on A 429, A 435, Spitalgate Lane and Dollar St – Swindon - Great Railway
Museum★ AC - Railway Village Museum★ AC, S : 17 m. on A 419, A 4312, A 4259 and
B 4289.
London 88 – Cirencester 9 – Oxford 29.

XXX **Allium,** 1 London St, Market Pl, GL7 4AH, ℰ (01285) 712200, *restaurant@allium.uk.net*,
Fax (01285) 712658 – ✦× ◎ 𝘝𝘐𝘚𝘈
closed 2 weeks January, 25-26 December, Sunday dinner-Tuesday – **Rest** 14.50/50.00 ♀.
♦ Pair of Cotswold stone cottages on a main road. Squashy sofas in lounge and bar. Food's
a serious matter here: modern dishes are prepared with skill and care. Personally run.

ENGLAND

FALMOUTH *Cornwall* **503** E 33 *The West Country G.* – *pop. 21 635.*

See : *Town*★ – *Pendennis Castle*★ (≤★★) *AC* B.

Env. : *Glendurgan Garden*★★ *AC* – *Trebah Garden*★, SW : 4½ m. by Swanpool Rd A – Mawnan Parish Church★ (≤★★) S : 4 m. by Swanpool Rd A – *Cruise along Helford River*★.

Exc. : *Trelissick*★★ (≤★★) NW : 13 m. by A 39 and B 3289 A – *Carn Brea* (≤★★) NW : 10 m. by A 393 A – *Gweek (Setting*★) – *Seal Sanctuary*★) SW : 8 m. by A 39 and Treverva rd – Wendron (Poldark Mine★) *AC*, SW : 12½ m. by A 39 – A and A 394.

🏌 Swanpool Rd ℰ (01326) 311262 A – 🏌 Budock Vean Hotel, Mawnan Smith ℰ (01326) 252102.

🛈 11 Market Strand, Prince of Wales Pier ℰ (01326) 312300.

London 308 – Penzance 26 – Plymouth 65 – Truro 11.

Plan on next page

Greenbank, Harbourside, TR11 2SR, ℰ (01326) 312440, sales@greenbank-hotel.com, Fax (01326) 211362, ≤ harbour – |☰| 🔟 ॐ⇔ ⇐ P. 🐵 AE ◑ VISA
A a
Harbourside : Rest (bar lunch Monday-Saturday)/dinner 29.50 ♀ – **57 rm** ☲ ✦70.00/100.00 – ✦✦120.00/215.00, 1 suite.
◆ Flagstones and sweeping staircase greet your arrival in this ex-17C coaching inn, just as they once did for Florence Nightingale and Kenneth Grahame. Rooms with harbour views. Fine vista of bay from modern restaurant.

Royal Duchy, Cliff Rd, TR11 4NX, ℰ (01326) 313042, info@royalduchy.com, Fax (01326) 319420, ≤, ♨, ⬛s, ▢, ☞ – |☰| ♨ P. 🐵 AE ◑ VISA. ঌ
B a
Restaurant : Rest 35.00 s. ♀ – **42 rm** ☲ ✦78.00/108.00 – ✦✦226.00/246.00, 1 suite.
◆ Located on clifftop next to beach with stunning views of Pendennis Castle on headland beyond. Indoor swimming pool and leisure area. Comfortable bedrooms, many with sea views. Restaurant has good choice menus promoting local, seasonal dishes.

Penmere Manor ঌ, Mongleath Rd, TR11 4PN, ℰ (01326) 211411, reservations@penmere.co.uk, Fax (01326) 317588, ₷, ⬛s, ▢ heated, ▢, ☞ – ✦ P. – ▨ 60. 🐵 AE ◑ VISA
A e
closed 24-27 December – **Bolitho's :** Rest (bar lunch)/dinner 36.00 and a la carte 24.75/27.00 s. ♀ – **37 rm** ☲ ✦60.00/95.00 – ✦✦160.00/180.00.
◆ Victorian whitewashed hotel in five acres of sub-tropical gardens and woodland. Well-kept lounge. Extensive leisure facilities. Immaculate rooms in varying styles. Formal dining in rural setting.

Dolvean without rest., 50 Melvill Rd, TR11 4DQ, ℰ (01326) 313658, reservations@dolvean.co.uk, Fax (01326) 313995 – ✦ P. 🐵 VISA. ঌ
B n
closed Christmas – **10 rm** ☲ ✦35.00/90.00 – ✦✦90.00.
◆ Smart cream property with local books and guides in parlour: exceptionally good detail wherever you look. Elegant, neatly laid breakfast room. Bright, well-kept bedrooms.

Prospect House without rest., 1 Church Rd, Penryn, TR10 8DA, Northwest : 2 m. by A 39 on B 3292 ℰ (01326) 373198, stay@prospecthouse.co.uk, ☞ – ✦ P. 🐵 VISA
3 rm ☲ ✦37.50/40.00 – ✦✦70.00.
◆ Large Georgian guesthouse on Penryn river, set within walled garden, run by welcoming owner. Super breakfasts with local produce in abundance. Individually styled rooms.

Rosemullion without rest., Gyllyngvase Hill, TR11 4DF, ℰ (01326) 314690, gail@rosemullionhotel.demon.co.uk, Fax (01326) 210098 – ✦ P. VISA. ঌ
B c
closed Christmas – **3 rm** ☲ ✦30.00/45.00 – ✦✦57.00/65.00.
◆ Spacious, whitewashed Tudor guesthouse. Wood panelled breakfast room and well-kept chintz lounge. Comfortable rooms. Personally run by pleasant owner.

Melvill House without rest., 52 Melvill Rd, TR11 4DQ, ℰ (01326) 316645, enquiries@melvill.eurobell.co.uk, Fax (01326) 211608 – ✦ P. 🐵 VISA. ঌ
B o
7 rm ☲ ✦25.00/52.00 – ✦✦52.00/60.00.
◆ Elegant Victorian house in pink, 200 yards from sandy beach. Guest lounge at the front; newspapers provided at breakfast. Well-kept, simple rooms.

Chelsea House without rest., 2 Emslie Rd, TR11 4BG, ℰ (01326) 212230, info@chelseahousehotel.com, ≤, ☞ – ✦ 🐵 VISA. ঌ
B e
restricted opening in winter – **8 rm** ☲ ✦35.00/45.00 – ✦✦60.00/75.00.
◆ Large Victorian house in quiet residential area with partial sea-view at front. Neat breakfast room; well-appointed bedrooms, two with their own balconies.

The Three Mackerel, Swanpool Beach, TR11 5BG, South : ¾ m. off Pennance Rd ℰ (01326) 311886, Fax (01326) 316014, ≤, ☞ – ✦. 🐵 AE ◑ VISA
A n
closed 25 and 31 December – **Rest** a la carte 16.40/23.85 ♀.
◆ Casually informal beachside restaurant with white clapperboard façade. Super terrace or light interior. Seasonal, local ingredients provide the core of modern menus.

ENGLAND

FALMOUTH

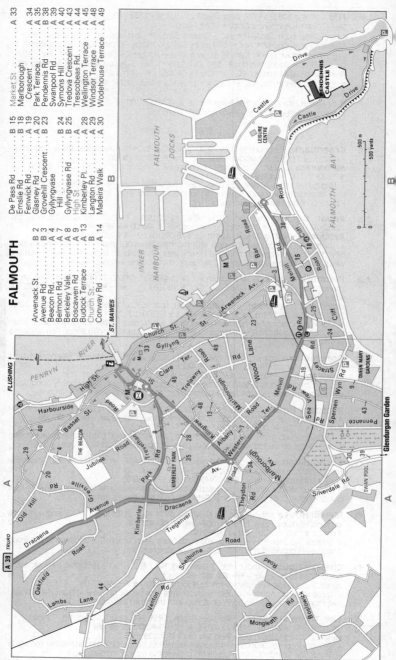

at Mylor Bridge North : 4½ m. by A 39 – A – and B 3292 on Mylor rd – ✉ Falmouth.

🏠 **Pandora Inn,** Restronguet Creek, TR11 5ST, Northeast : 1 m. by Passage Hill off Restronguet Hill *℘* (01326) 372678, Fax (01326) 378958, ≤, 🌧 – 🛗 **P.** ⇌ 8. **O₃** **VISA**
Rest (closed 25 December) a la carte 18.95/26.95 ♀.
◆ A very characterful thatched inn of 13C origins in stunning location next to harbour. Flagstone flooring, low ceilings, exposed beams. Dining room has more formal style.

at Mawnan Smith Southwest : 5 m. by Trescobeas Rd – A – ✉ Falmouth.

🏨 **Meudon** ≫, TR11 5HT, East : ½ m. by Carwinion Rd *℘* (01326) 250541, wecare@meudon.co.uk, Fax (01326) 250543, 🌧, 🔥 – ⇥ rest, **P.** **O₃** **VISA**
closed 31 December-January – Rest 29.50 a la carte 29.50/46.50 – **27 rm** ☑ ✝70.00/90.00 – ✝✝140.00/180.00, 2 suites.
◆ Landscaped sub-tropical gardens are the abiding allure of this elegant hotel. Antiques, oil paintings, log fires and fresh flowers abound. Comfy rooms, many with views. Conservatory restaurant highlighted by fruiting vine.

🏠 **Trelawne** ≫, Maenporth, TR11 5HS, East : ¾ m. by Carwinion Rd *℘* (01326) 250226, info@trelawnehotel.co.uk, Fax (01326) 250909, ≤, 🌧 – ⇥⇥ **P.** **O₃** **AE** **O** **VISA**
closed 20 November-10 February – **The Hutches :** Rest (bar lunch)/dinner 28.50 – **14 rm** ☑ ✝55.00/77.00 – ✝✝140.00/170.00.
◆ Purpose-built hotel with neat gardens in two acres of grounds. Good views across bay. Traditionally charming open lounge and very well-kept, individually furnished rooms. Smartly dressed dining room with fine bay views.

at Budock Water West : 2¼ m. by Trescobeas Rd – A – ✉ Falmouth.

🏨 **Crill Manor** ≫, TR11 5BL, South : ¾ m. *℘* (01326) 211880, info@crillmanor.com, Fax (01326) 211229, 🌧 – ⇥⇥ **P.** **O₃** **VISA**. 🎋
closed November-January except Christmas Rest (dinner only and Sunday lunch)/dinner 24.50 – **14 rm** (dinner included) ☑ ✝49.00/94.00 – ✝✝118.00/138.00.
◆ Small country house hotel in secluded location near Helford river. Spacious, well-furnished lounge. Individually styled, smartly appointed bedrooms. Smart dining room for meals featuring Cornish produce.

FAREHAM Hants. **503** **504** Q 31 Great Britain G. – pop. 56 160 (inc. Portchester).
Env. : Portchester castle★ AC, SE : 2½ m. by A 27.
🛈 Westbury Manor, 84 West St *℘* (01329) 221342.
London 77 – Portsmouth 9 – Southampton 13 – Winchester 19.

🏨 **Solent,** Rookery Ave, Whiteley, PO15 7AJ, Northwest : 5 m. by A 27 *℘* (01489) 880000, solent@shirehotels.co.uk, Fax (01489) 880007, 🌧, **I₄**, **≘s**, 🏊, 🎋 – 🛗 ⇥⇥ 🖥 **✆** 🚗 **P.** – 🏛 250. **O₃** **AE** **O** **VISA**. 🎋
Rest (bar lunch)/dinner a la carte 26.50/40.00 ♀ – **107 rm** ☑ ✝160.00 – ✝✝185.00, 4 suites.
◆ Nestling in acres of woodland. Beamed lounge and gallery; leisure facilities include sauna, solarium and hi-tech gym. Sizeable rooms boast sofa and ample work area. Timbered ceilings add to restaurant's warm and rustic feel.

🏨 **Lysses House,** 51 High St, PO16 7BQ, *℘* (01329) 822622, lysses@lysses.co.uk, Fax (01329) 822762, 🌧 – 🛗 ⇥⇥ **✆** **P.** – 🏛 100. **O₃** **AE** **O** **VISA**. 🎋
closed 24 December-2 January – **The Richmond :** Rest (closed Saturday lunch, Sunday lunch and Bank Holidays) 21.95 and a la carte 21.95/27.95 s. ♀ – **21 rm** ☑ ✝82.50/97.50 – ✝✝105.00.
◆ Former private residence built in the Georgian era. Elegant and stylish, in the heart of town. Quiet rear garden. Bright, smart bedrooms, practically appointed. Busy dining room caters for breakfasts to four course dinners.

🏠 **Springfield** without rest., 67 The Avenue, PO14 1PE, West : 1 m. on A 27 *℘* (01329) 828325, 🌧 – ⇥⇥ **P.** **O₃** **VISA**. 🎋
6 rm ✝45.00 – ✝✝55.00.
◆ Sizeable redbrick guesthouse, both comfortable and well-equipped - quieter rear bedrooms face a pleasant garden. The friendly owner cooks a hearty full breakfast at weekends.

✗ **Lauro's brasserie,** 8 High St, PO16 7AN, *℘* (01329) 234179, lauros@ntlworld.com, Fax (01329) 822776 – ⇥⇥ 🖥 **O₃** **AE** **O** **VISA**
closed 25 December, 1 January, Sunday dinner and Monday – Rest 11.50/19.50 (except Saturday) and a la carte 21.50/34.30 ♀.
◆ Picture-window façade; long narrow interior with red hued walls and open-plan kitchen. The unpretentious cooking has influences ranging from the Mediterranean to Japan.

ENGLAND

FARINGDON *Oxon.* 503 504 P 29.

🛈 *5 Market Pl* ℘ *(01367) 242191.*
London 81 – Newbury 29 – Oxford 19 – Swindon 12.

🍴 **The Trout at Tadpole Bridge** with rm, Buckland Marsh, SN7 8RF, Northeast : 4½ m.
by A 417 off A 420 on Bampton rd ℘ (01367) 870382, *info@troutinn.co.uk*, 🏡, 🌳 –
�️🛏 rm, & 🅿. 🐵 *VISA*
closed 25-26 and 31 December, 1 January and last week January – **Rest** *(closed Sunday
dinner)* a la carte 18.95/33.95 ♀ – **6 rm** ⌂ **†**55.00 – **††**80.00/110.00.
◆ Thames-side pub next to pretty bridge. Meat supplied by local farmer; marinated medallions of venison a speciality. Trout caught by local fisherman. Welcoming rooms.

at **Littleworth** *Northeast : 3 m. by A 417 off A 420* – ✉ *Faringdon.*

🍴 **The Snooty Fox Inn**, SN7 8PW, on A 420 ℘ (01367) 240549, 🌳 – 🅿. 🐵 *VISA*. ⅍
Rest *(closed Sunday dinner)* a la carte 18.00/27.00.
◆ Modern, cream painted pub on main road with minimalistic style and real fire. Friendly
service. Interesting signature dishes range from char-grills to fish and fresh pasta.

FARNBOROUGH *Hants.* 504 R 30 – *pop. 57 147.*
🔝 *Southwood, Ively Rd* ℘ *(01252) 548700.*
London 41 – Reading 17 – Southampton 44 – Winchester 33.

🏨 **Falcon**, 68 Farnborough Rd, GU14 6TH, South : ¾ m. on A 325 ℘ (01252) 545378, *ho
tel@falconfarnborough.com, Fax (01252) 522539* – ✖️ rest, 📞 🅿. 🐵 AE ① *VISA*. ⅍
Rest *(closed lunch Saturday, Sunday and Bank Holidays)* 19.95 (dinner) and a la carte
19.95/29.00 – **30 rm** ⌂ **†**98.00/108.00 – **††**112.00.
◆ Purpose-built whitewashed hotel offering traditional comfort. Ideal for business travellers. Rich oak panelling dominates Lobby bar. Neat bedrooms in bright colours. Well-kept,
efficiently run dining room.

FARNBOROUGH *Warks.* 503 504 P 27 *Great Britain G.*
Env. : *Upton House★, SW : 6 m. on B 4086 and A 422.*
London 83 – Banbury 6 – Birmingham 41.

🍴 **The Inn at Farnborough**, OX17 1DZ, ℘ (01295) 690615, *enquiries@innatfarnbor
ough.co.uk,* 🌳 – 🅿. 🐵 AE ① *VISA*. ⅍
closed 25 December – **Rest** 12.95 and a la carte 18.00/30.00 ♀.
◆ Solid 17C village centre pub. Inviting rustic interior typified by open fire and stone floor.
Tasty dishes: much time and effort is involved in sourcing local ingredients.

FARNHAM *Dorset* 503 N 31 – *see Blandford Forum.*

FARNHAM *Surrey* 504 R 30 – *pop. 36 298.*
🔝 *Farnham Park (Par Three)* ℘ *(01252) 715216.*
🛈 *Council Offices, South St* ℘ *(01252) 715109.*
London 45 – Reading 22 – Southampton 39 – Winchester 28.

🏨 **Bishop's Table**, 27 West St, GU9 7DR, ℘ (01252) 710222, *welcome@bishopstable.com,
Fax (01252) 733494,* 🌳 – ✖️. 🐵 AE *VISA*. ⅍
closed 24 December-5 January – **Rest** 17.50 (lunch) and a la carte 29.45/37.60 – ⌂ 12.50 –
15 rm †97.00/120.00 – **††**120.00/165.00.
◆ Stylish Georgian hotel once owned by the Marquis of Lothian and a former training
school for clergy. Take a drink in secluded walled garden. Individually decorated rooms.
Original dishes in pastel pink restaurant.

FARNHAM ROYAL *Bucks.* 503 504 S 29.
London 27.5 – Burnham 2 – Windsor 5.5.

🍴 **The King of Prussia**, Blackpond Lane, SL2 3EG, off A 355, by Cherry Tree Rd ℘ (01753)
643006, *info@tkop.co.uk, Fax (01753) 648645,* 🏡, 🌳 – ✖️ 🅿. 🐵 AE *VISA*. ⅍
Rest *(closed Sunday dinner)* a la carte 23.00/28.00.
◆ TV chef Phil Vickery part owns this charming village pub. Three dining areas - best of all
is the barn conversion - for constantly evolving menus full of fresh, local produce.

FARNINGHAM Kent 504 U 29.
London 22 – Dartford 7 – Maidstone 20.

⌂ **Beesfield Farm** ⤳ without rest., Beesfield Lane, DA4 0LA, off A 225 ☏ (01322) 863900, *kim.vingoe@btinternet.com*, Fax (01322) 863900, ☞ – ⇔ 🅿. ⚒
closed 16 December-16 January – **3 rm** ⌑ ✹55.00/70.00 – ✹✹80.00/90.00.
  ♦ Peaceful valley setting, with attractive garden. Exudes character: oldest part is 400 year-old Kentish longhouse. Comfy sitting room; bedrooms boast beams and garden outlook.

FAR SAWREY Cumbria 502 L 20 – see Hawkshead.

FAVERSHAM Kent 504 W 30 – pop. 18 222.
🛈 Fleur de Lis Heritage Centre, 13 Preston St ☏ (01795) 534542.
London 52 – Dover 26 – Maidstone 21 – Margate 25.

XXX **Read's** (Pitchford) with rm, Macknade Manor, Canterbury Rd, ME13 8XE, East : 1 m. on
ॐ A 2 ☏ (01795) 535344, *enquiries@reads.com*, Fax (01795) 591200, 🍴, ☞ – ⇔ rm, ❦ 🅿
⊕ 20. ⚋ 🄰 ⓪ *VISA*. ⚒
closed 25-26 December, first week January, first 2 weeks September, Sunday and Monday
– **Rest** 23.00/48.00 ⨅ ⅌ – **6 rm** ⌑ ✹125.00 – ✹✹155.00.
Spec. Tortellini of ham hock and chives, pea cream sauce and mint oil. Fillet of sea bass
with grilled polenta and pesto dressing. Plum soufflé, cinnamon shortbread.
  ♦ Georgian house with immaculate grounds and kitchen garden. Relax in bar before indulging in classic dishes making best use of delicious local produce. Very comfortable rooms.

at Dargate East : 6 m. by A 2 off A 299 – ⌧ Faversham.

🍴 **The Dove**, Plum Pudding Lane, ME13 9HB, ☏ (01227) 751360, ☞ – 🅿. ⚋ *VISA*
🐾 *closed Monday except Bank Holidays* – **Rest** *(closed dinner Tuesday and Sunday)* (booking
essential) a la carte 25.00/35.00 ⨅.
  ♦ Relaxed, well-run village pub: cosy interior of wooden tables, church-pew chairs and
black and white photos of old Dargate. Good, locally sourced food, affordably priced.

at Eastling Southwest : 5 m. by A 2 – ⌧ Faversham.

⌂ **Frith Farm House** ⤳ without rest., Otterden, ME13 0DD, Southwest : 2 m. by Otterden rd on Newnham rd ☏ (01795) 890701, *enquiries@frithfarmhouse.co.uk*, 🖥, ☞ – ⇔
🅿. ⚋ *VISA*. ⚒
3 rm ⌑ ✹50.00 – ✹✹85.00.
  ♦ Lovingly restored Georgian farmhouse in six acres of orchards which enhance the
wonderfully relaxed atmosphere. Plush sitting room with fireplace; exquisitely varied
rooms.

Red = Pleasant. Look for the red X and 🏠 symbols.

FAWKHAM GREEN Kent 504 U 29 – see Brands Hatch.

FENCE Blackburn – see Padiham.

FERMAIN BAY Guernsey (Channel Islands) 503 L 33 – see Channel Islands.

FERRENSBY N. Yorks. – see Knaresborough.

FINDON W. Sussex 504 S 31 – pop. 1 720 – ⌧ Worthing.
London 49 – Brighton 13 – Southampton 50 – Worthing 4.

🏨 **Findon Manor**, High St, BN14 0TA, off A 24 ☏ (01903) 872733, *hotel@findonma
nor.com*, Fax (01903) 877473, ☞ – ⇔ rest, ❦ 🅿 – 🔬 40. ⚋ 🄰 ⓪ *VISA*. ⚒
– **Rest** (bar lunch Monday-Saturday)/dinner a la carte 16.00/20.00 s. ⨅ – **11 rm** ⌑
✹64.00/75.00 – ✹✹100.00.
  ♦ Flint-built former rectory dating from the 16C. Characterful lounge with heavy drapes,
real fire and flagstones. Spacious, country house bedrooms. Elegant restaurant opening
onto secluded gardens.

FLAMSTEAD Herts. 504 S 28 – ✉ St Albans.
London 32 – Luton 5.

🏢 **Express by Holiday Inn** without rest., London Rd, AL3 8HT, Northeast : 1 m. on A 5 at junction 9 of M 1 ℘ (01582) 841332, ebhi-flamstead@btconnect.com, Fax (01582) 842486 – ♀ ♿ 🄿 – 🛦 30. 🐠 🚇 🖭 🚈 📨 ✓✗. ✗✗
75 rm ☑ ✦69.95 – ✦✦69.95.
◆ Modern, purpose-built lodge on busy M1 junction, sited just along from a Harvester grill restaurant. Informal breakfast area. Clean, well-kept bedrooms.

FLEETWOOD Lancs. 502 K 22 – pop. 26 841.
🄸 Fleetwood, Golf House, Princes Way ℘ (01253) 773573.
⛴ to Northern Ireland (Larne) (Stena Line).
🄱 Old Ferry Office, The Esplanade ℘ (01253) 773953.
London 245 – Blackpool 10 – Lancaster 28 – Manchester 53.

🏨 **North Euston,** The Esplanade, FY7 6BN, ℘ (01253) 876525, elizabeth.fleetwood@eliz abethhotels.co.uk, Fax (01253) 777842, ⩽ Wyre estuary and Lake District hills – 🕽 ✦✗ 🕻 🄿 – 🛦 200. 🐠 🖭 📨. ✗✗
Westerfields : Rest (closed Saturday lunch) 12.50/21.95 and dinner a la carte – **53 rm** ☑ ✦59.80/67.00 – ✦✦72.00/92.00.
◆ Impressive crescent-shaped Victorian hotel on fishing port esplanade with views to Lake District. Softly furnished bedrooms, most with sea views. Formal restaurant, with potted ferns, serves tasty local seafood.

FLETCHING E. Sussex 504 U 30/31.
London 45 – Brighton 20 – Eastbourne 24 – Maidstone 20.

🏠 **The Griffin Inn** with rm, TN22 3SS, ℘ (01825) 722890, info@thegriffininn.co.uk, Fax (01825) 722810, 🍴, ☞ – ✦✗ rm, 🄿. 🐠 🖭 📨. ✗✗
closed 25 December and dinner 1 January – **Rest** (meals in bar Sunday dinner) a la carte 20.00/32.00 ⨀ – **13 rm** ☑ ✦80.00 – ✦✦130.00.
◆ 16C coaching inn; rustic ambience with real fire, stone floor. Generous, traditional cooking. Beamed rooms with four-poster beds, rushmat flooring, hand-painted wall murals.

FLITWICK Beds. 504 S 27 – pop. 12 700.
London 45 – Bedford 13 – Luton 12 – Northampton 28.

🏯 **Flitwick Manor** ⧈, Church Rd, MK45 1AE, off Dunstable Rd ℘ (01525) 712242, flit wick@menzies-hotels.co.uk, Fax (01525) 718753, ⩽, ☞, ♤, ✖ – ✦✗ 🄿. 🐠 🖭 🚈 📨
Rest 25.00/60.00 and a la carte 29.00/49.50 – ☑ 19.00 – **18 rm** ✦125.00/175.00 – ✦✦145.00/195.00.
◆ Georgian manor house set in 27 acres. Elegant lounge. Individually decorated rooms: those on ground floor have garden seating areas, others overlook 300-year old cedar tree. Formal restaurant in Georgian house style.

FOLKESTONE Kent 504 X 30 Great Britain G. – pop. 45 273.
See : The Leas★ (⩽★) Z.
Channel Tunnel : Eurotunnel information and reservations ℘ (08705) 186186.
🄱 Harbour St ℘ (01303) 258594, tourism@folkestone.org.uk.
London 76 – Brighton 76 – Dover 8 – Maidstone 33.

Plan opposite

🏨 **Clifton,** The Leas, CT20 2EB, ℘ (01303) 851231, enquiries@thecliftonhotel.com, Fax (01303) 223949, ⩽, ☞ – 🕽. ✦✗ rm, 🕻 – 🛦 80. 🐠 🖭 🚈 📨. ✗✗   Z r
Rest 14.50/20.00 and a la carte 23.00/37.60 – ☑ 10.00 – **80 rm** ✦50.00/65.00 – ✦✦72.00/165.00.
◆ Seafront hotel with gardens and views over Channel. Traditional style; bar has sun terrace and flower-boxes. Comfortable bedrooms. Traditionally appointed restaurant.

🏢 **Relish** without rest., 4 Augusta Gardens, CT20 2RR, ℘ (01303) 850952, Fax (01303) 850958 – ✦✗ 🕻. 🐠 📨   Z n
closed 24 December-2 January – (minimum 2 night stay at weekends) **10 rm** ☑ ✦55.00/69.00 – ✦✦89.00/130.00.
◆ Large Regency townhouse overlooking private parkland. Stylish black canopy to entrance; modish furnishings. Handy food and drink area at foot of stairs. Light, airy rooms.

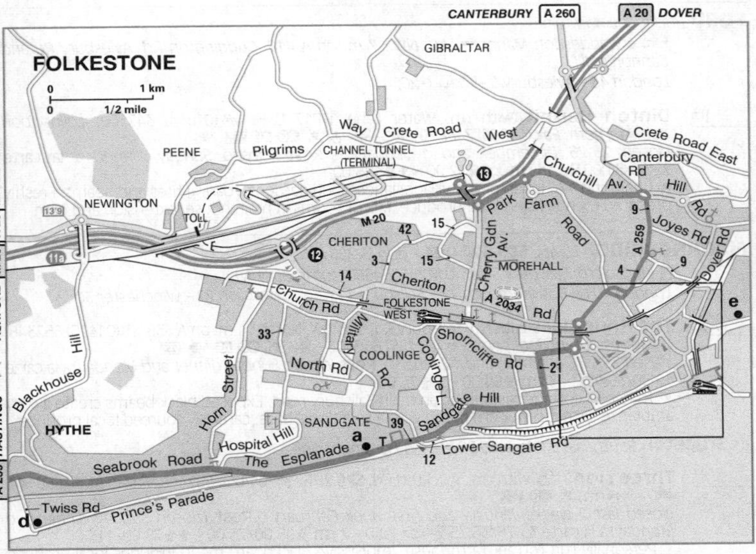

FOLKESTONE

Ashley Ave	X	3
Black Bull Rd	X, Y	4
Bouverie Pl.	Z	6
Bradstone Rd	Y	8
Canterbury Rd	X	9
Castle Rd	X	12
Cheriton High St	X	14
Cheriton Pl.	Z	13
Cherry Garden Lane	X	15
Clifton Crescent	Z	16
Clifton Rd.	Z	17
Durlocks (The)	Y	20
Earl's Ave	X	21
Grace Hill	Y	22
Guildhall St	YZ	23
Harbour App. Rd	Z	25
Harbour St.	Z	24
Langhorne Gardens	Z	27
Manor Rd	Z	28
Marine Terrace	Z	29
Middelburg Sq.	Z	30
North St	Y	32
Old High St	YZ	
Pond Hill Rd	X	33
Radnor Bridge Rd	Y	34
Remembrance (Rd of)	Z	35
Rendezvous St	Y	37
Ryland Pl.	Y	38
Sandgate High St	X	39
Sandgate Rd	Z	
Shorncliffe Rd	Y	41
Tilekiln Lane	X	42
Tontine St	Y	
Trinity Gardens	Z	43
Victoria Grove	Y	45
West Terrace	Z	47

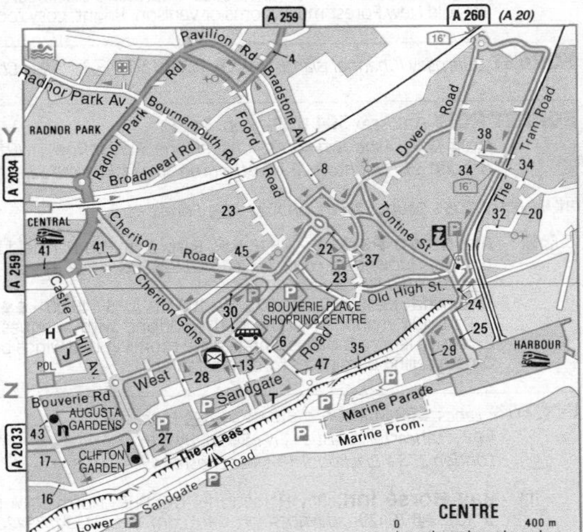

at Sandgate *West : 1¾ m. on A 259 – ✉ Folkestone.*

Sandgate, 8-9 Wellington Terrace, CT20 3DY, ☎ (01303) 220444, *info@sandgatehotel.com, Fax (01303) 220496,* ←, – 🛗 – ✂. MC AE VISA X a
closed 25-26 December – ***Restaurant:*** Rest a la carte 19.50/31.50 – **15 rm** ☕
†70.00/95.00 – ††80.00/95.00.

◆ 19C seafront hotel with smart beige and brown façade. Relaxed, modern boutique style public areas. Bedrooms have a crisp, simple freshness; some boast seaviews and balconies. Distinctively modern restaurant; very pleasant terrace.

FORD Bucks. Great Britain G.

Exc. : Waddesdon Manor★★ AC, NW : 7 m. on A 418, Cuddington Rd, Aylesbury Rd and Cannon's Hill.
London 43 – Aylesbury 5 – Oxford 20.

🏚 **Dinton Hermit** with rm, Water Lane, HP17 8XH, ✆ (01844) 347100, colinswood deb@aol.com, Fax (01296) 748819, 🌺 – 🍴 ⌖ 🕭 **P.** 🐵 **AE** **VISA**. ✀
closed 25-26 December and 1 January – **Rest** (closed Sunday dinner) a la carte 22.00/31.00 ♀ – **13 rm** ✚72.00 – ✚✚125.00.
♦ Charming 17C inn in pretty village; landscaped gardens, roaring fires and beams. Freshly prepared menus using local produce. Mix of rooms in main house, extension and barn.

FORDINGBRIDGE Hants. 503 504 O 31 – pop. 5 755.
🛈 Kings Yard, Salisbury St ✆ (01425) 654560 (summer only).
London 101 – Bournemouth 17 – Salisbury 11 – Southampton 22 – Winchester 30.

XX **The Hour Glass** with rm, Salisbury Rd, SP6 1LX, North : 1 m. on A 338 ✆ (01425) 652348, hglassrestaurant@aol.com, Fax (01425) 656002 – 🍴 **P.** 🐵 **AE** **①** **VISA**
closed 25-26 December and 1 January – **Rest** (closed Sunday dinner and Monday) a la carte 19.90/36.45 ♀ – **3 rm** ✚65.00 – ✚✚75.00.
♦ Thatched cottage restaurant on main Salisbury road. Exposed black beams create a cosy ambience. Eclectic modern menu with a traditional base; carefully sourced local produce.

at Stuckton Southeast : 1 m. by B 3078 – ✉ Fordingbridge.

X **Three Lions** ⌖ with rm, Stuckton Rd, SP6 2HF, ✆ (01425) 652489, Fax (01425) 656144, 🌺 – 🍴 rm, **P.** 🐵 **VISA**
closed last 2 weeks January and first week February – **Rest** (closed Sunday dinner and Monday) a la carte 31.75/36.75 ♀ – 🖂 7.50 – **7 rm** ✚65.00/75.00 – ✚✚75.00/115.00.
♦ Personally run former farmhouse. Impressive blackboard menu includes local produce like wild New Forest mushrooms or venison. Bright, cosy rooms with thoughtful extras.

FOREST Guernsey (Channel Islands) 503 P 33 and 517 ⑨ ⑩ – see Channel Islands.

FOREST ROW E. Sussex 504 U 30 – pop. 3 623.
🏌, 🏌 Royal Ashdown Forest, Chapel Lane, Forest Row ✆ (01342) 822018.
London 35 – Brighton 26 – Eastbourne 30 – Maidstone 32.

at Wych Cross South : 2½ m. on A 22 – ✉ Forest Row.

🏰 **Ashdown Park** ⌖, RH18 5JR, East : ¾ m. on Hartfield rd ✆ (01342) 824988, reservations@ashdownpark.com, Fax (01342) 826206, ≤, 🛁, 🚵, 🛎, 🏊, 🏌, 🌺, ⚘, ✗ – 🍴 🕭 **P.**
– 🚗 150. 🐵 **AE** **①** **VISA**. ✀
Anderida : Rest 23.95/46.00 s. ♀ – **100 rm** 🖂 ✚140.00 – ✚✚170.00, 6 suites.
♦ Part 19C manor in landscaped woodland with antiques, real fires. Former convent. Extensive leisure facilities. Immaculate rooms in two wings boast writing desks, armchairs. Ornate ceiling dominates formal restaurant.

FORTON Lancs. 502 M 25 Great Britain G. – ✉ Lancaster.
Env. : Lancaster - Castle★, N : 5½ m. by A 6.
London 236 – Blackpool 18 – Manchester 45.

🏚 **Bay Horse Inn**, Bay Horse Lane, LA2 0HR, North : 1 ¼ m. by A 6 on Quernmore rd ✆ (01524) 791204, bayhorseinfo@aol.com, Fax (01524) 791204 – **P.** 🐵 **AE** **VISA**. ✀
closed 25 December and 1 January – **Rest** (closed Sunday dinner and Monday) a la carte 20.00/30.00 ♀.
♦ Rurally set inn dating from 18C with open fires, exposed beams and enthusiastic owners. Good selection of real ales. Tasty, well-prepared, home-made dishes.

FOUR ELMS Kent 504 U 30 – see Edenbridge.

Undecided between two equivalent establishments?
Within each category, establishments are classified in our order of preference.

FOWEY Cornwall 503 G 32 The West Country G. – pop. 2 064.

See : Town★★.

Env. : Gribbin Head (≤★★) 6 m. rtn on foot – Bodinnick (≤★★) - Lanteglos Church★,
E : 5 m. by ferry – Polruan (≤★★) SE : 6 m. by ferry – Polkerris★, W : 2 m. by A 3082.

🛏 5 South St ℰ (01726) 833616, info@fowey.co.uk.

London 277 – Newquay 24 – Plymouth 34 – Truro 22.

Fowey Hall, Hanson Drive, PL23 1ET, West : ½ m. off A 3082 ℰ (01726) 833866,
info@fallhallhotel.co.uk, Fax (01726) 834100, ≤, 舒, 🔲, 溧 – ₩ ⊛ ✢ ₣ – 🏛 40. 🐠 🖭
VISA

Rest (light lunch Monday-Saturday)/dinner 35.00 ♀ – **24 rm** (dinner included) ☷
✦170.00/210.00 – ✦✦170.00/210.00, 12 suites.

* Imposing 19C country house within walled garden. Two spacious lounges with real fires,
wicker furnished garden room. Smart, plush rooms. Special facilities for children. Impressive oak-panelled restaurant.

Marina Villa Hotel, 17 The Esplanade, PL23 1HY, ℰ (01726) 833315, enquiries@the
marinahotel.co.uk, Fax (01726) 832779, ≤ Fowey river and harbour, 舒 – 🛗 ₩ ⇔, 🐠
AE VISA

Rest – (see **Waterside** below) – **17 rm** ☷ ✦120.00 – ✦✦120.00/200.00, 1 suite.

* Small house in tiny street with splendid views of river and quay. Attractive interior with
well-kept lounge, and rooms of varying size with a contemporary, individual feel.

Old Quay House, 28 Fore St, PL23 1AQ, ℰ (01726) 833302, info@theoldquay
house.com, Fax (01726) 833668, ≤, 舒 – ₩ ℰ, 🐠 🖭 **VISA**. ❀

Rest (closed lunch midweek in low season) 30.00 (dinner) and a la carte 24.00/35.00 –
12 rm ☷ ✦95.00/150.00 – ✦✦125.00/160.00.

* Former Victorian seamen's mission idyllically set on the waterfront. Stylish, contemporary lounge. Rear terrace overlooks the river. Smart, individually decorated bedrooms.
Spacious restaurant with wicker and wood furniture, serving modern British dishes.

Waterside (at Marina Villa H.), 17 The Esplanade, PL23 1HY, ℰ (01726) 833315,
Fax (01726) 832779, ≤ Fowey River and harbour, 舒 – 🛗 ₩, 🐠 🖭 **VISA**

Rest - Seafood specialities - 25.00/45.00 s. ♀.

* Smart, comfortable restaurant adding a stylish feel to well-established Georgian hotel.
Enjoy lovely river views to the accompaniment of very competent cooking.

FRAMLINGHAM Suffolk 504 Y 27 – pop. 2 839 – ✉ Woodbridge.

London 92 – Ipswich 19 – Norwich 42.

Colston Hall ⑤ without rest., Badingham, IP13 8LB, North : 4¼ m. by B 1120 off A 1120
ℰ (01728) 638375, lizjohn@colstonhall.com, Fax (01728) 638084, ⬐, 溧, ♨ – ₩ ₣. 🐠
VISA. ❀

6 rm ☷ ✦45.00 – ✦✦90.00.

* Part Elizabethan farmhouse in rural location with lakes and garden. Comfy rooms - three
of which are in stables - with character: plenty of timbers and small sitting areas.

FRAMPTON MANSELL Glos. Great Britain G.

Env. : Cirencester★ - Corinium Museum★, E : 7 m. by A 419.

London 106 – Bristol 34 – Gloucester 17.

The White Horse, Cirencester Rd, GL6 8HZ, on A 419 ℰ (01285) 760920, emmawhite
horse@aol.com, 舒 – ₩ ₣. 🐠 **VISA**

closed 1-4 January – **Rest** (closed Sunday dinner) a la carte 20.00/30.00 ♀.

* Stone-built public house on main road. Cosy small bar and attractive dining room.
Friendly service. Daily menu of classic and modern British dishes with original touches.

FREATHY Cornwall – see Millbrook.

FRESHWATER BAY I.O.W. 503 504 P 31 – see Wight (Isle of).

FRESSINGFIELD Suffolk 504 X 26.

London 104 – Ipswich 34 – Lowestoft 27.

The Fox & Goose Inn, Church Rd, IP21 5PB, ℰ (01379) 586247, foxandg
oose@uk2.net, Fax (01379) 586106, 舒 – ₩ ₣. 🐠 ⓞ **VISA**

closed 27-30 December, 13-27 April and Monday – **Rest** (booking essential) 13.95 (lunch)
and a la carte 24.50/31.25 ♀.

* Spacious black and white inn with leaded panes. Beams and wooden floor in dining
room. Extensive menu of traditional dishes with modern influence; some use of local
produce.

271

FRILSHAM Newbury – see Yattendon.

FRISTON Suffolk – see Aldeburgh.

FRITHSDEN Herts. – see Hemel Hempstead.

FRITTON Norfolk.

London 133 – Great Yarmouth 8 – Norwich 19.

 Fritton House ♨, Church Lane, NR31 9HA, ℰ (01493) 484008, frittonhouse@somer leyton.co.uk, ≤, 佘, 舞, 身 – ≒ tv P. ⑩⑧ VISA
Rest a la carte 23.00/32.00 – **7 rm** ☑ ✝85.00/130.00 – ✝✝120.00/160.00, 1 suite.
♦ Successful meeting point of 15C charm and contemporary boutique style. Elegant drawing room with sumptuous sofas and fresh flowers. No expense spared in sleek bedrooms. Dine on intriguing 21C dishes in relaxed, raftered surroundings.

FRODSHAM Ches. 502 503 L 24.

London 198 – Liverpool 20 – Runcorn 5.5.

Netherton Hall, Chester Rd, WA6 6UL, Southwest : ¾ m. on A 56 ℰ (01928) 732342, sharter@btconnect.com, Fax (01928) 739140, 舞 – ≒ P. ⑩⑧ AE VISA, ⌘
closed 25-26 December and 1 January – **Rest** a la carte 21.00/29.50.
♦ Converted Georgian farmhouse with spacious gardens. Homely interior: walls lined with books and curios. Four separate dining areas serving freshly prepared, eclectic menus.

FROGGATT EDGE Derbs. 502 503 504 P 24.

London 167 – Bakewell 6 – Sheffield 11.

The Chequers Inn with rm, Hope Valley, S32 3ZJ, ℰ (01433) 630231, info@chequers-froggatt.com, Fax (01433) 631072, 佘 – ≒ P. ⑩⑧ AE VISA, ⌘
closed 25 December – **Rest** a la carte 21.15/27.85 ☑ – **5 rm** ☑ ✝95.00 – ✝✝95.00.
♦ Refurbished 16C Grade II listed building, retaining many period features. Wide-ranging, modern menus enhanced by accomplished cooking. Pleasant, cosy bedrooms.

FROME Somerset 503 504 M/N 30.

London 118 – Bristol 24 – Southampton 52 – Swindon 44.

 Babington House ♨, Babington, BA11 3RW, Northwest : 6½ m. by A 362 on Vobster rd ℰ (01373) 812266, enquiries@babingtonhouse.co.uk, Fax (01373) 812112, 佘, ⑳, ƒ⑤, ≦s, ⌗ heated, ⌗, 舞, 身, ✕ – ✓ ✝✝ P – ▲ 45. ⑩⑧ AE ⑪ VISA
The Log Room : Rest (residents and members only) a la carte approx 28.00 ☑ – ☑ 12.50 – **23 rm** ✝310.00 – ✝✝395.00, 5 suites.
♦ Country house with vivid difference: Georgian exterior; cool, trendy interior. Laidback dining, health club, even a cinema: modern minimalism prevails. Trendy 21C rooms.

XX **The Settle**, 16 Cheap St, off Market Pl, BA11 1BN, ℰ (01373) 465975, Fax (01373) 465975 – ✓✕. ⑩⑧ AE VISA
closed 2 weeks Christmas-New Year, 2 weeks August, Sunday-Wednesday and Bank Holidays – **Rest** (dinner only) 25.00.
♦ First-floor restaurant above tea shop in town centre. Vivid red and blue linen colour scheme adds panache to compact dining area. Well-prepared dishes using local produce.

FRYERNING Essex.

London 33 – Brentwood 6 – Chelmsford 7.

XX **The Woolpack**, Mill Green Rd, CM4 0MS, ℰ (01277) 352189, info@thewoolpack-fryern ing.co.uk, Fax (01277) 356802, 佘 – ✓✕ ▤ P. ⑩⑧ AE VISA
closed 26 December - 7 January, Monday, Sunday dinner and Tuesday lunch – **Rest** a la carte 18.85/32.80.
♦ 19C inn located in a delightful rural village. Neighbourhood feel prevails with distinctive modish interior full of stylish charm. Accomplished cooking in the modern vein.

Your opinions are important to us:
please write and let us know about your discoveries and experiences – good and bad!

272

FUNTINGTON *W. Sussex* 504 R 31 – *see Chichester.*

GALMPTON *Devon* 503 J 32 – ⊠ *Brixham.*
London 229 – Plymouth 32 – Torquay 6.

↿   **Maypool Park** ⌂, Maypool, TQ5 0BJ, South : 1 m. ℰ (01803) 842442, *tilleyandco@tis
cali.co.uk,* ≤, ⌖ – ⥀⌖ ℙ. ⌖
    Rest (by arrangement) 25.00 s. – **3 rm** ⌸ ✟60.00 – ✟✟100.00.
    ◆ Guesthouse of converted 19C cottages in heart of estate bought by Agatha Christie in
    1938. Secluded, 300 feet above the Dart. Terrace with good views. Country style bed-
    rooms.

GALPHAY *N. Yorks. – see Ripon.*

GARFORTH *W. Yorks.* 502 P 22 – *see Leeds.*

The red ⌂ symbol?
This denotes the very essence of peace
– only the sound of birdsong first thing in the morning ...

ENGLAND

GARSTANG *Lancs.* 502 L 22 – pop. 6 293.
    🛈 *Discovery Centre, Council Offices, High St* ℰ (01995) 602125.
    London 233 – Blackpool 13 – Manchester 41.

🏛   **Garstang Country H. and Golf Club,** Bowgreave, PR3 1YE, South : 1 ¼ m. on
    B 6430 ℰ (01995) 600100, *reception@garstanghotelandgolf.co.uk,* Fax (01995) 600950, ⛳,
    ⌖ – ⬚ ⥀⌖ ℙ. ⌁ 250. ⓂⒸ ⒶⒺ 𝗩𝗜𝗦𝗔
    Rest (bar lunch Monday-Saturday)/dinner 16.50 and a la carte 21.70/27.40 ⌸ – **32 rm** ⌸
    ✟60.00 – ✟✟95.00.
    ◆ Stone-built hotel, privately owned. Rooms overlook golf course and driving range. Golf-
    ing breaks throughout year. Uniformly sized rooms with colourful fabrics and drapes.
    Restaurant with course outlook.

at Bilsborrow *South : 3¾ m. by B 6430 on A 6 – ⊠ Preston.*

↿   **Olde Duncombe House** without rest., Garstang Rd, PR3 0RE, ℰ (01995) 640500,
    oldedunc@aol.com, Fax (01995) 640336, ⌖ – ℙ. ⓂⒸ ⒶⒺ 𝗩𝗜𝗦𝗔
    9 rm ⌸ ✟39.50 – ✟✟59.00.
    ◆ Whitewashed, stonebuilt guesthouse, formerly three cottages dating back 400 years.
    Simple rooms with free-standing pine furniture. Rear rooms overlook the canal.

GATESHEAD *Tyne and Wear* 501 502 P 19 *Great Britain G. – pop. 78 403.*
    Exc. : *Beamish : North of England Open Air Museum*★★ *AC, SW : 6 m. by A 692 and A 6076*
    BX.
    ⛳ *Ravensworth, Moss Heaps, Wrekenton* ℰ (0191) 487 6014 – ⛳ *Heworth, Gingling Gate*
    ℰ (0191) 469 4424 *BX.*
    Tyne Tunnel (toll).
    🛈 *Central Library, Prince Consort Rd* ℰ (0191) 433 8420 *BX – Metrocentre, Portcullis, 7 The
    Arcade* ℰ (0191) 460 6345 *AX.*
    London 282 – Durham 16 – Middlesbrough 38 – Newcastle upon Tyne 1 – Sunderland 11.

Plan : see Newcastle upon Tyne

🏨   **Hilton Newcastle Gateshead,** Bottle Bank, NE8 2AR, ℰ (0191) 490 9700,
    Fax (0191) 490 9800, ≤, ⌖, ⌖, ⌧ – ⬚ ⥀⌖ ▤ ⌖ ⌖ ⌖ – ⌁ 500. ⓂⒸ ⒶⒺ ⓸
    𝗩𝗜𝗦𝗔   CZ e
    Windows on the Tyne : **Rest** (closed lunch Saturday and Sunday) a la carte 22.65/40.90 s.
    – ⌸ 16.95 – **251 rm** ✟105.00/185.00 – ✟✟105.00/185.00, 3 suites.
    ◆ Modern hotel on steep riverbank, with fine views across the Tyne. Well-equipped leisure
    centre. Extensive conference facilities. Stylish, modern rooms, many with river vistas. In-
    formal, modern restaurant overlooks the bridges.

273

ENGLAND

🏨 **Express by Holiday Inn** without rest., Riverside Way, Derwenthaugh, NE16 3BE, ℰ (0870) 720 0951, newcastle-metrocentre@morethanhotels.com, Fax (0870) 720 0952 – 🛗 ⁕ ℰ ♿ 🄿 – 🔬 25. 🐵 ⌷ ⌷ 🆅🆂🅰
134 rm ✦65.00/80.00 – ✦✦65.00/80.00.

AX a

♦ Conveniently positioned lodge hotel with economical, modern bedrooms. Competitively priced, purpose-built accommodation that is compact and comfortable.

✗✗ **McCoys at the Rooftop**, 6th Floor, Baltic Centre, South Shore Rd, NE8 3BA, ℰ (0191) 440 4949, reservations@mccoysbaltic.com, Fax (0191) 440 4950, ≤ City skyline – 🛗 ⁕ 🔙 ⌷ 🄴 🆅🆂🅰

BX c

closed 25-26 December, 1 January and Sunday dinner – **Rest** (booking essential) 19.95 (lunch) and a la carte 19.95/39.95 ⌷.

♦ Restaurant atop the Baltic Arts Centre; glass walls give fine city views. Stylish modern décor; original cooking to match the inventive art on show elsewhere in the building.

at Low Fell South : 2 m. on A 167 – BX – ✉ Gateshead.

🏨 **Eslington Villa**, 8 Station Rd, NE9 6DR, West : ¾ m. by Belle Vue Bank, turning left at T junction, right at roundabout then taking first turn right ℰ (0191) 487 6017, home@eslingtonvilla.co.uk, Fax (0191) 420 0667, ☞ – ⁕ 🄿 – 🔬 35. 🐵 🄴 ⌷ 🆅🆂🅰 ⌖
closed 4 days at Christmas – **Rest** – (see **The Restaurant** below) – **17 rm** ⌷ ✦69.50 – ✦✦84.50.

♦ Well-run, stylish, privately owned hotel 10 minutes' drive from city centre. Nicely furnished lounge bar leads from smart reception. Attractively styled, modern bedrooms.

✗✗ **The Restaurant** (at Eslington Villa), 8 Station Rd, NE9 6DR, West : ¾ m. by Belle Vue Bank, turning left at T junction, right at roundabout then taking first turn right ℰ (0191) 487 6017, home@eslingtonvilla.co.uk, Fax (0191) 420 0667, ☞ – ⁕ 🄿. 🐵 🄴 ⌷ 🆅🆂🅰
closed 4 days at Christmas, Saturday lunch and Sunday dinner – **Rest** 16.00/20.00 and a la carte 23.00/34.00 ⌷.

♦ Two separate dining areas, one of which is a conservatory. Both are classically decorated and serve good range of traditionally based dishes with modern twists.

at Whickham West : 4 m. by A 184, A 1, A 692 on B 6317 – ✉ Gateshead.

🏨 **Gibside**, Front St, NE16 4JG, ℰ (0191) 488 9292, reception@gibside-hotel.co.uk, Fax (0191) 488 8000 – ⁕ , 🍴 rest, ♿ ⇦ – 🔬 150. 🐵 🄴 ⌷ 🆅🆂🅰

AX s

Rest (bar lunch Monday-Saturday)/dinner a la carte 11.00/26.15 s. ⌷ – ⌷ 8.95 – **45 rm** ✦62.50 – ✦✦72.50.

♦ Purpose-built hotel in small town near Gateshead with views over Tyne Valley. Set on hill, so its up to date facilities are on different levels. Cosy, unfussy rooms. Newly refurbished modern restaurant.

The ✿ award is the crème de la crème.
This is awarded to restaurants
which are really worth travelling miles for!

GATWICK AIRPORT W. Sussex 504 T 30 – ✉ Crawley.
🛪 Gatwick Airport : ℰ (0870) 0002468.
London 29 – Brighton 28.

Plan opposite

🏨 **Hilton London Gatwick Airport**, South Terminal, RH6 0LL, ℰ (01293) 518080, londongatwick@hilton.com, Fax (01293) 528980, 🛁 – 🛗 ⁕ rm, 🍴 ℰ ♿ 🄿 – 🔬 500. 🐵 🄴 ⌷ 🆅🆂🅰 ⌖

Y u

Rest 16.95 (dinner) and a la carte 35.00/40.00 ⌷ – ⌷ 18.50 – **791 rm** ✦199.00/285.00 – ✦✦199.00/285.00.

♦ Large, well-established hotel, popular with business travellers. Two ground floor bars, lounge and leisure facilities. Older rooms co-ordinated, newer in minimalist style. Restaurant enlivened by floral profusions.

🏨 **Renaissance London Gatwick**, Povey Cross Rd, RH6 0BE, ℰ (01293) 820169, reservations.gatwick@renaissancehotels.com, Fax (01293) 820259, 🛁, ⇌, 🔲, squash – 🛗, ⁕ rm, 🍴 ℰ ♿ 🄿 – 🔬 220. 🐵 🄴 ⌷ 🆅🆂🅰

Y a

Rest (bar lunch)/dinner 26.95 s. ⌷ – ⌷ 16.50 – **253 rm** ✦115.00/135.00 – ✦✦115.00/165.00, 1 suites.

♦ Large red-brick hotel. Good recreational facilities including indoor pool, solarium. Bedrooms are spacious and decorated in smart, chintzy style. Small brasserie area open all day serving popular meals.

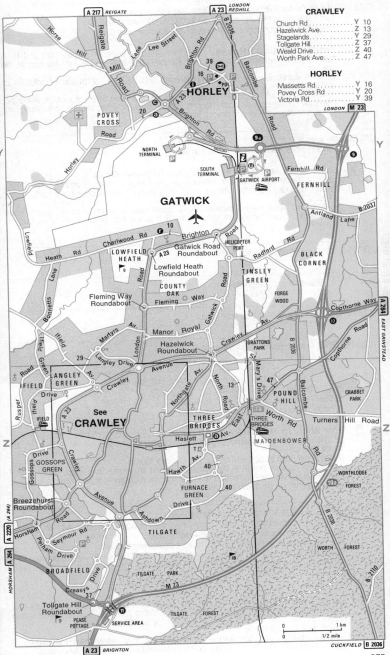

A 217 REIGATE   A 23 LONDON REDHILL   B 2036

Horse Hill

Reigate   Lee Street

Mill   Brighton Rd

Road   Balcombe

HORLEY   POL

POVEY CROSS

Road   Brighton Rd   LONDON M 23

Horley   A 23

NORTH TERMINAL   9a

Lowfield   Heath Rd   9

SOUTH TERMINAL   GATWICK AIRPORT   Fernhill Rd

FERNHILL

GATWICK

Charlwood Rd   Brighton   Road   HELICOPTER PORT   Radford   Rd   Antland Lane   B 2037

LOWFIELD HEATH   Gatwick Road Roundabout   BLACK CORNER

Heath   Rd   A 23   Lowfield Heath Roundabout   TINSLEY GREEN

Lowfield   Lane   COUNTY OAK   FORGE WOOD

Bonnetts   Road   Fleming Way Roundabout   Fleming   Way   Copthorne Way   A 264 EAST GRINSTEAD

Ifield   Green   Martyrs   Av.   Manor   Royal   Gatwick   Av.   Copthorne   Road   10

Ifield   Road   London   Hazelwick Roundabout   Crawley   GRATTONS PARK   CRABBET PARK

29   Langley Drive   Avenue   13   St. Mary's Drive   47   POUND HILL   Balcombe

LANGLEY GREEN   Langley   Av.

IFIELD   Rusper   Road   Ifield   Drive   A 23   Crawley   Northgate   Av.   North   Road   Worth   Rd   Turners   Hill   Road

See CRAWLEY   THREE BRIDGES   THREE BRIDGES   East   MAIDENBOWER

Gossops   Drive   GOSSOPS GREEN   Haslett   Av.   WORTHLODGE FOREST

A 2220 (A 264)   Breezehurst Roundabout   Crawley   Hawth   Av.   40   10a

HORSHAM A 264   Horsham   Road   Avenue   FURNACE GREEN   40   WORTH   FOREST

Pelham   Drive   Ashdown   Drive   TILGATE   B 2036

BROADFIELD   Seymour Rd   TILGATE   PARK   18   B 2110

Creasys   Drive   37   M 23   WORTH   FOREST

Tollgate Hill Roundabout   9   11   TILGATE   FOREST

PEASE POTTAGE   SERVICE AREA

0		1 km
0	1/2 mile	

A 23 BRIGHTON   CUCKFIELD B 2036

GILLINGHAM Dorset 503 504 N 30 *The West Country G.* – pop. 8 630.
Exc. : *Stourhead*★★★ *AC, N : 9 m. by B 3092, B 3095 and B 3092.*
London 116 – Bournemouth 34 – Bristol 46 – Southampton 52.

Stock Hill Country House 📎, Stock Hill, SP8 5NR, West : 1½ m. on B 3081 ℘ (01747) 823626, *reception@stockhillhouse.co.uk, Fax (01747) 825628,* ☎s, 📠, ℅ – ⇌ rest, 🅿. ⊙⊙
VISA. ℅
Rest *(closed Monday lunch)* (booking essential) 26.00/38.00 ⅋ – **9 rm** (dinner included) ⧄
♦135.00/175.00 – ♦♦240.00/300.00.
♦ Idyllically peaceful Victorian country house set in eleven acres of mature woodland. Classically furnished. Individually decorated bedrooms, including antique beds. Very comfortable restaurant with rich drapes, attentive service.

GISBURN Lancs. 502 N 22.
London 242.5 – Bradford 28.5 – Skipton 12.

✗ **La Locanda,** Main St, BB7 4HH, ℘ (01200) 445303 – ⇌. ⊙⊙ *VISA*
closed 25 December, 1 January, 1 week in winter, 2 weeks in summer and Monday – **Rest** -
Italian - (booking essential) (dinner only) 12.95 (except Saturday) and a la carte 15.40/
31.95.
♦ Snug 17C town centre osteria. Lovely stone interior augmented by superb joists and beams. Italian 'nonna' cooking of the first order: lots of comfort dishes from all regions.

GITTISHAM Devon 503 K 31 – see Honiton.

GLASTON Rutland – see Uppingham.

GLENRIDDING Cumbria 502 L 20 – see Ullswater.

GLEWSTONE Herefordshire – see Ross-on-Wye.

GLOSSOP Derbs. 502 503 504 O 23 – pop. 32 219 (inc. Hollingworth).
🏌 Sheffield Rd ℘ (01457) 865247.
🅱 Bank House, Henry St ℘ (01457) 855920.
London 194 – Manchester 18 – Sheffield 25.

🏠 **The Wind in the Willows** 📎, Derbyshire Level, SK13 7PT, East : 1 m. by A 57
℘ (01457) 868001, *info@windinthewillows.co.uk, Fax (01457) 853354,* ☞ – ⇌ ℅ 🅿. ⊙⊙
ℕ ⊙ *VISA*. ℅
Rest (dinner only) 29.00 ⅋ – **12 rm** ⧄ ♦88.00 – ♦♦150.00.
♦ Victorian country house in Peak District, named after trees in garden. Adjacent golf course. Snug, fully-panelled sitting room. Bedrooms individually styled with antiques. Eat on carved chairs at gleaming wooden tables.

GLOUCESTER Glos. 503 504 N 28 *Great Britain G.* – pop. 123 205.
See : *City*★ - *Cathedral*★★ Y – *The Docks*★ Y – *Bishop Hooper's Lodging*★ *AC* Y **M.**
🏌, 🏌 Gloucester Hotel, Matson Lane ℘ (01452) 525653.
🅱 28 Southgate St ℘ (01452) 396572, *tourism@gloucester.gov.uk.*
London 106 – Birmingham 52 – Bristol 38 – Cardiff 66 – Coventry 57 – Northampton 83 –
Oxford 48 – Southampton 98 – Swansea 92 – Swindon 35.

Plan opposite

🏠 **Express by Holiday Inn** without rest., Waterwells Business Park, Telford Way, Nr
Quedgeley, GL2 2AB, Southwest : 3 m. on A 38 ℘ (0870) 7200953, *gloucester@morethan
hotels.com, Fax (0870) 7200954* – 📧 ⇌ ℅ ⅁ 🅿 – ⅍ 30. ⊙⊙ ℕ ⊙ *VISA*
106 rm ♦69.00 – ♦♦69.00.
♦ Purpose-built lodge hotel conveniently located close to M5, three miles from cathedral. Designed for cost-conscious business or leisure travellers. Light, modern bedrooms.

GLOUCESTER

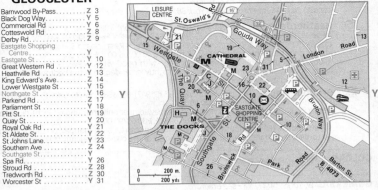

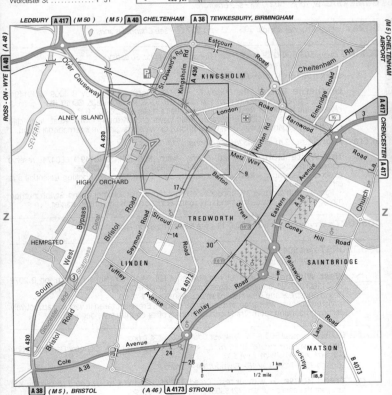

Hotels and restaurants change every year,
so change your Michelin guide every year!

GOATHLAND N. Yorks. 502 R 20 – ⊠ Whitby.
London 248 – Middlesbrough 36 – York 38.

Heatherdene ⊗, The Old Vicarage, The Common, YO22 5AN, ℰ (01947) 896334, info@heatherdenehotel.co.uk, Fax (01947) 896334, ≤, ☞ – ⊱≼ P. ⑩ Æ VISA. ℅
closed 25 December and restricted opening in winter – **Rest** (closed Sunday and Monday) (dinner only) (residents only) 18.95 ♀ – **7 rm** ☑ ✦40.00/65.00 – ✦✦95.00.
◆ Country house hotel in converted vicarage with good village views. Sitting room has contemporary styling, which is reflected to slightly lesser degree in the bedrooms. Hearty, home-cooked meals in modern dining room.

XX **Prudom House** with rm, YO22 5AN, ℰ (01947) 896368, info@prudomhouse.co.uk, Fax (01947) 896030, ☞ – ⊱≼ P. ⑩ Æ VISA. ℅
Rest (closed Sunday dinner, Monday and Tuesday) (dinner only and Sunday lunch)/dinner a la carte 28.00/33.00 – **6 rm** ☑ ✦40.00/65.00 – ✦✦80.00/90.00.
◆ Refurbished 18C longhouse: on one side are two smart, comfy lounges; on the other an up-to-date restaurant offering updated versions of the classics. Elegantly styled rooms.

GOLCAR W. Yorks. – see Huddersfield.

GOMERSAL W. Yorks. 502 O 22 – see Bradford.

GOREY Jersey (Channel Islands) 503 P 33 and 517 ⑪ – see Channel Islands.

GORING Oxon. 503 504 Q 29 Great Britain G. – pop. 3 934 (inc. Streatley).
Exc. : Ridgeway Path★★.
London 56 – Oxford 16 – Reading 12.

XX **Leatherne Bottel**, The Bridleway, RG8 0HS, North : 1 ½ m. by B 4009 ℰ (01491) 872667, leathernebottel@aol.com, Fax (01491) 875308, ≤, ☞ – ⬇ P. ⑩ Æ VISA
closed Sunday dinner – **Rest** (booking essential) a la carte 31.20/37.70 ◈.
◆ Charming Thames-side restaurant; idyllic views of Berkshire Downs. Neat, linen-clad round tables, sparkling windows, travel photos on walls. Imaginative international menu.

at Cray's Pond East : 2 m. on B 4526 – ⊠ Goring.

🍴 **The White Lion**, Goring Rd, Goring Heath, RG8 7SH, ℰ (01491) 680471, reservations@whitelioncrayspond.com, Fax (01491) 681654, ☞, ☞ – P. ⑩ VISA
closed 25 December – **Rest** (closed Sunday dinner and Monday) (booking essential) a la carte 20.00/30.00 ♀.
◆ Part 18C pub sporting 21C appearance. Front terrace for summer dining. Stylish interior: mix of old beams, low ceilings and soft lights. Eclectic dishes and British staples.

GOSFORTH Tyne and Wear 501 502 P 18 – see Newcastle upon Tyne.

GOUDHURST Kent 504 V 30.
London 50 – Hastings 25 – Maidstone 17.

⌂ **West Winchet** ⊗ without rest., Winchet Hill, TN17 1JX, North : 2 ½ m. on B 2079 ℰ (01580) 212024, annieparker@jpa-ltd.co.uk, Fax (01580) 212250, ☞ – ⊱≼ P.
closed Christmas and New Year – **3 rm** ☑ ✦50.00 – ✦✦70.00.
◆ Victorian house with large, attractive rear garden. Breakfast taken in vast and attractively decorated drawing room. Traditional bedrooms offer country style décor.

GRAMPOUND Cornwall 503 F 33 The West Country G. – ⊠ Truro.
Env. : Trewithen★★★ AC, W : 2 m. by A 390 – Probus★ (tower★, Country Demonstration Garden★ AC) W : 2½ m. by A 390.
London 287 – Newquay 16 – Plymouth 44 – Truro 8.

⌂ **Creed House** ⊗ without rest., Creed, TR2 4SL, South : 1 m. by Creed rd turning left just past the church ℰ (01872) 530372, ≤, ☞ – ⊱≼ P. ℅
3 rm ☑ ✦55.00/60.00 – ✦✦90.00.
◆ Smart Georgian rectory with restful gardens featured in several Cornish gardening books. Well-appointed sitting room. Fine art in breakfast room. Country house bedrooms.

XX **Eastern Promise**, 1 Moor View, TR2 4RT, ℰ (01726) 883033 – ⊱≼ P. ⑩ Æ ⑩ VISA
closed Wednesday – **Rest** - Chinese - (booking essential) (dinner only) 18.23 and a la carte.
◆ Cosy Chinese restaurant on busy main road close to Truro. Wall paintings in comfortable lounge. Lengthy menu with good, fresh cooking; clear flavours throughout.

GRANGE-OVER-SANDS *Cumbria* 502 L 21 *Great Britain G.* – pop. 4 835.

Env. : *Cartmel Priory★, NW : 3 m.*

🛇 *Meathop Rd* 𝒫 *(015395) 33180.*

🛈 *Victoria Hall, Main St* 𝒫 *(015395) 34026.*

London 268 – Kendal 13 – Lancaster 24.

Netherwood, Lindale Rd, LA11 6ET, 𝒫 (015395) 32552, *enquiries@netherwood-hotel.co.uk, Fax (015395) 34121,* ≤ Morecambe Bay, ⅃₅, ⬚, 🐾, ♨ – 🛗 ⤢, ▤ rest, ⅙ 🖭 – 🕍 150. ◍ 𝚅𝙸𝚂𝙰
Rest 22.00 (lunch) and a la carte 20.75/37.00 **s.** – **32 rm** ⊑ ♥75.00/115.00 – ♥♥150.00/190.00.
♦ Unusual, castellated late 18C hotel offering fine view of Morecambe Bay. Atmospheric wood-panelled lounges, each boasting open log fire. Comfy rooms with good mod cons. Dine formally and enjoy superb bay vistas.

Graythwaite Manor 🦢, Fernhill Rd, LA11 7JE, 𝒫 (015395) 32001, *enquiries@graythwaitemanor.co.uk, Fax (015395) 35549,* ≤, 🐾, ♨ – 🛗 ⤢ 🖭 ◍ 𝔸𝔼 𝚅𝙸𝚂𝙰 🛇
closed 5-19 January – **Rest** 15.00/25.00 – **21 rm** (dinner included) ⊑ ♥68.00/95.00 – ♥♥112.50/150.00.
♦ Victorian manor house. Extensive garden with distinctive floral base. Open fires enhance semi-panelled bar. Atmospheric billiard room. Very traditionally furnished bedrooms. Pervasive etched glass windows add gravitas to dining room.

Clare House, Park Rd, LA11 7HQ, 𝒫 (015395) 33026, *info@clarehousehotel.co.uk, Fax (015395) 34310,* ≤, 🐾 – ⤢ rest, 🖭. ◍ 𝚅𝙸𝚂𝙰 🛇
late March-early November – **Rest** (booking essential for non-residents) (dinner only) 28.00 – **19 rm** (dinner included) ⊑ ♥71.00 – ♥♥142.00.
♦ Longstanding family run hotel, its lovely lawned garden looking over Morecambe Bay. Two smartly furnished lounges. Traditionally styled rooms, most with bay views. Two pleasant dining rooms; daily changing five-course menus show care and interest.

at Lindale *Northeast : 2 m. on B 5277 –* ⌧ *Grange-over-Sands.*

Greenacres without rest., LA11 6LP, 𝒫 (015395) 34578, *greenacres-lindale@hotmail.com –* ⤢ 🖭. ◍ 𝚅𝙸𝚂𝙰 🛇
closed Christmas – **5 rm** ⊑ ♥29.00/35.00 – ♥♥64.00.
♦ Pleasant guesthouse with distinctive Cumbrian feel: small slate-lined sitting room with open log fire and adjacent, homely breakfast room. Good-sized, very well-kept rooms. Cosy lounge and conservatory.

at Cartmel *Northwest : 3 m –* ⌧ *Grange-over-Sands.*

Aynsome Manor 🦢, LA11 6HH, North : ¾ m. by Cartmel Priory rd on Wood Broughton rd 𝒫 (015395) 36653, *info@aynsomemanorhotel.co.uk, Fax (015395) 36016,* 🐾 – ⤢ 🖭. ◍ 𝔸𝔼 𝚅𝙸𝚂𝙰
closed 25-26 December and 2-26 January – **Rest** *(closed Sunday dinner to non-residents)* (dinner only and Sunday lunch)/dinner 23.00 ₤ – **12 rm** (dinner included) ⊑ ♥87.00/95.00 – ♥♥136.00/170.00.
♦ Country house, personally run by two generations of the same family. Open fired snug bar and lounge with fine clocks. Sitting room has Priory view. Airy, traditional rooms. Dine on candle-lit, polished wood tables with silver.

Hill Farm 🦢 without rest., LA11 7SS, Northwest : 1½ m. bearing to right of village shop in Market Square then left onto Cul-de-Sac rd after the racecourse 𝒫 (015395) 36477, *Fax (015395) 36477,* ≤, 🐾, ♨ – ⤢ 🖭
February-October – **3 rm** ⊑ ♥35.00/40.00 – ♥♥80.00/90.00.
♦ Superb hospitality a feature of this 16C farmhouse with cottagey interior and lovely gardens: a peaceful setting. Individual colour schemes enhance the pretty bedrooms.

L'Enclume (Rogan) with rm, Cavendish St, LA11 6PZ, 𝒫 (015395) 36362, *info@lenclume.co.uk, Fax (015395) 38907,* 🐾 – ⤢ 🖭 ◍ 𝔸𝔼 ◉ 𝚅𝙸𝚂𝙰
closed 1 week January and 1 week November – **Rest** *(closed Monday-Tuesday)* 25.00/38.00 ₤ – **10 rm** ♥59.00/69.00 – ♥♥170.00/200.00.
Spec. Breast of squab, blackcurrant and Darjeeling. Monkfish with prunes and basmati, citronnelle emulsion. White chocolate pudding, "gin and tonic".
♦ Delightfully set converted smithy. Rear garden overlooks superb Priory. Bags of original charm; modern, innovative cuisine: don't miss the tasting menu. Ultra stylish rooms.

ENGLAND

Look out for red symbols, indicating particularly pleasant establishments.

GRANTHAM *Lincs.* 502 504 S 25 *Great Britain G.* – pop. 34 592.

    See : *St Wulfram's Church*★.

    Env. : *Belton House*★ *AC, N* : 2½ m. by A 607.

    Exc. : *Belvoir Castle*★★ *AC, W* : 6 m. by A 607.

    ⓕ, ⓕ, ⓕ Belton Park, Belton Lane, Londonthorpe Rd ℘ (01476) 567399 – ⓘ₈, ⓘ₈, ⓕ Belton Woods H. ℘ (01476) 593200.

    🅭 The Guildhall Centre, St Peter's Hill ℘ (01476) 406166.

    London 113 – Leicester 31 – Lincoln 29 – Nottingham 24.

🏨   **Belton Woods,** Belton, NG32 2LN, North : 2 m. on A 607 ℘ (01476) 593200, *belton.woods@devere-hotels.com, Fax* (01476) 574547, ⚘, ⓥ, Ⅰ₆, 🛌, 🔲, ⓘ₈, ⓕ, ⚘, 🏊, ✖, squash – |🗎| ✦← ﹠ ♣ 🄿 – 🕭 245. 🆗 🆎 ⓞ 𝘝𝘐𝘚𝘈

    Manor : **Rest** *(closed Monday-Tuesday)* (dinner only) a la carte 31.00/42.00 ♀ – ***Stantons Brasserie :*** **Rest** 16.00/23.95 ♀ – **132 rm** ⚌ ✦69.00/78.00 – ✦✦79.00/155.00, 4 suites.

    ♦ Set in acres of countryside, this modern hotel offers impressive leisure facilities, including three golf courses. Range of conference suites. Spacious bedrooms. Manor has vast cocktail bar. Light, modern décor in Stantons Brasserie.

🏨   **Grantham Marriott,** Swingbridge Rd, NG31 7XT, South : 1¼ m. at junction of A 607 with A 1 southbound sliproad ℘ (01476) 593000, *mhrs.emamc.frontdesk@marriotthotels.com, Fax* (01476) 592592, ⚘, Ⅰ₆, 🛌, 🔲 – ✦←, ▤ rest, ﹠ 🄿 – 🕭 200. 🆗 🆎 ⓞ 𝘝𝘐𝘚𝘈

    Rest (bar lunch)/dinner 24.00 – ⚌ 14.95 – **89 rm** ✦85.00 – ✦✦85.00.

    ♦ Purpose-built hotel on A1 motorway, convenient for East Midlands airport. Impressive leisure facilities in light, airy surroundings. Smart, comfortable, modern bedrooms. Stylish restaurant with classic menus.

at Hough-on-the-Hill *North : 6¾ m. by A 607 – ⊠ Grantham.*

✕✕   **The Brownlow Arms** with rm, High Rd, NG32 2AZ, ℘ (01400) 250234, *armsinn@yahoo.co.uk*, ⚘ – ✦← rm, ▤ rest, ✆ 🄿. 🆗 🆎 𝘝𝘐𝘚𝘈 ✖

    closed 3 weeks January, 1 week in summer and 25-27 December – **Rest** *(closed Sunday dinner)* (dinner only and Sunday lunch) a la carte 25.00/38.00 – **4 rm** ⚌ ✦65.00 – ✦✦96.00.

    ♦ Attractive part 17/19C inn in heart of rural Lincolnshire. Wood-panelled bar with deep armchairs. Formal dining: well executed modern British dishes. Very tasteful rooms.

at Great Gonerby *Northwest : 2 m. on B 1174 – ⊠ Grantham.*

✕✕   **Harry's Place** (Hallam), 17 High St, NG31 8JS, ℘ (01476) 561780 – ✦← 🄿. 🆗 𝘝𝘐𝘚𝘈
❀   *closed Christmas-New Year, Sunday, Monday and Bank Holidays* – **Rest** (booking essential) a la carte 47.50/59.50.

    Spec. Foie gras with Sherry aspic, Cumberland sauce and watercress. Fillet of Scottish salmon, Sauternes sauce and chives. Prune and Armagnac ice cream with passion fruit.

    ♦ Discreet listed Georgian building with cerise interior. Just three tables, bedecked with lilies and candles. Charming and attentive service. Robust, exquisite modern cooking.

at Woolsthorpe-by-Belvoir *West : 7½ m. by A 607 – ⊠ Grantham.*

🍴   **The Chequers** with rm, Main St, NG32 1LU, ℘ (01476) 870701, *justinnabar@yahoo.co.uk*, ⚘, ⚘ – ✦← 🄿. 🆗 🆎 𝘝𝘐𝘚𝘈

    closed dinner 25 and 26 December – **Rest** *(closed Sunday dinner in winter)* 12.50/15.00 and a la carte 22.00/35.00 ♀ – **4 rm** ⚌ ✦49.00 – ✦✦59.00.

    ♦ Attractive pub, orginally built as 17C farmhouse. Various nooks, crannies, exposed bricks and beams. Traditional English cuisine with emphasis on game. Simple, clean rooms.

GRASMERE *Cumbria* 502 K 20 *Great Britain G.* – ⊠ *Ambleside.*

    See : *Dove Cottage*★ *AC* AY **A.**

    Env. : *Lake Windermere*★★, *SE* : by A 591 AZ.

    🅭 Redbank Rd ℘ (015394) 35245 *(summer only)* BZ.

    London 282 – Carlisle 43 – Kendal 18.

Plans : see Ambleside

🏨   **The Wordsworth,** Stock Lane, LA22 9SW, ℘ (015394) 35592, *enquiry@wordsworthhotel.co.uk, Fax* (015394) 35765, 🛌, 🔲, ⚘ – |🗎| ✦← rest, ▤ rest, ✆ 🄿 – 🕭 100. 🆗 🆎 ⓞ 𝘝𝘐𝘚𝘈

    BZ **s**

    Prelude : **Rest** 14.95/39.50 – **35 rm** ⚌ ✦60.00/115.00 – ✦✦130.00/195.00, 2 suites.

    ♦ This imposing Victorian hotel next to Wordsworth's burial ground has lovely rear gardens. Lily adorned sitting room and conservatory bar. Attractive, comfortable bedrooms. Immaculately traditional dining room.

ENGLAND

Gold Rill, Red Bank Rd, LA22 9PU, ℰ (015394) 35486, *reception@gold-rill.com,*
Fax (015394) 85486, ≤, ⬚ - *⟨⟩*, ≣ rest, **P**, **⬤⬤** **VISA** BZ **a**
closed 16-27 December – **Rest** (bar lunch)/dinner 24.00 ♀ – **31 rm** (dinner included) ⌂
★72.00/146.00 – ★★164.00, 1 suite.
* Liberally proportioned, privately owned hotel in quiet part of town. Good views, open
fires, slate based walls, traditional décor. Large bar with fine ales. Homely bedrooms. Quiet
rear dining room overlooking lake.

Red Lion, Red Lion Sq, LA22 9SS, ℰ (015394) 35456, *enquiries@hotelgrasmere.uk.com,*
Fax (015394) 35579, ≤, ⅃₄, ⬚, ⬚ - ▯ *⟨⟩*, ≣ rest, **P** – ▲ 60. **⬤⬤** **AE** **⬤** **VISA** BZ **c**
Rest (bar lunch)/dinner 24.00 ♀ – **47 rm** ⌂ 49.50/98.50 – ★★99.00/147.00, 1 suite.
* Centrally located hotel with good fell views. Squashy sofas in reception. Light, airy con-
servatory. Real ales in adjoining Lamb Inn. Most bedrooms boast jacuzzis. Central raised
atrium enhances restaurant.

White Moss House, Rydal Water, LA22 9SE, South : 1½ m. on A 591 ℰ (015394) 35295,
sue@whitemoss.com, Fax (015394) 35516, ⟍, ⬚ - *⟨⟩* rest, **P**, **⬤⬤** **VISA** ⬚ BY **v**
closed December and January – **Rest** *(closed Sunday)* (booking essential) (dinner only) (set
menu only) 39.50 ♀ – **6 rm** (dinner included) ⌂ 85.00/99.00 – ★★170.00/218.00, 1 suite.
* This small Lakeland house close to Rydal Water was once home to Wordsworth and his
family. Elegant lounge with antiques, oils, curios and slate tables. Well-kept bedrooms.
Dine at polished wooden tables with fine glassware.

Grasmere, Broadgate, LA22 9TA, ℰ (015394) 35277, *enquiries@grasmerehotel.co.uk,*
Fax (015394) 35277, ⬚ - *⟨⟩* **P**, **⬤⬤** **VISA** BZ **r**
closed 2 January-9 February – **Rest** (dinner only) 29.50 – **13 rm** ⌂ ★35.00/60.00 –
★★90.00/120.00.
* Small Victorian country house with pleasant acre of garden through which River Rothay
flows. Snug, open-fired bar with good malt whisky selection. Individually styled rooms.
Pleasant pine roofed rear dining room.

Woodland Crag ⬚ without rest., How Head Lane, LA22 9SG, Southeast : ¾ m. by
B 5287 ℰ (015394) 35351, *info@woodlandcrag.co.uk,* ≤, ⬚ - *⟨⟩* **P**, **⬤⬤** **VISA** ⬚ AY **s**
March-October – **4 rm** ⌂ ★55.00 – ★★80.00/90.00.
* Dove Cottage stands tantalisingly close to this solid stone guesthouse with its very
pleasant gardens and homely lounge. Cottage-style breakfast room. Comfortable rooms.

GRASSENDALE *Mersey.* **502 503** L 23 *– see Liverpool.*

GRASSINGTON *N. Yorks.* **502** O 21 *– ⬚ Skipton.*
🛈 *National Park Centre, Colvend, Hebden Rd* ℰ *(01756) 752774.*
London 240 – Bradford 30 – Burnley 28 – Leeds 37.

Ashfield House, Summers Fold, BD23 5AE, off Main St ℰ (01756) 752584, *sales@ash*
fieldhouse.co.uk, ⬚ - *⟨⟩* **⬤** **P**, **⬤⬤** **AE** **VISA** ⬚
closed 2 weeks January – **Rest** (booking essential for non-residents) (dinner only) 30.00 –
8 rm ⌂ 63.25/88.50 – ★★70.00/160.00.
* Sturdy 17C small stone hotel with beams and flagged floors: oozes period charm. Individually decorated, cottagey bedrooms with occasional exposed timber. Delightful garden. Tasty, locally-inspired dishes.

Grassington Lodge without rest., 8 Wood Lane, BD23 5LU, ℰ (01756) 752518,
relax@grassingtonlodge.co.uk, Fax (01756) 752518 – *⟨⟩* **P**, ⬚
10 rm ⌂ ★65.00/100.00 – ★★70.00/125.00.
* Modern guesthouse at gateway to Yorkshire Dales. Built over 100 years ago as home of
village doctor. Gallery of local photos on display around the house. Stylish, smart rooms.

GRAVESEND *Kent* **504** V 29 *– pop. 53 045.*
🛈 *18a St George's Sq* ℰ *(01474) 337600.*
London 25 – Dover 54 – Maidstone 16 – Margate 53.

Manor, Hever Court Rd, Singlewell, DA12 5UQ, Southeast : 2½ m. by A 227 off A 2 (eastbound carriageway) ℰ (01474) 353100, *manor@bestwestern.co.uk, Fax (01474) 354978,*
⅃₄, ⬚, ⬚ - *⟨⟩*, ≣ rest, **⬤** **P** – ▲ 200. **⬤⬤** **AE** **⬤** **VISA** ⬚
Rest *(closed Sunday)* (dinner only) 19.95 and a la carte 20.65/28.20 – **59 rm** ⌂
★89.00/99.00 – ★★109.00.
* Privately owned hotel close to A2 motorway. Useful for visitors to Bluewater shopping
complex. Bar, small health club. Comfortable bedrooms with limed oak style furniture.
Cosy, wood floored restaurant.

GRAVETYE *W. Sussex – see East Grinstead.*

ENGLAND

GREAT BADDOW *Essex 504* V 28 – *see Chelmsford.*

GREAT BIRCHAM *Norfolk 502 504* V 25.

London 115.5 – Hunstanton 10.5 – King's Lynn 15.

King's Head, PE31 6RJ, ℰ (01485) 578265, *welcome@the-kings-head-bircham.co.uk,* Fax (01485) 578635, ☞ – ☆☆, 🍽 rest, 🅿. ◍◍ 🆅🆂🅰
Rest a la carte 20.15/28.25 ℒ – **12 rm** �)⊃ ✸69.50/79.50 – ✸✸175.00.
◆ Sign saying '1860' denotes age of property. Smart interior: relaxed bar and stylish residents lounge with big leather chairs. Well-equipped rooms in striking, earthy tones. Modern menus in a contemporary restaurant boasting sheltered courtyard terrace.

GREAT BROUGHTON *N. Yorks. 502* Q 20 – ✉ *Middlesbrough.*

London 241 – Leeds 61 – Middlesbrough 10 – Newcastle upon Tyne 51 – York 54.

Wainstones, 31 High St, TS9 7EW, ℰ (01642) 712268, *reception@wainstoneshotel.co.uk,* Fax (01642) 711560 – ☆☆ rest, ♨ ㋡ 🅿 – 🔄 120. ◍◍ 🆎 ◍ 🆅🆂🅰. ✆
Rest *(closed Sunday dinner)* (dinner only and Sunday lunch)/dinner 28.50 – **24 rm** �)⊃ ✸65.00/95.00 – ✸✸90.00/110.00.
◆ Converted 17C farmhouse named after local outcrop of rocks. A good base for exploring North Yorkshire Moors. Large, atmospheric bar and sitting room. Good-sized bedrooms. Unfussy dining room.

GREAT DUNMOW *Essex 504* V 28 – *pop. 5 943.*

London 42 – Cambridge 27 – Chelmsford 13 – Colchester 24.

XXX **The Starr** with rm, Market Pl, CM6 1AX, ℰ (01371) 874321, *starrestaurant@btinternet.com,* Fax (01371) 876337 – ☆☆ ㋡ 🅿 – 🔄 35. ◍◍ 🆎 ◍ 🆅🆂🅰
closed 27 December-6 January – **Rest** *(closed Sunday dinner)* 35.00/42.50 ℒ – **8 rm** �)⊃ ✸80.00 – ✸✸120.00/145.00.
◆ Former 15C pub with rustic bar and fire. Characterful restaurant has exposed beams and conservatory. Strong, interesting cooking, traditionally inspired. Smart bedrooms.

X **Dish,** 15 High St, CM6 1AB, ℰ (01371) 859922, *Fax (01371) 859888* – ☆☆. ◍◍ 🆎 🆅🆂🅰
closed 25 December, 1 January and Sunday dinner – **Rest** 14.50 (lunch) and a la carte 25.15/29.75 ℒ.
◆ Modern family-run restaurant in 14C monastic reading room. Stylish interior with vibrant artwork and open plan kitchen. Contemporary menu with subtle Mediterranean feel.

GREAT GONERBY *Lincs. 502 504* S 25 – *see Grantham.*

GREAT MALVERN *Worcs. 503 504* N 27 – *pop. 35 588.*

� *21 Church St* ℰ (01684) 892289 B.
London 127 – Birmingham 34 – Cardiff 66 – Gloucester 24.

Plan opposite

Bredon House without rest., 34 Worcester Rd, WR14 4AA, ℰ (01684) 566990, *enquiries@bredonhouse.co.uk,* Fax (01684) 577530, ≤ Severn Valley, ☞ – 🅿. ◍◍ 🆅🆂🅰   B a
10 rm ☮ ✸45.00/70.00 – ✸✸90.00/110.00.
◆ Elegant, Grade II listed Regency house with spectacular views. Personable owners make breakfast a special event. Most of the individually styled rooms enjoy the fine vista.

Cowleigh Park Farm without rest., Cowleigh Rd, WR13 5HJ, Northwest : 1 ½ m. by B 4232 on B 4219 ℰ (01684) 566750, *cowleighpark@ukonline.co.uk,* ☞ – ☆☆ 🅿.   A r
closed 25-26 December – **4 rm** ☮ ✸45.00/60.00 – ✸✸70.00/75.00.
◆ Part 17C farmhouse nestling in rustic position by gurgling stream. Vast inglenook fireplace complements comfy, adjacent sitting room. Cosy, snug bedrooms with exposed beams.

at Malvern Wells *South : 2 m. on A 449 –* ✉ *Malvern.*

Cottage in the Wood ⚜, Holywell Rd, WR14 4LG, ℰ (01684) 575859, *reception@cottageinthewood.co.uk,* Fax (01684) 560662, ≤ Severn and Evesham Vales, ㋡, ☞ – ☆☆, 🍽 rest, 🅿. ◍◍ 🆎 🆅🆂🅰   A z
Rest 23.00 (lunch) and dinner a la carte 35.00/40.00 ℒ ❀ – ☮ 12.50 – **31 rm** ✸75.00/105.00 – ✸✸85.00/170.00.
◆ Early Victorian house, family owned and run, with superb view over surrounding vales. Very comfortable sitting room and bar. Individually furnished rooms in traditional style. Lovely restaurant with Oriental silk prints and Vale views.

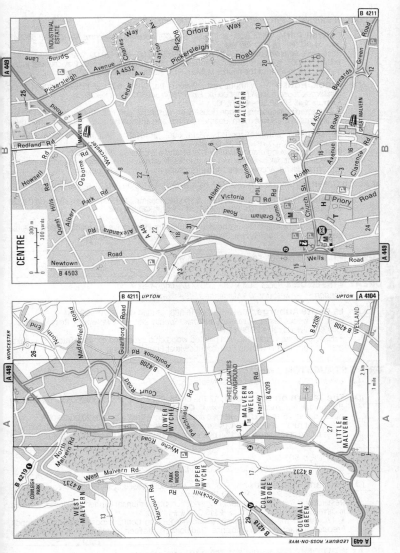

at Colwall *Southwest : 3 m. on B 4218 – ⊠ Great Malvern.*

🏛 **Colwall Park,** WR13 6QG, ℘ (01684) 540000, *hotel@colwall.com, Fax (01684) 540847,*
☞ – ⭑⭤ ✦ 🄿 – 🔏 120. 🆎 🆅🅸🆂🅰 A V
Rest – (see *Seasons* below) 🍴 – **20 rm** ⌲ ✦79.00/89.00 – ✦✦120.00, 2 suites.
   ◆ Built in 1903, this personally run hotel has a distinct Edwardian feel. Play croquet in the
garden or wander into the nearby Malvern Hills. Individually decorated bedrooms.

⌂ **Brook House** ⬙ without rest., Walwyn Rd, WR13 6QX, ℘ (01684) 540604, *mag
gie@brookhouse-colwall.fsnet.co.uk, Fax (01684) 540604,* ☞ – ⭑⭤ 🄿. ⬙
3 rm ⌲ ✦45.50/48.50 – ✦✦77.00.
   ◆ Characterful Jacobean manor house with delightful gardens, stream and arboretum.
Local prints in breakfast room. Beamed ceilings and antique furniture. All rooms individual.

❌❌ **Seasons** (at Colwall Park H.), WR13 6QG, ℘ (01684) 540000, *hotel@colwall.com,
Fax (01684) 540847,* ☞ – ⭑⭤ 🄿. A V
Rest (lunch booking essential)/dinner 26.95 and a la carte 30.25/35.40 s. 🍴.
   ◆ Predominant oak panelling merges seamlessly with modern styling in a spacious location
for formal dining. Accomplished and interesting modern British cooking.

at Acton Green *Northwest : 7 m. by A 449 – B –, B 4219, A 4103 on B 4220 – ⊠ Bromyard.*

⌂ **Hidelow House** ⬙ without rest., Acton Beauchamp, WR6 5AH, South : ¾ m. on B 4220
℘ (01886) 884547, *Fax (01886) 884658,* ☞ – ⭑⭤ 🄿. 🆎 🆅🅸🆂🅰. ⬙
3 rm ⌲ ✦41.95 – ✦✦73.90.
   ◆ Secluded, privately run guesthouse with pleasant views down the Leadon Valley. Sizeable
bedrooms with a homely feel. Boudoir grand piano in the firelit lounge.

GREAT MILTON *Oxon.* **503 504** Q 28 – *see Oxford.*

GREAT MISSENDEN *Bucks.* **504** R 28 – *pop. 7 070 (inc. Prestwood).*
   London 34 – Aylesbury 10 – Maidenhead 19 – Oxford 35.

❌❌ **La Petite Auberge,** 107 High St, HP16 0BB, ℘ (01494) 865370 – 🆎 🆅🅸🆂🅰
closed 2 weeks Easter, 2 weeks Christmas, Sunday and Bank Holidays – Rest - French -
(dinner only) a la carte 28.80/35.60.
   ◆ Neat, cottagey restaurant with painted wood chip paper and candles. Traditional chairs,
crisp and tidy linen. Fresh and confident style of French cooking.

GREAT STAUGHTON *Cambs..*
   London 62.5 – Huntingdon 12 – St Neots 5.5.

🍴 **The Tavern on the Green,** 12 The Green, PE19 5DG, ℘ (01480) 860336, *thetavenon
thegreen@btinternet.com,* ☞ – ⭑⭤ 🄿. 🆎 🆅🅸🆂🅰. ⬙
closed dinner 25 and 26 December, 1 and 2 January – Rest a la carte 20.00/26.00 🍴.
   ◆ Pleasant rural inn with distinctive modern feel, accentuated by comfy leather tub chairs.
Three dining areas: large selection of steaks, alongside appealing seasonal menus.

GREAT TEW *Oxon.* **503 504** P 28.
   London 75 – Birmingham 50 – Gloucester 42 – Oxford 21.

🍴 **Falkland Arms** with rm, OX7 4DB, ℘ (01608) 683653, *sjcourage@btconnect.com,
Fax (01608) 683656,* ☞ – ⬙. 🆎 🆁🅴 🆅🅸🆂🅰. ⬙
Rest *(closed Sunday dinner)* (bookings not accepted at lunch) (dinner booking essential) a
la carte 17.00/27.00 🍴 – **5 rm** ⌲ ✦115.00 – ✦✦115.00.
   ◆ 17C inn on the green in picturesque village. Flag floors, exposed beams, inglenook
fireplace guarantee warm ambience. Traditional, rustic food. Compact, cosy bedrooms.

GREAT WHITTINGTON *Northd.* **501 502** O 18 – *see Corbridge.*

GREAT WOLFORD *Warks.* **503 504** P 27.
   London 84 – Birmingham 37 – Cheltenham 26.

🍴 **The Fox & Hounds Inn** with rm, CV36 5NQ, ℘ (01608) 674220, *info@thefoxand
houndsinn.com –* ⭑⭤ rm, 🄿. 🆎 🆅🅸🆂🅰
closed first 2 weeks January and Monday – Rest *(closed Sunday dinner)* a la carte
18.50/30.00 – **3 rm** ⌲ ✦50.00 – ✦✦80.00.
   ◆ 16C inn occupying central position in pleasant village. Endearing interior, featuring exposed beams, hop vines and log fire. Hearty blackboard menus. Cosy, well-kept bedrooms.

GREAT YARMOUTH Norfolk 504 Z 26 Great Britain G. – pop. 58 032.

Env. : Norfolk Broads★.

🏌 Gorleston, Warren Rd ℘ (01493) 661911 – 🏌 Beach House, Caister-on-Sea ℘ (01493) 728699.

🖪 25 Marine Parade ℘ (01493) 846345.

London 126 – Cambridge 81 – Ipswich 53 – Norwich 20.

🏨🏨 **Imperial,** North Drive, NR30 1EQ, ℘ (01493) 842000, reception@imperialhotel.co.uk, Fax (01493) 852229, ≼ – 🛗 ⇄, 🍽 rest, 🅿 – 🛦 140. ⚫️⊘ ᴀᴇ ⓪ 𝓥𝓘𝓢𝓐

Rambouillet : Rest (closed Sunday dinner) (dinner only and Sunday lunch) 19.95 and a la carte 19.50/36.95 **s.** ♀ – **39 rm** ⊆ ✦78.00 – ✦✦98.00.

◆ Turn of 20C classic promenade hotel, still privately owned. Imposing exterior with large public areas. Pleasant bedrooms in light fabrics include four wine-themed rooms. French feel pervades basement restaurant.

✕✕ **Seafood,** 85 North Quay, NR30 1JF, ℘ (01493) 856009, seafood01@btconnect.com, Fax (01493) 332256 – 🍽. ⚫️⊘ ᴀᴇ ⓪ 𝓥𝓘𝓢𝓐

closed Christmas, May, Saturday lunch, Sunday and Bank Holidays – **Rest** - Seafood - a la carte 21.40/40.95.

◆ Run by a husband and wife team, a long-standing neighbourhood restaurant. Lobster tank, fish display, fresh, generous seafood, attentive service and home-made chocolates !

GREEN ISLAND Jersey (Channel Islands) – see Channel Islands.

GRETA BRIDGE Durham 502 O 20 – see Barnard Castle.

GREVE DE LECQ Jersey (Channel Islands) 503 P 33 and 517 ⑪ – see Channel Islands.

GRIMSTON Norfolk 504 V 25 – see King's Lynn.

GRINDLEFORD Derbs. 502 503 504 P 24 – ✉ Sheffield (S. Yorks.).

London 165 – Derby 31 – Manchester 34 – Sheffield 10.

🏨🏨 **Maynard Arms,** Main Rd, S32 2HE, on B 6521 ℘ (01433) 630321, info@themaynard.co.uk, Fax (01433) 630445, ≤ , 🌳 – 🍽 rest, 🅿 – 🛦 130. ⚫️⊘ 𝓥𝓘𝓢𝓐

Padley : Rest (closed Saturday lunch) 14.00/30.00 and a la carte 17.40/32.50 ♀ – **8 rm** ⊆ ✦75.00/85.00 – ✦✦85.00/95.00, 2 suites.

◆ Nestling in the Peak District, this late Victorian hotel has oak-panelled reception area and superb stained glass. Sepia photographs on walls. Open fires, immaculate bedrooms. Restaurant has imposing hill views.

GRINSHILL Shrops. 503 L 25 – see Shrewsbury.

GROUVILLE Jersey (Channel Islands) 503 M 33 – see Channel Islands.

GUERNSEY C.I. 503 OP 33 and 517 ⑨ ⑩ – see Channel Islands.

GUILDFORD Surrey 504 S 30 – pop. 69 400.

Env. : Clandon Park★★, E : 3 m. by A 246 Z – Hatchlands Park★, E : 6 m. by A 246 Z.

Exc. : Painshill★★, Cobham, NE : 10 m – Polesden Lacey★, E : 13 m. by A 246 Z and minor rd.

🖪 14 Tunsgate ℘ (01483) 444333 Y.

London 33 – Brighton 43 – Reading 27 – Southampton 49.

Plan on next page

✕✕ **Café de Paris,** 35 Castle St, GU1 3UQ, ℘ (01483) 534896, Fax (01483) 300411, 🌼 – ⚫️⊘ ᴀᴇ 𝓥𝓘𝓢𝓐
Y u
closed Sunday and Bank Holidays (except Good Friday) – **Rest** - French - (booking essential) a la carte 22.00/40.50 ☜.

◆ French-style backstreet eatery. Take your pick of brasserie in front or restaurant at back. Prix fixe or à la carte dishes with traditional twist and seasonal changes.

✕ **Zinfandel,** 4-5 Chapel St, GU1 3UH, ℘ (01483) 455155, mail@zinfandel.org.uk – 🍽. ⚫️⊘ ᴀᴇ 𝓥𝓘𝓢𝓐
Y v
closed 25-26 December, 1 January and Sunday dinner – **Rest** a la carte 17.95/27.20 ☜ ♀.

◆ Welcoming, modern and irresistibly laid back; Napa Valley cuisine mixes grills, Pacific Rim salads, full-flavoured, wood-fired pizzas and picket-fence classics like pecan pie.

285

GUILDFORD

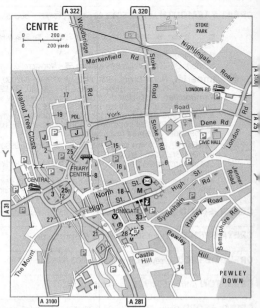

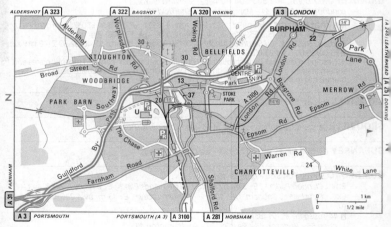

at Shere East : 6¾ m. by A 246 off A 25 – Z – ⊠ Guildford.

XX **Kinghams,** Gomshall Lane, GU5 9HE, ℘ (01483) 202168, paul@kinghams-restau
rant.co.uk – **P.** **M⑤** **AE** **①** **VISA**
closed 25 December-5 January, Sunday dinner and Monday – **Rest** (booking essential)
19.90 (lunch) and a la carte 23.85/31.85.
♦ Popular restaurant in 17C cottage in appealing village. Daily blackboard and fish specials
are particularly good value. Adventurous modern menus with bold combinations.

GUISBOROUGH Redcar and Cleveland **502** Q 20.
London 265 – Middlesbrough 9 – Newcastle upon Tyne 50 – Whitby 22.

Gisborough Hall, Whitby Lane, TS16 6PT, East : 1 m. on Whitby rd ℰ (0870) 400 8191, Fax (01287) 610844, 🕿, 🎠, ❊ – ▯ ❊ ❖ ⅃ ℗ – ⚙ 350. ⑳ ㏂ ① 𝘝𝘐𝘚𝘈
Tocketts : **Rest** 15.90/35.00 ⅄ – ⅁ 12.95 – **70 rm** ✹60.00 – ✹✹140.00, 1 suite.
◆ Imposing, ivy-clad 19C country house with modern wing. Very comfy drawing room; main hall has minstrel gallery; cosy library bar. Rooms more individually styled in main house. Restaurant, set in billiard room, infused with classical style.

GUITING POWER Glos. **503 504** O 28 – ⊠ Cheltenham.
London 95 – Birmingham 47 – Gloucester 30 – Oxford 39.

Guiting Guest House, Post Office Lane, GL54 5TZ, ℰ (01451) 850470, info@guiting guesthouse.com, Fax (01451) 850034 – ❊. ⑳ ① 𝘝𝘐𝘚𝘈
Rest (by arrangement) 30.00 – **6 rm** ⅄ ✹40.00/46.00 – ✹✹80.00.
◆ 16C stone-built former Cotswold farmhouse in centre of charming village. Cosy lounge, wood floors and original open fire. Two particularly comfortable converted cottage rooms. Intimate, low-beamed 'hop-strung' dining-room.

GUNNERSIDE N. Yorks. **502** N 20 – ⊠ Darlington.
London 268 – Newcastle upon Tyne 60 – Richmond 17.

Oxnop Hall 🐑 without rest., Low Oxnop, DL11 6JJ, West : 1½ m. on B 6270 ℰ (01748) 886253, Fax (01748) 886253, ≤, 🎠 – ❊ ℗. ❊
closed 25-26 December – **5 rm** ✹31.00/42.00 – ✹✹62.00/72.00.
◆ Pleasant stone-built 17C farmhouse and working sheep farm in agreeable hillside position. Cosy little lounge. Bedrooms feature beams, mullion windows and rural views.

GUNWALLOE Cornwall **503** E 33 – see Helston.

HACKNESS N. Yorks. **502** S 21 – see Scarborough.

HADDENHAM Bucks. **504** R 28 – pop. 4 720.
London 54 – Aylesbury 8 – Oxford 21.

Green Dragon, 8 Churchway, HP17 8AA, ℰ (01844) 291403, peteandsue@pmof fat.freeserve.co.uk, Fax (01844) 299532, 🎠 – ℗. ⑳ 𝘝𝘐𝘚𝘈. ❊
closed 25 December and 1 January – **Rest** (closed Sunday dinner) (booking essential) a la carte 24.50/32.00 ⅄.
◆ Warmly decorated, modern-style pub-restaurant with a friendly atmosphere and pleasant service. Very good value, from simple pub food to more elaborate restaurant-style dishes.

HADLEIGH Suffolk **504** W 27 – pop. 7 124.
🄱 Hadleigh Library, 29 High St ℰ (01473) 823778.
London 72 – Cambridge 49 – Colchester 17 – Ipswich 10.

Edge Hall without rest., 2 High St, IP7 5AP, ℰ (01473) 822458, r.rolfe@edgehall.co.uk, Fax (01473) 827751, 🎠 – ❊ ℗.
10 rm ⅄ ✹50.00/75.00 – ✹✹75.00/100.00.
◆ One of the oldest houses in the town (1590), with a Georgian façade. Spacious, comfy bedrooms are traditionally furnished, as are the communal areas. Very well-kept gardens.

HADLEY HEATH Worcs. – see Droitwich Spa.

Good food and accommodation at moderate prices?
Look for the Bib symbols:
red Bib Gourmand 🏵 for food, blue Bib Hotel 🏨 for hotels

HAILSHAM *E. Sussex* **504** U 31 – *pop. 19 177.*

Wellhurst G. & C.C., North St, Hellingly ℘ (01435) 813636.
London 57 – Brighton 23 – Eastbourne 7 – Hastings 20.

at Magham Down *Northeast : 2 m. by A 295 on A 271 – ⊠ Hailsham.*

Olde Forge, BN27 1PN, ℘ (01323) 842893, *theoldeforgehotel@tesco.net,*
Fax (01323) 842893 – ✻✻ 🅿 🐾 *VISA*
Rest (dinner only) 24.50 – **7 rm** ☲ ✦48.00 – ✦✦85.00.
♦ Privately owned timbered house with cottage feel, charmingly run by helpful, friendly
owners. Rooms are individually furnished in elegant pine; one boasts a four-poster bed.
Beamed restaurant with carefully compiled menu.

HALAM *Notts. Great Britain G.*

Env. : Southwell Minster★★ AC, E : 2 m. on Mansfield Rd, Halam Hill, Market Pl and A 612.
London 134 – Derby 8 – Nottingham 8.

Waggon and Horses, Mansfield Rd, NG22 8AE, ℘ (01636) 813109, *info@thewaggona*
thalam.co.uk, Fax (01636) 816228 – ✻✻ 🅿 🐾 *VISA* ✻
closed 25-26 December and 1 January – **Rest** *(closed Sunday dinner)* 14.50 and a la carte
23.00/28.00.
♦ Cosy, low-beamed pub with well-stocked bar and cricket themed curios. Owners are
members of 'Campaign For Real Food' and menus have emphasis on fresh, local, seasonal
produce.

If breakfast is included the ☲ symbol appears after the number of rooms.

HALFWAY BRIDGE *W. Sussex* **504** R 31 – *see Petworth.*

HALIFAX *W. Yorks.* **502** O 22 – *pop. 83 570.*

Halifax Bradley Hall, Holywell Green ℘ (01422) 374108 – Halifax West End, Paddock
Lane, Highroad Well ℘ (01422) 341878, Union Lane, Ogden ℘ (01422) 244171 –
Ryburn, Norland, Sowerby Bridge ℘ (01422) 831355 – Lightcliffe, Knowle Top Rd
℘ (01422) 202459.
Piece Hall ℘ (01422) 368725.
London 205 – Bradford 8 – Burnley 21 – Leeds 15 – Manchester 28.

Holdsworth House ⚶, Holmfield, HX2 9TG, North : 3 m. by A 629 and Shay Lane
℘ (01422) 240024, *info@holdsworthhouse.co.uk, Fax (01422) 245174,* ⇞, ⇘ – ✻✻ 🐾 ⚓
🅿 ⚶ 150. 🐾 AE ① *VISA* ✻
closed 23 December-3 January **Rest** *(closed lunch Saturday and Sunday)* 16.95 (lunch) and a
la carte 23.45/38.45 ☲ – **36 rm** ☲ ✦105.00/120.00 – ✦✦150.00, 4 suites.
♦ Characterful and extended part 17C manor house in a quiet location. Comfortable, traditionally decorated rooms with wood furniture. Country house-style throughout. Three-
roomed, wood-panelled restaurant overlooks garden.

Design House, Dean Clough (Gate 5), HX3 5AX, ℘ (01422) 383242, *enquiries@design*
houserestaurant.co.uk, Fax (01422) 322732 – ✻✻ 🔳 🅿, ⇗ 12. 🐾 AE ① *VISA*
closed 26 December-7 January, Saturday lunch, Sunday and Bank Holidays – **Rest** 15.00
(dinner) and a la carte 25.70/34.95.
♦ Located within converted mill on outskirts of town, an impressively stylish and modern
restaurant with Philippe Starck furniture. Varied menu of contemporary British cooking.

Shibden Mill Inn with rm, Shibden Mill Fold, HX3 7UL, Northeast : 2 ¼ m. by A 58 and
Kell Lane (turning left at Stump Cross public house) on Blake Hill Rd ℘ (01422) 365840,
Fax (01422) 362971, ⇞, ⇘ – 🅿 ⇗ 8. 🐾 AE *VISA*
Rest a la carte 16.95/27.45 ☲ – **12 rm** ☲ ✦68.00 – ✦✦130.00.
♦ Part 17C inn hidden away in wooded Shibden Valley. Beamed areas and open fires; first
floor restaurant. Classic or modern English dishes. Comfy rooms in converted barn.

at Shelf *Northeast : 3 m. on A 6036 – ⊠ Halifax.*

Bentley's, 12 Wadehouse Rd, HX3 7PB, ℘ (01274) 690992, *bentleys@btinternet.com,*
Fax (01274) 690011 – ✻✻ 🐾 *VISA*
closed first week January – **Rest** 10.95 (lunch) and a la carte 20.00/31.00.
♦ Converted terraced house with characterful interior, highlighted by rustic brickwork.
Appealing, wide-ranging blackboard menu serving hearty food with a Yorkshire base.

LOUIS ROEDERER

C H A M P A G N E

HALLAND *E. Sussex* 504 U 31 – ✉ *Lewes.*
London 59 – Brighton 17 – Eastbourne 15 – Maidstone 35.

⌂ **Shortgate Manor Farm** without rest., BN8 6PJ, Southwest : 1 m. on B 2192
🖉 (01825) 840320, *david@shortgate.co.uk, Fax (01825) 840320,* � – ५⋈ **P**. 🛠
3 rm 🖙 ✚40.00 – ✚✚80.00.
◆ Extended 18C shepherd's cottage with extensive, pretty gardens. Neat and spacious
bedrooms. Communal rooms decorated with home-grown dried flowers.

HALLATON *Leics.* 504 R 26.
London 95 – Leicester 17 – Market Harborough 9.

🍴 **Bewicke Arms** with rm, 1 Eastgate, LE16 8UB, 🖉 (01858) 555217, Fax (01858) 555598,
� – ५⋈ rm, **P**. 🐵 *VISA*. 🛠
closed Easter Monday – **Rest** *(closed Sunday dinner in winter)* (booking essential) a la carte
17.50/25.00 ⚏ **3 rm** 🖙 ✚40.00 – ✚✚55.00.
◆ Located in picturesque village, this part thatched 17C inn boasts hop vines, beams and a
crackling fire. Seasonal, regionally inspired dishes served by friendly staff.

HALL GREEN *W. Mids.* 502 503 504 O 26 – *see Birmingham.*

HALNAKER *W. Sussex – see Chichester.*

HALTWHISTLE *Northd.* 501 502 M 19 *Great Britain G. – pop. 3 811.*
Env. : *Hadrian's Wall*★★, N : 4½ m. by A 6079 – *Housesteads*★★ AC, NE : 6 m. by B 6318 –
Roman Army Museum★ AC, NW : 5 m. by A 69 and B 6318 – *Vindolanda (Museum*★*) AC,*
NE : 5 m. by A 69 – Steel Rig (≤★) NE : 5½ m. by B 6318.
🛆 *Wallend Farm, Greenhead* 🖉 *(01697) 747367.*
🄴 *Railway Station, Station Rd* 🖉 *(01434) 322002.*
London 335 – Carlisle 22 – Newcastle upon Tyne 37.

🏨 **Centre of Britain,** Main St, NE49 0BH, 🖉 (01434) 322422, *enquiries@centre-of-brit*
ain.org.uk, Fax (01434) 322655 – ५⋈ *rest,* **P**. – 🔏 25. 🐵 🄰🄴 ⓪ *VISA*
*closed 24-26 December***Rest** *(dinner only)* 21.95 and a la carte 16.45/25.00 **s.** – **12 rm** 🖙
✚60.00 – ✚✚100.00.
◆ Attractive hotel on busy main street. Oldest part, a pele tower, dates from 15C. Comfortable modern décor, including bedrooms, incorporates original architectural features.
Glass-roofed restaurant with light, airy feel.

⌂ **Ashcroft** without rest., Lantys Lonnen, NE49 0DA, 🖉 (01434) 320213, *ashcroft.1@btcon*
nect.com, Fax (01434) 321641, ≤, � – ५⋈ **P**. 🐵 🄰🄴 *VISA*. 🛠
closed 25 December – **7 rm** 🖙 ✚34.00/68.00 – ✚✚76.00/80.00.
◆ Imposing Victorian house, formerly a vicarage, with beautifully kept gardens. Family run
and attractively furnished throughout creating a welcoming atmosphere. Large bedrooms.

HAMBLE-LE-RICE *Southampton* 503 504 Q 31 – *see Southampton.*

HAMBLETON *Rutland – see Oakham.*

HAMPTON-IN-ARDEN *W. Mids.* 502 O 26.
London 114 – Birmingham 16 – Coventry 11.

🍴 **The White Lion** with rm, 10 High St, B92 0AA, 🖉 (01675) 442833, Fax (01675) 443168 –
५⋈ **P**. 🐵 *VISA*. 🛠
Rest *(closed Sunday dinner)* (booking essential) a la carte 19.50/23.95 ⚏ – 🖙 7.50 – **8 rm**
✚49.00 – ✚✚59.00.
◆ Pleasantly updated pub. Atmospheric front bar with lots of real ales. The rear dining
room is stylish and spacious, serving tasty, modern dishes. Retire to simple bedrooms.

HANLEY SWAN *Worcs.* 503 504 N 27 – *see Upton-upon-Severn.*

HANWELL *Oxon. – see Banbury.*

HARDWICK *Cambs. – see Cambridge.*

HARLOW *Essex 504* U 28 – *pop. 88 296.*

 Nazeing, Middle St ℘ *(01992) 893798.*
London 22 – Cambridge 37 – Ipswich 60.

🏨🏨 **Swallow Churchgate,** Churchgate St, Old Harlow, CM17 0JT, East : 3 ¼ m. by A 414 and B 183 ℘ (01279) 420246, *reservations.oldharlow@swallowhotels.com,* Fax (01279) 437720, *Ιΰ, ⇌s, ▣, ⚘ – ⅍ ᴥ [P] – 🔏 170. ⑩ ㏅ ⓞ ▓*
Rest *(closed lunch Saturday and Bank Holidays)* a la carte 22.95/30.50 **s.** – **83 rm** ⊐ ✝75.00/110.00 – ✝✝90.00/145.00, 2 suites.
♦ Modern hotel built around a Jacobean building. The bedrooms, many of which overlook the gardens, are modern and co-ordinated, and the executive rooms have oak furniture. Country house restaurant with inglenook.

🏨🏨 **Park Inn,** Southern Way, CM18 7BA, Southeast : 2 ¼ m. by A 1025 on A 414 ℘ (01279) 829988, *reservations.harlow@rezidorparkinn.com,* Fax (01279) 635094, *Ιΰ, ⇌s, ▣ – ⅍⅌,* ▤ rest, ℆ ⅙ [P] – 🔏 200. ⑩ ㏅ ⓞ ▓*
Rest *(bar lunch Monday-Saturday and Sunday)* a la carte approx 27.50 ℥ – ⊐ 11.50 – **119 rm** ✝65.00 – ✝✝120.00.
♦ Geared to the business traveller, a purpose-built hotel close to Stansted airport. Bedrooms are compact with modern fitted furniture. Coffee bar and business centre. Bistro-style dining.

🏨 **Green Man,** Mulberry Green, Old Harlow, CM17 0ET, East : 2 ¼ m. by A 414 and B 183 ℘ (0870) 609 6146, *reservations@corushotels.com,* Fax (01279) 626113, *⚘ – ⅍⅌ [P]* – 🔏 60. ⑩ ㏅ ▓ *⌘*
Rest *(closed Sunday dinner)* (bar lunch)/dinner a la carte 16.00/26.80 **s.** ℥ – ⊐ 10.75 – **55 rm** ✝79.00 – ✝✝79.00.
♦ Part timbered 14C coaching inn with bright, contemporary fabrics, furnishings and décor throughout, except in the bar which has a traditional, timbered pub style. Brightly coloured restaurant with timbered ceiling and joists.

HAROME *N. Yorks. – see Helmsley.*

HARPENDEN *Herts. 504* S 28 – *pop. 28 452.*

 Harpenden Common, East Commmon ℘ (01582) 711320 – ᴮ Hammonds End, ℘ (01582) 712580.
London 32 – Luton 6.

✕✕ **The Bean Tree,** 20A Leyton Rd, AL5 2HU, ℘ (01582) 460901, *enquiries@thebean tree.com,* Fax (01582) 460826, *⌂ – ⅍⅌. ⑩ ㏅ ▓*
closed Saturday lunch, Sunday dinner and Monday – **Rest** 21.75 and a la carte 23.50/46.00 ℥ *⌘.*
♦ Converted red-brick cottage with bean tree and smart terrace. Intimate, softly lit restaurant with sage green palette. Carefully sought ingredients; precise modern cooking.

🏚 **The White Horse,** Hatching Green, AL5 2JP, Southwest : 1 m. by A 1081 on B 487 ℘ (01582) 713428, *info@atouchofnovelli.com,* Fax (01582) 460148, *⌂ – ⅍⅌ [P] ⟳ 12. ⑩* ㏅ ▓
closed 24-25 December – **Rest** a la carte 20.00/30.00 ℥.
♦ Jean Christophe Novelli has major input to cuisine in this immaculate pub. Cutting edge interior to match the menus, which are ambitious and full of complex combinations.

🏚 **The Three Horseshoes,** 136 East Common, AL5 1AW, Southeast : 1 ¾ m. by A 1081 and Cross Lane, turning right at crossroads ℘ (01582) 713953, *satta13easy@yahoo.com,* *⌂, ⚘ – ⅍⅌ [P]. ⑩ ▓ *⌘*
Rest *(closed Sunday dinner)* a la carte 23.65/31.70.
♦ Set in wooded environs, this 17C pub has had a tasteful interior conversion around its solid inglenook. Restaurant oriented, modern European dishes benefit from herb garden.

🏚 **The Fox,** 469 Luton Rd, Kinsbourne Green, AL5 3QE, Northwest : 2 m. on A 1081 ℘ (01582) 713817, Fax (01582) 765206, *⌂ – ⅍⅌ [P]. ⑩ ㏅ ▓ *⌘*
Rest a la carte 24.00/30.00 ℥.
♦ Red-brick country dining pub enhanced by large al fresco terrace and a robust rustic interior with interesting stone and wood ornaments. Eclectic menus: popular rotisserie.

Do not confuse ✕ with ⌂!
✕ defines comfort, while stars are awarded for the best cuisine, across all categories of comfort.

ENGLAND

290

HARROGATE N. Yorks. 502 P 22 *Great Britain G.* – pop. 85 128.

See : Town★.

EXC. : *Fountains Abbey*★★★ *AC* :- *Studley Royal AC* (⩽★ *from Anne Boleyn's Seat*) - Fountains Hall (Façade★), N : 13 m. by A 61 and B 6265 AY – *Harewood House*★★ *(The Gallery★) AC*, S : 7½ m. by A 61 BZ.

ⁱ⁸ Forest Lane Head ℰ (01423) 863158 – ⁱ⁸ Follifoot Rd, Pannal ℰ (01423) 871641 – ⁱ⁸ Oakdale ℰ (01423) 567162 – ⁱ⁹ Crimple Valley, Hookstone Wood Rd ℰ (01423) 883485.

🛈 Royal Baths, Crescent Rd ℰ (01423) 537300, tic@harrogate.gov.uk.

London 211 – Bradford 18 – Leeds 15 – Newcastle upon Tyne 76 – York 22.

Plan on next page

Rudding Park, Rudding Park, Follifoot, HG3 1JH, Southeast : 3 ¾ m. by A 661 ℰ (01423) 871350, sales@ruddingpark.com, Fax (01423) 872286, 🍴, ⁱ₉, 🌳, 🎿-|🛗|, ⅙× rm, 🍽 rest, ✆ 🔥 🅿-🔏 300. 🆗 ㏂ ⑪ 𝚅𝙸𝚂𝙰. 🎿
The Clocktower : Rest a la carte 28.50/39.00 **s.** ⅌ – 48 rm ⊡ ✳150.00 – ✳✳180.00, 2 suites.
♦ Grade I listed Georgian house in rural location with modern extension. Comfortable, elegant style throughout. Rooms are simple and classical with modern, colourful fabrics. Smart, contemporary brasserie with oak floors.

Hotel du Vin, Prospect Pl, HG1 1LB, ℰ (01423) 856800, info@harrogate.hoteldu vin.com, Fax (01423) 856801, 🎿-|🛗| ✆ ✆ 🔥 🅿-🔏 60. 🆗 ㏂ 𝚅𝙸𝚂𝙰 BZ **a**
Bistro : Rest a la carte 28.00/32.00 ⅌ 🍷 – ⊡ 13.50 – 43 rm ✳95.00/345.00 – ✳✳95.00/345.00.
♦ Terrace of Georgian houses overlooking pleasant green. Individually appointed bedrooms with wine-theme decor and modern facilities. Buzzy, modern, stylish French bistro and private dining rooms. Good menu of Gallic influenced dishes.

Cedar Court, Queen Building, Park Parade, HG1 5AH, ℰ (01423) 858585, sales@cedar court.karoo.co.uk, Fax (01423) 504950, 🔥-|🛗| ⅙× 🍽 rest, ✆ 🔥 🅿-🔏 325. 🆗 ㏂ ⑪ 𝚅𝙸𝚂𝙰. 🎿 CZ **n**
Brasserie Tour d'Argent : Rest a la carte 24.00/34.00 **s.** – 97 rm ⊡ ✳110.00/140.00 – ✳✳155.00, 3 suites.
♦ Large, thoroughly modernised hotel with 17C origins, on edge of town but convenient for the centre. Modern rooms have largely chintz fabrics and furnishings. Compact, modern restaurant.

Grants, Swan Rd, HG1 2SS, ℰ (01423) 560666, enquiries@grantshotel-harrogate.com, Fax (01423) 502550-|🛗| ⅙×, 🍽 rest, ✆ 🅿-🔏 60. 🆗 ㏂ ⑪ 𝚅𝙸𝚂𝙰 AY **s**
Chimney Pots Bistro : Rest 10.95/27.00 and a la carte 17.70/27.00 – 41 rm ⊡ ✳70.00/130.00 – ✳✳110.00/165.00, 1 suite.
♦ Victorian terraced house in a residential area. Comfortable, traditionally decorated public areas. Bedrooms in varying styles, sizes and shapes. Close to conference centre. Brightly painted, basement bistro restaurant.

The Balmoral, Franklin Mount, HG1 5EJ, ℰ (01423) 508208, info@balmoralhotel.co.uk, Fax (01423) 530652 – ⅙×, 🍽 rest, ✆ 🅿. 🆗 𝚅𝙸𝚂𝙰 BY **v**
Villu Toots : Rest (dinner only) a la carte 21.00/28.00 – 20 rm ⊡ ✳65.00/100.00 – ✳✳110.00, 3 suites.
♦ Privately run, Gothic-style, Victorian property; charm accentuated by antique furnishings and individually decorated rooms. Bar with Harry Houdini memorabilia. Bustling informality in restaurant, where modern minimalism prevails.

Alexa House without rest., 26 Ripon Rd, HG1 2JJ, ℰ (01423) 501988, alexa house@msn.com, Fax (01423) 504086, 🌳 – ⅙× 🅿. 🆗 ⑪ 𝚅𝙸𝚂𝙰 AY **n**
13 rm ⊡ ✳48.00/70.00 – ✳✳85.00.
♦ Georgian house built in 1830 for Baron-de-Ferrier: contemporary interior touches provide a seamless contrast. Bedrooms in two buildings: more characterful in main house. Breakfast room with simplicity the key.

Ruskin without rest., 1 Swan Rd, HG1 2SS, ℰ (01423) 502045, ruskin.hotel@virgin.net, Fax (01423) 506131, 🌳 – ⅙× ✆ 🅿. 🆗 ㏂ 𝚅𝙸𝚂𝙰 AY **s**
7 rm ⊡ ✳65.00/85.00 – ✳✳140.00.
♦ Victorian house on quiet residential street. Comfortable period-style furnishings throughout with heavy drapes and open fires; individually decorated bedrooms.

Britannia Lodge without rest., 16 Swan Rd, HG1 2SA, ℰ (01423) 508482, info@bri tlodge.co.uk, Fax (01423) 526840, 🌳 – ⅙× 🅿. 🆗 𝚅𝙸𝚂𝙰. 🎿 AYZ **r**
closed 25-26 December – 3 rm ⊡ ✳85.00/90.00 – ✳✳85.00/90.00.
♦ Grade II listed Victorian house, close to the town centre. The décor is homely and warm. Modern, comfortable rooms, antique and pine furnished, vary in shape and size.

Alexandra Court without rest., 8 Alexandra Rd, HG1 5JS, ℰ (01423) 502764, of fice@alexandracourt.co.uk, Fax (01423) 850383, 🌳 – ⅙× ✆ 🅿. 🆗 ㏂ 𝚅𝙸𝚂𝙰 BY **o**
13 rm ⊡ ✳52.00/65.00 – ✳✳82.00.
♦ Detached, family owned Victorian house, retaining original features, in quiet residential area. Bedrooms and communal areas have a simple elegance in décor and ambience.

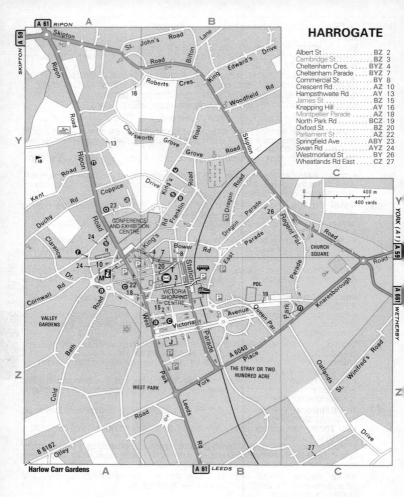

HARROGATE

⌂ **Brookfield House** without rest., 5 Alexandra Rd, HG1 5JS, ℘ (01423) 506646,
Fax (01423) 850383 – ⅓⅔ ✿ 🅟. 🌐 🅰🅴 🅓 *VISA*. ⅓⅔   BY **s**
closed Christmas and New Year – 6 rm ⌂ ✷55.00/65.00 – ✷✷68.00/85.00.
  ♦ Family owned Victorian property in a quiet, residential location close to the town centre.
Homely feel in communal areas and comfortable bedrooms with a mix of styles.

⌂ **Acacia** without rest., 3 Springfield Ave, HG1 2HR, ℘ (01423) 560752, *dee@acaciaharro
gate.co.uk* – ⅓⅔ 🅟. ⅓⅔   AY **o**
restricted opening November-March, minimum stay 2 nights – 4 rm ⌂ ✷55.00/85.00 –
✷✷75.00/85.00.
  ♦ Centrally located Victorian solid stone guesthouse, within a few minutes' walk of the
shops; very personably run. Immaculately kept throughout. Attractive, pine-clad bedrooms.

⌂ **Ashwood House** without rest., 7 Spring Grove, HG1 2HS, ℘ (01423) 560081, *ashwood
house@aol.com*, Fax (01423) 527928 – ⅓⅔ 🅟. 🌐 *VISA*. ⅓⅔   AY **a**
5 rm ⌂ ✷40.00/65.00 – ✷✷65.00.
  ♦ An Edwardian house minutes from the International Conference Centre. Simply decorated, pine furnished rooms and communal areas have a homely ambience.

XX **Quantro,** 3 Royal Par, HG1 2SZ, ✆ (01423) 503034, info@quantro.co.uk,
Fax (01423) 503034 – ✕⊷ 🔳 ◍◉ Æ 𝖵𝖨𝖲𝖠
AZ **a**
closed 25-26 December, 1 January and Sunday – Rest 12.95 and a la carte 18.25/28.30 🍴 ♈.
   ◆ Modern wall murals and mirrors adorn this smart restaurant. Comfy banquettes and black
tables. Good value mix of interesting dishes with Mediterranean underpinnings.

XX **Orchid,** 28 Swan Rd, HG1 2SE, ✆ (01423) 560425, info@orchidrestaurant.co.uk,
Fax (01423) 530967 – ✕⊷ ⇆ 16. ◍◉ Æ ① 𝖵𝖨𝖲𝖠
Rest - South East Asian - a la carte 18.00/39.00 ♈.
   ◆ Unfussy, uncluttered restaurant with Asian styling. Polite, friendly service adds to the
enjoyment of richly authentic dishes from a wide range of south-east Asian countries.

X **Courtyard,** 1 Montpellier Mews, HG1 2TQ, ✆ (01423) 530708, info@courtyardrestaur
ant.net, Fax (01423) 530708, ㋰ – ✕⊷. ◍◉ Æ 𝖵𝖨𝖲𝖠
AZ **c**
closed Sunday – Rest 12.95 (lunch) and a la carte 20.85/36.45 ♈.
   ◆ Former stables with Jacob's Ladder, set in Victorian mews area; cosy, contemporary
interior. Charming cobbled terrace. Modern English menus with sound Yorkshire ingredients.

X **Sasso,** 8-10 Princes Sq, HG1 1LX, ✆ (01423) 508838, Fax (01423) 508838 – ✕⊷. ◍◉
𝖵𝖨𝖲𝖠
BZ **c**
closed Sunday, Monday lunch and Bank Holidays – Rest - Italian - a la carte 22.65/33.40 ♈.
   ◆ In the basement of a 19C property. Antiques, ceramics and modern art embellish the
interior. The menu offers a good choice of authentic Italian dishes with modern influences.

at Kettlesing West : 6½ m. by A 59 – AY – ⊠ Harrogate.

⌂ **Knabbs Ash** without rest., Skipton Rd, HG3 2LT, on A 59 ✆ (01423) 771040,
sheila@knabbsash.co.uk, ≤, ㋰, ▣ – ✕⊷ ℙ. ⌘
closed Christmas and New Year – 3 rm �ₓ ⚹70.00 – ⚹⚹70.00.
   ◆ Stone built cottage with spacious gardens and grounds. Cosy lounge; pine furnished
breakfast room. Homely and simple, largely floral interior; rooms individually decorated.

HARTINGTON Derbs. 502 503 504 O 24 – ⊠ Buxton.
London 168 – Derby 36 – Manchester 40 – Sheffield 34 – Stoke-on-Trent 22.

🏠 **Biggin Hall** ❧, Biggin, SK17 0DH, Southeast : 2 m. by B 5054 ✆ (01298) 84451, enqui
ries@bigginhall.co.uk, Fax (01298) 84681, ≤, ㋰ – ✕⊷ ℙ. ⌘
Rest (booking essential for non-residents) (dinner only) 18.00 s. – ⊊ 3.80 – 20 rm
⚹47.00/84.00 – ⚹⚹116.00/156.00.
   ◆ Charming house with much rustic personality and individuality. Stone floored lounges
and open fires. Antique furnished bedrooms vary in size and shape. Elegant dining room
with low beams.

HARTLAND Devon 503 G 31.
London 221.5 – Bude 15.5 – Clovelly 4.5.

⌂ **Golden Park** ❧ without rest., EX39 6EP, Southwest : 5 m. following signs for Elmscott
and Bude ✆ (01237) 441254, lynda@goldenpark.co.uk, ㋰, ▣ – ✕⊷ ℙ. ⌘
closed 1 week in spring and Christmas – 3 rm ⊊ ⚹30.00/50.00 – ⚹⚹60.00/70.00.
   ◆ Walk to the North Devon coast from this delightfully set part 17C farmhouse. Style and
character prevail, particularly in guests' lounge and beamed, smartly decorated rooms.

HARWELL Oxon. 503 504 Q 29 – pop. 2 015.
London 64 – Oxford 16 – Reading 18 – Swindon 22.

🏠🏠 **Kingswell,** Reading Rd, OX11 0LZ, South : ¾ m. on A 417 ✆ (01235) 833043, king
swell@breathemail.net, Fax (01235) 833193 – ✕⊷ rm, 📺 ℙ. – ⚼ 30. ◍◉ Æ ① 𝖵𝖨𝖲𝖠. ⌘
closed 24-30 December – Rest 12.50/21.50 and a la carte 15.50/37.50 s. ♈ – 20 rm ⊊
⚹95.00 – ⚹⚹115.00.
   ◆ Large redbrick hotel located on the south Oxfordshire Downs. Convenient for Didcot
rail and Oxford. Spacious, uniform, traditional bedrooms and pubby public areas. Classic
menus served in traditional dining room.

HARWICH and DOVERCOURT Essex 504 X 28 – pop. 20 130 (Harwich).
   🚉 Station Rd, Parkeston ✆ (01255) 503616.
   ⛴ to Denmark (Esbjerg) (DFDS Seaways A/S) 1-3 weekly (20 h) – to The Netherlands
(Hook of Holland) (Stena Line) 2 daily (3 h 30 mn).
   🚪 Iconfield Park, Parkeston ✆ (01255) 506139.
London 78 – Chelmsford 41 – Colchester 20 – Ipswich 23.

🏠🏠 **Pier at Harwich,** The Quay, CO12 3HH, ✆ (01255) 241212, pier@milsomhotels.com,
Fax (01255) 551922, ≤ – 📺 ℙ. ◍◉ Æ ① 𝖵𝖨𝖲𝖠. ⌘
Harbourside : Rest - Seafood - a la carte 26.60/47.40 ♈ – 14 rm ⊊ ⚹70.00 – ⚹⚹115.00.
   ◆ Bright Victorian building located on the quayside giving many bedrooms views of the
area's busy sea lanes. Décor is comfortably stylish and contemporary with a nautical
theme. Seafood restaurant with North Sea outlook.

HASTINGS ST. LEONARDS

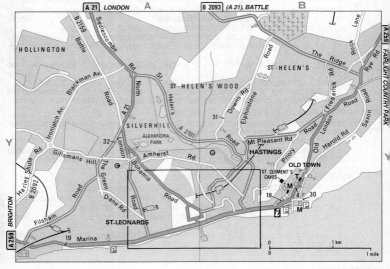

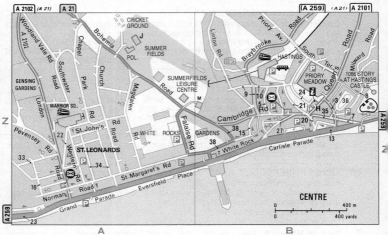

If breakfast is included the ☲ symbol appears after the number of rooms.

294

HASTINGS and ST LEONARDS E. Sussex 504 V 31 – pop. 85 828 (Hastings).

🐦 Beauport Park, Battle Rd, St Leonards-on-Sea ℘ (01424) 854243.

🛈 Town Hall, Queen's Sq, Priory Meadow ℘ (01424) 781111, hic-info@hastings.gov.uk – The Stade, Old Town Hall ℘ (01424) 781111.

London 65 – Brighton 37 – Folkestone 37 – Maidstone 34.

Plan on preceding page

Tower House, 26-28 Tower Road West, TN38 0RG, ℘ (01424) 427217, reservations@towerhousehotel.com, Fax (01424) 430165, 🐦 – ᐧᐧ ⚓, 🍴, ⓂⓈ VISA. 🌸 AY c
closed Christmas – **Rest** (residents only) (dinner only) (set menu only) 18.50 ♀ – 10 rm ☑
♣49.50/70.00 – ♣♣70.00/80.00.
• Friendly and well run, a redbrick Victorian house in a residential area. Comfortably furnished with individually decorated bedrooms and a conservatory bar lounge area.

Parkside House without rest., 59 Lower Park Rd, TN34 2LD, ℘ (01424) 433096, bkent.parksidehouse@talk21.com, Fax (01424) 421431 – ᐧᐧ. ⓂⓈ ⓄⒹ VISA. 🌸 BY e
5 rm ☑ ♣40.00/50.00 – ♣♣60.00/65.00.
• Detached Victorian house in quiet area of town overlooking a park. Traditionally decorated; the spacious bedrooms are smart and well kept.

HATCH BEAUCHAMP Somerset 503 K 30 – see Taunton.

HATFIELD HEATH Essex 504 U 28 – see Bishop's Stortford (Herts.).

HATFIELD PEVEREL Essex 504 V 28 Great Britain G. – pop. 3 258.
Exc. : Colchester - Castle and Museum★, E : 13 m. by A 12.
London 39 – Chelmsford 8 – Maldon 12.

Blue Strawberry Bistrot, The Street, CM3 2DW, ℘ (01245) 381333, reservations@bluestrawberrybistrot.co.uk, Fax (01245) 340498, 🍴 – 🅿. ⓂⓈ 🅰🅴 VISA
closed Saturday lunch and Sunday dinner – **Rest** 14.00 (lunch) and a la carte 19.95/31.95 ♀.
• Make your reservation by first name only in this characterful converted pub with inglenook and Victorian style. Rear dining terrace. Classic British cooking off large menus.

HATHERSAGE Derbs. 502 503 504 P 24 – pop. 1 582 – ⊠ Sheffield (S. Yorks.).
🐦 Sickleholme, Bamford ℘ (01433) 651306.
London 177 – Derby 39 – Manchester 34 – Sheffield 11 – Stoke-on-Trent 44.

George, S32 1BB, ℘ (01433) 650436, info@george-hotel.net, Fax (01433) 650099 – ᐧᐧ 🅿
– 🅰 70. ⓂⓈ 🅰🅴 ⓄⒹ VISA
George's : Rest a la carte 24.45/35.00 s. ♀ – 22 rm ☑ ♣83.00/93.00 – ♣♣133.00/135.00.
• Built in 14C as an inn to serve the packhorse route. Sympathetically restored in rustic style, with oak beams and stone walls. Bedrooms have a bright, more modern feel. Rustically decorated, vibrant-hued dining room.

LA HAULE Jersey (Channel Islands) 503 L 33 and 517 ⑪ – see Channel Islands.

HAWES N. Yorks. 502 N 21.
🛈 Dales Countryside Museum, Station Yard ℘ (01969) 666210.
London 253 – Kendal 27 – Leeds 72 – Newcastle upon Tyne 76 – York 65.

Simonstone Hall 📎, Simonstone, DL8 3LY, North : 1 ½ m. on Muker rd ℘ (01969) 667255, info@simonstonehall.co.uk, Fax (01969) 667741, ≤, 🍴, 🐟, 🐦 – ᐧᐧ 🅿. ⓂⓈ
VISA
Rest (bar lunch)/dinner 30.00 and a la carte 16.50/30.00 ♀ – 18 rm ☑ ♣60.00/120.00 –
♣♣120.00/240.00, 1 suite.
• Part 18C country house, with historic feel, amidst lovely countryside. Individually furnished bedrooms, many of which enjoy pleasant views from the front of the building. Dining room or tavern eating options.

Stone House 📎, Sedbusk, DL8 3PT, North : 1 m. by Muker rd ℘ (01969) 667571, daleshotel@aol.com, Fax (01969) 667720, ≤, 🐦 – ᐧᐧ 🅿. ⓂⓈ VISA
closed January and mid week in December – **Rest** (dinner only) 27.95 ♀ – 23 rm ☑
♣43.50/103.90 – ♣♣123.90.
• Built in 1908 as a family home. Interior decorated in traditional style; public areas include billiard room and oak panelled lounge. Some rooms with private conservatories. Dining room has exposed beams and wooden tables.

ENGLAND

Rookhurst Country House ⌂, Gayle, DL8 3RT, South : ½ m. by Gayle rd 𝒫 (01969) 667454, *enquiries@rookhurst.co.uk*, ⇄ – ⇌ 🅿 ⓜⓞ 𝘝𝘐𝘚𝘈 ⚘
closed 15 December - 15 January – **Rest** (booking essential) (residents only) (dinner only) 25.00 s. – 5 rm ⊡ ✦60.00 – ✦✦110.00/130.00.
◆ Spacious yet cosy country house with a very comfortable, smart, traditional atmosphere that's friendly and informal. Convenient for the Pennine Way. Uncluttered bedrooms.

Cockett's, Market Pl, DL8 3RD, 𝒫 (01969) 667312, *enquiries@cocketts.co.uk*, Fax (01969) 667162, ⌖ – ⇌ 🅿 ⓜⓞ Æ ⓞ 𝘝𝘐𝘚𝘈 ⚘
closed 25-26 December and January – **Rest** *(closed Tuesday)* (dinner only) 18.00 and a la carte 19.25/27.45 – 8 rm ⊡ ✦50.00/60.00 – ✦✦64.00/84.00.
◆ Grade II listed building with a historic inscribed door lintel - reputedly the most photographed doorway in the country. Cosy, traditional atmosphere throughout. Dining room with enticing, age-old ambience.

Bulls Head without rest., Market Pl, DL8 3RD, 𝒫 (01969) 667437, *rob@bullsheadhotel.co.uk*, Fax (01969) 667048 – ⇌ ⓜⓞ 𝘝𝘐𝘚𝘈
6 rm ⊡ ✦65.00 – ✦✦65.00.
◆ Substantial, listed 19C house, in former incarnations a bank and a pub. Lounge with original range and crackling fire. Pleasant rooms; two are vaulted and in the cellars.

East House ⌂ without rest., Gayle, DL8 3RZ, South : ½ m. by Gayle rd on Bainbridge rd 𝒫 (01969) 667405, *lornaward@lineone.net*, ≤, ⇄ – ⇌ 🅿 ⚘
closed Christmas and January – 3 rm ⊡ ✦28.00 – ✦✦56.00.
◆ Attractive, very tidily run stone house dating from early 1800s in peaceful hamlet: lovely views over Wensleydale. Combined breakfast and lounge area. Pleasant bedrooms.

HAWKSHEAD *Cumbria* 502 L 20 *Great Britain G.* – pop. 570 – ⊠ *Ambleside*.
See : *Village* ★.
Env. : *Lake Windermere* ★★ – *Coniston Water* ★ (*Brantwood* ★, on east side), SW : by B 5285.
🆔 *Main Car Park* 𝒫 (015394) 36525 (summer only).
London 283 – Carlisle 52 – Kendal 19.

Ivy House, Main St, LA22 0NS, 𝒫 (015394) 36204, *ivyhousehotel@btinternet.com*, Fax (015394) 36064, ⌐ – ⇌ 🅿 ⓜⓞ 𝘝𝘐𝘚𝘈
*closed 25-26 December***Rest** (by arrangement) a la carte 19.70/26.00 – 6 rm ⊡ ✦45.00/55.00 – ✦✦90.00/100.00.
◆ Georgian house, in centre of village, retains architectural features such as a period spiral staircase. Traditional style public areas; bedrooms feature four-poster beds. Simple dining room with fine Georgian furnishings.

at Near Sawrey *Southeast : 2 m. on B 5285 –* ⊠ *Ambleside.*

Sawrey House ⌂, LA22 0LF, 𝒫 (015394) 36387, *enquiries@sawreyhouse.com*, Fax (015394) 36010, ≤ Esthwaite Water and Grizedale Forest, ⬐, ⇄ – ⇌ 🅿 ⓜⓞ 𝘝𝘐𝘚𝘈
closed November-January except Christmas and New Year – **Rest** (booking essential) (dinner only) 39.00/45.00 – 12 rm ⊡ ✦65.00/130.00 – ✦✦90.000/160.00.
◆ Victorian house with idyllic views of Esthwaite Water and Grizedale Forest and adjacent to Beatrix Potter's house. Traditional interior with individually styled bedrooms. Restaurant with great views by day, candlelight by night.

Ees Wyke Country House ⌂, LA22 0JZ, 𝒫 (015394) 36393, *mail@eeswyke.co.uk*, ≤ Esthwaite Water and Grizedale Forest, ⇄ – ⇌ rest, 🅿 ⓜⓞ 𝘝𝘐𝘚𝘈
*restricted opening in winter***Rest** (booking essential) (dinner only) 31.00 – 8 rm (dinner included) ⊡ ✦73.00/103.00 – ✦✦158.00/180.00.
◆ Panoramic views of Esthwaite Water and Grizedale Forest from this large, impressive Georgian house. Good sized bedrooms with distinctive, homely charm. Dining room's large windows afford lovely views.

at Far Sawrey *Southeast : 2½ m. on B 5285 –* ⊠ *Ambleside.*

West Vale, LA22 0LQ, 𝒫 (015394) 42817, *enquiries@westvalecountryhouse.co.uk*, Fax (015394) 45302, ≤ – ⇌ 🅿 ⓜⓞ 𝘝𝘐𝘚𝘈 ⚘
closed 4 January-8 February and 25-26 December – **Rest** (by arrangement) 36.00 – 7 rm ⊡ ✦78.00/116.00 – ✦✦128.00/150.00.
◆ Victorian house on edge of hamlet with attractive country views. A warm welcome to an interior with open-fired, stone-floored sitting room and snug bedrooms. Meals locally sourced, proudly home cooked.

We try to be as accurate as possible when giving room rates.
But prices are susceptible to change,
so please check rates when booking.

HAWNBY N. Yorks. 502 Q 21 – ✉ Helmsley.
London 245 – Middlesbrough 27 – Newcastle upon Tyne 69 – York 30.

🏠 **Hawnby** ॐ, YO62 5QS, ℰ (01439) 798202, info@hawnbyhotel.co.uk, Fax (01439) 798344, ≼, ☜, ☞ – ⛾⛾ P. ⓜⓞ VISA. ❀
Closed 25 December/Rest a la carte 15.40/24.65 ♀ – **9 rm** ⚐ ♦59.00 – ♦♦79.00.
♦ Personally run small hotel in a very rural location with commanding views of nearby countryside - ideal for walking in the Dales. Snug bedrooms with a cottage feel. Tried-and-tested menus.

at Laskill Northeast : 2¼ m. by Osmotherley rd – ✉ Hawnby.

🏠 **Laskill Grange** without rest., Easterside, YO62 5NB, ℰ (01439) 798268, suesmith@laskillfarm.fsnet.co.uk, Fax (01439) 798498, ☞, ☚ – ⛾⛾ ☜ P. ⓜⓞ VISA
5 rm ⚐ ♦40.00/50.00 – ♦♦74.00/80.00.
♦ A working farm with four cottagey bedrooms set in two converted Victorian stable blocks, surrounded by 1000 acres of rolling farmland. Breakfast served in sunny conservatory.

HAWORTH W. Yorks. 502 O 22 Great Britain G. – pop. 6 078 – ✉ Keighley.
See : Brontë Parsonage Museum*AC*.
🅱 2-4 West Lane ℰ (01535) 642329, haworth@ytbtic.co.uk.
London 213 – Burnley 22 – Leeds 22 – Manchester 34.

🏠 **Hill Top Farmhouse** ॐ, Haworth Moor, BD22 0EL, West : 1 m. by Colne rd and Penistone Hill rd on Brontë Waterfall rd ℰ (01535) 643524, ≼ Haworth Moor, ☞ – ⛾⛾ P. ❀
Rest (by arrangement) 17.00 – **3 rm** ⚐ ♦40.00/56.00 – ♦♦61.00.
♦ Attractive 17C farmhouse wonderfully set on the moors, close to Brontë Parsonage Museum. Welcoming fires, wood carved furniture. Cosy rooms with fresh flowers and fine views. Good home cooking is assured.

🏠 **Rosebud Cottage,** 1 Belle Isle Rd, BD22 8QQ, ℰ (01535) 640321, info@rosebudcottage.co.uk, ☞ – ⛾⛾ P. ⓜⓞ ᴀᴇ VISA. ❀
closed 25-26 December – **Rest** (by arrangement) 15.00 – **5 rm** ⚐ ♦32.50/45.00 – ♦♦65.00/70.00.
♦ Compact, cosy sandstone end-of-terrace cottage built in 1752, next to station on preserved railway line. The homely bedrooms are all very different with individual themes. Pine-furnished dining room overlooks conservatory; home-cooked dishes.

🏠 **Aitches,** 11 West Lane, BD22 8DU, ℰ (01535) 642501, aitches@talk21.com – ⛾⛾. ⓜⓞ ᴀᴇ ⓞ VISA. ❀
closed January-February – **Rest** (by arrangement) 17.50 ♀ – **4 rm** ⚐ ♦37.00/40.00 – ♦♦60.00/65.00.
♦ Imposing Victorian house in centre of historic town: two minutes' walk from Brontë parsonage, and adjacent to famous cobbled streets. Distinctive homely feel; comfy rooms.

✕✕ **Weaver's** with rm, 15 West Lane, BD22 8DU, ℰ (01535) 643822, weaversinhaworth@aol.com, Fax (01535) 644832 – ⛾⛾ rest, ▤ rest. ⓜⓞ ᴀᴇ ⓞ VISA. ❀
closed 26 December-4 January – **Rest** (closed Saturday lunch, Sunday dinner and Monday) 18.95 (lunch) and a la carte 19.50/28.50 ♀ – **3 rm** ⚐ ♦60.00 – ♦♦95.00.
♦ Former weavers cottages with an informal atmosphere and some charm. Characterful cluttered lounge with ornaments and artefacts. Homely cooking, surroundings and bedrooms.

HAYDON BRIDGE Northd 501 502 N 19 – see Hexham.

HAYLING ISLAND Hants. 504 R 31 – pop. 14 842.
🅸🄶 Links Lane ℰ (023) 9246 3712.
🅱 Beachlands, Seafront ℰ (023) 9246 7111 (summer only).
London 77 – Brighton 45 – Southampton 28.

🏠 **Cockle Warren Cottage** without rest., 36 Seafront, PO11 9HL, ℰ (023) 9246 4961, cockle-warren@amserve.com, Fax (023) 9246 4838, ☒ heated, ☞ – ⛾⛾ P. ⓜⓞ VISA
6 rm ⚐ ♦40.00/50.00 – ♦♦70.00/85.00.
♦ A pleasant cottage just across the road from the beach. Conservatory breakfast room overlooks pool. Comfortable, well-kept bedrooms. Families particularly welcome.

HAYTOR VALE Devon – see Bovey Tracey.

HAYWARDS HEATH W. Sussex 504 T 31 Great Britain G. – pop. 29 110.

Env. : Sheffield Park Garden★, E : 5 m. on A 272 and A 275.

ris Paxhill Park, East Mascalls Lane, Lindfield ℘ (01444) 484467.

London 41 – Brighton 16.

XX **Jeremy's at Borde Hill,** Borde Hill Gdns, RH16 1XP, North : 1 ¾ m. by B 2028 on Balcombe Rd ℘ (01444) 441102, reservations@jeremysrestaurant.com, Fax (01494) 441355, 斉, 绿 – ⇔ P. ⚫⚫ AE ⓿ VISA

closed 1 week January, and Monday – Rest a la carte 26.50/38.00.

◆ Converted 19C stables with delightful views to Victorian walled garden. Contemporary interior with modern art. Confident, vibrant cooking in a light Mediterranean style.

HEACHAM Norfolk 504 V 25.

London 116 – Hunstanton 2.5 – King's Lynn 15.5.

个 **The Grove** without rest., 17 Collins Lane, PE31 7DZ, ℘ (01485) 570513, tm.shannon@tiscali.co.uk, 绿 – ⇔ P. ⚖

3 rm ⊐ ✚35.00/40.00 – ✚✚60.00.

◆ Victorian house set on high street continuation. Cosy, book-strewn guest lounge. Full cooked breakfasts with fruit plates. Two rooms homely and spotless; secluded stable room.

HEADLAM Durham 502 O 20 – see Darlington.

HEATHROW AIRPORT Middx. 504 S 29 – see Hillingdon (Greater London).

HEDDON ON THE WALL Northd..

London 288.5 – Blaydon 7.5 – Newcastle upon Tyne 8.5.

🏛 **Close House** ⚲, NE15 0HT, Southwest : 2 ¼ m. by B 6528 ℘ (01661) 852255, events@closehouse.co.uk, Fax (01661) 853322, ≤, ris, 绿, ⚘ – ⇔ P. – 🔏 80. ⚫⚫ AE ⓿ VISA ⚖

closed 25-26 December – Rest (closed Saturday lunch, Sunday and Monday dinner) 18.95 (lunch) and dinner a la carte 25.45/41.95 ⅅ – 7 rm ⊐ ✚92.50/105.00 – ✚✚140.00/165.00.

◆ Wedding oriented Georgian manor house in 300 acres of grounds in Hadrian's Wall country. Marble-floored reception leads to comfy lounge and bar. Stylish Regency rooms. Dining room in warm burgundy serves modern menus.

HELLAND Cornwall – see Bodmin.

HELMSLEY N. Yorks. 502 Q 21 Great Britain G. – pop. 1 559.

Env. : Rievaulx Abbey★★ AC, NW : 2½ m. by B 1257.

ris Ampleforth College, Castle Drive, Gilling East, York ℘ (01439) 788212.

🅱 Helmsley Castle, Castlegate ℘ (01439) 770173.

London 239 – Leeds 51 – Middlesbrough 28 – York 24.

🏛 **The Black Swan,** Market Pl, YO62 5BJ, ℘ (01439) 770466, blackswan@macdonaldhotels.co.uk, Fax (01439) 770174, 绿 – ⇔ P. ⚫⚫ AE ⓿ VISA

The Rutland Room : Rest 30.00 (dinner) and a la carte 29.75/37.00 ⅅ – 45 rm ⊐ ✚67.00/172.00 – ✚✚84.00/184.00.

◆ Part 16C coaching inn in a historic market town; indeed it overlooks the market. Charming rustic interior with exposed beams. Many bedrooms with period fittings and features. Formal dining in classically furnished restaurant.

🏛 **Feversham Arms,** YO62 5AG, on B 1257 ℘ (01439) 770766, info@fevershamarmshotel.com, Fax (01439) 770346, 斉, ⚗ heated, 绿, ⚑ – ⇔ P. – 🔏 35. ⚫⚫ AE VISA

Conservatory : Rest 32.00 (dinner) and a la carte 32.50/43.25 ⅅ – 24 rm ⊐ ✚130.00 – ✚✚235.00.

◆ A former coaching inn; its stone façade conceals surprisingly modern rooms of a quiet restful nature: walls, floors in muted colours, spot lighting, quality fabrics. Range of dining locations, including around the pool.

个 **No.54,** 54 Bondgate, YO62 5EZ, ℘ (01439) 771533, lizzie@no54.co.uk, Fax (01439) 771533, 绿 – ⇔ P.

Rest (by arrangement) (communal dining) – 4 rm ⊐ ✚35.00/45.00 – ✚✚80.00.

◆ Victorian terraced cottage, formerly the village vet's. Charming owner. Bedrooms are strong point: set around flagged courtyard, they're airy, bright and very well-equipped. Dine round antique communal table in homely lounge.

⌂ **Carlton Lodge** without rest., Bondgate, YO62 5EY, ☎ (01439) 770557, *b+b@carlton-lodge.com, Fax (01439) 770623 –* ⇔ **P.** 🌑🟢 *VISA*
8 rm � 🛏40.00/55.00 – 🛏🛏75.00/90.00.
* Late 19C house set just out of town. Homely and traditional air to the décor in the communal areas and the bedrooms, some of which have period features. Cosy breakfast room.

at Nawton *East : 3¼ m. on A 170 –* ⊠ *York.*

⌂ **Plumpton Court** without rest., High St, YO62 7TT, ☎ (01439) 771223, *mail@plumpton court.com, 🌹 –* ⇔ **P.** 🌑🟢 *AE VISA.* 🍸
March-October – **9 rm** ⊏ 🛏40.00 – 🛏🛏58.00.
* The emphasis here is on homeliness; this is well provided by cottage-style traditional décor, open fires and a friendly welcome. Top floor bedrooms have modern style.

at Harome *Southeast : 2¾ m. by A 170 –* ⊠ *York.*

🏨 **The Pheasant,** YO62 5JG, ☎ (01439) 771241, *Fax (01439) 771744,* 🔲, *🌹 –* ⇔ rest, **P.** 🌑🟢 *VISA*
closed Christmas - New Year – **Rest** *(bar lunch)/dinner* 25.00 – **12 rm** *(dinner included)* ⊏ 🛏78.00/87.00 – 🛏🛏156.00/170.00, 2 suites.
* Family run and hidden away in picturesque hamlet with a duck pond and mill stream close by. Open fires and beams in traditionally styled building with modern furniture. Conservatory dining room.

🏠 **Cross House Lodge at The Star Inn,** YO62 5JE, ☎ (01439) 770397, *Fax (01439) 771833, 🌹 –* ⇔ rm, 📶 **P.** 🌑🟢 *VISA*
closed 24 - 27 December **The Piggery :** **Rest** *(booking essential) (residents only) (set menu only)* 45.00 🍸 – *(see also* **The Star Inn** *below) –* **11 rm** ⊏ 🛏140.00/150.00 – 🛏🛏230.00.
* Converted farm building set opposite pub in pretty village. Open-plan, split-level lounge. Ultra-stylish, super-smart rooms in either main building, annex or local cottages.

🔲 **The Star Inn** (Pern), High St, YO62 5JE, ☎ (01439) 770397, *starinn@btopenworld.com, Fax (01439) 771833,* 🏞, *🌹 –* ⇔ **P.** 🌑🟢 *VISA.* 🍸
⟨꙰⟩ *closed 2 weeks in spring, 25 December and Bank Holidays –* **Rest** *(closed Sunday dinner and Monday) (booking essential)* a la carte 35.00/50.00 🍸 🍷.
Spec. Deep-fried Scarborough woof with scallops, plum tomato ketchup, caper butter. Roe deer and shepherd's pie. A celebration of Yorkshire rhubarb.
* Delightful thatched inn with appealing rustic character. Eat in the beamed bar or elegant dining room. Modern original cooking heavy with Yorkshire influences.

at Ampleforth *Southwest : 4½ m. by A 170 off B 1257 –* ⊠ *Helmsley.*

⌂ **Shallowdale House** 🐦, YO62 4DY, West : ½ m. ☎ (01439) 788325, *stay@shallowdale house.co.uk, Fax (01439) 788885,* ≤ *Gilling Gap, 🌹 –* ⇔ **P.** 🌑🟢 *VISA.* 🍸
closed Christmas - New Year – **Rest** *(by arrangement)* 32.50 – **3 rm** ⊏ 🛏67.50/77.50 – 🛏🛏85.00/105.00.
* Modern guesthouse with spectacular views of the Howardian Hills; an area of outstanding beauty. Spacious rooms with large picture windows for the scenery. Warm and relaxed. Owners proud of their home-cooked menus.

at Byland Abbey *Southwest : 6½ m. by A 170 –* ⊠ *Helmsley.*

⌂ **Oldstead Grange** 🐦 without rest., Oldstead, YO61 4BJ, Northwest : 1 ¼ m. on Oldstead rd ☎ (01347) 868634, *oldsteadgrange@yorkshireuk.com, 🌹, 🍷 –* ⇔ **P.** 🌑🟢 *VISA.* 🍸
3 rm ⊏ 🛏55.00/65.00 – 🛏🛏72.00/92.00.
* Comfort is paramount in this part 17C farmhouse on working farm. Cosy, warm lounge with real fire. Hand-made oak furniture adorns bedrooms which benefit from rural outlook.

🔲 **The Abbey Inn** with rm, YO61 4BD, ☎ (01347) 868204, *Fax (01347) 868678,* 🏞, *🌹 –* ⇔ rest, **P.** 🌑🟢 *VISA.* 🍸
closed 24-25 December – **Rest** *(closed Sunday dinner and Monday lunch) (booking essential)* a la carte 20.00/30.00 – **3 rm** ⊏ 🛏95.00/155.00 – 🛏🛏95.00/155.00.
* Characterful part 17C ivy-clad inn uniquely positioned overlooking Byland Abbey ruins. Tasty mix of modern and traditional food and very smart, stylish bedrooms.

(sidebar, right margin) **ENGLAND**

Undecided between two equivalent establishments?
Within each category, establishments are classified
in our order of preference.

HELSTON Cornwall 503 E 33 *The West Country G.* – *pop. 10 578.*

See : *The Flora Day Furry Dance* ★★.

Env. : *Lizard Peninsula* ★ – *Gunwalloe Fishing Cove* ★, S : 4 m. by A 3083 and minor rd – *Culdrose (Flambards Village Theme Park* ★ *)*, SE : 1 m. – *Wendron (Poldark Mine* ★ *)*, NE : 2½ m. by B 3297 – *Gweek (Seal Sanctuary* ★ *)*, E : 4 m. by A 394 and minor rd.

London 306 – Falmouth 13 – Penzance 14 – Truro 17.

at Trelowarren Southeast : 4 m. by A 394 and A 3083 on B 3293 – ✉ Helston.

✗ **New Yard** (at Trelowarren Estate), TR12 6AF, ✆ (01326) 221595, *newyardrestaurant@trelowarren.com, Fax (01326) 221595*, ✿ – ✸✻ P. ◉◉ ▨
closed 2 weeks February, 1 week November, Monday September-June and Sunday dinner – **Rest** 12.50 (lunch) and a la carte 24.70/38.25 ♀.
◆ Converted country house stable yard adjoining craft gallery. Terrace view from modern tables and chairs. Dinner offers full menus of locally inspired dishes; lunch is simpler.

at Nantithet Southeast : 4 m. by A 3083 on Cury Rd – ✉ Helston.

⌂ **Cobblers Cottage,** TR12 7RB, ✆ (01326) 241342, Fax (01326) 241342 – ✸✻ P. ✾
April-October – **Rest** (by arrangement) – 3 rm ⇆ ★56.00 – ★★60.00.
◆ Rurally set, converted 17C cobbler's shop, boasting an acre of mature, immaculately kept gardens. Homely style throughout; exposed beams enrich character. Superior bedrooms.

at Gunwalloe South : 5 m. by A 394 off A 3083 – ✉ Helston.

🍴 **The Halzephron Inn** ⚓ with rm, TR12 7QB, ✆ (01326) 240406, *halzephroninn@gunwalloe1.fsnet.co.uk, Fax (01326) 241442*, ≤, ✿ – ✸✻ rest, P. ◉◉ ▨. ✾
closed 25 December – **Rest** a la carte 17.00/28.00 ♀ – 2 rm ⇆ ★48.00 – ★★84.00.
◆ Country pub in pretty coastal setting. Gleaming copper, original paintings. Adventurous or traditional dishes using local produce. Selection of Cornish cheeses. Neat rooms.

HEMEL HEMPSTEAD Herts. 504 S 28 – *pop. 83 118.*

Env. : *Whipsnade Wild Animal Park* ★.

🏌 *Little Hay Golf Complex, Box Lane, Bovingdon* ✆ (01442) 833798 – 🏌 *Boxmoor, 18 Box Lane* ✆ (01442) 242434.

🛈 *Dacorum Information Centre, Marlowes* ✆ (01442) 234222.

London 30 – Aylesbury 16 – Luton 10 – Northampton 46.

at Frithsden Northwest : 4½ m. by A 4146 – ✉ Hemel Hempstead.

🍴 **The Alford Arms,** HP1 3DD, ✆ (01442) 864480, *info@alfordarmsfrithsden.co.uk, Fax (01442) 876893*, ✿ – P. ◉◉ ▨ ▨
Rest a la carte 18.00/26.00 ♀.
◆ Tucked away in a small hamlet, popular with cyclists and walkers. A pleasant, modern interior of terracotta and cream hues; stylish dishes with interesting combinations.

HEMINGFORD GREY Cambs. 504 T 27 – *see Huntingdon.*

HENFIELD W. Sussex 504 T 31 – *pop. 4 527.*

London 47 – Brighton 10 – Worthing 11.

at Wineham Northeast : 3½ m. by A 281, B 2116 and Wineham Lane – ✉ Henfield.

⌂ **Frylands** ⚓ without rest., BN5 9BP, West : ¼ m. taking left turn at telephone box ✆ (01403) 710214, *b+b@frylands.co.uk, Fax (01403) 711449*, ≤, ☷ heated, ⚓, ☞, ♨ – ✸✻ P. ✾
closed 21 December-2 January – 3 rm ⇆ ★30.00/35.00 – ★★55.00.
◆ Part Elizabethan farmhouse in 250 acres with woodlands and fishing. Fresh home-cooked breakfasts. Bedrooms exude charm and character with homely furnishings, original features.

HENLADE Somerset – *see Taunton.*

Your opinions are important to us:
please write and let us know about your discoveries and experiences –
good and bad!

HENLEY-IN-ARDEN Warks. 503 504 O 27 – pop. 2 797.
London 104 – Birmingham 15 – Stratford-upon-Avon 8 – Warwick 8.5.

Ardencote Manor H. & Country Club and Spa ⚶, Lye Green Rd, Claverdon, CV35 8LS, East : 3¾ m. by A 4189 on Shrewley rd ℘ (01926) 843111, *hotel@ardencote.com*, Fax (01926) 842646, ⚙, ℔, ⚖, ⬜, 🐎, ☂, ☀, ✎, squash – ⬛ ✦, ▤ rm, ⬛ ℗ – 🛎 200. 🆎 🆎 VISA 🆎
The Lodge : Rest a la carte 25.50/32.70 **s.** – **76 rm** 😊 ✦90.00/110.00 – ✦✦130.00/205.00.
◆ Secluded manor house with modern extension and spacious leisure facilities, in formal gardens and grounds. Bedrooms are generally large and traditionally furnished. Informal dining room.

Crabmill, Preston Bagot, Claverdon, B95 5EE, East : 1 m. on A 4189 ℘ (01926) 843342, *thecrabmill@lovelypubs.co.uk*, Fax (01926) 843989, ☂ – ℗, 🆎 🆎 VISA
closed 25 December – Rest *(closed Sunday dinner)* (booking essential) a la carte 25.00/30.00 ⚖.
◆ Stylish pub with a contemporary feel. Dining room has an intimate air, rustic décor and modern prints. Contemporary food with Mediterranean touches on a classic foundation.

at Tanworth-in-Arden Northwest : 4½ m. by A 3400 and Tanworth Rd – ✉ Henley-in-Arden.

The Bell with rm, The Green, B94 5AL, ℘ (01564) 742212, *ash@realcoolbars.com* – ✦ rm, ℗, 🆎 🆎 VISA 🆎
Rest *(closed Sunday dinner)* 10.50 (dinner) and a la carte 15.00/25.00 – **4 rm** 😊 ✦55.00/70.00 – ✦✦85.00/110.00.
◆ Very pleasant modern pub with rustic tones in pretty village; spacious bar. Intimate dining room serving good food with modish twists. Stylish rooms with designer touches.

HENLEY-ON-THAMES Oxon. 504 R 29 – pop. 10 513.
🏌 Huntercombe, Nuffield ℘ (01491) 641207.
⛴ to Reading (Salter Bros. Ltd) (summer only) daily (2 h 15 mn) – to Marlow (Salter Bros. Ltd) (summer only) daily (2 h 15 mn).
🛈 Kings Arms Barn, Kings Rd ℘ (01491) 578034.
London 40 – Oxford 23 – Reading 9.

Hotel du Vin, New St, RG9 2BP, ℘ (01491) 848400, *info@henley.hotelduvin.com*, Fax (01491) 848401, ☂ – ✦, ▤ rm, 📞 ⚖ ℗ – 🛎 35. 🆎 🆎 ⓞ VISA
Bistro : Rest a la carte approx 28.00 ⚖ ⬚ – ⬚ 13.50 – **43 rm** ✦115.00 – ✦✦115.00/175.00.
◆ Former brewery premises; now an easy-going, designer boutique hotel. Stunning rooms: studios with outdoor terrace and bath tub or airy doubles with great amenities. Bistro with resolutely Gallic style, French influenced menus and excellent wine list.

Red Lion, Hart St, RG9 2AR, ℘ (01491) 572161, *reservations@redlionhenley.co.uk*, Fax (01491) 410039, ⬝ – ℗ – 🛎 30. 🆎 🆎 VISA 🆎
Rest 14.50 (lunch) and a la carte 22.55/34.05 – ⬚ 13.50 – **26 rm** ✦99.00/135.00 – ✦✦125.00/155.00.
◆ Hostelry since 15C; has accommodated three kings and overlooks the regatta course. Rooms are well furnished with antiques; an elegant, traditional style pervades throughout. Dining room exudes crisp, light feel.

Thamesmead House without rest., Remenham Lane, RG9 2LR, ℘ (01491) 574745, *thamesmead@supanet.com*, Fax (01491) 579944 – ✦ 📞 ℗, 🆎 🆎 🆎 VISA 🆎
closed Christmas and New Year – **6 rm** 😊 ✦100.00/120.00 – ✦✦130.00/145.00.
◆ Victorian hotel with smart contemporary interiors. Comfy, informal breakfast lounge with stripey banquette seating. Bright, airy Scandinavian style rooms in pastel shades.

Alushta without rest., 23 Queen St, RG9 1AR, ℘ (01491) 636041, *sdr@alushta.co.uk*, Fax (01491) 636042 – ✦ ℗, 🆎
5 rm 😊 ✦40.00/50.00 – ✦✦65.00/85.00.
◆ Centrally located guesthouse, built in late 18C. Very pleasant breakfast room: display shelves boast Russian china. Well-appointed bedrooms with thoughtful extras.

Alftrudis without rest., 8 Norman Ave, RG9 1SG, ℘ (01491) 573099, *sue@alftrudis.co.uk* – ✦.
3 rm ⬚ ✦45.00/65.00 – ✦✦60.00/70.00.
◆ Grade II listed Victorian guesthouse in private cul-de-sac. Two well-furnished, comfortable lounges. Inviting breakfast room. Well-appointed, extremely spacious rooms.

Lenwade without rest., 3 Western Rd (off St Andrews Rd), RG9 1JL, ℘ (01491) 573468, *lenwadeuk@aol.com*, Fax (01491) 411664, ☂ – ✦ 📞 ℗, 🆎
closed 25-26 December – **3 rm** ⬚ ✦50.00/55.00 – ✦✦70.00/75.00.
◆ Late 19C home in a quiet residential area. Neatly kept throughout with modern appointments. Bedrooms are of a good size and pine furnished.

🍴 **The Three Tuns Foodhouse**, 5 Market Pl, RG9 2AA, ℰ (01491) 573260, *thefood house@btconnect.com*, 😊 – ❌. 🕦 🗺
Rest a la carte 25.00/45.00 ♀.
◆ Sandwiched between shops in attractive market place, this early 16C pub has a quirky front bar and cosy rear dining area. Market fresh produce employed on original menus.

at Binfield Heath *Southwest : 4 m. by A 4155* – ⌧ *Henley-on-Thames*.

⌂ **Holmwood** 🐾 *without rest.*, Shiplake Row, RG9 4DP, ℰ (0118) 947 8747, *wendy.cook@freenet.co.uk*, Fax (0118) 947 8637, 😊, 🔥, 🌳 – 🅿. 🕦 🗺. 🌿
closed 1 week Christmas – **5 rm** ⌧ ✚50.00/60.00 – ✚✚70.00.
◆ Part Georgian country house set in peaceful gardens. Charming drawing room facing south with extensive views of the Thames valley. Spacious bedrooms and good home comforts.

HEREFORD *Herefordshire* **503** L 27 *Great Britain G.* – pop. 56 373.
See : *City* ★ – *Cathedral* ★★ (*Mappa Mundi* ★) A **A** – *Old House* ★ A **B**.
Exc. : *Kilpeck* (*Church of SS. Mary and David* ★★) *SW : 8 m. by A 465* B.
🏌️ *Raven's Causeway, Wormsley* ℰ (01432) 830219 – 🏌️ *Belmont Lodge, Belmont* ℰ (01432) 352666 – 🏌️ *Burghill Valley, Tillington Rd, Burghill* ℰ (01432) 760456 – 🏌️ *Hereford Municipal, Holmer Rd* ℰ (01432) 344376 B.
🛈 *1 King St* ℰ (01432) 268430.
London 133 – Birmingham 51 – Cardiff 56.

HEREFORD

Aubrey St . . . . A 3
Berrington St . . . . A 5
Blueschool St. . . . . A 6
Broad St . . . . A 7
Church St. . . . . A 12
Commercial Rd . . . . A 14
Commercial St . . . . A 13
Eign St. . . . . B 16
Greyfriars Bridge . . . . A 17

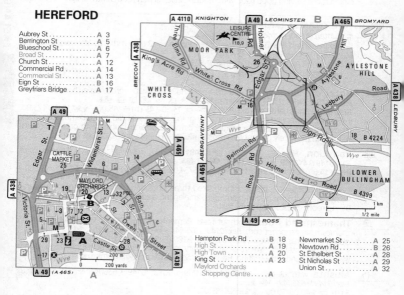

Hampton Park Rd . . . . . B 18
High St. . . . . A 19
High Town . . . . A 20
King St . . . . A 23
Maylord Orchards
  Shopping Centre . . . . . A

Newmarket St. . . . . A 25
Newtown Rd . . . . B 26
St Ethelbert St . . . . A 28
St Nicholas St . . . . A 29
Union St . . . . A 32

🏨 **Castle House**, Castle St, HR1 2NW, ℰ (01432) 356321, *info@castlehse.co.uk*, Fax (01432) 365909, 😊, 🌳 – 📶, ❌ rest, 📧 rest, 🕭, 🅿. 🕦 🗺 🗺   A **e**
La Rive : **Rest** a la carte 27.65/42.35 ♀ ⅊ – **15 rm** ⌧ ✚120.00/156.00 – ✚✚258.00.
◆ Stylish and exclusive air to this contemporary furnished, classically proportioned Georgian house, near the cathedral. Excellent quality and attention to detail throughout. Smart restaurant overlooks gardens and Wye.

🏠 **Aylestone Court**, 2 Aylestone Hill, HR1 1HS, ℰ (01432) 341891, *enquiries@aylestone court.com*, Fax (01432) 267691, 😊 – ❌ 🅿 – 🔬 40. 🕦 🗺 🕥 🗺. 🌿   B **a**
Rest 10.00 (lunch) and a la carte 18.75/27.40 – **10 rm** ⌧ ✚75.00/85.00 – ✚✚95.00/110.00.
◆ Characterful Georgian house, retaining many original features, a close walk from the city centre. Cosy bar. Bedrooms are decorated in a striking Louis XV style. Intimate dining room.

🏠 **Brandon Lodge** without rest., Ross Rd, HR2 8BH, South : 1 ¾ m. on A 49 ℰ (01432) 355621, info@brandonlodge.co.uk, Fax (01432) 355621, 🌳 – 🔲 **P**. **◑** **VISA**. ✀
10 rm ☲ ✿40.00/45.00 – ✿✿55.00/60.00.
❖ A good value hotel with 18C origins, charmingly overseen by owner. Bedrooms in main building and adjacent annex: all are spacious, boasting a cheery warmth and good facilities.

↑ **Grafton Villa Farm** without rest., Grafton, HR2 8ED, South : 2 ¼ m. on A 49 ℰ (01432) 268689, jennielayton@ereal.net, Fax (01432) 268689, 🌳, 🎝 – ✇✇ **P**. ✀
closed December and January – **3 rm** ☲ ✿40.00/50.00 – ✿✿60.00/70.00.
❖ Early 18C farmhouse, on a working farm with extensive grounds. Antique furnished homely bedrooms and fresh, substantial country breakfasts.

✕ **Floodgates Brasserie,** Left Bank Village, Bridge St, HR4 9DG, ℰ (01432) 349009, info@leftbank.co.uk, Fax (01432) 349012, 🍽 – 🔲 **P**. **◑** **AE** **VISA** ___A X
Rest 14.95 (lunch) and a la carte 20.85/30.30 ♀.
❖ Excellently located, with dining on the river terrace, in the Left Bank Village. A relaxed and informal, though smart, ambience matched by an internationally influenced menu.

at Kingstone Southwest : 6¾ m. by A 465 – B – and B 4349 – ✉ Hereford.

↑ **Mill Orchard** �´ without rest., HR2 9ES, ℰ (01981) 250326, relax@millorchard.co.uk, 🌳 – ✇✇ **P**
March-September – **3 rm** ☲ ✿36.00 – ✿✿64.00.
❖ An acre of lawned gardens accentuates the peaceful position of this personally run guesthouse. Cosy lounge and warmly welcoming breakfast room. Well-equipped bedrooms.

at Byford West : 7½ m. by A 438 – B – ✉ Hereford.

↑ **Old Rectory** without rest., HR4 7LD, ℰ (01981) 590218, info@theoldrectory.uk.com, 🌳 – ✇✇ **P**. ✀
March-October – **3 rm** ☲ ✿50.00 – ✿✿70.00.
❖ Rurally set Georgian-style 19C rectory with pleasant gardens. Spacious yet homely atmosphere and décor; the bedrooms are furnished in a simple, traditional style.

at Winforton Northwest : 15 m. on A 438 – ✉ Hereford.

↑ **Winforton Court** without rest., HR3 6EA, ℰ (01544) 328498, Fax (01544) 328498, 🌳 – ✇✇ **P**
closed 24-28 December – **3 rm** ☲ ✿55.00/60.00 – ✿✿60.00/90.00.
❖ Wonderfully characterful 16C house used as a circuit court by "Hanging" Judge Jeffries. Exudes personality with exposed beams, thick walls and uneven floors. Rustic rooms.

HERM 503 P 33 and 517 ⑩ – see Channel Islands.

HERMITAGE Dorset – see Sherborne.

HERSTMONCEUX E. Sussex 504 U 31.
London 63 – Eastbourne 12 – Hastings 14 – Lewes 16.

✕✕ **Sundial,** Gardner St, BN27 4LA, ℰ (01323) 832217, sundialrestaurant@hotmail.com, Fax (01323) 832909, 🌳 – ✇✇ **P**. **◑** **◑** **VISA**
closed Sunday dinner and Monday – **Rest** - French - 21.00/35.00 and a la carte 31.75/51.50.
❖ Converted 16C cottage retaining leaded windows and a beamed ceiling. Comfortable chairs in a well spaced dining room. Menu is French with a classic, familiar style.

at Wartling Southeast : 3¾ m. by A 271 and Wartling rd – ✉ Herstmonceux.

↑ **Wartling Place** without rest., BN27 1RY, ℰ (01323) 832590, accom@wartlingplace.pre stel.co.uk, Fax (01323) 831558, 🌳 – ✇✇ **◀** **P**. **◑** **AE** **VISA**. ✀
3 rm ☲ ✿70.00/105.00 – ✿✿145.00/190.00.
❖ Part Georgian house with three acres of gardens, sited in the village. Pleasantly furnished, with some antiques; two of the rooms have four-poster beds.

HERTFORD Herts. 504 T 28.
London 25 – Bishop's Stortford 16 – Stevenage 11.

🍴 **The Hillside,** 45 Port Hill, Bengeo, SG14 3EP, North : ¼ m. on B 158 ℰ (01992) 554556, justin624@hotmail.com, Fax (01992) 583709 – ✇✇ 🔲 **P**. **◑** **AE** **◑** **VISA**. ✀
Rest (closed Sunday dinner) a la carte 30.00/45.00 ♀.
❖ Refurbished 17C pub next to deli and farm shop. Intimate and cosy, with sofas by the fire. Dine in an airy, sunny environment. Fashionable brasserie dishes with global range.

HESSLE *Kingston-upon-Hull* 502 S 22 – *see Kingston-upon-Hull.*

HESWALL *Mersey.* 502 503 K 24 – *pop. 29 977.*
London 212 – Birkenhead 12 – Chester 14 – Liverpool 11.

XX **Gem,** 1 Milner Rd, CH60 5RT, ℰ (0151) 342 4811, *enquiries@gemrestaurant.co.uk,*
Fax (0151) 342 4811 – ✧ 14. 🟠🟢 *VISA*
closed 2 weeks September, Sunday and Monday – **Rest** (booking essential) (dinner only)
18.95 (mid week) and a la carte 24.85/31.70.
♦ Personally run, friendly neighbourhood restaurant; unassuming exterior and simple,
modern interior with intimate ambience. Country cooking with distinctive departures.

HETHERSETT *Norfolk* 504 X 26 – *see Norwich.*

HETTON *N. Yorks.* 502 N 21 – *see Skipton.*

HEXHAM *Northd.* 501 502 N 19 *Great Britain G.* – *pop. 10 682.*
See : *Abbey*★ *(Saxon Crypt*★★ *, Leschman chantry*★ *).*
Env. : *Hadrian's Wall*★★ *, N : 4½ m. by A 6079.*
Exc. : *Housesteads*★★ *, NW : 12½ m. by A 6079 and B 6318.*
🟦 *Spital Park* ℰ (01434) 603072 – 🟦 *De Vere Slaley Hall G. & C.C., Slaley* ℰ (01434) 673154 –
🟦 *Tynedale, Tyne Green* ℰ (01434) 608154.
🅱 *Wentworth Car Park* ℰ (01434) 652220.
London 304 – Carlisle 37 – Newcastle upon Tyne 21.

🏛 **Beaumont,** Beaumont St, NE46 3LT, ℰ (01434) 602331, *reservations@beaumontho*
tel.eclipse.co.uk, Fax (01434) 606184 – 📱 ✧ ✦ & 🅿 – 🔏 100. 🟠🟢 🄰🄴 ➀ *VISA* ✧
The Park : Rest 12.50/22.75 s. ☲ – 25 rm ☲ ✦75.00/88.00 – ✦✦105.00/110.00.
♦ Victorian building of local stone overlooking park and the town's ancient abbey - which
is visible from some of the comfortable rooms. Personally run with a warm atmosphere.
Park restaurant on the first floor with views of the abbey.

↑ **Hallbank,** Hallgate, NE46 1XA, ℰ (01434) 606656, Fax (01434) 605567 – ✧ 🅿. 🟠🟢 ➀
VISA. ✧
Rest (by arrangement) 25.00 – **8 rm** ☲ ✦50.00/90.00 – ✦✦60.00/110.00.
♦ Red-brick Georgian house close to market square, set in the shadow of the old gaol.
Fully refurbished rooms exhibit a warm, classic style with good modern facilities. Dine in
adjacent, informal café/bistro.

↑ **West Close House** ⌖ without rest., Hextol Terrace, NE46 2AD, Southwest : ½ m. off
B 6305 ℰ (01434) 603307, 🌼 – ✧ 🅿. ✧
4 rm ☲ ✦25.00 – ✦✦40.00.
♦ Detached house in a residential area providing a high standard of simple, good value
accommodation. Polished wood floors and immaculately kept.

↑ **Dene House** ⌖ without rest., Juniper, NE46 1SJ, South : 3 ¾ m. by B 6306 following
signs for Dye House ℰ (01434) 673413, *margaret@denehouse-hexham.co.uk,* 🌼 – ✧ 🅿.
✧
closed Christmas – **3 rm** ✦30.00/35.00 – ✦✦60.00.
♦ Attractive stone cottage in a quiet spot with pleasant views, numerous country walks in
the environs. Cosy feel throughout. Simple, homely rooms.

XX **Valley Connection 301,** Market Pl, NE46 3NX, ℰ (01434) 601234, Fax (01434) 606629
– ✧ 🟠🟢 🄰🄴 ➀ *VISA*
closed 25 December – **Rest** - Indian - (dinner only) a la carte approx 24.00.
♦ Near Hexham Abbey; views of the market place from both floors. Old favourites inter-
spersed with modern dishes in a tasty Indian menu.

X **The Green Room,** Hexham Railway Station, Station Rd, NE46 1EZ, ℰ (01434) 608800,
Fax (01434) 608800, 🌿 – ✧ 🟠🟢 🄰🄴 ➀ *VISA*
closed 2 weeks August, 1 week Christmas, Sunday dinner, Monday and Bank Holidays –
Rest a la carte 15.95/30.85 s.
♦ Located in former luggage room and named after 19C architect who designed Hexham
station. Pleasant rustic feel; accomplished, wide ranging menus exude eclectic appeal.

at Slaley *Southeast : 5½ m. by B 6306 –* ✉ *Hexham.*

Slaley Hall ⚜, NE47 0BY, Southeast : 2 ¼ m. ✆ (01434) 673350, *slaley.hall@devereho tels.com, Fax* (01434) 673962, ≼, 斎, ℗, ₧, ⩬, 🖼, 🎞, ⌨, 🏊, ₤ – 🛗 ⇆ ▤ ⚑ ₺ 🚶 ℙ – 🅰 400. 🆎 AE ① VISA. ⚒
Rest (bar lunch Monday-Saturday)/dinner 26.95 and a la carte 31.20/44.95 – **132 rm** ⊇ ✦175.00/195.00 – ✦✦210.00/235.00, 10 suites.
♦ Extended Edwardian manor house, now a leisure oriented hotel, grounds with woodland and two golf courses. Spacious bedrooms with up-to-date facilities and country views. Formal restaurant offering menus based on a modern English style.

at Haydon Bridge *West : 7½ m. on A 69 –* ✉ *Hexham.*

Langley Castle ⚜, Langley-on-Tyne, NE47 5LU, South : 2 m. by A 69 on A 686 ✆ (01434) 688888, *manager@langleycastle.com, Fax* (01434) 684019, 斎, ₤ – ⇆ rest, ₤ ℙ – 🅰 100. 🆎 AE ① VISA
Rest 18.95/32.95 – **19 rm** ⊇ ✦99.50 – ✦✦139.00, 1 suite.
♦ Turreted stone castle in 12 acres. Tapestry style fabrics, heraldic themed ornaments, open fire. Spacious rooms in castle or converted stables. Formal restaurant with beams and stone floor; classic dishes using local produce.

HEYTESBURY *Wilts.* 503 504 N 30 – *see Warminster.*

HIGHCLERE *Hants.* 503 P 29 – *pop. 2 409 –* ✉ *Newbury.*
London 69 – Newbury 5 – Reading 25.

The Yew Tree with rm, Hollington Cross, Andover Rd, RG20 9SE, South : 1 m. off A 343 ✆ (01635) 253360, *gareth.mcainsh@theyewtree.net, Fax* (01635) 255035, 斎 – ⇆ rest, ℙ. 🆎 AE VISA
Rest 16.50 (lunch) and a la carte 22.00/48.00 – **6 rm** ⊇ ✦60.00 – ✦✦60.00.
♦ 17C pub with smart front terrace, old rafters and no less than four elegant, candle-lit rear dining rooms with a classical style of modern cooking finding favour with locals.

HIGHCLIFFE *Dorset* 503 504 O 31.
London 112 – Bournemouth 10 – Salisbury 21 – Southampton 26 – Winchester 37.

Lord Bute, Lymington Rd, BH23 4JS, ✆ (01425) 278884, *mail@lordbute.co.uk, Fax* (01425) 279258 – ⇆ rest, ▤ ℙ – 🅰 25. 🆎 AE ① VISA
Rest (closed Sunday dinner and Monday) 16.95/22.95 and dinner a la carte 28.70/39.70 s. – **12 rm** ⊇ ✦78.00/88.00 – ✦✦108.00/180.00.
♦ Modern property with a traditional style. Well designed, light, airy lounge. Bedrooms are well appointed and include safes and spa baths. Formal dining room adjacent to Orangery lounge.

HIGHER BURWARDSLEY *Ches. – see Tattenhall.*

HIGH ONGAR *Essex.*
London 24 – Brentwood 11 – Chelmsford 10.

The Wheatsheaf Brasserie, King St, CM5 9NS, East : 2 m. by A 414 on Blackmore rd ✆ (01277) 822220, *Fax* (01277) 822441, 斎, 斎 – ℙ. 🆎 AE VISA. ⚒
closed 2 weeks from 26 December, 1 week May and 1 week October – **Rest** (closed Sunday dinner and Monday) (booking essential) a la carte 21.40/35.40 ⊈.
♦ Pretty, converted pub with large garden and terrace. Dine in four different rooms with open fires and homely ornamentation. Good value, accomplished British cuisine.

HIGH WYCOMBE *Bucks.* 504 R 29 *Great Britain G. – pop. 77 178.*
Env. : *Chiltern Hills★.*
🖼 *Hazlemere G & C.C., Penn Rd, Hazlemere* ✆ (01494) 719300 – 🖼, 🖼 *Wycombe Heights, Rayners Ave, Loudwater* ✆ (01494) 816686.
🖪 *Paul's Row* ✆ (01494) 421892.
London 34 – Aylesbury 17 – Oxford 26 – Reading 18.

Eat-Thai, 14-15 Easton St, HP11 1NJ, ✆ (01494) 532888, *Fax* (01494) 532889 – ⇆. 🆎 AE VISA
closed 25-28 December – **Rest** - Thai - 12.00/40.00 and a la carte 20.40/29.40 s.
♦ Modern restaurant with wood floors and well-spaced tables. Three distinct areas serving fresh, tasty dishes with ingredients flown regularly from Thailand. Attentive service.

HINCKLEY Leics. 502 503 504 P 26 – pop. 43 246.

🔼 Hinckley Library, Lancaster Rd 🖉 (01455) 635106.

London 103 – Birmingham 31 – Coventry 12 – Leicester 14.

🏨 **Sketchley Grange,** Sketchley Lane, LE10 3HU, South : 1 ½ m. by B 4109 (Rugby Rd) 🖉 (01455) 251133, reservations@sketchleygrange.co.uk, Fax (01455) 631384, ☜, ⅃₆, ☎, ⌣, ☞ – ⇕ ⅙, ≡ rest, ⅃₊ 🅿 – 🔏 280. 🐠 🆎 🚾
The Willow : Rest (closed Sunday-Monday) (dinner only and Sunday lunch)/dinner a la carte 20.00/35.00 – **The Terrace Bistro :** Rest a la carte 18.85/32.65 – 🖙 10.95 – **51 rm** ✹121.00 – ✹✹142.00, 1 suite.

◆ Privately owned, spacious hotel with good leisure and an array of conference facilities. Bedrooms are well proportioned, and furniture is comfortable and well chosen. The Willow exudes elegance and garden views. The Terrace Bistro is bright and spacious.

HINDON Wilts. 503 N 30.

London 103.5 – Shaftesbury 7.5 – Warminster 10.

🛏 **The Lamb Inn** with rm, High St, SP3 6DP, 🖉 (01747) 820573, info@lambathindon.co.uk, Fax (01747) 820605, ☞, ☞ – ⅙ rest, 🅿. 🐠 🆎 🚾
Rest a la carte 25.00/35.00 ☡ – **14 rm** 🖙 ✹70.00 – ✹✹99.00.

◆ 15C former coaching inn. Attractively creeper clad with picture-strewn rich red interior. Large blackboards offer heartily traditional British menus. Characterful rooms.

HINDRINGHAM Norfolk.

London 118.5 – Fakenham 8.5 – Holt 8.

🛏 **Field House** without rest., Moorgate Rd, NR21 0PT, 🖉 (01328) 878726, stay@fieldhou sehindringham.co.uk, ☞ – ⅙ ♿ 🅿. ⌣
closed Christmas and New Year – **3 rm** 🖙 ✹65.00/75.00 – ✹✹90.00/100.00.

◆ Well-kept flint stone house with pretty garden and summer house. Pristine lounge with books and magazines. Extensive breakfast menus. Carefully co-ordinated rooms with extras.

HINTLESHAM Suffolk 504 X 27 – see Ipswich.

HINTON ST GEORGE Somerset.

🛏 **Lord Poulett Arms** with rm, High St, TA17 8SE, 🖉 (01460) 73149, steveandmi chelle@lordpoulettarms.com, ☞, ⅍ – ⅙ 🅿. 🐠 🚾
Rest a la carte 17.50/28.50 – **4 rm** 🖙 ✹59.00 – ✹✹88.00.

◆ Beautifully restored 17C inn on delightful high street. Immense charm and character: stone floors, exposed brickwork. Accomplished, classical cooking. Immaculate rooms.

HISTON Cambs. 504 U 27 – see Cambridge.

HITCHIN Herts. 504 T 28 – pop. 33 352.

London 40 – Bedford 14 – Cambridge 26 – Luton 9.

✕ **Just 32,** 32 Sun St, SG5 1AH, 🖉 (01462) 455666 – 🐠 🆎 ① 🚾
closed 26 December, 1 January, Sunday and Monday – **Rest** a la carte 18.95/36.65 ☡.
◆ Friendly bistro, located just off the town square, with hatch to kitchen from which an interestingly eclectic range of dishes arrive at table. Keen service.

HOCKLEY HEATH W. Mids. 503 504 O 26 – pop. 13 616 – ✉ Solihull.

London 117 – Birmingham 11 – Coventry 17.

🏨 **Nuthurst Grange Country House,** Nuthurst Grange Lane, B94 5NL, South : ¾ m. by A 3400 🖉 (01564) 783972, info@nuthurst-grange.co.uk, Fax (01564) 783919, ☞ – 🅿 – 🔏 80. 🐠 🆎 🚾. ⌣
closed 1 week Christmas – **Rest** – (see **The Restaurant** below) – **15 rm** 🖙 ✹139.00 – ✹✹165.00/195.00.

◆ Part Edwardian manor house, overlooking M40 and convenient for Birmingham airport. Classic English country décor throughout. Spacious rooms with high level of comfort.

✕✕✕ **The Restaurant** (at Nuthurst Grange Country House), Nuthurst Grange Lane, B94 5NL, South : ¾ m. by A 3400 🖉 (01564) 783972, Fax (01564) 783919, ☞ – ⅙ 🅿 ⇆ 30. 🐠 🆎 🚾
closed 1 week Christmas and Saturday lunch – **Rest** 22.95/32.50 and a la carte 32.40/59.50 s. ☡.

◆ Thoroughly traditional tone in the dining room's décor which contributes to a formal ambience. Seasonal menu draws on British and French traditions.

at Lapworth *Southeast : 2 m. on B 4439 –* ⊠ *Warwick.*

🍴 **Boot Inn,** Old Warwick Rd, B94 6JU, on B 4439 ☎ (01564) 782464, *bootinn@hotmail.com,* Fax (01564) 784989, 🌤 , 🛋 – 🍴 ⚫⚫ Ⓐ🄴 *VISA*
closed 25 December – **Rest** (booking essential) a la carte 21.00/32.00 ⅊.
♦ Bustling modern dining pub, with traditional bucolic character at the front and spacious dining room to rear. Appealing rustic dishes supplemented by daily changing specials.

HOLBEACH *Lincs.* **502 504** U 25 *– pop. 7 247.*
London 117 – Kingston-upon-Hull 81 – Norwich 62 – Nottingham 60 – Peterborough 25.

⌂ **Pipwell Manor** *without rest.,* Washway Rd, Saracen's Head, PE12 8AL, Northeast : 1 ½ m. by A 17 ☎ (01406) 423119, *honnor@pipwellmanor.freeserve.co.uk,* Fax (01406) 423119, 🛋 – 🍴 🄿. 🕸
closed Christmas and New Year – **4 rm** ⚥ ✦36.00 – ✦✦50.00.
♦ Georgian manor built on site of Cisterian Grange, close to solitude of the Wash. Garden railway for train spotters. Complimentary tea, cake on arrival. Country style rooms.

HOLBETON *Devon.*
London 211.5 – Ivybridge 6 – Plymouth 10.5.

🍴 **The Dartmoor Union,** Fore St, PL8 1NE, ☎ (01752) 830288, *info@dartmoorunioninn.co.uk, Fax (01752) 830296,* 🌤 – 🍴 🄿. ⚫⚫ *VISA*
Rest 12.95 (lunch) and a la carte 18.85/27.95 ⅊.
♦ Hard to spot, but once inside, a conspicuous 19C log fire crackles in the bar and rose pink walls light up the restaurant. Seasonal dishes offer local flavours.

👀 Look out for red symbols, indicating particularly pleasant establishments.

HOLFORD *Somerset* **503** K 30 *Great Britain G. –* ⊠ *Bridgwater.*
Env. : Stogursey Priory Church★★*, W : 4½ m.*
London 171 – Bristol 48 – Minehead 15 – Taunton 22.

🏠 **Combe House** ⌂, TA5 1RZ, Southwest : ¾ m. by Youth Hostel rd ☎ (01278) 741382, *enquiries@combehouse.co.uk, Fax (01278) 741322,* 🚗, 🛋, ✕ – 🍴 ⚓ 🄿. ⚫⚫ *VISA*
Rest a la carte 25.15/31.15 – **18 rm** ⚥ ✦65.00/90.00 – ✦✦115.00/135.00.
♦ Interesting Edwardian country house with a water wheel in pleasant Quantock Hills location. Informal relaxed ambience with plenty of books and beams. Rooms overlook garden. Restaurant with spaced beams; locally sourced produce to the fore.

HOLKHAM *Norfolk* **504** W 25.
London 124 – King's Lynn 32 – Norwich 39.

🏨 **The Victoria,** Park Rd, NR23 1RG, ☎ (01328) 711008, *victoria@holkham.co.uk,* Fax (01328) 711009, 🌤 , 🛋 – 🍴 🄿. ⚫⚫ Ⓐ🄴 ⓪ *VISA*. 🕸
Rest *– (see **The Restaurant** below) –* **10 rm** ⚥ ✦95.00/120.00 – ✦✦115.00/210.00.
♦ Trendy, stylish hotel, built in 1838, overlooking Holkham nature reserve. Bedrooms are individually styled with much of the furniture sourced from Rajasthan.

🍽 **The Restaurant** (at The Victoria H.), Park Rd, NR23 1RG, ☎ (01328) 711008, *victoria@holkham.co.uk, Fax (01328) 711009,* 🌤 , 🛋 – 🍴 🄿. ⚫⚫ *VISA*
Rest a la carte 24.00/29.00 ⅊.
♦ Extensive dining areas, now including conservatory option, specialise in modish menus as well as fine fish and seafood dishes. The bar offers a buzzy alternative.

HOLMES CHAPEL *Ches.* **502 503 504** M 24 *– pop. 5 669.*
London 181 – Chester 25 – Liverpool 41 – Manchester 24 – Stoke-on-Trent 20.

🏠 **Cottage Restaurant and Lodge,** London Rd, Allostock, WA16 9LU, North : 3 m. on A 50 ☎ (01565) 722470, *reception@thecottagenutsford.co.uk, Fax (01565) 722749 –* 🍴 🄿 – 🛢 60. ⚫⚫ Ⓐ🄴 *VISA*. 🕸
closed 1 January – **Rest** *(closed Sunday dinner and Bank Holidays)* 16.95 (lunch) and dinner a la carte 21.95/31.40 – **12 rm** ⚥ ✦82.50 – ✦✦98.50.
♦ Brick-built cottage notable for an abundant degree of rustic allure and charm. Up-to-date, spacious bedrooms are the feature of its annex extension. Characterfully beamed restaurant is part of original cottage.

HOLT *Norfolk 504 X 25 – pop. 3 550.*
London 124 – King's Lynn 34 – Norwich 22.

🏛 **Byfords,** Shirehall Plain, NR25 6BG, ℰ (01263) 711400, *quenese@byfords.org.uk,* Fax (01263) 713520, 🍴 – 🖐 **P**. **OO** ① **VISA**. 🛠
closed 25 December – **Rest** a la carte 17.00/28.65 – **9 rm** ⊏ ✝85.00 – ✝✝160.00.
◆ Flint-fronted Grade II listed house that boasts something different: a well-stocked deli; rustic cellar café; and stunning rooms, with Egyptian cotton and under-floor heating.

XX **Yetman's,** 37 Norwich Rd, NR25 6SA, ℰ (01263) 713320 – 🖐. **OO** **AE** **VISA**
restricted opening in winter and closed Monday, Tuesday and Sunday dinner (except at Bank Holidays) – **Rest** (dinner only and Sunday lunch)/dinner 34.00 ♀ 🛠.
◆ A relaxed and cosy atmosphere in prettily painted Georgian cottages. Interesting and well balanced dishes, with a British feel, using local produce.

HOLT *Wilts. 503 504 N 29 – see Bradford-on-Avon.*

HONITON *Devon 503 K 31 The West Country G. – pop. 11 213.*
See : *All Hallows Museum★ AC.*
Env. : *Ottery St Mary★ (St Mary's★) SW : 5 m. by A 30 and B 3177.*
Exc. : *Faraway Countryside Park (≤★), SE : 6½ m. by A 375 and B 3174.*
🔢 *Lace Walk Car Park ℰ (01404) 43716.*
London 186 – Exeter 17 – Southampton 93 – Taunton 18.

🏛 **Deer Park** 🌳, Buckerell Village, Weston, EX14 3PG, West : 2 ½ m. by A 30 ℰ (01404) 41266, *admin@deerparkcountryhotel.com,* Fax (01404) 46598, ≤, 🏊 heated, 🐾, 🎾, �⃝, 🛠 – **P** – 🔙 70. **OO** **AE** ① **VISA**
Rest 17.95/31.95 – **25 rm** ⊏ ✝85.00/85.00 – ✝✝130.00.
◆ Characterful house pleasantly located down narrow country lane. Extensive rural sporting facilities and a country house feel throughout. Spacious, individually styled rooms. Dining room decorated in keeping with country house surroundings.

at Yarcombe *Northeast : 8 m. on A 30 – ⊠ Honiton.*

🏛 **Belfry Country H.,** EX14 9BD, on A 30 ℰ (01404) 861234, *stay@thebelfrycountryhotel.com,* Fax (01404) 861579, ≤ – 🖐 ✆ **P**. **OO** **VISA**. 🛠
closed Christmas-New Year – **Rest** (booking essential for non-residents) (dinner only) 28.00 **s.** – **6 rm** ⊏ ✝55.00 – ✝✝80.00.
◆ Pretty cottage, formerly the village school, opposite 14C church. Personally run and hospitable, with light, cosy bedrooms, named after poets, featuring stained glass windows. Comfy restaurant decorated with owner's world travel photos.

at Wilmington *East : 3 m. on A 35 – ⊠ Honiton.*

🏛 **Home Farm,** EX14 9JR, on A 35 ℰ (01404) 831278, *info@thatchedhotel.co.uk,* Fax (01404) 831411, 🍴, 🌳, 🐾 – 🖐 ✆ **P**. **OO** **AE** ① **VISA**
Rest a la carte 25.00/30.00 ♀ – **12 rm** ⊏ ✝50.00 – ✝✝57.00/110.00.
◆ Part 16C thatched farmhouse offering a simple and comfortable standard of accommodation. Characterful lounges and bedrooms with individual country personality. Snug, cosy dining room room with inglenook.

at Gittisham *Southwest : 3 m. by A 30 – ⊠ Honiton.*

🏛 **Combe House** 🌳, EX14 3AD, ℰ (01404) 540400, *stay@thishotel.com,* Fax (01404) 46004, ≤, 🌳, 🐾 – 🖐 **P**. – 🔙 60. **OO** **VISA**
closed 22-31 January – **Rest** (booking essential for non-residents) 27.00/41.00 – **13 rm** ⊏ ✝138.00 – ✝✝168.00/168.00, 2 suites.
◆ Elizabethan mansion set in glorious Devon countryside. See the original Victorian kitchen. Oak-panelling and 18C paintings. Individually designed rooms with fine antiques. Elegant restaurant with murals.

at Payhembury *Northwest : 7 m. by A 373 – ⊠ Honiton.*

↑ **Cokesputt House** 🌳, EX14 3HD, West : ¼ m. on Tale rd ℰ (01404) 841289, *aeac.forbes@virgin.net,* ≤, 🌳 – 🖐 **P**. **OO** **VISA**. 🛠
closed Christmas and January – **Rest** (booking essential) (communal dining) 27.00 – **3 rm** ⊏ ✝40.00/55.00 – ✝✝80.00.
◆ Part 17C and 18C house with gardens. Elegant antique furnished interior, in the best traditions of English country style. Charming bedrooms. Home-grown meals at welcoming communal table.

HOO GREEN Ches. – see Knutsford.

HOOK Hants. 504 R 30 – pop. 6 869 – ⊠ Basingstoke.
London 47 – Oxford 39 – Reading 13 – Southampton 31.

at Rotherwick North : 2 m. by A 30 and B 3349 on Rotherwick rd – ⊠ Basingstoke.

🏨🏨🏨 **Tylney Hall** ♨, RG27 9AZ, South : 1 ½ m. by Newnham rd on Ridge Lane ℘ (01256) 764881, sales@tylneyhall.com, Fax (01256) 768141, ⓥ, ↳, ⇌, ⌁ heated, ◪, ☞, ♨, ※ – ⇄ rm, 🄿 – 🛦 120. ⬛⬤ 🆅🆂🆐 ⓞ 🆅🆂🆐.
Rest 23.00/46.50 **s.** and a la carte ⓨ – **103 rm** ⊂⊃ ★140.00 – ★★235.00, 9 suites.
◆ Grand and beautifully restored 19C mansion in delightful, extensive Gertrude Jekyll gardens. Country house rooms, some with private conservatories or suites over two floors. Classically English dining room with oak panelling and garden views.

HOPE Derbs. 502 503 504 O 23 – ⊠ Sheffield.
London 180 – Derby 50 – Manchester 31 – Sheffield 15 – Stoke-on-Trent 40.

↑ **Underleigh House** ♨ without rest., Hope Valley, S33 6RF, North : 1 m. by Edale rd ℘ (01433) 621372, underleigh.house@btconnect.com, Fax (01433) 621324, ≼, ☞ – ⇄ 🄿. ⬛⬤ 🆅🆂🆐. ※
closed Christmas, New Year and January – **6 rm** ⊂⊃ ★55.00 – ★★75.00/90.00.
◆ Converted Victorian property, rurally located and personally run, well located for the Peak District. Countryside views and a welcoming country ambience.

HOPE COVE Devon 503 I 33 – see Salcombe.

HORLEY Surrey 504 T 30 – pop. 22 582.
London 27 – Brighton 26 – Royal Tunbridge Wells 22.

Plan : see Gatwick

🏨🏨 **Langshott Manor**, Langshott, RH6 9LN, North : by A 23 turning right at Thistle Gatwick H. onto Ladbroke Rd ℘ (01293) 786680, admin@langshottmanor.com, Fax (01293) 783905, ☞, ☞ – ⇄ ℅ 🄿. ⬛⬤ 🆐 ⓞ 🆅🆂🆐. ※
Mulberry : Rest (booking essential) 19.50/40.00 – **21 rm** ⊂⊃ ★148.00 – ★★310.00, 1 suite.
◆ Part Elizabethan manor house set amidst gardens of roses, vines and ponds. For centuries the home of aristocrats, now a refined and harmonious country house hotel. Country house-style dining room with intimate ambience.

↑ **Lawn** without rest., 30 Massetts Rd, RH6 7DF, ℘ (01293) 775751, info@lawnguest house.co.uk, Fax (01293) 821803, ☞ – ⇄ 🄿. ⬛⬤ 🆐 🆅🆂🆐   Y   r
12 rm ⊂⊃ ★40.00/50.00 – ★★58.00/63.00.
◆ Privately owned and personally run with home comforts and ambience. Close to the station and convenient for Gatwick airport. Chintz decorated bedrooms are pine furnished.

↑ **The Turret** without rest., 48 Massetts Rd, RH6 7DS, ℘ (01293) 782490, info@thetur ret.com, Fax (01293) 431492 – ⇄ 🄿. ⬛⬤ 🆅🆂🆐. ※   Y   i
10 rm ⊂⊃ ★39.00/54.00 – ★★54.00.
◆ Victorian home, with turrets, offering a warm welcome and simple comforts with homely style. Magnolia rooms with co-ordinated soft furnishings. Courtesy airport transport.

HORNCASTLE Lincs. 502 504 T 24 – pop. 6 090.
🄱 14 Bull Ring ℘ (01507) 526636.
London 143 – Lincoln 22 – Nottingham 62.

XX **Magpies**, 71-75 East St, LN9 6AA, ℘ (01507) 527004, Fax (01507) 525068 – ⇄ ▤. ⬛⬤ 🆅🆂🆐
closed New Year, Saturday lunch, Monday and Tuesday – **Rest** 25.00/32.00.
◆ Renowned, family run restaurant in a converted 18C house. Snug, comfortable, beamed interior. Local ingredients used in accomplished, refined dishes in a modern style.

HORNDON-ON-THE-HILL Essex 504 V 29.

London 25 – Chelmsford 22 – Maidstone 34 – Southend-on-Sea 16.

🔟 **The Bell** with rm, High Rd, SS17 8LD, ☎ (01375) 642463, *info@bell-inn.co.uk,*
Fax (01375) 361611, ☎ – ☼ **P**. **MC** **AE** **VISA** . ✄
closed 25-26 December – **Rest** *(closed Bank Holiday Monday)* a la carte 21.00/27.95 ♀ – ☐
9.00 – **5 rm** ✳85.00 – ✳✳85.00.
  ♦ 16C part timbered coaching inn. Log fire in bar and beamed ceiling in restaurant. Eclectically influenced range of menus. Comfortable, individually furnished bedrooms.

HORNINGSEA Cambs. – see Cambridge.

HORN'S CROSS Devon 503 H 31 Great Britain G. – ✉ Bideford.

Exc. : *Clovelly*✶✶, *W : 6½ m. on A 39 and B 3237 – Bideford : Bridge*✶✶ *- Burton Art Gallery*✶
AC - Lundy Island✶✶ *(by ferry), NE : 7 m. on a 39 and B 3235 – Hartland : Hartland Church*✶
- Hartland Quay✶ *(☀✶✶) - Hartland Point* ≼✶✶✶, *W : 9 m. on A 39 and B 3248 – Great
Torrington (Dartington Crystal*✶ *AC), SE 15 m. on A 39 and A 386 – Rosemoor*✶, *SE : 16 m.
on A 39, A 386 and B 3220.*
London 222 – Barnstaple 15 – Exeter 46.

⌂ **The Roundhouse** without rest., EX39 5DN, West : 1 m. on A 39 ☎ (01237) 451687,
enquiries@the-round-house.co.uk, Fax (01237) 451924, ☞ – ☼ **P**. **MC** **AE** **VISA**
3 rm ☐ ✳40.00 – ✳✳65.00.
  ♦ Located on site of 13C corn mill, this friendly guesthouse offers cream teas on arrival!
Spacious lounge and good quality breakfasts. Comfy, clean, well-kept bedrooms.

🔟 **The Hoops Inn** with rm, EX39 5DL, West : ½ m. on A 39 ☎ (01237) 451222, *sales@hoop
sinn.co.uk, Fax* (01237) 451247, ☎, ☞ – ☼ **P**. **MC** rest, **P** – ⣿ 160. **MC** **VISA**
Rest 25.00 and a la carte 15.00/35.00 ♀ – **13 rm** ☐ ✳55.00/65.00 – ✳✳95.00.
  ♦ Dating from 13C, this archetypal thatched Devonshire inn has timbers, thick cob walls
and oak panels. Menus feature quality local produce. Comfortable rooms.

HORRINGER Suffolk 504 W 27 – see Bury St Edmunds.

HORSHAM W. Sussex 504 T 30 – pop. 47 804.

📍₈, 📍₈ *Fullers, Hammerpond Rd, Mannings Heath* ☎ (01403) 210228.
🄱 *9 Causeway* ☎ (01403) 211661, *tourist.information@horsham.gov.uk.*
London 39 – Brighton 23 – Guildford 20 – Lewes 25 – Worthing 20.

🏨 **South Lodge** ☙, Brighton Rd, Lower Beeding, RH13 6PS, Southeast : 5 m. on A 281
☎ (01403) 891711, *enquiries@southlodgehotel.co.uk, Fax* (01403) 892289, ≼, ₁₆, 📍₈, ☜,
☞, 🔥, ⅍ – ☼ rest, **P** – ⣿ 160. **MC** **AE** **VISA**
Rest (booking essential for non-residents) 18.00/46.00 ♀ – ☐ 15.00 – **41 rm** ✳229.00 –
✳✳229.00, 3 suites.
  ♦ Victorian mansion in 93 acres of immaculate gardens and parkland, overlooking South
Downs. Opulent yet relaxed antique furnished public areas. Charming individual bedrooms.
Rich, refined dining room includes tapestry hung walls.

🍴🍴 **Les Deux Garçons**, Piries Pl, RH12 1DF, ☎ (01403) 271125, *info@lesdeuxgarcons.com,*
Fax (01403) 271022 – ☼ ▤. **MC** **AE** **VISA**
closed Sunday and Monday – **Rest** a la carte 19.10/41.90 ♀.
  ♦ A low sloped ceiling and candles enhance the appeal of this casually informal restaurant.
Menus range widely within a strong Gallic base: from menu rapide to gourmet.

🍴🍴 **Stan's Way House**, 3 Stans Way, East St, RH12 1HU, ☎ (01403) 255688, *sl@stansway
house.co.uk, Fax* (01403) 266144 – ☼. **MC** **AE** **VISA**
closed 2 weeks summer, 1 week Christmas, Sunday, Monday and Bank Holidays – **Rest**
19.95/28.50 ♀.
  ♦ Attractive part 15C building: upstairs restaurant is in striking, vaulted room with beamed
ceiling: rustic, yet modern. Relaxed service. Well-priced, modish European menus.

at Slinfold *West : 4 m. by A 281 off A 264 – ✉ Horsham.*

🏠 **Random Hall**, Stane St, RH13 0QX, West : ½ m. on A 29 ☎ (01403) 790558, *nigelrandom
hall@btconnect.com, Fax* (01403) 791046 – ☼ **P**. **MC** **VISA** . ✄
closed 2 weeks Christmas-New Year and last week August – **Rest** (residents only) (dinner
only) ♀ – **13 rm** ☐ ✳80.00 – ✳✳99.00.
  ♦ Restored part 16C farmhouse characterised by books, paintings, nooks and crannies.
The Tudor bar boasts oak beams and flagstone flooring; beams continue through to
bedrooms.

HORWICH Lancs. 502 504 M 23 – ⊠ Bolton.
London 217 – Liverpool 35 – Manchester 21 – Preston 16.

Whites, The Reebok Stadium, (Car Park A), De Havilland Way, BL6 6SF, Southeast : 2½ m. by A 673 on A 6027 ℰ (01204) 667788, *whites@devere-hotels.com, Fax* (01204) 673721, 🛎, 🕰, �, 📶 – 🕸 ✻, 🍴 rest, ↺ 🎽 – ⚿ 1700. 🆗 🆎 ⓪ 𝘝𝘐𝘚𝘈.
Brasserie at Whites : Rest 20.00 and a la carte 19.65/33.40 s. ♀ – (see also **Reflections** below) – **119 rm** ⚿ ✚89.00/135.00 – ✚✚99.00/155.00, 6 suites.
♦ Modern business hotel, uniquely part of Bolton Wanderers' football stadium. Well equipped all round with good, modern bedrooms. Corporate clients can use stadium facilities. Brasserie at Whites is a "must" for Wanderers fans.

Express by Holiday Inn without rest., 3 Arena Approach, BL6 6LB, Southeast : 2½ m. by A 673 on A 6027 ℰ (01204) 469111, *ebhi-bolton@btconnect.com, Fax* (01204) 469222 – 🕸 ✻ ↺ 🎽 – ⚿ 25. 🆗 🆎 ⓪ 𝘝𝘐𝘚𝘈. ✻
74 rm ✚59.95 – ✚✚59.95.
♦ Simple good quality furnishings in brightly decorated rooms with ample work space. Contemporary styling throughout and two popular grill restaurants adjacent.

Reflections (at Whites H.), The Reebok Stadium (car park A), De Havilland Way, BL6 6SF, ℰ (01204) 667788, *Fax* (01204) 673721 – 🕸 ✻ 🍴 🎽. 🆗 🆎 ⓪ 𝘝𝘐𝘚𝘈
closed Sunday-Tuesday – **Rest** (dinner only and Sunday lunch)/dinner a la carte 28.15/46.45 ♀.
♦ Notable for its elevated position overlooking the pitch at the Reebok Stadium. Formal dining experience, though dishes have a distinctly modern, original style.

> The ⦿ award is the crème de la crème.
> This is awarded to restaurants
> which are really worth travelling miles for!

HOUGH-ON-THE-HILL Lincs. – see Grantham.

HOUGHTON Cambs. – see Huntingdon.

HOUGHTON CONQUEST Beds. 504 S 27 – see Bedford.

HOVE Brighton and Hove 504 T 31 – see Brighton and Hove.

HOVINGHAM N. Yorks. 502 R 21 – ⊠ York.
London 235 – Leeds 47 – Middlesbrough 36 – York 25.

Worsley Arms, YO62 4LA, ℰ (01653) 628234, *worsleyarms@aol.com, Fax* (01653) 628130, 🌺 – ✻ 💺 🎽 – ⚿ 50. 🆗 🆎 𝘝𝘐𝘚𝘈
Cricketer's Bistro : Rest a la carte 21.75/28.70 s. ♀ – **The Restaurant :** Rest (dinner only and Sunday lunch) a la carte 21.75/28.70 s. ♀ – **19 rm** ⚿ ✚90.00/100.00 – ✚✚120.00.
♦ Part 19C coaching inn set in delightful Yorkshire stone village. Charm and character throughout the classically traditional public rooms. Comfortable individual bedrooms. Informal Cricketer's Bistro. Calm, refined Restaurant.

HUDDERSFIELD W. Yorks. 502 504 O 23 – pop. 146 234.
🏌, 🏌 Bradley Park, Bradley Rd ℰ (01484) 223772 – 🏌 Woodsome Hall, Fenay Bridge ℰ (01484) 602971 – 🏌 Outlane, Slack Lane ℰ (01422) 374762 A – 🏌 Meltham, Thick Hollins Hall ℰ (01484) 850227 – 🏌 Fixby Hall, Lightridge Rd ℰ (01484) 426203 B – 🏌 Crosland Heath, Felks Stile Rd ℰ (01484) 653216 A.
🛈 3 Albion St ℰ (01484) 223200.
London 191 – Bradford 11 – Leeds 15 – Manchester 25 – Sheffield 26.

Plans on following pages

at Thunder Bridge Southeast : 5¾ m. by A 629 – B – ⊠ Huddersfield.

Woodman Inn with rm, HD8 0PX, ℰ (01484) 605778, *thewoodman@connect free.co.uk, Fax* (01484) 604110 – ✻ rest, 🎽. 🆗 𝘝𝘐𝘚𝘈. ✻
Rest 10.50 (lunch) and a la carte 14.00/20.00 ♀ – **12 rm** ⚿ ✚45.00 – ✚✚65.00.
♦ A collection of 19C cottage style buildings, set in Last of the Summer Wine country. Freshly prepared dishes from bar or restaurant. Compact rooms in former weavers' cottages.

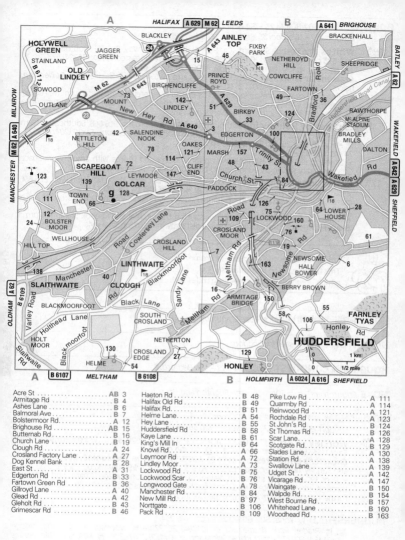

at Shelley *Southeast : 6¼ m. by A 629 – B – on B 6116 –* ⊠ *Huddersfield.*

    The Three Acres, Roydhouse, HD8 8LR, Northeast : 1½ m. on Flockton rd   ℰ *(01484)*
602606, *3acres@globalnet.co.uk, Fax (01484) 608411,* ⌂, ⇔ – ⇼ rest, ▤ rest, ℙ. ◑ ◐ ℍ
VISA. ✦

closed 25 December-3 January – **Rest** *(closed Saturday lunch)* (booking essential) a la carte
25.65/45.70 – **20 rm** ⊇ ✵70.00/100.00 – ✵✵100.00/120.00.
   ◆ Well-established stone inn in rural location. Annex rooms more spacious and
quiet; those in main house closer to the bar and dining room; all warm, modern and
comfortable. Agreeably busy restaurant with open fires: fish dishes prepared at open
seafood bar.

HUDDERSFIELD

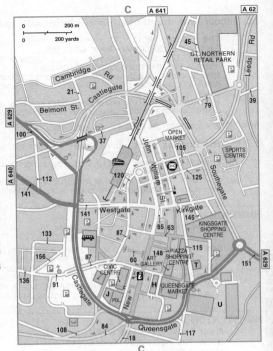

at Golcar West : 3½ m. by A 62 on B 6111 – ✉ Huddersfield.

XXX **The Weavers Shed** with rm, 88 Knowl Rd, via Scar Lane, HD7 4AN, ✆ (01484) 654284, info@weaversshed.co.uk, Fax (01484) 650980, �というロ – ⇔rest, 🅿, ⓂⓈ ΑΕ ① 𝘝𝘐𝘚𝘈   A g
closed Christmas-New Year – **Rest** (closed Saturday lunch, Sunday and Monday) 15.95
(lunch) and a la carte 33.15/48.40 ♀ – **5 rm** ⌂ ✦75.00 – ✦✦95.00.
◆ Converted 18C cloth finishing mill. Stone floored dining area with low beamed ceiling.
Select, modern British menu supplied by an extensive kitchen garden. Smart bedrooms.

The red 🐾 symbol?
This denotes the very essence of peace
– only the sound of birdsong first thing in the morning …

HULL Kingston-upon-Hull **502** S 22 – see Kingston-upon-Hull.

HUNGERFORD Newbury **503 504** P 29 *The West Country G.* – pop. 4 938.
EXC. : *Savernake Forest*★★ (*Grand Avenue*★★★), W : 7 m. by A 4 – Crofton Beam Engines★,
SW : 8 m. by A 338 and minor roads.
London 74 – Bristol 57 – Oxford 28 – Reading 26 – *Southampton* 46.

↑   **Fishers Farm** without rest., Shefford Woodlands, RG17 7AB, North : 4 m. by A 4 and
A 338 on B 4000 ✆ (01488) 648466, mail@fishersfarm.co.uk, Fax (01488) 648706, 🔲, 🌳,
♨ – ⇔ 🅿, 🌺
3 rm ⌂ ✦45.00/55.00 – ✦✦68.00/75.00.
◆ Attractive redbrick farmhouse in a rural spot on a working farm. Well-appointed sitting
room. Breakfast served family style. Individually styled rooms with country views.

at Lambourn Woodlands *North : 6 m. by A 338 on B 4000 –* ✉ *Hungerford.*

XX ❄ **The Hare,** RG17 7SD, ✆ (01488) 71386, *cuisine@theharerestaurant.co.uk,* *Fax (01488) 71186,* 🍴, 🌳 – ⇌ **P**. **MO** **AE** **VISA**
closed 25-27 December, 10 days July- August, Sunday dinner and Monday – **Rest** *(booking essential)* 25.00 (lunch) and a la carte 37.00/43.00 ☖.
Spec. Smoked duck with pickled wild mushrooms, foie gras trifle. Lobster with cannelloni, carrot and cardamom infusion. Banana Tart Tatin, caramelised walnut and parsley ice cream.
♦ Contemporary pub conversion with modish interior of three dining rooms and original beams. Building a strong local reputation based on innovative cooking of a high standard.

at Kintbury *Southeast : 3¾ m. by A 4 –* ✉ *Hungerford.*

🍴 **The Dundas Arms** with rm, Station Rd, RG17 9UT, ✆ (01488) 658263, *info@dunda sarms.co.uk, Fax (01488) 658568,* 🍴 – ⇌ **P**. **VISA** ⚥
closed 25-26 December – **Rest** *(closed Sunday and dinner Monday)* a la carte 17.00/26.00 ☖ – 5 rm 🛏 ✦80.00 – ✦✦90.00.
♦ Set on tiny island between river and canal. Unexceptional interior: the food's the thing here - tasty, accomplished, homecooked dishes. Bedrooms with small riverside terraces.

HUNSDON *Herts..*
London 26.5 – Bishop's Stortford 8.5 – Harlow 7.5.

🍴 **Fox and Hounds,** 2 High St, SG12 8NH, ✆ (01279) 843999, *info@foxandhounds-huns don.co.uk, Fax (01279) 841092,* 🍴, 🌳 – ⇌ **P**. **MO** **VISA**
closed 2 weeks late January-early February, 26 December and 1 January – **Rest** *(closed Sunday dinner and Monday)* 14.50/17.50 and a la carte 21.50/35.00 ☖.
♦ 300 year-old pub, rustic and characterful, with beams, soft sofas, open fire, books and guides. Loos accessed via trompe-l'oeil bookcases! Classical menus with global twists.

HUNSTANTON *Norfolk* 502 504 V 25 – *pop. 4 505.*
🅸🅸 *Golf Course Rd* ✆ (01485) 532811.
🅱 *Town Hall, The Green* ✆ (01485) 532610.
London 120 – Cambridge 60 – Norwich 45.

🏛 **Le Strange Arms,** Golf Course Rd, Old Hunstanton, PE36 6JJ, *North : 1 m. by A 149* ✆ (01485) 534411, *reception@lestrangearms.co.uk, Fax (01485) 534724,* ≤, 🌳 – ⇌ **P** – 🔼 150. **MO** **AE** **①** **VISA**
Rest *(bar lunch Monday-Saturday)/dinner* 25.00 and a la carte 26.00/33.00 – **44 rm** 🛏 ✦84.00 – ✦✦115.00/165.00.
♦ Imposing Georgian building with fine views across the Wash, immediate access to the beach and opposite an arts and crafts centre. Good sized, traditionally styled bedrooms. Sea view from restaurant.

⌂ **The Gables,** 28 Austin St, PE36 6AW, ✆ (01485) 532514, *bbatthegables@aol.com* – ⇌. **MO** **AE** **VISA**
Rest *(by arrangement)* 15.00 – **6 rm** 🛏 ✦33.00/46.00 – ✦✦50.00/70.00.
♦ Large Edwardian house built of traditional Norfolk stone: well located for beach and town centre. Neat guest lounge; family photos decorate hallway. Personally styled rooms. Cloth-clad dining room: extensive breakfasts and home-cooked meals.

⌂ **Claremont** without rest., 35 Greevegate, PE36 6AF, ✆ (01485) 533171, *clare montgh@tiscali.co.uk* – ⇌
mid March-mid November – **7 rm** 🛏 ✦28.00 – ✦✦56.00.
♦ Classic seaside guesthouse in a Victorian building close to beach, shops and gardens. Well-kept, traditional interior and a toaster on each table at breakfast.

at Ringstead *East : 3¾ m. by A 149 –* ✉ *Hunstanton.*

🍴 **The Gin Trap Inn** with rm, 6 High St, PE36 5JU, ✆ (01485) 525264, *gintra pinn@keme.co.uk, Fax (01485) 525321,* 🍴, 🌳 – ⇌ **P**. **MO** **VISA**
Rest a la carte 17.00/36.00 ☖ – **3 rm** 🛏 ✦80.00 – ✦✦170.00.
♦ Charming 17C inn with tasteful, uncluttered style, but with rural mainstays like beams and open fire. Lunchtime bar favourites; well executed gourmet evenings. Stylish rooms.

HUNSTRETE *Bath & North East Somerset* 503 504 M 29 – *see Bristol.*

HUNTINGDON *Cambs.* 504 T 26 – pop. 20 600 – ☞ *Hemingford Abbots, New Farm Lodge, Cambridge Rd ℰ (01480) 495000.*

🛈 *The Library, Princes St ℰ (01480) 388588.*

London 69 – Bedford 21 – Cambridge 16.

🏛 **Huntingdon Marriott,** Kingfisher Way, Hinchingbrooke Business Park, PE29 6FL, West : 1 ½ m. by A 141 at junction with A 14 ℰ (01480) 446000, *reservations.huntingdon@marriotthotels.co.uk, Fax (01480) 451111,* ɪ₆, ☎, 🔲 – ᛒ 🞲 ≒ 🖭 🗄 🄿 – 🛆 260. 🆖 🄰🄴 🄾 🆅🄸🅂🄰
Rest *(closed Saturday lunch)* (buffet lunch)/dinner 25.00 ☑ – **146 rm** � ✦125.00 – ✦✦135.00, 4 suites.
♦ Purpose-built 1990s hotel, well geared to the modern business traveller. Good standard of brand furniture in public areas and well-equipped rooms which include data ports. Smart, airy dining room.

🏛 **Old Bridge,** 1 High St, PE29 3TQ, ℰ (01480) 424300, *oldbridge@huntsbridge.co.uk, Fax (01480) 411017,* ⌂ – 🛆 50. 🆖🄰🄴 🄾 🆅🄸🅂🄰
Rest – (see **Terrace** below) – **24 rm** ⊠ ✦95.00/105.00 – ✦✦125.00/150.00.
♦ 18C former private bank overlooking the river. All bedrooms, some very contemporary, are decorated to a good standard and bathrooms often have deep Victorian-style baths.

XX **Terrace** (at Old Bridge H.), 1 High St, PE29 3TQ, ℰ (01480) 424300, *Fax (01480) 411017,* ⌂, ⌘ – 🄿. 🆖🄰🄴 🄾 🆅🄸🅂🄰
Rest 18.75 (lunch) and a la carte 23.25/33.45 s. ☑ ⌂.
♦ Two dining areas: a formal wood panelled room and a more casual conservatory with terrace. Hearty rustic Italian dishes provide the basis for menus.

at Broughton *Northeast : 6 m. by B 1514 off A 141 –* ✉ *Huntingdon.*

🍴 **The Crown,** Bridge Rd, PE28 3AY, ℰ (01487) 824428, *simon@thecrownbroughton.co.uk, Fax (01487) 824912,* ⌂, ⌘ – 🄿. 🆖 🆅🄸🅂🄰
closed first week January – **Rest** *(closed Monday-Tuesday)* 13.50 (lunch) and a la carte 19.50/27.00 ☑.
♦ Bay-windowed pub next to church in sleepy village. Uncluttered feel punctuated by bare tables and farmhouse chairs. Well-priced, modern meals with classic French base.

at Houghton *East : 3½ m. by B 1514 off A 1123 –* ✉ *Huntingdon.*

🏠 **Cheriton House** without rest., PE28 2AZ, ℰ (01480) 464004, *sales@cheritonhousecambs.co.uk, Fax (01480) 496960,* ⌘ – ≒ 🄿. 🆖 🆅🄸🅂🄰. ⌘
5 rm ✦62.00/68.00 – ✦✦68.00/88.00.
♦ Cream painted 19C house with lovely garden. Place your order overnight for memorable breakfast. Relaxing conservatory-lounge. Co-ordinated rooms with thoughtful touches.

at Hemingford Grey *Southeast : 5 m. by A 1198 off A 14 –* ✉ *Huntingdon.*

🏠 **The Willow** without rest., 45 High St, PE28 9BJ, ℰ (01480) 494748, *info@thewillowguesthouse.co.uk, Fax (01480) 464456 –* ≒ 🄿. 🆖 🆅🄸🅂🄰. ⌘
11 rm ⊠ ✦45.00 – ✦✦70.00/85.00.
♦ Very personally run guesthouse in picturesque village location: its vivid yellow exterior makes it easy to spot. Good value, and close to The Cock. Immaculately kept bedrooms.

🍴 **The Cock,** 47 High St, PE28 9BJ, ℰ (01480) 463609, *cock@cambscuisine.com, Fax (01480) 461747,* ⌂ – ≒ 🄿. 🆖 🆅🄸🅂🄰
Rest 12.95 (lunch) and a la carte 19.95/29.40 ☑.
♦ Real ale pub with spacious dining area that features a wood-burning stove and oil paintings for sale. Good choice of dishes: fresh fish or sausage selections are a speciality.

at Brampton *West : 2 m. by A 141 off A 14 on B 1514 –* ✉ *Huntingdon.*

XX **The Grange** with rm, 115 High St, PE28 4RA, ℰ (01480) 459516, *info@grangehotelbrampton.com, Fax (01480) 459391,* ⌂ – ≒ 🄿. 🆖 🆅🄸🅂🄰
closed 20-27 December and 1 week January – **Rest** *(closed Sunday and Bank Holidays)* a la carte 18.50/34.00 ☑ ⌂ – **7 rm** ⊠ ✦77.50/85.00 – ✦✦90.00/110.00.
♦ Red-brick Georgian house, once a girls' school. Light, airy dining room with trendy pale grey walls. Well executed classic and modern menus. Colourful, contemporary rooms.

at Spaldwick *West : 7½ m. by A 141 off A 14 –* ✉ *Huntingdon.*

🍴 **The George,** 5 High St, PE28 0TD, ℰ (01480) 890293, *Fax (01480) 896847,* ⌂ – ≒ 🖭 🄿. 🆖 🆅🄸🅂🄰. ⌘
closed dinner 25, 26 December and 1 January – **Rest** a la carte 20.00/32.00 ☑.
♦ Built in the early 1500s, now sporting lilac and aubergine walls and an imposing fireplace. Characterful beamed restaurant: menus mix modern European with home-grown classics.

HUNTON *Kent* 504 V 30 – ⊠ *Maidstone.*
   London 37 – Canterbury 28 – Folkestone 34 – Hastings 35 – Maidstone 5.

⌂   **Goldings** ⌘ without rest., ME15 0SG, Pass the school and sharp bend, left after Durrants Cottage down unmarked drive ℘ (01622) 820758, *goldingsoast@btinternet.com*, Fax (01622) 850754, 🌳, 🔌 – ⥲ **P**.
   closed 20 December-20 January – **3 rm** ⊐ ★50.00/60.00 – ★★75.00/85.00.
   ◆ Built in 1840 for drying hops; set in 100 riverside acres on arable working farm. Striking façade; simpler interior: relaxed guest lounge, and airy, modern, well-fitted rooms.

HURLEY *Berks..*
   London 35.5 – Maidenhead 5.5 – Reading 18.

🏮   **Black Boys Inn** with rm, Henley Rd, SL6 5NQ, Southwest : 1 ½ m. on A 4130 ℘ (01628) 824212, *info@blackboysinn.co.uk*, 🌳 – ⥲ 😾 **P**. 🐾
   closed 17-25 April, last week August and 1 week from 24 December – **Rest** *(closed Sunday dinner and Monday)* a la carte 22.50/31.70 ♀ – **8 rm** ⊐ ★65.00/75.00 – ★★95.00/105.00.
   ◆ 16C inn: delightful modernised interior, with sage walls and central fire. Restaurant ambience. Well-priced menus: Newlyn fish, game from Hambledon Estate. Characterful rooms.

HURST *Berks.* 503 504 Q 29 – *see Reading.*

HURSTBOURNE TARRANT *Hants.* 503 504 P 30 – ⊠ *Andover.*
   London 77 – Bristol 77 – Oxford 38 – Southampton 33.

🏛   **Esseborne Manor** ⌘, SP11 0ER, Northeast : 1 ½ m. on A 343 ℘ (01264) 736444, *info@esseborne-manor.co.uk*, Fax (01264) 736725, 🌳, ※ – ⥲ rest, 😾 **P** – 🔒 60. 🆗 ᴀᴇ
   ⓞ 🆅🅸🆂🅰
   Rest 18.00/22.00 and a la carte 25.00/40.50 s. ♀ – **20 rm** ⊐ ★95.00/105.00 – ★★180.00/240.00.
   ◆ 100 year old country house in attractive grounds with herb garden. Smart, well-appointed bedrooms, three in garden cottages. Ferndown room boasts a spa bath and private patio. Long, narrow dining room with large windows.

HURST GREEN *Lancs.* 502 M 22 – ⊠ *Clitheroe.*
   London 236 – Blackburn 12 – Burnley 13 – Preston 12.

🏛   **Shireburn Arms,** Whalley Rd, BB7 9QJ, on B 6243 ℘ (01254) 826518, *sales@shireburnarmshotel.com*, Fax (01254) 826208, 🌳, 🌳 – ⥲ rest, 😾 **P**. 🆗 ᴀᴇ 🆅🅸🆂🅰
   Rest 9.95 and a la carte 15.20/28.65 ♀ – **22 rm** ⊐ ★45.00/70.00 – ★★80.00/120.00, 1 suite.
   ◆ Ivy clad 17C former farmhouse located in a charming village. Traditional cottage décor and views of the Ribble valley. Reputedly haunted by a long deceased nun. Strong showing of local ingredients in dining room; good valley outlook, too.

HUSTHWAITE *N. Yorks. Great Britain G.*
   Exc. : *Castle Howard★★, E : 15 m. by minor roads.*
   London 230 – Easingwold 4 – Leeds 41 – Thirsk 8.

✕   **The Roasted Pepper,** Low St, YO61 4QA, ℘ (01347) 868007, *info@roastedpepper.co.uk*, Fax (01347) 868776, 🌳 – **P**. 🆗 🆅🅸🆂🅰 🐾
   Rest *(closed Sunday dinner and Monday)* a la carte 15.00/25.00 ♀.
   ◆ Immaculately whitewashed and refurbished village pub. Chunky wood tables give it the ambience of rustic restaurant. Good value, Mediterranean themed dishes. Friendly service.

HUTTON-LE-HOLE *N. Yorks.* 502 R 21.
   London 244 – Scarborough 27 – York 33.

⌂   **Burnley House** without rest., YO62 6UA, ℘ (01751) 417548, *info@burnleyhouse.co.uk*, 🌳 – ⥲ **P**
   6 rm ⊐ ★50.00 – ★★80.00.
   ◆ Attractive part 16C, part Georgian house, Grade II listed in a picturesque Moors village. Brown trout in beck winding through garden. Simple, individually styled bedrooms.

HUTTON MAGNA *Durham Great Britain G. – pop. 86.*
   Env. : *Raby Castle★, N : 5 m. by B 6274.*
   Exc. : *Richmond★, S : 8 m. by B 6274 – Bowes Museum★, W : 8 m. by A 66.*
   London 258 – Darlington 17 – Newcastle upon Tyne 53 – Scarborough 75.

🍴🛏 **Oak Tree Inn,** DL11 7HH, 𝒫 (01833) 627371 – **MC** **VISA**
🐌 *closed 25-26 December and 1 January* – **Rest** *(closed Monday)* (dinner only) a la carte 24.00/32.50.
◆ Part 18C inn in an unspoilt rural location. Interior beams and stone walls with homely décor. Blackboard menus offering a good range of modern pub dishes.

HUTTON ROOF *Cumbria – see Kirkby Lonsdale.*

HYTHE *Kent* 504 X 30 – *pop. 14 766.*
🏌 *Sene Valley, Sene, Folkestone 𝒫 (01303) 268513.*
🛈 *Visitor Centre, Railway Station 𝒫 (01303) 266421.*
London 68 – Folkestone 6 – Hastings 33 – Maidstone 31.

Plan : see Folkestone

🏰 **Hythe Imperial,** Prince's Parade, CT21 6AE, 𝒫 (01303) 267441, hytheimperial@mar stonhotels.com, Fax (01303) 264610, ≤, 🏡, 🕲, 𝕝₆, ☎, 🗔, 🏐, ⌖, 🔥, ⚒, squash – 📱 ✎
♿ 🖭 – 🕿 220. **MC** **AE** ① **VISA**. ✜
                                                                              X d
The Princes Room : **Rest** 14.50/25.50 and dinner a la carte approx 36.00 ⚑ – ⚌ 14.95 – 100 rm ⚌ ✦99.00/125.00 – ✦✦149.00/199.00.
◆ Set in a 50 acre estate, this classic Victorian hotel retains the elegance of a former age. Wide range of bedrooms cater for everyone from families to business travellers. Spacious restaurant with classic style and menus to match.

✗ **Hythe Bay,** Marine Parade, CT21 6AW, 𝒫 (01303) 233844, Fax (01303) 230651, ≤, 🏡 –
✜✎ 🖭, **MC** **AE** ① **VISA**
Rest - Seafood - (buffet lunch Sunday) a la carte 19.55/30.35.
◆ Originally built as tea rooms and in a great position just feet from the beach. Bright, airy room with views out to Channel. Seafood menus - ideal for lunch on a summer's day.

ICKLESHAM *E. Sussex* 504 V/W 31.
London 66 – Brighton 42 – Hastings 7.

🏠 **Manor Farm Oast** ⚘, Workhouse Lane, TN36 4AJ, South : ½ m. 𝒫 (01424) 813787, manor.farm.oast@lineone.net, Fax (01424) 813787, 🐜 – ✜✎ ⚒ **MC** ① **VISA**. ✜
closed Christmas and January – **Rest** (by arrangement) 29.50 – **3 rm** ⚌ ✦60.00/94.00.
◆ 19C former oast house retaining original features and surrounded by orchards. Welcoming beamed lounge with open fire. One of the comfy bedrooms is completely in the round! Home-cooked menus in circular dining room.

IFFLEY *Oxon. – see Oxford.*

IGHTHAM COMMON *Kent – see Sevenoaks.*

ILCHESTER *Somerset* 503 L 30 – *pop. 2 123.*
London 138 – Bridgwater 21 – Exeter 48 – Taunton 24 – Yeovil 5.

🍴🛏 **Ilchester Arms** with rm, The Square, BA22 8LN, 𝒫 (01935) 840220, Fax (01935) 841353, 🍽 – ✜✎ 🖭 **AE** **VISA**. ✜
closed 26 December – **Rest** *(closed Sunday dinner)* a la carte 17.50/26.50 ⚑ – **7 rm** ⚌ ✦60.00 – ✦✦75.00.
◆ Attractive-looking, ivy-covered 18C coaching inn. Relaxing, intimate public areas enhanced by flagstone flooring in bar. Hearty bistro menus. Clean and comfy bedrooms.

ILFRACOMBE *Devon* 503 H 30 *Great Britain G.*
Env. : *Mortehoe*★★ : *St Mary's Church - Morte Point*★, *SW : 5 ½ m. on B 3343 – Lundy Island*★★ (by ferry).
Exc. : *Braunton : St Brannock's Church*★, *Braunton Burrows*★, *S : 8 m. on A 361 – Barnstaple*★ : *Bridge*★, *S : 12 m. on A 3123, B 3230, A 39, A 361 and B 3233.*
London 218 – Barnstaple 13 – Exeter 53.

✗✗ **The Quay,** 11 The Quay, EX34 9EQ, 𝒫 (01271) 868090, info@11thequay.com, Fax (01271) 865599, ≤, 🏡 – ✜✎ **MC** **AE** ① **VISA**
– Atlantic Dining Room : **Rest** 17.50 (lunch) and dinner a la carte 23.50/35.00 ⚑ **– White Hart Bar :** **Rest** 13.50 and a la carte 15.00/30.00.
◆ Handsome 18C brick harbourside building, part owned by Damien Hirst. Cool, modish interior, typified by plethora of Hirst artworks. Sea views and modern cooking in Atlantic. White Hart Bar serves modern British dishes and offers harbour vistas.

ILKLEY W. Yorks. 502 O 22 – pop. 13 472.

Myddleton ♦ (01943) 607277.

Station Rd ♦ (01943) 602319.

London 210 – Bradford 13 – Harrogate 17 – Leeds 16 – Preston 46.

Rombalds, 11 West View, Wells Rd, LS29 9JG, ♦ (01943) 603201, reception@rombalds.demon.co.uk, Fax (01943) 816586 – ⇆ 🄿 – 🛗 70. 🆗 AE ⓪ 𝘝𝘐𝘚𝘈

closed 28 December-8 January – **Rest** 12.95 (lunch) and a la carte 15.50/31.00 **s**. – **15 rm** ⫩ ✦65.00/93.00 – ✦✦85.00/105.00, 4 suites.

♦ Privately owned Georgian town house on edge of Moor. Elegant fixtures and fittings adorn its sitting room. Individually styled bedrooms have matching fabrics and drapes. Yorkshire produce to fore in cool blue restaurant.

XXX **Box Tree** (Gueller), 37 Church St, LS29 9DR, on A 65 ♦ (01943) 608484, info@theboxtree.co.uk, Fax (01943) 607186 – ⇆ ≣ ⇔ 14. 🆗 ⓪ 𝘝𝘐𝘚𝘈

❀ closed 1-4 January, late July to early August, Sunday dinner and Monday – **Rest** (dinner only and lunch Friday-Sunday)/dinner 28.00 and a la carte 39.50/54.50 ⥥.

Spec. Nage of scallops with langoustine, cucumber, ginger and basil. Roast turbot with clam velouté. Fillet of Yorkshire beef, wild mushrooms, spinach, bacon and ceps.

♦ Stone farmhouse built in 1720. Antiques, ornaments and oils adorn lounges and restaurant. Light, delicate cuisine with classic French and English combinations.

ILLOGAN Cornwall 503 E 33 The West Country G. – ✉ Redruth.

Env. : Portreath★, NW : 2 m. by B 3300 – Hell's Mouth★, SW : 5 m. by B 3301.

London 305 – Falmouth 14 – Penzance 17 – Truro 11.

Aviary Court ♿, Mary's Well, TR16 4QZ, Northwest : ¾ m. by Alexandra Rd ♦ (01209) 842256, info@aviarycourthotel.co.uk, Fax (01209) 843744, 🌫, ✗ – ⇆ 🄿. 🆗 𝘝𝘐𝘚𝘈 ✻

Rest (closed Sunday dinner to non-residents) (dinner only and Sunday lunch)/dinner 17.75 – **6 rm** ⫩ ✦50.00/75.00 – ✦✦77.00.

♦ Tranquillity reigns at this cosy Cornish hotel with its neat, well-kept gardens. Traditional ambience prevails throughout with colourful furnishings and traditional rooms. Cornish ingredients dominate cuisine.

ILMINGTON Warks. 504 O 27 Great Britain G.

Env. : Hidcote Manor Garden★★, SW : 2 m. by minor rd – Chipping Campden★★, SW : 4 m. by minor rd.

London 91 – Birmingham 31 – Oxford 34 – Stratford-upon-Avon 9.

Folly Farm Cottage without rest., Back St, CV36 4LJ, ♦ (01608) 682425, Fax (01608) 682425, 🌫 – ⇆ 🄿. ✻

closed Christmas and New Year – **3 rm** ⫩ ✦45.00 – ✦✦60.00/84.00.

♦ Welcoming, cosy guesthouse with snug interior. Notable, sunny seating area in rear garden. Spacious breakfast room. Immaculate bedrooms, where breakfast may also be taken.

The Howard Arms with rm, Lower Green, CV36 4LT, ♦ (01608) 682226, info@howardarms.com, Fax (01608) 682226, 🍴, 🌫 – ⇆, ≣ rest, 🄿. 🆗 𝘝𝘐𝘚𝘈 ✻

closed 25 December – **Rest** a la carte 21.00/28.00 ⫩ ⥥ – **3 rm** ⫩ ✦85.00 – ✦✦130.00.

♦ Cotswold stone inn facing village green. Spacious pub with various rooms and snugs. Good British pub cooking; varied blackboard menu. Bright rooms with modern facilities.

ILMINSTER Somerset 503 L 31 The West Country G. – pop. 4 451.

See : Town★ – Minster★★.

Env. : Barrington Court Gardens★ AC, NE : 3½ m. by B 3168 – Chard (Museum★), S : 6 m. by B 3168 and A 358.

London 145 – Taunton 12 – Yeovil 17.

at Cricket Malherbie South : 2½ m. by Chard rd – ✉ Ilminster.

The Old Rectory ♿, TA19 0PW, ♦ (01460) 54364, info@malherbie.co.uk, Fax (01460) 57374, 🌫 – 🄿. 🆗 𝘝𝘐𝘚𝘈 ✻

closed Christmas – **Rest** (by arrangement) (communal dining) 30.00 – **5 rm** ⫩ ✦65.00 – ✦✦105.00.

♦ Warmly run 16C thatched house in enticingly tranquil spot off beaten track. Delightful gardens. Carved oak beams draw you into sitting room's deep sofas. Inviting bedrooms. Home-cooked meals.

ENGLAND

INGLETON N. Yorks. 502 M 21 – pop. 1 641 – ⊠ Carnforth (Lancs.).
🛈 The Community Centre 𝒫 (015242) 41049.
London 266 – Kendal 21 – Lancaster 18 – Leeds 53.

Pines Country House, Kendal Rd, LA6 3HN, Northwest : ¼ m. on A 65 𝒫 (015242) 41252, pineshotel@aol.com, Fax (015242) 41252, ⇌s, 🚗 – ⅍ 🅿 ◍◍ 𝓥𝓘𝓢𝓐. ⅍
February-October – **Rest** (booking essential) (residents only) (dinner only) 16.00 – **8 rm** ⊊ ✱45.00 – ✱✱60.00/64.00.
♦ Spacious early Victorian house, set on busy main road, near White Scar caves. Homely lounge. Good-sized, immaculately kept rooms. Conservatory dining room with fell views.

Riverside Lodge, 24 Main St, LA6 3HJ, 𝒫 (015242) 41359, info@riversideingle ton.co.uk, ⩽, ⇌s, 🚗 – ⅍ 🅿 ◍◍ 𝓥𝓘𝓢𝓐. ⅍
closed 24-25 December – **Rest** (by arrangement) 15.00 – **7 rm** ⊊ ✱37.00 – ✱✱54.00.
♦ Pleasant 19C house close to famous pot-holing caves. Conservatory dining room with great views across Yorkshire Dales. Informal gardens. Cosy sitting room and homely bedrooms.

Good food and accommodation at moderate prices?
Look for the Bib symbols:
red Bib Gourmand 🍴 for food, blue Bib Hotel 🏠 for hotels

INSTOW Devon 503 H 30 – see Bideford.

IPSWICH Suffolk 504 X 27 Great Britain G. – pop. 138 718.
Exc. : Sutton Hoo★, NE : 12 m. by A 12 Y and B 1083 from Woodbridge.
🐂 Rushmere, Rushmere Heath 𝒫 (01473) 725648
🐂, 🐂 Purdis Heath, Bucklesham Rd 𝒫 (01473) 727474
🐂, 🐂 Fynn Valley, Witnesham 𝒫 (01473) 785267.
🛈 St Stephens Church, St Stephens Lane 𝒫 (01473) 258070, ipswich@eetb.info.
London 76 – Norwich 43.

Plan on next page

Salthouse Harbour, 1 Neptune Quay, IP4 1AS, 𝒫 (01473) 226789, staying@salthouse harbour.co.uk, Fax (01473) 226927, ⩽, 🏠 – ▯, ⅍ rest, ✆ ⅍ 🅿 ◍◍ 𝓐𝓔 ◍ 𝓥𝓘𝓢𝓐 X a
Brasserie : Rest 14.95 (lunch) and a la carte 20.85/31.75 – **41 rm** ⊊ ✱100.00/135.00 – ✱✱130.00/145.00, 2 suites.
♦ Converted 7-storey warehouse overlooking the marina. Lounge with seagrass seats. Designer style bedrooms with modern facilities; some with good views; two penthouse suites. Modern brasserie with a Mediterranean touch.

The Gatehouse, 799 Old Norwich Rd, IP1 6LH, 𝒫 (01473) 741897, info@gatehouseho tel.co.uk, Fax (01473) 744236, 🚗 – ⅍ rest, 🅿 ◍◍ 𝓥𝓘𝓢𝓐. ⅍ Y c
closed Christmas – **Rest** (booking essential for non-residents) (dinner only) 24.00 – **9 rm** ⊊ ✱70.00/90.00 – ✱✱90.00/100.00.
♦ Regency style house in large garden on edge of town. Wood-panelled drawing room. Spacious rooms, including 4 singles, with individual colour schemes and attractive furniture. Smart dining room with cloth-clad tables at dinner.

Express by Holiday Inn without rest., Old Hadleigh Rd, Sproughton, IP8 3AR, West : 2½ m. by A 1214 and A 1071 on B 1113 𝒫 (01473) 222279, Fax (01473) 222297, 🚗 – ⅍ ⅍ 🅿 – ⅍ 30. ◍◍ 𝓐𝓔 ◍ 𝓥𝓘𝓢𝓐. ⅍
49 rm ✱46.95/64.95 – ✱✱46.95/64.95.
♦ A modern hotel within easy reach of the A12 and A14 junction, not far from the town centre. The Beagle Inn next door serves popular grill dishes. Well-equipped bedrooms.

Sidegate Guest House without rest., 121 Sidegate Lane, IP4 4JB, 𝒫 (01473) 728714, bookings@sidegateguesthouse.co.uk, 🚗 – ⅍ ✆ 🅿 Y a
closed Christmas – **5 rm** ⊊ ✱42.00/52.00 – ✱✱62.00.
♦ Compact, friendly guesthouse in residential area. Comfy lounge with terraced doors onto garden. Neatly laid breakfast room. Well-kept, cosy rooms.

319

IPSWICH

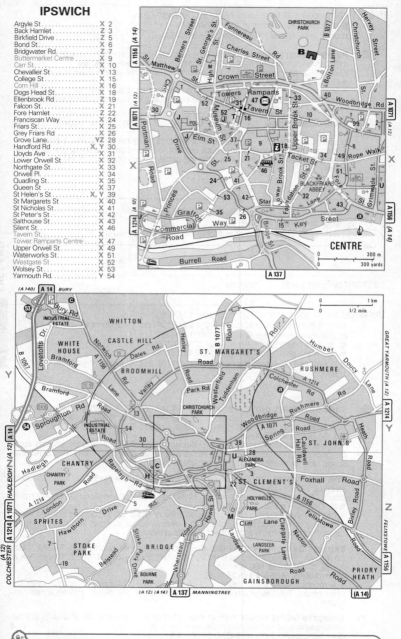

Look out for red symbols, indicating particularly pleasant establishments.

320

at Hintlesham West : 5 m. by A 1214 on A 1071 – Y – ⊠ Ipswich.

Hintlesham Hall ⊗, IP8 3NS, ℰ (01473) 652334, reservations@hintleshamhall.com, Fax (01473) 652463, ≼, ②, ₤₆, ≋s, ⊒ heated, ₁₆, ☞, ℗, ℀ – ᵗ⋇ rest, ℙ – 🚗 80. ◖◗ ◭ **VISA**
Rest 31.50/47.00 and a la carte 40.00/57.50 s. ♀ – ☟ 19.00 – **31 rm** ☟ ₮150.00 – ₮₮275.00, 2 suites.
♦ Grand and impressive Georgian manor house of 16C origins set in parkland with golf course. Stuart carved oak staircase. Ornate wedding room. Individually decorated rooms. Opulent room for fine dining.

IRONBRIDGE Wrekin 503 504 M 26 Great Britain G. – pop. 1 560.
See : Ironbridge Gorge Museum★★ AC (The Iron Bridge★★, Coalport China Museum★★, Blists Hill Open Air Museum★★, Museum of the Gorge and Visitor Centre★).
🛈 Ironbridge Gorge Museum Trust ℰ (01952) 884391, info@ironbridge.org.uk.
London 135 – Birmingham 36 – Shrewsbury 18.

Severn Lodge ⊗ without rest., New Rd, TF8 7AU, ℰ (01952) 432147, julia@severn lodge.com, Fax (01952) 432812, ☞ – ᵗ⋇ ℙ. ℀
closed 8 December-January – **3 rm** ☟ ₮65.00 – ₮₮95.00.
♦ Redbrick Georgian detached house with garden overlooking Iron Bridge, a World Heritage site. Quiet position. Cosy breakfast room. Antiques and pine furnishings in bedrooms.

The Library House without rest., 11 Severn Bank, TF8 7AN, ℰ (01952) 432299, info@li braryhouse.com, Fax (01952) 433967, ☞ – ᵗ⋇. ◖◗ **VISA**. ℀
4 rm ☟ ₮60.00/70.00 – ₮₮80.00.
♦ Nicely hidden, albeit tricky to find, guesthouse with rear terrace. Homely sitting room. Cottage style breakfast room. Compact, comfy rooms, with a touch of style about them.

Bridge House without rest., Buildwas Rd, TF8 7BN, West : 2 m. on B 4380 ℰ (01952) 432105, Fax (01952) 432105, ☞ – ℙ. ◖◗ **VISA**. ℀
closed December and January – **4 rm** ☟ ₮52.00/55.00 – ₮₮70.00/75.00.
♦ Characterful 17C cottage with interesting turn of 20C machines in garden. Comfy reception room, fine collection of local objects and photos. Individually decorated rooms.

da Vinci's, 26 High St, TF8 7AD, ℰ (01952) 432250 – ᵗ⋇. ◖◗ **VISA**
closed 1 week Christmas, 1 week spring, Sunday and Monday – **Rest** - Italian - (booking essential) (dinner only) 20.00 and a la carte 19.85/37.85.
♦ Buzzy, personally run town centre restaurant with its rustic interior, painted boards, exposed brickwork and framed Leonardo prints. Tasty, authentic Italian cooking.

ISLE OF MAN I.O.M. 502 FG 21 – see Man (Isle of).

ITTERINGHAM Norfolk – ⊠ Aylsham.
London 126 – Cromer 11 – Norwich 17.

Walpole Arms, The Common, NR11 7AR, ℰ (01263) 587258, goodfood@thewalpo learms.co.uk, Fax (01263) 587074, ☔, ☞ – ℙ. ◖◗ **VISA**
closed 25 December – **Rest** (closed Sunday dinner) a la carte 21.50/25.00 ♀.
♦ Charming, friendly, part 18C inn. Seasonal British menu draws intelligently on global ideas: dine at linen-clad parlour tables or in inviting, oak-beamed bar. Regional ale.

IVYCHURCH Kent 504 W 30 Great Britain G.
Exc. : Rye Old Town★★ : Mermaid St★ - St Mary's Church (≼★), SW : 9 m. on A 2070 and A 259.
London 67 – Ashford 11 – Rye 10.

Olde Moat House ⊗ without rest., TN29 0AZ, Northwest : ¾ m. on B 2070 ℰ (01797) 344700, oldemoathouse@hotmail.com, ☞ – ᵗ⋇ ℙ. ◖◗ **VISA**. ℀
3 rm ☟ ₮40.00/60.00 – ₮₮60.00/95.00.
♦ Blissfully characterful guesthouse with 15C origins, set in over three acres, encircled by small moat. Beamed sitting room with inglenook. Individual, homely styled rooms.

IXWORTH Suffolk 504 W 27 – see Bury St Edmunds.

JERSEY C.I. 503 OP 33 and 517 ⑩ ⑪ – see Channel Islands.

JEVINGTON E. Sussex 504 U 31 – see Eastbourne.

KEGWORTH *Derbs.* **502 503 405** Q 25 *Great Britain G.*

Exc. : Calke Abbey★, SW : 7 m. by A 6 (northbound) and A 453 (southbound) – Derby★ -
Museum and Art Gallery★, Royal Crown Derby Museum★, NW : 9 m. by A 50 – Nottingham
Castle Museum★, N : 11 m. by A 453 and A 52.
London 123 – Leicester 18 – Loughborough 6 – Nottingham 13.

▥ **Kegworth House,** 42 High St, DE74 2DA, ℘ (01509) 672575, tony@kegworth
house.co.uk, Fax (01509) 670645, 〰 – ✦ **P**. **MO** **AE** **VISA**
closed Christmas – **Rest** (by arrangement) 25.00 – **11 rm** ⇔ ✦75.00 – ✦✦125.00/195.00.
♦ Georgian manor house in village, secluded in walled garden. Fine interior with original
decorative features. Individually-decorated bedrooms of charm and character. Home
cooking by arrangement.

KELSALE *Suffolk* **504** Y 27 – ⊠ Saxmundham.
London 103 – Cambridge 68 – Ipswich 23 – Norwich 37.

⌂ **Mile Hill Barn** without rest., North Green, IP17 2RG, North : 1 ½ m. on (main) A 12
℘ (01728) 668519, mail@mile-hill-barn.co.uk, 〰 – ✦ **P**. ⅏
3 rm ⇔ ✦65.00/75.00 – ✦✦80.00/100.00.
♦ Converted 16C barn well placed for glorious Suffolk countryside. Timbered ceiling in-
vokes rustic feel in pleasant lounge. Comfy bedrooms with pine and chintz furnishings.

KENDAL *Cumbria* **502** L 21 *Great Britain G.* – pop. 28 030.
Env. : Levens Hall and Garden★ AC, S : 4½ m. by A 591, A 590 and A 6.
Exc. : Lake Windermere★★, NW : 8 m. by A 5284 and A 591.
▤ The Heights ℘ (01539) 723499.
🛈 Town Hall, Highgate ℘ (01539) 725758.
London 270 – Bradford 64 – Burnley 63 – Carlisle 49 – Lancaster 22 – Leeds 72 – Mid-
dlesbrough 77 – Newcastle upon Tyne 104 – Preston 44 – Sunderland 88.

⌂ **Beech House** without rest., 40 Greenside, LA9 4LD, by All Hallows Lane ℘ (01539)
720385, stay@beechhouse-kendal.co.uk, Fax (01539) 724082, 〰 – ✦ **V** **P**. **MO** **①** **VISA**.
⅏
closed 24-26 December – **6 rm** ⇔ ✦50.00/60.00 – ✦✦70.00/90.00.
♦ Tasteful and stylish semi-detached Georgian villa. Open-plan lounge; communal breakfasts. Individually decorated rooms are particularly tasteful and comfortable.

XX **One Bridge Street,** Bridge St, LA9 7DD, ℘ (01539) 738855, info@bridgehouseken
dal.co.uk, Fax (01539) 738855 – ✦. **P**. **MO** **AE** **VISA**
closed 25-26 December, Sunday dinner and Monday – **Rest** (lunch booking essential)
12.95/24.95.
♦ Sited within a Georgian building by the River Kent. Modern ground-floor lounge; dining
upstairs in two rooms. Menus boast a distinct local accent.

at Sizergh Southwest : 3 m. by A 391 – ⊠ Kendal.

▤ **Strickland Arms,** LA8 8DZ, ℘ (015395) 610101, Fax (015395) 61068, 🌫, 〰 – ✦ **P**.
MO **VISA**
Rest a la carte 17.90/26.90 ☺.
♦ A haven for hikers: proper refuelling guaranteed courtesy of huge portions of robust
traditional fare offered in the solid surroundings of this heartily rustic hostelry.

at Crosthwaite West : 5¼ m. by All Hallows Lane – ⊠ Kendal.

⌂ **Crosthwaite House,** LA8 8BP, ℘ (015395) 68264, bookings@crosthwaitehouse.co.uk,
Fax (015395) 68264, ≼, 〰 – ✦ **P**. **AE**
mid March-mid November – **Rest** (by arrangement) 17.00 – **6 rm** ⇔ ✦23.50/30.00 –
✦✦55.00.
♦ Comfortable Georgian style guesthouse in rural location with good views of nearby
valley and a large, rear damson orchard. Rustic décor. Spacious bedrooms have a cottage
feel. Cool dining room with shelves of curios; food from orchard.

▤ **The Punch Bowl Inn** with rm, LA8 8HR, ℘ (015395) 68237, info@the-punch
bowl.co.uk, Fax (015395) 68875, 🌫 – ✦ **P**. **MO** **AE** **VISA**. ⅏
Rest a la carte 30.00/45.00 ☺ – **9 rm** ⇔ ✦75.00/97.50 – ✦✦135.00/160.00.
♦ Superbly refurbished 17C inn with heart-warming rustic ambience. Dine at bar or in formal room: accomplished seasonal dishes strike the right note. Luxuriously stylish rooms.

Red = Pleasant. Look for the red X and ▥ symbols.

KENILWORTH Warks. 503 504 P 26 Great Britain G. – pop. 22 218.

See : Castle★ AC.

🖪 The Library, 11 Smalley Pl ℰ (01926) 748900.

London 102 – Birmingham 19 – Coventry 5 – Leicester 32 – Warwick 5.

Chesford Grange, Chesford Bridge, CV8 2LD, Southeast : 1 ¾ m. by A 452 on B 4115 ℰ (01926) 859331, chesfordgrangereservations@qhotels.co.uk, Fax (01926) 855272, ₤₅, ⬚, ≉, ₰ – 🛗 ⇔ ℃ P – 🔬 700. ⬚ 🖭 ⑩ 𝗩𝗜𝗦𝗔
Rest (closed Saturday lunch) 13.00/25.00 and dinner a la carte 13.00/35.00 s. – **209 rm** ⬚ ✦90.00/170.00 – ✦✦100.00/180.00
♦ Sizeable hotel in 17 acres of private gardens near Warwick Castle. Characterful foyer and staircase of oak. Extensive meeting facilities and leisure club. Spacious bedrooms. Smart dining room exudes comfy air.

Castle Laurels without rest., 22 Castle Rd, CV8 1NG, North : ½ m. on Stonebridge rd ℰ (01926) 856179, reception@castlelaurels.co.uk, Fax (01926) 854954 – ⇔ P. ⬚ 𝗩𝗜𝗦𝗔. ≉
– **11 rm** ⬚ ✦45.00/70.00 – ✦✦75.00/85.00.
♦ Characterful Victorian house adjacent to Kenilworth Castle. Semi-panelled entrance, stained glass windows, original tiled floor. Homely sitting room and ample sized rooms.

Victoria Lodge without rest., 180 Warwick Rd, CV8 1HU, ℰ (01926) 512020, info@victorialodgehotel.co.uk, Fax (01926) 858703, ≉ – ⇔ P. ⬚ 🖭 𝗩𝗜𝗦𝗔. ≉
closed 24 December - 2 February – **10 rm** ⬚ ✦47.00/62.00 – ✦✦70.00/80.00.
♦ Personally run hotel situated close to town centre. Small sitting room with adjacent bar. Simple and homely breakfast room. Immaculately kept, ample sized rooms.

Simply Simpsons, 101-103 Warwick Rd, CV8 1HL, ℰ (01926) 864567, info@simplysimpsons.co.uk, Fax (01926) 864510 – ⇔ 🍽 P. ⬚ 🖭 𝗩𝗜𝗦𝗔
closed 1 week Christmas, 1 week Easter, last 2 weeks August, Sunday and Monday – Rest 17.50 (lunch) and a la carte 24.15/32.00.
♦ Boasts contemporary feel, typified by striking mirrors and artwork. Good value, hearty, robust classically based dishes supplemented by tried-and-tested daily specials.

Bosquet, 97a Warwick Rd, CV8 1HP, ℰ (01926) 852463, rest.bosquet@aol.com, Fax (01926) 852463 – ⬚ 🖭 𝗩𝗜𝗦𝗔
closed 3 weeks July-August, 1 week Christmas, Sunday and Monday – Rest - French - (lunch by arrangement) 29.50 and a la carte approx 47.00.
♦ Well-established French restaurant near centre of town. Contemporary interior with wooden floor and well-spaced tables accommodating stylish leather chairs.

KENTON Exeter 503 J 31 – see Exeter.

KERNE BRIDGE Herefordshire 503 504 M 28 – see Ross-on-Wye.

KESWICK Cumbria 502 K 20 Great Britain G. – pop. 4 984.

Env. : Derwentwater★ X – Thirlmere (Castlerigg Stone Circle★), E : 1½ m. X A.

🏌 Threlkeld Hall ℰ (017687) 79324.

🖪 Moot Hall, Market Sq. ℰ (017687) 72645, seatoliertic@lake-district.gov.uk – at Seatoller, Seatoller Barn, Borrowdale ℰ (017687) 77294.

London 294 – Carlisle 31 – Kendal 30.

Plan on next page

Underscar Manor ⬚, Applethwaite, CA12 4PH, North : 1 ¾ m. by A 591 on Underscar rd ℰ (017687) 75000, Fax (017687) 74904, ≤ Derwent Water and Fells, ₤₅, ≋, ⬚, ≉, ₰ – P. ⬚ 🖭 𝗩𝗜𝗦𝗔. ≉
closed 2-4 January – Rest – (see The Restaurant below) – **11 rm** (dinner included) ⬚ ✦125.00 – ✦✦275.00.
♦ Blissfully located Victorian Italianate manor with commanding views of Derwent Water and Fells. Modern leisure centre. Large, well kept rooms.

Dale Head Hall Lakeside ⬚, Thirlmere, CA12 4TN, Southeast : 5 ¾ m. on A 591 ℰ (017687) 72478, onthelakeside@daleheadhall.co.uk, ≤ Lake Thirlmere, ≋, ≉ – ⇔ P. ⬚ 🖭 𝗩𝗜𝗦𝗔. ≉
closed 3-26 January – Rest (booking essential for non-residents) 19.50/40.00 s. ℤ – **12 rm** (dinner included) ⬚ ✦127.00/190.00 – ✦✦230.00/290.00.
♦ Wonderfully set 18C house on Lake Thirlmere. The family run friendliness lends a rich country house ambience. Log fired lounges, smart rooms. Daily changing dinner menu shows a careful touch; choose lake views or a rustic 16C dining room.

KESWICK

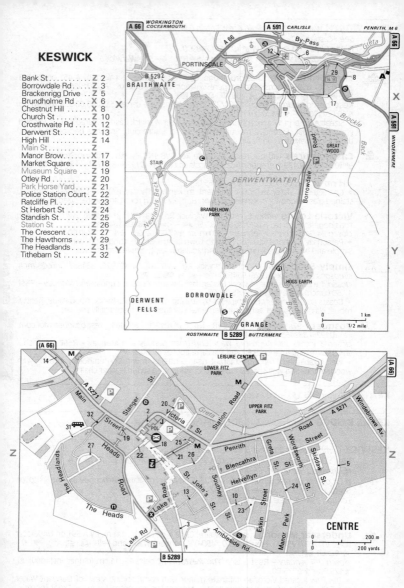

🏨 **Highfield,** The Heads, CA12 5ER, ✆ (017687) 72508, *info@highfield.co.uk,* ≼ Derwent Water and Borrowdale Valley, ♨ – ⇔⊱ 🅿, 🕮❻ 🆑 𝗩𝗜𝗦𝗔, ⋘   Z n
closed January - 13 February – **Rest** (dinner only) 32.50 🕮 – **18 rm** (dinner included) ⊆
✱65.00/120.00 – ✱✱140.00/160.00.
  ◆ Substantial, keenly run 19C house with fine views across Derwent Water to Borrowdale Valley. Most bedrooms offer the vista; all are spacious and individually decorated. Traditional restaurant has big windows and imaginatively created dishes.

Lyzzick Hall ⚐, Underskiddaw, CA12 4PY, Northwest : 2 ½ m. on A 591   ℰ (017687) 72277, *lyzzickhall@btconnect.com, Fax (017687) 72278*, ≤, ⇔s, ▣, ⬚, ☞ –⤢ ℙ. 🆖 VISA.
closed 24-26 December and January – **Rest** 27.00 (dinner) and lunch a la carte 13.75/21.50
– 31 rm ⚌ ✸54.00/74.00 – ✸✸108.00/118.00.
 ◆ Pleasant country house and gardens situated on slopes of Skiddaw. Welcoming lounge with plenty of plush chairs. Swimming pool and pretty terrace. Comfy, traditional bedrooms. L-shaped dining room filled with Lakeland pictures.

Lairbeck ⚐, Vicarage Hill, CA12 5QB,   ℰ (017687) 73373, *mg@lairbeckhotel-keswick.co.uk, Fax (017687) 73144*, ☞ –⤢ ℙ. 🆖 VISA. ℅   X a
closed December - mid March – **Rest** (residents only) (dinner only) 19.50 **– 14 rm** ⚌
✸41.00/74.00 – ✸✸82.00/112.00.
 ◆ Victorian country house with original fittings still in place: beautiful panelling and wooden staircase. Good views of Skiddaw. Homely bar and sitting room. Spacious bedrooms. Golden hued dining room with thick russet drapes.

Abacourt House without rest., 26 Stanger St, CA12 5JU,   ℰ (017687) 72967, *abacourt@btinternet.com* –⤢ ℙ. ℅   Z e
5 rm ⚌ ✸58.00 – ✸✸58.00.
 ◆ Converted Victorian town house close to town centre. Boasts original features such as pitch pine doors and staircase. Simple, cosy breakfast room. Immaculately kept bedrooms.

Claremont House without rest., Chestnut Hill, CA12 4LT,   ℰ (017687) 72089, *claremonthouse@btinternet.com*, ≤, ☞ –⤢ ℙ. ℅   X e
closed 24-26 December – **6 rm** ⚌ ✸35.00/65.00 – ✸✸50.00/65.00.
 ◆ Built 150 years ago, this former lodge house has good views over Keswick. Lounge filled with lovely prints and lithographs. Extensive breakfast menu. Spotless, homely rooms.

Acorn House without rest., Ambleside Rd, CA12 4DL,   ℰ (017687) 72553, *info@acornhousehotel.co.uk* –⤢ ℙ. 🆖 VISA. ℅   Z s
closed 1-26 December – **9 rm** ⚌ ✸45.00 – ✸✸76.00.
 ◆ Characterful Georgian house in residential part of town. Well cared for gardens are a step away from elegant, comfortable lounge. Very bright, traditional, spacious bedrooms.

The Restaurant (at Underscar Manor H.), Applethwaite, CA12 4PH, North : 1 ¾ m. by A 591 on Underscar rd   ℰ (017687) 75000, *Fax (017687) 74904*, ≤ Derwent Water and Fells, ☞, ▣ –⤢ ℙ. 🆖 AE VISA
closed 2-4 January – **Rest** 28.00/38.00 and a la carte 38.50/46.50.
 ◆ Conservatory dining room of impressive height. Formal ambience with lace clothed tables and elegant glassware. Traditional menus: à la carte with classic base.

Morrel's, 34 Lake Rd, CA12 5AQ,   ℰ (017687) 72666, *info@morrels.co.uk* –⤢. 🆖 VISA   Z x
closed 4 days Christmas and Monday – **Rest** (dinner only) a la carte 17.45/30.25.
 ◆ Pleasingly refurbished and personally run. Etched glass and vivid artwork dominate interior. Menus designed to appeal to all: an agreeable blend of traditional and modern.

at Threlkeld *East : 4 m. by A 66* – X – ✉ *Keswick.*

Scales Farm without rest., CA12 4SY, Northeast : 1 ½ m. off A 66   ℰ (017687) 79660, *scales@scalesfarm.com, Fax (017687) 79510*, ☞ –⤢ ዿ ℙ. 🆖 VISA
closed Christmas – **6 rm** ⚌ ✸35.00 – ✸✸60.00.
 ◆ Converted 17C farmhouse with much rustic charm. It boasts open stove, exposed beams and solid interior walls. Comfortable, homely sitting room. Spacious cottage style rooms.

at Borrowdale *South : on B 5289* – ✉ *Keswick.*

The Lodore Falls, CA12 5UX,   ℰ (017687) 77285, *lodorefalls@lakedistricthotels.net, Fax (017687) 77343*, ≤, ⅃₆, ⇔s, ⬚ heated, ⬚, ☞, 🜚, 🎾, squash – 🛗, ⤢ rest, ☏ ⚘ ⇔
ℙ – 🝕 120. 🆖 AE VISA   Y n
Rest (bar lunch Monday-Saturday)/dinner 32.50 ⚌ **– 72 rm** ⚌ ✸75.00/100.00 –
✸✸194.00/278.00.
 ◆ Swiss-styled exterior, in wonderfully commanding position overlooking Derwent Water; Lodore waterfalls in grounds. Leisure oriented. Choose west facing rooms overlooking lake. Llinen-clad dining room with classic Lakeland views.

at Grange-in-Borrowdale *South : 4¾ m. by B 5289* – ✉ *Keswick.*

Borrowdale Gates Country House ⚐, CA12 5UQ,   ℰ (017687) 77204, *hotel@borrowdale-gates.com, Fax (017687) 77254*, ≤ Borrowdale Valley, ☞ –⤢ rest, ℙ. 🆖 AE ⓪
VISA. ℅   Y s
restricted opening December-January – **Rest** (booking essential for non-residents) (light lunch Monday-Saturday)/dinner 34.50 and a la carte 29.75/47.75 ⚌ **– 27 rm** (dinner included) ⚌ ✸75.00/105.00 – ✸✸170.00/190.00.
 ◆ Sublime views of Borrowdale Valley greet guests at this early Victorian country house. Large slate reception leads to two open fired sitting rooms. Superior styled bedrooms. Fell views run length of pleasant dining room.

ENGLAND

at Rosthwaite South : 6 m. on B 5289 – Y – ⊠ Keswick.

🏛 **Hazel Bank Country House** ⤡, CA12 5XB, 𝄞 (017687) 77248, enquiries@hazel
bankhotel.co.uk, Fax (017687) 77373, ≤, 🌿 – ⫤ **P**. **M◎** **VISA**. ⫯
closed Christmas – **Rest** (booking essential for non-residents) (dinner only) (set menu only)
29.50 – **8 rm** (dinner included) ✦79.00/89.00. – ✦✦158.00/178.00.
♦ Panoramic fell views accentuate the isolated appeal of this very personally run 19C
country house. Original fittings; stained glass windows. Rooms have stamp of individuality.
Accomplished cuisine with daily changing set menus.

at Portinscale West : 1½ m. by A 66 – ⊠ Keswick.

🏛 **Swinside Lodge** ⤡, Newlands, CA12 5UE, South : 1 ½ m. on Grange Rd 𝄞 (017687)
72948, info@swinsidelodge-hotel.co.uk, Fax (017687) 73312, ≤ Catbells and Causey Pike,
🌿 – ⫤ **P**. **M◎** **VISA**. ⫯
X c
closed 3 weeks January – **Rest** (booking essential for non-residents) (set menu only) (dinner only) 35.00 s. – **7 rm** (dinner included) ⊡ – ✦✦196.00/216.00.
♦ Personally run 19C country house in beguilingly tranquil position close to extensive
walks with mountain views. Two comfortable lounges; well furnished, traditional rooms.
Intimate Victorian style dining room with large antique dresser.

at Braithwaite West : 2 m. by A 66 – X – ⊠ Keswick.

🏛 **Cottage in the Wood** ⤡, Whinllater Forest, CA12 5TW, Northwest : 1¾ m. on B 5292
𝄞 (017687) 78409, info@thecottageinthewood.co.uk, Fax (017687) 78064, ≤, 🌿 – ⫤ **P**.
M◎ **VISA**. ⫯
closed January – **Rest** (closed Monday) (dinner only) (set menu only) 27.50 s. – **9 rm** ⊡
✦43.00/48.00. – ✦✦66.00/110.00.
♦ Dramatically set 17C former coaching inn high up in large pine forest. Comfy, beamed
lounge with fire. Smart, updated bedrooms look out over Skiddaw or the forest. Proudly
local ingredients sourced for modern British cooking; mountain views.

KETTERING Northants. 504 R 26 – pop. 51 063.
🛈 The Coach House, Sheep St 𝄞 (01536) 410266.
London 88 – Birmingham 54 – Leicester 16 – Northampton 24.

at Rushton Northwest : 3½ m. by A 14 and Rushton Rd – ⊠ Kettering.

🏰 **Rushton Hall** ⤡, NN14 1RR, 𝄞 (01536) 713001, vhazelton@rushtonhall.com,
Fax (01536) 713010, ⤡, 🌿, ⯑, ⫯ – ⫥ ✦ **P** – 🏛 200. **M◎** **AE** **◎** **VISA**. ⫯
Rest 35.00 and a la carte 33.95/46.40 s. – **35 rm** ⊡ ✦140.00 – ✦✦140.00/280.00.
♦ Hugely imposing 15C house in quadrangle boasting delightful grounds, baronial style
sitting room of incredible proportions and immaculate bedrooms appointed most lux-
uriously. Spacious, formal dining room serving classical, wide-ranging menus.

KETTLESING N. Yorks. 502 P 21 – see Harrogate.

KETTLEWELL N. Yorks. 502 N 21.
London 246 – Darlington 42 – Harrogate 30 – Lancaster 42.

⌂ **Littlebeck** without rest., The Green, BD23 5RD, take turning at the Old Smithy shop by
the bridge 𝄞 (01756) 760378, stay@little-beck.co.uk – ⫤ **P**. ⫯
closed Christmas – **3 rm** ⊡ ✦64.00 – ✦✦64.00.
♦ Characterful stone house from 13C with Georgian façade overlooking village maypole.
Cosy lounge; extensive dales breakfast served. Attractively decorated bedrooms.

We try to be as accurate as possible when giving room rates.
But prices are susceptible to change,
so please check rates when booking.

ENGLAND

KEYSTON *Cambs.* 504 S 26 – ⊠ *Huntingdon.*
London 75 – Cambridge 29 – Northampton 24.

🍴 **Pheasant Inn,** Village Loop Rd, PE28 0RE, ℰ (01832) 710241, *thepheasant@cyber ware.co.uk, Fax (01832) 710340,* 🌭 – ⅹ P. ⓦⓞ ℀ ⓞ *VISA.* ⅹ
Rest *(closed Sunday dinner October-April)* (booking essential) a la carte 24.00/29.00 ⓨ ⅹ.
♦ Attractive thatched country inn with beams and open fires serving good monthly menu of eclectic dishes. Wood floors and country bric-a-brac complete the rustic feel.

KIBWORTH BEAUCHAMP *Leics.* – *pop. 4 788* – ⊠ *Leicester.*
London 85 – Birmingham 49 – Leicester 6 – Northampton 17.

XX **Firenze,** 9 Station St, LE8 0LN, ℰ (0116) 279 6260, *info@firenze.co.uk, Fax (0116) 279 3646* – ⓦⓞ *VISA*
closed 10 days Christmas-New Year, and Sunday – **Rest** - Italian - a la carte 18.50/55.50 ⓨ.
♦ Modern Italian restaurant in village centre. Beamed interior; contemporary décor. High-back wood-framed chairs. Expect king prawns with pancetta or quail with sage and garlic.

KIDDERMINSTER *Worcs.* 503 504 N 26 – *pop. 55 348.*
London 139 – Birmingham 17 – Shrewsbury 34 – Worcester 15.

at Chaddesley Corbett *Southeast : 4½ m. by A 448* – ⊠ *Kidderminster.*

🏰 **Brockencote Hall** ⊗, DY10 4PY, on A 448 ℰ (01562) 777876, *info@brockencote hall.com, Fax (01562) 777872,* ≤, 🌳, 🐾, Ⅹ – ⅹ ⓒ ⅽ P. – ⅔ 25. ⓦⓞ ℀ ⓞ *VISA.* ⅹ
closed 2-17 January – **Rest** – (see ***The Restaurant*** below) – **17 rm** ⊇ ★95.00/140.00 – ★★150.00/190.00.
♦ Reminiscent of a French château, a 19C mansion in extensive parkland. Pine and maple library, chintz furnished conservatory. Good-sized rooms, all unique in style and décor.

XXX **The Restaurant** (at Brockencote Hall), DY10 4PY, on A 448 ℰ (01562) 777876, *Fax (01562) 777872,* 🌳 – ⅹ P. ⓦⓞ ℀ ⓞ *VISA*
closed 2-17 January and Saturday lunch – **Rest** - French 19.00/34.50 and a la carte 30.30/44.50 **s.**
♦ Two adjacent dining rooms: impressive high ceilings, fine oak panelled walls, a formal but discreet and relaxed atmosphere and fine modern dishes from local produce.

KIDMORE END *Oxon.* – *see Reading.*

KILNSEY *N. Yorks.* 502 O 21 *Great Britain G.*
Exc. : *Skipton Castle★, S : 12 m. by B 6160 and B 6265 – Bolton Priory★, SE : 13 m. by B 6160.*
London 245 – Harrogate 31 – Skipton 14.

⌂ **Kilnsey Old Hall** ⊗ without rest., BD23 5PS, ℰ (01756) 753887, *oldhall.kilnsey@vir gin.net,* ≤ *Wharfdale Valley,* 🌳 – ⅹ P.
closed Christmas and New Year – **3 rm** ⊇ ★60.00 – ★★86.00.
♦ Stone-built 17C hall set below huge limestone crag. Inglenooks a highlight. "Pigeon Loft" crammed with maps, painting materials and books. Thoughtful touches in each bedroom.

KIMBOLTON *Herefordshire* 503 L 27 – *see Leominster.*

KINGHAM *Oxon.* 503 504 P 28.
London 81 – Gloucester 32 – Oxford 25.

🏠 **Mill House** ⊗, OX7 6UH, ℰ (01608) 658188, *stay@millhousehotel.co.uk, Fax (01608) 658492,* 🐾, 🌳 – ⅹ rest, 🌳 – ⅔ 70. ⓦⓞ ℀ ⓞ *VISA*
Rest 16.50/29.50 and lunch a la carte 16.40/22.95 – **23 rm** (dinner included) ⊇ ★114.50 – ★★179.00.
♦ Privately run house in 10 acres of lawned gardens with brook flowing through grounds. Spacious lounge with comfortable armchairs and books. Country house style bedrooms. Modern décor suffuses restaurant.

🏠 **The Tollgate Inn** with rm, Church St, OX7 6YA, ☎ (01608) 658389, *info@thetoll gate.com*, 🍴, 🌳 – ⇔ 🅿. 🐾 🖭 *VISA*
closed 25 December – **Rest** *(closed Sunday dinner and Monday)* a la carte 17.00/30.00 –
9 rm ⌂ ✱60.00 – ✱✱100.00.
◆ 17C Grade II listed Cotswold stone former farmhouse. Sympathetically modernised interior. Global influences on restaurant style dishes. Pleasant rooms in inn or annex.

KINGSBRIDGE Devon 503 I 33 *The West Country G.* – pop. 5 521.
See : *Town★ – Boat Trip to Salcombe★★ AC.*
Exc. : *Prawle Point (≤★★★) SE : 10 m. around coast by A 379.*
⛳ *Thurlestone ☎ (01548) 560405.*
🚹 *The Quay ☎ (01548) 853195.*
London 236 – Exeter 36 – Plymouth 24 – Torquay 21.

🏨 **Buckland-Tout-Saints** ⟋, Goveton, TQ7 2DS, Northeast : 2½ m. by A 381 ☎ (01548) 853055, *buckland@tout-saints.co.uk*, Fax (01548) 856261, ≤, 🌳 – ⇔ 📞 🅿 – 🔏 100. 🐾
🖭 *VISA*
Rest 19.00/25.00 and dinner a la carte 19.25/36.50 ♀ – **14 rm** ⌂ ✱85.00/120.00 –
✱✱165.00/215.00, 2 suites.
◆ Immaculate, impressive Queen Anne mansion with neat lawned gardens in rural location.
Wood panelled lounge; all other areas full of antiques. Well-furnished bedrooms. Accomplished cooking in beautiful wood-panelled country house restaurant.

KINGSDON Somerset 503 L 30 – *see Somerton.*

KINGSKERSWELL Devon 503 J 32 – ✉ Torquay.
London 199.5 – Exeter 18.5 – Torquay 4.5.

🏠 **Bickley Mill** with rm, Stoneycombe, TQ12 5LN, West : 2 m. ☎ (01803) 873201,
info@bickleymill.co.uk, Fax (01803) 875129, 🍴, 🌳 – ⇔ 🅿. 🐾 🖭 *VISA*
closed 25, 27 and 28 December – **Rest** a la carte 16.65/25.95 – 9 rm ⌂ ✱50.00 – ✱✱65.00.
◆ Dates back to 13C; delightful garden and decked terrace leads in to updated interior retaining beams and exposed stone walls. Modern British cooking; modish accommodation.

KING'S LYNN Norfolk 502 504 V 25 *Great Britain G.* – pop. 41 281.
Exc. : *Houghton Hall★★ AC, NE : 14½ m. by A 148 – Four Fenland Churches★ (Terrington St Clement, Walpole St Peter, West Walton, Walsoken) SW : by A 47.*
⛳ *Eagles, School Rd, Tilney All Saints ☎ (01553) 827147.*
🚹 *The Custom House, Purfleet Quay ☎ (01553) 763044, kings-lynn.tic@west-nor folk.gov.uk.*
London 103 – Cambridge 45 – Leicester 75 – Norwich 44.

🏠 **Old Rectory** without rest., 33 Goodwins Rd, PE30 5QX, ☎ (01553) 768544, *clive@theol directory-kingslynn.com*, 🌳 – ⇔ 📞 🅿
4 rm ⌂ ✱38.00 – ✱✱48.00.
◆ Personally run Georgian styled Victorian residence with garden. Bright breakfast room is matched by colourful bedrooms that are sizable and furnished in modern style.

XX **Maggie's,** 11 Saturday Market Pl, PE30 5DQ, ☎ (01553) 771483, *nickandersonchef@hot mail.com*, Fax (01553) 771483 – ⇔, 🐾 *VISA*
closed Sunday-Monday – **Rest** 21.00.
◆ Centrally located, in 17C house with vivid sitting room ceiling, exposed beams and bold artwork. Internationally influenced modern cooking with a distinctive seasonal base.

at Grimston East : 6¼ m. by A 148 – ✉ King's Lynn.

🏨 **Congham Hall** ⟋, Lynn Rd, PE32 1AH, ☎ (01485) 600250, *info@conghamhallho tel.co.uk*, Fax (01485) 601191, ≤, 🍴, 🌳, ⚘– ⇔ 🅿 – 🔏 30. 🐾 🖭 ⓞ *VISA*. ✖
Orangery : Rest 19.50/45.00 ♀ – **14 rm** ⌂ ✱95.00/130.00 – ✱✱230.00, 2 suites.
◆ Immaculately peaceful cream-washed part Georgian house with herb and salad garden.
Classic country house style lounges with many antiques. Elegant bedrooms of varying sizes. Pleasant, classic restaurant using herb garden produce.

KINGS MILLS Guernsey (Channel Islands) – *see Channel Islands.*

328

KINGSTON BAGPUIZE *Oxon.* 503 504 P 28 – *see Oxford.*

KINGSTON BLOUNT *Oxon.* – *see Chinnor.*

KINGSTONE *Herefordshire* 503 L 27 – *see Hereford.*

KINGSTON-UPON-HULL *Kingston-upon-Hull* 502 S 22 *Great Britain G.* – *pop. 301 416.*
  Exc. : *Burton Constable★ AC, NE : 9 m. by A 165 and B 1238* Z.
  ☐₁₈ *Springhead Park, Willerby Rd* ℘ *(01482) 656309 –* ☐₁₈ *Sutton Park, Salthouse Rd*
  ℘ *(01482) 374242.*
  Humber Bridge (toll).
  ✈ *Humberside Airport :* ℘ *(01652) 688456, S : 19 m. by A 63 –* **Terminal :** *Coach Service.*
  ⛴ *to The Netherlands (Rotterdam) (P & O North Sea Ferries) daily (11 h) – to Belgium (Zeebrugge) (P & O North Sea Ferries) daily (13 h 45 mn).*
  🛈 *1 Paragon St* ℘ *(01482) 223559 – King George Dock, Hedon Rd* ℘ *(01482) 702118.*
  London 183 – Leeds 61 – Nottingham 94 – Sheffield 68.

Plan on next page

🏨   **Village,** Henry Boot Way, Priory Park East, HU4 7DY, Southwest : 2 m. by A 63 ℘ (01482) 642422, *village.hull@village-hotels.com,* Fax (0870) 4215743, ☑, Ⅰₛ, ⇌, 🔲 – 🛗 ↔, 🍽 rest, 🄿 – 🏛 200. 🆎 🅰🅴 ① 𝚅𝙸𝚂𝙰
     Salingers : Rest *(closed Saturday lunch)* 19.00 (dinner) and a la carte 17.00/30.00 – **116 rm**
     ⊡ ♦75.00/125.00 – ♦♦85.00/135.00.
     ♦ Five minutes' drive from the Humber Bridge. Spacious, modern interior. Sports themed pub for snacks. Impressive state-of-the-art gym and pool area. Airy, functional rooms. Traditional British cooking in boothed restaurant.

✕   **Boars Nest,** 22 Princes Ave, HU5 3QA, Northwest : 1 m. by Ferensway off West Spring Bank Rd ℘ (01482) 445577, Fax (01482) 445577 – ↔. 🆎 𝚅𝙸𝚂𝙰
     closed Tuesday – **Rest** 12.00 (lunch) and a la carte 17.00/32.75.
     ♦ Early 20C butchers, with original tiles and carcass rails in situ. Comfy, cluttered first-floor lounge. Eat hearty English dishes downstairs at mismatched tables and chairs.

at Hessle *Southwest : 2 m. by A 63 –* ⊠ *Kingston-upon-Hull.*

✕✕   **Artisan,** 22 The Weir, HU13 0RU, ℘ (01482) 644906, *eat@artisanrestaurant.com –* ↔. 🆎 🆎 𝚅𝙸𝚂𝙰
     closed 2 weeks January and Sunday-Tuesday – **Rest** (booking essential) (dinner only) 35.95 ⊡.
     ♦ Homely, neighbourhood restaurant with vivid artwork on the walls. Formal tableware offset by cheerful, enthusiastic owner. Classical cooking utilising regional ingredients.

at Willerby *West : 5 m. by A 1079 –* Z *–, Spring Bank and Willerby Rd –* ⊠ *Kingston-upon-Hull.*

🏨   **Willerby Manor,** Well Lane (via Main St), HU10 6ER, ℘ (01482) 652616, *willerbyma nor@bestwestern.co.uk,* Fax (01482) 653901, 🍴, Ⅰₛ, ⇌, 🔲, ⇌ – ↔ rm, 🄿 – 🏛 500. 🆎 🅰🅴 ① 𝚅𝙸𝚂𝙰. ⋙
     closed 25 December – **Icon :** Rest (dinner only) 22.50 and a la carte 22.35/25.20 –
     Everglades : Rest a la carte 13.40/20.90 s. ⊡ – ⊡ 11.25 – **51 rm** ♦85.00/95.00 –
     ♦♦103.00.
     ♦ Modern hotel in residential area, with pleasantly laid-out landscaped grounds and rose gardens. Smart leisure facilities. Slightly functional bedrooms with colourful fabrics. Windowless Icon with contemporary menus. Everglades brasserie in hotel's lounge.

at Cottingham *Northwest : 5½ m. by A 1079 –* Z *– on B 1233 (Cottingham Rd) –* ⊠ *Kingston-upon-Hull.*

🏨   **Lazaat,** Woodhill Way, HU16 5SX, Northwest : 1 ½ m. by B 1233 on Skidby Lakes rd ℘ (01482) 847900, *info@lazaat.com,* Fax (01482) 844299, ⇌ – ↔, 🍽 rest, ✦ ⅙ 🄿 – 🏛 100. 🆎 🅰🅴 ① 𝚅𝙸𝚂𝙰. ⋙
     Rest a la carte 18.40/23.95 – **13 rm** ⊡ ♦75.00/95.00 – ♦♦85.00/110.00.
     ♦ Set in suburbs, this smart hotel boasts spacious public areas with a comfy lounge. Popular wedding venue. Bedrooms are a strong point: stylish, with high level of facilities. North African dishes - and themes - a speciality.

ENGLAND

Z a

329

KINGSTON-UPON-HULL

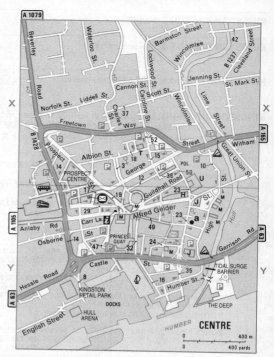

CENTRE

0   400 m
0   400 yards

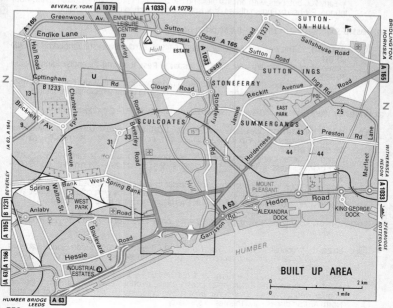

BUILT UP AREA

0   2 km
0   1 mile

KINGSWEAR Devon 503 J 32 – see Dartmouth.

KINGTON Herefordshire 503 K 27 – pop. 2 597.
London 152 – Birmingham 61 – Hereford 19 – Shrewsbury 54.

at Titley Northeast : 3½ m. on B 4355 – ⊠ Kington.

🍽️ **The Stagg Inn** (Reynolds) with rm, HR5 3RL, ℰ (01544) 230221, reservations@the
stagg.co.uk, Fax (01544) 231390, 🍴, 🌳 – ⇔ rest, 🅿️, 🆘 VISA
🎗️ closed 1 week in spring, first 2 weeks November, 25-26 December, 1 January and May Day
Bank Holiday Monday – Rest (closed Sunday dinner and Monday except at Bank Holidays
when closed Tuesday instead) (booking essential) a la carte 23.00/29.00 ♀ – 6 rm ⊊
★50.00/70.00 – ★★80.00/110.00.
Spec. Seared scallops with celeriac purée and cumin. Fillet of beef with horseradish mash
and red wine sauce. Vanilla, elderflower and lime crème brûlées.
♦ Modern pub cooking at its best in atmospheric inn; tasty, appealing dishes, full of local
ingredients. Comfy rooms in the old vicarage or the inn where breakfast is served.

KINTBURY Newbury 503 P 29 – see Hungerford.

KIRKBY LONSDALE Cumbria 502 M 21 – pop. 2 076 – ⊠ Carnforth (Lancs.).
🏌️ Scaleber Lane, Barbon ℰ (015242) 76365 – 🏌️ Casterton, Sedbergh Rd ℰ (015242)
71592.
🅱️ 24 Main St ℰ (015242) 71437.
London 259 – Carlisle 62 – Kendal 13 – Lancaster 17 – Leeds 58.

at Casterton Northeast : 1¼ m. by A 65 on A 683 – ⊠ Carnforth (Lancs.).

🍽️ **The Pheasant Inn** with rm, LA6 2RX, ℰ (015242) 71230, pheasantinn@fsbdial.co.uk,
Fax (015242) 74267, 🍴, 🌳 – ⇔ rest, 🕭, 🅿️, 🆘 VISA, 🛇
closed 2 weeks mid January – Rest a la carte 12.70/26.60 ♀ – 10 rm ⊊ ★37.00/45.00 –
★★70.00/100.00.
♦ 18C inn nestling beneath Fells. Bags of charm: open fire in bar, three sitting rooms, rural
artefacts. Full menus with grills and hearty stews. Warm, welcoming bedrooms.

at Cowan Bridge (Lancs.) Southeast : 2 m. on A 65 – ⊠ Kirkby Lonsdale.

❌❌ **Hipping Hall** with rm, LA6 2JJ, Southeast : ½ m. on A 65 ℰ (015242) 71187, info@hip
pinghall.com, Fax (015242) 72452, 🌳 – ⇔ 🕭 🛴 🅿️, 🆘 VISA
closed 2 weeks January – Rest (closed Saturday lunch) 25.00/42.50 – 9 rm (dinner included)
⊊ ★125.00 – ★★230.00.
♦ Charming part 15/16C house in mature grounds with stream and flagged terrace.
Modern, inventive cooking does justice to characterful hall dining room. Distinctly modish
rooms.

at Tunstall South : 3½ m. by A 65 on A 683 – ⊠ Kirkby Lonsdale.

🍽️ **Lunesdale Arms,** LA6 2QN, ℰ (015242) 74203, info@thelunesdale.co.uk,
Fax (015242) 74229, 🍴 – 🅿️, 🆘 ⓘ VISA
closed 25-26 December – Rest (closed Monday except Bank Holidays) a la carte
18.25/23.50 ♀.
♦ Stone-built 18C pub; now a modern dining establishment with bright, airy interior that
includes a vast fireplace and squashy sofas. Locally sourced dishes to fore.

at Hutton Roof West : 4½ m. by A 65 – ⊠ Kirkby Lonsdale.

⌂ **Pickle Farm** 🛇 without rest., LA6 2PH, North : ¼ m. ℰ (015242) 72104, stay@pickle
farm.co.uk, ≼, 🌳 🅿️, 🛇
3 rm ⊊ ★44.00/48.00 – ★★68.00/76.00.
♦ Attractive, renovated part 18C farmhouse in a tranquil location. Pleasant sitting room
opens onto walled garden. Organic breakfast. Simple but stylishly furnished rooms.

KIRKBYMOORSIDE N. Yorks. 502 R 21 – pop. 2 650.
🏌️ Manor Vale ℰ (01751) 431525.
London 244 – Leeds 61 – Scarborough 26 – York 33.

⌂ **Brickfields Farm** 🛇, Kirby Mills, YO62 6NS, East : ¾ m. by A 170 on Kirby Mills Industrial
Estate rd ℰ (01751) 433074, janet@brickfieldsfarm.co.uk, 🌳 – ⇔ 🅿️, 🛇
March-October – Rest (by arrangement) – 3 rm ⊊ ★40.00/45.00 – ★★70.00/80.00.
♦ Personally run 1850s red-brick former farmhouse set down private driveway. Rooms are
very comfortably appointed in rustic style with thoughtful extra touches. Homecooked
meals in pleasant conservatory overlooking gardens and fields.

⌂ **The Cornmill,** Kirby Mills, YO62 6NP, East : ½ m. by A 170 ℰ (01751) 432000, *corn mill@kirbymills.demon.co.uk*, Fax (01751) 432300, 🍸, 🚗 – ✦✦ 🐾 **P. ⑩ⓒ VISA JCB**. ⌖
Rest (by arrangement) 30.00 **s.** – **5 rm** ⌖ ✦55.00/62.50 – ✦✦100.00/105.00.
  ♦ Converted 18C cornmill, its millrace still visible through the glass floor of a beamed and flagged dining room. Individually decorated bedrooms in the Victorian farmhouse.

at Fadmoor *Northwest : 2¼ m.* – ⌧ *Kirkbymoorside*.

🍴 **The Plough Inn,** Main St, YO62 7HY, ℰ (01751) 431515, 😋, 🚗 – 🐾 **P. ⑩ⓒ VISA**. ⌖
closed 25-26 December and 1 January – **Rest** a la carte 17.95/27.00 ⚓.
  ♦ Pleasant rural pub with original tiled floor, rustic walls, scrubbed tables and real ales. Blackboard menu changes daily: traditional cooking with a modern twist.

KIRKBY STEPHEN *Cumbria 502* M 20 – *pop. 2 209.*
London 296 – Carlisle 46 – Darlington 37 – Kendal 28.

🏛 **Augill Castle** ⏏, CA17 4DE, Northeast : 4 ½ m. by A 685 ℰ (01768) 341937, *enqui ries@augillcastle.co.uk*, ⬱, 🚗, 🐾, ⚒ – 🐾 **P. ⑩ⓒ VISA**. ⌖
Rest *(weekends only)* (residents only) (communal dining) (dinner only) (set menu only) 35.00/40.00 ⚓ – **10 rm** ⌖ ✦70.00/100.00 – ✦✦120.00/140.00.
  ♦ Carefully restored Victorian folly in neo-Gothic style with extensive gardens; fine antiques and curios abound. Comfy music room and library. Individually decorated rooms. Expansive dining room with ornate ceiling and Spode tableware.

KIRKCAMBECK *Cumbria 501 502* L 18 – *see Brampton.*

KIRK DEIGHTON *W. Yorks.* – *see Wetherby.*

KIRKHAM *Lancs. 502* L 22 – *pop. 10 372* – ⌧ *Preston.*
London 240 – Blackpool 9 – Preston 7.

at Wrea Green *Southwest : 3 m. on B 5259* – ⌧ *Kirkham.*

🏛 **The Villa** ⏏, Moss Side Lane, PR4 2PE, Southwest : ½ m. on B 5259 ℰ (01772) 684347, *info@villah.tel-wreagreen.co.uk*, Fax (01772) 687647, 😋 – 🛗 ✦✦, 🛏 rm, **P.** – ⚒ 25. **⑩ⓒ AE VISA**
Rest 15.00/21.00 and a la carte 22.00/34.00 ⚓ – **25 rm** ⌧ ✦90.00 – ✦✦105.00.
  ♦ Imposing red brick manor house with sympathetic extensions. Original house with bar and lounge, open fire, objets d'art. Purpose-built block has smart, well-furnished rooms. Dining room made up of many snugs, small rooms and conservatory; themed style.

KIRKWHELPINGTON *Northd. 501 502* N/O 18 *Great Britain G.* – ⌧ *Morpeth.*
Env. : *Wallington House*★ *AC*, E : 3½ m. by A 696 and B 6342.
London 305 – Carlisle 46 – Newcastle upon Tyne 20.

⌂ **Shieldhall** ⏏, Wallington, NE61 4AQ, Southeast : 2½ m. by A 696 on B 6342 ℰ (01830) 540387, *robinson.gay@btinternet.com*, Fax (01830) 540490, 🚗, 🐾 – ✦✦ **P. ⑩ⓒ VISA**. ⌖
restricted opening in winter – **Rest** (by arrangement) 25.00 ⚓ – **4 rm** ⌖ ✦45.00/55.00 –
✦✦78.00.
  ♦ Converted 18C farm buildings with gardens. Well-furnished lounge/library. Spotless rooms in former stable block: furniture constructed by cabinet-making owner!

KIRTLINGTON *Oxon. 503* Q 28.
London 70.5 – Oxford 16 – Bicester 11.

🏛 **The Dashwood,** South Green, Heyford Rd, OX5 3HJ, ℰ (01869) 352707, *reserva tions@thedashwood.co.uk*, Fax (01869) 351432 – ✦✦ 🐾 🐾 **P. ⑩ⓒ AE VISA**. ⌖
closed 31 December - 9 January – **Rest** *(closed Sunday dinner to non-residents)* a la carte 18.50/25.45 ⚓ – **12 rm** ⌧ ✦85.00/120.00 – ✦✦110.00/150.00.
  ♦ Grade II listed 16C building in local soft stone. Lounge with comfy leather armchairs. Bedrooms, boasting super contemporary décor, divided between main building and barn. Exposed stone dining room: impressive menus with modern European slant.

KNAPTON *Norfolk 504* Y 25 – *see North Walsham.*

KNARESBOROUGH *N. Yorks.* 502 P 21 – *pop. 13 380.*

🏌 *Boroughbridge Rd* ℰ (01423) 862690.

🚩 *9 Castle Court, Market Pl* ℰ (0845) 3890177 (summer only).

London 217 – Bradford 21 – Harrogate 3 – Leeds 18 – York 18.

🏨 **Dower House,** Bond End, HG5 9AL, ℰ (01423) 863302, *enquiries@bwdower house.co.uk, Fax* (01423) 867665, ₤ぁ, ≘s, ◪, ℱ – ⇌ ∜ ₺ ℙ – 🔏 65. 🐠 ㏂
VISA
Rest 25.00 and a la carte 14.90/28.70 ℤ – **31 rm** ☑ ✱70.00/130.00 – ✱✱125.00/145.00.
✦ Part 15C, ivy clad, red brick house near town centre. Stone-floored reception and cosy bar. Small, well-equipped leisure centre. Good-sized, traditional bedrooms. Warmly toned restaurant overlooks the garden.

at Ferrensby *Northeast : 3 m. on A 6055.*

🍴 **The General Tarleton Inn** with rm, Boroughbridge Rd, HG5 0PZ, ℰ (01423) 340284, *gti@generaltarleton.co.uk, Fax* (01423) 340288 – ⇌ ℙ – 🔏 40. 🐠 ㏂ **VISA**
Rest *(closed Sunday dinner)* (dinner only and Sunday lunch)/dinner 29.50 – (see also below) – **14 rm** ☑ ✱85.00 – ✱✱97.00.
✦ Attractive stone building, an extension to original 18C coaching inn; surrounded by North Yorkshire countryside. Comfy rooms and dining room full of rustic style and ambience.

🍴 **The General Tarleton Inn,** Boroughbridge Rd, HG5 0PZ, ℰ (01423) 340284, *gti@generaltarleton.co.uk, Fax* (01423) 340288, ℱ – ℙ. 🐠 ㏂ **VISA** ✄
Rest a la carte 20.00/32.00 ℤ.
✦ Characterful, well run 18C coaching inn with stone décor, open fires and various snugs and seating areas. Robust British dishes with northern influence: excellent value.

KNIPTON *Leics.*
London 125 – Leicester 28.5 – Melton Mowbray 10.5.

🏨 **Manners Arms,** Croxton Rd, NG32 1RH, ℰ (01476) 879222, *info@mannersarms.com, Fax* (01476) 879228, ℱ, ℱ – ⇌ ₺ ℙ. 🐠 ㏂ **VISA**
Rest a la carte 21.75/34.95 – **10 rm** ☑ ✱55.00/70.00 – ✱✱80.00/120.00.
✦ Refurbished former hunting lodge originally built for sixth Duke of Rutland; a relaxing feel pervades. Locals gather round bar's roaring fire. Individually styled bedrooms. Spacious dining room offers hearty rustic cooking.

KNOSSINGTON *Rutland* 502 504 R 25 – *see Oakham.*

KNOWLE GREEN *Lancs. – see Longridge.*

KNOWSLEY BUSINESS PARK *Mersey. – see Liverpool.*

KNOWSTONE *Devon – see South Molton.*

KNUTSFORD *Ches.* 502 503 504 M 24 – *pop. 12 656.*
🚩 *Council Offices, Toft Rd* ℰ (01565) 632611.
London 187 – Chester 25 – Liverpool 33 – Manchester 18 – Stoke-on-Trent 30.

🏨 **Cottons,** Manchester Rd, WA16 0SU, Northwest : 1 ½ m. on A 50 ℰ (01565) 650333, *cottons@shirehotels.com, Fax* (01565) 755351, ☼, ₤ぁ, ≘s, ◪, ℱ – ▯ ⇌ ∜ ₺ ℙ –
🔏 200. 🐠 ㏂ ⓪ **VISA** ✄
Magnolia : Rest *(closed Saturday-Sunday)* (dinner only) 25.00 and a la carte 25.00/40.00 **s.**
ℤ – **109 rm** ☑ ✱145.00 – ✱✱165.00/225.00.
✦ Large purpose-built hotel aimed at business travellers. Two good-sized country house style lounges and clubby bar. Smart leisure complex; comfortable, up-to-date bedrooms. French New Orleans themed dining room.

🏨 **Longview,** 55 Manchester Rd, WA16 0LX, on A 50 ℰ (01565) 632119, *enquiries@longvie whotel.com, Fax* (01565) 652402 – ∜ ₺ ℙ. 🐠 ㏂ **VISA**
closed Christmas and New Year – **Rest** *(closed Sunday)* (dinner only) a la carte 17.95/30.45 **s.** ℤ – **28 rm** ☑ ✱86.00/89.00 – ✱✱113.00/149.00, 3 suites.
✦ Bay-windowed Victorian house, family run. Open log fire in reception. At foot of stone staircase lies cellar bar with soft lighting and low ceiling. Pleasant, comfy bedrooms. Mahogany furniture and chandeliers make for relaxed dining.

XX **Belle Epoque Brasserie** with rm, 60 King St, WA16 6DT, ℰ (01565) 633060, *info@the belleepoque.com, Fax* (01565) 634150, 🛱 – ⇆ ✆ ⑩ ⚑ ⑩ *VISA*.
– **Rest** *(closed Sunday dinner)* (dinner only and Sunday lunch) a la carte 23.85/35.90 **s**. ♀ –
6 rm ⌷ ✝99.00 – ✝✝99.00.
◆ Bustling brasserie with Art Nouveau décor. Traditional and modern dishes with international touches using local produce. Contemporary style bedrooms with modern facilities.

at Mobberley *Northeast : 2½ m. by A 537 on B 5085 – ⊠ Knutsford.*

⚪ **Laburnum Cottage,** Knutsford Rd, WA16 7PU, West : ¾ m. on B 5085 ℰ (01565) 872464, *laburnum.cottage@hotelmail.co.uk, Fax* (01565) 872464, 🌭 – ⇆ 🅿 ⑩ ⑩ *VISA*.
%
Rest (by arrangement) 17.00 – 5 rm ⌷ ✝46.00 – ✝✝61.00.
◆ Red-brick two storey cottage guesthouse with large garden. Homely ambience, with velvet furnishings in lounge and small conservatory to rear. Good sized, individual rooms. Home cooking proudly undertaken.

⚪ **Hinton,** Town Lane, WA16 7HH, on B 5085 ℰ (01565) 873484, *the.hinton@virgin.net,* 🌭
– ⇆ 🅿 ⑩ ⚑ ⑩ *VISA*. %
Rest (by arrangement) 17.00 – 6 rm ✝44.00 – ✝✝58.00.
◆ Bay-windowed guesthouse with rear garden. Homely lounge where you can play the organ if you wish! Simple, uncluttered bedrooms with floral theme. Local produce used in meals.

at Lach Dennis *Southwest : 7 m. by A 50, B 5081 and B 5082 – ⊠ Knutsford.*

🍴 **Duke of Portland,** Penny's Lane, CW9 7SY, ℰ (01606) 46264, *info@dukeofportland.com, Fax* (01606) 41724, 🛱, 🌭 – ⇆ 🅿 ⑩ ⚑ *VISA*. %
Rest a la carte 15.00/22.00 ♀.
◆ Airy, rural pub, its rustic ambience balanced by two lounges with a contemporary feel. Personally run by long-standing restaurant owners. Tasty, well-priced home-made dishes.

at Hoo Green *Northwest : 3½ m. on A 50 – ⊠ Knutsford.*

🏰 **Mere Court,** Warrington Rd, WA16 0RW, Northwest : 1 m. on A 50 ℰ (01565) 831000, *sales@merecourt.co.uk, Fax* (01565) 831001, 🌭 – ⇆ 🅿 – 🛦 75. ⑩ ⚑ ⑩ *VISA*. %
Arboreum : Rest *(closed Saturday lunch)* 24.95 and dinner a la carte 24.95/40.00 ♀ – ⌷
11.95 – 34 rm ✝125.00 – ✝✝145.00/185.00.
◆ Immaculate looking part Edwardian manor house with attractive gardens. Pleasant country house feel with large, comfy, well-equipped, individually decorated bedrooms. Elegant oak-beamed, panelled dining room with lake and garden vistas.

KYNASTON *Herefordshire – see Ledbury.*

LACH DENNIS *Ches. – see Knutsford.*

LACOCK *Wilts. 503 504 N 29 The West Country G. – ⊠ Chippenham.*
See : Village★★ - Lacock Abbey★ *AC* – High St★, St Cyriac★, Fox Talbot Museum of Photography★ *AC.*
London 109 – Bath 16 – *Bristol* 30 – Chippenham 3.

🏛 **At The Sign of the Angel,** 6 Church St, SN15 2LB, ℰ (01249) 730230, *angel@lacock.co.uk, Fax* (01249) 730527, 🛱, 🌭 – ⇆ rm, 🅿 ⑩ ⚑ ⑩ *VISA*
closed 1 week Christmas – **Rest** *(closed Monday lunch except Bank Holidays)* a la carte
23.70/33.25 – 11 rm ⌷ ✝72.00/72.00 – ✝✝132.00/155.00.
◆ Part 14C and 15C former wool merchant's house in charming National Trust village. Relaxed and historic atmosphere. Antique furnished rooms, four in the garden cottage. Tremendously characterful dining room of hotel's vintage: traditional English dishes served.

LADOCK *Cornwall 503 F 33.*
London 268 – Exeter 84 – Newquay 12 – Penzance 37 – Plymouth 51 – Truro 13.

⚪ **Bissick Old Mill** without rest., TR2 4PG, off B 3275 ℰ (01726) 882557, *enquiries@bissickoldmill.plus.com, Fax* (01726) 884057 – ⇆ 🅿 ⑩ ⚑ *VISA*. %
closed 2 weeks February – 4 rm ⌷ ✝45.00/50.00 – ✝✝65.00/85.00.
◆ Charming stone-built 17C former mill. Much historic character with low beamed ceilings and stone fireplaces. Comfortable bedrooms. Breakfast room has much period charm.

LAMBOURN WOODLANDS *Berks. – see Hungerford.*

LANCASTER *Lancs.* 502 L 21 *Great Britain G.* – *pop. 45 952.*

See : *Castle★ AC.*

 Ashton Hall, Ashton-with-Stodday ℘ *(01524) 752090 –* ℡ *Lansil, Caton Rd* ℘ *(01524) 39269.*

🛈 *29 Castle Hill* ℘ *(01524) 32878, tourism@lancaster.gov.uk.*

London 252 – Blackpool 26 – Bradford 62 – Burnley 44 – Leeds 71 – Middlesbrough 97 – Preston 26.

Lancaster House, Green Lane, Ellel, LA1 4GJ, South : 3¼ m. by A 6 ℘ (01524) 844822, *lancaster@elhmail.co.uk, Fax (01524) 844766,* ℔, ⇌, ▣ – ⇌ ♿ ℗ – 🕭 200. 🐵 🆎 ⓪ *VISA*

The Gressingham : **Rest** 24.95 s. ♈ – **80 rm** ⊑ ✦76.00/124.00 – ✦✦82.00/138.00, 19 suites.

◆ A purpose-built hotel set amidst lawned grounds and adjacent to Lancaster University, whose conference facilities can be used. Comfortable modern decor and country views. Split-level restaurant with views towards Morecambe Bay.

LANCING *W. Sussex* 504 S 31 – *pop. 30 360 (inc. Sompting).*

London 59 – Brighton 4 – Southampton 53.

Sussex Pad, Old Shoreham Rd, BN15 0RH, East : 1 m. off A 27 ℘ (01273) 454243, *reception@sussexpadhotel.co.uk, Fax (01273) 453010,* ☞ – ⇌ ♿ ℗, 🐵 ⓪ *VISA closed 24 December-3 January* – **Rest** a la carte 20.65/32.75 – **18 rm** ⊑ ✦75.00/90.00 – ✦✦90.00/110.00.

◆ Pubby modern hotel against the formidable backdrop of Lancing College. Co-ordinated rooms named after grand marque Champagnes: their namesakes in plentiful supply in the bar. Dine on seafood from nearby Brighton market.

LANGAR *Notts.* 502 R 25.

London 132 – Boston 45 – Leicester 25 – Lincoln 37 – Nottingham 14.

Langar Hall ⌂, NG13 9HG, ℘ (01949) 860559, *info@langarhall.co.uk,* *Fax (01949) 861045,* ≤, ☜, ☞, ⌨ – ⇌ rm, ℗, 🐵 *VISA* **Rest** 16.50 (lunch) and dinner a la carte 25.50/46.00 ♈ – **11 rm** ⊑ ✦75.00/95.00 – ✦✦175.00/210.00, 1 suite.

◆ Georgian manor in pastoral setting, next to early English church; overlooks park, medie-val fishponds. Antique filled rooms named after people featuring in house's history. Ele-gant, candle-lit, pillared dining room.

LANGHO *Lancs.* 502 M 22 – *see Blackburn.*

LANGTHWAITE *N. Yorks.* 502 O 20 – *see Reeth.*

LAPWORTH *Warks.* – *see Hockley Heath.*

LASKILL *N. Yorks.* – *see Helmsley.*

LASTINGHAM *N. Yorks.* 502 R 21 – *pop. 87 –* ✉ *York.*

London 244 – Scarborough 26 – York 32.

Lastingham Grange ⌂, YO62 6TH, ℘ (01751) 417345, *reservations@lastingham grange.com, Fax (01751) 417358,* ☞, ☞, ⌨ – ⇌ ℗, 🐵 *VISA March-November* – **Rest** (light lunch Monday-Saturday)/dinner 37.50/40.00 ♈ – **11 rm** (din-ner included) ⊑ ✦105.00/125.00 – ✦✦120.00/195.00.

◆ A delightfully traditional country house atmosphere prevails throughout this extended, pleasantly old-fashioned, 17C farmhouse. Lovely gardens; well-appointed bedrooms. Din-ing room with rustic fare and rose garden view.

Luxury pad or humble abode?
🏨 and ⌂ denote categories of comfort.

LAVENHAM *Suffolk* 504 W 27 *Great Britain G.* – ✉ *Sudbury.*
See : *Town*★★ – *Church of St Peter and St Paul*★.
🖼 *Lady St* ℰ *(01787) 248207.*
London 66 – Cambridge 39 – Colchester 22 – Ipswich 19.

🏠 **Swan,** High St, CO10 9QA, ℰ (01787) 247477, *info@theswanatlavenham.co.uk,*
Fax (01787) 248286, 🌳 – ⧉ **P** – 🍴 35. **AE ⓪ VISA**
Rest (bar lunch Monday-Saturday)/dinner 28.95 ♀ – **47 rm** ⌑ ★65.00/110.00 –
★★140.00/160.00, 2 suites.
♦ Well-restored, part 14C, half timbered house with an engaging historical ambience. Each
atmospheric bedroom is individually and stylishly decorated. Dining room has impressive
timbered ceiling verging on the cavernous.

🏠 **Lavenham Priory** without rest., Water St, CO10 9RW, ℰ (01787) 247404, *mail@laven*
hampriory.co.uk, Fax (01787) 248472, 🌳 – ⧉ 🐾 **P**. **AE VISA**. ⌖
closed Christmas-New Year – **6 rm** ⌑ ★70.00/85.00 – ★★95.00/155.00.
♦ A Jacobean oak staircase and Elizabethan wall paintings are just two elements of this
captivating part 13C former priory. Bedrooms stylishly furnished with antiques.

🍴🍴 **The Great House** with rm, Market Pl, CO10 9QZ, ℰ (01787) 247431, *info@great*
house.co.uk, Fax (01787) 248007, 🌳 – 🌳 – ⧉ 🐾 **AE VISA**
closed 3 weeks January – Rest - French - (closed Sunday dinner and Monday) 16.95/24.95
and a la carte 22.75/31.75 ♀ – ⌑ 9.50 – **3 rm** ★65.00/150.00 – ★★96.00/160.00, 2 suites
96.00/160.00.
♦ Timbered house with Georgian façade in town centre, dating from 14C. Rustic-style
restaurant serves good range of French dishes. Comfortable, antique furnished bedrooms.

🍴 **Angel** with rm, Market Pl, CO10 9QZ, ℰ (01787) 247388, *angellav@aol.com,*
Fax (01787) 248344, 🌳 – 🌳 – ⧉ **P**. **AE ⓪ VISA**
closed 25-26 December – Rest a la carte 15.00/25.00 ♀ – **8 rm** ★55.00 – ★★80.00.
♦ 15C inn on the market square. Residents' lounge has original early 17C ceiling. Comfortable, well-kept rooms are individually furnished and some are heavily timbered.

LEAFIELD *Oxon.* 503 504 P 28 – *see Witney.*

LEAMINGTON SPA *Warks.* 503 504 P 27 – *see Royal Leamington Spa.*

LECHLADE *Glos.* 503 504 O 28 *Great Britain G.*
Env. : *Fairford : Church of St Mary*★ *(stained glass windows*★★*), W : 4½ m. on A 417.*
London 84 – Cirencester 13 – Oxford 25.

at Southrop *Northwest : 3 m. on Eastleach rd* – ✉ *Lechlade.*

🍴 **The Swan,** GL7 2NU, ℰ (01367) 850205, *grazzer@gmail.com,* Fax (01367) 850517 – **AE**
VISA
closed 25 December – Rest 16.50 (lunch) and a la carte 21.00/32.00 ♀.
♦ Ivy covered 14C Cotswold inn. Characterful bar, popular with locals. Main dining room
boasts low beamed ceiling and log fires. Modern menus with subtle Mediterranean twist.

LEDBURY *Herefordshire* 503 504 M 27 – *pop. 8 491.*
London 119 – Hereford 14 – Newport 46 – Worcester 16.

🏠 **The Feathers,** High St, HR8 1DS, ℰ (01531) 635266, *mary@feathers-ledbury.co.uk,*
Fax (01531) 638955, 🌳, 🛁, 🗟 – 🐾 **P** – 🍴 120. **AE ⓪ VISA**
Quills : Rest a la carte 18.95/31.40 ♀ – **Fuggles :** Rest a la carte 18.95/31.40 ♀ – **19 rm** ⌑
★79.50 – ★★150.00.
♦ Impressive timbered 16C inn in centre of town. Much character with open fires and
antique furnishings. Rooms vary in design, though they all lay claim to a stylish modernity.
Fuggles is decorated with hops.

🏠 **The Barn House** without rest., New St, HR8 2DX, ℰ (01531) 632825, *barnhouseled*
bury@btconnect.com, 🌳 – ⧉ **P** – 🍴 60. **AE VISA**. ⌖
closed Christmas-New Year – **3 rm** ⌑ ★60.00 – ★★80.00.
♦ Parts date from 18C and the ancient "Barn Room", used for functions, from early 17C.
Homely traditional style throughout the communal areas and accommodation.

✗ **The Malthouse**, Church Lane, HR8 1DW, ☏ (01531) 634443, ♨ – ✦✦, ⓌⓈ 𝑽𝑰𝑺𝑨
closed Sunday and Monday – **Rest** (dinner only and Saturday lunch)/dinner 23.00 (mid-week) and a la carte 18.25/34.75 ♀.
• Tucked away behind the butter market; rustic décor and attractive courtyard lend a classic country cottage aura. Monthly menu of carefully prepared dishes using local produce.

at Much Marcle *Southwest : 4¼ m. on A 449 –* ✉ *Ledbury.*

✗ **Scrumpy House**, Westons Cider, The Bounds, HR8 2NQ, West : ¾ m. on Woolhope rd
☏ (01531) 660626, *matt@scrumpyhouse.co.uk*, ♨ – P, ⓌⓈ 𝐀𝐄 𝑽𝑰𝑺𝑨
closed 1-2 January and dinner Sunday-Tuesday – **Rest** (restricted opening in January) a la carte 16.40/27.70.
• Charmingly simple eatery boasting rafters and exposed stone: the essence of rusticity. Local ingredients, like Marcle beef or home-made ice-cream, feature prominently.

at Kynaston *West : 6½ m. by A 449, A 4172, Aylton Rd, on Fownhope Rd –* ✉ *Ledbury.*

⌂ **Hall End** ♨, HR8 2PD, ☏ (01531) 670225, *khjefferson@hallend91.freeserve.co.uk*,
Fax (01531) 670747, ⇐, ☒, ♨, ⌨, ✗ – ✦✦ P, ✗
closed Christmas and New Year – **Rest** (booking essential) (communal dining) (by arrangement) 29.50 – **3 rm** ☍ ✚60.00 – ✚✚95.00.
• Lovingly restored, personally run, part Georgian home and livery stable in the countryside. Relax in the orangery and, suitably reposed, retire to lavishly furnished bedrooms.

at Trumpet *Northwest : 3¼ m. on A 38 –* ✉ *Ledbury.*

✗✗ **The Verzon** with rm, Hereford Rd, HR8 2PZ, ☏ (01531) 670381, *info@theverzon.co.uk*,
Fax (01531) 670830, ♨, ♨ – ✦✦ P, ⓌⓈ 𝐀𝐄 𝑽𝑰𝑺𝑨, ✗
Rest 19.00 (lunch) and a la carte 20.00/30.00 ♀ – **8 rm** ☍ ✚65.00 – ✚✚110.00/150.00.
• Extended Georgian redbrick house with cool bar-brasserie interior. Relax in deep leather sofas; tuck into original dishes sourced from local ingredients. Airy, stylish rooms.

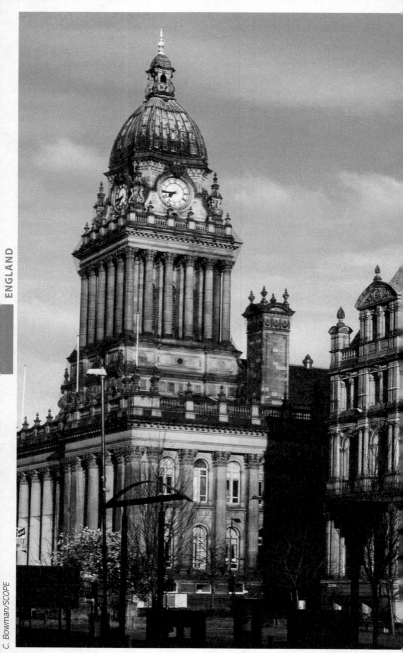

Leeds: Town Hall

LEEDS

W. Yorks. **502** P 22 *Great Britain G.* – *pop. 443 247.*

London 204 – Liverpool 75 – Manchester 43 – Newcastle upon Tyne 95 – Nottingham 74.

TOURIST INFORMATION

🛈 *The Arcade, City Station* ✆ *(0113) 242 5242; tourinfo@leeds.golf.uk*

PRACTICAL INFORMATION

🛇, 🛇 *Temple Newsam, Temple Newsam Rd, Halton* ✆ *(0113) 264 5624,* CT.
🛇 *Gotts Park, Armley Ridge Rd, Armley* ✆ *(0113) 234 2019,* BT.
🛇 *Middleton Park, Ring Rd, Beeston Park, Middleton* ✆ *(0113) 270 0449,* CU.
🛇, 🛇 *Moor Allerton, Coal Rd, Wike* ✆ *(0113) 266 1154.*
🛇 *Howley Hall, Scotchman Lane, Morley* ✆ *(01924) 350100.*
🛇 *Roundhay, Park Lane* ✆ *(0113) 266 2695* CT.
✈ *Leeds – Bradford Airport :* ✆ *(0113) 250 9696, NW : 8 m. by A 65 and A 658* BT.

SIGHTS

See : *City★ - Royal Armouries Museum★★★* GZ *– City Art Gallery★* AC GY **M**.

Env. : *Kirkstall Abbey★* **AC**, *NW : 3 m. by A 65* GY *– Temple Newsam★ (decorative arts★) AC, E : 5 m. by A 64 and A 63* CU **D**.

Exc. : *Harewood House★★ (The Gallery★) AC, N : 8 m. by A 61* CT *– Nostell Priory★ , SE : 18 m. by A 61 and A 638 – Yorkshire Sculpture Park★ , S : 20 m. by M 1 to junction 38 and 1 m. north off A 637 – Brodsworth Hall★ , SE : 25 m. by M 1 to junction 40, A 638 and minor rd (right) in Upton.*

ENGLAND

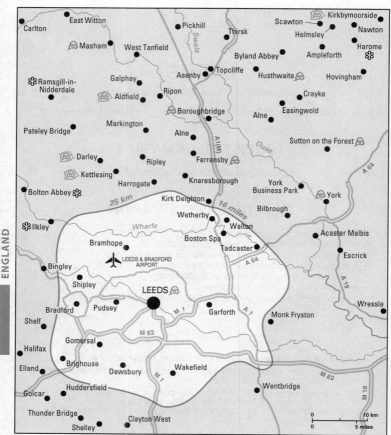

Thorpe Park H. and Spa, 1150 Century Way, Thorpe Park, LS15 8ZB, East : 6 m. by A 64 and A 63 on B 6120 *℘* (0113) 264 1000, *thorpepark@shirehotels.com,* Fax (0113) 264 1010, 龠, ⑩, *Iძ,* ⇌s, ▢ – ⫞ 吳 ▤ ❤ & 몓 – 益 200. ⑩⑨ 歴 *VISA* ⚘

closed 24-30 December
Rest 14.50/17.00 (lunch) and dinner a la carte approx 29.50 ♀
123 rm ⌖ ✚155.00 – ✚✚175.00/220.00.
♦ Smart, modish hotel, close to motorways. Open-fired reception and richly toned central atrium. Fully equipped leisure centre with spa. Immaculate rooms with host of extras. Spacious, modern restaurant.

The Queens, City Sq, LS1 1PJ, *℘* (0113) 243 1323, *thequeen@qhotels.co.uk,* Fax (0113) 242 5154 – ≒⤬ ▤ TV ❤ ⇌ – 益 600. ⑩⑨ 歴 ⑩ *VISA* FGZ **g**
Rest (carving dinner) 25.00 **s.**
⌖ 14.95 – **187 rm** ✚145.00 – ✚✚145.00, 30 suites.
♦ Fully restored to stunning proportions, this 30s Art Deco hotel has many original features in situ, including ballroom and splendid bar. Impressive rooms with period fittings. Basement dining room with carvery at its heart.

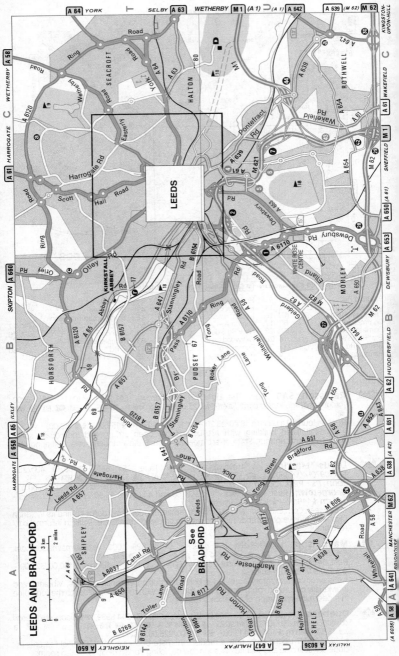

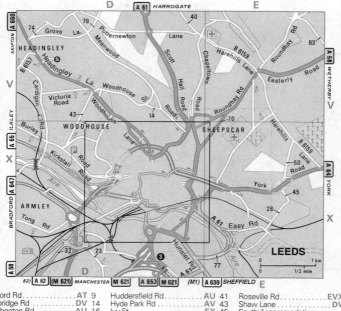

Radisson SAS, No.1 The Light, The Headrow, LS1 8TL, ℰ (0113) 236 6000, info.leeds@radissonsas.com, Fax (0113) 236 6100 – 園 ✻ ≡ ❤ & – 🔼 50. 🐱🕲 🖭 ⓞ 𝘝𝘐𝘚𝘈. ✻
GY **a**
Rest (in lounge) a la carte 18.40/23.20 – ⌒ 12.95 – **147 rm** ★139.00 – ★★139.00.
♦ Grade II listed building with Art Deco facia. Open atrium and individually styled furnishings throughout. State-of-art meeting rooms. Ultra modern, very well appointed rooms.

Leeds Marriott, 4 Trevelyan Sq, Boar Lane, LS1 6ET, ℰ (0870) 4007260, Fax (0870) 4007360, 𝐼₆, ⇆, 🔲 – 園 ✻ ≡ ❤ & – 🔼 320. 🐱🕲 🖭 ⓞ 𝘝𝘐𝘚𝘈. ✻ GZ **x**
John T's : Rest (closed lunch Saturday-Sunday) 24.00 and a la carte 23.00/29.00 ♀ – **Georgetown** : Rest - Malaysian - 10.00/21.50 and a la carte 15.50/23.50 **s.** – ⌒ 14.95 – **243 rm** ★119.00 – ★★129.00, 1 suite.
♦ Between Corn Exchange and station with smart, modern bedrooms behind its Victorian façade. Extensive conference facilities with an ample leisure centre. Relax in informal bar/restaurant.

Malmaison, 1 Swinegate, LS1 4AG, ℰ (0113) 398 1000, leeds@malmaison.com, Fax (0113) 398 1002, 𝐼₆ – 園 ✻ ≡ ❤ & – 🔼 45. 🐱🕲 🖭 ⓞ 𝘝𝘐𝘚𝘈. ✻ GZ **n**
Rest 14.50 (lunch) and a la carte 26.00/40.00 ♀ – ⌒ 13.95 – **100 rm** ★150.00/325.00 – ★★150.00/325.00, 1 suite.
♦ Relaxed, contemporary hotel hides behind imposing Victorian exterior. Vibrantly and individually decorated rooms are stylishly furnished, with modern facilities to the fore. Dine in modern interpretation of a French brasserie.

Quebecs without rest., 9 Quebec St, LS1 2HA, ℰ (0113) 244 8989, resquebecs@theeton collection.com, Fax (0113) 244 9090 – 園 ✻ ≡ ❤ & . 🐱🕲 🖭 ⓞ 𝘝𝘐𝘚𝘈. ✻ FZ **a**
⌒ 15.50 – **43 rm** ★104.00/115.00 – ★★125.00/225.00, 2 suites.
♦ 19C former Liberal Club, now a modish, intimate boutique hotel. Original features include oak staircase and stained glass window depicting Yorkshire cities. Stylish rooms.

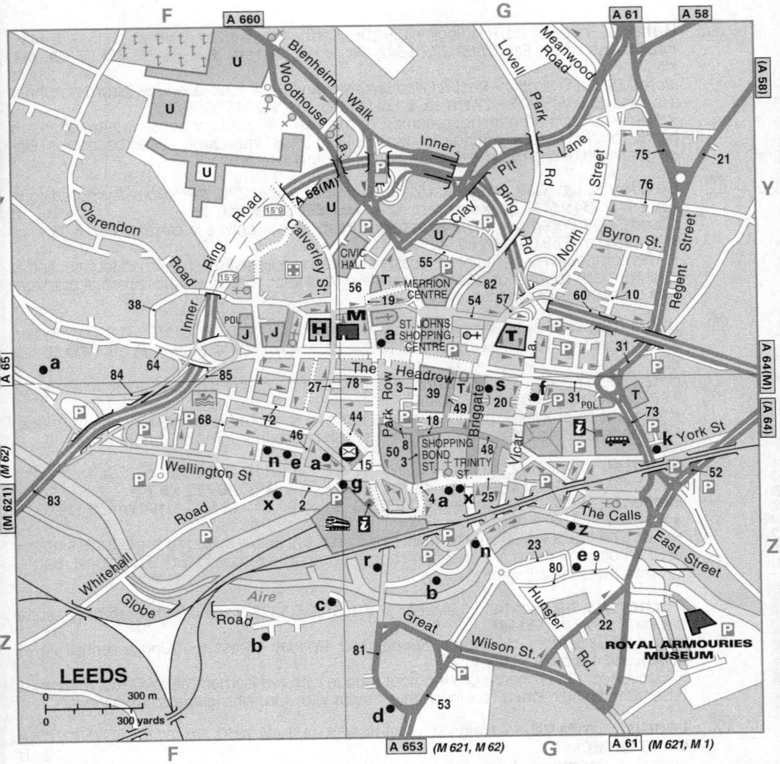

Aire St.	FZ	2	East Parade	FGZ	27	New York Rd.	GY	60
Albion St	GZ	3	Hanover Way	FY	38	Park Lane	FY	64
Boar Lane	GZ	4	Headrow Centre	GZ	39	Queen St	FZ	68
Bond St	GZ	8	Headrow (The)	GY		St John's Centre	GY	
Bowman Lane	GZ	9	Infirmary St	GZ	44	St Paul's St.	FZ	72
Bridge St	GY	10	King St	FZ	46	St Peter's St	GZ	73
Briggate	GZ		Kirkgate	GZ	48	Sheepscar St South	GY	75
City Square	GZ	15	Lands Lane	GZ	49	Skinner Lane	GY	76
Commercial St	GZ	18	Leeds Shopping Plaza	GZ	50	South Parade	FGZ	78
Cookridge St.	GY	19	Marsh Lane	GZ	52	Trinity St Shopping Centre	GZ	
County Arcade	GZ	20	Meadow Lane	GZ	53	Victoria Rd.	GZ	81
Cross Stamford St	GY	21	Merrion Centre	GY		Wade Lane	GY	82
Crown Point Rd	GZ	22	Merrion St	GY	54	Waterloo St.	GZ	80
Dock St	GZ	23	Merrion Way	GY	55	Wellington Rd	FZ	83
Duncan St	GZ	25	Millennium Square	GY	56	Westgate	FZ	85
Eastgate	GZ	31	New Briggate	GY	57	West St	FZ	84

42 The Calls, 42 The Calls, LS2 7EW, ✆ (0113) 244 0099, *hotel@42thecalls.co.uk,* *Fax (0113) 234 4100,* – – 70. MC AE VISA GZ z
closed 4 days Christmas – **Rest** – (see ***Brasserie Forty Four*** below) – 14.00 – **38 rm** 150.00/180.00 – 180.00/295.00, 3 suites.
◆ Stylish, contemporary converted quayside grain mill retaining many of the original workings. Rooms facing river have best views; all well equipped with a host of extras.

Hilton Leeds City, Neville St, LS1 4BX, ✆ (0113) 244 2000, *Fax (0113) 243 3577,* , – , rm, – 400. MC AE VISA GZ r
New World **:** **Rest** (bar lunch)/dinner 18.95 and a la carte 18.95/22.75 – 17.95 – **186 rm** 65.00/157.00 – 95.00/187.00, 20 suites.
◆ Proximity to station, business and commercial districts make this 1970s tower block a favourite for the corporate traveller. Neat rooms have views of city. Extensive brasserie menus with dishes from around the globe.

Haley's, Shire Oak Rd, Headingley, LS6 2DE, Northwest : 2 m. by A 660 ℰ (0113) 278 4446, info@haleys.co.uk, Fax (0113) 275 3342, ☞ – ℀, ▤ rest, ℙ – ≜ 25. ⚫ ⓐⓔ ⓞ ⚫

DV s

closed 26-30 December – **Rest** (closed Saturday lunch) (bar lunch Monday-Saturday)/dinner a la carte 40.00/45.00 ♀ – **27 rm** ☑ ✦125.00/135.00 – ✦✦145.00/280.00.

♦ Named after a prominent stonemason, this part 19C country house in a quiet area is handy for cricket fans. Antique furnished public areas. Individually styled bedrooms. Elegant, relaxed dining room with collection of original local artwork.

Bewley's, City Walk, Sweet St, LS11 9AT, ℰ (0113) 234 2340, leeds@bewleyshotels.com, Fax (0113) 234 2349 – |▤ ℀, ▤ rest, ℃ ⅊ ▱. ⚫ ⓐⓔ ⓞ ⚫⚫. ⚫

GZ d

closed 24-28 December – **The Brasserie** : Rest (dinner only) a la carte 13.85/26.95 – ♀ 6.95 – **334 rm** ✦69.00 – ✦✦69.00.

♦ This competitively priced hotel boasts a very spacious, stylishly furnished lounge, and is ideal for both tourists or business travellers. Well-kept rooms. Bright, informal brasserie with classically based menus.

Jurys Inn, Kendell St, Brewery Pl, Brewery Wharf, LS10 1NE, ℰ (0113) 283 8800, jurysinn leeds@jurysdoyal.com, Fax (0113) 283 8880 – |▤, ℀ rm, ▤ ℃ ⅊ ℙ – ≜ 100. ⚫ ⓐⓔ ⓞ ⚫⚫

GZ e

closed 24-26 December – **Innfusion** : Rest (bar lunch)/dinner a la carte approx 18.65 – ☑ 9.95 – **248 rm** ✦85.00 – ✦✦85.00.

♦ Adjacent to brewery, this good value 21C hotel is located near the Millennium Bridge. Airy, modern public areas. Well-equipped, stylish bedrooms. Informal, bright eatery.

Novotel, 4 Whitehall, Whitehall Quay, LS1 4HR, ℰ (0113) 242 6446, h3270@accor.com, Fax (0113) 242 6445, ⚫, ⚫ – |▤, ℀ rm, ▤ ℃ ⅊ ℙ – ≜ 90. ⚫ ⓐⓔ ⓞ ⚫⚫

FZ x

Elements : Rest a la carte 24.00/30.00 s. ♀ – ☑ 12.50 – **194 rm** ✦119.00 – ✦✦119.00/129.00, 1 suite.

♦ Just a minute's walk from the main railway station. Ideally suited to the business traveller, with desk modems and meeting rooms. Compact exercise facility. Functional rooms. Informal brasserie adjacent to lobby.

Anthony's, 19 Boar Lane, LS1 6EA, ℰ (0113) 245 5922, reservations@anthonysrestaur ant.co.uk – ℀. ▤. ⚫ ⚫⚫

GZ a

closed 25 December, 1 January, Sunday and Monday – **Rest** (booking essential) 22.95 (lunch) and a la carte 35.95/46.25.

♦ Converted 19C property; ground floor lounge with red leather Chesterfields; minimalist basement dining room offers innovative menus with some intriguing combinations.

Leodis, Victoria Mill, Sovereign St, LS1 4BA, ℰ (0113) 242 1010, Fax (0113) 243 0432, ☞ – ⚫ ⓐⓔ ⓞ ⚫⚫

GZ b

closed 26 December, 1 January, Saturday lunch, Sunday and Bank Holidays – **Rest** 16.95 and a la carte 19.40/40.40 ♀ ⚫.

♦ Appealing converted riverside storehouse offers hearty roasts, carving trolley and other generous British-style favourites in a bustling atmosphere. Friendly service.

No.3 York Place, 3 York Pl, LS1 2DR, ℰ (0113) 245 9922, dine@no3yorkplace.co.uk, Fax (0113) 245 9965 – ▤. ⚫ ⓐⓔ ⚫⚫

FZ e

closed 25 December-2 January, Saturday lunch and Bank Holidays – **Rest** 18.50 (lunch) and a la carte 20.00/32.00 ⚫.

♦ A minimalist and discreet environment keeps the spotlight on the appealing cuisine. Classic flavours reinterpreted in a tasty range of brasserie style dishes.

Simply Heathcotes, Canal Wharf, Water Lane, LS11 5PS, ℰ (0113) 244 6611, leeds@heathcotes.co.uk, Fax (0113) 244 0736, ← – ▤. ⚫ ⓐⓔ ⓞ ⚫⚫

FZ c

closed Bank Holidays – **Rest** 15.00 (lunch) and a la carte 17.25/33.45 ⚫ ♀.

♦ Converted grain warehouse by the canal. Distinctive modern feel with rich black banquettes. Effective contemporary cooking with prominent "northern" slant.

Aagrah Leeds City, St Peter's Sq, Quarry Hill, LS9 8AH, ℰ (0113) 245 5667 – ℀ ⚫ 40. ⚫ ⓐⓔ ⚫⚫

GZ k

closed 25 December – **Rest** - Indian (Kashmiri) - (dinner only) a la carte 13.55/19.90.

♦ On ground floor of BBC building in city centre, this stylish, open-plan restaurant gets very busy, but service invariably runs smoothly. Extensive, authentic Kashmiri menus.

The Foundry, 1 Saw Mill Yard, Round Foundry, LS11 5WH, ℰ (0113) 245 0390, Fax (0113) 243 8934, ☞ – ℀ ▤. ⚫ ⓞ ⚫⚫

FZ b

closed Saturday lunch, Sunday and Bank Holidays – **Rest** a la carte 21.00/28.00.

♦ Located in Industrial Revolution's cradle, this converted brick vaulted warehouse has a snug interior, offering unfussy seasonal cooking with a wide variety of daily specials.

XX **Plush,** 10 York Pl, LS1 2DS, 𝒫 (0113) 234 3344, *plushrestaurant@hotmail.com,*
Fax (0113) 242 7051 – ▤ ⇨ 16. **MC** **AE** **VISA**   FZ **n**
closed 25-26 December, 1 January, Saturday lunch and Bank Holidays – **Rest** a la carte
19.30/32.70 ♀.
   ◆ Based in the heart of Leeds: a modern, vibrant gathering place. Contemporary basement restaurant with fish tank containing lion fish. Eclectic menus invite close attention.

XX **Fourth Floor** (at Harvey Nichols), 107-111 Briggate, LS1 6AZ, 𝒫 (0113) 204 8000,
Fax (0113) 204 8080, ⌕ – 🛗 ▤. **MC** **AE** **①** **VISA**   GZ **s**
closed 25-26 December, Easter Sunday and dinner Sunday-Wednesday – **Rest** (lunch bookings not accepted on Saturday) 18.00 (lunch) and a la carte 21.00/30.20 🕮 ♀.
   ◆ Watch the chefs prepare the modern food with world-wide influences in these bright,
stylish, buzzy, contemporary surroundings. Advisable to get here early at lunch.

XX **Maxi's,** 6 Bingley St, LS3 1LX, off Kirkstall Rd 𝒫 (0113) 244 0552, *info@maxi-s.co.uk,*
Fax (0113) 234 3902 – ▤ **P.** **MC** **AE** **①** **VISA**   FY **a**
closed 25-26 December – **Rest** - Chinese (Canton, Peking) - a la carte 15.00/29.60 **s**.
   ◆ Savour the taste of the Orient in this ornately decorated and busy pagoda style restaurant. Specialises in the rich flavours of Canton and hot and spicy Peking dishes.

XX **Brasserie Forty Four** (at 42 The Calls H.), 44 The Calls, LS2 7EW, 𝒫 (0113) 234 3232,
info@brasserie44.com, Fax (0113) 234 3332 – ▤. **MC** **VISA**   GZ **z**
closed Sunday, Saturday lunch and Bank Holidays except Good Friday – **Rest** 16.00 (lunch)
and a la carte 24.75/28.95 🕮.
   ◆ Former riverside warehouse with stylish bar; exudes atmosphere of buzzy informality.
Smokehouse and char-grilled options in an eclectic range of menu dishes.

XX **Anthony's at Flannels,** Third Floor, 68 Vicar Lane, LS1 7JH, 𝒫 (0113) 242 8732,
reservations@anthonysatflannels.co.uk – ⅞ ▤   GZ **f**
closed 25 December, 1 January and Monday – **Rest** (lunch only) 16.00 and a la carte
15.50/18.50.
   ◆ Go to third floor of upmarket clothing store to find this sunny, stylish restaurant, adjacent to an art gallery. Friendly family service of good value, tasty, seasonal dishes.

X **The Mill Race,** 2-4 Commercial Rd, Kirkstall, LS5 3AQ, 𝒫 (0113) 275 7555, *enqui*
ries@themillrace-organic.com, Fax (0113) 275 0222 – ⅞ ▤. **MC** **VISA**   BT **r**
closed 25-26 December, 1 January and Monday – **Rest** - Organic - (dinner only and Sunday
lunch) a la carte 17.40/31.50 ♀.
   ◆ Former neighbourhood smithy offering an intimate, comfortable dining experience,
personally run by friendly owners. All meals are totally organic.

at Garforth *East : 7 m. by A 63* – CT – ✉ *Leeds.*

XX **Aagrah,** Aberford Rd, LS25 1BA, on A 642 (Garforth rd) 𝒫 (0113) 287 6606 – ⅞ ▤ **P.** **MC**
AE **VISA**
closed 25 December – **Rest** - Indian (Kashmiri) - (booking essential) (dinner only)
14.00/15.00 and a la carte 14.95/21.05 **s**.
   ◆ Part of a family owned and personally run expanding group. Classic regional Indian
cooking, specialising in the fragrant and subtly spiced dishes of the Kashmir region.

at Pudsey *West : 5¾ m. by A 647* – ✉ *Leeds.*

XX **Aagrah,** 483 Bradford Rd, LS28 8ED, on A 647 𝒫 (01274) 668818 – ▤ **P.** **MC** **AE**
VISA   BT **e**
closed 25 December – **Rest** - Indian (Kashmiri) - (booking essential) (dinner only)
14.00/15.00 and a la carte 14.95/21.05 **s**.
   ◆ Advance booking most definitely required here; a bustling Indian restaurant with modish styling. Offers an extensive range of carefully prepared authentic dishes.

at Bramhope *Northwest : 8 m. on A 660* – BT – ✉ *Leeds.*

⌂ **The Cottages** without rest., Moor Rd, LS16 9HH, South : ¼ m. on Cookridge rd 𝒫 (0113)
284 2754, *Fax (0113) 203 7496,* ⌗ – ⅞ **P.** ⅘
closed Christmas – **5 rm** ⊇ ✿45.00 – ✿✿55.00.
   ◆ A warm welcome awaits at this converted row of 18C stone cottages. Comfortable
lounge with open fire. Cosy, homely rooms are individually decorated. Good value accommodation.

ENGLAND

Your opinions are important to us:
please write and let us know about your discoveries and experiences –
good and bad!

LEICESTER Leicester 502 503 504 Q 26 *Great Britain G.* – pop. 330 574.

See : Guildhall★ BY B – Museum and Art Gallery★ CY M3 – St Mary de Castro Church★ BY D – Env. : National Space Centre★, N : 2 m. by A 6 – AX –, turning east into Corporation Rd and right into Exploration Drive.

🖫 Leicestershire, Evington Lane ℘ (0116) 273 8825 AY – 🖫 Western Park, Scudamore Rd ℘ (0116) 287 5211 – 🖫 Humberstone Heights, Gipsy Lane ℘ (0116) 299 5570 AX – 🖫 Oadby, Leicester Road Racecourse ℘ (0116) 270 0215 AY – 🖫 Lutterworth Rd, Blaby ℘ (0116) 278 4804.

✈ East Midlands Airport, Castle Donington : ℘ (0871) 9199000 NW : 22 m. by A 50 – AX – and M 1 – 🛈 7-9 Every St, Town Hall Sq ℘ (0906) 294 1113, info@goleicestershire.com. London 107 – Birmingham 43 – Coventry 24 – Nottingham 26.

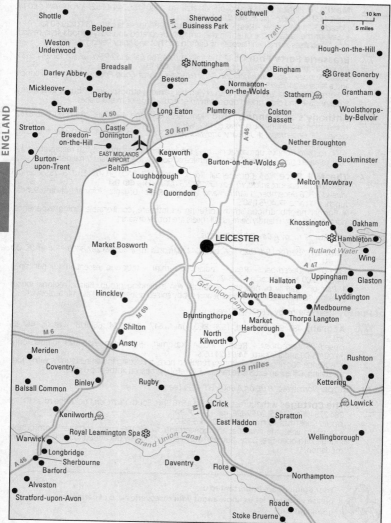

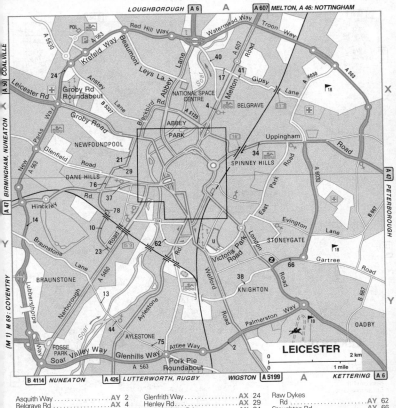

Holiday Inn Leicester City, 129 St Nicholas Circle, LE1 5LX, ℰ (0870) 4009048, *leices tercity.reservations@ichotelsgroup.com, Fax (0116) 251 3169*, ♣, ⌕, ▢ – ▯, ⟵ rm, ▤ ▣ – ▲ 250. ⏻⏻ ⏺⏺ ⏺ VISA BY c
Vermont : Rest a la carte 20.00/35.00 ♀ – ⌑ 14.95 – **187 rm** ✦149.00 – ✦✦159.00, 1 suite.
♦ Centrally located, imposing modern hotel convenient for the ring road. Comfortable brand style bedrooms with fitted furniture and particularly good Executive rooms. Stylish, modern restaurant and bar with American style menus.

Belmont House, De Montfort St, LE1 7GR, ℰ (0116) 254 4773, *info@belmontho tel.co.uk, Fax (0116) 247 0804* – ▯, ⟵ rm, ▣ – ▲ 160. ⏻⏻ ⏺⏺ ⏺ VISA CY c
closed 24 December - 2 January – **Cherry's :** Rest *(closed Saturday lunch, Sunday dinner and Bank Holidays)* a la carte 20.85/32.85 – ⌑ 10.50 – **77 rm** ✦110.00/115.00 – ✦✦120.00.
♦ Privately owned, centrally located and adjacent to a conservation area. Enlarged to provide a large bar and several function rooms. Spacious, comfortable bedrooms. Conservatory restaurant with formal air.

The Regency, 360 London Rd, LE2 2PL, Southeast : 2 m. on A 6 ℰ (0116) 270 9634, *info@the-regency-hotel.com, Fax (0116) 270 1375* – ⟵ rest, ▣, ⏻⏻ ⏺⏺ ⏺ VISA ⌖ AY z
Rest *(closed Saturday lunch and Bank Holidays)* 12.95 (lunch) and a la carte 15.50/28.95 ♀ – **32 rm** ⌑ ✦48.00/50.00 – ✦✦62.00/70.00.
♦ Attractive Victorian town house, formerly a convent. Character and historical notes in décor, especially in the individual bedrooms. Range of themed dinner-dance events. Restaurant or brasserie dining options.

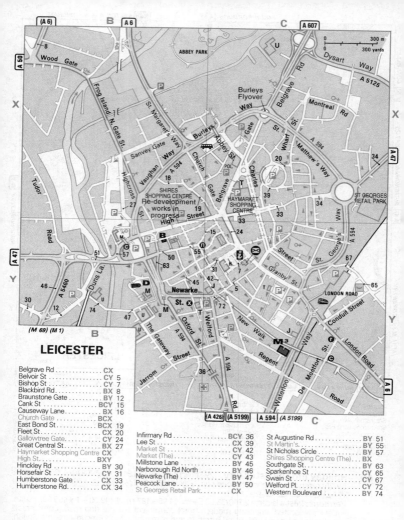

LEICESTER

XX **Watsons,** 5-9 Upper Brown St, LE1 5TE, ℰ (0116) 222 7770, *watsons.restaurant@vir gin.net*, Fax (0116) 222 7771 – ▤. 🕮 ㊂ ⒶⒺ *VISA*
BY **x**
closed 24 December- 4 January, Sunday and Bank Holidays – **Rest** 12.95 (lunch) and a la carte 23.40/28.95 ℥.
◆ Converted Victorian cotton mill in the centre of town. Vivid modern interior replete with chrome, glass and a cosmopolitan ambience. Wide ranging, competent, modern menu.

XX **Kabalou's** (at Comfort H.), 23-25 Loughborough Rd, LE4 5LJ, ℰ (0116) 268 2626, *reser vations@leicestercomforthotel.freeserve.co.uk*, Fax (0116) 268 2641 – ▤ Ⓟ. 🕮 ㊂ ⒶⒺ ①
VISA
AX **c**
Rest - Indian - a la carte 12.70/18.90.
◆ An opulent Indian restaurant with an unusual Egyptian themed bar and framed Indian gods in the dining area. Tasty, well-sourced regional Indian dishes.

XX **The Tiffin,** 1 De Montfort St, LE1 7GE, ☎ (0116) 247 0420, *thetiffin@msn.com*, Fax (0116) 255 3737 – ✜ 📧. 🆖 AE ① VISA CY r
closed 24-26 December, 1 January, Saturday and Sunday – **Rest** - Indian - (booking essential) 15.00/20.50 and a la carte 18.65/29.45.
* Busy, spacious and comfortable with a gentle Eastern theme to the décor. Tasty, authentic flavour in carefully prepared Indian dishes.

XX **The Case,** 4-6 Hotel St, St Martin's, LE1 5AW, ☎ (0116) 251 7675, Fax (0116) 251 7675 – ✜ 40. 🆖 AE ① VISA BY n
closed Sunday and Bank Holidays – **Rest** 12.95 (lunch) and a la carte 14.85/27.95 ②.
* Stylish modern restaurant in a converted Victorian luggage factory. Open main dining area and a small bar. Large, modern, seasonal menu. Champagne bar adjacent.

at Blaby South : 4¼ m. on A 426 – AY – ⊠ Leicester.

fff **Westfield House,** Enderby Rd, LE8 4GD, ☎ (0870) 609 6106, *reservations.leicester@corushotels.com*, Fax (01162) 781974, Ⅰ₆, ≘s, ☒ – ✜ rm, ▤ rest, ✇ ⅙ 🄿 – 🕰 70. 🆖 AE ① VISA
Rest 11.50/19.95 and a la carte 23.00/28.00 s. ② – ☲ 7.50 – **48 rm** ✹99.00 – ✹✹120.00.
* Distinctly modern atmosphere in this hotel based around a Victorian house. Smart, elegant rooms in contemporary style with co-ordinated soft furnishings. Smart bar/brasserie with stylish ambience.

LEIGH-ON-SEA Essex 504 W 29.
London 37 – Brighton 85 – Dover 86 – Ipswich 57.

XX **Boatyard,** 8-13 High St, SS9 2EN, ☎ (01702) 475588, Fax (01702) 475588, ≤, 🏤 – ⚓ ▤ 🄿. 🆖 VISA
closed Tuesday lunch and Monday – **Rest** 15.95 (lunch) and dinner a la carte 21.85/37.85 ②.
* Locally renowned, within a former boatyard by the Thames Estuary. Strikingly modern with floor to ceiling windows, deck terrace, oyster bar. Dishes have wide eclectic base.

LEINTWARDINE Shrops. 503 L 26 – ⊠ Craven Arms.
London 156 – Birmingham 55 – Hereford 24 – Worcester 40.

⌂ **Upper Buckton Farm** ⅗, Buckton, SY7 0JU, West : 2 m. by A 4113 and Buckton rd ☎ (01547) 540634, Fax (01547) 540634, ≤, 🏤, 🗷 – ✜ 🄿. ⅙
Rest (by arrangement) (communal dining) 25.00 – **3 rm** ☲ ✹52.00 – ✹✹84.00.
* Fine Georgian farmhouse, part of a working farm, surrounded by countryside. Comfortable, simple, country feel with open fires in the lounge and characterful bedrooms. Traditional dining; local produce.

🛏 **Jolly Frog,** SY7 0LX, Northeast : 1 m. on A 4113 ☎ (01547) 540298, Fax (01547) 540105, 🏤 – ✜ 🄿. 🆖 VISA. ⅙
Rest - Seafood specialities - *(closed Sunday dinner and Monday)* 16.50 (lunch) and a la carte 30.00/40.00 ②.
* Personally run, idiosyncratic rural pub with gloriously cluttered interior and useful deli annex! Rustic decor throughout. Extensive seafood menu and daily fixed price option.

LENHAM Kent 504 W 30 – pop. 2 191 – ⊠ Maidstone.
London 45 – Folkestone 28 – Maidstone 9.

fff **Chilston Park,** Sandway, ME17 2BE, South : 1 ¾ m. off Broughton Malherbe rd ☎ (01622) 859803, *chilstonpark@handpicked.co.uk*, Fax (01622) 858588, ≤, 🏤, 🗷, ⅍ – ⅋ ✜ ✇ ⅙ 🄿 – 🕰 110. 🆖 AE ① VISA
Rest *(closed Saturday lunch)* 22.50 (lunch) and a la carte 30.00/50.00 ② – ☲ 12.95 – **49 rm** ✹155.00 – ✹✹155.00, 4 suites.
* Part 17C mansion, set in parkland and furnished with antiques. Bedrooms are very individual and comfortable. Old stable conference facilities retain original stalls! Smart dining room and well-appointed sitting room.

Your opinions are important to us:
please write and let us know about your discoveries and experiences – good and bad!

ENGLAND

LEOMINSTER *Herefordshire* 503 L 27 *Great Britain G.* – pop. 10 440.

Env. : *Berrington Hall★ AC, N : 3 m. by A 49.*

🏌️ *Ford Bridge ℰ (01568) 612863.*

🛈 *1 Corn Sq ℰ (01568) 616460.*

London 141 – Birmingham 47 – Hereford 13 – Worcester 26.

at Kimbolton *Northeast : 3 m. by A 49 on A 4112.*

↑ **Lower Bache House** ◈, HR6 0ER, East : 1 ¾ m. by A 4112 ℰ (01568) 750304, *leslie.wiles@care4free.net*, ☞, ♨ – ⅙⇥ 🅿. ⅗

Rest (by arrangement) 24.50 – **4 rm** ☲ ✚44.50 – ✚✚69.00.

◆ A fine 17C farmhouse in a very quiet rural setting. Spacious, characterful, open feel throughout: bedrooms located in a charming converted granary. Converted cider barn dining room features original mill and press.

at Leysters *Northeast : 5 m. by A 49 on A 4112 – ⊠ Leominster.*

↑ **The Hills Farm** ◈ *without rest.*, HR6 0HP, ℰ (01568) 750205, *conolly@bigwig.net*, ≤, ☞, ♨ – ⅙⇥ 🅿. ⓿◎ ☒☒

closed mid November- March and 3 weeks June – **5 rm** ☲ ✚35.00/45.00 – ✚✚70.00.

◆ An attractive ivy-clad farmhouse on a working farm. The interior is delightfully comfortable, from the cosy lounge to the country-cottage rooms, three in the converted barns. Extensive country views from conservatory breakfast room.

at Pudleston *East : 5 m. by A 49 off A 44 – ⊠ Leominster.*

🏛 **Ford Abbey** ◈, HR6 0RZ, South : 1 m. on Pudleston rd ℰ (01568) 760700, *info@fordabbey.co.uk*, Fax (01568) 760264, ☞, ▨, ⸜, ☞, ♨ – ⅙⇥ & 🅿. ⓿◎ ﷼ ⓪ ☒☒. ⅗

Rest (booking essential for non-residents) (dinner only) (set menu only) 35.00 **s.** – **6 rm** ☲ – ✚✚125.00/180.00, 1 suite.

◆ Sumptuous, splendid isolation: a wonderful collection of medieval and 19C farmhouses and barns. Very characterful throughout. Luxurious rooms with low beams and hideaways. Dining room exudes appeal: 15C window frame still intact.

LETCHWORTH *Herts.* 504 T 28.

London 39.5 – Luton 18 – Stevenage 7.5.

at Willian *South : 1¾ m. by A 6141 – ⊠ Letchworth.*

🍴 **The Fox**, SG6 2AE, ℰ (01462) 480233, *restaurant@foxatwillian.co.uk*, Fax (01462) 676966, ☞ – 🅿. ⓿◎ ☒☒

Rest *(closed Sunday dinner and Monday)* a la carte 25.00/36.00.

◆ Refurbished pub in a pretty little village. Attractive pitched ceiling windows make restaurant feel like a conservatory. Interesting menus with emphasis on fish and shellfish.

LEVINGTON *Suffolk.*

London 75 – Ipswich 5 – Woodbridge 8.

🍴 **Ship Inn**, Church Lane, IP10 0LQ, ℰ (01473) 659573, ☞ – 🅿. ⓿◎ ☒☒. ⅗

closed 25-26 December and 1 January – **Rest** a la carte 16.00/25.00.

◆ Characterful, part 14C thatched and beamed pub with plenty of maritime curios and rustic charm. Fish a key element of dishes which range from traditional to rather innovative.

LEVISHAM *N. Yorks.* 502 R 21 – *see Pickering.*

LEWDOWN *Devon* 503 H 32 *The West Country G.*

Env. : *Lydford★★, E : 4 m.*

Exc. : *Launceston★ - Castle★ (≤★) St Mary Magdalene★, W : 8 m. by A 30 and A 388.*

London 238 – Exeter 37 – Plymouth 29.

🏛 **Lewtrenchard Manor** ◈, EX20 4PN, South : ¾ m. by Lewtrenchard rd ℰ (01566) 783222, *info@lewtrenchard.co.uk*, Fax (01566) 783332, ⸜, ☞, ♨ – ⅙⇥ 🅿. – ⬚ 40. ⓿◎ ﷼ ☒☒

Rest *(closed Monday lunch except Bank Holidays)* (booking essential for non-residents) 18.00/37.00 – **13 rm** ☲ ✚125.00/145.00 – ✚✚185.00/225.00, 1 suite.

◆ A grand historical atmosphere pervades this delightfully secluded 17C manor house. Plenty of personality with antiques, artworks, ornate ceilings and panelling throughout. Two elegant dining rooms with stained glass windows.

LEWES E. Sussex **504** U 31 *Great Britain G.* – pop. 15 988.

See : *Town★ (High St★, Keere St★) – Castle (≤★) AC.*

Exc. : *Sheffield Park Garden★ AC, N : 9½ m. by A 275.*

🏌 *Chapel Hill ℰ (01273) 473245.*

🖪 *187 High St ℰ (01273) 483448.*

London 53 – Brighton 8 – Hastings 29 – Maidstone 43.

🏰 **Shelleys,** High St, BN7 1XS, ℰ (01273) 472361, *info@shelleys-hotel-lewes.com,* Fax (01273) 483152, 🌇, 🐎 – 🛏 🛆 **P**, – 🕰 50. **◍◍ 🝙 VISA**
Rest 18.50/30.00 and lunch a la carte 17.20/21.75 ♀ – **18 rm** ⚏ ✚95.00/155.00 – ✚✚140.00/195.00, 1 suite.
◆ The great poet's family once owned this Georgian former inn. It has spacious bedrooms which are furnished and decorated in keeping with its historical connections. Smart restaurant exudes Georgian panache.

⌂ **Millers** without rest., 134 High St, BN7 1XS, ℰ (01273) 475631, *millers134@aol.com,* 🐎 – 🛏 🛆 🛆
closed 4-6 November and 19 December-7 January – **3 rm** ⚏ ✚68.00/73.00 – ✚✚75.00/80.00.
◆ Characterful, small family home in a row of 16C houses that lead to the high street. Appealing personal feel in the individual bedrooms with books, trinkets and knick-knacks.

at East Chiltington *Northwest : 5½ m. by A 275 and B 2116 off Novington Lane –* ⌂ *Lewes.*

🍴 **The Jolly Sportsman,** Chapel Lane, BN7 3BA, ℰ (01273) 890400, *info@thejollysports man.com,* Fax (01273) 890400, 🌇 – **P**, **◍◍ VISA**
closed 25-28 December – **Rest** *(closed Sunday dinner and Monday)* 15.75 (lunch) and a la carte 21.50/29.00 ♀.
◆ Brick and clapboard country pub with open, uncluttered interior and well cooked, contemporary dishes full of interest on regularly changing menu. Served with care.

LEYBURN N. Yorks. **502** O 21 – pop. 1 844.

🖪 *4 Central Chambers, Market Pl ℰ (01969) 623069.*

London 251 – Darlington 25 – Kendal 43 – Leeds 53 – Newcastle upon Tyne 62 – York 49.

⌂ **The Haven** without rest., Market Pl, DL8 5BJ, ℰ (01969) 623814, *warmwelcome@haven guesthouse.co.uk* – 🛏 **P**, **◍◍ VISA**. 🌸
closed 1 week February and 24-27 December – **6 rm** ⚏ ✚40.00/45.00 – ✚✚56.00/64.00.
◆ Neat and tidy house in village centre. Pleasant rural views from breakfast room, which also displays artwork from local gallery. Colourful rooms include DVD and CD players.

⌂ **Clyde House** without rest., Railway St, DL8 5AY, ℰ (01969) 623941, *info@clydehouseley burn.co.uk* – **◍◍ 🝙 ◍ VISA**
5 rm ⚏ ✚32.00/37.00 – ✚✚60.00.
◆ Former coaching inn dating from mid-18C: one of the oldest buildings in town. Two of the bedrooms are in the converted hayloft. Hearty Yorkshire breakfasts to start the day.

🍴 **The Sandpiper Inn** with rm, Market Pl, DL8 5AT, ℰ (01969) 622206, *hsand piper99@aol.com,* Fax (01969) 625367, 🌇 – 🛏 **P**, **◍◍ VISA**
closed 25 December and 1 January – **Rest** *(closed Monday)* a la carte 20.00/30.00 ♀ – **3 rm** ⚏ ✚65.00 – ✚✚70.00.
◆ Converted 16C stone house off market square. Rustic and simple with daily changing blackboard menu of tasty Yorkshire fare; good local ales. Pleasant pine furnished rooms.

at Constable Burton *East : 3½ m. on A 684 –* ⌂ *Leyburn.*

🍴 **Wyvill Arms** with rm, DL8 5LH, ℰ (01677) 450581, Fax (01677) 450829, 🌇, 🐎 – 🛏 rest, **P**, **◍◍ VISA**
Rest a la carte 20.00/29.00 ♀ – **3 rm** ⚏ ✚50.00 – ✚✚75.00.
◆ A classic Yorkshire pub with stone bar area and good choice of ales. Seasonally changing menu with steaks a speciality: eat in bar or formal dining room. Neat, tidy bedrooms.

LEYSTERS Herefordshire **503 504** M 27 – *see Leominster.*

The 🏵 award is the crème de la crème.
This is awarded to restaurants
which are really worth travelling miles for!

LICHFIELD Staffs. 502 503 504 O 25 Great Britain G. – pop. 28 435.

See : City★ - Cathedral★★ AC.

🏌 ,🏌 Seedy Mill, Elmhurst ℘ (01543) 417333.

🗓 Lichfield Garrick, Castle Dyke ℘ (01543) 412121.

London 128 – Birmingham 16 – Derby 23 – Stoke-on-Trent 30.

Swinfen Hall, WS14 9RE, Southeast : 2 ¼ m. by A 5206 on A 38 ℘ (01543) 481494, info@swinfenhallhotel.co.uk, Fax (01543) 480341, 🌳, ⬆, ※ – ⇔ rest, 🅿 – 🔏 160. 🕮 🎫 VISA. ※

Four Seasons : Rest (closed Saturday lunch and Sunday dinner to non-residents) 22.50/39.50 s. ♀ - ⚌ 5.00 – **16 rm** ✦125.00/140.00 – ✦✦160.00/175.00, 1 suite.

◆ Very fine 18C house in 100 acres with beautiful façade, impressive stucco ceilings and elegant lounges furnished with taste and style. Bedrooms offer high levels of comfort. Modern menus served in superb oak-panelled restaurant with Grinling Gibbons carvings.

Express By Holiday Inn without rest., Wall Island, Birmingham Rd, Shenstone, WS14 0QP, South : 2 ¼ m. on A 5127 ℘ (0870) 7201078, lichfield@morethanhotels.com, Fax (0870) 7201079 – 📶 ⇔ & 🅿 – 🔏 30. 🕮 🎫 ⓞ VISA. ※

102 rm ✦45.00/125.00 – ✦✦45.00/125.00.

◆ A standard lodge with simply furnished rooms. Well placed for Lichfield Cathedral and Alton Towers. Strategically placed close to A5 and M6.

Thrales, 40-44 Tamworth St, WS13 6JJ, (corner of Backcester Lane) ℘ (01543) 255091, Fax (01543) 415352 – ⇔, 🕮 🎫 ⓞ VISA

closed Sunday dinner, Monday and Saturday lunch – Rest a la carte 25.00/40.00 ♀.

◆ Busy, popular restaurant with a rustic style; building has 16C origins. Wide-ranging menu of simple homely dishes using mainly local produce.

Chandlers Grande Brasserie, Corn Exchange, Conduit St, WS13 6JU, ℘ (01543) 416688, Fax (01543) 417887 – ⇔ ▤. 🕮 🎫 ⓞ VISA

closed 26 December, 1-4 January, May and August Bank Holiday – Rest 13.50/16.50 and a la carte 21.25/26.50 ♀.

◆ On two floors in old cornmarket building. Tiled floors, prints and pin lights; a pleasant, relaxed atmosphere in which to enjoy a brasserie menu with good value lunch options.

LICKFOLD W. Sussex – see Petworth.

LIDGATE Suffolk 504 V 27 – see Newmarket.

LIFTON Devon 503 H 32 The West Country G. – pop. 964.

Env. : Launceston★ - Castle★ (≤★) St Mary Magdalene★, W : 4½ m. by A 30 and A 388.

London 238 – Bude 24 – Exeter 37 – Launceston 4 – Plymouth 26.

Arundell Arms, Fore St, PL16 0AA, ℘ (01566) 784666, reservations@arundellarms.com, Fax (01566) 784494, 🌳 , 🎣, 🌳 – ⇔ rest, 🕿 🅿 – 🔏 100. 🕮 🎫 ⓞ VISA

closed 24-25 December – Rest 22.00/42.00 ♀ s – **21 rm** ⚌ ✦99.00/114.00 – ✦✦160.00/190.00.

◆ Coaching inn, in a valley of five rivers, dating back to Saxon times. True English sporting hotel - popular with shooting parties and fishermen. Good country lodge style. English and French cuisine in opulently grand dining room.

Tinhay Mill with rm, Tinhay, PL16 0AJ, ℘ (01566) 784201, tinhay.mill@talk21.com, Fax (01566) 784201, 🌳 – ⇔ 🅿. 🕮 VISA

Rest (closed Sunday and Monday) (dinner only) 28.50 and a la carte 24.50/36.00 – **4 rm** ⚌ ✦58.50 – ✦✦85.00/89.50.

◆ Small converted mill: furnishings a mix of rustic and traditional, creating a cosy feel. Locally based, tasty cuisine from renowned Devonian owner/cook. Cottagey bedrooms.

The red 🕊 symbol?

This denotes the very essence of peace

– only the sound of birdsong first thing in the morning …

LINCOLN *Lincs.* 502 504 S 24 *Great Britain G.* – pop. 85 963.

See : *City*★★ – *Cathedral and Precincts*★★★ *AC* Y – *High Bridge*★★ Z 9 – *Usher Gallery*★ *AC* YZ **M1** – *Jew's House*★ Y – *Castle*★ *AC* Y.

Env. : *Doddington Hall*★ *AC*, W : 6 m. by B 1003 – Z – and B 1190.

Exc. : *Gainsborough Old Hall*★ *AC*, NW : 19 m. by A 57 – Z – and A 156.

[18] Carholme, Carholme Rd ℰ (01522) 523725.

✈ Humberside Airport : ℰ (01652) 688456, N : 32 m. by A 15 – Y – M 180 and A 18.

🛈 9 Castle Hill ℰ (01522) 873213.

London 140 – Bradford 81 – Cambridge 94 – Kingston-upon-Hull 44 – Leeds 73 – Leicester 53 – Norwich 104 – Nottingham 38 – Sheffield 48 – York 82.

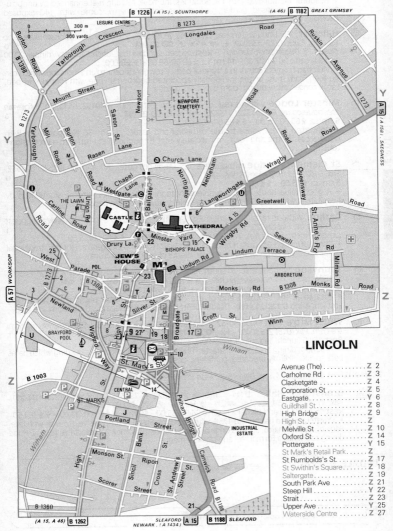

LINCOLN

🏠🏠 **Bentley,** Newark Rd, South Hykeham, LN6 9NH, Southwest : 5 ¾ m. by A 15 on B 1434 at junction with A 46 _&_ (01522) 878000, _infothebentleyhotel@btconnect.com_, Fax (01522) 878001, 🛌, ₤₅, ≘₅, ⬜ – 📶 ₩ , ▤ rest, 📞 ₺ 🄿 – 🔬 300. 🆑🅾 🄰🄴 🆅🅸🆂🄰. 🔉
Rest (carvery lunch)/dinner 19.20/25.00 **s.** and a la carte 28.95/36.50 – **80 rm** ⬜
†85.00/95.00 – **††**100.00/110.00.
• New purpose-built hotel. Smart, modern feel with traditional touches throughout. Well kept bedrooms including Executive and more traditional styles. Well-run leisure club. Formal or relaxed dining alternatives.

🏠🏠 **Bailhouse** without rest., 34 Bailgate, LN1 3AP, _&_ (01522) 520883, _info@bailhouse.co.uk_, Fax (01522) 521829, ⬜ heated, 🌾 – 📶 🄿, 🆑🅾 🄰🄴 🆅🅸🆂🄰. 🔉   Y c
⬜ 9.50 – **14 rm †**94.50 – **††**165.00/185.00.
• Beautiful 14C building with 19C additions. Intimate, relaxing feel enhanced by unobtrusive service, enclosed garden, and rooms oozing charm, some with 14C exposed beams.

🏠 **Hillcrest,** 15 Lindum Terrace, LN2 5RT, _&_ (01522) 510182, _reservations@hillcrest-ho tel.com_, Fax (01522) 538009, <, 🌾 – 📶 🄿. 🆑🅾 🄰🄴 🆅🅸🆂🄰   Y o
closed 23 December-5 January – **Rest** (closed Sunday) (bar lunch Saturday)/dinner 20.00 and a la carte 20.00/27.00 – **14 rm** ⬜ **†**60.00/69.00 – **††**89.00.
• Victorian former rectory in a tranquil part of town. Adjacent to an arboretum which can be seen from most of the traditionally appointed bedrooms - one with four-poster bed. Large conservatory dining room overlooks garden.

🏠 **Minster Lodge** without rest., 3 Church Lane, LN2 1QJ, _&_ (01522) 513220, _info@min sterlodge.co.uk_, Fax (01522) 513220 – 📶 📞 🄿. 🔉   Y a
6 rm ⬜ **†**60.00/75.00 – **††**85.00/105.00.
• Converted house, close to the cathedral and castle, just by 3C Newport Arch with good access to the ring road. Immaculately kept throughout and run with a professional touch.

🏠 **St Clements Lodge** without rest., 21 Langworthgate, LN2 4AD, _&_ (01522) 521532, Fax (01522) 521532 – 📶 🄿. 🔉   Y u
3 rm ⬜ **†**45.00 – **††**60.00.
• A good value house in a convenient location, a short walk from the sights. Run by hospitable owners who keep three large, pleasantly decorated bedrooms.

🏠 **Carline** without rest., 1-3 Carline Rd, LN1 1HL, _&_ (01522) 530422, _sales@carlineguest house.co.uk_, Fax (01522) 530422 – 📶 🄿. 🔉   Y i
closed Christmas and New Year – **9 rm** ⬜ **†**35.00/40.00 – **††**50.00/65.00.
• Double fronted Edwardian house a short walk from the city centre. Homely, traditional décor and style. Large sitting room with plenty of tourism literature.

🏠 **Tennyson** without rest., 7 South Park, LN5 8EN, South : 1 ¼ m. on A 15 _&_ (01522) 521624, _tennyson.hotel@virgin.net_, Fax (01522) 521355 – 🄿. 🆑🅾 🄰🄴 🆅🅸🆂🄰. 🔉
closed 24 December-2 January – **8 rm** ⬜ **†**30.00/40.00 – **††**50.00.
• Located at the southern end of the city, adjacent to large public park. Welcoming ambience and traditional feel. Delightful Art Deco tiled fireplace in sitting room.

🍴 **Wig & Mitre,** First Floor, 30-32 Steep Hill, LN2 1TL, _&_ (01522) 535190, _email@wigandmi tre.com_, Fax (01522) 532402 – 📶. 🆑🅾 🄰🄴 🅾 🆅🅸🆂🄰. 🔉   Y r
Rest 13.95 (lunch) and a la carte 22.00/36.50 ⬜.
• First floor dining area, with characterful almost medieval decor, in a building which dates back to 14C. Skilfully prepared, confident, classic cooking.

at Branston Southeast : 3½ m. by A 15 – Z – on B 1188 – ✉ Lincoln.

🏠🏠 **Branston Hall,** LN41 1PD, _&_ (01522) 793305, _info@branstonhall.com_, Fax (01522) 790734, ≘₅, ⬜, 🌾, 🌡 – 📶 📶 🄿 – 🔬 120. 🆑🅾 🄰🄴 🅾 🆅🅸🆂🄰. 🔉
Rest 15.95/24.00 and dinner a la carte 24.00/35.00 – **50 rm** ⬜ **†**70.00/99.00 – **††**164.50.
• Privately owned hall built in 1736, with additions. Stands in impressive grounds with lake. Bags of period charm, such as original wood panelling. Homely, comfortable rooms. Huge dining room has a formal feel and classical menus.

LINDALE Cumbria 502 L 21 – see Grange-over-Sands.

😊 Red = Pleasant. Look for the red 🍴 and 🏠 symbols.

LISKEARD Cornwall 503 G 32 The West Country G. – pop. 8 478.

See : Church★.

Exc. : Lanhydrock★★, W : 11½ m. by A 38 and A 390 – NW : Bodmin Moor★★ - St Endellion Church★★ - Altarnun Church★ - St Breward Church★ - Blisland★ (church★) - Camelford★ – Cardinham Church★ - Michaelstow Church★ - St Kew★ (church★) - St Mabyn Church★ - St Neot★ (Parish Church★★) - St Sidwell's, Laneast★ - St Teath Church★ - St Tudy★ – Launceston★ – Castle★ (≼★) St Mary Magdalene★, NE : 19 m. by A 390 and A 388.

London 261 – Exeter 59 – Plymouth 19 – Truro 37.

🏨 **The Well House** ◈, St Keyne, PL14 4RN, South : 3½ m. by B 3254 on St Keyne Well rd *℘* (01579) 342001, enquiries@wellhouse.co.uk, Fax (01579) 343891, ≼, ⅗ heated, ☞, ℀ – ≼⊁ rest, **P.** **◍** **VISA**

closed 25-26 and 31 December and 2 weeks January – **Rest** (booking essential for non-residents)/dinner 23.50/37.50 and lunch a la carte 23.85/30.85 – **9 rm** ⊆ ✦105.00 – ✦✦170.00/205.00.

◆ Large 19C country house surrounded by extensive grounds; personally run by friendly owner. Individual rooms have winning outlooks; those by the garden have private patios. Stylish, modern country house restaurant looks out over the countryside.

🏨 **Pencubitt Country House** ◈, Station Rd, PL14 4EB, South : ½ m. by B 3254 on Lamellion rd *℘* (01579) 342694, hotel@pencubitt.com, Fax (01579) 342694, ☞ – ≼⊁ **✆** **P.** **◍** **VISA**, ℀

closed 17 December-8 January – **Rest** (booking essential) (dinner only) 25.00 – **9 rm** ⊆ ✦55.00/75.00 – ✦✦80.00/110.00.

◆ Late Victorian mansion, with fine views of East Looe Valley. Spacious drawing room with open fire, plus sitting room, bar and veranda. Comfy rooms, most with rural views. Attractive, candlelit dining room.

LITTLE BARROW Ches. – see Chester.

LITTLE BEDWYN Newbury 503 504 P 29 – see Marlborough.

> We try to be as accurate as possible when giving room rates.
> But prices are susceptible to change,
> so please check rates when booking.

LITTLE BOLLINGTON Gtr Manchester – see Altrincham.

LITTLEBOROUGH Gtr Manchester 502 504 N 23 – see Rochdale.

LITTLE BUDWORTH Ches. 502 503 M 24 – see Tarporley.

LITTLEBURY GREEN Essex – see Saffron Walden.

LITTLE CHALFONT Bucks. 504 S 29.

London 33 – Amersham 2 – Watford 11.

🍴 **Sugar Loaf Inn**, Station Rd, HP7 9PN, *℘* (01494) 765579, info@thesugarloafinn.com, ☞ – ≼⊁ **P.** **◍** **VISA**. ℀

closed 26 December and 1 January – **Rest** a la carte 20.00/26.00 ℤ.

◆ Restored 1930s roadside pub in heart of Chilterns village. Characterful interior with oak panelled walls and mood lighting. Fresh, unfussy cooking with modern British edge.

LITTLEHAMPTON W. Sussex 504 S 31 – pop. 55 716.

🛈 The Look and Sea Centre, 63-65 Surrey St *℘* (01903) 721866.

London 64 – Brighton 18 – Portsmouth 31.

🏨 **Bailiffscourt & Spa** ◈, Climping St, Climping, BN17 5RW, West : 2 ¾ m. by A 259 *℘* (01903) 723511, bailiffscourt@hshotels.co.uk, Fax (01903) 723107, ☞, ℗, ℉, ≘s, ⅗ heated, ☒, ☞, ℀, ℀ – ≼⊁ rest, **✆ P.** – **♨** 35. **◍** **AE** **VISA**

Rest 16.00/44.50 ℤ – **39 rm** (dinner included) ⊆ ✦155.00/295.00 – ✦✦235.00/395.00.

◆ Alluring reconstructed medieval house basking in acres of utterly peaceful grounds. Rich antiques and fine period features in an enchanting medieval ambience. Superb spa. Split-room dining area nestling amidst warmly tapestried walls.

Amberley Court ⬧ without rest., Crookthorn Lane, Climping, BN17 5SN, West : 1 ¾ m. by B 2187 off A 259 ℰ (01903) 725131, Fax (01903) 725131, 🐎 – ⇔ 🅿. ⬥
9 rm ⊑ ✦45.00/50.00 – ✦✦75.00.

♦ Converted farm barn with a tidy, homely atmosphere. Exposed beams, flourishing plants and a warm welcome. Simply decorated rooms, some in grounds, with traditional chintz.

LITTLE LANGDALE *Cumbria* 502 K 20 – *see Ambleside.*

LITTLE LANGFORD *Wilts.* – *see Salisbury.*

LITTLE PETHERICK *Cornwall* 503 F 32 – *see Padstow.*

LITTLE SHELFORD *Cambs.* 504 U 27 – *see Cambridge.*

LITTLE THETFORD *Cambs.* – *see Ely.*

LITTLETON *Hants.* 503 504 P 30 – *see Winchester.*

LITTLE WILBRAHAM *Cambs.* – *see Cambridge.*

LITTLEWORTH *Oxon.* 503 504 P 28 – *see Faringdon.*

On the docks of Liverpool

LIVERPOOL

Mersey. **502 503** L 23 *Great Britain G. – pop. 469 017.*

London 219 – Birmingham 103 – Leeds 75 – Manchester 35.

TOURIST INFORMATION

🛈 *36-38 Whitechapel ℘ (0151) 233 2008; askme@visitliverpool.com – Atlantic Pavilion, Albert Dock ℘ (0906) 680 6886.*

PRACTICAL INFORMATION

ENGLAND

📷, 📷 *Allerton Municipal, Allerton Rd ℘ (0151) 428 1046.*
📷 *Liverpool Municipal, Ingoe Lane, Kirkby ℘ (0151) 546 5435,* BV.
📷 *Bowring, Bowring Park, Roby Rd ℘ (0151) 489 1901.*
Mersey Tunnels (toll) AX.
✈ *Liverpool John Lennon Airport : ℘ (0870) 129 8484, SE : 6 m. by A 561* BX.
Terminal : *Pier Head.*
⛴ *to Isle of Man (Douglas) (Isle of Man Steam Packet Co. Ltd) (2 h 30 mn/4 h) – to Northern Ireland (Belfast) (Norfolkline Irish Sea Ltd) 1-2 daily (11 h) – to Dublin (NorseMerchant Ferries Ltd) 2 daily (approx. 7 h 45 mn) – to Dublin (P & O Irish Sea) daily (8 h) – to Dublin (P & O Irish Sea) daily February-November (3 h 45 mn).*
⛴ *to Birkenhead and Wallasey (Mersey Ferries) frequent services daily.*

SIGHTS

See: *City★ – The Walker★★* DY **M3** *– Liverpool Cathedral★★ (Lady Chapel★)* EZ *– Metropolitan Cathedral of Christ the King★★* EY *– Albert Dock★* CZ *(Merseyside Maritime Museum★* AC **M2** *- Tate Liverpool★).*
Exc. : *Speke Hall★* AC, *SE : 8 m. by A 561* BX.

359

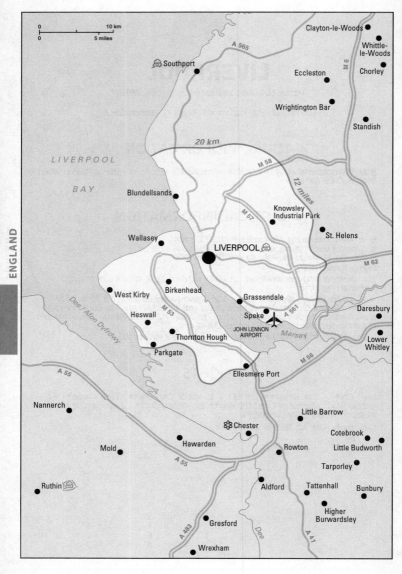

Your opinions are important to us:
please write and let us know about your discoveries and experiences –
good and bad!

L'infini pluriel

Route du Fort-de-Brégançon - 83250 La Londe-les-Maures - Tél. 33 (0)4 94 01 53 53
Fax 33 (0)4 94 01 53 54 - domaines-ott.com - ott.particuliers@domaines-ott.com

the MICHELIN guide

a collection to savour !

Belgique & Luxembourg
Deutschland
España & Portugal
France
Great Britain & Ireland
Italia
Nederland
Österreich
Portugal
Suisse

Also :

Paris
London
New York City
San Francisco
Main Cities of Europe

INDEX OF STREET NAMES IN LIVERPOOL

361

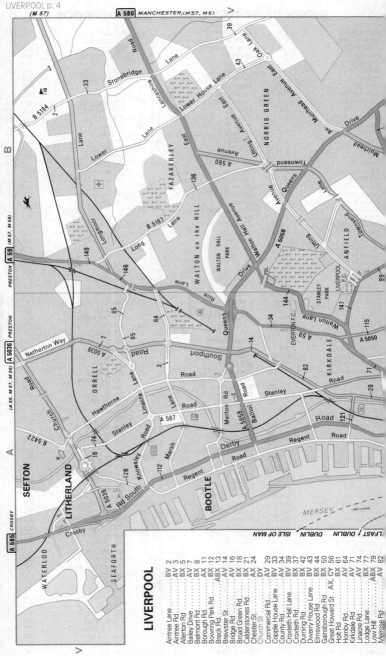

(M 57)

A 580 MANCHESTER,(M57, M6)

B 5194

PRESTON **A 59** (M 57, M 58)

A 5036 PRESTON (A 59, M 57, M 58)

A 565 CROSBY

A 5058

NORRIS GREEN

FAZAKERLEY

WALTON on the HILL

WALTON HALL PARK

ANFIELD

STANLEY PARK

LIVERPOOL F.C.

EVERTON F.C.

KIRKDALE

SEFTON

LITHERLAND

ORRELL

BOOTLE

WATERLOO

SEAFORTH

MERSEY

BELFAST / DUBLIN   DUBLIN   ISLE OF MAN

362

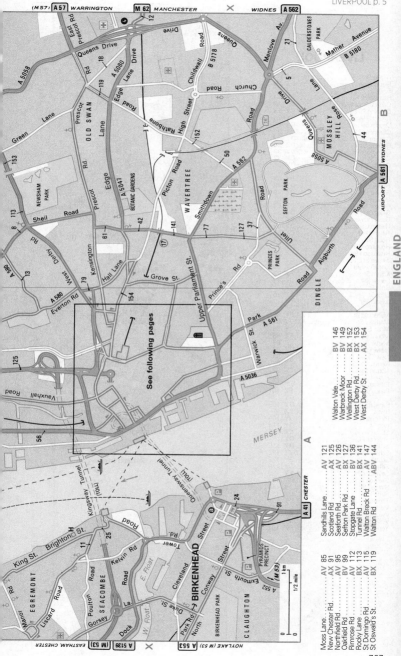

ENGLAND

(M 57) A 57 WARRINGTON   M 62 MANCHESTER   WIDNES A 562

East Prescot Rd
Queens Drive
A 5058
A 5080
Edge Lane Drive
Green Lane
Queens Drive
Childwall Road
Queens Drive
Menlove Av.
Mather Avenue
CALDERSTONES PARK
B 5180
21
119
18
5
OLD SWAN
Prescot Rd.
Edge Lane
High Street
Rathbone Road
Church Road
Queens Drive
MOSSLEY HILL
A 5058
B 5178
153
Green Lane
NEWSHAM PARK
A 5047
BOTANIC GARDENS
Prescot Road
Sheil Road
Picton Road
WAVERTREE
A 562
Smithdown Road
Road
SEFTON PARK
152
50
44
113
8
61
42
141
77
127
37
Rd
A 580
West Derby Rd
Kensington
Hall Lane
Grove St.
ULLET
PRINCES PARK
Aigburth
DINGLE
13
79
17
154
A 580
Everton Rd
Upper Parliament St.
Prince's
Rd
Park
Road
A 561
125
See following pages
Warwick St.
A 5036
56
Vauxhall Road
Kingsway Tunnel (Toll)
Queensway Tunnel (Toll)
MERSEY
A 41 CHESTER
AIRPORT A 561 WIDNES
B

HOYLAKE (M 53) A 540   EASTHAM, CHESTER

King St.
Brighton St.
Manor Rd
EGREMONT
Liscard
SEACOMBE
Kelvin Rd
Poulton Road
Gorsey La.
Dock Road
W. Float
E. Float
BIRKENHEAD PARK
CLAUGHTON
Conway Street
Cleveland Street
Exmouth St.
Duke St.
Park Rd
North
PYRAMIDS PRECINCT
BIRKENHEAD
Tower Rd
A 552 (M 53)
A 553
X
25
11
24
91
A 5139 A 553

0   1 km
0   1/2 mile

LIVERPOOL

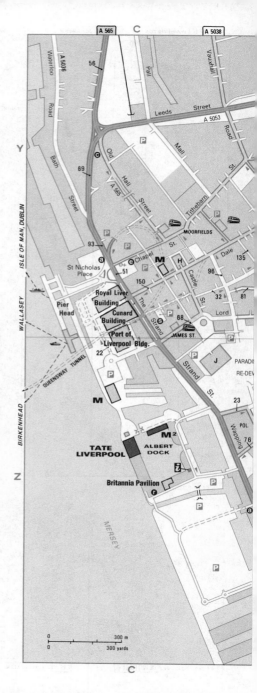

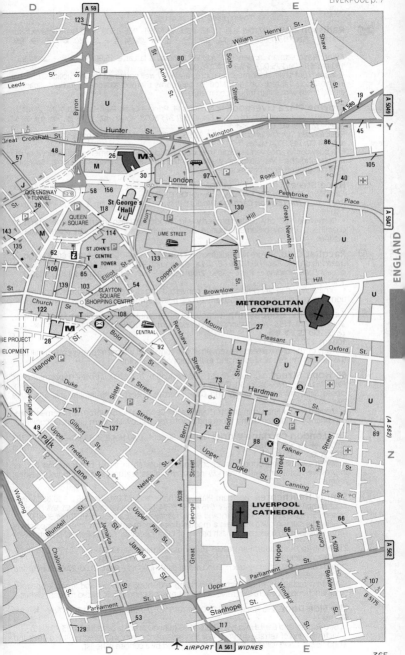

ENGLAND

AIRPORT A 561 WIDNES

Town plans: Liverpool pp. 3-7

Radisson SAS, 107 Old Hall St, L3 9BD, ✆ (0151) 966 1500, *info.liverpool@radisson sas.com*, Fax (0151) 966 1501, 🛏, 🍴, 🖵 – 📶 ✕ ➡ ☎ 🚷 – 🔼 180. 🆎 🆎 🆎 🆎
⚡
CY c

Filini : Rest - Italian influences - *(closed Sunday)* a la carte 16.90/31.40 ♀ – ☞ 14.95 – **189 rm** ✦99.00/275.00 – ✦✦99.00/275.00, 5 suites.
✦ Waterfront style: sleek meeting rooms and very well equipped leisure facilities. Chic bar in two Grade II listed cottages. Modern bedrooms themed "ocean" or "urban". Spacious dining room with Italian influenced menus.

Crowne Plaza Liverpool, St Nicholas Pl, Princes Dock, Pier Head, L3 1QN, ✆ (0151) 243 8000, *sales@cpliverpool.co.uk*, Fax (0151) 243 8008, ≼, 🛏, 🍴, 🖵 – 📶, ✕ rm, ☎ ☎
🚷 🅿 – 🔼 500. 🆎 🆎 🆎. ⚡
CY a

Rest *(closed Sunday lunch)* a la carte 23.95/37.20 – ☞ 14.95 – **155 rm** ✦124.00/139.00 – ✦✦134.00/149.00, 4 suites.
✦ A busy conference venue within the popular dockside development. Enjoys views of the Mersey and the Liver Building. Well-appointed and very comfortable rooms. Spacious, informal ground floor brasserie.

Hope Street, 40 Hope St, L1 9DA, ✆ (0151) 709 3000, *sleep@hopestreethotel.co.uk*, Fax (0151) 709 2454 – 📶 ✕ ☎ 🚷 – 🔼 60. 🆎 🆎 🆎
EZ o

Rest – (see **The London Carriage Works** below) – ☞ 14.50 – **41 rm** ✦140.00 – ✦✦140.00, 7 suites.
✦ Converted 19C city centre property with modern, stylish interior: leather furniture prominent. Trendy basement lounge bar. Contemporary rooms with state-of-the-art facilities.

Racquet Club, Hargreaves Buildings, 5 Chapel St, L3 9AA, ✆ (0151) 236 6676, *info@rac quetclub.org.uk*, Fax (0151) 236 6870, 🛏, 🍴, squash – 📶 ✕ – 🔼 80. 🆎 🆎 🆎 🆎 CY c closed Bank Holidays – Rest – (see **Ziba** below) – ☞ 12.00 – **8 rm** ✦120.00/180.00 – ✦✦120.00/180.00.
✦ Ornate Victorian city centre building converted into club offering unusual accommodation. Leisure facilities are a particularly strong point. Simple, well-equipped rooms.

Express by Holiday Inn without rest., Britannia Pavilion, Albert Dock, L3 4AD, ✆ (0151) 709 1133, *reservations@exliverpool.com*, Fax (0151) 709 1144, ≼ – 📶 ✕ 🚷 – 🔼 35. 🆎 🆎 🆎 🆎
CZ r

100 rm ✦70.00 – ✦✦125.00.
✦ Many of the original features remain at this converted Victorian former cotton mill near the 'Beatles' museum. Modern and well-equipped bedrooms.

60 Hope Street, 60 Hope St, L1 9BZ, ✆ (0151) 707 6060, *info@60hopestreet.com*, Fax (0151) 707 6016 – 🍴 ➡ 30. 🆎 🆎 🆎
EZ x

closed Saturday lunch, Sunday and Bank Holidays – Rest 16.95 (lunch) and a la carte 29.85/42.40 🍴 ♀.
✦ Modern restaurant within an attractive Grade II Georgian house. Informal basement café-bar, brightly decorated dining room and private room above. Modern European cooking.

The London Carriage Works (at Hope Street H.), 40 Hope St, L1 9DA, ✆ (0151) 705 2222 – ✕ 🍴, 🆎 🆎 🆎
EZ o

Rest 20.00/55.00 🍴 ♀.
✦ Stylish twin dining options in eponymous venue: an informal brasserie and bar, or impressive restaurant with strikingly prominent glass feature, and ambitious, seasonal menus.

Simply Heathcotes, Beetham Plaza, 25 The Strand, L2 0XL, ✆ (0151) 236 3536, *liver pool@simplyheathcotes.co.uk*, Fax (0151) 236 3534, 🍴 – ✕ 🍴 ➡ 30. 🆎 🆎 🆎 🆎 CY s closed 25-26 December, 1 January and Bank Holidays – Rest a la carte 15.70/31.50 🍴 ♀.
✦ Behind a sloping glass façade is a modish dining room where staff in emblemed shirts serve variations on the classics: hash brown of black pudding. Views of water sculpture.

Ziba (at Racquet Club), Hargreaves Buildings, 5 Chapel St, L3 9AA, ✆ (0151) 236 6676, *info@racquetclub.org.uk*, Fax (0151) 236 6870 – 🍴 ➡ 35. 🆎 🆎 🆎
CY e

closed Christmas, Saturday lunch, Sunday and Bank Holidays – Rest 18.00/27.00 (lunch) and a la carte 26.65/39.70 s. ♀.
✦ Modern restaurant in old Victorian building with huge windows and artwork on walls. Small lunch menus, more extensive dinner menus, offering classic-based modern dishes.

The Side Door, 29a Hope St, L1 9BQ, ✆ (0151) 707 7888, Fax (0151) 707 7888 – ✕ 🍴.
🆎 🆎
EZ a

closed Sunday and Bank Holidays – Rest 14.95 (dinner) and a la carte 16.70/23.70 🍴 ♀.
✦ Victorian end of terrace ground floor and basement eatery with green painted brick and wood floors. Good value dishes are supplemented by a concise wine list.

at Blundellsands North : 7½ m. by A 565 – CY – ⊠ Liverpool.

⌂ **The Blundellsands** without rest., 9 Elton Ave, L23 8UN, ℰ (0151) 924 6947, bsbb@blueyonder.co.uk, Fax (0151) 924 6947 – ✦✦ **P**, **QS** **AE** **VISA**, **S%**
4 rm ⊇ ✦39.00/55.00 – ✦✦65.00/75.00.
   ✦ Large semi-detached guesthouse with residential setting. Comfortable guests' lounge; the bedrooms, chintz in style, are clean, well-kept and have lots of extra touches.

at Knowsley Business Park Northeast : 8 m. by A 580 – BV – ⊠ Liverpool.

🏨 **Suites H.**, Ribblers Lane, L34 9HA, ℰ (0151) 549 2222, enquiries@suiteshotelgroup.com, Fax (0151) 549 1116, **I₺**, **☎**, **⊠** – **⋈** ✦✦ **≡** **₺** **P** – **益** 300. **QS** **AE** **OD** **VISA**
Rest (closed lunch Saturday and Sunday) 18.50 (dinner) and a la carte 21.45/31.90 s., 80 suites ⊇ 75.00/102.00.
   ✦ Adjoins a business park, with smartly designed work areas. A well-equipped, privately owned hotel, ideal for corporate clients. All rooms are comfortably furnished suites. Upbeat, vibrantly decorated dining room.

at Grassendale Southeast : 4½ m. on A 561 – BX – ⊠ Liverpool.

XX **Gulshan**, 544-548 Aigburth Rd, L19 3QG, on A 561 ℰ (0151) 427 2273, Fax (0151) 427 2111 – ✦✦ **≡**, **QS** **AE** **VISA**
Rest - Indian - (dinner only) 17.00 and a la carte 16.30/20.70.
   ✦ A richly decorated and comfortable traditional Indian restaurant within a parade of shops. Smart and efficient service of an extensive menu of authentic dishes.

at Speke Southeast : 8¾ m. by A 561 – BX – ⊠ Liverpool.

🏨 **Liverpool Marriott H. South**, Speke Aerodrome, Speke Rd, L24 8QD, West : 1 ¾ m. on A 561 ℰ (0151) 4945000, mhrs.lplms.eventsorganiser@marriotthotels.com, Fax (0151) 4945050, **I₺**, **☎**, **⊠**, **X**, squash – **⋈** ✦✦ **₺** **P** – **益** 280. **QS** **AE** **VISA**, **S%**
Starways : Rest a la carte 19.00/25.00 **₎** – ⊇ 14.95 – **163 rm** ✦99.00/200.00 – ✦✦99.00/200.00, 1 suite.
   ✦ Converted Art Deco airport terminal building, built 1937. Aviation and 1930s era the prevailing themes throughout. The modern, well-equipped bedrooms have a stylish appeal. Smart brasserie within original airport terminal; in keeping with hotel's style.

ENGLAND

Good food without spending a fortune?
Look out for the Bib Gourmand ☺

LIZARD Cornwall 503 E 34 The West Country G.
   Env. : Lizard Peninsula★ - Mullion Cove★★ (Church★) - Kynance Cove★★ - Cadgwith★ - Coverack★ - Cury★ (Church★) – Gunwalloe Fishing Cove★ - St Keverne (Church★) – Landewednack★ (Church★) – Mawgan-in-Meneage (Church★) - Ruan Minor (Church★) - St Anthony-in-Meneage★.
   London 326 – Penzance 24 – Truro 29.

🏠 **Housel Bay** ❧, Housel Bay, TR12 7PG, ℰ (01326) 290417, info@houselbay.com, Fax (01326) 290359, ≼ Housel Cove, **☞** – **⋈** ✦✦ **P**, **QS** **AE** **VISA**, **S%**
Rest (bar lunch Monday-Saturday)/dinner a la carte 20.50/26.50 – **21 rm** ⊇ ✦33.50/44.50 – ✦✦67.00/89.00.
   ✦ Britain's most southerly mainland hotel, with spectacular views of Atlantic and Channel: the Cornish coastal path runs through its gardens. Comfortable bedrooms. Dining room affords dramatic sea and lighthouse views.

⌂ **Landewednack House** ❧, Church Cove, TR12 7PQ, East : 1 m. by A 3083 ℰ (01326) 290877, luxurybandb@landewednackhouse.com, Fax (01326) 290192, **🛋** heated, **☞** – ✦✦ rm, **P**, **QS** **AE** **OD** **VISA**
Rest (communal dining) 38.00/45.00 – **6 rm** ⊇ ✦60.00/120.00 – ✦✦125.00/150.00.
   ✦ Part 17C former rectory and garden, overlooking Church Cove. Smart interiors stylishly furnished with antiques. Diners encouraged to discuss menus: best local produce to hand.

⌂ **Tregullas House** ❧ without rest., Housel Bay, TR12 7PF, ℰ (01326) 290351, ≼, **☞** – ✦✦ **P**
restricted opening in winter – **3 rm** ⊇ ✦32.00/48.00 – ✦✦56.00.
   ✦ Simple guesthouse in a charming location with mature garden and sea vista. Spotlessly kept with a cottagey style. Uncluttered bedrooms. At breakfast, take in the garden view.

LLANGARRON Herefordshire 503 504 L 28 – see Ross-on-Wye.

London: Big Ben

LONDON

504 *folds* S 29 *to* U 29 – *London G.* – *pop.* 6679699

SIGHTS

HISTORIC BUILDINGS AND MONUMENTS

Palace of Westminster★★★ : *House of Lords*★★, *Westminster Hall*★ *(hammerbeam roof*★★★*), Robing Room*★*, Central Lobby*★*, House of Commons*★*, Big Ben*★*, Victoria Tower*★*, 39* ALX – *Tower of London*★★★ *(Crown Jewels*★★★*, White Tower or Keep*★★★*, St. John's Chapel*★★ – *British Airways London Eye (views*★★★*)32* AMV.

Banqueting House★★ *31* ALV – *Buckingham Palace*★★ *(Changing of the Guard, Royal Mews*★★*, Queen's Gallery*★★*)38* AIX – *Kensington Palace*★★ *27* ABV – *Lincoln's Inn*★★ *32* AMT – *Lloyds Building*★★ *34* ARU – *Royal Hospital Chelsea*★★ *37* AGZ – *St. James's Palace*★★ *30* AJV – *Somerset House*★★ *32* AMU – *South Bank Arts Centre*★★ *(Royal Festival Hall*★*, National Theatre Royal*★*, County Hall*★*)32* AMV – *Spencer House*★★ *30* AIV – *The Temple*★★ *(Middle Temple Hall*★★*)32* ANU – *Tower Bridge*★★ *34* ASV.

Albert Memorial★ *36* ADX – *Apsley House*★ *30* AHV – *Burlington House*★ *30* AIV – *Charterhouse*★ *19* UZD – *George Inn*★*, Southwark 33* AQV – *Gray's Inn*★ *32* AMV – *Guildhall*★ *(Lord Mayor's Show)33* AQT – *Shakespeare's Globe*★ *33* APV – *Dr Johnson's House*★ *32* ANT – *Leighton House*★ *35* AAX – *Linley Sambourne House*★ *35* AAX – *London Bridge*★ *34* ARV – *Mansion House*★ *(plate and insignia*★★*) 33* AQV – *The Monument*★ *(*✳*★*) 34* ARU – *Old Admiralty*★ *31* AKV – *Royal Albert Hall*★ *36* ADX – *Royal Exchange*★ *34* ARU – *Royal Opera House*★ *(Covent Garden)31* ALU – *Staple Inn*★ *32* ANT – *Theatre Royal*★ *(Haymarket), 31* AKV – *Westminster Bridge*★ *39* ALX.

CHURCHES

The City Churches

St. Paul's Cathedral★★★ *(Dome* ⩽★★★*)* 33 APU.

St. Bartholomew the Great★★ *(choir*★*)* 33 APT – *St. Dunstan-in-the-East*★ *(Tower*★*)* 34 ARU – *St. Mary-at-Hill*★★ *(plan*★*)* 34 ARU – *Temple Church*★★ 32 ANU.

All Hallows-by-the-Tower (font cover★★*, brasses*★*)* 33 ARU – *Christ Church*★ 33 APT – *Cole Abbey Presbyterian Church (spire*★*)* 33 APU – *St. Andrew Undershaft (monuments*★*)* 34 ARU – *St. Bride*★ *(steeple*★★*)* 32 ANU – *St. Clement Eastcheap (pulpit*★*)* 34 ARU – *St. Edmund the King and Martyr (spire*★*)* 34 ARU – *St-Giles Cripplegate*★ 33 AQT – *St. Helen Bishopsgate*★ *(monuments*★★*)* 34 ART – *St. James Garlickhythe (spire*★*, sword rests*★*)* 33 AQU – *St. Magnus the Martyr (tower*★*, sword rest*★*)* 34 ARU – *St. Margaret Lothbury*★ *(spire*★*, woodwork*★*, screen*★*, font*★*)* 33 AQT – *St. Margaret Pattens (spire*★*, woodwork*★*)* 34 ARU – *St. Martin-within-Ludgate (spire*★*, door cases*★*)* 33 APU – *St. Mary Abchurch*★ *(reredos*★★*, spire*★*, dome*★*)* 33 AQU – *St. Mary-le-Bow (steeple*★★*)* 33 AQU – *St. Michael Paternoster Royal (spire*★*)* 35 AQU – *St. Olave*★ 34 ARU – *St. Peter upon Cornhill (screen*★*)* 34 ARU – *St. Stephen Walbrook*★ *(steeple*★*, dome*★*)* 33 AQU.

Other Churches

Westminster Abbey★★★ *(Henry VII Chapel*★★★*, Chapel of Edward the Confessor*★★*, Chapter House*★★*, Poets' Corner*★*)* 39 ALX.

Southwark Cathedral★★ 33 AQV.

Queen's Chapel★ 30 AJV – *St. Clement Danes*★ 32 AMU – *St. James's*★ 30 AJV – *St. Margaret's*★ 39 ALX – *St. Martin-in-the-Fields*★ 31 ALV – *St. Paul's*★ *(Covent Garden)* 31 ALU – *Westminster Roman Catholic Cathedral*★ 39 ALX.

PARKS

Regent's Park★★★ 11 QZC *(terraces*★★*, Zoo*★★*)*.

Hyde Park 29 AFV – *Kensington Gardens*★★ 28 ACV *(Orangery*★*)* 27 ABV – *St. James's Park*★★ 31 AKV.

STREETS AND SQUARES

The City★★★ 33 AQT.

Bedford Square★★ 31 AKT – *Belgrave Square*★★ 37 AGX – *Burlington Arcade*★ 30 AIV – *Covent Garden*★★ *(The Piazza*★★*)* 31 ALU – *The Mall*★★ 31 AKV – *Piccadilly*★ 30 AIV – *Trafalgar Square*★★ 31 AKV – *Whitehall*★★ *(Horse Guards*★*)* 31 ALV.

Barbican★ 33 AQT – *Bond Street*★ 30 AIU – *Canonbury Square*★ 13 UZB – *Carlton House Terrace*★ 31 AKV – *Cheyne Walk*★ 23 PZG – *Fitzroy Square*★ 18 RZD – *Jermyn Street*★ 30 AJV – *Leicester Square*★ 31 AKU – *Merrick Square*★ 19 VZE – *Montpelier Square*★ 37 AFX – *Neal's Yard*★ 31 ALU – *Piccadilly Arcade*★ 30 AIV – *Piccadilly Circus*★ 31 AKU – *Portman Square*★ 29 AGT – *Regent Street*★ 30 AIU – *Royal Opera Arcade*★ 31 AKV – *St. James's Square*★ 31 AJV – *St. James's Street*★ 30 AIV – *Shepherd Market*★ 30 AHV – *Trinity Church Square*★ 19 VZE – *Victoria Embankment Gardens*★ 31 ALV – *Waterloo Place*★ 31 AKV.

MUSEUMS

British Museum★★★ 31 AKL – *Imperial War Museum*★★★ 40 ANY – *National Gallery*★★★ 31 AKV – *Science Museum*★★★ 36 ADX – *Tate Britain*★★★ 39 ALY – *Victoria and Albert Museum*★★★ 36 ADY – *Wallace Collection*★★★ 29 AGT.

Courtauld Institute Galleries★★ *(Somerset House)* 32 AMU – *Gilbert Collection*★★ *(Somerset House)* 32 AMU – *Museum of London*★★ 33 APT – *National Portrait Gallery*★★ 31 AKU – *Natural History Museum*★★ 36 ADY – *Sir John Soane's Museum*★★ 32 AMT – *Tate Modern*★★ *(views*★★★ *from top floors)* 33 APV.

Clock Museum★ *(Guildhall)* 33 AQT – *London's Transport Museum*★ 31 ALU – *Madame Tussaud's Waxworks*★ 17 QZD – *National Army Museum*★ 37 AGZ – *Percival David Foundation of Chinese Art*★ 18 SZD – *Wellington Museum*★ *(Apsley House)* 30 AHV.

OUTER LONDON

Blackheath 8 HX *terraces and houses*★, *Eltham Palace*★ **A**
Brentford 5 BX *Syon Park*★★, *gardens*★
Bromley 7 GXY *The Crystal Palace Park*★
Chiswick 6 CV *Chiswick Mall*★★, *Chiswick House*★ **D**, *Hogarth's House*★ **E**
Dulwich 11 *Picture Gallery*★ FX **X**
Greenwich 7 *and* 8 GHV *Cutty Sark*★★ GV **F**, *Footway Tunnel* (≤ ★★), *Fan Museum*★ 10 GV **A**, *National Maritime Museum*★★ *(Queen's House*★★*)* GV **M²** *Royal Naval College*★★ *(Painted Hall*★, *the Chapel*★ *)* GV **G**, *The Park and Old Royal Observatory*★ *(Meridian Building : collection*★★ *)* HV **K**, *Ranger's House*★ *(Wernher Collection)* GX **N**
Hampstead *Kenwood House*★★ *(Adam Library*★★, *paintings*★★ *)* 2 EU **P**, *Fenton House*★★ 11 PZA
Hampton Court 5 BY *(The Palace*★★★, *gardens*★★★, *Fountain Court*★, *The Great Vine*★ *)*
Kew 6 CX *Royal Botanic Gardens*★★★ *: Palm House*★★, *Temperate House*★, *Kew Palace or Dutch House*★★, *Orangery*★, *Pagoda*★, *Japanese Gateway*★
Hendon ★ 2 *Royal Air Force Museum*★★ CT **M³**
Hounslow 5 BV *Osterley Park*★★
Lewisham 7 GX *Horniman Museum*★ **M⁴**
Richmond 5 *and* 6 CX *Richmond Park*★★, ⁎★★★ CX, *Richmond Hill*⁎★ CX, *Richmond Bridge*★★ R, *Richmond Green*★★ BX **S**, *(Maids of Honour Row*★★, *Trumpeter's House*★ *)*, *Asgill House*★ BX **B**, *Ham House*★★ BX **V**
Shoreditch 14 XZ *Beffrye Museum*★ **M**
Tower Hamlets 7 GV *Canary Wharf*★★ B, *Isle of Dogs*★ *St. Katharine Dock*★ 34 ASV
Twickenham 5 BX *Marble Hill House*★ **Z**, *Strawberry Hill*★ **A** .

The maps in this section of the Guide are based upon the Ordnance Survey of Great Britain with the permission of the Controller of Her Majesty's Stationery Office. © Crown Copyright 100000247

PRACTICAL INFORMATION

🛈 *Britain Visitor Centre, 1 Regent St, W1* ☎ *(020) 8846 9000*

Airports

🛬 *Heathrow* ☎ *08700 000123* 12 **AX** *Terminal: Airbus (A1) from Victoria, Airbus (A2) from Paddington Underground (Piccadilly line) frequent service daily.*
🛬 *Gatwick* ☎ *08700 002468* 13: *by A23* **EZ** *and M23 – Terminal: Coach service from Victoria Coach Station (Flightline 777, hourly service) - Railink (Gatwick Express) from Victoria (24 h service).*
🛬 *London City Airport* ☎ *(020) 7646 0000* 11 **HV**
🛬 *Stansted, at Bishop's Stortford* ☎ *08700 000303, NE: 34m* 11 *by M11* **JT** *and A120.*
British Airways, Ticket sales and reservations Paddington Station London W2 ☎ *0870 8509850* 36 **BX**

Banks

Open, generally 9.30 am to 4.30 pm weekdays (except public holidays). You need ID (passport) for cashing cheques. Banks levy smaller commissions than hotels.
Many 'Bureaux de Change' around Piccadilly open 7 days.

Medical Emergencies

To contact a doctor for first aid, emergency medical advice and chemists night service: 07000 372255.
Accident & Emergency: dial 999 for Ambulance, Police or Fire Services.

Post Offices

Open Monday to Friday 9 am to 5.30 pm. Late collections made from Leicester Square.

Shopping

Most stores are found in Oxford Street (Selfridges, M & S), Regent Street (Hamleys, Libertys) and Knightsbridge (Harrods, Harvey Nichols). Open usually Monday to Saturday 9 am to 6 pm. Some open later (8 pm) once a week; Knightsbridge Wednesday, Oxford Street and Regent Street Thursday. Other areas worth visiting include Jermyn Street and Savile Row (mens outfitters), Bond Street (jewellers and haute couture).

Theatres

The "West End" has many major theatre performances and can generally be found around Shaftesbury Avenue. Most daily newspapers give details of performances. A half-price ticket booth is located in Leicester Square and is open Monday-Saturday 1 - 6.30 pm, Sunday and matinée days 12 noon - 6.30 pm. Restrictions apply.

Tipping

When a service charge is included in a bill it is not necessary to tip extra. If service is not included a discretionary 10% is normal.

Travel

As driving in London is difficult, it is advisable to take the Underground, a bus or taxi. Taxis can be hailed when the amber light is illuminated.

Congestion Charging

The congestion charge is £8 per day on all vehicles (except motor cycles and exempt vehicles) entering the central zone between 7.00 am and 6.00 pm - Monday to Friday except on Bank Holidays.

Payment can be made in advance, on the day, by post, on the Internet, by telephone (0845 900 1234) or at retail outlets.

A charge of up to £100 will be made for non-payment.

Further information is available on the Transport for London website - www.cclondon.com.

Localities outside the Greater London limits are listed alphabetically throughout the guide.

Les localités situées en dehors des limites de Greater London se trouvent à leur place alphabetique dans le guide.

Alle Städte und Gemeinden außerhalb von Greater London sind in alphabetischer Reihenfolge aufgelistet.

Le località situate al di fuori dei confini della Greater London sono ordinate alfabeticamente all'interno della Guida.

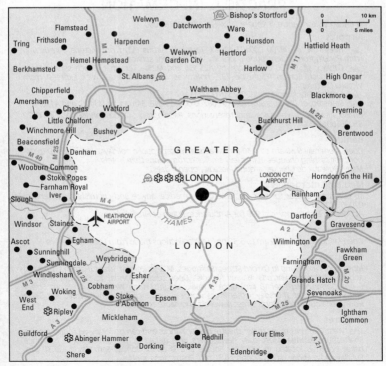

372

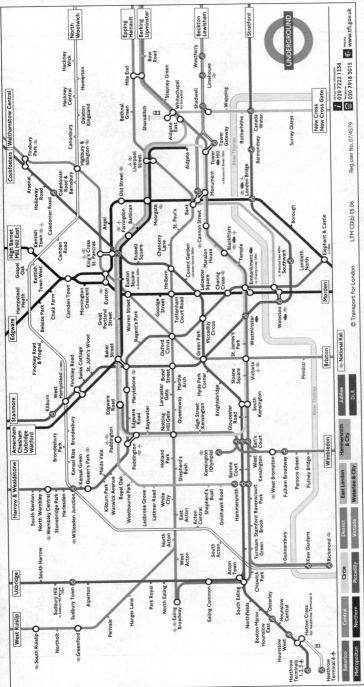

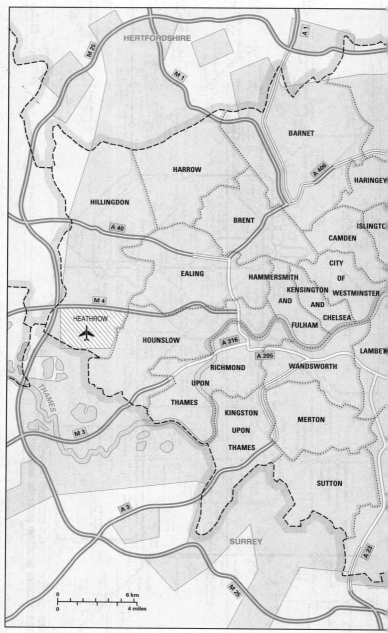

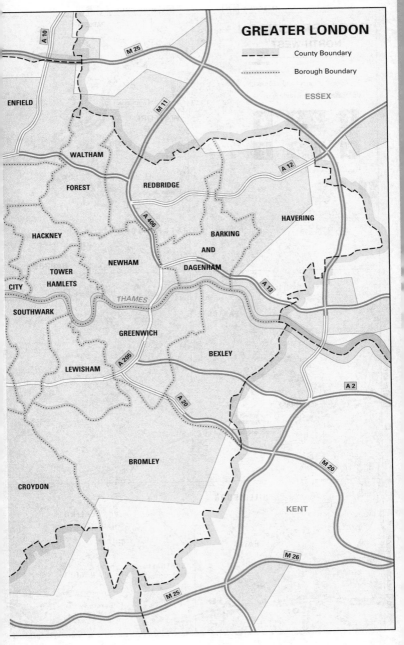

GREATER LONDON

- – – – County Boundary
- ·········· Borough Boundary

ESSEX

A 10

M 25

M 11

ENFIELD

WALTHAM

FOREST

REDBRIDGE

A 12

HAVERING

HACKNEY

A 406

BARKING

AND

DAGENHAM

TOWER

HAMLETS

NEWHAM

CITY

SOUTHWARK

THAMES

A 13

GREENWICH

BEXLEY

A 2

LEWISHAM

A 205

A 20

M 20

BROMLEY

CROYDON

KENT

M 26

M 25

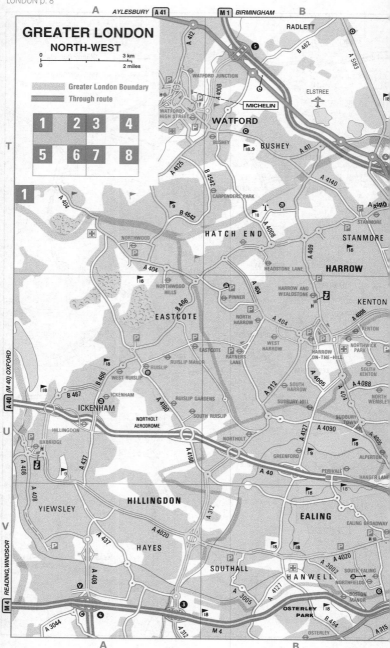

GREATER LONDON
NORTH-WEST

0   3 km
0   2 miles

Greater London Boundary

Through route

| 1 | 2 | 3 | 4 |
| 5 | 6 | 7 | 8 |

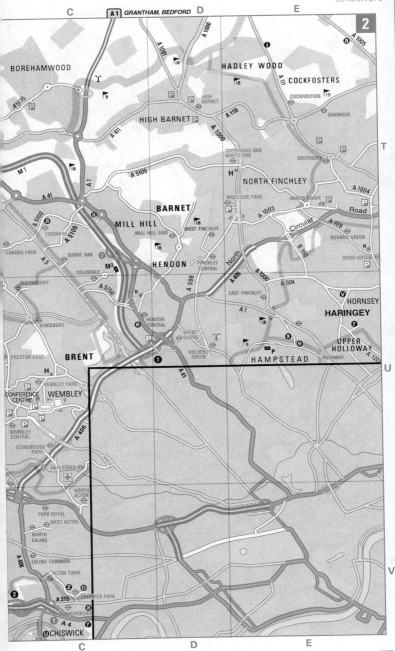

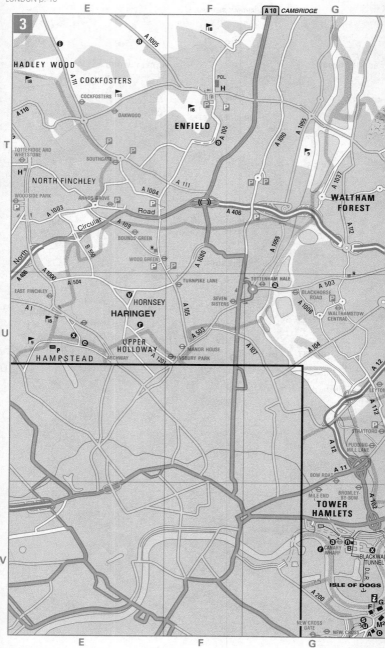

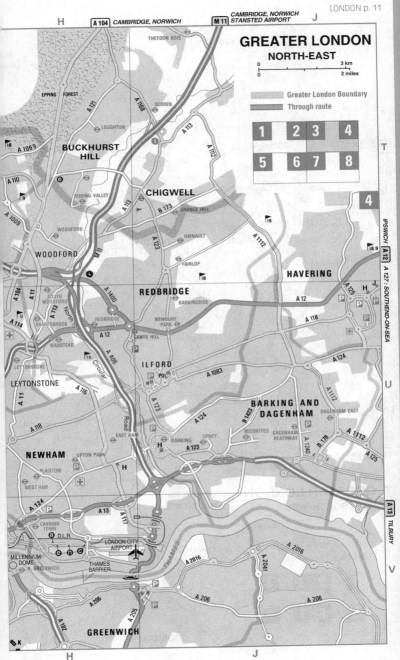

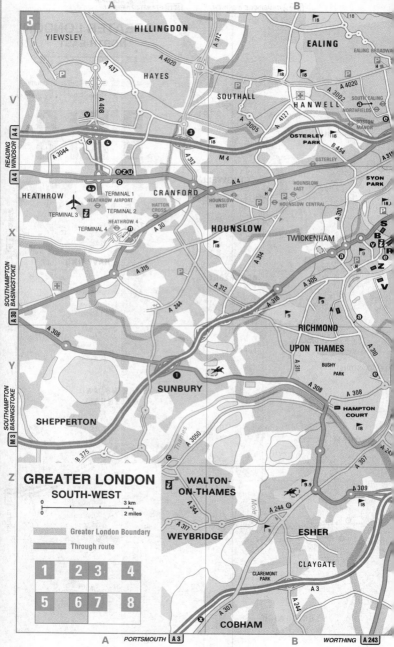

GREATER LONDON
SOUTH-WEST

0 ——— 3 km
0 ——— 2 miles

Greater London Boundary

Through route

| 1 | 2 | 3 | 4 |
| 5 | 6 | 7 | 8 |

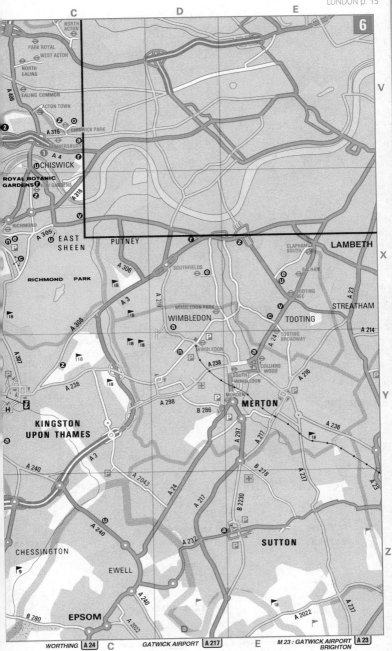

C   D   E

V

X

Y

Z

NORTH ACTON
PARK ROYAL   WEST ACTON
NORTH EALING
EALING COMMON
A 406
ACTON TOWN
A 315   CHISWICK PARK
GUNNERSBURY
A 4
CHISWICK
ROYAL BOTANIC
GARDENS   KEW GARDENS
A 316
RICHMOND
A 305   EAST SHEEN
PUTNEY   LAMBETH
RICHMOND PARK
A 306   SOUTHFIELDS   CLAPHAM SOUTH
BALHAM
A 3   A 219   WIMBLEDON PARK   TOOTING BEC
A 308   WIMBLEDON   TOOTING   STREATHAM
A 23
A 307   A 24   A 214
A 238   WIMBLEDON   TOOTING BROADWAY
A 238   COLLIERS WOOD
SOUTH WIMBLEDON
A 298   MORDEN   A 216
B 286   MERTON
KINGSTON
UPON THAMES   A 297   A 217   A 236
A 240   A 3   B 278   A 237   A 23
A 2043   A 24
A 217   B 2230
A 240
A 232   SUTTON
CHESSINGTON   A 240
EWELL
EPSOM   A 2022   A 2022   A 237
B 280   A 2022

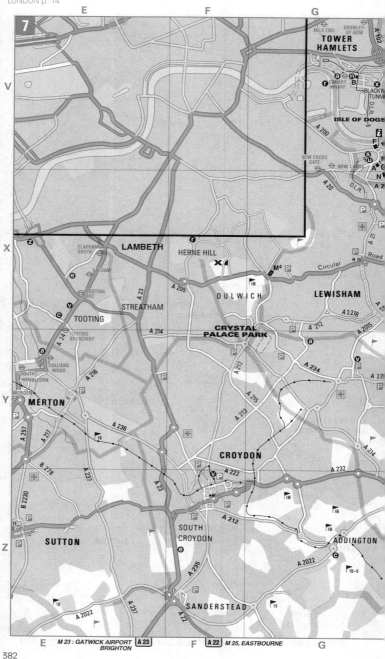

E   F   G

V

MILE END   BROMLEY-BY-BOW   A 102

TOWER HAMLETS

CANARY WHARF

BLACKW TUNNE

ISLE OF DOGS

A 200

NEW CROSS GATE   NEW CROSS

A 20

DLR   A 2

X

LAMBETH   HERNE HILL

CLAPHAM SOUTH

BALHAM

A 23   A 205   M⁴

STREATHAM   **DULWICH**   **LEWISHAM**

TOOTING BEC

TOOTING   A 214   **CRYSTAL PALACE PARK**

A 24   TOOTING BROADWAY

A 2 218   A 2015

A 212   A 234   A 22

COLLIERS WOOD

SOUTH WIMBLEDON   A 216   A 215

Y

MORDEN

MERTON   A 213

A 297   A 217   A 236

A 214

B 278   18   **CROYDON**   A 232

B 2230   A 237   A 23   A 222

18

Z

SUTTON   **SOUTH CROYDON**   A 212   **ADDINGTON**

18

A 235   A 2022   18-9

18   A 2022   A 237   A 72   **SANDERSTEAD**   18

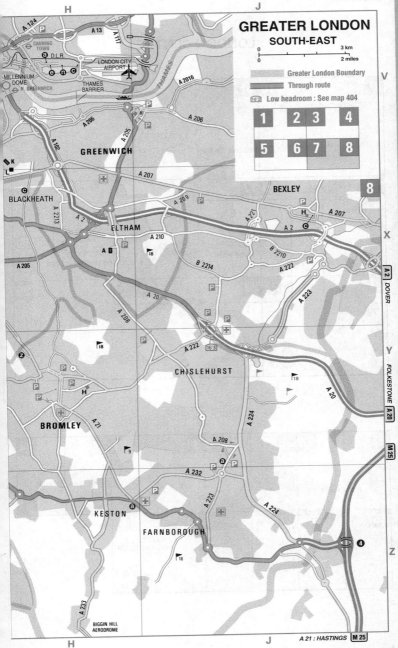

GREATER LONDON
SOUTH-EAST

	3 km
0	
0	2 miles

Greater London Boundary
Through route
16·2 Low headroom : See map 404

1	2	3	4
5	6	7	8

A 124

CANNING TOWN
D.L.R.
A 13
A 117
LONDON CITY AIRPORT
THAMES

MILLENNIUM DOME
N. GREENWICH
THAMES BARRIER

A 2016

A 206

A 1102

A 205

GREENWICH

A 206

A 207

BLACKHEATH

A 2213

A 2

A 205

ELTHAM

A 210

B 2214

A 20

A 208

BEXLEY

A 209

A 2

A 207

A 22

B 2210

A 222

A 223

CHISLEHURST

A 222 16·3

A 20

BROMLEY

A 21

A 224

A 208

KESTON

A 232

A 223

FARNBOROUGH

A 224

A 233

BIGGIN HILL AERODROME

V

8

X

Y

Z

A 2 DOVER

FOLKESTONE A 20

M 25

LONDON CENTRE

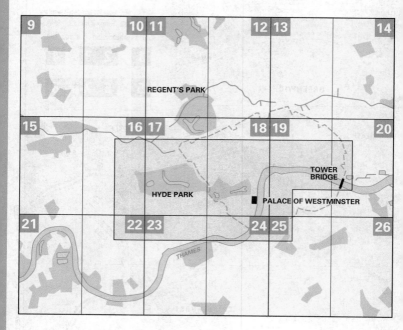

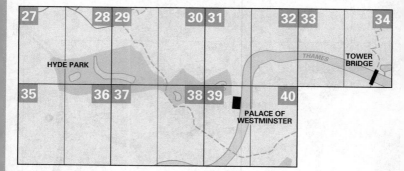

INDEX OF STREET NAMES IN LONDON CENTRE

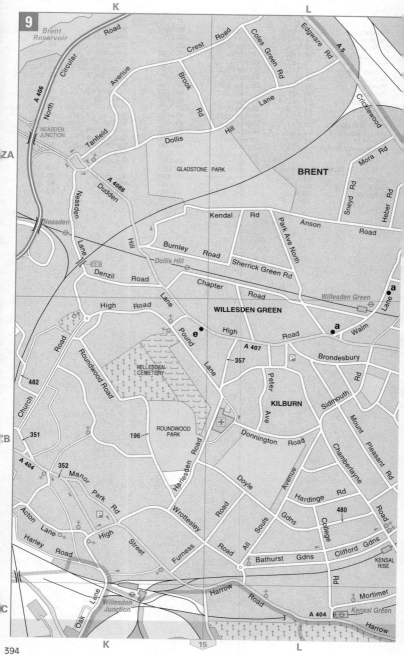

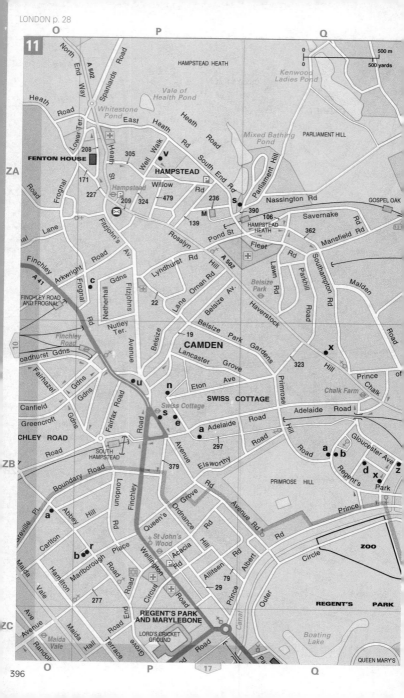

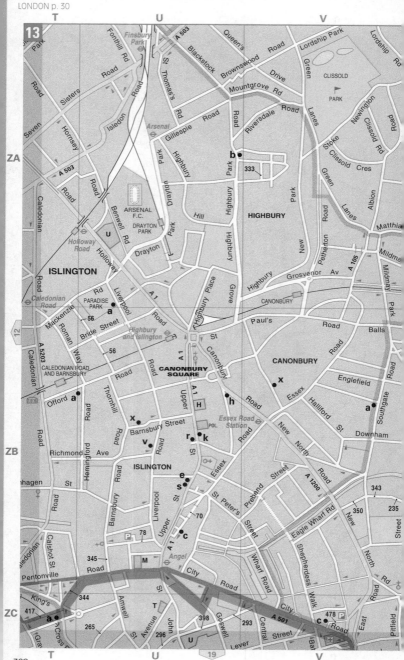

14

X   Y

STOKE
NEWINGTON

Mount Pleasant Hill

0   500 m

0   500 yards

A 107

A 104

Kyverdale   Road

Upper   Clapton

Cleveleys   Road

Bridge

Chatsworth   Road

Northwold   Road

Maury   Road

Clapton   Road

Lea

e ✕

STOKE
NEWINGTON

church St

Rd

A 10   High   Street

Rectory   Road

Brooke   Road

Evering   Road

RECTORY
ROAD

Kenninghall   Road

Lower

ZA

Millfields   Road

Powerscroft   Road

Clifden   Rd

Median

Rd

Clapton

Road

A 102

Homerton   High

Barbauld
Rd

Nevill   Road

Walford   Rd

Prince

George   Rd

Barretts   Grv

Rd

Road

Boleyn

Road

Amhurst   Road

HACKNEY

Shacklewell   La

Cecilia

Newington   Road

Sandringham   Road

Road

Downs   Road

HACKNEY
DOWNS

Downs   Park   Road

Amhurst   Road

Pembury   Rd

Clapton   Way

Rd

Dalston
Lane

Road

Street

378

13'8

15'6

337

DALSTON
KINGSLAND

Ridley   Rd

Stoke

Road

HACKNEY
DOWNS

HACKNEY
CENTRAL

Lane

Morning

Pond

Road

A 10   Kingsland

Dalston   Lane

Forest   Road

Richmond   Road

Graham   Road

Richmond   Road

Lansdowne   Drive

Queensbridge   Road

LONDON
FIELDS

A 107   Mare

Park   Rd

Frampton

Street

Well   Street

Cassland
Rd

13'9

13'0

Beauvoir

Road

Middleton

Albion   Drive

Road

Pownall   Rd

Well   Street

Victoria

Park   Road

ZB

16'0

DALSTON

a

Mare   Street

Sheep   Lane

15'9

464

Nuttall   St

Whiston   Road

Queensbridge   Road

Pritchard's   Rd

HAGGERSTON
PARK

VICTORIA
PARK

Sewardstone   Rd

Bishop's   Way

Bonner   Rd

13'9

Street

Kingsland

**GEFFRYE
MUSEUM**

Warner   Pl

Hackney   Road

CAMBRIDGE
HEATH

Road

Ford   Rd

Old

16'3

Hoxton

16'

r

v S**m**

Hackney

Columbia   Road

Old   Bethnal   Green

Turin   St

A 1209

Green

Carrobert   St

Road

M

Roman   Road

B 119

Globe

Bethnal
Green

ZC

20

X   Y

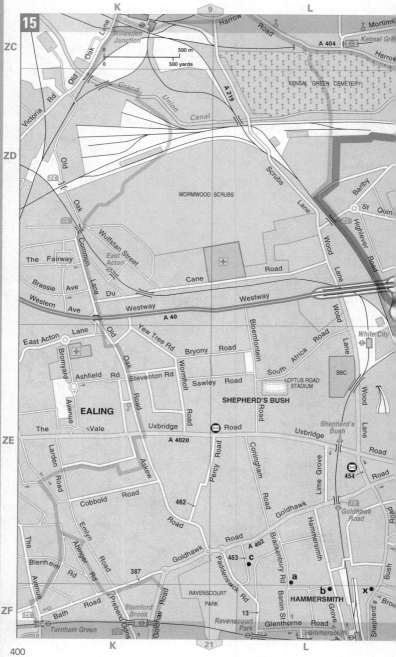

15

ZC

ZD

ZE

ZF

K

L

9

21

Willesden Junction

Oak Lane

Harrow Road

A 404

Kensal Green

Mortime

Harrow

500 m

500 yards

Victoria Rd

Old

Grand

Union

Canal

A 219

KENSAL GREEN CEMETERY

Old

Oak

Common Lane

Wulfstan Street

East Acton

The Fairway

Brassie Ave

Western Ave

Du

Westway

Cane

WORMWOOD SCRUBS

Scrubs

Lane

Wood

Lane

Highlever Road

Barlby

St Quin

Road

Westway

A 40

East Acton Lane

Bromyard

Ashfield Rd

Avenue

EALING

The

Vale

Larden

Road

Cobbold

Road

Emlyn

Road

Abinger Rd

The

Blenheim

Rd

Avenue

Bath

Road

Turnham Green

Old

Oak

Road

Yew Tree Rd

Bryony

Road

Steventon Rd

Wornholt

Road

Sawley

Road

Uxbridge

Road

A 4020

Askew

Road

Goldhawk

Road

462

387

Goldhawk

Road

Stamford Brook

Prebend Gdns

Bloemfontein

Road

South Africa

Road

LOFTUS ROAD STADIUM

SHEPHERD'S BUSH

Percy Road

Coningham

Road

Road

A 402

463

Paddenswick Rd

RAVENSCOURT PARK

13

Ravenscourt Park

Glenthorne

Banim St

Goldhawk Road

White City

BBC

Wood

Lane

Shepherd's Bush

Uxbridge

Road

Lime Grove

Goldhawk

Road

Hammersmith

Brackenbury Rd

c

a

b

HAMMERSMITH

Road

x

Shepherd's

Bro

454

Shepherd's

Bush

Wood

Lane

Road

Road

400

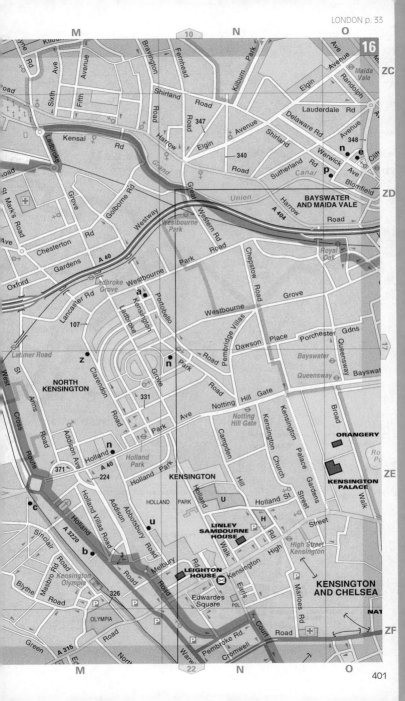

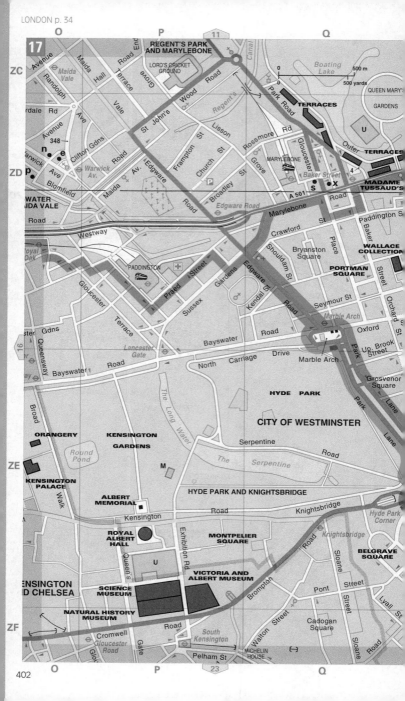

19

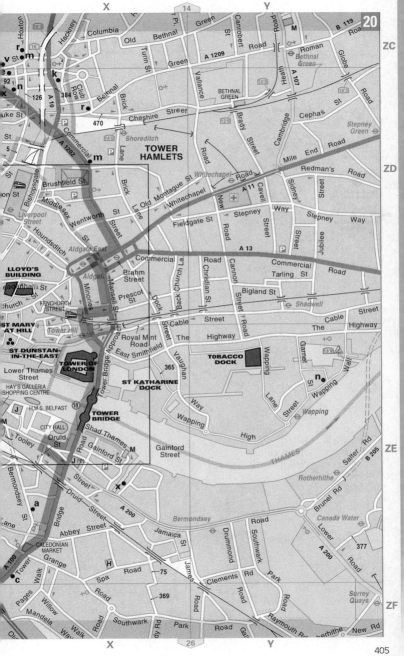

20

ZC

ZD

ZE

ZF

Hoxton

Columbia

Old

Bethnal

Green

Canrobert

St

Road

M

B 119

Roa

Roman

Road

Bethnal

Green

Globe

St

Turin

St

A 1209

Green

A 107

Vallance

BETHNAL
GREEN

Road

Cambridge

Cephas

Bethnal

Brick

Road

St

Cheshire

Street

Brady

Mile

End

Road

Stepney
Green

470

Shoreditch

Commercial

Road

Whitechapel

Road

Redman's

Road

ZD

Brushfield St

Brick

Old

Montague St

Whitechapel

New

Cavell

Sidney

Street

Stepney

Way

Stepney

Way

Jubilee

Liverpool
Street

Middlesex

Wentworth

St

Street

Lane

Fieldgate St

Stepney

Street

Street

Road

A 13

Houndsditch

Aldgate East

Commercial

Road

Cannon

Commercial

Tarling St

Road

LLOYD'S
BUILDING

Aldgate

Brahm
Street

Christian St

Bigland St

Shadwell

eadenhall St

FENCHURCH
STREET

Prescot
St

Back Church La.

Street

Cable

Street

church

Minories

Mansell

Dock

Street

Street

Road

Cable

Highway

ST MARY
AT HILL

Tower Hill

Cable

Street

The

Highway

ST DUNSTAN-
IN-THE-EAST

Royal Mint
Road

The

Highway

Garnet

Lower Thames
Street

East Smithfield

365

Vaughan

TOBACCO
DOCK

Wapping

n

St

Wapping

HAY'S GALLERIA
SHOPPING CENTRE

TOWER OF
LONDON

ST KATHARINE
DOCK

Way

Lane

Street

Wapping

J

H.M.S. BELFAST

18

TOWER
BRIDGE

Wapping

High

CITY HALL

Druid
St

Shad Thames

M

Gainford
Street

THAMES

ZE

Tooley

Road

Gainford St

J PB

Rotherhithe

Salter Rd

B 205

Bermondsey

St

Druid

Street

X

Brunel Rd

Canada Water

Lower

a

Bridge

A 200

Bermondsey

Road

Southwark

A 200

Road

377

Lane

Abbey

Street

Jamaica

St

Drummond

Park

CALEDONIAN
MARKET

Grange

H

Spa

Road

75

James

Clements Rd

Park

A100

Tower

Walk

Road

Surrey
Quays

c

Pages

Willow

369

Road

Road

Southwark

Road

ZF

Mandela

Walk

Southwark

Rd Ap

Park

Road

Ga

Raymouth R

herhithe

New Rd

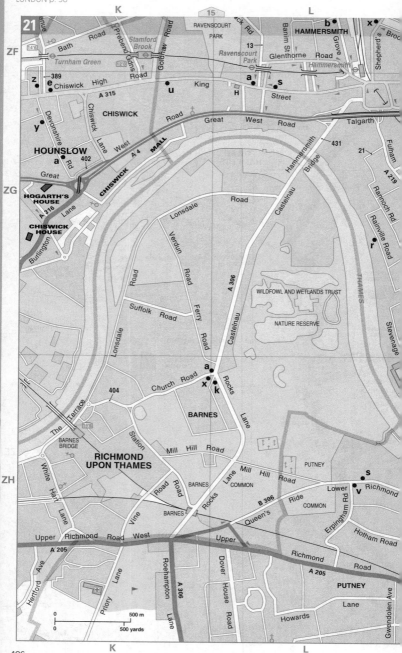

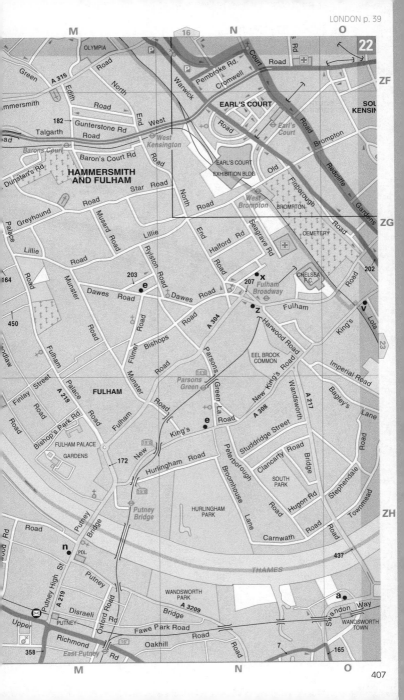

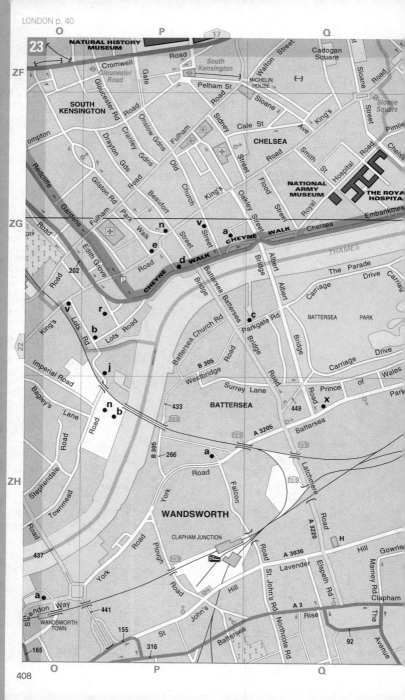

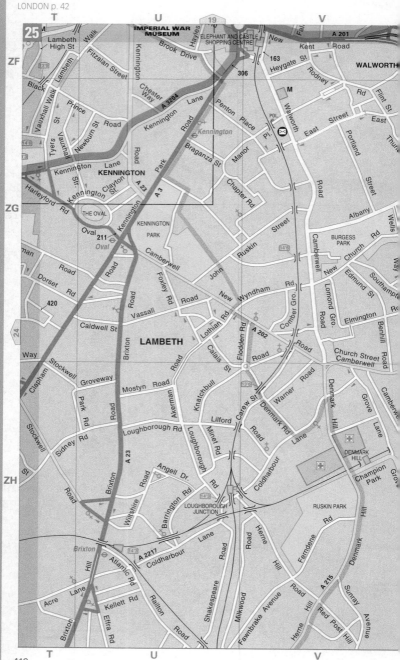

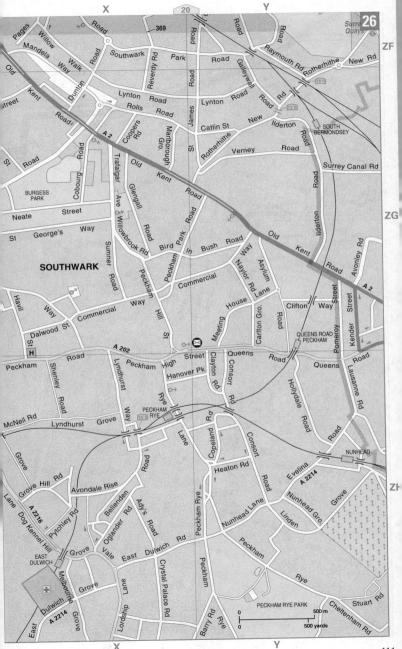

Surrey Quays

ZF

ZG

ZH

X   Y

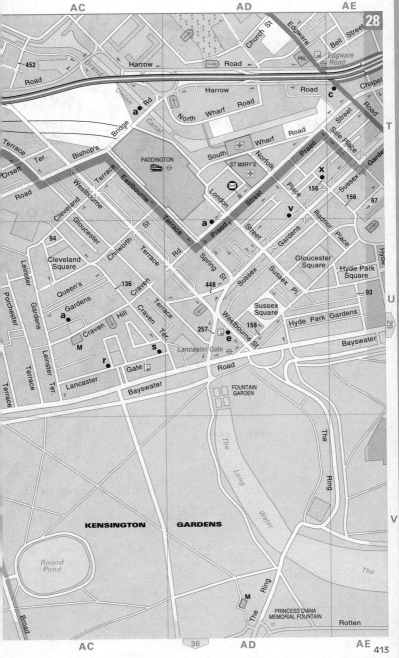

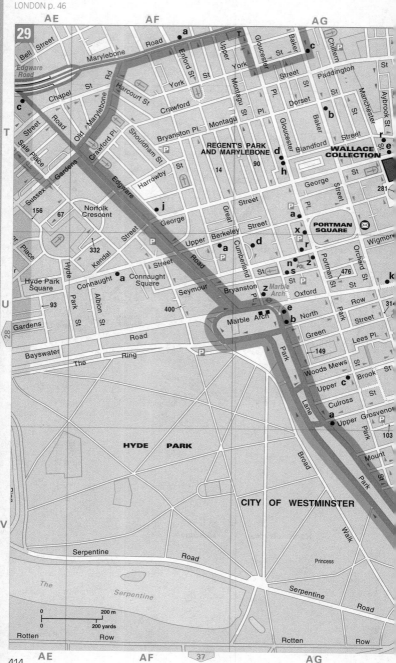

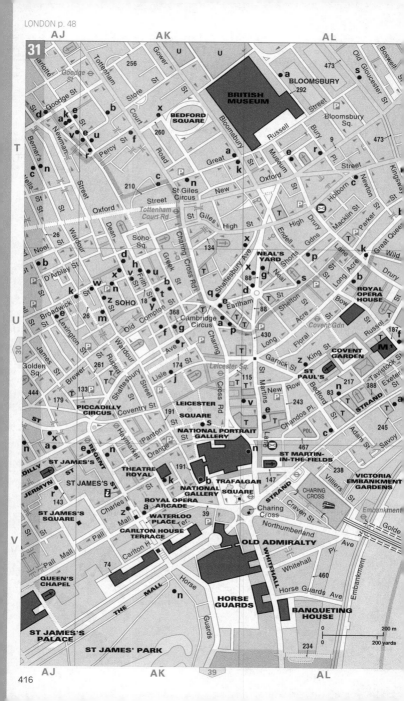

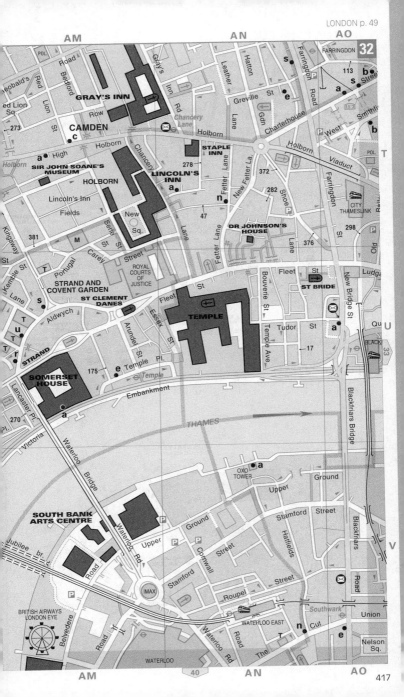

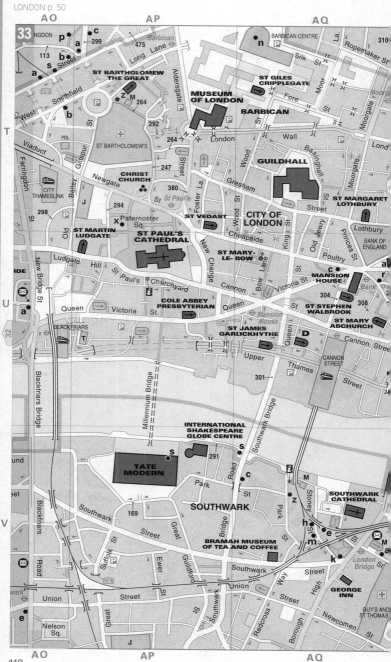

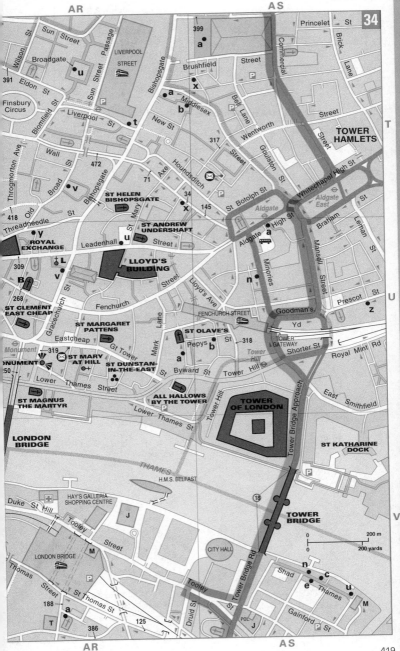

AR

AS

Sun Street
Broadgate
Sun Street Passage
391 Eldon St
Wilson
LIVERPOOL STREET
Bishopsgate
u
399
a
Brushfield
Street
Princelet St
Commercial
Brick
Lane
x
Middlesex
a
b
Bell Lane
Wentworth
Street
TOWER HAMLETS
T
Finsbury Circus
Blomfield
Liverpool St
New St
t
317
Goulston
Street
Whitechapel High St
Throgmorton Ave
Wall St
Broad St
Bishopsgate
472
71
Axe
Houndsditch
Street
St Botolph
St
Aldgate East
Braham
Leman St
418
Old
Threadneedle
ST HELEN BISHOPSGATE
St Mary
34
145
x
Aldgate
Aldgate High St
a
Mansell
y
ROYAL EXCHANGE
309
L
u
ST ANDREW UNDERSHAFT
Leadenhall
Street
Minories
n
Prescot St
z
U
B
V
v
LLOYD'S BUILDING
Lloyd's Ave
FENCHURCH STREET
Goodman's
Yd
268
ST CLEMENT EAST CHEAP
Fenchurch
Gracechurch St
Street
Lane
Shorter St
Royal Mint Rd
ST MARGARET PATTENS
Eastcheap
Gt Tower
Mark
ST OLAVE'S
Pepys St
b
318
TOWER GATEWAY
Monument
319
MONUMENT
50
ST MARY AT HILL
St Dunstan's
a
Byward St
Tower Hill
Tower Hill
East
Smithfield
ST DUNSTAN-IN-THE-EAST
Lower Thames Street
ALL HALLOWS BY THE TOWER
Lower Thames St
Tower Hill
Tower Bridge Approach
ST MAGNUS THE MARTYR
LONDON BRIDGE
TOWER OF LONDON
ST KATHARINE DOCK
THAMES
H.M.S. BELFAST
HAY'S GALLERIA SHOPPING CENTRE
Duke St Hill
Tooley
Street
J
M
18
TOWER BRIDGE
LONDON BRIDGE
Thomas
St Thomas St
P
CITY HALL
Tooley
0   200 m
0   200 yards
V
188
a
T
386
125
Druid St
POL
St
Shad
Thames
n
c
e
u
Gainford
St
P
J
M

AR

AS

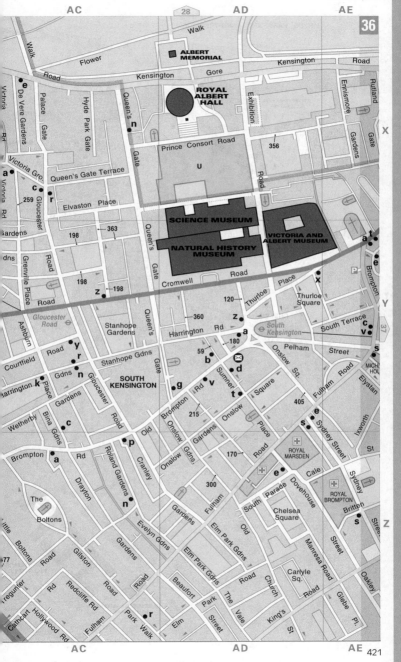

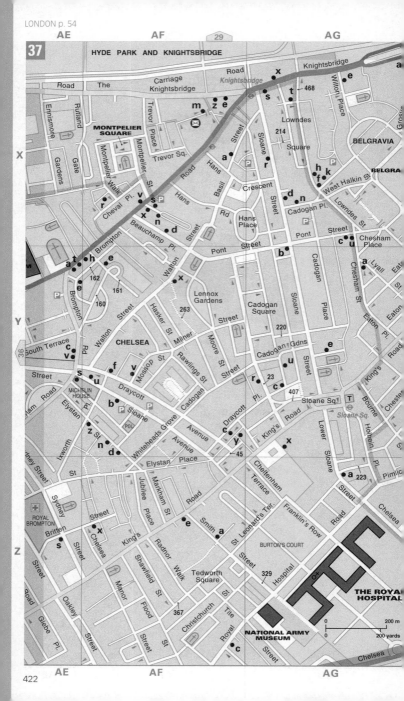

AE

AF

29

AG

a

37

HYDE PARK AND KNIGHTSBRIDGE

Road

Knightsbridge

Road

The

Carriage

Knightsbridge

x

Knightsbridge

e

Road

Ennismore

Rutland

Gate

MONTPELIER
SQUARE

Trevor Place

m

z

e

s

t ←468

Wilton Place

Grosve

Montpellier Walk

Montpelier St.

Trevor Sq.

Street

Sloane

Lowndes

214

Square

BELGRAVIA

X

Gate
Gardens

a

r

h

BELGRA

Hans

Crescent

Basil

d

n

f

k

West Halkin St.

Lowndes St.

Chesham St.

r

Cheval Pl.

v

s

Hans

Rd

P

Street

Cadogan Pl.

P

a

Lyall

Eat

Brompton

x

n

Beauchamp Pl.

d

Street

Hans
Place

Pont

Street

Pont

Street

c

u

Chesham
Place

Eaton
Pl.

Eaton

a

t

h

e

Brompton

162

e

161

Walton

Street

x

Lennox
Gardens

b

Cadogan

Place

Sloane

Road

Y

160

Hasker St.

263

CHELSEA

Walton

Street

Milner

Moore

St.

Cadogan
Square

220

Cadogan Gdns

Street

e

South Terrace

36

c

v

s

u

f

v

Mossop St.

Rawlings St.

Cadogan

Street

r

23

c

u

407

e

King's

MICHELIN
HOUSE

b

Draycott

Sloane

P

POL

Avenue

Pl.

Sloane Sq.

T

Sloane Sq.

Bourne

Chester

z

St

Whiteheads Grove

Avenue

c

King's

Road

Lower

Sloane

Holbein

Pl.

S

ROYAL
BROMPTON

Ixworth

n

d

Elystan

Place

y

45

x

Draycott

Cheltenham

Terrace

Franklin's Row

Road

a

223

Pimlic

Chelsea

Sydney Street

St

Jubilee

Markham St.

Radnor Walk

King's

Smith

e

a

St. Leonard's Ter.

St.

Street

BURTON'S COURT

Britten

x

Chelsea

Shawfield St.

329

Hospital

THE ROYAL
HOSPITAL

Z

s

Street

King's

Manor

Street

Flood

Street

Tedworth
Square

367

Christchurch St.

Tile

Royal

NATIONAL ARMY
MUSEUM

0   200 m

0   200 yards

Oakley

Glebe
Pl.

Street

c

Chelsea

AE

AF

AG

422

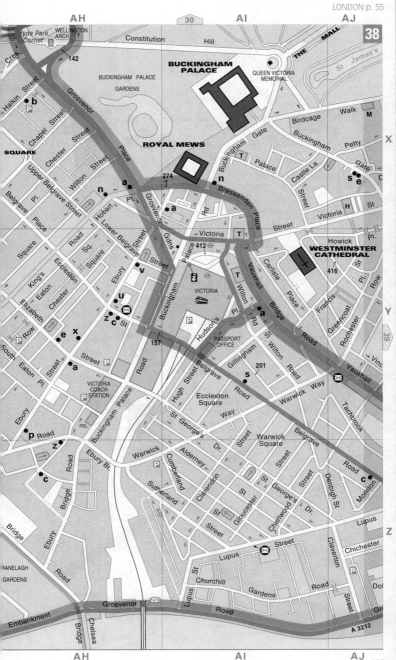

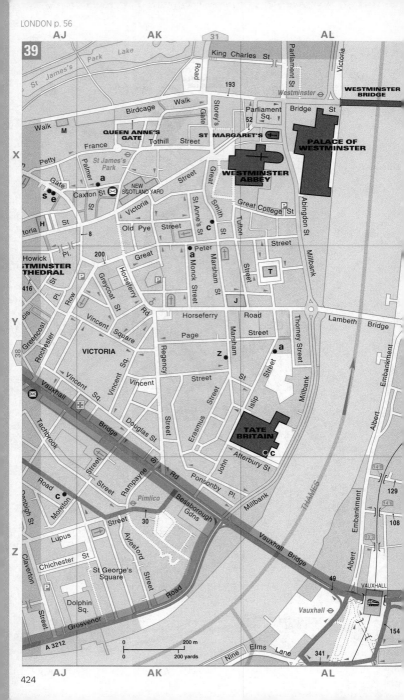

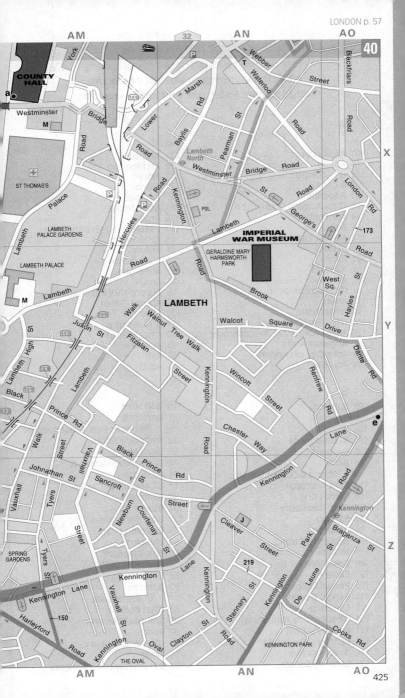

York

Westminster
COUNTY HALL
a

M
Bridge

Road

ST THOMAS'S

Palace

LAMBETH PALACE GARDENS

LAMBETH PALACE

M
Lambeth

Lambeth High St

Black

Prince Rd

Walk

Johnathan St

Vauxhall

SPRING GARDENS

Tyers St

Harleyford

Road

Hercules

Lower

Road

Road

Baylis

Marsh

Rd

Lambeth North

Westminster Bridge Road

POL

Kennington

Road

Road

LAMBETH

Juxon St

Fitzalan

Walnut Tree Walk

Walk

Street

Vauxhall

Tyers

Street

Newburn

Sancroft

Black Prince

Courtenay St

St

Kennington Lane

Vauxhall St

Prince Rd

Walk

Street

-150

Road

Lane

Kennington

Clayton St

Oval

THE OVAL

Webber

Waterloo Street

Pearman

St

St

Bridge Road

IMPERIAL WAR MUSEUM

GERALDINE MARY HARMSWORTH PARK

Brook

Kennington

Road

Walcot Square

Wincott Street

Chester Way

Cleaver

219

Kennington

Lane

Stannary St

Road

London Rd

Road

George's

-173

Road

West Sq.

Hayles St

Drive

Renfrew Rd

Lane

Kennington

Park

St

J

Street

Blackfriars Road

Dante Rd

e

Braganza St

Kennington

De Laune

Cooks Rd

KENNINGTON PARK

Alphabetical list of hotels and restaurants
Liste alphabétique des hôtels et restaurants
Elenco alfabetico degli alberghi e ristoranti
Alphabetisches Hotel- und Restaurantverzeichnis

Park City (handwritten annotation)

Starred establishments in London
Les établissements à étoiles de Londres
Gli esercizi con stelle a Londra
Die Stern-Restaurants in London

✿ ✿ ✿

✿ ✿

❀

Good food at moderate prices
Repas soignés à prix modérés
Pasti accurati a prezzi contenuti
Sorgfältig zubereitete, preiswerte Mahlzeiten

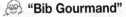 "Bib Gourmand"

433

Particularly pleasant hotels and restaurants
Hôtels et restaurants agréables
Alberghi e ristoranti ameni
Angenehme Hotels und Restaurants

🏨🏨🏨🏨🏨

🏨🏨🏨🏨

🏨🏨🏨

🏨🏨

XXXXX

XXXX

XXX

XX

X

Restaurants classified according to type
Restaurants classés suivant leur genre
Ristoranti classificati secondo il loro genere
Restaurants nach Art und Einrichtung geordnet

American

page
| 124 | Mayfair | ✕ | Automat |

Asian

123	Mayfair	✕✕	Cocoon	83	Hoxton	✕✕	Great Eastern Dining Room
75	Bloomsbury	✕✕	Crazy Bear				
101	North Kensington	✕✕	E&O	123	Mayfair	✕✕	Taman Gang
97	Chelsea	✕✕	Eight over Eight	109	Bermondsey	✕	Champor-Champor
				91	Finsbury	✕	Cicada

Bangladeshi

| 115 | Bayswater & Maida Vale | ✕ | Ginger |

British

120	Mayfair	✕✕✕✕	(The) Grill (at Brown's)	112	Spitalfields	✕	Canteen
121	Mayfair	✕✕✕	Bentley's (Grull)	134	Strand & Covent Garden	✕	(The) National Dining Rooms
121	Mayfair	✕✕✕	Brian Turner Mayfair	81	City of London	✕	Paternoster Chop House
136	Victoria	✕✕✕	Shepherd's				
136	Victoria	✕✕	Boisdale	83	Greenwich	✕	Rivington
80	City of London	✕✕	Boisdale of Bishopgate	84	Shoreditch	✕	Rivington
				90	Smithfield	✕	St John
109	Southwark	✕✕	Roast	111	Spitalfields	✕	St John Bread and Wine
133	Strand & Covent Garden	✕✕	Rules				
109	Bermondsey	✕	Butlers Wharf Chop House	89	Canonbury	🍴	(The) Marquess Tavern

Chinese

120	Mayfair	✕✕✕✕	China Tang	117	Hyde Park & Knightsbridge	✕✕	Mr Chow
122	Mayfair	✕✕✕	Kai				
97	Chelsea	✕✕	Good Earth	128	Regent's Park & Marylebone	✕✕	Phoenix Palace
72	Mill Hill	✕✕	Good Earth	77	Holborn	✕✕	Shangai Blues
75	Bloomsbury	✕✕	✿ Hakkasan	73	Orpington	✕✕	Xian
136	Victoria	✕✕	Ken Lo's Memories of China	85	Fulham	✕✕	Yi-Ban
				132	Soho	✕	Bar Shu
85	Fulham	✕✕	Mao Tai	132	Soho	✕	Chinese Experience
82	Ealing	✕✕	Maxim				
100	Kensington	✕✕	Memories of China	132	Soho	✕	Fung Shing
				132	Soho	✕	✿ Yauatcha

Danish

| 103 | South Kensington | ✕✕ | Lundum's |

Eastern European

109 *Southwark*	XX Baltic	100 *Kensington*	XX Wódka

French

120 *Mayfair*	XXXXX ✿✿ (Le) Gavroche	75 *Bloomsbury*	XX Mon Plaisir
79 *City of London*	XXX Coq d'Argent	89 *Barnsbury*	XX Morgan M
136 *Victoria*	XXX ✿ Roussillon	96 *Chelsea*	XX Papillon
92 *Islington*	XX Almeida	77 *Primrose Hill*	XX (Le) Petit Train
113 *Putney*	XX (L') Auberge	96 *Chelsea*	XX Poissonnerie de l'Avenue (Seafood)
127 *Regent's Park & Marylebone*	XX L'Aventure		
107 *Twickenham*	XX (La) Brasserie McClements	95 *Chelsea*	XX 🍴 Racine
		83 *Greenwich*	XX Spread Eagle
130 *St. James's*	XX 🍴 Brasserie Roux	131 *Soho*	XX (La) Trouvaille
96 *Chelsea*	XX (Le) Cercle	134 *Strand and Covent Garden*	X ✿ L'Atelier de Joël Robuchon
85 *Hammersmith*	XX Chez Kristof		
134 *Strand & Covent Garden*	XX Clos Maggiore	97 *Chelsea*	X Aubaine
		86 *Crouch End*	X Bistro Aix
80 *City of London*	XX ✿ Club Gascon	108 *Twickenham*	X 🍴 Brula Bistrot
96 *Chelsea*	XX (Le) Colombier	90 *Clerkenwell*	X 🍴 Comptoir Gascon
112 *Battersea*	XX (The) Food Room		
104 *Surbiton*	XX (The) French Table	104 *Kennington*	X Lobster Pot (Seafood)
126 *Regent's Park & Marylebone*	XX Galvin	107 *Kew*	X 🍴 Ma Cuisine
		108 *Twickenham*	X 🍴 Ma Cuisine
		137 *Victoria*	X (La) Poule au Pot

Greek

83 *Hoxton*	XX Real Greek	110 *Southwark*	X (The) Real Greek Bankside
84 *Hoxton*	X Mezedopolio		

Indian

116 *Belgravia*	XXX ✿ Amaya	115 *Bayswater & Maida Vale*	XX Jamuna
121 *Mayfair*	XXX ✿ Benares		
103 *South Kensington*	XXX Bombay Brasserie	103 *South Kensington*	XX Khan's of Kensington
95 *Chelsea*	XXX Chutney Mary	129 *St James's*	XX Mint Leaf
136 *Victoria*	XXX (The) Cinnamon Club	77 *Holborn*	XX Moti Mahal
		96 *Chelsea*	XX Painted Heron
85 *Fulham*	XXX Memsaab	81 *Addington*	XX Planet Spice
136 *Victoria*	XXX Quilon	127 *Regent's Park & Marylebone*	XX (La) Porte des Indes
131 *Soho*	XXX Red Fort		
121 *Mayfair*	XXX ✿ Tamarind	127 *Regent's Park & Marylebone*	XX Rasa Samudra (Seafood) (Vegetarian)
108 *Bermondsey*	XX Bengal Clipper		
111 *Spitalfields*	XX Bengal Trader		
131 *Soho*	XX Café Lazeez	95 *Chelsea*	XX ✿ Rasoi
112 *Whitechapel*	XX 🍴 Café Spice Namaste	113 *Southfields*	XX 🍴 Sarkhel's
		104 *Herne Hill*	XX 3 Monkeys
123 *Mayfair*	XX Chor Bizarre	96 *Chelsea*	XX Vama
126 *Regent's Park & Marylebone*	XX Deya	123 *Mayfair*	XX Veeraswamy
78 *Swiss Cottage*	XX Eriki	99 *Kensington*	XX Zaika
97 *Chelsea*	XX Haandi	86 *Hammersmith*	X 🍴 Agni
72 *Edgware*	XX Haandi	103 *South Kensington*	X Café Lazeez
85 *Hammersmith*	XX Indian Zing		

132	*Soho*	✗	Imli
113	*Tooting*	✗	Kastoori (Vegetarian)
100	*Kensington*	✗ 🍴	Malabar
76	*Bloomsbury*	✗	Mela
89	*Archway*	✗ 🍴	(The) Parsee
84	*Stoke Newington*	✗	Rasa (Vegetarian)
84	*Stoke Newington*	✗	Rasa Travancore
73	*Willesden Green*	✗	Sabras (Vegetarian)
108	*Twickenham*	✗ 🍴	Tangawizi

Italian

122	*Mayfair*	✗✗✗	Cecconi's
129	*St James's*	✗✗✗	Fiore
126	*Regent's Park & Marylebone*	✗✗✗	Latium
126	*Regent's Park & Marylebone*	✗✗✗	✿ Locanda Locatelli
129	*St James's*	✗✗✗	Luciano
131	*Soho*	✗✗✗	Quo Vadis
136	*Victoria*	✗✗✗	Santini
121	*Mayfair*	✗✗✗	Sartoria
95	*Chelsea*	✗✗✗	Toto's
117	*Belgravia*	✗✗✗	✿ Zafferano
108	*Twickenham*	✗✗	A Cena
122	*Mayfair*	✗✗	Alloro
113	*Wandsworth*	✗✗	Amici
127	*Regent's Park & Marylebone*	✗✗	Bertorelli
127	*Regent's Park & Marylebone*	✗✗	Caldesi
96	*Chelsea*	✗✗	Caraffini
97	*Chelsea*	✗✗	Carpaccio
97	*Chelsea*	✗✗	C Garden
78	*Primrose Hill*	✗✗	(La) Collina
136	*Victoria*	✗✗	(Il) Convivio
95	*Chelsea*	✗✗	Daphne's
101	*North Kensington*	✗✗	Edera
113	*Putney*	✗✗	Enoteca Turi
130	*St James's*	✗✗	Franco's
122	*Mayfair*	✗✗	Giardinetto
92	*Islington*	✗✗ 🍴	Metrogusto
75	*Bloomsbury*	✗✗	Neal Street
96	*Chelsea*	✗✗	Pellicano
111	*Canary Wharf*	✗✗	Quadrato
85	*Hammersmith*	✗✗	✿ River Café
127	*Regent's Park & Marylebone*	✗✗	Rosmarino
75	*Bloomsbury*	✗✗	Sardo
77	*Primrose Hill*	✗✗	Sardo Canale
122	*Mayfair*	✗✗	Teca
100	*Kensington*	✗✗	Timo
131	*Soho*	✗✗	Vasco and Piero's Pavillion
123	*Mayfair*	✗ 🍴	Via Condotti
115	*Bayswater & Maida Vale*	✗ 🍴	(L') Accento
130	*St. James's*	✗ 🍴	Al Duca
115	*Bayswater & Maida Vale*	✗	Arturo
115	*Bayswater & Maida Vale*	✗	✿ Assaggi
132	*Soho*	✗	Bertorelli
128	*Regent's Park & Marylebone*	✗	Caffè Caldesi
76	*Bloomsbury*	✗	Camerino
108	*Bermondsey*	✗	Cantina Del Ponte
100	*Kensington*	✗	Cibo
86	*Crouch End*	✗	Florians
97	*Chelsea*	✗	Manicomio
137	*Victoria*	✗	Olivo
76	*Bloomsbury*	✗	Passione
106	*Barnes*	✗	Riva

Japanese

136	*Victoria*	✗✗	Atami
96	*Chelsea*	✗✗	Benihana
77	*Holborn*	✗✗	Matsuri-High Holborn
130	*St James's*	✗✗	Matsuri-St James's
123	*Mayfair*	✗✗	✿ Nobu
123	*Mayfair*	✗✗	✿ Nobu Berkeley St.
96	*Chelsea*	✗✗	Nozomi
127	*Regent's Park & Marylebone*	✗✗	Roka
81	*City of London*	✗✗	Saki
123	*Mayfair*	✗✗	Sumosan
81	*City of London*	✗✗	Tatsuso
111	*Canary Wharf*	✗✗	Ubon by Nobu
122	*Mayfair*	✗✗	✿ Umu
115	*Bayswater & Maida Vale*	✗✗	Yakitoria
117	*Hyde Park & Knightsbridge*	✗✗	Zuma
76	*Bloomsbury*	✗	Abeno
124	*Mayfair*	✗	Chisou
132	*Soho*	✗	itsu
107	*Richmond*	✗	Matsuba
73	*Willesden Green*	✗	Sushi-Say
104	*Clapham*	✗	Tsunami

Korean

| 77 | *Holborn* | ✗✗ | Asadal |

437

Kosher

Latin American

Lebanese

Malaysian

Moroccan

North African

Pubs

Seafood

95	*Chelsea*	XXX One-O-One	124	*Mayfair*	X Bentley's (Oyster *Bar*)

95 *Chelsea*	XXX One-O-One	124 *Mayfair*	X Bentley's (Oyster *Bar*)
81 *City of London*	XX Chamberlain's	97 *Chelsea*	X Bibendum Oyster Bar
85 *Fulham*	XX Deep		
133 *Strand & Covent Garden*		88 *Chiswick*	X Fish Hook
96 *Chelsea*	XX J. Sheekey	89 *Chiswick*	X Fishworks
	XX Poissonnerie de l'Avenue (French)	128 *Regent's Park & Marylebone*	X Fishworks
127 *Regent's Park & Marylebone*		104 *Kennington*	X Lobster Pot (French)
	XX Rasa Samudra (Indian) (Vegetarian)	90 *Clerkenwell*	X Rudland Stubbs
		110 *Southwark*	X Wright Brothers

Spanish

103 *South Kensington*	XX Cambio De Tercio	76 *Bloomsbury*	X Cigala
75 *Bloomsbury*	XX Fino	110 *Southwark*	X Tapas Brindisa
100 *Kensington*	XX L Restaurant & Bar		

Thai

84 *Fulham*	XXX Saran Rom	103 *South Kensington*	X Bangkok
85 *Fulham*	XX Blue Elephant		
112 *Battersea*	XX Chada	128 *Regent's Park & Marylebone*	X Chada Chada
117 *Belgravia*	XX Mango Tree	113 *Tooting*	X Oh Boy
117 *Belgravia*	XX ❀ Nahm		
115 *Bayswater & Maida Vale*	XX Nipa		

Turkish

127 *Regent's Park & Marylebone*   XX Ozer

Vegetarian

127 *Regent's Park & Marylebone*	XX Rasa Samudra (Indian) (Seafood)	84 *Stoke Newington*	X Rasa (Indian)
113 *Tooting*	X Kastoori (Indian)	73 *Willesden Green*	X Sabras (Indian)

Vietnamese

91 *Highbury*   X Au Lac

Boroughs and areas

Greater London *is divided, for administrative purposes, into 32 boroughs plus the City: these sub-divide naturally into minor areas, usually grouped around former villages or quarters, which often maintain a distinctive character.*

BARNET *Gtr London.*

Child's Hill *Gtr London –* ⊠ *NW2.*

XX **Philpott's Mezzaluna,** 424 Finchley Rd, NW2 2HY, ℰ (020) 7794 0455, Fax (020) 7794 0452, ㋰ – ▤. ◍⑨ *VISA*
10 NZA **c**
closed 25-26 December, 1 January, Saturday lunch and Monday – **Rest** - Italian influences - 20.00/29.50.
♦ Homely Italian restaurant, affably run by patrons. Huge lunar artefacts complement the plain walls. Weekly changing menus offer tasty, modern cuisine at moderate prices.

Edgware *Gtr London –* ⊠ *HA8.*

XX **Haandi,** 301-303 Hale Lane, HA8 7AX ⊖ *Edgware,* ℰ (020) 8905 4433, haandirestaur ant@btconnect.com, Fax (020) 8905 4646 – ▤. ◍⑨ ℀ ⓞ *VISA*
2 CT **a**
closed 25 December, lunch Monday and Tuesday – **Rest** - Indian - a la carte 14.00/26.90.
♦ In the middle of a busy high street, this brightly lit restaurant boasts skylight, small central fountain, vivid colours and flavoursome dishes from North India.

Hendon *Gtr London –* ⊠ *NW4.*

XX **Gallery,** 407-411 Hendon Way, NW4 3LH ⊖ *Hendon Central,* ℰ (020) 8202 4000, reserva tions@galleryhendon.com, Fax (020) 8202 4433 – ▤. ◍⑨ ℀ *VISA*
2 CU **e**
closed Monday – **Rest** (dinner only and Sunday lunch) 24.00 and a la carte 24.50/47.50.
♦ A touch of opulence on Hendon Way courtesy of quality artworks ranging from pastels to lithographs and seascapes to portraits. British ingredients prepared with French flair.

Mill Hill *Gtr London –* ⊠ *NW7.*

🚡 *100 Barnet Way, Mill Hill* ℰ (020) 8959 2339 CT.

XX **Good Earth,** 143 The Broadway, NW7 4RN, ℰ (020) 8959 7011, Fax (020) 8959 1464 – ▤. ◍⑨ ℀ *VISA*
2 CT **a**
closed 23-30 December – **Rest** - Chinese - a la carte 28.00/50.00.
♦ Smart, well-kept Chinese restaurant set slightly back from the busy A1 outside. Spacious and comfortable with efficient staff. Authentic menu; extensive vegetarian choice.

BEXLEY *Gtr London.*

Bexleyheath *Kent –* ⊠ *Kent.*

🏨 **Bexleyheath Marriott,** 1 Broadway, DA6 7JZ, ℰ (020) 8298 1000, Fax (020) 8298 1234, 𝄑, ⬚ – ▮, ⟿ rm, ▤ ⅑ ℙ – 🔏 250. ◍⑨ ℀ ⓞ *VISA*. ❀
8 JX **c**
Copper : Rest *(closed Sunday lunch)* a la carte 17.50/37.50 **s.** ℤ – � 14.95 – **142 rm** ★114.00/119.00 – ★★114.00/154.00.
♦ A group hotel offering extensive conference facilities as well as a leisure club in a Graeco-Roman theme. Comfortable and spacious bedrooms with marble bathrooms. Popular carvery restaurant.

BRENT *Gtr London.*

Kensal Rise *Middx –* ⊠ *Middx.*

🍴 **The Greyhound,** 64-66 Chamberlayne Rd, NW10 3JJ ⊖ *Kensal Green,* ℰ (020) 8969 8080, thegreyhound@needtoeat.co.uk, Fax (020) 8969 8081, ㋰ – ▤. ◍⑨ *VISA*
❀
10 MZB **a**
closed 25-26 December and 1 January – **Rest** *(closed Sunday dinner and Monday)* a la carte 16.00/27.00 ℤ.
♦ Trendy gastropub, popular with locals. On one side: bar with leather sofas; on other: restaurant with reclaimed furniture, black oak floors and modern British cooking.

Willesden Green *Middx – ⊠ Middx.*

✗ **Sabras,** 263 High Rd, NW10 2RX ⊖ *Dollis Hill,* ℘ (020) 8459 0340, Fax (020) 8459 0541 –
✦✕ ⊙ 🕩 ◎ *VISA*   9 KZB e
closed 25-26 December and Monday – **Rest** - Indian Vegetarian - (dinner only) a la carte
15.25/22.20.
♦ Tasty Indian vegetarian food served in modest, but friendly, surroundings. Framed
awards and write-ups garnered since opening in 1973 bear testament to its popularity.

✗ **Sushi-Say,** 33B Walm Lane, NW2 5SH ⊖ *Willesden Green,* ℘ (020) 8459 2971,
Fax (020) 8907 3229 – ◎ *VISA*   9 LZB a
closed 25-26 December, 1 January, Easter, 1 week August and Monday – **Rest** - Japanese -
(dinner only and lunch Saturday and Sunday)/dinner 19.80/31.00 and a la carte 13.40/34.70.
♦ Friendly service provided by the owner in traditional dress. From bare wooden tables,
watch her husband in the open-plan kitchen carefully prepare authentic Japanese food.

🍴 **The Green,** 110 Walm Lane, NW2 4RS ⊖ *Willesden Green,* ℘ (020) 8452 0171, *info@the*
greennw2.com, Fax (020) 8452 0774, 🛱 – ◎ *VISA*   9 LZA a
closed 1 January – **Rest** 17.50 and a la carte 25.00/40.00.
♦ Large bustling bar with high ceiling conveying airy feel: light menus served here. Rear
dining room: chef adds subtle Caribbean twists to modern dishes in generous portions.

BROMLEY *Gtr London.*

  📍₁₈, 📍₉ Cray Valley, Sandy Lane, St Paul's Cray, Orpington ℘ (01689) 837909 JY.

Beckenham *Kent – ⊠ Kent.*

✗✗ **Mello,** 2 Southend Rd, BR3 1SD, ℘ (020) 8663 0994, *info@mello.uk.com,*
Fax (020) 8663 3674 – ▤ 🅿. – 🔼 35. ◎ ⏃ *VISA*   7 GY v
closed 2-9 January, 2 weeks August and Sunday dinner – **Rest** a la carte 24.50/36.45.
♦ Unassuming and welcomingly run neighbourhood restaurant; walls hung with multi-
coloured modern oils. Good value, seasonally sensitive dishes enhanced by precise execution.

Bromley *Kent – ⊠ Kent.*

  📍₉ Magpie Hall Lane ℘ (020) 8462 7014 HY.

🏨 **Bromley Court,** Bromley Hill, BR1 4JD, ℘ (020) 8461 8600, *enquiries@bromleycourtho*
tel.co.uk, Fax (020) 8460 0899, 🛱, 📍₆, 🖈 – 📶, ✦✕ rm, ▤ ✆ 🅿 – 🔼 150. ◎ ⏃ ⓪
VISA   8 HY z
Rest (closed Saturday lunch) 19.95 – **112 rm** �$ ✚89.00/109.00 – ✚✚105.00/120.00,
2 suites.
♦ A grand neo-Gothic mansion in three acres of well-tended garden. Popular with corporate guests for the large conference space, and the bedrooms with modems and voice-
mail. Conservatory or terrace dining available.

Farnborough *Kent – ⊠ Kent.*

✗✗✗ **Chapter One,** Farnborough Common, Locksbottom, BR6 8NF, ℘ (01689) 854848,
info@chaptersrestaurants.com, Fax (01689) 858439 – ✦✕ ▤ 🅿. ◎ ⏃ ⓪ *VISA*   8 HZ a
closed first 2 weeks January – **Rest** 19.95/26.95 ⬒.
♦ The mock Tudor exterior belies a stylish, light and contemporary interior. Smooth service; well executed modern European menus at a keen price.

Orpington *Kent – ⊠ Kent.*

  📍₈ High Elms, High Elms Rd, Downe, Orpington ℘ (01689) 858175.

✗✗ **Xian,** 324 High St, BR6 0NG, ℘ (01689) 871881 – ▤. ◎ ⏃ ⓪ *VISA*   8 JY a
closed 25-26 December, 1 week September, and Sunday lunch – **Rest** - Chinese (Peking,
Szechuan) - 9.50/25.00 and a la carte 11.70/17.70.
♦ Modern, marbled interior with oriental artefacts make this personally run Chinese restaurant a firm favourite with locals. Specialises in the hotter dishes of Peking.

Penge *Gtr London – ⊠ SE20.*

🏠 **Melrose House** without rest., 89 Lennard Rd, SE20 7LY, ℘ (020) 8776 8884, *mel*
rose.hotel@virgin.net, Fax (020) 8778 6366, 🖈 – ✦✕ ✆ 🕭 🅿. ◎ *VISA*. ✿   7 GY a
closed 24 December-2 January – **9 rm** ✚ 35.00/45.00 – ✚✚65.00.
♦ An imposing Victorian house with a conservatory sitting room. Breakfast is taken "en
famille" and the older bedrooms still have their original fireplaces.

CAMDEN *Gtr London.*

Belsize Park *Gtr London –* ✉ *NW3.*

🍴 **The Hill,** 94 Haverstock Hill, NW3 2BD ⊖ *Chalk Farm,* ℰ (020) 7267 0033, *thehill@gero nimo-inns.co.uk,* 🍽 – ⓦⓢ *VISA*
11 QZB x
closed 25 December – **Rest** a la carte 18.00/25.00 ℤ.
♦ Large 19C pub; lively main bar with twinkling fairy lights, old sofas, deep red walls and dining tables. Menus offer a good choice with a Mediterranean or Asian influence.

Bloomsbury *Gtr London –* ✉ *W1/WC1/WC2.*

🏛 **Covent Garden,** 10 Monmouth St, WC2H 9HB ⊖ *Covent Garden,* ℰ (020) 7806 1000, *covent@firmdale.com,* Fax (020) 7806 1100, ⅃₅ – 🛗, 🕺 rm, 🔲 📺 🖁 ⇔ 10 – ⚹ 50. ⓦⓢ ⒶⒺ *VISA.* ✄
31 ALU x
Brasserie Max : **Rest** (booking essential) a la carte 29.00/50.00 ℤ – � 19.50 – **56 rm** ✴258.00/311.40 – ✴✴358.00/364.30, 2 suites.
♦ Individually designed and stylish bedrooms, with CDs and VCRs discreetly concealed. Boasts a very relaxing first floor oak-panelled drawing room with its own honesty bar. Informal restaurant.

🏛 **Marlborough,** 9-13 Bloomsbury St, WC1B 3QD ⊖ *Tottenham Court Road,* ℰ (020) 7636 5601, *resmarl@radisson.com,* Fax (020) 7636 0532 – 🛗, 🕺 rm, 🔲 rest, 🖁 🕹 – ⚹ 250. ⓦⓢ ⒶⒺ ⓪ *VISA.* ✄
31 AKT k
Glass : **Rest** *(closed lunch Saturday-Sunday)* a la carte 25.00/33.50 – ⊏ 16.50 – **171 rm** ✴154.00/220.00 – ✴✴216.00/257.00, 2 suites.
♦ A Victorian building around the corner from the British Museum. The lobby has been restored to its original marbled splendour and the bedrooms offer good comforts. Bright, breezy restaurant with suitably modish cooking.

🏛 **Mountbatten,** 20 Monmouth St, WC2H 9HD ⊖ *Covent Garden,* ℰ (020) 7836 4300, *resmoun@radisson.com,* Fax (020) 7240 3540, ⅃₅ – 🛗, 🕺 rm, 🔲 🖁 – ⚹ 90. ⓦⓢ ⒶⒺ *VISA.* ✄
31 ALU d
Dial : **Rest** *(closed lunch Friday-Sunday)* 25.00 dinner and a la carte 25.00/33.50 – ⊏ 16.50 – **149 rm** ✴171.00/245.00 – ✴✴220.00/282.00, 2 suites.
♦ Photographs and memorabilia of the eponymous Lord Louis adorn the walls and corridors. Ideally located in the heart of Covent Garden. Compact but comfortable bedrooms. Bright, stylish restaurant.

🏛 **Grafton,** 130 Tottenham Court Rd, W1P 9HP ⊖ *Warren Street,* ℰ (020) 7388 4131, *resgraf@radisson.com,* Fax (020) 7387 7394, ⅃₅ – 🛗, 🕺 rm, 🔲 🖁 🕹 – ⚹ 100. ⓦⓢ ⒶⒺ ⓪ *VISA.* ✄
18 RZC n
Aston's : **Rest** *(closed lunch Saturday-Sunday)* 25.00 (dinner) and a la carte 25.00/33.00 – ⊏ 16.50 – **326 rm** ✴142.00/208.00 – ✴✴203.00/246.00, 4 suites.
♦ Just yards from Warren Street tube. Discreet Edwardian charm that belies its location in one of London's busier streets. Bedrooms to becalm in soft beige tones. Open-plan restaurant and bar.

🏛 **Kenilworth,** 97 Great Russell St, WC1B 3BL ⊖ *Tottenham Court Road,* ℰ (020) 7637 3477, *reskent@radisson.com,* Fax (020) 7631 3133, ⅃₅ – 🛗, 🕺 rm, 🔲 🕹 – ⚹ 100. ⓦⓢ ⒶⒺ ⓪ *VISA.* ✄
31 AKT a
Rest *(closed lunch Saturday-Sunday)* 19.50/25.00 and dinner a la carte 25.00/33.50 – ⊏ 16.50 – **186 rm** ✴154.00/220.00 – ✴✴216.00/257.00.
♦ Usefully placed for the shops of Oxford Street. Stylish interiors and modern designer hi-tech bedrooms, equipped to meet the needs of the corporate traveller. Smart dining room with a modern style.

🏛 **Jurys Gt Russell St,** 16-22 Gt Russell St, WC1B 3NN ⊖ *Tottenham Court Road,* ℰ (020) 7347 1000, *gtrussellstreet@jurysdoyle.com,* Fax (020) 7347 1001 – 🛗, 🕺 rm, 🔲 🖁 🕹 – ⚹ 220. ⓦⓢ ⒶⒺ ⓪ *VISA.* ✄
31 AKT n
Lutyens : **Rest** (bar lunch)/dinner a la carte 27.90/42.40 s – ⊏ 16.00 – **169 rm** ✴240.00 – ✴✴240.00, 1 suite.
♦ Neo-Georgian building by Edward Lutyens, built for YMCA in 1929. Smart comfortable interior decoration from the lounge to the bedrooms. Facilities include a business centre. Restaurant has understated traditional style.

🏛 **Montague on the Gardens,** 15 Montague St, WC1B 5BJ ⊖ *Holborn,* ℰ (020) 7637 1001, *bookmt@rchmail.com,* Fax (020) 7637 2516, 🍽, ⅃₅, 🖽, 🌿 – 🛗, 🕺 rm, 🔲 🖁 🕹 – ⚹ 100. ⓦⓢ ⒶⒺ ⓪ *VISA*
31 ALT a
The Chef's Table : **Rest** 15.50/19.50 and a la carte 24.95/48.85 ℤ – ⊏ 16.50 – **93 rm** ✴159.00/288.00 – ✴✴217.00/311.00, 6 suites.
♦ A period townhouse with pretty hanging baskets outside. The hushed conservatory overlooks a secluded garden. The clubby bar has a Scottish golfing theme. Rich bedroom décor. Restaurant divided into two small, pretty rooms.

Myhotel Bloomsbury, 11-13 Bayley St, Bedford Sq, WC1B 3HD ⊖ *Tottenham Court Road*, ℘ (020) 7667 6000, *res@myhotels.co.uk*, Fax (020) 7667 6001, ╔ – ╗ ∺ ≡ ☎ – ⚙ 40. **MC AE** *VISA*. ※
31 AKT x

Yo! Sushi : Rest - Japanese - a la carte 15.00/21.50 – ☲ 18.00 – **77 rm** ✦147.00/266.00 – ✦✦266.00/305.00.

♦ The minimalist interior is designed on the principles of feng shui; even the smaller bedrooms are stylish and uncluttered. Mybar is a fashionable meeting point. Diners can enjoy Japanese food from conveyor belt.

Pied à Terre (Osborn), 34 Charlotte St, W1T 2NH ⊖ *Goodge Street*, ℘ (020) 7636 1178, *info@pied-a-terre.co.uk*, Fax (020) 7916 1171 – ∺ ≡ ⇔ 12. **MC AE** *VISA*
31 AJT e
closed last week December-first week January, Saturday lunch and Sunday – Rest 30.00/60.00 ♀ ఊ.

Spec. Ceviche of scallop, avocado and crème fraîche purée, sesame filo. Warm terrine of pig's head with crispy belly, apricot and vanilla. Chocolate tart with stout ice cream and macadamia nuts.

♦ Understated, discreet exterior; intimate, stylish interior, incorporating sleek first floor lounge. Elaborate yet refined modern cuisine complemented by accomplished service.

Origin, The Hospital, 24 Endell St, WC2H 9HQ ⊖ *Covent Garden*, ℘ (020) 7170 9200, *reservations@origin-restaurant.com*, Fax (020) 7170 9221 – ╗ ∺ ≡ ⇔ 18. **MC AE O**
VISA
31 ALU p
closed Saturday lunch, Sunday and Bank Holidays – Rest a la carte 33.00/49.00 ఊ ♀.

♦ Located on the first floor of a former hospital. Buzzy lounge/bar leads to smart dining room with original Hockneys on the wall. Modern British cooking with global reach.

Mon Plaisir, 21 Monmouth St, WC2H 9DD ⊖ *Covent Garden*, ℘ (020) 7836 7243, *eatafrog@mail.com*, Fax (020) 7240 4774 – **MC AE** *VISA*
31 ALU g
closed Saturday lunch, Sunday and Bank Holidays – Rest - French - 15.95 (lunch) and a la carte 26.20/41.75 ఊ ♀.

♦ London's oldest French restaurant and family-run for over fifty years. Divided into four rooms, all with a different feel but all proudly Gallic in their decoration.

Incognico, 117 Shaftesbury Ave, WC2H 8AD ⊖ *Tottenham Court Road*, ℘ (020) 7836 8866, *incognicorestaurante@mail.com*, Fax (020) 7240 9525 – ≡. **MC AE O**
VISA
31 AKU q
closed 1 week Christmas, Sunday and Bank Holidays – Rest a la carte 20.50/32.00 ♀.

♦ Firmly established with its robust décor of wood panelling and brown leather chairs. Downstairs bar has a window into the kitchen, from where French and English classics derive.

Neal Street, 26 Neal St, WC2H 9QW ⊖ *Covent Garden*, ℘ (020) 7836 8368, Fax (020) 7240 3964 – **MC AE O** *VISA*
31 ALU s
closed Christmas, Easter, Sunday and Bank Holidays – Rest - Italian - 25.00 and a la carte 31.00/47.50 ఊ ♀ ఊ.

♦ Light, bright and airy; tiled flooring and colourful pictures. Dishes range from the simple to the more complex. Mushrooms a speciality. Has its own shop next door.

Sardo, 45 Grafton Way, W1T 5DQ ⊖ *Warren Street*, ℘ (020) 7387 2521, *info@sardo-restaurant.com*, Fax (020) 7387 2559. **MC AE O** *VISA*
18 RZD c
closed Saturday lunch and Sunday – Rest - Italian (Sardinian specialities) - a la carte 24.90/34.00.

♦ Simple, stylish interior run in a very warm and welcoming manner with very efficient service. Rustic Italian cooking with a Sardinian character and a modern tone.

Hakkasan, 8 Hanway Pl, W1T 1HD ⊖ *Tottenham Court Road*, ℘ (020) 7927 7000, *mail@hakkasan.com*, Fax (020) 7907 1889 – ≡. **MC AE** *VISA*
31 AKT c
closed 24-25 December – Rest - Chinese (Canton) - a la carte 34.00/101.10 ♀.

Spec. Peking duck with Beluga caviar. Stir-fry black pepper rib-eye beef. Pan-fried silver cod in XO sauce.

♦ A distinctive, modern interpretation of Cantonese cooking in an appropriately contemporary and cavernous basement. The lively, bustling bar is an equally popular nightspot.

Fino, 33 Charlotte St (entrance on Rathbone St), W1T 1RR ⊖ *Goodge Street*, ℘ (020) 7813 8010, *info@finorestaurant.com*, Fax (020) 7813 8011 – **MC AE** *VISA*
31 AJT a
closed 25 December and Bank Holidays – Rest - Spanish - a la carte 21.00/32.50 s. ♀.

♦ Spanish-run basement bar with modern style décor and banquette seating. Wide-ranging menu of authentic dishes; 2 set-price selections offering an introduction to tapas.

Crazy Bear, 26-28 Whitfield St, W1T 2RG ⊖ *Goodge Street*, ℘ (020) 7631 0088, *enquiries@crazybeargroup.co.uk*, Fax (020) 7631 1188 – ≡. **MC AE** *VISA*
31 AKT b
closed Saturday lunch, Sunday and Bank Holidays – Rest - South East Asian - a la carte 23.00/34.00.

♦ Exotic destination: downstairs bar geared to fashionable set; ground floor dining room is art deco inspired. Asian flavoured menus, with predominance towards Thai dishes.

XX **Archipelago,** 110 Whitfield St, W1T 5ED ⊖ *Goodge Street,* ℰ (020) 7383 3346, *archipe lago@onetel.com, Fax (020) 7383 7181* – ✗✗ 🚇 AE 🚇 VISA   18 RZD c
closed 24-29 December, Saturday lunch and Sunday – **Rest** a la carte 31.50/37.00.
* Eccentric in both menu and décor and not for the faint hearted. Crammed with knick-knacks from cages to Buddhas. Menu an eclectic mix of influences from around the world.

X **Passione,** 10 Charlotte St, W1T 2LT ⊖ *Tottenham Court Road,* ℰ (020) 7636 2833, *liz@passione.co.uk, Fax (020) 7636 2889* – 🚇 AE 🚇 VISA   31 AKT u
closed Christmas, Saturday lunch and Sunday – **Rest** - Italian - (booking essential) a la carte 40.00/49.00.
* Compact but light and airy. Modern Italian cooking served in informal surroundings, with friendly and affable service. Particularly busy at lunchtime.

X **Cigala,** 54 Lamb's Conduit St, WC1N 3LW ⊖ *Holborn,* ℰ (020) 7405 1717, *tasty@ci gala.co.uk, Fax (020) 7242 9949* – 🚇 AE 🚇 VISA   19 TZD a
closed 24-26 December, 1 January, Easter Sunday and Monday – **Rest** - Spanish - 18.00 (lunch) and a la carte 22.50/34.50 ☯.
* Spanish restaurant on the corner of attractive street. Simply furnished with large win-dows and open-plan kitchen. Robust Iberian cooking. Informal tapas bar downstairs.

X **Camerino,** 16 Percy St, W1T 1DT ⊖ *Tottenham Court Road,* ℰ (020) 7637 9900, *info@camerinorestaurant.com, Fax (020) 7637 9696* – ▤. 🚇 AE 🚇 VISA   31 AKT f
closed 25 December, 1 January, Saturday lunch and Sunday – **Rest** - Italian - 23.50 and a la carte 27.50/36.50 ☯☯ ☯.
* Personally run, wood floored restaurant where bold red drapes contrast with crisp white linen-clad tables. Menus take the authentic taste of Italy's regions for inspiration.

X **Salt Yard,** 54 Goodge St, W1T 4NA ⊖ *Goodge Street,* ℰ (020) 7637 0657, *info@salt yard.co.uk, Fax (020) 7580 7435* – ✗✗ ▤. 🚇 AE VISA   31 AJT d
closed 2 weeks Christmas-New Year, Sunday, Saturday lunch and Bank Holidays – **Rest** - Spanish and Italian tapas - a la carte 20.00/40.00 ☯.
* Vogue destination with buzzy downstairs restaurant specialising in inexpensive sharing plates of tasty Italian and Spanish dishes: try the freshly cut hams. Super wine list.

X **Mela,** 152-156 Shaftesbury Ave, WC2H 8HL ⊖ *Leicester Square,* ℰ (020) 7836 8635, *info@melarestaurant.co.uk, Fax (020) 7379 0527* – ▤. 🚇 AE 🚇 VISA   31 AKU e
closed 25-26 December – **Rest** - Indian - 10.95/34.95 and a la carte 13.90/33.20 s.
* Vibrantly decorated dining room with a simple style in a useful location close to Theatre-land. Enjoy thoroughly tasty Indian food in a bustling, buzzy environment.

X **Abeno,** 47 Museum St, WC1A 1LY ⊖ *Tottenham Court Road,* ℰ (020) 7405 3211, *oko nomi@abeno.co.uk, Fax (020) 7405 3212* – ▤. 🚇 AE 🚇 VISA   31 ALT e
closed 25-26 and 31 December and 1 January – **Rest** - Japanese (Okonomi-Yaki) - 7.50/19.80 (lunch) and a la carte 14.00/33.80.
* Specialises in okonomi-yaki: little Japanese "pancakes" cooked on a hotplate on each table. Choose your own filling and the size of your pancake.

Hampstead *Gtr London –* ✉ *NW3.*

🏌 *Winnington Rd, Hampstead* ℰ *(020) 8455 0203.*

🏛 **Langorf** without rest., 20 Frognal, NW3 6AG ⊖ *Finchley Road,* ℰ (020) 7794 4483, *info@langorfhotel.com, Fax (020) 7435 9055* – 🛗. 🚇 AE 🚇 VISA. ✗   11 PZA c
41 rm ✦82.00 – ✦✦110.00/150.00, 5 suites.
* Converted Edwardian house in a quiet residential area. Bright breakfast room overlooks secluded walled garden. Fresh bedrooms, many of which have high ceilings.

🍽 **The Wells,** 30 Well Walk, NW3 1BX ⊖ *Hampstead Heath,* ℰ (020) 7794 3785, *info@the wellshampstead.co.uk, Fax (020) 7794 6817,* 🌫 – ✗✗ rest, ▤. 🚇 VISA   11 PZA v
closed 1 January – **Rest** 15.95/28.50 and a la carte 17.00/22.00 ☯.
* Attractive 18C inn with modern interior. Ground floor bar and a few tables next to open-plan kitchen; upstairs more formal dining rooms. Classically-based French cooking.

🍽 **The Magdala,** 2A South Hill Park, NW3 2SB ⊖ *Belsize Park,* ℰ (020) 7435 2503, *Fax (020) 7435 6167,* 🌫 – 🚇 AE 🚇   11 PZA s
closed 25 December – **Rest** a la carte 20.00/25.00 ☯.
* Located on the edge of the Heath. Two bars popular with locals, one with open-plan kitchen. Upstairs dining room, open at weekends, offers robust cooking. Simpler lunch menu.

Hatton Garden *Gtr London –* ✉ *EC1.*

XX **Bleeding Heart,** Bleeding Heart Yard, EC1N 8SJ, off Greville St ⊖ *Farringdon,* ℰ (020) 7242 8238, *bookings@bleedingheart.co.uk, Fax (020) 7831 1402,* 🌫 – 🚇 AE 🚇 VISA   32 ANT e
closed 23 December-3 January, Saturday, Sunday and Bank Holidays – **Rest** a la carte 23.85/39.85 ☯ ⊞.
* Wood panelling, candlelight and a heart motif; a popular romantic dinner spot. By contrast, a busy City restaurant at lunchtime. French influenced menu. Weighty wine list.

Holborn *Gtr London –* ✉ *WC1/WC2.*

🏨🏨🏨 **Renaissance Chancery Court**, 252 High Holborn, WC1V 7EN ⊖ *Holborn,* 𝒫 (020) 7829 9888, *sales.chancerycourt@renaissancehotels.com, Fax (020) 7829 9889,* 🕗, ₤₆, 🚗 – 📱, 🔆 rm, 🖥 ✆ ≐ – 🛎 400. 🆗 🆎 ⓪ 𝚅𝙸𝚂𝙰. 🛠
                                                        32 AMT a
Rest – (see *Pearl* below) – � 22.50 – **354 rm** 🛏276.00 – 🛏🛏347.00, 2 suites.
  ◆ Striking building built in 1914, now an imposing place to stay. Impressive marbled lobby and grand central courtyard. Very large bedrooms with comprehensive modern facilities.

🏨🏨 **Kingsway Hall**, Great Queen St, WC2B 5BX ⊖ *Holborn,* 𝒫 (020) 7309 0909, *sales@king swayhall.co.uk, Fax (020) 7309 9129,* ₤₆ – 📱, 🔆 rm, 🖥 ✆ ≐ – 🛎 150. 🆗 🆎 ⓪ 𝚅𝙸𝚂𝙰.
                                                        31 ALT b
Harlequin : **Rest** *(closed lunch Saturday and Sunday)* 19.95 and a la carte 25.75/34.50 – ⊒ 15.25 – **168 rm** 🛏316.00 – 🛏🛏316.00, 2 suites.
  ◆ Large, corporate-minded hotel. Striking glass-framed and marbled lobby. Stylish ground floor bar. Well-appointed bedrooms with an extensive array of mod cons. European menus in smart, minimalist restaurant.

✗✗✗ **Pearl** (at Renaissance Chancery Court H.), 252 High Holborn, WC1V 7EN ⊖ *Holborn,* 𝒫 (020) 7829 7000, *Fax (020) 7829 9889* – ⇄ 10. 🆗 🆎 ⓪ 𝚅𝙸𝚂𝙰
                                                        32 AMT a
closed Saturday lunch and Sunday – **Rest** 26.50/45.00 and a la carte 30.20/45.00 🍷 ⌀.
  ◆ Impressive dining room with walls clad in Italian marble; Corinthian columns. Waiters provide efficient service at well-spaced tables ; original menus.

✗✗ **Matsuri - High Holborn**, Mid City Pl, 71 High Holborn, WC1V 6EA ⊖ *Holborn,* 𝒫 (020) 7430 1970, *eat@matsuri-restaurant.com, Fax (020) 7430 1971* – 🆗 🆎 ⓪ 𝚅𝙸𝚂𝙰 **32 AMT c**
closed 25 December, Sunday and Bank Holidays – **Rest** - Japanese - 15.00/70.00 and a la carte 24.50/43.00 🍷.
  ◆ Spacious, airy Japanese restaurant. Authentic menu served in main dining room, in basement teppan-yaki bar and at large sushi counter, where chefs demonstrate their skills.

✗✗ **Shanghai Blues**, 193-197 High Holborn, WC1V 7BD ⊖ *Holborn,* 𝒫 (020) 7404 1668, *info@shanghaiblues.co.uk, Fax (020) 7404 1448* – 🖥 ⇄ 28. 🆗 🆎 𝚅𝙸𝚂𝙰 **31 ALT c**
closed 25 December – **Rest** - Chinese - a la carte 30.00/50.00.
  ◆ Set in Grade II listed former St Giles Library, this spacious, moody Chinese restaurant is offset by cool bar and mezzanine lounge. Wide range of specialities to choose from.

✗✗ **Asadal**, 227 High Holborn, WC1V 7DA ⊖ *Holborn,* 𝒫 (020) 7430 9006, *info@asadal.co.uk* – 🖥. 🆗 🆎 𝚅𝙸𝚂𝙰 **31 ALT n**
closed 25 December, 1 January and Sunday lunch – **Rest** - Korean - 17.50 and a la carte 8.50/25.00.
  ◆ A hectic, unprepossessing location, but delivers the authenticity of a modest Korean café with the comfort and service of a proper restaurant. Good quality Korean cooking.

✗✗ **Moti Mahal**, 45 Great Queen St, WC2B 5AA ⊖ *Covent Garden,* 𝒫 (020) 7240 9329, *reservations@motimahal-uk.com, Fax (020) 7836 0790* – 🖥 ⇄ 35. 🆗 🆎 𝚅𝙸𝚂𝙰 **31 ALU k**
closed 25-26 December, 1 January and Sunday – **Rest** - Indian - 14.95 (lunch) and a la carte 28.00/36.00.
  ◆ Elegant stone fronted restaurant. Bar with huge whisky selection; cool contemporary dining room where concise, modern Indian dishes using well prepared ingredients are served.

Primrose Hill *Gtr London –* ✉ *NW1.*

✗✗ **Odette's**, 130 Regent's Park Rd, NW1 8XL ⊖ *Chalk Farm,* 𝒫 (020) 7586 5486, *odettes@vpmg.net, Fax (020) 7722 5388* – 🆗 𝚅𝙸𝚂𝙰 **11 QZB b**
closed 24-31 December, Sunday dinner and Monday – **Rest** 21.95/40.00 and a la carte 25.90/43.90.
  ◆ Identified by the pretty hanging baskets outside. A charming interior with mirrors of various sizes covering the walls. Detailed service. Contemporary cuisine.

✗✗ **Sardo Canale**, 42 Gloucester Ave, NW1 8JD ⊖ *Chalk Farm,* 𝒫 (020) 7722 2800, *info@sardocanale.com, Fax (020) 7722 0802,* 🌳 – 🔆 🖥. 🆗 🆎 ⓪ 𝚅𝙸𝚂𝙰 **12 RZB a**
closed 25-26 December and Monday lunch – **Rest** - Italian (Sardinian specialities) - a la carte 22.90/33.40.
  ◆ A series of five snug but individual dining rooms in conservatory style; delightful terrace with 200 year old olive tree. Appealing Italian menus with strong Sardinian accent.

✗✗ **Le Petit Train**, 40 Chalcot Rd, NW1 8LS ⊖ *Chalk Farm,* 𝒫 (020) 7483 0077, *leeo rion@btconnect.com* – 🔆 🖥. 🆗 𝚅𝙸𝚂𝙰 **11 QZB d**
closed 25-26 December and Sunday – **Rest** - French - (booking essential) (dinner only and Saturday lunch) 14.75 a la carte 23.00/31.50 🍷.
  ◆ An eye-catching green exterior announces this cosy restaurant near the Roundhouse. Closely set tables invite a buzzy ambience; menus born in Southern France are the backbone.

XX **La Collina,** 17 Princess Rd, NW1 8JR ⊖ *Camden Town*, 𝒫 (020) 7483 0192, �af – ✖️. **MO**
VISA   11 QZB x
closed Bank Holidays – **Rest** - Italian - (dinner only and lunch Friday-Sunday) 22.50.
  ◆ Neighbourhood restaurant over two floors: downstairs is a more intimate place to dine.
Well cooked, great value Piedmontese dishes are the reason the locals keep coming back.

🛏 **The Queens,** 49 Regent's Park Rd, NW1 8XD ⊖ *Chalk Farm*, 𝒫 (020) 7586 0408,
Fax (020) 7586 5677, �af – **MO** **VISA**. ✖️   11 QZB a
closed 25 December – **Rest** a la carte 20.00/26.00 ♀.
  ◆ One of the original "gastropubs". Very popular balcony overlooking Primrose Hill and the
high street. Robust and traditional cooking from the blackboard menu.

🛏 **The Engineer,** 65 Gloucester Ave, NW1 8JH ⊖ *Chalk Farm*, 𝒫 (020) 7722 0950,
Fax (020) 7483 0592, �af – **MO** **VISA**   11 QZB z
closed 25-26 December – **Rest** a la carte 18.00/45.00 ♀.
  ◆ Busy pub that boasts a warm, neighbourhood feel. Dining room, decorated with modern pictures, has modish appeal. Informal, chatty service. Modern cuisine.

Swiss Cottage *Gtr London* – ⊠ NW3.

🏨 **Marriott Regents Park,** 128 King Henry's Rd, NW3 3ST ⊖ *Swiss Cottage*, 𝒫 (020)
7722 7711, *Fax (020) 7586 5822,* 🛁, 🈂️, 🔲 – 🛗, ✖️ rm, 🔲 📞 & 🅿️ – 🔬 300. **MO AE ⓞ**
VISA. ✖️   11 PZB a
Meditterano : **Rest** a la carte 22.00/33.00 s. ♀ – � 16.95 – **298 rm** ✚163.30/165.00 –
✚✚163.30/193.90, 5 suites.
  ◆ Large writing desks and technological extras attract the corporate market to this purpose-built group hotel. The impressive leisure facilities appeal to weekend guests. Large,
open-plan restaurant and bar.

🏨 **Swiss Cottage** without rest., 4 Adamson Rd, NW3 3HP ⊖ *Swiss Cottage*, 𝒫 (020) 7722
2281, *reservations@swisscottagehotel.co.uk, Fax (020) 7483 4588* – 🛗 ✖️ 📞 – 🔬 35. **MO**
AE ⓞ VISA. ✖️   11 PZB n
� 6.95 **53 rm** ✚65.00/99.50 – ✚✚69.50/135.00, 6 suites.
  ◆ Made up of four Victorian houses in a residential conservation area. Bedrooms vary in
size and shape, reflecting the age of the house. Basement breakfast room.

XX **Bradley's,** 25 Winchester Rd, NW3 3NR ⊖ *Swiss Cottage*, 𝒫 (020) 7722 3457, ssjbrad
leys@aol.com, *Fax (020) 7435 1392* – 🔲. **MO AE VISA**   11 PZB e
closed 1 week Christmas, Monday, Sunday dinner, Saturday lunch and Bank Holidays – **Rest**
13.95 (lunch) and a la carte 23.50/35.50 🍷♀.
  ◆ Warm pastel colours and modern artwork add a Mediterranean touch to this neighbourhood restaurant. The theme is complemented by the cooking of the chef patron.

XX **Eriki,** 4-6 Northways Parade, Finchley Rd, NW3 5EN ⊖ *Swiss Cottage*, 𝒫 (020) 7722 0606,
info@eriki.co.uk, *Fax (020) 7722 8866* – 🔲. **MO AE VISA**   11 PZB u
closed 25-26 December and Saturday lunch – **Rest** - Indian - a la carte 13.85/18.85.
  ◆ A calm and relaxing venue, in spite of the bright interior set off by vivid red walls.
Obliging service of carefully presented, flavoursome dishes from southern India.

Tufnell Park *Gtr London* – ⊠ NW5.

🛏 **Junction Tavern,** 101 Fortess Rd, NW5 1AG ⊖ *Tufnell Park*, 𝒫 (020) 7485 9400,
Fax (020) 7485 9401, �af – **MO** **VISA**   12 RZA x
closed 24-26 December and 1 January – **Rest** a la carte 20.00/30.00 ♀.
  ◆ Typical Victorian pub with wood panelling. Eat in the bar or in view of the open plan
kitchen. Robust cooking using good fresh ingredients, served in generous portions.

CITY OF LONDON *Gtr London* – ⊠ E1/EC1/EC2/EC3/EC4.

🏨 **Great Eastern,** Liverpool St, EC2M 7QN ⊖ *Liverpool Street*, 𝒫 (020) 7618 5000,
info@great-eastern-hotel.co.uk, *Fax (020) 7618 5001,* 🛁 – 🛗, ✖️ rm, 🔲 & – 🔬 250. **MO**
AE ⓞ VISA   34 ART t
Fishmarket : **Rest** - Seafood - *(closed Saturday-Sunday)* a la carte 25.00/47.50 ♀ – *Miyabi :*
Rest - Japanese - *(closed Christmas, Saturday lunch and Sunday)* (booking essential) 18.00
(lunch) and a la carte 23.50/43.50 – (see also *Aurora* below) – � 22.00 – **264 rm**
✚117.50/370.10 – ✚✚117.50/370.10, 3 suites.
  ◆ A contemporary and stylish interior hides behind the classic Victorian façade of this
railway hotel. Bright and spacious bedrooms with state-of-the-art facilities. Fishmarket
based within original hotel lobby. Miyabi is compact Japanese restaurant.

Crowne Plaza London - The City, 19 New Bridge St, EC4V 6DB ⊖ *Blackfriars*, ℰ (0870) 4009190, *loncy.info@ichotelsgroup.com*, *Fax (020) 7438 8080*, ₤₅, ⥱ – |ṡ|, ⥱ rm, ▤ ℃ ♨ – 🚻 180. 🐠 🆎 ⑩ 𝘝𝘐𝘚𝘈.
32 AOU a
Refettorio : Rest– Italian - *(closed Sunday, Saturday lunch and Bank Holidays)* 20.00 (dinner) and a la carte 32.50/36.50 – *Spicers :* Rest a la carte 22.00/27.95 – 🖙 17.00 – **201 rm** ★358.00 – ★★358.00, 2 suites.
• Art deco façade by the river; interior enhanced by funky chocolate, cream and brown palette. Compact meeting room; well equipped fitness centre. Sizable, stylish rooms. Modish Refettorio for Italian cuisine. British dishes with a modern twist at Spicers.

Threadneedles, 5 Threadneedle St, EC2R 8AY ⊖ *Bank*, ℰ (020) 7657 8080, *resthread needles@theetoncollection.com*, *Fax (020) 7657 8100* – |ṡ| ⥱ ▤ ℃ ♨ – 🚻 35. 🐠 🆎 ⑩ 𝘝𝘐𝘚𝘈. ⁂
34 ARU y
Rest – (see *Bonds* below) – 🖙 16.50 – **68 rm** ★346.60 – ★★346.60, 1 suite.
• A converted bank, dating from 1856, with a stunning stained-glass cupola in the lounge. Rooms are very stylish and individual featuring CD players and Egyptian cotton sheets.

Apex City of London, No 1, Seething Lane, EC3N 4AX ⊖ *Fenchurch Street*, ℰ (020) 7702 2020, *Fax (020) 7702 2020*, ₤₅, ⥱ – |ṡ| ⥱ ▤ 📺 ℃ ♨ – 🚻 80. 🐠 🆎 ⑩ 𝘝𝘐𝘚𝘈. ⁂
34 ARU a
Addendum Bar : Rest a la carte 17.40/27.40 – (see also *Addendum* below) – 🖙 16.95 – **129 rm** ★287.90 – ★★287.90, 1 suite.
• Tucked away behind Tower of London, overlooking leafy square. Smart meeting facilities, well-equipped gym and treatment rooms. Bedrooms are super sleek with bespoke extras. Open plan bar/brasserie serves interesting modern dishes; al fresco in summer.

The Chamberlain, 130-135 Minories, EC3N 1NU ⊖ *Aldgate*, ℰ (020) 7680 1500, *the chamberlain@fullers.co.uk*, *Fax (020) 7702 2500* – |ṡ| ⥱ ▤ ℃ ♨ – 🚻 50. 🐠 🆎 ⑩ 𝘝𝘐𝘚𝘈. ⁂
34 ASU n
closed Christmas – Rest (in bar Saturday-Sunday) a la carte 19.85/31.35 ₤ – 🖙 14.95 – **64 rm** ★225.00 – ★★255.00.
• Modern hotel aimed at business traveller, two minutes from the Tower of London. Warmly decorated bedrooms with writing desks. All bathrooms have inbuilt plasma TVs. Popular range of dishes.

Novotel London Tower Bridge, 10 Pepys St, EC3N 2NR ⊖ *Tower Hill*, ℰ (020) 7265 6000, *h3107@accor.com*, *Fax (020) 7265 6060*, ₤₅, ⥱ – |ṡ|, ⥱ rm, ▤ rest, ♨ – 🚻 100. 🐠 🆎 ⑩ 𝘝𝘐𝘚𝘈
34 ASU b
The Garden Brasserie : Rest (bar lunch Saturday-Sunday) (buffet lunch)/dinner a la carte 20.70/29.85 s. ₤ – 🖙 13.50 – **199 rm** ★185.00 – ★★205.00, 4 suites.
• Modern, purpose-built hotel with carefully planned, comfortable bedrooms. Useful City location and close to Tower of London which is visible from some of the higher rooms. Informally styled brasserie.

Aurora (at Great Eastern H.), Liverpool St, EC2M 7QN ⊖ *Liverpool Street*, ℰ (020) 7618 7000, *restaurants@great-eastern-hotel.co.uk*, *Fax (020) 7618 5035* – ▤. 🐠 🆎 ⑩ 𝘝𝘐𝘚𝘈
34 ART t
closed Saturday-Sunday – Rest 28.50/50.00 and a la carte 35.00/45.00 🕙 ₤ ♨.
• Vast columns, ornate plasterwork and a striking glass dome feature in this imposing dining room. Polished and attentive service of an elaborate and modern menu.

Rhodes Twenty Four, 24th floor, Tower 42, 25 Old Broad St, EC2N 1HQ ⊖ *Liverpool Street*, ℰ (020) 7877 7703, *reservations@rhodes24.co.uk*, *Fax (020) 7877 7788*, ≤ London – |ṡ| ▤ 🐠 🆎 ⑩ 𝘝𝘐𝘚𝘈
34 ART u
closed Christmas-New Year, Saturday, Sunday and Bank Holidays – Rest a la carte 33.80/49.50 ₤.
Spec. Seared scallops with mashed potato and shallot mustard sauce. Steamed oxtail suet pudding, buttered carrots and oxtail jus. Bread and butter pudding.
• Modern restaurant on the 24th floor of the former Natwest building with panoramic views of the city. Modern, refined cooking of classic British recipes. Booking advised.

Coq d'Argent, No.1 Poultry, EC2R 8EJ ⊖ *Bank*, ℰ (020) 7395 5000, *coqdargent@con ran-restaurants.co.uk*, *Fax (020) 7395 5050*, 🌳 – |ṡ| ▤ 🐠 🆎 ⑩ 𝘝𝘐𝘚𝘈
33 AQU c
closed Saturday lunch, Sunday dinner, Christmas, Easter and Bank Holidays – Rest - French - (booking essential) 27.00 (lunch) and a la carte 29.50/44.00 🕙 ₤.
• Take the dedicated lift to the top of this modern office block. Tables on the rooftop terrace have city views; busy bar. Gallic menus highlighted by popular shellfish dishes.

447

XXX **1 Lombard Street (Restaurant),** 1 Lombard St, EC3V 9AA ⊖ *Bank*, ℰ (020) 7929
6611, hb@1lombardstreet.com, Fax (020) 7929 6622 – ⇥ ▤ ⇔ 40. **MC AE ①**
VISA
33 AQU **r**

closed 24 December- 3 January, Saturday, Sunday and Bank Holidays – **Rest** (lunch booking
essential) 39.00/45.00 and a la carte 52.50/61.50 ♀.

Spec. Carpaccio of tuna with Oriental spices, ginger and lime vinaigrette. Beef tournedos
with wild mushrooms, parsley purée and oxtail sauce. Feuillantine of apple, Guinness ice
cream and glazed hazelnuts.

◆ A haven of tranquillity behind the forever busy brasserie. Former bank provides the
modern and very comfortable surroundings in which to savour the accomplished cuisine.

XXX **Prism,** 147 Leadenhall, EC3V 4QT ⊖ *Aldgate*, ℰ (020) 7256 3888, Fax (0870) 191 6025 –
▤. **MC AE ① VISA**
34 ARU **u**

closed Saturday and Sunday – **Rest** a la carte 21.50/39.50 ♀.

◆ Enormous Corinthian pillars and a busy bar feature in this capacious and modern restaurant. Efficient service of an eclectic menu. Quieter tables in covered courtyard.

XXX **Addendum,** No 1, Seething Lane, EC3N 4AX ⊖ *Fenchurch Street*, ℰ (020) 7977 9500,
londonevents@apexhotels.co.uk – ⇥ ▤. **MC AE ① VISA**
34 ARU **a**

closed 23 December-3 January, Saturday, Sunday and Bank Holidays – **Rest** a la carte
38.50/54.50 ♀.

◆ Intimate and elegant with chocolate leather banquettes, fresh flowers and modern
mirrors. Precise service of robust, earthy dishes which often rejoice in the use of offal.

XXX **Bonds** (at Threadneedles H.), 5 Threadneedle St, EC2R 8AY ⊖ *Bank*, ℰ (020) 7657 8088,
bonds@theetongroup.com, Fax (020) 7657 8089 – ⇥ ▤ ⇔ 16. **MC AE ① VISA** 34 ARU **y**

closed Saturday and Sunday – **Rest** 24.50 (lunch) and a la carte 35.50/60.00 ♀.

◆ Modern interior juxtaposed with the grandeur of a listed city building. Vast dining room
with high ceiling and tall pillars. Attentive service of hearty, contemporary food.

XX **Club Gascon** (Aussignac), 57 West Smithfield, EC1A 9DS ⊖ *Barbican*, ℰ (020) 7796 0600,
info@clubgascon.com, Fax (020) 7796 0601 – ▤. **MC AE VISA**
33 APT **z**

closed 24 December - 6 January, Sunday, Saturday lunch and Bank Holidays – **Rest** - French
(Gascony specialities) - (booking essential) 35.00 (lunch) and a la carte 28.50/49.00 ♀ ﹩.

Spec. Saffron duck foie gras, crispy chicory. Grilled wild salmon, smoked violet tea and
aubergine. Glazed veal sweetbread, Bergamot and artichoke barigoule.

◆ Intimate restaurant on the edge of Smithfield Market. Specialises in both the food and
wines of Southwest France. Renowned for its tapas-sized dishes.

XX **Sauterelle,** The Royal Exchange, EC3V 3LR ⊖ *Bank*, ℰ (020) 7618 2483 – ⇥ ▤ ⇔ 24.
MC AE ① VISA
33 AQU **a**

closed Christmas-New Year, Saturday and Sunday – **Rest** a la carte 28.20/40.50.

◆ Located on mezzanine level of Royal Exchange, a stunning 16C property with ornate
columns and pillars. Typically Conran rustic French menus attract smart lunchtime diners.

XX **The Chancery,** 9 Cursitor St, EC4A 1LL ⊖ *Chancery Lane*, ℰ (020) 7831 4000, reserva
tions@thechancery.co.uk, Fax (020) 7831 4002 – ▤. **MC AE ① VISA**
32 ANT **a**

closed 22 December-8 January, Saturday and Sunday – **Rest** 32.00 ♀.

◆ Near Law Courts, a small restaurant with basement bar. Contemporary interior with
intimate style. Quality ingredients put to good use in accomplished, modern dishes.

XX **Lanes,** 109-117 Middlesex St, E1 7JF ⊖ *Liverpool Street*, ℰ (020) 7247 5050, info@lanes
restaurant.co.uk, Fax (020) 7247 8071 – ▤ ⇔ 28. **MC AE ① VISA**
34 ART **b**

closed 25 December, Saturday lunch, Sunday and Bank Holidays – **Rest** 21.50 (dinner) and a
la carte 27.50/43.50 ♀.

◆ Busy lunchtimes and more sedate evenings at this bright destination with subterranean
bar, where art displays are a regular backdrop. Modern British/European menus hold sway.

XX **Boisdale of Bishopgate,** Swedeland Court, 202 Bishopgate, EC2M 4NR ⊖ *Liverpool
Street*, ℰ (020) 7283 1763, Fax (020) 7283 1664 – ▤. **MC AE VISA**
34 ART **a**

closed 25 December, 1 January, Saturday, Sunday and Bank Holidays – **Rest** - Scottish - a la
carte 22.95/35.55 ♀.

◆ Through ground floor bar, serving oysters and champagne, to brick vaulted basement
with red and tartan décor. Menu featuring Scottish produce. Live jazz most evenings.

XX **Bevis Marks,** Bevis Marks, EC3A 5DQ ⊖ *Aldgate*, ℰ (020) 7283 2220, enquiries@bevis
markstherestaurant.com, Fax (020) 7283 2221, ㎡ – ⇥ ▤. **MC AE VISA**
34 ART **x**

closed Saturday, Sunday, Friday dinner and Jewish Holidays – **Rest** - Kosher - a la carte
26.50/33.40 ♀.

◆ Glass-roofed extension to city's oldest synagogue: limestone flooring, modern murals
on wall. Regularly changing Kosher menus; influences from Mediterranean and Middle
East.

XX **Searcy's,** Barbican Centre, Level 2, Silk St, EC2Y 8DS ⊖ *Barbican*, ☎ (020) 7588 3008, *searcys@barbican.org.uk, Fax (020) 7382 7247* – ▤. MC AE ① VISA 33 **AQT** n
closed 24-26 December, Sunday, Saturday lunch and Bank Holidays – **Rest** a la carte 26.40/39.85 ♀.
◆ Stylish modern surroundings, smooth effective service and seasonal modern British cooking. Unique location ideal for visitors to Barbican's multi-arts events.

XX **Chamberlain's,** 23-25 Leadenhall Market, EC3V 1LR ⊖ *Bank*, ☎ (020) 7648 8690, *info@chamberlains.org, Fax (020) 7648 8691* – ▤. MC AE VISA 34 **ARU** v
closed 25-26 December, Saturday, Sunday and Bank Holidays – **Rest** - Seafood - 16.95 (dinner) and a la carte 32.95/53.25 **s.** ♀.
◆ Bright, modern restaurant in ornate Victorian indoor market. Top quality seafood from fish and chips to mousse of lobster. There's even a fish tank in the lavatories!

XX **Tatsuso,** 32 Broadgate Circle, EC2M 2QS ⊖ *Liverpool Street*, ☎ (020) 7638 5863, *info.tatsuso@btinternet.com, Fax (020) 7638 5864* – ▤ ⇔ 18. MC AE ① VISA 34 **ART** u
closed Saturday, Sunday and Bank Holidays – **Rest** - Japanese - (booking essential) a la carte 30.00/97.00 **s.**
◆ Dine in the busy teppan-yaki bar or in the more formal restaurant. Approachable staff in traditional costume provide attentive service of authentic and precise dishes.

XX **The White Swan,** 1st Floor, 108 Fetter Lane, EC4A 1ES ⊖ *Temple*, ☎ (020) 7242 9696, *info@thewhiteswanlondon.com, Fax (020) 7404 2250* – ▤. MC AE VISA. ✈ 32 **ANT** n
closed 24-26 and 31 December, 1 January and Bank Holidays – **Rest** *(closed Saturday, Sunday and dinner Monday)* 25.00 (lunch) and a la carte 20.00/30.00 ♀.
◆ Smart dining room above pub just off Fleet Street: mirrored ceilings, colourful paintings on wall. Modern, daily changing menus, are good value for the heart of London.

XX **Saki,** 4 West Smithfield, EC1A 9JX ⊖ *Barbican*, ☎ (020) 7489 7033, *info@saki-food.com, Fax (020) 7489 1658* – ⇔ ▤ ⇔ 12. MC VISA 33 **AOT** b
closed Christmas-New Year, Sunday and Bank Holidays – **Rest** - Japanese - 25.00/55.00 and a la carte 22.30/59.70.
◆ Uber-stylish bar/restaurant below a Japanese deli. Incorporates a sushi bar, communal 'garden table' and impressive Japanese dishes based on seasonality and healthy eating.

X **Paternoster Chop House,** Warwick Court, Paternoster Square, EC4N 7DX ⊖ *St Paul's*, ☎ (020) 7029 9400, *paternosterr@conran-restaurants.co.uk, Fax (020) 7029 9409*,
☂ – ⇔ ▤. MC AE ① VISA 33 **APT** x
closed 22 December-2 January, Saturday and Sunday dinner – **Rest** - British - a la carte 31.50/46.00 ♀.
◆ A modern ambience holds sway, while there's a reassuringly resolute British classic style to the dishes. Back to basics menu relies on seasonality and sourcing of ingredients.

Your opinions are important to us:
please write and let us know about your discoveries and experiences – good and bad!

CROYDON *Gtr London.*

Addington – ✉ *Surrey.*

⛳18, ⛳18, ⛳9 *Addington Court, Featherbed Lane* ☎ *(020) 8657 0281* **GZ** – ⛳18 *The Addington, 205 Shirley Church Rd* ☎ *(020) 8777 1055* **GZ.**

XX **Planet Spice,** 88 Selsdon Park Rd, CR2 8JT, ☎ (020) 8651 3300, *emdad@planet-spice.com, Fax (020) 8651 4400* – ▤ P. MC AE VISA 7 **GZ** c
closed 25-26 December – **Rest** - Indian - a la carte 23.65/27.40 ♀.
◆ Brasserie style Indian restaurant with fresh, vibrant décor and a modern feel. Attentive and helpful service. Traditional cooking with some innovative touches.

Coulsdon *Surrey* – ✉ *Surrey.*

Coulsdon Manor ⛰, Coulsdon Court Rd, via Stoats Nest Rd (B 2030), CR5 2LL, ☎ (020) 8668 0414, *coulsdon@oluml.com, Fax (020) 8668 3118*, ≤, Ⅎ6, ≘s, ⛳18, ✂, squash – ⇅ ⇔ ♿ P – 🏛 180. MC AE VISA. ✈
Manor House **:** **Rest** 19.50/32.50 **s.** and a la carte 18.50/28.00 ♀ – **35 rm** ☕ 🚹115.00/138.00 – 🚹🚹158.00.
◆ A secluded Victorian country house, extended over the years. Set in 140 acres, much of which is taken up by the popular golf course. Smart bedrooms, restful sitting room. Softly-lit dining room with cocktail bar.

Croydon *Surrey –* ⊠ *Surrey.*

🖪 *Croydon Clocktower, Katharine St* ℰ *(020) 8253 1009.*

🏨 **Hilton Croydon,** Waddon Way, Purley Way, CR9 4HH, ℰ *(020) 8680 3000, reserva tions.croydon@hilton.com, Fax (020) 8681 6171,* 🛵, ⌂, 🖾 – 🛊 ⇄ ≡ 🕭 🕭, ₽ – 🔬 400. ◑◐ 🕭 ◍ 𝘝𝘐𝘚𝘈, ⅗
⠀⠀⠀7 FZ e
closed 25-31 December – **Rest** *(closed Sunday) (dinner only)* 18.00 **s.** ⅞ – ⌇ 15.25 – **168 rm** ✶139.00 – ✶✶169.00.
⠀◆ A modern hotel where the relaxing café in the open-plan lobby is open all day. Internet access is available in all bedrooms, which are decorated to a good standard. Open-plan dining room; informal char-grill concept.

🏨 **Jurys Inn,** Wellesley Road, CR0 9XY, ℰ *(020) 8448 6000, jurysinncroydon@jurys doyle.com, Fax (020) 8448 6111 –* 🛊, ⇄ rm, ≡ 🕭 🕭 – 🔬 120. ◑◐ 🕭 ◍ 𝘝𝘐𝘚𝘈, ⅗
⠀⠀⠀7 FZ v
closed 24-25 December **Rest** *(bar lunch)/dinner* 16.95 **s.** – ⌇ 9.95 – **240 rm** ✶65.00/99.00 – ✶✶65.00/99.00.
⠀◆ Along main dual carriageway in town centre. Informal coffee bar in foyer. Conference facilities on first and second floors. Bright, modern rooms with good facilities. Restaurant near foyer; very relaxed informality.

EALING *Gtr London.*

Acton Green *Gtr London –* ⊠ *W4.*

🍴 **The Bollo,** 13-15 Bollo Lane, W4 5LR ⊖ *Chiswick Park,* ℰ *(020) 8994 6037, sullivanash ley@hotmail.com, Fax (020) 8743 5810,* 🍽 – ◑◐ ◍ 𝘝𝘐𝘚𝘈⠀⠀⠀⠀⠀⠀⠀⠀⠀⠀⠀⠀⠀6 CV z
closed 25 December – **Rest** *a la carte* 18.00/30.00 ⅞.
⠀◆ Attractive redbrick pub with dining area under a domed glass rotunda. Daily changing menu - mixture of traditional and eclectic dishes - served throughout the pub.

Ealing *Gtr London –* ⊠ *W13.*

 West Middlesex, Greenford Rd, Southall ℰ *(020) 8574 3450* BV – 🏌 *Horsenden Hill, Woodland Rise, Greenford* ℰ *(020) 8902 4555* BU.

✕✕ **Maxim,** 153-155 Northfield Ave, W13 9QT ⊖ *Northfields,* ℰ *(020) 8567 1719, Fax (020) 8932 0717 –* ≡. ◑◐ 🕭 𝘝𝘐𝘚𝘈⠀⠀⠀⠀⠀⠀⠀⠀⠀⠀⠀⠀⠀⠀⠀⠀⠀⠀⠀⠀⠀⠀⠀⠀⠀⠀⠀⠀1 BV a
closed 25-28 December and Sunday lunch – **Rest** *- Chinese (Peking) -* 15.00/35.00 and a la carte 17.00/30.00.
⠀◆ Decorated with assorted oriental ornaments and pictures. Well-organised service from smartly attired staff. Authentic Chinese cooking from the extensive menu.

South Ealing *Gtr London –* ⊠ *W5.*

🍴 **The Ealing Park Tavern,** 222 South Ealing Rd, W5 4RL ⊖ *South Ealing,* ℰ *(020) 8758 1879, Fax (020) 8560 5269,* 🍽 – ◑◐ 🕭 𝘝𝘐𝘚𝘈⠀⠀⠀⠀⠀⠀⠀⠀⠀⠀⠀⠀⠀⠀⠀⠀⠀⠀⠀⠀1 BV e
closed 25-26 December and Monday lunch except Bank Holidays – **Rest** *a la carte* 20.00/25.00 ⅞.
⠀◆ Victorian building with an atmospheric, cavernous interior. Characterful beamed dining room and an open-plan kitchen serving modern dishes from a daily changing menu.

ENFIELD *Gtr London.*

🏌 *Lee Valley Leisure, Picketts Lock Lane, Edmonton* ℰ *(020) 8803 3611* GT.

Enfield *Middx –* ⊠ *Middx.*

🏌 *Whitewebbs, Beggars Hollow, Clay Hill* ℰ *(020) 8363 2951, N : 1 m.* FT.

🏠 **Oak Lodge** without rest., 80 Village Rd, Bush Hill Park, EN1 2EU, ℰ *(020) 8360 7082, oaklodge@fsmail.net,* 🍽 – ⇄ 🕭, ◑◐ 🕭 ◍ 𝘝𝘐𝘚𝘈⠀⠀⠀⠀⠀⠀⠀⠀⠀⠀⠀⠀⠀⠀⠀⠀⠀3 FT a
6 rm ✶79.50 – ✶✶89.50.
⠀◆ An Edwardian house personally run by the hospitable owner and located in a residential area. Individually decorated bedrooms are compact but well equipped.

Hadley Wood *Herts. –* ⊠ *Herts.*

🏨 **West Lodge Park** ⑊, off Cockfosters Rd, EN4 0PY, ℰ *(020) 8216 3900, westlodge park@bealeshotel.co.uk, Fax (020) 8216 3937,* ≼, 🍽, 🍽, 🛵 – 🛊 ⇄ 🕭 🕭 ₽ – 🔬 80. ◑◐ 🕭 ◍ 𝘝𝘐𝘚𝘈, ⅗
⠀⠀⠀3 ET i
The Cedar : **Rest** *(closed Saturday lunch)* 25.95 *(lunch) and a la carte* 31.25/41.70 – ⌇ 14.50 – **59 rm** ✶115.00/135.00 – ✶✶155.00.
⠀◆ Family owned for over half a century, a country house in sweeping grounds with arbor- etum. Comfortable sitting rooms; neat, spacious bedrooms. Use of nearby leisure centre. Dining room boasts large windows and exposed brick walls.

GREENWICH Gtr London.

Greenwich Gtr London – ⊠ SE10.

XX **North Pole,** 131 Greenwich High Rd, SE10 8JA ⊖ Greenwich (DLR), ℰ (020) 8853 3020, north-pole@btconnect.com, Fax (020) 8853 3501 – 🝏🝐 🝐 𝗩𝗜𝗦𝗔   7 GV u
Rest (bar lunch Monday-Saturday)/dinner 25.00 and a la carte 21.00/35.00 ♀.
  • Rat-pack themed former pub with popular bar: piano played most evenings. Upstairs dining room benefits from large windows and bright colours. Relaxed service; robust cooking.

XX **Spread Eagle,** 1-2 Stockwell St, SE10 9JN ⊖ Greenwich (DLR), ℰ (020) 8853 2333, Fax (020) 8293 1024 – ✻⟝ ▤, 🝏🝐 𝗩𝗜𝗦𝗔   7 GV c
closed January – **Rest** - French - a la carte 25.00/35.00 ♀.
  • This converted pub is something of an institution. Cosy booth seating, wood panelling and a further upstairs room. Traditional French-influenced menu with attentive service.

X **Rivington,** 178 Greenwich High Rd, SE10 8NN ⊖ Greenwich (DLR), ℰ (020) 8293 9270, office@rivingtongrill.co.uk – ▤, 🝏🝐 🝐 𝗩𝗜𝗦𝗔   7 GV s
closed 25-26 December and 1 January – **Rest** - British - 16.00 (lunch) and a la carte 18.50/33.00 ♀.
  • Part of the Picturehouse complex; 21C rustic interior with closely set tables. Firmly English menus in bar and galleried restaurant. Banquets and market breakfasts on offer.

HACKNEY Gtr London.

Hackney Gtr London – ⊠ E8.

🝑 **Cat & Mutton,** 76 Broadway Market, E8 4QJ ⊖ Bethnal Green, ℰ (020) 7254 5599, info@catandmutton.co.uk – 🝏🝐 🝐 𝗩𝗜𝗦𝗔   14 YZB a
closed 25-26 December – **Rest** (closed Sunday dinner and Monday lunch) a la carte 19.00/29.00 ♀.
  • 19C corner pub with vast windows, school chairs and wood-panelled ceiling. Menu on a slate board: robust gastro pub fare with ingredients from the Saturday farmers' market.

Hoxton Gtr London – ⊠ E1/EC1/EC2/N1.

🏨 **Saint Gregory,** 100 Shoreditch High St, E1 6JQ ⊖ Shoreditch, ℰ (020) 7613 9800, sales@saintgregoryhotel.com, Fax (020) 7613 9811, 🛵 – 🛗 ✻⟝ ▤ 🚗 – 🝰 110. 🝏🝐 🝐 🝐 𝗩𝗜𝗦𝗔. ❀
Rest a la carte 29.70/33.40 – � 13.95 – **200 rm** ✚155.00 – ✚✚155.00.   20 XZD k
  • Purpose-built hotel on the edge of the Square Mile. Clean-lined, co-ordinated rooms with smart mod cons and king-size beds. Stylish 'Saints' bar. The Globe bar and restaurant has great views over The City.

🏨 **The Hoxton,** 81 Great Eastern St, EC2A 3HU ⊖ Old Street, ℰ (020) 7550 1000, info@hoxtonhotels.com, Fax (020) 7550 1090, ☕ – 🛗 ✻⟝ ▤ 🍷 🕭 – 🝰 60. 🝏🝐 🝐 🝐 𝗩𝗜𝗦𝗔. ❀   20 XZD x
Hoxton Grille : Rest a la carte 19.50/31.00 ♀ – **205 rm** ✚79.00/99.00 – ✚✚79.00/149.00.
  • Urban lodge: industrial styled, clean lined modernism. "No ripoffs" mantra: cheap phone rate, free internet, complimentary 'lite pret' breakfast. Carefully considered rooms. Cooking style: New York deli meets French brasserie.

🏨 **Express by Holiday Inn** without rest., 275 Old St, EC1V 9LN ⊖ Old Street, ℰ (020) 7300 4300, reservationsfc@holidayinnlondon.com, Fax (020) 7300 4555 – 🛗 ✻⟝ 🕭 – 🝰 80. 🝏🝐 🝐 🝐 𝗩𝗜𝗦𝗔. ❀   20 XZC a
224 rm ✚95.00/149.00 – ✚✚95.00/149.00.
  • Large purpose-built property close to the tube and the financial district. Brightly decorated bedrooms are all generously sized and offer good value accommodation.

XX **Great Eastern Dining Room,** 54 Great Eastern St, EC2A 3QR ⊖ Old Street, ℰ (020) 7613 4545, Fax (020) 7613 4137 – ✻⟝ ▤, 🝏🝐 🝐 🝐 𝗩𝗜𝗦𝗔   20 XZD n
closed Christmas and Sunday – **Rest** - South East Asian - a la carte 23.50/36.50 ♀.
  • Half the place is a bar that's heaving in the evening. Dining area has candle-lit tables, contemporary chandeliers, and carefully prepared, seriously tasty pan-Asian cooking.

XX **Real Greek,** 15 Hoxton Market, N1 6HG ⊖ Old Street, ℰ (020) 7739 8212, admin@there algreek.co.uk, Fax (020) 7739 4910, ☕ – 🝏🝐 𝗩𝗜𝗦𝗔   20 XZC v
closed 25-26 December, Sunday and Bank Holidays – **Rest** - Greek - a la carte 22.70/34.35 ♀.
  • A former Victorian pub in a pleasant square. Plain wooden tables with open-plan kitchen. Very tasty, wholly Greek menu and wine list with unaffected and pleasant service.

X **Fifteen,** 13 Westland Pl, N1 7LP ⊖ Old Street, ℘ (0871) 3301515, Fax (020) 7251 2749 –
■. ⍟⍟ ⍜Ⓔ VISA   13 VZC c
closed 25 December - 1 January – **Rest** 25.00/60.00 and lunch a la carte 34.00/41.50 ⍭.
♦ Jamie Oliver's TV restaurant. Open plan kitchen showing the trainee chefs at work.
Typical menu of robust earthy flavours using carefully-sourced ingredients.

X **Cru,** 2-4 Rufus St, N1 6PE ⊖ Old Street, ℘ (020) 7729 5252, info@cru.uk.com,
Fax (020) 7729 1070 – ■, ⍟⍟ ⍜Ⓔ VISA   20 XZC m
closed 25-30 December – **Rest** a la carte 19.00/25.00 ⍭ ⍅.
♦ Converted 19C warehouse trendily located with artwork for sale. Bar and delicatessen
leading past open kitchen to restaurant. Modern menu with Asian influences. Good value.

X **Hoxton Apprentice,** 16 Hoxton Sq, N1 6NT ⊖ Old Street, ℘ (020) 7749 2828,
info@hoxtonapprentice.com, ⇗ – ■ ↔ 30. ⍟⍟ VISA   20 XZC r
Rest 13.00 (lunch) and a la carte 21.30/31.65 ⍭.
♦ Set up as charitable enterprise in 19C former primary school; now stands on its own as
accomplished restaurant where apprentices and pros cook interesting, seasonal dishes.

X **Mezedopolio,** 15 Hoxton Market, N1 6HG ⊖ Old Street, ℘ (020) 7739 8212, ad
min@therealgreek.demon.co.uk, Fax (020) 7739 4910 – ⍟⍟ VISA   20 XZC v
closed 25-26 December, 1 January, Sunday and Bank Holidays – **Rest** - Greek meze -
(bookings not accepted) a la carte 10.00/16.70.
♦ Greek meze bar, part of The Real Greek, though with a more informal style. High ceilings,
marble memorials. Large menu of authentic dishes from Greece and the Aegean.

Shoreditch Gtr London – ✉ EC2.

X **Rivington,** 28-30 Rivington St, EC2A 3DZ ⊖ Old Street, ℘ (020) 7729 7053, shore
ditch@rivingtongrill.co.uk – ■, ⍟⍟ ⍜Ⓔ VISA   20 XZD e
closed 25-26 December and 1 January – **Rest** - British - (brunch at weekends) a la carte
25.00/36.00 ⍭.
♦ Ex-button factory with a local buzz. Airy main restaurant has school chairs, well worn
floor. There's also a comfy lounge and an intimate front area. Solid English cooking.

🍴 **The Princess,** (first floor) 76-78 Paul St, EC2A 4NE ⊖ Old Street, ℘ (020) 7729 9270,
theeaston@btconnect.com – ⍟⍟ ⍜Ⓔ VISA, ⍅⍅   19 VZD a
closed 24 December-8 January and Bank Holidays – **Rest** (closed Saturday lunch) a la carte
22.00/26.00 ⍭.
♦ Traditional corner pub given a gastro makeover. Dining room, above busy bar, has a
stylish appeal matched by interesting international dishes underpinned by strong cooking.

🍴 **The Fox,** 28 Paul St, EC2A 4LB ⊖ Old Street, ℘ (020) 7729 5708, fox.ph@virgin.net – ⍟⍟
⍜Ⓔ VISA   19 VZD c
closed Easter, 23 December-3 January and Bank Holidays – **Rest** (closed Saturday-Sunday)
(booking essential) 21.50.
♦ Rough and ready pub with a great menu: this is found upstairs in the rather serene, but
Gothic, restaurant. No nonsense dishes with bold, seasonal, unfussy, fresh flavours.

Stoke Newington Gtr London – ✉ N16.

X **Rasa,** 55 Stoke Newington Church St, N16 0AR, ℘ (020) 7249 0344, Fax (02) 7637 0224 –
⍅⍬ ■, ⍟⍟ ⍜Ⓔ VISA   14 XZA e
Rest - Indian Vegetarian - (booking essential) (dinner only and Saturday and Sunday lunch)
16.00 and a la carte 9.20/11.95.
♦ Busy Indian restaurant, an unpretentious environment in which to sample authentic,
sometimes unusual, dishes. The "Feast" offers a taste of the range of foods on offer.

X **Rasa Travancore,** 56 Stoke Newington Church St, N16 0NB, ℘ (020) 7249 1340 – ⍅⍬
■, ⍟⍟ ⍜Ⓔ VISA   20 XZA x
Rest - Indian - (dinner only and Sunday lunch) a la carte 16.00/20.70 s..
♦ Friendly, knowledgable service a distinct bonus to diners getting to know Keralan cook-
ing. Good value dishes: 'feast' menu recommended by staff offers the full experience.

HAMMERSMITH and FULHAM Gtr London.

Fulham Gtr London – ✉ SW6.

XXX **Saran Rom,** The Boulevard, Imperial Wharf, Townmead Rd, SW6 2UB ⊖ Fulham Broadway, ℘ (020) 7751 3111, info@saranrom.com, ⇗ – ■ ↔ 35. ⍟⍟ ⍜Ⓔ VISA   23 PZH b
Rest - Thai - a la carte 29.00/38.00.
♦ In a recently constructed "village", with super river views. Ornately carved interior with
series of rooms, including bar with Thames outlook. Authentic, fresh Thai menus.

XXX **Memsaab,** 7 The Boulevard, Imperial Wharf, SW6 2UB ⊖ *Fulham Broadway*, ℰ (020) 7736 0077, *Fax (020) 7731 5222,* ㎡ – ▤. ☯☯ AE *VISA*　35 PZH n
closed 25 December – **Rest** - Indian - 9.95 and a la carte 23.45/35.35 ㉟.
* Indian fabrics adorn this slinky restaurant in a spanking new wharf complex. Vast palm useful for getting your bearings: interesting, original, well-presented Indian dishes.

XX **Yi-Ban,** 5 The Boulevard, Imperial Rd, Imperial Wharf, SW6 2UB ⊖ *Fulham Broadway*, ℰ (020) 7731 6606, *Fax (020) 7731 7584* – ▤. ☯☯ AE ☯ *VISA*　23 PZH n
closed Sunday – **Rest** - Chinese - 15.00/45.00 and a la carte 30.00/60.00.
* Very stylish and contemporary with dark, seductice interior divided by opaque nets; cocktail bar adds to the mix. Modern Chinese dishes meet tried-and-tested favourites.

XX **Deep,** The Boulevard, Imperial Wharf, SW6 2UB ⊖ *Fulham Broadway*, ℰ (020) 7736 3337, info@deeplondon.co.uk, *Fax (020) 7736 7578,* ㎡ – ✴✴ ▤. ☯☯ AE *VISA*　23 PZH n
closed first 2 weeks January and August, Monday, Sunday dinner and Saturday lunch – **Rest** - Seafood - 17.50 (lunch) and a la carte 24.50/78.00 ㉟.
* Slick, modern restaurant on rejuvenated riverside wharf. Linen-clad tables; floor-to-ceiling windows. Modern seafood dishes with Scandinavian feel; large aquavit selection.

XX **Blue Elephant,** 4-6 Fulham Broadway, SW6 1AA ⊖ *Fulham Broadway*, ℰ (020) 7385 6595, london@blueelephant.com, *Fax (020) 7386 7665* – ▤. ☯☯ AE *VISA*　22 NZG z
closed Saturday lunch – **Rest** - Thai - (booking essential) 15.00 (lunch) and a la carte approx 28.75 ㉟㍿.
* Elaborately ornate, unrestrained décor: fountains, bridges, orchids and ponds with carp. Authentic Thai food served by attentive staff in national costumes.

XX **Mao Tai,** 58 New Kings Rd, Parsons Green, SW6 4LS ⊖ *Parsons Green*, ℰ (020) 7731 2520, info@maotai.co.uk – ▤. ☯☯ AE ☯ *VISA*　22 NZH e
closed 25-26 December – **Rest** - Chinese (Szechuan) - a la carte 21.50/31.00 s ㉟.
* A light and modern interior with wood flooring and framed artwork with an eastern theme. Well organised service. Chinese cuisine with Szechuan specialities.

🍴 **The Farm,** 18 Farm Lane, SW6 1PP ⊖ *Fulham Broadway*, ℰ (020) 7381 3331, info@the farmfulham.co.uk – ▤. ☯☯ AE *VISA*. ✴✴　22 NZG x
closed 25 December – **Rest** a la carte 18.00/35.00 ㉟.
* Red brick pub with leather sofas and contemporary fireplaces. Rear dining room is ultra stylish, and the menus are suitably modern British with a French accent.

Hammersmith *Ctr London* – ✉ *W6/W14.*

XX **River Café** (Ruth Rogers/Rose Gray), Thames Wharf, Rainville Rd, W6 9HA ⊖ *Barons Court*, ℰ (020) 7386 4200, info@rivercafe.co.uk, *Fax (020) 7386 4201,* ㎡ – ✴✴. ☯☯ AE ☯ *VISA*　21 LZG r
✿
closed Christmas-New Year, Sunday dinner and Bank Holidays – **Rest** - Italian - (booking essential) a la carte 42.00/57.00 ㉟.
Spec. Chargrilled squid with rocket and red chilli. Wood roasted turbot with capers and marjoram. "Chocolate nemesis".
* Longstanding cosmopolitan landmark with full length windows and open plan kitchen. Canteen-style atmosphere. Accomplished rustic Italian cooking employing the finest produce.

XX **Chez Kristof,** 111 Hammersmith Grove, Brook Green, W6 0NQ ⊖ *Hammersmith*, ℰ (020) 8741 1177, info@chezkristof.co.uk, ㎡ – ▤ ⇄ 50. ☯☯ AE *VISA*　21 LZF b
closed Christmas – **Rest** - French - 15.00 (lunch) and a la carte 22.50/29.50 ㉟.
* Well worth seeking out in Brook Green: there's a luxurious deli, delightful terrace, and unmistakable Gallic ambience to this serious French restaurant where classics reign.

XX **Indian Zing,** 236 King St, W6 0RF ⊖ *Ravenscourt Park*, ℰ (020) 8748 5959, indianz ing@aol.com, *Fax (020) 8748 2332,* ㎡ – ▤. ☯☯ AE *VISA*　21 LZG a
Rest - Indian - a la carte 20.60/26.00.
* Sophisticated, modern restaurant with crisp white walls adorned with photos of life on the subcontinent. Traditional Indian menus are jettisoned for modish, original dishes.

X **Snows on the Green,** 166 Shepherd's Bush Rd, Brook Green, W6 7PB ⊖ *Hammersmith,* ℰ (020) 7603 2142, sebastian@snowsonthegreen.freeserve.co.uk, *Fax (020) 7602 7553* – ▤. ☯☯ AE ☯ *VISA*　15 LZF x
closed 24-28 December, Saturday lunch, Sunday and Bank Holiday Mondays – **Rest** 17.50 (lunch) and a la carte 25.00/28.00 ㉟.
* Name refers to the chef patron, not the inclement weather found in west London. Mediterranean influenced decoration matched by the style of the cooking.

X **The Brackenbury,** 129-131 Brackenbury Rd, W6 0BQ ⊖ *Ravenscourt Park*, ℰ (020) 8748 0107, *Fax (020) 8748 6159,* ㎡ – ☯☯ AE *VISA*　15 LZE a
closed August Bank Holiday, 25-26 December, 1 January, Saturday lunch and Sunday dinner – **Rest** 14.50 (lunch) and a la carte 24.00/32.50 ㉟.
* The closely set wooden tables, pavement terrace and relaxed service add to the cosy, neighbourhood feel. Cooking is equally unfussy; modern yet robust.

X **Azou,** 375 King St, W6 9NJ ⊖ *Stamford Brook*, ℘ (020) 8563 7266, *info@azou.co.uk*, Fax (020) 8741 1425 – ◍◍ ◔ *VISA*   21 KZG u
closed 25 December and 1 January – **Rest** - North African - a la carte 15.35/24.05.
   ◆ The North African theme is not confined to the menu; the room is decorated with hanging lanterns, screens and assorted knick-knacks. Friendly service and well priced dishes.

X
◉ **Agni,** 160 King St, W6 0QU ⊖ *Ravenscourt Park*, ℘ (020) 8846 9191, *info@agnirestaurant.com*, Fax (0870) 1996940 – ⤨⤨ ◍ ⇔ 35. ◍◍ *VISA*   21 LZG s
closed 25 December and 1 January – **Rest** - Indian - a la carte 14.40/21.50 ℒ.
   ◆ Modest façade hides a clean, bright interior. Dishes are 'home' style from Hyderabad with biryani to the fore, and are notably good value.

⏚ **Anglesea Arms,** 35 Wingate Rd, W6 0UR ⊖ *Ravenscourt Park*, ℘ (020) 8749 1291, *anglesea.events@gmail.com*, Fax (020) 8749 1254, 🍴 – ◍◍ *VISA*. ℅   15 LZE c
closed 1 week Christmas – **Rest** (bookings not accepted) 12.95 (lunch) and a la carte 20.00/35.00 ℒ.
   ◆ The laid-back atmosphere and local feel make this pub a popular venue. Worth arriving early as bookings are not taken. Modern cooking from blackboard menu.

⏚
◉ **The Havelock Tavern,** 57 Masbro Rd, W14 0LS ⊖ *Kensington Olympia*, ℘ (020) 7603 5374, *info@thehavelocktavern.co.uk*, Fax (020) 7602 1163, 🍴 – ▤   16 MZE e
closed 22-26 December and Easter Sunday – **Rest** (bookings not accepted) a la carte 21.00/26.00 ℒ.
   ◆ West London take on rusticity, with no-frills service and smoky atmosphere. Food is the priority: hearty portions of British and European dishes, both tasty and nourishing

Shepherd's Bush *Gtr London* – ✉ *W14*.

🏨 **K West,** Richmond Way, W14 0AX ⊖ *Kensington Olympia*, ℘ (0870) 027 4343, *bookit@k-west.co.uk*, Fax (0870) 811 2612, 𝄢, ⇆ – ▮ ⤨⤨ ▤ ☏ & ℙ – 🔥 50. ◍◍ ◭ ◔ *VISA*.
℅   16 MZE c
Kanteen : **Rest** a la carte 20.00/31.00 – ⊡ 22.00 – **214 rm** ⚿151.60/294.00 – ⚿⚿151.60/294.00, 6 suites.
   ◆ Former BBC offices, the interior is decorated in a smart, contemporary fashion. Bedrooms in understated modern style, deluxe rooms with work desks and DVD and CD facilities. Modish menus in trendy dining room.

HARINGEY *Gtr London*.

Crouch End *Gtr London* – ✉ *N4/N8*.

⏠ **Mountview** without rest., 31 Mount View Rd, N4 4SS, ℘ (020) 8340 9222, *mountviewbb@aol.com*, ⬜ – ⤨⤨ ◍◍ ◔ *VISA*. ℅   3 EU r
3 rm ⊡ ⚿45.00/50.00 – ⚿⚿80.00.
   ◆ Redbrick Victorian house with a warm and stylish ambience engendered by the homely décor. One bedroom features an original fireplace and two overlook the quiet rear garden.

X **Florians,** 4 Topsfield Parade, Middle Lane, N8 8RP, ℘ (020) 8348 8348, Fax (020) 8292 2092, 🍴 – ▤. ◍◍ *VISA*   3 EU c
– **Rest** - Italian - a la carte 28.25/30.95 ℒ.
   ◆ Light room with tiled flooring and large paintings, nestling behind a busy front bar. Italian menu with blackboard daily specials. Efficient and obliging service.

X **Bistro Aix,** 54 Topsfield Parade, Tottenham Lane, N8 8PT, ℘ (020) 8340 6346, Fax (020) 8348 7236 – ⤨⤨ ◍◍ ◭ ◔ *VISA*   3 EU v
closed 26 December, 1 January and Monday – **Rest** - French - a la carte 15.00/34.50.
   ◆ The simple wood furniture is complemented by plants and pictures. The owner chef's experience in France is reflected in the menu and the robust and hearty cooking.

Highgate *Gtr London* – ✉ *N6*.

⏚ **The Bull,** 13 North Hill, N6 4AB ⊖ *Highgate*, ℘ (0845) 4565053, *info@inthebull.biz*, Fax (0845) 4565034, 🍴 – ◇ 20. ◍◍ ◔ *VISA*   2 EU x
Rest *(closed Monday lunch)* 17.95 (lunch) and a la carte 27.00/40.00 ℒ.
   ◆ Grade II listed pub with large terrace and interior, spread over two floors. Appealing dishes - a mix of British and classical French - are very much reliant on the seasons.

Tottenham *Gtr London* – ✉ *N17*.

XX **The Lock,** Heron House, Hale Wharf, Ferry Lane, N17 9NF ⊖ *Tottenham Hale*, ℘ (020) 8885 2829, *thelock06@btconnect.com*, Fax (020) 8885 1618 – ℙ. ◍◍ ◭ *VISA* 3 GU a
closed 1-8 January, 28 May-6 June, Saturday lunch, Sunday dinner and Monday – **Rest** 14.50 (lunch) and a la carte 21.95/31.95.
   ◆ An oasis of cool in N17. By the side of a lock, there's a long bar with sofas, and restaurant with wood or mosaic tables. Original touches enhance tasty French/Italian mix.

HARROW *Gtr London.*

Harrow Weald *Middx – ⊠ Middx.*

🏛 **Grim's Dyke** ⌂, Old Redding, HA3 6SH, ℰ (020) 8385 3100, *reservations@grims dyke.com, Fax (020) 8954 4560,* ℮ – ✲⊷ rm, ₺ 🅿 – 🔬 100. ⓌⓄ 🄰🄴 ① 𝘝𝘐𝘚𝘈   1 BT a
Gilberts : Rest *(closed Saturday lunch)* 26.50 and a la carte 28.20/43.95 ♀ – **46 rm** ☷ 🛉100.00 – 🛉🛉125.00/175.00.
♦ Victorian mansion, former country residence of W.S.Gilbert. Rooms divided between main house and lodge, the former more characterful. Over 40 acres of garden and woodland. Restaurant with ornately carved fireplace.

Pinner *Middx – ⊠ Middx.*

%% **Friends,** 11 High St, HA5 5PJ ⊖ *Pinner,* ℰ (020) 8866 0286, *info@friendsrestaur ant.co.uk, Fax (020) 8866 0286 –* ✲⊷ ▦. 🄰🄴 ① 𝘝𝘐𝘚𝘈   a
closed 25-26 December, Monday, 2 weeks August, 3 days end May, Sunday dinner and Bank Holidays – **Rest** 19.50/26.50 and a la carte 26.15/41.50 ♀.
♦ Pretty beamed cottage, with some parts dating back 400 years. Inside, a welcoming glow from the log fire; personal service from owners and a fresh, regularly-changing menu.

HILLINGDON *Gtr London.*

🏌 Haste Hill, The Drive, Northwood ℰ (01923) 825224 AU.

Heathrow Airport *Middx.*

🏨 **London Heathrow Marriott,** Bath Rd, Hayes, UB3 5AN, ℰ (020) 8990 1100, *sales admin.heathrow@marriotthotels.com, Fax (020) 8990 1110,* ₲, ⇌, 🗔 – |𝖘|, ✲⊷ rm, ▦ ₺ 🅿 – 🔬 540. ⓌⓄ 🄰🄴 ① 𝘝𝘐𝘚𝘈 . ✲   5 AX z
Tuscany : Rest - Italian - *(closed Sunday)* (dinner only) a la carte 25.45/37.95 s. ♀ – *Allie's grille :* Rest 22.00 and a la carte 19.00/33.45 s. ♀ – **391 rm** 🛉145.00 – 🛉🛉145.00, 2 suites.
♦ Built at the end of 20C, this modern, comfortable hotel is centred around a large atrium, with comprehensive business facilities: there is an exclusive Executive floor. Tuscany is bright and convivial.

🏨 **Crowne Plaza London - Heathrow,** Stockley Rd, West Drayton, UB7 9NA, ℰ (0870) 400 9140, *reservations.cplhr@ichotelsgroup.com, Fax (01895) 445122,* ₲, ⇌, 🗔, 🏌 – |𝖘|, ✲⊷ rm, ▦ ₺ 🅿 – 🔬 200. ⓌⓄ 🄰🄴 ① 𝘝𝘐𝘚𝘈 . ✲   1 AV v
Concha Grill : Rest 15.00/20.00 ♀ – (see also *Simply Nico Heathrow* below) – ☷ 15.50 – **457 rm** 🛉210.00 – 🛉🛉210.00, 1 suite.
♦ Extensive leisure, aromatherapy and beauty salons make this large hotel a popular stopover for travellers. Club bedrooms are particularly well-equipped. Bright, breezy Concha Grill with lively bar.

🏨 **Radisson Edwardian,** 140 Bath Rd, Hayes, UB3 5AW, ℰ (020) 8759 6311, *resreh@rad isson.com, Fax (020) 8759 4559,* ₲, ⇌ – |𝖘|, ✲⊷ rm, ▦ ₢ 🅿 – 🔬 550. ⓌⓄ 🄰🄴 ① 𝘝𝘐𝘚𝘈 . ✲   5 AX e
Henleys : Rest (dinner only Monday-Friday) 29.50 – **Brasserie :** Rest a la carte 19.00/27.50 – ☷ 15.00 – **442 rm** 🛉142.00/208.00 – 🛉🛉178.00/246.00, 10 suites.
♦ Capacious group hotel with a huge atrium over the leisure facilities. Plenty of comfortable lounges, well-appointed bedrooms and attentive service. Henleys boasts oil paintings and cocktail bar.

🏨 **Sheraton Skyline,** Bath Rd, Hayes, UB3 5BP, ℰ (020) 8759 2535, *res268-skyline@sher aton.com, Fax (020) 8750 9150,* ₲, 🗔 – |𝖘| ✲⊷ ▦ ₢ ₺ 🅿 – 🔬 500. ⓌⓄ 🄰🄴 ① 𝘝𝘐𝘚𝘈   5 AX u
Sage : Rest a la carte 14.50/32.00 ♀ – ☷ 17.00 – **348 rm** 🛉257.00 – 🛉🛉257.00, 2 suites.
♦ Well known for its unique indoor swimming pool surrounded by a tropical garden which is overlooked by many of the bedrooms. Business centre available. Classically decorated dining room.

🏨 **Hilton London Heathrow Airport,** Terminal 4, TW6 3AF, ℰ (020) 8759 7755, *sales.heathrow@hilton.com, Fax (020) 8759 7579,* ₲, ⇌, 🗔 – |𝖘|, ✲⊷ rm, ▦ ₢ ₺ 🅿 – 🔬 250. ⓌⓄ 🄰🄴 ① 𝘝𝘐𝘚𝘈 . ✲   5 AX n
Brasserie : Rest *(closed lunch Saturday and Sunday)* (buffet lunch) 26.50/44.00 and a la carte 29.50/52.00 s ♀ – **Zen Oriental :** Rest - Chinese - 29.80 and a la carte 22.50/52.40 – ☷ 19.95 – **390 rm** 🛉209.00 – 🛉🛉209.00/255.56, 5 suites.
♦ Group hotel with a striking modern exterior and linked to Terminal 4 by a covered walkway. Good sized bedrooms, with contemporary styled suites. Spacious Brasserie in vast atrium. Zen Oriental offers formal Chinese experience.

Holiday Inn London Heathrow, Sipson Rd, West Drayton, UB7 0JU, (M 4 junction 4) ℘ (0870) 4008595, *Fax (020) 8897 8659*, ₤₅ – |ф|, ✵ rm, ▣ ✆ ᔕ ℙ – ᔐ 140. ☻☺ ㏑ ⓪ *VISA*. ✆
1 AV c
Sampans : **Rest** - Asian - (dinner only) a la carte 17.00/27.00 – ***Rotisserie :*** **Rest** (buffet meals) 17.95/19.95 – ☞ 17.50 – **604 rm** ★232.70 – ★★232.70, 4 suites.
♦ Busy group hotel where the Academy conference suite attracts the business community. Bedrooms come in a variety of styles. Popular Irish bar. Sampans offers regional Chinese dishes. Spacious Rotisserie with chef carving to order.

Renaissance London Heathrow, Bath Rd, TW6 2AQ, ℘ (020) 8897 6363, *lhrrenaissance@aol.com, Fax (020) 8897 1113*, ₤₅, ⩫ – |ф|, ✵ rm, ▣ ᕓ ℙ – ᔐ 400. ☻☺ ㏑ ⓪ *VISA*. ✆
5 AX c
Rest (bar lunch)/dinner a la carte 21.25/32.00 ☿ – ☞ 16.00 – **643 rm** ★182.00 – ★★182.00, 6 suites.
♦ Low level façade belies the size of this easily accessible hotel. Large lounge and assorted shops in the lobby. Some of the soundproofed bedrooms have views of the runway. Open-plan restaurant with buffet or à la carte.

Simply Nico Heathrow (at Crowne Plaza London - Heathrow H.), Stockley Rd, West Drayton, UB7 9NA, ℘ (01895) 437564, *heathrow.simplynico@corushotels.com, Fax (01895) 437565* – ▣ ℙ. ☻☺ ㏑ ⓪ *VISA*
5 AV v
closed Sunday – **Rest** (dinner only) a la carte 23.40/44.40 ☿.
♦ Located within the hotel but with its own personality. Mixes modern with more classically French dishes. Professional service in comfortable surroundings.

Ickenham *Middx.*

Jospens, 15 Long Lane, UB10 8QU ⊖ *Ickenham*, ℘ (01895) 632519, *Fax (01895) 272284* – ▣. ☻☺ ㏑ ⓪ *VISA*
1 AU a
closed 25 December, 1 week summer, Saturday lunch and Monday – **Rest** 13.50/20.00 and a la carte 22.45/30.45.
♦ Neighbourhood restaurant with window boxes. Smart interior boasts deep lilac ceiling. Simple, well executed dishes with modern influences.

Ruislip *Middx.*

Hawtrey's (at The Barn H.), West End Rd, HA4 6JB ⊖ *Ruislip*, ℘ (01895) 679999, *info@thebarnhotel.co.uk, Fax (01895) 638379*, ⌀ – ✵ ▣ ℙ ᔐ 30. ☻☺ ㏑ ⓪ *VISA*
1 AU e
closed Sunday dinner – **Rest** 19.50/29.00 a la carte 42.50/49.00 ☿.
♦ Jacobean styled baronial hall: an extension to 16C Barn Hotel. Cloth clad tables, bright chandeliers. Fine dining - modern cooking that's confident and assured.

HOUNSLOW *Gtr London.*

ᕲ Wyke Green, Syon Lane, Isleworth ℘ (020) 8560 8777 BV – ᕲ Airlinks, Southall Lane ℘ (020) 8561 1418 ABV – ᕲ Hounslow Heath, Staines Rd ℘ (020) 8570 5271 BX.
🛈 24 The Treaty Centre, High St ℘ (0845) 456 2929 *(closed Sunday)*.

Chiswick *Middx.* – ⊠ W4.

High Road House, 162 Chiswick High Rd, W4 1PR ⊖ *Turnham Green*, ℘ (020) 8742 1717, *reservation@highroadhouse.co.uk, Fax (020) 8987 8762* – ✆. ☻☺ ㏑ *VISA* 21 KZG f
Rest – (see **High Road Brasserie** below) – ☞ 8.00 – **14 rm** ★160.00 – ★★160.00.
♦ Cool, sleek hotel and club, the latter a slick place to lounge around or play games. Light, bright bedrooms with crisp linen. A carefully appointed, fair-priced destination.

La Trompette, 5-7 Devonshire Rd, W4 2EU ⊖ *Turnham Green*, ℘ (020) 8747 1836, *reception@latrompette.co.uk, Fax (020) 8995 8097*, ㏒ – ✵ ▣. ☻☺ ㏑ *VISA* 21 KZG y
closed 24-26 December and 1 January – **Rest** 29.50/35.00 ☿ ✿.
♦ Terraced property on smart residential street. Open-plan restaurant with linen laid tables and a bustling atmosphere. Daily menus of French influenced robust modern dishes.

High Road Brasserie, 162 Chiswick High Rd, W4 1PR ⊖ *Turnham Green*, ℘ (020) 8742 7474, ㏒ – ▣. ☻☺ ㏑ *VISA* 21 KZG f
Rest a la carte 28.00/36.00 ☿.
♦ Confidently stylish place to eat. Marble-topped bar and Belgian tiled dining area provide sleek backdrop to well-priced, satisfying menus full of interesting brasserie dishes.

Fish Hook, 6-8 Elliott Rd, W4 1PE ⊖ *Turnham Green*, ℘ (020) 8742 0766, *Fax (020) 8742 3374* – ✵ ▣. ☻☺ ㏑ *VISA* 21 KZG z
closed Christmas – **Rest** - Seafood - 18.50 (lunch) and a la carte 24.00/34.00 ☿.
♦ Carnivores, steer clear: fish is exclusively on the menu here, either as starter or main course. Bright, simple interior. Well conceived dishes cooked with dextrous aplomb.

✗ **Sam's Brasserie,** 11 Barley Mow Passage, W4 4PH ⊖ *Turnham Green*, ℰ (020) 8987 0555, *info@samsbrasserie.co.uk*, Fax (020) 8987 7389 – ⊱✗ ▦, 🕼 ꞏ ⫧ **VISA**　　2　**CV** a
closed Christmas – **Rest** 15.00 (lunch) and a la carte 20.25/31.50 ℤ.
 ꞏ Former paper mill by Turnham Green. 'Industrial', open plan feel with concrete and stainless steel. Robust brasserie dishes seem to be in keeping with the surroundings.

✗ **Fishworks,** 6 Turnham Green Terrace, W4 1QP ⊖ *Turnham Green*, ℰ (020) 8994 0086, *chiswick@fishworks.co.uk*, Fax (020) 8994 0778, 🕼 – 🕼 ꞏ ⫧ **VISA**　　21　**KZG** e
closed 25 December-5 January, Sunday dinner, Monday and Bank Holidays – **Rest** - Seafood - (booking essential) a la carte 26.40/41.40 ℤ.
 ꞏ Well-run branded restaurant opening onto delightful rear terrace with olive trees. Daily blackboard menu of grills and popular seafood dishes.

🍴 **The Devonshire House,** 126 Devonshire Rd, W4 2JJ ⊖ *Turnham Green*, ℰ (020) 8987 2626, *info@thedevonshirehouse.co.uk*, Fax (020) 8995 0152, 🕼 – 🕼 ꞏ ⫧ **VISA**　　21　**KZG** a
closed 24-30 December and Monday lunch – **Rest** a la carte 14.95/25.95 ℤ.
 ꞏ Period pub conversion retaining original features. Leather banquettes and chairs; bare tables. Daily menu of modern cooking, slightly simpler at lunchtime. Attentive service.

ISLINGTON *Gtr London.*

Archway – ✉ *N19.*

✗　**The Parsee,** 34 Highgate Hill, N19 5NL ⊖ *Archway*, ℰ (020) 7272 9091, Fax (020) 7687 1139 – ▦. 🕼 ⫧ **VISA**　　3　**EU** e
closed Christmas-New Year, Sunday and Bank Holidays – **Rest** - Indian (Parsee) - (dinner only) a la carte 16.50/23.95 ℤ.
 ꞏ Two brightly painted rooms, one non smoking and featuring a painting of a Parsee Angel. Good value, interesting, carefully spiced cuisine, Persian and Indian in inspiration.

🍴 **St John's,** 91 Junction Rd, N19 5QU ⊖ *Archway*, ℰ (020) 7272 1587, Fax (020) 7687 2247 – 🕼 ⫧ **VISA**. 🕼　　12　**RZA** s
closed 25-26 December and 1 January – **Rest** (closed lunch Monday-Thursday) a la carte 20.00/30.00 ℤ.
 ꞏ Busy front bar enjoys a lively atmosphere; dining room in a large rear room. Log fire at one end, open hatch into kitchen the other. Blackboard menu; rustic cooking.

Barnsbury *Gtr London* – ✉ *N1/N7.*

✗✗　**Morgan M,** 489 Liverpool Rd, N7 8NS ⊖ *Highbury and Islington*, ℰ (020) 7609 3560, Fax (020) 8292 5699 – ⊱✗ ▦. 🕼 ꞏ ⫧ **VISA**　　13　**UZA** a
closed 24-30 December, lunch Tuesday and Saturday, Sunday dinner and Monday – **Rest** - French - 23.50/32.00 ℤ.
 ꞏ Simple restaurant in a converted pub. Smartly-laid tables complemented by formal service. Modern dishes based on classical French combinations.

✗　**Fig,** 169 Hemingford Rd, N1 1DA ⊖ *Caledonian Road*, ℰ (020) 7609 3009, *figrestaurant@btconnect.com*, 🕼 – ⊱✗. 🕼 **VISA**　　13　**UZB** a
closed 22 December-3 January, last 2 weeks August, Monday and Tuesday – **Rest** (dinner only and Sunday lunch)/dinner a la carte 19.00/29.00 ℤ.
 ꞏ Attractive and cosy neighbourhood restaurant with fig tree leaning over garden terrace. Original combinations move the weekly changing menu away from the modern European norm.

Canonbury *Gtr London* – ✉ *N1.*

🍴 **The House,** 63-69 Canonbury Rd, N1 2DG ⊖ *Highbury and Islington*, ℰ (020) 7704 7410, *info@inthehouse.biz*, Fax (020) 7704 9388, 🕼 – 🕼 ꞏ **VISA**　　13　**UZB** h
closed Christmas – **Rest** (closed Monday lunch) 17.95 (lunch) and a la carte 45.00/66.00 ℤ.
 ꞏ This pleasant pub, on a street corner and popular with locals, has a restaurant with linen-covered tables, ceiling fans, art for sale, and modern menus with a classical base.

🍴 **The Marquess Tavern,** 32 Canonbury St, N1 2TB ⊖ *Highbury and Islington*, ℰ (020) 7354 2975, *sarah@marquesstavern.co.uk* – 🕼 ⫧ **VISA**　　13　**VZB** x
Rest - British - a la carte 22.00/27.50 ℤ.
 ꞏ Pillared exterior dominates a cosy corner. Stools and sofas in front bar. Far end dining area resoundingly British with all produce from the UK including wines from Cornwall.

Clerkenwell Gtr London – ✉ EC1.

Malmaison, Charterhouse Sq, EC1M 6AH ⊖ Barbican, ℘ (020) 7012 3700, london@malmaison.com, Fax (020) 7012 3702, 𝑓Ɑ – |𝑔|, ⅀← rm, ■ 𝒞 & – 𝔄 30. ⑳ Ⅲ ⑩ ⅤⅠⓈⒶ
19 UZD o

closed 23-27 December **Brasserie :** Rest 14.50/17.95 and a la carte 26.95/37.45 ⅀ – ⯁ 16.95 – **97 rm** ★229.00/276.00 – ★★276.00/358.00.

• Striking early 20C redbrick building overlooking pleasant square. Stylish, comfy public areas. Bedrooms in vivid, bold colours, with extras such as stereo and free broadband. Modern brasserie employing meats from Smithfield.

The Rookery without rest., 12 Peters Lane, Cowcross St, EC1M 6DS ⊖ Barbican, ℘ (020) 7336 0931, reservations@rookery.co.uk, Fax (020) 7336 0932 – ⅀← ■ 𝒞, ⑳ Ⅲ ⑩ ⅤⅠⓈⒶ, ⯑
33 AOT p

⯑ 9.95 **32 rm** ★205.00 – ★★240.00/288.00, 1 suite.

• A row of charmingly restored 18C houses. Wood panelling, stone-flagged flooring, open fires and antique furniture. Highly individual bedrooms, with Victorian bathrooms.

Smiths of Smithfield, Top Floor, 67-77 Charterhouse St, EC1M 6HJ ⊖ Barbican, ℘ (020) 7251 7950, reservations@smithsofsmithfield.co.uk, Fax (020) 7236 5666, <, 🍴 – |𝑔| ■. ⑳ Ⅲ ⑩ ⅤⅠⓈⒶ
33 AOT s

closed 25-26 December, 1 January and Saturday lunch – Rest a la carte 27.50/45.50 ⅀ – **The Dining Room :** Rest (Sunday) a la carte 19.75/23.00 ⅀.

• On three floors where the higher you go the more formal it becomes. Busy, bustling atmosphere and modern menu. Good views of the market from the top floor terrace. The Dining Room with mirrors and dark blue walls.

St John, 26 St John St, EC1M 4AY ⊖ Barbican, ℘ (020) 7251 0848, reservations@stjohnrestaurant.com, Fax (020) 7251 4090 – ■ ⯑ 18. ⑳ Ⅲ ⑩ ⅤⅠⓈⒶ
33 APT c

closed Christmas, Easter, Saturday lunch and Sunday – Rest - British - a la carte 34.10/46.00 ⅀.

• Deservedly busy converted 19C former smokehouse. Popular bar, simple comforts. Menu specialises in offal and an original mix of traditional and rediscovered English dishes.

Vinoteca, 7 St John St, EC1M 4AA ⊖ Farringdon, ℘ (020) 7253 8786, enquiries@vinoteca.co.uk, Fax (020) 7490 4282 – ■. ⑳ ⅤⅠⓈⒶ
33 APT a

closed Christmas-New Year, Sunday and Bank Holidays – Rest (booking essential at lunch) (bookings not accepted at dinner) a la carte 18.50/24.45 ⅀ ⯑.

• Bold, modern dishes with perfect wine pairing in this thoroughly informal 'wine bar' eatery. Well-stocked shelves a great attraction: take out your favourite or drink within.

Comptoir Gascon, 61-63 Charterhouse St, EC1M 6HJ ⊖ Barbican, ℘ (020) 7608 0851, comptoirgascon@btconnect.com, Fax (020) 7608 0871 – ⅀← ■. ⑳ Ⅲ ⅤⅠⓈⒶ 33 AOT a

closed Christmas-New Year, Sunday and Monday – Rest - French - a la carte 19.50/25.50 ⅀.

• Half restaurant, half deli, situated opposite Smithfield. Rustic notions enhanced by exposed brick. Well priced, French based dishes form the mainstay of a simple restaurant.

Rudland Stubbs, 35-37 Green Hill Rents, Cowcross St, EC1M 6BN ⊖ Farringdon, ℘ (020) 7253 0148, reservations@rudlandstubbs.co.uk – ⑳ Ⅲ ⅤⅠⓈⒶ
33 AOT b

closed 1 week Christmas, Saturday-Sunday and Bank Holidays – Rest - Seafood - a la carte 27.45/39.75 ⅀.

• Eponymous duo set up sausage factory in late 1970s; now a seriously popular lunchtime venue with Art Deco style, ceiling fans and seafood dishes cooked with care and finesse.

Flâneur, 41 Farringdon Rd, EC1M 3JB ⊖ Farringdon, ℘ (020) 7404 4422, mail@flaneur.com, Fax (020) 7831 4532 – ⅀←. ⑳ Ⅲ ⅤⅠⓈⒶ
32 ANT s

closed Sunday dinner and Bank Holidays – Rest (Sunday brunch) 20.00 (dinner) and a la carte 22.80/29.95 ⅀.

• Pleasant food store and eatery: the former has immaculately lined shelves of deli products, the latter is surrounded by succulent aromas; cooking is robust modern European.

The Coach & Horses, 26-28 Ray St, EC1R 3DJ ⊖ Farringdon, ℘ (020) 7278 8990, info@thecoachandhorses.com, Fax (020) 7278 1478, 🍴 – ⑳ Ⅲ ⅤⅠⓈⒶ 19 UZD a

closed Easter, Christmas-New Year and Bank Holidays – Rest (closed Saturday lunch and Sunday dinner) a la carte 20.00/28.00 ⅀.

• Ornate exterior in red and cream; down-to-earth interior. Daily changing menus are fiercely seasonal and carefully compiled. 'Untypical' ingredients, interesting flavours.

Finsbury Gtr London – ✉ EC1.

The Zetter, 86-88 Clerkenwell Rd, EC1M 5RJ ⊖ Farringdon, ℘ (020) 7324 4444, info@thezetter.com, Fax (020) 7324 4445 – |𝑔|, ⅀← rm, ■ 𝒞 & – 𝔄 50. ⑳ Ⅲ ⅤⅠⓈⒶ, ⯑
19 UZD s

Rest a la carte 23.50/35.00 ⅀ – ⯑ 16.50 – **59 rm** ★176.25 – ★★176.25/264.00.

• Discreetly trendy modern design in the well-equipped bedrooms and rooftop studios of a converted 19C warehouse:pleasant extras from old paperbacks to flat-screen TV/DVDs. Light, informal restaurant serves modern Mediterranean dishes and weekend brunches.

XX **The Clerkenwell Dining Room**, 69-73 St John St, EC1M 4AN ⊖ *Farringdon*, ℰ (020) 7253 9000, *reservations@theclerkenwell.com, Fax (020) 7253 3322* – ⧉ ⇦ 30. ⊙⊙
AE ⊙ VISA
19 UZD h
closed Christmas, Saturday lunch, Sunday dinner and Bank Holidays – **Rest** 19.50 and a la carte 29.50/39.50 ⟨⟩.
♦ Former pub, now a stylish modern restaurant with etched glass façade. Three adjoining dining areas with bar provide setting for contemporary British cooking.

XX **Portal**, 88 St John St, EC1M 4EH ⊖ *Farringdon*, ℰ (020) 7253 6950, *antonio@portalres taurant.com, Fax (020) 7490 5836* – ⧉ ⇦ 12. ⊙⊙ AE ⊙ VISA
19 UZD r
closed Christmas-New Year, and Sunday – **Rest** a la carte 24.50/39.00 ⟨⟩.
♦ Set in Grade II listed building with entrance to the 'industrial chic' restaurant via busy, bustling bar. The influence of Spain and Portugal highlighted in interesting menus.

X **Quality Chop House**, 94 Farringdon Rd, EC1R 3EA ⊖ *Farringdon*, ℰ (020) 7837 5093, *enquiries@qualitychophouse.co.uk, Fax (020) 7833 8748* – ⧉. ⊙⊙ AE VISA
19 UZD n
closed 25-26 December and Saturday lunch – **Rest** 9.95 (lunch) and a la carte 25.75/30.50.
♦ On the window is etched "Progressive working class caterers". This is borne out with the individual café-style booths and a menu ranging from jellied eels to caviar.

X **Moro**, 34-36 Exmouth Market, EC1R 4QE ⊖ *Farringdon*, ℰ (020) 7833 8336, *info@moro.co.uk, Fax (020) 7833 9338* – ⟨⟩ ⧉. ⊙⊙ AE VISA
19 UZD b
closed Christmas, New Year, Sunday and Bank Holidays – **Rest** (booking essential) a la carte 24.00/30.50 ⟨⟩ ⟨⟩.
♦ Daily changing menu an eclectic mix of Mediterranean, Moroccan and Spanish. Friendly T-shirted staff. Informal surroundings with bare tables and a large zinc bar.

X **The Ambassador**, 55 Exmouth Market, EC1R 4QL ⊖ *Farringdon*, ℰ (020) 7837 0009, *clive@theambassadorcafe.co.uk*
19 UZD c
closed Christmas and Sunday dinner – **Rest** 16.00 (lunch) and a la carte 18.50/33.50 ⟨⟩.
♦ Lino and melamine give a refreshing retro appeal to this cool, buzzy diner. Seasonal, honest, earthy ingredients inform all-day Eurocentric menus that tend towards the Gallic.

X **Medcalf**, 40 Exmouth Market, EC1R 4QE ⊖ *Farringdon*, ℰ (020) 7833 3533, *mail@med calfbar.co.uk, Fax (020) 7833 1321*, ⟨⟩. ⊙⊙ VISA
19 UZD b
closed 25 December-1 January – **Rest** (booking essential) a la carte 25.00/32.00 ⟨⟩.
♦ Former butchers', now a 'rough-and-ready' eatery where ragged and chic charmingly collide. Precise, skilful cooking mixes a rustic style with global overtones. Very popular.

X **Cicada**, 132-136 St John St, EC1V 4JT ⊖ *Farringdon*, ℰ (020) 8608 1550, *reservations@ci cada.nu, Fax (020) 8608 1551* – ⟨⟩ ⟨⟩ 23. ⊙⊙ AE ⊙ VISA
19 UZD a
closed 23 December-2 January, Saturday lunch and Sunday – **Rest** - South East Asian - 22.50/27.00 and a la carte 17.00/29.50.
♦ Set in a culinary hotbed, this buzzy restaurant and vibrant bar is spacious, lively and popular for its South East Asian dishes: pop in for one course and a beer if you like.

⟨⟩ **The Peasant**, 240 St John St, EC1V 4PH ⊖ *Farringdon*, ℰ (020) 7336 7726, *eat@thepeasant.co.uk, Fax (020) 7490 1089* – ⟨⟩. ⊙⊙ AE ⊙ VISA. ⟨⟩
19 UZD e
Rest (booking essential) a la carte 35.00/45.00 ⟨⟩.
♦ Large, busy pub with half of the ground floor given over as a bar. Dining continues in the high-ceilinged room upstairs. Robust and rustic cooking with generous portions.

⟨⟩ **The Well**, 180 St John St, EC1V 4JY ⊖ *Farringdon*, ℰ (021) 7251 9363, *drink@down thewell.co.uk, Fax (020) 7404 2250* – ⊙⊙ AE VISA. ⟨⟩
19 UZD x
closed 24-26 December – **Rest** a la carte 18.00/25.00 ⟨⟩.
♦ Rather predictable looking pub distinguished by big black canopies. Food lifts it above the average: everything from 'pie of the week' to sophisticated modern British dishes.

Highbury *Gtr London* – ✉ N5.

X **Au Lac**, 82 Highbury Park, N5 2XE ⊖ *Arsenal*, ℰ (020) 7704 9187, *Fax (020) 7704 9187* – ⧉. ⊙⊙ ⊙ VISA
13 VZA b
closed 25 December and Bank Holidays – **Rest** - Vietnamese - (dinner only and lunch Thursday and Friday) a la carte 12.00/16.00.
♦ Cosy Vietnamese restaurant, with brightly coloured walls and painted fans. Large menus with authentic dishes usefully highlighted. Fresh flavours; good value.

Islington *Gtr London* – ✉ N1.

🏨 **Hilton London Islington**, 53 Upper St, N1 0UY ⊖ *Angel*, ℰ (020) 7354 7700, *reserva tions.islington@hilton.com, Fax (020) 7354 7711*, ⟨⟩, ⟨⟩, ⟨⟩ – ⟨⟩ ⟨⟩ ⟨⟩ ⟨⟩ ⟨⟩ – ⟨⟩ 35. ⊙⊙ AE ⊙ VISA. ⟨⟩
13 UZB s
Rest a la carte 19.00/33.00 ⟨⟩ – ⟨⟩ 17.50 – **184 rm** ✹157.45/216.20 – ✹✹157.45/216.20.
♦ Benefits from its location adjacent to the Business Design Centre. A purpose-built hotel with all bedrooms enjoying the appropriate creature comforts. Open-plan brasserie with small bar.

459

XX **Frederick's,** Camden Passage, N1 8EG ⊖ *Angel*, ℰ (020) 7359 2888, *eat@fredericks.co.uk, Fax (020) 7359 5173*, ⇗, ⌺ – ▤, ◍◉ *VISA* 13 UZB c
closed 25 December- 1 January, Easter, Sunday and Bank Holidays – **Rest** 17.00 (lunch) and a la carte 28.00/37.00 ⬚ ⵕ.
♦ Long-standing restaurant among the antique shops of Camden Passage. Attractive garden and al fresco dining; main room with large, plant-filled conservatory.

XX **Almeida,** 30 Almeida St, N1 1AD ⊖ *Angel*, ℰ (020) 7354 4777, *oliviere@conran-restaurants.co.uk, Fax (020) 7354 2777* – ▤. ◍◉ ◭ ◉ *VISA* 13 UZB r
Rest - French - 17.50/27.00 ⵕ.
♦ Spacious, open plan restaurant with pleasant contemporary styling adjacent to Almeida Theatre. Large à la carte: a collection of classic French dishes.

XX **Metrogusto,** 13 Theberton St, N1 0QY ⊖ *Angel*, ℰ (020) 7226 9400,
🍴 *Fax (020) 7226 9400* – ⵕ✕ ▤, ◍◉ ◭ *VISA* 13 UZB e
closed 25 December, 1 January, Easter, Sunday and Bank Holidays – **Rest** - Italian - (dinner only and lunch Friday-Saturday) a la carte 22.95/31.50 ⬚ ⵕ.
♦ Stylish and smart with a contemporary feel. Dining in two rooms with striking modern art on the walls and a relaxed atmosphere. Modern, carefully prepared Italian food.

X **Ottolenghi,** 287 Upper St, N1 2TZ ⊖ *Highbury and Islington*, ℰ (020) 7288 1454, *upper@ottolenghi.co.uk, Fax (020) 7704 1456* – ▤. ◍◉ ◉ *VISA* 13 UZB k
closed Christmas, New Year, Sunday dinner and Bank Holidays – **Rest** a la carte 25.50/30.50.
♦ Cool, contemporary restaurant behind a smart deli. Two long tables accommodate most diners. Grazing style dishes are fresh, vibrant and tasty with a subtle Eastern spicing.

🍴 **The Drapers Arms,** 44 Barnsbury St, N1 1ER ⊖ *Highbury and Islington*, ℰ (020) 7619 0348, *info@thedrapersarms.co.uk, Fax (020) 7619 0413*, ⇗ – ◍◉ ◭ *VISA*. ✕ 13 UZB x
closed 24-28 December – **Rest** a la carte 22.00/35.00 ⵕ.
♦ Real presence to the façade of this Georgian pub tucked away in a quiet residential area. Spacious modern interior where competent, contemporary dishes are served.

🍴 **The Northgate,** 113 Southgate Rd, N1 3JS ⊖ *Old Street*, ℰ (020) 7359 7392, *thenorthgate@hppubs.co.uk, Fax (020) 7359 7393*, ⇗ – ◍◉ *VISA* 13 VZB a
closed 25 December – **Rest** (dinner only and lunch Saturday and Sunday) a la carte 18.00/24.00 ⵕ.
♦ Corner pub with wood flooring and modern art on display. Rear dining area with a large blackboard menu offering a cross section of internationally influenced modern dishes.

🍴 **The Barnsbury,** 209-211 Liverpool Rd, N1 1LX ⊖ *Highbury and Islington*, ℰ (020) 7607 5519, *info@thebarnsbury.co.uk, Fax (020) 7607 3256*, ⇗ – ◍◉ ◭ *VISA*. ✕ 13 UZB v
closed 24-26 December and 1 January – **Rest** a la carte 21.00/30.00 ⵕ.
♦ Former public house with pine tables and chairs arranged round central counter bar; art work for sale on the walls. Robust and hearty food in generous portions.

King's Cross *Gtr London* – ✉ WC1.

X **Konstam at the Prince Albert,** 2 Acton St, WC1X 9NA ⊖ *King's Cross St Pancras*, ℰ (020) 7833 5040, *princealbert@konstam.co.uk, Fax (020) 7833 5045* – ⵕ✕ ⬚ 24. ◍◉ ◭ *VISA* 18 TZC a
closed Christmas and Sunday – **Rest** a la carte 23.00/32.00 ⵕ.
♦ Avert your gaze from the hugely wondrous light display to enjoy interesting dishes sourced totally from within boundaries of London Transport network! Chef has own allotment.

KENSINGTON and CHELSEA (Royal Borough of) *Gtr London*.

Chelsea *Gtr London* – ✉ SW1/SW3/SW7/SW10.

🏨🏨🏨🏨 **Jumeirah Carlton Tower,** Cadogan Pl, SW1X 9PY ⊖ *Knightsbridge*, ℰ (020) 7235 1234, *jctinfo@jumeirah.com, Fax (020) 7235 9129*, ≤, ⓦ, *Ƒб*, ⇌, ⬚, ⌗, ⚲ – ⧎, ⵕ✕ rm, ▤ ⚲ ↺ ⇌ – 🔏 400. ◍◉ ◭ ◉ *VISA*. ✕ 37 AGX n
Rib Room : **Rest** a la carte 44.50/76.00 ⵕ – ⬚ 30.00 – **190 rm** ✦410.00/563.00 – ✦✦563.00, 30 suites.
♦ Imposing international hotel overlooking a leafy square. Well-equipped roof-top health club has funky views. Generously proportioned rooms boast every conceivable facility. Rib Room restaurant has a clubby atmosphere.

🏨🏨🏨 **Conrad London,** Chelsea Harbour, SW10 0XG ⊖ *Fulham Broadway*, ℰ (020) 7823 3000, *londoninfo@conradhotels.com, Fax (020) 7352 8174*, ≤, ⓦ, *Ƒб*, ⇌, ⌗ – ⧎, ⵕ✕ rm, ▤ ⚲ ⚲ ↺ ⇌ – 🔏 250. ◍◉ ◭ ◉ *VISA*. ✕ 23 PZG j
Rest – (see *Aquasia* below) – ⬚ 22.50, **160 suites** 558.00.
♦ Modern, all-suite hotel within an exclusive marina and retail development. Many of the spacious and well-appointed rooms have balconies and views across the Thames.

Sheraton Park Tower, 101 Knightsbridge, SW1X 7RN ⊖ *Knightsbridge*, ℘ (020) 7235 8050, *central.london.reservations@sheraton.com*, Fax (020) 7235 8231, ≤, ₁₄ – |⋛|, ⋈ rm, ☰ ⅙, ⇔ – ⅙ 100. ⅏ ⅙ ⅌ ⅦⅨⅤ.
37 AGX t
Rest – (see *One-O-One* below) – ⊡ 21.95 – **275 rm** ♦294.00/476.00 – ♦♦294.00/476.00, 5 suites.
♦ Built in the 1970s in a unique cylindrical shape. Well-equipped bedrooms are all identical in size. Top floor executive rooms have commanding views of Hyde Park and City.

Capital, 22-24 Basil St, SW3 1AT ⊖ *Knightsbridge*, ℘ (020) 7589 5171, *reservations@capitalhotel.co.uk*, Fax (020) 7225 0011 – |⋛| ⋈ ☰ ⅙, ⇔ – ⅙ 25. ⅏ ⅙ ⅌ ⅦⅨⅤ 37 AFX a
Rest – (see *The Capital Restaurant* below) – ⊡ 18.50 – **49 rm** ♦247.00/335.00 – ♦♦385.00.
♦ Discreet and privately owned town house with distinct English charm. Individually decorated rooms with plenty of thoughtful touches.

Draycott, 26 Cadogan Gdns, SW3 2RP ⊖ *Sloane Square*, ℘ (020) 7730 6466, *reservations@draycotthotel.com*, Fax (020) 7730 0236, ⋈ – |⋛|, ☰ rm, ⅙, ⅏ ⅙ ⅌ ⅦⅨⅤ
37 AGY c
Rest (room service only) – ⊡ 19.95 – **31 rm** ♦147.00/206.00 – ♦♦288.00/347.00, 4 suites.
♦ Charmingly discreet 19C house with elegant sitting room overlooking tranquil garden. Smart breakfast room or 24-hour service. Individual rooms in a country house style.

The Cadogan, 75 Sloane St, SW1X 9SG ⊖ *Knightsbridge*, ℘ (020) 7235 7141, *reservations@cadogan.com*, Fax (020) 7245 0994, ₁₄, ⋈, ⅘ – |⋛| ⋈ ☰ ⅙ – ⅙ 40. ⅏ ⅙ ⅌ ⅦⅨⅤ. ⅘
Mes'anges : Rest *(closed Sunday dinner)* 23.00 (lunch) and a la carte 38.00/50.00 – ⊡ 19.50 – **62 rm** ♦347.00 – ♦♦347.00, 2 suites.
♦ An Edwardian town house, where Oscar Wilde was arrested; modernised and refurbished with a French accent. Contemporary drawing room. Stylish bedrooms; latest facilities. Discreet, stylish restaurant.

Millennium Knightsbridge, 17-25 Sloane St, SW1X 9NU ⊖ *Knightsbridge*, ℘ (020) 7235 4377, *reservations.knightsbridge@mill-cop.com*, Fax (020) 7235 3705 – |⋛| ⋈ ☰ ⅙ – ⅙ 120. ⅏ ⅙ ⅌ ⅦⅨⅤ. ⅘
37 AGX r
Mju : Rest *(closed dinner 25 December, 26-27 December, 1-3 January and Sunday)* 24.00/36.00 – ⊡ 15.00 – **218 rm** ♦259.00/282.00 – ♦♦341.00, 4 suites.
♦ Modern, corporate hotel in the heart of London's most fashionable shopping district. Executive bedrooms are well-appointed and equipped with the latest technology.

Franklin without rest., 22-28 Egerton Gdns, SW3 2DB ⊖ *South Kensington*, ℘ (020) 7584 5533, *bookings@franklinhotel.co.uk*, Fax (020) 7584 5449, ⋈ – |⋛|, ⋈ rest, ☰ ⅙, ⅏ ⅙ ⅌ ⅦⅨⅤ. ⅘ – ⊡ 18.50 – **46 rm** ♦176.00/347.00 – ♦♦347.00/464.00. 37 AEY e
♦ Attractive Victorian town house in an exclusive residential area. Charming drawing room overlooks a tranquil communal garden. Well-furnished rooms in a country house style.

Knightsbridge, 10 Beaufort Gdns, SW3 1PT ⊖ *Knightsbridge*, ℘ (020) 7584 6300, *knightsbridge@firmdale.com*, Fax (020) 7584 6355 – |⋛| ⋈ ☰ ⅙ ⅙. ⅏ ⅙ ⅦⅨⅤ. ⅘
37 AFX s
Rest (room service only) – **44 rm** ♦176.25/211.50 – ♦♦305.50.
♦ Attractively furnished town house with a very stylish, discreet feel. Every bedroom is immaculately appointed and has an individuality of its own; fine detailing throughout.

San Domenico House, 29-31 Draycott Pl, SW3 2SH ⊖ *Sloane Square*, ℘ (020) 7581 5757, *info@sandomenicohouse.com*, Fax (020) 7584 1348 – |⋛|, ⋈ rm, ☰ ⅙, ⅏ ⅙ ⅌ ⅦⅨⅤ. ⅘
37 AFY c
Rest (room service only) – ⊡ 14.10 – **15 rm** ♦229.00 – ♦♦264.00/335.00.
♦ Intimate and discreet Victorian town house with an attractive rooftop terrace. Individually styled and generally spacious rooms with antique furniture and rich fabrics.

Parkes without rest., 41 Beaufort Gdns, SW3 1PW ⊖ *Knightsbridge*, ℘ (020) 7581 9944, *info@parkeshotel.com*, Fax (020) 7581 1999 – |⋛| ⅙ ⅏ ⅙ ⅌ ⅦⅨⅤ. ⅘ 37 AFX x
⊡ 27.50 – **19 rm** ♦234.00/417.00 – ♦♦311.00/417.00, 14 suites 382.00/558.00.
♦ Behind the portico entrance one finds a well-kept private hotel. The generally spacious and high ceilinged rooms are pleasantly decorated. Friendly and personally run.

The London Outpost of Bovey Castle without rest., 69 Cadogan Gdns, SW3 2RB ⊖ *Sloane Square*, ℘ (020) 7589 7333, *info@londonoutpost.co.uk*, Fax (020) 7581 4958, ⋈ – |⋛| ⋈ ☰ ⅙. ⅏ ⅙ ⅌ ⅦⅨⅤ. ⅘
37 AGY r
closed 23-27 December – ⊡ 16.95 – **11 rm** ♦235.00 – ♦♦273.00/387.00.
♦ Classic town house in a most fashionable area. Relaxed and comfy lounges full of English charm. Bedrooms, named after local artists and writers, full of thoughtful touches.

Egerton House, 17-19 Egerton Terrace, SW3 2BX ⊖ *South Kensington*, ℘ (020) 7589 2412, *bookings@egertonhousehotel.co.uk*, Fax (020) 7584 6540 – |⋛| ⋈ ☰ ⅙. ⅏ ⅙ ⅌ ⅦⅨⅤ. ⅘
37 AFY e
Rest (room service only) – ⊡ 17.00 – **29 rm** ♦276.00 – ♦♦300.00/464.00.
♦ Stylish redbrick Victorian town house close to the exclusive shops. Relaxed drawing room. Antique furnished and individually decorated rooms.

Beaufort without rest., 33 Beaufort Gdns, SW3 1PP ⊖ Knightsbridge, ℰ (020) 7584 5252, reservations@thebeaufort.co.uk, Fax (020) 7589 2834 – ⏐≡⏐ ⇔⍒ ≡ ℰ. ▥▨ ΑΕ ① VISA ⫯⫯
37 AFX **n**

⇌ 11.50 **29 rm** ⚦135.00/182.00 – ⚦⚦206.00/305.50.
◆ World's largest collection of English floral watercolours adorn this 19C town house. Modern and co-ordinated rooms. Tariff includes all drinks and continental breakfast.

Myhotel Chelsea, 35 Ixworth Pl, SW3 3QX ⊖ South Kensington, ℰ (020) 7225 7500, mychelsea@myhotels.com, Fax (020) 7225 7555, ℔ – ⏐≡⏐ ≡ ℰ – 🛋 60. ▥▨ ΑΕ ① VISA ⫯⫯
37 AFY **z**

Rest a la carte 17.85/25.15 s. – ⇌ 18.00 – **44 rm** ⚦241.00/276.00 – ⚦⚦276.00/417.00, 1 suite.
◆ Restored Victorian property in a fairly quiet and smart side street. Conservatory breakfast room. Modern and well-equipped rooms are ideal for the corporate traveller. Smart dining room for modern menus.

Eleven Cadogan Gardens, 11 Cadogan Gdns, SW3 2RJ ⊖ Sloane Square, ℰ (020) 7730 7000, reservations@number-eleven.co.uk, Fax (020) 7730 5217, ℔, ⇔, ⇜ – ⏐≡⏐ ℰ. ▥▨ ΑΕ ① VISA ⫯⫯
37 AGY **u**

Rest (residents only) a la carte 26.00/33.00 – ⇌ 13.50 – **55 rm** ⚦182.00/276.00 – ⚦⚦381.00, 5 suites.
◆ Occupying four Victorian houses, one of London's first private town house hotels. Traditionally appointed bedrooms vary considerably in size. Genteel atmosphere. Light and airy basement dining room exclusively for residents.

Sydney House, 9-11 Sydney St, SW3 6PU ⊖ South Kensington, ℰ (020) 7376 7711, info@sydneyhousechelsea.com, Fax (020) 7376 4233 – ⏐≡⏐ ⇔⍒ ≡ ℰ. ▥▨ ΑΕ ① VISA ⫯⫯
36 ADY **s**

closed 25-29 December – **Rest** (room service only) – ⇌ 9.95 – **21 rm** ⚦125.00/175.00 – ⚦⚦145.00/250.00.
◆ Two usefully located Victorian town houses. Basement breakfast room; small lounge near entrance. Compact contemporary style bedrooms; one on top floor with own roof terrace.

Gordon Ramsay, 68-69 Royal Hospital Rd, SW3 4HP ⊖ Sloane Square, ℰ (020) 7352 4441, Fax (020) 7352 3334 – ⇔⍒ ≡. ▥▨ ΑΕ ① VISA
37 AFZ **c**

closed 2 weeks Christmas-New Year, Saturday and Sunday – Rest (booking essential) 40.00/85.00 ♀ ⌕.
Spec. Ballottine and sautéed foie gras. Fillets of John Dory with crab, caviar and crushed new potatoes. Chocolate and amaretto biscuit soufflé with cinnamon ice cream.
◆ Elegant and sophisticated room. The eponymous chef creates some of Britain's finest, classically inspired cooking. Detailed and attentive service. Book two months in advance.

La Noisette, 164 Sloane St, SW1X 9QB ⊖ Knightsbridge, ℰ (020) 7750 5000, lanoisette@gordonramsay.com, Fax (020) 7750 5001 – ⏐≡⏐ ⇔⍒ ≡. ▥▨ ΑΕ ① VISA
37 AGX **d**

closed Saturday lunch and Sunday – Rest 21.00/50.00 ♀.
Spec. Seared foie gras with coffee and Amaretto. Slow cooked Atlantic cod with Jabugo ham and squid. Fromage blanc soufflé, apricots and toasted almond ice cream.
◆ From the Ramsay portfolio, with Art Deco and hazelnut meeting at the top of the stairs. Confident service of highly accomplished original/classical dishes with bold flavours.

The Capital Restaurant (at Capital H.), 22-24 Basil St, SW3 1AT ⊖ Knightsbridge, ℰ (020) 7589 5171, caprest@capitalhotel.co.uk, Fax (020) 7225 0011 – ⇔⍒ ≡ ⇜. ▥▨ ΑΕ ① VISA
37 AFX **a**

Rest (booking essential) 29.50/55.00 ⌕.
Spec. Salmon with deep-fried soft shell crab. Honey roast pork belly with horseradish pommes mousseline. Iced coffee parfait with chocolate fondant.
◆ A hotel restaurant known for its understated elegance, discretion and graceful service. Cooking blends the innovative with the classic to create carefully crafted dishes.

Bibendum, Michelin House, 81 Fulham Rd, SW3 6RD ⊖ South Kensington, ℰ (020) 7581 5817, reservations@bibendum.co.uk, Fax (020) 7823 7925 – ≡. ▥▨ ΑΕ ① VISA 37 AEY **s**

closed dinner 24-26 December and 1 January – **Rest** 28.50 (lunch) and dinner a la carte 36.75/59.75 ♀ ⌕.
◆ A fine example of Art Nouveau architecture; a London landmark. 1st floor restaurant with striking stained glass 'Michelin Man'. Attentive service of modern British cooking.

Tom Aikens, 43 Elystan St, SW3 3NT ⊖ South Kensington, ℰ (020) 7584 2003, info@tomaikens.co.uk, Fax (020) 7584 2001 – ⇔⍒ ≡. ▥▨ ΑΕ VISA
37 AFY **n**

closed last two weeks August, 10 days Christmas-New Year, Saturday, Sunday and Bank Holidays – Rest 29.00/60.00 ♀ ⌕.
Spec. Frogs legs with chervil, white onion velouté and morels. Roast pork cutlet with pork lasagna and pearl barley. Passion fruit jelly and mousse with passion fruit syrup.
◆ Smart restaurant; minimalist style decor with chic tableware. Highly original menu of individual and inventive dishes; smooth service. Book one month in advance.

XXX ❀
Aubergine, 11 Park Walk, SW10 0AJ ⊖ *South Kensington*, ℰ (020) 7352 3449, *Fax (020) 7352 1770* – ❀⊨ ▤. ⬤◎ 𝐀𝐄 ◎ 𝘝𝘐𝘚𝘈   36 ACZ r
closed Saturday lunch, Sunday and Bank Holidays – Rest (booking essential) 64.00 ₤.
Spec. Mousse of salmon and langoustine, basil and tomato emulsion. Roast grouse with blackberries and thyme. Dark chocolate chiboust with poached cherries.
◆ Intimate, refined restaurant where the keen staff provide well drilled service. French influenced menu uses top quality ingredients with skill and flair. Extensive wine list.

XXX
One-O-One (at Sheraton Park Tower H.), William St, SW1X 7RN ⊖ *Knightsbridge*, ℰ (020) 7290 7101, *Fax (020) 7235 6196* – ▤. ⬤◎ 𝐀𝐄 ◎ 𝘝𝘐𝘚𝘈   37 AGX t
Rest - Seafood - 25.00/48.00 and a la carte 35.00/58.00 ₤.
◆ Modern and very comfortable restaurant overlooking Knightsbridge decorated in cool blue tones. Predominantly seafood menu offers traditional and more adventurous dishes.

XXX
Aquasia (at Conrad London H.), Chelsea Harbour, SW10 0XG ⊖ *Fulham Broadway*, ℰ (020) 7300 8443, ≤, 🍽 – ▤ 𝐏. ⬤◎ 𝐀𝐄 ◎ 𝘝𝘐𝘚𝘈   23 PZG j
Rest a la carte 24.50/45.00 ₤.
◆ Modern restaurant located within Conrad London hotel. Views over Chelsea Harbour. Cuisine captures the essence of the Mediterranean and Asia.

XXX
Drones, 1 Pont St, SW1X 9EJ ⊖ *Knightsbridge*, ℰ (020) 7235 9555, *sales@whitestar line.org.uk, Fax (020) 7235 9566* – ▤ ↔ 40. ⬤◎ 𝐀𝐄 ◎ 𝘝𝘐𝘚𝘈   37 AGX c
closed 26 December, 1 January, Saturday lunch and Sunday dinner – Rest 17.95 (lunch) and a la carte 31.50/46.50 ₤.
◆ Smart exterior with etched plate-glass window. U-shaped interior with moody film star photos on walls. French and classically inspired tone to dishes.

XXX
Fifth Floor (at Harvey Nichols), Knightsbridge, SW1X 7RJ ⊖ *Knightsbridge*, ℰ (020) 7235 5250 – |♿| ▤. ⬤◎ 𝐀𝐄 ◎ 𝘝𝘐𝘚𝘈   37 AGX s
closed Christmas and Sunday dinner – Rest 19.50/39.50 and a la carte 28.00/43.50 🕯🍸 ₤ ⚘.
◆ On Harvey Nichols' top floor; elevated style sporting a pink-hued oval shaped interior with green frosted glass. Chic surroundings with food to match and smooth service.

XXX
Toto's, Walton House, Walton St, SW3 2JH ⊖ *Knightsbridge*, ℰ (020) 7589 0075, *Fax (020) 7581 9668* – ⬤◎ 𝐀𝐄 ◎ 𝘝𝘐𝘚𝘈   37 AFY x
closed 3 days Christmas – Rest - Italian - 23.00 (lunch) and a la carte 35.00/50.00 ₤.
◆ Converted mews house in tucked away location. Ornately decorated and bright restaurant with additional balcony area. Professional service of an extensive Italian menu.

XXX
Awana, 85 Sloane Ave, SW3 3DX ⊖ *South Kensington*, ℰ (020) 7584 8880, *info@awana.co.uk, Fax (020) 7584 6188* – ❀⊨ ▤. ⬤◎ 𝐀𝐄 ◎ 𝘝𝘐𝘚𝘈   37 AFY b
Rest - Malaysian - 15.00 (lunch) and a la carte 23.00/31.50 ₤.
◆ Enter into stylish cocktail bar. Traditional Malay elements adorn restaurant. Satay chef cooks to order. Malaysian dishes authentically prepared and smartly presented.

XXX
Chutney Mary, 535 King's Rd, SW10 0SZ ⊖ *Fulham Broadway*, ℰ (020) 7351 3113, *chutneymary@realindianfood.com, Fax (020) 7351 7694* – ▤ ↔ 24. ⬤◎ 𝐀𝐄 ◎
𝘝𝘐𝘚𝘈   22 OZG v
Rest - Indian - (dinner only and lunch Saturday and Sunday)/dinner a la carte 33.35/43.00 ₤.
◆ Soft lighting and sepia etchings hold sway at this forever popular restaurant. Extensive menu of specialities from all corners of India. Complimentary wine list.

XX
Daphne's, 112 Draycott Ave, SW3 3AE ⊖ *South Kensington*, ℰ (020) 7589 4257, *of fice@daphnes-restaurant.co.uk, Fax (020) 7225 2766* – ▤ ↔ 40. ⬤◎ 𝐀𝐄 ◎ 𝘝𝘐𝘚𝘈 37 AFY j
closed dinner 24 December and 25-26 December – Rest - Italian - (booking essential) 21.75 (lunch) and a la carte 22.75/41.75 ₤.
◆ Positively buzzes in the evening, the Chelsea set gelling smoothly and seamlessly with the welcoming Tuscan interior ambience. A modern twist updates classic Italian dishes.

XX ❀
Rasoi (Bhatia), 10 Lincoln St, SW3 2TS ⊖ *Sloane Square*, ℰ (020) 7225 1881, *ra soi.vineet@btinternet.com, Fax (020) 7581 0220* – ❀⊨ ▤. ⬤◎ 𝐀𝐄 ◎ 𝘝𝘐𝘚𝘈   37 AFY y
closed 25 December, Saturday lunch and Sunday and Bank Holidays – Rest - Indian - a la carte 31.00/66.00 ₤.
Spec. Chicken tikka flavoured with mustard seeds and curry leaves. Ginger and chilli lobster dusted with spiced cocoa powder. Chocolate and almond samosa, walnut and coffee mousse.
◆ Elegant mid-19C townhouse off Kings Road with L-shaped dining room and attractive friezes. Seamlessly crafted mix of classic and contemporary Indian flavour combinations.

XX ✿
Racine, 239 Brompton Rd, SW3 2EP ⊖ *South Kensington*, ℰ (020) 7584 4477, *Fax (020) 7584 4900* – ❀⊨ ▤. ⬤◎ 𝐀𝐄 ◎ 𝘝𝘐𝘚𝘈   37 AEY t
closed 25 December – Rest - French - 17.50 (lunch) and a la carte 25.50/35.25 🕯🍸 ₤.
◆ Dark leather banquettes, large mirrors and wood floors create the atmosphere of a genuine Parisienne brasserie. Good value, well crafted, regional French fare.

XX **Papillon,** 96 Draycott Ave, SW3 3AD ⊖ *South Kensington*, ℘ (020) 7225 2555, *info@papillonchelsea.co.uk, Fax (020) 7225 2554* – ■ ⟷ 16. **◍◎** **AE** **VISA**
37 AFY f
closed 24-26 December – **Rest** - French - 16.50 (lunch) and a la carte 27.00/36.00 ♈.
♦ Feels like a Parisian brasserie: large arched windows, brown décor, fleur-de-lys green banquettes and leather chairs. Classic French menus please the smart Chelsea set.

XX **Nozomi,** 15 Beauchamp Pl, SW3 1NQ ⊖ *Knightsbridge*, ℘ (020) 7838 1500, *Fax (020) 7838 1001* – ■ ⟷ 24. **◍◎** **AE** **VISA**
37 AFX d
closed Sunday – **Rest** - Japanese - a la carte 40.00/55.00 ♈.
♦ DJ mixes lounge music at the front bar; up the stairs in the restaurant the feeling is minimal with soft lighting. Innovative Japanese menus provide an interesting choice.

XX **Bluebird,** 350 King's Rd, SW3 5UU ⊖ *Sloane Square*, ℘ (020) 7559 1000, *enquiries@bluebird-store.co.uk, Fax (020) 7559 1115* – 🛗 ■ ⟷ 32. **◍◎** **AE** **VISA**
37 PZG n
closed 23-30 December, 12-27 August and Sunday – **Rest** (dinner only) 30.00 ☖♈.
♦ A foodstore, café and homeware shop also feature at this impressive skylit restaurant. Much of the modern British food is cooked in wood-fired ovens. Lively atmosphere.

XX **Poissonnerie de l'Avenue,** 82 Sloane Ave, SW3 3DZ ⊖ *South Kensington*, ℘ (020) 7589 2457, *info@poissonnerie.co.uk, Fax (020) 7581 3360* – ■ ⟷ 20. **◍◎** **AE** **◍** **VISA**
37 AFY u
closed dinner 25-26 December, and Sunday – **Rest** - French Seafood - 28.00 (lunch) and a la carte 26.50/38.50 ♈.
♦ Long-established and under the same ownership since 1965. Spacious and traditional French restaurant offering an extensive seafood menu. An institution favoured by locals.

XX **Le Cercle,** 1 Wilbraham Pl, SW1X 9AE ⊖ *Sloane Square*, ℘ (020) 7901 9999, *info@lecercle.co.uk, Fax (020) 7901 9111* – ■. **◍◎** **AE** **VISA**
37 AGY e
closed 23 December-8 January and Sunday-Monday – **Rest** - French - 19.50 (lunch) and a la carte 29.00/47.00 ♈.
♦ Discreetly signed basement restaurant down residential side street. High, spacious room with chocolate banquettes. Tapas style French menus; accomplished cooking.

XX **Le Colombier,** 145 Dovehouse St, SW3 6LB ⊖ *South Kensington*, ℘ (020) 7351 1155, *Fax (020) 7351 5124* – ⇆ ⟷ 28. **◍◎** **AE** **VISA**
36 ADZ e
Rest - French - 19.00 (lunch) and a la carte 26.60/37.30 ☖♈.
♦ Proudly Gallic corner restaurant in an affluent residential area. Attractive enclosed terrace. Bright and cheerful surroundings and service of traditional French cooking.

XX **Painted Heron,** 112 Cheyne Walk, SW10 0DJ ⊖ *Gloucester Road*, ℘ (020) 7351 5232, *Fax (020) 7351 5313*, ☆ – ■. **◍◎** **AE** **VISA**
40 PZG s
closed 25 December, 1 January and Saturday lunch – **Rest** - Indian - a la carte 25.00/35.00 ♈.
♦ Just off Cheyne Walk near the river. Contemporary in style, exemplified by oil paintings. Modern Indian dishes with eclectic ingredients drawn from around the sub-continent.

XX **Pellicano,** 19-21 Elystan St, SW3 3NT ⊖ *South Kensington*, ℘ (020) 7589 3718, *pellicano@btconnect.com, Fax (020) 7584 1789*, ☆ – ■ ⟷ 20. **◍◎** **AE** **VISA**
37 AFY d
closed Christmas-New Year – **Rest** - Italian - 18.50 (lunch) and a la carte 25.00/40.00 ♈.
♦ Dark blue canopy announces attractive neighbourhood restaurant. Contemporary interior with wood floors. Tasty and interesting modern Italian dishes; Sardinian specialities.

XX **Brasserie St Quentin,** 243 Brompton Rd, SW3 2EP ⊖ *South Kensington*, ℘ (020) 7589 8005, *reservations@brasseriestquentin.co.uk, Fax (020) 7584 6064* – ■ ⟷ 20. **◍◎** **AE** **◍** **VISA**
37 AEY a
closed 1 week Christmas – **Rest** 17.50 (lunch) and a la carte approx 29.70 ☖♈.
♦ Authentic Parisien brasserie, with rows of closely set tables, banquettes and ornate chandeliers. Attentive service and a lively atmosphere. French classics aplenty.

XX **Benihana,** 77 King's Rd, SW3 4NX ⊖ *Sloane Square*, ℘ (020) 7376 7799, *chelsea@benihana.co.uk, Fax (020) 7376 7377* – ■. **◍◎** **AE** **◍** **VISA**
37 AFZ e
closed 25 December – **Rest** - Japanese (Teppan-Yaki) - 11.50/58.00 s.
♦ Vast basement restaurant. Be prepared to share your table with other guests; teppan-yakis sit up to eight. Theatrical preparation and service of modern Japanese cooking.

XX **Caraffini,** 61-63 Lower Sloane St, SW1W 8DH ⊖ *Sloane Square*, ℘ (020) 7259 0235, *info@caraffini.co.uk, Fax (020) 7259 0236*, ☆ – ■. **◍◎** **AE** **VISA**
37 AGZ a
closed 25 December, Easter, Sunday and Bank Holidays – **Rest** - Italian - (booking essential) a la carte 25.15/33.00.
♦ The omnipresent and ebullient owner oversees the friendly service in this attractive neighbourhood restaurant. Authentic and robust Italian cooking; informal atmosphere.

XX **Vama,** 438 King's Rd, SW10 0LJ ⊖ *Sloane Square*, ℘ (020) 7565 8500, *admin@vama.co.uk, Fax (020) 7565 8501* – **◍◎** **AE** **◍** **VISA**
37 PZG e
closed 25-26 December and 1 January – **Rest** - Indian - (booking essential) (dinner only and lunch Saturday-Sunday) 14.95/45.00 and a la carte 20.00/34.50 s. ♈.
♦ Adorned with traditional artefacts, a modern and bright restaurant. Keen and eager service of an elaborate and seasonally changing menu of Northwest Indian specialities.

XX **Carpaccio,** 4 Sydney St, SW3 6PP ⊖ *South Kensington,* ✆ (020) 7352 3433, *eat@carpaccio.uk.com, Fax (020) 7352 3435* – ▤ ⇔ 25. MO AE ① VISA 36 ADY e
closed Sunday – **Rest** - Italian - a la carte 32.00/40.00 ♀.
◆ Fine Georgian exterior housing James Bond stills, 1920s silent Italian comedies, Ayrton Senna's Honda cockpit, witty waiters, and enjoyable, classical Trattoria style cooking.

XX **The Collection,** 264 Brompton Rd, SW3 2AS ⊖ *South Kensington,* ✆ (020) 7225 1212, *office@the-collection.co.uk, Fax (020) 7225 1050* – ▤. MO AE VISA 37 AEY v
closed 25-26 December, 1 January and Sunday – **Rest** (dinner only) 40.00 and a la carte 29.00/41.00 ♀.
◆ Beyond the impressive catwalk entrance one will find a chic bar and a vast split level, lively restaurant. The eclectic and global modern menu is enjoyed by the young crowd.

XX **Eight over Eight,** 392 King's Rd, SW3 5UZ ⊖ *Gloucester Road,* ✆ (020) 7349 9934, *Fax (020) 7351 5157* – ▤ ⇔ 12. MO AE ① VISA 23 PZG n
closed 25-26 December, 1 January and Sunday lunch – **Rest** - South East Asian - a la carte 22.00/39.50 ♀.
◆ Lively modern restaurant in converted theatre pub; bar in front and dining room at rear. Enthusiastic service. Eclectic Asian menu: strong flavours and unusual combinations.

XX **Good Earth,** 233 Brompton Rd, SW3 2EP ⊖ *Knightsbridge,* ✆ (020) 7584 3658, *goodearthgroup@aol.com, Fax (020) 7823 8769* – ▤. MO AE VISA 37 AFY h
closed 22-31 December – **Rest** - Chinese - 11.50/42.00 and a la carte 21.40/31.10 ♀.
◆ Ornately decorated, long-established and comfortable restaurant. Polite and efficient service. Extensive and traditional Chinese menu.

XX **C Garden,** 119 Sydney St, SW3 6NR ⊖ *South Kensington,* ✆ (020) 7352 2718, 🏠 – ⇔ 12. MO AE VISA 37 AEZ s
closed Sunday dinner – **Rest** - Italian - a la carte approx 28.00 ♀.
◆ A tent-like conservatory with fine sheltered terrace, a warm fawn and light chocolate makeover and simply prepared, good quality Italian dishes add up to a tasty concoction.

XX **Haandi,** 136 Brompton Rd, SW3 1HY ⊖ *Knightsbridge,* ✆ (020) 7823 7373, *haandirestaurant@btconnect.com, Fax (020) 7823 9696* – ▤. MO AE ① VISA 37 AFX v
Rest - Indian - a la carte 16.15/38.30 ♀.
◆ Spacious basement restaurant, though with natural light in some sections. Live jazz in the bar and chefs very much on display. Flavoursome, succulent north Indian food.

X **Bibendum Oyster Bar,** Michelin House, 81 Fulham Rd, SW3 6RD ⊖ *South Kensington,* ✆ (020) 7589 1480, *reservations@bibendum.co.uk, Fax (020) 7823 7148* – MO AE ① VISA 37 AEY s
closed 25-26 December and 1 January – **Rest** - Seafood specialities - (bookings not accepted) a la carte 20.50/50.00.
◆ Dine in either the busy bar, or in the light and relaxed foyer of this striking landmark. Concise menu of mainly cold dishes focusing on fresh seafood and shellfish.

X **Manicomio,** 85 Duke of York Sq, King's Rd, SW3 4LY ⊖ *Sloane Square,* ✆ (020) 7730 3366, *Fax (020) 7730 3377,* 🏠 – ▤. MO AE VISA 37 AGY x
closed 25-26 December and 1 January – **Rest** - Italian - a la carte 23.00/40.50.
◆ Outside, a delightful terrace overlooks the trendy Square. Inside, a clean, modern, informal style prevails. Rustic Italian menus. Next door, a café and superbly stocked deli.

X **Aubaine,** 260-262 Brompton Rd, SW3 2AS ⊖ *South Kensington,* ✆ (020) 7052 0100, *info@aubaine.co.uk, Fax (020) 7052 0622* – ⇹ ▤. MO AE VISA 37 AEY c
closed 25 December and 1 January – **Rest** - French - 21.00 (dinner) and a la carte 20.45/37.00.
◆ 'Boulangerie, patisserie, restaurant'. Pass the bakery aromas to an all-day eatery with 'distressed' country feel. Well-judged menus range from croque monsieur to coq au vin.

🍺 **The Admiral Codrington,** 17 Mossop St, SW3 2LY ⊖ *South Kensington,* ✆ (020) 7581 0005, *admiralcodrington@longshotplc.com, Fax (020) 7589 2452* – ▤. MO AE VISA. ⚘ 37 AFY v
closed 24-26 December – **Rest** a la carte 22.95/31.15 ♀.
◆ Aproned staff offer attentive, relaxed service in this busy gastropub. A retractable roof provides alfresco dining in the modern back room. Cosmopolitan menu of modern dishes.

🍺 **Chelsea Ram,** 32 Burnaby St, SW10 0PL ⊖ *Gloucester Road,* ✆ (020) 7351 4008, *bookings@chelsearam.co.uk, Fax (020) 7349 0885* – MO VISA 23 PZG r
Rest a la carte 16.00/24.50 ♀.
◆ Wooden floors, modern artwork and books galore feature in this forever popular pub. Concise menu of modern British cooking with daily changing specials. Friendly atmosphere.

🍴 **Swag and Tails,** 10-11 Fairholt St, SW7 1EG ⊖ *Knightsbridge*, ℰ (020) 7584 6926, *theswag@swagandtails.com*, Fax (020) 7581 9935 – 🐼 AE VISA . ※
  37 **AFX** r
closed 1 week Christmas-New Year, Saturday, Sunday and Bank Holidays – **Rest** a la carte 21.25/32.00 ♀.
  ◆ Attractive Victorian pub close to Harrods and the fashionable Knightsbridge shops. Polite and approachable service of a blackboard menu of light snacks and seasonal dishes.

🍴 **Builders Arms,** 13 Britten St, SW3 3TY ⊖ *South Kensington*, ℰ (020) 7349 9040 – ▣.
🐼 AE VISA
  37 **AFZ** x
closed 25 December and 1 January – **Rest** (bookings not accepted) a la carte 22.00/40.00 ♀.
  ◆ Extremely busy modern 'gastropub' favoured by the locals. Eclectic menu of contemporary dishes with blackboard specials. Polite service from a young and eager team.

🍴 **The Pig's Ear,** 35 Old Church St, SW3 5BS ⊖ *Sloane Square*, ℰ (020) 7352 2908, *thepig sear@hotmail.com*, Fax (020) 7352 9321 – ฿✗▣. 🐼 VISA
  23 **PZG** v
closed 25-26 December and 1 January – **Rest** a la carte 22.00/35.75 ♀.
  ◆ Corner pub that gets very busy, particularly for downstairs bar dining. Upstairs, more sedate wood panelled dining room. Both menus are rustic, robust and seasonal in nature.

🍴 **The Phoenix,** 23 Smith St, SW3 4EE ⊖ *Sloane Square*, ℰ (020) 7730 9182, *thephoe nix@geronimo-inns.co.uk*, ㄹ – ฿✗ ▣. 🐼 VISA
  37 **AFZ** a
closed 25-26 December – **Rest** a la carte 15.00/25.00 ♀.
  ◆ Tile-fronted pub with al fresco seating area, very popular in summer. Shabby chic décor that's been modernised but feels retro. Modern British repertoire on extensive menus.

🍴 **The Cross Keys,** 1 Lawrence St, SW3 5NB ⊖ *South Kensington*, ℰ (020) 7349 9111, *cross.keys@fsmail.net*, Fax (020) 7349 9333 – ▣. 🐼 AE ① VISA. ※
  23 **PZG** a
closed 24-30 December and Bank Holidays – **Rest** 12.50 (lunch) and a la carte 20.65/27.80 ♀.
  ◆ Hidden away near the Embankment, this 18C pub has period furniture and impressive carved stone fireplaces. Interesting, modern menus include blackboard of daily specials.

🍴 **Lots Road Pub and Dining Room,** 114 Lots Rd, SW10 0RJ ⊖ *Fulham Broadway*, ℰ (020) 7352 6645, Fax (020) 7376 4975 – ▣. 🐼 VISA
  23 **PZG** b
Rest a la carte 35.00/60.00 ♀.
  ◆ Traditional corner pub with an open-plan kitchen, flowers at each table and large modern pictures on the walls. Contemporary menus change daily.

Earl's Court *Gtr London* – ⊠ *SW5.*

🏨 **K + K George,** 1-15 Templeton Pl, SW5 9NB ⊖ *Earl's Court*, ℰ (020) 7598 8700, *hotel george@kkhotels.co.uk*, Fax (020) 7370 2285, ㄹ – ฿ ✗ ▣ ㄹ 🄿. ㄹ 30. 🐼 AE ①
VISA
  35 **AAY** s
Rest (in bar) a la carte 16.95/28.50 s. ♀ – **154 rm** ㅁ ✦182.00 – ✦✦217.00.
  ◆ Five converted 19C houses overlooking large rear garden. Scandinavian style to rooms with low beds, white walls and light wood furniture. Breakfast room has the garden view. Informal dining in the bar.

🏨 **Twenty Nevern Square** without rest., Nevern Sq, SW5 9PD ⊖ *Earl's Court*, ℰ (020) 7565 9555, *hotel@twentynevernsquare.co.uk*, Fax (020) 7565 9444 – ฿ ✗ ㄹ 🄿. 🐼 VISA. ※
  35 **AAY** u
ㅁ 9.00 – **20 rm** ✦99.00/110.00 – ✦✦175.00/270.00.
  ◆ In an attractive Victorian garden square, an individually designed, privately owned town house. Original pieces of furniture and some rooms with their own terrace.

🏨 **Mayflower** without rest., 26-28 Trebovir Rd, SW5 9NJ ⊖ *Earl's Court*, ℰ (020) 7370 0891, *info@mayflower-group.co.uk*, Fax (020) 7370 0994 – ฿ ✗ ㄹ. 🐼 AE VISA.
※
  35 **ABY** n
ㅁ 9.00 – **47 rm** ✦65.00/99.00 – ✦✦89.00/109.00.
  ◆ Conveniently placed, stylish establishment with a secluded rear breakfast terrace, juice bar and basement breakfast room. Individualistic rooms have Indian/ Asian influence.

🏨 **Amsterdam** without rest., 7 and 9 Trebovir Rd, SW5 9LS ⊖ *Earl's Court*, ℰ (020) 7370 2814, *reservations@amsterdam-hotel.com*, Fax (020) 7244 7608, ㄹ – ฿ ✗ ㄹ. 🐼 AE ①
VISA. ※
  35 **ABY** c
ㅁ 2.75 **19 rm** ✦68.00/88.00 – ✦✦88.00/94.00, 8 suites.
  ◆ Basement breakfast room and a small secluded garden. The brightly decorated bedrooms are light and airy. Some have smart wood floors; some boast their own balcony.

🏨 **Rushmore** without rest., 11 Trebovir Rd, SW5 9LS ⊖ *Earl's Court*, ℰ (020) 7370 3839, *rushmore-reservations@london.com*, Fax (020) 7370 0274 – ✗. 🐼 AE ① VISA.
※
  35 **ABY** a
22 rm ✦59.00/75.00 – ✦✦79.00/129.00.
  ◆ Behind its Victorian façade lies an hotel popular with tourists. Individually decorated bedrooms in a variety of shapes and sizes. Piazza-styled conservatory breakfast room.

XX **Langan's Coq d'Or**, 254-260 Old Brompton Rd, SW5 9HR ⊖ *Earl's Court*, ℰ *(020) 7259 2599, admin@langansrestaurant.co.uk, Fax (020) 7370 7735* – 🖃. 🐿️🐿️ 🝐 ⓘ 𝗩𝗜𝗦𝗔 35 ABZ **e** *closed 25-26 December* – **Rest** 21.50 and a la carte approx 25.50.
  ♦ Classic, buzzy brasserie and excellent-value menu to match. Walls adorned with pictures of celebrities: look out for more from the enclosed pavement terrace. Smooth service.

Kensington *Gtr London* – ✉ SW7/W8/W11/W14.

🏨🏨 **Royal Garden**, 2-24 Kensington High St, W8 4PT ⊖ *High Street Kensington*, ℰ *(020) 7937 8000, sales@royalgardenhotel.co.uk, Fax (020) 7361 1991,* ≤, 𝐼₆, 🝐 – 🛗, 🙌 rm, 🖃 📞 ⭑ 🍴 – 🔬 550. 🐿️🐿️ 🝐 ⓘ 𝗩𝗜𝗦𝗔 35 ABX **c**
  Park Terrace : **Rest** a la carte 23.75/33.00 **s** – *The Tenth :* **Rest** *(closed Saturday lunch, Sunday and Bank Holidays)* 23.00/65.00 and a la carte 36.00/45.00 **s**. – ⌁ 18.00 – **376 rm** ♦317.00/388.00 – ♦♦388.00/476.00, 20 suites.
  ♦ A tall, modern hotel with many of its rooms enjoying enviable views over the adjacent Kensington Gardens. All the modern amenities and services, with well-drilled staff. Bright, spacious, large-windowed Park Terrace. Great views from The Tenth.

🏨🏨 **The Milestone**, 1-2 Kensington Court, W8 5DL ⊖ *High Street Kensington*, ℰ *(020) 7917 1000, bookms@rchmail.com, Fax (020) 7917 1010,* 𝐼₆, 🝐 – 🛗 🙌 🖃 📞. 🐿️🐿️ 🝐 ⓘ 𝗩𝗜𝗦𝗔 35 ABX **u**
  Rest (booking essential for non-residents) 18.50/23.50 and a la carte 45.80/58.00 ⓨ – ⌁ 21.50 – **52 rm** ♦235.00/294.00 – ♦♦235.00/294.00, 5 suites.
  ♦ Elegant 'boutique' hotel with decorative Victorian façade and English feel. Charming oak panelled lounge and snug bar. Meticulously decorated bedrooms with period detail. Panelled dining room with charming little oratory for privacy seekers.

🏨🏨 **Baglioni**, 60 Hyde Park Gate, SW7 5BB ⊖ *High Street Kensington*, ℰ *(020) 7368 5711, info@baglionihotellondon.com, Fax (020) 7368 5701,* 🍴 , 𝐼₆, 🝐 – 🛗, 🙌 rm, 🖃 📞 – 🔬 60. 🐿️🐿️ 🝐 ⓘ 𝗩𝗜𝗦𝗔. 🌟 36 ACX **v**
  Brunello : **Rest** - Italian - 24.00/48.00 and a la carte 47.00/72.00 – ⌁ 25.00 – **53 rm** ♦370.00 – ♦♦370.00/529.00, 15 suites.
  ♦ Opposite Kensington Palace: ornate interior, trendy basement bar. Impressively high levels of service. Small gym/sauna. Superb rooms in cool shades boast striking facilities. Restaurant specialises in rustic Italian cooking.

XXX **Belvedere**, Holland House, off Abbotsbury Rd, W8 6LU ⊖ *Holland Park*, ℰ *(020) 7602 1238, infos@belvedererestaurant.co.uk, Fax (020) 7610 4382,* 🍴 , 🝐 – 🍴 ⇔ 20. 🐿️🐿️ 🝐 ⓘ 𝗩𝗜𝗦𝗔 16 MZE **u**
  closed 26 December, 1 January and Sunday dinner – **Rest** 17.95 (lunch) and a la carte 30.00/42.45 🝐 ⓨ.
  ♦ Former 19C orangery in a delightful position in the middle of the Park. On two floors with a bar and balcony terrace. Huge vases of flowers. Modern take on classic dishes.

XXX **Babylon** (at The Roof Gardens), 99 Kensington High St (entrance on Derry St), W8 5SA ⊖ *High Street Kensington*, ℰ *(020) 7368 3993, babylon@roofgardens.virgin.co.uk, Fax (020) 7368 3995,* ≤, 🍴 – 🙌 🖃 ⇔ 14. 🐿️🐿️ 𝗩𝗜𝗦𝗔 35 ABX **n** *closed Christmas, New Year and Sunday dinner* – **Rest** 21.00 (lunch) and a la carte 29.75/58.50 ⓨ.
  ♦ Situated on the roof of this pleasant London building affording attractive views of the London skyline. Stylish modern décor in keeping with the contemporary, British cooking.

XX **Ribbands**, 147-149 Notting Hill Gate, W11 3LF ⊖ *Notting Hill Gate*, ℰ *(020) 7034 0301, eat@ribbandsrestaurant.com, Fax (020) 7229 4259* – 🖃. 🐿️🐿️ 𝗩𝗜𝗦𝗔 27 AAV **a** *closed Sunday, Monday and Bank Holidays* – **Rest** 25.00/48.00 and a la carte 39.50/55.50 ⓨ.
  ♦ Coffee shop/bar at the front; step down to the serious eating areas. Range of menus to wade through. Dishes are elaborately detailed, buttressed by first-rate ingredients.

XX **Clarke's**, 124 Kensington Church St, W8 4BH ⊖ *Notting Hill Gate*, ℰ *(020) 7221 9225, restaurant@sallyclarke.com, Fax (020) 7229 4564* – 🙌 🖃. 🐿️🐿️ 🝐 ⓘ 𝗩𝗜𝗦𝗔 27 ABV **c** *closed 10 days Christmas-New Year, Monday dinner, Sunday and Bank Holidays* – **Rest** 39.75/49.50 (dinner) and lunch a la carte 26.50/31.50 ⓨ.
  ♦ Forever popular restaurant, now serving a choice of dishes boasting trademark fresh, seasonal ingredients and famed lightness of touch. Loyal following for over 20 years.

XX **Zaika**, 1 Kensington High St, W8 5NP ⊖ *High Street Kensington*, ℰ *(020) 7795 6533, info@zaika-restaurant.co.uk, Fax (020) 7937 8854* – 🖃. 🐿️🐿️ 𝗩𝗜𝗦𝗔 35 ABX **r** *closed 25-26 December and Saturday lunch* – **Rest** - Indian - 19.00 (lunch) and a la carte 24.75/37.25 ⓨ.
  ♦ A converted bank, sympathetically restored, with original features and Indian artefacts. Well organised service of modern Indian dishes.

467

XX **Whits,** 21 Abingdon Rd, W8 6AH ⊖ *High Street Kensington*, ℰ (020) 7938 1122, *eva@whits.co.uk, Fax (020) 7937 6121* – 🔟, **MC AE VISA**
35 AAX d
closed last 2 weeks August, 24 December- 3 January, Sunday, Monday and Saturday lunch.
– **Rest** 17.50/22.50 and a la carte 25.95/35.95 ♈.
   ✦ Buzzy destination: bar runs length of lower level. Most diners migrate upstairs with its modish art work, intimate tables and modern dishes: do check out the souffles!

XX **Launceston Place,** 1a Launceston Pl, W8 5RL ⊖ *Gloucester Road*, ℰ (020) 7937 6912, *lpr@egami.co.uk, Fax (020) 7938 2412* – 🔟 ⇔ 14. **MC AE ⓞ VISA**
35 ACX a
closed 24-26 December, 1-2 January, Saturday lunch and some Bank Holidays – **Rest** 24.50 (lunch) and a la carte 30.50/38.75 ♈.
   ✦ Divided into a number of rooms, this corner restaurant is lent a bright feel by its large windows and gilded mirrors. Chatty service and contemporary cooking.

XX **Memories of China,** 353 Kensington High St, W8 6NW ⊖ *High Street Kensington*, ℰ (020) 7603 6951, *Fax (020) 7603 0848* – 🔟, **MC VISA**
35 AAY v
closed Easter and Christmas – **Rest** - Chinese - (booking essential) 19.50/39.50 and a la carte 21.55/34.65 ♈.
   ✦ Subtle lighting and brightly coloured high-back chairs add to the modern feel of this Chinese restaurant. Screens separate the tables. Plenty of choice from extensive menu.

XX **11 Abingdon Road,** 11 Abingdon Rd, W8 6AH ⊖ *High Street Kensington*, ℰ (020) 7937 0120, *eleven@abingdonroad.co.uk* – 🔟, **MC VISA**
35 AAX a
closed Bank Holidays – **Rest** a la carte 20.95/29.50 ♈.
   ✦ Part of a little 'eating oasis' off Ken High Street. Stylish frosted glass façade with a clean, white interior. Cooking's from the modern British stable with Euro accents.

XX **L Restaurant & Bar,** 2 Abingdon Rd, W8 6AF ⊖ *High Street Kensington*, ℰ (020) 7795 6969, *info@l-restaurant.co.uk, Fax (020) 7795 6699* – ✖ 🔟 ⇔ 14. **MC AE VISA**   35 AAX x
closed 1 January, 25-26 December, Sunday dinner and Monday lunch – **Rest** - Spanish - a la carte 24.50/36.50 ♈.
   ✦ Wonderfully airy glass-roofed dining room with tastefully designed wood work and mirrors. Authentic Iberian menus with an emphasis on tapas matched by good-value wine list.

XX **Timo,** 343 Kensington High St, W8 6NW ⊖ *High Street Kensington*, ℰ (020) 7603 3888, *timorestaurant@fsmail.net, Fax (020) 7603 8111* – 🔟, **MC AE VISA**
35 AAY c
closed 25-26 December, Easter, Saturday lunch and Sunday dinner – **Rest** - Italian - 16.50 (lunch) and dinner la carte 26.50/28.90 ♈.
   ✦ Modern, personally run restaurant with unadorned walls and comfortable seating in brown suede banquettes. Italian menus of contemporary dishes and daily changing specials.

X **Kensington Place,** 201 Kensington Church St, W8 7LX ⊖ *Notting Hill Gate*, ℰ (020) 7727 3184, *kpr@egami.co.uk, Fax (020) 7229 2025* – 🔟. **MC AE ⓞ VISA**
27 AAV z
closed 25-26 December and 1 January – **Rest** (booking essential) 19.50/39.50 and a la carte 31.00/39.50 ♈.
   ✦ A cosmopolitan crowd still head for this establishment that set the trend for large, bustling and informal restaurants. Professionally run with skilled modern cooking.

X **Cibo,** 3 Russell Gdns, W14 8EZ ⊖ *Kensington Olympia*, ℰ (020) 7371 6271, *Fax (020) 7602 1371* – **MC AE VISA**
16 MZE b
closed Easter, Christmas, Saturday lunch, Sunday dinner and Bank Holidays – **Rest** - Italian - 22.50 (lunch) and a la carte 23.00/35.50.
   ✦ Smoothly run Italian restaurant that combines style with the atmosphere of a neighbourhood favourite. Unaffected service with robust and tasty food.

X **Malabar,** 27 Uxbridge St, W8 7TQ ⊖ *Notting Hill Gate*, ℰ (020) 7727 8800, *feedback@malabar-restaurant.co.uk* – 🔟, **MC AE VISA**
27 AAV e
closed 1 week Christmas – **Rest** - Indian - (booking essential) (buffet lunch Sunday) 15.00 and a la carte 18.00/33.00 **s**.
   ✦ Indian restaurant in a residential street. Three rooms with individual personalities and informal service. Extensive range of good value dishes, particularly vegetarian.

X **Wódka,** 12 St Albans Grove, W8 5PN ⊖ *High Street Kensington*, ℰ (020) 7937 6513, *info@wodka.co.uk, Fax (020) 7937 8621* – ⇔ 30. **MC AE VISA**
35 ABX c
closed 25 December, 1 January and lunch Saturday and Sunday – **Rest** - Polish - 14.50 (lunch) and a la carte 23.90/29.00 ♈.
   ✦ Unpretentious Polish restaurant with rustic, authentic menu. Assorted blinis and flavoured vodkas a speciality. Simply decorated, with wooden tables and paper napkins.

North Kensington – ✉ W2/W11.

🏠 **The Portobello** without rest., 22 Stanley Gdns, W11 2NG ⊖ *Notting Hill Gate*, ℰ (020) 7727 2777, *info@portobello-hotel.co.uk, Fax (020) 7792 9641* – 🛗 ✎ **MC AE VISA**
16 NZE n
🍴 12.00 **24 rm** ✿140.00/180.00 – ✿✿180.00/290.00.
   ✦ An attractive Victorian town house in an elegant terrace. Original and theatrical décor. Circular beds, half-testers, Victorian baths: no two bedrooms are the same.

Abbey Court without rest., 20 Pembridge Gdns, W2 4DU ⊖ Notting Hill Gate, ℘ (020) 7221 7518, info@abbeycourthotel.co.uk, Fax (020) 7792 0858 – ✕, 🐾. **MO** **AE** **①** **VISA**. ✕

27 AAV u

⊡ 8.00 **22 rm** ★75.00/125.00 – ★★110.00/145.00.

♦ Five-storey Victorian town house with individually decorated bedrooms, with many thoughtful touches. Breakfast served in a pleasant conservatory. Friendly service.

Guesthouse West, 163-165 Westbourne Grove, W11 2RS ⊖ Notting Hill Gate, ℘ (020) 7792 9800, reception@guesthousewest.com, Fax (020) 7792 9797, 🍴 – ✕ rm, ≣ ✆. **MO**

AE **①** **VISA**. ✕

27 AAU x

Rest (closed lunch Monday-Wednesday) a la carte 17.50/21.50 – ⊡ 8.00 – **20 rm** ★147.00/170.00 – ★★147.00/200.00.

♦ Attractive Edwardian house in the heart of Notting Hill, close to its shops and restaurants. Contemporary bedrooms boast the latest in audio visual gadgetry. Chic Parlour Bar for all-day light dishes in a tapas style.

The Ledbury, 127 Ledbury Rd, W11 2AQ ⊖ Notting Hill Gate, ℘ (020) 7792 9090, info@theledbury.com, Fax (020) 7792 9191, 🍴 – ✕ ≣. **MO** **AE** **VISA**

27 AAT a

closed 24-26 December and August Bank Holiday – Rest 29.50/45.00 🏵.

Spec. Scallops roasted in liquorice with fennel and white onion purée. Lamb baked in hay with creamed potato, truffle and celery. Chicory crème brûlée with coffee ice cream and chocolate Madeleine.

♦ Converted pub whose cool décor fits seamlessly into the neighbourhood it serves. Confident, highly accomplished cooking using first-rate ingredients; portions are generous.

Notting Hill Brasserie, 92 Kensington Park Rd, W11 2PN ⊖ Notting Hill Gate, ℘ (020) 7229 4481, enquiries@nottinghillbrasserie.com, Fax (020) 7221 1246 – ≣ ⇔ 20. **MO** **AE**

VISA

27 AAU a

closed Sunday dinner – Rest 19.50/30.00 (lunch) and dinner a la carte 34.50/44.50 🏵.

♦ Modern, comfortable restaurant with quiet, formal atmosphere set over four small rooms. Authentic African artwork on walls. Contemporary dishes with European influence.

Edera, 148 Holland Park Ave, W11 4UE ⊖ Holland Park, ℘ (020) 7221 6090, Fax (020) 7313 9700 – ≣. **MO** **AE** **VISA**

16 MZE n

closed 25 December and 1 January – Rest - Italian - a la carte 27.00/35.00 🏵.

♦ Split level restaurant with 4 outdoor tables. Attentive service by all staff. Interesting menus of modern Italian cooking with some unusual ingredients and combinations.

E&O, 14 Blenheim Crescent, W11 1NN ⊖ Ladbroke Grove, ℘ (020) 7229 5454, info@eando.nu, Fax (020) 7229 5522 – ✕ ≣ ⇔ 18. **MO** **AE** **①** **VISA**

16 MZD a

closed Sunday-Monday and Bank Holidays – Rest - South East Asian - a la carte 22.00/34.00 🏵.

♦ Mean, dark and moody: never mind the exterior, we're talking about the A-list diners. Minimalist chic meets high sound levels. Menus scour Far East: cutlery/chopstick choice.

Notting Grill, 123A Clarendon Rd, W11 4JG ⊖ Holland Park, ℘ (020) 7229 1500, not tinggrill@aol.com, Fax (020) 7229 8889, 🍴 – **AE** **①** **VISA**

16 MZE z

closed 24 December-3 January and Monday lunch – Rest - Steak specialities - 17.50 (lunch) a la carte 27.50/42.00 🏵.

♦ Converted pub that retains a rustic feel, with bare brick walls and wooden tables. Specialises in well sourced, quality meats.

South Kensington Gtr London – ✉ SW5/SW7.

The Bentley Kempinski, 27-33 Harrington Gdns, SW7 4JX ⊖ Gloucester Road, ℘ (020) 7244 5555, info@thebentley-hotel.com, Fax (020) 7244 5566, ⌼, ⛴ – ⧉ ✕ ≣ ✆ – 🔏 70. **MO** **AE** **①** **VISA**.

36 ACY k

Peridot : Rest (lunch and dinner Sunday-Monday) 26.50/52.00 and a la carte 28.50/52.50 – (see also **1880** below) – ⊡ 19.50 – **52 rm** ★340.00/458.00 – ★★458.00, 12 suites.

♦ A number of 19C houses have been joined to create this opulent, lavish, hidden gem, decorated with marble, mosaics and ornate gold leaf. Bedrooms with gorgeous silk fabrics. Airy, intimate Peridot offers brasserie menus.

Millennium Gloucester, 4-18 Harrington Gdns, SW7 4LH ⊖ Gloucester Road, ℘ (020) 7373 6030, reservations.gloucester@mill-cop.com, Fax (020) 7373 0409, ⌼ – ⧉ ✕ ≣ ⅙ 🄿 – 🔏 500. **MO** **AE** **①** **VISA**. ✕

36 ACY r

Bugis Street : Rest - Chinese (Singaporean) - 16.50 and a la carte – **South West 7 :** Rest (closed Sunday-Monday) (dinner only) a la carte – ⊡ 15.50 – **604 rm** ★223.00 – ★★223.00, 6 suites.

♦ A large international group hotel. Busy marbled lobby and vast conference facilities. Smart and well-equipped bedrooms are generously sized, especially the 'Club' rooms. Dinner or buffet at South West 7. Informal, compact Bugis Street.

The Pelham, 15 Cromwell Pl, SW7 2LA ⊖ *South Kensington*, ℘ (020) 7589 8288, *pelham@firmdale.com, Fax (020) 7584 8444, ♣ – 劇 ⓦ ⒶⒺ *VISA*. ﹠ 36 ADY z
Kemps : Rest 17.95 and a la carte 24.50/32.50 ♀ – ⇨ 17.50 – **50 rm** ✦188.00/229.00 –
✦✦294.00, 2 suites.
 ♦ Attractive Victorian town house with a discreet and comfortable feel. Wood panelled
drawing room and individually decorated bedrooms with marble bathrooms. Detailed service. Warm basement dining room.

Blakes, 33 Roland Gdns, SW7 3PF ⊖ *Gloucester Road*, ℘ (020) 7370 6701, *blakes@blake shotels.com, Fax (020) 7373 0442*, 🌡, ♣ – 劇, ▤ rest, ✆, ⓦ ⒶⒺ ⓞ *VISA*. ﹠ 36 ACZ n
Rest *(closed 25-26 December and 1 January)* a la carte 63.00/80.00 – ⇨ 25.00 – **45 rm**
✦206.00/323.00 – ✦✦417.00, 3 suites.
 ♦ Behind the Victorian façade lies one of London's first 'boutique' hotels. Dramatic, bold
and eclectic décor, with oriental influences and antiques from around the globe. Fashionable restaurant with bamboo and black walls.

Harrington Hall, 5-25 Harrington Gdns, SW7 4JB ⊖ *Gloucester Road*, ℘ (020) 7396 9696, *book.london@nh-hotels.com, Fax (020) 7396 1719*, ♣, ⇌ – 劇 ✦ ▤ ✆ – 🕭 200.
ⓦ ⒶⒺ ⓞ *VISA*. ﹠ 36 ACY n
closed 25 December **Wetherby's :** Rest 19.50 (lunch) and dinner a la carte 30.45/40.00 s.
♀ – ⇨ 17.00 – **200 rm** ✦215.00 – ✦✦215.00.
 ♦ A series of adjoined terraced houses, with an attractive period façade that belies the
size. Tastefully furnished bedrooms, with an extensive array of facilities. Classically decorated dining room.

Vanderbilt, 68-86 Cromwell Rd, SW7 5BT ⊖ *Gloucester Road*, ℘ (020) 7761 9000, *resvand@radisson.com, Fax (020) 7761 9001*, ♣ – 劇 ✦ ▤ ✆ ♿ – 🕭 100. ⓦ ⒶⒺ ⓞ *VISA*. ﹠ 36 ACY z
6886 : Rest *(closed lunch Saturday-Sunday)* 25.00 and a la carte 25.00/33.50 ♀ – ⇨ 15.00 –
215 rm ✦122.00/183.00 – ✦✦158.00/245.00.
 ♦ A Victorian town house, once home to the Vanderbilt family. Retains many original
features such as stained glass windows and fireplaces. Now a modern, group hotel. Restaurant has unusual objets d'art and striking cracked glass bar.

London Marriott Kensington, 147 Cromwell Rd, SW5 0TH ⊖ *Gloucester Road*, ℘ (020) 7973 1000, *london.regional.reservations@marriott.com, Fax (0870) 400 7366*, ♣, ⇌, ▥ – 劇 ✦ ▤ ✆ ♿ – 🕭 200. ⓦ ⒶⒺ *VISA*. ﹠ 35 ABY s
Fratelli : Rest - Italian - a la carte 26.00/32.00 ♀ – ⇨ 17.95 – **215 rm** ✦198.00 – ✦✦198.00,
1 suite.
 ♦ Modern seven-storey hotel around atrium with good leisure centre. Coffee bar and
Spanish tapas bar. Spacious, comfortable, well-equipped bedrooms with many extras. In-
formal Italian restaurant with open kitchen and wide ranging menu.

Rembrandt, 11 Thurloe Pl, SW7 2RS ⊖ *South Kensington*, ℘ (020) 7589 8100, *rembrandt@sarova.co.uk, Fax (020) 7225 3476*, ♣, ⇌, ▥ – 劇, ✦ rm, ▤ rest, ✆ ♿ – 🕭 200.
ⓦ ⒶⒺ ⓞ *VISA*. ﹠ 36 ADY x
Rest (carving lunch) (booking essential) 19.95 s. ♀ – **195 rm** ✦220.00/235.00 – ✦✦235.00.
 ♦ Built originally as apartments in the 19C, now a well-equipped hotel opposite the Victoria
and Albert museum. Comfortable lounge, adjacent leisure club, well appointed rooms.
Spacious dining room.

Jurys Kensington, 109-113 Queen's Gate, SW7 5LH ⊖ *South Kensington*, ℘ (020) 7589 6300, *kensington@jurysdoyle.com, Fax (020) 7589 7659* – 劇 ✦ ▤ ✆ ♿ – 🕭 80. ⓦ ⒶⒺ ⓞ *VISA*. ﹠ 36 ADY g
Rest (dinner only) 18.00/35.00 s. – ⇨ 14.95 – **174 rm** ✦195.00 – ✦✦195.00.
 ♦ A row of 18C town houses that were converted into a hotel in the 1920s. Spacious lobby
lounge and busy basement Irish pub. Well-equipped, comfortable bedrooms. Dining room
exudes a traditional appeal.

Number Sixteen, 16 Sumner Pl, SW7 3EG ⊖ *South Kensington*, ℘ (020) 7589 5232, *sixteen@firmdale.com, Fax (020) 7584 8615*, 🌡 – 劇 ✆. ⓦ ⒶⒺ *VISA*. ﹠ 36 ADY d
Rest (room service only) – ⇨ 13.00 – **42 rm** ✦118.00/206.00 – ✦✦300.00.
 ♦ Enticingly refurbished 19C town houses in smart area. Discreet entrance, comfy sitting
room and charming breakfast terrace. Bedrooms in English country house style.

The Cranley, 10 Bina Gdns, SW5 0LA ⊖ *Gloucester Road*, ℘ (020) 7373 0123, *info@the cranley.com, Fax (020) 7373 9497* – 劇 ✆. ⓦ ⒶⒺ ⓞ *VISA*. ﹠ 36 ACY c
Rest (room service only) – ⇨ 10.00 – **38 rm** ✦159.00/258.00 – ✦✦241.00/276.00, 1 suite.
 ♦ Delightful Regency town house that artfully combines charm and period details with
modern comforts and technology. Individually styled bedrooms; some with four-posters.

The Gore, 190 Queen's Gate, SW7 5EX ⊖ *Gloucester Road*, ℘ (020) 7584 6601, *reserva tions@gorehotel.com, Fax (020) 7589 8127* – ⧈, ⟲ rm, ▤ ⟲ – ⧈ 70. ◉◉ ᴀᴇ ꕤ
36 ACX n

190 Queensgate : Rest (booking essential) 15.95 (lunch) and a la carte 30.90/50.95 ♀ – ☲ 16.95 – **50 rm** ✦170.00/235.00 – ✦✦211.00/235.00.
◆ Opened its doors in 1892; has retained its individual charm. Richly decorated with anti- ques, rugs and over 4,000 pictures that cover every inch of wall. 190 Queensgate boasts French-inspired décor.

Aster House without rest., 3 Sumner Pl, SW7 3EE ⊖ *South Kensington*, ℘ (020) 7581 5888, *asterhouse@btinternet.com, Fax (020) 7584 4925*, ⩜ – ⟲ ▤ ⟲. ◉◉ ᴠɪꜱᴀ.
36 ADY t

13 rm ✦93.00/159.00 – ✦✦128.00/182.00.
◆ End of terrace Victorian house with a pretty little rear garden and first floor conserva- tory. Ground floor rooms available. A wholly non-smoking establishment.

1880 (at The Bentley Kempinski H.), 27-33 Harrington Gdns, SW7 4JX ⊖ *Gloucester Road*, ℘ (020) 7244 5555, *info@thebentley-hotel.com, Fax (020) 7244 5566* – ⟲ ▤. ◉◉ ᴀᴇ ꕤ ᴠɪꜱᴀ
36 ACY k

closed Sunday-Monday – Rest (dinner only) 54.00.
◆ Luxurious, opulently decorated room in Bentley basement: silk panels, gold leaf, Italian marble, chandeliers. Extensive "grazing" menu up to 10 courses.

Bombay Brasserie, Courtfield Rd, SW7 4QH ⊖ *Gloucester Road*, ℘ (020) 7370 4040, *bombay1brasserie@aol.com, Fax (020) 7835 1669* – ▤. ◉◉ ᴀᴇ ꕤ ᴠɪꜱᴀ
36 ACY y

closed 25-26 December – Rest - Indian - (buffet lunch)/dinner 35.00/45.00 and dinner a la carte 29.35/38.75 ♀.
◆ Something of a London institution: an ever busy Indian restaurant with Raj-style décor. Ask to sit in the brighter plant-filled conservatory. Popular lunchtime buffet.

Lundum's, 119 Old Brompton Rd, SW7 3RN ⊖ *Gloucester Road*, ℘ (020) 7373 7774, *Fax (020) 7373 4472*, ⩜ – ⇔ 18. ◉◉ ᴀᴇ ꕤ ᴠɪꜱᴀ
36 ACZ p

closed 23 December-4 January and Sunday dinner – Rest - Danish - 16.50/24.50 and a la carte 28.10/55.75 ♀.
◆ A family run Danish restaurant offering an authentic, traditional lunch with a more expansive dinner menu. Comfortable room, with large windows. Charming service.

L'Etranger, 36 Gloucester Rd, SW7 4QT ⊖ *Gloucester Road*, ℘ (020) 7584 1118, *sa sha@etranger.co.uk, Fax (020) 7584 8886* – ▤ ⟲. ◉◉ ᴀᴇ ꕤ ᴠɪꜱᴀ
35 ACX c

closed lunch Saturday and Sunday – Rest (booking essential) 16.50 (lunch) and a la carte 33.50/77.50 ⩜.
◆ Corner restaurant with mosaic entrance floor and bay window. Modern décor. Tables extend into adjoining wine shop. French based cooking with Asian influences.

Pasha, 1 Gloucester Rd, SW7 4PP ⊖ *Gloucester Road*, ℘ (020) 7589 7969, *info@pasha- restaurant.co.uk, Fax (020) 7581 9996* – ▤ ⇔ 20. ◉◉ ᴀᴇ ꕤ ᴠɪꜱᴀ
36 ACX r

closed Sunday lunch – Rest - Moroccan - a la carte 35.00/40.00 ♀.
◆ Relax over ground floor cocktails, then descend to mosaic floored restaurant where the rose-petal strewn tables are the ideal accompaniment to tasty Moroccan home cooking.

Khan's of Kensington, 3 Harrington Rd, SW7 3ES ⊖ *South Kensington*, ℘ (020) 7584 4114, *info@khansofkensington.co.uk, Fax (020) 7581 2900* – ⟲ ▤. ◉◉ ᴀᴇ
36 ADY a

closed 25 December and dinner 26 December – Rest - Indian - 20.00/25.00 and a la carte 19.90/26.80 ♀.
◆ Bright room with wood flooring and a large mural depicting scenes from old India. Basement bar in a colonial style. Authentic Indian cooking with attentive service.

Cambio de Tercio, 163 Old Brompton Rd, SW5 0LJ ⊖ *Gloucester Road*, ℘ (020) 7244 8970, *alusa@btconnect.com, Fax (020) 7373 8817* – ▤ ⇔ 18. ◉◉ ᴀᴇ ᴠɪꜱᴀ
36 ACZ a

closed 20 December- 3 January – Rest - Spanish - a la carte 26.25/32.00.
◆ The keen young owners have created a vibrant destination offering a mix of traditional and sophisticated Spanish cooking complemented by a well-sourced regional wine list.

Café Lazeez, 93-95 Old Brompton Rd, SW7 3LD ⊖ *South Kensington*, ℘ (020) 7581 6996, *southkensington@cafelazeez.com, Fax (020) 7581 8200* – ▤. ◉◉ ᴀᴇ ꕤ ᴠɪꜱᴀ
36 ADY v

Rest - North Indian - 25.00/30.00 and a la carte 18.50/25.00 ♀.
◆ Glass-topped tables and tiled flooring add an air of modernity to this Indian restaurant; reflected in the North Indian cooking. Willing service. Upstairs room more formal.

Bangkok, 9 Bute St, SW7 3EY ⊖ *South Kensington*, ℘ (020) 7584 8529 – ▤. ◉◉ ᴠɪꜱᴀ
36 ADY b

closed Christmas-New Year and Sunday – Rest - Thai Bistro - a la carte 18.50/31.45.
◆ This simple Thai bistro has been a popular local haunt for many years. Guests can watch the chefs at work, preparing inexpensive dishes from the succinct menu.

KINGSTON UPON THAMES *Gtr London.*

⑱ Home Park, Hampton Wick ℰ *(020) 8977 6645,* BY.

Surbiton *Surrey –* ✉ *Surrey.*

XX **The French Table,** 85 Maple Rd, KT6 4AW, ℰ *(020) 8399 2365, Fax (020) 8390 5353 –*
🍴, **MO AE ⓪** *VISA*
6 CY **a**
closed 25-26 December, 1-10 January, Monday, Sunday dinner and lunch Saturday – **Rest** -
French-Mediterranean - 16.50 (lunch) and dinner a la carte 26.10/33.50 ⚚.
   ◆ The lively atmosphere makes this narrow room with wooden tables and modern art a
popular local. Attentive and relaxed service of a concise French-Mediterranean menu.

LAMBETH *Gtr London.*

Clapham Common *Gtr London –* ✉ *SW4.*

X **Tsunami,** Unit 3, 5-7 Voltaire Rd, SW4 6DQ ⊖ *Clapham North,* ℰ *(020) 7978 1610,*
Fax (020) 7978 1591 – 🍴, **MO AE** *VISA*
24 SZH **a**
closed 25-26 December and Easter – **Rest** - Japanese - (dinner only and Saturday-Sunday
lunch) a la carte 15.95/40.40 ⚚.
   ◆ Trendy, mininalist-style restaurant. Interesting Japanese menu with many dishes designed for sharing and plenty of original options. Good Sushi and Sashimi selection.

Herne Hill *Gtr London –* ✉ *SE24.*

XX **3 Monkeys,** 136-140 Herne Hill, SE24 9QH, ℰ *(020) 7738 5500, info@3monkeysrestaur
ant.com, Fax (020) 7738 5505 –* ✦✖ 🍴, **MO AE ⓪** *VISA*
7 FX **r**
Rest - Indian - a la carte 18.85/29.10 ⚚.
   ◆ 'New wave' Indian restaurant in a converted bank. Dining room in bright white reached
via a bridge over the bar and kitchen. Menu uses influences from all over India.

Kennington *Gtr London –* ✉ *SE11.*

X **Lobster Pot,** 3 Kennington Lane, SE11 4RG ⊖ *Kennington,* ℰ *(020) 7582 5556 –* 🍴, **MO**
AE *VISA*
40 AOY **e**
closed 24 December-8 January, Sunday and Monday – **Rest** - French Seafood - 21.50/43.50
and a la carte 26.30/40.10.
   ◆ A nautical theme so bold you'll need your sea legs: fishing nets, shells, aquariums,
portholes, even the sound of seagulls. Classic French seafood menu is more restrained.

Waterloo *Gtr London –* ✉ *SE1.*

Channel Tunnel : *Eurostar information and reservations* ℰ *(08705) 186186.*

🏨 **London Marriott H. County Hall,** Westminster Bridge Rd, SE1 7PB ⊖ *Westmin-*
ster, ℰ *(020) 7928 5200, mhrs.lonch.salesadmin@marriotthotels.com, Fax (020) 7928 5300,*
≤, ⚗, 🛠, ≘s, ⧄ – ∣🛉∣, ✦✖ rm, 🍴 ✆ ⅙ – 🔬 70. **MO AE ⓪** *VISA*. ⚒
40 AMX **a**
County Hall : Rest 23.00 and a la carte 25.50/44.00 ⚚ – ⚏ 20.95 – **195 rm** ✦281.00/327.00
– ✦✦281.00/327.00, 5 suites.
   ◆ Occupying the historic County Hall building. Many of the spacious and comfortable
bedrooms enjoy river and Parliament outlook. Impressive leisure facilities. World famous
views from restaurant.

LEWISHAM *Gtr London.*

Blackheath *Gtr London –* ✉ *SE3.*

XX **Chapter Two,** 43-45 Montpelier Vale, SE3 0TJ, ℰ *(020) 8333 2666, fiona.chap
ter2@talk21.com, Fax (020) 8355 8399 –* ✦✖ 🍴, **MO AE ⓪** *VISA*
8 HX **c**
Rest 19.00/23.00 and a la carte 19.95/26.00 ⚚.
   ◆ Smart and contemporary interior. Decorated in primary colours, with pine flooring.
Formal service of a well-priced, well-judged European-influenced modern menu.

LONDON HEATHROW AIRPORT *– see Hillingdon, London p. 87.*

 Look out for red symbols, indicating particularly pleasant establishments.

MERTON Gtr London.

Colliers Wood Gtr London – ⊠ SW19.

🏨 **Express by Holiday Inn** without rest., 200 High St, SW19 2BH, on A 24 ⊖ Colliers Wood, ℰ (020) 8545 7300, info@exhiwimbledon.co.uk, Fax (020) 8545 7301 – |≢| ⇔ ⚓ ♿
⟺ – 🚗 50. 🐵 🖭 ⓪ VISA
7 EY a
83 rm ✦92.00/99.00 – ✦✦92.00/99.00.
♦ Modern, corporate budget hotel. Spacious and well-equipped bedrooms; power showers in en suite bathrooms. Ideal for the business traveller. Continental breakfast included.

Wimbledon Gtr London – ⊠ SW19.

🏨 **Cannizaro House** ⑤, West Side, Wimbledon Common, SW19 4UE ⊖ Wimbledon, ℰ (020) 8879 1464, info@cannizarohouse.com, Fax (020) 8879 7338, ≤, ☞, ℛ – |≢| ⇔ rm,
🄿 – 🚗 120. 🐵 🖭 ⓪ VISA
6 DXY x
Rest a la carte 22.50/38.00 ♀ – **43 rm** ⬚ ✦135.00/330.00 – ✦✦135.00/330.00, 2 suites.
♦ Part Georgian mansion in a charming spot on the Common. Appealing drawing room popular for afternoon tea. Rooms in original house are antique furnished, some with balconies. Refined restaurant overlooks splendid formal garden.

✕ **Light House,** 75-77 Ridgway, SW19 4ST ⊖ Wimbledon, ℰ (020) 8944 6338, info@light housewimbledon.com, Fax (020) 8946 4440 – 🐵 🖭 VISA
6 DY n
closed 25-26 December, 1 January and Sunday dinner – **Rest** 16.50 (lunch) and a la carte 22.70/32.20 ♀.
♦ Bright and modern neighbourhood restaurant with open plan kitchen. Informal service of a weekly changing and diverse menu of progressive Italian/fusion dishes.

🍴 **The Fire Stables,** 27-29 Church Rd, SW19 5DQ ⊖ Wimbledon, ℰ (020) 8946 3197, thefirestables@thespiritgroup.com, Fax (020) 8946 1101 – ▤. 🐵 VISA. ✑
6 DX a
Rest 15.50 (lunch) and a la carte 22.00/33.00 ♀.
♦ Modern gastropub in village centre. Open-plan kitchen. Polished wood tables and banquettes. Varied modern British dishes. Expect fishcakes, duck confit salad or risotto.

If breakfast is included the ⬚ symbol appears after the number of rooms.

NEWHAM Gtr London.

ExCel Gtr London – ⊠ E16.

🏨 **Crowne Plaza Docklands,** Royal Victoria Dock, Western Gateway, E16 1AL ⊖ Royal Victoria, ℰ (0870) 9909692, sales@crowneplazadocklands.co.uk, Fax (0870) 9909693, ℔,
⇔, ▦ – |≢| ⇔ ▤ ⚓ ♿ 🄿 – 🚗 275. 🐵 🖭 ⓪ VISA. ✑
8 HV a
Terra: Rest (dinner only) 25.00 and a la carte 25.85/33.90 – ⬚ 14.50 – **205 rm**
✦163.00/175.00 – ✦✦163.00/175.00, 5 suites.
♦ Spacious and stylish hotel with emphasis on the business traveller. State-of-the-art meeting rooms; snazzy, compact leisure centre. Ultra-smart, well-equipped rooms. Modish dining room with funky bar.

🏨 **Ramada H. & Suites - London Docklands,** 2 Festoon Way, Royal Victoria Dock, E16 1RH ⊖ Prince Regent, ℰ (0870) 1118779, Fax (0870) 1118789, ℔ – |≢| ▤ ⚓ ♿
🚗 25. 🐵 🖭 VISA. ✑
8 HV c
The Waterfront: Rest a la carte 18.50/35.10 s. – **153 rm** ⬚ ✦108.00/141.00 –
✦✦129.00/229.00, 71 suites.
♦ Plush, purpose-built hotel five minutes from City Airport and ExCel. Two small, well-equipped meeting rooms. The bedrooms are a strong point with impressive facilities. Modern dining room with al fresco option for fine weather.

🏨 **Novotel London ExCel,** 7 Western Gateway, Royal Victoria Dock, E16 1AA ⊖ Royal Victoria, ℰ (020) 7540 9700, h3656@accor.com, Fax (020) 7540 9710, ℔, ⇔ – |≢| ⇔ ▤ ⚓
♿ 🄿 – 🚗 80. 🐵 🖭 ⓪ VISA
8 HV e
The Upper Deck: Rest 15.00/40.00 and a la carte 23.50/37.90 s. – ⬚ 13.50 – **250 rm**
✦140.00 – ✦✦160.00, 7 suites.
♦ Capacious purpose-built hotel adjacent to ExCel Centre. Ultra modish bar and coffee area exudes minimalism. Up-to-date meeting facilities. Well-appointed, comfortable rooms. Formal dining room with menus influenced by the seasons.

🏨 **Sunborn Yacht H.,** Royal Victoria Dock, E16 1SL ⊖ *Prince Regent*, ☎ (020) 7059 9100,
reservations.london@sunbornhotels.com, Fax (020) 7059 9432 – 📶 🌀 ⬛ 📞 📮 – 🛗 90.
🆗 AE ⑩ VISA. ⅜   8 HV n
Rest (bar lunch)/dinner 30.00/60.00 and a la carte 28.70/56.40 – ☷ 13.50 – **102 rm**
🛏82.00/276.00 – 🛏🛏82.00/276.00, 2 suites.
   ◆ Permanently moored next to ExCel, this glitzy yacht hotel offers unique, water-borne
accommodation. The sizable rooms have a distinct 'cabin' feel: two suites boast a sauna.
European menus in the formal, airy dining room.

RICHMOND-UPON-THAMES *Gtr London.*

Barnes *Gtr London – ✉ SW13.*

XX **Sonny's,** 94 Church Rd, SW13 0DQ, ☎ (020) 8748 0393, *manager@sonnys.co.uk,*
Fax (020) 8748 2698 – ⬛ ⇔ 20. 🆗 AE VISA   21 KZH x
closed Sunday dinner and Bank Holidays – **Rest** 21.50 (lunch and dinner Monday-Thursday)
a la carte 21.50/33.50 ☟.
   ◆ Dine in the bright, modern and informal restaurant or the equally relaxed café-bar.
Attentive service of imaginative modern dishes.

X **Riva,** 169 Church Rd, SW13 9HR, ☎ (020) 8748 0434, *Fax (020) 8748 0434* – 🆗 AE
VISA   21 LZH a
closed last 2 weeks August, 24 December-4 January, Saturday lunch and Bank Holidays –
Rest - Italian - a la carte 26.50/40.00 ☟.
   ◆ The eponymous owner manages the polite service in this unassuming restaurant. Rustic
and robust cooking uses some of Italy's finest produce. Extensive all-Italian wine list.

X **Barnes Grill,** 2-3 Rocks Lane, SW13 0DB, ☎ (020) 8878 4488 – 🌀 ⬛ 🆗 AE
VISA   21 LZH k
closed Monday lunch – **Rest** - Steak specialities - (booking essential) a la carte
22.00/45.00 ☟.
   ◆ Popular neighbourhood addition: eye-catching wall-mounted feather displays and
mounted bull's head. Steaks, hung for 35 days, typify the heartily old-fashioned British
dishes.

East Sheen *Gtr London – ✉ SW14.*

XX **Redmond's,** 170 Upper Richmond Road West, SW14 8AW, ☎ (020) 8878 1922,
pippa@redmonds.org.uk – 🌀 ⬛ 🆗 VISA   6 CX v
closed 3 days Christmas, Sunday and Bank Holidays – **Rest** (dinner only) 15.50/32.00.
   ◆ Bright, spacious and relaxed restaurant. Friendly and approachable service of modern
British cooking prepared with care. Mid-week set-price menu is good value.

🍴 **The Victoria,** 10 West Temple Sheen, SW14 7RT, ☎ (020) 8876 4238, *bookings@thevic*
toria.net, Fax (020) 8878 3464, 🌁 – 🌀 📮 🆗 AE VISA ⅜   6 CX u
closed 24-27 December – **Rest** a la carte 25.00/35.00 ☟.
   ◆ Traditional pub near Richmond Park with bright modern décor. Large conservatory,
terrace and children's play area. Daily menu of interesting modern and traditional dishes.

Hampton Wick *Surrey – ✉ Surrey.*

🏠 **Chase Lodge,** 10 Park Rd, KT1 4AS, ☎ (020) 8943 1862, *info@chaselodgehotel.com,*
Fax (020) 8943 9363 – 🆗 AE ⑩ VISA   5 BY e
Rest 15.00/25.00 – **13 rm** 🛏65.00/85.00 – 🛏🛏98.00/105.00.
   ◆ Personally-run small hotel in mid-terrace Victorian property in an area of outstanding
architectural and historical interest. Individually furnished, comfortable rooms. Bright, airy
conservatory restaurant.

Kew *Surrey – ✉ Surrey.*

XX **The Glasshouse,** 14 Station Parade, TW9 3PZ ⊖ *Kew Gardens*, ☎ (020) 8940 6777,
🍃 *info@glasshouserestaurant.co.uk, Fax (020) 8940 3833* – 🌀 ⬛ 🆗 AE VISA   6 CX z
closed 24-26 December and 1 January – **Rest** 23.50/35.00 s. ☟ ⅊.
Spec. Warm salad of duck magret with deep-fried truffled egg. Slow roast pork belly with
apple tart, choucroute and crispy ham. Vanilla yoghurt with red fruit compote.
   ◆ Light pours in through the glass façade of this forever busy, contemporary restaurant.
Assured, knowledgeable service of imaginative dishes that employ a skilful, light touch.

XX **Kew Grill,** 10b Kew Green, TW9 3BH ⊖ *Kew Gardens*, ☎ (020) 8948 4433, *kew*
grill@aol.com, Fax (020) 8605 3532 – 🌀 ⬛ 🆗 AE VISA   6 CX u
closed 25-26 December and Monday lunch – **Rest** - Beef specialities - (booking essential)
14.95 (lunch) and a la carte 25.00/43.00 ☟.
   ◆ Just off Kew Green, this long, narrow restaurant has a Mediterranean style and feel.
Grilled specialities employing top-rate ingredients: the beef is hung for 35 days.

✗ **Ma Cuisine,** The Old Post Office, 9 Station Approach, TW9 3QB ⊖ *Kew Gardens*, ℘ (020) 8332 1923, 🐾 – 📧 *VISA* 6 CX r

Rest - French - 15.50 (lunch) and dinner a la carte 18.25/23.70 ☻.
* Formerly Kew's post office building; features tables on the pavement, arched roof and red gingham tablecloths. Good value, classic French dishes. Truly, "le petit bistrot".

Richmond *Surrey* – ⊠ *Surrey*.

🏌, 🏌 *Richmond Park,* Roehampton Gate ℘ *(020) 8876 3205* CX – 🏌 *Sudbrook Park* ℘ *(020) 8940 1463* CX.

🅷 *Old Town Hall,* Whittaker Ave ℘ *(020) 8940 9125.*

🏰 **Petersham,** Nightingale Lane, TW10 6UZ, ℘ (020) 8940 7471, *enq@petershamho tel.co.uk,* Fax *(020) 8939 1002,* ≤, 🌳 – 🛗 📞 🖲 – 🔏 35. 🐾 🔤 ⊙ *VISA* 🛥 6 CX c

closed 25-26 December – **Rest** – (see *Restaurant* below) – 60 rm ☲ ✦135.00/160.00 – ✦✦170.00/275.00, 1 suite.
* Extended over the years, a fine example of Victorian Gothic architecture. Impressive Portland stone, self-supporting staircase. Most comfortable rooms overlook the Thames.

🏰 **Richmond Gate,** 158 Richmond Hill, TW10 6RP, ℘ (020) 8940 0061, *richmondgate@fo liohotels.com,* Fax *(020) 8332 0354,* 📠, 🚌, 🔲, 🌳 – 🚿 📞 ♨ 🖲 – 🔏 45. 🐾 🔤 *VISA* 🛥 6 CX c

Gates On The Park : Rest *(closed Saturday lunch)* 22.50/28.00 and a la carte approx 33.40 s. ☻ – 67 rm ☲ ✦160.00 – ✦✦160.00/180.00, 1 suite.
* Originally four elegant Georgian town houses and now a very comfortable corporate hotel. Cosy lounges have a period charm. Well-appointed deluxe rooms have thoughtful extras. Comfortable restaurant has intimate feel.

⌂ **Doughty Cottage** without rest., 142A Richmond Hill, TW10 6RN, ℘ (020) 8332 9434, *deniseoneill425@aol.co.uk,* Fax *(020) 8948 3716,* 🌳 – 🚿 🖲. 🐾 🔤 *VISA* 6 CX c

closed 25-26 December – 4 rm ✦55.00/65.00 – ✦✦75.00/120.00.
* Positioned high above the river, this attractive 18C Regency house is discreetly set behind a picturesque walled garden. Thoughtfully equipped rooms, two with patio gardens.

⌂ **Chalon House** without rest., 8 Spring Terrace, Paradise Rd, TW9 1LW ⊖ *Richmond,* ℘ (020) 8332 1121, *chalonhouse@hotmail.com,* Fax *(020) 8332 1131,* 🌳 – 🚿 🖲. 🛥 6 CX e

3 rm ✦70.00/80.00 – ✦✦90.00/95.00.
* Carefully renovated Georgian house a couple of minutes from town centre. Comfy, well furnished lounge; organic breakfasts shared with fellow guests. Individually styled rooms.

XXX **Restaurant** (at Petersham H.), Nightingale Lane, TW10 6UZ, ℘ (020) 8939 1084, Fax *(020) 8939 1002,* ≤, 🌳 – 🖲 🖲 ⟳ 16. 🐾 🔤 ⊙ *VISA* 6 CX c

closed 25-26 December – **Rest** 25.00 (lunch) and a la carte 34.00/45.50 ☻ 🍷.
* Tables by the window have spectacular views across royal parkland and the winding Thames. Formal surroundings in which to enjoy classic and modern cooking. See the cellars.

✗ **Matsuba,** 10 Red Lion St, TW9 1RW, ℘ (020) 8605 3513, *matsuba10@hotmail.com* – 🚿 📧. 🐾 🔤 *VISA* 6 CX n

closed 25-26 December, 1 January and Sunday – **Rest** - Japanese - a la carte approx 35.00.
* Family-run restaurant with slick, contemporary interior featuring a rear sushi bar and authentic, market fresh, super value Japanese menus. Gets packed in the evenings!

Teddington *Middx* – ⊠ *Middx.*

XX **The Wharf,** 22 Manor Rd, TW11 8BG, ℘ (020) 8977 6333, *the.wharf@walk-on-wa ter.co.uk,* Fax *(020) 8977 9444,* ≤, 🐾 – 🎏 📧 🖲. 🐾 🔤 *VISA* 5 BX a

closed 25-26 December, first week January, Sunday dinner and Monday – **Rest** 16.00/19.00 and dinner a la carte 23.00/32.00 ☻.
* Riverside restaurant with large heated terrace opposite Teddington lock. Modern menu of good value dishes; fixed price menu in the week; modern music.

Twickenham *Middx* – ⊠ *Middx.*

XX **La Brasserie McClements,** 2 Whitton Rd, TW1 1BJ, ℘ (020) 8744 9598, *john mac21@aol.com* – 🚿 📧. 🐾 🔤 ⊙ *VISA* 5 BX a

closed 1 January, and Sunday-Monday – **Rest** - French - 20.00 (lunch) and a la carte 28.00/34.50 ☻.
* Middle 'brioche' of a McClements triple decker, this restyled stalwart now has a French brasserie feel. Sizable menus of classic bourgeoise dishes prepared with refinement.

XX **A Cena,** 418 Richmond Rd, TW1 2EB ⊖ *Richmond,* ℘ (020) 8288 0108, Fax (020) 8940 5346 – ▤. **MC AE VISA**   5 **BX** x
closed last 2 weeks August, Christmas, Sunday dinner and Monday – **Rest** - Italian - a la carte 21.00/33.50 ℒ.
◆ Smart, neighbourhood style restaurant with pleasant bar boasting extensive cocktail list and dining room festooned with mirrors. Accomplished dishes from all regions of Italy.

X **Tangawizi,** 406 Richmond Rd, Richmond Bridge, TW1 2EB ⊖ *Richmond,* ℘ (020) 8891 3737, tangawizi-richmond@hotmail.com, Fax (020) 8891 3737 – ✸ ▤. **MC AE VISA**   5 **BX** e
closed 25 December and 1 January – **Rest** - Indian - (dinner only) a la carte 14.95/22.40.
◆ Name means Ginger in Swahili. Sleek décor in warm purple with subtle Indian touches. Well priced, nicely balanced, slowly evolving menus take their influence from North India.

X **Brula Bistrot,** 43 Crown Rd, St Margarets, TW1 3EJ, ℘ (020) 8892 0602, info@brulabistrot.com, Fax (020) 8892 7727 – ✸ ⇔ 25. **MC AE VISA**   5 **BX** v
closed 25-26 December and 1 January – **Rest** - French - (booking essential) 14.50 (lunch) and a la carte 20.50/34.00.
◆ Behind the stained glass windows and the rose arched entrance, you'll find an intimate and cosy bistro. Friendly and relaxed service of a weekly changing, rustic menu.

X **Ma Cuisine,** 6 Whitton Rd, TW1 1BJ, ℘ (020) 8607 9849 – ✸. **MC VISA**   5 **BX** a
closed Sunday – **Rest** - French - 15.50 (lunch) and a la carte 18.25/23.70 ℒ.
◆ Small neighbourhood bistro style restaurant offering good value. Classic French country cooking with blackboard specials; concise wine list.

SOUTHWARK Gtr London.

🖪 Vinopolis, 1 Bank End ℘ (020) 7357 9168, tourisminfo@southwark.gov.uk.

Bermondsey Gtr London – ✉ SE1.

🏨 **London Bridge,** 8-18 London Bridge St, SE1 9SG ⊖ *London Bridge,* ℘ (020) 7855 2200, sales@londonbridgehotel.com, Fax (020) 7855 2233, ᴵ♨ – ▐♯▌, ✸ rm, ▤ ♿ – ▵ 85. **MC AE Ⓞ VISA** ✸   33 **AQV** a
Georgetown : Rest 25.00 (lunch) and a la carte 19.75/28.70 – ⊇ 14.95 – **135 rm** ✸209.00 – ✸✸209.00, 3 suites.
◆ In one of the oldest parts of London, independently owned with an ornate façade dating from 1915. Modern interior with classically decorated bedrooms and an impressive gym. Restaurant echoing the colonial style serving Malaysian dishes.

XXX **Le Pont de la Tour,** 36d Shad Thames, Butlers Wharf, SE1 2YE ⊖ *London Bridge,* ℘ (020) 7403 8403, lepontres@conran-restaurants.co.uk, Fax (020) 7940 1835, ≤, 綶 – ⇔ 24. **MC AE Ⓞ VISA**   34 **ASV** c
closed 25 December and 1 January – **Rest** 30.00 (lunch) and dinner a la carte 42.00/65.00 ℒ ☕.
◆ Elegant and stylish room commanding spectacular views of the Thames and Tower Bridge. Formal and detailed service. Modern menu with an informal bar attached.

XX **Bengal Clipper,** Cardamom Building, Shad Thames, Butlers Wharf, SE1 2YR ⊖ *London Bridge,* ℘ (020) 7357 9001, mail@bengalclipper.co.uk, Fax (020) 7357 9002 – ▤. **MC AE VISA**   34 **ASV** e
Rest - Indian - 27.00 (dinner) and a la carte 12.50/27.40.
◆ Housed in a Thames-side converted warehouse, a smart Indian restaurant with original brickwork and steel supports. Menu features Bengali and Goan dishes. Evening pianist.

X **Blueprint Café,** Design Museum, Shad Thames, Butlers Wharf, SE1 2YD ⊖ *London Bridge,* ℘ (020) 7378 7031, Fax (020) 7357 8810, ≤ Tower Bridge – **MC AE Ⓞ VISA**   34 **ASV** u
closed 25-26 December, 1 January and Sunday dinner – **Rest** a la carte 24.00/39.00 ℒ.
◆ Above the Design Museum, with impressive views of the river and bridge: handy binoculars on tables. Eager and energetic service, modern British menus: robust and rustic.

X **Village East,** 171 Bermondsey St, SE1 3UW ⊖ *London Bridge,* ℘ (020) 7357 6082, info@villageeast.co.uk, Fax (020) 7403 3360 – ✸ ▤ ⇔ 18. **MC AE Ⓞ VISA**   20 **XZE** a
Rest a la carte 24.00/36.20 ℒ.
◆ In a glass fronted block sandwiched between Georgian townhouses, this trendy restaurant has two loud, buzzy bars and dining areas serving ample portions of modern British fare.

X **Cantina Del Ponte,** 36c Shad Thames, Butlers Wharf, SE1 2YE ⊖ *London Bridge,* ℘ (020) 7403 5403, Fax (020) 7940 1845, ≤, 綶 – **MC AE Ⓞ VISA**   34 **ASV** c
closed 25-26 December – **Rest** - Italian - 13.50 and a la carte 23.50/32.00 ℒ.
◆ Quayside setting with a large canopied terrace. Terracotta flooring; modern rustic style décor, simple and unfussy. Tasty, refreshing Mediterranean-influenced cooking.

X **Butlers Wharf Chop House,** 36e Shad Thames, Butlers Wharf, SE1 2YE ⊖ *London Bridge*, ℘ (020) 7403 3403, bwchophouse@conran-restaurants.co.uk, Fax (020) 7940 1855, ≼ Tower Bridge, ✿ – ⓂⓈ ⒶⒺ ⓋⒾⓈⒶ
34 ASV n
closed 25-26 December, 1 January and Sunday dinner – **Rest** - English - 26.00 (lunch) and dinner a la carte 30.00/46.00 ℤ.
◆ Book the terrace in summer and dine in the shadow of Tower Bridge. Rustic feel to the interior, with obliging service. Menu focuses on traditional English dishes.

X **Champor-Champor,** 62-64 Weston St, SE1 3QJ ⊖ *London Bridge*, ℘ (020) 7403 4600, mail@champor-champor.com – ▣ ↻ 8. ⓂⓈ ⒶⒺ ⓋⒾⓈⒶ
34 ARV a
closed Easter, Christmas and Monday – **Rest** - Asian - (booking essential) (dinner only) 27.00/31.00.
◆ Brims over with colourful Asian décor and artefacts including serene Buddha and sacred cow. Two intimate dining rooms: tasty, appealing mix of Malay, Chinese and Thai cuisine.

🍴 **The Hartley,** 64 Tower Bridge Rd, SE1 4TR ⊖ *Borough*, ℘ (020) 7394 7023, enqui ries@thehartley.com – ⓂⓈ ⒶⒺ ⓪ ⓋⒾⓈⒶ
20 XZE c
closed Christmas, 27 December and 1 January – **Rest** a la carte 16.00/30.00 ℤ.
◆ Classic 19C red brick pub, named after former Hartley jam factory opposite: jam jars even adorn the walls! Interesting menus offer five daily changing blackboard specials.

Rotherhithe *Gtr London* – ✉ *SE16.*

🏨 **Hilton London Docklands,** 265 Rotherhithe St, Nelson Dock, SE16 5HW, ℘ (020) 7231 1001, sales-docklands@hilton.com, Fax (020) 7231 0599, ≼, ✿, ℔, ☎, ▢ – ▮ ⬆, ⇆ rm, ▤ ₰ ▣ – ▲ 350. ⓂⓈ ⒶⒺ ⓪ ⓋⒾⓈⒶ
7 GV r
closed 22-30 December – **Traders Bistro :** Rest (dinner only) 23.95 ℤ – ⇌ 14.95 – **361 rm** ✱112.00/194.00 – ✱✱112.00/194.00, 4 suites.
◆ Redbrick group hotel with glass façade. River-taxi from the hotel's own pier. Extensive leisure facilities. Standard size rooms with all mod cons. Eat on board Traders Bistro, a reconstructed galleon moored in dry dock.

Southwark *Gtr London* – ✉ *SE1.*

🏨 **Novotel London City South,** 53-61 Southwark Bridge Rd, SE1 9HH ⊖ *London Bridge*, ℘ (020) 7089 0400, h3269@accor.com, Fax (020) 7089 0410, ℔, ☎ – ▮, ⇆ rm, ▤ ✆ ₰ – ▲ 100. ⓂⓈ ⒶⒺ ⓪ ⓋⒾⓈⒶ
34 AQV c
The Garden Brasserie : Rest 19.50/25.00 and a la carte 16.70/31.85 ℤ – ⇌ 13.50 – **178 rm** ✱180.00/200.00 – ✱✱200.00/220.00, 4 suites.
◆ The new style of Novotel with good business facilities. Triple glazed bedrooms, furnished in the Scandinavian style with keyboard and high speed internet. Brasserie style dining room with windows all down one side.

🏨 **Southwark Rose,** 43-47 Southwark Bridge Rd, SE1 9HH ⊖ *London Bridge*, ℘ (020) 7015 1480, info@southwarkrosehotel.co.uk, Fax (020) 7015 1481 – ▮ ⇆ ▤ ✆ ₰ ▣ – ▲ 60. ⓂⓈ ⒶⒺ ⓋⒾⓈⒶ, ✢
34 AQV c
Rest (dinner only) a la carte 13.35/18.85 – ⇌ 12.95 – **78 rm** ✱170.00 – ✱✱170.00, 6 suites.
◆ Purpose built budget hotel south of the City, near the Globe Theatre. Top floor dining room with bar. Uniform style, reasonably spacious bedrooms with writing desks.

XXX **Oxo Tower,** (8th floor), Oxo Tower Wharf, Barge House St, SE1 9PH ⊖ *Southwark*, ℘ (020) 7803 3888, oxo.reservations@harveynichols.co.uk, Fax (020) 7803 3838, ≼ London skyline and River Thames, ✿ – ▮ ▤. ⓂⓈ ⒶⒺ ⓪ ⓋⒾⓈⒶ
32 ANV a
closed 24-26 December – **Rest** 29.50 (lunch) and dinner a la carte 42.00/56.75 ℤ ☙ – (see also *Oxo Tower Brasserie* below).
◆ Top of a converted factory, providing stunning views of the Thames and beyond. Stylish, minimalist interior with huge windows. Smooth service of modern cuisine.

XX **Roast,** The Floral Hall, Borough Market, SE1 1TL ⊖ *London Bridge*, ℘ (020) 7940 1300, info@roast-restaurant.com, Fax (020) 7940 1301 – ▮ ⇆ ▤. ⓂⓈ ⒶⒺ ⓋⒾⓈⒶ
33 AQV a
closed Sunday dinner and Bank Holidays – **Rest** - British - 21.00 (lunch) and a la carte 32.00/46.50 ▨ ☙ ℤ.
◆ Set into the roof of Borough Market's Floral Hall. Extensive cocktail list in bar; split-level restaurant has views to St. Paul's. Robust English cooking using market produce.

XX **Baltic,** 74 Blackfriars Rd, SE1 8HA ⊖ *Southwark*, ℘ (020) 7928 1111, info@balticrestaur ant.co.uk, Fax (020) 7928 8487 – ⓂⓈ ⒶⒺ ⓪ ⓋⒾⓈⒶ
33 AOV e
closed 25 December and 1 January – **Rest** - East European with Baltic influences - 13.50 (lunch) and a la carte 25.00/29.50 ℤ.
◆ Set in a Grade II listed 18C former coach house. Enjoy authentic and hearty east European and Baltic influenced food. Interesting vodka selection and live jazz on Sundays.

Oxo Tower Brasserie, (8th floor), Oxo Tower Wharf, Barge House St, SE1 9PH ⊖ Southwark, ✆ (020) 7803 3888, Fax (020) 7803 3838, ≤ London skyline and River Thames, 🈺 – 🛗 🗐. 🐠 🖭 ⑩ VISA 32 ANV a
closed 24-26 December – Rest 21.50 (lunch) and a la carte 31.50/42.25 ♈.
♦ Same views but less formal than the restaurant. Open-plan kitchen, relaxed service, the modern menu is slightly lighter. In summer, try to secure a table on the terrace.

Cantina Vinopolis, No.1 Bank End, SE1 9BU ⊖ London Bridge, ✆ (020) 7940 8333, cantina@vinopolis.co.uk, Fax (020) 7089 9339 – 🗐. 🐠 🖭 ⑩ VISA 33 AQV z
closed 24 December-2 January and Sunday – Rest 29.95 (lunch) and a la carte 22.35/36.90 ♈ ☺.
♦ Large, solid brick vaulted room under Victorian railway arches, with an adjacent wine museum. Modern menu with a huge selection of wines by the glass.

Tate Modern (Restaurant), 7th Floor, Tate Modern, Bankside, SE1 9LS ⊖ Southwark, ✆ (020) 7401 5020, modern.restaurant@tate.org.uk, ≤ London skyline and River Thames – 🐠 VISA 33 APV s
closed 25 December – Rest (lunch only and dinner Friday-Saturday) a la carte 21.15/30.85 ♈.
♦ Modernity to match the museum, with vast murals and huge windows affording stunning views. Canteen-style menu at a sensible price with obliging service.

Tapas Brindisa, 18-20 Southwark St, Borough Market, SE1 1TJ ⊖ London Bridge, ✆ (020) 7357 8880, office@tapasbrindisa.com. 🐠 VISA 33 AQV k
closed Sunday and Bank Holidays – Rest - Spanish (Tapas) - (bookings not accepted) a la carte 8.75/18.00.
♦ Primary quality Spanish produce sold in owner's shops and this bustling eatery on edge of Borough Market. Freshly prepared, tasty tapas: waiters will assist with your choice.

The Real Greek (Bankside), Units 1-2, Riverside House, 2A Southwark Bridge Rd, SE1 9HA ⊖ Southwark, ✆ (020) 7620 0162, bankside@therealgreek.com, Fax (020) 7620 0262, ≤, 🈺 – 🗐. 🐠 VISA 33 AQV s
Rest - Greek - a la carte 10.55/17.45.
♦ Overlooking the Thames, two minutes from Globe Theatre: a casual, modern restaurant with excellent value menus featuring totally authentic Greek dishes and beers.

Wright Brothers, 11 Stoney St, Borough Market, SE1 9AD ⊖ London Bridge, ✆ (020) 7403 9554, reservations@wrightbros.eu.com, Fax (020) 7403 9558 – 🍴. 🐠 🖭 VISA 33 AQV m
closed 25-26 December and Sunday – Rest - Oyster specialities - a la carte 23.00/43.00 ♈.
♦ Classic style oyster and porter house - a large number of porter ales on offer. Simple settings afford a welcoming ambience to enjoy huge range of oysters and prime shellfish.

Brew Wharf, Brew Wharf Yard, Stoney St, SE1 9AD ⊖ London Bridge, ✆ (020) 7378 6601, Fax (020) 7940 8336, 🈺 – 🗐. 🐠 🖭 ⑩ VISA 33 AQV h
closed Christmas-New Year – Rest a la carte 19.45/29.00 ♈.
♦ Bustling market eatery and micro-brewery housed in three huge railway arches. The beers and concise wine list are the reasons most people come here; menus are quite simple.

The Anchor and Hope, 36 The Cut, SE1 8LP ⊖ Southwark, ✆ (020) 7928 9898, Fax (020) 7928 4595 – 🐠🕑
32 ANV n
closed Christmas-New Year and Bank Holidays – Rest (closed Sunday and Monday lunch) (bookings not accepted) a la carte 18.00/35.00 ♈.
♦ Close to Waterloo, the distinctive dark green exterior lures visitors in droves. Bare floorboards, simple wooden furniture. Seriously original cooking with rustic French base.

SUTTON Gtr London.

Sutton Surrey – ✉ Surrey.

🏌, 🏌 Oak Sports Centre, Woodmansterne Rd, Carshalton ✆ (020) 8643 8363.

Holiday Inn, Gibson Rd, SM1 2RF, ✆ (0870) 4009113, Fax (020) 8770 1995, 🛋, ⇌, 🗐 – 🛗, 🍴 rm, 🗐 🖐 🖭. 🔏 180. 🐠 🖭 ⑩ VISA. 🛠 6 DZ a
Rest (dinner only) 20.00/35.00 s. and a la carte 19.50/34.25 – ☑ 14.95 – 115 rm ✚60.00/160.00 – ✚✚60.00/160.00, 1 suite.
♦ Centrally located and modern. Offers comprehensive conference facilities. Spacious and well-equipped bedrooms. An ideal base for both corporate and leisure guests. Bright, modern, relaxed bar and restaurant.

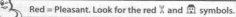
Red = Pleasant. Look for the red 🍴 and 🏨 symbols.

TOWER HAMLETS *Gtr London.*

Canary Wharf *Gtr London –* ⊠ *E14.*

Four Seasons, Westferry Circus, E14 8RS ⊖ *Canary Wharf*, ℰ (020) 7510 1999, *sales.caw@fourseasons.com, Fax (020) 7510 1998,* ≼, ₤₅, ≋, ⊠ – ﹖ ⚡ ⊨ ⚫ ⇔,
⚴ 200. ⑩⑧ AE ⑩ VISA
3 GV a
Rest – (see *Quadrato* below) – ⚏ 21.50 – **128 rm** ⚛388.00/447.00 – ⚛⚛408.00/467.00,
14 suites.
* Sleek and stylish with striking river and city views. Atrium lobby leading to modern bedrooms boasting every conceivable extra. Detailed service.

Circus Apartments without rest., 39 Westferry Circus, E14 8RW ⊖ *Canary Wharf*,
ℰ (020) 7719 7000, *res@circusapartments.co.uk, Fax (020) 7719 7001 –* ﹖ ⚡ ⊨ ⚫ ⇔.
⑩⑧ AE ⑩ VISA. ⚘
7 GV a
⚏ 7.50, **45 suites** 229.00/276.00.
* Smart, contemporary, fully serviced apartment block close to Canary Wharf: rooms, comfortable and spacious, can be taken from one day to one year.

Plateau (Restaurant), Canada Place, Canada Square, E14 5ER ⊖ *Canary Wharf*,
ℰ (020) 7715 7122, *Fax (020) 7715 7110 –* ﹖ ⊨ ⇔ 24. ⑩⑧ AE ⑩ VISA
3 GV n
closed Sunday – **Rest** 24.75 (dinner) and a la carte 27.00/37.00.
* Fourth floor restaurant overlooking Canada Square and The Big Blue art installation. Glass-sided kitchen; well-spaced, uncluttered tables. Modern menus with classical base.

Ubon by Nobu, 34 Westferry Circus, E14 8RR ⊖ *Canary Wharf*, ℰ (020) 7719 7800, *ubon@noburestaurants.com, Fax (020) 7719 7801,* ≼ River Thames and city skyline – ﹖ ⊨
P, ⑩⑧ AE ⑩ VISA
7 GV a
closed 25-26 and 31 December, 1 January, Saturday lunch, Sunday and Bank Holidays –
Rest - Japanese - 55.00/90.00 and a la carte 35.00/50.50 ⚹.
* Light, airy, open-plan restaurant, with floor to ceiling glass and great Thames views. Informal atmosphere. Large menu with wide selection of modern Japanese dishes.

Quadrato (at Four Seasons H.), Westferry Circus, E14 8RS ⊖ *Canary Wharf*, ℰ (020) 7510
1999, *Fax (020) 7510 1998,* ⚞ – ⊨ ⇔. ⑩⑧ AE ⑩ VISA
3 GV a
Rest - Italian - a la carte 34.00/50.00 ⚹.
* Striking, modern restaurant with terrace overlooking river. Sleek, stylish dining room with glass-fronted open-plan kitchen. Menu of northern Italian dishes; swift service.

Plateau (Grill), Canada Place, Canada Square, E14 5ER ⊖ *Canary Wharf*, ℰ (020) 7715
7000, *Fax (020) 7715 7110 –* ﹖ ⊨. ⑩⑧ AE ⑩ VISA
3 GV n
closed 25 December, 1 January and Sunday dinner – **Rest** 20.00/24.75 and a la carte
27.00/37.00.
* Situated on fourth floor of 21C building; adjacent to Plateau Restaurant, with simpler table settings. Classical dishes, with seasonal base, employing grill specialities.

The Gun, 27 Coldharbour, E14 9NS ⊖ *Blackwall (DLR),* ℰ (020) 7515 5222, *info@thegun docklands.com, Fax (020) 7515 4407,* ⚞ – ⑩⑧ AE VISA. ⚘
7 GV x
closed 26 December – **Rest** a la carte 22.00/35.00 ⚹.
* Restored historic pub with a terrace facing the Dome: tasty dishes, including Billingsgate market fish, balance bold simplicity and a bit of French finesse. Efficient service.

Spitalfields *Gtr London –* ⊠ *E1.*

Les Trois Garcons, 1 Club Row, E1 6JX ⊖ *Shoreditch,* ℰ (020) 7631 1924, *info@les troisgarcons.com, Fax (020) 7012 1236 –* ⊨ ⇔ 10. ⑩⑧ AE ⑩ VISA
20 XZD r
closed Sunday – **Rest** (dinner only) 28.00 (Monday and Wednesday) and a la carte
34.00/44.00 ⚹.
* Extraordinarily eccentric, with stuffed animals, twinkling beads, assorted chandeliers and ceiling handbags. The cooking? Original and detailed, served by bow-tied staff.

Bengal Trader, 44 Artillery Lane, E1 7NA ⊖ *Liverpool Street,* ℰ (020) 7375 0072, *mail@bengalclipper.co.uk, Fax (020) 7247 1002 –* ⊨. ⑩⑧ AE VISA
34 AST x
Rest - Indian - a la carte 13.25/22.50.
* Contemporary Indian paintings feature in this stylish basement room beneath a ground floor bar. Menu provides ample choice of Indian dishes.

St John Bread and Wine, 94-96 Commercial St, E1 6LZ ⊖ *Shoreditch,* ℰ (020) 7251
0848, *reservations@stjohnbreadandwine.com, Fax (020) 7247 8924 –* ⊨. ⑩⑧ AE
VISA
20 XZD m
closed Christmas, Sunday dinner and Bank Holidays – **Rest** - British - a la carte 19.10/32.20.
* Very popular neighbourhood bakery providing wide variety of home-made breads. Appealing, intimate dining section: all day menus that offer continually changing dishes.

X **Canteen,** 2 Crispin Pl, E1 6DW ⊖ *Liverpool Street*, ℘ (0845) 6861122, *info@can teen.co.uk* – ⇔ ≣. **M© AE VISA**
34 AST **a**
closed 25 December – **Rest** - British - a la carte 16.50/29.00 ♀.
◆ All-glass modernist restaurant in 'new' Spitalfields. Sit on blond wood benches at communal refectory tables and enjoy well-sourced, well-priced classic British options.

Wapping *Gtr London* – ⊠ *E1.*

X **Wapping Food,** Wapping Wall, E1W 3ST ⊖ *Wapping*, ℘ (020) 7680 2080, *info@wap ping-wpt.com*, ☆ – **P. M© AE VISA**
20 YZE **n**
closed 24 December-3 January, Sunday dinner and Bank Holidays – **Rest** a la carte 23.75/33.00.
◆ Something a little unusual; a combination of restaurant and gallery in a converted hydraulic power station. Enjoy the modern menu surrounded by turbines and TV screens.

Whitechapel *Gtr London* – ⊠ *E1.*

XX **Cafe Spice Namaste,** 16 Prescot St, E1 8AZ ⊖ *Tower Hill*, ℘ (020) 7488 9242, *info@ca fespice.co.uk*, Fax (020) 7481 0508 – ≣. **M© AE ① VISA**
34 ASU **z**
closed Christmas-New Year, Saturday lunch, Sunday and Bank Holidays – **Rest** - Indian - a la carte 22.25/33.70 ♀.
◆ A riot of colour from the brightly painted walls to the flowing drapes. Sweet-natured service adds to the engaging feel. Fragrant and competitively priced Indian cooking.

The ✿ award is the crème de la crème.
This is awarded to restaurants
which are really worth travelling miles for!

WANDSWORTH *Gtr London.*

Battersea *Gtr London* – ⊠ *SW8/SW11/SW18.*

🏨 **Express by Holiday Inn** without rest., Smugglers Way, SW18 1EG, ℘ (0870) 7201298, *wandsworth@morethanhotels.com*, Fax (0870) 7201299 – 🛗 ⇔ ≣ ℆ ㄟ. **P** – ♨ 35. **M© AE ① VISA**
22 OZH **a**
148 rm ✿79.00/109.00 – ✿✿79.00/109.00.
◆ Modern, purpose-built hotel on major roundabout, very much designed for the cost-conscious business guest or traveller. Adjacent steak house. Sizeable, well-kept bedrooms.

XX **The Food Room,** 123 Queenstown Rd, SW8 3RH, ℘ (020) 7622 0555, *info@thefood room.com*, Fax (020) 7627 5440 – ≣. **M© VISA**
24 RZH **c**
closed 1-3 January, 25-26 December, Sunday and Monday – **Rest** - French - (dinner only) 26.50.
◆ Attractive eatery with a relaxed feel and attentive service. Concise French/Mediterranean menus with Italian and North African flavours, utilising very good quality produce.

XX **Chada,** 208-210 Battersea Park Rd, SW11 4ND, ℘ (020) 7622 2209, *enquiry@chada thai.com*, Fax (020) 7924 2178 – ≣. **M© AE ① VISA**
23 QZH **x**
closed Sunday and Bank Holidays – **Rest** - Thai - (dinner only) a la carte 15.90/36.90 ♀.
◆ Weather notwithstanding, the Thai ornaments and charming staff in traditional silk costumes transport you to Bangkok. Carefully prepared and authentic dishes.

X **Ransome's Dock,** 35-37 Parkgate Rd, SW11 4NP, ℘ (020) 7223 1611, *chef@ransom esdock.co.uk*, Fax (020) 7924 2614, ☆ – **M© AE ① VISA**
23 QZG **c**
closed Christmas, August Bank Holiday and Sunday dinner – **Rest** a la carte 21.00/42.00 ♀ ♨.
◆ Secreted in a warehouse development, with a dock-side terrace in summer. Vivid blue interior, crowded with pictures. Chef patron produces reliable brasserie-style cuisine.

X **The Butcher & Grill,** 39-41 Parkgate Rd, SW11 4NP, ℘ (020) 7924 3999, *info@the butcherandgrill.com*, Fax (020) 7223 7977, ☆ – ⇔ . **M© AE VISA**
23 QZG **c**
closed 25-26 December, 1 January and Sunday dinner – **Rest** a la carte 21.45/47.50 ♀.
◆ Shop at the master butcher for prime cuts, or dine at former riverside warehouse with rear terrace. Industrial interior matched by hearty, traditional, unfussy meat dishes.

🍺 **The Greyhound,** 136 Battersea High St, SW11 3JR, ℘ (020) 7978 7021, *eat@thegrey houndatbattersea.co.uk*, Fax (020) 7978 0599, ☆ – ⇔ ⇔ 25. **M© VISA**
27 PZH **a**
closed Christmas and New Year – **Rest** (closed Sunday dinner and Monday) 27.00/31.00 (dinner) and lunch a la carte 14.00/16.00 ♀ ♨.
◆ Attractive tile-and-glass fronted pub with superb wine list and range of beers. Leather pouffes in stylish bar. Cosy restaurant serves concise, organically inspired menus.

Putney – ⊠ SW15.

XX Enoteca Turi, 28 Putney High St, SW15 1SQ ⊖ *Putney Bridge*, ℰ (020) 8785 4449, Fax (020) 8780 5409 – ▦. 🍴 AE ① VISA
22 MZH n
closed 25-26 December, 1 January and Sunday – **Rest** - Italian - 16.50 (lunch) and a la carte 24.30/36.30 ♀.
◆ A friendly neighbourhood Italian restaurant, overseen by the owner. Rustic cooking, with daily changing specials. Good selection of wine by the glass.

XX L'Auberge, 22 Upper Richmond Rd, SW15 2RX, ℰ (020) 8874 3593 – ✳⇨. 🍴 VISA
6 DX r
closed 1-15 January, 2 weeks August, Sunday and Monday – **Rest** - French - (dinner only) a la carte 23.00/30.00.
◆ Locally renowned neighbourhood restaurant. Art Nouveau prints of famous Champagne houses set tone for frequently changing, authentic French dishes; personable service assured.

X The Phoenix, Pentlow St, SW15 1LY, ℰ (020) 8780 3131, thephoenix@sonnys.co.uk, Fax (020) 8780 1114, 余 – ▦. 🍴 AE VISA
21 LZH s
closed 25-26 December and Bank Holidays – **Rest** - Italian influences - 15.50 (lunch) and a la carte 23.00/29.50 ♀.
◆ Light and bright interior with French windows leading out on to a spacious terrace. Unfussy and considerate service. An eclectic element to the modern Mediterranean menu.

⑩ The Spencer Arms, 237 Lower Richmond Rd, SW15 1HJ, ℰ (020) 8788 0640, Fax (020) 8780 0816 – ▦. 🍴 VISA
21 LZH v
closed 25-26 December – **Rest** a la carte 20.00/27.50.
◆ Attractive Victorian corner pub on Putney Common. Library area with books, games and leather sofas. Rustic bar/restaurant serves concise, seasonal, daily changing menus.

Southfields *Gtr London* – ⊠ SW18.

XX Sarkhel's, 199 Replingham Rd, SW18 5LY ⊖ *Southfields*, ℰ (020) 8870 1483, info@sar khels.co.uk – ▦. 🍴 VISA
6 DX e

closed 25-26 December and Monday – **Rest** - Indian - 9.95 (lunch) and a la carte 12.70/23.40 ♀.
◆ Recently expanded Indian restaurant with a large local following. Authentic, carefully prepared and well-priced dishes from many different Indian regions. Obliging service.

Tooting *Gtr London* – ⊠ SW17.

X Kastoori, 188 Upper Tooting Rd, SW17 7EJ ⊖ *Tooting Bec*, ℰ (020) 8767 7027 – ▦. 🍴 VISA
6 EX v
closed 25-26 December and lunch Monday and Tuesday – **Rest** - Indian Vegetarian - a la carte 12.75/15.50.
◆ Specialising in Indian vegetarian cooking with a subtle East African influence. Family-run for many years, a warm and welcoming establishment with helpful service.

X Oh Boy, 843 Garratt Lane, SW17 0PG ⊖ *Broadway*, ℰ (020) 8947 9760, Fax (020) 8879 7867 – ▦. 🍴 AE ① VISA
6 EX c
closed 1 week Christmas and Monday – **Rest** - Thai - (dinner only) a la carte 13.50/19.00.
◆ Long-standing neighbourhood Thai restaurant. Extensive menu offers authentic and carefully prepared dishes, in simple but friendly surroundings.

Wandsworth *Gtr London* – ⊠ SW17/SW18.

XX Chez Bruce (Poole), 2 Bellevue Rd, SW17 7EG ⊖ *Tooting Bec*, ℰ (020) 8672 0114, enqui ries@chezbruce.co.uk, Fax (020) 8767 6648 – ✳⇨ ▦. 🍴 AE ① VISA
6 EX e
❀ *closed 24-26 December and 1 January* – **Rest** (booking essential) 23.50/37.50 ♀ ⌂.
Spec. Tuna ceviche with prawn tempura, pine nuts and coriander. Roast pigeon with foie gras, Savoy cabbage and caramelised onions. Cherry and almond croustade with almond ice cream.
◆ An ever-popular restaurant, overlooking the Common. Simple yet considered modern British cooking. Convivial and informal, with enthusiastic service.

XX Amici, 35 Bellevue Rd, SW17 7EF ⊖ *Balham*, ℰ (020) 8672 5888, info@amiciitalian.co.uk, Fax (020) 8672 8856, 余 – ✳⇨ ▦. 🍴 AE ① VISA
6 EX u
closed 25-28 December – **Rest** - Italian - a la carte 18.75/26.00 ♀.
◆ Ornate Georgian exterior; inside is a restaurant with rich wood panelling and leather chairs. Valentina Harris a consultant on clean, unfussy and spot-on Italian cooking.

X Ditto, 55-57 East Hill, SW18 2QE, ℰ (020) 8877 0110, will@doditto.co.uk, Fax (020) 8875 0110 – ⇔ 20. 🍴 AE VISA
6 EX z
Rest a la carte 17.00/27.50 ♀.
◆ Beware: it's easy to drive past this sofa-strewn, laid-back but lively bar and restaurant. A clever, flexible menu merges Spanish, Italian and French elements.with success.

WESTMINSTER (City of) *Gtr London.*

Bayswater and Maida Vale *Gtr London –* ⊠ *NW6/W2/W9.*

Hilton London Paddington, 146 Praed St, W2 1EE ⊖ *Paddington,* ℰ *(020) 7850 0500, sales.paddington@hilton.com, Fax (020) 7850 0600,* ₤₆, ⇔s – |♯|, ⇖ rm, ≡ ⚓ ₺ – ᴁ 350. ◍◑ ᴀᴇ ◑ ᴠᴵˢᴬ. ⅌
28 ADU a
The Brasserie : Rest a la carte 20.00/54.00 ⅌ – � 19.95 – **344 rm** ★140.00/311.00 – ★★140.00/311.00, 20 suites.
◆ Early Victorian railway hotel, sympathetically restored in contemporary style with Art Deco details. Co-ordinated bedrooms with high tech facilities continue the modern style. Contemporarily styled brasserie offering a modern menu.

Hilton London Metropole, Edgware Rd, W2 1JU ⊖ *Edgware Road,* ℰ *(020) 7402 4141, cbs-londonmet@hilton.com, Fax (020) 7724 8866,* ≤, ₤₆, ⇔s, ⬚ – |♯|, ⇖ rm, ≡ ₺ ᴁ ᴘ – ᴁ 1600. ◍◑ ᴀᴇ ◑ ᴠᴵˢᴬ. ⅌
28 AET c
Nippon Tuk : Rest - South East Asian - a la carte 21.70/40.95 – *Fiamma :* Rest a la carte 17.00/28.20 – ⊆ 17.95 – **1033 rm** – ★★627.00/294.00, 25 suites.
◆ One of London's most popular convention venues by virtue of both its size and transport links. Well-appointed and modern rooms have state-of-the-art facilities. Vibrant Nippon Tuk. Italian favourites at Fiamma.

Royal Lancaster, Lancaster Terrace, W2 2TY ⊖ *Lancaster Gate,* ℰ *(020) 7262 6737, sales@royallancaster.com, Fax (020) 7724 3191,* ≤ – |♯| ⇖ ≡ ⚓ ₺ ᴘ – ᴁ 1200. ◍◑ ᴀᴇ ◑ ᴠᴵˢᴬ.
28 ADU e
Rest – (see *Island* and *Nipa* below) – ⊆ 19.00 – **394 rm** ★304.00 – ★★304.00, 22 suites.
◆ Imposing 1960s purpose-built hotel overlooking Hyde Park. Some of London's most extensive conference facilities. Well-equipped bedrooms are decorated in traditional style.

The Hempel ⚘, 31-35 Craven Hill Gdns, W2 3EA ⊖ *Queensway,* ℰ *(020) 7298 9000, hotel@the-hempel.co.uk, Fax (020) 7402 4666,* ⇝ – |♯| ≡ ⚓ ₺. ◍◑ ᴀᴇ ◑ ᴠᴵˢᴬ. ⅌
28 ACU a
closed Christmas – *I-Thai :* Rest - Italian-Japanese-Thai - (closed Sunday) a la carte 35.00/56.00 – ⊆ 15.00 – **37 rm** ★194.00/335.00 – ★★247.00/347.00, 4 suites.
◆ A striking example of minimalist design. Individually appointed bedrooms are understated yet very comfortable. Relaxed ambience. Modern basement restaurant.

Marriott, Plaza Parade, NW6 5RP ⊖ *Kilburn Park,* ℰ *(020) 7543 6000, mhrs.lonwh.reser vations@marriotthotels.com, Fax (020) 7543 2100,* ₤₆, ⇔s, ⬚ – |♯| ⇖ ≡ ⚓ ₺ ⇆ – ᴁ 200. ◍◑ ᴀᴇ ◑ ᴠᴵˢᴬ. ⅌
10 NZB c
Fratelli : Rest - Italian - (closed Sunday) (dinner only) 18.00 and a la carte 21.00/32.00 s. ⅌ – ⊆ 16.95 – **226 rm** ★99.00/149.00 – ★★99.00/149.00, 11 suites.
◆ A capacious hotel, away from the busier city centre streets. Well equipped with both business and leisure facilities including 12m pool. Suites have small kitchens. Informal restaurant and brasserie.

Colonnade Town House without rest., 2 Warrington Crescent, W9 1ER ⊖ *Warwick Avenue,* ℰ *(020) 7286 1052, rescolonnade@theetoncollection.com, Fax (020) 7286 1057 –* |♯| ⇖ ≡ ⚓. ◍◑ ᴀᴇ ◑ ᴠᴵˢᴬ.
17 OZD e
⊆ 15.00 – **43 rm** ★164.00/211.00 – ★★188.00/211.00.
◆ Two Victorian townhouses with comfortable well-furnished communal rooms decorated with fresh flowers. Stylish and comfortable bedrooms with many extra touches.

Commodore, 50 Lancaster Gate, Hyde Park, W2 3NA ⊖ *Lancaster Gate,* ℰ *(020) 7402 5291, reservations@commodore-hotel.com, Fax (020) 7262 1088,* ₤₆ – |♯|, ⇖ rm, ≡ ⚓. ◍◑ ᴀᴇ ◑ ᴠᴵˢᴬ. ⅌
28 ACU u
Rest (closed Sunday and Bank Holidays) (dinner only) a la carte 26.50/35.00 s. – ⊆ 7.50 – **77 rm** ★100.00/140.00 – ★★160.00/170.00, 2 suites.
◆ Three converted Georgian town houses in a leafy residential area. Bedrooms vary considerably in size and style. Largest rooms decorated with a Victorian theme. Relaxed, casual bistro.

Mornington without rest., 12 Lancaster Gate, W2 3LG ⊖ *Lancaster Gate,* ℰ *(020) 7262 7361, london@mornington.co.uk, Fax (020) 7706 1028 –* |♯| ⇖. ◍◑ ᴀᴇ ◑ ᴠᴵˢᴬ. ⅌
28 ACU s
closed Christmas – **66 rm** ⊆ ★125.00/140.00 – ★★150.00.
◆ The classic portico facade belies the cool and modern Scandinavian influenced interior. Modern bedrooms are well-equipped and generally spacious. Duplex rooms available.

New Linden without rest., 58-60 Leinster Sq, W2 4PS ⊖ *Bayswater,* ℰ *(020) 7221 4321, newlindenhotel@mayflower-group.co.uk, Fax (020) 7727 3156 –* |♯| ⇖ ᴛᴠ. ◍◑ ᴀᴇ ᴠᴵˢᴬ. ⅌
27 ABU e
⊆ 7.00 **46 rm** ★69.00/85.00 – ★★85.00/95.00.
◆ Smart four storey white stucco façade. Basement breakfast room with sunny aspect. Bedrooms are its strength: flat screen TVs and wooden floors; two split level family rooms.

Delmere, 130 Sussex Gdns, W2 1UB ⊖ *Paddington*, ☎ (020) 7706 3344, *delmereho tel@compuserve.com, Fax (020) 7262 1863* – |♦|, ⇔ rm, ☎. MC AE ① VISA. ✂ 28 ADT v
Rest *(closed August, Christmas, New Year and Sunday)* (dinner only) 16.00 and a la carte 15.00/29.50 – ☕ 9.00 – **38 rm** ★62.00/115.00 – ★★115.00/129.00.
◆ Attractive stucco fronted and porticoed Victorian property. Now a friendly private hotel. Compact bedrooms are both well-equipped and kept. Modest prices. Bright, relaxed restaurant and adjacent bar.

Miller's without rest., 111A Westbourne Grove (entrance on Hereford Rd), W2 4UW ⊖ *Bayswater*, ☎ (020) 7243 1024, *enquiries@millersuk.com, Fax (020) 7243 1064* – ☎. MC AE VISA. ✂ 27 ABU a
7 rm ☕ ★176.00/194.00 – ★★217.00/270.00.
◆ Victorian house brimming with antiques and knick-knacks. Charming sitting room provides the setting for a relaxed breakfast. Individual, theatrical rooms named after poets.

Jamuna, 38A Southwick St, W2 1JQ ⊖ *Edgware Road*, ☎ (020) 7723 5056, *info@jamuna.co.uk, Fax (020) 7706 1870* – ⇔ ▤. MC AE VISA 28 ADT x
closed 25-26 December, 1 January and Sunday – **Rest** - Indian - a la carte 23.45/42.95.
◆ Don't be put off by the unprepossessing nature of the area: this is a modern out of the ordinary Indian restaurant with cooking that's well presented, refined and flavoursome.

Island (at Royal Lancaster H.), Lancaster Terrace, W2 2TY ⊖ *Lancaster Gate*, ☎ (020) 7551 6070, *eat@islandrestaurant.co.uk, Fax (020) 7551 6071* – ▤. MC AE ① VISA 28 ADU e
Rest 21.00 (lunch) and a la carte 24.00/36.00 ♀.
◆ Modern, stylish restaurant with buzzy open kitchen. Full length windows allow good views of adjacent Hyde Park. Seasonally based, modern menus with wide range of dishes.

Yakitoria, 25 Sheldon Sq, W2 6EY ⊖ *Paddington*, ☎ (020) 3214 3000 – |♦| ⇔ ▤ ⇔ 60. MC AE VISA 28 ACT a
closed Christmas, Saturday lunch and Sunday – **Rest** - Japanese - a la carte 26.25/35.50 ♀.
◆ Funky, sleek interior accessible from platform 8 at Paddington. Appealing blend of old and new Japanese menus with a distinctive American edge. Bento boxes to take away.

Nipa (at Royal Lancaster H.), Lancaster Terrace, W2 2TY ⊖ *Lancaster Gate*, ☎ (020) 7262 6737, *Fax (020) 7724 3191* – ▤ P. MC AE ① VISA 28 ADU e
closed Saturday lunch, Sunday and Bank Holidays – **Rest** - Thai - 14.90/32.00 and a la carte 21.50/28.00 **s.**
◆ On the 1st floor and overlooking Hyde Park. Authentic and ornately decorated restaurant offers subtly spiced Thai cuisine. Keen to please staff in traditional silk costumes.

Assaggi (Sassu), 39 Chepstow Pl, (above Chepstow pub), W2 4TS ⊖ *Bayswater*, ☎ (020) 7792 5501, *nipi@assaggi.demon.co.uk* – ▤. MC ① VISA 27 AAU c
closed 2 weeks Christmas, Sunday and Bank Holidays – **Rest** - Italian - (booking essential) a la carte approx 36.70 ♀.
Spec. Pecorino con carpegna & rucola. Tagliolini alle erbe. Fegato di vitello.
◆ Polished wood flooring, tall windows and modern artwork provide the bright surroundings for this forever busy restaurant. Concise menu of robust Italian dishes.

Ginger, 115 Westbourne Grove, W2 4UP ⊖ *Bayswater*, ☎ (020) 7908 1990, *info@gingerrestaurant.co.uk, Fax (020) 7908 1991* – ▤. MC AE VISA 27 ABU v
closed 25 December – **Rest** - Bangladeshi - (dinner only and lunch Saturday and Sunday) a la carte 15.00/30.00.
◆ Bengali specialities served in contemporary styled dining room. True to its name, ginger is a key flavouring; dishes range from mild to spicy and are graded accordingly.

L'Accento, 16 Garway Rd, W2 4NH ⊖ *Bayswater*, ☎ (020) 7243 2201, *laccentorest@aol.com, Fax (020) 7243 2201* – MC AE VISA 27 ABU b
closed Sunday – **Rest** - Italian - 19.50 and a la carte 25.50/30.00.
◆ Rustic surroundings and provincial, well priced, Italian cooking. Menu specialises in tasty pasta, made on the premises, and shellfish. Rear conservatory for the summer.

Arturo, 23 Connaught St, W2 2AY ⊖ *Marble Arch*, ☎ (020) 7706 3388, *enquiries@arturorestaurant.co.uk, Fax (020) 7402 9195* – ▤. MC AE VISA 29 AFU a
closed Christmas, Easter and lunch Bank Holidays – **Rest** - Italian - 15.95 (lunch) and a la carte 15.95/27.00 ♀.
◆ On a smart street near Hyde Park: sleek, modish feel imbues interior with intimate, elegant informality. Tuscan and Sicilian dishes cooked with confidence and originality.

Prince Alfred & Formosa Dining Room, 5A Formosa St, W9 1EE ⊖ *Warwick Avenue*, ☎ (020) 7286 3287, *princealfred@youngs.co.uk, Fax (020) 7286 3383* – ▤. MC AE VISA 17 OZD n
Rest a la carte 18.50/30.50 ♀.
◆ Traditional pub appearance and a relaxed dining experience on offer behind the elegant main bar. Contemporary style of cooking.

The Waterway, 54 Formosa St, W9 2JU ⊖ *Warwick Avenue*, ℘ (020) 7266 3557, *info@thewaterway.co.uk*, ㍿, ⓦⓞ ⒜ⓔ ⓞ ⓥⓘⓢⓐ, ⅏
Rest a la carte 20.00/28.00 ℤ.
17 OZD p
◆ Pub with a thoroughly modern, metropolitan ambience. Spacious bar and large decked terrace overlooking canal. Concise, well-balanced menu served in open plan dining room.

Belgravia *Gtr London – ⊠ SW1.*

The Berkeley, Wilton Pl, SW1X 7RL ⊖ *Knightsbridge*, ℘ (020) 7235 6000, *info@theberkeley.co.uk*, Fax (020) 7235 4330, ⓦ, ⅛, ≘ₛ, ⊡ – ▯, ⅙≠ rm, ≡ ⓥ ⇔ – 益 250. ⓦⓞ ⒜ⓔ ⓞ ⓥⓘⓢⓐ. ⅏
37 AGX e
Boxwood Café (℘ (020) 7235 1010) : Rest a la carte 28.00/35.50 ℤ – (see also *Pétrus* below) – ⌣ 29.00 – **189 rm** ✱539.00 – ✱✱598.00, 25 suites.
◆ A gracious and discreet hotel. Relax in the gilded and panelled Lutyens lounge or enjoy a swim in the roof-top pool with its retracting roof. Opulent bedrooms. Split-level basement restaurant, divided by bar with modern stylish décor; New York-style dining.

The Lanesborough, Hyde Park Corner, SW1X 7TA ⊖ *Hyde Park Corner*, ℘ (020) 7259 5599, *info@lanesborough.com*, Fax (020) 7259 5606, ⅙ – ▯, ⅙≠ rm, ≡ ⓥ ⅘ ℙ – 益 90. ⓦⓞ ⒜ⓔ ⓞ ⓥⓘⓢⓐ
37 AGX a
The Conservatory : Rest 24.00/48.00 and a la carte 45.50/79.00 s. ℤ – ⌣ 28.00 – **86 rm** ✱370.00/511.00 – ✱✱511.00, 9 suites.
◆ Converted in the 1990s from 18C St George's Hospital. A grand and traditional atmosphere prevails. Butler service offered. Regency-era decorated, lavishly appointed rooms . Ornate, glass-roofed dining room with palm trees and fountains.

The Halkin, 5 Halkin St, SW1X 7DJ ⊖ *Hyde Park Corner*, ℘ (020) 7333 1000, *res@halkin.como.bz*, Fax (020) 7333 1100 – ▯ ≡ ⓥ ⓦⓞ ⒜ⓔ ⓞ ⓥⓘⓢⓐ. ⅏
38 AHX b
closed 25-26 December and 1 January – Rest – (see *Nahm* below) – ⌣ 25.00 – **35 rm** ✱288.00/411.00 – ✱✱370.00/500.00, 6 suites.
◆ One of London's first minimalist hotels. The cool, marbled reception and bar have an understated charm. Spacious rooms have every conceivable facility.

Sheraton Belgravia, 20 Chesham Pl, SW1X 8HQ ⊖ *Knightsbridge*, ℘ (020) 7235 6040, *reservations.sheratonbelgravia@sheraton.com*, Fax (020) 7259 6243 – ▯, ⅙≠ rm, ≡ ⓥ ⅘ ℙ – 益 25. ⓦⓞ ⒜ⓔ ⓞ ⓥⓘⓢⓐ. ⅏
37 AGX u
The Dining Room : Rest 20.00 (lunch) and a la carte 24.00/33.00 ℤ – ⌣ 19.50 – **82 rm** ✱199.00/329.00 – ✱✱247.00/376.00, 7 suites.
◆ Modern corporate hotel overlooking Chesham Place. Comfortable and well-equipped for the tourist and business traveller alike. A few minutes' walk from Harrods. Modern, international menus.

Jumeirah Lowndes, 21 Lowndes St, SW1X 9ES ⊖ *Knightsbridge*, ℘ (020) 7823 1234, *jutinto@jumeirah.com*, Fax (020) 7235 1154, ㍿ – ▯, ⅙≠ rm, ≡ ⓥ ℙ – 益 25. ⓦⓞ ⒜ⓔ ⓞ ⓥⓘⓢⓐ
37 AGX h
Mimosa : Rest a la carte ℤ – ⌣ 23.50 – **86 rm** ✱382.00 – ✱✱382.00, 1 suite.
◆ Compact yet friendly modern corporate hotel within this exclusive residential area. Good levels of personal service offered. Close to the famous shops of Knightsbridge. Modern restaurant opens onto street terrace.

Diplomat without rest., 2 Chesham St, SW1X 8DT ⊖ *Sloane Square*, ℘ (020) 7235 1544, *diplomat.hotel@btinternet.com*, Fax (020) 7259 6153 – ▯, ⓦⓞ ⒜ⓔ ⓞ ⓥⓘⓢⓐ. ⅏
37 AGY a
26 rm ⌣ ✱95.00/115.00 – ✱✱175.00.
◆ Imposing Victorian corner house built in 1882 by Thomas Cubitt. Attractive glass-domed stairwell and sweeping staircase. Spacious and well-appointed bedrooms.

%%%% **Pétrus** (Wareing) (at The Berkeley H.), Wilton Pl, SW1X 7RL ⊖ *Knightsbridge*, ℘ (020) 7235
❀❀ 1200, *petrus@marcuswareing.com*, Fax (020) 7235 1266 – ⅙≠ ≡ ✿ 12. ⓦⓞ ⒜ⓔ ⓞ ⓥⓘⓢⓐ
37 AGX e
closed 1 week Christmas, Sunday, Saturday lunch and Bank Holidays – Rest 30.00/80.00 ℤ ⍊.
Spec. Roast veal sweetbread with garden peas and black olives. Braised turbot with wild asparagus, poached quail egg and caviar. Peanut parfait with rice crisp crunch and chocolate mousse.
◆ Elegantly appointed restaurant named after one of the 40 Pétrus vintages on the wine list. One table in the kitchen to watch the chefs at work. Accomplished modern cooking.

%%% **Amaya,** Halkin Arcade, 19 Motcomb St, SW1X 8JT ⊖ *Knightsbridge*, ℘ (020) 7823 1166,
❀ *info@realindianfood.com*, Fax (020) 7259 6464 – ≡ ✿ 14. ⓦⓞ ⒜ⓔ ⓞ ⓥⓘⓢⓐ
37 AGX k
Rest - Indian - 26.75 (lunch) and a la carte 30.25/50.25.
Spec. Punjabi chicken wing "lollipops" with chilli, lime and cinnamon. Tandoori tiger prawn, scallops in herb sauce and grilled oyster. Grilled lamb chops with ginger, lime and coriander.
◆ Light, piquant and aromatic Indian cooking specialising in kebabs from a tawa skillet, sigri grill or tandoor oven. Chic comfortable surroundings, modern and subtly exotic.

XXX ❀ **Zafferano,** 15 Lowndes St, SW1X 9EY ⊖ *Knightsbridge,* ℰ (020) 7235 5800, Fax (020) 7235 1971 – ✕✕ 🍽 ✧ 20. 🆗❸ 🆎 ① 𝚟𝙸𝚂𝙰   37 AGX f
closed Christmas-New Year – **Rest** - Italian - 34.50/49.50 ∑ ☆.
Spec. Scallops in saffron vinaigrette. Veal shank ravioli in saffron. Chargrilled monkfish with courgettes and sweet chilli.
◆ Forever busy and relaxed. No frills, robust and gutsy Italian cooking, where the quality of the produce shines through. Wholly Italian wine list has some hidden treasures.

XX ❀ **Nahm** (at The Halkin H.), 5 Halkin St, SW1X 7DJ ⊖ *Hyde Park Corner,* ℰ (020) 7333 1234, Fax (020) 7333 1100 – 🍽 ✧ 30. 🆗❸ 🆎 ① 𝚟𝙸𝚂𝙰   38 AHX b
closed lunch Saturday and Sunday and Bank Holidays – **Rest** - Thai - (booking essential) 26.00/49.50 and a la carte 36.50/42.50 ∑.
Spec. Red curry of minced quail with ginger and Thai basil. Crunchy prawn cake salad with green mango. Lychees, mangosteens and rambutans in perfumed syrup.
◆ Teak furniture and honey-coloured walls add up to sleek, understated decor. Menu offers the best of Thai cooking with modern interpretations and original use of ingredients.

XX **Mango Tree,** 46 Grosvenor Pl, SW1X 7EQ ⊖ *Victoria,* ℰ (020) 7823 1888, *info@mango tree.org.uk,* Fax (020) 7838 9275 – 🍽 . 🆗❸ 🆎 ① 𝚟𝙸𝚂𝙰   38 AHX a
closed 25 December, 1 January and Saturday lunch – **Rest** - Thai - a la carte 25.00/40.00 ☷ ∑.
◆ Thai staff in regional dress in contemporarily styled dining room of refined yet minimalist furnishings sums up the cuisine: authentic Thai dishes with modern presentation.

XX **Noura Brasserie,** 16 Hobart Pl, SW1W 0HH ⊖ *Victoria,* ℰ (020) 7235 9444, *noura@noura.co.uk,* Fax (020) 7235 9244 – 🍽 . 🆗❸ 🆎 ① 𝚟𝙸𝚂𝙰   38 AHX n
Rest - Lebanese - 16.50/38.00 and a la carte approx 23.00/33.00.
◆ Dine in either the bright bar or the comfortable, contemporary restaurant. Authentic, modern Lebanese cooking specialises in char-grilled meats and mezzes.

Hyde Park and Knightsbridge *Gtr London –* ⊠ *SW1/SW7.*

🏨🏨 **Mandarin Oriental Hyde Park,** 66 Knightsbridge, SW1X 7LA ⊖ *Knightsbridge,* ℰ (020) 7235 2000, *molon-info@mohg.com,* Fax (020) 7235 2001, ≤, ⓥ, 𝐼₅, ⟲ – 📶, ✕✕ rm, 🍽 ✆ ੬ – 🔬 220. 🆗❸ 🆎 ① 𝚟𝙸𝚂𝙰   37 AGX x
The Park: **Rest** 33.00 (lunch) and a la carte 20.00/47.00 – (see also **Foliage** below) – ☷ 26.00 – **177 rm** ✦464.00/488.00 – ✦✦587.00/617.00, 23 suites.
◆ Built in 1889 this classic hotel, with striking façade, remains one of London's grandest. Many of the luxurious bedrooms enjoy Park views. Immaculate and detailed service. Smart ambience in The Park.

🏨 **Knightsbridge Green** without rest., 159 Knightsbridge, SW1X 7PD ⊖ *Knightsbridge,* ℰ (020) 7584 6274, *reservations@thekghotel.com,* Fax (020) 7225 1635 – 📶 ✕✕ 🍽 🆗❸ 🆎 ① 𝚟𝙸𝚂𝙰 . ✆   37 AFX z
closed Christmas – – ☷ 12.00 – **16 rm** ✦105.00/160.00 – ✦✦145.00/170.00, 12 suites.
◆ Privately owned hotel, boasting peaceful sitting room with writing desk. Breakfast - sausage and bacon from Harrods! - served in the generously proportioned bedrooms.

XXX ❀ **Foliage** (at Mandarin Oriental Hyde Park H.), 66 Knightsbridge, SW1X 7LA ⊖ *Knightsbridge,* ℰ (020) 7201 3723, Fax (020) 7201 4552 – 🍽 . 🆗❸ 🆎 ① 𝚟𝙸𝚂𝙰   37 AGX x
Rest 25.00 (lunch) and a la carte 47.50/50.00 ∑.
Spec. Smoked belly of ham, date marmalade, black pudding and cauliflower cream. Roast loin of venison, wild mushrooms and smoked artichoke purée. Pumpkin treacle tart with pecans and orange marmalade mousse.
◆ Reached via a glass-enclosed walkway that houses the cellar. Hyde Park outside the window reflected in the foliage-themed décor. Gracious service, skilled modern cooking.

XX **Zuma,** 5 Raphael St, SW7 1DL ⊖ *Knightsbridge,* ℰ (020) 7584 1010, *info@zumarestaur ant.com,* Fax (020) 7584 5005 – 🍽 . 🆗❸ 🆎 𝚟𝙸𝚂𝙰   37 AFX m
Rest - Japanese - a la carte 35.00/55.00 ∑.
◆ Strong modern feel with exposed pipes, modern lighting and granite flooring. A theatrical atmosphere around the Sushi bar and a varied and interesting modern Japanese menu.

XX **Mr Chow,** 151 Knightsbridge, SW1X 7PA ⊖ *Knightsbridge,* ℰ (020) 7589 7347, *mrchow@aol.com,* Fax (020) 7584 5780 – 🍽 . 🆗❸ 🆎 ① 𝚟𝙸𝚂𝙰   37 AFX e
closed 24-26 December, 1 January and Easter Monday – **Rest** - Chinese - 26.00 (lunch) and a la carte 35.50/44.50 ∑.
◆ Cosmopolitan Chinese restaurant with branches in New York and L.A. Well established ambience. Walls covered with mirrors and modern art. House specialities worth opting for.

Mayfair *Gtr London –* ✉ *W1.*

Dorchester, Park Lane, W1A 2HJ ⊖ *Hyde Park Corner,* ℰ (020) 7629 8888, *info@the dorchester.com, Fax (020) 7409 0114,* 🌮, ㎘, ≋ – 🛗, ⤢ rm, 🖥 ✆ & ⇦ – 🔬 500. ⬤⬤ ⒶⒺ ⓪ 𝒱𝐼𝑆𝐴, ✺
30 AHV **a**
The Grill : Rest 27.50 and a la carte 40.00/80.00 – (see also **China Tang** below) – ⌚ 28.00 –
200 rm ✸423.00 – ✸✸617.00, 49 suites.
♦ A sumptuously decorated, luxury hotel offering every possible facility. Impressive marbled and pillared promenade. Rooms quintessentially English in style. Faultless service.

Claridge's, Brook St, W1A 2JQ ⊖ *Bond Street,* ℰ (020) 7629 8860, *info@claridges.co.uk, Fax (020) 7499 2210,* ㎘ – 🛗, ⤢ rm, 🖥 ✆ & – 🔬 200. ⬤⬤ ⒶⒺ ⓪ 𝒱𝐼𝑆𝐴, ✺ 30 AHU **c**
Rest 32.50/35.00 and a la carte 47.50/73.50 ⒵ – (see also **Gordon Ramsay at Claridge's**
below) – ⌚ 27.00 – **143 rm** ✸480.00/562.00 – ✸✸598.00/621.00, 60 suites.
♦ The epitome of English grandeur, celebrated for its Art Deco. Exceptionally well-appointed and sumptuous bedrooms, all with butler service. Magnificently restored foyer. Relaxed, elegant restaurant.

Grosvenor House, Park Lane, W1K 7TN ⊖ *Marble Arch,* ℰ (020) 7499 6363, *grosvenor.house@marriotthotels.com, Fax (020) 7493 3341,* ㎘, ≋, ◻ – 🛗, ⤢ rm, 🖥 ✆ & ⇦
– 🔬 1500. ⬤⬤ ⒶⒺ ⓪ 𝒱𝐼𝑆𝐴, ✺
29 AGU **a**
La Terrazza : Rest - Italian influences - 25.50 and a la carte 27.00/44.50 ⒵ – ⌚ 21.50 –
378 rm ✸282.00/317.00 – ✸✸282.00/317.00, 74 suites.
♦ Over 70 years old and occupying an enviable position by the Park. Edwardian-style décor. The Great Room, an ice rink in the 1920s, is Europe's largest banqueting room. Bright, relaxing dining room with contemporary feel.

Four Seasons, Hamilton Pl, Park Lane, W1A 1AZ ⊖ *Hyde Park Corner,* ℰ (020) 7499 0888, *fsh.london@fourseasons.com, Fax (020) 7493 1895,* ㎘ – 🛗, ⤢ rm, 🖥 ✆ & ⇦ –
🔬 400. ⬤⬤ ⒶⒺ ⓪ 𝒱𝐼𝑆𝐴, ✺
30 AHV **b**
Lanes : Rest 28.00/38.00 and a la carte 46.50/68.00 s. ⒵ – ⌚ 24.50 – **193 rm**
✸394.00/429.00 – ✸✸458.00, 26 suites.
♦ Set back from Park Lane so shielded from the traffic. Large, marbled lobby; its lounge a popular spot for light meals. Spacious rooms, some with their own conservatory. Restaurant's vivid blue and stained glass give modern yet relaxing feel.

Le Meridien Piccadilly, 21 Piccadilly, W1J 0BH ⊖ *Piccadilly Circus,* ℰ (020) 7734 8000, *piccadilly.sales@lemeridien.com, Fax (020) 7437 3574,* 🌮, ㎘, ≋, ◻, squash – 🛗, ⤢ rm, 🖥 ✆ & – 🔬 250. ⬤⬤ ⒶⒺ ⓪ 𝒱𝐼𝑆𝐴, ✺
31 AJV **a**
Terrace : Rest a la carte 33.50/37.50 – ⌚ 22.50 – **248 rm** ✸364.00 – ✸✸364.00/411.00,
18 suites.
♦ Comfortable international hotel, in a central location. Boasts one of the finest leisure clubs in London. Individually decorated bedrooms with first class facilities. Modern cuisine in comfortable surroundings.

London Hilton, 22 Park Lane, W1K 1BE ⊖ *Hyde Park Corner,* ℰ (020) 7493 8000, *reservations.parklane@hilton.com, Fax (020) 7208 4142,* ≼ London, ㎘, ≋ – 🛗, ⤢ rm, 🖥 ✆ &
– 🔬 1000. ⬤⬤ ⒶⒺ ⓪ 𝒱𝐼𝑆𝐴, ✺
30 AHV **e**
Trader Vics (ℰ (020) 7208 4113) : Rest *(closed lunch Saturday and Sunday)* a la carte
31.50/47.00 ⒵ – **Park Brasserie :** Rest a la carte 28.50/39.50 ⒵ – (see also **Galvin at Windows** below) – ⌚ 22.00 – **395 rm** ✸269.00/434.00 – ✸✸269.00/434.00, 55 suites.
♦ This 28 storey tower is one of the city's tallest hotels, providing impressive views from the upper floors. Club floor bedrooms are particularly comfortable. Exotic Trader Vics with bamboo and plants. A harpist adds to the relaxed feel of Park Brasserie.

Connaught, 16 Carlos Pl, W1K 2AL, (planned closure March-September for renovations)
⊖ *Bond Street,* ℰ (020) 7499 7070, *info@the-connaught.co.uk, Fax (020) 7495 3262,* ㎘ –
🛗 ✆ & ⬤⬤ ⒶⒺ ⓪ 𝒱𝐼𝑆𝐴, ✺
30 AHU **e**
Rest – (see **Angela Hartnett at The Connaught** below) – ⌚ 29.25 – **68 rm**
✸363.00/480.00 – ✸✸504.00, 24 suites.
♦ 19C quintessentially English hotel with country house feel. The grand mahogany staircase leads up to antique furnished rooms. One of the capital's most exclusive addresses.

Brown's, Albemarle St, W1S 4BP ⊖ *Green Park,* ℰ (020) 7493 6020, *reservations@brownsroccofortehotels.com, Fax (020) 7493 9381,* ㎘ – 🛗 🖥 📺 ✆ & ⬤⬤ ⒶⒺ ⓪ 𝒱𝐼𝑆𝐴,
✺
30 AIV **d**
Rest – (see **The Grill** below) – ⌚ 27.50 – **105 rm** ✸364.00 – ✸✸723.00, 12 suites.
♦ After a major refit, this urbane hotel offers a swish bar featuring Terence Donovan prints, up-to-the-minute rooms and, of course, a quintessentially English lounge for tea.

Park Lane, Piccadilly, W1J 7BX ⊖ Green Park, ℰ (020) 7499 6321, reservations.theparklane@sheraton.com, Fax (020) 7499 1965, ₺₆ – |≋|, ⅀← rm, ▤ ℰ ₺ ⇔ – 🔏 500. ⑩ ⓪ 𝔸𝔼 ⓪ 𝕍𝕀𝕊𝔸
30 AHV x
Citrus (ℰ (020) 7290 7364) : **Rest** a la carte 28.00/35.00 ⅄ – ⚏ 21.00 – **285 rm** ✱222.00/341.00 – ✱✱222.50, 20 suites.
◆ The history of the hotel is reflected in the elegant 'Palm Court' lounge and ballroom, both restored to their Art Deco origins. Bedrooms vary in shape and size. Summer pavement tables in restaurant opposite Green Park.

London Marriott Park Lane, 140 Park Lane, W1K 7AA ⊖ Marble Arch, ℰ (020) 7493 7000, Fax (020) 7493 8333, ₺₆, ⊠ – |≋| ⅀← ⚏ ₺ ₺ – 🔏 75. ⑩ ⓪ 𝔸𝔼 𝕍𝕀𝕊𝔸 ※ 29 AGU b
140 Park Lane : Rest (bar lunch Saturday) 18.50 (lunch) and a la carte 29.50/46.50 ⅄ – ⚏ 20.95 – **148 rm** ✱276.00/335.00 – ✱✱276.00/335.00, 9 suites.
◆ Superbly located 'boutique' style hotel at intersection of Park Lane and Oxford Street. Attractive basement health club. Spacious, well-equipped rooms with luxurious elements. Attractive restaurant overlooking Marble Arch.

Westbury, Bond St, W1S 2YF ⊖ Bond Street, ℰ (020) 7629 7755, sales@westburymayfair.com, Fax (020) 7495 1163, ₺₆ – |≋|, ⅀← rm, ▤ ℰ ₺ – 🔏 120. ⑩ ⓪ 𝔸𝔼 ⓪ 𝕍𝕀𝕊𝔸 ※
30 AIU a
Rest (closed Sunday and Saturday lunch) 24.50 and a la carte 32.50/49.00 – ⚏ 24.00 – **230 rm** ✱152.00/311.00 – ✱✱152.00/311.00, 19 suites.
◆ Surrounded by London's most fashionable shops; the renowned Polo bar and lounge provide soothing sanctuary. Some suites have their own terrace. Bright, fresh restaurant enhanced by modern art.

The Metropolitan, Old Park Lane, W1K 1LB ⊖ Hyde Park Corner, ℰ (020) 7447 1000, res.lon@metropolitan.como.bz, Fax (020) 7447 1100, ≤, ₺₆ – |≋|, ⅀← rm, ▤ ℰ ⇔, ⑩ ⓪ 𝔸𝔼
30 AHV c
⓪ 𝕍𝕀𝕊𝔸
Rest – (see **Nobu** below) – ⚏ 25.00 – **147 rm** ✱376.00/411.00 – ✱✱411.00, 3 suites.
◆ Minimalist interior and a voguish reputation make this the favoured hotel of pop stars and celebrities. Innovative design and fashionably attired staff set it apart.

Athenaeum, 116 Piccadilly, W1J 7BS ⊖ Hyde Park Corner, ℰ (020) 7499 3464, info@athenaeumhotel.com, Fax (020) 7493 1860, ₺₆, ⊕ – |≋|, ⅀← rm, ▤ ℰ – 🔏 55. ⑩ ⓪ 𝔸𝔼
30 AHV g
⓪ 𝕍𝕀𝕊𝔸
Damask : Rest (closed lunch Saturday and Sunday) 21.00 (lunch) and a la carte 33.00/42.50 s. ⅄ – ⚏ 22.00 – **145 rm** ✱347.00 – ✱✱452.00, 12 suites.
◆ Built in 1925 as a luxury apartment block. Comfortable bedrooms with video and CD players. Individually designed suites are in an adjacent Edwardian townhouse. Conservatory roofed dining room renowned for its mosaics and malt whiskies.

Chesterfield, 35 Charles St, W1J 5EB ⊖ Green Park, ℰ (020) 7491 2622, bookch@rchmail.com, Fax (020) 7491 4793 – |≋|, ⅀← rm, ▤ ℰ – 🔏 110. ⑩ ⓪ 𝔸𝔼 ⓪
30 AHV f
𝕍𝕀𝕊𝔸
Rest 18.50/24.50 and a la carte 30.00/44.00 ⅄ – ⚏ 19.00 – **106 rm** ✱264.00/346.00 – ✱✱381.00, 4 suites.
◆ An assuredly English feel to this Georgian house. Discreet lobby leads to a clubby bar and wood panelled library. Individually decorated bedrooms, with some antique pieces. Classically decorated restaurant.

Washington Mayfair, 5-7 Curzon St, W1J 5HE ⊖ Green Park, ℰ (020) 7499 7000, info@washington-mayfair.co.uk, Fax (020) 7495 6172, ₺₆ – |≋|, ⅀← rm, ▤ ℰ – 🔏 90. ⑩ ⓪ 𝔸𝔼
30 AHV d
⓪ 𝕍𝕀𝕊𝔸 ※
Rest 18.95 and a la carte 25.45/35.40 ⅄ – ⚏ 18.95 – **166 rm** ✱176.00/352.00 – ✱✱176.00/352.00, 5 suites.
◆ Successfully blends a classical style with modern amenities. Relaxing lounge with traditional English furniture and bedrooms with polished, burred oak. Piano bar annex to formal dining room.

London Marriott Grosvenor Square, Grosvenor Sq, W1K 6JP ⊖ Bond Street, ℰ (020) 7493 1232, mhrs.londt.sales.exec@marriotthotels.com, Fax (020) 7514 1528, ₺₆ – |≋|, ⅀← rm, ▤ ℰ ₺ – 🔏 600. ⑩ ⓪ 𝔸𝔼 ⓪ 𝕍𝕀𝕊𝔸 ※
30 AHU s
Rest a la carte 27.50/31.50 ⅄ – ⚏ 24.00 – **209 rm** ✱264.00/311.00 – ✱✱276.00/311.00, 12 suites.
◆ A well-appointed international group hotel that benefits from an excellent location. Many of the bedrooms specifically equipped for the business traveller. Formal dining room with its own cocktail bar.

Hilton London Green Park, Half Moon St, W1J 7BN ⊖ Green Park, ℰ (020) 7629 7522, reservations.greenpark@hilton.com, Fax (020) 7491 8971 – |≋| ⅀← ℰ ₺ – 🔏 130. ⑩ ⓪
30 AIV a
𝔸𝔼 ⓪ 𝕍𝕀𝕊𝔸 ※
Rest (bar lunch)/dinner a la carte 24.95/42.95 s. ⅄ – ⚏ 19.95 – **162 rm** ✱245.00/304.00 – ✱✱304.00.
◆ A row of sympathetically adjoined townhouses, dating from the 1730s. Discreet marble lobby. Bedrooms share the same décor but vary in size and shape. Monet prints decorate light, airy dining room.

Park Lane Mews, 2 Stanhope Row, W1J 7BS ⊖ Hyde Park Corner, ℰ (020) 7493 7222, mail@parklanemewslondon.com, Fax (020) 7629 9423 – 劇 ⚡ ▤ 戋 – ᔕ 50. ⑩⓪ Æ 🆅🆂🅰
🏤
30 AHV u

Rest a la carte 23.00/34.00 ♀ – **72 rm** ⊃ ★229.00/264.00 – ★★264.00.
♦ Tucked away in a discreet corner of Mayfair. This modern, group hotel manages to retain a cosy and intimate feel. Well-equipped bedrooms to meet corporate needs. Meals in cosy dining room or lounge.

XXXX ❀❀ **Le Gavroche** (Roux), 43 Upper Brook St, W1K 7QR ⊖ Marble Arch, ℰ (020) 7408 0881, bookings@le-gavroche.com, Fax (020) 7491 4387 – ⚡ ▤. ⑩⓪ Æ ⓪ 🆅🆂🅰
29 AGU c
closed Christmas-New Year, Sunday, Saturday lunch and Bank Holidays – **Rest** - French - (booking essential) 48.00 (lunch) and a la carte 58.60/129.80 ⅋.
Spec. Foie gras chaud et pastilla de canard à la cannelle. Râble de lapin et galette au parmesan. Le palet au chocolat amer et praline croustillant.
♦ Long-standing, renowned restaurant with a clubby, formal atmosphere. Accomplished classical French cuisine, served by smartly attired and well-drilled staff.

XXXX ❀ **Angela Hartnett at The Connaught,** 16 Carlos Pl, W1K 2AL ⊖ Bond Street, ℰ (020) 7592 1222, reservations@angelahartnett.com, Fax (020) 7592 1223 – ⚡ ▤. ⑩⓪ Æ ⓪ 🆅🆂🅰
30 AHU e
Rest (booking essential) 30.00/70.00 ♀ ⅋.
Spec. Farfalle with roasted ceps and langoustine, truffle shavings. Veal fillet, parmesan cream, new season peas and leeks. Coconut parfait, exotic fruit salsa and pineapple.
♦ Stylishly updated landmark, respectful of its history: mahogany panelling softened by enticing artwork. Accomplished modern European cooking with elegant Italian overlay.

XXXX ❀ **Gordon Ramsay at Claridge's,** Brook St, W1K 4HR ⊖ Bond Street, ℰ (020) 7499 0099, reservations@gordonramsay.com, Fax (020) 7499 3099 – ⚡ ▤. ⑩⓪ Æ ⓪ 🆅🆂🅰
30 AHU c
Rest (booking essential) 30.00/75.00 ♀ ⅋.
Spec. Roast foie gras with cherries, pickled ginger, cauliflower and almond cream. Braised turbot with caviar, lettuce, root vegetables and coriander sauce. Assiette of pineapple.
♦ A thoroughly comfortable dining room with a charming and gracious atmosphere. Serves classically-inspired food executed with a high degree of finesse.

XXXX ❀❀ **The Square** (Howard), 6-10 Bruton St, W1J 6PU ⊖ Green Park, ℰ (020) 7495 7100, info@squarerestaurant.com, Fax (020) 7495 7150 – ⚡ ▤ ⇔ 18. ⑩⓪ Æ ⓪ 🆅🆂🅰 30 AIU v
closed 25-26 December, 1 January and lunch Saturday, Sunday and Bank Holidays – **Rest** 30.00/65.00 ♀ ⅋.
Spec. Lasagne of crab with shellfish and basil cappuccino. Saddle of lamb with shallot purée and rosemary. Assiette of chocolate.
♦ Varnished wood and bold abstract canvasses add an air of modernity. Extensive menus offer French-influenced cooking of the highest order. Prompt and efficient service.

XXXX **The Grill (at Brown's)** (at Brown's H.), Albemarle St, W1S 4BP ⊖ Green Park, ℰ (020) 7518 4004, Fax (020) 7518 4064 – ▤. ⑩⓪ Æ ⓪ 🆅🆂🅰
30 AIV d
Rest - British - 25.00 (lunch) and a la carte 37.95/50.50 ♀.
♦ Cavernous room decorated by Olga Polizzi to reflect hotel's heritage: dark wood panelling, lime green banquettes. Well executed and unashamedly traditional English cooking.

XXXX ❀ **Sketch (The Lecture Room),** First Floor, 9 Conduit St, W1S 2XG ⊖ Oxford Street, ℰ (0870) 7774488, Fax (0870) 7774400 – ▤. ⑩⓪ Æ ⓪ 🆅🆂🅰
30 AIU h
closed 23-30 December, 1 January, Sunday, Monday, Saturday lunch and Bank Holidays – **Rest** (booking essential) 35.00/65.00 and a la carte 57.00/102.00 ⅋.
Spec. Custard of foie gras, crab and eel, broccoli and cauliflower. Grilled sea bass with dried fruit marmalade. Chocolate dessert.
♦ Stunning venue, combining art and food, creating an experience of true sensory stimulation. Vibrant dining options: Lecture Room or Library. Highly original, complex cooking.

XXXX **China Tang** (at Dorchester H.), Park Lane, W1A 2HJ ⊖ Hyde Park Corner, ℰ (020) 7629 9988, Fax (020) 7629 9595 – ▤ ⇔ 16. ⑩⓪ Æ ⓪ 🆅🆂🅰
30 AHV a
closed 25 December – **Rest** - Chinese (Cantonese) - a la carte 40.00/75.00.
♦ A striking mix of Art Deco, Oriental motifs, hand-painted fabrics, mirrors and marbled table tops. Carefully prepared, traditional Cantonese dishes using quality ingredients.

XXXX **Galvin at Windows** (at London Hilton H.), 22 Park Lane, W1K 1BE ⊖ Hyde Park Corner, ℰ (020) 7208 4021, ⚡ City skyline – ▤. ⑩⓪ Æ ⓪ 🆅🆂🅰
30 AHV e
closed Saturday lunch and Sunday dinner – **Rest** 28.00/65.00 and a la carte 33.00/55.50 ♀.
♦ On the 28th floor, so the views are spectacular. Contemporary makeover includes silk curtains and opulent gold leaf effect sculpture on ceiling. Upmarket brasserie dishes.

XXX **The Greenhouse**, 27a Hay's Mews, W1J 5NY ⊖ *Hyde Park Corner*, ℰ (020) 7499 3331,
✿ reservations@greenhouserestaurant.co.uk, Fax (020) 7499 5368 – ✸✖ ■ ✿ 10. ⚙ AE ⑩
VISA   30 AHV **m**
closed 25-26 and 31 December, 1 January, Saturday lunch and Sunday – Rest 32.00/60.00 ♀
☼.
Spec. Atlantic cod with hummus, chickpeas and chicken jus. Anjou pigeon, pomegranate
and baby daikon. Poularde de Bresse with black truffle and chestnut.
✦ A pleasant courtyard, off a quiet mews, leads to this stylish, discreet restaurant where
an elaborate, innovative blend of flavours is much in evidence on inventive menus.

XXX **Mirabelle**, 56 Curzon St, W1J 8PA ⊖ *Green Park*, ℰ (020) 7499 4636, sales@whitestar
✿ line.org.uk, Fax (020) 7499 5449, ✿ – ■ ✿ 48. ⚙ AE ⑩ **VISA**   30 AIV **x**
closed 26 December – Rest 21.00 (lunch) and a la carte 32.50/54.95 ♀ ☼.
Spec. Tarte Tatin of endive with scallops, beurre à l'orange. Bresse pigeon with foie gras
and Madeira sauce. Lemon tart.
✦ As celebrated now as it was in the 1950s. Stylish bar with screens and mirrors, leather
banquettes and rows of windows. Modern interpretation of some classic dishes.

XXX **Maze**, 10-13 Grosvenor Sq, W1K 6JP ⊖ *Bond Street*, ℰ (020) 7107 0000, maze@gordon
✿ ramsay.com, Fax (020) 7107 0001 – ✸✖ ■ ✿ 10. ⚙ AE ⑩ **VISA**   30 AHU **z**
Rest a la carte 32.50/49.50.
Spec. Bacon and onion cream, lettuce velouté and tomato. Beef "tongue 'n cheek" with
capers, raisins and ginger carrots. Peanut butter and cherry jam sandwich with salted nuts
and cherry sorbet.
✦ Part of the Gordon Ramsay empire; a stylish, sleek restaurant. Kitchen eschews usual
three-course menus by offering a number of small dishes of variety, precision and flair.

XXX **Benares** (Kochhar), 12 Berkeley House, Berkeley Sq, W1J 6BS ⊖ *Green Park*, ℰ (020)
✿ 7629 8886, reservations@benaresrestaurant.com, Fax (020) 7499 2430 – ■ ✿ 22. ⚙ AE
⑩ **VISA**   30 AIU **q**
closed 25-26 December, 1 January, lunch Saturday and Bank Holidays – Rest - Indian - 20.00
(lunch) and a la carte 33.40/67.45 ♀.
Spec. Crispy soft shell crab with spicy squid, passion fruit dressing. Ground lamb kebabs
with mint and tamarind chutney and green mango salad. Sea bass in coconut milk with
coconut kedgeree.
✦ Indian restaurant where pools of water scattered with petals and candles compensate
for lack of natural light. Original Indian dishes; particularly good value at lunch.

XXX **Embassy**, 29 Old Burlington St, W1S 3AN ⊖ *Green Park*, ℰ (020) 7851 0956, em
bassy@embassylondon.com, Fax (020) 7734 3224, ✿ – ■. ⚙ AE **VISA**   30 AIU **u**
closed Sunday, Monday and Bank Holidays – Rest (dinner only) 39.50 and a la carte
27.00/58.00 ♀.
✦ Marble floors, ornate cornicing and a long bar create a characterful, moody dining room.
Tables are smartly laid and menus offer accomplished, classic dishes.

XXX **Tamarind**, 20 Queen St, W1J 5PR ⊖ *Green Park*, ℰ (020) 7629 3561, manager@tamarin
✿ drestaurant.com, Fax (020) 7499 5034 – ■, ⚙ AE ⑩ **VISA**   30 AHV **h**
closed 25-26 December, lunch and lunch Saturday and Bank Holidays – Rest - Indian -
18.95 (lunch) and a la carte 34.70/59.90 ♀.
Spec. Fillet of John Dory with coconut and coriander, wrapped in banana leaf. Grilled
scallops with green, pink and black peppercorns and fenugreek. Leg of lamb with cinnamon, bayleaf, rose petals and spices.
✦ Gold coloured pillars add to the opulence of this basement room. Windows allow diners
the chance to watch the kitchen prepare original and accomplished Indian dishes.

XXX **Bentley's (Grill)**, 11-15 Swallow St, W1B 4DG ⊖ *Piccadilly Circus*, ℰ (020) 7734 4756,
info@bentleys.org – ✸✖ ■ ✿ 6. ⚙ AE **VISA**   30 AJU **n**
closed 25-26 December – Rest - British - a la carte 34.00/49.00 ♀.
✦ Entrance into striking bar; panelled staircase to richly decorated restaurant. Carefully
sourced seafood or meat dishes enhanced by clean, crisp cooking. Unruffled service.

XXX **Sartoria**, 20 Savile Row, W1S 3PR ⊖ *Green Park*, ℰ (020) 7534 7000, sartoriareserva
tions@conran-restaurants.co.uk, Fax (020) 7534 7070 – ■ ✿ 45. ⚙ AE ⑩ **VISA** 30 AIU **b**
closed 25-27 December, 1 January, Sunday, Saturday lunch and Bank Holidays – Rest -
Italian - 24.50 and a la carte 28.50/38.50 ☼♀ ♀.
✦ In the street renowned for English tailoring, a coolly sophisticated restaurant to suit
those looking for classic Italian cooking with modern touches.

XXX **Brian Turner Mayfair** (at Millennium Mayfair H.), 44 Grosvenor Sq, W1K 2HP ⊖ *Bond
Street*, ℰ (020) 7596 3444, turner.mayfair@mill-cop.com, Fax (020) 7596 3443 – ■ ✿ 60.
⚙ AE ⑩ **VISA**   30 AHU **x**
closed 1 week Christmas, Sunday, Saturday lunch and Bank Holidays – Rest - British - 26.50
(lunch) and a la carte 28.75/46.25 ♀.
✦ Located within the Millennium Mayfair overlooking Grosvenor Square. Restaurant on
several levels with sharp modern décor. Good English dishes with modern twist.

XXX **Cecconi's,** 5a Burlington Gdns, W1S 3EP ⊖ *Green Park,* ℘ (020) 7434 1500, *gia como@cecconis.co.uk, Fax (020) 7434 2020* – ▤. ☻☺ ▧ ▧ ▧   30 AIU d
closed 25 December – **Rest** - Italian - a la carte 27.50/47.50 ☼.
  ◆ A chic bar and a stylish, modern dining venue, invariably busy; the menus call on the Italian classics with unusual touches.

XXX **Berkeley Square,** 7 Davies St, W1K 3DD ⊖ *Bond Street,* ℘ (020) 7629 6993, *info@the berkeleysquare.com, Fax (020) 7491 9719,* ♔ – ☻☺ ▧ ▧ ▧   30 AHU w
closed last 2 weeks August, 24-30 December, Saturday, Sunday and Bank Holidays – **Rest** 21.95/49.95 ☼.
  ◆ Smart contemporary restaurant with pavement terrace and recordings of famous novels in the loos! Modern British food with original touches.

XXX **Kai,** 65 South Audley St, W1K 2QU ⊖ *Hyde Park Corner,* ℘ (020) 7493 8988, *kai@kaimay fair.com, Fax (020) 7493 1456* – ▤ ⟷ 10. ☻☺ ▧ ▧ ▧   30 AHV n
closed 25-26 December and 1 January – **Rest** - Chinese - (booking essential) 22.00/75.00 and a la carte 27.50/72.00 ☼.
  ◆ Marble flooring and mirrors add to the opulent feel of this smoothly run Chinese restaurant. Extensive menu offers dishes ranging from the luxury to the more familiar.

XX **Umu,** 14-16 Bruton Pl, W1J 6LX ⊖ *Bond Street,* ℘ (020) 7499 8881, *enquiries@umures taurant.com, Fax (020) 7499 5120* – ⟷ ▤. ☻☺ ▧ ▧ ▧   30 AIU k
✿ *closed between Christmas and New Year, Saturday lunch, Sunday and Bank Holidays* – **Rest** - Japanese - 22.00/38.00 (lunch) and a la carte 60.00/70.00 ✎.
Spec. Sesame tofu with wasabi and sea urchin. Rice with marinated sea bream and pickled vegetables. Grilled toro teriyaki with radish and wasabi.
  ◆ Exclusive neighbourhood location: stylish, discreet interior with central sushi bar. Japanese dishes, specialising in Kyoto cuisine, employing highest quality ingredients.

XX **Bellamy's,** 18 Bruton Pl, W1J 6LY ⊖ *Bond Street,* ℘ (020) 7491 2727, *info@bellamysres taurant.com, Fax (020) 7491 9990* – ▤. ☻☺ ▧ ▧ ▧   30 AIU c
closed Saturday lunch, Sunday and Bank Holidays – **Rest** 28.50 and a la carte 35.25/56.75.
  ◆ French deli/brasserie tucked down a smart mews. Go past the caviar and cheeses into the restaurant proper for a very traditional, but well-executed, range of Gallic classics.

XX **Giardinetto,** 39-40 Albemarle St, W1S 4TE ⊖ *Green Park,* ℘ (020) 7493 7091, *info@giar dinetto.co.uk, Fax (020) 7493 7096* – ▤. ☻☺ ▧ ▧ ▧   30 AIV p
closed 25 December, Saturday lunch, Sunday and Bank Holidays – **Rest** - Italian - 25.00 (lunch) and a la carte 31.50/67.00 ☼.
  ◆ Manages to mix a smart, stylish interior with a neighbourhood intimacy. Three dining areas, front being largest. Genoese chef/owner conjures up well-presented Ligurian dishes.

XX **Patterson's,** 4 Mill St, W1S 2AX ⊖ *Oxford Street,* ℘ (020) 7499 1308, *pattersonmay fair@btconnect.com, Fax (020) 7491 2122* – ▤ ⟷ 30. ☻☺ ▧ ▧   30 AIU p
closed 25-26 December, Sunday and Saturday lunch – **Rest** 25.00/40.00 ☼.
  ◆ Stylish modern interior in black and white. Elegant tables and attentive service. Modern British cooking with concise wine list and sensible prices.

XX **Teca,** 54 Brooks Mews, W1Y 2NY ⊖ *Bond Street,* ℘ (020) 7495 4774, *Fax (020) 7491 3545* – ▤. ☻☺ ▧ ▧   30 AHU f
closed Christmas-New Year, Sunday, Saturday lunch and Bank Holidays – **Rest** - Italian - 37.50 (dinner) and lunch a la carte 30.00/45.00 ☼.
  ◆ A glass-enclosed cellar is one of the features of this modern, slick Italian restaurant. Set price menu with the emphasis on fresh, seasonal produce.

XX **Alloro,** 19-20 Dover St, W1S 4LU ⊖ *Green Park,* ℘ (020) 7495 4768, *alloro@hotmail.co.uk, Fax (020) 7629 5348* – ▤ ⟷ 16. ☻☺ ▧ ▧ ▧   30 AIV r
closed 24 December-2 January, Saturday lunch, Sunday and Bank Holidays – **Rest** - Italian - 29.00/33.00 and lunch a la carte 31.00/38.00 ☼.
  ◆ One of the new breed of stylish Italian restaurants with contemporary art and leather seating. A separate, bustling bar. Smoothly run with modern cooking.

XX **Hush,** 8 Lancashire Court, Brook St, W1S 1EY ⊖ *Bond Street,* ℘ (020) 7659 1500, *info@hush.co.uk, Fax (020) 7659 1501,* ♔ – ▮▮ ▤ ⟷ 80. ☻☺ ▧ ▧   30 AHU v
closed 24-26 December, 31 December-3 January, Saturday lunch, Sunday and Bank Holidays – **Rest** (booking essential) 26.50 (lunch) and a la carte 33.00/48.00 ☼ – **Le Club** : **Rest** *(closed lunch September-May)* a la carte 26.00/44.00 ☼.
  ◆ Tucked away down a delightful mews courtyard, this brasserie - with sunny courtyard terrace - is an informal and lively little place to eat rustic Mediterranean fare. Upstairs, Le Club serves slightly more refined dining menus.

XX **Fakhreldine,** 85 Piccadilly, W1J 7NB ⊖ *Green Park,* ℘ (020) 7493 3424, *info@fakhrel dine.co.uk, Fax (020) 7495 1977* – ▤. ☻☺ ▧ ▧ ▧   30 AIV e
Rest - Lebanese - a la carte 29.00/45.00 ☼.
  ◆ Long-standing Lebanese restaurant with great view of Green Park. Large selection of classic mezze dishes and more modern European styled menu of original Lebanese dishes.

XXX **Nobu** (at The Metropolitan H.), 19 Old Park Lane, W1Y 4LB ⊖ *Hyde Park Corner*, ℰ (020)
7447 4747, confirmations@noburestaurants.com, Fax (020) 7447 4749, ≼ – ☰ ✦ 40. 🐠 🞂
30 AHV **c**
VISA
closed 25-26 December and 1 January – Rest - Japanese with South American influences -
(booking essential) 50.00/70.00 and a la carte 33.50/40.00 ☙.
Spec. Yellowtail with jalapeño. Black cod with miso. Scallop tiradito.
♦ Its celebrity clientele has made this one of the most glamorous spots. Staff are fully
conversant in the unique menu that adds South American influences to Japanese cooking.

XXX **Via Condotti**, 23 Conduit St, W1S 2XS ⊖ *Oxford Circus*, ℰ (020) 7493 7050, info@via
condotti.co.uk, Fax (020) 7409 7985 – ☰ ✦ 18. 🐠 🞂 **VISA**
30 AIU **f**
closed Sunday and Bank Holidays – Rest - Italian - 24.50 ☙.
♦ Chic bar-room leads to restaurant with Italian prints and leather banquettes. Full-flavoured rustic dishes with most ingredients from Italy; chef/owner makes his own breads.

XXX **Taman Gang**, 141 Park Lane, W1K 7AA ⊖ *Marble Arch*, ℰ (020) 7518 3160, info@taman
gang.com, Fax (020) 7518 3161 – ☰. 🐠 🞂 🞂 **VISA**
29 AGU **e**
closed Sunday – Rest - South East Asian - (dinner only) a la carte 22.50/45.00 ☙.
♦ Basement restaurant with largish bar and lounge area. Stylish but intimate décor. Informal and intelligent service. Pan-Asian dishes presented in exciting modern manner.

XXX **Sumosan**, 26 Albemarle St, W1S 4HY ⊖ *Green Park*, ℰ (020) 7495 5999, info@sumo
san.co.uk, Fax (020) 7355 1247 – ☰. 🐠 🞂 🞂 **VISA**
30 AIU **e**
closed 25-26 and 31 December, 1 January, and lunch Saturday and Sunday – Rest - Japanese - 22.50 (lunch) and a la carte 29.30/51.00 **s**. ☙.
♦ A very smart interior in which diners sit in comfy banquettes and armchairs. Sushi bar to
the rear with some semi-private booths. Extensive menus of Sushi and Sashimi.

XXX **Mews of Mayfair**, 10-11 Lancashire Court, New Bond St, W1S 1EY ⊖ *Bond Street*,
ℰ (020) 7518 9388, Fax (020) 7518 9389 – ✦. 🐠 🞂 🞂 **VISA**
30 AHU **a**
Rest 19.50/40.00 and a la carte 28.00/41.50 ☙.
♦ Converted mews houses once used as storage rooms for Savile Row. Ground floor bar
with French windows. Pretty first floor restaurant where eclectic modern menus are
served.

XXX **Chor Bizarre**, 16 Albemarle St, W1S 4HW ⊖ *Green Park*, ℰ (020) 7629 9802, chorbizar
relondon@oldworldhospitality.com, Fax (020) 7493 7756 – ✦ ☰. 🐠 🞂 🞂
30 AIV **s**
VISA
closed 25-26 December, 1 January, Sunday lunch and Bank Holidays – Rest - Indian - 16.50
(lunch) and a la carte 17.00/27.00.
♦ Translates as 'thieves market' and the décor is equally vibrant; antiques, curios, carvings
and ornaments abound. Cooking and recipes chiefly from north India and Kashmir.

XXX **Sketch (The Gallery)**, 9 Conduit St, W1S 2XG ⊖ *Oxford Street*, ℰ (0870) 7774488,
info@sketch.uk.com, Fax (020) 7774400 – ☰. 🐠 🞂 **VISA**
30 AIU **h**
closed 24-26 December, 1 January, Sunday and Bank Holidays – Rest (booking essential)
(dinner only) a la carte 32.50/52.50.
♦ On the ground floor of the Sketch building: daytime video art gallery metamorphoses
into evening brasserie with ambient wall projections and light menus with eclectic range.

XXX **Cocoon**, 65 Regent St, W1B 4EA ⊖ *Piccadilly Circus*, ℰ (020) 7494 7600, reserva
tions@cocoon-restaurants.com, Fax (020) 7494 7607 – ✦ ☰ ✦ 12. 🐠 🞂 **VISA** 30 AJU **x**
closed Saturday lunch and Sunday – Rest - Asian - a la carte 35.00/70.00 ☙ ☙.
♦ Trendy restaurant, based on a prime Regent Street site. Silk nets cleverly divide long,
winding room. Bold, eclectic menus cover a wide spectrum of Asian dishes.

XXX **Nobu Berkeley St**, 15 Berkeley St, W1J 8DY ⊖ *Green Park*, ℰ (020) 7290 9222, nobu
berkeley@noburestaurants.com, Fax (020) 7290 9223 – ✦ ☰. 🐠 🞂 🞂 **VISA**
30 AIV **b**
closed lunch Saturday-Sunday and Bank Holidays – Rest - Japanese with South American
influences - a la carte 42.75/78.50 ☙.
Spec. Wood roasted steak with truffles. Toro with miso and jalapeño salsa. Crispy pork belly
with spicy miso.
♦ In a prime position off Berkeley Square: downstairs 'destination' bar and above, a top
quality, soft-hued restaurant. Innovative Japanese dishes with original combinations.

XXX **Momo**, 25 Heddon St, W1B 4BH ⊖ *Oxford Circus*, ℰ (020) 7434 4040, info@momor
esto.com, Fax (020) 7287 0404, ☆ – ☰. 🐠 🞂 🞂 **VISA**
30 AIU **n**
closed 25-26 and 31 December, 1 January, Sunday and Bank Holidays – Rest -
Moroccan - 16.00 (lunch) and dinner a la carte 28.50/40.00.
♦ Elaborate adornment of rugs, drapes and ornaments mixed with Arabic music lend an
authentic feel to this busy Moroccan restaurant. Helpful service. Popular basement bar.

XXX **Veeraswamy**, Victory House, 99 Regent St, W1B 4RS, entrance on Swallow St ⊖ *Piccadilly Circus*, ℰ (020) 7734 1401, veeraswamy@realindianfood.com, Fax (020) 7439 8434 – ☰
✦ 36. 🐠 🞂 🞂 **VISA**
30 AIU **t**
Rest - Indian - 16.00 (lunch) and a la carte 28.50/54.00 ☙ ☙.
♦ The country's oldest Indian restaurant enlivened by vivid coloured walls and glass
screens. The menu also combines the familiar with some modern twists.

✗ **Chisou,** 4 Princes St, W1B 2LE ⊖ *Oxford Circus*, 𝒫 (020) 7629 3931 – ▤. **MO** **AE** **VISA**
30 AIU m
closed 21-31 August, 23 December-4 January, Sunday and Bank Holidays – **Rest** - Japanese - 17.00 (lunch) and a la carte 20.40/37.50.
♦ In Mayfair's Japanese quarter; simple slate flooring and polished wood tables. Cosy sushi bar to rear. Elaborate menus of modern/classic Japanese dishes. Gets very busy.

✗ **Bentley's (Oyster Bar),** 11-15 Swallow St, W1B 4DG ⊖ *Piccadilly Circus*, 𝒫 (020) 7734 4756, info@bentleys.org – ✗ ▤. **MO** **AE** **VISA**
30 AJU n
closed 25-26 December – **Rest** - Seafood - a la carte 27.00/39.25.
♦ Ground floor location, behind the busy bar. White-jacketed staff open oysters by the bucket load. Interesting seafood menus feature tasty fish pies. Hearty Sunday roasts.

✗ **Automat,** 33 Dover St, W1S 4NF ⊖ *Green Park*, 𝒫 (020) 7499 3033, info@automat-london.com, Fax (020) 7499 2682 – ▤. **MO** **AE** **VISA**
30 AIV r
closed Sunday dinner – **Rest** - American - a la carte 23.00/39.00. ⌾.
♦ Buzzing New York style brasserie in three areas: a café, a 'dining car' with deep leather banquettes, and actual brasserie itself. Classic dishes from burgers to cheesecake.

✗ **The Cafe** (at Sotheby's), 34-35 New Bond St, W1A 2AA ⊖ *Bond Street*, 𝒫 (020) 7293 5077, ken.hall@sotheby's.com, Fax (020) 7293 6993 – ✗ ▤. **MO** **AE** **VISA**
30 AIU y
closed last 2 weeks August, 22 December-3 January, Saturday, Sunday and Bank Holidays – **Rest** (booking essential) (lunch only) a la carte 22.00/32.00 ⌾.
♦ A velvet rope separates this simple room from the main lobby of this famous auction house. Pleasant service from staff in aprons. Menu is short but well-chosen and light.

Regent's Park and Marylebone *Gtr London* – ⊠ NW1/NW8/W1.

🏨🏨🏨🏨 **Landmark London,** 222 Marylebone Rd, NW1 6JQ ⊖ *Edgware Rd*, 𝒫 (020) 7631 8000, reservations@thelandmark.co.uk, Fax (020) 7631 8080, ⓥ, Ⅰ₆, ⇌, ▭ – ▯, ✗ rm, ▤ ✓ ⅙ ⇌ – 🔏 350. **MO** **AE** **①** **VISA** ✗
29 AFT a
Winter Garden : **Rest** 25.75/33.45 and dinner a la carte 29.00/47.00 ⌾ – ⌚ 25.00 – **290 rm** ✦217.00/288.00 – ✦✦247.00/305.00, 9 suites.
♦ Imposing Victorian Gothic building with a vast glass enclosed atrium, overlooked by many of the modern, well-equipped bedrooms. Winter Garden popular for afternoon tea.

🏨🏨🏨 **Langham,** 1c Portland Pl, Regent St, W1B 1JA ⊖ *Oxford Circus*, 𝒫 (020) 7636 1000, loninfo@langhamhotels.com, Fax (020) 7323 2340, ⓥ, Ⅰ₆, ⇌, ▭ – ▯, ✗ rm, ▤ ✓ ⅙ – 🔏 250. **MO** **AE** **①** **VISA** ✗
30 AIT e
Rest 37.50/45.00 and a la carte 38.50/46.50 – ⌚ 24.95 – **407 rm** ✦411.00 – ✦✦411.00, 20 suites.
♦ Opposite the BBC, with Colonial inspired décor. Polo themed bar and barrel vaulted Palm Court. Concierge Club rooms offer superior comfort and butler service. Memories is a bright, elegant dining room.

🏨🏨🏨 **The Cumberland,** Great Cumberland Pl, W1A 4RF ⊖ *Marble Arch*, 𝒫 (0870) 3339280, enquiries@thecumberland.co.uk, Fax (0870) 3339281 – ▯ ✗ ▤ ✓ ⅙ – 🔏 300. **MO** **AE** **①** **VISA**
29 AGU z
Rest – (see *Rhodes W1* below) – ⌚ 16.95 – **1019 rm** ✦370.00 – ✦✦382.00.
♦ Fully refurbished, conference oriented hotel whose vast lobby boasts modern art, sculpture and running water panels. Distinctive bedrooms with a host of impressive extras.

🏨🏨🏨 **Hyatt Regency London-The Churchill,** 30 Portman Sq, W1A 4ZX ⊖ *Marble Arch*, 𝒫 (020) 7486 5800, london.churchill@hyattintl.com, Fax (020) 7486 1255, Ⅰ₆, ⇌, ✗ – ▯, ✗ rm, ▤ ✓ ⅙ – 🔏 250. **MO** **AE** **①** **VISA** ✗
29 AGT x
The Montagu : **Rest** 22.50 (lunch) and a la carte 34.50/46.50 ⌾ – ⌚ 15.00 – **397 rm** ✦399.00 – ✦✦423.00, 40 suites.
♦ Modern property overlooking attractive square. Elegant marbled lobby .Cigar bar open until 2am for members. Well-appointed rooms have the international traveller in mind. Restaurant provides popular Sunday brunch entertainment.

🏨🏨 **Charlotte Street,** 15 Charlotte St, W1T 1RJ ⊖ *Goodge Street*, 𝒫 (020) 7806 2000, charlotte@firmdale.com, Fax (020) 7806 2002, Ⅰ₆ – ▯ ▤ ✓ ⅙ – 🔏 65. **MO** **AE** **①** **VISA** ✗
31 AKT e
Rest – (see *Oscar* below) – ⌚ 18.50 – **44 rm** ✦229.00/240.00 – ✦✦335.00, 8 suites.
♦ Interior designed with a charming and understated English feel. Welcoming lobby laden with floral displays. Individually decorated rooms with CDs and mobile phones.

🏨🏨 **Sanderson,** 50 Berners St, W1T 3NG ⊖ *Oxford Circus*, 𝒫 (020) 7300 1400, sanderson@morganshotelgroup.com, Fax (020) 7300 1401, ☕, Ⅰ₆ – ▯, ✗ rm, ▤ ✓ **MO** **AE** **①** **VISA** ✗
31 AJT c
Spoon+ : **Rest** a la carte 36.00/84.00 ⌾ – ⌚ 21.50 – **150 rm** ✦264.00/441.00 – ✦✦294.00/499.00.
♦ Designed by Philipe Starck: the height of contemporary design. Bar is the place to see and be seen. Bedrooms with minimalistic white décor have DVDs and striking bathrooms. Stylish Spoon+ allows diners to construct own dishes.

The Leonard, 15 Seymour St, W1H 7JW ⊖ Marble Arch, ℰ (020) 7935 2010, reserva tions@theleonard.com, Fax (020) 7935 6700, ₲ – 🛗 🖙 🚬 📞 📶 🌣 AE ⓞ VISA 🛠
29 AGU n

Rest (room service only) – ⊆ 19.50 – **25 rm** ✶176.00 – ✶✶276.00, **20 suites** 311.00/464.00.

◆ Around the corner from Selfridges, an attractive Georgian townhouse: antiques and oil paintings abound. Informal, stylish café bar offers light snacks. Well-appointed rooms.

Radisson SAS Portman, 22 Portman Sq, W1H 7BG ⊖ Marble Arch, ℰ (020) 7208 6000, sales.london@radissonsas.com, Fax (020) 7208 6001, ₲, 🍴, 🛠 – 🛗, 🖙 rm, 🖥 📞 🛎 650. 📶 AE ⓞ VISA 🛠
29 AGT a

Rest (buffet lunch)/dinner a la carte 24.00/33.00 ♀ – ⊆ 17.50 – **265 rm** ✶222.00 – ✶✶234.00, 7 suites.

◆ This modern, corporate hotel offers check-in for both British Midland and SAS airlines. Rooms in attached towers decorated in Scandinavian, Chinese and Italian styles. Restaurant renowned for its elaborate buffet lunch.

Montcalm, Great Cumberland Pl, W1H 7TW ⊖ Marble Arch, ℰ (020) 7402 4288, mon tcalm@montcalm.co.uk, Fax (020) 7724 9180 – 🛗, 🖙 rm, 🖥 📞 – 🛎 80. 📶 AE ⓞ VISA 🛠
29 AGU d

The Crescent : Rest (closed lunch Saturday-Sunday and Bank Holidays) 26.00/29.50 s. – ⊆ 17.95 – **110 rm** ✶176.00/294.00 – ✶✶200.00/294.00, 10 suites.

◆ Named after the 18C French general, the Marquis de Montcalm. In a charming crescent a short walk from Hyde Park. Spacious bedrooms with a subtle oriental feel.

London Marriott Marble Arch, 134 George St, W1H 5DN ⊖ Marble Arch, ℰ (020) 7723 1277, salesadmin.marblearch@marriott.co.uk, Fax (020) 7402 0666, ₲, 🍴, ⬜ – 🛗 🖙 🚬 📞 🕭 🅿 – 🛎 150. 📶 AE ⓞ
29 AFT j

Mediterrano : Rest (dinner only) 37.50/45.00 and a la carte 20.00/25.00 s. ♀ – ⊆ 18.95 – **240 rm** ✶222.00/257.00 – ✶✶222.00/293.00.

◆ Centrally located and modern. Offers comprehensive conference facilities. Leisure centre underground. An ideal base for both corporate and leisure guests. Mediterranean-influenced cooking.

Berkshire, 350 Oxford St, W1N 0BY ⊖ Bond Street, ℰ (020) 7629 7474, resberk@radi sson.com, Fax (020) 7629 8156 – 🛗, 🖙 rm, 🖥 📞 – 🛎 40. 📶 AE ⓞ VISA 🛠
30 AHU n

Ascots : Rest (closed Sunday) (dinner only) 25.00 and a la carte 25.00/33.50 ♀ – ⊆ 16.50 – **145 rm** ✶171.00/245.00 – ✶✶220.00/282.00, 2 suites.

◆ Above the shops of Oxford St. Reception areas have a pleasant traditional charm. Comfortably appointed modern bedrooms have plenty of style. Personable staff. Stylish, relaxed dining room.

Durrants, 26-32 George St, W1H 5BJ ⊖ Bond Street, ℰ (020) 7935 8131, enquiries@dur rantshotel.co.uk, Fax (020) 7487 3510 – 🛗, 🖥 rest, 📞 – 🛎 55. 📶 AE VISA 🛠
29 AGT e

Rest 19.50/22.00 (lunch) and a la carte 28.50/37.75 – ⊆ 14.50 – **88 rm** ✶105.00/155.00 – ✶✶175.00, 4 suites.

◆ First opened in 1790 and family owned since 1921. Traditionally English feel with the charm of a bygone era. Cosy wood panelled bar. Attractive rooms vary somewhat in size. Semi-private booths in quintessentially British dining room.

The Mandeville, Mandeville Pl, W1V 2BE ⊖ Bond Street, ℰ (020) 7935 5599, info@mandeville.co.uk, Fax (020) 7935 9588 – 🛗 🖙 🖥 📞 🕭 – 🛎 40. 📶 AE ⓞ VISA 🛠
30 AHT x

de Ville : Rest (closed Sunday) 19.00/23.00 and a la carte 30.00/38.50 – ⊆ 20.00 – **135 rm** ✶250.00/275.00 – ✶✶275.00/450.00, 7 suites.

◆ Fashionably located hotel, refurbished in 2005 with marbled reception and strikingly colourful bar. Stylish rooms have flatscreen TVs and make good use of the space available. Informal restaurant serving modern British cuisine.

Dorset Square, 39-40 Dorset Sq, NW1 6QN ⊖ Marylebone, ℰ (020) 7723 7874, reser vations@dorsetsquare.co.uk, Fax (020) 7724 3328, 🌳 – 🛗 🖙 📞 📶 AE ⓞ VISA 🛠
17 QZD s

The Potting Shed : Rest (closed Saturday lunch and Sunday dinner) (booking essential) 21.95/24.85 and a la carte 25.00/36.00 ♀ – ⊆ 15.75 – **37 rm** ✶176.00/258.00 – ✶✶305.50/411.00.

◆ Converted Regency townhouses in a charming square and the site of the original Lord's cricket ground. A relaxed country house in the city. Individually decorated rooms. The Potting Shed features modern cuisine and a set business menu.

The Sumner without rest., 54 Upper Berkeley St, W1H 7QR ⊖ Marble Arch, ℰ (020) 7723 2244, enquiry@thesumner.com, Fax (0870) 705 8679 – 🛗 🖙 📺 📞 🕭 📶 AE ⓞ VISA 🛠
17 AFU a

20 rm ⊆ ✶116.00/152.00 – ✶✶116.00/152.00.

◆ Two Georgian terrace houses in developing area of town. Comfy, stylish sitting room; basement breakfast room. Largest bedrooms, 101 and 201, have sunny, full-length windows.

Sherlock Holmes, 108 Baker St, W1U 6LJ ⊖ *Baker Street*, ℰ (020) 7486 6161, *info@sherlockholmeshotel.com, Fax (020) 7958 5211*, ₤₅, ☎ – ∣᠔∣ ⇥ ≣ ✆ – ⚊ 45. ⬛⑨ ⚿ ᴀᴇ ⑩ VISA
29 AGT c

Rest 14.50 (lunch) and a la carte 25.00/44.00 ♀ – ⚌ 16.50 – **116 rm** ✦176.00/294.00 – ✦✦176.00/294.00, 3 suites.
♦ A stylish building with a relaxed contemporary feel. Comfortable guests' lounge with Holmes pictures on the walls. Bedrooms welcoming and smart, some with wood floors. Brasserie style dining.

Hart House without rest., 51 Gloucester Pl, W1U 8JF ⊖ *Marble Arch*, ℰ (020) 7935 2288, *reservations@harthouse.co.uk, Fax (020) 7935 8516* – ⇥ . ⬛⑨ VISA . ✀
29 AGT d
15 rm ⚌ ✦70.00/95.00 – ✦✦95.00/110.00.
♦ Once home to French nobility escaping the 1789 Revolution. Now an attractive Georgian, mid-terraced private hotel. Warm and welcoming service. Well kept bedrooms.

St George without rest., 49 Gloucester Pl, W1U 8JE ⊖ *Marble Arch*, ℰ (020) 7486 8586, *reservations@stgeorge-hotel.net, Fax (020) 7486 6567* – ⇥ ✆. ⬛⑨ ᴀᴇ VISA . ✀ 29 AGT h
⚌ 5.00 **19 rm** ✦75.00/90.00 – ✦✦95.00/100.00.
♦ Terraced house on a busy street, usefully located within walking distance of many attractions. Offers a warm welcome and comfortable bedrooms which are spotlessly maintained.

Orrery, 55 Marylebone High St, W1U 5RB ⊖ *Regent's Park*, ℰ (020) 7616 8000, *orrery@conran-restaurants.co.uk, Fax (020) 7616 8080* – ∣᠔∣. ⬛⑨ ᴀᴇ ⑩ VISA 18 RZD a
closed Christmas and New Year – Rest (booking essential) 23.50 (lunch) and a la carte 31.00/50.00 ♀ ⍟.
Spec. Poached scallops with Vermouth cream, broad beans and girolles. Poached breast of chicken, truffle bouillon and thyme gnocchi. Chocolate fondant, pistachio ice cream.
♦ Contemporary elegance: a smoothly run 1st floor restaurant in converted 19C stables, with a Conran shop below. Accomplished modern British cooking.

Locanda Locatelli, 8 Seymour St, W1H 7JZ ⊖ *Marble Arch*, ℰ (020) 7935 9088, *info@locandalocatelli.com, Fax (020) 7935 1149* – ≣. ⬛⑨ ᴀᴇ VISA
29 AGU r
closed Bank Holidays – Rest - Italian - a la carte 30.50/59.50 ♀ ⍟.
Spec. Fillet of sea bass baked in a salt and herb crust. Tagliatelle with kid goat ragu. Medallions of venison with ceps and radicchio.
♦ Very stylishly appointed restaurant with banquettes and cherry wood or glass dividers which contribute to an intimate and relaxing ambience. Accomplished Italian cooking.

Latium, 21 Berners St, Fitzrovia, W1T 3LP ⊖ *Oxford Circus*, ℰ (020) 7323 9123, *info@latiumrestaurant.com, Fax (020) 7323 3205* – ≣. ⬛⑨ ᴀᴇ ⑩ VISA 31 AJT n
closed Saturday lunch, Sunday and Bank Holidays – Rest - Italian - 32.50 ♀.
♦ Welcoming restaurant owned by affable chef. Smart feel with well-spaced linen-clad tables, tiled floors and rural pictures. Italian country cooking in the heart of town.

Deya, 34 Portman Sq, W1H 7BY ⊖ *Marble Arch*, ℰ (020) 7224 0028, *reservation@deya-restaurant.co.uk, Fax (020) 7224 0411* – ≣. ⬛⑨ ᴀᴇ VISA
29 AGU z
closed 2 weeks August, 26 and 31 December, Sunday and Saturday lunch – Rest - Indian - 32.50 and a la carte 23.50/32.45 ♀.
♦ Has its own pillared entrance, though part of Mostyn hotel. Grand 18C Grade II listed room with ornate ceiling. Modern, stylish makeover. Interesting, original Indian menus.

Rhodes W1 (at The Cumberland H.), Great Cumberland Pl, W1A 4RF ⊖ *Marble Arch*, ℰ (020) 7479 3838, *rhodesw1@thecumberland.co.uk, Fax (020) 7479 3888* – ≣. ⬛⑨ ᴀᴇ ⑩ VISA
29 AGU z
Rest 20.00 (lunch) and a la carte 23.15/36.60 ♀.
♦ In the heart of the Cumberland Hotel, a very stylish dining experience with impressively high ceiling and classical Gary Rhodes dishes bringing out the best of the seasons.

Galvin, 66 Baker St, W1U 7DN ⊖ *Baker Street*, ℰ (020) 7935 4007, *info@galvinbistrotdeluxe.co.uk, Fax (020) 7486 1735* – ≣. ⬛⑨ ᴀᴇ VISA
29 AGT b
closed 25-26 December and 1 January – Rest - French - 15.50 (lunch) and a la carte 23.00/36.50 ⍟ ♀.
♦ A modern take on the classic Gallic bistro with ceiling fans, globe lights, rich wood panelled walls and French influenced dishes where precision and good value are paramount.

Six13, 19 Wigmore St, W1H 9LA ⊖ *Bond Street*, ℰ (020) 7629 6133, *inquiries@six13.com, Fax (020) 7629 6135* – ≣ ⟷ 22. ⬛⑨ ᴀᴇ VISA
30 AHT n
closed Jewish Holidays, Friday and Saturday – Rest - Kosher - 24.50 (lunch) and a la carte 27.50/45.00 ♀.
♦ Stylish and immaculate with banquette seating. Strictly kosher menu supervised by the Shama offering interesting cooking with a modern slant.

Oscar (at Charlotte Street H.), 15 Charlotte St, W1T 1RJ ⊖ *Goodge Street*, ℰ (020) 7907 4005, *charlotte@firmdale.com, Fax (020) 7806 2002* – ≣. ⬛⑨ ᴀᴇ ⑩ VISA 31 AKT e
closed Sunday lunch – Rest (booking essential) a la carte 33.00/48.50 ♀.
♦ Adjacent to hotel lobby and dominated by a large, vivid mural of contemporary London life. Sophisticated dishes served by attentive staff: oysters, wasabi and soya dressing.

XX **The Providores**, 109 Marylebone High St, W1U 4RX ⊖ *Bond Street*, ℰ (020) 7935 6175, anyone@theprovidores.co.uk, Fax (020) 7935 6877 – ✒ ⊟, ⬤❶ 🆎 𝘝𝘐𝘚𝘈   30 **AHT** y
closed 25-26 and 31 December and 1 January – **Rest** a la carte 23.20/46.70 ♈.
  ♦ Swish, stylish restaurant on first floor; unusual dishes with New World base and fusion of Asian, Mediterranean influences. Tapas and light meals in downstairs Tapa Room.

XX **La Porte des Indes**, 32 Bryanston St, W1H 7EG ⊖ *Marble Arch*, ℰ (020) 7224 0055, london.reservation@laportedesindes.com, Fax (020) 7224 1144 – ⊟ ⇔ 14, ⬤❶ 🆎 ⓪ 𝘝𝘐𝘚𝘈   29 **AGU** s
closed 25-28 December and Saturday lunch – **Rest** - Indian - a la carte 21.40/39.50 ♈.
  ♦ Don't be fooled by the discreet entrance: inside there is a spectacularly unrestrained display of palm trees, murals and waterfalls. French influenced Indian cuisine.

XX **Rosmarino**, 1 Blenheim Terrace, NW8 0EH ⊖ *St John's Wood*, ℰ (020) 7328 5014, rosmarinouk@yahoo.co.uk, Fax (020) 7625 2779, 🍽 – ⊟, ⬤❶ 🆎 𝘝𝘐𝘚𝘈   11 **PZB** r
closed 25 December, 1 January and lunch Friday-Sunday – **Rest** - Italian - a la carte 24.45/31.50 ♈.
  ♦ Modern, understated and relaxed. Friendly and approachable service of robust and rustic Italian dishes. Set priced menu is carefully balanced.

XX **Ozer**, 4-5 Langham Pl, Regent St, W1B 3DG ⊖ *Oxford Circus*, ℰ (020) 7323 0505, info@so fra.co.uk, Fax (020) 7323 0111 – ⊟, ⬤❶ 🆎 𝘝𝘐𝘚𝘈   30 **AIT** z
Rest - Turkish - la carte 14.85/28.15 ⬛♈.
  ♦ Behind the busy and vibrantly decorated bar you'll find a smart modern restaurant. Lively atmosphere and efficient service of modern, light and aromatic Turkish cooking.

XX **Roka**, 37 Charlotte St, W1T 1RR ⊖ *Tottenham Court Road*, ℰ (020) 7580 6464, info@ro karestaurant.com, Fax (020) 7580 0220 – ✒ ⊟, ⬤❶ 🆎 𝘝𝘐𝘚𝘈   31 **AJT** k
closed 25-26 December and 1 January – **Rest** - Japanese - 25.00/50.00 and a la carte 28.00/39.00 s. ♈.
  ♦ Striking glass and steel frontage. Airy, atmospheric interior of teak, oak and paper wall screens. Authentic, flavoursome Japanese cuisine with variety of grill dishes.

XX **Rasa Samudra**, 5 Charlotte St, W1T 1RE ⊖ *Goodge Street*, ℰ (020) 7637 0222, Fax (020) 7637 0224 – ✒ ⬤❶ 🆎 𝘝𝘐𝘚𝘈   31 **AKT** r
closed 24-30 December, 1 January and Sunday lunch – **Rest** - Indian Seafood and Vegetarian - 22.50/30.00 and a la carte 13.00/23.95.
  ♦ Comfortably appointed, richly decorated and modern Indian restaurant. Authentic Keralan (south Indian) cooking with seafood and vegetarian specialities.

XX **Levant**, Jason Court, 76 Wigmore St, W1U 2SJ ⊖ *Bond Street*, ℰ (020) 7224 1111, info@levant.co.uk, Fax (020) 7486 1216 – ⊟, ⬤❶ 🆎 ⓪ 𝘝𝘐𝘚𝘈   30 **AHT** c
closed 25 December – **Rest** - Lebanese - 15.00 (lunch) and a la carte 24.00/44.50 ♈.
  ♦ The somewhat unpromising entrance leads down to a vibrantly decorated basement. Modern Lebanese cooking featuring subtly spiced dishes.

XX **Caldesi**, 15-17 Marylebone Lane, W1U 2NE ⊖ *Bond Street*, ℰ (020) 7935 9226, tus can@caldesi.com, Fax (020) 7935 9228 – ⊟ ⇔ 20, ⬤❶ 🆎 ⓪ 𝘝𝘐𝘚𝘈   30 **AHT** e
closed Sunday, Saturday lunch and Bank Holidays – **Rest** - Italian - a la carte 33.50/39.50 ♈.
  ♦ A traditional Italian restaurant that continues to attract a loyal clientele. Robust and authentic dishes with Tuscan specialities. Attentive service by established team.

XX **Villandry**, 170 Great Portland St, W1W 5QB ⊖ *Regent's Park*, ℰ (020) 7631 3131, book atable@villandry.com, Fax (020) 7631 3030 – ✒ ⊟, ⬤❶ 🆎 ⓪ 𝘝𝘐𝘚𝘈   30 **AIT** s
closed Sunday dinner and Bank Holidays – **Rest** a la carte 22.75/34.50 ♈.
  ♦ The senses are heightened by passing through the well-stocked deli to the dining room behind. Bare walls, wooden tables and a menu offering simple, tasty dishes.

XX **Bertorelli**, 19-23 Charlotte St, W1T 1RL ⊖ *Goodge Street*, ℰ (020) 7636 4174, bertorel lisc@groupechezgerard.co.uk, Fax (020) 7467 8902 – ⊟, ⬤❶ 🆎 ⓪ 𝘝𝘐𝘚𝘈   31 **AJT** v
closed 24-27 December, 1 January and Sunday – **Rest** - Italian - 18.50 (lunch) and a la carte 20.00/45.00 ⬛♈.
  ♦ Above the informal and busy bar/café. Bright and airy room with vibrant décor and informal atmosphere. Extensive menu combines traditional and new wave Italian dishes.

XX **Blandford Street**, 5-7 Blandford St, W1U 3DB ⊖ *Bond Street*, ℰ (020) 7486 9696, info@blandford-street.co.uk, Fax (020) 7486 5067 – ⊟ ⇔ 18, ⬤❶ 🆎 𝘝𝘐𝘚𝘈   30 **AHT** v
closed Sunday, Saturday lunch and Bank Holidays – **Rest** 22.95 (lunch) and dinner a la carte 26.85/36.85 ⬛♈.
  ♦ Understated interior with plain walls hung with modern pictures and subtle spot-lighting. Contemporary menu with a notably European character.

XX **L'Aventure**, 3 Blenheim Terrace, NW8 0EH ⊖ *St John's Wood*, ℰ (020) 7624 6232, Fax (020) 7625 5548, 🍽 – ⬤❶ 🆎 𝘝𝘐𝘚𝘈   11 **PZB** b
closed Easter, Sunday, Saturday lunch and Bank Holidays – **Rest** - French - 18.50/32.50.
  ♦ Behind the pretty tree lined entrance you'll find a charming neighbourhood restaurant. Relaxed atmosphere and service by personable owner. Authentic French cuisine.

XX **Phoenix Palace,** 3-5 Glentworth St, NW1 5PG ⊖ *Baker Street*, ℰ (020) 7486 3515, phoenixpalace@btconnect.com, Fax (020) 7486 3401 – 📺 ⟷ 30. ◑◉ ᴀᴇ 𝗩𝗜𝗦𝗔   17 QZD x
closed 25 December – **Rest** - Chinese - 15.80/26.80 and a la carte 19.70/55.00.
♦ Tucked away near Baker Street station; lots of photos of celebrities who've eaten here. Huge room for 200 diners where authentic, fresh, well prepared Chinese dishes are served.

X **Union Café,** 96 Marylebone Lane, W1U 2QA ⊖ *Bond Street*, ℰ (020) 7486 4860, union cafe@brinkleys.com, Fax (020) 7935 1537 – ◑◉ ᴀᴇ 𝗩𝗜𝗦𝗔   30 AHT d
closed 25-26 December, 1 January and Sunday dinner – **Rest** a la carte 22.00/35.00 ℤ.
♦ No standing on ceremony at this bright, relaxed restaurant. The open kitchen at one end produces modern Mediterranean cuisine. Ideal for visitors to the Wallace Collection.

X **Michael Moore,** 19 Blandford St, W1U 3DH ⊖ *Baker Street*, ℰ (020) 7224 1898, info@michaelmoorerestaurant.com, Fax (020) 7224 0970 – ✸ ⟷ 14. ◑◉ ᴀᴇ ◉
𝗩𝗜𝗦𝗔   29 AGT r
closed Christmas-New Year, Saturday lunch, Sunday and Bank Holidays – **Rest** 19.95 (lunch) and a la carte 24.70/39.25 ℤ.
♦ Warm glow emanates not just from mustard façade but also effusive welcome within. Cosy, locally renowned favourite, with global cuisine served by friendly, efficient staff.

X **Caffè Caldesi,** 1st Floor, 118 Marylebone Lane, W1U 2QF ⊖ *Bond Street*, ℰ (020) 7935 1144, people@caldesi.com, Fax (020) 7935 8832 – 📺 ◑◉ ᴀᴇ 𝗩𝗜𝗦𝗔   30 AHT s
closed Christmas, Sunday and Bank Holidays – **Rest** - Italian - a la carte 28.00/34.00 ℤ.
♦ Converted pub with a simple modern interior in which to enjoy tasty, uncomplicated Italian dishes. Downstairs is a lively bar with a deli counter serving pizzas and pastas.

X **Chada Chada,** 16-17 Picton Pl, W1U 1BP ⊖ *Bond Street*, ℰ (020) 7935 8212, en quiry@chadathai.com, Fax (020) 7924 2178 – 📺. ◑◉ ᴀᴇ ◉ 𝗩𝗜𝗦𝗔   30 AHU b
closed Sunday and Bank Holidays – **Rest** - Thai - 12.50 (lunch) and a la carte 15.90/36.90 ℤ.
♦ Authentic and fragrant Thai cooking; the good value menu offers some interesting departures from the norm. Service is eager to please in the compact and cosy rooms.

X **Fishworks,** 89 Marylebone High St, W1U 4QW ⊖ *Baker Street*, ℰ (020) 7935 9796, marylebone@fishworks.co.uk, Fax (020) 7935 8796 – ✸ 📺. ◑◉ ᴀᴇ 𝗩𝗜𝗦𝗔   30 AHT k
closed Monday – **Rest** - Seafood - (booking essential) a la carte 24.80/48.50 ℤ.
♦ Go through the fish shop to bright, unfussy restaurant where a blackboard lists the daily specials. Extensive menus offer simply prepared seafood straight from front-of-house!

🍺 **The Salt House,** 63 Abbey Rd, NW8 0AE ⊖ *St John's Wood*, ℰ (020) 7328 6626, jack westhead@majol.co.uk, Fax (020) 7604 4804, 🍴 – ◑◉ ◉ 𝗩𝗜𝗦𝗔   11 OZB a
closed 25 December – **Rest** a la carte 18.00/30.00 ℤ.
♦ Grand Victorian pub appearance in bottle green. Busy bar at the front; main dining room, in calm duck egg blue, to the rear. Modern menus boast a distinct Mediterranean style.

St James's *Gtr London –* ⊠ *NW1/W1/SW1.*

🏨🏨🏨 **The Ritz,** 150 Piccadilly, W1J 9BR ⊖ *Green Park*, ℰ (020) 7493 8181, enquire@theritzlon don.com, Fax (020) 7493 2687, ₣ᵟ – 📶, ✸ rm, 📺 ✆ – 🔒 50. ◑◉ ᴀᴇ ◉ 𝗩𝗜𝗦𝗔.
✸   30 AIV c
Rest – (see **The Restaurant** below) – ☷ 30.00 – **116 rm** ✱294.00/470.00 –
✱✱352.00/470.00, 17 suites.
♦ Opened 1906, a fine example of Louis XVI architecture and decoration. Elegant Palm Court famed for afternoon tea. Many of the lavishly appointed rooms overlook the park.

🏨🏨 **Sofitel St James London,** 6 Waterloo Pl, NW1Y 4AN ⊖ *Piccadilly Circus*, ℰ (020) 7747 2200, Fax (020) 7747 2210, ₣ᵟ – 📶, ✸ rm, 📺 ✆ 占 – 🔒 180. ◑◉ ᴀᴇ ◉
𝗩𝗜𝗦𝗔   31 AKV a
Rest – (see **Brasserie Roux** below) – ☷ 21.00 – **179 rm** ✱417.00/464.00 – ✱✱493.00, 7 suites.
♦ Grade II listed building in smart Pall Mall location. Classically English interiors include floral Rose Lounge and club-style St. James bar. Comfortable, well-fitted bedrooms.

🏨🏨 **Stafford** ⌂, 16-18 St James's Pl, SW1A 1NJ ⊖ *Green Park*, ℰ (020) 7493 0111, info@thestaffordhotel.co.uk, Fax (020) 7493 7121 – 📶 📺 ✆ – 🔒 40. ◑◉ ᴀᴇ ◉ 𝗩𝗜𝗦𝗔.
✸   30 AIV u
Rest *(closed Saturday lunch)* 29.50 (lunch) and dinner a la carte 49.50/61.50 s. ℤ – ☷ 19.50
– **75 rm** ✱282.00/323.00 – ✱✱376.00/393.00, 6 suites.
♦ A genteel atmosphere prevails in this elegant and discreet country house in the city. Do not miss the famed American bar. Well-appointed rooms created from 18C stables. Refined, elegant, intimate dining room.

Dukes ⮬, 35 St James's Pl, SW1A 1NY ⊖ Green Park, ℰ (020) 7491 4840, bookings@dukeshotel.com, Fax (020) 7493 1264, Ⅰ₅ – ▐�‌§▌, ✕⇌ rest, ▤ ✆ – ▵ 60. ◑◐ ▨ ⓪ 𝗩𝗜𝗦𝗔. ✇
30 AIV f

Rest (closed Saturday lunch) 20.00 (lunch) and a la carte approx 37.50 ⁎ – � 19.50 – **82 rm** ⁑346.00/370.00 – ⁑⁑493.00, 7 suites.
◆ Privately owned, discreet and quiet hotel. Traditional bar, famous for its martinis and Cognac collection. Well-kept spacious rooms in a country house style. Refined dining.

De Vere Cavendish, 81 Jermyn St, SW1Y 6JF ⊖ Piccadilly Circus, ℰ (020) 7930 2111, cavendish.reservations@devere-hotels.com, Fax 7600) 7930 2125 – ▐‌§▌, ✕⇌ rm, ▤ ✆ ⅋ ⟿ – ▵ 100. ◑◐ ▨ ⓪ 𝗩𝗜𝗦𝗔. ✇
30 AIV v

Rest (closed lunch Saturday-Sunday and Bank Holidays) a la carte 26.00/37.50 s. ⁎ – ⊡ 21.00 – **227 rm** ⁑305.00 – ⁑⁑305.00, 3 suites.
◆ Modern hotel in heart of Piccadilly. Contemporary, minimalist style of rooms with moody prints of London; top five floors offer far-reaching views over and beyond the city. Classic-styled restaurant overlooks Jermyn Street.

22 Jermyn Street, 22 Jermyn St, SW1Y 6HL ⊖ Piccadilly Circus, ℰ (020) 7734 2353, office@22jermyn.com, Fax (020) 7734 0750 – ▐‌§▌ ▤ ✆. ◑◐ ▨ ⓪ 𝗩𝗜𝗦𝗔. ✇
31 AKV e

closed 24-25 December – **Rest** (room service only) – ⊡ 13.20 – **5 rm** ⁑258.00 – ⁑⁑258.00, 13 suites 364.00/411.00.
◆ Discreet entrance amid famous shirt-makers' shops leads to this exclusive boutique hotel. Stylishly decorated bedrooms more than compensate for the lack of lounge space.

The Restaurant (at The Ritz H.), 150 Piccadilly, W1V 9DG ⊖ Green Park, ℰ (020) 7493 8181, Fax (020) 7493 2687, ☞ – ▤. ◑◐ ▨ ⓪ 𝗩𝗜𝗦𝗔
30 AIV c

Rest (dancing Friday and Saturday evening) 37.00/80.00 and a la carte 48.00/80.00 s. ⁎.
◆ The height of opulence: magnificent Louis XVI décor with trompe l'oeil and ornate gilding. Delightful terrace over Green Park. Refined service, classic and modern menu.

The Wolseley, 160 Piccadilly, W1J 9EB ⊖ Green Park, ℰ (020) 7499 6996, Fax (020) 7499 6888 – ▤. ◑◐ ▨ ⓪ 𝗩𝗜𝗦𝗔
30 AIV q

closed dinner 24-25 December, 1 January and August Bank Holiday – **Rest** (booking essential) a la carte 28.00/48.00 ⁎.
◆ Has the feel of a grand European coffee house: pillars, high vaulted ceiling, mezzanine tables. Menus range from caviar to a hot dog. Also open for breakfasts and tea.

W'Sens, 12 Waterloo Pl, SW1Y 4AU ⊖ Piccadilly Circus, ℰ (020) 7484 1355, reservations@wsens.co.uk, Fax (020) 7484 1366 – ▤ ✿ 12. ◑◐ ▨ 𝗩𝗜𝗦𝗔
31 AKV z

closed lunch Saturday and Sunday – **Rest** 23.50 (lunch) and a la carte 26.50/39.00 ✇ ⁎.
◆ Impressive 19C façade; contrastingly cool interior: dive bar is a destination in its own right and the wildly eclectic restaurant is matched by three intriguing menu sections.

Fiore, 33 St James's St, SW1A 1HD ⊖ Green Park, ℰ (020) 7930 7100, info@fiore-restaurant.co.uk, Fax (020) 7930 4070 – ▤. ◑◐ ▨ ⓪ 𝗩𝗜𝗦𝗔
30 AIV k

closed Saturday lunch and Sunday – **Rest** - Italian - a la carte 23.00/41.00 ⁎.
◆ Formal restaurant with affluent feel appropriate to its setting: full linen cover and smart banquettes. Traditional Italian regional cooking with contemporary embellishments.

Luciano, 72-73 St James's St, SW1A 1PH ⊖ Green Park, ℰ (020) 7408 1440, info@lucianorestaurant.co.uk – ▤ ✿ 16. ◑◐ ▨ ⓪ 𝗩𝗜𝗦𝗔
30 AIV m

closed Easter, 24-26 December, 1 January, Sunday and Bank Holidays – **Rest** - Italian - 22.50 (lunch) and a la carte 33.50/45.50 ⁎.
◆ Art Deco, David Collins styled bar leads to restaurant sympathetic to its early 19C heritage. Mix of Italian and English dishes cooked in rustic, wholesome and earthy manner.

Le Caprice, Arlington House, Arlington St, SW1A 1RJ ⊖ Green Park, ℰ (020) 7629 2239, reservation@le-caprice.co.uk, Fax (020) 7493 9040 – ▤. ◑◐ ▨ ⓪ 𝗩𝗜𝗦𝗔
30 AIV h

closed 24-26 December, 1 January and August Bank Holiday – **Rest** (Sunday brunch) a la carte 31.25/49.25 s. ⁎.
◆ Still attracting a fashionable clientele and as busy as ever. Dine at the bar or in the smoothly run restaurant. Food combines timeless classics with modern dishes.

Quaglino's, 16 Bury St, SW1Y 6AL ⊖ Green Park, ℰ (020) 7930 6767, Fax (020) 7839 2866 – ▤ ✿ 45. ◑◐ ▨ 𝗩𝗜𝗦𝗔
30 AIV j

closed 26 December and 1 January – **Rest** (booking essential) 17.50 (lunch) and a la carte 24.50/46.00 ✇ ⁎.
◆ Descend the sweeping staircase into the capacious room where a busy and buzzy atmosphere prevails. Watch the chefs prepare everything from osso bucco to fish and chips.

Mint Leaf, Suffolk Pl, SW1Y 4HX ⊖ Piccadilly Circus, ℰ (020) 7930 9020, reservations@mintleafrestaurant.com, Fax (020) 7930 6205 – ▐‌§▌ ▤. ◑◐ ▨ ⓪ 𝗩𝗜𝗦𝗔
31 AKV k

closed Bank Holidays and lunch Saturday and Sunday – **Rest** - Indian - a la carte 26.20/41.00 ✇ ⁎.
◆ Basement restaurant in theatreland. Cavernous dining room incorporating busy, trendy bar with unique cocktail list and loud music. Helpful service. Contemporary Indian dishes.

XX **Brasserie Roux**, 8 Pall Mall, SW1Y 5NG ⊖ *Piccadilly Circus*, ℰ (020) 7968 2900, h3144-fb4@accor.com, Fax (020) 7747 2251 – ■. **MC AE VISA**   31 AKV **a**
Rest - French - 24.50 and a la carte approx 33.50 s. ⊠ ⅀.
• Informal, smart, classic brasserie style with large windows making the most of the location. Large menu of French classics with many daily specials; comprehensive wine list.

XX **Franco's**, 61 Jermyn St, SW1Y 6LX ⊖ *Green Park*, ℰ (020) 7499 2211, reserve@franco slondon.com, Fax (020) 7495 1375 – ✄ ■. **MC AE VISA**   30 AIV **d**
closed 24-30 December, Sunday and Bank Holidays – **Rest** - Italian - (booking essential) a la carte 29.50/34.50 s. ⊠ ⅀.
• Great all-day menu at 'the café'. Further in, regulars have taken to smart refurbishment. Classic/modern Italian cooking allows bold but refined flavours to shine through.

XX **The Avenue**, 7-9 St James's St, SW1A 1EE ⊖ *Green Park*, ℰ (020) 7321 2111, ave nue@egami.co.uk, Fax (020) 7321 2500 – ■. **MC AE ① VISA**   30 AIV **y**
closed 25-26 December, 1 January, Saturday lunch and Sunday – **Rest** 21.95 and a la carte 28.00/36.50 ⊠ ⅀.
• The attractive and stylish bar is a local favourite. Behind is a striking, modern and busy restaurant. Appealing and contemporary food. Pre-theatre menu available.

XX **Matsuri - St James's**, 15 Bury St, SW1Y 6AL ⊖ *Green Park*, ℰ (020) 7839 1101, dine@matsuri-restaurant.com, Fax (020) 7930 7010 – ⊄ 18. **MC AE ① VISA**   30 AIV **w**
closed 25 December and 1 January – **Rest** - Japanese (Teppan-Yaki, Sushi) - 15.00/35.00 and a la carte 23.00/34.00 ⊠ ⅀.
• Specialising in theatrical and precise teppan-yaki cooking. Separate restaurant offers sushi delicacies. Charming service by traditionally dressed staff.

XX **Noura Central**, 22 Lower Regent St, SW1Y 4UJ ⊖ *Piccadilly Circus*, ℰ (020) 7839 2020, Fax (020) 7839 7700 – ■. **MC AE VISA**   31 AKV **n**
Rest - Lebanese - 14.50/34.00 and a la carte 15.00/35.00.
• Eye-catching Lebanese façade, matched by sleek interior design. Buzzy atmosphere enhanced by amplified background music. Large menus cover all aspects of Lebanese cuisine.

X **Al Duca**, 4-5 Duke of York St, SW1Y 6LA ⊖ *Piccadilly Circus*, ℰ (020) 7839 3090, info@al duca-restaurants.co.uk, Fax (020) 7839 4050 – ■. **MC AE VISA**   31 AJV **r**
closed 25 December-2 January, Sunday and Bank Holidays – **Rest** - Italian - 22.50/24.50 ⊠ ⅀.
• Relaxed, modern, stylish restaurant. Friendly and approachable service of robust and rustic Italian dishes. Set priced menu is good value.

X **Inn the Park**, St James's Park, SW1A 2BJ ⊖ *Charing Cross*, ℰ (020) 7451 9999, info@in nthepark.co.uk, Fax (020) 7451 9998, ≤, 斧 – ■ **MC AE VISA**   31 AKV **n**
closed 25 December – **Rest** 27.50 and a la carte 27.00/40.00 ⅀.
• Eco-friendly restaurant with grass covered roof; pleasant views across park and lakes. Super-heated dining terrace. Modern British menus of tasty, wholesome dishes.

Soho Gtr London – ⊠ W1/WC2.

🏠🏠 **The Soho**, 4 Richmond Mews, W1D 3DH ⊖ *Tottenham Court Road*, ℰ (020) 7559 3000, soho@firmdale.com, Fax (020) 7559 3003, Ⅰ₆ – ▐ ■ ⤫ ₺ – ▵ 100. **MC AE VISA** ⅍   31 AKU **n**
Refuel : Rest 19.95 (lunch) and a la carte 26.50/34.50 ⅀ – ⊊ 18.50 – **83 rm** ✦282.00 – ✦✦346.00, 2 suites.
• Opened in autumn 2004: stylish hotel with two screening rooms, comfy drawing room and up-to-the-minute bedrooms, some vivid, others more muted, all boasting hi-tec extras. Contemporary bar and restaurant.

🏠🏠 **Hampshire**, Leicester Sq, WC2H 7LH ⊖ *Leicester Square*, ℰ (020) 7839 9399, re shamp@radisson.com, Fax (020) 7930 8122, 斧, Ⅰ₆ – ▐, ✄ rm, ■ ⤫ – ▵ 100. **MC AE ① VISA** ⅍   31 AKU **s**
The Apex : Rest (closed Sunday) (dinner only) 29.50 and a la carte 25.00/33.50 – ⊊ 19.00 – **119 rm** ✦208.00/282.00 – ✦✦270.00/320.00, 5 suites.
• The bright lights of the city are literally outside and many rooms overlook the bustling Square. Inside it is tranquil and comfortable with well-appointed bedrooms. Formal yet relaxing dining room with immaculately dressed tables.

🏛️ **Courthouse Kempinski**, 19-21 Great Marlborough St, W1F 7HL ⊖ *Oxford Circus*, ℰ (020) 7297 5555, info@courthouse-hotel.com, Fax (020) 7297 5566, Ⅰ₆, ≦s, ☒ – ▐, ✄ rm, ■ ⤫ ₺ – ▵ 180. **MC AE ① VISA**   30 AIU **z**
The Carnaby : Rest 15.95/18.95 and a la carte 21.90/29.90 – (see also **Silk** below) – ⊊ 18.90 – **107 rm** ✦317.00 – ✦✦317.00, 5 suites.
• Striking Grade II listed ex magistrates' court: interior fused imaginatively with original features; for example, the bar incorporates three former cells. Ultra stylish rooms. Informal Carnaby offers extensive French, modern and British menu.

Hazlitt's without rest., 6 Frith St, W1D 3JA ⊖ *Tottenham Court Road*, 𝒫 (020) 7434 1771, *reservations@hazlitts.co.uk, Fax (020) 7439 1524* – 🖥 📞, 🌐 AE ⓞ VISA   31 AKU u
22 rm ✿206.00/240.00 – ✿✿240.00, 1 suite.
♦ A row of three adjoining early 18C town houses and former home of the eponymous essayist. Individual and charming bedrooms, many with antique furniture and Victorian baths.

L'Escargot, 48 Greek St, W1D 4EF ⊖ *Tottenham Court Road*, 𝒫 (020) 7437 2679, *sales@whitestarline.org.uk, Fax (020) 7437 0790* – 🖥 🌐 AE ⓞ VISA   31 AKU b
Rest *(closed 25-26 December, 1 January, Sunday and Saturday lunch)* 18.00 (lunch) and a la carte 26.50/30.95 🍷 ⅼ – *Picasso Room* : Rest *(closed August, Sunday, Monday and Saturday lunch)* 25.50/42.00.
Spec. Escargots en coquille Bordelaise. Smoked haddock with crushed Jersey potatoes, poached egg, mustard sauce. Chocolate fondant, milk ice cream.
♦ Soho institution. Ground Floor is chic, vibrant brasserie with early-evening buzz of theatre-goers. Finely judged modern dishes. Intimate and more formal upstairs Picasso Room famed for its limited edition art.

Quo Vadis, 26-29 Dean St, W1D 3LL ⊖ *Tottenham Court Road*, 𝒫 (020) 7437 9585, *sales@whitestarline.org.uk, Fax (020) 7734 7593* – 🖥, 🐾, 🌐 AE ⓞ VISA   31 AKU v
closed 24-25 December, 1 January, Sunday and Saturday lunch – Rest - Italian - 17.95 (lunch) and a la carte 20.75/35.50 🍷 ⅼ.
♦ Stained glass windows and a neon sign hint at the smooth modernity of the interior. Modern artwork abounds. Contemporary cooking and a serious wine list.

Red Fort, 77 Dean St, W1D 3SH ⊖ *Tottenham Court Road*, 𝒫 (020) 7437 2525, *info@red fort.co.uk, Fax (020) 7434 0721* – 🖥. 🌐 AE VISA   31 AKU x
closed lunch Saturday, Sunday and Bank Holidays – Rest - Indian - a la carte 25.50/46.00 🍷 ⅼ.
♦ Smart, stylish restaurant with modern water feature and glass ceiling to rear. Seasonally changing menus of authentic dishes handed down over generations.

Richard Corrigan at Lindsay House, 21 Romilly St, W1D 5AF ⊖ *Leicester Square*, 𝒫 (020) 7439 0450, *richardcorrigan@lindsayhouse.co.uk, Fax (020) 7437 7349* – ✂ 🖥 ⟨⟩ 18. 🌐 AE ⓞ VISA   31 AKU f
closed Saturday lunch and Sunday – Rest 27.00/52.00 🍷 ⅼ.
Spec. Roast scallops with pea gnocchi and crispy bacon. Smoked eel and foie gras terrine with sour apple. Grouse en croute with wild mushroom duxelle.
♦ One rings the doorbell before being welcomed into this handsome 18C town house, retaining many original features. Skilled and individual cooking with a subtle Irish hint.

Floridita, 100 Wardour St, W1F 0TN ⊖ *Tottenham Court Road*, 𝒫 (020) 7314 4000, *Fax (020) 7314 4040* – 🖥 ⟨⟩ 8. 🌐 AE ⓞ VISA   31 AKU z
Rest - Latin American - (live music and dancing) (dinner only and lunch mid November-December) a la carte 31.75/60.75 ⅼ.
♦ Buzzy destination where the Latino cuisine is a fiery accompaniment to the vivacious Cuban dancing. Slightly less frenetic upstairs in the Spanish tapas and cocktail bar.

Silk (at Courthouse Kempinski H.), 19-21 Great Marlborough St, W1F 7HL ⊖ *Oxford Circus*, 𝒫 (020) 7297 5555, *Fax (020) 7297 5566* – 🖥. 🌐 AE VISA   30 AIU z
(closed Sunday-Monday) – Rest (dinner only) a la carte 18.00/34.50.
♦ Stunningly unique former courtroom with original panelling, court benches and glass roof. Menu follows the journey of the Silk Route with Asian, Indian and Italian influences.

Café Lazeez, 21 Dean St, W1D 3TN ⊖ *Tottenham Court Road*, 𝒫 (020) 7434 9393, *soho@cafelazeez.com, Fax (020) 7434 0022* – 🖥. 🌐 AE ⓞ VISA   31 AKU d
closed Sunday – Rest - North Indian - 20.00/35.00 and a la carte 26.50/34.50 🍷 ⅼ.
♦ In the same building as Soho Theatre; the bar hums before shows, restaurant is popular for pre- and post-theatre meals of modern Indian fare. Refined décor; private booths.

Vasco and Piero's Pavilion, 15 Poland St, W1F 8QE ⊖ *Tottenham Court Road*, 𝒫 (020) 7437 8774, *eat@vascosfood.com, Fax (020) 7437 0467* – 🖥 ⟨⟩ 30. 🌐 AE ⓞ VISA   31 AJU b
closed Saturday lunch, Sunday and Bank Holidays – Rest - Italian - (lunch booking essential) 27.00 (dinner) and lunch a la carte 24.75/34.25.
♦ A long standing, family run Italian restaurant with a loyal local following. Pleasant service under the owners' guidance. Warm décor and traditional cooking.

La Trouvaille, 12A Newburgh St, W1F 7RR ⊖ *Piccadilly Circus*, 𝒫 (020) 7287 8488, *Fax (020) 7434 4170*, 🌲 – 🌐 AE VISA   30 AIU g
closed 25 December, Sunday and Bank Holidays – Rest - French - 18.00/33.00 🍷.
♦ Atmospheric restaurant located just off Carnaby Street. Hearty, robust French cooking with a rustic character. French wine list with the emphasis on southern regions.

X **Arbutus** (Demetre), 63-64 Frith St, W1D 3JW ⊖ *Tottenham Court Road*, ℘ (020) 7734
❀ 4545, *info@arbutusrestaurant.co.uk*, Fax (020) 7287 8624 – ✸ ≡.
VISA
31 AKU n
closed 24-26 December and 1 January – **Rest** 15.50 (lunch) and a la carte 26.45/
33.45 ♨ ♇.
Spec. Chicken oysters with macaroni, lemon thyme and hazelnuts. Saddle of rabbit, cottage pie of shoulder and mustard sauce. Floating Island with pink pralines.
◆ Dining room and bar that's bright and stylish without trying too hard. Bistro classics turned on their head: poised, carefully crafted cooking - but dishes still pack a punch.

X **Yauatcha**, 15 Broadwick St, W1F 0DL ⊖ *Tottenham Court Road*, ℘ (020) 7494 8888,
❀ *mail@yauatcha.com*, Fax (020) 7494 8889 – ✸ ≡. ◍◉ ﾑ **VISA**
31 AJU k
closed 25-26 December – **Rest** - Chinese (Dim Sum) a la carte 25.40/70.50.
Spec. Scallop shumai. Chilean sea bass mooli roll. Stir fry of Mongolian rib-eye beef.
◆ Converted 1960s post office in heart of Soho. Choose between darker, atmospheric basement or lighter, brighter ground floor. Refined Chinese dishes served on both levels.

X **Bertorelli**, 11-13 Frith St, W1D 4RB ⊖ *Tottenham Court Road*, ℘ (020) 7494 3491,
bertorelli-soho@groupechezgerard.co.uk, Fax (020) 7439 9431, ⇷ – ≡. ◍◉ ﾑ
VISA
31 AKU t
closed 25-26 December – **Rest** - Italian - a la carte 25.00/40.00 ♇.
◆ A haven of tranquillity from the bustling street below. Discreet and professionally run first floor restaurant with Italian menu. Popular ground floor café.

X **Alastair Little**, 49 Frith St, W1D 5SG ⊖ *Tottenham Court Road*, ℘ (020) 7734 5183,
Fax (020) 7734 5206 – ≡. ◍◉ ﾑ ◍ **VISA**
31 AKU y
closed Sunday, Saturday lunch and Bank Holidays – **Rest** (booking essential) 35.00/
38.00.
◆ The eponymous owner was at the vanguard of Soho's culinary renaissance. Tasty, daily changing British based cuisine; the compact room is rustic and simple.

X **Bar Shu**, 28 Frith St, W1D 5LF ⊖ *Leicester Square*, ℘ (020) 7287 8822,
Fax (020) 7287 8858 – ≡ ⇩ 15. ◍◉ ﾑ **VISA**
31 AKU g
closed 25-26 December – **Rest** - Chinese (Sichuan) - 19.50/24.50.
◆ Three floors decorated in carved wood and lanterns. Truly authentic Sichuan cooking typified by intense heat generated by peppers and chillies. Not for the faint hearted!

X **Chinese Experience**, 118 Shaftesbury Ave, W1D 5EP ⊖ *Leicester Square*, ℘ (020)
7437 0377, *info@chineseexperience.com* – ≡. ◍◉ ﾑ **VISA**
31 AKU r
Rest - Chinese - 23.00 (dinner) and a la carte approx 17.00.
◆ Bright, airy restaurant: sit at long bench or chunky wood tables. Large, good value menus cover a wide range of Chinese dishes. Knowledgable service. A buzzy, informal place.

X **Imli**, 167-169 Wardour St, W1F 8WR ⊖ *Tottenham Court Road*, ℘ (020) 7287 4243,
info@imli.co.uk, Fax (020) 7287 4245 – ✸ ≡ ⇩ 40. ◍◉ ﾑ ◍ **VISA**
31 AKU w
Rest - Indian - a la carte 14.00/18.00.
◆ Long, spacious interior is a busy, buzzy place to be: not the venue to while away an evening! Good value, fresh and tasty Indian tapas style dishes prove a popular currency.

X **itsu**, 103 Wardour St, W1F 0UQ ⊖ *Piccadilly Circus*, ℘ (020) 7479 4790,
Fax (020) 7479 4795 – ✸ ≡. ◍◉ ﾑ **VISA**
31 AKU m
closed 25 December – **Rest** - Japanese - (bookings not accepted) a la carte approx
20.00.
◆ Japanese dishes of Sushi, Sashimi, handrolls and miso soup turn on a conveyor belt in a pleasingly hypnotic fashion. Hot bowls of chicken and coconut soup also appear.

X **Aurora**, 49 Lexington St, W1F 9AP ⊖ *Piccadilly Circus*, ℘ (020) 7494 0514, ⇷ – ⇩ 18.
◍◉ ﾑ **VISA**
31 AJU e
closed 23 December-3 January, Sunday and Bank Holidays – **Rest** (booking essential) a la carte 18.95/26.65 ♨.
◆ An informal, no-nonsense, bohemian style bistro with a small, but pretty, walled garden terrace. Short but balanced menu; simple fresh food. Pleasant, languid atmosphere.

X **Fung Shing**, 15 Lisle St, WC2H 7BE ⊖ *Leicester Square*, ℘ (020) 7437 1539,
Fax (020) 7734 0284 – ≡ ⇩ 50. ◍◉ ﾑ ◍ **VISA**
31 AKU j
closed 24-26 December and lunch Bank Holidays – **Rest** - Chinese (Canton) - 17.00/35.00
and a la carte 14.70/28.55 ♇.
◆ A long-standing Chinese restaurant on the edge of Chinatown. Chatty and pleasant service. A mix of authentic, rustic dishes and the more adventurous chef's specials.

Strand and Covent Garden *Gtr London –* ⊠ *WC2.*

Savoy, Strand, WC2R 0EU ⊖ *Charing Cross,* ℰ (020) 7836 4343, *Fax (020) 7240 6040,* ₤₅, ⚏, ☒ – ▐§▌, ⇔ rm, ■ ❤ ⇔ – ☒ 500. ⓂⓈ ☒ ⑩ 𝓥𝓘𝓢𝓐
31 ALU a
Banquette : Rest a la carte 19.00/40.00 𝒴 – (see also ***The Savoy Grill*** below) – ⇨ 25.50 – **236 rm** ✦246.00/457.00 – ✦✦269.00/480.00, 27 suites.
◆ Famous the world over, since 1889, as the epitome of English elegance and style. Celebrated for its Art Deco features and luxurious bedrooms. Banquette is bright, airy, upmarket American diner.

Swissôtel The Howard, Temple Pl, WC2R 2PR ⊖ *Temple,* ℰ (020) 7836 3555, *reser vations.london@swissotel.com, Fax (020) 7379 4547,* ⇐, ⇔ – ▐§▌, ⇔ rm, ■ ❤ ⇔ – ☒ 120. ⓂⓈ ☒ ⑩ 𝓥𝓘𝓢𝓐. ⅋
32 AMU e
Rest – (see ***Jaan*** below) 𝒴 – ⇨ 23.50 – **177 rm** ✦370.00/541.00 – ✦✦370.00/541.00, 12 suites.
◆ Cool elegance is the order of the day at this handsomely appointed hotel. Many of the comfortable rooms enjoy balcony views of the Thames. Attentive service.

The Waldorf Hilton, Aldwych, WC2B 4DD ⊖ *Covent Garden,* ℰ (020) 7836 2400, *wal dorflondon@hilton.com, Fax (020) 7836 7244,* ₤₅, ⚏, ☒ – ▐§▌, ⇔ rm, ■ ❤ ♿ – ☒ 400. ⓂⓈ ☒ ⑩ 𝓥𝓘𝓢𝓐. ⅋
32 AMU u
Homage : Rest *(closed lunch Saturday and Sunday)* 19.50 (lunch) and a la carte 29.00/43.50 – ⇨ 22.00 – **289 rm** ✦233.00/375.00 – ✦✦233.00/375.00, 10 suites.
◆ Impressive curved and columned façade: an Edwardian landmark. Basement leisure club. Ornate meeting rooms. Two bedroom styles: one contemporary, one more traditional. Large, modish brasserie with extensive range of modern menus.

One Aldwych, 1 Aldwych, WC2B 4RH ⊖ *Covent Garden,* ℰ (020) 7300 1000, *sales@onealdwych.com, Fax (020) 7300 1001,* ₤₅, ⚏, ☒ – ▐§▌, ⇔ rm, ■ ❤ ♿ ▣ – ☒ 50. ⓂⓈ ☒ ⑩ 𝓥𝓘𝓢𝓐. ⅋
r
Indigo : Rest a la carte 29.25/39.00 𝒴 – (see also ***Axis*** below) – ⇨ 21.95 – **96 rm** ✦400.00 – ✦✦423.00, 9 suites.
◆ Decorative Edwardian building, former home to the Morning Post newspaper. Now a stylish and contemporary address with modern artwork, a screening room and hi-tech bedrooms. All-day restaurant looks down on fashionable bar.

St Martins Lane, 45 St Martin's Lane, WC2N 4HX ⊖ *Charing Cross,* ℰ (020) 7300 5500, *sml@morganshotelgroup.com, Fax (020) 7300 5501,* ⇔, ₤₅ – ▐§▌, ⇔ rm, ■ ❤ ⇔ – ☒ 40. ⓂⓈ ☒ ⑩ 𝓥𝓘𝓢𝓐. ⅋
31 ALU e
Asia de Cuba : Rest - Asian - a la carte 36.00/84.00 – ⇨ 19.00 – **202 rm** ✦235.00/370.00 – ✦✦259.00/394.00, 2 suites.
◆ The unmistakable hand of Philippe Starck evident at this most contemporary of hotels. Unique and stylish, from the starkly modern lobby to the state-of-the-art rooms. 350 varieties of rum at fashionable Asia de Cuba.

The Savoy Grill (at Savoy H.), Strand, WC2R 0EU ⊖ *Charing Cross,* ℰ (020) 7592 1600, *savoygrill@marcuswareing.com, Fax (020) 7592 1601-* ⇔ ■ ⇔ 55. ⓂⓈ ☒ 𝓥𝓘𝓢𝓐 31 ALU a
Rest 30.00/65.00 🍴 𝒴 ⅋.
Spec. Omelette Arnold Bennett with Scottish lobster and hollandaise. Fillet of beef with potato galette and truffle sauce. Earl Grey tea cream and Garibaldi biscuits.
◆ Seamlessly conserving its best traditions, the Grill buzzes at midday and in the evening. Formal service; menu of modern European dishes and the Savoy classics.

Ivy, 1 West St, WC2H 9NQ ⊖ *Leicester Square,* ℰ (020) 7836 4751, *Fax (020) 7240 9333 –* ■. ⓂⓈ ☒ 𝓥𝓘𝓢𝓐
31 AKU p
closed 25-26 December, 1 January and August Bank Holiday – Rest a la carte 26.25/ 56.75 𝒴.
◆ Wood panelling and stained glass combine with an unpretentious menu to create a veritable institution. A favourite of 'celebrities', so securing a table can be challenging.

Axis, 1 Aldwych, WC2B 4RH ⊖ *Covent Garden,* ℰ (020) 7300 0300, *axis@onealdwych.com, Fax (020) 7300 0301–* ■. ⓂⓈ ☒ ⑩ 𝓥𝓘𝓢𝓐
31 AMU r
closed 24 December-4 January, Easter, Sunday, Saturday lunch and Bank Holidays – Rest (live music at dinner Tuesday and Wednesday) 20.50 (lunch) and a la carte 27.85/ 36.70 🍴 𝒴.
◆ Lower-level room overlooked by gallery bar. Muted tones, black leather chairs and vast futuristic mural appeal to the fashion cognoscenti. Globally-influenced menu.

Jaan (at Swissôtel The Howard), Temple Pl, WC2R 2PR ⊖ *Temple,* ℰ (020) 7300 1700, *jaan.london@swissotel.com, Fax (020) 7240 7816,* ⇔ – ■. ⓂⓈ ☒ ⑩ 𝓥𝓘𝓢𝓐
32 AMU e
closed Saturday lunch and Sunday – Rest 22.00/38.00 𝒴.
◆ Bright room on the ground floor of the hotel with large windows overlooking an attractive terrace. Original cooking - modern French with Cambodian flavours and ingredients.

XX **J. Sheekey,** 28-32 St Martin's Court, WC2N 4AL ⊖ *Leicester Square*, ℘ (020) 7240 2565, reservations@j-sheekey.co.uk, Fax (020) 7497 0891 – ▤. **⑩⑥ ⴷⴼ ① VISA**
31 **ALU v**
closed 25-26 December, 1 January and August Bank Holiday – **Rest** - Seafood - (booking essential) a la carte 22.00/49.25 ঊⴷ ⵛ.
♦ Festooned with photographs of actors and linked to the theatrical world since opening in 1890. Wood panels and alcove tables add famed intimacy. Accomplished seafood cooking.

XX **Rules,** 35 Maiden Lane, WC2E 7LB ⊖ *Leicester Square*, ℘ (020) 7836 5314, info@rules.co.uk, Fax (020) 7497 1081 – ⵛ✕ ▤. **⑩⑥ ⴷⴼ VISA**
31 **ALU n**
closed 4 days Christmas – **Rest** - British - (booking essential) a la carte 29.85/40.85 ঊⴷ ⵛ.
♦ London's oldest restaurant boasts a fine collection of antique cartoons, drawings and paintings. Tradition continues in the menu, specialising in game from its own estate.

XX **Clos Maggiore,** 33 King St, WC2 8JD ⊖ *Leicester Square*, ℘ (020) 7379 9696, enqui ries@maggiores.uk.com, Fax (020) 7379 6767 – ⵛ✕ ▤ ⇔ 20. **⑩⑥ ⴷⴼ VISA**
31 **ALU z**
closed Saturday lunch, Sunday and Bank Holidays – **Rest** - French - 19.50/24.50 and a la carte 27.00/41.00 ঊⴷ ⵛ ⵙ.
♦ Walls covered with flowering branches create delightful woodland feel to rear dining area with retractable glass roof. Seriously accomplished, original, rustic French cooking.

XX **Admiralty,** Somerset House, The Strand, WC2R 1LA ⊖ *Temple*, ℘ (020) 7845 4646, Fax (020) 7845 4658 – ⵛ✕ ▤. **⑩⑥ ⴷⴼ ① VISA**
32 **AMU a**
closed 24-27 December and dinner Sunday and Bank Holiday Mondays – **Rest** 19.50 (lunch) and a la carte approx 40.00 ⵛ.
♦ Interconnecting rooms with bold colours and informal service contrast with its setting within the restored Georgian splendour of Somerset House. 'Cuisine de terroir'.

XX **Bank,** 1 Kingsway, Aldwych, WC2B 6XF ⊖ *Covent Garden*, ℘ (020) 7379 9012, ald wych.restaurant@bankrestaurants.com, Fax (020) 7379 9014 – ▤. **⑩⑥ ⴷⴼ ①
VISA**
32 **AMU s**
closed Sunday dinner – **Rest** 16.00 (lunch) and a la carte 26.40/41.75 ঊⴷ ⵛ.
♦ Ceiling decoration of hanging glass shards creates a high level of interest in this bustling converted bank. Open-plan kitchen provides an extensive array of modern dishes.

XX **Le Deuxième,** 65a Long Acre, WC2E 9JH ⊖ *Covent Garden*, ℘ (020) 7379 0033, Fax (020) 7379 0066 – ▤. **⑩⑥ ⴷⴼ VISA**
31 **ALU b**
closed 24-25 December – **Rest** 15.50 (lunch) and a la carte 25.25/29.25 ঊⴷ ⵛ.
♦ Caters well for theatregoers: opens early, closes late. Buzzy eatery, quietly decorated in white with subtle lighting. Varied international menu: Japanese to Mediterranean.

X **L'Atelier de Joël Robuchon,** 13-15 West St, WC2H 9NE ⊖ *Leicester Square*, ℘ (020)
⊛ 7010 8600, Fax (020) 7010 8601 – ▯ ⵛ✕ ▤. **⑩⑥ ⴷⴼ ① VISA**
31 **AKU a**
Rest - French - 30.00/60.00 and a la carte 33.00/79.00 ঊⴷ ⵛ – *La Cuisine :* **Rest** - French - (booking essential) 30.00/80.00 and a la carte 36.00/82.00 ⵛ.
Spec. Warm foie gras with roasted peaches. Lamb cutlets with fresh thyme. Crispy frog's legs with sweet garlic mash and parsley coulis.
♦ Entrance into trendy atelier with counter seating; upstairs the more structured La Cuisine has wonderfully delicate, precise modern French cooking. Cool top floor lounge bar.

X **Le Café du Jardin,** 28 Wellington St, WC2E 7BD ⊖ *Covent Garden*, ℘ (020) 7836 8769, Fax (020) 7836 4123 – ▤. **⑩⑥ ⴷⴼ VISA**
31 **ALU f**
closed 24-25 December – **Rest** 15.00 (lunch) and a la carte 24.75/28.75 ঊⴷ ⵛ ⵙ.
♦ Divided into two floors with the downstairs slightly more comfortable. Light and contemporary interior with European-influenced cooking. Ideally placed for the Opera House.

X **Portrait,** 3rd Floor, National Portrait Gallery, St Martin's Pl, WC2H 0HE ⊖ *Charing Cross*, ℘ (020) 7312 2490, portrait.restaurant@searcys.co.uk, Fax (020) 7925 0244, ≤ – ▯ ⵛ✕ ▤. **⑩⑥ ⴷⴼ VISA**
31 **ALV n**
closed 25 December, 1 January and Sunday – **Rest** (booking essential) (lunch only and dinner Thursday and Friday) a la carte 25.40/38.50 ঊⴷ ⵛ.
♦ On the top floor of National Portrait Gallery with rooftop local landmark views: a charming spot for lunch. Modern British/European dishes find favour with hungry tourists.

X **The National Dining Rooms,** Sainsbury Wing, The National Gallery, Trafalgar Sq, WC2N 5DN ⊖ *Charing Cross*, ℘ (020) 7747 2525, enquiries@thenationaldiningrooms.co.uk
– ▯ ⵛ✕ ▤. **⑩⑥ ⴷⴼ VISA**
31 **AKV b**
closed Christmas – **Rest** - British - (lunch only and dinner Wednesday) 19.95 and a la carte 23.00/37.50 ⵛ.
♦ Set on the East Wing's first floor, you can tuck into cakes in the bakery or grab a prime corner table in the restaurant for great views and proudly seasonal British menus.

X **Bedford & Strand,** 1a Bedford St, WC2E 9HH ⊖ *Charing Cross*, ℘ (020) 7836 3033 –
⑩⑥ ⴷⴼ VISA
31 **ALU c**
closed 25-26 December, 1 January, Saturday lunch, Sunday and Bank Holidays – **Rest** (booking essential) 15.50 and a la carte 17.40/26.50 ⵛ.
♦ Basement bistro/wine bar with simple décor and easy-going (if somewhat smokey) atmosphere; kitchen sources well and has a light touch with Italian, French and British dishes.

Victoria *Gtr London –* ⊠ *SW1.*
🚺 *Victoria Station Forecourt.*

🏛 **The Goring,** 15 Beeston Pl, Grosvenor Gdns, SW1W 0JW ⊖ Victoria, ℰ (020) 7396 9000, *reception@goringhotel.co.uk, Fax (020) 7834 4393,* ☞ – |📶| ▤ 📞 – 🔏 50. 🆎 🆎 🅾 𝗩𝗜𝗦𝗔.
✦
38 AIX **a**
Rest - British - *(closed Saturday lunch)* 31.00/46.00 ⊈ � – ⊑ 24.00 – **65 rm** ✦347.00/405.00
– ✦✦541.00, 6 suites.
♦ Opened in 1910 as a quintessentially English hotel. The fourth generation of Goring is now at the helm. Many of the attractive rooms overlook a peaceful garden. Elegantly appointed restaurant provides memorable dining experience.

🏛 **Crowne Plaza London - St James,** 45 Buckingham Gate, SW1E 6AF ⊖ St James's, ℰ (020) 7834 6655, *sales@cplonsj.co.uk, Fax (020) 7630 7587,* ℔, ☎ – |📶|, ✦rm, ▤ ⅊ – 🔏 180. 🆎 🆎 🅾 𝗩𝗜𝗦𝗔. ✦
39 AJX **e**
Bistro 51 : Rest 15.00 (lunch) and a la carte 20.55/46.20 ⊈ – (see also *Quilon* and *Bank* below) – ⊑ 16.00 – **323 rm** ✦323.00 – ✦✦323.00, 19 suites.
♦ Built in 1897 as serviced accommodation for visiting aristocrats. Behind the impressive Edwardian façade lies an equally elegant interior. Quietest rooms overlook courtyard. Bright and informal café-style restaurant.

🏛 **51 Buckingham Gate,** 51 Buckingham Gate, SW1E 6AF ⊖ St James's, ℰ (020) 7769 7766, *info@51-buckinghamgate.co.uk, Fax (020) 7828 5909,* ℔, ☎ – |📶| ▤ 📞. 🆎 🆎 🅾 𝗩𝗜𝗦𝗔. ✦
39 AJX **s**
Rest – (see *Quilon* and *Bank* below) – ⊑ 19.00 –, **86 suites** 360.00/975.00.
♦ Canopied entrance leads to luxurious suites: every detail considered, every mod con provided. Colour schemes echoed in plants and paintings. Butler and nanny service.

🏛 **41** without rest., 41 Buckingham Palace Rd, SW1W 0PS ⊖ Victoria, ℰ (020) 7300 0041, *book41@rchmail.com, Fax (020) 7300 0141* – |📶| ▤ 📞. 🆎 🆎 🅾 𝗩𝗜𝗦𝗔
38 AIX **n**
⊑ 17.50 **27 rm** ✦264.00/347.00 – ✦✦288.00/382.00, 1 suite.
♦ Discreet appearance; exudes exclusive air. Leather armchairs; bookcases line the walls. Intimate service. State-of-the-art rooms where hi-tec and fireplace merge appealingly.

🏛 **The Rubens at The Palace,** 39 Buckingham Palace Rd, SW1W 0PS ⊖ Victoria, ℰ (020) 7834 6600, *bookrb@rchmail.com, Fax (020) 7828 5401* – |📶| ✦rm ▤ 📞 – 🔏 90. 🆎 🆎 🅾 𝗩𝗜𝗦𝗔
38 AIX **n**
Rest *(closed lunch Saturday and Sunday)* (carvery) 22.50/29.00 and a la carte 34.00/40.00 ⊈
– ⊑ 17.50 – **170 rm** ✦153.00/259.00 – ✦✦188.00/317.00, 2 suites.
♦ Traditional hotel with an air of understated elegance. Tastefully furnished rooms: the Royal Wing, themed after Kings and Queens, features TVs in bathrooms. Smart carvery restaurant. Intimate, richly decorated Library restaurant has sumptuous armchairs.

🏛 **Victoria Park Plaza,** 239 Vauxhall Bridge Rd, SW1V 1EQ ⊖ Victoria, ℰ (020) 7769 9999, *vppsales@parkplazahotels.co.uk, Fax (020) 7769 9998,* ℔, ☎ – |📶| ✦rm ▤ 📞 & 🅿 – 🔏 750. 🆎 🆎 🅾 𝗩𝗜𝗦𝗔. ✦
38 AIY **a**
J.B.'s : Rest *(closed Saturday lunch and Bank Holidays)* 18.50 and a la carte 19.40/31.90 –
⊑ 17.00 – **299 rm** ✦294.00 – ✦✦335.00.
♦ Conveniently located for Victoria station. Spacious modern interior filled with modish artwork. State-of-the-art meeting rooms. Well-equipped rooms boast a host of facilities. Appealing dining room offers modern European cuisine.

🏛 **Jolly St Ermin's,** Caxton St, SW1H 0QW ⊖ St James's, ℰ (020) 7222 7888, *stermin suk@jollyhotels.com, Fax (020) 7222 6914* – |📶|, ✦rm, ▤ rm – 🔏 150. 🆎 🆎 🅾 𝗩𝗜𝗦𝗔. ✦
39 AKX **a**
Rest 22.50/26.50 and a la carte 37.00/45.80 – ⊑ 16.00 – **272 rm** ✦199.00/281.00 –
✦✦199.00/304.00, 8 suites.
♦ Ornate plasterwork to both the lobby and the balconied former ballroom are particularly striking features. Club rooms have both air conditioning and a private lounge. Grand brasserie with ornate ceiling.

🏛 **City Inn,** 30 John Islip St, SW1P 4DD ⊖ Pimlico, ℰ (020) 7630 1000, *westminster@cit yinn.com, Fax (020) 7932 4609,* ℔ – |📶| ✦rm ▤ 📞 & – 🔏 150. 🆎 🆎 🅾 𝗩𝗜𝗦𝗔. ✦
39 ALY **a**
City Cafe : Rest 17.50 and a la carte 22.00/33.00 ⊈ – ⊑ 19.00 – **444 rm** ✦311.00 –
✦✦311.00, 16 suites.
♦ Modern hotel five minutes' walk from Westminster Abbey and Tate Britain. Well-appointed bedrooms with high-tech equipment and some with pleasant views of London. Brasserie serving modern-style food next to a glass-covered terrace with artwork feature.

🏛 **B + B Belgravia** without rest., 64-66 Ebury St, SW1W 9QD ⊖ Victoria, ℰ (020) 7259 8570, *info@bb-belgravia.com, Fax (020) 7259 8591,* ☞ – ✦rm 📺 📞 & 🆎 🆎 𝗩𝗜𝗦𝗔
18 RZF **x**
17 rm ⊑ ✦94.00 – ✦✦99.00.
♦ Two houses, three floors, and, considering the location, some of the best value accommodation in town. Sleek, clean-lined rooms. Breakfast overlooking little garden terrace.

Winchester without rest., 17 Belgrave Rd, SW1V 1RB ⊖ *Victoria*, ℘ (020) 7828 2972, *winchesterhotel17@hotmail.com, Fax (020) 7828 5191 –* ⊗
18 rm ⊐ ✦75.00 – ✦✦85.00.
38 AIY s
◆ Behind the portico entrance one finds a friendly, well-kept private hotel. The generally spacious rooms are pleasantly appointed. Comprehensive English breakfast offered.

Express by Holiday Inn without rest., 106-110 Belgrave Rd, SW1V 2BJ ⊖ *Pimlico*, ℘ (020) 7630 8888, *info@hiexpressvictoria.co.uk, Fax (020) 7828 0441 –* 🛗 ⊗ ㅎ. ◍ 🝑 ① 𝖵𝖨𝖲𝖠 ⊗
52 rm ✦99.00/135.00 – ✦✦99.00/135.00.
39 AJZ c
◆ Converted Georgian terraced houses a short walk from station. Despite property's age, all rooms are stylish and modern with good range of facilities including TV movies.

The Cinnamon Club, Great Smith St, SW1P 3BU ⊖ *St James's*, ℘ (020) 7222 2555, *info@cinnamonclub.com, Fax (020) 7222 1333 –* ▤ 🅿 ⇦ 50. ◍ 🝑 ① 𝖵𝖨𝖲𝖠
39 AKY c
closed Sunday and Bank Holidays – **Rest** - Indian - 22.00 (lunch) and a la carte 26.50/51.50 ♧.
◆ Housed in former Westminster Library: exterior has ornate detail, interior is stylish and modern. Walls are lined with books. New Wave Indian cooking with plenty of choice.

Quilon (at Crowne Plaza London - St James H.), 45 Buckingham Gate, SW1 6AF ⊖ *St James's*, ℘ (020) 7821 1899, *info@quilonrestaurant.co.uk, Fax (020) 7233 9597 –* ⊗ ▤. ◍ 🝑 ① *closed Saturday lunch* – **Rest** - Indian - 15.95 (lunch) and dinner a la carte 27.00/35.50 ♈.
39 AJX e
◆ A selection of Eastern pictures adorn the walls in this smart, modern and busy restaurant. Specialising in progressive south coast Indian cooking.

Santini, 29 Ebury St, SW1W 0NZ ⊖ *Victoria*, ℘ (020) 7730 4094, *info@santini-restaurant.com, Fax (020) 7730 0544,* ㅈ – ▤. ◍ 🝑 𝖵𝖨𝖲𝖠
38 AHY v
closed 25 December, 1 January, lunch Saturday and Sunday – **Rest** - Italian - a la carte 35.50/55.50 ♈.
◆ Discreet, refined and elegant modern Italian restaurant. Assured and professional service. Extensive selection of modern dishes and a more affordable set lunch menu.

Shepherd's, Marsham Court, Marsham St, SW1P 4LA ⊖ *Pimlico*, ℘ (020) 7834 9552, *admin@langansrestaurants.co.uk, Fax (020) 7233 6047 –* ▤ ⇦ 24. ◍ 🝑 ① 𝖵𝖨𝖲𝖠
39 AKY z
closed 25-26 December, Saturday, Sunday and Bank Holidays – **Rest** - British - (booking essential) 33.00.
◆ A truly English restaurant where game and traditional puddings are a highlight. Popular with those from Westminster - the booths offer a degree of privacy.

Roussillon, 16 St Barnabas St, SW1W 8PE ⊖ *Sloane Square*, ℘ (020) 7730 5550, *alexis@roussillon.co.uk, Fax (020) 7824 8617 –* ▤. ◍ 🝑 𝖵𝖨𝖲𝖠
38 AHZ c
closed 1 week August, 25 December, Saturday lunch, Sunday and Bank Holidays – **Rest** - French - 35.00/48.00 ♈ ♤.
Spec. Wild asparagus with poached quail eggs and lemon zest. Venison with caramelised pumpkin and poached pear. Apricot soufflé with dark chocolate sauce.
◆ Tucked away in a smart residential area. Cooking clearly focuses on the quality of the ingredients. Seasonal menu with inventive elements and a French base.

Atami, 37 Monck St (entrance on Great Peter St), SW1P 2BL ⊖ *St James's Park*, ℘ (020) 7222 2218, *mail@atami-restaurant.com, Fax (020) 7222 2788 –* ⊗ ▤. ◍ 🝑 𝖵𝖨𝖲𝖠
39 AKY a
closed Sunday – **Rest** - Japanese - a la carte 18.50/40.50.
◆ Clean, modern lines illuminated by vast ceiling orbs induce a sense of calm. Menus true to Japanese roots feature sushi and sashimi turning down interesting modern highways.

Il Convivio, 143 Ebury St, SW1W 9QN ⊖ *Sloane Square*, ℘ (020) 7730 4099, *comments@etruscarestaurants.com, Fax (020) 7730 4103,* ㅈ – ▤ ⇦ 14. ◍ 🝑 ① 𝖵𝖨𝖲𝖠
38 AHY a
closed 25 December and Sunday – **Rest** - Italian - 26.50/38.50 (lunch) and a la carte approx 30.00 ♈.
◆ A retractable roof provides alfresco dining to part of this comfortable and modern restaurant. Contemporary and traditional Italian menu with home-made pasta specialities.

Bank, 45 Buckingham Gate, SW1E 6BS ⊖ *St James's*, ℘ (020) 7379 9797, *westres@bankrestaurants.com, Fax (020) 7240 7001,* ㅈ – ▤. ◍ 🝑 ① 𝖵𝖨𝖲𝖠
39 AJX e
closed Saturday lunch and Sunday – **Rest** 17.95 (lunch) and a la carte 26.85/40.25 ♧ ♈.
◆ The understated entrance belies the vibrant contemporary interior. One of Europe's longest bars has a lively atmosphere. Conservatory restaurant, modern European cooking.

RAMOS PINTO

Est. 1880

Little Red Riding Hood

But Little Red Riding Hood had her regional map with her, and so she did not fall into the trap. She did not take the path through the wood and she did not meet the big bad wolf. Instead, she chose the picturesque touring route straight to Grandmother's house, and arrived safely with her cake and her little pot of butter.

The End

XX **Boisdale,** 15 Eccleston St, SW1W 9LX ⊖ *Victoria*, ℘ (020) 7730 6922, *info@bois
dale.co.uk, Fax (020) 7730 0548*, 🎺 – 🔲 ⇔ 20. 🐵 🖭 ⓞ *VISA*   38 AHY c
closed Christmas and Sunday – **Rest** - Scottish - (live jazz at dinner) a la carte 28.95/
47.95 ♀.
♦ Popular haunt of politicians; dark green, lacquer red panelled interior. Run by a Scot of
Clanranald, hence modern British dishes with Scottish flavour.

XX **Rex Whistler,** Tate Britain, Millbank, SW1P 4RG ⊖ *Pimlico*, ℘ (020) 7887 8825, *tate.res
taurant@tate.org.uk, Fax (020) 7887 8902* – 🔲. 🐵 🖭 ⓞ *VISA*   39 ALY c
closed 25 December – **Rest** (booking essential) (lunch only) a la carte 27.70/32.20 ♀ 🌣.
♦ Continue your appreciation of art when lunching in this basement room decorated with
original Rex Whistler murals. Forever busy, it offers modern British fare.

XX **Ken Lo's Memories of China,** 65-69 Ebury St, SW1W 0NZ ⊖ *Victoria*, ℘ (020) 7730
7734, *Fax (020) 7730 2992* – 🔲. 🐵 🖭 ⓞ *VISA*   38 AHY u
closed 25-26 December and Sunday lunch – **Rest** - Chinese - a la carte approx 28.00 ♀.
♦ An air of tranquillity pervades this traditionally furnished room. Lattice screens add extra
privacy. Extensive Chinese menu: bold flavours with a clean, fresh style..

X **Olivo,** 21 Eccleston St, SW1W 9LX ⊖ *Victoria*, ℘ (020) 7730 2505, *maurosanna@oli
veto.fsnet.co.uk, Fax (020) 7823 5377* – 🔲. 🐵 🖭 ⓞ *VISA*   38 AHY z
closed lunch Saturday and Sunday and Bank Holidays – **Rest** - Italian (Sardinian specialities) -
19.50 (lunch) and a la carte 27.50/35.00.
♦ Rustic, informal Italian restaurant. Relaxed atmosphere provided by the friendly staff.
Simple, non-fussy cuisine with emphasis on best available fresh produce.

X **La Poule au Pot,** 231 Ebury St, SW1W 8UT ⊖ *Sloane Square*, ℘ (020) 7730 7763,
Fax (020) 7259 9651, 🎺 – 🔲. 🐵 🖭 ⓞ *VISA*   38 AHY p
closed 25 December – **Rest** - French - 16.50 (lunch) and a la carte 25.50/41.00.
♦ The subdued lighting and friendly informality make this one of London's more romantic
restaurants. Classic French menu with extensive plats du jour.

🍺 **The Ebury,** Ground Floor, 11 Pimlico Rd, SW1W 8NA ⊖ *Sloane Square*, ℘ (020) 7730
6784, *info@theebury.co.uk, Fax (020) 7730 6149* – 🔲. 🐵 🖭 *VISA*. ⋙   38 AHZ z
closed 25-26 December – **Rest** a la carte 23.00/29.00 ♀.
♦ Victorian corner pub restaurant with walnut bar, simple tables and large seafood bar.
Friendly service. Wide-ranging menu from snacks to full meals.

🍺 **The Thomas Cubitt,** First Floor, 44 Elizabeth St, SW1W 9PA ⊖ *Sloane Square*, ℘ (020)
7730 6060, *reservations@thethomascubitt.co.uk, Fax (020) 7730 6055* – ⋙. 🐵 🖭
VISA   18 RZF e
closed 4 days Easter, 25 December and 1 January – **Rest** (booking essential) 21.50 (lunch)
and a la carte 26.50/47.00 ♀.
♦ Georgian pub refurbished and renamed after master builder. He'd approve of elegant,
formal dining room. Carefully supplied ingredients underpin tasty, seasonal English
dishes.

Do not confuse X with ❀!
X defines comfort, while stars are awarded for the best cuisine,
across all categories of comfort.

LONGBRIDGE *Warks. – see Warwick.*

LONG CRENDON *Bucks.* 503 504 R 28 – *pop. 2 383* – ⊠ *Aylesbury.*
London 50 – Aylesbury 11 – *Oxford 15.*

✗ **Angel** with rm, 47 Bicester Rd, HP18 9EE, ℰ (01844) 208268, *angelrestaurant@aol.co.uk*,
Fax (01844) 202497, ☆ – ⇌ rm, **P.** **⓪⓪** **VISA**. ⅍
Rest *(closed Sunday dinner)* 19.95 (lunch) and a la carte 30.00/45.00 ℤ – **3 rm** ⊇ ✦65.00 –
✦✦85.00.
◆ Part 16C building with a pubby feel - leather furnished lounge bar, tiled floors and low
ceilings. Seasonally changing menus with fresh seafood a speciality. Stylish rooms.

LONGHORSLEY *Northd.* 501 502 O 18 – *see Morpeth.*

LONG MELFORD *Suffolk* 504 W 27 *Great Britain G.* – *pop. 2 734.*
See : *Melford Hall*★ *AC.*
London 62 – Cambridge 34 – Colchester 18 – Ipswich 24.

🏨 **Black Lion,** The Green, CO10 9DN, ℰ (01787) 312356, *enquiries@blacklionhotel.net*,
Fax (01787) 374557, ☆ – ⇌ **P.** **⓪⓪** **AE** **①** **VISA**
Rest a la carte 20.40/32.45 ℤ – **9 rm** ⊇ ✦90.50 – ✦✦170.00, 1 suite.
◆ 17C inn overlooking the village green and beyond to the Tudor Melford Hall. Individual
rooms have a mix of furnishings with much use of antique pine. Stylish restaurant with
walled garden terrace.

✗✗ **Chimneys,** Hall St, CO10 9JR, ℰ (01787) 379806, *sam.chalmers@chimneyslongmel*
ford.co.uk, Fax (01787) 312294 – **⓪⓪** **AE** **VISA**
closed Sunday – **Rest** (lunch booking essential) 21.50 and a la carte 27.65/37.35 ℤ.
◆ Part 16C timbered cottage in village centre. Something of a quaint country atmosphere
amidst exposed beams. British and Continental food with international touches.

✗ **Scutchers,** Westgate St, CO10 9DP, on A 1092 ℰ (01787) 310200, *eat@scutchers.com*,
Fax (01787) 375700 – ⇌ ▤. **⓪⓪** **AE** **VISA**
closed Christmas, 10 days March, 10 days August, Sunday and Monday – **Rest** a la carte
27.00/38.00 ℤ.
◆ Former medieval Hall House now contains an informal and unpretentious restaurant
serving a range of creative modern dishes using good quality ingredients.

LONGRIDGE *Lancs.* 502 M 22 – *pop. 7 491.*
London 241 – Blackburn 12 – Burnley 18.

✗✗ **The Longridge Restaurant,** 104-106 Higher Rd, PR3 3SY, Northeast : ½ m. by
B 5269 following signs for Jeffrey Hill ℰ (01772) 784969, *longridge@heathcotes.co.uk*,
Fax (01772) 785713 – ⇌ ▤ ⇔ 18. **⓪⓪** **VISA**
closed 1 January, 27-28 December, Saturday lunch and Monday – **Rest** 22.00 (lunch) and a
la carte 23.25/39.00 ℤ.
◆ Contemporary styling in a modern pub with modern cooking boasting a decidedly Lancastrian bias throughout the contemporary, seasonal menus. Friendly service.

✗ **Thyme,** 1-3 Inglewhite Rd, PR3 3SR, ℰ (01772) 786888, Fax (01772) 786888 – ⇌. **⓪⓪** **AE**
VISA
closed 2-9 January and Monday – **Rest** 10.95/23.90 ℤ.
◆ Modern restaurant near roundabout; wooden floors and modern lighting; artwork on
the walls. Locally sourced produce used as much as possible. Good value, especially at
lunch.

at Knowle Green *East : 2¼ m. by A 5269 on B 6243* – ⊠ *Longridge.*

⌂ **Oak Lea** without rest., Clitheroe Rd, PR3 2YS, East : ½ m. on B 6243 ℰ (01254) 878486,
tandm.mellor@tiscali.co.uk, Fax (01254) 878486, ☞ – ⇌ **P.** ⅍
closed Christmas – **3 rm** ⊇ ✦24.00/34.00 – ✦✦50.00/52.00.
◆ Neat little guesthouse in the heart of the Ribble Valley with fine all-round views. Conservatory with access to mature garden. Pleasantly furnished bedrooms.

LONG SUTTON *Somerset* 503 L 30 – ⊠ *Langport.*
London 132.5 – Bridgwater 16 – Yeovil 10.

🏚 **The Devonshire Arms** with rm, TA10 9LP, ℰ (01458) 241271, *mail@thedevonshir*
earms.com, Fax (01458) 241037, ☆, ☞ – ⇌ **P.** **⓪⓪** **VISA**
Rest *(closed Sunday dinner October-May)* a la carte 20.00/30.00 – **9 rm** ⊇ ✦60.00/75.00 –
✦✦75.00/120.00.
◆ 17C ivy-clad ex-hunting lodge on the green. Sun-trap terrace and walled garden. Modern sofa-strewn interior in tune with refined, flavoursome menus. Boldly appointed
rooms.

LONGTOWN *Cumbria* 501 502 L 18.
London 326 – Carlisle 9 – Newcastle upon Tyne 61.

⌂
Bessiestown Farm ⊗, Catlowdy, CA6 5QP, Northeast : 8 m. by Netherby St on B 6318
🏠 *ℰ* (01228) 577219, *info@bessiestown.co.uk*, Fax (01228) 577019, ⬛, ⚘, 🐾 – ✜⚬ **P**. **⓪** **AE**
VISA. ✦
closed 25 December – **Rest** (by arrangement) 16.50 – 6 rm ⊐ ✜45.00 – ✜✜70.00/120.00.
◆ Comfortable, warm accommodation in homely, modern farmhouse conversion in a
rural location on a working farm. Décor has a traditional British tone, well-kept throughout.
Home-cooked food served in airy dining room.

LOOE *Cornwall* 503 G 32 *The West Country G.* – *pop. 5 280.*
See : Town★ – Monkey Sanctuary★ *AC.*
🏌 *Bin Down ℰ* (01503) 240239 – 🏌 *Whitsand Bay Hotel, Portwrinkle, Torpoint ℰ* (01503)
230276.
🅱 *The Guildhall, Fore St ℰ* (01503) 262072.
London 264 – Plymouth 23 – Truro 39.

🏛
Barclay House, St Martins Rd, East Looe, PL13 1LP, East : ½ m. by A 387 on B 3253
ℰ (01503) 262929, *info@barclayhouse.co.uk*, Fax (01503) 262632, ≤, ⬛, ⚘ – ✜⚬ **P**. **⓪**
AE **VISA**. ✦
closed 5 days Christmas and 2 weeks mid January – **Rest** – (see **The Restaurant** below) –
10 rm ⊐ ✜40.00/90.00 – ✜✜100.00/150.00.
◆ Smart but relaxed and welcoming hotel near harbour. Gardens overlooking estuary.
Snug sitting room and bar. Individually decorated bedrooms.

⌂
Bucklawren Farm ⊗ *without rest.,* St Martin-by-Looe, PL13 1NZ, Northeast : 3 ½ m.
by A 387 and B 3253 turning right onto single track road signposted to Monkey Sanctuary
ℰ (01503) 240738, *bucklawren@btopenworld.com*, Fax (01503) 240481, ≤, ⚘, 🐾 – ✜⚬ **P**.
⓪ **VISA**. ✦
March-October – 6 rm ⊐ ✜30.00/50.00 – ✜✜54.00/60.00.
◆ Characterful farmhouse within 500 acre working farm. Large conservatory overlooks
pleasant garden. Spotlessly kept interior with simple, country house-style bedrooms.

✕✕
The Restaurant (at Barclay House), St Martin's Rd, East Looe, PL13 1LP, East : ½ m. by
A 387 on B 3253 *ℰ* (01503) 262929, Fax (01503) 262632, ≤, ⚘ – ✜⚬ **P**. **⓪** **AE** **VISA**
closed Christmas, 2 weeks mid January, Saturday and Sunday – **Rest** (lunch only) a la carte
20.00/30.00 ♀.
◆ Extensive views of estuary. Matching mustard coloured walls and table cloths. Attentive
well-informed service. Eclectic menu using fresh local produce, particularly seafood.

✕
Trawlers on the Quay, The Quay, East Looe, PL13 1AH, *ℰ* (01503) 263593,
info@trawlersrestaurant.co.uk – ✜⚬. **⓪** **AE** **VISA**
closed 25-26 December, and Sunday-Monday – **Rest** (dinner only) a la carte 23.50/31.95.
◆ Personally run restaurant in a pretty setting on the quay. Faux marble table tops; clean,
neutral décor. Balanced menu of local seafood and meat dishes. Home-made bread, too.

at Talland Bay *Southwest : 4 m. by A 387 –* ⊠ *Looe.*

🏨
Talland Bay ⊗, PL13 2JB, *ℰ* (01503) 272667, *reception@tallandbayhotel.co.uk*,
Fax (01503) 272940, ≤, ⬛ heated, ⚘ – ✜⚬ **P**. **⓪** **VISA**
Terrace : Rest 18.00/32.50 ♀ – 20 rm ⊐ ✜75.00/130.00 – ✜✜150.00/195.00, 3 suites.
◆ 16C house in secluded position with lovely gardens. Well chosen fabrics and furniture
create a warm and comfortable environment. Many rooms with sea views. Modern fine
dining from interesting menu.

LORTON *Cumbria* 502 K 20 – *see Cockermouth.*

LOUGHBOROUGH *Leics.* 502 503 504 Q 25 – *pop. 55 258.*
🏌 *Lingdale, Joe Moore's Lane, Woodhouse Eaves ℰ* (01509) 890703.
🅱 *Town Hall, Market Pl ℰ* (01509) 218113.
London 117 – Birmingham 41 – Leicester 11 – Nottingham 15.

🏛
The Old Manor *without rest.,* 11-14 Sparrow Hill, LE11 1BT, off Baxter Gate *ℰ* (01509)
211228, *bookings@oldmanor.com*, Fax (01509) 211128 – ✜⚬ **℃**. **⓪** **AE** **VISA**. ✦
⊐ 10.50 – 8 rm ⊐ ✜92.00 – ✜✜120.00.
◆ Charming part 15C house close to a church and away from the town centre. Spacious
breakfast room with Hispanic feel and characterful bedrooms.

at Burton-on-the-Wolds *East : 3¾ m. by A 60 on B 676 – ⊠ Loughborough.*

Lang's, Horse Leys Farm, LE12 5TQ, East : 1 m. on B 676 *℘* (01509) 880980, *langsrestaur ant@amserve.net, Fax (01509) 889018 – ⇌ P̄. ◍◐ VISA*
closed Sunday dinner and Monday – **Rest** 15.50 (lunch) and a la carte 22.00/32.00 **s**..
♦ Converted barn in a rural location. Snug, simple and homely rustic feel. Good, tasty and unpretentious menu built around a strong seasonal foundation.

at Quorndon *Southeast : 3 m. by A 6 – ⊠ Loughborough.*

Quorn Country H., 66 Leicester Rd, LE12 8BB, *℘* (01509) 415050, *Fax (01509) 415557, 🌭 – ⇌ rm, ☰ rm, ♨ P̄ – 🏛 300. ◍◐ ☎ ◑ VISA. ⚘*
Shires : Rest *(closed Saturday lunch)* 24.00 and a la carte 22.00/39.70 ⚎ – **Orangery :** Rest *(closed Saturday lunch)* 23.50 and a la carte 22.50/39.20 ⚎ – ⚏ 10.95 – **28 rm** ⚗110.00/150.00 – ⚗⚗125.00/150.00, 2 suites.
♦ Personally run hotel based around a listed 17C building, once a private club. Very comfortable and appealingly traditional, individually decorated bedrooms. Classic, intimate, traditionally styled Shires. Spacious Orangery features hanging plants and rural art

Quorn Grange, 88 Wood Lane, LE12 8DB, Southeast : ¾ m. *℘* (01509) 412167, *mail@quorngrangehotel.co.uk, Fax (01509) 415621, 🌭 – ⇌ ♿ P̄ – 🏛 100. ◍◐ ☎ VISA. ⚘*
closed 1 week Christmas – **Rest** (bar lunch Monday-Saturday)/dinner 22.00 and a la carte 22.40/29.90 **s.** – **38 rm** ⚗72.00/92.00 – ⚗⚗92.00/112.00.
♦ Spacious 18th century building in landscaped garden. Owned by a media union and used, though not exclusively, for union business. Agreeable, uniformly decorated bedrooms. Bright conservatory dining room with pleasant garden views.

at Belton *West : 6 m. by A 6 on B 5324 – ⊠ Loughborough.*

The Queen's Head, 2 Long St, LE12 9TP, *℘* (01530) 222359, *enquiries@thequeens head.org, Fax (01530) 224860, 🍴, 🌭 – ⇌ P̄ ⇄ 24. ◍◐ VISA*
closed 25 December – **Rest** *(closed Sunday dinner)* 16.00 and a la carte 25.00/34.00 ⚎ – **6 rm** ⚗60.00 – ⚗⚗100.00.
♦ Early 19C pub, with extension, now embraces a sleek modernity. Restaurant boasts chocolate suede chairs. Serious dining menus evolve constantly. Modish, bright, airy rooms.

LOUTH *Lincs.* **502 504** U 23 – pop. 15 930.
🄳 *The New Market Hall, off Cornmarket ℘* (01507) 609289.
London 156 – Boston 34 – Great Grimsby 17 – Lincoln 26.

Kenwick Park ⚐, LN11 8NR, Southeast : 2 ¼ m. by B 1520 on A 157 *℘* (01507) 608806, *enquiries@kenwick-park.co.uk, Fax (01507) 608027, ≼, ◔, ⚕, ⇌s, ☐, 🏌, 🌭, ⚕, ⚘, squash – ⇌ ♿ ✛ P̄ – 🏛 250. ◍◐ ☎ ◑ VISA*
Rest 25.95 ⚎ – **34 rm** ⚗89.50/99.00 – ⚗⚗100.00/120.00.
♦ Privately owned Victorian house in rural location. Focus is on very comprehensive and up-to-date leisure facilities. Uniform rooms to a high standard. Popular for weddings. Conservatory dining room filled with natural light.

Brackenborough Arms, Cordeaux Corner, Brackenborough, LN11 0SZ, North : 2 m. by A 16 *℘* (01507) 609169, *info@brackenborough.co.uk, Fax (01507) 609413 – ⇌ rm, ♨ P̄ – 🏛 35. ◍◐ ☎ VISA.*
closed 25 December – **Signature :** Rest a la carte 17.25/26.50 ⚎ – **24 rm** ⚗69.00/82.00 – ⚗⚗82.00.
♦ Family owned hotel run with a warm and personal style. Public areas have a relaxed feel and bedrooms are spacious, individually designed and boast a host of extras. Homely dining.

The Beaumont, 66 Victoria Rd, LN11 0BX, by Eastgate off Ramsgate Rd *℘* (01507) 605005, *beaumonthotel@aol.com, Fax (01507) 607768 – 📶 P̄. ◍◐ ☎ VISA*
Rest *(closed Sunday)* 17.95 and a la carte 17.35/30.25 **s.** – **16 rm** ⚗57.00/80.00 – ⚗⚗90.00/130.00.
♦ Conveniently located close to the town centre. A comfy, settled atmosphere in the public areas and especially the bar. Uniformly fitted, comfortable bedrooms. Cosy dining room.

LOVINGTON *Somerset* **503** M 30 – see Castle Cary.

LOWER HARDRES *Kent* **504** X 30 – see Canterbury.

LOWER ODDINGTON *Glos. – see Stow-on-the-Wold.*

LOWER QUINTON Warks. – see Stratford-upon-Avon.

LOWER SLAUGHTER Glos. 503 504 O 28 – see Bourton-on-the-Water.

LOWER SWELL Glos. – see Stow-on-the-Wold.

LOWER WHITLEY Ches. 502 M 24.
London 199 – Liverpool 25 – Manchester 24 – Warrington 7.

🏠 **Chetwode Arms** with rm, Street Lane, WA4 4EN, ℰ (01925) 730203, info@chetwo dearms.com, Fax (01925) 730870, 🌳 – ✖ rest, 🅿. ⓜⓢ ⒶⒺ ⓪ 𝐕𝐈𝐒𝐀
closed 25 December and 1 January – **Rest** 20.00 and a la carte 20.00/35.00 � – **3 rm** 🖙 ✹60.00/100.00 – ✹✹85.00/120.00.
♦ Redbrick 17C coaching inn and lawned garden. Variety of panelled rooms and snugs. Large menus and blackboard specials of classic British dishes. Simple, homely bedrooms.

LOWESTOFT Suffolk 504 Z 26 Great Britain G. – pop. 62 907.
Env. : Norfolk Broads★.
🇮🇸, 🇮🇸 Rookery Park, Carlton Colville ℰ (01502) 509190.
🄳 East Point Pavillion, Royal Plain ℰ (01502) 533600, touristinfo@wavernly.gov.uk.
London 116 – Ipswich 43 – Norwich 30.

at Oulton Broad West : 2 m. by A 146 – ✉ Lowestoft.

🏨 **Ivy House** ⑤, Ivy Lane, NR33 8HY, Southwest : 1 ½ m. by A 146 ℰ (01502) 501353, michelin@ivyhousecountryhotel.co.uk, Fax (01502) 501539, 🌳, ☯ – ♿ 🅿. – 🛎 50. ⓜⓢ ⓪ 𝐕𝐈𝐒𝐀
closed 2 weeks Christmas- New Year – **Rest** – (see **The Crooked Barn** below) – **19 rm** 🖙 ✹95.00 – ✹✹159.00, 1 suite.
♦ Converted farm in rural seclusion down an unmade lane. Well kept gardens and grounds. Spacious bedrooms, in converted barns, have bright, fresh décor.

🍽🍽 **The Crooked Barn** (at Ivy House), Ivy Lane, NR33 8HY, Southwest : 1 ½ m. by A 146 ℰ (01502) 501353, michelin@ivyhousecountryhotel.co.uk, Fax (01502) 501539 – ✖ 🅿. ⓜⓢ ⒶⒺ ⓪ 𝐕𝐈𝐒𝐀
closed 2 weeks Christmas-New Year – **Rest** 15.00/27.50 and a la carte 26.85/38.85 **s**.
♦ Thatched part 18C former hay loft, the focus of Ivy House Farm's characterful setting. Delightful crooked beamed interior. Modern British fare using fresh, local produce.

LOW FELL Tyne and Wear – see Gateshead.

LOWICK Northants.
London 92 – Leicester 39 – Peterborough 23.

🏠 **The Snooty Fox**, 16 Main St, NN14 3BH, ℰ (01832) 733434, thesnootyfox@btinter net.com, Fax (01832) 733931 – 🅿. ⓜⓢ ⓪ 𝐕𝐈𝐒𝐀
🕊 closed dinner 25-26 December and 1-2 January – **Rest** 14.90 (lunch) and a la carte 20.00/28.00 �.
♦ Locally renowned stone-built village inn. Main bar with appealing blackboard menu and elegant dining room. Noteworthy, accomplished rotisserie.

LUDLOW Shrops. 503 L 26 Great Britain G. – pop. 9 548.
See : Town★ Z – Castle★ AC – Feathers Hotel★ – St Laurence's Parish Church★ (Miseri-cords★) S.
Exc. : Stokesay Castle★ AC, NW : 6½ m. by A 49.
🄳 Castle St ℰ (01584) 875053.
London 162 – Birmingham 39 – Hereford 24 – Shrewsbury 29.

Plan on next page

🏨 **Overton Grange**, Hereford Rd, SY8 4AD, South : 1 ¾ m. by B 4361 ℰ (01584) 873500, info@overtongrangehotel.com, Fax (01584) 873524, ≤, 🌳 – ✖ 🅿. ⓜⓢ ⒶⒺ 𝐕𝐈𝐒𝐀. ✼
closed 28 December - 7 January – **Rest** (booking essential for non-residents) (lunch by arrangement) 32.50/39.50 � – **14 rm** 🖙 ✹95.00/140.00 – ✹✹140.00/240.00.
♦ Edwardian country house with good views of the surrounding countryside. Comfortable lounges. Attentive service and well-kept, individual rooms. Accomplished, inventive mod-ern cuisine with a French base.

ENGLAND

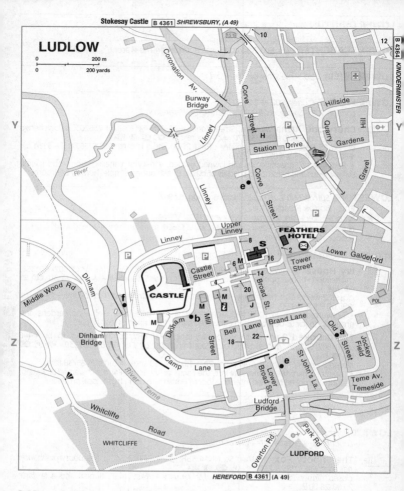

LUDLOW

0   200 m
0   200 yards

FEATHERS HOTEL

CASTLE

HEREFORD B 4361 (A 49)

Dinham Hall, Dinham, SY8 1EJ, ℰ (01584) 876464, info@dinhamhall.co.uk, Fax (01584) 876019, ⚞ – ⚞ rest, ℙ – ⚞ 40. ⚞ ⚞ ⚞ VISA
Z b
Rest 38.50 (dinner) and lunch a la carte 24.50/31.50 ♀ – **13 rm** ⚞ ✝95.00/150.00 – ✝✝140.00/190.00.
♦ 18C manor house, with pretty walled garden, situated by Ludlow Castle in the heart of charming medieval town. Period furnishings and individual rooms. Crisp, bright décor and creative menu.

Bromley Court without rest., 73-74 Lower Broad St, SY8 1PH, ℰ (01584) 876996, ⚞ – ⚞ ⚞ VISA
Z e
minimum stay 2 nights at weekend – **3 rm** ⚞ ✝90.00/110.00 – ✝✝105.00/115.00.
♦ Delightful Tudor cottage converted to provide three well-furnished suites of bed and living room: high quality comfort. Breakfast and check-in opposite at 73 Lower Broad St.

XXX ✿✿ **Hibiscus** (Bosi), 17 Corve St, SY8 1DA, (possible relocation during 2007) ℘ (01584) 872325, Fax (01584) 874024 – ✂ **P.** **M©** **VISA**   Y e
closed 23 December-15 January, 10-18 July, Sunday, Monday and lunch Tuesday – Rest (booking essential) 25.00/45.00 s. ♀.
Spec. Foie gras ice cream with brioche emulsion, balsamic vinegar caramel. Crispy pork belly with eel, white bean and pineapple purée. Iced sweet olive oil parfait with local strawberries.
♦ Two dining rooms, one with 17C oak panelling and the other with exposed stone walls. Precise cooking with some original and innovative touches; attentive formal service.

XX ✿ **Mr Underhill's at Dinham Weir** (Bradley) with rm, Dinham Bridge, SY8 1EH, ℘ (01584) 874431, ≤, 㵘, ♁, 㲍 – ✂ **P.** 㸝   Z f
closed 25-26 December – Rest *(closed Monday-Tuesday)* (booking essential) (set menu only) (dinner only) 45.00/55.00 – **7 rm** ⚏ ✦110.00/150.00 – ✦✦140.00/175.00, 2 suites.
Spec. Asparagus with chervil pasta and sorrel cream. Fillet of beef with ox cheek pie and pickled vegetables. Highland parfait with Drambuie, caramel and flapjack wafers.
♦ Yellow painted riverside house, away from town centre. Daily set menu: unfussy, simple cooking with good flavours, prepared with skill. Smart bedrooms with wood and inlay décor.

X **Koo**, 127 Old St, SY8 1NU, ℘ (01584) 878462, Fax (01584) 878 462 – **M©** **AE** **VISA**   Z a
closed 25 December, 1 January, Sunday and Monday – Rest - Japanese - (light lunch)/dinner 18.95/22.95.
♦ Friendly atmosphere in a simply styled interior decorated with banners and artefacts. Good value meals from a regularly changing menu of authentic and tasty Japanese dishes.

at Woofferton *South : 4 m. by B 4361 – Z – and A 49 –* ✉ *Ludlow.*

⌂ **Ravenscourt Manor** without rest., SY8 4AL, on A 49 ℘ (01584) 711905, *elizabeth@ravenscourtmanor.plus.com, Fax (01584) 711905,* 㵘 – ✂ **P.** 㸝
April-December – **3 rm** ⚏ ✦45.00/55.00 – ✦✦70.00.
♦ Characterful black and white timbered 16C manor house in two and a half acres of lawned gardens. Friendly welcome; comfy lounge. Individually decorated, period style rooms.

at Brimfield *South : 4½ m. by B 4361 – Z – and A 49 –* ✉ *Ludlow.*

⌂ **The Marcle** without rest., SY8 4NE, ℘ (01584) 711459, *marcle@supanet.com, Fax (01584) 711459,* 㵘 – ✂ **P.** 㸝
March-November – **3 rm** ⚏ ✦45.00/75.00 – ✦✦75.00/85.00.
♦ 16C cottage with attractive gardens in the heart of the village. Characterful feel to the interior with its beams and open fires. Compact, comfortable bedrooms.

|◎ **The Roebuck Inn** with rm, SY8 4NE, ℘ (01584) 711230, 㶣 – ✂ **P.** **M©** **①** **VISA**
closed 25-26 December – Rest a la carte 22.00/29.00 ♀ – **3 rm** ⚏ ✦45.00 – ✦✦80.00.
♦ Country pub filled with rustic objects and curios. Well prepared, locally sourced, traditional-style food in bar and formal dining room. Warm, homely bedrooms.

at Orleton *South : 5½ m. by B 4361 – Y –* ✉ *Ludlow.*

⌂ **Line Farm** 㲦 without rest., Tunnel Lane, SY8 4HY, Southeast : ¾ m. ℘ (01568) 780400, *linefarm@lineone.net, Fax (01568) 780995,* ≤, 㵘, ♄ – ✂ **P.** 㸝
March-October – **3 rm** ⚏ ✦65.00 – ✦✦70.00.
♦ Purpose-built house in a relaxing location on a working farm. Pleasant views across a pretty garden to open countryside from each of the comfortable bedrooms.

at Bromfield *Northwest : 2½ m. on A 49 – Y –* ✉ *Ludlow.*

XX **The Clive** with rm, SY8 2JR, ℘ (01584) 856565, *info@theclive.co.uk, Fax (01584) 856661,* 㶣 – ✂ ♿ **P.** 㺉 40. **M©** **AE** **VISA**
closed 25-26 December – Rest 25.00 and a la carte ♀ – **15 rm** ⚏ ✦50.00/75.00 – ✦✦70.00/95.00.
♦ Large converted pub with modern décor in vivid colours. Restaurant, bar, café and bistro areas. Menu of internationally inspired traditional dishes. Very good modern bedrooms.

LUTON *Luton 504* S 28 *Great Britain G. – pop. 185 543.*

Exc. : *Whipsnade Wild Animal Park★, West : 8 m. by B 489, signed from M 1 (junction 9) and M 25 (junction 21)* X.

🏌 *Stockwood Park, London Rd* ℘ (01582) 413704, X – 🄵, 🄵 *South Beds, Warden Hill Rd* ℘ (01582) 575201.

✈ *Luton International Airport :* ℘ (01582) 405100, E : 1½ m. X – **Terminal :** Luton Bus Station.

🅱 *Central Library, St George's Sq* ℘ (01582) 401579.
London 35 – Cambridge 36 – Ipswich 93 – Oxford 45 – Southend-on-Sea 63.

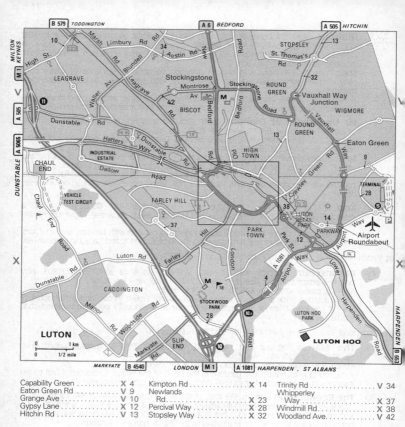

🏨 **St Lawrence,** 40A Guildford St, LU1 2PA, ℰ (01582) 482119, *reservations@hotelstlawrence.co.uk*, Fax (01582) 482818 – ⇇, ▤ rest, ✆. 🕼 ᴀᴇ ① *VISA*. ❀ Y x
Fields : Rest *(closed Sunday, and lunch Saturday* a la carte 19.00/23.00 ♀ – **28 rm** ⌂
✿62.00/77.00 – ✿✿72.00/82.00.
   ◆ Red-brick hotel next to the station. A former hat factory; some decorate the lounge wall. Elsewhere, modern leather prevails. Refurbished bedrooms are smart and clean-lined. Informal restaurant boasts vivid colours and modern, Mediterranean inspired dishes.

at Luton Airport *East : 2 m. by A 505 –* ⊠ *Luton.*

🏨 **Express by Holiday Inn** without rest., 2 Percival Way, LU2 9GP, ℰ (0870) 4448920, *lutonairport@expressbyholidayinn.net*, Fax (0870) 4448930 – ▐ ⇇ ▤ & ᴘ. – 🖾 50. 🕼 ᴀᴇ ① *VISA* X s
147 rm ✿95.00 – ✿✿95.00.
   ◆ Purpose-built hotel handily placed beside the airport. Inclusive contenental breakfasts, plus 24 hour snack menus. Rooms are modern and well-equipped.

> **Your opinions are important to us:**
> please write and let us know about your discoveries and experiences –
> good and bad!

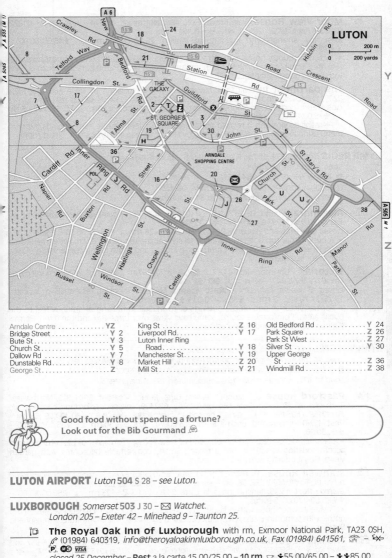

LUTON

0 200 m
0 200 yards

Good food without spending a fortune?
Look out for the Bib Gourmand ⊛

LUTON AIRPORT *Luton* 504 S 28 – *see Luton.*

LUXBOROUGH *Somerset* 503 J 30 – ⊠ *Watchet.*
London 205 – Exeter 42 – Minehead 9 – Taunton 25.

🏠 **The Royal Oak Inn of Luxborough** with rm, Exmoor National Park, TA23 0SH,
📞 (01984) 640319, info@theroyaloakinnluxborough.co.uk, Fax (01984) 641561, ☂ – ⤝⤞
P. ◖◗ *VISA*
closed 25 December – **Rest** a la carte 15.00/25.00 – **10 rm** �

 ✦55.00/65.00 – ✦✦85.00.
♦ Rural inn with bags of character and lots of real ale. Home-cooked food, including fresh
fish and game, served in numerous beamed rooms. Tastefully furnished bedrooms.

LYDDINGTON *Rutland* – *see Uppingham.*

LYDFORD *Devon* 503 H 32 *The West Country G.* – *pop. 1 734* – ⊠ *Okehampton.*
See : *Village*★★.
Env. : *Dartmoor National Park*★★.
London 234 – Exeter 33 – Plymouth 25.

↑ **Moor View House**, Vale Down, EX20 4BB, Northeast : 1 ½ m. on A 386 ℰ (01822) 820220, Fax (01822) 820220, ⇔ – ⇔ **P**. ⚆
Rest (by arrangement) (communal dining) 20.00 – **4 rm** ⇌ ✦45.00/50.00 – ✦✦70.00/80.00.
• Victorian country house with attractive garden. Relaxed and friendly atmosphere with real fires; traditionally furnished with antique pieces. Thoughtful, personal touches. Dine with fellow guests at antique table.

⓾ **The Dartmoor Inn** with rm, Moorside, EX20 4AY, East : 1 m. on A 386 ℰ (01822) 820221, info@dartmoorinn.co.uk, Fax (01822) 820494, ⇔ – ⇔ **P**. ⚆⚆ ஊ 𝘝𝘐𝘚𝘈. ⚆
closed Sunday dinner and Monday – **Rest** 16.95 (lunch) and a la carte 26.50/35.00 ♀ – **3 rm** ⇌ ✦75.00/80.00 – ✦✦100.00/120.00.
• Pleasant service and a relaxed ambience amidst gently rustic surroundings. Modern menu using local ingredients influenced by Mediterranean and local styles. Smart rooms.

LYME REGIS Dorset 503 L 31 The West Country G. – pop. 4 406.
See : Town★ – The Cobb★.
⓲ Timber Hill ℰ (01297) 442963.
🅱 Guildhall Cottage, Church St ℰ (01297) 442138.
London 160 – Dorchester 25 – Exeter 31 – Taunton 27.

🏨 **Alexandra**, Pound St, DT7 3HZ, ℰ (01297) 442010, enquiries@hotelalexandra.co.uk, Fax (01297) 443229, ≤, ⇔ – ⇔ rest, **P**. ⚆⚆ 𝘝𝘐𝘚𝘈
closed Christmas and January – **Rest** 17.50/29.95 – **26 rm** ⇌ ✦65.00/90.00 – ✦✦150.00.
• A busy, family run hotel with traditional style at the top of the town. Set in manicured gardens with views of the sea. Comfortable lounge and south facing conservatory. Tasty, home-cooked menus.

🏨 **Victoria**, Uplyme Rd, DT7 3LP, ℰ (01297) 444801, info@vichotel.co.uk, Fax (01297) 442949 – ⇔ rest, **P**. ⚆⚆ 𝘝𝘐𝘚𝘈. ⚆
closed 2 weeks February – **Rest** (closed Monday) (booking essential) a la carte 15.75/27.70 s. ♀ – **7 rm** ⇌ ✦35.00/70.00 – ✦✦60.00/70.00.
• Former Victorian pub on the outskirts of town. Still something of a pubby feel to the public areas. Comfortable rooms; some have views over Lyme Bay and the town. Formal dining room and brightly coloured bar.

LYMINGTON Hants. 503 504 P 31 – pop. 14 227.
🚢 to the Isle of Wight (Yarmouth) (Wightlink Ltd) frequent services daily (30 mn).
🅱 St Barb Museum & Visitor Centre, New St ℰ (01590) 689000.
London 103 – Bournemouth 18 – Southampton 19 – Winchester 32.

🏨 **Passford House** ⚶, Mount Pleasant Lane, Mount Pleasant, SO41 8LS, Northwest : 2 m. by A 337 and Sway Rd ℰ (01590) 682398, sales@passfordhousehotel.co.uk, Fax (01590) 683494, ≤, ₤₅, ⚌, ⚏ heated, 🔲, ⇔, ♘, ⚒ – ⇔ **P** – 🕭 80. ⚆⚆ ஊ ⓪ 𝘝𝘐𝘚𝘈
Rest 32.50 (dinner) and lunch a la carte 34.00/42.50 s. ♀ – **50 rm** ⇌ ✦85.00/120.00 – ✦✦350.00.
• Classically decorated mansion on edge of New Forest in 10 acres of peaceful grounds accommodating various leisure activities. Smart, comfortable bedrooms with garden views. Elegant dining with pleasant vista.

🏨 **Stanwell House**, 15 High St, SO41 9AA, ℰ (01590) 677123, sales@stanwellhousehotel.co.uk, Fax (01590) 677756, ⇔ – ⇔ rm, ♟ – 🕭 40. ⚆⚆ ஊ 𝘝𝘐𝘚𝘈
Bistro : **Rest** 15.95 (lunch) and a la carte 23.85/27.85 ♀ – **23 rm** ⇌ ✦50.00/85.00 – ✦✦85.00/170.00, 5 suites.
• Privately owned hotel with individual style in Georgian building. Rich décor verges on the gothic with sumptuous silks, crushed velvets and an eclectic mix of furniture. Atmospheric Bistro in dramatic, rich colours.

🏨 **The Mill at Gordleton**, Silver St, Hordle, SO41 6DJ, Northwest : 3 ½ m. by A 337 and Sway Rd ℰ (01590) 682219, info@themillatgordleton.co.uk, Fax (01590) 683073, ⇔ – ⇔, ▦ rest, **P**. ⚆⚆ 𝘝𝘐𝘚𝘈. ⚆
closed 25 December – **Rest** (closed Sunday dinner) 15.50 (lunch) and a la carte 23.25/38.65 ♀ – **6 rm** ⇌ ✦65.00/85.00 – ✦✦125.00/195.00, 1 suite.
• Delightfully located part 17C water mill on edge of New Forest, in well-kept gardens. Comfortable, traditionally styled interior with a pubby bar and clean-lined rooms. Terrace available for alfresco dining.

↑ **Efford Cottage** without rest., Everton, SO41 0JD, West : 2 m. on A 337 ℰ (01590) 642315, effordcottage@aol.com, Fax (01590) 641030 – ⇔ **P**.
closed 25 December – **3 rm** ⇌ ✦55.00 – ✦✦80.00.
• Family run guesthouse in Georgian cottage with garden. Traditional-style interiors include a spacious drawing room with large windows and well-equipped bedrooms.

✗ **Egan's,** 24 Gosport St, SO41 9BG, ℰ (01590) 676165, *johnegan@dsl.pipex.com*, *Fax (01590) 670133 –* ✷✷ ⬤⬤ VISA
closed 26 December-8 January, Sunday and Monday – **Rest** - Bistro - (booking essential) 13.95 (lunch) and dinner a la carte 22.45/30.85.
♦ Bustling bistro style restaurant near the High Street. Warm yellow walls give it a Mediterranean feel. Pleasant, efficient service. Fresh, simple cooking with modern elements.

at Downton *West : 3 m. on A 337 –* ✉ *Lymington.*

⌂ **The Olde Barn** without rest., Christchurch Rd, SO41 0LA, East : ½ m. on A 337 ℰ (01590) 644939, *julie@theoldebarn.co.uk, Fax (01590) 644939 –* ✷✷ P. ⬤⬤ VISA ✍
3 rm ⌯ ✦45.00/70.00 – ✦✦60.00/70.00.
♦ Unsurprisingly, a converted 17C barn with large, chintzy lounge and wood burner. Some bedrooms in barn annex: a mix of modern style and exposed brick, all spotlessly clean.

LYNDHURST *Hants.* 503 504 P 31 *Great Britain G.*
Env. : *New Forest*★★ *(Bolderwood Ornamental Drive*★★ *, Rhinefield Ornamental Drive*★★ *).*
⛳, ⛳ *Dibden Golf Centre, Main Rd* ℰ (023) 8020 7508 – ⛳ *New Forest, Southampton Rd* ℰ (023) 8028 2752.
🅱 *New Forest Museum & Visitor Centre, Main Car Park* ℰ (023) 8028 2269.
London 95 – Bournemouth 20 – Southampton 10 – Winchester 23.

🏨 **Crown,** 9 High St, SO43 7NF, ℰ (023) 8028 2922, *reception@crownhotel-lyndhurst.co.uk, Fax (023) 8028 2751, ☞ –* 📺 ✷✷ ✆ P. – 🅰 70. ⬤⬤ ⓞ VISA
Rest (bar lunch Monday-Saturday)/dinner a la carte 15.95/25.50 s. ♀ – **37 rm** ⌯ ✦77.50/87.50 – ✦✦145.00/185.00, 1 suite.
♦ Extended house with 19C façade in the middle of town - a classically English hotel. Spacious public areas include a wood panelled bar. Bedrooms vary in shapes and sizes. "Decidedly fattening" puddings a dining room speciality.

🏨 **Beaulieu,** Beaulieu Rd, SO42 7YQ, Southeast : 3 ½ m. on B 3056 ℰ (023) 8029 3344, *beaulieu@newforesthotels.co.uk, Fax (023) 8029 2729,* 🖼, ☞ – ✷✷ rest, P. – 🅰 250. ⬤⬤ AE VISA
– **Rest** (dinner only) 21.50 – **23 rm** ⌯ ✦80.00/85.00 – ✦✦130.00/140.00.
♦ Small country hotel in terrific location deep in New Forest, giving some rooms great views. Traditional interior and well-equipped rooms. Dining room is divided into partitioned areas.

🏨 **Ormonde House,** Southampton Rd, SO43 7BT, ℰ (023) 8028 2806, *enquiries@ormondehouse.co.uk, Fax (023) 8028 2004, ☞ –* ✷✷ P. ⬤⬤ VISA
closed Christmas – **Rest** (by arrangement) (residents only) (dinner only) 21.00 – **25 rm** ⌯ ✦40.00/70.00 – ✦✦80.00/125.00.
♦ Privately owned hotel on edge of the New Forest. Decorated in warm pastel colours throughout, including the well-kept bedrooms. Public areas include conservatory lounge. Locally sourced menus.

⌂ **Whitemoor House** without rest., Southampton Rd, SO43 7BU, ℰ (023) 8028 2186, *whitemoor@aol.com –* ✷✷ P. ⬤⬤ VISA ✍
closed 1 week Christmas – **7 rm** ⌯ ✦35.00/50.00 – ✦✦55.00/80.00.
♦ Detached house overlooking the New Forest, a short walk from town. Bright, modern drawing room. Simple, sunny, spacious bedrooms.

LYNMOUTH *Devon* 503 I 30 – *see Lynton.*

LYNTON *Devon* 503 I 30 *The West Country G.*
See : *Town*★ *(*⩽★ *).*
Env. : *Valley of the Rocks*★ *, W : 1 m. – Watersmeet*★ *, E : 1½ m. by A 39.*
Exc. : *Exmoor National Park*★★ *– Doone Valley*★ *, SE : 7½ m. by A 39 (access from Oare on foot).*
🅱 *Town Hall, Lee Rd* ℰ (0845) 6603232, *info@lyntourism.co.uk.*
London 206 – Exeter 59 – Taunton 44.

🏨 **Lynton Cottage** ✍, North Walk Hill, EX35 6ED, ℰ (01598) 752342, *mail@lyntoncottage.co.uk, Fax (01598) 754016,* ⩽ bay and Countisbury Hill, ☺, ☞ – ✷✷ P. ⬤⬤ AE VISA
closed 15 December-February – **Rest** (bar lunch)/dinner 24.00/29.00 s. – **16 rm** ⌯ ✦51.00/58.00 – ✦✦80.00/128.00.
♦ Stunning vistas of the bay and Countisbury Hill from this personally run, cliff top hotel. All bedrooms to a good standard - superior rooms command the best views. Outside the restaurant, stunning sea views. Inside, local art on the walls.

ENGLAND

Hewitt's - Villa Spaldi ⓢ, North Walk, EX35 6HJ, ℰ (01598) 752293, *hewitts.ho tel@talk21.com, Fax (01598) 752489*, ≤ bay and Countisbury Hill, 🍴, 🌳, 🐾 – 🐜 📞 🅿. 🆗 ఔ ⓞ 🆅🆂🅰

February-October – **Rest** 25.00/45.00 s. ♀ – **8 rm** ⚏ ✦65.00/85.00 – ✦✦180.00/240.00, 1 suite.
  ◆ Splendid 19C Arts & Crafts house in tranquil wooded cliffside setting. Stained glass window by Burne Jones and library filled with antiques. Stylish rooms with sea views. Oak panelled dining room; charming service.

Highcliffe House, Sinai Hill, EX35 6AR, ℰ (01598) 752235, *info@highcliffehouse.co.uk, Fax (01598) 753815*, ≤ bay and Countisbury Hill, 🌳 – 🐜 📞 🅿. 🆗 ఔ 🆅🆂🅰. 🌿
closed December-January – **Rest** *(closed Monday-Thursday)* (residents only) (dinner only) 24.95 – **6 rm** ⚏ ✦58.00/80.00 – ✦✦98.00/110.00.
  ◆ Intimate, friendly atmosphere in former Victorian gentleman's residence. Authentic period-style rooms with panoramic views and ornate antique beds. Modern dining room has lovely views from panoramic windows.

Victoria Lodge without rest., 30-31 Lee Rd, EX35 6BS, ℰ (01598) 753203, *info@victor ialodge.co.uk, Fax (01598) 753203*, 🌳 – 🐜 📞 🅿. 🆗 🆅🆂🅰. 🌿
mid March-October – **8 rm** ⚏ ✦63.75 – ✦✦110.00.
  ◆ Large 19C house decorated with period photographs, prints and Victoriana. Traditional décor in communal areas and bedrooms which are comfortable and inviting.

Seawood ⓢ, North Walk, EX35 6HJ, ℰ (01598) 752272, *seawoodhotel@aol.com*, ≤ bay and headland, 🌳 – 🐜 📞 🅿. 🆗 🆅🆂🅰
April-October – **Rest** (dinner only) 25.00 – **12 rm** ⚏ ✦45.00 – ✦✦90.00.
  ◆ Victorian house with marvellous views of bay and headland. Spacious lounges with tranquil, comfy feel. Traditional rooms in floral and pastel shades with four-poster beds. Neatly kept dining room overlooking the sea.

St Vincent ⓢ, Castle Hill, EX35 6JA, ℰ (01598) 752244, *welcome@st-vincent-hotel.co.uk, Fax (01598) 752244*, 🌳 – 🐜 📞. 🆗 🆅🆂🅰. 🌿
Easter - mid December – **Rest** *closed Monday* (booking essential for non-residents) (dinner only) 26.00 – **5 rm** ⚏ ✦60.00 – ✦✦70.00.
  ◆ Grade II listed building with charming Belgian owners 200 metres from Coastal Path. Lovely Edwardian lounge with crackling fire. Neat, simple, clean bedrooms. Cloth-clad dining room: owners proud of French/Mediterranean menus.

at Lynmouth.

Tors ⓢ, EX35 6NA, ℰ (01598) 753236, *torshotel@torslynmouth.co.uk, Fax (01598) 752544*, ≤ Lynmouth and bay, 🏊 heated, 🌳 – 🛗, 🐜 rest, 📞 – 🅿 60. 🆗 ఔ ⓞ 🆅🆂🅰
closed 2 January-2 February – **Rest** (bar lunch)/dinner 30.00 – **31 rm** ⚏ ✦73.00/98.00 – ✦✦106.00/136.00.
  ◆ Perched above Lynmouth and the bay, affording splendid views. Unashamedly traditional: spacious lounges and popular bar. Well-appointed, bright rooms in light tones. Traditional restaurant; tea served on the terrace.

Shelley's without rest., 8 Watersmeet Rd, EX35 6EP, ℰ (01598) 753219, *info@shelley shotel.co.uk, Fax (01598) 753219*, ≤ – 🐜 🆗 🆅🆂🅰. 🌿
March-October – **11 rm** ⚏ ✦60.00/75.00 – ✦✦69.50/109.50.
  ◆ Centrally located hotel named after eponymous poet who honeymooned here in 1812. Stylish public areas. Very comfortable bedrooms with good views of picturesque locale.

Bonnicott House, Watersmeet Rd, EX35 6EP, ℰ (01598) 753346, *bonnicott@aol.com*, ≤, 🌳 – 🐜. 🆗 ఔ 🆅🆂🅰. 🌿
Rest (by arrangement) 26.00 – **8 rm** ⚏ ✦62.00/93.00 – ✦✦70.00/104.00.
  ◆ Former 19C rectory in elevated setting. Spacious lounge with log fire: large windows offer good views to sea. Bright rooms, two with four poster, all with sherry decanter. Fresh, traditional meals cooked on the Aga.

Rising Sun, Harbourside, EX35 6EG, ℰ (01598) 753223, *reception@specialplace.co.uk, Fax (01598) 753480*, ≤, 🌳 – 🐜. 🆗 🆅🆂🅰
closed 25 December **Rest** (bar lunch)/dinner a la carte 26.70/35.45 s. ♀ – **14 rm** ⚏ ✦60.00/85.00 – ✦✦160.00, 1 suite.
  ◆ Part 14C thatched and whitewashed harbourside smuggler's inn. Warm, intimate style. Pubby bar with tiled floor and exposed beams. Well furnished, individually styled rooms. Balanced modern meals making good use of local game and seafood.

The Heatherville ⓢ, Tors Park, EX35 6NB, by Tors Rd ℰ (01598) 752327, *Fax (01598) 752634*, ≤ – 🐜 📞. 🆗 ఔ 🆅🆂🅰
closed December-January – **Rest** (by arrangement) 24.00 – **6 rm** ⚏ ✦84.00 – ✦✦84.00.
  ◆ Victorian house perched above the town. Well kept throughout with bright, warm décor. Rooms with bold fabrics and woodland views: room 6 has the best outlook. Home-cooked meals employ fresh, local produce.

⌂ **Sea View Villa**, 6 Summer House Path, EX35 6ES, ✆ (01598) 753460, *reservations@sea viewvilla.co.uk, Fax* (01598) 753496, ↩ – ⅍ ⅍ ⅍
closed 3 January- 12 February and first 2 weeks November – **Rest** (communal dining) (by arrangement) 27.50 – **5 rm** ☂ ⅍30.00/70.00 – ✦✦100.00/110.00.
✦ Grade II listed Georgian house a stone's throw from harbour. Luxurious interior filled with owners' mementoes. Stylish rooms furnished with taste; all boast enviable sea view. Dinner party style evening meals with fellow guests.

at Martinhoe *West : 4¼ m. via Coast rd (toll)* – ✉ *Barnstaple.*

🏠 **Old Rectory** ⌖, EX31 4QT, ✆ (01598) 763368, *reception@oldrectoryhotel.co.uk, Fax* (01598) 763567, ↩ – ⅍ ⅍ ⅍ ☁ ℙ. ⑩ **VISA**. ⅍
Easter-October – **Rest** (residents only) (dinner only) 33.00 **s.** – **9 rm** (dinner included) ☂ ✦110.00/130.00 – ✦✦180.00/210.00.
✦ Built in 19C for rector of Martinhoe's 11C church. Quiet country retreat in charming three acre garden with cascading brook. Bright and co-ordinated bedrooms. Classic country house dining room.

LYTHAM ST ANNE'S *Lancs.* 502 L 22 – *pop.* 41 327.

🏌 *Fairhaven, Lytham Hall Park, Ansdell* ✆ (01253) 736741 – 🏌 *St Annes Old Links, Highbury Rd* ✆ (01253) 723597.
🛈 *67 St Annes Rd West* ✆ (01253) 725610, *touristinfo@flyde.gov.uk.*
London 237 – Blackpool 7 – Liverpool 44 – Preston 13.

at Lytham.

🏰 **Clifton Arms**, West Beach, FY8 5QJ, ✆ (01253) 739898, *welcome@cliftonarms-lytham.com, Fax* (01253) 730657, ← – ▐ ⅍ ⅍ ℙ. – ⅍ 200. ⑩ ⑩ **VISA**. ⅍
Rest (bar lunch Monday-Saturday)/dinner 25.00 and a la carte 22.00/35.50 ♀ – **45 rm** ☂ ✦100.00 – ✦✦135.00/165.00, 3 suites.
✦ Former coaching inn with strong associations with local championship golf course. Traditional country house public areas. Cottage-style rooms, front ones with great views. Restaurant's popular window tables overlook Lytham Green.

at St Anne's.

🏰 **The Grand**, South Promenade, FY8 1NB, ✆ (01253) 721288, *book@the-grand.co.uk, Fax* (01253) 714459, ←, 🎗, 🏊, 🖼 – ▐ ⅍ ⅍ ℙ – ⅍ 100. ⑩ ⑩ **VISA**. ⅍
closed 24-26 December – **The Bay : Rest** (bar lunch Monday-Saturday)/dinner a la carte 24.00/34.95 ♀ – **53 rm** ☂ ✦120.00/140.00 – ✦✦160.00, 2 suites.
✦ Impressive, turreted Victorian hotel on promenade. Warm, country house-style décor. Spacious rooms, most with good views, turret rooms have particularly good aspect. Rich crimson restaurant overlooks the sea.

🏰 **Dalmeny**, 19-33 South Promenade, FY8 1LX, ✆ (01253) 712236, *reservations@dalmeny hotel.co.uk, Fax* (01253) 724447, ←, 🍴, ⑦, 🎗, 🛎, 🖼, squash – ▐ ⅍ ⅍ ℙ – ⅍ 200. ⑩ ⑩ ⑩ **VISA**. ⅍
closed 24-26 December – **Rest** – (see *Atrium* below) – **127 rm** ☂ ✦77.00/107.50 – ✦✦89.00/162.00.
✦ 1970s building with most rooms overlooking sea. Range of lounges, games rooms, and three restaurants to suit a range of styles and pockets. Well geared up for children.

🏨 **Glendower**, North Promenade, FY8 2NQ, ✆ (01253) 723241, *glendower@bestwestern.co.uk, Fax* (01253) 640069, ←, 🎗, 🛎, 🖼 – ▐ ⅍ ⅍ ℙ – ⅍ 150. ⑩ ⑩ ⑩ **VISA**. ⅍
– **The Clifton : Rest** (bar lunch)/dinner 20.00 – **61 rm** ☂ ✦50.00/120.00 – ✦✦80.00/140.00.
✦ Family owned hotel consisting of 19C buildings overlooking the beach and Irish Sea. Comfortable, traditional style throughout. Choose the west facing rooms for best views. Comfortable, welcoming restaurant.

🏠 **Bedford**, 307-313 Clifton Drive South, FY8 1HN, ✆ (01253) 724636, *reservations@bedford-hotel.com, Fax* (01253) 729244, 🎗 – ▐ ⅍ ⅍ ℙ – ⅍ 120. ⑩ ⑩ **VISA**. ⅍
Rest 25.50 (dinner) and a la carte 20.70/31.40 – **45 rm** ☂ ✦55.00/67.50 – ✦✦114.00.
✦ Privately owned traditional hotel in town centre. Large, comfy public areas include a basement pub with live music most days. Well-kept, simple rooms; those to rear quieter. Daily, fresh, local produce used in restaurant.

✕✕ **Atrium** (at Dalmeny H.), 19-33 South Promenade, FY8 1LX, ✆ (01253) 716009, *Fax* (01253) 724447, – 🍴 ℙ. ⑩ ⑩ ⑩ **VISA**
closed 24-26 December – **Rest** (dinner only) 19.95 and a la carte 23.85/35.40 **s.**
✦ Contemporarily styled open-plan restaurant: bright décor and modern fitted bar. Bustling atmosphere with informality and piped jazz. Regularly changing British menu.

ENGLAND

XX **Greens Bistro,** 3-9 St Andrews Road South - Lower Ground Floor, FY8 1SX, ℰ (01253) 789990, info@greensbistro.co.uk – ◍◍ VISA

closed 1 week spring, 1 week autumn, 25 December, Sunday and Monday – **Rest** (dinner only) 15.95 (Tuesday-Friday) and a la carte 22.25/25.20 ℤ.

♦ Worth the effort to find, this simple, pleasant bistro, hidden beneath some shops, has linen clad tables, friendly service, and good value, well executed modern British menus.

MACCLESFIELD Ches. 502 503 504 N 24 – pop. 50 688.

ꜞ8 *The Tytherington Club* ℰ (01625) 506000 – ꜞ8 *Shrigley Hall, Shrigley Park, Pott Shrigley* ℰ (01625) 575757.

🚩 *Town Hall* ℰ (01625) 504114.

London 186 – Chester 38 – Manchester 18 – Stoke-on-Trent 21.

🏠 **Chadwick House** without rest., 55 Beech Lane, SK10 2DS, North : ¼ m. on A 538 ℰ (01625) 615558, chadwickhouse@ntlworld.com, Fax (01625) 610265 – ⇔ ➿ P. ◍◍ VISA. ✺

14 rm � ✾30.00/40.00 – ✾✾55.00.

♦ Two converted terraced houses away from the town centre. Bedrooms vary in shapes and sizes and all are traditionally decorated and pine furnished.

at Pott Shrigley *Northeast : 4¾ m. by A 523 on B 5090 –* ⊠ *Macclesfield.*

🏰 **Shrigley Hall** ⍉, Shrigley Park, SK10 5SB, North : ¼ m. ℰ (01625) 575757, shrigleyre servations@paramount-hotels.co.uk, Fax (01625) 573323, ⌂, ♁, ⇔s, ⬚, ꜞ8, ⍩, ♨, ⅍ – 📶 ⇔ ➿ P – ▵ 250. ◍◍ AE ⓞ VISA

Oakridge : **Rest** (dinner only) 25.00 and a la carte 24.50/47.50 – **148 rm** � ✾175.00/195.00 – ✾✾195.00.

♦ Peaceful setting for impressive part Edwardian country house with grand staircase and plush lounges. Conference facilities and leisure centre. Rooms with quality décor. Neo-classically styled restaurant.

MADINGLEY Cambs. 504 U 27 – see Cambridge.

MAGHAM DOWN E. Sussex – see Hailsham.

MAIDENCOMBE Devon 503 J 32 – see Torquay.

MAIDENHEAD Windsor & Maidenhead 504 R 29 – pop. 58 848.

ꜞ8 *Bird Hills, Drift Rd, Hawthorn Hill* ℰ (01628) 771030 – ꜞ8 *Shoppenhangers Rd* ℰ (01628) 624693 X.

⛴ *to Marlow, Cookham and Windsor (Salter Bros. Ltd) (summer only) (3 h 45 mn).*

🚩 *The Library, St Ives Rd* ℰ (01628) 796502.

London 33 – Oxford 32 – Reading 13.

Plan opposite

🏨 **Fredrick's,** Shoppenhangers Rd, SL6 2PZ, ℰ (01628) 581000, reservations@fredricks-hotel.co.uk, Fax (01628) 771054, ⌂, ⍩, ♁, ⇔s, ⬚ heated, ⬚, ⍏ – ⇔ ⬚ ➿ P – ▵ 150. ◍◍ AE ⓞ VISA. ✺

X c

Rest – (see **Fredrick's** below) – 33 rm ⍰ ✾215.00 – ✾✾285.00, 1 suite.

♦ Redbrick former inn with well-equipped spa facilities. Ornate, marble reception with smoked mirrors. Conservatory with wicker chairs. Very comfy, individually styled rooms.

🏨 **Holiday Inn Maidenhead,** Manor Lane, SL6 2RA, off Shoppenhangers Rd ℰ (0870) 400 9053, reservations-maidenhead@ichotelsgroup.com, Fax (01628) 506001, ♁, ⇔s, ⬚ – 📶 ⇔ ⬚ ➿ P – ▵ 400. ◍◍ AE ⓞ VISA. ✺

X n

Rest a la carte 19.90/28.85 s. – **193 rm** ⍰ ✾69.00/140.00 – ✾✾105.00/195.00.

♦ 1970s purpose-built hotel. Convenient for M4 motorway. Ideal for business guests with extensive conference facilities and spacious, well-equipped leisure centre.

🏨 **Walton Cottage,** Marlow Rd, SL6 7LT, ℰ (01628) 624394, res@waltoncottageho tel.co.uk, Fax (01628) 773851 – 📶, ⇔ rest, ➿ P – ▵ 40. ◍◍ AE ⓞ VISA. ✺

Y e

closed 24 December-2 January – **Rest** (closed Friday-Sunday and Bank Holidays) (dinner only) 18.75 – **69 rm** ⍰ ✾110.00/120.00 – ✾✾150.00/180.00, 3 suites.

♦ A collection of brick built, bay-windowed houses and annexed blocks near town centre. Poet's Parlour lounge is cosy with beams and brick. Aimed at the business traveller. Restaurant prides itself in traditional home cooking.

ENGLAND

MAIDENHEAD

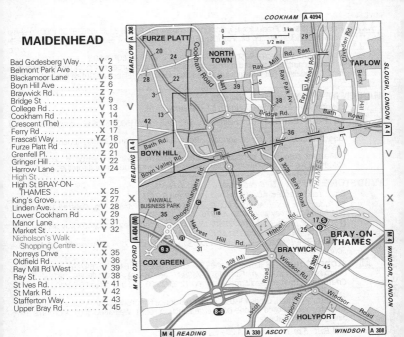

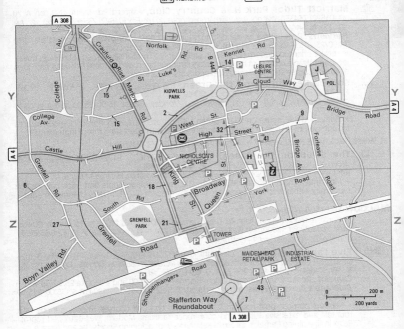

XXX **Fredrick's** (at Fredrick's H.), Shoppenhangers Rd, SL6 2PZ, _(01628) 581000, reserva tions@fredricks-hotel.co.uk, Fax (01628) 771054, 😤, 🌳 – ⤢ ▤ 🅿 🛱 14. ◍ ⒶⒺ ⓞ_
VISA
X c
closed Saturday lunch – **Rest** 29.50/39.50 and a la carte 44.50/56.50 ⒴.
◆ Ornate paintings, smoked mirrors and distressed pine greet diners in this large restaurant. Chandeliers, full-length windows add to classic feel. Elaborate British menus.

MAIDEN NEWTON Dorset 503 504 M 31.

London 144 – Exeter 55 – Taunton 37 – Weymouth 16.

XX **Le Petit Canard**, Dorchester Rd, DT2 0BE, _(01300) 320536, craigs@le-petit-canard.co.uk, Fax (01300) 321286_ – ⤢. ◍ ⒶⒺ VISA
closed Monday and dinner Sunday – **Rest** (dinner only and Sunday lunch by arrangement)/dinner 29.00/33.50 ⒴.
◆ Pleasant stone-built cottage in middle of charming village. Plenty of candles, well-spaced tables and soft music. English dishes with French and Oriental touches.

MAIDSTONE Kent 504 V 30 Great Britain G. – pop. 89 684.

Env. : Leeds Castle★ AC, SE : 4½ m. by A 20 and B 2163.

🛆 Tudor Park Hotel, Ashford Rd, Bearsted _(01622) 734334_ – 🛆 Cobtree Manor Park, Chatham Rd, Boxley _(01622) 753276._

🄳 Town Hall, High St _(01622) 602169, tic@maidstone.gov.uk_ – Motorway Service Area, junction 8, M 20, Hollingbourne _(01622) 739029._

London 36 – Brighton 64 – Cambridge 84 – Colchester 72 – Croydon 36 – Dover 45 – Southend-on-Sea 49.

🏠 **Stone Court**, 28 Lower Stone St, ME15 6LX, _(01622) 769769, swallow.stonecourt@swallowhotels.com, Fax (01622) 769888_ – ⤢ 🅿. – 🛆 80. ◍ ⒶⒺ VISA. 🛇
Chambers : Rest (closed Sunday dinner) 12.95/25.00 and a la carte 25.00/40.50 – **16 rm** ⊡ ✸70.00/95.00 – ✸✸95.00.
◆ Centrally located, Grade II listed former residence for Crown Court judges. Characterful, intimate, oak-panelled lounge bar. Large function room. Well-appointed bedrooms. Fine dining in smart restaurant.

at Bearsted East : 3 m. by A 249 off A 20 – ⊠ Maidstone.

🏛 **Marriott Tudor Park H. & Country Club**, Ashford Rd, ME14 4NQ, on A 20 _(01622) 734334, events.tudor@marriotthotels.co.uk, Fax (01622) 735360_, ≤, 😤, 🌤, Ⅰ₅, ⤢s, 🏊, 🛆, 🌳, 🅿, 🎾 – ⧉ ⤢ ▤ rm, ♿ 🛌 🅿 – 🛆 250. ◍ ⒶⒺ ⓞ VISA. 🛇
Fairviews : Rest (dinner only and Sunday lunch) 27.00 ⒴ – **LongWeekend : Rest** a la carte 14.90/23.20 ⒴ – ⊡ 14.95 – **119 rm** ✸115.00/130.00 – ✸✸115.00/130.00, 1 suite.
◆ Leisure oriented modern hotel set in park near M20 motorway. Aimed at business traveller. Comfortable rooms, many overlooking tranquil courtyard garden. Fairviews has views onto golf course and pool. LongWeekend is casual café-bar.

XX **Soufflé Restaurant on the Green**, The Green, ME14 4DN, _(01622) 737065, Fax (01622) 737065_, 😤 – ⤢ 🅿 ⇆ 25. ◍ ⒶⒺ VISA
closed Saturday lunch, Sunday dinner and Monday – **Rest** 16.50/25.00 and a la carte 32.00/37.00.
◆ Converted 16C house on village green with terrace. Timbered interior. Period features include old bread oven in one wall. Modern dishes with interesting mix of ingredients.

at West Peckham Southwest : 7¾ m. by A 26 off B 2016 – ⊠ Maidstone.

🍴 **The Swan on the Green**, ME18 5JW, _(01622) 812271, info@swan-on-the-green.co.uk, Fax (0870) 0560556_, 😤 – 🅿. ◍ ⒶⒺ ⓞ VISA
Rest (closed 25 December and dinner Sunday and Monday) a la carte 18.00/26.00.
◆ Pleasantly ornate, gabled 16C pub on the green. Village prints and hops balance the modernity within. Micro brewery to rear. Tasty, modern dishes on daily changing menus.

MALDON Essex 504 W 28 – pop. 20 731.

🛆 Forrester Park, Beckingham Rd, Great Totham _(01621) 891406_ – 🛆, 🛆 Bunsay Downs, Little Baddow Rd, Woodham Walter _(01245) 412648_ – 🄳 Coach Lane _(01621) 856503._
London 42 – Chelmsford 9 – Colchester 17.

🏠 **Five Lakes**, Colchester Rd, Tolleshunt Knights, CM9 8HX, Northeast : 8 ¼ m. by B 1026 _(01621) 868888, enquiries@fivelakes.co.uk, Fax (01621) 869696_, 😤, 🌤, Ⅰ₅, ⤢s, 🏊, 🛆, 🌤, 🎾, squash – ⧉ ⤢ 📞 ♿ 🅿 – 🛆 400. ◍ ⒶⒺ VISA. 🛇
Camelot : Rest (closed Sunday-Monday) (dinner only) 27.00 and a la carte 23.50/36.50 ⒴ – **Bejerano's Brasserie : Rest** a la carte 14.90/25.50 ⒴ – ⊡ 13.95 – **190 rm** ✸135.00/215.00 – ✸✸330.00, 4 suites.
◆ Massive, purpose-built hotel in 320 acres with two golf courses, imposing lobby with fountain and extensive leisure and conference facilities. Modern, well-equipped rooms. Relax in fine dining Camelot. Informal Bejerano's with adjoining Sports Bar and terrace.

ENGLAND

MALMESBURY Wilts. 503 504 N 29 *The West Country G.* – pop. 5 094.

See : *Town★ – Market Cross★★ – Abbey★* .

🅱 *Town Hall, Market Lane* ℘ *(01666) 823748.*

London 108 – Bristol 28 – Gloucester 24 – Swindon 19.

Whatley Manor ⌕, Easton Grey, SN12 0RB, West : 2 ¼ m. on B 4040 ℘ (01666) 822888, *reservations@whatleymanor.com, Fax (01666) 826120,* ≤, 🏵, 🕏, 🐾, ⇌s, 🌫, 🐾 – 🛗 ⇄ ♿ & ℙ – ⛟ 40. 🅜🅞 🅐🅔 🆅🅘🆂🅐

The Dining Room : Rest *(closed Monday-Tuesday)* (booking essential for non-residents) (dinner only) 60.00/75.00 s. ⅌ – (see also *Le Mazot* below) – **15 rm** ⊇ – ✦✦280.00/450.00, 8 suites.

Spec. Smoked eel, warm duck and cured foie gras, radish and walnuts. Roast pigeon with foie gras, Sherry and bitter chocolate. Mango cannelloni with lime curd and pink grapefruit jelly.

♦ Extended Cotswold stone manor in its own grounds. Luxurious décor; superb hydrotherapy treatment spa. Elegant, well-appointed, stylish bedrooms in varying sizes. Refined, well-judged and accomplished cooking in The Dining Room overlooking terrace and gardens.

The Old Bell, Abbey Row, SN16 0BW, ℘ (01666) 822344, *info@oldbellhotel.com, Fax (01666) 825145,* 🏵, 🌫 – ✦✦ ♿ ℙ – 🕏 55. 🅜🅞 🅐🅔 🆅🅘🆂🅐

Rest – (see *The Restaurant* below) – **31 rm** ⊇ ✦85.00/95.00 – ✦✦125.00.

♦ Part 13C former abbots hostel with gardens. Elegant public areas with hugely characterful bar and lounge. Handsome, well-kept rooms in coach-house or inn.

Le Mazot (at Whatley Manor), Easton Grey, SN12 0RB, West : 2 ¼ m. on B 4040 ℘ (01666) 822888, *lemazot@whatleymanor.com, Fax (01666) 826120* – ✦✦ ▤ ℙ. 🅜🅞 🅐🅔 🅞 🆅🅘🆂🅐

Rest 21.50 (lunch) and a la carte 25.50/32.00 s. ⅌.

♦ Wood carving and alpine tones recreate a Swiss ambience. Interesting modern menus prevail. Disarmingly relaxed and intimate with assured, friendly service.

The Restaurant (at The Old Bell), Abbey Row, SN16 0BW, ℘ (01666) 822344, *info@old bellhotel.com, Fax (01666) 825145* – ✦✦ ℙ. 🅜🅞 🅐🅔 🆅🅘🆂🅐

Rest a la carte 20.00/38.95.

♦ Charming restaurant with accomplished modern cooking; local ingredients are very much to the fore. Outside terrace with peaceful garden allows for relaxed summer dining.

---

at Crudwell *North : 4 m. on A 429 –* ✉ *Malmesbury.*

The Rectory, SN16 9EP, ℘ (01666) 577194, *info@therectoryhotel.com, Fax (01666) 577853,* 🌫 – ✦✦ ♿ ℙ. 🅜🅞 🅐🅔 🆅🅘🆂🅐

Rest 18.50 (lunch) and dinner a la carte 23.50/31.75 – **11 rm** ⊇ ✦85.00/135.00 – ✦✦155.00, 1 suite.

♦ 17C stone-built former Rectory with formal garden and mature trees. Personally run. Comfortable, individually-styled bedrooms with many modern extras, some with spa baths. Airy oak-panelled dining room; modern seasonal cooking.

MALPAS Ches. 502 503 L 24.

London 177 – Birmingham 60 – Chester 15 – Shrewsbury 26 – Stoke-on-Trent 30.

Tilston Lodge without rest., Tilston, SY14 7DR, Northwest : 3 m. on Tilston Rd ℘ (01829) 250223, Fax (01829) 250223, 🌫, 🐾 – ✦✦ ℙ. ⌗

closed 25 December – **3 rm** ⊇ ✦45.00/50.00 – ✦✦70.00/80.00.

♦ A former Victorian hunting lodge with delightful gardens and grounds, personally run in a very pleasant style by the charming owner. Cosy, individually appointed bedrooms.

MALVERN Worcs. 503 504 N 27 – see Great Malvern.

MALVERN WELLS Worcs. 503 504 N 27 – see Great Malvern.

Douglas: on the seafront

MAN (Isle of)

502 F/G 21 *Great Britain G. – pop. 76 315.*

PRACTICAL INFORMATION

⛴ from Douglas to Belfast (Isle of Man Steam Packet Co. Ltd) (summer only) (2 h 45 mn) – from Douglas to Republic of Ireland (Dublin) (Isle of Man Steam Packet Co. Ltd) (2 h 45 mn/ 4 h) – from Douglas to Heysham (Isle of Man Steam Packet Co.) (2 h 30 mn) – from Douglas to Liverpool (Isle of Man Steam Packet Co. Ltd) (2 h 30 mn/4 h).

SIGHTS

See : *Laxey Wheel*★★ – *Snaefell*★ (☀★★★) – *Cregneash Folk Museum*★.

ENGLAND

Douglas *I.O.M. – pop. 25 347.*

⌐ᵧ₈ Douglas Municipal, Pulrose Park ℰ (01624) 675952 – ⌐ᵧ₈ King Edward Bay, Groudle Rd, Onchan ℰ (01624) 620430.

✈ Ronaldsway Airport : ℰ (01624) 821600, SW : 7 m. – **Terminal** : Coach service from Lord St.

🛈 Sea Terminal Buildings ℰ (01624) 686766.

🏨🏨 **Sefton,** Harris Promenade, IM1 2RW, ℰ (01624) 645500, info@seftonhotel.co.im, Fax (01624) 676004, ₤₆, ⬛s, ⬛ – ⬛ ⇄⇄ rm, ⬛ ⬛ 🅿 – ⬛ 80. ⬛ ⬛ ⬛ ⬛
The Gallery : **Rest** (lunch residents only) 9.95/21.95 and dinner a la carte 28.75/38.85 – ⬚ 9.95 – **97 rm** ✦90.00/100.00 – ✦✦120.00/170.00, 3 suites.
• Enviable promenade position: behind the 19C façade lies a stunning atrium with water features and flora; marble reception. The well-appointed bedrooms overlook the bay. Modish, bright eatery with modern Manx art on the walls.

🏨🏨 **The Regency,** Queens Promenade, IM2 4NN, ℰ (01624) 680680, regency@iom-1.net, Fax (01624) 680690, ⇐ – ⬛⬛, ⇄⇄ rm, ⬛ – ⬛ 30. ⬛ ⬛ ⬛ ⬛. ⬛
Five Continents : **Rest** 22.95 and a la carte 28.20/42.00 ⬛ ⬛ – ⬚ 8.90 – **42 rm** ✦54.00/74.00 – ✦✦82.00, 3 suites.
• Grand-looking, four storey hotel with appealing traditional style. Sea front position with good views over Douglas Bay. Rooms equipped with latest technology. Wood-panelled restaurant with sea outlook.

🏨🏨 **Mount Murray H. & Country Club,** Santon, IM4 2HT, Southwest : 4 ¾ m. by A 5 ℰ (01624) 661111, hotel@mountmurray.com, Fax (01624) 611116, ₤₆, ⬛s, ⬛, ⌐ᵧ₈, squash – ⬛⬛ ⇄⇄ ⬛ ⬛ 🅿 – ⬛ 300. ⬛ ⬛ ⬛ ⬛. ⬛
Charlotte's Bistro : **Rest** (closed Sunday lunch) 22.95 (dinner) and a la carte 16.40/32.45 – **90 rm** ⬚ ✦103.00 – ✦✦175.00.
• Surrounded by vast grounds and golf course. Large sports bar and two lounges. Extensive leisure and conference facilities. Comfortable, modern rooms. Large, formal Murray's overlooks golf course. Charlotte's Bistro offers monthly themed cuisine.

🏨 **Admirals House** without rest., 12 Loch Promenade, IM1 2LX, ℰ (01624) 629551, enqui ries@admiralhouse.com, Fax (01624) 675021 – ⬛ ⇄⇄ ⬛ – ⬛ 40. ⬛ ⬛ ⬛. ⬛
26 rm ⬚ ✦75.00/95.00 – ✦✦120.00/150.00.
• Impressively situated Victorian building on promenade and only two minutes from ferry terminal. Split-level café-bar. Particularly large, modern bedrooms.

🏨 **Empress,** Central Promenade, IM2 4RA, ℰ (01624) 661155, gm@theempresshotel.net, Fax (01624) 6735543, ₤₆, ⬛s – ⬛⬛, ⬛ rest, ⬛ – ⬛ 150. ⬛ ⬛ ⬛ ⬛. ⬛
La Brasserie : **Rest** (bar lunch Monday-Saturday)/dinner a la carte 16.45/26.50 – **100 rm** ⬚ ✦70.00/75.00 – ✦✦75.00/130.00.
• Large Victorian hotel in prominent position on promenade overlooking Douglas Bay. Lounge and bar with jazz style pianist at weekends. Small leisure centre. Modern rooms. Informal, colourful basement brasserie.

🏠 **Penta** without rest., Queens Promenade, IM9 4NE, ℰ (01624) 680680, penta@iom-1.net, Fax (01624) 680690 – ⬛ ⬛ ⬛. ⬛ ⬛ ⬛ ⬛. ⬛
22 rm ✦49.00 – ✦✦57.00/57.00.
• Victorian property with bay windows on the town's main promenade. By way of contrast, spacious and up-to-date bedrooms which include a computer in each room.

XXX **Ciappelli's,** 12-13 Loch Promenade, IM1 2LK, ℰ (01624) 677442, enquiries@ciappel lis.com, Fax (01624) 671305 – ⇄⇄. ⬛ ⬛ ⬛ ⬛
closed 25-26 December, 1 January, Saturday lunch and Sunday – **Rest** 24.50 (lunch) and a la carte 39.50/52.50.
• Sleek promenade destination. Funky basement bar. Split level restaurant enhanced by wall-hung glassware. Immaculate tables; smooth service; locally inspired seasonal dishes.

Port Erin *I.O.M. – pop. 3 369.*

⌂ **Rowany Cottier** without rest., Spaldrick, IM9 6PE, ℰ (01624) 832287, rowanycot tier@manx.net, Fax (01624) 835685, ⇐ Port Erin Bay, ⬛ – ⇄⇄ 🅿. ⬛
5 rm ⬚ ✦40.00/55.00 – ✦✦70.00/76.00.
• Detached house with spectacular views over Port Erin Bay. Homely lounge with open fires. Oak floor and pine tables in breakfast room. Bright, colourful bedrooms.

Port St Mary *I.O.M. – pop. 1 941.*

⌂　**Aaron House** without rest., The Promenade, IM9 5DE, ℰ (01624) 835702 – ⇔, ⚘
　　closed Christmas-New Year – **5 rm** ⊇ ✦69.00/98.00 – ✦✦78.00/98.00.
　　◆ High degree of hospitality guaranteed in this imposing 19C property - owner wears
　　Victorian dresses. Substantial breakfasts. Very comfortable rooms with winning touches.

Ramsey *I.O.M. – pop. 7 322.*

⌂　**The River House** ⚘ without rest., IM8 3DA, North : ¼ m. turning left after bridge
　　before Bridge Inn on Bowring Rd ℰ (01624) 816412, ≤, ⚘ – **P**
　　closed February – **3 rm** ⊇ ✦49.50/75.00 – ✦✦77.00/97.00.
　　◆ Part Georgian house in delightful location along riverside. Peaceful ambience. Country
　　house style lounge. Scrubbed wood breakfast room. Individually styled bedrooms.

Manchester, the Museum of Science and Industry

MANCHESTER

Gtr Manchester **502 503 504** N 23 *Great Britain G.* – pop. 394 269.

London 202 – Birmingham 86 – Glasgow 221 – Leeds 43 – Liverpool 35 – Nottingham 72.

TOURIST INFORMATION

🛈 *Manchester Visitor Centre, Town Hall Extension, Lloyd St ℰ (0161) 234 3158; manchester_ visitor_centre@notes.manchester.gov.uk*
🛈 *Manchester Airport, International Arrivals Hall, Terminal 1 ℰ (0161) 436 3344 – Manchester Airport, International Arrivals Hall, Terminal 2 ℰ (0871) 222 8223 – Salford T.I.C., Pier 8, Salford Quays ℰ (0161) 848 8601.*

PRACTICAL INFORMATION

🏊 *Heaton Park, Prestwich ℰ (0161) 654 9899, ABV.*
🏊 *Houldsworth Park, Houldsworth St, Reddish, Stockport ℰ (0161) 442 1712.*
🏊 *Chorlton-cum-Hardy, Barlow Hall, Barlow Hall Rd ℰ (0161) 881 3139.*
🏊 *William Wroe, Pennybridge Lane, Flixton ℰ (0161) 748 8680.*
✈ *Manchester International Airport : ℰ (0161) 489 3000, S : 10 m. by A 5103 – AX – and M 56.*
Terminal : *Coach service from Victoria Station.*

SIGHTS

See : *City★ - Castlefield Heritage Park★ CZ – Town Hall★ CZ – Manchester Art Gallery★ CZ* **M2** *– Cathedral★ (stalls and canopies★) CY – Museum of Science and Industry★ CZ M. – Urbis★ CY – Imperial War Museum North★ , Trafford Park AX* **M.**

Env. : *Whitworth Art Gallery★ , S : 1½ m.*

Exc. : *Quarry Bank Mill★ , S : 10 m. off B 5166, exit 5 from M 56.*

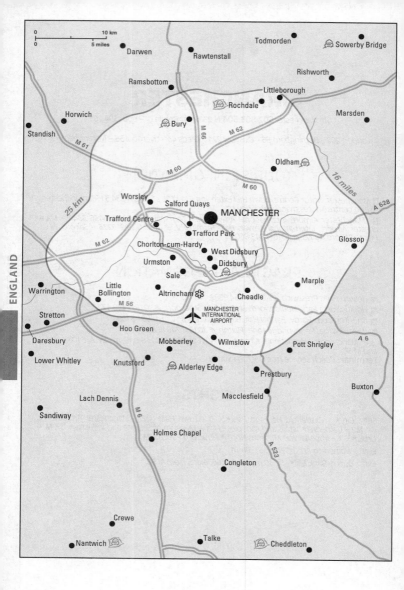

ENGLAND

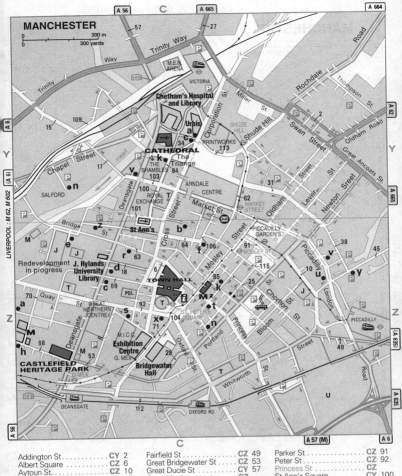

MANCHESTER

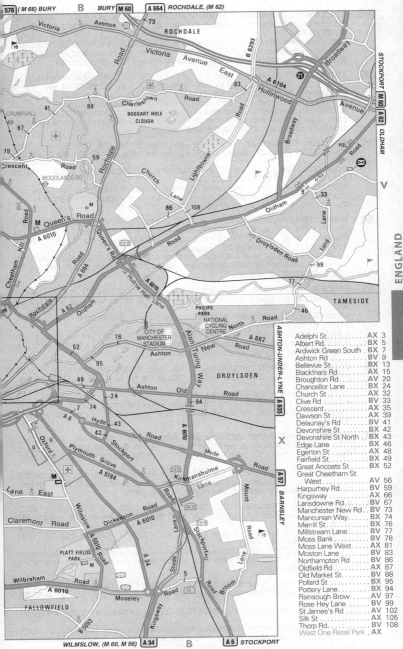

ROCHDALE

STOCKPORT M 60 A 62 OLDHAM

ENGLAND

TAMESIDE

ASHTON-UNDER-LYNE A 635

DROYLSDEN

BARNSLEY A 57

FALLOWFIELD

531

ENGLAND

The Lowry, 50 Dearmans Pl, Chapel Wharf, Salford, M3 5LH, *℘* (0161) 827 4000, *enqui ries@roccofortehotels.com, Fax (0161) 827 4001, ⓜ, ʃჳ, ☎ – ᵗ⫶ 宐 ↩ ﴾ ﴿ ᴾ – ᴀ 400.
ⓜⓒ ᴀᴇ ⓞ ᴠɪsᴀ
CY n
Rest – (see *River* below) – ☲ 17.50 – **158 rm** ✦235.00/270.00 – ✦✦270.00/300.00, 7 suites.
♦ Stylish contemporary design with a minimalist feel. Smart spacious bedrooms have high levels of comfort and facilities; some overlook River Irwell. State-of-the-art spa.

The Midland, 16 Peter St, M60 2DS, *℘* (0161) 236 3333, *themidland@qhotels.co.uk,* Fax (0161) 932 4100, ʃჳ, ☎, ⬛, squash – ᵗ⫶ 宐 ⬛ ﴾ ﴿ – ᴀ 450. ⓜⓒ ᴀᴇ ⓞ ᴠɪsᴀ CZ x
The Colony : Rest *(closed Saturday)* 18.95 (lunch) and dinner a la carte 23.40/35.35 – (see also **The French** below) – ☲ 14.95 – **298 rm** ✦165.00 – ✦✦165.00, 14 suites.
♦ Edwardian splendour on a vast scale in the heart of the city. Period features and a huge open lobby combine with up-to-date facilities to create a thoroughly grand hotel. Brasserie menus take pride of place at the restaurant.

Radisson Edwardian, Free Trade Hall, Peter St, M2 5GP, *℘* (0161) 835 9929, Fax (0161) 835 9979, 宐, ⓜ, ʃჳ, ☎, ⬛ – ᵗ⫶ 宐 rm, ⬛ ﴾ ﴿ ᴾ – ᴀ 425. ⓜⓒ ᴀᴇ ⓞ ᴠɪsᴀ ﴿
CZ s
Opus One : Rest 25.00 (lunch) and a la carte 25.00/33.50 – ☲ 19.00 – **233 rm** ✦167.00/196.00 – ✦✦188.00/240.00, 30 suites.
♦ Smart, modern hotel incorporating impressive façade of Free Trade Hall. Grand surroundings of stone, marble and sculptures. Conference and leisure facilities. Stylish rooms. Chic fine dining, with strong Japanese influences, in Opus One.

Malmaison, Piccadilly, M1 3AQ, *℘* (0161) 278 1000, *manchester@malmaison.com,* Fax (0161) 278 1002, ʃჳ, ☎ – ᵗ⫶, 宐 rm, ⬛ ﴾ ﴿ – ᴀ 75. ⓜⓒ ᴀᴇ ⓞ ᴠɪsᴀ CZ u
Brasserie : Rest 15.95/19.95 and a la carte 24.00/41.00 ﹖ – ☲ 12.75 – **154 rm** ✦99.00/165.00 – ✦✦99.00/165.00, 13 suites.
♦ A more modern brand of hotel that combines contemporary design and fresh décor with an informal and unstuffy atmosphere. Bedrooms are bright, stylish and hi-tech. Bright, characterful brasserie.

Arora International, 18-24 Princess St, M1 4LY, *℘* (0161) 236 8999, *manchesterreser vations@arorainternational.com, Fax (0161) 236 3222 – ᵗ⫶ 宐 ⬛ ﴾ ﴿ – ᴀ 80. ⓜⓒ ᴀᴇ ⓞ ᴠɪsᴀ
CZ t
closed 25 December **Obsidian :** Rest 16.00/19.00 and a la carte 30.00/43.00 – ☲ 13.50 – **141 rm** ✦145.00/175.00 – ✦✦145.00/209.00.
♦ Part owned by Sir Cliff Richard, this Grade II listed building has been refurbished with distinctive modern décor throughout. Very comfy rooms, four with a "Cliff" theme! Stylish basement dining room with eclectic mix of dishes.

Great John Street without rest., Great John St, M3 4FD, *℘* (0870) 2202277, *info@greatjohnstreet.co.uk, Fax (0161) 831 3212, ʃჳ – ᵗ⫶ 宐 ﴾ ﴿ – ᴀ 40. ⓜⓒ ᴀᴇ ⓞ ᴠɪsᴀ ﴿
CZ a
☲ 16.50 – **30 rm** ✦155.00/235.00 – ✦✦235.00.
♦ Revamped 19C school featuring many stylish, elegant touches. Rooftop terrace with champagne bar, hot tub, and city views. State-of-art rooms boast duplex style and vivid hues.

Marriott Manchester Victoria and Albert, Water St, M3 4JQ, *℘* (0161) 832 1188, Fax (0161) 834 2484 – ᵗ⫶, 宐 rm, ⬛ ﴾ ﴿ ᴾ – ᴀ 250. ﴿
AX u
Rest (bar lunch) dinner a la carte 26.50/31.90 ﹖ – ☲ 16.95 – **143 rm** ✦129.00 – ✦✦129.00, 4 suites.
♦ Restored 19C warehouses on the banks of the River Irwell, with exposed brick and original beams and columns. Bedrooms take their themes from Granada Television productions. Restaurant proud of its timbered warehouse origins.

Renaissance, Blackfriars St, Deansgate, M3 2EQ, *℘* (0161) 831 6000, *rhi.manbr.gm@renaissancehotels.com, Fax (0161) 835 3077 – ᵗ⫶ 宐 ⬛ ﴾ ﴿ ᴾ – ᴀ 400. ⓜⓒ ᴀᴇ ⓞ ᴠɪsᴀ ﴿
CY v
Robbies : Rest (dinner only) a la carte 15.00/20.50 ﹖ – ☲ 14.00 – **201 rm** ✦115.00/139.00 – ✦✦135.00/189.00, 4 suites.
♦ Converted 15-storey office block with large, marbled lobby well sited at top of Deansgate. Spacious, well-equipped bedrooms, most enjoying city skyline views. Airy dining room with adjacent bar.

Rossetti (closed for refurbishment until spring 2007), 107 Piccadilly, M1 2DB, *℘* (0161) 247 7744, *reservationsmanchester@abodehotels.co.uk, Fax (0161) 247 7747 – ᵗ⫶ 宐 ﴾ ﴿ ⓜⓒ ᴀᴇ ᴠɪsᴀ
CZ v
Cafe Paradiso : Rest a la carte 25.00/33.00 ﹖ – ☲ 12.00 – **57 rm** ✦125.00 – ✦✦125.00, 4 suites.
♦ Former 19C textile factory with original features: tiled staircases, cast iron pillars. Staff, by contrast, in casual attire. Chic basement bar. Rooms exude designer style. Informal restaurant with wood-burning stove, flexible menu arrangement.

Novotel, 21 Dickinson St, M1 4LX, *(0161) 235 2200, h3145@accor.com, Fax (0161) 235 2210*, ♨, ☎ – ⧉, ⇖ rm, ☎ ⌖ ⌖ – ⚷ 90. ⓶⓪ ΑΕ ⓪ VISA   CZ **n**
Rest *closed Saturday and Sunday lunch* a la carte 18.75/26.85 **s.** ⅋ – ⌓ 12.50 – **164 rm** ✦89.00/119.00 – ✦✦89.00/119.00.
❖ The open-plan lobby boasts a spacious, stylish bar and residents can take advantage of an exclusive exercise area. Decently equipped, tidily appointed bedrooms. Compact dining room with grill-style menus.

The French (at The Midland H.), Peter St, M60 2DS, *(0845) 074 0053, Fax (0161) 932 4100* – ⇖ ☰ P. ⓶⓪ ΑΕ ⓪ VISA   CZ **x**
closed Sunday and Bank Holidays – **Rest** (dinner only) 25.00/41.00 and a la carte 31.00/45.85 ⅋.
❖ As grand as the hotel in which it is housed, with gilded paintings, large mirrors and heavy drapes. Attentively formal service, classically French-based cooking.

Le Mont, Urbis, Levels 5 and 6, Cathedral Gardens, M4 3BG, *(0161) 605 8282, info@le-mont.co.uk, Fax (0161) 605 8283*, ⇐ – ⧉ ⇖ ☰. ⓶⓪ VISA   CY **a**
closed 22 December-2 January, Saturday lunch, Sunday and Monday – **Rest** 19.95 (lunch) and a la carte 28.50/53.00 ⅋.
❖ Set on top of the Urbis Museum, boasting spectacular views of the city: formal dining in dramatic surroundings. Imaginative modern cuisine based around a classic French style.

River (at The Lowry H.), 50 Dearmans Pl, Chapel Wharf, Salford, M3 5LH, *(0161) 827 4003, enquiries@thelowryhotel.com, Fax (0161) 827 4001*, ⌂ – ☰ P. ⓶⓪ ΑΕ ⓪ VISA CY **n**
Rest 25.00 (lunch) and a la carte 40.85/46.20 ⅋.
❖ Matching its surroundings, this is a stylish modern restaurant serving, in a precise manner, classic dishes that have stood the test of time. Irwell views, for good measure.

Cotton House, Ducie St, M1 2TP, *(0161) 237 5052, info@thecottonhouse.net, Fax (0161) 237 5072* – ☰. ⓶⓪ ΑΕ VISA   CZ **y**
closed 25 December, 1-3 January and Sunday dinner – **Rest** a la carte 13.00/29.00 **s.** ☺⅋.
❖ Situated on ground floor of 19C warehouse; stylish Champagne bar. Huge dining room with original styling, affording atmospheric dinners. Well executed modern menus.

Wings, 1 Lincoln Sq, M2 5LN, *(0161) 834 9000, wing@wingsrestaurant.co.uk* – ☰. ⓶⓪ ΑΕ VISA   CZ **d**
closed 25 December – **Rest** - Chinese (Canton) - a la carte 12.60/22.40.
❖ Chinese restaurant hidden off busy square, its smart exterior exuding an up-to-date feel. Carefully prepared, top quality dishes washed down with wide range of champagnes.

Establishment, 43-45 Spring Gdns, M2 2BG, *(0161) 839 6300, Fax (0161) 839 6353* – ⇖ ☰. ⓶⓪ ΑΕ VISA   CZ **f**
closed Saturday lunch and Sunday – **Rest** 21.50 and a la carte 35.50/50.50 ⅋.
❖ Converted Victorian building in city centre: marble columns, ornate glass domed ceilings. Precise, modern dishes, with a classical base, cooked in accomplished fashion.

Second Floor - Restaurant (at Harvey Nichols), 21 New Cathedral St, M1 1AD, *(0161) 828 8898, Fax (0161) 828 8815* – ⇖ ☰. ⓶⓪ ΑΕ VISA   CY **k**
closed 25-26 December, 1 January, Easter Sunday and dinner Sunday and Monday – **Rest** a la carte 27.50/43.50 ⅋.
❖ Central location on second floor of famous department store. Well-designed restaurant with immaculate linen-clad tables. Brasserie style cooking.

Pacific, 58-60 George St, M1 5HF, *(0161) 228 6668, enquiries@pacificrestaurant.co.uk, Fax (0161) 236 0191* – ⧉ ☰. ⓶⓪ ΑΕ VISA   CZ **k**
Rest - Chinese and Thai - 9.50/38.50 and a la carte 17.00/36.00.
❖ Located in Chinatown: Chinese cuisine on first floor, Thai on the second; modern décor incorporating subtle Asian influences. Large menus boast high levels of authenticity.

Simply Heathcotes, Jackson Row, Deansgate, M2 5WD, *(0161) 835 3536, manchester@simplyheathcotes.co.uk, Fax (0161) 835 3534* – ⧉ ⇖ ☰ ⟐ 60. ⓶⓪ ΑΕ ⓪ VISA   CZ **c**
closed 25-26 December and Bank Holidays – **Rest** a la carte 18.25/35.50 ☺⅋.
❖ Contemporary interior, with live jazz in the wine bar, contrasts with the original oak panels of this Victorian former register office. Robust menu is equally à la mode.

Koreana, Kings House, 40a King St West, M3 2WY, *(0161) 832 4330, alexkoreana@aol.com, Fax (0161) 832 2293* – ⓶⓪ ⓪ VISA   CZ **z**
closed 25-26 December, 1 January, Sunday, lunch Saturday and Bank Holidays – **Rest** - Korean - 12.40 and a la carte 11.50/29.50 ☺.
❖ Family run basement restaurant, bustling yet still relaxed, offers authentic, balanced Korean cuisine. Novices are guided gently through the menu by staff in national dress.

XX **Palmiro,** 197 Upper Chorlton Rd, M16 0BH, South : 2 m. by A 56 off Chorlton Rd
    ℰ (0161) 860 7330, *bookings@palmiro.net*, Fax (0161) 861 7464, 🍽 – **①③** **VISA**   AX **b**
closed 25-28 December and 1-3 January – Rest - Italian - (dinner only and Sunday
lunch)/dinner a la carte 19.25/25.55 **s**.
   ◆ Spartan interior with grey mottled walls and halogen lighting: a highly regarded neighbourhood Italian eatery boasting good value rustic dishes cooked with maximum simplicity.

X **The Restaurant Bar and Grill,** 14 John Dalton St, M2 6JR, ℰ (0161) 839 1999,
manchester@rbgltd.co.uk, Fax (0161) 835 1886 – 🍴. **①③** **①** **VISA**   CZ **r**
closed 25 December – Rest a la carte 15.00/35.00 ♀.
   ◆ Stylish ground floor lounge bar and lively first floor eatery. Extensive international repertoire from an open kitchen. Very busy with business community at lunch.

X **Second Floor - Brasserie** (at Harvey Nichols), 21 New Cathedral St, M1 1AH, ℰ (0161)
828 8898, *secondfloor.reservations@harveynichols.com*, Fax (0161) 828 8815 – 🍽 🍴. **①③**
① **VISA**   CY **k**
closed 25 December, 1 January, and dinner Sunday and Monday – Rest a la carte
21.00/29.50 ♀.
   ◆ Open and lively restaurant with minimalist décor. Wide range of cocktails available at the
large bar. Attractive menu with a European eclectic mix of dishes.

X **Brasserie Blanc,** 55 King St, M2 4LQ, ℰ (0161) 832 1000, *manchester@brasserie*
blanc.co.uk, Fax (0161) 832 1001 – 🍴 ⟷ 30. **①③** **①** **VISA**   CZ **b**
closed 25-26 December and 1 January – Rest 12.50/17.50 and a la carte 19.95/34.20 🕒 ♀.
   ◆ Busy, group-owned brasserie with large bar and polished tables. Extensive menus of
classic and modern British dishes as well as regional French options. Attentive service.

X **Shimla Pinks,** Dolefield Crown Sq, M3 3HA, ℰ (0161) 831 7099, *enquiries@shimlapinks*
manchester.com, Fax (0161) 832 2202 – 🍴. **①③** **①** **VISA**   CZ **e**
closed 25 December, 1 January, lunch Saturday and Sunday – Rest - Indian - 8.95/14.95
and a la carte 16.85/26.85 🕒.
   ◆ Centrally located Indian restaurant. Colourful artwork and murals and a bustling modern
ambience. Extensive menus of authentic Indian dishes and regional specialities.

X **Zinc Bar and Grill,** The Triangle, Hanging Ditch, M4 3ES, ℰ (0161) 827 4200, *zincman*
chester-reservations@conran-restaurants.co.uk, Fax (0161) 827 4212, 🍽 – **①③** **①**
VISA   CY **c**
closed 25-26 December – Rest 13.00 (lunch) and a la carte 16.00/27.00 🕒 ♀.
   ◆ Converted 19C corn exchange with bustling atmosphere, background jazz and a late-
night bar. Tables available on pavement and in shopping centre. Modern international
menu.

🍷 **The Ox,** 71 Liverpool Rd, Castlefield, M3 4NQ, ℰ (0161) 839 7760, *gmtheox@baabar.co.uk*
– **①③** **①** **VISA**. 🍸   CZ **h**
Rest 15.00/18.00 and a la carte 19.00/29.00.
   ◆ Central, homely pub, ideal after local museum trip. Cooking style is eclectic, featuring
many well-tried or original dishes. Spot a celebrity from nearby Granada TV studios!

at Didsbury South : 5½ m. by 5103 – AX – on A 5145 – ✉ Manchester.

🏨 **Didsbury House,** Didsbury Park, M20 5LJ, South : 1½ m. on A 5145 ℰ (0161) 448 2200,
enquiries@didsburyhouse.co.uk, Fax (0161) 448 2525, 🛁 – 🍽 **P.** **①③** **①** **VISA**. 🍸
Rest (room service only) – ☲ 14.50 – **23 rm** 🛏88.00 – 🛏🛏145.00, 4 suites.
   ◆ Grade II listed 19C house: grand wooden staircase, superb stained glass window. Other-
wise, stylish and modern with roof-top hot tubs. Spacious, individually designed rooms.

🏨 **Eleven Didsbury Park,** 11 Didsbury Park, M20 5LH, South : ½ m. by A 5145 ℰ (0161)
448 7711, *enquiries@didsburyhouse.co.ukom*, Fax (0161) 448 8282, 🌲 – 🍽 **P.** **①③** **①**
VISA. 🍸
Rest (room service only) – ☲ 14.50 – **20 rm** 🛏95.00/195.00 – 🛏🛏95.00/255.00.
   ◆ The cool contemporary design in this Victorian town house creates a serene and relaxing
atmosphere. Good-sized bedrooms decorated with flair and style. Personally run.

X **Café Jem&I,** 1c School Lane, M20 6SA, ℰ (0161) 445 3996, *jemosullivan@aol.com*,
Fax (0161) 448 8661 – **①③** **①** **VISA**
closed 25-26 December, Monday lunch and Bank Holidays – Rest a la carte 18.65/31.40 **s**.
   ◆ Simple, unpretentious cream coloured building tucked away off the high street. Open-
plan kitchen; homely, bistro feel. Good value, tasty modern classics.

at West Didsbury *South : 5½ m. by A 5103 – AX – and A 5145 – ✉ Manchester.*

✗ **Rhubarb,** 167 Burton Rd, M20 2LN, ✆ (0161) 448 8887, *info@rhubarbrestaurant.co.uk* – ✖ ▬ ◙◙ ஊ *VISA*
closed 25 December, 1 January and Monday – **Rest** (dinner only and Sunday lunch) a la carte 25.40/29.85 ♀.
◆ An eye-catching exterior draws in a loyal local following. Yes, there are rhubarb walls, but the cooking, not so locally inspired, features tasty dishes from far and wide.

at Manchester Airport *South : 9 m. by A 5103 – AX – off M 56 – ✉ Manchester.*

🏨 **Radisson SAS Manchester Airport,** Chicago Ave, M90 3RA, ✆ (0161) 490 5000, *sales.manchester.airport@radissonsas.com*, Fax (0161) 490 5100, ≼, ⌘, ⇌, ☒ – ▐, ✖ rm, ▬ ❄ & ₽ – ▵ 250. ◙◙ ஊ ⓞ *VISA*, ✻
Phileas Fogg : Rest (dinner only) 27.50 and a la carte 25.25/42.50 s. ♀ – *Runway Brasserie :* Rest a la carte 17.20/26.60 s. ♀ – ☲ 16.95 – **354 rm** ✦143.00/155.00 – ✦✦143.00/155.00, 6 suites.
◆ Vast, modern hotel linked to airport passenger walkway. Four room styles with many extras. Ideal for business clients or travellers. Phileas Fogg is curved restaurant with eclectic menus and runway views. All-day Runway with arrivals/departures info.

🏨 **Hilton Manchester Airport,** Outwood Lane (Terminal One), M90 4WP, ✆ (0161) 435 3000, *reservations.manchester@hilton.com*, Fax (0161) 435 3040, ₷, ⇌ – ▐, ✖ rm, ▬ ❄ & ₽ – ▵ 300. ◙◙ ஊ ⓞ *VISA*, ✻
Rest *(closed Sunday lunch)* 14.95/27.95 and dinner a la carte 32.85/44.55 s. – ☲ 17.95 – **224 rm** ✦96.00/193.00 – ✦✦96.00/193.00, 1 suite.
◆ Popular with corporate travellers for its business centre and location 200 metres from the airport terminal. Comfortable, soundproofed bedrooms. Restaurant exudes pleasant, modern style.

🏨 **Etrop Grange,** Thorley Lane, M90 4EG, ✆ (0161) 499 0500, *etropgrange@corushotels.com*, Fax (0161) 499 0790 – ✖ ₽ – ▵ 80. ◙◙ ஊ ⓞ *VISA*
Rest 35.95/44.50 and a la carte 19.20/28.15 s. – ☲ 13.50 – **62 rm** ✦99.00/149.00 – ✦✦99.00/149.00, 2 suites.
◆ Sympathetically extended Georgian house that retains a period feel. Rooms vary in size; all are pleasantly decorated with some boasting four-posters, others cast-iron beds. Intimate, traditionally styled dining room.

🏨 **Bewley's,** Outwood Lane, (Terminal Three), M90 4HL, ✆ (0161) 498 0333, *man@bewleyshotels.com*, Fax (0161) 498 0222 – ▐, ✖ rm, ▬ rest, ❄ & ₽ – ▵ 90. ◙◙ ஊ ⓞ *VISA*, ✻
Rest (bar lunch)/dinner a la carte 17.85/31.85 ♀ – ☲ 6.95 – **365 rm** ✦69.00 – ✦✦69.00.
◆ Good value, four-storey, purpose-built group hotel with modern, open lobby. Brightly decorated bedrooms that all have either one double bed and sofa or two double beds. Appealing, popular dishes in restaurant or lobby café.

✗✗✗ **Moss Nook,** Ringway Rd, Moss Nook, M22 5WD, East : 1 ¼ m. on Cheadle rd ✆ (0161) 437 4778, Fax (0161) 498 8089, ⌗ – ₽. ◙◙ ஊ *VISA*
closed 2 weeks Christmas, Saturday lunch, Sunday and Monday – **Rest** 19.50/37.50 and a la carte 32.50/44.00.
◆ Decorated in a combination of Art Nouveau, lace and panelling. Long-standing owners provide polished and ceremonial service; cooking is robust and classically based.

at Trafford Park *Southwest : 2 m. by A 56 and A 5081 – ✉ Manchester.*

🏨 **Golden Tulip,** Waters Reach, M17 1WS, ✆ (0161) 873 8899, *info@goldentulipmanchester.co.uk*, Fax (0161) 872 6556 – ▐ ✖ ❄ & ₽ – ▵ 180. ◙◙ ஊ ⓞ *VISA*, ✻   AX c
Rest – (see *Watersreach* below) – ☲ 12.00 – **157 rm** ✦75.00/155.00 – ✦✦75.00/155.00, 3 suites.
◆ Manchester United fans will not only appreciate the proximity to the ground but also the football paraphernalia in the lobby. Uniformly decorated bedrooms are a good size.

🏨 **Old Trafford Lodge** without rest., Lancashire County Cricket Club, Talbot Rd, Old Trafford, M16 0PX, ✆ (0161) 874 3333, *lodge@lccc.co.uk*, Fax (0161) 874 3399, ≼ – ▐ ✖ ₽. ◙◙ ஊ *VISA*, ✻   AX k
closed 24 December-2 January – **68 rm** ✦49.00/79.00 – ✦✦49.00/79.00.
◆ Purpose-built lodge within Lancashire County Cricket Club; half the rooms have balconies overlooking the ground. Good value accommodation in smart, colourful bedrooms.

✗✗ **Watersreach,** Waters Reach, M17 1WS, ✆ (0161) 868 1900, *watersreach@goldentulipmanchester.co.uk*, Fax (0161) 868 1901 – ✖ ▬ ₽. ◙◙ ஊ *VISA*, ✻   AX c
closed lunch Saturday, Sunday and Bank Holidays – **Rest** a la carte 22.35/30.85 ♀.
◆ Modern, stylish, David Collins designed restaurant, adjacent to Old Trafford. Smart bar area has comfortable seating. Good, eclectic mix of precisely cooked dishes.

at Salford Quays *Southwest : 2¼ m. by A 56 off A 5063 – ⊠ Manchester.*

Copthorne Manchester, Clippers Quay, M50 3SN, ☎ (0161) 873 7321, *room sales.manchester@mill-cop.com*, Fax (0161) 877 8112 – |📶|, ✳ rm, 🍴 rest, ♿ 🅿 – 🔬 150. 🆗 AE ⓞ VISA ⚬⚬

AX n

Chandlers : Rest *(closed Saturday-Sunday)* (dinner only) 37.50/42.50 and a la carte ♀ –
Clippers : Rest *(bar lunch Saturday)*/dinner a la carte 18.35/33.20 ♀ – ⧄ 15.75 – **166 rm** ✱175.00 – ✱✱175.00.

♦ Part of the redeveloped Quays, overlooking the waterfront, with a Metrolink to the City. Connoisseur bedrooms are particularly well-appointed. Chandlers offers diners enjoyable waterfront views. Informal, pleasantly busy Clippers with open kitchen.

Express by Holiday Inn without rest., Waterfront Quay, M5 2XW, ☎ (0161) 868 1000, *managersalfordquays@expressholidayinn.co.uk*, Fax (0161) 868 1068, ⇐ – |📶| ✳ ☎ ♿ 🅿 – 🔬 25. 🆗 AE ⓞ VISA

AX a

120 rm ✱90.00/100.00 – ✱✱90.00/100.00.

♦ Its pleasant quayside position and modern, well-equipped bedrooms make it a popular choice with both business and leisure travellers. Complimentary breakfast provided.

at Chorlton-Cum-Hardy *Southwest : 5 m. by A 5103 – AX – on a 6010 – ⊠ Manchester.*

Abbey Lodge without rest., 501 Wilbraham Rd, M21 0UJ, ☎ (0161) 862 9266, *info@abbey-lodge.co.uk*, Fax (0161) 862 9266, ⚘ – ✳ 🅿. 🆗 AE VISA. ⚬⚬

AX z

⧄ 5.00 **4 rm** ✱40.00/45.00 – ✱✱60.00.

♦ Attractive Edwardian house boasting many original features including stained glass windows. Owners provide charming hospitality and pine fitted rooms are immaculately kept.

Marmalade, 60 Beech Rd, Chorlton Green, M21 9EG, ☎ (0161) 862 9665, *jqmarmalade@tiscali.co.uk* – 🆗 ⓞ VISA. ⚬⚬

closed 25-26 December – Rest *(closed lunch Monday-Wednesday)* 11.95/14.95 (dinner) and a la carte 17.95/25.00.

♦ Three tier cake stands, crutches and antique suitcases define this eye-catching pub. Food's a serious matter: cracking local menus. Yes, homemade marmalade's on offer, too.

at Trafford Centre *Southwest : 5¼ m. by A 56 – AX – and A 5081 – ⊠ Manchester.*

Tulip Inn, Old Park Lane, M17 8PG, on B 5214 ☎ (0161) 755 3355, *info@tulipinnmanchester.co.uk*, Fax (0161) 755 3344 – |📶|, ✳ rm, 🍴 rest, ♿ 🅿. 🆗 AE ⓞ VISA. ⚬⚬
Rest (dinner only) a la carte approx 15.00 **s.** – ⧄ 8.95 – **160 rm** ✱90.00 – ✱✱90.00.

♦ Large, modern hotel within a stone's throw of the Trafford Centre and M60. Good value accommodation. Bedrooms are notably spacious, well-equipped and up-to-date. Relaxed, informal bistro.

at Worsley *West : 7¼ m. by M 602 – AV – and M 60 (eastbound) on A 572 – ⊠ Manchester.*

Marriott Worsley Park H. & Country Club, Worsley Park, M28 2QT, on A 575 ☎ (0161) 975 2000, *mhrs.mangs.dys@marriotthotels.co.uk*, Fax (0161) 975 2033, ⚘, ♣, ⅃, 🔲, ▯, 🏊 – |📶|, ✳ rm, 🍴 rest, ♿ 🅿 – 🔬 250. 🆗 AE ⓞ VISA. ⚬⚬
Brindley's : Rest *(closed Saturday lunch)* (carving lunch)/dinner 28.00 and a la carte 25.25/39.75 **s.** ♀ – ⧄ 14.95 – **153 rm** ✱109.00/125.00 – ✱✱149.00/159.00, 5 suites.

♦ Built around restored Victorian farm buildings in over 200 acres. Excellent leisure facilities including a championship standard golf course. Large, well-equipped bedrooms. Restaurant is former farm building with high beamed ceiling.

MANCHESTER AIRPORT *Gtr Manchester 502 503 504 N 23 – see Manchester.*

MANSFIELD *Notts. 502 503 504 Q 24.*
London 143 – Chesterfield 12.5 – Worksop 14.5.

No.4 Wood Street, No.4 Wood St, NG18 1QA, ☎ (01623) 424824 – ✳ 🍴 🅿. 🆗 AE VISA

closed 26 December, 1 January, Monday, Sunday dinner and Saturday lunch – Rest 18.95 (lunch) and a la carte 21.15/38.40.

♦ Solid brick restaurant hidden away in town centre. Relax in lounge bar with comfy armchairs before enjoying well-executed, modern, seasonal dishes in rustic dining room.

Do not confuse ✗ with ✿!
✗ defines comfort, while stars are awarded for the best cuisine, across all categories of comfort.

ENGLAND

MARAZION *Cornwall 503* D 33 *The West Country G.* – ✉ *Penzance.*

Env. : St Michael's Mount★★ (≤★★) – Ludgvan★ (Church★) N : 2 m. by A 30 – Chysauster Village★ , N : 2 m. by A 30 – Gulval★ (Church★) W : 2½ m – Prussia Cove★ , SE : 5½ m. by A 30 and minor rd.

📷 *Praa Sands, Penzance* ℰ *(01736) 763445.*

London 318 – Penzance 3 – Truro 26.

🏨 **Mount Haven,** Turnpike Rd, TR17 0DQ, East : ¼ m. ℰ (01736) 710249, *reception@mounthaven.co.uk, Fax (01736) 711658,* ≤ St Michael's Mount and bay, 🍴, 🌳 – 📶 **P.** 🅌 🆅🆂🅰
closed 20 December - February – **Rest** (bar lunch)/dinner a la carte 25.95/30.95 – **18 rm** 🍽 ✸60.00/80.00 – ✸✸70.00/120.00.
 ♦ Small hotel overlooking St Michael's Bay. Spacious bar and lounge featuring Indian crafts and fabrics. Contemporary rooms with modern amenities, some with balcony and view. Bright attractive dining room; menu mixes modern and traditional.

🏠 **Ennys** 🌿 without rest., Trewhella Lane, St Hilary, TR20 9BZ, East : 2½ m. by Turnpike Rd, on B 3280 ℰ (01736) 740262, *ennys@ennys.co.uk, Fax (01736) 740055,* ⛲ heated, 🌳, 🏡, 🎾 – 📶 📶 **P.** 🅌 🅰🅴 🆅🆂🅰. 🌸
20 March-October – **5 rm** 🍽 ✸60.00/100.00 – ✸✸95.00/110.00.
 ♦ Blissful 17C manor house on working farm. Spacious breakfast room and large farmhouse kitchen for afternoon tea. Modern country house style lounge. Elegant, classical rooms.

at Perranuthnoe *Southeast : 1¾ m. by A 394* – ✉ *Penzance.*

🏠 **Ednovean Farm** 🌿 without rest., TR20 9LZ, ℰ (01736) 711883, *info@ednovean farm.co.uk, Fax (01736) 710480,* ≤ St Michaels Mount and Bay, 🌳, 🏡 – 📶 **P.** 🅌 🆅🆂🅰 🌸
closed Christmas and New Year – **3 rm** 🍽 ✸90.00/100.00 – ✸✸85.00/100.00.
 ♦ Very spacious, characterful converted 17C granite barn offering peace, tranquillity and Mounts Bay views. Fine choice at breakfast on oak table. Charming, individual rooms.

MARDEN *Wilts.* – *see Devizes.*

MARKET BOSWORTH *Leics. 502 503 504* P 26 – *pop. 1 906* – ✉ *Nuneaton.*
London 109 – Birmingham 30 – Coventry 23 – Leicester 22.

🏨 **Softleys,** Market Pl, CV13 0LE, ℰ (01455) 290464, *softleysrestaurant@tiscali.co.uk, Fax (01455) 292532* – 📶 📶 🅌 🆅🆂🅰. 🌸
closed 25-26 December and Bank Holidays – **Rest** *(closed Monday lunch, and Sunday)* 13.95 (lunch) and a la carte 19.20/30.95 🍽 – **3 rm** 🍽 ✸65.00 – ✸✸75.00.
 ♦ Solid stone hotel in centre of historic town close to famous battlefield. Snug bar area; first floor dining room used for parties. Good-sized bedrooms exude homely charm. Pleasantly spacious dining room; good use of appealing seasonal ingredients.

MARKET DRAYTON *Shrops. 502 503 504* M 25.
London 159.5 – Nantwich 13.5 – Shrewsbury 21.

🏨 **Goldstone Hall** 🌿, TF9 2NA, South : 4½ m. on A 529 ℰ (01630) 661202, *info@gold stonehall.com, Fax (01630) 661585,* ≤, 🌳 – 📶 📶 **P.** 🅌 🆅🆂🅰
Rest 20.00/29.00 – **11 rm** 🍽 ✸80.00/98.00 – ✸✸120.00/150.00.
 ♦ 16C red-brick country house that's been extensively added to over the ages. Five acres of formal garden: PG Wodehouse enjoyed its shade! Modern rooms with huge beds. Contemporary twists on daily changing menus.

MARKET HARBOROUGH *Leics. 504* R 26 – *pop. 20 127.*
📷 *Great Oxendon Rd* ℰ *(01858) 463684.*
🅱 *Council Offices, Adam and Eve St* ℰ *(01858) 828282.*
London 88 – Birmingham 47 – Leicester 15 – Northampton 17.

🏨 **The Angel,** 37 High St, LE16 7AF, ℰ (01858) 462702, *theangel@theangelhotel.net, Fax (01858) 410464* – 📶 **P.** 🚗 50. 🅌 🅰🅴 🆅🆂🅰. 🌸
Rest (dinner only and Sunday lunch)/dinner 20.95 – 🍽 9.95 – **16 rm** ✸48.00/62.50 – ✸✸58.00/68.00.
 ♦ Centrally located former coaching inn dating from 1746. Sophisticated yet informal feel throughout. Ostlers lounge bar has open fire. Good-sized, comfortable bedrooms. Tasty modern dishes in the restaurant.

at Thorpe Langton *North : 3¾ m. by A 4304 via Great Bowden – ⊠ Market Harborough.*

🍴 **The Bakers Arms,** Main St, LE16 7TS, 𝒫 (01858) 545201 – **P**, **MO** **VISA**. ⊁

Rest *(closed Sunday dinner and Monday)* (booking essential) (dinner only and lunch Saturday and Sunday) a la carte 20.00/30.00.

◆ Atmospheric thatched pub with deep red walls, exposed timbers and pew seats. Scrubbed wooden tables add to the relaxed feel. Tasty, well-priced, tried-and-tested dishes.

MARKINGTON N. Yorks. 502 P 21 – *see Ripon.*

MARLBOROUGH Wilts. 503 504 O 29 *The West Country G. – pop. 7 713.*

See : *Town★.*

Env. : *Savernake Forest★★ (Grand Avenue★★★), SE : 2 m. by A 4 – Whitehorse (≼★), NW : 5 m – West Kennett Long Barrow★, Silbury Hill★, W : 6 m. by A 4.*

Exc. : *Ridgeway Path★★ – Avebury★★ (The Stones★, Church★), W : 7 m. by A 4 – Crofton Beam Engines★ AC, SE : 9 m. by A 346 – Wilton Windmill★ AC, SE : 9 m. by A 346, A 338 and minor rd.*

🛝 *The Common* 𝒫 *(01672) 512147.*

🖪 *The Library, High St* 𝒫 *(01672) 513989.*

London 84 – Bristol 47 – Southampton 40 – Swindon 12.

✗ **Coles,** 27 Kingsbury Hill, SN8 1JA, 𝒫 (01672) 515004, Fax (01672) 512069, 🏠 – ⊁⇜ ▤. **MO** **VISA**

closed 25-26 December, 1 January, Sunday and Bank Holidays – **Rest** a la carte 22.50/30.00 ℧.

◆ Shots of 70s film stars adorn a busy, bay-windowed former pub which retains its firelit bar. Friendly staff and elaborate but robust cuisine with an array of daily specials.

at Little Bedwyn *East : 9½ m. by A 4 – ⊠ Marlborough.*

✗✗ **The Harrow at Little Bedwyn** (Jones), SN8 3JP, 𝒫 (01672) 870871, *dining@harro* ❀ *winn.co.uk,* 🏠 – ⊁⇜. **MO** **VISA**

closed 14-31 August, 22 December-18 January, Sunday dinner, Monday and Tuesday – **Rest** 25.00 (lunch) and a la carte 38.00/44.00 ℧ ⚞.

Spec. Timbale of crab. Roast new season grouse with neeps and haggis. Blackberry crumble with vanilla ice cream.

◆ Cosy, intimate former village pub. Daily changing menus offer well crafted, locally sourced dishes. A variety of tasting menus also feature, accompanied by impressive wines.

We try to be as accurate as possible when giving room rates.
But prices are susceptible to change,
so please check rates when booking.

MARLDON Devon 503 J 32.

London 193.5 – Newton Abbott 7 – Paignton 3.

🍴 **Church House Inn,** Village Rd, TQ3 1SL, 𝒫 (01803) 558279, Fax (01803) 664865, 🏠, ⇜ – ⊁⇜ **P**, **MO** **VISA**

Rest a la carte 26.00/30.00 ℧.

◆ Tricky to find, but worth the effort. Characterful interior of beams and flags, and lots of informal areas to enjoy tasty, locally based dishes that are all home made.

MARLOW Bucks. 504 R 29 – *pop. 17 552.*

⛴ *to Henley-on-Thames (Salter Bros. Ltd) (summer only) (2 h 45 mn) – to Maidenhead, Cookham and Windsor (Salter Bros. Ltd) (summer only).*

🖪 *31 High St* 𝒫 *(01628) 483597.*

London 35 – Aylesbury 22 – Oxford 29 – Reading 14.

🏰 **Danesfield House** ⬧, Henley Rd, SL7 2EY, Southwest : 2 ½ m. on A 4155 𝒫 (01628) 891010, *sales@danesfieldhouse.co.uk,* Fax (01628) 890408, ≼ Terraced gardens and River Thames, 🏠, ⚛, **Fô**, ⇌, 🏊, ⇜, ⚘, ✗ – 🖷 🛗, ⊁⇜ rest, ▤ rest, ✆ **P** – 🔬 100. **MO** **AE** **①** **VISA**. ⊁

Oak Room : **Rest** (dinner only and Saturday lunch)/dinner 49.00/70.00 ℧ – *Orangery :* **Rest** 28.50 – **86 rm** ⊒ ✦215.00/220.00 – ✦✦260.00, 1 suite.

◆ Stunning house and gardens in Italian Renaissance style with breathtaking views of Thames. Grand lounge with country house feel. Comfy rooms; state-of-art health spa. Intimate Oak Room restaurant. Orangery is a charming terrace brasserie.

Crowne Plaza Marlow, Fieldhouse Lane, SL7 1GJ, East : 2 m. by A 4155 off Parkway Rd *𝒫* (0870) 4448940, *enquiries@crowneplazamarlow.co.uk*, Fax (0870) 4448950, 🛋, ᵴₒ, ⬛, 🌲 – 🛗, ᵡ rm, 🖥 🎮 & 🅿 – 🕍 350. 🆗 🆎 ⓞ 𝘝𝘐𝘚𝘈 ⬛
Glaze : **Rest** *(closed lunch Saturday and Sunday)* 28.00 and a la carte 19.50/26.50 – *Agua* : **Rest** a la carte 14.25/20.50 – **162 rm** ⟷ ✳155.00/235.00 – ✳✳180.00/260.00, 6 suites.
♦ Purpose built hotel near business park. Spacious lobby, leisure club and meeting rooms. Bedrooms well equipped with large desk. Glaze with conservatory overlooking the artificial lake. More informal Agua.

Compleat Angler, Marlow Bridge, Bisham Rd, SL7 1RG, *𝒫* (0870) 4008100, *general.compleatangler@macdonald-hotels.co.uk*, Fax (01628) 486388, ≤ River Thames, 🌲, ⬛ – 🛗 ᵡ & 🅿 – 🕍 120. 🆗 🆎 ⓞ 𝘝𝘐𝘚𝘈
Riverside : **Rest** 27.50/37.50 ♀ – *Alfresco* : **Rest** *(closed Sunday dinner)* a la carte 22.45/32.50 ♀ – ⟷ 17.50 – **61 rm** ✳220.00/260.00 – ✳✳220.00/450.00, 3 suites.
♦ Picturesque riverside hotel; spectacular view of Marlow weir. Well-furnished lounges. Rooms are very comfortable; those on river side have four-poster beds and balcony. Formal Riverside restaurant; fine views. Alfresco is a relaxed conservatory brasserie.

The Vanilla Pod, 31 West St, SL7 2LS, *𝒫* (01628) 898101, *allmail@thevanillapod.co.uk*, Fax (01628) 898108 – ⟷ 8. 🆗 🆎 𝘝𝘐𝘚𝘈
closed Easter, 1 week August, Christmas, Sunday and Monday – **Rest** *(booking essential)* 19.50/40.00 s.
♦ Distinctly comfy restaurant in town centre. Richly hued dining room with snug, intimate feel and courteous service. Modern cooking, classically underpinned.

The Hand & Flowers (Kerridge), 126 West St, SL7 2BP, *𝒫* (01628) 482277, 🌲, 🌱 – 🅿. 🆗 𝘝𝘐𝘚𝘈 ⬛
closed dinner 24-26 December – **Rest** a la carte 20.00/50.00 ♀.
Spec. Potted crab. Braised shin of beef with bone marrow. Vanilla crème brûlée.
♦ Series of 19C cottages with timbered exterior. Unspoilt within: original bar and adjacent chunky wood tables for diners. Appealing dishes use only best quality local produce.

The Royal Oak, Frieth Rd, Bovingdon Green, SL7 2JF, West : 1¼ m. by A 4155 *𝒫* (01628) 488611, *info@royaloakmarlow.co.uk*, Fax (01628) 478680, 🌲, 🌱 – 🅿. 🆗 🆎 𝘝𝘐𝘚𝘈
closed 25-26 December – **Rest** a la carte 18.00/26.75 ♀.
♦ Characterful pub with redbrick exterior and smart interior. Full-length window area at back faces spacious garden terrace. Modern menus plus specials board.

MARPLE *Gtr Manchester* **502 503 504** N 23 – *pop. 18 475.*
London 190 – Chesterfield 35 – Manchester 11.

Springfield without rest., 99 Station Rd, SK6 6PA, *𝒫* (0161) 449 0721, Fax (0161) 449 0766, 🌱 – ᵡ 🅿. 🆗 🆎 𝘝𝘐𝘚𝘈 ⬛
8 rm ⟷ ✳45.00/50.00 – ✳✳65.00/70.00.
♦ Part Victorian house with sympathetic extensions. Useful for visits to Peak District. Two homely lounges, one with good views to Derbyshire hills. Individually styled rooms.

MARSDEN *W. Yorks.* **502 504** O 23 – *pop. 3 499* – ✉ *Huddersfield.*
London 195 – Leeds 22 – Manchester 18 – Sheffield 30.

Olive Branch with rm, Manchester Rd, HD7 6LU, Northeast : 1 m. on A 62 *𝒫* (01484) 844487, *mail@olivebranch.uk.com*, 🌲 – 🅿. 🆗 𝘝𝘐𝘚𝘈 ⬛
closed first 2 weeks January and 26 December – **Rest** - Seafood specialities - *(closed Monday-Tuesday and lunch Saturday)* 18.50 (lunch) and a la carte 22.50/37.00 ♀ – ⟷ 10.50 – **3 rm** ✳55.00 – ✳✳70.00.
♦ In a secluded valley, a part 16C drovers inn, run with real warmth. Open fire and wide-ranging menus in smart restaurant with outside decking; seafood specials. Modern rooms.

MARSH BENHAM *West Berks. – see Newbury.*

MARSTON MONTGOMERY *Derbs. – see Ashbourne.*

MARTINHOE *Devon – see Lynton.*

MARTOCK Somerset 503 L 31 The West Country G. – pop. 4 309.

See : Village★ – All Saints★★.

Env. : Montacute House★★ AC, SE : 4 m. – Muchelney★★ (Parish Church★★), NW : 4½ m. by B 3165 – Ham Hill (≤★★), S : 2 m. by minor roads.

Exc. : – Barrington Court★ AC, SW : 7½ m. by B 3165 and A 303.

London 148 – Taunton 19 – Yeovil 6.

The Hollies, Bower Hinton, TA12 6LG, South : 1 m. on B 3165 ✆ (01935) 822232, info@thehollieshotel.com, Fax (01935) 822249, 🐾 – ☆ ✆ ⚓ 🅿 – ▲ 100. 🐵 🗚 ⓪ ⚡.
🛳

Rest (closed Sunday) (dinner only) a la carte 21.95/25.95 s ♀ – **39 rm** ⊆ ✦78.00/83.00 – ✦✦88.00/98.00, 3 suites.
• Impressive former 17C farmhouse in small village near grand Montacute House. Separate annex has large, well-equipped, up-to-date bedrooms with good comforts and facilities. Characterful oak beamed, boothed restaurant and lounge in the farmhouse.

MARTON Lincs. 502 504 R 24 – pop. 508.

London 155 – Doncaster 27 – Lincoln 14 – Nottingham 40.

Black Swan without rest., 21 High St, DN21 5AH, ✆ (01427) 718878, reservations@blackswanguesthouse.co.uk, Fax (01427) 718878, 🐾 – ☆ ⚓ 🅿. 🐵 🗚 ⚡
10 rm ⊆ ✦45.00 – ✦✦75.00.
• Village centre coaching inn. Homely lounge has velvet furniture; breakfast room with pine table. Six rooms in main house, two in converted stables: all individually styled.

Your opinions are important to us:
please write and let us know about your discoveries and experiences – good and bad!

MARTON N. Yorks. 502 R 21 – see Pickering.

MARTON Shrops. Great Britain G.

Env. : Powis Castle★★★, NW : 7 m. by B 4386 and A 490.

London 174 – Birmingham 57 – Shrewsbury 16.

The Sun Inn, SY21 8JP, ✆ (01938) 561211, info@suninn.biz – ☆ 🅿. 🐵 ⚡. 🛳
Rest (closed Monday, Tuesday lunch and Sunday dinner) a la carte 15.00/30.00.
• Rural pub where keen young owners serve good value, tasty, traditional dishes heavily influenced by local ingredients. Choose to eat in bar or beech-furnished dining room.

MASHAM N. Yorks. 502 P 21 – ✉ Ripon.

London 231 – Leeds 38 – Middlesbrough 37 – York 32.

Swinton Park 🦢, Swinton, HG4 4JH, Southwest : 1 m ✆ (01765) 680900, enquiries@swintonpark.com, Fax (01765) 680901, ≤, 🐓, 🐟, 🐾, ☎ – 🛗 ☆ ✆ ⚓ 🅿 – ▲ 120. 🐵 🗚 ⓪ ⚡
Samuels : Rest 21.50/50.00 ♀ – **26 rm** ⊆ ✦150.00 – ✦✦150.00/350.00, 4 suites.
• 17C castle with Georgian and Victorian additions, on a 20,000 acre estate and deer park. Luxurious, antique filled lounges. Very comfortable, individually styled bedrooms. Grand dining room with ornate gold leaf ceiling and garden views.

King's Head, Market Pl, HG4 4EF, ✆ (01765) 689295, kings.head6395@thespiritgroup.com, Fax (01765) 689070, 🍽 – ☆ rest, ⚓ – ▲ 50. 🐵 🗚 ⚡
Rest a la carte 16.15/31.85 s. ♀ – 🔹 6.95 – **23 rm** ✦55.00/70.00 – ✦✦80.00.
• Dominant Georgian building on main market square. Atmospheric bar with old church pews, beams and vivid walls. Individually styled, well furnished rooms, some in smart annex. Characterful dining room with oak panelling.

Bank Villa, HG4 4DB, on A 6108 ✆ (01765) 689605, bankvilla@btopenworld.com, 🐾 – ☆ 🅿. 🐵 ⚡. 🛳
Rest (by arrangement) a la carte 18.50/26.00 – **6 rm** ⊆ ✦45.00/60.00 – ✦✦75.00/95.00.
• Stone-built Georgian villa with Victorian additions. Two lounges and conservatory; delightful, "sun-trap" stepped garden. Cosy, cottagey rooms: some are in the eaves! Home-cooked menus in pastel dining room/tea room.

XX / ☺ **Vennell's,** 7 Silver St, HG4 4DX, ℰ (01765) 689000, *info@vennellsrestaurant.co.uk* – ✗. ⬚⬚ AE VISA
closed 1-14 January, 26-30 December, Sunday, Monday and lunch Tuesday-Thursday and restricted opening September-April – Rest 24.90 **s**.
♦ Smart restaurant with comfy basement bar; linen-clad dining room enhanced by local artwork. Warm service of good value, seasonal dishes prepared with flair and a flourish.

MATFEN Northd. 501 502 O 18.
London 309 – Carlisle 42 – Newcastle upon Tyne 24.

🏠 **Matfen Hall** ⌂, NE20 0RH, ℰ (01661) 886500, *info@matfenhall.com*, Fax (01661) 886055, ≤, ⌕, Ⅰ₆, ⌬, ⬚, Ⅰ₈, ⌨, ☎ – ⬚ ✗ ⚒ ♿ P. – 🔒 120. ⬚⬚ AE ⬚ VISA
Library and Print Room : Rest (dinner only and Sunday lunch)/dinner 25.00 and a la carte 31.00/42.95 ♀ – **53 rm** ⌂ ✦110.00/135.00 – ✦✦245.00.
♦ 19C country mansion built by Thomas Ruckman, master of Gothic design. Set in 500 acres with superb Grand Hall, fine paintings, plush drawing room and mix of bedroom styles. Characterful Library dining room has display of original books.

MATLOCK Derbs. 502 503 504 P 24 Great Britain G. – pop. 11 265.
Exc. : Hardwick Hall★★ AC, E : 12½ m. by A 615 and B 6014 – Crich Tramway Village★ AC, S : 12 m. by A 6 and B 5036.
🛈 Crown Sq ℰ (01629) 583388 – The Pavilion, Matlock Bath ℰ (01629) 55082.
London 153 – Derby 17 – Manchester 46 – Nottingham 24 – Sheffield 24.

🏠 **Riber Hall** ⌂, Riber Village, DE4 5JU, Southeast : 3 m. by A 615 ℰ (01629) 582795, *info@riber-hall.co.uk*, Fax (01629) 580475, ⌨, ✗ – ✗ P. ⬚⬚ AE ⬚ VISA
closed 25 December – Rest 40.00 (dinner) and lunch a la carte 20.65/26.95 – ⌂ 12.00 – **14 rm** ✦85.00/98.00 – ✦✦125.00/188.00.
♦ Part Elizabethan manor house on hilltop hamlet. Wonderfully peaceful setting. Leaded windows, Elizabethan styling, exposed beams, stone walls. Four posters in rooms. Period style restaurant with gold drapes.

at Birchover Northeast : 7½ m. by A 6 – ✉ Matlock.

🍴 **The Druid Inn,** Main St, DE4 2BL, ℰ (01629) 650302, ⌨ – ✗ P. ⬚⬚ VISA. ✗
Rest *(closed Monday October-March and Sunday dinner)* 16.00 and a la carte 22.00/30.00 ♀.
♦ Early 19C stone-built pub in Peak District, providing Derbyshire tradition in contemporary style. Huge menus offer a vast choice of sensibly priced modern dishes.

MAULDS MEABURN Cumbria – see Appleby-in-Westmorland.

MAWNAN SMITH Cornwall 503 E 33 – see Falmouth.

MEDBOURNE Leics. 504 R 26.
London 93 – Corby 9 – Leicester 16.

XX **Horse & Trumpet** with rm, Old Green, LE16 8DX, ℰ (01858) 565000, *info@horse andtrumpet.com*, Fax (01858) 565551, ⌨ – ✗ ⚒ ⬚⬚ ⬚ VISA
closed 1 week January, Sunday dinner and Monday – Rest 20.00 (lunch) and dinner a la carte 30.00/42.45 ♀ – **4 rm** ⌂ ✦75.00 – ✦✦75.00.
♦ 18C thatched inn with bowling green. Stylish well-furnished bedrooms. Linen clad tables in the dining rooms; al fresco eating in courtyard. Modern menu using local produce.

The ✿ award is the crème de la crème.
This is awarded to restaurants
which are really worth travelling miles for!

541

ENGLAND

MELBOURN *Cambs.* 504 U 27 – *pop. 4 298 –* ⊠ *Royston (Herts.).*
London 44 – Cambridge 10.

↑ **Melbourn Bury,** Royston Rd, SG8 6DE, Southwest : ¾ m. ℰ (01763) 261151, *melbourn bury@biztobiz.co.uk, Fax* (01763) 262375, ≤, 舜, 氐 – ✳✕ **P**, **MO** **VISA**, ⅍
closed Easter and 24 December-2 January – **Rest** *(by arrangement) (communal dining)* 26.00 – **3 rm** ⊡ ⁑85.00 – ⁑⁑130.00.
• Country house of Tudor origins with good views of surrounding countryside. Drawing room with antiques and lovely oil paintings. Spacious rooms have period furnishings. Dine communally at antique table.

XX **Sheene Mill** with rm, Station Rd, SG8 6DX, ℰ (01763) 261393, *info@sheenemill.co.uk,* Fax (01763) 261376, ≤, 舜, 舜 – ✳✕, ▤ rest, **P**, **MO** **AE** **VISA**, ⅍
closed 26 December and 1 January – **Rest** *(closed Sunday dinner)* 20.00/35.00 and a la carte 25.00/36.00 ♀ – **9 rm** ⊡ ⁑85.00/95.00 – ⁑⁑120.00.
• Restored 17C watermill with gardens, terraces and good views of millpond. Log fire and flagstones; friendly service. Modern à la carte menu. Designer themed bedrooms.

MELKSHAM *Wilts.* 503 504 N 29 *The West Country G. – pop. 14 372.*
Env. : *Corsham Court*★★ *AC, NW : 4½ m. by A 365 and B 3353 – Lacock*★★ *(Lacock Abbey*★ *AC, High Street*★*, St Cyriac*★*, Fox Talbot Museum of Photography*★ *AC) N : 3 ½ m. by A 350.*
🛈 *Church St* ℰ (01225) 707424.
London 113 – Bristol 25 – Salisbury 35 – Swindon 28.

at Whitley *Northwest : 2 m. by A 365 on B 3353 –* ⊠ *Melksham.*

🛏 **The Pear Tree Inn** with rm, Top Lane, SN12 8QX, by First Lane ℰ (01225) 709131, *enquiries@thepeartreeinn.com,* Fax (01225) 702276, 舜, 舜 – ✳✕ ❤ **P**, **MO** **VISA**, ⅍
closed 25-26 December and 1 January – **Rest** 16.00 *(lunch) and a la carte* 21.50/32.50 ♀ – **8 rm** ⊡ ⁑75.00 – ⁑⁑105.00.
• Characterful Bath stone pub with lovely gardens and terrace. Modish restaurant to rear: assured, tasty cooking. Very smart, modern, stylish bedrooms in house and conversion.

The red 🦋 symbol?
This denotes the very essence of peace
– only the sound of birdsong first thing in the morning …

MELLOR *Lancs. – see Blackburn.*

MELTON MOWBRAY *Leics.* 502 504 R 25 – *pop. 25 554.*
🛅 *Waltham Rd, Thorpe Arnold* ℰ (01664) 562118.
🛈 *7 King St* ℰ (01664) 480992.
London 113 – Leicester 15 – Northampton 45 – Nottingham 18.

🏛 **Stapleford Park** ❧, LE14 2EF, East : 5 m. by B 676 on Stapleford rd ℰ (01572) 787000, *reservations@stapleford.co.uk, Fax* (01572) 787001, ≤, ⊘, ᵼ₆, ➭, ⬚, ⛳, ⛵, 舜, 氐, ⅍ – 🍴 ✳✕ **P** – 🔬 200. **MO** **AE** **VISA**
Grinling Gibbons Dining Room : **Rest** *(booking essential) (dinner only and Sunday lunch)* 46.50 and a la carte 44.50/57.50 – **Pavilion Brasserie :** **Rest** a la carte 21.00/28.00 – **53 rm** ⊡ ⁑195.00/250.00 – ⁑⁑250.00, 2 suites.
• Astoundingly beautiful stately home in 500 glorious acres, exuding a grandeur rarely surpassed. Extensive leisure facilities; uniquely designed rooms of sumptuous elegance. Ornate rococo dining room a superb example of master craftsman's work. Smart brasserie.

🏠 **Quorn Lodge,** 46 Asfordby Rd, LE13 0HR, West : ½ m. on A 6006 ℰ (01664) 566660, *quornlodge@aol.com, Fax* (01664) 480660 – ✳✕ ❤ **P** – 🔬 80. **MO** **VISA**, ⅍
closed 26 December-2 January – **The Laurels :** **Rest** a la carte 9.95/19.95 ♀ – **19 rm** ⊡ ⁑62.00 – ⁑⁑65.00/88.00.
• Former hunting lodge, privately owned, situated just outside town centre. Spacious sitting room and bar leads on to small conference room. Spacious, neatly kept rooms. Homely restaurant with pretty garden to rear.

at Stathern *North : 8 m. by A 607 –* ⊠ *Melton Mowbray.*

🛏 **Red Lion Inn,** 2 Red Lion St, LE14 4HS, ℘ (01949) 860868, *info@theredlioninn.co.uk,*
🍴 *Fax (01949) 861579,* 🌳 – 🄿 🆇🅾 𝘝𝘐𝘚𝘈
closed 1 January and dinner 25 and 26 December – **Rest** *(closed Sunday dinner)* (booking
essential) 15.95 (lunch) and a la carte 20.00/29.00 ☉.
   ✦ Rural pub with a predominant "country" feel: solid stone floors, wooden antiques, rustic
ornaments, solid fireplaces, skittle alley. Daily changing, modern menus.

at Nether Broughton *Northwest : 5¾ m. on A 606 –* ⊠ *Melton Mowbray.*

🏠 **The Red house,** 23 Main St, LE14 3HB, ℘ (01664) 822429, *bookings@the-red*
house.co.uk, Fax (01664) 823805, 🌳 – ⤢ 🄿 🆇🅾 🅰🅴 🅾 𝘝𝘐𝘚𝘈
Rest *(closed Sunday dinner)* a la carte 20.50/30.50 ☉ – ☷ 5.00 – **8 rm** ✦65.00 – ✦✦130.00.
   ✦ Stylish, smart bedrooms with plenty of extras are the highlight of this 15C former
coaching inn. Brightly painted, modern public areas. Delightful terrace and bar. Popular
favourites to fore in dining room; local produce much in evidence.

MERIDEN *W. Mids.* 503 504 P 26 – *see Coventry.*

MEVAGISSEY *Cornwall* 503 F 33 *The West Country G. – pop. 2 221.*
   See : *Town*★★.
   Env. : *NW : Lost Gardens of Heligan*★.
   London 287 – Newquay 21 – Plymouth 44 – Truro 20.

🏨 **Trevalsa Court,** School Hill, PL26 6TH, East : ½ m. on B 3273 (St Austell rd) ℘ (01726)
842468, *stay@trevalsa-hotel.co.uk, Fax (01726) 844482,* ≤, 🌳 – ⤢ 🕊 🄿 🆇🅾 𝘝𝘐𝘚𝘈
🍴
closed December and January – **Rest** (dinner only) 28.00 and a la carte ☉ – **12 rm** ☷
✦70.00/150.00 – ✦✦110.00/190.00.
   ✦ Charming 1930s building with lovely garden which has access to Polstreath
Beach. Homely morning room; quirky, 'Continental'-style bar. Autumnal shades enhance
tasteful rooms. Oak-panelled dining room with daily menu, devised using best available
produce.

⌂ **Kerryanna** 🍴 without rest., Treleaven Farm, PL26 6RZ, ℘ (01726) 843558, *enqui*
ries@kerryanna.co.uk, Fax (01726) 843558, 🗗 heated, 🌳, 🏋 – ⤢ 🄿 🆇🅾 𝘝𝘐𝘚𝘈 🍴
Easter-October – **4 rm** ☷ ✦45.00 – ✦✦70.00.
   ✦ Purpose-built bungalow within farm providing pleasant ambience. Useful for Lost Gardens of Heligan. Spacious front sitting room. Immaculately kept, sizeable, chintz bedrooms.

MICKLEHAM *Surrey* 504 T 30.
   London 21 – Brighton 32 – Guildford 14 – Worthing 34.

🛏 **The King William IV,** Byttom Hill, RH5 6EL, North : ½ m. by A 24 ℘ (01372) 372590, 🌳
   – 🆇🅾 🅾 𝘝𝘐𝘚𝘈. 🍴
closed 25 and 31 December – **Rest** *(closed Sunday dinner)* a la carte 18.00/25.00.
   ✦ Once a beer house for Lord Beaverbrook's staff, this part 19C hillside pub looks
over Mole Valley from lounge and terrace. Large blackboard menu: wholesome and
homely.

MICKLEOVER *Derbs.* 502 503 504 P 25 – *see Derby.*

MICKLETON *Glos.* 503 504 O 27 – *see Chipping Campden.*

   Good food and accommodation at moderate prices?
   Look for the Bib symbols:
   red Bib Gourmand 🍴 **for food, blue Bib Hotel** 🛏 **for hotels**

ENGLAND

MIDDLEHAM N. Yorks. 502 O 21.

London 233 – Kendal 45 – Leeds 47 – Newcastle upon Tyne 63 – York 45.

Waterford House, 19 Kirkgate, DL8 4PG, ℘ (01969) 622090, *info@waterfordhouseho tel.co.uk, Fax (01969) 624020*, 🌳 – ✸ 🄿, ◍◎ *VISA*. ✋
closed 23 December-3 January – **Rest** *(closed Sunday)* (residents only) (dinner only) 31.00 s. ☲ 5 rm ☲ ✦65.00/80.00 – ✦✦110.00/115.00.
♦ Elegant Georgian house, just off cobbled market square, with neat walled garden. Drawing room boasts cluttered charm. Individually appointed rooms with thoughtful touches. Formal restaurant: home cooked menus use much local produce.

Middleham Grange without rest., Market Pl, DL8 4NR, ℘ (01969) 622630, *tammi.t@tiscali.co.uk, Fax (01969) 625437*, 🌳 – ✸ 🄿. ✋
3 rm ☲ ✦60.00 – ✦✦80.00.
♦ Beautifully restored part-Georgian manor house. Comfy period style lounge; bright breakfast room in conservatory overlooking garden. Snug bedrooms exude a classical style.

The White Swan with rm, Market Pl, DL8 4PE, ℘ (01969) 622093, *whiteswan@easy net.co.uk, Fax (01969) 624551*, �️, 🌳 – ◍◎ *VISA*
closed dinner 25 December – **Rest** 13.95 (lunch) and a la carte 15.00/25.00 ☲ – **17 rm** ☲ ✦55.00/69.00 – ✦✦99.00.
♦ Former coaching inn in the market place. Traditional flagged floor bar with wood-burning stove and inglenook. Hearty English dishes with local ingredients. Comfy rooms.

at Carlton-in-Coverdale Southwest : 4½ m. by Coverham rd – ⊠ Leyburn.

Abbots Thorn ⬙, DL8 4AY, ℘ (01969) 640620, *abbots.thorn@virgin.net*, ⪡ – ✸
closed 23 December-8 January – **Rest** (by arrangement) (communal dining) 18.00 – **3 rm** ☲ ✦44.00 – ✦✦54.00.
♦ Well priced, comfortable, quiet guesthouse in attractive rural village. Handy for visits to Moors. Cosy sitting room. Sizeable bedrooms which are homely and well-kept. Fresh, local produce to fore at dinner.

Foresters Arms with rm, DL8 4BB, ℘ (01969) 640272, *chambersmic@hotmail.co.uk, Fax (01969) 640272*, 🌴 – ✸ 🄿, ◍◎ *VISA*
closed lunch November-April except Friday-Sunday – **Rest** *(closed Sunday dinner, Monday and Tuesday lunch)* a la carte 15.50/27.60 ☲ – **3 rm** ☲ ✦65.00 – ✦✦79.00.
♦ Compact 17C stone-built inn. Flagged floor bar with beams and open fire. Timbered restaurant where modern dishes utilise fresh, local produce. Pleasant, cottagey rooms.

Your opinions are important to us:
please write and let us know about your discoveries and experiences – good and bad!

MIDDLESBROUGH Middlesbrough 502 Q 20 – pop. 142 691.

🏌 Middlesbrough Municipal, Ladgate Lane ℘ (01642) 315533 – 🏌 Brass Castle Lane, Marton ℘ (01642) 311515.
Cleveland Transporter Bridge (toll) BY.
✈ Durham Tees Valley Airport : ℘ (01325) 332811, SW : 13 m. by A 66 – AZ – and A 19 on A 67.
🛈 Town Hall Box Office, 99-101 Albert Rd ℘ (01642) 729700.
London 246 – Kingston-upon-Hull 89 – Leeds 66 – Newcastle upon Tyne 41.

Plan opposite

Thistle, Fry St, TS1 1JH, ℘ (0870) 3339141, *middlesbrough@thistle.co.uk, Fax (0870) 3339241*, ⪡, ₤₆, ⪡ˢ, ▧ – ▯ ✸, ▤ rest, ዿ, 🄿 – 🔏 400. ◍◎ 🄰🄴 ◍ *VISA* BY e
Gengis : **Rest** 17.00/24.00 (dinner) and a la carte approx 23.95 s. – ☲ 11.50 – **132 rm** ✦155.00 – ✦✦155.00.
♦ Tower block hotel in a convenient central location. Well-planned modern style and décor throughout public areas and compact, well-equipped bedrooms. East meets west cuisine in bright, informal restaurant.

MIDDLESBROUGH

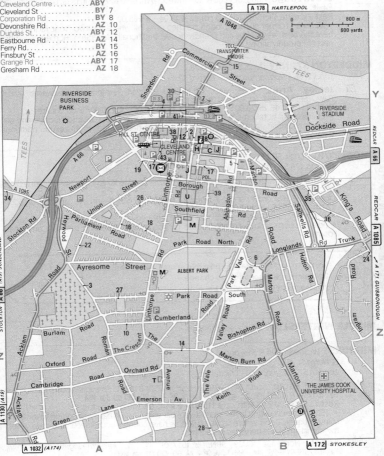

🛏 **Express by Holiday Inn** without rest., Marton Rd, TS4 3BS, 𝒫 (01642) 814444,
Fax (01642) 819999 – 📱 ⟡ ᗕ ₤ – 🔬 30. 🆎 🆎 ⓪ 𝑽𝑰𝑺𝑨. ⟡   **BZ** a
74 rm 🕇58.00 – 🕇🕇58.00.
◆ Purpose-built lodge on main road into city opposite South Cleveland Hospital. Smart
modern rooms decorated in bright, well-ordered style. Well suited to business travellers.

Do not confuse 🍴 with ✿!
🍴 defines comfort, while stars are awarded for the best cuisine,
across all categories of comfort.

MIDDLETON *N.Yorks. – see Pickering.*

MIDDLETON-IN-TEESDALE *Durham 502 N 20 – pop. 1 143.*
🛈 *Market Pl ℰ (01833) 641001.*
London 447 – Carlisle 91 – Leeds 124 – Middlesbrough 70 – Newcastle upon Tyne 65.

⌂ **Grove Lodge,** Hude, DL12 0QW, Northwest : ½ m. on B 6277 ℰ (01833) 640798, ≤, ☞ – ⊱⇔ **P**
Rest a la carte 14.15/27.70 ℤ – **3 rm** ⊯ ✝40.00 – ✝✝65.00.
   ♦ Victorian former shooting lodge perched on a hill where the two front facing rooms have the best views. Neat and friendly house, traditionally decorated. Home-cooked dinners are proudly served.

MIDDLETON STONEY *Oxon. 503 504 Q 28.*
London 66 – Northampton 30 – Oxford 12.

🏨 **Jersey Arms,** OX25 4AD, ℰ (01869) 343234, *jerseyarms@bestwestern.co.uk*, Fax (01869) 343565, ☞ – ⊱⇔ 🌜 **P**, 🌃 **AE ⓪** **VISA**, ⊱
Rest a la carte 16.25/26.00 ℤ – **17 rm** ⊯ ✝79.00/95.00 – ✝✝95.00/99.00, 3 suites.
   ♦ Characterful hotel on site of old coaching inn. Comfortable, beamed lounge and bar. Modern rooms in courtyard have rust and cream décor; older rooms exude traditional style. Small dining room with beams.

MIDDLEWICH *Ches. 502 503 504 M 24.*
London 176.5 – Crewe 13 – Northwich 7.5.

✗ **Kinderton's** with rm, Kinderton St, CW10 0JE, ℰ (01606) 834325, Fax (01606) 832323, 🈺, ☞ – ⊱⇔, ▤ rest, **P** ⇆ 10. **🌃 VISA**
closed 25-27 December and 1-2 January – **Rest** 11.95 (lunch) and a la carte 18.50/33.25 – **12 rm** ⊯ ✝65.00 – ✝✝65.00.
   ♦ Personally run restaurant in pleasantly refurbished hotel with garden and terrace. The simple, modern style is complemented by good value, appealing menus. Comfy bedrooms.

We try to be as accurate as possible when giving room rates.
But prices are susceptible to change,
so please check rates when booking.

MIDDLE WINTERSLOW *Wilts. – see Salisbury.*

MIDHURST *W. Sussex 504 R 31 – pop. 6 120.*
🛈 *North St ℰ (01730) 817322.*
London 57 – Brighton 38 – Chichester 12 – Southampton 41.

🏫 **Spread Eagle,** South St, GU29 9NH, ℰ (01730) 816911, *spreadeagle@hshotels.co.uk*, Fax (01730) 815668, ⓩ, **£₅**, ☎, ▦ – ⊱⇔ 🌜 **P** – 🛎 80. **🌃 AE ⓪ VISA**
Rest 18.50/35.00 ℤ – **37 rm** ⊯ ✝110.00 – ✝✝145.00/240.00, 2 suites.
   ♦ 15C hostelry boasting lovely characterful bar with uneven oak flooring and roaring fire. Many antiques. Good leisure facilities. Rooms have country house décor and style. A very traditional ambience pervades restaurant.

🏨 **Angel,** North St, GU29 9DN, ℰ (01730) 812421, *info@theangelmidhurst.co.uk*, Fax (01730) 815928, ☞ – ⊱⇔ ♿ **P** – 🛎 60. **🌃 AE ⓪ VISA**
Brasserie : **Rest** (lunch booking essential)/dinner a la carte 15.45/30.40 ℤ – **28 rm** ⊯ ✝59.00/110.00 – ✝✝69.00/150.00.
   ♦ 16C coaching inn with a country house feel on main road in town centre. Georgian façade and Tudor origins. Neatly furnished lounge. Well kept, chintz bedrooms. Informal brasserie with distinctive mahogany furniture.

at Bepton Southwest : 2½ m. by A 286 on Bepton rd – ⊠ Midhurst.

🏨 **Park House** ⏍, Bepton, GU29 0JB, ℰ (01730) 819000, *reservations@parkhouseho tel.com*, Fax (01730) 819099, ⏋ heated, **F₅**, ☞, ✗ – ⊱⇔ ♿ **P** – 🛎 70. **🌃 VISA**
Rest (booking essential) 25.00/32.00 – **14 rm** ⊯ ✝85.00/155.00 – ✝✝125.00/290.00, 1 suite.
   ♦ Comfortable, privately owned country house. Charming lounge with chintz armchairs, antique paintings, heavy drapes. Bar with honesty policy. Rooms are bright and colourful. Classical dining room with antique tables and chairs.

at Elsted *Southwest : 5 m. by A 272 on Elsted rd –* ⊠ *Midhurst.*

🍴 **Three Horseshoes,** GU29 0JY, ℰ (01730) 825746, 🌿 – **P**. **M◎** **VISA**
Rest a la carte 20.00/25.00.
♦ Lovely, informal 16C drovers inn with wood burners, stone floors and low ceiling. Honest pub cooking, fresh and tasty. Expect cottage or fish pie with a little extra twist.

at Stedham *West : 2 m. by A 272 –* ⊠ *Midhurst.*

✗ **Nava Thai at The Hamilton Arms,** School Lane, GU29 0NZ, ℰ (01730) 812555, hamiltonarms@hotmail.com, Fax (01730) 817459 – ✗⊱ **P**. **M◎** **AE** **VISA**
closed 1 week January – **Rest** - Thai - *(closed Monday except lunch Bank Holidays)* 19.50/21.50 and a la carte 15.00/25.00 ℿ.
♦ Busy Thai restaurant in bustling pub. Mahogany tables, wicker chairs. Thai royalty adorns the walls. Lanterns lighten your way. Colourful cooking, fragrant and flavoursome.

MIDSOMER NORTON *Somerset* 503 504 M 30.
London 125 – Bath 11 – Wells 12.

✗✗ **The Moody Goose at the Old Priory** with rm, Church Sq, BA3 2HX, ℰ (01761) 416784, info@theoldpriory.co.uk, Fax (01761) 417851, 🌿 – ✗⊱ **P**. **M◎** **AE** **◎** **VISA**
closed Christmas Sunday and Bank Holidays except Good Friday – **Rest** 19.50/25.00 and dinner a la carte 36.00/39.50 ℿ – **7 rm** ⊊ ✦80.00 – ✦✦135.00.
♦ 12C former priory, by a chuch, with enviable walled garden. Flagged floors, beams and vast fireplaces create impressive interior. Interesting modern cooking. Comfy rooms.

MILFORD-ON-SEA *Hants.* 503 504 P 31 – *pop. 4 229 –* ⊠ *Lymington.*
London 109 – Bournemouth 15 – Southampton 24 – Winchester 37.

🏨 **Westover Hall** ⤢, Park Lane, SO41 0PT, ℰ (01590) 643044, info@westoverhallhotel.com, Fax (01590) 644490, ≼ Christchurch Bay, Isle of Wight and The Needles, 🌳, 🌿 – ✗⊱ **P**. **AE** **VISA**
Rest 25.00/38.50 – **11 rm** (dinner included) ⊊ ✦130.00/215.00 – ✦✦190.00/330.00, 1 suite.
♦ Characterful 19C family-owned mansion in stunning spot overlooking Christchurch Bay. Very comfortable sitting room. Magnificent hall and minstrels gallery. Sumptuous rooms. Ornate dining room: decorative ceiling, stained glass, panelling.

MILLBROOK *Cornwall* 503 H 32.
London 235 – Liskeard 16 – Plymouth 23.5.

at Freathy *West : 3 m. by B 3247, Whitsand Bay Rd and Treninnow Cliff Rd –* ⊠ *Millbrook.*

✗ **The View,** PL10 1JY, East : 1 m. ℰ (01752) 822345, ≼ Whitsand Bay and Rame Head, 🌳 – **P**. **M◎** **AE** **VISA**
closed 7 January-7 March, 1-14 November, Monday and Tuesday at Bank Holidays – **Rest** - Seafood specialities - 19.00/29.00.
♦ Converted café: best views are from front terrace. Basic interior smartened up in evenings. Interesting, understated, seafood oriented menus: cooking is clean and delicious.

MILLOM *Cumbria* 502 K 21 *Great Britain G.* – *pop. 6 103.*
Exc. : *Hard Knott Pass*★★ , *N : 23 m. by A 595 and minor rd (eastbound).*
London 299 – Barrow-in-Furness 22 – Ulverston 17.

🏠 **Underwood,** The Hill, LA18 5EZ, North : 2 m. on A 5093 ℰ (01229) 771116, andrew.miller@aggregate.com, Fax (01229) 719900, ≼, 🔲, 🌿, ✗ – ✗⊱ ✔ **P**. **M◎** **◎** **VISA** 🌿
closed 2 weeks in February and 1 week in November – **Rest** (booking essential) (dinner only) 25.00 – **5 rm** ⊊ ✦35.00/55.00 – ✦✦110.00.
♦ Built in classic Lakeland grey, a Victorian former vicarage boasting two comfortable lounges and a large indoor pool. Well-kept, spacious double rooms with countryside views. Pleasant dining room overlooks gardens; tasty home cooking.

MILTON ABBOT *Devon* 503 H 32 – *see Tavistock.*

MILTON BRYAN *Beds.* 504 S 28 – *see Woburn.*

MILTON ERNEST *Beds.* 504 S 27 – *see Bedford.*

ENGLAND

MILTON KEYNES *Milton Keynes 504 R 27 – pop. 184 506.*

᠍ Abbey Hill, Monks Way, Two Mile Ash ₰ (01908) 563845 AV – ᠍ Windmill Hill, Tattenhoe Lane, Bletchley ₰ (01908) 631113 BX – ᠍, ᠍ Wavendon Golf Centre, Lower End Rd, Wavendon ₰ (01908) 281811 CV, askvic@powernet.com.

London 56 – Bedford 16 – Birmingham 72 – Northampton 18 – *Oxford 37.*

🏛 **Holiday Inn Milton Keynes,** 500 Saxon Gate West, Central Milton Keynes, MK9 2HQ, ₰ (0870) 400 9057, *reservations-miltonkeynes@ichotelsgroup.com, Fax (01908) 698693,* ᵇ, ⬱, ◻ – ⑂, ⬱ rm, ⬱ 🅿 – 🔏 100. ⓂⓄ 🅰🅴 ⓄⒾ 𝘝𝘐𝘚𝘈, ⬱   EYZ **a**
Rest 20.00/31.85 and dinner a la carte 15.00/25.00 – ⬱ 14.95 – **164 rm** ✸170.00 – ✸✸170.00, 2 suites.
♦ Commercial business hotel, with public areas set in modern atrium. Opposite main shopping area. Good leisure club with above average sized pool. Well-kept, clean rooms. Informal, family-friendly restaurant.

MILTON KEYNES

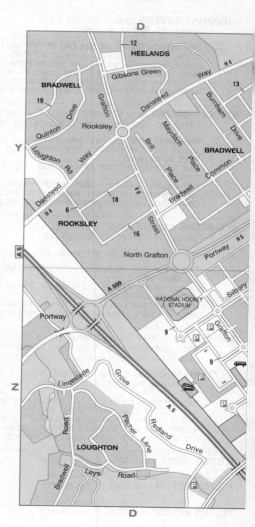

Hilton Milton Keynes, Timbold Drive, Kents Hill Park, MK6 7AH, Southeast : 4 m. by B 4034 and A 421 off Brickhill St. (V10) ℰ (01908) 694433, *miltonkeynes@hilton.com*, Fax (01908) 695533, ₤₅, ≋, ⊠ – ☆←, ⊟ rest, ✦ ₺ ⲡ – 🛅 300. 🆖 🆎 ⑩ 𝗩𝗜𝗦𝗔, ⫽ CVX **d**
Britisserie : Rest *(closed lunch Saturday and Sunday)* 12.75/19.50 and dinner a la carte 23.25/32.40 **s.** – ⊡ 15.95 – **138 rm** ✦70.00/180.00 – ✦✦80.00/190.00.
♦ Modern, commercial group hotel with comprehensive business facilities. Large lounge and bar. Comfortable rooms in three different grades varying slightly by size. Informal dining room aimed at business traveller.

Express by Holiday Inn without rest., Eastlake Park, Tongwell St, Fox Milne, MK15 0YA, ℰ (01908) 681000, *exhimiltonkeynes@aol.com*, Fax (01908) 609429 – 🛗 ☆← ⊟ ✦ ₺ ⲡ – 🛅 60. 🆖 🆎 ⑩ 𝗩𝗜𝗦𝗔, ⫽
CV **a**
178 rm ✦49.00/99.95 – ✦✦49.00/99.95.
♦ Large modern lodge hotel offering a superior range of accommodation. Spacious bedrooms boast all amenities and carefully planned modern style. Good motorway access.

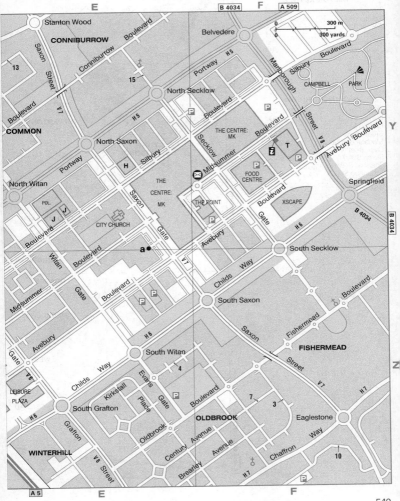

HORIZONTAL ROADS

Bletcham Way (H10) . . . . **CX**
Chaffron Way (H7) . . . . **BX, CV**
Childs Way (H6) . . . . **BX, CV**
Dansteed Way (H4) . . . . **ABV**
Groveway (H9) . . . . **CVX**
Millers Way (H2). . . . . **AV**
Monks Way (H3). . . . . **ABV**
Portway (H5) . . . . **BCV**
Ridgeway (H1) . . . . **AV**
Standing Way (H8) . . . . . . **BX, CV**

MILTON KEYNES

Buckingham Rd . . . . **BX**
London Rd. . . . . **CUV**
Manor Rd . . . . **CX**
Marsh End Rd . . . . **CU**
Newport Rd . . . . **BV**
Northampton Rd . . . . **AU**
Stoke Rd. . . . . **CX**
Stratford Rd . . . . **AV**
Whaddon Way . . . . **BX**
Wolverton Rd. . . . . **BU**

VERTICAL ROADS

Brickhill St (V10) . . . . **BU, CX**
Fulmer St (V3) . . . . **ABX**
Grafton St (V6). . . . . **BVX**
Great Monks St (V5) . . . . **AV**
Marlborough St (V8). . . . . **BV, CX**
Overstreet (V9) . . . . **BV**
Saxon St (V7) . . . . **BVX**
Snelshall St (V1) . . . . **BX**
Tattenhoe St (V2). . . . . **ABX**
Tongwell St (V11) . . . . **CVX**
Watling St (V4) . . . . **AV, BX**

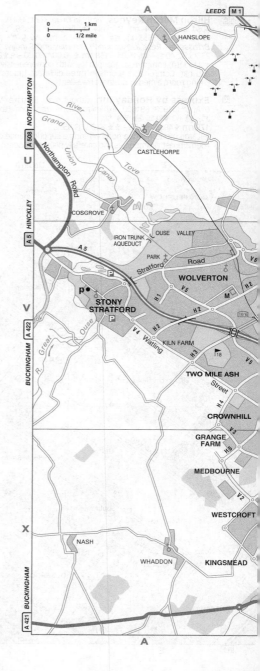

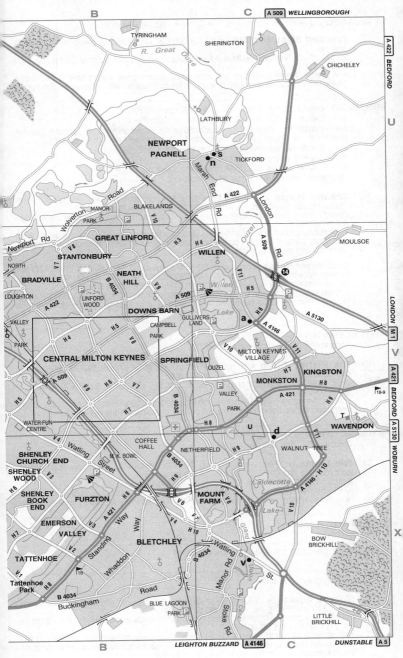

at Newton Longville *Southwest : 6 m. by A 421 – AX – ⊠ Milton Keynes.*

Crooked Billet, MK17 0DF, ℘ (01908) 373936, *john@thebillet.co.uk*, 🌳 – **P.** **⓪⑩** **AE** **VISA** . ❄
closed 25-26 December – **Rest** *(closed Sunday dinner and Monday lunch)* a la carte 25.00/40.00 ♀ ❧.
♦ A pretty, thatched exterior and large front garden greet visitors to this village pub. Dining in two areas on scrubbed pine and mahogany tables. Tasty, modern English menus.

MINEHEAD *Somerset* **503** J 30 *The West Country G. – pop. 11 699.*
See : *Town★ - Higher Town (Church Steps★, St Michael's★).*
Env. : *Dunster★★ - Castle★★ AC (upper rooms ≤★) Water Mill★ AC, St George's Church★, Dovecote★, SE : 2½ m. by A 39 – Selworthy★ (Church★, ≤★★) W : 4½ m. by A 39.*
Exc. : *Exmoor National Park★★ – Cleeve Abbey★★ AC, SE : 6½ m. by A 39.*
🏌 *The Warren, Warren Rd* ℘ (01643) 702057.
🚹 *17 Friday St* ℘ (01643) 702624, *mineheadtic@visit.org.uk.*
London 187 – Bristol 64 – Exeter 43 – Taunton 25.

Channel House ⬎, Church Path, TA24 5QG, off Northfield Rd ℘ (01643) 703229, *channel.house@virgin.net*, Fax (01643) 708925, ≤, 🌳 – ⇥✕ **P.** **⓪⑩** **VISA** . ❄
closed January-February – **Rest** *(dinner only)* 26.00 – **8 rm** *(dinner included)* ⊇ ✸96.00 – ✸✸162.00.
♦ Pleasantly located Edwardian hotel in rural location surrounded by mature yet carefully manicured gardens. Small, homely style lounge and fair sized, immaculate bedrooms. Home-cooked meals using local ingredients.

Glendower House *without rest.,* 30-32 Tregonwell Rd, TA24 5DU, ℘ (01643) 707144, *info@glendower-house.co.uk*, Fax (01643) 708719, 🌳 – ⇥✕ **P.** **⓪⑩** **AE** **VISA** . ❄
closed mid December-mid February – **12 rm** ⊇ ✸40.00/50.00 – ✸✸70.00.
♦ Good value, warmly run guesthouse, convenient for seafront and town; boasts original Victorian features. Snug bar/sitting room. Immaculately kept bedrooms with a homely feel.

MISTLEY *Essex* **504** X 28.
London 69 – Colchester 11 – Ipswich 14.

The Mistley Thorn *with rm,* High St, CO11 1HE, ℘ (01206) 392821, *info@mistley thorn.co.uk*, Fax (01206) 390122 – ⇥✕ **P.** **⓪⑩** **VISA**
Rest 13.95 *(lunch)* and a la carte 16.00/23.00 ♀ – ⊇ 6.95 – **5 rm** ✸70.00/75.00 – ✸✸80.00/85.00.
♦ Attractive yellow painted Georgian pub with modern interior: sitting area has cosy sofas. Interesting dishes, cooked with care, full of local, organic ingredients. Neat rooms.

MITCHELL *Cornwall* **503** E 32 – ⊠ *Truro.*
London 265 – Plymouth 47 – Truro 9.

The Plume of Feathers *with rm,* TR8 5AX, ℘ (01872) 510387, *lewinnich@btcon nect.com*, Fax (01872) 83940, 🌳 – ⇥✕ **P.** **⓪⑩** **VISA**
Rest a la carte 41.25/48.75 – **5 rm** ⊇ ✸65.00/75.00.
♦ 16C pub in village centre. Rustic, beamed interior. Pleasant dining area with fresh flowers and small candles. Modern food with fine Cornish ingredients. Airy, modish rooms.

MITTON *Lancs. - see Whalley.*

MOBBERLEY *Ches.* **502 503 504** N 24 *- see Knutsford.*

MOCCAS *Herefordshire* **503** L 27.

Moccas Court ⬎, HR2 9LH, ℘ (019851) 500019, *benemaster@btconnect.com*, Fax (01981) 500098, ⬎, 🍴 – ⇥✕ **P.** **⓪⑩** **AE** **VISA** . ❄
Rest *(by arrangement) (communal dining) (dinner only) (set menu only)* 35.00 s. – **5 rm** ⊇ ✸112.00/148.00 – ✸✸145.00/195.00.
♦ Breathtakingly beautiful Grade I listed Georgian house in 100 acres of grounds on terraced banks over the Wye. Antique filled interior; bedrooms furnished to high standard. Estate sourced produce served in ornate Round Room.

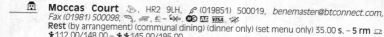

MONK FRYSTON *N. Yorks.* **502** Q 22 – ⊠ *Lumby.*
London 190 – Kingston-upon-Hull 42 – Leeds 13 – York 20.

🏨 **Monk Fryston Hall,** Main St, LS25 5DU, ✆ (01977) 682369, *reception@monkfryston-hotel.co.uk, Fax (01977) 683544,* 🏛, 🌳, ₤ – ✦ P – 🔥 50. 🅾🎖 AE VISA
Rest 27.50 (dinner) and lunch a la carte 17.75 approx ♈ – **29 rm** ✱85.00/105.00 –
✱✱140.00.
◆ Very characterful, possibly haunted, manor house dating from the 1300s with many later additions. Spacious grounds. Baronial style hall with antiques. Imposing rooms. Comfortable dining room with baronial touches.

MONKLEIGH *Devon – see Bideford.*

MONKS ELEIGH *Suffolk* **504** W 27.
London 72 – Cambridge 47 – Colchester 17 – Ipswich 16 – Norwich 49.

🍴 **Swan Inn,** The Street, IP7 7AU, ✆ (01449) 741391, *swan@monkseleigh.com,* 🌳 – ✦ P.
🅾🎖 VISA 🌿
closed 25-26 December and 1 January – **Rest** *(closed Monday-Tuesday)* a la carte 18.50/32.00 ♈.
◆ Charming, friendly ambience in 16C whitewashed village inn with thatched roof. Daily changing blackboard menus of modern British pub food using fresh local ingredients.

MONTACUTE *Somerset* **503 504** L 31 – *see Yeovil.*

MORETONHAMPSTEAD *Devon* **503** I 32 *The West Country G.* – ⊠ *Newton Abbot.*
Env. : Dartmoor National Park★★.
🏌 Bovey Castle, North Bovey ✆ (01647) 445009.
London 213 – Exeter 13 – Plymouth 30.

🏨 **The White Hart,** The Square, TQ13 8NF, ✆ (01647) 441340, *enquiries@whitehartdartmoor.co.uk, Fax (01647) 441341,* 🏛 – ✦ – 🔥 50. 🅾🎖 AE ① VISA
Rest *(bar lunch)/dinner* a la carte 22.00/30.00 – **28 rm** ⊇ ✱50.00/70.00 – ✱✱90.00/120.00.
◆ 17C Grade II listed former coaching inn in the town. Charming country furnished residents lounge. Pleasant 'locals' bar. Attractively refurbished rooms are strong point. Clothed dining room with Glorious Devon posters on the wall.

⌂ **Moorcote** without rest., TQ13 8LS, Northwest : ¼ m. on A 382 ✆ (01647) 440966, *moorcote@smartone.co.uk,* ⇐, 🌳 – ✦ P. 🌿
March-October – **4 rm** ⊇ ✱40.00 – ✱✱54.00.
◆ Perched on hill above Moretonhampstead, this Victorian guesthouse has mature gardens and well-kept bedrooms with stunning views of Dartmoor. Cosy breakfast room and lounge.

⌂ **Great Sloncombe Farm** ⏏ without rest., TQ13 8QF, Northwest : 1 ½ m. by A 382 ✆ (01647) 440595, *hmerchant@sloncombe.freeserve.co.uk, Fax (01647) 440595,* ₤ – ✦ P.
3 rm ⊇ ✱36.00 – ✱✱64.00.
◆ Cottagey part 13C farmhouse on vast working farm. Atmospheric beamed lounge with woodburning stove. Airy pine-furnished rooms. Pleasant breakfast room with rustic feel.

MORETON-IN-MARSH *Glos.* **503 504** O 28 *Great Britain G.* – *pop. 3 198.*
Env. : Chastleton House★★, SE : 5 m. by A 44.
London 86 – Birmingham 40 – Gloucester 31 – Oxford 29.

🏨 **Manor House,** High St, GL56 0LJ, ✆ (01608) 650501, *info@manorhousehotel.info,* Fax (01608) 651481, 🏛, 🌳 – 🛗 ✦, 🍽 rest, 🕯 P – 🔥 120. 🅾🎖 AE VISA
Mulberry : Rest *(light lunch)/dinner* 32.50 – **36 rm** ⊇ ✱115.00/135.00 –
✱✱155.00/170.00, 2 suites.
◆ Part 16C manor house in town centre. Walled lawns to rear. Two country house style low-beamed lounges with open fires. Sympathetically styled rooms; luxurious fabrics. Contemporary restaurant with bold style and cooking.

at Bourton-on-the-Hill *West : 2 m. on A 44* – ⊠ *Moreton-in-Marsh.*

🍴 **Horse and Groom** with rm, GL56 9AQ, ✆ (01386) 700413, *greenstocks@horseandgroom.info, Fax (01386) 700413,* 🏛, 🌳 – ✦ P. 🅾🎖 VISA 🌿
closed 25 and 31 December – **Rest** *(closed Sunday dinner and Monday lunch)* (booking essential) a la carte 18.00/25.00 ♈ – **5 rm** ⊇ ✱65.00 – ✱✱115.00.
◆ Attractive 18C former coaching inn of yellowing local stone. Big, welcoming, beamed bar. 'Proper' English cooking on menus that change up to twice a day. Large, comfy rooms.

MORPETH Northd. 501 502 O 18 – pop. 13 555.

🏌 The Common ℘ (01670) 504942.

🅱 The Chantry, Bridge St ℘ (01670) 500700.

London 301 – Edinburgh 93 – Newcastle upon Tyne 15.

at Eshott North : 6 m. by A 1 – ⊠ Morpeth.

🏠 **Eshott Hall** ⟿, Eshott Hall Estate, NE65 9EP, by unmarked drive just before entering village ℘ (01670) 787777, thehall@eshott.co.uk, Fax (01670) 787999, ⟿, ₤, ⋇ – ⇥ ℙ –
🏛 120. ℗❸ 🆎 ⓪ 𝚅𝙸𝚂𝙰
closed Christmas - New Year**Rest** (by arrangement) (communal dining) 18.00/27.50 – **6 rm**
⌖ ✦66.00 – ✦✦108.00.
• Impressive Georgian mansion in a private drive with mature grounds. A smart country house feel is evident all around. Popular for weddings. Rooms exude spotless quality. Owner cooks and serves at an antique table.

at Longhorsley Northwest : 6½ m. by A 192 on A 697 – ⊠ Morpeth.

🏨 **Linden Hall** ⟿, NE65 8XF, North : 1 m. on A 697 ℘ (01670) 500000, lindenhall@macdonald-hotels.co.uk, Fax (01670) 500001, ≼, 🍴, ᴵ₅, 🏊, 🗙, 🏌, ⟿, ₤, ⋇ – 🖹 ⇥ ⚓ 🍴
ℙ – 🏛 300. ℗❸ 𝚅𝙸𝚂𝙰
Dobson : Rest (dinner only and lunch Saturday and Sunday)/dinner 32.50 s. ♀ – **Linden Tree :** Rest a la carte approx 20.00 – **50 rm** ⌖ ✦82.00 – ✦✦94.00/174.00.
• Imposing, ivy clad Georgian house in extensive grounds. Numerous lounges refurbished with contemporary edge and a real fire. Well-kept, modernised, stylish rooms. Formal dining in comfy Dobson. Modish Linden Tree.

🏠 **Thistleyhaugh Farm** ⟿, NE65 8RG, Northwest : 3 ¾ m. by A 697 and Todburn rd taking first right turn ℘ (01665) 570629, stay@thistleyhaugh.com, Fax (01665) 570629, ⟿, ₤ – ⋇ ℙ. ⋇
restricted opening in winter – **Rest** (by arrangement) (communal dining) 17.00 – 5 rm ⌖ ✦42.00 – ✦✦65.00.
• Attractive Georgian farmhouse on working farm in a pleasant rural area. The River Coquet flows through the grounds. Comfortable, cosy bedrooms in traditional style. Communal dining overlooking garden.

MORSTON Norfolk – see Blakeney.

MORTEHOE Devon 503 H 30 – see Woolacombe.

MOTCOMBE Dorset 503 504 N 30 – see Shaftesbury.

MOULSFORD Oxon.
London 53.5 – Newbury 16 – Reading 13.5.

🍴🍴 **The Beetle & Wedge Boathouse**, Ferry Lane, OX10 9JF, ℘ (01491) 651381, boathouse@beetleandwedge.co.uk, Fax (01491) 651376, ≼, 🍴, ⟿ – 🚻 ℙ. ℗❸ 🆎 𝚅𝙸𝚂𝙰
Rest (booking essential) a la carte 26.95/42.20.
• Beautifully located by the Thames and enhanced by lovely terrace. Two dining options: bare-brick char-grill or conservatory dining room. Daily changing, wide-ranging menus.

MOULTON N. Yorks. 502 P 20 – ⊠ Richmond.
London 243 – Leeds 53 – Middlesbrough 25 – Newcastle upon Tyne 43.

🍴🍴 **Black Bull Inn**, DL10 6QJ, ℘ (01325) 377289, sarah@blackbullinn.demon.co.uk, Fax (01325) 377422 – ℙ. ℗❸ 🆎 𝚅𝙸𝚂𝙰
closed 24-26 December and Sunday – **Rest** - Seafood specialities - 19.95 (lunch) and a la carte 35.00/45.00.
• Old country pub with variety of dining areas, including an original Brighton Belle Pullman carriage from 1932 and conservatory with huge grapevine. Seafood a speciality.

Undecided between two equivalent establishments?
Within each category, establishments are classified
in our order of preference.

MOUSEHOLE Cornwall 503 D 33 The West Country G. – ✉ Penzance.

See : Village★.
Env. : Penwith★★ – Lamorna (The Merry Maidens and The Pipers Standing Stone★)
SW : 3 m. by B 3315.
Exc. : Land's End★ (cliff scenery★★★) W : 9 m. by B 3315.
London 321 – Penzance 3 – Truro 29.

🏠 **The Old Coastguard,** The Parade, TR19 6PR, ℰ (01736) 731222, bookings@oldcoast
guardhotel.co.uk, Fax (01736) 731720, ≤, 佘, 록 – 🔆 🄿 🐠 🄰🄴 🆅🅸🆂🅰 . ✺
Rest (closed 25 December) a la carte 23.00/33.50 🍸 – **20 rm** 🖙 ✦40.00/100.00 –
✦✦80.00/160.00.
♦ Creamwash hotel in unspoilt village with good views of Mounts Bay. Spacious lounge has
sun terrace overlooking water. Modern rooms: Premier variety are best for the vista. Watch
the bay as you eat freshly caught seafood..

✗ **Cornish Range** with rm, 6 Chapel St, TR19 6SB, ℰ (01736) 731488, info@corni
shrange.co.uk – 🔆 rm. 🐠 🆅🅸🆂🅰
closed Sunday lunch – **Rest** - Seafood - (booking essential) a la carte 20.40/33.45 🍸 – **3 rm**
🖙 – ✦✦85.00/100.00.
♦ Converted 18C pilchard processing cottage hidden away in narrow street. Cottagey
inner filled with Cornish artwork. Excellent local seafood dishes. Very comfortable rooms.

MUCH MARCLE Herefordshire 503 504 M 28 – see Ledbury.

MUCH WENLOCK Shrops. 502 503 M26 Great Britain G. – pop. 1 959.

See : Priory★ AC.
Env. : Ironbridge Gorge Museum★★ AC (The Iron Bridge★★ - Coalport China Museum★★ -
Blists Hill Open Air Museum★★ – Museum of the Gorge and Visitor Centre★) NE : 4½ m. by
A 4169 and B 4380.
🅱 The Museum, The Square, High St ℰ (01952) 727679 (summer only).
London 154 – Birmingham 34 – Shrewsbury 12 – Worcester 37.

🏨 **Raven,** Barrow St, TF13 6EN, ℰ (01952) 727251, enquiry@ravenhotel.com,
Fax (01952) 728416, 佘 – 🔆 rest, 🄿 🐠 🄰🄴 🄾 🆅🅸🆂🅰 . ✺
closed 25 December – **The Restaurant :** Rest 28.00 and a la carte 20.90/24.95 – **14 rm** 🖙
✦75.00 – ✦✦150.00.
♦ Hotel spread across range of historic buildings with 17C coaching inn at its heart. Pleasant inner courtyard and conservatory. Good sized bedrooms with chintz fabrics. Dining
room exudes homely rustic charm.

at Brockton Southwest : 5 m. on B 4378 – ✉ Much Wenlock.

🍴 **The Feathers Inn,** TF13 6JR, ℰ (01746) 785202, kayiatou@hotmail.com,
Fax (01746) 785202, 佘 – 🔆 🄿 🐠 🄰🄴 🆅🅸🆂🅰 . ✺
closed 26 December-3 January, Monday, Tuesday-Friday lunch and Bank Holidays – **Rest**
14.95 (dinner) and a la carte 14.95/40.00.
♦ Characterful part 16C pub near Wenlock Edge: whitewashed stone walls, beams and vast
inglenooks. Constantly changing blackboard menus provide plethora of interesting dishes.

MUDEFORD Dorset 503 504 O 31 – see Christchurch.

MULLION Cornwall 503 E 33 The West Country G. – pop. 1 834 – ✉ Helston.

See : Mullion Cove★★ (Church★) – Lizard Peninsula★.
Env. : Kynance Cove★★, S : 5 m. – Cury★ (Church★), N : 2 m. by minor roads.
Exc. : Helston (The Flora Day Furry Dance★★) (May), N : 7½ m. by A 3083 – Culdrose
(Flambards Village Theme Park★) AC, N : 6 m. by A 3083 – Wendron (Poldark Mine★),
N : 9½ m. by A 3083 and B 3297.
London 323 – Falmouth 21 – Penzance 21 – Truro 26.

🏨 **Mullion Cove,** TR12 7EP, Southwest : 1 m. by B 3296 ℰ (01326) 240328, mul
lion.cove@btinternet.com, Fax (01326) 240998, ≤ Mullion Cove and Mount's Bay, 佘, ⇆,
⌧, 록 – 🔆 rest, 🄿 🐠 🄰🄴 🆅🅸🆂🅰
Atlantic View : Rest dinner only 25.95 🍸 – **Bistro :** Rest a la carte 14.40/40.90 s. – **30 rm**
(dinner included) 🖙 ✦85.50/221.50 – ✦✦104.00/240.00.
♦ Dramatic Victorian hotel, personally run, standing in spectacular position on cliffs above
Mullion Cove. Terrific views along coastline. Comfortable, modern rooms. Cream painted,
welcoming Atlantic View. Bistro with terrace perfect for lunch.

555

MUNSLOW *Shrops. 503* L 26.

London 166 – Ludlow 10 – Shrewsbury 21.

🏠 **The Crown Country Inn** with rm, SY7 9ET, on B 4378 ℰ (01584) 841205, *info@crowncountryinn.co.uk, Fax (01584) 841255,* 🏠 – ☜ 🅿. 🐾 🎟 – 🖘 **P. ⬛⬛ ⯈⯈**. ⯈
closed 25 December – Rest (closed Monday) a la carte 20.00/29.00 – 3 rm ⯈ ✦45.00 –
✦✦65.00/70.00.
♦ Hugely characterful, heavily beamed bar, crackling fire and hops hanging from the rafters. Well executed dishes served here or in linen clad restaurant. Simple, comfy rooms.

MYLOR BRIDGE *Cornwall 503* E 33 – see Falmouth.

NAILSWORTH *Glos. 503 504* N 28 – pop. 5 276.

London 110 – Bristol 30 – Swindon 28.

🏨 **Egypt Mill,** GL6 0AE, ℰ (01453) 833449, *reception@egyptmill.com, Fax (01453) 839919,* 🏠, 🍴 – ☜ 🐾 🅿 – 🔬 60. 🐾 **⬛⬛ ⯈⯈**.
Rest a la carte 17.90/27.90 ⯈ – 28 rm ⯈ ✦65.00 – ✦✦95.00.
♦ Hugely characterful former 16C mill on the Frome, once used for cloth manufacture. Bedrooms are in three blocks; some with original features and river views. Comfy bistro style restaurant with watery vistas; mill workings surround diners.

NANTITHET *Cornwall – see Helston.*

NANTWICH *Ches. 502 503 504* M 24 – pop. 13 447.

🏌 *Alvaston Hall, Middlewich Rd* ℰ (01270) 628473.
🎫 *Church House, Church Walk* ℰ (01270) 610983.
London 176 – Chester 20 – Liverpool 45 – Manchester 40 – Stoke-on-Trent 17.

🏨 **Rookery Hall** 🌿, Worleston, CW5 6DQ, North : 2 ½ m. by A 51 on B 5074 ℰ (01270) 610016, *rookery@handpicked.co.uk, Fax (01270) 626027,* ≤, 🐾, 🍴, ♨ – 🖩, 🖘 rest, 🐾 &
🅿 – 🔬 70. 🐾 🎟 **⬛⬛ VISA**
Rest (closed Saturday lunch) (booking essential) 19.50/29.50 and dinner a la carte 32.50/45.50 ⯈ – ⯈ 12.50 – 44 rm ✦140.00 – ✦✦150.00, 2 suites.
♦ Originally built in 1816 in Georgian style; enjoys a peacefully set, smart country house ambience. The individually decorated bedrooms offer a very good level of comfort. Wood panelled restaurant with polished tables.

🏠 **The Limes** without rest., 5 Park Rd, CW5 7AQ, on A 530 (Whitchurch rd) ℰ (01270) 624081, *thelimesparkroad@aol.com, Fax (01270) 624081,* 🍴 – 🖘 🅿. ⯈
March-October – 3 rm ⯈ ✦50.00/55.00 – ✦✦55.00/60.00.
♦ Redbrick Victorian house in Queen Anne style. The large bedrooms have been individually decorated and benefit from a warm personality. Friendly and personally run.

🏠 **Oakland House** without rest., 252 Newcastle Rd, Blakelow, Shavington, CW5 7ET, East : 2 ½ m. by A 51 on A 500 ℰ (01270) 567134, *enquiries@oaklandhouseonline.co.uk,* 🍴 – 🖘
🅿. 🐾 ⯈ **VISA**
9 rm ⯈ ✦39.00 – ✦✦54.00.
♦ Private guesthouse with family photos adding personal touch. Homely lounge, warmly decorated breakfast room and conservatory. Comfy rooms in house and converted outbuildings.

NATIONAL EXHIBITION CENTRE *W. Mids. 503 504* O 26 – see Birmingham.

NAWTON *N. Yorks. – see Helmsley.*

NAYLAND *Suffolk 504* W 28.

London 64 – Bury St Edmunds 24 – Cambridge 54 – Colchester 6 – Ipswich 19.

XX **White Hart Inn** with rm, 11 High St, CO6 4SF, ℰ (01206) 263382, *nayhart@aol.com, Fax (01206) 263638,* 🏠 – 🖘 rm, 🅿. 🐾 🎟 ⯈ **VISA**. ⯈
closed 26 December-10 January – Rest (closed Monday) (booking essential) 15.50 (lunch)
and a la carte 20.00/32.00 **s.** ⯈ – 6 rm ⯈ ✦69.00/87.00 – ✦✦85.00/110.00.
♦ Accomplished food served in terracotta tiled dining room of part 15C coaching inn. Floodlit cellars and comfortable beamed bedrooms.

NEAR SAWREY *Cumbria 502* L 20 – see Hawkshead.

NETHER BROUGHTON *Leics. 502 504* R 25 – see Melton Mowbray.

NETHER WASDALE Cumbria.
London 309 – Ambleside 24 – Blackpool 85 – Carlisle 52 – Whitehaven 17.

XX **Low Wood Hall** ⌂ with rm, CA20 1ET, ℰ (019467) 26100, *reservations@lowwood hall.co.uk*, Fax (019467) 26111, ≤, ☞ – ⅔⊱ **P**, ⏍ ⏃ **VISA**
closed Christmas and Sunday – **Rest** (dinner only) 25.00 s. – 6 rm ☺ ✝60.00/60.00 –
✝✝110.00/120.00.
♦ Split-level dining room with garden views within fine Victorian country house boasting tiled floor and stained glass. Tasty, fresh, well-cooked modern menus. Homely rooms.

NETTLEBED Oxon. 504 R 29.
London 44 – Oxford 20 – Reading 10.

血 **White Hart**, 28 High St, RG9 5DD, ℰ (01491) 641245, *info@whitehartnettlebed.com*, Fax (01491) 649018 – ⅔⊱ **♥ P**, – ⊿ 30. ⏍ ⏃ **VISA**. ⅘
Bistro : Rest 14.95 and a la carte 17.70/28.20 s. ⏃ – **Number 28 : Rest** (dinner only Thursday-Saturday) 35.00 – **12 rm** ☺ ✝85.00/125.00 – ✝✝95.00/125.00.
♦ Recently refurbished part 17C inn boasts spacious, modern bedrooms, all uniquely styled with a certain "designer" appeal, some in original hotel, others in adjacent new block. Minimalist Bistro. Number 28 for contemporary cooking.

NETTLETON SHRUB Wilts. 503 504 N 29 – see Castle Combe.

NEWARK-ON-TRENT Notts. 502 504 R 24 Great Britain G. – pop. 35 454.
See : St Mary Magdalene★.
ᴎ Kelwick, Coddington ℰ (01636) 626282.
London 127 – Lincoln 16 – Nottingham 20 – Sheffield 42.

血 **Grange**, 73 London Rd, NG24 1RZ, South : ½ m. on Grantham rd (B 6326) ℰ (01636) 703399, *info@grangenewark.co.uk*, Fax (01636) 702328, ☞ – ⅔⊱ **P**, ⏍ ⏃ ⏀ **VISA**. ⅘
closed 24 December-3 January – **Cutlers : Rest** (bar lunch Monday-Saturday)/dinner a la carte 21.95/27.95 – **19 rm** ☺ ✝72.00/85.00 – ✝✝130.00/150.00.
♦ Situated in a residential area but not far from town centre, this small hotel is fitted with functional, simply decorated bedrooms and miniature pulpit-style bar. Compact dining room boasts cadlelit dinners.

XX **Reeds**, 13-15 Castlegate, NG24 1AL, ℰ (01636) 704500, *food@reedrestaurants.com*, Fax (01636) 611139 – ⏍ ⏃ **VISA**
closed Sunday dinner – **Rest** a la carte 18.70/36.30.
♦ Intimate, brick vaulted, Georgian house cellar with original ceiling meat hooks in situ. Mix of linen-clad and plain tables. Seasonal ingredients to the fore in varied menus.

at Caunton Northwest : 4½ m. by A 616 – ✉ Newark-on-Trent.

洷 **Caunton Beck**, Main St, NG23 6AB, ℰ (01636) 636793, Fax (01636) 636828, ☞ – ⅔⊱ **P**, ⏍ ⏃ ⏀ **VISA**. ⅘
Rest 13.95 and a la carte 22.50/32.00 ⏃.
♦ Period pub by stream; sparkling menus singing with flavour: modern with oriental, Mediterranean touches. Sample elderflower blancmange with shortbread and rose petal syrup.

NEWBIGGIN Cumbria 502 L 19 – see Penrith.

NEWBURY Newbury 503 504 Q 29 – pop. 33 273.
ᴎ Newbury and Crookham, Bury's Bank Rd, Greenham Common ℰ (01635) 40035 AX – ᴎ Donnington Valley, Old Oxford Rd ℰ (01635) 568140 AX.
🖪 The Wharf ℰ (01635) 30267, tourism@westberks.gov.uk.
London 67 – Bristol 66 – Oxford 28 – Reading 17 – Southampton 38.

Plan on next page

 Vineyard, Stockcross, RG20 8JU, Northwest : 2 m. by A 4 on B 4000 ℰ (01635) 528770, *general@the-vineyard.co.uk*, Fax (01635) 528398, ℔, ≘s, ◻, ☞ – ⴲ, ⅔⊱ rm, ▤ **♥ P** –
⊿ 100. ⏍ ⏃ ⏀ **VISA**. ⅘
❀❀ AV b
Rest 24.00/65.00 ⏃ ☞ – ☺ 18.50 – **34 rm** ☺ ✝170.00 – ✝✝270.00, 15 suites ☺ 350.00/525.00.
Spec. Scallops with parsley root, horseradish and "chicken biscuit". Wild venison with parsnip purée and pickled pears. Parfait with jasmine, mandarin, thyme and ginger.
♦ Outside, a pool bearing bowls of fire encapsulates bright art-filled interiors. Luxurious suites with woven fabrics. Very good service. Super spa. Modern or classic rooms. Indulge in accomplished original cuisine and exceptional wine list.

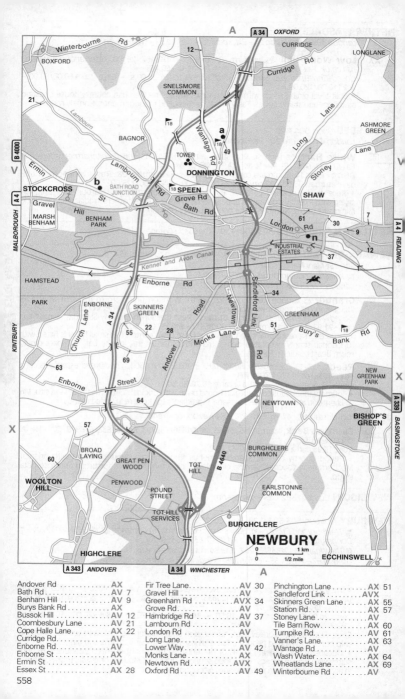

558

NEWBURY

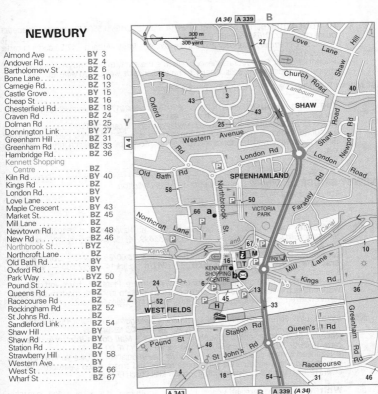

🏯 Donnington Valley H. & Spa, Old Oxford Rd, Donnington, RG14 3AG, North : 1 ¾ m.
by A 4 off B 4494 ℰ (01635) 551199, *general@donningtonvalley.co.uk, Fax (01635) 551123,*
⑫, ℾₛ, ⚿ – |✦| ✦⟵ ☰ ℰ ₫ Ᵽ – ⫝̸ 140. ⓜ◉ Ⓐ🄴 ⓘ *VISA*. ✦ᵧ
AV **a**
Winepress : Rest 22.00/26.00 and a la carte 32.00/42.00 ♀ ✿ – ☲ 14.50 – **113 rm** ✦170.00
– ✦✦250.00.
◆ Smart executive and family rooms in purpose-built country hotel with 18-hole golf
course. Artwork abounds: sculptures and paintings as well as concerts and other events.
Dine in conservatory or gallery.

🏯 Newbury Manor, London Rd, RG14 2BY, ℰ (01635) 528838, *enquiries@newbury-
manor-hotel.co.uk, Fax (01635) 523406,* 🌇, ⚄, ✿ – ✦⟵, ☰ rest, ℰ Ᵽ – ⫝̸ 100. ⓜ◉ Ⓐ🄴
AV **n**
ⓘ *VISA* ✦ᵧ
Rest 22.50 (lunch) and dinner a la carte 23.45/28.45 ♀ – **33 rm** ☲ ✦80.00/120.00 –
✦✦80.00/165.00.
◆ Close to Newbury racecourse and on banks of river Kennett, this listed building boasts
soft furnished rooms, some with balconies. Deep sofas in conservatory to relax in. Restaurant has glass wall which opens for alfresco dining.

XX The Square, 5-6 Weavers Walk, Northbrook St, RG14 1AL, ℰ (01635) 44805, *enqui
ries@thesquarenewbury.co.uk, Fax (01635) 523114,* 🌇 – ☰ ⟷ 30. ⓜ◉ ⓘ *VISA*
BZ **a**
closed Sunday – **Rest** 21.95 (dinner) and a la carte 25.50/36.70 ♀.
◆ Tucked away in a little high street mews. French influenced artwork enlivens walls.
Adventurous gastronomic excursions: expect unusual combinations with vivid presentation.

※ **Le Petit Square**, 17 The Market Pl, RG14 5AA, ℰ (01635) 550770, *enquiries@lepetits quare.co.uk, Fax (01635) 529669*
BZ **b**
closed 25 December, 1 January and Sunday dinner – **Rest** *-* French *- 17.50 and a la carte 20.95/29.50* 🕃 ⏧.
♦ Identikit classic French brasserie: opposite the theatre with pre- and post-performance choice. Gallic posters line walls. Menus in French alongside well-priced wine list.

at Marsh Benham *West :* 3½ *m. by A 4 – AV –* ⊠ *Newbury.*

🍴 **The Red House**, RG20 8LY, ℰ (01635) 582017, *cyrilgrell@btconnect.com, Fax (01635) 581621*, 🎘, 🐖 – ⁜⊱ ℙ ⟡ 20. **⃝O ⃝O** 𝗔𝗘 𝗩𝗜𝗦𝗔. 🕱
closed 25-26 December – **Rest** *(closed Sunday dinner)* a la carte 19.45/32.95.
♦ Redbrick thatched house, once an inn. Interior is a tiled, beamed pub and adjacent dining room with modern fabrics and furnishings. Accomplished French influenced cooking.

NEWBY BRIDGE *Cumbria* 502 L 21 *Great Britain G. –* ⊠ *Ulverston.*
Env. : *Lake Windermere*★★.
London 270 – Kendal 16 – Lancaster 27.

🏨 **Lakeside**, Lakeside, LA12 8AT, Northeast : 1 m. on Hawkshead rd ℰ (015395) 30001, *reservations@lakesidehotel.co.uk, Fax (015395) 31699*, ≤, ⑩, 𝗜ₛ, ⛉ₛ, ⛆, ↝, 🐖 – 🛗 ⬆ ⁜⊱ & ℙ – 🛆 100. **⃝O ⃝O** 𝗩𝗜𝗦𝗔. 🕱
Lakeview : Rest 27.00/50.00 and lunch a la carte 23.00/28.00 s. ⏧ – *John Ruskins* **Brasserie :** Rest (dinner only) 36.00 ⏧ – **74 rm** ⊑ ✦145.00/175.00 – ✦✦265.00, 3 suites.
♦ Delightfully situated on the shores of Lake Windermere. Plenty of charm and character. Work out at the state-of-the-art leisure centre then sleep in fitted, modern bedrooms. Lakeview offers smart ambience. Bright, informal John Ruskins Brasserie.

🏨 **Swan**, LA12 8NB, ℰ (01539) 531681, *enquiries@swanhotel.com, Fax (01539) 531917*, ≤, 𝗜ₛ, ⛉ₛ, ⛆, ↝, 🐖 – 🛗 ⬆ ⁜⊱ ℙ – 🛆 70. **⃝O ⃝O** 𝗔𝗘 𝗩𝗜𝗦𝗔. 🕱 – 🖻 rest, � ℙ – 🛆 120. **⃝O ⃝O** 𝗔𝗘 𝗩𝗜𝗦𝗔. 🕱
Revell's : Rest (dinner only and Sunday lunch) 32.50 – **Mail Coach Brasserie :** Rest a la carte 16.45/26.30 – **55 rm** ⊑ ✦67.00/96.00 – ✦✦134.00/178.00.
♦ Extended former coaching inn on the River Leven adjacent to Lake Windermere. Extensive range of well-equipped conference rooms and smart, fitted bedrooms. Revell's offers formal dining experience. Bright, breezy Mail Coach Brasserie.

🏠 **Whitewater**, The Lakeland Village, LA12 8PX, Southwest : 1½ m. by A 590 ℰ (01539) 531133, *enquiries@whitewater-hotel.co.uk, Fax (01539) 531881*, ⑩, 𝗜ₛ, ⛉ₛ, ⛆, ※, squash – 🖻 ⁜⊱ ℙ – 🛆 70. **⃝O ⃝O** 𝗔𝗘 𝗩𝗜𝗦𝗔. 🕱
Riverside : Rest *(bar lunch Monday-Saturday)/dinner* 25.50/30.50 s. and a la carte 26.90/35.35 ⏧ – **35 rm** ⊑ ✦97.50/100.00 – ✦✦130.00.
♦ Converted mill of lakeland stone on banks of fast-flowing River Leven. Traditionally appointed interior with good sized bedrooms. Up-to-date leisure and treatment rooms. Restaurant or pubby bar dining options.

🏠 **The Knoll**, Lakeside, LA12 8AU, Northeast : 1¼ m. on Hawkshead rd ℰ (015395) 31347, *info@theknoll-lakeside.co.uk, Fax (015395) 30850*, 🐖 – ⁜⊱ ℙ. **⃝O ⃝O** 𝗔𝗘 𝗩𝗜𝗦𝗔. 🕱
closed 25-26 December – **Rest** *(closed Sunday-Monday)* (booking essential for non-residents) (dinner only) 26.00/30.00 s. – **8 rm** ⊑ ✦55.00/90.00 – ✦✦122.00.
♦ Late Victorian country house close to popular lakeside. Original stained glass, cornices and staircase. Welcoming lounge. Extensive breakfast menu. Cosy, comfortable bedrooms. Linen clad dining room; local produce proudly used.

NEWBY WISKE *N. Yorks.* 502 P 21 *– see Northallerton.*

Your opinions are important to us:
please write and let us know about your discoveries and experiences – good and bad!

ENGLAND

NEWCASTLE-UNDER-LYME *Staffs.* 502 503 504 N 24 *Great Britain G. – pop. 74 247.*

Exc. : *Wedgwood Visitor's Centre★ AC, SE : 6½ m. by A 34 Z.*

🛉 *Keele Golf Centre, Keele Rd* ℰ *(01782) 627596.*

🅱 *Newcastle Library, Ironmarket* ℰ *(01782) 297313, tic.newcastle@staffordshire.gov.uk.*

London 161 – Birmingham 46 – Liverpool 56 – Manchester 43.

Plan of Built up Area : see Stoke-on-Trent

NEWCASTLE-UNDER-LYME

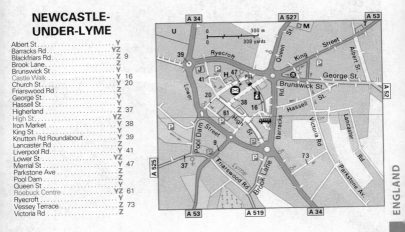

XX　**Ivory,** 13A Brunswick St, ST5 1HF, ℰ (01782) 710580 – ✸✖ 📠 　　　　　　a
closed Sunday – **Rest** a la carte 17.00/26.00 ♀.
　◆ Smart, canopied restaurant on busy street. Modish creams, blacks and browns provide a
fitting background for modern British cooking venturing down interesting avenues.

Newcastle upon Tyne: Millennium Bridge

NEWCASTLE UPON TYNE

Tyne and Wear **501 502** O 19 *Great Britain G. – pop. 189 863.*

London 276 – Edinburgh 105 – Leeds 95.

ENGLAND

TOURIST INFORMATION

🛈 *132 Grainger St 🕿 (0191) 277 8000; tourist.info@newcastle.gov.uk.*
🛈 *Guild Hall Visitors Centre, Quayside;*
🛈 *Newcastle International Airport 🕿 (0191) 214 4422.*

PRACTICAL INFORMATION

🅱 *Broadway East, Gosforth 🕿 (0191) 285 6710,* BV.
🅱 *City of Newcastle, Three Mile Bridge, Gosforth 🕿 (0191) 285 1775.*
🅱 *Wallsend, Rheydt Ave, Bigges Main 🕿 (0191) 262 1973, NE : by A 1058* BV.
🅱 *Whickham, Hollinside Park, Fellside Rd 🕿 (0191) 488 7309.*
Tyne Tunnel (toll).
✈ *Newcastle Airport : 🕿 (0870) 122 1488, NW : 5 m. by A 696* AV.
Terminal : *Bus Assembly : Eldon Sq.*
🛳 *to Norway (Bergen, Haugesund and Stavanger) (Fjord Line) (approx. 26 h) – to Sweden (Gothenburg) (via Kristiansand, Norway) (Scandinavian Seaways) (summer only) 2 weekly (approx. 26 h) – to The Netherlands (Amsterdam) (DFDS Seaways A/S) daily (15 h).*

SIGHTS

See : *City★ – Grey Street★* CZ *– Quayside★* CZ *: Composition★, All Saints Church★ (interior★) – Castle Keep★* AC CZ *– Laing Art Gallery and Museum★* AC CY **M1** *– Museum of Antiquities★* CY **M2** *– LIFE Interactive World★* CZ *– Gateshead Millennium Bridge★* CZ.

Env. : *Hadrian's Wall★★ , W : by A 69* AV.

Exc. : *Beamish : North of England Open-Air Museum★★* AC, *SW : 7 m. by A 692 and A 6076* AX *– Seaton Delaval Hall★* AC, *NE : 11 m. by A 189 –* BV *– and A 190.*

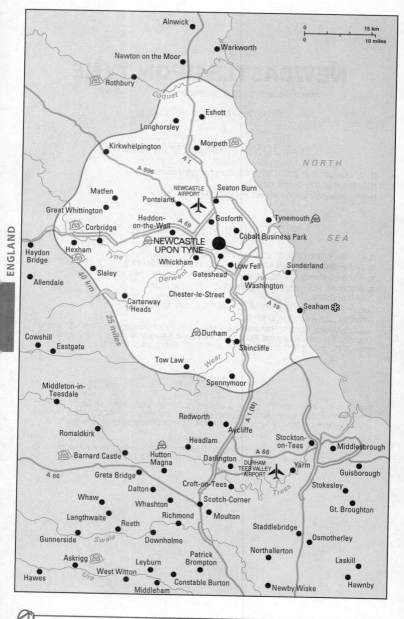

ENGLAND

If breakfast is included the ☕ symbol appears after the number of rooms.

564

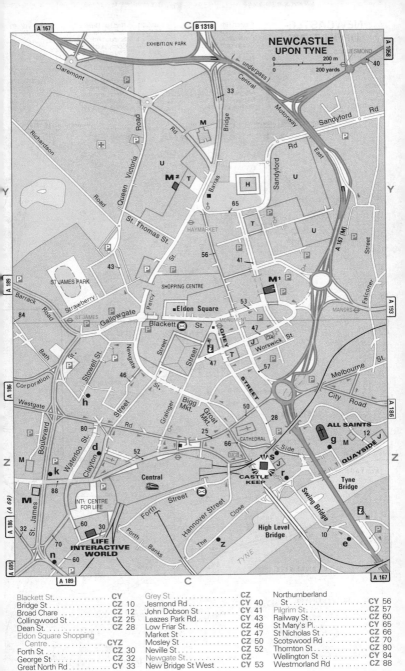

NEWCASTLE-UPON-TYNE

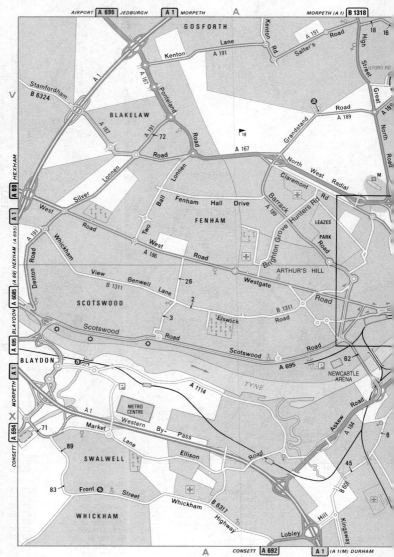

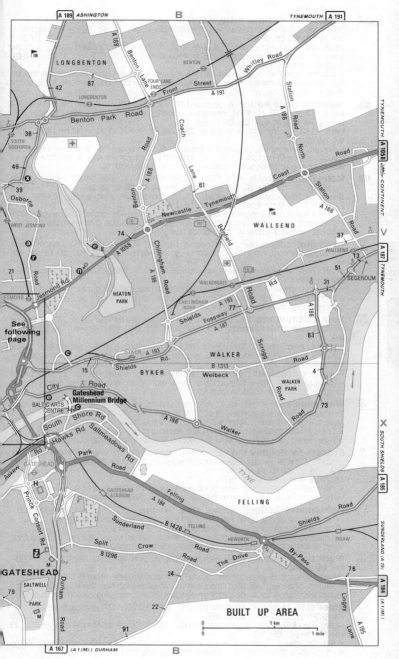

Copthorne H. Newcastle, The Close, Quayside, NE1 3RT, ℘ (0191) 222 0333, sales.newcastle@mill-cop.com, Fax (0191) 260 3033, ≤, 霜, ℔, ⌂, ☒ – ₪ ♔, ▤ rest, ⓺ ℙ – 쇼 200. ⬤⬤ ஈ ⓞ 𝘷𝘪𝘴𝘢
CZ z
Le Rivage : Rest *(dinner only)* a la carte 30.35/41.45 ♀ – *Harry's :* Rest *(closed Saturday lunch and Bank Holidays)* 10.00/21.95 and a la carte 21.95/35.45 ♀ – ⌚ 15.75 – **156 rm** ✦190.00 – ✦✦190.00.
♦ Modern hotel beside the Tyne. Bright and airy lounges within an imposing atrium. Well-appointed rooms have river views; ask for one with a balcony. Ornately decorated Le Rivage overlooks the Tyne. Bright, modern Harry's.

Jesmond Dene House ⌂, Jesmond Dene Rd, NE2 2EY, Northeast: 1½ m. by B 1318 and A 189 ℘ (0191) 212 3000, info@jesmonddenehouse.co.uk, Fax (0191) 212 3001, 霜, ☞ – ₪ ♔ ⓺ ⓻ ℙ – 쇼 120. ⬤⬤ ஈ 𝘷𝘪𝘴𝘢. ℠
BV x
Rest 20.50 (lunch) and a la carte 35.00/48.50 – ⌚ 15.00 – **40 rm** ✦150.00 – ✦✦195.00/295.00.
♦ Stylishly refurbished 19C Grade II listed house in tranquil city dene.Two very smart lounges, one with cocktail bar. Eclectic range of modish rooms with hi-tech feel. Formal dining room with conservatory style extension overlooks garden.

Malmaison, Quayside, NE1 3DX, ℘ (0191) 245 5000, newcastle@malmaison.com, Fax (0191) 245 4545, ℔, ⌂ – ₪ ♔ ▤ ⓺ ⓻ ℙ – 쇼 30. ⬤⬤ ஈ ⓞ 𝘷𝘪𝘴𝘢
BX e
Brasserie : Rest *(bar lunch Saturday)* 12.75/15.95 (weekdays) and a la carte 22.40/40.50 s. ♀ – ⌚ 12.75 – **120 rm** ✦140.00 – ✦✦140.00, 2 suites.
♦ Unstuffy and contemporary hotel hides within this quayside former Co-operative building. Vibrantly and individually decorated rooms; some overlook Millennium Bridge. Brasserie has modern interpretation of French style.

Jurys Inn, St James Gate, Scotswood Rd, NE4 7JH, ℘ (0191) 201 4400, jurysinnnewcastle@jurysdoyle.com, Fax (0191) 201 4411 – ₪ ♔, ▤ rest, ⓺ – 쇼 100. ⬤⬤ ஈ ⓞ 𝘷𝘪𝘴𝘢 ℠
CZ n
closed 24-26 December – Rest *(bar lunch)/dinner* a la carte approx 15.95 – ⌚ 9.50 – **274 rm** ✦89.00 – ✦✦89.00.
♦ Modern hotel well placed for visiting the district. Large reception area with small lounge and coffee shop. Well-appointed uniform rooms, some with view of the city. Informal wood-panelled ground floor restaurant.

New Northumbria, 61-73 Osborne Rd, Jesmond, NE2 2AN, ℘ (0191) 281 4961, reservations@newnorthumbriahotel.co.uk, Fax (0191) 281 8588, 霜 – ₪ ♔ – 쇼 50. ⬤⬤ ஈ 𝘷𝘪𝘴𝘢
BV a
Scalini's : Rest - Italian - 8.95 (lunch) and a la carte 11.65/20.40 ♀ – *Louis :* Rest *closed Saturday lunch* 13.95 (lunch) and a la carte 17.85/35.85 – **57 rm** ⌚ ✦70.00/95.00 – ✦✦85.00/95.00.
♦ Welcoming hotel with bright yellow exterior and metro access to city. Bustling bar: its lively ground floor lounge gives immediate access to buzzy nightspots. Well-equipped, comfy rooms. Large restaurant with Italian specialities.

Waterside without rest., 48-52 Sandhill, Quayside, NE1 3JF, ℘ (0191) 230 0111, enquiries@watersidehotel.com, Fax (0191) 230 1615 – ₪ ♔ ℙ. ⬤⬤ ஈ ⓞ 𝘷𝘪𝘴𝘢. ℠
CZ r
closed 24-26 December – **24 rm** ✦60.00/70.00 – ✦✦75.00/80.00.
♦ Grade II listed quayside conversion close to most of the city's attractions. Compact yet well-furnished and cosy bedrooms. Top floor rooms benefit from air-conditioning.

Express by Holiday Inn without rest., Waterloo Sq, St James Boulevard, NE1 4DN, ℘ (0870) 4281488, newcastle@expressbyholidayinn.net, Fax (0870) 4281477 – ₪ ♔ ▤ ⓣⓥ ⓺ ⓺ – 쇼 25. ⬤⬤ ஈ ⓞ 𝘷𝘪𝘴𝘢. ℠
CZ i
130 rm ✦89.95 – ✦✦89.95/149.00.
♦ Impressive purpose built lodge hotel in city centre location close to St James' Park and Metro Radio Arena. Rich, warm rooms are inviting for leisure or business travellers.

Fisherman's Lodge, Jesmond Dene, Jesmond, NE7 7BQ, ℘ (0191) 281 3281, info@fishermanslodge.co.uk, Fax (0191) 281 6410, 霜 – ♔ ℙ ⇌ 40. ⬤⬤ ஈ 𝘷𝘪𝘴𝘢
BV e
closed 25 December and Sunday-Tuesday – Rest 17.50/50.00 s. ♀.
♦ Attractive Victorian house secreted in a narrow wooded valley yet close to city centre. Series of well-appointed, stylish rooms. Modern British cooking with seafood bias.

Black Door, 32 Clayton Street West, NE1 5DZ, ℘ (0191) 261 6295, Fax (0191) 261 6295 – ♔. ⬤⬤ ஈ 𝘷𝘪𝘴𝘢
CZ d
closed 1 January, 25-26 December, Sunday and Monday – Rest 19.00/39.50 ♀.
♦ Set in Georgian terrace, with smart and contemporary interior. There's a wood floored lounge with leather sofas and a cosy dining room serving intriguing modern combinations.

Amer's, 34 Osborne Rd, Jesmond, NE2 2AJ, ℘ (0191) 281 5377, jesmondhotel@aol.com, Fax (0191) 212 0789 – ♔. ⬤⬤ ஈ 𝘷𝘪𝘴𝘢
BV d
closed 1 week Christmas, Monday lunch and Sunday – Rest *(booking essential)* 15.95/25.75 and a la carte 13.85/29.15.
♦ Popular ground floor restaurant in smart location. Cosy, stylish lounge/bar sets you up for good value dishes that are modern in style and prepared with skill and flair.

ENGLAND

XX **Brasserie Black Door,** The Biscuit Factory, 16 Stoddart St, NE2 1AN, ☏ (0191) 260 5411 – ✗✗, **MC** **AE** **VISA**
BV **c**
closed 25-26 December, 1 January and Sunday – Rest 16.95 (lunch) and a la carte 26.40/38.85 ☰.
◆ Art gallery restaurant set in a 1930s former biscuit factory. Through modish lounge to airy dining space with industrial ambience, wall art and recognisable brasserie dishes.

XX **Vujon,** 29 Queen St, Quayside, NE1 3UG, ☏ (0191) 221 0601, *matab@vujon.com*, Fax (0191) 221 0602 – ☰, **MC** **AE** **①** **VISA**
CZ **g**
closed 25 December and Sunday lunch – Rest - Indian - a la carte 22.90/38.90.
◆ A friendly and authentic Indian restaurant can be found behind the striking Victorian façade with modern etched windows. Menu of traditional and more contemporary dishes.

X **Barn under a Wandering Star,** 217 Jesmond Rd, Cradlewell, NE2 1LA, ☏ (0191) 281 7179, Fax (0191) 281 7082, ☆ – ✗✗, **MC** **AE** **VISA**
BV **b**
closed Sunday dinner, Monday lunch and Bank Holidays – Rest (booking essential) 16.50 (lunch) and a la carte 24.00/34.00.
◆ A busy and popular eatery near city centre. Set on three floors, waiting staff are obviously used to being on their toes. Original dishes employ interesting combinations.

X **Blackfriars,** Friars St, NE1 4XN, ☏ (0191) 261 5945, *info@blackfriarscafebar.co.uk*, Fax (0191) 261 9432, ☆ – ✗✗ ☰, **MC** **AE** **VISA**
CZ **h**
closed 25-26 December, 1 January, Sunday dinner and Bank Holiday Mondays – Rest 12.50 (lunch) and a la carte 20.00/30.00 ☰.
◆ Late 13C stone built monks' refectory still serving food in a split level beamed restaurant. Relaxed atmosphere with friendly informal service. Interesting and original menu.

at Gosforth *North : 2½ m. by B 1318 – AV – ⊠ Newcastle upon Tyne.*

🏨 **Newcastle Marriott H. Gosforth Park,** High Gosforth Park, NE3 5HN, North : 2 m. on B 1318 at junction with A 1056 ☏ 0870 400 7288, *events.gosforth@marriotthotels.com*, Fax (0191) 236 8192, ≤, ⑦, ₤₆, ⓩ, ☒, ☞, ₤, ✗, squash – 🛗 ✗✗ ☰ ☏ 🚷 ☑ –
🏛 800. **MC** **AE** **VISA**. ✗
Chats : Rest a la carte 16.85/27.85 s. ☰ – *Park :* Rest (dinner only and Sunday lunch)/dinner 27.60/28.00 and a la carte 27.60/36.65 ☰ – ☷ 14.95 – **173 rm** ✦99.00/150.00 – ✦✦99.00/150.00, 5 suites.
◆ Ideal for both corporate and leisure guests. Extensive conference and leisure facilities. Well-equipped bedrooms with up-to-date décor. Close to the racecourse and the A1 . Relaxed Park overlooks the grounds. Informal Chats for light snacks.

X **Open Kitchen,** 3rd Floor, Gosforth Squash Club, Moor Court Annexe, NE3 4YD, Southwest : 1¼ m. by B 1318, A 189 and Kenton Rd on Westfield Rd ☏ (0191) 285 2909, *eat@the openkitchen.co.uk* – ✗✗, **MC** **AE** **VISA**
AV **a**
closed 25-26 and 31 December, 1st week January, Sunday, Monday and lunch Tuesday – Rest (booking essential) 14.00 (lunch) and a la carte 18.50/33.00 ☰.
◆ Intimate restaurant on top floor of a squash club. Kitchen is, indeed, on show behind the bar. Polite, knowledgable service underpins original cooking using Fairtrade produce.

at Seaton Burn *North : 8 m. by B 1318 – AV – ⊠ Newcastle upon Tyne.*

🏨 **Horton Grange,** NE13 6BU, Northwest : 3 ½ m. by Blagdon rd on Ponteland rd ☏ (01661) 860686, *enquiries@horton-grange.co.uk*, Fax (01661) 860308, ☞ – ✗✗ **P**, **MC** **VISA**. ✗
Rest *(closed Sunday dinner)* (booking essential) 27.50/38.00 (dinner) and a la carte 26.00/35.00 ☰ – ☷ 9.95 – **9 rm** ☷ ✦95.00 – ✦✦135.00◆ Attractive, personally run Edwardian country house with contemporary edge. Bedrooms in main house have more character and space than those in annex. Dine in pleasant conservatory overlooking ornamental garden.

at Cobalt Business Park *Northeast : 8 m. by A 1058 – BV –, A 19 off A 191 – ⊠ Newcastle upon Tyne.*

🏨 **Village H. and Leisure Club,** NE27 0BY, ☏ (0191) 270 1414, *village.newcastle@village-hotels.com*, Fax (0191) 270 1515, ₤₆, ☷, ☒ – 🛗 ✗✗, ☰ rest, ☑ **P** – 🏛 300. **MC** **AE** **①** **VISA**
Rest (grill rest.) 8.90/16.95 and a la carte 15.35/23.85 ☰ – ☷ 9.95 – **127 rm** ✦99.00 – ✦✦109.00.
◆ A modern hotel on business park with an excellent, extensive and well-equipped leisure club. Bright, light and airy modern bedrooms. Popular menus in the grill restaurant, the village pub or the cafe in the leisure club.

at Ponteland *Northwest : 8¼ m. by A 167 on A 696 – AV –* ⊠ *Newcastle upon Tyne.*

✗ **Cafe Lowrey,** 33-35 Broadway, Darras Hall Estate, NE20 9PW, Southwest : 1 ½ m. by B 6323 and Darras Hall Estate rd ℰ (01661) 820357, *Fax (01661) 820357 –* ▤. ⓿ 🅐🅔 𝘝𝘐𝘚𝘈
closed 25-26 December, Sunday and Bank Holidays – **Rest** *(booking essential) (dinner only and Saturday lunch)* 15.50 *(lunch) and a la carte* 22.00/36.00 ♀.
♦ Small restaurant in shopping parade with wooden chairs and cloth-laid tables. Black-board menus offering modern British cooking using local produce.

NEWICK *E. Sussex 504 U 31 – pop. 2 129.*
London 57 – Brighton 14 – Eastbourne 20 – Hastings 34 – Maidstone 30.

🏛 **Newick Park** ⟍, BN8 4SB, Southeast : 1 ½ m. following signs for Newick Park ℰ (01825) 723633, *bookings@newickpark.co.uk, Fax (01825) 723969,* ≼, ⌁ heated, ⟍, ⊶, 🐾, ✶ – ✝ ⅙ ㊒ P. ⓿ 🅐🅔 𝘝𝘐𝘚𝘈
closed 31 December- 5 January – **Rest** *(booking essential for non-residents)* 18.00/35.00 –
15 rm ⌲ ✝125.00 – ✝✝165.00/285.00, 1 suite.
♦ Georgian manor in 200 acres; views of Longford river and South Downs. Stately hallway and lounge. Unique rooms, some with original fireplaces, all with Egyptian cotton sheets. Dine in relaxed formality on high-back crimson chairs.

✗✗ **272,** 20-22 High St, BN8 4LQ, ℰ (01825) 721272, *twoseventwo@hotmail.co.uk, Fax (01825) 724698 –* ▤ P. ⓿ 🅐🅔 𝘝𝘐𝘚𝘈
closed 25-26 December, 1 January, Monday, Sunday dinner and Tuesday lunch – **Rest** 15.00/19.95 *and a la carte* 22.85/36.00 ♀.
♦ Well-run restaurant with an easy-going, relaxed feel. Chairs from Italy, modern art on walls. Frequently changing menus offer a winning blend of British and European flavours.

NEWMARKET *Suffolk 504 V 27 – pop. 16 947.*
🏌 *Links, Cambridge Rd* ℰ (01638) 663000.
🛈 *Palace House, Palace St* ℰ (01638) 667200.
London 64 – Cambridge 13 – Ipswich 40 – Norwich 48.

🏛 **Bedford Lodge,** Bury Rd, CB8 7BX, Northeast : ½ m. on A 1304 ℰ (01638) 663175, *info@bedfordlodgehotel.co.uk, Fax (01638) 667391,* ⅙, ⇋, ⌁, ✶ – ⧉ ⅙ ▤ ㊒ P. –
🅰 200. ⓿ 🅐🅔 ⓞ 𝘝𝘐𝘚𝘈. ⊶
Orangery : **Rest** 20.00/25.00 *and a la carte* 29.95/41.50 s. ♀ – **55 rm** ⌲ ✝135.00/200.00 –
✝✝170.00/240.00.
♦ Extended Georgian hunting lodge built for Duke of Bedford, set in three acres of seclu-ded gardens, close to racecourse. Racing theme pursued in stylish contemporary rooms. Characterful dining room with chandelier and large windows.

🏛 **Rutland Arms,** High St, CB8 8NB, ℰ (01638) 664251, *Fax (01638) 666298,* ㊟ – ⅙ rm, ㊒ P. – 🅰 80. ⓿ 🅐🅔 𝘝𝘐𝘚𝘈
Rest *(bar lunch Monday-Saturday) a la carte* 22.15/28.00 ♀ – **46 rm** ⌲ ✝49.00/135.00 –
✝✝60.00/145.00.
♦ Constructed round a central courtyard, this Georgian coaching inn has warm interiors of patterned carpets and wallpapers. Bedrooms are similarly traditional. Rustic dining room with racing theme.

at Lidgate *Southeast : 7 m. on B 1063 –* ⊠ *Newmarket.*

🍴 **The Star Inn,** The Street, CB8 9PP, ℰ (01638) 500275, *Fax (01638) 500275,* ㊟ – P. ⓿
🅐🅔 𝘝𝘐𝘚𝘈. ⊶
closed 25-26 December and 1 January – **Rest** *- Spanish - (closed Sunday dinner)* 12.50 *(lunch) and a la carte* 26.00/30.00.
♦ Pink washed part 16C inn, oozing charm with beams and inglenooks, in pretty village. Original, predominantly Iberian menus: local game cooked in a hearty, fresh Spanish style.

at Six Mile Bottom *(Cambs.) Southwest : 6 m. on A 1304 –* ⊠ *Newmarket.*

🏛 **Swynford Paddocks,** CB8 0UE, ℰ (01638) 570234, *events@swynfordpaddocks.com, Fax (01638) 570283,* ≼, ✶ – ⅙ rest, P. – 🅰 80. ⓿ 🅐🅔 ⓞ 𝘝𝘐𝘚𝘈
Rest 24.50 *and a la carte* 20.00/43.00 ♀ – **15 rm** ⌲ ✝110.00/135.00 – ✝✝110.00/195.00.
♦ Hotel in pastures with a past: Lord Byron stayed here, penning poetry and having an affair with half-sister: their portraits on stairs. Elegant rooms. Softly lit, oak-panelled res-taurant.

Your opinions are important to us:
please write and let us know about your discoveries and experiences –
good and bad!

ENGLAND *(side margin)*

NEW MILTON *Hants.* 503 504 P 31 – *pop. 26 681 (inc. Barton-on-Sea).*

  📍 📍 *Barton-on-Sea, Milford Rd* 🖉 *(01425) 615308.*
  London 106 – Bournemouth 12 – Southampton 21 – Winchester 34.

🏨 **Chewton Glen** 🦢, Christchurch Rd, BH25 6QS, West : 2 m. by A 337 and Ringwood Rd
   on Chewton Farm Rd 🖉 (01425) 275341, *reservations@chewtonglen.com*,
   Fax (01425) 272310, ≤, 🏡, ⚙, Ⅰ₆, ≋, ⬚ heated, 🔲, 📍, 🛋, ✻indoor/outdoor – ✦ rest,
   🖥 ☎ 📞 – 🏛 120. **◍ 🖾 VISA** ✦
   Marryat Room and Conservatory : Rest 24.50/62.50 and a la carte 46.00/56.50 **s.** ♈ 🍽 –
   ☷ 25.00 – **36 rm** ✿290.00 – ✿✿445.00/435.00, 22 suites 545.00/820.00.
   ✦ A byword in luxury: 19C house where Captain Marryat wrote novels. Sherry and shortbread await in huge rooms of jewel colours; balconies overlook grounds. Scented steam
   room. Accomplished cooking in cool smooth conservatory and bright dining room.

NEWPORT *Shrops.* 502 503 504 M 25.
   London 148 – Stafford 12.5 – Telford 9.5.

🍺 **The Fox**, Pave Lane, Chetwynd Aston, TF10 9LQ, South : 1 ½ m. by Wolverhampton rd
   (A 41) 🖉 (01952) 815940, *fox@brunningandprice.co.uk, Fax (01952) 815941*, 🏡, 🌳 – ✦
   📍 **◍ VISA**
   closed 26 December – **Rest** a la carte 16.95/32.15 ♈.
   ✦ Updated pub with lawned garden and terrace. Light, airy interior: walls filled with old
   pictures and posters. Big tables predominate for family get-togethers. Modern menus.

   The red 🦢 symbol?
   This denotes the very essence of peace
   – only the sound of birdsong first thing in the morning …

NEWPORT PAGNELL *Milton Keynes* 504 R 27 – *pop. 14 739.*
   London 57 – Bedford 13 – Luton 21 – Northampton 21 – Oxford 46.

   Plan : see Milton Keynes

🏨 **Swan Revived**, High St, MK16 8AR, 🖉 (01908) 610565, *info@swanrevived.co.uk,
   Fax (01908) 210995* – 🛗, ✦ rest, 🖥 rest, 📍 – 🏛 70. **◍ 🖾 ⓞ VISA**
                                                                          CU **s**
   Rest *closed Saturday lunch* 14.95 (lunch) and a la carte 21.15/35.15 ♈ – **40 rm** ☷
   ✿60.00/88.95 – ✿✿75.00/95.00, 2 suites.
   ✦ You no longer need a horse to stay at this 15C coaching inn, known for its stabling.
   Rooms are welcoming, many in pine, one has four-poster. A naturopathic clinic is nearby.
   Oak-panelled dining room enhanced by soft lighting.

🍴🍴 **Robinsons**, 18-20 St John St, MK16 8HJ, 🖉 (01908) 611400, *info@robinsonsrestaur
   ant.co.uk, Fax (01908) 216900* – ✦ **◍ 🖾 ⓞ VISA**
                                                                          CU **n**
   closed Saturday lunch, Sunday and Bank Holidays – **Rest** 6.50/18.95 (weekdays) and a la
   carte 27.35/33.65.
   ✦ A bright façade defines sunny nature of Mediterranean style cuisine. An upbeat eatery
   in which to sample an eclectic blend of dishes which range from modern to traditional.

NEWQUAY *Cornwall* 503 E 32 *The West Country G.* – *pop. 19 562.*
   Env. : Penhale Point and Kelsey Head★ (≤★★), SW : by A 3075 Y – Trerice★ *AC*, SE : 3½ m.
   by A 392 – Y – and A 3058.
   Exc. : St Agnes – St Agnes Beacon★★ (☀★★), SW : 12½ m. by A 3075 – Y – and B 3285.
   📍 *Tower Rd* 🖉 (01637) 872091, Z – 📍 *Treloy* 🖉 (01637) 878554 – 📍 *Merlin, Mawgan Porth*
   🖉 (01841) 540222.
   ✈ *Newquay Airport :* 🖉 (01637) 860600 Y.
   🛈 *Municipal Offices, Marcus Hill* 🖉 (01637) 854020, *info@newquay.co.uk.*
   London 291 – Exeter 83 – Penzance 34 – Plymouth 48 – Truro 14.

   Plan on next page

🏨 **Trebarwith**, Trebarwith Crescent, TR7 1BZ, 🖉 (01637) 872288, *enquiry@trebarwith-ho
   tel.co.uk, Fax (01637) 875431*, ≤ bay and coast, ≋, 🔲, 🌳 – ✦ 📞 📍 **◍ VISA** ✦ Z **a**
   April-October – **Rest** (bar lunch)/dinner 18.00/33.00 **s.** ♈ – **42 rm** (dinner included) ☷
   ✿39.00/144.00 – ✿✿100.00/144.00.
   ✦ Superb bay and coastline views from this renowned seaside hotel. Has its own cinema,
   plus evening discos and dances. You'll get the stunning vistas from traditional bedrooms.
   Dine by the sea beneath Wedgwood-style ceiling.

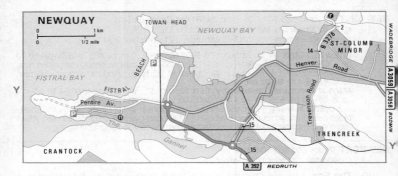

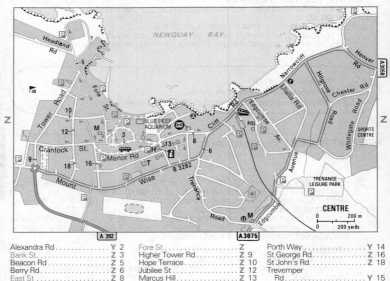

Alexandra Rd	Y 2	Fore St	Z	Porth Way	Y 14
Bank St	Z 3	Higher Tower Rd	Z 9	St George Rd	Z 16
Beacon Rd	Z 5	Hope Terrace	Z 10	St John's Rd	Z 18
Berry Rd	Z 6	Jubilee St	Z 12	Trevemper	
East St	Z 8	Marcus Hill	Z 13	Rd	Y 15

🏨 **The Bristol,** Narrowcliff, TR7 2PQ, ℰ (01637) 870275, *info@hotelbristol.co.uk,*
Fax (01637) 879347, ≤, ⛫, ☒ – ▮⬛, ⥺ rest, 🅿 – 🔥 200. 🆎 🆎 ⓞ 𝘝𝘐𝘚𝘈   Z r
Rest (bar lunch Monday-Saturday)/dinner 22.00 and a la carte 25.00/32.50 ♀ – **73 rm**
★75.00/110.00 – ★★150.00/114.00, 1 suite.
  • Classic Victorian seaside hotel, well established and family run. Wide range of bedrooms from singles
to family suites. Extensive conference facilities. Large windowed dining room overlooks Atlantic.

🏨 **Trenance Lodge,** 83 Trenance Rd, TR7 2HW, ℰ (01637) 876702, *info@trenance-*
lodge.co.uk, Fax (01637) 878772, ⋘ – ⥺ 🅿. 🆎 𝘝𝘐𝘚𝘈. ⋘   Z u
restricted opening in winter – **Rest** (booking essential) (dinner only) a la carte 21.45/29.95 –
5 rm ⌑ ★45.00/50.00 – ★★60.00/80.00.
  • Purpose-built, personally run hotel. Modern feel to the interior with well-maintained and
comfortable guest areas. Provides neat accommodation. Wide-ranging menu with strong
Cornish flavour.

🏨 **Corisande Manor** ⋙, Riverside Ave, Pentire, TR7 1PL, ℰ (01637) 872042, *relax@cori*
sande.com, Fax (01637) 874557, ≤ Gannel Estuary, ⋘ – ⥺ rest, 🅿. 🆎 𝘝𝘐𝘚𝘈   Y n
January-10 September – **Rest** (set menu only) (dinner only) 26.00 s. ⅏ – **9 rm** ⌑
★89.00/99.00 – ★★185.00.
  • Attractive manor house, built for an Austrian count, perched above, and with supreme
views, of, Gannel Estuary. Bedrooms with a fine, co-ordinated, modern elegance. Dining
room boasts historic beamed ceiling.

572

🏠 **Whipsiderry**, Trevelgue Rd, Porth, TR7 3LY, Northeast : 2 m. by A 392 off B 3276
🖉 (01637) 874777, info@whipsiderry.co.uk, Fax (01637) 874777, ≤, ≊, ⏄ heated, 🚗 –
✗ 🅿, ⓂⓈ 𝘝𝘐𝘚𝘈
closed January-February and November – **Rest** (bar lunch)/dinner 18.00 ♀ – **20 rm** (dinner
included) ⊆ ✦54.00/66.00 – ✦✦104.00/132.00.
• Simple, whitewashed building; family run, in a residential area. Communal areas include
two lounges with a small bar and panoramic views. Pine furnished bedrooms. Tried-and-
tested menus.

🏠 **The Windward** without rest., Alexandra Rd, Porth Bay, TR7 3NB, 🖉 (01637) 873185,
enquiries@windwardhotel.co.uk, Fax (01637) 851400 – ✗ 🅿, ⓂⓈ ⅋ⅇ 𝘝𝘐𝘚𝘈. ⅍   Y r
– **12 rm** ⊆ ✦54.00/84.00 – ✦✦74.00/104.00.
• Small hotel with large windows overlooking the sea; a super place to have breakfast.
Simply appointed, pine furnished bedrooms, some with large balconies.

at Watergate Bay Northeast : 3 m. by A 3059 on B 3276 – ✉ Newquay.

🍴🍴 **Fifteen Cornwall**, On The Beach, TR8 4AA, 🖉 (01637) 861000, ≤ Watergate Bay – ▤
⇆ 12. ⓂⓈ 𝘝𝘐𝘚𝘈
Rest 24.50 (lunch) and a la carte 27.00/40.00 ♀.
• Phenomenally successful converted café in a golden idyll. Jamie Oliver's academy
youngsters offer Cornwall-meets-Italy menus in a cavernous room bathed in West Coast
hues.

at Crantock Southwest : 4 m. by A 3075 – Y – ✉ Newquay.

🏠 **Crantock Bay** ⅍, West Pentire, TR8 5SE, West : ¾ m. 🖉 (01637) 830229, stay@cran
tockbayhotel.co.uk, Fax (01637) 831111, ≤ Crantock Bay, 𝟤⅙, ≊, ⏄, 🚗, ⅍ – ✗ rest, 🅿,
ⓂⓈ ⅋ⅇ ⓞ 𝘝𝘐𝘚𝘈
closed January, 11-30 November and Christmas – **Rest** (buffet lunch)/dinner 25.00 ♀ –
32 rm (dinner included) ⊆ ✦59.00/118.50 – ✦✦118.00/158.00.
• Delightfully sited hotel affording exceptional views of Crantock Bay. Good leisure facilities, gala evenings and children's parties. Comfortable, traditional rooms. Dining room
enhanced by the views.

NEW ROMNEY Kent 504 W 31.
London 71 – Brighton 60 – Folkestone 17 – Maidstone 36.

🏠 **Romney Bay House** ⅍, Coast Rd, Littlestone, TN28 8QY, East : 2 ¼ m. off B 2071
🖉 (01797) 364747, Fax (01797) 367156, ≤, 🚗 – ✗ 🅿, ⓂⓈ ⅋ⅇ 𝘝𝘐𝘚𝘈. ⅍
closed 1 week Christmas – **Rest** (closed Sunday-Monday and Thursday) (booking essential
for non-residents) (set menu only) (dinner only) 37.50 – **10 rm** ⊆ ✦60.00 – ✦✦155.00.
• Beach panorama for late actress Hedda Hopper's house, built by Portmeirion architect
Clough Williams-Ellis. Individual rooms; sitting room with telescope and bookcases. Enjoy
drinks on terrace before conservatory dining.

NEWTON LONGVILLE Bucks. 504 R 28 – see Milton Keynes.

NEWTON ON THE MOOR Northd. 501 502 O 17 – see Alnwick.

NEWTON POPPLEFORD Devon 503 K 31 – see Sidmouth.

NOMANSLAND Wilts. 503 504 P 31 – ✉ Salisbury.
London 96 – Bournemouth 26 – Salisbury 13 – Southampton 14 – Winchester 25.

🍴🍴 **Les Mirabelles**, Forest Edge Rd, SP5 2BN, 🖉 (01794) 390205, Fax (01794) 390106, 🍽 –
▤. ⓂⓈ ⅋ⅇ 𝘝𝘐𝘚𝘈
closed Sunday and Monday – **Rest** - French - a la carte 22.20/39.60 ⅍.
• Unpretentious little French restaurant overlooking the village common. Superb wine list.
Extensive menu of good value, classic Gallic cuisine.

NORMANTON-ON-THE-WOLDS Notts. 502 Q 25 – see Nottingham.

The ❀ award is the crème de la crème.
This is awarded to restaurants
which are really worth travelling miles for!

ENGLAND

NORTHALLERTON *N. Yorks.* 502 P 20 – *pop. 15 517.*

🅩 *The Applegarth Car Park* 𝒫 *(01609) 776864.*

London 238 – Leeds 48 – Middlesbrough 24 – Newcastle upon Tyne 56 – York 33.

at Staddlebridge *Northeast : 7½ m. by A 684 on A 19 at junction with A 172 – ⊠ Northallerton.*

✗ **McCoys Bistro at The Tontine** with rm, DL6 3JB, on southbound carriageway (A 19) 𝒫 (01609) 882671, *enquiries@mccoysatthetontine.co.uk*, Fax (01609) 882660 – 🛏 rm, ✸ **P.** 🐾 🖭 ⓿ *VISA*
closed 25-26 December and 1-3 January – **Rest** (booking essential) 16.95 (lunch) and a la carte 28.65/37.25 – **6 rm** � ✱95.00 – ✱✱120.00.
◆ Yorkshire meets France in long-standing restaurant with mirrors, wood panelling, framed memorabilia. Snug bar to plot coups in. Large bedrooms, unique in decorative style.

at Newby Wiske *South : 2½ m. by A 167 – ⊠ Northallerton.*

🏛 **Solberge Hall** ⌂, DL7 9ER, Northwest : 1 ¼ m. on Warlaby rd 𝒫 (01609) 779191, *reservations@solbergehall.co.uk*, Fax (01609) 780472, ≼, 🐎, 🖭 – ✸✱ **P.** – 🏛 80. 🐾 🖭 *VISA*
Rest 15.95/22.50 and dinner a la carte 25.30/38.90 **s.** – **23 rm** � ✱80.00/100.00 – ✱✱120.00/160.00, 1 suite.
◆ Tranquil grounds surround this graceful Georgian house, situated in the heart of the countryside. Popular for weddings; bedrooms in main house or stable block. Local ingredients well employed in flavoursome menus.

NORTHAMPTON *Northants.* 504 R 27 *Great Britain G. – pop. 189 474.*

Exc. : *All Saints, Brixworth★, N : 7 m. on A 508* Y.

🏌, 🏌 *Delapre, Eagle Drive, Nene Valley Way* 𝒫 *(01604) 764036* Z – 🏌 *Collingtree Park, Windingbrook Lane* 𝒫 *(01604) 700000.*

🅩 *The Guildhall, St Giles Square* 𝒫 *(01604) 838800, tic@northampton.gov.uk.*

London 69 – Cambridge 53 – Coventry 34 – Leicester 42 – Luton 35 – Oxford 41.

Plan opposite

🏨 **Northampton Marriott,** Eagle Drive, NN4 7HW, Southeast : 2 m. by A 428 off A 45 𝒫 (01604) 768700, *events.northampton@marriotthotels.co.uk*, Fax (01604) 769011, 🏋, ≦s, 🏊, 🐎 – ✸✱, 🛏 rest, ॐ **P.** – 🏛 220. 🐾 🖭 ⓿ *VISA*   Z a
Mediterrano : **Rest** – *Mediterranean - (closed Saturday lunch)* (buffet lunch)/dinner a la carte 20.00/40.00 **s.** ⟡ – **120 rm** � ✱140.00 – ✱✱150.00/660.00.
◆ Modern hotel in riverside setting. Neat trim rooms, very practical, with well-lit work desks, some have disabled facilities and sofa beds. Silverstone race track is nearby. Pleasing dining room with bright brasserie feel.

🏨 **Hilton Northampton,** 100 Watering Lane, Collingtree, NN4 0XW, South : 3 m. on A 508 𝒫 (01604) 700666, *reservations.northampton@hilton.com*, Fax (01604) 702850, 🍴, 🏋, ≦s, 🏊, 🐎 – 🛏 rm, 🛏 rest, ✸ ॐ **P.** – 🏛 300. 🐾 🖭 ⓿ *VISA*
closed 27-30 December – **Rest** *(closed Saturday lunch)* (carving lunch) 12.50/21.75 **s.** and a la carte ⟡ – � 14.95 – **136 rm** ✱86.00/240.00 – ✱✱86.00/240.00, 3 suites.
◆ Built by the motorway, this clean-lined hotel greets with open-plan foyer and café area. Terrace on which to enjoy barbecues. Sizeable rooms; well-equipped leisure centre. Restaurant offers international choice.

🏛 **Northampton Courtyard,** Bedford Rd, NN4 7YF, Southeast : 1 ½ m. on A 428 𝒫 (0870) 4007214, *meetings.northampton@courtyardhotels.co.uk*, Fax (0870) 4007314, 🏋 – 🛗 ✸✱ 🛏 ✸ & **P.** – 🏛 40. 🐾 🖭 ⓿ *VISA*. ✂   Z c
Rest a la carte 18.15/28.85 ⟡ – � 12.95 – **104 rm** ✱65.00/130.00 – ✱✱75.00/140.00.
◆ Purpose-built, modern hotel. Smart interior with a branded style. Comfortable bedrooms are simply appointed and well-kept. Suited to business and leisure travellers. Relaxing restaurant and adjacent lounge.

at Spratton *North : 7 m. by A 508 off A 5199 – Y – ⊠ Northampton.*

🏛 **Broomhill Country House** ⌂, Holdenby Rd, NN6 8LD, Southwest : 1 m. on Holdenby rd 𝒫 (01604) 845959, *broomhillhotel@aol.com*, Fax (01604) 845834, ≼, 🏊, 🐎, 🖭 – ✸✱ rest, **P.** 🐾 🖭 ⓿ *VISA*
closed 26 December - 8 January – **Rest** *(closed Sunday dinner and Bank Holidays)* 21.50/23.50 and dinner a la carte 27.95/36.15 **s.** – **13 rm** � ✱75.00 – ✱✱95.00.
◆ Peacocks strut in grounds of grand red Victorian house; patterned carpets, wall lamps enhance warm interiors. Spacious rooms with panoramic views. Croquet for enthusiasts. Fine dining room with large mirror, grandfather clock and lovely vistas.

574

ENGLAND

NORTHAMPTON

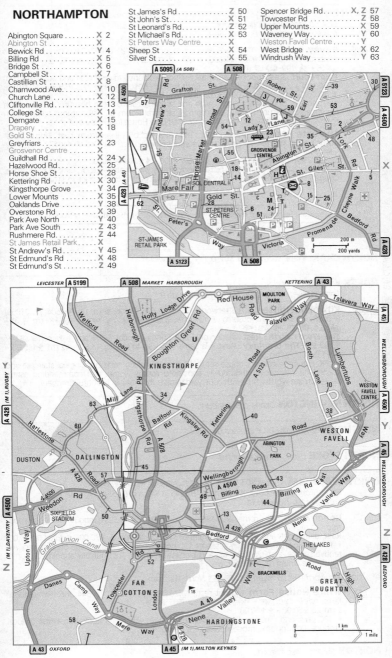

NORTH BOVEY Devon 503 I 32 The West Country G. – ⊠ Newton Abbot.
Env. : Dartmoor National Park★★.
London 214 – Exeter 13 – Plymouth 34 – Torquay 21.

Bovey Castle ⑤, TQ13 8RE, West : 1 m. on B 3212 𝒫 (01647) 445000, *enquiries@bo veycastle.com*, Fax (01647) 445020, ≤, 斎, ⑫, 𝕝ᵇ, ᗡ, ⋐, 18, ⍂, ☞, ⍨, ℀ – ⑮ ⥂ ℃ ⍾⍾ ℙ – ⚿ 100. ◐◑ ⒶⒺ 𝑽𝑰𝑺𝑨
Palm Court : **Rest** (booking essential for non-residents) (dinner only and Sunday lunch) 38.50 and a la carte 38.95/57.25 **s.** – **Club House :** **Rest** a la carte 22.50/38.50 – **62 rm** ⍰ ✸155.00/221.25 – ✸✸195.00/850.00, 3 suites.
♦ Stunningly opulent property: castle and sporting estate set in beautiful grounds with incomparable leisure facilities, awesome Cathedral Room and sumptuous, stylish bedrooms. Formal, cloth-clad Palm Court Relaxed Club House includes a golf shop!

The Gate House ⍩ without rest., TQ13 8RB, just off village green, past "Ring of Bells" public house 𝒫 (01647) 440479, *srw.gatehouse@virgin.net*, Fax (01647) 440479, ≤, ⌕, ☞ – ⥂ ℙ
closed 25-26 December – **3 rm** ⍰ ✸46.00/50.00 – ✸✸70.00/76.00.
♦ 15C white Devon hallhouse; picturebook pretty with thatched roof, pink climbing rose. Country style rooms; some have views of moor. Large granite fireplace in sitting room.

If breakfast is included the ⍰ symbol appears after the number of rooms.

NORTH CHARLTON Northd. 501 502 O 17 – see Alnwick.

NORTH KILWORTH Leics.
London 95 – Leicester 20 – Market Harborough 9.

Kilworth House ⍩, Lutterworth Rd, LE17 6JE, West : ½ m. on A 4304 𝒫 (01858) 880058, *info@kilworthhouse.co.uk*, Fax (01858) 880349, 𝕝ᵇ, ⍂, ☞, ⍨ – ⑮, ⥂ rm, ⅄ ℙ – ⚿ 100. ◐◑ ⒶⒺ ⓪ 𝑽𝑰𝑺𝑨 ⍟
The Wordsworth : **Rest** (dinner only and Sunday lunch) 34.00 and a la carte 38.00/ 53.00 **s.** – *The Orangery :* **Rest** a la carte 22.50/30.40 **s.** – ⍰ 13.50 – **42 rm** ✸135.00 – ✸✸135.00, 2 suites.
♦ 19C extended country house set in 38 acres of rolling parkland. Original staircase and stained glass windows. Individually appointed rooms, some with commanding estate views. Ornate Wordsworth with courtyard vista. Light meals in beautiful Orangery.

NORTH NEWINGTON Oxon. – see Banbury.

NORTHREPPS Norfolk 504 Y 25 – see Cromer.

NORTH STOKE Oxon. – see Wallingford.

NORTH WALSHAM Norfolk 503 504 Y 25 Great Britain G. – pop. 11 845.
Exc. : Blicking Hall★★ AC, W : 8½ m. by B 1145, A 140 and B 1354.
London 125 – Norwich 16.

Beechwood, 20 Cromer Rd, NR28 0HD, 𝒫 (01692) 403231, *enquiries@beechwood-hotel.co.uk*, Fax (01692) 407284, ☞ – ⥂ ℙ. ◐◑ 𝑽𝑰𝑺𝑨
Rest (dinner only and Sunday lunch)/dinner 34.00 ⍰ – **17 rm** ⍰ ✸70.00 – ✸✸90.00/160.00.
♦ Privately owned, peacefully set, part 19C hotel where Agatha Christie once stayed. Attentive service, as typified by tea and biscuits on arrival. Thoughtfully appointed rooms. Handsome dining room with flowers.

at Knapton Northeast : 3 m. on B 1145 – ⊠ North Walsham.

White House Farm without rest., NR28 0RX, 𝒫 (01263) 721344, *info@whitehouse farmnorfolk.co.uk*, ☞ – ⥂ ℙ. ◐◑ ⒶⒺ ⓪ 𝑽𝑰𝑺𝑨 ⍟
3 rm ⍰ ✸50.00 – ✸✸60.00.
♦ 18C brick and flint farmhouse. Spacious lounge with many books. Breakfast of local produce. Comfortable, modern, well-kept bedrooms.

NORTON Shrops. – see Telford.

Live in Italian

At finer restaurants in Paris, London, New York and of course, Milan.

For the best little places, follow the leader.

Looking for the latest news on today's best hotels and restaurants? Pick up the Michelin Guide and look for the Bib Gourmand and Bib Hotel symbols. With 45,000 addresses in Europe, in every category and price range, the perfect place to dine or stay is never far away.

A better way forward

NORTON ST PHILIP *Somerset* 503 504 N 30 – ⊠ *Bath.*
London 113 – Bristol 22 – Southampton 55 – Swindon 40.

🏠 **George Inn,** High St, BA2 7LH, ℰ (01373) 834224, *georgeinnsp@aol.com*,
Fax (01373) 834861, 斧, 畢 – 씆 🅿. 🝳 🖭 𝗩𝗜𝗦𝗔
accommodation closed 25-26 December amd 1 January – **Rest** a la carte 15.95/26.40 ♈ –
8 rm ⊊ ✦60.00 – ✦✦90.00.
   ◆ Spectacular timber framed medieval inn built for merchants attending wool fairs. Popular now as a film set. Unique rooms: wall paintings, 15C fireplaces and leaded windows. Rustic dining.

🏠 **Bath Lodge** without rest., BA2 7NH, East : 1¼ m. by A 366 on A 36 ℰ (01225) 723040,
info@bathlodge.com, Fax (01225) 723737, 畢 – 씆 📞 🅿. 🝳 🖭 ① 𝗩𝗜𝗦𝗔. 🛇
closed Christmas – **7 rm** ⊊ ✦55.00/75.00 – ✦✦100.00/145.00.
   ◆ Grade II listed lodge with a charming exterior of towers and battlements once served as a gatehouse to the Farleigh estate. Country house décor, spacious, comfortable rooms.

🏠 **The Plaine** without rest., BA2 7LT, ℰ (01373) 834723, *theplaine@easynet.co.uk*,
Fax (01373) 834101 – 씆 🅿. 🝳 𝗩𝗜𝗦𝗔
closed 24 December-2 January – **3 rm** ⊊ ✦48.00/52.00 – ✦✦65.00/80.00.
   ◆ 16C stone cottages opposite George Inn on site of original market place. Beams, stone walls denote historic origins. Four-posters, pine furnishings in bedrooms. Family run.

NORWICH *Norfolk* 504 Y 26 *Great Britain G.* – **pop. 174 047.**
   See : *City★★ - Cathedral★★* Y *- Castle (Museum and Art Gallery★ AC)* Z *- Market Place★* Z.
   Env. : *Sainsbury Centre for Visual Arts★ AC, W : 3 m. by B 1108* X.
   Exc. : *Blicking Hall★★ AC, N : 11 m. by A 140 – V – and B 1354 – NE : Norfolk Broads★*.
   🛆 *Royal Norwich, Drayton High Rd, Hellesdon* ℰ *(01603) 425712,* V – 🛆 *Marriott Sprowston Manor Hotel, Wroxham Rd* ℰ *(0870) 4007229 –* 🛆 *Costessey Park, Costessey* ℰ *(01603) 746333 –* 🛆 *Bawburgh, Glen Lodge, Marlingford Rd* ℰ *(01603) 740404.*
   ✈ *Norwich Airport :* ℰ *(01603) 411923, N : 3½ m. by A 140* V.
   🖪 *The Forum, Millennium Plain* ℰ *(01603) 727927.*
   London 109 – Kingston-upon-Hull 148 – Leicester 117 – Nottingham 120.

Plans on following pages

🏨 **Marriott Sprowston Manor H. & Country Club,** Wroxham Rd, NR7 8RP, Northeast : 3¼ m. on A 1151 ℰ (01603) 410871, *mhrs.nwigs.frontdesk@marriotthotels.co.uk*,
Fax (01603) 423911, ⑫, 🖫, ≊, 🏊, 🛆, 畢, 厽 – ⫴ 씆, 🝳 rest, ♿ 🅿. – 🅰 120. 🝳 🖭 ①
𝗩𝗜𝗦𝗔. 🛇
Manor : Rest *(closed Saturday lunch)* 16.95/22.50 and dinner a la carte 30.85/39.35 ♈ –
⊊ 14.95 – **93 rm** ✦200.00 – ✦✦200.00, 1 suite.
   ◆ Part Elizabethan manor house set in 10 acres of parkland and golf course. Pleasant lounge. Extensive leisure facilities. Many of the bedrooms overlook the picturesque grounds. Restaurant with Gothic arched windows, ancient mahogany columns and oil paintings.

🏨 **Dunston Hall H. Golf & Country Club,** Ipswich Rd, NR14 8PQ, South : 4 m. on
A 140 ℰ (01508) 470444, *dhreception@devere-hotels.com*, Fax (01508) 471499, 斧, 🖫,
≊, 🔍, 🏊, 畢, 厽 – ⫴ 씆, 🝳 rest, ♿ 🅿. – 🅰 300. 🝳 🖭 ① 𝗩𝗜𝗦𝗔. 🛇
Rest *(carvery lunch)* a la carte 18.95/36.40 s. ♈ – **127 rm** ✦145.00 – ✦✦165.00/225.00,
2 suites.
   ◆ Built in 1859, a wealth of original features remain in this imposing Elizabethan style country mansion. Most characterful rooms in the main house have golf course views. Restaurant overlooks magnificent golf course.

🏨 **Beeches,** 2-6 Earlham Rd, NR2 3DB, ℰ (01603) 621167, *beeches@mjbhotels.com*,
Fax (01603) 620151, 畢 – 씆 🅿. 🝳 🖭 𝗩𝗜𝗦𝗔. 🛇   VX e
Rest *(dinner only)* 24.95 and a la carte 15.00/21.95 ♈ – **42 rm** ⊊ ✦74.00/79.00 – ✦✦95.00,
1 suite.
   ◆ Personally run series of Grade II listed properties overlooking terraced Victorian gardens. Spacious rooms may have Cathedral views. Popular with business guests. Dining room with Plantation Garden outlook.

🏨 **Annesley House,** 6 Newmarket Rd, NR2 2LA, ℰ (01603) 624553, *annesleyhouse@best*
western.co.uk, Fax (01603) 621577, 畢 – 씆 📞 🅿. 🝳 🖭 ① 𝗩𝗜𝗦𝗔. 🛇   Z c
closed 24 December-3 January – **Rest** *(light lunch)/dinner* 24.00 ♈ – **26 rm** ⊊
✦80.00/95.00 – ✦✦101.00.
   ◆ A relaxed atmosphere prevails at this established hotel set in a pair of Georgian houses. Some of the generously proportioned bedrooms overlook the feature water garden. Conservatory restaurant.

ENGLAND

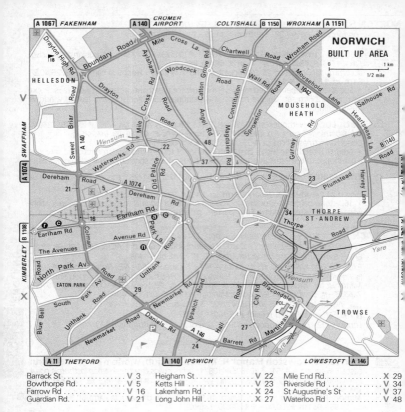

Catton Old Hall without rest., Lodge Lane, Old Catton, NR6 7HG, North : 3 ¼ m. by Catton Grove Rd and St Faiths Rd ℰ (01603) 419379, *enquiries@catton-hall.co.uk*, Fax (01603) 400339, ⌖ – ⇔ **P**. ⓐⓑ **AE** ⓪ **VISA**
closed Christmas-New Year – **7 rm** ⌂ ✦70.00/75.00 – ✦✦120.00.
♦ 17C flint fronted farmhouse in a residential area. Antique furnished lounge with log fire. Individually and attractively furnished rooms have plenty of thoughtful extras.

The Gables without rest., 527 Earlham Rd, NR4 7HN, ℰ (01603) 456666, Fax (01603) 250320, ⌖ – ⇔ **P**. ⓐⓑ **VISA**. ⌘   **X c**
closed 20 December-2 January – **11 rm** ⌂ ✦46.00 – ✦✦73.00.
♦ Modern detached house close to university Enjoy a game of snooker before retiring to the well-kept and homely bedrooms. Breakfast served in the conservatory.

Beaufort Lodge without rest., 62 Earlham Rd, NR2 3DF, ℰ (01603) 627928, *beaufor tlodge@aol.com*, Fax (01603) 440712, ⌖ – ⇔ **P**. ⌘   **VX a**
4 rm ⌂ ✦50.00/60.00 – ✦✦65.00.
♦ Within easy walking distance of the Market Place, a pretty Victorian terraced house run by a husband and wife team. Good-sized bedrooms in modern pine.

Arbor Linden Lodge without rest., 557 Earlham Rd, NR4 7HW, ℰ (01603) 451303, *info@guesthousenorwich.com*, Fax (01603) 250641, ⌖ – ⇔ **Ⓒ P**. ⓐⓑ **VISA**. ⌘   **X r**
6 rm ⌂ ✦40.00/45.00 – ✦✦60.00.
♦ Close to both university and hospitals. Friendly and family run guesthouse. Enjoy a relaxed breakfast in the conservatory. A non smoking establishment.

578

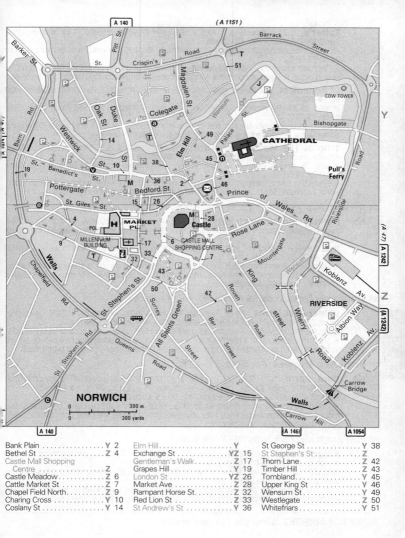

XX **Adlard's**, 79 Upper St Giles St, NR2 1AB, ℰ (01603) 633522, *bookings@adlards.co.uk* –
✂ ▤, Ⓜ️Ⓒ Ⓐ Ⓔ Ⓞ *VISA*   YZ e
closed 25-26 December, 1 week January, Sunday and Monday – **Rest** 21.00 (lunch) and a la
carte 37.00/50.00.
⬩ Personally run, well-established restaurant - relaxed, classic style. Upper area also incorporates a bar. Refined dishes with a distinct French base.

XX **By Appointment** with rm, 25-29 St Georges St, NR3 1AB, ℰ (01603) 630730,
Fax (01603) 630730 – ✂ ℗, Ⓜ️Ⓒ *VISA*. ✴️   Y a
closed 25 December – **Rest** *(closed Sunday-Monday)* (dinner only) a la carte 33.40/36.40 –
5 rm ⌸ ✱70.00/85.00 – ✱✱130.00.
⬩ Pretty, antique furnished restaurant. Interesting, traditional dishes off blackboard with
theatrical service. Characterful bedrooms include a host of thoughtful extras.

✗ **Tatler's,** 21 Tombland, NR3 1RF, ✆ (01603) 766670, *info@tatlers.com,*
Fax (01603) 766625 – ✸✕. 🌐🕲 🄰🄴 *VISA*   Y n
closed 25 December, Sunday and Bank Holidays – **Rest** 18.00 (lunch) and dinner a la carte
24.50/31.50 ♀.
◆ Georgian townhouse near cathedral comprising small rooms on several floors set off by
period detail. Relaxed atmosphere. Modern menu; inventive cooking using local produce.

✗ **St Benedicts,** 9 St Benedicts St, NR2 4PE, ✆ (01603) 765377, Fax (01603) 624541 – 🌐🕲
🄰🄴 🄾 *VISA*   Y v
closed 25-31 December, Sunday and Monday – **Rest** 8.95/15.95 and a la carte
19.00/23.95 ♀.
◆ Informal and personally run bistro. Interesting menus of both traditional British and
adventurous heart-warming dishes. Booking advisable for dinner.

✗ **1 Up at The Mad Moose Arms,** 2 Warwick St, NR2 3LD, off Dover St ✆ (01603)
⊕ 627687, *madmoose@animalinns.co.uk –* ✸✕. 🌐🕲 🄰🄴 🄾 *VISA*. ✸✕   X n
closed 25 December – **Rest** (dinner only and Sunday lunch) 18.50 and a la carte
20.00/28.00 ♀.
◆ Enjoy the relaxed atmosphere in this converted Victorian pub. Friendly service, occasional live music. Rustic and modern food guarantees great choice in the menus.

at Norwich Airport *North : 3½ m. by A 140 –* V *–* ⌧ *Norwich.*

🏨 **Holiday Inn Norwich City Airport,** Cromer Rd, NR6 6JA, ✆ (01603) 410544,
sales@hinorwich.com, Fax (01603) 789935, 🛌, 🚰, 🖾 *–* 🛗 ✸✕ ⅙ 🄿 *–* 🕍 450. 🌐🕲 🄰🄴 🄾
VISA. ✸✕
Rest (carvery) 14.95/21.50 and a la carte approx 25.00 *–* ⌧ 13.95 *–* **121 rm** ✱89.00/129.00
– ✱✱89.00/129.00.
◆ Purpose built and benefits from easy access to terminal. Aimed at the corporate sector,
the well-proportioned rooms have ample work space. Extensive conference and leisure.
Informal carvery and lounge bar.

at Stoke Holy Cross *South : 5¾ m. by A 140 –* X *–* ⌧ *Norwich.*

🍴 **Wildebeest Arms,** 82-86 Norwich Rd, NR14 8QJ, ✆ (01508) 492497, *wildebees*
⊕ *tarms@animalinns.co.uk, Fax (01508) 494946,* 🍽 *–* 🍴 *–* 🌐🕲 🄰🄴 *VISA.* ✸✕
closed 25-26 December – **Rest** (booking essential) 15.95/18.95 and a la carte 25.00/35.00 ♀.
◆ Modern-rustic pub in a pretty village. Inventive, seasonal, contemporary menus served
at tree-trunk tables. Garden dining recommended. Attentive service from bright staff.

at Hethersett *Southwest : 6 m. by A 11 –* X *–* ⌧ *Norwich.*

🏨 **Park Farm,** NR9 3DL, on B 1172 ✆ (01603) 810264, *enq@parkfarm-hotel.co.uk,*
Fax (01603) 812104, 🛌, 🚰, 🖾, 🍽 *–* ✸✕, 🍴 rest, 🄿 *–* 🕍 120. 🌐🕲 🄰🄴 🄾 *VISA.* ✸✕
Rest 15.45/24.00 ♀ *–* **42 rm** ⌧ ✱99.00/145.00 *–* ✱✱128.00/195.00.
◆ Extended Georgian farmhouse set in 200 acres of gardens and parkland. Comprehensive
leisure and conference facilities. Executive rooms in cottages are most comfortable. Well-
appointed conservatory restaurant.

at Bawburgh *West : 5 m. by B 1108 –* X *–* ⌧ *Norwich.*

🍴 **Kings Head,** Harts Lane, NR9 3LS, ✆ (01603) 744977, *anton@kingshead-baw*
burgh.co.uk, Fax (01603) 744990, 🍽 *–* ✸✕ 🄿. 🌐🕲 🄰🄴 *VISA*
closed 25 December and dinner 26 December and 1 January – **Rest** *(closed Sunday dinner*
and Monday) a la carte 23.50/33.00 ♀.
◆ Family-owned pub with stylish interior, its timbered bar most inviting in winter. Modern
menu with international influences: take a seat by the fire or in the dining room.

NORWICH AIRPORT *Norfolk* **504** X 25 *– see Norwich.*

NOSS MAYO *Devon The West Country G.*
Exc. : *Saltram House*★★, *NW : 7 m. by B 3186 and A 379 – Plymouth*★, *NW : 9 m. by B 3186*
and A 379.
London 242 – Plymouth 12 – Yealmpton 3.

🍴 **The Ship Inn,** PL8 1EW, ✆ (01752) 872387, *ship@nossmayo.com,* 🍽 *–* ✸✕ 🄿. 🌐🕲 *VISA*
Rest a la carte 10.00/25.00 ♀.
◆ On two floors with a terrific terrace; beside the water in delightful coastal village. Oldest
part dates from 1700s. Extensive menus from the simple to the adventurous.

Red = Pleasant. Look for the red ✗ and 🏠 symbols.

ENGLAND

NOTTINGHAM Nottingham 502 503 504 Q 25 *Great Britain G. – pop. 249 584.*

See : *Castle Museum★ (alabasters★) AC, CZ* **M.**

Env. : *Wollaton Hall★ AC, W : 2½ m. by Ilkeston Rd, A 609 AZ* **M.**

Exc. : *Southwell Minster★★, NE : 14 m. by A 612 BZ – Newstead Abbey★ AC, N : 11 m. by A 60, A 611 - AY - and B 683 – Mr Straw's House★, Worksop, N : 20 m. signed from B 6045 (past Bassetlaw Hospital) – St Mary Magdalene★, Newark-on-Trent, NE : 20 m. by A 612 BZ.*

🔙 *Bulwell Forest, Hucknall Rd & (0115) 977 0576, AY – 🔙 Wollaton Park & (0115) 978 7574, AZ – 🔙 Mapperley, Central Ave, Plains Rd & (0115) 955 6672, BY – 🔙 Nottingham City, Lawton Drive, Bulwell & (0774) 028 8694 – 🔙 Beeston Fields, Beeston & (0115) 925 7062 – 🔙 Ruddington Grange, Wilford Rd, Ruddington & (0115) 984 6141, BZ – 🔟, 🔟 Edwalton & (0115) 923 4775, BZ – 🔟, 🔟, 🔟 Cotgrave Place G. & C.C., Stragglethorpe & (0115) 933 3344.*

✈ *Nottingham East Midlands Airport, Castle Donington : & (0871) 9199000 SW : 15 m. by A 453 AZ.*

🗓 *1-4 Smithy Row & (0115) 915 5330, touristinfo@nottinghamcity.gov.uk – at West Bridgford : County Hall, Loughborough Rd & (0115) 977 3558.*

London 135 – Birmingham 50 – Leeds 74 – Leicester 27 – Manchester 72.

Plans on following pages

🏨 **Park Plaza,** 41 Maid Marian Way, NG1 6GD, & (0115) 947 7200, info@parkplazanotting ham.com, Fax (0115) 947 7300, 🔡 – 🛗, 🚭 rm, 🔳 ⚐ – 🏛 175. 🕦 🕮 AE ⓪ VISA . 🕬   CY v
Chino Latino : Rest - Japanese influences - *(closed Sunday and Bank Holidays)* a la carte 26.50/50.00 🍷 – 🖙 12.00 – **178 rm** ✸90.00/150.00 – ✸✸185.00/260.00, 6 suites.
◆ Converted city centre office block with stylish and contemporary decor. Choice of meeting rooms. Spacious stylish bedrooms with many extras. Formal Chino Latino Japanese restaurant.

🏨 **Welbeck,** Talbot St, NG1 5GS, & (0115) 841 1000, info@welbeck-hotel.co.uk, Fax (0115) 841 1001 – 🛗, 🚭 rm, 🔳 ⚐ – 🏛 60. 🕦 🕮 AE ⓪ VISA . 🕬   CY s
closed 24 December - 2 January – **Rest** a la carte 18.40/27.85 – 🖙 9.95 – **96 rm** ✸115.00 – ✸✸115.00.
◆ Bright modern hotel in city centre close to theatre. Colourful cushions and pared-down style in bedrooms. Three conference rooms for hire. Fifth floor dining room gives fine views of city.

🏨 **Hart's,** Standard Hill, Park Row, NG1 6FN, & (0115) 988 1900, ask@hartsnotting ham.co.uk, Fax (0115) 947 7600, ≼, 🚗 – 🛗 🚭 ⚒ ⚐ P. 🕦 🕮 AE VISA   CZ e
Rest – (see *Harts* below) – 🖙 13.50 – **30 rm** ✸120.00 – ✸✸165.00/255.00, 2 suites.
◆ Stylish modern hotel. Breakfast in contemporary style bar serving light snacks. Modern bedrooms; ground floor rooms open onto patio; good views from higher floors.

🏨 **Lace Market,** 29-31 High Pavement, NG1 1HE, & (0115) 852 3232, stay@lacemarketho tel.co.uk, Fax (0115) 852 3223 – 🛗 🚭 – 🏛 35. 🕦 🕮 AE VISA   DZ a
closed 24-27 December – **Rest** – (see *Merchants* below) – 🖙 14.95 – **42 rm** ✸95.00/119.00 – ✸✸119.00/239.00.
◆ Located in old lacemaking quarter, but nothing lacy about interiors; crisp rooms with minimalist designs, unpatterned fabrics. A stylish place to rest one's head.

🏨 **Express by Holiday Inn** without rest., 7 Chapel Quarter, Chapel Bar, Maid Marian Way, NG1 6JS, & (0870) 4176000, nottingham@kewgreen.co.uk, Fax (0115) 941 5764 – 🛗 🚭 ⚒ – 🏛 25. 🕦 🕮 AE ⓪ VISA . 🕬   CY a
120 rm ✸69.00/85.00 – ✸✸69.00/85.00.
◆ Lodge accommodation opened in 2004, located in the heart of Nottingham. Uniform bedrooms of good size, comfort and value. Close to city's facilities and attractions.

🏠 **Greenwood Lodge City** without rest., 5 Third Ave, Sherwood Rise, NG7 6JH, & (0115) 962 1206, pdouglas71@aol.com, Fax (0115) 962 1206, 🚗 – 🚭 P. 🕦 🕮 VISA . 🕬   AY n
closed 24-28 December – **6 rm** 🖙 ✸43.00/55.00 – ✸✸80.00.
◆ Regency house with elegant reception offset by paintings, antiques. Conservatory breakfast room from which to view birdlife. Period beds, lovely fabrics in pretty rooms.

🍴🍴🍴 **Restaurant Sat Bains** with rm, Trentside, Lenton Lane, NG7 2SA, & (0115) 986 6566, info@restaurantsatbains.net, Fax (0115) 986 0343, 🚗 – 🚭, 🔳 rest, P. 🕦 VISA . 🕬   AZ n
🏵 *closed first 2 weeks January and 2 weeks August –* Rest *(closed Sunday-Monday)* (dinner only) 55.00/85.00 🍷 – **8 rm** 🖙 ✸114.00 – ✸✸129.00/200.00, 2 suites.
Spec. Veal bread, broccoli purée, pineapple and noisette jus. Anjou pigeon with melon, feta, mint chocolate and grapefruit. Chocolate, cherries, orange and marzipan.
◆ Converted 19C farmhouse in hidden location off the city ring road. Stylish dining room where innovative cooking is very much to the fore. Spacious, rustic rooms.

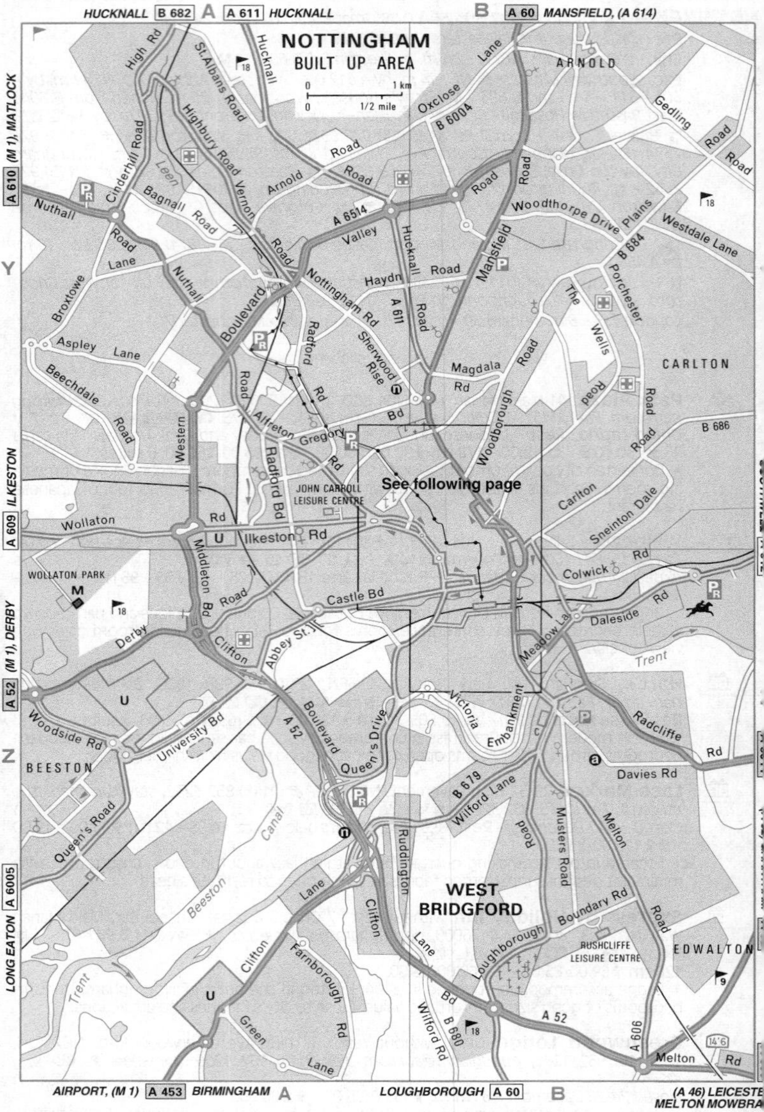
HUCKNALL B 682 A A 611 HUCKNALL
B A 60 MANSFIELD, (A 614)
NOTTINGHAM
BUILT UP AREA
0 1 km
0 1/2 mile
A 610 (M 1), MATLOCK
A 609 ILKESTON
A 52 (M 1), DERBY
LONG EATON A 6005
AIRPORT, (M 1) A 453 BIRMINGHAM A
LOUGHBOROUGH A 60 B
(A 46) LEICESTE
MELTON MOWBRA
Y
Z
ARNOLD
CARLTON
BEESTON
WEST
BRIDGFORD
EDWALTON
WOLLATON PARK
JOHN CARROLL
LEISURE CENTRE
RUSHCLIFFE
LEISURE CENTRE
See following page
High Rd
St.Albans Road
Hucknall
Highbury Road
Vernon
Cinderhill Road
Bagnall Road
Nuthall
Leen
Arnold
Road
A 6514
Valley
Road
Nottingham Rd
Oxclose
Lane
B 6004
Gedling
Road
Woodthorpe Drive
Plains
Westdale Lane
B 684
Porchester
Road
Mansfield
Road
Hucknall
Road
A 611
Haydn
Road
Sherwood
Rise
Radford
Rd
Boulevard
Broxtowe
Lane
Aspley
Lane
Beechdale
Road
Western
Magdala
Rd
Woodborough
Road
The
Wells
Road
Alfreton
Gregory
Bd
Radford Bd
Wollaton
Rd
Ilkeston
Rd
Carlton
Sneinton Dale
B 686
Colwick
Rd
Daleside
Rd
Middleton
Bd
Road
Castle Bd
Derby
Clifton
Abbey St.
Meadow La
Trent
Radcliffe
Rd
Davies Rd
Victoria
Embankment
Woodside Rd
University Bd
A 52
Boulevard
Queen's Drive
B 679
Wilford Lane
Road
Musters Road
Melton
Queen's Road
Canal
Ruddington
Beeston
Lane
Clifton
Lane
Boundary Rd
Loughborough
Road
Clifton
Farnborough
Rd
Green
Lane
Bd
Wilford Rd
B 680
A 52
A 606
Melton
Rd
Trent

XX **Merchants** (at Lace Market H.), 29-31 High Pavement, The Lace Market, NG1 1HE, ✆ (0115) 852 3232, *stay@lacemarkethotel.co.uk, Fax (0115) 852 3223* – ⇹ ▤. MC AE VISA DZ a

closed 24-27 December, lunch Saturday-Monday and Sunday dinner – **Rest** 14.95/29.50 and a la carte 27.50/46.00 ♀.

◆ Located within Lace Market hotel, entered via trendy Saints bar. Stylish, modern eatery typified by deep red banquettes. Modish British cooking with a spark of originality.

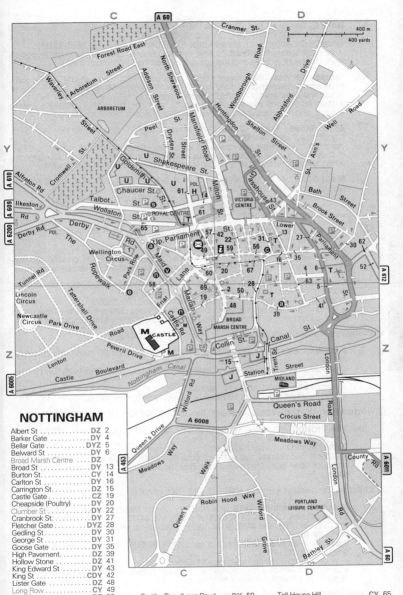

NOTTINGHAM

XX **Hart's,** Standard Court, Park Row, NG1 6GN, ℰ (0115) 988 1900, *ask@hartsnotting
ham.co.uk, Fax (0115) 911 0611,* ⌨ – ✿ 12. 🆗 🆎 🆅🅸🆂🅰   CZ e
closed 26 December and 1 January – **Rest** 15.95 (lunch) and a la carte 28.00/42.00 ⚏.
♦ Designer setting for vibrant cooking. Brightly coloured seats, oil paintings, impressive
vases of flowers. Truffles on plates with coffee. Dashing mix of modern meals.

XX **World Service,** Newdigate House, Castlegate, NG1 6AF, ℰ (0115) 847 5587,
info@worldservicerestaurant.com, Fax (0115) 847 5584, ⌨ – 🆗 🆎 🆅🅸🆂🅰   CZ n
closed first week January – **Rest** 16.50 (lunch) and a la carte 30.50/35.50 ⚏.
♦ Spacious Georgian mansion close to castle, with chic glass tanks containing Eastern
artefacts and huge ceiling squares with vivid silks. Effective, tasty fusion food.

XX **4550 Miles from Delhi,** 41 Mount St, NG1 6HE, ℰ (0115) 947 5111,
Fax (0115) 947 4555 – ▤. 🆗 🆎 🆅🅸🆂🅰   CY n
closed 25-26 December, Saturday lunch and Sunday – **Rest** - Indian - a la carte 12.35/27.85.
♦ Stylish, up-to-date and very spacious restaurant incorporating a three storey glazed
atrium and modish bar. Freshly prepared, skilfully cooked, authentic Indian cuisine.

XX **Mem-Saab,** 12-14 Maid Marian Way, NG1 6HS, ℰ (0115) 957 0009, *contact@mem-
saab.co.uk, Fax (0115) 941 2724* – ▤. 🆗 🆎 🆅🅸🆂🅰   CY n
closed 25 December – **Rest** - Indian - (dinner only) 20.95 and a la carte 15.00/23.00.
♦ Large, spacious and relaxed restaurant away from town centre. Vivid oils on plain white
walls. Authentic Indian cuisine: expect tasty, unusual regional dishes.

XX **The Monkey Tree,** 70 Bridgford Rd, West Bridgford, NG2 6AP, ℰ (0115) 981 1419,
info@themonkeytree.co.uk – 🆗 🆅🅸🆂🅰   BZ a
closed 25 December – **Rest** a la carte 11.85/25.70 ⚏.
♦ Near Trent Bridge cricket ground; a relaxed, "neighbourhood" air prevails with very
comfy leather-backed chairs. Freshly prepared dishes with distinctive Mediterranean base.

🍴 **Cock and Hoop,** 25 High Pavement, NG1 1HE, ℰ (0115) 852 3231, *cockandhoop@lace
markethotel.co.uk, Fax (0115) 852 3223* – ✖ ▤. 🆗 🆎 🆅🅸🆂🅰   DZ a
closed 25-26 December and 1 January – **Rest** a la carte 17.90/22.00 ⚏.
♦ Set on cobbled street in redeveloped lace market area. Basement, now a large dining
room, is a former cock fighting pit. Modern British cooking served in substantial portions.

at Plumtree *Southeast : 5¾ m. by A 60* – BZ – *off A 606* – ✉ *Nottingham.*

X **Perkins,** Old Railway Station, Station Rd, NG12 5NA, ℰ (0115) 937 3695, *info@perkinsres
taurant.co.uk, Fax (0115) 937 6405,* ⌨ – 🅿. 🆗 🆎 🆅🅸🆂🅰
closed 25-26 December, 1 January, Sunday dinner and Monday – **Rest** 16.95 (lunch) and a
la carte 20.75/30.95 ⚏.
♦ Named after owners; once a railway station. Pot roast quails, pithivier of walnuts remove
it from its origins. Dine in conservatory or relax in bar, a former waiting room.

at Normanton-on-the-Wolds *Southeast : 6 m. by A 60* – BZ – *off A 606* – ✉ *Nottingham.*

🍴 **The Plough,** Old Melton Rd, NG12 5NN, ℰ (0115) 937 2401, *Fax (0115) 937 2401,* ⌨,
🍴 – ✖ 🅿 ✿ 16. 🆅🅸🆂🅰
Rest 12.95 and a la carte 12.95/30.00.
♦ Creeper-clad country pub with two petanque pitches in garden. Simple interior with
plenty of open fires. Cheap lunchtime fixed price menus. Evening: more adventurous
dishes.

at Beeston *Southwest : 4¼ m. on A 6005* – AZ – ✉ *Nottingham.*

🏨 **Village H. & Leisure Club,** Brailsford Way, Chilwell Meadows, Chilwell Retail Park, NG9
6DL, Southwest : 2 ¾ m. by A 6005 ℰ (0115) 946 4422, *village.nottingham@village-ho
tels.com, Fax (0115) 946 4428,* ⚫, 🛏, 🍸, 🏊, squash – 🖕 ✖ ▤ rest, & ⛹ 🅿 – 🔔 400.
🆗 🆎 🆂 🆅🅸🆂🅰
Rest (grill rest.) 15.50/28.00 and a la carte 15.15/28.35 ⚏ – **154 rm** ✦85.00/120.00 –
✦✦95.00/100.00.
♦ Modern hotel with impressive leisure facilities: large pool, toning tables, cardio vascular
area, gym, squash courts. After exercising, unwind in neat, comfortable rooms. A couple
of traditionally based restaurant alternatives.

at Sherwood Business Park *Northwest : 10 m. by A 611* – AY – *off A 608* – ✉ *Nottingham.*

🏨 **Dakota,** Lakeview Drive, NG15 0DA, ℰ (0870) 4422727, *enquiries@dakotahotels.co.uk,
Fax (01623) 727677,* ⌨, 🛏 – 🖕, ✖ rm, 🗓 & 🅿 – 🔔 60. 🆗 🆎 🆅🅸🆂🅰 ✂
Grill : Rest a la carte approx 25.00 ⚏ – ⚌ 10.00 – **92 rm** ✦84.50/89.50 – ✦✦89.50.
♦ Hard-to-miss hotel just off the M1 - it's a big black cube! Lobby with plush sofas,
bookshelves and Dakota aircraft montage. Spacious rooms with kingsize beds and plasma
TVs. Modern British grill style menus.

NOTTINGHAM EAST MIDLANDS AIRPORT *Leics. 502 503 504* P/Q 25 – ⊠ *Derby.*
London 125 – Birmingham 40 – Derby 13 – Leicester 24 – Nottingham 15.

🏨 **Hilton East Midlands Airport,** Derby Rd, Castle Donnington, DE74 2YW, Northeast :
2 ¾ m. by A 453 on A 50 at junction 24 of M 1 ℘ (01509) 674000, Fax (01509) 672412, 🛁,
🛋, 🔲 – 🛌, ⇄ rm, 🖥 🚹 🗜 🅿 – 🔬 300. 🐧 🅰🅴 ◑ 🆅🅸🆂🅰
Rest (carvery lunch/dinner 25.00 and a la carte 24.00/33.00 s. 🍷 – ⊡ 15.95 – **150 rm** ⊡
✝76.00/146.00 – ✝✝76.00/146.00, 2 suites.
♦ Purpose-built hotel close to the airport and major motorway links, well suited to the
business traveller. Comfortable, modern bedrooms and complimentary airport transport.
Restaurant or café dining options.

🏨 **Thistle East Midlands Airport,** DE74 2SH, ℘ (0870) 333 9132, east.midlandsair
port@thistle.co.uk, Fax (0870) 333 9232, 🛁, 🛋, 🔲 – 🛌 🚹 🗜 🅿 – 🔬 220. 🐧 🅰🅴 ◑ 🆅🅸🆂🅰
Rest (closed Saturday lunch) (bar lunch)/dinner 24.95 and a la carte 28.85/45.85 s. 🍷 –
⊡ 13.95 – **164 rm** ✝195.00 – ✝✝215.00.
♦ Spacious and carefully designed modern, purpose-built hotel on the airport doorstep.
Rooms are smart and bright with contemporary furnishings. Light, airy dining room; popular menu suiting all tastes.

OAKHAM *Rutland 502 504* R 25 – pop. 9 620.
See : *Oakham Castle★.*
Env. : *Rutland Water★*, E : *by A 606 – Normanton Church★ AC*, SE : *5 m. by A 603 and minor
road East.*
🅱 *Victoria Hall, 39 High St* ℘ (01572) 724329.
London 103 – Leicester 26 – Northampton 35 – Nottingham 28.

🏨 **Barnsdale Lodge,** The Avenue, Rutland Water, LE15 8AH, East : 2 ½ m. on A 606
℘ (01572) 724678, reservations@barnsdalelodge.co.uk, Fax (01572) 724961, 🌺 – ⇄ 📞 🗜
🅿 – 🔬 300. 🐧 🅰🅴 ◑ 🆅🅸🆂🅰
Restaurant : Rest 14.95 (lunch) and a la carte 19.85/28.25 – **Conservatory :** Rest a la
carte 19.85/28.25 – **44 rm** ✝70.00/80.00 – ✝✝80.00/85.00.
♦ Privately owned, converted farmhouse with mature gardens. Ample, modern rooms, a
large bar flagged in York stone and extensive meeting facilities in renovated stables. Flavours of the season to fore in the Restaurant. More informal Conservatory.

🏨 **Whipper-In** with rm, Market Pl, LE15 6DT, ℘ (01572) 756971, whipperin@brook-ho
tels.co.uk, Fax (01572) 757759 – ⇄ rest, 📞 – 🔬 60. 🐧 🅰🅴 ◑ 🆅🅸🆂🅰
No.5 (℘ (01572) 740774) : Rest a la carte 21.95/30.00 🍷 – ⊡ 10.95 – **24 rm** ✝85.00/95.00 –
✝✝95.00/105.00.
♦ 17C inn on the Market Square has retained its coaching yard and much of its traditional
feel. Rooms in understated country style and firelit lounge with inviting armchairs. No 5 is
clean-lined brasserie.

🍴🍴 **Lord Nelson's House H. and Nicks Restaurant** with rm, Market Pl, LE15 6DT,
℘ (01572) 723199, simon@nicksrestaurant.co.uk, Fax (01572) 723199 – 🐧 🅰🅴 🆅🅸🆂🅰. 🌸
closed 1 week Christmas – **Rest** 18.95 (lunch) and a la carte 24.95/39.40 s. 🍷 – **4 rm** ⊡
✝70.00 – ✝✝95.00.
♦ Imaginative modern interiors in 17C town house: choose nautical dark wood, zebra-skin
throws or an elegant chaise longue. Classic seasonal dishes with a flavourful flourish.

at Hambleton *East : 3 m. by A 606 – ⊠ Oakham.*

🏨 **Hambleton Hall** 🌸, LE15 8TH, ℘ (01572) 756991, hotel@hambletonhall.com,
Fax (01572) 724721, ≤ Rutland Water, 🌊 heated, 🌺, 👗, 🎾 – 🛌 ⇄ 📞 🗜 🐧 🅰🅴 ◑ 🆅🅸🆂🅰
❀ Rest 27.00/40.00 and a la carte 58.00/78.00 🍷 ☕ – ⊡ 14.00 – **16 rm** ✝165.00/220.00 –
✝✝295.00/360.00, 1 suite.
Spec. Seared scallops with aubergine purée and tomatoes. Fillet of beef with slow roasted
onions and chou farci. Poached peach with raspberries and Champagne sorbet.
♦ Lovingly appointed period interiors in a peaceful and sumptuous Victorian manor. Draw-
ing room with fine objets d'art. Antique filled bedrooms, immaculate in every respect.
Confident, harmoniously balanced menus; abundant local produce.

🍴 **Finch's Arms** with rm, Oakham Rd, LE15 8TL, ℘ (01572) 756575, finch
sarms@talk21.com, Fax (01572) 771142, ≤, 🏯, 🌺 – ⇄ 🗜 🐧 🆅🅸🆂🅰. 🌸
closed 25 December – **Rest** 11.95 (lunch) and a la carte 16.95/26.95 🍷 – **6 rm** ⊡ ✝65.00 –
✝✝75.00.
♦ Sandstone pub overlooking Rutland Water: rustic interior, flagged floors, rattan chairs.
Real ales accompany tasty modern menus, brimming with Asian flavours. Cosy bedrooms.

at Wing South : 5 m. by A 6003 – ⊠ Oakham.

Kings Arms with rm, 13 Top St, LE15 8SE, ℰ (01572) 737634, info@thekingsarms-wing.co.uk, Fax (01572) 737255, ☞ – ⵂ← rm, 🅿. ⓂⓈ 🄰🄴 𝗩𝗜𝗦𝗔. ⁒
Rest (closed Monday lunch November-March) a la carte 17.00/32.00 – **8 rm** ⌂ ✝60.00/65.00 – ✝✝70.00/75.00.
♦ Cosy, rural 17C pub in pleasant hamlet near Rutland Water. Well furnished interior with flag floor, rafters and fire. Fresh, seasonally inspired dishes. Warm, welcoming rooms.

at Knossington West : 4 m. by A 606 and Braunston rd – ⊠ Oakham.

The Fox and Hounds, 6 Somerby Rd, LE15 8LY, ℰ (01664) 454676, Fax (01664) 454031, ☞ – ⵂ← 🅿. ⓂⓈ ⓞ 𝗩𝗜𝗦𝗔
Rest (closed Sunday dinner and Monday) (booking essential) a la carte 19.95/30.00.
♦ Welcoming 18C, ivy-clad former coaching inn set in pretty village. Low ceiling, beams and log fires enhance delightful ambience. Tasty dishes brimming with local fare.

OAKSEY Wilts. 503 N 29.
London 98 – Cirencester 8.5 – Stroud 20.

The Wheatsheaf at Oaksey, Wheatsheaf Lane, SN16 9TB, ℰ (01666) 577348, ☞ – ⵂ← 🅿. ⓂⓈ 𝗩𝗜𝗦𝗔. ⁒
Rest (closed Monday) 15.95 and a la carte 21.00/27.00 ⁒.
♦ Rurally set traditional pub in the heart of the country. Rafters; exposed stone walls covered with farming implements above inglenook. Assured, ambitious, modern cooking.

OBORNE Dorset 503 504 M 31 – see Sherborne.

OCKLEY Surrey 504 S 30.
🗒 Gatton Manor Hotel G. & C.C., Standon Lane ℰ (01306) 627555.
London 31 – Brighton 32 – Guildford 23 – Lewes 36 – Worthing 29.

Bryce's, The Old School House, RH5 5TH, on A 29 ℰ (01306) 627430, bryces.fish@virgin.net, Fax (01306) 628274 – ⵂ← rm, 🅿. ⓂⓈ 🄰🄴 ⓞ 𝗩𝗜𝗦𝗔
closed 25-26 December and 1 January – **Rest** - Seafood - 29.00 and a la carte 19.15/25.15 ⁒.
♦ Busy, redbrick former school, locally renowned for flavourful, home-smoked and market-fresh seafood from Thai fricassee to swordfish mille feuille. Attentive, dapper staff.

ODIHAM Hants. 504 R 30 – pop. 2 908 – ⊠ Hook.
London 51 – Reading 16 – Southampton 37 – Winchester 25.

George, 100 High St, RG29 1LP, ℰ (01256) 702081, reception@georgehotelodiham.com, Fax (01256) 704213 – ⵂ← rm, 🅿. ⓂⓈ 🄰🄴 ⓞ 𝗩𝗜𝗦𝗔
closed 25-26 December – **Cromwell's** : Rest - Seafood specialities - (closed Saturday lunch, Sunday dinner and Bank Holidays) 15.95 and a la carte 27.40/33.50 ⁒ – **Next door at the George** : Rest a la carte 17.85/26.25 ⁒ – **28 rm** ⌂ ✝90.00/100.00 – ✝✝125.00.
♦ 15C inn at the heart of the town; cosy lounge bar and comfortable rooms. Those in the main building have greater rural character than more recent, if smartly fitted ones. Cromwells is impressively oak-panelled. Informality rules Next door at the George.

St John, 83 High St, RG29 1LB, ℰ (01256) 702697, reuben.evans@st-john-restaurant.co.uk, Fax (01256) 702697 – ⵂ← 🍴 ♦ 12. ⓂⓈ 🄰🄴 𝗩𝗜𝗦𝗔
closed 25-28 December and Sunday – **Rest** 18.95 (lunch) and a la carte 22.80/38.50.
♦ Refurbished and stylish restaurant boasts vivid artwork, suspended arcs of wood from the ceiling and comfy leather banquettes. Eclectic menus with classical base.

Grapevine, 121 High St, RG29 1LA, ℰ (01256) 701122, grapevine701122@tiscali.co.uk – ▪. ⓂⓈ 🄰🄴 𝗩𝗜𝗦𝗔
closed 2 weeks Christmas, Saturday lunch, Sunday and Bank Holidays – **Rest** 14.95 (lunch) and a la carte 21.85/32.85 ⁒.
♦ Bright, airy, relaxed neighbourhood restaurant. Local produce used to good effect in generous modern British dishes, plus flavourful, more elaborate blackboard specialities.

OLD BURGHCLERE Hants. 504 Q 29 – ⊠ Newbury.
London 77 – Bristol 76 – Newbury 10 – Reading 27 – Southampton 28.

Dew Pond, RG20 9LH, ℰ (01635) 278408, Fax (01635) 278580, ≤ – ⵂ← 🅿. ⓂⓈ 𝗩𝗜𝗦𝗔
closed 2 weeks Christmas, Sunday and Monday – **Rest** (dinner only) 32.00/40.00 ⁒.
♦ This traditionally decorated cottage, set in fields and parkland, overlooks Watership Down and houses a collection of local art. Tasty Anglo-gallic menu.

OLDHAM *Gtr Manchester* 502 504 N 23 – *pop. 103 544.*

🏌 *Crompton and Royton, High Barn, Royton* ℰ *(0161) 624 2154 –* 🏌 *Werneth, Green Lane, Garden Suburb* ℰ *(0161) 624 1190 –* 🏌 *Lees New Rd* ℰ *(0161) 624 4986.*

🛈 *12 Albion St* ℰ *(0161) 627 1024.*

London 212 – Leeds 36 – Manchester 7 – Sheffield 38.

Plan : see Manchester

🏨🏨 **Smokies Park,** Ashton Rd, Bardsley, OL8 3HX, South : 2 ¾ m. on A 627 ℰ *(0161) 785 5000, enquiries@smokies.co.uk, Fax (0161) 785 5010,* 🛌, 🐕🐾 – 🛗, 🍴 rm, 🍽 rest, 💛 ₺ 🅿 – 🛎 110. 🐵🖸 🖭 ⑩ 𝘝𝘐𝘚𝘈. 🛇
Cosi Fan Tutti : Rest - Italian - (dinner only) 25.00 and a la carte 22.95/30.00 s. ♀ – **72 rm** ☲ ✹95.00 – ✹✹105.00/160.00, 1 suite.
♦ Purpose-built hotel in the southern suburbs. Executive rooms in particular are modern and handsomely equipped. Regular music in the nightclub or more relaxing lounge bar. Trattoria styling in airy restaurant.

🍴 **The White Hart Inn** with rm, 51 Stockport Rd, Lydgate, OL4 4JJ, East : 3 m. by A 669
🅰 on A 6050 ℰ *(01457) 872566, bookings@thewhitehart.co.uk, Fax (01457) 875190 –* 🍽 🅿 –
🛎 200. 🐵🖸 🖭 𝘝𝘐𝘚𝘈. 🛇
Rest (booking essential) 18.00/35.00 and a la carte 24.00/30.00 ♀ – **12 rm** ☲
✹90.00/100.00 – ✹✹120.00/135.00.
♦ Busy, yet laid-back pub with old timber and exposed brick. On the walls are sepia photos of Lydgate; open fires add to the rich, welcoming mix. Hearty modern dishes.

OLD WARDEN *Beds.* 504 S 27 – *see Biggleswade.*

OLTON *W. Mids.* 502 503 504 O 26 – *see Solihull.*

OMBERSLEY *Worcs.* 503 504 N 27 – *pop. 2 089.*

🏌 *Bishopswood Rd* ℰ *(01905) 620747.*
London 148 – Birmingham 42 – Leominster 33.

🍴🍴 **The Venture In,** Main St, WR9 0EW, ℰ *(01905) 620552, Fax (01905) 620552 –* 🍽 🍽 🅿.
🐵🖸
closed 1 week Christmas, 2 weeks February, 2 weeks August, Sunday dinner and Monday –
Rest 18.95/32.50.
♦ Charming, restored Tudor inn, traditional from its broad inglenook to its fringed Victorian lights. Modern, flavourful menu, well judged and locally sourced. Friendly staff.

ORFORD *Suffolk* 504 Y 27 – ✉ *Woodbridge.*
London 103 – Ipswich 22 – Norwich 52.

🏨 **Crown and Castle,** IP12 2LJ, ℰ *(01394) 450205, info@crownandcastle.co.uk,* 🌳 – 🍽
🅿. 🐵🖸 𝘝𝘐𝘚𝘈
closed 19-22 December and 3-4 January – Rest - (see **The Trinity** below) – **18 rm** ☲
✹72.00/95.00 – ✹✹135.00/145.00.
♦ 19C redbrick hotel with garden and terrace standing proudly next to 12C Orford Castle. Cosy lounges with soft suites and sofas. Stylish modern rooms, some facing the Ness.

🍴 **The Trinity** (at Crown and Castle H.), IP12 2LJ, ℰ *(01394) 450205, info@crownandcas*
🅰 *tle.co.uk,* 🍴, 🌳 – 🍽 🅿. 🐵🖸 𝘝𝘐𝘚𝘈. 🛇
closed 19-22 December and 3-4 January – Rest (booking essential) a la carte 23.50/31.50 ♀
🅱.
♦ Stylish and relaxed - lovely al fresco dining on fine summer days. Full-flavoured dishes blend wide-ranging modern British cooking and Italian undertones. Well-chosen wines.

ORLETON *Shrops.* 503 L 23 – *see Ludlow.*

OSMOTHERLEY *N. Yorks.* 502 Q 20 – ✉ *Northallerton.*
London 245 – Darlington 25 – Leeds 49 – Middlesbrough 20 – Newcastle upon Tyne 54 – York 36.

🍴 **The Golden Lion,** 6 West End, DL6 3AA, ℰ *(01609) 883526 –* 🍽. 🐵🖸 𝘝𝘐𝘚𝘈
closed 25 December – Rest a la carte 15.00/25.00 ♀.
♦ Unpretentious, beamed, firelit alehouse; plant-filled upper dining room; large menu of satisfying, full-flavoured cooking, Yorkshire beers and sprightly, engaging service.

OSWESTRY *Shrops.* 502 503 K 25 – *pop. 16 660.*

🏌 *Aston Park* ℘ *(01691) 610535* – 🏌 *Llanymynech, Pant* ℘ *(01691) 830983.*

🛈 *Mile End Services* ℘ *(01691) 662488* – *The Heritage Centre, 2 Church Terr* ℘ *(01691) 662753.*

London 182 – Chester 28 – Shrewsbury 18.

🏛 **The Wynnstay,** Church St, SY11 2SZ, ℘ (01691) 655261, *info@wynnstayhotel.com,* Fax (01691) 670606, 🆗, 🍽, 🔲 – 🌬, 🍴 rest, 🅿 – 🔏 250. 🆖 🆔 ⓞ 🆚🆂🅰
Four Seasons : Rest *(closed Sunday dinner)* 21.95 ⓢ – 🍽 10.45 – **28 rm** 🚹60.00/85.00 –
🚹🚹100.00, 1 suite.
◆ Town centre former posting inn with its own bowling green and a gym in the old stables. Behind a fine Georgian façade, sizeable rooms have kept traces of original character. Smart dining room for tasty, traditional dishes.

🏛 **Lion Quays,** Moreton, SY11 3EN, North: 4 m. on A 5 ℘ (01691) 684300, *sales@lion quays.co.uk,* Fax (01691) 684313, 🍽 – 🛗 🌬, 🍽 rm, 🅑 🅿 – 🔏 400. 🆖 🆔 🆚🆂🅰
Bridge 17 : Rest a la carte 19.50/29.75 **s.** – **79 rm** 🍽 🚹105.00/185.00, 3 suites.
◆ 21C hotel with two buildings in a tranquil canalside location: most public areas take in this view. There's a cosy little lounge bar and bedrooms which each boast a balcony. Conservatory restaurant beside the canal.

🍴 **The Walls,** Welsh Walls, SY11 1AW, ℘ (01691) 670970, *info@the-walls.co.uk,* Fax (01691) 653820, 🍽 – 🌬 🅿 ⇄ 40. 🆖 🆔 🆚🆂🅰
closed 26-28 December, 1-3 January and Sunday dinner – Rest 17.00 and a la carte 18.50/31.50 ⓢ.
◆ Built in 1841 as a school; now a buzzy restaurant. High ceiling with wooden rafters; original wood flooring. Friendly atmosphere. Varied menu offers some adventurous options.

at Trefonen *Southwest : 2½ m. on Trefonen rd* – ✉ *Oswestry.*

🏠 **The Pentre** 🌿, SY10 9EE, Southwest : 1 ¾ m. by Treflach rd off New Well Lane ℘ (01691) 653952, *helen@thepentre.com,* ≤ Tanat Valley, 🍽, 🅑 – 🌬 🅿. 🌿
closed 1 week Christmas – **Rest** (communal dining) 18.00 – **3 rm** 🍽 🚹80.00 – 🚹🚹80.00.
◆ Restored 16C farmhouse with superb views over Tanat Valley. Heavily timbered inglenook and wood-burning stove in lounge. Sloping floors enhance rooms of tremendous character. Home-cooked dinners served with fellow guests.

at Rhydycroesau *West : 3¼ m. on B 4580* – ✉ *Oswestry.*

🏛 **Pen-Y-Dyffryn Country H.** 🌿, SY10 7JD, ℘ (01691) 653700, *stay@peny.co.uk,* ≤, 🍽, 🍽 – 🌬 🅿. 🆖 🆚🆂🅰
Rest (booking essential for non-residents) (dinner only) 34.00 – **12 rm** 🍽 🚹82.00/84.00 – 🚹🚹114.00/138.00.
◆ Peaceful 19C listed rectory in five-acre informal gardens near Offa's Dyke. Cosy lounge, friendly ambience; good-sized, individually styled rooms, four in the coach house. Home-cooked dishes utilising organic ingredients.

OULTON BROAD *Suffolk* 504 Z 26 – *see Lowestoft.*

OUNDLE *Northants.* 504 S 26 – *pop. 5 219* – ✉ *Peterborough.*

🏌 *Benefield Rd* ℘ *(01832) 273267.*

🛈 *14 West St* ℘ *(01832) 274333.*

London 89 – Leicester 37 – Northampton 30.

🏠 **Castle Farm** without rest., Fotheringhay, PE8 5HZ, North : 3 ¾ m. by A 427 off A 605 ℘ (01832) 226200, Fax (01832) 226200, 🍽, 🍽 – 🅿. 🌿
5 rm 🍽 🚹39.00/68.00 – 🚹🚹64.00/68.00.
◆ Wisteria-clad, gabled 19C house in the Nene Valley; lawned gardens beside the river. Ample, pine furnished rooms, two in the adjacent wing, with open fire.

🍴 **The Falcon Inn,** Fotheringhay, PE8 5HZ, North : 3 ¾ m. by A 427 off A 605 ℘ (01832) 226254, *falcon@cyberware.co.uk,* Fax (01832) 226046, 🍽, 🍽 – 🌬 🅿. 🆖 🆔 🆚🆂🅰 🌿
Rest a la carte 25.00/35.00 ⓢ 🌿.
◆ Popular village inn: pretty bouquets, framed prints and airy, spacious conservatory. Mediterranean flavours to the fore in robust dishes from the modern British menu.

OVERSTRAND *Norfolk* 504 Y 25 – *see Cromer.*

OVINGTON *Hants.* – *see Winchester.*

OXFORD Oxon. 503 504 Q 28 Great Britain G. – pop. 143 016.

See : City★★★ - Christ Church★★ (Hall★★ AC, Tom Quad★, Tom Tower★, Cathedral★ AC - Choir Roof★) BZ – Merton College★★ AC BZ - Magdalen College★★ BZ – Ashmolean Museum★★ BY **M1** – Bodleian Library★★ (Ceiling★★, Lierne Vaulting★) AC BZ **A1** – St John's College★ BY - The Queen's College★ BZ – Lincoln College★ BZ - Trinity College (Chapel★) BY – New College (Chapel★) AC, BZ – Radcliffe Camera★ BZ **P1** – Sheldonian Theatre★ AC, BZ **T** – University Museum of National History★ BY **M4** – Pitt Rivers Museum★ BY **M3.**

Env. : Iffley Church★ AZ A.

Exc. : Woodstock : Blenheim Palace★★★ (Park★★★) AC, NW : 8 m. by A 4144 and A 34 AY. Swinford Bridge (toll).

⤸ to Abingdon Bridge (Salter Bros. Ltd) (summer only) daily (2 h).

🛈 15-16 Broad St ℘ (01865) 726871, tic@oxford.gov.uk.

London 59 – Birmingham 63 – Brighton 105 – Bristol 73 – Cardiff 107 – Coventry 54 – Southampton 64.

Plans on following pages

Plans on following pages

Randolph, Beaumont St, OX1 2LN, ℘ (0870) 4008200, sales.randolph@macdonald-hotels.co.uk, Fax (01865) 791678 – 📶 ⇄ 📞 – ⚿ 250. 🆗 🆎 ⑩ 𝐕𝐈𝐒𝐀   BY **n**
🍴 **The Restaurant at the Randolph** (℘ (01865) 256410) **:** Rest 22.00/27.00 and a la carte 29.45/61.45 – ⇄ 15.95 – **146 rm** ★210.00 – ★★220.00, 5 suites.
◆ Grand Victorian edifice. Lounge bar: deep burgundy, polished wood and chandeliers. Handsome rooms in a blend of rich fabrics; some, more spacious, have half-tester beds. Spacious, linen-clad Restaurant.

Malmaison, 3 Oxford Castle, OX1 1AY, ℘ (01865) 268400, oxford@malmaison.com, Fax (01865) 268402, 🍴, **I₆** – 📶 ⇄, ▤ rest, 📞 🅖. 🆗 🆎 𝐕𝐈𝐒𝐀   BZ
Brasserie : Rest (Sunday brunch) a la carte 26.45/33.25 🍷 ⯎ – ⇄ 13.95 – **91 rm** ★150.00 – ★★150.00, 3 suites.
◆ Unique accommodation by castle: this was a prison from 13C to 1996! Former visitors' room now residents' lounge. Stunning rooms in converted cells or ex-house of correction! Brasserie in old admin area: modern British menu with fine French edge.

Old Bank, 92-94 High St, OX1 4BN, ℘ (01865) 799599, info@oldbank-hotel.co.uk, Fax (01865) 799598, 🍴 – 📶 ▤ 📞 🅑 🅿. 🆗 🆎 ⑩ 𝐕𝐈𝐒𝐀. ⯎   BZ **s**
closed 24-26 December – **Quod :** Rest a la carte 16.85/32.65 – ⇄ 12.95 – **41 rm** ★150.00 – ★★165.00, 1 suite.
◆ Elegantly understated, clean-lined interiors and the neo-Classical façade of the city's first bank - an astute combination. Rooms in modern wood and leather with CD players. Lively Italian-influenced brasserie.

Oxford Spires, Abingdon Rd, OX1 4PS, ℘ (01865) 324324, spires@four-pillars.co.uk, Fax (01865) 324325, **I₆**, ⇋, 🔲 – 📶 ⇄ 📞 🅑 🅿 – ⚿ 230. 🆗 🆎 ⑩ 𝐕𝐈𝐒𝐀. ⯎   AZ **e**
Deacons : Rest (closed Saturday lunch) (buffet lunch Monday-Friday) (carvery lunch Sunday) 12.95/25.95 s. 🍷 ⯎ – ⇄ 12.95 – **158 rm** ★119.00/149.00 – ★★149.00/169.00, 4 suites.
◆ Follow the river path to this imposing modern hotel; comprehensive gymnasium overlooks the pool; spacious rooms, some with iron-framed four-poster beds and parkland views. Pleasantly formal, spacious dining room.

Holiday Inn, Peartree Roundabout, OX2 8JD, ℘ (0870) 4009086, reservations-oxford@ichotels.com, Fax (01865) 888333, **I₆**, ⇋, 🔲 – 📶, ⇄ rm, ▤ 🅑 🅿 – ⚿ 150. 🆗 🆎 ⑩ 𝐕𝐈𝐒𝐀. ⯎   AY **n**
Rest 20.00 and dinner a la carte 19.85/27.85 – **154 rm** ⇄ ★98.00/195.00 – ★★98.00/195.00.
◆ Bright, well-soundproofed rooms, all with mini-bars and computer consoles, in a group hotel on the edge of the city. A useful address for the business traveller. The Junction Restaurant offers modern British cooking.

Old Parsonage, 1 Banbury Rd, OX2 6NN, ℘ (01865) 310210, info@oldparsonage-hotel.co.uk, Fax (01865) 311262, 🍴, – ⇄ rm, ▤ 📞 🅿. 🆗 🆎 𝐕𝐈𝐒𝐀   BY **e**
Rest 15.95 (lunch) and a la carte 21.50/34.95 🍷 – ⇄ 12.50 – **30 rm** ★155.00 – ★★160.00/225.00.
◆ Part 17C house, creeper-clad and typically Oxfordian; dedicated staff; pristine rooms: antiques, modern and traditional fabrics and, in some cases, views of the roof garden. Meals in cosy lounge bar with antique prints and paintings.

Cotswold Lodge, 66a Banbury Rd, OX2 6JP, ℘ (01865) 512121, info@cotswoldlodgehotel.co.uk, Fax (01865) 512490, 🍴 – ⇄ 🅿 – ⚿ 80. 🆗 🆎 ⑩ 𝐕𝐈𝐒𝐀. ⯎   AY **x**
Rest a la carte 19.00/31.00 – **48 rm** ⇄ ★85.00/115.00 – ★★140.00/160.00, 1 suite.
◆ Large 19C house in a quiet suburb. Relaxing, handsomely furnished drawing room with log fire; comfortable rooms, all individually styled, are named after colleges. Gallic influenced cuisine; immaculate layout.

ENGLAND

589

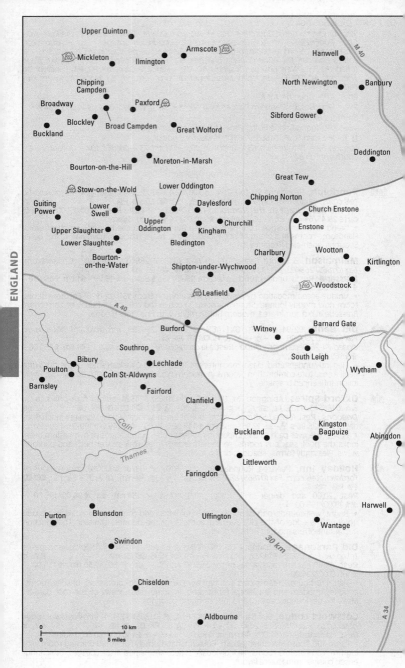

ENGLAND

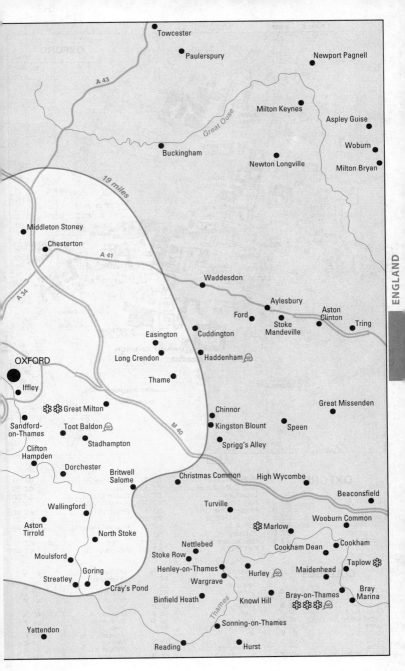

Towcester
Paulerspury
Newport Pagnell
Milton Keynes
Aspley Guise
Woburn
Buckingham
Newton Longville
Milton Bryan
A 43
Great Ouse
19 miles
Middleton Stoney
Chesterton
A 41
Waddesdon
A 34
Aylesbury
Ford
Aston Clinton
Cuddington
Stoke Mandeville
Tring
Easington
Long Crendon
Haddenham
OXFORD
Thame
Iffley
Great Missenden
❄️❄️ Great Milton
Chinnor
Sandford-on-Thames
Toot Baldon
Kingston Blount
Speen
Stadhampton
Clifton Hampden
Sprigg's Alley
Dorchester
Britwell Salome
Christmas Common
High Wycombe
Beaconsfield
Wallingford
Turville
Wooburn Common
Aston Tirrold
North Stoke
❄️ Marlow
Cookham Dean
Cookham
Moulsford
Nettlebed
Taplow ❄️
Stoke Row
Cookham Dean
Maidenhead
Goring
Henley-on-Thames
Hurley
Streatley
Wargrave
Bray-on-Thames
Bray Marina
Cray's Pond
Binfield Heath
Knowl Hill
❄️❄️❄️
Yattendon
Thames
Sonning-on-Thames
Reading
Hurst

ENGLAND

M 40

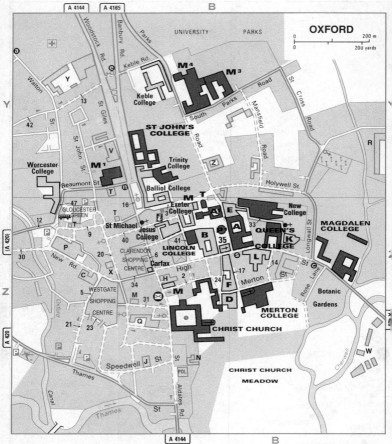

OXFORD

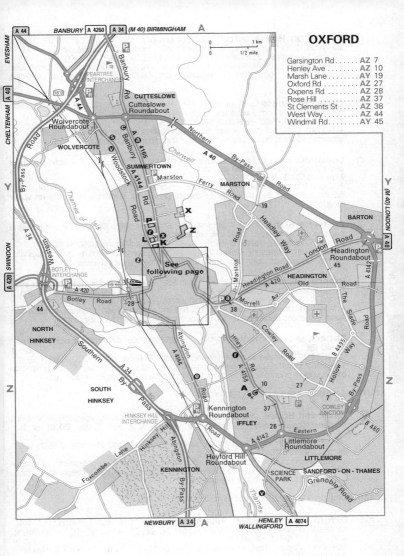

OXFORD

🏨 **Eastgate** without rest., 73 High St, OX1 4BE, ℰ (0870) 4008201, *events.eastgate@mac donald-hotels.co.uk, Fax (01865) 794163* – 📶, ✸ rm, ✆ 🄿. 🕔🅾 🅰🅴 🄾 𝘝𝘐𝘚𝘈 . ✼
⊆ 13.95 – **63 rm** ✸109.00/129.00 – ✸✸129.00/139.00.   BZ **c**
   ◆ Near the botanical gardens and the Boathouse's punt moorings, a former coaching inn offering comfortable, traditionally styled rooms decorated in plaid and floral patterns.

🏠 **Marlborough House** without rest., 321 Woodstock Rd, OX2 7NY, ℰ (01865) 311321, *enquiries@marlbhouse.co.uk, Fax (01865) 515329* – ✸ ✆ 🕔🅾 🅰🅴 🄾 𝘝𝘐𝘚𝘈 . ✼   AY **v**
17 rm ⊆ ✸77.00/80.00 – ✸✸90.00.
   ◆ Three-storey modern house. Simple yet spacious rooms - some in bold chintz, all with a small kitchenette - in the northern suburb of Summertown.

ENGLAND

↑ **Burlington House** without rest., 374 Banbury Rd, OX2 7PP, ℰ (01865) 513513, stay@burlington-house.co.uk, Fax (01865) 311785 – ⅋✕ ℂ ℙ. ⓂⓈ 𝗩𝗜𝗦𝗔. ⅍
AY a
closed 24 December- 2 January – **12 rm** ⌷ ✝45.00/75.00 – ✝✝80.00/90.00.
♦ Contemporary rooms, stylish and intelligently conceived, in a handsome 1889 house. Tasty breakfasts - omelettes, home-made bread and granola - presented on Delft-blue china.

↑ **Cotswold House** without rest., 363 Banbury Rd, OX2 7PL, ℰ (01865) 310558, d.r.walker@talk21.com, Fax (01865) 310558 – ⅋✕ ℙ. ⓂⓈ 𝗩𝗜𝗦𝗔. ⅍
AY c
8 rm ⌷ ✝52.00/65.00 – ✝✝80.00/105.00.
♦ Modern, Cotswold stone house, hung with baskets of flowers in summer. Affordable, spotless en suite rooms in pretty, traditional style; friendly ambience. Non smoking.

↑ **Chestnuts** without rest., 45 Davenant Rd, OX2 8BU, ℰ (01865) 553375, stay@chestnuts guesthouse.co.uk – ⅋✕ ℙ. ⓂⓈ 𝗩𝗜𝗦𝗔. ⅍
AY s
7 rm ⌷ ✝55.00 – ✝✝85.00.
♦ Under friendly personal management; co-ordinated décor and thoughtful details like mineral water and bathrobes in ensuite bedrooms. A short walk to the Isis water meadows.

✕ **Brasserie Blanc**, 71-72 Walton St, OX2 6AG, ℰ (01865) 510999, oxford@brasserie blanc.co.uk, Fax (01865) 510700 – ⅋✕ ▤. ⓂⓈ ⒜ 𝗩𝗜𝗦𝗔
AY z
closed 25 December – **Rest** - Brasserie - 12.50/17.50 and a la carte 20.50/34.95 🕦 ℤ.
♦ Busy, informal brasserie; striking interior and sharp service; French regional recipes with the new-wave touch: John Dory with coriander or ribeye steak in béarnaise.

✕ **Branca**, 111 Walton St, OX2 6AJ, ℰ (01865) 556111, info@brancarestaurants.com, Fax (01865) 556501 – ▤. ⓂⓈ ⒜ ⓪ 𝗩𝗜𝗦𝗔
BY a
closed 24-25 December – **Rest** - Italian influences - a la carte 19.35/25.25 ℤ.
♦ Modern restaurant with casual, friendly feel and minimalist décor. Vibrant, simple, fresh Italian influenced dishes: antipasti taster plates, pasta and pizza are specialities.

✕ **Fishers**, 36-37 St Clements, OX4 1AB, ℰ (01865) 243003, dining@fishers-oxford.co.uk – ▤. ⓂⓈ 𝗩𝗜𝗦𝗔
AZ a
closed 24-29 December and Monday lunch – **Rest** - Seafood - a la carte 20.00/40.00 ℤ.
♦ Informal, bright restaurant near Magdalen Bridge. Tables covered with fish and chip style paper. Market-oriented dishes include Mediterranean and Pacific Rim influences.

at Iffley Southeast : 2 m. by A 4158 – ✉ Oxford.

🏢 **Hawkwell House**, Church Way, OX4 4DZ, ℰ (01865) 749988, reservations@hawkwell househotel.co.uk, Fax (01865) 748525, ☞ – 📶 ⅋✕ ℂ ✧ ℙ. – 🏛 200. ⓂⓈ ⒜ ⓪ 𝗩𝗜𝗦𝗔. ⅍
AZ c
closed 27-29 December – **Rest** (closed Sunday) 16.15/28.45 and a la carte 13.95/29.95 ℤ – **66 rm** ⌷ ✝89.00/109.00 – ✝✝135.00.
♦ Victorian in origin, a group-owned hotel in a quiet suburb. Co-ordinated and smartly fitted modern rooms, suited to business travel. Bright lounge bar in checks and tartans. Airy, atmospheric conservatory restaurant.

at Sandford-on-Thames Southeast : 5 m. by A 4158 – ✉ Oxford.

🏨 **Oxford Thames Four Pillars**, Henley Rd, OX4 4GX, ℰ (01865) 334444, thames@four-pillars.co.uk, Fax (01865) 334400, 🗗, ☎, 🖼, ☞, 🅟, ✕ – 🔟 ⅋✕, ▤ rest, ℂ ✧ ℙ. – 🏛 150. ⓂⓈ ⓪ 𝗩𝗜𝗦𝗔. ⅍
AZ v
The River Room : **Rest** 12.50/36.00 s. ℤ – ⌷ 12.95 – **62 rm** ⌷ ✝139.00/164.00 – ✝✝172.00/245.00.
♦ Modern sandstone hotel around a 13C barn, though the pool is more reminiscent of a Roman bath; spacious lounge with medieval style chandelier, spotless, comfortable rooms. Restaurant overlooks lawned grounds and river.

at Toot Baldon Southeast : 5½ m. by B 480 – AZ – ✉ Oxford.

🍴 **The Mole Inn**, OX44 9NG, ℰ (01865) 340001, info@themoleinn.com, Fax (01865) 343011 – ℙ. ⓂⓈ ⒜ 𝗩𝗜𝗦𝗔. ⅍
closed 25 December and 1 January – **Rest** a la carte 20.00/30.00.
♦ Much refurbished pub in tiny hamlet. Beams galore, stone tiles, cosy lounge with leather sofas, pine/oak tables. Tasty, assured menus: rustic and earthy or appealingly mod-ish.

at Great Milton *Southeast : 12 m. by A 40 off A 329 –* AY *–* ⊠ *Oxford.*

🏛️ 🏛️
❀ ❀

Le Manoir aux Quat' Saisons (Blanc) ⬧, Church Rd, OX44 7PD, ☏ (01844) 278881, *lemanoir@blanc.co.uk*, Fax (01844) 278847, ≼, ☞, ⌖ – ⤝ rest, ▤ P ↻ 50. ⓪ AE ⓪ VISA
❀

closed 2-7 January – Rest *-* French *- 45.00 (lunch weekdays) and a la carte 87.00/91.00* s. ⓨ
– **25 rm** ✱380.00/575.00 – ✱✱380.00/515.00, 7 suites 550.00/1275.00.
Spec. Salad of Cornish crab, curry and mango, natural yoghurt and caviar. White asparagus with hen's egg and pancetta. Pigeon with coco beans, garden vegetables and Madeira sauce.
♦ Refined elegance at every turn, resulting in picture perfect harmony. Sumptuous lounges and rooms, classic and modern, surrounded by Japanese, ornamental and kitchen gardens. Virtuoso classic French menu of precision and flair, inspired by the seasons.

at Kingston Bagpuize *Southwest : 10 m. by A 420 –* AY *– off A 415 –* ⊠ *Oxford.*

🏛️

Fallowfields Country House ⬧, Faringdon Rd, OX13 5BH, ☏ (01865) 820416, *stay@fallowfields.com*, Fax (01865) 821275, ☞ , ☞ – ⤝ P ⓪ AE VISA
closed 1 week January – **Wellingtonia :** Rest *20.50 (lunch) and a la carte 29.00/44.00 –*
10 rm ⌑ ✱95.00/105.00 – ✱✱170.00.
♦ Elephants are everywhere - in paintings, wood and china - in this privately run 19C manor. Cosy lounge, fireside chintz armchairs. Canopy beds in thoughtfully appointed rooms. Classically elegant restaurant views sweeping lawns.

at Wytham *Northwest : 3¼ m. by A 420 –* AY *– off A 34 (northbound carriageway) –* ⊠ *Oxford.*

🍴

The White Hart, OX2 8QA, ☏ (01865) 244372, *whitehartwytham@aol.com*, Fax (01865) 248595, ☞ – ⤝ P ⓪ VISA
Rest *(closed dinner 25 December)* a la carte 18.00/30.00 ⓨ.
♦ Mellow 18C inn located in a pretty hamlet. Delightful courtyard terrace; inside are roaring fires, flagged floors, scrubbed pine tables. Menus mix classics with contemporary.

OXHILL *Warks.* 503 504 P 27.
London 90 – Banbury 11 – Birmingham 37.

⌂
🖼️

Oxbourne House ⬧, CV35 0RA, ☏ (01295) 688202, *graememcdonald@msn.com*, ≼, ☞, ⌖ – ⤝ P ❀
Rest *(by arrangement)* (communal dining) *20.00 –* **3 rm** ⌑ ✱40.00/50.00 – ✱✱70.00.
♦ Late 20C house oozing charm, individuality and fine rural views; splendid gardens. Antiques abound, complemented by the finest soft furnishings. Stylishly appointed bedrooms. Spacious dining room: plenty of ingredients grown in house grounds.

PADIHAM *Blackburn* 502 N 22.
London 230 – Burnley 6 – Clitheroe 8.5.

at Fence *Northeast : 3 m. by A 6068 –* ⊠ *Burnley.*

🍴

The Fence Gate Inn, Wheatley Lane Rd, BB12 9GG, ☏ (01282) 618101, *info@fence gate.co.uk* – ⤝ rest, P ⓪ VISA
Rest a la carte 20.00/25.60 ⓨ – **The Topiary :** Rest a la carte 25.00/33.00.
♦ High on the moors, a cavernous 17C inn renowned for locally sourced ingredients such as tasty home-made sausages. Bar or brasserie dining: service with a sense of humour.

🍴

The Forest Inn, Cuckstool Lane, BB12 9PA, *Southwest :* ½ m. on A 6248 ☏ (01282) 613641, Fax (01282) 698140, ☞ – ⤝ P ⓪ VISA
closed Monday except Bank Holidays – **Rest** *9.95 (dinner) and a la carte 9.95/27.00.*
♦ Rural pub with fine country views. Modish interior includes stripped wooden floors and comfy leather tub chairs. Main dining area serves hearty, seasonal, rustic dishes.

The red ⬧ symbol?
This denotes the very essence of peace
– only the sound of birdsong first thing in the morning ...

Cornwall 503 F 32 *The West Country G. – pop. 2 449.*

See : *Town★ – Prideaux Place★.*
Env. : *Trevone (Cornwall Coast Path★★) W : 3 m. by B 3276 – Trevose Head★ (≤★★) W : 6 m. by B 3276.*
Exc. : *Bedruthan Steps★, SW : 7 m. by B 3276 – Pencarrow★, SE : 11 m. by A 389.*
🐾, 🐾, 🐾 *Trevose, Constantine Bay ℘ (01841) 520208.*
🅱 *Red Brick Building, North Quay ℘ (01841) 533449, padstowtic@visit.org.uk.*
London 288 – Exeter 78 – Plymouth 45 – Truro 23.

🏨 **The Metropole,** Station Rd, PL28 8DB, ℘ (01841) 532486, *info@the-metropole.co.uk,* Fax (01841) 532867, ≤ Camel Estuary, ☲ heated, – 🛗 ✸✸ 🅿 🐾 🆎 ⓪ 𝘝𝘐𝘚𝘈
Rest (bar lunch Monday-Saturday)/dinner 29.95 ♀ – **53 rm** ☲ ♦59.00/100.00 – ♦♦158.00/190.00.
◆ Grand 19C hotel perched above this quaint fishing town. Exceptional views of Camel Estuary. Well-furnished sitting room. Comfortable bedrooms in smart, co-ordinated style. Traditional dining; local produce.

🏨 **Old Custom House Inn,** South Quay, PL28 8BL, ℘ (01841) 532359, *oldcustom house@smallandfriendly.co.uk,* Fax (01841) 533372, ≤ Camel Estuary and harbour – ✸✸, ▤ rest, ✸✸
Pescadou : Rest (booking essential) a la carte 28.65/33.50 – **24 rm** ☲ ♦65.00/85.00 – ♦♦100.00/180.00.
◆ Listed, slate-built former grain store and exciseman's house: spacious and comfortable throughout. Front and side rooms have views of the quayside and Camel Estuary. Seafood emphasis in bustling, glass-fronted restaurant.

🏠 **Cross House** without rest., Church St, PL28 8BG, ℘ (01841) 532391, *info@cross house.co.uk,* Fax (01841) 533633 – ✸✸, 🐾 𝘝𝘐𝘚𝘈, ✸✸
11 rm ☲ ♦80.00/90.00 – ♦♦105.00/125.00.
◆ Charming, centrally located, Grade II listed Georgian house. Two lounges with real fires and a comfortable feel. Varying room sizes, all with co-ordinated fabrics.

🏠 **Woodlands Country House** without rest., Treator, PL28 8RU, West : 1 ¼ m. on B 3276 ℘ (01841) 532426, *info@woodlands-padstow.co.uk,* Fax (01841) 533353, ≤, 🌳 – ✸✸ 🕭 🅿 🐾 🆎 𝘝𝘐𝘚𝘈
closed 22 December- 1 February – **9 rm** ☲ ♦60.00 – ♦♦110.00/132.00.
◆ Personally run Victorian country house with well-kept garden. Large lounge in classic traditional style; views sweeping down to Trevone Bay. Co-ordinated bedrooms.

🏠 **Treverbyn House** without rest., Station Rd, PL28 8DA, ℘ (01841) 532855, Fax (01841) 532855, ≤, 🌳 – ✸✸ 🅿. ✸✸
closed Christmas – **5 rm** ☲ ♦50.00 – ♦♦90.00/100.00.
◆ Something of a grand style with views of the Camel Estuary. Large rooms retain open fireplaces and have comfortable, uncluttered décor: Turret rooms are the ones to ask for.

🏠 **Althea Library** without rest., 27 High St, PL28 8BB, ℘ (01841) 532717, *enquiries@al thealibrary.co.uk,* Fax (01841) 532717 – ✸✸ 🅿. 🐾 𝘝𝘐𝘚𝘈. ✸✸
closed 22-27 December – **4 rm** ☲ – ♦♦82.00/116.00.
◆ Grade II listed former school library with very friendly feel. Neat terrace; homely break-fast room/lounge with food cooked on the Aga. Cosy, individually styled beamed rooms.

✕✕ **The Seafood** with rm, Riverside, PL28 8BY, ℘ (01841) 532700, *reservations@rick stein.com,* Fax (01841) 532942 – ✸✸, ▤ rest, 🅿. 🐾 𝘝𝘐𝘚𝘈
closed 24-26 December and 1 May – **Rest** - Seafood - (booking essential) a la carte 35.50/58.00 ♀ – **20 rm** ☲ ♦115.00 – ♦♦250.00.
◆ Bold artwork and a buzz of enthusiasm animate Rick Stein's converted granary and conservatory. Flavourful Cornish seafood. Stylish rooms in a cool modern palette.

✕✕ **St Petroc's** with rm, 4 New St, PL28 8EA, ℘ (01841) 532700, *reservations@rick stein.com,* Fax (01841) 532942, 🌳 – ✸✸ 🅿. 🐾 𝘝𝘐𝘚𝘈
closed 24-26 December and 1 May – **Rest** (booking essential) a la carte 33.00/33.90 ♀ – **10 rm** ☲ – ♦♦190.00/195.00.
◆ Handsome white-fronted house on a steep hill, where confidently prepared modern dishes with local, seasonal produce take centre stage. Stylish, individual bedrooms.

✕✕ **No.6,** 6 Middle St, PL28 8AP, ℘ (01841) 532093, *enquiries@number6inpadstow.co.uk,* Fax (01841) 533941 – ✸✸ ⟲ 20. 🐾 𝘝𝘐𝘚𝘈
closed 23-26 December, 2 January-9 February, Mondays from 1 November-31 May and Sunday – **Rest** (dinner only) a la carte 39.50/53.00 ♀.
◆ Targeting the top end of the market, this converted cottage has striking black and white floors, early evening as well as ambitious menus featuring elaborate, complex dishes.

✗ **Rick Stein's Café** with rm, 10 Middle St, PL28 8AP, ℰ (01841) 532700, *reservations@rickstein.com, Fax (01841) 532942* – ✦✦. ⓂⓈ
closed 24-26 December, 1 May and dinner Sunday and Monday November-February –
Rest (booking essential) 19.95 (dinner) and a la carte 22.25/29.70 – **3 rm** ☲ – ✦✦110.00/
115.00.
♦ Contemporary, unfussy bistro with modern, well-priced Mediterranean influenced cuisine employing the best local and seasonal ingredients. Well-appointed bedrooms.

✗ **Margot's**, 11 Duke St, PL28 8AB, ℰ (01841) 533441, *enquiries@margots.co.uk* – ✦✦. ⓂⓈ
ⒶⒺ ⓄⒾ 𝗩𝗜𝗦𝗔
closed January, Sunday-Monday and lunch Tuesday – Rest (dinner booking essential) 25.00
(dinner) and a la carte 24.00/33.00.
♦ Informal bistro-style restaurant with a friendly welcoming atmosphere. Varied menu
capitalises on finest, fresh, local ingredients and bold, characterful flavours.

at Little Petherick South : 3 m. on A 389 – ✉ Wadebridge.

🏠 **Molesworth Manor** without rest., PL27 7QT, ℰ (01841) 540292, *molesworthma
nor@aol.com*, ≤, 🖘 – ✦✦. 🅿. ✘
February-October – **9 rm** ☲ ✦60.00/65.00 – ✦✦80.00/105.00.
♦ Part 17C and 19C former rectory. Charming individual establishment with inviting country house atmosphere amid antique furniture and curios. Rooms furnished in period style.

⌂ **Old Mill House**, PL27 7QT, ℰ (01841) 540388, *enquiries@theoldmillhouse.com,
Fax (01841) 540406*, 🖘 – ✦✦. ⓂⓈ 𝗩𝗜𝗦𝗔. ✘
April-October – Rest (by arrangement) 29.50 – **7 rm** ☲ ✦70.00/80.00 – ✦✦80.00/115.00.
♦ Rural curios on display in a listed, family owned 16C cornmill with working water wheel.
Homely, individually decorated rooms, some overlooking the millrace and neat garden.

at St Issey South : 3½ m. on A 389 – ✉ Wadebridge.

⌂ **Olde Tredore House** ✎ without rest., PL27 7QS, North : ¼ m. off A 389 ℰ (01841)
540291, ≤, 🖘 – ✦✦. 🅿. ✘
closed Christmas and New Year – **3 rm** ☲ ✦60.00 – ✦✦65.00.
♦ Large, grand house in a tranquil and secluded location. Well-furnished guest areas and
bedrooms all in traditional country house style.

at St Merryn West : 2½ m. on B 3276 – ✉ Padstow.

✗✗ **Ripley's**, PL28 8NQ, ℰ (01841) 520179, *chefripley@aol.com* – ✦✦. ⓂⓈ 𝗩𝗜𝗦𝗔
✿ *restricted opening in January and closed 1 week Christmas, Sunday and Monday* – Rest
(booking essential) (dinner only) a la carte 29.00/36.50 ☲.
Spec. House terrine and rillette plate with prune and Armagnac jam. Breast of duck with
plum purée and Pinot Noir sauce. Passion fruit and nougat parfait.
♦ Obeys the first rule of cooking: don't over-elaborate when you have great ingredients.
Exposed beams and brickwork provide the ideal backdrop.

at Constantine Bay West : 4 m. by B 3276 – ✉ Padstow.

🏨 **Treglos** ✎, PL28 8JH, ℰ (01841) 520727, *stay@tregloshotel.com, Fax (01841) 521163*,
≤, 🖾, ▣, 🖘 – 🛗 ✦✦, 🗖 rest, 🕿 🕭 🖘 🅿. ⓂⓈ 𝗩𝗜𝗦𝗔
March-November – Rest (bar lunch Monday-Saturday)/dinner 26.00 ☲ – **39 rm** ☲
✦61.50/77.50 – ✦✦139.00/167.00, 3 suites.
♦ An extensive, family run building surrounded by garden. Facilities include games rooms,
children's play area and a lounge bar. Consistently decorated, bright, neat bedrooms.
Smart attire the code in very comfortable dining room.

PAIGNTON Torbay 503 J 32 *The West Country G.* – pop. 47 398.
See : Torbay★ - Kirkham House★ AC Y B.
Env. : Paignton Zoo★★ AC, SW : ½ m. by A 3022 AY *(see Plan of Torbay)* – Cockington★, N :
3 m. by A 3022 and minor roads.
🄱 The Esplanade (08707) 070 010, tourist.board@torbay.gov.uk.
London 226 – Exeter 26 – Plymouth 29.

Plan of Built up Area : see Torbay

Plan on next page

🏨 **Redcliffe**, 4 Marine Drive, TQ3 2NL, ℰ (01803) 526397, *redclfe@aol.com,
Fax (01803) 528030*, ≤ Torbay, 🖪, 🖾s, 🖾 heated, 🖾, 🖘 – 🛗, ✦✦ rest, 🗖 rest, 🅿 –
🖾 120. ⓂⓈ ⒶⒺ 𝗩𝗜𝗦𝗔. ✘   Y n
Rest (bar lunch Monday-Saturday)/dinner 17.50 and a la carte 19.50/25.50 – **68 rm** ☲
✦55.00/112.00 – ✦✦110.00/120.00.
♦ Smoothly run family owned hotel, handily set on the seafront, a favourite of auther Dick
Francis. Children's play area and putting green options. Airy, pine furnished rooms. Admire
the sea views from spacious, neat restaurant.

ENGLAND

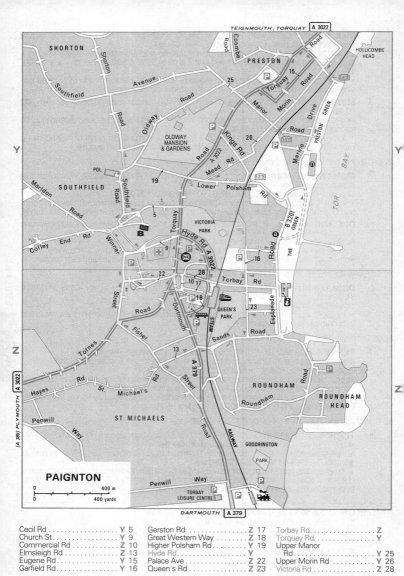

Palace, Esplanade Rd, TQ4 6BJ, ℘ (01803) 555121, info@palacepaignton.com, Fax (01803) 527974, ≤, ₤₅, ≡s, ◄, ☞ – ⧣, ✖ rest, ✆ ℙ. ◑◐ ㏈ **VISA**. ✖ **Y a** closed 2-27 January **Rest** (bar lunch)/dinner 16.75 ☿ – **54 rm** ☿ ✦40.00/66.00 – ✦✦80.00/112.00.

♦ Mid-19C hotel: its white façade dominates the esplanade. Large public areas: comfy sun lounge has bay views. Smart, up-to-date leisure facilities. Well-equipped bedrooms. Comfortable dining room with traditional appeal.

PAINSWICK Glos. 503 504 N 28 Great Britain G. – pop. 1 666.

See : Town★.

London 107 – Bristol 35 – Cheltenham 10 – Gloucester 7.

🏛 **Painswick** ⅀, Kemps Lane, GL6 6YB, Southeast : ½ m. by Bisley St, St Marys St, The Cross and Tibbiwell Lane ℰ (01452) 812160, reservations@painswickhotel.com, Fax (01452) 814059, 🝮, ☞ – ⇌ ☏ 🄿. 🐠 🄰🄴 𝓥𝓘𝓢𝓐

Rest (closed Monday) 30.00/35.00 and a la carte 35.00/39.50 ⅀ – Ⲍ 17.00 – **19 rm** ✦160.00/180.00 – ✦✦260.00.

◆ Tranquil, extended Palladian rectory in pretty village. Well-appointed rooms, most charming in the old house, mix modern and period furniture; good views from upper floors. Panelled dining room; terrace by croquet lawn.

↟ **Cardynham House** without rest., The Cross, GL6 6XX, by Bisley St and St Marys St ℰ (01452) 814006, info@cardynham.co.uk, Fax (01452) 812321 – 🐠 🄰🄴 𝓥𝓘𝓢𝓐 . ⲷ

9 rm Ⲍ ✦50.00/59.00 – ✦✦89.00.

◆ Part 15C house with a stylish, relaxed, even Bohemian feel to its elegant, firelit lounge. Themed, uniquely styled rooms: eight have four-poster beds, one a private pool.

PARKGATE Mersey. 502 503 K 24.

London 212 – Birkenhead 10 – Chester 16 – Liverpool 12.

✕ **Marsh Cat,** 1 Mostyn Sq, CH64 6SL, ℰ (0151) 336 1963, info@marshcat.com, Fax (0151) 336 4998, ≤ – ▤. 𝓥𝓘𝓢𝓐

closed 25-26 December and 1 January – **Rest** (booking essential) a la carte 13.45/26.75 ⅀.

◆ Brightly painted, lively village bistro overlooking Wirral marshes. British, Cajun, French, Jamaican and Oriental flavours in worldwide repertoire - ask about set menus.

PARKHAM Devon 503 H 31 – ✉ Bideford.

London 229 – Barnstaple 14 – Exeter 87 – Plymouth 58.

🏠 **Penhaven Country House** ⅀, Rectory Lane, EX39 5PL, ℰ (01237) 451711, reception@penhaven.co.uk, Fax (01237) 451878, ☞, 🝮 – ⇌ rest, 🄿. 🐠 🄰🄴 𝓥𝓘𝓢𝓐

Rest (dinner only and Sunday lunch)/dinner a la carte 20.95/27.25 **s.** – **12 rm** (dinner included) Ⲍ – ✦✦140.00/160.00.

◆ Ducks and badgers potter around grounds of this old rectory, traditional from the cosy chairs and stone fireplace in the lounge to well-kept rooms, seven in cottage annexes. Dining room's tall conservatory windows overlook gardens and woods.

PARTRIDGE GREEN W. Sussex 504 T 31 – ✉ Horsham.

London 47 – Horsham 9.5 – Worthing 16.

🍽 **The Green Man Inn,** Church Rd, Jolesfield, RH13 8JT, on B 2135 ℰ (01403) 710250, info@thegreenman.org, Fax (01403) 713212, 🝤 – ⇌ 🄿. 🐠 🄰🄴 𝓥𝓘𝓢𝓐 . ⲷ

Rest (closed Sunday dinner and Monday except Bank Holidays) 14.95 (lunch) and a la carte 18.00/32.00 ⅀.

◆ Appealing 19C roadside pub with pleasant terrace. Stylish interior: rustic overtones and many Sussex prints. Locally sourced produce: fresh cooking with renowned tapas option.

PATCHWAY South Gloucestershire 503 504 M 29 – see Bristol.

PATELEY BRIDGE N. Yorks. 502 O 21 Great Britain G. – pop. 2 504 – ✉ Harrogate.

Exc. : Fountains Abbey★★★ AC - Studley Royal AC (≤★ from Anne Boleyn's Seat) - Fountains Hall (Façade★), NE : 8½ m. by B 6265.

🅳 18 High St ℰ (08453) 890179.

London 225 – Leeds 28 – Middlesbrough 46 – York 32.

at Ramsgill-in-Nidderdale Northwest : 5 m. by Low Wath Rd – ✉ Harrogate.

✕✕ **Yorke Arms** (Frances Atkins) ⅀ with rm, HG3 5RL, ℰ (01423) 755243, enquiries@yorke-arms.co.uk, Fax (01423) 755330, 🝤, ☞ – ⇌ 🄿. 🐠 🄰🄴 ⓞ 𝓥𝓘𝓢𝓐 . ⲷ
ⓈⓈ
Rest (closed Sunday dinner for non-residents) 21.00/50.00 and a la carte 30.00/50.00 ⅀ ⅋ – **14 rm** (dinner included) Ⲍ ✦120.00/150.00 – ✦✦150.00/240.00.

Spec. Potted beef, ham hock and foie gras terrine, asparagus velouté. Cheese soufflé, seared scallops, vanilla and salsify. Blanquette of mutton, black pudding, cider and apples.

◆ Part 17C former shooting lodge, now a quintessentially English Inn by Gouthwaite reservoir. Classically based seasonal dishes with a modern touch. Lavishly furnished bedrooms.

PATRICK BROMPTON *N. Yorks.* **502** P 21 – ⊠ *Bedale.*
London 242 – Newcastle upon Tyne 58 – York 43.

🏛 **Elmfield House** ⌂, Arrathorne, DL8 1NE, Northwest : 2 ¼ m. by A 684 on Richmond rd
𝒫 (01677) 450558, *stay@elmfieldhouse.co.uk, Fax (01677) 450557*, 🐟, 🌳, 🏊 – ⇆ 👆 **P.**
🐾 🗚 **VISA** . ⌘
closed 24-26 December, 31 December and 1 January – **Rest** *(booking essential) (residents
only) (dinner only)* 18.50 – **7 rm** ☇ ♦45.00 – ♦♦78.00.
♦ Spacious, neatly fitted accommodation in a peaceful, personally run hotel, set in acres
of gardens and open countryside. Try your luck at the adjacent fishing lake. Tasty, home-
cooked meals.

PAULERSPURY *Northants.* **503 504** R 27 – *see Towcester.*

PAXFORD *Glos.* **503 504** O 27 – *see Chipping Campden.*

PAYHEMBURY *Devon – see Honiton.*

PEASMARSH *E. Sussex* **504** W 31 – *see Rye.*

PEMBRIDGE *Herefordshire* **503** L 27.
London 162 – Hereford 15.5 – Leominster 7.5.

⌂ **Lowe Farm,** HR6 9JD, West : 3 ¼ m. by A 44 following signs through Marston village
𝒫 (01544) 388395, *wiliams–family@lineone.net, Fax (01544) 388395*, ≤, 🌳, 🏊 – ⇆ **P.**
⌘
– **Rest** *(by arrangement)* 21.00 – **5 rm** ☇ ♦37.00 – ♦♦70.00.
♦ Working farm: farmhouse dates from 13C; renovated barn from 14C with pleasant
lounge and countryside views. Rooms in house and barn are cosy, comfortable and of a
good size. Dining room boasts chunky pine tables, exposed brick and beams.

PEMBURY *Kent* **504** U 30 – *see Royal Tunbridge Wells.*

PENRITH *Cumbria* **501 502** L 19 – *pop. 14 471.*
🏌 *Salkeld Rd* 𝒫 (01768) 891919.
🅳 *Robinsons School, Middlegate* 𝒫 (01768) 867466, *pen.tic@eden.gov.uk – Rheged, Red-
hills, Penrith* 𝒫 (01768) 860034.
London 290 – Carlisle 24 – Kendal 31 – Lancaster 48.

🏨 **North Lakes,** Ullswater Rd, CA11 8QT, South : 1 m. by A 592 at junction 40 of M 6
𝒫 (01768) 868111, *nlakes@shirehotels.com, Fax (01768) 868291*, 🌳, 🏖, **I₅**, 😄, 🖥, 🔲 – 🕸
⇆ 📞 👆 ⚓ **P.** – 🔬 200. **🐾** 🗚 ⓪ **VISA** . ⌘
The Martindale : **Rest** *(bar lunch Saturday and Sunday)* 19.00 *(lunch) and dinner a la carte*
24.95/37.00 **s.** ♀ – **84 rm** ☇ ♦117.00/123.00 – ♦♦155.00/195.00.
♦ Comprehensive leisure club, up-to-date meeting suites and comfortable, usefully ap-
pointed rooms in this group hotel; practically located and ideal for the working traveller.
Medieval tapestry reproduction is restaurant's focal point.

⌂ **Brooklands** *without rest.,* 2 Portland Pl, CA11 7QN, 𝒫 (01768) 863395, *enquiries@broo
klandsguesthouse.com, Fax (01768) 863395* – ⇆, **🐾** ⓪ **VISA** . ⌘
closed 1 week Christmas – **7 rm** ☇ ♦30.00/60.00 – ♦♦65.00/70.00.
♦ Traditonal Victorian terraced house a minute's walk from the shops: many original features restored. Pleasantly furnished breakfast room. Locally made pine enhances bedrooms.

at Temple Sowerby *East :* 6¾ *m. on A 66 –* ⊠ *Penrith.*

🏨 **Temple Sowerby House,** CA10 1RZ, 𝒫 (01768) 361578, *stay@templesowerby.com,
Fax (01768) 361958*, 🌳 – ⇆ **P. 🐾** 🗚 **VISA**
closed 10 days Christmas – **Rest** *(dinner only) a la carte* 26.70/34.00 – **12 rm** ☇ ♦85.00 –
♦♦115.00/165.00.
♦ Part 16C, part 18C listed building with Georgian frontage and walled garden, run with
enthusiasm and charm. Individually styled rooms exude either a period or rustic ambience.
Elegant dining in 18C part of the house.

at Yanwath *Southwest :* 2½ *m. by A 6 and B 5320 –* ⊠ *Penrith.*

🍴 **The Yanwath Gate Inn,** CA10 2LF, 𝒫 (01768) 862386, *enquiries@yanwathgate.com,
Fax (01768) 899892* – ⇆ rest, **P. 🐾** 🗚 ⓪ **VISA**
Rest *a la carte* 24.00/36.85.
♦ Charming, characterful 17C inn with intimate, open-fired interior. Adjacent dining room
with panelled walls. Locally sourced dishes full of organic and free-range ingredients.

ENGLAND

at Tirril Southwest : 3 m. by A 6 on B 5320 – ⊠ Penrith.

🏠 **The Queens Head Inn** with rm, CA10 2JF, ℰ (01768) 863219, bookings@queen sheadinn.co.uk, Fax (01768) 863243 – ❧❤ **P**. **MO** **VISA**. ❧
Rest a la carte 15.00/30.00 – **7 rm** ⊇ ✦40.00 – ✦✦70.00.
◆ Characterful 18C inn once owned by the Wordsworth family; open fires, heavily beamed. Local produce features prominently on tried-and-tested menus. Cosy bedrooms.

at Newbiggin West : 3½ m. by A 66 – ⊠ Penrith.

🏠 **The Old School**, CA11 0HT, ℰ (01768) 483709, info@theold-school.com, Fax (01768) 483709, ⊕ – ❧❤ **P**. **MO** **VISA**
closed 11-18 June and Christmas – **Rest** (by arrangement) 20.00 – **3 rm** ⊇ ✦35.00/55.00 – ✦✦60.00/70.00.
◆ Well sited off two major roads, this 19C former school house has been tastefully converted with an open-fired lounge and rooms individually decorated to a high standard.

PENZANCE Cornwall 503 D 33 The West Country G. – pop. 20 255.

See : Town★ - Outlook★★★ – Western Promenade (≤★★★) YZ – National Lighthouse Centre★ AC Y – Chapel St★ Y – Maritime Museum★ AC Y M1 – Penlee House Gallery and Museum★, AC.

Env. : St Buryan★★ (church tower★★), SW : 5 m. by A 30 and B 3283 – Penwith★★ – Trengwainton Garden★★, NW : 2 m. – Sancreed - Church★★ (Celtic Crosses★★) – Carn Euny★, W : 3½ m. by A 30 Z – St Michael's Mount★★ (≤★★★), E : 4 m. by B 3311 – Y – and A 30 – Gulval★ (Church★), NE : 1 m. – Ludgvan★ (Church★), NE : 3½ m. by A 30 – Chysauster Village★, N : 3½ m. by A 30, B 3311 and minor rd – Newlyn★ - Pilchard Works★, SW : 1½ m. by B 3315 Z - Lanyon Quoit★, NW : 3½ m. by St Clare Street – Men-an-Tol★, NW : 5 m. by B 3312 – Madron Church★, NW : 1½ m. by St Clare Street Y.

Exc. : Morvah (≤★★★), NW : 6½ m. by St Clare Street Y – Zennor (Church★), NW : 6 m. by B 3311 Y – Prussia Cove★, E : 8 m. by B 3311 – Y – and A 394 – Land's End★ (cliff scenery★★★), SW : 10 m. by A 30 Z – Porthcurno★, SW : 8½ m. by A 30, B 3283 and minor rd.

Access to the Isles of Scilly by helicopter, British International Heliport (01736) 364296, Fax (01736) 363871.

≈ to the Isles of Scilly (Hugh Town) (Isles of Scilly Steamship Co. Ltd) (summer only) (approx. 2 h 40 mn).

🛈 Station Rd ℰ (01736) 362207.
London 319 – Exeter 113 – Plymouth 77 – Taunton 155.

Plan on next page

🏨 **Hotel Penzance,** Britons Hill, TR18 3AE, ℰ (01736) 363117, enquiries@hotelpen zance.com, Fax (01736) 350970, ≤, 🍽, ⤬ heated, ⊕ – ❧❤, ▤ rest, ✆ **P**. **MO** **AE** **VISA**
Y c
Bay : Rest (booking essential for non-residents) (dinner only and lunch in summer) a la carte 20.00/30.00 – **24 rm** ⊇ ✦55.00/92.00 – ✦✦99.00/155.00.
◆ Well-established hotel with modern interior in elevated spot with views to St. Michaels Mount. Comfortable lounge. Bedrooms are immaculately kept and equipped with mod cons. Bright, modern restaurant with local artwork and bar.

🏛 **The Abbey** without rest., Abbey St, TR18 4AR, ℰ (01736) 366906, hotel@theabbeyon line.com, Fax (01736) 351163, ⊕ – ❧❤ **P**. **MO** **VISA**
Y u
closed 25 December – **6 rm** ⊇ ✦65.00/150.00 – ✦✦145.00/180.00, 2 suite.
◆ Powder blue painted 17C house with lovely Victorian gardens. Attractive antique furnishings include historical pictures. Country house atmosphere and characterful bedrooms.

🏛 **Beachfield,** The Promenade, TR18 4NW, ℰ (01736) 362067, office@beachfield.co.uk, Fax (01736) 331100, ≤ – ❧❤. **MO** **AE** **VISA**
Z a
closed Christmas-New Year – **Rest** (dinner only) 22.95 and a la carte 19.00/31.00 s. – **18 rm** ⊇ ✦52.50/82.50 – ✦✦105.00/125.00.
◆ Classic seaside hotel with good views. Well-kept public areas include traditional lounge. Comfy bedrooms are well maintained and have a neat, bright feel. Traditional, varied menus, featuring fish specials.

🏠 **Chy-An-Mor** without rest., 15 Regent Terrace, TR18 4DW, ℰ (01736) 363441, info@chyanmor.co.uk, Fax (01736) 363441, ≤, ⊕ – ❧❤ **P**. **MO** **VISA**. ❧
Y e
mid February-October – **10 rm** ⊇ ✦35.00/65.00 – ✦✦73.00/87.00.
◆ Located on a terrace of houses overlooking the promenade. Thoroughly well kept throughout. Comfy, well-furnished bedrooms. Wake up to a good choice at breakfast.

🏠 **Estoril** without rest., 46 Morrab Rd, TR18 4EX, ℰ (01736) 362468, enquiries@estorilho tel.co.uk, Fax (01736) 367471 – ❧❤. **MO** **VISA**. ❧
Y o
9 rm ⊇ ✦32.00/50.00 – ✦✦64.00/70.00.
◆ In a quiet suburb near Morrab and Penlee Gardens, a characterful bay windowed Victorian house with a comfortable, traditional lounge and spotless rooms at modest rates.

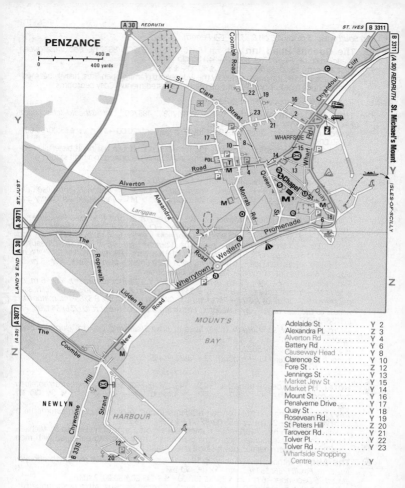

XX
❀
The Abbey (Tunnicliffe), Abbey St, TR18 4AR, ℘ (01736) 330680, *kinga@theabbeyon
line.com* – ✕ ≡ ◫◎ ◭ **VISA**
　　　　　　　　　Y u
closed Tuesday-Thursday lunch, Monday and mid December-February – **Rest** 23.00 and
dinner a la carte 29.50/41.50 ♀.
Spec. Seared scallops with chilli jam and herb couscous. Rack of lamb with sweetbreads
and ceps. Chocolate tart with Bailey's ice cream.
　◆ Enter into vivid bar/lounge and watch chefs at work via wall-mounted TV! Upstairs
restaurant has dramatic mono photos, and the unerringly precise cooking is equally of
note.

XX
Harris's, 46 New St, TR18 2LZ, ℘ (01736) 364408, *contact@harrissrestaurant.co.uk*,
Fax (01736) 333273 – ✕ ◫◎ ◭ **VISA**
　　　　　　　　　Y a
closed 3 weeks in winter, 25-26 December, 1 January, Monday in winter and Sunday – **Rest**
a la carte 28.95/43.50 ♀.
　◆ Friendly and well-established restaurant, tucked away on a cobbled street. Brightly
decorated interior with smart linen clothed tables. Cornish menu with a French
overlay.

XX **The Summer House** with rm, Cornwall Terrace, TR18 4HL, ✆ (01736) 363744, *reception@summerhouse-cornwall.com, Fax (01736) 360959,* – **P**. VISA. Z s
31 March-4 November – **Rest** *(closed Monday-Wednesday)* (dinner only) 28.50 – **5 rm** ★85.00/110.00 – ★★90.00/110.00.
◆ Listed Regency rooms and restaurant in bright blues and yellows. Relaxed, friendly ambience. Mediterranean influenced seafood; modern and flavourful. Leafy patio garden.

X **The Lime Tree,** Trevelyan House, 16 Chapel St, TR18 4AQ, ✆ (01736) 332555, *bookings@the-lime-tree.co.uk, Fax (01736) 332555* – . AE VISA Y s
closed last 2 weeks January and Sunday-Monday – **Rest** (light lunch) a la carte 16.95/27.85.
◆ Central three-storey Georgian townhouse comprising two dining rooms, comfy lounge and tiny lunchtime roof terrace. Adventurous dinner menus and good value lunches of interest.

X **Bakehouse,** Old Bakehouse Lane, Chapel St, TR18 4AE, ✆ (01736) 331331, *carrjasper@aol.com* – . VISA Y z
closed 25-26 December, 1 January and Sunday – **Rest** (booking essential) (dinner only) a la carte 22.45/31.95 ♀.
◆ Penzance's original bakery, now a stylish restaurant on two floors, with old bakers oven in situ downstairs. Modern menus boast good choice of local seafood and produce.

at Drift *Southwest : 2½ m. on A 30 – Z – ✉ Penzance.*

Rose Farm without rest., Chyenhal, Buryas Bridge, TR19 6AN, Southwest : ¾ m. on Chyenhal rd ✆ (01736) 731808, *penny@rosefarmcornwall.co.uk, Fax (01736) 731808,* – **P**. VISA
closed 24-25 December – **3 rm** ★40.00/45.00 – ★★60.00.
◆ In the heart of the countryside, a tranquil working farm. Cosy, rustic farmhouse ambience with neatly kept bedrooms including large barn room.

Look out for red symbols, indicating particularly pleasant establishments.

PERRANUTHNOE *Cornwall* 503 D 33 – *see Marazion.*

PERSHORE *Worcs.* 503 504 N 27 – *pop. 7 104.*
London 106 – Birmingham 33 – Worcester 8.

The Barn without rest., Pensham Hill House, Pensham, WR10 3HA, Southeast : 1 m. by B 4084 ✆ (01386) 555270, *ghorton@pensham-barn.co.uk, Fax (01386) 552894,* ←, – **P**
3 rm ★50.00 – ★★85.00.
◆ Stylish barn renovation in enviable hillside location. Attractive open-plan lounge and breakfast area with exposed roof timbers. Rooms individually styled to a high standard.

XX **Belle House,** Bridge St, WR10 1AJ, ✆ (01386) 555055, *mail@belle-house.co.uk, Fax (01386) 555377* – 36. AE VISA
closed first 2 weeks January, 1 week August, 25-26 December, Sunday and Monday – **Rest** 18.00/26.00 ♀.
◆ 16C and 18C high street building with some very characterful parts, including heavily beamed bar. Accomplished cooking on modern menus using carefully sourced ingredients.

PETERBOROUGH *Peterborough* 502 504 T 26 *Great Britain G.* – *pop. 136 292.*
See : *Cathedral★★ AC* Y.
18 Thorpe Wood, Nene Parkway ✆ (01733) 267701, BX – *18 Peterborough Milton, Milton Ferry ✆ (01733) 380489,* BX – *18 Orton Meadows, Ham Lane ✆ (01733) 237478,* BX.
3-5 Minster Precinct ✆ (01733) 452336.
London 85 – Cambridge 35 – Leicester 41 – Lincoln 51.

Plan on next page

Orton Hall, The Village, Orton Longueville, PE2 7DN, Southwest : 2½ m. by Oundle Rd (A 605) ✆ (01733) 391111, *reception@ortonhall.co.uk, Fax (01733) 231912,* – **P** – 120. AE VISA BX c
The Huntly Restaurant : **Rest** *(closed 24-26 and 31 December)* (bar lunch Monday-Saturday)/dinner 27.00 and a la carte 28.00/36.00 – 13.00 – **65 rm** ★75.00/95.00 – ★★150.00.
◆ Smartly run, part 17C house in 20 acres, once the seat of the Marquess of Huntly. Spacious, comfortable rooms: State rooms particularly impressive. Pub in former stables. Pleasantly set dining room offers richly varied cuisine.

ENGLAND

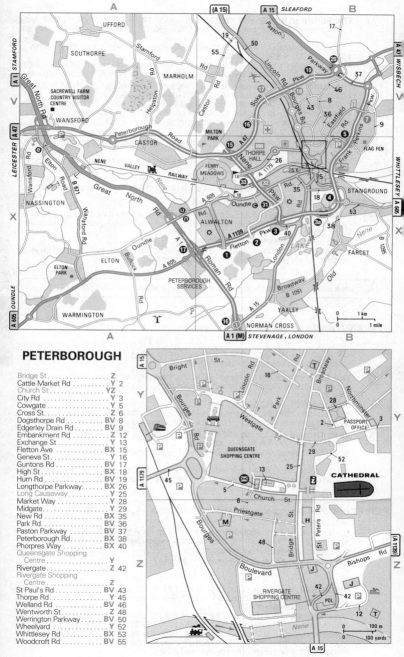

PETERBOROUGH

at Alwalton *Southwest : 5¾ m. on Oundle Rd (A 605) –* ✉ *Peterborough.*

🏨 **Peterborough Marriott**, Peterborough Business Park, Lynch Wood, PE2 6GB, (opposite East of England Showground) ☎ (0870) 4007258, *events.peterborough@marriottho tels.co.uk, Fax (0870) 4007358,* ⑤, ⇔, 🖥, 🌇 – ⇄ 🍽 🛏 ⬛ 🛠 – 🔺 300. ⬛ 🅰🅴 ⓐ ⬛ 𝑽𝑰𝑺𝑨 ⬚
AX u
Rest (buffet lunch)/dinner 22.00 and a la carte 23.65/32.95 s. 🍷 – 🍽 14.95 – **161 rm** ✸85.000/105.00 – ✸✸95.000/115.00, 2 suites.
* Modern group hotel located opposite the East of England Showground providing well-equipped bedrooms, smart leisure club and plenty of up-to-date conference space. Formal dining with international range.

🏨 **Express by Holiday Inn** without rest., East of England Way, PE2 6HE, ☎ (01733) 284450, *expressby@oriel-leisure.co.uk, Fax (0870) 7201198* – ⇄ ✆ 🛠 ⬛ – 🔺 25. ⬛
🅰🅴 ⓐ 𝑽𝑰𝑺𝑨
AX n
80 rm ✸69.00 – ✸✸75.00.
* Purpose-built hotel under group management, providing trim, bright rooms, spacious and practically designed. A popular choice for East of England Show.

at Wansford *West : 8½ m. by A 47 –* ✉ *Peterborough.*

🏨 **Haycock**, PE8 6JA, ☎ (01780) 782223, *sales@thehaycock.co.uk, Fax (01780) 783031,* 🌇,
🍽 – ⇄ ✆ 🛠 ⬛ – 🔺 250. ⬛ 🅰🅴 ⓐ 𝑽𝑰𝑺𝑨
AX e
Bentley : Rest *(closed Sunday-Wednesday)* (set menu only at dinner) a la carte approx 19.15/35.15 🍷 – **Orchards : Rest** *(closed Sunday-Wednesday and Saturday lunch)* 15.95/45.00 – 🍽 12.50 – **48 rm** ✸85.00/50.00 – ✸✸119.00.
* Extended part 17C coaching inn with neat gardens by the River Nene. Traditionally cosy, flagged lounge. Bedrooms, in a stylish theme, exude a good feeling of comfort. Orchards is breezy conservatory dining room. More formal dining in Bentley.

If breakfast is included the 🍽 symbol appears after the number of rooms.

PETERSFIELD *Hants.* **504** R 30.
London 60 – Brighton 45 – Portsmouth 21 – *Southampton 34.*

🏠 **Langrish House** ♨, Langrish, GU32 1RN, West : 3 ½ m. by A 272 ☎ (01730) 266941, *frontdesk@langrishhouse.co.uk, Fax (01730) 260543,* 🌇, ♨ – 🛠 ⬛ – 🔺 60. ⬛ ⓐ 𝑽𝑰𝑺𝑨
– **Rest** (lunch by arrangement)/dinner 29.95 – **13 rm** 🍽 ✸72.00/90.00 – ✸✸94.50/145.00.
* Peaceful country house in wooded grounds, dating from 17C and family owned for seven generations. Characterful lounge in old Civil War cellars. Bright bedroom décor. Modish cuisine, proudly served.

XXX **JSW** (Watkins), 20 Dragon St, GU31 4JJ, ☎ (01730) 262030, 🌇 – ⬛ ⟳ 20. ⬛ 𝑽𝑰𝑺𝑨
❀ *closed 2 weeks Christmas and New Year, 2 weeks August, Sunday and Monday* – **Rest** 29.50/40.50 🍷 🖺.
Spec. Scallops with pea purée and asparagus. Suckling pig cooked two ways. Trio of elderflower with raspberries.
* Sympathetically restored coaching inn with attractive enclosed rear courtyard for summer dining. Contemporary cooking: flavourful, well-sourced and confident.

PETERSTOW *Herefordshire* **503 504** M 28 – *see Ross-on-Wye.*

PETWORTH *W. Sussex* **504** S 31 *Great Britain G.* – *pop. 2 298.*
See : *Petworth House*★★ *AC.*
🛆 *Osiers, London Rd* ☎ (01798) 344097.
London 54 – Brighton 31 – Portsmouth 33.

🏠 **Old Railway Station** without rest., GU28 0JF, South : 1 ½ m. off A 285 ☎ (01798) 342346, *info@old-station.co.uk, Fax (01798) 343066,* 🌇 – ⇄ ⬛ ⬛ 🅰🅴 𝑽𝑰𝑺𝑨 ⬚
closed 24-26 and 31 December and 1 January – **8 rm** 🍽 ✸52.00/107.00 –
✸✸108.00/160.00.
* Elegant converted 1894 waiting room and ticket hall, full of charming details from the age of steam. Six rooms in handsome Pullman carriages. Summer breakfast on platform.

XX **The Grove Inn**, Grove Lane, GU28 0HY, South : ½ m. by High St and Pulborough rd ☎ (01798) 343659, 🌇, ♨ – ⇄ ⬛ ⬛ 🅰🅴 ⓐ 𝑽𝑰𝑺𝑨
closed 8-14 January, Sunday dinner and Monday – **Rest** (light lunch)/dinner a la carte 21.75/33.70.
* Restored farmhouse: conservatory bar and beamed restaurant. Dinner menu with modern influence, simpler lunch menu. Attentive service.

🏠 **Badgers** with rm, Coultershaw Bridge, GU28 0JF, South : 1 ½ m. on A 285 ℰ (01798) 342651, 🍴 – 📺 📶 📶⊖ 💳 ❄
closed 25 December and Bank Holidays – **Rest** *(closed Sunday dinner in winter)* a la carte 13.00/29.00 – **3 rm** ☲ ✸80.00 – ✸✸80.00.
♦ Lovely pub next to Old Railway Station. Beautiful oak panelled bar has old photos and 'badger and honey' theme. Log fire; intimate alcove. Eclectic, robust menus. Comfy rooms.

at Halfway Bridge *West : 3 m. on A 272 –* ✉ *Petworth.*

🏠 **The Halfway Bridge Inn** with rm, GU28 9BP, ℰ (01798) 861281, *hwb@thesussex pub.co.uk*, 🌼 – ❄⊷ rm, 📶 📶⊖ 🅰🅴 ⓞ 💳
closed 25 December – **Rest** a la carte 22.00/35.00 – **6 rm** ☲ ✸65.00/90.00 – ✸✸110.00/140.00.
♦ Affable staff, balanced cooking and fine local ales in an instantly likeable 17C coaching inn. Brick interior festooned with hops, warmed by stoves and log fires. Comfy rooms.

at Lickfold *Northwest : 6 m. by A 272 –* ✉ *Petworth.*

🏠 **Lickfold Inn**, GU28 9EY, ℰ (01798) 861285, *thelickfoldinn@aol.com*, 🍴, 🌼 – 📶 📶⊖ 💳 ❄
closed 25-26 December – **Rest** *(closed Sunday dinner and Monday except Bank Holiday Monday)* a la carte 25.00/30.00 ☲.
♦ Handsome, oak-beamed pub in a quiet Downs village. Cosy ambience and easygoing, helpful staff. Concise modern repertoire, with a Mediterranean twist, from wood-fired ovens.

> Red = Pleasant. Look for the red ✗ and 🏠 symbols.

PHILLEIGH *Cornwall –* ✉ *Truro.*
London 273 – Falmouth 26 – Truro 14.

🏠 **Roseland Inn**, TR2 5NB, ℰ (01872) 580254, *stallardsimon@yahoo.co.uk*, Fax (01872) 580966 – 📶
closed 25 December – **Rest** a la carte 14.00/25.00 ☲.
♦ Family run, rurally set 16C inn with lovely rustic interior. Exposed beams, solid stone floor and open fires aid relaxation. Wide-ranging menu with Cornish base.

PICKERING *N. Yorks.* **502** R 21 – *pop. 6 616.*
🛈 *The Ropery* ℰ (01751) 473791.
London 237 – Middlesbrough 43 – Scarborough 19 – York 25.

🏠 **White Swan Inn**, Market Pl, YO18 7AA, ℰ (01751) 472288, *welcome@white-swan.co.uk*, Fax (01751) 475554 – ❄⊷ ☎ 📶 📶⊖ 🅰🅴 💳 ❄
Rest – *(see The Restaurant below)* – 18 rm ☲ ✸89.00 – ✸✸169.00, 3 suites.
♦ Personally run former coaching halt in a popular market town. Welcoming, antique filled sitting room and comfortable, stylish bedrooms full of individual details.

🏠 **17 Burgate** without rest., 17 Burgate, YO18 7AU, ℰ (01751) 473463, *info@17-bur gate.co.uk*, Fax (01751) 473463, 🌼 – ❄⊷ 📺 📶 📶⊖ 💳 ❄
5 rm ☲ ✸65.00/75.00 – ✸✸85.00/99.00.
♦ Painstakingly restored 17C town house, the décor smoothly spanning 400 years. Sitting room bar; sizzling breakfasts; superbly appointed rooms, two with larger seating areas.

🏠 **Bramwood**, 19 Hall Garth, YO18 7AW, ℰ (01751) 474066, *bramwood@fsbdial.co.uk*, 🌼 – ❄⊷ 📶 📶⊖ 💳 ❄
closed January – **Rest** *(by arrangement)* 17.50 – 8 rm ☲ ✸32.00/50.00 – ✸✸70.00.
♦ Georgian town house with sheltered garden. Personally run with curios of rural life dotted around a firelit lounge. Cosy bedrooms in homely, cottagey style.

🏠 **Old Manse**, Middleton Rd, YO18 8AL, ℰ (01751) 476484, *info@oldmansepickering.co.uk*, Fax (01751) 477124, 🌼 – ❄⊷ 📶 📶⊖ 💳
Rest 21.00 ☲ – **10 rm** ☲ ✸35.00/55.00 – ✸✸75.00/85.00.
♦ A welcoming ambience and modestly priced rooms, spacious and spotless, make this personally run house an ideal base for touring the moors. Secluded rear garden and orchard. Informal conservatory dining room.

✗✗ **The Restaurant** (at White Swan Inn), Market Pl, YO18 7AA, ℰ (01751) 472288, *wel come@white-swan.co.uk*, Fax (01751) 475554, 🍴 – ❄⊷ 📶 📶⊖ 🅰🅴 💳
Rest a la carte 17.90/36.15.
♦ Set in the coaching inn, with comfy lounge for pre-prandials. Restaurant boasts roaring fire, tapestry screens, modern décor, and modish menus with local produce to the fore.

at Levisham *Northeast : 6½ m. by A 169 –* ✉ *Pickering.*

⌂ **The Moorlands Country House** ⌖, YO18 7NL, ℘ (01751) 460229, *ronaldoleo nardo@aol.com, Fax (01751) 460470,* ≤, ☞ – ✦✕ **P**, **VISA**, ✦
March-November, minimum 2 night stay – **Rest** (by arrangement) 36.00 – **7 rm** ☐
✦60.00/100.00 – ✦✦110.00/140.00.
 ◆ Restored 19C house with attractive gardens in the heart of the North York Moors National Park. There are fine views to be enjoyed here. Rooms furnished to high standard. Traditional, home-cooked meals in pretty dining room.

at Marton *West : 5¼ m. by A 170 –* ✉ *Pickering.*

⌂ **The Appletree,** YO62 6RD, ℘ (01751) 431457, *appletreeinn@supanet.com, Fax (01751) 430190,* ☞, ☞ – ✦✕ **P**, **OO** **VISA**, ✦
closed 2 weeks January and 25 December – **Rest** (closed Monday-Tuesday) a la carte 20.00/35.00 ☐.
 ◆ Large, part 18C inn in quiet village. Plenty of recently added beams. Small, comfy, sofa-strewn lounge. The modern British cooking provides originality and interest.

at Middleton *Northwest : 1½ m. on A 170 –* ✉ *Pickering.*

⌂ **The Leas** ⌖, Nova Lane, YO18 8PN, North : 1 m. via Church Lane ℘ (01751) 472129, *enquiries@cottageleashotel.co.uk, Fax (01751) 474930,* ≤, ☞, ☞ – ✦✕ **P**, **OO** **AE** **VISA**
Rest (lunch by arrangement)/dinner a la carte 21.50/33.50 – **17 rm** ☐ ✦44.50/54.50 –
✦✦68.00/88.00.
 ◆ Get away from it all to an extended period house in the hills above Middleton. Large lounge with open fire. Simple, sizeable rooms looking to quiet, unspoilt fields. Bistro menus in heavily wood-furnished restaurant.

at Sinnington *Northwest : 4 m. by A 170 –* ✉ *York.*

⌂ **Fox and Hounds** with rm, Main St, YO62 6SQ, ℘ (01751) 431577, *foxhoundsinn@easy net.co.uk, Fax (01751) 432791,* ☞ – ✦✕ **P**, **OO** **VISA**
closed 25-26 December – **Rest** a la carte 20.00/28.00 ☐ – **10 rm** ☐ ✦49.00/69.00 –
✦✦80.00/120.00.
 ◆ At the heart of this sleepy village on the river Seven, an extended coaching house, beamed and panelled in ancient oak. Well-proportioned, cottagey rooms; hearty breakfasts. Modern restaurant or rustic bar offer dining options.

PICKHILL *N. Yorks.* **502** P 21 – ✉ *Thirsk.*
London 229 – Leeds 41 – Middlesbrough 30 – York 34.

⌂ **Nags Head Country Inn,** YO7 4JG, ℘ (01845) 567391, *reservations@nagsheadpick hill.freeserve.co.uk, Fax (01845) 567212,* ☞, ☞ – ✦✕ rest, **P** – ⌂ 30. **OO** **VISA**
closed 25th December **Rest** a la carte 17.95/26.95 ☐ – **14 rm** ☐ ✦55.00 – ✦✦80.00/90.00, 1 suite.
 ◆ Atmospheric 300 year old inn in an ancient hamlet, an easy drive to Thirsk and Ripon races. Neat rooms in soft floral fabrics. Over 800 ties on display in the rustic bar. Rural restaurant adorned with bookshelves and patterned rugs.

PILLERTON HERSEY *Warks.*
London 91 – Birmingham 33 – Stratford-upon-Avon 8.

⌂ **Dockers Barn Farm** ⌖ without rest., Oxhill Bridle Rd, CV35 0QB, Southeast : 1 m.
℘ (01926) 640475, *jwhoward@onetel.com, Fax (01926) 641747 –* ✦✕ **P**
closed 4 days Christmas – **3 rm** ☐ ✦38.00/40.00 – ✦✦54.00/58.00.
 ◆ Restored 18C barn in charmingly rural location close to Stratford. Stone floors and hop vines enhance rustic character. Attractive rooms: four-poster in former threshing barn.

PILLING *Lancs.* **502** L 22 – *pop. 2 204 –* ✉ *Preston.*
London 243 – Blackpool 11 – Burnley 43 – Manchester 49.

⌂ **Springfield House** ⌖, Wheel Lane, PR3 6HL, ℘ (01253) 790301, *recep@springfield househotel.co.uk, Fax (01253) 790907,* ≤, ☞ – ✦✕ **P**, **OO** **AE** **VISA**
accommodation closed 24-27 December **Rest** (closed Monday) 10.95/15.95 – **8 rm** ☐
✦55.00 – ✦✦80.00.
 ◆ 1840s house surrounded by tranquil walled gardens. Handsome façade in Georgian style, period inspired rooms and country house interiors make it a popular wedding venue. Traditionally inspired dining room.

PLUCKLEY *Kent* 504 W 30.

London 53 – Folkestone 25 – Maidstone 18.

The Dering Arms, Station Rd, TN27 0RR, South : 1 ½ m. on Bethersden rd ✆ (01233) 840371, *jim@deringarms.com, Fax (01233) 840498,* – P. MO AE VISA
closed 25-28 December and 1 January – **Rest** - Seafood specialities - *(closed Sunday dinner and Monday)* a la carte 17.95/32.50 ♀.
◆ Well-established, personally run 19C gabled lodge; informal, flagged bar hung with hunting trophies. Robust dishes, seafood specials, farm ciders and a real "local" feel.

PLUMTREE *Notts. – see Nottingham.*

PLUSH *Dorset* 503 M 31.

London 142 – Bournemouth 35 – Salisbury 44 – Taunton 52 – Weymouth 15 – Yeovil 23.

Brace of Pheasants, DT2 7RQ, ✆ (01300) 348357, *info@braceofpheasants.co.uk*, , – P. MO AE VISA
closed 25 December and Monday except Bank Holidays – **Rest** *(closed Sunday dinner in winter)* a la carte 18.00/31.00 ♀.
◆ Secluded 16C inn, once two thatched cottages and smithy; Robust modern and classic dishes in a spacious bar or more formal parlour. Rear garden, woods and bridleways beyond.

PLYMOUTH *Plymouth* 503 H 32 *The West Country G. – pop. 243 795.*

See : *Town★ – Smeaton's Tower (≤★★) AC* BZ **T1** – *Plymouth Dome★ AC* BZ – *Royal Citadel (ramparts ≤★★) AC* BZ – *City Museum and Art Gallery★* BZ **M1**.
Env. : *Saltram House★★ AC, E : 3 ½ m.* BY **A** – *Tamar River★★ – Anthony House★ AC, W : 5 m. by A 374 – Mount Edgcumbe (≤★) AC, SW : 2 m. by passenger ferry from Stonehouse* AZ.
Exc. : *NE : Dartmoor National Park★★ – Buckland Abbey★★ AC, N : 7½ m. by A 386* ABY.
18 *Staddon Heights, Plymstock ✆ (01752) 402475* – 9 *Elfordleigh Hotel G. & C.C., Colebrook, Plympton ✆ (01752) 348425.*
Tamar Bridge (toll) AY.
✈ *Plymouth City (Roborough) Airport : ✆ (01752) 204090, N : 3½ m. by A 386* ABY.
to France (Roscoff) (Brittany Ferries) 1-3 daily (6 h) – to Spain (Santander) (Brittany Ferries) 2 weekly (approx 24 h).
Mayflower Centre, 3-5 The Barbican ✆ (01752) 304849 – Plymouth Discovery Centre, Crabtree ✆ (01752) 266030.
London 242 – Bristol 124 – Southampton 161.

Plans opposite

Holiday Inn, Armada Way, PL1 2HJ, ✆ (01752) 639988, *hiplymouth@qmh-hotels.com, Fax (01752) 673816,* ≤ city and Plymouth Sound, , , – , – 425. MO AE VISA. BZ s
Rest (bar lunch)/dinner 19.95 and a la carte 25.00/31.00 s. ♀ – 13.50 – **211 rm** ★120.00/150.00 – ★★120.00/150.00.
◆ Substantial purpose-built hotel enjoys a panorama of the city skyline and the Plymouth Sound. Neatly laid-out, well-equipped bedrooms; extensive leisure club. Modern restaurant on top floor to make most of view.

Copthorne H. Plymouth, Armada Centre, Armada Way, PL1 1AR, (via Western Approach southbound) ✆ (01752) 224161, *sales.plymouth@mill-cop.com, Fax (01752) 670688* – , rest, P – 250. MO AE VISA. BZ e
Rest (bar lunch Monday-Saturday)/dinner a la carte 23.25/30.25 ♀ – 15.75 – **135 rm** ★155.00 – ★★190.00.
◆ Popular with business travellers, a group-owned hotel in easy reach of the station. Smartly kept accommodation - quieter corner rooms look across the gardens or the city. Bentley's offers spacious, modern comforts.

The Duke of Cornwall, Millbay Rd, PL1 3LG, ✆ (01752) 275850, *info@thedukeofcornwallhotel.com, Fax (01752) 275854* – , rest, P – 300. MO AE VISA AZ c
closed 27-30 December – **Rest** (bar lunch)/dinner a la carte 21.50/32.00 s. ♀ – **69 rm** ★99.00/120.00 – ★★240.00, 3 suites.
◆ Panelled bar with deep sofas and a relaxing atmosphere and individually styled rooms - some modern, some traditional - behind a locally famous, listed Victorian façade. Dining room centred on high-domed ceiling and sparkling chandelier.

ENGLAND

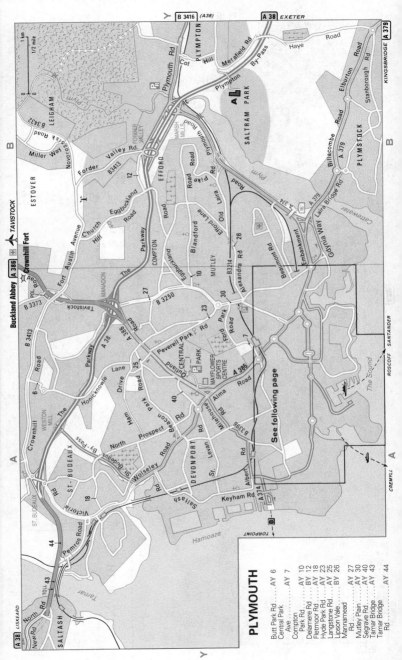

PLYMOUTH

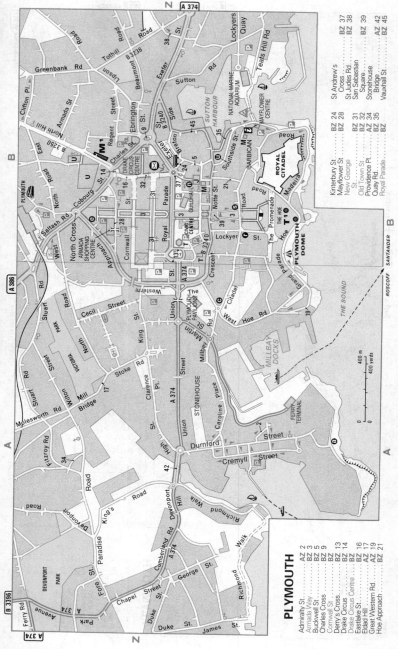

PLYMOUTH

🏠 **Bowling Green** without rest., 9-10 Osborne Pl, Lockyer St, The Hoe, PL1 2PU, ℘ (01752) 209090, info@bowlinggreenhotel.co.uk, Fax (01752) 209092 – ✳✳ 🐾 ⑳ ⓪
VISA
BZ r
12 rm ⊃ ✝45.00 – ✝✝55.00/62.00.

◆ Georgian house, half overlooking Hoe, near site of Drake's legendary game. High-ceilinged rooms in pine and modern fabrics; some have power showers. Stroll to promenade.

XX **Tanners**, Prysten House, Finewell St, PL1 2AE, ℘ (01752) 252001, goodfood@tanners
restaurant.co.uk, Fax (01752) 252105, 霜 – ✳✳. ⑳ 🆎 ⓪ **VISA**
BZ n
closed 25-26 and 31 December, first week January, Sunday and Monday – **Rest** (booking essential) 16.00/35.00.

◆ Characterful 15C house, reputedly Plymouth's oldest building: mullioned windows, tapestries, exposed stone and an illuminated water well. Modern, interesting cooking.

XX **Artillery Tower**, Firestone Bay, PL1 3QR, ℘ (01752) 257610, ≼ – ✳✳ ✧14. ⑳ 🆎
VISA
AZ a
closed Christmas-New Year, Sunday and Monday – **Rest** 28.50/36.50 ♀.

◆ Uniquely located in 500 year-old circular tower, built to defend the city. Courteous service of mostly well executed local dishes: blackboard fish specialities.

X **Barbican Kitchen**, Black Friars Distillery, 60 Southside St, PL1 2LQ, ℘ (01752) 604448,
info@barbicankitchen.com, Fax (01752) 604445 – ✳✳. ⑳ 🆎 **VISA**
BZ u
closed 25-26 and 31 December, 1 January, dinner Sunday and Bank Holidays – **Rest** a la carte 15.95/27.40 ⓧⓖ ♀.

◆ Set within the famous Plymouth Gin Distillery, this stylish restaurant, in vivid lime green and lilac, is split between two upper rooms, offering good value brasserie fare.

> Good food and accommodation at moderate prices?
> Look for the Bib symbols:
> red Bib Gourmand 🏮 for food, blue Bib Hotel 🏠 for hotels

ENGLAND

POLPERRO Cornwall 503 G 33 The West Country G. – ✉ Looe.
See : Village★.
London 271 – Plymouth 28.

🏠 **Trenderway Farm** ॐ without rest., PL13 2LY, Northeast : 2 m. by A 387 ℘ (01503)
272214, trenderwayfarm@hotmail.com, Fax (01503) 272991, ≼, 霜, 𝄪 – ✳✳ 🅿. ⑳ **VISA**.
❀
closed Christmas – **6 rm** ⊃ ✝35.00/50.00 – ✝✝70.00.

◆ Charming 16C farmhouse on working farm with converted outbuildings: modish ambience in a traditional setting. Breakfast over the lake. Stylish rooms with modern fabrics.

PONTELAND Tyne and Wear 501 502 O 19 – see Newcastle upon Tyne.

POOLE Poole 503 504 O 31 The West Country G. – pop. 144 800.
See : Town★ (Waterfront M1 , Scaplen's Court M2).
Env. : Compton Acres★★, (English Garden ≼★★★) AC, SE : 3 m. by B 3369 BX (on Bournemouth town plan) – Brownsea Island★ (Baden-Powell Stone ≼★★) AC, by boat from Poole Quay or Sandbanks BX (on Bournemouth town plan).
🖥 Parkstone, Links Rd ℘ (01202) 707138 – 🖥 The Bulbury Club, Bulberry Lane, Lytchett Matravers ℘ (01929) 459574.
⛴ to France (Cherbourg) (Brittany Ferries) 1-2 daily May-September (4 h 15 mn) day (5 h 45 mn) night – to France (St Malo) (Brittany Ferries) 4/7 weekly (8 h) – to France (St Malo) (Condor Ferries Ltd).
🛈 Welcome Centre, Enefco House, Poole Quay ℘ (01202) 253253.
London 116 – Bournemouth 4 – Dorchester 23 – Southampton 36 – Weymouth 28.

Plan on next page

Plan of Built up Area : see Bournemouth

🏨 **Haven**, 161 Banks Rd, Sandbanks, BH13 7QL, Southeast : 4 ¼ m. on B 3369 ℘ (01202)
707333, enquiries@havenhotel.co.uk, Fax (01202) 708796, ≼ Ferry, Old Harry Rocks and Poole Bay, 霜, ⑳, 𝄪₆, 🈴, 🈯 heated, 🈯, ✕ – 🛗, ✳✳ rest, 🍽 rest, 🐾🅿 – 🔬 160. ⑳ 🆎
⓪ **VISA**. ❀
on Bournemouth town plan BX c
Seaview : **Rest** (closed lunch Saturday and Sunday) 15.50/28.50 ♀ – (see **La Roche** below)
– **76 rm** ⊃ ✝95.00/155.00 – ✝✝280.00/320.00, 2 suites.

◆ Sweeping white façade and heated seawater pool. Smart modern rooms. Lounge on site of Marconi's laboratory has fireside leather wing chairs. Candlelit Seaview overlooks bay.

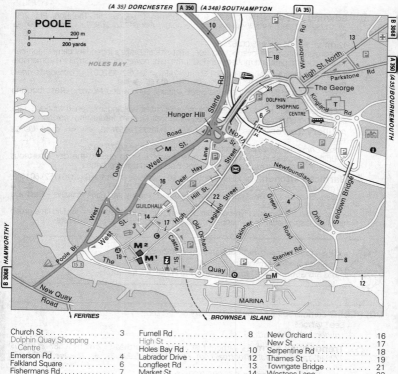

POOLE

Harbour Heights, Haven Rd, Sandbanks, BH13 7LW, Southeast : 3 m. by B 3369 ℰ (01202) 707272, *enquiries@harbourheights.net,* Fax (01202) 708594, ≤ Poole Harbour, 佘, 秝 – ⧄ 쓪 ☰ ☎ 🅿 – 🔏 50. 🅜🅒 🅐🅔 ⓪ 🆅🆂🅰. ⅝
harbar bistro : Rest a la carte 25.00/40.00 – **38 rm** ☲ ✲145.00/155.00 –
✲✲240.00/270.00.   on Bournemouth town plan BX n
♦ 1920s hotel stylishly updated in 2003; walls decorated with vibrant modern art. Swanky, smart bedrooms boast modern interiors and all mod cons: request room with a sea view. Bistro-styled restaurant with very popular terrace.

Mansion House, 7-11 Thames St, BH15 1JN, off Poole Quay ℰ (01202) 685666, *enqui ries@themansionhouse.co.uk,* Fax (01202) 665709 – ☰ rest, ☎ 🅿 – 🔏 40. 🅜🅒 🅐🅔 ⓪ 🆅🆂🅰.
⅝   a
closed 28-30 December – **The Restaurant :** Rest *(closed lunch Saturday, and Sunday dinner, except at Bank Holidays)* 22.00/29.95 ♀ – **Bistro :** Rest *(closed Sunday lunch and Monday)* (residents only) 19.00 (dinner) and lunch a la carte approx 16.00 ♀ – **32 rm** ☲
✲75.00/105.00 – ✲✲135.00/150.00.
♦ Attractive, ivy-covered 18C town house in a narrow cobbled mews near the quay. An impressive staircase leads to Georgian-styled rooms, some with antique lamps and bed-steads. Cosy cherrywood-panelled Restaurant has paintings and naval prints. Informal Bis-tro.

Thistle Poole, The Quay, BH15 1HD, ℰ (0870) 333 9143, *poole@thistle.co.uk,* Fax (0870) 333 9243, ≤ – ⧄ 쓪 🅿 – 🔏 60. 🅜🅒 🅐🅔 ⓪ 🆅🆂🅰
                                                                                    e
Rest (bar lunch Monday-Saturday) a la carte 25.85/34.85 s. – ☲ 12.25 – **70 rm**
✲175.00/185.00 – ✲✲195.00.
♦ Purpose-built, redbrick, group hotel on the quay; informal bar; neatly laid-out rooms - half of which have views over the water - in sober blue fabrics and pine furniture. Fine outlook from wide-windowed restaurant.

Express by Holiday Inn without rest., Walking Field Lane, BH15 1RZ, ✆ (01202) 649222, poole@khl.uk.com, Fax (01202) 649666 – 📱 ✻✖ ✔ & 🖪 . – 🏊 30. 🆀🔞 🝙 ⓪ 𝖵𝖨𝖲𝖠.
🈯
i
85 rm ✿79.00/85.00 – ✿✿79.00/85.00.
◆ Modern lodge accommodation in central location within walking distance of shops and restaurants. Complimentary continental breakfast. Well appointed, comfy rooms.

La Roche (at Haven H.), 161 Banks Rd, Sandbanks, BH13 7QL, Southeast : 4 ¼ m. on B 3369 ✆ (01202) 707333, Fax (01202) 708796, ≤ Ferry, Old Harry Rocks and Poole Bay, 🏤 – ✻✖ 🖪 . 🆀🔞 🝙 ⓪ 𝖵𝖨𝖲𝖠 on Bournemouth town plan BX c
closed Sunday dinner and Monday – **Rest** a la carte 29.00/37.00 s. 🍷.
◆ Perched at the side of the Haven, overlooking the bay. Watch the fishing boats from wonderful adjacent terrace. Eclectic menus with seafood base and tasty local ingredients.

Isabel's, 32 Station Rd, Lower Parkstone, BH14 8UD, ✆ (01202) 747885, isabels@onetel. com, Fax (01202) 747885 – ✻✖ ⇔ 28. 🆀🔞 🝙 𝖵𝖨𝖲𝖠 on Bournemouth town plan BX a
– **Rest** (booking essential) (dinner only) 32.00 and a la carte 25.90/31.90.
◆ Long-established neighbourhood restaurant; old shelves recall its origins as a Victorian pharmacy. Intimate wooden booths. Classically inspired menu with a rich Gallic tone.

POOLEY BRIDGE Cumbria 501 502 L 20 – see Ullswater.

PORLOCK Somerset 503 J 30 The West Country G. – ✉ Minehead.
See : Village★ – Porlock Hill (≤★★) – St Dubricius Church★.
Env. : Dunkery Beacon★★★ (≤★★★), S : 5½ m. – Exmoor National Park★★ – Selworthy★ (≤★★, Church★), E : 2 m. by A 39 and minor rd – Luccombe★ (Church★), E : 3 m. by A 39 – Culbone★ (St Beuno), W : 3½ m. by B 3225, 1½ m. on foot – Doone Valley★, W : 6 m. by A 39, access from Oare on foot.
London 190 – Bristol 67 – Exeter 46 – Taunton 28.

Porlock Vale House 🐾, Porlock Weir, TA24 8NY, Northwest : 1 ¼ m. ✆ (01643) 862338, info@porlockvale.co.uk, Fax (01643) 863338, ≤, 🏤, 🌿, 🝙, – ✻✖ 🖪 . 🆀🔞 🝙 𝖵𝖨𝖲𝖠
restricted opening in winter – **Rest** (closed Monday dinner) (booking essential for non-residents) (light lunch)/dinner 29.00 – **15 rm** ⚌ ✿60.00/110.00 – ✿✿130.00/170.00.
◆ Attractive Edwardian house and equestrian centre with grounds stretching to sea. Cosy bar, three lounges and delightful terrace; lots of Arts and Crafts features. Smart rooms. Enjoy traditional menus and sea vistas in enchanting wood-panelled dining room.

Oaks, TA24 8ES, ✆ (01643) 862265, info@oakshotel.co.uk, Fax (01643) 863131, ≤ Porlock Bay, 🌿 – ✻✖ 🖪 . 🆀🔞 𝖵𝖨𝖲𝖠 . 🈯
March-October and Christmas-New Year – **Rest** (booking essential for non-residents) (dinner only) 32.50 – **7 rm** ⚌ ✿90.00 – ✿✿130.00.
◆ Traditionally styled Edwardian country house in pretty gardens, very well run by most hospitable owners. Stunning rural views. Cosy, individual rooms in co-ordinated colours. Neat dining room: all land produce from a 20 mile radius.

PORT ERIN Isle of Man 502 F 21 – see Man (Isle of).

PORTHLEVEN Cornwall.
London 284.5 – Helston 3 – Penzance 12.5.

Kota with rm, Harbour Head, TR13 9JA, ✆ (01326) 562407, kota@btconnect.com, Fax (01326) 562407 – 🆀🔞 𝖵𝖨𝖲𝖠
closed January, 1 week February and 25 December – **Rest** (closed Sunday dinner) a la carte 21.95/31.50 🍷 – **2 rm** ⚌ ✿60.00/80.00 – ✿✿65.00/85.00.
◆ Cottagey converted 18C harbourside granary. Characterful restaurant - thick walls, tiled floors - serves modern Asian inspired dishes with local fish specials. Simple rooms.

PORTINSCALE Cumbria – see Keswick.

PORTLOE Cornwall 503 F 33 – ✉ Truro.
London 296 – St Austell 15 – Truro 15.

Lugger, TR2 5RD, ✆ (01872) 501322, office@luggerhotel.com, Fax (01872) 501691, ≤, 🏤 – ✻✖ 🖪 . 🆀🔞 𝖵𝖨𝖲𝖠 . 🈯
Rest (light lunch)/dinner 37.50 🍷 – **22 rm** ⚌ ✿135.00/190.00 – ✿✿220.00/290.00.
◆ Former inn in a beautiful location within pretty Cornish cove. Stylish public areas. The bedrooms are created with a tasteful palette in strikingly contemporary vein. Restaurant enjoys blissful outlook over the cove.

PORT ST MARY *I.O.M.* 502 F/G 21 – *see Man (Isle of)*.

PORTSCATHO *Cornwall* 503 F 33 *The West Country G.* – ⊠ *Truro*.
Env. : *St Just-in-Roseland Church*★★, *W : 4 m. by A 3078 – St Anthony-in-Roseland* (≤★★) *S : 3½ m*.
London 298 – Plymouth 55 – Truro 16.

🏨 **Rosevine**, Rosevine, TR2 5EW, North : 2 m. by A 3078 ℰ (01872) 580206, *info@rose vine.co.uk, Fax* (01872) 580230, ≤, ⇗, 🔲, 🐾, ✕ – ⇤ 🅿. 🆎 🖭 *VISA*
closed January – **Rest** *(bar lunch)/dinner* 38.00 *and a la carte* 32.90/47.95 ♀ – **17 rm** 🖙
✹86.00/187.00 – ✹✹204.00/260.00.
♦ Surrounded by attractive gardens, this family owned hotel offers traditional, homely comforts. Rooms are well looked after and a friendly air prevails. Pretty restaurant makes use of local ingredients.

🏠 **Driftwood** ⌂, Rosevine, TR2 5EW, North : 2 m. by A 3078 ℰ (01872) 580644, *info@driftwoodhotel.co.uk, Fax* (01872) 580801, ≤ Gerrans Bay, 🐾 – ⇤ 🅿. 🆎 🖭 *VISA*. 🐾
closed January – **Rest** *(closed Sunday dinner to non-residents)* (booking essential) *(dinner only)* 39.00 ♀ – **15 rm** 🖙 ✹150.00 – ✹✹220.00/210.00.
♦ Stylish décor and a neutral, contemporary feel make this an enviable spot to lay one's head. Attractive decking affords fine sea views. Smart bedrooms with pristine style. Distinctive modern dining room with fine vistas.

> Look out for red symbols, indicating particularly pleasant establishments.

ENGLAND

PORTSMOUTH and SOUTHSEA *Portsmouth* 503 504 Q 31 *Great Britain G.* – *pop. 187 056*.
See : *City*★ – *Naval Portsmouth* BY : *H.M.S. Victory*★★★ *AC, The Mary Rose*★★, *Royal Naval Museum*★★ *AC – Old Portsmouth*★ BYZ : *The Point* (≤★★) *- St Thomas Cathedral*★ – *Southsea (Castle*★ *AC)* AZ – *Royal Marines Museum, Eastney*★ *AC,* AZ **M1**.
Env. : *Portchester Castle*★ *AC, NW : 5½ m. by A 3 and A 27* AY.
🏌 *Great Salterns, Portsmouth Golf Centre, Burrfields Rd* ℰ (023) 9266 4549 AY – 🏌 *Crookhorn Lane, Widley, Waterlooville* ℰ (023) 9237 2210 – 🏌 *Southwick Park, Pinsley Drive, Southwick* ℰ (023) 9238 0131.
🚢 *to France (St Malo) (Brittany Ferries) daily (8 h 45 mn) day (10 h 45 mn) night – to France (Caen) (Brittany Ferries) 2-3 daily (6 h) day (6 h 45 mn) night – to France (Cherbourg) (Brittany Ferries) 3-4 daily (5 h) day, (7 h) night – to France (Le Havre) (LD Lines) daily (5 h 30 mn/7 h 30 mn) – to France (Cherbourg) (Brittany Ferries) 2-3 daily (2 h 45 mn) – to France (Caen) (Brittany Ferries) 2-3 daily (3 h 25 mn) – to Spain (Bilbao) (P & O European Ferries Ltd) 1-2 weekly (35 h) – to Guernsey (St Peter Port) and Jersey (St Helier) (Condor Ferries Ltd) daily except Sunday (10 hrs) – to the Isle of Wight (Fishbourne) (Wightlink Ltd) frequent services daily (35 mn)*.
🚢 *to the Isle of Wight (Ryde) (Wightlink Ltd) frequent services daily (15 mn) – from Southsea to the Isle of Wight (Ryde) (Hovertravel Ltd) frequent services daily (10 mn)*.
🛈 *The Hard* ℰ (023) 9282 6722, *tic@portsmouthcc.gov.uk – Clarence Esplanade* ℰ (023) 9282 6722.
London 78 – Brighton 48 – Salisbury 44 – Southampton 21.

Plan opposite

🏠 **Beaufort**, 71 Festing Rd, Southsea, PO4 0NQ, ℰ (023) 9282 3707, *enq@beauforthotel.co.uk, Fax* (023) 9287 0270 – ⇤ 📞 🅿. 🆎 🖭 ⓪ *VISA*. 🐾   AZ **n**
closed 25-26 December – **Rest** *(dinner only)* 19.50 s. ♀ – **20 rm** 🖙 ✹48.00/70.00 – ✹✹60.00/100.00.
♦ Privately owned Southsea hotel, a few minutes from the water. Sizeable and well-kept bedrooms in smart modern décor. Cosy sitting room with leather chesterfields. Sprays of flowers brighten traditional dining room.

🏠 **Upper Mount House** without rest., The Vale, Clarendon Rd, PO5 2EQ, ℰ (023) 9282 0456, *Fax* (023) 9282 0456 – ⇤ 🅿. 🆎 *VISA*. 🐾   CZ **e**
closed 2 weeks Christmas – **16 rm** 🖙 ✹36.00/42.00 – ✹✹60.00.
♦ Privately managed, gabled Victorian villa, set in a quiet suburb. Handsomely sized rooms in varying styles, some with four poster beds, all simply appointed.

🏠 **Fortitude Cottage** without rest., 51 Broad St, Old Portsmouth, PO1 2JD, ℰ (023) 9282 3748, *fortcott@aol.com, Fax* (023) 9282 3748 – ⇤ 🅿. 🆎 *VISA*. 🐾   BY **c**
closed Christmas and New Year – **4 rm** 🖙 ✹35.00/75.00 – ✹✹75.00/80.00.
♦ Pretty little quayside townhouse named after an 18C battleship. Watch yachts rounding the Point from a cosy bow windowed lounge. Simple, well-priced rooms, charming owners.

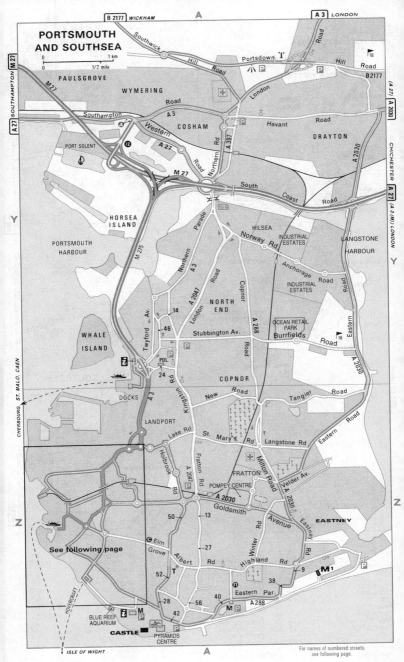

PORTSMOUTH AND SOUTHSEA

0   1 km
1/2 mile

PAULSGROVE

WYMERING

COSHAM

DRAYTON

PORT SOLENT

HORSEA ISLAND

PORTSMOUTH HARBOUR

HILSEA

LANGSTONE HARBOUR

NORTH END

WHALE ISLAND

Stubbington Av.

OCEAN RETAIL PARK

Burrfields

INDUSTRIAL ESTATES

INDUSTRIAL ESTATES

Eastern

COPNOR

DOCKS

LANDPORT

New   Road

Tangier   Road

St. Mary's   Rd.

Langstone Rd.

Lake Rd.

POMPEY CENTRE

FRATTON

Milton Road

Velder Av.

Goldsmith   Avenue

EASTNEY

See following page

Elm Grove

Albert   Rd.

Highland   Rd.

Winter   Rd.

Eastern   Rd.

Eastern   Par.

BLUE REEF AQUARIUM

CASTLE

PYRAMIDS CENTRE

ISLE OF WIGHT

HOVERCRAFT

CHERBOURG, ST. MALO, CAEN

ST. MALO, CAEN

A 27 SOUTHAMPTON M 27

B 2177 WICKHAM

A 3 LONDON

(A 27) A 2030

CHICHESTER A 27 (A 3 (M)) LONDON

B 2177

Southwick   Hill   Road

Portsdown

Hill   Road

Southampton   Road

A 3

Western

Road

Northern   Rd.

A 397

Havant

Road

A 27

A 2030

M 27

South   Coast

Road

Parade

Northern

A 3

A 2047

London

Road

Copnor

Road

Norway   Rd.

Anchorage   Road

Road

A 288

Road

Twyford   Av.

POL

Kingston   Rd.

A 3

Holbrook

Rd.

A 2047

Fratton Rd.

A 2030

A 2030

A 288

12

14

46

24

15.6

18

18

50   13

27

52   T

28   56

42

40

9

38

1

For names of numbered streets,
see following page.

615

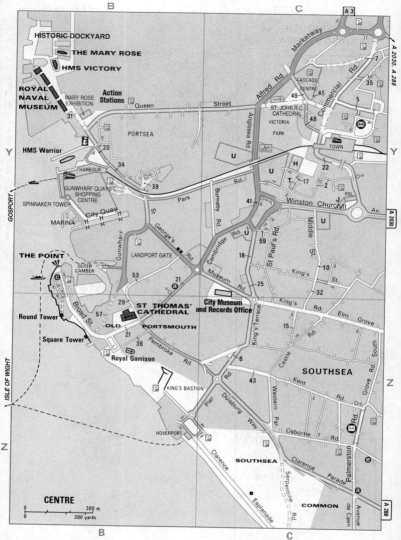

616

XX **Tang's,** 127 Elm Grove, Southsea, PO5 1LJ, 𝒫 (023) 9282 2722, Fax (023) 9283 8323 – ▤.
MO AE VISA
AZ c
closed 25-26 December and Monday – **Rest** - Chinese - (dinner only) 22.50 and a la carte
12.50/20.00.
• Smooth presentation at every turn at this neighbourhood Chinese restaurant - rattan
chairs, neat linen, impeccably attired staff and authentic, delicately composed cuisine.

X **Bistro Montparnasse,** 103 Palmerston Rd, Southsea, PO5 3PS, 𝒫 (023) 9281 6754 –
✦ ⇄ 30. **MO AE VISA**
CZ a
closed 25-26 December, 1 week January, Sunday and Monday – **Rest** 17.50/27.50 ♀.
• Behind a trim shop front, a vivid interior of tangerine and blue. The menu is just as
colourful: tuna, prawn and papaya, Campari orange mousse. Friendly, informal service.

X **Lemon Sole,** 123 High St, Old Portsmouth, PO1 2HW, 𝒫 (023) 9281 1303, *lemon*
soles@btconnect.com, Fax (023) 9281 1345 – **MO AE ⓞ VISA**
BY a
closed 25 December, Sunday and Bank Holidays – **Rest** - Seafood specialities - 16.00/35.00
and a la carte 22.95/27.95 ♀.
• Seafood motifs abound in a bright, informal restaurant. Choose a tasty, simple recipe
and market-fresh fish from the slab. Likeable, helpful staff. Part 14C wine cellar.

at Cosham North : 4½ m. by A 3 – AY – and M 275 on A 27 – ✉ Portsmouth.

▲▲▲ **Portsmouth Marriott,** Southampton Road, PO6 4SH, 𝒫 (0800) 4007285,
events.portsmouth@marriotthotels.co.uk, Fax (0800) 4007385, ɭ₅, ≋, ▨ – ▮, ⇆ rm, ▤
✆ & ₱ – ▵ 300. **MO AE ⓞ VISA**
AY a
Mediterrano : **Rest** (bar lunch)/dinner a la carte 19.75/28.75 ♀ – ⇌ 14.95 – **174 rm**
★129.00 – ★★129.00/195.00.
• Modern, open-plan lounge and invariably smart, spacious rooms, all with writing desks
and useful mod cons, in a substantial, well-run group hotel. A short drive to the port. Tasty
Mediterranean menus.

▥ **Tulip Inn,** Binnacle Way, PO6 4FB, 𝒫 (023) 9237 3333, *reservations@tulipinnports*
mouth.co.uk, Fax (023) 9237 3335 – ▮ ⇆ ✆ & ₱ – ▵ 30. **MO AE VISA**. ⋇
Bibo Bistro : **Rest** (dinner only) (residents only) a la carte 13.15/27.50 s. – ⇌ 7.95 – **108 rm**
★90.00 – ★★90.00.
• This smart, good value hotel has convenient motorway connections and very stylish
bedrooms with lots of handy extras to complement the designer flourishes. Modern bar/
grill with wide-ranging menus.

ENGLAND

Do not confuse X with ⇔!
X defines comfort, while stars are awarded for the best cuisine,
across all categories of comfort.

POSTBRIDGE Devon 503 I 32.
London 207 – Exeter 21 – Plymouth 21.

▥ **Lydgate House** ⟋, PL20 6TJ, 𝒫 (01822) 880209, *lydgatehouse@email.com,*
Fax (01822) 880202, ≤, ⟿, ⚘ – ⇆ ₱, **MO VISA**
weekends only November-February – **Rest** (by arrangement) (residents only) 28.50 – **7 rm**
⇌ ★60.00/85.00 – ★★130.00.
• In an idyllic secluded location high up on the moors within woodland and overlooking
the East Dart River. Comfortable sitting room with log fires and neat, snug bedrooms.
Candlelit conservatory dining room.

POTTERNE Wilts. 503 O 29 – see Devizes.

POTT SHRIGLEY Ches. – see Macclesfield.

POULTON Glos. 503 504 O 28.
London 91 – Bristol 43 – Oxford 33.

 The Falcon Inn, London Rd, GL7 5HN, 𝒫 (01285) 850844, *info@thefalconpoulton.co.uk*
– ⇆ ₱. **MO VISA**. ⋇
Rest *(closed 25-26 December, 1 January and Sunday dinner)* a la carte 20.00/30.00 ♀.
• Easy going pub, contemporary in design, with super wine list. Divided into three rooms,
one with large log fire, all with old church pews. Locally underpinned modern menus.

⌷ₐ *De Vere Mottram Hall, Wilmslow Rd, Mottram St Andrews* ℘ *(01625) 820064.*
London 184 – Liverpool 43 – Manchester 17 – Stoke-on-Trent 25.

🏨 **De Vere Mottram Hall,** Wilmslow Rd, Mottram St Andrew, SK10 4QT, Northwest :
2¼ m. on A 538 ℘ (01625) 828135, *dmh.sales@devere-hotels.com, Fax (01625) 828950,* ≤,
Ⅰₖ, ≋, ⬜, ⌷ₐ, ☂, 魡, ※, squash – 劃 ⅙⊁ ✆ & ⅌ – 🕮 200. 🐧 🖭 ⓞ 🚾 ⅙
Nathaniel's : Rest (live music Saturday evening) (bar lunch)/dinner a la carte 20.70/40.50
s. ⅌ – **128 rm** ⅏ ⅙105.00/150.00 – ⅙⅙115.00/160.00, 3 suites.
  ♦ Imposing part 18C mansion. Traditional rooms are larger in the manor. Lovely cocktail
bar. Championship golf course crosses wooded parkland. Classically decorated dining
room named after the original owner of the house; modern cooking.

🏨 **White House Manor** without rest., The Village, SK10 4HP, ℘ (01625) 829376,
info@thewhitehouse.uk.com, Fax (01625) 828627, ☂ – ⅙⊁ ✆ ⅌. 🐧 🖭 🚾 ⅙
closed 25-26 December – ⅏ 11.50 – **11 rm** ⅙80.00/110.00 – ⅙⅙150.00.
  ♦ Privately run 18C redbrick house with stylish, unique and individually decorated rooms
which provide every luxury. Breakfast in your room or in the conservatory.

🏨 **The Bridge,** The Village, SK10 4DQ, ℘ (01625) 829326, *reception@bridge-hotel.co.uk,*
Fax (01625) 827557, ☈, ☂ – ⅙⊁ rm, ✆ & ⅌ – 🕮 100. 🐧 🖭 ⓞ 🚾 ⅙
Rest *(closed Sunday dinner)* 12.95/17.95 and a la carte 20.85/29.95 – ⅏ 9.75 – **23 rm**
⅙50.00/60.00 – ⅙⅙88.00/115.00.
  ♦ Dating back to the 1600s, a sympathetically extended hotel on the river Bollin. Classic,
subtly co-ordinated décor in rooms, more characterful in the old timbered house. Live
music at weekends in the beamed, galleried hall of the restaurant.

⌷ₐ *Fulwood Hall Lane, Fulwood* ℘ (01772) 700011 – ⌷ₐ *Ingol, Tanterton Hall Rd* ℘ (01772)
734556 – ⌷ₐ *Aston & Lea, Tudor Ave, Blackpool Rd* ℘ (01772) 735282 – ⌷ₐ *Penwortham,
Blundell Lane* ℘ (01772) 744630.
🛈 *The Guildhall, Lancaster Rd* ℘ (01772) 253731.
*London 226 – Blackpool 18 – Burnley 22 – Liverpool 30 – Manchester 34 – Stoke-on-Trent
65.*

🏨 **The Park,** 209 Tulketh Rd, PR2 1ES, Northwest: 2¼ m. by A 6 off ℘ (01772) 726250,
parkrestauranthotel@hotmail.com, Fax (01772) 723743 – ⅙⊁ ⅌. 🐧 🖭 🚾 ⅙
closed 25 December – **Rest** *(closed Sunday)* (dinner only) a la carte 18.35/33.45 s. – **14 rm**
⅏ ⅙50.00/60.00 – ⅙⅙75.00/95.00.
  ♦ Built in 1903, a turreted, redbrick villa in a quiet suburb. Original hall - antique tiling and
stained glass. Traditional rooms with greater personality in the old house. Light dining
room dominated by black marble fireplace.

XX **Winckley Square Chop House,** 23 Winckley Sq, PR1 3JJ, ℘ (01772) 252732, *pres*
🏵 *ton@heathcotes.co.uk, Fax (01772) 203433 –* ⅙⊁ ▤. 🐧 🖭 🚾
closed 25-26 December and 1 January – Rest a la carte 15.70/31.50 ⅌ – **Olive Press :** Rest
(closed Bank Holidays) a la carte 16.50/27.00 ⅌.
  ♦ Chic and contemporary restaurant with a cuisine style that handsomely matches the
surroundings. Robust, balanced, classic British cooking with some regional input. Spacious
basement bar-bistro serving pizzas and pastas.

XX **Inside Out,** 100 Higher Walton Rd, Walton-le-Dale, PR5 4HR, Southeast : 1¾ m. by A 6
🏵 on A 675 ℘ (01772) 251366, *Fax (01772) 258918,* ☈, ☂ – ⅌. 🐧 🖭 🚾
*closed 25-26 December, first 2 weeks January, 3rd week October, Saturday lunch and
Monday –* Rest 13.50/16.50 and a la carte 20.50/22.50 ⅌.
  ♦ Inside - a chic and stylish restaurant; 'out' - a lovely decked terrace with heaters overlooking a garden. Well sourced, quality ingredients assembled with love and flair.

at Broughton *North : 3 m. on A 6 –* ⊠ *Preston.*

🏨 **Preston Marriott,** 418 Garstang Rd, PR3 5JB, ℘ (01772) 864087, *frontdesk.pres*
ton@marriotthotels.co.uk, Fax (01772) 861327, Ⅰₖ, ≋, ⬜, ☂ – 劃 ⅙⊁ ▤ & ⅌ – 🕮 200.
🐧 🖭 ⓞ 🚾
Rest (bar lunch Monday-Saturday)/dinner 23.50 and a la carte 23.50/40.00 ⅌ – **Broughton
Brasserie :** Rest (dinner only and Sunday lunch) a la carte 22.90/35.85 ⅌ – ⅏ 14.95 –
149 rm ⅙102.00/112.00 – ⅙⅙102.00/112.00.
  ♦ Sympathetically extended 19C redbrick house in wooded grounds offers airy modern
accommodation: more traditional comfort in original house rooms. Up-to-date leisure
club. Easy-going lounge/restaurant. Formal, linen-clad Broughton Brasserie.

🏨 **Ibis** without rest., Garstang Rd, PR3 5JE, South : ¾ m. off A 6 ℘ (01772) 861800,
h3162@accor.com, Fax (01772) 861900 – 劃 ⅙⊁ & ⅌ – 🕮 30. 🐧 🖭 ⓞ 🚾
82 rm ⅙47.95/50.00 – ⅙⅙47.95/50.00.
  ♦ Excellent motorway connections from this purpose-built lodge. Neatly laid-out and simply fitted accommodation in contemporary style: the rear-facing bedrooms are quieter.

PUDLESTON *Herefordshire – see Leominster.*

PUDSEY *W. Yorks. 502 P 22 – see Leeds.*

LA PULENTE *Jersey (Channel Islands) 503 P 33 and 517 ⑪ – see Channel Islands.*

PULFORD *Ches. 502 503 L 24 – see Chester.*

PULHAM MARKET *Norfolk 504 X 26 – pop. 919 – ⊠ Diss.*
London 106 – Cambridge 58 – Ipswich 29 – Norwich 16.

 Old Bakery without rest., Church Walk, IP21 4SL, ℘ (01379) 676492, *jean@theoldbak
ery.net*, Fax (01379) 676492, 🌳 – ⥂ 🏠 ⥬
closed Christmas and New Year – 3 rm ⊇ ✶45.00/55.00 – ✶✶64.00/70.00.
• Characterful Elizabethan house on village green: spacious timbered rooms hold antiques
or comfy armchairs; toiletries by local herbalist. Pretty garden with summer house.

We try to be as accurate as possible when giving room rates.
But prices are susceptible to change,
so please check rates when booking.

PURTON *Wilts. 503 504 O 29 – pop. 3 328 – ⊠ Swindon.*
London 94 – Bristol 41 – Gloucester 31 – Oxford 38 – Swindon 5.

 Pear Tree at Purton, Church End, SN5 4ED, South : ½ m. by Church St on Lydiard
Millicent rd ℘ (01793) 772100, *stay@peartreepurton.co.uk*, Fax (01793) 772369, 🌳 – ⥂
🏠 – 🔏 50. ⬤⬤ 🅰🅴 ⓞ 𝘝𝘐𝘚𝘈
closed 26-30 December – **Rest** *(closed lunch Saturday and Bank Holidays)* 18.50/34.50 ♀ –
15 rm ⊇ ✶115.00 – ✶✶145.00/155.00, 2 suites.
• Personally run, extended 16C sandstone vicarage in mature seven-acre garden. Spacious
flower-filled lounge. Rooms with traditional comforts and thoughtful extras. Conservatory
restaurant overlooks wild flower borders.

QUITHER *Devon – see Tavistock.*

QUORNDON *Leics. 502 503 504 Q 25 – see Loughborough.*

RAINHAM *Essex 504 U 29.*
London 14 – Basildon 16 – Dartford 9.

🏠🏠 **The Manor,** Berwick Pond Rd, RM13 9EL, North : ¾ m. ℘ (01708) 555586, *info@thema
noressex.co.uk*, Fax (01708) 630055, 🌳 – 📳 ⥂, 🍴 rest, ✆ 👌 🏠 – 🔏 100. ⬤⬤ 🅰🅴 𝘝𝘐𝘚𝘈.
⥬
*closed 26 December and 1 January***Rest** *(closed Sunday dinner)* a la carte 23.00/39.90 –
14 rm ⊇ ✶90.00 – ✶✶90.00/120.00.
• This ultra stylish hotel, opened in 2004, has a distinctive, contemporary feel and a lovely
rear garden; smart, compact conference facility. Elegant and modish bedrooms. Appealing
menus with wide-ranging modern dishes.

RAMSBOTTOM *Gtr Manchester 502 N 23 – pop. 17 352.*
London 223 – Blackpool 39 – Burnley 12 – Leeds 46 – Manchester 13 – Liverpool 39.

✗ **Ramsons,** 18 Market Pl, BL0 9HT, ℘ (01706) 825070 – ⥂. ⬤⬤ 𝘝𝘐𝘚𝘈
*closed first week January, 2 weeks May, 1 week September, Sunday dinner, Monday and
Tuesday* – **Rest** - Italian influences - 25.00/40.00 ♀ 🏵.
• Passionately run and slightly quirky, this well-regarded eatery offers mostly Italian influenced cooking utilising refined ingredients. Accompanying fine wine list.

RAMSEY *Isle of Man 502 G 21 – see Man (Isle of).*

RAMSGILL-IN-NIDDERDALE *N. Yorks. 502 O 21 – see Pateley Bridge.*

ENGLAND

RAWTENSTALL *Lancs.* 502 N 22.

London 232.5 – Accrington 9.5 – Burnley 12.5.

XX **The Dining Room,** 8-12 Burnley Rd, BB4 8EW, ℰ (01706) 210567, *thedining room@hotmail.co.uk* – ✦✦, **MC AE VISA**
closed 25-26 December, 1 January, Monday and Tuesday – **Rest** *(booking essential)* 14.95 (lunch) and a la carte 25.40/38.40.
♦ Bland façade hides slick, neutral interior. Semi-split level dining room hosts good value, understated, seasonal cooking where texture, balance and flavours gel seamlessly.

RAYLEIGH *Essex* 504 V 29 – pop. 30 629.

London 35 – Chelmsford 13 – Southend-on-Sea 6.

🏠 **Express by Holiday Inn** without rest., Rayleigh Weir, Arterial Rd, SS6 7SP, South : ½ m. by A 129 at junction with A 127 ℰ (01268) 775001, *express-rayleigh@btconnect.com,* Fax (01268) 777505 – ✦✦ & **P** – ⚑ 30. **MC AE OD VISA**, ✦✦
49 rm ✦59.95 – ✦✦59.95.
♦ Compact, purpose-built hotel in a useful location near major road junction; complimentary continental buffet breakfast. Comfortable family rooms with all mod cons.

at Thundersley *South : 1¼ m. on A 129 –* ✉ *Rayleigh.*

🍴 **The Woodmans Arms,** Rayleigh Rd, SS7 3TA, ℰ (01268) 775799, *thewoodmans@hot mail.co.uk*, Fax (01268) 590689, 🌳 – ✦✦ **P**, **MC VISA**, ✦✦
Rest a la carte 17.00/25.00.
♦ Updated 19C pub in gastronomic desert. Cosy lounge with comfy leather sofas. Dining areas, separated by screens, serve impressive range of dishes - eg: Thai, French, British.

READING *Reading* 503 504 Q 29 – pop. 232 662.

🏌 *Calcot Park, Bath Rd, Calcot* ℰ (0118) 942 7124.
Whitchurch Bridge (toll).
⛴ *to Henley-on-Thames (Salter Bros. Ltd) (summer only).*
🛈 *Church House, Chain St* ℰ (0118) 956 6226.
London 43 – Brighton 79 – Bristol 78 – Croydon 47 – Luton 62 – Oxford 28 – Portsmouth 67 – Southampton 46.

Plan opposite

🏨 **Crowne Plaza Reading,** Caversham Bridge, Richfield Ave, RG1 8BD, ℰ (0118) 925 9988, *info@cp-reading.co.uk*, Fax (0118) 939 1665, ≤, 🌳, **I₅, ≘s, 🌊 – 劇 ✦✦ 🔳 ✓ & P –** ⚑ 160. **MC AE OD VISA**, ✦✦
X e
Rest 19.00 and a la carte 23.00/30.50 **s.** ♀ – ⚏ 13.95 – **122**/165.00 – ✦✦165.00/165.00, 2 suites.
♦ Modern purpose-built hotel just out of centre on banks of Thames. Spacious public areas with large windows which look towards river. Executive rooms boast extra touches. Bright restaurant with terrace and atrium roof.

🏨 **Millennium Madejski,** Madejski Stadium, RG2 0FL, South : 1½ m. by A 33 ℰ (0118) 925 3500, *sales.reading@mill-cop.com*, Fax (0118) 925 3501, **I₅, ≘s, 🌊 – 劇 ✦✦ 🔳 ✓ & P –** ⚑ 80. **MC AE OD VISA**, ✦✦
X v
Cilantro : Rest *(closed Sunday)* (dinner only) 49.50 ♀ – **Le Café :** Rest *(closed Saturday lunch)* 13.50 (lunch) and a la carte 24.25/35.50 **s.** ♀ – ⚏ 15.75 – **132 rm** ✦200.00 – ✦✦200.00, 8 suites.
♦ Purpose-built hotel, in modern retail park; part of the Madejski sports stadium. Imposing Atrium lounge-bar and marble floored lobby. Stylish, inviting rooms. Impressively smart Cilantro. Informal Le Café is open plan to Atrium lounge.

🏛 **The Forbury,** 26 The Forbury, RG1 3EJ, ℰ (0800) 0789789, *info@theforburyhotel.co.uk,* Fax (0118) 959 0806 – 劇 ✦✦, ▤ rest, ✓ & P – ⚑ 40. **MC AE VISA**, ✦✦
Y c
Cerise : Rest 17.95 (lunch) and dinner a la carte 29.00/39.50 – ⚏ 10.50 – **24 rm** ✦230.00/260.00 – ✦✦230.00/260.00.
♦ Former civic hall overlooking Forbury Square Gardens; now a very stylish town house hotel. Eye-catching artwork features in all the stunningly individualistic bedrooms. Stylish basement cocktail bar/restaurant where clean, crisp, modern cooking holds sway.

🏛 **Renaissance Reading,** Oxford Rd, RG1 7RH, ℰ (0118) 958 6222, Fax (0118) 959 7842, **I₅, ≘s, 🌊 – 劇,** ✦✦ rm, ▤ ✓ & P – ⚑ 220. **MC AE OD VISA**, ✦✦
Z i
Rest a la carte 14.05/23.40 **s.** ♀ – ⚏ 15.95 – **195 rm** ✦150.00 – ✦✦150.00, 1 suite.
♦ Bustling, centrally located hotel, adjacent to Hexagon Theatre. Views improve with altitude. Business emphasis; leisure facilities a highlight. Well Kept uniform rooms. Restaurant has comfortable, well organised air.

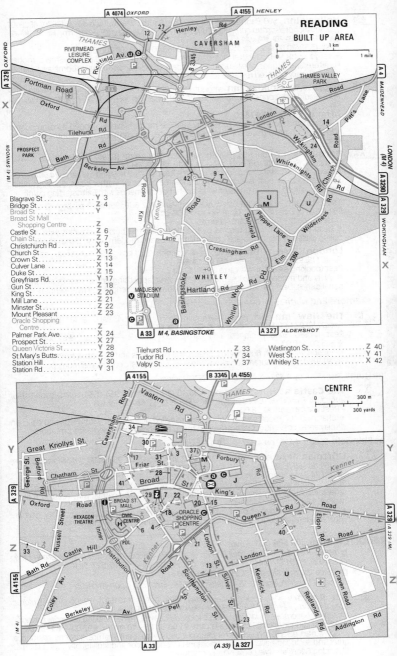

Holiday Inn, 500 Basingstoke Rd, RG2 0SL, South : 2 ½ m. by A 33 ℘ (0870) 4009067, reading@ichotelsgroup.com, Fax (0118) 931 1958, ㎅, ⬛, ☐ – 🗝 rm, ▥ ✆ ⚓ 🅿 – 🏛 110. ⓪❸ ⒶⒺ ⓪ VISA. ⬗
X a
Rest 13.50/20.00 s. 🍷 – ☲ 15.95 – **202 rm** ✸160.00 – ✸✸160.00/135.00.
♦ Large purpose-built hotel out of the city centre in residential area. Smart, modern furniture and fittings. Well suited to business travellers; also family rooms available. Informal, family oriented restaurant.

Express by Holiday Inn without rest., Richfield Ave, RG1 8EQ, ℘ (0118) 958 2558, ebhi-reading@btconnect.com, Fax (0118) 958 2858 – 🛗 🗝 ✆ ⚓ 🅿 – 🏛 30. ⓪❸ ⒶⒺ VISA. ⬗
X u
74 rm ☲ ✸76.00 – ✸✸76.00.
♦ Conveniently located next to Holiday Inn. The modern, well-equipped accommodation is ideal for business travellers. Good weekend rates and complimentary continental breakfast.

Forbury's, 1 Forbury Sq, The Forbury, RG1 3BB, ℘ (0118) 957 4044, forburys@btconnect.com, Fax (0118) 956 9191, ㎡ – ▤ ⇄ 16. ⓪❸ ⒶⒺ VISA
Y a
closed 25-27 December and Sunday dinner – **Rest** 17.75/21.00 and a la carte 24.50/32.70 🍷.
♦ Modern eatery near law courts. Relaxing area of comfy leather seats. Spacious dining room enhanced by bold prints of wine labels. Eclectic menus with Gallic starting point.

1sq2, Lime Sq., 220 South Oak Way, Green Park, RG2 6UP, South : 2 m. by A 33 ℘ (0118) 987 3702, info@lsq2.co.uk, ㎡ – 🗝 🅿 ⓪❸ ⒶⒺ VISA
X c
closed Sunday – **Rest** a la carte approx 27.00.
♦ Head towards the wind turbine by the M4 to find this buzzy restaurant with floor-to-ceiling glass serving 'corporate' style lunch menus and modern British dishes for dinner.

London Street Brasserie, 2-4 London St, RG1 4SE, ℘ (0118) 950 5036, Fax (0118) 950 5031, ㎡ – 🗝 ⓪❸ ⒶⒺ ⓪ VISA
Z c
Rest (booking essential) a la carte 23.50/32.00 🍷.
♦ Lively and modern: a polite, friendly team serve appetising British classics and international dishes. Deck terrace and first-floor window tables overlook the river Kennett.

at Kidmore End North : 5 m. by A 4155 – X – off B 481 – ✉ Reading.

The New Inn with rm, Chalkhouse Green Rd, RG4 9AU, ℘ (0118) 972 3115, Fax (0118) 972 3115, ㎡ – ⬅ 🗝 🅿 ⓪❸ ⒶⒺ VISA
Rest (closed Sunday dinner) a la carte 20.00/25.00 🍷 – **6 rm** ☲ ✸65.00/110.00 – ✸✸65.00/110.00.
♦ 16C inn with rough floorboards, beams and open fires and delightful canopied terrace. Smart, updated restaurant serves adventurous fare. Stylish, comfy, well-equipped rooms.

at Hurst East : 5 m. by A 329 – X – on B 3030 – ✉ Reading.

The Castle at Hurst, Church Hill, RG10 0SJ, ℘ (0118) 934 0034, info@castlerestaurant.co.uk, Fax (0118) 934 0334, ㎡, ⬅ – 🗝 🅿 ⇄ 13. ⓪❸ ⒶⒺ ⓪ VISA
– **Rest** a la carte 19.50/28.00.
♦ Charming 16C monk's wash-house. Part panelled dining room with wattle and daub on display and a cosy snug. Classical French menu enhanced by modern interpretations.

at Shinfield South : 4¼ m. on A 327 – X – ✉ Reading.

L'Ortolan (Murchison), Church Lane, RG2 9BY, ℘ (0118) 988 8500, info@lortolan.com, Fax (0118) 988 9338, ㎡ – 🗝 🅿 ⇄ 16. ⓪❸ ⒶⒺ
⸎
closed 24 December- 8 January, Sunday and Monday – **Rest** 21.00/55.00 🍷.
Spec. Scallops with cauliflower purée, Alsace bacon and curry oil. Suckling pig tasting plate, sage gnocchi, Savoy cabbage, smoked apple purée. Vanilla parfait with toasted marshmallow, wild strawberry sorbet.
♦ The ivy-clad exterior of this former vicarage contrasts with the contemporary interior. Service is detailed; cooking is classically based overlaid with modern influences.

REDDITCH Worcs. 503 504 O 27 – pop. 74 803.
㊀ Abbey Park G. & C.C., Dagnell End Rd ℘ (01527) 406600 – ㊀ Lower Grinsty, Green Lane, Callow Hill ℘ (01527) 543079 – ㊂ Pitcheroak, Plymouth Rd ℘ (01527) 541054.
🅑 Palace Theatre, Alcester St ℘ (01527) 60806.
London 111 – Birmingham 15 – Cheltenham 33 – Stratford-upon-Avon 15.

Old Rectory ⬱, Ipsley Lane, Ipsley, B98 0AP, ℘ (01527) 523000, ipsleyoldrectory@aol.com, Fax (01527) 517003, ㎡ – 🗝 🅿 ⓪❸ ⒶⒺ VISA
closed 25 December, 1 January – **Rest** (closed Friday-Sunday) (booking essential for non-residents) (dinner only) 23.50 and a la carte 21.00/30.00 – **10 rm** ☲ ✸97.00 – ✸✸133.00.
♦ Converted early Georgian rectory surrounded by pleasant mature gardens creating a quiet and secluded haven. Smart, traditional interior décor and individually styled rooms. Charming Georgian style conservatory restaurant.

REDHILL _Surrey_ **504** _T 30 – pop. 50 436 (inc. Reigate)._

     Redhill & Reigate, Clarence Lodge, Pendleton Rd _&_ (01737) 770204 – Canada Ave _&_ (01737) 770204.

     London 22 – Brighton 31 – Guildford 20 – Maidstone 34.

Nutfield Priory, Nutfield, RH1 4EL, East : 2 m. on A 25 _&_ (01737) 824400, _nutfield priory@handpicked.co.uk,_ Fax (01737) 824410, ≤, 🛋, 🏖, ₤⑤, ≦S, 🗔, 🕳, 🖎, squash – 🛗 🚼 🕭 ✦ 🛏 🕭 – 🕭 80. ⓂⓈ 🄰🄴 ⓄⒾ **VISA**
   Cloisters : Rest _(closed Saturday lunch)_ 22.00/36.00 and a la carte 36.25/54.50 – ☷ 14.50 – **59 rm** 🕭165.00/185.00 – 🕭🕭225.00/245.00, 1 suite.
   ◆ Restored Victorian mansion boasting intricate stonework, stained glass and neo-Gothic cloisters. Tasteful country house décor throughout including the comfortable rooms. Characterful dining room with stained glass and views across countryside.

REDWORTH _Durham – see Darlington._

REETH _N. Yorks._ **502** _O 20 – ⊠ Richmond._

     🄳 Hudson House, The Green _&_ (01748) 884059.

     London 253 – Leeds 53 – Middlesbrough 36 – Newcastle upon Tyne 61.

The Burgoyne, On The Green, DL11 6SN, _&_ (01748) 884292, _enquiries@thebur goyne.co.uk,_ Fax (01748) 884292, ≤, 🛋 – 🚼 🕭 🅿. ⓂⓈ **VISA**
   closed 2 January-14 February – **Rest** (booking essential for non-residents) (dinner only) 29.50 ☷ – **8 rm** 🕭89.00/116.50 – 🕭🕭102.50/160.00.
   ◆ Late Georgian hotel overlooking the green with views of the Dales. A charming, person-ally run, traditionally furnished house with well-appointed, individually styled rooms. Deep green dining room complements surrounding fells.

Arkleside, DL11 6SG, Northeast corner of the green _&_ (01748) 884200, _info@arkleside hotel.co.uk,_ Fax (01748) 884200, ≤, 🛋 – 🚼 🅿. ⓂⓈ **VISA**
   closed January and 25-26 December**Rest** (booking essential for non-residents) (dinner only) 27.00 – **9 rm** ☷ 🕭62.00 – 🕭🕭110.00.
   ◆ Just off Reeth's village green, a row of modernised former lead miners' cottages. Com-fortable décor throughout with a conservatory and bar area. Simple, traditional rooms. Dining room has vivid stone walls.

at Langthwaite _Northwest : 3¼ m. on Langthwaite rd – ⊠ Reeth._

The Charles Bathurst Inn 🛌 _with rm,_ DL11 6EN, _&_ (01748) 884567, _info@cbinn.co.uk,_ Fax (01748) 884599, ≤, 🛋 – 🚼 🅿. ⓂⓈ **VISA**
   closed 25 December – **Rest** a la carte 17.50/30.00 – **19 rm** ☷ 🕭85.00 – 🕭🕭105.00.
   ◆ 18C inn sited high in the hills. Open fires provide appealing atmosphere. Fresh, locally sourced menus mixing classic with modern. Large, timbered rooms with country views.

at Whaw _Northwest : 5¼ m. by Langthwaite rd on Tan Hill rd – ⊠ Reeth._

Chapel Farm 🛌, DL11 6RT, _&_ (01748) 884062, _chapelfarmbb@aol.com,_ ≤, 🖎 – 🚼 🅿. **VISA**. 🞓
   Rest (by arrangement) (communal dining) 15.00 – **3 rm** ☷ 🕭43.00 – 🕭🕭60.00.
   ◆ Restored, peaceful 18C lead miners' cottages in remote hamlet: dales are literally out-side the front door. Beamed lounge with open fire. Attractive rural styled bedrooms.

   A good night's sleep without spending a fortune?
   Look for a Bib Hotel 🏠

REIGATE _Surrey_ **504** _T 30 – pop. 50 436 (inc. Redhill)._

     London 26 – Brighton 33 – Guildford 20 – Maidstone 38.

Tony Tobin @ The Dining Room, 59a High St, RH2 9AE, _&_ (01737) 226650, Fax (01737) 226650 – 🚼 🍽. ⓂⓈ 🄰🄴 **VISA**
   closed 23 January-3 January, Saturday lunch, Sunday dinner and Bank Holidays – **Rest** 19.50/42.00 and a la carte 36.45/41.95.
   ◆ Top floor of a building on the High Street with a smart modern interior. Busy, bustling atmosphere. International menus with a modern style of cooking.

La Barbe, 71 Bell St, RH2 7AN, _&_ (01737) 241966, _restaurant@labarbe.co.uk,_ Fax (01737) 226387 – 🚼 🍽. ⓂⓈ 🄰🄴 **VISA**
   closed 23-26 December, Saturday lunch, Sunday dinner – **Rest** - French - 22.95/29.95.
   ◆ Friendly bistro with Gallic atmosphere and welcoming ambience. Regularly changing menus offer good choice of traditional French cuisine - classical and provincial in style.

ENGLAND

RETFORD Notts. 502 503 504 R 24 – pop. 21 314.

🏛 40 Grove St (01777) 860780.

London 148 – Lincoln 23 – Nottingham 31 – Sheffield 27.

⌂ **The Barns** ⌂ without rest., Morton Farm, Babworth, DN22 8HA, Southwest : 2¼ m. by A 6420 🖉 (01777) 706336, enquiries@thebarns.co.uk, � – ⇔ 🅿. ⚫⚫ VISA

closed Christmas and New Year – **6 rm** ⌷ ✦38.00 – ✦✦60.00.

♦ Privately owned and run converted part 18C farmhouse on a quiet country road. Informal, old-fashioned, cottage décor throughout. Beams within and lawned gardens without.

RHYDYCROESAU Shrops. 502 503 K 25 – see Oswestry.

RICHMOND N. Yorks. 502 O 20 Great Britain G. – pop. 8 178.

See : Town★ – Castle★ AC – Georgian Theatre Royal and Museum★.

Exc. : The Bowes Museum★, Barnard Castle, NW : 15 m. by B 6274, A 66 and minor rd (right) – Raby Castle★, NE : 6 m. of Barnard Castle by A 688.

🛇 Bend Hagg 🖉 (01748) 825319 – 🛇 Catterick, Leyburn Rd 🖉 (01748) 833268.

🏛 Friary Gardens, Victoria Rd 🖉 (01748) 850252.

London 243 – Leeds 53 – Middlesbrough 26 – Newcastle upon Tyne 44.

🏨 **The King's Head,** Market Pl, DL10 4HS, 🖉 (01748) 850220, res@kingsheadrichmond.co.uk, Fax (01748) 850635 – ⇔ 🅿 – 🔏 150. ⚫⚫ AE ① VISA

Rest (bar lunch Monday-Saturday)/dinner a la carte 23.85/30.90 s. ⚚ – **30 rm** ⌷ ✦80.00/88.00 – ✦✦138.00.

♦ Built in 1718, later to become a coaching inn, located on the main square. Classic, traditional style; a lounge with carriage and case clocks and simple, elegant bedrooms. Restaurant has views across square to Norman castle.

⌂ **Millgate House** without rest., 3 Millgate, DL10 4JN, 🖉 (01748) 823571, oztim@millgatehouse.demon.co.uk, Fax (01748) 850701, � – ⇔ 🤍 🅿

3 rm ⌷ ✦65.00 – ✦✦85.00/95.00.

♦ Georgian townhouse with fine elevated views of river Swale and Richmond Castle. Award winning terraced garden. Antique furnished interior. Bedrooms are tastefully restrained.

⌂ **West End** without rest., 45 Reeth Rd, DL10 4EX, West : ½ m. on A 6108 🖉 (01748) 824783, westend@richmond.org, 🌫 – ⇔ 🅿. ✂

closed December-January – **5 rm** ⌷ ✦30.00/45.00 – ✦✦60.00.

♦ Fine mid 19C house, away from town centre, with gardens. Homely lounge with plenty of maps and walking guides. Simple, neat and tidy rooms. Adjacent self-catering cottages.

at Downholme Southwest : 5½ m. on A 6108 – ✉ Richmond.

⌂ **Walburn Hall** without rest., DL11 6AF, South : 1½ m. on A 6108 🖉 (01748) 822152, walburnhall@farmersweekly.net, Fax (01748) 822152, ≼, 🌫 – ⇔ 🅿. ⚫⚫ VISA. ✂

March-October – **3 rm** ⌷ ✦40.00/45.00 – ✦✦64.00/76.00.

♦ Mary Queen of Scots reputedly stayed in this part 14C fortified farmhouse. Cottage-style lounge; dining room serves traditional Yorkshire breakfasts. Beamed bedrooms.

at Whashton Northwest : 4½ m. by Ravensworth rd – ✉ Richmond.

⌂ **Whashton Springs Farm** ⌂ without rest., DL11 7JS, South : 1½ m. on Richmond rd 🖉 (01748) 822884, whashtonsprings@btconnect.com, Fax (01748) 826285, 🌫, 🐾 – ⇔ 🅿. ✂

closed Christmas-New Year – **8 rm** ⌷ ✦35.00/40.00 – ✦✦58.00/64.00.

♦ A working farm with a spacious, pleasantly converted, period farmhouse; surrounded by attractive countryside. Cottagey rooms, some in converted stable block.

at Dalton Northwest : 6¾ m. by Ravensworth rd and Gayles rd – ✉ Richmond.

🍴 **The Travellers Rest,** DL11 7HU, 🖉 (01833) 621225 – 🅿. ⚫⚫ VISA

closed 25-26 December and 1 January – **Rest** (closed dinner Sunday and Monday) (dinner only and Sunday lunch) a la carte 15.95/24.00 ⚚.

♦ Characterful country inn in tiny hamlet. Blackboard menu offers a wide-ranging menu where traditional meets the up-to-date. Linen-laid restaurant also available.

RIDGEWAY Derbs. – see Sheffield (S. Yorks.).

RILLA MILL Cornwall – see Callington.

RINGSTEAD Norfolk 504 V 25 – see Hunstanton.

RINGWOOD Hants. 503 504 O 31 – pop. 13 387.

🧳 *The Furlong* ℰ *(01425) 470896.*
London 102 – Bournemouth 11 – Salisbury 17 – Southampton 20.

🏛 **Moortown Lodge** without rest., 244 Christchurch Rd, BH24 3AS, South : 1 m. on B 3347 ℰ (01425) 471404, *hotel@moortownlodge.co.uk, Fax* (01425) 476527 – ↜✕ 📞 📍.
🕸 🆅🅸🆂🅰. ⌗
7 rm ⌑ ✦64.00 – ✦✦80.00/90.00.
◆ House dating from the 1760s, located on the edge of the New Forest. Family run, traditional atmosphere with a cosy lounge and chintz-furnished rooms of varying sizes.

RIPLEY N. Yorks. 502 P 21 – ✉ Harrogate.
London 213 – Bradford 21 – Leeds 18 – Newcastle upon Tyne 79.

🏛🏛 **The Boar's Head,** HG3 3AY, ℰ (01423) 771888, *reservations@boarsheadripley.co.uk, Fax* (01423) 771509, 🔨, ⌗ – ↜✕ 📍. 🕸 🆅🅸🆂🅰 🅰🅴 ① 🆅🅸🆂🅰
The Restaurant : Rest 19.00/40.00 and a la carte 20.00/31.00 ⌇ – **The Bistro :** Rest 16.95/30.00 and a la carte 20.00/26.00 ⌇ – **25 rm** ⌑ ✦105.00 – ✦✦150.00.
◆ 18C coaching inn within estate village of Ripley Castle, reputedly furnished from castle's attics. Comfy, unique rooms, some in courtyard or adjacent house. The Restaurant, in deep burgundy, has period paintings. The Bistro boasts impressive flagged floors.

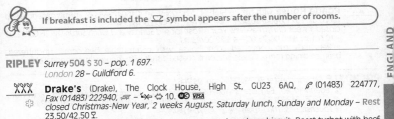

If breakfast is included the ⌑ symbol appears after the number of rooms.

ENGLAND

RIPLEY Surrey 504 S 30 – pop. 1 697.
London 28 – Guildford 6.

🍴🍴🍴 **Drake's** (Drake), The Clock House, High St, GU23 6AQ, ℰ (01483) 224777, *Fax* (01483) 222940, 🌳 – ↜✕ ✿ 10. 🕸 🆅🅸🆂🅰
❀ *closed Christmas-New Year, 2 weeks August, Saturday lunch, Sunday and Monday –* Rest 23.50/42.50 ⌇.
Spec. Poached egg with pea cream, cep casserole and cep biscuit. Roast turbot with beef cheek, asparagus and mushroom velouté. Crème renversée with Granny Smith sorbet.
◆ Large illuminated clock announces this smart restaurant of Georgian red brick. Local gallery art nestles on walls. Refined cooking on a classical base; good value lunches.

RIPON N. Yorks. 502 P 21 Great Britain G. – pop. 16 468.
See : Town★ - Cathedral★ (Saxon Crypt) AC.
Env. : Fountains Abbey★★★ AC :- Studley Royal AC (≼★ from Anne Boleyn's Seat) - Fountains Hall (Façade★), SW : 2½ m. by B 6265 – Newby Hall (Tapestries★) AC, SE : 3½ m. by B 6265.
🏌 Ripon City, Palace Rd ℰ (01765) 603640.
🧳 Minster Rd ℰ (08453) 890178.
London 222 – Leeds 26 – Middlesbrough 35 – York 23.

🏛🏛 **The Old Deanery,** Minster Rd, HG4 1QS, ℰ (01765) 600003, *reception@theolddeanery.co.uk, Fax* (01765) 600027, 🌳 – ↜✕ 📞 📍. – 🛎 50. 🕸 🆅🅸🆂🅰
closed 25 December – Rest (*closed Sunday dinner*) 12.50/24.50 and dinner a la carte 29.50/41.70 s ⌇ – **11 rm** ⌑ ✦95.00 – ✦✦140.00.
◆ Eponymously named hotel opposite cathedral. Stylish interior blends seamlessly with older charms. Afternoon tea in secluded garden. 18C oak staircase leads to modern rooms. Appealing seasonal cooking in spacious dining room.

⌂ **Sharow Cross House,** Dishforth Rd, Sharow, HG4 5BQ, Northeast : 1 ¾ m. by A 61 on Sharow rd ℰ (01765) 609866, *sharowcrosshouse@btinternet.com,* 🌳 – ↜✕ 📍. ⌗
closed Christmas and New Year – Rest (by arrangement) 20.00 – **3 rm** ⌑ ✦50.00/60.00 – ✦✦65.00/75.00.
◆ Idyllically set 19C house, built for mill owner. Capacious hall with welcoming fire. Spacious bedrooms: the master room is huge and offers Cathedral views on clear days.

at Aldfield Southwest : 3¾ m. by B 6265 – ✉ Ripon.

⌂ **Bay Tree Farm** 🐄 without restaurant, HG4 3BE, ℰ (01765) 620394, *val@btfarm.entadsl.com, Fax* (01765) 620394, 🌳 – ↜✕ 🖧 📍. 🕸 🆅🅸🆂🅰
restricted opening in winter – – **6 rm** ⌑ ✦40.00/60.00 – ✦✦70.00/75.00.
◆ Comfortable and characterful farmhouse conversion with pleasant gardens. Homely rooms, some beamed, in 17C stone barn; all accommodation boasts serene views over pasture.

at Markington *Southwest : 5 m. by A 61 – ✉ Harrogate.*

Hob Green, HG3 3PJ, Southwest : ½ m. ✆ (01423) 770031, *info@hobgreen.com, Fax (01423) 771589*, ←, ⊄, ⚘ – ⇔ P. MC AE ⊙ VISA
Rest 16.95/26.50 – **11 rm** ☐ ☆85.00/95.00 – ☆☆110.00/120.00, 1 suite.
◆ 18C country house in a rural position surrounded by extensive parkland. A true country house hotel furnished with antiques and curios. Each room unique and characterful. Dining room with country views; garden produce prominently used.

at Galphay *West : 4½ m. by B 6265 – ✉ Ripon.*

Galphay Inn, HG4 3NJ, ✆ (01765) 650133, *info@galphayinn.co.uk, Fax (01765) 658992* – P. MC VISA
Rest *(closed Tuesday)* 15.95 (lunch) and a la carte 19.00/26.00.
◆ Pleasantly set in charming rural spot; a distinctive, homely feel prevails. Snug interior with open fire. Tasty, accomplished cooking propelled by a taste of the seasons.

RISHWORTH *W. Yorks. – see Sowerby Bridge.*

ROADE *Northants.* 504 R 27 – *pop. 2 254.*

London 66 – Coventry 36 – Leicester 42 – Northampton 5.5.

XX **Roade House** with rm, 16 High St, NN7 2NW, ✆ (01604) 863372, *info@roadehousehotel.co.uk, Fax (01604) 862421* – ⇔, ▤ rest, P. MC AE VISA. ⚘
closed 1 week Christmas-New Year – **Rest** *(closed Sunday and lunch Saturday)* 26.00/32.00 – **10 rm** ☐ ☆60.00/75.00 – ☆☆70.00/83.00.
◆ Personally run converted schoolhouse with comfortable bedrooms. Uncluttered, beamed dining room. Classic, seasonally based dishes with modern international elements.

ROCHDALE *Gtr Manchester* 502 N 23 – *pop. 95 796.*

18 Edenfield Rd, Bagslate ✆ (01706) 646024 – 18 Marland, Springfield Park, Bolton Rd ✆ (01706) 649801 – 18, 9 Castle Hawk, Chadwick Lane, Castleton ✆ (01706) 640841.
Touchstones, The Esplanade ✆ (01706) 864928.
London 224 – Blackpool 40 – Burnley 11 – Leeds 45 – Liverpool 40 – Manchester 12.

Hindle Pastures, Highgate Lane, Whitworth, OL12 0TS, North : 2½ m. by A 671 off Tonacliffe Rd ✆ (01706) 643310, *hindlepastures@tiscali.co.uk*, ←, ⊜, ⊄, ⚘ – ⇔ P. ⚘
Rest (by arrangement) (communal dining) 18.00 – **3 rm** ☐ ☆30.00/40.00 – ☆☆60.00.
◆ Superbly located barn high in the Pennines with views over four counties. Special attention paid to extensive breakfasts with freshly laid eggs. Brightly decorated rooms. Open plan dining room; imaginative meals served with fellow guests.

XX **Nutters**, Edenfield Rd, Norden, OL12 7TT, West : 3½ m. on A 680 ✆ (01706) 650167, *enquiries@nuttersrestaurant.com, Fax (01706) 650167*, ← – ⇔ P. ⇔ 20. MC AE VISA
closed 27-28 December, 2-3 January and Bank Holiday Mondays – **Rest** 15.95/34.00 and a la carte 22.25/35.30 ♀.
◆ Views of the lyrical gardens contrast with a menu of often complex modern British dishes with international twists and influences. Best views at either end of the room.

XX **After Eight**, 2 Edenfield Rd, OL11 5AA, West : 1 m. on A 680 ✆ (01706) 646432, *ataylor@aftereight.uk.com, Fax (01706) 646432*, ⊄ – ⇔. MC AE ⊙ VISA
closed 24 and 31 December, Sunday dinner and Monday-Wednesday – **Rest** (dinner only and Sunday lunch) a la carte 20.50/27.95.
◆ Substantial 19C house, personally run, offering a relaxed neighbourhood ambience. Concise menu offers a broad range of traditional dishes with vegetarians well catered for.

at Littleborough *Northeast : 4½ m. by A 58 on B 6225 – ✉ Rochdale.*

Hollingworth Lake without rest., 164 Smithybridge Rd, OL15 0DB, ✆ (01706) 376583, ⊄ – ⇔ ✆ P. MC ⊙ VISA
5 rm ☐ ☆32.50/37.50 – ☆☆50.00.
◆ A short distance from country park, lake and the moors. A comfortable, friendly, good value house with well equipped, attractively furnished bedrooms.

ROCHESTER *Medway* 504 V 29 *Great Britain G.* – *pop. 17 125* – ✉ *Chatham.*

See : *Castle★ AC – Cathedral★ AC.*
Env. : *World Naval Base★★, Chatham, NE : 2 m. of the Cathedral.*
Exc. : *Leeds Castle★, SE : 11 m. by A 229 and M 20.*
95 High St ✆ (01634) 843666, visitor.centre@medway.gov.uk.
London 30 – Dover 45 – Maidstone 8 – Margate 46.

ENGLAND

Bridgewood Manor, Bridgewood Roundabout, ME5 9AX, Southeast : 3 m. by A 2 and A 229 on Walderslade rd *ℰ* (01634) 201333, *reservationsbm@marstonhotels.com*, Fax (01634) 201330, ☯, ℉, ⇔, ⬚, ℀ – 🕴 ⇔, ▦ rest, & **P.** – 🔁 250. ⚫❸ 🄰🄴 🄾 *VISA*. ✿

Squires : Rest 13.95/25.00 **s.** and a la carte 25.00/34.00 ♀ – **96 rm** �byꜛ *✦*132.50 – *✦✦*171.00, 4 suites.
 ◆ Purpose-built hotel with central courtyard and fitted modern interior. Bedrooms have a well-kept, comfortable feel. Geared to business travellers. Imposingly formal Squires.

ROCK Cornwall 503 F 32 *The West Country G.* – pop. 3 433 – ✉ Wadebridge.
 Exc. : Pencarrow★, SE : 8½ m. by B 3314 and A 389.
 London 266 – Newquay 24 – Tintagel 14 – Truro 32.

St Enodoc, PL27 6LA, *ℰ* (01208) 863394, *info@enodoc-hotel.co.uk*, Fax (01208) 863970, ⩽, 佘, ℉, ⇔, ⬚ heated, 🌹 – ⇔ rm, ❤ **P.** ⚫❸ 🄰🄴 *VISA*. ✿
 closed 10 December-9 February except New Year – **Restaurant :** Rest (light lunch)/dinner a la carte 26.45/35.65 – **16 rm** ⊆ *✦*90.00/170.00 – *✦✦*115.00/220.00, 4 suites.
 ◆ A refreshingly modern take on the seaside hotel; neutral fabrics, sandwashed pine and contemporary oil paintings in stylish rooms, many facing the Camel Estuary.

L'Estuaire, Rock Rd, PL27 6JS, *ℰ* (01208) 862622, *lestuairerest@btconnect.com*, Fax (01208) 862622, 佘 – ⇔ ⚫❸ *VISA*
 closed Christmas, 2 weeks January, 2 weeks November and Monday-Tuesday except Bank Holidays – **Rest** - French - 23.00 (lunch) and a la carte 25.00/51.00.
 ◆ Oddly shaped building has been a dance hall and garage in its day! Now a family run restaurant, its tastefully restrained interior is matched by serious modern French menus.

ROCKBEARE Devon – see Exeter.

LA ROCQUE Jersey (Channel Islands) 517 ⑪ – see Channel Islands.

ROGATE W. Sussex 504 R 30 – ✉ Petersfield (Hants.).
 London 63 – Brighton 42 – Guildford 29 – Portsmouth 23 – Southampton 36.

Mizzards Farm ⌀ without rest., GU31 5HS, Southwest : 1 m. by Harting rd *ℰ* (01730) 821656, *francis@mizzards.co.uk*, Fax (01730) 821655, ⩽, ⬚ heated, 🌹, ꭫ – ⇔ **P.** ✿
 closed Christmas and New Year – **3 rm** ⊆ *✦*55.00 – *✦✦*80.00/85.00.
 ◆ 17C farmhouse with delightful landscaped gardens, which include a lake, bordered by river Rother. Views of woods and farmland. Fine fabrics and antiques in appealing rooms.

ROMALDKIRK Durham 502 N 20 – see Barnard Castle.

ROMSEY Hants. 503 504 P 31 *Great Britain G.* – pop. 17 386.
 See : Abbey★ (interior★★).
 Env. : Broadlands★ AC, S : 1 m.
 ᴛ₈ Dunwood Manor, Danes Rd, Awbridge *ℰ* (01794) 340549 – ᴛ₈ Nursling *ℰ* (023) 8073 2218 – ᴛ₈, ℡ Wellow, Ryedown Lane, East Wellow *ℰ* (01794) 322872.
 🄱 13 Church St *ℰ* (01794) 512987.
 London 82 – Bournemouth 28 – Salisbury 16 – Southampton 8 – Winchester 10.

Ranvilles Farm House without rest., Ower, SO51 6AA, Southwest : 2 m. on A 3090 (southbound carriageway) *ℰ* (023) 8081 4481, *info@ranvilles.com*, Fax (023) 8081 4481, 🌹 – ⇔ **P.**
 4 rm ⊆ *✦*30.00/40.00 – *✦✦*60.00/65.00.
 ◆ Attractive part 16C farmhouse set within five acres of garden and fields. Welcoming country style décor and furniture throughout, including the well-kept bedrooms.

Highfield House ⌀, Newtown Rd, Awbridge, SO51 0GG, Northwest : 3½ m. by A 3090 (old A 31) and A 27 *ℰ* (01794) 340727, *highfield-house@btinternet.com*, Fax (01794) 340727, 🌹 – ⇔ **P.** ✿
 Rest (by arrangement) (communal dining) 17.50 – **3 rm** ⊆ *✦*45.00 – *✦✦*65.00.
 ◆ Modern house with gardens, in a tranquil location just out of Awbridge village. Accommodation is comfortable with good facilities. Real fires in the guest lounge. Communal dining with garden views.

The Three Tuns, 58 Middlebridge St, SO51 8HL, *ℰ* (01794) 512639 – ⇔ **P.** ⚫❸ *VISA*
 Rest (closed Monday) a la carte 15.00/25.00.
 ◆ 18C town centre pub with period feel supplied by beams and log fire, though rest of interior is understated. Modern, well-judged cooking using first-rate ingredients.

ROSEDALE ABBEY *N. Yorks.* 502 R 20 *Great Britain G.* – ✉ *Pickering.*
   Env. : ≤★ *on road to Hutton-le-Hole.*
   London 247 – Middlesbrough 27 – Scarborough 25 – York 36.

🏛 **Milburn Arms,** YO18 8RA, ℰ (01751) 417312, *info@milburnarms.co.uk,*
   Fax (01751) 417541, 佘 – 圏 **P.** – 🔏 300. ◯◯ **AE** **VISA**. ✼
   – Priory : Rest 20.00 and a la carte 16.90/28.40 **– 13 rm** ⊆ ✟47.50/62.50 **– ✟✟**80.00.
   ✦ Neatly kept, comfy bedrooms in pastel shades, cosy little sitting room and traditional
   real ale bar in a well-run village inn: a good base for walking the North York Moors. Split-
   level dining room with subtle country styling.

ROSS-ON-WYE *Herefordshire* 503 504 M 28 *Great Britain G.* – *pop. 10 085.*
   See : *Market House★ – Yat Rock* (≤★).
   Env. : *SW : Wye Valley★ – Goodrich Castle★ AC, SW : 3½ m. by A 40.*
   🖪 *Swan House, Edde Cross St* ℰ (01989) 562768.
   London 118 – Gloucester 15 – Hereford 15 – Newport 35.

🏛🏛 **The Chase,** Gloucester Rd, HR9 5LH, ℰ (01989) 763161, *res@chasehotel.co.uk,*
   Fax (01989) 768330, 佘 – 圏 圏 **P.** – 🔏 300. ◯◯ **AE** ◯ **VISA**. ✼
   closed 24-29 December **– Rest** 15.00/25.00 and a la carte 23.00/39.95 ♈ **– 36 rm** ⊆ ✟79.00
   – ✟✟95.00/175.00.
   ✦ Elegant Georgian country house, close to town centre. Original architectural features
   such as impressive tiled reception area. Range of room styles with traditional décor. Restaurant exudes airy, period feel.

🏛 **Wilton Court,** Wilton Lane, HR9 6AQ, West : ¾ m. by B 4260 (A 49 Hereford) ℰ (01989)
   562569, *info@wiltoncourthotel.com, Fax* (01989) 768460, 佘, 佘 – 圏 ℭ **P.** ◯◯ **AE** **VISA**
   Mulberry : Rest *(closed Sunday dinner)* (dinner only and Sunday lunch)/dinner 27.50 and a
   la carte 23.70/31.40 **– 10 rm** ⊆ ✟70.00/110.00 **– ✟✟**90.00/130.00.
   ✦ Attractive, part-Elizabethan house on the banks of the river Wye. 16C wood panelling in
   situ in bar and two of the bedrooms: others have a distinctly William Morris influence.
   Light, airy conservatory restaurant boasts Lloyd Loom furniture and garden views.

✕✕ **Bridge House** with rm, Wilton, HR9 6AA, ℰ (01989) 567655, *info@bridge-house-ho*
   tel.com, Fax (01989) 567652, ✎, 佘 – 圏 **P.** ◯◯ **AE** **VISA**
   Rest a la carte 26.00/36.20 **– 9 rm** ⊆ ✟65.00 **–** ✟✟96.00/120.00.
   ✦ On the banks of the Wye, boasting a kitchen garden supplying ingredients for the
   owners' passionate belief in home cooking. Also, a homely bar and well-maintained bedrooms.

🍴 **The Lough Pool Inn,** Sellack, HR9 6LX, Northwest : 3 ¼ m. by B 4260 and A 49 on
   Hoarwithy rd ℰ (01989) 730236, *david@loughpool.co.uk, Fax* (01432) 880055, 佘, 佘 –
   圏 **P.** ◯◯ **VISA**. ✼
   closed 25 December and Sunday dinner and Monday November and January **– Rest** a la
   carte 16.00/30.00 ♈.
   ✦ Ancient beams and wattle walls in this personally run 16C inn. Seasonal cooking, served
   at scrubbed farmhouse tables, is well-priced, unfussy and full of local flavour.

at Kerne Bridge *South : 3¾ m. on B 4234 –* ✉ *Ross-on-Wye.*

↑ **Lumleys** without rest., HR9 5QT, ℰ (01600) 890040, *helen@lumleys.force9.co.uk,* 佘 –
   圏 ℭ **P.**
   3 rm ⊆ ✟45.00/55.00 **– ✟✟**70.00.
   ✦ Welcoming and personally run guesthouse in sympathetically converted Victorian
   house. Ideally located for Wye valley and Forest of Dean. Pine decorated cottage style
   rooms.

at Glewstone *Southwest : 3¼ m. by A 40 –* ✉ *Ross-on-Wye.*

🏛 **Glewstone Court,** HR9 6AW, ℰ (01989) 770367, *glewstone@aol.com,*
   Fax (01989) 770282, ≤, 佘 – 圏 rest, **P.** ◯◯ **AE** **VISA**
   closed 25-28 December **– Rest** a la carte 22.25/30.95 **s.** **– 8 rm** ⊆ ✟57.50/79.00 **–**
   ✟✟115.00.
   ✦ Part Georgian and Victorian country house with impressive cedar of Lebanon in grounds.
   Sweeping staircase leads to uncluttered rooms. Family run with charming eccentricity.
   Antique-strewn dining room.

at Llangarron *Southwest : 5½ m. by A 40 –* ✉ *Ross-on-Wye.*

↑ **Trecilla Farm** 🌿 without rest., HR9 6NQ, ℰ (01989) 770647, *info@trecillafarm.co.uk,*
   ✎, 佘, 🐴 – 圏 **P.**
   closed Christmas and New Year **– 3 rm** ⊆ ✟50.00/75.00 **–** ✟✟85.00/100.00.
   ✦ 16C farmhouse with babbling brook. Beautiful lounge typifies smart, country house
   style. Breakfast locations dependent on time of year. Book the four-poster room if possible!

at **Peterstow** *West : 2½ m. on A 49 – ⊠ Ross-on-Wye.*

🏨 **Pengethley Manor** ⌂, HR9 6LL, Northwest : 1 ½ m. on A 49 ℰ (01989) 730211,
reservations@pengethleymanor.co.uk, Fax *(01989) 730238,* ≤, ⌸ heated, ☞, 🅿 – ⭐ 🅿 –
🔔 50. 🐵 🎗 🎗 ⓪ 𝗩𝗜𝗦𝗔
Georgian Restaurant : Rest 18.00 (lunch) and a la carte 26.00/40.50 ♀ – **22 rm** ⊈ ♦79.00
– ♦♦120.00, 3 suites.
   ◆ Fine period house set in a prominent position affording country views. Grounds include
vineyard and giant chess set. Rooms vary in size and all are comfy and characterful. Spacious dining room with country house feel.

ROSTHWAITE *Cumbria 502 K 20 – see Keswick.*

ROTHBURY *Northd. 501 502 O 18 Great Britain G. – pop. 1 963 – ⊠ Morpeth.*
   See : *Cragside House★ (interior★) AC.*
   🛈 National Park Centre, Church House, Church St ℰ *(01669) 620887.*
   London 311 – Edinburgh 84 – Newcastle upon Tyne 29.

⌂ **Farm Cottage,** Thropton, NE65 7NA, West : 2 ¼ m. on B 6341 ℰ (01669) 620831,
joan@farmcottageguesthouse.co.uk, Fax *(01669) 620831,* ☞ – ⭐ 🅿. 🐵 𝗩𝗜𝗦𝗔. ⌖
Rest (by arrangement) – 5 rm ☶ ♦45.00/45.00 – ♦♦60.00/72.00.
   ◆ 18C stone cottage and gardens; owner was actually born here. Two comfy lounges filled
with family prints and curios. Individually styled rooms with plenty of extra touches. Glass-
roofed, garden styled dining room serves home cooked menus.

⌂ **Thropton Demesne Farmhouse** ⌂ without rest., Thropton, NE65 7LT, West :
2 ¼ m. on B 6341 ℰ (01669) 620196, *thropton–demesne@yahoo.co.uk,* ≤, ☞ – ⭐ 🅿.
⌖
Easter-October – 3 rm ☶ ♦50.00 – ♦♦60.00.
   ◆ Early 19C stone-built former farmhouse; unbroken Coquet Valley views. Lounge defined
by quality décor. Artwork on walls by owner. Individually styled rooms with lovely vistas.

⌂ **Lee Farm** ⌂ without rest., NE65 8JQ, South : 3 ¼ m. by B 6342 on The Lee rd ℰ (01665)
570257, *enqs@leefarm.co.uk,* Fax *(01665) 570257,* ≤, ☞, 🅿 – ⭐ 🅿.
closed Christmas and New Year – 3 rm ☶ ♦45.00/50.00 – ♦♦65.00/70.00.
   ◆ Family-run house in a peaceful valley; firelit lounge, trim, pretty rooms in pastel tones,
breakfasts at a communal table. Guests are free to explore the livestock farm.

ROTHERHAM *S. Yorks. 502 503 504 P 23 – pop. 117 262.*
   🛆 Thrybergh Park ℰ *(01709) 850466 –* 🛆 Grange Park, Upper Wortley Rd, Kimberworth
   ℰ *(01709) 558884 –* 🛆 Phoenix, Pavilion Lane, Brinsworth ℰ *(01709) 363788.*
   🛈 40 Bridgegate ℰ *(01709) 835904.*
   London 166 – Kingston-upon-Hull 61 – Leeds 36 – Sheffield 6.

🏨 **Courtyard by Marriott,** West Bawtry Rd, S60 4NA, South : 2 ¼ m. on A 630 ℰ (0870)
400 7235, *res.rthcourtyard@kewgreen.co.uk,* Fax *(0870) 400 7335,* Ⅰ₆, ⌧ – 📶 ⭐, 🍴 rest,
📶 🅿 – 🔔 300. 🐵 🎗 🎗 ⓪ 𝗩𝗜𝗦𝗔. ⌖
Capistrano : Rest (bar lunch Saturday) (carving lunch)/dinner 19.95 ♀ – **102 rm** ⊈
♦102.00 – ♦♦110.00, 2 suites.
   ◆ Modern purpose-built hotel out of town centre. Uniform rooms have a bright tone.
Features, such as work desks and ergonomic chairs, are well suited to business travellers.
Restaurant boasts smoked glass conservatory extension.

🏨 **Elton,** Main St, Bramley, S66 2SF, East : 4 ¼ m. by A 6021, A 631 and Cross St. ℰ (01709)
545681, *bestwestern.eltonhotel@btinternet.com,* Fax *(01709) 549100 –* ⭐, 🍴 rest, 🖉 🅿 –
🔔 50. 🐵 🎗 ⓪ 𝗩𝗜𝗦𝗔
Rest 13.50/22.50 and a la carte 22.85/28.15 s. ♀ – **29 rm** ☶ ♦75.00/90.00 –
♦♦98.00/95.00.
   ◆ Solid stone house with extensions, in the centre of village. Traditionally styled public
areas include conservatory lounge. Extension rooms have a more modern style. Richly
styled dining room with warm burgundy walls.

ROTHERWICK *Hants. – see Hook.*

ROUGHAM GREEN *Suffolk – see Bury St Edmunds.*

ROWDE *Wilts. 503 504 N 29 – see Devizes*

ENGLAND

629

ROWSLEY *Derbs.* 502 503 504 P 24 *Great Britain G.* – ⊠ *Matlock.*
Env. : *Chatsworth*★★★ *(Park and Garden*★★★*) AC, N : by B 6012.*
London 157 – Derby 23 – Manchester 40 – Nottingham 30.

East Lodge ⌂, DE4 2EF, ℘ (01629) 734474, *info@eastlodge.com, Fax (01629) 733949,*
🍽, 🚗, 🛏 – ⇔ 👍 ⓟ, ☎ ☎ VISA. ✦
Rest 16.00/40.00 – **12 rm** ⌂ ✦110.00/130:00 – ✦✦160.00/210.00.
● Elegant 17C country house set in ten acres of well kept grounds, once the lodge to
Haddon Hall. Rooms are each individually decorated and superior rooms have garden
views. Simple dining room with terrace.

The Peacock, Bakewell Rd, DE4 2EB, ℘ (01629) 733518, *reception@thepeacockatrows*
ley.com, Fax (01629) 732671, ⌂, 🚗 – ⇔ rest, ⓟ, ☎ ☎ ☎ VISA
*closed 2-8 January*Rest 21.50 (lunch) and a la carte 25.25/45.95 ♀ – ⌂ 6.25 – **16 rm**
✦75.00/125.00 – ✦✦165.00/200.00.
● Characterful, antique furnished, 17C house with gardens leading down to the river
Derwent. Rooms, a variety of shapes and sizes, are antique or reproduction furnished.
Restaurant divided between three smart rooms.

ROWTON *Ches.* 502 503 L 24 – *see Chester.*

ROYAL LEAMINGTON SPA *Warks.* 503 504 P 27 – *pop. 61 595.*
🏌 *Leamington and County, Golf Lane, Whitnash* ℘ (01926) 425961 *(on plan of Warwick).*
🚺 *The Royal Pump Rooms, The Parade* ℘ (01926) 742762.
London 99 – Birmingham 23 – Coventry 9 – Leicester 33 – Warwick 3.

ROYAL
LEAMINGTON SPA

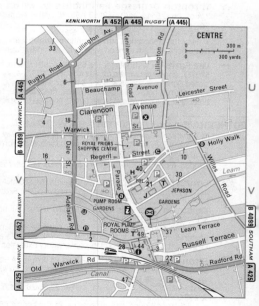

Mallory Court ⌂, Harbury Lane, Bishop's Tachbrook, CV33 9QB, South : 2 ¼ m. by
B 4087 (Tachbrook Rd) ℘ (01926) 330214, *reception@mallory.co.uk, Fax (01926) 451714,*
⇐, ⛳, ⚒, ✎ – 📶 – 🔬 160. ☎ ☎ ☎ VISA
Rest (booking essential) 25.00/49.50 ♀ –(see also **The Brasserie at Mallory** below) – 30 rm
⌂ ✦95.00/250.00 – ✦✦350.00/400.00.
Spec. Marinated tuna, dressed crab and roasted scallops. Fillet of veal with sweetbread and
wild mushroom cannelloni. Strawberry and white chocolate soufflé with strawberry trifle.
● Part Edwardian country house in Lutyens style; extensive landscaped gardens. Finest
quality antiques and furnishings throughout public areas and individually styled bedrooms.
Refined country house style dining in elegant restaurant.

Courtyard by Marriott, Olympus Ave, Tachbrook Park, CV34 6RT, Southwest : 1 ½ m. by A 452 ℘ (01926) 425522, *res.lspcourtyard@kewgreen.co.uk, Fax (01926) 881332* – rm, rest, P – 70. MC AE VISA
on Warwick town plan Z v
Rest (bar lunch)/dinner 20.00 and a la carte 26.00/33.00 **s.** – **91 rm** 118.00/145.00 – 128.00/175.00.
◆ Modern hotel in the conveniently located Tachbrook business park. Smart modern fixtures and fittings provide good levels of comfort. Well suited to business travellers. Bright, brasserie-style restaurant.

The Angel, 143 Regent St, CV32 4NZ, ℘ (01926) 881296, *angelhotel143@hotmail.com, Fax (01926) 313853* – P – 40. MC AE VISA U c
The Print Room : **Rest** *(closed Sunday dinner)* (bar lunch Monday-Saturday)/dinner 18.00 – **46 rm** 75.00/85.00 – 85.00/100.00.
◆ Centrally located Regency hotel which once provided stabling for a hundred horses. Traditional public areas. Rooms have an uncluttered air with simple, elegant furnishings. Classic ambience defines restaurant.

Episode, 64 Upper Holly Walk, CV32 3JL, ℘ (01926) 883777, *Fax (01926) 330467*, – rest, P – 40. MC AE VISA. U o
Rest (bar lunch)/dinner a la carte 19.90/31.45 – **30 rm** 85.00/90.00 – 100.00/115.00.
◆ Characterful Victorian house with spacious and well-decorated interior featuring high ceilings and parquet flooring. Good comfort levels in the sizeable bedrooms. Bistro dining room has smart, elegant, period feel.

Adams without restaurant, 22 Avenue Rd, CV31 3PQ, ℘ (01926) 450742, *bookings@adams-hotel.co.uk, Fax (01926) 313110*, – P. MC VISA V n
closed Christmas and New Year – **14 rm** 55.00/76.00 – 78.00/85.00.
◆ Delightful house of the Regency period with plenty of charm and character: original features include ceiling mouldings. Immaculate and similarly attractive bedrooms.

York House without rest., 9 York Rd, CV31 3PR, ℘ (01926) 424671, *reservations@yorkhousehotel.biz, Fax (01926) 832272* – . MC VISA V u
closed 2 weeks Christmas – **8 rm** 25.00/52.00 – 52.00/68.00.
◆ Victorian house on a pleasant parade, retains characterful fittings such as stained glass windows. Views of River Leam. Simply furnished rooms in period style.

The Brasserie at Mallory (at Mallory Court H.), Harbury Lane, Bishop's Tachbrook, CV33 9QB, South : 2 ¼ m. by B 4087 (Tachbrook Rd) ℘ (01926) 453939, *thebrasserie@mallory.co.uk, Fax (01926) 451714*, , – P 25. MC AE VISA
closed Sunday dinner – **Rest** a la carte 18.45/36.50 **s.**
◆ In hotel annex; step into bar with eye-catching Art Deco style. Conservatory dining room overlooks pretty walled garden and terrace. Modern British cooking in a buzzy setting.

The Emperors, Bath Pl, CV31 3BP, ℘ (01926) 313030, *Fax (01926) 435966* – . MC AE VISA V i
closed 25-26 December, 1 January and Sunday – **Rest** - Chinese (Canton and Peking) - a la carte 18.00/28.00.
◆ Large warehouse conversion adjacent to railway station. Decorated with traditional war banners and framed oriental prints. Authentic, tasty Chinese cuisine.

Restaurant 23, 23 Dormer Place, CV32 5AA, ℘ (01926) 422422, *info@restaurant23.co.uk, Fax (01926) 422246* – . MC VISA V a
closed 2 weeks August, 1-7 January, 25 December, Sunday and Monday – **Rest** 21.00 (lunch) and dinner a la carte 26.85/33.45 **s.**
◆ Ever spoken to a working chef in a restaurant? You can here, in elegantly appointed surroundings, where classically based, seasonal, modern dishes are concocted by the owner.

Oscar's, 39 Chandos St, CV32 4RL, ℘ (01926) 452807, *enquiries@oscarsfrenchbistro.co.uk* – . MC AE VISA U x
closed Sunday-Monday – **Rest** (booking essential) 16.00/23.00.
◆ Bustling, informal and unpretentious, set in three rooms on two floors; upstairs smoking area. Good value, accomplished French bistro cooking; notable steak specialities.

Undecided between two equivalent establishments?
Within each category, establishments are classified in our order of preference.

ENGLAND

ROYAL TUNBRIDGE WELLS Kent 504 U 30 *Great Britain G.* – *pop.* 60 095.

See : *The Pantiles★* B 26 – *Calverley Park★* B.

🛇 Langton Rd 𝒫 (01892) 523034 A.

🛈 The Old Fish Market, The Pantiles 𝒫 (01892) 515675.

London 36 – *Brighton* 33 – *Folkestone* 46 – *Hastings* 27 – *Maidstone* 18.

ROYAL TUNRIDGE WELLS

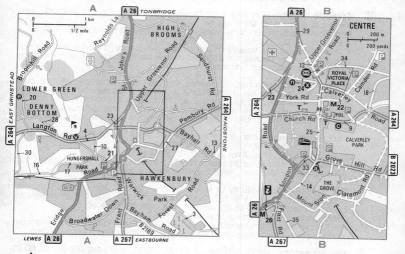

🏛🏛🏛 **Hotel du Vin,** Crescent Rd, TN1 2LY, 𝒫 (01892) 526455, *info@tunbridgewells.hotel duvin.com,* Fax (01892) 512044, ≤, 🐦 – 📳 ↔ 🗏 📞 🅿 – 🔬 80. 🆎 🅐 🅥🅸🆂🅰. ⅏   B c
Rest – (see **Bistro** below) – ⌑ 13.50 – **34 rm** ✦105.00/120.00 – ✦✦175.00/195.00.
◆ Delightful Georgian house with a contemporary styled interior themed around wine; provides a stylish, comfortable feel throughout. Occasional wine-based events.

🏛🏛🏛 **Spa,** Mount Ephraim, TN4 8XJ, 𝒫 (01892) 520331, *reservations@spahotel.co.uk,* Fax (01892) 510575, Ⅰ₆, ≘ₛ, 🖾, 🐦, 🖭, ⅏ – 📳, ↔ rest, 📞 ♿ 🅿 – 🔬 350. 🆎 🅐 🅥🅸🆂🅰   A v
Chandelier : Rest *(closed Saturday lunch)* 19.50/35.00 s. ⅋ – ⌑ 14.50 – **66 rm** ✦103.00/150.00 – ✦✦210.00, 3 suites.
◆ Classic Georgian mansion set in 14 acres of gardens and parkland with lakes. An old-fashioned, English style of hospitality. Comfortable, well-furnished bedrooms. Dining options in formal restaurant or lounge.

⌂ **Danehurst** without rest., 41 Lower Green Rd, Rusthall, TN4 8TW, West : 1¾ m. by A 264 𝒫 (01892) 527739, *info@danehurst.net,* Fax (01892) 514804, 🐦 – ↔ 🅿. 🆎 🅐 🅥🅸🆂🅰. ⅏   A e
closed 1-14 February – **4 rm** ⌑ ✦50.00/69.50 – ✦✦69.50/95.00.
◆ Victorian family home, with koi carp in the garden, located in residential area of town. Mix of homely furniture and furnishings and a conservatory breakfast room.

✕✕ **Thackeray's,** 85 London Rd, TN1 1EA, 𝒫 (01892) 511921, *reservations@thackeraysres taurant.co.uk,* Fax (01892) 527561, 🍽 – ↔ 🆎 🅥🅸🆂🅰   B n
closed 26 December, 1 January, Sunday dinner and Monday – Rest 15.95 (lunch) and a la carte 38.00/49.95 ⅋.
◆ Grade II listed 17C house with handsome Oriental terrace. Modern interior contrasts pleasingly with façade. The classically based cooking employs first rate ingredients.

XX **Signor Franco**, 5a High St, TN1 1UL, ℰ (01892) 549199, *Fax (01892) 541378* – ▤. ◍◍
◍◍ *VISA*   B **a**
closed Sunday and Bank Holidays – **Rest** - Italian - a la carte 23.10/36.40.
♦ On first floor in high street. Several dining areas with good-sized, well-spaced tables.
Classic Italian feel in the broad range of dishes and the welcoming ambience.

XX **Bistro** (at Hotel du Vin), TN1 2LY, ℰ (01892) 526455, *Fax (01892) 512044*, 余, 余 – ❖❖ ℙ.
⇔ 14. ◍◍ Æ ◉ *VISA*   B **c**
Rest (booking essential) a la carte 27.75/35.25 ♀ ➘.
♦ Classically styled with dark wood floors and furniture and wine memorabilia. Terrace for
lunch. Interesting modern menu. Informal and efficient service.

X **Blanc Brasserie**, Fiveways, Lime Hill Rd, TN1 1LJ, ℰ (01892) 559170, *tunbridge*
wells@lepetitblanc.co.uk, Fax (01892) 559171 – ❖❖ ▤. ◍◍ Æ *VISA*   B **x**
closed 25 December – **Rest** - Brasserie - a la carte 20.50/31.00 ➘➘.
♦ Simple, modern décor: banquette seats and full-length glass windows. Extensive selection of menus with a French base, prepared with trademark Blanc expertise.

at Speldhurst *North : 3½ m. by A 26* – A – ✉ *Royal Tunbridge Wells.*

🏠 **George & Dragon**, Speldhurst Hill, TN3 0NN, ℰ (01892) 863125, *julian@leefe-grif*
fiths.freeserve.co.uk, Fax (01892) 863216, 余, 余 – ℙ. ◍◍ *VISA*
🛋 **Rest** *(closed Sunday dinner)* a la carte 25.00/35.00 ♀.
♦ Locally renowned black-and-white fronted pub where fresh Kentish ingredients from
small, local suppliers are proudly employed in good value dishes with a classic French base.

at Pembury *Northeast : 4 m. by A 264* – A – *off B 2015* – ✉ *Royal Tunbridge Wells.*

🏨 **Ramada Tunbridge Wells**, 8 Tonbridge Rd, TN2 4QL, ℰ (01892) 823567, *salestun*
wells@ramadajarvis .co.uk, Fax (01892) 823567, 🍴, ▦ – ❖❖ ♿ ℙ – 🔬 180. ◍◍ Æ ◉
VISA
Rest 14.95/21.95 ♀ – ⊻ 11.95 – **82 rm** ✦110.00 – ✦✦110.00, 2 suites.
♦ Well-fitted, bright, modern furniture and furnishings throughout. Room selection in-
cludes Studio range, particularly geared to business travellers, with desks and modems.
Bright, warmly toned restaurant.

ROYSTON *Herts.* **504** T 27.

🏠 **The Cabinet at Reed**, High St, Reed, SG8 8AH, *South : 3 m. by A 10* ℰ (01763) 848366,
thecabinet@btinternet.com, Fax (01763) 849407, 余 – ❖❖ ℙ. ◍◍ *VISA*
Rest 18.50/25.50 and a la carte 22.00/41.00 ♀ ➘.
♦ 16C clapperboard country pub with a smart, contemporary restaurant and welcoming
ambience. Interesting choice of modern British dishes; good wine list, many by the glass.

ROZEL BAY *Jersey (Channel Islands)* **503** P 33 and **517** ⑪ – *see Channel Islands.*

RUAN-HIGH-LANES *Cornwall* **503** F 33 – *see Veryan.*

RUCKHALL *Herefordshire* – *see Hereford.*

RUGBY *Warks.* **503 504** Q 26 – *pop. 61 988.*

🏌 *Whitefields H., Coventry Rd, Thurlaston* ℰ (01788) 815555 – 🏌 *Clifton Rd* ℰ (01788)
544637.
🎫 *Art Gallery, Museum & Library, Little Elborow St* ℰ (01788) 533217, *visitor.cen*
tre@rugby.gov.uk.
London 88 – Birmingham 33 – Leicester 21 – Northampton 20 – Warwick 17.

🏨 **Brownsover Hall**, Brownsover Lane, CV21 1HU, *North : 2 m. by A 426 and Brownsover*
Rd ℰ (0870) 6096104, *brownsoverhall@corushotels.com, Fax (01788) 535367*, 余, ⇱ – ❖❖
ℙ – 🔬 70. ◍◍ Æ ◉ *VISA*. ❀
Rest *(closed Saturday lunch)* (buffet lunch)/dinner 22.50 and a la carte 26.45/34.45 **s.** –
45 rm ⊻ ✦88.00/138.00 – ✦✦138.00/158.00, 2 suites.
♦ 19C Gothic building designed by Gilbert Scott. Interiors include a main hall of dramatic
proportions and vast ornate fireplaces. Newer courtyard rooms particularly smart. Tall
Gothic windows define dining room on a grand scale.

at Crick *Southeast : 6 m. on A 428.*

🏨 **Ibis** without rest., Parklands, NN6 7EX, *West : 1 ¼ m. on A 428* ℰ (01788) 824331,
h3588@accor.com, Fax (01788) 824332 – 🛗 ❖❖ ♿ ℙ – 🔬 35. ◍◍ Æ ◉ *VISA*
111 rm ✦52.00/70.00 – ✦✦52.00/70.00.
♦ Simply furnished and brightly decorated with well-proportioned modern bedrooms.
Conveniently located lodge hotel suited to business and family stopovers.

RUNSWICK BAY *N. Yorks.* – ✉ *Whitby.*

London 285 – Middlesbrough 24 – Whitby 9.

Cliffemount, TS13 5HU, ✆ (01947) 840103, *info@cliffemounthotel.co.uk, Fax (01947) 841025,* ←, – rest, P. MC VISA

Rest a la carte 15.00/36.50 – **20 rm** ☕ ★35.00/65.00 – ★★123.00.

◆ Enviably located hotel which has benefitted hugely from refurbishment. Cosy bar with blackboard menu. Balanced mix of luxurious or cosy bedrooms, 10 of which have balconies. Light, airy dining room boasts fantastic views of bay. Strong seafood base.

RUSHLAKE GREEN *E. Sussex* **504** U 31 – ✉ *Heathfield.*

London 54 – Brighton 26 – Eastbourne 13.

Stone House, TN21 9QJ, Northeast corner of the green ✆ (01435) 830553, *Fax (01435) 830726,* ←, , , – P. MC VISA

closed 24 December-1 January – **Rest** (residents only) (dinner only and lunch May-August) 24.95 **s.** – **5 rm** ☕ ★85.00/120.00 – ★★195.00/245.00, 1 suite.

◆ Charming part 15C, part Georgian country house surrounded by parkland. All interiors delightfully furnished with antiques and fine art. Garden produce features on menu.

RUSHTON *Northants.* – *see Kettering.*

RYDE *I.O.W.* **503 504** Q 31 – *see Wight (Isle of).*

RYE *E. Sussex* **504** W 31 *Great Britain G.* – *pop. 4 195.*

See : *Old Town*★★ : *Mermaid Street*★, *St Mary's Church* (←★).

The Heritage Centre, Strand Quay ✆ *(01797) 226696, ryetic@rother.gov.uk.*

London 61 – Brighton 49 – Folkestone 27 – Maidstone 33.

Mermaid Inn, Mermaid St, TN31 7EY, ✆ (01797) 223065, *info@mermaidinn.com, Fax (01797) 225069* – rest, P. MC AE VISA.

Rest 23.00/38.50 and a la carte 36.50/51.50 ♀ – **31 rm** (dinner included) ☕ ★115.00/280.00 – ★★280.00.

◆ Historic inn dating from 15C. Immense character from the timbered exterior on a cobbled street to the heavily beamed, antique furnished interior warmed by roaring log fires. Two dining options: both exude age and character.

Rye Lodge, Hilders Cliff, TN31 7LD, ✆ (01797) 223838, *info@ryelodge.co.uk, Fax (01797) 223585,* , – rest, P. MC AE VISA

Rest (dinner only) 29.50 and a la carte 20.00/35.00 ♀ – **18 rm** ☕ ★75.00/125.00 – ★★100.00/200.00.

◆ Family run house located close to historic town centre yet with Romney Marsh in sight. Welcoming guest areas and comfortable, smartly fitted rooms, three in the courtyard. Enjoy dining in candlelight.

Jeake's House without rest., Mermaid St, TN31 7ET, ✆ (01797) 222828, *stay@jeakeshouse.com, Fax (01797) 222623* – P. MC VISA

11 rm ☕ ★70.00/79.00 – ★★122.00.

◆ Down a cobbled lane, a part 17C house, once a wool store and a Quaker meeting place. Welcoming atmosphere amid antiques, sloping floors and beams. Pretty, traditional rooms.

Durrant House without rest., 2 Market St, TN31 7LA, ✆ (01797) 223182, *info@durranthouse.com, Fax (01797) 226940,* – . MC VISA

closed 22 January- 8 February – **6 rm** ☕ ★55.00/78.00 – ★★75.00/90.00.

◆ Grade I listed house of unknown age. Neat breakfast room with daily breakfast specials. Bright lounge looks down East Street. Carefully appointed, immaculate modern rooms.

Little Orchard House without rest., West St, TN31 7ES, ✆ (01797) 223831, *info@littleorchardhouse.com, Fax (01797) 223831,* – . MC VISA.

minimum 2 night stay at weekends – **3 rm** ☕ ★60.00/70.00 – ★★100.00/110.00.

◆ Charming cottage in quiet street, rebuilt 1745. Surrounded by peaceful garden. Pleasantly cluttered atmosphere with paintings and objets d'art in communal areas and rooms.

The Benson without rest., 15 East St, TN31 7JY, ✆ (01797) 225131, *info@bensonhotel.co.uk, Fax (01797) 225512,* ← – . MC VISA.

closed January – **3 rm** ★80.00 – ★★104.00.

◆ Former wool merchant's house and vicarage, built in 1707. Comfortable sitting room. Rooms have four-posters or half-testers: two have views of Romney Marsh and River Rother.

Flushing Inn, 4 Market St, TN31 7LA, ✆ (01797) 223292, *j.e.flynn@btconnect.com* – . MC VISA

closed first 2 weeks January, first 2 weeks June, Monday dinner and Tuesday – **Rest** - Seafood - 18.50/37.00 and lunch a la carte 15.30/22.50.

◆ A neighbourhood institution, this 15C inn with heavily timbered and panelled dining area features a superb 16C fresco. The seafood oriented menu has a local, traditional tone.

✗ **Webbes at The Fish Café**, 17 Tower St, TN31 7AT, ✆ (01797) 222226, *info@thefish cafe.com, Fax (01797) 229260* – ❦ 🖳 ⊜ 65. **MC AE VISA**
closed first week January – **Rest** - Seafood - (dinner booking essential) a la carte 18.50/28.50 ⌹.
♦ Large converted warehouse: terracotta painted ground floor for seafood lunches and eclectic options. Dinner upstairs features more serious piscine menus. Tangible buzziness.

✗ **Landgate Bistro**, 5-6 Landgate, TN31 7LH, ✆ (01797) 222829 – **MC VISA**
closed 25 December, 1 January, Sunday and Mondays except before Bank Holidays – **Rest** (dinner only) a la carte 20.30/26.75 s. ⌹.
♦ Well established, personally run, unpretentious bistro: a local favourite. Classic and modern cooking is fresh and tasty with good choice seafood reassuringly to the fore.

at Camber Southeast : 4¼ m. by A 259 – ⊠ Rye.

🏨 **The Place**, New Lydd Rd, Camber Sands, TN31 7RB, ✆ (01797) 225057, *enquiries@the placecambersands.co.uk, Fax (01797) 227003*, ☜, ✿ – ❦ rm, ⊜ rest, ☎ 🖳 – ♨ 30. **MC AE VISA**. ✿
closed 25-26 December – **Rest** a la carte 19.75/30.25 ⌹ – **18 rm** ✦72.50/82.50 – ✦✦110.00/120.00.
♦ Immaculately whitewashed, converted former seaside motel located over the dunes. Smart, stylish rooms with a good level of facilities and charming extra touches. Informal brasserie style restaurant with emphasis on local ingredients.

at Peasmarsh Northwest : 4 m. on A 268 – ⊠ Rye.

🏨 **Flackley Ash**, London Rd, TN31 6YH, on A 268 ✆ (01797) 230651, *enquiries@flack leyashhotel.co.uk, Fax (01797) 230510*, 🛁, ☞, ⬜, ✿ – ❦ rest, ☎ ৬ 🖳 – ♨ 100. **MC AE VISA**
Rest (bar lunch Monday-Saturday)/dinner 28.50 ⌹ – **41 rm** ⊊ ✦87.00/89.00 – ✦✦168.00/172.00, 4 suites.
♦ Extended Georgian country house of red brick. Traditional style throughout with comfortable lounge and bar areas. Each well-equipped bedroom is of a unique size and shape. Dining room has sunny conservatory extension.

SAFFRON WALDEN Essex 504 U 27 – pop. 14 313.
London 43 – Bishop's Stortford 12 – Cambridge 18.

✗ **the restaurant**, Victoria House, 2 Church St, CB10 1JW, ✆ (01799) 526444, *restau rant526444@aol.com* – **MC VISA**
closed 1 week January, Sunday and Monday – **Rest** (dinner only) 16.95 and a la carte 22.85/30.85 s. ⌹.
♦ Stylishly converted cellar with an informal feel: candles light the brick and flint walls and etched glass tables. Original, contemporary menu; relaxed style and service.

✗ **Dish**, 13a King St, CB10 1HE, ✆ (01799) 513300, *dishrestaurant@btinternet.com, Fax (01799) 531699* – ❦ 🖳 ⊜. **MC AE VISA**
closed 25-27 December, 1 January and Sunday dinner – **Rest** 14.95 (lunch) and dinner a la carte 23.95/28.45 ⌹.
♦ First floor restaurant within characterful beamed house in town centre. Modern oil paintings exude jazzy theme. Classically based dishes take on adventurous note at dinner.

at Littlebury Green West : 4½ m. by B 1383 – ⊠ Saffron Walden.

↑ **Chaff House** without rest, Ash Grove Barns, CB11 4XB, ✆ (01763) 836278, *diana duke@btopenworld.com, Fax (01763) 837340*, ✿, ⬚ – ❦ rest, 🖳. **MC VISA**. ✿
closed Christmas – **3 rm** ⊊ ✦40.00/45.00 – ✦✦70.00/75.00.
♦ Lovely barn conversion on 900 acre estate. Excellent craftsmanship: exposed beams, well appointed lounge. Very smart rooms, two with their own stable doors, all with rafters.

ST AGNES Cornwall 503 E 33 The West Country G. – pop. 2 759.
See : St Agnes Beacon★★ (✿★★).
Env. : Portreath★, SW : 5½ m.
🏌 Perranporth, Budnic Hill ✆ (01872) 572454.
London 302 – Newquay 12 – Penzance 26 – Truro 9.

🏨 **Rose-in-Vale Country House** ✿, Mithian, TR5 0QD, East : 2 m. by B 3285 ✆ (01872) 552202, *reception@rose-in-vale-hotel.co.uk, Fax (01872) 552700*, ⬛ heated, ✿ – ❦ 🖳. **MC AE ⓘ VISA**
The Valley : **Rest** (light lunch Monday-Saturday)/dinner 18.00 s. and a la carte 15.00/35.00 – **18 rm** ⊊ ✦75.00/80.00 – ✦✦200.00.
♦ Handsome Georgian manor clad in climbing roses; outdoor pool and peaceful gardens with summer house and dovecote. Classically styled lounge bar and library; well-kept rooms. Neat, formal dining room with local specials.

ENGLAND

ST ALBANS Herts. 504 T 28 *Great Britain G.* – pop. 82 429.

See : *City★* - *Cathedral★* BZ – *Verulamium★ (Museum★ AC* AY).

Env. : *Hatfield House★★ AC, E : 6 m. by A 1057.*

🏌 *Batchwood Hall, Batchwood Drive ℰ (01727) 833349 –* 🏌₁₈, 🏌₉ *Redbourn, Kinsbourne Green Lane ℰ (01582) 793493.*

🅱 *Town Hall, Market Pl ℰ (01727) 864511.*

London 27 – Cambridge 41 – Luton 10.

🏨 **Sopwell House** ⬥, Cottonmill Lane, AL1 2HQ, Southeast : 1 ½ m. by A 1081 and Mile House Lane ℰ (01727) 864477, enquiries@sopwellhouse.co.uk, Fax (01727) 844741, 🏖, ⑦, 🏊, 🛬, 🔍, 🚘, ♨ – 🕸 ⚡ 🗔 🄿 – 🔬 450. ⬢⬢ 🄰🄴 ⑪ *VISA*. ⬥
Magnolia : Rest *(closed Saturday and Monday lunch)* 19.50/29.50 and a la carte 26.95/42.30 ♀ – *Bejerano's Brasserie :* Rest a la carte 18.00/29.50 ♀ – ⬇ 14.00 – **127 rm** ⬇ ✚99.00/185.00 – ✚✚169.00/185.00, 2 suites.

♦ Everything denotes peace and seclusion: pretty gardens, leather furnished lounge, modern spa with Japanese treatments, pool and gym. Modern rooms and apartments. Magnolia features eponymous 100 year-old trees. Bejerano's Brasserie with swimming pool views.

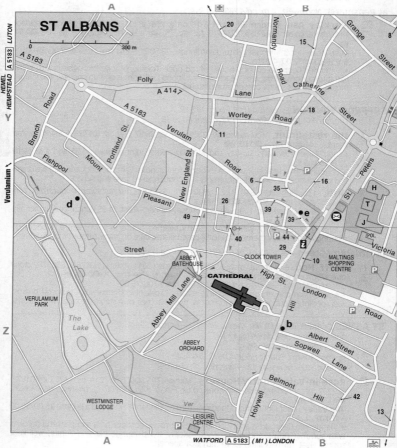

St Michael's Manor, St Michael's Village, Fishpool St, AL3 4RY, ✆ (01727) 864444, *reservations@stmichaelsmanor.com*, Fax (01727) 848909, ≤, ✿ – ⁱ✗ rest, ✔ P, ⓜ AE ⑪ VISA

AY **d**

Rest *(closed dinner 25 December)* 19.65 (lunch) and a la carte 25.00/42.40 ♀ – **29 rm** ⌷ ♦145.00 – ♦♦250.00/335.00, 1 suite.

♦ This part 16C, part William and Mary manor house overlooks a lake. Elegant bedrooms are named after trees; some are suites with sitting rooms, all are luxurious and stylish. Conservatory dining room with splendid vistas.

Thistle St Albans, Watford Rd, AL2 3DS, Southwest : 2 ½ m. at junction of A 405 with B 4630 ✆ (0870) 3339144, *reservations.stalbans@thistle.co.uk*, Fax (0870) 3339244, ₤₅, ≦ₛ, ⌸ – ⁱ✗, ▤ rest, P, – ⩺ 50. ⓜ AE ⑪ VISA

Noke : Rest *(closed Sunday dinner and Monday)* 18.00/26.95 s. and a la carte ♀ – ⌷ 12.95 – **109 rm** ♦160.00 – ♦♦160.00, 2 suites.

♦ A busy, business hotel with country house charm. Leisure facilities include pool, jacuzzi and fitness centre. Rooms are solidly stylish with wall lamps and patterned fabrics. Restaurant with conservatory and floral drapes.

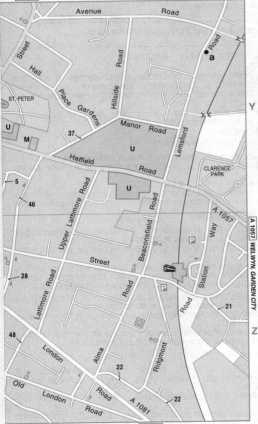

Comfort, Ryder House, Holywell Hill, AL1 1HG, ☎ (01727) 848849, *admin@gb055.u-net.com, Fax (01727) 812210* – 📶 ✦, ▤ rest, ♿, ⬚ – 🔬 35. 🆗 AE ⓞ *VISA* BZ b
Rest *(closed Bank Holidays)* (dinner only) and a la carte 16.00/23.00 ♀ – ☞ 8.95 – **60 rm**
✚75.00/79.00 – ✚✚75.00/79.00.
◆ Built by Samuel Ryder, donor of golf's Ryder cup. Defined by Edwardian features: stained glass dome and carved fireplace. The bedrooms, though, are of practical bent. Meals served in restaurant or your room.

Ardmore House, 54 Lemsford Rd, AL1 3PR, ☎ (01727) 859313, *info@ardmorehouse hotel.co.uk, Fax (01727) 859313*, ☞ – ✦ P. 🆗 AE *VISA*. ✿ CY a
Rest 19.95/29.95 s. – **40 rm** ☞ 63.00/68.00 – ✚✚78.00/125.00.
◆ Edwardian residence with Victorian annex: this is a traditional, family owned hotel. Homely bedrooms have the feel of a lounge, boasting sofas and wall lamps. Traditional dining room with menu to match.

Sukiyaki, 6 Spencer St, AL3 5EG, ☎ (01727) 865009 – 🆗 AE ⓞ *VISA* BY e
closed 2 weeks in summer, 1 week Christmas, Sunday and Monday – **Rest** - Japanese - 9.80/25.00 and a la carte 14.25/19.50.
◆ A pared-down style, minimally decorated restaurant with simple, precise helpings of Japanese food. No noodles or sushi, expect instead sukiyaki (a beef dish), and tempura.

ST ANNE *Alderney (Channel Islands)* 503 Q 33 and 517 ⑨ – *see Channel Islands.*

ST ANNE'S *Lancs.* 502 K 22 – *see Lytham St Anne's.*

ST AUBIN *Jersey (Channel Islands)* 503 P 33 and 517 ⑪ – *see Channel Islands.*

ST AUSTELL *Cornwall* 503 F 32 *The West Country G.* – *pop. 22 658.*
See : *Holy Trinity Church★.*
Env. : *St Austell Bay★★ (Gribbin Head★★) E : by A 390 and A 3082 – Carthew : Wheal Martyn China Clay Heritage Centre★★ AC, N : 2 m. by A 391 – Mevagissey★★ - Lost Gardens of Heligan★, S : 5 m. by B 3273 – Charlestown★, SE : 2 m. by A 390 – Eden Project★★, NE : 3 m. by A 390 at St Blazey Gate.*
Exc. : *Trewithen★★★ AC, NE : 7 m. by A 390 – Lanhydrock★★, NE : 11 m. by A 390 and B 3269 – Polkerris★, E : 7 m. by A 390 and A 3082.*
🏌 *Carlyon Bay* ☎ (01726) 814250.
London 281 – Newquay 16 – Plymouth 38 – Truro 14.

Poltarrow Farm without rest., St Mewan, PL26 7DR, Southwest : 1 ¾ m. by A 390 ☎ (01726) 67111, *enquire@poltarrow.co.uk, Fax (01726) 67111*, 🏊, ☞, 🐴 – ✦ P. 🆗 *VISA*. ✿
closed Christmas and New Year – **5 rm** ☞ – ✚✚66.00/70.00.
◆ Tucked away down a tree-lined drive stands this working farm equipped with indoor pool, elegant sitting room and conservatory serving Cornish breakfasts. Rooms have views.

at Tregrehan *East : 2½ m. by A 390* – ✉ *St Austell.*

Boscundle Manor, PL25 3RL, ☎ (01726) 813557, *stay@boscundlemanor.co.uk, Fax (01726) 814997*, 🏊 heated, 🏊, ☞ – ✦ ♿ P. 🆗 AE *VISA*
closed January **Rest** 25.00/40.00 and a la carte 30.00/50.00 – **12 rm** ✚60.00/120.00 – ✚✚180.00/200.00, 2 suites.
◆ A converted 18C manor house one mile from sea, in beautiful wild flower gardens. Clean-lined rooms; simply painted and sunny games room with table tennis and snooker table. Dining room with 170 bin wine list, bone china, silver cutlery and antique tables.

Anchorage House, Nettles Corner, Boscundle, PL25 3RH, ☎ (01726) 814071, *info@an choragehouse.co.uk, Fax (01726) 813462*, ☞ – ✦ P. 🆗 AE *VISA*. ✿
March- November – **Rest** (by arrangement) (communal dining) 35.00 – **4 rm** ☞ ✚90.00/100.00 – ✚✚150.00/160.00.
◆ Intriguing mix of modern and period styles in welcoming house set in peaceful position. Antique beds in spacious rooms plus extras: flowers, fruit, hot water bottles.

at Carlyon Bay *East : 2½ m. by A 3601* – ✉ *St Austell.*

Carlyon Bay, PL25 3RD, ☎ (01726) 812304, *reservations@carlyonbay.com, Fax (01726) 814938*, ≤ Carlyon Bay, ≋s, 🏊 heated, 🏊, 🏌, ☞, ♨, ✾ – 📶 ✦, ▤ rest, ⚽ P. – 🔬 65. 🆗 AE ⓞ *VISA*. ✿
Rest 16.50/35.00 and dinner a la carte 30.00/47.00 ♀ – **86 rm** ☞ ✚70.00/152.50 – ✚✚210.00/316.00.
◆ With superb views across bay and well-positioned pool as suntrap, this family friendly hotel has golf course access and lays on programmes for children. Spacious, neat rooms. Dining room with live music and handsome vistas.

🏠 **Porth Avallen**, Sea Rd, PL25 3SG, ✆ (01726) 812802, *info@porthavallen.co.uk*, *Fax (01726) 817097*, ≼ Carlyon Bay, 🍴, 🌳 – ⇔ 🅿 – 🔥 100. 🔘 🆎 VISA. ✻
Rest (bar lunch)/dinner 29.50/41.50 ♀ – **28 rm** ⬜ ✦61.00/91.00 – ✦✦126.00/152.00.
  ◆ Built as a family home in 1928; enjoys a commanding position overlooking Carlyon Bay. Warmly decorated interiors with wood panelling, rich coloured carpets and furnishings. Restaurant with fine sea views.

at Charlestown *Southeast : 2 m. by A 390 –* ⊠ *St Austell.*

🏠 **T' Gallants** without rest., 6 Charlestown Rd, PL25 3NJ, ✆ (01726) 70203, *enquiries@tgallants.co.uk*, 🌳 – ⇔ 🔘 VISA. ✻
8 rm ✦45.00 – ✦✦65.00/120.00.
  ◆ Georgian house in quiet fishing port. Benches in walled garden for sunning yourself. Good value accommodation: try and book Room 5, which boasts four poster and the best view.

✕ **Revival**, PL25 3NJ, ✆ (01726) 879053, *info@cornwall-revival.co.uk*, 🍴 – ⇔. 🔘 VISA
closed 2 weeks January, Monday and Sunday except lunch in summer. – **Rest** a la carte 26.15/33.85 ♀.
  ◆ Once a cooperage; reputedly Charlestown's second oldest building, it overlooks 19C tall ships in the harbour. Local, seasonal ingredients used to good effect on all-day menus.

 Red = Pleasant. Look for the red ✕ and 🏠 symbols.

ST BLAZEY *Cornwall 503* F 32 *The West Country G. – pop. 9 256 (inc. Par).*
  Env. : *Eden Project*★★, *NW ; 1½ m. by A 390 and minor roads.*
  London 276 – Newquay 21 – Plymouth 33 – Truro 19.

🏠 **Nanscawen Manor House** 🦢 without rest., Prideaux Rd, PL24 2SR, West : ¾ m. by Luxulyan rd ✆ (01726) 814488, *keith@nanscawen.com*, ≼, 🌊 heated, 🌳 – ⇔ 🅿. 🔘 VISA. ✻
3 rm ⬜ ✦86.00 – ✦✦120.00.
  ◆ Sumptuous country house, until 1520 the home of Nanscawen family. Conservatory breakfast room set in fragrant gardens. Welcoming bedrooms; outdoor spa bath. Non smoking.

ST BRELADE'S BAY *Jersey (Channel Islands) 503* P 33 and **517** ⑪ – *see Channel Islands.*

ST HELENS *Mersey. 502 503* L 23 – *pop. 106 293.*
  🏌 Sherdley Park Municipal, Sherdley Park ✆ (01744) 813149.
  London 207 – Liverpool 16 – Manchester 27.

🏠 **Hilton St Helens**, Linkway West, WA10 1NG, ✆ (01744) 453444, *reservations.sthelens@hilton.com*, *Fax (01744) 454655*, 🗜, ⇌, 🔲 – 🛗 ⇔ 🍴 🛗 🅿 – 🔥 250. 🔘 🆎 ⓞ VISA
Rest (bar lunch)/dinner 16.95 and a la carte 24.70/28.15 – ⬜ 14.95 – **81 rm** ✦99.00/160.00 – ✦✦99.00/160.00, 3 suites.
  ◆ Built by Pilkington Glass, hence many glass features to the hotel, such as the atrium, and the consequent light ambience. Comfortable, unfussy rooms with air conditioning. Modern restaurant with glass pyramid ceiling.

ST HELIER *Jersey (Channel Islands) 503* P 33 and **517** ⑪ – *see Channel Islands.*

ST ISSEY *Cornwall 503* F 32 – *see Padstow.*

ST IVES *Cambs. 504* T 27 – *pop. 9 866 –* ⊠ *Huntingdon.*
  London 75 – Cambridge 14 – Huntingdon 6.

🏠 **Slepe Hall**, Ramsey Rd, PE27 5RB, ✆ (01480) 463122, *mail@slepehall.co.uk*, *Fax (01480) 300706*, 🌳 – ⇔ 🅿 – 🔥 200. 🔘 🆎 ⓞ VISA
closed 26-27 December – **Rest** a la carte 17.45/24.25 ♀ – **16 rm** ⬜ ✦80.00/90.00 – ✦✦99.00.
  ◆ Constructed in 1848 as girls' boarding school. Rooms are far from institutional: simple décor, brightly emulsioned walls, canopy beds. The four-poster room is very popular. Restaurant boasts garden views.

See : Town★★ - Barbara Hepworth Museum★★ AC Y M1 – Tate St Ives★★ (≤★★) - St Nicholas Chapel (≤★★) Y – Parish Church★ Y A.

Env. : S : Penwith★★ Y.

Exc. : St Michael's Mount★★ (≤★★) S : 10 m. by B 3306 – Y – B 3311, B 3309 and A 30.

🏌 Tregenna Castle H. ℘ (01736) 795254 ext: 121 Y – 🏌 West Cornwall, Lelant ℘ (01736) 753401.

🚹 The Guildhall, Street-an-Pol ℘ (01736) 796297, ivtic@penwith.gov.uk.

London 319 – Penzance 10 – Truro 25.

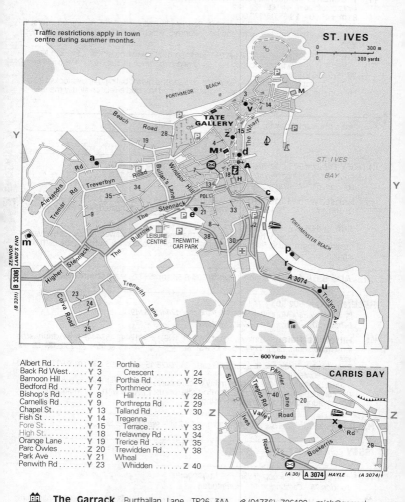

🏨 **The Garrack,** Burthallan Lane, TR26 3AA, ℘ (01736) 796199, mich@garrack.com, Fax (01736) 798955, ≤, ≦s, ◻, 龠 – ℗, 閧🅾 🅰🅴 ⓪ 𝐕𝐈𝐒𝐀 Y a
closed Christmas – **The Restaurant :** Rest (dinner only) 25.50 and a la carte 19.20/56.25 ♀ – **18 rm** ⊆ ✝75.00/144.00 – ✝✝174.00/190.00.

♦ Well-established hotel with pleasant gardens close to Tate. Plenty of homely touches. Spacious pool and sauna. Individually designed bedrooms, many with feature beds. Very popular dining room serves Cornish specialities.

Pedn-Olva, West Porthminster Beach, TR26 2EA, ✆ (01736) 796222, *pednolva@small andfriendly.co.uk*, Fax (01736) 797710, ≤ Harbour and bay, ㊝ – ✕ **P**, **MO** **AE** **VISA**, ✼
Y c
The Lookout: Rest (bar lunch)/dinner 32.50 – **31 rm** ⌂ ✝60.00/93.00 – ✝✝140.00/166.00.
♦ Meaning "lookout on the headland" in Cornish; boasts commanding views of harbour and bay. Sheltered sun terrace and pool. Neutral décor typified by simple bedrooms. Restaurant offers diners splendid outlook.

Blue Hayes without rest., Trelyon Ave, TR26 2AD, ✆ (01736) 797129, *info@blue hayes.co.uk*, Fax (01736) 799098, ≤, ㊝, ☞ – ✕ ❤ **P**, **MO** **AE** **VISA**, ✼
Y u
closed December-January – **6 rm** ⌂ ✝120.00/130.00 – ✝✝170.00/190.00.
♦ 19C house with super view from terrace over the harbour; access to coast path from garden. Hi-tech interior. Single course supper available. Well-appointed bedrooms.

Primrose Valley, Porthminster Beach, TR26 2ED, ✆ (01736) 794939, *info@primro seonline.co.uk*, Fax (01736) 794939, ≤ – ✕ **P**, **MO** **VISA**, ✼
Y r
closed December and January – Rest (by arrangement in summer only) – **10 rm** ✝80.00/95.00 – ✝✝115.00/180.00.
♦ Edwardian villa with unrivalled proximity to beach. Stylish café bar and lounge; relaxing front patio. Local suppliers ensure good breakfast choice. Individually styled rooms. Summer-time meals arranged with the owners.

Old Vicarage without rest., Parc-an-Creet, TR26 2ES, ✆ (01736) 796124, *stay@old vicarage.com*, ☞ – ✕ **P**, **MO** **VISA**
Y m
Easter-October – **7 rm** ⌂ ✝54.00 – ✝✝72.00.
♦ Former vicarage built of granite and slate retains Victorian charm and character, especially in bar lounge furnished in red velvet, gilt and mahogany. Rooms in uniform style.

Pebble without rest., 4 Parc Ave, TR26 2DN, ✆ (01736) 794168, *info@pebble-hotel.co.uk*, ≤ – ✕ ❤ **P**, **MO** **VISA**, ✼
Y e
restricted opening in winter – **6 rm** ⌂ ✝30.00/55.00 – ✝✝60.00/100.00.
♦ Small family run hotel; superb views of harbour and bay. Make yourself at home in lounge stocked with local information books. Simply furnished bedrooms in cottage style.

Alba, Old Lifeboat House, The Wharf, TR26 1LF, ✆ (01736) 797222, Fax (01736) 798937, ≤ – ✕ 🍽 **MO** **AE** **VISA**
Y d
closed 25-26 December – Rest - Seafood - 16.00 (lunch) and a la carte 27.40/32.70 ⅀.
♦ Ideally situated in centre of town, on both floors of Old Lifeboat House; good harbour views. Modern feel; artwork on walls. Tasty, extensive menus with a modern slant.

Russets, 18a Fore St, TR26 1AB, ✆ (01736) 794700, *info@russets.co.uk*, Fax (01736) 794700 – ✕, **MO** **AE** **①** **VISA**
Y z
Restricted opening in winter – Rest - Seafood specialities - (light lunch)/dinner a la carte 22.90/29.45 ⅀.
♦ Steamed monkfish wrapped in banana leaf sums up the seafood bias of the menus in a spacious town centre restaurant. Also boasts comfortable bar furnished with Chesterfields.

Porthminster Cafe, Porthminster Beach, TR26 2EB, ✆ (01736) 795352, *p.min ster@btopenworld.com*, Fax (01736) 795352, ≤ St Ives Bay and town, ㊝ – ✕, **MO** **VISA**
Y p
March-October – Rest - Seafood - a la carte 22.85/42.20 ⅀.
♦ 1930s beach house on Porthminster sands. Super views: large terrace for al fresco dining. Colourful local artwork on walls. Seafood oriented dishes plus eclectic dinner menus.

Blue Fish, Norway Lane, TR26 1LZ, ✆ (01736) 794204, ≤, ㊝ – **MO** **VISA**
Y v
restricted opening in winter) – Rest - Seafood - a la carte 23.85/38.85.
♦ Welcoming, family run eatery in the centre of town with a charming sunny terrace affording views of the town. Local and Mediterranean seafood in a simple, relaxed style.

at Carbis Bay *South : 1¾ m. on A 3074* – ✉ St Ives.

Boskerris, Boskerris Rd, TR26 2NQ, ✆ (01736) 795295, *reservations@boskerrisho tel.co.uk*, ≤, ☞ – ✕ ❤ **P**, **MO** **AE** **VISA**, ✼
Z x
closed December and January – Rest (dinner only) 20.00/30.00 ⅀ – **15 rm** ⌂ ✝65.00/105.00 – ✝✝85.00/190.00.
♦ Hotel with panoramic views of Carbis Bay and coastline. Lounge, separate TV room and bar serving light lunches. Outdoor pool overlooking the sea. Restaurant serving local fish, produce and herbs from hotel garden.

ENGLAND

Your opinions are important to us:
please write and let us know about your discoveries and experiences – good and bad!

ST JUST *Cornwall* 503 C 33 *The West Country G.* – pop. 1 890.

See : *Church★*.

Env. : *Penwith★★* – *Sancreed – Church★★ (Celtic Crosses★★)*, SE : 3 m. by A 3071 – *St Buryan★★ (Church Tower★★)*, SE : 5½ m. by B 3306 and A 30 – *Land's End★ (cliff scenery★★★)*, S : 5½ m. by B 3306 and A 30 – *Cape Cornwall★* (≤★★), W : 1½ m. – *Morvah* (≤★★), NE : 4½ m. by B 3306 – *Geevor Tin Mine★ AC*, N : 3 m. by B 3306 – *Carn Euny★* , SE : 3 m. by A 3071 – *Wayside Cross★* – *Sennen Cove★*, (≤★), S : 5½ m. by B 3306 and A 30.

Exc. : *Porthcurno★*, S : 9½ m. by B 3306, A 30 and B 3315.

ⓘ *Cape Cornwall G. & C.C.* ℘ (01736) 788611.

London 325 – Penzance 7.5 – Truro 35.

🏠 **Boscean Country** ⚬, TR19 7QP, Northwest : ½ m. by Boswedden Rd ℘ (01736) 788748, *info@bosceancountryhotel.co.uk*, ≤, 🌿 – ⁎⇥ 🅿. 🕪 🕪
Rest (residents only) (dinner only) – 12 rm ⚏ ✝49.00/53.00 – ✝✝64.00/70.00.
• Originally a doctor's residence; this Edwardian house is surrounded by 3 acres of walled gardens, a haven for wildlife. Wealth of oak panelling indoors; most rooms have views.

ST KEVERNE *Cornwall* 503 E 33.

London 302 – Penzance 26 – Truro 28.

🏠 **Old Temperance House** without rest., The Square, TR12 6NA, ℘ (01326) 280986, *info@oldtemperancehouse.co.uk*, Fax (01326) 280986 – ⁎⇥ 🅿
4 rm ⚏ ✝32.00/38.00 – ✝✝76.00/90.00.
• 'Roses round the door' charm, in idyllic spot on pretty square. Spotlessly neat lounge. Excellent, out-of-the-ordinary breakfasts. Fresh, bright, carefully co-ordinated rooms.

ST LAWRENCE *Channel Islands – see Jersey.*

ST LAWRENCE *I.O.W.* 503 504 Q 32 – *see Wight (Isle of).*

ST LEONARDS *E. Sussex* 504 V 31 – *see Hastings and St Leonards.*

ST MARGARET'S AT CLIFFE *Kent* 504 Y 30 – *see Dover.*

ST MARTIN *Guernsey (Channel Islands)* 503 P 33 and 517 ⑩ – *see Channel Islands.*

ST MARTIN'S *Cornwall* 503 B 34 – *see Scilly (Isles of).*

ST MARY'S *Cornwall* 503 B 34 – *see Scilly (Isles of).*

ST MAWES *Cornwall* 503 E 33 *The West Country G.* – ✉ *Truro.*

See : *Town★ - Castle★ AC* (≤★).

Env. : *St Just-in-Roseland Church★★*, N : 2½ m. by A 3078.

London 299 – Plymouth 56 – Truro 18.

🏨 **Tresanton** ⚬, 27 Lower Castle Rd, TR2 5DR, ℘ (01326) 270055, *info@tresanton.com*, Fax (01326) 270053, ≤ St Mawes bay, St Anthony's Head and lighthouse, 🏖 – ⁎⁎ 🅿 – 🔼 50. 🕪 🄰🄴 *VISA*. 🕪
Rest - Seafood specialities - (booking essential for non-residents) 28.00/39.00 ⚏ – **27 rm** ⚏ ✝170.00/350.00 – ✝✝170.00/350.00, 2 suites.
• Enduringly trendy former 1940s yachtsman's club with cinema. Watercolours on pale walls; gleaming crisp rooms with views; contemporary lounge and attentive service. Dining room boasts open terrace with harbour views and modern seafood dishes.

🏨 **Idle Rocks,** Harbourside, 1 Tredenham Rd, TR2 5AN, ℘ (01326) 270771, *reception@idlerocks.co.uk*, Fax (01326) 270062, ≤ harbour and estuary – ⁎⇥. 🕪 🄰🄴 🄾 *VISA*
The Water's Edge : Rest (light lunch)/dinner 38.00/45.00 – **33 rm** ⚏ ✝64.00/118.50 – ✝✝218.00/278.00.
• Fine waterfront hotel with splendid views of the harbour and fishermen's cottages. Deep comfortable chairs in lounge and bright bedrooms, many with sea views. Restaurant with terrace overlooks the sea.

🏠 **Rising Sun,** The Square, TR2 5DJ, ☎ (01326) 270233, *info@risingsunstmawes.co.uk,*
Fax (01326) 270198 – ⇔ rest. **MC** **VISA**
Rest (bar lunch Monday-Saturday)/dinner 38.00 ♀ – **8 rm** ⌑ ♦55.00/120.00 –
♦♦110.00/150.00.
✦ Renovated 17C house on harbour. Immaculately furnished bedrooms with a stylish feel.
Lively, open-fired bar. A friendly place to rest your head. Buzzy conservatory restaurant
with seascapes on the walls.

ST MAWGAN *Cornwall* **503** F 32 – ✉ *Newquay.*
London 262 – Plymouth 41 – St Austell 3.

🍴 **The Falcon Inn,** TR8 4EP, ☎ (01637) 860225, *enquiries@thefalconinn-newquay.co.uk,*
Fax (01637) 860884, 🍴, 🌳 – ⇔ **P.** **MC** **VISA**
closed dinner 25 December – **Rest** a la carte 14.00/20.00 – **3 rm** ⌑ ♦37.00 – ♦♦37.00.
✦ Characterful 16C pub with cosy terrace. Warm interior in keeping with age of property;
well maintained rustic décor. Popular menus, with seafood the highlight. Comfy rooms.

ST MERRYN *Cornwall* **503** F 32 – *see Padstow.*

ST MICHAELS-ON-WYRE *Lancs.* **502** L 22.
London 235 – Blackpool 24 – Burnley 35 – Manchester 43.

🏠 **Compton House** without rest., Garstang Rd, PR3 0TE, ☎ (01995) 679378, *dave@comp
ton-hs.co.uk,* Fax (01995) 679378, 🌳 – ⇔ **P.** **MC** **VISA**. ⇔
April-October – **3 rm** ⌑ ♦30.00 – ♦♦40.00/50.00.
✦ Redbrick house on busy road. Attractive garden; abundance of flowers in hanging baskets. Village location; riverside walks. Cottage style rooms; one to rear is quieter.

ST PETER *Jersey (Channel Islands)* **503** P 33 *and* **517** ⑪ – *see Channel Islands.*

ST PETER PORT *Guernsey (Channel Islands)* **503** P 33 *and* **517** ⑩ – *see Channel Islands.*

ST SAVIOUR *Guernsey (Channel Islands)* **503** P 33 *and* **517** ⑨ – *see Channel Islands.*

ST SAVIOUR *Jersey (Channel Islands)* **503** P 33 *and* **517** ⑪ – *see Channel Islands.*

SALCOMBE *Devon* **503** I 33 *The West Country G.* – *pop. 1 893.*
Env. : *Sharpitor (Overbecks Museum and Garden★) (≤★★) AC, S : 2 m. by South Sands* Z.
Exc. : *Prawle Point (≤★★★) E : 16 m. around coast by A 381 –* Y *– and A 379.*
🛈 *Council Hall, Market St* ☎ (01548) 843927, *info@salcombeinformation.co.uk.*
London 243 – Exeter 43 – Plymouth 27 – Torquay 28.

Plan on next page

🏨 **Marine,** Cliff Rd, TQ8 8JH, ☎ (01548) 844444, Fax (01548) 843109, ≤ estuary, 🍴, **Ⅰ₅**, ➘,
▱ – ⧉ ⬇ ⇔ **P.** **MC** **AE** **VISA**   Y e
Rest 16.50/29.50 and a la carte 32.00/47.50 – **52 rm** (dinner included) ♦55.00/225.00 –
♦♦110.00/300.00, 1 suite.
✦ Spectacular position on water's edge overlooking the estuary. Hotel makes the most of
this; many bedrooms have balconies whilst centrally located rooms share the best views.
Bright, roomy restaurant looks onto the water.

🏠 **Tides Reach,** South Sands, TQ8 8LJ, ☎ (01548) 843466, *enquire@tidesreach.com,*
Fax (01548) 843954, ≤ estuary, **Ⅰ₅**, ➘, ▱, 🍴, squash – ⧉ ⇔ **P.** **MC** **AE** **VISA**   Z x
closed December-January – **Rest** (bar lunch) 35.00 ♀ – **35 rm** (dinner included) ⌑
♦66.00/125.00 – ♦♦130.00/250.00.
✦ Traditional, personally run hotel set in pleasant sandy cove on Salcombe Estuary.. Lilac
and green rooms boast floral fabrics and flowers; many have balconies and a fine view.
Restaurant overlooks attractive gardens and pond.

🍽 **Restaurant 42,** Fore St, TQ8 8JG, ☎ (01548) 843408, *jane@restaurant42.demon.co.uk,*
Fax (01548) 842854, ≤ – ⇔. **MC** **VISA**   Y n
*closed 25-26 December, 1 January-14 February, Tuesday and Wednesday February-Easter
and Monday* – **Rest** (dinner only) a la carte 33.30/42.70.
✦ Things you may not know about 42: it has a delightful terrace/garden; fabulous views of
the estuary; comfy lounge with squashy sofas; and interesting use of local ingredients.

SALCOMBE

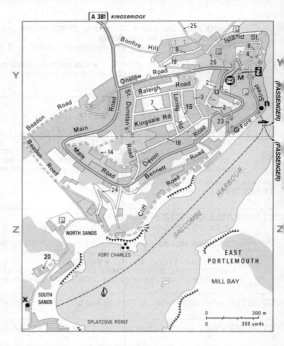

at Soar Mill Cove *Southwest : 4¼ m. by A 381 – Y – via Malborough village – ⊠ Salcombe.*

🏨 **Soar Mill Cove** ⌂, TQ7 3DS, ℰ (01548) 561566, *info@soarmillcove.co.uk*, Fax (01548) 561223, ≤, 余, ≋, ⤢ heated, 🔲, 帚, ℀ – ⇔ 🅿. ⚫⊙ 𝘝𝘐𝘚𝘈
closed 2 January-9 February**Rest** (booking essential for non-residents) 28.00/39.00 and lunch a la carte 20.00/31.00 s. ♀ – **22 rm** ⊇ ✻80.00/160.00 – ✻✻150.00/200.00.
◆ Family run local stone and slate hotel on one level in delightful and secluded coastal setting; rooms have terraces and chintz furnishings. Geared for families. Classically styled dining room.

at Hope Cove *West : 4 m. by A 381 – Y – via Malborough village – ⊠ Kingsbridge.*

🏠 **Lantern Lodge** ⌂, TQ7 3HE, by Grand View Rd ℰ (01548) 561280, *lantern lodge@hopecove.wanadoo.co.uk*, Fax (01548) 561736, ≤, ≋, 🔲, 帚 – ⇔ rest, 🅿. ⚫⊙ 𝘝𝘐𝘚𝘈. ℀
March-21 November – **Rest** (booking essential for non-residents) (dinner only) 20.00 – **14 rm** (dinner included) ⊇ ✻85.00/105.00 – ✻✻130.00/160.00.
◆ Named after its lantern window, reputedly designed to guide sailors home, this welcoming, traditional clifftop hotel overlooks Hope Cove. Front bedrooms have views. Pretty dining room with small, adjacent bar.

SALE *Gtr Manchester* **502 503 504** N 23 – *pop. 55 234 – ⊠ Manchester.*
🏌 *Sale Lodge, Golf Rd ℰ (0161) 973 1638.*
London 212 – Liverpool 36 – Manchester 6 – Sheffield 43.

🏨 **Belmore**, 143 Brooklands Rd, M33 3QN, off A 6144 ℰ (0161) 973 2538, *belmore-ho tel@hotmail.com*, Fax (0161) 973 2665, 帚 – ⇔ ℂ 🅿. – ⚐ 80. ⚫⊙ 𝘈𝘌 ① 𝘝𝘐𝘚𝘈
Classic : Rest *(closed Monday dinner)* (booking essential for non-residents) a la carte 28.95/38.00 s. ♀ – **Cada's :** Rest *(closed Sunday)* (dinner only) a la carte 16.55/25.70 s. – **18 rm** ⊇ ✻85.00/95.00 – ✻✻110.00, 2 suites.
◆ Victorian origins: built by the local landowner for his daughter. Impressive conference facilities. Bedrooms decked in quality drapes and fabrics; rear rooms are quieter. Classic overlooks terrace and Victorian garden. Cada's is informal basement brasserie.

⌂ **Cornerstones** without rest., 230 Washway Rd, M33 4RA, ☎ (0161) 283 6909, info@cor
nerstonesguesthouse.com, Fax (0161) 2831754, ⇘ – ⇔ **P**. **♨** **⊙** **VISA**. ⊗
closed Christmas-New Year – ⊡ 6.00 – **9 rm** ⚿30.00/38.00 – ⚿⚿55.00.
◆ Built in 1871 for the Lord Mayor, this restored Victorian house is family run. A medley of
rooms: spacious with varied décor and fabrics. Homely breakfast room.

SALFORD QUAYS Gtr. Manchester – see Manchester.

SALISBURY Wilts. 503 504 O 30 The West Country G. – pop. 43 355.

See : City★★ – Cathedral★★★ AC Z – Salisbury and South Wiltshire Museum★ AC Z M2 –
Close★ Z : Mompesson House★ AC Z A – Sarum St Thomas Church★ Y B – Redcoats in the
Wardrobe★ Z M1.
Env. : Wilton Village★ (Wilton House★★ AC, Wilton Carpet Factory★ AC), W : 3 m. by A 30 Y
– Old Sarum★ AC, N : 2 m. by A 345 Y – Woodford (Heale House Garden★) AC, NW : 4½ m.
by Stratford Rd Y.
Exc. : Stonehenge★★★ AC, NW : 10 m. by A 345 – Y – and A 303 – Wardour Castle★ AC, W :
15 m. by A 30 Y.
◪, ◪ Salisbury & South Wilts., Netherhampton ☎ (01722) 742645 – ◪ High Post, Great
Durnford ☎ (01722) 782356.
🛈 Fish Row ☎ (01722) 334956.
London 91 – Bournemouth 28 – Bristol 53 – Southampton 23.

Plan on next page

🏨 **White Hart,** 1 St John's St, SP1 2SD, ☎ (01722) 327476, whitehartsalisbury@macdonald-
hotels.co.uk, Fax (01722) 412761, ⇘ – ⇔ ✆ **P**. – ⚿ 100. **♨** **AE** **⊙** **VISA** Z s
Squire's : Rest (closed lunch Saturday and Bank Holiday Mondays) (bar lunch)/dinner a la
carte 17.70/29.20 **s**. ⅌ – **68 rm** ⊡ ⚿80.00/115.00 – ⚿⚿120.00/160.00.
◆ The elegant portico façade of this 17C hotel hints at formality whilst interior is relaxed
and comfortable with plenty of sofas and armchairs in lounge and plush bedrooms. Dine al
fresco on foliage-filled terrace.

🏨 **Milford Hall,** 206 Castle St, SP1 3TE, ☎ (01722) 417411, reservations@milfordhallho
tel.com, Fax (01722) 419444, ⇘, ⇘ – ⇔ **P**. – ⚿ 100. **♨** **AE** **⊙** **VISA** Y a
closed 24-26 December – **Brasserie at 206 :** Rest a la carte 19.70/29.50 – ⊡ 9.50 – **35 rm**
⚿106.00 – ⚿⚿136.00.
◆ A Georgian house, built 1780s; four period rooms in main building and in extension a
variety of modern rooms, some with sofa beds. A predominantly commercial establishment. Outside decking for terrace dining.

🏨 **Grasmere House,** 70 Harnham Rd, SP2 8JN, ☎ (01722) 338388, grasmerehotel@mis
tral.co.uk, Fax (01722) 333710, ≤, ⇘ – ⇔ ✆ ♿ **P**. – ⚿ 110. **♨** **AE** **VISA** Z a
Rest a la carte 24.50/29.50 **s**. – **38 rm** ⊡ ⚿75.50/105.50 – ⚿⚿110.50/145.00.
◆ A deep redbrick house built for Salisbury merchants in 1896 and set in lawned gardens
that go down to the rivers Avon and Nadder. Canopied beds in smartly furnished rooms.
Conservatory restaurant with splendid views.

🏠 **Cricket Field House** without rest., Wilton Rd, SP2 9NS, West : 1 ¼ m. on A 36
☎ (01722) 322595, cricketfieldcottage@btinternet.com, Fax (01722) 322595, ⇘ – ⇔ ✆ ♿
P. – ⚿ 25. **♨** **AE** **VISA**. ⊗
14 rm ⊡ ⚿58.00/70.00 – ⚿⚿85.00.
◆ Personally run extended house overlooking the County Cricket Ground. Bedrooms are
prettily decorated with pictures and floral touches; majority of rooms are in the annex.

⌂ **Old House** without rest., 161 Wilton Rd, SP2 7JQ, West : 1 m. on A 36 ☎ (01722) 333433,
Fax (01722) 335551, ⇘ – ⇔ **P**. **♨** **VISA**. ⊗
6 rm ⊡ ⚿35.00/55.00 – ⚿⚿60.00/90.00.
◆ 17C house with homely rooms and character: cosy lounge, basement bar, stone flagged
breakfast room, spacious bedrooms, antique artefacts. There's a rather nice garden, too.

⌂ **Websters** without rest., 11 Hartington Rd, SP2 7LG, (off A 360 Devizes Rd) ☎ (01722)
339779, enquiries@websters-bed-breakfast.com – ⇔ ♿ **P**. **♨** **VISA** Y n
closed New Year – **5 rm** ⊡ ⚿40.00/60.00 – ⚿⚿55.00/65.00.
◆ Secluded Victorian terrace house, with own parking, close to town centre. Friendly
owner. Cosy breakfast room. Homely style bedrooms, immaculately kept; very good value.

⌂ **Malvern** without rest., 31 Hulse Rd, SP1 3LU, ☎ (01722) 327995, malvern–gh@madasa
fish.com, Fax (01722) 327995, ⇘ – ⇔ ✆ **P**. ⊗ Y x
3 rm ⊡ ⚿50.00 – ⚿⚿65.00.
◆ A terrace house in a cul-de-sac which backs onto the river Avon, a short walk from city
centre. Well-sized bedrooms, in homely decorative style. A non smoking establishment.

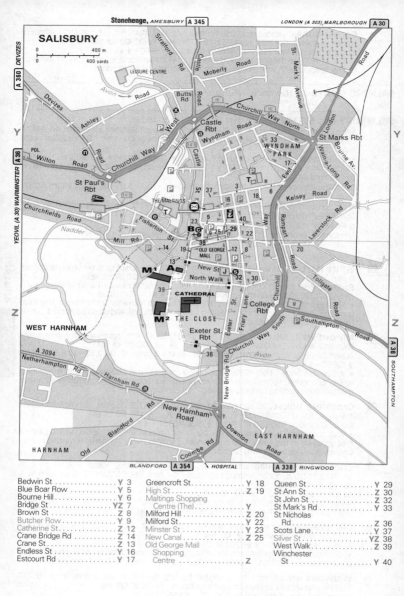

SALISBURY

Stonehenge, AMESBURY A 345

LONDON (A 303), MARLBOROUGH A 30

DEVIZES A 360

YEOVIL (A 30) WARMINSTER A 36

A 36 SOUTHAMPTON

BLANDFORD A 354 — HOSPITAL | A 338 RINGWOOD

XX **Anokaa**, 60 Fisherton St, SP2 7RB, ℰ (01772) 414142, *enquiry@anokaa.com*, Fax (01772) 414142 – ⧖⧖ ▤, ◍◍ ◫ *VISA*   Y e
closed 25-26 December – **Rest** - Indian - (buffet lunch) 10.50/15.00 and a la carte 21.05/42.15.
  ♦ Lives up to being "something out of the ordinary", with eye-catching interior and staff in silky full-length gowns. Indian dishes mix modern and classical styles with aplomb.

One Minster Street @ The Haunch of Venison, 1 Minster St, SP1 1TB, ℰ (01772) 411313, oneminsterstreet@aol.com, Fax (01772) 341774 – ⁕⤫ ⟡ 10. ◍◉ VISA
Y C
Rest 9.90 and a la carte 15.00/40.00 ♀.
  • Immensely charming and characterful 14C inn: check out 'The House of Lords' with its mummified hand! Bags of individuality in main dining room: eclectic menus; hearty fare.

at Middle Winterslow Northeast : 6½ m. by A 30 – Y – ⊠ Salisbury.

The Beadles ⤫ without rest., Middleton, SP5 1QS, ℰ (01980) 862922, winter bead@aol.com, Fax (01980) 863565, ⇗ – ⁕⤫ P. ◍◉ ⤫
restricted opening in winter – **3 rm** ⊒ ✦45.00 – ✦✦70.00.
  • Recently built from 100-year old bricks and Georgian in style; geese clack in garden. Flower-filled rooms with extra touches: pictures, reading lamps, comfortable chairs. Celebration breakfasts served on antique table.

at Whiteparish Southeast : 7½ m. by A 36 – Z – on A 27 – ⊠ Salisbury.

Newton Farmhouse without rest., Southampton Rd, SP5 2QL, Southwest : 1½ m. on A 36 ℰ (01794) 884416, enquiries@newtonfarmhouse.co.uk, ⤼, ⇗ – ⁕⤫ P. ⤫
– **9 rm** ⊒ ✦50.00/80.00 – ✦✦90.00.
  • Step back in time in this 16C farmhouse, gifted to Nelson's family after Battle of Trafalgar. Original bread oven in inglenook fireplace, oak beams and well. Cottagey rooms.

at Burcombe West : 5¼ m. by A 36 – Y – off A 30 – ⊠ Salisbury.

The Ship Inn, Burcombe Lane, SP2 0EJ, ℰ (01722) 743182, theshipbur combe@mail.com, ⇗, ⇗ – P. ◍◉ ⒜Ⓔ VISA
closed 2 weeks January – **Rest** a la carte 17.95/29.40.
  • Attractive part 17C pub: a tributary of river Nadder gurgles along at garden's end. Beams, open fires, plus sprinkling of modernity. Ample choice menus with seasonal variety.

at Teffont West : 10¼ m. by A 36 – Y – and A 30 on B 3089 – ⊠ Salisbury.

Howard's House ⤫, Teffont Evias, SP3 5RJ, ℰ (01722) 716392, enq@howardshouse hotel.co.uk, Fax (01722) 716820, ⇗ – ⁕⤫ rest, ✆ P. ◍◉ ⒜Ⓔ VISA
closed Christmas – **Rest** (closed lunch Monday and Friday) (booking essential for nonresidents) 25.00/42.00 and dinner a la carte 25.95/42.00 ♀ – **9 rm** ⊒ ✦100.00 – ✦✦175.00.
  • Personally run, part 17C dower house boasting fine gardens in a quaint, quiet village. Comfortable lounge and pleasant bedrooms with village/ garden vistas. Garden herbs and vegetables grace accomplished cooking.

at Stapleford Northwest : 7 m. by A 36 – Y – on B 3083 – ⊠ Salisbury.

Elm Tree Cottage without rest., Chain Hill, SP3 4LH, ℰ (01722) 790507, jaw.sykes@vir gin.net, ⇗ – ⁕⤫ P.
restricted opening in winter – **3 rm** ⊒ ✦45.00 – ✦✦60.00.
  • Pretty, redbrick, quintessentially English cottage; the lounge boasts inglenook fireplace. Conservatory overlooks garden. Self-contained, chintz rooms with cottagey décor.

at Little Langford Northwest : 8 m. by A 36 – Y – and Great Wishford rd – ⊠ Salisbury.

Little Langford Farmhouse without rest., SP3 4NP, ℰ (01722) 790205, bandb@lit tlelangford.co.uk, Fax (01722) 790086, ≤, ⇗, ⤼ – ⁕⤫ P. ◍◉ VISA ⤫
restricted opening in winter – **3 rm** ✦50.00/60.00 – ✦✦65.00/75.00.
  • An unusual Victorian Gothic farmhouse with turret, crenellations and lancet windows. Period style interiors throughout. Spacious, well-furnished bedrooms with rural views.

SANDFORD-ON-THAMES Oxon. – see Oxford.

SANDGATE Kent 504 X 30 – see Folkestone.

SANDIWAY Ches. 502 503 504 M 24 – ⊠ Northwich.
London 191 – Liverpool 34 – Manchester 22 – Stoke-on-Trent 26.

Nunsmere Hall, Tarporley Rd, CW8 2ES, Southwest : 1½ m. by A 556 on A 49 ℰ (01606) 889100, reservations@nunsmere.co.uk, Fax (01606) 889055, ⇗, ⇗, ⤼ – ▯ ⁕⤫ P. – ⒜ 50. ◍◉ ⒜Ⓔ ⓪ VISA ⤫
Crystal : **Rest** 26.50 (lunch) and a la carte 32.50/53.00 ♀ – ⊒ 19.50 – **36 rm** ✦152.50 – ✦✦210.00.
  • Secluded, on a wooded peninsular, originally built in 1900. Deep-seated sofas and sumptuous drawing rooms. Tasteful, individually furnished bedrooms exude quality and comfort. Dine in the classical style on imaginative and accomplished cuisine.

ENGLAND

SANDSEND *N. Yorks.* 502 R/S 20 – *see Whitby.*

SANDWICH *Kent* 504 Y 30 *Great Britain G.* – *pop. 4 398.*
See : *Town★.*
🛈 *Guildhall* 𝒫 *(01304) 613565.*
London 72.5 – Canterbury 13 – Dover 12.

  The Bell at Sandwich, The Quay, CT13 9EF, 𝒫 (01304) 613388, *reservations@sandwich.theplacehotels.co.uk, Fax (01304) 615308* – ⇆⊁ 🅿 – ♨ 150. 🆗 🆎 *VISA*. 🛠
closed 25-26 December – **The Place Brasserie** : Rest a la carte 19.95/30.65 – **34 rm** ⊡
⚡85.00/105.00 – ⚡⚡115.00/185.00.
   ◆ Situated by River Stour with original Victorian fittings in situ. Refurbishment has resulted in stunning transformation of bedrooms: now cool, elegant, stylish and welcoming. Pleasant brasserie with strong seafood base.

SANDY *Beds.* 504 T 27 – *pop. 10 887.*
🛈 *5 Shannon Court, High St* 𝒫 *(01767) 682728.*
London 49 – Bedford 8 – Cambridge 24 – Peterborough 35.

 Holiday Inn Garden Court, Girtford Bridge, London Rd, SG19 1DH, West : ¾ m. by B 1042 at junction of A 1 with A 603 𝒫 (01767) 692220, *Fax (01767) 680452* – ⇆⊁ rm, 🍽 rest, ✆ 🅿 – ♨ 150. 🆗 🆎 ⓞ *VISA*. 🛠
Rest *(closed Saturday lunch)* (dinner only) 15.00/20.00 **s.** – ⊡ 10.95 – **57 rm** ⚡72.00/88.00 – ⚡⚡72.00/88.00.
   ◆ Located on A1; Bedford museums are among local attractions. Comfortable rooms of uniform shape and size accommodating up to three people (sofa beds available). Well staffed. Pleasant, family-friendly dining room.

⚘ **Highfield Farm** without rest., Great North Rd, SG19 2AQ, North : 2 m. by B 1042 on A 1 (southbound carriageway) 𝒫 (01767) 682332, *margaret@highfield-farm.co.uk, Fax (01767) 692503, �ᵉ, ♨ – ⇆⊁ 🅿. 🆗 🆎 VISA*
8 rm ⊡ ⚡53.00/70.00 – ⚡⚡70.00/75.00.
   ◆ Working arable farm with gardens and 300 acres of land. Light, airy breakfast room, homely lounge and immaculately kept bedrooms, three of which are outside in coach house.

SANDYPARK *Devon* 503 I 31 – *see Chagford.*

SAPPERTON *Glos.* 503 504 N 28 – *see Cirencester.*

SARK *C.I.* 503 P 33 and 517 ⑩ – *see Channel Islands.*

SAUNTON *Devon* 503 H 30 *The West Country G.* – ✉ *Braunton.*
Env. : *Braunton★ – St Brannock's Church★, E : 2½ m. on B 3231 – Braunton Burrows★, E :* ½ *m. on B 3231.*
🛐₈, 🛐₈ *Saunton, Braunton* 𝒫 *(01271) 812436.*
London 230 – Barnstaple 8 – Exeter 48.

 Saunton Sands, EX33 1LQ, 𝒫 (01271) 890212, *info@sauntonsands.com, Fax (01271) 890145,* ≼ Saunton Sands and Bideford Bay, 🌀, *ℐₛ,* ≋ₛ, 🔲 heated, 🔳, 🌳, 🎾, squash – 🛗, ⇆⊁ rest, 🍽 rest, 🚼 🅿 – ♨ 150. 🆗 🆎 ⓞ *VISA*. 🛠
Rest 19.50/30.00 – **73 rm** (dinner included) ⊡ ⚡95.00/154.50 – ⚡⚡266.00/376.00.
   ◆ Imposing and busy 1930s seaside hotel in a prominent elevated position. Airy, spacious deluxe rooms have sea vistas. Families are well catered for; staffed crèche available. Classic dining room has sweeping sea views.

SAWDON *N. Yorks.* – *see Scarborough.*

The ✿ award is the crème de la crème.
This is awarded to restaurants
which are really worth travelling miles for!

A WATER THAT BELONGS ON THE WINE LIST.

SAWLEY Lancs. 502 M 22.

London 242 – Blackpool 39 – Leeds 44 – Liverpool 54.

XX **Spread Eagle**, BB7 4NH, ℰ (01200) 441202, Fax (01200) 441973 – ⅋ P. ◍ ◍ VISA
closed 1 week January, Sunday dinner and Monday – **Rest** 16.75 (lunch) and a la carte
20.00/28.40 ♀.
♦ Former pub overlooking the Ribble and surrounding countryside; this busy restaurant
serves well-priced dishes with a modern twist and strong local influences.

SAXMUNDHAM Suffolk 504 Y 27 – pop. 2 712 – ⊠ Ipswich.

London 95 – Aldeburgh 7 – Ipswich 20.

🏠 **The Bell**, 31 High St, IP17 1AF, ℰ (01728) 602331, thebell@saxhighstreet.fsnet.co.uk,
Fax (01728) 602331 – ⅋ P. ◍ ◍ VISA
Rest *(closed 1 week in spring, 1 week in autumn, Sunday and Monday except Bank Holidays)* 14.50 (lunch) and a la carte 24.70/28.60 s. ♀ – ⌷ 5.95 – 10 rm ⌷ ✦40.00 – ✦✦75.00.
♦ 17C former coaching inn, retaining much original visual character. Striking wall mural in
hall. Local ale flows in cosy public bar. Spacious bedrooms offer stylish comforts. Accomplished cooking in smart dining room.

SCALBY N. Yorks. 502 S 21 – see Scarborough.

SCARBOROUGH N. Yorks. 502 S 21 Great Britain G. – pop. 38 364.

Exc. : Robin Hood's Bay★, N : 16 m. on A 171 and minor rd to the right (signposted) –
Whitby Abbey★, N : 21 m. on A 171 – Sledmere House★, S : 21 m. on A 645, B 1249 and
B 1253 (right).

🏌 Scarborough North Cliff, North Cliff Ave, Burniston Rd ℰ (01723) 360786, NW : 2 m. by
A 165 Y – 🏌 Scarborough South Cliff, Deepdale Ave, off Filey Rd ℰ (01723) 374737, S : 1 m.
by A 165 Z.

🛈 Unit 15A, Brunswick Shopping Centre, Westborough ℰ (01723) 383636 – Harbourside,
Sandside ℰ (01723) 383637 (except November-Easter Sunday only).

London 253 – Kingston-upon-Hull 47 – Leeds 67 – Middlesbrough 52.

Plan on next page

🏛 **Beiderbecke's**, 1-3 The Crescent, YO11 2PW, ℰ (01723) 365766, info@beider
beckes.com, Fax (01723) 367433 – ⅋ ⅋ ⅋. ✺   Z s
Rest (live jazz Friday-Saturday)(dinner only) 20.50 and a la carte 24.35/31.30 – **26 rm** ⌷
✦65.00/75.00 – ✦✦130.00/140.00, 1 suite.
♦ Named after the jazz musician. Although housed in a restored Georgian building, the
rooms' décor is balanced between period style and contemporary feel with bright colours.
Themed restaurant with nightclub feel.

🏛 **The Royal**, St Nicholas St, YO11 2HE, ℰ (01723) 364333, royalhotel@englishroseho
tels.co.uk, Fax (01723) 500618, ⅃, ▣ – ⅋ ⅋ ⅋ ⅋ – 🔺 275. ◍ ◍ ◍ VISA   Z a
Rest 18.95/27.50 and a la carte 19.85/28.85 – **118 rm** ⌷ ✦69.00/99.00 –
✦✦130.00/140.00.
♦ Make-up recently re-applied to one of the town's grand old ladies; 1830s elegance
exemplified by unforgettable main staircase. Mix of original or contemporary bedroom
styles. Formal ambience in grand dining room.

🏛 **The Crown Spa H.**, 7-11 Esplanade, YO11 2AG, ℰ (01723) 357400, info@crownspaho
tel.com, Fax (01723) 357404, ←, ⅃, ⊜, ▣ – ⅋ ⅋ ⅋ P. – 🔺 200. ◍ ◍ ◍ VISA   Z i
Jewels : **Rest** (dinner only) 15.95/26.95 – **Café Bar :** **Rest** 15.95/24.95 (dinner) and a la
carte 16.00/24.00 s. – **85 rm** ⌷ ✦51.00/120.00 – ✦✦101.00/150.00, 1 suite.
♦ 19C landmark – the town's first resort hotel, on the esplanade overlooking the bay.
Spacious lounges in the classic style. Large bedrooms, many with fine sea views. Popular
Jewels serves family favourites. Informal dining in Café Bar.

🏠 **Ox Pasture Hall** ⌖, Lady Edith's Drive, Raincliffe Woods, YO12 5TD, West : 3 ¼ m. by
A 171 following signs for Raincliffe Woods ℰ (01723) 365295, oxpasturehall@btcon
nect.com, Fax (01723) 355156, ←, ⌖, ⌖, ⅋ – ⅋ ⅋ P. – 🔺 200. ◍ ◍ ◍ VISA
Rest (bar lunch)/dinner 24.95 and a la carte 24.95/34.95 ♀ – **22 rm** ⌷ ✦50.00/70.00 –
✦✦130.00/160.00.
♦ Deep in the countryside, yet close to the sea. A charming part-17C farmhouse: most
bedrooms offer pleasant views, some around an attractive wisteria-clad courtyard. Dining
room has uniform feel.

🏠 **Alexander**, 33 Burniston Rd, YO12 6PG, ℰ (01723) 363178, enquiries@alexanderhotels
carburgh.co.uk, Fax (01723) 354821 – ⅋ P. ◍ ◍ VISA. ✺   Y a
March-October – **Rest** *(closed Sunday)* (residents only) (dinner only) 17.00 s. ♀ – **10 rm** ⌷
✦31.00/42.00 – ✦✦60.00/66.00.
♦ Red-brick 1930s house situated close to North Bay attractions. Smartly furnished
lounge. Bedrooms vary in size and are all pleasantly decorated and comfortable.

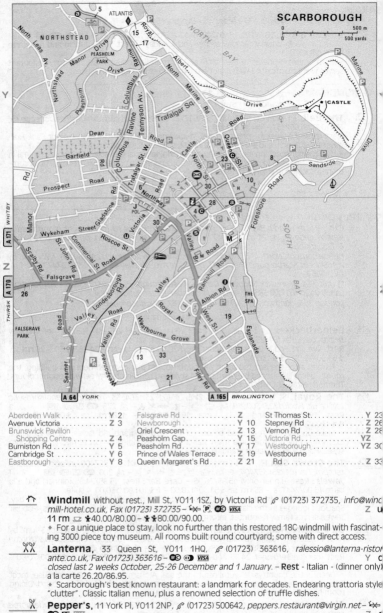

SCARBOROUGH

⚓ **Windmill** without rest., Mill St, YO11 1SZ, by Victoria Rd ℘ (01723) 372735, *info@windmill-hotel.co.uk*, Fax (01723) 372735 – ⇆ 🅿. 🕮🕄 𝘝𝘐𝘚𝘈   Z **u**
11 rm ⇆ ✸40.00/80.00 – ✸✸80.00/90.00.
  ◆ For a unique place to stay, look no further than this restored 18C windmill with fascinating 3000 piece toy museum. All rooms built round courtyard; some with direct access.

XX **Lanterna,** 33 Queen St, YO11 1HQ, ℘ (01723) 363616, *ralessio@lanterna-ristorante.co.uk*, Fax (01723) 363616 – 🕮🕄 ⓞ 𝘝𝘐𝘚𝘈   Y **c**
closed last 2 weeks October, 25-26 December and 1 January. – **Rest** - Italian - (dinner only) a la carte 26.20/86.95.
  ◆ Scarborough's best known restaurant: a landmark for decades. Endearing trattoria style "clutter". Classic Italian menu, plus a renowned selection of truffle dishes.

X **Pepper's,** 11 York Pl, YO11 2NP, ℘ (01723) 500642, *peppers.restaurant@virgin.net* – ⇆ 🕮🕄 🄰🄴 𝘝𝘐𝘚𝘈   Z **c**
closed 24-29 December, Sunday and lunch Monday-Wednesday – **Rest** a la carte 25.50/32.50.
  ◆ Set in a Victorian terrace, and run by a husband and wife team. Unfussy ambience with humorous local artwork on the walls. Locally landed fish and shellfish a speciality.

650

at Sawdon *Southwest : 9¾ m. by A 170 – Z – ⊠ Scarborough.*

🍴 **The Anvil Inn,** Main St, YO13 9DY, ℘ (01723) 859896, 🌳 – ⅍ **P.** 🐄 **VISA**. ⅍
closed 25 December – **Rest** *(closed Sunday dinner and Monday)* a la carte 14.35/21.65.
♦ Locally renowned pub, an ex-forge with old furnace, bellows and tools providing a sense of place. Intimate restaurant serves serious, hearty Yorkshire fare in good portions.

at Scalby *Northwest : 3 m. by A 171 – Z – ⊠ Scarborough.*

🏨 **Wrea Head Country House** ⌂, Barmoor Lane, YO13 0PB, North : 1 m. by A 171
℘ (01723) 378211, *sales@englishrosehotels.co.uk*, Fax (01723) 371780, ≼, 🌳, ₤ – ⅍ **P.** – 🔼 30. 🐄 🗚 ⓞ **VISA**. ⅍
Rest 16.95/25.00 – **19 rm** ⊠ ✦49.50/120.00 – ✦✦90.00/140.00, 1 suite.
♦ Close to North York Moors National Park and flanked by gardens, this Victorian manor promises a peaceful stay: oak panelling, stained glass, spacious rooms. Elegant dining room renowned for its local produce.

at Hackness *Northwest : 7 m. by A 171 – Z – ⊠ Scarborough.*

🏨 **Hackness Grange** ⌂, YO13 0JW, ℘ (01723) 882345, *hacknessgrange@englishroseho tels.co.uk*, Fax (01723) 882391, 🗋, 🌳, ₤, ℀ – ⅍ **P.** 🐄 🗚 ⓞ **VISA**. ⅍
Rest (bar lunch)/dinner 25.00 – **33 rm** ⊠ ✦49.50/110.00 – ✦✦135.00/170.00.
♦ A grand 18C house, part of Lord Derwent's estate, set in attractive grounds. Indoor pool with floor to ceiling windows; bedrooms in main house have good views. Restaurant diners can contemplate views of lake.

 If breakfast is included the ⊠ symbol appears after the number of rooms.

ENGLAND

SCILLY (Isles of) *Cornwall 503 A/B 34 The West Country G.*
See : *Islands★ - The Archipelago (≼★★★).*
Env. : *St Agnes : Horsepoint★.*
Helicopter service from St Mary's and Tresco to Penzance : ℘ (01736) 363871.
✈ *St Mary's Airport : ℘ (01720) 422677, E : 1½ m. from Hugh Town.*
⛴ *from Hugh Town to Penzance (Isles of Scilly Steamship Co. Ltd) (summer only) (2 h 40 mn).*
🛈 *Hugh Town, St Mary's ℘ (01720) (Scillonia) 422536.*

Bryher *Cornwall The West Country G. – pop. 78 – ⊠ Scillonia.*
See : *Watch Hill (≼★) – Hell Bay★.*

🏨 **Hell Bay** ⌂, TR23 0PR, ℘ (01720) 422947, *contactus@hellbay.co.uk*, Fax (01720) 423004, ≼, 🌳, ₤, ⌂, ⅃ heated, 🌳 – ⅍ **P.** 🐄 **VISA**
closed 2 January-mid February – **Rest** (booking essential to non-residents) (bar lunch)/dinner 35.00 ℀ – **11 rm** (dinner included) ⊠ – ✦✦240.00/380.00, 14 suites 280/500.
♦ Totally renovated, with a charming style that's relaxed, modern, comfy and colourful. Courtyard terraces, a vast lounge/bar and clean-lined rooms add to an idyllic appeal. Dining room with garden views and daily changing menu.

🏠 **Bank Cottage** ⌂ without rest., TR23 0PR, ℘ (01720) 422612, *macmace@patrol.i-way.co.uk*, Fax (01720) 422612, ≼, 🌳 – ⅍. ⅍
April-November – **4 rm** – ✦✦80.00/90.00.
♦ A modern guesthouse in lush sub-tropical gardens, complete with koi fish pond. A peaceful haven with floral bedrooms and a cosy little boxroom where you can buy seafood.

St Martin's *Cornwall The West Country G. – pop. 113.*
See : *St Martin's Head (≼★★).*

🏨 **St Martin's on the Isle** ⌂, TR25 0QW, ℘ (01720) 422092, *stay@stmartinshotel.co.uk*, Fax (01720) 422298, ≼ Tean Sound and islands, 🌳, 🗋, 🌳, ℀ – ⎏, ⅍ rest, ☆. 🐄 🗚 ⓞ **VISA**
April-October – **Tean : Rest** (booking essential) (dinner only) 39.50 s. ℀ – **Bistro : Rest** *(closed Monday dinner)* – **27 rm** (dinner included) ⊠ ✦150.00/188.00 – ✦✦300.00/560.00, 3 suites.
♦ Set on the quayside with unrivalled views of white beaches and blue sea; a truly idyllic island setting. Snooze extremely peacefully in snug bedrooms. Skilfully prepared seasonal dishes in Tean. Bistro, with terrace and eclectic menu, is perfect for lunch.

St Mary's Cornwall *The West Country G.* – *pop. 1 607.*

See : *Gig racing*★★ – *Garrison Walk*★ (≤ ★★) – *Peninnis Head*★ – *Hugh Town - Museum*★.
🇫🇸 ℱ *(01720) 422692.*

🏛️ **Star Castle** ≫, The Garrison, TR21 0JA, ℱ *(01720) 422317, info@star-castle.co.uk,*
Fax (01720) 422343, ≤, 🖼️, 🌳, ※ – ⇥= 🔞 ᴀᴇ 𝖵𝖨𝖲𝖠
closed 2 January-9 February – **Castle dining room :** Rest (dinner only) 29.50 ♀ –
Conservatory : Rest - Seafood - *(April-October)* (dinner only) ♀ – **34 rm** (dinner included)
□ ★65.00/200.00 – ★★110.00/296.00, 4 suites.
  ◆ Elizabethan castle built in 1593 in the shape of an eight pointed star, surrounded by
dry moat. There are harbour views; palms, echiums in garden. Airy rooms; subtle
colours. Medieval wall tapestry highlight of Castle Dining Room. Seafood menus in Conservatory

🏛️ **Atlantic,** Hugh St, Hugh Town, TR21 0PL, ℱ *(01720) 422417, atlantichotel@smalland
friendly.co.uk, Fax (01720) 423009,* ≤ St Mary's Harbour – ⇥= 🛗 🔞 ᴀᴇ 𝖵𝖨𝖲𝖠
3 February - December – **Rest** (dinner only) 25.00 and a la carte 18.00/25.00 – **25 rm** (dinner
included) □ ★99.00/119.00 – ★★158.00/188.00.
  ◆ A traditional white hotel with views of St Mary's harbour and bobbing boats. Cottage
charm in older rooms - low ceilings, floral fabrics; modern rooms in extension. Scillian
ingredients in dining room with harbour views.

🏠 **Amaryllis** ≫, Buzza Hill, TR21 0NQ, ℱ *(01720) 423387, earlsamaryllis@aol.com,* ≤, 🌳 –
⇥= 📺
Easter-October – **Rest** *(high season only on alternate nights)* – **3 rm** (dinner included),
weekly stays ★800.00/920.00 – ★★800.00/920.00.
  ◆ Stroll down sloping garden and take in super views to beach and across to St. Agnes.
Family style breakfast table. Immaculate sitting room. Co-ordinated, pretty bedrooms.
Home-cooked meals featuring fresh Scillian ingredients.

🏠 **Carntop,** Church Rd, TR21 0NA, ℱ *(01720) 423763* – ⇥= 📺
Rest – **3 rm** (dinner included) □ ★108.00 – ★★108.00.
  ◆ Chalet style house run by friendly owners: husband born and bred on the island. Bedrooms are modern with light, fresh co-ordination and boast good amenities. Vegetables
grown 'at the back' are the backbone of proudly home-cooked meals.

🏠 **Evergreen Cottage** without rest., Parade, High Town, TR21 0LP, ℱ *(01720) 422711,
evergreen.scilly@btinternet.com* – ⇥= 📺
March-December – **5 rm** □ ★34.50/73.00 – ★★69.00/73.00.
  ◆ A 300-year old captain's cottage; very pleasant, with window boxes, a few minutes walk
from the quay. Plenty of local literature in low beamed lounge. Compact, tidy rooms.

Tresco Cornwall *The West Country G.* – *pop. 167* – ✉️ *New Grimsby.*
See : *Island*★ - *Abbey Gardens*★★ AC *(Lighthouse Way* ≤ ★★).

🏨 **The Island** ≫, Old Grimsby, TR24 0PU, ℱ *(01720) 422883, islandhotel@tresco.co.uk,*
Fax (01720) 423008, ≤ St Martin's and islands, 🌊 heated, 🌳, 🏹, ※ – 🔼 ⇥= 🚗🚗 🔞 𝖵𝖨𝖲𝖠.
※
12 February-October – **Rest** (terrace lunch)/dinner 38.00 ♀ – **45 rm** (dinner included) □
★130.00/330.00 – ★★340.00/450.00, 3 suites.
  ◆ A heated pool, sub-tropical gardens, panoramic views to be had at this luxurious hotel.
Enthusiastic owners collect art for interiors. Well appointed garden rooms. Light, welcoming dining room boasts sea vistas and friendly staff..

🏛️ **New Inn,** TR24 0QQ, ℱ *(01720) 422844, newinn@tresco.co.uk, Fax (01720) 423200,* ≤,
🌳, 🌊 heated – ⇥= 🔞 𝖵𝖨𝖲𝖠. ※
Rest (booking essential for non-residents) a la carte 20.00/30.00 ♀ – **16 rm** (dinner included) □ ★135.00/150.00 – ★★192.00/228.00.
  ◆ This stone built former inn makes a hospitable stopping off point. Friendly, bustling
ambience in lounges and bars; very pleasant garden terrace. Comfortable bedrooms. Bistro-style dining room's more refined cooking a good alternative to bar menu.

The red ≫ symbol?
This denotes the very essence of peace
– only the sound of birdsong first thing in the morning …

ENGLAND

SCUNTHORPE North Lincolnshire 502 S 23 – pop. 72 669.

📍 Ashby Decoy, Burringham Rd ℘ (01724) 842913 – 📍 Kingsway ℘ (01724) 840945 – 📍,
📍 Grange Park, Butterwick Rd, Messingham ℘ (01724) 762945.

✈ Humberside Airport : ℘ (01652) 688456, E : 15 m. by A 18.

London 167 – Leeds 54 – Lincoln 30 – Sheffield 45.

Forest Pines, Ermine St, Broughton, DN20 0AQ, Southeast : 5 m. by A 1029 off A 18
℘ (01652) 650770, forestpines@qhotels.co.uk, Fax (01652) 650495, 🌤, ⏱, ↕, 🏊, 🔲, 📍,
📍, 🌳 – 🗐 ✙, 🗏 rest, ☎ ఉ 📍 – 🔬 250. 🆎 🎫 ⓞ 𝘝𝘐𝘚𝘈. 🛠
Beechtree : Rest a la carte 14.00/24.00 – **Garden Room :** Rest a la carte 14.00/24.00 ℤ –
112 rm ⇆ ✸119.00 – ✸✸129.00, 2 suites.
♦ A luxury hotel in woodland with 27 hole golf course and smart, well-equipped leisure
complex; includes beauty treatments. Bedrooms are all spacious with modern facilities.
Fine dining at the Beech Tree. The Garden Room features a lovely decked terrace.

SEAHAM Durham 501 502 P/Q 19 – pop. 21 153.

London 284 – Carlisle 77 – Leeds 84 – Middlesbrough 24 – Newcastle upon Tyne 17.

Seaham Hall, ⚘, Lord Byron's Walk, SR7 7AG, North : 1 ¼ m. by B 1287 ℘ (0191) 516
1400, reservations@seaham-hall.com, Fax (0191) 516 1410, ≤, ⏱, ↕, 🏊, 🔲, 🌳, ⚑ – ✙
🗐 ☎ ఉ 📍 – 🔬 120. 🆎 🎫 𝘝𝘐𝘚𝘈. 🛠
The White Room : Rest (booking essential for non-residents) 17.50/30.00 and a la carte
45.00/65.00 s. – **16 rm** ⇆ ✸225.00 – ✸✸360.00/535.00, 3 suites.
Spec. Crab ravioli with crab consommé, tarragon and tomato. Poached and roasted
chicken, mushroom purée and truffle gnocchi. Passion fruit soufflé with banana sorbet.
♦ Imposing 17C and 19C mansion with ultra-modern technology in spacious rooms. Contemporary sculpture and décor. Unique Oriental spa has relaxing, Far Eastern ambience.
Crisp linen and fine china define restaurant.

SEAHOUSES Northd. 501 502 P 17 Great Britain G.

Env. : Farne Islands★ (by boat from harbour).

📍 Beadnell Rd ℘ (01665) 720794.

🛈 Car Park, Seafield Rd ℘ (01665) 720884 (Easter-October).

London 328 – Edinburgh 80 – Newcastle upon Tyne 46.

Olde Ship, 9 Main St, NE68 7RD, ℘ (01665) 720200, theoldeship@seahouses.co.uk,
Fax (01665) 721383 – ✙ 📍 – 🔬 40. 🆎 𝘝𝘐𝘚𝘈. 🛠
February-November – **Rest** (bar lunch Monday-Saturday)/dinner 20.00 and a la carte
18.25/20.00 ℤ – **13 rm** ⇆ ✸48.00/110.00 – ✸✸96.00/110.00, 5 suites.
♦ Built in 1745 as a farmhouse but has left origins far behind, proudly showing nautical
links. Harbour views and marine artefacts throughout. Cosy, comfortable rooms. Dine in
characterful bar at lunch or classic dining room for dinner.

SEASALTER Kent 504 X 29 – see Whitstable.

SEATON BURN Tyne and Wear 502 P 18 – see Newcastle upon Tyne.

SEAVIEW I.O.W. 503 504 Q 31 – see Wight (Isle of).

SEDLESCOMBE E. Sussex 504 V 31 – ✉ Battle.

London 56 – Hastings 7 – Lewes 26 – Maidstone 27.

Brickwall, The Green, TN33 0QA, ℘ (01424) 870253, info@brickwallhotel.com,
Fax (01424) 870785, 🌤, 🏊 heated, 🌳 – ✙ 📍 🆎 🎫 ⓞ 𝘝𝘐𝘚𝘈
Rest 18.00/28.50 and a la carte 21.00/28.50 ℤ – **25 rm** ⇆ ✸65.00/100.00 –
✸✸88.00/110.00.
♦ Part Tudor mansion at top of village green, built for local ironmaster in 1597. Well placed
for beauty spots. Range of rooms include family, four-poster and ground floor. Dining
room boasts characterful low beamed ceiling.

SEMINGTON Wilts. 503 504 N 29 – see Trowbridge.

SETTLE N. Yorks. 502 N 21 – pop. 3 621.

🖫 Giggleswick ℰ (01729) 825288.
🖪 Town Hall, Cheapside ℰ (01729) 825192.
London 238 – Bradford 34 – Kendal 30 – Leeds 41.

🏨 **Falcon Manor**, Skipton Rd, BD24 9BD, ℰ (01729) 823814, enquiries@thefalconma
nor.com, Fax (01729) 822087, ☞ – ⇔ 🅿 – 🔬 100. ◑◎ 🆅🅸🆂🅰. ℁
📞110.00.
Ingfield : Rest (dinner only and Sunday lunch) 24.95 – **18 rm** ☑ ✝75.00/85.00 –
✝✝★110.00.
◆ Built in 1842 as a rectory; sits on the fringe of Dales National Park. A grand hall with
chandelier and sweeping wooden staircase leads to traditionally furnished rooms. Elegant
dining room: ornate ceiling, large leaded window.

⌂ **Husband's Barn** without rest., Stainforth, BD24 9PB, North : 2 m. on B 6479 ℰ (01729)
822240, Fax (01729) 822240 – ⇔ 🅿. ℁
closed January-February and 25- 26 December – **3 rm** ☑ ✝40.00/55.00 – ✝✝55.00/65.00.
◆ Recently converted barn, surrounded by attractive dales scenery. Comfy beamed
lounge with open fire. Light, airy breakfast room with views. Bedrooms have exposed
rafters.

✕ **Little House**, 17 Duke St, BD24 9DJ, ℰ (01729) 823963 – ⇔. ◑◎ 🆅🅸🆂🅰
closed 2 weeks Spring and 2 weeks Autumn – **Rest** (booking essential) (dinner only Wednesday-Saturday) a la carte 19.40/27.30.
◆ Former 19C gate house, a 'little house' of stone that was once a cobblers. Well-kept,
rustic style within a compact space. Traditional and classic styles of cooking prevail.

SEVENOAKS Kent 504 U 30 Great Britain G. – pop. 26 699.

Env. : Knole★★ AC, SE :½ m. – Ightham Mote★★ AC, E : 5 m. by A 25.
🖫 Woodlands Manor, Tinkerpot Lane ℰ (01959) 523806 – 🖫 Darenth Valley, Station Rd,
Shoreham ℰ (01959) 522944.
🖪 Buckhurst Lane ℰ (01732) 450305, tic@sevenoakstown.gov.uk.
London 26 – Guildford 40 – Maidstone 17.

✕✕ **Sun Do**, 61 High St, TN13 1JF, ℰ (01732) 453299, Fax (01732) 454860 – ▤. ◑◎ 🅰🅴 🆅🅸🆂🅰
closed 25-26 December – **Rest** - Chinese - a la carte approx 21.00.
◆ Meaning "Happiness", with attentive staff and oriental setting, you can expect authentic
Chinese food here. Extensive choice, including various set menus.

at Ightham Common Southeast : 5 m. by A 25 on Common Rd – ⊠ Sevenoaks.

🏠 **Harrow Inn**, Common Rd, TN15 9EB, ℰ (01732) 885912, Fax (01732) 885912, ☞ – ⇔
🅿. ◑◎ 🆅🅸🆂🅰. ℁
closed 26 December, 1 January, Sunday dinner and Monday – **Rest** a la carte 18.00/30.00.
◆ Attractive 17C stone and brick inn on sleepy narrow lane. Oozing character: flags, beams,
open fire. Appealing and inventive dishes are enhanced by honest, rustic cooking.

SHAFTESBURY Dorset 503 504 N 30 The West Country G. – pop. 6 665.

See : Gold Hill★ (≤★) – Local History Museum★ AC.
Env. : Wardour Castle★ AC, NE : 5 m.
🖪 8 Bell St ℰ (01747) 853514.
London 115 – Bournemouth 31 – Bristol 47 – Dorchester 29 – Salisbury 20.

🏨 **Royal Chase**, Royal Chase Roundabout, SP7 8DB, Southeast : at junction of A 30 with
A 350 ℰ (01747) 853355, royalchasehotel@btinternet.com, Fax (01747) 851969, 🖳, ☞ –
⇔ 🅿 – 🔬 180. ◑◎ 🅰🅴 ◑ 🆅🅸🆂🅰
Byzant : Rest 12.95 (lunch) and a la carte 22.95/29.45 s. – ☑ 9.50 – **33 rm** ✝95.00 –
✝✝110.00.
◆ Located in "Thomas Hardy" country and once a training school for the Order of Mis-
sionary Priests. Possesses a Turkish steam room, indoor pool. Individually styled bedrooms.
Cosy, atmospheric dining room.

⌂ **The Retreat** without rest., 47 Bell St, SP7 8AE, ℰ (01747) 850372, info@the-re
treat.org.uk, Fax (01747) 850372 – ⇔ ⦸ & 🅿. ◑◎ 🆅🅸🆂🅰. ℁
closed January – **10 rm** ☑ ✝37.00/65.00 – ✝✝70.00/80.00.
◆ Georgian townhouse in good location - central but not noisy. Spotlessly clean throughout. Individually decorated bedrooms; several overlook the rear, so particularly quiet.

✕✕ **La Fleur de Lys** with rm, Bleke St, SP7 8AW, ℰ (01747) 853717, info@lafleurdelys.co.uk,
Fax (01747) 853130, ☞ – ⇔ 🅿. ◑◎ 🅰🅴 🆅🅸🆂🅰
closed 3 weeks January, Sunday dinner and Monday and Tuesday lunch – **Rest** 28.50 (lunch)
and dinner a la carte 30.00/39.00 ☉ – **7 rm** ☑ ✝65.00/75.00 – ✝✝95.00/110.00.
◆ Owners relocated to this address in 2003: smart restaurant in an 1870s ivy-covered
house. Comfy bar with plenty of sofas. Well-kept bedrooms, named after grape varieties.

XX **Wayfarers,** Sherborne Causeway, SP7 9PX, West : 2½ m. on A 30 ℘ (01747) 852821 – 🅿.
🅼🅾 𝘝𝘐𝘚𝘈
*closed 26 December-17 January, 1week June, Monday, Tuesday lunch, Saturday lunch and
Sunday dinner* – **Rest** (lunch booking essential) 20.00/32.00 ℞.
◆ A 200-year old cottage with an Old England interior of exposed stone walls, beams hung
with china plates and a lovely log fire. Broad à la carte with simpler lunch menus.

at Donhead St Andrew *East : 5 m. by A 30* – ⊠ *Shaftesbury.*

🏠 **Forester Inn** with rm, Lower St, SP7 9EE, ℘ (01747) 828038, enquiries@foresterinndon
headstandrew.co.uk, Fax (01747) 828050, 🈺, 🈺, ↳✦ 🅿. 🅼🅾 𝘝𝘐𝘚𝘈
Rest a la carte 20.00/30.00 ℞ – **2 rm** ⊊ ✦57.50/95.00 – ✦✦65.00/110.00.
◆ Attractive thatched pub with 13C origins. Lovely rustic bar with beams and inglenooks.
Dine in barn style extension where much locally sourced produce enhances modern
dishes.

at Compton Abbas *South : 4 m. on A 350* – ⊠ *Shaftesbury.*

🏠 **Old Forge** without rest., Chapel Hill, SP7 0NQ, ℘ (01747) 811881, theoldforge@hot
mail.com, Fax (01747) 811881, 🈺 – ↳✦ 🅿. 🈺
3 rm ⊊ ✦40.00/50.00 – ✦✦70.00.
◆ Thatched cottage dating from 1700; once a wheelwright, carriage builder. Tradition
continues in car restoration business. Rooms all slightly different; pretty, characterful.

at Motcombe *Northwest : 2½ m. by B 3081* – ⊠ *Shaftesbury.*

🏨 **Coppleridge Inn** 🈺, SP7 9HW, North : 1 m. on Mere rd ℘ (01747) 851980, thecop
pleridgeinn@btinternet.com, Fax (01747) 851858, 🈺, 🈺, 🈺, 🈺 – 🅿 – 🛏 50. 🅼🅾 🄰🄴 🅾
𝘝𝘐𝘚𝘈
Rest a la carte 15.50/24.00 ℞ – **10 rm** ⊊ ✦45.00 – ✦✦80.00.
◆ A converted 18C farmhouse in 15 acres of meadow. Bedrooms, in a separate courtyard,
with views, are a particular strength - bright and airy. Magnificent barn for functions.

ENGLAND

> Good food and accommodation at moderate prices?
> Look for the Bib symbols:
> red Bib Gourmand 🍴 for food, blue Bib Hotel 🛏 for hotels

SHANKLIN *I.O.W.* **503 504** Q 32 – *see Wight (Isle of).*

SHEDFIELD *Hants.* **503 504** Q 31 – *pop. 3 558* – ⊠ *Southampton.*
🛈, 🛈 *Marriott Meon Valley H. & C.C., Sandy Lane, off A 334* ℘ *(01329) 833455.*
London 75 – Portsmouth 13 – Southampton 10.

🏨 **Marriott Meon Valley H. & Country Club,** Sandy Lane, SO32 2HQ, off A 334
℘ (01329) 833455, events.meon@marriotthotels.co.uk, Fax (01329) 834411, 🈺, 🈺, 🛏,
🈺, 🈺, 🛈, 🈺, 🈺 – 🛗 ↳✦, 🈺 rest, 🅱. 🅿 – 🛏 80. 🅼🅾 🄰🄴 🅾 𝘝𝘐𝘚𝘈. 🈺
Treetops : Rest (dinner only and Sunday lunch) 28.00 and a la carte 26.00/43.00 ℞ – **The
Long Weekend :** Rest a la carte 15.20/34.35 ℞ – ⊊ 14.95 – **113 rm** ✦119.00/129.00 –
✦✦129.00/164.00.
◆ Set in 225 acres of Hampshire countryside with extensive leisure facilities: championship
golf course, all weather tennis courts, cardiovascular suite. Well-equipped rooms. Treetops
overlooks the golf course. The Long Weekend is sports oriented brasserie.

SHEFFIELD *S. Yorks.* **502 503 504** P 23 *Great Britain G.* – *pop. 439 866.*
See : *Cutlers' Hall*★ *CZ* **A** – *Cathedral Church of SS. Peter and Paul CZ* **B** : *Shrewsbury
Chapel (Tomb*★*).*
Env. : *Magna*★ *AC, NE : 3 m. by A 6178* – **BY** – *and Bessemer Way.*
🛈 *Tinsley Park, High Hazel Park, Darnall* ℘ *(0114) 203 7435 BY* – 🛈 *Beauchief Municipal,
Abbey Lane* ℘ *(0114) 236 7274 AZ* – 🛈 *Birley Wood, Birley Lane* ℘ *(0114) 264 7262 BZ* –
🛈 *Concord Park, Shiregreen Lane* ℘ *(0114) 257 7378 BY* – 🛈 *Abbeydale, Twentywell
Lane, Dore* ℘ *(0114) 236 0763 AZ* – 🛈 *Lees Hall, Hemsworth Rd, Norton* ℘ *(0114)
255 4402 AZ.*
🄳 *Winter Garden* ℘ *(0114) 221 1900.*
London 174 – Leeds 36 – Liverpool 80 – Manchester 41 – Nottingham 44.

Plans on following pages

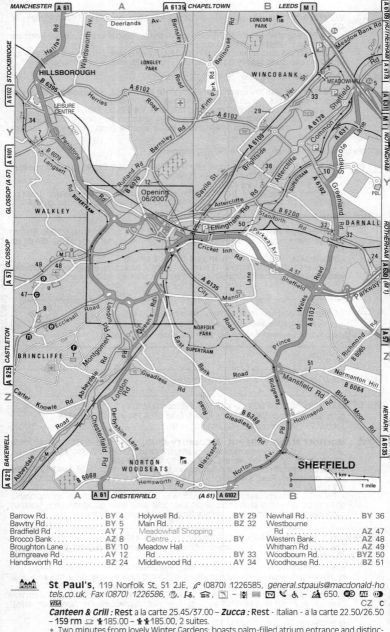

Barrow Rd . . . . **BY** 4	Holywell Rd . . . . **BY** 29	Newhall Rd . . . . **BY** 36
Bawtry Rd . . . . **BY** 5	Main Rd . . . . **BZ** 32	Westbourne
Bradfield Rd . . . . **AY** 7	Meadowhall Shopping	Rd . . . . **AZ** 47
Brocco Bank . . . . **AZ** 8	Centre . . . . **BY**	Western Bank . . . . **AZ** 48
Broughton Lane . . . . **BY** 10	Meadow Hall	Whitham Rd . . . . **AZ** 49
Burngreave Rd . . . . **AY** 12	Rd . . . . **BY** 33	Woodbourn Rd . . . . **BYZ** 50
Handsworth Rd . . . . **BZ** 24	Middlewood Rd . . . . **AY** 34	Woodhouse Rd . . . . **BZ** 51

St Paul's, 119 Norfolk St, S1 2JE, ☏ (0870) 1226585, *general.stpauls@macdonald-hotels.co.uk*, Fax (0870) 1226586, ⌖, ℉₆, ⇆s, ☒ − ✦ ☰ ☎ ☚ & − ⚂ 650. ⦿◉ �credit ⓪ ⓿
VISA
CZ c
Canteen & Grill : Rest a la carte 25.45/37.00 − ***Zucca :*** Rest - Italian - a la carte 22.50/26.50
− **159 rm** ⌕ ✦185.00 − ✦✦185.00, 2 suites.
   ♦ Two minutes from lovely Winter Gardens; boasts palm-filled atrium entrance and distinctive, designer touches throughout. State-of-the-art gym. Sleek and spacious rooms. Italian dishes in Zucca. Steaks to the fore in Canteen & Grill.

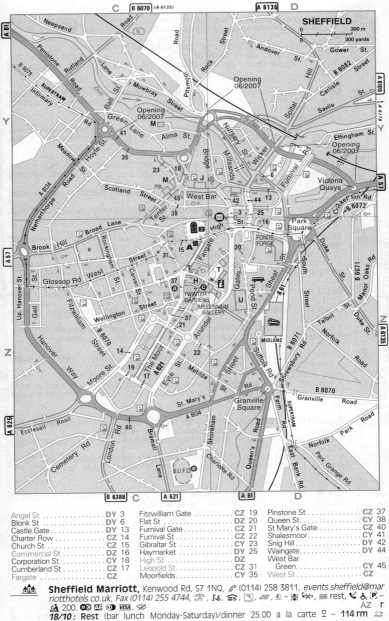

SHEFFIELD

🏨 **Sheffield Marriott,** Kenwood Rd, S7 1NQ, ☎ (0114) 258 3811, *events.sheffield@mar riotthotels.co.uk, Fax (0114) 255 4744*, 😤, 🔥, ⥄s, 🔲, 🔊, ♨ – 🛗 🖙, 🍴 rest, 📶 & 🅿 – 🕍 200. 🆖 🖭 ⓪ **VISA**. 🛇
AZ r
18/10 : Rest (bar lunch Monday-Saturday)/dinner 25.00 a la carte 🍷 – **114 rm** ⌨
🛏120.00/140.00 – 🛏🛏140.00/160.00.
  ♦ Refurbished part Victorian mansion in quiet suburb. Whilst rooms in original house have character, the more modern rooms overlook the landscaped gardens and ornamental lake. Relaxing views a feature of the restaurant.

🏠 **Westbourne House** without rest., 25 Westbourne Rd, S10 2QQ, ℰ (0114) 266 0109, guests@westbournehousehotel.com, Fax (0114) 266 7778, 🌳 – ⇔ 🄿, 🐼 🖭 🕦 VISA
⌖
AZ **c**

closed 2 weeks August and Christmas – **8 rm** ⇆ ✦50.00/70.00 – ✦✦95.00.
• 19C former gentleman's residence full of character. Overlooks tree-lined garden. Friendly, personal service by affable owners. Individually decorated, well-appointed rooms.

⌂ **Quarry House** without rest., Rivelin Glen Quarry, Rivelin Valley Rd, S6 5SE, Northwest : 4½ m. by A 61 on A 6101 ℰ (0114) 234 0382, penelopeslack@aol.com, Fax (0114) 234 7630, 🌳 – ⇔ 🦮 🄿.
4 rm ⇆ ✦40.00/80.00 – ✦✦80.00.
• Sited in a disused 19C quarry - check out the local stonemason! Bohemian style prevails; thespians stay regularly. Individually styled rooms with plenty of hospitable touches. Supper tray available.

XX **Rafters**, 220 Oakbrook Rd, Nether Green, S11 7ED, Southwest : 2 ½ m. by A 625 and Fulwood rd, turning left at mini roundabout, on right at traffic lights ℰ (0114) 230 4819, Fax (0114) 230 4819 – 🗐. 🐼 🖭 VISA
closed 25 December, 1 week January, 1 week August, Sunday, Tuesday and Bank Holidays. – **Rest** (dinner only) 28.95.
• Discreetly located above a parade of shops and definitely worth seeking out. Friendly and approachable service of a classically influenced modern British menu.

XX **Bluefin**, 85 Junction Rd, Hunters Bar, S11 8XA, ℰ (0114) 266 0805 – ⇔ 🗐. 🐼 VISA
AZ **n**
closed Sunday – **Rest** - Seafood - a la carte 23.00/31.00 s.
• Suburban twin level restaurant: downstairs dining in the bar, upstairs includes local artists' work for sale on walls. Eclectic seafood menus: modern and Asian influences.

XX **Delhi Junction**, The Old Station, Abbeydale Road South, S17 3LB, Southwest : 4 m. on A 621 ℰ (0114) 262 0675 – 🗐 🄿. 🐼 🖭 VISA
closed 25-26 December, 1 January and Sunday – **Rest** - Indian - (dinner only) a la carte 14.15/21.85 s.
• Pleasantly converted Victorian railway station. Spacious, open dining rooms with Eastern feel; proceedings orchestrated by larger-than-life owner. Tasty Indian menus.

XX **Artisan**, 32-34 Sandygate Rd, S10 5RY, West : 2 ¼ m. by A 57, turning left at Crosspool
⊕ Tavern ℰ (0114) 266 6096, Fax (0114) 266 0279 – ⇔ 🗐 🐼 🖭 VISA
closed 25-26 December – **Rest** 16.00/25.00 and a la carte 25.00/32.00 ♀.
• Burgundy leather seats and banquettes create a really smart ambience enhanced by lots of wine racks and mirrors. Classical menu of bistro favourites; themed evenings aplenty.

XX **Bosworths at Bramall Lane**, Global Windows South Stand, Bramall Lane, S2 4SU, ℰ (0114) 292 2777, bosworths@bramalllane.com – ⇔ 🗐. 🐼 VISA
CZ **e**
closed 25 December, Sunday dinner and Monday – **Rest** (dinner only and Sunday lunch) a la carte 19.00/36.00.
• Handily opened in time for Sheffield United's Premiership adventure, this 'Blades' dominated restaurant serves an appealing mix of hearty dishes, both classic and modern.

X **Catch**, (first floor) 32-34 Sandygate Rd, S10 5RY, West : 2 ¾ m. by A 57 turning left at Crosspool Tavern ℰ (0114) 266 6096 – ⇔ 🗐. 🐼 🖭 VISA
closed 25-26 December – **Rest** - Seafood - 15.00 and a la carte 22.00/48.00.
• Intimate eatery; chef goes to market every day to select the best, freshest fish and seafood available, written up on daily blackboard menu. Fruits de mer are a speciality.

X **Thyme Cafe**, 490 Glossop Rd, S10 2QA, ℰ (0114) 267 0735, 🌳 – ⇔. 🐼 VISA AZ **a**
closed 25-26 December and Bank Holidays – **Rest** (bookings not accepted) a la carte 11.00/28.00 ♀.
• Snug, though bustling, bistro located outside city centre. Rustic interior with wooden school chairs and church pews. Appealing range of hearty dishes, ordered from the bar.

X **Nonna's**, 535-541 Ecclesall Rd, S11 8PR, ℰ (0114) 268 6166, enquiries@nonnas.co.uk, Fax (0114) 266 6122 – 🐼 VISA
AZ **e**
Rest - Italian - a la carte 19.45/39.70 ♀.
• Take a walk through the deli before sitting down to savour the robust and authentic Italian dishes in busy surroundings. Speciality home-made pastas.

🛏 **Lions Lair,** 31 Burgess St, S1 2HF, 𝒸 (0114) 263 4264, *info@lionslair.co.uk,* Fax (0114) 263 4265, 🌣 – 𝟎𝟎 𝐀𝐄 *VISA* . ✗
closed 25 December and 1 January – **Rest** a la carte 7.50/10.50.   **CZ a**
  • Hidden away in the city centre; compact rear terrace, cosy interior with leather banquettes, and a winning mixture of simple, fresh, carefully prepared, popular dishes.

at Chapeltown *North : 6 m. on A 6135 – AY –* ✉ *Sheffield.*

XX **Greenhead House,** 84 Burncross Rd, S35 1SF, 𝒸 (0114) 246 9004, Fax (0114) 246 9004, 🌣 – ✗ **P**. 𝟎𝟎 𝐀𝐄 *VISA*
closed 2 weeks Easter, 2 weeks mid August, Christmas-New Year, Sunday-Tuesday, lunch Wednesday, Thursday and Saturday – **Rest** (booking essential) 39.00/45.00 ♉.
  • Cosy and attractive restaurant in country house style where hospitable owners offer traditional, tasty and home-cooked fare. A local favourite for many a year.

at Ridgeway *(Derbs.) Southeast : 6¾ m. by A 6135 (signed Hyde Park) – BZ – on B 6054 turning right at Ridgeway Arms –* ✉ *Sheffield.*

XXX **Old Vicarage** (Tessa Bramley), Ridgeway Moor, S12 3XW, on Marsh Lane rd 𝒸 (0114) 247 5814, *eat@theoldvicarage.co.uk,* Fax (0114) 248 3743, 🌣 – ✗ **P**. 𝟎𝟎 *VISA*
  ✿ closed first two weeks August, Christmas, Sunday and Monday – **Rest** (lunch by arrangement) 40.00/60.00 ♉ ⌂.
Spec. Griddled scallops with bacon, langoustine and saffron fondant potatoes. Fillet of beef, sautéed porcini on celeriac and thyme. Sweet woodruff ice cream in pistachio wafer with cherry.
  • Personally run Victorian vicarage, its kitchen garden providing much of the produce. Formal yet unobtrusive service of an accomplished seasonal menu in elegant surroundings.

at Totley *Southwest : 5½ m. on A 621 – AZ –* ✉ *Sheffield.*

🛏 **The Cricket,** Penny Lane, S17 3AZ, Southwest : 1 m. by A 621 and Lane Head Rd 𝒸 (0114) 236 5256, *enquiries@the.cricket.com,* 🌣 , 🌣 – ✗ **P**. 𝟎𝟎 *VISA*
closed 25 December and Monday October-April – **Rest** (closed Sunday dinner and Monday) (bar lunch only Tuesday-Saturday) a la carte 14.00/30.00 ♉.
  • Stone built pub boasts cricket paraphernalia within, and village pitch to rear. Dine at pubby bar with pews or in linen-clad restaurant. Dishes range from simple to classic.

SHEFFORD *Beds.* **504** S 27 – *pop. 3 319.*
London 48 – Bedford 10 – Luton 16 – Northampton 37.

🛏 **The Black Horse** with rm, Ireland, SG17 5QL, Northwest : 1¾ m. by Northbridge St and B 658 on Ireland rd 𝒸 (01462) 811398, 🌣 , 🌣 – ✗ **P**. 𝟎𝟎 𝐀𝐄 *VISA* . ✗
closed 25-26 December and 1 January – **Rest** (closed Sunday dinner) 24.95 and a la carte 22.00/29.00 ♉ – **2 rm** ✶55.00 – ✶✶55.00.
  • Part 18C brick and timbered pub with garden and chalet-style bedrooms. Confident cooking, interesting menus based round old favourites. Eat in traditional bar or restaurant.

SHELF *W. Yorks.* **502** O 22 – *see Halifax.*

SHELLEY *W. Yorks.* **502 504** O 23 – *see Huddersfield.*

SHEPTON MALLET *Somerset* **503 504** M 30 *The West Country G. – pop. 8 830.*
See : Town★ - SS. Peter and Paul's Church★.
Env. : Downside Abbey★ (Abbey Church★) N : 5½ m. by A 37 and A 367.
Exc. : Longleat House★★★ AC, E : 15 m. by A 361 and B 3092 – Wells★★ - Cathedral★★★, Vicars' Close★, Bishop's Palace★ AC (≤★★) W : 6 m. by A 371 – Wookey Hole★ (Caves★ AC, Papermill★) W : 6½ m. by B 371 – Glastonbury★★ - Abbey★★ (Abbot's Kitchen★) AC, St John the Baptist★★, Somerset Rural Life Museum★ AC – Glastonbury Tor★ (≤★★★) SW : 9 m. by B 3136 and A 361 - Nunney★, E : 8½ m. by A 361.
🛆 The Mendip, Gurney Slade 𝒸 (01749) 840570.
London 127 – Bristol 20 – Southampton 63 – Taunton 31.

🏛 **Charlton House,** BA4 4PR, East : 1 m. on A 361 (Frome rd) 𝒸 (01749) 342008, *enquiry@charltonhouse.com,* Fax (01749) 346362, 🌣 , 🗇 , 🖀 , 🌣 – ✗ , 🍽 rest, ♺ 𝔤 **P** – 🎪 100. 𝟎𝟎 𝐀𝐄 𝟎 *VISA*
Rest 27.00/49.50 – **26 rm** ⚏ ✶140.00 – ✶✶180.00/465.00.
  • Grand 17C house owned by founders of Mulberry Company; a smart, boutique style prevails touched by informality. Antiques in luxury bedrooms: Adam and Eve carved four-poster. Well used local produce to the fore in conservatory dining room.

SHERBORNE Dorset 503 504 M 31 *The West Country G. – pop. 7 606.*

See : *Town★ - Abbey★★ - Castle★ AC.*

Env. : *Sandford Orcas Manor House★ AC, NW : 4 m. by B 3148 – Purse Caundle Manor★ AC, NE : 5 m. by A 30.*

Exc. : *Cadbury Castle (≼★★) N : 8 m. by A 30 – Parish Church★, Crewkerne, W : 14 m. on A 30.*

🏌 *Higher Clatcombe ℰ (01935) 812274.*

🅱 *3 Tilton Court, Digby Rd ℰ (01935) 815341.*

London 128 – Bournemouth 39 – Dorchester 19 – Salisbury 36 – Taunton 31.

🏨 **Eastbury,** Long St, DT9 3BY, ℰ (01935) 813131, enquiries@theeastburyhotel.co.uk, Fax (01935) 817296, �, – ✦ ❤ P. – 🄰 👪 🐾 AE VISA ۞.
Rest (bar lunch)/dinner 28.00 and a la carte 28.00/36.50 ☍ – **23 rm** ☍ ✦58.00/85.00 – ✦✦120.00/155.00.
◆ Traditional town house, a former gentleman's residence, built in 1740 with peaceful walled garden. Well-kept rooms named after country flowers. 15C abbey is nearby. Bright restaurant looking onto garden.

✕✕ **The Green,** On The Green, DT9 3HY, ℰ (01935) 813821 – ✦❤ ✧ 20. 👪 AE VISA
closed 2 weeks February, 1 week June, 1 week September, 24-26 December, Sunday and Monday – **Rest** 16.95/28.95 (dinner) and lunch a la carte 19.95/28.90 ☍.
◆ Pretty Grade II listing at the top of the hill in town centre with stone floor and inglenook. A bistro feel predominates; dishes are traditional with a strong seasonal base.

at Corton Denham North : 3¾ m. by B 3145 – ✉ Sherborne.

🛏 **The Queens Arms** with rm, DT9 4LR, ℰ (01963) 220317, relax@thequeensarms.com, � – ✦❤ P. 👪 VISA
Rest a la carte 16.00/20.00 ☍ – **5 rm** ☍ ✦60.00/70.00 – ✦✦90.00/120.00.
◆ The essence of this pub is relaxed informality, engendered by sofas and armchairs inside, and an attractively sunny rear terrace. Locally inspired dishes; luxurious bedrooms.

at Oborne Northeast : 2 m. by A 30 – ✉ Sherborne.

🏨 **The Grange** 🐾, DT9 4LA, ℰ (01935) 813463, reception@thegrange.co.uk, Fax (01935) 817464, 🌫 – ✦❤ P. 👪 AE ① VISA. ۞
Rest *(closed Sunday dinner)* (light lunch)/dinner 29.50 – **18 rm** ☍ ✦85.00 – ✦✦140.00.
◆ A 200-year old country house in floodlit gardens. Rooms are a treat: five modern, five traditional, all large; some have patio access; some have balconies. Friendly owner. Dorset and Somerset ingredients zealously used in dining room.

at Hermitage South : 7½ m. by A 352 – ✉ Sherborne.

⌂ **Almshouse Farm** 🐾 without rest., DT9 6HA, ℰ (01963) 210296, Fax (01963) 210296, ≼, 🌫 – ✦❤ P. ۞
March-October – **3 rm** ☍ ✦30.00/35.00 – ✦✦52.00/60.00.
◆ Part 16C former monastery, now a working farm, surrounded by rural landscape. Original features include inglenook fireplace in cosy breakfast room. Pretty, neat bedrooms.

at Alweston Southeast : 2½ m. by A 352 A 3030 – ✉ Sherborne.

⌂ **Munden House** 🐾 without rest., Munden Lane, DT9 5HU, ℰ (01963) 23150, admin@mundenhouse.demon.co.uk, Fax (01963) 23153, 🌫 – ✦❤ P. 👪 AE VISA
7 rm ☍ ✦55.00/65.00 – ✦✦85.00/100.00.
◆ Peacefully located guesthouse: originally a small complex of stone cottages. Modern country house furnishings. Breakfast room with 300 year old fireplace. Elegant bedrooms.

SHERE Surrey 504 S 30 – *see Guildford.*

SHERINGHAM Norfolk 504 X 25 – *pop. 7 143.*
London 136 – Cromer 5 – Norwich 27.

🏨 **The Dales Country House** 🐾, Lodge Hill, Upper Sheringham, NR26 8TJ, Southwest : 1 ¼ m. by A 149 on B 1157 ℰ (01263) 824555, dales@mackenziehotels.com, Fax (01263) 822647, 🌫 – 📶 ✦❤ P. – 🄰 60. 👪 VISA. ۞
Upchers : **Rest** 14.95/17.95 (lunch) and a la carte 24.65/30.85 ☍ – **17 rm** ☍ ✦87.00/146.00 – ✦✦134.00/156.00.
◆ Substantial 19C country house whose rich décor affords much comfort. Famous gardens conveniently adjacent. Original oak staircase in situ. Smart bedrooms overlook the grounds. Wood-panelled restaurant with superb oak-carved inglenook.

⌂ **Willow Lodge** without rest., 6 Vicarage Rd, NR26 8NH, off B 1157 ℰ (01263) 822204, Fax (01263) 824424, 🌫 – ✦❤ P. 👪 VISA. ۞
5 rm ☍ ✦38.00/40.00 – ✦✦56.00/60.00.
◆ Late 19C house in quiet residential area not far from town. Comfy lounge overlooking garden. Attractively decorated, spacious bedrooms with handmade pine furniture.

SHILTON *W. Mids.* 503 504 P 26 – *see Coventry.*

SHINCLIFFE *Durham – see Durham.*

SHINFIELD *Reading* 504 R 29 – *see Reading.*

SHIPLEY *W. Yorks.* 502 O 22 – *pop. 28 162.*
   ⛳ Northcliffe, High Bank Lane ℰ (01274) 584085 – ⛳ Beckfoot Lane, Cottingley Bridge,
   Bingley ℰ (01274) 568652.
   London 216 – Bradford 4 – Leeds 12.

🏰 **Marriott Hollins Hall H. and Country Club** ⏍, Hollins Hill, Baildon, BD17 7QW,
   Northeast : 2 ½ m. on A 6038 ℰ 760274) 530053, *mhrs.l6ags.eventorganiser@marriottho
   tels.com, Fax (0870) 4007327*, ≤, ₤₆, ≘, ⬛, ⛳, ☞, ₤–₤ ↦, ▤ rest, ₤ ₽ – 🔺 170. 🆎
   🆎 ⓪ 𝘝𝘐𝘚𝘈. ⚘
   Heathcliffe's : Rest (bar lunch Monday-Saturday) 27.50 ♀ – ☲ 14.95 – **121 rm**
   ♥99.00/115.00 – ♥♥99.00/115.00, 1 suite.
   ◆ In the heart of Yorkshire with excellent leisure facilities including 20m pool and 18 hole
   golf course overlooking Aire Valley. Sandstone façade conceals restful rooms. Roomy,
   modern restaurant; good views over gardens.

XX **Beeties Gallery** with rm, 7 Victoria Rd, Saltaire Village, BD18 3LA, ℰ (01274) 595988,
   jayne.dixon39@blueyonder.co.uk, Fax (01274) 582118 – ↦ rm, ✆, 🆎 𝘝𝘐𝘚𝘈
   closed 27 December- 1 January – **Rest** (dinner only) 16.95 and a la carte 22.85/28.85 ♀ –
   5 rm ☲ ♥47.00/53.00 – ♥♥60.00.
   ◆ Grade II listed Victorian building with regularly changing art on walls: 50 yards from
   Hockney collection at Salt Mills. Well executed modern British cuisine. Cottagey rooms.

XX **Aagrah**, Ground Floor, 4 Saltaire Rd, BD18 3HN, ℰ (01274) 530880, *Fax (01274) 599105* –
   ▤ ₽. 🆎 🆎 𝘝𝘐𝘚𝘈. ⚘
   closed lunch Saturday and Sunday – **Rest** - Indian (Kashmiri) - 15.00 and a la carte
   14.95/21.05 **s**.
   ◆ Spacious, modern first floor buffet/carvery with cooking and char-grilling to order. Sit
   at funky red leather seats. Cuisine includes delicious Dahi dishes from Kashmir.

Do not confuse X with ❀!
X defines comfort, while stars are awarded for the best cuisine,
across all categories of comfort.

SHIPTON GORGE *Dorset – see Bridport.*

SHIPTON-UNDER-WYCHWOOD *Oxon.* 503 504 P 28.
   London 81 – Birmingham 50 – Gloucester 37 – Oxford 25.

↑ **Shipton Grange House** without rest., OX7 6DG, ℰ (01993) 831298, *veronica@ship
   tongrangehouse.com*, ☞ – ↦ ₽. ⚘
   3 rm ☲ ♥50.00/55.00 – ♥♥65.00/80.00.
   ◆ An arched gateway leads to a charming walled garden, converted Georgian coach house
   and stables. Handsomely furnished sitting room, spotless bedrooms, welcoming atmosphere.

SHOBDON *Herefordshire* 503 L 27 – ✉ Leominster.
   London 158 – Birmingham 55 – Hereford 18 – Shrewsbury 37 – Worcester 33.

↑ **The Paddock** without rest., HR6 9NQ, ℰ (01568) 708176, *thepaddock@talk21.com,
   Fax (01568) 708829* – ↦ ₽. ⚘
   March-October – **4 rm** ☲ ♥35.00/38.00 – ♥♥52.00/54.00.
   ◆ Well-priced, ground floor accommodation in this pleasant, village centre bungalow. All
   rooms are comfy and immaculately kept. Well run by hospitable owner.

SHOTTLE *Derbs. – see Belper.*

ENGLAND

SHREWSBURY *Shrops.* 502 503 L 25 *Great Britain G.* – pop. 67 126.

See : Abbey★ D.

Exc. : *Ironbridge Gorge Museum*★★ *AC (The Iron Bridge*★★ - *Coalport China Museum*★★ - *Blists Hill Open Air Museum*★★ – *Museum of the Gorge and Visitor Centre*★ *) SE : 12 m. by A 5 and B 4380.*

🔞 *Condover* ♟ (01743) 872976 – 🏐 *Meole Brace* ♟ (01743) 364050.

🛈 *The Music Hall, The Square* ♟ (01743) 281200, tic@shrewsburytourism.co.uk.

London 164 – Birmingham 48 – Chester 43 – Derby 67 – Gloucester 93 – Manchester 68 – Stoke-on-Trent 39 – Swansea 124.

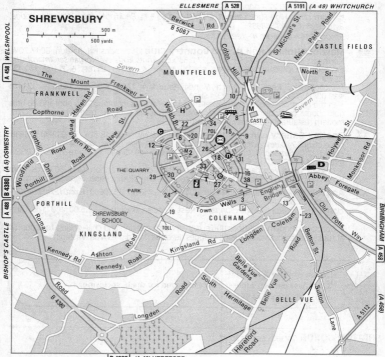

🏨 **Prince Rupert,** Butcher Row, SY1 1UQ, ♟ (01743) 499955, *post@prince-rupert-ho tel.co.uk, Fax (01743) 357306,* ⨎, ⇔s – ⧉ ⬥, ▦ rest, ⧉. ℙ. – ⚊ 120. 🆚 🆎 ⓞ 🚷

VISA n

Royalist : Rest *(closed Sunday dinner and Monday)* a la carte 24.20/31.85 **s.** ♀ – *Chambers :* Rest a la carte 17.45/24.65 **s.** – ⌥ 10.50 – **68 rm** ✸85.00/95.00 – ✸✸105.00, 2 suites.

◆ 12C home of Prince Rupert, in the shadow of the cathedral. A collection of old buildings, some 15C, affords tremendous character. Rooms vary in age: the oldest are the best. Baronial style Royalist. Olde Worlde atmosphere of Chambers.

↑ **Pinewood House** without rest., Shelton Park, The Mount, SY3 8BL, Northwest : 1½ m. on A 458 ℰ (01743) 364200, ⟶ - 🅿.
closed 2 weeks January and 24-26 December – **4 rm** ⌑ ✶44.00/48.00 - ✶✶56.00/62.00.
◆ A Regency house surrounded by wooded gardens. A homely, intimate atmosphere pervades the drawing room with its sofas, fresh flowers whilst bedrooms are charmingly decorated.

↑ **Tudor House** without rest., 2 Fish St, SY1 1UR, ℰ (01743) 351735, *enquire@tudorhou seshrewsbury.co.uk*, Fax (01743) 351735 – ⇔. ⋘   e
3 rm ⌑ ✶69.00/95.00 - ✶✶89.00/120.00.
◆ On a picturesque medieval street in a historic part of Shrewsbury, this compact 15C house retains its antiquated charm in its cosy sitting room and simple bedrooms.

⌂ **The Armoury**, Victoria Quay, Welsh Bridge, SY1 1HH, ℰ (01743) 340525, *ar moury@brunningandprice.co.uk*, Fax (01743) 340526 – ⓂⓄ ⒶⒺ 𝘝𝘐𝘚𝘈. ⋘   c
Rest a la carte 19.00/30.00 ⌑.
◆ Former 18C riverside warehouse with huge open-plan interior; sturdy brick walls full of old pictures and bookshelves. Daily changing menus offer an eclectic range of dishes.

at Albrighton *North : 3 m. on A 528 – ✉ Shrewsbury.*

🏨 **Albrighton Hall**, Ellesmere Rd, SY4 3AG, ℰ (01939) 291000, *albrighton@macdonald-hotels.co.uk*, Fax (01939) 291123, ⓘ, 𝄪, 🛁, 🖳, 🖼, 🖈, squash – 🖆 ⇔ 🅱 🖿 𝖯 – 🔬 400.
ⓂⓄ ⒶⒺ 𝘝𝘐𝘚𝘈
***Oak Room* : Rest** (dinner only) 28.50 ⌑ – **87 rm** ⌑ ✶85.00/115.00 - ✶✶110.00/170.00.
◆ Extended 17C manor house with ornamental lake and lovely gardens. Impressive spa. Characterful panelled lounge. Individualistic rooms in old house; spacious and modern in new. Dine in oak-panelled formality.

🏨 **Albright Hussey Manor** ⤳, Ellesmere Rd, SY4 3AF, ℰ (01939) 290571, *info@albrigh thussey.co.uk*, Fax (01939) 291143, ≼, ⟶ – ⇔ 🖆 🅱 🖿 𝖯 – 🔬 200. ⓂⓄ ⒶⒺ ⓄⒹ 𝘝𝘐𝘚𝘈
Rest 20.00/35.00 and a la carte 25.00/35.00 – **25 rm** ⌑ ✶65.00/85.00 - ✶✶120.00/130.00, 1 suite.
◆ Most impressive part 16C moated manor house. Fountains, stone walls and bridge in lawned gardens. The five rooms in the original house have oak panelling and huge fire-places. Hugely characterful, heavily beamed 16C dining room.

at Grinshill *North : 7¾ m. by A 49 – ✉ Shrewsbury.*

XX **The Inn at Grinshill** with rm, The High St, SY4 3BL, ℰ (01939) 220410, *info@theinnat grinshill.co.uk*, Fax (01939) 220327, 🏛 – ⇔ 🖆 𝖯. ⓂⓄ 𝘝𝘐𝘚𝘈
closed Sunday dinner and Bank Holidays – **Rest** 9.95 (lunch) and a la carte 19.00/26.00 ⌑ – ⌑ 10.00 – **6 rm** ✶50.00/82.50 - ✶✶100.00/110.00.
◆ 18C stable block in small village: a cosy bar with sofas awaits, while beyond a light and airy, modern restaurant serves a wide range of menus. Spacious, stylish bedrooms.

at Atcham *Southeast : 3 m. by A 5064 on B 4380 – ✉ Shrewsbury.*

🏨 **The Mytton and Mermaid**, SY5 6QG, ℰ (01743) 761220, *admin@myttonandmer maid.co.uk*, Fax (01743) 761292, ⟶, ⤳, ⟶ – ⇔ 𝖯. ⓂⓄ ⓄⒹ 𝘝𝘐𝘚𝘈. ⋘
closed 25 December – **Rest** a la carte 21.00/30.00 ⌑ – **18 rm** ⌑ ✶75.00/85.00 - ✶✶155.00.
◆ Impressive, ivy clad 18C house on the banks of the Severn. Quirky bar with log fire and sofas. Riverside drawing room. Smart rooms divided between main house and courtyard. Informal restaurant dining: seasonal menus.

at Acton Burnell *Southeast : 7½ m. by A 458 – ✉ Shrewsbury.*

↑ **Acton Pigot** ⤳, Acton Pigot, SY5 7PH, Northeast : 1¾ m. by Kenley rd ℰ (01694) 731209, *acton@farmline.com*, Fax (01694) 731399, 🖳 heated, ⤳, ⟶, 🎾 – ⇔ 𝖯. ⋘
closed 25-26 December – **Rest** (by arrangement) (communal dining) 15.00/25.00 – **3 rm** ⌑ ✶45.00 - ✶✶70.00.
◆ 17C farmhouse on working farm. Wealth of pursuits includes heated pool, fishing lake and tennis court. Age of house handsomely apparent in guest areas. Pleasant, cosy rooms. Huge oak dining table for dinner with fellow guests; adventurous cooking.

SHURDINGTON *Glos. 503 504 N 28 – see Cheltenham.*

SIBFORD GOWER *Oxon. – see Banbury.*

SIDFORD *Devon 503 K 31 – see Sidmouth.*

 Look out for red symbols, indicating particularly pleasant establishments.

ENGLAND

SIDMOUTH *Devon* 503 K 31 *The West Country G. – pop. 12 066.*

Env. : *Bicton★ (Gardens★) AC, SW : 5 m.*

🏌 *Cotmaton Rd ℰ (01395) 513023.*

🎫 *Ham Lane ℰ (01395) 516441.*

London 176 – Exeter 14 – Taunton 27 – Weymouth 45.

🏨🏨 **Victoria,** The Esplanade, EX10 8RY, ℰ (01395) 512651, *info@victoriahotel.co.uk,* Fax *(01395) 579154,* ≤, ⊆s, ⊒ heated, 🏊, ☞, ℅ – 📶, ⅙ rest, ▤ rest, 🅿. 🐵 🖭 ⓪ 𝘝𝘐𝘚𝘈 ℅
Rest *(dancing Saturday evening)* 18.00/32.00 **s.** – � 15.00 – **62 rm** ✦90.00/230.00 – ✦✦130.00/230.00, 3 suites.
◆ An imposing Edwardian house on Esplanade; most rooms are south facing with coastal views. Sun lounge, games room, dancing every Saturday night are among its attractions. Menus run on traditional lines.

🏨🏨 **Riviera,** The Esplanade, EX10 8AY, ℰ (01395) 515201, *enquiries@hotelriviera.co.uk,* Fax *(01395) 577775,* ≤, 🍴 – 📶 ⅙, ▤ rest, ⇦ – ▨ 85. 🐵 🖭 ⓪ 𝘝𝘐𝘚𝘈
Rest 23.00/35.00 and a la carte 40.00/44.95 – **26 rm** *(dinner included)* � ✦104.00/156.00 – ✦✦208.00/334.00.
◆ An established seafront hotel with fine Regency façade and bow fronted windows. Peach and pink bedrooms with floral touches and friendly staff make for a comfortable stay. Formal dining salon affords views across Lyme Bay.

🏨🏨 **Belmont,** The Esplanade, EX10 8RX, ℰ (01395) 512555, *reservations@belmont-hotel.co.uk, Fax (01395) 579101,* ≤, 🍴, ☞ – 📶 ⅙, ▤ rest, 🅿. 🐵 🖭 ⓪ 𝘝𝘐𝘚𝘈. ℅
Rest *(dancing Saturday evening)* 17.50/33.00 and a la carte 41.00/48.00 **s.** – � 14.00 – **50 rm** ✦85.00/200.00 – ✦✦120.00/200.00.
◆ A former 19C family summer residence situated on seafront with attendant views. Spacious lounge; traditional bedrooms. Guests can use leisure facilities at Victoria hotel. Stylish dining room with resident pianist.

↥ **Old Farmhouse,** Hillside Rd, EX10 8JG, off Salcombe Rd ℰ (01395) 512284 – ⅙ 🅿.
April-October – Rest *(by arrangement)* 14.00 – **6 rm** ✦56.00 – ✦✦66.00/66.00.
◆ Utterly charming 16C ex-cider mill and farmhouse with low ceilings, heavy beams, numerous inglenooks, cosy lounge and pleasant rooms that boast rafters and sloping roofs. Dinner served in rustic dining room.

at Sidford *North : 2 m. –* ✉ *Sidmouth.*

✗✗ **Salty Monk** with rm, Church St, EX10 9QP, on A 3052 ℰ (01395) 513174, *salty monk@btconnect.com,* 🍴, ☞ – ⅙ 🅿 ⟳ 14. 🐵 𝘝𝘐𝘚𝘈
closed 8-30 November and 8-31 January – Rest *(booking essential)* *(lunch by arrangement Thursday-Saturday)/dinner* 31.00/40.00 and lunch a la carte 23.50/33.50 – **5 rm** � ✦60.00/65.00 – ✦✦150.00/180.00.
◆ Former 16C salt house where monks stayed en route to Exeter Cathedral. Fine lounge with deep leather armchairs. Modern cooking in conservatory restaurant. Pleasant bedrooms.

at Newton Poppleford *Northwest : 4 m. by B 3176 on A 3052 –* ✉ *Sidmouth.*

✗✗ **Moores',** 6 Greenbank, High St, EX10 0EB, ℰ (01395) 568100, *mooresrestaurant@aol.com, Fax (01395) 568092,* 🍴 – ⅙ 🐵 ⓪ 𝘝𝘐𝘚𝘈
closed Christmas, 2 weeks January, Sunday dinner, Monday and Bank Holidays – Rest 14.00/24.50 ⅄.
◆ Two pretty 18C cottages set back from the main road are the setting for this busy, personally run restaurant with conservatory extension. Modern, locally sourced dishes.

SILCHESTER *Hants.* 503 504 Q 29 – ✉ *Reading (Berks.).*
London 62 – Basingstoke 8 – Reading 14 – Southampton 37 – Winchester 26.

🏨 **Romans,** Little London Rd, RG7 2PN, ℰ (0118) 970 0421, *romanhotel@hotmail.com, Fax (0118) 970 0691,* 🍴, 🛏, ⊆s, ⊒ heated, ☞, ℅ – ⅙ rest, 🅿 – ▨ 80. 🐵 🖭 ⓪ 𝘝𝘐𝘚𝘈
Rest *(closed Saturday lunch)* 22.95/26.00 and a la carte 28.30/46.90 ⅄ – **25 rm** � ✦105.00 – ✦✦165.00.
◆ A Lutyens-style manor set in well-kept gardens, close to the historic village. Boasts strong leisure and conference facilities. Rooms divided between main house and annex. Dining room, adjacent to garden, is hung with century old oil painting.

SINGLETON Lancs. 502 L 22 – see Blackpool.

SINNINGTON N. Yorks. 502 R 21 – see Pickering.

SISSINGHURST Kent 504 V 30 – see Cranbrook.

SITTINGBOURNE Kent 504 W 29.
London 44 – Canterbury 18 – Maidstone 15 – Sheerness 9.

🏠 **Hempstead House**, London Rd, Bapchild, ME9 9PP, East : 2 m. on A 2 ℰ (01795) 428020, info@hempsteadhouse.co.uk, Fax (01795) 436362, ㉑, ⌁ heated, ☞ – ↩✖ ♨ 🅿 – ♿ 150. 🕥 🖭 ⑩ 𝘝𝘐𝘚𝘈
Lakes : Rest (Sunday dinner residents only) 15.00/24.50 and a la carte 15.25/34.95 ℤ – 27 rm ⊇ ✶80.00 – ✶✶130.00.
◆ Part Victorian manor, a former estate house for surrounding farmland. Original sitting room in situ; outdoor heated pool. Cheerful, individually designed, modern bedrooms. Sunny restaurant with terrace.

> We try to be as accurate as possible when giving room rates.
> But prices are susceptible to change,
> so please check rates when booking.

ENGLAND

SIX MILE BOTTOM Cambs. – see Newmarket (Suffolk).

SIZERGH Cumbria – see Kendal.

SKELWITH BRIDGE Cumbria 502 K 20 – see Ambleside.

SKIPTON N. Yorks. 502 N 22 Great Britain G. – pop. 14 313.
See : Castle★ AC.
🔟 off NW Bypass ℰ (01756) 793922.
🛈 35 Coach St ℰ (01756) 792809.
London 217 – Kendal 45 – Leeds 26 – Preston 36 – York 43.

⌂ **Carlton House** without rest., 46 Keighley Rd, BD23 2NB, ℰ (01756) 700921, carlton house@rapidial.co.uk, Fax (01756) 700921 – ↩✖. 🕥 𝘝𝘐𝘚𝘈. ✀
5 rm ⊇ ✶25.00/40.00 – ✶✶50.00/55.00.
◆ Victorian terraced house near centre of town. Pleasantly furnished in sympathetic style. Attractive dining room serves full English breakfast. Individually decorated bedrooms.

🍴 **The Bull**, Broughton, BD23 3AE, West : 3 m. on A 59 ℰ (01756) 792065, janeneil@thebul latbroughton.co.uk, Fax (01756) 792065, ㉑ – ↩✖ 🅿. 🕥 🖭 𝘝𝘐𝘚𝘈
Rest (closed Sunday and Bank Holiday Monday) a la carte 15.00/24.00 ℤ.
◆ Set on busy main road, this delightful country pub has open log fire and its own specially brewed beer. Intimate dining room serving varied, tasty menus full of local produce.

at Hetton North : 5¾ m. by B 6265 – ✉ Skipton.

XXX **Angel Inn and Barn Lodgings** with rm, BD23 6LT, ℰ (01756) 730263, info@angel hetton.co.uk, Fax (01756) 730363 – ↩✖ 🖵 🅿. 🕥 🖭 𝘝𝘐𝘚𝘈
closed 25 December, 1 week January and Sunday dinner – Rest (booking essential) (dinner only and Sunday lunch)/dinner a la carte 27.00/34.15 ℤ ☞ – (see also below) – 5 rm ⊇ ✶130.00 – ✶✶155.00/180.00.
◆ Well regarded restaurant with stone walls, beams and roaring log fire. Fine quality, locally sourced produce. Bedrooms with antique furniture and modern appointments.

🍴 **The Angel Inn**, BD23 6LT, ℰ (01756) 730263, info@angelhetton.co.uk, Fax (01756) 730363, ㉑ – ↩✖ 🅿. 🕥 🖭 𝘝𝘐𝘚𝘈. ✀
closed 25 December and 1 January – Rest (booking essential) a la carte 20.00/34.50 ℤ ☞.
◆ Ancient beams and inglenooks in hugely characterful pubby part of renowned 18C inn. Fine modern British cooking. Shares rooms with restaurant in converted farmbuildings.

665

SLALEY *Northd.* **501 502** N 19 – *see Hexham.*

SLAPTON *Devon* **503** J 33 *The West Country G.*
Exc. : *Dartmouth★★, N : 7 m. by A 379 – Kingsbridge★, W : 7 m. by A 379.*
London 223 – Dartmouth 7 – Plymouth 29.

🍴 **The Tower Inn** with rm, Church Rd, TQ7 2PN, ℰ (01548) 580216, *towerinn@slapton.org*, 😊, 🍽, – ⇔ 🅿, ⬤ 🄰🄴 *VISA*
closed 25 December, Sunday dinner and Monday in winter – **Rest** a la carte 18.00/25.00 ♀ –
3 rm ⊑ ✦40.00 – ✦✦60.00.
♦ Built in 1347 as cottages for men working on local chantry. Beams, flag floors, stone walls: all very characterful. Surprisingly modern menus. Simple annex bedrooms.

SLEAFORD *Lincs.* **502 504** S 25 – *pop. 15 219.*
🏌 *Willoughby Rd, South Rauceby* ℰ (01529) 488273.
🅵 *Money's Yard, Carre St* ℰ (01529) 414294.
London 119 – Leicester 45 – Lincoln 17 – Nottingham 39.

🏨 **Lincolnshire Oak,** East Rd, NG34 7EH, Northeast : ¾ m. on B 1517 ℰ (01529) 413807,
reception@lincolnshire-oak.co.uk, Fax (01529) 413710, 🌳 – ⇔ 🅿 – 🛦 140. ⬤ 🄰🄴 *VISA*
🦢
Rest (booking essential) 19.95 – **17 rm** ⊑ ✦59.00/72.00 – ✦✦72.50/87.50.
♦ A hospitable Victorian house on the edge of town, once used as an officer's mess.
Outside are small, pleasant gardens; inside are amply sized, comfortably furnished rooms.
Homely dining room.

> Undecided between two equivalent establishments?
> Within each category, establishments are classified
> in our order of preference.

SLINFOLD *W. Sussex – see Horsham.*

SLOUGH *Slough* **504** S 29 – *pop. 126 276.*
London 29 – Oxford 39 – Reading 19.

🏨 **Slough/Windsor Marriott,** Ditton Rd, Langley, SL3 8PT, Southeast : 2 ½ m. on A 4
ℰ (0870) 4007244, *events.sloughwindsor@marriotthotels.co.uk*, Fax (0870) 4007344, 🛌,
🛁🅂, 🔲, 🛠 – 🛗 ⇔ rm, 🔳 📞 & 🅿 – 🛦 400. ⬤ 🄰🄴 ⓞ *VISA* 🦢
Rest (buffet lunch) a la carte 22.45/33.05 s. – ⊑ 14.95 – **381 rm** ✦159.00/189.00 –
✦✦159.00/189.00, 1 suite.
♦ A five-storey hotel, 15 minutes from Heathrow airport, with well-equipped leisure club.
Bedrooms are furnished with good quality fabrics; Executive rooms have private lounge.
All-day restaurant option.

🏨 **Copthorne,** 400 Cippenham Lane, SL1 2YE, Southwest : 1 ¼ m. by A 4 on A 355 off M 4
junction 6 ℰ (01753) 516222, *event.slough@mill-cop.com*, Fax (01753) 516237, 🛌, 🛁🅂, 🔲
– 🛗 ⇔, 🔳 rest, 📞 & 🅿 – 🛦 280. ⬤ 🄰🄴 ⓞ *VISA* 🦢
Zig Zag : Rest (closed lunch Saturday and Sunday) a la carte 21.00/34.50 ♀ – **Turner's Grill :**
Rest (closed Saturday lunch and Sunday) a la carte 23.75/31.90 – **217 rm** ⊑ ✦190.00 –
✦✦230.00, 2 suites.
♦ The marble floored reception leads to split-level lounge, bar, leisure club. Rooms with
mini-bars; some overlook Windsor Castle. Good business facilities in Executive rooms.
Turner's Grill for British classics. Zig Zag is informal modern eatery.

🏨 **Courtyard by Marriott Slough/Windsor,** Church St, Chalvey, SL1 2NH, Southwest : 1 ¼ m. by A 4 on A 355 off M 4 junction 6 ℰ (0870) 4007215, *events.slcourt
yard@kewgreen.co.uk*, Fax (0870) 4007315, 🛌 – 🛗 ⇔ 🔳 & 🅿 – 🛦 80. ⬤ 🄰🄴 ⓞ *VISA*
🦢
Rest (bar lunch)/dinner 18.00 and a la carte 18.20/27.85 s. ♀ – ⊑ 12.95 – **150 rm**
✦80.00/165.00 – ✦✦80.00/165.00.
♦ Modern hotel, ideal for leisure and business travellers, close to Windsor Castle. All mod
cons and services readily available. Executive rooms have work area. Smart mezzanine level
restaurant.

SNAINTON N. Yorks. **502** S 21.
London 241 – Pickering 8.5 – Scarborough 10.

XX **Coachman Inn** with rm, Pickering Road West, YO13 9PL, West : ½ m. by A 170 on B 1258   ℰ (01723) 859231, james@coachmanninn.co.uk, Fax (01723) 850008, 斎 , 龗 – ★★ ℗ ⇔ 10.
  觟⑤ ℀ℰ VISA . ℀
  Rest (closed Monday) a la carte 14.00/25.00 ♀ – **2 rm** ★40.00 – ★★66.00.
  ♦ Classically Georgian former coaching inn. Eat in the cosy bar with fire or the modern dining room. Prominent Yorkshire produce on modern British menus. Individual bedrooms.

SNAPE Suffolk **504** Y 27.
London 113 – Ipswich 19 – Norwich 50.

⌂ **The Crown Inn** with rm, Bridge Rd, IP17 1SL, ℰ (01728) 688324, 斎 , 龗 – ★★ rm, ℗.
  觟⑤ VISA . ℀
  closed 25 December and dinner 26 December – **Rest** a la carte 18.00/26.00 ♀ – **3 rm** ⇌
  ★70.00 – ★★80.00.
  ♦ 15C inn with antique settle, log fire and exposed beams. Agricultural artefacts and paintings fill the small dining rooms where seasonal dishes are served. Comfortable rooms.

SNETTISHAM Norfolk **504** V 25 – pop. 2 145.
London 113 – King's Lynn 13 – Norwich 44.

⌂ **The Rose and Crown** with rm, Old Church Rd, PE31 7LX, ℰ (01485) 541382, info@ro
  seandcrownsnettisham.co.uk, Fax (01485) 543172, 斎 , 龗 – ★★ rm, ℗. 觟⑤ VISA
  Rest a la carte 17.00/25.00 – **16 rm** ⇌ ★50.00/80.00 – ★★85.00/95.00.
  ♦ Cosy, rustic pub in centre of town: open fires, antique furniture, bustling ambience. Original menus with Asiatic and Italian influences. Vibrant, well-maintained rooms.

SOAR MILL COVE Devon – see Salcombe.

SOLIHULL W. Mids. **503 504** O 26 – pop. 94 753.
  🛈 Central Library, Homer Rd ℰ (0121) 704 6130.
London 109 – Birmingham 7 – Coventry 13 – Warwick 13.

🏨 **Renaissance Solihull**, 651 Warwick Rd, B91 1AT, ℰ (0121) 711 3000, reservations.sol
  ihull@marriotthotels.co.uk, Fax (0121) 705 6629, Ⅰ₆, 🛋 , 🏊 , 龗 – ♯ ★★ 🖻 ₺ ℗ – 🔬 700.
  觟⑤ ℀ℰ ◑ VISA
  651 : Rest 21.95 and a la carte 23.00/28.00 s. ♀ – ⇌ 14.95 – **176 rm** ★130.00/210.00 –
  ★★140.00/220.00, 4 suites.
  ♦ Well placed for road and rail links and the airport. Behind an unpromising façade, modern rooms are usefully equipped and extensive conference facilities are much in demand. Restaurant with garden outlook.

XX **The Town House**, 727 Warwick Rd, B91 3DA, ℰ (0121) 704 1567, hospitalityengi
  neers@btinternet.com, Fax (0121) 713 2189 – ℗. 觟⑤ VISA
  closed Sunday dinner – **Rest** 15.25 (lunch) and a la carte 25.20/37.40 ♀.
  ♦ Once a salubrious nightclub with town centre location. Stylish open-plan interior boasts large dining area with leather banquettes. Soundly prepared modern dishes.

XX **Shimla Pinks**, 44 Station Rd, B91 3RX, ℰ (0121) 704 0344, Fax (0121) 643 3325 – 🖻. 觟⑤
  ℀ℰ ◑ VISA
  Rest - Indian - (dinner only) a la carte 17.40/28.40.
  ♦ Well regarded Indian cuisine in distinctly modern surroundings. A popular venue: regulars return for the original, interesting cooking that ventures away from the traditional.

X **Metro Bar and Grill**, 680-684 Warwick Rd, B91 3DX, ℰ (0121) 705 9495,
  Fax (0121) 705 4754 – 🖻. 觟⑤ ℀ℰ VISA
  closed 25-26 December, 1 January and Sunday – **Rest** a la carte 19.20/29.95 ♀.
  ♦ Locally renowned town centre bar/restaurant that combines buzzy informality with appealing range of brasserie dishes. Dine alongside busy bar: don't expect a quiet night out!

at Olton Northwest : 2½ m. on A 41 – ✉ Solihull.

XX **Rajnagar**, 256 Lyndon Rd, B92 7QW, ℰ (0121) 742 8140, info@rajnagar.com,
  Fax (0121) 743 3147 – 🖻. 觟⑤ ℀ℰ ◑ VISA
  Rest - Indian - (dinner only) a la carte 13.45/19.95.
  ♦ A busy, modern neighbourhood favourite, privately owned, offering authentic, regional specialities of Indian cuisine. Service is flexible and friendly.

SOMERLEYTON Suffolk.

London 134.5 – Great Yarmouth 10.5 – Norwich 20.5.

Duke's Head, Slugs Lane, NR32 5QR, West : ¾ m. off B 1074 *ℰ* (01502) 730281, *dukes head@somerleyton.co.uk, Fax* (01493) 733931, 😤 – **P. ⑳ VISA**
Rest a la carte 20.00/30.00.
* Part of the Somerleyton Estate; boasts a super sundrenched terrace "down by the river". Appetizing modern dishes employ tasty fresh cooking with ingredients from the estate.

SOMERTON Somerset 503 L 30 The West Country G. – pop. 4 133.

See : Town★ - Market Place★ (cross★) – St Michael's Church★.
Env. : Long Sutton★ (Church★★) SW : 2½ m. by B 3165 – Huish Episcopi (St Mary's Church Tower★★) SW : 4½ m. by B 3153 – Lytes Cary★, SE : 3½ m. by B 3151 – Street - The Shoe Museum★, N : 5 m. by B 3151.
Exc. : Muchelney★★ (Parish Church★★) SW : 6½ m. by B 3153 and A 372 – High Ham (≼★★, St Andrew's Church★), NW : 9 m. by B 3153, A 372 and minor rd – Midelney Manor★ AC, SW : 9 m. by B 3153 and A 378.
London 138 – Bristol 32 – Taunton 17.

Lynch Country House without rest., 4 Behind Berry, TA11 7PD, *ℰ* (01458) 272316, *the–lynch@talk21.com, Fax* (01458) 272590, ≼, 🌱, 🏊–⇆✦ **P. ⑳ ℍ ⓞ VISA**
9 rm ⌷ ✦60.00 – ✦✦95.00.
* Stands on a crest overlooking the Cary Valley. The grounds of this Regency house are equally rich with unusual shrubs, trees and lake. Antique four-poster; spotless rooms.

at Kingsdon Southeast : 2½ m. by B 3151 – ✉ Somerton.

Kingsdon Inn, TA11 7LG, *ℰ* (01935) 840543, *robert@rhorler.freeserve.co.uk,* 😤, 🌱 – ⇆✦ **P. ⑳ VISA**
Rest a la carte 14.00/26.00 ⚲ – **2 rm** ⌷ ✦45.00 – ✦✦70.00.
* Thatched inn with bags of character. Modernised interior retains beams, wood-burning stove, colourful scatter cushions. Daily changing menus full of traditional favourites.

The 🟔 award is the crème de la crème.
This is awarded to restaurants
which are really worth travelling miles for!

SONNING-ON-THAMES Wokingham 504 R 29.

London 48 – Reading 4.

French Horn with rm, RG4 6TN, *ℰ* (01189) 692204, *info@thefrenchhorn.co.uk, Fax* (01189) 442210, ≼ River Thames and gardens – 🔟, 🍽 rm, ✆ 👌 **P.** 🕿 24. **⑳ ℍ ⓞ VISA**
🟔
closed Christmas-New Year – **Rest** (booking essential) 33.00/45.00 (lunch) and a la carte 45.00/141.00 **s.** ⚲ – **16 rm** ⌷ ✦120.00 – ✦✦205.00, 5 suites.
* Personally run former 19C coaching inn. Warm, comfy lounges with open fires. Accomplished cooking of classics; professional service in formal environment. Individual rooms.

SOUTHAMPTON Southampton 503 504 P 31 Great Britain G. – pop. 234 224.

See : Old Southampton AZ : Bargate★ B - Tudor House Museum★ M1.
🏌, 🏌 Southampton Municipal, Golf Course Rd, Bassett *ℰ* (023) 8076 8407, AY – 🏌 Stoneham, Monks Wood Close, Bassett *ℰ* (023) 8076 9272, AY – 🏌 Chilworth Golf Centre, Main Rd, Chilworth *ℰ* (023) 8074 0544, AY.
Itchen Bridge (toll) AZ.
✈ Southampton/Eastleigh Airport : *ℰ* (0870) 040 0009, N : 4 m. BY.
⛴ to France (Cherbourg) (Brittany Ferries) 4 weekly (5 h) – to the Isle of Wight (East Cowes) (Red Funnel Ferries) frequent services daily (55 mn).
⛴ to Hythe (White Horse Ferries Ltd) frequent services daily (12 mn) – to the Isle of Wight (Cowes) (Red Funnel Ferries) frequent services daily (approx. 22 mn).
🛈 9 Civic Centre Rd *ℰ* (023) 8083 3333, city.information@southampton.gov.uk.
London 87 – Bristol 79 – Plymouth 161.

Plans on following pages

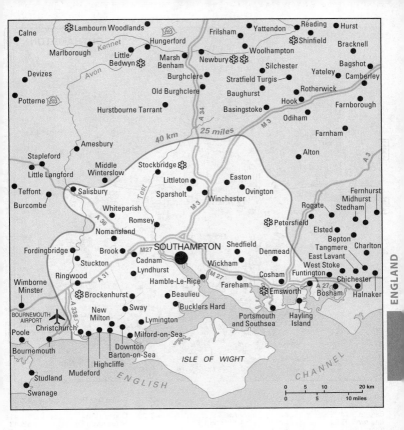

De Vere Grand Harbour, West Quay Rd, SO15 1AG, ℘ (023) 8063 3033, *grand harbour@devere-hotels.com, Fax (023) 8063 3066*, 🕭, ʰ⌕, ⇌, ▨ – 🕭 ⤫, ▤ rest, ₺ 🅿 –
🔏 500. 🅜🅞 🄰🄴 🄾 *VISA* . ⅍   **AZ a**
Allerton's : Rest *(dinner only and Sunday lunch)/dinner* (booking essential) 42.50 ♈ –
Number 5 : Rest 28.95 and a la carte 22.50/33.25 s. ♈ – **169 rm** � ♛139.00 –
♛♛149.00/229.00, 4 suites.
◆ Modern and stylish. The split-level pavilion leisure club boasts a Finnish sauna, Turkish
steam room and bar. Well furnished rooms; some with balconies and king-size beds.
Allerton's is arcaded, with screens. Chic, informal Number 5.

Hilton Southampton, Bracken Pl, Chilworth, SO16 3RB, ℘ (023) 8070 2700,
Fax (023) 8076 7233, ʰ⌕, ⇌, ▨ – 🕭 ⤫ ▤ ₺ & 🅿 – 🔏 180. 🅜🅞 🄰🄴 🄾 *VISA* . ⅍   **AY e**
Rest *(lunch booking essential)/dinner* 27.50/37.50 and a la carte 26.50/41.50 ♈ – ⊃ 15.95 –
133 rm ♛179.00 – ♛♛179.00/229.00, 2 suites.
◆ A purpose-built hotel with smart marbled lobby and individual reception desks. Extensive leisure facilities and good size bedrooms, well furnished to a high standard. Informal, family-oriented restaurant.

Jurys Inn, 1 Charlotte Pl, SO14 0TB, ℘ (023) 8037 1111, *jurysinnsouthampton@jurys
doyle.com, Fax (023) 8037 1100* – 🕭 ⤫ ₺ & 🅿 – 🔏 120. 🅜🅞 🄰🄴 🄾 *VISA*   **AZ c**
Innfusion : Rest *(bar lunch)/dinner a la carte 24.00/34.00 s.* – ⊃ 9.95 – **270 rm**
♛99.00/114.00 – ♛♛99.00/114.00.
◆ Up-to-date hotel, handily placed close to city centre. Well-equipped conference facilities; spacious coffee shop/bar. Good value, ample sized accommodation. Modern dining
room with modish menus.

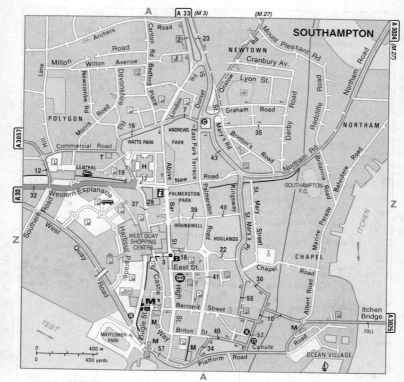

Dockgate 4, 1 South Western House, SO14 3AS, ℰ (023) 8033 9303, info@dock
gate4.com, Fax (023) 8033 6999 – ▤ ❖ 12. 🅜🅢 🄰🄴 𝗩𝗜𝗦𝗔
AZ n
Rest a la carte 23.95/37.40 ♀.
* Set in elegantly apportioned Wedgwood ballroom with beautifully ornate ceiling. Smart, well-spaced tables mirror surroundings. Tasty, appealing menus boast plenty of choice.

Oxfords, 35-36 Oxford St, SO14 3DS, ℰ (023) 8022 4444, bookings@oxfordsrestaur
ant.com, Fax (023) 8022 2284 – 🅜🅢 🄰🄴 𝗩𝗜𝗦𝗔
AZ x
closed 25-26 December – **Rest** and a la carte 20.25/28.95 ♀.
* Well-run, modern eatery in lively part of town. Entrance bar has impressively vast wall of wines. Restaurant features bold, fresh brasserie cuisine with extensive choice.

White Star Tavern and Dining Rooms, 28 Oxford St, SO14 3DJ, ℰ (023) 8082
1990, manager@whitestartavern.co.uk, Fax (023) 8090 4982 – ▤. 🅜🅢 🄰🄴 🄾 𝗩𝗜𝗦𝗔
🍴
AZ x
closed 25-26 December and 1 January – **Rest** a la carte 20.00/29.95 ♀.
* Smartly attired town centre pub. Spacious, comfortable premises with antique tables. Small lounge with leather armchairs. Good range of contemporary cuisine.

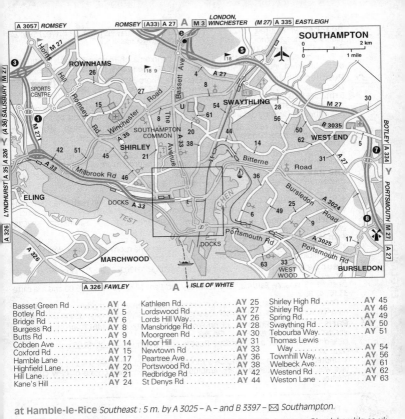

Top map labels:

A 3057 ROMSEY — ROMSEY (A33) A 27 — A — M 3 — LONDON, WINCHESTER (M 27) A 335 EASTLEIGH

SOUTHAMPTON

0 — 2 km
0 — 1 mile

ROWNHAMS
SPORTS CENTRE
SWAYTHLING
WEST END
SOUTHAMPTON COMMON
SHIRLEY
The Avenue
Bitterne
Road
Bursledon
Road
ELING
DOCKS A 33
TEST
ITCHEN
Portsmouth Rd
DOCKS
MARCHWOOD
WEST WOOD
BURSLEDON
Portsmouth Rd

A 326 FAWLEY — A — ISLE OF WHITE

Basset Green Rd	AY 4	Kathleen Rd	AY 25	Shirley High Rd	AY 45
Botley Rd	AY 5	Lordswood Rd	AY 27	Shirley Rd	AY 46
Bridge Rd	AY 6	Lords Hill Way	AY 26	Spring Rd	AY 49
Burgess Rd	AY 8	Mansbridge Rd	AY 28	Swaything Rd	AY 50
Butts Rd	AY 9	Moorgreen Rd	AY 30	Tebourba Way	AY 51
Cobden Ave	AY 14	Moor Hill	AY 31	Thomas Lewis	
Coxford Rd	AY 15	Newtown Rd	AY 33	Way	AY 54
Hamble Lane	AY 17	Peartree Ave	AY 36	Townhill Way	AY 56
Highfield Lane	AY 20	Portswood Rd	AY 38	Welbeck Ave	AY 61
Hill Lane	AY 21	Redbridge Rd	AY 42	Westend Rd	AY 62
Kane's Hill	AY 24	St Denys Rd	AY 44	Weston Lane	AY 63

at Hamble-le-Rice Southeast : 5 m. by A 3025 – A – and B 3397 – ⊠ Southampton.

🏠 **The Bugle,** High St, SO31 4HA, ℰ (023) 8045 3000, manager@buglehamble.co.uk, Fax (023) 8045 3051, 🈺 – ⇔ 10. 🐵 🅰🅴 🆅🅸🆂🅰. ⬌
closed 25 December – **Rest** a la carte 16.85/26.20 .**s** ⬌.
♦ Part 12C inn on Southampton Water. Carefully restored: original beams, wattle walls, open fire with brick lining, stone and oak floor. Freshly prepared range of favourites.

SOUTH CADBURY Somerset 503 M 30 – see Castle Cary.

SOUTH DALTON East Riding – see Beverley.

SOUTHEND-ON-SEA Southend 504 W 29 – pop. 160 257.
📍 Belfairs, Eastwood Road North, Leigh-on-Sea ℰ (01702) 525345 – 📍 Ballards Gore G. & C.C., Gore Rd, Canewdon, Rochford ℰ (01702) 258917 – 📍, 📍 The Essex Golf Complex, Garon Park, Eastern Ave ℰ (01702) 601701.
✈ Southend-on-Sea Airport : ℰ (01702) 608100, N : 2 m.
🛈 Western Esplanade ℰ (01702) 215120.
London 39 – Cambridge 69 – Croydon 46 – Dover 85.

🏠 **Camelia,** 178 Eastern Esplanade, Thorpe Bay, SS1 3AA, ℰ (01702) 587917, enquiries@cameliahotel.com, Fax (01702) 585704 – ❄✖, 🍽 rest. 🐵 🅰🅴 🅾 🆅🅸🆂🅰. ⬌
Rest (residents only Sunday dinner) (dinner only and Sunday lunch) 14.95 and a la carte 13.75/19.20 **s** – **34 rm** ⬌ ✦49.00/55.00 – ✦✦90.00/120.00.
♦ A white hotel on the seafront at Thorpe Bay with good views of the Thames Estuary. Comfortable, well-kept bedrooms, particularly Superior rooms in the new extension. Popular menus in front dining room.

⌂ **Beaches** without rest., 192 Eastern Esplanade, Thorpe Bay, SS1 3AA, ℰ (01702) 586124, *mark@beachesguesthouse.co.uk*, ⇐ – 🍴 📞, 🐾 🖭 *VISA*. ⅏
7 rm ⚹35.00 – ⚹⚹70.00/80.00.
◆ A sunny guesthouse on Thorpe Bay with panorama of Thames Estuary. Continental buffet breakfast. Individually styled rooms: four have sea views; two have balconies.

⌂ **Pebbles** without rest., 190 Eastern Esplanade, Thorpe Bay, SS1 3AA, ℰ (01702) 582329, *pebbles-guesthouse@yahoo.co.uk*, Fax (01702) 582329, ⇐ – 🍴. 🐾 *VISA*. ⅏
5 rm ⌸ ⚹35.00/55.00 – ⚹⚹55.00/65.00.
◆ Friendly guesthouse on the Esplanade overlooking estuary; away from bustle of town but within easy walking distance. Rooftop garden and sea views from most bedrooms.

⌂ **Atlantis** without rest., 63 Alexandra Rd, SS1 1EY, ℰ (01702) 332538, *atlantisguest house@eurotelbroadband.com*, Fax (01702) 392736 – 🍴. 🅿. 🐾 *VISA*. ⅏
closed 25-26 December – **10 rm** ⌸ ⚹45.00 – ⚹⚹65.00.
◆ Centrally located Victorian terraced house; pretty cloth-clad dining room with good traditional breakfast choice. Thoughtfully decorated bedrooms are all very well maintained.

⌂ **The Bay** without rest., 187 Eastern Esplanade, Thorpe Bay, SS1 3AA, ℰ (01702) 588415, *thebayguesthouse@hotmail.com* – 🍴. 🐾 🖭 ① *VISA*. ⅏
4 rm ⌸ ⚹35.00 – ⚹⚹60.00.
◆ Spruce Edwardian house on seafront; a flint wall and pretty tiled path leads to roomy interiors. Generous breakfasts served in light, mirrored breakfast room. Neat bedrooms.

⌂ **Moorings** without rest., 172 Eastern Esplanade, SS1 3AA, ℰ (01702) 587575, *emma@themooringsbedandbreakfast.com* – ⅏
3 rm ⌸ ⚹30.00/40.00 – ⚹⚹50.00/55.00.
◆ An Edwardian terraced house overlooking the sea; one room with a view. Well-kept and comfortable with affable owner. Simple, modern breakfast room.

XX **Fleur de Provence**, 52 Alexandra St, SS1 1BJ, ℰ (01702) 352987, *marcel@fleurdepro vence.co.uk*, Fax (01702) 431123 – 🐾 🖭 *VISA*
closed 1-15 January, Saturday lunch, Sunday and Bank Holidays – **Rest** 15.00 and a la carte 33.85/42.85 ⅊.
◆ Personally run restaurant, a classical French inspiration with a modern edge underpinning flavourful menus. Friendly service and continental style; well regarded in the area.

XX **Paris**, 719 London Rd, Westcliff-on-Sea, SS0 9ST, ℰ (01702) 344077, *info@parisrestaur ant.net*, Fax (01702) 349238 – 🍽. 🐾 *VISA*
closed Sunday dinner and Monday – **Rest** (lunch booking essential) 18.95 and dinner a la carte 31.85/35.85 ⅊.
◆ Unprepossessing façade conceals a modern restaurant with well-spaced, well-sized tables waited on by attentive staff. Ambitious cooking on good choice of daily changing menus.

The red 🐦 symbol?
This denotes the very essence of peace
– only the sound of birdsong first thing in the morning …

SOUTH LEIGH Oxon. 503 504 P 28 – see Witney.

SOUTH MOLTON Devon 503 I 30.
London 197 – Barnstaple 11 – Bristol 81.

⌂ **Kerscott Farm** 🐦, Ash Mill, EX36 4QG, Southeast : 5 m. by A 361 on B 3227 ℰ (01769) 550262, *kerscott.farm@virgin.net*, Fax (01769) 550910, ⇐, ⇆, 🖭 – 🍴 🅿. ⅏
closed 24-26 and 31 December and 1 January–**Rest** (communal dining) 14.00 – **3 rm** ⌸ ⚹35.00 – ⚹⚹56.00/60.00.
◆ Beautiful, personally run 14C/17C farmhouse with fine views to Exmoor. Watch out for lambs and geese. Bags of internal character: beams and vast inglenooks. Charming rooms. Communal farmhouse dinners using farm's own produce.

at Knowstone Southeast : 9½ m. by A 361 – ✉ South Molton.

🏠 **The Masons Arms** (Dodson), EX36 4RY, ℰ (01398) 341231, *dodsonmason sarms@aol.com*, 🎋, ⇆ – 🍴 🅿. 🐾 *VISA*
closed first 2 weeks January – **Rest** (closed Sunday dinner and Monday) (booking essential) a la carte 28.50/36.00.
Spec. Ham hock and mushroom terrine, grain mustard dressing. Fillet of Devon beef, pea purée and smoked bacon, Madeira sauce. Chocolate and caramelised hazelnut mousse.
◆ Delightful, thatched 13C inn, with beams, vast fireplace and exquisite ceiling mural in restaurant. Superb, flavourful, modern dishes, employing quality seasonal ingredients.

SOUTH NORMANTON Derbs. 502 503 504 Q 24 – pop. 14 044 (inc. Pinxton).
London 130 – Derby 17 – Nottingham 15 – Sheffield 31.

🏨 **Renaissance Derby/Nottingham,** Carter Lane East, DE55 2EH, on A 38 ☎ (0870) 400 7262, Fax (0870) 400 7362, 🛌, ☎, 🖵 – ⅍ 🕭 ⅃. ₽ – 🕭 220. 🕭 🕭 🕭 🕭
Rest (closed Saturday lunch) 20.00/22.50 and a la carte 19.65/37.35 s. ⅌ – **157 rm** ⌹
✦70.00/119.00 – ✦✦70.00/119.00.
  ✦ Located close to M1; a modern hotel offering comfortable, well-equipped rooms; those away from motorway are quieter. Usefully, newspapers, toiletries available at reception. Capacious restaurant.

SOUTHPORT Mersey. 502 K 23 – pop. 91 404.
🛆 Southport Municipal Golf Links, Park Road West ☎ (01704) 535286.
🎫 112 Lord St ☎ (01704) 533333.
London 221 – Liverpool 25 – Manchester 38 – Preston 19.

🏨 **Cambridge House,** 4 Cambridge Rd, PR9 9NG, Northeast : 1½ m. on A 565 ☎ (01704) 538372, info@cambridgehousehotel.co.uk, Fax (01704) 547183, 🐎 – ⅍ ₽. 🕭 🕭 🕭
🈂
closed 25 December–Rest (dinner only and Sunday lunch)/dinner 17.50/25.00 s. – **16 rm**
✦58.00/80.00 – ✦✦90.00/160.00.
  ✦ Personally run Victorian town house; lavishly furnished lounge and cosy bar. Very comfortably appointed period rooms in original house; large, more modern style in extension. Regency-style dining room with elegant chairs.

🏨 **The Waterford** without rest., 37 Leicester St, PR9 0EX, ☎ (01704) 530559, reception@waterford-hotel.co.uk, Fax (01704) 542630 – ⅍ ₽. 🕭 🕭 🈂
closed December and January – **8 rm** ⌹ ✦45.00/55.00 – ✦✦75.00/85.00.
  ✦ Pleasantly located close to the promenade, this personally run seaside hotel features a cosy bar for residents and decently sized, neatly decorated bedrooms.

🏠 **Lynwood** without rest., 11A Leicester St, PR9 0ER, ☎ (01704) 540794, info@lynwoodhotel.com, Fax (01704) 500724 – ⅍ ₽. 🕭 🕭 🈂
– **10 rm** ⌹ ✦35.00/45.00 – ✦✦65.00/80.00.
  ✦ Only a couple of minutes' walk from busy Lord Street, this 19C terraced house retains period style in its lounge and neat breakfast room. Pleasantly individual bedrooms.

🍴🍴 **Warehouse Brasserie,** 30 West St, PR8 1QN, ☎ (01704) 544662, info@warehouse brasserie.co.uk, Fax (01704) 500074 – ⅍ ▤. 🕭 🕭
closed 25-26 December, 1 January and Sunday – Rest 13.95 (lunch) and a la carte 19.40/34.40.
  ✦ Former warehouse, now a sleek modern restaurant with Salvador Dali prints and buzzy atmosphere. The open-plan kitchen offers modern cooking with interesting daily specials.

SOUTHROP Glos. 503 504 O 28 – see Lechlade.

SOUTHSEA Portsmouth 503 504 Q 31 – see Portsmouth and Southsea.

SOUTHWELL Notts. 502 504 R 24 Great Britain G. – pop. 6 285.
See : Minster★★ AC.
London 135 – Leicester 35 – Lincoln 24 – Nottingham 14 – Sheffield 34.

🏠 **Old Forge** without rest., 2 Burgage Lane, NG25 0ER, ☎ (01636) 812809, theoldforge southwell@yahoo.co.uk, Fax (01636) 816302, 🐎 – ⅍ ₽. 🕭 🕭
closed 25 December – **4 rm** ⌹ ✦45.00 – ✦✦75.00.
  ✦ Quaint, converted forge with stable looks out to rear Minster. Sunny conservatory leads off from breakfast room. Relax on patio with tiny pond. Homely, well-sized rooms.

SOUTHWOLD Suffolk 504 Z 27 – pop. 3 858.
🛆 The Common ☎ (01502) 723234.
🎫 69 High St ☎ (01502) 724729.
London 108 – Great Yarmouth 24 – Ipswich 35 – Norwich 34.

🏨 **Swan,** Market Pl, IP18 6EG, ☎ (01502) 722186, swan.hotel@adnams.co.uk, Fax (01502) 724800, 🏤, 🐎 – 🛗, ⅍ rest, ₽ – 🕭 40. 🕭 🕭 🈂
Rest 25.00/35.00 ⅌ – **40 rm** ⌹ ✦83.00/113.00 – ✦✦146.00/156.00, 2 suites.
  ✦ Restored coaching inn by Adnams Brewery. Antique filled interiors: 17C portrait of local heiress in hallway. Vintage rooms in main house; garden rooms built round the green. Tall windows define elegant restaurant.

The Crown, 90 High St, IP18 6DP, ℰ (01502) 722275, *crown.hotel@adnams.co.uk*, Fax (01502) 727263 – ✲✲ ℙ. ℳ◎ ◎ – **14 rm** ⚏ ✚80.00/90.00 – ✚✚170.00/180.00, 1 suite.
• Whitewashed inn combines a smart bar with buzzy dining area and locally popular real ale pub. Unfussy rooms are furnished in contemporary style. Smart, elegant restaurant with impressive wine list.
Rest 29.00 (dinner) and a la carte 25.00/29.00 ♀ ⌖

Northcliffe without rest., 20 North Parade, IP18 6LT, ℰ (01502) 724074, *north cliffe.southwold@virgin.net*, ← – ✲✲. ✲
– **6 rm** ⚏ ✚80.00 – ✚✚95.00.
• Keenly run 19C house commands fine clifftop views; contemporary en suite rooms: ask for one facing the sea. Model boats and nautical curios decorate a cosy, firelit lounge.

The Randolph with rm, 41 Wangford Rd, Reydon, IP18 6PZ, Northwest : 1 m. by A 1095 on B 1126 ℰ (01502) 723603, *reception@therandolph.co.uk*, Fax (01502) 722194, ⇞ – ✲✲ ℙ. ℳ◎ VISA. ✲
Rest a la carte 25.00/30.00 ♀ – **10 rm** ⚏ ✚55.00/65.00 – ✚✚80.00/105.00.
• Renovated in bright contemporary style, a substantial turn of 20C inn named in honour of Randolph Churchill. Heartwarming, modern food. Spacious rooms with distinctive décor.

The Kings Head with rm, 25 High St, IP18 6AD, ℰ (01502) 724517, *reception@south woldkingshead.co.uk* – ✲✲ ⇆ 30. ℳ◎ VISA. ✲
Rest a la carte 18.00/25.00 – **3 rm** ⚏ ✚50.00/65.00 – ✚✚80.00/100.00.
• Smartly refurbished town centre pub; 'proper' bar with carpet, tiles and real fire. Two dining areas serve locally inspired, appealing menus. Bright, fresh and spacious rooms.

Good food and accommodation at moderate prices?
Look for the Bib symbols:
red Bib Gourmand ⊛ for food, blue Bib Hotel 🏠 for hotels

SOWERBY BRIDGE W. Yorks. 502 O 22 – pop. 9 901 – ✉ Halifax.
London 211 – Bradford 10 – Burnley 35 – *Manchester 32* – Sheffield 40.

The Millbank, Mill Bank Rd, HX6 3DY, Southwest : 2 ¼ m. by A 58 ℰ (01422) 825588, *eat@themillbank.com*, ⇞ – ✲✲. ℳ◎ VISA. ✲
closed first 2 weeks October and first week January – **Rest** *(closed Monday lunch)* (booking essential) a la carte 18.50/34.50 ♀.
• A stone inn, now a modernised dining pub with wooden and flagstone floors. Smart conservatory from which views of valley can be savoured over interesting modern cooking.

at Rishworth Southwest : 4 m. by A 58 and A 672 – ✉ Sowerby Bridge.

The Old Bore, Oldham Rd, HX6 4QU, South : ½ m. on A 672 ℰ (01422) 822291, *chefhes sel@aol.com*, ⇞ – ✲✲ ℙ. ℳ◎ VISA
closed 2 weeks January and 25 December – **Rest** *(closed Monday)* a la carte 18.95/40.00 ♀.
• Remote pub with pleasantly landscaped terrace. Three roomed interior includes warm, rustic bar and formal dining room. Interesting and original dishes full of local flavours.

SPALDING Lincs. 502 T 25.
London 108 – Peterborough 23 – Stamford 19.

at Surfleet Seas End North : 5¾ m. by A 16 – ✉ Spalding.

The Ship Inn with rm, 154 Reservoir Rd, PE11 4DH, ℰ (01775) 680547, *info@shipinnsur fleet.com*, Fax (01775) 680541, ←, ⇞ – ✲✲ ⱴ ℙ. ℳ◎ ΑΕ ◎ VISA. ✲
Rest *(closed Sunday dinner and Monday)* a la carte 20.00/30.00 – **4 rm** ⚏ ✚50.00 – ✚✚65.00.
• Actually, a dozen miles from the briny! Refurbished part 17C inn with nautical themed bar. First floor: adventurous dishes and a wonderful balcony. Comfy rooms with views.

SPALDWICK Cambs. 504 S 26 – see Huntingdon.

SPARSHOLT Hants. 503 504 P 30 – see Winchester.

SPEEN *Bucks.* 504 R 28 – ⊠ *Princes Risborough.*
London 41 – Aylesbury 15 – Oxford 33 – Reading 25.

XX **Old Plow (Restaurant),** Flowers Bottom, HP27 0PZ, West : ½ m. by Chapel Hill and
Highwood Bottom ℰ (01494) 488300, Fax (01494) 488702, ⌖ – **P**, **⬤⬤** **AE** **VISA**
*closed Christmas-New Year, August, Monday, Saturday lunch, Sunday dinner and Bank
Holidays except Good Friday* – **Rest** 25.95/33.95 – (see also **Bistro** below).
◆ A fine, oak beamed restaurant at back of the bistro; more formal in style with linen table
cover and high-back chairs. Set menus show French influence with classic sauces.

X **Bistro** (at Old Plow), Flowers Bottom, HP27 0PZ, West : ½ m. by Chapel Hill and Highwood
Bottom ℰ (01494) 488300, Fax (01494) 488702, ⌖, ⌖, ⬤ – **P**, **⬤⬤** **AE** **VISA**
*closed Christmas-New Year, August, Monday, Saturday lunch, Sunday dinner and Bank
Holidays except Good Friday* – **Rest** (booking essential) a la carte 26.85/35.85.
◆ A cosy little bistro: low ceiling, tiled floors; log fire in the lounge. Blackboards announce
simple à la carte menus; includes separate Brixham fish board. Affable owners.

SPEKE *Mersey.* 502 503 L 23 – *see Liverpool.*

SPELDHURST *Kent* 504 U 30 – *see Royal Tunbridge Wells.*

SPENNYMOOR *Durham* 501 502 P 19 – *pop. 17 207* – ⊠ *Darlington.*
London 275 – Durham 6 – Leeds 75 – Newcastle upon Tyne 24.

🏛 **Whitworth Hall Country Park H.** ⬤, DL16 7QW, Northwest : 1 ½ m. by Middle-
stone Moor rd on Brancepeth rd ℰ (01388) 811772, *enquiries@whitworthhall.co.uk,*
Fax (01388) 818669, ⬤, ⬤, ⌖, ⬤ – ⌖ **P**, – 🛏 120. **⬤⬤** **AE** **VISA**. ⬤
Library : Rest *(closed Sunday dinner)* (dinner only and Sunday lunch) a la carte 22.00/35.00
– **Silver Buckles Brasserie :** Rest 15.95 (lunch) and dinner a la carte 20.75/35.90 – **29 rm**
⬤ ✦115.00 – ✦✦200.
◆ Part 19C country house, sympathetically converted; fine views over deer park and vineyard. Orangery lounge; larger rooms, in the original house, are in period style. The Library
handsomely set in eponymous room. Conservatory dining in Silver Buckles Brasserie.

SPRATTON *Northants.* 504 R 27 – *see Northampton.*

SPRIGG'S ALLEY *Oxon.* – *see Chinnor.*

STADDLEBRIDGE *N. Yorks.* – *see Northallerton.*

STADHAMPTON *Oxon.* 503 504 Q 28.
London 53 – Aylesbury 18 – Oxford 10.

🛏 **Crazy Bear** with rm, Bear Lane, OX44 7UR, off Wallingford rd ℰ (01865) 890714, *enqui
ries@crazybeargroup.co.uk,* Fax (01865) 400481, ⌖, ⌖ – **P** ⬤ 20. **⬤⬤** **VISA**. ⬤
Rest 15.50 and a la carte 22.00/32.00 ⬤ – **Thai Thai :** Rest (booking essential) a la carte
22.00/32.00 ⬤ – **17 rm** ⬤ ✦80.00 – ✦✦325.00.
◆ Behind unassuming stone pub exterior are wacky rooms to hit you between the eyes:
zebra striped carpets, walls of peacock blue and purple. Vibrant, contemporary bedrooms.
Either modern British or Thai cuisine where exotic fish swim in tanks.

STAFFORD *Staffs.* 502 503 504 N 25 – *pop. 63 681.*
🏰 Stafford Castle, Newport Rd ℰ (01785) 223821.
🄱 Market St ℰ (01785) 619619.
London 142 – Birmingham 26 – Derby 32 – Shrewsbury 31 – Stoke-on-Trent 17.

🏰 **Moat House,** Lower Penkridge Rd, Acton Trussell, ST17 0RJ, South: 3 ¾ m. by A 449
ℰ (01785) 712217, *info@moathouse.co.uk,* Fax (01785) 715344, ⌖ – ⌖, ▦ rest, ⬤ **P** –
🛏 200. **⬤⬤** **AE** **⬤** **VISA**. ⬤
closed 24-25 December and 1 January – **The Conservatory :** Rest 20.00/37.50 and dinner
a la carte 27.75/38.25 s. ⬤ – **40 rm** ⬤ ✦125.00 – ✦✦140.00, 1 suite.
◆ Timbered 15C moated manor house with modern extensions and lawned gardens,
within sight of the M6. Characterful rustic bar. Colourful rooms with individual style. Bright,
airy conservatory restaurant overlooks canal.

The Swan, 46-46A Greengate St, ST16 2JA, *℘* (01785) 258142, *info@theswanstaf
ford.co.uk, Fax* (01785) 225372 – 📶 ✏️, 🍽 rest, ಈ 🅿️ 🐨 🗷 ✏️
closed 25 December – *The Brasserie at The Swan :* Rest 8.95/15.00 and a la carte
17.15/27.75 **s.** 🍷 – **31 rm** 🖂 ✦✦80.00/90.00 – ✦✦95.00/130.00.
 • Part 17C coaching inn with modern décor throughout. Convenient central location.
Stylish reception. Well-equipped bedrooms with good facilities. Light, airy brasserie is open
all day.

Express by Holiday Inn without rest., Acton Court, Acton Gate, ST18 9AR, South :
3 m. on A 449 *℘* (01785) 212244, *stafford@morethanhotels.com, Fax* (01785) 212377 – 📶
✏️ ✆ ಈ 🅿️ – 🔬 40. 🐨 🗷 🔘 🗷
103 rm ✦69.00/95.00 – ✦✦69.00/95.00.
 • A good value hotel, ideal as a stopover for those travelling both North and South and
close to the famous Staffordshire Potteries. Comfortable bedrooms.

STAINES *Middx.* **504** S 29 – *pop. 50 538.*
London 26 – Reading 25.

Thames Lodge, Thames St, TW18 4SJ, *℘* (01784) 464433, *sales.thameslodge@macdon
ald-hotels.co.uk, Fax* (01784) 454858, ≤ – ✏️, 🍽 rest, ✆ ಈ 🅿️ – 🔬 50. 🐨 🗷 🔘 🗷
The Brasserie : Rest a la carte 20.00/29.00 **s.** 🍷 – 🖂 15.95 – **78 rm** ✦100.00/160.00 –
✦✦110.00/170.00.
 • Once used as a stopover for horse-pulled barges, this riverside hotel has moorings on
the Thames. A mix of rooms: some with traditional décor, some more modern in style.
Terrace brasserie overlooks river.

STAITHES *N. Yorks.* **502** R 20 – ✉ *Saltburn (Cleveland).*
London 269 – Middlesbrough 22 – Scarborough 31.

Endeavour with rm, 1 High St, TS13 5BH, *℘* (01947) 840825, *endeavour.restaurant@vir
gin.net* – ✏️ 🅿️ 🐨 🔘 🗷
closed 25-26 December, 1 January, Sunday and Monday – **Rest** - Seafood - (dinner only) a
la carte 22.15/28.95 – **4 rm** 🖂 – ✦✦95.00.
 • Named after Captain Cook's sailing ship: a compact former fisherman's cottage serving
tasty menus, with emphasis on locally caught fish. Neat, well-appointed bedrooms.

STAMFORD *Lincs.* **502 504** S 26 *Great Britain G.* – *pop. 19 525.*
See : *Town★★ - St Martin's Church★ – Lord Burghley's Hospital★ – Browne's Hospital★ AC.*
Env. : *Burghley House★★ AC, SE : 1½ m. by B 1443.*
🚩 *The Arts Centre, 27 St Mary's St ℘* (01780) 755611.
London 92 – Leicester 31 – Lincoln 50 – Nottingham 45.

The George of Stamford, 71 St Martin's, PE9 2LB, *℘* (01780) 750750, *reserva
tions@georgehotelofstamford.com, Fax* (01780) 750701, 🌳, 🌳 – 🅿️ – 🔬 50. 🐨 🗷 🔘
🗷
The George : Rest 17.50 (lunch) and a la carte 32.50/50.00 **s.** 🍷 – **Garden Lounge :** Rest -
Seafood specialities - a la carte 26.30/47.65 **s.** 🍷 – **46 rm** 🖂 ✦78.00/98.00 – ✦✦225.00,
1 suite.
 • Historic inn, over 900 years old. Crusading knights stayed here en route to Jerusalem.
Walled garden and courtyard with 17C mulberry tree. Original bedrooms; designer décor.
Oak panelled dining room exudes elegance. Garden Lounge with leafy courtyard.

Garden House, 42 High St, St Martin's, PE9 2LP, *℘* (01780) 763359, *enquiries@garden
househotel.com, Fax* (01780) 763339, 🌳, 🌳 – ✏️ rest, 🅿️ 🐨 🗷 🗷
closed 26-29 December and 1-7 January – **Rest** (closed Sunday dinner) a la carte
22.70/28.20 – **20 rm** 🖂 ✦65.00/80.00 – ✦✦90.00.
 • Next to Burghley Park, dating from 1796, this fine hotel with garden and conservatory
makes a good base for exploring Stamford. Variety of rooms; includes large family ones.
Dining room with graceful chairs and Belgian tapestries.

Jim's Yard, 3 Ironmonger St, PE9 1PL, off Broad St *℘* (01780) 756080, *jim@jimsyard.biz,
Fax* (01780) 480848, 🌳 – ✏️ 🐨 🗷
closed last week July and first week August, 2 weeks Christmas, and Sunday and Monday –
Rest a la carte 20.50/25.95 🍷.
 • Two 18C houses in a courtyard: conservatory or first-floor dining options. Smart
tableware enhances enjoyment of great value menus employing well-executed, classic
cooking.

at Collyweston *Southwest : 3½ m. on A 43 –* ✉ *Stamford.*

🏠 **The Collyweston Slater** with rm, 87-89 Main Rd, PE9 3PQ, ℰ (01780) 444288, info@collywestonslater.co.uk, Fax (01780) 444270 – ❧✖ 📺 🅿. 🆖 *VISA*
closed 25 December and dinner Sunday and Bank Holidays – **Rest** *a la carte 17.70/29.40 –* 5 rm ☷ ✦60.00/70.00 – ✦✦120.00/120.00.
♦ Vastly refurbished pub with a 'modern rustic' feel, and floodlit boules alley! Well presented mix of modern/traditional dishes served in dining room or bar. Elegant rooms.

at Stretton *(Rutland) Northwest : 8 m. by B 1081 off A 1 –* ✉ *Stamford.*

🏠 **The Jackson Stops Inn,** Rookery Rd, LE15 7RA, ℰ (01780) 410237, info@thejackson stops.co.uk, 🏤, 🏤 – ❧✖ 🅿. 🆖 *VISA*
closed first 2 weeks January, 25 December, Sunday dinner and Monday – **Rest** 18.00/23.95 and a la carte 26.50/38.50 ☷.
♦ 17C stone inn with thatched roof and garden and rural decor. Low wood bar and four eating areas. Daily menu of good British cooking with blackboard specials.

at Clipsham *(Rutland) Northwest : 9½ m. by B 1081 off A 1 –* ✉ *Stamford.*

🏠 **The Olive Branch & Beech House** (Hope) with rm, Main St, LE15 7SH, ℰ (01780) 410355, info@theolivebranchpub.com, Fax (01780) 410000, 🏤 – ❧✖ 📺 🅿. 🆖 *VISA*
❀ *closed 1 January, dinner 25-26 December and lunch 31 December –* **Rest** (booking essential) 16.00 (lunch) and a la carte 20.00/31.50 ☷ – **6 rm** ☷ ✦95.00 – ✦✦150.00.
Spec. Tiger prawn tempura, sweet chilli dip. Braised oxtail, horseradish gratin, mashed carrots. Marmalade pudding with clotted cream.
♦ Soundly judged, flavoursome cooking, varied and modern, in cosy firelit pub with simple pews and sepia prints. Rooms, over the road in Georgian house, are sassy and stylish.

Do not confuse ✕ with ❀!
✕ defines comfort, while stars are awarded for the best cuisine, across all categories of comfort.

ENGLAND

STANDISH *Gtr Manchester* 502 504 M 23 – *pop. 14 350 –* ✉ *Wigan.*
London 210 – Liverpool 25 – Manchester 21 – Preston 15.

at Wrightington Bar *Northwest : 3½ m. by A 5209 on B 5250 –* ✉ *Wigan.*

🏠 **The Mulberry Tree,** 9 Wood Lane, WN6 9SE, ℰ (01257) 451400, Fax (01257) 451400 – ❧✖ 🅿. 🆖 *VISA*. 🏵
closed 26 December and 1 January – **Rest** *a la carte 25.00/45.00.*
♦ Foody-themed modern pub with warm, buzzy atmosphere. Modern cooking, generous portions and lots of blackboard specials. Eat in the bar or slightly more expensive dining room.

STANNERSBURN *Northd.* 501 502 M 18 – ✉ *Hexham.*
London 363 – Carlisle 56 – Newcastle upon Tyne 46.

🏠 **The Pheasant Inn** 🌫 with rm, Falstone, NE48 1DD, ℰ (01434) 240382, enquiries@thepheasantinn.com, Fax (01434) 240382, 🏤 – ❧✖ 📺 🅿. 🆖 *VISA*. 🏵
closed 25-26 December and Monday-Tuesday November-Easter – **Rest** *a la carte 14.00/23.00 ☷ –* **8 rm** ☷ ✦45.00/60.00 – ✦✦75.00/85.00.
♦ Set in Northumberland National Park, near Kielder reservoir; epitome of a traditional inn. Pine dining room serves homecooked local fare. Cottagey rooms in converted stables.

STANSTED AIRPORT *Essex* 504 U 28 – ✉ *Stansted Mountfitchet.*
✈ *Stansted International Airport :* ℰ (0870) 0000303 – **Terminal :** *to Liverpool St Station, London.*
London 37 – Cambridge 29 – Chelmsford 18 – Colchester 29.

🏨 **Radisson SAS,** Waltham Close, CM24 1PP, ℰ (01279) 661012, info.stansted@radisson sas.com, Fax (01279) 661013, 🗗, 🎴, 🔒, 🛁 – 🛗 ❧✖ 🔳 🔥 🅿 – 🕍 400. 🆖 ⒶⒺ ① *VISA*. 🏵
New York Grill Bar : Rest a la carte 23.40/31.40 s. – **Wine Tower :** Rest a la carte 10.70/13.00 s. – **Filini :** Rest - Italian - a la carte 15.70/24.95 s. – ☷ 14.95 – **484 rm** ✦125.00 – ✦✦125.00, 16 suites.
♦ Impressive hotel just two minutes from main terminal; vast open atrium housing 40 foot wine cellar. Extensive meeting facilities. Very stylish bedrooms in three themes. Small, formal New York Grill Bar. Impressive Wine Tower. Filini for Italian dishes.

Hilton London Stansted Airport, Round Coppice Rd, CM24 1SF, ℘ (01279) 680800, *reservations.stansted@hilton.com*, Fax (01279) 680890, ₤ₐ, ☎, ☒ – ▤, ↔ rm, ▤ rest, ₺ ℙ – ♨ 250. ⦿ ⸰ ⦿ ₘₐ. ⸰
Rest *(closed lunch Saturday, Sunday and Bank Holidays)* 13.95/19.50 and dinner a la carte 24.45/34.85 ♀ – ☜ 17.95 – **237 rm** ⚐94.00/145.50 – ⚐⚐94.50/145.50, 2 suites.
♦ Bustling hotel whose facilities include leisure club, hairdressers and beauty salon. Modern rooms, with two of executive style. Transport can be arranged to and from terminal. Restaurant/bar has popular menu; sometimes carvery lunch as well.

Express by Holiday Inn without rest., Thremhall Ave, CM24 1PY, ℘ (01279) 680015, *stansted@kewgreen.co.uk*, Fax (01279) 680838 – ▤ ↔ ₺ ℙ – ♨ 60. ⦿ ₘₐ ⸰ ₘₐ. ⸰
183 rm ⚐79.95/96.00 – ⚐⚐79.95/96.00.
♦ Adjacent to the airport and medium term parking facilities, so useful for leisure and business travellers. Functional rooms provide good value accommodation.

STANSTED MOUNTFITCHET *Essex* 504 U 28 – *see Bishop's Stortford (Herts.).*

STANTON *Suffolk* 504 W 27 – *pop. 2 073.*
London 88 – Cambridge 38 – Ipswich 40 – King's Lynn 38 – Norwich 39.

Leaping Hare, Wyken Vineyards, IP31 2DW, South : 1 ¼ m. by Wyken Rd ℘ (01359) 250287, Fax (01359) 253022, ㎡, ㎡ – ↔ ℙ. ⦿ ₘₐ
– **Rest** (booking essential) (lunch only and dinner Friday and Saturday) 19.95 (lunch) and a la carte 21.85/30.40 ♀ ㎡.
♦ 17C long barn in working farm and vineyard. Hare-themed pictures and tapestries decorate a beamed restaurant and café. Tasty dishes underpinned by local, organic produce.

STANTON SAINT QUINTIN *Wilts.* 503 504 N 29 – *see Chippenham.*

STANTON WICK *Bath & North East Somerset* 503 504 M 29 – *see Bristol.*

STAPLEFORD *Wilts.* 503 504 O 30 – *see Salisbury.*

STATHERN *Leics.* – *see Melton Mowbray.*

STAVERTON *Devon* 503 I 32 – *pop. 682 – ✉ Totnes.*
London 220 – Exeter 20 – Torquay 33.

Kingston House ⬎, TQ9 6AR, Northwest : 1 m. on Kingston rd ℘ (01803) 762235, *info@kingston-estate.com*, Fax (01803) 762444, ≼, ₤ₐ, ☎, ㎡, ▤ – ↔ ℂ ℙ – ♨ 100. ⦿ ₘₐ ⸰ ₘₐ. ⸰
closed 22 December-3 January – **Rest** (residents only) (set menu only) (dinner only) 35.00/40.00 – **3 rm** ☜ ⚐105.00/115.00 – ⚐⚐190.00.
♦ A spectacular Georgian mansion in sweeping moorland. Unique period details include painted china closet, marquetry staircase, authentic wallpapers. Variety of antique beds.

STAVERTON *Northants.* 504 Q 27 – *see Daventry.*

STEDHAM *W. Sussex* 504 R 31 – *see Midhurst.*

STEPPINGLEY *Beds.*
London 44.5 – Luton 12.5 – Milton Keynes 13.5.

The French Horn, MK45 5AU, ℘ (01525) 712051, *paul@thefrenchhorn.com*, Fax (08717) 334305, ㎡ – ↔ ℙ. ⦿ ₘₐ. ⸰
Rest *(closed Sunday dinner)* (booking essential) a la carte 24.00/50.00 ♀.
♦ Refurbished late 18C pub with restaurant in pretty hamlet. Characterful front bar and smart restaurant where contemporary style and well-regarded seasonal menus hold sway.

We try to be as accurate as possible when giving room rates.
But prices are susceptible to change,
so please check rates when booking.

STEVENAGE Herts. **504** T 28 *Great Britain G.* – pop. 81 482.

Env. : Knebworth House★ *AC*, S : 2½ m.

F_18, F_9 Aston Lane   *🅀* (01438) 880424 – F_18, F_9 Chesfield Downs, Jack's Hill, Graveley *🅀* (01462) 482929.

London 36 – Bedford 25 – Cambridge 27.

🏠 **Novotel Stevenage,** Knebworth Park, SG1 2AX, Southwest : 1½ m. by A 602 at junction 7 of A 1(M) *🅀* (01438) 346100, h0992@accor.com, Fax (01438) 723872, 🔲 heated – 🛗, ↔ rm, 🍽 rest, ♥ ♿ 🅿 – 🔼 120. 🆎 🆎 🅾 **VISA**
Rest a la carte 18.40/28.15 **s.** ♀ – 🖵 11.00 – **100 rm** ✝95.00 – ✝✝95.00.
◆ Modern hotel not far from Knebworth Park and Hatfield House. Large rooms with family facilities, some with sofa beds. Outdoor playground available and babysitting on request. Dining room with open kitchen area.

STEYNING W. Sussex **504** T 31 – pop. 9 501 (inc. Upper Beeding).

London 52 – Brighton 12 – Worthing 10.

🏠 **The Old Tollgate,** The Street, Bramber, BN44 3WE, Southwest : 1 m. *🅀* (01903) 879494, info@oldtollgatehotel.com, Fax (01903) 813399, 🌿 – 🛗 ↔ ♥ ♿ 🅿 🆎 🆎 🅾 **VISA**. ❀
Rest (carvery) 18.25/23.95 – 🖵 9.95 – **30 rm** ✝82.00 – ✝✝110.00.
◆ Once travellers had to stop here to pay toll; now it is a pleasant hotel offering hospitality and resting place. Spic and span rooms; pine furnishings. Renowned three-roomed carvery restaurant.

🏠 **Springwells** without rest., 9 High St, BN44 3GG, *🅀* (01903) 812446, contact@spring wells.co.uk, Fax (01903) 879823, ☎, 🔲 heated, 🌿 – 🅿 🆎 🆎 🅾 **VISA**
closed Christmas-New Year – **11 rm** 🖵 ✝59.00 – ✝✝95.00.
◆ Built in 1772, a picturesque former merchant's house in the heart of town. Tidy accommodation in pretty chintz; four-poster rooms on the first floor face the High Street.

at Ashurst North : 3½ m. on B 2135 – ✉ Steyning.

🍽 **The Fountain Inn,** BN44 3AP, *🅀* (01403) 710219, 🌿 – 🅿 🆎 **VISA**. ❀
restricted opening 25-26 December – **Rest** (closed Sunday dinner) a la carte 14.00/25.00 ♀.
◆ Former farmhouse dating from 1572, now an attractive pub with garden and pond. Interior oozes charm with low ceilings and beams galore. Freshly prepared traditional fare.

> Undecided between two equivalent establishments?
> Within each category, establishments are classified
> in our order of preference.

STILTON Cambs. **504** T 26 – pop. 2 500 – ✉ Peterborough.

London 76 – Cambridge 30 – Northampton 43 – Peterborough 6.

🏠 **Bell Inn,** Great North Rd, PE7 3RA, *🅀* (01733) 241066, reception@thebellstilton.co.uk, Fax (01733) 245173, 🌿 – ↔ 🅿 – 🔼 100. 🆎 🆎 🅾 **VISA**. ❀
closed 25 and 31 December – **Rest** (closed Saturday dinner) 25.95 ♀ – (see also **Village Bar** below) – **22 rm** 🖵 ✝72.50/79.50 – ✝✝129.50.
◆ A swinging red bell pub sign hangs outside this part 16C inn with garden. Deluxe bedrooms are individually styled; some retain original rafters and stonework. Nook-and-cranny galleried dining room with exposed stone walls.

🍽 **Village Bar** (at Bell Inn), Great North Rd, PE7 3RA, *🅀* (01733) 241066, reception@thebell stilton.co.uk, 🍴 – 🅿 🆎 **VISA**
Rest a la carte 19.20/27.20 **s.** ♀.
◆ As one would expect, Stilton cheese is used to full effect in this rustic bar, appearing in soups, dumplings, quiche and dressings. Blackboard specials to tickle tastebuds.

STOCK Essex **504** V 29.

London 38.5 – Brentwood 12 – Chelmsford 8.

🍴🍴 **Bear,** 16 The Square, CM4 9LH, *🅀* (01277) 829100, info@thebearinn.biz, Fax (01277) 841300, 🍴 – 🅿 🆎 🆎 **VISA**
closed 25 December, Sunday dinner and Monday – **Rest** 19.95 and a la carte 37.50/60.00 ♀.
◆ 16C former inn, featuring a noteworthy duck pond and terrace. Thick walls enhance rustic interior. Frequently changing modern menus in ground and first floor restaurants.

ENGLAND

679

STOCKBRIDGE *Hants.* 503 504 P 30.

> *London 75 – Salisbury 14 – Southampton 19 – Winchester 9.*

🛏 ❄ **The Greyhound** with rm, 31 High St, SO20 6EY, ✆ (01264) 810833, *heleneschoe man777@yahoo.co.uk, Fax (0870) 8912897,* 🍴, 🌳 – 📺 🅿. 🏧 *VISA* 🐾
closed 25-26 December, 1 January and dinner Bank Holidays – **Rest** *(closed Sunday dinner)* a la carte 20.00/38.50 ♀ – **8 rm** 🖵 ♦65.00 – ♦♦100.00.
Spec. Warm salad of ham hock and Puy lentils, broad bean dressing. Pan-fried halibut with boulangère potatoes, wild mushrooms and creamed leeks. Cinnamon rice pudding, candied orange zest.
♦ Characterful, low-beamed, yellow brick pub with aged wooden tables beside Test on smart high street.Contemporary dishes of carefully sourced ingredients. Sleek, airy bedrooms.

STOCKTON-ON-TEES *Stockton-on-Tees* 502 P 20 – pop. 80 060.

> 🏌 *Eaglescliffe, Yarm Rd* ✆ (01642) 780098 – 🏌 *Knotty Hill Golf Centre, Sedgefield* ✆ (01740) 620320 – 🏌 *Norton, Junction Rd* ✆ (01642) 676385.
> ✈ *Durham Tees Valley Airport :* ✆ (01325) 332811, SW : 6 m. by A 1027, A 135 and A 67.
> 🛈 *Stockton Central Library, Church Road* ✆ (01642) 521830.
> *London 251 – Leeds 61 – Middlesbrough 4 – Newcastle upon Tyne 39.*

🏨 **Parkmore,** 636 Yarm Rd, Eaglescliffe, TS16 0DH, South: 3 ½ m. on A 135 ✆ (01642) 786815, *enquiries@parkmorehotel.co.uk, Fax (01642) 790485,* 🛁, 🚲, 🏊 – 🌳 ✆ 🅿. – 🅰 120. 🏧 🅰🅴 *VISA*
Reeds at Six Three Six : Rest 18.75 (dinner) and a la carte 13.45/29.45 s. – 🖵 7.95 – **54 rm** ♦72.00/79.00 – ♦♦95.00/118.00, 1 suite.
♦ Built in 1896 for shipbuilding family; combines a sense of the old and new. Rooms are furnished in modern style; leisure and conference facilities also available. Dining room specialises in steak options.

STOKE BRUERNE *Northants.* 504 R 27 – ✉ *Towcester.*

> *London 69 – Coventry 33 – Leicester 44 – Northampton 9 – Oxford 33.*

✕✕ **Bruerne's Lock,** 5 The Canalside, NN12 7SB, ✆ (01604) 863654, *enquiries@bruernes lock.com, Fax (01604) 863330,* 🌳 – 🅿. 🏧 🅰🅴 *VISA*
closed Sunday dinner and Monday – **Rest** 16.50 (lunch) and a la carte 22.20/27.45 ♀.
♦ Georgian house overlooking the busy Grand Union Canal. Restaurant is modern in style with well-spaced tables. Flexible menus with Mediterranean base; themed gourmet evenings.

STOKE BY NAYLAND *Suffolk* 504 W 28.

> *London 70 – Bury St Edmunds 24 – Cambridge 54 – Colchester 11 – Ipswich 14.*

🏨 **The Stoke by Nayland,** Keepers Lane, Leavenheath, CO6 4PZ, Northwest : 1½ m. on B 1068 ✆ (01206) 262836, *hotelbookings@stokebynayland.com, Fax (01206) 263356,* 🛁, 🍴, 🏊, 🏌, 🍴 – 📶 🌳 ✆ 🕭 🅿. – 🅰 500. 🏧 🅰🅴 ⓪ *VISA* 🐾
closed 25 December**Rest** (bar lunch Monday-Saturday) (carvery lunch Sunday)/dinner 23.95 – **30 rm** 🖵 ♦99.00/109.00 – ♦♦129.00/139.00.
♦ Golfers will be in their element with a pro-shop, driving range and two courses tacking through 300 acres of woods and lakes. Neat, modern rooms; well-equipped spa and gym. Dining room overlooks the fairway.

🛏 **The Crown,** CO6 4SE, ✆ (01206) 262001, *thecrown@eoinns.co.uk, Fax (01206) 264026,* 🍴, 🌳 – 🅿. 🏧 *VISA*
closed 25-26 December – **Rest** (booking essential) a la carte 17.85/27.70 ♀ 🍷.
♦ 16C pub with smart terrace, huge garden and 21C style: spacious rooms offer variety of cool dining options. Locally renowned menus: a seasonal, modern take on classic dishes.

🛏 **The Angel Inn** with rm, Polstead St, CO6 4SA, ✆ (01206) 263245, *the.angel@tis cali.co.uk, Fax (01206) 263373,* 🍴 – 🌳 🅿. 🏧 🅰🅴 *VISA*
Rest a la carte 16.00/25.00 ♀ – **6 rm** 🖵 ♦70.00 – ♦♦85.00.
♦ 16C timbered inn, its original well is the dining room centrepiece; Speciality griddle dishes are well worth tucking into. Traditional rooms available.

STOKE CANON *Devon* 503 J 31 – see Exeter.

STOKE D'ABERNON *Surrey* 504 S 30 – see Cobham.

STOKE HOLY CROSS *Norfolk* 504 X 26 – see Norwich.

ENGLAND (side margin)

STOKEINTEIGNHEAD *Devon – see Torquay.*

STOKE MANDEVILLE *Bucks.* 504 R 28.
   London 41 – Aylesbury 4 – Oxford 26.

🏠 **The Wool Pack**, 21 Risborough Rd, HP22 5UP, 𝒫 (01296) 615970, *Fax (01296) 615971*,
   ➕ – **P.** **🅐🅔** **ⒶⒺ** **ⓄⒹ** **VISA**
   Rest a la carte 15.00/45.00 ℥.
   ◆ Attractive, part-thatched pub with pretty terrace. Low beams, roaring fire in front bar;
   airy rear restaurant serves appealing, well-priced menus with subtle Italian twists.

STOKENHAM *Devon* 503 I 33 *The West Country G.* – ✉ *Kingsbridge.*
   Env. : *Kingsbridge★, W : 5 m. by A 379.*
   Exc. : *Dartmouth★★, N : 9 m. by A 379.*
   London 225 – Plymouth 26 – Salcombe 11.

🏠 **The Tradesman's Arms**, TQ7 2SZ, 𝒫 (01548) 580313, *nick@thetradesmansarms.com*,
   Fax (01548) 580657, ➕ , 🌿 – 🚫 **P.** **🅐🅔** **VISA**
   Rest (booking essential) a la carte 17.95/25.00 ℥.
   ◆ Charming, personally run part-14C thatched inn with beamed bar and stone fireplace in
   delightful coastal village. Lots of character; neat garden. Local fish and game feature.

STOKE-ON-TRENT *Stoke-on-Trent* 502 503 504 N 24 *Great Britain G.* – *pop. 259 252.*
   See : *The Potteries Museum and Art Gallery★* Y **M** – *Gladstone Pottery Museum★* AC V.
   Env. : *The Wedgwood Story★ AC, S : 7 m. on A 500, A 34 and minor rd* V.
   Exc. : *Little Moreton Hall★★ AC, N : 10 m. by A 500 on A 34* U – *Biddulph Grange Garden★,*
   N : 7 m. by A 52, A 50 and A 527 U.
   🏌 *Greenway Hall, Stockton Brook* 𝒫 (01782) 503158, U – 🏌 *Parkhall, Hulme Rd, Weston*
   Coyney 𝒫 (01782) 599584, V.
   🛈 *Victoria Hall, Bagnall St, Hanley* 𝒫 (01782) 236000, *stoke.tic@virgin.net.*
   London 162 – Birmingham 46 – Leicester 59 – Liverpool 58 – Manchester 41 – Sheffield 53.

ENGLAND

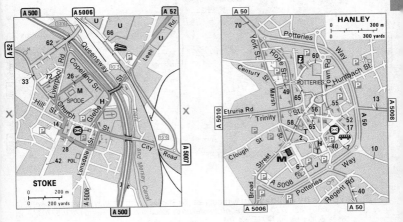

STOKE-ON-TRENT
NEWCASTLE-
UNDER-LYME

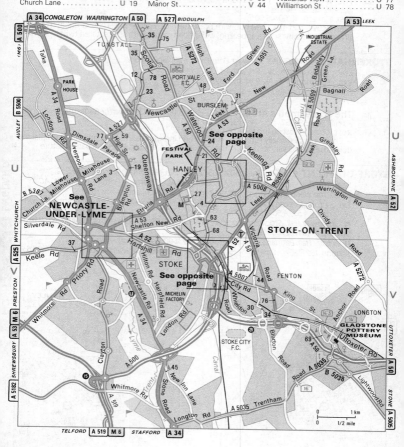

Express by Holiday Inn without rest., Sir Stanley Matthews Way, Trentham Lakes, ST4 4EG, *℘* (01782) 377000, *stokeontrent@expressholidayinn.co.uk*, Fax (01782) 377037 – 🏊
🌊 📞 🔥 🖵 – 🏛 30. 🐗 🖭 ⓪ **VISA**   V **a**
123 rm 🍴72.50/74.00 – 🍴🍴72.50/74.00.
   ◆ Purpose-built lodge in outskirts and next to Britannia Stadium. Fitted modern style throughout and a good level of facilities in the bedrooms.

Red = Pleasant. Look for the red 🍴 and 🏛 symbols.

STOKE POGES Bucks. 504 S 29 – pop. 4 112.

    📙₁₈, 📙₉ *Park Rd* ℰ (01753) 643332.

    London 30 – Aylesbury 28 – Oxford 44.

Stoke Park Club ⬥, Park Rd, SL2 4PG, ℰ (01753) 717171, *info@stokeparkclub.com*, Fax (01753) 717181, ⬚, ₣₅, 🖳, 📙₁₈, 📙₉, ⬦, ⬧, 🍴, ⬨ – 📶, ⬤ rest, 🖥 rest, 🄿 – 🔬 70. ⬤⬤ AE VISA ⬥

closed 24-26 December and 1-5 January – **Park :** Rest (residents only) (dinner only and Sunday lunch)/dinner 39.50 ⓨ – ⬚ 18.50 – **20 rm** ★285.00 – ★★400.00, 1 suite.

♦ A palatial hotel, all pillars, balconies and cupola with golf course where James Bond played Goldfinger in film. Rooms are impressive: antiques, marble baths, heated floors. Snug, plush chairs in relaxed brasserie with French posters on walls.

Stoke Place, Stoke Green, SL2 4HT, South : ½ m. by B 416 ℰ (01753) 534790, *enquiries@stokeplace.co.uk*, Fax (01753) 512743, ⬚, ₤, ⬧ ⬤ ⬦ 🄿 – 🔬 400. ⬤⬤ AE ⑩ VISA

Rest 25.00/35.00 and dinner a la carte 36.50/45.00 ⓨ – **29 rm** ⬚ ★150.00/180.00 – ★★150.00/180.00.

♦ 17C extended Queen Anne mansion in 22 acres with lake and geese. Boutique makeover has particularly benefitted Gloucester and Queen Anne rooms with their cool, sleek lines. Chic garden room restaurant serves fresh, local modern menus.

STOKE PRIOR Worcs. – see Bromsgrove.

STOKE ROW Oxon..

    London 45.5 – Henley-on-Thames 6 – Reading 10.

The Cherry Tree Inn with rm, RG9 5QA, ℰ (01491) 680430, *info@thecherrytreeinn.com*, Fax (01491) 682168, ⬩, ⬦ – ⬧ 🄿 ⬤⬤ VISA ⬥

closed 25-26 December and 1 January – **Rest** a la carte 20.00/25.00 ⓨ – **4 rm** ⬚ ★65.00 – ★★85.00.

♦ 17C inn with an impressive 21C refurbishment: bags of charm and character typified by low ceiling and beams. Platefuls of good value dishes offering eclectic mix. Plush rooms.

STOKESLEY N. Yorks. 502 Q 20 Great Britain G. – pop. 4 725 – ✉ Middlesbrough.

    Env. : Great Ayton (Captain Cook Birthplace Museum★ AC), NE : 2½ m. on A 173.

    London 239 – Leeds 59 – Middlesbrough 8 – Newcastle upon Tyne 49 – York 52.

Chapter's with rm, 27 High St, TS9 5AD, ℰ (01642) 711888, *enquiries@chaptershotel.co.uk*, Fax (01642) 713387, ⬚ – ⬧ ⬤, 🖥 rest, ⬦ ⬤⬤ AE VISA

closed 17-24 September, 25-26 December and 1 January – **Rest** (closed Sunday-Monday) (dinner only) a la carte 22.15/34.75 ⓨ – **13 rm** ⬚ ★66.00/70.00 – ★★80.00.

♦ Solid, mellow brick Victorian house with colour washed rooms. Bistro style dining with strong Mediterranean colour scheme. Eclectic menu: classics and more modern dishes.

STOKE SUB HAMDON Somerset 503 L 31 – see Yeovil.

STON EASTON Somerset 503 504 M 30 – ✉ Bath (Bath & North East Somerset).

    London 131 – Bath 12 – Bristol 11 – Wells 7.

Ston Easton Park ⬥, BA3 4DF, ℰ (01761) 241631, *info@stoneaston.co.uk*, Fax (01761) 241377, ⬰, ₤, ⬧ – ⬧ ⬦ 🄿 ⬤⬤ AE VISA

The Cedar Tree : Rest (booking essential for non-residents) 22.50/44.50 ⓨ – **21 rm** ⬚ ★125.00/356.00 – ★★155.00/420.00, 1 suite.

♦ Aristocratic Palladian mansion; grounds designed by Humphrey Repton, through which river Norr flows. Lavish rooms: Grand Saloon with Kentian plasterwork. 18C style bedrooms. Formal restaurant served by a Victorian kitchen garden.

STORRINGTON W. Sussex 504 S 31 – pop. 7 727.

    London 54 – Brighton 20 – Portsmouth 36.

Old Forge, 6 Church St, RH20 4LA, ℰ (01903) 743402, *enquiry@oldforge.co.uk*, Fax (01903) 742540 – ⬤⬤ AE VISA

closed 2 weeks in spring and autumn, Saturday lunch, Sunday dinner and Monday-Wednesday – **Rest** 18.00/34.00 ⬚.

♦ Appealing whitewashed and brick cottages with three dining rooms bearing all hallmarks of flavoursome traditional cuisine. Array of cheeses; fine wine from small producers.

STOURPORT-ON-SEVERN Worcs. 503 504 N 26 – pop. 18 899.
London 137 – Birmingham 21 – Worcester 12.

Stourport Manor, Hartlebury Rd, DY13 9JA, East : 1¼ m. on B 4193 *✆ (01299) 289955, stourport@menzies-hotels.co.uk, Fax (01299) 878520,* **Ⅰ₆, ≘ₛ, ⬜, ☞, ☜, ✼,** squash – ‡⇆ **P** – **益** 350. **🐼 🎫 ⒶⒺ ⓪ 𝘝𝘐𝘚𝘈**
The Brasserie : Rest 13.95/19.95 and a la carte 24.00/32.00 s. ♀ – ☑ 14.95 – **66 rm** ✿125.00 – ✿✿125.00, 2 suites.
◆ Gracious country house, once home to former prime minister, Stanley Baldwin. Lovely, warm-hued lounge; wide-ranging indoor leisure facilities. Bedrooms are nicely spacious. Brasserie overlooks the garden; wide ranging menus.

STOURTON Wilts.
London 112 – Shaftesbury 12 – Wincanton 10.

The Spread Eagle Inn with rm, Church Lawn, BA12 6QE, *✆ (01747) 840954,* ☞ – ‡⇆ **P. 🐼 𝘝𝘐𝘚𝘈. ✼**
closed 25 December – Rest a la carte 19.20/22.00 – **5 rm** ☑ ✿60.00/70.00 – ✿✿70.00/98.00.
◆ Located within the stunning grounds of Stourhead House, this 18C pub has a front bar and two rear burgundy rooms, serving locally sourced menus. Simple, well-kept rooms.

STOW-ON-THE-WOLD Glos. 503 504 O 28 Great Britain G. – pop. 2 074.
Exc. : Chastleton House★★, NE : 6½ m. by A 436 and A 44.
🅱 Hollis House, The Square *✆ (01451) 831082.*
London 86 – Birmingham 44 – Gloucester 27 – Oxford 30.

Wyck Hill House ⟡, GL54 1HY, South : 2¼ m. by A 429 on A 424 *✆ (01451) 831936, enquiries@wyckhillhouse.com, Fax (01451) 832243,* ⟨, ☞, ≘ₛ, ☞, ☜ – 🛗 ‡⇆, ▦ rest, ✆ Ꮽ **P** – **益** 150. **🐼 ⒶⒺ 𝘝𝘐𝘚𝘈**
Rest 12.50/32.50 – **31 rm** ☑ ✿129.00 – ✿✿180.00/287.00, 1 suite.
◆ Handsome 18C mansion set in 100-acre grounds above Windrush Valley. Panelled drawing rooms; quiet and characterful rooms in the old wing, coach house and modern orangery. Conservatory restaurant with wold views.

Grapevine, Sheep St, GL54 1AU, *✆ (01451) 830344, enquiries@vines.co.uk, Fax (01451) 832278,* ☞ – ‡⇆ ⚲ **P.** – **益** 25. **🐼 ⒶⒺ ⓪ 𝘝𝘐𝘚𝘈**
The Conservatory : Rest 19.50/33.00 ♀ – *Lavigna :* Rest a la carte 16.95/23.45 – **22 rm** ☑ ✿85.00 – ✿✿160.00.
◆ Among the antique shops, two extended 17C houses. Rooms in bright, modern décor with a nod to tradition, half with beams and bare stone. Timbered bar; sepia photos of Stow. In Conservatory black grapes hang from spreading vine. Easy-going, informal Lavigna.

The Royalist, Digbeth St, GL56 1BN, *✆ (01451) 830670, enquiries@theroyalistho tel.com, Fax (01451) 870048* – ‡⇆ ⚲ **P. 🐼 ⒶⒺ 𝘝𝘐𝘚𝘈**
947 AD : Rest *(closed Sunday-Wednesday in winter)* 15.95 (lunch) and a la carte 18.00/35.00 ♀ – (see also *Eagle & Child* below) – **14 rm** ☑ ✿99.00 – ✿✿130.00.
◆ Historic high street inn - reputedly England's oldest. Comfortable, stylish rooms, individual in shape and décor and quieter at the rear. Two-room bar in exposed stone. Intimate, beamed restaurant offers fine dining: inglenook fireplace.

Fosse Manor, Fosse Way, GL54 1JX, South : 1¼ m. on A 429 *✆ (01451) 830354, enqui ries@fossemanor.co.uk, Fax (01451) 832486,* ☞, ☞ – ‡⇆ **P.** – **益** 45. **🐼 ⒶⒺ 𝘝𝘐𝘚𝘈**
Rest a la carte 22.50/33.50 ♀ – **19 rm** ☑ ✿95.00 – ✿✿130.00.
◆ Former coaching inn on the main road. Contemporary public areas with informal feel. Up-to-date bedrooms, some of which are set in the coach house. Lunch available in bar. Classically proportioned dining room with menu of Mediterranean favourites.

Crestow House without rest., GL54 1JX, at junction of A 429 on B 4068 Lower Swell rd *✆ (01451) 830969, fsimonetti@btinternet.com,* ⟨, ≘ₛ, ☒ heated, ☞ – ‡⇆ **P. 🐼 𝘝𝘐𝘚𝘈. ✼**
closed 24-25 December – **4 rm** ☑ ✿50.00 – ✿✿75.00.
◆ Victorian manor house with conservatory, garden and pool. Breakfast served in family style. Well-appointed rooms larger at front or smaller at rear overlooking the garden.

Number Nine without rest., 9 Park St, GL54 1AQ, *✆ (01451) 870333, enquiries@num ber-nine.info* – ‡⇆. **🐼 𝘝𝘐𝘚𝘈. ✼**
3 rm ☑ ✿45.00/50.00 – ✿✿60.00/70.00.
◆ Ivy-clad 18C Cotswold stone house run by friendly owners on the high street. Winding staircase leads to the large bedrooms which occupy each floor.

X
The Old Butchers, 7 Park St, GL54 1AQ, ℰ (01451) 831700, *louise@theoldbutch ers.com, Fax (01451) 831388,* 🍴 – 🔲. 🐼 *VISA*
closed 1 week May and 1 week October – Rest a la carte 19.00/26.50 **s.** ⅋.
♦ Former butcher's shop of Cotswold stone: closely set tables in a very busy, modern restaurant. Daily changing, affordable, modish menus feature prominent use of local produce.

🏠
Eagle & Child (at The Royalist H.), Digbeth St, GL54 1BN, ℰ (01451) 830670, *enqui ries@theroyalisthotel.com, Fax (01451) 870048* – 🍴. 🐼 🗚 *VISA*
Rest a la carte 20.00/35.00 ⅋.
♦ Stone pub attached to an inn; conservatory to the rear. Atmospheric dining room: soft lighting, flagstones, beams. Robust cooking: plenty of choice.

at Upper Oddington *East : 2 m. by A 436* – ⊠ *Stow-on-the-Wold.*

🏠
Horse and Groom with rm, GL56 0XH, ℰ (01451) 830584, *info@horseand groom.uk.com,* 🍴 , 🌳 – 🍴 P. 🐼 *VISA*. 🍴
Rest a la carte 18.00/25.00 ⅋ – **7 rm** ⌖ 60.00/70.00 – ★★78.00/89.00.
♦ Part 16C former coaching inn in rural hamlet. Long, split-level interior with beams and open fires. Modern pub food from a regularly changing menu. Cottage-style bedrooms.

at Lower Oddington *East : 3 m. by A 436* – ⊠ *Stow-on-the-Wold.*

🏠
The Fox Inn with rm, GL56 0UR, ℰ (01451) 870555, *info@foxinn.net, Fax (01451) 870669,* 🍴 , 🌳 – 🍴 rm, P. 🐼 *VISA*
closed 25 December – Rest (booking essential) a la carte 17.95/27.65 – **3 rm** ⌖ 68.00 – ★★95.00.
♦ 16C ivy dressed pub in a charming village. Flag floors, beams, fireplaces, nooks, crannies, books and candlelight. Hearty English fare. Sumptuously decorated rooms.

at Daylesford *East : 3½ m. by A 436* – ⊠ *Stow-on-the-Wold.*

X
The Cafe at Daylesford Organic, GL56 0YG, ℰ (01608) 731700, *enquiries@day lesfordorganic.com, Fax (01608) 731701,* 🍴 – 🍴 P. 🐼 🗚 ⓪ *VISA*
closed 1 January and 25-27 December – Rest - Organic - (lunch only) (bookings not accepted) a la carte 18.85/30.85.
♦ Beautifully designed farm shop, spa, yoga centre and two-floor café, which becomes very busy, as punters tuck into tasty dishes where all ingredients are organically sourced.

at Bledington *(Oxon.) Southeast : 4 m. by A 436 on B 4450* – ⊠ *Kingham.*

🏠
The Kings Head Inn, The Green, OX7 6XQ, ℰ (01608) 658365, *kingshead@orr-ew ing.com, Fax (01608) 658902,* 🍴 – 🍴 rm, P. 🐼 *VISA*
closed 25-26 December – Rest a la carte 23.00/30.00 ⅋ – **12 rm** ⌖ 55.00/60.00 – ★★70.00/125.00.
♦ 15C inn on the green, oozing style, charm and personality: stone floors, beams, open fires. Confident cooking with good flavour combinations. Timbered or modern annex rooms.

at Lower Swell *West : 1¼ m. on B 4068* – ⊠ *Stow-on-the-Wold.*

🏠
Rectory Farmhouse without rest., GL54 1LH, by Rectory Barns Rd ℰ (01451) 832351, *rectory.farmhouse@cw-warwick.co.uk,* 🌳 – 🍴 P. 🍴
closed Christmas and New Year – **3 rm** ⌖ 55.00 – ★★85.00/90.00.
♦ 17C former farmhouse of Cotswold stone. Bedrooms are very comfortable and decorated in distinctive cottage style. Communal breakfast at family table.

STRATFIELD TURGIS *Hants.* 503 504 Q 29 – ⊠ *Basingstoke.*
London 46 – Basingstoke 8 – Reading 11 – Southampton 37.

🏨
Wellington Arms, RG27 0AS, on A 33 ℰ (01256) 882214, *wellington.arms@virgin.net, Fax (01256) 882934,* 🌳 – P. 🛎 200. 🐼 🗚 ⓪ *VISA*
Rest a la carte 16.45/30.00 ⅋ – **30 rm** ⌖ 98.00/120.00 – ★★140.00/160.00.
♦ 17C farmhouse on the Duke of Wellington Estate. The "pièce de résistance" is the lounge-bar with log fire and sofas. Bedrooms are pine furnished in quiet colour schemes. Homely dining room; window seats are particularly popular.

> Your opinions are important to us:
> please write and let us know about your discoveries and experiences –
> good and bad!

STRATFORD-UPON-AVON *Warks. 503 504* P 27 *Great Britain G. – pop. 22 187.*

See : *Town★★ - Shakespeare's Birthplace★ AC,* AB.
Env. : *Mary Arden's House★ AC, NW : 4 m. by A 3400 A.*
Exc. : *Ragley Hall★ AC, W : 9 m. by A 422 A.*

ⁿ⁸ *Tiddington Rd ℰ (01789) 205749,* B
ⁿ⁸ *Welcombe Hotel, Warwick Rd ℰ (01789) 413800,* B
ⁿ⁸ *Stratford Oaks, Bearley Rd, Snitterfield ℰ (01789) 731980,* B.
🛈 *Bridgefoot ℰ (0870) 1607930, stratfordtic@shakespeare-country.co.uk.*
London 96 – Birmingham 23 – Coventry 18 – Leicester 44 – Oxford 40.

STRATFORD-
UPON-AVON

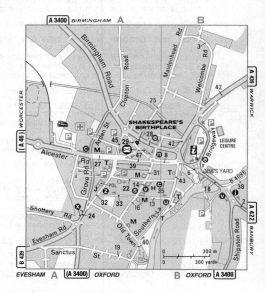

🏨 **Ettington Park** ⌂, Alderminster, CV37 8BU, Southeast : 6 ¼ m. on A 3400 ℰ (01789) 450123, *ettingtonpark@handpicked.co.uk,* Fax (01789) 450472, ⓢ, ◲, ⌇, 🐎, ⌛, ※ – 📶, ✲ rest, ఉ, 🅿 – 🕍 100, ✲ 🅰🅴 🆅🅸🆂🅰
Rest (dinner only and Sunday lunch) 30.00 and a la carte 39.00/45.50 ♀ – **43 rm** ⌕ ✦110.00/130.00 – ✦✦129.00/179.00, 5 suites.
 ◆ Imposing, corporate friendly, Gothic mansion with sympathetic extensions in attractive grounds. Ornate ceilings, classic country house feel. Comfy, well-equipped bedrooms. Oak-panelled dining room with medieval feel.

🏨 **Welcombe H. & Golf Course,** Warwick Rd, CV37 0NR, Northeast : 1 ½ m. on A 439 ℰ (01789) 295252, *welcombe@menzies-hotels.co.uk,* Fax (01789) 414666, ⟨, ⓠ, ℔, ⓢ, ◲, ⌇, 🐎, ⌛ – ✲ 🅿 – 🕍 100. 🅼🅾 🅰🅴 🆅🅸🆂🅰 ✄
Trevelyan : Rest *(closed Saturday lunch)* a la carte 28.25/35.50 – **73 rm** ⌕ ✦95.00/155.00 – ✦✦95.00/175.00, 5 suites.
 ◆ Jacobean house built 1869; sweeping Italian gardens and gracious, oak panelled interiors. Grand rooms in main house with many antique features. Golf course overlooks Avon. Savour views of gardens, fountain and waterfall from restaurant.

🏨 **Alveston Manor,** Clopton Bridge, CV37 8EA, ℰ (0870) 4008181, *sales.alvestonmanor@macdonald-hotels.co.uk,* Fax (01789) 414095, 🌳, ⓠ, ℔, ⓢ, ◲, 🐎 – ✲ ⓦ 🅿 – 🕍 120. ⓠ 🅼🅾 🅰🅴 ⓞ 🆅🅸🆂🅰   B i
The Manor Grill : Rest (bar lunch Monday-Saturday)/dinner 28.00 and a la carte 35.00/46.00 s. ♀ – **109 rm** ⌕ ✦70.00/195.00 – ✦✦80.00/205.00, 4 suites.
 ◆ Part Elizabethan manor where "A Midsummer's Night Dream" was first performed beneath the cedar tree in the grounds. Richly decorated period rooms; modern rooms in extension. Seasoned oak panelling in medieval dining room.

Holiday Inn, Bridgefoot, CV37 6YR, ℰ (0870) 2254701, *stratford@qmh-hotel.com,* Fax (01789) 298589, ₣ₔ, ⇌, 🔲, – 📱 – |🛎| ✦ rm, 📶 📞 ♿ 🅿 – 🎖 600. 🆗 ⓐ 🆎 ⑩ *VISA*
🍽️
B e
The Riverside : Rest (bar lunch Monday-Saturday) (carving rest.) 20.00 – **257 rm** ⚏ ✦75.00/180.00 – ✦✦75.00/180.00, 2 suites.
◆ Overlooking the river Avon with imposing open reception area. Close to all sights, including Warwick Castle, for which discounts are available. Spacious, comfortable rooms. Spacious informality at The Riverside.

Stratford Victoria, Arden St, CV37 6QQ, ℰ (01789) 271000, *stratfordvictoria@mar* stonhotels.com, Fax (01789) 271001, ₣ₔ – |🛎| ✦, 🍽 rest, 🅿 – 🎖 140. 🆗 ⓐ 🆎 ⑩
🍽️
A c
Rest (carvery lunch Sunday) 15.50 and a la carte 25.00/30.00 **s.** 🍷 – **101 rm** ⚏ ✦89.00/115.00 – ✦✦85.00/130.00, 1 suite.
◆ Situated near a train station; built on site of a former 19C hospital and designed in Victorian style. Retains original gardens; modern, nicely decorated rooms. Discreet dining room where British classics play centre stage.

The Shakespeare, Chapel St, CV37 6ER, ℰ (0870) 400 8182, *general.shake* speare@macdonald-hotels.co.uk, Fax (01789) 415411 – |🛎| ✦ 📞 🅿 – 🎖 100. 🆗 ⓐ 🆎 ⑩
VISA
A v
David Garrick : Rest (dinner only and Sunday lunch) 25.00/38.00 and a la carte 29.00/38.00 **s.** 🍷 – **73 rm** ⚏ ✦85.00/135.00 – ✦✦130.00/230.00, 1 suite.
◆ Exudes atmosphere with gabled façade, leaded windows; this 18C inn was once a writers' watering hole. Afternoon tea served in vintage lounge; rooms with modern furnishings. Medieval styled restaurant; abundance of tried-and-tested dishes.

Thistle Stratford-Upon-Avon, Waterside, CV37 6BA, ℰ (01789) 294949, *stratfor* duponavon@thistle.co.uk, Fax (0870) 333 9246, 🌳, – ✦ 🅿 – 🎖 50. 🆗 ⓐ 🆎 ⑩
VISA
B u
Bards : Rest 12.95 (lunch) and a la carte approx 25.00 – ⚏ 10.50 – **63 rm** ✦162.00/182.00 – ✦✦182.00/170.00.
◆ A compact hotel opposite the renowned RSC and birthplace of the bard. Themed weekends such as murder mysteries are popular. Well-equipped bedrooms. Bustling restaurant with a formal, elegant style.

Stratford Manor, Warwick Rd, CV37 0PY, Northeast : 3 m. on A 439 ℰ (01789) 731173, *stratfordmanor@marstonhotels.com,* Fax (01789) 731131, ₣ₔ, ⇌, 🔲, 🏊, 🎾 – |🛎| ✦, 🍽 rest, 🅿 – 🎖 350. 🆗 ⓐ 🆎 ⑩ *VISA*. 🍽️
Rest (closed Saturday lunch) 24.50/33.50 **s.** 🍷 – **104 rm** ⚏ ✦132.50 – ✦✦171.00.
◆ Three miles from Stratford and Warwick, this modern, well located hotel enjoys 21 acres of surrounding countryside. Murals, arresting meeting room and ample bedrooms within. Popular restaurant with traditional palette.

Swans Nest without rest., Bridgefoot, CV37 7LT, ℰ (01789) 266804, Fax (01789) 414547, 🌳 – ✦ 📞 🅿 – 🎖 150. 🆗 ⓐ 🆎 ⑩ *VISA*. 🍽️
B v
⚏ 13.95 – **67 rm** ✦65.00/130.00 – ✦✦75.00/140.00.
◆ Part 17C house in pleasant setting with courtyard garden and river frontage close to town centre and Royal Shakespeare Theatre. Rooms boast minibar, interactive television.

The Payton without rest., 6 John St, CV37 6UB, ℰ (01789) 266442, *info@payton.co.uk,* Fax (01789) 266442 – ✦. 🆗 *VISA*. 🍽️
A e
closed 24 December - 2 January – **5 rm** ⚏ ✦59.00/65.00 – ✦✦59.00/72.00.
◆ Pretty, white Grade II listed Georgian town house built in 1832 in quiet conservation area. Pale, pastel coloured bedrooms and small neat breakfast room.

Victoria Spa Lodge without rest., Bishopton Lane, CV37 9QY, Northwest : 2 m. by A 3400 on Bishopton Lane turning left at roundabout with A 46 ℰ (01789) 267985, ptozer@victoriaspalodge.demon.co.uk, Fax (01789) 204728, 🌳 – ✦ 🅿. 🆗 *VISA*. 🍽️
closed 24-26 and 31 December and 1 January – **7 rm** ⚏ ✦50.00 – ✦✦65.00.
◆ Built as spa, hotel and pump room; Queen Victoria stayed as one of its many guests, testified by the gables which bear her coat of arms. Pristine rooms are among its charms.

Virginia Lodge without rest., 12 Evesham Pl, CV37 6HT, ℰ (01789) 292157, pamela83@btinternet.com, Fax (01789) 292157, 🌳 – ✦ 🆗 *VISA*. 🍽️
A x
closed 23-27 December – **7 rm** ⚏ ✦20.00/55.00 – ✦✦60.00.
◆ Family friendly Victorian house; pretty lounge in cottage style; individually decorated rooms named after furnishings: Laura Ashley and Country Manor.

Malbec, 6 Union St, CV37 6QT, ℰ (01789) 269106, *eatmalbec@aol.com,* Fax (01789) 269106 – ✦. 🆗 *VISA*
A n
closed 1 week Easter, 1 week May/June, 1 week October, Christmas, Sunday, Monday, and Tuesday following Bank Holidays – **Rest** a la carte 14.00/28.00 **s.** 🍷.
◆ Pleasant modern restaurant with atmospheric barrel ceiling in intimate basement. Good value set menus: accomplished à la carte with season's larder bolstering a classic base.

X **Lambs**, 12 Sheep St, CV37 6EF, *℘* (01789) 292554, *eat@lambsrestaurant.co.uk,*
Fax (01789) 293372 – **①⊙** **VISA**   B C
closed 25-26 December – **Rest** 15.00/20.00 and a la carte 21.40/32.15 ⓥ⊙ ♀.
* 16C town house with zesty bistro-style cooking in old-world surrounds of white wattle
walls, rafters and well-spaced wooden tables.

at Alveston *East : 2 m. by B 4086* – B – ⊠ *Stratford-upon-Avon.*

🍴 **The Baraset Barn**, 1 Pimlico Lane, CV37 7RF, on B 4086 *℘* (01789) 295510, *baraset*
barn@lovelypubs.co.uk, Fax (01789) 292961, ⌂ – ↞ ▤ **P.**⟱ 14. **①⊙** **VISA**. ⅋
closed 25 December – **Rest** *(closed Sunday dinner)* 14.00 (lunch) and a la carte
20.00/40.00 ♀.
* 200 year-old pub given a sumptuous contemporary makeover. Decked terrace; stylish lounge
conservatory; family dining in barn or mezzanine: bold, freshly prepared modern cooking.

at Lower Quinton *Southwest : 6½ m. by A 3400* – B – *and B 4632* – ⊠ *Stratford-upon-Avon.*

🍴 **The College Arms** with rm, CV37 8SG, *℘* (01789) 720342, *mail@collegearms.co.uk,*
Fax (01789) 720392, ⌂ , ⋘ – ↞ **P.**⟱ 12. **①⊙** **VISA**. ⅋
Rest *(closed Sunday dinner)* 17.00 and a la carte 20.00/35.00 ♀ – **4 rm** ⊃ ✦55.00/65.00 –
✦✦65.00/70.00.
* Part 16C pub with beams, inglenook and solid stone surrounds. Ideal watering hole for
those on the tourist trail. Menus offer plenty of choice. Cosy, well maintained bedrooms.

at Ardens Grafton *Southwest : 5 m. by A 46* – A – ⊠ *Stratford-upon-Avon.*

🍴 **The Golden Cross**, Wixford Rd, B50 4LG, South : ¼ m. *℘* (01789) 772420, *steve@the*
goldencross.net, Fax (01789) 491358, ⌂ – **P.** **①⊙** **AE** **①** **VISA**. ⅋
Rest *(closed Sunday dinner)* a la carte 16.00/25.00.
* Solid stone floor, exposed beams, open fire, scrubbed wooden furnishing: all the winning ingredients for a welcoming pub. Freshly prepared dishes with tasty seasonal base.

at Billesley *West : 4½ m. by A 422* – A – *off A 46* – ⊠ *Stratford-upon-Avon.*

🏰 **Billesley Manor** ॐ, B49 6NF, *℘* (01789) 279955, *info@billesleymanor.co.uk,*
Fax (01789) 764145, ⩽, ⓓ, **I₅,** ⇌, ◨, ⋘, ⅌ – ↞ ℂ **P.** – ▲ 120. **①⊙** **AE** **①** **VISA**. ⅋
The Stuart : **Rest** 17.50/37.50 and dinner a la carte 24.00/41.00 s. ♀ – **70 rm** ⊃
✦125.00/195.00 – ✦✦295.00/350.00, 2 suites.
* Topiary garden and ornamental pond complements lovely 16C manor. The oak panelled
interior evokes its past: Shakespeare reputedly used the library. Modern and period rooms.
Original 16C oak panelling in restaurant.

STREATLEY *Newbury* **503 504** Q 29 *Great Britain G.* – *pop. 3 924 (inc. Goring)* – ⊠ *Goring.*
Env. : *Basildon Park*★ **AC**, SE : 2½ m. by A 329 – *Mapledurham*★ **AC**, E : 6 m. by A 329, B 471
and B 4526.
Exc. : *Ridgeway Path*★★.
🏌 *Goring & Streatley, Rectory Rd* *℘* (01491) 873229.
London 56 – Oxford 16 – Reading 11.

🏰 **The Swan at Streatley**, High St, RG8 9HR, *℘* (01491) 878800, *sales@swan-at-streat*
ley.co.uk, Fax (01491) 872554, ⩽ River Thames, ⌂, **I₅,** ⇌, ◨, ⇌ – ↧ ↞ ⅋ **P.** – ▲ 120.
①⊙ **AE** **①** **VISA**
Cygnetures : **Rest** a la carte 30.40/42.95 ♀ – **44 rm** ⊃ ✦110.00/140.00 –
✦✦138.00/150.00, 1 suite.
* Attractive riverside views to be savoured from large windows of most bedrooms, some
having patios and balconies. Hotel's business nature benefits from Thames-side location.
Nautically themed restaurant overlooking the water.

STRETE *Devon* – *see Dartmouth.*

STRETTON *Ches.* **502 503 504** M 23 – *see Warrington.*

STRETTON *Rutland* – *see Stamford.*

STRETTON *Staffs.* **502 503 504** P 25 – *see Burton-upon-Trent.*

STROUD *Glos.* **503 504** N 28 – *pop. 32 052.*
🏌₁₈, 🏌₁₈, 🏌₁₈ *Minchinhampton* *℘* (01453) 832642 (old course) (01453) 833840 (new course) –
🏌₁₈ *Painswick* *℘* (01452) 812180.
🅱 *Subscription Rooms, George St* *℘* (01453) 760960.
London 113 – Bristol 30 – Gloucester 9.

at Brimscombe *Southeast : 2¼ m. on A 419 –* ☒ *Stroud.*

🏠 **Burleigh Court** ⌂, Burleigh Lane, GL5 2PF, South : ½ m. by Burleigh rd via The Roundabouts ℘ (01453) 883804, *info@burleighcourthotel.co.uk,* Fax (01453) 886870, ≤, ⌂, ☞
– ⇔ 🅿. ⓜⓞ ⓞ 𝘝𝘐𝘚𝘈
Rest 22.95/29.50 and a la carte 19.50/29.50 ☲ – **18 rm** ☲ ✝85.00 – ✝✝125.00/170.00.
♦ 18C manor house on edge of a steep hill overlooking Golden Valley. Swimming pool in closeted garden of hidden pathways and stone walls. Homely bedrooms with views. Regency style dining room overlooks terraced gardens.

STUCKTON *Hants. – see Fordingbridge.*

STUDLAND *Dorset 503 504 O 32.*
London 135 – Bournemouth 25 – Southampton 53 – Weymouth 29.

✗ **Shell Bay,** Ferry Rd, BH19 3BA, North : 3 m. or via car ferry from Sandbanks ℘ (01929) 450363, *Fax (01929) 450570,* ≤ Poole Harbour and Brownsea Island, ☞ – ⬛. ⓜⓞ ⒶⒺ 𝘝𝘐𝘚𝘈
closed January and weekends only in winter – **Rest** - Seafood - a la carte 27.00/36.45.
♦ Hut-like appearance, but in a spectacular location with views of Poole Harbour and Brownsea Island. Inside, large windows and mirrors make the most of this. Seafood emphasis.

STUDLEY *Warks. 503 504 O 27 – pop. 6 257 –* ☒ *Redditch.*
London 109 – Birmingham 15 – Coventry 33 – Gloucester 39.

✗✗ **Peppers,** 45 High St, B80 7HN, ℘ (01527) 853183 – ▤. ⓜⓞ 𝘝𝘐𝘚𝘈
closed 25 December – **Rest** - Indian - (dinner only) 28.50 and a la carte 11.65/22.60.
♦ Fresh, authentic Indian food served by committed, friendly staff. Balance of flavour and spice in "something for everyone" dishes. Speciality cocktails.

STURMINSTER NEWTON *Dorset 503 504 N 31 The West Country G. – pop. 2 317.*
See : *Mill*★ *AC.*
London 123 – Bournemouth 30 – Bristol 49 – Salisbury 28 – Taunton 41.

✗✗✗ **Plumber Manor** ⌂ with rm, DT10 2AF, Southwest : 1 ¾ m. by A 357 on Hazelbury Bryan rd ℘ (01258) 472507, *book@plumbermanor.com,* Fax (01258) 473370, ≤, ☞, ☲, ✗✗
– 🅿 – ⅍ 25. ⓜⓞ ⒶⒺ 𝘝𝘐𝘚𝘈
closed February – **Rest** (dinner only and Sunday lunch)/dinner 26.00 – **16 rm** ☲
✝95.00/110.00 – ✝✝170.00.
♦ Secluded 18C manor house owned by the same family since it was first built. Three dining rooms where assured, popular dishes are served. Well-kept rooms, some with antiques.

SUMMERCOURT *Cornwall 503 F 32 –* ☒ *Newquay.*
London 263 – Newquay 9 – Plymouth 45.

✗ **Viners,** Carvynick (Golf & Country Club), TR8 5AF, Northwest : 1 ½ m. of the junction of
A 30 and A 3058 ℘ (01872) 510544, *Fax (01872) 510468,* ☞ – ⇔ 🅿 ⅍ 25. ⓜⓞ 𝘝𝘐𝘚𝘈. ✑
closed 4 weeks in winter – **Rest** *(closed Sunday dinner late October-Whitsun and Monday dinner mid September-mid July)* (dinner only and Sunday lunch)/dinner a la carte 26.85/33.75 ☲.
♦ 17C pub with grey stone exterior and rustic interior boasting original beams. Welcoming ambience. Buzzy restaurant offers a creative, but very affordable, style of cooking.

SUNDERLAND *Tyne and Wear 501 502 P 19 – pop. 280 807.*
See : *National Glass Centre*★ A.
🅶 *Whitburn, Lizard Lane, South Shields* ℘ *(0191) 529 2144.*
🅱 *50 Fawcett St* ℘ *(0191) 553 2000, tourist.info@sunderland.gov.uk.*
London 272 – Leeds 92 – Middlesbrough 29 – Newcastle upon Tyne 12.

Plan on next page

🏠 **Sunderland Marriott,** Queens Parade, Seaburn, SR6 8DB, ℘ (0870) 4007287, *mhrs.nclsl.reservations@marriotthotels.com,* Fax (0870) 4007387, ≤, ♨, ☎, ▧ – ⧈ ⇔,
▤ rest, ⅋ 🅿 – ⅍ 300. ⓜⓞ ⒶⒺ ⓞ 𝘝𝘐𝘚𝘈
A e
Rest a la carte 19.85/34.65 **s.** – ☲ 14.95 – **82 rm** ✝135.00 – ✝✝160.00.
♦ Overlooks Whitburn Sands. A smart, contemporary, branded commercial hotel. Equally modern bedrooms with stylish, comfortable facilities. Restaurant and bar dining alternatives.

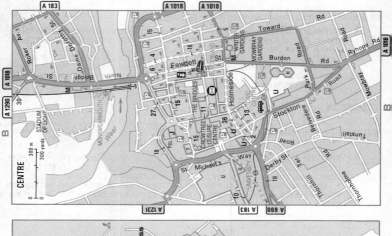

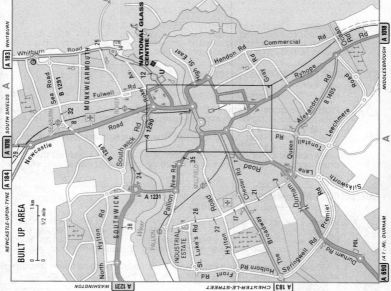

SUNDERLAND

SUNNINGDALE _Berks._ 504 S 29.

%%% **Bluebells,** Shrubbs Hill, London Rd, SL5 0LE, Northeast : ¾ m. on A 30 _&_ (01344) 622722, _info@bluebells-restaurant.com, Fax_ (01344) 620990, 🌳 – ✂ 🖥 📺 ✿ 14. 📶 ﹝AE﹞ **VISA**
closed 25-26 December and Monday – **Rest** 19.95 (lunch) and dinner a la carte 28.75/44.65 ♀.
   ♦ Smart, well-manicured façade matched by sophisticated interior of deep green. Large rear terrace, deck and garden. Modern British cooking with original starting point.

SUNNINGHILL _Windsor & Maidenhead_ 504 S 29 – _see Ascot._

SURFLEET SEAS END _Lincs. – see Spalding._

SUTTON COLDFIELD _W. Mids._ 503 504 O 26 – _pop._ 105 452.
   ⛳ _Pype Hayes, Eachelhurst Rd, Walmley &_ (0121) 351 1014, DT – ⛳ _Boldmere, Monmouth Dr. &_ (0121) 353 3379, DT – ⛳ _110 Thornhill Rd &_ (0121) 580 7878, DT – ⛳, ⛳ _The Belfry, Lichfield Rd, Wishaw &_ (01675) 470301 DT.
   London 124 – Birmingham 8 – Coventry 29 – Nottingham 47 – Stoke-on-Trent 40.

   Plan : see Birmingham pp. 4 and 5

🏨 **The Belfry,** Wishaw, B76 9PR, East : 6 ½ m. by A 453 on A 446 _&_ (01675) 470301, _enquiries@thebelfry.com, Fax_ (01675) 470256, ≤, ⊘, ⅃₆, ≋s, ⬜, ⬜₂₇, 🌹, 🐾, 🎾, squash – ❘⃝ ✂, 🖥 rest, ⅃, ◻ – ⚖ 450. 📶 ﹝AE﹞ ⓞ **VISA**. ✁
French Restaurant : **Rest** (dinner only and Sunday lunch) a la carte 31.95/58.85 **s.** ♀ – **Atrium : Rest** (dinner only and Sunday lunch)/dinner 24.95 ♀ – ☲ 13.95 – **311 rm** ✹179.00 – ✹✹199.00/239.00, 13 suites.
   ♦ Famed for championship golf course, this large hotel has an unashamedly leisure oriented slant, including a superb AquaSpa. Sizeable rooms; superior variety overlook courses. Atrium dominated by glass dome ceiling. Formal French Restaurant has golfing vistas.

🏨 **New Hall** ⊱, Walmley Rd, B76 1QX, Southeast : 1 ½ m. by Coleshill St, Coleshill Rd and Reddicap Hill on B 4148 _&_ (0121) 378 2442, _Fax (0121) 378 4637,_ 🌳, ⊘, ⅃₆, ≋s, ⬜, ⬜₉,
🌹, 🐾, 🎾 – ◻ ✂, ⅃, ◻ – ⚖ 50. 📶 ﹝AE﹞ ⓞ **VISA**. ✁   DT i
The Bridge : Rest _(closed Sunday- Monday)_ (dinner only and Sunday lunch) 45.00 ♀ – **The Terrace Room : Rest** a la carte 20.50/27.00 – **55 rm** ☲ ✹105.00/135.00 – ✹✹170.00/270.00, 5 suites.
   ♦ Reputedly the oldest moated manor in England, dating from 13C; once the Earl of Warwick's shooting lodge. Superb gardens. Bedrooms named after moat-floating lilies. Very formal dining at The Bridge. Informal Terrace Room serves tried-and-tested favourites.

🏨 **Moor Hall,** Moor Hall Drive, B75 6LN, Northeast : 2 m. by A 453 and Weeford Rd _&_ (0121) 308 3751, _mail@moorhallhotel.co.uk, Fax_ (0121) 308 8974, ⅃₆, ≋s, ⬜, 🌹 – ❘⃝ ✂ ⅃, ◻ –
⚖ 200. 📶 ﹝AE﹞ ⓞ **VISA**. ✁   DT r
Oak Room : Rest _(closed Sunday dinner)_ 16.95/23.00 **s.** – **Country Kitchen : Rest** (carvery rest.) (dinner only and lunch Saturday and Sunday) 13.50 **s.** – **82 rm** ☲ ✹120.00 – ✹✹120.00/150.00.
   ♦ Imposing, commercially oriented manor house featuring 19C/early 20C fixtures and fittings, set in quiet parkland. Fine range of rooms: some look over sunken gardens. Refined Oak Room. Carvery at Country Kitchen.

🍴 **The Cock Inn,** Bulls Lane, Wishaw, B76 9QL, East : 7 m. by A 453 off A 446 following signs to Grove End _&_ (0121) 313 3960, 🌳 – ◻. 📶 ﹝AE﹞ **VISA**. ✁
Rest _(closed Sunday dinner)_ a la carte 18.50/31.00.
   ♦ Modern, spacious pub adorned by wood carvings and log fires; separate cigar bar adds an air of exclusivity. Seasonally changing, robust modern cooking with eclectic twists.

SUTTON GAULT _Cambs._ 504 U 26 – _see Ely._

The ✿ award is the crème de la crème.
This is awarded to restaurants
which are really worth travelling miles for!

SUTTON-ON-THE-FOREST N. Yorks. 502 P 21.

London 230 – Kingston-upon-Hull 50 – Leeds 52 – Scarborough 40 – York 12.

XX **The Blackwell Ox Inn** with rm, Huby Rd, YO61 1DT, ℰ (01347) 810328, *info@black welloxinn.co.uk, Fax* (01347) 812738 – ⬛ ⬆ 🅿, ⓒⓢ 𝗩𝗜𝗦𝗔. ⬧
Rest 10.50/13.50 and a la carte 17.50/27.50 – **5 rm** ⊑ ✱95.00 – ✱✱95.00.
◆ Stylish destination in very pleasant village. Open-fired bar with cosy sofas. Two comfy, snug dining rooms: tasty menus with Spanish and French accent. Individual rooms.

🏠 **Rose & Crown,** Main St, YO61 1DP, ℰ (01347) 811333, *andymiddleton@btconnect.com,*
Fax (01347) 811333, ☞ – ⬆ 🅿, ⓒⓢ 𝗔𝗘 𝗩𝗜𝗦𝗔. ⬧
closed first 2 weeks January and 25 December – Rest *(closed Sunday dinner and Monday)*
(booking essential) a la carte 15.00/35.00 ⓨ.
◆ Lovely enclosed rear terrace and garden. Rustic bar ambience made all the warmer by roaring fires. Modern menu plus blackboard specials with imaginative, stylish twists.

SWANAGE Dorset 503 504 O 32 The West Country G. – pop. 11 097.

See : *Town*★.
Env. : *St Aldhelm's Head*★★ *(≤★★★), SW : 4 m. by B 3069 – Durlston Country Park (≤★★),*
S : 1 m. – Studland (Old Harry Rocks★★, Studland Beach (≤★), St Nicholas Church★),
N : 3 m. – Worth Matravers (Anvil Point Lighthouse ≤★★), S : 2 m. – Great Globe★, S : 1¼ m.
Exc. : *Corfe Castle★ (≤★★) AC, NW : 6 m. by A 351 – Blue Pool★, NW : 9 m. by A 351 and*
minor roads – Lulworth Cove★, W : 18 m. by A 351 and B 3070.
🛆, 🛆 *Isle of Purbeck, Studland* ℰ (01929) 450361.
🅱 *The White House, Shore Rd* ℰ (01929) 422885.
London 130 – Bournemouth 22 – Dorchester 26 – Southampton 52.

X **Cauldron Bistro,** 5 High St, BH19 2LN, ℰ (01929) 422671 – ⓒⓢ 𝗩𝗜𝗦𝗔
closed 2 weeks January, 2 weeks November and Monday-Wednesday – Rest (light lunch)/dinner a la carte 22.95/31.50.
◆ Quaint and cosy; boothed tables, mix and match furniture. Quality ingredients, local fish, generous portions cooked with care. Unusual vegetarian dishes.

The red 🍂 symbol?
This denotes the very essence of peace
– only the sound of birdsong first thing in the morning …

SWAY Hants. 503 504 P 31 – see Brockenhurst.

SWINDON Swindon 503 504 O 29 The West Country G. – pop. 155 432.

See : *Great Western Railway Museum★ AC – Railway Village Museum★ AC* Y **M.**
Env. : *Lydiard Park (St Mary's★) W : 4 m.* U.
Exc. : *Ridgeway Path★★, S : 8½ m. by A 4361 – Whitehorse (≤★)E : 7½ m. by A 4312, A 420*
and B 400 off B 4057.
🛆, 🛆 *Broome Manor, Pipers Way* ℰ (01793) 532403 – 🛆 *Shrivenham Park, Penny Hooks,*
Shrivenham ℰ (01793) 783853 – 🛆 *The Wiltshire, Vastern, Wootton Bassett* ℰ (01793)
849999 – 🛆 Wrag Barn G & C.C., Shrivenham Rd, Highworth ℰ (01793) 861327.
🅱 *37 Regent St* ℰ (01793) 530328.
London 83 – Bournemouth 69 – Bristol 40 – Coventry 66 – Oxford 29 – Reading 40 –
Southampton 65.

Plan opposite

🏨 **Swindon Marriott,** Pipers Way, SN3 1SH, South : 1 ½ m. by Marlborough Road off
B 4006 ℰ (0870) 4007281, *Fax* (0870) 4007381, ⓐ, 🏋, ⬌⬌, 🏊, ⬧ – ⬛ ⬆ ⬇ ⬧ 🛆 🅿 –
🔒 250. ⓒⓢ 𝗔𝗘 ⓞ 𝗩𝗜𝗦𝗔. ⬧
Mediterrano : Rest 21.00 and a la carte 18.00/24.00 s. ⓨ – ⊑ 14.95 – **156 rm** ✱119.00 –
✱✱119.00.
V   S
◆ A modern, four storey business hotel in woodland yet close to the business park. Double beds in standard rooms; king size in executives: all have up-to-date mod cons. Restaurant exudes Mediterranean ambience.

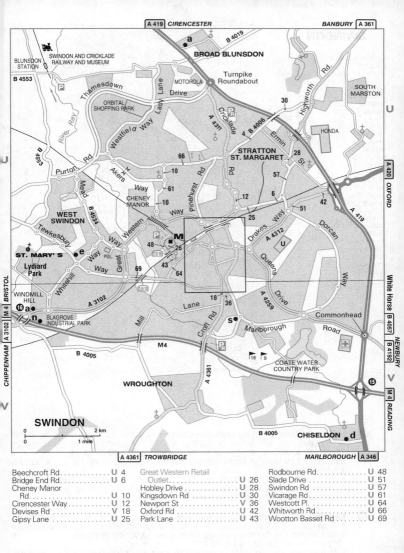

BROAD BLUNSDON

BLUNSDON STATION

SWINDON AND CRICKLADE RAILWAY AND MUSEUM

B 4553

Turnpike Roundabout

MOTOROLA

Thamesdown   Drive

ORBITAL SHOPPING PARK

Westfield Way   Lady Lane   A 4311   B 4006

River Ray

Purton   Rd

SOUTH MARSTON

HONDA

Cricklade   Rd

30

Ermin   St.

STRATTON ST. MARGARET

66

28

B 4553

Mead   B 4534

Akers   Way

10

61

Pinehurst   Rd

57

Way

CHENEY MANOR

10

12

6

42

A 419

WEST SWINDON

Tewkesbury   Way

51

25

Drakes   Way

A 4312

Dorcan   Way

ST. MARY'S

Lydiard Park

e

Western   Way   Great   Way

P   M

48   26

POL.

43

U

Queens   Drive

WINDMILL HILL

Whitehill   Way

69

64

a

n

BLAGROVE INDUSTRIAL PARK

A 3102

18

36

A 4259

Commonhead

Road

Mill   Lane

Croft   Rd

s

Marlborough

B 4005

M4

A 4361

P   18   9

COATE WATER COUNTRY PARK

15

WROUGHTON

SWINDON

0   2 km
0   1 mile

B 4005

CHISELDON   d

Beechcroft Rd	**U** 4	Great Western Retail		Rodbourne Rd .... **U** 48
Bridge End Rd	**U** 6	Outlet .... **U** 26		Slade Drive .... **U** 51
Cheney Manor		Hobley Drive ...... **U** 28		Swindon Rd .... **U** 57
Rd	**U** 10	Kingsdown Rd ..... **U** 30		Vicarage Rd .... **U** 61
Cirencester Way	**U** 12	Newport St .... **V** 36		Westcott Pl .... **U** 64
Devises Rd	**V** 18	Oxford Rd .... **U** 42		Whitworth Rd ...... **U** 66
Gipsy Lane	**U** 25	Park Lane .... **U** 43		Wootton Basset Rd ... **U** 69

De Vere Shaw Ridge Swindon, Shaw Ridge Leisure Park, Whitehill Way, SN5 7DW, West : 2 ¾ m. by A 3102 off B 4553 ℘ (01793) 878785, *dvs.sales@devere-hotels.com*, Fax (01793) 877822, 佘, ⁊, ⌶, ⇌, ⬚ – |創 ⇔, ▦ rest, ⚓ & ℗ – 逢 400. ⬤❾ AE ⬤ **U** e
VISA

The Park Brasserie : Rest *(bar lunch Saturday)* 14.95 and a la carte 24.00/32.70 s. ⁊ – ⬚ 12.95 – **148 rm** ⬧125.00 – ⬧⬧155.00, 4 suites.

♦ Large, corporate, well-equipped hotel on out-of-town leisure site ; a good range of well-equipped, up-to-date rooms, from suites and four-posters to family rooms. Brasserie with theatre kitchen, walk-in cellar and fish tanks.

SWINDON

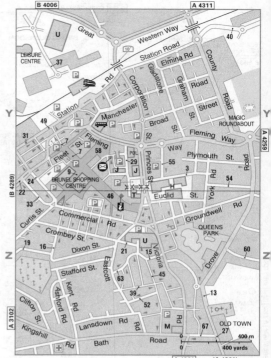

🏨 **Hilton Swindon,** Lydiard Fields, Great Western Way, SN5 8UZ, West : 3 ½ m. by A 3102 at junction 16 of M 4 ℰ (01793) 881777, *reservations.swindon@hilton.com,* *Fax (01793) 881881,* ₺₅, ⇌₅, ◲, –|≢| ✦✕ ≡ ❤ & ℙ, – ⚿ 350. ◑❸ 延 ◍ VISA　　　V a
Minsky's : Rest (buffet lunch) (carving dinner) 20.95 s. ♀ – **171 rm** ⌷ ✚135.00 – ✚✚145.00/165.00.
◆ Corporate hotel usefully located to west of town, making an excellent base from which to explore the West Country. The Living Well health club is also on hand. Spacious rooms. Dining options: buffet lunch, carvery dinner.

🏨 **Express by Holiday Inn** without rest., Frankland Rd, Blagrove, SN5 8UD, West : 3 ½ m. by A 3102 at junction 16 of M 4 ℰ (01793) 818800, *swindon@expressby* *holidayinn.net, Fax (01793) 818888* – |≢| ✦✕ & ℙ, – ⚿ 70. ◑❸ 延 ◍ VISA　　　V n
121 rm ⌷ ✚65.00/90.00 – ✚✚65.00/90.00.
◆ Modern purpose-built lodge accommodation in handy position next to M4 motorway. Smart, contemporary rooms for business or leisure customers.

at Blunsdon *North : 4½ m. by A 4311 on A 419 –* ✉ *Swindon.*

🏨 **Blunsdon House,** SN26 7AS, ℰ (01793) 721701, *info@blunsdonhouse.co.uk,* *Fax (01793) 721056,* ₺₅, ⇌₅, ◲, ₨, ☂, ♨, ✵, squash – |≢| ✦✕, ≡ rest, ❤ & ℙ, – ⚿ 300. ◑❸ 延 ◍ VISA, ✦✕　　　U a
The Ridge : Rest (dinner only and Sunday lunch)/dinner 26.50/41.00 s. ♀ – *Christophers :* Rest (carving lunch) 14.50/16.50 s. ♀ – **114 rm** ⌷ ✚130.00 – ✚✚140.00, 3 suites.
◆ Built as a farmhouse, this vast family-owned establishment now offers conference rooms and excellent leisure facilities. Large bedrooms with patios or balconies are popular. The Ridge is elegant and stylish. Christophers offers lively carvery - and discos!

at Chiseldon South : 6¼ m. by A 4259, A 419 and A 346 on B 4005 – ⊠ Swindon.

Chiseldon House, New Rd, SN4 0NE, ℰ (01793) 741010, chishoho@hotmail.com, Fax (01793) 741059, ☞ – ⁜ rm, ℭ P – 🔬 50. ⬤ ⠀ ⠀ ⠀ VISA ⠀ ⠀ v d
Orangery : Rest 20.00/28.00 and a la carte 15.50/33.25 s. ⚲ – 21 rm � ♦90.00 –
♦♦110.00/130.00.
◆ The gardens are one of the strongest aspects of this extended Georgian house. Rooms are a particularly good size with all mod cons. Close to motorway and easily accessible. Ornate, split-level restaurant decorated with murals.

SYMONDS YAT WEST Herefordshire 503 504 M 28 Great Britain G. – ⊠ Ross-on-Wye.
See : Town★ – Yat Rock (≤★).
Env. : S : Wye Valley★.
London 126 – Gloucester 23 – Hereford 17 – Newport 31.

Norton House without rest., Whitchurch, HR9 6DJ, ℰ (01600) 890046, enquiries@nor ton-house.com, Fax (01600) 890045, ☞ – ⁜ P
closed 24-26 December – **3 rm** � ♦41.00/46.00 – ♦♦76.00.
◆ Built of local stone, this 18C farmhouse of 15C origins boasts quaint interiors. Rooms with antique beds in patchwork quilts and flowers. Tea, cake on arrival.

TADCASTER N. Yorks. 502 Q 22 – pop. 6 548.
London 206 – Harrogate 16 – Leeds 14 – York 11.

Hazlewood Castle ⑤, Paradise Lane, Hazlewood, LS24 9NJ, Southwest : 2 ¾ m. by A 659 off A 64 ℰ (01937) 535353, info@hazlewood-castle.co.uk, Fax (01937) 530630, ≤, ☞, ♨, ⁜ ℭ P – 🔬 120. ⬤ ⠀ ⬤ VISA ⠀
Restaurant Anise (ℰ (01937) 535317) : Rest 25.00/30.00 (dinner) and lunch a la carte 17.40/23.40 ⚲ – 12 rm ⊒ ♦155.00 – ♦♦195.00, **9 suites** ⊒ 225.00/295.00.
◆ Impressive part 13C fortified manor house in parkland. Panelled entrance hall, ornate lounges. Extensive conference facilities. Spacious rooms, individually styled. Dine in former orangery.

Aagrah, York Rd, Steeton, LS24 8EG, Northeast : 2½ m. on A 64 (westbound carriageway) ℰ (01937) 530888 – ▤ P. ⬤ ⠀ ⠀
closed 25 December – Rest - Indian (Kashmiri) - (booking essential) (dinner only) 15.00 and a la carte 14.95/21.05 s.
◆ Tasty and authentic Kashmiri specialities in a spacious, busy Indian restaurant with orna ments and friezes inspired by the subcontinent. Large menus and quality ingredients.

TALLAND BAY Cornwall 503 G 32 – see Looe.

TANGMERE W. Sussex 504 R 31 – see Chichester.

TANWORTH-IN-ARDEN Warks. 503 504 O 26/27 – see Henley-in-Arden.

TAPLOW Windsor & Maidenhead 504 R 29.
London 33 – Maidenhead 2 – Oxford 36 – Reading 12.

Cliveden ⑤, SL6 0JF, North : 2 m. by Berry Hill ℰ (01628) 668561, info@cliveden house.co.uk, Fax (01628) 661837, ≤ National Trust Gardens, parterre and River Thames, ⓐ, ₤₅, ≦s, ⑤ heated, ▨, ♨, ☞, ♨, ✻indoor/outdoor, squash – ▯ ⁜ ℭ P – 🔬 40. ⬤ ⠀ ⬤ VISA
Terrace : Rest 29.50/55.00 s. and a la carte 55.00/58.00 – (see also *Waldo's* below) – **31 rm** ⊒ 225.00/335.00 – ♦♦225.00/335.00, 7 suites 495.00/610.00.
◆ Breathtakingly stunning 19C stately home in National Trust gardens. Ornate, sumptuous public areas, filled with antiques. Exquisitely appointed rooms the last word in luxury. View parterre and Thames in top class style from Terrace.

Taplow House, Berry Hill, SL6 0DA, ℰ (01628) 670056, reception@ta plow.wrensgroup.com, Fax (01628) 783985, ☞, ☞ – ⁜ ℭ P – 🔬 120. ⬤ ⠀ ⬤ VISA
Stroks : Rest (closed Saturday lunch) 18.95 (lunch) and dinner a la carte 31.95 ⚲ – ⊒ 12.95 – **31 rm** ♦108.00/135.00 – ♦♦112.00/185.00, 1 suite.
◆ Part 16C mansion with Europe's tallest tulip tree, planted by Elizabeth I. Set in mature woodland. Warm, cosy décor throughout. Plush suites and sofas. Well-equipped rooms. Intimate dining room, overlooking lawned gardens.

XXXX

✿

Waldo's (at Cliveden H.), SL6 0JF, North : 2 m. by Berry Hill ℰ (01628) 668561, *info@clive denhouse.co.uk, Fax (01628) 661837* – ✦✕ ≡ 🅿, ⓶ ⒜Ⓔ ⓪ 𝘝𝘐𝘚𝘈 *closed, 2 weeks Christmas-New Year, first week January, 2 weeks August, Sunday,Monday and Tuesday following Bank Holidays* – **Rest** (booking essential) (dinner only) 68.00.
Spec. Langoustine with caramelised cauliflower purée and seaweed cracker. Anjou pigeon with sautéed potatoes and buttered spinach. Bitter chocolate box with caramel and cumin mousse.
♦ Exquisitely upholstered restaurant, seamlessly weaving into the grand tapestry of Cliveden. Superbly prepared ingredients contribute to seasonal menus served with flair.

TARPORLEY *Ches.* 502 503 504 L/M 24 – *pop. 2 634.*

🄖 *Portal G & C.C., Cobblers Cross Lane ℰ (01829) 733933 –* 🄖 *Portal Premier, Forest Rd ℰ (01829) 733884.*
London 186 – Chester 11 – Liverpool 27 – Shrewsbury 36.

🏥 **The Swan,** 50 High St, CW6 0AG, ℰ (01829) 733838, Fax (01829) 732932, �& – ✦✕ 🅿, ⓶ 60. ⓶⓪ ⒜Ⓔ 𝘝𝘐𝘚𝘈, 🌦
Rest 11.95 (lunch) and a la carte 19.80/39.30 ♀ – **16 rm** ⌷ ✚64.50/77.00 – ✚✚87.50/135.00.
♦ 16C former coaching inn with hanging baskets, located in pleasant village. Original beams, open fires and oak panelling adorn guest areas. Bedrooms retain period feel of inn. Informality the key to relaxed dining room.

at Cotebrook *Northeast : 2½ m. on A 49 –* ✉ *Tarporley.*

🍴 **Fox and Barrel,** Forrest Rd, CW6 9DZ, ℰ (01829) 760529, Fax (01829) 760192, 🌦, 🌱 – ✦✕ 🅿, ⓶ ⒜Ⓔ ⓪ 𝘝𝘐𝘚𝘈, 🌦
closed 25 December – **Rest** (live music Monday evening) a la carte 15.95/22.25 ♀.
♦ Wood floors, beamed ceiling and character aplenty. Busy and friendly pub offers an extensive menu of hearty traditional fare. Book early for the Monday live Jazz evenings.

at Little Budworth *Northeast : 3½ m. on A 49 –* ✉ *Tarporley.*

XX **Cabbage Hall,** CW6 9ES, ℰ (01829) 760292, Fax (01829) 760292, 🌱 – ✦✕ 🅿, ⓶⓪ 𝘝𝘐𝘚𝘈
closed Monday – **Rest** 12.00 (lunch) and a la carte 27.00/41.00.
♦ Sleek former pub in 11 acres of land. Beautiful interior with gilded mirrors and startling copies of Picasso and Van Gogh. Impressively comprehensive range of bistro dishes.

at Bunbury *South : 3¼ m. by A 49 –* ✉ *Tarporley.*

🍴 **Dysart Arms,** Bowes Gate Rd, CW6 9PH, by Bunbury Mill rd ℰ (01829) 260183, *dysart.arms@brunningandprice.co.uk, Fax (01829) 261286,* 🌦, 🌱 – 🅿, ⓶⓪ 𝘝𝘐𝘚𝘈
closed 25 and 31 December – **Rest** a la carte 17.20/27.70 ♀.
♦ Characterful village pub, in the shadow of impressive Bunbury Church. Open fire, beams and lots of clutter. Interesting, original, hearty British food.

at Willington *Northwest : 3½ m. by A 51 –* ✉ *Tarporley.*

🏥 **Willington Hall** 🦉, CW6 0NB, ℰ (01829) 752321, *enquiries@willingtonhall.co.uk, Fax (01829) 752596,* ≤, 🌦, 🌱 – ✦✕ rest, 🅿 – ⓶ 200. ⓶⓪ ⒜Ⓔ 𝘝𝘐𝘚𝘈
closed 25-26 December – **Rest** (closed Sunday dinner) 9.80/24.00 and dinner a la carte approx 28.00 – **10 rm** ⌷ ✚70.00 – ✚✚120.00.
♦ Imposing 19C country house with ornate façade in mature grounds; many original features remain, including vast hall and impressive staircase. Most rooms have rural outlook. Intimate dinners served in classically proportioned surroundings.

TARR STEPS *Somerset* 503 J 30.

See : *Tarr Steps★★ (Clapper Bridge★★).*
London 191.5 – Taunton 31 – Tiverton 20.

🍴 **Tarr Farm Inn** with rm, TA22 9PY, ℰ (01643) 851507, *enquiries@tarrfarm.co.uk, Fax (01643) 851111,* 🌦, 🌱, 🅰 – ✦✕ ☎ 🅿, ⓶⓪ 𝘝𝘐𝘚𝘈
closed 1-10 February – **Rest** a la carte 18.00/27.00 ♀ – **9 rm** ⌷ ✚80.00 – ✚✚130.00.
♦ On beautiful Exmoor, overlooking ancient clapper bridge. Hugely characterful, beamed interior. Accomplished, modish menus in intimate restaurant. Bedrooms exude luxury.

Good food and accommodation at moderate prices?
Look for the Bib symbols:
red Bib Gourmand 🍽 for food, blue Bib Hotel 🏨 for hotels

ENGLAND

TATTENHALL *Ches.* 502 503 504 L 24 – *pop. 1 860.*
London 200 – Birmingham 71 – Chester 10 – Liverpool 29 – Manchester 38 – Stoke-on-Trent 30.

⌂ **Higher Huxley Hall** ⟋, CH3 9BZ, North : 2 ¼ m. on Huxley rd ℘ (01829) 781484, *info@huxleyhall.co.uk*, ⟨, ⟨⟩ ⬛ 🅿 ⓜ 🅰🅴 𝘝𝘐𝘚𝘈 ⟩⟩
booking essential – **Rest** (by arrangement) (communal dining) 30.00 – **5 rm** ⊠ ✶50.00/65.00 – ✶✶90.00/95.00.
♦ This historic manor house, sited on a former farm, dates from 13C and is attractively furnished with antiques. Bedrooms are comfortable and well equipped. Homely, communal dining room serving local produce.

at Higher Burwardsley *Southeast : 1 m. –* ⊠ *Tattenhall.*

🝊 **The Pheasant Inn** ⟋ *with rm*, CH3 9PF, ℘ (01829) 770434, *info@thepheasantinn.co.uk*, *Fax* (01829) 771097, ⟨ Cheshire plain, ⟨⟩ ⟨⟩ 🅿 ⓜ 🅰🅴 ⓞ 𝘝𝘐𝘚𝘈. ⟩⟩
Rest a la carte 22.00/30.00 ⟓ – **12 rm** ⊠ ✶65.00 – ✶✶80.00/130.00.
♦ Appealing part-timber pub with superb views over Cheshire Plain. Accomplished, original food on offer. Attractively stylish rooms in adjacent, converted sandstone barn.

TAUNTON *Somerset* 503 K 30 *The West Country G. – pop. 58 241.*

See : *Town★ – St Mary Magdalene★* V *– Somerset County Museum★* AC V M *– St James'★* U *– Hammett St★* V 25 *– The Crescent★* V *– Bath Place★* V 3.
Env. : *Trull* (Church★), S *: 2½ m. by A 38 – Hestercombe Gardens★*, N *: 5 m. by A 3259* BY *and minor roads to Cheddon Fitzpaine.*
Exc. : *Bishops Lydeard★* (Church★), NW *: 6 m. – Wellington : Church★, Wellington Monument* (⟨★★⟩), SW *: 7½ m. by A 38 – Combe Florey★, NW : 8 m. – Gaulden Manor★* AC, NW *: 10 m. by A 358 and B 3227.*
🛦, 🛦 *Taunton Vale, Creech Heathfield* ℘ (01823) 412220 – 🛦 *Vivary, Vivary Park* ℘ (01823) 289274 – 🛦 *Taunton and Pickeridge, Corfe* ℘ (01823) 421537.
🅱 *Paul St* ℘ (01823) 336344.
London 168 – Bournemouth 69 – Bristol 50 – Exeter 37 – Plymouth 78 – Southampton 93 – Weymouth 50.

Plan on next page

🏛 **The Castle,** Castle Green, TA1 1NF, ℘ (01823) 272671, *reception@the-castle-hotel.com,* *Fax* (01823) 336066, ⟨⟩, ⟨⟩ – 🛗 ⟨⟩ 🅿 – 🔬 100. ⓜ 🅰🅴 ⓞ V a
Rest *(closed Sunday dinner)* 23.00/43.00 s. ⟓ ⟨⟩ – **44 rm** ⊠ ✶110.00/135.00 – ✶✶180.00/255.00.
Spec. Scrambled duck egg with smoked eel and spiced oil. Fillet of turbot with gnocchi, peas and broad beans. Dark chocolate tart with marinated cherries.
♦ Traditionally renowned, family owned British hotel: afternoon tea a speciality. 12C origins with Norman garden. Wisteria-clad and castellated. Individually styled rooms. Top quality West Country produce underpins inventive cuisine.

🏠 **Meryan House,** Bishop's Hull Rd, TA1 5EG, West : ¾ m. by A 38 ℘ (01823) 337445, *meryanhouse@btclick.com, Fax* (01823) 322355, ⟨⟩ – ⟨⟩ ⟨⟩ 🅿, ⓜ 𝘝𝘐𝘚𝘈 AZ c
Rest *(closed Sunday)* (booking essential for non-residents) (dinner only) 24.00 and a la carte 16.00/24.00 ⟓ – **12 rm** ⊠ ✶50.00/58.00 – ✶✶80.00.
♦ Privately owned extended house on town outskirts. Comfortable sitting room has adjacent patio garden and small bar with jukebox. Well-kept, individually styled rooms. Intimate dining room with large inglenook.

🏠 **Express by Holiday Inn** *without rest.,* Blackbrook Business Park, TA1 2PX, ℘ (01823) 624000, *taunton@expressholidayinn.co.uk, Fax* (01823) 624024 – 🛗 ⟨⟩ ⟨ 🅿 – 🔬 30. ⓜ 🅰🅴 ⓞ 𝘝𝘐𝘚𝘈 BY a
92 rm ✶69.95/85.00 – ✶✶69.95/85.00.
♦ Purpose-built hotel with cosy bar. Bedrooms have a Scandinavian feel and boast good extras. Next door is a Harvester restaurant.

XX **The Willow Tree,** 3 Tower Lane, TA1 4AR, ℘ (01823) 352835 – ⟨⟩ ⟨⟩ 10. ⓜ 𝘝𝘐𝘚𝘈 V c
closed January, August, Sunday and Monday – **Rest** (dinner only) 22.50/29.50.
♦ Converted 17C town house in central location. Exposed beams and large inglenook fireplaces. Friendly service. Appealing menu of modern seasonal cooking with a classical base.

X **Brazz,** Castle Bow, TA1 1NF, ℘ (01823) 252000, *taunton@brazz.co.uk, Fax* (01823) 336066 – ⟨⟩ ☰ 🅿, ⓜ 🅰🅴 ⓞ 𝘝𝘐𝘚𝘈 V e
closed 25 December – **Rest** 12.95 and a la carte 13.00/28.50 ⟓.
♦ Bright and breezy bistro style eatery to rear of The Castle hotel. Large, bustling bar area. Main restaurant has large aquarium, concave ceiling and brasserie favourites.

TAUNTON

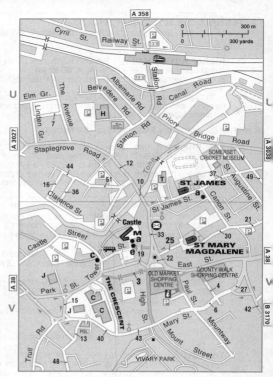

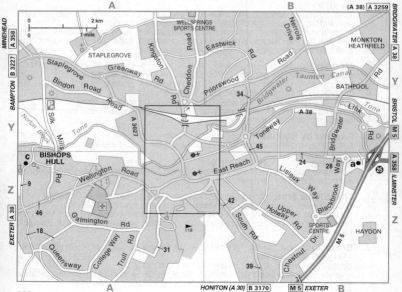

✕ **The Sanctuary**, Middle St, TA1 1SJ, ℰ (01823) 257788, Fax (01823) 257788, 斎 – ✖✕, U a **♨** **VISA**
closed 24 December - 2 January, Saturday lunch, and Sunday – **Rest** a la carte 19.30/29.50 ♈.
♦ Long-standing, popular eatery of exposed brick and beams tucked away down a side street. Search out charming little landscaped roof terrace. Simple and eclectic modern menus.

at West Monkton Northeast : 3½ m. by A 38 – BY – ✉ Taunton.

⌂ **Springfield House** without rest., Walford Cross, TA2 8QW, on A 38 ℰ (01823) 412116, melanie@springfieldhse.co.uk, 斎 – ✖✕ **P.** ✖
5 rm ☷ ✲40.00 – ✲✲60.00.
♦ Guesthouse with annex of quite recent vintage with attractive, spacious gardens. Main building has simple breakfast room and conservatory lounge. Cottage style bedrooms.

at Henlade East : 3½ m. on A 358 – BZ – ✉ Taunton.

🏰 **Mount Somerset** ⚘, Lower Henlade, TA3 5NB, South : ½ m. by Stoke Rd ℰ (01823) 442500, info@mountsomersethotel.co.uk, Fax (01823) 442900, ≼, 斎 – ᴙ ✖✕ **P** – 🏛 50. **♨** **AE** **①** **VISA**
Rest 28.50/37.00 and dinner a la carte 28.50/37.00 ♈ – **11 rm** ☷ ✲105.00/120.00 – ✲✲145.00/205.00.
♦ Imposing Regency mansion with good views of Vale of Taunton. Exotic peacocks in landscaped gardens. Comfortable, spacious drawing rooms. Elegant bedrooms, most with views. Oak panelled, formal dining room.

at Hatch Beauchamp Southeast : 6 m. by A 358 – BZ – ✉ Taunton.

🏠 **Farthings**, TA3 6SG, ℰ (01823) 480664, farthing1@aol.com, Fax (01823) 481118, 斎 – ✖✕ **P.** **♨** **AE** **VISA**
Rest (dinner only) a la carte 23.95/36.40 ♈ – **9 rm** ☷ ✲80.00/90.00 – ✲✲110.00/130.00.
♦ Georgian country house with pleasant, spacious gardens in pretty village. Personally run, with small lounge and well-stocked bar. Sizeable, individually decorated rooms. Smart dining room; local produce to fore.

at West Bagborough Northwest : 10½ m. by A 358 – AY – ✉ Taunton.

⌂ **Tilbury Farm** ⚘ without rest., TA4 3DY, East : ¾ m. ℰ (01823) 432391, ≼ Vale of Taunton, 斎, ♞ – ✖✕ **P.** ✖
3 rm ☷ ✲60.00 – ✲✲60.00.
♦ Impressively characterful 18C house with terrific views of Vale of Taunton. Welcoming lounge boasts log fire. Well- kept, spacious bedrooms all with beams and good views.

🍴 **The Rising Sun Inn** with rm, TA4 3EF, ℰ (01823) 432575, rob@theriser.co.uk – ✖✕, **♨** **VISA**
closed Monday except Bank Holidays – **Rest** (closed Sunday dinner) a la carte 21.00/26.00 ♈ – **2 rm** ☷ ✲75.00 – ✲✲85.00.
♦ 16C pub, rebuilt after a fire, seemingly tumbling off the edge of the Quantocks! Modernity alongside oak and slate; interesting locally sourced dishes. Two stylish bedrooms.

at Triscombe Northwest : 11 m. by A 358 – AY – ✉ Taunton.

🍴 **The Blue Ball Inn** with rm, TA4 3HE, ℰ (01984) 618242, info@blueballinn.co.uk, Fax (01984) 618371, 斎, ♞ – ✖✕ & **P.** **♨** **VISA**. ✖
Rest (closed 25 December) (booking essential) a la carte 20.00/30.00 ♈ – **2 rm** ☷ ✲40.00/52.50 – ✲✲60.00/85.00.
♦ Wonderfully characterful pub with thatched roof and stepped gardens: former 15C stable block. Wood burning stoves and charmingly sloping floors. Robust, rustic food.

TAVISTOCK Devon 503 H 32 The West Country G. – pop. 11 018.
Env. : Morwellham★ AC, SW : 4½ m.
Exc. : E : Dartmoor National Park★★ – Buckland Abbey★★ AC, S : 7 m. by A 386 – Lydford★★, N : 8½ m. by A 386.
🏌 Down Rd ℰ (01822) 612344 – 🏌 Hurdwick, Tavistock Hamlets ℰ (01822) 612746.
🛈 Town Hall, Bedford Sq ℰ (01822) 612938, tavistocktic@visit.org.uk.
London 239 – Exeter 38 – Plymouth 16.

🏨 **Browns**, 80 West St, PL19 8AQ, ℰ (01822) 618686, enquiries@brownsdevon.co.uk, Fax (01822) 618646, 斎, ♨ – ᴙ ✖✕ **P.** **♨** **AE** **VISA**. ✖
Rest 18.50 (lunch) and a la carte 19.00/37.00 s – ☷ 12.50 – **20 rm** ✲75.00/95.00 – ✲✲160.00.
♦ Former coaching inn and oldest licensed premises in town; now a stylish and contemporary hotel. The mews rooms have a particularly comfortable feel to them. Busy, friendly, informal brasserie.

⌂ **April Cottage,** Mount Tavy Rd, PL19 9JB, ℘ (01822) 613280 – ⇔⇔ 🅿.
Rest 17.00 – 3 rm ⊊ ✦40.00/45.00 – ✦✦55.00/60.00.
  • Compact but homely Victorian cottage. Meals taken in rear conservatory overlooking River Tavy. Curios adorn small lounge. Carefully furnished rooms with varnished-
pine.

XXX **The Horn of Plenty** ⤴ with rm, Gulworthy, PL19 8JD, West : 4 m. by A 390 off
Chipshop rd ℘ (01822) 832528, enquiries@thehornofplenty.co.uk, Fax (01822) 834390, ≤
Tamar Valley and Bodmin Moor, 🍴, 🌳 – ⇔⇔ 🅿 ⇆ 12. 🆎 🆎 VISA
closed 25-26 December – Rest (closed Monday lunch) 26.00/42.50 ♀ – 10 rm ⊊ ✦130.00 –
✦✦230.00.
  • Smart, individually styled bedrooms enhance enchanting creeper-clad Tamar Valley
country house. Choose to dine in house or stables: good use of local ingredients.

at Quither Northwest : 5¾ m. by Chillaton rd on Quither rd – ✉ Tavistock.

⌂ **Quither Mill** ⤴, PL19 0PZ, ℘ (01822) 860160, quither.mill@virgin.net,
Fax (01822) 860160, ≤, 🌳, 🎱 – ⇔⇔ 🅿. 🆎 VISA. ✀
closed Christmas-New Year – Rest (communal dining) 25.00 – 3 rm ⊊ ✦55.00 – ✦✦80.00.
  • 18C converted water mill in peaceful rural location. Characterful stone appearance. Fine
antiques. Utter peacefulness pervades beamed, country style rooms. Communal dining
room employing fine china and silver.

at Milton Abbot Northwest : 6 m. on B 3362 – ✉ Tavistock.

🏨 **Hotel Endsleigh** ⤴, PL19 0PQ, Southwest : 1 m. ℘ (01822) 870000, mail@hotelend
sleigh.com, Fax (01822) 870578, ≤, 🍴, 🐾, 🌳, 🎱 – ⇔⇔ rest, 🅿. 🆎 🆎 VISA
closed 12-23 January – Rest 27.00/39.00 and a la carte 27.00/45.00 – 13 rm ⊊ ✦210.00 –
✦✦300.00/400.00, 3 suites.
  • Painstakingly restored Regency lodge in magnificent Devonian gardens and grounds.
Stylish lounge and refined bedrooms are imbued with an engaging, understated elegance.
Interesting, classically based dishes served in two minimalist dining rooms.

at Chillaton Northwest : 6¼ m. by Chillaton rd – ✉ Tavistock.

⌂ **Tor Cottage** ⤴ without rest., PL16 0JE, Southwest : ¼ m. by Tavistock rd, turning right
at bridle path sign, down unmarked track for ½ m. ℘ (01822) 860248, info@torcot
tage.co.uk, Fax (01822) 860126, ≤, 🎱 – ⇔⇔ 🅿. 🆎 VISA. ✀
closed mid December-6 January – 5 rm ⊊ ✦94.00 – ✦✦140.00.
  • Lovely cottage and peaceful gardens in 18 hillside acres. Terrace or conservatory
breakfast. Individual rooms, most spread around garden, with tremendous attention to
detail.

Do not confuse X with ☺!
X defines comfort, while stars are awarded for the best cuisine,
across all categories of comfort.

TEFFONT Wilts. – see Salisbury.

TEIGNMOUTH Devon 503 J 32 – pop. 14 799.
🚉 The Den, Sea Front ℘ (01626) 215666.
London 216 – Exeter 16 – Torquay 8.

🏨 **Thomas Luny House** without rest., Teign St, TQ14 8EG, follow signs for the Quays, off
the A 381 ℘ (01626) 772976, alisonandjohn@thomas-luny-house.co.uk, 🌳 – ⇔⇔ 🅿. 🆎
VISA. ✀
4 rm ⊊ ✦55.00/65.00 – ✦✦70.00/92.00.
  • Personally run Georgian house with sheltered walled garden. Smart breakfast room
with antique pieces. Well furnished drawing room. Stylish, individually appointed
bedrooms.

⌂ **Britannia House** without rest., 26 Teign St, TQ14 8EG, ℘ (01626) 770051, gilletbritan
nia@aol.com, Fax (01626) 776302, 🌳 – ⇔⇔. 🆎 🆎 VISA. ✀
closed January – 3 rm ⊊ ✦50.00/60.00 – ✦✦70.00/80.00.
  • Intimate 17C Grade II listed townhouse enhanced by many original features. Tuck into an
organic breakfast and relax in walled garden or cosy upstairs lounge. Homely rooms.

ENGLAND

TELFORD Wrekin 502 503 504 M 25 *Great Britain G.* – *pop. 138 241.*

Env. : *Ironbridge Gorge Museum★★ AC (The Iron Bridge★★, Coalport China Museum★★, Blists Hill Open Air Museum★★, Museum of the River and Visitor Centre★) S : 5 m. by B 4373.*

Exc. : *Weston Park★★ AC, E : 7 m. by A 5.*

🏌️, 🏌️ *Telford, Great Hay, Sutton Heights* ℘ *(01952) 429977* – 🏌️ *Wrekin, Wellington* ℘ *(01952) 244032* – 🏌️, 🏌️, 🏌️ *The Shropshire, Muxton Grange, Muxton* ℘ *(01952) 677866.*

🚊 *Management Suite, The Telford Centre* ℘ *(01952) 238008.*

London 152 – Birmingham 33 – Shrewsbury 12 – Stoke-on-Trent 29.

🏛️ **Hadley Park House,** Hadley, TF1 6QS, North : 3 ¼ m. by A 442 ℘ (01952) 677269, info@hadleypark.co.uk, Fax (01952) 676938, 斋, 🌿 – ⇥ rest, 🍴 rest, **P**. **⃝⃝** **AE** **VISA**
The Conservatory : **Rest** *(closed Sunday dinner and Bank Holidays)* 16.00 *(lunch)* and dinner a la carte 20.45/31.00 – **12 rm** ☑ ✦70.00/90.00 – ✦✦110.00/125.00.
◆ Georgian house with good communications if you're coming by road. Cosy bar lounge with an attractive "English" style. Bedrooms on two floors are comfortable and up-to-date. Very appealing conservatory restaurant with its own summer terrace.

at Norton *South : 7 m. on A 442* – ✉ *Shifnal.*

🍺 **Hundred House** with rm, Bridgnorth Rd, TF11 9EE, ℘ (01952) 730353, *reservations@hundredhouse.co.uk, Fax (01952) 730355,* 斋, 🌿 – **P**. **⃝⃝** **AE** **VISA**. ✦
accommodation closed 25-26 December – **Rest** a la carte 24.00/35.00 ☑ – **10 rm** ☑ ✦85.00 – ✦✦125.00.
◆ Characterful, family run redbrick inn with herb garden. Carefully sourced dishes, robust and original. Sizable rooms in 19C style, some with canopied beds and swings.

at Bratton *Northwest : 6¾ m. by A 442 and B 5063 (following signs for Admaston) off the B 4394* – ✉ *Telford.*

🏠 **Dovecote Grange** without rest., Bratton Rd, TF5 0BT, ℘ (01952) 243739, mandy@dovecotegrange.co.uk, Fax (01952) 243739, 🌿 – ⇥ 🐾 **P**. **⃝⃝** **VISA**. ✦
5 rm ☑ ✦45.00/60.00 – ✦✦70.00/75.00.
◆ Attractive guesthouse, garden and terrace enjoying views over the local fields. Combined lounge and breakfast area with modern leather furniture. Large, comfy, modish rooms.

TEMPLE SOWERBY Cumbria 502 M 20 – *see Penrith.*

TENBURY WELLS Worcs. 503 504 M 27 – *pop. 3 316.*
London 144 – Birmingham 36 – Hereford 20 – Shrewsbury 37 – Worcester 28.

🏨 **Cadmore Lodge** ⤬, St Michaels, WR15 8TQ, Southwest : 2 ¾ m. by A 4112 ℘ (01584) 810044, *info@cadmorelodge.co.uk, Fax (01584) 810044,* ≤, 🏌️, 🗔, 🏌️, 🎣, ♨ – ⇥ **P**. – 🏛️ 100. **⃝⃝** **VISA**. ✦
closed 25 December – **Rest** *(bar lunch Monday)* 14.00/22.50 ☑ – **15 rm** ☑ ✦47.50/56.00 – ✦✦85.00/125.00.
◆ Family run hotel in pleasant location. Lakeside setting. Plenty of outdoor activities, including golf and fishing. Well-planned rooms: some larger ones have antique furniture. Restaurant overlooks the lake.

TENTERDEN Kent 504 W 30 – *pop. 6 977.*
🚊 *Town Hall, High St* ℘ (01580) 763572 *(summer only).*
London 57 – Folkestone 26 – Hastings 21 – Maidstone 19.

🏨 **Little Silver Country H.,** Ashford Rd, St Michaels, TN30 6SP, North : 2 m. on A 28 ℘ (01233) 850321, *enquiries@little-silver.co.uk, Fax (01233) 850647,* 🌿 – ⇥ **P** – 🏛️ 120. **⃝⃝** **AE** **VISA**. ✦
Rest *(light lunch)*/dinner a la carte 21.45/28.95 – **16 rm** ☑ ✦60.00 – ✦✦95.00/95.00.
◆ Extended mock-Tudor country house hotel with smart gardens. Large function room ideal for weddings. Cosy conservatory breakfast room. Clean and spacious bedrooms. Dining room with table lamps, candelabra and Kentish watercolours.

🏨 **Collina House,** 5 East Hill (via Oaks Rd), TN30 6RL, ℘ (01580) 764852, *enquiries@collina househotel.co.uk, Fax (01580) 762224* – ⇥ **P**. **⃝⃝** **AE** **VISA**. ✦
closed 23 December-12 January – **Rest** *(dinner only)* 21.50/25.00 and a la carte 23.50/30.00 s. – **15 rm** ☑ ✦40.00/55.00 – ✦✦75.00/85.00.
◆ Family run detached house with annex. In good position for visits to Sissinghurst and Leeds Castle. Small, cosy bar and very spacious rooms with neat, simple style. Cosy, family friendly restaurant.

TETBURY *Glos.* 503 504 N 29 *Great Britain G.* – pop. 5 250.
Env. : *Westonbirt Arboretum★ AC, SW : 2½ m. by A 433.*
☞ *Westonbirt* ☎ *(01666) 880242.*
🛈 *33 Church St* ☎ *(01666) 503552, tourism@tetbury.com.*
London 113 – Bristol 27 – Gloucester 19 – Swindon 24.

🏛 **Calcot Manor,** Calcot, GL8 8YJ, West : 3 ½ m. on A 4135 ☎ *(01666) 890391, recep tion@calcotmanor.co.uk, Fax (01666) 890394,* 🍴, ⑩, *Ⅰ₆,* ⇌, ⌇ heated, ☒, ☞, ⌁, ⚘ – ⇌ rest, ℅ ⚘ **P** – 🔒 100. **⓪** **Ⅲ** **Ⅷ**. ⚘
Conservatory : Rest *(booking essential)* a la carte 32.75/40.15 ⚏ – (see also **The Gumstool Inn** below) – **26 rm** ⚏ ✦180.00 – ✦✦235.00, 4 suites.
◆ Impressive Cotswold farmhouse, gardens and meadows with converted ancient barns and stables. Superb spa. Variety of luxuriously appointed rooms with contemporary flourishes. Stylish Conservatory serves interesting modern dishes.

🏛 **Snooty Fox,** Market Pl, GL8 8DD, ☎ *(01666) 502436, res@snooty-fox.co.uk, Fax (01666) 503479,* 🍴 – ⇌ ℅. **⓪** **Ⅲ** **Ⅷ**
Rest a la carte 17.50/30.00 – **12 rm** ⚏ ✦69.00/74.00 – ✦✦94.00/165.00.
◆ Stone built former 17C wool factory, with extensions, opposite Tudor market place. Characterful bar with inglenook. Individualistic rooms with superior drapes and fabrics. Cosy wood panelled bistro with all-day menu.

🍴 **The Trouble House** (Bedford), Cirencester Rd, GL8 8SG, Northeast : 2 m. on A 433
❀ ☎ *(01666) 502206, enquiries@troublehouse.co.uk, Fax (01666) 504508,* 🍴 – ⇌ **P**. **⓪** **Ⅲ**
Ⅷ
closed 25 December-3 January, Sunday dinner, Monday and Bank Holidays – **Rest** a la carte 27.00/37.50 ⚏.
Spec. Roast scallops with crayfish and Parma ham. Braised ox cheeks and oxtail in red wine with lardons and creamy mash potato. Dessert plate.
◆ Some of England's best pub food is served here! Robust, hearty classics cooked with care and fine local ingredients in a cordial atmosphere of low-beamed bars and big fires.

🍴 **The Gumstool Inn** (at Calcot Manor H.), Calcot, GL8 8YJ, West : 3 ½ m. on A 4135
🍴 ☎ *(01666) 890391, reception@calcotmanor.co.uk, Fax (01666) 890394,* 🍴, ☞ – ⇌ **P**.
⓪ **Ⅲ** **⑩** **Ⅷ**
Rest *(booking essential)* a la carte 20.00/50.00 ⚏.
◆ Cheerful, flagstoned pub incorporated into Calcot Manor. Low ceiling creates atmosphere. Large menus with daily blackboard specials. Classic pub dishes.

at Willesley *Southwest : 4 m. on A 433 –* ⊠ *Tetbury.*

⌂ **Tavern House,** GL8 8QU, ☎ *(01666) 880444, robertson@tavernhouse.co.uk,* ☞ – ⇌
P. ⚘
Rest *(by arrangement)* a la carte approx 17.45 ⚏ **4 rm** ⚏ ✦50.00/75.00 – ✦✦65.00/95.00.
◆ Part 17C former inn and staging post with an attractive and secluded rear garden, which is overlooked by lounge and little breakfast room. Pretty, cottagey bedrooms.

TEWKESBURY *Glos.* 503 504 N 28 *Great Britain G.* – pop. 9 978.
See : *Town★ – Abbey★★ (Nave★★, vault★).*
Env. : *St Mary's, Deerhurst★, SW : 4 m. by A 38 and B 4213.*
☞ *Tewkesbury Park Hotel, Lincoln Green Lane* ☎ *(01684) 295405.*
🛈 *64 Barton St* ☎ *(01684) 295027.*
London 108 – Birmingham 39 – Gloucester 11.

🏨 **Hilton Puckrup Hall,** Puckrup, GL20 6EL, North : 2 ½ m. by A 38 ☎ *(01684) 296200, events-tewkesbury@hilton.com, Fax (01684) 850788, Ⅰ₆,* ⇌, ☒, ☞, ☞ – ⿱ ⇌, ▤ rest, ℅ ⅋ **P** – 🔒 200. **⓪** **Ⅲ** **Ⅷ**
Balharries : Rest *(closed Saturday lunch)* (buffet lunch)/dinner 23.95 and a la carte 25.85/34.85 – ⚏ 15.95 – **110 rm** ✦79.00/199.00 – ✦✦79.00/199.00, 2 suites.
◆ Vast, modern hotel with emphasis on business traveller, built around 17C manor house. Strong leisure facilities. Rooms in main hotel offer all that the business guest needs. Restaurant offers good views across golf course.

⌂ **Evington Hill Farm** without rest., Tewkesbury Rd, The Leigh, GL19 4AQ, South : 5 m. on A 38 ☎ *(01242) 680255, evingtonfarm@gmail.com,* ☞, ⚘ – ⇌ **P**. ⚘
3 rm ⚏ ✦55.00 – ✦✦90.00/100.00.
◆ Converted farmhouse with 16C origins and small conservatory extension. Set in four acres. Characterful, low beamed lounge with real fire. Antique and pine furnished rooms.

⌂ **Alstone Fields Farm** without rest., Stow Rd, Teddington Hands, GL20 8NG, East : 5 m. by A 438 and A 46 on B 4077 ☎ *(01242) 620592, janeandrobin@yahoo.co.uk,* ≤, ☞, ⌁ – ⇌ ℅ **P**. ⚘
– **6 rm** ⚏ ✦45.00 – ✦✦60.00/70.00.
◆ Farmhouse in well-tended garden. Communal breakfast room with view; local ingredients and fruit from the garden. Bright, clean, chintzy rooms, two on the ground floor.

at Corse Lawn Southwest : 6 m. by A 38 and A 438 on B 4211 – ⊠ Gloucester.

Corse Lawn House, GL19 4LZ, ℰ (01452) 780771, enquiries@corselawn.com, Fax (01452) 780840, 🔲, 🐾, ✗ – ❤ 🄿 – 🔬 40. 🐠 🄬 🄰🄴 🄳 𝘝𝘐𝘚𝘈
closed 24-26 December – **Bistro :** Rest 14.50/17.50 (lunch) and a la carte 17.50/27.50 s. 🍷 – (see also **The Restaurant** below) – **17 rm** ⌑ ✦90.00/95.00 – ✦✦140.00/150.00, 2 suites.
♦ Elegant Queen Anne Grade II listed house, set back from village green and fronted by former "coach wash". Two comfortable lounges and classic country house style rooms. Informal brasserie style eatery in atmospheric bar.

The Restaurant (at Corse Lawn House H.), GL19 4LZ, ℰ (01452) 780771, Fax (01452) 780840, 🖼, 🍴 – ❤ 🄿 🐠 🄰🄴 🄳 𝘝𝘐𝘚𝘈
Rest 22.50/29.50 and a la carte 30.00/40.00 s. 🍷 🖼.
♦ Formal restaurant with period décor and framed prints, nicely set overlooking rear garden. Extensive à la carte and set menu. Classic style of dishes; quality wine list.

THAME Oxon. 504 R 28 Great Britain G. – pop. 10 886.
Exc. : Ridgeway Path★★.
🄱 Market House, North St ℰ (01844) 212834.
London 48 – Aylesbury 9 – Oxford 13.

Spread Eagle, 16 Cornmarket, OX9 2BW, ℰ (01844) 213661, enquiries@spreadeagle thame.co.uk, Fax (01844) 261380 – ❤, 🔳 rest, 🄿 – 🔬 250. 🐠 🄰🄴 🄳 𝘝𝘐𝘚𝘈, 🛠
Rest 24.00/28.00 and a la carte 24.00/35.00 s. 🍷 – **31 rm** ⌑ ✦99.95/120.95 – ✦✦115.95/140.95, 2 suites.
♦ Well established market town hotel. In use since 16C and host to writers and politicians over the years. Immaculate lounge bar. Pink and green rooms with antique pine. Informal, relaxed restaurant.

THAXTED Essex 504 V 28 – pop. 2 066.
London 44 – Cambridge 24 – Colchester 31 – Chelmsford 20.

Crossways without rest., 32 Town St, CM6 2LA, ℰ (01371) 830348, info@crosswaysthax ted.co.uk, 🍴 – 🛠
3 rm ⌑ ✦40.00 – ✦✦60.00.
♦ 16C house in picturesque, largely timbered village. Breakfast room is tea room during day. Small lounge with fireplace and beams. Rooms in keeping with age of property.

THIRSK N. Yorks. 502 P 21 – pop. 9 099.
🄵 Thornton-Le-Street ℰ (01845) 522170.
🄱 49 Market Pl ℰ (01845) 522755.
London 227 – Leeds 37 – Middlesbrough 24 – York 24.

Golden Fleece, 42 Market Pl, YO7 1LL, ℰ (01845) 523108, reservations@goldenfleece hotel.com, Fax (01845) 523996 – ❤ 🄿 – 🔬 70. 🐠 🄰🄴 🄳 𝘝𝘐𝘚𝘈
Rest (bar lunch Monday-Saturday)/dinner a la carte 16.70/23.70 s. – **23 rm** ⌑ ✦65.00/75.00 – ✦✦100.00/115.00.
♦ Sizeable Grade II listed 16C coaching inn located in centre of market town. Dick Turpin was a regular visitor. Spacious, comfortable lounge. Well-kept, inviting rooms. Yorkshire flavours are a staple of restaurant.

Spital Hill, York Rd, YO7 3AE, Southeast : 1 ¾ m. on A 19, entrance between 2 white posts ℰ (01845) 522273, spitalhill@amserve.net, Fax (01845) 524970, 🍴, 🐾 – ❤ 🄿 🐠 🄰🄴 𝘝𝘐𝘚𝘈, 🛠
Rest (by arrangement) (communal dining) 29.00 – **3 rm** ⌑ ✦63.00/64.00 – ✦✦98.00.
♦ Expansive early Victorian house surrounded by nearly two acres of secluded gardens. Fully tiled entrance hall and comfortable sitting room. Spacious rooms, warmly furnished. Communal dining at mealtimes.

Laburnum House without rest., 31 Topcliffe Rd, YO7 1RX, Southwest : ¾ m. by A 61 on Wetherby rd ℰ (01845) 524120, 🍴 – ❤ 🄿 🛠
mid March-October – **3 rm** ⌑ – ✦✦50.00.
♦ Modern house on the road into this busy market town, famous for its connection with vet and author James Herriot. Spacious, well-maintained bedrooms at affordable rates.

Oswalds with rm, Church Farm, Front St, Sowerby, YO7 1JF, South : ¾ m. by A 61, Wetherby rd on Sowerby Rd ℰ (01845) 523655, bookings@oswaldsrestaurantwith rooms.co.uk, Fax (01845) 524120, 🍴 – ❤ 🄿 🔬 22. 🐠 𝘝𝘐𝘚𝘈
closed 25 December and Monday lunch – Rest 12.00 (lunch) and a la carte 17.65/26.85 s. 🍷 – **8 rm** ⌑ ✦65.00 – ✦✦95.00.
♦ Collection of red-brick former farm buildings. Characterful rusticity prevails within both dining rooms. Traditionally based cooking with an old-fashioned feel. Comfy rooms.

at Topcliffe Southwest : 4½ m. by A 168 – ⊠ Thirsk.

🏠 **Angel Inn,** Long St, YO7 3RW, ℰ (01845) 577237, res@angelinn.co.uk, Fax (01845) 578000, ⇌, ⇌ rest, **P** – 🔏 150. 🆗 ﷼ 𝘝𝘐𝘚𝘈.
Rest a la carte 17.80/25.50 ♀ – **15 rm** ⊇ ✷55.00/60.00 – ✷✷75.00.
  • Enlarged hostelry dating back to early 17C in tiny village. Spacious lounge and character-ful bar. Popular with business travellers. Sizeable bedrooms have pine furniture. Bright décor enlivens dining room.

at Asenby Southwest : 5¼ m. by A 168 – ⊠ Thirsk.

🏠🏠 **Crab Manor,** Dishforth Rd, YO7 3QL, ℰ (01845) 577286, info@crabandlobster.co.uk, Fax (01845) 577109, ⇌, ⇌ – **P**. 🆗 ﷼ 𝘝𝘐𝘚𝘈. ⚘
Rest – (see **Crab and Lobster** below) – **14 rm** ⊇ ✷150.00/200.00 – ✷✷150.00/200.00, 2 suites.
  • Part Georgian manor filled with quality objects and Victoriana. Highly individual bed-rooms, themed around world famous hotels. Some rooms have outdoor hot tubs.

❌❌ **Crab and Lobster,** Dishforth Rd, YO7 3QL, ℰ (01845) 577286, reservations@craband lobster.co.uk, Fax (01845) 577109, ⇌, ⇌ – ⇌ **P**. 🆗 ﷼ 𝘝𝘐𝘚𝘈. ⚘
Rest – Seafood - 14.50/17.50 (lunch) and a la carte 24.30/37.95 ♀.
  • Atmospheric and individual eating place filled with memorabilia. Choose the informal bar or formal Pavilion restaurant. Seafood oriented menus with blackboard specials.

> We try to be as accurate as possible when giving room rates.
> But prices are susceptible to change,
> so please check rates when booking.

THORNBURY South Gloucestershire 503 504 M 29 – pop. 11 969 – ⊠ Bristol.
London 128 – Bristol 12 – Gloucester 23 – Swindon 43.

🏨🏨🏨 **Thornbury Castle** ⊛, Castle St, BS35 1HH, ℰ (01454) 281182, info@thornburycas tle.co.uk, Fax (01454) 416188, ⇌, ₤ – ⇌ rest, ⚫**P** – 🔏 75. 🆗 ﷼ ① 𝘝𝘐𝘚𝘈
Rest 25.00/42.50 ♀ – **22 rm** ⊇ ✷90.00/195.00 – ✷✷155.00/225.00, 3 suites.
  • 16C castle built by Henry VIII with gardens and vineyard. Two lounges boast plenty of antiques. Rooms of stately comfort; several bathrooms resplendent in marble. Restaurant exudes formal aura.

THORNHAM MAGNA Suffolk 504 X 27 – ⊠ Eye.
London 96 – Cambridge 47 – Ipswich 20 – Norwich 30.

🏠 **Thornham Hall** ⊛, IP23 8HA, ℰ (01379) 783314, hallrestaurant@aol.com, Fax (01379) 788347, ⇌, ⇌, ⇌, ₤, ⚘ – **P**. 🆗 ﷼ ① 𝘝𝘐𝘚𝘈
Rest (by arrangement) (communal dining) 15.00/17.75 and a la carte 18.00/23.00 – **3 rm** ⊇ ✷55.00 – ✷✷90.00.
  • 20C incarnation of former Tudor, Georgian and Victorian homes. House party atmos-phere. Lovely paintings throughout. Comfortable, welcoming rooms. Dining room of char-acter in converted coach house.

at Yaxley West : 2 m. on A 140 – ⊠ Eye.

❌❌ **The Bull Auberge** with rm, Ipswich Rd, IP23 8BZ, ℰ (01379) 783604, deesten house@fsmail.net, Fax (01379) 788486 – ⇌ 🔲 **P**. 🆗 ﷼ ① 𝘝𝘐𝘚𝘈. ⚘
closed Saturday lunch, Sunday, and Monday – **Rest** (dinner only) a la carte 15.65/31.40 – **4 rm** ⊇ ✷65.00/75.00 – ✷✷100.00.
  • 15C inn by busy road; rustic origins enhanced by brick walls, beams and open fire. Original, well presented, modern menus prepared with care. Stylish, well appointed rooms.

THORNTON Lancs 502 K 22 –see Blackpool.

THORNTON HOUGH Mersey. 502 503 K 24 – ⊠ Wirral.
London 215 – Birkenhead 12 – Chester 17 – Liverpool 12.

🏨🏨🏨 **Thornton Hall,** CH63 1JF, on B 5136 ℰ (0151) 336 3938, reservations@thorntonhallho tel.com, Fax (0151) 336 7864, ☜, ₤₅, ⇌, ⬜, ⇌ – ⇌ rm, ₺ **P** – 🔏 400. 🆗 ﷼ ① 𝘝𝘐𝘚𝘈
closed 1 January **The Italian Room :** Rest (bar lunch Saturday) 11.95/28.00 and a la carte 27.00/34.00 s. ♀ – ⊇ 13.50 – **62 rm** ✷119.00 – ✷✷119.00, 1 suite.
  • Family owned, extended manor house with lawned gardens in rural location. Atmos-pheric wood panelled lounges with heavy drapes. Excellent leisure club. Spacious bed-rooms. Rich, warmly decorated dining room with chandelier.

THORPE Derbs. 502 503 504 O 24 Great Britain G. – ✉ Ashbourne.
See : Dovedale★★ (Ilam Rock★).
London 151 – Birmingham 50 – Sheffield 33 – Stoke-on-Trent 26.

🏠 **Peveril of the Peak** ⌘, DE6 2AW, ✆ (01335) 350396, frontdesk@peverilofthe
peak.co.uk, Fax (01335) 350507, ≤, 舜, ※ – 🗝 📞 P – 🅰 150. ◑◐ 🄰🄴 VISA
Rest 13.95/25.00 – **45 rm** � (dinner included) ✿82.50 – ✿✿110.00.
  • Charming Peak District inn hotel at foot of Thorpe Cloud in Dovedale Valley. Set in its
own farmland and country gardens. Rustic lounge. Rooms richly hued with heavy drapes.
Local ingredients to fore in spacious dining room.

THORPE LANGTON Leics. – see Market Harborough.

THORPE MARKET Norfolk 504 X 25 – ✉ North Walsham.
London 130 – Norwich 21.

🏠 **Elderton Lodge** ⌘, Gunton Park, NR11 8TZ, South : 1 m. on A 149 ✆ (01263) 833547,
enquiries@eldertonlodge.co.uk, Fax (01263) 834673, ≤, 舜 – 🗝 📞 ◑◐ 🄰🄴 VISA
Rest 15.00/27.00 – **11 rm** ⊇ ✿65.00 – ✿✿100.00/120.00.
  • Late 18C former shooting lodge on large estate and deer park. Tranquil air. Favoured
retreat of Lillie Langtry. Modern bedrooms are individually styled and comfortable. Local
ingredients used widely in restaurant; particularly good value lunches.

THRELKELD Cumbria 502 K 20 – see Keswick.

THUNDER BRIDGE W. Yorks. – see Huddersfield.

THUNDERSLEY Essex 504 V 29 – see Rayleigh.

THURSFORD GREEN Norfolk.
London 120 – Fakenham 7 – Norwich 29.

🏠 **Holly Lodge** ⌘, The Street, NR21 0AS (01328) 878465, ✆ (01328) 878465, info@holly
lodgeguesthouse.co.uk, 舜 – 🗝 P. ◑◐ VISA. ※
closed 25 December-February – **Rest** 17.50 – **3 rm** ⊇ ✿60.00/70.00 – ✿✿80.00/120.00.
  • Stylishly furnished 18C house set in delightful garden. Welcome includes Pimms by the
pond or afternoon tea. Excellent breakfast. Well appointed bedrooms in converted stables.
Home-cooked evening meals.

THWING East Riding.
London 228 – Bridlington 10 – York 16.

※ **The Falling Stone,** Main St, YO25 3DS, ✆ (01262) 470403 – 🗝 P. ◑◐ VISA. ※
Rest (closed Monday-Tuesday) (dinner only and lunch Saturday-Sunday) a la carte
18.00/25.00 ☒.
  • A relaxed local, typified by owners' friendly mastiff. Snug rooms with low-level sofas. Fine
selection of local beers. Rustic dining room specialises in classical French fare.

TICEHURST E. Sussex 504 V 30 – pop. 3 118 – ✉ Wadhurst.
🏌, 🏌 Dale Hill ✆ (01580) 200112.
London 49 – Brighton 44 – Folkestone 38 – Hastings 15 – Maidstone 24.

🏠 **King John's Lodge** ⌘, Sheepstreet Lane, Etchingham, TN19 7AZ, South : 2 m. by
Church St ✆ (01580) 819232, kingjohnslodge@aol.com, Fax (01580) 819562, ≤, ⌁ heated,
舜, ※ – 🗝 rm, P. ◑◐ 🄰🄴 ◑ VISA. ※
– **Rest** (by arrangement) (communal dining) 25.00 – **4 rm** ⊇ ✿55.00 – ✿✿90.00.
  • Part Tudor hunting lodge with Jacobean additions and stunning gardens. King John II
imprisoned here in 1350. Cosy sitting rooms with log fire. Cottagey bedrooms. Communal
dining room exudes great rustic charm.

TIRRIL Cumbria – see Penrith.

TITLEY Herefordshire 503 L 27 – see Kington.

TIVERTON *Devon 503 J 31 – pop. 16 772.*
London 191 – Bristol 64 – Exeter 15 – Plymouth 63.

⌂ **Hornhill** ⑭ without rest., Exeter Hill, EX16 4PL, East : ½ m. by A 396 and Butterleigh rd
🖉 (01884) 253352, *hornhill@tinyworld.co.uk*, Fax (01884) 253352, ≤, 🐾, 🏠 – 🙌 **P**. ❀
closed Christmas-New Year – **3 rm** 🖂 ✴35.00 – ✴✴58.00.
 ● Georgian house on hilltop boasting pleasant views of the Exe Valley. Well-furnished
drawing room with real fire. Attractively styled bedrooms with antiques.

TODMORDEN *W. Yorks. 502 N 22.*
London 217 – Burnley 10 – Leeds 35 – Manchester 22.

XX **The Old Hall** with rooms, Hall St, OL14 7AD, off A 6033 🖉 (01706) 815998,
Fax (01706) 810669, 🏠, 🐾 – 🙌 **VISA**
closed 25 December, first week January, last 2 weeks August, Sunday dinner and Monday –
Rest (dinner only and Sunday lunch)/dinner a la carte 23.65/27.85 🖵 **2 rm** 🖂 – ✴✴95.00.
 ● Impressive example of an Elizabethan manor house. Three rooms in which to dine: one
boasts a vast fireplace and period grandeur. Sound cooking with global twists.

TOOT BALDON *Oxon. – see Oxford.*

TOPCLIFFE *N. Yorks. 502 P 21 – see Thirsk.*

TOPSHAM *Devon 503 J 31 – ✉ Exeter.*

X **The Galley** with rm, 41 Fore St, EX3 0HU, 🖉 (01392) 876078, *fish@galleyrestaur
ant.co.uk*, Fax (01392) 876333 – 🙌 ⚓, 🍴 ⚪ **VISA**
closed Christmas-New Year, Sunday and Monday – **Rest** - Seafood - a la carte 36.40/41.85 –
2 rm 🖂 ✴87.50/95.00 – ✴✴150.00.
 ● Idiosyncratic and gloriously eccentric, every nook and cranny filled with bric-a-brac or
foody paraphernalia. Original, tasty, locally sourced piscine dishes. Comfy bedrooms.

TORQUAY *Torbay 503 J 32 The West Country G. – pop. 62 968.*
See : *Torbay*★ *– Kent's Cavern*★ *AC* CX **A**.
Env. : *Paignton Zoo*★★ *AC, SE : 3 m. by A 3022 – Cockington*★, *W : 1 m.* AX.
🏌 Petitor Rd, St Marychurch 🖉 (01803) 327471, CX.
🅱 Vaughan Parade 🖉 (08707) 070010, *torquay.tic@torbay.gov.uk.*
London 223 – Exeter 23 – Plymouth 32.

Plans on following pages

🏨 **The Imperial,** Park Hill Rd, TQ1 2DG, 🖉 (01803) 294301, *imperialtorquay@paramoun
thotels.co.uk*, Fax (01803) 298293, ≤ Torbay, ⑭, 🛠, 🚿, 🏊 heated, 🔲, 🐾, ❀, squash –
🖩 🙌, 🍴 rest, ❀ 🔥 🚃 **P** – 🙌 350. ⚪⚪ 🄰🄴 ⚪ **VISA**. ❀   CZ **a**
Regatta : **Rest** (dinner only) 28.50/40.50 🖵 – 🖵 12.50 – **135 rm** ✴160.00/180.00 –
✴✴180.00, 17 suites.
 ● Landmark hotel's super clifftop position is part of Torquay skyline. Palm Court lounge
has classic style. Excellent leisure facilities. Rooms provide stunning bay views. Regatta's
style emulates cruise liner luxury.

🏨 **The Palace,** Babbacombe Rd, TQ1 3TG, 🖉 (01803) 200200, *info@palacetorquay.co.uk*,
Fax (01803) 299899, 🛠, 🛠, 🚿 heated, 🔲, 🐾, ❀, ❀ indoor/outdoor, squash – 🖩,
🙌 rest, ❀ 🚃 **P** – 🙌 350. ⚪⚪ 🄰🄴 ⚪ **VISA**. ❀   CX **u**
Rest (dinner only) 27.00 and a la carte 27.25/38.50 **s.** – **135 rm** 🖂 ✴69.00/94.00 –
✴✴168.00, 6 suites.
 ● Large, traditional hotel in 25 acres of gardens with sub-tropical woodland and charming
terraces. Well-furnished lounge. Excellent leisure facilities. Comfortable rooms. Spacious
restaurant exudes air of fine dining.

🏨 **The Grand,** Sea Front, TQ2 6NT, 🖉 (01803) 296677, *reservations@grandtorquay.co.uk*,
Fax (01803) 213462, ≤, 🛠, 🚿, 🏊 heated, 🔲 – 🖩 🙌 🚃 – 🙌 300. ⚪⚪ 🄰🄴 **VISA**.
❀   BZ **z**
Rest (bar lunch Monday-Saturday)/dinner 30.00 – **124 rm** 🖂 ✴60.00/125.00 –
✴✴120.00/180.00, 7 suites.
 ● All-time classic seaside hotel with famously imposing blue and white exterior. Impressive
basement leisure facilities. Riviera bar, sunny terrace, comfortable rooms. Resplendent
restaurant with heavy drapes, crisp white tablecloths.

ENGLAND

The Osborne, Hesketh Crescent, Meadfoot, TQ1 2LL, ✆ (01803) 213311, enq@osborne-torquay.co.uk, Fax (01803) 296788, ≤, 🏠, 🏋, 🎾, 🏊 heated, 🎾, 🦋, ✗ – 🖐 🍸 📞 📺 –
🏛 30. 🍴 🔘 VISA ✗ CX n
Langtry's : Rest (dinner only) a la carte 21.25/29.50 s. – *The Brasserie :* Rest a la carte 13.50/21.35 s. 🍸 – **33 rm** 🛏 ✦60.00/100.00 – ✦✦120.00/170.00.
✦ Smart hotel situated within elegant Regency crescent. Charming terrace and garden with views over Torbay. Well-appointed rooms: those facing sea have telescope and balcony. Langtry's has classic deep green décor. Informal Brasserie with terrace.

Corbyn Head, Seafront, TQ2 6RH, ✆ (01803) 213611, info@corbynhead.com, Fax (01803) 296152, ≤ – 🍴✗ 📞 📺, 🔘 AE VISA BX a
Harbour View : Rest (lunch booking essential)/dinner 24.95 🍸 – (see also *Orchid* below) –
45 rm 🛏 ✦60.00/100.00 – ✦✦120.00/180.00.
✦ Boasts sea views across Torbay. Pleasant, enthusiastic staff. Very large, comfy sitting room and cosy bar. Bright, airy bedrooms, prettily created from a pastel palette. A friendly atmosphere pervades the main Harbour View dining room.

Marstan, Meadfoot Sea Rd, TQ1 2LQ, ✆ (01803) 292837, enquiries@marstanhotel.co.uk, Fax (01803) 299202, 🏊 heated, 🦋, ✗ – 🍴✗ 📞 📺, 🔘 AE VISA ✗ CX a
closed 12-16 April – **Rest** (Wednesday-Sunday) (dinner only) 20.00/30.00 – **9 rm** 🛏
✦55.00/65.00 – ✦✦130.00.
✦ Substantial 19C house in quiet area; given a 21C edge with hot tub, sun deck and pool. Opulent interior with gold coloured furniture and antiques. Room décor of high standard. Dinner served in sumptuous surroundings.

Colindale without restaurant, 20 Rathmore Rd, Chelston, TQ2 6NY, ✆ (01803) 293947, rathmore@blueyonder.co.uk – 🍴✗ 📞, 🔘 AE ⓞ VISA ✗ BZ a
8 rm 🛏 ✦35.00/45.00 – ✦✦65.00/70.00.
✦ Yellow hued 19C terraced house with pretty front garden. Particularly attractive sitting room with deep sofas and books. Welsh dresser in breakfast room. Immaculate bedrooms.

Cranborne House, 58 Belgrave Rd, TQ2 5HY, ✆ (01803) 298046, info@cranborneho tel@co.uk – 🍴✗ 📞, 🔘 VISA BY i
Rest 22.50 – **10 rm** 🛏 ✦35.00/70.00 – ✦✦60.00/80.00.
✦ Victorian house close to shops and seafront. Light, airy, pastel hued dining room; rear 'clubby' bar dotted with Victoriana. Tasteful rooms boast bathrobes.

Kingston House, 75 Avenue Rd, TQ2 5LL, ✆ (01803) 212760, stay@kingstonhouseho tel.co.uk, Fax (01803) 201425 – 🍴✗ 📞, 🔘 VISA BY n
Restricted opening in winter – **Rest** 18.00/25.00 – **5 rm** 🛏 ✦54.00/64.00 – ✦✦61.00/72.00.
✦ Sunny yellow Victorian house enhanced by vivid summer floral displays; run by friendly Italian husband and wife. Convivial sitting room; bedrooms of individual character. Popular, well crafted evening meals have an Italian slant.

Fairmount House, Herbert Rd, Chelston, TQ2 6RW, ✆ (01803) 605446, stay@fair mounthousehotel.co.uk, Fax (01803) 605446, 🦋 – 🍴✗ 📞, 🔘 VISA AX a
Rest (dinner only) 15.00 s. 🍸 – **8 rm** 🛏 ✦26.00/33.00 – ✦✦58.00/76.00.
✦ Yellow-hued Victorian house above picturesque Cockington Valley. Small bar in conservatory. Spotless, chintz bedrooms: two have doors leading onto secluded rear garden.

The Orchid (at Corbyn Head H.), Seafront, TQ2 6RH, ✆ (01803) 296366, dine@orchid restaurant.net, ≤ – 🍴✗ 📞, 🔘 AE VISA BX a
closed Sunday and Monday – **Rest** (lunch by arrangement)/dinner 34.95 🍸.
✦ On first floor of hotel; benefits from plenty of windows making most of sea view. Immaculate linen cover. Elaborate, modern dishes using top quality ingredients.

The Elephant, 3-4 Beacon Terrace, TQ1 2BH, ✆ (01803) 200044, theelephant@ore stone.co.uk – 🍴✗ ↔ 20. 🔘 AE VISA CZ e
🌸 closed first 2 weeks January, Sunday and Wednesday October-April – **Rest** 19.95 (lunch) and dinner a la carte 30.75/39.75 🍸.
Spec. Roast John Dory on parsnip emulsion with baby artichoke. Crab and creamed avocado "martini" with crab beignet. Dark chocolate tart with espresso ice cream.
✦ Quality cuisine in 19C setting by the harbour. Relax in smart, modish upstairs bar then indulge in wonderfully accomplished modern dishes executed with originality and flair.

Mulberry House with rm, 1 Scarborough Rd, TQ2 5UJ, ✆ (01803) 213639, stay@mul berryhousetorquay.co.uk – 🍴✗, 🔘 VISA CY x
Rest (booking essential) (residents only Monday-Tuesday) a la carte 20.00/27.00 – **3 rm** 🛏
✦45.00/52.00 – ✦✦60.00/80.00.
✦ Personally run, with notable hospitality and a country style feel. Daily changing menu offers very tasty dishes using fresh market produce. Individually styled bedrooms.

Number 7, Beacon Terrace, TQ1 2BH, ✆ (01803) 295055, enquiries@no7-fish.com – 📠.
🔘 AE VISA CZ e
closed 2 weeks Christmas-New Year, 2 weeks February, 1 week November, Tuesday lunch, Sunday and Monday in winter – **Rest** - Seafood - a la carte 23.75/33.50 🍸.
✦ On harbour front in centre of town: modest, friendly, family run restaurant specialising in simply prepared fresh fish, mostly from Brixham. Fishing themes enhance ambience.

ENGLAND

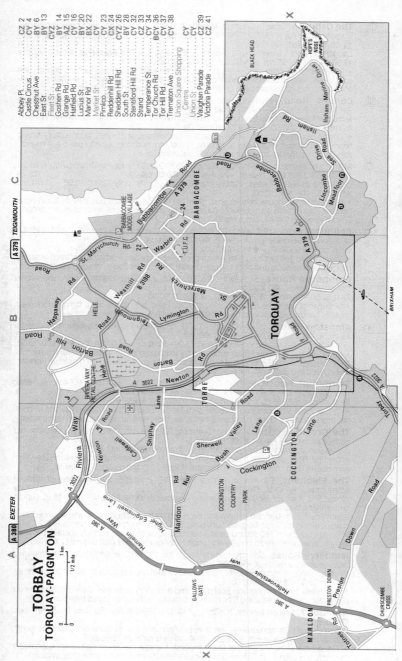

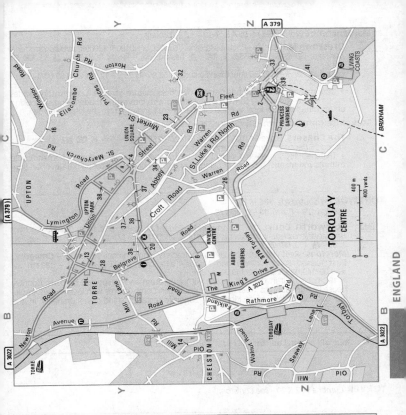

N

TORQUAY
CENTRE

0   400 m
0   400 yards

UPTON

Lymington

TORRE

The
King's Drive
A 3022

RIVIERA
CENTRE

ABBEY
GARDENS

Rathmore Rd

Falkland

Walnut Road

TORQUAY

Torbay Rd

Seaway Lane

CHELSTON

PIO

PIO

Newton   Avenue

Mill   Lane

Belgrave   Road

Croft   Road

Warren   Road

St. Luke's Rd North

St. Marychurch   Rd

Ellacombe   Rd

Princes   Rd

Church   Rd

Windsor   Road

Hoxton

Market   St.

Union   Street

Abbey   Road

Warren   Road

Fleet

UNION
SQUARE

UPTON PARK

Union   Road

Mill   Road

PRINCESS
GARDENS

LIVING
COASTS

ENGLAND

16   23   32   33   41   39   2   1   4   13   28   36   37   38   20   26   37   6   34   15

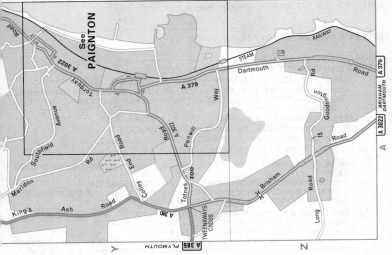

See PAIGNTON

Road

A 3022   Torquay   Way

A 379

STEAM   RAILWAY

Dartmouth   Road

Southfield   Avenue

Maridon   Rd

King's   Ash   Road

Colley   End   Road

A 3022   Road

Totnes   Road

A 380

TWEENAWAYS
CROSS

ZOO

Penwill   Way

Brixham   Road

Goodrington   Rd

Long   Road

N

15

at Maidencombe North : 3½ m. by A 379 – BX – ✉ Torquay.

🏛 **Orestone Manor** ❦, Rockhouse Lane, TQ1 4SX, ✆ (01803) 328098, info@orestonema
nor.com, Fax (01803) 328336, ≤, 斎, ⌁ heated, ☞ – ❧ ✆ ℙ ⇔ 18 – 🏛 30. ◑ ℗
VISA

closed January**Rest** 22.50 (lunch) and a la carte 32.95/45.25 ♀ – **12 rm** ⌖ ✦89.00/149.00 –
✦✦125.00/190.00.

* Country house in the woods! Terrace overlooks mature gardens. Conservatory exudes
exotic charm. Individual rooms. Pleasant dining with interesting modern English cooking
underpinned by tasty local seafood plus herbs, fruit and veg from the kitchen garden.

at Stokeinteignhead North : 5¾ m. by A 379 – BX – ✉ Torquay.

🍴 **The Chasers**, Stoke Rd, TQ12 4QS, ✆ (01626) 873670, 斎 – ❧ ℙ. ◑ **VISA**
closed 26 December and 1 January – **Rest** 21.00/26.50 ♀.
* Thatched 16C inn given a vibrant 21C gastro style makeover including framed foodie
pictures and menus. Top class cooking: chef's touch brings out best from Devonian supplies.

TORTWORTH South Glos. 503 M 29.
London 128 – Bristol 19 – Stroud 18.

🏛 **Tortworth Court** ❦, Wotton-under-Edge, GL12 8HH, ✆ (01454) 263000, tortwor
threservations@four-pillars.co.uk, Fax (01454) 263001, 斎, Ⅰ₄, ☎, ▦, ⌁, ☞, ♫ – ▯ ❧
& ℙ – 🏛 400. ◑ ℗ **VISA**. ✿
Moretons : **Rest** (closed Saturday lunch) (carvery lunch)/dinner 25.95 s. ♀ – **Orangery :**
Rest (closed Sunday dinner and Monday) a la carte 21.85/27.45 s. ♀ – **189 rm** ⌖
✦59.00/149.00 – ✦✦69.00/149.00, 1 suite.
* 19C hotel built in the Gothic style with arboretum and sculptured gardens. Country
house lounges abound. Glass ceilinged atrium bar. Comfy rooms with lovely views. Inspiring outlook to lake from Moretons. Superbly restored stand-alone Orangery in the
grounds.

> Red = Pleasant. Look for the red 🍴 and 🏛 symbols.

TORVER Cumbria 502 K 20 – see Coniston.

TOTLAND I.O.W. 503 504 P 31 – see Wight (Isle of).

TOTLEY S. Yorks. 502 503 504 P 24 – see Sheffield.

TOTNES Devon 503 I 32 The West Country G. – pop. 7 929.
See : Town★ – Elizabethan Museum★ – St Mary's★ – Butterwalk★ – Castle (≤ ★★★) AC.
Env. : Paignton Zoo★★ AC, E : 4½ m. by A 385 and A 3022 – British Photographic Museum,
Bowden House★ AC, S : 1 m. by A 381 – Dartington Hall (High Cross House★), NW : 2 m. on
A 385 and A 384.
Exc. : Dartmouth★★ (Castle ≤ ★★★) SE : 12 m. by A 381 and A 3122.
🏌, 🏌 Dartmouth G & C.C., Blackawton ✆ (01803) 712686.
🛈 The Town Mill, Coronation Rd ✆ (01803) 863168.
London 224 – Exeter 24 – Plymouth 23 – Torquay 9.

🍴🍴 **Wills,** 2-3 The Plains, TQ9 5DR, ✆ (01803) 865192, philsil@btconnect.com – ❧ ⇔ 12. ◑
℗ **VISA**
closed 25 December and Sunday dinner – **Rest** a la carte 19.85/35.85 ♀.
* Smart Regency townhouse restaurant, named after local explorer William Wills. Bold
Georgian décor and antique chairs for dining. Modern British dishes.

🍴 **The Steam Packet Inn** with rm, St Peters Quay, TQ9 5EW, ✆ (01803) 863880, steam
packet@buccaneer.co.uk, Fax (01803) 862754, 斎 – ▯ ❧ ℙ. ◑ ℗ **VISA**
Rest a la carte 23.00/25.50 – **4 rm** ⌖ ✦55.00 – ✦✦79.50.
* 19C inn delightfully set in the quay in the centre of town. Rustic bar is cosy, but most
people come for conservatory, terrace and River Dart. Versatile menus. Sleek bedrooms.

TOWCESTER *Northants.* **503 504** R 27 – *pop. 8 073.*

📍, 📍 *Whittlebury Park G. & C.C., Whittlebury* ℘ (01327) 850000 – 📍 *Farthingstone Hotel, Farthingstone* ℘ (01327) 361291.

London 70 – Birmingham 50 – Northampton 9 – Oxford 36.

at Paulerspury *Southeast : 3¼ m. by A 5 –* ✉ *Towcester.*

XX **Vine House,** 100 High St, NN12 7NA, ℘ (01327) 811267, *info@vinehousehotel.com,* Fax (01327) 811309, 🌳 – 🍴 **P.** **⑩** **VISA**. 🍴
closed Christmas and lunch Monday and Sunday – **Rest** 29.95.
◆ Converted 17C stone building with cottage garden in old village. Pleasantly rustic sitting room, bar with log fire. Quality cooking with traditional base.

TRAFFORD CENTRE *Gtr Manchester – see Manchester.*

TRAFFORD PARK *Gtr Manchester – see Manchester.*

TREFONEN *Shrops.* **502 503** K 25 – *see Oswestry.*

TREGREHAN *Cornwall* **503** F 32 – *see St Austell.*

TRELOWARREN *Cornwall – see Helston.*

TRESCO *Cornwall* **503** B 34 – *see Scilly (Isles of).*

TRING *Herts.* **504** S 28 – *pop. 11 835.*
London 38 – Aylesbury 7 – Luton 14 – Oxford 31.

🏰 **Pendley Manor,** Cow Lane, HP23 5QY, East : 1½ m. by B 4635 off B 4251 ℘ (01442) 891891, *info@pendley-manor.co.uk,* Fax (01442) 890687, ≤, 🛁, 🚪, 🖼, 🌳, 🏊, ❊ – 🛗, 🍴 rest, 🚗 **P.** – 🔔 250. **⑩** **①** **VISA**
Rest 25.00/31.00 and a la carte 27.70/35.25 **s.** – **73 rm** 🛏 ❊95.00/140.00 – ❊❊125.00/150.00.
◆ Attractive manor house in 35 acres of parkland. Good outdoor leisure facilities. Charming, wicker furnished lounge in the modern conservatory. Spacious, functional rooms. Smart, comfy air pervades dining room.

TRINITY *Jersey (Channel Islands)* **503** P 33 and **517** ⑪ – *see Channel Islands.*

TRISCOMBE *Somerset* **503** K 30 – *see Taunton.*

TROUTBECK *Cumbria* **502** L 20 – *see Windermere.*

TROWBRIDGE *Wilts.* **503 504** N 30 *The West Country G. – pop. 34 401.*
Env. : *Westwood Manor★ , NW : 3 m. by A 363 – Farleigh Hungerford★ (St Leonard's Chapel★) AC, W : 4 m.*
Exc. : *Longleat House★★★ AC, SW : 12 m. by A 363, A 350 and A 362 - Bratton Castle (≤★★) SE : 7½ m. by A 363 and B 3098 – Steeple Ashton★ (The Green★) E : 6 m. – Edington (St Mary, St Katherine and All Saints★) SE : 7½ m.*
🛈 *St Stephen's Pl* ℘ (01225) 710535, *visittrowbridge@westwiltshire.gov.uk.*
London 115 – Bristol 27 – Southampton 55 – Swindon 32.

🏨 **Old Manor,** Trowle Common, BA14 9BL, Northwest : 1 m. on A 363 ℘ (01225) 777393, *romanticbeds@oldmanorhotel.com,* Fax (01225) 765443, 🌳 – 🍴 👍 **P.** **⑩** **①** **VISA**
closed 23-30 December – **Rest** *(closed Sunday dinner)* (dinner only and Sunday lunch) 21.00/27.00 – **19 rm** 🛏 ❊70.00/90.00 – ❊❊130.00.
◆ Attractive Grade II listed Queen Anne house with 15C origins. Lovely gardens and pleasant lounges: wealth of beams adds to charm. Most bedrooms - some four poster - in annex. Spacious restaurant with welcoming ambience.

X **Red or White,** Evolution House, 46 Castle St, BA14 8AY, ℘ (01225) 781666, *info@redorwhite.biz,* Fax (01225) 776505 – 🍴 🖼 **P.** ✂ 34. **⑩** **VISA**
closed Sunday and Bank Holidays – **Rest** 8.95/14.75 and a la carte 18.00/27.00 ♀ ☙.
◆ Modern personally-run restaurant at the rear of wine shop where you choose what to drink with your meal. Seasonal food cooked with flair; good value for lunch.

at Semington *Northeast : 2½ m. by A 361 – ⊠ Trowbridge.*

🍴 **The Lamb on the Strand,** 99 The Strand, BA14 6LL, East : 1½ m. on A 361 ✆ (01380) 870263, *philip@cbcc.fsworld.co.uk*, Fax (01380) 871203, 🌳, 🍴 – ✦ 🅿, ⓂⓈ ⒶⒺ 𝑉𝐼𝑆𝐴. 🚭
closed 25 December and 1 January – **Rest** *(closed Sunday dinner)* (booking essential) a la carte 18.00/22.00 ♀.
◆ Attractive ivy-clad pub with 18C origins. Spacious bar affords plenty of seating while dining area has exposed bricks and tasty, original dishes on blackboard menu.

TRUMPET *Herefordshire – see Ledbury.*

TRURO *Cornwall 503 E 33 The West Country G. – pop. 20 920.*
See : *Royal Cornwall Museum*★★ *AC.*
Env. : *Trelissick Garden*★★ *(≤★★) AC, S : 4 m. by A 39 – Feock (Church*★*) S : 5 m. by A 39 and B 3289.*
Exc. : *Trewithen*★★★*, NE : 7½ m. by A 39 and A 390 – Probus (tower*★ *- garden*★*) NE : 9 m. by A 39 and A 390.*
🏌 *Treliske ✆ (01872) 272640 –* 🏌 *Killiow Park, Killiow, Kea ✆ (01872) 270246.*
🅱 *Municipal Buildings, Boscawen St ✆ (01872) 274555.*
London 295 – Exeter 87 – Penzance 26 – Plymouth 52.

🏨 **Royal,** Lemon St, TR1 2QB, ✆ (01872) 270345, *reception@royalhotelcornwall.co.uk*, Fax (01872) 242453 – ✦ 🕭 🅿. ⓂⓈ ⒶⒺ ⓄⒹ 𝑉𝐼𝑆𝐴. 🚭
closed 24-28 December – **Mannings : Rest** *(closed Sunday lunch)* a la carte 27.60/43.70 ♀ – **26 rm** ⊊ ✦75.00/99.00 – ✦✦99.00, 9 suites.
◆ The name came after Prince Albert stayed in 1846: the Royal Arms stands proudly above the entrance. Comfortable, stylish lounges; modern bedrooms. Cuisine with global influences.

❌ **Saffron,** 5 Quay St, TR1 2HB, ✆ (01872) 263771, *saffronrestaurant@btconnect.com* – ✦. ⓂⓈ
closed 25-26 December, Bank Holidays, Sunday and Monday dinner in winter – **Rest** a la carte 27.00/35.50 **s.** ♀.
◆ Bright exterior with colourful hanging baskets and attractive brightly coloured interior with a rustic tone. Varied Cornish menus to be enjoyed at any hour of the day.

TUNBRIDGE WELLS *Kent 504 U 30 – see Royal Tunbridge Wells.*

TUNSTALL *Cumbria – see Kirkby Lonsdale.*

TURNERS HILL *W. Sussex 504 T 30 – pop. 1 534.*
London 33 – Brighton 24 – Crawley 7.

🏰 **Alexander House** 🔆, East St, RH10 4QD, East : 1 m. on B 2110 ✆ (01342) 714914, *info@alexanderhouse.co.uk*, Fax (01342) 717328, ≤, ⑩, 🌳, 🌡, ❌ – 🛗, ✦ rest, 🕭 🅿 – 🔆 120. ⓂⓈ ⒶⒺ ⓄⒹ 𝑉𝐼𝑆𝐴
Alexanders : Rest *(closed Sunday dinner and Monday)* (dinner only and Sunday lunch)/dinner a la carte 34.00/45.50 – **Reflections brasserie : Rest** a la carte 25.00/32.00 – ⊊ 15.00 – **36 rm** ✦155.00 – ✦✦350.00, 2 suites.
◆ Set in extensive gardens, a stunning, classically comfortable country house, once owned by the family of poet Percy Shelley. Luxuriously appointed rooms in rich chintz. Sumptuous Alexanders. Informal air at Reflections.

TURVILLE *Bucks. – ⊠ Henley-on-Thames.*
London 45 – Oxford 22 – Reading 17.

🍴 **The Bull & Butcher,** RG9 6QU, ✆ (01491) 638283, *info@thebullandbutcher.com*, Fax (01491) 638836, 🌳 – ✦ 🅿. ⓂⓈ 𝑉𝐼𝑆𝐴
Rest a la carte 21.00/28.00 ♀.
◆ Small pub in charming 'Vicar of Dibley' village. Flagstone flooring, log fires and scrubbed pine. Slightly different modern and traditional menus served in all dining areas.

Undecided between two equivalent establishments?
Within each category, establishments are classified
in our order of preference.

ENGLAND

TWO BRIDGES *Devon 503* I 32 *The West Country G.* – ⊠ *Yelverton.*
Env. : *Dartmoor National Park*★★.
London 226 – Exeter 25 – Plymouth 17.

🏛 **Prince Hall** ♨, PL20 6SA, East : 1 m. on B 3357 ℰ (01822) 890403, *info@prince hall.co.uk, Fax (01822) 890676, ≼, ♋, ⇔ – ⇔ ⚓ P. ⓌⓄ ஊ VISA*
closed January – **Rest** *(booking essential for non-residents) (dinner only)* 27.95/35.00 **s.** –
9 rm *(dinner included)* ⊡ ✸95.00/175.00 – ✸✸220.00/250.00.
♦ Unique 18C country house, traditional in style, set alone in heart of Dartmoor. Magnificent view over West Dart River to rolling hills. Individually styled rooms. Local dishes proudly served in rustic restaurant.

TYNEMOUTH *Tyne and Wear 501 502* P 18 – *pop. 17 056.*
London 290 – Newcastle upon Tyne 8 – Sunderland 7.

🏛 **Grand,** Grand Parade, NE30 4ER, ℰ (0191) 293 6666, *info@grandhotel-uk.com, Fax (0191) 293 6665, ≼ – ⮹ ⇔ – ⚐ 130. ⓌⓄ ஊ VISA ✺*
Rest *(closed Sunday dinner)* a la carte 29.85/33.40 – **45 rm** ⊡ ✸85.00 – ✸✸95.00.
♦ Impressive Victorian hotel built as home for Duchess of Northumberland. Commanding views over coastline. Atmospheric lounges and bars. Well-equipped rooms with fine views. Classical dining room with imposing drapes, floral displays and ceiling cornices.

⌂ **Martineau Guest House** *without rest.,* 57 Front St, NE30 4BX, ℰ (0191) 296 0746, *martineau.house@ukgateway.net, ⇔ – ⇔. ✺*
3 rm ⊡ ✸45.00/55.00 – ✸✸70.00.
♦ 18C Georgian stone terraced house in main street, named after Harriet Martineau. Breakfast in open plan kitchen. Homely spacious individually styled rooms, two with view.

✗ **Sidney's,** 3-5 Percy Park Rd, NE30 4LZ, ℰ (0191) 257 8500, *bookings@sidneys.co.uk, Fax (0191) 257 9800 – ⇔. ⓌⓄ ஊ VISA*
closed 25-26 December, Sunday and Bank Holidays – **Rest** *(booking essential)* 12.00 *(lunch)*
and a la carte 20.50/29.95 ☯.
♦ Fine painted, wood floored, busy little restaurant with two dining areas. The modern British cooking is interesting with plenty of variety and choice.

ENGLAND

> 😊 Look out for red symbols, indicating particularly pleasant establishments.

UCKFIELD *E. Sussex 504* U 31 – *pop. 15 374.*
London 45 – Brighton 17 – Eastbourne 20 – Maidstone 34.

🏨 **Horsted Place** ♨, Little Horsted, TN22 5TS, South : 2½ m. by B 2102 and A 22 on A 26
ℰ (01825) 750581, *hotel@horstedplace.co.uk, Fax (01825) 750459, ≼, ⌗, ⌘, ⇔, 𝟃, ✺ –*
⮹ ⇔ rest, P. – ⚐ 80. ⓌⓄ ஊ ⓞ VISA. ✺
closed first week January – **Rest** *(closed Saturday lunch)* 18.95 *(lunch)* and a la carte 36.00 ☯
– **15 rm** ⊡ ✸130.00/170.00 – ✸✸130.00/170.00, 5 suites.
♦ Imposing country house from the height of the Victorian Gothic revival; handsome Pugin-inspired drawing rooms and luxurious bedrooms overlook formal gardens and parkland. Pristine restaurant with tall 19C archways and windows.

🏨 **Buxted Park** ♨, Buxted, TN22 4AY, Northeast : 2 m. on A 272 ℰ (01825) 733333, *buxtedpark@handpicked.co.uk, Fax (01825) 732770, ≼, ⌗, 𝕝ₐ, ⇌ₛ, ♋, ⇔, ♨ – ⇔ ⚓ ⅋*
P. – ⚐ 130. ⓌⓄ ஊ ⓞ VISA
Orangery : **Rest** *(closed Saturday lunch)* 17.95/39.50 lunch and dinner a la carte
38.50/46.50 – ⊡ 12.95 – **43 rm** ✸155.00 – ✸✸165.00, 1 suite.
♦ 18C Palladian mansion in 300 acres with ornate public areas exuding much charm: spacious, period lounges. Rooms, modern in style, in original house or garden wing. Beautiful all-glass Orangery restaurant with large terrace.

UFFINGTON *Oxon. 503 504* P 29.
London 75 – Oxford 29 – Reading 32 – Swindon 17.

⌂ **Craven** ♨, Fernham Rd, SN7 7RD, ℰ (01367) 820449, *carol@thecraven.co.uk, Fax (01367) 820351, ⇔ – ⇔ P. ⓌⓄ ⓞ VISA. ✺*
Rest *(by arrangement) (communal dining)* 25.00 – **5 rm** ⊡ ✸45.00/55.00 –
✸✸65.00/105.00.
♦ 17C thatched hostelry; some rooms in brewhouse, stables. Quaint features: winding passageways, antique weighing machine in bathroom, four-poster with Victorian pillowslips. Dine in huge scarlet-walled kitchen with pretty china on dresser.

713

ULLINGSWICK *Herefordshire* 503 504 M 27 – ⊠ *Hereford.*
London 134 – Hereford 12 – Shrewsbury 52 – Worcester 19.

▷ **Three Crowns Inn,** Bleak Acre, HR1 3JQ, East : 1 ¼ m. ℰ (01432) 820279, *info@three crownsinn.com, Fax (08700) 515338,* ⇔, ⇒ – ⇔ **P.** ⬛ **VISA**. ⬤
closed 2 weeks after lunch 25 December and Monday – **Rest** 14.95 (lunch) and a la carte 14.95/24.75 ☘.
♦ Pleasant part-timbered pub on a quiet country road: hops hang from the beams. Eclectic assortment of benches and pews. Rustic, robust dishes on daily changing menus.

ULLSWATER *Cumbria* 502 L 20 – ⊠ *Penrith.*
🔼 *Beckside Car Park, Glenridding, Penrith* ℰ *(017684) 82414.*
London 296 – Carlisle 25 – Kendal 31 – Penrith 6.

at Pooley Bridge *on B 5320 –* ⊠ *Penrith.*

🏛 **Sharrow Bay Country House** ⬦, CA10 2LZ, South : 2 m. on Howtown rd
ℰ (017684) 86301, *info@sharrowbay.co.uk, Fax (017684) 86349,* < Ullswater and fells, ⬦,
⇒ – ⇔, ⬛ rest, **P.** ⬛ ⬛ **VISA**
Rest (booking essential) 39.50/52.50 ☘ ⬦ – **20 rm** (dinner included) ⬦ ⬤135.00/210.00 –
⬤⬤350.00/420.00, 4 suites.
Spec. Braised pork belly with foie gras and sweetbread black pudding. Fillet of sea bass with parsnip purée and scallop velouté. Sticky toffee pudding soufflé with toffee sauce.
♦ Quintessential country house on the shores of Ullswater: marvellous lake views. Traditional rooms, some in grounds and formal gardens, retain a charming, very English feel. Antique-filled restaurant plus tables overlooking the water. Refined classical cooking.

at Watermillock *on A 592 –* ⊠ *Penrith.*

🏛 **Rampsbeck Country House** ⬦, CA11 0LP, ℰ (017684) 86442, *enquiries@ramps beck.fsnet.co.uk, Fax (017684) 86688,* < Ullswater and fells, ⇒, ⬤ – ⇔ rest, **P.** ⬛ **VISA**
closed 3 January- 9 February – **Rest** – (see **The Restaurant** below) – **18 rm** ⬦
⬤75.00/90.00 – ⬤⬤120.00/250.00, 1 suite.
♦ Classically proportioned 18C country house with attractive terraced gardens and spectacular views across Lake Ullswater; some rooms have balconies to make the most of this.

🏛 **Leeming House** ⬦, CA11 0JJ, on A 592 ℰ (017684) 86622, *leeminghouse@macdon ald-hotels.co.uk, Fax (017684) 86443,* <, ⇔, ⬦, ⇒, ⬤ – ⇔ **P.** – ⬛ 24. ⬛ ⬛ **VISA**
Regency : Rest (dinner only) 17.50/36.00 ☘ – **41 rm** (dinner included) ⬦ ⬤136.00/186.00 – ⬤⬤185.00/225.00.
♦ Built as private residence in 19C for local family; in stepped gardens leading down to Lake Ullswater. A rural retreat with croquet lawn; appropriately styled country rooms. Georgian dining room brightened by mirrors and chandelier.

🏠 **Old Church** ⬦, CA11 0JN, ℰ (017684) 86204, *info@oldchurch.co.uk, Fax (017684) 86368,* < Ullswater and fells, ⬦, ⇒ – ⬇ ⇔ **P.** ⬛ ⬛ **VISA**. ⬤
Easter-October – **Rest** *(closed Sunday-Monday)* (booking essential) (dinner only) 35.00 s. –
10 rm ⬦ ⬤70.00 – ⬤⬤180.00.
♦ Beautifully located Georgian house looks out on austere fells the shores of Ullswater. Charming, traditionally appointed lounge and cosy rooms in tasteful fabrics. Polished wood tables and simple, locally sourced cooking in the dining room.

XX **The Restaurant** (at Rampsbeck Country House H.), CA11 0LP, ℰ (017684) 86442, *Fax (017684) 86688,* < Ullswater and fells, ⇒, ⬤ – ⇔ **P.** ⬛ **VISA**
closed 3 January- 9 February – **Rest** (booking essential) (lunch by arrangement Monday-Saturday)/dinner 39.50.
♦ Choose from classic staples - salmon and spinach - to more creative options - beef fillet with roast veal sweetbreads, kumquat soufflé. Savour the flavour; admire the view.

▷ **Brackenrigg Inn** with rm, CA11 0LP, ℰ (017684) 86206, *enquiries@brackenrig ginn.co.uk, Fax (017684) 86945,* < Ullswater and fells, ⇔, ⇒ – ⇔ rest, ⬤ **P.** ⬛ **VISA**
Rest a la carte 16.00/24.95 ☘ – **17 rm** ⬦ ⬤33.00/38.00 – ⬤⬤61.00/79.00.
♦ 18C coaching inn in prime position overlooking lake and fells. Tasty, traditional cooking served in the bar or the restaurant. Fine selection of ales. Cosy rooms.

at Glenridding *on A 592 –* ⊠ *Penrith.*

🏛 **The Inn on the Lake,** CA11 0PE, ℰ (017684) 82444, *info@innonthelakeullswa ter.co.uk, Fax (017684) 82303,* < Ullswater and fells, ⛱, ⬛, ⇒, ⬤ – ⬥ ⬇ ⇔ **P.** – ⬛ 50.
⬛ ⬛ ⬤ **VISA**
Rest 15.95/32.95 ☘ – **46 rm** ⬦ ⬤71.00 – ⬤⬤164.00/184.00.
♦ This busy Lakeland hotel on the shores of Ullswater is popular with families. Pleasant terrace. Sizeable bedrooms, most with grand views. Ramblers Bar pub. Restaurant takes in lovely vistas of lake and fells.

ENGLAND

ULVERSTON *Cumbria 502* K 21 – *pop. 11 210.*
🛈 *Coronation Hall, County Sq* ℰ *(01229) 587120.*
London 278 – Kendal 25 – Lancaster 36.

⌂ **Church Walk House** without rest., Church Walk, LA12 7EW, ℰ (01229) 582211, *mar tinchadd@btinternet.com –* ⇥⇤
restricted opening in winter – **3 rm** ⇄ ✝25.00/35.00 – ✝✝60.00/65.00.
◆ Converted, privately owned Georgian town house; bedrooms and sitting room alike are spacious and comfortably furnished. A short walk from the Laurel and Hardy Museum.

XX **The Bay Horse** ⌖ with rm, Canal Foot, LA12 9EL, East : 2 ¼ m. by A 5087, turning left at Morecambe Tavern B&B and beyond Industrial area, on the coast ℰ (01229) 583972, *reservations@thebayhorsehotel.co.uk*, Fax (01229) 580502, ≤ Morecambe Bay – ⇥⇤ rest, **P**. **⍟** **AE** **VISA**
Rest *(closed Monday lunch)* (booking essential) 31.50 (dinner) and a la carte 21.00/40.00 – **9 rm** ⇄ ✝80.00 – ✝✝85.00/117.50.
◆ Well-established inn by Ulverston Sands. Smart conservatory, flavourful seasonal menu and friendly staff. Cosy rooms, some equipped with binoculars and birdwatching guides.

UMBERLEIGH *Devon 503* I 31.
London 196 – Barnstaple 8 – Bideford 15.5.

⌂ **Eastacott Barton** ⌖ without rest., EX37 9AJ, Southeast : 1 ½ m. by B 3227 and Warkleigh rd on Eastercott rd ℰ (01769) 540545, *stay@eastacott.com*, ≤, 🦢, ⚑ – ⇥⇤ **P**. **⍟** **VISA**
closed 25 December - 12 January – **5 rm** – ✝✝85.00/125.00.
◆ 19C country house with peaceful views over the hills and plentiful grounds to roam. Run by experienced ex-hoteliers. Delightful breakfast conservatory. Enticing mix of rooms.

If breakfast is included the ⇄ symbol appears after the number of rooms.

UPPER HARBLEDOWN SERVICE AREA *Kent – see Canterbury.*

UPPER ODDINGTON *Glos. – see Stow-on-the-Wold.*

UPPER SLAUGHTER *Glos. 503* O 28 – *see Bourton-on-the-Water.*

UPPINGHAM *Rutland 504* R 26 – *pop. 3 947.*
London 101 – Leicester 19 – Northampton 28 – Nottingham 35.

X **Lake Isle** with rm, 16 High St East, LE15 9PZ, ℰ (01572) 822951, *info@lakeislehotel.com*, Fax (01572) 824400 – ⇥⇤ **⚞** **P**. **⍟** **AE** **VISA**
Rest *(closed Sunday dinner and Monday lunch)* a la carte 19.95/32.25 ⴲ – **10 rm** ⇄ ✝60.00 – ✝✝75.00/120.00, 2 suites.
◆ Converted 18C shop; old scales, pine dresser and tables. Simple, well-judged seasonal menu, fine half-bottle cellar. Rooms in pretty cottage style, named after wine regions.

at Glaston *East : 2½ m. on A 47 –* ✉ *Uppingham.*

🏠 **The Old Pheasant** with rm, 15 Main Rd, LE15 9BP, ℰ (01572) 822326, *info@the oldpheasant.co.uk*, Fax (01572) 823316, �─ – ⇥⇤ **P**. **⍟** **VISA**. ⌖
closed 25 December – **Rest** *(closed Sunday dinner)* a la carte 19.85/29.95 ⴲ – **9 rm** ⇄ ✝45.00/60.00 – ✝✝75.00/100.00.
◆ 18C former coaching inn, refurbished sympathetically with building's age. Classic pub cooking underpinned by Rutland ingredients. Updated rooms are comfortable and pleasant.

at Lyddington *South : 2 m. by A 6003 –* ✉ *Uppingham.*

🏠 **Old White Hart** with rm, 51 Main St, LE15 9LR, ℰ (01572) 821703, *mail@oldwhite hart.co.uk*, Fax (01572) 821965, ⚑ – ⇥⇤ rest, **P**. **⍟** **VISA**. ⌖
closed 25 December – **Rest** *(closed Sunday dinner)* 12.95 (lunch) and a la carte 18.75/32.15 – **6 rm** ⇄ ✝55.00 – ✝✝80.00/85.00.
◆ Very pleasant 17C pub in pretty village; rural memorabilia within and huge petanque court without. Tasty, carefully prepared dishes. Welcoming rooms with a country feel.

UPTON SCUDAMORE *Wilts. 503* N 30 – *see Warminster.*

UPTON-UPON-SEVERN *Worcs.* 503 504 N 27 – *pop. 1 789.*

 🛈 *4 High St* ℰ *(01684) 594200, upton.tic@malvernhills.gov.uk.*
 London 116 – Hereford 25 – Stratford-upon-Avon 29 – Worcester 11.

⌂ **Tiltridge Farm and Vineyard** ⌂ without rest., Upper Hook Rd, WR8 0SA, West : 1
 ½ m. by A 4104 and Greenfields Rd following B&B signs ℰ *(01684) 592906, info@til
 tridge.com, Fax (01684) 594142,* 🌿 – ⇖ **P**, **MO** **VISA**.
 closed 24 December-1 January – **3 rm** ⇆ ✸40.00 – ✸✸60.00.
 ◆ Extended 17C farmhouse at the entrance to a small vineyard. Homely lounge, dominated by a broad inglenook fireplace, and spacious bedrooms, one with original timbers.

at Hanley Swan *Northwest : 3 m. by B 4211 on B 4209* – ⊠ *Upton-upon-Severn.*

⌂ **Yew Tree House** without rest., WR8 0DN, ℰ *(01684) 310736, info@yewtree
 house.co.uk, Fax (01684) 311709,* 🌿 – ⇖ **P**, **MO** **VISA**. ⌖
 3 rm ⇆ ✸40.00/45.00 – ✸✸65.00/70.00.
 ◆ Imposing cream coloured Georgian guesthouse, built in 1780, in centre of pleasant
 village. One mile from Three Counties Showground. Cosy lounge; individually styled rooms.

URMSTON *Gtr Manchester* 502 M 23.
 London 204.5 – Manchester 9.5 – Sale 4.5.

✗ **Isinglass,** 46 Flixton Rd, M40 1AB, ℰ *(0161) 749 8400, isinglass@ntlworld.com* – ⇖. **MO**
 AE **VISA**
 closed Monday – **Rest** (dinner only and Sunday lunch) a la carte 17.35/24.10.
 ◆ Hidden away in Manchester suburb, this is a neighbourhood favourite. Very personally
 run, with warm rustic interior. Unusual dishes underpinned by a strong Lancastrian base.

UTTOXETER *Staffs.* 503 504 O 25 – *pop. 12 023.*
 London 150 – Birmingham 41 – Stafford 16.

at Beamhurst *Northwest : 3 m. on A 522* – ⊠ *Uttoxeter.*

✗✗ **Gilmore at Strine's Farm,** ST14 5DZ, ℰ *(01889) 507100, paul@restaurantgil
 more.com, Fax (01889) 507238,* 🌿 – ⇖ **P**, **MO** **VISA**
 *closed 1 week January, 1 week Easter, 2 weeks August, Monday, Tuesday, Saturday lunch
 and Sunday dinner* – **Rest** (booking essential) 19.50/32.50.
 ◆ Personally run converted farmhouse in classic rural setting. Three separate, beamed,
 cottage style dining rooms. New approach to classic dishes: fine local ingredients used.

VAZON BAY *Guernsey (Channel Islands)* 503 P 33 and 517 ⑨ – *see Channel Islands.*

VENTNOR *I.O.W.* 503 504 Q 32 – *see Wight (Isle of).*

VERYAN *Cornwall* 503 F 33 *The West Country G.* – ⊠ *Truro.*
 See : Village★.
 London 291 – St. Austell 13 – Truro 13.

🏨 **Nare** ⌂, Carne Beach, TR2 5PF, Southwest : 1 ¼ m. ℰ *(01872) 501111, office@nareho
 tel.co.uk, Fax (01872) 501856,* ≤ Carne Bay, 🍴, ƒ♨, ⇆, ⌁ heated, ⌸, 🌿, ✗ – ⅼ,
 ⇖ rest, **P**, **MO** **VISA**. ⌖
 The Dining Room : **Rest** (dinner only and Sunday lunch) 41.00 – **Quarterdeck :** **Rest** a la
 carte 22.20/57.70 ⌐ – **35 rm** ⇆ ✸105.00/239.75 – ✸✸306.00/380.00, 4 suites.
 ◆ On the curve of Carne Bay, surrounded by National Trust land; superb beach. Inside,
 owner's Cornish art collection in evidence. Most rooms have patios and balconies. The
 Dining Room boasts high windows and sea views; dinner dress code. Informal Quarterdeck.

at Ruan High Lanes *West : 1¼ m. on A 3078* – ⊠ *Truro.*

🏛 **The Hundred House,** TR2 5JR, ℰ *(01872) 501336, enquiries@hundredhouseho
 tel.co.uk, Fax (01872) 501151,* 🌿 – ⇖ **P**, **MO** **AE** **VISA**. ⌖
 closed 2 January - 12 February **Fish in the Fountain :** **Rest** (booking essential for non-
 residents) (dinner only) 30.00 – **10 rm** ⇆ ✸60.00 – ✸✸120.00.
 ◆ Personally run small hotel: its period furnished hallway with fine staircase, ornate wallpaper sets tone of care and attention to detail. Mirrors, flowers, fine china abound. Comfortable dining room serves West Country fare.

VIRGINSTOW Devon 503 H 31.
London 227 – Bideford 25 – Exeter 41 – Launceston 11 – Plymouth 33.

🏛 **Percy's,** Coombeshead Estate, EX21 5EA, Southwest : 1 ¼ m. on Tower Hill rd ℰ (01409)
211236, *info@percys.co.uk, Fax (01409) 211460*, ≤, 🌦, 🔊 – ⤫ ✦ 📞 ⬛ 🆚
Rest – (see below) – **8 rm** ⬜ †110.00 – ††190.00.
  • Rural location surrounded by 130 acres of land and forest which include woodland trails
and animals. Airy, modern rooms in granary or bungalow boast range of charming extras.

XX **Percy's,** Coombeshead Estate, EX21 5EA, Southwest : 1 ¼ m. on Tower Hill rd ℰ (01409)
211236, *info@percys.co.uk, Fax (01409) 211460*, 🌦 – ⤫ 📞 ⬛ 🆚
Rest *(dinner only)* 40.00 ⚎.
  • Modern rear extension with deep sofas alongside chic ash and zinc bar. Restaurant has
an understated style. Locally sourced, organic produce and homegrown vegetables.

WADDESDON Bucks. 504 R 28 *Great Britain G.* – pop. 1 865 – ✉ Aylesbury.
See : *Chiltern Hills*★.
Env. : *Waddesdon Manor*★★ , S :½ m. by a 41 and minor rd – *Claydon House*★ , N : by minor
rd.
London 51 – Aylesbury 5 – Northampton 32 – Oxford 31.

🍴 **The Five Arrows** with rm, High St, HP18 0JE, ℰ (01296) 651727, *bookings@thefivear
rowshotel.fsnet.co.uk, Fax (01296) 658596*, 🌦 , 🌦 – ⤫ ✦ 📞 ⬛ 🆚 🆎 🆚 . ⤫
Rest *(closed Sunday dinner)* 19.50 (lunch) and a la carte 20.00/36.00 ⚎ – ⬜ 5.00 – **11 rm**
†75.00 – ††150.00.
  • 19C inn on the Rothschild estate, an influence apparent in pub crest and wine cellar.
Stylish dining, relaxed ambience, Anglo-Mediterranean menu. Classic rooms.

Your opinions are important to us:
please write and let us know about your discoveries and experiences –
good and bad!

WAKEFIELD W. Yorks. 502 P 22 *Great Britain G.* – pop. 76 886.
Env. : *Nostell Priory*★ *AC*, SE : 4½ m. by A 638.
🏌 *City of Wakefield, Lupset Park, Horbury Rd* ℰ (01924) 367442 – 🏌 *28 Woodthorpe Lane,
Sandal* ℰ (01924) 258778 – 🏌 *Painthorpe House, Painthorpe Lane, Crigglestone* ℰ (01924)
255083.
🅱 *9 The Bull Ring* ℰ (0845) 6018353, tic@wakefield.gov.uk.
London 188 – Leeds 9 – Manchester 38 – Sheffield 23.

🏛 **Express by Holiday Inn** without rest., Denby Dale Rd, WF4 3BB, Southwest : 2 m. on
A 636 at junction with M 1 ℰ (01924) 257555, *Fax (01924) 249888* – 🛏 ⤫ ✦ & 📞 – 🔒 30.
⬛ 🆎 ⬀ 🆚 . ⤫
74 rm †59.95 – ††59.95.
  • A short distance from the M1, and 10 minutes' drive from centre of town. Good value,
up-to-date budget accommodation for the business traveller with well-equipped rooms.

XX **Aagrah,** 108 Barnsley Rd, Sandal, WF1 5NX, South : 1 ¼ m. on A 61 ℰ (01924) 242222,
Fax (01924) 240562 – ▤ 📞 ⬛ 🆎 🆚
closed 25 December – **Rest** - Indian (Kashmiri) - (booking essential) (dinner only) 15.00 and
a la carte 14.95/21.05 **s**.
  • Ornate Eastern curios and furnishings catch the eye in this ever-lively restaurant; good
choice of genuine Indian dishes; friendly service from a smartly dressed team.

WALBERTON W. Sussex – see Arundel.

WALCOTT Norfolk – ✉ Norwich.
London 134 – Cromer 12 – Norwich 23.

⌂ **Holly Tree Cottage** 🌿 without rest., Walcott Green, NR12 0NS, South : 2 m. by B
1159 and Stalham rd taking 2nd left after Lighthouse Inn ℰ (01692) 650721, 🌦 – ⤫ 📞.
⤫
May-September – **3 rm** ⬜ †40.00 – ††60.00.
  • A hospitable couple keep this traditional Norfolk flint cottage in excellent order. Snug
lounge with wood-fired stove and neat rooms overlooking fields. Good breakfasts.

WALLASEY *Mersey.* 502 503 K 23 – *pop. 58 710 –* ✉ *Wirral.*

⛳ *Wallasey, Bayswater Rd* ℘ *(0151) 691 1024.*

London 222 – Birkenhead 3 – Liverpool 4.

🏛 **Grove House,** Grove Rd, CH45 3HF, ℘ (0151) 639 3947, *reception@thegrove house.co.uk, Fax (0151) 639 0028,* 🌳 – ▤ rest, 🅿. – 🔏 100. ⓌⒸ 🄰🄴 ⓞ 𝐕𝐈𝐒𝐀. ❤️
Rest 14.95/18.95 lunch and a la carte 16.40/27.85 – 🖙 7.95 – **14 rm** ✦64.75/79.75 –
✦✦79.75/89.75.
◆ Part Victorian house in a residential street. Meeting room with conservatory. Bedrooms in different shapes and sizes: quieter rear accommodation overlooks garden. Oak-panelled dining room.

WALLINGFORD *Oxon.* 503 504 Q 29 *Great Britain G. – pop. 8 019.*

Exc. : *Ridgeway Path★★.*

🔼 *Town Hall, Market Pl* ℘ *(01491) 826972.*

London 54 – Oxford 12 – Reading 16.

🏛 **George,** High St, OX10 0BS, ℘ (01491) 836665, *info@george-hotel-wallingford.com, Fax (01491) 825359 –* ❤️ ❤️ 🅿. – 🔏 140. ⓌⒸ 🄰🄴 ⓞ 𝐕𝐈𝐒𝐀. ❤️
Rest 13.75 and dinner a la carte 16.95/25.10 s. ♀ – 🖙 11.85 – **39 rm** ✦118.00/148.00 –
✦✦125.00/135.00.
◆ Part 16C coaching inn with well-run ambience in market town centre. Bustling beamed public bar with real fire. Cosy, well-kept lounge. Characterful, stylish bedrooms. Appealing restaurant with memorable pink décor.

at North Stoke *South : 2¾ m. by A 4130 and A 4074 on B 4009 –* ✉ *Wallingford.*

🏛 **The Springs** 🦢, Wallingford Rd, OX10 6BE, ℘ (01491) 836687, *info@thespringsho tel.com, Fax (01491) 836877,* ≤, ⌘s, ⬛, ⛳, 🦢, 🌳, ♨ – ❤️ ❤️ 🅿. – 🔏 70. ⓌⒸ 🄰🄴 ⓞ 𝐕𝐈𝐒𝐀
Rest (carving lunch Sunday) 16.50/25.00 and dinner a la carte 29.50/36.50 ♀ – **30 rm** 🖙
✦95.00 – ✦✦110.00/155.00, 2 suites.
◆ Sympathetically extended Victorian mock-Tudor house incorporates spacious bed-rooms, oak-panelled front lounge with fireside leather armchairs and several meeting rooms. Ducks bob past restaurant on lake fed by local spring.

👨‍🍳 The ✿ award is the crème de la crème.
This is awarded to restaurants
which are really worth travelling miles for!

WALTHAM ABBEY *Essex* 504 U 28 *– pop. 17 675.*

🔼 *4 Highbridge St* ℘ *(01992) 652295.*

London 15 – Cambridge 44 – Ipswich 66 – Luton 30 – Southend-on-Sea 35.

🏛 **Waltham Abbey Marriott,** Old Shire Lane, EN9 3LX, Southeast : 1 ½ m. on A 121
℘ (01992) 717170, *events.waltham@marriotthotels.co.uk, Fax (01992) 711841,* 🗲, ⌘s, 🔳
– ❤️ ▤ & 🅿. – 🔏 280. ⓌⒸ 🄰🄴 ⓞ 𝐕𝐈𝐒𝐀
Rest a la carte 25.85/37.40 s. – 🖙 14.95 – **162 rm** ✦129.00 – ✦✦129.00/209.00.
◆ Useful motorway links from this group hotel, a few minutes' drive from the town cen-tre; Well-equipped bedrooms, designed for business travel, plus modern meeting rooms. Capacious restaurant conveniently open all day.

WALTON *W. Yorks.* 502 Q 22 *– see Wetherby.*

WANSFORD *Peterborough* 504 S 26 *– see Peterborough.*

WANTAGE *Oxon.* 503 504 P 29 *– pop. 17 913.*

🔼 *Vale and Downland Museum, 19 Church St* ℘ *(01235) 760176.*

London 71 – Oxford 16 – Reading 24 – Swindon 21.

🏠 **The Boar's Head** with rm, Church St, Ardington, OX12 8QA, East : 2 ½ m. by A 417
℘ (01235) 833254, *info@boarsheadardington.co.uk, Fax (01235) 833254,* 🌳 – ❤️ rm, 🅿.
ⓌⒸ 🄰🄴 𝐕𝐈𝐒𝐀. ❤️
Rest 14.50 (lunch) and a la carte 20.00/35.00 ♀ – **3 rm** 🖙 ✦75.00/105.00 –
✦✦85.00/130.00.
◆ Pretty, timbered pub: pine tables, hunting curios and rural magazines. Locally-grown salad, modern British dishes, good wine and ale draw the locals. Bright modern bedrooms.

WARE Herts. 504 T 28 – pop. 17 193.

🏌 Whitehill, Dane End ℘ (01920) 438495.

London 24 – Cambridge 30 – Luton 22.

🏨 **Marriott Hanbury Manor H. & Country Club,** Thundridge, SG12 0SD, North : 1 ¾ m. by A 1170 on A 10 ℘ (01920) 487722, Fax (01920) 487692, ≤, ㈜, ⑫, Ⅰ₆, ≦s, ⬜, 🏌, ㈜, 垒, ❀ – 🛗 ❄, 🍽 rest, ⅙, ✦ P – 🛎 120. ⓦ ℗ ① VISA
Zodiac : Rest *(closed first 2 weeks January, Monday, Sunday dinner and Bank Holidays)* 20.00/30.00 (lunch) and dinner a la carte 47.95/59.40 – **Oakes :** Rest 25.00/32.00 and a la carte 34.15/46.20 – �) 17.50 – **156 rm** ✦159.00/169.00 – ✦✦159.00/169.00, 5 suites.
◆ 1890s neo-Jacobean mansion, a former convent, in 220 acres. Tea in firelit, oak-beamed hall. Classically luxurious rooms; many overlook golf course and lake. Walled garden. Formal, fine dining Zodiac. Mediterranean menus in spacious Oakes.

✗ **Jacoby's,** Churchgate House, 15 West St., SG12 9EE, ℘ (01920) 469181, info@jaco bys.co.uk, Fax (01920) 469182, ㈜ – ✦ 🍽. ⓦ ℗ VISA
closed Monday – Rest 7.95 (lunch) and a la carte 25.00/40.00.
◆ Carefully renovated 15C Grade II listed timber framed house with tremendous character. Front bar with leather armchairs. Twin level dining: British or Mediterranean classics.

WAREHAM Dorset 503 504 N 31 *The West Country G.* – pop. 2 568.

See : Town★ – St Martin's★★.

Env. : *Blue Pool★ AC, S : 3½ m. by A 351 – Bovington Tank Museum★ AC, Woolbridge Manor★, W : 5 m. by A 352.*

Exc. : *Moreton Church★★, W : 9½ m. by A 352 – Corfe Castle★ (≤★★) AC, SE : 6 m. by A 351 – Lulworth Cove★, SW : 10 m. by A 352 and B 3070 – Bere Regis★ (St John the Baptist Church★), NW : 6½ m. by minor rd.*

🅱 Holy Trinity Church, South St ℘ (01929) 552740.

London 123 – Bournemouth 13 – Weymouth 19.

🏨 **Springfield Country H.,** Grange Rd, BH20 5AL, South : 1 ¼ m. by South St and West Lane ℘ (01929) 552177, enquiries@springfield-country-hotel.co.uk, Fax (01929) 551862, Ⅰ₆, ≦s, ⬜ heated, ⬜, ㈜, 垒, squash – 🛗, ✦ rest, ☎ P – 🛎 200. ⓦ ℗ ① VISA
Millview : Rest (bar lunch)/dinner 24.50 and a la carte 19.95/34.00 ♀ – **Springers :** Rest *(closed Friday-Sunday)* (dinner only) a la carte 18.70/30.00 ♀ – **57 rm** �) ✦85.00/99.00 – ✦✦125.00/165.00.
◆ Privately owned hotel in sight of the Purbeck Hills. Neatly laid-out rooms; landscaped gardens. Comprehensive spa treatments and a state-of-the-art gym. Regional flavours abound in Millview. Informal, unfussy Springers.

🏨 **Priory** ⬎, Church Green, BH20 4ND, ℘ (01929) 551666, reservations@theprioryho tel.co.uk, Fax (01929) 554519, ≤, ㈜, ⬎, ㈜ – 🛗, ✦ rest, ☎ P. ⓦ ℗ ① VISA. ❀
Rest 35.00 (dinner) and lunch a la carte 25.70/32.40 ♀ – **16 rm** �) ✦168.00 – ✦✦280.00/340.00, 2 suites.
◆ Charming, privately run part 16C priory, friendly and discreetly cosy. Well-equipped rooms. Manicured four-acre gardens lead down to River Frome: luxury suites in boathouse. Charming restaurant beneath stone vaults of undercroft.

🏠 **Gold Court House,** St John's Hill, BH20 4LZ, ℘ (01929) 553320, info@goldcourt house.co.uk, Fax (01929) 553320, ㈜ – P.
Rest *(winter only)* (by arrangement) (communal dining) 15.00 – 3 rm �) ✦45.00 – ✦✦70.00.
◆ Affable hosts are justly proud of this pretty 1760s house on a quiet square. Classically charming sitting room and bedrooms; well-chosen books and antiques. Dine communally while viewing delightful courtyard garden.

WAREN MILL Northd. 501 502 O 17 – see Bamburgh.

WARGRAVE Windsor & Maidenhead 504 R 29 – pop. 2 876.

London 37 – Henley-on-Thames 4 – Oxford 27.

🏠 **St George & Dragon,** High St, RG10 8HY, ℘ (0118) 940 5021, Fax (0118) 940 5024, ≤, ㈜, ㈜ – P. ⓦ ℗ ① VISA. ❀
Rest a la carte 20.00/30.00.
◆ Modernised yet still characterful beamed pub with lovely decked terrace overlooking Thames. Text-book modern interior. Stone-fired oven provides range of modern dishes.

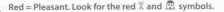

Red = Pleasant. Look for the red ✗ and 🏠 symbols.

London 316 – Alnwick 7.5 – Morpeth 24.

⌂ **Roxbro House,** 5 Castle Terrace, NE65 0UP, ℰ (01665) 711416, info@roxbro house.co.uk – ⇔ **P**, **MC** **VISA**
Rest (by arrangement) 20.00 – **3 rm** ⚹75.00 – ⚹⚹80.00.
* A discreet style enhances this 19C stone house in the shadow of Warkworth castle. Stylish lounge in harmony with very smart boutique bedrooms, two of which face the castle. Delightful home cooking in garden dining room.

Env. : Longleat House★★★ AC, SW : 3 m.
Exc. : Stonehenge★★★ AC, E : 18 m. by A 36 and A 303 – Bratton Castle (≼★★) NE : 6 m. by A 350 and B 3098.
🛈 Central Car Park ℰ (01985) 218548.
London 111 – Bristol 29 – Exeter 74 – Southampton 47.

🏛 **Bishopstrow House,** BA12 9HH, Southeast : 1 ½ m. on B 3414 ℰ (01985) 212312, info@bishopstrow.co.uk, Fax (01985) 216769, ≼, 🍽, 🍸, F₆, ⇘, ⅃ heated, ⬚, 🐾, 🚲, 🏊indoor/outdoor – ⇔ rest, **P**, – 🅰 60. **MC** **AE** **①** **VISA**
The Mulberry : Rest 16.50/38.00 ♀ – **29 rm** ⊆ ⚹99.00/135.00 – ⚹⚹199.00/330.00, 3 suites.
* Dignified, ivy-clad Georgian manor; 22-acre gardens along the river Wylye. Large modern rooms. Clubby, panelled bar with log fire; popular leisure club for the more active. Wall lanterns lend a warm feel to restaurant, which overlooks the garden.

at Upton Scudamore North : 2½ m. by A 350 – ⊠ Warminster.

🏚 **The Angel Inn** with rm, BA12 0AG, ℰ (01985) 213225, mail@theangelinn.co.uk, Fax (01985) 218182, 🍽 – ⇔ **P**, **MC** **VISA**
closed 25-26 December and 1 January – Rest a la carte 20.00/30.00 – **10 rm** ⊆ ⚹72.00 – ⚹⚹85.00.
* Refurbished 16C inn with a warm personal style. Sunny rear terrace. Rustic interior of scrubbed wood and pine. Fish specials highlight of appealing menus. Immaculate rooms.

at Heytesbury Southeast : 3¾ m. by B 3414 – ⊠ Warminster.

🏚 **The Angel Inn** with rm, High St, BA12 0ED, ℰ (01985) 840330, admin@theangelheytes bury.co.uk, Fax (01985) 840931, 🍽 – ⇔ **P**, **MC** **VISA**
closed 25 December – Rest - Steak specialities - 16.95 (lunch) and a la carte 25.00/35.00 ♀ – **8 rm** ⊆ ⚹60.00 – ⚹⚹75.00.
* 17C village inn with a delightful courtyard terrace. Dine at well-spaced tables in an elegant restaurant or the friendly real-ale bar. Cosy, well-appointed bedrooms.

at Corsley Northwest : 5 m. by A 362 – ⊠ Warminster.

🏚 **The Cross Keys,** Lyes Green, BA12 7PB, ℰ (01373) 832406, Fax (01373) 832934, 🌳 – ⇔ **P** ⇄ 50. **VISA**
closed dinner 25, 26 December and 1 January – Rest a la carte 15.25/25.75 ♀.
* Very personally run rural pub with large garden; local pictures and prints adorn walls. Extensive, freshly prepared menus utilise local suppliers: try renowned fish specials.

🏌 Hill Warren, Appleton ℰ (01925) 261620 – 🏌 Walton Hall, Warrington Rd, Higher Walton ℰ (01925) 266775 – 🏌 Birchwood, Kelvin Close ℰ (01925) 818819 – 🏌 Leigh, Kenyon Hall, Broseley Lane, Culcheth ℰ (01925) 763130 – 🏌 Alder Root, Alder Root Lane, Winwick ℰ (01925) 291919.
🛈 The Market Hall, Academy Way ℰ (01925) 632571.
London 195 – Chester 20 – Liverpool 18 – Manchester 21 – Preston 28.

at Stretton South : 3½ m. by A 49 on B 5356 – ⊠ Warrington.

🏛 **Park Royal,** Stretton Rd, WA4 4NS, ℰ (01925) 730706, parkroyalreservations@qho tels.co.uk, Fax (01925) 730740, 🍸, F₆, ⇘, ⬚, 🏊 – 📶 ⇔, 🍽 rest, ᴖ **P**, – 🅰 400. **MC** **AE** **①** **VISA**. 🍽
Topiary in the Park: Rest a la carte 27.75/38.75 s. ♀ – **139 rm** ⚹75.00/200.00 – ⚹⚹210.00, 3 suites.
* Busy, well-equipped business hotel with motorway access. Well-appointed rooms in co-ordinated patterns, facing open countryside at rear. Excellent leisure centre and café-bar. Traditionally formal restaurant.

ENGLAND

Nespresso. What else ?

Personalized gifts are an important part of any relationship.

Your company's name here

For reaching your customers, driving sales to your business, go for Michelin customized road maps and travel guides. Contact us via **www.b2b-cartesetguides.michelin.com** and we will work out with you a business solution to meet your needs.

at Daresbury *Southwest : 4 m. on A 56 –* ✉ *Warrington.*

🏨 **Daresbury Park,** Chester Rd, WA4 4BB, Southwest : 1½ m. by A 56 ℰ (01925) 267331, *reservations.daresbury@devere-hotels.com,* Fax (01925) 265615, 𝓕𝓼, ≒s, ◻, 🐎, squash – 🛗 ⇆, ▤ rest, ☎ & 🅿 – 🕍 300. ◕◙ 🅰🅴 ⓘ 𝐕𝐈𝐒𝐀
The Looking Glass : Rest (carving lunch Sunday) 25.00 ⅌ – **171 rm** ⇆ ✝82.00 – ✝✝82.00, 12 suites.
♦ In a modern business park near Lewis Carroll's birthplace. An impressively modish entrance leads into this well-equipped and up-to-date business and leisure hotel. Informal styling at The Looking Glass.

WARTLING *E. Sussex* 504 V 31 – *see Herstmonceux.*

WARWICK *Warks.* 503 504 P 27 *Great Britain G. – pop. 23 350.*
See : *Town★ – Castle★★ AC Y – Leycester Hospital★ AC Y B – Collegiate Church of St Mary★ (Tomb★) Y A.*
🐦 *Warwick Racecourse* ℰ (01926) 494316 Y.
🅱 *The Court House, Jury St* ℰ (01926) 492212.
London 96 – Birmingham 20 – Coventry 11 – Leicester 34 – Oxford 43.

Plan on next page

🏠 **Old Fourpenny Shop,** 27-29 Crompton St, CV34 6HJ, ℰ (01926) 491360, *fourpenny shop@aol.com,* Fax (01926) 411892 – ⇆ 🅿. ◕◙ 𝐕𝐈𝐒𝐀. ⋙   Y a
Rest (closed Sunday dinner) a la carte 19.00/29.95 s. ⅌ – **11 rm** ⇆ ✝50.00/70.00 – ✝✝87.00/92.00.
♦ One-time pub has retained its inn sign and local reputation for real ale. Simple yet comfortable and neatly kept bedrooms, some in the rear courtyard extension. Smart bar and dining room.

⌂ **Charter House** without rest., 87 West St, CV34 6AH, ℰ (01926) 496965, 🐎 – ⇆ 🅿. ◕◙ ⓘ 𝐕𝐈𝐒𝐀. ⋙   Y c
closed 25-26 December – **3 rm** ⇆ ✝56.00/65.00 – ✝✝95.00.
♦ Timbered 15C house not far from the castle. Comfortable, delicately ordered rooms with a personal touch: pretty counterpanes and posies of dried flowers. Tasty breakfasts.

⌂ **Park Cottage** without rest., 113 West St, CV34 6AH, ℰ (01926) 410319, *janet@parkcot tagewarwick.co.uk,* Fax (01926) 497994 – ⇆ 🅿. ◕◙ 🅰🅴 𝐕𝐈𝐒𝐀. ⋙   Y e
5 rm ⇆ ✝49.50/55.00 – ✝✝65.00/80.00.
♦ Between the shops and restaurants of West Street and the River Avon, a listed part Tudor house offering a homely lounge and sizeable, traditionally appointed bedrooms.

✕✕ **Saffron,** Unit 1, Westgate House, Market St, CV34 4DE, ℰ (01926) 402061 – ▤. ◕◙ 🅰🅴 ⓘ 𝐕𝐈𝐒𝐀   Y n
closed 25-26 December – **Rest** - Indian - (dinner only) a la carte 10.30/17.40.
♦ Split-level dining room hung with sitars and prints from the subcontinent. Piquant seafood and Goan dishes are the specialities of a freshly prepared Indian repertoire.

✕ **Prym's,** 48 Brook St, CV34 4BL, ℰ (01926) 493504, Fax (01926) 493322 – ◕◙ 𝐕𝐈𝐒𝐀   Y z
closed 1 Christmas, 1 week October, Sunday and Monday and lunch Tuesday and Wednesday – **Rest** a la carte 20.00/30.00.
♦ Bright, modern restaurant in the heart of the city. Stripped wooden floor, exposed beams, lots of wrought iron. Simple, tasty and well-cooked British fare on offer.

✕ **Art Kitchen,** 7 Swan St, CV34 4BJ, ℰ (01926) 494303, *reservations@theartkitchen.com,* Fax (01926) 494304 – ⇆ ▤. ◕◙ 🅰🅴 𝐕𝐈𝐒𝐀   Y r
closed 25 December - mid January – **Rest** - Thai - 12.95 (lunch) and a la carte 15.85/26.05.
♦ Unpretentious town centre restaurant with upstairs dining area featuring artwork for sale by owners' daughter. Authentic Thai cooking with attention paid to originality.

at Barford *South : 3½ m. on A 429 – Z –* ✉ *Warwick.*

🏨 **Glebe,** Church St, CV35 8BS, on B 4462 ℰ (01926) 624218, *sales@glebehotel.co.uk,* Fax (01926) 624625, 𝓕𝓼, ≒s, ◻, 🐎 – 🛗, ▤ rest, 🅿 – 🕍 120. ◕◙ 🅰🅴 ⓘ 𝐕𝐈𝐒𝐀
Rest 25.95 – **38 rm** ⇆ ✝105.00 – ✝✝175.00, 1 suite.
♦ On the edge of a quiet hamlet by St Peter's church, a classically proportioned manor in late Georgian redbrick. Neatly-equipped bedrooms in smart co-ordinated prints. Arch-roofed conservatory restaurant with views of evergreen borders.

WARWICK-ROYAL LEAMINGTON SPA

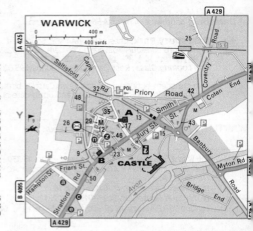

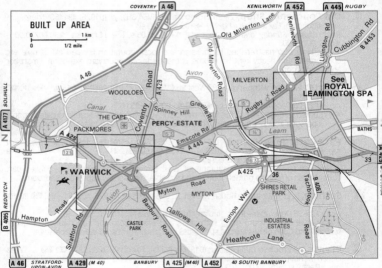

at Longbridge Southwest : 2 m. on A 429 – **Z** – ⊠ Warwick.

Hilton Warwick, Stratford Rd, CV34 6RE, on A 429 at junction 15 of M 40 ℘ (01926) 499555, Fax (01926) 410020, *Ló*, ≦ѕ, ⌧ – |ф| ↔, ≡ rest, & **P** – ≙ 250. **©** **AE** **①** **VISA**
Rest 24.95 s. – ☑ 15.50 – **181 rm** ✦99.00/159.00 – ✦✦98.00/151.00.
   ♦ Substantial group hotel, outside the city centre. Handsomely equipped, contemporary rooms; open-plan foyer and popular conference rooms. Restaurant or café-bar dining alternatives.

Express by Holiday Inn without rest., Stratford Rd, CV34 6TW, on A 429 at junction 15 of M 40 ℘ (01926) 483000, Fax (01926) 483033 – |ф| ↔ ≡ & **P** – ≙ 30. **©** **AE** **①** **VISA**
138 rm ✦94.95 – ✦✦94.95.
   ♦ Purpose-built lodge with useful motorway links. Trim, modern rooms with work desks and power showers; low-fat and take-away light breakfasts - ideal for business stopovers.

WASHINGTON *Tyne and Wear 501 502 P 19 – pop. 53 388.*

🏨 *Washington Moat House, Stone Cellar Rd, Usworth ℰ (0191) 417 8346.*
London 278 – Durham 13 – Middlesbrough 32 – Newcastle upon Tyne 7.

🏨 **Express by Holiday Inn** without rest., Emerson Rd, District 5, NE37 1LB, ℰ (0191) 416 9416, *ebhi-washington@btconnect.com, Fax (0191) 416 3123* – 📶 ⅍ 🕭 ₧ – 🔬 30. 🌐 🖭 ① VISA 🛠
74 rm ✦55.00/58.00 – ✦✦55.00/58.00.
♦ Recently built, comfortable lodge accommodation in a useful location close to A1 motorway and Angel of the North. An ideal stop-over address for business travellers.

WATERGATE BAY *Cornwall 503 E 32 – see Newquay.*

WATERMILLOCK *Cumbria 502 L 20 – see Ullswater.*

WATFORD *Herts. 504 S 29 – pop. 120 960.*

🏨 *West Herts., Cassiobury Park ℰ (01923) 236484 –* 🏨 *Oxhey Park, Prestwick Rd, South Oxhey ℰ (01923) 248213,* AT.
London 21 – Aylesbury 23.

Plan : see Greater London (North-West) 2

🏨🏨🏨 **The Grove,** Chandler's Cross, WD3 4TG, Northwest : 2 m. on A 411 ℰ (01923) 807807, *info@thegrove.co.uk, Fax (01923) 221008,* ⓜ, ⚡, ➡ ⩥, ⨋ heated, ⬜, 🏨, ⅍, ♨, ⅍ – 📶, ⅍ rm, ▤ ⅍ ♨♨ ₧ – 🔬 500. 🌐 🖭 ① VISA 🛠
Glasshouse : Rest (buffet) 27.50/39.50 ⅍ – **Stables** *(ℰ (01923) 296015)* **:** Rest a la carte 28.50/43.50 ⅍ – (see also **Colette's** below) – ⊡ 23.50 – **215 rm** ✦250.00 – ✦✦250.00, 12 suites.
♦ Converted country house with walled garden and golf course. Modern décor in public rooms. Extensive new spa facility. Hi-tech bedrooms and suites in modern extension. Glasshouse for stylish buffet meals. Informal dining in golfer-friendly Stables.

🏨🏨 **Hilton Watford,** Elton Way, WD25 8HA, Watford Bypass, East : 3 ½ m. on A 41 at junction with B 462 ℰ (01923) 235881, *reservations.watford@hilton.com, Fax (01923) 220836,* ⚡, ➡, ⬜ – 📶 ⅍, ▤ rest, ⚒ ⅍ ₧ – 🔬 375. 🌐 🖭 ① VISA 🛠 BT e
Patio : Rest *(closed Saturday lunch)* (live music and dancing Saturday) 19.95 – ⊡ 14.95 – **199 rm** ✦140.00 – ✦✦140.00, 2 suites.
♦ Behind the austere façade of this group-owned block are rooms with work spaces, internet access and contemporary minimalist décor. Comfortable if busy first-floor lounge. Spacious Patio rest. has jazz Sunday lunch.

✗✗✗ **Colette's** (at The Grove), WD3 4TG, Northwest : 2 m. on A 411 ℰ (01923) 296015, *restaurants@thegrove.co.uk, Fax (01923) 221008* – ⅍ ▤ ₧. 🌐 🖭 ① VISA
closed 1-15 January, first 2 weeks August, Monday and Sunday dinner except at Bank Holidays – **Rest** *(dinner only and Sunday lunch)* 54.00 ⅍.
♦ Elegant dining under stylish chandeliers and original artwork; overlooks golf course. Snazzy bar and comfy lounge. Accomplished, original cooking boasting luxury ingredients.

WATTON *Norfolk 504 W 26.*
London 95 – Norwich 22 – Swaffham 10.

✗✗ **The Café at Brovey Lair** ☞ with rm, Carbrooke Rd, Ovington, IP25 6SD, Northeast : 1 ¾ m. by A 1075 ℰ (01953) 882706, *champagne@broveylair.com, Fax (01953) 885365,* ☞, ⨋ heated, ☞ – ⅍, ▤ rest, ₧. 🌐 🖭 VISA 🛠
closed 25 December - 1 January – **Rest** - Seafood - (booking essential) (set menu only) 35.00/45.00 – **2 rm** ⊡ ✦125.00 – ✦✦140.00.
♦ Unique dining experience, within chef's own house: you're encouraged to watch her cook an accomplished four-course, no choice set seafood menu. Personally run. Smart rooms.

WEDMORE *Somerset 503 L 30.*
London 155.5 – Cheddar 4.5 – Glastonbury 9.5.

🏨 **The Sexey's Arms,** Sexey's Rd, Blackford, BS28 4NT, West : 1 ¾ m. on B 3139 ℰ (01934) 712487, *enquiries@thesexeysarms.co.uk, Fax (01934) 712447,* ☞ – ⅍ ₧. 🌐 🖭 VISA 🛠
Rest *(closed Sunday dinner and Monday)* a la carte 19.00/30.00.
♦ A cider house that evolved into a pub, with a locals snug and a dining room featuring tiled floor, beams and inglenook. French owner/chef serves accomplished modern classics.

ENGLAND

723

WELFORD-ON-AVON Warks..
London 109.5 – Alcester 9.5 – Stratford-upon-Avon 4.5.

🏠 **The Bell Inn,** Binton Rd, CV37 8EB, ℘ (01789) 750353, info@thebellwelford.co.uk, Fax (01789) 750893, 佘, ㎡ – ⇔ℙ. ⑩ 𝘝𝘐𝘚𝘈. ⅍
Rest a la carte 18.15/25.85.
♦ Part 17C inn in neat village near Stratford. Attractive dining terrace. Flagged and beamed bar with open fire. Eclectic mix of dishes: local suppliers printed on back of menu.

WELLINGBOROUGH Northants. 504 R 27 – pop. 46 959.
🛈 Library, Pebble Lane ℘ (01933) 276412.
London 73 – Cambridge 43 – Leicester 34 – Northampton 10.

🏨 **Ibis** without rest., Enstone Court, NN8 2DR, Southwest : 2½ m. by A 5128 (Northampton rd) on A 509 at junction with A 45 ℘ (01933) 228333, h3164@accor.com, Fax (01933) 228444 – 🖃 ⇔ 🕭 ℙ. – 🔏 25. ⑩ 🄰🄴 ⑩ 𝘝𝘐𝘚𝘈.
78 rm ✦54.00 – ✦✦54.00.
♦ Modern purpose-built hotel offering simple and well-maintained lodge accommodation. Good value and convenient for business and leisure travellers.

WELLINGHAM Norfolk.
London 120 – King's Lynn 29 – Norwich 28.

🏠 **Manor House Farm** ⌖ without rest., PE32 2TH, ℘ (01328) 838227, Fax (01328) 838348, ㎡, ♨ – ⇔ ℙ. ⅍
3 rm ⊑ ✦45.00/60.00 – ✦✦70.00/90.00.
♦ Idyllic setting beside church, surrounded by gardens and working farm. Family style breakfast; home grown bacon and sausage. Charming rooms in the house or comfortable annexe.

WELLINGTON Somerset 503 K 31 – pop. 10 599.
London 176 – Barnstaple 42 – Exeter 32 – Taunton 10.

🏰 **Bindon Country House** ⌖, Langford Budville, TA21 0RU, Northwest : 4½ m. by B 3187 via Langford Budville village following signs for Wiveliscombe ℘ (01823) 400070, stay@bindon.com, Fax (01823) 400071, ≼, 佘, ⌇ heated, ㎡, ℀ – ⇔ ⌦ ℙ – 🔏 45. ⑩ 🄰🄴 ⑩ 𝘝𝘐𝘚𝘈
The Wellesley : Rest 16.95/39.00 ⌁ – **12 rm** ⊑ ✦95.00/115.00 – ✦✦115.00/215.00.
♦ A rural idyll; splendid part 17C house with distinctive Flemish gables, rose garden; personally run with tasteful style. Individually designed rooms in refined, quiet colours. Fine views from restaurant; accomplished cooking in modern style.

WELLS Somerset 503 504 M 30 The West Country G. – pop. 10 406.
See : City★★ – Cathedral★★★ – Bishop's Palace★ (≼★★★) AC – St Cuthbert★.
Env. : Glastonbury★★ – Abbey★★ (Abbot's Kitchen★) AC, St John the Baptist★★, Somerset Rural Life Museum★ AC, Glastonbury Tor★ (≼★★★), SW : 5½ m. by A 39 – Wookey Hole★ (Caves★ AC, Papermill★), NW : 2 m.
Exc. : Cheddar Gorge★★ (Gorge★★, Caves★, Jacob's Ladder ⁂★) – St Andrew's Church★, NW : 7 m. by A 371 – Axbridge★★ (King John's Hunting Lodge★, St John the Baptist Church★), NW : 8½ m. by A 371.
🏌 East Horrington Rd ℘ (01749) 675005.
🛈 Town Hall, Market Pl ℘ (01749) 672552, wells.tic@ukonline.co.uk.
London 132 – Bristol 20 – Southampton 68 – Taunton 28.

🏨 **The Swan,** 11 Sadler St, BA5 2RX, ℘ (01749) 836300, swan@bhere.co.uk, Fax (01749) 836301, 佘 – ⇔ 🕭 ℙ. – 🔏 120. ⑩ 🄰🄴 ⑩ 𝘝𝘐𝘚𝘈. ⅍
Rest a la carte 22.40/34.95 ⌁ – **49 rm** ⊑ ✦90.00/102.00 – ✦✦134.00/170.00.
♦ Refurbished to a very good standard, this friendly former posting inn faces the Cathedral's west front. Two relaxing, firelit lounges; stylish individually decorated rooms. Restaurant boasts framed antique clothing and oak panelling.

🏨 **Beryl** ⌖ without rest., BA5 3JP, East : 1¼ m. by B 3139 off Hawkers Lane ℘ (01749) 678738, stay@beryl-wells.co.uk, Fax (01749) 670508, ≼, ⌇ heated, ㎡, ♨ – ⇔ ℙ. ⑩ 𝘝𝘐𝘚𝘈
closed 24-26 December – **9 rm** ⊑ ✦60.00/75.00 – ✦✦115.00.
♦ Neo-gothic former hunting lodge in formal gardens run in idiosyncratic style. Impeccable antique-filled drawing room. Traditional rooms, larger on first floor. Charming hosts.

⋔ **Littlewell Farm** without rest., Coxley, BA5 1QP, Southwest : 1 ½ m. on A 39 ℘ (01749) 677914, enquiries@littlewellfarm.co.uk, ⛵ – ⋈ **P**. ⅍
4 rm ⛵ ✸35.00/40.00 – ✸✸56.00.
♦ Restored 18C farmhouse set in a broad lawned garden. Cosy, attractively furnished sitting room and pristine, individually decorated bedrooms. Breakfasts at communal table.

✗ **The Old Spot**, 12 Sadler St, BA5 3TT, ℘ (01749) 689099 – ⋈. **M⊘ AE** ***VISA***
closed 25 December, Sunday dinner, Monday and Tuesday lunch – Rest 15.00/25.00 �.
♦ Restaurant's rear leads straight onto stunning Cathedral grounds. Relaxing interior "spot on" for enjoying gloriously unfussy, mouth-wateringly tasty dishes. Good value, too.

at Wookey Hole Northwest : 1¾ m. by A 371 – ⊠ Wells.

🏠 **Glencot House** ⅍, Glencot Lane, BA5 1BH, ℘ (01749) 677160, relax@glencot house.co.uk, Fax (01749) 670210, ☎, ⛵, ⌀ – ⋈ **P**. **M⊘ AE ⓞ** ***VISA***
Rest (booking essential for non-residents) (dinner only) 29.50 s. – **15 rm** ⛵ ✸90.00/115.00 – ✸✸150.00.
♦ Set in mature gardens by the river Axe, a 19C mansion in Jacobean style. Preserved walnut panelling, carved ceilings and comfortable rooms with decorative touches. Dining room with mullioned windows, chandelier, river views.

at Easton Northwest : 3 m. on A 371 – ⊠ Wells.

⋔ **Beaconsfield Farm** without rest., BA5 1DU, on A 371 ℘ (01749) 870308, carol5ll@aol.com, ⛵ – ⋈ **P**. ⅍

closed 20 December - New Year – 3 rm ⛵ ✸57.00/58.00 – ✸✸65.00/70.00.
♦ In the foothills of the Mendips, a renovated farmhouse offering well-fitted, cottage-style rooms. Generous breakfasts in the parlour overlooking the four-acre grounds.

WELLS-NEXT-THE-SEA Norfolk 504 W 25 – pop. 2 451.
London 122 – Cromer 22 – Norwich 38.

🏠 **The Crown**, The Buttlands, NR23 1EX, ℘ (01328) 710209, reception@thecrownhotel wells.co.uk, Fax (01328) 711432, ⅋ – ⋈ **M⊘ AE ⓞ** ***VISA***. ⅍
Restaurant : Rest (dinner only) 29.95 – **Bar** : Rest (bookings not accepted) a la carte 17.75/26.15 � – **12 rm** ⛵ ✸100.00 – ✸✸160.00.
♦ 16C coaching inn with smart Georgian façade, overlooking the village green. Bedrooms are contemporary in style; service is informal and friendly. Light, airy Restaurant with bright décor. Modern conservatory Bar with terrace.

🍴 **The Globe Inn** with rm, The Buttlands, NR23 1EU, ℘ (01328) 710206, globe@holk ham.co.uk, Fax (01328) 713249, ⅋ – ⋈ **TV** ⅍. **M⊘** ***VISA***
Rest a la carte 15.00/25.00 � – 7 rm ⛵ ✸40.00/90.00 – ✸✸55.00/105.00.
♦ Updated Georgian pub with terrace facing town green. Sleek, modern bar. Large dining room: excellent local photos enliven walls. Modern British cooking. Stylish rooms.

WELWYN Herts. 504 T 28 – pop. 10 700 (inc. Codicote).
London 31 – Bedford 31 – Cambridge 31.

🏠🏠 **Tewin Bury Farm**, AL6 0JB, Southeast : 3½ m. by A 1000 on B 1000 ℘ (01438) 717793, hotel@tewinbury.co.uk, Fax (01438) 840440, ⛵, ⌀ – ⋈ rest, ▤ rest, **P**. – **▲** 150. **M⊘ AE ⓞ** ***VISA***. ⅍
Rest 19.95 (dinner) and a la carte 17.00/22.00 – **30 rm** ⛵ ✸111.00/131.00 – ✸✸119.00/139.00.
♦ Consisting of a range of converted farm buildings on 400-acre working farm. 17C tythe barn used as function room located next to river. Individual rooms have beamed ceilings. Restaurant located in timbered farm building.

WELWYN GARDEN CITY Herts. 504 T 28.
🏌, 🏌 Panshanger Golf Complex, Old Herns Lane ℘ (01707) 333312.
London 22 – Luton 21.

✗✗✗ **Auberge du Lac** ⅍, Brocket Hall, AL8 7XG, West : 3 m. by A 6129 on B 653 ℘ (01707) 368888, auberge@brocket-hall.co.uk, Fax (01707) 368898, ⅋, ⌀ – ▤ **P**. **M⊘ AE ⓞ** ***VISA***
closed 27 December-4 January Sunday dinner and Monday – Rest 29.50 (lunch) and a la carte 43.50/58.50 � ⅍.
♦ Part 18C former hunting lodge with lakeside terrace in the grounds of Brocket Hall - an idyllic setting for confident, classic cooking with a firm French base.

WENDLING Norfolk 504 W 25 – see East Dereham.

WENTBRIDGE *W. Yorks.* 502 504 Q 23 – ⊠ *Pontefract.*
London 183 – Leeds 19 – Nottingham 55 – Sheffield 28.

Wentbridge House, Old Great North Rd, WF8 3JJ, ℘ (01977) 620444, *info@went bridgehouse.co.uk, Fax (01977) 620148,* 🌳, ♨ – 🅿 – 🔬 120. 🕥🕥 ㎺ ⓪ *VISA*. ✺
closed 25 December – **Fleur de Lys :** Rest *(closed Sunday dinner)* (dinner only and Sunday lunch) 28.00 and a la carte 30.75/42.45 – **Wentbridge Brasserie :** Rest *(closed Sunday lunch)* a la carte 19.40/30.45 ♀ – **18 rm** ⊠ ✦89.00 – ✦✦160.00.
  • Once owned by the late Queen Mother's family, a part 18C bay-windowed house decorated in traditional colours. Sizeable rooms, some overlooking the lawned grounds. Fleur de Lys adjacent to smart firelit bar. Informal Wentbridge Brasserie.

WEOBLEY *Herefordshire* 503 L 27 – ⊠ *Hereford.*
London 145 – Brecon 30 – Hereford 12 – Leominster 9.

Broxwood Court 🌳, Broxwood, HR6 9JJ, Northwest : 3 ¼ m. by A 4112, Broxwood rd on Lyonshall rd ℘ (01544) 340245, *mikeanne@broxwood.kc3.co.uk, Fax (01544) 340573,* ≤, 🌳 heated, 🌳, ♨, ✺ – ✦✦ rm, 🅿 🕥🕥 *VISA*. ✺
closed 24 December - 4 January – Rest *(by arrangement)* (communal dining) 27.50 ♀ – **4 rm** ⊠ ✦40.00/60.00 – ✦✦95.00.
  • 1950s house set in wonderfully tranquil location: vast grounds and formally laid-out gardens. Spacious drawing room, cosy library. Individually styled rooms with views.

The Salutation Inn with rm, Market Pitch, HR4 8SJ, ℘ (01544) 318443, *salutatio ninn@btinternet.com, Fax (01544) 318405,* 🍴 – ✦✦ 🅿 🕥🕥 ㎺ *VISA*. ✺
closed 25 December – Rest a la carte 18.00/30.00 ♀ – **4 rm** ⊠ ✦53.00/58.00 – ✦✦80.00/86.00.
  • In the heart of this pretty village, a charming, part 16C former cider house with a rustic real ale bar. Traditionally decorated bedrooms, two in the next-door cottage. Attractive dining room.

Look out for red symbols, indicating particularly pleasant establishments.

WEST BAGBOROUGH *Somerset* 503 K 30 – *see Taunton.*

WEST BEXINGTON *Dorset* 503 504 M 31 – ⊠ *Dorchester.*
London 150 – Bournemouth 43 – Bridport 6 – Weymouth 13.

Manor, Beach Rd, DT2 9DF, ℘ (01308) 897616, *themanorhotel@btconnect.com, Fax (01308) 897704,* ≤, – 🅿 🕥🕥 *VISA*
Rest 17.95/28.00 – **13 rm** (dinner included) ⊠ ✦95.00/120.00 – ✦✦125.00/170.00.
  • A short walk from the beach, a personally run and pleasantly unfussy country house of 11C origin. Neat, traditional rooms and a convivial cellar bar popular with the locals. Pretty flag-floored dining room decorated with rural curios.

WEST BURTON *N. Yorks.* 502 O 21 – ⊠ *Leyburn.*
London 260 – Carlisle 81 – Darlington 34 – Kendal 40 – Leeds 62 – York 58.

The Grange, DL8 4JR, ℘ (01969) 663348, *ashfordpaul5@aol.com,* 🌳, 🌳 – ✦✦ ✦ 🅿 🕥🕥 *VISA*
Rest 20.00 – **3 rm** ⊠ ✦45.00 – ✦✦70.00/75.00.
  • 19C house: preserved tiling, staircase and antiques. Well-proportioned bedrooms, firelit drawing room. Mature riverside gardens. Impressive mahogany breakfast table.

WESTBURY *Wilts.* 503 N 30.
London 111 – Trowbridge 5.5 – Warminster 4.5.

Garden House with rm, 26 Edward St, BA13 3BD, North : 4 m. by A 350 ℘ (01373) 859995, *reception@thegardenhouse-hotel.co.uk, Fax (01373) 858586,* 🍴, 🌳 – ✦✦, ▤ rest, ✦ 🕥🕥 ㎺ *VISA*
closed 24 December - 4 January – Rest *(closed Sunday dinner)* (dinner only and Sunday lunch) a la carte 20.40/31.20 s. – **8 rm** ⊠ ✦65.00/95.00 – ✦✦100.00/115.00.
  • Very personally run former post office in centre of town, with lovely enclosed rear garden. Modern, tasty menus with strong seasonal base. Cosy bedrooms.

WEST DIDSBURY *Gtr Manchester* – *see Manchester.*

726

WEST END Surrey 504 S 29 – pop. 4 135 – ⊠ Guildford.
London 37 – Bracknell 7 – Camberley 5 – Guildford 8 – Woking 6.

⭑☐ **The Inn @ West End,** 42 Guildford Rd, GU24 9PW, on A 322 ℘ (01276) 858652, greatfood@the-inn.co.uk, 🍴 – **P.** **MO** **AE** **VISA**
Rest a la carte 19.95/32.15 ♀.
♦ Well-prepared modern British standards and good-value lunches in this smartly renovated Victorian roadside pub; occasional wine tastings from a diverse cellar.

WESTFIELD E. Sussex 504 V 31 – pop. 1 509.
London 66 – Brighton 38 – Folkestone 45 – Maidstone 30.

XX **The Wild Mushroom,** Woodgate House, Westfield Lane, TN35 4SB, Southwest : ½ m. on A 28 ℘ (01424) 751137, info@wildmushroom.co.uk, Fax (01424) 753405, 🍴 – ⤙⤙ **P.** **MO** **AE** **VISA**
closed 2 weeks January, 2 weeks August, Monday, Saturday lunch and Sunday dinner – Rest (booking essential) 17.95 (lunch) and dinner a la carte 22.00/32.40 ♀.
♦ Bustling and hospitable with modern interior and conservatory lounge. Flavourful, well-priced dishes from a varied, interesting menu. Loyal local following: be sure to book.

WEST KIRBY Wirral 502 504 K 23 Great Britain G.
EXC. : Liverpool★ – Cathedrals★★, The Walker★★, Merseyside Maritime Museum★ and Albert Dock★, E : 13½ m. by A 553.
London 219 – Chester 19 – Liverpool 12.

🏠 **Peel Hey** without rest., Frankby Rd, Frankby, CH48 1PP, East : 2¼ m. by A 540 on B 5139 ℘ (0151) 677 9077, enquiries@peelhey.com, Fax (0151) 625 4115, 🍴 – ⤙⤙ **&** **P.** **MO** **AE** **VISA**. 🌸
9 rm ⊆ ✝59.00/79.00 – ✝✝79.00/89.00.
♦ Modernised 19C house that offers a good standard of accommodation. Attractive, comfortable rooms. Smart dining room with linen-clad tables and chunky wooden chairs.

WESTLETON Suffolk 504 Y 27 – ⊠ Saxmundham.
London 97 – Cambridge 72 – Ipswich 28 – Norwich 31.

🏠 **Pond House** without rest., The Hill, IP17 3AN, ℘ (01728) 648773, 🍴 – ⤙⤙ **P.** 🌸
closed 1 week Christmas and minimum stay 2 nights – **3 rm** ⊆ ✝30.00 – ✝✝56.00.
♦ A welcoming atmosphere prevails in this neatly maintained 1700s cottage beside the village green. Simple, pine furnished bedrooms. Convenient for Minsmere Nature Reserve.

WEST LULWORTH Dorset 503 504 N 32 The West Country G. – ⊠ Wareham.
See : Lulworth Cove★.
London 129 – Bournemouth 21 – Dorchester 17 – Weymouth 19.

🏠 **Gatton House** without rest., Main Rd, BH20 5RL, ℘ (01929) 400252, avril@gatton house.co.uk, Fax (01929) 400252, 🍴 – ⤙⤙ **P.** **MO** **AE** **VISA**. 🌸
March-September – **8 rm** ⊆ ✝52.00/62.00 – ✝✝64.00/84.00.
♦ Follow the winding garden path to a smart gabled house in the middle of this pleasant village. Comfy accommodation in co-ordinated décor; neat front-facing breakfast room.

WEST MALLING Kent 504 V 30 – pop. 2 144.
📍, 📍 Addington, Maidstone ℘ (01732) 844785.
London 35 – Maidstone 7 – Royal Tunbridge Wells 14.

🏠 **Scott House** without rest., 37 High St, ME19 6QH, ℘ (01732) 841380, mail@scott-house.co.uk, Fax (01732) 522367 – ⤙⤙ **&** **MO** **AE** **①** **VISA**. 🌸
closed Christmas-New Year – **5 rm** ⊆ ✝65.00 – ✝✝85.00.
♦ Comfy rooms in period style and a relaxing first-floor lounge share this part Georgian town house with a fine interior décor shop, run by the same warm husband and wife team.

X **The Swan,** 35 Swan St, ME19 6JU, ℘ (01732) 521910, info@theswanwestmalling.co.uk, Fax (01732) 522898, 🍴 – ⤙⤙ **≡** ⇔ **28.** **MO** **AE** **VISA**
closed 26 and 28 December, 1 January and lunch 31 December and 2 January – Rest 15.00 and a la carte 25.00/36.00 ♀.
♦ Radically renovated 16C pub in modern pine. Stylish lounge: leopard-print carpet, purple cushions. Modish menu at sensible prices; informal, very efficient service.

WESTON-SUPER-MARE North Somerset 503 K 29 The West Country G. – pop. 78 044.

See : Seafront (≤★★) BZ.

Exc. : Axbridge★★ (King John's Hunting Lodge★, St John the Baptist Church★) SE : 9 m. by A 371 – BY – and A 38 – Cheddar Gorge★★ (Gorge★★, Caves★, Jacob's Ladder ✳★) – Clevedon★ (≤★★, Clevedon Court★), NE : 10 m. by A 370 and M 5 – St Andrew's Church★, SE : 10½ m. by A 371.

🇷 Worlebury, Monks Hill ℘ (01934) 625789 BY.

🇮 Beach Lawns ℘ (01934) 888800.

London 147 – Bristol 24 – Taunton 32.

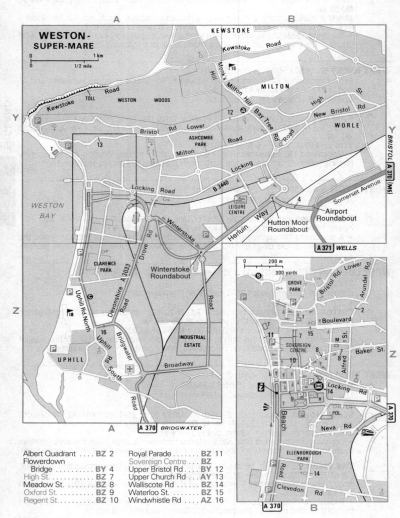

The Beachlands, 17 Uphill Road North, BS23 4NG, ☏ (01934) 621401, *info@beachland shotel.com*, Fax (01934) 621966, ⌖, ▨, ⇜ – ⇤ ⅙ ℙ – 🅰 40. ⓂⓄ 🅰🅴 Ⓞⅅ *VISA*. ⅏ AZ c
closed 24 December-4 January – **Rest** (bar lunch Monday-Saturday)/dinner 21.00 – **23 rm** ⌕ ✶59.50/82.50 – ✶✶110.00.
♦ Well-established and family run, convenient for beach and golf course. Rooms in traditional prints; some, south-facing, have veranda doors giving on to a secluded garden. Formal dining room overlooks pleasant gardens.

🏠 **Queenswood,** Victoria Park, BS23 2HZ, off Upper Church Rd ☏ (01934) 416141, Fax (01934) 621759 – ⇤, ▤ rest. ⓂⓄ 🅰🅴 *VISA* BZ s
closed Christmas and New Year – **Rest** (bar lunch)/dinner 19.50 ℤ – **19 rm** ⌕ ✶57.50/70.00 – ✶✶80.00/110.00.
♦ Sizeable, 19C-style house, well kept by friendly, long-standing owners. Red velour lounge sofas and neat rooms in the time-honoured tradition of the British seaside holiday. Tried-and-tested menus.

%% **Duets,** 103 Upper Bristol Rd, BS22 8ND, ☏ (01934) 413428 – ⓂⓄ *VISA* BY a
closed 1 week August, 1 week January, Sunday dinner and Monday – **Rest** (dinner only and Sunday lunch)/dinner 28.95 and a la carte 28.95/31.40.
♦ Diligent and unfussy service sets the tone in this traditionally styled restaurant, deservedly a neighbourhood favourite. Ably judged cooking on a tasty classical base.

The red 🕊 symbol?
This denotes the very essence of peace
– only the sound of birdsong first thing in the morning ...

WESTON UNDERWOOD Derbs. – see Derby.

WESTOW N. Yorks.
London 224.5 – Malton 8 – York 15.

🛏 **The Blacksmiths Inn** with rm, Main St, YO60 7NE, ☏ (01653) 618365, *info@black smithsinn.co.uk*, Fax (01653) 618394, ⇝ – ⇤ ⅙ ℙ. ⓂⓄ *VISA*
closed 1 week January and Monday – **Rest** (closed Tuesday) (dinner only and Sunday lunch)/dinner a la carte 21.40/30.95 ℤ – **6 rm** ⌕ ✶40.00 – ✶✶70.00.
♦ Fully refurbished country dining pub; log-burning stove, beams and flagged floor. Ingredients from local Manor Farm proudly used in winningly modish menus with daily specials.

WEST PECKHAM Kent – see Maidstone.

WEST RUNTON Norfolk 504 X 25 – ✉ Cromer.
🛏 Links Country Park Hotel ☏ (01263) 838383.
London 135 – King's Lynn 42 – Norwich 24.

🏠 **Links Country Park H.,** Sandy Lane, NR27 9QH, ☏ (01263) 838383, *sales@links-ho tel.co.uk*, Fax (01263) 838264, ℔, ⌖, ▨, 🛏, ⇜, %% – 🛏 ⇤, ▤ rest, ☎ ℙ – 🅰 150. ⓂⓄ 🅰🅴 Ⓞⅅ *VISA*
Rest (bar lunch Monday-Saturday)/dinner 25.95 and a la carte approx 30.00 – **49 rm** ✶60.00/70.00 – ✶✶150.00.
♦ Gabled Victorian house offering sizeable accommodation, most smartly decorated on the third floor. Nine-hole golf course meanders through 40 acres of coastal parkland. Spacious dining room using locally sourced ingredients.

WEST STOKE W. Sussex – see Chichester.

WEST TANFIELD N. Yorks. 502 P 21 – ✉ Ripon.
London 237 – Darlington 29 – Leeds 32 – Middlesbrough 39 – York 36.

🛏 **The Bruce Arms** with rm, Main St, HG4 5JJ, ☏ (01677) 470325, *geoff@brucearms.com*, ⇝ – ⇤ rm, ℙ. ⓂⓄ *VISA*. ⅏
Rest (closed Sunday dinner, Monday and lunch Tuesday) 12.95 (lunch) and a la carte 12.95/28.50 ℤ – **2 rm** ⌕ ✶60.00 – ✶✶80.00.
♦ Stone-built village pub: log fire, local ales, leather sofas. Vine covered, decked terrace. Well-spaced candlelit pub tables. Satisfying blackboard menu.. Rustic bedrooms.

WEST WITTON N. Yorks. 502 O 21 – ⊠ *Leyburn*.
London 241 – Kendal 39 – Leeds 60 – Newcastle upon Tyne 65 – York 53.

⌂ **Ivy Dene,** DL8 4LP, ℰ (01969) 622785, info@ivydeneguesthouse.co.uk, Fax (01969) 622785 – ⇔ ℙ. ⋘
closed 1 December-6 January – **Rest** (by arrangement) 16.50 – **4 rm** ⊊ ✦58.00/60.00 – ✦✦60.00.
♦ Cosy, cottage-style rooms, one with four-poster bed, others with brass bedsteads, in this 300-year-old house. Firelit sitting room with a collection of clocks and antiques. Dining room offers renowned sticky toffee pudding.

WETHERAL Cumbria 501 502 L 19 – *see Carlisle.*

WETHERBY W. Yorks. 502 P 22 *Great Britain G. – pop. 10 562.*
Env. : Harewood House★★ *(The Gallery★) AC, SW : 5½ m. by A 58 and A 659.*
🛆 Linton Lane, Linton ℰ (01937) 580089.
🛈 The Library, 17 Westgate ℰ (01937) 582151.
London 208 – Harrogate 8 – Leeds 13 – York 14.

🏛 **Wood Hall** ⊗, Trip Lane, Linton, LS22 4JA, Southwest : 3 m. by A 661 and Linton Rd ℰ (01937) 587271, enquiries@woodhall.co.uk, Fax (01937) 584353, ≤, ₤₅, ⬜, ⬎, 🐾, ♨ – ⦙, ⇔ rest, ℃ ℙ – ⚐ 140. ⓪⓪ Æ ⓪ *VISA*. ⋘
Rest (bar lunch Monday-Saturday)/dinner 35.00 and a la carte 39.50/70.00 ⊊ – **44 rm** ⊊ ✦190.00 – ✦✦240.00/360.00.
♦ Peacefully set part Jacobean and Georgian manor in 100 acres of woods and gardens. Refurbished contemporary public areas; well-appointed bedrooms. Popular wedding venue. Elegant dining room with candelabras and tall sash windows.

at Walton East : 4 m. by B 1224 – ⊠ Wetherby.

🍽 **The Fox and Hounds,** Hall Park Rd, LS23 7DQ, ℰ (01937) 842192 – ⇔ ℙ. ⓪⓪ *VISA*
Rest (closed Sunday dinner) (booking essential) a la carte 17.50/30.00.
♦ Hidden away in a sleepy village. Snug bar with stuffed fox in basket, framed sepia prints and dried flowers. Wide-ranging, homemade menus from rustic bread to ice-cream.

at Kirk Deighton Northwest : 1½ m. on B 6164 – ⊠ Wetherby.

🍽 **The Bay Horse Inn,** Main St, LS22 4DZ, ℰ (01937) 580058 – ⇔. ⓪⓪ *VISA*
Rest (closed Sunday dinner and Monday lunch) (booking essential) a la carte 17.50/30.00.
♦ Pub exuding real country character: fishing rods on ceiling, sepia prints, solid stone floors. Buy home-made jams and pickles. Eat tasty dishes with strong Yorkshire accent.

If breakfast is included the ⊊ symbol appears after the number of rooms.

WEYBRIDGE Surrey 504 S 29 – *pop. 52 890 (inc. Walton).*
London 23 – Crawley 27 – Guildford 17 – Reading 33.

🏛 **The Ship,** Monument Green, High St, KT13 8BQ, off A 317 ℰ (01932) 848364, reservations@desboroughhotels.com, Fax (01932) 857153 – ⇔, ▤ rest, ℙ – ⚐ 150. ⓪⓪ Æ ⓪ *VISA*
Rest (bar lunch Monday-Saturday)/dinner a la carte 25.00/45.00 s. ⊊ – **75 rm** ⊊ ✦155.00/170.00 – ✦✦170.00.
♦ This former coaching inn is pleasingly decorated throughout: pictures and plates on walls, floral furnishings, soft lighting, welcoming fire in lounge. Rooms in quiet hues. Dining room defined by flowers and mellow tones.

WEYMOUTH Dorset 503 504 M 32 *The West Country G. – pop. 48 279.*
See : Town★ – Timewalk★ AC – Nothe Fort (≤★) AC – Boat Trip★ (Weymouth Bay and Portland Harbour) AC.
Env. : Chesil Beach★★ – Portland★ - Portland Bill (⋇★★) S : 2½ m. by A 354.
Exc. : Maiden Castle★★ (≤★) N : 6½ m. by A 354 – Sub-Tropical Gardens★ AC, St Catherine's Chapel★) NW : 9 m. by B 3157.
🛆 Links Rd ℰ (01305) 773981.
⛴ to Guernsey (St Peter Port) and Jersey (St Helier) (Condor Ferries Ltd).
🛈 The King's Statue, The Esplanade ℰ (01305) 785747, tic@weymouth.gov.uk.
London 142 – Bournemouth 35 – Bristol 68 – Exeter 59 – Swindon 94.

Moonfleet Manor ⊗, DT3 4ED, Northwest : 4 ½ m. by B 3157 ℘ (01305) 786948, info@moonfleetmanor.co.uk, Fax (01305) 774395, ≤, ⇌, 🖼, ⇌, ✗, squash – ⇌ rest, ✗ ✗ P – 🔒 60. ⬛ AE ① VISA
Rest (bar lunch Monday-Saturday)/dinner 34.00 – **36 rm** ✱130.00/170.00 – ✱✱270.00/410.00, 2 suites.
 • Georgian in origin, an extended country house with stunning coastal views. Well equipped rooms, cosy lounges hung with oils. Games room and special facilities for families. Subtle Mediterranean styling imbues restaurant.

Chatsworth, 14 The Esplanade, DT4 8EB, ℘ (01305) 785012, stay@thechatsworth.co.uk, Fax (01305) 766342, ≤, 🍽 – ✆. ⬛ VISA. ✗
Rest (by arrangement) 24.00 ♀ – **8 rm** ♀ ✱35.00/80.00 – ✱✱80.00/110.00.
 • Seafront terraced house; brightly coloured bedrooms, modern and well-maintained. A pretty terrace, facing south over the quay, overflows with hanging baskets in summer. Combined bay-windowed dining room and fire-lit lounge.

Bay View without rest., 35 The Esplanade, DT4 8DH, ℘ (01305) 782083, info@bayview-weymouth.co.uk, Fax (01305) 782083, ≤ – P. ⬛ ① VISA. ✗
closed December – **8 rm** ♀ ✱45.00/50.00 – ✱✱60.00/70.00.
 • Generously sized en suite rooms, many with four-poster beds or broad bay windows, in a sizeable townhouse with views over the bay. Neatly kept basement lounge.

✗ **Perry's**, 4 Trinity Rd, The Old Harbour, DT4 8TJ, ℘ (01305) 785799, Fax (01305) 787002 – ⇌. ⬛ VISA
closed 25-27 December, 1-3 January, lunch Monday and Saturday and Sunday dinner in winter – **Rest** 19.95 (lunch) and a la carte 24.40/31.40.
 • Simple, family-run local favourite by the old harbour. Friendly staff, tasty cooking and plenty of seafood specials: shellfish soup, Portland crab, citrus-dressed bass.

WHALLEY Lancs. 502 M 22 – pop. 3 230 – ✉ Blackburn.
  🏌 Long Leese Barn, Clerkhill ℘ (01254) 822236.
  London 233 – Blackpool 32 – Burnley 12 – Manchester 28 – Preston 15.

at Mitton Northwest : 2½ m. on B 6246 – ✉ Whalley.

🍴 **The Three Fishes**, Mitton Rd, BB7 9PQ, ℘ (01254) 826888, Fax (01254) 826026, 🍽 – ⇌ P. ⬛ AE ① VISA
closed 25 December – **Rest** (bookings not accepted) a la carte 18.00/23.00.
 • Huge, 140 cover modern dining pub, once a coaching inn. Lancashire and north-west England regional specialities dominate the menu. Perenially busy: remember, you can't book!

WHASHTON N. Yorks. – see Richmond.

WHAW N. Yorks. 502 O 20 – see Reeth.

WHICKHAM Tyne and Wear 501 502 O/P 19 – see Gateshead.

WHITBY N. Yorks. 502 S 20 Great Britain G. – pop. 13 594.
  See : Abbey★.
  🏌 Sandsend Rd, Low Straggleton ℘ (01947) 600660.
  🚊 Langborne Rd ℘ (01723) 383637.
  London 257 – Middlesbrough 31 – Scarborough 21 – York 45.

🏛 **Bagdale Hall**, 1 Bagdale, YO21 1QL, ℘ (01947) 602958, Fax (01947) 820714 – ⇌ rest, P. ⬛ AE ① VISA. ✗
Rest (dinner only) a la carte approx 25.20 ♀ – **14 rm** ♀ ✱70.00 – ✱✱138.00.
 • Tudor manor with fine fireplaces in carved wood and 19C Delft tiles; panelled rooms with mullioned windows; four-posters in period style bedrooms. Annex for more modern rooms. Dining room boasts timbered ceiling and massive wooden fireplace.

🏛 **Cross Butts Stable**, Guisborough Rd, YO21 1TL, West : 1 ¾ m. on A 171 (Teeside rd) ℘ (01947) 820986, info@cross-butts, Fax (01947) 825665, 🍽, 🌿, 🐴 – ⇌ ✆ & P. ⬛ VISA. ✗
Rest a la carte 19.00/29.50 – **9 rm** ♀ ✱80.00/90.00 – ✱✱140.00/160.00.
 • Extended farmhouse on working farm personally run by a welcoming family. Superb bedrooms, set round courtyard with water feature, have flag floors and warm, sumptuous aura. Smart, informal restaurant areas over two floors: a mix of suites, sofas and tables.

ENGLAND

✗ **Greens**, 13 Bridge St, YO22 4BG, ℰ (01947) 600284, *info@greensofwhitby.com* – ⟲ ▦. ⁕⊕ VISA
closed 25-26 December and 1 January – **Rest** - Seafood specialities - (booking essential) (dinner only and lunch Friday-Sunday) a la carte 22.00/36.25.
◆ Set in town centre, close to quayside, with a rustic, informal ambience. Constantly changing seafood menus are simply cooked and employ much produce freshly landed at Whitby.

at Briggswath *Southwest : 3½ m. by A 171 (Teesdie rd), A 169 on B 1410* – ⊠ *Whitby.*

⌂ **The Lawns**, 73 Carr Hill Lane, YO21 1RS, ℰ (01947) 810310, *lorton@onetel.com*, Fax (01947) 810310, ≤, 🌳 – ⁕⊕ P. ✗
closed Christmas - New Year – **Rest** (by arrangement) 20.00 – 3 rm ⊒ ✦64.00 – ✦✦64.00.
◆ Sizeable, converted house above a south-facing garden and verge of evergreens. Stripped wooden floors, understated décor. Spotless rooms. Fine views of moors and Esk valley.

⌂ **The Olde Ford** without rest, 1 Briggswath, YO21 1RU, ℰ (01947) 810704, *gray.theolde ford@btinternet.com*, 🗨, 🌳 – ⁕⊕ P. ⁕⊕ AE VISA
closed 2 weeks June – **3 rm** ⊒ ✦40.00 – ✦✦55.00.
◆ Appealing little stone cottage on the banks of the river Esk: former village post office. Traditional Yorkshire breakfasts. All rooms look out over garden and river.

at Dunsley *West : 3¼ m. by A 171* – ⊠ *Whitby.*

🏛 **Dunsley Hall Country House** 🦮, YO21 3TL, ℰ (01947) 893437, *reception@dunsley hall.com*, Fax (01947) 893505, ≤, ♨, ☎, 🗌, 🌳, ✗ – ⁕⊕ P. – 🏊 100. ⁕⊕ AE VISA
Rest (bar lunch Monday-Saturday)/dinner 27.95 ⊒ – **18 rm** ⊒ ✦95.00/115.00 – ✦✦180.00.
◆ Behind pillared gates, a personally run late Victorian house: intricately oak panelled lounge with leather furnished bar. Comfortable, period styled rooms with country views. Dining room boasts Whitby seafood.

at Sandsend *Northwest : 3 m. on A 174* – ⊠ *Whitby.*

✗✗ **Estbek House** with rm, East Row, YO21 3SY, ℰ (01947) 893424, *reservations@estbek house.co.uk*, Fax (01947) 893625 – ⁕⊕. ⁕⊕ VISA
closed 3 January - 1 February – **Rest** - Seafood specialities - (dinner only) a la carte 25.40/39.40 ⊒ – **4 rm** ✦50.00 – ✦✦100.00.
◆ This personally run Regency house, adjacent to beach, boasts delightful terrace, basement bar, smart restaurant serving local, wild seafood, and utterly charming rooms.

WHITCHURCH *Shrops. 502 503 L 25.*
London 168.5 – Nantwich 11 – Wrexham 15.5.

at Burleydam *East : 4¼ m. on A 525* – ⊠ *Whitchurch.*

🍴 **The Combermere Arms**, SY13 4AT, ℰ (01948) 871223, *combermere.arms@brunnin gandprice.co.uk*, Fax (01948) 661371, 🌳, 🌳 – ⁕⊕ P. ⁕⊕ VISA
Rest a la carte 17.65/26.90 ⊒.
◆ Rurally located pub with smart terrace ideal for al fresco refreshment. Interior skylights lend an open, airy feel. Informal, eclectic menus. Some vast tables for big parties.

WHITEHAVEN *Cumbria 502 J 20.*
London 332 – Carlisle 39 – Keswick 28 – Penrith 47.

✗✗ **Zest**, Low Rd, CA28 9HS, South : ½ m. on B 5345 (St Bees) ℰ (01946) 692848, Fax (01946) 66984 – P. ⁕⊕ ⓞ VISA
closed 25 December - 2 January and Sunday-Tuesday – **Rest** (dinner only) a la carte 17.00/29.50 ⊒.
◆ Don't be put off by the unprepossessing exterior: inside is a smart, stylish eatery and bar with brown leather sofas. Eclectic range of modern menus with numerous influences.

WHITEPARISH *Wilts. 503 504 P 30* – *see Salisbury.*

WHITEWELL *Lancs. 502 M 22* – ⊠ *Clitheroe.*
London 281 – Lancaster 31 – Leeds 55 – Manchester 41 – Preston 13.

🏛 **The Inn at Whitewell**, Forest of Bowland, BB7 3AT, ℰ (01200) 448222, *reception@in natwhitewell.com*, Fax (01200) 448298, ≤, 🗨, 🌳 – P. ⁕⊕ VISA
Rest (bar lunch)/dinner a la carte 15.50/35.00 ⊒ – **23 rm** ⊒ ✦70.00 – ✦✦96.00, 1 suite.
◆ Once home to the Royal Keeper of the Forest, a popular inn with considerable charm, full of eyecatching curios. Stylish rooms with CD players; some have real peat fires. Intimate dining room overlooks river Hodder and Trough of Bowland.

WHITLEY *Wilts. – see Melksham.*

WHITSTABLE *Kent* 504 X 29 – *pop. 30 195.*

🏛 *7 Oxford St* ℘ *(01227) 275482, whitstableinformation@canterbury.gov.uk.*
London 68 – Dover 24 – Maidstone 37 – Margate 12.

🏛🏛 **Continental,** 29 Beach Walk, CT5 2BP, East : ½ m. by Sea St and Harbour St ℘ (01227) 280280, *jamie@hotelcontinental.co.uk, Fax (01227) 284114,* ←, 😋 – 🍴 ✦ **P.** 🐵 **VISA**. 🛇
Rest (bar lunch)/dinner 21.00 and a la carte 23.85/34.95 – **24 rm** 🍽 ✦56.50 – ✦✦142.00/150.00.
♦ Laid-back, privately owned hotel with an unadorned 30s-style façade overlooking the sea; simply furnished, plain-walled rooms - picture windows and warm colours. Split-level bistro with "no frills" approach.

✗ **Whitstable Oyster Fishery Co.,** Royal Native Oyster Stores, The Horsebridge, CT5 1BU, ℘ (01227) 276856, *Fax (01227) 770829,* ← – 😋 – 🛇. 🐵 **VISA**. 🛇
closed 25-26 and 31 December, and Monday except Bank Holidays – **Rest** - Seafood - (booking essential in winter) a la carte 26.95/35.45 🍷.
♦ Relaxed and unfussy converted beach warehouse; seafood on display in open kitchen; oysters and moules-frites draw a trendy young set at weekends. Arthouse cinema upstairs.

✗ **Jo Jo's,** 209 Tankerton Rd, CT5 2AT, East : 1½ m. by Sea St and Harbour St ℘ (01227) 274591, – 😋
closed mid December-early January, Monday-Tuesday and Sunday dinner – **Rest** (booking essential) a la carte approx 18.00.
♦ Charmingly laid back eatery with snug interior and mix of bar stools and rustic wooden tables. There's a simple terrace, too. Appealing mix of tapas and meze to graze over.

at Seasalter *Southwest : 2 m. by B 2205 –* ✉ *Whitstable.*

🍴 **The Sportsman,** Faversham Rd, CT5 4BP, Southwest : 2 m. following coast rd ℘ (01227) 273370, 🌿 – **P.** 🐵 **VISA**.
closed 25-26 December – **Rest** *(closed Sunday dinner and Monday)* a la carte 25.00/35.00 🍷.
♦ Set along the coast road with shingle and beach to one side, acres of marshland to the other. Tasty classic and modern menus. Local farmer supplies best seasonal ingredients.

WHITTLE-LE-WOODS *Lancs.* 502 M 23 – *see Chorley.*

WHITTLESFORD *Cambs.* 504 U 27.
London 50 – Cambridge 11 – Peterborough 46.

✗✗ **The Tickell Arms,** 1 North Rd, CB2 4NZ, ℘ (01223) 833128, *Fax (01223) 835907,* 😋 – 😋 **P.** 🐵 **VISA**
closed Sunday dinner and Monday – **Rest** a la carte 23.15/42.20 🍷 ♨.
♦ Richly ornate 300 year-old exterior with conservatory and terrace. Quirky feel pervades: emerald green walls, yellow ceiling. Rich, classic meals from the Gallic repertoire.

WHITWELL-ON-THE-HILL *N. Yorks.* 502 R 21 – ✉ *York.*
London 240 – Kingston-upon-Hull 47 – Scarborough 29 – York 13.

🍴 **The Stone Trough Inn,** Kirkham Abbey, YO60 7JS, East : 1¾ m. by A 64 on Kirkham Priory rd ℘ (01653) 618713, *info@stonetroughinn.co.uk, Fax (01653) 618819,* 😋 – 😋 **P.** 🐵 **VISA**. 🛇
closed 25 December – **Rest** *(closed Sunday dinner and Monday)* a la carte 23.00/26.00 🍷.
♦ Friendly rustic pub, two minutes from the striking ruins of Kirkham Abbey. Wide-ranging menu on a sound local base: satisfying and full of flavour. Warm, attentive service.

WICKFORD *Essex* 504 V 29 – *see Basildon.*

WICKHAM *Hants.* 503 504 Q 31 – *pop. 1 915.*
London 74 – Portsmouth 12 – Southampton 11 – Winchester 16.

✗✗ **The Old House** with rm, The Square, PO17 5JG, ℘ (01329) 833049, *oldhouseho tel@aol.com, Fax (01329) 833672,* 😋, 🌿 – 😋 **P.** 🐵 **AE** **VISA**. 🛇
closed 26-30 December – **Rest** *(closed Sunday dinner)* a la carte 23.85/35.15 🍷 – 🍽 10.00 – **15 rm** ✦65.00/75.00 – ✦✦150.00.
♦ Handsome Queen Anne house in town centre. Eat in pretty conservatory or on delightful terrace. Unfussy, accomplished, seasonal cooking. Smarter bedrooms in the garden wing.

WIGHT (Isle of) *I.O.W. 503 504 P/Q 31 32 Great Britain G.* – pop. 124 577.

> See : *Island★★*.
>
> Env. : *Osborne House, East Cowes★★ AC – Carisbrooke Castle, Newport★★ AC (Keep ≤★) – Brading★ (Roman Villa★ AC, St Mary's Church★, Nunwell House★ AC) – Shorwell : St Peter's Church★ (wall paintings★)*.
>
> 🚢 *from East Cowes to Southampton (Red Funnel Ferries) frequent services daily (1 h) – from Yarmouth to Lymington (Wightlink Ltd) frequent services daily (30 mn) – from Fishbourne to Portsmouth (Wightlink Ltd) frequent services daily (35 mn).*
>
> 🚢 *from Ryde to Portsmouth (Hovertravel Ltd) frequent services daily (10 mn) – from Ryde to Portsmouth (Wightlink Ltd) frequent services daily (15 mn) – from East Cowes to Southampton (Red Funnel Ferries) frequent services daily (22 mn).*

Brighstone.

⌂ **The Lodge** ⌷ without rest., Main Rd, PO30 4DJ, ℰ (01983) 741272, thelodgeb@hotmail.com, Fax (01983) 741272, ⌗, ⌷ – ⌷ ⌷ ⌷
restricted opening in winter – **7 rm** ⌷ ★50.00/70.00 – ★★70.00.
  ♦ Victorian country house set in two and a half acres: quiet location. Real fire centrepiece of large sitting room. Completely co-ordinated rooms of varnished pine.

Freshwater *I.O.W. – pop. 7 317 (inc. Totland) – ⌷ Isle of Wight.*
Newport 13.

🏠 **Sandpipers,** Coastguard Lane (via public car park), Freshwater Bay, PO40 9QX, South : 1 ½ m. by A 3055 ℰ (01983) 758500, info@sandpipershotel.com, ⌷, ⌗ – ⌷ ⌷ ⌷ ⌷ ⌷
VISA
Rest a la carte 22.95/46.45 ⌷ – **26 rm** ⌷ ★40.00/65.00 – ★★90.00/120.00.
  ♦ Detached Victorian house with a friendly, family run atmosphere. Close to the cliffs, beach and Afton nature reserve. Good sized, modern-style rooms. Garden conservatory restaurant set around variety of water features.

⌂ **Rockstone Cottage** without rest., Colwell Chine Rd, PO40 9NR, Northwest : ¾ m. by A 3055 off A 3054 ℰ (01983) 753723, enquiries@rockstonecottage.co.uk, ⌗ – ⌷ ⌷ ⌷
5 rm ★36.00/40.00 – ★★52.00/60.00.
  ♦ Simple, pretty cottage, with small garden, dating from the 1790s. Well-kept domestic feel with a traditional and homely standard of décor.

🍴 **The Red Lion,** Church Pl, PO40 9BP, via Hooke Hill ℰ (01983) 754925, Fax (01983) 754925, ⌗ – ⌷ ⌷ **VISA**
Rest (closed 25 December) a la carte 20.00/25.00 ⌷.
  ♦ Bustling part 14C pub with much charm. Located at the top of a hill and next to the church. Stone floors, open fires and a couple of sofas. Blackboard menu of seasonal fare.

Ryde *I.O.W. – ⌷ Isle of Wight.*
🏌 *Binstead Rd ℰ (01983) 614809.*
🛈 *81-83 Union St ℰ (01983) 813818.*
Newport 7.

🍴🍴 **Beijing Palace,** Appley Rise, PO33 1LE, ℰ (01983) 811888, Fax (01983) 562888 – ⌷ ⌷ AE ① **VISA**
Rest - Chinese - a la carte approx 15.00.
  ♦ Sizable thatched roofed façade belied by narrow interior with simple décor that's highlighted by life-sized central Buddha. Good value menus, full of tasty, regional dishes.

St Lawrence *I.O.W. – ⌷ Isle of Wight.*
Newport 16.

⌂ **Little Orchard** without rest., Undercliffe Drive, PO38 1YA, West : 1 m. on A 3055 ℰ (01983) 731106, ⌗ – ⌷ ⌷ ⌷
3 rm ⌷ ★42.00 – ★★60.00.
  ♦ A pretty, detached stone cottage with secluded rear garden and some views of the sea. Large, welcoming lounge with piano. Simple, comfortable bedrooms.

Seaview *I.O.W. – pop. 2 181 – ⌷ Isle of Wight.*

🏨 **Priory Bay** ⌷, Priory Drive, PO34 5BU, Southeast : 1½ m. by B 3330 ℰ (01983) 613146, enquiries@priorybay.co.uk, Fax (01983) 616539, ⌗, ⌷, ⌗, ⌷, ⌷ – ⌷ rest, ⌷ ⌷ AE ①
VISA
The Restaurant : Rest 29.50 (dinner) and a la carte approx 25.00 – **18 rm** ⌷ ★65.00/130.00 – ★★190.00/260.00, 2 suites.
  ♦ Medieval priory with Georgian additions, surrounded by woodland. High ceilinged drawing room and bar area with leaded windows. Characterful rooms. Main Restaurant has views of the garden.

🏠 **Seaview,** High St, PO34 5EX, ℰ (01983) 612711, *reception@seaviewhotel.co.uk,* Fax (01983) 613729, 🍴 – ✗, 🍽 rest, ♨ **P**, 🅼🅾 🅰🅴 ① 🆅🅸🆂🅰
– *The Restaurant and Sunshine Room :* **Rest** (booking essential) (in bar Sunday dinner except Bank Holidays) a la carte 28.95/42.20 – **15 rm** ⌗ ✦70.00/180.00 – ✦✦137.00/180.00, 2 suites.
• Victorian hotel with smart genuine style. Integral part of the community, on street leading to seafront. Bold modern bedrooms and nautically styled, welcoming public areas. Twin eateries, full of clocks and rare model ship collection.

Shanklin *I.O.W. – pop. 17 305 (inc. Sandown) – ⊠ Isle of Wight.*
🖪 The Fairway, Lake Sandown ℰ (01983) 403217.
🖪 67 High St ℰ (01983) 813818.
Newport 9.

🏠 **Rylstone Manor** ⌂, Rylstone Gdns, PO37 6RG, ℰ (01983) 862806, *rylstonemanor iow@btinternet.com,* Fax (01983) 862806, 🍴 – ✗ 🐾 **P**, 🅾 🅰🅴 🆅🅸🆂🅰. 🍴
Rest (dinner only) 25.00 – **9 rm** ⌗ ✦52.00/100.00 – ✦✦119.00.
• Part 19C former gentleman's residence set in the town's cliff-top gardens. Interior has a comfortable period feel. Well furnished, individually styled bedrooms. Characterful Victorian hued dining room.

🏠 **Foxhills** without rest., 30 Victoria Ave, PO37 6LS, ℰ (01983) 862329, *info@foxhillsho tel.co.uk,* Fax (01983) 866666, 🍴 – ✗ **P**, 🅾 🆅🅸🆂🅰. 🍴
closed January – **8 rm** ⌗ ✦49.00/70.00 – ✦✦78.00/98.00.
• Attractive house in leafy avenue with woodland to the rear. Bright lounge with fireplace. Bedrooms in pastel shades. Unusual jacuzzi, spa and beauty treatments. Breakfast room opens onto terrace.

🏠 **Grange Bank,** Grange Rd, PO37 6NN, ℰ (01983) 862337, *grangebank@btinternet.com* – ✗ **P**, 🅾 ① 🆅🅸🆂🅰. 🍴
Easter-October – **Rest** (booking essential) (residents only) (dinner only) (unlicensed) 10.50 – **9 rm** ⌗ ✦26.00/41.00 – ✦✦52.00/62.00.
• Extended Victorian house near high street. Comfortable, simple and immaculately kept with friendly, domestic ambience. Good value accommodation.

Totland *I.O.W. – pop. 7 317 (inc. Freshwater) – ⊠ Isle of Wight.*
Newport 13.

🏠 **Sentry Mead,** Madeira Rd, PO39 0BJ, ℰ (01983) 753212, *info@sentrymead.co.uk,* Fax (01983) 754710, 🍴 – ✗ **P**, 🅾 🅰🅴 🆅🅸🆂🅰
Rest (bar lunch)/dinner 19.50 – **14 rm** ⌗ ✦45.00/90.00 – ✦✦90.00/120.00.
• Detached Victorian house with quiet garden 100 yards from beach. Traditional interiors include bar area and conservatory lounge. Comfortable rooms furnished with light wood. Popular menus in dining room.

Ventnor *I.O.W. – pop. 5 978 – ⊠ Isle of Wight.*
🖪 Steephill Down Rd ℰ (01983) 853326.
🖪 Coastal Visitors Centre, Salisbury Gdns, Dudley Rd ℰ (01983) 813818 (summer only).
Newport 10.

🏠🏠🏠 **Royal,** Belgrave Rd, PO38 1JJ, ℰ (01983) 852186, *enquiries@royalhoteliow.co.uk,* Fax (01983) 855395, ⌗, 🍴 – 📶 ✗ **P**, 🏊 40. 🅾 🅰🅴 ① 🆅🅸🆂🅰
closed 2 weeks January – **Rest** (bar lunch Monday-Saturday)/dinner 35.00/45.00 s. – **55 rm** ⌗ ✦80.00/140.00 – ✦✦140.00/160.00.
• Largest hotel on the island, a Victorian property, in the classic style of English seaside hotels. Traditional décor throughout the public areas and comfortable bedrooms. Light lunches in conservatory; classic meals in capacious dining room.

🏠🏠 **Wellington,** Belgrave Rd, PO38 1JH, ℰ (01983) 856600, *enquiries@thewellingtonho tel.net,* Fax (01983) 856611, ≼ Ventnor and English Channel, 🍴 – ✗ rest, 🐾 **P**, 🅾 🅰🅴 ① 🆅🅸🆂🅰. 🍴
Rest (dinner only) a la carte 21.65/29.25 – **28 rm** ⌗ ✦80.00/88.00 – ✦✦125.00/135.00.
• Totally refurbished Victorian hotel with commanding town and sea views. Modish lines throughout. Most rooms have a balcony; all are imbued with a stunning sense of modernity. Spacious dining room with dramatic views and beautiful decked terrace.

🏠 **Lake** ⌂, Shore Rd, Bonchurch, PO38 1RF, ℰ (01983) 852613, *mich@lakehotel.co.uk,* 🍴 – ✗ **P**
closed December-6 February – **Rest** (dinner only) 12.00 s. – **20 rm** ⌗ ✦42.00/76.00 – ✦✦70.00/80.00.
• 19C private residence, run as hotel by one family since 1960s. South facing public rooms in traditional style. Bedrooms in annex and main house have simple country feel. Garden views from dining room.

XX **Hambrough** with rm, Hambrough Rd, PO38 1SQ, ℰ (01983) 856333, *info@theham brough.com, Fax (01983) 857260,* ≤, 屛 – ✤, ▤ rest, 🅿 ✿ 25. ⑩ 🆅🆂🅰
Rest *(closed Tuesday and Sunday dinner)* 14.50/35.00 – **7 rm** ⌂ ✚95.00/110.00 – ✚✚145.00/205.00.
● Victorian house with contrastingly modish bar and avant-garde restaurant. Well-conceived menus enjoy contemporary starting point. State-of-the-art rooms with neutral hues.

XX **The Pond Café**, Bonchurch, PO38 1RG, ℰ (01983) 855666, *info@thepondcafe.com,* Fax (01983) 855666, 屛 – ✤, 🆅🆂🅰
closed Monday – **Rest** a la carte 20.20/30.45.
● Intimate restaurant, with duck pond, in sleepy hamlet. Cosy sunlit terrace. Island's larder utilised to the full for seasonal dishes in unfussy, halogen lit surroundings.

Yarmouth *I.O.W.* – ✉ *Isle of Wight.*
Newport 10.

🏤 **The George**, Quay St, PO41 0PE, ℰ (01983) 760331, *res@thegeorge.co.uk,*
✿ *Fax (01983) 760425,* ≤, 屛 – ✤ rm, ▤ rest. ⑩ 🅰🅴 🆅🆂🅰
The Restaurant : **Rest** *(closed Sunday-Monday)* (booking essential) (dinner only) 46.50 ♀ –
(see also **The Brasserie** below) – **16 rm** ⌂ ✚130.00 – ✚✚255.00/265.00, 1 suite.
Spec. Mackerel with crab salad, watermelon and beetroot syrup. Duck with nougatine, endive and jasmine tea sauce. Trio of chocolate desserts on raspberry sauce.
● Splendid 17C quayside hotel. Relaxed, intimate style engendered by gracious comfort and attentive service. Superb individually decorated rooms. Memorable cooking: highly competent and inventive skills; fine traditional ingredients.

X **The Brasserie** (at The George H.), Quay St, PO41 0PE, ℰ (01983) 760331, Fax (01983) 760425, 屛 – ⑩ 🅰🅴 🆅🆂🅰
Rest a la carte 28.40/34.50 ♀.
● French bistro-style restaurant. Warm yellow walls, wood furniture and views of the garden create a sunny ambience. Modern menu offers exciting choice of eclectic dishes.

WILLERBY *East Riding* 502 S 22 – *see Kingston-upon-Hull.*

WILLESLEY *Glos.* 503 504 N 29 – *see Tetbury.*

WILLIAN *Herts.* – *see Letchworth.*

WILLINGTON *Ches.* – *see Tarporley.*

WILMINGTON *Devon* 503 K 31 – *see Honiton.*

WILMINGTON *E. Sussex* 504 U 31 – *see Eastbourne.*

WILMINGTON *Kent* 504 V 29 – *see Dartford.*

WILMSLOW *Ches.* 502 503 504 N 24 – *pop. 34 087.*
🏌 *Great Warford, Mobberley* ℰ (01565) 872148.
London 189 – Liverpool 38 – Manchester 12 – Stoke-on-Trent 27.

🏨 **Holiday Inn Manchester Airport**, Oversley Ford, Altrincham Rd, SK9 4LR, Northwest : 2 ¾ m. on A 538 ℰ (01625) 889988, *Fax (01625) 531876,* 🛁, 🆂, 🏊, squash – 📶 ✤
▤ 🗪 🅿 – 🔏 300. ⑩ 🆅🆂🅰 ✂
The Terrace : **Rest** *(bar lunch)/dinner* a la carte 20.00/26.00 **s.** – ⌂ 13.95 – **126 rm**
✚129.00/149.00 – ✚✚129.00/149.00.
● Group hotel, at first sight suggestive of a large cream-painted villa. Bright rooms, busy meeting suites plus coffee shop and extensive leisure club for relaxing time-outs. Bright modern décor. Extensive menu of popular dishes to suit all tastes.

🏨 **Stanneylands**, Stanneylands Rd, SK9 4EY, North : 1 m. by A 34 ℰ (01625) 525225, *enquiries@stanneylandshotel.co.uk, Fax (01625) 537282,* 屛 – ✤ rm, 🕻 🅿 – 🔏 120. ⑩
🅰🅴 ⓞ 🆅🆂🅰 ✂
The Restaurant : **Rest** *(residents only Sunday dinner)* 13.50/27.50 ♀ – ⌂ 11.50 – **54 rm**
✚110.00/125.00 – ✚✚135.00, 1 suite.
● Attractive 19C redbrick hotel standing in mature grounds; exudes pleasant, country house style. Two characterful lounges and comfortable, traditional bedrooms. Comfy oak-panelled surroundings for diners.

ENGLAND

⌂ **Marigold House** without rest., 132 Knutsford Rd, SK9 6JH, Southwest : 1 m. on B 5086
℘ (01625) 584414, ☞ – P.
closed Christmas – **3 rm** ⌷ ✸38.00 – ✸✸50.00.
♦ 18C former farmhouse, 10 minutes from Manchester Airport; flagged floors throughout
with log fires and antiques. Oak beams in bedrooms. Communal breakfast at superb oak
table.

WIMBORNE MINSTER *Dorset 503 504 O 31 The West Country G. – pop. 14 884.*
See : *Town★ – Minster★ – Priest's House Museum★ AC.*
Env. : *Kingston Lacy★★ AC, NW : 3 m. by B 3082.*
🛈 *29 High St ℘ (01202) 886116, wimbornetic@eastdorsetdc.gov.uk.*
London 112 – Bournemouth 10 – Dorchester 23 – Salisbury 27 – Southampton 30.

XXX **Les Bouviers** with rm, Arrowsmith Rd, Canford Magna, BH21 3BD, South : 2 ¼ m. by A
349 and A 341 ℘ (01202) 889555, *info@lesbouviers.co.uk, Fax (01202) 639428,* ☞ – ☼ P.
🕮 AE ⑩ VISA
Rest 21.95/31.95 ⚥ – ⌷ 12.50 – **6 rm** ✸100.00/120.00 – ✸✸160.00/225.00.
♦ Plush yet homely restaurant affording views to acres of mature grounds. Formal feel
lightened by personable service. Complex dishes with modern twists. Well-appointed
rooms.

WINCANTON *Somerset 503 504 M 30.*
London 118 – Bruton 5 – Glastonbury 20.

🏛 **Holbrook House** ⌂, BA9 8BS, West : 2 ¼ m. on A 371 ℘ (01963) 824466, *enqui*
ries@holbrookhouse.co.uk, Fax (01963) 32681, 🏊, ₤₅, ☎₅, 🎾, ☞, ☟, ✾ – ☼ rest, P. –
🕮 220. 🕮 AE VISA
Cedar : Rest *(closed Sunday dinner)* 16.95 (lunch) and dinner a la carte 26.40/42.90 **s** –
19 rm ⌷ ✸140.00/195.00 – ✸✸250.00/175.00, 2 suites.
♦ Substantial 19C country house in mature grounds. Dramatic proportions prevail, but
intimate spaces - like the wood-panelled bar - gel seamlessly. Smart spa; individual rooms.
Classic dining room overlooks gardens.

WINCHCOMBE *Glos. 503 504 O 28 – pop. 3 682.*
🛈 *Town Hall, High St ℘ (01242) 602925.*
London 100 – Birmingham 43 – Gloucester 26 – Oxford 43.

⌂ **Isbourne Manor House** without rest., Castle St, GL54 5JA, ℘ (01242) 602281, *fe*
licity@isbourne-manor.co.uk, Fax (01242) 602281, ☞ – ☼ P. ✾
closed Christmas – **3 rm** ⌷ ✸50.00/60.00 – ✸✸90.00/95.00.
♦ Wisteria-clad Georgian and Elizabethan manor. Cosy drawing room: antique furniture
and open fire. One room has a four-poster bed, one a roof top terrace. Riverside garden.

⌂ **Westward** ⌂ without rest., Sudeley Lodge, GL54 5JB, East : 1 ½ m. by Castle St on
Sudeley Lodge/Parks/Farm rd ℘ (01242) 604372, *jimw@haldon.co.uk, Fax (01242) 604640,*
≤, ☞, ☟ – ☼ rest, P. VISA. ✾
closed Christmas-New Year – **3 rm** ⌷ ✸55.00/65.00 – ✸✸90.00/100.00.
♦ Secluded, personally run 18C farmhouse: elegant, wood-floored drawing room and
charming sitting room, bedrooms share fine views of 550-acre estate and mature gardens.

XX **Wesley House** with rm, High St, GL54 5LJ, ℘ (01242) 602366, *enquiries@wesley*
house.co.uk, Fax (01242) 609046 – ☼ ▤. 🕮 AE VISA
closed 25-26 December – **Rest** *(closed Sunday dinner)* 18.00/38.00 and lunch a la carte
24.45/29.95 **s.** ⚥ – **5 rm** ⌷ ✸65.00 – ✸✸95.00.
♦ Hugely characterful part 15C house: dine amongst the beams or in the stylish glass-
roofed extension. Tasty modern British cooking with original twists. Smilingly quaint
rooms.

XX **5 North St** (Ashenford), 5 North St, GL54 5LH, ℘ (01242) 604566, *marcusashenford@ya*
🕸 *hoo.co.uk, Fax (01242) 603788* – ☼. 🕮 AE VISA
closed 3 weeks January, 1 week August, Sunday lunch, Tuesday lunch and Monday –
Rest 22.50/37.00.
Spec. Terrine of lemon sole, trout and crab with sweet pepper. Braised pig cheek, choucroute ravioli, onion and sage marmalade. Lemon thyme parfait, mango and hazelnut salad.
♦ Personally run, cosy, 17C timbered restaurant with low-beamed ceiling and a pleasantly
relaxed, friendly atmosphere. Good value menus offer flavoursome and refined cooking.

X **Bar & Tapas**, 20 High St, GL54 5LJ, ℘ (01242) 604360, *enquiries@wesleyhouse.co.uk,*
Fax (01242) 609046 – ☼. 🕮 AE VISA
closed 25-26 December – **Rest** - Tapas - 9.99 (lunch) and a la carte 10.00/22.50 **s.**.
♦ Located on busy high street, this is a buzzy place to be, with trendy bar, comfy lounge,
and wood-floored dining area serving authentic Spanish tapas beneath the big mirrors.

ENGLAND

WINCHELSEA E. Sussex 504 W 31 Great Britain G.

See : Town★ – St Thomas Church (effigies★).
London 64 – Brighton 46 – Folkestone 30.

⌂ **Strand House** without rest., Tanyard's Lane, TN36 4JT, East : ¼ m. on A 259 ℘ (01797)
🖼 226276, info@thestrandhouse.co.uk, Fax (01797) 224806, 🐾 – 🗝️ **P**. **⬤** **AE** **①** **VISA**. 🛇
10 rm ⊃ ✦50.00 – ✦✦85.00.
♦ 14C and 15C half-timbered house of low beams and inglenook fireplaces: carefully
tended rear garden shaded by tall trees, snug lounge; well-kept rooms in traditional style.

WINCHESTER Hants. 503 504 P 30 Great Britain G. – pop. 41 420.

See : City★★ - Cathedral★★★ AC B – Winchester College★ AC B B – Castle Great Hall★ B D –
God Begot House★ B A.
Env. : St Cross Hospital★★ AC A.
🖪 Guildhall, The Broadway ℘ (01962) 840500, tourism@winchester.gov.uk.
London 72 – Bristol 76 – Oxford 52 – Southampton 12.

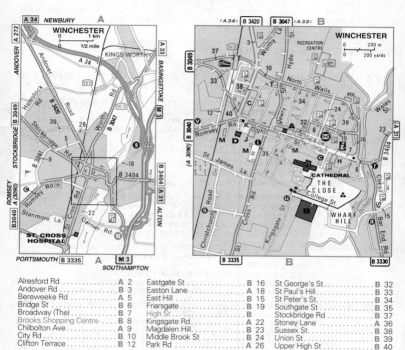

Alresford Rd	**A** 2	Eastgate St	**B** 16	St George's St	**B** 32
Andover Rd	**B** 3	Easton Lane	**A** 18	St Paul's Hill	**B** 33
Bereweeke Rd	**A** 5	East Hill	**B** 15	St Peter's St	**B** 34
Bridge St	**B** 6	Friarsgate	**B** 19	Southgate St	**B** 35
Broadway (The)	**B** 7	High St	**B**	Stockbridge Rd	**B** 37
Brooks Shopping Centre	**B** 8	Kingsgate Rd	**B** 22	Stoney Lane	**A** 36
Chilbolton Ave	**A** 9	Magdalen Hill	**B** 23	Sussex St	**B** 38
City Rd	**B** 10	Middle Brook St	**B** 24	Union St	**B** 39
Clifton Terrace	**B** 12	Park Rd	**A** 26	Upper High St	**B** 40

🏨 **Wessex**, Paternoster Row, SO23 9LQ, ℘ (0870) 4008126, gm.wessex@macdonald-ho
tels.co.uk, Fax (01962) 841503, ⇐ – ❘♦❘ 🗝️, ▤ rest, **P**. – 🔼 100. **⬤** **AE** **①** **VISA**. 🛇   B c
Walkers : Rest (bar lunch)/dinner 28.00 s. ♀ – **93 rm** ⊃ ✦79.00/169.00 –
✦✦100.00/180.00, 1 suite.
♦ Smartly run group hotel. Enviable cathedral view from the lounge - a pleasant spot for
tea - and many of the rooms, all well appointed and decorated in traditional patterns. Wide
windowed restaurant with floodlit views of cathedral by night.

🏨 **Hotel du Vin**, 14 Southgate St, SO23 9EF, ℘ (01962) 841414, info@winchester.hotel
duvin.com, Fax (01962) 842458, 🐾 – ☎ **P**. – 🔼 30. **⬤** **AE** **VISA**. 🛇   B i
Rest – (see **Bistro** below) – ⊃ 13.95 – **24 rm** ✦120.00/175.00 – ✦✦120.00/175.00.
♦ Elegant bedrooms, each with CD player, mini bar and distinct décor reflecting its wine
house sponsors, in a 1715 redbrick house. Smart Champagne bar with inviting sofas.

Giffard House without rest., 50 Christchurch Rd, SO23 9SU, *℘* (01962) 852628, *giffard hotel@aol.com, Fax (01962) 856722,* ≈ – ♦ **P**, **MO** **AE** **VISA**, ✿ B s
closed 24 December-1 January – **13 rm** ♦**69.00/79.00** – ♦♦**105.00/115.00.**
♦ Imposing part Victorian, part Edwardian house. Spacious breakfast room and comfortable sitting room with large fireplace. Immaculate rooms with good facilities.

Dawn Cottage without rest., Romsey Rd, SO22 5PQ, *℘* (01962) 869956, *dawncot tage@hotmail.com, Fax (01962) 869956,* ≪, ≈ – ♦✗ **P**, ✿ A c
3 rm ⊡ ♦**50.00/55.00** – ♦♦**65.00/68.00.**
♦ Attractive, spotlessly kept cottage; friendly hosts. Simply decorated rooms; all have views across the Itchen Valley. Secluded rear garden flanked by tall trees.

Chesil Rectory, Chesil St, SO23 0HU, *℘* (01962) 851555, *info@chesilrectory.co.uk, Fax (01962) 869704* – **MO** **AE** **VISA** B r
closed 2 weeks Christmas, 2 weeks August, Sunday, Monday and lunch Tuesday – **Rest** 23.00/49.00 �*.*
♦ Formal white linen blends well with a part 15C interior of low beams and leaded windows. Attentive service; modern cooking in marked contrast with the surroundings.

Bistro (at Hotel du Vin), 14 Southgate St, SO23 9EF, *℘* (01962) 841414, *Fax (01962) 842458,* ✾, ≈ – **P**, **MO** **AE** **VISA** B i
Rest (booking essential) 28.40 ⌖.
♦ Oenophile memorabilia covers panelled cream walls; hops crown tall sash windows. Terrace under broad sunshades. Classic modern flavours set off the carefully chosen wines.

The Wykeham Arms with rm, 75 Kingsgate St, SO23 9PE, *℘* (01962) 853834, *wykeha marms@accommodating-inns.co.uk, Fax (01962) 854411,* ✾, ≈ – ♦✗ rm, **P**, **MO** **AE** **①** **VISA**, ✿ B u
closed 25 December – **Rest** *(closed Sunday dinner)* (booking essential) a la carte 14.50/28.50 ⌖ – **14 rm** ⊡ ♦**57.00/105.00** – ♦♦**95.00/135.00.**
♦ 18C inn; cosy snugs off a bar crammed with tankards, sporting curios and old school desks. Full-flavoured cooking. Cottage-style rooms, larger in annex: a city institution.

The Black Boy, 1 Wharf Hill, SO23 9NQ, *℘* (01962) 861754, *blackboypub@ntlworld.com,* ✾ – **MO** **VISA** B a
closed 2 weeks September-October, 2 weeks Christmas-New Year, Monday and Sunday dinner – **Rest** (booking essential) (light lunch) a la carte 24.25/29.40.
♦ Gloriously quirky pub: feast your eyes on a multitude of disparate items. Loaf around in intimate nooks, one boasting an Aga. In evening, dine on cutting-edge concoctions.

at Easton *Northeast : 4 m. by A 3090* – A – *off B 3047* – ⊠ *Winchester.*

Chestnut Horse, SO21 1EG, *℘* (01962) 779257, *Fax (01962) 779037,* ✾ – **P**, **MO** **VISA**
Rest *(closed Sunday dinner in winter)* a la carte 16.00/30.00 ⌖.
♦ Characterful 16C pub in rural village near M3. Welcoming interior with log fires, beams and hanging pots and jugs. Two dining rooms serve tasty, classic pub favourites.

at Ovington *East : 5¾ m. by B 3404* – A – *and A 31* – ⊠ *Winchester.*

Bush Inn, SO24 0RE, *℘* (01962) 732764, *thebushinn@wadworth.co.uk, Fax (01962) 735130,* ✾, ≈ – ♦✗ **P**, **MO** **AE** **VISA**
closed 25 December – **Rest** *(closed Sunday dinner)* a la carte 19.50/31.50.
♦ 17C country inn, hidden down winding country road along river Itchen, with delightful garden and engaging rural décor. Four intimate dining rooms serve tasty country dishes.

at Littleton *Northwest : 2½ m. by B 3049* – A – ⊠ *Winchester.*

The Running Horse with rm, 88 Main Rd, SO22 6QS, *℘* (01962) 880218, *runni nghorse@btconnect.com, Fax (01962) 886596,* ✾ – ♦✗ **P**, **MO** **VISA**
closed 25 December – **Rest** a la carte 19.50/25.00 ⌖ – **9 rm** ⊡ ♦**65.00** – ♦♦**65.00.**
♦ Yellow hued hostelry boasting a rear restaurant with stone floors, wicker chairs and a sophisticated range of dishes. Two terraces for summer dining. Smart rooms.

at Sparsholt *Northwest : 3½ m. by B 3049* – A – ⊠ *Winchester.*

Lainston House ≫, SO21 2LT, *℘* (01962) 863588, *enquiries@lainstonhouse.com, Fax (01962) 776672,* ≪, ✾, ♣, ≈, ⅛ – rest, **P**, **⚿** 80, **MO** **AE** **①** **VISA**
Avenue : **Rest** 28.00/50.00 and a la carte 35.50/49.20 ⌖ – ⊡ 17.50 – **48 rm** ♦125.00/225.00 – ♦♦325.00, 2 suites.
♦ Charming 17C manor with pretty grounds, parks and old herb garden. Traditionally styled lounge, cedar-panelled bar and up-to-date gym. Rooms, some more modern, vary in size. Dark wood dining room overlooks lawn.

Plough Inn, Main Rd, SO21 2NW, *℘* (01962) 776353, *Fax (01962) 776400,* ✾, ≈ – **P**, **MO** **VISA**
closed 25 December – **Rest** (booking essential) a la carte 18.00/28.00 ⌖.
♦ Friendly, unassuming pub - book early for a varied blackboard menu combining the modern and traditional, all served at pine tables. Real ales.

ENGLAND

739

London 11 – Brookmans Park 10 – Potters Bar 7.5.

🍴 **The Plough,** The Hill, HP7 0PA, ℰ (01494) 721001, *ploughamersham@btconnect.com*, 🍴, ☞ – ⇌ ᴘ. ⬜ ᴀᴇ ⓪ 𝘝𝘐𝘚𝘈. ⬚
Rest 11.90 (lunch) and a la carte 20.00/30.00 ⬚.
◆ Neatly whitewashed pub on the green in peaceful village. Flagstoned bar with beams and leather sofas. Split-level dining: evolving menus where fine dining meets pub classics.

WINDERMERE *Cumbria 502* L 20 *Great Britain G.* – *pop. 7 941.*
Env. : *Lake Windermere*★★ – *Brookhole National Park Centre*★ *AC, NW : 2 m. by A 591.*
🛈 *Victoria St* ℰ (015394) 46499.
London 274 – Blackpool 55 – Carlisle 46 – Kendal 10.

Plan opposite

🏰 **Langdale Chase,** LA23 1LW, Northwest : 3 m. on A 591 ℰ (015394) 32201, *sales@lang dalechase.co.uk*, Fax (015394) 32604, ⩽ Lake Windermere and mountains, ☞ – 🔟 ⇌, ☰ rest, ᴘ. ⬜ ᴀᴇ ⬜
Rest 18.95/34.00 ⬚ – **26 rm** ⊡ ✦80.00/104.00 – ✦✦150.00/198.00, 1 suite.
◆ Substantial 19C house with beautiful gardens and wonderful lakeside setting boasting a wealth of ornate Victoriana and superbly preserved carvings. Pleasantly styled rooms. Formal dining in a classic room; sweeping views across the lake.

🏨 **Holbeck Ghyll** ⬚, Holbeck Lane, LA23 1LU, Northwest : 3 ¼ m. by A 591 ℰ (015394) 32375, *stay@holbeckghyll.com*, Fax (015394) 34743, ⩽ Lake Windermere and mountains, ╏ᴓ, ⩶, ☞, ⚞% – ⚙ ᴘ. ⬜ ᴀᴇ ⬜ 𝘝𝘐𝘚𝘈.
closed 2 weeks January – Rest (lunch booking essential) 27.50/55.00 ⬚ ☞ – **20 rm** (dinner included) ⊡ ✦170.00/240.00 – ✦✦220.00/490.00, 1 suite.
Spec. A taste of duck, pear and foie gras. John Dory with spiced cauliflower, pickled beetroot and horseradish velouté. Assiette of chocolate.
◆ In lovely gardens; breathtaking mountain vistas. A Victorian hunting lodge formerly owned by Lord Lonsdale; exudes luxury from oak panelled hall to fine fabrics in rooms. Refined dining: exquisite flavours in opulent surroundings, complete with mountain views.

🏠 **Cedar Manor,** Ambleside Rd, LA23 1AX, ℰ (015394) 43192, *info@cedarmanor.co.uk*, ☞ – ⇌ ᴘ. ⬜ 𝘝𝘐𝘚𝘈.   Y i
Rest (dinner only) 22.50 **s.** – **10 rm** ⊡ ✦60.00/63.00 – ✦✦100.00/110.00, 1 suite.
◆ 1860s house, its mature garden shaded by an ancient cedar. Sizeable bedrooms, including the Coniston Room with views of Langdale Pike, and lounge with ornate stained glass. Locally sourced menus.

🏠 **Glenburn,** New Rd, LA23 2EE, ℰ (015394) 42649, *glen.burn@virgin.net*, Fax (015394) 88998 – ⇌ ᴘ. ⬜ 𝘝𝘐𝘚𝘈. ⬚   Y u
Rest (dinner only) 24.50 and a la carte 18.50/28.00 **s.** – **16 rm** ⊡ ✦54.00/64.00 – ✦✦68.00/88.00.
◆ Well-placed for exploring the central Lakes, a privately run hotel offering homely rooms in soft-toned décor plus a small bar and lounge with an open fire. Neatly set dining room with peach and white linen.

🏠 **Woodlands,** New Rd, LA23 2EE, ℰ (015394) 43915, *enquiries@woodlands-winder mere.co.uk*, Fax (015394) 43915 – ⇌ ᴘ. ⬜ ⬜ 𝘝𝘐𝘚𝘈. ⬚   Y u
Rest (dinner only) 15.00/18.50 **s.** ⬚ – **15 rm** ⊡ ✦40.00/50.00 – ✦✦60.00/80.00.
◆ Personally run hotel with spacious sitting room centred on the fireplace and affordable bedrooms - homely and immaculate - in cheerful floral décor. Neat dining room; fresh local produce served.

⌂ **Boston House** without rest., The Terrace, LA23 1AJ, ℰ (015394) 43654, *stay@boston house.co.uk* – ⇌ ᴘ. ⬜ 𝘝𝘐𝘚𝘈. ⬚   Y e
5 rm ⊡ ✦39.00/53.00 – ✦✦78.00/84.00.
◆ Personally run Victorian house: a tasteful style prevails throughout. Nicely appointed lounge and breakfast room. Individually decorated rooms exhibit quality furnishings.

⌂ **Beaumont House** without rest., Holly Rd, LA23 2AF, ℰ (015394) 47075, *thebeaumon thotel@btinternet.com*, Fax (015394) 88311 – ⇌ ᴘ. ⬜ 𝘝𝘐𝘚𝘈. ⬚   Y n
11 rm ⊡ ✦40.00/75.00 – ✦✦80.00/120.00.
◆ Substantial Victorian house, its period stained glass and tiling still intact. Good-sized en suite bedrooms, comfortably furnished with a traditional feel.

⌂ **Glencree** without rest., Lake Rd, LA23 2EQ, ℰ (015394) 45822, *h.butterworth@btinter net.com* – ⇌ ᴘ. ⬜ ⬜ 𝘝𝘐𝘚𝘈. ⬚   Z s
6 rm ⊡ ✦35.00/60.00 – ✦✦55.00/80.00.
◆ Personally managed, detached guesthouse built of local slate. Spotless, individually decorated - and affordable - rooms in co-ordinated fabrics offer a good level of comfort.

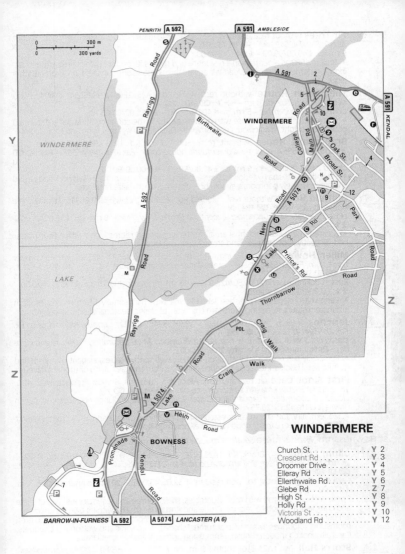

WINDERMERE

↑ **Newstead** without rest., New Rd, LA23 2EE, ℰ (015394) 44485, *info@newstead-guest house.co.uk*, Fax (015394) 88904 – ⇔⋯ 🅿. ⋯   Y **a**
closed 1 week Christmas – **7 rm** ⊇ ✚45.00/65.00 – ✚✚50.00/90.00.
◆ A warm welcome is assured at this restored Victorian residence. Original features aplenty; fireplaces in all the cosy, spotless bedrooms. Hearty breakfasts a speciality.

↑ **The Howbeck,** New Rd, LA23 2LA, ℰ (015394) 44739, *relax@howbeck.co.uk* – ⇔⋯ ⋯ 🅿.
🆎 VISA ⋯   Y **o**
Rest (by arrangement) 27.95 – **11 rm** ⊇ ✚50.00/69.00 – ✚✚67.00/127.00.
◆ Victorian slate house on the outskirts. Well appointed lounge with maritime theme. Spacious bedrooms, some boasting four-posters, stylishly painted in up-to-date palette. Attractive dining room with well-laid tables: home-cooked, daily changing dinners.

⌂ **Fir Trees** without rest., Lake Rd, LA23 2EQ, ✆ (015394) 42272, *enquiries@fir-trees.com*, Fax (015394) 42512, ✍ – ⇔ **P**. ⓌⓄ **VISA**. ⅏
Z x
9 rm ⚌ ✝40.00/90.00 – ✝✝40.00/90.00.
♦ Built in 1888 as a gentleman's residence and retains its original pine staircase. Contrastingly modern bedrooms. Broad-windowed breakfast room surveyed by a grandfather clock.

⌂ **The Coach House** without rest., Lake Rd, LA23 2EQ, ✆ (015394) 44494, *enquiries@lakedistrictbandb.com* – ⇔ **P**. ⓌⓄ **VISA**. ⅏
Z s
closed 25-26 December – **5 rm** ⚌ ✝40.00/55.00 – ✝✝65.00/80.00.
♦ Converted 19C coach house with modern twists: in the compact, individually decorated bedrooms, bright, vivid colours predominate. Outside is a weather vane and front clock.

⌂ **Braemount House** without rest., Sunny Bank Rd, LA23 2EN, by Queens Drive ✆ (015394) 45967, *enquiries@braemount-house.co.uk*, Fax (015394) 45967 – ⇔ **P**. ⓌⓄ **VISA**
Z u
closed 24-25 December – **9 rm** ⚌ ✝40.00/50.00 – ✝✝60.00/90.00.
♦ Extended 1870s bay-windowed house: original tiles and decorative glasswork add period character. Homely bedrooms; simple breakfast room with slate fireplace.

⌂ **Oldfield House** without rest., Oldfield Rd, LA23 2BY, ✆ (015394) 88445, *info@oldfieldhouse.co.uk* – ⇔ **P**. ⓌⓄ **VISA**. ⅏
Y c
closed January and December except Christmas-New Year – **8 rm** ⚌ ✝36.00/66.00 – ✝✝72.00/76.00.
♦ Located in a quiet residential area; pretty, well-priced rooms - one with a four poster bed, all neatly kept - in a lakeland stone house run by a husband and wife team.

※※ **Miller Howe** with rm, Rayrigg Rd, LA23 1EY, ✆ (015394) 42536, *lakeview@millerhowe.com*, Fax (015394) 45664, < Lake Windermere and mountains, ✍ – ⇔ rest, ▤ rest, **P**. ⓌⓄ ᴀᴇ **VISA**
Y s
Rest (booking essential) 21.50/42.50 ♨ – **13 rm** (dinner included) ⚌ ✝125.00/220.00 – ✝✝260.00/290.00, 2 suites.
♦ Renowned, elegantly furnished lakeside villa with handsomely fitted rooms. Modern Italianate restaurant; distinct Northern character to classic, seasonal dishes. Smart rooms.

※※ **Jerichos**, Birch St, LA23 1EG, ✆ (015394) 42522, *enquiries@jerichos.co.uk*, Fax (015394) 42522 – ⇔. ⓌⓄ **VISA**
Y z
closed last 2 weeks November-first week December, 24-26 December, 1 January and Monday – **Rest** (dinner only) a la carte 29.95/33.00 ℤ.
♦ Personally run restaurant with open kitchen; well-spaced tables, elegant glassware and framed Beryl Cook prints. Local produce enhances rich, complex blend of modern flavours.

✕ **First Floor Cafe** (at Lakeland Ltd), Alexandra Buildings, Station Precinct, LA23 1BQ, ✆ (015394) 88200, *email@firstfloorcafe.co.uk* – ▤ ⇔ ▤ **P**. ⓌⓄ **VISA**
Y r
closed 25 December, 1 January and Easter Sunday – **Rest** (bookings not accepted) (lunch only) a la carte 12.75/20.75.
♦ Modern, airy and stylish cafe/restaurant on first floor of Lakeland Ltd's store. A smart setting for coffee, cake or good value, well prepared hot dishes.

at Bowness-on-Windermere South : 1 m. – Z – ⊠ Windermere.

🏨 **Gilpin Lodge** ⊱, Crook Rd, LA23 3NE, Southeast : 2 ½ m. by A 5074 on B 5284 ✆ (015394) 88818, *hotel@gilpinlodge.co.uk*, Fax (015394) 88058, <, 🌳, ✍, ⌘ – ⇔ ❦ **P**. ⓌⓄ ᴀᴇ Ⓞ **VISA**. ⅏
Rest (booking essential for non-residents) 32.00/45.00 ℤ – **20 rm** (dinner included) ⚌ ✝175.00 – ✝✝350.00.
Spec. Best end of lamb with root vegetables, shallot purée and rosemary jus. Tian of skate and crab, leek and potato velouté. Prune and Armagnac soufflé with its own ice cream.
♦ Friendly, family run Edwardian country house rightly proud of its luxuriously appointed rooms. Firelit lounges awash with autumnal shades, deep sofas and welcoming bouquets. Carefully cooked modern British dishes using prime Lakeland ingredients.

🏨 **Storrs Hall** ⊱, LA23 3LG, South : 2 m. on A 592 ✆ (015394) 47111, *storrshall@elhmail.co.uk*, Fax (015394) 47555, <, ⍟, ✍, ⌘ – 📧 ⇔ **P**. – 🅿 40. ⓌⓄ ᴀᴇ Ⓞ **VISA**. ⅏
The Terrace : Rest 19.75/39.50 ℤ – **29 rm** ⚌ ✝110.00 – ✝✝295.00, 1 suite.
♦ Oils, antiques and fine fabrics fill an elegant Georgian mansion. Traditional orangery, 19C bar in dark wood and stained glass and comfortable, individually decorated rooms. Ornate dining room overlooks lawns and lake.

🏨 **Linthwaite House** ⊱, Crook Rd, LA23 3JA, South : ¾ m. by A 5074 on B 5284 ✆ (015394) 88600, *stay@linthwaite.com*, Fax (015394) 88601, < Lake Windermere and fells, ⍟, ⌘ – ⇔ **P**. ⓌⓄ Ⓞ **VISA**. ⅏
Rest (light lunch Monday-Saturday)/dinner 46.00 s. ℤ – **27 rm** ⚌ ✝120.00/200.00 – ✝✝150.00/320.00.
♦ Set in superb elevated position with stunning views of Lake Windermere. Chic, modern rooms. Cane chairs and louvred blinds give conservatory teas an almost colonial feel. Refined modern cooking in restaurant boasting vast mirror collection!

Lindeth Howe, Storrs Park, LA23 3JF, South : 1¼ m. by A 592 off B 5284 (015394) 45759, *hotel@lindeth-howe.co.uk, Fax (015394) 46368*, ≤, , , – ♿ P. VISA.
closed 1 week January – ***The Dining Room :*** **Rest** (light lunch Monday-Saturday)/dinner 36.00 **s.** ♀ – **36 rm** ☕ ✝70.00/110.00 – ✝✝150.00/230.00.
◆ Once owned by Beatrix Potter, this extended and updated house surveys a broad sweep of Lakeland scenery. Smart, spacious rooms in traditional style, some with useful extras. Spacious dining room with wonderful fell views.

Fayrer Garden House, Lyth Valley Rd, LA23 3JP, South : 1 m. on A 5074 (015394) 88195, *lakescene@fayrergarden.com, Fax (015394) 45986*, ≤, – , rest, P. VISA.
closed 2-19 January – ***The Terrace :*** **Rest** (booking essential for non-residents) (dinner only) 35.00 ♀ – **29 rm** (dinner included) ☕ ✝75.00/134.00 – ✝✝124.00/164.00.
◆ Extensive house with five acres of grounds and beautiful gardens. Clubby bar and pleasantly homely lounge. Cosy rooms show the owners' feel for thoughtful detail. Wonderful views to be gained from The Terrace.

Lindeth Fell, Lyth Valley Rd, LA23 3JP, South : 1 m. on A 5074 (015394) 43286, *kennedy@lindethfell.co.uk, Fax (015394) 47455*, ≤ Lake Windermere and mountains, , – P. VISA.
closed 2-26 January – **Rest** 15.00/30.00 – **14 rm** (dinner included) ☕ ✝70.00/110.00 – ✝✝140.00/180.00.
◆ In landscaped gardens with bowls and croquet lawns, a privately owned 1907 house with neat, bright rooms, oak-panelled hall and curios and watercolours in the drawing room. Elegantly set dining room with superb Lakeland views.

Angel Inn, Helm Rd, LA23 3BU, (015394) 44080, *rooms@the-angelinn.com, Fax (015394) 46003*, – P. VISA Z v
closed 25 December **Rest** a la carte 18.85/27.95 ♀ – **11 rm** ☕ ✝50.00/80.00 – ✝✝85.00/150.00.
◆ Homely, good-sized rooms in an enlarged early 18C cottage, set in a secluded spot yet close to town. Cosy, unpretentious bar, its armchairs centred on an open fire. Dining room has columned archway and landscape murals.

Oakbank House without rest., Helm Rd, LA23 3BU, (015394) 43386, *enquiries@oakbankhousehotel.co.uk, Fax (015394) 47965*, ≤ – P. VISA. Z n
12 rm ☕ ✝50.00/90.00 – ✝✝98.00/110.00.
◆ Privately run house off the main street. Affordable bedrooms, stylish and individually decorated. Ferns and chandeliers lend grandeur to substantial Cumbrian breakfasts.

Fair Rigg without rest., Ferry View, LA23 3JB, South : ½ m. on A 5074 (015394) 43941, *stay@fairrigg.co.uk*, ≤ – P.
restricted opening in winter – **6 rm** ☕ ✝40.00/70.00 – ✝✝70.00/90.00.
◆ 19C property with pleasing views over the lake to the hills. Hearty Cumbrian breakfasts guaranteed, accompanied by the fine vista. Original fireplaces enhance comfy rooms.

at Troutbeck *North : 4 m. by A 592 – Y – ✉ Windermere.*

Broadoaks, Bridge Lane, LA23 1LA, South : 1 m. on Windermere rd (015394) 45566, *trev@broadoaksf9.co.uk, Fax (015394) 88766*, ≤, – P. VISA
Rest 14.95/42.50 and a la carte 18.15/49.85 **s.** ♀ – **14 rm** ☕ ✝59.50/75.00 – ✝✝120.00/160.00.
◆ Extended 19C manor in mature 10-acre garden. Victoriana fills the panelled hall and a handsome Music Room with Bechstein piano. Individual rooms, many with four-poster beds. Imposing period fireplace is dining room's focal point.

Queens Head with rm, LA23 1PW, North : ¾ m. on A 592 (015394) 32174, *enquiries@queensheadhotel.com, Fax (015394) 31938*, ≤, – rm, P. VISA.
closed 25 December – **Rest** 15.50 and a la carte 22.00/29.00 ♀ – **16 rm** ☕ ✝67.50/75.00 – ✝✝100.00/150.00.
◆ 17C posting inn with charm to spare: beamed, panelled interior, unique four-poster bar. Tasty blackboard menu; real ale. Cosy rooms, many have antique beds and furniture.

WINDLESHAM *Surrey* **504** S 29 – *pop. 4 103.*
London 40 – Reading 18 – Southampton 53.

The Brickmakers, Chertsey Rd, GU20 6HT, East : 1 m. on B 386 (01276) 472267, *thebrickmakers@4cinns.co.uk*, – P. VISA
Rest 25.95 and a la carte 25.00/35.00 ♀.
◆ Appropriately redbrick pub with bright, modern dining room and conservatory. Tasty menu with a new-British slant plus daily fish specials. Friendly staff; good ale.

ENGLAND

WINDSOR

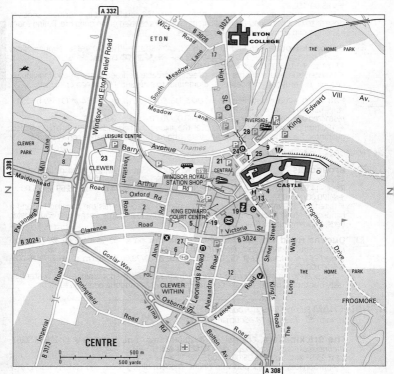

WINDSOR *Windsor & Maidenhead* **504** S 29 *Great Britain G. – pop. 30 568 (inc. Eton).*

See : *Town★ – Castle★★★ : St George's Chapel★★★ AC (stalls★★★), State Apartments★★ AC, North Terrace (≤★★) Z – Eton College★★ AC (College Chapel★★, Wall paintings★) Z.*

Env. : *Windsor Park★ AC* Y.

≈ *to Marlow, Maidenhead and Cookham (Salter Bros. Ltd) (summer only).*

🖪 *24 High St ℰ (01753) 743900, windsor.tic@86wm.gov.uk.*

London 28 – Reading 19 – Southampton 59.

Plan opposite

Oakley Court, Windsor Rd, Water Oakley, SL4 5UR, West : 3 m. on A 308 ℰ (01753) 609988, *reservations@oakleycourt.com, Fax (01753) 609939,* ≤, *Ⅰₛ,* ≋ₛ, 🔲, 🔟, 🚗, ♨, ✵ – 🔟 ✵≈ 🔲 ℃ ₺ 🄿 – 🖎 160. 🐠 🖭 VISA. ✵
The Oakleaf : Rest (closed Saturday lunch) 29.50 and a la carte 34.95/48.90 **s.** ⚱ – **118 rm** ⚬ ✵160.00/190.00 – ✵✵170.00/200.00.
♦ Impressive part Gothic mansion on banks of river Thames. Spacious public areas in classic country house style. Many bedrooms in annex, most characterful ones in main house. Large dining room provides pleasant views of gardens and river.

The Castle, High St, SL4 1LJ, ℰ (0870) 4008300, *castle@macdonald-hotels.co.uk, Fax (01753) 856930 –* ⭤ ✵≈ ℃ 🄿 – 🖎 400. 🐠 🖭 VISA. ✵　　　　　　　　　**Z c**
Eighteen : Rest 18.50/27.50 and a la carte 23.40/37.85 ⚱ – ⚬ 15.95 – **104 rm** ✵210.00/225.00 – ✵✵235.00/270.00, 4 suites.
♦ Former inn built by monks, now a terraced property with Georgian façade. Décor in traditional style. Modern rooms in converted stables, more characterful ones in old building. Very comfortable Eighteen with modern menus.

Sir Christopher Wren's House, Thames St, SL4 1PX, ℰ (01753) 442429, *reservations@windsorwrensgroup.com, Fax (01753) 442490,* 🍴, *Ⅰₛ,* ≋ₛ – 🔟 ✵≈, 🔲 rest, ℃ – 🖎 120. 🐠 🖭 ⓞ VISA. ✵　　　　　　　　　　　　　　　　　　　　　　　　　　　　**Z e**
Strok's : Rest a la carte approx 35.50 ⚱ – ⚬ 9.50 – **90 rm** ✵165.00/220.00 – ✵✵220.00/300.00, 5 suites.
♦ Built by Wren as his family home in 1676, he supposedly haunts his old rooms. On banks of Thames close to station and Windsor Castle. Antique furnished in original building. Restaurant has views of Thames and elegant dining terrace.

Royal Adelaide, 46 Kings Rd, SL4 2AG, ℰ (01753) 863916, *royaladelaide@meridianleisure.com, Fax (01753) 830682 –* ⭤ ✵≈ 🄿 – 🖎 120. 🐠 🖭 ⓞ VISA. ✵　　　　　　　　**Z v**
Rest a la carte 20.95/27.70 **s.** ⚱ – **42 rm** ⚬ ✵105.00/150.00 – ✵✵125.00/160.00.
♦ Three adjoining Georgian houses with light blue painted façade. Just outside town centre. Rooms vary in shapes and sizes, all in individual traditional style. Dining room offers daily changing, international menus.

The Christopher without rest., 110 High St, Eton, SL4 6AN, ℰ (01753) 852359, *sales@thechristopher.co.uk, Fax (01753) 830914 –* ✵≈ ℃ 🄿. 🐠 🖭 ⓞ VISA　　　**Z a**
33 rm ✵110.00/145.00 – ✵✵145.00/175.00.
♦ Refurbished 17C former coaching inn close to Eton College and perfect for walking to the castle. Contemporary bedrooms split between main building and mews annex.

The Dorset without rest., 4 Dorset Rd, SL4 3BA, ℰ (01753) 852669, *Fax (01753) 852669 –* ✵≈ 🄿. 🐠 VISA. ✵　　　　　　　　　　　　　　　　　　　　　**Z x**
closed 20 December-6 January – **4 rm** ⚬ ✵60.00/65.00 – ✵✵75.00/80.00.
♦ Bay windowed, late Victorian detached house on quiet residential street, just out of town centre. Traditional décor with large and comfortable bedrooms.

Al Fassia, 27 St Leonards Rd, SL4 3BP, ℰ (01753) 855370, *Fax (01753) 855370 –* ✵≈ 🔲 ✵ 30. 🐠 🖭 ⓞ VISA　　　　　　　　　　　　　　　　　　　　　　　**Z n**
closed 25 December and 1 January – **Rest** - Moroccan - (booking essential) 12.95/19.95 and a la carte 16.95/21.95.
♦ The name means "a lady from Fez" and the food has an authentic fresh Moroccan flavour with subtle spicing and fragrant flavours. Friendly and well run.

WINEHAM *W. Sussex* **504** T 31 *– see Henfield.*

WINFORTON *Herefordshire* **503** K 27 *– see Hereford.*

WING *Rutland* **504** R 28 *– see Oakham.*

Good food without spending a fortune?
Look out for the Bib Gourmand 🍃

WINSFORD *Somerset 503 J 30 The West Country G.* – ✉ *Minehead.*

See : *Village★.*

Env. : *Exmoor National Park★★.*

London 194 – Exeter 31 – Minehead 10 – Taunton 32.

The Royal Oak Inn, Exmoor National Park, TA24 7JE, ℰ (01643) 851455, *enqui ries@royaloak-somerset.co.uk, Fax (01643) 851009,* ❦ , ☞ – ⇔ rest, **P**. **◍ ⅀ Ⅵ⅀⅄**. ✕✕
Rest (in bar Monday-Saturday lunch and Sunday dinner)/dinner a la carte 15.00/75.00 –
12 rm ⌗ ✦75.00/116.00 – ✦✦116.00/136.00.
♦ Attractive part 12C thatched inn overlooking the village green. Quaint cottage atmosphere, especially in those rooms in the main house; annex rooms of more recent vintage. Out-and-out English cooking prevails.

Karslake House, Halse Lane, TA24 7JE, ℰ (01643) 851242, *enquiries@karslake house.co.uk, Fax (01643) 851242,* ☞ – ⇔ **P**. **Ⅵ⅀⅄**
closed February-March and 1 week Christmas – **Rest** *(closed Sunday-Monday and Tuesday-Thursday to non-residents)* (dinner only) 29.50 – **6 rm** ⌗ ✦70.00 – ✦✦111.00.
♦ Personally run 15C malthouse with lovely gardens. Good home-cooked fare on varied menus with fine use of local produce. Welcoming accommodation including four-poster comfort.

WINTERBOURNE STEEPLETON *Dorset 503 504 M 31 – see Dorchester.*

WINTERINGHAM *North Lincolnshire 502 S 22 –* ✉ *Scunthorpe.*
London 176 – Kingston-upon-Hull 16 – Sheffield 67.

XXXX **Winteringham Fields** with rm, Silver St, DN15 9PF, ℰ (01724) 733096, *wint fields@aol.com, Fax (01724) 733898* – ⇔ ℰ **P** ⇔ 10. **◍ ⅀ Ⅵ⅀⅄**
❀   *closed Christmas, first 2 weeks January, 1 week April and 3 weeks August* – **Rest** *(closed Sunday-Monday)* (booking essential for non-residents) 36.00/75.00 and a la carte 68.00/82.50 ⅀ ⌗ – ⌗ 12.00 – **7 rm** ✦140.00 – ✦✦210.00, 2 suites.
Spec. Langoustine with quail egg in crisp baguette and wild mushrooms. Pot roasted squab pigeon with cannelloni of crab. Peach and plum roasted with lemongrass and honey, peach sorbet.
♦ 16C house with beamed ceilings, and original range with fire. Cosy, cottagey atmosphere. Carefully executed menu, served in choice of dining rooms. Characterful bedrooms.

WITCOMBE *Glos. – see Cheltenham.*

WITNEY *Oxon. 503 504 P 28 – pop. 22 765.*
🛈 *26A Market Sq* ℰ (01993) 775802.
London 69 – Gloucester 39 – Oxford 13.

Witney Four Pillars, Ducklington Lane, OX28 4TJ, South : 1½ m. on A 415 ℰ (01993) 779777, *witney@fourpillars.co.uk, Fax (01993) 703467,* ❦, ☎, ▦ – ⇔ rm, ℰ ⅄ **P** – 逾 160. **◍ ⅀ ◍ Ⅵ⅀⅄**. ✕✕
Rest (dinner only) 19.50 ⅀ – ⌗ 9.25 – **86 rm** ✦89.00 – ✦✦148.00.
♦ Situated at the edge of the Cotswolds. Built in traditional style, accommodating business and leisure visitors. Modern rooms with, in the deluxe category, extra comforts. Convivial, popular restaurant.

at Barnard Gate *East : 3¼ m. by B 4022 off A 40 –* ✉ *Eynsham.*

The Boot Inn, OX29 6XE, ℰ (01865) 881231, *info@theboot-inn.com, Fax (01865) 880762,* ❦ – **P**. **◍ Ⅵ⅀⅄**. ✕✕
Rest a la carte 20.00/35.00 ⅀.
♦ Friendly pub in Cotswold stone. Snug interior with memorabilia and boot collection, including footwear from Bee Gees and Stanley Matthews. Traditional menu, informal service.

at South Leigh *Southeast : 3 m. by B 4022 –* ✉ *Witney.*

X   **Mason Arms** with rm, OX29 6XN, ℰ (01993) 702485, ☞ – **P**. **Ⅵ⅀⅄**. ✕✕
closed 3 weeks August, 1 week in spring and 4 days Christmas – **Rest** *(closed Sunday dinner and Monday)* a la carte 20.00/50.00 – **2 rm** ✦35.00 – ✦✦65.00.
♦ Privately owned 15C thatched inn with unique style and much individuality. Comfortable rooms and public areas. French influenced traditional cooking and extensive wine list.

at Leafield *Northwest : 5¾ m. by B 4022 (Charlbury Rd) –* ⊠ *Witney.*

🗔 **The Navy Oak,** Lower End, OX29 9QQ, ℘ (01993) 878496, *thenavyoak@aol.com,*
🕭 *Fax (01993) 878496,* 🏤 *– ⊱ ᗭ P. ᗯᑎ VISA. ※*
closed first 2 weeks January, Monday and Sunday dinner – **Rest** a la carte 20.00/30.00.
   ◆ Refurbished solid stone pub in rural village; pleasant outside seating and cosy bar with
   open fire. Good value, appealing, modern menus in rustic or formal dining areas.

WIX *Essex 504 X 28 –* ⊠ *Manningtree.*
    London 70 – Colchester 10 – Harwich 7 – Ipswich 16.

🏠 **Dairy House Farm** ⊗ *without rest.,* Bradfield Rd, CO11 2SR, Northwest : 1 m.
   ℘ (01255) 870322, *bridgetwhitworth@btinternet.com, Fax (01255) 870186,* ≤, ⌾, ᗭ *– ⊱⊱*
   P. ※
   3 rm ⊑ ✦38.00 – ✦✦58.00.
   ◆ Victorian farmhouse, delightfully secluded in 700 acres of working arable and fruit farmland. Friendly and welcoming. Simple, comfortable style and well-kept throughout.

WOBURN *Beds. 504 S 28 Great Britain G. –* ⊠ *Milton Keynes.*
    See : *Woburn Abbey★★.*
    London 49 – Bedford 13 – Luton 13 – Northampton 24 – Oxford 47.

🏯 **Inn at Woburn,** George St, MK17 9PX, ℘ (01525) 290441, *enquiries@theinnatwo*
   burn.com, Fax (01525) 290432 – ⊱ᗭ, ▤ rest, ᕲ P. *– ᴬ 60.* ᗯᑎ ᴀᴇ ⓞ VISA
   Rest 15.00 (lunch) and dinner a la carte 17.10/29.40 ♀ **– 52 rm** ⊑ ✦115.00/120.00 –
   ✦✦165.00/205.00, 5 suites.
   ◆ 18C coaching inn, part of Woburn Estate with its abbey and 3000 acre park. Pleasant
   modern furnishings and interior décor. Tastefully decorated rooms: book a Cottage suite.
   Brasserie open throughout the day.

XXX **Paris House,** Woburn Park, MK17 9QP, Southeast : 2 ¼ m. on A 4012 ℘ (01525) 290692,
   info@parishouse.co.uk, Fax (01525) 290471, ⌾, *– ᗭ.* ᗯᑎ ᴀᴇ VISA
   closed 1-15 January, Sunday dinner and Monday – **Rest** 22.00/55.00 ♀.
   ◆ Built 1878 for Paris Exhibition, dismantled and rebuilt on Woburn Estate, this striking
   timbered house provides an august setting for classic French-inspired cuisine.

🗔 **The Birch,** 20 Newport Rd, MK17 9HX, North : ½ m. on A 5130 ℘ (01525) 290295, *eta*
   verns@aol.com, Fax (01525) 290899, 🏤 *– ⊱ ᗭ P.* ᗯᑎ ᴀᴇ VISA. ※
   closed 25-26 December and 1 January – **Rest** (closed Sunday dinner) (booking essential) a
   la carte 17.95/23.95 ♀.
   ◆ Established modern dining pub. Stylish décor in the smart restaurant and bar. Modern
   menu specialising in meat and fish from an open grill. Attentive service.

at Milton Bryan *Southeast : 2½ m. by A 4012 –* ⊠ *Woburn.*

🗔 **The Red Lion,** Toddington Rd, MK17 9HS, ℘ (01525) 210044, *paul@redlion-mil*
   tonbryan.co.uk, 🏤 *– ⊱⊱ P.* ᗯᑎ VISA. ※
   closed 25-26 December and 1 January – **Rest** (closed Monday dinner in winter and Sunday
   dinner) a la carte approx 25.00 ♀.
   ◆ Open fires and exposed beams define the lovely old world charm of this tastefully
   furnished pub. Carefully sourced ingredients underpin tasty, home cooked dishes.

WOKING *Surrey 504 S 30.*
    London 34 – Guildford 7 – Farnborough 14.

🏯 **Holiday Inn,** Victoria Way (A 320), GU21 8EW, ℘ (01483) 221000, *f&b@wokingholiday-*
   inn.com, Fax (01483) 221021, 🏤 *, ⨍₅ – ▤ᐧ, ⊱⊱* rm, ▤ ᕲ ᕲ P. *– ᴬ 50.* ᗯᑎ ᴀᴇ ⓞ VISA
   Rest (closed Saturday lunch, and Sunday) 12.95/20.00 and dinner a la carte 27.00/32.00 ♀ *–*
   ⊑ 13.50 **– 161 rm** ✦139.00/169.00 – ✦✦139.00/169.00.
   ◆ Two minutes from the high street, a modern group hotel in redbrick and glass, geared
   to the corporate market. Usefully equiped bedrooms with bright fabrics and work desks.
   Tried-and-tested menus.

WOLD NEWTON *East Riding.*
    London 229.5 – Bridlington 25 – Scarborough 13.5.

🏠 **Wold Cottage** ⊗, YO25 3HL, South : ½ m. on Thwing rd ℘ (01262) 470696, *ka*
   trina@woldcottage.com, Fax (01262) 470696, ≤, ⌾, ᗭ *– ⊱ᗭ P.* ᗯᑎ VISA
   Rest (by arrangement) 18.50 **– 5 rm** ⊑ ✦40.00/55.00 – ✦✦70.00/110.00.
   ◆ Georgian former farmhouse set in many rural acres; a country house style prevails with
   antique furniture in all areas. Spacious, individually named rooms: two in barn annex.
   Home-cooked dishes in two-roomed dining area.

ENGLAND

WOLVERHAMPTON W. Mids. 502 503 504 N 26 – pop. 254 623.

18 18 Queen Sq ℰ (01902) 556110, wolverhampton.tic@dial.pipex.com.
London 132 – Birmingham 15 – Liverpool 89 – Shrewsbury 30.

Plan of Enlarged Area : see Birmingham pp. 4 and 5

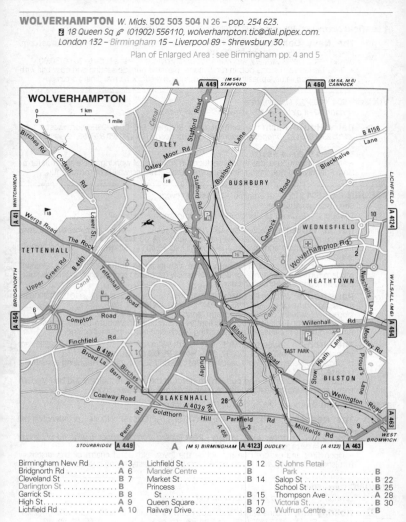

Birmingham New Rd . . . . A 3	Lichfield St. . . . . B 12	St Johns Retail
Bridgnorth Rd . . . . A 6	Mander Centre . . . . B	Park . . . . B
Cleveland St . . . . B 7	Market St. . . . . B 14	Salop St . . . . B 22
Darlington St . . . . B	Princess	School St . . . . B 25
Garrick St . . . . B 8	St . . . . B 15	Thompson Ave . . . . A 28
High St. . . . . A 9	Queen Square . . . . B 17	Victoria St. . . . . B 30
Lichfield Rd . . . . A 10	Railway Drive. . . . . B 20	Wulfrun Centre . . . . B

🏨 **Novotel**, Union St, WV1 3JN, ℰ (01902) 871100, h1188@accor.com, Fax (01902) 870054,
🏊 heated – |🛗|, 🛏 rm, ℰ 🔥 🅿 – 🔧 200. 🆘 🆎 ⓞ 𝗩𝗜𝗦𝗔   B a
The Garden Brasserie : Rest *(dinner only)* a la carte 22.00/30.95 s. ♀ – ⌖ 11.00 – **132 rm**
✱52.00/120.00 – ✱✱52.00/120.00.
  ♦ Conveniently located in the centre of town near to train station. Purpose-built lodge
hotel with well fitted modern furnishings. Suitable for business and leisure stopovers.
Large windows give bright feel to restaurant.

XX **Bilash**, No 2 Cheapside, WV1 1TU, ℰ (01902) 427762, enquiries@thebilash.co.uk,
Fax (01902) 311991 – 🛏 ≣ ⇔ 14. 🆘 🆎 ⓞ 𝗩𝗜𝗦𝗔   B c
closed 25-26 December and Sunday – **Rest** - Indian Bangladeshi - 14.95/35.95 and a la carte
20.30/39.70 ⌖ ♀.
  ♦ In a pleasant square, and easily identified by its bright yellow façade and modish interior.
Family owned; well established, locally renowned Indian/Bangladeshi cooking.

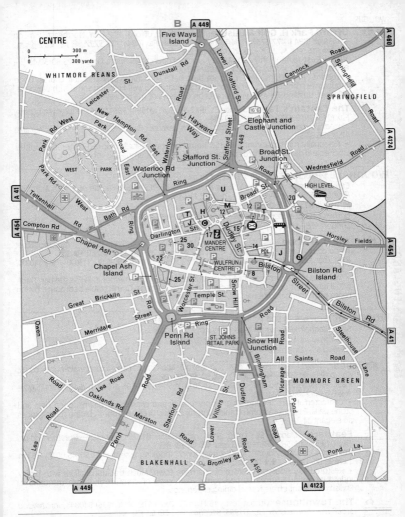

WOOBURN COMMON Bucks. – see Beaconsfield.

WOODBRIDGE Suffolk 504 X 27 – pop. 10 965.

    Cretingham, Grove Farm *(01728) 685275* – Seckford, Seckford Hall Rd, Great Bealings *(01394) 388000.*

    London 81 – Great Yarmouth 45 – Ipswich 8 – Norwich 47.

    Seckford Hall , IP13 6NU, Southwest : 1 ¼ m. by A 12 *(01394) 385678, reception@seckford.co.uk, Fax (01394) 380610,* ≤, ₁₆, ⬛, ₁₈, ⬛, ⬛, ⬛ – ⬛, ⬛ rest, ⬛ ⬛ ⬛ – ⬛ 120. ⬛ ⬛ ⬛ ⬛ ⬛

    closed 25 December – **Rest** *(closed Monday lunch)* a la carte 28.50/38.50 ⬛ – **32 rm** ⬛ ⬛ 90.00/110.00 – ⬛ ⬛ 220.00, 7 suites.

    ♦ Reputedly once visited by Elizabeth I, a part Tudor country house set in attractive gardens. Charming traditionally panelled public areas. Comfortable bedrooms. Local lobster proudly served in smart dining room.

Ufford Park H. Golf & Leisure, Yarmouth Rd, Ufford, IP12 1QW, Northeast : 2 m. on B 1438 *&* (0844) 477 3737, mail@uffordpark.co.uk, Fax (0844) 477 3727, ≤, ♣, ⇔, ☒, ⓝ, ♨ – ⅏ℵ, ▤ rest, ☎ & ℙ – ♨ 200. ◍◍ ◍ 𝘝𝘐𝘚𝘈. ℅
Vista : Rest (dinner only and Sunday lunch)/dinner 19.95 and a la carte 23.80/30.40 ♀ – **87 rm** ♀ **†**100.00/165.00 – **††**120.00/170.00.
♦ Leisure oriented, modern, purpose-built hotel set amidst park and golf course. Good modern feel throughout. Variety of room standards, all well-kept and some with balconies. Informal, bustling Carvery. Vista boasts broad views of the fairways.

The Captain's Table, 3 Quay St, IP12 1BX, *&* (01394) 383145, food2enjoy@aol.com, Fax (01394) 388508, ⇔ – ⅏ℵ. ◍◍ 𝘝𝘐𝘚𝘈
closed 25 December, Sunday and Monday except Bank Holidays – Rest a la carte 17.00/23.95 **s**.
♦ Personally run restaurant in a 16C house offers classically inspired dishes plus lighter lunches and daily blackboard specials, all confident, generous and very well priced.

WOODHALL SPA Lincs. 502 504 T 24 Great Britain G. – pop. 4 133.
   Env. : *Tattershall Castle*★ AC, SE : 4 m. by B 1192 and A 153 – *Battle of Britain Memorial Flight, RAF Coningsby*★, SE : 3½ m. on B 1192.
   ⓝ Woodhall Spa *&* (01526) 351835.
   🄱 The Cottage Museum, Iddesleigh Rd *&* (01526) 353775 (summer only).
   London 138 – Lincoln 18.

The Petwood ☟, Stixwould Rd, LN10 6QF, *&* (01526) 352411, reception@pet wood.co.uk, Fax (01526) 353473, ≤, ⓝ, ♨ – ▯ ⅏ℵ & ℙ – ♨ 200. ◍◍ ◍ 𝘝𝘐𝘚𝘈
Rest (bar lunch Monday-Saturday)/dinner 22.50 – **52 rm** ♀ **†**95.00/119.00 – **††**140.00, 1 suite.
♦ Wartime officers' mess for 617 "Dambusters" Squadron - memorabilia fills the bar. Traditional interiors include panelled reception. Lovely gardens. Comfortable bedrooms. Dining room with strong traditional feel.

WOODSTOCK Oxon. 503 504 P 28 Great Britain G. – pop. 2 589.
   See : *Blenheim Palace*★★★ *(Park*★★★*) AC.*
   🄱 Oxfordshire Museum, Park St *&* (01993) 813276.
   London 65 – Gloucester 47 – Oxford 8.

Bear, Park St, OX20 1SZ, *&* (0870) 4008202, bear@macdonald-hotels.co.uk, Fax (01993) 813380 – ⅏ℵ ☎ & ℙ – ♨ 60. ◍◍ ᴀᴇ ◍ 𝘝𝘐𝘚𝘈
Rest 19.95/35.95 and a la carte 21.00/28.00 **s**. ♀ – ♀ 15.95 – **51 rm** ♀165.00/175.00 – **††**175.00/250.00, 3 suites.
♦ Characterful part 16C inn. Original personality and charm; oak beams, open fires and stone walls. Particularly comfortable contemporary furnished rooms. Dining room exudes an elegant air.

Feathers, Market St, OX20 1SX, *&* (01993) 812291, enquiries@feathers.co.uk, Fax (01993) 813158 – ⅏ℵ rest, ▤ rest. ◍◍ ᴀᴇ ◍ 𝘝𝘐𝘚𝘈
Rest (closed Sunday dinner and Monday lunch) (booking essential) 21.50/45.00 ♀ – **16 rm** ♀ **†**99.00/199.00 – **††**145.00/275.00, 4 suites.
♦ Restored 17C houses in centre of charming town. Much traditional allure with highly individual, antique furnished bedrooms. High levels of comfort and style throughout. Stylish restaurant offers formal dining experience.

The Townhouse without rest., 15 High St, OX20 1TE, *&* (01993) 810843, info@wood stock-townhouse.com, Fax (01993) 810864 – ⅏ℵ. ◍◍ ᴀᴇ 𝘝𝘐𝘚𝘈. ℅
5 rm ♀ **†**55.00 – **††**80.00.
♦ Charming town house in the centre of this attractive market town. Friendly owner and bright bedrooms with all amenities. Breakfast is served in the garden conservatory.

The Laurels without rest., Hensington Rd, OX20 1JL, *&* (01993) 812583, stay@laurels guesthouse.co.uk, Fax (01993) 810041 – ⅏ℵ. ◍◍ 𝘝𝘐𝘚𝘈. ℅
closed Christmas and New Year – **3 rm** ♀ **†**55.00/65.00 – **††**65.00/75.00.
♦ Fine Victorian house just off the town centre. Personally run home with pretty guest rooms and private room facilities.

at Wootton North : 2½ m. by A 44 – ✉ Woodstock.

Kings Head with rm, Chapel Hill, OX20 1DX, *&* (01993) 811340, t.fay@kings-head.co.uk – ⅏ℵ ℙ. ◍◍ 𝘝𝘐𝘚𝘈. ℅
closed 25-26 December – Rest (closed Sunday dinner and Monday except Bank Holiday Monday) a la carte 18.00/28.00 ♀ – **3 rm** ♀ **†**60.00/70.00 – **††**75.00/110.00.
♦ Pubby appearance in quaint village. Personally run and a traditional ambience. Cooking has a varied and eclectic style with several fish specials. Tidy, simple bedrooms.

WOOFFERTON Shrops. – see Ludlow.

WOOKEY HOLE Somerset 503 L 30 – see Wells.

WOOLACOMBE Devon 503 H 30 The West Country G.

Env. : Exmoor National Park★★ – Mortehoe★★ (St Mary's Church★, Morte Point – vantage point★) N :½ m. – Ilfracombe : Hillsborough (≼★★) AC, Capstone Hill★ (≼★), St Nicholas' Chapel (≼★) AC, NE : 5½ m. by B 3343 and A 361.

Exc. : Braunton★ (St Brannock's Church★, Braunton Burrows★), S : 8 m. by B 3343 and A 361.

🗎 The Esplanade ℘ (01271) 870553.

London 237 – Barnstaple 15 – Exeter 55.

🏨 **Woolacombe Bay,** South St, EX34 7BN, ℘ (01271) 870388, woolacombe.bayhotel@btinternet.com, Fax (01271) 870613, ≼, ♨, ⊆s, ⊒ heated, 🔲, ☞, ⅍, squash – 🛗 ⅍, 🍽 rest, ♣♣ 🅿 – 🔬 150. 🐵 🗚 ⓪ 𝘝𝘐𝘚𝘈. ⅍
closed 2 January-9 February – **Doyles** : Rest (dinner only) 30.00 s. ♀ – **Maxwell's** : Rest (lunch only) a la carte approx 15.00 ♀ – **63 rm** (dinner included) ⇌ ✝65.00/115.00 – ✝✝87.00/137.00.
♦ Large, traditional, family oriented Victorian seaside hotel with gardens and beach access. Activities from board games to health suite. Well-kept, bright bedrooms. Classic Doyles dining room. Informal Maxwell's bistro.

at Mortehoe North :½ m. – ✉ Woolacombe.

🏨 **Watersmeet,** The Esplanade, EX34 7EB, ℘ (01271) 870333, info@watersmeethotel.co.uk, Fax (01271) 870890, ≼ Morte Bay, ⊒ heated, 🔲, ☞ – ⅍ ♿ 🅿 – 🔬 40. 🐵 𝘝𝘐𝘚𝘈. ⅍
Rest 15.95/36.00 ♀ – **27 rm** (dinner included) ⇌ ✝72.00/198.00 – ✝✝160.00/260.00.
♦ Edwardian house on the National Trust's rugged North Atlantic coastline. Superb views of Morte Bay. Smart country house style, large lounges and steps to the beach. Stylish restaurant offers tremendous sea views.

🏠 **Cleeve House,** EX34 7ED, ℘ (01271) 870719, info@cleevehouse.co.uk, Fax (01271) 870719, ☞ – ⅍ ♿ 🅿. 🐵 𝘝𝘐𝘚𝘈. ⅍
March-October – Rest (by arrangement) 19.00 and a la carte 22.00/32.00 s. – **6 rm** ⇌ ✝50.00/52.00 – ✝✝70.00/74.00.
♦ Bright and welcoming feel in décor and atmosphere. Very comfortable lounge and individually styled bedrooms with co-ordinated fabrics. Rear rooms with great country views. Neat dining room; walls hung with local artwork.

WOOLAVINGTON Somerset 503 L 30 – see Bridgwater.

WOOLER Northd. 502 N 17.

London 330 – Alnwick 17 – Berwick-on-Tweed 17.

🏠 **Firwood** ⌖ without rest., Middleton Hall, NE71 6RD, South : 1 ¾ m. by Earle rd on Middleton Hall rd ℘ (01668) 283699, welcome@firwoodhouse.co.uk, ☞ – ⅍ 🅿. 🐵 𝘝𝘐𝘚𝘈
3 rm ✝50.00/60.00 – ✝✝66.00/74.00.
♦ Victorian former hunting lodge in the Cheviot. Homely lounge and open-fired breakfast rooms boast bay windows with country views. Good sized rooms with individual style.

🏠 **Tallet Country** without rest., Coldmartin, NE71 6QN, South : 1 ¾ m. by A 697 on Coldmartin rd ℘ (01668) 283488, stay@coldmartin.co.uk – ⅍ 🅿
March - October – **3 rm** ✝45.00 – ✝✝70.00.
♦ Rurally located converted farmbuildings benefitting from impressive refurbishment, including a warmly appointed lounge, cosy communal breakfast room and airy, stylish rooms.

WOOLHAMPTON Berks. 503 504 Q 29 Great Britain G.

Exc. : Basildon Park★, NE : 10 m. by A 4, A 340 and A 417.

London 56 – Newbury 8 – Thatcham 4.

🍴 **The Angel,** Bath Rd, RG7 5RT, ℘ (0118) 971 3307, mail@a4angel.com, ☞ – ⅍ 🅿. 🐵 𝘝𝘐𝘚𝘈. ⅍
closed 1 week Christmas – Rest (closed Monday) a la carte 19.00/25.00 ♀.
♦ Technicolored interior, vividly dressed with elaborate vases and rows of bottles. Fireplaces divide rooms. Well-spaced tables. Interesting dishes from modern British range.

WOOLSTHORPE-BY-BELVOIR *Lincs.* **502 504** R 25 – *see Grantham.*

WOOTTON *Oxon.* **503 504** P 28 – *see Woodstock.*

WORCESTER *Worcs.* **503 504** N 27 *Great Britain G.* – *pop. 94 029.*

See : *City★ – Cathedral★★ – Royal Worcester Porcelain Works★ (Museum of Worcester Porcelain★)* **M.**

Exc. : *The Elgar Trail★.*

Perdiswell Park, Bilford Rd ✆ (01905) 754668.

The Guildhall, High St ✆ (01905) 726311.

London 124 – Birmingham 26 – Bristol 61 – Cardiff 74.

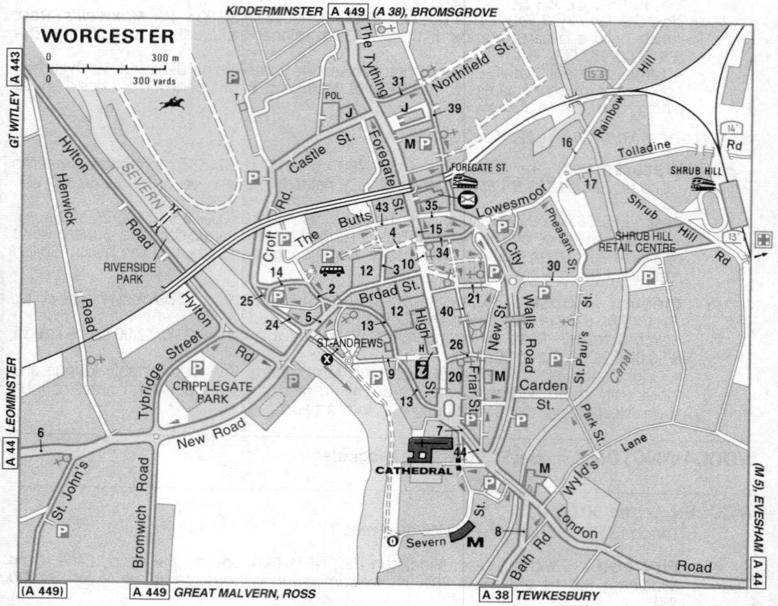

Diglis House, Severn St, WR1 2NF, ✆ (01905) 353518, *diglishouse@yahoo.com, Fax (01905) 767772,* ≤, , – ⇹ 🅿 – 🏛 50. MC AE ⓓ VISA. O
closed 26 December-3 January – **Rest** (bar lunch)/dinner 25.00 – **25 rm** ☕ ★90.00/100.00 – ★★130.00, 1 suite.

◆ Georgian house on banks of river Severn. Close to Royal Worcester factory. Attractive bar terrace. Characterful rooms in main house, those in annex more modern. Conservatory dining room with river outlook.

XX **Brown's,** 24 Quay St, WR1 2JJ, ℰ (01905) 26263, *Fax (01905) 25768* – ⊱. ⓂⒸ ⒶⒺ
ⓋⒾⓈⒶ   x
closed 1 week Christmas, Sunday dinner and Monday – **Rest** 27.50/39.50 (dinner) and lunch
a la carte approx. 23.50 ♀.
  ◆ Converted riverside corn mill. Spacious, open interior as befits the building's origins.
Impressive collection of modern artwork. Mainly British dishes are renowned locally.

at Bransford *West : 4 m. by A 44 on A 4103* – ✉ *Worcester.*

🏠 **Bear and Ragged Staff,** Station Rd, WR6 5JH, Southeast : ½ m. on Powick rd
ℰ (01886) 833399, *enquiries@bear.uk.com, Fax (01886) 833106*, 🍴 , 🌳 – ⊱ Ⓟ. ⓂⒸ ⒶⒺ
Ⓞ ⓋⒾⓈⒶ .
closed dinner 25, 26 December and 1 January – **Rest** a la carte 19.70/31.00.
  ◆ Two oak trees dominate the front of this traditional pub in quiet country
lane. Huge blackboard menus offer plenty of interest: vegetables travel from rear garden
to kitchen.

WORFIELD *Shrops. – see Bridgnorth.*

> Do not confuse X with ✿!
> X defines comfort, while stars are awarded for the best cuisine,
> across all categories of comfort.

ENGLAND

WORSLEY *Gtr Manchester* **502 503 504** M/N 23 *– see Manchester.*

WORTHING *W. Sussex* **504** S 31 *– pop. 96 964.*
  🏌 Hill Barn, Hill Barn Lane ℰ (01903) 237301 BY – 🏌, 🏌 Links Rd ℰ (01903) 260801 AY .
  ✈ Shoreham Airport : ℰ (01273) 296900, E : 4 m. by A 27 BY .
  🏢 Chapel Rd ℰ (01903) 221307, tic@worthing.gov.uk – Marine Parade ℰ (01903) 221307.
  London 59 – Brighton 11 – Southampton 50.

Plan on next page

🏨 **Beach,** Marine Parade, BN11 3QJ, ℰ (01903) 234001, *info@thebeachhotel.co.uk,*
Fax (01903) 234567, ≤ – 🛗 ⊱ ℅ ㅺ Ⓟ – 🅰 100. ⓂⒸ ⒶⒺ Ⓞ ⓋⒾⓈⒶ .   AZ e
closed 24-25 December – **Rest** (light lunch)/dinner 19.75 and a la carte approx 38.00 **s.** –
75 rm � ✲50.00/85.00 – ✲✲90.00/125.00, 4 suites.
  ◆ On town's marine parade with front rooms all boasting clear Channel views. Large public
areas decorated in Art Deco style. Bedrooms of a good size and well kept. Popular, family-
friendly restaurant.

🏨 **The Windsor,** 14-20 Windsor Rd, BN11 2LX, ℰ (01903) 239655, Reservations (Freephone) 0800 9804242, *reception@thewindsor.co.uk, Fax (01903) 210763*, 🌳 – ⊱ 📺 ℅ Ⓟ
– 🅰 120. ⓂⒸ ⒶⒺ Ⓞ ⓋⒾⓈⒶ .   BY i
closed 23-31 December – **Rest** (bar lunch Monday-Saturday) (carvery Saturday)/dinner
18.95 and a la carte 21.50/29.00 – **30 rm** ✲86.00/110.00 – ✲✲105.00/130.00.
  ◆ At eastern entrance to town in quiet residential area. Well suited to business or leisure
traveller with a wide range of rooms. Front rooms particularly spacious and bright. Large
dining room with welcoming atmosphere.

🏨 **Berkeley,** 86-95 Marine Parade, BN11 3QD, ℰ (01903) 820000, *reservations@berkeley*
hotel-worthing.co.uk, Fax (01903) 821234, ≤ – 🛗 ⊱, 🍴 rest, ℅ ㅺ Ⓟ – 🅰 100. ⓂⒸ ⒶⒺ Ⓞ
ⓋⒾⓈⒶ . ℅   BZ a
Rest (bar lunch Monday-Saturday)/dinner 21.95 and a la carte 22.00/26.20 **s.** – **80 rm** �
✲60.00/100.00 – ✲✲80.00/126.00.
  ◆ Overlooking the Channel and well located for visiting the famous South Downs. First
floor rooms boast original Victorian splendour of high ceilings and larger windows. Dining
room boasts pleasant sea views.

🏨 **Chatsworth,** Steyne, BN11 3DU, ℰ (01903) 236103, *hotel@chatsworthworthing.co.uk,*
Fax (01903) 823726 – 🛗, ⊱ rest, 🍴 rest, ℅ ㅺ – 🅰 150. ⓂⒸ ⒶⒺ ⓋⒾⓈⒶ   BZ x
Rest (dinner only) 16.95 – **98 rm** ⊎ ✲95.00 – ✲✲130.00.
  ◆ In a Georgian terrace overlooking Steyne Gardens and ideally located for a range of the
town's resort activities. Attentive service and good sized bedrooms. Simple, uncluttered
dining room.

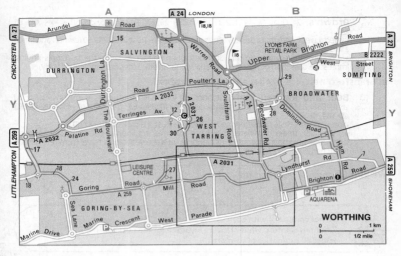

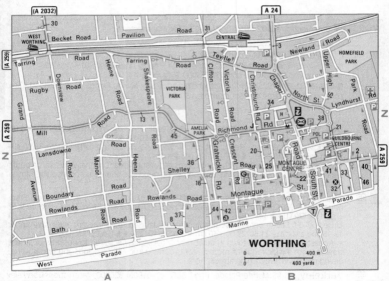

⟰ **Beacons** without rest., 18 Shelley Rd, BN11 1TU, ℘ (01903) 230948 – ✜ 🅿 ⓶ VISA.
⸜⸝
BZ e

8 rm ⊆ ✝36.00/42.00 – ✝✝66.00/76.00.
• Friendly traditional home providing classic English seaside accommodation. In the centre of town close to parks. Ideal base for visiting historic Arundel and Chichester.

XX **The Parsonage,** 6-10 High St, Tarring, BN14 7NN, ℘ (01903) 820140, *parsonage.book ings@ntlworld.com,* Fax (01903) 523233, 🛋 – ✧ 18. ⓶ ℡ VISA
AY c
closed 26 December-4 January, Saturday lunch, Sunday and Bank Holidays – **Rest** 21.00/24.00 and a la carte 25.85/30.50 ⓩ.
• Within one of Tarring high street's original 15C cottages. Exposed beams and framed photographs. Good international cuisine and a friendly, comfortable atmosphere.

WREA GREEN *Lancs.* 502 L 22 – see Kirkham.

WRESSLE *East Riding* 502 R 22 *Great Britain G.* – ✉ *Selby (N. Yorks.).*
Env. : *Selby (Abbey Church★), W : 5 m. by minor road and A 63.*
London 208 – Kingston-upon-Hull 31 – Leeds 31 – York 19.

🏨 **Loftsome Bridge Coaching House,** YO8 6EN, South : ½ m. ℘ (01757) 630070, *reception@loftsomebridge-hotel.co.uk,* Fax (01757) 633900, 🛋 – ✜, ▤ rest, 🅿 ⓶ ℡ VISA.
closed 25 December – **Rest** *(closed Sunday dinner)* (dinner only and Sunday lunch)/dinner 24.95 **s.** – **17 rm** ⊆ ✝50.00 – ✝✝70.00/80.00, 1 suite.
• One-time coaching inn from 1782, with converted former farm outbuildings and lawned garden. Adjacent to River Derwent. Comfortable rooms in main house and annexes. Smart dining room echoing house's light style.

We try to be as accurate as possible when giving room rates.
But prices are susceptible to change,
so please check rates when booking.

WRIGHTINGTON BAR *Gtr Manchester* 502 504 L 23 – see Standish.

WRINEHILL *Staffs..*
London 167 – Nantwich 10.5 – Stoke-on-Trent 10.

▯ **The Hand & Trumpet,** Main Rd, CW3 9BJ, ℘ (01270) 820048, 🛋 , 🛋 – ✜ 🅿 ⓶ VISA.
⸜⸝
closed 25-26 December – **Rest** a la carte 20.00/25.00 ⓩ.
• Refurbished country pub with delightful terrace overlooking gardens and duck pond. Relaxing country style interior with book shelves. Traditional dishes recognisable to all.

WROXHAM *Norfolk* 504 Y 25 *Great Britain G.*
Env. : *Norfolk Broads★.*
London 118 – Great Yarmouth 21 – Norwich 7.

⟰ **Coach House** without rest., 96 Norwich Rd, NR12 8RY, ℘ (01603) 784376, *bishop@worldonline.co.uk,* Fax (01603) 783734 – ✜ 🅿 ⓶ VISA.
closed 25-26 December – **3 rm** ⊆ ✝35.00/40.00 – ✝✝50.00/60.00.
• Converted Georgian coach house. Interior décor retains an English country feel with a snug lounge and good-sized, well-kept bedrooms.

WYCH CROSS *E. Sussex* 504 U 30 – see Forest Row.

WYE *Kent* 504 W 30 – pop. 11 420 – ✉ Ashford.
London 60 – Canterbury 10 – Dover 28 – Hastings 34.

XX **Wife of Bath** with rm, 4 Upper Bridge St, TN25 5AF, ℘ (01233) 812540, *reserva tions@wifeofbath.com,* Fax (01233) 813033, 🛋 – ✜ 🅿 ⓶ ℡ ① VISA. ⸜⸝
closed 2 weeks Christmas and 2 weeks August – **Rest** *(closed Sunday-Monday)* 19.00/24.50 and a la carte 28.00/44.00 – ⊆ 7.50 – **5 rm** ✝55.00 – ✝✝95.00.
• A lovely timber-framed house built in 1760. Fine cloth tables. Well chosen menu of satisfying dishes. Full or Continental breakfast after staying in comfy, soft-toned rooms.

WYMONDHAM Norfolk 504 X 26.

London 102 – Cambridge 55 – King's Lynn 49 – Norwich 12.

Wymondham Consort, 28 Market St, NR18 0BB, ✆ (01953) 606721, *wymond ham@bestwestern.co.uk, Fax* (01953) 601361, ⌂, 🍴 – ⇔ 🅿, 🐵 🆎 ⓪ 𝘝𝘐𝘚𝘈
Rest 8.95/15.95 and a la carte 13.85/29.70 ♀ – **20 rm** ⊡ ✦60.00/85.00 – ✦✦75.00/95.00.
 ♦ 18C town house in heart of historic, pretty town. Classic traditional style of décor throughout with well-kept bedrooms decorated in cosy cottage style. Restaurant and café which doubles up as wine bar in the evening.

Old Thorn Barn without rest., Corporation Farm, Wymondham Rd, Hethel, NR14 8EU, Southeast : 3 ½ m. on B 1135 (following signs to Mulbarton) ✆ (01953) 607785, *enqui ries@oldthornbarn.co.uk, Fax* (01953) 601909 – ⇔ 🅿, 🐵 𝘝𝘐𝘚𝘈. 🛇
7 rm ⊡ ✦33.00/56.00 – ✦✦52.00/56.00.
 ♦ Simple, rural guesthouse sited on farm and utilising former outbuildings as bedrooms with hand-built wood furniture. Rustic lounge and breakfast area with wood-burning stove.

WYTHAM Oxon. – see Oxford.

Red = Pleasant. Look for the red 🍴 and 🏨 symbols.

YANWATH Cumbria – see Penrith.

YARCOMBE Devon 503 K 31 – see Honiton.

YARM Stockton-on-Tees 502 P 20 – pop. 8 929.

London 242 – Middlesbrough 8 – Newcastle upon Tyne 47.

Crathorne Hall 🛇, Crathorne, TS15 0AR, South : 3 ½ m. by A 67 ✆ (01642) 700398, *crathornehall@handpicked.co.uk, Fax* (01642) 700814, ≤, 🛋, 🍴, 🕭 – ⇔ 📞 🅿 – 🔬 80. 🐵 🆎 ⓪ 𝘝𝘐𝘚𝘈
Leven : Rest 22.50/37.50 and a la carte 30.00/36.40 ♀ – **36 rm** ✦95.00/140.00 – ✦✦110.00/180.00, 1 suite.
 ♦ One of the last stately homes of the Edwardian period. Plenty of original features such as wood panelling and ornate fireplaces. Antique furnished bedrooms and public areas. Formal dining room with an air of classic elegance and tables clothed in crisp linen.

Judges Country House 🛇, Kirklevington Hall, Kirklevington, TS15 9LW, South : 1 ½ m. on A 67 ✆ (01642) 789000, *enquiries@judgeshotel.co.uk, Fax* (01642) 787692, ≤, 🕭, 🍴, 🕮 – ⇔ rest, 📞 🅿 – 🔬 220. 🐵 🆎 ⓪ 𝘝𝘐𝘚𝘈
Rest 17.50/37.50 and a la carte 37.50/45.00 ♀ – **21 rm** ⊡ ✦130.00/163.00 – ✦✦174.00/189.00.
 ♦ Former Victorian judge's residence surrounded by gardens. Welcoming panelled bar and spacious lounge filled with antiques and curios. Attractive rooms with a host of extras. Conservatory dining room overlooks the gardens.

YARMOUTH I.O.W. 503 504 P 31 – see Wight (Isle of).

YARPOLE Herefordshire.

The Bell Inn, Green Lane, HR6 0BD, ✆ (01568) 780359, ⌂, 🍴 – ⇔ 🅿, 🐵 𝘝𝘐𝘚𝘈
Rest *(closed Monday except Bank Holidays)* a la carte 22.00/27.50 ♀.
 ♦ Traditional country pub: black and white timbered façade, original stone cider press, roaring fire. Converted barn dining room for robust amalgam of classic and modern dishes.

YATELEY Hants. 504 R 29 – pop. 15 395 – ⊠ Camberley.

London 37 – Reading 12 – Southampton 58.

Casa Dei Cesari, Handford Lane, Cricket Hill, GU46 6BT, ✆ (01252) 873275, *reserva tions@casadeicesari.co.uk, Fax* (01252) 870614, 🍴 – 📞 🅿, 🐵 🆎 ⓪ 𝘝𝘐𝘚𝘈. 🛇
Rest - Italian - a la carte 24.50/40.50 – **42 rm** ⊡ ✦98.50 – ✦✦120.00, 2 suites.
 ♦ An attractive extended 17C house with surrounding gardens. Offers well-run, uncompli cated, uncluttered accommodation with few frills. Beamed ceilings adorn cosy restaurant.

YATTENDON
Newbury 503 504 Q 29 – ✉ *Newbury*.
London 61 – Oxford 23 – Reading 12.

🏠 **The Royal Oak** with rm, The Square, RG18 0UG, 🖊 (01635) 201325, *info@royaloakyat tendon.com*, Fax (01635) 201926, 🌳, ⇔ – ⇔ ♦ 🅿 🕮 🎫 *VISA*. ⬧
closed 1 January – **Rest** (booking essential) 15.00 (lunch) and a la carte 24.00/35.00 ⬧ – **5 rm** ⬚ ⚒85.00/105.00 – ⚒⚒130.00.
◆ Personally run part 16C former coaching inn in attractive village. Quintessentially English style. Classic or modern dishes in beamed bar or cosy restaurant. Chintzy bedrooms.

at Frilsham *South : 1 m. by Frilsham rd on Bucklebury rd* – ✉ *Yattendon*.

🏠 **The Pot Kiln**, RG18 0XX, 🖊 (01635) 201366, *info@potkiln.co.uk*, 🌳, ⇔ – ⇔ 🅿 🕮 🎫 *VISA*. ⬧
closed 25 December and Sunday dinner – **Rest** a la carte 23.00/28.00 ⬧ ⬧.
◆ 350-year old pub: tiny, wonderfully characterful bar with centuries-old benches. Micro-brewery to rear. Totally local food: owner shoots game; veg from garden and woods.

YAXLEY
Suffolk – see Thornham Magna.

YEALMPTON
Devon 503 H/I 32.
London 211 – Ivybridge 7.5 – Plymouth 8.

%% **The Seafood** (at Rose & Crown), Market St, PL8 2EB, 🖊 (01752) 880502, *info@thero seandcrown.co.uk*, Fax (01752) 881058 – ⇔ 🅿 🕮 *VISA*
closed 25 December, Sunday dinner and Monday – **Rest** - Seafood - 12.95 (lunch) and a la carte 18.95/33.40.
◆ Converted barn opposite Rose & Crown. Exudes a welcoming New England feel, with local fishing photos. Fittingly, the delicious seafood dishes are interesting and ambitious.

🏠 **Rose & Crown**, Market St, PL8 2EB, 🖊 (01752) 880223, *info@theroseandcrown.co.uk*, Fax (01752) 881058, 🌳 – ⇔ 🅿 🕮 *VISA*
Rest *(closed 25 December)* 12.95 (lunch) and a la carte 19.50/28.00 ⬧.
◆ Neat exterior and smart rear walled terrace and water feature. Big leather sofas and long benches in open-plan interior where modern dishes make use of seafood proximity.

YEOVIL
Somerset 503 504 M 31 *The West Country G.* – pop. 41 871.
See : *St John the Baptist★*.
Env. : *Monacute House★★ AC, W : 4 m. on A 3088 – Fleet Air Arm Museum, Yeovilton★★ AC, NW : 5 m. by A 37 – Tintinhull House Garden★ AC, NW : 5½ m. – Ham Hill (⩽★★) W : 5½ m. by A 3088 – Stoke sub-Hamdon (parish church★) W : 5¼ m. by A 3088.*
Exc. : *Muchelney★★ (Parish Church★★) NW : 14 m. by A 3088, A 303 and B 3165 – Lytes Cary★, N : 7½ m. by A 37, B 3151 and A 372 – Sandford Orcas Manor House★, NW : 8 m. by A 359 – Cadbury Castle (⩽★★) NE : 10½ m. by A 359 – East Lambrook Manor★ AC, W : 12 m. by A 3088 and A 303.*
🏌, 🏌 Sherborne Rd 🖊 (01935) 422965.
🚉 Hendford 🖊 (01935) 845946, *yeoviltic@southsomerset.gov.uk* – at Cart Gate : Picnic Site 🖊 (01935) 829333.
London 136 – Exeter 48 – Southampton 72 – Taunton 26.

🏛 **Lanes**, West Coker, BA22 9AJ, Southwest : 3 m. on A 30 🖊 (01935) 862555, *stay@lanesho tel.net*, Fax (01935) 864260, 🌳, ⇔, ⇔ – ⇔ rest, 🅿 – 🚗 45. 🕮 🎫 *VISA*. ⬧
Rest a la carte 15.25/25.75 – **27 rm** ⬚ ⚒90.00 – ⚒⚒110.00.
◆ 18C stone former rectory in walled grounds. Stylish modern interior with chocolate and red leather predominant. Stretch out in relaxed lounge. Airy, modish bedrooms. Modern classics and lots of glass in the Brasserie.

at Barwick *South : 2 m. by A 30 off A 37* – ✉ *Yeovil*.

%% **Little Barwick House** ⬧ with rm, BA22 9TD, 🖊 (01935) 423902, *reservations@bar wick7.fsnet.co.uk*, Fax (01935) 420908, ⇔ – ⇔ rest, 🅿 🕮 *VISA*. ⬧
closed 2 weeks Christmas – **Rest** *(closed Sunday dinner, Tuesday lunch and Monday)* (booking essential) 18.95/34.95 – **6 rm** ⬚ ⚒75.00/115.00 – ⚒⚒140.00.
◆ Dignified Georgian dower house in a secluded spot. Though cosy rooms are available, the focus is on the restaurant with its menu of satisfying regionally based menus.

at Montacute *Northwest : 5 m. by A 3088* – ✉ *Yeovil*.

🏠 **Phelips Arms**, The Borough, TA15 6XB, 🖊 (01935) 822557, *info@phelips.co.uk*, Fax (01935) 822557, 🌳, ⇔ – 🕮 🎫 *VISA*
closed 1 week January – **Rest** *(closed Sunday dinner and Monday)* a la carte 15.00/25.00 ⬧.
◆ Sand coloured 17C pub with traditional décor and furnishings. Modern, interesting menus, underpinned by accomplished cooking, have an eclectic range.

at Stoke sub Hamdon *Northwest : 5½ m. by A 3088 –* ⊠ *Yeovil.*

XX **The Priory House,** 1 High St, TA14 6PP, ℰ (01935) 822826, *reservations@thepriory houserestaurant.co.uk, Fax (01935) 825822 –* ⅙⅙ ⓪⓪ ᴀᴇ ꟾꟾꟾꟾꟾ
closed last week May-first week June, first 2 weeks November, Sunday, Monday and Bank Holidays – **Rest** (dinner only and Saturday lunch) a la carte 29.50/35.00 s. ℒ.
♦ Village centre restaurant that sticks firmly to traditions with tried and tested classics to the fore: a quiet and relaxing experience. Swallow a cider brandy after dinner!

YORK *N. Yorks.* **502** Q 22 *Great Britain G. – pop. 137 505.*

See : *City*★★★ – *Minster*★★★ (*Stained Glass*★★★ , *Chapter House*★★, *Choir Screen*★★) CDY – *National Railway Museum*★★★ CY – *The Walls*★★ CDXYZ – *Castle Museum*★ AC DZ **M2** – *Jorvik Viking Centre*★ AC DY **M1** – *Fairfax House*★ AC DY A – *The Shambles*★ DY **54**.

🛦 *Lords Moor Lane, Strensall* ℰ (01904) 491840 BY – 🛦 *Heworth, Muncaster House, Muncastergate* ℰ (01904) 424618 BY.

🖪 *The De Grey Rooms, Exhibition Sq* ℰ (01904) 621756, *tic@york.tourism.co.uk* – *York Railway Station, Outer Concourse* ℰ (01904) 621756.

London 203 – Kingston-upon-Hull 38 – Leeds 26 – Middlesbrough 51 – Nottingham 88 – Sheffield 62.

Plan opposite

ENGLAND

▲▲▲ **Middlethorpe Hall,** Bishopthorpe Rd, YO23 2GB, South : 1 ¾ m. ℰ (01904) 641241, *info@middlethorpe.com, Fax (01904) 620176,* ≼, ⓥ, ᴵ₆, ⇌, ▢, ☞, ♬ – ▯ ⅙⅙ ⅙ 🅿 – 🛦 50. ⓪⓪ ᴀᴇ ꟾꟾꟾꟾꟾ
Rest (booking essential for non-residents) 23.00/39.00 s. ℒ – ⥢ 6.95 – **21 rm** ♦115.00/175.00 – ♦♦180.00/315.00, 8 suites.
♦ Impressive William and Mary country house dating from 1699. Elegantly and carefully restored; abundantly furnished with antiques. Most characterful rooms in main house. Wood-panelled, three-roomed restaurant with period feel.

▲▲▲ **The Grange,** Clifton, YO30 6AA, ℰ (01904) 644744, *info@grangehotel.co.uk, Fax (01904) 612453 –* ⅙⅙ rest, ⅏ 🅿 ⇆ 16 – 🛦 60. ⓪⓪ ᴀᴇ ⓪ ꟾꟾꟾꟾꟾ
CX u
The Ivy Brasserie : Rest (closed Sunday dinner) (dinner only and Sunday lunch) a la carte 25.20/35.50 ℒ – **The Cellar Bar: Rest** (closed Sunday lunch) a la carte approx 25.00 – **29 rm** ⥢ ♦115.00/135.00 – ♦♦150.00, 1 suite.
♦ Elegant Regency town house with stylish period furniture throughout. Comfortable lounges and marble columned entrance hall. Excellently kept rooms vary in shapes and sizes. Ivy Brasserie boasts grand ceiling mural. Cellar Bar exudes much character.

▲▲▲ **Marriott,** Tadcaster Rd, YO24 1QQ, ℰ (01904) 701000, *york@marriotthotels.co.uk, Fax (01904) 702308,* ᴵ₆, ⇌, ▢, ☞, ℀ – ▯ ⅙⅙ 🖳 ⅙ 🅿 – 🛦 170. ⓪⓪ ᴀᴇ ⓪ ꟾꟾꟾꟾꟾ.
℀
AZ a
Ridings : Rest (closed Sunday lunch) 15.00/25.00 and dinner a la carte approx 35.00 s. ℒ – ⥢ 14.95 – **148 rm** ♦120.00/140.00 – ♦♦140.00/150.00, 3 suites.
♦ Large, group owned property on the edge of the racecourse with purpose-built extensions. Grandstand rooms, featuring large balconies and terraces, overlook course. Dining room with racecourse outlook.

▲▲ **York Pavilion,** 45 Main St, Fulford, YO10 4PJ, South : 1½ m. on A 19 ℰ (01904) 622099, *help@yorkpavilionhotel.com, Fax (01904) 626939,* ☞ – ⅙⅙ ⅏ 🅿 – 🛦 150. ⓪⓪ ᴀᴇ ⓪ ꟾꟾꟾꟾꟾ.
℀
Langtons Brasserie : Rest 16.95 (lunch) and dinner a la carte 21.55/31.85 s. ℒ – **57 rm** ⥢ ♦75.00/100.00 – ♦♦90.00/140.00.
♦ Georgian house on main road in suburbs. Wood panelled reception and period-style lounge. Older, more individual rooms in main house and uniform, chintzy style in extension. Informal dining.

▲▲ **Dean Court,** Duncombe Pl, YO1 7EF, ℰ (01904) 625082, *info@deancourt-york.co.uk, Fax (01904) 620305 –* ▯ ⅙⅙, 🖳 rest, ⅏ 🅿 – 🛦 50. ⓪⓪ ᴀᴇ ⓪ ꟾꟾꟾꟾꟾ. ℀
CY c
DCH : Rest 16.50 (lunch) and dinner a la carte 24.75/30.75 – **36 rm** ⥢ ♦80.00/130.00 – ♦♦120.00/210.00, 1 suite.
♦ Built in the 1850s to house clerics visiting the Minster, visible from most rooms. Now a very modern feel pervades the public areas. Aforementioned rooms more traditional. Minster outlook from smart restaurant.

▲▲ **Monkbar,** St Maurice's Rd, YO31 7JA, ℰ (01904) 638086, *sales@monkbarhotel.co.uk, Fax (01904) 629195 –* ▯ ⅙⅙ ⅏ 🅿 – 🛦 160. ⓪⓪ ᴀᴇ ⓪ ꟾꟾꟾꟾꟾ
DX a
Rest 12.50/21.00 and dinner a la carte approx 30.00 s. ℒ – **99 rm** ⥢ ♦105.00/125.00 – ♦♦145.00/175.00.
♦ Purpose-built and close to impressive Monkbar Gate. Modern décor throughout. Two room types: traditional, cottage-style in annex and uniform, modern rooms in main building. Restaurant exudes medieval atmosphere.

YORK

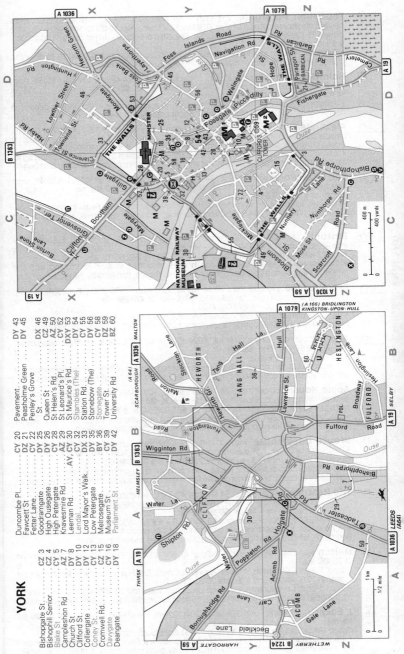

759

Four High Petergate, 2-4 High Petergate, YO1 7EH, ✆ (01904) 658516, *enquiries@fourhighpetergate.co.uk, Fax (01904) 634573,* – ⅍ P. MO AE VISA. ✂ CX e
closed 25 December – **Rest** – (see also ***The Bistro*** below) – **14 rm** ☐ ★65.00/85.00 – ★★110.00/125.00.
◆ Early 18C house, just inside old city walls. Antiques and racing pictures in all areas. Tranquil enclosed garden to rear. Bedrooms are sleek, minimalist and modern.

Holmwood House without rest., 114 Holgate Rd, YO24 4BB, ✆ (01904) 626183, *holmwood.house@dial.pipex.com, Fax (01904) 670899* – ⅍ P. MO VISA. ✂ AZ x
14 rm ☐ ★60.00/80.00 – ★★90.00/100.00.
◆ Informal atmosphere in well-kept terraced Victorian property. Individually decorated bedrooms include William Morris styling. Bright basement breakfast room.

Alexander House without rest., 94 Bishopthorpe Rd, YO23 1JS, ✆ (01904) 625016, *info@alexanderhouseyork.co.uk* – ⅍ P. MO VISA. ✂ CZ v
closed Christmas and New Year – **4 rm** ☐ ★55.00/75.00 – ★★65.00/85.00.
◆ Classic Victorian terraced house, immaculately refurbished by experienced owners. Delightful sitting room with porcelain and artworks. Hearty breakfasts. Attractive bedrooms.

The Hazelwood without rest., 24-25 Portland St, YO31 7EH, ✆ (01904) 626548, *reservations@thehazelwoodyork.com, Fax (01904) 628032* – ⅍ P. MO VISA. ✂ CX c
13 rm ☐ ★50.00/105.00 – ★★120.00.
◆ Two 19C town houses with characterful basement sitting room featuring original cooking range. Welcoming breakfast room in blue. Individual bedrooms, some with four posters.

Easton's without rest., 90 Bishopthorpe Rd, YO23 1JS, ✆ (01904) 626646, *bookings@eastons.ws, Fax (01904) 626646* – ⅍ P. ✂ CZ s
closed 2 weeks Christmas – **10 rm** ☐ ★42.00/46.00 – ★★52.00/76.00.
◆ Two joined end-of-terrace Victorian houses carefully furnished in keeping with the property's age. Period style throughout with well-chosen, comfortable furniture.

Crook Lodge without rest., 26 St Mary's, Bootham, YO30 7DD, ✆ (01904) 655614, *crooklodge@hotmail.com, Fax (01904) 625915* – ⅍ P. MO VISA. ✂ CX z
6 rm ☐ ★60.00/70.00 – ★★70.00/80.00.
◆ Privately owned, attractive Victorian redbrick house in quiet location. Basement breakfast room with original cooking range. Some rooms compact, all pleasantly decorated.

Acer without rest., 52 Scarcroft Hill, YO24 1DE, ✆ (01904) 653839, *info@acerhotel.co.uk, Fax (01904) 677017* – ⅍. MO VISA. ✂ CZ x
5 rm ☐ ★45.00 – ★★90.00.
◆ Terraced Victorian house with a creeper covered exterior. Warm welcome into homely and immaculately kept surroundings. Individually styled, traditionally appointed rooms.

Apple House without rest., 74-76 Holgate Rd, YO24 4AB, ✆ (01904) 625081, *pamelageorge1@yahoo.co.uk, Fax (01904) 628918* – ⅍ P. MO VISA AZ c
restricted opening at Christmas – **10 rm** ☐ ★35.00/55.00 – ★★60.00/80.00.
◆ 19C terraced house that's been refurbished to a neat and tidy standard. Rooms vary in shape and size; all have good modern facilities. A friendly address to lay your head.

Bronte Guesthouse without rest., 22 Grosvenor Terrace, YO30 7AG, ✆ (01904) 621066, *enquiries@bronte-guesthouse.com, Fax (01904) 653434* – ⅍. MO VISA. ✂ CX n
closed 24-26 December – **5 rm** ☐ ★38.00/50.00 – ★★70.00/80.00.
◆ Cosy little Victorian terraced house with pretty exterior, decorated in keeping with period nature of property. Charming breakfast room has antique furnishings. Comfy rooms.

The Heathers without rest., 54 Shipton Rd, Clifton-Without, YO30 5RQ, Northwest : 1 ½ m. on A 19 ✆ (01904) 640989, *reservations@heathers-guest-house.co.uk, Fax (01904) 640989,* – ⅍ P. MO AE VISA. ✂ AY n
closed 24-26 December – **6 rm** ☐ ★60.00/86.00 – ★★76.00/120.00.
◆ A personally run guesthouse in an extended 1930s property overlooking meadowland. Bedrooms, which vary in size, are colourfully decorated and well furnished.

Melton's, 7 Scarcroft Rd, YO23 1ND, ✆ (01904) 634341, *Fax (01904) 635115* – ⅍ ▤ ⇔ 20. MO VISA CZ c
closed 3 weeks Christmas, 1 week August, Monday lunch and Sunday – **Rest** (booking essential) 19.00 (lunch) and a la carte 26.00/39.00 ♀.
◆ Glass fronted restaurant with mural decorated walls and neighbourhood feel. Smart, crisp tone in both service and table cover. Good modern British food with some originality.

J. Baker's, 7 Fossgate, YO1 9TA, ✆ (01904) 622688, *Fax (01904) 671931* – ⅍ ▤. MO AE ⓓ VISA DY c
closed 1-8 January and Sunday-Monday – **Rest** (light lunch)/dinner 24.50 s.
◆ Contemporary restaurant in city centre. Spacious first floor 'chocolate' lounge for coffee and truffles. Modern dining room matched by good value, funky, cutting edge dishes.

X **Blue Bicycle**, 34 Fossgate, YO1 9TA, ℰ (01904) 673990, *info@thebluebicycle.com*, Fax (01904) 677688 – ⛏. **M© VISA**   DY e
closed 25-26 December and 1-2 January – **Rest** (booking essential) a la carte 31.00/41.00 ℚ.
• Delightfully cluttered, atmospheric restaurant full of objets d'art, ornaments and pictures. Wood floors and heavy, old, pine tables. Bustling and busy; British cuisine.

X **31 Castlegate**, 31 Castlegate, YO1 9RN, ℰ (01904) 621404 – ⛏. **M© AE VISA**   DY r
closed 25 December and Monday – **Rest** 11.95 (lunch) and dinner a la carte 19.90/25.15.
• Superbly located former home of Georgian architect. Impressive period décor in situ. First floor, high ceilinged dining room for well-priced, tasty dishes on eclectic menus.

X **The Bistro** (at Four High Petergate H.), 2-4 High Petergate, YO1 7EH, ℰ (01904) 658516, *enquiries@fourhighpetergate.co.uk*, Fax (01904) 634573 – ⛏ ▤. **M© AE VISA**   CX e
Rest (booking essential) 16.95 (lunch) and a la carte 28.00/33.00.
• Set in a former doll's house repair shop, this smart, compact bistro has a friendly, welcoming ambience. Modern cooking strikes the right chord after a visit to the sights.

X **Vanilla Black**, 26 Swinegate, YO1 8AZ, ℰ (01904) 676750 – ⛏. **M© VISA**   DY o
closed 1 week January, 1 week June, 25-26 December, Sunday, Monday and Tuesday lunch – **Rest** - Vegetarian - (light lunch) a la carte 21.20/23.80.
• Vegetarian restaurant with eye-catching exterior, close to the Minster. Spacious interior dotted with scrubbed wooden tables. Very interesting dishes with host of influences.

X **The Tasting Room**, 13à Swinegate Court East, YO1 8AJ, ℰ (01904) 627879, *book ings@thetastingroom.co.uk* – ⛏. **M© VISA**   DY n
closed 25 December, 1 January and Sunday – **Rest** 14.95 (lunch) and dinner a la carte 21.45/27.90 ℚ.
• Near the Minster with outdoor tables in good weather. Refurbished in 2005: smart fabrics and mood lighting. Simple, tasty, approachable cooking based upon a few good flavours.

X **Melton's Too**, 25 Walmgate, YO1 9TX, ℰ (01904) 629222, *greatfood@melton stoo.co.uk*, Fax (01904) 636677 – ⛏. **M© VISA**   DY a
closed 25-26 and 31 December and 1 January – **Rest** a la carte 17.30/24.90 ℚ.
• Café-bistro 'descendant' of Melton's restaurant. Located in former saddlers shop with oak beams and exposed brick walls. Good value eclectic dishes, with tapas a speciality.

at Acaster Malbis South : 4¾ m. by Bishopthorpe Rd – BZ – ✉ York.

🏠 **The Manor Country House** ⌖ without rest., Mill Lane, YO23 2UL, ℰ (01904) 706723, *manorhouse@selcom.co.uk*, Fax (01904) 706723, ⌇, 🌳 – ⛏ ♥ **P**. **M© VISA**
closed mid December- mid February – **10 rm** ⬚ ✷50.00/60.00 – ✷✷72.00/80.00.
• A quiet location in picturesque village on River Ouse, 15 minutes from city centre. River bus in summer. Parts date from 1700s. Snug, elegant country house atmosphere.

at Escrick South : 5¾ m. on A 19 – BZ – ✉ York.

🏨 **Parsonage Country House**, Main St, YO19 6LF, ℰ (01904) 728111, *reserva tions@parsonagehotel.co.uk*, Fax (01904) 728151, 🌳 – 📶 ⛏ **P** – 🔔 150. ⛏ **M© AE VISA**. 🍴
Rest (closed Saturday) 15.00/39.95 – **48 rm** ⬚ ✷75.00/120.00 – ✷✷120.00/140.00.
• Ivy-clad former parsonage with gardens; dating from 1848 and located adjacent to the parish church of St. Helen. Main house rooms most characterful, all are well appointed. Dining room with palpable country house feel.

at York Business Park Northwest : 3¾ m. by A 59 – AY – on A 1237 – ✉ York.

XX **Maxi's**, Ings Lane, Nether Poppleton, YO26 6RA, ℰ (01904) 783898, *info@maxi-s.co.uk*, Fax (01904) 783818 – ▤ **P**. **M© AE ① VISA**
closed 25-26 December – **Rest** - Chinese (Canton, Peking) - a la carte 17.80/20.00.
• Purpose-built property with an ornate exterior. Chinese theme throughout including a feature pagoda in the dining room. Authentic food and attentive, friendly service.

ZENNOR Cornwall 503 D 33.
London 305.5 – Penzance 11 – St Ives 5.

🍴 **The Gurnard's Head** with rm, Treen, TR26 3DE, West : 1 ½ m. on B 3306 ℰ (01736) 796928, *enquiries@gurnardshead.co.uk*, Fax (01736) 795313, 🌳 – **TV P**. **M© VISA**
closed January-February – **Rest** (restricted lunch Monday) a la carte 18.50/27.00 ℚ – **7 rm** ⬚ ✷45.00/52.50 – ✷✷72.50/82.50.
• Roughly textured, mustard hued pub. Shelves of books give it a shabby chic edge. Eat in restaurant or bar: clever, satisfying, carefully balanced combinations. Smart rooms.

ENGLAND

Your opinions are important to us:
please write and let us know about your discoveries and experiences – good and bad!

Castle of Scotland: flowers and towers

Towns
from A to Z

Villes
de A à Z

Città
de A a Z

Städte
von A bis Z

Scotland

Place with at least _____

a hotel or restaurant ● Tongue
a pleasant hotel or restaurant 🏨, ⬆, X
Good accommodation at moderate prices 🏠
a quiet, secluded hotel 🦮
a restaurant with ❀, ❀❀, ❀❀❀, ☙ Rest
Town with a local map ●

La località possiede come minimo _____

una risorsa alberghiera ● Tongue
Albergo o ristorante ameno 🏨, ⬆, X
Buona sistemazione a prezzi contenuti 🏠
un albergo molto tranquillo, isolato 🦮
un'ottima tavola con ❀, ❀❀, ❀❀❀, ☙ Rest
Città con carta dei dintorni ●

Localité offrant au moins _____

une ressource hôtelière ● Tongue
un hôtel ou restaurant agréable 🏨, ⬆, X
Bonnes nuits à petits prix 🏠
un hôtel très tranquille, isolé 🦮
une bonne table à ❀, ❀❀, ❀❀❀, ☙ Rest
Carte de voisinage : voir à la ville choisie ●

Ort mit mindestens _____

einem Hotel oder Restaurant ● Tongue
einem angenehmen Hotel oder Restaurant 🏨, ⬆, X
Hier übernachten Sie gut und preiswert 🏠
einem sehr ruhigen und abgelegenen Hotel 🦮
einem Restaurant mit ❀, ❀❀, ❀❀❀, ☙ Rest
Stadt mit Umgebungskarte ●

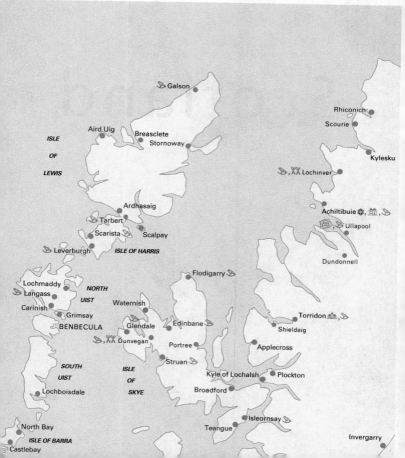

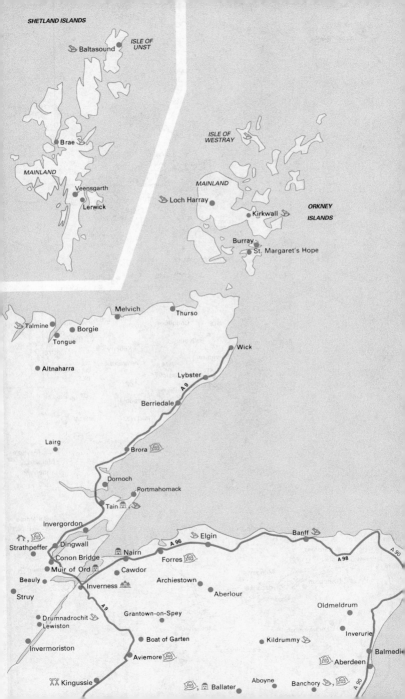

ABERDEEN Aberdeen 501 N 12 Scotland G. – pop. 184 788.

See : City★★ – Old Aberdeen★★ X – St Machar's Cathedral★★ (West Front★★★, Heraldic Ceiling★★★) X **A** – Art Gallery★★ (Macdonald Collection★★) Y **M** – Mercat Cross★★ Y **B** – King's College Chapel★ (Crown Spire★★★, medieval fittings★★★) X **D** – Provost Skene's House★ (painted ceilings★★) Y **E** – Maritime Museum★ Z **M1** – Marischal College★ Y **U**.

Env. : Brig o' Balgownie★, by Don St X.

Exc. : SW : Deeside★★ – Crathes Castle★★ (Gardens★★★) AC, SW : 16 m. by A 93 X – Dunnottar Castle★★ AC (site★★★), S : 18 m. by A 90 X – Pitmedden Garden★★, N : 14 m. by A 90 on B 999 X – Castle Fraser★ (exterior★★) AC, W : 16 m. by A 944 X – Fyvie Castle★, NW : 26½ m. on A 947.

🛈, 🛈, 🛈 Hazelhead, Hazelhead Park ℰ (01224) 321830 – 🛈, 🛈 Royal Aberdeen, Balgownie, Bridge of Don ℰ (01224) 702571, X – 🛈 Balnagask, St Fitticks Rd ℰ (01224) 871286, X – 🛈 King's Links, Golf Rd ℰ (01224) 632269, X – 🛈 Portlethen, Badentoy Rd ℰ (01224) 781090, X – 🛈, 🛈 Murcar, Bridge of Don ℰ (01224) 704354, X – 🛈 Auchmill, Bomyview Rd, West Heatheryfold ℰ (01224) 715214, X.

✈ Aberdeen Airport, Dyce : ℰ (0870) 0400006, NW : 7 m. by A 96 X – **Terminal** : Bus Station, Guild St (adjacent to Railway Station).

🚢 to Shetland Islands (Lerwick) and via Orkney Islands (Stromness) (P & O Scottish Ferries) 1-2 daily.

🛈 23 Union St ℰ (01224) 288828.

Edinburgh 130 – Dundee 67.

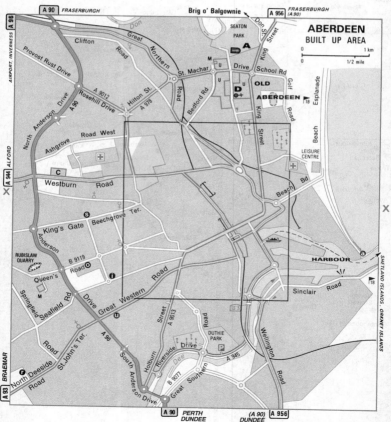

The Marcliffe at Pitfodels, North Deeside Rd, AB15 9YA, ℰ (01224) 861000, *enquiries@marcliffe.com*, Fax (01224) 868860, ⌂, ☒, ≡ – |☰| ⇖, ≣ rest, ⛷ & ℙ – ☒ 400. ⚫⚫
🆎 ⓪ VISA

X r

Conservatory : Rest a la carte 30.00/43.00 s. ♀ ☒ – **40 rm** ☒ ✦140.00/175.00 –
✦✦150.00/215.00, 2 suites.
♦ Family owned and professionally run modern country house set amidst 8 acres of pleasant grounds. Spacious, individually decorated rooms with antique furniture. Light, airy conservatory dining.

Ardoe House, South Deeside Rd, Blairs, AB12 5YP, Southwest : 5 m. on B 9077
ℰ (01224) 860600, *ardoe@macdonald-hotels.co.uk*, Fax (01224) 860644, ≤, ☒, ☎, ▢,
☒, ♨, ✂ – |☰| ⇖ ⛷ & ℙ – ☒ 500. ⚫⚫ 🆎 ⓪ VISA

Blairs : Rest 33.50 and a la carte 28.90/42.45 ♀ – ☒ 15.95 – **107 rm** ✦200.00 – ✦✦200.00,
2 suites.
♦ Imposing 18C Scottish baronial style mansion with annexes. Country house character aligned to excellent leisure facilities. Modern bedrooms, many overlooking the grounds. Formal, wood-panelled Blairs.

Simpson's, 59 Queen's Rd, AB15 4YP, ℰ (01224) 327777, *reservations@simpsonshotel.co.uk*, Fax (01224) 327700 – |☰| ⇖ ⛷ & ℙ. ⚫⚫ 🆎 ⓪ VISA

X o

closed 25 December-3 January – **Brasserie** (ℰ (01224) 327799) : Rest 15.50/29.50 and a la carte 13.75/31.20 – **48 rm** ☒ ✦130.00/140.00 – ✦✦155.00, 2 suites.
♦ Period granite façade belies vibrantly decorated and contemporary interior. Family owned and relaxed "boutique" hotel. Stylish and modern bedrooms with business facilities. Roman bath house styled brasserie.

Skene House Holburn without rest., 6 Union Grove, AB10 6SY, ℰ (01224) 580000,
holburn@skene-house.co.uk, Fax (01224) 585193 – ⇖ ⛷ ℙ. ⚫⚫ 🆎 ⓪ VISA. ✂

Z v

☒ 8.25, **39 suites** 99.00/149.00.
♦ Row of five granite former tenements. Not your conventional hotel, but a number of serviced apartments. Each suite benefits from its own kitchen. Ideal for long stays.

The Mariner, 349 Great Western Rd, AB10 6NW, ℰ (01224) 588901, *info@themariner hotel.co.uk*, Fax (01224) 571621 – ⇖ ⛷ & ℙ. ⚫⚫ 🆎 ⓪ VISA. ✂

X u

closed 26 December **Atlantis** : Rest - Seafood - (bar lunch Saturday) 15.00/18.00 and a la carte 22.50/36.50 – **25 rm** ☒ ✦70.00/85.00 – ✦✦105.00/130.00.
♦ A nautical theme prevails through the ground floor of this commercial hotel. Spacious, colourfully decorated bedrooms with extensive facilities. More seclusion in annex rooms. Long established restaurant with wood panelling and maritime themed décor.

Atholl, 54 King's Gate, AB15 4YN, ℰ (01224) 323505, *info@atholl-aberdeen.co.uk*,
Fax (01224) 321555 – ⇖ ⛷ & ℙ – ☒ 60. ⚫⚫ 🆎 VISA. ✂

X s

closed 1 January – Rest a la carte 15.95/28.35 ♀ – **34 rm** ☒ ✦75.00/95.00 – ✦✦120.00.
♦ Baronial style hotel set in leafy suburbs; well run by friendly staff. Traditional lounge bar; well-priced, up-to-date rooms. A useful address for visitors to the city. Dining room specialises in tried-and-tested Scottish cooking.

Express by Holiday Inn without rest., Chapel St, AB10 1SQ, ℰ (01224) 623500,
info@hieaberdeen.co.uk, Fax (01224) 623523 – |☰| ⇖ ⛷ & – ☒ 35. ⚫⚫ 🆎 ⓪ VISA

Z u

155 rm ✦85.00 – ✦✦85.00.
♦ Located in the heart of the city; well-equipped, up-to-date bedrooms for the business traveller. Plenty of restaurants are located nearby.

Penny Meadow without rest., 189 Great Western Rd, AB10 6PS, ℰ (01224) 588037,
frances@pennymeadow.freeserve.co.uk, Fax (01224) 573639, ☒ – ⇖ ℙ. ⚫⚫ VISA.
✂

Z x

3 rm ☒ ✦40.00/55.00 – ✦✦60.00/100.00.
♦ Attractive Victorian house built of local granite. Welcoming service by owners. Light and airy bedrooms have some thoughtful touches and are well-appointed.

Silver Darling, Pocra Quay, North Pier, AB11 5DQ, ℰ (01224) 576229,
Fax (01224) 588119, ≤ Aberdeen Harbour and Bay, ⌂ – ⚫⚫ 🆎 ⓪ VISA

X a

closed 2 weeks Christmas-New Year, Saturday lunch and Sunday – Rest - French Seafood -
a la carte 21.50/34.50 ♀.
♦ Former customs house attractively set at port entrance; panoramic views across harbour and coastline. Attentive service of superb quality seafood prepared in imaginative ways.

The Eating Room, 239 Great Western Rd, AB10 6PS, ℰ (01224) 212125, *info@eating room.com* – ⇖. ⚫⚫ 🆎 ⓪ VISA

Z a

closed 25-26 December, 1 January, Sunday, and Monday – Rest a la carte 19.55/31.15 ♀.
♦ Small, contemporary restaurant in a granite house. Neatly laid, polished lacquered tables. Modern cooking style incorporates complex twists with feel for Asian flavours.

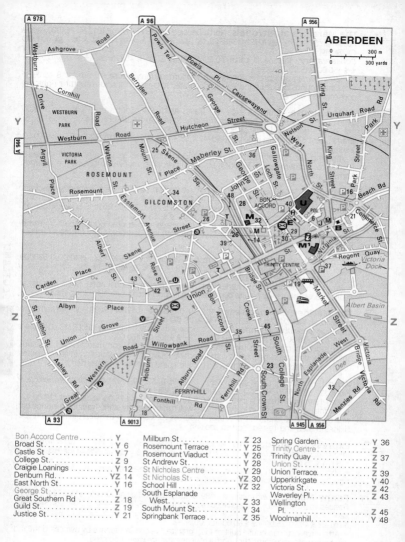

XX **Nargile,** 77-79 Skene St, AB10 1QD, ℘ (01224) 636093, Fax (01224) 636202 – 🍽️, ⓂⓈ AE
① VISA
                                                                 Y a
closed 25-26 December and 1 January – **Rest** - Turkish - (dinner only and lunch in December) 21.95 and a la carte 16.20/25.15 🍴.
   ◆ Traditionally decorated Turkish restaurant with subdued lighting from Turkish lamps. Open-plan kitchen allows the diner to watch the chefs prepare the authentic dishes.

X **Rendezvous at Nargile,** 106-108 Forest Ave, AB15 4UP, ℘ (01224) 323700, narg
ile@freeserve.co.uk, Fax (01224) 312202 – 🍽️, ⓂⓈ AE ① VISA
                                                                X l
closed 25-26 December and 1-2 January – **Rest** - Turkish/Mediterranean - a la carte 17.85/32.85 s.
   ◆ Corner restaurant with contemporary décor. Mediterranean - predominantly Turkish - menu from snacks to a full a la carte meal; fixed price menu between 5-7pm.

at Aberdeen Airport *(Aberdeenshire) Northwest : 6 m. by A 96 – ✕ – ✉ Aberdeen.*

🏨 **Thistle Aberdeen Airport,** Argyll Rd, AB21 0AF, ℘ (0870) 3339149, *aberdeenair port@thistle.co.uk, Fax (0870) 3339249,* ₤₅ – ✕ ✆ ₺ 🅿 – 🛆 600, 🐵 🖭 🛈 *VISA closed lunch Saturday and Sunday –* **Rest** *(closed lunch Saturday and Sunday)* 13.95/22.00 and dinner a la carte 20.50/29.75 – � 11.00 – **146 rm** ✝150.00 – ✝✝175.00, 1 suite.
♦ Busy commercial hotel within walking distance of the terminal. Extensive conference and banqueting facilities. Well-appointed and boldly decorated modern bedrooms. Restaurant combines international cuisine with traditional Scottish dishes.

ABERDEEN AIRPORT *Aberdeenshire* 501 N 12 – *see Aberdeen.*

ABERFELDY *Perth and Kinross* 501 I 14.
Edinburgh 75 – Dunkeld 17.5 – Pitlochry 14.5.

↑ **Guinach House** ⊗ *without rest., Urlar Rd, PH15 2ET, South : ½ m. by A 826* ℘ (01887) 820251, *info@guinachhouse.co.uk,* ☞ – ✕ ✆ 🅿. ✾
3 rm ✝85.00 – ✝✝95.00/105.00.
♦ Personally run Edwardian house in mature grounds. Dressers on landing house DVD library, books and games. Modish, individually appointed rooms. Continental breakfast in bed.

Your opinions are important to us:
please write and let us know about your discoveries and experiences – good and bad!

ABERFOYLE *Stirling* 501 G 15.
🇧 *Trossachs Discovery Centre, Main St* ℘ (08707) 200604, *info@aberfoylevisitscot land.com.*
Edinburgh 57 – Glasgow 30 – Perth 49.

🏨 **Forest Hills** ⊗, *Kinlochard, FK8 3TL, West : 4 ¼ m. on B 829* ℘ (0870) 1942105, *for est-hills@macdonald-hotels.co.uk, Fax (01877) 387307,* ≤ Loch Ard, ₤₅, ⩩, 🔲, 🏊, ☞, 🏌, ✾ – ᵇ🛢 ⅃ ✕ ₺ 🅿 – 🛆 150. 🐵 🖭 *VISA.* ✾
Garden : **Rest** *(dinner only)* 26.95/35.95 **s.** – **Rafters :** **Rest** a la carte 13.00/25.00 s. ♀ –
49 rm *(dinner included)* ⊒ ✝130.00/160.00 – ✝✝180.00/240.00, 1 suite.
♦ Lovely location overlooking Loch Ard. Country house ambience with open fires and pleasant views. Extensive leisure club: haggis hurling on offer too. Well-furnished rooms. Glorious views from Garden restaurant. Informal Rafters.

ABERLOUR *Aberdeenshire* 501 K 11 *Scotland G.*
Env. : *Dufftown (Glenfiddich Distillery★), SE : 6 m. by A 95 and A 941.*
🇫₉ *Rothes, Blackhall* ℘ (01340) 831443.
Edinburgh 192 – Aberdeen 60 – Elgin 15 – Inverness 55.

🏨 **Dowans,** AB38 9LS, *Southwest : ¾ m. by A 95* ℘ (01340) 871488, *enquiries@dowansho tel.com, Fax (01340) 871038,* 🏊, ☞ – ✕ ✆ 🅿. 🐵 🖭 *VISA.*
Rest a la carte 17.20/35.50 **s.** – **19 rm** ⊒ ✝55.00/75.00 – ✝✝140.00.
♦ Welcoming, informal establishment with classic Scottish country house style. Inviting public areas. Comfortably smart rooms, refurbished in 2006; best views from the front. Two roomed restaurant.

ABOYNE *Aberdeenshire* 501 L 12 *Scotland G. – pop. 2 202 (inc. Cromar).*
Exc. : *Craigievar Castle★ AC, NE : 12 m. by B 9094, B 9119 and A 980.*
🇫ₙ *Formanston Park* ℘ (013398) 86328.
Edinburgh 131 – Aberdeen 30 – Dundee 68.

↑ **Struan Hall** *without rest., Ballater Rd, AB34 5HY,* ℘ (013398) 87241, *struanhall@zet net.co.uk, Fax (013398) 87241,* ☞ – ✕ 🅿. 🐵 *VISA.* ✾
April-September – **3 rm** ⊒ ✝38.00/45.00 – ✝✝90.00.
♦ An agreeable and welcoming guesthouse with attractive garden. Well kept throughout. Large sitting room and antique breakfast table. Simple, comfy bedrooms.

ACHILTIBUIE *Highland* **501** D 9.

Edinburgh 243 – Inverness 84 – Ullapool 25.

Summer Isles 🦢, IV26 2YG, *☎ (01854) 622282, info@summerisleshotel.co.uk, Fax (01854) 622251,* ≤ Summer Isles, 🌱 – ☆ **P. ⑩ VISA**. ❄
April-15 October – **Rest** (booking essential) (set menu at dinner) (light seafood lunch)/dinner 50.00 ♀ – (see also **Summer Isles Bar** below) – **10 rm** ☑ ✱82.00 – ✱✱198.00, 3 suites.
Spec. Fillet of salmon with bearnaise sauce and oatmeal loaf. Breast of wood pigeon with toasted brioche and local chanterelles. Seared scallops with champ, basil and mixed herb pesto.
◆ Exceedingly well run with a picturesque setting and fantastic views of Summer Isles. Very comfortable lounges and real fire. Superb duplex suite and cosy log cabin rooms. Very pleasant restaurant boasts exacting cooking to a very high standard; local seafood to the fore.

Summer Isles Bar (at Summer Isles H.), IV26 2YG, *☎ (01854) 622205, info@summerisleshotel.co.uk, Fax (01854) 622251,* 🍴 – **P. ⑩ VISA**. ❄
April-October – **Rest** - Seafood - (bookings not accepted) a la carte 10.50/25.00.
◆ Simple, informal bar with outside seating for sunny days and snug interior for more bracing weather. Seafood oriented blackboard menu and puddings from the restaurant.

AIRD UIG *Western Isles (Outer Hebrides)* – see Lewis and Harris (Isle of).

ALLOWAY *South Ayrshire* **501 502** G 17 – see Ayr.

ALTNAHARRA *Highland* **501** G 9 *Scotland G.* – ✉ Lairg.

Exc. : Ben Loyal★★, N : 10 m. by A 836 – Ben Hope★ (≤★★★) NW : 14 m.
Edinburgh 239 – Inverness 83 – Thurso 61.

Altnaharra 🦢, IV27 4UE, *☎ (01549) 411222, office@altnaharra.co.uk, Fax (01549) 411233,* ≤, 🌱 – ☆ **P. ⑩ AE VISA**
Rest 28.50/32.50 s. – **13 rm** (dinner included) ☑ ✱105.00/150.00 – ✱✱210.00/260.00.
◆ Refurbished rural hunting lodge with abundance of local wildlife. Stylishly decorated, cosy interiors include a cocktail bar and library. Simple, good-sized bedrooms. Local, seasonal menus in smart, formally set restaurant oozing charm and character.

ALYTH *Perthshire and Kinross* **501** J 14 – pop. 2 301.

🏌 Pitcrocknie *☎ (01828) 632268.*
Edinburgh 63 – Aberdeen 69 – Dundee 16 – Perth 21.

Lands of Loyal 🦢, Loyal Rd, PH11 8JQ, North : ½ m. by B 952 *☎ (01828) 633151, enq@landsofloyal.com, Fax (01828) 633313,* ≤, � – **P. ⑩ AE ⑩ VISA**
Rest a la carte 21.50/32.40 s. – **16 rm** ☑ ✱79.00/89.00 – ✱✱136.00.
◆ Victorian mansion with an impressive reproduction salon from the SS Mauritania. Individually decorated bedrooms blend a pleasant traditional style with antiques. Appealing restaurant spans three different rooms.

ANNBANK *South Ayrshire* **501** G 17.

Edinburgh 84 – Glasgow 38 – Ayr 6 – Dumfries 54.

Enterkine 🦢, KA6 5AL, Southeast : ½ m. on B 742 (Coylton rd) *☎ (01292) 520580, mail@enterkine.com, Fax (01292) 521582,* ≤, 🌱, �, ♨ – ☆ ♥ **P. ⑩ AE ⑩ VISA**
Rest (booking essential) 16.50/40.00 – **6 rm** (dinner included) ☑ ✱90.00/110.00 – ✱✱140.00/180.00.
◆ 1930s country house in utterly peaceful location surrounded by extensive gardens and woodlands. Log fires and a charming library. Excellent bedrooms with a luxurious feel. Crystal glassware embodies style of attractive dining room.

 Look out for red symbols, indicating particularly pleasant establishments.

ANSTRUTHER Fife 501 L 15 *Scotland G. – pop. 3 442.*

See : *Scottish Fisheries Museum*★★ *AC.*
Env. : *The East Neuk*★★ *– Crail*★★ *(Old Centre*★★*, Upper Crail*★*) NE : 4 m. by A 917.*
Exc. : *Kellie Castle*★ *AC, NW : 7 m. by B 9171, B 942 and A 917.*
⌕ *Marsfield Shore Rd* ℘ *(01333) 310956.*
🔋 *Scottish Fisheries Museum, Harbourhead* ℘ *(01333) 311073 (April-October).*
Edinburgh 46 – Dundee 23 – Dunfermline 34.

⌂ **The Spindrift,** Pittenweem Rd, KY10 3DT, ℘ (01333) 310573, *info@thespindrift.co.uk,*
Fax (01333) 310573 – 🛏️ 📮 🅫 🆎 💳
closed 5-25 January, 2 weeks November and Christmas – **Rest** (by arrangement) 20.00 –
8 rm �െ ★38.00/48.00 – ★★56.00/76.00.
• Victorian house originally owned by tea clipper captain whose bedroom replicates a
master's cabin. Comfortable period style throughout and local kippers for breakfast. 19C
style dining room reflects house's age.

⌂ **The Grange** without rest., 45 Pittenweem Rd, KY10 3DT, ℘ (01333) 310842, *grange@pa*
mela-rae.com, Fax (01333) 310842, 🚗 – 🛏️ 📮 💳
Closed January-February – **4 rm** ⊑ ★30.00/45.00 – ★★60.00/70.00.
• Spacious Edwardian house on main road into this delightful coastal village. Snug lounges
including charming sun room. Neatly kept, traditional bedrooms.

XX **Cellar**, 24 East Green, KY10 3AA, ℘ (01333) 310378, Fax (01333) 312544 – 🅫 🆎 ① 💳
closed Christmas, Sunday and Monday – **Rest** - Seafood - (booking essential) (dinner only
and Saturday lunch) 21.50/35.00 ⊻.
• Located through an archway on quiet back streets. Warm ambience with fires and
exposed brick and stone. Bold, original cooking, more elaborate at dinner.

APPLECROSS Highland 501 C 11.

🏠 **Applecross Inn,** Shore St, IV54 8LR, ℘ (01520) 744262, *applecrossinn@globalnet.co.uk,*
Fax (01520) 744400, ⩽ Islands of Raasay and Skye, 🌤️, 🚗 – 🛏️ ♿ 📮 🅫 💳
closed 25 December and 1 January – **Rest** (booking essential) a la carte 15.00/25.00 – **7 rm**
⊑ ★80.00 – ★★90.00.
• An unforgettable coastal road journey of 24 miles ends at this cosy row of stone fishermen's cottages with lots of windows to enjoy the stupendous views. Smart, comfy rooms.
Blackboard menus feature local seafood.

X **The Potting Shed,** Applecross Walled Garden, IV54 8ND, Northeast : ½ m. ℘ (01520)
744440, *mail@eatinthewalledgarden.co.uk,* 🌤️, 🚗 – 📮 💳
restricted opening in winter – **Rest** (lunch only and dinner Wednesday-Saturday) a la carte
18.85/28.85.
• Lovely 17C walled kitchen garden whose restaurant has grown from a tearoom. Its
simple structure belies its tasty dishes, fresh from owner's fishing boat or the garden itself.

ARBROATH Angus 501 M 14.
Edinburgh 72.5 – Dundee 17.5 – Montrose 12.

⌂ **The Old Vicarage** without rest., 2 Seaton Rd, DD11 5DX, Northeast : ¾ m. by A 92 and
Hayshead Rd ℘ (01241) 430475, *loris@theoldvicaragebandb.co.uk,* 🚗 – 🛏️ 📮 💳
3 rm ⊑ ★40.00/45.00 – ★★55.00/60.00.
• Detached 19C house, of large proportions, clothed in Victorian style throughout. Eye-
catching dolls house in lounge. Antique furnished rooms: ask for view of Arbroath Abbey.

ARCHIESTOWN Moray 501 K 11 – ✉ *Aberlour (Aberdeenshire).*
Edinburgh 194 – Aberdeen 62 – Inverness 49.

🏠 **Archiestown,** The Square, AB38 7QL, ℘ (01340) 810218, *jah@archiestownhotel.co.uk,*
Fax (01340) 810239, 🌤️, 🎣, 🚗 – 🛏️ 📮 🅫 💳
closed 3 January-8 February and 23-28 December – **Bistro :** **Rest** a la carte 19.50/36.00 –
11 rm ⊑ ★72.50 – ★★80.00/115.00.
• Privately owned little hotel appealing to all with its characterful, comfortable lounges
and nearby golf and distilleries. Comfy, individual rooms, prettily decorated. Informal bistro with daily changing menu.

ARDEONAIG Perth and Kinross 501 H 14 – *see Killin (Stirling).*

ARDHASAIG Western Isles (Outer Hebrides) 501 Z 10 – *see Lewis and Harris (Isle of).*

Edinburgh 132 – Glasgow 86 – Oban 40.

⌂ **Allt-na-Craig,** Tarbert Rd, PA30 8EP, on A 83 ℘ (01546) 603245, *information@allt-na-craig.co.uk, Fax (01546) 603255, ≤, ᾔ – ⅙⇐ ☎ ☒, ◍◐ 𝘝𝘐𝘚𝘈*
closed Christmas – **Rest** (by arrangement) 21.50 – **5 rm** ⊑ ✝40.00/57.50 – ✝✝110.00.
♦ Spacious, modernised Victorian house with lovely gardens, once the childhood home of author Kenneth Grahame. Front bedrooms have good views over loch. Simple, traditional dining room where breakfasts and evening meals are served.

ARDUAINE *Argyll and Bute* **501** D 15 *Scotland G.* – ⊠ *Oban*.
Exc.: *Loch Awe*★★, E : 12 m. by A 816 and B 840.
Edinburgh 142 – Oban 20.

🏨 **Loch Melfort** ≫, PA34 4XG, ℘ (01852) 200233, *reception@lochmelfort.co.uk, Fax (01852) 200214,* ≤ Asknish bay and Islands of Jura, Shuna and Scarba, ᾔ, ⌑ – ⬚ ⅙⇐ ☎ – ⚿ 45. ◍◐ ⒶⒺ 𝘝𝘐𝘚𝘈
closed 3 January-15 February – **Rest** - Seafood specialities - (bar lunch)/dinner 16.50/24.00 – **25 rm** ⊑ ✝69.00/89.00 – ✝✝118.00/138.00.
♦ Next to Arduaine Gardens and with glorious, captivating views of the Sound of Jura, the hotel has spacious public areas including a bistro bar. Largest rooms in main house. Formal atmosphere in the main restaurant with a focus on quality local seafood.

ARRAN (Isle of) *North Ayrshire* **501 502** DE 16 17 *Scotland G.*
See : *Island*★★ - *Brodick Castle*★★ *AC*.
⛴ from Brodick to Ardrossan (Caledonian MacBrayne Ltd) 4-6 daily (55 mn) – from Lochranza to Kintyre Peninsula (Claonaig) (Caledonian MacBrayne Ltd) frequent services daily (30 mn) – from Brodick to Isle of Bute (Rothesay) (Caledonian MacBrayne Ltd) 3 weekly (2 h 5 mn).

Brodick *North Ayrshire – pop. 822.*
🇮🇸 Brodick ℘ (01770) 302349 – 🇮🇸 Machrie Bay ℘ (01770) 850232.
🇧 The Pier ℘ (0845) 2255121.

🏨 **Kilmichael Country House** ≫, Glen Cloy, KA27 8BY, West : 1 m. by Shore Rd, taking left turn opposite Golf Club ℘ (01770) 302219, *enquiries@kilmichael.com, Fax (01770) 302068,* ᾔ – ⅙⇐ ☎, ◍◐ ① 𝘝𝘐𝘚𝘈
April-October – **Rest** *(closed Tuesday)* (booking essential) (dinner only) 38.50 – **4 rm** ⊑ ✝95.00 – ✝✝136.00/195.00, 3 suites.
♦ Arran's oldest building in its delightfully tranquil country setting creates a very fine small hotel. Individually styled, antique furnished rooms. Cosy elegance throughout. Daily changing menus in conservatory extension to main house.

⌂ **Dunvegan House,** Shore Rd, KA27 8AJ, ℘ (01770) 302811, *dunveganhouse@hotmail.com, Fax (01770) 302811,* ≤, ᾔ – ⅙⇐ ☎
closed Christmas and New Year – **Rest** 18.00/25.00 – **9 rm** ⊑ ✝30.00/40.00 – ✝✝60.00/70.00.
♦ Located on the Brodick seafront with a pleasant outlook over the bay. Lawned garden area and comfortable lounge. Bedrooms are modern and well kept. Locally sourced menus.

Lamlash *North Ayrshire – pop. 900 –* ⊠ *Brodick*.
🇮🇸 Lamlash ℘ (01770) 600296.

⌂ **Lilybank** without rest., Shore Rd, KA27 8LS, ℘ (01770) 600230, *colin369.richardson@virgin.net, Fax (01770) 600230,* ≤, ᾔ – ⅙⇐ ☎, ⌗
April-October – **6 rm** ⊑ ✝30.00/40.00 – ✝✝60.00/65.00.
♦ Whitewashed late 18C cottage on shores of Lamlash Bay overlooking Holy Island. Tidy, snug bedrooms and atmosphere throughout. A good value base for touring the island.

Lochranza *North Ayrshire.*
🇮🇸 Lochranza ℘ (0177083) 0273.

⌂ **Apple Lodge,** KA27 8HJ, Southeast : ½ m. on Brodick rd ℘ (01770) 830229, *Fax (01770) 830229,* ≤, ᾔ – ⅙⇐ ☎, ⌗
closed Christmas and New Year, minimum 3 night stay – **Rest** (by arrangement) 23.00 – **4 rm** ⊑ ✝51.00 – ✝✝76.00/84.00.
♦ Extended period house with small garden and pleasing views, in centre of quiet village. Homely cottage-style decor with antique furniture and a welcoming atmosphere. Food is home-cooked and uses island and home produce in good, hearty, varied dishes.

SCOTLAND

Whiting Bay North Ayrshire – ⊠.
> ⓘ Whiting Bay, Golf Course Rd ℘ (01770) 700775.

⌂ **Royal Arran** without rest., Shore Rd, KA27 8PZ, ℘ (01770) 700286, royalarran@btinter net.com, Fax (01770) 700286, ≤, 爫 – ⇔ 戋 **P**. **MO** **AE** **①** **VISA**
Easter-October – **Rest** 19.50 – **4 rm** � 42.50 – ✦✦95.00.
◆ Large sandstone Victorian house, almost on the seashore, with fine views to the mainland. Welcoming interiors with open fires. Comfy bedrooms with pleasant aspects.

ASCOG Argyll and Bute **501** E 16 – see Bute (Isle of).

AUCHENCAIRN Dumfries and Galloway **501** **502** I 19 – ⊠ Castle Douglas.
Edinburgh 94 – Dumfries 21 – Stranraer 60.

🏨 **Balcary Bay** ♨, DG7 1QZ, Southeast : 2 m. on Balcary rd ℘ (01556) 640217, reserva tions@balcary-bay-hotel.co.uk, Fax (01556) 640272, ≤ Balcary Bay and Solway Firth, 爫 – ⇔ 戋 **P**. **MO** **VISA**
closed 3 December-6 February – **Rest** (lunch by arrangement)/dinner 32.50 and a la carte 16.60/33.00 s. – **20 rm** � 60.00/120.00 – ✦✦140.00/160.00.
◆ Perched on the eponymous bay with magnificent views of Auchencairn Bay and Solway Firth. Comfortable, family run hotel. Bedrooms have bay or garden views. Restaurant decorated in keeping with the hotel's traditional style; window tables much in request.

⌂ **Balcary Mews** ♨ without rest., Balcary Bay, DG7 1QZ, Southwest : 2 m. on Balcary rd
℘ (01556) 640276, pamelavaughan@yahoo.com, Fax (01556) 640276, ≤ Balcary Bay and Solway Firth, 爫 – ⇔ 戋 **P**. ❀
February-November – **3 rm** ✦45.00/50.00 – ✦✦70.00/80.00.
◆ Well-priced, smuggler-built 18C property with lovely views. Warm welcome enhances overall homely feel, typified by comfy lounge overlooking pretty garden. Quality rooms.

> The ✿ award is the crème de la crème.
> This is awarded to restaurants
> which are really worth travelling miles for!

AUCHTERARDER Perth and Kinross **501** I 15 Scotland G. – pop. 3 945.
Env. : Tullibardine Chapel★ , NW : 2 m.
ⓘ Ochil Rd ℘ (01764) 662804 – ⓘ Dunning, Rollo Park ℘ (01764) 684747.
ⓘ 90 High St ℘ (01764) 663450 (closed half day Wednesday October-March), auchterar dertic@perthshire.co.uk.
Edinburgh 55 – Glasgow 45 – Perth 14.

🏰 **Gleneagles**, PH3 1NF, Southwest : 2 m. by A 824 on A 823 ℘ (01764) 662231, re sort.sales@gleneagles.com, Fax (01764) 662134, ≤, 斎, ☀, ㎘, 拏, 🏓, ㉮, ⓘ, ⅀, ⌲, 爫, ♪, ✎, squash – ▯, ⇔ rm, ✓ &, 拏 **P** – 🕍 360. **MO** **AE** **①** **VISA**
Strathearn : **Rest** (dinner only and Sunday lunch)/dinner 50.00 ⅀ – **The Club** : **Rest** a la carte 21.00/37.00 – (see also **Andrew Fairlie at Gleneagles** below) – **230 rm** � ✦285.00/430.00 – ✦✦395.00/500.00, 13 suites.
◆ World renowned hotel. Graceful Art Deco and country house décor within impressive grandeur of early 20C mansion. Championship golf courses and extensive leisure facilities. Strathearn is elegant Art Deco dining room. The Club offers informal dining.

🏨 **Coll Earn House**, PH3 1DF, ℘ (01764) 663553, reservations@collearnhousehotel.co.uk, Fax (01764) 662376, 爫 – ⇔ **P** – 🕍 50. **MO** **AE** **VISA**, ❀
closed 23 December-3 January – **Rest** a la carte 18.70/25.60 – **8 rm** � ✦85.00/95.00 – ✦✦130.00/140.00.
◆ Striking Victorian country house with large lawned gardens, just off town's main street. Bedrooms are capacious and well furnished with antique and reproduction furniture. The restaurant has a light ambience with plain walls with light wood half-panelling.

❀❀❀❀ **Andrew Fairlie at Gleneagles**, PH3 1NF, Southwest : 2 m. by A 824 on A 823
✿ ✿ ℘ (01764) 694267, andrew.fairlie@gleneagles.com, Fax (01764) 694163 – ▤ **P**. **MO** **AE** **①** **VISA**
closed 3 weeks January, 24-25 December and Sunday – **Rest** (dinner only) 65.00 ⅀.
Spec. Home-smoked lobster, lime and herb butter sauce. Assiette of pork. Raspberry soufflé, fromage blanc sorbet.
◆ Stylish dining room with a discreet, contemporary feel on the ground floor of this world renowned hotel. Accomplished modern style applied to excellent Scottish ingredients.

SCOTLAND

AVIEMORE *Highland 501 I 12 Scotland G. – pop. 2 397 –Winter sports.*

See : *Town★*.

Exc. : *The Cairngorms★★ (≤★★★) – ※★★★ from Cairn Gorm, SE : 11 m. by B 970 – Land-mark Visitor Centre (The Highlander★) AC, N : 7 m. by A 9 – Highland Wildlife Park★ AC, SW : 7 m. by A 9.*

🖪 *Grampian Rd ℰ (0845) 2255121, aviemoretic@host.co.uk.*

Edinburgh 129 – Inverness 29 – Perth 85.

🏠 **Corrour House** ⌂, *Inverdruie, PH22 1QH, Southeast : 1 m. on B 970 ℰ (01479) 810220, enquiries@corrourhouse.co.uk, Fax (01479) 811500, ≤, 🞮 – ⥱ P. ꣑ VISA*
closed mid November-30 December – **Rest** *(booking essential for non-residents) (dinner only) 28.50/31.50* **s.** *– 8 rm ☑ ★40.00/55.00 – ★★80.00/100.00.*

• Victorian dower house in charming setting surrounded by neat lawned garden. Rooms are comfortably furnished with reproduction furniture - those on top floor have best views. Good sized dining room with a slightly more modern feel than the rest of the house.

🛖 **The Old Minister's Guest House** *without rest., Rothiemurchus, PH22 1QH, South-east : 1 m. on B 970 ℰ (01479) 812181, kate@theoldministershouse.co.uk, Fax (0871) 661 9324, 🞮 – ⥱ P. ꣑ VISA.*
closed 25 December – 4 rm ☑ ★42.00/50.00 – ★★70.00/80.00.

• Early 20C house on outskirts of town, recently vacated by minister. River at bottom of pretty garden. Nicely-laid breakfast room. Spacious bedrooms, finished to high standard.

AYR *South Ayrshire 501 502 G 17 Scotland G. – pop. 46 431.*

Env. : *Alloway★ (Burns Cottage and Museum★ AC) S : 3 m. by B 7024 BZ.*

Exc. : *Culzean Castle★ AC (setting★★★, Oval Staircase★★) SW : 13 m. by A 719 BZ.*

🖪 *Belleisle, Belleisle Park, Doonfoot Rd ℰ (01292) 441258, BZ – 🖪 Dalmilling, Westwood Ave ℰ (01292) 263893, BZ – 🖪 Doon Valley, Hillside, Patna ℰ (01292) 531607, BZ.*

🖪 *22 Sandgate ℰ (01292) 288688.*

Edinburgh 81 – Glasgow 35.

Plan opposite

🏛 **Fairfield House**, *12 Fairfield Rd, KA7 2AS, ℰ (01292) 267461, manager@fairfieldho tel.co.uk, Fax (01292) 261456, Ib, ☎, ⬚ – ⥱ ℰ P. – 🔏 140. ꣑ AE ⓞ VISA. ⅍* **AY a**
Martins Bar & Grill : Rest a la carte 19.40/31.85 **s.** – **44 rm** ☑ ★69.00/149.00 – ★★99.00/169.00.

• Extended Victorian house on seafront, well equipped with leisure and function facilities. Newer bedrooms with a fitted modern feel and older rooms more traditional in tone. Popular favourites at Martin's Bar & Grill.

🏛 **Western House**, *Ayr Racecourse, 2 Craigie Rd, KA8 0HA, ℰ (0870) 0555510, info@west ernhousehotel.co.uk, Fax (0870) 0555515, 🞮 – 🕼 ⥱ ℰ & P. – 🔏 180. ꣑ AE VISA.*
⅍ **BZ a**
The Jockey Club : Rest (dinner only) a la carte 15.70/20.45 **s.** – **48 rm** ☑ ★80.00/140.00 – ★★80.00/140.00, 1 suite.

• Charm and luxury - all within 60 metres of Ayr racecourse! Stylish, 21C interior harmo-nises with 18C/19C period detail. Bedrooms offer a high degree of space and luxury. Smart restaurant offers traditional Scottish cuisine.

🛖 **No.26 The Crescent** *without rest., 26 Bellevue Crescent, KA7 2DR, ℰ (01292) 287329, carrie@26crescent.freeserve.co.uk, Fax (01292) 286779 – ⥱. ꣑ VISA. ⅍* **BZ c**
closed 3 weeks October, Christmas and New Year – 5 rm ☑ ★45.00 – ★★60.00/70.00.

• Located in a smart Victorian terrace in a quiet residential area. Tastefully and comfortably furnished and decorated throughout. Bedrooms finished to a high standard.

🛖 **Coila** *without rest., 10 Holmston Rd, KA7 3BB, ℰ (01292) 262642, hazel@coila.co.uk – ⥱ P. ꣑ VISA. ⅍* **AY u**
closed Christmas and New Year – 4 rm ☑ ★35.00/40.00 – ★★55.00/60.00.

• Friendly family home within walking distance of town centre. Simple, comfortably styled interior with golfing memorabilia. Good sized bedrooms, all with en suite facilities.

✗ **Fouters**, *2a Academy St, KA7 1HS, ℰ (01292) 261391, qualityfood@fouters.co.uk, Fax (01292) 619323 – ▤. ꣑ VISA* **AY e**
closed first 2 weeks January and Sunday-Monday – **Rest** a la carte 24.00/39.00 **s.**.

• Down a little alleyway is a modern entrance leading to the vaulted basements of this 18C building. Modern British cooking with good use of locally sourced ingredients.

at Alloway *South : 3 m. on B 7024 – BZ – ⌧ Ayr.*

🏛 **Brig O'Doon House**, *KA7 4PQ, ℰ (01292) 442466, brigodoon@costleyhotels.co.uk, Fax (01292) 441999, ⌖, 🞮 – ⥱ – 🔏 220. ꣑ AE VISA. ⅍*
Rest a la carte 17.15/31.15 ♈ – **5 rm** ☑ ★85.00 – ★★120.00.

• Attractive 19C inn in the pretty village where Robbie Burns was born. Cosy, warm atmos-phere amidst tartan and timbers. Atmospheric bedrooms with dark wood furnishings. Heavily timbered, open fired restaurant.

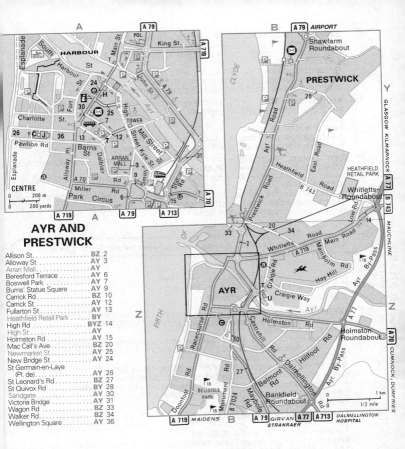

AYR AND PRESTWICK

at Dunfoot/Doonfoot Southwest : 2½ m. on A 719 – BZ – ⊠ Ayr.

⌂ **Greenan Lodge** without rest., 39 Dunure Rd, Doonfoot, KA7 4HR, on A 719 ℘ (01292) 443939, helen@greenanlodge.com – ⊁⊁ 🅿. ⊁
3 rm ⊾ ✦40.00/45.00 – ✦✦56.00/60.00.
♦ The birthplace of Robert Burns is just five minutes away from this personally run, homely guesthouse. Sitting room with open fire. Immaculately kept bedrooms.

BALLACHULISH Highland 501 E 13 Scotland G.
Exc. : Glen Coe★★, E : 6 m. by A 82.
🖪 Albert Rd ℘ (01855) 811866.
Edinburgh 117 – Inverness 80 – Kyle of Lochalsh 90 – Oban 38.

🏨 **Isles of Glencoe**, PH49 4HL, ℘ (0871) 2223417, reservations@swallowhotels.com, Fax (0871) 2223418, ≤ Loch Leven and the Pap of Glencoe, 🗗, 🖙, 🔲, 🐾, 🖭 – ⊁⊁ ᇰ ᚕ
🅿 – 🔬 40. 🕥 🟠 Æ 𝘝𝘐𝘚𝘈
Rest 20.00 (dinner) and a la carte 20.00/35.00 ⊻ – **59 rm** ⊾ ✦65.00/100.00 – ✦✦120.00/170.00.
♦ Family-friendly modern hotel in peninsular with fine views to Glencoe. Relax in extensive grounds. Spacious lounge and bar. Leisure facilities. Well-equipped rooms with views. Conservatory restaurant is a bistro by day and offers casual fine dining by night.

Ballachulish House ⌖, PH49 4JX, West : 2 ½ m. by A 82 off A 828 ☎ (01855) 811266, *mclaughlins@btconnect.com, Fax (01855) 811498*, ≤, ⌖, ⌖, –⌖ P. ⌖ AE VISA ⌖
Rest (booking essential for non-residents) 23.50/47.50 s. – **8 rm** ⌖ ✦80.00/147.00 –
✦✦221.00.

◆ Attractive, whitewashed, 17C former laird's house with colourful history that inspired Stevenson's "Kidnapped". Drawing room with honesty bar. Large rooms with loch views. The formal, draped dining room belies the tasty modern cooking on offer.

Ardno House without rest., Lettermore, Glencoe, PH49 4JD, West : 3 ½ m. by A 82 on A 828 ☎ (01855) 811830, *pam@ardnohouse.co.uk*, ≤ Loch Linnhe and Morven Hills, ⌖ –⌖ P. ⌖
3 rm ⌖ 50.00 – ✦✦60.00.

◆ Purpose-built guesthouse with fine view of Loch Linnhe and the Morven Hills. Personally run and providing good value, comfortable accommodation. Spacious bedrooms.

Lyn Leven, West Laroch, PH49 4JP, ☎ (01855) 811392, *macleodcilla@aol.com*, Fax (01855) 811600, ≤, ⌖ –⌖ P. ⌖ VISA ⌖
closed 25 December – **Rest** (by arrangement) 10.00 – **8 rm** ⌖ ✦30.00/35.00 –
✦✦50.00/64.00.

◆ Spacious bungalow with attractive gardens a mile from Glencoe overlooking Loch Leven. Comfortable lounge and rooms offering good standard of homely accommodation. Traditional dining room with panoramic views.

If breakfast is included the ⌖ symbol appears after the number of rooms.

BALLANTRAE South Ayrshire 501 502 E 18 – ⌖ Girvan.
Edinburgh 115 – Ayr 33 – Stranraer 18.

Glenapp Castle ⌖, KA26 0NZ, South : 1 m. by A 77 taking first right turn after bridge ☎ (01465) 831212, *enquiries@glenappcastle.com, Fax (01465) 831000*, ≤, ⌖, ⌖, ⌖, ⌖ –
⌖ –⌖ ⌖ P. ⌖ AE VISA
April-November and New Year – **Rest** (booking essential for non-residents) (set menu only) (light lunch)/dinner 55.00 ⌖ – **14 rm** (dinner included) ⌖ 255.00/275.00 –
✦✦375.00/475.00, 3 suites.
Spec. Roast scallops with cauliflower and pancetta. Fillet of beef with Anna potatoes, ceps, celeriac and red wine sauce. White and dark chocolate pavé with cherries.
◆ Stunning Victorian Baronial castle in extensive gardens and woodland. Grand sitting rooms with rich fabrics and fine antiques. Peaceful library. Luxuriously furnished rooms. Elaborate, refined dining.

Cosses Country House ⌖, KA26 0LR, East : 2 ¼ m. by A 77 (south) taking first turn left after bridge ☎ (01465) 831363, *booking@cossescountryhouse.com*, Fax (01465) 831598, ⌖, ⌖ –⌖ P. ⌖ VISA
Restricted opening in winter – **Rest** (by arrangement) (communal dining) 27.00/33.00 ⌖ –
3 rm ⌖ ✦55.00 – ✦✦80.00/95.00.
◆ Part 16C former shooting lodge with most agreeable rural ambience. Wood-floored hall and well-furnished country house style drawing room. Bedrooms of taste and quality. Own garden produce in elegant dining room.

BALLATER Aberdeenshire 501 K 12 – pop. 1 446.
⌖ Victoria Rd ☎ (013397) 55567.
⌖ The Old Royal Station ☎ (013397) 55306, ballater@agtb.org.
Edinburgh 111 – Aberdeen 41 – Inverness 70 – Perth 67.

Hilton Craigendarroch, Braemar Rd, AB35 5XA, on A 93 ☎ (013397) 55858, *reservations.craigendarroch@hilton.com, Fax (013397) 55447*, ≤ Dee Valley and Grampians, ⌖, ⌖, ⌖, ⌖, ⌖, ⌖, ⌖, squash – ⌖ –⌖ ⌖ P. – ⌖ 130. ⌖ AE ⌖ VISA ⌖
Oaks : Rest (dinner only) 27.95/32.95 s. ⌖ – **The Club House : Rest** (dinner only) a la carte 15.00/29.95 s. ⌖ – **40 rm** (dinner included) ⌖ 159.00 – ✦✦179.00/259.00, 5 suites.
◆ Substantial leisure based hotel in a wooded location. Extensive spa facilities. Comfortable bedrooms: some enhanced to notable degree with balconies. Formal Oaks restaurant with smart wood furnishing. Club House Grill is informal with a popular menu.

Darroch Learg, Braemar Rd, AB35 5UX, ☎ (013397) 55443, *info@darrochlearg.co.uk*, Fax (013397) 55252, ≤ Dee Valley and Grampians, ⌖, ⌖ –⌖ P. ⌖ AE ⌖ VISA
closed last 3 weeks January and Christmas – **Rest** – (see **The Conservatory** below) – **17 rm** (dinner included) ⌖ ✦85.00/125.00 – ✦✦170.00/250.00.
◆ Country house hotel: enjoy superb views from its elevated position. Plush lounges with soft suites, open fires and antiques. Enticing bedrooms: upper floors have best outlook.

🏠 **Balgonie Country House** ⚐, Braemar Pl, AB35 5NQ, West : ½ m. by A 93 ℰ (013397) 55482, *balgoniech@aol.com, Fax* (013397) 55497, ≼, ℱ – ⇝ **P**. **M③** **AE** **VISA**. ℅
closed 6 January-March – **Rest** (booking essential for non-residents) (lunch by arrangement)/dinner 37.50/45.00 – **9 rm** ⊇ ✵60.00/80.00 – ✵✵100.00/160.00.
◆ Personally run, peaceful Edwardian style country house with relaxed atmosphere in mature gardens with fine hill views. Individually furnished bedrooms boast admirable outlook. Restaurant renowned for its use of fine Scottish produce and accomplished cooking.

⌂ **Moorside House** without rest., 26 Braemar Rd, AB35 5RL, ℰ (013397) 55492, *info@moorsidehouse.co.uk, Fax* (013397) 55492, ℱ – ⇝ **P**. **M③** **VISA**. ℅
April-October – **9 rm** ⊇ ✵45.00 – ✵✵60.00.
◆ Detached Victorian pink stone guesthouse on main road just outside town centre. Neat garden. Vividly coloured breakfast room. Sizeable, well-furnished rooms.

⌂ **Morvada House** without rest., 28 Braemar Rd, AB35 5RL, ℰ (013397) 56334, *mor vada@aol.com, Fax* (013397) 56092 – ⇝ **P**. **M③** **VISA**. ℅
5 rm ⊇ ✵35.00 – ✵✵60.00.
◆ Attractive stone built house. Personally run. Notable for its collection of Russel Flint pictures. Immaculately kept, individually decorated rooms, some with mountain views.

XX **The Conservatory** (at Darroch Learg H.), Braemar Rd, AB35 5UX, ℰ (013397) 55443, *info@darrochlearg.co.uk, Fax* (013397) 55252, ≼, ℱ – **P**. **M③** **AE** **①** **VISA**
closed Christmas and last 3 weeks January – **Rest** (dinner only and Sunday lunch) 40.00/48.00 **s**. ℤ ⌖.
◆ Attractive conservatory restaurant with a fine view from its garden location: comfortable dining enhanced by attentive service. Notably impressive wine list.

XX **The Green Inn** with rm, 9 Victoria Rd, AB35 5QQ, ℰ (013397) 55701, *info@green-inn.com* – **M③** **AE** **VISA**
closed 2 weeks late January, 25 December, Sunday and Monday – **Rest** (dinner only) 29.50/35.00 ℤ – ⊇ 8.00 – **3 rm** ✵35.00/40.00 – ✵✵50.00/60.00.
◆ Former temperance hall, opposite the green, boasting comfy lounges and pleasant conservatory. Interesting, well sourced and accomplished modern British cooking. Cosy rooms.

BALLOCH West Dunbartonshire **501** G 15 *Scotland G.* – ✉ *Alexandria*.
Env. : N : *Loch Lomond*★★.
🛈 *The Old Station Building, Balloch Rd ℰ* (08707) 200607 (April-October), *info@balloch.vis itscotland.com.*
Edinburgh 72 – Glasgow 20 – Stirling 30.

🏨 **De Vere Cameron House** ⚐, Loch Lomond, G83 8QZ, Northwest : 1 ½ m. by A 811 on A 82 ℰ (01389) 755565, *reservations@cameronhouse.co.uk, Fax* (01389) 759522, ≼ Loch Lomond, ②, ⅃♨, ⓢ, ⊠, ▮⅋, ⚲, ℱ, 凪, ✼, squash – ▯ ⅃ ⇝, ▤ rest, ⚘ ♿ ♣♣ **P** – 🚗 300. **M③** **AE** **①** **VISA**. ℅
Smolletts : **Rest** (dinner only) 29.50 and a la carte 25.85/40.85 **s**. ℤ – *Marina :* **Rest** - Mediterranean - a la carte 18.15/36.85 **s**. ℤ – (see also *Georgian Room* below) – **89 rm** ⊇ ✵99.00/149.00 – ✵✵129.00/199.00, 7 suites.
◆ Extensive Victorian house superbly situated on shores of Loch Lomond. Impressive leisure facilities. Luxurious rooms with four posters and panoramic views. Stylish Smolletts with superb views. Delightfully set Marina for Mediterranean cuisine.

XXXX **Georgian Room** (at De Vere Cameron House H.), Loch Lomond, G83 8QZ, Northwest : 1 ½ m. by A 811 on A 82 ℰ (01389) 755565, *reservations@cameronhouse.co.uk, Fax* (01389) 759522, ≼ Loch Lomond, ℱ – ⅃ **P**. **M③** **AE** **①** **VISA**
closed Monday-Tuesday – **Rest** (booking essential) (dinner only and Sunday lunch) 49.00/59.50 **s**.
◆ Elegant refurbishment guarantees a refined and formal dining experience that utilises notably fine ingredients in a well-executed, precisely prepared style.

BALLYGRANT Argyll and Bute **501** B 16 – *see Islay (Isle of).*

BALMEDIE Aberdeenshire **501** N 12.
Edinburgh 137 – Aberdeen 7.5 – Peterhead 24.

🍴 **Cock and Bull,** Ellon Rd, Blairton, AB23 8XY, North : 1 m. on A 90 ℰ (01358) 743249, *Fax* (01358) 742466, 佘 – **P**. **M③** **VISA**. ℅
Rest a la carte 18.00/28.00 ℤ.
◆ Whitewashed 19C pub and conservatory with North Sea views. Bar and restaurant have bags of atmosphere, courtesy of characterful artefacts. Hearty dishes cover wide range.

BALTASOUND Shetland Islands **501** R 1 – *see Shetland Islands (Island of Unst).*

BANAVIE Highland **501** E 13 – see Fort William.

BANCHORY Aberdeenshire **501** M 12 Scotland G. – pop. 6 034.

Env. : Crathes Castle★★ (Gardens★★★) AC, E : 3 m. by A 93 – Cairn o'Mount Road★ (≤★★), S : by B 974.

Exc. : Dunnottar Castle★★ (site★★★) AC, SW : 15½ m. by A 93 and A 957 – Aberdeen★★, NE : 17 m. by A 93.

🅸🆂 Kinneskie 🖉 (01330) 822365 – 🅸🆂 Torphins 🖉 (013398) 82115.

🅱 Bridge St 🖉 (01330) 822000 (Easter-October).

Edinburgh 118 – Aberdeen 17 – Dundee 55 – Inverness 94.

Raemoir House ⮥, AB31 4ED, North : 2½ m. on A 980 🖉 (01330) 824884, relax@raemoir.com, Fax (01330) 822171, ≤, 🐴, 🍷, ☆ – ⇆ 🛎 🅿 – 🔬 50. 🐵 🅰🅴 🟠 𝗩𝗜𝗦𝗔
closed 25-29 December – **Rest** 34.00/38.00 ⊈ – **20 rm** ⬜ ★70.00/90.00 – ★★140.00/145.00.
♦ Enviably located 18C Highland mansion with 17C "ha-hoose" (hall house) as popular alternative to main house. Country house ambience: antiques abound. Very comfortable rooms. The "Oval" dining room luxuriates with Victorian tapestry walls.

Banchory Lodge ⮥, Dee St, AB31 5HS, 🖉 (01330) 822625, enquiries@banchorylodge.co.uk, Fax (01330) 825019, ≤, 🐟, 🐴 – ⇆ 🅿 – 🔬 30. 🐵 𝗩𝗜𝗦𝗔
Rest (bar lunch)/dinner 28.50 a la carte 15.95/29.25 s. – **22 rm** ⬜ ★75.00/85.00 – ★★150.00.
♦ Part 16C former coaching inn delightfully situated on River Dee. Country house style accentuated by antiques and china. Individually decorated bedrooms. Dee views and floral displays enhance the attraction of the dining room.

The Old West Manse without rest., 71 Station Rd, AB31 5YD, on A 93 🖉 (01330) 822202, westmanse@btinternet.com, Fax (01330) 822202, 🐴 – ⇆ 🅿. 🐵 𝗩𝗜𝗦𝗔
3 rm ⬜ ★40.00 – ★★60.00.
♦ Immaculately distinctive guesthouse just outside village. Bright yellow exterior, lovely gardens and homely lounge with warm décor. Spotlessly kept, bright bedrooms.

BANFF Aberdeenshire **501** M 10 Scotland G. – pop. 3 991.

See : Town★ – Duff House★★ (baroque exterior★) AC – Mercat Cross★.

🅸🆂 Royal Tarlair, Buchan St, Macduff 🖉 (01261) 832897 – 🅸🆂 Duff House Royal, The Barnyards 🖉 (01261) 812062.

🅱 Collie Lodge 🖉 (01261) 812419 (Easter-October).

Edinburgh 177 – Aberdeen 47 – Fraserburgh 26 – Inverness 74.

The Orchard ⮥ without rest., Duff House, AB45 3TA, by Duff House rd and Wrack Wood rd 🖉 (01261) 812146, orchardbanff@aol.com, Fax (01261) 812146, 🐴 – ⇆ 🅿. ☆
5 rm ⬜ ★30.00/40.00 – ★★60.00.
♦ Good value, purpose-built guesthouse in tranquil, wooded location in grounds of Duff House Gallery and Country House. Cosy lounge and breakfast room. Simple, spotless rooms.

BARCALDINE Argyll and Bute **501** E 14 – ✉ Oban.

Edinburgh 128 – Dundee 122 – Glasgow 105 – Inverness 103 – Oban 13.

Barcaldine House ⮥ without rest., PA37 1SG, 🖉 (01631) 720219, enquiries@barcaldinehouse.co.uk, 🐴 – ⇆ 🅿. 🐵 𝗩𝗜𝗦𝗔. ☆
8 rm ⬜ ★75.00/85.00 – ★★96.00/130.00.
♦ Fine 18C country house in quiet location. Communal areas include two spacious lounges, one in Louis XVI-style, and a billiard room. Comfortable, traditional bedrooms.

BARRA (Isle of) Western Isles **501** X 12/13 – ✉ Castlebay.

Castlebay Western Isles.

Castlebay, HS9 5XD, 🖉 (01871) 810223, bookings@castlebayhotel.com, Fax (01871) 810455, ≤ Kisimul Castle and Island of Vatersay – ⇆ 🅿. 🐵 𝗩𝗜𝗦𝗔
closed Christmas-February – **Rest** (bar lunch) a la carte 15.35/27.95 s. – **10 rm** ⬜ ★50.00/95.00 – ★★85.00/95.00.
♦ Personally run, early 20C hotel situated in prominent position overlooking Kisimul Castle and Isle of Vatersay. Cosy sitting room and spacious bar. Homely, well-kept rooms. Linen-clad dining room with excellent bay view and traditional fare.

⌂ **Grianamul** without rest., HS9 5XD, ℰ (01871) 810416, *macneilronnie@aol.com*, Fax (01871) 810319, ≤, ⛭ – ⇥ 🅿, 🆖 𝘝𝘐𝘚𝘈, ⅏
3 rm ⧄ ✦40.00/50.00 – ✦✦56.00.
♦ Purpose-built guesthouse, convenient for local amenities; adjacent to heritage centre. Comfortable, homely lounge. Very sunny breakfast room. Sizeable, well-kept rooms.

North Bay *Western Isles.*

🏠 **Heathbank,** HS9 5YQ, ℰ (01871) 890266, *info@barrahotel.co.uk*, Fax (01871) 890266, ≤, 🏠, ⛭ – ⇥ 🅿, 🆖 𝘝𝘐𝘚𝘈, ⅏
Rest (booking essential in winter) (bar lunch) a la carte 9.80/26.30 s. – 5 rm ⧄ ✦48.00/80.00 – ✦✦76.00/84.00.
♦ Former 19C schoolhouse on a quiet road. Relax in ample space, including a terrace to admire the landscape. Airy bedrooms, in light lemon hues with DVDs, are the strong point. Home-cooked menus in bar and intimate dining room.

BATHGATE *West Lothian* 501 J 16 – pop. 15 068.
Edinburgh 24 – Dundee 62 – Glasgow 29 – Perth 50.

🏠 **Express by Holiday Inn** without rest., Starlaw Rd, EH48 1LQ, ℰ (01506) 650650, Fax (01506) 650651 – 📶 ⇥ ⅖ 🅿 – 🔬 20, 🆖 𝔸𝔼 ⓞ 𝘝𝘐𝘚𝘈, ⅏
74 rm ✦59.95 – ✦✦59.95.
♦ Purpose-built corporate hotel close to motorway junction providing good standard of accommodation at fair price. Open plan breakfast-cum-bar area. Sizeable, modern rooms.

The red 🐦 symbol?
This denotes the very essence of peace
– only the sound of birdsong first thing in the morning …

SCOTLAND

BEAULY *Highland* 501 G 11 – pop. 1 164.
Edinburgh 169 – Inverness 13 – Wick 125.

🏨 **Lovat Arms,** High St, IV4 7BS, ℰ (01463) 782313, *info@lovatarms.com*, Fax (01463) 782862 – ⇥ 🅿 – 🔬 60, 🆖 𝘝𝘐𝘚𝘈
Rest (bar lunch Monday-Saturday) a la carte 16.20/27.25 – 28 rm ⧄ ✦35.00/60.00 – ✦✦50.00/90.00.
♦ Stylish, family owned hotel in village centre with distinctive Scottish feel: full tartan décor abounds. Spacious sitting room, busy bar. Smart rooms with clan influence. All-enveloping tartan curtains dominate warmly hued dining room.

BELLANOCH *Argyll and Bute* 501 D 15 *Scotland G.*
Env. : *Crinan★, W : 2 m. by B 841.*
Exc. : *Auchindrain Township Open Air Museum★, E : 25 m. by B 841 and A 83.*
Edinburgh 134 – Arduaine 16 – Oban 34.

⌂ **Bellanoch House,** Bellanoch Bay, Crinan Canal, PA31 8SN, ℰ (01546) 830149, *stay@bellanochhouse.co.uk*, ≤, ⛭ – ⚡ ⇥ ⅖ 🅿, ⅏
Rest (by arrangement) 30.00 – 4 rm ⧄ ✦55.00 – ✦✦90.00.
♦ Former church and school-house with gardens. Stylish lounge boasts stone fireplace from Italy. Owners' family paintings on walls. Airy rooms; front two with good views. Home-cooked food served in dining area.

BENDERLOCH *Argyll and Bute* 501 D 14 – *see Connel.*

BISHOPTON *Renfrewshire* 501 G 16.
Edinburgh 59 – Dumbarton 9 – Glasgow 13.

🏰 **Mar Hall** 🐦, Earl of Mar Estate, PA7 5NW, Northeast : 1 m. on B 815 ℰ (0141) 812 9999, *info@marhall.com*, Fax (0141) 812 9997, ≤, ⚕, 🛁, ⛷, 🏊, 🎾, ⛭, 🞰 – 📶 ⇥ 🐕 ⅖ 🅿 – 🔬 120, 🆖 𝔸𝔼 𝘝𝘐𝘚𝘈, ⅏
closed 2-4 January **Cristal :** Rest (dinner only and Sunday lunch) a la carte 23.00/38.00 ℗ – ⧄ 15.50 – 50 rm ✦135.00/150.00 – ✦✦150.00/190.00, 3 suites.
♦ Impressive Gothic mansion, overlooking Clyde and Kilpatrick Hills. Excellent leisure club incorporating Asian influenced spa. Period and contemporary mix to bedrooms. Formal fine dining in The Cristal.

BLAIR ATHOLL *Perth and Kinross* 501 I 13.

⌐₉ *Blair Atholl, Invertilt Rd ℰ (01796) 481407.*
Edinburgh 79 – Inverness 83 – Perth 35.

XX **The Loft,** Golf Course Rd, PH18 5TE, ℰ (01796) 481377, *daniel@theloftrestaurant.co.uk,*
Fax (01796) 481511 – 🗐 **P**. **AO** **VISA**
closed 8 January-8 February – **Rest** (dinner only Thursday-Saturday and Sunday lunch) a la
carte 22.50/28.00 ♀.
◆ Modern restaurant set on first floor of former hayloft, with beamed ceilings in situ.
Bright décor; lots of natural light. Good value, freshly prepared modern menus.

BLAIRGOWRIE *Perth and Kinross* 501 J 14 *Scotland G. – pop. 7 965.*

Exc. : *Scone Palace★★ AC, S : 12 m. by A 93.*
🗓 *26 Wellmeadow ℰ (01250) 872960, blairgowrietic@perthshire.co.uk.*
Edinburgh 60 – Dundee 19 – Perth 16.

🏛 **Kinloch House** ♨, PH10 6SG, West : 3 m. on A 923 ℰ (01250) 884237, *reception@kin*
lochhouse.com, Fax (01250) 884333, ≤, **I₅**, **⩧**, **▨**, **☞**, **⌖** – **⁒** **P**. **AO** **AE** **VISA**. **⋇**
closed 2 weeks Christmas – **Rest** 30.00/50.00 ♀ – **17 rm** ⊇ ✦100.00/250.00 –
✦✦250.00/310.00, 1 suite.
◆ Wonderfully tranquil, ivy-clad 19C country house set in its own grounds. Appealingly
traditional lounges. Conservatory and leisure centre. Large, smart, well-furnished rooms.
Restaurant with bright yellow décor and Scottish influenced cooking.

⌂ **Heathpark House** without rest., Coupar Angus Rd, Rosemount, PH10 6JT, Southeast :
¾ m. on A 923 ℰ (01250) 870700, *lori@forsyth12.freeserve.co.uk, Fax (01250) 870700,* **☞**
– **⁒** **P**. **AO** **VISA**. **⋇**
closed 25-26 December – **3 rm** ⊇ ✦40.00 – ✦✦70.00.
◆ Substantial Victorian guesthouse in a quiet residential spot with mature gardens. Spacious lounge; breakfasts taken in welcoming dining room. Large, individually styled rooms.

⌂ **Gilmore House** without rest., Perth Rd, PH10 6EJ, Southwest : ½ m. on A 93 ℰ (01250)
872791, *jill@gilmorehouse.co.uk, Fax (01250) 872791* – **⁒** **P**. **⋇**
closed 24-26 December – **3 rm** ⊇ ✦25.00/50.00 – ✦✦45.00/50.00.
◆ Traditional stone-built guesthouse only a few minutes' walk from town, keenly run by
owners. Comfortable front lounge and breakfast room. Cosy bedrooms with tartan flourishes.

⌂ **Laurels,** Golf Course Rd, PH10 6LH, Southwest : 1 ¼ m. on A 93 ℰ (01250) 874920,
laurel-blairgowrie@talk21.com, Fax (01250) 874920, **☞** – **⁒** **P**. **AO** **VISA**. **⋇**
closed mid November-mid January – **Rest** (by arrangement) 13.50 – **6 rm** ⊇ ✦22.00/30.00 –
✦✦44.00/46.00.
◆ Stone built extended cottage just out of town centre and useful base for touring Perthshire. Comfortable, homely lounge with soft velvet suites. Simple, spotless rooms.

BOAT OF GARTEN *Highland* 501 I 12.

⌐₈ *Boat of Garten ℰ (01479) 831282.*
Edinburgh 133 – Inverness 28 – Perth 89.

🏨 **The Boat,** PH24 3BH, ℰ (01479) 831258, *info@boathotel.co.uk, Fax (01479) 831414,* **☞**
– **⁒** **⫞** **P**. – **⩘** 30. **AO** **VISA**
closed last 3 weeks January – **Capercaillie :** **Rest** (dinner only) 34.50 s. – **The Osprey Bar :**
Rest a la carte 20.85/27.50 – **24 rm** ⊇ ✦64.50/84.50 – ✦✦100.00/185.00, 1 suite.
◆ An evocative hiss of steam from adjacent Strathspey railway line adds character to this
19C hotel, run by keen, friendly young team. Pleasant traditional or modern rooms.. Busy
Osprey bar/bistro overlooks the trains.

BONNYRIGG *Lothian* 501 K 16.

Edinburgh 8 – Galashiels 27 – Glasgow 50.

🏛 **Dalhousie Castle** ♨, EH19 3JB, Southeast : 1 ¼ m. on B 704 ℰ (01875) 820153,
dalhousiecastle.co.uk, Fax (01875) 821936, ≤, **⊘**, **⩧**, **⬟**, **☞**, **⌖** – **⁒** **P** – **⩘** 120.
AO **AE** **①** **VISA**
Dungeon : **Rest** (booking essential for non-residents) (dinner only) 38.00 – **The Or-**
angery : **Rest** a la carte 22.15/29.20 – **36 rm** ⊇ ✦150.00/160.00 – ✦✦195.00/220.00.
◆ 13C castle in woodland on the South Esk. Period-style furnishing in the spacious rooms,
eclipsed by the library's 19C panelling and rococo ceiling. Falconry centre in grounds.
Classic menus in characterful Dungeon. Orangery overlooks river and parkland.

BORGIE *Highland 501* H 8.
Edinburgh 262 – Inverness 93 – Thurso 31.

🏨 **Borgie Lodge** 🦌, KW14 7TH, ℰ (01641) 521332, *info@borgielodgehotel.co.uk*, Fax (01641) 521889, ≼, 🦐, 🚗 – ⚡ P. **◑◐** **VISA**
closed 25 December – **Rest** *(closed Monday lunch)* (bar lunch)/dinner 32.00 s. ⵚ – **8 rm** ⵣ ✝50.00/65.00 – ✝✝80.00/95.00.
◆ Small, detached hotel in peaceful Highland setting. Simple "locals" bar and residents lounge with coal fire and deep sofas. Rooms with characterful older style furnishings. Cosy dining room.

BOWMORE *Argyll and Bute 501* B 16 – *see Islay (Isle of).*

BRAE *Shetland Islands 501* P 2 – *see Shetland Islands (Mainland).*

BRAEMAR *Aberdeenshire 501* J 12 *Scotland G.*
Env. : *Lin O'Dee*★, W : 5 m.
🛝 *Cluniebank Rd* ℰ (013397) 41618.
🛈 *The Mews, Mar Rd* ℰ (013397) 41600.
Edinburgh 85 – Aberdeen 58 – Dundee 51 – Perth 51.

⌂ **Callater Lodge** without rest., 9 Glenshee Rd, AB35 5YQ, ℰ (013397) 41275, *hamp sons@hotel-braemar.co.uk*, Fax (013397) 41345, 🚗 – ⚡ P. **◑◐** **VISA**. 🛇
closed November-December – **6 rm** ⵣ ✝32.00/50.00 – ✝✝60.00/60.00.
◆ Stone house in large garden on the road to Glenshee. Lounge with leather chairs and library with inglenook. Pleasant spacious bedrooms, some with view across the valley.

BREASCLETE *Western Isles (Outer Hebrides) 501* Z 9 – *see Lewis and Harris (Isle of).*

BRIDGEND OF LINTRATHEN *Angus 501* K 13 – ✉ *Kirriemuir.*
Edinburgh 70 – Dundee 20 – Pitlochry 37.

✗✗ **Lochside Lodge and Roundhouse Restaurant** with rm, DD8 5JJ, ℰ (01575) 560340, *enquiries@lochsidelodge.com*, Fax (01575) 560251, 🦐 – P. **◑◐** **VISA**. 🛇
closed 1-21 January and 25-26 December – **Rest** *(closed Sunday dinner and Monday)* a la carte 16.00/32.00 – **6 rm** ⵣ ✝45.00/85.00 – ✝✝45.00/65.00.
◆ Converted farmstead in tiny hamlet at gateway to Angus Glens by Loch Lintrathen. Elaborate modern cooking in former grain grinding room. Comfy rooms in hayloft conversion.

BROADFORD *Highland 501* C 12 – *see Skye (Isle of).*

BRODICK *North Ayrshire 501 502* E 17 – *see Arran (Isle of).*

BRORA *Highland 501* I 9 – *pop. 1 140.*
🛝 *Golf Rd* ℰ (01408) 621417.
Edinburgh 234 – Inverness 78 – Wick 49.

🏨🏨 **Royal Marine**, Golf Rd, KW9 6QS, ℰ (01408) 621252, *info@highlandescape.com*, Fax (01408) 621181, 👗, ≋s, 🏊, 🦐, 🚗 – ⚡ ✆ ⅙ P. – ⚖ 70. **◑◐** **AE** **◐** **VISA**
Rest a la carte 16.00/30.00 s. ⵚ – **22 rm** ⵣ ✝79.00/99.00 – ✝✝120.00.
◆ Originally a laird's home. Traditional lounge with log fire. Good leisure facilities plus snooker room and unlimited golf. Spacious bedrooms with antique furnishings. Cuisine reflects Highland location.

⌂ **Glenaveron** without rest., Golf Rd, KW9 6QS, ℰ (01408) 621601, *glenaveron@hot mail.com*, 🚗 – ⚡ ⅙ P. **◑◐** **VISA**. 🛇
closed 2 weeks mid October, Christmas and New Year – **3 rm** ⵣ ✝45.00/55.00 – ✝✝60.00/66.00.
◆ Agreeable looking, detached, stone guesthouse with gardens. Spick and span lounge. Pleasant communal breakfast room. Very spacious rooms with superior pine furnishings.

BROUGHTY FERRY *Dundee City 501* L 14 – *see Dundee.*

BUNCHREW *Highland* – *see Inverness.*

BUNESSAN *Argyll and Bute 501* B 15 – *see Mull (Isle of).*

BURRAY *Orkney Islands 501* L 7 – *see Orkney Islands.*

BUTE (Isle of) *Argyll and Bute 501 502* E 16 – *pop. 7 354.*
🚢 from Rothesay to Wemyss Bay (Mainland) (Caledonian MacBrayne Ltd) *frequent services daily (35 mn)* – from Rhubodach to Colintraive (Mainland) (Caledonian MacBrayne Ltd) *frequent services daily (5 mn).*

Ascog *Argyll and Bute.*

⌂ **Balmory Hall** ⚭ without rest., Balmory Rd, PA20 9LL, ℘ (01700) 500669, *enquiries@balmoryhall.com*, Fax (01700) 500669, ≤, 🞀, 🖭 – 🞀 🄿, 🅬🅭 *VISA*. 🞀
closed February-November – **3 rm** ⌷ ✦80.00 – ✦✦160.00.
◆ Impressive, carefully restored mid 19C Italianate mansion. Columned hall and well-furnished lounge. Tastefully furnished bedrooms. Breakfast at an antique table.

Rothesay *Argyll and Bute.*

🛈 Canada Hill ℘ (01700) 503554 – 🛈 Sithean, Academy Rd ℘ (01700) 504369 – 🛈 Port Bannatyne, Bannatyne Mains Rd ℘ (01700) 504544.
🅱 Isle of Bute Discovery Centre, Winter Garden ℘ (08707) 200619, *info@rothesay.visitscotland.com.*

🏨 **Cannon House,** 5 Battery Pl, PA20 9DP, ℘ (01700) 502819, *cannon.house@btinternet.com*, Fax (01700) 505725, ≤, 🞀 – 🞀 🄿, 🅬🅭 *VISA*. 🞀
Restricted opening in winter – **Rest** (booking essential for non-residents) (dinner only) a la carte 14.45/22.20 – **7 rm** ⌷ ✦42.50/45.00 – ✦✦95.00/100.00.
◆ Attractive late Georgian house on Rothesay promenade with panoramic view of bay and harbour. Furnished in keeping with house's age. Individually styled rooms. Elegant, clean-lined dining room with daily changing menu of Scottish based dishes.

CADBOLL *Highland – see Tain.*

CAIRNBAAN *Argyll and Bute 501* D 15 – *see Lochgilphead.*

CALLANDER *Stirling 501* H 15 *Scotland G. – pop. 2 754.*
See : *Town★.*
Exc. : *The Trossachs★★★ (Loch Katrine★★) – Hilltop Viewpoint★★★ (❄★★★) W : 10 m. by A 821.*
🛈 Aveland Rd ℘ (01877) 330090.
🅱 Rob Roy & Trossachs Visitor Centre, Ancaster Sq ℘ (08707) 200628, *robroyandt@eillst.ossian.net.*
Edinburgh 52 – Glasgow 43 – Oban 71 – Perth 41.

🏨 **Roman Camp** ⚭, Main St, FK17 8BG, ℘ (01877) 330003, *mail@romancamphotel.co.uk*, Fax (01877) 331533, ≤, 🞀, 🞀, 🖭 – 🞀 🄿, 🅬🅭 🄰🄴 🅪 *VISA*
Rest – (see **The Restaurant** below) – **10 rm** ⌷ ✦75.00/125.00 – ✦✦165.00/185.00, 4 suites.
◆ Part 17C hunting lodge in extensive gardens. Replete with antiques and fine objets d'art. Public rooms include a hidden chapel. Comfortable, country house-style bedrooms.

🏨 **Lubnaig** without rest., Leny Feus, FK17 8AS, ℘ (01877) 330376, *info@lubnaighouse.co.uk*, Fax (01877) 330376, 🞀 – 🞀 🄿, 🅬🅭 *VISA*. 🞀
May-October – **8 rm** ⌷ ✦45.00/55.00 – ✦✦60.00/78.00.
◆ Built in 1864, a characterful Victorian house on the outskirts of town. Well-kept mature gardens visible from communal rooms. Homely bedrooms, two in converted stables.

⌂ **Dunmor House** without rest., Leny Rd, FK17 8AL, ℘ (01877) 330756, *reservations@dunmorhouse.co.uk* – 🞀 🄿.
closed 18 December-7 January – **4 rm** ⌷ ✦40.00 – ✦✦60.00.
◆ Large Victorian house conveniently situated on Callander's high street. Good sized sitting room and bedrooms. Decorated in comfortable, homely style throughout.

⌂ **Brook Linn** ⚭ without rest., Leny Feus, FK17 8AU, ℘ (01877) 330103, *derek@blinn.freeserve.co.uk*, Fax (01877) 330103, ≤, 🞀 – 🞀 🄿, 🅬🅭 *VISA*
Easter-mid October – **6 rm** ⌷ ✦25.00/28.00 – ✦✦60.00/70.00.
◆ Victorian house in a fairly secluded rural location. Homely style lounge and wood furnished dining room for breakfast. Traditional, well-kept bedrooms.

XXX **The Restaurant** (at Roman Camp H.), Main St, FK19 8BG, ℘ (01877) 330003, mail@ro mancamphotel.co.uk, Fax (01877) 331533 – **P**. **MC** **AE** **①** **VISA**
Rest 28.00/46.00 and dinner a la carte 40.50/59.50 ⬆.
* Crisp linen covered tables with simple, elegant place settings in vibrant modern room. Attentive staff serve carefully and skilfully prepared modern Scottish cuisine.

CAMPBELTOWN Argyll and Bute **501** D 17 – see Kintyre (Peninsula).

CARDROSS Argyll and Bute **501** G 16 Scotland G.
Env. : The Clyde Estuary★.
Edinburgh 63 – Glasgow 17 – Helensburgh 5.

⌂ **Kirkton House** ⌂ without rest., Darleith Rd, G82 5EZ, ℘ (01389) 841951, mich@kirk tonhouse.co.uk, Fax (01389) 841868, ≤, ☞ – 🔲 **P**. **MC** **AE** **①** **VISA**
closed December-January – **6 rm** ⬜ ✲40.00 – ✲✲60.00.
* Former farmhouse with origins in 18C; quiet, elevated spot overlooking North Clyde. Ideal stop-off between Glasgow airport and Highlands. Bedrooms all have country views.

CARINISH Western Isles **501** Y 11 – see Uist (Isles of).

CARNOUSTIE Angus **501** L 14 – pop. 10 561.
🏌, 🏌 Monifieth Golf Links, Medal Starter's Box, Princes St, Monifieth ℘ (01382) 532767 – 🏌 Burnside, Links Par ℘ (01241) 855344 – 🏌 Panmure, Barry ℘ (01241) 855120 – 🏌 Buddon Links, Links Par ℘ (01241) 853249.
🅱 1B High St ℘ (01241) 852258 (Easter-September).
Edinburgh 68 – Aberdeen 59 – Dundee 12.

⌂ **The Old Manor** ⌂ without rest., Panbride, DD7 6JP, Northeast : 1 ¼ m. by A 930 on Panbride Rd ℘ (01241) 854804, stay@oldmanorcarnoustie.com, Fax (01241) 855327, ≤, ☞ – ✲✲ **P**. **MC** **VISA**. ⌖
closed 13-23 July – **5 rm** ⬜ ✲50.00 – ✲✲70.00.
* Substantial 18C house five minutes' drive from championship golf course. Good views of Tay Estuary. Hearty Scottish breakfast guaranteed. Smart rooms, some with brass beds.

XX **11 Park Avenue**, 11 Park Ave, DD7 7JA, ℘ (01241) 853336 – **P**. **MC** **AE** **VISA**
closed Monday, lunch Tuesday, Wednesday and Sunday – **Rest** a la carte 25.30/36.20 **s.**.
* A former Masonic hall tucked away off the High Street. Comfortable, traditional surroundings and accomplished modern cooking from classic Scottish ingredients.

CARRADALE Argyll and Bute **501** D 17 – see Kintyre Peninsula.

CASTLEBAY Western Isles **501** X 12/13 – see Barra (Isle of).

CASTLE DOUGLAS Dumfries and Galloway **501** **502** I 19 Scotland G. – pop. 3 671.
Env. : Threave Garden★★ AC, SW : 2½ m. by A 75 – Threave Castle★ AC, W : 1 m.
🏌 Abercromby Rd ℘ (01556) 502801.
🅱 Market Hill ℘ (01556) 502611 (Easter-October).
Edinburgh 98 – Ayr 49 – Dumfries 18 – Stranraer 57.

⌂ **Douglas House**, 63 Queen St, DG7 1HS, ℘ (01556) 503262, info@douglas-house.com – ✲✲ ⌖. **MC** **VISA**. ⌖
Rest (by arrangement) (communal dining) – **4 rm** ⬜ ✲27.00/50.00 – ✲✲75.00.
* Attractive stone built house (1880) with some original features near the high street. Communal breakfast table in guest lounge. Comfortable individually decorated bedrooms. Home cooked evening meals served round communal table.

⌂ **Smithy House** without rest., The Buchan, DG7 1TH, Southwest : ¾ on A 75 (Stranraer rd) ℘ (01556) 503841, enquiries@smithyhouse.co.uk, ☞ – ✲✲ **P**. **MC** **VISA**. ⌖
3 rm ⬜ ✲55.00/65.00 – ✲✲65.00/75.00.
* Converted 14C smithy in large garden 10 minutes walk from town. Communal breakfast table. Guests' lounge featuring original forge. Pleasant bedrooms facing garden or loch.

at Kirkpatrick Durham Northeast : 5½ m. by A 75 and B 794 – ⌧ Castle Douglas.

⌂ **Chipperkyle** ⌂ without rest., DG7 3EY, ℘ (01556) 650223, Fax (01556) 650223, ☞, 🐾, ⌖ – ✲✲ **P**. **MC** **VISA**. ⌖
closed 15 December - 28 January – **3 rm** ⬜ ✲60.00 – ✲✲90.00.
* Georgian manor house in rural location. Charming country house atmosphere in a family style environment. Comfortable, spacious rooms.

CAWDOR Highland 501 I 11 – ⊠ Inverness.
Edinburgh 170 – Aberdeen 100 – Inverness 14.

 Cawdor Tavern, The Lane, IV12 5XP, 𝒫 (01667) 404777, cawdortavern@btopen
world.com, Fax (01667) 404777, ㈜ – 🅿. 🕪 🖭 ⓪ 𝘝𝘐𝘚𝘈. ※
closed 25 December and 1 January – **Rest** (booking essential Saturday-Sunday) a la carte
16.95/24.50 ℤ.
♦ Country inn within stone's throw of castle. Well run with an emphasis on the food.
Friendly staff serve dishes from large menu offering traditional or more adventurous fare.

CHIRNSIDE Borders 501 N 16 – pop. 1 204 – ⊠ Duns.
Edinburgh 52 – Berwick-upon-Tweed 8 – Glasgow 95 – Newcastle upon Tyne 70.

🏛 **Chirnside Hall** ⌂, TD11 3LD, East: 1 ¼ m. on A 6105 𝒫 (01890) 818219, chirnside
hall@globalnet.co.uk, Fax (01890) 818231, ≤, 𝟒𝟔, ⌘, ㈜ – ✁ 🅿. 🕪 🖭 𝘝𝘐𝘚𝘈
closed March – **Rest** (booking essential for non-residents) (dinner only) 30.00 s. – **10 rm** ⊇
✦85.00 – ✦✦205.00.
♦ Large, imposing, Victorian country house in a rural location. Well appointed interiors
with good quality period atmosphere. Individually decorated bedrooms. Smart place settings in a traditionally appointed dining room.

> Red = Pleasant. Look for the red ※ and 🏛 symbols.

SCOTLAND

CLACHAN SEIL Argyll and Bute 501 D 15 – see Seil (Isle of).

CLYDEBANK West Dunbartonshire 501 G 16 – pop. 29 858.
🇮🇸 Clydebank Municipal, Overtoun Rd, Dalmuir 𝒫 (0141) 952 2070.
Edinburgh 52 – Glasgow 6.

🏛 **The Beardmore**, Beardmore St, G81 4SA, off A 814 𝒫 (0141) 951 6000, info@beard
more.scot.nhs.uk, Fax (0141) 951 6019, ⓥ, 𝟒𝟔, ≋s, ▢, ㈜ – ⧈ ✁ ▤ 🕹 🅿. – 🅢 170. 🕪
🖭 ⓪ 𝘝𝘐𝘚𝘈. ※
Arcoona : **Rest** (closed Sunday and Monday) (dinner only) a la carte 23.15/35.15 s. ℤ – **B
bar cafe** : **Rest** a la carte 15.50/22.50 s. ℤ – ⊇ 12.95 – **160 rm** ✦99.00 – ✦✦99.00, 6 suites.
♦ Large purpose-built building immediately adjacent to Clydebank hospital. Good leisure
and beauty facility and open-plan lounge. Smart, well-equipped, large bedrooms. Arcoona
offers smart formality. B bar café provides bright setting in open-plan lounge bar.

COLONSAY (Isle of) Argyll and Bute 501 B 15.
🇮🇸 Isle of Colonsay 𝒫 (019512) 316.
🚢 – from Scalasaig to Oban (Caledonian MacBrayne Ltd) 3 weekly (2 h) – from Scalasaig
to Kintyre Peninsula (Kennacraig) via Isle of Islay (Port Askaig) (Caledonian MacBrayne Ltd)
weekly.

Scalasaig Argyll and Bute – ⊠ Colonsay.

🏛 **The Colonsay** ⌂, PA61 7YP, ≤, – 🕹 🅿. 🕪 🖭 𝘝𝘐𝘚𝘈
Fax (01951) 200353, ≤, ㈜ – 🕹 🅿. 🕪 🖭 𝘝𝘐𝘚𝘈
March-October – **Rest** (bar lunch)/dinner a la carte 17.50/24.25 ℤ – ⊇ 9.95 – **9 rm**
✦50.00/105.00. – ✦✦115.00/135.00.
♦ Listed building from mid-18C; a thoroughly rural, remote setting. Public areas include
excellent photos of local scenes and the only bar on the island. Bright, modern rooms.
Welcoming, informal dining room.

COMRIE Perthshire 501 I 14 – pop. 1 839.
🇮🇸 Comrie, Laggan Braes 𝒫 (01764) 670055.
Edinburgh 66 – Glasgow 56 – Oban 70 – Perth 24.

🏛 **The Royal**, Melville Sq, PH6 2DN, 𝒫 (01764) 679200, reception@royalhotel.co.uk,
Fax (01764) 679219, ⌘, ㈜ – 🕹 🅿. 🕪 ⓪ 𝘝𝘐𝘚𝘈
closed 25-26 December – **Royal** : **Rest** a la carte 15.70/28.95 – **13 rm** ⊇ ✦80.00 –
✦✦130.00/170.00.
♦ 18C coaching inn in centre of town: Queen Victoria once stayed here. Stylish, contemporary feel, especially individually decorated bedrooms, with four posters and antiques. Restaurant with two rooms: conservatory brasserie or intimate dining room.

CONNEL Argyll and Bute **501** D 14 – ⌧ Oban.
Edinburgh 118 – Glasgow 88 – Inverness 113 – Oban 5.

⌂ **Ards House** without rest., PA37 1PT, on A 85 ℰ (01631) 710255, ardsconnel@aol.com,
Fax (01631) 710857, ≤, 🞮 – ⇆ ℙ. 🞮🞮 ᴠɪsᴀ
closed 12 December - 5 January – **4 rm** ⌧ ♦50.00/60.00 – ♦♦80.00/88.00.
♦ Victorian house overlooking Loch Etive. Well run with a smart and elegant atmosphere.
Traditional décor and appointments throughout communal areas and bedrooms. Cosy
breakfast room.

⌂ **Ronebhal** without rest., PA37 1PJ, on A 85 ℰ (01631) 710310, ronebhal@btinter
net.com, Fax (01631) 710310, ≤, 🞮 – ⇆ ℙ. 🞮🞮 ᴠɪsᴀ. 🞮
April - mid October – **6 rm** ⌧ ♦24.00/60.00 – ♦♦60.00/70.00.
♦ Victorian house built in granite, with fine views over Loch Etive. Attractive guests' lounge
with plenty of local information. Individually decorated bedrooms.

▥ **The Oyster Inn** with rm, PA37 1PJ, ℰ (01631) 710666, stay@oysterinn.co.uk,
Fax (01631) 710042, ☎ – ℙ. 🞮🞮 ᴀᴇ ⓞ ᴠɪsᴀ
Rest a la carte 15.75/30.15 s. ♀ – **16 rm** ⌧ ♦52.00/65.00 – ♦♦84.00/114.00.
♦ Three in one: a modern restaurant with loch view; adjacent bar/pub, The Ferryman's;
comfy, modish bedrooms. Fresh, home-made dishes throughout: seafood specials prevail.

at Benderloch North : 2½ m. by A 828 – ⌧ Connel.

⌂ **Dun Ma Mara** without rest., PA37 1RT, ℰ (01631) 720233, stay@dunnamara.com, ≤
Ardmucknish Bay and Isle of Mull, 🞮 – ⇆ ℙ. 🞮
February-November – **5 rm** ⌧ ♦48.00/68.00 – ♦♦96.00.
♦ Fully restored Edwardian home with fine views. Minimalistic, intimate interior. Pleasant
gardens lead to idyllic private beach. Individual, modish rooms boast clean lines.

CONON BRIDGE Highland **501** G 11.
Edinburgh 168 – Inverness 12.

🏠 **Kinkell House** ⌖, Easter Kinkell, IV7 8HY, Southeast : 3 m. by B 9163 and A 835 on B
9169 ℰ (01349) 861270, info@kinkellhousehotel.com, Fax (01349) 867240, ≤, 🞮 – ⇆ &
ℙ. 🞮🞮 ⓞ ᴠɪsᴀ
closed 22 December-8 January – **Rest** (lunch by arrangement Monday-Saturday) 23.95 ♀ –
9 rm ⌧ ♦60.00/100.00 – ♦♦100.00/120.00.
♦ Peacefully located house in a rural location makes for a welcoming country house atmosphere, keenly overseen by a young team. Homely bedrooms. Traditional dining room
overlooks the garden.

CRAIGHOUSE Argyll and Bute **501** C 16 – see Jura (Isle of).

CRAIGNURE Argyll and Bute **501** C 14 – see Mull (Isle of).

CRAILING Borders **501 502** M 17 – see Jedburgh.

CRIEFF Perth and Kinross **501** I 14 Scotland G. – pop. 6 579.
See : Town★.
Env. : Drummond Castle Gardens★ AC, S : 2 m. by A 822.
Exc. : Scone Palace★★ AC, E : 16 m. by A 85 and A 93.
🞮, 🞮 Perth Rd ℰ (01764) 652909 – 🞮 Muthill, Peat Rd ℰ (01764) 681523.
🞮 Town Hall, High St ℰ (01764) 652578, criefftic@perthshire.co.uk.
Edinburgh 60 – Glasgow 50 – Oban 76 – Perth 18.

⌂ **Merlindale**, Perth Rd, PH7 3EQ, on A 85 ℰ (01764) 655205, merlin.dale@virgin.net,
Fax (01764) 655205, 🞮 – ⇆ ℙ. ᴠɪsᴀ. 🞮
closed mid December-mid January – **Rest** (by arrangement) (communal dining)
25.00/35.00 – **3 rm** ⌧ ♦40.00/60.00 – ♦♦60.00/80.00.
♦ Traditional, stone-built house close to the town. Well-equipped bedrooms are individually decorated and very comfortable. Accomplished evening meals at a communal table.

⌂ **Glenearn House** without rest., Perth Rd, PH7 3EQ, on A 85 ℰ (01764) 650000,
john@glenearnhouse.com, 🞮 – ⇆ ℙ. 🞮🞮 ᴠɪsᴀ. 🞮
closed 20 December- February – **5 rm** ⌧ ♦40.00/60.00 – ♦♦64.00/80.00.
♦ Personally run former school house, built in Victorian times. Extremely comfy, modern
lounge. Neat and tidy garden complements the immaculate nature of the accommodation.

✗
☞ **The Bank,** 32 High St, PH7 3BS, ✆ (01764) 656575, *mail@thebankrestaurant.co.uk,*
Fax (01764) 656575 – **⑳** **AE** **VISA**
closed 2 weeks January, 1 week July, 25-26 December, Sunday and Monday – Rest a la
carte 17.75/26.95 s. ☯.
♦ Impressive, Gothic, former bank dating from 1901 which dominates the high street.
Traditional, good value cooking using fine ingredients and an informal, friendly atmosphere.

CRINAN Argyll and Bute 501 D 15 Scotland G. – ⊠ Lochgilphead.
See : Hamlet★.
Exc. : Kilmory Knap (Macmillan's Cross★) SW : 14 m.
Edinburgh 137 – Glasgow 91 – Oban 36.

🏨 **Crinan,** PA31 8SR, ✆ (01546) 830261, *nryan@crinanhotel.com,* Fax (01546) 830292, ≼
Loch Crinan and Sound of Jura, ☛ – 🛗 ⇟⋉ **P,** **⑳** **VISA**
closed Christmas – Rest 45.00 (dinner) and a la carte 19.85/30.85 – **20 rm** (dinner included)
☷ ✦85.00/130.00 – ✦✦170.00/260.00.
♦ Superbly located in a commanding setting with exceptional views of Loch Crinan and
Sound of Jura. Cosy, wood panelled, nautically themed bar. Bright, pleasant bedrooms.
Restaurant provides wonderful views and interesting cuisine with seafood predominance.

CROCKETFORD Dumfries and Galloway 501 502 I 18 Scotland G. – ⊠ Castle Douglas.
Exc. : Sweetheart Abbey★, SE : 10 m. by minor rd – Threave Garden★★ and Threave Castle★, S : 10 m. by A 75.
Edinburgh 89 – Dumfries 9 – Kirkcudbright 18.

🏠 **Craigadam** ⌂, DG7 3HU, West : 2 m. on A 712 ✆ (01556) 650233, *inquiry@craigadam.com,* Fax (01556) 650233, ⬱, ☛, ☐-⇟⋉ **P,** **⑳** **①** **VISA**
closed 24 December-6 January – Rest (communal dining) (residents only) (dinner only)
21.00 – **10 rm** ☷ ✦50.00/80.00 – ✦✦80.00.
♦ 18C country house on working farm. Comfortable, spacious rooms, some with south-facing view. Communal meals. Distinctively themed bedrooms in house or rear courtyard.

CROSSFORD Fife 501 J 15 – see Dunfermline.

CULLODEN Highland 501 H 11 – see Inverness.

CUPAR Fife 501 K 15 – pop. 8 506.
Edinburgh 45 – Dundee 15 – Perth 23.

🏠 **Westfield House** without rest., Westfield Rd, KY15 5AR, West : ½ m. by A 91 off
Westfield Ave ✆ (1334) 655699, *westfieldhouse@standrews4.freeserve.co.uk,*
Fax (01334) 650075, ☛ – ⇟⋉ **P,** ⌘
3 rm ☷ ✦59.00 – ✦✦98.00.
♦ Georgian house with the feeling of a comfy private home. Extensive gardens. Traditionally decorated communal areas and great care taken over details in the well-kept bed-
rooms.

✗ **Ostler's Close,** 25 Bonnygate, KY15 4BU, ✆ (01334) 655574, Fax (01334) 654036 – **⑳**
AE **VISA**
*closed 1-2 January, 2 weeks Easter, 2 weeks October, 25-26 December, Sunday, Monday
and lunch Tuesday-Friday* – Rest a la carte 22.50/36.00 ☯.
♦ Welcoming restaurant with snug atmosphere and low ceilings. Very personally run, with
cottage feel throughout. Particular attention to prime Scottish meat and local fish.

DALRY North Ayrshire 501 502 F 16.
Edinburgh 70 – Ayr 21 – Glasgow 25.

🏠 **Langside Farm,** KA24 5JZ, North : 2 m. by B 780 (Kilbirnie rd) on B 784 (Largs rd)
✆ (01294) 834402, *mail@langsidefarm.co.uk,* Fax (0870) 0569380, ≼, ☛ – ⇟⋉ **P,** **⑳** **AE**
VISA
restricted opening in winter – Rest (by arrangement) (communal dining) 24.50 – **4 rm** ☷
✦35.00 – ✦✦80.00.
♦ Converted farmhouse, dating from 1745, set on hillside affording panoramic views.
Classic furnishings throughout. Comfortable bedrooms exude a homely, relaxing ambience.

SCOTLAND

⭑ **Lochwood Farm Steading** ⌂ without rest., KA21 6NG, Southwest : 5 m. by A 737 on Saltcoats rd ℰ (01294) 552529, *info@lochwoodfarm.co.uk*, ≤ – ⇥ **P**. **◑◉ VISA** ⁄⁄ *February-November* – **8 rm** ⊆ ✦45.00 – ✦✦60.00.
* Excellent hospitality at a good value farmhouse on one hundred acres of dairy farm. Fine views of country and coast from outside hot tub. Pleasant, well-kept little bedrooms.

XX **Braidwoods**, Drumastle Mill Cottage, KA24 4LN, Southwest : 1 ½ m. by A 737 on Saltcoats rd ℰ (01294) 833544, *keithbraidwood@btconnect.com*, Fax (01294) 833553 – **P**. **◑◉**
✿ **AE ◑ VISA**
closed first 3 weeks January, first 2 weeks September, 25-26 December, Monday, Tuesday lunch and Sunday except lunch October-April – **Rest** (booking essential) 20.00/39.00.
Spec. Crab and avocado salad with spiced Bloody Mary dressing. Grilled turbot on crushed Jersey potatoes. Caramelised lime cream with a Champagne rhubarb compote.
* Personally run, cosy, cottagey restaurant off the beaten track. Chef patron prides himself on use of local produce: prime ingredients used with care. Well-flavoured dishes.

DINGWALL *Highland* 501 G 11 – *pop. 5 026.*
Edinburgh 172 – Inverness 14.

XX **Cafe India Brasserie**, Lockhart House, Tulloch St, IV15 9JZ, ℰ (01349) 862552 – ▤.
◑◉ AE VISA
closed 25 December – **Rest** - Indian - 28.00 and a la carte 19.55/30.90 s..
* Bustling, locally regarded Indian restaurant, handily located in town centre. Updated décor is fresh and modern. Authentically prepared, tasty regional Indian food.

Good food and accommodation at moderate prices?
Look for the Bib symbols:
red Bib Gourmand 🅑 for food, blue Bib Hotel 🅑 for hotels

SCOTLAND

DOONFOOT *Sth Ayrshire* 501 502 G 17 – *see Ayr.*

DORNOCH *Highland* 501 H 10 *Scotland G.* – *pop. 1 206.*
See : *Town★*.
🅛, 🅛 *Royal Dornoch, Golf Rd* ℰ (01862) 810219.
🅱 *The Coffee Shop, The Square* ℰ (0845) 2255121.
Edinburgh 219 – Inverness 63 – Wick 65.

⭑ **Highfield House** without rest., Evelix Rd, IV25 3HR, ℰ (01862) 810909, *enqui ries@highfieldhouse.co.uk*, Fax (01862) 811605, ≤, ⌇ – ⇥ **P**
May - mid October. – **3 rm** ⊆ ✦45.00/50.00 – ✦✦60.00/65.00.
* Purpose-built guesthouse with garden and fine Highland views. Small, spruce lounge; neat and tidy breakfast room. Bedrooms offer ample comforts: one has whirlpool bath.

XX **2 Quail** with rm, Castle St, IV25 3SN, ℰ (01862) 811811, *bookings@2quail.com* – **◑◉ AE**
VISA
closed 2 weeks spring, Christmas and restricted opening October-April – **Rest** *(closed Sunday-Monday)* (dinner only) (set menu only) 37.00 ⊻ – **3 rm** ⊆ ✦90.00 – ✦✦100.00.
* Elegant, book-lined restaurant in town house. Interesting dishes with high levels of skill and sensitivity brought to tasty, well-prepared ingredients. Pleasant guest rooms.

DRUMNADROCHIT *Highland* 501 G 11 *Scotland G.* – ✉ *Milton.*
Env. : *Loch Ness★★ – Loch Ness Monster Exhibition★ AC – The Great Glen★*.
Edinburgh 172 – Inverness 16 – Kyle of Lochalsh 66.

⭑ **Drumbuie Farm** without rest., Drumbuie, IV63 6XP, East : ¾ m. by A 82 ℰ (01456) 450634, *drumbuie@loch-ness-farm.bandb.co.uk*, Fax (01456) 450595, ≤, ⌂ – ⇥ **P**. **◑◉**
VISA ⁄⁄
3 rm ⊆ ✦32.00/36.00 – ✦✦50.00/54.00.
* Immaculate purpose-built guesthouse on working farm with Highland cattle. Conservatory breakfast room has Loch Ness views. Good collection of malt whiskies. Spacious bedrooms.

DUFFUS *Moray* 501 K 11 – *see Elgin.*

DULNAIN BRIDGE *Highland* 501 J 12 – *see Grantown-on-Spey.*

DUMFRIES Dumfries and Galloway 501 502 J 18 Scotland G. – pop. 31 146.

See : Town★ – Midsteeple★ A **A**.

Env. : Lincluden College (Tomb★) AC, N : 1½ m. by College St **A**.

Exc. : Drumlanrig Castle★★ (cabinets★) AC, NW : 16½ m. by A 76 **A** – Shambellie House Museum of Costume (Costume Collection★) S : 7¼ m. by A 710 **A** – Sweetheart Abbey★ AC, S : 8 m. by A 710 **A** – Caerlaverock Castle★ (Renaissance façade★★) AC, SE : 9 m. by B 725 **B** – Glenkiln (Sculptures★) W : 9 m. by A 780 – **A** – and A 75.

▸ Dumfries & Galloway, 2 Laurieston Ave, Maxwelltown ℰ (01387) 253582 **A** – ▸ Dumfries & County, Nunfield, Edinburgh Rd ℰ (01387) 253585 – ▸ Crichton, Bankend Rd ℰ (01387) 247894, **B**.

🅱 64 Whitesands ℰ (01387) 253862, **A**.

Edinburgh 80 – Ayr 59 – Carlisle 34 – Glasgow 79 – Manchester 155 – Newcastle upon Tyne 91.

↟ **Redbank House** ⌕ without rest., New Abbey Rd, DG2 8EW, South : 1½ m. on A 710
🖾 ℰ (01387) 247034, redbankhouse@talk21.com, Fax (01387) 266220, ⇆s, ⇆ – ⇆⇆ 🅿. ⬤⬤
VISA ⛝

6 rm ⇆ ★45.00/55.00 – ★★65.00.

♦ Spacious Victorian villa with formally laid, mature gardens. Large sitting room with adjacent conservatory. Sizeable breakfast room. Homely rooms with floral furnishings.

SCOTLAND

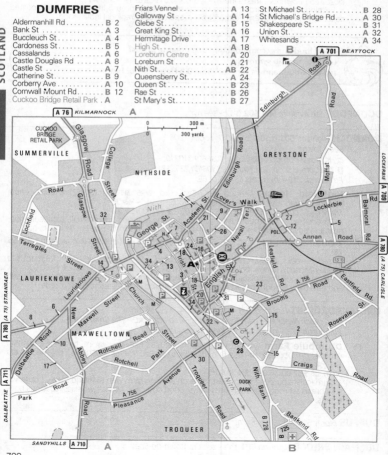

⌂ **Hazeldean House** without rest., 4 Moffat Rd, DG1 1NJ, ℰ (01387) 266178, *info@hazel deanhouse.com*, Fax (01387) 266178, *☞ – ╳≒ ℃ P. ◍◎ VISA. ⅏*   **B u**
closed Christmas – **6 rm** ⊆ ♦30.00/40.00 – ♦♦52.00/54.00.
◆ Interestingly furnished 19C villa. Entrance door has original stained glass. Characterful antiques and Victoriana in lounge. Conservatory breakfast room. Spacious bedrooms.

⌂ **Rivendell** without rest., 105 Edinburgh Rd, DG1 1JX, ℰ (01387) 252251, *info@riven dellbnb.co.uk*, Fax (01387) 263084, *☞ – ╳≒ P. ◍◎ VISA. ⅏*   **B i**
6 rm ⊆ ♦25.00/50.00 – ♦♦48.00/54.00.
◆ Attractive Rennie Mackintosh style villa with parquet floors, decorative woodwork and brass fittings. Comfortable, pleasant bedrooms with view of large garden.

XX **The Linen Room**, 53 St Michael St, DG1 2QB, ℰ (01387) 255689, *thelinenroom@ yahoo.co.uk*, Fax (01387) 253387 – ◍◎ ⌶ VISA   **B c**
closed 2 weeks January, 2 weeks October and Monday – **Rest** 15.95 (lunch) and a la carte 25.00/32.50 **s**. ⅏.
◆ Don't be put off by unprepossessing exterior: a young team run a serious restaurant where tasting menus are prominent and original dishes use good quality local produce.

Do not confuse X with ✿!
X defines comfort, while stars are awarded for the best cuisine, across all categories of comfort.

SCOTLAND

DUNAIN PARK *Highland – see Inverness.*

DUNBLANE *Stirling 501 I 15 Scotland G. – pop. 7 911 (inc. Lecropt).*
See : Town★ – Cathedral★★ (west front★★).
Env. : Doune★ (castle★ AC) W : 4½ m. by A 820.
🛈 Stirling Rd ℰ (08707) 200613 (May-September).
Edinburgh 42 – Glasgow 33 – Perth 29.

🏛 **Cromlix House** ⌂, Kinbuck, FK15 9JT, North : 3 ½ m. on B 8033 ℰ (01786) 822125, *reservations@cromlixhouse.com*, Fax (01786) 825450, ≤, ☜, ☞, ⚘ – ╳≒ P. ◍◎ ⌶ VISA
Rest (booking essential) 39.00/49.00 and a la carte 38.50/51.50 ⅋ – **6 rm** ⊆ ♦175.00/195.00 – ♦♦250.00/280.00, **8 suites** ⊆ 250.00/390.00.
◆ Effortlessly relaxing 19C mansion in extensive grounds with ornate private chapel. Charming morning room; spacious conservatory with plants. Definitive country house rooms. Two elegant, richly furnished dining rooms.

DUNDEE *Dundee 501 L 14 Scotland G. – pop. 154 674.*
See : Town★ – The Frigate Unicorn★ AC Y A – Discovery Point★ AC Y B – Verdant Works★ Z D – McManus Galleries★ Y M.
🛇₁₈, 🛇₉, 🛇 Caird Park, Mains Loan ℰ (01382) 453606 – 🛇 Camperdown, Camperdown Park ℰ (01382) 623398 – 🛇 Downfield, Turnberry Ave ℰ (01382) 825595.
Tay Road Bridge (toll) Y.
✈ Dundee Airport : ℰ (01382) 662200, SW : 1½ m. Z.
🛈 21 Castle St ℰ (01382) 527527.
Edinburgh 63 – Aberdeen 67 – Glasgow 83.

Plan on next page

🏛 **Apex City Quay**, 1 West Victoria Dock Rd, DD1 3JP, ℰ (01382) 202404, *reserva tions@apexhotels.co.uk*, Fax (01382) 201401, ≤, ◎, ⅙, ⊆s, ⬚ – ⧈ ╳≒, ▤ rest, ℃ ぐ P. – ❧ 600. ◍◎ ⌶ ◍ VISA. ⅏   **Y a**
Metro Brasserie : **Rest** 17.50/20.00 and a la carte 15.35/28.35 ⅋ – **Alchemy :** **Rest** (dinner only Thursday-Saturday) 17.50/20.00 and a la carte 15.35/28.35 – ⊆12.50 **150 rm** ♦89.00/200.00 – ♦♦99.00/210.00, 2 suites.
◆ Modern hotel on the waterfront. Business and leisure facilities to the fore, the smart spa offering plenty of treatments. Airy, up-to-date rooms all with views. Fine dining in Alchemy. Informal feel suffuses Metro: both restaurants look out over dockside.

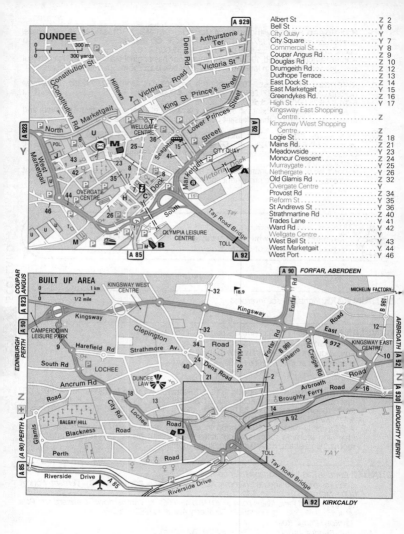

at Broughty Ferry *East : 4½ m. by A 930 –* Z *–* ⊠ *Dundee.*

🏨 **Broughty Ferry,** 16 West Queen St, DD5 1AR, ℰ (01382) 480027, *enquiries@hotel broughtyferry.co.uk, Fax* (01382) 739426, ♫, ⇌s, ◧ – ⅛⇔ ⅋ ℙ, ◍◉ 𝔸𝔼 𝒱𝐼𝒮𝐀. ⋘
Bombay Brasserie : Rest - Indian - a la carte 18.00/30.00 s. – **16 rm** ⊆ ✚68.00/80.00 – ✚✚88.00.
 ♦ Family owned and friendly modern hotel beside the main road. The spacious, individually decorated bedrooms are furnished to a high standard. Brasserie serves elaborate, authentic Indian menus.

⌂ **Invermark House** without rest., 23 Monifieth Rd, DD5 2RN, ℰ (01382) 739430, *enqui ries@invermarkhotel.co.uk, Fax* (01382) 220834, ♫ – ⅛⇔ ℙ, ◍◉ ◍ 𝒱𝐼𝒮𝐀. ⋘
6 rm ⊆ ✚25.00/30.00 – ✚✚40.00/50.00.
 ♦ Imposing, detached Victorian house retains a period charm. Welcoming owners and relaxed atmosphere. Individually decorated rooms with thoughtful touches.

792

DUNDONNELL Highland 501 E 10 Scotland G. – ⊠ Garve.

    Env. : Wester Ross★★★ – Loch Broom★★, N : 4½ m. via Allt na h–Airbhe.
    Exc. : Falls of Measach★★, SE : 10 m. by A 832 – Corrieshalloch Gorge★, SE : 11½ m. by A 832 and A 835.
    Edinburgh 215 – Inverness 59.

🏨 **Dundonnell,** Little Loch Broom, IV23 2QR, ℰ (01854) 633204, enquiries@dundonnellhotel.co.uk, Fax (01854) 633366, ≤ Dundonnell Valley – ⇅⇄ ₺ ℙ – 🕰 90. ⓂⓈ 𝑉𝐼𝑆𝐴
    March-October – **Rest** (bar lunch)/dinner a la carte 13.13/29.20 s. – **32 rm** ⇆ ✦35.00/50.00 – ✦✦70.00/90.00.
    ♦ Up-to-date, comfortable hotel where the mountains meet the sea with views over Dundonnell Valley. Bustling bar and two well-furnished lounges. Clean, spruce rooms. Home baking makes use of finest local produce.

DUNFERMLINE Fife 501 J 15 Scotland G. – pop. 39 229.

    See : Town★ – Abbey★ (Abbey Church★★) AC.
    Env. : Forth Bridges★★, S : 5 m. by A 823 and B 980.
    Exc. : Culross★★ (Village★★★, Palace★★ AC, Study★ AC), W : 7 m. by A 994 and B 9037.
    🟦 Canmore, Venturefair Ave ℰ (01383) 724969 – 🟦 Pitreavie, Queensferry Rd ℰ (01383) 722591 – 🟦 Pitfirrane, Crossford ℰ (01383) 723534 – 🟦 Saline, Kinneddar Hill ℰ (01383) 852591.
    🚩 1 High St ℰ (01383) 720999 (April-October).
    Edinburgh 16 – Dundee 48 – Motherwell 39.

🏨 **Garvock House,** St John's Drive, Transy, KY12 7TU, East : ¾ m. by A 907 off Garvock Hill ℰ (01383) 621067, sales@garvock.co.uk, Fax (01383) 621168, 🌳 – ⇅⇄ ℙ – 🕰 150. ⓂⓈ 𝐴𝐸 ① 𝑉𝐼𝑆𝐴
    Rest 20.00 (lunch) and dinner a la carte 22.00/33.95 – **26 rm** ⇆ ✦79.50/90.00 – ✦✦85.00/135.00.
    ♦ Privately owned Victorian house in woodland setting with classically decorated public areas. Contrastingly, most of the attractive, modish rooms are in a modern extension. Comfortable, smartly decorated dining room.

at Crossford Southwest : 1¾ m. on A 994 – ⊠ Dunfermline.

🏨 **Keavil House,** Main St, KY12 8QW, ℰ (01383) 736258, sales@keavilhouse.co.uk, Fax (01383) 621600, 𝐹₆, 🛏, ▣, 🌳, ♨ – ⇅⇄ ✆ ₺ ℙ – 🕰 300. ⓂⓈ 𝐴𝐸 ① 𝑉𝐼𝑆𝐴. ※
    Cardoon : **Rest** 25.00/34.00 (dinner) and a la carte 21.00/33.00 s. ♀ – **47 rm** ⇆ ✦90.00/170.00 – ✦✦110.00/180.00.
    ♦ Busy, part 16C country house in woods and gardens on edge of estate. Useful for business traveller. Small bar, extensive leisure facilities. Well-equipped rooms. Elegant, linen-clad conservatory restaurant offering verdant surroundings in which to dine.

Your opinions are important to us:
please write and let us know about your discoveries and experiences – good and bad!

DUNFOOT South Ayrshire 501 502 G 17 – see Ayr.

DUNKELD Perth and Kinross 501 J 14 Scotland G. – pop. 1 005.

    See : Village★ – Cathedral Street★.
    🟦 Dunkeld & Birnam, Fungarth ℰ (01350) 727524.
    🚩 The Cross ℰ (01350) 727688 (April-October), dunkeldtic@perthshire.co.uk.
    Edinburgh 58 – Aberdeen 88 – Inverness 98 – Perth 14.

🏨 **Kinnaird** ⌖, PH8 0LB, Northwest : 6 ¾ m. by A 9 on B 898 ℰ (01796) 482440, enquiry@kinnairdestate.com, Fax (01796) 482289, ≤ Tay valley and hills, 🐟, 🌳, ♨, ※ – 📶 ⇅⇄ ℙ. ⓂⓈ 𝐴𝐸 𝑉𝐼𝑆𝐴
    Rest 20.00/55.00 ♀ – **8 rm** (dinner included) ✦195.00/375.00 – ✦✦275.00/475.00, 1 suite.
    ♦ Imposing Georgian mansion with superb Tay Valley views and sprawling gardens. Antiques, framed oils and country house drapes throughout. Immaculately kept, luxurious rooms. Formal restaurant with hand painted frescoes and ornate ceilings.

SCOTLAND

793

Hilton Dunkeld House ⌘, PH8 0HT, ℰ (01350) 727771, *reservations.dunkeld@hilton.com, Fax (01350) 728924*, ≤, ஃ, ₤₅, ⌁, ▣, ◥, ⋒, ₤, ⋇ – ▮⋈ ✦ ℰ ₺ ₧ – ⚏ 120. ⏀⊘ ␃ ⓪ *VISA*. ⋘
The Garden : Rest *(bar lunch)/dinner* 29.00/35.00 **s.** ⥹ – **91 rm** *(dinner included)* ⥲ ✝142.00/230.00 – ✝✝162.00/250.00, 7 suites.
• Edwardian country house on banks of Tay. Two good sized drawing rooms with Scottish décor. Modern leisure centre. Warmly inviting rooms, with lush fabrics and soft suites. Rich, Scottish themed restaurant overlooking river.

Letter Farm ⌘ without rest., Loch of the Lowes, PH8 0HH, Northeast : 3 m. by A 923 on Loch of Lowes rd ℰ (01350) 724254, *letterlowe@aol.com, Fax (01350) 724341*, ⌬ – ⋇ ₧. ⏀⊘ *VISA*. ⋘
early May-mid November – 3 rm ⥲ ✝35.00 – ✝✝60.00.
• Attractive, traditional farm house close to the Loch of Lowes Nature Reserve. Welcoming, homely atmosphere and comfortable bedrooms.

DUNOON *Argyll and Bute* **501** F 16 *Scotland G.* – *pop. 8 251.*
Env. : *The Clyde Estuary*★.
ฦ Cowal, Ardenslate Rd ℰ (01369) 705673 – ฦ Innellan, Knockamillie Rd ℰ (01369) 830242.
⛴ *from Dunoon Pier to Gourock Railway Pier (Caledonian MacBrayne Ltd) frequent services daily (20 mn) – from Hunters Quay to McInroy's Point, Gourock (Western Ferries (Clyde) Ltd) frequent services daily (20 mn).*
🛈 7 Alexandra Parade ℰ (08707) 200629, *info@dunoon.visitscotland.com.*
Edinburgh 73 – *Glasgow 27* – Oban 77.

Dhailling Lodge, 155 Alexandra Parade, PA23 8AW, North : ¾ m. on A 815 ℰ (01369) 701253, *donald@dhaillinglodge.com*, ⌬ – ▮ ⋇ ✦ ℰ ₧. ⏀⊘ ␃ *VISA*. ⋘
March-October – **Rest** *(booking essential for non-residents) (dinner only)* 17.00 – **7 rm** ⥲ ✝36.00 – ✝✝70.00.
• Victorian villa with neat and tidy gardens, overlooking Firth of Clyde. Homely lounge boasts books and local guides. Individually decorated rooms with welcoming extra touches. Smart dining room with good views from all tables.

DUNVEGAN *Highland* **501** A 11 – *see Skye (Isle of).*

DUROR *Argyll and Bute* **501** E 14.
Edinburgh 131.5 – Ballachulish 7.5 – Oban 26.

Bealach House ⌘, Salachan Glen, PA38 4BW, Southeast : 4½ m. by A 828 ℰ (01631) 740298, *info@bealach-house.co.uk*, ⌬ – ⋇ ₧. ⏀⊘ *VISA*. ⋘
Closed 18 December - 12 January – **Rest** *(by arrangement) (communal dining)* 25.00 – 3 rm ⥲ ✝40.00/55.00 – ✝✝80.00.
• Down a one-and-a-half mile rural track for total privacy. This former crofter's house, set in eight acres, is immaculate, with snug conservatory and smart, well-kept rooms. Communal dining: daily changing menus have strong local base.

DYKE *Moray* **501** J 11 – *see Forres.*

EAST KILBRIDE *South Lanarkshire* **501 502** H 16 – *pop. 73 796.*
ฦ Torrance House, Strathaven Rd ℰ (01355) 248638.
Edinburgh 46 – Ayr 35 – *Glasgow 10.*

Crutherland House, Strathaven Rd, G75 0QZ, Southeast : 2 m. on A 726 ℰ (01355) 577000, *crutherland@macdonald-hotels.co.uk, Fax (01355) 220855*, ₤₅, ⌁, ▣, ⌬, ₤ – ▮ ✦ ℰ ₺ ₧ – ⚏ 500. ⏀⊘ ␃ ⓪ *VISA*
The Restaurant : Rest *(closed Saturday lunch)* 26.50 *(dinner)* and a la carte 27.25/41.95 ⥹ – **75 rm** ⥲ ✝135.00/145.00 – ✝✝155.00.
• Recently extended country house amidst woodland. Business traveller oriented. Comfortable furnishings and décor throughout. Impressive meeting facilities and well run leisure. Elegant, comfortable dining room: fresh, local produce in tried-and-tested dishes.

Look out for red symbols, indicating particularly pleasant establishments.

EDDLESTON *Peebleshire* 501 K 16.
Edinburgh 20 – Galashiels 22 – Peebles 4.5.

XX **The Horseshoe Inn** with rm, EH45 8QP, ℰ (01721) 730225, *reservations@thehorse shoe.inn.co.uk, Fax (01721) 730268* – 📞 🅿. 🆎 💳
closed 1 week January, 1 week October and dinner Sunday-Monday – **Rest** a la carte approx 38.00 – ***Bistro :* Rest** 20.00 (lunch) and a la carte approx 25.00 ♀ – **8 rm** ☕ ✸75.00/90.00 – ✸✸150.00/180.00.
✦ It's easy to drive past this roadside former pub, but stop off for serious cooking from experienced French chef or lighter dishes in adjacent bistro. Simple, comfy bedrooms

EDINBANE *Highland* 501 A 11 – *see Skye (Isle of).*

Edinburgh: old building on the Royal Mile

EDINBURGH

501 K 16 *Scotland G.* – pop. 430 082.

Glasgow 46 – Newcastle upon Tyne 105.

TOURIST INFORMATION

⌘ Edinburgh & Scotland Information Centre, 3 Princes St ℘ (0845) 2255121; info@visit scotland.co.uk
⌘ Edinburgh Airport, Tourist Information Desk ℘ (0845) 2255121.

PRACTICAL INFORMATION

ⁿ₈, ⁿ₁₈ Braid Hills, Braid Hills Rd ℘ (0131) 447 6666, BX.
ⁿ₁₈ Carrick Knowe, Glendevon Park ℘ (0131) 337 1096, AX.
ⁿ₁₈ Duddingston, Duddingston Road West ℘ (0131) 661 7688, BV.
ⁿ₁₈ Silverknowes, Parkway ℘ (0131) 336 3843, AV.
ⁿ₁₈ Liberton, 297 Gilmerton Rd ℘ (0131) 664 3009, BX.
ⁿ₈, ⁿ₁₈ Marriott Dalmahoy Hotel & C.C., Kirknewton ℘ (0131) 335 8010, AX.
ⁿ₉ Portobello, Stanley St ℘ (0131) 669 4361, BV.
✈ Edinburgh Airport : ℘ (0870) 040 0007, W : 6 m. by A 8 AV.
Terminal : Waverley Bridge.

SIGHTS

See : City★★★ – Edinburgh International Festival★★★ (August) – Royal Museum of Scotland★★★ EZ **M2** – National Gallery of Scotland★★ DY **M4** – Royal Botanic Garden★★★ AV – The Castle★★ AC DYZ : Site★★★ – Palace Block (Honours of Scotland★★★) – St Margaret's Chapel (❋★★★) – Great Hall (Hammerbeam Roof★★) – ≼★★ from Argyle and Mill's Mount DZ – Abbey and Palace of Holyroodhouse★★ AC (Plasterwork Ceilings★★★, ❋★★ from Arthur's Seat) BV – Royal Mile★★ : St Giles' Cathedral★★ (Crown Spire★★★) EYZ – Gladstone's Land★ AC EYZ A – Canongate Talbooth★ EY B – New Town★★ (Charlotte Square★★★ CY **14** – The Georgian House★ AC CY **D** – Scottish National Portrait Gallery★ EY **M6** – Dundas House★ EY **E**) – Scottish National Gallery of Modern Art★ AV **M1** – Victoria Street★ EZ **84** – Scott Monument★ (≼★) AC EY **F** – Craigmillar Castle★ AC, SE: 3 m by A7 BX – Calton Hill (❋★★★ AC from Nelson's Monument) EY – Dean Gallery★ AV opposite **M1** – Royal Yacht Britannia★ BV.

Env. : Edinburgh Zoo★★ AC AV – Hill End Ski Centre (❋★★) AC, S : 5½ m. by A 702 BX – The Royal Observatory (West Tower ≼★) AC BX – Ingleston, Scottish Agricultural Museum★, W : 6½ m. by A 8 AV.

Exc. : Rosslyn Chapel★★ AC (Apprentice Pillar★★★) S : 7½ m. by A 701 BX and B 7006 – Forth Bridges★★, NW : 9½ m. by A 90 AV – Hopetoun House★★ AC, NW : 11½ m. by A 90 AV and A 904 – Dalmeny★ – Dalmeny House★ AC, St Cuthbert's Church★ (Norman South Doorway★★) NW : 7 m. by A 90 AV – Crichton Castle (Italianate courtyard range★) AC, SE : 10 m. by A 7 X and B 6372.

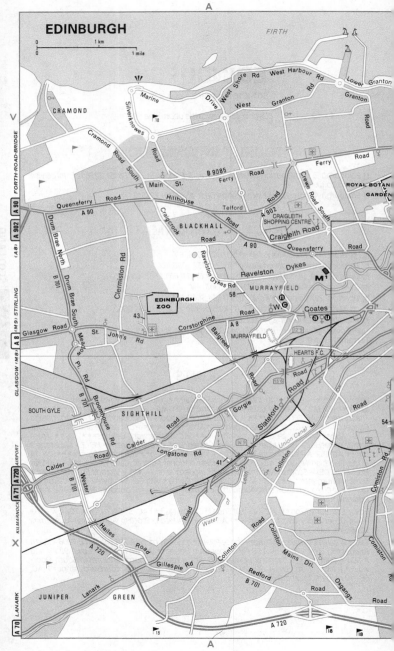

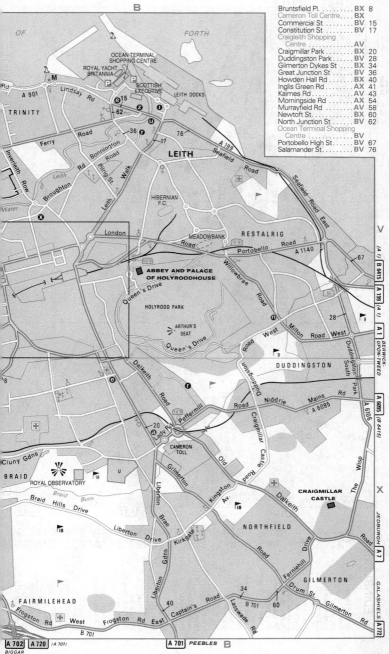

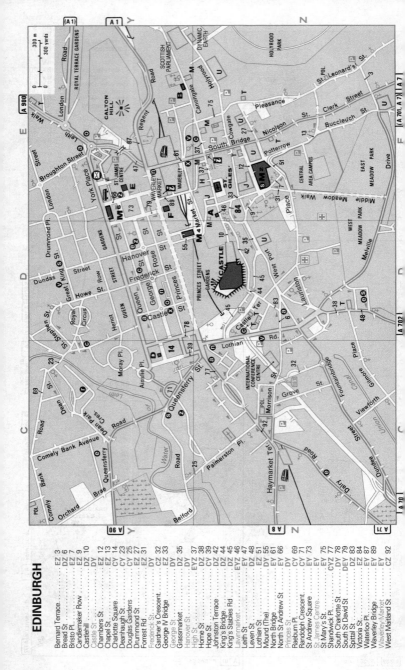

EDINBURGH

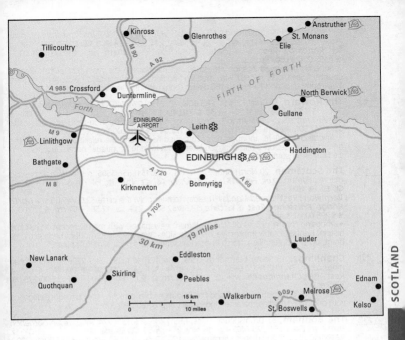

Balmoral, 1 Princes St, EH2 2EQ, ℘ (0131) 556 2414, *thebalmoral@roccoforteho tels.com*, Fax (0131) 557 8740, 🗖, ⇌, 🖃 – 🛊 ⇌ ▤ ✔ ⅙ ⟵ – 🛆 350. ⬥ 🎟 𝘝𝘐𝘚𝘈.
※
EY n
Rest – (see *Number One* and *Hadrian's* below) – ⌧ 18.50 – **167 rm** ✦290.00/450.00 –
✦✦345.00/510.00, 21 suites.
 ◆ Richly furnished rooms in grand baronial style complemented by contemporary furnish-
ings in the Palm Court exemplify this de luxe Edwardian railway hotel and city landmark.

Caledonian Hilton, Princes St, EH1 2AB, ℘ (0131) 222 8888, *guest.caledonian@hil ton.com*, Fax (0131) 222 8889, 🗖, ⇌, 🖃 – 🛊, ⇌ rm, ▤ rest, ✔ ⅙ 🄿 – 🛆 300. ⬥ 🎟 ⓞ
𝘝𝘐𝘚𝘈. ※
CY Y
The Pompadour: Rest *(closed Saturday lunch, Sunday and Monday)* 15.00/21.00 (lunch)
and a la carte 30.40/40.85 ⅌ – **Chisholms:** Rest a la carte 26.85/34.15 ⅌ – ⌧ 19.50 – **238 rm**
✦150.00/245.00 – ✦✦180.00/275.00, 13 suites.
 ◆ A city landmark, affectionately known locally as "The Cally". Overlooked by the castle,
with handsomely appointed rooms and wood-panelled halls behind an imposing 19C façade. The Pompadour boasts elegant dining. Informal Chisholms serves popular brasserie
fare.

Sheraton Grand, 1 Festival Sq, EH3 9SR, ℘ (0131) 229 9131, *grandedinburgh.shera ton@sheraton.com*, Fax (0131) 229 9631, ⓠ, 🗖, ⇌, 🖃 – 🛊, ⇌ rm, ▤ ✔ ⅙ 🄿 – 🛆 500.
⬥ 🎟 ⓞ 𝘝𝘐𝘚𝘈. ※
CDZ v
Terrace: Rest (buffet only) 20.95/21.95 ⅌ – (see also *Grill Room* and *Santini* below) – ⌧
18.00 – **244 rm** ✦245.00 – ✦✦275.00, 16 suites.
 ◆ A modern, centrally located and smartly run hotel. A popular choice for the working
traveller, as it boasts Europe's most advanced urban spa. Comfy, well-kept rooms. Glass
expanse of Terrace restaurant overlooks Festival Square.

The George, 19-21 George St, EH2 2PB, ℘ (0131) 225 1251, Fax (0131) 240 7119 – 🛊,
⇌ rm – 🛆 200. ⬥ 🎟 ⓞ 𝘝𝘐𝘚𝘈. ※
DY z
The Tempus: Rest a la carte 24.00/33.00 ⅌ – ⌧ 15.50 – **192 rm** ✦80.00/165.00 –
✦✦100.00/175.00, 3 suites.
 ◆ Grade II listed Georgian classic in the heart of the city's most chic street; makes the most
of Robert Adam's listed design. Modern decor allied to smartly refurbished rooms. Interesting modern menus at The Tempus.

Prestonfield ⚜, Priestfield Rd, EH16 5UT, ℘ (0131) 225 7800, *mail@prestonfield.com*, *Fax (0131) 220 4392*, ≤, 🏠, ☂, ←–🛏–🚪 ♥ ☎ 🅟 – 🏛 900. 🖭 🝙 🅰🅴 ➀ *VISA*.   BX **r**
🕭 **Rhubarb :** Rest a la carte 32.00/45.00 ♀ – **20 rm** ☲ ⚿195.00/255.00 –
⚿⚿195.00/295.00, 2 suites.
◆ Superbly preserved interior, tapestries and paintings in the main part of this elegant country house, built in 1687 with modern additions. Set in parkland below Arthur's Seat. Two-roomed, period-furnished 18C dining room with fine views of the grounds.

The Howard, 34 Great King St, EH3 6QH, ℘ (0131) 274 7402, *reserve@thehoward.com*, *Fax (0131) 274 7405* – 🛗 ♥ 🅟 – 🏛 30. 🖭 🅰🅴 *VISA*. 🛠   DY **s**
closed Christmas – **The Atholl :** Rest (booking essential for non-residents) a la carte 33.00/42.50 ♀ – ☲ 16.50 – **14 rm** ⚿108.00/175.00 – ⚿⚿180.00/265.00, 4 suites.
◆ Crystal chandeliers, antiques, richly furnished rooms and the relaxing opulence of the drawing room set off a fine Georgian interior. An inviting "boutique" hotel. Elegant, linen-clad tables for sumptuous dining.

The Scotsman, 20 North Bridge, EH1 1YT, ℘ (0131) 556 5565, *reservations@thescots manhotelgroup.co.uk, Fax (0131) 652 3652*, 🔳, 🎏, 🚵, 🔲 – 🛗, ←– rm, ♥ 🅟 – 🏛 80. 🖭 🅰🅴 ➀ *VISA*   EY **x**
Vermilion : Rest *(closed Monday-Tuesday)* (dinner only) a la carte 32.00/45.00 s. – **North Bridge Brasserie :** Rest a la carte 18.50/32.50 s. ♀ – ☲ 17.50 – **57 rm** ⚿270.00 – ⚿⚿295.00, 12 suites.
◆ Imposing former offices of "The Scotsman" newspaper, with marble reception hall and historic prints. Notably impressive leisure facilities. Well-equipped modern bedrooms. Vibrant, richly red Vermilion. North Bridge Brasserie boasts original marble pillars.

Channings, 15 South Learmonth Gdns, EH4 1EZ, ℘ (0131) 315 2226, *reserve@chan nings.co.uk, Fax (0131) 332 9631*, 🎏, 🎏 – 🛗 ←– ♥ – 🏛 35. 🖭 🅰🅴 ➀ *VISA*. 🛠   CY **e**
Rest – (see **Channings** below) – ☲ 12.50 – **41 rm** ☲ ⚿125.00/195.00 – ⚿⚿235.00/275.00, 3 suites.
◆ Sensitively refurbished rooms and fire-lit lounges blend an easy country house elegance with original Edwardian character. Individually appointed bedrooms.

The Bonham, 35 Drumsheugh Gdns, EH3 7RN, ℘ (0131) 274 7400, *reserve@thebon ham.com, Fax (0131) 274 7405* – 🛗 ←– ♥ 🅟 – 🏛 50. 🖭 🅰🅴 *VISA*. 🛠   CY **z**
Rest 16.00 (lunch) and dinner a la carte 26.10/37.10 ♀ – ☲ 11.50 – **46 rm** ⚿145.00/165.00 – ⚿⚿195.00, 2 suites.
◆ A striking synthesis of Victorian architecture, eclectic fittings and bold, rich colours of a contemporary décor. Numerous pictures by "up-and-coming" local artists. Chic dining room with massive mirrors and "catwalk" in spotlights.

The Glasshouse without rest., 2 Greenside Pl, EH1 3AA, ℘ (0131) 525 8200, *resglass house@theetongroup.com, Fax (0131) 525 8205*, ≤, 🎏 – 🛗 ←– ♥ 🅟 – 🏛 70. 🖭 🅰🅴 ➀ *VISA*. 🛠   EY **o**
☲ 16.50 – **65 rm** ⚿250.00 – ⚿⚿270.00.
◆ Glass themes dominate the discreet style. Modern bedrooms, with floor to ceiling windows, have views of spacious roof garden or the city below. Breakfast room to the rear.

The Roxburghe, 38 Charlotte Sq, EH2 4HG, ℘ (0131) 240 5500, *roxburghe@macdon ald-hotels.co.uk, Fax (0131) 240 5555*, 🎏, 🚵, 🔲 – 🛗 ←–, 🛏 rest, ♥ 🅟 – 🏛 300. 🖭 🅰🅴 ➀ *VISA*. 🛠   DY **i**
The Melrose : Rest *(closed Saturday lunch)* (dinner only and Sunday lunch) 21.50/26.50 and a la carte 25.00/32.00 ♀ – ☲ 15.95 – **197 rm** ⚿90.00/200.00 – ⚿⚿90.00/250.00, 1 suite.
◆ Attentive service, understated period-inspired charm and individuality in the British style. Part modern, part Georgian but roomy throughout; welcoming bar. Restaurant reflects the grandeur of architect Robert Adam's exterior.

Edinburgh Marriott, 111 Glasgow Rd, EH12 8NF, West : 4½ m. on A 8 ℘ (0131) 334 9191, *mhrs.edieb.frontdesk@marriotthotels.com, Fax (0131) 316 4507*, 🔳, 🚵, 🚵, 🔲 – 🛗 ←– 🛏 ♥ 🅟 – 🏛 250. 🖭 🅰🅴 *VISA*. 🛠
Mediterrano : Rest (dinner only and lunch Saturday-Sunday) a la carte 21.90/33.45 ♀ – ☲ 14.95 – **241 rm** ⚿105.00/145.00 – ⚿⚿105.00/145.00, 4 suites.
◆ Excellent road connections for the airport and Glasgow and well-equipped rooms make this large, group-operated hotel a practical choice for business travel. Modern restaurant with Mediterranean twist.

Point, 34 Bread St, EH3 9AF, ℘ (0131) 221 5555, *Fax (0131) 221 9929* – 🛗, ←– rm, ♥ 🅟 – 🏛 120. 🖭 🅰🅴 ➀ *VISA*. 🛠   DZ **a**
Rest 12.50/19.50 ♀ – ☲ 10.00 – **134 rm** ⚿135.00 – ⚿⚿155.00, 4 suites.
◆ Formerly the Co-operative offices, converted in daring minimalist style. Boldly toned lobby and light, clean-lined rooms. Castle views over the rooftops from the upper floors. Strikingly lit avant-garde restaurant.

🏛 **Christopher North House** without rest., 6 Gloucester Pl, EH3 6EF, ℘ (0131) 225 2720, reservations@christophernorth.co.uk, Fax (0131) 220 4706 – ‰ rm, 🍴, 🌐🏧 ⁝ ⒶⒺ ⓪
▒ VISA. ‰
                                                                                 CY c
30 rm ⊇ ✦88.00/110.00 – ✦✦98.00/220.00.
◆ Georgian house on cobbled street in quiet residential area; a chintzy feel overlays the contemporary interior. Eclectically styled bedrooms feature homely extra touches.

🏛 **Clarendon** without rest., 25-33 Shandwick Pl, EH2 4RG, ℘ (0131) 229 1467, res@claren donhotelei.co.uk, Fax (0131) 229 7549 – 📳 ‰ &, 🌐🏧 ⒶⒺ VISA. ‰
                                                                               CZ a
66 rm ⊇ ✦40.00/130.00 – ✦✦60.00/160.00.
◆ Two minutes' walk from Princes Street, tastefully updated, this smart hotel boasts bright, vivid colours, a cosy, contemporary bar and well-presented rooms.

🏛 **The Lodge** (without rest.), 6 Hampton Terrace, West Coates, EH12 5JD, ℘ (0131) 337 3682, info@thelodgehotel.co.uk, Fax (0131) 313 1700, ☞ – ‰ 🍴 🅿. 🌐🏧 ⒶⒺ VISA.
                                                                        AV u
– 12 rm ⊇ ✦60.00/80.00 – ✦✦80.00/135.00.
◆ A converted Georgian manse, family owned and immaculately kept. Individually designed bedrooms and lounge decorated with taste and care; close to Murrayfield rugby stadium.

🏛 **Kildonan Lodge** without rest., 27 Craigmillar Park, EH16 5PE, ℘ (0131) 667 2793, info@kildonanlodgehotel.co.uk, Fax (0131) 667 9777 – ‰ 🍴 🅿. 🌐🏧 ⒶⒺ VISA.
                                                BX a
closed 25 December – **15 rm** ⊇ ✦58.00/98.00 – ✦✦78.00/138.00.
◆ Privately managed, with a cosy, firelit drawing room which feels true to the Lodge's origins as a 19C family house. One room has a four-poster bed and a fine bay window.

🏛 **Express by Holiday Inn** without rest., Picardy Pl, EH1 3JT, ℘ (0131) 558 2300, info@hieedinburgh.co.uk, Fax (0131) 558 2323 – 📳 ‰ 🍴 &, – 🚗 30. 🌐🏧 ⒶⒺ ⓪ VISA EY a
161 rm ✦95.00 – ✦✦95.00.
◆ Converted Georgian house offering trim, bright, reasonably priced accommodation. Great position for Princes Street and the other central city tourist attractions.

🏠 **Kew House** without rest., 1 Kew Terr, Murrayfield, EH12 5JE, ℘ (0131) 313 0700, info@kewhouse.com, Fax (0131) 313 0747 – ‰ 🅿. 🌐🏧 ⒶⒺ VISA. ‰
                                                                     AV a
8 rm ⊇ ✦70.00/120.00 – ✦✦85.00/150.00.
◆ Secure private parking and good road access for the city or Murrayfield Stadium. Neat, carefully kept rooms which are modern and well-proportioned.

🏠 **Elmview** without rest., 15 Glengyle Terrace, EH3 9LN, ℘ (0131) 228 1973, nici@elm view.co.uk – ‰. 🌐🏧 VISA. ‰
                                                                           DZ e
April-October – **3 rm** ⊇ ✦65.00/95.00 – ✦✦85.00/115.00.
◆ Basement of a Victorian house in pretty terrace overlooking The Meadows. Bedrooms are spotlessly kept and feature a host of extras: videos, fridges, sherry and more.

🏠 **Davenport House** without rest., 58 Great King St, EH3 6QY, ℘ (0131) 558 8495, daven porthouse@btinternet.com, Fax (0131) 558 8496 – ‰ 🍴. 🌐🏧 ⓪ VISA. ‰
                                                                   DY v
closed Christmas – **6 rm** ⊇ ✦65.00/75.00 – ✦✦75.00/110.00.
◆ Three-storey Georgian townhouse on cobbled street. Welcoming period style lounge; chintzy breakfast room. The bedrooms are of varying styles and sizes; all are well equipped.

🏠 **The Beverley** without rest., 40 Murrayfield Ave, EH12 6AY, ℘ (0131) 337 1128, enqui ries@thebeverley.com, Fax (0131) 313 3275 – ‰ 🍴. 🌐🏧 ⒶⒺ VISA. ‰
                                                                 AV n
closed 22-28 December – **8 rm** ⊇ ✦35.00/80.00 – ✦✦70.00/90.00.
◆ Elegant 19C bay windowed house in quiet, tree-lined avenue close to the rugby stadium. Good value, individually appointed rooms with modern facilties and thoughtful extras.

🏠 **16 Lynedoch Place** without rest., 16 Lynedoch Pl, EH3 7PY, ℘ (0131) 225 5507, susie.lynedoch@btinternet.com – ‰. 🌐🏧 VISA
                                                                       CY s
closed Christmas – **3 rm** ⊇ ✦35.00/80.00 – ✦✦70.00/120.00.
◆ Under charming family management for over 20 years, a listed Georgian residence close to the West End with cosy and well maintained en suite rooms.

🏠 **Seven Danube Street** without rest., 7 Danube St, EH4 1NN, ℘ (0131) 332 2755, seven.danubestreet@virgin.net, Fax (0131) 343 3648, ☞ – ‰. 🌐🏧 VISA
                                                                      CY r
closed Christmas – **3 rm** ⊇ ✦60.00/90.00 – ✦✦100.00/150.00.
◆ Bright, traditionally styled rooms with antique furnishings in a residential street. Breakfasts taken around one large table add to a feeling of engaging hospitality.

🏠 **Castle View** without rest., 30 Castle St, EH2 3HT, ℘ (0131) 226 5784, coranne@castle viewgh.co.uk, Fax (0131) 226 1603 – ‰. 🌐🏧 VISA. ‰
                                                                   DY x
closed 23-29 December – **7 rm** ⊇ ✦45.00/100.00 – ✦✦70.00/100.00.
◆ As name implies, set in great position for tourists. Lounge with comfy sofas. Well-kept, individual rooms in a terraced house; those at front have castle views.

SCOTLAND

XXXX **Number One** (at Balmoral H.), 1 Princes St, EH2 2EQ, ℰ (0131) 622 8831, *number
one@roccofortehotels.com*, *Fax (0131) 557 8740* – ⊟. ☯☺ ᴁ ① VISA   EY **n**
Rest (dinner only and lunch in December) 55.00/65.00 ℤ ᐅᐧ.
Spec. Seared scallops with chestnut purée, smoked bacon and shellfish velouté. Poached
fillet of beef with horseradish glaze and mushroom emulsion. Caramelised hazelnut and
chocolate frangipane with banana cream.
  ♦ Edinburgh's nonpareil for polished fine dining and immaculate service; spacious basement setting. Original dishes with a well-balanced flair showcase Scottish produce.

XXX **Oloroso,** 33 Castle St, EH2 3DN, ℰ (0131) 226 7614, *info@oloroso.co.uk*,
Fax (0131) 226 7608, ≼, ᐂ – ⊟ ⇄ 14. ☯☺ ᴁ VISA   DY **o**
closed first week January and 25-26 December – **Rest** a la carte 28.95/45.45 ℤ.
  ♦ Modish third floor restaurant in heart of city. Busy, atmospheric bar. Lovely terrace with
good castle views to the west. Stylish, modern cooking with Asian influence.

XXX **Grill Room** (at Sheraton Grand H.), 1 Festival Sq, EH3 9SR, ℰ (0131) 221 6422,
Fax (0131) 229 6254 – ⊟ ℙ. ☯☺ ᴁ VISA   CDZ **v**
closed Saturday lunch, Sunday and Monday – **Rest** a la carte 29.00/50.00 ℤ.
  ♦ Ornate ceilings, wood panels and modern glass make an ideal setting for imaginative,
well presented cooking. Local ingredients with a few European and Pacific Rim elements.

XXX **Santini** (at Sheraton Grand H.), 8 Conference Sq, EH3 8AN, ℰ (0131) 221 7788,
Fax (0131) 221 7789 – ⊟ ℙ. ☯☺ ᴁ ① VISA   CDZ **v**
closed Saturday lunch and Sunday – **Rest** - Italian - 25.00 (lunch) and a la carte
27.50/46.50 **s.**.
  ♦ The personal touch is predominant in this stylish restaurant appealingly situated under a
superb spa. Charming service heightens the enjoyment of tasty, modern Italian food.

XXX **Cosmo,** 58A North Castle St, EH2 3LU, ℰ (0141) 226 6743, *info@cosmo-restaurant.co.uk*
– ☯☺ ᴁ ① VISA   DY **a**
closed first 2 weeks January, Saturday lunch, Sunday dinner and Bank Holidays – **Rest** 21.50
(lunch) and dinner a la carte 33.50/49.50 ℤ.
  ♦ Off busy city centre street into a vividly red, leather furnished lounge and dining room
in similar opulent style. Traditional menus served in pleasant, relaxing ambience.

XX **Off The Wall,** 105 High St, EH1 1SG, ℰ (0131) 558 1497, *otwedinburgh@aol.com* – ☯☺
ᴁ VISA   EY **c**
closed 24-26 December, 1-3 January, Sunday and Monday – **Rest** 16.50/19.95 (lunch) and
dinner a la carte 35.15/41.85 ℤ.
  ♦ Located on the Royal Mile, though hidden on first floor away from bustling crowds.
Vividly coloured dining room. Modern menus underpinned by a seasonal Scottish base.

XX **Channings** (at Channings H.), 12-16 South Learmonth Gdns, EH4 1EZ, ℰ (0131) 623
9302, *Fax (0131) 623 9306*, ᐂ – ☯☺ ᴁ ① VISA   CY **e**
Rest 15.00 (lunch) and dinner a la carte 21.00/33.00 **s.** ℤ.
  ♦ A warm, contemporary design doesn't detract from the formal ambience pervading this
basement restaurant in which classic Gallic flavours hold sway.

XX **Forth Floor (at Harvey Nichols),** 30-34 St Andrew Sq, EH2 2AD, ℰ (0131) 524
8350, *fourthfloorreservations@harveynichols.com*, *Fax (0131) 524 8351*, ≼ Castle and city
skyline, ᐂ – ▤ ☰. ☯☺ ᴁ ① VISA   EY **z**
closed 25 December, 1 January and dinner Sunday-Monday – **Rest** 17.50/31.00 and a la
carte 23.50/35.50 ℃ᐼ ℤ.
  ♦ Stylish restaurant with delightful outside terrace affording views over the city. Half the
room in informal brasserie-style and the other more formal. Modern, Scottish menus.

XX **Atrium,** 10 Cambridge St, EH1 2ED, ℰ (0131) 228 8882, *eat@atriumrestaurant.co.uk*,
Fax (0131) 228 8808 – ⊟. ☯☺ ᴁ ① VISA   DZ **c**
*closed 25-26 December, 1-2 January, Sunday and Saturday lunch except during Edinburgh
Festival* – **Rest** 17.50/27.00 and a la carte 30.50/43.50 ℤ ᐅᐧ.
  ♦ Located inside the Traverse Theatre, an adventurous repertoire enjoyed on tables made
of wooden railway sleepers. Twisted copper lamps subtly light the ultra-modern interior.

XX **Duck's at Le Marche Noir,** 2-4 Eyre Pl, EH3 5EP, ℰ (0131) 558 1608, *enqui
ries@ducks.co.uk*, *Fax (0131) 556 0798* – ⇄ 24. ☯☺ ᴁ ① VISA   BV **x**
closed 25-26 December and lunch Saturday-Monday – **Rest** 12.00/15.00 (lunch) and a la
carte 22.00/38.00 ℤ.
  ♦ Confident, inventive cuisine with a modern, discreetly French character, served with
friendly efficiency in bistro-style surroundings - intimate and very personally run.

XX **Hadrian's** (at Balmoral H.), 2 North Bridge, EH1 1TR, ℰ (0131) 557 5000,
Fax (0131) 557 3747 – ⊟. ☯☺ ᴁ ① VISA   EY **n**
Rest 16.95/20.95 and a la carte 24.45/39.20 **s.** ℃ᐼ ℤ.
  ♦ Drawing on light, clean-lined styling, reminiscent of Art Deco, and a "British new wave"
approach; an extensive range of contemporary brasserie classics and smart service.

XX **Roti,** 70 Rose St, North Lane, EH2 3DX, ✆ (0131) 225 1233, *info@roti.uk.com*, DY n
Fax (0131) 225 5374 – **MC** **AE** **VISA**
closed Saturday lunch, Sunday and Monday – **Rest** - Indian - a la carte 22.50/26.00 ⌺.
♦ Though set in an unprepossessing backstreet, this is an out-of-the-ordinary Indian restaurant in two sparse rooms serving authentic dishes with satisfyingly original elements.

XX **La Garrigue,** 31 Jeffrey St, EH1 1DH, ✆ (0131) 557 3032, *pugarrigue@btconnect.com*, EY v
Fax (0131) 5573032 – **MC** **AE** **VISA**
closed 1 week January, 25-26 December and Sunday except July-September – **Rest** -
French - 14.50/25.00 and a la carte 17.00/29.00.
♦ Very pleasant restaurant near the Royal Mile: beautiful handmade wood tables add warmth to rustic décor. Authentic French regional cooking with classical touches.

XX **The Tower,** Museum of Scotland (5th floor), Chambers St, EH1 1JF, ✆ (0131) 225 3003, EZ s
mail@tower-restaurant.com, Fax (0131) 220 4392, ≤, 斉 – 崑. **MC** **AE** **①** **VISA**
closed 25-26 December – **Rest** a la carte 28.00/44.00 ⌺.
♦ Game, grills and seafood feature in a popular, contemporary brasserie style menu. On the fifth floor of the Museum of Scotland - ask for a terrace table and admire the view.

X **Le Café Saint-Honoré,** 34 North West Thistle Street Lane, EH2 1EA, ✆ (0131) 226 DY c
2211 – **MC** **AE** **①** **VISA**
closed 3 days Christmas and 3 days New Year – **Rest** (booking essential) a la carte
24.00/35.00 ⌺⌺ ⌺.
♦ Tucked away off Frederick St, a bustling, personally run bistro furnished in the classic French style of a century ago. Good-value cuisine with a pronounced Gallic flavour.

X **First Coast,** 97-101 Dalry Rd, EH11 2AB, ✆ (0131) 313 4404, *info@first-coast.co.uk*, CZ e
Fax (0131) 346 7811 – ▤. **MC** **AE** **VISA**
closed Sunday, 25-26 December and 1-2 January – **Rest** a la carte 19.50/27.85 ⌺⌺.
♦ Informal restaurant near Haymarket station. The exposed stone walls in one of the rooms lend a rustic aspect. Sizeable menus boast a classic base with modern twists.

X **Fenwicks,** 15 Salisbury Pl, EH9 1SL, ✆ (0131) 667 4265, *enquiries@fenwicks-restaurant.co.uk, Fax (0131) 667 4285.* **MC** **AE** **①** **VISA** BX e
closed 25-26 December and 2 January – **Rest** 12.50/20.00 and a la carte approx 20.00.
♦ Cosy and unpretentious with a neighbourhood feel. Colourful French posters on the walls. Good value menus: the cooking is rustic Scottish with dashes of French inspiration.

X **Nargile,** 73 Hanover St, EH2 1EE, ✆ (0131) 225 5755, *info@nargile.co.uk* – **MC** **AE**
VISA DY e
closed 25-26 December, 1 January, Monday lunch and Sunday – **Rest** - Turkish - a la carte
15.95/25.70.
♦ Unpretentious and welcoming restaurant with simple décor and enthusiastic service. A la carte, set menus and lunch time mezes of tasty, well-prepared Turkish cuisine.

X **Blue,** 10 Cambridge St, EH1 2ED, ✆ (0131) 221 1222, *eat@bluebarcafe.com*, DZ c
Fax (0131) 228 8808 – ▤. **MC** **AE** **VISA**
closed 25-26 December, 1-2 January and Sunday except during Edinburgh Festival – **Rest**
13.95 (lunch) and a la carte 17.45/25.75 ⌺⌺ ⌺.
♦ Strikes a modern note with bright, curving walls, glass and simple settings. A café-bar with a light, concise and affordable menu drawing a young clientele. Bustling feel.

Leith *Edinburgh*.

🏛🏛 **Malmaison,** 1 Tower Pl, EH6 7DB, ✆ (0131) 468 5000, *edinburgh@malmaison.com*, BV i
Fax (0131) 468 5002, 斉, ₣₅ – 崑, ⇥ rm, ✆ & 曽 – 益 70. **MC** **AE** **①** **VISA**. ⌗
Brasserie : Rest 13.95/14.95 and a la carte 26.45/40.50 ⌺ – ⌷ 12.75 – **95 rm** ✦145.00 –
✦✦145.00, 5 suites.
♦ Imposing quayside sailors' mission converted in strikingly elegant style. Good-sized rooms, thoughtfully appointed, combine more traditional comfort with up-to-date overtones. Sophisticated brasserie with finely wrought iron.

🏛 **Express by Holiday Inn** without rest., Britannia Way, Ocean Drive, EH6 6JJ, ✆ (0131)
555 4422, *info@hiex-edinburgh.com, Fax (0131) 555 4646* – 崑 ⇥ ✆ & 曽 – 益 25. **MC** **AE**
① **VISA** BV e
145 rm ✦76.00 – ✦✦89.00.
♦ Modern, purpose-built hotel offering trim, bright, reasonably-priced accommodation. Convenient for Leith centre restaurants and a short walk from the Ocean Terminal.

XXX **Martin Wishart,** 54 The Shore, EH6 6RA, ✆ (0131) 553 3557, *info@martin-wishart.co.uk, Fax (0131) 467 7091* – **MC** **AE** **VISA** BV u
❀ *closed 1 week January, 1 week September, Christmas-New Year, Sunday and Monday* –
Rest (booking essential) 22.50/50.00 s. ⌺.
Spec. Lobster and smoked haddock soufflé, lobster cappuccino. John Dory with almonds and leeks, poached apricots and curry jus. Braised cheek and rib of beef, veal sweetbreads, wild mushroom ravioli.
♦ Simply decorated dockside conversion with a fully formed reputation. Modern French-accented menus characterised by clear, intelligently combined flavours.

XX **The Kitchin,** 78 Commercial Quay, EH6 6LX, ℰ (0131) 555 1755, *info@thekitchin.com,* Fax (0131) 553 0608, ☜ – ◍◎ ﾑᴇ ⓪ *VISA* BV z
❀ closed 2-4 January, 1-15 July and Sunday-Monday – Rest 20.00 (lunch) and a la carte 34.50/45.00 ♀.
Spec. Langoustine with braised pork belly with Mesclun salad. Seared halibut with ginger tomato chutney and herb beurre blanc. Poached pear with mint and chocolate sorbet.
♦ Former dockside warehouse, the industrial feel enhanced by original metal supports and battleship grey décor. Well-priced menus offering skilful, accomplished, modern cooking.

XX **The Vintners Rooms,** The Vaults, 87 Giles St, EH6 6BZ, ℰ (0131) 554 6767, *enqui ries@thevintnersrooms.com,* Fax (0131) 555 5653 – ◍◎ ﾑᴇ *VISA* BV r
closed 25-26 December, Sunday and Monday – Rest 19.00 (lunch) and a la carte 32.50/38.00 ♀.
♦ Atmospheric 18C bonded spirits warehouse with high ceilings, stone floor, rug-covered walls and candlelit side-room with ornate plasterwork. French/Mediterranean cooking.

at Kirknewton Southwest : 7 m. on A 71 – AX – ⊠ Edinburgh.

🏨 **Dalmahoy H. & Country Club** ♨, EH27 8EB, ℰ (0131) 333 1845, *mhrs.edigs.front desk@marriotthotels.com,* Fax (0131) 333 1433, ≪, ⑫, ⅙, ≋, 🖳, ▥, ☞, ⚘, ℀ – ⓵ ↝,
▤ rest, ⚓ ⅚ 🅿 – 🏛 300. ◍◎ ﾑᴇ *VISA* ℀
Pentland : Rest (dinner only) a la carte 31.00/35.00 ♀ – **The Long Weekend :** Rest (grill rest.) a la carte 19.00/32.00 ♀ – ☲ 14.95 – **212 rm** ☲ ✴105.00/165.00 – ✴✴105.00/165.00, 3 suites.
♦ Extended Georgian mansion in 1000 acres with 2 Championship golf courses. Comprehensive leisure club, smart rooms and a clubby cocktail lounge. Tranquil atmosphere with elegant comfort in Pentland restaurant. Informal modern dining at The Long Weekend.

EDNAM Borders 501 502 M 17 – see Kelso.

EDZELL Angus 501 M 13 Scotland G. – pop. 783.
Env. : Castle★ AC (The Pleasance★★★) W : 2 m.
Exc. : Glen Esk★, NW : 7 m.
Edinburgh 94 – Aberdeen 36 – Dundee 31.

🏨 **Glenesk,** High St, DD9 7TF, ℰ (01356) 648319, *gleneskhotel@btconnect.com,* Fax (01356) 647333, ⅙, ≋, 🖳, ☞ – ↝ 🅿 – 🏛 150. ◍◎ ﾑᴇ *VISA*
Rest (bar lunch)/dinner 25.00/35.00 s. and a la carte 19.45/37.35 – **23 rm** ☲ ✴60.00/90.00 – ✴✴90.00/120.00.
♦ Well run and family owned, a substantial 19C hotel with the pleasant village on its doorstep. Friendly atmosphere prevails; simple rooms of varying shapes and sizes. Restaurant overlooks golf course and gardens.

ELGIN Moray 501 K 11 Scotland G. – pop. 20 829.
See : Town★ – Cathedral★ (Chapter house★★)AC.
Exc. : Glenfiddich Distillery★, SE : 10 m. by A 941.
▥ Moray, Stotfield Rd, Lossiemouth ℰ (01343) 812018 – ▥ Hardhillock, Birnie Rd ℰ (01343) 542338 – ▥ Hopeman, Moray ℰ (01343) 830578.
🛈 17 High St ℰ (01343) 542666.
Edinburgh 198 – Aberdeen 68 – Fraserburgh 61 – Inverness 39.

🏨 **Mansion House,** The Haugh, IV30 1AW, via Haugh Rd ℰ (01343) 548811, *recep tion@mhelgin.co.uk,* Fax (01343) 547916, ⅙, ≋, 🖳, ☞ – ↝ 🅿 – 🏛 200. ◍◎ ﾑᴇ *VISA*, ℀
Rest 18.50/29.95 – **23 rm** ☲ ✴85.00/98.00 – ✴✴175.00.
♦ 19C Baronial mansion surrounded by lawned gardens. Country house-style interior. Rooms in main house most characterful, those in purpose-built annex more modern. The formal restaurant is decorated in warm yellows and blues.

⌂ **The Pines** without rest., East Rd, IV30 1XG, East : ½ m. on A 96 ℰ (01343) 552495, *enquiries@thepinesguesthouse.com,* Fax (01343) 552495, ☞ – ↝ 🅿 ◍◎ *VISA* ℀
6 rm ☲ ✴40.00/45.00 – ✴✴52.00/60.00.
♦ Detached Victorian house with a friendly and warm ambience amidst comfy, homely décor. Bedrooms are of a good size and furnished with colourful, modern fabrics.

↑ **The Croft** without rest., 10 Institution Rd, IV30 1QX, via Duff Ave ℘ (01343) 546004, thecroftelgin@hotmail.com, Fax (01343) 546004, � – ❄️ **P**. ♨
closed mid December- mid January – **3 rm** 🖙 ✚33.00/50.00 – ✚✚62.00/64.00.
♦ Victorian family home with delightful garden. Large, comfortable, library-style lounge and a breakfast room with fine dining suite. Comfy, pine furnished rooms.

↑ **The Lodge**, 20 Duff Ave, IV30 1QS, ℘ (01343) 549981, info@thelodge-elgin.com, Fax (01343) 540527, � – ❄️ **P**. **MO** **VISA**. ♨
Rest (by arrangement) a la carte 16.05/23.80 – **8 rm** 🖙 ✚32.00/50.00 – ✚✚56.00/66.00.
♦ Victorian house with a distinctive facade. Antique furnished hall and homely lounge with open fires. Comfortable bedrooms with dark wood furniture. Tasty home-cooked meals.

at Urquhart *East : 5 m. by A 96* – ⊠ *Elgin.*

↑ **Parrandier** ♨, The Old Church of Urquhart, Meft Rd, IV30 8NH, Northwest : ¼ m. by Main St and Meft Rd ℘ (01343) 843063, parrandier@freeuk.com, Fax (01343) 843063, ≤, � – ❄️ **P**. **MO** **VISA**
Rest (by arrangement) (communal dining) 12.00 – **3 rm** 🖙 ✚34.00/36.00 – ✚✚48.00/52.00.
♦ Former 19C church in quiet rural location converted to provide open plan lounge and split level dining area. Comfortable bedrooms with original church features.

at Duffus *Northwest : 5½ m. by A 941 on B 9012* – ⊠ *Elgin.*

↑ **Burnside House** without rest., IV30 5QS, Northwest : 1 ¾ m. by B 9012 on B 9040 ℘ (01343) 835165, burnside@begga.fsnet.co.uk, Fax (01343) 835165, ≤, ☎, 🌻 – ❄️ **P**
3 rm 🖙 ✚34.00 – ✚✚56.00.
♦ 19C house with garden; the residence of the founder of Gordonstoun School nearby. Attractive rooms with view; snooker table. Large bedrooms with tartan themes.

ELIE *Fife* 501 L 15.
Edinburgh 44 – Dundee 24 – St Andrews 13.

XX **Sangster's**, 51 High St, KY9 1BZ, ℘ (01333) 331001, bruce@sangsters.co.uk, Fax (01333) 331001 – **MO** **O** **VISA**
closed first 4 weeks January, 1 week November, 25-26 December, Saturday lunch, Sunday dinner and Monday – **Rest** (booking essential) 20.00/32.50.
♦ Husband and wife team run this homely, modern restaurant with local artwork for sale on the walls. The classical style of cooking employs notable use of good, local produce.

ERISKA (Isle of) *Argyll and Bute* 501 D 14 – ⊠ *Oban.*
Edinburgh 127 – Glasgow 104 – Oban 12.

🏨 **Isle of Eriska** ♨, Benderloch, PA37 1SD, ℘ (01631) 720371, office@eriska-hotel.co.uk, Fax (01631) 720531, ≤ Lismore and mountains, 🐾, ₤₃, ☎, ☐, 🏌, 🌻, 🏊, ❀ – ❄️, 🍴 rest, ♨ ₺ **P**. **MO** **AE** **VISA**
closed January – **Rest** (booking essential) (light lunch residents only)/dinner 39.00 – **18 rm** 🖙 ✚220.00 – ✚✚345.00, 4 suites.
♦ On a private island, a wonderfully secluded 19C Scottish Baronial mansion with dramatic views of Lismore and mountains. Highest levels of country house comfort and style. Elegant dining.

ESKDALEMUIR *Dumfries and Galloway* 501 K 18.
Edinburgh 71 – Dumfries 27 – Hawick 32.

🏠 **Hart Manor** ♨, DG13 0QQ, Southeast : 1 m. on B 709 ℘ (01387) 373217, visit@hartmanor.co.uk, ≤, 🌻 – ❄️ **P**. **MO** **VISA**. ♨
Rest (booking essential for non-residents) (dinner only) 30.00 – **5 rm** (dinner included) 🖙 ✚87.50 – ✚✚155.00.
♦ Former shooting lodge in an attractive rural location and dating from the 19C. Most of the comfortable bedrooms have countryside views, superior rooms are notably larger. Cosy restaurant offers daily changing, home-made, traditional fare.

FAIRLIE *North Ayrshire* 501 502 F 16.
Edinburgh 75 – Ayr 50 – Glasgow 36.

X **Fins**, Fencebay Fisheries, Fencefoot Farm, KA29 0EG, South : 1 ½ m. on A 78 ℘ (01475) 568989, fencebay@aol.com, Fax (01475) 568921 – **P**. **MO** **VISA**
closed 25-26 December, 1-2 January, Sunday dinner and Monday – **Rest** - Seafood - (booking essential) a la carte 22.00/43.50.
♦ Converted farm buildings house a simple, flag-floored restaurant, craft shops and a traditional beech smokery. Friendly service and fresh seasonal seafood.

FASNACLOICH *Argyll and Bute –* ⊠ *Appin.*
Edinburgh 133 – Fort William 34 – Oban 19.

⌂ **Lochside Cottage** ≫, PA38 4BJ, ℰ (01631) 730216, broadbent@lochsidecottage.fsnet.co.uk, Fax (01631) 730216, ≤ Loch Baile Mhic Chailen and mountains, ✿ – ⇔
P.

Rest (by arrangement) (communal dining) 26.00 – **3 rm** ⊡ ✸36.00 – ✸✸72.00.
* Captivating views of surrounding mountains and Loch Baile Mhic Chailen, on whose shore it stands in idyllic seclusion. Log fires in the lounge and inviting, cosy bedrooms. Dinners take place with a house party atmosphere as guests dine together at one table.

FIONNPHORT *Argyll and Bute 501* A 15 *– Shipping Services : see Mull (Isle of).*

FLODIGARRY *Highland 501* B 11 *– see Skye (Isle of).*

FORGANDENNY *Perth 501* J 14 *– see Perth.*

FORRES *Moray 501* J 11 *Scotland G. – pop. 8 967.*
Env. : *Sueno's Stone*★★, N :½ m. by A 940 on A 96 – *Brodie Castle*★ *AC*, W : 3 m. by A 96.
Exc. : *Elgin*★ (*Cathedral*★, chapter house★★ *AC*), E : 10¼ m. by A 96.
☗ Muiryshade ℰ (01309) 672949.
🛈 116 High St ℰ (01309) 673783 (Easter-October).
Edinburgh 165 – Aberdeen 80 – Inverness 27.

🏛 **Knockomie** ≫, Grantown Rd, IV36 2SG, South : 1 ½ m. on A 940 ℰ (01309) 673146, stay@knockomie.co.uk, Fax (01309) 673290, ✿, ♨ – ⇔ ✆ ₺ **P.** – 🖴 40. ◍◎ 🕮 ◑ 𝘝𝘐𝘚𝘈
closed 25-26 December – **The Grill Room** : Rest 25.00/37.00 and a la carte 25.00/36.95 ☿ –
16 rm ⊡ ✸110.00/200.00.
* Extended Arts and Crafts house in comfortable seclusion off a country road. Country house atmosphere. Bedrooms in main house older and more characterful. The Grill baronial style restaurant specializes in Scottish beef.

🏛 **Ramnee**, Victoria Rd, IV36 3BN, ℰ (01309) 672410, info@ramneehotel.com, Fax (01309) 673392, ✿ – ⇔ ✆ **P.** – 🖴 80. ◍◎ 🕮 ◑ 𝘝𝘐𝘚𝘈
closed 25 December and 1-3 January – **Hamlyns** : Rest a la carte 14.30/27.40 s. ☿ – **18 rm**
⊡ ✸75.00/105.00 – ✸✸105.00/155.00, 1 suite.
* Family owned Edwardian building in town centre with extensive lawned grounds. Welcoming public areas include panelled reception and pubby bar. Warmly traditional bedrooms. Formal dining room in traditional style.

🏠 **Cluny Bank**, St Leonard's Rd, IV36 1DW, South :½ m. by Tolbooth St ℰ (01309) 674304, mtb@clunybankhotel.co.uk, Fax (01309) 601444, ✿ – ⇔ **P.** ◍◎ 𝘝𝘐𝘚𝘈
closed 2 weeks January – **Rest** (dinner only) a la carte 20.40/32.40 s – **10 rm** ⊡
✸70.00/80.00 – ✸✸99.00.
* Personally run 19C listed house, nestling beneath Cluny Hill. Extended in 1910, it boasts antiques, oak staircase, original floor tiling and simple, pleasant, airy bedrooms. Dining room features much work by local artist.

at Dyke *West : 3¾ m. by A 96 –* ⊠ *Forres.*

⌂ **The Old Kirk** ≫ without rest., IV36 2TL, Northeast : ½ m. ℰ (01309) 641414, old kirk@gmx.net, Fax (01309) 641144 – ⇔ **P.** ◍◎ 𝘝𝘐𝘚𝘈
3 rm ⊡ ✸30.00/40.00 – ✸✸60.00.
* Former 19C church in country location. Stained glass window in first floor lounge; wood furnished breakfast room. Pleasantly furnished bedrooms with original stonework.

FORT WILLIAM *Highland 501* E 13 *Scotland G. – pop. 9 908.*
See : *Town*★.
Exc. : *The Road to the Isles*★★ (Neptune's Staircase (≤★★), Glenfinnan★ ≤★, Arisaig★, Silver Sands of Morar★, Mallaig★), NW : 46 m. by A 830 – Ardnamurchan Peninsula★★ – Ardnamurchan Point (≤★★), NW : 65 m. by A 830, A 861 and B 8007 – SE : Ben Nevis★★ (≤★★) - Glen Nevis★.
☗ North Rd ℰ (01397) 704464.
🛈 Cameron Sq ℰ (0845) 2255121.
Edinburgh 133 – Glasgow 104 – Inverness 68 – Oban 50.

Inverlochy Castle ⬙, Torlundy, PH33 6SN, Northeast : 3 m. on A 82 𝒫 (01397) 702177, *info@inverlochy.co.uk*, Fax (01397) 702953, ≤ loch and mountains, ⬙, 🖾, 🛋, ✗ – ✎ 🚗 **P**. 🆗 **AE** **VISA**
Rest (dinner booking essential for non-residents) 35.00/65.00 ♀ ⓐ – **17 rm** ⬙ ✦250.00/490.00 – ✦✦390.00/490.00, 1 suite.
Spec. Scallops with chicken oysters, thyme velouté and braised shallots. Pigeon stuffed artichoke heart with broad beans and summer truffle. Hazelnut praline with Champagne truffle beignet.
 ♦ A world renowned hotel set in a Victorian castle with extensive parkland and stunning views of the loch and mountains. Impressive luxury and detailed yet friendly service. Three classic dining rooms ensure that meals are a special experience.

Distillery House without rest., Nevis Bridge, North Rd, PH33 6LR, 𝒫 (01397) 700103, *disthouse@aol.com*, Fax (01397) 702980, 🚗 – ✎ 🚗 **P**. 🆗 **AE** **VISA**. ✾
10 rm ⬙ ✦40.00/70.00 – ✦✦90.00/90.00.
 ♦ Conveniently located a short walk from the centre of town, formerly part of Glenlochy distillery. Cosy guests' lounge and comfortable rooms, some with views of Ben Nevis.

The Grange ⬙ without rest., Grange Rd, PH33 6JF, South : ¾ m. by A 82 and Ashburn Lane 𝒫 (01397) 705516, *info@grangefortwilliam.com*, Fax (01397) 701595, ≤, 🚗 – ✎ 🚗 **P**. 🆗 **VISA**
March-October – **4 rm** ⬙ ✦85.00 – ✦✦110.00.
 ♦ Large Victorian house with attractive garden, in an elevated position in a quiet residential part of town. Very comfortable and tastefully furnished with many antiques.

Crolinnhe ⬙ without rest., Grange Rd, PH33 6JF, South : ¾ m. by A 82 and Ashburn Lane 𝒫 (01397) 702709, *crolinnhe@yahoo.com*, Fax (01397) 700506, ≤, 🚗 – ✎ 🚗 **P**. 🆗 **VISA**. ✾
Easter-October – **3 rm** ⬙ ✦110.00 – ✦✦125.00.
 ♦ Very comfortably and attractively furnished Victorian house, run with a real personal touch. Relaxing guests' sitting room and well furnished bedrooms.

Lochan Cottage without rest., Lochyside, PH33 7NX, North : 2 ½ m. by A 82, A 830 on B 8006 𝒫 (01397) 702695, *lochanco@btopenworld.com*, Fax (01397) 700506, ✾
Restricted opening November-December – **6 rm** ⬙ ✦24.00/60.00 – ✦✦48.00/60.00.
 ♦ Spotlessly kept, whitewashed cottage with homely public areas. Breakfast taken in conservatory overlooking delightfully landscaped gardens. Neat, well-kept rooms.

Ashburn House without rest., 18 Achintore Rd, PH33 6RQ, South : ½ m. on A 82 𝒫 (01397) 706000, *christine@no-1.fsworld.co.uk*, Fax (01397) 702024, 🚗 – ✎ 🚗 **P**. 🆗 **VISA**. ✾
7 rm ⬙ ✦45.00/50.00 – ✦✦90.00/100.00.
 ♦ Attractive Victorian house overlooking Loch Linnhe, on the main road into town which is a short walk away. Well furnished bedrooms and a comfortable conservatory lounge.

Lawriestone without rest., Achintore Rd, PH33 6RQ, South : ½ m. on A 82 𝒫 (01397) 700777, *susan@lawriestone.co.uk*, Fax (01397) 700777, ≤, 🚗 – ✎ 🚗 **P**. 🆗 **VISA**. ✾
closed 25-26 December and 1-2 January – **5 rm** ⬙ ✦60.00/80.00 – ✦✦60.00/80.00.
 ♦ Victorian house overlooking Loch Linnhe; not far from town centre, ideal for touring Western Highlands. Especially proud of Scottish breakfasts. Airy rooms; some with views.

✗ **Crannog**, The Underwater Centre, An Aird, PH33 6AN, 𝒫 (01397) 705589, *enqui ries@crannog.net*, Fax (01397) 708666, ≤ Loch Linnhe – 🆗 **VISA**
closed dinner 24-26 and 31 December and 1 January – **Rest** - Seafood - (booking essential) a la carte 25.10/34.45 s.
 ♦ Name reflects philosophy of catching and preparing local seafood. The owner, a former fisherman, has converted a bait store into a lochside restaurant; wonderful views.

at Banavie North : 3 m. by A 82 and A 830 on B 8004 – ⬚ Fort William.

Moorings, PH33 7LY, 𝒫 (01397) 772797, *reservations@moorings-fortwilliam.co.uk*, Fax (01397) 772441, ≤, 🚗 – ✎ 🚗 **P**. ⯐ 100. 🆗 **AE** ⬤ **VISA**
closed 24-26 December – **Rest** (bar lunch)/dinner 26.00 and a la carte 20.00/32.00 – **27 rm** ⬙ ✦60.00/94.00 – ✦✦90.00/134.00.
 ♦ Modern accommodation in traditional style. Adjacent to Caledonian Canal and at start of "Road to the Isles". Most rooms boast views of mountains and Neptune's Staircase. Meals served in panelled lounge bar with views of Ben Nevis.

GALSON *Western Isles (Outer Hebrides)* 501 A 8 – *see Lewis and Harris (Isle of).*

We try to be as accurate as possible when giving room rates.
But prices are susceptible to change,
so please check rates when booking.

SCOTLAND

GATEHEAD *East Ayrshire* 501 502 G 17 – ✉ *Kilmarnock*.
Edinburgh 72 – Ayr 10 – Glasgow 25 – Kilmarnock 5.

 Cochrane Inn, 45 Main Rd, KA2 0AP, ℰ (01563) 570122 – **P**. **☎☉ ⓘ** *VISA*. ﹪
Rest (booking essential) a la carte 16.00/20.00 ♀.
* Neat and tidy pub in tiny hamlet near Kilmarnock. Traditional establishment with beams and open fire. Mixture of popular and modern dishes. Perennially busy.

GATEHOUSE OF FLEET *Dumfries and Galloway* 501 502 H 19 – *pop. 919*.
🛅 *Gatehouse, Innisfree, Lauriestown, Castle Douglas* ℰ (01557) 814766.
🛈 *Car Park* ℰ (01557) 814212 (Easter-October).
Edinburgh 113 – Dumfries 33 – Stranraer 42.

Cally Palace ﹪, DG7 2DL, East : ½ m. on B 727 ℰ (01557) 814341, *info@callypalace.co.uk*, Fax (01557) 814522, ≤, ⑫, Ⅰぁ, ⓢ, 🔲, Ⅰ℠, ⌬, ﹩, ﹪ – ﹩ **P** – 🚗 40. **☎☉ ⅀ꜜ** *VISA*. ﹪
closed 3 January-mid February – **Rest** 30.00 (dinner) and lunch a la carte 20.20/21.95 ♀ –
50 rm (dinner included) ﹡104.00/131.00 – ﹡﹡218.00/230.00, 5 suites.
* Highly impressive 18C mansion with golf course. Sitting room with fantastically ornate ceiling of original gilding. Small leisure centre. Large rooms with delightful views. Elegant dining room serving Galloway produce. Pianist in attendance.

GATTONSIDE *Borders* – see Melrose.

GIGHA (Isle of) *Argyll and Bute* 501 C 16.
 to Tayinloan (Caledonian MacBrayne Ltd) 8-10 daily (20 mn).
Edinburgh 168.

🏠 **Gigha** ﹪, PA41 7AA, ℰ (01583) 505254, *hotel@gigha.org.uk*, Fax (01583) 505244, ≤
Sound of Gigha and Kintyre Peninsula, 🍴, ⌬ – ﹩ **P**. **☎☉** *VISA*
closed Christmas – **Rest** (booking essential for non-residents) (bar lunch)/dinner 26.95 –
13 rm ⌸ ﹡49.95/78.45 – ﹡﹡99.90/139.90.
* 18C whitewashed house on island owned by residents; views over Ardminish Bay to Kintyre. Cosy pine-panelled bar. Elegant lounge. Simple, clean and tidy rooms. Inviting restaurant with exposed stone walls and pine tables.

GLAMIS *Angus* 501 K/L 14 – ✉ *Forfar*.
See : *Town*★ – *Castle*★★.
Exc. : *Meigle Museum*★ *AC W : 7 m. by A 94.*
Edinburgh 69 – Dundee 13 – Forfar 7.

🏠 **Castleton House**, DD8 1SJ, West : 3 ¼ m. on A 94 ℰ (01307) 840340, *hotel@castleton glamis.co.uk*, Fax (01307) 840506, ⌬, ⌬ – ﹩﹦ **☪ P**. **☎☉ ⅀ꜜ ⓘ** *VISA*
The Conservatory : **Rest** 35.00 and a la carte 35.00/60.00 **s**. ♀ – **6 rm** ⌸ ﹡130.00/150.00
– ﹡﹡200.00.
* Moat still visible in gardens of this 20C country house built on site of medieval fortress. Appealing lounges, cosy bar. Individually designed, attractively appointed rooms. Stylish conservatory restaurant looks out to garden.

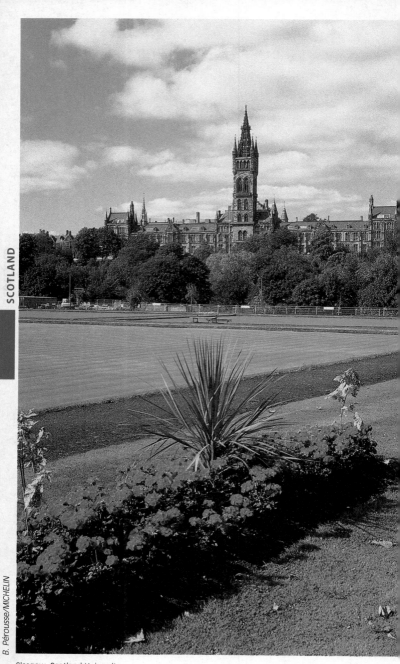

Glasgow: Scotland University

GLASGOW

501 502 H 16 *Scotland G.* – *pop. 624 501.*

Edinburgh 46 – Manchester 221.

TOURIST INFORMATION

🖪 *11 George Sq ℘ (0141) 204 4400; enquiries@seeglasgow.com*
🖪 *Glasgow Airport, Tourist Information Desk, ℘ (0141) 848 4440.*

PRACTICAL INFORMATION

🖫 *Littlehill, Auchinairn Rd ℘ (0141) 772 1916.*
🖫 *Rouken Glen, Stewarton Rd, Thornliebank ℘ (0141) 638 7044,* AX.
🖫 *Linn Park, Simshill Rd ℘ (0141) 633 0377,* BX.
🖫 *Lethamhill, Cumbernauld Rd ℘ (0141) 770 6220,* BV.
🖫 *Alexandra Park, Dennistoun ℘ (0141) 556 1294,* BV.
🖫 *King's Park, 150a Croftpark Ave, Croftfoot ℘ (0141) 630 1597,* BX.
🖫 *Knightswood, Lincoln Ave ℘ (0141) 959 6358,* AV.
🖫 *Ruchill Park, Brassey St ℘ (0141) 946 7676.*
Access to Oban by helicopter.
✈ *Glasgow Airport : ℘ (0870) 0400008, W : 8 m. by M 8,* AV.
Terminal : *Coach service from Glasgow Central and Queen Street main line Railway Stations and from Anderston Cross and Buchanan Bus Stations.*
✈ *see also Prestwick.*

SIGHTS

See : *City*★★★ – *Cathedral*★★★ *(*≼★*)* DZ – *The Burrell Collection*★★★ AX **M1** – *Hunterian Art Gallery*★★ *(Whistler Collection*★★★ – *Mackintosh Wing*★★★*) AC* CY **M4** – *Museum of Transport*★★ *(Scottish Built Cars*★★★*, The Clyde Room of Ship Models*★★★*)* AV **M6** – *Art Gallery and Museum Kelvingrove*★★ CY – *Pollok House*★ *(The Paintings*★★*)* AX **D** – *Tolbooth Steeple*★ DZ – *Hunterian Museum (Coin and Medal Collection*★*)* CY **M5** – *City Chambers*★ DZ **C** – *Glasgow School of Art*★ *AC* CY **M3** – *Necropolis (*≼★ *of Cathedral)* DYZ – *Gallery of Modern Art*★ – *Glasgow (National) Science Centre*★*, Pacific Quay* AV.

Env. : *Paisley Museum and Art Gallery (Paisley Shawl Section*★*), W : 4 m. by M 8* AV.

Exc. : *The Trossachs*★★★*, N : 31 m. by A 879* BV*, A 81 and A 821 – Loch Lomond*★★*, NW : 19 m. by A 82* AV *– New Lanark*★★*, SE : 20 m. by M 74 and A 72* BX.

SCOTLAND

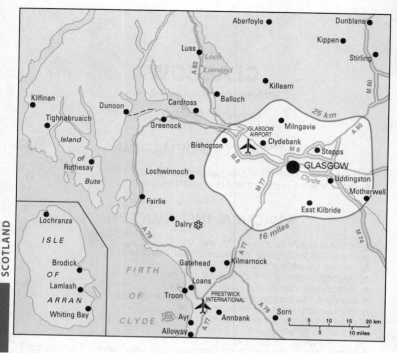

Hilton Glasgow, 1 William St, G3 8HT, ☎ (0141) 204 5555, *reservations.glasgow@hilton.com*, Fax (0141) 204 5004, ≤, ℐ₆, ⊑, ⊠ – |♦| ⅙ ≡ ⅏ ₺ ⇔ 🅟 – 🖾 1000. 🐾 🆎 ⓞ *VISA*. ⅜
CZ s
Minsky's : Rest 18.95/24.95 and a la carte 27.40/36.85 ♀ – (see also *Camerons* below) – ⊑ 17.95 – **315 rm** ♦179.00/230.00 – ♦♦179.00/230.00, 4 suites.
♦ A city centre tower with impressive views on every side. Comfortable, comprehensively fitted rooms. Extensive leisure and conference facilities. Spacious, modern Minsky's has the style of a New York deli.

Radisson SAS, 301 Argyle St, G2 8DL, ☎ (0141) 204 3333, *reservations.glasgow@radissonsas.com*, Fax (0141) 204 3344, ℐ₆, ⊑, ⊠ – |♦| ⅙ rm, ≡ ⅏ ₺ 🅟 – 🖾 800. 🐾 🆎 ⓞ *VISA*. ⅜
DZ o
Collage : Rest - Mediterranean - 18.95/25.95 and a la carte 22.65/35.40 S. ♀ – *TaPaell'Ya :* Rest - Tapas - (closed Saturday lunch and Sunday) a la carte 20.40/31.40 ♀ – ⊑ 13.75 – **246 rm** ♦198.00 – ♦♦198.00, 1 suite.
♦ A stunning, angular, modish exterior greets visitors to this consummate, modern commercial hotel. Large, stylish, eclectically furnished bedrooms. Collage is a bright modern restaurant. Ta Paell'Ya serves tapas.

Hotel du Vin, 1 Devonshire Gardens, G12 0UX, ☎ (0141) 339 2001, Fax (0141) 337 1663, ℐ₆ – ⅙ ⅏ – 🖾 50. 🐾 🆎 ⓞ *VISA*
AV a
Bistro : Rest (closed Saturday lunch) 17.50 (lunch) and a la carte 24.95/45.95 – ⊑ 17.00 – **32 rm** ♦140.00/305.00 – ♦♦140.00/305.00, 3 suites.
♦ Collection of adjoining 19C houses in terrace, furnished with attention to detail. Elegantly convivial drawing room, comfortable bedrooms and unobtrusive service. Smart Bistro.

Malmaison, 278 West George St, G2 4LL, ☎ (0141) 572 1000, *glasgow@malmaison.com*, Fax (0141) 572 1002, ℐ₆ – |♦|, ⅙ rm, ⅏ ₺ – 🖾 25. 🐾 🆎 ⓞ *VISA*
CY c
🍽 *The Brasserie* (☎ (0141) 572 1001) : Rest 14.50 (lunch) and a la carte 32.00/41.00 ♀ – ⊑ 12.75 – **64 rm** ♦140.00 – ♦♦140.00, 8 suites.
♦ Visually arresting former Masonic chapel. Comfortable, well-proportioned rooms seem effortlessly stylish with bold patterns and colours and thoughtful extra attentions. Informal Brasserie with French themed menu and Champagne bar.

Glasgow Marriott, 500 Argyle St, Anderston, G3 8RR, ✆ (0141) 226 5577, *front desk.glasgow@marriotthotels.co.uk*, Fax (0141) 221 9202, ≤, ⅙, ≋, ☐ – ⅛ ✦ ▤ ⬛ ⬛ ⅙ – ⬛ 600. ⬟⬟ ⬛ ⬛ **VISA**. ✦
Mediterrano : Rest - Mediterranean - (dinner only) a la carte 16.50/22.95 s. ♀ – ⬜ 14.95 – 300 rm ★95.00/105.00 – ★★105.00/115.00.
◆ Internationally owned city centre hotel with every necessary convenience for working travellers and an extensive lounge and café-bar. Upper floors have views of the city. Strong Mediterranean feel infuses restaurant.

CZ a

Abode Glasgow, 129 Bath St, G2 2SZ, ✆ (0141) 221 6789, *reservationsglasgow@abo dehotels.co.uk*, Fax (0141) 221 6777 – ⅛ ✦ ✦ ⬛ – ⬛ 70. ⬟⬟ ⬛ ⬛ **VISA**. ✦
Rest – (see *Michael Caines* below) – ⬜ 12.95 – 60 rm ★125.00 – ★★125.00.
◆ Near Mackintosh's School of Art, an early 20C building decorated with a daring modern palette: striking colour schemes and lighting in the spacious, elegantly fitted rooms. Basement grill restaurant, plus seafood and Teppan-Yaki bar.

DY v

Millennium Glasgow, 40 George Sq, G2 1DS, ✆ (0141) 332 6711, *reservations.glas gow@mill-cop.com*, Fax (0141) 332 4264 – ⅛ ✦ ✦ ▤ ⬛ ⬛ ⬛ ✦
closed 25-26 December *Brasserie on George Square* : Rest *(closed Sunday lunch)* 12.00/19.75 and a la carte 22.25/40.25 ♀ – ⬜ 15.75 – 111 rm ★79.00/175.00 – ★★89.00/185.00, 5 suites.
◆ Group-owned hotel aimed at business travellers, nicely located overlooking George Square and adjacent to main railway station. Contemporary interior in a Victorian building. Brasserie with airy, columned interior and views to Square.

DZ v

Carlton George, 44 West George St, G2 1DH, ✆ (0141) 353 6373, *resgeorge@carlton hotels.co.uk*, Fax (0141) 353 6263 – ⅛ ✦ ✦ ▤ ⬛ ⬛. ✦
closed 23/27 December and 1-2 January – ⬚⬚ *Windows* : Rest 16.50/21.50 and dinner a la carte 21.85/34.15 s. ♀ – ⬜ 13.50 – 64 rm ★185.00 – ★★185.00.
◆ A quiet oasis away from the city bustle. Attractive tartan decorated bedrooms bestow warm tidings. Comfortable 7th floor business lounge. An overall traditional ambience. Ask for restaurant table with excellent view across city's rooftops.

DZ a

Sherbrooke Castle, 11 Sherbrooke Ave, Pollokshields, G41 4PG, ✆ (0141) 427 4227, *mail@sherbrooke.co.uk*, Fax (0141) 427 5685, ⬛ – ✦, ▤ rest, ✦ ⬛ – ⬛ 300. ⬟⬟ ⬛ ⬛ **VISA**
Morrisons : Rest a la carte 16.00/34.00 ♀ – 22 rm ⬜ ★95.00/110.00 – ★★160.00, 2 suites.
◆ Late 19C baronial Romanticism given free rein inside and out. The hall is richly furnished and imposing; rooms in the old castle have a comfortable country house refinement. Panelled Victorian dining room with open fire.

AX r

City Inn, Finnieston Quay, G3 8HN, ✆ (0141) 240 1002, *glasgow.reservations@cit yinn.com*, Fax (0141) 248 2754, ≤, ⬛ – ⅛ ✦ ▤ ✦ ⬛ ⬛ – ⬛ 50. ⬟⬟ ⬛ ⬛ **VISA**.
closed 26 December – *City Café* : Rest 14.95/16.50 and a la carte 18.70/33.15 ♀ – ⬜ 12.50 – 164 rm ★135.00 – ★★135.00.
◆ Quayside location and views of the Clyde. Well priced hotel with a "business-friendly" ethos; neatly maintained modern rooms with sofas and en suite power showers. Restaurant fronts waterside terrace.

CZ u

Bewley's, 110 Bath St, G2 2EN, ✆ (0141) 353 0800, *gla@bewleyshotels.com*, Fax (0141) 353 0900 – ⅛, ✦ rm, ▤ rest, ✦ ⬛ ⬟⬟ ⬛ ⬛ **VISA**. ✦
closed 24-29 December – *Loop* : Rest (dinner only) a la carte 17.85/21.85 – ⬜ 6.95 – 103 rm ★69.00 – ★★69.00.
◆ A well-run group hotel, relaxed but professional in approach, in the middle of Glasgow's shopping streets. Upper rooms boast rooftop views and duplex apartments. People-watch from glass-walled eatery.

DY i

Tulip Inn, 80 Ballater St, G5 0TW, ✆ (0141) 429 4233, *info@tulipinnglasgow.co.uk*, Fax (0141) 429 4244 – ⅛ ✦, ▤ rest, ✦ ⬛ – ⬛ 180. ⬟⬟ ⬛ ⬛ **VISA**
Bibo Bar and Bistro : Rest (dinner only) a la carte 15.70/25.50 – ⬜ 7.95 – 114 rm ★59.50/85.00 – ★★59.50/85.00.
◆ Sensibly priced hotel appealing to cost-conscious business travellers. Good access to motorway and city centre. Bedrooms have working space and most modern conveniences. Informal, bright eatery serves a varied menu.

BX a

Express by Holiday Inn without rest., Theatreland, 165 West Nile St, G1 2RL, ✆ (0141) 331 6800, *express@higlasgow.com*, Fax (0141) 331 6828 – ⅛ ✦ ✦ ⬛ ⬟⬟ ⬛ ⬛ **VISA**. ✦
closed 25-26 December – 118 rm ★65.00 – ★★77.00.
◆ Modern accommodation - simple and well arranged with adequate amenities. Equally suitable for business travel or leisure tourism.

DY o

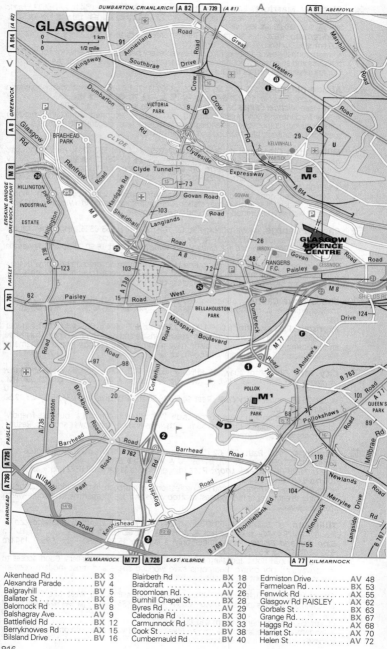

Aikenhead Rd . . . . BX 3
Alexandra Parade . . . . BV 4
Balgrayhill . . . . BV 5
Ballater St . . . . BX 6
Balornock Rd . . . . BV 8
Balshagray Ave . . . . AV 9
Battlefield Rd . . . . BX 12
Berryknowes Rd . . . . AX 15
Bilsland Drive . . . . BV 16

Blairbeth Rd . . . . BX 18
Braidcraft . . . . AX 20
Broomloan Rd . . . . AV 26
Burnhill Chapel St . . . . BX 28
Byres Rd . . . . AV 29
Caledonia Rd . . . . BX 30
Carmunnock Rd . . . . BX 33
Cook St . . . . BV 38
Cumbernauld Rd . . . . BV 40

Edmiston Drive . . . . AV 48
Farmeloan Rd . . . . BX 53
Fenwick Rd . . . . AX 55
Glasgow Rd PAISLEY . . . . . AX 62
Gorbals St . . . . BX 63
Grange Rd . . . . BX 67
Haggs Rd . . . . AX 68
Harriet St . . . . AX 70
Helen St . . . . AV 72

816

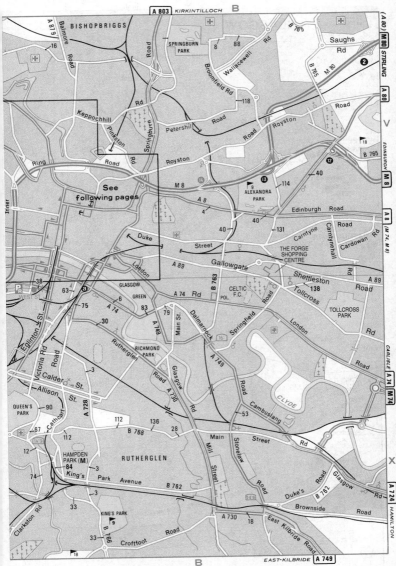

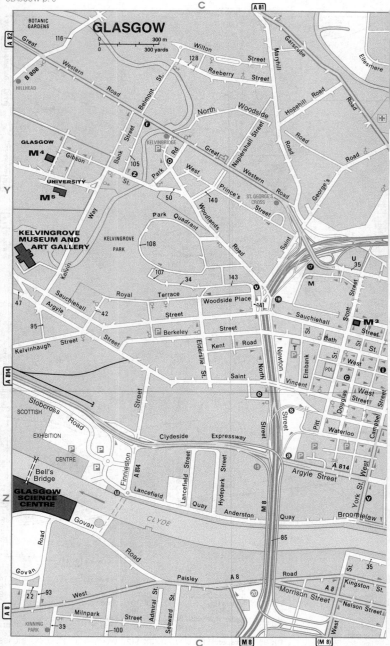

GLASGOW

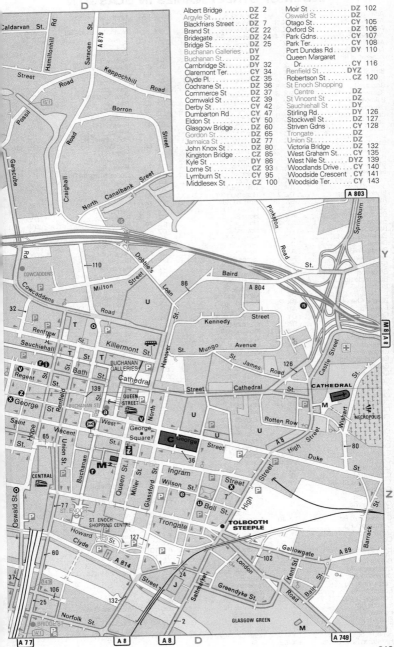

819

↑ **Park House**, 13 Victoria Park Gardens South, G11 7BX, ✆ (0141) 339 1559, *mail@par khouseglasgow.co.uk* – ✦✦ **P**. **🆖** **VISA**. ❀
AV n
closed 2 weeks spring, Christmas and New Year – **Rest** (by arrangement) 25.00 – **3 rm** ⊑ ✦40.00/60.00 – ✦✦70.00/80.00.
♦ An extensive, smartly kept suburban house retaining much of its Victorian character. Comfortable, classically stylish bedrooms combine period furniture with CD systems. Dining room with neatly set 19C ambience.

↑ **The Town House** without rest., 4 Hughenden Terrace, G12 9XR, ✆ (0141) 357 0862, *hospitality@thetownhouseglasgow.com, Fax (0141) 339 9605* – ✦✦. **🆖** **AE** **VISA**. ❀ AV i
10 rm ⊑ ✦60.00 – ✦✦72.00.
♦ Elegant, personally run town house with fine Victorian plasterwork: spacious, pleasantly decorated rooms and an inviting firelit lounge. Hearty breakfasts.

XXXX **Camerons** (at Hilton Glasgow H.), 1 William St, G3 8HT, ✆ (0141) 204 5511, *Fax (0141) 204 5004* – ■ **P**. **🆖** **AE** **VISA**
CZ s
closed Saturday lunch, Sunday and Bank Holidays – **Rest** 19.50 (lunch) and dinner a la carte 29.85/44.85 ⊑.
♦ Carefully prepared and full-flavoured modern cuisine with strong Scottish character. Very formal, neo-classical styling and smart staff have advanced its local reputation.

XXX **Buttery**, 652 Argyle St, G3 8UF, ✆ (0141) 221 8188, *the–buttery@hotmail.co.uk, Fax (0141) 204 4639* – **P**. **🆖** **AE** **VISA**
CZ e
closed Sunday, Monday and Saturday lunch – **Rest** 22.00/38.00 🍷 ⊑.
♦ Established, comfortable restaurant away from the bright lights; red velour and ageing bric-a-brac reveal its past as a pub. Ambitiously composed modern Scottish repertoire.

XXX **étain**, The Glass House, Springfield Court, G1 3JN, ✆ (0141) 225 5630, *etain@zinc bon.co.uk, Fax (0141) 225 5640* – 🎶 ■. **🆖** **AE** **VISA**
DZ r
closed 25 December, 1 January, Saturday lunch and Sunday dinner – **Rest** 29.00/32.00 ⊑.
♦ Comfortable, contemporary restaurant in unusual glass extension to Princes Square Centre. Well-sourced Scottish ingredients prepared in a modern, interesting way.

XXX **Rococo**, 202 West George St, G2 2NR, ✆ (0141) 221 5004, *info@rococoglasgow.co.uk, Fax (0141) 221 5006* – ■. **🆖** **AE** **VISA**
DYZ z
closed 26 December and 1 January – **Rest** 18.95/39.50 and lunch a la carte 19.40/33.85 🍷 ⊑ 🌿.
♦ In style, more like studied avant-garde: stark, white-walled cellar with vibrant modern art and high-backed leather chairs. Accomplished, fully flavoured contemporary menu.

XXX **Lux**, 1051 Great Western Rd, G12 0XP, ✆ (0141) 576 7576, *enquiries@luxstazione.co.uk, Fax (0141) 576 0162* – ■ **P**. **🆖** **AE** **①** **VISA**
AV o
closed 25-26 December, 1-2 January and Sunday – **Rest** (dinner only) 29.50/33.50.
♦ 19C railway station converted with clean-lined elegance: dark wood, subtle lighting and vivid blue banquettes. Fine service and flavourful, well-prepared modern menus.

XX **Michael Caines** (at Abode Glasgow), 129 Bath St, G2 2SZ, ✆ (0141) 572 6011 – ✦✦ ■. **🆖** **AE** **①** **VISA**. ❀
DY v
closed Sunday – **Rest** 12.50/17.50 and a la carte 30.00/40.00 ⊑.
♦ Smart, stylish restaurant in boutique hotel, a mirrored wall creating impression of size. Quality décor matched by clean, unfussy cooking prepared with finesse and skill.

XX **Brian Maule at Chardon d'Or**, 176 West Regent St, G2 4RL, ✆ (0141) 248 3801, *info@brianmaule.com, Fax (0141) 248 3901* – **🆖** **AE** **①** **VISA**
CY i
closed 2 weeks January, 25-26 December, 1 January, Saturday lunch, Sunday and Bank Holidays – **Rest** 15.50/18.50 (lunch) and a la carte approx 36.00 🍷 ⊑.
♦ Large pillared Georgian building. Airy interior with ornate carved ceiling and hung with modern art. Modern dishes with fine Scottish produce; substantial wine list.

XX **Gamba**, 225a West George St, G2 2ND, ✆ (0141) 572 0899, *info@gamba.co.uk, Fax (0141) 572 0896* – **🆖** **AE** **VISA**
DZ x
closed 25-26 December, 1-2 January and Sunday – **Rest** - Seafood - 15.95/18.95 (lunch) and a la carte 34.00/40.00 🍷.
♦ Seafood specialists: an enterprising diversity of influences and well-priced lunches. Compact, brightly decorated basement in hot terracotta with a pleasant cosy bar.

XX **La Parmigiana**, 447 Great Western Rd, Kelvinbridge, G12 8HH, ✆ (0141) 334 0686, *s.giovanazzi@btclick.com, Fax (0141) 357 5595* – ■. **🆖** **AE** **①** **VISA**
CY r
closed 25-26 December, 1-2 January and Sunday – **Rest** - Italian - 11.50 (lunch) and a la carte 24.20/32.70 s. 🍷.
♦ Compact, pleasantly decorated traditional eatery with a lively atmosphere and good local reputation. Obliging, professional service and a sound, authentic Italian repertoire.

SCOTLAND

XX **Manna,** 104 Bath St, G2 2EN, ℰ (0141) 332 6678, *info@mannarestaurant.co.uk,*
Fax (0141) 332 6549 – **⓪ℬ** **AE** **VISA**
DY r
closed 25-26 December, 1-2 January and Sunday lunch – **Rest** 14.95 (lunch) and a la carte
29.00/39.00 ✦☒ ☑.
• Parrot motifs recur everywhere, even on the door handles! Well-spaced tables and
mirrored walls add a sense of space to the basement. A free-ranging fusion style prevails.

XX **Zinc Bar and Grill,** Princes Sq, G1 3JN, ℰ (0141) 225 5620, *reservationsglasgow@zinc*
bar.co.uk, Fax (0141) 225 5640 – ⧉ ⊟. **⓪ℬ** **AE** **①** **VISA**
DZ r
closed 25 December, 1 January and Sunday dinner – **Rest** a la carte 16.95/27.00 ☑.
• Contemporary dining on second floor atrium of Princes Square Centre. Stylish décor
and tableware. Modern menu offering popular dishes; good value lunches.

XX **Ho Wong,** 82 York St, G2 8LE, ℰ (0141) 221 3550, *ho.wong@amserve.com,*
Fax (0141) 248 5330 – ⊟. **⓪ℬ** **AE** **VISA**
CZ v
closed Sunday lunch – **Rest** - Chinese (Peking) - 9.50/42.50 and a la carte approx 23.90.
• In an up-and-coming part of town, a long-established restaurant with a modern style.
Authentic Chinese cuisine with the emphasis on Peking dishes.

XX **Amber Regent,** 50 West Regent St, G2 2QZ, ℰ (0141) 331 1655, *Fax (0141) 353 3398* –
⊟, **⓪ℬ** **AE** **VISA**
DY e
closed Chinese New Year and Sunday – **Rest** - Chinese - 9.95/35.95 and a la carte
24.75/39.00.
• Traditional Chinese dishes served by conscientious staff. Comfy, personally managed
restaurant in a 19C office building in the heart of the city. Good value lunch.

XX **Shish Mahal,** 60-68 Park Rd, G4 9JF, ℰ (0141) 3398256, *reservations@shishmahal.co.uk,*
Fax (0141) 572 0800 – ⊟. **⓪ℬ** **AE** **VISA**
CY o
closed 25 December and Sunday lunch – **Rest** - Indian - 5.50/11.95 and a la carte
12.85/22.40.
• Tandoori specialities in a varied pan-Indian menu, attentive service and an evocative
modern interior of etched glass, oak and Moorish tiles have won city-wide recognition.

X **The Ubiquitous Chip,** 12 Ashton Lane, G12 8SJ, off Byres Rd ℰ (0141) 334 5007,
mall@ubiquitouschip.co.uk, Fax (0141) 337 1302 – ⊟. **⓪ℬ** **AE** **①** **VISA**
AV e
closed 25 December and 1 January – **Rest** 28.65/39.85 and a la carte 11.65/31.00 ☑ ✦.
• A long-standing favourite, "The Chip" mixes Scottish and fusion styles. Well known for its
glass-roofed courtyard, with a more formal but equally lively warehouse interior.

X **Stravaigin,** 28 Gibson St, (basement), G12 8NX, ℰ (0141) 334 2665, *stravaigin@btinter*
net.com, Fax (0141) 334 4099 – ⊟. **⓪ℬ** **AE** **①** **VISA**
CY z
closed 25 December, and 1 January – **Rest** 13.95 (lunch) and a la carte 21.50/31.00 ✦☒.
• Basement restaurant with bright murals. A refined instinct for genuinely global cuisine
produces surprising but well-prepared combinations - ask about pre-theatre menus.

X **Stravaigin 2,** 8 Ruthven Lane, G12 9BG, off Byres Rd ℰ (0141) 334 7165, *stravai*
gin@btinternet.com, Fax (0141) 357 4785 – ⊟. **⓪ℬ** **AE** **①** **VISA**
AV s
closed 25 December and 1 January – **Rest** 13.95 (lunch) and a la carte 26.30/33.30 ✦☒.
• Lilac painted cottage tucked away in an alley off Byres Rd. Simple, unfussy, modern
bistro-style interior. Contemporary menu offering eclectic range of original dishes.

X **The Dhabba,** 44 Candleriggs, G1 1LE, ℰ (0141) 553 1249, *info@thedhabba.com,*
Fax (0141) 553 1730 – **⓪ℬ** **AE** **VISA**
DZ u
Rest - North Indian - 10.00 (lunch) and a la carte 22.00/25.00.
• In the heart of the Merchant City, this large, modern restaurant boasts bold colours and
huge wall photos. Concentrates on authentic, accomplished North Indian cooking.

X **Mao,** 84 Brunswick St, G1 1TD, ℰ (0141) 564 5161, *glasgow@cafemao.com,*
Fax (0141) 564 5161 – ⊟. **⓪ℬ** **AE** **VISA**
DZ e
closed 24-26 December – **Rest** - South East Asian - 11.50 (lunch) and a la carte
14.00/21.00 **s.** ☑.
• Eatery located on two floors, decorated in bright, funky style with vivid, modern colours;
centrally located, buzzy atmosphere. Thoroughly tasty South East Asian food.

🍺 **Babbity Bowster,** 16-18 Blackfriars St, G1 1PE, ℰ (0141) 552 5055,
Fax (0141) 552 7774, ⌂ – **⓪ℬ** **AE** **①** **VISA**, ✂
DZ x
closed 25 December – **Rest** a la carte 12.95/25.85 ☑.
• Well regarded pub of Georgian origins with columned façade. Paradoxically simple ambi-
ence: gingham-clothed tables, hearty Scottish dishes, slightly more formal in evenings.

at Glasgow Airport (Renfrewshire) West : 8 m. by M 8 – AV – ✉ Paisley.

🏨 **Express by Holiday Inn,** St Andrews Drive, PA3 2TJ, ℰ (0141) 842 1100, *info@hiex-*
glasgow.com, Fax (0141) 842 1122 – ⧉ ✿, ⊟ rest, ✆ ₺ ▣ – ⚤ 75. **⓪ℬ** **AE** **①** **VISA**
Rest (dinner only) a la carte 16.00/21.50 – **143 rm** ✸99.00/109.00 – ✸✸99.00/109.00.
• Ideal for both business travellers and families. Spacious, carefully designed, bright and
modern bedrooms with plenty of work space. Complimentary continental breakfast. Traditional and busy buffet-style restaurant.

SCOTLAND

GLENDALE Highland – see Skye (Isle of).

GLENDEVON Perth and Kinross 501 I/J 15.
Edinburgh 37 – Perth 26 – Stirling 19.

🍴 **Tormaukin Country Inn** with rm, FK14 7JY, ℘ (01259) 781252, enquiries@tormaukin.co.uk, Fax (01259) 781526, 斎, ◄ – 🅿. ℳ⑩ ﹢ ﹢ VISA
closed 5 days January – **Rest** a la carte 16.85/30.00 ♀ – **12 rm** ⊈ ✱55.00/65.00 –
✱✱75.00/95.00.
♦ Extended 18C drovers' inn tucked away in this picturesque glen. Traditional Scottish fare is served in the atmospheric bar or in the cosy restaurant. Comfortable bedrooms.

GLENROTHES Fife 501 K 15 Scotland G. – pop. 38 679.
Env. : Falkland★ (Palace of Falkland★ AC, Gardens★ AC) N : 5½ m. by A 92 and A 912.
ᐟ₈ Thornton, Station Rd ℘ (01592) 771173 – ᐟ₈ Golf Course Rd ℘ (01592) 758686 – ᐟ₈
Balbirnie Park, Markinch ℘ (01592) 612095 – ᐟ₉ Auchterderran, Woodend Rd, Cardenden
℘ (01592) 721579 – ᐟ₉ Leslie, Balsillie Laws ℘ (01592) 620040.
Edinburgh 33 – Dundee 25 – Stirling 36.

🏨 **Balbirnie House** ⟫, Markinch, KY7 6NE, Northeast : 1 ¾ m. by A 911 and A 92 on B
9130 ℘ (01592) 610066, info@balbirnie.co.uk, Fax (01592) 610529, ᐟ₈, 斎, ♮ – ﹢﹢ ﹢ 🅿.
🅐⟩ 250. ℳ⑩ ﹢ ﹢ ⑩ VISA
Orangery : Rest 15.50/35.00 ♀ – **28 rm** ⊈ ✱135.00/165.00 – ✱✱230.00/250.00, 2 suites.
♦ Highly imposing part Georgian mansion in Capability Brown-styled grounds. Several lounges and library bar with period style and individually furnished country house rooms. Glass-roofed restaurant; friendly service from kilted staff.

🏨 **Express by Holiday Inn** without rest., Leslie Roundabout, Leslie Rd, KY7 3EP, West :
2 m. on A 911 ℘ (01592) 745309, ebhi-glenrothes@btconnect.com, Fax (01592) 745577 –
﹢﹢ ﹢ ﹢ 🅿 – 🅐⟩ 30. ℳ⑩ ﹢ ﹢ ⑩ VISA. ﹢
49 rm ✱59.95 – ✱✱59.95.
♦ Modern lodge accommodation in the heart of Fife within close proximity of Dundee, Perth and St. Andrews. Ideal for business travellers.

GRANTOWN-ON-SPEY Highland 501 J 12 – pop. 2 166.
ᐟ₈ Golf Course Rd ℘ (01479) 872079 – ᐟ₉ Abernethy, Nethy Bridge ℘ (01479) 821305.
🛈 54 High St ℘ (0845) 2255121 (April-October).
Edinburgh 143 – Inverness 34 – Perth 99.

🏨 **Culdearn House**, Woodlands Terrace, PH26 3JU, ℘ (01479) 872106, enquiries@culdearn.com, Fax (01479) 873641, 斎 – ﹢﹢ ﹢ 🅿. ℳ⑩ VISA. ﹢
closed February – **Rest** (booking essential for non-residents) (dinner only) 30.00 **s.** – **6 rm**
(dinner included) ⊈ ✱85.00/88.00 – ✱✱170.00/176.00.
♦ Personally run Victorian granite stone hotel offering a high degree of luxury, including beautifully furnished drawing room and very tastefully furnished bedrooms. Formally attired dining room; good Scottish home cooking.

🏨 **The Pines**, Woodside Ave, PH26 3JR, ℘ (01479) 872092, info@thepinesgrantown.co.uk,
斎 – ﹢﹢ 🅿. ℳ⑩ VISA
March-October – **Rest** (dinner only) (residents only) (set menu only) 30.00 – **7 rm** ⊈
✱50.00/70.00 – ✱✱120.00/130.00.
♦ Top level hospitality in an attractive 19C house with lovely rear garden leading onto woods and Spey. Elegant lounges display fine pieces of art. Individually appointed rooms. Candlelit dinners, full of Scottish flavours, are a special event!

🏨 **Ravenscourt House**, Seafield Ave, PH26 3JG, ℘ (01479) 872286, info@ravenscourthouse.co.uk, 斎 – ﹢﹢ ﹢ 🅿. ℳ⑩ VISA. ﹢
Rest (booking essential for non-residents) (dinner only) a la carte 23.00/27.00 **s.** ♀ – **8 rm**
⊈ ✱43.00 – ✱✱86.00.
♦ 19C former manse. Solid stone exterior. Interiors designed to enhance original house. Two comfortable drawing rooms; very welcoming, spacious bedrooms. Huge conservatory dining room with menu of locally sourced produce.

XX **The Glass House**, Grant Rd, PH26 3LD, ℘ (01479) 872980, Fax (01479) 872980, 斎 – 🅿.
ℳ⑩ ﹢ ﹢ VISA
closed 2 weeks November, 1-2 January, 25-26 December, Sunday dinner, Monday and Tuesday lunch – **Rest** a la carte 27.15/33.40.
♦ Conservatory style dining in a house extension near the high street. Light-filled interior overlooks the garden. Amiable owner serves tasty, seasonal modern British dishes.

SCOTLAND

at Dulnain Bridge *Southwest : 3 m. by A 95 on A 938 –* ⊠ *Grantown-on-Spey.*

🏠 **Muckrach Lodge** ♧, PH26 3LY, West : ½ m. on A 938 ℰ (01479) 851257, *info@muck rach.co.uk, Fax (01479) 851325,* ≤, 🐎, 🔊 – ⅓⅔ ℃ & P – 🖾 35. ㎝ 𝔸𝔼 ⓘ 𝘝𝘐𝘚𝘈
closed 2-16 January and Monday and Tuesday in winter – **Finlarig :** Rest (dinner only)
37.50 s. – **Conservatory Bistro :** Rest 15.50/21.00 (lunch) and dinner a la carte
18.95/28.95 ♈ – **10 rm** ⌖ ★75.00/150.00 – ★★170.00, 2 suites.
   ◆ 19C country house whose name translates as "haunt of the wild boar". Log fires and soft
sofas in lounges. Bedrooms with fresh flowers and old books. Modern, original dining in
Finlarig. Vast Conservatory offers enviable views and lighter dishes.

🏠 **Auchendean Lodge**, PH26 3LU, South : 1 m. on A 95 ℰ (01479) 851347, *hotel@au chendean.com,* ≤ Spey Valley and Cairngorms, 🐎 – ⅓⅔ P, ㎝ 𝔸𝔼 𝘝𝘐𝘚𝘈
26 March-29 October – Rest (booking essential for non-residents) (dinner only) 34.00 –
5 rm ⌖ ★56.50/69.50 – ★★122.00.
   ◆ Early 20C lodge with Arts and Crafts style architecture. Superb views over Spey Valley to
Cairngorms. Log-fired drawing room. Comfortable rooms with elegant pine furniture.
Enviably located restaurant facing the mountains.

GREENOCK *Inverclyde* 501 F 16 – *pop. 45 467.*
   🏌, 🏌 *Forsyth St* ℰ *(01475) 720793.*
   Edinburgh 70 – Ayr 48 – Glasgow 24.

🏠 **Express by Holiday Inn** *without rest.,* Cartsburn, PA15 4RT, East : ¾ m. off A 8
ℰ (01475) 786666, *greenock@expressbyholidayinn.net, Fax (01475) 786777* – 🛗 ⅓⅔ ℃ &
P – 🖾 80. ㎝ 𝔸𝔼 ⓘ 𝘝𝘐𝘚𝘈
71 rm ★39.95/69.95 – ★★42.50/69.95.
   ◆ Large, purpose-built hotel aimed at business traveller. Reception with multi-purpose bar
and breakfast room. Light snacks in evening. Spacious, modern, lodge style rooms.

GRETNA GREEN *Dumfries and Galloway.*
   Edinburgh 88 – Annan 10.5 – Carlisle 11.

🏠🏠 **Smiths**, DG16 5EA, ℰ (01461) 337007, *info@gretnagreen.com* – 🛗 ⅓⅔ 🖳 ℃ & P –
🖾 200. ㎝ 𝔸𝔼 ⓘ 𝘝𝘐𝘚𝘈 . ♧
Rest 20.00 and dinner a la carte 15.20/32.60 – **49 rm** ⌖ ★75.00/115.00 – ★★85.00/125.00,
1 suite.
   ◆ Family owned hotel near famous Blacksmiths Shop. Airy, open-plan lounge/bar. Rooms
and suites are the strength - all are modern and well equipped: revolving bed in penthouse. Brasserie dishes in bright, spacious restaurant.

GRIMSAY *Western Isles (Outer Hebrides)* 501 Y 11 – *see Uist (Isles of).*

GRULINE *Argyll and Bute – see Mull (Isle of).*

GULLANE *East Lothian* 501 L 15 *Scotland G. – pop. 2 172.*
   Env. : *Dirleton★ (Castle★) NE : 2 m. by A 198.*
   Edinburgh 19 – North Berwick 5.

🏠 **Greywalls** ♧, Duncur Rd, Muirfield, EH31 2EG, ℰ (01620) 842144, *hotel@grey walls.co.uk, Fax (01620) 842241,* ≤ Gardens and Muirfield golf course, 🐎, ⅔ – P – 🖾 30.
㎝ 𝔸𝔼 𝘝𝘐𝘚𝘈
closed January-February – Rest (booking essential for non-residents) 25.00/45.00 – **23 rm**
⌖ ★130.00/260.00 – ★★250.00/295.00.
   ◆ Crescent shaped Edwardian country house by Lutyens; formal gardens by Jekyll. Superb
views of Muirfield golf course. Beautifully kept sitting room. Charming, stylish rooms.
Inviting dining room with warm, pretty country house style, view of golf course.

Look out for red symbols, indicating particularly pleasant establishments.

SCOTLAND

HADDINGTON *East Lothian 501* L 16 *Scotland G. – pop. 8 851.*

See : *Town★ - High Street★.*
Env. : *Lennoxlove★ AC, S : 1 m – Gifford★, SE : 5 m. by B 6369.*
Exc. : *Tantallon Castle★★ (clifftop site★★★) AC, NE : 12 m. by A 1 and A 198 – Northern foothills of the Lammermuir Hills★★, S : 14 m. by A 6137 and B 6368 – Stenton★, E : 7 m.*
🏌 *Amisfield Park ℰ (01620) 823627.*
Edinburgh 17 – Hawick 53 – Newcastle upon Tyne 101.

XX **Bonars,** Poldrate, Tyne House, EH41 4DA, South : ¼ m. on B 6368 ℰ (01620) 822100, dabonar@aol.com – 🆎 **VISA**
closed 26 December, 1 January, Monday and Tuesday – **Rest** a la carte 18.35/32.65 ₤.
♦ In charming surroundings adjacent to burn and 18C mill. Interior in warm Mediterranean style. Regularly changing menus of elaborate dishes using Scottish produce.

HARRIS (Isle of) *Western Isles (Outer Hebrides) 501* Z 10 – *see Lewis and Harris (Isle of).*

HAWICK *Borders 501 502* L 17 *Scotland G. – pop. 14 573.*

Exc. : *Jedburgh★ - Abbey★★, Mary Queen of Scots Visitor Centre★, NE : 11 m. by A 698 and B 6358 – Bowhill★★, N : 15 m. by A 7, B 7009 and B 7039.*
Edinburgh 51 – Galashiels 18 – Jedburgh 12.

🏠 **Glenteviot Park** ॐ, Hassendeanburn, TD9 8RU, Northeast : 3 ¾ m. by A 698 ℰ (01450) 870660, info@glenteviotpark.com, Fax (01450) 870154, ≤, ≋, ⌘, 🌷 – ⊁ 🅿. 🆎 🆎 **VISA**
Rest (dinner only) (residents only) 29.00 – **5 rm** ⌂ ✱78.00 – ✱✱135.00.
♦ Purpose-built hotel idyllically sited overlooking River Teviot and surrounding hills. Rustic bar/lounge, sauna and snooker room. Individually furnished, well-equipped rooms. Cosy dining room offering homecooked menus.

INVERGARRY *Highland 501* F 12 *Scotland G.* – ✉ *Inverness.*

Env. : *The Great Glen★.*
Edinburgh 159 – Fort William 25 – Inverness 43 – Kyle of Lochalsh 50.

🏰 **Glengarry Castle** ॐ, PH35 4HW, on A 82 ℰ (01809) 501254, castle@glengarry.net, Fax (01809) 501207, ≤, ⌘, 🌷, 🕭, ⅋ – 🔟 ⊁ ⌘ 🅿. 🆎 **VISA**
mid March- mid November – **Rest** (light lunch Monday-Saturday)/dinner 28.00 **s.** ₤ – **26 rm** ⌂ ✱61.00/90.00 – ✱✱146.00/160.00.
♦ On shores of Loch Oich, and named after eponymous Victorian castle whose ruin stands in grounds. Warm country house feel throughout; many bedrooms retain original fittings. Dining room shares the warm, country house style of the hotel.

INVERGORDON *Ross-shire 501* H 10.

🏠 **Kincraig House,** IV18 0LF, on A 9 ℰ (01349) 852587, info@kincraig-house-hotel.co.uk, Fax (01349) 852193, ≤, ⌘ – ⊁ ⌘ & 🅿 – ⅍ 60. 🆎 🆎 **VISA** ⌘
Rest 16.50/32.50 – **15 rm** ⌂ ✱65.00/110.00 – ✱✱110.00/130.00.
♦ In an enviably elevated position, this Georgian house has been restored with style, retaining wood panelling and Adams fireplaces. Some of the comfy rooms are four-postered. Smart restaurant serves locally sourced, traditional dishes.

INVERKEILOR *Angus 501* M 14 – ✉ *Arbroath.*
Edinburgh 85 – Aberdeen 32 – Dundee 22.

XX **Gordon's** with rm, 32 Main St, DD11 5RN, ℰ (01241) 830364, gordonsrest@aol.com – 🅿. 🆎 **VISA** ⌘
closed 2 weeks January – **Rest** (closed Monday and Sunday dinner to non-residents) (booking essential) 25.00/39.00 – **3 rm** ⌂ ✱60.00 – ✱✱90.00.
♦ Family owned restaurant in small village. Welcoming atmosphere, beams, open fires and rugs on the wood floors. Classic cooking with modern twists. Pleasant, pine fitted rooms.

INVERMORISTON *Inverness 501* G 12.

⌂ **Tigh na Bruach** without rest., IV63 7YE, Southwest : ½ m. on A 82 ℰ (01320) 351349, tighnabruach@btconnect.com, ⌘, ⌘ – 🔟 ⊁ ⌘ 🅿. 🆎 ⓞ **VISA**. ⌘
3 rm ⌂ ✱60.00/80.00 – ✱✱80.00/90.00.
♦ Don't be put off by rather unprepossessing exterior: located by Loch Lomond, it has beautiful gardens, and very comfy rooms with pleasant little terraces overlooking a lake.

INVERNESS Highland 501 H 11 *Scotland G.* – *pop. 40 949.*

See : *Town*★ – *Museum and Art Gallery*★ Y **M.**

Exc. : *Loch Ness*★★ , *SW : by A 82 Z* – *Clava Cairns*★ , *E : 9 m. by Culcabock Rd, B 9006 and B 851 Z* – *Cawdor Castle*★ *AC, NE : 14 m. by A 96 and B 9090* Y.

🇮🇸 *Culcabock Rd* ℘ *(01463) 239882 Z* – 🇮🇸 *Torvean, Glenurquhart Rd* ℘ *(01463) 711434.*

✈ *Inverness Airport, Dalcross :* ℘ *(01667) 464000, NE : 8 m. by A 96* Y.

🅱 *Castle Wynd* ℘ *(0845) 2255121* Y, *invernesstic@host.co.uk.*

Edinburgh 156 – Aberdeen 107 – Dundee 134.

Plans opposite

🏨 **Rocpool Reserve**, Culduthel Rd, IV2 4AG, ℘ (01463) 240089, *info@rocpool.com*, Fax (01463) 248431, 🍴 – 🍽 🛏 ℃ & 🄿. **⬤S** 🄰🄴 *VISA*. 	Z r
Reserve : Rest a la carte 25.50/38.00 – **11 rm** ⊇ ✝115.00/180.00 – ✝✝115.00/180.00.
♦ 19C house reborn as a boutique hotel - the talk of the city! Look cool in sexy, stylish bar and sleep in rooms the ultimate in chic design, with breathtaking bathrooms. Italian twists enhance accomplished modern dishes in sleek restaurant.

🏨 **Glenmoriston Town House**, 20 Ness Bank, IV2 4SF, ℘ (01463) 223777, *reception@glenmoristontownhouse.com*, Fax (01463) 712378 – 🍽 ℃ 🄿. **⬤S** 🄰🄴 🄳 *VISA*. 🛇	Z x
Contrast : Rest a la carte approx 18.00 – (see also **Abstract** below) – **30 rm** ⊇ ✝95.00/115.00 – ✝✝130.00/170.00.
♦ Chic, stylish town house. Modern cocktail bar a trendy meeting point. Bedrooms are individualistic, those on the front enjoying river views; those at the rear are quieter. Locally sourced cooking at Contrast.

🏠 **Glendruidh House** 🐾, Old Edinburgh Rd South, IV2 6AR, South : 3 m. by B 865, B 9006 off B 8082 ℘ (01463) 226499, *michael@cozzee-nessie-bed.co.uk*, Fax (01463) 710745, 🌳 – 🍽 ℃ 🄿. **⬤S** 🄰🄴 🄳 *VISA*. 🛇
closed 23-28 December – **Rest** (booking essential) (residents only) (dinner only) 33.00 **s.** ⅌ – **5 rm** ⊇ ✝69.00/99.00 – ✝✝99.00/149.00.
♦ An oasis on city outskirts! Mature gardens outside; smartly updated 200 year old personally run comforts inside. Unusual circular shaped drawing room. Stylish bedrooms.

🏠 **Express by Holiday Inn** without rest., Stoneyfield, IV2 7PA, East : 1½ m. by B 865 on A 96 (eastbound carriageway) ℘ (01463) 732700, *managerinverness@expressholidayinn.co.uk*, Fax (01463) 732732 – 📶 🍽 ℃ & 🄿 – 🔬 30. **⬤S** 🄰🄴 🄳 *VISA*
94 rm ✝80.00/90.00 – ✝✝80.00/90.00.
♦ Purpose-built lodge-style accommodation at an out-of-town retail park. Fully equipped bedrooms, ideal for the business traveller.

🏡 **Millwood House** without rest., 36 Old Mill Rd, IV2 3HR, ℘ (01463) 237254, *enquiries@millwoodhouse.co.uk*, Fax (01463) 719400, 🌳 – 🍽 ℃ 🄿. **⬤S** *VISA*. 🛇	Z z
closed Christmas-New Year – **3 rm** ⊇ ✝70.00 – ✝✝93.00/96.00.
♦ A warm welcome is assured by the charming owner of this delightful house. Relax in front of a log fire in the antique furnished drawing room. Cosy, warm and bright bedrooms.

🏡 **Ballifeary House** without rest., 10 Ballifeary Rd, IV3 5PJ, ℘ (01463) 235572, *info@ballifearyguesthouse.co.uk*, Fax (01463) 717583 – 🍽 🄿. **⬤S** *VISA*. 🛇	Z n
closed 24-28 December – **7 rm** ⊇ ✝30.00/70.00 – ✝✝60.00/76.00.
♦ Immaculately kept Victorian house with a pretty rear garden. Peaceful and relaxing feel as no children under 15 years are taken. A wholly non-smoking establishment.

🏡 **Moyness House** without rest., 6 Bruce Gdns, IV3 5EN, ℘ (01463) 233836, *stay@moyness.co.uk*, Fax (01463) 233836, 🌳 – 🍽 🄿. **⬤S** 🄰🄴 *VISA*. 🛇	Z c
closed Christmas – **7 rm** ⊇ ✝36.00/70.00 – ✝✝72.00/80.00.
♦ Immaculately clipped hedges frame this attractive Victorian villa. Bedrooms vary in shape and size but all are comfortable, individually decorated and fully en suite.

🏡 **Eden House** without rest., 8 Ballifeary Rd, IV3 5PJ, ℘ (01463) 230278, *edenhouse@btinternet.com*, Fax (01463) 230278 – 🍽 🄿. **⬤S** *VISA*. 🛇	Z o
closed mid December-March – **4 rm** ⊇ ✝40.00/60.00 – ✝✝60.00/74.00.
♦ Pleasant ten minute walk into the city centre. Friendly proprietors run a neat and spotless house. Pretty little conservatory and good sized bedrooms.

XXX **Abstract** (at Glenmoriston Town House), 20 Ness Bank, IV2 4SF, ℘ (01463) 223777, Fax (01463) 712378 – 🄿. **⬤S** 🄰🄴 🄳 *VISA*	Z x
closed Monday – **Rest** (dinner only) 42.00 **s.** ⅌.
♦ Restaurant, bar and conservatory with considerable style. Vast wall mirror offsets abstract ink pictures. Accomplished cooking with Gallic accent is impressively original.

XX **Rocpool Rendezvous**, 1 Ness Walk, IV3 5NE, ℘ (01463) 717274, *info@rocpool.com* – 🍴 *VISA*	Y i
closed 25 December, 1 January and Sunday lunch – **Rest** a la carte 20.00/34.00 ⅌.
♦ On the banks of the river Ness, this modern, cosmopolitan restaurant has a stylish ambience, popular with business diners. Modern cooking with a British/Mediterranean axis.

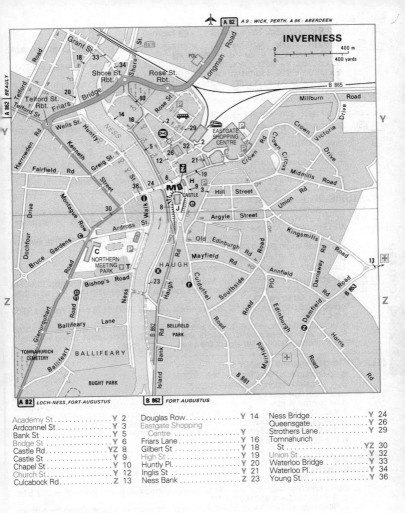

INVERSENESS

A 82 A 9 : WICK, PERTH, A 96 : ABERDEEN

0 400 m
0 400 yards

A 82 LOCH-NESS, FORT-AUGUSTUS

B 862 FORT-AUGUSTUS

Academy St. . . . . **Y** 2
Ardconnel St . . . . **Y** 3
Bank St . . . . **Y** 5
Bridge St . . . . **Y** 6
Castle Rd. . . . . **YZ** 8
Castle St . . . . **Y** 9
Chapel St . . . . **Y** 10
Church St . . . . **Y** 12
Culcabock Rd. . . . . **Z** 13

Douglas Row . . . . **Y** 14
Eastgate Shopping
   Centre . . . . **Y**
Friars Lane . . . . **Y** 16
Gilbert St . . . . **Y** 18
High St . . . . **Y** 19
Huntly Pl. . . . . **Y** 20
Inglis St . . . . **Y** 21
Ness Bank . . . . **Z** 23

Ness Bridge. . . . . **Y** 24
Queensgate. . . . . **Y** 26
Strothers Lane. . . . . **Y** 29
Tomnahurich
   St . . . . **YZ** 30
Union St . . . . **Y** 32
Waterloo Bridge . . . . **Y** 33
Waterloo Pl. . . . . **Y** 34
Young St . . . . **Y** 36

✗ **Café 1,** Castle St, IV2 3EA, ℰ (01463) 226200, *info@cafe1.net, Fax (01463) 716363* – **Ⓜ⒪ AE**
VISA   Y e
closed Sunday – **Rest** 12.00 (lunch) and a la carte 15.00/28.00 **s.** ⌷.
   ◆ Personally run bistro opposite the castle with an informal touch, enhanced by tiled flooring and modish chairs. Local ingredients feature in regularly changing modern menus.

at Culloden *East : 3 m. by A 96* – Y – ✉ *Inverness.*

🏛 **Culloden House** ⌂, IV2 7BZ, ℰ (01463) 790461, *info@cullodenhouse.co.uk, Fax (01463) 792181,* ≤, ⌷, 🐟, ⌷ – ✦ ℙ, **Ⓜ⒪ AE ⒪ VISA**
closed Christmas and 2 weeks January – **Adams Dining Room :** **Rest** a la carte 32.00/41.50
⌷ – **25 rm** ⌷ ✦100.00/175.00 – ✦✦140.00/240.00, 3 suites.
   ◆ Imposing Georgian country house in 40 acres, requisitioned by Bonnie Prince Charlie in 1746. Drawing rooms boast ornate wall-hung plaster friezes. Antique-furnished rooms. Adam's plaster reliefs adorn walls and ceiling of grand dining room; traditional menu.

827

at Dunain Park *Southwest : 2½ m. on A 82 – Z –* ⊠ *Inverness.*

🏨 **Dunain Park** ॐ, IV3 8JN, ℰ (01463) 230512, *info@dunainparkhotel.co.uk,*
Fax (01463) 224532, ≤, 畑 – ❖ **P. ⑩ⓢ ⒶⒺ VISA**
closed January – **Rest** (dinner only) a la carte 25.00/33.00 – **5 rm** ⊈ ✱99.00/125.00 –
✱✱138.00/198.00, **8 suites** ⊈ 138.00/198.00.
◆ Secluded Georgian country house, surrounded by gardens and woodland. Nicely furnished sitting rooms. Marbled bathrooms and spacious bedrooms, some with four-poster
beds. Dining room is warmly decorated and the tables highly polished.

at Bunchrew *West : 3 m. on A 862 – Y –* ⊠ *Inverness.*

🏨 **Bunchrew House** ॐ, IV3 8TA, ℰ (01463) 234917, *welcome@bunchrew-inver*
ness.co.uk, Fax (01463) 710620, ≤, 畑, ♤ – ❖ ⅙ **P. ⑩ⓢ ⒶⒺ VISA. ⅛**
closed 4 days Christmas – **Rest** 26.50/36.50 **s.** – **16 rm** ⊈ ✱97.50/170.00 –
✱✱145.00/240.00.
◆ Unhurried relaxation is assured at this 17C Scottish mansion nestling in a tranquil spot
on the shores of Bealy Firth. Drawing room is wood panelled; bedrooms restful. Gardens
seen through the windows provide a pleasant backdrop to spacious dining room.

INVERURIE *Aberdeenshire* 501 M 12 *Scotland G.* – *pop. 10 882.*

Exc. : *Castle Fraser★ (exterior★★) AC, SW : 6 m. by B 993 – Pitmedden Gardens★★, NE : 10
m. by B 9170 and A 920 – Haddo House★, N : 14 m. by B 9170 and B 9005 – Fyvie Castle★,
N : 13 m. by B 9170 and A 947.*

🛇 *Blackhall Rd* ℰ (01467) 624080 – 🛇 *Kintore, Balbithan Rd* ℰ (01467) 632631 – 🛇 *Kemnay,
Monymusk Rd* ℰ (01467) 642060.

🚪 *18 High St* ℰ (01467) 625800.

Edinburgh 147 – Aberdeen 17 – Inverness 90.

🏨 **Strathburn,** Burghmuir Drive, AB51 4GY, Northwest : 1 ¼ m. by Inverness rd (A 96)
ℰ (01467) 624422, *strathburn@btconnect.com,* Fax (01467) 625133, 畑 – ❖, ▦ rest, ⚹
P – 🕰 30. **⑩ⓢ ⒶⒺ ① VISA**
closed 25-26 December and 1-2 January – **Rest** a la carte 14.50/31.75 **s.** – **25 rm** ⊈ ✱80.00
– ✱✱110.00.
◆ Uncluttered purpose-built hotel in a residential area of town and conveniently located
for A96. Well-planned modern interiors. Rooms in uniform fitted style. Dining available in
the comfortable lounge-bar area or the adjacent dining room.

ISLAY (Isle of) *Argyll and Bute* 501 B 16.

🛇 *25 Charlotte St, Port Ellen* ℰ (01496) 300094.

✈ *Port Ellen Airport :* ℰ (01496) 302022.

⛴ *from Port Askaig to Isle of Jura (Feolin) (Caledonian MacBrayne Ltd) frequent services
daily (approx. 4 mn) – from Port Ellen or Port Askaig to Kintyre Peninsula (Kennacraig)
(Caledonian MacBrayne Ltd) 1-2 daily – from Port Askaig to Oban via Isle of Colonsay (Scalasaig) (Caledonian MacBrayneLtd) weekly – from Port Askaig to Isle of Colonsay (Scalasaig)
and Kintyre Peninsula (Kennacraig) (Caledonian MacBrayne Ltd) weekly.*

🚪 *The Square, Main St, Bowmore* ℰ (08707) 200617.

Ballygrant *Argyll and Bute.*

🏠 **Kilmeny** ॐ, PA45 7QW, Southwest : ½ m. on A 846 ℰ (01496) 840668, *info@kil*
meny.co.uk, Fax (01496) 840668, ≤, 畑, ♤ – ❖ **P. ⅛**
closed Christmas and New Year – **Rest** (by arrangement) (communal dining) 28.00 – **5 rm**
⊈ ✱50.00/70.00 – ✱✱100.00/140.00.
◆ 19C converted farmhouse on a working farm. Its elevated position affords far reaching
countryside views. Best of Scottish hospitality, home-cooking and comfort.

Bowmore *Argyll and Bute.*

✕✕ **Harbour Inn** with rm, The Square, PA43 7JR, ℰ (01496) 810330, *info@harbour-inn.com,*
Fax (01496) 810990, ≤ – **⑩ⓢ VISA. ⅛**
Rest a la carte 26.40/42.20 ♀ – **7 rm** ⊈ ✱65.00/85.00 – ✱✱145.00.
◆ Attractive whitewashed inn in busy little town, short walk from distillery. Panelled bar
and a dining room with bay views. Menus centre on Islay produce. Bright bedrooms.

Port Charlotte *Argyll and Bute.*

🏨 **Port Charlotte,** Main St, PA48 7TU, ℰ (01496) 850360, *info@portcharlottehotel.co.uk,*
Fax (01496) 850361, ≤, 畑, ♤ – ❖ **P. ⑩ⓢ VISA**
closed 24-26 December – **Rest** (bar lunch)/dinner a la carte approx 33.00 **s.** – **10 rm** ⊈
✱70.00 – ✱✱115.00.
◆ Simple, well-modernised, Victorian building in attractive conservation village. Pine panelled bar and relaxing lounge with open fires. Rooms furnished with fine old pieces. Attractive wood furnished restaurant with stone walls and views over the bay.

Port Ellen *Argyll and Bute.*

🏠 **Glenegedale House**, PA42 7AS, Northwest : 4 ¾ m. on A 846 ℘ (01496) 500400, *info@glenegedalehouse.com*, 🚗 – ⇔⬚ 🅿 🚾 AE ① VISA
  Rest (by arrangement) – **9 rm** (dinner included) ♨ ✦95.00 – ✦✦150.00.
  ✦ Refurbished in elegantly sympathetic style, this stalwart house proffers neutral tones with quality soft furnishings. Antiques abound. Well-equipped rooms. Handy for airport. Spacious dining room with homely cooked fare.

↑ **Glenmachrie Farmhouse** without rest., PA42 7AQ, Northwest : 4 ½ m. on A 846 ℘ (01496) 302560, *glenmachrie@lineone.net*, Fax (01496) 302560, 🐦, 🚗, ♨ – ⇔⬚ 🅿
  5 rm ♨ ✦65.00 – ✦✦80.00.
  ✦ Modern farmhouse on a working farm a short drive from a number of Islay's distilleries and Duich Nature Reserve. Run on "green" low-impact policies. Warm welcoming rooms.

ISLEORNSAY *Highland* **501** C 12 – *see Skye (Isle of).*

JEDBURGH *Borders* **501 502** M 17 *Scotland G.* – *pop. 4 090.*
  See : Town★ – Abbey★★ *AC* – *Mary Queen of Scots House Visitor Centre★ AC* – *The Canongate Bridge★.*
  Env. : Waterloo Monument (※★★) N : 4 m. by A 68 and B 6400.
  🛆 Jedburgh, Dunion Rd ℘ (01835) 863587.
  🇮 Murray's Green ℘ (0870) 608 0404.
  Edinburgh 48 – Carlisle 54 – Newcastle upon Tyne 57.

🏠🏠 **Jedforest** ♨, Camptown, TD8 6PJ, South : 4 m. on A 68 ℘ (01835) 840222, *info@jedforesthotel.com*, Fax (01835) 840226, 🐦, 🚗, ♨ – ⇔⬚ 📞 & 🅿 🚾 AE VISA
  Rest (dinner only and lunch Friday-Sunday)/dinner a la carte approx 29.40 – **12 rm** ♨ ✦70.00 – ✦✦140.00/160.00.
  ✦ Extended country house with outbuildings and attractive views. Public areas include spacious and comfortable drawing room. Bedrooms in varying co-ordinated styles and sizes. Formal dining room decorated to have an intimate feel with alcoves and low lighting.

↑ **The Spinney** without rest., Langlee, TD8 6PB, South : 2 m. on A 68 ℘ (01835) 863525, *thespinney@btinternet.com*, Fax (01835) 864883, 🚗 – ⇔⬚ & 🅿 🚾 ① VISA . ✦
  March-November – ♨ 5.00 **3 rm** ✦54.00/58.00 – ✦✦54.00/58.00.
  ✦ Good value accommodation with homely atmosphere and ambience. Traditional feel from the gardens to the lounge. Bedrooms of a good size overlooking the attractive gardens.

↑ **Hundalee House** ♨ without rest., TD8 6PA, South : 1½ m. by A 68 ℘ (01835) 863011, *sheila.whittaker@btinternet.com*, Fax (01835) 863011, ≼, 🚗, ♨ – ⇔⬚ 🅿 ✦
  mid March-October – **5 rm** ♨ ✦28.00/40.00 – ✦✦46.00/46.00.
  ✦ 18C country lodge in a rural location, with good gardens featuring mature topiary. County house feel and a warm welcome. Distinctive period décor and some antiques.

at Crailing *Northeast : 4 m. by A 68 on A 698* – ✉ Jedburgh.

↑ **Crailing Old School**, TD8 6TL, on B 6400 ℘ (01835) 850382, *info@crailingoldschool.co.uk*, Fax (01835) 850382, 🚗 – ⇔⬚ 🅿 🚾 AE VISA . ✦
  closed Christmas-New Year, 2 weeks February and 2 weeks November – **Rest** (by arrangement) (communal dining) 25.00 – **3 rm** ♨ ✦28.50/37.50 – ✦✦57.00/70.00.
  ✦ Former village school well sited for touring and golfing. Attractive guests' lounge also used for communal breakfast. Comfortable bedrooms in the house and the garden lodge. Home-cooked dinners.

JOHN O'GROATS *Highland* **501** K 8 – *Shipping Services : see Orkney Islands.*

JURA (Isle of) *Argyll and Bute* **501** C 15.
  ⛴ from Feolin to Isle of Islay (Port Askaig) (Caledonian MacBrayne Ltd) frequent services daily (approx. 4 mn).

Craighouse *Argyll and Bute* – ✉ Jura.

🏠 **Jura**, PA60 7XU, ℘ (01496) 820243, *jurahotel@aol.com*, Fax (01496) 820249, ≼ Small Isles Bay, 🚗 – ⇔⬚ 🅿 🚾 AE VISA
  closed February - November – **Rest** (bar lunch)/dinner a la carte 11.95/23.70 s. – **16 rm** ♨ ✦42.00/60.00 – ✦✦90.00, 1 suite.
  ✦ The only hotel on one of the wildest and quietest of the Scottish islands. Next door to the distillery. Relaxed, traditional and simple in style. Many rooms with fine views. Dining room shares the feel of the establishment with wooden chairs and fine views.

KELSO Borders 501 502 M 17 Scotland G. – pop. 5 116.

See : Town★ – The Square★★ – ≼★ from Kelso Bridge.

Env. : Tweed Valley★★ – Floors Castle★ *AC*, NW : 1½ m. by A 6089.

Exc. : Mellerstain★★ (Ceilings★★★, Library★★★) *AC*, NW : 6 m. by A 6089 – Waterloo Monument (※★★), SW : 7 m. by A 698 and B 6400 – Jedburgh Abbey★★ *AC*, SW : 8½ m. by A 698 – Dryburgh Abbey★★ *AC* (setting★★★), SW : 10½ m. by A 6089, B 6397 and B 6404 – Scott's View★★, W : 11 m. by A 6089, B 6397, B 6404 and B 6356 – Smailholm Tower★ (※★★), NW : 6 m. by A 6089 and B 6397 – Lady Kirk (Kirk o'Steil★), NE : 16 m. by A 698, A 697, A 6112 and B 6437.

🛅 Berrymoss Racecourse Rd ℰ (01573) 23009.

🛈 Town House, The Square ℰ (0870) 6080404 (mornings only in winter).

Edinburgh 44 – Hawick 21 – Newcastle upon Tyne 68.

🏨 **The Roxburghe** ⏦, Heiton, TD5 8JZ, Southwest : 3 ½ m. by A 698 ℰ (01573) 450331, hotel@roxburghe.net, Fax (01573) 450611, ≼, 🎇, 🛅, 🗬, 🛋, 🏊, ※ – 🔆 P. – 🛎 60. 🅰🅾 🅰🄴 🆅🅸🆂🅰

Rest 37.00 (dinner) and lunch a la carte 12.00/20.00 s. ♀ – **20 rm** ⊆ ✦140.00 – ✦✦210.00, 2 suite.

♦ Wonderfully characterful Jacobean style mansion built in 1853. Sitting rooms with log fires and fresh flowers. Lovely conservatory, attractive library bar. Luxurious rooms. Warmly hued, formal restaurant with collection of horse racing pictures.

🏨 **Ednam House**, Bridge St, TD5 7HT, ℰ (01573) 224168, contact@ednamhouse.com, Fax (01573) 226319, ≼, 🗬, 🎇 – 🔆 P. – 🛎 200. 🅰🅾 🆅🅸🆂🅰

closed Christmas and New Year – **Rest** (bar lunch Monday-Saturday)/dinner a la carte approx 25.00 ♀ – **32 rm** ⊆ ✦76.00 – ✦✦76.00.

♦ Dominant Georgian mansion on Tweed. Distinctive décor exudes period appeal. Three impressively ornate lounges. Bar with fishing theme. Traditional rooms. Spacious dining room with relaxed atmosphere, overlooking gardens and river.

🏠 **Bellevue House** without rest., Bowmont St, TD5 7DZ, North : ½ m. on A 6089 ℰ (01573) 224588, bellevuekelso@aol.com – 🔆 P. 🅰🅾 🆅🅸🆂🅰

closed 2 weeks November and 24 December-2 January – **6 rm** ⊆ ✦37.50 – ✦✦58.00/60.00.

♦ Victorian house 5 minutes from the Market Square. Individually decorated bedrooms. Good hospitality and range of breakfast dishes.

at Ednam North : 2¼ m. on B 6461 – ✉ Kelso.

🏠 **Edenwater House** ⏦, TD5 7QL, off Stichill rd ℰ (01573) 224070, relax@edenwaterhouse.co.uk, Fax (01573) 226615, ≼, 🎇 – 🔆 P. 🅰🅾 🆅🅸🆂🅰 ⚘

closed first 2 weeks January and May – **Rest** (closed Sunday-Wednesday for non-residents) (booking essential) (dinner only) 35.00 ♀ – **4 rm** ⊆ ✦65.00 – ✦✦95.00.

♦ Charming house in rural location next to 17C kirk. Beautiful gardens with stream and meadows beyond. Antique filled lounges. Rooms boast fine quality furnishings. Elegant dining room serving traditionally based meals using local produce.

> **Your opinions are important to us:**
> please write and let us know about your discoveries and experiences –
> good and bad!

KENMORE Perth and Kinross 501 I 14 Scotland G.

See : Village★.

Env. : Loch Tay★★.

Exc. : Ben Lawers★★, SW : 8 m. by A 827.

🛅 Taymouth Castle, Aberfeldy ℰ (01887) 830228 – 🛅, 🛅 Mains of Taymouth ℰ (01887) 830226.

Edinburgh 82 – Dundee 60 – Oban 71 – Perth 38.

🏨 **Kenmore**, The Square, PH15 2NU, ℰ (01887) 830205, reception@kenmorehotel.co.uk, Fax (01887) 830262, 🛅, 🛅 – 🛊 🔆, ▤ rest, P. – 🛎 70. 🅰🅾 🅰🄴 🆅🅸🆂🅰

Taymouth : Rest a la carte 20.15/30.85 s. – **40 rm** ⊆ ✦50.00/67.00 – ✦✦70.00/104.00.

♦ Scotland's oldest inn. Standing on the Tay, it is now a smart, white-fronted hotel with Poet's Parlour featuring original pencilled verse by Burns. Cosy, well-kept rooms. Restaurant with panoramic river views.

KILBERRY Argyll and Bute 501 D 16 – see Kintyre (Peninsula).

SCOTLAND

KILCHRENAN *Argyll and Bute* **501** E 14 *Scotland G.* – ⊠ *Taynuilt.*
>
> Env. : *Loch Awe*★★, *E : 1¼ m.*
> *Edinburgh 117 – Glasgow 87 – Oban 18.*

🏛️ **Ardanaiseig** 🦢, PA35 1HE, Northeast : 4 m. *℘* (01866) 833333, *ardanaiseig@clara.net*, Fax (01866) 833222, ≤ gardens and Loch Awe, 🐟, 🐎, ⚖, ☆ – 🔽 ⇄ 🎧 📮 🐾🐾 ₳₤ ⓪ **VISA**
> *closed 2 January-9 February* – **Rest** (booking essential for non-residents) (light lunch)/dinner 42.00 – **17 rm** 🖙 ✶85.00/188.00 – ✶✶188.00/316.00, 1 suite.
> ◆ Substantial country house in extensive informal gardens beside Loch Awe. Undisturbed peace. Impressively elegant interior; antiques to the fore. Tasteful bedrooms. Dining room boasts views to loch; classic country house cooking.

⌂ **Roineabhal** 🦢, PA35 1HD, *℘* (01866) 833207, *maria@roineabhal.com*, Fax (01866) 833477, 🐎 – ⇄ 🎧 🕭 📮 🐾🐾 **VISA**
> *closed Christmas* – **Rest** (by arrangement) (communal dining) 30.00 – **3 rm** 🖙 ✶60.00 – ✶✶90.00.
> ◆ Large stone house, built by the owners, enviably located by rushing stream and close to Loch Awe. Rusticity prevails in welcoming interior; spacious rooms with homely extras. By arrangement five-course communal dinner, home-cooked using local produce.

KILDRUMMY *Aberdeenshire* **501** L 12 *Scotland G.* – ⊠ *Alford.*
>
> See : *Castle*★ *AC.*
> Exc. : *Huntly Castle (Heraldic carvings*★★★*) N : 15 m. by A 97 – Craigievar Castle*★, *SE : 13 m. by A 97, A 944 and A 980.*
> *Edinburgh 137 – Aberdeen 35.*

🏛️ **Kildrummy Castle** 🦢, AB33 8RA, South : 1 ¼ m. on A 97 *℘* (019755) 71288, *bookings@kildrummycastlehotel.co.uk*, Fax (019755) 71345, ≤ gardens and Kildrummy Castle, 🐟, 🐎, ⚖ – 📮 🐾🐾 **VISA**
> *closed January* – **The Dining Room :** Rest 21.00/35.50 s. – **16 rm** 🖙 ✶80.00/90.00 – ✶✶190.00.
> ◆ Imposing, stone built 19C mansion in superb grounds with fine view of original 13C castle. Baronial, country house style abounds: lounges flaunt antiques. Variable rooms. Delightfully wood-panelled dining room; homely Scottish cooking.

KILLEARN *Stirling* **501** G 15 – ⊠ *Glasgow.*
>
> *Edinburgh 60 – Glasgow 19 – Perth 55 – Stirling 22.*

🏨 **Black Bull,** 2 The Square, G63 9NG, *℘* (01360) 550215, *sales@blackbullhotel.com*, Fax (01360) 550143, 🌇, 🐎 – ⇄ 📮 🐾🐾 ₳₤ **VISA**
> **The Grill :** Rest 14.95/19.95 and a la carte 17.45/30.15 ⓨ – **12 rm** 🖙 ✶55.00/95.00 – ✶✶95.00, 1 suite.
> ◆ Pleasant little inn in centre of small village close to Campsie Fells. Local artwork is on display in all areas. Contemporary bar and rooms that offer neat and tidy comforts. Trendy, modern brasserie.

KILLIECRANKIE *Perth and Kinross* **501** I 13 – *see Pitlochry.*

KILLIN *Stirling* **501** H 14 *Scotland G.* – *pop. 666.*
>
> Exc. : *Loch Tay*★★, *Ben Lawers*★★, *NE : 8 m. by A 827.*
> 🏌 *Killin ℘* (01567) 820312.
> 🛈 *Breadalbane Folklore Centre, Falls of Dochart ℘* (0870) 200627.
> *Edinburgh 72 – Dundee 64 – Perth 43 – Oban 54.*

🏨 **Dall Lodge Country House** without rest., Main St, FK21 8TN, on A 827 *℘* (01567) 820217, *connor@dalllodge.co.uk*, Fax (01567) 820726, 🐟, 🐎 – 🔽 ⇄ 📮 🐾🐾 **VISA**
> *Easter-September* – **9 rm** 🖙 ✶35.00/40.00 – ✶✶76.00.
> ◆ Victorian hotel of stone, proudly overlooking river Lochay. Walls adorned by foreign artefacts and local oils. Conservatory with exotic plants. Stylish, halogen lit rooms.

⌂ **Breadalbane House,** Main St, FK21 8UT, *℘* (01567) 820134, *info@breadalbane house.com*– ⇄ 📮 🐾🐾 **VISA**, ⚘
> **Rest** (by arrangement) 17.50 – **5 rm** 🖙 ✶30.00/45.00 – ✶✶46.00/60.00.
> ◆ Surrounded by Ben Lawers, Loch Tay, Glen Lochay and the Falls of Dochart, this cosy guesthouse offers simple, homely comforts. Clean, well-kept rooms with good views. Evening meals available by prior arrangement in the simple, pine furnished dining room.

at Ardeonaig *(Perth and Kinross) Northeast : 6¾ m. –* ⊠ *Killin (Stirling).*

Ardeonaig ⌂, South Loch Tay, FK21 8SU, ✆ (01567) 820400, *info@ardeonaigho tel.co.uk*, Fax (01567) 820282, ⇐, ⌐, ➪, ⌑ – ⌑ ⇄ **P.** **⑩** **VISA**
Rest – (see ***The Restaurant*** below) – **20 rm** (dinner included) ⌸ ♦135.00 – ♦♦180.00.
♦ 17C inn and super, modern, airy lochside suite, in wooded meadows on shore of Loch Tay. Cheery, well-stocked bar. Cosy sitting room. Library with fine views. Smart rooms.

XX **The Restaurant** (at Ardeonaig H.), South Loch Tay, FK21 8SU, ✆ (01567) 820400, *info@ardeonaighotel.co.uk*, Fax (01567) 820282, ⌂, ⌐, ➪ – **P.** **⑩** **VISA**
Rest 26.50 and a la carte 26.50/37.50.
♦ Located in Ardeonaig hotel extension. Rennie Mackintosh style chairs, white linen-clad tables. Good value dishes: South African influences merge well with local ingredients.

KILMARNOCK *East Ayrshire* **501 502** G 17 *Scotland G.*
See : *Dean Castle (arms and armour★, musical instruments★).*
Edinburgh 64 – Ayr 13 – Glasgow 25.

🏨 **The Park**, Kilmarnock Football Club, Rugby Park, KA1 2DP, off Dundonald Rd ✆ (01563) 545999, *enquiries@theparkhotel.uk.com*, Fax (01563) 545322, **₭₅** – ▯ ⇄ ♦ ⅋ **P.** – **⚿** 600. **⑩** **AE** **VISA**. ⌀
Blues : Rest a la carte 16.75/30.00 – **50 rm** ⌸ ♦65.00/120.00 – ♦♦75.00/132.00.
♦ Adjacent to Kilmarnock Football Club, who are its owners, this stylish, glass structured hotel offers up-to-date facilities. Spacious, well-equipped and comfortable bedrooms. Mezzanine-level restaurant boasts tables with views of the pitch.

The ✿ award is the crème de la crème.
This is awarded to restaurants
which are really worth travelling miles for!

KINCLAVEN *Perth and Kinross* **501** J 14 *– pop. 394 –* ⊠ *Stanley.*
Edinburgh 56 – Perth 12.

🏰 **Ballathie House** ⌂, Stanley, PH1 4QN, ✆ (01250) 883268, *email@ballathiehouseho tel.com*, Fax (01250) 883396, ⇐, ⌐, ➪, ⌑ – ⇄ ♦ **P.** – **⚿** 50. **⑩** **VISA**
Rest 18.00/39.00 ⌾ – **39 rm** ⌸ ♦86.00/130.00 – ♦♦178.00/196.00, 3 suites.
♦ Imposing mid 19C former shooting lodge on banks of Tay, imbued with tranquil, charming atmosphere. Elegant, individually furnished bedrooms with a floral theme. Richly alluring restaurant overlooking river.

KINFAUNS *Perth and Kinross* **501** J 14 *– see Perth.*

KINGUSSIE *Highland* **501** H 12 *Scotland G. – pop. 1 410.*
Env. : *Highland Wildlife Park★ AC, NE : 4 m. by A 9.*
Exc. : *Aviemore★, NE : 11 m. by A 9 – The Cairngorms★★ (⇐★★★) – ☀★★★ from Cairn Gorm, NE : 18 m. by B 970.*
🖥 *Gynack Rd* ✆ (01540) 661600.
Edinburgh 117 – Inverness 41 – Perth 73.

⌂ **Hermitage**, Spey St, PH21 1HN, ✆ (01540) 662137, *thehermitage@clara.net*, Fax (01540) 662177, ⌐ – ⇄ ♦ **⑩** **VISA**. ⌀
Rest (by arrangement) 18.00 ⌾ – **5 rm** ⌸ ♦30.00/45.00 – ♦♦54.00/70.00.
♦ Pleasant Victorian detached house with views of Cairngorms. Attractive lawned garden. Homely, welcoming lounge with log fire. Colourful, floral rooms. Garden views from conservatory style dining room.

⌂ **Homewood Lodge** ⌂, Newtonmore Rd, PH21 1HD, ✆ (01540) 661507, *jenni ferander5@hotmail.com*, ⌐ – ⇄ ♦ **P.** ⌀
Rest (by arrangement) 13.00 – **4 rm** ⌸ ♦25.00 – ♦♦50.00/60.00.
♦ An immaculate whitewashed exterior and a prominent hilltop position attract the visitor's eye to this Victorian villa guesthouse with its uncluttered feel and simple rooms.

XX **The Cross at Kingussie** ⌂ with rm, Tweed Mill Brae, Ardbroilach Rd, PH21 1LB, ✆ (01540) 661166, *relax@thecross.co.uk*, Fax (01540) 661080 – ♦ **P.** **⑩** **AE** **VISA**. ⌀
restricted opening in winter – **Rest** (closed Sunday-Monday) (booking essential) (dinner only) 39.00 ⌀ – **8 rm** (dinner included) ⌸ ♦120.00/150.00 – ♦♦180.00/200.00.
♦ Personally run converted tweed mill restaurant in four acres of waterside grounds with beamed ceilings and modern artwork. Modish Scottish cuisine. Comfortable rooms.

KINROSS *Perth and Kinross* 501 J 15 – *pop. 4 681.*

🗠, 🗠 *Green Hotel, 2 The Muirs* 𝒫 *(01577) 863407 –* 🗠 *Milnathort, South St* 𝒫 *(01577) 864069 –* 🗠 *Bishopshire, Kinnesswood* 𝒫 *(01592) 780203.*

🛈 *Heart of Scotland Visitor Centre, junction 6, M 90* 𝒫 *(01577) 863680 (closed weekends October-April).*

Edinburgh 28 – Dunfermline 13 – Perth 18 – Stirling 25.

🏛 **The Green,** 2 Muirs, KY13 8AS, 𝒫 (01577) 863467, *reservations@green-hotel.com,* Fax (01577) 863180, 🚅, 🔲, 🗠, ☞, �, squash – ※❦ 🄿 – ♨ 130. 🕮 🄰🄴 🄾 𝘝𝘐𝘚𝘈 accommodation closed 24-29 December – **Basil's** : Rest (dinner only) 29.50 s. ⌿ – **46 rm** ⌸ ✸100.00/115.00 – ✸✸170.00.
   ◆ 18C former coaching inn in neat grounds off village high street. Spacious, welcoming lounge. Leisure complex includes curling rink. Comfortable, modern rooms. Bright, airy modern restaurant with modish menus to match.

🏠 **Burnbank** without rest., 79 Muirs, KY13 8AZ, North : ¾ m. on A 922 𝒫 (01577) 861931, *bandb@burnbank-kinross.co.uk,* ☞ – ※❦ 🄿. 🕮 𝘝𝘐𝘚𝘈. ✄
   3 rm ⌸ ✸40.00 – ✸✸70.00.
   ◆ Well-kept, proudly run guesthouse: cosy reception room full of maps and local info. Owners make their own breakfast bread and preserves. Lomond Hills vistas from smart rooms.

KINTYRE (Peninsula) *Argyll and Bute* 501 D 16 *Scotland G.*

See : *Carradale★ – Saddell (Collection of grave slabs★).*

🗠, 🗠 *Machrihanish, Campbeltown* 𝒫 *(01586) 810213 –* 🗠 *Dunaverty, Southend, Campbeltown* 𝒫 *(01586) 830677 –* 🗠 *Gigha, Isle of Gigha* 𝒫 *(01583) 505242.*

✈ *Campbeltown Airport :* 𝒫 *(01586) 553797.*

⛴ *from Claonaig to Isle of Arran (Lochranza) (Caledonian MacBrayne Ltd) frequent services daily (30 mn) – from Kennacraig to Isle of Islay (Port Ellen or Port Askaig) (Caledonian MacBrayne Ltd) 1-3 daily – from Kennacraig to Oban via Isle of Colonsay (Scalasaig) and Isle of Islay (Port Askaig) 3 weekly.*

Campbeltown *Argyll and Bute.*

🛈 *Mackinnon House, The Pier* 𝒫 *(08707) 200609, info@campbeltown.visitscotland.com.*
Edinburgh 176.

🏛 **Craigard House,** Low Askomil, PA28 6EP, East : ¾ m. by B 842 on no through rd 𝒫 (01586) 554242, *info@craigard-house.co.uk,* Fax (01586) 551137, ≤, ☞ – ※❦ 🄿. 🕮 🄰🄴 𝘝𝘐𝘚𝘈
   Rest (booking essential for non-residents) (lunch by arrangement) a la carte 16.50/27.20 – **14 rm** ⌸ ✸50.00/60.00 – ✸✸70.00/120.00.
   ◆ Built 1882 by distillery owner on shores of Campbeltown Loch. Fine hallway with stained -glass window. Individually decorated rooms named after local geographical features. Tables at bow window looking out to loch are popular in period styled dining room.

Carradale *Argyll and Bute.*

🏛 **Dunvalanree** 🍃, Port Righ Bay, PA28 6SE, 𝒫 (01583) 431226, *eat@dunvalanree.com,* Fax (01583) 431 339, ≤, ☞ – ※❦ ᕦ 🄿. 🕮 𝘝𝘐𝘚𝘈
   closed 3 January-2 March – **Rest** 25.00 – **7 rm** (dinner included) ⌸ ✸45.00/77.00 – ✸✸135.00.
   ◆ 1930s house on the bay facing Arran and Kilbrannan Sound. Comfortable firelit lounge, "Arts and Crafts" stained glass entrance and well-fitted rooms, one in Mackintosh style. Intimate dining room takes up the period style.

Kilberry *Argyll and Bute.*
Edinburgh 165 – Glasgow 121 – Oban 75.

🍴 **Kilberry Inn** 🍃 with rm, PA29 6YD, 𝒫 (01880) 770223, *relax@kilberryinn.com* – 🄿. 🕮
🍽 𝘝𝘐𝘚𝘈
   closed January-mid March – **Rest** (closed Monday and Tuesday-Thursday November-December) a la carte 18.70/29.10 – **3 rm** ⌸ ✸39.50 – ✸✸45.00.
   ◆ Characterful, cosy, red tin-roofed cottage incorporating open fires, beams, exposed stone. Walls hung with local artists' work. Well-priced dishes. Stylish, modern bedrooms.

KIPPEN *Stirlingshire* 501 H 15 *Scotland G. – pop. 934.*

Exc. : *Doune★ - Castle★ , NE : 8 m. by A 811, B 8075 and A 84 – Dunblane★ - Cathedral★★ , NE : 13 m. by A 811 and M 9 – Stirling★★ - Castle★★ , Argyll and Sutherland Highlanders Regimental Museum★ , Argyll's Lodging★ , Church of the Holy Rude★ , E : 9 m. by A 811.*
Edinburgh 75 – Glasgow 62 – Stirling 16.

🍴 **The Inn at Kippen** with rm, Fore Rd, FK8 3DT, ℰ (01786) 871010, *info@theinnatkippen.co.uk*, Fax (01786) 871011, ☕ – ᴘ. ⓂⓈ *VISA*
closed 25 December and 1 January – **Rest** a la carte 16.00/40.00 � – **4 rm** �㎡ ✹50.00 – ✹✹70.00/80.00.
 ◆ Village inn with modern interior and photos of former village life. Large lunch and dinner menu of popular pub and restaurant style dishes. Simple wood-furnished bedrooms.

KIRKBEAN Dumfries and Galloway **501 502** J 19 *Scotland G.*
Env. : *Sweetheart Abbey★, N : 5 m. by A 710.*
Exc. : *Threave Garden★★ and Threave Castle★ , W : 20 m. by A 710 and A 745.*
Edinburgh 92 – Dumfries 13 – Kirkcudbright 29.

🏛 **Cavens** ঔ, DG2 8AA, ℰ (01387) 880234, *enquiries@cavens.com*, Fax (01387) 880467, ≼, ☕ – ﹠ ᴘ. ⓂⓈ *VISA*
closed January- March – **Rest** (dinner only) 25.00 **s.** – **6 rm** �㎡ ✹80.00/120.00 – ✹✹120.00/160.00.
 ◆ 18C house with extensions set in mature gardens. Very comfortable lounges opening onto terrace. Spacious well furnished bedrooms. Simple refreshing meals using local produce.

KIRKCOLM Dumfries and Galloway **501 502** E 19 – *see Stranraer.*

KIRKCUDBRIGHT Dumfries and Galloway **501 502** H 19 *Scotland G. – pop. 3 447.*
See : *Town★.*
Env. : *Dundrennan Abbey★ AC, SE : 5 m. by A 711.*
🏌 *Stirling Crescent* ℰ (01557) 330314.
🛈 *Harbour Sq* ℰ (01557) 330494 (Easter-October).
Edinburgh 108 – Dumfries 28 – Stranraer 50.

🏨 **Selkirk Arms,** High St, DG6 4JG, ℰ (01557) 330402, *reception@selkirkarmshotel.co.uk*, Fax (01557) 331639, ☕ – ﹠ ✆ ᴘ. ⓂⓈ ᴀ̲ʟ̲ᴇ̲ *VISA*
Rest (bar lunch)/dinner a la carte 16.50/28.25 – **16 rm** �㎡ ✹60.00/95.00 – ✹✹90.00/100.00.
 ◆ Traditional coaching inn in centre of quaint town; Burns reputedly wrote "The Selkirk Grace" here. Rustic interior. Large bar serving simple food. Good sized rooms. Comfortable dining room with seasonal, classically based menu.

↑ **Gladstone House,** 48 High St, DG6 4JX, ℰ (01557) 331734, *hilarygladstone@aol.com*, Fax (01557) 331734, ☕ – ﹠. ⓂⓈ *VISA*. ⅏
Rest (by arrangement) 18.00 **3 rm** �㎡ ✹41.00 – ✹✹64.00.
 ◆ Attractive Georgian house. Spacious, comfortably furnished sitting room and breakfast room. Evening meals offered. Traditional rooms with stripped wooden furnishings.

KIRKMICHAEL Perth and Kinross **501** J 13.
Edinburgh 73 – Aberdeen 85 – Inverness 102 – Perth 29.

↑ **Cruachan Country Cottage,** PH10 7NZ, on A 924 ℰ (01250) 881226, *cruachan@kirkmichael.net*, ☕ – ﹠ ᴘ.
Rest (by arrangement) a la carte 14.85/22.60 **s.** – **3 rm** �㎡ ✹35.50/40.50 – ✹✹61.00/71.00.
 ◆ Extended stone cottage with neat garden, overlooking River Ardle. Homely lounge with open fire and interesting, local prints. Individually decorated bedrooms. Dinners home-cooked proudly by owners.

KIRKNEWTON Edinburgh **501** J 16 – *see Edinburgh.*

KIRKPATRICK DURHAM Dumfries and Galloway **501 502** I 18 – *see Castle Douglas.*

KIRKTON OF GLENISLA Perthshire **501** K 13 – ✉ Blairgowrie.
Edinburgh 73 – Forfar 19 – Pitlochry 24.

↑ **Glenmarkie Health Spa and Riding Centre** ঔ, PH11 8QB, East : 3 ¾ m. by B 951 ℰ (01575) 582295, *holidays@glenmarkie.freeserve.co.uk*, Fax (01575) 582295, ≼, ☕, ⌧ – ﹠ ᴘ. ⅏
Rest (by arrangement) 20.00 – **3 rm** �㎡ ✹40.00 – ✹✹56.00.
 ◆ Stunningly located, cosy little farmhouse in beautiful glen. Horse riding and massages available, not necessarily in that order. Simple, individually decorated bedrooms.

KIRKWALL Orkney Islands **501** L 7 – *see Orkney Islands (Mainland).*

KIRK YETHOLM *Borders.*

⌂ **Mill House** without rest., Main St, TD5 8PE, ☎ (01573) 420604, *millhousebb@tis cali.co.uk*, 🞰 – ⚐ 🅿
3 rm ⊂⊃ ✱45.00 – ✱✱80.00.
◆ Converted grain mill with a spacious and immaculately presented interior, full of homely, warm touches. Well appointed bedrooms add the final touch to a most appealing house.

KIRRIEMUIR *Angus* 501 K 13 – *pop. 5 963.*
🛈 *1 Cumberland Close* ☎ (01575) 574097 *(Easter-September).*
Edinburgh 65 – Aberdeen 50 – Dundee 16 – Perth 30.

⌂ **Purgavie Farm** ⑳, Lintrathen, DD8 5HZ, West : 5 ½ m. on B 951 ☎ (01575) 560213, *purgavie@aol.com*, Fax (01575) 560213, ≤, 🞰 – ⚐ 🅿, ⓜ VISA
Rest (by arrangement) (communal dining) 13.00 – **3 rm** ⊂⊃ ✱30.00 – ✱✱52.00.
◆ Farmhouse on working farm at foot of Glen Isla, part of lovely Glens of Angus. Homely lounge with open fire. Large, comfortable rooms with panoramic views. Meals are taken communally in the comfortable dining room.

KYLE OF LOCHALSH *Highland* 501 C 12 – *pop. 739.*
🛈 *Car park* ☎ (01599) 534276 *(April-October).*
Edinburgh 207 – Dundee 177 – Inverness 81 – Oban 123.

✕ **The Seafood,** Railway Station, IV40 8AE, ☎ (01599) 534813, *jann@the-seafood-restau rant.co.uk*, Fax (01599) 577230 – ⓜ AE ⓞ VISA
Easter-mid October – **Rest** - Seafood - *(closed Sunday except summer)* (dinner only and lunch Thursday-Friday) a la carte 16.45/24.50 **s.**
◆ Popular restaurant on main platform of railway station. Light, airy dining room with fishy prints. Wide ranging menus, very strong on local seafood. Fresh, unfussy cooking.

KYLESKU *Highland* 501 E 9 *Scotland G.*
Env. : *Loch Assynt*★★ , *S : 6 m. by A 894.*
Edinburgh 256 – Inverness 100 – Ullapool 34.

🏨 **Kylesku** with rm, IV27 4HW, ☎ (01971) 502231, *info@kyleskuhotel.co.uk*, Fax (01971) 502313, ≤ Loch Glencoul and mountains, 🞰, 🞰 VISA, 🞰
16 October-February – **Rest** (in bar Monday dinner and lunch)/dinner 29.00 and a la carte 15.00/25.00 – **8 rm** ⊂⊃ ✱50.00 – ✱✱80.00.
◆ Stunningly located inn, at the end of the pier overlooking loch, mountain and country-side. Spacious establishment with interesting, intriguing, individual rooms. Restaurant in superb spot with great views: local, seasonal ingredients with strong seafood slant.

LADYBANK *Fife* 501 K 15 *Scotland G.* – *pop. 1 487.*
Env. : *Falkland*★ – *Palace of Falkland*★ – *Gardens*★ – *Village*★, *S :½ m. by A 914 on A 912.*
🛈 *Ladybank, Annsmuir* ☎ (01337) 830814.
Edinburgh 38 – Dundee 20 – Stirling 40.

⌂ **Redlands Country Lodge** ⑳ without rest., Pitlessie Rd, KY15 7SH, East : ¾ m. by Kingskettle rd taking first left after railway bridge ☎ (01337) 831091, *info@redland slodge.com*, 🞰 – ⚐ 🅿, ⓜ ⓞ VISA
4 rm ⊂⊃ ✱35.00/40.00 – ✱✱56.00/66.00.
◆ Detached cottage on a quiet country lane in a rural location. Bedrooms, which have a simple snug air, are located in an adjacent pine lodge. Breakfast in the main cottage and with a sun terrace for warmer days.

LAIRG *Highland* 501 G9 – *pop. 857.*
🛈 *Ferrycroft Countryside Centre, Sutherland* ☎ (01549) 402160 *(April-October).*
Edinburgh 218 – Inverness 61 – Wick 72.

⌂ **Park House,** IV27 4AU, ☎ (01549) 402208, *david-walker@park–house@freeserve.co.uk*, Fax (01549) 402693, ≤, 🞰, 🞰 – ⚐ 🅿, ⓜ VISA
closed Christmas and New Year – **Rest** (by arrangement) 19.00 – **3 rm** ⊂⊃ ✱32.00/48.00 – ✱✱54.00/72.00.
◆ Victorian house on the banks of Loch Shin, comfortable and well furnished with high ceilings and views of the loch. Good spacious bedrooms. Country pursuits organised. Hunting and fishing activities of the establishment reflected in the home-cooked menus.

LAMLASH *North Ayrshire* 501 E 17 – *see Arran (Isle of).*

LANGASS *Western Isles – see Uist (Isles of).*

LARGOWARD *Fife* **501** L 15 – ⊠ *St Andrews.*
Edinburgh 44 – Glenrothes 14 – St Andrews 7.

XX **The Inn at Lathones** with rm, KY9 1JE, Northeast : ¾ m. on A 915 ℰ (01334) 840494, *lathones@theinn.co.uk, Fax (01334) 840694* – ❤, ௧, 🅿, ⇔ 22. 🆎 🆎 ⓪ *VISA*
closed 2 weeks January – **Rest** 18.50/45.00 and a la carte 29.40/39.20 ♀ – **13 rm** ⊊ ♦80.00/150.00 – ♦♦150.00/225.00.
* Early 17C inn; now a restaurant where modern styles and adventurous combinations are the order of the day: bold diners can try the innovative 'Trilogy' menu. Stylish rooms.

LAUDER *Berwickshire* **501** L 16 – *pop. 1 108.*
🏌 *Galashiels Rd* ℰ *(01578) 722526.*
Edinburgh 27 – Berwick-upon-Tweed 34 – Carlisle 74 – Newcastle upon Tyne 77.

🏠 **The Lodge,** Carfraemill, TD2 6RA, Northwest : 4 m. by A 68 on A 697 ℰ (01578) 750750, *enquiries@carfraemill.co.uk, Fax (01578) 750751,* 🏡 – ⇔⊁ 🅿, ♠ 150. 🆎 🆎 ⓪ *VISA* ✎
Jo's Kitchen : Rest (grill rest.) a la carte 18.00/26.00 – **10 rm** ⊊ ♦60.00 – ♦♦90.00.
* Family run hotel, once a coaching inn, just off the Newcastle-Edinburgh road. Warmly traditional style of décor and a welcoming ambience. Well-equipped bedrooms. A choice of informal eating areas with a traditional farmhouse feel.

🍴 **Black Bull** with rm, 13-15 Market Pl, TD2 6SR, ℰ (01578) 722208, *enquiries@blackbull-lauder.com, Fax (01578) 722419,* ☜ – 🅿. 🆎 *VISA*
Rest a la carte 15.20/28.90 **s.** ♀ – **8 rm** ⊊ ♦55.00/60.00 – ♦♦90.00.
* Hanging baskets catch the eye outside this former coaching inn. Various snugs provide a cosy welcome. Extensive menus of popular, home-cooked dishes. Clean, well-kept rooms.

LEITH *Edinburgh* **501** K 16 – *see Edinburgh.*

LERWICK *Shetland Islands* **501** Q 3 – *see Shetland Islands (Mainland).*

LESLIE *Fife* **501** K 15 – *pop. 2 998.*
Edinburgh 35 – Dundee 26 – Perth 25 – Stirling 33.

🏠 **Rescobie House,** 6 Valley Drive, KY6 3BQ, ℰ (01592) 749555, *rescobiehotel@compu serve.com, Fax (01592) 620231,* 🏡 – ⇔⊁ 🅿, 🆎 🆎 *VISA*
closed 1 week January – **Rest** (booking essential) (dinner only and Sunday lunch)/dinner 24.95 **s.** – **10 rm** ⊊ ♦49.95/67.50 – ♦♦99.50.
* Listed house, dating from 1930s, in extensive gardens. Smart, uncluttered feel throughout. Rooms in soft creams and browns; spacious and comfortable with a simple elegance. Bay-windowed dining room, intimate and formally set.

LEVERBURGH *Western Isles (Outer Hebrides)* **501** Y 10 – *see Lewis and Harris (Isle of).*

LEWIS and HARRIS (Isle of) *Western Isles (Outer Hebrides)* **501** A 9 *Scotland G.*
See : *Callanish Standing Stones*★★ – *Carloway Broch*★ – *St Clement's Church, Rodel (tomb*★ *).*
🚢 *from Stornoway to Ullapool (Mainland) (Caledonian MacBrayne Ltd) 2 daily (2 h 40 mn) – from Kyles Scalpay to the Isle of Scalpay (Caledonian MacBrayne Ltd) (10 mn) – from Tarbert to Isle of Skye (Uig) (Caledonian MacBrayne Ltd) 1-2 daily (1 h 45 mn) – from Tarbert to Portavadie (Caledonian MacBrayne Ltd) (summer only) frequent services daily (25 mn) – from Leverburgh to North Uist (Otternish) (Caledonian MacBrayne Ltd) (3-4 daily) (1 h 10 mn).*

LEWIS *Western Isles.*

Aird Uig *Western Isles.*

X **Bonaventure** ☜ with rm, HS2 9JA, ℰ (01851) 672474, *jo@bonaventurelewis.co.uk, Fax (01851) 672474,* ⇐ – 🅿.
Rest *(closed Sunday and Monday)* (booking essential) (dinner only) 30.50 – **5 rm** ⊊ ♦30.00 – ♦♦50.00.
* Former 1950s RAF radar station in a stunning setting converted to spacious bistro style dining room with Scottish/French menu serving local produce. Basic bedrooms.

SCOTLAND

Breasclete *Western Isles.*

⚲ **Eshcol** ⚲, 21 Breasclete, HS2 9ED, *℘ (01851) 621357*, *neil@eshcol.com*, *Fax (01851) 621357*, ≤, ⚘ – ⤫ P. ⚸
March-October – **Rest** (by arrangement) 22.00 – **3 rm** ⚌ ✱35.00/45.00 – ✱✱70.00.
◆ Friendly, family run house in rural location, set against a backdrop of delightful scenery. Immaculately kept throughout with a homely atmosphere and views from most rooms. Dinners served at Loch Roag next door.

⚲ **Loch Roag** ⚲, 22A Breasclete, HS2 9EF, *℘ (01851) 621357*, *donald@lochroag.com*, *Fax (01851) 621357*, ⚘ – ⤫ P. ⚸
March-October – **Rest** (by arrangement) 22.00 – **4 rm** ⚌ ✱35.00/45.00 – ✱✱70.00/88.00.
◆ Charming rural location with super views. Run by same family as Eshcol! Bedrooms are decorated in traditional style and the house as a whole has a snug welcoming atmosphere. Simple uncluttered dining room with lovely loch view.

Galson *Western Isles.*

⚲ **Galson Farm** ⚲, South Galson, HS2 0SH, *℘ (01851) 850492*, *galsonfarm@yahoo.com*, *Fax (01851) 850492*, ≤, ⚘, ⚐ – ⤫ P. ⓂⓄ VISA
Rest (by arrangement) (communal dining) 25.00 – **4 rm** ⚌ ✱45.00/85.00.
◆ Characterful working farm in a very remote location. Close to the ocean and ideally placed for exploring the north of the island. Cosy, comfortable, well-kept bedrooms. Traditionally styled dining room where meals are taken communally at a large central table.

Stornoway *Western Isles.*

🛈 Lady Lever Park *℘ (01851) 702240.*
🛈 26 Cromwell St *℘ (01851) 703088*, *witb@visitthehebrides.co.uk.*

🏨 **Cabarfeidh**, Manor Park, HS1 2EU, North : ½ m. on A 859 *℘ (01851) 702604*, *cabar feidh@calahotels.com, Fax (01851) 705572*, ⚘ – |⧉| ⤫, ▤ rest, ☎ P. – 🔺 300. ⓂⓄ AE Ⓞ VISA
Rest 15.95/25.50 and a la carte 22.85/29.15 s. – **46 rm** ⚌ ✱88.00/98.00 – ✱✱118.00/128.00.
◆ Modern purpose-built hotel surrounded by gardens and close to golf course. Up-to-date, well-equipped bedrooms. Range of banqueting and conference facilities. Restaurant is divided into four areas including conservatory, bistro and garden rooms.

⚲ **Braighe House** without rest., 20 Braighe Rd, HS2 0BQ, Southeast : 3 m. on A 866 *℘ (01851) 705287, alison@braighehouse.co.uk*, ⚘ – ⤫ ☎ P. ⓂⓄ VISA. ⚸
5 rm ⚌ ✱45.00/55.00 – ✱✱70.00/80.00.
◆ Spacious proportions allied to enviable coastal outlook. Style and taste predominate in the large, comfy lounge and airy bedrooms. Hearty breakfasts set you up for the day.

HARRIS *Western Isles.*

Ardhasaig *Western Isles.*

XX **Ardhasaig House** ⚲ with rm, HS3 3AJ, *℘ (01859) 502500, accommodation@ardha saig.co.uk, Fax (01859) 502077*, ≤ Ardhasaig bay and North Harris mountains – P. ⓂⓄ AE VISA
April-October – **Rest** (booking essential for non-residents) (dinner only) (set menu only) 35.00/48.00 ⚌ – **6 rm** ⚌ ✱60.00/75.00 – ✱✱150.00/180.00.
◆ Smart dining room with daily changing menu featuring seasonal island produce. Purpose-built house with wild, dramatic views. In the smart dining room the young owner/chef serves accomplished dishes featuring seasonal island produce. Well-kept rooms.

Leverburgh *Western Isles.*

⚲ **Carminish** ⚲, 1a Strond, HS5 3UD, South : 1 m. on Srandda rd *℘ (01859) 520400, info@carminish.com*, ≤ Carminish Islands and Sound of Harris, ⚘ – ⤫ P.
Rest (by arrangement) (communal dining) 19.00 – **3 rm** ⚌ ✱23.00/45.00 – ✱✱46.00/58.00.
◆ Idyllically located guesthouse with spectacular views of the Carminish Islands and Sound of Harris. Comfortable lounge. Well-kept rooms. Hearty meals in communal setting.

Scalpay *Western Isles.*

⚲ **Hirta House** without rest., HS4 3XZ, *℘ (01859) 540394, m.mackenzie@tiscali.co.uk, Fax (01859) 540394*, ≤ – ⤫ P. ⚸
3 rm ⚌ ✱50.00.
◆ Enter Scalpay by impressive modern bridge and admire the hills of Harris from this stylish guesthouse with its bold wall colours, vivid artwork and nautically inspired rooms.

Scarista *Western Isles.*

ᵣ₉ ℰ *(01859) 550226.*

🏠 **Scarista House** ⌂, HS3 3HX, ℰ *(01859) 550238, timandpatricia@scaristahouse.com,*
Fax *(01859) 550277,* ≤ *Scarista Bay,* 🍴 – ⅍ 🄿 ⓌⓈ 𝗩𝗜𝗦𝗔
booking essential in winter – **Rest** (booking essential for non-residents) (dinner only) (set
menu only) 39.50/48.50 – **5 rm** ⌂ ✦110.00/150.00 – ✦✦180.00/199.50.
♦ Sympathetically restored part 18C former manse, commanding position affords delightful views of Scarista Bay. Elegant library and inviting antique furnished bedrooms. Strong
local flavour to the daily changing menu.

Tarbert *Western Isles – pop. 795 – ⊠ Harris.*

⌂ **Ceol na Mara** ⌂, 7 Direcleit, HS3 3DP, ℰ *(01859) 502464, midgie@madasafish.com,*
🍴 ⅍ ✔ 🄿 ⓌⓈ 𝗩𝗜𝗦𝗔
Rest (by arrangement) (communal dining) 22.50 – **4 rm** ⌂ ✦40.00/45.00 –
✦✦60.00/70.00.
♦ Wonderful views and a loch's edge setting enhance the allure of this idyllically set house
with smart decking area, peaceful garden, lovely lounge and simple, spacious rooms. Share
home-cooked meals with your fellow guests.

⌂ **Hillcrest** without rest., HS3 3AH, Northwest : 1 ¾ m. on A 859 ℰ *(01859) 502119, angusa*
hillcrest@tiscali.co.uk, Fax *(01859) 502119,* ≤, 🍴 – ⅍ 🄿 ⓌⓈ 𝗔𝗘 Ⓞ 𝗩𝗜𝗦𝗔. ⌂
3 rm ⌂ ✦40.00 – ✦✦50.00.
♦ A private house, family run, in a commanding position overlooking Loch Tarbert. Small
cosy sitting room and spacious bedrooms, most enjoying sea views.

LEWISTON *Highland 501 G 12 Scotland G.*
Env. : *Loch Ness★★ – The Great Glen★ .*
Edinburgh 173 – Inverness 17.

⌂ **Woodlands** without rest., East Lewiston, IV63 6UJ, ℰ *(01456) 450356, stay@woodlands-*
lochness.co.uk, Fax *(01456) 459343,* 🍴 – ⅍ 🕭 🄿 ⓌⓈ 𝗩𝗜𝗦𝗔. ⌂
February-19 November and New Year – **5 rm** ⌂ ✦30.00/38.00 – ✦✦48.00/60.00.
♦ Spacious, purpose-built guesthouse with large garden and decked terrace situated just
away from the town. Airy, immaculately kept and comfortable bedrooms.

⌂ **Glen Rowan** without rest., West Lewiston, IV63 6UW, ℰ *(01456) 450235, info@glenro*
wan.co.uk, Fax *(01456) 450817,* 🍴 – ⅍ ✔ 🄿 ⓌⓈ 𝗩𝗜𝗦𝗔. ⌂
3 rm ⌂ ✦22.00/37.50 – ✦✦44.00/55.00.
♦ Purpose-built house in a quiet spot with pleasant garden bordering a mountain stream.
Tea served to arriving guests. Compact but charming and well-kept bedrooms.

LINLITHGOW *West Lothian 501 J 16 Scotland G. – pop. 13 370.*
See : *Town★★ – Palace★★ AC : Courtyard (fountain★★), Great Hall (Hooded Fireplace★★),*
Gateway★ – St Michael's★ .
Env. : *Cairnpapple Hill★ AC, SW : 5 m. by A 706 – House of the Binns (plasterwork ceilings★)*
AC, NE : 4½ m. by A 803 and A 904.
Exc. : *Hopetoun House★★ AC, E : 7 m. by A 706 and A 904 – Abercorn Parish Church*
(Hopetoun Loft★★) NE : 7 m. by A 803 and A 904.
ᵣ₁₈ *Braehead* ℰ *(01506) 842585 –* ᵣ₁₈ *West Lothian, Airngath Hill* ℰ *(01506) 826030.*
🄱 *Burgh Hall, The Cross* ℰ *(08452) 255121 (April-October).*
Edinburgh 19 – Falkirk 9 – Glasgow 35.

🏨 **Champany Inn,** Champany, EH49 7LU, Northeast : 2 m. on A 803 at junction with A 904
ℰ *(01506) 834532, reception@champany.com,* Fax *(01506) 834302,* 🍴 – 🕭 🄿 ⓌⓈ 𝗔𝗘
ⓄⓄ 𝗩𝗜𝗦𝗔. ⌂
closed 25-26 December and 1 January – **The Chop and Ale House :** Rest (grill rest.) a la
carte 17.95/29.50 – (see also *The Restaurant* below) – **16 rm** ⌂ ✦115.00 – ✦✦135.00.
♦ Comfortable lounges, a rustic breakfast room with kitchen range and handsomely
equipped rooms themed around tartan colour schemes. The Chop and Ale House is set in
inn's original bar.

⌂ **Arden House** ⌂ without rest., Belsyde, EH49 6QE, Southwest : 2 ¼ m. on A 706
ℰ *(01506) 670172, info@ardencountryhouse.com,* Fax *(01506) 670172,* 🍴 – ⅍ ✔ 🄿 ⓌⓈ
𝗔𝗘 𝗩𝗜𝗦𝗔. ⌂
closed 25 December – 3 rm ⌂ ✦45.00/70.00 – ✦✦68.00/84.00.
♦ Charmingly run guesthouse set in peaceful location with lovely rural views. Thoughtful
extras include scones and shortbread on arrival. Rooms boast a luxurious style.

XXX **The Restaurant** (at Champany Inn), Champany, EH49 7LU, Northeast : 2 m. on A 803 at junction with A 904 ☏ (01506) 834532, Fax (01506) 834302, ☂ – 🅿, 🆆🅲 🅰🅴 ① 𝗩𝗜𝗦𝗔
closed 25-26 December, 1 January, Saturday lunch and Sunday – **Rest** - Beef specialities - 27.00 (lunch) and a la carte 38.50/55.00 ♀ ☂.
❖ Personally run converted horse mill. Superb South African wines in a charming cellar, fine china and twinkling glass in the roundhouse restaurant, specialising in prime beef.

XX **Livingston's**, 52 High St, EH49 7AE, ☏ (01506) 846565, *contact@livingstons-restau rant.co.uk*, ☂, ☁ – 🆆🅲 ① 𝗩𝗜𝗦𝗔
closed first 2 weeks January, 1 week June, 1 week October, Sunday and Monday – **Rest** 19.95/33.50.
❖ Friendly restaurant tucked away off high street. Menus offer good value meals using fresh regional produce; comfortable dining room, conservatory and summer terrace.

LOANS *South Ayrshire* **501 502** G 17 – *see Troon.*

LOCHALINE *Argyll and Bute* **501** C 14.
Edinburgh 162 – Craignure 6 – Oban 7.5.

X **Whitehouse**, PA34 5XT, ☏ (01967) 421777, *info@whitehouserestaurant.co.uk*, Fax 01967 421 220, ☂, 🆆🅲 𝗩𝗜𝗦𝗔
Easter-October and restricted opening November-December – **Rest** *(closed Sunday dinner and Monday)* a la carte 21.00/32.50.
❖ Remote setting adds to welcoming feel endorsed by hands-on owners. Two lovely, cosy, wood-lined dining rooms where the ethos of seasonal and local cooking shines through.

LOCHBOISDALE *Western Isles (Outer Hebrides)* **501** Y 12 – *see Uist (Isles of).*

LOCHEARNHEAD *Stirling* **501** H 14 *Scotland G.*
Edinburgh 65 – Glasgow 56 – Oban 57 – Perth 36.

 Mansewood Country House, FK19 8NS, South : ½ m. on A 84 ☏ (01567) 830213, *stay@mansewoodcountryhouse.co.uk*, Fax (01567) 830485, ☁ – ❖ 🅿, 🆆🅲 𝗩𝗜𝗦𝗔
March-October – **Rest** (residents only) (dinner only) 20.00 s. – 5 rm ⌑ ✦30.00/40.00 – ✦✦60.00.
❖ An attractive stone building, once a toll house and later a manse. Comfortable lounge and a bar area, well stocked with whiskies. Bedrooms have a cosy snug feel.

LOCHGILPHEAD *Argyll and Bute* **501** D 15 *Scotland G.* – *pop. 2 326.*
Env. : *Loch Fyne*★★, E : 3½ m. by A 83.
⛳ *Blarbuie Rd* ☏ (01546) 602340.
🄴 *Lochnell St* ☏ (08707) 200618 *(April-October), info@lochgilphead.visitscotland.org.*
Edinburgh 130 – Glasgow 84 – Oban 38.

🏛 **Empire Travel Lodge** without rest., Union St, PA31 8JS, ☏ (01546) 602381, *enquiries @empirelodge.co.uk*, Fax (01546) 606606 – ♿ 🅿, 🆆🅲 ① 𝗩𝗜𝗦𝗔, ✂
closed Christmas-New Year – **9 rm** ⌑ ✦30.00 – ✦✦55.00/55.00.
❖ Former cinema whose interior walls are decorated with classic posters of screen stars. Provides simple, spacious, good value accommodation.

at Cairnbaan *Northwest : 2¼ m. by A 816 on B 841* – ✉ *Lochgilphead.*

🏨 **Cairnbaan**, PA31 8SJ, ☏ (01546) 603668, *info@cairnbaan.com*, Fax (01546) 606045, ☂ – ❖ 🅿 – 🔏 100. 🆆🅲 𝗩𝗜𝗦𝗔
closed Christmas – **Rest** (bar lunch)/dinner a la carte 18.50/30.50 – **12 rm** ⌑ ✦72.50/79.50 – ✦✦145.00.
❖ 18C former coaching inn overlooking the Crinan Canal. Comfortable lounges and panelled bar. Well-equipped, individually decorated rooms, some in attractive contemporary style. Light, airy restaurant with modern art decorating the walls.

LOCH HARRAY *Orkney Islands* **501** K 6 – *see Orkney Islands (Mainland).*

LOCHINVER *Highland* **501** E 9 *Scotland G.* – ✉ *Lairg.*
See : *Village*★.
Env. : *Loch Assynt*★★, E : 6 m. by A 837.
🄴 *Assynt Visitor Centre, Main St* ☏ (08452) 255121 *(April-October).*
Edinburgh 251 – Inverness 95 – Wick 105.

SCOTLAND

🏨 **Inver Lodge,** Iolaire Rd, IV27 4LU, $\mathcal{C}$ (01571) 844496, stay@inverlodge.com, Fax (01571) 844395, $\leqslant$ Loch Inver Bay, Suilven and Canisp mountains, ⏏s, 🐾, 🌳 – 🗱 ✓ 📞 ♻ 🅰🅴 ⓘ 💳

4 April-October – **Rest** (bar lunch)/dinner 40.00 s. – **20 rm** ⊠ ✱80.00 – ✱✱160.00.
♦ Comfy, modern hotel set in hillside above the village, surrounded by unspoilt wilderness. Choice of spacious lounges. Superior bedrooms with ocean views are particularly good. Restaurant boasts wonderful outlook.

⋔ **Veyatie** ⌇ without rest., 66 Baddidarroch, IV27 4LP, West : 1 ¼ m. by Baddidarroch rd $\mathcal{C}$ (01571) 844424, veyatie-lochinver@tiscali.co.uk, Fax (01571) 844424, $\leqslant$ Loch Inver Bay, Suilven and Canisp mountains, 🌳 – 🗱 📞 ♻
3 rm ⊠ ✱35.00/40.00 – ✱✱58.00.
♦ An idyllic secluded haven with stunning views of Loch Inver Bay and mountains. Lovely conservatory. Friendly welcome, relaxing gardens and simple, snug bedrooms.

⋔ **Davar** without rest., Baddidarroch Rd, IV27 4LJ, West : ½ m. on Baddidarroch rd $\mathcal{C}$ (01571) 844501, jean@davar36.fsnet.co.uk, $\leqslant$ Loch Inver Bay and Suilven – 🗱 📞 ♻
March-November – **3 rm** ⊠ ✱25.00/40.00 – ✱✱50.00/58.00.
♦ Modern guesthouse in an excellent position which affords wonderful views of Loch Inver Bay and Suilven. Homely and simple with well-kept bedrooms and communal breakfast.

XX **The Albannach** ⌇ with rm, Baddidarroch, IV27 4LP, West : 1 m. by Baddidarroch rd $\mathcal{C}$ (01571) 844407, info@thealbannach@co.uk, Fax (01571) 844285, $\leqslant$ Loch Inver Bay, Suilven and Canisp mountains, 🌳, ♻ – 🗱 rm, 📞 📞 ♻ 💳 ♻
closed November-March – **Rest** (closed Monday) (booking essential for non-residents) (dinner only and lunch Wednesday-Sunday)(set menu only at dinner) 47.00 and lunch a la carte 19.00/32.00 ⊈ – **5 rm** (dinner included) ⊠ ✱165.00 – ✱✱240.00/260.00.
♦ Pleasant restaurant and conservatory with predominantly Scottish feel and exceptional views. Daily changing menu makes fine use of Highland produce. Warm inviting bedrooms.

LOCHMADDY Western Isles (Outer Hebrides) 501 Y 11 – see Uist (Isles of).

LOCHRANZA North Ayrshire 501 502 E 16 – see Arran (Isle of).

LOCHWINNOCH Renfrewshire 501 502 G 16 – pop. 2 570 – ⊠ Paisley.
Edinburgh 61 – Ayr 37 – Glasgow 15 – Greenock 20.

⋔ **East Lochhead Country House** without rest., Largs Rd, PA12 4DX, Southwest : 1 ¼ m. on A 760 $\mathcal{C}$ (01505) 842610, admin@eastlochhead.co.uk, Fax (01505) 842610, 🌳, ♻ – 🗱 📞 📞 ♻ 🅰🅴 💳
3 rm ⊠ ✱40.00/45.00 – ✱✱70.00/90.00.
♦ Within striking distance of Glasgow airport yet firmly rural with views of Barr Loch and Renfrewshire hills. Comfy rooms in the farmhouse and outbuildings; lovely rear garden.

LOCKERBIE Dumfries and Galloway 501 502 J 18 – pop. 4 009.
🛏 Corrie Rd $\mathcal{C}$ (01576) 203363 – 🛏 Lochmaben, Castlehill Gate $\mathcal{C}$ (01387) 810552.
Edinburgh 74 – Carlisle 27 – Dumfries 13 – Glasgow 73.

🏨 **Dryfesdale Country House,** DG11 2SF, Northwest : 1 m. by Glasgow rd off B 7076 $\mathcal{C}$ (01576) 202427, reception@dryfesdalehotel.co.uk, Fax (01576) 204187, $\leqslant$, 🌳 – 🗱 ✓ ♿ 📞 – 🔏 120. ♻ 🅰🅴 💳
Rest 16.95/29.50 and a la carte 20.00/29.00 s. ⊈ – **27 rm** (dinner included) ⊠ ✱65.00/85.00 – ✱✱100.00/150.00.
♦ Extended, commercially oriented 17C house in a rural setting with pleasant countryside views. Lounge bar with fine selection of malts. Refurbished rooms are modish and smart. Enjoy the vistas from renovated dining room.

LUSS Argyll and Bute 501 G 15 Scotland G. – pop. 402.
See : Village★.
Env. : E : Loch Lomond★★.
Edinburgh 89 – Glasgow 26 – Oban 65.

🏨 **Lodge on Loch Lomond,** G83 8PA, $\mathcal{C}$ (01436) 860201, res@loch-lomond.co.uk, Fax (01436) 860203, $\leqslant$ – 🗱 ♿ 📞 – 🔏 175. ♻ 🅰🅴 💳
Rest (light lunch Monday-Saturday)/dinner 27.95 and a la carte 13.55/27.95 ⊈ – **46 rm** ⊠ ✱113.00/154.00 – ✱✱133.00/174.00, 1 suite.
♦ Busy family run establishment in a superb spot on the shores of Loch Lomond. Most of the cosy pine panelled rooms have balconies; all of them can boast a sauna. Restaurant and bar lounge carefully designed on two levels, opening the view to every table.

SCOTLAND

LYBSTER Highland **501** K 9 Scotland G.

Env. : The Hill o'Many Stanes★ , NE : 3½ m. by A 9 – Grey Cairns of Camster★ , N : 6 m. by A 9 and minor rd.

Edinburgh 251 – Inverness 94 – Thurso 28 – Wick 14.

🏨 **Portland Arms,** Main St, KW3 6BS, on A 9 ℘ (01593) 721721, swallow.lybster@swallow hotels.com, Fax (01593) 721722 – 🙏 🛏 🅿 – 🔬 200. 🍴🌑 AE ① VISA . 🛞

closed 30 December - 3 January – **Rest** (bar lunch Monday-Saturday)/dinner a la carte 16.00/28.00 – **22 rm** 🖵 ✦50.00/75.00 – ✦✦63.00/100.00.

◆ Former coaching inn dating from mid-19C. Informal atmosphere: spacious country house style lounge. Bedrooms are modern, comfortable and brightly decorated. Library dining room.

MAIDENS South Ayrshire **501 502** F 18.

Edinburgh 99 – Glasgow 53 – Maybole 7.

🍴 **Wildings** with rm, 21 Harbour Rd, KA26 9NR, ℘ (01655) 331401, Fax (01655) 331330, ⇐ – 🅿. 🍴🌑 ① VISA . 🛞

closed 25-26 December and 1-2 January – **Rest** - Seafood specialities - 14.50/22.50 🏵 – **10 rm** 🖵 ✦45.00 – ✦✦80.00/130.00.

◆ Adjacent to harbour in coastal hamlet, visible from many bedrooms. Very hearty robust food from extensive menus which include excellent seafood. Simple rooms available.

MAYBOLE South Ayrshire **501** 402 F 17 Scotland G. – pop. 4 552.

Env. : Culzean Castle★ AC (setting★★★), Oval Staircase★★) W : 5 m. by B 7023 and A 719.
🛠 Memorial Park ℘ (01655) 889770.
Edinburgh 93 – Ayr 10 – New Galloway 35 – Stranraer 42.

🏠 **Ladyburn** 🐦, KA19 7SG, South : 5 ½ m. by B 7023 off B 741 (Girvan rd) ℘ (01655) 740585, jh@ladyburn.co.uk, Fax (01655) 740580, ⇐, 🌳, 🏡 – 🙏 🅿. 🍴🌑 VISA . 🛞

closed Christmas-New Year and restricted opening in winter – **Rest** (closed Sunday-Monday) (booking essential for non-residents) (light lunch)/dinner 32.50/45.00 – **5 rm** 🖵 ✦80.00/100.00 – ✦✦160.00/200.00.

◆ Friendly and relaxed family run dower house in beautiful rose gardens. Elegant, bay windowed drawing room, firelit library, charming rooms with antique furniture and prints. Richly flavoured Scottish or Gallic dishes served at candlelit tables.

MELROSE Borders **501 502** L 17 Scotland G. – pop. 11 656.

See : Town★ - Abbey★★ (decorative sculpture★★★) AC.

Env. : Eildon Hills (⬆★★★) – Scott's View★★ – Abbotsford★★ AC, W : 4½ m. by A 6091 and B 6360 – Dryburgh Abbey★★ AC (setting★★★), SE : 4 m. by A 6091 – Tweed Valley★★.

Exc. : Bowhill★★ AC, SW : 11½ m. by A 6091, A 7 and A 708 – Thirlestane Castle (plasterwork ceilings★★) AC, NE : 21 m. by A 6091 and A 68.

🛠 Melrose, Dingleton ℘ (01896) 822855.
🚩 Abbey House, Abbey St ℘ (0870) 6080404.
Edinburgh 38 – Hawick 19 – Newcastle upon Tyne 70.

🏨 **Burts,** Market Sq, TD6 9PL, ℘ (01896) 822285, burtshotel@aol.com, Fax (01896) 822870, 🏡, 🌳 – 🙏 🅿 – 🔬 30. 🍴🌑 VISA

closed 26 December – **Rest** 24.75/31.75 – **20 rm** 🖵 ✦56.00/85.00 – ✦✦75.00/106.00.

◆ One-time coaching inn on main square - traditionally appointed and family run. Unpretentious rooms behind a neat black and white façade, brightened by pretty window boxes. Cosy, clubby restaurant.

🏠 **The Townhouse,** Market Sq, TD6 9PQ, ℘ (01896) 822645, enquiries@thetownhouse melrose.co.uk, Fax (01896) 823474, 🏡 – 🙏 🅿 – 🔬 60. 🍴🌑 VISA . 🛞

closed 25-26 December – **Rest** 21.50/28.50 and a la carte 17.50/28.45 – **Brasserie :** Rest 21.50/28.50 and a la carte 17.25/28.20 – **11 rm** 🖵 ✦65.00/85.00 – ✦✦120.00/80.00.

◆ Refreshed and refurbished, this 17C townhouse has a spruce, clean-lined appeal throughout. The bedrooms continue the theme of simple, well-kept attention to detail. Warm and intimate restaurant or informal brasserie options.

at Gattonside North : 2 m. by B 6374 on B 6360 – ✉ Melrose.

↑ **Fauhope House** 🐦 without rest., TD6 9LU, East : ¼ m. by B 6360 taking unmarked lane to the right of Monkswood Rd at edge of village ℘ (01896) 823184, fauhope@border net.co.uk, Fax (01896) 823184, ⇐, 🌳, 🏡 – 🙏 🅿. 🍴🌑 VISA . 🛞

3 rm 🖵 ✦60.00 – ✦✦80.00.

◆ Melrose Abbey just visible through the trees of this charming 19C country house with its antiques and fine furniture. Valley views at breakfast. Flower strewn, stylish rooms.

MELVICH _Highland_ 501 I 8 _Scotland G._ – ✉ _Thurso._

    Env. : Strathy Point★ (≤★★★, Ben Loyal★★), NW : 5 m. by A 836 and minor rd.
    Edinburgh 267 – Inverness 110 – Thurso 18 – Wick 40.

⌂   **The Sheiling** without rest., KW14 7YJ, on A 836 _℘_ (01641) 531256, _thesheiling@btinter
    net.com, Fax_ (01641) 531256, _≤, ☞ – ⇔ P. ◍◉ VISA. ※_
    May-September – **3 rm** ⊑ ✱70.00 – ✱✱70.00.
    ◆ Pebble-dashed 1950s house run by husband and wife team. Spotless, thoughtfully fur-
    nished rooms overlook countryside. Extensive breakfast choice at family style table.

METHVEN _Perth and Kinross_ 501 J 14 – _see Perth._

MILNGAVIE _East Dunbarton_ 501 H 16.
    Edinburgh 52 – Glasgow 8 – Dumfries 83 – Stirling 28.

✗   **The Wild Bergamot**, 1 Hillhead St, G62 8AF, _℘_ (0141) 956 6515, _info@thewildberga
    mot.co.uk_ – ◍◉ ◭ VISA
    closed 3 weeks January, 25-26 December, Monday and Tuesday – **Rest** (dinner only and
    lunch Friday and Saturday) 35.00/45.00 ☼.
    ◆ Compact, unfussy first-floor restaurant on a pedestrianised town centre street. Friendly
    service adds to the enjoyment of well executed dishes with pronounced Scottish accent.

> Good food without spending a fortune?
> Look out for the Bib Gourmand 🔴

MOFFAT _Dumfries and Galloway_ 501 502 J 17 _Scotland G._ – _pop. 2 135._

    Exc. : Grey Mare's Tail★★, NE : 9 m. by A 708.
    ▮₁₈ _Coatshill_ _℘_ (01683) 220020.
    🄱 _Churchgate_ _℘_ (01683) 220620 (Easter-October).
    Edinburgh 61 – Carlisle 43 – Dumfries 22 – Glasgow 60.

⌂   **Bridge House**, Well Rd, DG10 9JT, East : ¾ m. by Selkirk rd (A 708) taking left hand turn
    before bridge _℘_ (01683) 220558, _info@bridgehousemoffat.co.uk, ☞ – ⇔ P. ◍◉ VISA_
    closed 25-27 December – **Rest** (by arrangement) 19.95 – **7 rm** ⊑ ✱35.00/40.00 –
    ✱✱75.00.
    ◆ Personally run early Victorian guesthouse. Lots of room to stretch out in comfy, modish
    lounge overlooking garden. Front two bedrooms have best views, one boasts four poster.
    Local, seasonal menus in linen-laid dining room.

⌂   **Well View**, Ballplay Rd, DG10 9JU, East : ¾ m. by Selkirk rd (A 708) _℘_ (01683) 220184,
    info@wellview.co.uk, Fax (01683) 220088, _☞ – ⇔ rm, P. ◍◉ ◭ VISA. ※_
    closed 1 week May and 1 week October – **Rest** (by arrangement) (communal dining) 35.00
    – **3 rm** ⊑ ✱65.00/80.00 – ✱✱100.00/120.00.
    ◆ Well established, family run 19C house. The bedrooms are the strong point: traditionally
    furnished, they're of a good size and most comfortable.

✗   **The Limetree**, High St, DG10 9HG, _℘_ (01683) 221654, _Fax_ (01683) 221721 – ◍◉ VISA
    closed 2 weeks October, 25 December, Sunday dinner and Monday – **Rest** (booking essen-
    tial) (dinner only and Sunday lunch) 18.50/23.50.
    ◆ Simple, informal, invariably popular restaurant in cosy High Street cottage. Small, con-
    stantly changing menus, employing well sourced local produce, take on a global reach.

MONTROSE _Angus_ 501 M 13 _Scotland G._ – _pop. 10 845._

    _Exc. : Edzell Castle★ (The Pleasance★★★) AC, NW : 17 m. by A 935 and B 966 – Cairn
    O'Mount Road★ (≤★★) N : 17 m. by B 966 and B 974 – Brechin (Round Tower★) W : 7 m. by
    A 935 – Aberlemno (Aberlemno Stones★, Pictish sculptured stones★) W : 13 m. by A 935
    and B 9134._
    ▮₁₈, ▮₁₈ _Traill Drive_ _℘_ (01674) 672932.
    🄱 _Bridge St_ _℘_ (01674) 672000 (Easter-September).
    Edinburgh 92 – Aberdeen 39 – Dundee 29.

⌂   **36 The Mall** without rest., 36 The Mall, DD10 8SS, North : ½ m. by A 92 at junction with
    North Esk Road _℘_ (01674) 673646, _enquiries@36themall.co.uk, Fax_ (01674) 673646, _☞ –
    ⇔ ◍◉ ◭ ◉ VISA. ※_
    3 rm ⊑ ✱35.00/45.00 – ✱✱50.00/70.00.
    ◆ Bay windowed 19C former manse with pleasant conservatory lounge to rear. Impressive
    plate collection the talking point of communal breakfast room. Sizable, well-kept rooms.

MOTHERWELL North Lanarkshire **501** I 16.
  Edinburgh 38 – Glasgow 12.

🏨🏨🏨 **Hilton Strathclyde,** Phoenix Crescent, Bellshill, ML4 3JQ, Northwest : 4 m. by A 721 on
  A 725 ℰ (01698) 395500, reservations.strathclyde@hilton.com, Fax (01698) 395511, ⚅, ₅,
  ≘s, ⬜ – 🛉 ⤨, 🍴 rest, 🍷 & 🄿 – 🔬 400. 🆗 🄰🄴 ℀ 𝘝𝘐𝘚𝘈. ❀
  Rest (closed lunch Saturday and Bank Holidays) 9.50/22.95 and dinner a la carte ⛏ – ⚌
  15.95 – **111 rm** ✵63.00/145.00 – ✵✵63.00/145.00.
  ◆ Group owned and smoothly run; a regular choice for business travellers, drawn by
  smartly laid-out modern rooms, open-plan lounge and coffee shop and superb leisure
  complex. Restaurant sets out to put a subtle new spin on classic dishes.

🏨🏨 **Alona,** Strathclyde Country Park, ML1 3RT, Northwest : 4½ m. by A 721 and B 7070 off A
  725 ℰ (01698) 333888, julian@alonahotel.co.uk, Fax (01698) 338720 – 🛉, ⤨ rm, 🍴 rest,
  🍷 & 🄿, 🆗 🄰🄴 ℀ 𝘝𝘐𝘚𝘈
  Rest (carving lunch)/dinner 19.95 and a la carte 19.25/40.00 – **51 rm** ⚌ ✵84.00/120.00 –
  ✵✵89.00/130.00.
  ◆ Attractively set modern hotel in 1500 acres of Strathclyde Country Park. Conservatory
  atrium with open-plan lounge and bar. Good-sized bedrooms exuding contemporary
  taste. Restaurant affords pleasant lakeside views.

🏨 **Express by Holiday Inn** without rest., Strathclyde Country Park, Hamilton Rd, ML1
  3RB, Northwest : 4 ¼ m. by A 721 and B 7070 off A 725 ℰ (01698) 858585,
  Fax (01698) 852375 – 🛉 ⤨ & 🄿 – 🔬 30. 🆗 🄰🄴 ℀ 𝘝𝘐𝘚𝘈
  120 rm ✵49.00 – ✵✵69.95.
  ◆ Good motorway connections from this purpose-built hotel offering trim rooms in contemporary style plus a small lounge and bar: a useful address for business stopovers.

MUIR OF ORD Highland **501** G 11 – pop. 1 812.
  🏌 Great North Rd ℰ (01463) 870825.
  Edinburgh 173 – Inverness 10 – Wick 121.

🏠 **Dower House** ⟡, Highfield, IV6 7XN, North : 1 m. on A 862 ℰ (01463) 870090, enqui
  ries@thedowerhouse.co.uk, Fax (01463) 870090, ⪪ – ⤨ 🍷 🄿. 🆗 𝘝𝘐𝘚𝘈
  closed Christmas – **Rest** (booking essential for non-residents) (set menu only) (lunch by
  arrangement)/dinner 38.00 s. – **3 rm** ⚌ ✵55.00/85.00 – ✵✵120.00/135.00, 1 suite.
  ◆ Personally run, part 17C house in mature garden. Stacked bookshelves, soft fireside
  armchairs, cosy bedrooms and fresh flowers: a relaxed but well-ordered country home.
  Dining room offers careful cooking of fine fresh ingredients.

MULL (Isle of) Argyll and Bute **501** B/C 14/15 Scotland G. – pop. 2 838.
  See : Island★ - Calgary Bay★★ – Torosay Castle **AC** (Gardens★ ≤★).
  Env. : Isle of Iona★ (Maclean's Cross★, St Oran's Chapel★, St Martin's High Cross★, Infirmary
  Museum★ **AC** (Cross of St John★)).
  🏌 Craignure, Scallastle ℰ (01680) 302517.
  🚢 from Craignure to Oban (Caledonian MacBrayne Ltd) frequent services daily (45 mn) –
  from Fishnish to Lochaline (Mainland) (Caledonian MacBrayne Ltd) frequent services daily
  (15 mn) – from Tobermory to Isle of Tiree (Scarinish) via Isle of Coll (Arinagour) (Caledonian
  MacBrayne Ltd) 3 weekly (2 h 30 mn) – from Tobermory to Kilchoan (Caledonian MacBrayne
  Ltd) 4 daily (summer only) (35 mn).
  🚢 from Fionnphort to Isle of Iona (Caledonian MacBrayne Ltd) frequent services daily (10
  mn) – from Pierowall to Papa Westray (Orkney Ferries Ltd) (summer only) (25 mn).
  🚩 The Pier, Craignure ℰ (08707) 200610 – Main Street, Tobermory ℰ (01688) 302182
  (April-October).

Bunessan Argyll and Bute.

🍴 **The Reef,** Main St, PA67 6DG, ℰ (01681) 700291, Fax (01681) 700534 – 🆗 𝘝𝘐𝘚𝘈
  April-September – **Rest** - Seafood specialities - a la carte 21.95/28.40.
  ◆ Don't be put off by simple tea-room façade and standard menu. Come here to enjoy
  the supremely fresh, excellent value daily blackboard seafood specials - owner is a fisherman.

Craignure Argyll and Bute.

🏠 **Birchgrove** ⟡ without rest., Lochdon, PA64 6AP, Southeast : 3 m. on A 849 ℰ (01680)
  812364, birchgrove@isle-of-mull.demon.co.uk, ≤, ⪪ – ⤨ 🄿. 🆗 𝘝𝘐𝘚𝘈. ❀
  25 March- 6 October – **3 rm** ⚌ ✵43.00/46.00 – ✵✵56.00/60.00.
  ◆ Modern guesthouse with landscaped gardens in peaceful setting with good views. Close
  to ferry pier. Clean, well-kept rooms, all boasting pleasant island outlook.

Gruline *Argyll and Bute.*

⌂ **Gruline Home Farm** ⌖, PA71 6HR, ℘ (01680) 300581, boo@gruline.com, Fax (01680) 300573, ≼, – ⊱✕ P. ⬥⊙ VISA
Rest (by arrangement) (communal dining) 32.50 – **3 rm** (dinner included) ⌷ ✦148.00 – ✦✦170.00.
◆ Spot deer, eagles and buzzards in utter tranquillity at this delightful farm, located off the beaten track with fine views over nearby mountains. Beautifully appointed rooms. Creative cooking brings out true flavour of island produce.

Tiroran *Argyll and Bute.*

🏠 **Tiroran House** ⌖, PA69 6ES, ℘ (01681) 705232, info@tiroran.com, Fax (01681) 705240, ≼ Loch Scridain, ☞, ⬥ – ⊱✕ P. ⬥⊙ AE VISA. ⬥✕
Rest (booking essential) (residents only) (dinner only) 35.00 **s.** – **6 rm** ⌷ ✦78.00/86.00 – ✦✦116.00/132.00.
◆ Attractive whitewashed hotel sited in remote location with superb views across Loch Scridain. Well-decorated lounges with country house style. Individually appointed rooms. Home-cooked dinners in vine-covered dining room or conservatory.

Tobermory *Argyll and Bute – pop. 2 708.*
🛈 Erray Rd ℘ (01688) 302387.

🏠 **Tobermory,** 53 Main St, PA75 6NT, ℘ (01688) 302091, tobhotel@tinyworld.co.uk, Fax (01688) 302254, ≼ – ⊱✕ ৬. ⬥⊙ VISA
closed 13 January - 9 February and 1 week Christmas – **Waters Edge :** **Rest** (booking essential for non-residents) (dinner only) 25.00/32.50 – **16 rm** ⌷ ✦37.00/98.00 – ✦✦84.00/114.00.
◆ Pink-painted, converted fishing cottages - cosy, well-run and informal - on the pretty quayside. Soft toned bedrooms in cottage style, most overlooking the bay. Intimate setting: linen-clad tables and subtly nautical décor.

⌂ **Ptarmigan House,** The Fairways, PA75 6PS, North : ½ m. by Back Brae and Erray Rd ℘ (01688) 302863, suefink@btopenworld.com, Fax (01688) 302913, ≼, ⬚, 🛈, ☞ – ⊱✕ TV P. ⬥⊙ VISA
restricted opening in winter – **Rest** (by arrangement) 27.00 – **4 rm** ⌷ ✦65.00/85.00 – ✦✦75.00/95.00.
◆ Immaculately nuanced, with super Sound of Mull views from smart decked terrace. Enjoy a swim in the pool, then take in vista from your room: one has terrace, one a balcony. Freshly prepared, very tasty cooking from set menu.

⌂ **Brockville** without rest., Raeric Rd, PA75 6RS, by Back Brae ℘ (01688) 302741, helen@brockville-tobermory.co.uk, Fax (01688) 302741, ≼, ☞ – ⊱✕ P. ⬥✕
3 rm ⌷ ✦35.00/45.00 – ✦✦56.00/70.00.
◆ Modern guesthouse in the residential part of town. The communal breakfast room has good views over the sea. Cottagey rooms have extra touches including videos and CDs.

✕✕ **Highland Cottage** with rm, Breadalbane St, PA75 6PD, via B 8073 ℘ (01688) 302030, davidandjo@highlandcottage.co.uk – ⊱✕ rm, P. ⬥⊙ VISA
March-October – **Rest** (booking essential for non-residents) (dinner only) 39.50 ⌷ – **6 rm** ⌷ ✦120.00 – ✦✦175.00.
◆ Modern cottage near the harbour. Prettily set dining room shows the same care and attention as the locally sourced menu. Individually styled rooms with good views.

NAIRN *Highland* **501** I 11 *Scotland G.* – *pop. 8 418.*
Env. : *Forres (Sueno's Stone★★) E : 11 m. by A 96 and B 9011 – Cawdor Castle★ AC, S : 5½ m. by B 9090 – Brodie Castle★ AC, E : 6 m. by A 96.*
Exc. : *Fort George★, W : 8 m. by A 96, B 9092 and B 9006.*
🛈, 🛈 Seabank Rd ℘ (01667) 453208 – 🛈 Nairn Dunbar, Lochloy Rd ℘ (01667) 452741.
Edinburgh 172 – Aberdeen 91 – Inverness 16.

🏛 **Golf View,** The Seafront, IV12 4HD, ℘ (01667) 458800, reservations.golfview@swallow hotels.com, Fax (01667) 458818, ≼, ₰, ⌷, ⬚, ☞, ✕ –|✦ ⊱✕, ▦ rest, ⬥ ✦✦ P. – 🏛 120. ⬥⊙ AE VISA
Restaurant : **Rest** 27.00 – **Conservatory :** **Rest** a la carte 18.05/27.85 **s.** – **41 rm** ⌷ ✦94.00/150.00 – ✦✦142.00/240.00, 1 suite.
◆ Non-golfers may prefer the vista of the Moray Firth from one of the sea-view rooms or a poolside lounger. Smart, traditional accommodation, up-to-date gym and beauty salon. Half-panelled dining room. Stylish, spacious conservatory restaurant.

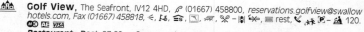

Swallow Newton ⚜, Inverness Rd, IV12 4RX, ℰ (01667) 453144, *swallow.new ton@swallowhotels.com*, Fax (01667) 454026, ☞, ♨ – 📶 ✸✦ ✆ ♿ 📷 – 🔏 500. ◍◒ 亜 ◑ *VISA*

The Restaurant : Rest (dinner only) 26.00 ♀ – *Chaplins :* Rest a la carte 16.95/28.95
– 53 rm ♿ ✹60.00/150.00 – ✹✹128.00/200.00, 3 suites.
◆ Enlarged mansion bounded by woods. Surprisingly contemporary interiors; state-of-the-art conference centre. Period styled rooms in the old house have greater character. Formal dining in Restaurant. Chaplins is informal bistro style diner.

Claymore House, 45 Seabank Rd, IV12 4EY, ℰ (01667) 453731, *claymore house@btconnect.com*, Fax (01667) 455290, ☞ – ✸✦ ♿ 📷 ◍◒ 亜 ◑ *VISA*
Rest (bar lunch)/dinner a la carte 17.20/31.65 s. – 15 rm ♿ ✹47.50/65.00 –
✹✹75.00/125.00, 1 suite.
◆ A privately-run, extended 19C house in a residential area. Comfortable lounge and conservatory. Modern rooms in warm colours are quieter at the rear. Neatly laid-out dining room: choose from a range of traditional Scottish favourites.

Boath House, Auldearn, IV12 5TE, East : 2 m. on A 96 ℰ (01667) 454896, *wendy@boath-house.com*, Fax (01667) 455469, ⇐, ⚘, ☞, ♨ – ✸✦ ♿ 📷 ◍◒ *VISA*
closed 1 week Christmas – Rest (closed for non-residents Monday-Wednesday lunch) (booking essential) 32.00/48.00 s. ♀ – 6 rm ♿ ✹120.00 – ✹✹250.00/280.00.
◆ 1820s neo-classical mansion, owned by a charming couple, hosts modern Highland art collections. Intimate, elegant rooms may have half-tester beds or views of the trout lake. Dining room with 18C garden views: precise, accomplished cooking in a modern style.

Sunny Brae, Marine Rd, IV12 4EA, ℰ (01667) 452309, *reservations@sunnybraeho tel.com*, Fax (01667) 454860, ⇐, ⚘, ☞ – ✸✦ ♿ 📷 *VISA*. ✸
closed January and November – Rest (closed lunch Saturday and Sunday) 20.00/35.00 ♀ –
8 rm ♿ ✹69.00/118.00 – ✹✹90.00/130.00.
◆ Behind an unassuming façade, this family-owned hotel offers sizeable, neatly kept bedrooms in cheerful patterns - many, like the terrace, have views of the shore. Light, summery dining room; traditional Scottish menus.

Bracadale House without rest., Albert St, IV12 4HF, ℰ (01667) 452547, *hannah@bra cadalehouse.com*, ☞ – ✸✦ 📷 ◍◒ *VISA*. ✸
March-October – 3 rm ♿ ✹30.00/50.00 – ✹✹50.00/60.00.
◆ This elegant Victorian house, near the beach, is enthusiastically run by a friendly owner. There's an attractive first floor lounge and rooms finished with a tasteful palette.

The Classroom, 1 Cawdor St, IV12 4QD, ℰ (01667) 455999, Fax (01667) 455999 – ◍◒ 亜
◑ *VISA*
closed 25-26 December and 1-2 January – Rest a la carte 14.70/27.40 ♀.
◆ Extended former school house in town centre. Split level modern brasserie style with L-shaped bar and pictures of pupils on the walls. Extensive menu with daily specials.

NETHERLEY Aberdeenshire 501 N 13 – see Stonehaven.

NEW LANARK Lanarkshire 501 I 17.
See : Town★★.
Edinburgh 44 – Dumfries 55 – Glasgow 31.

New Lanark Mill, Mill One, New Lanark Mills, ML11 9DB, ℰ (01555) 667200, *hotel@new lanark.org*, Fax (01555) 667222, ⇐ – 📶 ✸✦ ♿ 📷 – 🔏 150. ◍◒ 亜 ◑ *VISA*
Mill One : Rest (carving lunch Sunday) (bar lunch Monday-Saturday)/dinner 25.50 s. –
38 rm ♿ ✹69.50 – ✹✹109.00/134.00.
◆ Converted Clydeside cotton mill on the riverside in this superbly restored Georgian village, a World Heritage site. Usefully equipped, modern accommodation. Formal restaurant overlooking the river.

NEWTON STEWART Dumfries and Galloway 501 502 G 19 Scotland G. – pop. 3 573.
Env. : Galloway Forest Park★, Queen's Way★ (Newton Stewart to New Galloway) N : 19 m. by A 712.
🏌, Kirroughtree Ave, Minnigaff ℰ (01671) 402172 – 🏌 Wigtownshire County, Mains of Park, Glenluce ℰ (01581) 300420.
🛈 Dashwood Sq ℰ (01671) 402431 (Easter-October).
Edinburgh 131 – Dumfries 51 – Glasgow 87 – Stranraer 24.

SCOTLAND

Kirroughtree House ⚘, DG8 6AN, Northeast : 1 ½ m. by A 75 on A 712 ☏ (01671) 402141, *info@kirroughtreehouse.co.uk, Fax (01671) 402425*, ≤ woodland and Wigtown Bay, *☞*, ✖ – ⬛ ✦ ⬗ 🄿 ⬛ 🄰🄴 🆅🅸🅂🄰
closed 2 January-mid February – **Rest** (booking essential for non-residents) 32.50 (dinner) and lunch a la carte 17.25/24.25 – **15 rm** ☲ ✱90.00/125.00 – ✱✱180.00/200.00, 2 suites.
◆ Grand 1719 mansion dominates acres of sculpted garden. Well-proportioned bedrooms; firelit lounge with antiques, period oils and French windows leading to the croquet lawn. Elegant fine dining, in keeping with formal grandeur of the house.

Rowallan, Corsbie Rd, DG8 6JB, via Jubilee Rd off Dashwood Sq ☏ (01671) 402520, *enquiries@rowallan.co.uk, Fax (01671) 402520*, *☞* – ✦✖ 🄿. ⬗
closed 25-26 December – **Rest** (by arrangement) 12.00 – **6 rm** ☲ ✱36.00/39.00 – ✱✱60.00.
◆ Victorian house in attractive large garden not far from town centre. Large lounge with bar; meals served in conservatory. Brightly decorated bedrooms.

NORTH BAY *Western Isles – see Barra (Isle of).*

NORTH BERWICK *East Lothian 501 L 15 Scotland G. – pop. 5 871.*

Env. : *North Berwick Law (⬗★★★) S : 1 m. - Tantallon Castle★★ (clifftop site★★★) AC, E : 3 ½ m. by A 198 – Dirleton★ (Castle★ AC) SW : 2½ m. by A 198.*
Exc. : *Museum of Flight★ , S : 6 m. by B 1347 – Preston Mill★, S : 8½ m. by A 198 and B 1047 – Tyninghame★, S : 7 m. by A 198 – Coastal road from North Berwick to Portseton★, SW : 13 m. by A 198 and B 1348.*
🅢 North Berwick, West Links, Beach Rd ☏ (01620) 895040 – 🅢 The Glen, East Links ☏ (01620) 892726.
🄱 Quality St ☏ (01620) 892197.
Edinburgh 24 – Newcastle upon Tyne 102.

Glebe House ⚘ without rest., Law Rd, EH39 4PL, ☏ (01620) 892608, *gwenscott@gle behouse-nb.co.uk, Fax (01620) 893588, ☞* – ✦✖ 🄿. ⬗
closed 25-26 December – **3 rm** ☲ ✱50.00/60.00 – ✱✱80.00/90.00.
◆ Owned by a likeable couple, a classically charming 1780s manse in secluded gardens. En suite rooms are pleasantly unfussy and well-kept. Breakfasts at a long communal table.

Beach Lodge without rest., 5 Beach Rd, EH39 4AB, ☏ (01620) 892257, ≤ – ✦✖. ⬗
🄰 3 rm ☲ ✱50.00/55.00 – ✱✱70.00/80.00.
◆ Friendly and well-run: breakfast room and compact, modern bedrooms share an appealing, clean-lined style. All rooms have fridges and videos, one overlooks the sea.

NORTH UIST *Western Isles (Outer Hebrides) 501 X/Y 10/11 – see Uist (Isles of).*

OBAN *Argyll and Bute 501 D 14 Scotland G. – pop. 8 120.*

Exc. : *Loch Awe★★, SE : 17 m. by A 85 – Bonawe Furnace★, E : 12 m. by A 85 – Cruachan Power Station★ AC, E : 16 m. by A 85 – Seal and Marine Centre★ AC, N : 14 m. by A 828.*
🅢 Glencruitten, Glencruitten Rd ☏ (01631) 562868.
Access to Glasgow by helicopter.
⛴ to Isle of Mull (Craignure) (Caledonian MacBrayne Ltd) (45 mn) – to Isle of Tiree (Scarinish) via Isle of Mull (Tobermory) and Isle of Coll (Arinagour) (Caledonian MacBrayne Ltd) – to Isle of Islay (Port Askaig) and Kintyre Peninsula (Kennacraig) via Isle of Colonsay (Scalasaig) (Caledonian MacBrayne Ltd) (summer only) – to Isle of Lismore (Achnacroish) (Caledonian MacBrayne Ltd) 2-3 daily (except Sunday) (55 mn) – to Isle of Colonsay (Scalasaig) (Caledonian MacBrayne Ltd) 3 weekly (2 h).
🄱 Church Building, Argyll Sq ☏ (08707) 200630, info@oban.org.uk.
Edinburgh 123 – Dundee 116 – Glasgow 93 – Inverness 118.

Oban Caledonian, Station Sq, PA34 5RF, ☏ (01631) 563133 – ⬛ ✦✖ 📺 – 🄰 40. 🄲🄾 🄰🄴 🄳 🆅🅸🅂🄰 🄹🄲🄱
Rest *a la carte* 20.00/30.00 – **59 rm** ✱55.00/85.00 – ✱✱110.00/260.00.
◆ Well located near harbour. Modish interior includes spacious bar displaying vivid artwork. Pleasant rooms: ask for one with four poster and rewarding front facing views. Seasonal local fish a highlight of smart dining room's menu.

Manor House, Gallanach Rd, PA34 4LS, ☏ (01631) 562087, *info@manorhouseo ban.com, Fax (01631) 563053*, ≤ Oban harbour and bay, *☞* – ✦✖ 🄿. 🄲🄾 🄰🄴 🆅🅸🅂🄰
closed 25-26 December – **Rest** (lunch by arrangement)/dinner 35.00 – **11 rm** (dinner included) ☲ ✱85.00/140.00 – ✱✱132.00/185.00.
◆ Period furniture and colour schemes bring out the character of this 18C dower house, once part of the Argyll ducal estate. Individual rooms, most with fine views of the bay. Green and tartan restaurant warmed by an ancient range.

⌂ **Polrudden** without rest., Peerie Sea Loan, KW15 1UH, West : 1 m. by Pickaquoy Rd
 𝒫 (01856) 874761, *linda@polrudden.com* – ↻↻ **P**. **⑩⑩** *VISA*. ⁂
 closed 24 December - 3 January – **7 rm** ⊆ ✹40.00 – ✹✹60.00.
 ✦ Well-kept en suite accommodation - over two floors - with matching fabrics and var-
 nished pine in a sizeable converted house just outside the town centre. Friendly owner.
 Breakfast room: picture windows give on to quiet fields.

⌂ **Brekk-Ness** without rest., Muddisdale Rd, KW15 1RS, West : ¾ m. by Pickaquoy Rd
 𝒫 (01856) 874317, *sandrabews@aol.com*, Fax (01856) 874317 – ↻↻ **P**. **⑩⑩** *VISA*
 closed 24 December - 3 January – **11 rm** ⊆ ✹40.00 – ✹✹60.00.
 ✦ In the fields on the edge of the town, an unassuming guesthouse, neatly maintained by
 a likeable couple. Bedrooms are practically fitted and en suite.

❀❀ **Foveran** ⌖ with rm, St Ola, KW15 1SF, Southwest : 3 m. on A 964 *𝒫* (01856) 872389,
 foveranhotel@aol.com, Fax (01856) 876430, ← – ↻↻ rm, **P**. **⑩⑩** *VISA*. ⁂
 restricted opening in winter – **Rest** (dinner only) a la carte 15.65/31.70 – **8 rm** ⊆
 ✹59.50/80.00 – ✹✹99.00.
 ✦ Modern restaurant enjoys a beautiful view of Scapa Flow. Simple, soft-toned bedrooms,
 furnished in warm wood and a firelit lounge, in the same style, where apéritifs are served.
 Orkney fudge cheesecake a dining room regular.

Loch Harray *Orkney Islands.*

🏠 **Merkister** ⌖, KW17 2LF, off A 986 *𝒫* (01856) 771366, *merkister-hotel@ecosse.net*,
 Fax (01856) 771515, ← Loch Harray, ↝, ← – 🔟 ↻↻ ♦ **P**. **⑩⑩** *AE* *VISA*
 closed 23 December-4 January – **Rest** *(booking essential in winter)* (bar lunch Monday-
 Saturday)/dinner 17.50/22.50 and a la carte 21.50/28.45 – **16 rm** ⊆ ✹35.00/65.00 –
 ✹✹70.00/120.00.
 ✦ In a peaceful spot above Loch Harray, a popular angling base, family run with friendly
 efficiency. Trim bedrooms; public bar with a quiet buzz of far-fetched fishing tales. Restaurant offers an extensive menu on a distinctly Scottish base.

St Margaret's Hope *Orkney Islands.*

❀❀ **Creel** with rm, Front Rd, KW17 2SL, *𝒫* (01856) 831311, *alan@thecreel.freeserve.co.uk*, ←
 – **P**. **⑩⑩** *VISA*. ⁂
 April-mid October – **Rest** - Seafood specialities - *(closed Monday except June-August and
 Tuesday)* (dinner only) 32.50/45.50 – **3 rm** ⊆ ✹65.00/75.00 – ✹✹95.00/120.00.
 ✦ Smart, family run restaurant; flavourful local dishes without culinary curlicues: menu
 devised daily based upon the best seasonal produce. Friendly staff. Neat, homely rooms.

Westray (Island of).

🏠 **Cleaton House** ⌖, KW17 2DB, *𝒫* (01857) 677508, *cleaton@orkney.com*,
 Fax (01857) 677442, ← Papa Westray, ☞ – ↻↻ ♦ **P**. **⑩⑩** *VISA*
 Rest (booking essential for non-residents) (bar lunch)/dinner a la carte 15.00/38.00 ⟓ –
 6 rm ⊆ ✹55.00/60.00 – ✹✹100.00/110.00.
 ✦ Originally built as mansion for Laird of Cleat in 1850, this charming guesthouse is idyllically situated halfway up the island. Charming lounge. Individually appointed rooms. Country house dining room overlooks garden.

PEAT INN *Fife.*

❀❀❀ **Peat Inn** with rm, KY15 5LH, *𝒫* (01334) 840206, *stay@thepeatinn.co.uk*,
 Fax (01334) 840530, ☞ – **P**. **⑩⑩** *AE* *VISA*
 closed 1-2 January, 25-26 December and Sunday-Monday – **Rest** (booking essential)
 22.00/32.00 and dinner a la carte 31.50/43.50 – **8 rm** ✹95.00/125.00 – ✹✹145.00/165.00.
 ✦ Former coaching inn with a homely country house style. Three dining rooms serve tasty,
 traditional dishes. Annex bedrooms are very strong and full of charming extra touches.

The red ⌖ symbol?
This denotes the very essence of peace
– only the sound of birdsong first thing in the morning …

SCOTLAND

PEEBLES *Borders* 501 502 K 17 *Scotland G.* – pop. 8 065.

Env. : *Tweed Valley*★★.

Exc. : *Traquair House*★★ *AC, SE* : 7 m. by B 7062 – *Rosslyn Chapel*★★ *AC, N* : 16½ m. by A 703, A 6094, B 7026 and B 7003.

🏌 *Kirkland St ℰ (01721) 720197.*

🛈 *High St ℰ (0870) 608 0404.*

Edinburgh 24 – Glasgow 53 – Hawick 31.

Cringletie House ⚲, Edinburgh Rd, EH45 8PL, North : 3 m. on A 703 ℰ (01721) 725750, enquiries@cringletie.com, Fax (01721) 725751, ≤, ≈, ⚖ – ∣≸∣ ⧱ ⧳ 🅿, ⓂⓄ 🆀 𝓥𝓘𝓢𝓐
closed 2 January-3 February – **Rest** 19.50/37.50 – **13 rm** ⊆ ✦130.00/165.00 –
✦✦190.00/230.00.
◆ Smoothly run and handsomely furnished Victorian hotel in country house style with contemporary edge. Rooms are modern, well-equipped and peaceful. Spacious, formal restaurant with a trompe l'oeil ceiling.

Peebles Hydro, Innerleithen Rd, EH45 8LX, ℰ (01721) 720602, info@peebleshydro.com, Fax (01721) 722999, ≤, ⓥ, ⅙, ⇌, ☒, ≈, ⚖, ⅍ – ∣≸∣ ⧱ ⧳ ⅋, ⅍⅍ 🅿 – ⚖ 450.
ⓂⓄ 🆀 𝓥𝓘𝓢𝓐
Rest 19.50/29.00 – **126 rm** (dinner included) ⊆ ✦125.00/144.00 – ✦✦269.00/311.00, 3 suites.
◆ Grand Edwardian spa hotel, now offering everything from aromatherapy to reflexology plus a crèche and supervised activities to keep children busy. Modern, soft-toned bedrooms. High ceilinged, classically styled restaurant.

Castle Venlaw ⚲, Edinburgh Road, EH45 8QG, North : 1 ¼ m. by A 703 ℰ (01721) 720384, stay@venlaw.co.uk, Fax (01721) 724066, ≤, ≈ – ⧱ ⧳ ⅋ – ⚖ 35. ⓂⓄ 𝓥𝓘𝓢𝓐
Rest (booking essential for non-residents) 30.00 s. ♀ – **12 rm** (dinner included) ⊆ ✦93.00/105.00 – ✦✦166.00/190.00.
◆ Renovated 18C Scottish baronial style house in wooded gardens: friendly and privately run. Well-appointed rooms; family suite in tower. Afternoon tea in firelit Library bar. Parquet-floored dining room with pleasant views through the trees.

Park, Innerleithen Rd, EH45 8BA, ℰ (01721) 720451, reserve@parkpeebles.co.uk, Fax (01721) 723510, ≈ – ∣≸∣ ⧱ ⧳ ⅋, ⓂⓄ 🆀 𝓥𝓘𝓢𝓐
Rest 27.40 (dinner) and lunch a la carte 13.15/22.30 s. – **24 rm** (dinner included) ✦81.00/100.00 – ✦✦174.00/208.00.
◆ Extended town-centre hotel - tidy and unpretentious - overlooks a well-tended lawn. Simple bar with tartan sofas, neatly kept rooms: a good address for the mature traveller. Wood-panelled restaurant continues the traditional décor and atmosphere of the hotel.

Rowanbrae without rest., 103 Northgate, EH45 8BU, ℰ (01721) 721630, john@rowanbrae.freeserve.co.uk, Fax (01721) 723324- ⧱, ≈
closed Christmas-New Year – **3 rm** ⊆ ✦30.00/35.00 – ✦✦48.00/50.00.
◆ Built for the manager of a 19C woollen mill. Pleasant, affordable rooms, well kept by a cheerful couple. Fortifying breakfasts with posies of garden flowers on each table.

Halcyon, 39 Eastgate, EH45 8AD, ℰ (01721) 725100, mail@halcyonrestaurant.com – ⓂⓄ
🆀 𝓥𝓘𝓢𝓐
closed 1 week March, 1 week November, 25-27 December and Sunday-Monday – **Rest** 15.00 (lunch) and a la carte 20.50/35.50 s..
◆ Chef/owner prepares and cooks alone in kitchen; regulars at this cosy restaurant appreciate his constantly evolving menus featuring skilfully prepared, excellent value dishes.

PERTH *Perth and Kinross* 501 J 14 *Scotland G.* – pop. 43 450.

See : *City*★ – *Black Watch Regimental Museum*★ Y **M1** – *Georgian Terraces*★ Y – *Museum and Art Gallery*★ Y **M2**.

Env. : *Scone Palace*★★ *AC, N* : 2 m. by A 93 Y – *Branklyn Garden*★ *AC, SE* : 1 m. by A 85 Z – *Kinnoull Hill* (≤★) *SE* : 1¼ m. by A 85 Z – *Huntingtower Castle*★ *AC, NW* : 3 m. by A 85 Y – *Elcho Castle*★ *AC, SE* : 4 m. by A 912 – Z – and Rhynd rd.

Exc. : *Abernethy (11C Round Tower*★), *SE* : 8 m. by A 912 – Z – and A 913.

🏌 *Craigie Hill, Cherrybank ℰ (01738) 620829 Z – 🏌 King James VI, Moncreiffe Island ℰ (01738) 625170 Z – 🏌 Murrayshall, New Scone ℰ (01738) 554804 Y – 🏌 North Inch, c/o Perth & Kinross Council, 5 High St ℰ (01738) 636481 Y.*

🛈 *Lower City Mills, West Mill St ℰ (01738) 450600, perthtic@perthshire.co.uk.*

Edinburgh 44 – Aberdeen 86 – Dundee 22 – Dunfermline 29 – Glasgow 64 – Inverness 112 – Oban 94.

Plan opposite

850

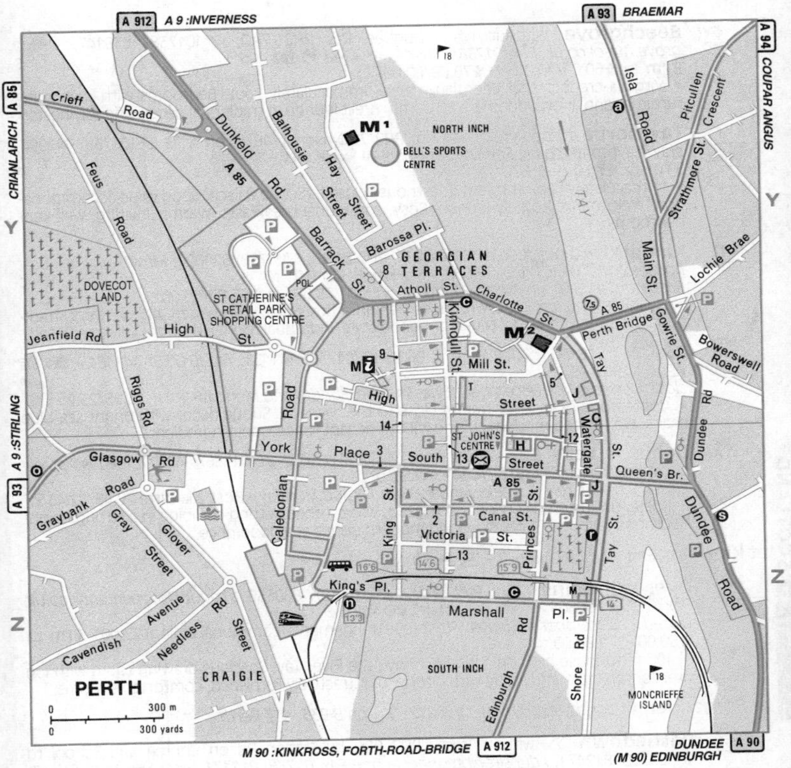

Charterhouse Lane . . . . Z 2
County Pl. . . . . Z 3
George St . . . . Y 5
High St . . . . Y
Melville St . . . . Y 8
North Methven St . . . . Y 9
St Catherine's Retail Park . . . . Y
St John St . . . . Z 12
St John's Centre . . . . Z
Scott St . . . . Z 13
South Methven St. . . . . Y 14
South St . . . . Z

Huntingtower , Crieff Rd, PH1 3JT, West : 3½ m. by A 85 (01738) 583771, *reservations@huntingtowerhotel.co.uk, Fax (01738) 583777*, , – – 250. AE VISA
Oak Room : **Rest** (bar lunch)/dinner 27.50 and a la carte 25.00/32.00 **s.** – **34 rm** 99.00/109.00 – 159.00.
◆ Late Victorian half-timbered country house named after nearby castle. Choose bedrooms in the more traditional old house or modern, executive rooms. Restaurant with views towards lawn and stream.

Parklands, 2 St Leonard's Bank, PH2 8EB, (01738) 622451, *info@theparklandshotel.com, Fax (01738) 622046*, , – . VISA Z n
Acanthus : **Rest** (dinner only) 27.95/32.95 – ***No.1 The Bank :*** **Rest** a la carte 18.40/31.85 – **15 rm** 79.00/129.00 – 109.00/169.00.
◆ Privately run, these two well-kept houses are handily positioned opposite railway station. Rooms, in co-ordinated patterns, are named after local places: most face garden. New-British dishes in contemporary Acanthus. Conservatory bistro fare at No 1 The Bank.

Express by Holiday Inn without rest., 200 Dunkeld Rd, Inveralmond, PH1 3AQ, Northwest : 2 m. on A 912 (01738) 636666, *info@hiexpressperth.co.uk, Fax (01738) 633363* – – 40. AE VISA
81 rm 65.00/72.00 – 65.00/72.00.
◆ Outside the city centre, a group-owned lodge, modern in style, providing practical, simply planned accommodation in cheerful colours. Excellent road connections.

↑ **Beechgrove** without rest., Dundee Rd, PH2 7AQ, ℰ (01738) 636147, *beech grove.h@sol.co.uk, Fax (01738) 636147*, ⊯ – 🛏 **P. VISA**. ⊗
8 rm ☑ ✸60.00/70.00 – ✸✸75.00/80.00.
Z s
♦ Virginia creeper clad Georgian manse, immaculately kept. Bedrooms with mahogany furniture and a few added extras; comfy firelit lounge in traditional décor. Friendly hosts.

↑ **Taythorpe** without rest., Isla Rd, PH2 7HQ, North : 1 m. on A 93 ℰ (01738) 447994, *stay@taythorpe.co.uk, Fax (01738) 447994* – 🛏 **P.** ⊗
3 rm ☑ ✸70.00 – ✸✸70.00.
Y a
♦ Immaculately kept, modern guesthouse close to Scone Palace. Good value accommodation. Welcoming, homely lounge. Cosy, communal breakfasts. Warmly inviting, well-kept bedrooms.

↑ **Kinnaird** without rest., 5 Marshall Pl, PH2 8AH, ℰ (01738) 628021, *info@kinnaird-guest house.co.uk, Fax (01738) 444056*, ⊯ – 🛏 **P. ◖◗ VISA**. ⊗
Restricted opening in winter – 7 rm ☑ ✸35.00/50.00 – ✸✸55.00/65.00.
Z c
♦ Neatly kept Georgian town house behind a tidy front lawn edged with flowers. Traditional sitting room with a touch of period style. Individual rooms, thoughtfully appointed.

✕✕ **63 Tay Street**, 63 Tay St, PH2 8NN, ℰ (01738) 441451, Fax (01738) 441461 – **◖◗ AE VISA**
r
closed 2 weeks late December, 2 weeks June, Sunday and Monday – Rest 15.95/25.95 � .
♦ Contemporary style restaurant close to the riverside. Subtle décor with bright sea-blue chairs. Well-priced modern cuisine with penchant for seasonal ingredients.

✕✕ **Deans @ Let's Eat**, 77-79 Kinnoull St, PH1 5EZ, ℰ (01738) 643377, *deans@letseat perth.co.uk, Fax (01738) 621464* – **◖◗ AE VISA**
Y c
closed 2 weeks July, 2 weeks January, Sunday and Monday – Rest a la carte 20.45/32.45 � .
♦ Polite, unflustered service and relaxed, warm-toned setting combine in a strong neighbourhood favourite. Robust, varied modern dishes at a good price.

at Kinfauns East : 4 m. by A 90 – Z – ✉ Perth.

↑ **Over Kinfauns** ⊗, PH2 7LD, ℰ (01738) 860538, *bandb@overkinfauns.co.uk, Fax (01738) 860803*, ≤, ⊯, ⊞ – 🛏 **P**. ⊗
closed 23 December - 5 January Rest (by arrangement) (communal dining) 27.00 – 3 rm ☑
✸50.00 – ✸✸80.00.
♦ 19C farmhouse high on a hillside above the River Tay. Spacious drawing room with log fire; conservatory and study with local info. Attractively furnished, comfortable rooms.

at Forgandenny Southwest : 6½ m. by A 912 – Z – on B 935 – ✉ Perth.

↑ **Battledown** ⊗ without rest., PH2 9EL, by Station Rd on Church and School rd ℰ (01738) 812471, *i.dunsire@btconnect.com, Fax (01738) 812471*, ⊯ – 🛏 ⏚ **P. ◖◗ ◖◗**
VISA
3 rm ☑ ✸35.00 – ✸✸60.00.
♦ Immaculately whitewashed, part 18C cottage in quiet village. Homely lounge full of local info. Cosy, pine-furnished breakfast room. Neat, tidy rooms, all on ground level.

at Methven West : 6½ m. on A 85 – Y – ✉ Perth.

✕ **Hamish's**, Main St, PH1 3PU, ℰ (01738) 840505, *info@hamishs.co.uk* – **◖◗ ◖◗ VISA**
closed 2 weeks January, Monday and Tuesday – Rest a la carte 15.95/24.95 s.
♦ Former Victorian school-house with smart, modish interior accentuated by striking red leather chairs. Accomplished modern cooking with classical base and Scottish bias.

PITLOCHRY Perth and Kinross 501 I 13 Scotland G. – pop. 2 564.
See : Town★.
Exc. : Blair Castle★★ AC, NW : 7 m. by A 9 A – Queen's View★★, W : 7 m. by B 8019 A – Falls of Bruar★, NW : 11 m. by A 9 A.
🇷 Golf Course Rd ℰ (01796) 472792.
🄱 22 Atholl Rd ℰ (01796) 472215, pitlochrytic@perthshire.co.uk.
Edinburgh 71 – Inverness 85 – Perth 27.

Plan opposite

🏛 **Green Park**, Clunie Bridge Rd, PH16 5JY, ℰ (01796) 473248, *bookings@thegreen park.co.uk, Fax (01796) 473520*, ≤, 🌳, ⊯ – 🛏 📞 ⏚ **P. ◖◗ VISA**
A a
closed 25-26 December – Rest (booking essential for non-residents) (light lunch residents only)/dinner 21.00/25.00 � – 51 rm (dinner included) ☑ ✸60.00/85.00 – ✸✸120.00/170.00.
♦ Family run 1860s summer retreat on Loch Faskally. Rooms in the old house are decorated in floral patterns; impressive up-to-date wing has good, contemporary facilities. Unhurried dinners at lochside setting.

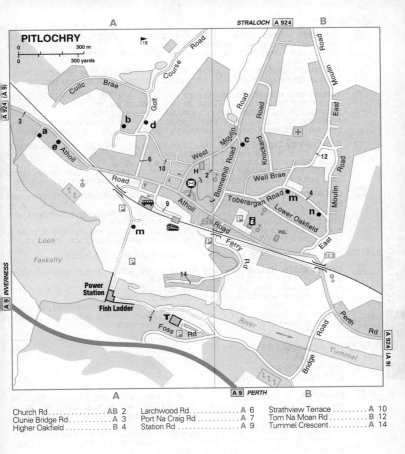

Church Rd.	AB 2	Larchwood Rd.	A 6	Strathview Terrace	A 10
Clunie Bridge Rd.	A 3	Port Na Craig Rd.	A 7	Tom Na Moan Rd.	B 12
Higher Oakfield	B 4	Station Rd.	A 9	Tummel Crescent	A 14

🏨 **Pine Trees** ॐ, Strathview Terrace, PH16 5QR, ℘ (01796) 472121, *info@pinetreesho tel.co.uk*, Fax (01796) 472460, <, 雫 – ⅜⊶ 🅿. ⑩© 🆎 💳
                                                               A b
Rest 21.50/25.50 and a la carte 13.40/25.50 – **20 rm** (dinner included) ⊇ ✸56.00/120.00 –
✸✸132.00/168.00.
  ◆ Extended 1892 mansion: superb wood-panelled hall with open fire, period prints and antiques. Modern rooms in warm décor; those at front have best views of 8-acre gardens. Two eating alternatives: dining room or bistro area.

🏠 **Craigatin House and Courtyard** without rest., 165 Atholl Rd, PH16 5QL, ℘ (01796) 472478, *enquiries@craigatinhouse.co.uk*, Fax (01796) 470167, 雫 – ⅜⊶ ௯ 🅿. ⑩© 💳 ⅗
                                                                   A e
closed 15 December - 5 January – **12 rm** ⊇ ✸35.00/65.00 – ✸✸80.00/90.00, 1 suite.
  ◆ 19C detached house with converted stables. Smart, stylish décor, including comfy conservatory lounge and breakfast room. Eye-catchingly inviting rooms, some in the annexe.

🏠 **Knockendarroch House**, 2 Higher Oakfield, PH16 5HT, ℘ (01796) 473473, *book ings@knockendarroch.co.uk*, Fax (01796) 474068, <, ⅜⊶ ⑩© 💳   **B m**
March-October – **Rest** (dinner only) 26.50 – **12 rm** (dinner included) ⊇ ✸79.00/97.00 –
✸✸116.00/156.00.
  ◆ A handsome late Victorian house in a neat garden. Most of the large, light bedrooms have good views; comfortably furnished, bright, airy, two-room lounge. Cosy, homely dining room.

853

🏛 **Balrobin,** Higher Oakfield, PH16 5HT, ☎ (01796) 472901, *info@balrobin.co.uk,* Fax (01796) 474200, ≤, 🐾 – ⇎ **P.** ⬛ *VISA* ⬛   **B n**
April-October – **Rest** (residents only) (dinner only) 18.75 – **14 rm** ⊇ ✦39.50/49.50 –
✦✦68.00/94.00.
♦ Affordable, simply furnished, spacious bedrooms - with good town views from front -
in a local stone house of late 19C origin. Impressive range of whiskies in residents' bar.

🏠 **Torrdarach House** without rest., Golf Course Rd, PH16 5AU, ☎ (01796) 472136, *torr darach@.msn.com, Fax (01796) 472136,* 🐾 – ⇎ **P.** ⬛ ⬛ *VISA* ⬛   **A d**
restricted opening in winter – **7 rm** ⊇ ✦24.00/50.00 – ✦✦48.00/64.00.
♦ Pleasant, well-priced rooms in bright colours and traditionally cosy sitting room behind
the deep red façade of this Edwardian country house. Beautifully kept, ornate gardens.

🏠 **Dunmurray Lodge** without rest., 72 Bonnethill Rd, PH16 5ED, ☎ (01796) 473624, *tony@dunmurray.co.uk, Fax (01796) 473624,* 🐾 – ⇎ **P.**   **B c**
closed 25 December – **4 rm** ⊇ ✦30.00/50.00 – ✦✦50.00/64.00.
♦ Pretty, immaculately kept 19C cottage, once a doctor's surgery. Relax in homely sitting
room's squashy sofas. Bedrooms are small and cosy with soothing cream colour scheme.

✕✕ **Old Armoury,** Armoury Rd, PH16 5AP, ☎ (01796) 474281, *info@theoldarmouryrestaur ant.com, Fax (01796) 473157,* ⛭, 🐾 – **P.** ⬛ ⓪ *VISA*   **A m**
closed 2 January-1 February, 24-28 December and Monday-Wednesday November-March
– **Rest** 13.95/16.25 (lunch) and dinner a la carte 18.35/37.75 ⅗.
♦ 18C former Black Watch armoury. Smart al fresco dining area and wishing well. Inside: a
bright lounge, three dining rooms and traditional menus with distinct Scottish accent.

at Killiecrankie Northwest : 4 m. by A 924 – A – and B 8019 on B 8079 – ✉ Pitlochry.

🏨 **Killiecrankie House** ⬙, PH16 5LG, ☎ (01796) 473220, *enquiries@killiecrankieho tel.co.uk, Fax (01796) 472451,* ≤, 🐾 – ⇎ **P.** ⬛ *VISA*
April- 2 January – **Rest** (bar lunch)/dinner 28.00 and a la carte 18.50/28.00 s. ♀ – **9 rm**
(dinner included) ✦84.00/168.00 – ✦✦168.00/198.00, 1 suite.
♦ Quiet and privately run, a converted 1840 vicarage with a distinct rural feel. Mahogany
panelled bar; sizeable rooms in co-ordinated patterns overlook pleasant countryside.
Warm, red dining room; garden produce prominent on menus.

SCOTLAND

PLOCKTON Highland 501 D 11 Scotland G.
     See : Village★.
     Env. : Wester Ross★★★.
     Edinburgh 210 – Inverness 88.

🏛 **Plockton,** 41 Harbour St, IV52 8TN, ☎ (01599) 544274, *info@plocktonhotel.co.uk,* Fax (01599) 544475, ≤ Loch Carron and mountains, ⛭, 🐾 – ⇎ ✿ ⬩, ⬛ ⬛ *VISA* ⬛
closed 25 December and 1 January – **Courtyard :** Rest a la carte 15.00/35.00 ♀ – **15 rm** ⊇
✦45.00 – ✦✦90.00/100.00.
♦ Enlarged traditional inn commands fine views of the mountains and Loch Carron. Convivial, half-panelled bar; local ale. New rooms in particular have a simple, stylish feel. Popular menu served in the spacious modern restaurant.

🍴 **Plockton Inn** with rm, Innes St, IV52 8TW, ☎ (01599) 544222, *stay@plocktoninn.co.uk,* Fax (01599) 544487, ⛭, 🐾 – ⬩ **P.** ⬛ *VISA*
closed 25-26 December – **Rest** - Seafood - a la carte 14.00/22.00 – **14 rm** ⊇ ✦40.00 –
✦✦80.00.
♦ Family run converted manse, with a cosy locals bar refreshingly short on airs and graces.
Welcoming lounges for dining on local fish and shellfish. Trim, cheerful bedrooms.

PORT APPIN Argyll and Bute 501 D 14 – ✉ Appin.
     Edinburgh 136 – Ballachulish 20 – Oban 24.

🏨 **Airds** ⬙, PA38 4DF, ☎ (01631) 730236, *airds@airds-hotel.com, Fax (01631) 730535,* ≤ Loch Linnhe and mountains of Kingairloch, 🦢, 🐾 – ⇎ ✿ **P.** ⬛ *VISA*
closed 8-28 January – **Rest** (booking essential for non-residents) 49.50 s. (dinner) and lunch
a la carte 20.25/29.95 ♀ – **12 rm** (dinner included) ⊇ ✦180.00/230.00 – ✦✦245.00/355.00.
♦ Former ferry inn with superb views of Loch Linnhe and mountains. Charming rooms -
antiques and floral fabrics. Firelit, old-world sitting rooms hung with landscapes. Smartly
set tables, picture windows looking across the water in the restaurant.

PORT CHARLOTTE Argyll and Bute 501 A 16 – see Islay (Isle of).

PORT ELLEN Argyll and Bute 501 B 17 – see Islay (Isle of).

PORTMAHOMACK Highland 501 I 10.
Edinburgh 194.5 – Dornoch 21 – Tain 12.5.

XX **The Oystercatcher** with rm, Main St, IV20 1YB, *ℰ* (01862) 871560, *gordon@burtonro
bertson.fsnet.co.uk*, Fax (01862) 871777 – **P**. **CO AE VISA**
restricted opening in Winter – **Rest** - Seafood - (closed Monday-Tuesday) (booking essential) a la carte 28.75/66.00 **s**. – **3 rm** ⬜ ✦42.50/70.00 – ✦✦97.50.
◆ Personally run bistro and piscatorially themed main dining room in a lovely setting, ideal
for sunsets. Enjoyable local fish dishes, with lobster a speciality. Homely rooms.

PORTPATRICK Dumfries and Galloway 501 502 E 19 – *pop. 585 –* ✉ *Stranraer.*
🏌, 🏌 *Golf Course Rd ℰ* (01776) 810273.
Edinburgh 141 – Ayr 60 – Dumfries 80 – Stranraer 9.

🏨 **Knockinaam Lodge** ⬚, DG9 9AD, Southeast : 5 m. by A 77 off B 7042 *ℰ* (01776)
810471, *reservations@knockinaamlodge.com*, Fax (01776) 810435, ≤, ⬚, ⬚, ⬚ – ✦✦ **P**.
CO AE VISA
Rest (booking essential for non-residents) (set menu only) 40.00/50.00 ⬚ ⬚ – **9 rm** (dinner
included) ⬜ ✦145.00/165.00 – ✦✦270.00/360.00.
Spec. Ravioli of sweetbreads with lemon, chicken and thyme reduction. Baked scallops
with root vegetables, Champagne butter sauce. Hot passion fruit soufflé with its own ice
cream.
◆ 19C shooting lodge in a picturesque coastal setting. Panelled bar with superb rare single
malts. Comfy, individualistic rooms. Personally managed. Ornate ceilings, pristine tables
enhance the enjoyment of carefully prepared, skilled modern Scottish dishes.

🏨 **Fernhill**, Heugh Rd, DG9 8TD, *ℰ* (01776) 810220, *info@fernhillhotel.co.uk*,
Fax (01776) 810596, ≤ Portpatrick and the North Channel, ⬚ – ✦✦ ✦ & **P**. **CO AE ⓞ**
VISA
closed January – **Rest** 16.00/32.50 **s**. – **36 rm** (dinner included) ⬜ ✦76.00/90.00 –
✦✦76.00/103.00.
◆ Family owned hotel in an elevated position; comfortable lounge and bar with fine view
of the harbour and sea. Rooms vary in size; the more luxurious have balconies. Unpretentious restaurant and conservatory with menu which changes with the seasons.

🏨 **The Waterfront**, North Crescent, DG9 8SX, *ℰ* (01776) 810800, *waterfrontho
tel@aol.com*, Fax (01776) 810850, ≤, ⬚ – ✦✦, ⬛ rest, ✦. **CO AE VISA**
closed 1 week Christmas – **Rest** (bar lunch)/dinner 22.50/32.50 and a la carte 16.50/40.00 –
8 rm ⬜ ✦60.00/68.00 – ✦✦86.00/96.00.
◆ 18C harbourside hotel with good views and pleasant terraced seating. Modern, stylish
décor with a light, arty feel. Compact, contemporary styled rooms overlooking the harbour. Pleasant, pine-panelled dining room with extensive menu.

XX **Campbells**, 1 South Cres, DG9 8JR, *ℰ* (01776) 810314, *dianecampbell@campbellsres
taurant.wanadoo.co.uk*, Fax (01776) 810361, ≤ Portpatrick harbour, ⬚ – ✦✦. **CO VISA**
closed 2 weeks February, 25 December and 1 January – **Rest** - Seafood specialities - a la
carte 17.15/29.70.
◆ Personally run attractive harbourside restaurant with modern rustic feel throughout.
Tasty, appealing menus, full of seafood specialities and Scottish ingredients.

Good food and accommodation at moderate prices?
Look for the Bib symbols:
red Bib Gourmand ⬚ **for food, blue Bib Hotel** ⬚ **for hotels**

PORTREE Highland 501 B 11 – *see Skye (Isle of).*

QUOTHQUAN South Lanarkshire 501 J 27 Scotland G. – ✉ *Biggar.*
Env. : *Biggar★ (Gladstone Court Museum★ AC – Greenhill Covenanting Museum★ AC) SE :
4½ m. by B 7016.*
Edinburgh 32 – Dumfries 50 – Glasgow 36.

🏨 **Shieldhill Castle** ⬚, ML12 6NA, Northeast : ¾ m. *ℰ* (01899) 220035, *enquiries@shield
hill.co.uk*, Fax (01899) 221092, ≤, ⬚ – ✦✦ **P**. ⬚ 250. **CO AE VISA**
Chancellors : Rest 19.95 and a la carte 22.35/42.85 ⬚ ⬚ – **16 rm** ⬜ ✦85.00/95.00 –
✦✦100.00/248.00.
◆ Part 12C fortified manor with 16C additions and invitingly comfortable panelled lounge.
Large rooms, individually furnished, some with vast sunken baths. Popular for weddings.
Accomplished cooking in 16C dining room with high carved ceilings.

RANNOCH STATION Perth and Kinross 501 G 13.

Edinburgh 108 – Kinloch Rannoch 17 – Pitlochry 36.5.

🏠 **Moor of Rannoch** ⌂, PH17 2QA, 𝒞 (01882) 633238, bookings@moorofran noch.co.uk, ⩽ Rannoch Moor, 🚗 – ⤋⤋ **P**, **⓿** **VISA**
14 February-5 November – **Rest** (closed Monday to non-residents) (booking essential for non-residents) a la carte 15.45/26.45 s. – **5 rm** ⌗ ✦48.00 – ✦✦80.00.
◆ Immaculately whitewashed 19C property "in the middle of nowhere", next to railway station with link to London! Comfy, sofa-strewn lounges. Rustic rooms with antiques. Home-cooked menus in characterful dining room with conservatory.

RHICONICH Highland 501 F 8 Scotland G. – ⊠ Lairg.

Exc. : Cape Wrath★★★ (⩽★★) AC, N : 21 m. (including ferry crossing) by A 838 and minor rd.
Edinburgh 249 – Thurso 87 – Ullapool 57.

🏠 **Rhiconich,** IV27 4RN, 𝒞 (01971) 521224, rhiconichhotel@aol.com, Fax (01971) 521732, ⩽ Loch Inchard, 🚗 – ⤋⤋ **P**, **⓿** **VISA**
closed Christmas and New Year – **Rest** (bar lunch)/dinner 20.00 and a la carte 14.00/22.00 – **11 rm** ⌗ ✦42.00/50.00 – ✦✦82.00.
◆ White-fronted hotel sitting majestically at the head of Loch Inchard. Stylish rooms offer loch views; larger, well located superior rooms feature pastel co-ordinated décor. Dining room, with stunning views and serving local produce.

ROTHESAY Argyll and Bute 501 502 E 16 – see Bute (Isle of).

ST ANDREWS Fife 501 L 14 Scotland G. – pop. 14 209.

See : City★★ – Cathedral★ (⩘★★) AC B – West Port★ A.
Env. : Leuchars (parish church★), NW : 6 m. by A 91 and A 919.
Exc. : The East Neuk★★, SE : 9 m. by A 917 and B 9131 B – Crail★★ (Old Centre★★, Upper Crail★) SE : 9 m. by A 917 B – Kellie Castle★ AC, S : 9 m. by B 9131 and B 9171 B – Ceres★, SW : 9 m. by B 939 - E : Inland Fife★ A.
⚑₁₈ (x4), Eden, Jubilee, New, Strathyrum and ⚑₅ Balgove Course 𝒞 (01334) 466666 – ⚑₁₈ Duke's, Craigtoun Park 𝒞 (01334) 474371.
🄱 70 Market St 𝒞 (01334) 472021.
Edinburgh 51 – Dundee 14 – Stirling 51.

Plan opposite

🏨🏨🏨🏨 **The Old Course H. Golf Resort and Spa,** Old Station Rd, KY16 9SP, 𝒞 (01334) 474371, reservations@oldcoursehotel.co.uk, Fax (01334) 477668, ⩽ Championship golf course and St Andrews Bay, ⌀, ⚓, ⥁⥁, ⬚, ⚑₁₈ – |≣|, ⤋⤋ rm, 📞 ⅃ **P** – ⚑ 500. **⓿** **AE** **⑪** **VISA**
A b
Road Hole Grill : **Rest** (dinner only) a la carte 35.50/52.00 ⚏ – **Sands : Rest** a la carte 18.75/31.50 ⚏ – **116 rm** ⌗ ✦165.00/214.00 – ✦✦181.00/445.00, 28 suites ⌗ 325.00/720.00.
◆ Relax into richly composed formal interiors and comprehensive luxury with a fine malt or a spa mudpack. Bright, stylish rooms. Unrivalled views of the bay and Old Course. Road Hole Grill has a fine view of the 17th hole. Worldwide flavours at Sands brasserie.

🏨🏨🏨 **St Andrews Bay,** KY16 8PN, Southeast : 3 m. on A 917 𝒞 (01334) 837000, stand rews.scotland@fairmont.com, Fax (01334) 471115, ⩽, ⌀, ⚓, ⥁⥁, ⚑₁₈, 🚗, ⚏ – |≣|, ⤋⤋ rm, ≣ 📞 ⅃ **P** – ⚑ 700. **⓿** **AE** **⑪** **VISA**
The Squire : Rest (closed Monday-Tuesday) (dinner only) 32.00/44.00 **s.** and a la carte 32.00/44.00 ⚏ – **Esperante : Rest** (closed Monday-Tuesday) (dinner only) 43.50/85.00 **s.** – **192 rm** ⌗ ✦169.00/310.00 – ✦✦169.00/310.00, 17 suites.
◆ Golf oriented modern, purpose-built hotel on clifftop site with wonderful Tayside views and pristine fairways. Extensive conference facilities. Stylish, modern rooms. Golf chat to the "fore" in informal Squire. Mediterranean influenced Esperante.

🏠🏠 **Rufflets Country House** ⌂, Strathkinness Low Rd, KY16 9TX, West : 1½ m. on B 939 𝒞 (01334) 472594, reservations@rufflets.co.uk, Fax (01334) 478703, ⩽, 🚗, ⚏ – ⤋⤋ 📞 ⅃ **P** – ⚑ 25. **⓿** **AE** **⑪** **VISA**. ⥁
closed 2 weeks January-February – **Garden : Rest** (dinner only and Sunday lunch) 38.00/40.00 ⚏ – **Music Room : Rest** (lunch only) a la carte 13.00/20.50 ⚏ – **22 rm** ⌗ ✦125.00/210.00 – ✦✦198.00/220.00, 2 suite.
◆ Handsome 1920s house set in ornamental gardens. Traditional drawing room with cosy fireside sofas, thoughtfully appointed rooms are pristine and characterful. Garden restaurant offers fine vantage point to view the lawns. Informal Music Room for lunch.

ST ANDREWS

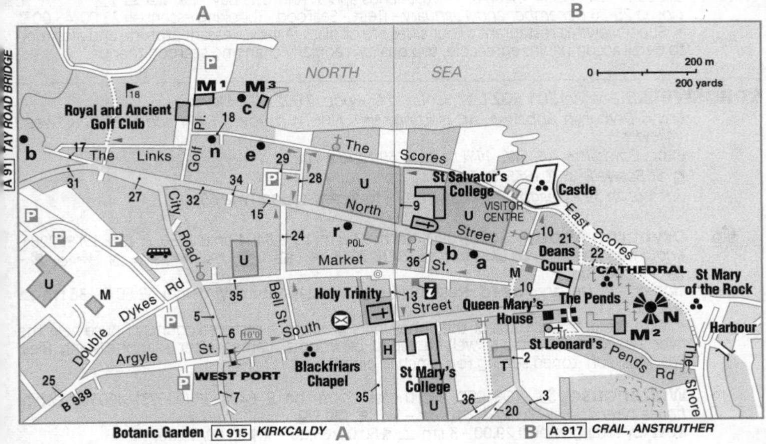

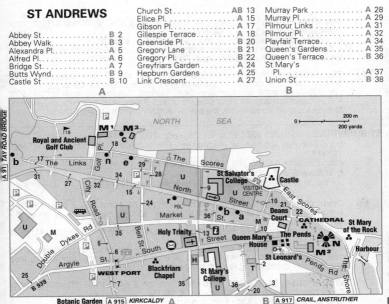

SCOTLAND

St Andrews Golf, 40 The Scores, KY16 9AS, ✆ (01334) 472611, *reception@standrews-golf.co.uk, Fax (01334) 472188,* ≤ – |‡| 🅿 – 🚶 200. MC AE ⊙ VISA   A e
closed 24-29 December – **Rest** 15.00 (lunch) and dinner a la carte 21.00/27.00 ♀ – **21 rm** ☐ ✝135.00/200.00 – ✝✝250.00.
◆ Two converted 19C town houses: well-established and family run. Cellar bar is a local favourite. Traditional, pastel-toned rooms vary in size, with sea views from the front. Oak panelled, firelit dining room.

The Scores, 76 The Scores, KY16 9BB, ✆ (01334) 472451, *reception@scoreshotel.co.uk, Fax (01334) 473947,* ≤, – |‡| ⇔ ✆ 🅿 – 🚶 160. MC AE ⊙ VISA. ✂   A n
***Alexanders :* Rest** (dinner only) a la carte 19.35/30.85 ♀ – **29 rm** ☐ ✝91.00/138.00 – ✝✝122.00/182.00, 1 suite.
◆ Practically equipped rooms in a handsome 1880s terrace by the Old Course and facing the bay. Bar celebrates Scots heroes and the filming of "Chariots of Fire" on the beach. Formal, classic restaurant; views out to sea.

Albany without rest., 56-58 North St, KY16 9AH, ✆ (01334) 477737, *enq@standrewsalbany.co.uk, Fax (01334) 477742,* – ⇔ ✆. MC AE ⊙ VISA. ✂   B a
22 rm ☐ ✝55.00/100.00 – ✝✝80.00/130.00.
◆ Well-kept, pleasingly unfussy rooms - quieter at the rear - in a family run 1790s house. Homely, firelit lounge with stacked bookshelves, antique sideboards and deep sofas.

Aslar House without rest., 120 North St, KY16 9AF, ✆ (01334) 473460, *enquiries@aslar.com, Fax (01334) 477540,* – ⇔ ✆. MC VISA. ✂   A r
closed 1-20 January, 23-31 December – **6 rm** ☐ ✝38.00/75.00 – ✝✝76.00/84.00.
◆ Victorian house, privately run in a welcoming spirit. Homely, pine furnished rooms, all en suite, are larger on the top floor; most overlook a quiet rear garden. Good value.

18 Queens Terrace without rest., 18 Queens Terrace, KY16 9QF, by Queens Gardens ✆ (01334) 478849, *stay@18queensterrace.com, Fax (01334) 470283,* – ⇔ ✆. MC VISA. ✂
4 rm ☐ ✝60.00/65.00 – ✝✝80.00/85.00.
◆ Characterful Victorian guesthouse in smart street next to one of the colleges. Very well-furnished lounge with antiques. Stunning rooms in period and sympathetic style.

⌂ **Deveron House** without rest., 64 North St, KY16 9AH, ℰ (01334) 473513, book
ings@deveronhouse.com – ✦✦. **MC** **VISA**. ✦
B b
closed 16 December-6 January – **6 rm** �. ✦53.00/72.00 – ✦✦87.00.
* Centrally located Victorian guesthouse. Cosy, clean lounge. Sunny, bright and modern
breakfast room with smart wicker chairs. Flowery bedrooms with varnished pine.

XXX **The Seafood**, The Scores, KY16 9AB, ℰ (01334) 479475, info@theseafoodrestaur
ant.com, Fax (01334) 479476, ≤ West Sands and St Andrews Bay – ▤. **MC** **AE** **VISA**
A C
closed 25-26 December and 1 January – **Rest** - Seafood - (booking essential) 25.00/45.00 ℤ.
* Super views as restaurant's four sides are of glass. A very pleasant attitude and attention
to detail accompanies agreeable, top quality, regularly changing seafood menus.

ST BOSWELLS Borders 501 502 L 17 Scotland G. – pop. 2 092 – ⊠ Melrose.
Env. : Dryburgh Abbey★★ AC (setting★★★), NW : 4. m. by B 6404 and B 6356 – Tweed
Valley★★.
Exc. : Bowhill★★ AC, SW : 11½ m. by A 699 and A 708.
🏌 St Boswells ℰ (01835) 823527.
Edinburgh 39 – Glasgow 79 – Hawick 17 – Newcastle upon Tyne 66.

🏛 **Dryburgh Abbey** ⌂, TD6 0RQ, North : 3½ m. by B 6404 on B 6356 ℰ (01835) 822261,
enquiries@dryburgh.co.uk, Fax (01835) 823945, ≤, ☎, ▢, ⬟, ☞, ♨ – ▯ ✦✦ ♿ ℗ –
🚿 110. **MC** **VISA**
closed 7-18 January **Tweed** : **Rest** (bar lunch Monday-Saturday)/dinner 32.50 ℤ – **36 rm** ☱
✦60.00/73.00 – ✦✦180.00/220.00, 2 suites.
* With the dramatic ruins of the abbey in its grounds, a restored country house near the
river Tweed. Comfortable, well-equipped bedrooms, named after salmon-fishing flies.
Spacious, soft-toned setting for armchair dining.

⌂ **Whitehouse** ⌂, TD6 0ED, Northeast : 3 m. on B 6404 ℰ (01573) 460343, white
house.tyrer@tiscali.co.uk, ≤, ⬟, ☞ – ✦✦ ℗, **MC** **VISA**
Rest (by arrangement) 29.00 – **3 rm** ☱ ✦60.00/65.00 – ✦✦90.00/95.00.
* Appreciate the good rural views from enticingly comfortable country house style lounge
in this 19C former dower house. Nourishing breakfast specials. Airy, welcoming rooms.
Home-cooked meals in dining room overlooking the fields.

⌂ **Clint Lodge**, TD6 0DZ, North : 2 ¼ m. by B 6404 on B 6356 ℰ (01835) 822027, clin
tlodge@aol.com, Fax (01835) 822656, ≤ River Tweed and Cheviot Hills, ☞ – ✦✦ ✌ ℗, **MC**
AE **VISA**
Rest 25.00/35.00 – **5 rm** ☱ ✦45.00/65.00 – ✦✦90.00/110.00.
* Personally run Victorian shooting lodge with sweeping prospects of the Tweed Valley
and Cheviots. Antiques, open fires, fishing memorabilia and comfortable, classic rooms. A
choice of tables allows for private or communal dining.

ST CYRUS Aberdeenshire 501 M 13 Scotland G. – pop. 1 365.
Exc. : Dunnottar Castle★★, N : 15 m. by A 92.
Edinburgh 93 – Aberdeen 32 – Montrose 5.

⌂ **Woodston Fishing Station** ⌂ without rest., DD10 0DG, Northeast : 1 m. by A 92
ℰ (01674) 850226, info@woodstonfishingstation.co.uk, Fax (01674) 850343, ≤ St Cyrus
Bay, ☞ – ✦✦ ℗. **MC** **VISA**
March-November – **6 rm** ☱ ✦40.00/60.00 – ✦✦80.00.
* Superbly sited on an isolated wind-swept cliff top. High degree of comfort. Simple
Victorian style rooms with fine views of bay and nature reserve. Communal breakfast
room.

ST FILLANS Perth & Kinross 501 H 14.
Edinburgh 65 – Lochearnhead 8 – Perth 29.

🏠 **Achray House**, PH6 2NF, ℰ (01764) 685231, info@achray-house.co.uk,
Fax (01764) 685320, ≤ Loch Earn, ☞ – ✦✦ ℗. **MC** **①** **VISA**
closed 4-25 January – **Rest** a la carte 18.20/25.85 – **8 rm** ☱ ✦50.00/65.00 –
✦✦70.00/110.00.
* Well run, former Edwardian villa with a stunning Loch Earn view. A homely warmth
pervades all areas. Bedrooms are clean and simple; some are suitable for families. Freshly
prepared seafood a feature of dining room menus.

ST MARGARET'S HOPE Orkney Islands 501 K 6 – see Orkney Islands.

ST MONANS Fife 501 L 15 – pop. 3 965 (inc. Elie and Pinttenweem).
Edinburgh 47 – Dundee 26 – Perth 40 – Stirling 56.

XX **The Seafood,** 16 West End, KY10 2BX, ℰ (01333) 730327, info@theseafoodrestaur
ant.com, Fax (01333) 730508, ≤, 😊 – ◍⬛ ⬛ **VISA**
closed 25-26 December, 1 January, Monday - Tuesday in winter – **Rest** - Seafood - (booking
essential) 24.00/35.00 ⵜ.
  ◆ Informal former pub in a quiet fishing village; nautical memorabilia abounds. Smart
lounge bar leads into a neatly set restaurant with sea views. Tasty, locally caught dishes.

SCALASAIG Argyll and Bute 501 B 15 – see Colonsay (Isle of).

SCALPAY Western Isles 501 A 10 – see Lewis and Harris (Isle of).

SCARISTA Western Isles (Outer Hebrides) 501 Y 10 – see Lewis and Harris (Isle of).

SCOURIE Highland 501 E 8 Scotland G. – ✉ Lairg.
Exc. : Cape Wrath★★★ (≤★★) AC, N : 31 m. (including ferry crossing) by A 894 and A 838 –
Loch Assynt★★, S : 17 m. by A 894.
Edinburgh 263 – Inverness 107.

🏛 **Eddrachilles** ⌂, Badcall Bay, IV27 4TH, South : 2 ½ m. on A 894 ℰ (01971) 502080,
enq@eddrachilles.com, Fax (01971) 502477, ≤ Badcall Bay and islands, 🐟, 🌿 – ⬛. ◍⬛ **VISA**.
🌿
mid March-mid October – **Rest** (bar lunch)/dinner 25.00/45.00 s. – **11 rm** (dinner included) ⵜ ✦79.90/83.95 – ✦✦119.80/127.90.
  ◆ Isolated hotel, converted from small part 19C building, magnificently set at the head of
Badcall Bay and its islands. Conservatory lounge. Traditional, well-kept rooms. Dining room
with stone walls and flagstone floors.

Do not confuse X with ⭐!
X defines comfort, while stars are awarded for the best cuisine,
across all categories of comfort.

SEIL (Isle of) Argyll and Bute 501 D 15 – ✉ Oban.

Clachan Seil Argyll and Bute – ✉ Oban.

🏛 **Willowburn** ⌂, PA34 4TJ, ℰ (01852) 300276, willowburn.hotel@virgin.net, ≤, 🌿 – ↔
🐾 ⬛. ◍⬛ **VISA**
mid March- mid November – **Rest** (booking essential for non-residents) (dinner only) 37.00
– **7 rm** (dinner included) ⵜ ✦84.00/124.00 – ✦✦168.00.
  ◆ Simple, white-painted hotel overlooking Clachan Sound. Comfortable lounge with birdwatching telescope. Cosy bedrooms show an individual, personal touch. Airy dining room
overlooks the water.

SELKIRK Borders 501 502 L 17 Scotland G. – pop. 5 772.
Env. : Bowhill★★ AC, W : 3½ m. by A 708 – Abbotsford★★ AC, NE : 5½ m. by A 7 and B 6360
– Tweed Valley★★.
Exc. : Melrose Abbey★★ (decorative sculpture★★★) AC, NE : 8½ m. by A 7 and A 6091 –
Eildon Hills (❅★★★) NE : 7½ m. by A 699 and B 6359.
🏌 The Hill ℰ (01750) 20621.
🛈 Halliwell's House ℰ (0870) 6080404 (Easter-October), selkirk@scot-borders.co.uk.
Edinburgh 48 – Hawick 11 – Newcastle upon Tyne 77.

🏛🏛 **Philipburn Country House** ⌂, TD7 5LS, West : 1 m. by A 707 at junction with A 708
ℰ (01750) 20747, info@philipburnhousehotel.co.uk, Fax (01750) 721690, 🏊 heated, 🌿 –
↔ ⬛ – 🔒 30. ◍⬛ **VISA**. 🌿
1745 : Rest 29.50 (dinner) and lunch a la carte 18.85/28.40 **s.** – **Charleys Bistro :** Rest
(dinner only) 26.95 **s.** – **14 rm** ⵜ ✦85.00/95.00 – ✦✦120.00/199.00.
  ◆ Extended 18C house along private driveway with smart gardens. Eclectic variety of
rooms, most having pleasant rural outlook, two overlooking outdoor pool. Linen-laid 1745
has fine dining menu. Informal Charleys for bistro favourites.

SHETLAND ISLANDS Shetland Islands 501 P/Q 3 Scotland G. – pop. 22 522.

See : Islands★ - Up Helly Aa (last Tuesday in January) – Mousa Broch★★★ AC (Mousa Island) – Jarlshof★★ - Lerwick to Jarlshof★ (←★) – Shetland Croft House Museum★ AC.

✈ Tingwall Airport : ℘ (01595) 840306, NW : 6½ m. of Lerwick by A 971.

⚓ from Lerwick (Mainland) to Aberdeen and via Orkney Islands (Stromness) (P & O Scottish Ferries) – from Vidlin to Skerries (Shetland Islands Council) booking essential 3-4 weekly (1 h 30 mn) – from Lerwick (Mainland) to Skerries (Shetland Islands Council) 2 weekly (booking essential) (2 h 30 mn) – from Lerwick (Mainland) to Bressay (Shetland Islands Council) frequent services daily (7 mn) – from Laxo (Mainland) to Isle of Whalsay (Symbister) (Shetland Islands Council) frequent services daily (30 mn) – from Toft (Mainland) to Isle of Yell (Ulsta) (Shetland Islands Council) frequent services daily (20 mn) – from Isle of Yell (Gutcher) to Isle of Fetlar (Oddsta) and via Isle of Unst (Belmont) (Shetland Islands Council) – from Fair Isle to Sumburgh (Mainland) (Shetland Islands Council) 3 weekly (2 h 40 mn).

⚓ from Foula to Walls (Shetland Islands Council) 1-2 weekly (2 h 30 mn) – from Fair Isle to Sumburgh (Shetland Islands Council) 1-2 weekly (2 h 40 mn).

MAINLAND Shetland Islands

Brae Shetland Islands.

🏠 **Busta House** ⚘, ZE2 9QN, Southwest : 1 ½ m. by A 970 ℘ (01806) 522506, reservations@bustahouse.com, Fax (01806) 522588, ←, ☞ – ⬇ ⇖ ℙ, ⓂⓈ ᴀᴇ ⓄⒹ ᴠɪsᴀ. ⋘
closed 23 December-6 January – **Rest** (bar lunch Monday-Saturday)/dinner 30.00 and a la carte 17.85/25.85 ⤢ – **22 rm** ⊡ ✦65.00/85.00 – ✦✦110.00/130.00.
♦ Part 16C and 18C house on Busta Voe. Good-sized traditional rooms, some have canopy beds. Elegant "long room" with ancestral portraits. House of Commons gargoyles in garden. Garden views add balance to sober dining room.

Lerwick Shetland Islands Scotland G. – pop. 7 590.

See : Clickhimin Broch★.
Env. : Gulber Wick (←★), S : 2 m. by A 970.
🏌 Shetland, Dale, Gott ℘ (01595) 840369.
🛈 The Market Cross, Lerwick ℘ (08701) 999440.

🏠 **Kveldsro House,** Greenfield Pl, ZE1 0AQ, ℘ (01595) 692195, reception@kveldsrohotel.co.uk, Fax (01595) 696595 – ℙ, ⓂⓈ ᴀᴇ ⓄⒹ ᴠɪsᴀ. ⋘
closed 1-2 January, 25-26 December – **Rest** (carving lunch Sunday) (bar lunch Monday-Saturday)/dinner a la carte 15.95/26.45 ⤢. – **17 rm** ⊡ ✦95.00 – ✦✦110.00.
♦ Neat, modern style in evidence throughout this smoothly run hotel - its name comes from the Norse for "evening peace". Tidy rooms, well-equipped and furnished in pale wood. Classically smart and formally set restaurant.

🏠 **Grand,** 149 Commercial St, ZE1 0EX, ℘ (01595) 692826, info@kgqhotels.co.uk, Fax (01595) 694048 – ⓂⓈ ᴀᴇ ⓄⒹ ᴠɪsᴀ. ⋘
closed 24 December-4 January – **Rest** (bar lunch)/dinner 17.95 and a la carte approx 13.25 ⤢. – **24 rm** ⊡ ✦72.50/88.50 – ✦✦98.50.
♦ Handsome period hotel with turret and stepped gables. Above the row of ground-floor shops are neatly kept rooms with modern fittings, a simple lounge bar and a night-club. Comfortably furnished dining room with a formal atmosphere.

🏠 **Shetland,** Holmsgarth Rd, ZE1 0PW, ℘ (01595) 695515, reception@shetlandhotel.co.uk, Fax (01595) 695828, ← – ⧆ ⇖ ⅊ ℙ – ⬱ 250. ⓂⓈ ᴀᴇ ⓄⒹ ᴠɪsᴀ. ⋘
closed 25-26 December and 1-2 January – **Rest** (bar lunch)/dinner a la carte 14.10/25.75 ⤢. ⴲ – **63 rm** ⊡ ✦79.95/98.50 – ✦✦98.50/112.00, 1 suite.
♦ Purpose-built hotel near the harbourside. Mahogany furnished bar, a choice of modern conference rooms and usefully fitted rooms in co-ordinated fabrics. Simply but formally arranged dining room.

🏠 **Glen Orchy House,** 20 Knab Rd, ZE1 0AX, ℘ (01595) 692031, glenorchy.house@virgin-net, Fax (01595) 692031 – ⇖ ⅊ ℙ, ⓂⓈ ᴠɪsᴀ
Rest - Thai - (booking essential) (residents only) (dinner only) 17.00/20.00 ⤢. – **24 rm** ⊡ ✦47.00/50.00 – ✦✦74.00/80.00.
♦ Built as a convent in the 1900s and sympathetically extended. Colourful public areas. Bright honesty bar. Spotless bedrooms with neat modern fabrics and fittings. Restaurant offers authentic Thai menus.

Veensgarth *Shetland Islands.*

🏛 **Herrislea House**, ZE2 9SB, ℘ (01595) 840208, *hotel@herrisleahouse.co.uk,*
Fax (01595) 840630, 🗺 – ↬ ⛻ 🄿 ⬤🅢 ⓘ 𝘝𝘐𝘚𝘈
closed 23 December-6 January – **Rest** *(closed Sunday)* (booking essential for non-residents)
(bar lunch)/dinner a la carte 11.00/27.75 s. ♀ – **13 rm** ⊊ ✸50.00/85.00 – ✸✸90.00/110.00.
◆ Purpose-built hotel run by native islanders; a homely hall, with mounted antlers, leads
to tidy bedrooms, pleasantly furnished in solid pine, and an angling themed bar. Neatly laid
out but fairly informal restaurant.

ISLAND OF UNST *Shetland Islands*

Baltasound *Shetland Islands.*

⌂ **Buness House** 🗺, ZE2 9DS, East : ½ m. by A 968 and Springpark Rd ℘ (01957) 711315,
buness-house@zetnet.co.uk, Fax (01957) 711815, ≤ Balta Sound, 🗺, 🚗 – 🄹 ↬ 🄿 ⬤🅢
𝘝𝘐𝘚𝘈
restricted opening December-February – **Rest** (by arrangement) (communal dining) 30.00
– **3 rm** ⊊ ✸60.00 – ✸✸100.00.
◆ Whitewashed house of 16C origin. Cosy, well-stocked library. Comfortable rooms facing
Balta Sound, one decorated with Victorian prints and découpages. Nearby nature reserve.
Willow-pattern china and sea views from the conservatory dining room.

SHIELDAIG *Highland* 501 D 11 *Scotland G.* – ✉ Strathcarron.
Env. : *Wester Ross*★★★.
Edinburgh 226 – Inverness 70 – Kyle of Lochalsh 36.

🏛 **Tigh An Eilean**, IV54 8XN, ℘ (01520) 755251, *tighaneileanhotel@shieldaig.fsnet.co.uk,*
Fax (01520) 755321, ≤ Shieldaig Islands and Loch – ↬ ⛿. ⬤🅢 🄰🄴 𝘝𝘐𝘚𝘈
mid March-October – **Rest** (booking essential for non-residents) (bar lunch)/dinner 41.00 –
11 rm ⊊ ✸68.00 – ✸✸144.00.
◆ In a sleepy lochside village, an attractive, personally run 19C inn with fine views of the
Shieldaig Islands. Cosy, well-kept bedrooms and a comfy lounge with a homely feel. Linen-
clad dining room showing eclectic variety of art; Scottish produce to the fore.

SKIRLING *Peeblesshire* 501 502 J 17 *Scotland G.* – ✉ Biggar.
Env. : *Biggar*★ - *Gladstone Court Museum*★, *Greenhill Covenanting Museum*★, S : 3 m. by
A 72 and A 702.
Exc. : *New Lanark*★★, NW : 16 m. by A 72 and A 73.
Edinburgh 29 – Glasgow 45 – Peebles 16.

⌂ **Skirling House**, ML12 6HD, ℘ (01899) 860274, *enquiry@skirlinghouse.com,*
Fax (01899) 860255, 🚗, 🄵, 🎾 – ↬ 🄿 ⬤🅢 𝘝𝘐𝘚𝘈
closed January-February – **Rest** (by arrangement) 27.50/30.00 – **5 rm** ⊊ ✸55.00/60.00 –
✸✸90.00/100.00.
◆ Attractive Arts and Crafts house (1908). 16C Florentine carved ceiling in drawing room.
Comfortable bedrooms with modern conveniences. Daily dinner menu using fresh produce.

SKYE (Isle of) *Highland* 501 B 11 /12 *Scotland G.* – *pop. 8 868.*
See : *Island*★★ – *The Cuillins*★★★ – *Skye Museum of Island Life*★ *AC.*
Env. : N : *Trotternish Peninsula*★★ – W : *Duirinish Peninsula*★ – *Portree*★.
🚢 from Mallaig to Armadale (Caledonian MacBrayne Ltd) 1-5 daily (30 mn) – from Uig to
North Uist (Lochmaddy) or Isle of Harris (Tarbert) (Caledonian MacBrayne Ltd) 1-3 daily (1 h
50 mn) – from Sconser to Isle of Raasay (Caledonian MacBrayne Ltd) 9-10 daily (except
Sunday) (15 mn).
🚢 from Mallaig to Isles of Eigg, Muck, Rhum and Canna (Caledonian MacBrayne Ltd)
(summer only) – from Mallaig to Armadale (Caledonian MacBrayne Ltd) (summer only) 1-2
weekly (30 mn).

Broadford *Highland.*

⌂ **Tigh an Dochais** without rest., 13 Harrapool, IV49 9AQ, on A 87 ℘ (01471) 820022,
hopeskye@btinternet.com, ≤ Broadford Bay and Applecross peninsular, 🚗 – ↬ ⛿ 🄿 ⬤🅢
🄰🄴 𝘝𝘐𝘚𝘈 🎾
closed Christmas-New Year – **3 rm** ⊊ ✸40.00/45.00 – ✸✸60.00/70.00.
◆ Stylish, award-winning architecture; this is a striking house, full of glass, in a fabulous
setting. Superb views at breakfast and stark, clean-lined surroundings at night.

Dunvegan *Highland.*

↑ **Roskhill House,** Roskhill, IV55 8ZD, Southeast : 2 ½ m. by A 863 ℰ (01470) 521317, *stay@roskhillhouse.co.uk, Fax (01470) 521827, ⇌ – ⇌ P. ◍ VISA. ✻*
closed January-February – **Rest** (by arrangement) 20.00 – **5 rm** ⊆ ✲45.00/50.00 – ✲✲72.00.
♦ In friendly personal ownership, an extended, traditional 19C croft house which preserves its exposed brick walls and peat fires. Bedrooms are homely and unpretentious. Once a post office, the dining room offers homely cooking at simple wooden tables.

XX **The Three Chimneys & The House Over-By** ⌛ with rm, Colbost, IV55 8ZT, Northwest : 5 ¾ m. by A 884 (Glendale) ℰ (01470) 511258, *eatandstay@three chimneys.co.uk, Fax (01470) 511358, ≼, ⇌ – &, P. ◍ ◍ VISA*
closed 7-26 January – **Rest** - Seafood specialities - *(closed Sunday lunch)* (booking essential) (dinner only in winter) 27.50/52.00 ⊆ – **6 rm** ⊆ – ✲✲250.00.
♦ Internationally renowned crofter's cottage restaurant on Loch Dunvegan shores. Accomplished Skye seafood dishes, plus Highland lamb, beef and game. Sumptuous bedrooms.

Edinbane *Highland.*

🏨 **Greshornish House** ⌛, IV51 9PN, North : 3 ¾ m. by A 850 in direction of Dunvegan ℰ (01470) 582266, *info@greshornishhouse.com, Fax (01470) 582245, ≼, ⇌, ▣, ✻ – ⇌ P. ◍ ◍ VISA*
restricted opening in winter – **Rest** (lunch booking essential)/dinner 32.50 – **8 rm** ⊆ ✲65.00/110.00 – ✲✲130.00/160.00.
♦ Utter tranquillity: a beautifully sited hotel in 10 acres of grounds, with cluttered sitting rooms, snooker room, smart bedrooms with a view - and Skye's only tennis court! Conservatory breakfasts; Western Isle ingredients to fore in the dining room.

Flodigarry *Highland – ⊠ Staffin.*

🏨 **Flodigarry Country House** ⌛, IV51 9HZ, ℰ (01470) 552203, *info@flodigarry.co.uk, Fax (01470) 552301, ≼ Staffin Island and coastline, ◔, ⇌ – ⇌ &, P. ◍ ◍ VISA*
Rest (bar lunch Monday-Saturday)/dinner 30.00/36.00 and a la carte 19.90/27.40 – **18 rm** ⊆ ✲45.00/130.00 – ✲✲80.00/130.00.
♦ With views of Staffin and the coast, a curio-filled country house once home to Flora Macdonald. Traditional down to its old-world rooms, peat fire and 19C conservatory. Semi-panelled candlelit restaurant.

Glendale *Highland.*

↑ **Clach Ghlas** ⌛ without rest., Lower Milovaig, IV55 8WR, ℰ (01470) 511205, *info@clachghlas.co.uk, Fax (01470) 511205, ≼ Loch Pooltiel and Dunvegan Head, ⇌ – ⇌ ✆ P. ✻*
closed Christmas-New Year – **3 rm** ⊆ ✲120.00 – ✲✲120.00.
♦ Modern house commanding superb hillside spot and vistas to lochs and headlands. Attractive breakfast conservatory; relaxing sitting room. Quiet bedrooms and super Jacuzzis.

Isleornsay *Highland – ⊠ Sleat.*

🏨 **Kinloch Lodge** ⌛, IV43 8QY, North : 3 ½ m. by A 851 ℰ (01471) 833214, *bookings@kin loch-lodge.co.uk, Fax (01471) 833277, ≼ Loch Na Dal, ◔, ⇌, ▣ – ⇌ P. ◍ ◍ VISA*
15 March-15 November – **Rest** (booking essential for non-residents) 42.00 (dinner) and lunch a la carte 12.00/21.00 ⊆ – **14 rm** ⊆ ✲50.00/280.00 – ✲✲100.00/280.00.
♦ Historic 17C hunting lodge on Loch Na Dal run by Lord and Lady Macdonald. Handsome, comfortable drawing room with family antiques; sizeable rooms, some of great character. Gilt-framed ancestral oils and candlelit wooden dining tables with fine silverware.

Portree *Highland – pop. 2 126.*
🛈 Bayfield House, Bayfield Rd ℰ (08452) 255121.

🏨 **Cuillin Hills** ⌛, IV51 9QU, Northeast : ¾ m. by A 855 ℰ (01478) 612003, *info@cuillinhills-hotel-skye.co.uk, Fax (01478) 613092, ≼ Portree bay and the Cuillins, ⇌, ▣ – ⇌ &, P. – 🏛 180. ◍ ◍ VISA. ✻*
Rest (bar lunch Monday-Saturday) (buffet lunch Sunday)/dinner 32.50 – **27 rm** ⊆ ✲60.00/140.00 – ✲✲120.00/160.00.
♦ Enlarged 19C hunting lodge in 15-acre grounds above lochside with fine views. Well-proportioned drawing room with broad Chesterfields; usefully equipped rooms vary in size. Smart and spacious dining room with views of Portree Bay.

SCOTLAND

Bosville, Bosville Terrace, IV51 9DG, ℰ (01478) 612846, bosville@macleodhotels.co.uk, Fax (01478) 613434, ≤ – ✤✤ ✦ 🅲🅰 🅰🅴 🅾 ⓋⒾⓈⒶ
Bistro : Rest a la carte approx 15.00 – (see also **Chandlery** below) – **19 rm** ⌲ ✦59.00/105.00 – ✦✦78.00/110.00.
✦ Well-established, busy hotel overlooking harbour and hills. First-floor sitting room and tidy, modern accommodation in co-ordinated décor. Buzzy ground floor bistro.

Rosedale, Beaumont Crescent, IV51 9DB, ℰ (01478) 613131, Fax (01478) 612531, ≤ harbour, ✿ – ✤✤ 🅲🅰 🅾 ⓋⒾⓈⒶ
March-October – Rest (dinner only) 18.00/30.00 Ⓨ – **18 rm** ⌲ ✦30.00/80.00 – ✦✦60.00/140.00.
✦ Converted quayside terrace of fishermen's houses with fine views over the water. Neat and cosy lounge and compact but immaculately kept bedrooms in floral prints. First-floor, linen-clad restaurant with a traditionally based, seasonal menu.

Almondbank without rest., Viewfield Rd, IV51 9EU, Southwest : ¾ m. on A 87 ℰ (01478) 612696, jansvans@aol.com, Fax (01478) 613114, ≤ Portree Bay, ✿ – 🅿 🅼🅲 ⓋⒾⓈⒶ
4 rm ⌲ ✦35.00/55.00 – ✦✦60.00/70.00.
✦ Situated away from the town centre, a converted modern house, well maintained by the friendly owner. Spotless bedrooms; superb views across Portree Bay.

The Chandlery (at Bosville H.), Bosville Terrace, IV51 9DG, ℰ (01478) 612846, Fax (01478) 613434 – 🅼🅲 🅰🅴 🅾
Rest - Seafood - (booking essential) (dinner only) 29.00/39.00.
✦ Purple colour scheme distinguishes this formal but relaxed restaurant from adjacent bistro. Skilfully executed seafood dishes display a proven touch of orginality and flair.

Struan Highland.

Ullinish Country Lodge ⌁, IV56 8FD, West : 1 ½ m. by A 863 ℰ (01470) 572214, ullinish@theisleofskye.co.uk, Fax (01470) 572341, ≤ Loch Harport and Cuillin Hills, ✿ – ✤✤ 🅿 🅼🅲 ⓋⒾⓈⒶ ⌁
closed January – Rest (booking essential for non-residents) 39.50 – **6 rm** ⌲ ✦90.00 – ✦✦160.00.
✦ Country lodge comforts in superb windswept spot with fine views. Chilled sitting room; each bedroom has a distinct style with luxury fabrics and character beds built of wood. Skye ingredients put to compelling, highly original use on creative modern dishes.

Teangue Highland.

Toravaig House, Knock Bay, IV44 8RE, on A 851 ℰ (01471) 820200, info@skyeho tel.co.uk, Fax (01471) 833231, ≤, ✿ – ✤✤ 🅿 🅼🅲 🅰🅴 🅾 ⓋⒾⓈⒶ ⌁
Rest (closed for lunch in winter) (booking essential for non-residents) 29.50/32.50 – **9 rm** ⌲ ✦95.00 – ✦✦130.00/160.00.
✦ Quality range of fabrics and furniture in a whitewashed house on road to Mallaig ferry. Small but perfectly formed lounge. Rooms designed to a high standard. Hearty sea views. Dine on best Skye produce in attractive surroundings.

Waternish Highland.

Stein Inn ⌁, MacLeod Terrace, Stein, IV55 8GA, ℰ (01470) 592362, angus.teresa@stei ninn.co.uk, ≤ Loch bay, 🍴 – ✤✤ 🅿 🅼🅲 ⓋⒾⓈⒶ
closed 25 December and 1 January – Rest - Seafood specialities - (residents only Monday dinner except Bank Holidays) a la carte 12.75/22.00 – **5 rm** ⌲ ✦26.00 – ✦✦72.00.
✦ The oldest inn on Skye with dramatic waterfront views. Charming friendly place serving locally brewed ale and over 90 malt whiskies. Comfy well-kept rooms with seaview. Solid traditional fare in the dining room.

Loch Bay Seafood, 1 MacLeod Terrace, Stein, IV55 8GA, ℰ (01470) 592235, da vid@lochbay-seafood-restaurant.co.uk, Fax (01470) 592235 – 🅿 🅼🅲 🅰🅴 ⓋⒾⓈⒶ ⌁
Easter-October and New Year – Rest - Seafood - (closed Saturday lunch and Sunday) (booking essential) a la carte 17.55/31.25 Ⓨ.
✦ Cottage restaurant with simple wooden tables and benches. Tiny, atmospheric room where the freshest local seafood, including halibut, sole and turbot, is prepared faultlessly.

SORN East Ayrshire 501 H 17.
Edinburgh 67 – Ayr 15 – Glasgow 35.

Sorn Inn with rm, 35 Main St, KA5 6HU, ℰ (01290) 551305, craig@sorninn.com, Fax (01290) 553470 – 🅿 🅼🅲 ⓋⒾⓈⒶ
closed 2 weeks mid January – Rest (closed Monday) 13.95/23.50 and a la carte 14.00/23.50 – **4 rm** ⌲ ✦40.00 – ✦✦90.00.
✦ Family run, traditional pub in small village. Its hub is the dining room, where good value, locally sourced modern dishes are cooked in an accomplished way. Comfy rooms.

SPEAN BRIDGE *Highland* 501 F 13.

🏌 *ℰ (01397) 703907.*
🛈 *ℰ (08452) 255121 (April-October).*
Edinburgh 143 – Fort William 10 – Glasgow 94 – Inverness 58 – Oban 60.

🏛 **Corriegour Lodge,** Loch Lochy, PH34 4EA, North : 8 ¾ m. on A 82 *ℰ (01397) 712685, info@corriegour-lodge-hotel.com, Fax (01397) 712696,* ≤, *☞ –* 🛗 *🛎 P. 🅼🅾 🅰🅴 🅾 VISA. 🛳*
closed December-January except New Year – **Rest** *(weekends only February and November) (booking essential for non-residents) (dinner only)* 48.50 – **11 rm** ✦59.50/69.50 –
✦✦119.00/139.00.
♦ Enthusiastically run 19C hunting lodge in woods and gardens above Loch Lochy. Bright, individually decorated rooms and a cosy bar and lounge share a warm, traditional feel. Formally set dining room with wide picture windows.

↑ **Spean Lodge** without rest., PH34 4EP, *ℰ (01397) 712004, welcome@speanlodge.co.uk,*
☞ – ⬟ P. 🅼🅾 VISA. 🛳
3 rm ⊊ ✦45.00/60.00 – ✦✦60.00/75.00.
♦ 19C former shooting lodge whose gardens are filled with mature trees. Antiques and period furnishings abound. Utterly restful sitting room. Pleasantly individual rooms.

↑ **Corriechoille Lodge** ≤, PH34 4EY, East : 2 ¾ m. on Corriechoille rd *ℰ (01397) 712002,* ≤, *☞ –* ⬠✦ 🛎 P. 🅼🅾 VISA. 🛳
closed November-March, Monday and Tuesday – **Rest** *(by arrangement)* 20.00 – **4 rm** ⊊
✦45.00 – ✦✦70.00.
♦ Off the beaten track in quiet estate land, a part 18C lodge: stylishly modern lounge, spacious en suite rooms: those facing south have fine views of the Grey Corries.

✗ **Russel's at Smiddy House** with rm, Roybridge Road, PH34 4EU, *ℰ (01397) 712335, enquiry@smiddyhouse.co.uk, Fax (01397) 712043 –* P. 🅼🅾 VISA. 🛳
closed 2 weeks January and 2 weeks November **Rest** *(booking essential) (dinner only)*
26.95/31.00 s. – **4 rm** ⊊ ✦50.00/70.00 – ✦✦70.00/80.00.
♦ Large Victorian house with three dining rooms; all exude simple bistro feel. Strong, local seafood base and welcoming service. Immaculate bedrooms boast personalised feel.

✗ **Old Pines** 🛳 with rm, PH34 4EG, Northwest : 1 ½ m. by A 82 on B 8004 *ℰ (01397) 712324, enquiries@oldpines.co.uk,* ≤, 🅿 *– ⬠ P. 🅼🅾 🅾 VISA*
– **Rest** *(booking essential for non-residents) (light lunch)/dinner* 34.50/37.50 ⊊ – **8 rm** ⊊
✦45.00/67.50 – ✦✦90.00/105.00.
♦ You're encouraged to share tables in this restaurant which favours a dinner party atmosphere. Emphasis on the seasonal and the organic. Friendly staff. Well-kept rooms.

SPITTAL OF GLENSHEE *Perth and Kinross* 501 J 13 *Scotland G.* – ✉ *Blairgowrie.*
Env. : *Glenshee (*※★★*) (chairlift AC).*
Edinburgh 69 – Aberdeen 74 – Dundee 35.

🏨 **Dalmunzie House** 🛳, PH10 7QG, *ℰ (01250) 885224, reservations@dalmunzie.com, Fax (01250) 885225,* ≤, 🏌, 🐟, *☞, 🅿, ※ – 🕴 ⬠✦ P. 🅼🅾 VISA. 🛳*
closed 29 November - 29 December – **Rest** *(bar lunch)/dinner a la carte approx* 36.00 –
17 rm ⊊ ✦80.00/120.00 – ✦✦150.00/190.00.
♦ Edwardian hunting lodge in a magnificent spot, encircled by mountains. Traditional rooms mix antique and pine furniture. Bar with cosy panelled alcove and leather chairs. Modern dining room with views down the valley.

STIRLING *Stirling* 501 I 15 *Scotland G.* – *pop. 32 673.*
See : *Town★★ – Castle★★ AC (Site★★★, external elevations★★★, Stirling Heads★★, Argyll and Sutherland Highlanders Regimental Museum★)* B *– Argyll's Lodging★ (Renaissance decoration★)* B A *– Church of the Holy Rude★* B B.
Env. : *Wallace Monument (*※★★*) NE : 2½ m. by A 9 –* A *– and B 998.*
Exc. : *Dunblane★ (Cathedral★★, West Front★★), N : 6½ m. by A 9* A.
🛈 *Dumbarton Rd ℰ (08707) 200621, stirlingtic@aillst.ossian.net – Royal Burgh Stirling Visitor Centre ℰ (01786) 479901 – Pirnhall, Motorway Service Area, junction 9, M 9 ℰ (01786) 814111 (April-October).*
Edinburgh 37 – Dunfermline 23 – Falkirk 14 – Glasgow 28 – Greenock 52 – Motherwell 30 – Oban 87 – Perth 35.

SCOTLAND

Plan opposite

864

STIRLING

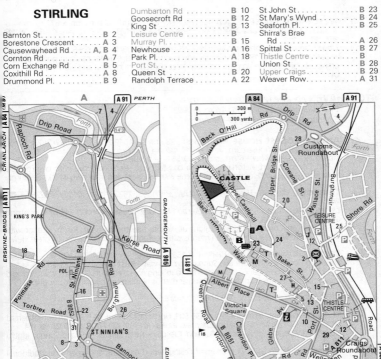

Park Lodge, 32 Park Terrace, FK8 2JS, ☏ (01786) 474862, info@parklodge.net, Fax (01786) 449748, 🌲 – ⇆🛏 📞 📶 – 🔬 50. 🅒🅞 🄰🄴 𝚅𝙸𝚂𝙰   B a
closed Christmas and New Year – **Rest** (closed Sunday) 15.00/28.00 and a la carte 20.50/29.00 – **9 rm** ⚏ ✶65.00/90.00 – ✶✶100.00/120.00.
  ♦ Creeper-clad Georgian and Victorian house, still in private hands and furnished with an enviable collection of antiques. Compact but well-equipped rooms with a stylish feel. Intimate dining room overlooking a pretty garden.

Express by Holiday Inn without rest., Springkerse Business Park, FK7 7XH, East : 2 m. by A 905 off A 91 ☏ (01786) 449922, info@hiex-stirling.com, Fax (01786) 449932 – 📼, ⇆🛏 rm, 📞 & 📞 – 🔬 30. 🅒🅞 🄰🄴 🅞 𝚅𝙸𝚂𝙰
78 rm ✶67.00 – ✶✶79.00.
  ♦ Purpose-built hotel on the periphery of the town. Neat, contemporary bedrooms, a simple but up-to-date meeting room and buffet breakfast bar: useful for business stop-overs.

Number 10 without rest., Gladstone Pl, FK8 2NN, ☏ (01786) 472681, cameron-10@ tinyonline.co.uk, Fax (01786) 472681, 🌲 – ⇆🛏. 🛩   B v
3 rm ⚏ ✶50.00 – ✶✶50.00.
  ♦ Surprisingly spacious 19C terrace house in a pleasant suburb. Pine furnished en suite bedrooms are characteristically well kept and comfortable. Friendly owner.

⚕ **West Plean House** ⌂ without rest., FK7 8HA, South : 3 ½ m. on A 872 (Denny rd) ℘ (01786) 812208, *moira@westpleanhouse.com*, Fax (01786) 480550, ☞, 〓 – ⇥⇤ **P.** ⓶
VISA. ⅍
closed January and Christmas-New Year – **3 rm** ⌂ **†**40.00/45.00 – **††**60.00/64.00.
◆ Dating back to the 1800s, a homely and traditional house under pleasant personal ownership. Simple en suite accommodation. Neat gardens, duckpond and working farm close
by.

STONEHAVEN *Aberdeenshire* 501 N 13 *Scotland G.*
Env. : *Dunnottar Castle*★★, *S : 1½ m. by A 92.*
Edinburgh 109 – Aberdeen 16 – Montrose 22.

⚕ **Arduthie Guest House** without rest., 28 Ann St, AB39 2DA, ℘ (01569) 762381, *mar
tin@arduthieguesthouse.com*, ☞ – ⇥⇤ ✆, ⓶ **VISA**. ⅍
26 December – 6 rm ⌂ **†**25.00/55.00 – **††**55.00.
◆ Part Georgian/part Victorian house in coastal town. Personally run with comfortable
lounge. Individually decorated rooms, some with sea view, and your own whisky decanter.

XX **Tolbooth**, Old Pier, Harbour, AB39 2JU, ℘ (01569) 762287, *Fax (01569) 762287* – ⓶
VISA
closed 25 December-12 January, Sunday and Monday – **Rest** - Seafood - 15.00 (lunch) and
a la carte 25.55/31.95.
◆ Stonehaven's oldest building, delightfully located by the harbour. Rustic interior with
lovely picture window table. Varied menus with seafood base accompanied by great views.

XX **Carron**, 20 Cameron St, AB39 2HS, ℘ (01569) 760460, *Fax (01569) 760460*, 斤 – ⓶ **VISA**
closed 25 December-12 January, Sunday and Monday – **Rest** a la carte 19.25/28.35.
◆ 1930s Art Deco elegance fully restored to its original splendour. Panelled walls with old
mono photos. Sunny front terrace. Popular menus highlighted by daily lobster dishes.

as Netherley *North : 6 m. by B 979* – ✉ *Aberdeenshire.*

XX **The Crynoch** (at Lairhillock Inn), AB39 3QS, Northeast : 1 ½ m. by B 979 on Portlethen rd
℘ (01569) 730220, *lairhillock@breathemail.net, Fax (01569) 731175* – **P.** ⓶ AE ⓪ **VISA**
closed 1-2 January, 25-26 December and Tuesday – **Rest** (dinner only and Sunday lunch)
22.75.
◆ Converted cattle shed with beamed ceiling, wood panelling and open fire. Traditional
dishes using locally sourced ingredients.

STORNOWAY *Western Isles (Outer Hebrides)* 501 A 9 – *see Lewis and Harris (Isle of).*

STRACHUR *Argyll and Bute* 501 E 15 – *pop. 628.*
Edinburgh 112 – Glasgow 66 – Inverness 162 – Perth 101.

⛪ **The Creggans Inn**, PA27 8BX, ℘ (01369) 860279, *info@creggans-inn.co.uk,
Fax (01369) 860637,* ≤ Loch Fyne, ☞ – ⇥⇤ **P.** ⓶ **VISA**
closed 25-26 December – **Rest** a la carte 18.00/30.00 ♀ – **14 rm** ⌂ **†**75.00/85.00 –
††110.00/130.00, 1 suite.
◆ Locally renowned inn, with splendid views over Loch Fyne. Cosy bar with busy pub dining
trade and two lounges, one with fine outlook. Individually styled, comfy rooms. Large
dining room with wood floor and warm colour scheme.

X **Inver Cottage** ⌂, Strathlaclan, PA27 8BU, Southwest : 6 ½ m. by A 886 on B 8000
℘ (01369) 860537, ≤ Loch Fyne and mountains, 斤 – **P.** ♿ 20
*April-September, weekends October-Christmas, lunch only except Thursday-Saturday July,
August and October* – **Rest** *(closed Monday except July-August and Bank Holidays)* a la
carte 12.50/24.50.
◆ Wonderfully located former crofters' cottage with fine views over lake and mountains.
The simple little restaurant, with its own craft shop, serves tasty Scottish based menus.

We try to be as accurate as possible when giving room rates.
But prices are susceptible to change,
so please check rates when booking.

STRANRAER Dumfries and Galloway 501 502 E 19 Scotland G. – pop. 10 851.

    Exc. : Logan Botanic Garden★ AC, S : 11 m. by A 77, A 716 and B 7065.

    🏌 Creachmore, Leswalt ℘ (01776) 870245.

    ⛴ to Northern Ireland (Belfast) (Stena Line) (1 h 45 mn) – to Northern Ireland (Belfast) (Stena Line) 4-5 daily (1 h 45 mn/3 h 15 mn).

    🛈 28 Harbour St ℘ (01776) 702595.

    Edinburgh 132 – Ayr 51 – Dumfries 75.

⌂ **Glenotter** without rest., Leswalt Rd, DG9 0EP, Northwest : 1 m. on A 718 ℘ (01776) 703199, enquiries@glenotter.co.uk, 🚗 – ⇔✗ 🅿. ✵
    closed 25-26 December and 1 January – 3 rm ⚏ ✝38.00/49.00 – ✝✝52.00/58.00.
    ♦ Homely guesthouse run by a husband and wife team, on main road just out of town, convenient for ferry. Well-kept rooms in co-ordinated colours are simple and sensibly priced.

at Kirkcolm Northwest : 6 m. by A 718 – ✉ Stranraer.

🏛 **Corsewall Lighthouse** ⌘, Corsewall Point, DG9 0QG, Northwest : 4 ¼ m. by B 738 ℘ (01776) 853220, lighthousehotel@btinternet.com, Fax (01776) 854231, ≤, 🛥 – ⇔✗ 🐶 ஃ
    🅿. 🅜🅞 🄰🄴 🄾 VISA
    Rest 32.50 (dinner) and a la carte 28.25/31.75 – 6 rm (dinner included) ⚏ ✝110.00/130.00 – ✝✝220.00/250.00, 3 suites.
    ♦ Sensitively converted and family run, a 19C working lighthouse at the mouth of Loch Ryan. Snug bedrooms in traditional fabrics - views of the sea or the windswept promontory. Simple, characterful restaurant with seascapes and old black beams.

STRATHPEFFER Highland 501 G 11 – pop. 918.

    🏌 Strathpeffer Spa ℘ (01997) 421219.

    🛈 The Square ℘ (08452) 255121 (April-October).

    Edinburgh 174 – Inverness 18.

⌂ **Craigvar** without rest., The Square, IV14 9DL, ℘ (01997) 421622, craigvar@talk21.com, Fax (01997) 421622, 🚗 – ⇔✗ 🐶 🅿. 🅜🅞 VISA. ✵
    closed Christmas and New Year – 3 rm ⚏ ✝30.00/40.00 – ✝✝60.00/68.00.
    ♦ Georgian house overlooking main square of pleasant former spa town. Charming owner guarantees an agreeable stay. Bedrooms are crammed with antiques and original fittings.

STRATHYRE Stirling 501 H 15 Scotland G. – ✉ Callander.

    Exc. : The Trossachs★★★ (Loch Katrine★★) SW : 14 m. by A 84 and A 821 – Hilltop viewpoint★★★ (🌅 ★★★) SW : 16½ m. by A 84 and A 821.

    Edinburgh 62 – Glasgow 53 – Perth 42.

⌂ **Ardoch Lodge** ⌘, FK18 8NF, West : ¼ m. ℘ (01877) 384606, ardoch@btinternet.com, Fax (01877) 384666, ≤, 🐶, 🚗, 🕭 – ⇔✗ 🅿. 🅜🅞 VISA
    mid March - mid September – Rest (by arrangement) 26.00 – 3 rm ⚏ ✝50.00/60.00 – ✝✝70.00/90.00.
    ♦ Victorian in origin, a family-owned country house set in wooded hills above Strathyre's river. Simple accommodation and traditionally decorated sitting room. Home cooking prepared with pride.

XX **Creagan House** with rm, FK18 8ND, on A 84 ℘ (01877) 384638, eatandstay@creagan house.co.uk, Fax (01877) 384319, ≤ – 🕭 🅿. 🄰🄴 VISA
    closed February and 4-23 November – Rest (closed Thursday) (booking essential) (dinner only) 28.00 ⚏ – 5 rm ⚏ ✝65.00 – ✝✝110.00.
    ♦ Surrounded by hills which inspired Sir Walter Scott; a feast for the eye to be enjoyed in baronial style dining room. French classics with Scottish overtones. Cosy rooms.

STRONTIAN Highland 501 D 13.

    🛈 Acharacle ℘ (08452) 255121 (April-October).

    Edinburgh 139 – Fort William 23 – Oban 66.

🏛 **Kilcamb Lodge** ⌘, PH36 4HY, ℘ (01967) 402257, enquiries@kilcamblodge.co.uk, Fax (01967) 402041, ≤, 🐶, 🚗, 🕭 – ↓ ⇔✗ 🅿. 🅜🅞 VISA
    closed January-February – Rest (closed Monday-Tuesday) (light lunch) (dinner booking essential for non-residents)/dinner 45.00 ⚏ – 10 rm ⚏ ✝95.00/130.00 – ✝✝175.00/225.00.
    ♦ A spectacular location in 19 acres of lawn and woodland, leading down to a private shore on Loch Sunart. The idyll continues indoors: immaculate bedrooms; thoughtful extras. Savour views from large windows and tuck into roast grouse.

STRUAN Highland – see Skye (Isle of).

STRUY Highland 501 F 11.
  Edinburgh 180 – Inverness 19 – Kyle of Lochalsh 82.

⚔ **The Glass at the Struy Inn**, IV4 7JS, ℮ (01463) 761219, info@glassrestaurant.info –
P. M© ①) VISA
  closed Monday and Tuesday lunch and October-mid March except Christmas – **Rest** (dinner
  booking essential) 21.95 (dinner) and a la carte 23.40/27.40.
  ♦ Converted inn retains a traditional, almost homely feel. Wide-ranging menu of wholesome, satisfying dishes, plus a blackboard listing daily specials and fresh seafood.

SWINTON Borders 501 502 N 16 – pop. 472 – ✉ Duns.
  Edinburgh 49 – Berwick-upon-Tweed 13 – Glasgow 93 – Newcastle upon Tyne 66.

❚❚ **The Wheatsheaf** with rm, TD11 3JJ, ℮ (01890) 860257, reception@wheatsheaf-swin
ton.co.uk, Fax (01890) 860688, ☗, ※ – ⌂, **P. M© VISA**. ⛌
  closed 25-27 December – **Rest** (closed Sunday dinner December-February) a la carte
  22.00/35.00 ☆ – **7 rm** ⊜ ✱67.00 – ✱✱102.00.
  ♦ A village inn with firelit real ale bar and comfortable, well-furnished rooms. Classic,
  unfussy seasonal dishes bring out the distinctive flavour of local produce.

TAIN Highland 501 H 10.
  ℹ Tain, Chapel Rd ℮ (01862) 892314 – ℹ Tarbat, Portmahomack ℮ (01862) 871486.
  Edinburgh 191 – Inverness 35 – Wick 91.

⌂ **Golf View House** without rest., 13 Knockbreck Rd, IV19 1BN, ℮ (01862) 892856, golf
view@hotmail.co.uk, Fax (01862) 892856, ≤, ※ – ⌂➞ **P. M© VISA**. ⛌
  March-October – **5 rm** ⊜ ✱35.00/50.00 – ✱✱56.00/65.00.
  ♦ Built as a vicarage, a local sandstone house overlooking the Firth and the fairways.
  Simple rooms are well kept and tidy. Lawn and flowers shaded by beech trees.

at Cadboll Southeast : 8½ m. by A 9 and B 9165 (Portmahomack rd) off Hilton rd – ✉ Tain.

⌂ **Glenmorangie House** ☗, Fearn, IV20 1XP, ℮ (01862) 871671, relax@glenmoran
gieplc.co.uk, Fax (01862) 871625, ≤, ☗, ※, ⌂ – ⌂➞ **P. M© AE VISA**
  closed 2-25 January – **Rest** (booking essential for non-residents) (dinner only) (communal
  dining) (set menu only) 45.00 **s.** – **9 rm** (dinner included) ⊜ ✱185.00 – ✱✱320.00.
  ♦ Restored part 17C house owned by the famous distillery. Tasteful, old-world morning
  room and more informal firelit lounge; house party ambience prevails. Smart, comfy
  rooms. Imposing communal dining room: gilt-framed portraits, eastern rugs and a long
  table.

TALMINE Highland 501 G 8 – ✉ Lairg.
  Edinburgh 245 – Inverness 86 – Thurso 48.

⌂ **Cloisters** ☗ without rest., Church Holme, IV27 4YP, ℮ (01847) 601286, recep
tion@cloistertal.demon.co.uk, Fax (01847) 601286, ≤ Rabbit Islands and Tongue Bay, ※ –
⌂➞ ⌂ **P.**
  3 rm ⊜ ✱30.00 – ✱✱50.00.
  ♦ Purpose-built guesthouse, by a converted church, offers simple but trim and spotless
  rooms in bright fabrics and superb view of Rabbit Islands and Tongue Bay. Friendly host.

TARBERT Western Isles (Outer Hebrides) 501 Z 10 – see Lewis and Harris (Isle of).

TARBET Argyll and Bute 501 F 15 – ✉ Arrochar.
  Edinburgh 88 – Glasgow 42 – Inverness 138 – Perth 78.

⌂ **Lomond View** without rest., G83 7DG, on A 82 ℮ (01301) 702477, lomondview
house@aol.com, Fax (01301) 702477, ≤ Loch Lomond, ※ – ⌂➞ **P. M© ①) VISA**. ⛌
  3 rm ⊜ ✱55.00/70.00 – ✱✱70.00/80.00.
  ♦ Purpose-built guesthouse which lives up to its name: there are stunning loch views.
  Spacious sitting room. Light and airy breakfast room. Sizeable, modern bedrooms.

TAYVALLICH Argyll and Bute 501 D 15 – ✉ Lochgilphead.
  Edinburgh 148 – Glasgow 103 – Inverness 157.

❚❚ **Tayvallich Inn**, PA31 8PL, ℮ (01546) 870282, rfhanderson@aol.com,
Fax (01546) 870354, ≤, ☗ – **P. M© AE ①) VISA**
  closed Monday-Wednesday November-February and 25 December – **Rest** a la carte
  20.00/30.00.
  ♦ Well-regarded pub in little coastal hamlet close to the shores of Loch Sween. Interior of
  pine panelling and log fires. Simple or creative seafood dishes are the speciality.

TEANGUE Highland – see Skye (Isle of).

THORNHILL Dumfries and Galloway 501 502 I 18 Scotland G. – pop. 1 512.
  Env. : Drumlanrig Castle★★ (cabinets★) AC, NW : 4 m. by A 76.
  Edinburgh 64 – Ayr 44 – Dumfries 15 – Glasgow 63.

🏠 **Trigony House,** Closeburn, DG3 5EZ, South : 1 ½ m. on A 76 ℰ (01848) 331211,
  info@trigonyhotel.co.uk, ⚲, ☞, 🛰 ✦ P. 🞳 VISA
  closed 24-27 December – **Rest** (dinner only) a la carte 14.65/22.50 s. ♀ – **10 rm** (dinner
  included) ⚌ ✦62.50 – ✦✦160.00.
  • Ivy-clad Victorian shooting lodge, family owned, mixes period décor and modern art.
  Cosy bar with an open fire. Traditional rooms overlook four acres of woodland and garden.
  Tasty, locally inspired dishes.

🏠 **Gillbank House** without rest., 8 East Morton St, DG3 5LZ, ℰ (01848) 330597,
  hanne@gillbank.co.uk, Fax (01848) 331713, ☞ – ✦ P. 🞳 VISA
  6 rm ⚌ ✦40.00 – ✦✦60.00.
  • Victorian stone built personally run house just off town square. Guests' sitting room and
  airy breakfast room. Spacious, well-furnished bedrooms with bright décor.

THURSO Highland 501 J 8 Scotland G. – pop. 7 737.
  Exc. : Strathy Point★ (≤★★★) W : 22 m. by A 836.
  🛈 Newlands of Geise ℰ (01847) 893807.
  ⚓ from Scrabster to Stromness (Orkney Islands) (P & O Scottish Ferries) (2 h).
  🛈 Riverside ℰ (08452) 255121 (April-October).
  Edinburgh 289 – Inverness 133 – Wick 21.

🏨 **Forss House** ⚲, Forss, KW14 7XY, West : 5 ½ m. on A 836 ℰ (01847) 861201, anne@
  forsshousehotel.co.uk, Fax (01847) 861301, ⚲, ☞, 🛰 ✦ P. 🞳 AE ① VISA
  closed 23 December-3 January – **Rest** (closed Sunday dinner) (dinner only and Sunday
  lunch) dinner a la carte 24.85/33.40 – **12 rm** ⚌ ✦70.00/85.00 – ✦✦135.00, 1 suite.
  • Traditional décor sets off the interior of this 19C house, smoothly run in a friendly style.
  Good-sized, comfy rooms. Angling themed bar, drying room and warm atmosphere. Vast
  choice of malts in restaurant bar.

🏠 **Station,** 54 Princes St, KW14 7DH, ℰ (01847) 892003, stationhotel@northhotels.co.uk,
  Fax (01847) 891820 – ✦ P. 🞳 AE VISA
  Rest a la carte 12.00/25.00 ♀ – **30 rm** ⚌ ✦45.00/70.00 – ✦✦80.00/90.00.
  • Personally run with care and immaculate housekeeping. Co-ordinated bedrooms are
  bright, attractive and well-appointed. Some rooms in Coach House annex are slightly
  larger. Simple, neat restaurant with traditional menus.

🏠 **Murray House,** 1 Campbell St, KW14 7HD, ℰ (01847) 895759, enquiries@murrayhou
  sebb.com – ✦ P. ⚲
  closed Christmas and New Year – **Rest** 15.00 – **5 rm** ⚌ ✦25.00/50.00 – ✦✦50.00/56.00.
  • A centrally located and family owned Victorian town house. Pine furnished bedrooms,
  half en suite, are simple but carefully maintained. Modern dining room where home-
  cooked evening meals may be taken.

TIGHNABRUAICH Argyll and Bute 501 E 16.
  Edinburgh 113 – Glasgow 63 – Oban 66.

🏨 **Royal,** PA21 2BE, ℰ (01700) 811239, info@royalhotel.org.uk, Fax (01700) 811300, ≤ – 🛅
  ✦ P. 🞳 VISA
  closed Christmas – **Rest** (meals in bar lunch and Sunday-Tuesday dinner) a la carte approx
  26.00 ♀ – **11 rm** ⚌ ✦100.00/190.00 – ✦✦100.00/190.00.
  • Privately owned 19C hotel in an unspoilt village overlooking the Kyles of Bute. Firelit
  shinty bar and bistro option. Well-equipped rooms in strong individual styles. Fine loch
  views and an interesting modern art collection in a pleasant formal dining room.

TILLICOULTRY Clackmannanshire 501 I 15 – pop. 5 400.
  🛈 Alva Rd ℰ (01259) 50124.
  Edinburgh 35 – Dundee 43 – Glasgow 38.

🏠 **Harviestoun Country Inn,** Dollar Rd, FK13 6PQ, East : ¼ m. by A 91 ℰ (01259)
  752522, harviestounhotel@aol.com, Fax (01259) 752523, ☞ – ✦ ⚫ P. – 🛖 70. 🞳 VISA
  ⚲
  Rest a la carte 16.20/26.25 – **11 rm** ⚌ ✦60.00 – ✦✦80.00.
  • Converted Georgian stable block, now a smoothly run modern hotel. Neat, unfussy, pine
  furnished bedrooms, half facing the Ochil hills; coffees and home baking in the lounge.
  Beams and flagstones hint at the restaurant's rustic past.

TIRORAN *Argyll and Bute – see Mull (Isle of).*

TOBERMORY *Argyll and Bute* 501 B 14 *– see Mull (Isle of).*

TONGUE *Highland* 501 G 8 *Scotland G. –* ⊠ *Lairg.*
Exc. : *Cape Wrath*★★★ (≤★★) *W : 44 m. (including ferry crossing) by A 838 – Ben Loyal*★★, *S : 8 m. by A 836 – Ben Hope*★ (≤★★★) *SW : 15 m. by A 838 – Strathy Point*★ (≤★★★) *E : 22 m. by A 836 – Torrisdale Bay*★ (≤★★) *NE : 8 m. by A 836.*
Edinburgh 257 – Inverness 101 – Thurso 43.

🏦 **Tongue,** Main St, IV27 4XD, ℰ (01847) 611206, *info@tonguehotel.co.uk,* *Fax* (01847) 611345, ≤, 🐾 – ⅍ 🅿 🐠 ① 𝘝𝘐𝘚𝘈. 🕸
April-October – **Rest** (bar lunch)/dinner a la carte 14.00/28.00 – **19 rm** ⊊ ✝40.00/60.00 – ✝✝70.00/120.00.
◆ Former hunting lodge of the Duke of Sutherland overlooking Kyle of Tongue. Smart interiors include intimate bar and beamed lounge. Individually styled rooms with antiques. Restaurant with fireplace and antique dressers.

🏠 **Ben Loyal,** Main St, IV27 4XE, ℰ (01847) 611216, *stay@btinternet.com,* *Fax* (01847) 611212, ≤ Ben Loyal and Kyle of Tongue – ⅍ 📞 🅿 🐠 𝘝𝘐𝘚𝘈
March-October – **Rest** a la carte 18.90/26.45 **s.** – **11 rm** ⊊ ✝40.00/55.00 – ✝✝80.00.
◆ Unassuming hotel in the village centre enjoys excellent views of Ben Loyal and the Kyle of Tongue - a useful hiking or fishing base. Rooms are unfussy, modern and well kept. Pine furnished restaurant overlooks the hills and sea.

TORRIDON *Highland* 501 D 11 *Scotland G. –* ⊠ *Achnasheen.*
Env. : *Wester Ross*★★★.
Edinburgh 234 – Inverness 62 – Kyle of Lochalsh 44.

🏯 **Loch Torridon** 🌀, IV22 2EY, South : 1 ½ m. on A 896 ℰ (01445) 791242, *enquiries@lochtorridonhotel.com, Fax* (01445) 712253, ≤ Upper Loch Torridon and mountains, 🐾, 🌾, ♨ – ⅋ ⅍ 📞 🅿 🐠 🅰🅴 𝘝𝘐𝘚𝘈. 🕸
closed 2-28 January and Monday-Tuesday February-March – **Rest** (booking essential) (bar lunch)/dinner 40.00/50.00 ⅀ – **18 rm** (dinner included) ⊊ ✝115.00/160.00 – ✝✝658.00/245.00, 1 suite.
◆ 19C hunting lodge; idyllic view of Loch Torridon and mountains. Ornate ceilings, peat fires and Highland curios add to a calm period feel shared by the more luxurious rooms. Formal, pine-panelled restaurant uses fine local produce, some from the grounds.

🏠 **Ben Damph Inn** 🌀, IV22 2EY, South : 1 ½ m. on A 896 ℰ (01445) 791242, *bendamph@lochtorridonhotel.com, Fax* (01445) 712253, 🍴, 🐾, 🌾, ♨ – ⅍ 🅰 🅿 🐠 🅰🅴 𝘝𝘐𝘚𝘈. 🕸
April-October – **Rest** (grill rest.) 17.00 and a la carte 21.75/26.25 – **12 rm** ⊊ ✝49.00 – ✝✝74.00.
◆ Simple, modern, affordable rooms - some sleeping up to six - in a converted stable block, set in a quiet rural spot and named after the mountain nearby. Spacious pubby bar. Traditionally styled and informal restaurant.

TROON *South Ayrshire* 501 502 G 17 – *pop. 14 766.*
🏌, 🏌, 🏌 *Troon Municipal, Harling Drive* ℰ (01292) 312464.
⛴ *to Northern Ireland (Larne) (P & O Irish Sea) 2 daily.*
Edinburgh 77 – Ayr 7 – Glasgow 31.

🏯 **Lochgreen House** 🌀, Monktonhill Rd, Southwood, KA10 7EN, Southeast : 2 m. on B 749 ℰ (01292) 313343, *lochgreen@costley-hotels.co.uk, Fax* (01292) 318661, 🌾, 🕸 – ⅋ ⅍ 📞 🅰 🅿 – 🅰 80. 🐠 🅰🅴 𝘝𝘐𝘚𝘈. 🕸
Rest – (see **The Tapestry Restaurant** below) – **43 rm** ⊊ ✝99.00/125.00 – ✝✝150.00/180.00, 1 suite.
◆ Attractive, coastal Edwardian house in mature grounds. Lounges exude luxurious country house feel. Large rooms, modern or traditional, have a good eye for welcoming detail.

🏦 **Piersland House,** 15 Craigend Rd, KA10 6HD, ℰ (01292) 314747, *reservations@piersland.co.uk, Fax* (01292) 315613, 🌾 – ⅍ 🅰 🅿 – 🅰 70. 🐠 🅰🅴 ① 𝘝𝘐𝘚𝘈
Restaurant 1820 : Rest *(closed lunch Monday-Saturday)*/dinner a la carte 13.50/26.00 **s.** – **15 rm** ⊊ ✝70.00/98.00 – ✝✝130.00/187.50, **15 suites** ⊊ 130.00/154.00.
◆ Built for the family of Johnnie Walker; Jacobean and 19C in style: fine original panelling, stonework and Arts and Crafts garden. Well-equipped rooms, 15 in courtyard annex. Tastefully replicated period dining room of dark wood and neat linen.

XXX **The Tapestry Restaurant** (at Lochgreen House H.), Monktonhill Rd, Southwood, KA10 7EN, Southeast : 2 m. on B 749 ℰ (01292) 313343, Fax (01292) 318661, 🐎 – 🗐 **P.** ◖◗ 〇 **VISA**
Rest (dinner only and Sunday lunch)/dinner 37.50 and lunch a la carte 20.00/35.00 s. ♊.
♦ Spacious dining room with baronial feel. Elegant chandeliers; large pottery cockerels. Classical, modern cooking, with a strong Scottish base.

X **The Apple Inn,** 89 Portland St, KA10 6QU, ℰ (01292) 318819 – ◖◗ 〇 **VISA**
Rest a la carte 16.95/25.40.
♦ Former High Street bar, now a popular little eatery with pale green, cool and tidy décor; simple pine tables and chairs. Tasty, modish British menus.

at Loans East : 2 m. on A 759 – ✉ Troon.

XX **Highgrove House** with rm, Old Loans Rd, KA10 7HL, East : ¼ m. on Dundonald rd ℰ (01292) 312511, highgrove@costleyhotels.co.uk, Fax (01292) 318228, ≤, 🐎 – **P.** ◖◗ 〇
VISA 🏶
Rest 19.95/25.95 and a la carte 16.00/32.00 – **9 rm** � ✸69.00/75.00 – ✸✸110.00/120.00.
♦ Elevated position, offering superb coastal panorama. Open plan dining area with lounge and bar. Seafood, and local meat and game, to the fore. Comfy rooms with fine views.

TURNBERRY South Ayrshire **501 502** F 18 Scotland G. – ✉ Girvan.
Env. : Culzean Castle★ AC (setting★★★, Oval Staircase★★) NE : 5 m. by A 719.
Edinburgh 97 – Ayr 15 – Glasgow 51 – Stranraer 36.

🏨🏨🏨 **The Westin Turnberry Resort** ⛳, KA26 9LT, on A 719 ℰ (01655) 331000, turn berry@westin.com, Fax (01655) 331706, ℰ – golf courses, bay, Ailsa Craig and Mull of Kintyre, 🍴, ◉, 🎿, ⇄s, 🔲, 🏌, 🐎, 🎾 – 🛗 ⇄, 🗐 rest, ℰ & **P.** – ⚖ 275. ◖◗ 〇 ◑ **VISA**
closed 18-28 December – **Turnberry** : Rest (dinner only) a la carte 38.00/65.00 ♊ – **The Terrace Brasserie :** Rest (closed Tuesday-Wednesday) 26.00 and a la carte 26.00/40.50 ♊ – **Tappie Toorie :** Rest a la carte 12.20/25.65 ♊ – **211 rm** � ✸185.00/340.00 – ✸✸230.00/395.00, 8 suites.
♦ Impeccably run part Edwardian hotel with panoramic views of coast and world famous golf courses. Much original charm intact. Superbly equipped with every conceivable facility. Fine diningTurnberry. Smart Terrace Brasserie. Informal Tappie Toorie Grill.

UDDINGSTON South Lanarkshire **501 502** H 16 – pop. 5 576 – ✉ Glasgow.
🏌 Coatbridge, Townhead Rd ℰ (01236) 28975.
Edinburgh 41 – Glasgow 10.

🏨 **Redstones,** 8-10 Glasgow Rd, G71 7AS, ℰ (01698) 813774, info@redstoneshotel.com, Fax (01698) 815319, 🐎 – ⇄ rm, ℰ **P.** – ⚖ 30. ◖◗ 〇 ◑ **VISA**. 🏶
Rest 11.45/23.00 and a la carte 12.85/24.90 – **12 rm** � ✸85.00 – ✸✸95.00.
♦ Renovated Victorian houses in distinctive red sandstone - the conservatory lounge is a later addition; usefully-equipped bedrooms feel stylish and modern. Formal dining room.

UIST (Isles of) Western Isles (Outer Hebrides) **501** X/Y 10 /11/12 – pop. 3 510.
🛬 see Liniclate.
🛳 – from Lochmaddy to Isle of Skye (Uig) (Caledonian MacBrayne Ltd) 1-3 daily (1 h 50 mn) – from Otternish to Isle of Harris (Leverburgh) (Caledonian MacBrayne Ltd) (1 h 10 mn).

NORTH UIST Western Isles

Carinish Western Isles.

🏠 **Temple View,** HS6 5EJ, ℰ (01876) 580676, templeviewhotel@aol.com, Fax (01876) 580682, ≤, 🐎 – ⇄ **P.** ◖◗ **VISA**
Rest (bar lunch) 21.50/24.00 and a la carte 15.50/26.50 s. – **10 rm** � ✸55.00/70.00 – ✸✸95.00/105.00.
♦ Extended Victorian house on main route from north to south. Pleasantly refurbished, it offers a smart sitting room, cosy bar with conservatory, and up-to-date bedrooms. Extensive local specialities the highlight of small dining room.

Grimsay Western Isles.

🏠 **Glendale** ⛳ without rest., 7 Kallin, HS6 5HY, ℰ (01870) 602029, glendale@ecosse.net, ≤, 🐎 – ⇄ **P.** 🏶
closed Christmas and New Year – **3 rm** � ✸40.00 – ✸✸50.00.
♦ Overlooking picturesque Kallin harbour, a simple converted house with a friendly atmosphere. Homely lounge and compact but pleasant and affordable bedrooms.

SCOTLAND

UIST (Isles of)

Langass *Western Isles.*

🏨 **Langass Lodge** ⌕, HS6 5HA, ℰ (01876) 580285, *langasslodge@btconnect.com,*
Fax (01876) 580385, ≤ Ben Eaval and Langass Loch, ⌀, 🌿, ℟ – ⌖⌖ ✦ P. ⫸ VISA
Rest a la carte approx 29.00 – **12 rm** ⫷ ✦60.00 – ✦✦120.00.
◆ Former Victorian shooting lodge boasting superb views, classical comforts, a modish
conservatory extension, and bedrooms styled from traditional to clean-lined modernity.
Superior cooking of fine Hebridean produce from land and sea.

Lochmaddy *Western Isles.*

🏨 **Tigh Dearg,** HS6 5AE, ℰ (01876) 500700, *info@tighdearghotel.co.uk,*
Fax (01876) 500701, ☕, 🛋, ⛺ – ⌖⌖ ✦ P. ⫸ VISA. ⌀
Rest a la carte 14.45/25.25 s. – **8 rm** ⫷ ✦80.00/120.00 – ✦✦110.00/140.00.
◆ 'The Red House', visible from a long distance, is an outpost of utterly stylish chic. Modish
bar matched by well-equipped gym, sauna and steam room, and sleek 21C bedrooms.
Hebridean produce well sourced in designer-style restaurant.

SOUTH UIST *Western Isles*

Lochboisdale *Western Isles.*

⌂ **Brae Lea** ⌕, Lasgair, HS8 5TH, Northwest : 1 m. by A 865 ℰ (01878) 700497, *braelea@su*
panet.com, Fax (01878) 700497, ⌀ – ⌖⌖ P. ⌀
Rest (by arrangement) 15.00/20.00 – **6 rm** ⫷ ✦30.00/40.00 – ✦✦60.00/70.00.
◆ In a quiet spot yet convenient for the ferry, a purpose-built guesthouse, well-estab-
lished and family run. Neat, pine-fitted rooms, homely lounge with wide picture windows.
Unpretentious home-cooked dinners in a suitably simple setting.

ULLAPOOL *Highland* 501 E 10 *Scotland G.* – pop. 1 308.

See : *Town*★.

Env. : *Wester Ross*★★★ – *Loch Broom*★★.

Exc. : *Falls of Measach*★★, S : 11 m. by A 835 and A 832 - *Corrieshalloch Gorge*★, SE : 10 m.
by A 835 – *Northwards to Lochinver*★★, *Morefield* (≤★★ of *Ullapool*), ≤★ *Loch Broom*.
⛴ to *Isle of Lewis (Stornoway) (Caledonian MacBrayne Ltd) (2 h 40 mn).*
🚹 *Argyle St* ℰ (08452) 255121.
Edinburgh 215 – Inverness 59.

🏠 **Ardvreck** ⌕ without rest., Morefield Brae, IV26 2TH, Northwest : 2 m. by A 835
ℰ (01854) 612028, *ardvreck.guesthouse@btinternet.com,* Fax (01854) 613000, ≤ Loch
Broom and mountains, ⌀ – ⌖⌖ P. ⫸ VISA. ⌀
February-November – **10 rm** ⫷ ✦30.00/65.00 – ✦✦76.00/70.00.
◆ Peacefully located hotel boasting fine views of loch and mountains. Well appointed
breakfast room with splendid vistas. Spacious rooms: some with particularly fine outlooks.

⌂ **Tanglewood House** ⌕, IV26 2TB, on A 835 ℰ (01854) 612059, *tanglewood*
house@ecosse.net, ≤ Loch Broom, ⌀ – ⌖⌖ P. ⫸ VISA
closed Christmas, New Year and Easter – **Rest** (by arrangement) (communal dining) 33.00 –
3 rm ⫷ ✦66.00 – ✦✦96.00.
◆ Blissfully located guesthouse on heather covered headland. Drawing room has a 20 foot
window overlooking loch. Homely, pastel shaded rooms, all with vistas. Meals taken at
communal table.

⌂ **The Sheiling** without rest., Garve Rd, IV26 2SX, ℰ (01854) 612947, Fax (01854) 612947,
≤ Loch Broom, ⛺, ⌀, ⌀ – ⌖⌖ P. ⫸ VISA. ⌀
closed Christmas and New Year – **6 rm** ⫷ ✦40.00 – ✦✦56.00/64.00.
◆ Welcoming guesthouse by the shores of Loch Broom. Renowned breakfasts include a
platter of locally smoked fish. Homely lounge and comfortable bedrooms.

⌂ **Point Cottage** without rest., West Shore St, IV26 2UR, ℰ (01854) 612494, *stay@point*
cottage.co.uk, ≤ Loch Broom, ⌀ – ⌖⌖ P. ⌀
14 February - March – **3 rm** ⫷ ✦25.00/50.00 – ✦✦44.00/60.00.
◆ Converted fisherman's cottage of 18C origin. Rooms in bright modern fabrics enjoy
beautiful views across Loch Broom to the hills. Substantial breakfasts.

⌂ **Dromnan** without rest., Garve Rd, IV26 2SX, ℰ (01854) 612333, *info@dromnan.com,* ≤,
⌀ – ⌖⌖ P. ⫸ ⓞ VISA. ⌀
7 rm ⫷ ✦28.00 – ✦✦40.00/60.00.
◆ Family run, modern house overlooking Loch Broom. Television lounge with deep leather
chairs. Practically equipped rooms vary in décor from patterned pastels to dark tartan.

UNST (Island of) *Shetland Islands* 501 R 1 – *see Shetland Islands.*

URQUHART *Moray – see Elgin.*

VEENSGARTH *Shetland Islands – see Shetland Islands (Mainland).*

WALKERBURN *Borders.*
Edinburgh 30 – Galashiels 23.5 – Peebles 8.5.

 Windlestraw Lodge ⚜, Tweed Valley, EH43 6AA, on A 72 ℘ (01896) 870636, *reception@windlestraw.co.uk*, Fax (01896) 870639, ≤, ⌬, ☞ – ⊁ ℗. ⑩⑳ 𝘝𝘐𝘚𝘈
closed 23 December - 10 January – **Rest** (booking essential for non-residents) (residents only Sunday-Wednesday) (dinner only) 34.00/45.00 ♀ – **6 rm** ⊑ (dinner included) ✦110.00 – ✦✦190.00/250.00.
♦ Edwardian country house in picturesque Tweed Valley: lovely views guaranteed. Period style lounges serviced by well-stocked bar. Half the good-sized rooms enjoy the vista. Linen-clad dining room.

WATERNISH *Highland – see Skye (Isle of).*

Undecided between two equivalent establishments?
Within each category, establishments are classified
in our order of preference.

SCOTLAND

WESTRAY (Island of) *Orkney Islands 501 K/L 6/7 – see Orkney Islands.*

WHITING BAY *North Ayrshire 501 502 E 17 – see Arran (Isle of).*

WICK *Highland 501 K 8 Scotland G. – pop. 7 333.*
Exc. : *Duncansby Head★ (Stacks of Duncansby★★) N : 14 m. by A 9 – Grey Cairns of Camster★ (Long Cairn★★) S : 17 m. by A 9 – The Hill O'Many Stanes★, S : 10 m. by A 9.*
☗₈ *Reiss ℘ (01955) 602726.*
✈ *Wick Airport : ℘ (01955) 602215, N : 1 m.*
🅱 *Whitechapel Rd ℘ (01955) 602596.*
Edinburgh 282 – Inverness 126.

🏠 **The Clachan** without rest., South Rd, KW1 5NJ, South : ¾ m. on A 99 ℘ (01955) 605384, *enquiry@theclachan.co.uk*, ☞ – ⊁. ⅏
closed Christmas and New Year – **3 rm** ⊑ ✦35.00 – ✦✦45.00/48.00.
♦ This detached 1930s house on the town's southern outskirts provides homely en suite accommodation in pastels and floral patterns. Charming owner.

✗ **Bord De L'Eau**, 2 Market St (Riverside), KW1 4AR, ℘ (01955) 604400, 🍴 – ⑩⑳ 𝘝𝘐𝘚𝘈
closed first 3 weeks January, 25-26 December, Sunday lunch and Monday – **Rest** - French Bistro - a la carte 19.15/35.85.
♦ Totally relaxed little riverside eatery with French owner. Friendly, attentive service of an often-changing, distinctly Gallic repertoire. Keenly priced dishes.

WORMIT *Fife 501 L 14 – ✉ Newport-on-Tay.*
☗₈ *Scotscraig, Golf Rd, Tayport ℘ (01382) 552515.*
Edinburgh 53 – Dundee 6 – St Andrews 12.

🏨 **Sandford Country House** ⚜, DD6 8RG, South : 2 m. on B 946 ℘ (01382) 541802, *sandford.hotel@btinternet.com*, Fax (01382) 542136, ≤, ☞ – ⊁ ℗, 🔒 45. ⑩⑳ ⒶⒺ 𝘝𝘐𝘚𝘈
Rest (bar lunch)/dinner 27.50 ♀ – **13 rm** ⊑ ✦40.00/58.00 – ✦✦65.00/84.00.
♦ Designed by Baillie Scott, a 20C country house in wooded gardens. Comfy lounge with minstrels gallery; rooms, contrasting with exterior, are modern and minimalist in style. Restaurant boasts tall church candles and Mackintosh-style chairs.

873

Caernarfon: the pier and the medieval walls of the castle

Towns
from A to Z

Villes
de A à Z
Città
de A a Z
Städte
von A bis Z

Wales

Place with at least

a hotel or restaurant — ● Cardiff

a pleasant hotel or restaurant — 🏨🏨🏨, ⛪, X

Good accommodation at moderate prices — 🏨

a quiet, secluded hotel — 🏨

a restaurant with — ⛄, ⛄⛄, ⛄⛄⛄, 🍴, Rest

Town with a local map — ●

Localité offrant au moins

une ressource hôtelière — ● Cardiff

un hôtel ou restaurant agréable — 🏨🏨🏨, ⛪, X

Bonnes nuits à petits prix — 🏨

un hôtel très tranquille, isolé — 🏨

une bonne table à — ⛄, ⛄⛄, ⛄⛄⛄, 🍴, Rest

Carte de voisinage : voir à la ville choisie — ●

La località possiede come minimo

una risorsa alberghiera — ● Cardiff

Albergo o ristorante ameno — 🏨🏨🏨, ⛪, X

Buona sistemazione a prezzi contenuti — 🏨

un albergo molto tranquillo, isolato — 🏨

un'ottima tavola con — ⛄, ⛄⛄, ⛄⛄⛄, 🍴, Rest

Città con carta dei dintorni — ●

Ort mit mindestens

● einem Hotel oder Restaurant

● einem angenehmen Hotel oder Restaurant

Hier übernachten Sie gut und preiswert

einem sehr ruhigen und abgelegenen Hotel

einem Restaurant mit

⬤ Stadt mit Umgebungskarte

● Cardiff

ABERAERON Ceredigion 503 H 27.
Cardiff 90 – Aberystwyth 16 – Fishguard 41.

Ty Mawr Mansion Country House ⟍, Cilcennin, SA48 8DB, East : 4½ m. by A 482 ℰ (01570) 470033, info@tymawrmansion.co.uk, Fax (01570) 471502, ☞, ♨ – ⇥ ⟍ P. ₥Ⓞ AE VISA ⟍

Closed 24 December - 15 January – Rest (closed Monday-Tuesday lunch, Sunday and Monday dinner to non-residents) (lunch booking essential) a la carte 29.85/43.40 ♀ – 8 rm ☐ ✸80.00/160.00 – ✸✸120.00/220.00, 1 suite.

◆ Grade II listed Georgian stone mansion in 12 acres of grounds. Three sumptuous reception rooms matched by luxurious bedrooms, which are oversized and full of top facilities. Chefs rear pigs for locally renowned restaurant boasting bold edge to cooking.

Llys Aeron without rest., Lampeter Rd, SA46 0ED, on A 482 ℰ (01545) 570276, enquiries@llysaeron.co.uk, ☞ – ⇥ TV P. ₥Ⓞ VISA ⟍
3 rm ☐ ✸40.00/50.00 – ✸✸60.00/70.00.

◆ Imposing Georgian house on main road. Hearty Aga cooked breakfasts overlooking well established rear walled garden. Comfy lounge; light, airy rooms in clean pastel shades.

Harbour Master with rm, Quay Parade, SA46 0BA, ℰ (01545) 570755, info@harbour-master.com, ⟨ – ⇥ ⟍ P. ₥Ⓞ VISA ⟍
closed 24 December-10 January – Rest (closed Sunday dinner and Monday lunch) 16.50 (lunch) and a la carte 21.00/30.00 ♀ – 9 rm ☐ 55.00 – ✸✸120.00.

◆ Good value, former harbour master's house, located on attractive quayside. Stylish décor throughout and run in a relaxing style. Snug bar; individually styled bedrooms. Contemporary dining room with a seafood grounding.

ABERDOVEY (Aberdyfi) Gwynedd 503 H 26 Wales G.
Env. : Snowdonia National Park★★★.
London 230 – Dolgellau 25 – Shrewsbury 66.

Llety Bodfor without rest., Bodfor Terrace, LL35 0EA, ℰ (01654) 767475, info@lletybodfor.co.uk, Fax (01654) 767850, ⟨ – ⇥ P. ₥Ⓞ AE VISA ⟍
closed 23-29 December – 8 rm ☐ ✸45.00/60.00 – ✸✸145.00.

◆ Two 19C seafront terraces painted pale mauve with modish interior featuring sitting/breakfast room with piano and hi-fi; luxurious bedrooms have blue/white seaside theme.

Penhelig Arms with rm, LL35 0LT, ℰ (01654) 767215, info@penheligarms.com, Fax (01654) 767690, ⟨ Dyfi Estuary, 🍽 – ⇥ , ▤ rest, P. ₥Ⓞ VISA
closed 25-26 December – Rest 28.00 (dinner) and a la carte 17.50/25.75 ♀ ♨ – 15 rm ☐ ✸49.00/55.00 – ✸✸78.00/130.00, 1 suite.

◆ Standing by the harbour, looking across Dyfi Estuary, this part 18C inn boasts superior bedrooms, with views from most, and strongly seafood based menus, mostly local.

at Pennal Northeast : 6½ m. on A 493 – ⊠ Aberdovey.

Penmaendyfi ⟍ without rest., Cwrt, SY20 9LD, Southwest : 1¼ m. by A 493 ℰ (01654) 791246, shana@penmaendyfi.co.uk, Fax (01654) 791616, ⟨, ⟰ heated, ☞, ♨, ⟍ – ⇥ ⅊ P. ₥Ⓞ VISA ⟍
closed Christmas and New Year – 7 rm ☐ ✸50.00/55.00 – ✸✸80.00/100.00.

◆ Impressive late 16C mansion with elegant sweeping grounds and ancient trees: a peaceful location. Sumptuous lounge. Spacious, smartly appointed rooms with fine country views.

ABERGAVENNY (Y-Fenni) Monmouthshire 503 L 28 Wales G. – pop. 14 055.
See : Town★ – St Mary's Church★ (Monuments★★).
Env. : Brecon Beacons National Park★★ – Blaenavon Ironworks★, SW : 5 m. by A 465 and B 4246.
Exc. : Raglan Castle★ AC, SE : 9 m. by A 40.
🏌 Monmouthshire, Llanfoist ℰ (01873) 852606.
🚪 Swan Meadow, Monmouth Rd ℰ (01873) 857588.
London 163 – Cardiff 31 – Gloucester 43 – Newport 19 – Swansea 49.

Llansantffraed Court, Llanvihangel Gobion, NP7 9BA, Southeast : 6½ m. by A 40 and B 4598 off old Raglan rd ℰ (01873) 840678, reception@llch.co.uk, Fax (01873) 840674, ⟨, ☞, ♨ – ⅼ ⇥ ⟍ P. ₥Ⓞ AE Ⓞ VISA
Rest 20.00/35.00 and a la carte 26.00/41.00 – 21 rm ☐ ✸86.00/115.00 – ✸✸130.00/170.00.

◆ 12C hotel, set in 19 acres of land with ornamental trout lake; built in country house style of William and Mary; popular for weddings. Magnolia rooms with mahogany furniture. Welsh seasonal fare in chintz dining room.

The Angel, 15 Cross St, NP7 5EN, ℰ (01873) 857121, *mail@angelhotelabergavenny.com*, Fax (01873) 858059, 🍴 – 🕏 🖰 🖥 – 🛗 180. 🐧 🖾 📧 *VISA*
closed 25 December – **Rest** a la carte 16.00/28.80 s. 🍷 ♀ – **30 rm** ⇌ ★60.00 – ★★85.00.
♦ Updated Georgian building with a warm and cosy bar lit by real fire. Impressive public areas; locally renowned afternoon tea. Cocktails taken before dinner. Functional rooms. Stylish restaurant offers classic French and British blend.

The Hardwick, Old Raglan Rd, NP7 9AA, Southeast : 2 m. by A 40 on B 4598 ℰ (01873) 854220, *stephen@thehardwick.co.uk*, Fax (01873) 854623, 🍴 – 🖰 🐧 📧
closed 22-30 January, 2-9 October, 25 December, dinner 26 December, Sunday dinner and Monday except lunch Bank Holidays – **Rest** a la carte 17.95/29.85 ♀.
♦ Unassuming façade belies 'feelgood' interior with beams and wood burner. Talented kitchen: former Walnut Tree owner/chef offers great choice of neat, wholesome, modern dishes.

at Llandewi Skirrid Northeast : 3¼ m. on B 4521 (Skenfrith rd) – ✉ Abergavenny.

The Walnut Tree Inn, NP7 8AW, ℰ (01873) 852797, *francesco@thewalnut treeinn.com*, Fax (01873) 859764, 🍴 – 🖰 🐧 *VISA*
closed Sunday dinner and Monday – **Rest** - Italian - (booking essential) a la carte 23.00/34.00 ♀.
♦ Renowned inn displays work by Welsh artists. A full-flavoured seasonal blend of rustic Italian and Welsh cooking employs best local produce. Booking ahead is essential.

at Nant Derry Southeast : 6½ m. by A 40 off A 4042 – ✉ Abergavenny.

The Foxhunter, NP7 9DN, ℰ (01873) 881101, *info@thefoxhunter.com*, Fax (01873) 881377 – 🕏 🖰 🐧 📧
closed 25-26 December, 2 weeks February, Sunday and Monday – **Rest** 20.00 (lunch) and a la carte 20.00/30.00.
♦ Bright, contemporary feel within flint-stone former 19C station master's house. Light and airy in summer and cosy in winter. Modern menus using fine local ingredients.

at Llanwenarth Northwest : 3 m. on A 40 – ✉ Abergavenny.

Llanwenarth, Brecon Rd, NP8 1EP, ℰ (01873) 810550, *info@llanwenarthhotel.com*, Fax (01873) 811880, ≤, 🍴, 🐧 – 🕏 🖰 🐧 🖾 *VISA*. 🛇
Rest (closed dinner 26 December and 1 January) 12.95 (lunch) and a la carte 21.50/26.40 ♀ – **17 rm** ⇌ ★63.00 – ★★85.00.
♦ Part 16C inn; perches on banks of river Usk, famed for salmon, trout fishing. Most bedrooms have balconies from which to enjoy panoramas of Blorenge Mountain and Usk Valley. Tall-windowed dining room with fine valley views and varied menus.

WALES *(side tab)*

Your opinions are important to us:
please write and let us know about your discoveries and experiences – good and bad!

ABERSOCH Gwynedd 502 503 G 25 Wales G. – ✉ Pwllheli.
Env. : Lleyn Peninsula★★ – Plas-yn-Rhiw★ AC, W : 6 m. by minor roads.
Exc. : Bardsey Island★, SW : 15 m. by A 499 and B 4413 – Mynydd Mawr★, SW : 17 m. by A 499, B 4413 and minor roads.
🏌 Golf Rd ℰ (01758) 712636.
London 265 – Caernarfon 28 – Shrewsbury 101.

Neigwl, Lon Sarn Bach, LL53 7DY, ℰ (01758) 712363, *relax@neigwl.com*, Fax (01758) 712544, ≤ Cardigan Bay – 🖰 🐧 *VISA*. 🛇
closed January – **Rest** (booking essential) (dinner only) 29.00 s. ♀ – **9 rm** (dinner included) ⇌ ★75.00/110.00 – ★★130.00/165.00.
♦ A comfortable, family owned hotel close to town yet with fine sea vistas. Rooms are perfectly neat and individually decorated whilst the lounge is the ideal place to relax. The restaurant overlooks sea and mountains.

at Bwlchtocyn South : 2 m. – ✉ Pwllheli.

Porth Tocyn 🛇, LL53 7BU, ℰ (01758) 713303, *bookings@porthtocyn.fsnet.co.uk*, Fax (01758) 713538, ≤ Cardigan Bay and mountains, 🌊 heated, 🌳, 🎾 – 🕏 🖰 🐧 *VISA*. 🛇
Easter-October – **Rest** (bar lunch Monday-Saturday) (buffet lunch Sunday)/dinner 38.50 – ⇌ 5.75 – **17 rm** ★65.00/107.00 – ★★120.00/184.00.
♦ Originally a row of miners' cottages; family run for three generations and family orientated. A pleasant headland location: panoramas of bay and mountains. Pretty bedrooms. Sunday buffet lunch, described as a family event. Interesting, varied menus.

ABERYSTWYTH *Ceredigion 503* H 26 *Wales G.* – pop. 15 935.

See : *Town*★★ – *The Seafront*★ – *National Library of Wales (Permanent Exhibition*★*)*.
Env. : *Vale of Rheidol*★★ *(Railway*★★ *AC)* – *St. Padarn's Church*★, SE : 1 m. by A 44.
Exc. : *Devil's Bridge (Pontarfynach)*★, E : 12 m. by A 4120 – *Strata Florida Abbey*★ *AC (West Door*★*)*, SE : 15 m. by B 4340 and minor rd.

🏌 *Bryn-y-Mor* ℘ (01970) 615104.
🛈 *Terrace Rd* ℘ (01970) 612125, aberystwythtic@ceredigion.gov.uk.
London 238 – Chester 98 – Fishguard 58 – Shrewsbury 74.

⌂ **Bodalwyn** without rest., Queen's Ave, SY23 2EG, ℘ (01970) 612578, hilary.d@line one.net, Fax (01970) 639261 – ✺, ⅍
closed 24 December-1 January – 8 rm ⌷ ✦35.00/45.00 – ✦✦55.00/65.00.
♦ Victorian house, run enthusiastically and to a very good standard by a young owner. Rooms blend modern and traditional, numbers 3 and 5 being particularly enticing

XX **Le Vignoble,** 31 Eastgate St, SY23 2AR, ℘ (01970) 630800, enquiries@levignoble.co.uk, Fax (01970) 617606 – ✺, ◍◍ VISA, ⅍
closed Christmas, Sunday, Monday and Tuesday lunch – **Rest** 16.00 (lunch) and dinner a la carte 21.50/34.00.
♦ Love of things Gallic evident from fine photos of vineyards brightening up the walls. Best local and seasonal produce from small suppliers in modern cooking with French edge.

at Chancery (Rhydgaled) *South : 4 m. on A 487* – ⌧ *Aberystwyth*.

🏨 **Conrah Country House** ॐ, SY23 4DF, ℘ (01970) 617941, enquiries@conrah.co.uk, Fax (01970) 624546, ≼, ⅍, ♨ – ⅜ ✺ P. – 🕿 50. ◍◍ VISA, ⅍
Rest 25.00/30.00 (dinner) and lunch a la carte 16.45/26.95 – **17 rm** ⌷ ✦65.00/95.00 – ✦✦160.00.
♦ Part 18C mansion, elegant inside and out. Lovely grounds, kitchen garden, pleasant views. Airy country house rooms include three very smart new ones in converted outbuildings. Scenic vistas greet restaurant diners.

BARMOUTH (Abermaw) *Gwynedd 502 503* H 25 *Wales G.* – pop. 2 251.

See : *Town*★ – *Bridge*★ *AC*.
Env. : *Snowdonia National Park*★★★.

🛈 *The Old Library, Station Rd* ℘ (01341) 280787, barmouth.tic@gwynedd.gov.uk.
London 231 – Chester 74 – Dolgellau 10 – Shrewsbury 67.

🏨 **Bae Abermaw,** Panorama Rd, LL42 1DQ, ℘ (01341) 280550, enquiries@baeaber maw.com, Fax (01341) 280346, ≼ Mawddach estuary and Cardigan Bay, ℛ – ✺ P. ◍◍ VISA. ⅍
Rest (closed Monday) (dinner only) a la carte 26.50/34.50 – **14 rm** ⌷ ✦83.00/107.00 – ✦✦132.00/158.00.
♦ Victorian house with inspiring views over Cardigan Bay. Classic façade allied to minimalist interior, typified by an uncluttered, airy lounge. Brilliant white bedrooms. Pleasant, comfy restaurant with appealing modern menus.

⌂ **Llwyndû Farmhouse** ॐ, LL42 1RR, Northwest : 2 ¼ m. on A 496 ℘ (01341) 280144, intouch@llwyndu-farmhouse.co.uk, ℛ – ✺ P. ◍◍ VISA
closed 24-26 December – **Rest** (by arrangement) 23.95 – **6 rm** ⌷ ✦49.00 – ✦✦82.00.
♦ Characterful part 16C farmhouse and 18C barn conversion on a hillside overlooking Cardigan Bay. Bunk beds and four-posters amidst stone walls and wood beams. An eclectic style of home-cooking using traditional regional ingredients.

BARRY (Barri) *Vale of Glamorgan 503* K 29 – pop. 50 661.

🏌 *RAF St Athan* ℘ (01446) 751043.
🛈 *The Promenade, The Triangle, Barry Island* ℘ (01446) 747111, tourism@valeofglamor gan.gov.uk.
London 167 – Cardiff 10 – Swansea 39.

🏨 **Egerton Grey Country House** ॐ, CF62 3BZ, Southwest : 4 ½ m. by B 4226 and A 4226 and Porthkerry rd via Cardiff Airport ℘ (01446) 711666, info@egertongrey.co.uk, Fax (01446) 711690, ≼, ℛ – ✺ ✆ P. ◍◍ AE VISA
Rest 27.50/33.00 s. – **10 rm** ⌷ ✦90.00 – ✦✦120.00/160.00.
♦ A secluded country house with a restful library and drawing room. Part Victorian rectory. Bedrooms overlook gardens with views down to Porthkerry Park and the sea. Intimate dining room with paintings and antiques.

🏨 **Express by Holiday Inn** without rest., Port Rd, Cardiff Airport, CF62 3BT, Southwest : 4 ¼ m. by B 4226 and A 4226 on Porthkerry rd ℘ (01446) 711117, gm@exhicardiffair port.co.uk, Fax (01446) 713290 – ⅜ ✺ ▤ ✆ ⅋ P. – 🕿 25. ◍◍ AE ⓞ VISA
111 rm ✦59.95/79.95 – ✦✦59.95/79.95.
♦ Great new accommodation for plane spotters: rooms on 2nd and 3rd floors have fine views of the runway. Breakfast offered from as early as 4am. Good, modern family rooms.

BEAUMARIS *Anglesey* 502 503 H 24 *Wales G. – pop. 1 513.*

See : *Town★★ – Castle★* AC.
Env. : *Anglesey★★ – Penmon Priory★, NE : 4 m. by B 5109 and minor roads.*
Exc. : *Plas Newydd★* AC, SW : 7 m. by A 545 and A 4080.
🏌 *Baron Hill* ℰ *(01248) 810231.*
London 253 – Birkenhead 74 – Holyhead 25.

🏠 **Ye Olde Bull's Head Inn,** Castle St, LL58 8AP, ℰ (01248) 810329, *info@bullshea dinn.co.uk, Fax (01248) 811294 –* ✤ 🅿. 🛐 25. 🟥 🆎 *VISA*. ❀
closed 25-26 December and 1 January – *The Brasserie :* Rest (bookings not accepted) a la carte 13.50/21.50 ♀ – (see also *The Loft* below) – **13 rm** ⌕ ✦75.00/77.00 –
✦✦98.50/100.00.
♦ Part 17C inn on the high street. Cosy pubby bar area sets the tone with period charm, brasses and bric-a-brac. Well decorated bedrooms, most named after Dickens characters. Less formal dining facility decorated in an attractive modern style.

🏠 **Bishopsgate House,** 54 Castle St, LL58 8BB, ℰ (01248) 810302, *hazel@johnson-ol lier.freeserve.co.uk, Fax (01248) 810166 –* ✤ 🅿. 🟥 🆎 *VISA*
Rest (booking essential for non-residents) 16.95 and a la carte 24.20/27.20 – **9 rm** ⌕
✦55.00/62.00 – ✦✦85.00.
♦ Georgian townhouse on the high street. Chesterfields in the lounge, a rare Chinese Chippendale staircase and a small bar area. Individually decorated bedrooms. Neatly decorated dining room in keeping with the character of the establishment.

🏠 **Cleifiog** without rest., Townsend, LL58 8BH, ℰ (01248) 811507, *liz@cleifiogbandb.com,*
≤ Menai Strait and Snowdonia, 🌿 – ✤ 📞. 🟥 *VISA*. ❀
closed Christmas - New Year – **3 rm** ⌕ ✦45.00/65.00 – ✦✦65.00/85.00.
♦ Lovely views from this seafront part Georgian house with 16C origins. Comfy, relaxing period style lounge. Bedrooms mix Arts and Crafts with up-to-date style and facilities.

✕✕ **The Loft** (at Ye Olde Bull's Head Inn H.), Castle St, LL58 8AP, ℰ (01248) 810329,
Fax (01248) 811294 – ✤. 🟥 🆎 *VISA*
closed Sunday – Rest (dinner only) 35.00/37.50.
♦ In contrast to the inn, The Loft has a contemporary feel and style engendered by bold décor and modern lighting. Modish menus: a fresh approach to traditional ingredients.

If breakfast is included the ⌕ symbol appears after the number of rooms.

BEDDGELERT *Gwynedd* 502 503 H 24 *Wales G. – pop. 535.*

Env. : *Snowdonia National Park★★★ – Aberglaslyn Pass★, S : 1½ m. on A 498.*
London 249 – Caernarfon 13 – Chester 73.

🏠 **Sygun Fawr Country House** ❧, LL55 4NE, Northeast : ¾ m. by A 498 ℰ (01766) 890258, *sygunfawr@aol.com, Fax (01766) 890258,* ≤ Snowdon and Gwynant valley, 🌿, 🏊 –
✤ 🅿. 🟥 *VISA*
closed January – Rest (booking essential to non-residents) (dinner only) 22.00 s. – **11 rm**
⌕ ✦74.00/74.00.
♦ Part 16C stone built house in Gwynant Valley. Superbly located, an elevated spot which affords exceptional views of Snowdon, particularly from double deluxe rooms. Dine in new conservatory extension or traditional room in house.

BENLLECH *Anglesey* 502 503 H 24.
London 277 – Caernarfon 17 – Chester 76 – Holyhead 29.

🏠 **Hafod** without rest., Amlwch Rd, LL74 8SR, ℰ (01248) 853092, 🌿 – ✤ 📞. ❀
closed 25 December – **4 rm** ⌕ ✦40.00 – ✦✦60.00.
♦ Sensitively renovated 19C house with lawned garden and views of sea and bays. Comfortably finished bedrooms, well maintained by the charming owner.

BETWS GARMON *Gwynedd.*
Cardiff 194.5 – Betws-y-Coed 25 – Caernarfon 5.

🏠 **Betws Inn,** LL54 7YY, Northwest : 1 m. on A 4085 ℰ (01286) 650324, *stay@betwys-inn.co.uk,* 🌿 – ✤ 📞. *VISA*. ❀
Rest (by arrangement) 17.95/22.95 – **3 rm** ⌕ ✦50.00/60.00 – ✦✦60.00/70.00.
♦ Former village coaching inn with characterful beamed lounge. After a day's trekking, sleep in well-priced, good sized rooms with quality wood furniture and smart fabrics. Home-cooked local produce proudly served in rustic dining room.

WALES

BETWS-Y-COED Conwy 502 503 I 24 Wales G. – pop. 848.

See : Town★.

Env. : Snowdonia National Park★★★.

Exc. : Blaenau Ffestiniog★ (Llechwedd Slate Caverns★ AC), SW : 10½ m. by A 470 – The Glyders and Nant Ffrancon (Cwm Idwal★), W : 14 m. by A 5.

🛅 Clubhouse ☎ (01690) 710556.

🖪 Royal Oak Stables ☎ (01690) 710426.

London 226 – Holyhead 44 – Shrewsbury 62.

🏛 **Tan-y-Foel Country House** ⌂, LL26 0RE, East : 2 1/2 m. by A 5, A 470 and Capel Garmon rd on Llanrwst rd ☎ (01690) 710507, enquiries@tyfhotel.co.uk, Fax (01690) 710681, ≤ Vale of Conwy and Snowdonia, 🌣 – ⇆ 🄿 🕭 VISA. ⌘
Restricted opening December-January – **Rest** (booking essential) (dinner only) 42.00 ♀ –
6 rm ⌚ ✦99.00/155.00 – ✦✦140.00/160.00.
✦ Part 16C country house, stylishly decorated in modern vein. Stunning views of Vale of Conwy and Snowdonia. Lovely rooms revel in the quality and elegance of the establishment. Contemporary rear room makes up the restaurant.

🏛 **Henllys The Old Courthouse** without rest., Old Church Rd, LL24 0AL, ☎ (01690) 710534, gillian.bidwell@btconnect.com, Fax (01690) 710884, 🌣 – ⇆ 🄿 🕭 VISA. ⌘
closed January and 25-26 December – 9 rm ⌚ ✦30.00/84.00 – ✦✦60.00/84.00.
✦ Former Victorian magistrates' court and police station overlooking the River Conwy. Comfortable rooms with homely feel. Police memorabilia all around.

↑ **Bryn Bella** without rest., Lôn Muriau, Llanrwst Rd, LL24 0HD, Northeast : 1 m. by A 5 on A 470 ☎ (01690) 710627, welcome@bryn-bella.co.uk, ≤ Vale of Conwy – ⇆ 🖔 🄿 🕭 VISA. ⌘
closed Christmas-New Year – 5 rm ⌚ ✦45.00 – ✦✦55.00/60.00.
✦ Smart guesthouse in an elevated position with splendid views of the Vale of Conwy. Affordable accommodation; modern colours. Convenient base for touring the Snowdonia region.

↑ **Pengwern** without rest., Allt Dinas, LL24 0HF, Southeast : 1 ½ m. on A 5 ☎ (01690) 710480, gwawr.pengwern@btopenworld.com, 🌣 – ⇆ 🄿 🕭 VISA. ⌘
closed Christmas – 3 rm ⌚ ✦50.00/70.00 – ✦✦68.00/80.00.
✦ Former Victorian artist 'colony' with a comfy, homely and stylish lounge, warmly decorated breakfast room and individually appointed bedrooms, two with superb valley vistas.

↑ **Llannerch Goch** ⌂ without rest., Capel Garmon, LL26 0RL, East : 2 m. by A 5 and A 470 on Capel Gorman rd ☎ (01690) 710261, eirian@betwsycoed.co.uk, ≤, 🌣 – ⇆ 🄿. ⌘
February-October – 3 rm ⌚ ✦40.00/45.00 – ✦✦58.00/64.00.
✦ Very peaceful 17C country house with original features. Pleasant sun lounge overlooking the garden. Set in four idyllic acres. Cosy sitting room, smart bedrooms.

↑ **Glyntwrog House** without rest., LL24 0SG, Southeast : ¾ m. on A 5 ☎ (01690) 710930, glyntwrog@betws-y-coed.org, 🌣 – ⇆ 🄿 🕭 VISA. ⌘
4 rm ⌚ ✦38.00/42.00 – ✦✦56.00/66500.
✦ Victorian stone house set just off the road and surrounded by woodland. Pleasantly renovated to a homely and attractive standard. Comfortable bedrooms in varying sizes.

at Penmachno Southwest : 4¾ m. by A 5 on B 4406 – ✉ Betws-y-Coed.

↑ **Penmachno Hall** ⌂, LL24 0PU, on Ty Mawr rd ☎ (01690) 760410, stay@penmachno hall.co.uk, Fax (01690) 760410, ≤, 🌣 – ⇆ 🄿 🕭 VISA. ⌘
closed Christmas-New Year – **Rest** (by arrangement) (communal dining) 28.00/30.00 – 3 rm ⌚ ✦90.00 – ✦✦90.00.
✦ Former rectory built in 1862 with neat garden; super country setting. Sunny morning room where breakfast is served. Modern, bright bedrooms personally styled by the owners. Tasty home-cooking in deep burgundy communal dining room.

BODUAN Gwynedd 502 503 G 25 – see Pwllheli.

BONVILSTON (Tresimwn) Vale of Glamorgan 503 J 29.

London 164 – Cardiff 9 – Swansea 25.

↑ **The Great Barn** ⌂ without rest., Lillypot, CF5 6TR, Northwest : 1 m. by A 48 off Tre-Dodridge rd ☎ (01446) 781010, nina@greatbarn.com, Fax (01446) 781185, ≤, 🌣 – ⇆ 🄿. 🕭 VISA
closed 25 December – 6 rm ⌚ ✦35.00/38.00 – ✦✦60.00/65.00.
✦ Converted corn barn, personally run in simple country home style. Pleasant antiques, pine and white furniture in rooms. Great traditional breakfasts; relax in conservatory.

WALES

BRECON (Aberhonddu) *Powys 503* J 28 *Wales G. – pop. 7 901.*

See : *Town★ – Cathedral★ AC – Penyclawdd Court★*.

Env. : *Brecon Beacons National Park★★*.

Exc. : *Llanthony Priory★★, S : 8 m. of Hay-on-Wye by B 4423 – Dan-yr-Ogof Showcaves★ AC, SW : 20 m. by A 40 and A 4067 – Pen-y-Fan★★, SW : by A 470*.

🏌 *Cradoc, Penoyre Park ℰ (01874) 623658 –* 🏌 *Newton Park, Llanfaes ℰ (01874) 622004.*

🗿 *Cattle Market Car Park ℰ (01874) 622485, brectic@powys.gov.uk.*

London 171 – Cardiff 40 – Carmarthen 31 – Gloucester 65.

⭡ **Canal Bank** without rest., LD3 7HG, off B 4601 over bridge on unmarked rd ℰ (01874) 623464, *enquiries@accommodation-breconbeacons.co.uk*, � – ✖ **P**. ⚘
closed Christmas – 3 rm ☲ ✿45.00/60.00 – ✿✿79.00.
* Delightfully stylish and peaceful 18C canalside cottage. Charming garden with pergola and access to Usk. Organic breakfasts. Immaculate rooms with extra attention to detail.

⭡ **Cantre Selyf** without rest., 5 Lion St, LD3 7AU, ℰ (01874) 622904, *enquiries@cantrese lyf.co.uk, Fax (01874) 622315*, � – ✖ **P**. ⚘
closed December-January – 3 rm ☲ ✿48.00 – ✿✿70.00.
* An engaging 18C townhouse in town centre. Georgian fireplaces and beamed ceilings. Lovely quiet rooms with period feel. Attractive rear walled garden with sun house.

⭡ **Felin Glais** ⚘, Aberyscir, LD3 9NP, West : 4 m. by Upper Chapel rd off Cradoc Golf Course rd turning right immediately after bridge ℰ (01874) 623107, *felin glais@kerne.co.uk, Fax (01874) 623107*, � – 📺 **P**.
Rest (by arrangement) (communal dining) – 4 rm ☲ ✿60.00 – ✿✿70.00.
* Mid-17C house in a tranquil hamlet with a wonderfully relaxing sitting room and comfy rooms that boast many thoughtful extras, such as cosy seating areas with magazines. Seriously considered menus: fresh, country cooking on large-choice menus.

⭡ **Coach House**, Orchard St, LD3 8AN, ℰ (07050) 691216, *info@coachhousebrecon.co.uk, Fax (07050) 691217*, � – ✖ 📺 📞 **P**. **⓪** **VISA**. ⚘
Rest (dinner only) a la carte 19.00/28.95 – 8 rm ☲ ✿35.00/50.00 – ✿✿55.00/70.00.
* 17C building just over Usk Bridge a short walk from town. Rear garden and terrace. The bedrooms are modern, co-ordinated and well-equipped, with stylish fabrics and Wi-Fi. Dining room offers best local produce on a classic Welsh base.

🍴 **Felin Fach Griffin** with rm, Felin Fach, LD3 0UB, Northeast : 4¾ m. by B 4602 off A 470 ℰ (01874) 620111, *enquiries@eatdrinksleep.ltd.uk, Fax (01874) 620120*, 🍽, � – ✖ rm, **P**. **⓪** **VISA**
closed 25-26 December – **Rest** (closed Monday lunch except Bank Holidays) 27.90 (dinner) and a la carte 17.00/30.00 ♀ – 7 rm ☲ ✿67.50 – ✿✿97.50/125.00.
* Terracotta hued traditional pub, once a farmhouse. Characterful interior boasts log fire with sofas, antiques and reclaimed furniture. Modern menus and smart bedrooms.

BRIDGEND (Pen-y-Bont) *Bridgend 503* J 29 – *pop. 39 427.*

🗿 *McArthur Glen Design Outlet Village, The Derwen, junction 36, M 4 ℰ (01656) 654906, bridgendtic@bridgend.gov.uk.*

London 177 – Cardiff 20 – Swansea 23.

at Coychurch (Llangrallo) *East : 2¼ m. by A 473 – ✉ Bridgend.*

🏨 **Coed-y-Mwstwr** ⚘, CF35 6AF, North : 1 m. by Bryn Rd ℰ (01656) 860621, *enqui ries@coed-y-mwstwr.com, Fax (01656) 863122*, ≼, 🛏, ≘s, ⌶ heated, �, ⚖, ✗ – ⫚ ✖ 📞 **P** – ⚒ 175. **⓪** **AE** **VISA**. ⚘
Eliots : Rest 12.95/28.95 – 28 rm ☲ ✿105.00 – ✿✿195.00, 2 suites.
* Meaning "whispering trees", this Victorian mansion overlooks Vale of Glamorgan and woodland. Local golf courses, comfortable lounge bar. Sizeable country house rooms. Well-kept restaurant with a formal, traditional ambience.

at Southerndown *Southwest : 5½ m. by A 4265 on B 4524 – ✉ Bridgend.*

🍴🍴 **Frolics**, Beach Rd, CF32 0RP, ℰ (01656) 880127, *dougwindsor34@aol.com* – ✖ **P**. **⓪** **VISA**
closed Sunday dinner and Monday – **Rest** 13.95/16.95 and a la carte 20.30/30.30 ♀.
* Personally run restaurant named after 17C ship wrecked on nearby coast. Cosy neigh-bourhood style. Inventive touches enliven menus that make full use of area's ingredients.

at Laleston *West : 2 m. on A 473 – ✉ Bridgend.*

🏨 **Great House**, High St, CF32 0HP, on A 473 ℰ (01656) 657644, *enquiries@great-house-laleston.co.uk, Fax (01656) 668892*, 🛏, ≘s, 🌫 – ✖ **P**. **⓪** **AE** **⓪** **VISA**. ⚘
Rest – (see **Leicester's** below) – 19 rm ☲ ✿90.00 – ✿✿140.00.
* 15C Grade II listed building, believed to have been a gift from Elizabeth I to the Earl of Leicester. Personally run - attention to detail particularly evident in the rooms.

XX **Leicester's** (at Great House H.), High St, CF32 0HP, on A 473 $\mathscr{E}$ (01656) 657644, *enquiries@great-house-laleston.co.uk*, Fax (01656) 668892, 舜 – ⤋ 🅿, ⑩ ⟨ AE ⑩ VISA, ⟨
closed Sunday dinner – **Rest** 14.95 (lunch) and a la carte 15.65/30.50.
◆ Comfortable dining courtesy of exposed beams, original windows and owner's personal touches and nuances. Imaginative, seasonal menus using finest local and Welsh produce.

BUILTH WELLS (Llanfair-ym-Muallt) *Powys* 503 J 27.
London 191.5 – Cardiff 63.5 – Brecon 20.5.

XX **The Drawing Room** with rm, Twixt Cwmbach, Newbridge-on-Wye, LD2 3RT, North : 3 ½ m. on A 470 $\mathscr{E}$ (01982) 552493, *post@the-drawing-room.co.uk*, 舜 – ⤋ ⟨ 🅿 ⟨ 8. ⑩ VISA
closed 2 weeks January, Sunday and Monday – **Rest** (booking essential) a la carte 31.50/41.95 ₤ – **3 rm** ⟨ (dinner included) ✦120.00 – ✦✦190.00/220.00.
◆ Delightful Georgian house with 19C additions: sumptuous country style at every turn. Carefully sourced seasonal menu with distinct French classic emphasis. Very stylish rooms.

BWLCHTOCYN *Gwynedd* 502 503 G 25 – *see Abersoch.*

CAERNARFON *Gwynedd* 502 503 H 24 *Wales G. – pop. 9 695.*
See : *Town*★★ – *Castle*★★★ *AC.*
Env. : *Snowdonia National Park*★★★.
🛆 Aberforeshore, Llanfaglan $\mathscr{E}$ (01286) 673783.
🛈 Oriel Pendeitsh, Castle St. $\mathscr{E}$ (01286) 672232, *caernarfon.tic@gwynedd.gov.uk.*
London 249 – Birkenhead 76 – Chester 68 – Holyhead 30 – Shrewsbury 85.

🏛 **Celtic Royal,** Bangor St, LL55 1AY, $\mathscr{E}$ (01286) 674477, *admin@celtic-royal.co.uk*, Fax (01286) 674139, ⎙, 🕿, 🖥 – 🕙 ⤋ & 🅿 – ⚖ 250. ⑩ AE VISA. ⟨
Rest (bar lunch)/dinner 16.95 and a la carte 17.85/26.15 s. – **110 rm** ⟨ ✦77.00 – ✦✦110.00.
◆ Updated Victorian hotel which now caters primarily for the corporate market. Good access to Holyhead and Bangor. Strong leisure and conference facilities. Modern rooms. Comfortable, split-level restaurant with classic style.

at Llanrug *East : 3 m. on A 4086 –* ⊠ *Caernarfon.*

↑ **Plas Tirion Farm** ⟨ without rest., LL55 4PY, South : 1 m. by Ffordd Glanmoelyn Rd on Waenfawr rd $\mathscr{E}$ (01286) 673190, *cerid@plastirion.plus.com*, Fax (01286) 671883, 舜, 🐾 – ⤋ 🅿, ⟨
April-October – **3 rm** ⟨ ✦30.00/40.00 – ✦✦60.00.
◆ Stone built farmhouse on dairy farm surrounded by 300 acres. Relaxing, homely sitting room. Generous portions served in airy breakfast room with log burner. Cottagey rooms.

at Saron *Southwest : 3¼ m. by A 487 on Saron rd –* ⊠ *Caernarfon.*

↑ **Pengwern** ⟨, LL54 5UH, Southwest : ¼ m. $\mathscr{E}$ (01286) 831500, *janepengwern@aol.com*, Fax (01286) 830741, 舜, 🐾 – 🅿 AE VISA. ⟨
April-October – **Rest** (by arrangement) 22.50 – **3 rm** ⟨ ✦49.00 – ✦✦70.00.
◆ Charming farmhouse on working farm, picturesquely situated between mountains and sea. Snowdonia views. Neat and tidy guest areas. Bedrooms of traditional quality. Owner serves fresh, robust farmhouse cuisine including home-reared beef and lamb.

CAERSWS *Powys* 502 503 J 26.
London 194 – Aberystwyth 39 – Chester 63 – Shrewsbury 42.

at Pontdolgoch *Northwest : 1½ m. on A 470 –* ⊠ *Newtown.*

🛏 **Talkhouse** with rm, SY17 5JE, $\mathscr{E}$ (01686) 688919, *info@talkhouse.co.uk*, 🍽, 舜 – ⤋ 🅿, ⑩ VISA. ⟨
closed first 2 weeks January – **Rest** *(closed Sunday dinner and Monday)* (booking essential Tuesday, Wednesday and Thursday lunch in winter) a la carte 21.95/29.50 ₤ – **3 rm** ⟨ ✦70.00 – ✦✦95.00.
◆ Owner-run 17C coaching inn on Aberystwyth-Shrewsbury road. Ornate rustic bar. Dining room opening onto terrace and gardens. Locally-based blackboard menu. Stylish bedrooms.

CARDIFF (Caerdydd) *Cardiff* 503 K 29 *Wales G.* – pop. 292 150.

See : *City*★★★ – *National Museum and Gallery*★★★ *AC (Evolution of Wales*★★ , *Picture galleries*★★) BY – *Castle*★ *AC* BZ – *Llandaff Cathedral*★ AV B – *Cardiff Bay*★ *(Techniquest*★ *AC)* AX.

Env. : *Museum of Welsh Life*★★ *AC, St. Fagan's, W : 5 m. by A 4161* AV – *Castell Coch*★★ *AC, NW : 5 m. by A 470* AV.

Exc. : *Caerphilly Castle*★★ *AC, N : 7 m. by A 469* AV – *Dyffryn Gardens*★ *AC, W : 8 m. by A 48* AX.

🏌 *Dinas Powis, Old Highwalls* ✆ *(029) 2051 2727,* AX.

✈ *Cardiff (Wales) Airport :* ✆ *(01446) 711111, SW : 8 m. by A 48* AX – **Terminal :** *Central Bus Station.*

🛈 *The Old Library, The Hayes* ✆ *(029) 2022 7281.*

London 155 – Birmingham 110 – Bristol 46 – Coventry 124.

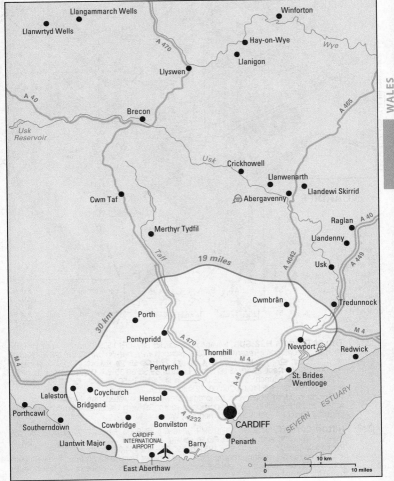

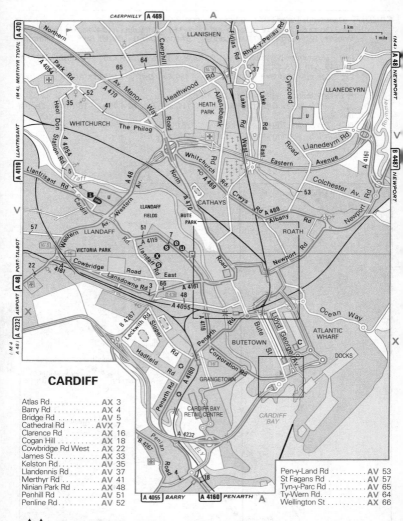

CARDIFF

Atlas Rd. . . . . AX 3
Barry Rd . . . . AX 4
Bridge Rd . . . . AV 5
Cathedral Rd . . . . AVX 7
Clarence Rd . . . . AX 16
Cogan Hill . . . . AX 18
Cowbridge Rd West . . AX 22
James St. . . . . AX 33
Kelston Rd. . . . . AV 35
Llandennis Rd . . . . AV 37
Merthyr Rd . . . . AV 41
Ninian Park Rd . . . . . . AX 48
Penhill Rd . . . . AV 51
Penline Rd . . . . AV 52

Pen-y-Land Rd . . . . AV 53
St Fagans Rd . . . . AV 57
Tyn-y-Parc Rd . . . . AV 65
Ty-Wern Rd. . . . . AV 64
Wellington St . . . . AX 66

The St David's H. & Spa, Havannah St, Cardiff Bay, CF10 5SD, South : 1 ¾ m. by Bute St ℘ (029) 2045 4045, *reservations.stdavids@roccofortehotels.com, Fax (029) 2031 3075,* ≤, 佘, ⑫, ƒ₆, ⇔, ⊠ – ﹪ ✝ ▤ ℃ ₺ ℙ – ₳ 270. 🆖 🆎 ⓪ *VISA* . ⅜   CU a
🐾 *Tides Grill :* Rest 22.50/35.00 and a la carte 35.50/58.50 ♀ – *Waves :* Rest (booking essential) (buffet lunch)/dinner 35.00 and a la carte 35.50/58.50 – ☷ 17.50 – **120 rm** ✝110.00/260.00 – ✝✝110.00/260.00, 12 suites.
♦ Striking modern hotel with panoramic views across waterfront. High-tech meeting rooms and fitness club. Well-proportioned rooms, all with balconies, in minimalist style. Informal Tides Grill. Welsh sourced menus at Waves.

Hilton Cardiff, Kingsway, CF10 3HH, ℘ (0800) 8568000, *Fax (029) 2064 6333,* ƒ₆, ⇔, ⊠ – ✝⇔ rm, ▤ ₺ ℙ – ₳ 340. 🆖 🆎 ⓪ *VISA* . ⅜   BZ x
Rest 16.95/26.50 s. ♀ – ☷ 17.95 – **193 rm** ✝90.00 – ✝✝104.00, 4 suites.
♦ State-of-the-art meeting rooms and leisure facilities feature in this imposingly modern corporate hotel. Spacious, comfy bedrooms boast fine views of castle or City Hall. Popular menu in conservatory-style restaurant.

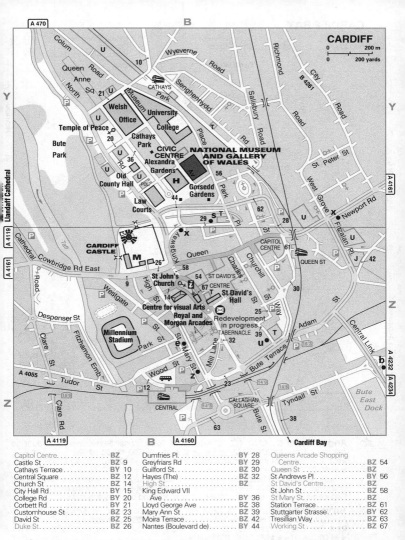

CARDIFF

0 — 200 m
0 — 200 yards

Park Plaza, Greyfriars Rd, CF10 3AL, ☎ (029) 2011 1111, *ppinfo@parkplazahotels.co.uk,* Fax (029) 2011 1112, 斎, ☻, ₤₺, ◨ – ⧉ ⤢ ▤ ☏ ₺ – ⤴ 160. ◍ 应 *VISA*   BY **s**
Rest – (see ***Laguna Kitchen and Bar*** below) – 129 rm ⬜ ♥90.00/190.00 – ♥♥100.00/210.00.
  ♦ Central hotel, opened early 2005. Vast leisure centre boasts stainless steel pool. Impressive meeting rooms. Spacious, contemporary bedrooms, with good, up-to-date amenities.

MacDonald Holland House, 24-26 Newport Rd, CF24 0DD, ☎ (0870) 1220020, *reve nue.holland@macdonald-hotels.co.uk, Fax (029) 2048 8894,* ≤, ☻, ₤₺, 🗲, ◨ – ⧉ ⤢ ▤ ☏ ₺ ⇔ ◨ – ⤴ 700. ◍ 应 ◍ *VISA*. ⅍   BY **x**
Rest 18.50/22.00 and a la carte 20.70/34.65 – **160 rm** ⬜ ♥90.00/230.00 – ♥♥126.00/255.00, 5 suites.
  ♦ 14-storey converted office block that opened as an hotel in 2004. Large marbled lobby; spacious busy bar. State-of-the-art gym and therapy rooms. Airy, well-equipped rooms. Modern menus with local produce to fore in informal restaurant.

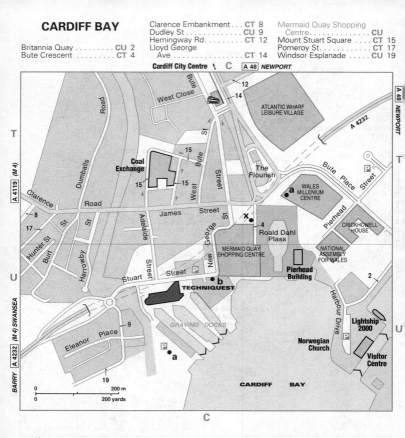

CARDIFF BAY

Cardiff City Centre \ C A 48 NEWPORT

Angel, Castle St, CF10 1SZ, ℘ (029) 2064 9200, *angelreservations@paramount-ho tels.co.uk, Fax (029) 2039 6212* – ❘ ❨ 늏 ❩ ☰ rest, ✆ & ℗ – 🕿 300. ● ▨ ● *VISA* ☆   BZ a
Rest (bar lunch Monday-Saturday)/dinner 21.50 s. ♀ – **100 rm** ☲ ✸180.00/230.00 –
✸✸280.00, 2 suites.
◆ Restored Victorian hotel near Millennium Stadium. Magnificent Waterford Crystal foyer chandelier and sweeping staircase. Some of the airy, well-equipped rooms overlook castle. Elegant and intimate restaurant ideal for both social and business entertaining.

Jurys Cardiff, Mary Ann St, CF10 2JH, ℘ (029) 2034 1441, *cardiff@jurysdoyle.com, Fax (029) 2022 3742* – ❘ ❨ 늏 ❩ ☰ rest, ✆ & ℗ – 🕿 300. ● ▨ ● *VISA* ☆   BZ u
Rest (bar lunch Monday-Saturday)/dinner a la carte 22.40/28.40 s. – ☲ 12.50 – **143 rm**
✸75.00/285.00 – ✸✸85.00/285.00, 3 suites.
◆ Corporate hotel opposite the International Arena. Impressive Victorian-style lobby over-looked by many of the well-equipped bedrooms. Executive rooms have thoughtful extras. Snug dining room with cosy, intimate feel; busy bar alternative.

Royal without rest., 10 St Mary St, CF10 5DW, ℘ (029) 2055 0750, *enquiries@theroyalho telcardiff.com, Fax (029) 2055 0760* – ❘ ❨ 늏 ❩ ☰ 📺 ✆ & – 🕿 120. ● ▨ ● *VISA*   BZ e
64 rm ✸124.00 – ✸✸134.00.
◆ Don't be put off by stark entrance. This central hotel has an extensive continental breakfast buffet and sleek rooms with bold fabrics, crisp Egyptian bedding and DVD library.

Jolyon's without rest., 5 Bute Crescent, Cardiff Bay, CF10 5AN, ℘ (029) 2048 8775, *info@jolyons.co.uk, Fax (029) 2048 8775* – ❨ ✆ ● ▨ ● *VISA* ☆   CT x
6 rm ☲ ✸85.00/140.00 – ✸✸85.00/140.00.
◆ Georgian townhouse within Cardiff Bay's oldest terrace. Boutique style prevails. Rustic, slate-floored bar with log stove, red leather sofas. Light, modern, stylish bedrooms.

Lincoln House without rest., 118 Cathedral Rd, CF11 9LQ, ℘ (029) 2039 5558, *reservations@lincolnhotel.co.uk, Fax (029) 2023 0537* – 🍴 📞 **P**, 🐵 **AE** ⓪ **VISA**. 🛠
AV **e**
23 rm 🖂 🛏60.00/75.00 – 🛏🛏85.00/95.00.
♦ Sympathetically restored Victorian house close to the attractive Bute Gardens. Friendly service by eager-to-please owners. Four-poster room in period style most comfortable.

The Lodge by Macdonald without rest., Wharf Rd East, Tyndall St, CF10 4BB, ℘ (0870) 1942134, *rec.thelodgecardiff@macdonald-hotels.co.uk, Fax (029) 20 488894* – 🛗 🍴 🔲 📞 ⚙ **P**, 🐵 **AE** **VISA**. 🛠
BZ **b**
🖂 8.95 – **100 rm** 🛏85.00/150.00 – 🛏🛏85.00/150.00.
♦ Purpose-built lodge accommodation opened in 2006 close to all amenities. Evening meals delivered to rooms, which are spacious and well equipped with safes and flat screen TVs.

The Town House without rest., 70 Cathedral Rd, CF11 9LL, ℘ (029) 2023 9399, *thetownhouse@msn.com, Fax (029) 2022 3214* – 🍴 **P**, 🐵 **AE** **VISA**
AV **u**
8 rm 🖂 🛏49.50/72.50 – 🛏🛏62.50/82.50.
♦ Carefully restored Victorian house, hospitably run by owners. Light and airy bedrooms have some thoughtful touches and are well appointed: ones at front are the most spacious.

Annedd Lon without rest., 157 Cathedral Rd, CF11 9PL, ℘ (029) 2022 3349, *Fax (029) 2064 0885* – 🍴 **P**, 🐵 **VISA**. 🛠
AV **s**
closed 24-30 December – **6 rm** 🖂 🛏40.00/55.00 – 🛏🛏70.00.
♦ Victorian house with Gothic influences located within a conservation area. Genuine hospitality in a friendly house. Portmeirion China at breakfast. Comfortable bedrooms.

XX **Le Gallois**, 6-10 Romilly Cres, CF11 9NR, ℘ (029) 2034 1264, *info@legallois-ycymro.com, Fax (029) 2023 7911* – 🍴 🔲, 🐵 **VISA**
AX **x**
closed Christmas-New Year and Sunday – **Rest** 19.95/35.00 🍷.
♦ Bright and relaxed restaurant where keen owners provide both the friendly service and the assured modern European cooking. Gallic and Welsh combinations with inventive edge.

XX **Laguna Kitchen and Bar** (at Park Plaza H.), Greyfriars Rd, CF10 3AL, ℘ (029) 2011 1103, *ppc-lkb@parkplazahotels.co.uk*, 🍽 – 🍴 🔲, 🐵 **AE** **VISA**
BY **s**
Rest 15.00/21.00 and a la carte 15.25/31.50 🍷.
♦ On ground floor of hotel, this smart, modern restaurant serves an intriguing mix of local or international dishes.There's a bar, too, with an area of booths for casual dining.

XX **Da Castaldo**, 5 Romilly Crescent, CF11 9NP, ℘ (029) 2022 1905, *Fax (029) 2022 1920* – 🍴 🔲, 🐵 **VISA**
AX **s**
closed Christmas, Sunday and Monday – **Rest** - Italian - 13.50 (lunch) and a la carte 22.40/29.40 🍷.
♦ Appealingly modern ambience in a residential setting; charming owners add to the relaxed air. Tasty Italian influences enhance the classical cooking. Good value lunch.

X **Woods Brasserie**, The Pilotage Building, Stuart St, Cardiff Bay, CF10 5BW, South : 1½ m. by Bute St ℘ (029) 2049 2400, *gilles@woodsbrasserie.com, Fax (029) 2048 1998* – 🔲. 🐵 **AE** ⓪ **VISA**
CU **b**
closed 25-26 December, and Sunday dinner – **Rest** (booking essential at dinner) 12.50/15.50 (lunch) and dinner a la carte 20.40/33.90 🍷 🍷.
♦ Modern brasserie dishes and European influences from an open kitchen. Bay view from the first-floor terrace. Popular for business lunches and bay visitors in the evening.

X **Brazz**, Wales Millennium Centre, Bute Place, Cardiff Bay, CF10 5AL, ℘ (029) 2045 9000, *cardiff@brazz.co.uk, Fax (029) 2044 0270* – 🍴 🔲, 🐵 ⓪ **VISA**
CT **a**
closed 25 December – **Rest** 15.95 and a la carte 21.00/25.20 🍷 🍷.
♦ Based in the stunning Wales Millennium Centre. In two sections: the intimate Club or more spacious Brasserie. Eclectic, daily changing menus offer a modern and classic blend.

at Thornhill North : 5¼ m. by A 470 – AV – on A 469 – 🖂 Cardiff.

New House Country, Thornhill Rd, CF14 9UA, on A 469 ℘ (029) 2052 0280, *enquiries@newhousehotel.com, Fax (029) 2052 0324*, ≤, 🏋, 🌳, 🏊 – 🍴 **P** – 🕍 200. 🐵 **AE** **VISA**. 🛠
Rest 27.95 🍷 – **33 rm** 🖂 🛏98.00 – 🛏🛏195.00, 3 suites.
♦ Extended Edwardian country house in secluded spot commanding views over Vale of Glamorgan. Popular for weddings, ideal for corporate or leisure guests. Traditional rooms. Classically appointed, Regency-styled dining room.

Manor Parc, Thornhill Rd, CF14 9UA, on A 469 ℘ (029) 2069 3723, *enquiry@manorparc.com, Fax (029) 2061 4624*, 🌳, 🎾 – 🍴 📞 **P** – 🕍 120. 🐵 **AE** **VISA**. 🛠
closed 24 and 26 December-2 January – **Rest** (closed Sunday dinner) 16.95/25.00 – **21 rm** 🖂 🛏45.00/72.00 – 🛏🛏95.00/130.00.
♦ Personally run country house set in attractive terraced gardens. Some of the well-appointed rooms have south facing balconies and views over the Bristol Channel. Bright, airy orangery restaurant with Continental menu.

WALES

at Penarth *South : 3 m. by A 4160 – AX – ⊠ Cardiff.*

※※ **The Olive Tree**, 21 Glebe St, CF64 1EE, ℰ (029) 2070 7077 – ⇌, **MO** AE *VISA*
closed Sunday dinner-Monday – **Rest** (dinner only and Sunday lunch) a la carte
21.75/33.75 **s**. 🗒.
* Rewarding discovery tucked away in the centre of town. Relaxing feel augmented by
vivid artwork. Warm, friendly service of good value, seasonal, frequently changing dishes.

at Pentyrch *Northwest : 7 m. by A 4119 – AV – ⊠ Cardiff.*

※※※※ **De Courcey's**, Tyla Morris Ave (off Church Rd), CF15 9QN, South : 1 m. ℰ (029) 2089
2232, dinedecourceys@aol.com, Fax (029) 2089 1949, 🌳 – ⇌ **P** ⇕ 24 – 🏛 100. **MO** AE ⓪
VISA
closed first week January – **Rest** (dinner only and Sunday lunch)/dinner 29.95 and a la carte
30.50/37.50 🗒.
* Long-standing restaurant in an ornately decorated neo-Georgian house. Formal yet
homely atmosphere. Accomplished traditional cuisine, served by smartly attired staff.

CARDIGAN (Aberteifi) *Ceredigion* 503 *G 27 Wales G. – pop. 4 082.*
Env. : *Pembrokeshire Coast National Park*★★.
📇 *Gwbert-on-Sea ℰ (01239) 612035.*
🛈 *Theatr Mwldan, Bath House Rd ℰ (01239) 613230, cardigan.tic@ceredigion.gov.uk.*
London 250 – Carmarthen 30 – Fishguard 19.

at Gwbert on Sea *Northwest : 3 m. on B 4548 – ⊠ Cardigan.*

 Gwbert, SA43 1PP, on B 4548 ℰ (01239) 612638, gwbert@enterprise.net,
Fax (01239) 621474, ≤ Cardigan Bay, 🍴, 🛦, 🖴 – |🛗| ⇌, ☰ rest, 🗨 **P**. **MO** AE ⓪ *VISA*
Rest a la carte 11.50/24.00 **s**. – **17 rm** ⊡ ✟40.00/50.00 – ✟✟97.00.
* Traditional seaside hotel on banks of Teifi with inspiring views of Cardigan Bay. Con-
temporary public areas and smart bar. Well-kept rooms with co-ordinated neutral scheme.
Bistro/brasserie with panoramic views of Pembroke National Park coastline.

CARMARTHEN (Caerfyrddin) *Carmarthenshire* 503 *H 28 Wales G. – pop. 14 648.*
See : *Kidwelly Castle*★ – *National Botanic Garden*★.
🛈 *113 Lammas St ℰ (01267) 231557, tourism@carmarthenshire.gov.uk.*
London 219 – Fishguard 47 – Haverfordwest 32 – Swansea 27.

at Felingwm Uchaf *Northeast : 8 m. by A 40 on B 4310 – ⊠ Carmarthen.*

⋔ **Allt y Golau Uchaf** without rest., SA32 7BB, North : ½ m. on B 4310 ℰ (01267) 290455,
alltygolau@btinternet.com, Fax (01267) 290743, 🌳 – ⇌ **P**. ⅍
closed Christmas – **3 rm** ⊡ ✟40.00 – ✟✟60.00.
* Georgian farmhouse in uplifting elevated position, perfect for walkers. Tranquil garden
bursts into life in spring. Home-baked breakfasts of repute. Neat, pretty, compact rooms.

at Nantgaredig *East : 5 m. on A 40 – ⊠ Carmarthen.*

🕍 **Y Polyn**, SA32 7LH, South : 1 m. by B 4310 on B 4300 ℰ (01267) 290000, ypolyn@hot
mail.com, 🍴, 🌳 – ⇌ **P**. **MO** AE *VISA*. ⅍
closed 2 weeks September or October and 1 week Christmas – **Rest** *(closed Monday,
Saturday lunch and Sunday dinner)* a la carte 20.00/26.00.
* Roadside hostelry enhanced by pleasant summer terrace and stream. Bright, fresh interior with rich, rose-painted walls. Classic, rustic menus with Gallic/Welsh starting point.

CEMAES (Cemais) *Anglesey* 502 503 *G 23 Wales G.*
Env. : *Anglesey*★★.
London 272 – Bangor 25 – Caernarfon 32 – Holyhead 16.

⋔ **Hafod Country House** without rest., LL67 0DS, South : ½ m. on Llanfechell rd
ℰ (01407) 711645, hbr1946@aol.com, ≤, 🌳 – ⇌ **P**. **MO** *VISA*. ⅍
April-September – **3 rm** ⊡ ✟35.00/40.00 – ✟✟55.00/60.00.
* Pleasant Edwardian guesthouse with very welcoming owner on outskirts of picturesque
fishing village. Comfortable sitting room. The bedrooms are in immaculately kept order.

CHANCERY (Rhydgaled) *Ceredigion* 503 *H 26 – see Aberystwyth.*

CHEPSTOW (Cas-gwent) *Monmouthshire* 503 504 M 29 *Wales G.* – *pop. 10 821.*
See : *Town★ – Castle★★ AC.*
Env. : *Wynd Cliff★, N : 2½ m. by A 466 – Caerwent★ (Roman Walls★), SW : 4 m. by A 48.*
🛈 Castle Car Park, Bridge St ℘ (01291) 623772.
London 131 – Bristol 17 – Cardiff 28 – Gloucester 34.

at Shirenewton *East : 5 m. by B 4293 off B 4235 – ⊠ Chepstow.*

⌂ **Coalpits Farm** without rest., NP16 6LS, South : 1 m. on Crick rd ℘ (01291) 641820,
Fax (01291) 641820, 🌾, 🏠 – ⇔ **P**. **MO** **VISA**. 🌼
3 rm ⊑ **†**35.00 – **††**60.00.
♦ Extended stone farmhouse, extraordinarily welcoming owner, horses at the window, woodland walks, charming garden, fine breakfasts, immaculate rooms...what more can we add?

CLYNNOG-FAWR *Gwynedd* 503 G 24.

🏠 **Bryn Eisteddfod** 🦢, LL54 5DA, ℘ (01286) 660431, *info@bryneisteddfod.com*, ≤, 🌾
– ⇔ **P**. **MO** **VISA**. 🌼
closed 23 December-5 January – **Rest** *(closed Monday-Tuesday)* (dinner only) (residents only) 18.00/20.00 **s**. – ⊑ 4.00 – **8 rm** **†**36.00/45.00 – **††**55.00/75.00.
♦ Owner of this 19C former rectory is local guide, full of useful info. Enjoy breakfast in the conservatory, and relax in homely lounge. Front rooms look to bay and mountains. Dining room has views through conservatory and offers tasty home-cooked dishes.

COLWYN BAY (Bae Colwyn) *Conwy* 502 503 I 24 *Wales G.* – *pop. 30 269.*
See : *Welsh Mountain Zoo★ AC (≤★).*
Env. : *Bodnant Garden★★ AC, SW : 6 m. by A 55 and A 470.*
🏌 Abergele, Tan-y-Goppa Rd ℘ (01745) 824034 – 🏌 Old Colwyn, Woodland Ave ℘ (01492) 515581.
🛈 Imperial Buildings, Station Sq, Princes Drive ℘ (01492) 530478 – The Promenade, Rhos-on-Sea ℘ (01492) 548778 (summer only).
London 237 – Birkenhead 50 – Chester 42 – Holyhead 41.

⌂ **Rathlin Country House** without rest., 48 Kings Rd, LL29 7YH, Southwest : 1/4 m. on
B 5113 ℘ (01492) 532173, *enquiries@rathlincountryhouse.co.uk, Fax* (0871) 661 9887, **≋s**,
🏊 heated, 🌾 – ⇔ **℃** **P**. **MO** **VISA**. 🌼
3 rm ⊑ **†**55.00/85.00 – **††**78.00/85.00.
♦ Surrounded by almost an acre of mature gardens, this personally run guesthouse has a large summer pool, inglenook fireplace, oak panelling and slightly modish rooms of style.

🍴 **Pen-y-Bryn,** Pen-y-Bryn Rd, Upper Colwyn Bay, LL29 6DD, Southwest : 1 m. by B 5113
℘ (01492) 534902, *pen.y.bryn@brunningandprice.co.uk, Fax* (01492) 536127, 🌾 – ⇔ **P**.
MO **VISA**. 🌼
closed dinner 25, 26 December and 1 January – **Rest** a la carte 17.00/24.00 ⅋.
♦ Built in the 1970s, with lawned garden and bay view. Spacious interior with large, polished wood tables. Extensive menus feature Welsh dishes with eclectic influences.

at Rhos-on-Sea *Northwest : 1 m. – ⊠ Colwyn Bay.*

⌂ **Plas Rhos** without rest., Cayley Promenade, LL28 4EP, ℘ (01492) 543698, *info@plasr hos.co.uk, Fax* (01492) 540088, ≤, 🌾 – ⇔ **℃** **P**. **MO** **AE** **VISA**. 🌼
closed 20 December-February – **8 rm** ⊑ **†**40.00/60.00 – **††**80.00/90.00.
♦ 19C house on first promenade from Colwyn Bay. Homely front lounge with bay view. Breakfasts feature local butcher's produce. Immaculately kept rooms: superior ones to front.

CONWY *Conwy* 502 503 I 24 *Wales G.* – *pop. 3 847.*
See : *Town★★ – Castle★★ AC – Town Walls★★ – Plas Mawr★★.*
Env. : *Snowdonia National Park★★★ – Bodnant Garden★★ AC, S : 8 m. by A 55 and A 470 – Conwy Crossing (suspension bridge★).*
🏌 Penmaenmawr, Conway Old Rd ℘ (01492) 623330.
🛈 Conwy Castle Visitor Centre ℘ (01492) 592248.
London 241 – Caernarfon 22 – Chester 46 – Holyhead 37.

🏛 **Sychnant Pass House** 🦢, Sychnant Pass Rd, LL32 8BJ, Southwest : 2 m. by A 547 and Sychnant rd, turning right at T junction ℘ (01492) 596868, *bre@sychnant-pass-house.co.uk, Fax* (01492) 585486, ≤, **[**⌂**]**, **≋s**, 🏊, 🌾 – ⇔ **P**. **MO** **VISA**. 🌼
closed January and 24-26 December – **Rest** (booking essential for non-residents) (dinner only) 30.00 ⅋ – **10 rm** ⊑ **†**70.00 – **††**95.00/180.00, 1 suite.
♦ Country house with Snowdonia National Park providing utterly peaceful backdrop. Charming sitting room with attractive décor. Comfy rooms, named after cats from T.S. Elliott. Informal dining room with rustic style and seasonal menus.

🏠🏠 **Castle,** High St, LL32 8DB, ℰ (01492) 582800, *mail@castlewales.co.uk*, Fax (01492) 582300 – ⇆ ⚓ **P** – 🔬 25. **MO** **AE** ***VISA***
closed 26 December – **Shakespeare's** : Rest 14.95/16.95 (lunch) and dinner a la carte 28.65/31.45 – **27 rm** ⊑ ✦70.00/110.00 – ✦✦130.00/150.00, 1 suite.
◆ Two eye-catching ex-coaching inns on site of former Cistercian abbey. Characterful interior with original features in situ. Refurbished rooms have a stylish period feel. Dining room features paintings of Shakespearean characters by John Dawson-Watson.

at Llansanffraid Glan Conwy *Southeast : 2½ m. A 547 on A 470* – ⊠ *Conwy.*

🏠 **Old Rectory Country House** ⤴ *without rest.,* Llanrwst Rd, LL28 5LF, on A 470 ℰ (01492) 580611, *info@oldrectorycountryhouse.co.uk*, Fax (01492) 584555, ≼ Conwy estuary, 🐎 – ⇆ **P**. **MO** ***VISA***
Restricted opening in Winter – **6 rm** ⊑ ✦99.00/129.00 – ✦✦139.00/159.00.
◆ Enjoys fine position on estuary; once home to parish rectors, renovated in Georgian style. House motto: "beautiful haven of peace"; antiques throughout, watercolours abound.

at Tyn-y-Groes *(Gwynedd) South : 4 m. on B 5106* – ⊠ *Conwy.*

🏠 **The Groes Inn,** LL32 8TN, North : 1½ m. on B 5106 ℰ (01492) 650545, *enquiries@the groes.com*, Fax (01492) 650855, ≼, 🏠, 🐎 – **P**. **MO** **AE** **①** ***VISA***. ⤴
Rest 16.95/28.00 and a la carte 15.00/30.00 ⊑ – **14 rm** ⊑ ✦79.00/95.00 – ✦✦95.00/175.00.
◆ Part 16C inn, Wales' first licensed house. Beamed ceilings, log fires and historic bric-a-brac. Immaculately sumptuous bedrooms, some with super rural views. Georgian-style dining room.

COWBRIDGE (Y Bont Faen) *Vale of Glamorgan* 503 J 29 – *pop. 3 616.*
London 170 – Cardiff 15 – Swansea 30.

XX **Huddarts,** 69 High St, CF71 7AF, ℰ (01446) 774645, Fax (01446) 772215 – ⇆ . **MO** ***VISA***
closed 1 week spring, 1 week autumn, 26 December-8 January, Sunday dinner and Monday
– Rest a la carte 27.15/31.85.
◆ Intimate, family run restaurant located on high street of this ancient market town. Welsh tapestries on wall. Skilfully executed traditional dishes with modern influences.

COYCHURCH (Llangrallo) *Bridgend* 503 J 29 – *see Bridgend.*

CRICCIETH *Gwynedd* 502 503 H 25 *Wales G. – pop. 1 826.*
Env. : *Lleyn Peninsula*★★ *– Ffestiniog Railway*★★.
🏌 *Ednyfed Hill* ℰ (01766) 522154.
London 249 – Caernarfon 17 – Shrewsbury 85.

🏠 **Mynydd Ednyfed Country House** ⤴, Caernarfon Rd, LL52 0PH, Northwest : ¾ m.
on B 4411 ℰ (01766) 523269, *mynedd-ednyfed@criccieth.net*, Fax (01766) 522929, ≼, 🐎,
⤴ – ⇆ **P**. **MO** ***VISA***
closed 22 December-5 January – Rest (dinner only) a la carte approx 24.40 – **9 rm** ⊑
✦50.00/70.00 – ✦✦100.00.
◆ Idyllically located 17C country house in eight acres of gardens and woods overlooking Tremadog Bay. Refurbished lounge bar. Airy conservatory for breakfasts. Homely rooms. Small, cosy, comfortable dining room.

CRICKHOWELL (Crucywel) *Powys* 503 K 28 *Wales G.*
Env. : *Brecon Beacons National Park*★★.
Exc. : *Llanthony Priory*★★, *NE : 10 m. by minor roads.*
🛈 *Beaufort Chambers, Beaufort St* ℰ (01873) 812105.
London 169 – Abergavenny 6 – Brecon 14 – Cardiff 40 – Newport 25.

🏠🏠 **Gliffaes Country House** ⤴, NP8 1RH, West : 3 ¾ m. by A 40 ℰ (01874) 730371, *calls@gliffaeshotel.com*, Fax (01874) 730463, ≼, 🐟, 🎾, ⤴ – ⇆ **P** – 🔬 40. **MO** **AE** **①** ***VISA***. ⤴
closed 2-30 January – Rest (light lunch Monday-Saturday)/dinner 24.50/30.75 s. ⊑ – **23 rm**
⊑ ✦80.00/100.00 – ✦✦220.00.
◆ 19C country house and gardens on banks of Usk, offering great tranquillity. Welcoming bar, lounge and conservatory. Popular for outdoor pursuits. Luxuriously individual rooms. Bold, country house dining room has pleasant garden views.

Bear, High St, NP8 1BW, ℰ (01873) 810408, *bearhotel@aol.com*, Fax (01873) 811696, ⟵ – ⤫ ⟵ ⓟ – ⚿ 50. ⓜ ⒜ⓔ *VISA*
Rest (in bar) a la carte 20.00/35.00 ♀ – (see also **The Restaurant** below) – **32 rm** �

🛏65.00/115.00 – 🛏🛏80.00/150.00, 2 suites.
◆ Imposing, part 15C former coaching inn with maze of public areas. Bustling bar and lounges. Good conference facilities. Plush, spacious bedrooms with individual furnishings. Tried-and-tested, hearty bar menus.

Ty Croeso ⟝, The Dardy, NP8 1PU, West : 1½ m. by A 4077 off Llangynidr rd ℰ (01873) 810573, *info@ty-croeso.co.uk*, Fax (01873) 810573, ≤, ⟵ – ⤫ ⓟ, ⓜ ⒜ⓔ *VISA*. ⟱
Rest (dinner only and lunch July-August) 18.00 and a la carte 17.75/27.00 ♀ – **8 rm** ⊡

🛏42.00/50.00 – 🛏🛏68.00/85.00.
◆ Small hotel of Welsh stone, originally part of a Victorian workhouse. Personally run by pleasant owners. Large bar with log fire. Neatly designed rooms have rewarding views. Interesting menus feature well-sourced ingredients.

Glangrwyney Court, NP8 1ES, South : 2 m. on A 40 ℰ (01873) 811288, *info@glan court.co.uk*, Fax (01873) 810317, ⟵, ⟱ – ⤫ ⓟ, ⓜ *VISA*. ⟱
Rest (by arrangement) 30.00 – **5 rm** ⊡ 🛏50.00/80.00 – 🛏🛏65.00/95.00.
◆ Spacious Georgian house with sizeable garden and warm welcome. Large front lounge in chintz with antiques and trinkets. Pleasantly cluttered, well-kept rooms.

The Restaurant (at Bear H.), High St, NP2 1BN, ℰ (01873) 810408, *bearhotel@aol.com*, Fax (01873) 811696 – ⤫ ⓟ, ⓜ ⒜ⓔ *VISA*
closed Monday – Rest (dinner only and Sunday lunch) a la carte 23.45/30.00 ♀.
◆ Charming dining rooms - with polite service, wide-ranging menus employing classical base underpinned by Welsh ingredients - are a sedate option to the ever busy bar.

Nantyffin Cider Mill Inn, Brecon Rd, NP8 1SG, West : 1½ m. on A 40 ℰ (01873) 810775, *info@cidermill.co.uk*, ⟵ – ⓟ, ⓜ ⒜ⓔ *VISA*
closed Monday except Bank Holidays – Rest 16.95 and a la carte 12.95/30.00 ♀.
◆ Converted 16C cider mill, its working parts still in situ. Choose between bars or Mill Room. Local farm meat, fish and - yes - cider on offer on Drovers menu or blackboard.

CROSSGATES *Powys* 503 J 27 – *see Llandrindod Wells.*

CWMBRAN (Cwmbrân) *Torfaen* 503 K 29 – *pop. 47 254.*
London 149 – Bristol 35 – Cardiff 17 – Newport 5.

Parkway, Cwmbran Drive, NP44 3UW, South : 1 m. by A 4051 ℰ (01633) 871199, *enqui ries@parkwayhotel.co.uk*, Fax (01633) 869160, 🛢, ☎, 🔳 – ⤫, 🍽 rest, ⚹ ⓟ – ⚿ 500. ⓜ ⒜ⓔ ⓞ *VISA*
Ravello's : Rest (dinner only and Sunday lunch)/dinner 19.95 and a la carte 20.05/29.85 **s.** – ⊡ 13.95 – **69 rm** 🛏90.00/110.00 – 🛏🛏100.00/125.00, 1 suite.
◆ Purpose-built hotel aimed at the business traveller with extensive conference facilities. Spacious lounge. Smart, well-kept bedrooms benefit from refurbishment. Small, comfortable restaurant with formal chairs and water fountain in centre.

CWM TAF *Merthyr Tydfil* 503 J 28 – *see Merthyr Tydfil.*

DEGANWY *Conwy* 502 503 I 24 – *see Llandudno.*

DOLGELLAU *Gwynedd* 502 503 I 25 *Wales G. – pop. 2 407.*
See : *Town*★.
Env. : *Snowdonia National Park*★★★ – *Cadair Idris*★★★ – *Precipice Walk*★, *NE : 3 m. on minor roads.*
🛢 *Hengwrt Estate, Pencefn Rd* ℰ (01341) 422603.
🅱 *Ty Meirion, Eldon Sq* ℰ (01341) 422888.
London 221 – Birkenhead 72 – Chester 64 – Shrewsbury 57.

Penmaenuchaf Hall ⟝, Penmaenpool, LL40 1YB, West : 1¾ m. on A 493 (Tywyn Rd) ℰ (01341) 422129, *relax@penhall.co.uk*, Fax (01341) 422787, ≤ Rhinog mountains and Mawddach estuary, ⟱, ⟲, ⟵, ⚹ – ⤫ ⟵ ⓟ, ⓜ ⓞ *VISA*
Rest 17.95/35.00 and a la carte 34.45/42.50 – **14 rm** ⊡ 🛏75.00/135.00 – 🛏🛏130.00/200.00.
◆ From a handsome drawing room, enjoy the enviable position of this Victorian mansion with its Rhinog Mountain and Mawddach Estuary vistas. Bedrooms are tastefully furnished. Dine in smart garden room with outside terrace.

WALES

⌂ **Tyddyn Mawr** ⌂ without rest., Islawdref, Cader Rd, LL40 1TL, Southwest : 2 ½ m. by
Tywyn rd on Cader Idris rd ℰ (01341) 422331, ≤ Cader Idris, ⌖, ⌖, ⌖ – ⌖ **P**. ⌖
February-November – 3 rm ⌖ **†**64.00 – **† †**64.00.
♦ Part 18C farmhouse with sympathetic extension: boasts breath-taking views from breath-taking position. Timbered breakfast room. Superb rooms: one with patio, one with balcony.

EAST ABERTHAW (Aberddawan) *Vale of Glamorgan* 503 J 29 – ✉ *Barry*.
London 180 – Cardiff 20 – Swansea 33.

⌂ **Blue Anchor Inn**, CF62 3DD, ℰ (01446) 750329, Fax (01446) 750077 – **P**. **◯** **VISA**
Rest 17.95 (dinner) and a la carte 13.00/25.00.
♦ Characterful thatched and creeper covered inn, dating back to 1380. Nooks, crannies and warrens invoke charming atmosphere. Wide-ranging menus with traditional dishes.

FELINGWM UCHAF *Carmarthenshire – see Carmarthen.*

FISHGUARD (Abergwaun) *Pembrokeshire* 503 F 28 *Wales G. – pop. 3 193.*
Env. : *Pembrokeshire Coast National Park★★.*
⌖ to Republic of Ireland (Rosslare) (Stena Line) 2-4 daily (1 h 50 mn/3 h 30 mn).
🄱 *Town Hall, The Square* ℰ *(01348) 873484 – Ocean Lab, The Parrog, Goodwick* ℰ *(01348) 872037.*
London 265 – Cardiff 114 – Gloucester 176 – Holyhead 169 – Shrewsbury 136 – Swansea 76.

⌂ **Manor Town House**, 11 Main St, SA65 9HG, ℰ (01348) 873260, enquiries@manor
townhouse.com, Fax (01348) 873260, ≤, ⌖ – ⌖ **P**. ⌖
Rest (by arrangement) 19.50 ⌖ – **6 rm** ⌖ **†**30.00/45.00 – **† †**70.00/80.00.
♦ Georgian Grade II listed house. Bedrooms are individually styled and furnished with antiques, choose from Victorian and Art Deco; some with harbour and sea views. Welsh ingredients intrinsic to proudly served home-cooked dishes.

at Welsh Hook *Southwest : 7½ m. by A 40 – ✉ Haverfordwest.*

XX **Stone Hall** ⌖ with rm, SA62 5NS, ℰ (01348) 840212, Fax (01348) 840815, ⌖ – ⌖ **P**.
◯ **AE** **◯** **VISA**. ⌖
closed 2 weeks January, 1 week Spring, 25-26 and 31 December – **Rest** (closed Sunday-Monday) (booking essential) (dinner only) 28.90 and a la carte 27.65/33.00 – **5 rm** ⌖
†70.00/85.00 – **† †**105.00.
♦ Charming part-14C manor house with 17C additions. Tranquil setting and personal hospitality. Home-cooked, French-style dishes using prime seasonal produce. Comfy rooms.

GELLILYDAN *Gwynedd – see Llan Ffestiniog.*

GRESFORD (Groes-ffordd) *Wrexham* 502 503 L 24 – see Wrexham.

GUILSFIELD (Cegidfa) *Powys* 502 503 K 26 – see Welshpool.

GWBERT ON SEA *Ceredigion* 503 F 27 – see Cardigan.

HARLECH *Gwynedd* 502 503 H 25 *Wales G. – pop. 1 233.*
See : *Castle★★ AC.*
Env. : *Snowdonia National Park★★★.*
🄸 *Royal St. David's* ℰ *(01766) 780203.*
🄱 *Llys y Graig, High St* ℰ *(01766) 780658.*
London 241 – Chester 72 – Dolgellau 21.

⌂ **Hafod Wen**, LL46 2RA, South : ¾ m. on A 496 ℰ (01766) 780356, enquiries@harlech
guesthouse.co.uk, Fax (01766) 780356, ≤ Tremadoc Bay and Snowdonia, ⌖ – ⌖ **P**. **◯**
VISA
March-December – **Rest** (by arrangement) 27.00 – **6 rm** ⌖ **†**68.00 – **† †**96.00.
♦ Unusual house with Dutch colonial architectural references. Superb views of Tremadoc Bay and Snowdonia from most of the antique and curio filled bedrooms. Footpath to beach. The dining room shares in the establishment's delightful views.

WALES

⌂ **Gwrach Ynys** without rest., LL47 6TS, North : 2 ¼ m. on A 496   ℰ (01766) 780742, *info@gwrachynys.co.uk*, Fax (01766) 781199, 🐾 – ⇔ 🅿. 🌫
7 rm ☑ ✱26.00/50.00 – ✱✱60.00/70.00.
♦ Edwardian house in good location for exploring Snowdonia and Cardigan Bay. Welcoming owners. Traditional bedrooms, two of which are ideal for families.

XX **Castle Cottage** with rm, Pen Llech, LL46 2YL, off B 4573   ℰ (01766) 780479, *glyn@cas tlecottageharlech.co.uk* – ⇔ 🆘 🆅🆂🅰. 🌫
closed 3 weeks January – **Rest** (booking essential) (dinner only) 32.00 – **7 rm** ☑ ✱70.00 – ✱✱130.00.
♦ A little cottage just a short distance from the imposing Harlech Castle. Stylish, modern restaurant where Welsh food with a modern twist is served. Smart contemporary rooms.

HAVERFORDWEST (Hwlffordd) Pembrokeshire 503 F 28 Wales G. – pop. 13 367.

See : *Scolton Museum and Country Park*★.
Env. : *Pembrokeshire Coast National Park*★★.
Exc. : *Skomer Island and Skokholm Island*★, SW : 14 m. by B 4327 and minor roads.
🅕 Arnolds Down   ℰ (01437) 763565.
🛈 Old Bridge   ℰ (01437) 763110.
London 250 – Fishguard 15 – Swansea 57.

⌂ **Lower Haythog Farm** 🐾, Spittal, SA62 5QL, Northeast : 5 m. on B 4329   ℰ (01437) 731279, *nesta@lowerhaythogfarm.co.uk*, Fax (01437) 731279, 🐾, 🐴 – ⇔ 🅿
Rest (by arrangement) 25.00 – **6 rm** ☑ ✱35.00/45.00 – ✱✱55.00/80.00.
♦ Friendly atmosphere, traditional comforts and a warm welcome at this 250 acre working dairy farm with accessible woodland walks. Well kept and comfortable throughout. Dining room in homely, country style reflected in hearty, home-cooked food.

HAWARDEN (Penarlâg) Flintshire 502 K 24.

London 205 – Chester 9 – Liverpool 17 – Shrewsbury 45.

X **The Brasserie,** 68 The Highway, CH5 3DH,   ℰ (01244) 536353, Fax (01244) 520888 – 🍽.
🆘 🆀🅴 🆅🆂🅰
Rest (booking essential) a la carte 17.85/28.15 ♀.
♦ Neutral walls, wood floors and spot lighting contribute to the busy, modern ambience in this good value, small restaurant; well reputed locally. Cuisine with a Welsh tone.

HAY-ON-WYE (Y Gelli) Powys 503 K 27 Wales G. – pop. 1 846.

See : *Town*★.
Env. : *Brecon Beacons National Park*★★.
Exc. : *Llanthony Priory*★★, SE : 12 m. by minor roads.
🅕 Rhosgoch, Builth Wells   ℰ (01497) 851251.
🛈 Craft Centre, Oxford Rd   ℰ (01497) 820144.
London 154 – Brecon 16 – Cardiff 59 – Hereford 21 – Newport 62.

🏛 **The Swan,** Church St, HR3 5DQ,   ℰ (01497) 821188, *info@swanathay.co.uk*, Fax (01497) 821424, 🐾 – ⇔ 🅿. – 🔏 80. 🆘 🆀🅴 🛈 🆅🆂🅰
Rest (bar lunch)/dinner a la carte 18.50/33.50 s. – **19 rm** ☑ ✱72.00/95.00 – ✱✱95.00/140.00.
♦ Constantly evolving 18C former coaching inn bordered by neat book-lovers' garden. Restyled front bar is light, airy and inviting. Guest lounge with 21C makeover. Spruce rooms. French influenced modern menus in the restaurant.

⌂ **Hardwicke Green** without rest., HR3 5HA, East : 3 m. by B 4348 on B 4352   ℰ (01497) 831051, *info@hardwickegreen.co.uk*, 🐾 – ⇔ 🅿. 🌫
closed Christmas-New Year, 1 week February-March – **3 rm** ☑ ✱22.00/46.00 – ✱✱56.00.
♦ Ex-farmhouse built in 1740 with later addition. Charming garden in six acres. Comfy conservatory lounge. Stay in Farmhouse or Victorian rooms: immaculately smart rustic chic.

🏠 **Old Black Lion** with rm, 26 Lion St, HR3 5AD,   ℰ (01497) 820841, *info@oldblack lion.co.uk*, Fax (01497) 822960, 🍴 – ⇔ 🅿. 🆘 🆅🆂🅰. 🌫
closed 24-26 December – **Rest** a la carte 19.40/28.50 ♀ – **10 rm** ☑ ✱50.00 – ✱✱85.00.
♦ Inn with parts dating back to 13C and 17C when it reputedly hosted Oliver Cromwell. A friendly place with a traditional atmosphere, popular menu and comfortable bedrooms.

at Llanigon *Southwest : 2½ m. by B 4350* – ✉ *Hay-on-Wye.*

⌂ **Old Post Office** without rest., HR3 5QA,   ℰ (01497) 820008 – ⇔ 🅿
closed January and minimum 2 night stay at weekends – **3 rm** ☑ ✱35.00/60.00 – ✱✱70.00.
♦ Dating from 17C, a converted inn. Near the "book town" of Hay-on-Wye. Smart modern ambience blends with characterful charm. Pine furnished rooms with polished floors.

HENSOL *Rhondda Cynon Taff Wales G.*

Exc. : *Museum of Welsh Life*★★, E : 8 m. by minor rd north to Miskin, A 4119 and minor rd south.

London 161 – Bridgend 10 – Cardiff 8 – Cowbridge 7.

⌂ **Llanerch Vineyard** without rest., CF72 8GG, ℘ (01443) 225877, *enquiries@llanerch-vineyard.co.uk, Fax* (01443) 225546 – ⇔ ✆. ⦿⦿. ⨯

10 rm ⊡ ✝59.00 – ✝✝79.00.

♦ Rurally set, fully functioning vineyard in woodland with 20 acres of vines. The modern breakfast area is furnished with Welsh art. Immaculate, state of the art bedrooms.

HOLYHEAD (Caergybi) *Anglesey* 502 503 G 24 *Wales G.* – pop. 11 237.

Env. : *South Stack Cliffs*★, W : 3 m. by minor roads.

⛴ to Republic of Ireland (Dun Laoghaire) (Stena Line) 4-5 daily (1 h 40 mn) – to Republic of Ireland (Dublin) (Irish Ferries) 2 daily (3 h 15 mn) – to Republic of Ireland (Dublin) (Stena Line) 1-2 daily (3 h 45 mn).

🛈 *Terminal 1, Stena Line* ℘ (01407) 762622.

London 269 – Birkenhead 94 – Cardiff 215 – Chester 88 – Shrewsbury 105 – Swansea 190.

⌂ **Yr Hendre** without rest., Porth-y-Felin Rd, LL65 1AH, Northwest : ½ m. turning left at war memorial and by Thomas St ℘ (01407) 762929, *rita@yrhendre.freeserve.co.uk, Fax* (01407) 765936, ☞ – ⇔ ℙ. ⨯

closed 25-26 December – **3 rm** ⊡ ✝40.00 – ✝✝60.00.

♦ Detached house dating from the 1920s in a pleasant, residential area of town and ideally located for the ferry terminus. Comfortable and well-furnished bedrooms. Breakfast overlooking the garden and with views of the sea.

HOWEY *Powys – see Llandrindod Wells.*

KNIGHTON (Trefyclawdd) *Powys* 503 K 26 *Wales G.* – pop. 2 743.

See : *Town*★.

Exc. : *Offa's Dyke*★, NW : 9½ m.

🛦 *Little Ffrydd Wood* ℘ (01547) 528646.

🛈 *Offa's Dyke Centre, West St* ℘ (01547) 529424.

London 162 – Birmingham 59 – Hereford 31 – Shrewsbury 35.

🏨 **Milebrook House,** Ludlow Rd, Milebrook, LD7 1LT, East : 2 m. on A 4113 ℘ (01547) 528632, *hotel@milebrook.kc3ltd.co.uk, Fax* (01547) 520509, ☜, ☞ – ⇔ ℙ. ⦿⦿ 🆅🅸🆂🅰 ⨯

Rest *(closed Monday lunch)* 30.50 **s.** ⨯. ⊡ – **10 rm** ⊡ ✝67.50 – ✝✝104.00.

♦ Located in the Teme Valley; good for exploring the Welsh Marches. Possesses a fine, formal garden well stocked with exotic plants. Rooms are large and pleasingly decorated. The kitchen garden provides most of the vegetables which appear in the restaurant.

LAKE VYRNWY *Powys* 502 503 J 25 *Wales G.* – ✉ *Llanwddyn.*

See : *Lake*★.

🛈 *Unit 2, Vyrnwy Craft Workshops* ℘ (01691) 870346, *laktic@powys.gov.uk.*

London 204 – Chester 52 – Llanfyllin 10 – Shrewsbury 40.

🏨 **Lake Vyrnwy** ☜, SY10 0LY, ℘ (01691) 870692, *res@lakevyrnwy.com, Fax* (01691) 870259, ≤ Lake Vyrnwy, ☜, ☞, ♨, ⨯ – ⇔ rest, ℙ – ⛬ 120. ⦿⦿ 🅰🅴 🆅🅸🆂🅰

Rest 34.00 **s.** – **37 rm** ⊡ ✝75.00/175.00 – ✝✝100.00/195.00, 1 suite.

♦ Victorian country house built from locally quarried stone overlooking the lake; an RSPB sanctuary and sporting estate, ideal for game enthusiasts. Rooms have timeless chic. Spectacular lakeside views from the restaurant are matched by accomplished cooking.

LALESTON *Bridgend* 503 J 29 – see Bridgend.

LAMPHEY (Llandyfai) *Pembrokeshire* 503 F 28 – see Pembroke.

LAUGHARNE *Carmarthenshire* 503 G 28.

London 230 – Cardiff 80 – Carmarthen 13.

🏨 **Hurst House** ☜, East Marsh, SA33 4RS, South : 3 m. by A 4066 taking left turn on unmarked road opposite Hill Crest house ℘ (01994) 427417, *Fax* (01994) 427840, ☞, ⦿, ☞ – ✆ ℙ. ⦿⦿ 🅰🅴 ⓪ 🆅🅸🆂🅰

Rest 16.95/42.00 – **18 rm** ⊡ ✝265.00 – ✝✝265.00/350.00.

♦ Converted farmhouse and outbuildings in Dylan Thomas country: epitomises new wave of trendy, informal country hotels. Rooms boast vivid colour schemes and up-to-date extras. Modish menus in restaurant with reclaimed tables and contemporary artwork.

LLANARMON DYFFRYN CEIRIOG Wrexham 502 503 K 25 – ⊠ Llangollen (Denbighshire).
London 196 – Chester 33 – Shrewsbury 32.

🏠 **West Arms**, LL20 7LD, ℰ (01691) 600665, gowestarms@aol.com, Fax (01691) 600622,
🍴, 🌳 – ⋙ 🅿 – 🕳 50. 🆖 🆅🆂🅰
Rest (bar lunch Monday-Saturday)/dinner 32.90 and a la carte 20.35/28.85 – **13 rm** 🖵
⋆70.00 – ⋆⋆153.00, 2 suites.
  • Set in Ceiriog Valley; enjoys many original fixtures associated with a part 16C country inn
  - slate-flagged floors, inglenooks, timberwork. Bedrooms with matching ambience. A concise but well-balanced menu offered in atmospheric dining room.

LLANBEDR Gwynedd 502 503 H 25 Wales G. – pop. 1 101.
Env. : Harlech Castle★★, N : 3 m. by A 496.
Cardiff 150 – Dolgellau 18 – Harlech 3.

⌂ **Pensarn Hall** without rest., LL45 2HS, North : ¾ m. on A 496 ℰ (01341) 241236, wel
come@pensarn-hall.co.uk, 🌳 – ⋙ 🅿 🆖 🆅🆂🅰
February-October – **7 rm** 🖵 ⋆50.00 – ⋆⋆75.00/80.00.
  • Late 19C house on an estuary. Impressive entrance with original tiled floor. Pleasant
  front conservatory. Breakfast room has good view. Simple, well-kept rooms.

If breakfast is included the 🖵 symbol appears after the number of rooms.

LLANBERIS Gwynedd 503 H 24 Wales G. – pop. 1 842.
See : Town★ – Welsh Slate Museum★ AC.
Env. : Snowdonia National Park★★★ (Snowdon★★★, Snowdon Mountain Railway★★ AC –
panorama★★★).
🛈 41 High St ℰ (01286) 870765, llanberis.tic@gwynedd.gov.uk.
London 243 – Caernarfon 7 – Chester 65 – Shrewsbury 78.

XX **Y Bistro**, 43-45 High St, LL55 4EU, ℰ (01286) 871278, ybistro@fsbdial.co.uk – ⋙. 🆖
🆅🆂🅰
closed 2 weeks January, 1 week June-July, Sunday and Monday except Bank Holidays – **Rest**
(booking essential) (dinner only) a la carte 23.50/31.50.
  • Long established, in lakeside village at foot of Snowdonia. Brush up on your Welsh when
  perusing menus of Eidion Badell (beef flamed in Cognac), Cawl Tomato Ceiros, (soup).

LLANDEILO Carmarthenshire 503 I 28 Wales G. – pop. 1 731.
See : Town★ – Dinefwr Park★ AC.
Env. : Brecon Beacons National Park★★ – Black Mountain★, SE : by minor roads – Carreg
Cennen Castle★ AC, SE : 4 m. by A 483 and minor roads.
London 218 – Brecon 34 – Carmarthen 15 – Swansea 25.

🏠 **Cawdor**, Rhosmaen St, SA19 6EN, ℰ (01558) 823500, fdesk@thecawdor.com,
Fax (01558) 822399 – ⋙ 🍴 ৬, 🆖 🆅🆂🅰 🌳
Rest 15.00/25.00 and a la carte 23.00/32.00 – **25 rm** 🖵 ⋆65.00 – ⋆⋆200.00.
  • Vividly hued coaching inn on main street. Public areas are leather furnished, 'loungey',
  relaxed and modern. Main strength lies in bedrooms: contemporary, sleek and sassy.
  Menus add Mediterranean edge to prominent Welsh base.

🏠 **Plough Inn**, Rhosmaen, SA19 6NP, North : 1 m. on A 40 ℰ (01558) 823431, enqui
ries@ploughrhosmaen.co.uk, Fax (01558) 823969, ≤, 𝕝𝕤, 🍴, 🌳 – ⋙ 🍴 ৬ 🅿 – 🕳 45. 🆖
🅰🅴 🆅🆂🅰. 🌳
Rest a la carte 17.00/20.50 – **14 rm** 🖵 ⋆60.00 – ⋆⋆80.00.
  • Once a farmhouse, the perfect base for country pursuits. Rooms, named after characters from Mabinogion, are well-kept and co-ordinated; large windows for views. Wholesome favourites to fore in light, airy and relaxed modern dining room.

at Salem North : 3 m. by A 40 off Pen y banc rd – ⊠ Llandeilo.

🍴 **The Angel Inn**, SA19 7LY, ℰ (01558) 823394, 🌳 – ⋙ 🅿 🆖 🆅🆂🅰 🌳
closed 1 week January, Sunday and Monday – **Rest** a la carte 20.00/35.00.
  • Cream coloured pub next to chapel in small village. Inviting bar lounge with chair and
  sofa assortment. Edwardian style dining room: elaborate cooking utilising local fare.

LLANDENNY Monmouthshire 503 L 28 – see Usk.

LLANDEWI SKIRRID Monmouthshire – see Abergavenny.

LLANDRILLO Denbighshire 502 503 J 25 – ⊠ Corwen.
London 210 – Chester 40 – Dolgellau 26 – Shrewsbury 46.

XXX **Tyddyn Llan** ⑤ with rm, LL21 0ST, ℰ (01490) 440264, tyddynllan@compuserve.com, Fax (01490) 440414, ☞ – ✜ P. ⓂⓄ VISA
closed 2 weeks January – **Rest** (booking essential) (dinner only and lunch Friday-Sunday) 28.00/40.00 ♀ ☞ – **13 rm** ☷ ✦75.00/105.00 – ✦✦170.00/240.00.
♦ Charming sitting areas for pre-dinner drinks. Two dining rooms with blue painted wood panels. Classic menus employing local produce. Fine selection of country house rooms.

LLANDRINDOD WELLS Powys 503 J 27 Wales G. – pop. 5 024.
Exc. : Elan Valley★★ (Dol-y-Mynach and Claerwen Dam and Reservoir★★, Caban Coch Dam and Reservoir★, Garreg-ddu Viaduct★, Pen-y-Garreg Reservoir and Dam★, Craig Goch Dam and Reservoir★), NW : 12 m. by A 4081, A 470 and B 4518.
ᐧ₈ Llandrindod Wells ℰ (01597) 823873.
🚹 Old Town Hall, Memorial Gardens ℰ (01597) 822600, llandtic@powys.gov.uk.
London 204 – Brecon 29 – Carmarthen 60 – Shrewsbury 58.

🏛 **Metropole,** Temple St, LD1 5DY, ℰ (01597) 823700, info@metropole.co.uk, Fax (01597) 824828, ⇌s, ▨, ☞ – ▐ ✜ ఈ P. – ᇫ 300. ⓂⓄ ᴁ VISA
Rest (bar lunch)/dinner 25.00/30.00 ♀ – **120 rm** ☷ ✦50.00/102.00 – ✦✦80.00/160.00, 2 suites.
♦ Run by Baird-Murray family for 100 years and popular for hosting vintage car rallies. Leisure complex is in 19C style conservatory. Eight "Tower" rooms with adjoining lounge. Expect to find cuisine committed to using local ingredients.

at Crossgates Northeast : 3½ m. on A 483 – ⊠ Llandrindod Wells.

⌂ **Guidfa House,** LD1 6RF, ℰ (01597) 851241, guidfa@globalnet.co.uk, Fax (01597) 851875, ☞ – ✜ P. ⓂⓄ VISA. ⨯
Rest (by arrangement) 22.00 – **6 rm** ☷ ✦40.00/50.00 – ✦✦72.00.
♦ Georgian house with white painted façade and pleasant garden to relax in. Indoors, find spacious, bright bedrooms. A friendly welcome is given with tips on local activities. Seasonally changing menu of zesty home cooking in traditionally decorated dining room.

at Howey South : 1½ m. by A 483 – ⊠ Llandrindod Wells.

⌂ **Acorn Court Country House** ⑤ without rest., Chapel Rd, LD1 5PB, Northeast : ½ m. ℰ (01597) 823543, info@acorncourt.co.uk, Fax (01597) 823543, ☞, ⅏ – ✜ P. ⨯
closed 15 December-1 February – **4 rm** ☷ ✦30.00/35.00 – ✦✦55.00/65.00.
♦ Chalet-style house in lovely countryside; guests can fish in the lake. Bedrooms are large with many extra touches: hairdryers, stationery, soft toys - homely and welcoming.

LLANDUDNO Conwy 502 503 I 24 Wales G. – pop. 14 872.
See : Town★ – Pier★ B – The Great Orme★ (panorama★★, Tramway★, Ancient Copper Mines★ AC) AB.
Exc. : Bodnant Garden★★ AC, S : 7 m. by A 470 B.
ᐧ₈ Rhos-on-Sea, Penrhyn Bay ℰ (01492) 549641 A – ᐧ₈ 72 Bryniau Rd, West Shore ℰ (01492) 875325 A – ᐧ₈ Hospital Rd ℰ (01492) 876450 B.
🚹 1-2 Chapel St ℰ (01492) 876413.
London 243 – Birkenhead 55 – Chester 47 – Holyhead 43.

Plan opposite

🏛 **Bodysgallen Hall** ⑤, LL30 1RS, Southeast : 2 m. on A 470 ℰ (01492) 584466, info@bodysgallen.com, Fax (01492) 582519, ≼ gardens and mountains, ⑦, ⅙, ⇌s, ▨, ☞, ⅏, ⨯ – ✜ ⓥ ఈ P. – ᇫ 40. ⓂⓄ ᴁ VISA. ⨯
Rest (booking essential) 27.00/40.00 s. – **18 rm** ✦125.00/135.00 – ✦✦375.00, 16 suites 215.00/375.00.
♦ Majestic and rare sums up this part 17C-18C hall with tower, once a soldier's lookout, now a place to take in views of mountains and terraced gardens. Antique filled dining room. Formal dining room with tall windows; serves fine and distinctive dishes.

🏛 **The Empire,** 73 Church Walks, LL30 2HE, ℰ (01492) 860555, reservations@empirehotel.co.uk, Fax (01492) 860791, ⇌s, ▨ heated, ▨ – ▐ ✜ rest, ▤ ⓥ ఈ P. – ᇫ 40. ⓂⓄ ᴁ ⓪ VISA. ⨯
A e
closed 16-28 December – **Watkins and Co. : Rest** (dinner only and Sunday lunch)/dinner 19.75/25.00 – **38 rm** ☷ ✦55.00/85.00 – ✦✦125.00/130.00, 7 suites.
♦ A porticoed façade sets the Victorian tone found in bedrooms with original cast iron beds, antiques and Russell Flint prints on walls. 21C mod cons bring them bang up-to-date. Fine menus with a mix and match of the Celtic and the Continental.

WALES

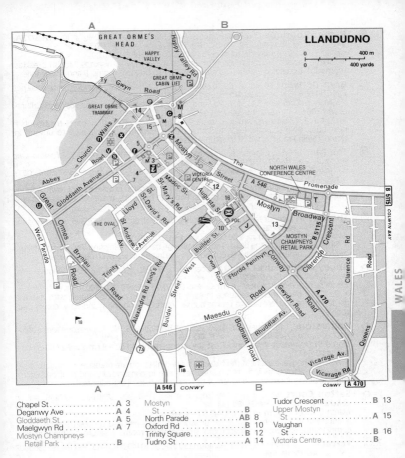

Osborne House, 17 North Parade, LL30 2LP, ℰ (01492) 860330, *sales@osborne house.com*, Fax (01492) 860791, ← – ▤ 🕻 🄿. ⬛🄾 🄰🄴 🄾 🆅🅸🆂🄰. ❀   **A** c
closed 16-28 December – Rest – (see ***Osborne's Cafe Grill*** below) – 6 rm ✹145.00/200.00 – ✹✹145.00/200.00.
♦ Sumptuous interior: huge rooms extend length of house; bedrooms epitomise Victorian luxury - original wood flooring, elaborate silk drapes, fine antiques. Richly hued lounge.

St Tudno, North Parade, LL30 2LP, ℰ (01492) 874411, *sttudnohotel@btinternet.com*, Fax (01492) 860407, ←, ◰ – ▯ ✕⇢ ⇔. ⬛🄾 🄰🄴 🄾 🆅🅸🆂🄰   **A** c
Rest – (see ***Terrace*** below) – 17 rm ⊊ ✹75.00/95.00 – ✹✹94.00/115.00, 1 suite.
♦ Prime position on the promenade opposite a Victorian pier; boasts sitting room, lounge in charming period style with seafront vistas. Comfortable rooms with fine fabrics.

Dunoon, Gloddaeth St, LL30 2DW, ℰ (01492) 860787, *reservations@dunoonhotel.co.uk*, Fax (01492) 860031 – ▯, ✕⇢ rest, ⅙. 🄿. ⬛🄾 🆅🅸🆂🄰   **A** r
11 March- mid December – Rest (bar lunch Monday-Saturday)/dinner 20.50 ⊊ – 49 rm (dinner included) ⊊ ✹66.00/98.00 – ✹✹132.00/128.00.
♦ A hospitable hotel; a panelled hallway leads to the "Welsh Dresser Bar" furnished with an antique cooking range. Bygone era ambience. Rooms are individually styled. Restaurant, modernised in a traditional style, with menu to match.

899

Escape Boutique B & B without rest., 48 Church Walks, LL30 2HL, ✆ (01492) 877776, *info@escapebandb.co.uk, Fax (01492) 878777*, ≤, ⩲ – ✦⊱ ⚓ **P**, **MC** **VISA** . ⌘
       A n
closed 3 days Christmas – **9 rm** ⊠ ✦75.00/105.00 – ✦✦85.00/120.00.
* Ornate, elevated Victorian villa with ultra contemporary furnishings. Modish breakfast room with fine choice. Cool beige/brown or 'French boudoir' rooms. B and B with style.

Bryn Derwen, 34 Abbey Rd, LL30 2EE, ✆ (01492) 876804, *brynderwen@fsmail.net, Fax (01492) 876804* – ✦⊱ **P**, **MC** **VISA** . ⌘
       A v
February-November – **Rest** *(closed Sunday)* (booking essential for non-residents) (dinner only) 19.00 s. – **9 rm** ⊠ ✦50.00 – ✦✦92.00.
* Built in 1878 with welcoming owners. A beauty salon offering range of treatments is next door. Pine staircase leads to immaculate bedrooms. Quiet lounge to unwind in. Homely dining room in which to sample classic dishes.

Tan Lan, 14 Great Orme's Rd, West Shore, LL30 2AR, ✆ (01492) 860221, *info@tanlanho tel.co.uk, Fax (01492) 870219* – ✦⊱ **P**, **MC** **VISA** . ⌘
       A u
19 March-28 October – **Rest** (dinner only) 17.50 s. – **17 rm** ⊠ ✦37.00/40.00 – ✦✦54.00/60.00.
* Detached, neat and tidy house, personally run and located in quiet part of town. A sunny lounge in yellow and comfortable rooms, two with balconies, make for a pleasant stay. A bright dining room delivers varied set meals.

The Wilton without rest., 14 South Parade, LL30 2LN, ✆ (01492) 878343, *info@wiltonho tel.com* – ✦⊱ **P**, **AE** **VISA** . ⌘
       AB z
April-November – **14 rm** ⊠ ✦30.00/42.00 – ✦✦60.00/70.00.
* Situated adjacent to the beach and pier. Lounge bar with interesting Victorian prints; the bedrooms, some of which have four-posters, are in bright, warm colour schemes.

Abbey Lodge without rest., 14 Abbey Rd, LL30 2EA, ✆ (01492) 878042, *enquiries@ab beylodgeuk.com, Fax (01492) 878042*, ⩲ – ✦⊱ **P**. ⌘
       A x
Restricted opening in winter – **4 rm** ⊠ ✦45.00/50.00 – ✦✦70.00/75.00.
* Built as a gentlemen's residence in early 1850s; a pretty, gabled house with terraced garden where you're made to feel at home. Smart drawing room and cosy, comfy bedrooms.

Epperstone, 15 Abbey Rd, LL30 2EE, ✆ (01492) 878746, *epperstonehotel@btcon nect.com, Fax (01492) 871223* – ✦⊱ **P**, **MC** **VISA**
       A s
closed 31 December-4 January – **Rest** (by arrangement) 19.50 – **8 rm** ⊠ ✦27.00/32.00 – ✦✦54.00/64.00.
* A period house, evident in the fixtures: stained glass, ornate fireplace, mahogany staircase. Other attractions include a marine aquarium in conservatory and neat bedrooms. Intimate dining room serving varied dishes using fresh, local ingredients.

Sefton Court without rest., 49 Church Walks, LL30 2HL, ✆ (01492) 875235, *sefton court@aol.com*, ⩲ – ✦⊱ **P**, **MC** **VISA** . ⌘
       A n
March-October – **11 rm** ⊠ ✦35.00/45.00 – ✦✦65.00.
* Imposing Victorian house, fully refurbished in 2006, perched on quiet hillside. Large, comfy lounge; spacious breakfast room. Smart, homely rooms. Near Great Orme Tramway.

XXX **Terrace** (at St Tudno H.), North Parade, LL30 2LP, ✆ (01492) 874411, *Fax (01492) 860407* – ✦⊱ ▤, **MC** **AE** **VISA**
       A c
Rest 18.00 (lunch) and dinner a la carte 29.50/40.00 s. ♀ ⌘.
* Smart and formal dining room incorporating blown-up photograph of Lake Como and, on a smaller scale, a neat little water feature. Accomplished and precise modern cooking.

XX **Osborne's Cafe Grill** (at Osborne House H.), 17 North Parade, LL30 2LP, ✆ (01492) 860330, *sales@osbornehouse.com* – ✦⊱ ▤, **MC** **AE** **①** **VISA**
       A c
closed 16-18 December – **Rest** a la carte 20.00/30.50 ⌘ ♀.
* Impressive, ornate main dining room with velvet drapes and ornate gold lighting. Eclectic, modern menus, and the bustling informal style of a bistro; enthusiastic service.

at Deganwy South : 2¾ m. on A 546 – A – ⌂ Llandudno.

X **Nikki Ip's**, 57 Station Rd, LL31 9DF, ✆ (01492) 596611, *Fax (01492) 596600* – ▤, **MC** **VISA**
closed Monday in winter – **Rest** - Chinese - (booking essential) (dinner only) 23.00/40.00 and a la carte 21.50/30.00.
* Good value, stylish and unconventional, but beware: no signage outside. Particularly welcoming owners. Coral interior; Cantonese, Peking and Szechuan specialities are served.

> The ✿ award is the crème de la crème.
> This is awarded to restaurants
> which are really worth travelling miles for!

LLANDYRNOG Denbighshire 503 J/K 24.
Cardiff 158 – Denbigh 7.5 – Ruthin 6.

↑ **Pentre Mawr** ⌂, LL16 4LA, North : 1 ¼ m. by B 5429 taking left hand fork after ¾ m. ℰ (01824) 790732, bre@sychnant-pass-house.co.uk, ≤, ⌐ heated, ⌐, ⌐, ⌐, ⌐ – ⌐ P. restricted opening November-February – **Rest** (by arrangement) (communal dining) 22.50 – **3 rm** ⌐ ✦80.00/90.00 – ✦✦110.00/120.00.
♦ Spacious, rebuilt 17C former farmhouse in nearly 200 acres. Very comfortable, with period style lounges, morning room, pool, terrace and tastefully individualistic rooms. Communal dining room offers classic décor and homely touches.

LLANELLI Carmarthenshire 503 H 28.
London 202.5 – Cardiff 54.5 – Swansea 12.5.

⌂ **Llwyn Hall** without rest., Llwynhendy, SA14 9LJ, East : 3 ½ m. by A 484 ℰ (01554) 777754, richardburrows@hotmail.com, Fax (01554) 777754, ⌐ – ⌐ ⌐ P. ⌐ ⌐ ⌐ ⌐ VISA ⌐
6 rm ⌐ ✦50.00/70.00 – ✦✦70.00/85.00.
♦ Pretty yellow-and-white 19C gabled house with extension. Country style soft furnishings. Chintzy rooms of pleasant individuality: those at front face garden and North Gower. Cloth-clad dining room; traditional, well-priced menus.

✗ **Fairyhill Bar and Brasserie**, Machynys Golf Club, Nicklaus Ave, Machynys, SA15 2DG, South : 3 m. by A 484 off Machynys rd ℰ (01554) 744944, machynys@fairyhill.net, ≤ golf course, Loughor estuary and Gower Peninsula, ⌐ – ⌐ ⌐ ⌐ ⌐ VISA
Rest a la carte 16.35/29.50.
♦ On first floor of golf clubhouse with pleasant views of course and estuary. Choose between lounge bar with leather sofas or bustling brasserie for well prepared modern dishes.

LLANERCHYMEDD Anglesey 502 503 G 24 Wales G.
Env. : Anglesey★★.
London 262 – Bangor 18 – Caernarfon 23 – Holyhead 15.

↑ **Llwydiarth Fawr** ⌂ without rest., LL71 8DF, North : 1 m. on B 5111 ℰ (01248) 470321, llwydiarth@hotmail.com, ≤, ⌐, ⌐, ⌐ – ⌐ P. ⌐ VISA. ⌐
closed Christmas – **4 rm** ⌐ ✦35.00/55.00 – ✦✦75.00/80.00.
♦ Part of an 800-acre cattle and sheep farm, Georgian in style with picturesque vistas. Guests can enjoy nature walks, fishing on lake; welcoming owner. Airy, well-kept rooms.

↑ **Drws-Y-Coed** ⌂ without rest., LL71 8AD, East : 1 ½ m. by B 5111 on Benllech rd ℰ (01248) 470473, drwsycoed2@hotmail.com, ≤, ⌐, ⌐ – ⌐ P. ⌐ VISA. ⌐
closed 25 December – **3 rm** ⌐ ✦40.00/45.00 – ✦✦60.00/70.00.
♦ Meaning "Door of the Wood"; 1960s house, run by Welsh speaking family in 550-acre farm of cattle and cereal crops. Countryside views add to enjoyment of neat and tidy rooms.

LLAN FFESTINIOG Gwynedd.
Env. : Llechwedd Slate Caverns★ AC N : 4 m. by A 470.
London 234 – Bangor 35 – Wrexham 52.

↑ **Cae'r Blaidd Country House** ⌂, LL41 4PH, North : ¾ m. by A 470 on Blaenau Rd ℰ (01766) 762765, info@caerblaidd.fsnet.co.uk, Fax (01766) 762765, ≤ Vale of Ffestiniog and Moelwyn mountains, ⌐ – ⌐ P. ⌐ VISA. ⌐
closed January – **Rest** (communal dining) 17.50 – **3 rm** ⌐ ✦45.00 – ✦✦70.00.
♦ Spacious Victorian country house in wooded gardens; spectacular views of Ffestiniog and Moelwyn Mountains. Smart, uncluttered rooms. Guided tours and courses are organised. A huge dining room; large refectory table where communal dinners are served.

at Gellilydan Southwest : 2¾ m. by A 470 off A 487 – ✉ Ffestiniog.

↑ **Tyddyn du Farm**, LL41 4RB, East : ½ m. by A 487 on A 470 ℰ (01766) 590281, mich/paula@snowdoniafarm.com, ≤, ⌐, ⌐ – ⌐ P.
Rest (by arrangement) 17.50 – **5 rm** ⌐ ✦45.00/70.00 – ✦✦78.00/95.00.
♦ 400-year old farmhouse set against Moelwyn Mountains. Guests can participate in farming activities or visit Roman site. Some rooms have large jacuzzis; all are very spacious. Cooking takes in free-range farm eggs; soups and rolls are home-made.

LLANFIHANGEL Powys 502 503 J 25 – see Llanfyllin.

LLANFYLLIN Powys 502 503 K 25 Wales G.

Exc. : Pistyll Rhaeadr★ , NW : 8 m. by A 490, B 4391, B 4580 and minor roads.

London 188 – Chester 42 – Shrewsbury 24 – Welshpool 11.

X **Seeds**, 5 Penybryn Cottages, High St, SY22 5AP, ℰ (01691) 648604 – ✦✤, **◑⊙** **VISA**

closed 1 week March, 1 week October, 25 December, Monday, Tuesday, Wednesday and Sunday dinner – **Rest** (restricted opening in winter) 24.75/26.70 (dinner) and lunch a la carte 17.45/26.40.

✦ Converted 16C rustic cottages with eclectic décor: souvenirs from owner's travels. Blackboard menu offers modern or traditional dishes. Local seasonal ingredients to the fore.

at Llanfihangel Southwest : 5 m. by A 490 and B 4393 on B 4382 – ✉ Llanfyllin.

⌂ **Cyfie Farm** ♠, SY22 5JE, South : 1 ½ m. by B 4382 ℰ (01691) 648451, info@cyfie farm.co.uk, Fax (01691) 648363, ⇐ Meifod valley, ≋s, ☞, ♨, – ✦✤ P, **◑⊙** AE **VISA**, ✦✤

restricted opening in winter **Rest** (by arrangement) (communal dining) 25.00 – **4 rm** ⊑

✦75.00/90.00 – ✦✦90.00/105.00.

✦ 17C longhouse, now a sheep farm, with super views of Meifod Valley. One room has distinctly quaint feel. Luxurious new cottages: outdoor hot tub affords great vistas. Cordon Bleu trained owners serve at communal table.

LLANGAMMARCH WELLS Powys 503 J 27.

London 200 – Brecon 17 – Builth Wells 8 – Cardiff 58.

▦ **Lake Country House and Spa** ♠, LD4 4BS, East : ¾ m. ℰ (01591) 620202, info@lakecountryhouse.co.uk, Fax (01591) 620457, ⇐, ⑩, Fₔ, ▢, Ƒ₉, ⌇, ☞, ♨, ✦ – ✦✤ ⚒ ♿ P, – ⚚ 40. **◑⊙** AE ① **VISA**

Rest (booking essential) 24.50/39.50 s. ♀ ☞ – **17 rm** ⊑ ✦110.00 – ✦✦170.00/250.00, **11 suites** ⊑ 210.00.

✦ 19C country house in mature grounds. Welsh teas a speciality. Rooms in house or Lodge full of antiques, flowers and extravagant fabrics. Tranquil spa adds to the experience. Candlelit dining; super wine list.

LLANGOLLEN Denbighshire 502 503 K 25 Wales G. – pop. 2 930.

See : Town★ – Railway★ AC – Plas Newydd★ AC.

Env. : Pontcysyllte Aqueduct★★ , E : 4 m. by A 539 – Castell Dinas Bran★ , N : by footpath – Valle Crucis Abbey★ AC, N : 2 m. by A 542.

Exc. : Chirk Castle★★ AC (wrought iron gates★), SE : 7½ m. by A 5 – Rug Chapel★ AC, W : 11 m. by A 5 and A 494.

▯ß Vale of Llangollen, Holyhead Rd ℰ (01978) 860613.

🛈 Y Capel, Castle St ℰ (01978) 860828.

London 194 – Chester 23 – Holyhead 76 – Shrewsbury 30.

▦ **Bryn Howel** ♠, LL20 7UW, East : 2 ¾ m. by A 539 ℰ (01978) 860331, hotel @brynhowel.com, Fax (01978) 860119, ⇐, ≋s, ☞ – ⼚ P – ⚚ **◑⊙** **VISA** ✦✤

Cedar Tree : Rest 15.95/19.95 and a la carte 20.85/30.85 ♀ – **35 rm** ⊑ ✦69.95/79.95 – ✦✦99.90/119.90, 1 suite.

✦ Built 1896 for owner of Ruabon brick company, mock Jacobean in style with Vale of Llangollen views. Bar has unique "Anthem Fireplace". Rooms in main house and modern wing. Admire panoramas and dine on classic Welsh cuisine.

▥ **Gales**, 18 Bridge St, LL20 8PF, ℰ (01978) 860089, richard@galesoflangollen.co.uk, Fax (01978) 861313, ♨ – ✦✤ ✦ P, – ⚚ 25. **◑⊙** AE ① **VISA** ✦✤

closed 23 December-2 January – **Rest** (closed Sunday) (in bar) a la carte 12.95/24.70 ♀ – ⊑ 5.00 – **13 rm** ✦50.00/60.00, 2 suites.

✦ Part 17C and 18C town house; rooms are divided between two buildings and display many historic features: wattle and daub walls, brass and walnut beds, beams and inglenooks. A wooden floored dining room and bar with inn-like ambience.

⌂ **Oakmere** without rest., Regent St, LL20 8HS, on A 5 ℰ (01978) 861126, oakmer egh@aol.com, ☞ – ✦✤ P, ✦✤

6 rm ⊑ ✦45.00/55.00 – ✦✦60.00.

✦ A restored Victorian house with an immaculate garden. Indoors are polished pitch pine furnishings, a breakfast room with conservatory area and tidy bedrooms.

⌂ **Hillcrest** without rest., Hill St, LL20 8EU, on Plas Newydd rd ℰ (01978) 860208, d–ray ment@btconnect.com, Fax (01978) 860208, ☞ – ✦✤ P, **◑⊙** **VISA**

7 rm ⊑ ✦30.00/38.00 – ✦✦50.00.

✦ A semi-detached house with large garden, close to the town centre. Homely and tidy inside with nicely decorated bedrooms and some original features: a slate fireplace.

The Corn Mill, Dee Lane, LL20 8PN, ℰ (01978) 869555, *cornmill@bandp.co.uk*, Fax (01978) 869930, 🏠 – ✳ rest. **⑩⑨ ⒶⒺ VISA**
closed 25-26 December – **Rest** a la carte approx 15.00 ♀.
* Imposing corn mill on banks of the Dee with large decked seating area extending into the river. Inside are two restored water wheels, slate and brick rooms. Rustic cuisine.

LLANGRANNOG *Ceredigion* 503 G 27.

The Grange ⤫, Pentregat, SA44 6HW, Southeast : 3 m. by B 4321 on A 487 ℰ (01239) 654121, *theresesexton@freenetname.co.uk*, Fax (01239) 654121, 🌳 – ✳ 📺 🅿
Rest (by arrangement) 20.00 – 4 rm 🍽 ♦50.00 – ♦♦70.00.
* Pink washed Georgian house with most welcoming owner. Afternoon tea trolley in real silver. Immaculate room décor in keeping with house age. Very handy for coast and country. Breakfast and country dinner proudly served: honest, fresh home cooking.

LLANIGON *Powys* 503 K 27 – *see Hay-on-Wye.*

LLANRHIAN *Pembrokeshire* – *see St Davids.*

LLANRHIDIAN *Swansea* 503 H 29 – *see Swansea.*

LLANRUG *Gwynedd* 502 503 H 24 – *see Caernarfon.*

LLANSANFFRAID GLAN CONWY *Conwy* 502 503 I 24 – *see Conwy.*

LLANTWIT MAJOR (Llanilltud Fawr) *Vale of Glamorgan* 503 J 29 – *pop. 13 366.*
London 175 – Cardiff 18 – Swansea 33.

West House Country, West St, CF61 1SP, ℰ (01446) 792406, *enq@westhouse-ho tel.co.uk*, Fax (01446) 796147, 🌳 – ✳ 📞 🅿 **⑩⑨ ⒶⒺ VISA**
Rest 17.00/25.00 and a la carte 17.00/31.95 **s.** – 20 rm 🍽 ♦56.50/64.50 – ♦♦68.00/72.00.
* 16C hotel in Vale of Glamorgan. After a bracing cliff top walk, relax in the welcoming bar. Rooms vary in style; traditional dominates. Conservatory used for small weddings. Light, clean Heritage restaurant with seasonal, local produce to fore.

LLANUWCHLLYN *Gwynedd* 503 I/J 25.
Cardiff 147.5 – Dolgellau 13 – Llangollen 27.

Eifionydd ⤫ *without rest.*, LL23 7UB, ℰ (01678) 540622, *stay@eifionydd.com*, ≤, 🌳 – ✳ 🅿
closed 20 December-2 January – 3 rm 🍽 ♦40.00 – ♦♦64.00/70.00.
* Good value guesthouse with lovely gardens and inspiring mountain views. Comfy lounge; linen-clad breakfast room; relaxing conservatory. Individual rooms with homely touches.

LLANWENARTH *Monmouthshire* – *see Abergavenny.*

LLANWRTYD WELLS *Powys* 503 J 27 *Wales G.* – *pop. 649.*
EXC. : Abergwesyn-Tregaron Mountain Road★, NW : 19 m. on minor roads.
🖪 Ty Barcud, The Square ℰ (01591) 610666, *tic@celt.rural.wales.org.*
London 214 – Brecon 32 – Cardiff 68 – Carmarthen 39.

Lasswade Country House, Station Rd, LD5 4RW, ℰ (01591) 610515, *info@lasswade hotel.co.uk*, Fax (01591) 610611, ≤, 🍃, 🌳 – ✳ 🅿 **⑩⑨ ⒶⒺ VISA**
Rest (dinner only) 28.00 – 8 rm 🍽 ♦49.00/60.00 – ♦♦95.00.
* Personally run Edwardian country house, with fine views of mid-Wales countryside from the breakfast conservatory. Cosy lounge. Bedrooms in traditional style. Proudly pro-organic meals on the daily menu.

New Hall, Victoria Rd, LD5 4SU, ℰ (01591) 610265, *newhallhouse@aol.com* – ✳ ♿ 🅿 ⤫
Rest (by arrangement) 13.00 – 4 rm 🍽 ♦45.00 – ♦♦65.00/80.00.
* Converted early 20C church hall; now a well-priced 'new era' B&B with board games in comfy lounge, and spacious, well-equipped rooms that exude a light, relaxed style. Dining room has short menus with choice; eg: Mexican, Thai or steak and kidney pie.

WALES

XX **Carlton House** with rm, Dolycoed Rd, LD5 4RA, *℘* (01591) 610248, *info@carltonres taurant.co.uk* – ⟲ ✦ **MC** **VISA**
closed December – Rest *(closed Sunday)* (booking essential) (lunch by arrangement)/din-ner a la carte 33.50/45.00 – **6 rm** ⟷ ✦40.00/50.00 – ✦✦60.00/90.00.
• Personally run Victorian house with an unpretentious and relaxing feel. Tasty seasonal dishes made with local ingredients on daily changing menu. Traditional rooms.

LLYSWEN *Powys 503* K 27 *Wales G.* – ⊠ *Brecon.*
Env. : *Brecon Beacons National Park★★*.
London 188 – Brecon 8 – *Cardiff* 48 – Worcester 53.

🏰🏰 **Llangoed Hall** 🛏, LD3 0YP, Northwest : 1 ¼ m. on A 470 *℘* (01874) 754525, *enqui ries@llangoedhall.com*, Fax (01874) 754545, ≤, ☜, ⇗, 𝄞 – ⟲✦ **P** **MC** **AE** **①** **VISA**, ⋙
Rest (booking essential for non-residents) 25.00/45.00 – **20 rm** ⟷ ✦150.00 – ✦✦350.00/315.00, 3 suites.
• Set up by Sir Bernard Ashley of Laura Ashley group: rooms furnished accordingly. River Wye to rear. Tennis court, gardens, carved staircase; guests can arrive by helicopter. Dining room menu has classic Welsh roots; Rex Whistler etchings in adjoining room.

MACHYNLLETH *Powys 502 503* I 26 *Wales G.* – pop. 2 147.
See : *Town★ – Celtica★ AC.*
Env. : *Snowdonia National Park★★★ – Centre for Alternative Technology★★ AC, N : 3 m. by A 487.*
🎅 Ffordd Drenewydd *℘* (01654) 702000.
🇧 Canolfan Owain Glyndwr *℘* (01654) 702401, *machtic@powys.gov.uk.*
London 220 – Shrewsbury 56 – Welshpool 37.

🏛 **Ynyshir Hall** 🛏, Eglwysfach, SY20 8TA, Southwest : 6 m. on A 487 *℘* (01654) 781209, *info@ynyshir-hall.co.uk*, Fax (01654) 781366, ≤, ☞, 𝄞, ⋙ – ⟲✦ **P** **MC** **AE** **①** **VISA**, ⋙
closed January – Rest (booking essential) 36.00/65.00 s. ⊻ – **6 rm** ⟷ ✦125.00/175.00 – ✦✦180.00/300.00, 3 suites.
• Part Georgian house set within 1000 acre RSPB reserve; bright, individually appointed bedrooms, classically cosy drawing room with art, antiques and Welsh pottery. Modern cooking with a refined style.

MENAI BRIDGE (Porthaethwy) *Anglesey 502 503* H 24.
London 270 – Caernarfon 10 – Chester 69 – Holyhead 22.

⌂ **Neuadd Lwyd** 🛏, Penmynydd, LL61 5BX, Northwest : 4 ¾ m. by B 5420 on Eglwys St Gredifael Church rd *℘* (01248) 715005, *post@neuaddlwyd.co.uk*, ≤, ☞ – ⟲✦ **P** **MC** **VISA**, ⋙
closed 25-26 December – Rest (by arrangement) 35.00 – **4 rm** ⟷ ✦90.00/100.00 – ✦✦135.00.
• This fine 19C rectory, set in a beautiful rural location, has had a sleek and stylish refit, lending it a luxurious air. Elegant interiors are matched by stunning bedrooms. Freshest Welsh ingredients incorporated into tasty evening meals.

⌂ **Wern Farm** without rest., Pentraeth Rd, LL59 5RR, North : 2 ¼ m. by B 5420 off A 5025 *℘* (01248) 712421, *wernfarmanglesey@onetel.com*, Fax (01248) 712421, ≤, ☞, 𝄞, ⋙ – ⟲✦ **P** **MC** **VISA**, ⋙
March-October – **3 rm** ⟷ ✦45.00/75.00 – ✦✦65.00/75.00.
• Attractive Georgian farmhouse run by a friendly couple. Bedrooms are spacious and comfortable. Enjoy countryside views in conservatory where vast breakfast is offered.

XX **Ruby,** Dale St, LL59 5AW, *℘* (01248) 714999, Fax (01248) 717888 – ⟲✦ ☷ **MC** **VISA**
closed 26 December, 1 January and Saturday lunch – Rest 12.95/15.95 and a la carte 15.95/26.00 ⊻.
• Former firestation and council offices; now a lively, bustling eatery on two floors with good local reputation. Eclectic, global menus employing flavoursome, vibrant cooking.

MERTHYR TYDFIL *Merthyr Tydfil 503* J 28 *Wales G.* – pop. 30 483.
Env. : *Brecon Beacons National Park★★*.
Exc. : *Ystradfellte★, NW : 13 m. by A 4102, A 465, A 4059 and minor roads.*
🎅 Morlais Castle, Pant, Dowlais *℘* (01685) 722822 – 🎅 Cilsanws Mountain, Cefn Coed *℘* (01685) 723308.
🇧 14a Glebeland St *℘* (01685) 379884.
London 179 – *Cardiff* 25 – Gloucester 59 – Swansea 33.

WALES

at Cwm Taf *Northwest : 6 m. on A 470 –* ✉ *Merthyr Tydfil.*

Nant Ddu Lodge, CF48 2HY, on A 470 ℰ (01685) 379111, *enquiries@nant-ddu-lodge.co.uk, Fax (01685) 377088, Ⅰ₆, ☎, ⬜, ⚐ – ⅙ rest, 🅿 🐾 🆎 VISA*
closed 25 December – **Rest** (in bar Monday-Saturday lunch) a la carte 20.45/22.45 **s.** ♀ – ⌑ 4.95 – **31 rm** ♦69.50 – ♦♦99.50/125.00.
♦ Family run hotel, Georgian in origin, named after the nearby "black stream". Sizeable, spotless rooms in an eye-catching blend of modern fabrics. Bustling, buzzy bar. Colourful bistro where blackboard specials complement a tasty and satisfying selection.

MOLD (Yr Wyddgrug) *Flintshire* 502 503 K 24 *Wales G. – pop. 9 586.*

See : *St Mary's Church★.*

Ⅰ₈ *Clicain Rd, Pantmywyn* ℰ (01352) 740318 – Ⅰ₈, Ⅰ₉ *Clicain Rd, Old Padeswood, Station Rd* ℰ (01244) 547701 – Ⅰ₈ *Padeswood & Buckley, The Caia, Station Lane, Padeswood* ℰ (01244) 550537 – Ⅰ₅ *Caerwys* ℰ (01352) 721222.
🅱 *Library, Museum and Art Gallery, Earl Rd* ℰ (01352) 759331.
London 211 – Chester 12 – Liverpool 22 *– Shrewsbury 45.*

Tower ⚐ *without rest., Nercwys, CH7 4EW, South : 1 m. by B 5444, Nercwys rd on Treuddyn rd* ℰ (01352) 700220, *Fax* (01352) 700220, ≤, ⚐ – ⅙ 🅿 🐾 VISA ⚙
closed Christmas-New Year – **3 rm** ⌑ 50.00 – ♦♦90.00.
♦ Last of the Welsh fortified border houses, owned by the same family for 500 years. Combined lounge/breakfast room. Spacious, simply furnished rooms overlook private parkland.

The Stables (at Soughton Hall H.), CH7 6AB, *North : 2 ½ m. by A 5119 and Alltami Rd* ℰ (01352) 840577, *info@soughtonhall.co.uk, Fax* (01352) 840872, ☂, ⚐ – ⅙ 🅿 🐾 🆎 VISA
Rest (booking essential) a la carte 24.20/31.40 ♀.
♦ 17C stable block in grounds of wedding venue hotel; bar and first-floor brasserie in bare brick and scrubbed pine. Tasty classics from open kitchen. Terrace for summer lunch.

Glas Fryn, *Raikes Lane, Sychdyn, CH7 6LR, North : 1 m. by A 5119 on Civic Centre rd* (Theatr Clwyd) ℰ (01352) 750500, *glasfryn@bandp.co.uk, Fax* (01352) 751923, ☂, ⚐ – 🅿 🐾 🆎 VISA
closed 25-26 December – **Rest** a la carte 15.95/29.70 ♀.
♦ Informal and open-plan; sepia prints, crammed bookshelves and rows of old bottles surround wooden tables. Varied brasserie menu draws a lively young set.

MONMOUTH (Trefynwy) *Monmouthshire* 503 L 28 *– pop. 8 547.*

See : *Town★.*
London 135 – Abergavenny 19 – Cardiff 40.

at Whitebrook *South : 8¼ m. by A 466 –* ✉ *Monmouth.*

The Crown at Whitebrook ⚐ *with rm, NP25 4TX,* ℰ (01600) 860254, *info@crownatwhitebrook.co.uk, Fax* (01600) 860607, ⚐ – ⅙ ⚑ 🅿 🐾 VISA
closed 26 December-9 January, Sunday dinner and Monday – **Rest** (booking essential) 22.50/39.50 **s.** ♀ – **8 rm** ⌑ ♦85.00 – ♦♦130.00.
Spec. Pan-fried scallops with cauliflower, Alsace jelly and cumin. Canon of lamb with wild mushrooms, gherkin purée and Port jus. Bubblegum panna cotta with cinnamon doughnut.
♦ Attentively run, with a modern feel, in an area of outstanding natural beauty. Local produce given an inventive, modish edge. Very comfy Executive rooms with immense style.

at Rockfield *Northwest : 2½ m. on B 4233 –* ✉ *Monmouth.*

Stone Mill, NP25 5SN, *West : 1 m. on B 4233* ℰ (01600) 716273, *Fax* (01600) 715257, ⚐ – ⅙ 🅿 🐾 VISA
closed 2 weeks January, Sunday dinner and Monday – **Rest** 12.95/16.95 and a la carte 26.40/33.95 ♀.
♦ Converted 16C stone cider mill with exposed timbers; leather sofa in sitting area/bar. Attentive service. Well sourced modern seasonal dishes using small local suppliers.

MONTGOMERY (Trefaldwyn) *Powys* 503 K 26 *Wales G.*

See : *Town★.*
London 194 – Birmingham 71 – Chester 53 – Shrewsbury 30.

Little Brompton Farm ⚐ *without rest., SY15 6HY, Southeast : 2 m. on B 4385* ℰ (01686) 668371, *gaynor.brompton@virgin.net, Fax* (01686) 668371, Ⅾ – ⅙ 🅿 ⚙
3 rm ⌑ ♦30.00/35.00 – ♦♦50.00/60.00.
♦ Part 17C cottage on working farm, run by friendly couple: husband's lived here all his life! Cosy beamed lounge and inglenook. Hearty breakfast. Traditionally appointed rooms.

WALES

MUMBLES (The) Swansea 503 I 29 – see Swansea.

NANNERCH Flintshire 502 503 K 24 – ⊠ Mold.
London 218 – Chester 19 – Liverpool 29 – Shrewsbury 52.

⌂ **Old Mill** without rest., Melin-y-Wern, Denbigh Rd, CH7 5RH, Northwest : ¾ m. on A 541
ℰ (01352) 741542, mail@old-mill.co.uk, 🐎 – ⅝ P. ⬛ AE ⓪ VISA. ⅝
6 rm ⊊ ✷50.00 – ✷✷74.50.
◆ Renovated stone-built Victorian stables set in well-kept gardens on a busy road. The
beamed bedrooms are comfortable, modern and pine-fitted.

NANTGAREDIG Carmarthenshire 503 H 28 – see Carmarthen.

NANT DERRY Monmouthshire – see Abergavenny.

NEWPORT (Casnewydd-Ar-Wysg) Newport 503 L 29 Wales G. – pop. 116 143.
See : Museum and Art Gallery★ AX M – Transporter Bridge★ AC AY – Civic Centre (murals★)
AX.
Env. : Caerleon Roman Fortress★★ AC (Fortress Baths★ – Legionary Museum★ – Amphi-
theatre★), NE : 2½ m. by B 4596 AX – Tredegar House★★ (Grounds★ – Stables★), SW : 2½
m. by A 48 AY.
Exc. : Penhow Castle★ , E : 8 m. by A 48 AX.
🞖 Caerleon, Broadway *ℰ* (01633) 420342 – 🞖 Parc, Church Lane, Coedkernew *ℰ* (01633)
680933.
🞖 Museum and Art Gallery, John Frost Sq *ℰ* (01633) 842962.
London 145 – Bristol 31 – Cardiff 12 – Gloucester 48.

Plan opposite

🏨 **Celtic Manor Resort,** Coldra Woods, NP18 1HQ, East : 3 m. on A 48 *ℰ* (01633) 413000,
postbox@celtic-manor.com, Fax (01633) 412910, ⑫, 🞖₆, ⩙s, 🞖, 🞖ₐ, ᴥ, ⅏ – ⛁, ⅝ rm, 🞖
⛲ ⴴ ⵒ⯎ P – 🞖 1500. ⬛ AE ⓪ VISA. ⅝
Owens : Rest (closed Sunday) (dinner only) 45.00/60.00 ☟ – *The Olive Tree* : Rest 25.00
(dinner) and lunch a la carte 19.00/25.00 ☟ – ⊊ 15.00 – **298 rm** ✷235.00 – ✷✷235.00,
32 suites 410.00/1500.00.
◆ Classical, Celtic and country house motifs on a grand modern scale. Smart contemporary
rooms boast hi-tech mod cons. State-of-the-art gym, golf academy and spa. Elaborate
Welsh-derived fusion food at Owens. Buffets sometimes served in the Olive Tree bistro.

✗ **The Chandlery,** 77-78 Lower Dock St, NP20 1EH, *ℰ* (01633) 256622, Fax (01633) 256633
⊛ – ▤. ⬛ AE VISA
AY **a**
closed 24 December-3 January, Saturday lunch, Sunday and Monday – Rest 12.95 (lunch)
and a la carte 18.40/32.40 S. ☟.
◆ Converted 18C chandler's store by the Usk. Spacious split-level restaurant. Polite service.
Wide-ranging menu of freshly prepared dishes: confident, good-value modern cooking.

at Tredunnock Northeast : 8¾ m. by A 4042 – AX –, B 4596 and B 4236, off Usk rd, turning right
at Cwrt Bleddyn Hotel – ⊠ Newport.

🞖 **The Newbridge** with rm, NP15 1LY, East : ¼ m. *ℰ* (01633) 451000, thenewbridge@ti
nyonline.co.uk, Fax (01633) 451001, ≼, 🞖 – ⅝ rm, P. ⬛ AE ⓪ VISA. ⅝
closed 26 December – Rest a la carte 20.00/32.00 ☟ – **6 rm** ⊊ ✷110.00 – ✷✷150.00.
◆ Bright, comfy pub idyllically set by bridge overlooking Usk. Modern and classical techniques applied to locally based dishes. Superb contemporary bedrooms exude immense
style.

at Redwick Southeast : 9½ m. by M 4 – AY – off B 4245 – ⊠ Magor.

⌂ **Brick House Country** 🞖 without rest., North Row, NP26 3DX, *ℰ* (01633) 880230,
brickhouse@compuserve.com, Fax (01633) 882441, 🐎 – ⅝ P. ⬛ AE VISA. ⅝
7 rm ⊊ ✷35.00/50.00 – ✷✷55.00/60.00.
◆ Ivy-covered Georgian house under long-standing family management. Faultlessly neat
bedrooms with traditional floral décor and a spacious front lounge and bar.

WALES

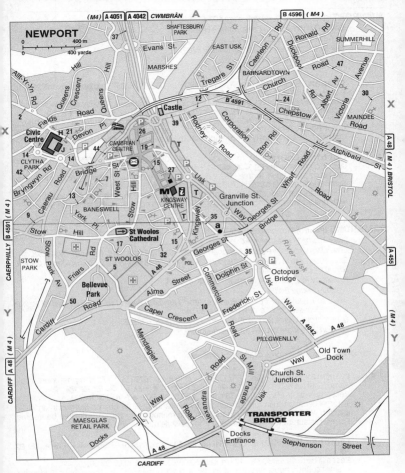

NEWPORT

at St Brides Wentlooge *Southwest : 4½ m. by A 48 –* **AY** *– on B 4239 –* ⊠ *Newport.*

🏠 **The Inn at The Elm Tree**, NP10 8SQ, 𝒫 (01633) 680225, *inn@the-elm-tree.co.uk,*
Fax (01633) 681055, 🍴 – ⇌⇥ **P. MO AE VISA**
Rest 12.50/25.00 and a la carte approx 36.00 – **10 rm** ⊑ ✦60.00/80.00 – ✦✦90.00/130.00.
♦ Converted 19C barn. Pristine, pine-furnished rooms in bright fabrics thoughtfully sup-
plied with 21C mod cons; all individually styled. Lounge bar serves Champagne on ice.
Immaculately set dining room; wide-ranging, Welsh-based dishes.

NEWPORT (Trefdraeth) *Pembrokeshire* 503 F 27 *Wales G.* – *pop. 1 162.*
Env. : *Pembrokeshire Coast National Park*★★.
🟦 Newport ℰ (01239) 820244.
🅱 2 Bank Cottages, Long St ℰ (01239) 820912.
London 258 – Fishguard 7.

🏛 **Cnapan,** East St, SA42 0SY, on A 487 ℰ (01239) 820575, *cnapan@ukonline.co.uk,*
Fax (01239) 820878, 🌳 – ⚟ 🅿 🕮 🅼🅾 *VISA.* 🦫
closed January-February and 25-26 December – **Rest** *(closed Tuesday and lunch Sunday)*
(booking essential) (light lunch)/dinner 22.00/27.50 – **5 rm** ☷ ★47.00 – ★★80.00.
♦ Pine-fitted bedrooms with floral fabrics and individual character in a genuinely friendly
guest house, family run for over 15 years. Homely lounge has a wood-burning stove.
Clothed tables and family photographs set the tone in the traditional dining room.

XX **Doctor's Court** with rm, East St, SA42 0SY, ℰ (01239) 820008, *contact@doctor*
scourt.com, 🌳 – ⚟ 📺 📞 🅿 🅼🅾 *VISA*
restricted opening in winter – **Rest** *(closed Sunday dinner and Monday)* (light lunch May-
October)/dinner a la carte 21.95/31.95 ♀ – **6 rm** ☷ ★75.00 – ★★120.00.
♦ Earnestly laid-back style; lunch offered in Mediterranean herb kitchen garden. Dinner,
with fine art surroundings, has modern Welsh/Italian edge. Superbly stylish bedrooms.

PEMBROKE (Penfro) *Pembrokeshire* 503 F 28 *Wales G.* – *pop. 7 214.*
See : *Town*★★ – *Castle*★★ *AC.*
Env. : *Pembrokeshire Coast National Park*★★ – *Carew Castle*★ *AC, NE : 4 m. by A 4075.*
Exc. : *Bosherston (St Govan's Chapel*★), *S : 7 m. by A 4319 and minor roads – Stack Rocks*★,
SW : 9 m. by B 4319 and minor roads.
🟦 Military Rd, Pembroke Dock ℰ (01646) 621453.
Cleddau Bridge (toll).
🚢 to Republic of Ireland (Rosslare) (Irish Ferries) 2 daily (4 h) – to Republic of Ireland
(Cork) (Swansea Cork Ferries) daily (8 h 30 mn).
🅱 Pembroke Visitor Centre, Commons Rd ℰ (01646) 622388.
London 252 – Carmarthen 32 – Fishguard 26.

at Lamphey *East : 1¾ m. on A 4139 –* ✉ *Pembroke.*

🏰 **Lamphey Court** ⑤, SA71 5NT, ℰ (01646) 672273, *info@lampheycourt.co.uk,*
Fax (01646) 672480, �, 🍸, ⬛, 🌳, ♨, ❊ – ⚟ 📞 🅿 – 🔺 70. 🅼🅾 🅰🅴 🅾 *VISA.* 🦫
Rest a la carte 26.00/32.00 **s.** – **38 rm** ☷ ★82.00/95.00 – ★★115.00/165.00.
♦ Large Georgian mansion surrounded by parkland, built by Charles Mathias in an idyllic
location. Well furnished throughout with fine mahogany in the co-ordinated bedrooms.
Formal restaurant with a good country house-style menu.

🏛 **Lamphey Hall,** SA71 5NR, ℰ (01646) 672394, Fax (01646) 672369, 🌳 – ⚟ 🅿 🅼🅾 🅰🅴
🅾 *VISA*
Rest a la carte 19.35/30.35 – **12 rm** ☷ ★55.00/65.00 – ★★80.00/95.00.
♦ Small country house with a neat garden and a rich style of décor throughout. Bedrooms
are a mix of shapes and sizes and all are individually styled. The restaurant or bar offers
spacious, comfortable surroundings in which to enjoy Welsh produce.

PENALLY (Penalun) *Pembrokeshire* 503 F 29 – *see Tenby.*

PENARTH *Cardiff* 503 K 29 – *see Cardiff.*

PENMACHNO *Conwy* 502 503 I 24 – *see Betws-y-Coed.*

PENNAL *Gwynedd* 503 I 26 – *see Aberdovey.*

PENTYRCH *Cardiff* 503 K 29 – *see Cardiff.*

PONTDOLGOCH *Powys – see Caersws.*

PONTYPRIDD *Rhondda Cynon Taff* 503 K 29 *Wales G.* – pop. 29 781.
Env. : *Rhondda Heritage Park★ AC, NW : 4 m. by A 4058.*
Exc. : *Caerphilly Castle★★ AC, SE : 7 m. by A 470 and A 468 – Llancaiach Fawr Manor★ AC,*
NE : 6½ m. by A 4054, A 472, B 4255 and B 4254.
🛈 *Pontypridd Museum, Bridge St* ☎ *(01443) 490748.*
London 164 – Cardiff 9 – Swansea 40.

🏫 **Llechwen Hall** ⌖, Llanfabon, CF37 4HP, Northeast : 4 ¼ m. by A 4223 off A 4054
☎ (01443) 742050, llechwen@aol.com, Fax (01443) 742189, ☞ – ⌖ ℙ – 🏄 80. 🆎 🆎 ⓞ
𝗩𝗜𝗦𝗔
closed 25-29 December – **Rest** a la carte 21.50/29.00 – ⌖ 8.95 – **20 rm** ⌖60.00 – ⌖⌖95.00.
♦ 17C house with Victorian frontage, overlooks the Aberdare and Merthyr Valleys. Smart
country house style and comforts. Spotless bedrooms in either the main or coach house.
Two dining options, both decorated in similar traditional style.

PORTH *Rhondda Cynon Taff* 503 J 29 *Wales G.* – pop. 6 225 – ✉ *Pontypridd.*
Env. : *Trehafod (Rhondda Heritage Park★), E : 1½ m. by A 4058.*
London 168 – Cardiff 13 – Swansea 45.

🏫 **Heritage Park,** Coed Cae Rd, Trehafod, CF37 2NP, on A 4058 ☎ (01443) 687057, *reser*
vations@heritageparkhotel.co.uk, Fax (01443) 687060, 🎣, ☎, ◳ – ⌖, ▤ rest, ☏ ⌖ ℙ –
🏄 200. 🆎 🆎 𝗩𝗜𝗦𝗔
closed 24-26 December – **The Loft :** Rest 17.50 and a la carte 14.65/26.60 – **44 rm** ⌖
⌖84.00/94.00 – ⌖⌖107.00.
♦ Brick-built hotel in Rhondda Valley, adjacent to Heritage Park Centre; Museum of Mining
close by. Countryside location, yet not far from Cardiff. Co-ordinated, classic rooms. Loft
dining with verandah or conservatory options.

PORTHCAWL *Bridgend* 503 I 29 *Wales G.* – pop. 15 640.
Env. : *Glamorgan Heritage Coast★.*
🛈 *The Old Police Station, John St* ☎ *(01656) 786639, porthcawltic@bridgend.gov.uk.*
London 183 – Cardiff 28 – Swansea 18.

🏩 **Fairways,** West Drive, CF36 3LS, ☎ (01656) 782085, *info@thefairwayshotel.co.uk,*
Fax (01656) 785351, ⇐ – ▦ ⌖ ☏ ℙ. 🆎 🆎 𝗩𝗜𝗦𝗔 ✁
Rest a la carte 14.40/25.40 **s.** – **18 rm** ⌖ ⌖70.00/90.00 – ⌖⌖100.00/150.00.
♦ Traditionally attired 18C seafront hotel. Relaxed, easy-going public areas. Half the rooms
have sea views: check out Room 1, which is particularly airy and boasts Jacuzzi. 'Safe'
classics in cloth-clad dining room.

🛏 **Foam Edge** without rest., 9 West Drive, CF36 3LS, ☎ (01656) 782866, *hywelandhe*
len@aol.com, ⇐ – ⌖ 📺 ℙ. ✁
3 rm ⌖ ⌖30.00/50.00 – ⌖⌖50.00/70.00.
♦ Enjoy original breakfast dishes and Bristol Channel views. Impressive front bedrooms:
one's a four poster with sun lounge, other's nicely co-ordinated in neutral shades.

✗✗ **Coast,** 2-4 Dock St, CF36 3BL, ☎ (01656) 782025, *james@coastrestaurants.co.uk* – ⌖. 🆎
🆎 𝗩𝗜𝗦𝗔
closed 2-14 January, Sunday dinner and Monday except July and December – **Rest** a la
carte 15.85/28.20 ⌖.
♦ Locally renowned, this airy, up-to-date restaurant has a front lounge and rear dining
room, where you can choose between the tried-and-tested or dishes with an original
edge.

PORTHGAIN *Pembrokeshire – see St Davids.*

Do not confuse ✗ with ✧!
✗ defines comfort, while stars are awarded for the best cuisine,
across all categories of comfort.

PORTHMADOG Gwynedd 503 H 25.
Cardiff 162 – Blanau Ffestiniog 12 – Caernarfon 19.

🏛 **Plas Tan-yr-Allt** ♨, Tremadog, LL49 9RG, North : 1½ m. by A 487 on A 498 ℰ (01766) 514545, info@tanyrallt.co.uk, ≤ Tremadog Bay and countryside, �, 🔥 – ⚡ 🄿. 🕥⊙ 🄰🄴 𝗩𝗜𝗦𝗔. ⅋
closed Christmas 1 week February, and Monday-Tuesday in winter – **Rest** (booking essential) (communal dining) (dinner only) 32.00 **s.** – **6 rm** ⊐ ✚70.00/100.00 – ✚✚130.00.
♦ Fully refurbished, this former home of Shelley, built into wooded cliffside, has an airy, stylish and comfy feel bordering on the luxurious. Charming, individualistic rooms. Dine en-famille style: a Welsh Country House menu prevails.

PORTMEIRION Gwynedd 502 503 H 25 Wales G.
See : Village★★★ AC.
Env. : Snowdonia National Park★★★ – Lleyn Peninsula★★ – Ffestiniog Railway★★ AC.
London 245 – Caernarfon 23 – Colwyn Bay 40 – Dolgellau 24.

🏚🏚 **Portmeirion** ♨, LL48 6ET, ℰ (01766) 770000, hotel@portmeirion-village.com, Fax (01766) 771331, ≤ village and estuary, �, 🔥 heated, 🌳 – ⚡ rest, 🄿. – 🄰 50. 🕥⊙ 🄰🄴 ⊙ 𝗩𝗜𝗦𝗔. ⅋
closed 2 weeks January **Rest** (booking essential for non-residents) 19.50/39.50 and dinner a la carte 21.00/43.50 ⵦ – **35 rm** ⊐ ✚132.00 – ✚✚167.00, 16 suites.
♦ Set in private Italianate village in extensive gardens and woodland designed by Sir Clough Williams-Ellis. Delightful views of village and estuary. Antique furnished rooms. Restaurant offers lovely views of the estuary and an open and light style of décor.

🏚🏚 **Castell Deudraeth**, LL48 6EN, ℰ (01766) 772400, hotel@portmeirion-village.com, Fax (01766) 771771, ≤, 🌻, 🌳 – ▐◣, ⚡ rest, ☰ rest, ☎ 🄿. – 🄰 40. 🕥⊙ 🄰🄴 ⊙ 𝗩𝗜𝗦𝗔. ⅋
closed 21 January - 2 February – **Grill : Rest** 19.00/24.00 ⵦ – **9 rm** ⊐ ✚174.00 – ✚✚277.00, 2 suites.
♦ Crenellated 19C manor, its modern decor in harmony with the original Welsh oak, slate and stone. Superbly stylish rooms in blues, greys and pale wood. Restored walled garden. Victorian solarium, converted into a modish minimalist restaurant.

PWLLHELI Gwynedd 502 503 G 25 Wales G. – pop. 3 861.
Env. : Lleyn Peninsula★★.
🞖 Golf Rd ℰ (01758) 701644.
🄱 MinyDon, Station Sq ℰ (01758) 613000, pwllheli.tic@gwynedd.gov.uk.
London 261 – Aberystwyth 73 – Caernarfon 21.

🞫🞫 **Plas Bodegroes** (Chown) ♨ with rm, LL53 5TH, Northwest: 1 ¾ m. on A 497
🕸 ℰ (01758) 612363, gunna@bodegroes.co.uk, Fax (01758) 701247, 🌳 – ⚡ 🄿. 🕥⊙ 𝗩𝗜𝗦𝗔
8 March-17 November – **Rest** (closed Sunday-Monday, except Bank Holidays) (booking essential) (dinner only and Sunday lunch)/dinner 42.50 ⍺ – **11 rm** ⊐ ✚50.00/100.00 – ✚✚170.00.
Spec. Seared John Dory and scallops with caramelised chicory, vanilla sauce. Fillet of Welsh beef with a steak and oyster pie. Chocolate soufflé with white chocolate ice cream.
♦ Georgian mansion in peaceful seclusion amidst charming gardens. Cottagey bedrooms. Spacious dining room with assorted artwork in which to relish stylish, inventive dishes.

at Boduan Northwest : 3¾ m. on A 497 – ✉ Pwllheli.

🏠 **The Old Rectory** without rest., LL53 6DT, ℰ (01758) 721519, thepollards@theoldrectory.net, Fax (01758) 721519, 🌳 – ⚡ 🄿.
closed 1 week Christmas – **3 rm** ⊐ ✚60.00/90.00 – ✚✚90.00.
♦ Part Georgian house with garden and paddock, adjacent to church. Well restored providing comfortable, individually decorated bedrooms and attractive sitting room.

RAGLAN Monmouthshire 503 L 28 Wales G. – ✉ Abergavenny.
See : Castle★ AC.
London 154 – Cardiff 32 – Gloucester 34 – Newport 18 – Swansea 58.

🍴 **Clytha Arms** with rm, NP7 9BW, West : 3 m. on Clytha rd (old Abergavenny Rd)
ℰ (01873) 840206, theclythaarms@tiscali.co.uk, Fax (01873) 840209, 🌳 – ⚡ 📺 🄿. 🕥⊙ 🄰🄴 ⊙ 𝗩𝗜𝗦𝗔
Rest (closed Sunday dinner and Monday lunch) 19.95 and a la carte approx 28.00 ⵦ – **4 rm** ⊐ ✚60.00 – ✚✚100.00.
♦ Personally run converted dower house. Welcoming, open fires; traditional games sprinkled around tapas-serving bar. Generous, eclectic menus utilise the best of Welsh produce.

REDWICK Newport 503 L 29 – see Newport (Newport).

WALES

RHAYADER (Rhaeadr) *Powys* 503 J 27 – *pop. 1 783.*
🔲 *The Leisure Centre, North Street* 𝒫 *(01597) 810591.*
London 195 – Aberystwyth 39 – Carmarthen 67 – Shrewsbury 60.

↑ **Beili Neuadd** ⤷ *without rest., LD6 5NS, Northeast : 2 m. by A 44 off Abbey-cwm-hir rd*
𝒫 *(01597) 810211, rhayaderbreaks@yahoo.co.uk, ⩽, ⛭ – P*
closed 16 December- 13 January – **3 rm** ☲ ✝25.00 – ✝✝50.00.
♦ Part 16C stone-built farmhouse in a secluded rural setting with countryside views. Personally run with comfortable bedrooms. Close to Rhayader and the "Lakeland of Wales".

RHOS-ON-SEA (Llandrillo-yn-Rhos) *Conwy* 502 503 I 24 – *see Colwyn Bay.*

RHYL *Denbighshire* 502 503 J 24 *Wales G. – pop. 25 390.*
Env. : *Rhuddlan Castle★★ , S : 3 m. by A 525 – Bodelwyddan★★ , S : 5 m. by A 525 and minor rd – St Asaph Cathedral★ , S : 5 m. by A 525.*
Exc. : *Llandudno★ , W : 16 m. by A 548, A 55 and B 5115.*
Cardiff 182 – Chester 34 – Llandudno 18.5.

XX **Barratt's at Ty'n Rhyl** *with rm, 167 Vale Rd, LL18 2PH, South : ½ m. on A 525*
𝒫 *(01745) 344138, ebarratt5@aol.com, Fax (01745) 344138, ⇗ – ⛭⩽ P. ◍◉ VISA. ⅋*
Rest (booking essential) (dinner only and Sunday lunch) a la carte 25.00/28.00 – **3 rm** ☲
✝55.00 – ✝✝75.00.
♦ Rhyl's oldest house boasts comfortable lounges with rich oak panelling. Dine in either new conservatory or original house. Ambitious cooking on classic base. Individual rooms.

Do not confuse X with ⁕!
X defines comfort, while stars are awarded for the best cuisine,
across all categories of comfort.

ROCKFIELD *Monmouthshire* 503 L 28 – *see Monmouth.*

RUTHIN (Rhuthun) *Denbighshire* 502 503 K 24 *Wales G. – pop. 5 218.*
Env. : *Llandyrnog (St Dyfnog's Church★), Llanrhaeder-yng-Nghinmeirch (Jesse Window★★), N : 5½ m. by A 494 and B 5429.*
Exc. : *Denbigh★, NW : 7 m. on A 525.*
🏌 *Ruthin-Pwllglas* 𝒫 *(01824) 702296.*
🔲 *Ruthin Craft Centre, Park Rd* 𝒫 *(01824) 703992.*
London 210 – Birkenhead 31 – Chester 23 – Liverpool 34 – Shrewsbury 46.

↑ **Firgrove,** *Llanfwrog, LL15 2LL, West : 1 ¼ m. by A 494 on B 5105* 𝒫 *(01824) 702677,*
 meadway@firgrovecountryhouse.co.uk, Fax (01824) 702677, ⇗ – ⛭⩽ ⍟ P. ◍◉ VISA. ⅋
February-November – **Rest** (by arrangement) (communal dining) 35.00 – **3 rm** ☲ ✝45.00 –
✝✝68.00.
♦ Well-furnished house with tasteful interiors set within attractive gardens. Bedrooms are comfortable; one is a self-contained cottage with a small kitchen. Close to the town. Traditionally furnished dining room with meals taken at a communal table.

↑ **Eyarth Station** ⤷, *Llanfair Dyffryn Clwyd, LL15 2EE, South : 1¾ m. by A 525* 𝒫 *(01824)*
703643, stay@eyarthstation.com, Fax (01824) 707464, ⩽, ⤴ heated, ⇗ – ⛭⩽ P. ◍◉ VISA
closed 25 December – **Rest** (by arrangement) 15.00 – **6 rm** ☲ ✝45.00 – ✝✝70.00.
♦ Former railway station with a fine collection of photographs of its previous life. Pleasant country location. Traditional décor in bedrooms, sitting room and a small bar. Views over the countryside and hearty home-cooked food in the dining room.

ST BRIDES WENTLOOGE *Newport* 503 K 29 – *see Newport.*

ST CLEARS *Carmarthenshire* 503 G 28.

↑ **Coedllys Country House** ⤷ *without rest., Llangynin, SA33 4JY, Northwest : 3 ½ m.*
 by A 40 on Glyn-car Paradise Valley track in village 𝒫 *(01994) 231455, enquiries@coedlly scountryhouse.co.uk, Fax (01944) 231441, ⩽, ⩬, ⇗, ⚘ – ⛭⩽ P. ◍◉ VISA*
closed Christmas – **3 rm** ☲ ✝45.00/47.50 – ✝✝75.00/80.00.
♦ Idyllic country house and animal sanctuary with picture-perfect façade. Delightful owner keeps everything immaculate. Superb breakfasts. Rooms with unerring eye for detail.

ST DAVIDS (Tyddewi) *Pembrokeshire* 503 E 28 *Wales G.* – pop. 1 959 – ⊠ *Haverfordwest.*
See : Town★ – Cathedral★★ – Bishop's Palace★ *AC.*
Env. : Pembrokeshire Coast National Park★★.
🍃 *St Davids City, Whitesands Bay* ℰ (01437) 721751.
🖪 *National Park Visitor Centre, The Grove* ℰ (01437) 720392, enquiries@stdavids.pembro keshirecoast.org.uk.
London 266 – Carmarthen 46 – Fishguard 16.

🏠 **Warpool Court** ॐ, SA62 6BN, Southwest : ½ m. by Porth Clais rd ℰ (01437) 720300, info@warpoolcourthotel.com, Fax (01437) 720676, ≤, ⬛, 🐎, ✻ – ⇔ P. ⬛ 🔵 AE ① VISA
closed January – **Rest** 29.00/49.00 – **25 rm** �) ✚90.00/180.00 – ✚✚180.00/240.00.
♦ Over 3000 hand-painted tiles of Celtic or heraldic design decorate the interior of this 19C house. Modern bedrooms, some with views over neat lawned gardens to the sea. Daily changing classic menus accompanied by fine views.

🏠 **Old Cross,** Cross Sq, SA62 6SP, ℰ (01437) 720387, enquiries@oldcrosshotel.co.uk, Fax (01437) 720394, 🐎 – ⇔ P. 🔵 VISA
closed January – **Rest** (bar lunch Monday-Saturday)/dinner 20.00 and a la carte 19.75/27.95 ℥ – **16 rm** �) ✚40.00/85.00 – ✚✚70.00/110.00.
♦ Overlooking the old market square, a long-established, ivy-clad hotel: rooms are modern and simply decorated. Beamed lounge - club chairs grouped around a brick fireplace. Wheelback chairs and yellow linen-clad tables in an unassuming, traditional restaurant.

🏠 **Crug-Glas** ॐ, Abereiddy, SA62 6XX, Northeast : 5 ½ m. on A 487 ℰ (01348) 831302, janet@crugglas.wanadoo.co.uk, Fax (01348) 831302, 🐎, ₤ – ⇔ TV P. 🔵 VISA
closed Christmas and New Year – **Rest** (by arrangement) 25.00 – **5 rm** �) ✚60.00 – ✚✚100.00/130.00.
♦ Imposing family run Georgian house on a farm believed to have been worked since 12/13C. Partake of honesty bar then retire to one of the luxurious bedrooms: ask for no. 5. Good local choice on tried-and-tested evening menu.

🏠 **Ramsey House** without rest., Lower Moor, SA62 6RP, Southeast : ½ m. on Porthclais rd ℰ (01437) 720321, info@ramseyhouse.co.uk, 🐎 – ⇔ P. ✼
March-October – **5 rm** �) ✚40.00 – ✚✚70.00/75.00.
♦ Detached house just outside town centre. Spotlessly kept, homely interior. Fine breakfasts employ tasty home baking; small bar overlooks gardens. Compact, neat and tidy rooms.

🏠 **The Waterings** ॐ without rest., Anchor Drive, High St, SA62 6QH, East : ¼ m. on A 487 ℰ (01437) 720876, enquiries@waterings.co.uk, Fax (01437) 720876, 🐎 – ⇔ P. ✼
5 rm �) ✚50.00/80.00 – ✚✚75.00/80.00.
♦ Set in peaceful landscaped gardens and named after a sheltered cove on Ramsey Island. Spacious rooms, furnished in solid pine, around a central courtyard. Likeable hosts.

🏠 **Y-Gorlan** without rest., 77 Nun St, SA62 6NU, ℰ (01437) 720837, mikebohlen@aol.com, Fax (01437) 721148 – ⇔ P. 🔵 VISA ✼
closed 2 weeks February and Christmas – **5 rm** �) ✚35.00/50.00 – ✚✚62.00/70.00.
♦ Run by a friendly couple, Y-Gorlan - "the fold" - offers comfortable, spotless modern rooms, all en suite. Homely lounge looks towards Whitesands Bay. Good breakfasts.

at Llanrhian *Northeast : 6½ m. by A 487 – ⊠ St Davids.*

🏠 **Trevaccoon** without rest., SA62 6DP, ℰ (01348) 831438, flynn@trevaccoon.co.uk, ≤, 🐎 – ⇔ TV ₤ P. 🔵 VISA ✼
closed 3 weeks late January-mid February and Christmas – **5 rm** ☺ ✚55.00/80.00 – ✚✚80.00/115.00.
♦ Pale pink coastal Georgian house with fine rural views. Its spacious and original proportions are augmented by modern furnishings. Organic breakfasts. Light, airy rooms.

at Porthgain *Northeast : 7¾ m. by A 487 – ⊠ St Davids.*

✗ **The Shed,** The Quay, SA62 5BN, ℰ (01348) 831518, Fax (01348) 831803, 🏠 – ⇔ P. 🔵 VISA
restricted opening in winter – **Rest** - Seafood - *(closed Monday dinner)* (booking essential) a la carte 30.95/43.85 ℥.
♦ At the tip of the harbour in a charming spot, this locally renowned rustic eatery started life as a lobster pot store and now serves simply prepared, tasty seafood dishes.

SALEM *Carmarthenshire – see Llandeilo.*

SARON *Gwynedd – see Caernarfon.*

SAUNDERSFOOT Pembrokeshire 503 F 28.
London 241 – Cardiff 90 – Pembroke 12.

 St Brides Spa H., St Brides Hill, SA69 9NH, ℰ (01834) 812304, *reservations@stbridesho tel.com*, Fax (01834) 811766, ≤ Harbour and Carmarthen Bay, 斧, ℗, ≦ – ⎸ ⇶ ℃ & ℙ – 函 60. ⓒ ⒶⒺ *VISA* –
Cliff : Rest a la carte 26.50/38.00 s. ⊈ – **35 rm** ⋆100.00/160.00 – ⋆⋆140.00/260.00.
♦ Occupying a great position over Carmarthen Bay, with breathtaking spa equipped to the highest spec. Fabulous terraces and outdoor infinity pool. Superbly designed bedrooms. Modern European cooking in fine dining restaurant with informal style.

Gower, Milford Terrace, SA69 9EL, ℰ (01834) 813452, *tim.rowe@rotels.com*, Fax (01834) 813452 – ⎸ ⇶ ℃ ℙ. ⓒ *VISA*
Rest (dinner only and Sunday lunch) 21.95 and a la carte 20.40/29.35 s. – **20 rm** ⋥ ⋆56.00/58.00 – ⋆⋆92.00/94.00.
♦ Four-storey yellow hued hotel, refurbished in 2004, close to the beach. Leather chester-fields enhance wood-floored bar. Immaculate bedrooms in a uniform style. Bright, spacious dining room with conservatory extension; good choice of fish.

SHIRENEWTON Monmouthshire 503 L 29 – see Chepstow.

SKENFRITH Monmouthshire.
London 135 – Hereford 16 – Ross-on-Wye 11.

The Bell at Skenfrith with rm, NP7 8UH, ℰ (01600) 750235, *enquiries@sken frith.co.uk*, Fax (01600) 750525, 斧, ℀, 庭 – ⇶ ℙ ⇔ 40. ⓒ ⒶⒺ *VISA*
closed late January-early February and Mondays in winter – Rest (booking essential) a la carte 25.00/30.00 ⊈ ⊘ – **8 rm** ⋥ ⋆75.00 – ⋆⋆180.00.
♦ Michelin's 2007 Pub of the Year is a charming 17C coaching inn with antiques, curios, open fires and tasty modern menus. Very comfy rooms have state-of-the-art appointments.

SOUTHERNDOWN Bridgend 503 J 29 – see Bridgend.

SWANSEA (Abertawe) Swansea 503 I 29 Wales G. – pop. 169 880.
See : Town★ – Maritime Quarter★ B – Maritime and Industrial Museum★ B – Glynn Vivian Art Gallery★ B – Guildhall (British Empire Panels★ A H).
Env. : Gower Peninsula★★ (Rhossili★★), W : by A 4067 A.
Exc. : The Wildfowl and Wetlands Trust★, Llanelli, NW : 6½ m. by A 483 and A 484 A.
🛆 Morriston, 160 Clasemont Rd ℰ (01792) 771079, A – 🛆 Clyne, 120 Owls Lodge Lane, Mayals ℰ (01792) 401989, A – 🛆 Langland Bay ℰ (01792) 366023, A – 🛆 Fairwood Park, Blackhills Lane, Upper Killay ℰ (01792) 297849, A – 🛆 Inco, Clydach ℰ (01792) 841257, A – 🛆 Allt-y-Graban, Allt-y-Graban Rd, Pontlliw ℰ (01792) 885757 – 🛆 Palleg, Lower Cwmtwrch, Swansea Valley ℰ (01639) 842193.
🚢 to Republic of Ireland (Cork) (Swansea Cork Ferries) (10 h).
🛈 Plymouth St ℰ (01792) 468321, *tourism@swansea.gov.uk*.
London 191 – Birmingham 136 – Bristol 82 – Cardiff 40 – Liverpool 187 – Stoke-on-Trent 175.

Plan on next page

 Morgans, Somerset Place, SA1 1RR, ℰ (01792) 484848, *reception@morganshotel.co.uk*, Fax (01792) 484847, ᑫ – ⎸ ⇶ ⊜ & ℙ – 函 40. ⓒ ⒶⒺ *VISA*. ✻ B b
Rest 16.50/20.00 and dinner a la carte 20.00/35.00 ⊈ – **41 rm** ⋥ ⋆80.00 – ⋆⋆250.00.
♦ Converted hotel near docks. Contemporary feel: neutral colours, leather sofas. Splendid original features include soaring cupola. Very stylish rooms. Modish cooking in sleek surroundings.

Ramada Encore, Fabian Way, SA1 8LD, on A 483 ℰ (0870) 4422825, *enquiries@encor eswanseabay.co.uk*, Fax (0870) 4422826 – ⎸ ⇶ ℃ & ℙ – 函 30. ⓒ ⒶⒺ ⓄⒹ *VISA*. ✻ A b
Rest (grill rest.) (dinner only) a la carte 15.85/24.90 s. ⊈ – **99 rm** ⋆59.95/69.95 – ⋆⋆69.95/99.95.
♦ Colourful, light and modern hotel by Swansea's docks. Contemporary rooms with up-to-date amenities.

XX **Didier & Stephanie's,** 56 St Helens Rd, SA1 4BE, ℰ (01792) 655603, Fax (01792) 470563 – ⇶ ⊜. ⓒ *VISA* A a
closed late December-mid January, Sunday and Monday – Rest - French - (booking essential) a la carte approx 27.30.
♦ Cosy, neighbourhood-styled restaurant with a strong Gallic influence. Welcoming owners provide tasty, good value, seasonally changing menus with lots of French ingredients.

WALES

SWANSEA

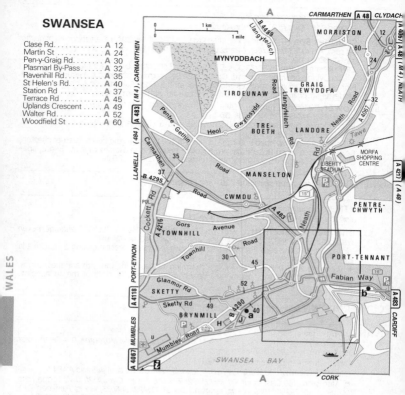

✗ **The Restaurant,** Pilot House Wharf, Trawler Rd, Swansea Marina, SA1 1UN, ✆ (01792) 466200, *therestaurant@aol.com, Fax (01792) 281528* – ℙ. ✕⊘ – **℗. ⓂⓈ ⒶⒺ ⓪ 𝘝𝘐𝘚𝘈**   **C a** *closed 24-26 December, Sunday dinner, Monday lunch and Bank Holidays* – **Rest** - Seafood specialities - (booking essential) 14.95 (lunch) and a la carte 19.85/34.85.
   ◆ Friendly, easygoing restaurant above a tackle shop and in sight of the harbour. Black-board fish specials are the pick of a carefully sourced repertoire. Good value lunch.

at The Mumbles *Southwest : 7¾ m. by A 4067 –* **A** *–* ✉ *Swansea.*

🏠 **Norton House,** 17 Norton Rd, SA3 5TQ, ✆ (01792) 404891, *nortonhouse@btcon nect.com, Fax (01792) 403210,* 🍽 *–* ✕← rest, ℙ *–* 🔬 25. ⓂⓈ ⒶⒺ ⓪ 𝘝𝘐𝘚𝘈. ✕ *closed 22-29 December –* **Rest** (dinner only) 25.00/27.50 and a la carte 25.00/39.20 *–* **15 rm** ⌧ ✦85.00 *–* ✦✦125.00.
   ◆ Georgian former master mariner's house, run with personable ease by a husband and wife team. Tidy rooms in traditional fabrics and furnishings - some have four-poster beds. Elegant, classically proportioned dining room, offset by French etched glassware.

at Llanrhidian *West : 10½ m. by A 4118 –* **A** *– and B 4271 –* ✉ *Reynoldston.*

🏠 **Fairyhill** ⌂, Reynoldston, SA3 1BS, West : 2½ m. by Llangennith Rd ✆ (01792) 390139, *postbox@fairyhill.net, Fax (01792) 391358,* 🍽, 🍴, 🌳 *–* ✕← rest, ℙ *–* 🔬 30. ⓂⓈ 𝘝𝘐𝘚𝘈. ✕ *closed 1-24 January –* **Rest** 19.95/37.50 and lunch a la carte approx 23.00 ♀ 🍷 *–* **8 rm** ⌧ ✦130.00 *–* ✦✦150.00.
   ◆ Georgian country house in extensive parkland and gardens. Mix includes sleek lounge, eclectic bedrooms, treatment and meeting rooms, all set within general modish ambience. Gower produce dominates seasonal menus.

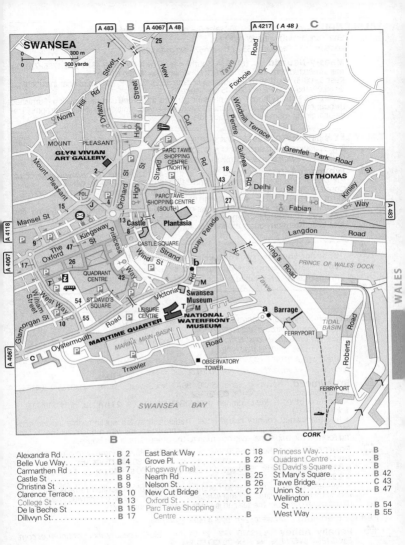

SWANSEA

0 ___ 300 m
0 ___ 300 yards

WALES

XX **The Welcome To Town**, SA3 1EH, ℘ (01792) 390015, *enquiries@thewelcometo town.co.uk*, Fax (01792) 390015 – ✦✕ **P**, **❻❻** **VISA**
closed 25-26 December, last 2 weeks February, 1 January, Sunday dinner and Monday except June-August – **Rest** (booking essential) 17.95/32.50 and a la carte 15.95/41.00.
◆ Converted pub set on picturesque peninsula. Cosy, traditional interior with good service of seasonal dishes cooked with real quality from wide choice menu.

> We try to be as accurate as possible when giving room rates.
> But prices are susceptible to change,
> so please check rates when booking.

TALSARNAU Gwynedd 502 503 H 25 Wales G. – pop. 647 – ⊠ Harlech.

Env. : Snowdonia National Park★★★.

London 236 – Caernafon 33 – Chester 67 – Dolgellau 25.

🏨 **Maes-y-Neuadd** ⑤, LL47 6YA, South : 1½ m. by A 496 off B 4573 ℘ (01766) 780200, maes@neuadd.com, Fax (01766) 780211, ≤, ㈜ – ⁴⑲ 🅿, ⑩⑨ 🖭 𝘝𝘐𝘚𝘈
Rest 33.00/37.00 (dinner) and lunch a la carte 15.25/22.00 𝟡 – **14 rm** (dinner included) ⊷ ✝165.00/165.00 – ✝✝190.00/245.00, 1 suite.
◆ Part 14C country house with pleasant gardens in delightful rural seclusion. Furnished throughout with antiques and curios. Charming service. Individually styled bedrooms. Traditional dining room with linen-clad tables.

TAL-Y-LLYN Gwynedd 502 503 I 25 Wales G. – ⊠ Tywyn.

Env. : Snowdonia National Park★★★ – Cadair Idris★★★.

London 224 – Dolgellau 9 – Shrewsbury 60.

🏨 **Tynycornel**, LL36 9AJ, on B 4405 ℘ (01654) 782282, reception@tynycornel.co.uk, Fax (01654) 782679, ≤ Tal-y-Llyn Lake and Cadair Idris, ⬭, ㈜ – ⁴⑲ 🅿, ⑩⑨ 𝘝𝘐𝘚𝘈
Closed 24-26 December/**Rest** (bar lunch Monday-Saturday)/dinner a la carte 15.50/27.00 – **21 rm** ⊷ ✝35.00/65.00 – ✝✝50.00/110.00, 1 suites.
◆ Extended former inn with fine views of Tal-y-Llyn Lake, renowned for its fishing, and Cadair Idris. Comfortable rooms with good facilities, some in converted outbuildings. Purpose-built extension houses modern restaurant.

> Undecided between two equivalent establishments?
> Within each category, establishments are classified
> in our order of preference.

WALES

TENBY (Dinbych-Y-Pysgod) Pembrokeshire 503 F 28 Wales G. – pop. 4 934.

See : Town★★ – Harbour and seafront★★.

Env. : Pembrokeshire Coast National Park★★ – Caldey Island★, S : by boat.

📍₁₈ The Burrows ℘ (01834) 842978.

🗓 The Croft ℘ (01834) 842402.

London 247 – Carmarthen 27 – Fishguard 36.

🏨 **Broadmead**, Heywood Lane, SA70 8DA, Northwest : ¾ m. ℘ (01834) 842641, Fax (01834) 845757, ㈜ – ⁴⑲ 🅿, ⑪
March-November – **Rest** (dinner only) 18.00/25.00 s. – **23 rm** ⊷ ✝31.00/47.00 – ✝✝62.00/74.00.
◆ Privately owned country house hotel. Traditionally styled public rooms include conservatory overlooking gardens. Individually decorated rooms with modern amenities. Dining room in the traditional style common to the other parts of the house.

🏨 **Fourcroft**, North Beach, SA70 8AP, ℘ (01834) 842886, staying@fourcroft-hotel.co.uk, Fax (01834) 842888, ≤, ⇌₅, ☐ heated, ㈜ – ▯ ⁴⑲ – 🅰 80. ⑩⑨ 🖭 ⑩ 𝘝𝘐𝘚𝘈
Rest (bar lunch)/dinner 25.00 and a la carte 25.00/40.00 s. – **40 rm** ⊷ ✝45.00/115.00 – ✝✝90.00/140.00.
◆ Well-established, family owned hotel forming part of a Georgian terrace. Sea facing rooms benefit from large original windows. Attractions and water activities nearby. The dining room overlooks the sea and is decorated in traditional style.

at Penally (Penalun) Southwest : 2 m. by A 4139 – ⊠ Tenby.

🏨 **Penally Abbey** ⑤, SA70 7PY, ℘ (01834) 843033, penally.abbey@btinternet.com, Fax (01834) 844714, ≤, ㈜ – ⁴⑲ 🅿, ⑩⑨ 🖭 𝘝𝘐𝘚𝘈, ⑪
Rest (lunch booking essential) 22.00/36.00 – **17 rm** ⊷ ✝124.00/158.00 – ✝✝134.00/168.00.
◆ Gothic style, stone built house with good views of Carmarthen Bay and surrounded by woodland. Calm, country house décor and atmosphere. Lodge rooms are particularly pleasant. Candlelit dining room, decorated in the country style of the establishment.

🏠 **Wychwood House**, SA70 7PE, ℘ (01834) 844387, wychwoodbb@aol.com, Fax (01834) 844425, ㈜ – ⁴⑲ 🅿, ⑩⑨ 𝘝𝘐𝘚𝘈, ⑪
Rest (by arrangement) – **3 rm** ⊷ ✝45.00/50.00 – ✝✝70.00.
◆ Large 1940s house with a comfy, friendly ambience. Well-appointed guest drawing room. Individually styled bedrooms exude a winningly retro 'Noel Coward' feel. Serious dining: far eastern and modern European dominate owner's repertoire.

THORNHILL Cardiff 503 K 29 – see Cardiff.

TINTERN (Tyndyrn) *Monmouthshire* 503 504 L 28 *Wales G.* – ✉ *Chepstow.*
See : *Abbey★★ AC.*
London 137 – Bristol 23 – Gloucester 40 – Newport 22.

🏠 **Parva Farmhouse,** NP16 6SQ, on A 466 ℰ (01291) 689411, *parva-hoteltintern@hot mail.com,* Fax (01291) 689941 – ⇄ ✿ ℙ. ⓜⓞ 𝚅𝙸𝚂𝙰.
Rest (dinner only) 16.50/25.95 – **8 rm** ⚏ ✦55.00/60.00 – ✦✦73.00/85.00.
♦ Mid 17C stone farmhouse adjacent to River Wye; refurbished to country standard. Traditional cooking, warm hospitality and a pleasant ambience. Comfortable rooms.

TREARDDUR BAY *Anglesey* 502 503 G 24 *Wales G.* – ✉ *Holyhead.*
Env. : *Anglesey★★.*
Exc. : *Barclodiad y Gawres Burial Chamber★, SE : 10 m. by B 4545, A 5 and A 4080.*
London 269 – Bangor 25 – Caernarfon 29 – Holyhead 3.

🏨 **Trearddur Bay,** LL65 2UN, ℰ (01407) 860301, *enquiries@trearddurbayhotel.co.uk,* Fax (01407) 861181, ≼, 🔄, 🐾 – 🚽 – 🖪 160. ⓜⓞ 𝙰𝙴 ⓞ 𝚅𝙸𝚂𝙰. ✿
closed Christmas – **Rest** (bar lunch Monday-Saturday)/dinner a la carte 22.40/29.40 – **40 rm** ⚏ ✦96.50 – ✦✦144.50/171.50.
♦ Situated next to "Blue Flag" beach. Well run with good facilities, including pool and spacious, comfortable rooms: go for balcony rooms with bay window seating. Modern dining room; drinks in cocktail lounge before dining.

TREDUNNOCK *Newport* 503 L 29 – *see Newport.*

TREMEIRCHION *Denbighshire* 502 503 J 24 – ✉ *St Asaph.*
London 225 – Chester 29 – Shrewsbury 59.

🏠 **Bach-Y-Graig** ⬙ *without rest.,* LL17 0UH, Southwest : 2 m. by B 5429 off Denbigh rd ℰ (01745) 730627, *anwen@bachygraig.co.uk,* Fax (01745) 730971, ⬍, 🐾, ⬚ – 🚽 ℙ. ✿
closed 25 December – **3 rm** ⚏ ✦39.00/49.00 – ✦✦68.00/74.00.
♦ Attractive brick-built farmhouse dating from 16C, on working farm. In quiet spot with woodland trails nearby. Large open fires and wood furnished rooms with cast iron beds.

TYN-Y-GROES *Gwynedd – see Conwy (Aberconwy and Colwyn).*

USK (Brynbuga) *Monmouthshire* 503 L 28 *Wales G.* – *pop. 2 318.*
Exc. : *Raglan Castle★ AC, NE : 7 m. by A 472, A 449 and A 40.*
🮲₁₈, 🮲₁₈ *Alice Springs, Bettws Newydd* ℰ (01873) 880708.
London 144 – Bristol 30 – Cardiff 26 – Gloucester 39 – Newport 10.

🏨 **Glen-yr-Afon House,** Pontypool Rd, NP15 1SY, ℰ (01291) 672302, *enquiries@glen-yr-afon.co.uk,* Fax (01291) 672597, 🐾 – 🛗 🚽, ▤ rest, ✆ ⬧ ℙ – 🖪 200. ⓜⓞ 𝙰𝙴 ⓞ 𝚅𝙸𝚂𝙰
closed 25 December **Rest** 15.00 and a la carte 22.75/32.25 s. ⅌ – **28 rm** ⚏ ✦85.70 – ✦✦143.00.
♦ Across bridge from town is this warmly run 19C villa with relaxing country house ambience. Several welcoming lounges and comfy, warm, well-kept bedrooms. Friendly welcome. Stylish restaurant.

at Llandenny *Northeast : 4¼ m. by A 472 off B 4235* – ✉ *Usk.*

🍴 **Raglan Arms,** NP15 1DL, ℰ (01291) 690800, Fax (01291) 690155, 🍽 – 🚽 ℙ. ⓜⓞ 𝚅𝙸𝚂𝙰
closed Sunday dinner and Monday – **Rest** a la carte 19.00/27.00 ⅌.
♦ Stone-faced pub in the middle of small village. Busy central bar; eating area includes big leather sofas in front of the fire, and good value dishes enhanced by sharp cooking.

WELSH HOOK *Pembrokeshire* 503 F 28 – *see Fishguard.*

WELSHPOOL (Trallwng) *Powys* 502 503 K 26 *Wales G.* – *pop. 5 539.*
See : *Town★.*
Env. : *Powis Castle★★ AC, SW : 1½ m. by A 483.*
🮲₁₈ *Golfa Hill* ℰ (01938) 850249.
🮮 *Vicarage Garden, Church St* ℰ (01938) 552043, *weltic@powys.gov.uk.*
London 182 – Birmingham 64 – Chester 45 – Shrewsbury 19.

at Guilsfield *North : 3 m. by A 490 on B 4392 –* ⊠ *Welshpool.*

⌂ **Lower Trelydan** ⟠ *without rest.,* SY21 9PH, *South : ¾ m. by B 4392 on unmarked road* 𝒫 *(01938) 553105, stay@lowertrelydan.com, Fax (01938) 553105,* 🌂, 🔔 *–* ⊱✗ **P**. **VISA**. ⚘
February-November – **3 rm** ⊊ ✝35.00 *–* ✝✝58.00.

• Sheep and fine horses graze the quiet fields around this warmly run, listed 16C timbered farmhouse. Comfortable lounge and neatly kept bedrooms in traditional style.

WHITEBROOK *Monmouthshire – see Monmouth.*

WOLF'S CASTLE (Cas-Blaidd) *Pembrokeshire* 503 F 28 *Wales G. –* ⊠ *Haverfordwest.*
Env. : *Pembrokeshire Coast National Park*★★.
London 258 – Fishguard 7 – Haverfordwest 8.

🏛 **Wolfscastle Country H.,** SA62 5LZ, 𝒫 *(01437) 741225, enquiries@wolfscastle.com, Fax (01437) 741383,* 🌂 *–* ⊱✗ **P** *–* 🔊 150. **MC** **AE** **VISA**
closed 24-26 December – **Rest** (lunch by arrangement Monday-Saturday)/dinner a la carte 16.25/32.40 ⊊ *–* **20 rm** ⊊ ✝60.00 *–* ✝✝115.00.

• Spacious, family run country house; tidy rooms in traditional soft chintz, modern conference room and simply styled bar with a mix of cushioned settles and old wooden chairs. Dining room with neatly laid tables in pink linens.

WALES

Your opinions are important to us:
please write and let us know about your discoveries and experiences – good and bad!

WREXHAM (Wrecsam) *Wrexham* 502 503 L 24 *Wales G. – pop. 42 576.*
See : *St Giles Church*★.
Env. : *Erddig*★★ *AC (Gardens*★★*), SW : 2 m – Gresford (All Saints Church*★*), N : 4 m. by A 5152 and B 5445.*
ⁱ₈, ⁱ₅ *Chirk* 𝒫 *(01691) 774407 –* ⁱ₈ *Clays, Bryn Estyn Rd* 𝒫 *(01978) 661406 –* ⁱ₉ *Moss Valley, Moss Rd* 𝒫 *(01978) 720518 –* ⁱ₉ *Pen-y-Cae, Ruabon Rd* 𝒫 *(01978) 810108 –* ⁱ₉ *The Plassey, Eyton* 𝒫 *(01978) 780020.*
🛈 *Lambpit St* 𝒫 *(01978) 292015, tic@wrexham.gov.uk.*
London 192 – Chester 12 – Liverpool 35 – Shrewsbury 28.

🏛 **Ramada Plaza,** Elice Way, LL13 7YH, *West : 1 ¼ m. by A 541 and B 5101 off Technology Park rd* 𝒫 *(01978) 291400, info@ramadaplazawrexham.co.uk, Fax (01978) 291401,* 𝄜, ⇌ *–* |🛗| ⊱✗ 📺 ℂ 🔥 **P** *–* 🔊 220. **MC** **AE** **①** **VISA**
Rest (bar lunch)/dinner a la carte 18.95/23.70 **s.** *–* ⊊ 12.50 *–* **85 rm** ⊊ ✝75.00/120.00 *–* ✝✝75.00/120.00.

• Modern purpose-built hotel just out of town centre. Business oriented: conference operation; gym, sauna and plunge pool. High level of facilities enhances impressive rooms. Welsh-based menus dominate informal restaurant.

at Gresford *Northeast : 3 m. by A 483 on B 5445.*

🍴 **Pant-yr-Ochain,** Old Wrexham Rd, LL12 8TY, *South : 1 m.* 𝒫 *(01978) 853525, pantyrochain@brunningandprice.co.uk, Fax (01978) 853505,* 🍽, 🌂 *–* ⊱✗ **P**. **MC** **VISA**. ⚘
closed 25-26 December – **Rest** (booking essential) a la carte 16.95/25.00 ⊊.

• Bustling part 16C inn overlooking a lake with pleasant gardens and terrace. Open-plan dining rooms, bar and library. Blackboard menu and real ales.

Ireland

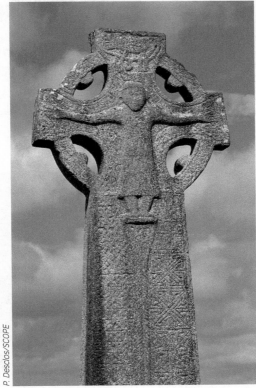

Kilfenora: Celtic cross

Giant's Causeway

Towns
from A to Z

Villes
de A à Z

Città
de A a Z

Städte
von A bis Z

Northern Ireland

Place with at least _____

a hotel or restaurant   ● Belfast
a pleasant hotel or restaurant   🏨🏨, 🏠, 🏶
Good accommodation at moderate prices   🏶
a quiet, secluded hotel   🏶
a restaurant with   ❀, ❀❀, ❀❀❀, 🏶 **Rest**
Town with a local map   ●

La località possiede come minimo

una risorsa alberghiera   ● Belfast
Albergo o ristorante ameno   🏨🏨, 🏠, 🏶
Buona sistemazione a prezzi contenuti   🏶
un albergo molto tranquillo, isolato   🏶
un'ottima tavola con   ❀, ❀❀, ❀❀❀, 🏶 **Rest**
Città con carta dei dintorni   ●

Localité offrant au moins _____

une ressource hôtelière   ● Belfast
un hôtel ou restaurant agréable   🏨🏨, 🏠, 🏶
Bonnes nuits à petits prix   🏶
un hôtel très tranquille, isolé   🏶
une bonne table à   ❀, ❀❀, ❀❀❀, 🏶 **Rest**
Carte de voisinage : voir à la ville choisie   ●

Ort mit mindestens _____

einem Hotel oder Restaurant   ● Belfast
einem angenehmen Hotel oder Restaurant   🏨🏨, 🏠, 🏶
Hier übernachten Sie gut und preiswert   🏶
einem sehr ruhigen und abgelegenen Hotel   🏶
einem Restaurant mit   ❀, ❀❀, ❀❀❀, 🏶 **Rest**
Stadt mit Umgebungskarte   ●

ANNAHILT *Down* **712** N/O 4 – *see Hillsborough.*

ARMAGH *Armagh* **712** M 4.

See : *St Patrick's Cathedral★ (Anglican) – St Patrick's Cathedral★ (Roman Catholic) – The Mall★ : Armagh County Museum★ AC, Royal Irish Fusiliers Museum★ AC.*
Env. : *Navan Fort★ AC W : 2 m. by A 28.*
Exc. : *The Argory★ AC N : 10 m. by A 29 and minor road right.*
Belfast 39 – Dungannon 13 – Portadown 11.

Armagh City H., 2 Friary Rd, BT60 4FR, ℰ (028) 3751 8888, *info@armaghcityhotel.com*, Fax (028) 3751 2777, 🖪, 🛬, 🖾 – 🛗 🕭 🦺 🖪 – 🕍 1200. 🐠 🖭 ⓪ 🖾. 🛠
closed 25 December – **Rest** (dinner only and Sunday lunch) 22.00/26.00 and a la carte 16.65/25.20 – **82 rm** � ✿84.00 – ✿✿97.00.
◆ Modern purpose-built hotel well geared-up to the business traveller. Stylish, wood furnished bedrooms, the city's two cathedrals visible from those to the front. Large, split-level restaurant serving traditional dishes.

BALLYCLARE *Antrim* **712** N/O 3.

XX **Oregano**, 29 Ballyrobert Rd, BT39 9RY, South : 3¼ m. by A 57 on B 56 ℰ (028) 9084 0099, *oregano.rest@btconnect.com*, Fax (028) 9084 0033 – 🍴 🖃 🖪 ↻ 22. 🐠 🖾
closed 12-13 July, 25-26 December, Monday and Saturday lunch – **Rest** 17.95 (lunch) and a la carte 19.40/27.95 ₤.
◆ Traditional facade contrasts with modish interior. Light, bright dining room is spacious and contemporary, in keeping with the flavoursome, modern European dishes on offer.

BALLYMENA (An Baile Meánach) *Antrim* **712** N 3 *Ireland G.* – pop. 58 610.

Exc. : *Antrim Glens★★★ – Murlough Bay★★★ (Fair Head ≤★★★), NE : 32 m. by A 26, A 44, A 2 and minor road – Glengariff Forest Park★★ AC (Waterfall★★), NW : 13 m. by A 43 – Glengariff★, NE : 18 m. by A 43 – Glendun★, NE : 19 m. by A 43, B 14 and A2 – Antrim (Round Tower★) S : 9½ m. by A 26.*
🖈 *128 Raceview Rd* ℰ (028) 2586 1207.
🛈 *76 Church St* ℰ (028) 2563 8494, *ballymenatic@hotmail.com.*
Belfast 27 – Dundalk 78 – Larne 21 – Londonderry 51 – Omagh 53.

Rosspark, 20 Doagh Rd, BT42 3LZ, Southeast : 6 m. by A 36 on B 59 ℰ (028) 2589 1663, *info@rosspark.com*, Fax (028) 2589 1477, 🖪, 🐎, 🍴, 🖃 rest, 🕭 🦺 🖪 – 🕍 300. 🐠 🖭 🖾. 🛠
closed 25 December – **Rest** a la carte 14.50/23.50 **s.** – **39 rm** ⊒ ✿75.00 – ✿✿95.00, 1 suite.
◆ Off the beaten track, yet fully equipped with all mod cons. Rooms are smart and contemporarily styled, some with sofas. Executive rooms have large working areas. Restaurant in the heart of the hotel decorated in terracotta colours.

↥ **Marlagh Lodge**, 71 Moorfields Rd, BT42 3BU, Southeast : 2¼ m. on A 36 ℰ (028) 2563 1505, *info@marlaghlodge.com*, Fax (028) 2564 1590, 🐎 – 🍴 🖪. 🐠 🖾. 🛠
Rest (by arrangement) 31.50 – **3 rm** ⊒ ✿40.00 – ✿✿80.00.
◆ Substantial 19C house with immediate, if busy, road connection. Many original features restored; stained glass in front door and hall. Tasteful, individually furnished rooms. Guests treated to seasonally changing five course dinner, upon arrangement.

BANGOR (Beannchar) *Down* **712** O/P 4 *Ireland G.*

See : *North Down Heritage Centre★.*
Env. : *Ulster Folk and Transport Museum★★ AC, W : 8 m. by A 2.*
Exc. : *Newtownards : Movilla Priory (Cross Slabs★) S : 4 m. by A 21 – Mount Stewart★★★ AC, SE : 90 m. by A 21 and A 20 – Scrabo Tower (≤★★) S : 6½ m. by A 21 – Ballycopeland Windmill★, SE : 10 m. by B 21 and A 2, turning right at Millisle – Strangford Lough★ (Castle Espie Centre★ AC - Nendrum Monastery★) – Grey Abbey★ AC, SE : 20 m. by A 2, A 21 and A 20.*
🛈 *34 Quay St* ℰ (028) 9127 0069, *bangor@nitic.net.*
Belfast 15 – Newtownards 5.

Clandeboye Lodge, 10 Estate Rd, Clandeboye, BT19 1UR, Southwest : 3 m. by A 2 and Dundonald rd following signs for Blackwood Golf Centre ℰ (028) 9185 2500, *info@clandeboyelodge.co.uk*, Fax (028) 9185 2772, 🖪, 🐎 – 🛗 🍴 🕭 🦺 🖪 – 🕍 450. 🐠 🖭 ⓪ 🖾. 🛠
closed 25-26 December – **Lodge :** **Rest** (bar lunch Monday-Saturday)/dinner 45.00 and a la carte 18.40/31.95 ₤ – **43 rm** ⊒ ✿85.00/110.00 – ✿✿95.00/115.00.
◆ On site of former estate school house, surrounded by 4 acres of woodland. Well placed for country and coast. Meetings and weddings in separate extension. Contemporary rooms. Restaurant boasts minimal, stylish décor. Modish menus.

Cairn Bay Lodge, 278 Seacliffe Rd, BT20 5HS, East : 1 ¼ m. by Quay St ✆ (028) 9146 7636, *info@cairnbaylodge.com, Fax (028) 9145 7728,* ≼, ⌖ – ⇆ **P**. **MO** ⓘ *VISA*. ⌖
Rest (by arrangement) 20.00 – 3 rm ⌧ ✦35.00/60.00 – ✦✦70.00/75.00.
• Built in 1913; retains lots of period charm: Dutch fireplaces, stained glass, panelling. Beach views; individually styled rooms. Attractive garden. Health/beauty treatments.

Hebron House, 68 Princetown Rd, BT20 3TD, ✆ (028) 9146 3126, *reception@hebron-house.com, Fax (028) 9146 3126* – ⇆ **TV P**. **MO** *VISA*. ⌖
closed 21-31 December – **Rest** (by arrangement) (communal dining) 20.00 – 3 rm ⌧ ✦45.00/70.00 – ✦✦70.00.
• Redbrick double fronted 19C property in elevated location. Immaculate styling, yet in keeping with age of house. Ultra stylish rooms offer every conceivable facility. Very neat communal dining room; good choice of homecooked meals.

Shelleven House, 59-61 Princetown Rd, BT20 3TA, ✆ (028) 9127 1777, *shelleven house@aol.com, Fax (028) 9127 1777* – ⇆ **P**. **MO** *VISA*. ⌖
Rest (by arrangement) 30.00 – 11 rm ⌧ ✦33.00/15.00 – ✦✦70.00.
• Personally run, end of terrace, double front Victorian house; short stroll to marina. Large, uniformly appointed rooms: ask for a large one at the front. Homely, good value.

Coyle's, 44 High St, BT20 5AZ, ✆ (028) 9127 0362, *Fax (028) 9127 0362* – **MO** ⓘ *VISA*
closed 25 December and Monday – **Rest** a la carte 14.00/18.00.
• Black exterior advertising real music and hard liquor! Also serves super dishes in an Art Deco upstairs restaurant: safe steaks meet ambitious, well executed surprises.

→ *Discover the best restaurant ?*
→ *Find the nearest hotel ?*
→ *Find your bearings using our maps and guides ?*
→ *Understand the symbols used in the guide...*

Follow the red Bibs !

Advice on restaurants from **Chef Bib**.

Tips and advice from **Clever Bib** on finding your way around the guide and on the road.

Advice on hotels from **Bellboy Bib**.

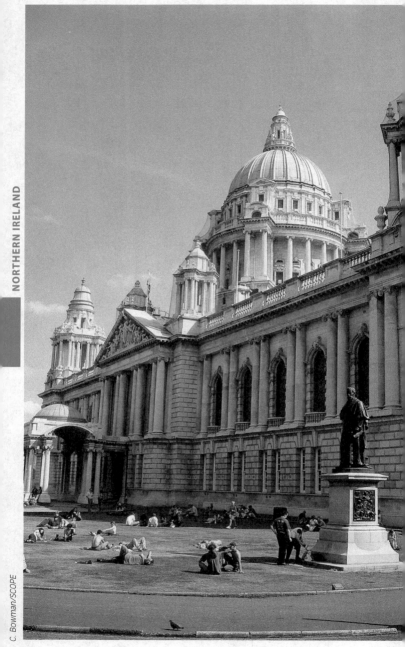

Belfast: City Hall

BELFAST - (Béal Feirste)

Antrim **712** O 4 *Ireland G. – pop. 277 391*

Dublin 103 – Londonderry 70.

TOURIST INFORMATION

🛈 *47 Donegal Pl ℘ (028) 9024 6609; info@nitic.com.*
🛈 *Belfast International Airport, Information desk ℘ (028) 9442 2888.*
🛈 *Belfast City Airport, Sydenham Bypass ℘ (028) 9093 9093.*

PRACTICAL INFORMATION

🛝 *Balmoral, 518 Lisburn Rd ℘ (028) 9038 1514,* AZ.
🛝 *Belvoir Park, Church Rd, Newtonbreda ℘ (028) 9049 1693,* AZ.
🛝 *Fortwilliam, Downview Ave ℘ (028) 9037 0770,* AY.
🛝 *The Knock Club, Summerfield, Dundonald ℘ (028) 9048 2249.*
🛝 *Shandon Park, 73 Shandon Park ℘ (028) 9079 3730.*
🛝 *Cliftonville, Westland Rd ℘ (028) 9074 4158,* AY.
🛝 *Ormeau, 50 Park Rd ℘ (028) 9064 1069,* AZ
🛫 *Belfast International Airport, Aldergrove : ℘ (028) 9448 4848, W : 15½ m. by A 52* AY *–*
Belfast City Airport : ℘ (028) 9093 9093.
Terminal : *Coach service (Ulsterbus Ltd) from Belfast Europe Bus Centre (40 mn).*
⛴ *to Isle of Man (Douglas) (Isle of Man Steam Packet Co. Ltd) (summer only) (2 h 45 mn) –*
to Stranraer (Stena Line) 4-5 daily (1 h 30 mn/3 h 15 mn), (SeaCat Scotland) March-January
(90 mn) – to Liverpool (Norfolkline Irish Sea) daily (18 h 30 mn).

SIGHTS

See : *City★ - Ulster Museum★★ (Spanish Armada Treasure★★, Shrine of St Patrick's Hand★)*
AZ **M1** *– City Hall★* BY *– Donegall Square★* BY **20** *– Botanic Gardens (Palm House★)* AZ *–*
St Anne's Cathedral★ BX *– Crown Liquor Saloon★* BY *– Sinclair Seamen's Church★* BX *–*
St Malachy's Church★ BY.
Env. : *Belfast Zoological Gardens★★ AC, N : 5 m. by A 6* AY.
Exc. : *Carrickfergus (Castle★★ AC, St Nicholas' Church★) NE : 9½ m. by A 2.*

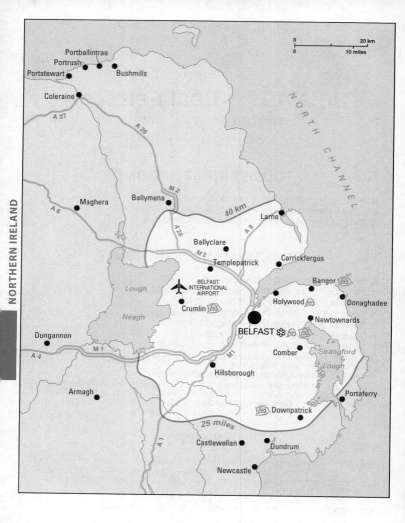

NORTHERN IRELAND

Good food and accommodation at moderate prices?
Look for the Bib symbols:
red Bib Gourmand 🍴 for food, blue Bib Hotel 🏨 for hotels

INDEX OF STREET NAMES IN BELFAST

NORTHERN IRELAND

Hilton Belfast, 4 Lanyon Pl, BT1 3LP, ℰ (028) 9027 7000, hilton.belfast@hilton.com, Fax (028) 9027 7277, ₤₅, ≦s, ◲ – ﹩, ⅏ rm, 🖩 ₡ ♿ 🅿 – 🕭 400. 🕮 🆎 ⓞ VISA   BY s
Sonoma : Rest (closed lunch Saturday and Sunday) 19.50/21.00 (dinner) and a la carte 28.40/34.45 ♀ – ☲ 16.50 – **189 rm** ★165.00 – ★★225.00/305.00, 6 suites.
♦ Modern branded hotel overlooking river and close to concert hall. Spacious and brightly decorated rooms with all mod cons. Upper floors with good city views. Striking California-style décor and good choice menus from Sonoma.

Europa, Great Victoria St, BT2 7AP, ℰ (028) 9027 1066, res@eur.hastingshotels.com, Fax (028) 9032 7800 – ﹩| ⅏ rest, ₡ ♿ – 🕭 750. 🕮 🆎 ⓞ VISA. ⅏   BY e
closed 24-25 December – **The Piano Bar Restaurant** : Rest (closed Sunday) (dinner only) 22.00 and a la carte 24.00/28.00 ♀ – **The Brasserie** : Rest a la carte 15.00/24.00 ♀ – ☲ 16.00 – **235 rm** ★125.00/155.00 – ★★180.00, 5 suites.
♦ Busy hotel in the heart of the lively Golden Mile area. Extensive meeting facilities. Executive rooms are particularly well equipped and modern. Formal Piano Bar restaurant has immaculate feel. Pleasant feel suffuses informal Brasserie; international choice.

The Merchant, 35-39 Waring St, BT1 2DY, ℰ (028) 9023 4888, info@themerchantho tel.com, Fax (028) 9024 4775 – ﹩| ⅏ 🖩 ₡ ♿ 🅿. 🕮 🆎 VISA. ⅏   BX x
The Great Room : Rest a la carte 30.00/45.50 ♀ **24 rm** ☲ ★120.00/220.00 – ★★120.00/220.00, 2 suites.
♦ Ornate former HQ of Ulster Bank imbued with rich, opulent interior. Cocktail bar a destination in itself. Hotel's comforts exemplified by sumptuous, highly original bedrooms. Tremendous detail in former main banking hall dining room; French based dishes.

Radisson SAS, 3 Cromac Pl, Cromac Wood, BT7 2JB, ℰ (028) 9043 4065, info.bel fast@radissonsas.com, Fax (028) 9043 4066, ≼ – ﹩| ⅏ rm, 🖩 ₡ ♿ 🅿 – 🕭 150. 🕮 🆎 ⓞ VISA. ⅏   BY z
Filini : Rest - Italian influences - (closed Sunday lunch) 12.00/15.00 and a la carte 22.75/32.50 – ☲ 13.95 – **119 rm** ★89.00/140.00 – ★★89.00/140.00, 1 suite.
♦ Stylish, modern hotel on the site of former gasworks. Smart, up-to-date facilities. Two room styles - Urban or Nordic; both boast fine views over city and waterfront. Restaurant/bar with floor-to-ceiling windows and part-open kitchen.

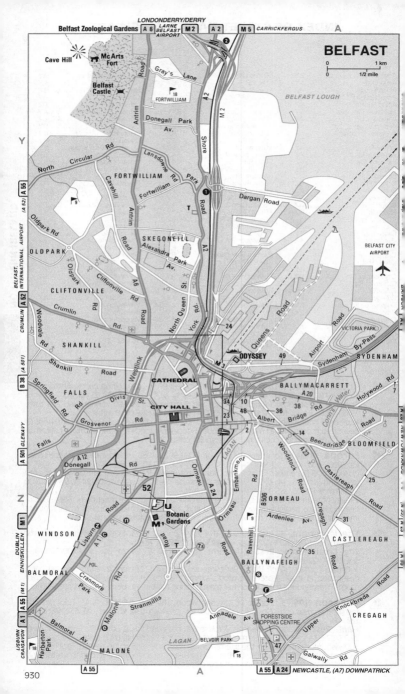

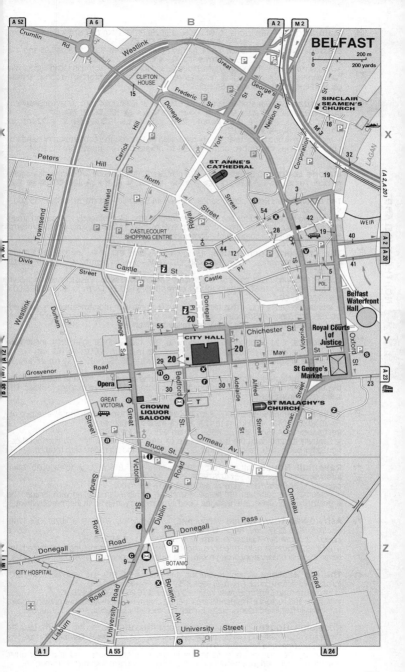

Malmaison, 34-38 Victoria St, BT1 3GH, ℘ (028) 9022 0200, *belfast@malmaison.com*, Fax (028) 9022 0220, ₺₅ – |፱|, ⅙↔, ▤ rest, ✆ ₺, ⅏ AE VISA

BY **v**

Brasserie : Rest *(closed lunch 11-14 July and Christmas-New Year)* 14.95/15.95 and a la carte 18.95/31.45 – ⊇ 12.95 – **62 rm** ✦140.00 – ✦✦140.00, 2 suites.

◆ An unstuffy, centrally located hotel hides behind its intricate Victorian façade. Originally two warehouses, many original features remain. Modern, comfortable rooms. Stylish, comfortable, modern dining in Brasserie.

Ten Square, 10 Donegall Square South, BT1 5JD, ℘ (028) 9024 1001, *reservations@tens square.co.uk, Fax (028) 9024 3210* – |፱|, ⅙↔ rm, ▤ ✆ ₺ – ⅍ 100. ⅏ AE VISA

BY **x**

closed 25 December – **Grill Room :** Rest a la carte 19.00/29.00 **s.** – **22 rm** ⊇ ✦165.00/250.00 – ✦✦165.00/250.00.

◆ Victorian mill building in heart of city renovated to a thoroughly contemporary standard. Notably spacious deluxe bedrooms. Access to private bar for guests. Smart, stylish Grill Room.

Malone Lodge, 60 Eglantine Ave, BT9 6DY, ℘ (028) 9038 8000, *info@malonelodgeho tel.com, Fax (028) 9038 8088*, ₺₅, ⅏ – |፱| ⅙↔, ▤ rest, ✆ ₺ ⅊ – ⅍ 120. ⅏ AE ⅁ VISA

AZ **n**

The Green Door : Rest *(closed Sunday dinner)* 14.50/22.50 – **51 rm** ⊇ ✦80.00/130.00 – ✦✦115.00/140.00.

◆ Imposing hotel in 19C terrace in quiet residential area. Elegant lobby lounge and smart bar. Conference facilities. Basement gym. Stylish, modern rooms with good comforts. Restaurant provides a comfortable, contemporary environment.

The Crescent Townhouse, 13 Lower Crescent, BT7 1NR, ℘ (028) 9032 3349, *info@crescenttownhouse.com, Fax (028) 9032 0646* – ⅙↔, ▤ rest, ✆ ₺ – ⅍ 36. ⅏ AE VISA

BZ **x**

closed 11-13 July, 25 December and 1 January – **Metro Brasserie :** Rest *(closed lunch Sunday to Wednesday)* 16.50 *(dinner)* and a la carte 18.95/31.20 ⅒ – **17 rm** ⊇ ✦85.00/125.00 – ✦✦85.00/145.00.

◆ Intimate Regency house that blends original features with modern amenities. Relaxed, discreet atmosphere. Spacious and luxurious rooms with interior designed period feel. Modern classic brasserie with a lively and relaxed ambience.

Benedicts, 7-21 Bradbury Pl, Shaftsbury Sq, BT7 1RQ, ℘ (028) 9059 1999, *info@bene dictshotel.co.uk, Fax (028) 9059 1990* – |፱|, ⅙↔ rm, ▤ rest, ✆ ₺. ⅏ AE ⅁ VISA. ⅍ BZ **c**

Benedicts Restaurant : Rest 18.00/22.00 and a la carte 16.15/21.85 ⅒ – **32 rm** ⊇ ✦60.00 – ✦✦70.00.

◆ A lively, strikingly designed bar with nightly entertainment can be found at the heart of this busy commercial hotel. Well-appointed bedrooms above offer modern facilities. Relaxed, popular restaurant.

Days H., 40 Hope St, BT12 5EE, ℘ (028) 9024 2494, *reservations@dayshotelbelfast.co.uk, Fax (028) 9024 2495* – |፱| ⅙↔, ▤ rest, ₺ ⅊ – ⅍ 60. ⅏ AE VISA. ⅍

BY **a**

Rest a la carte 14.95/17.85 – ⊇ 7.95 – **250 rm** ✦75.00 – ✦✦75.00.

◆ Centrally located, with the bonus of free parking. Large, "no frills", low cost hotel designed for business traveller or tourist. Sizable, bright, modern rooms with mod cons.

Ravenhill House without rest., 690 Ravenhill Rd, BT6 0BZ, ℘ (028) 9020 7444, *info@ravenhillhouse.com, Fax (028) 9028 2590* – ⅙↔ ⅊. ⅏ VISA. ⅍

AZ **s**

closed 1 week Christmas – 5 rm ⊇ ✦45.00/50.00 – ✦✦70.00.

◆ Personally run detached 19C house, attractively furnished in keeping with its age. The largely organic breakfast is a highlight. Good sized rooms with bold shades predominant.

Ash Rowan Town House without rest., 12 Windsor Ave, BT9 6EE, ℘ (028) 9066 1758, Fax (028) 9066 3227, ⅌ – ⅙↔ ⅊. ⅏ VISA. ⅍

AZ **c**

closed 22 December-7 January – 5 rm ⊇ ✦59.00/66.00 – ✦✦96.00.

◆ Late 19C house in quiet tree-lined avenue. Personally run; interestingly "cluttered" interior. Comfy conservatory sitting room. Well-judged bedrooms with thoughtful touches.

The Old Rectory without restaurant, 148 Malone Rd, BT9 5LH, ℘ (028) 9066 7882, *info@anoldrectory.co.uk, Fax (028) 9068 3759*, ⅌ – ⅙↔ ⅊. ⅍

AZ **e**

closed Easter and Christmas-New Year –– 5 rm ⊇ ✦36.00/48.00 – ✦✦70.00.

◆ Former 19C rectory in residential area; period charm retained. Attractive drawing room. Traditionally furnished rooms. Super breakfasts: speciality sausages, organic produce.

Roseleigh House without rest., 19 Rosetta Park, BT6 0DL, South : 1 ½ m. by A 24 (Ormeau Rd) ℘ (028) 9064 4414, *info@roseleighhouse.co.uk* – ⅙↔ ⅊. ⅏ VISA. ⅍

AZ **r**

closed Christmas and New Year – 9 rm ⊇ ✦40.00/50.00 – ✦✦60.00.

◆ Imposing Victorian house close to the Belvoir Park golf course and in a fairly quiet residential suburb. Brightly decorated and well-kept bedrooms with modern amenities.

XXX **Restaurant Michael Deane**, 34-40 Howard St, BT1 6PF, ✆ (028) 9033 1134,
ℰℰℰ *info@michaeldeane.co.uk, Fax (028) 9056 0001* – ✦ ▤, **MC AE VISA**　　　　BY **n**
closed 7-18 July, 22 December - 3 January and Sunday-Tuesday – **Rest** (dinner only) 46.00 ♀
▱ – (see also **Deanes Brasserie** below).
Spec. Carpaccio of beef with cress salad and truffle dressing, oyster beignet. Roast turbot
with Savoy cabbage, oxtail ravioli and red wine jus. A tasting of chocolate and cherry.
◆ Elegant 1st floor restaurant with rich, plush décor. Polished and professional service by
approachable team. Concise menu of refined, classically based modern Irish dishes.

XX **Roscoff Brasserie**, 7-11 Linenhall St, BT2 8AA, ✆ (028) 9031 1150, *Fax (028) 9031 1151*
– ▤, **MC AE ① VISA**　　　　　　　　　　　　　　　　　　　　　　BY **r**
closed 25-26 December, Sunday and Saturday lunch – **Rest** 19.50 (lunch) and a la carte
31.00/40.00 ♀.
◆ Not your typical brasserie - more formal and a little quieter than most, but stylish and
modern. Confidently prepared modish cooking with classic base. Good value lunches.

XX **James Street South**, 21 James Street South, BT2 7GA, ✆ (028) 9043 4310,
info@jamesstreetsouth.co.uk, Fax (028) 9043 4310 – ✦ ▤, **MC AE VISA**　　　　BY **o**
closed 1 January, 12 July, 25-26 December and Sunday lunch – **Rest** 15.50 (lunch) and a la
carte 22.00/34.40 🗟.
◆ Tucked away down back alley in heart of the city. 19C façade hides distinctly modish
interior. Good value menus; modern cooking based upon well-sourced, fine quality produce.

XX **Cayenne**, 7 Ascot House, Shaftesbury Sq, BT2 7DB, ✆ (028) 9033 1532, *reserva*
⊛ *tions@cayennerestaurant.com, Fax (028) 9026 1575* – ✦ ▤ ↔ 16. **MC AE ① VISA**　BZ **r**
closed 25-26 December, 1 January, 12 July and lunch Saturday and Sunday – **Rest** (booking
essential) 15.50 (lunch) and a la carte 20.50/37.45 ♀.
◆ Striking modern artwork and a lively atmosphere feature in this busy, relaxed and stylish
restaurant. Carefully prepared selection of creative Asian influenced dishes.

XX **Shu**, 253 Lisburn Rd, BT9 7EN, ✆ (028) 9038 1655, *eat@shu-restaurant.com,*
Fax (028) 9068 1632 – ▤ ↔ 24. **MC AE VISA**　　　　　　　　　　　　　AZ **z**
closed 1 January, 12-13 July, 24-26 December and Sunday – **Rest** 13.00 (lunch) and a la
carte 20.75/30.00 ♀.
◆ Trendy, modern restaurant on the Lisburn Road. Converted from terraced houses, it is
spacious and uncluttered with neutral and black décor. Eclectic, contemporary dishes.

XX **Aldens**, 229 Upper Newtownards Rd, BT4 3JF, East : 2 m. on A 20 ✆ (028) 9065 0079,
info@aldensrestaurant.com, Fax (028) 9065 0032 – ▤ **MC AE ① VISA**
closed, Saturday lunch, Sunday and Bank Holidays – **Rest** (booking essential) 18.95 (dinner)
and a la carte 19.50/32.00 ♀.
◆ Well established, spacious and contemporary restaurant in "up-and-coming" area. Extensive menus of classic and modern dishes. Moderately priced midweek menu, friendly
service.

XX **The Wok**, 126 Great Victoria St, BT2 7BG, ✆ (028) 9023 3828 – ▤. **MC VISA**　　BZ **a**
closed 25-26 December and lunch Saturday-Sunday – **Rest** - Chinese - 18.80/23.00 (dinner)
and a la carte 13.50/25.20.
◆ Smart, modern Chinese restaurant with pleasant ambience. Menus feature classic interpretations and less well-known authentic dishes: most regions of China are represented.

X **Deanes Brasserie**, 36-40 Howard St, BT1 6PF, ✆ (028) 9056 0000, *info@michael*
⊛ *deane.co.uk, Fax (028) 9056 0001* – ▤ **MC AE VISA**　　　　　　　　　　　BY **n**
closed 12-13 July, Christmas and Sunday – **Rest** 15.95 (lunch) and a la carte 23.00/31.50 ♀.
◆ Ornately decorated, lively and modern street level brasserie continues to attract a loyal
regular following. Robust and cosmopolitan cooking with a traditional Irish base.

X **Nick's Warehouse**, 35-39 Hill St, BT1 2LB, ✆ (028) 9043 9690, *info@nickswhare*
house.co.uk, Fax (028) 9023 0514 – ▤, **MC AE ① VISA**　　　　　　　　　　BX **a**
closed 3 days Easter, 1 May, 12-13 July, 1 January, Saturday lunch, Monday dinner and
Sunday – **Rest** a la carte 18.40/29.35 ♀.
◆ Built in 1832 as a bonded whiskey store. On two floors, the ground floor Anix is relaxed
and buzzy. Upstairs more formal. Well informed service of an eclectic menu.

X **The Ginger Tree**, 23 Donegall Pass, BT7 1DQ, ✆ (028) 9032 7151 – ✦ ▤. **MC**
VISA　　　　　　　　　　　　　　　　　　　　　　　　　　　　BZ **e**
closed Saturday lunch – **Rest** - Japanese - 18.95/23.50 and a la carte 12.50/35.00.
◆ Cosy Japanese eatery boasting distinctive black tables and chairs with red cushions. One
wall highlighted by striking Japanese dress. Endearing service of authentic dishes.

X **Ginger**, 7-8 Hope St, BT12 5EE, ✆ (028) 9024 4421 – ✦. **MC VISA**　　　　BYZ **i**
closed 2 weeks July, 2 weeks December, Sunday and Monday – **Rest** 13.00 (lunch) and a la
carte 26.00/30.50 🗟.
◆ Simple, intimate neighbourhood diner with chocolate ceiling and aluminium duct pipes;
modern art for sale. Local produce to fore on eclectic menus with distinct global twists.

NORTHERN IRELAND

933

Molly's Yard, 1 College Green Mews, Botanic Ave, BT7 1LW, ℰ (028) 9032 2600, 🌫 –
✻⚊, 🆖 VISA
BZ s
closed 1 January, 11-13 July, 25-27 December and Sunday – **Rest** (booking essential)
22.50/27.50 (dinner) and a la carte 16.35/30.00.
♦ Converted stables and coach house with popular summer courtyard. Downstairs a cosy
bistro; upstairs a casual restaurant. Both serve fresh, earthy and robust seasonal dishes.

at Belfast International Airport *West : 15½ m. by A 52* – AY – ⊠ *Belfast.*

Park Plaza Belfast, BT29 4ZY, ℰ (028) 9445 7000, *reception@parkplazabelfast.com*,
Fax (028) 9442 3500 – 📶 ✻⚊ ▤ 🛏 **P** – 🔬 250. 🆖 🆎 ⓞ VISA. ✂
Circles : **Rest** (booking essential) (dinner only) 20.00 **s.** – � 12.00 – **106 rm** ✻105.00 –
✻✻120.00, 2 suites.
♦ Imposingly up-to-date hotel with sun-filled lobby, 50 metres from terminal entrance.
Terrace, secluded garden, cocktail bar; conference facilities. Distinctively modern rooms.
Formal restaurant with smart, cosmopolitan ambience.

BELFAST INTERNATIONAL AIRPORT (Aerphort Béal Feirste) *Antrim* 712 N 4 – *see Belfast.*

BELLEEK (Béal Leice) *Fermanagh* 712 H 4.
See : *Belleek Pottery AC.*
Belfast 117 – Londonderry 56.

Carlton, Main St, BT93 3FX, ℰ (028) 6865 8282, *reception@hotelcarlton.co.uk*,
Fax (028) 6865 9005 – 📶 ✻⚊ & **P** – 🔬 100. 🆖 🆎 ⓞ VISA. ✂
closed 24-25 December – **Rest** (carvery lunch Monday-Saturday)/dinner 22.65 and a la carte
11.00/23.00 ⊉ – **35 rm** ⊆ ✻60.00 – ✻✻90.00.
♦ Located in the heart of Ireland's Lake District, bordering the river Erne and ideal for
fishing enthusiasts. Bedrooms are in soft pastel colours and most have river views. Classic
styled daily menu in contemporary restaurant.

BUSHMILLS (Muileann na Buaise) *Antrim* 712 M 2 *Ireland G.* – ⊠ *Bushmills.*
Exc. : *Giant's Causeway*★★★ *(Hamilton's Seat* ⊰★★*)* N : 2 m. by A 2 and minor road –
Dunluce Castle★★ *AC* W : 3 m. by A 2 – Carrick-a-rede Rope Bridge★★★ *AC*, E : 8 m. by A 2 –
Magilligan Strand★★, W : 18 m. by A 2, A 29 and A 2 – Gortmore Viewpoint★★, SW : 23 m.
by A 2, A 29, A 2 and minor road from Downhill – Downhill★ *(Mussenden Temple★)*, W : 15
m. by A 2, A 29 and A 2.
🏌 *Bushfoot, 50 Bushfoot Rd, Portballintrae* ℰ (028) 2073 1317.
Belfast 57 – Ballycastle 12 – Coleraine 10.

Bushmills Inn, 9 Dunluce Rd, BT57 8QG, ℰ (028) 2073 3000, *mail@bushmillsinn.com*,
Fax (028) 2073 2048 – ✻⚊ 📶 **P** – 🔬 40. 🆖 🆎 VISA. ✂
closed 24-25 December – **The Restaurant :** **Rest** (carving lunch Sunday) a la carte
25.00/32.00 ⊉ – **32 rm** ⊆ ✻68.00/158.00 – ✻✻148.00/168.00.
♦ Very characterful part 18C inn near famous whiskey distillery. Period features include
turf fires, oil lamps, grand staircase and circular library. Rooms in house and mill. Try Irish
coffee with Bushmills in restaurant overlooking courtyard.

Craig Park 🍃 without rest., 24 Carnbore Rd, BT57 8YF, Southeast : 2½ m. by B 66 and
Ballycastle rd (B 17), off Billy rd ℰ (028) 2073 2496, *jan@craigpark.co.uk*, ⊰, 🌫 – ✻⚊ **P**, 🆖
VISA. ✂
3 rm ⊆ ✻40.00 – ✻✻65.00.
♦ Pleasant country house with views of Donegal mountains, Antrim Hills, dramatic coastal
scenery. Communal breakfast room to start the day; bright, airy bedrooms await at night.

Distillers Arms, 140 Main St, BT57 8QE, ℰ (028) 2073 1044, *simon@distillersarms.com*,
Fax (028) 2073 2843 – ✻⚊ **P**, 🆖 VISA
Rest *(closed lunch Monday-Friday and Monday dinner in winter)* a la carte 15.00/25.00 ⊉.
♦ Modern rusticity in village centre. Sit in squashy sofas in peat fired sitting area. Eat tasty
dishes from frequently changing menus with a seasonal Irish base.

NORTHERN IRELAND

CARRICKFERGUS (Carraig Fhearghais) *Antrim* **712** O 3.

See : *Castle*★ *AC – St Nicholas' Church*★ *AC*.

🏠 *35 North Rd* ℰ *(028) 9336 3713*.

🈂 *Heritage Plaza, Antrim Street* ℰ *(028) 9336 8049 (April-September), touristinfo@carrick fergus.org.*

Belfast 11 – Ballymena 25.

🏨 **Clarion**, 75 Belfast Rd, BT38 8PH, on A 2 ℰ (028) 9336 4556, *reservations1@clarioncar rick.com*, Fax (028) 9335 1620 – 📶 ✆, 🍴 rest, ✆ ♿ 🅿 – 🔼 470. 🎴 🎫 ⓐ *VISA* ✆
Red Pepper : Rest (dinner only) 25.00 and a la carte 18.00/28.70 **s.** ♀ – **67 rm** ⊂ ♦67.50 – ♦♦75.00.

◆ A large, purpose-built hotel with trim, neatly furnished bedrooms; some suites have jacuzzis and views of Belfast Lough; the Scottish coastline can be seen on a clear day. Expect modern French 'prestige' and à la carte menu.

CASTLEDAWSON *Londonderry* **712** M 3.

Belfast 34 – Antrim 17 – Ballymena 23.5.

🍴🍴 **The Inn at Castledawson** with rm, 47 Main St, BT45 8AA, ℰ (028) 7946 9777, *info@theinnatcastledawson.co.uk*, Fax (028) 7946 9888, 🍷 – ✆ 📺 ✆ ♿ 🅿 ✛ 20. 🎴
VISA
closed 26 December, 1 January and Saturday lunch – Rest a la carte 14.00/29.50 ♀ – **12 rm** ⊂ ♦49.95 – ♦♦69.00.

◆ Stylishly updated restaurant, with pine rafters, in 200 year-old inn. Accomplished cooking blends classic and modern styles with finesse. Sleek rooms; fine views from rear.

CASTLEWELLAN *Down* **712** O 5 – pop. 2 496.

See : *Castlewellan Forest Park*★★ *AC*.

Exc. : *Mourne Mountains*★★ *(Silent Valley Reservoir*★ *), SW : 15 m. by A 50, B 180 and B 27 – Dundrum Castle*★ *AC E : 6 m. by A 50 and A 180.*

Belfast 32 – Downpatrick 12 – Newcastle 4.

🏠 **Slieve Croob Inn** 🔽, 119 Clanvaraghan Rd, BT31 9LA, North : 5½ m. by A 25 off B 175 ℰ (028) 4377 1412, *info@slievecroobinn.com*, Fax (028) 4377 1162, ≤, 🚗, ♨ – ✆ 🅿 – 🔼 80. 🎴 ⓐ *VISA*
Restricted opening in winter – Rest (closed Monday) (bar lunch Monday-Saturday)/dinner 19.95 and a la carte 14.15/23.15 **s** – **5 rm** ⊂ ♦40.00 – ♦♦75.00.

◆ Pleasant inn in stunningly attractive mountainous area with panoramic sea views. Modern, rustic style. Bedrooms with simple comforts. Peace and quiet aplenty. Roof timbers and fine views in open, buzzy dining room: same menu also in bar.

COLERAINE (Cúil Raithin) *Londonderry* **712** L 2 *Ireland G.* – pop. 56 315.

Exc. : *Giant's Causeway*★★★ *(Hamilton's Seat* ≤★★ *), NE : 14 m. by A 29 and A2 – Dunluce Castle*★★ *AC, NE : 8 m. by A 29 and A 2 – Carrick-a-rede-Rope Bridge*★★★ *AC, NE : 18 m. by A 29 and A2 – Benvarden*★ *AC E : 5 m. by B 67 – Magilligan Strand*★★, *NW : 8 m. by A 2 – Gortmore Viewpoint*★★, *NW : 12 m. by A 2 and minor road from Downhill – Downhill*★ *AC (Mussenden Temple*★ *), NE : 7 m. by A 2.*

🏠, 🏴 Castlerock, Circular Rd ℰ (028) 7084 8314 – 🏴 Brown Trout, 209 Agivey Rd ℰ (028) 7086 8209.

🈂 *Railway Rd* ℰ *(028) 7034 4723, colerainetic@btconnect.com.*

Belfast 53 – Ballymena 25 – Londonderry 31 – Omagh 65.

🏨 **Bushtown House**, 283 Drumcroone Rd, BT51 3QT, South : 2½ m. on A 29 ℰ (028) 7035 8367, *reception@bushtownhotel.com*, Fax (028) 7032 0909, 🏋, 🚿, 🏊, 🚗 – ✆ 🅿 – 🔼 250. 🎴 *VISA*
closed 26 December – Rest (bar lunch Monday-Saturday)/dinner a la carte 15.75/22.00 **s.** – **39 rm** (dinner included) ⊂ ♦60.00/65.00 – ♦♦90.00/95.00.

◆ Set in mature gardens on outskirts of university town. Indoors, comfortable and homely with various rooms to relax in. Traditional, co-ordinated bedrooms in muted colours. Intimately lit, cosy restaurant with wide variety of simple menus.

🏠 **Brown Trout Golf and Country Inn**, 209 Agivey Rd, Aghadowey, BT51 4AD, Southeast : 9 m. on A 54 ℰ (028) 7086 8209, *bill@browntroutinn.com*, Fax (028) 7086 8878, 🏋, 🏴, 🚿, ♨ – ✆ rest, ♿ 🅿 – 🔼 40. 🎴 🎫 ⓐ *VISA*
Rest a la carte 12.00/20.00 ♀ – **15 rm** ⊂ ♦55.00/65.00 – ♦♦70.00/100.00.

◆ A farm and blacksmith's forge was here in 1600s; now an inn well set up for those with an active disposition - fishing, golf, shooting are on hand. Simple rooms in annexe. Traditionally styled restaurant offers fresh home-cooked meals.

⌂ **Greenhill House** ⤳ without rest., 24 Greenhill Rd, Aghadowey, BT51 4EU, South : 9 m. by A 29 on B 66 ℘ (028) 7086 8241, *greenhill.house@btinternet.com, Fax (028) 7086 8365,* ⛲, 🅿 – ⇔ 🅿, 🆔 AE VISA. ⤳
March-October – **6 rm** ⊇ **†**40.00 – **††**60.00.
♦ An agreeably clean-lined Georgian house with large windows overlooking fields. Game and course fishing available locally. Neat bedrooms replete with extra touches.

COMBER Down 712 O 4.

⌂ **Anna's House** ⤳ without rest., Tullynagee, 35 Lisbarnett Rd, BT23 6AW, Southeast : 3 ½ m. by A 22 ℘ (028) 9754 1566, *anna@annashouse.com, Fax (028) 9754 1566,* ≤, ⛲, 🅡 – ⇔ 📞 🅿, 🆔 VISA. ⤳
closed Christmas-New Year – **3 rm** ⊇ **†**45.00/50.00 – **††**70.00/90.00.
♦ 100 year old farmhouse with 100 per cent organic breakfasts utilising produce from two acre garden. Idyllic lake and panoramic rural views. Comfy bedrooms with lovely vistas.

CRUMLIN (Cromghlinn) Antrim 712 N 4 – pop. 2 697.
Belfast 14 – Ballymena 20.

⌂ **Caldhame Lodge** without rest., 102 Moira Rd, Nutts Corner, BT29 4HG, Southeast : 1 ¼ m. on A 26 ℘ (028) 9442 3099, *info@caldhamelodge.co.uk, Fax (028) 9442 3315,* ⛲ – ⇔ 🅿, 🆔 AE ① VISA. ⤳
8 rm ⊇ **†**35.00/40.00 – **††**50.00/70.00.
♦ Spic and span, with thoroughly polished, wood furnished hall, complete with grandfather clock. Immaculate, co-ordinated, individualistic rooms; bridal suite with whirlpool.

DERRY Londonderry 712 K 2/3 – see Londonderry.

DONAGHADEE (Domhnach Daoi) Down 712 P 4.
Env. : *Ballycopeland Windmill★ AC S : 4 m. by A 2 and B 172.*
Exc. : *Mount Stewart★★★ AC, SW : 10 m. by A 2 and minor road SW – Movilla (cross slabs★), Newtownards, SW : 7 m. by B 172.*
🏌 *Warren Rd* ℘ (028) 9188 3624.
Belfast 18 – Ballymena 44.

❚⃝ **Grace Neill's,** 33 High St, BT21 0AH, ℘ (028) 9188 4595, *info@graceneills.com, Fax (028) 9188 9631,* 🍴 – ⇔ 🅿, 🆔 AE VISA
closed 25 December – **Rest** a la carte 17.00/21.50 ⓨ.
♦ Reputedly Ireland's oldest pub; dates from 1611. Thoroughly traditional bar; contemporary restaurant. Modern dishes full of freshness. Good value early evening meals for two.

❚⃝ **Pier 36** with rm, 36 The Parade, BT21 0HE, ℘ (028) 9188 4466, *info@pier36.co.uk, Fax (028) 9188 4636,* 🍴 – ⇔ TV, 🆔 AE VISA
closed 25 December – **Rest** - Seafood specialities - a la carte 14.00/35.00 ⓨ – **4 rm** ⊇ **†**80.00/90.00 – **††**80.00/90.00.
♦ Personally run spacious pub by the harbour. Appealing rustic feel with stone flooring, curios and wood panelling. Extensive menus with an global range. Modern, comfy bedrooms.

DOWNPATRICK (Dún Pádraig) Down 712 O 4/5.
See : *Cathedral★ AC – Down County Museum★ AC.*
Env. : *Struell Wells★ AC, SE : 2 m. by B 1 – Ardglass★ (Jordan's Castle AC), SE : 7 m. by B 1 – Inch Abbey★ AC, NW : 2 m. by A 7 – Quoile Countryside Centre★ AC, E : 2 m. by A 25 – Castle Ward★★ AC (Audley's Castle★), E : 8 m. by A 25.*
Belfast 23 – Newtownards 22 – Newry 31.

⌂ **Pheasants' Hill Farm** without rest., 37 Killyleagh Rd, BT30 9BL, North : 3 m. on A 22 ℘ (028) 4461 7246, *info@pheasantshill.com, Fax (028) 4461 7246,* ⛲, 🅡 – ⇔ 🅿, 🆔 AE VISA. ⤳
17 March-October – **5 rm** ⊇ **†**40.00/44.00 – **††**60.00/64.00.
♦ Purpose-built house surrounded by an organic smallholding with livestock which provides many ingredients for hearty breakfasts. Homely, pine furnished bedrooms.

NORTHERN IRELAND

DUNDRUM *Down* **712** O 5.

See : *Castle* ★ *AC.*

Env. : *Castlewellan Forest Park* ★★ *AC, W : 4 m. by B 180 and A 50 – Tollymore Forest Park* ★ *AC, W : 3 m. by B 180 – Drumena Cashel and Souterrain* ★ *, W : 4 m. by B 180.*

Belfast 29 – Downpatrick 9 – Newcastle 4.

⌂   **The Carriage House** without rest., 71 Main St, BT33 0LU, *𝒫* (028) 4375 1635, *in box@carriagehousedundrum.com,* 🐾 – ⅍⊨ 🖵 🅿. 🕸

    3 rm � ★40.00 – ★★60.00/70.00.

    ◆ Charming owner runs super, comfy guesthouse: lilac exterior, very well-appointed guest areas. Breakfast sources local organic ingredients. Warm bedrooms with personal touches.

⌶🖵   **Buck's Head Inn,** 77 Main St, BT33 0LU, *𝒫* (028) 4375 1868, *buckshead1@aol.com,* Fax (028) 4481 1033, 🍸, 🐾 – ⅍⊨ 🐠 ⅍⅃ 𝗩𝗜𝗦𝗔. 🕸

    closed 24-25 December and Monday October-March – **Rest** - Seafood specialities - 25.50 (dinner) and a la carte 15.50/25.50 ⅀.

    ◆ Traditional high street bar. Interesting, well-cooked dishes with strong seafood base served in conservatory or cosy front room. Early evening high tea popular with walkers.

⌶🖵   **Mourne Seafood Bar,** 10 Main St, BT33 0LU, *𝒫* (028) 4375 1377, Fax (028) 4375 1161, 🍸 – ⅍⊨ 🐠 𝗩𝗜𝗦𝗔

    closed Monday-Tuesday in winter – **Rest** - Seafood - (booking essential in summer) a la carte 18.00/28.00.

    ◆ Simple, casual seafood pub featuring the day's local catch. Tasty, out-of-ordinary menus based on fish with healthy stocks, rather than threatened species. Reasonably priced.

DUNGANNON (Dún Geanainn) *Tyrone* **712** L 4 *Ireland G.*

Env. : *The Argory* ★ *, S : 5 m. by A 29 and east by minor rd.*

Exc. : *Ardboe Cross* ★ *, NW : 17 m. by A 45, B 161 and B 73 – Springhill* ★ *AC, NE : 24 m. by A 29 – Sperrin Mountains* ★ *: Wellbrook Beetling Mill* ★ *AC, NW : 22 m. by A 29 and A 505 – Beaghmore Stone Circles* ★ *, NW : 24 m. by A 29 and A 505.*

Belfast 42 – Ballymena 37 – Dundalk 47 – Londonderry 60.

⌂   **Grange Lodge** 🌿, 7 Grange Rd, Moy, BT71 7EJ, Southeast : 3 ½ m. by A 29 *𝒫* (028) 8778 4212, *grangelodge@nireland.com,* Fax (028) 8778 4313, 🐾 – ⅍⊨ 🅿. 🐠 𝗩𝗜𝗦𝗔. 🕸

    closed 15 December-1 February – **Rest** (by arrangement) 28.00/35.00 – **5 rm** ⊯ ★55.00/59.00 – ★★78.00.

    ◆ Attractive Georgian country house surrounded by well-kept mature gardens with a peaceful ambience. Fine hospitality and period furnishings. Tastefully decorated bedrooms. Large dining room furnished with elegant antiques and fine tableware.

ENNISKILLEN (Inis Ceithleann) *Fermanagh* **712** J 4 *Ireland G. – pop. 11 436.*

Env. : *Castle Coole* ★★★ *AC, SE : 1 m. – Florence Court* ★★ *AC, SW : 8 m. by A 4 and A 32 – Marble Arch Caves and Forest Nature Reserve* ★ *AC, SW : 10 m. by A 4 and A 32.*

Exc. : *NW by A 26 : Lough Erne* ★★ *: Cliffs of Magho Viewpoint* ★★★ *AC– Tully Castle* ★ *AC – N by A 32, B 72, A 35 and A 47 : Devenish Island* ★ *AC – Castle Archdale Forest Park* ★ *AC – White Island* ★ *– Janus Figure* ★ *.*

⛳ *Castlecoole 𝒫* (028) 6632 5250.

🛈 *Wellington Rd 𝒫* (028) 6632 3110, *tourism@fermanagh.gov.uk.*

Belfast 87 – Londonderry 59.

🏛   **Manor House** 🌿, Killadeas, BT94 1NY, North : 7 ½ m. by A 32 on B 82 *𝒫* (028) 6862 2200, *info@manor-house-hotel.com,* Fax (028) 6862 1545, ≤, 𝐼ᵇ, 🐎, 🏊, 🐾, 🕸 – 📶 🛗 ⅍⊨ ৬. 🅿 – 🔏 400. 🐠 ⅍⅃ 𝗩𝗜𝗦𝗔. 🕸

    Rest 13.95/28.00 and dinner a la carte 25.00/29.00 **s.** – **81 rm** ⊯ ★100.00/120.00 – ★★125.00/165.00.

    ◆ In a commanding position overlooking Lough Erne. Noted for fine Italian plasterwork evident in guest areas. Relaxing conservatory lounge. Spacious, comfortable bedrooms. Classically appointed dining room featuring chandeliers and ornate plasterwork.

⌂   **Cedars,** BT94 1PG, North : 10 m. by A 32 on B 82 *𝒫* (028) 6862 1493, *info@cedarsguest house.com,* Fax (028) 6862 8335, 🐾 – ৬. 🅿. 🐠 𝗩𝗜𝗦𝗔. 🕸

    closed Christmas – **Rectory Bistro :** **Rest** *(closed Monday-Tuesday in winter)* (dinner only and Sunday lunch)/dinner a la carte 18.90/31.90 – **10 rm** ⊯ ★40.00 – ★★180.00.

    ◆ Good value, converted 19C former rectory with pleasant gardens. Exudes impression of spaciousness; country style décor. Individually styled bedrooms: ask for numbers 2 or 5. Country style bistro serves hearty cuisine.

⬜ **Rossahilly House** ⬥ without rest., BT94 2FP, North : 4½ m. by A 32 off B 82 ℘ (028) 6632 2352, *enquiries@rossahilly.com, Fax (028) 6632 0277*, ≤ Lower Lough Erne, 🦢, 🏕, ⌘ – ⋦ **P**. **⑩ VISA**. ⋘
7 rm ⌂ ✱45.00 – ✱✱70.00/90.00.
* Superbly sited 1930s guesthouse, with supreme views of Lower Lough Erne. Comfortable sitting room and conservatory. Individually styled rooms, one with its own sitting room.

XX **Ferndale** with rm, Irvinestown Rd, BT74 4RN, ℘ (028) 6632 8374, *ferndale chandr@gmail.com* – ⋦ **P**. **⑩ VISA**
Rest *(closed Monday-Tuesday and Sunday dinner)* (dinner only and Sunday lunch) 28.00/34.00 – **6 rm** ⌂ ✱37.50/47.50 – ✱✱75.00.
* Laid-back, personally run restaurant in 17C/19C building. Owner/chef encourages a relaxed visit with time to enjoy abstract art on walls and fine modern cooking. Simple rooms.

X **Café Merlot** (at Blake's of the Hollow), 6 Church St, BT74 7EJ, ℘ (028) 6632 0918 – ⋦ ▦. **⑩ VISA**
closed 25 December – **Rest** (restricted lunch) 22.95 (dinner) and a la carte 18.95/26.40 **s**. ⥅ 🍷.
* Pleasant basement restaurant to the rear of Blake's of the Hollow pub. Vaulted ceilings and ornate stone work surroundings; dine on interesting menus with international scope.

🐦 Look out for red symbols, indicating particularly pleasant establishments.

HILLSBOROUGH (Cromghlinn) *Down* **712** N 4 *Ireland G.*
See : *Town★ – Fort★*.
Env. : *Rowallane Gardens★ AC, Saintfield, E : 10 m. by B 178 and B 6*.
Exc. : *The Argory★, W : 25 m. by A 1 and M 1*.
🛈 *Courthouse ℘ (028) 9268 9717, hillsborough@nitic.net*.
Belfast 12.

🍴 **The Plough Inn,** 3 The Square, BT26 6AG, ℘ (028) 9268 2985, *Fax (028) 9268 2472* – ⋦ **P**. **⑩ AE ①** **VISA**
closed 25 December – **Rest** 14.95/21.95 and a la carte 15.00/20.00 🍷 – **Bar Retro :** **Rest** *(closed Monday)* a la carte 20.00/30.00 🍷.
* Characterful looking pub in lovely small town. Traditionally decorated pub bistro-style dining in two rooms. Cavernous portions of good Irish pub cooking. Wide range of menus.

at Annahilt *Southeast : 4 m. on B 177* – ⊠ *Hillsborough*.

⬜ **Fortwilliam** without rest., 210 Ballynahinch Rd, BT26 6BH, Northwest : ¼ m. on B 177 ℘ (028) 9268 2255, *info@fortwilliamcountryhouse.com, Fax (028) 9268 9608*, 🏕, ⚘ – ⋦ **P**. **⑩ VISA**. ⋘
3 rm ⌂ ✱40.00 – ✱✱65.00.
* Large house on a working farm with attractive gardens. Charming hospitality amidst traditional farmhouse surroundings. Characterful bedrooms with a range of extras.

🍴 **The Pheasant,** 410 Upper Ballynahinch Rd, BT26 6NR, North : 1 m. on Lisburn rd ℘ (028) 9263 8056, *pheasantinn@aol.com, Fax (028) 9263 8026*, ⥮ – ⋦ **P**. **⑩ AE ①** **VISA**
closed 12-13 July and 25-26 December – **Rest** a la carte 12.00/23.00 🍷.
* Modern rustic feel with peat fires and wood floors. Extensive menu offers hearty portions of classic country dishes. Live music on Fridays. A local favourite.

HOLYWOOD (Ard Mhic Nasca) *Down* **712** O 4 *Ireland G.* – pop. 9 252.
Env. : *Cultra : Ulster Folk and Transport Museum★★ AC, NE : 1 m. by A 2*.
🏌 *Holywood, Nuns Walk, Demesne Rd ℘ (028) 9042 2138*.
Belfast 7 – Bangor 6.

🏨 **Culloden,** 142 Bangor Rd, BT18 0EX, East : 1½ m. on A 2 ℘ (028) 9042 1066, *res@cull.hastingshotel.com, Fax (028) 9042 6777*, ≤, ⥮, ℔, ⬛, 🏕, ⚘ – ⬥, ⋦ rm, ▤ rest, ⌘ **P** – ⥟ 1000. **⑩ AE ①** **VISA**. ⋘
Mitre : **Rest** (dinner only and Sunday lunch)/dinner 40.00/50.00 – **Cultra Inn :** **Rest** a la carte 20.00/26.00 – ⌂ 18.00 – **76 rm** ✱170.00 – ✱✱210.00, 3 suites.
* Part Victorian Gothic manor, originally built as an official residence for the Bishops of Down. Top class comfort amid characterful interiors. Smart, comfortable bedrooms. The Mitre has a smart and well-kept air. Timbered, flagged Cultra Inn.

🏠 **Rayanne House**, 60 Demesne Rd, BT18 9EX, by My Lady's Mile Rd 🖉 (028) 9042 5859, *rayannehouse@hotmail.com, Fax (028) 9042 5859*, ≼, –≍≺– 🅿 🝋 *VISA* 🝋 – closed 24 December-4 January – **Rest** (booking essential) 30.00/39.50 ♀ – **11 rm** ⋆70.00/75.00 – ⋆⋆90.00/100.00.
♦ Redbrick house with attractive views of town. Very personally run with smart, alluring interiors. Individually styled rooms feature hand-painted murals and personal trinkets. Warm, attentive service and fine choice menu.

🏠 **Beech Hill** ॐ without rest., 23 Ballymoney Rd, Craigantlet, BT23 4TG, Southeast : 4½ m. by A 2 on Craigantlet rd 🖉 (028) 9042 5892, *info@beech-hill.net, Fax (028) 9042 5892*, ≼, 🚗 – ≍≺ 🅿 🝋 🝋 *VISA*
3 rm ⋄ ⋆50.00/55.00 – ⋆⋆70.00/75.00.
♦ Country house in rural location. Pleasant clutter of trinkets and antiques in guest areas which include a conservatory. Neat, traditionally styled bedrooms: a very fine home.

✗ **Fontana**, 61A High St, BT18 9AE, 🖉 (028) 9080 9908, *Fax (028) 9080 9912*, 🍴 – 🝋 *VISA*
closed 25-26 December, 1 January, 12 July, Monday, Sunday dinner and Saturday lunch – **Rest** (booking essential) (Sunday brunch) 12.50 (lunch) and a la carte 17.10/29.85 ♀.
♦ Modish dining room. Friendly staff. Tasty, unfussy, modern Irish food with refreshing Californian and Mediterranean influences. Choose between main or 'mini' good value menus.

KIRCUBBIN (Cill Ghobáin) *Down* 712 P 4.
Belfast 20.5 – Donaghadee 12.5 – Newtownards 10.5.

✗✗ **Paul Arthurs** with rm, 66 Main St, BT22 2SP, 🖉 (028) 4273 8192, *info@paularthurs.com*, 🚗 – ≍≺ rm. 🝋 *VISA*
closed January, 25-26 December, Monday and Sunday dinner – **Rest** (dinner only and Sunday lunch) a la carte 21.25/32.50 ♀ – **7 rm** ⋄ ⋆50.00 – ⋆⋆70.00.
♦ Distinctive salmon/coral façade. Cosy ground floor lounge. Upstairs dining room flaunts modern Belfast art. Confident, unfussy menus exude bold, classic flavours. Comfy rooms.

LARNE (Latharna) *Antrim* 712 O 3 *Ireland G.* – *pop. 30 832.*
Env. : SE : Island Magee (Ballylumford Dolmen★), by ferry and 2 m. by B 90 or 18 m. by A 2 and B 90.
Exc. : NW : Antrim Glens★★★ – Murlough Bay★★★ (Fair Head ≼★★★), N : 46 m by A 2 and minor road – Glenariff Forest Park★★ AC (Waterfall★★), N : 30 m. by A 2 and A 43 – Glenariff★, N : 25 m. by A 2 – Glendun★, N : 30 m. by A 2 – Carrickfergus (Castle★★ – St Nicholas' Church★), SW : 15 m. by A 2.
🏌 Cairndhu, 192 Coast Rd, Ballygally 🖉 (028) 2858 3324.
⛴ to Fleetwood (Stena Line) daily (8 h) – to Cairnryan (P & O Irish Sea) 3-5 daily (1 h/2 h 15 mn).
🛈 Narrow Gauge Rd 🖉 (028) 2826 0088.
Belfast 23 – Ballymena 20.

🏠 **Manor House** without rest., 23 Olderfleet Rd, Harbour Highway, BT40 1AS, 🖉 (028) 2827 3305, *welcome@themanorguesthouse.com, Fax (028) 2826 0505* – ≍≺ 🅿 🝋 *VISA* 🐾
8 rm ⋄ ⋆25.00/26.00 – ⋆⋆45.00/48.00.
♦ Spacious Victorian terraced house two minutes from ferry terminal. Well-furnished lounge with beautifully varnished wood floors. Small breakfast room. Cosy, homely bedrooms.

LIMAVADY (Léim an Mhadaidh) *Londonderry* 712 L 2.
Env. : Sperrin Mountains★ : Roe Valley Country Park★ AC, S : 2 m. by B 68– Glenshane Pass★, S : 15 m. by B 68 and A 6.
🏌 Benone Par Three, 53 Benone Ave, Benone 🖉 (028) 7775 0555.
🛈 Council Offices, 7 Connell St 🖉 (028) 7776 0307, tourism@limavady.gov.uk.
Belfast 62 – Ballymena 39 – Coleraine 13 – Londonderry 17 – Omagh 50.

🏛 **Radisson SAS Roe Park H. & Golf Resort** ॐ, Roe Park, BT49 9LB, West : ½ m. on A 2 🖉 (028) 7772 2222, *reservations@radissonroepark.com, Fax (028) 7772 2313*, 🛁, ≋, 🖼, 🏌, ⚘, ≐–≋ ≍≺, ▤ rest, 📶 ♨ ⚐⚐ 🅿 – 🛎 450. 🝋 🝋 ① *VISA* 🐾
Greens : **Rest** (closed Sunday and Monday except Bank Holidays) (dinner only and Sunday lunch) a la carte 25.15/31.85 s. ♀ – **The Coach House :** **Rest** a la carte 17.95/24.15 s. ♀ – **117 rm** ⋄ ⋆100.00 – ⋆⋆146.00, 1 suite.
♦ A golfer's idyll with academy and driving range in the grounds of Roe Park. Good leisure centre. Spacious modern bedrooms. Complimentary broadband. Greens is formal in character with menu to match. Brasserie Coach House with open fire and all day service.

✗ **Lime Tree**, 60 Catherine St, BT49 9DB, ☎ (028) 7776 4300, *info@limetreerest.com* – ⊱.
⑩ AE VISA
closed 25-26 December, 12 July, Sunday and Monday – **Rest** (dinner only) a la carte
22.50/30.50.
❖ Well regarded, contemporary neighbourhood restaurant, personally run by friendly husband and wife team. Seasonal produce often includes seafood and a Mediterranean influence.

LONDONDERRY/DERRY (Doire) Londonderry **712** K 2/3 Ireland G. – pop. 72 334.

See : *Town*★ – *City Walls and Gates*★★ – *Guildhall*★ *AC* – *Long Tower Church*★ – *St Columb's Cathedral*★ *AC* – *Tower Museum*★ *AC*.

Env. : *Grianan of Aileach*★★ (⩽★★) (Republic of Ireland) NW : 5 m. by A 2 and N 13.

Exc. : *Ulster-American Folk Park*★★, S : 33 m. by A 5 – *Ulster History Park*★ *AC*, S : 32 m. by A 5 and minor road – *Sperrin Mountains*★ : *Glenshane Pass*★ (⩽★★), SE : 24 m. by A 6 – *Sawel Mountain Drive*★ (⩽★★), S : 22 m. by A 5 and minor roads via Park – *Roe Valley Country Park*★ *AC*, E 15 m. by A 2 and B 68 – *Beaghmore Stone Circles*★, S : 52 m. by A 5, A 505 and minor road.

🏌, 🏌 *City of Derry*, 49 Victoria Rd ☎ (028) 7134 6369.

✈ *City of Derry Airport* : ☎ (028) 7181 0784, E : 6 m. by A 2.

🛈 *44 Foyle St* ☎ (028) 7126 7284, *info@derry.visitor.com*.

Belfast 70 – Dublin 146.

🏛 **City**, Queens Quay, BT48 7AS, ☎ (028) 7136 5800, *res@derry-gsh.com*,
Fax (028) 7136 5801, ⩽, ₤₆, ☒ – 🔌, ⊱ rm, 🔲 rest, ♦ & 🅿 – ₄ 250. **⑩ AE VISA**. ⅍
closed 24-26 December – **Thompson's on the River** : **Rest** (carving lunch/dinner 19.95
and a la carte 19.95/26.95 s. ♀ – ☷ 10.00 – **144 rm** ₤130.00 – ₤₤130.00, 1 suite.
❖ Hotel in purpose-built modern style. Well located, close to the city centre and the quay.
Smart rooms ordered for the business traveller. Useful conference facilities. Modern restaurant overlooks water; carvery lunch very popular.

🏛 **Hastings Everglades**, Prehen Rd, BT47 2NH, South : 1½ m. on A 5 ☎ (028) 7132 1066,
info@egh.hastingshotels.com, Fax (028) 7134 9200 – 🔌 ⊱, 🔲 rest, ♦ & 🅿 – ₄ 500. **⑩ AE ⓞ VISA**. ⅍
Satchmo : **Rest** (dinner only and Sunday lunch) 22.00 and a la carte approx 24.00 ♀ – **64 rm**
☷ ₤78.00/100.00 – ₤₤90.00/130.00.
❖ This modern hotel on the banks of the Foyle makes a useful base for exploring the 17C
city of Derry. Golf facilities nearby. Uniformly decorated rooms. Vibrant painting of Louis
Armstrong hangs in eponymous restaurant.

🏛 **Beech Hill Country House** ⅍, 32 Ardmore Rd, BT47 3QP, Southeast : 3½ m. by A 6
☎ (028) 7134 9279, *info@beech-hill.com*, Fax (028) 7134 5366, ₤₆, ⩮, ⅍, ⩰, ⅌, ⅍ –
⊱ rest, ♦ & 🅿 – ₄ 80. **⑩ AE VISA**
closed 24-25 December – **The Ardmore** : **Rest** 17.95/27.95 ♀ – **25 rm** ☷ ₤80.00 –
₤₤110.00, 2 suites.
❖ 18C country house, now personally run but once a US marine camp; one lounge is filled
with memorabilia. Accommodation varies from vast rooms to more traditional, rural ones.
Restaurant housed within conservatory and old billiard room. Fine garden.

🏛 **Ramada H. Da Vinci's**, 15 Culmore Rd, BT48 8JB, North : 1 m. following signs for
Foyle Bridge ☎ (028) 7127 9111, *info@davincishotel.com*, Fax (028) 7127 9222 – 🔌 ⊱,
🔲 rest, ♦ & 🅿. **⑩ AE ⓞ VISA**. ⅍
closed 24-25 December – **The Grill Room** : **Rest** (dinner only and Sunday lunch) 17.95
(dinner) and a la carte 21.15/27.70 s. – **70 rm** ☷ ₤55.00/65.00 – ₤₤65.00/85.00.
❖ Modern purpose-built hotel at northern end of city's quayside close to major through
routes. Stylish lobby area. Large, atmospheric bar. Good sized, well-equipped bedrooms.
Spacious restaurant has an elegant ambience.

✗✗ **Mandarin Palace**, Lower Clarendon St, BT48 7AW, ☎ (028) 7137 3656, *stan
ley.lee1@btinternet.com*, Fax (028) 7137 3636 – 🔲. **⑩ AE ⓞ VISA**
closed 25-26 December and Saturday lunch – **Rest** - Chinese - a la carte 17.00/30.00 s.
❖ Oriental restaurant, with good views of Foyle river and bridge. Smart staff oversee the
service of unfussy, well-executed Chinese cuisine, featuring good value set menus.

The ❀ award is the crème de la crème.
This is awarded to restaurants
which are really worth travelling miles for!

MAGHERA (Machaire Rátha) *Londonderry* 712 L 3.

Belfast 40 – Ballymena 19 – Coleraine 21 – Londonderry 32.

Ardtara Country House ⌂, 8 Gorteade Rd, Upperlands, BT46 5SA, North : 3 ¼ m. by A 29 off B 75 *℘* (028) 7964 4490, *Fax* (028) 7964 5080, *☞*, *✗* – *rest*, *☎ & P. ⓂⓈ ⒶⒺ* *VISA*
Rest (booking essential for non-residents) (lunch by arrangement)/dinner 35.00 – **9 rm** ⊇ *♦*85.00/100.00 – *♦♦*130.00/150.00.
* 19C house with a charming atmosphere. The interior features "objets trouvés" collected from owner's travels; original fireplaces set off the individually styled bedrooms. Restaurant set in former billiard room with hunting mural and panelled walls.

NEWCASTLE (An Caisleán Nua) *Down* 712 O 5 *Ireland G.* – pop. 7 214.

Env. : *Castlewellan Forest Park★★ AC, NW : 4 m. by A 50 – Tolymore Forest Park★ AC, W : 3 m. by B 180 – Dundrum Castle★ AC, NE : 4 m. by A 2.*
Exc. : *– Silent Valley Reservoir★ (≤★) – Spelga Pass and Dam★ – Kilbroney Forest Park (viewpoint★) – Annalong Marine Park and Cornmill★ AC, S : 8 m. by A 2 – Downpatrick : Cathedral★ AC, Down Country Museum★ AC, NE : 20 m. by A 2 and A 25.*
🛈 *10-14 Central Promenade ℘ (028) 4372 2222, newcastletic@downdc.gov.uk.*
Belfast 32 – Londonderry 101.

Slieve Donard, Downs Rd, BT33 0AH, *℘* (028) 4372 1066, *gm@sdh.hastingshotels.com,* *Fax* (028) 4372 1166, *≤, ☜, ɪ₅, ☎, ◻, ☞ – |𝄐| ✗ ☎ & P. – 🔬 850. ⓂⓈ ⒶⒺ ⓄⒹ VISA*
Oak : Rest 25.00/32.50 ♈ – **Percy French :** Rest a la carte 9.95/12.00 s. ♈ – **178 rm** ⊇ *♦*165.00/190.00 – *♦♦*190.00.
* Victorian grand old lady with sea views. Domed lobby with open fire. Highly impressive spa and leisure. Chaplins bar named after Charlie, who stayed here. Modern rooms. Grand style dining in semi-panelled Oak. Percy French bar-restaurant has easy-going menu.

Burrendale H. & Country Club, 51 Castlewellan Rd, BT33 0JY, North : 1 m. on A 50 *℘* (028) 4372 2599, *reservations@burrendale.com, Fax* (028) 4372 2328, *ɪ₅, ☎, ◻, ☞ – |𝄐| ✗, ▤ rest, & P. – 🔬 300. ⓂⓈ ⒶⒺ ⓄⒹ VISA ✗*
Vine : Rest (dinner only and Sunday lunch) 26.50 s. ♈ – **Cottage Kitchen :** Rest a la carte 13.15/18.75 s. ♈ – **69 rm** ⊇ *♦*80.00 – *♦♦*120.00, 1 suite.
* Set between the Mourne Mountains and Irish Sea, with the Royal Country Down Golf Course nearby. Leisure oriented. Range of rooms from small to very spacious. Linen-clad Vine for traditional dining. Homely cooking to the fore at Cottage Kitchen.

NEWTOWNARDS (Baile Nua na hArda) *Down* 712 O 4.

Belfast 10 – Bangor 144 – Downpatrick 22.

Edenvale House ⌂ without rest., 130 Portaferry Rd, BT22 2AH, Southeast : 2 ¾ m. on A 20 *℘* (028) 9181 4881, *edenvalehouse@hotmail.com, Fax* (028) 9182 6192, *≤, ☞ – P. ⓂⓈ ✗*
closed Christmas – **3 rm** ⊇ *♦*50.00 – *♦♦*80.00.
* Attractive Georgian house with fine views of the Mourne Mountains. Elegant sitting room. Communal breakfasts featuring home-made bread and jams. Individually styled rooms.

PORTAFERRY (Port an Pheire) *Down* 712 P 4 *Ireland G.*

See : *Exploris★ AC.*
Env. : *Castle Ward★★ AC (Audley's Castle★), W : 4 m. by ferry and A 25.*
🛈 *The Stables, Castle St ℘ (028) 4272 9882 (Easter-September).*
Belfast 29 – Bangor 24.

Portaferry, 10 The Strand, BT22 1PE, *℘* (028) 4272 8231, *info@portaferryhotel.com, Fax* (028) 4272 8999, *≤ – ✗ rest. ⓂⓈ ⒶⒺ VISA ✗*
closed 24-25 December – **Rest** (bar lunch Monday-Saturday)/dinner a la carte 18.00/30.75 – **14 rm** ⊇ *♦*55.00/95.00 – *♦♦*110.00/130.00.
* Formerly private dwellings, this personally run hotel dates from 18C. Located on Strangford Lough, most rooms have waterside views. Lounge features Irish paintings. Crisp and fresh dining room with strong emphasis on local produce.

PORTBALLINTRAE (Port Bhaile an Trá) *Antrim* 712 M 2 *Ireland G.*

Env. : *Giant's Causeway***, E : 3 m. by A 2 – Benvarden*, S : 5 m. by B 66 – Dunluce Castle**, W : 2 m. by A 2.*

Belfast 57 – Coleraine 11 – Portrush 5.

🏨 **Bayview**, 2 Bayhead Rd, BT57 8RZ, *℘ (028) 2073 4100, info@bayviewhotelni.com, Fax (028) 2073 4330,* <, – 🛗 🕭 🅿. – 🔏 60. ◉◉ 🏧 ◉ 𝘝𝘐𝘚𝘈, ✼
closed 25 December **Porthole** : Rest a la carte 20.00/30.00 s. – 25 rm ⊊ ✝55.00/85.00 –
✝✝60.00/170.00.
• Situated in centre of pretty village and, as the name suggests, commanding good views of the bay. Well-equipped meeting room. Very comfy rooms, three in appealing 'turret'. Basement dining room with open, spacious feel.

PORTRUSH (Port Rois) *Antrim* 712 L 2 *Ireland G.* – pop. 5 703.

Exc. : *Giant's Causeway*** (Hamilton's Seat* <**, E : 9 m by A 2) – Carrick-a-rede Rope Bridge***, E : 14 m. by A 2 and B 15 – Dunluce Castle** AC, E : 3 m. by A 2 – Gortmore Viewpoint**, E : 14 m. by A 29 , A 2 and minor road – Magilligan Strand**, E : 13 m. by A 29 and A 2 – Downhill* (Mussenden Temple*), E : 12 m. by A 29 and A 2.*

🏌₁₈, 🏌₁₈, 🏌 Royal Portrush, Dunluce Rd *℘ (028) 7082 2311.*

🚩 *Dunluce Centre, Sandhill Drive ℘ (028) 7082 3333 (March-October), portrush@nitic.net.*

Belfast 58 – Coleraine 4 – Londonderry 35.

🏨 **Comfort**, 73 Main St, BT56 8BN, *℘ (028) 7082 6100, info@comforthotelportrush.com, Fax (028) 7082 6160,* <, – 🛗, ✼ rm, ≣ rest, ✆ – 🔏 100. ◉◉ 🏧 ◉ 𝘝𝘐𝘚𝘈, ✼
closed 25 December – **The Counties** : Rest a la carte 20.00/30.00 s. – 69 rm ⊊
✝55.00/120.00 – ✝✝60.00/120.00.
• Located in the heart of town, but just two minutes' walk from blue flag beach. Plenty of small meeting rooms. Well-equipped bedrooms, many being useful for family groups. Contemporary, appealing cafe/restaurant serving popular menus.

⌂ **Beulah**, 16 Causeway St, BT57 8TU, *℘ (028) 7082 2413, stay@beulahguesthouse.com –* ✼✿ 🆃🆅 🅿. ◉◉ ◉ 𝘝𝘐𝘚𝘈, ✼
closed Christmas – Rest (by arrangement) – 9 rm ⊊ ✝35.00/50.00 – ✝✝100.00/110.00.
• Terraced Victorian house in perfect central location. Sound Irish breakfasts. Homely guest lounge. Colourful, co-ordinated and immaculately kept modern bedrooms. Country style meals by arrangement.

✗ **The Harbour Bistro**, 6 Harbour Rd, BT56 8DF, *℘ (028) 7082 2430, Fax (028) 7082 3194* – ◉◉ 𝘝𝘐𝘚𝘈
closed 25 December – Rest (bookings not accepted) (dinner only and Sunday lunch) a la carte 19.90/25.40 ⽟.
• Buzzy bistro in the old part of town near to popular beach. Modern décor. Wide ranging menus providing generous servings. Expect to order and carry your own drinks from bar.

> 😊 Red = Pleasant. Look for the red ✗ and 🏨 symbols.

PORTSTEWART (Port Stióbhaird) *Londonderry* 712 L 2.

Belfast 60 – Ballymena 32 – Coleraine 6.

🏨 **Cromore Halt Inn**, 158 Station Rd, BT55 7PU, East : ½ m. by A 2 (Portrush rd) on B 185 (Coleraine rd) *℘ (028) 7083 6888, info@cromore.com, Fax (028) 7083 1910 –* 🛗 ✼, ≣ rest, ✆ 🕭 🅿. – 🔏 30. ◉◉ 𝘝𝘐𝘚𝘈, ✼
closed 24-26 December – Rest a la carte 14.45/23.45 ⽟ – 19 rm ⊊ ✝55.00 –
✝✝70.00/85.00.
• Modern hotel sited on road into town. Bright, airy, open-plan bar and lounge area. Bedrooms are spacious and well-equipped with attractive, modern colour schemes. Eat in restaurant or Galvally bistro.

TEMPLEPATRICK (Teampall Phádraig) *Antrim* 712 N 3 – ✉ *Ballyclare.*

Belfast 13 – Ballymena 14 – Dundalk 65 – Larne 16.

🏨 **Templeton**, 882 Antrim Rd, BT39 0AH, *℘ (028) 9443 2984, reception@templetonho tel.com, Fax (028) 9443 3406,* 🌿 – ✼✿ 🕭 🅿. – 🔏 350. ◉◉ 🏧 ◉ 𝘝𝘐𝘚𝘈, ✼
closed 25-26 December – **Raffles** : Rest *(closed Monday-Tuesday)* (dinner only and Sunday lunch)/dinner 27.45 and a la carte 23.25/32.60 s. ⽟ – **Upton Grill** : Rest (grill rest.) a la carte 10.95/23.15 ⽟ – 24 rm ⊊ ✝65.00/90.00 – ✝✝90.00/130.00.
• Large and distinctive pine "chalet" appearance. Inside, a swish atrium leads you to a pillared lounge; bedrooms are warm and light. Very popular for weddings. Peaceful library themed Raffles for fine dining. Buzzy Upton Grill with popular menu.

XX **Copper,** 4 Duke St, BT34 3JY, ℘ (028) 4175 3047, *info@copperrestaurant.co.uk* – ⇔ 🗐.
🆇 AE ① *VISA*
closed Christmas, Saturday lunch and Monday – **Rest** 25.00 and a la carte 15.00/25.00.
◆ Modish restaurant with an eye-catching blood red interior and high ceiling.
Chatty, attentive service. Interestingly balanced menus: classic repertoire with ambitious
touches.

X **Restaurant 23,** 23 Church St, BT34 3HN, ℘ (028) 4175 3222, *restaurant23@btcon
nect.com, Fax (028) 4175 2992* – ⇔ 🆇 AE ① *VISA*
closed 2-9 January, 25 December and Monday-Tuesday – **Rest** a la carte 20.00/28.00 **s**.
◆ A very stylish interior makes most of intimate space. Easy-going, good value brasserie
style lunches; evening dishes - adopting a more original slant - are more serious.

B. Pérousse/MICHELIN

Dingle peninsula

Towns
from A to Z

Villes
de A à Z

Città
de A a Z

Städte
von A bis Z

Republic
of Ireland

Place with at least

- a hotel or restaurant   ● Dublin
- a pleasant hotel or restaurant   🏠, ⌂, ✗, 🏠
- Good accommodation at moderate prices   🏠
- a quiet, secluded hotel   🦢
- a restaurant with   ❁, ❁❁, ❁❁❁, 🦢   Rest
- Town with a local map   ●

Ballyliffin
Portsalon
Dunfanaghy
Bunbeg
Rathmullan
Gweedore
Rathmelton
Letterkenny
Ballybofey
N 15
Dunkineely
Killybegs
Donegal
Rossnowlagh
Bundoran
Ballyshannon
Kinlough
Ballycastle
Inishcrone
Rosses Point
N 16
Blacklion
Bangor
Sligo
Crossmolina
Ballina
Ballymote
Riverstown
Ballyconnell
Keel
Doogort
Castlebaldwin
Keshcarrigan
Cava
ACHILL ISLAND
Drumshanbo
Pontoon
Boyle
Killashandra
Mulranny
Newport
Carrick-on-Shannon
Cava
Westport
Knock
Termonbarry
Longford
Tully Cross
Leenane
Ballinlough
Letterfrack
Clonbur
Cong
N 17
Roscommon
Clifden
Ballynahinch
Mullingar
Recess
Caherlistrane
Roundstone
Oughterard
Athlone
Cashel
Moycullen
Carna
Spiddal
Galway
Ballinasloe
Inishmore
Furbogh
Barna
Clarinbridge
Craughwell
ARAN
Kilcolgan
ISLANDS
Ballyvaughan
Kinvarra
Tullamore
New Quay
Doolin
Liscannor
Lisdoonvarna
Birr
Ennistimon
Terryglass
Portlaoise
Lahinch
Corofin
Borrisokane
N 7
Spanish Point
Ennis
N 18
Killaloe
Nenagh
Roscrea
Abbeyleix
Newmarket-
on-Fergus
Durrow
Carlo
Kilkee
Kilrush
Shannon
Bunratty
Thurles
Bagenalstown
Limerick
Glin
N 21
Horse and Jockey
Kilkenny
Ballybunion
Adare
N 24
Graiguenamanag
Listowel
Cashel
Thomastown
Ballingarry
Fethard
Ballydavid
Castlegregory
Kilmallock
Clonmel
New Ros
Ballyferriter
Tralee
Ardfinnan
Dingle
Kanturk
Ballymacarbry
Camp
Killorglin
Mallow
Lismore
Waterford
Caragh Lake
Killarney
Ballynamult
Arthurstow
VALENCIA
Cahirsiveen
Castlelyons
Cappoquin
Tramore
ISLAND
Dungarvan
Knights
Portmagee
Kenmare
Blarney
Youghal
Dunmore East
Town
Tahilla
Macroom
Cork
Killeagh
Waterville
Killeagh
Duncannon
Caherdaniel
Garryvoe
Shanagarry
Castletownbere
Ballycotton
Toormore
Crookhaven

Localité offrant au moins

une ressource hôtelière   ● Dublin
un hôtel ou restaurant agréable   𝕗𝕚𝕟𝕟, ⌂, ✗, 🍴
Bonnes nuits à petits prix   🏠
un hôtel très tranquille, isolé   ⑤
une bonne table à   ✿, ✿✿, ✿✿✿, 🏛 **Rest**

Carte de voisinage : voir à la ville choisie ●

La località possiede come minimo

una risorsa alberghiera   ● Dublin
Albergo o ristorante ameno   𝕗𝕚𝕟𝕟, ⌂, ✗, 🍴
Buona sistemazione a prezzi contenuti   🏠
un albergo molto tranquillo, isolato   ⑤
un'ottima tavola con   ✿, ✿✿, ✿✿✿, 🏛 **Rest**

Città con carta dei dintorni ●

Ort mit mindestens

einem Hotel oder Restaurant   ● Dublin
einem angenehmen Hotel oder Restaurant   𝕗𝕚𝕟𝕟, ⌂, ✗, 🍴
Hier übernachten Sie gut und preiswert   🏠
einem sehr ruhigen und abgelegenen Hotel   ⑤
einem Restaurant mit   ✿, ✿✿, ✿✿✿, 🏛 **Rest**

Stadt mit Umgebungskarte ●

- *Prices quoted in this section of the guide are in euro*
- *Dans cette partie du guide, les prix sont indiqués en euros*
- *I prezzi indicati in questa parte della guida sono in euro*
- *Die Preise in diesem Teil sind in Euro angegeben*

ABBEYLEIX (Mainistir Laoise) *Laois* 712 J 9.

Exc. : *Emo Court*★★ *AC, N : 17 km by R 425 and R 419 – Rock of Dunamase*★ *, NE : 10km by R 425 and N 80 – Stradbally Steam Museum*★ *AC, NE : 19km by R 425 and R 427 – Timahoe Round Tower*★ *, NE : 15km by R 430 and a minor road.*

⊞ *Abbeyleix, Rathmoyle* ℰ *(0502) 31450.*
Dublin 96.5 – Kilkenny 35.5 – Limerick 108.

Abbeyleix Manor, Cork Rd, Southwest : ¾ km on N 8 ℰ (0502) 30111, *info@abbeyleix manorhotel.com*, Fax (0502) 30220 – ✦✦ ▤ ✦ ♿ 🅿 – 🔏 400. 🕮 🆎 ⓞ 𝘝𝘐𝘚𝘈 . ✦
closed 25 December – **Rest** *(closed Sunday-Tuesday dinner)* (carving lunch Monday-Friday) (bar lunch Saturday)/dinner 33 and a la carte 17/31 s. ♀ – **46 rm** �} ✦65/75 – ✦✦110/130.
◆ Modern purpose-built hotel painted a distinctive yellow. Mural decorated public areas. Well-kept bar and a games room. Uniform bedrooms with simple, comfortable style. Restaurant has a bright modern feel.

ACHILL ISLAND (Acaill) *Mayo* 712 B 5/6 *Ireland G.*

See : *Island*★.
⊞ *Achill Island, Keel* ℰ *(098) 43456.*
🛈 *Achill* ℰ *(098) 47353 (July-August).*

Doogort (Dumha Goirt) – ✉ *Achill Island.*

Gray's ⟡, ℰ (098) 43244, ⌗ – ✦✦ 🅿
closed Christmas – **Rest** *(by arrangement)* 32 – **14 rm** ✦55/61 – ✦✦110.
◆ A row of tranquil whitewashed cottages with a homely atmosphere; popular with artists. Cosy sitting rooms with fireplaces and simple but spotless bedrooms. Local scene paintings adorn dining room walls.

Keel (An Caol) – ✉ *Achill Island.*

Achill Cliff House, ℰ (098) 43400, *info@achillcliff.com*, Fax (098) 43007, ≼, ⌂ – ✦✦ ♿ ♿ 🅿 🕮 🆎 𝘝𝘐𝘚𝘈 . ✦
Rest (bar lunch Monday-Saturday)/dinner 26/30 and a la carte 28/37 ♀ – **10 rm** �} ✦40/120 – ✦✦70/120.
◆ Whitewashed modern building against a backdrop of countryside and ocean. Within walking distance of Keel beach. Well-kept, spacious bedrooms with modern furnishings. Spacious restaurant with sea views.

ADARE (Áth Dara) *Limerick* 712 F 10 *Ireland G.*

See : *Town*★ *– Adare Friary*★ *– Adare Parish Church*★.
Exc. : *Rathkeale (Castle Matrix*★ *AC – Irish Palatine Heritage Centre*★ *) W : 12 km by N 21 – Newcastle West*★ *, W : 26 km by N 21 – Glin Castle*★ *AC, W : 46½ km by N 21, R 518 and N 69.*

🛈 *Heritage Centre, Mains St* ℰ *(061) 396255.*
Dublin 210 – Killarney 95 – Limerick 16.

Adare Manor ⟡, ℰ (061) 396566, *reservations@adaremanor.com*, Fax (061) 396124, ≼, ⌗, ⬚, 🐾, ⟍, ⌗, ♨–🛗 ✦✦ ✦ 🅿 – 🔏 80. 🕮 🆎 ⓞ 𝘝𝘐𝘚𝘈 . ✦
The Oakroom : Rest (dinner only) 59 and a la carte 47/65 – **The Carriagehouse :** Rest a la carte 24/49 – �} 23 – **62 rm** ✦260/375 – ✦✦565/675.
◆ Part 19C Gothic mansion on banks of River Maigue in extensive parkland. Impressively elaborate interiors and capacious lounges. Most distinctive rooms in the oldest parts. Oak-panelled dining room overlooks river. Informal Carriagehouse.

Dunraven Arms, Main St, ℰ (061) 396633, *reservations@dunravenhotel.com*, Fax (061) 396541, 🛌, ⬚, ⌗ – 🛗 ✦✦ 🅿 – 🔏 350. 🕮 🆎 ⓞ 𝘝𝘐𝘚𝘈 . ✦
The Inn Between : Rest *(closed January-April, Sunday and Monday)* (bar lunch) a la carte 25/34 – (see also **Maigue** below) – �} 20 – **86 rm** ✦135/180 – ✦✦155/200.
◆ Considerably extended 18C building opposite town's charming thatched cottages. Understated country house style. Comfortable bedrooms in bright magnolia. Well-equipped gym. Welcoming bistro in charming thatched cottage.

⌂ **Carrabawn Guesthouse** without rest., Killarney Rd, Southwest : ¾ km on N 21
℘ (061) 396067, carrabawnhouse@eircom.net, Fax (061) 396925, ≉ – ⇥ P, ◼◎ VISA ⊁
March-October–– ⊇ 11 8 rm ✦55 – ✦✦60.
♦ Well-established guesthouse with genuine homely style and large mature garden. Sitting room with games and books and comfortable sun lounge. Well-kept co-ordinated bedrooms.

⌂ **Berkeley Lodge** without rest., Station Rd, ℘ (061) 396857, berlodge@iol.ie,
Fax (061) 396857 – ⇥ P, ◼◎ VISA ⊁
6 rm ⊇ ✦55/60 – ✦✦70/80.
♦ Good value accommodation with a friendly and well-run ambience. Hearty breakfast choices include pancakes and smoked salmon. Simply furnished traditional bedrooms.

XX **The Wild Geese,** Rose Cottage, ℘ (061) 396451, wildgeese@indigo.ie, Fax (061) 396451
– ◼◎ AE ◎ VISA
closed 24 December - 2 January, Monday in winter and Sunday – **Rest** (booking essential) (dinner only) 38 and a la carte approx 48.
♦ Traditional 18C cottage on main street. Friendly service and cosy welcoming atmosphere. Varied menu with classic and international influences uses much fresh local produce.

XX **Maigue** (at Dunraven Arms H.), Main St, ℘ (061) 396633, Fax (061) 396541, ≉ – ◼ P, ◼◎
AE ◎ VISA
Rest (dinner only and Sunday lunch) a la carte 32/39.
♦ Burgundy décor, antique chairs and historical paintings create a classic traditional air. Menus offer some eclectic choice on an Irish backbone. Formal yet friendly service.

ARAN ISLANDS (Oileáin Árann) Galway **712** CD 8 Ireland G.
See : Islands★ – Inishmore (Dún Aonghasa★★★).
Access by boat or aeroplane from Galway city or by boat from Kilkieran, Rossaveel or Fisherstreet (Clare) and by aeroplane from Inverin.
🖪 Aran Kilronan ℘ (099) 61263.

Inishmore Galway – ⊠ Aran Islands.

🏠 **Pier House** ⑤, Kilronan, ℘ (099) 61417, pierh@iol.ie, Fax (099) 61122, ≤, ≉ – ⇥ P, ◼◎ VISA ⊁
March-October – **Rest** – (see **The Restaurant** below) – 10 rm ⊇ ✦50/100 – ✦✦120.
♦ Purpose-built at the end of the pier with an attractive outlook. Spacious, planned interiors and spotlessly kept bedrooms furnished in a comfortable modern style.

⌂ **Ard Einne Guesthouse** ⑤, Killeany, ℘ (099) 61126, ardeinne@eircom.net, Fax (099) 61388, ≤ Killeany Bay – P, ◼◎ VISA ⊁
February-October – **Rest** (by arrangement) 25 – 14 rm ⊇ ✦60/90 – ✦✦80/100.
♦ Purpose-built chalet-style establishment in isolated spot with superb views of Killeany Bay. Homely atmosphere amidst traditional appointments. Simple, comfortable bedrooms. Spacious dining room provides home-cooked meals.

⌂ **Kilmurvey House** ⑤, Kilmurvey, ℘ (099) 61218, kilmurveyhouse@eircom.net, Fax (099) 61397, ≤, ᇤ – ◼◎ VISA ⊁
April-October – **Rest** (by arrangement) 30/35 – 12 rm ⊇ ✦60/90 – ✦✦100/120.
♦ Extended stone-built house in tranquil, secluded location with the remains of an ancient fort in grounds. Well-kept traditional style throughout. Simply decorated bedrooms. Traditional dining room. Good use of fresh island produce.

X **The Restaurant** (at Pier House H.), Kilronan, ℘ (099) 61417, pierh@iol.ie, Fax (099) 61122 – ◼◎ VISA
March-October – **Rest** - Seafood specialities - (light lunch) a la carte 20/45.
♦ Cosy, snug, cottagey restaurant, typified by its rustic, wooden tables. Light lunches are replaced by more serious dinner menus with strong selection of local fish dishes.

ARDEE (Baile Atha Fhirdhia) Louth **712** M 6 Ireland G. – pop. 3 791.
Exc. : St Mochta's House★, N : 11 km by R 171 – Dún a'Rí Forest Park★, NW : 21 km by N 52 and R 165 – Mellifont Old Abbey★, S : 21 km by N 2 and minor rd – Monasterboice★★, S : 24 km by N 2, R 168 and minor rd.
Dublin 66 – Drogheda 29 – Dundalk 27.

X **Rolf's Bistro**, 52 Market St, ℘ (041) 685 7949, rolfsbistro@eircom.net, Fax (041) 685 7949 – ◼◎ VISA
closed Sunday – **Rest** (dinner only) a la carte 25/45 **s.**
♦ Georgian townhouse in main street. Bar and restaurant hung with local artists' work for sale. Early bird and main menu, a mixture of Irish, Swedish and Asian dishes.

ARDFINNAN (Ard Fhíonáin) Tipperary 712 I 11.

Dublin 185 – Caher 9.5 – Waterford 63.

⌂ **Kilmaneen Farmhouse** ⬧, East : 3 ¼ km by Goatenbridge rd ℰ (052) 36231, *kilmaneen@eircom.net*, Fax (052) 36231, ⬧, 🍴, ♨ – ⚡ P. ⬛ VISA
16 March - October – **Rest** (communal dining) 25 – **3 rm** ⚏ ♦40/50 – ♦♦80.
◆ Traditional farmhouse on dairy farm hidden away in the countryside. Cosy and neat, with a welcoming lounge. Comfortable bedrooms are well kept and individually furnished. Tasty menus with a rural heart.

ARTHURSTOWN (Colmán) Wexford 712 L 11.

Dublin 166 – Cork 159 – Limerick 162.5 – Waterford 42.

🏨 **Dunbrody Country House** ⬧, ℰ (051) 389600, *dunbrody@indigo.ie*, Fax (051) 389601, ≤, 🍴, ⬧, ♨ – ⚡ ♦ ♨ P. ⬛ AE ⓞ VISA. ⬧
closed 1 week Christmas – **Rest** (booking essential for non-residents) (residents only Sunday dinner) (bar lunch Monday-Saturday)/dinner 60 ⚡ – **17 rm** ⚏ ♦135/153 – ♦♦260/345, 5 suites.
◆ A fine country house hotel with a pristine elegant style set within a part Georgian former hunting lodge, affording much peace. Smart comfortable bedrooms. Elegant dining room in green damask and burgundy.

ASHBOURNE (Cill Dhéagláin) Meath 712 M 7.

Dublin 21 – Drogheda 26 – Navan 27.5.

⌂ **Broadmeadow Country House** ⬧ without rest., Bullstown, Southeast : 4 km by N 2 on R 125 (Swords rd) ℰ (01) 835 2823, *info@irishcountryhouse.com*, Fax (01) 835 2819, 🍴, ♨, ⬧ – P. ⬛ VISA. ⬧
closed 23 December-2 January – **8 rm** ⚏ ♦50/80 – ♦♦100/120.
◆ Substantial ivy-clad guesthouse and equestrian centre in rural area yet close to airport. Light and airy breakfast room overlooks garden. Spacious rooms have country views.

ASHFORD (Áth na Fuinseoge) Wicklow 712 N 8 – pop. 1 215.

Dublin 43.5 – Rathdrum 17.5 – Wicklow 6.5.

⌂ **Ballyknocken House**, Glenealy, South : 4 ¾ km by N 11 ℰ (0404) 44627, *cfulvio@ballyknocken.com*, Fax (0404) 44696, 🍴, ♨, ⬧ – ⚡ P. ⬛ VISA. ⬧
February-14 December – **Rest** (by arrangement) 40 – **9 rm** ⚏ ♦69/95 – ♦♦104/130.
◆ Part Victorian guesthouse on a working farm: the comfy bedrooms are furnished with antiques, and some have claw foot baths: most are in the new wing. Charming owner proud of home cooking.

ATHLONE (Baile Átha Luain) Westmeath 712 I 7 Ireland G. – pop. 15 544.

Exc. : Clonmacnois★★★ (Grave Slabs★, Cross of the Scriptures★) S : 21 km by N 6 and N 62 – N : Lough Ree (Ballykeeran Viewpoint★).*
🛈 Hodson Bay ℰ (0902) 92073.
🛈 Athlone Castle ℰ (090) 649 4630 (April-October).
Dublin 120.5 – Galway 92 – Limerick 120.5 – Roscommon 32 – Tullamore 38.5.

🏨 **Radisson SAS,** Northgate St, ℰ (090) 6442600, *info.athlone@radissonsas.com*, Fax (090) 6442655, ≤, 🛁, ≋, ⬚ – ⬛ ⬚ ⚡ ▦ ♨ & P. – 🅿 700. ⬛ AE ⓞ VISA. ⬧
Rest (buffet lunch Monday-Saturday)/dinner 38 and a la carte 30/47 ⚡ – **127 rm** ⚏ ♦130 – ♦♦155.
◆ Overlooks River Shannon, cathedral and marina. Quayside bar with super terrace. Impressive leisure and meeting facilities. Very modern rooms with hi-tech mod cons. Modish restaurant serving buffet or à la carte.

🏨 **Hodson Bay,** Northwest : 7 ¾ km by N 61 ℰ (090) 6442000, *info@hodsonbayhotel.com*, Fax (090) 6442020, 🛁, ≋, ⬚, 🛈, ⬧, 🍴, ♨ – ⬚ ⚡ ⬚ ♨ & ♨ P. – 🅿 700. ⬛ AE ⓞ VISA. ⬧
L'Escale : Rest 20/40 and dinner a la carte 26/56 – **182 rm** ⚏ ♦195 – ♦♦300.
◆ Purpose-built hotel appealingly sited on shores of Lough Ree. Plenty of indoor and outdoor leisure activities: busy conference facility. Most bedrooms with views of the lough. Shoreside ambience is pleasant at dinner.

⌂ **Shelmalier House** without rest., Retreat Rd, Cartrontroy, East : 2½ km by Dublin rd (N 6) ℰ (090) 6472245, *shelmalier@eircom.net*, Fax (090) 6473190, ≋, 🍴 – ⚡ P. ⬛ VISA. ⬧
closed January – **7 rm** ⚏ ♦45/49 – ♦♦66/70.
◆ Modern house with large garden in a quiet residential area of town. Homely décor throughout, including comfortable bedrooms which are well kept.

↑ **Riverview House** without rest., Summerhill, Galway Rd, West : 4 km on N 6 ℘ (090) 6494532, riverviewhouse@hotmail.com, Fax (090) 6494532, � – ⇔ P. ◑◐ Æ VISA . ✗
March-18 December – **4 rm** ⊆ ✹45 – ✹✹64.
  ♦ Modern house with well-kept garden. Homely, comfortable lounge and wood furnished dining room. Uniformly styled fitted bedrooms. Good welcome.

✗ **Left Bank Bistro,** Fry Pl, ℘ (090) 6494446, info@leftbankbistro.com, Fax (090) 6494509 – ▤. ◑◐ VISA
closed 25 December-6 January, Sunday and Monday – **Rest** (light lunch)/dinner a la carte 25/44 ℥.
  ♦ Glass-fronted with open-plan wine store and bright, modern bistro buzzing with regulars. Salads and foccacias, plus modern Irish dishes and fish specials in the evening.

at Glassan *Northeast : 8 km on N 55* – ✉ *Athlone.*

🏨 **Wineport Lodge** ≼, Southwest : 1 ½ km ℘ (090) 6439010, lodge@wineport.ie, Fax (090) 6485471, ≼ Lough Ree, 🍴 – 📱 🛁 ⇔ ▤ ✆ ⇘ ⇔ 12. ◑◐ Æ VISA
closed 24-26 December – **Rest** (dinner only) 65 and a la carte 48/60 s. ℥ – **29 rm** ⊆ ✹140 – ✹✹275/295.
  ♦ Beautifully located by Lough Ree. Come in from the delightful terrace and sip champagne in stylish bar. Superb rooms of limed oak and ash boast balconies and lough views. Smart restaurant with separate galleried area for private parties.

🏨 **Glasson Golf H. & Country Club** ≼, West : 2 ¾ km ℘ (090) 6485120, info@glassongolf.ie, Fax (090) 6485444, ≼ Golf course and Lough Ree, 🍴, ┌•, 🌳, ⊞– 🛁 ⇔ ✆ ⇘ & ✗ – 🏌 80. ◑◐ Æ ◑ VISA . ✗
closed 25 December – **Rest** (bar lunch)/dinner 30/55 and a la carte 21/47 s. ℥ – **28 rm** ⊆ ✹80/210 – ✹✹120/400, 1 suite.
  ♦ Family owned hotel commands fine views of Lough Ree and its attractive golf course. Modern bedrooms are spacious with superior rooms making most of view. Original Georgian house restaurant with wonderful outlook.

↑ **Glasson Stone Lodge** without rest., ℘ (090) 6485004, glassonstonelodge@eircom.net, 🌳 – ⇔ P. ◑◐ VISA . ✗
April-November – **6 rm** ⊆ ✹45/65.00 – ✹✹70/80.00.
  ♦ A warm welcome and notable breakfasts with home-baked breads and locally sourced organic bacon. Bedrooms and communal areas are airy and tastefully furnished.

↑ **Harbour House** ≼ without rest., Southwest : 2 km ℘ (090) 6485063, ameade@indigo.ie., 🌳 – ⇔ P. ◑◐ VISA . ✗
May-October – **6 rm** ⊆ ✹45 – ✹✹70.
  ♦ Sited in quiet rural spot a stone's throw from Lough Ree. Traditionally styled lounge with stone chimney breast; adjoining breakfast room. Comfy bedrooms overlook garden.

ATHY **(Baile Átha Í)** *Kildare* **712** L 9 *Ireland G.* – *pop. 5 306.*
  Exc. : *Emo Court*★★ , *N : 32 km by R 417 (L 18), west by N 7 (T 5) and north by R 422 – Stradbally Steam Museum★ AC, W : 13 km by R 428 – Castledermot High Crosses★ , SE : 15 ¼ km by R 418 – Moone High Cross★ , E : 19¼ km by Ballitore minor rd and south by N9 – Rock of Dunamase★ (≼★), NW : 19¼ km by R 428 (L109) and N80 (T16) – Timahoe Round Tower★ , W : 16 km by R 428 (L 109) and N 80 (T 16).*
  ┌• *Athy, Geraldine ℘ (059) 863 1729.*
  Dublin 64.5 – Kilkenny 46.5 – Wexford 95.

🏨 **Clanard Court,** Dublin Rd, Northeast : 2 km on N 78 ℘ (059) 8640666, sales@clanardcourt.ie, Fax (059) 8640888, 🌳 – 📱 ⇔, ▤ rest, ✆ & P. – 🏌 350. ◑◐ Æ VISA . ✗
closed 25 December – **Courtyard Bistro : Rest** (closed Sunday dinner and Monday) (carvery lunch)/dinner 45/55 – **38 rm** ⊆ ✹79/129 – ✹✹790/198.
  ♦ Commercially oriented modern hotel in bright yellow which opened in 2005. Well-equipped meeting rooms. Large bar to snack, sup and unwind. Comfy, smart bedrooms. Restaurant offers Mediterranean/North African style and menus.

AUGHRIM **(Eachroim)** *Wicklow* **712** N 9.
  🈯 *The Battle of Aughrim Visitors Centre, Ballinasloe ℘ (0909) 742604 (summer only).*
  Dublin 74 – Waterford 124 – Wexford 96.5.

🏨 **Brooklodge** ≼, Macreddin Village, North : 3 ¼ km ℘ (0402) 36444, brooklodge@macreddin.ie, Fax (0402) 36580, 🍷, Ⅰ₄, ≋, 🏊, 🌳, ⊞– 📱 ⇔ P. – 🏌 220. ◑◐ Æ ◑ VISA
Orchard Cafe : Rest (lunch only) a la carte 14/18 – **Strawberry Tree : Rest** (dinner only and Sunday lunch)/dinner 60 s. – **42 rm** ⊆ ✹135/260 – ✹✹220/380, 12 suites.
  ♦ Very individual hotel in idyllic parkland setting. Self-contained microbrewery, smokehouse and bakery. Well-appointed bedrooms and a friendly comfortable style throughout. Orchard Cafe is relaxed, informal eatery. Organic ingredients in Strawberry Tree.

AVOCA (Abhóca) *Wicklow* **712** N 9 *Ireland G.*
Exc. : *Avondale★, N : by R 752 – Meeting of the Waters★, N : by R 752.*
Dublin 75.5 – Waterford 116 – Wexford 88.5.

⌂ **Keppel's Farmhouse** ⬡ without rest., Ballanagh, South : 3 ¼ km by unmarked rd
ℰ (0402) 35168, *keppelsfarmhouse@eircom.net*, Fax (0402) 30950, <, ⬡, ⬡ – ⬡ **P**. **⬡⬡**
VISA. ⬡
June-September – **5 rm** ⬡ **†**50/55 – **††**65/75.
 ♦ Farmhouse set in seclusion at end of long drive on working dairy farm. Attractively
simple modern and traditional bedrooms; those in front have far-reaching rural views.

BAGENALSTOWN (Muine Bheag) *Carlow* **712** L 9.
Dublin 101.5 – Carlow 16 – Kilkenny 21 – Wexford 59.5.

▥ **Kilgraney Country House** ⬡, South : 6 ½ km by R 705 (Borris Rd) ℰ (059) 9775283,
info@kilgraneyhouse.com, Fax (059) 9775595, <, ⬡, ⬡ – ⬡ **P**. **⬡⬡** **AE** **VISA**. ⬡
March-October – **Rest** *(closed Monday-Tuesday except July-August)* (booking essential)
(residents only) (communal dining) (dinner only) 48 s. – **8 rm** ⬡ **†**100 – **††**240.
 ♦ 18C house with individual interiors featuring Far Eastern artefacts from owners' travels.
Sitting room in dramatic colours, paintings resting against wall. Stylish rooms. Communal
dining in smart surroundings.

> Your opinions are important to us:
> please write and let us know about your discoveries and experiences –
> good and bad!

BALLINA (Béal an Átha) *Mayo* **712** E 5 *Ireland G.* – *pop. 8 762.*
Env. : *Rosserk Abbey★, N : 6 ½ km by R 314.*
Exc. : *Moyne Abbey★, N : 11 ¼ km by R 314 – Pontoon Bridge View (≤★), S : 19 ¼ km by*
N 26 and R 310 – Downpatrick Head★, N : 32 km by R 314.
🛈 *Mossgrove, Shanaghy* ℰ (096) 21050.
🛈 *Cathedral Rd* ℰ (096) 70848 *(April-October).*
Dublin 241.5 – Galway 117.5 – Roscommon 103 – Sligo 59.5.

▥ **Downhill Inn,** Sligo Rd, East : 1 ½ km off N 59 ℰ (096) 73444, *thedownhillinn@eir*
com.net, Fax (096) 73411 – ⬡ **P**. **⬡⬡** **AE** **VISA**. ⬡
closed 21-28 December – **Rest** (bar lunch Monday-Saturday)/dinner 27/35 and a la carte
26/38 s. ⬡ – **45 rm** ⬡ **†**65/120 – **††**100/150.
 ♦ Purpose-built lodge-style hotel on Ballina outskirts in heart of Moy Valley, with superb
salmon fishing nearby. Comfortable, warm interiors enhance the rooms. Simply decorated
restaurant with a welcoming atmosphere.

BALLINADEE (Baile na Daidhche) *Cork* **712** G 12 – *see Kinsale.*

BALLINASLOE (Béal Átha na Sluaighe) *Galway* **712** H 8 *Ireland G.* – *pop. 5 723.*
Env. : *Clonfert Cathedral★ (west doorway★★), SW : by R 355 and minor roads.*
Exc. : *Turoe Stone, Bullaun★, SW : 29 km by R 348 and R 350 – Loughrea (St Brendan's*
Cathedral★), SW : 29 km by N 6 – Clonmacnoise★★★ (grave slabs★, Cross of the Script-ur-
es★) E : 21km by R 357 and R 444.
🛈 *Rossgloss* ℰ (0905) 42126 – 🛈 *Mountbellew* ℰ (0905) 79259.
🛈 ℰ (0909) 742604 *(July-August).*
Dublin 146.5 – Galway 66 – Limerick 106 – Roscommon 58 – Tullamore 55.

✕ **Tohers,** 18 Dunlo St, ℰ (090) 9644848, Fax (090) 9644844 – **⬡⬡** **VISA**
closed 2 weeks October, 1 week February, 25-26 December, Good Friday, Monday dinner
and Sunday – **Rest** (bar lunch)/dinner 38 and a la carte 25/42.
 ♦ Converted pub in a busy market town; simple restaurant and bustling lower bar. Tasty
dishes. Charming, friendly service.

BALLINCLASHET (Baile na Claise) *Cork* **712** G 12 – *see Kinsale.*

BALLINGARRY (Baile an Gharraí) *Limerick* **712** F 10 *Ireland G.*

Exc. : *Kilmallock★ (Kilmallock Abbey★, Collegiate Church★), SE : 24 km by R 518 – Lough Gur Interpretive Centre★ AC, NE : 29 km by R 519, minor road to Croom, R 516 and R 512 – Monasteranenagh Abbey★, NE : 24 km by R 519 and minor road to Croom.*
Dublin 227 – Killarney 90 – Limerick 29.

🏨 **Mustard Seed at Echo Lodge** ⟨S⟩, ℰ (069) 68508, *mustard@indigo.ie*,
Fax (069) 68511, ⟨⟩, ♠ – ⟨⟩ ♿ P – ⟨A⟩ 25. 🐵 🅰🅴 Ⓞ 🆅🅸🆂🅰. ⟨⟩
closed 20 January- 10 February and 24-26 December – **Rest** *(closed Monday in winter)*
(booking essential for non-residents) (dinner only) 57/60 – **13 rm** ⟨⟩ ★115 – ★★230,
2 suites.
  ◆ Converted convent with very neat gardens and peaceful appeal. Cosy lounge with fire-place and beautiful fresh flowers. Individually furnished rooms with mix of antiques. Meals enlivened by home-grown herbs and organic farm produce.

BALLINLOUGH (Baile an Locha) *Roscommon* **712** G 6.

Dublin 183.5 – Galway 64.5 – Roscommon 38.5 – Sligo 82.

🏨 **White House,** ℰ (094) 9640112, *thewhitehousehotel@eircom.net*, Fax (094) 9640993 –
⟨⟩ ⟨⟩, 🍽 rest, ⟨⟩ ♿ – ⟨A⟩ 250. 🐵 🅰🅴 🆅🅸🆂🅰. ⟨⟩
closed 25 December – **The Blue Room :** **Rest** *(closed Monday-Wednesday)* (carvery
lunch)/dinner a la carte 18/35 **s. – 19 rm** ⟨⟩ ★55/69 – ★★109/165.
  ◆ On the village square; popular bar with live music at weekends; conference room, lav-ishly decorated honeymoon suite and smartly furnished rooms. Intimate dining room with rich décor and antique furniture.

BALLSBRIDGE (Droichead na Dothra) *Dublin* **712** N 8 – see Dublin.

BALLYBOFEY (Bealach Féich) *Donegal* **712** I 3 – pop. 3 047 (inc. Stranorlar).

🏌 *Ballybofey & Stranorlar, The Glebe* ℰ (074) 31093.
Dublin 238 – Londonderry 48 – Sligo 93.

🏨 **Kee's,** Main St, Stranorlar, Northeast : ¾ km on N 15 ℰ (074) 9131018, *info@keeshotel.ie*,
Fax (074) 9131917, ⟨⟩, ⟨⟩, 🔲 – ⟨⟩ ♠ P – ⟨A⟩ 300. 🐵 🅰🅴 ⓄⓄ 🆅🅸🆂🅰. ⟨⟩
Looking Glass : **Rest** *(restricted opening in winter)* (dinner only and Sunday lunch)/dinner
36/45 – **Old Gallery :** **Rest** a la carte 20/36 **s. – 53 rm** ⟨⟩ ★100/120 – ★★200.
  ◆ Very comfortable hotel established over 150 years ago. Smart lobby with plush sofas. Atmospheric bar and raised lounge area. Comfortable rooms. Intimate Looking Glass offer-ing international menus. Popular favourites in uncluttered Old Gallery bistro.

🏨 **Villa Rose,** Main St, ℰ (074) 9132266, *info@villarose.net*, Fax (074) 9130666 – ⟨⟩ ⟨⟩,
🍽 rest, ♿, 🐵 🅰🅴 🆅🅸🆂🅰. ⟨⟩
closed 25-26 December – **Rest** a la carte 25/35 – **60 rm** ⟨⟩ ★70/75 – ★★110/160.
  ◆ Under private ownership, a modern hotel in the centre of the town. Neat, well-appoin-ted accommodation, furnished in co-ordinated colours and fabrics. Bright, airy dining room with contemporary style and wide international choice.

BALLYBUNION (Baile an Bhuinneánaigh) *Kerry* **712** D 10 *Ireland G.*

Env. : *Rattoo Round Tower★, S : 10 km by R 551.*
Exc. : *Ardfert★, S : 29 km by R 551, R 556 and minor road W – Banna Strand★, S : 28 km by R 551 – Carrigafoyle Castle★, NE : 21 km by R 551 – Glin Castle★ AC, E : 30½ km by R 551 and N 69.*
🏌, 🏌 *Ballybunnion, Sandhill Rd* ℰ (068) 27146.
Dublin 283 – Limerick 90 – Tralee 42.

🏨 **Iragh Ti Connor,** Main St, ℰ (068) 27112, *iraghticonnor@eircom.net*, Fax (068) 27787,
⟨⟩ – ⟨⟩ P. 🐵 🅰🅴 🆅🅸🆂🅰. ⟨⟩
April-first week November – **Rest** (dinner only and Sunday lunch) a la carte 25/35 **s. – 17 rm**
⟨⟩ ★155 – ★★195.
  ◆ Locals gather in the cosy front bar of this rustic 19C inn with an ivy-clad modern wing. Very spacious bedrooms in smart reproduction furnishings. Keen, friendly owner. Baby grand piano accompanies diners.

🏨 **Harty Costello Townhouse,** Main St, ℰ (068) 27129, *hartycostello@eircom.net*,
Fax (068) 27489 – ⟨⟩. 🐵 🅰🅴 🆅🅸🆂🅰. ⟨⟩
April- October – **Rest** *(closed Sunday)* (dinner only) 23/26 42 **s.** ⟨⟩ – **8 rm** ⟨⟩ ★60/85 –
★★120/185.
  ◆ This personally run hotel, set around and above the pub downstairs, is smart, stylish and contemporary. A popular choice for visitors to this golfing town. Local fish in spruce, welcoming restaurant.

Teach de Broc Country House, Link Rd, South : 2 ½ km on Golf Club rd ✆ (068) 27581, *info@ballybunniongolf.com, Fax (068) 27919* – VISA.
April-October – **Rest** *(closed Monday)* a la carte 22/38 – **14 rm** 80/140 – 140/170.
◆ Clean, tidy guesthouse with coastal proximity and great appeal to golfers as it's adjacent to the famous Ballybunion golf course. Home cooked meals. Neat, spacious rooms.

The 19th Lodge without rest., Golf Links Rd, South : 2 ¾ km by Golf Club rd ✆ (068) 27592, *the19thlodge@eircom.net, Fax (068) 27830,* – , rm, VISA.
March - November – **12 rm** 80/150 – 130/200.
◆ Orange washed house aimed at golfers playing at adjacent course. First floor lounge with honesty bar and comfy sofas. Linen-clad breakfast room. Luxurious rooms.

Cashen Course House without rest., Golf Links Rd, South : 2 ¾ km by Golf Club rd ✆ (068) 27351, *golfstay@eircom.net, Fax (068) 28934,* – , rm, AE VISA.
15 March-October – **10 rm** 80/120 – 130/180.
◆ Overlooks first hole at the Cashen Course: clubhouse just one minute away. Bright, breezy breakfast room; quality furnishings in comfy lounge. Spacious, colourful rooms.

REPUBLIC OF IRELAND

BALLYCASTLE (Baile an Chaisil) *Mayo* 712 D 5.

Exc. : *Céide Fields*★, *AC, NE 8 Km by R 314.*
Dublin 267 – Galway 140 – Sligo 88.5.

Stella Maris , Northwest : 3 km by R 314 ✆ (096) 43322, *info@stellamarisireland.com, Fax (096) 43965,* ≤ Bunatrahir Bay, – VISA.
April-September – **Rest** *(closed to non-residents Monday dinner)* (dinner only) a la carte 32/46 – **11 rm** 155 – 250.
◆ Former coastguard station and fort in a great spot overlooking the bay. Public areas include a long conservatory. Attractive rooms with antique and contemporary furnishings. Modern menus in stylish dining room.

The ✿ award is the crème de la crème.
This is awarded to restaurants
which are really worth travelling miles for!

BALLYCONNELL (Béal Atha Conaill) *Cavan* 712 J 5.

18 *Slieve Russell* ✆ *(049) 952 6458.*
Dublin 143 – Drogheda 122.5 – Enniskillen 37.

Slieve Russell, Southeast : 2 ¾ km on N 87 ✆ (049) 952 6444, *slieve-russell@quinn-hotels.com, Fax (049) 952 6474,* 18, – , rest, – 1200. AE VISA.
Conall Cearnach : **Rest** (dinner only and Sunday lunch) 25/45 – ***Setanta :*** **Rest** 18 (lunch) and dinner a la carte 30/42 – **217 rm** 140 – 250, 2 suites.
◆ Purpose-built hotel set in extensive gardens and golf course. Marbled entrance, large lounges, leisure and conference facilities. Spacious, modern rooms. Conall Cearnach has sophisticated appeal. Modern, informal, Mediterranean menu in Setanta.

Carnagh House without rest., Clinty, West : 3 km on N 87 ✆ (049) 952 3300, *caraghhouse@eircom.net, Fax (049) 952 3300,* – .
10 rm 40/50 – 65/70.
◆ Modern guesthouse with pleasant rural aspect. Warmly run by owners: tea and sandwiches await guests on arrival. Comfortable lounge with views. Good-sized bedrooms.

BALLYCOTTON (Baile Choitín) *Cork* 712 H 12 *Ireland G.*

Exc. : *Cloyne Cathedral*★, *NW : by R 629.*
Dublin 265.5 – Cork 43.5 – Waterford 106.

Bayview, ✆ (021) 4646746, *res@thebayviewhotel.com, Fax (021) 4646075,* ≤ Ballycotton Bay and harbour, – AE VISA.
4 April-October – **Rest** (bar lunch Monday-Saturday)/dinner a la carte 44/54 – **33 rm** 118/139 – 198, 2 suites.
◆ A series of cottages in an elevated position with fine views of bay, harbour and island. Bar and lounge in library style with sofas. Spacious, comfy rooms with ocean views. Warm, inviting dining room.

BALLYDAVID (Baile na nGall) *Kerry* 712 A 11 – ✉ *Dingle.*
Dublin 362 – Dingle 11.5 – Tralee 58.

🏠 **Gorman's Clifftop House** ⌂, Glaise Bheag, North : 2 km 𝒸 (066) 9155162, *info@gormans-clifftophouse.com*, Fax (066) 9155003, ≤ Smerwick Harbour, Ballydavid Head and the Three Sisters, 🍴 – ⇆✕ 🅟 ⓂⓄ 𝚅𝙸𝚂𝙰 ✁
restricted opening in winter – **Rest** *(closed Sunday)* (dinner only) 39 – **9 rm** ⚏ ✝85/125 – ✝✝120/190.
♦ Fine views of Ballydavid Head and the Three Sisters from this peaceful modern house. Cosy sitting room with log fire; stylish, spacious rooms in vibrant colours and old pine. Bright restaurant invites diners to look out over the water.

🏠 **Old Pier** ⌂, An Fheothanach, North : 3 km 𝒸 (066) 9155242, *info@oldpier.com*, ≤ Smerwick Harbour, Ballydavid Head and the Three Sisters, 🍴 – ⇆✕ 🅟 ⓂⓄ 𝚅𝙸𝚂𝙰
closed 25 December – **Rest** (by arrangement) 33 – **5 rm** ⚏ ✝40/55 – ✝✝70/90.
♦ Run by the charming owner, a pretty clifftop house surveying the harbour and the Three Sisters. Immaculate rooms with bright bedspreads and cherrywood floors.

BALLYFERRITER (Baile an Fheirtéaraigh) *Kerry* 712 A 11 – ✉ *Dingle.*
See : *Corca Dhuibhne Regional Museum*★ **AC** *Gallarus Oratory*★★, E : 4 km by F 559 – *Kilmalkedar*★, E : 8 km by R 559 – *Slea Head*★★ (*beehive huts*★), S : 14 km by R 559 *Blasket Islands*★, S : 8 km by R 559 and by boat from Dunquin – *Connor Pass*★★, NE : 24 km by R 559 and minor road.
🏌 Ceann Sibeal 𝒸 (066) 9156255.
Dublin 363.5 – Killarney 85.5 – Limerick 167.5.

🏨 **Smerwick Harbour,** East : 4 ½ km on R 559 𝒸 (066) 9156470, *info@smerwickho tel.com*, Fax (066) 9156473, ≤ – 🛗 ⇆✕ 🕭 🅟 ⒶⒺ 𝚅𝙸𝚂𝙰 ✁
March-October and New Year – **Rest** a la carte 26/38 s. – **33 rm** ⚏ ✝40/85 – ✝✝80/165.
♦ Purpose-built hotel in dramatic Dingle Peninsula, Ireland's most westerly point. Large, atmospheric oak tavern with local artefacts. Sizeable rooms have spectacular views. Inviting dining room has fire with large brick surround.

BALLYLICKEY (Béal Átha Leice) *Cork* 712 D 12 *Ireland G.* – ✉ *Bantry.*
Env. : *Bantry Bay*★ – *Bantry House*★ **AC**, S : 5 km by R 584.
Exc. : *Glengarriff*★ (*Ilnacullin*★★, access by boat) NW : 13 km by N 71 – *Healy Pass*★★ (≤★★) W : 37 km by N 71, R 572 and R 574 – *Slieve Miskish Mountains* (≤★★) W : 46¾ km by N 71 and R 572 – *Lauragh* (*Derreen Gardens*★ **AC**) NW : 44 km by N 71, R 572 and R 574 – *Allihies* (*copper mines*★) W : 66¾ km by N 71, R 572 and R 575 – *Garnish Island* (≤★) W : 70¾ km by N 71 and R 572.
🏌 Bantry Bay, Donemark 𝒸 (027) 50579.
Dublin 347.5 – Cork 88.5 – Killarney 72.5.

🏨 **Ballylickey House** *without rest.*, 𝒸 (027) 50071, *ballymh@eircom.net*, Fax (027) 56725, ⌧ heated, ⌀, 🍴, ⌀ – ⇆✕ 🅟 ⓂⓄ ⓄⒾ 𝚅𝙸𝚂𝙰 ✁
late March-mid October – **6 rm** ⚏ ✝85/95 – ✝✝120/185.
♦ Impressive hotel with attractive gardens set amongst Bantry Bay's ragged inlets. Well-appointed sitting rooms with antiques. Rooms include luxurious garden cottage suites.

🏨 **Seaview House,** 𝒸 (027) 50462, *info@seaviewhousehotel.com*, Fax (027) 51555, 🍴 – ⇆✕ & 🅟 ⓂⓄ ⒶⒺ ⓄⒾ 𝚅𝙸𝚂𝙰 ✁
mid March-mid November – **Rest** (dinner only and Sunday lunch)/dinner 35/50 and a la carte 30/40 ♀ – **25 rm** ⚏ ✝95 – ✝✝105.
♦ Tall, well-run, whitewashed Victorian house set amidst lush gardens which tumble down to Bantry Bay. Traditional lounges with bar and spacious, individually designed rooms. Warmly decorated dining room.

BALLYLIFFIN *Donegal* 712 J 2.

🏨 **Ballyliffin Lodge,** Shore Rd, 𝒸 (074) 9378200, *info@ballyliffinlodge.com*, Fax (074) 9378985, ⌀, ℉₅, ≘₅, ⌧ – 🛗 ⇆✕, 🍴 rest, 📺 ✓ & 🅟 – 🕭 350. ⓂⓄ ⒶⒺ ⓄⒾ 𝚅𝙸𝚂𝙰
closed 25 December – **Rest** (bar lunch Monday-Saturday)/dinner a la carte 25/47 – **40 rm** ⚏ ✝105 – ✝✝190.
♦ Nick Faldo part-designed golf course set close to this new hotel with rural/beach views. Well-appointed lounge and good quality spa. Well-equipped rooms, some with sea vistas. Fine dining restaurant inspired by classical cuisine.

BALLYMACARBRY (Baile Mhac Cairbre) *Waterford* 712 I 11 *Ireland G.* – ✉ *Clonmel.*

Exc. : *Clonmel★ (St Mary's Church★, County Museum★ AC), N 16 km by R 671 – Lismore★ (Castle Gardens★ AC, St Carthage's Cathedral★), SW : 26 km by R 671 and N 72 – W : Nier Valley Scenic Route★★.*

Dublin 190 – Cork 79 – Waterford 63.

Hanora's Cottage ॐ, Nire Valley, East : 6½ km by Nire Drive rd and Nire Valley Lakes rd ℘ (052) 36134, hanorascottage@eircom.net, Fax (052) 36540, ≤, 綿 – ✗ **P**. **⬤⬤** **VISA**. ✗

closed 1 week Christmas – **Rest** *(closed Sunday)* (booking essential for non-residents) (dinner only) 47 – **10 rm** ☲ ✦85 – ✦✦125.

♦ Pleasant 19C farmhouse with purpose-built extensions in quiet location at foot of mountains. Very extensive and impressive breakfast buffet. Stylish rooms, all with jacuzzis. Locally renowned menus, brimming with fresh produce.

↑ Cnoc-na-Ri ॐ without rest., Nire Valley, East : 6 km on Nire Drive rd ℘ (052) 36239, richardharte@eircom.net, ≤, 綿 – ✗ **P**. **VISA**. ✗

February-October – **5 rm** ☲ ✦45 – ✦✦70/80.

♦ Purpose-built guesthouse situated in the heart of the unspoilt Nire Valley, a perfect location for walking holidays. Immaculately kept, clean and spacious bedrooms. Comfy breakfast room doubles as lounge at other times of day.

↑ Glasha Farmhouse ॐ, Northwest : 4 km by R 671 ℘ (052) 36108, glasha@eircom.net, Fax (052) 36108, ≤, 綿 – ✗ **P**. **⬤⬤** **VISA**. ✗

closed 1-28 December – **Rest** (by arrangement) 35 – **6 rm** ☲ ✦60/65 – ✦✦100/120.

♦ Immaculate farmhouse rurally set on working farm. Garden water feature is focal point. Spacious conservatory. Wonderful breakfasts with huge choice. Neat, tidy rooms.

BALLYMOTE (Baile an Mhóta) *Sligo* 712 G 5 – ✉ *Sligo.*

᠉ Ballymote, Ballinascarrow ℘ (071) 83504.

Dublin 199.5 – Longford 77 – Sligo 24.

↑ Mill House without rest., Keenaghan, ℘ (071) 9183449, millhousebb@eircom.net, 綿, ✗ – ✗ **P**. ✗

closed 18 December-10 January – **6 rm** ☲ ✦35 – ✦✦68.

♦ Simple guesthouse situated on edge of busy market town. Very friendly welcome. Small, comfortable sitting room. Light, airy breakfast room. Spacious, immaculate bedrooms.

BALLYNABOLA *Wexford* 712 L 10 – see New Ross.

BALLYNAGALL *Westmeath* – see Mullingar.

BALLYNAHINCH (Baile na hInse) *Galway* 712 C 7 – ✉ *Recess.*

Exc. : *Connemara★★★ – Roundstone★, S : by R 341 – Cashel★, SE : by R 341 and R 340.*

Dublin 225 – Galway 66 – Westport 79.

Ballynahinch Castle ॐ, ℘ (095) 31006, bhinch@iol.ie, Fax (095) 31085, ≤ Owenmore River and woods, ❀, 綿, ❀, ✗ – ✗ **P**. **⬤⬤** **①** **VISA**. ✗

closed February and 1 week Christmas – **Rest** (booking essential for non-residents) (bar lunch)/dinner a la carte approx 50 ☲ – **37 rm** ☲ ✦182/230 – ✦✦297/396, 3 suites.

♦ Grey stone, part 17C castle in magnificent grounds with fine river views. Two large sitting rooms, characterful bar frequented by fishermen. Spacious rooms with antiques. Inviting dining room with stunning river views.

BALLYNAMULT (Béal na Molt) *Waterford.*

Dublin 194.5 – Clonmel 21 – Waterford 63.

↑ Sliabh gCua Farmhouse without rest., Tooraneena, Southeast : 2 km ℘ (058) 47120, breedacullinan@sliabhgcua.com, ≤, 綿 – ✗ **P**

April-October – **4 rm** ☲ ✦45 – ✦✦80.

♦ Creeper clad early 20C house in quiet hamlet with rural views. Tea and scones on arrival. Comfy lounge with real fire. Individually decorated rooms boast period furniture.

The red ॐ symbol?
This denotes the very essence of peace
– only the sound of birdsong first thing in the morning …

BALLYSHANNON (Béal Atha Seanaidh) *Donegal* **712** H 4 – *pop. 2 775.*
Dublin 53 – Donegal 272 – Letterkenny 283 – Sligo 215.5.

🏠 **Heron's Cove,** Creevy, Northwest : 3 km on R 231 ℘ (071) 9822070, *info@heron scove.ie, Fax (071) 9822075 –* ⇔ 📺 **P. MO VISA**
closed 7 January- 10 February – **Rest** *(closed Sunday-Tuesday in winter)* (dinner only and Sunday lunch) a la carte 26/60 – **10 rm** ⇨ ✦75/85 – ✦✦120/140.
◆ A well priced, friendly and informal destination on the road to Rossnowlagh. Identical bedrooms are clean and light with contemporary soft furnishings. An informal dining room offers a good choice menu with local seafood specialities.

BALLYVAUGHAN (Baile Uí Bheacháin) *Clare* **712** E 8 *Ireland G. – pop. 257.*
Env. : *The Burren*★★ *(Scenic Route*★★*, – Kilfenora (Crosses*★ *, Burren Centre*★ *AC), S : 25 km N 67 and R 476.*
Exc. : *Cliffs of Moher*★★★ *, S : 32 km by N 67 and R 478.*
Dublin 240 – Ennis 55 – Galway 46.5.

🏰 **Gregans Castle** ⌂, Southwest : 6 km on N 67 ℘ (065) 707 7005, *stay@gregans.ie, Fax (065) 707 7111,* ≤ countryside and Galway Bay, 🌳, ✿ – ⇔ **P. MO AE VISA**. ✗
April-27 October – **Rest** (bar lunch)/dinner a la carte 46/58 s. ♀ – **17 rm** ⇨ ✦150/190 – ✦✦190/230, 4 suites.
◆ Idyllically positioned, family owned hotel with fine views to The Burren and Galway Bay. Relaxing sitting room, cosy bar lounge, country house-style bedrooms. Sizeable conservatory dining room specialising in seasonal, regional dishes.

🏠 **Drumcreehy House** without rest., Northeast : 2 km on N 67 ℘ (065) 7077377, *info@drumcreehyhouse.com, Fax (065) 7077379,* ≤, 🌳 – ⇔ ✆ **P. MO VISA**
booking essential in winter – **10 rm** ⇨ ✦55/66 – ✦✦76/100.
◆ Pristine house overlooking Galway Bay. Bedrooms are excellent value: spacious, comfortable and furnished in German stripped oak.

🏠 **Rusheen Lodge** without rest., Southwest : 1 km on N 67 ℘ (065) 7077092, *rus heen@iol.ie, Fax (065) 7077152,* – ⇔ **P. MO VISA**. ✗
mid February-mid November – **8 rm** ⇨ ✦57/70 – ✦✦80/100, 1 suite.
◆ Cheery yellow façade decked with flowers, lounge with fine sofas and rooms in pale woods and floral patterns. Pretty gardens complete the picture. Charming, welcoming owner.

🏠 **Ballyvaughan Lodge** without rest., ℘ (065) 7077292, *ballyvau@iol.ie, Fax (065) 7077287 –* ⇔ **P. MO VISA**
closed 25-26 December – **11 rm** ⇨ ✦45/60 – ✦✦75/80.
◆ Red hued guesthouse, attractively furnished throughout. Light and airy sitting room with large windows. Home-made bread and jams for breakfast. Clean, tidy bedrooms.

🏠 **Cappabhaile House** without rest., Southwest : 1 ½ km on N 67 ℘ (065) 7077260, *cappabhaile@oceanfree.net,* ≤, 🌳 – ⇔ **P. MO AE VISA**. ✗
March-October – **8 rm** ⇨ ✦55/75 – ✦✦84/98.
◆ Stone clad bungalow with pleasant gardens and good views across the Burren. Spacious open-plan lounge-cum-breakfast room with central fireplace. Very large, spotless rooms.

BALTIMORE (Dún na Séad) *Cork* **712** D 13 *Ireland G.*
Exc. : *Sherkin Island*★ *(by ferry) – Castletownshend*★ *, E : 20 km by R 595 and R 596 – Glandore*★ *, E : 26 km by R 595, N 71 and R 597.*
Dublin 344.5 – Cork 95 – Killarney 124.

🏠 **Casey's of Baltimore,** East : ¾ km on R 595 ℘ (028) 20197, *info@caseysofbalti more.com, Fax (028) 20509,* ≤ – ⇔ 🍽️, ▤ rest, **P. MO AE ◉ VISA**. ✗
closed 20-27 December – **Rest** a la carte 29/45 – **14 rm** ⇨ ✦98/116 – ✦✦154/182.
◆ Popular hotel near sea-shore. Cosy bar with open fires and traditional music at weekends, with beer garden overlooking bay. Large, well-decorated rooms with pine furniture. Great sea views from dining room.

🏠 **Slipway** ⌂ without rest., The Cove, East : ¾ km ℘ (028) 20134, *theslipway@hot mail.com, Fax (028) 20134,* ≤ Baltimore Harbour, 🌳 – ⇔ **P.** ✗
Easter - October – **4 rm** ⇨ ✦60/70 – ✦✦68/75.
◆ Relaxed, informal guesthouse with yellow façade and lovely views of local harbour, particularly from veranda outside breakfast room. Simple, individualistic, well-kept rooms.

🍴 **Customs House,** Main St, ℘ (028) 20200, *oliva405@aol.com*
April-October – **Rest** - Seafood - (booking essential) (dinner only) 35/45.
◆ Converted customs house, consisting of three small rooms with a painted wood floor. Good value, innovative seafood menu: all dishes are tasty and carefully prepared.

BANGOR (Baingear) Mayo 712 C 5.

Exc. : Céide Fields★ AC, NE : 30 km by minor road and R 314.
Dublin 281.5 – Ballina 42 – Westport 63.

🏛 **Teach Iorrais,** Geesala, Southwest : 12 km on Geesala rd ℘ (097) 86888, teachlor@iol.ie, Fax (097) 86855, ≤ – ⇆, 🛏 rest, ✆ 🕭 ₧ – 🏛 250. 🐵 🖭 *VISA*, ⅘
An Neifin : Rest (bar lunch Monday-Saturday)/dinner 25/35 and a la carte 33/40 – **31 rm** ⊈ ✦46/80 – ✦✦92/120.
  ♦ Purpose-built hotel with views of Neifin mountains. Public bar with live music at weekends and quieter residents lounge. Bright bedrooms, those to the front with best views. Charming views from window tables of Gothic styled restaurant.

BARNA (Bearna) Galway 712 E 8.

Dublin 227 – Galway 9.5.

✗ **O'Grady's on the Pier,** ℘ (091) 592223, ogradysonthepier@hotmail.com, Fax (091) 590677, ≤ Galway Bay – 🐵 🖭 *VISA*
closed 1 week Christmas – **Rest** - Seafood - (booking essential) (dinner only and Sunday lunch) a la carte 28/50.
  ♦ Converted quayside pub on two floors with great views of Galway Bay. Cheerful, attentive staff and daily menus of simple, flavourful seafood have earned good local reputation.

BARRELLS CROSS Cork – see Kinsale.

BEAUFORT (Lios an Phúca) Kerry 712 D 11 – see Killarney.

BIRR (Biorra) Offaly 712 I 8 Ireland G. – pop. 4 193.

See : Town★ – Birr Castle Demesne★★ AC (Telescope★★).
Exc. : Clonfert Cathedral★ (West doorway★★), NW : 24 km by R 439, R 356 and minor roads – Portumna★ (Castle★ AC), W : 24 km by R 489 – Roscrea★ (Damer House★ AC) S : 19¼ km by N 62 – Slieve Bloom Mountinas★, E : 21 km by R 440.
🛆 The Glenns ℘ (0509) 20082.
🖪 Brendon St ℘ (0509) 20110.
Dublin 140 – Athlone 45 – Kilkenny 79 – Limerick 79.

🏛 **County Arms,** Railway Rd, South : ¾ km on N 62 ℘ (057) 9120791, info@countyarmshotel.com, Fax (057) 9121234, 🖪, ≲, 🖾, 🖛 – ‖ ⇆ 🕭 ₧ – 🏛 400. 🐵 🖭 ① *VISA*, ⅘
Rest a la carte 21/38 s. ♀ – **70 rm** ⊈ ✦60/160 – ✦✦120/320.
  ♦ Sizeable, late Georgian hotel secluded in its own wooded grounds. Period furniture and old prints abound. Large conservatory bar. Flowery fabrics enrich the bedrooms. Dining room uses produce from its own gardens and greenhouse.

🏛 **The Maltings,** Castle St, ℘ (057) 91 21345, themaltingsbirr@eircom.net, Fax (057) 91 22073 – ⇆ ₧. 🐵 🖭 *VISA*, ⅘
closed 24-27 December – **Rest** (closed dinner in winter) 30 (dinner) and a la carte – **13 rm** ⊈ ✦50/55 – ✦✦76/80.
  ♦ Characterful 19C hotel on riverside near Birr Castle, originally built to store malt for Guinness. Cosy bar and lounge. Bedrooms enriched by flowery fabrics and drapes. Sizeable, bustling restaurant with chintz fabrics and spot lighting.

BLACKLION (An Blaic) Cavan 712 I 5.

🛆 Blacklion, Toam ℘ (072) 53024.
Dublin 194.5 – Drogheda 170.5 – Enniskillen 19.5.

✗✗ **Mac Nean House** with rm, Main St, ℘ (071) 9853022, Fax (071) 9853404 – 🐵 🖭 *VISA*
closed 1 week October and 2 weeks Christmas – **Rest** (closed Monday-Wednesday in winter) (dinner only and Sunday lunch)/dinner a la carte approx 44 s. ♀ – **6 rm** ⊈ ✦45/50 – ✦✦70/80.
  ♦ Family run restaurant in the heart of border town. Antique chairs and fine tableware. Local produce to the fore in high quality, original menus. Homely rooms.

BLACKWATER Wexford 712 M 10.

Dublin 117.5 – Kilkenny 92 – Waterford 75.5 – Wexford 21.

🏠 **Blackwater Lodge**, The Square, ☏ (053) 27222, blackwaterlodgeres@eircom.net, Fax (053) 27496 – ⊱⊱ **P**, **MO AE VISA**. ⋇
closed 24 December-1 January – **Rest** (closed Monday, Tuesday and Wednesday in winter) (dinner only and Sunday lunch) 55 and a la carte approx 44 **s**. ♀ – **6 rm** ☑ ✦60 – ✦✦120.
◆ Colourful, competitively priced lodge accommodation in pretty village close to Wexford's coastal attractions. Pine decorated bar. Modern, pale wood rooms with all amenities. Local ingredients well used in menus.

BLARNEY (An Bhlarna) Cork 712 G 12 Ireland G. – pop. 1 963 – ⊠ Cork.

See : Blarney Castle★★ AC – Blarney Castle House★ AC.
🖪 ☏ (021) 4381624.
Dublin 268.5 – Cork 9.5.

⌂ **Killarney House** without rest., Station Rd, Northeast : 1 ½ km ☏ (021) 4381841, info@killarneyhouseblarney.com, Fax (021) 4381841, � – ⊱⊱ **P**. ⋇
6 rm ☑ ✦45/55 – ✦✦66/76.
◆ Spacious, modern guesthouse set above attractive village. Very comfortable lounge. Breakfast room equipped to high standard. Sizeable, immaculately kept rooms.

at Tower West : 3¼ km on R 617 – ⊠ Cork.

🏠 **Ashlee Lodge**, ☏ (021) 4385346, info@ashleelodge.com, Fax (021) 4385726, ☎s – ⊱⊱ ▤ ℃ & **P**. **MO AE O VISA**
closed 20 December-20 January **Rest** (closed Sunday-Monday) (dinner only) a la carte 25/41 **s**. – **10 rm** ☑ ✦80/100 – ✦✦100/150.
◆ Relaxing modern house, ideally located for Blarney Castle. Breakfast room with extensive menu. Outdoor Canadian hot tub. Very well-equipped rooms, some with whirlpool baths.

⌂ **Maranatha Country House** ⋟ without rest., East : ¾ km on R 617 ☏ (021) 4385102, info@maranathacountryhouse.com, Fax (021) 4382978, 🌫, ☝ – ⊱⊱ ℃ **P**. **MO VISA**. ⋇
March-November – **6 rm** ☑ ✦45/90 – ✦✦120.
◆ Charming Victorian house in acres of peaceful grounds. Antique furnished drawing room. Relaxing, individual bedrooms, one lined with books, another with a large circular bath.

Good food and accommodation at moderate prices?
Look for the Bib symbols:
red Bib Gourmand 🏮 for food, blue Bib Hotel 🏨 for hotels

BORRISOKANE Tipperary 712 H 8/9 – pop. 850.

Env. : Portumna★ (Castle★ AC), NW : 15 km by N 65.
Exc. : Birr★ : Castle Demesne★★ AC (Telescope★★), NE : 21 km by N 52 – Roscrea★ (Damer House★ AC), E : 31 km by R 490 and R 491.
Dublin 162.5 – Galway 85.5 – Limerick 59.5.

⌂ **Dancer Cottage** ⋟ without rest., Curraghmore, West : 3 ¼ km by Ballinderry rd ☏ (067) 27414, dcr@eircom.net, Fax (067) 27414, 🌫 – ⊱⊱ **P**. **MO AE VISA**. ⋇
closed December-8 January – **4 rm** ☑ ✦40 – ✦✦66.
◆ Modern guesthouse with spacious garden in wonderfully peaceful country location. Comfy lounge and extremely well-kept bedrooms with chintz fabrics; some four-posters.

BOYLE (Mainistir na Búille) Roscommon 712 H 6 – pop. 1 690.

See : King House★ AC.
Env. : Boyle Abbey★ AC, E : 2 km by N 4 – Lough Key Forest Park★ AC, E : 3.2 km by N 4.
Exc. : Arigna Scenic Drive★ (≼★), NE : 20 km by N 4, R 280 and R 207 – Curlew Mountains (≼★), NW : 3½ km by N 4.
Dublin 175 – Longford 53 – Sligo 45.

⌂ **Rosdarrig House** without rest., Dublin Rd, ☏ (071) 9662040, rosdarrig@yahoo.co.uk, 🌫 – **P**. **VISA**
February-November – **6 rm** ☑ ✦45/50 – ✦✦68/70.
◆ Comfortable, well-kept guesthouse with friendly owners. Attractive lounge and appealing wood-floored breakfast room. Good sized, smartly decorated rooms overlooking garden.

BRAY (Bré) *Wicklow* 712 N 8 *Ireland G.* – pop. 27 923.

Env. : *Powerscourt*★★ *(Waterfall*★★ *AC)* W : 6½ km – *Killruddery House and Gardens*★ *AC,*
S : 3¼ km by R 761.

Exc. : *Wicklow Mountains*★★.

🏌 Woodbrook, Dublin Rd 𝒫 (01) 282 4799 – 🏌 Old Conna, Ferndale Rd 𝒫 (01) 282 6055 –
🏌 Greystones Rd 𝒫 (01) 276 3200.
Dublin 21 – Wicklow 32.

🏨 **Ramada Woodland Court,** Southern Cross, South : 4 km by R 761 on Greystones rd
𝒫 (01) 276 0258, *ramadawoodlandcourt.com, Fax (01) 276 0298* – ⇖, 🍽 rest, ✆ & 🅿 –
🔒 60. 🆗 🆎 *VISA*. 🛏
closed 24-25 December – **Rest** (bar lunch)/dinner 25 and a la carte 21/30 s. – ⚏ 10 – **86 rm**
♦75 – ♦♦75.

♦ Bright, yellow painted hotel and smart garden. Warm lounge and bar boasts burgundy
and dark green sofas and chairs. Comfortable rooms with thick carpeting and rich décor.
Afternoon tea a staple of airy restaurant.

BUNBEG (An Bun Beag) *Donegal* 712 H 2 *Ireland G.*

Exc. : *The Rosses*★, *S : by R 257.*
Dublin 314 – Donegal 106 – Londonderry 88.5.

🏨 **Ostan Gweedore** ⤴, 𝒫 (074) 9531177, *reservations@ostangweedore.com,*
Fax (074) 9531726, ⇐ *Gweedore Bay,* 🛐, 🚡, 🔲, 🏊–🅿 – 🔒 200. 🆗 🆎 *VISA*. 🛏
9 February-6 November and New Year – **Restaurant** : Rest (dinner only) a la carte 48/62 s.
⚏ – **Sundowner** : Rest - Tapas - *(closed Monday-Wednesday and Thursday in winter)* (dinner only) a la carte 23/33 s. ⚏ – **33 rm** ⚏ ♦96/105 – ♦♦169/185, 3 suites.

♦ Traditional hotel in a prominent position commanding spectacular views over Gweedore
Bay. Large bar and pleasant sitting room. Treatment room. Classic, spacious bedrooms.
Fresh, local produce to fore in Restaurant. Tapas menus in informal Sundowner.

BUNCLODY *Co. Wexford* 712 M 10.

🏨 **The Carlton Millrace,** Carrigduff, 𝒫 (053) 9375100, *info@millrace.ie,*
Fax (053) 9375124, 🛐, 🚡, 🔲, – 🛏 ⇖ ✆ & 🅿 – 🔒 250. 🆗 *VISA*. 🛏
Lady Lucys : Rest (dinner only) 37 and a la carte 30/47 s. – **Bistro** : Rest a la carte 22/28 –
56 rm ⚏ ♦59/160 – ♦♦118/170, 16 suites.

♦ A family friendly hotel of vivid hues which also incorporates meeting facilties and sizable
leisure centre. Spacious family apartments and suites are in adjacent block. Panoramic
views from fourth floor Lady Lucys; formal menus. All-day, popular Bistro.

BUNDORAN (Bun Dobhráin) *Donegal* 712 H 4 – pop. 1 796.

Env. : *Creevykeel Court Cairn*★, *S : 5 km by N 15* – *Rossnowlagh Strand*★★, *N : 8.5km by N*
15 and R 231.

🅳 *The Bridge, Main St* 𝒫 (071) 9841350 *(April-October).*
Dublin 259 – Donegal 27.5 – Sligo 37.

🏨 **Allingham Arms,** Main St, 𝒫 (071) 9841075, *allinghamarmshotel1@eircom.net,*
Fax (071) 9841171 – 🛐 ⇖ & 🅿 – 🔒 400. 🆗 🆎 🅾 *VISA*. 🛏
closed Christmas and weekends only January-February – **Rest** (bar lunch)/dinner 35 –
132 rm ⚏ ♦75/80 – ♦♦120/150.

♦ Sizeable hotel named after poet William Allingham. Country and Western music weekends. Quay West bar offers contemporary styled dining. Ask for Seaview deluxe rooms.
Restaurant is light and airy with daily changing international menu.

🏨 **Fitzgerald's,** 𝒫 (071) 9841336, *info@fitzgeraldshotel.com, Fax (071) 9842121,* ⇐ – 🛐
⇖ 🅿 🆗 *VISA*. 🛏
restricted opening in winter – **The Bistro** : Rest *(closed Monday-Tuesday except residents*
July-August) (dinner only) a la carte 28/33 s. – **16 rm** ⚏ ♦55/85 – ♦♦100/140.

♦ Family owned hotel in centre of popular seaside town overlooking Donegal Bay. Reception rooms warmed by wood-burning stove. Sumptuous sofas abound. Sea-facing front
bedrooms. Linen-clad, informal Bistro with carefully compiled menu.

BUNRATTY (Bun Raite) *Clare* **712** F 9 *Ireland G.*
  See : *Town*★★ – *Bunratty Castle*★★.
  Dublin 207.5 – Ennis 24 – Limerick 13.

Bunratty Shannon Shamrock H., ℰ (061) 361177, *reservations@dunneho*
tels.com, Fax (061) 364863, *Ⅰ♣, ≲s, ◻, ≈ – ✦✗ ☏ ᴘ. – 🏊 1200. 🐵 🖭 VISA. ※*
closed 24-25 December – **Rest** (bar lunch Monday-Saturday)/dinner 29 **s**. – ☷ 13 – **115 rm**
✦170 – ✦✦215.
  ◆ Large, purpose-built hotel close to Limerick ideal for business travellers. Extensive conference and leisure facilities. Well-kept, contemporary rooms with mod cons. Dining room decorated with modern art, very popular at weekends.

Bunratty Manor, ℰ (061) 707984, *bunrattymanor@eircom.net*, Fax (061) 360588, ㎡,
≈ – ✦✗ ☏ ᴘ. 🐵 🖭 VISA. ※
closed 22 December-6 January – **Rest** *(closed Sunday)* (dinner only) 45 and a la carte
39/49 ☷ – **23 rm** ☷ ✦90/105 – ✦✦120/150.
  ◆ Purpose-built, tourist-oriented hotel in village centre. Comfy lounge with chintz suites; Neat, modern rooms in colourful fabrics and drapes. Smart terrace fringed by pleasant garden. Popular menus.

Bunratty Grove ⏍ without rest., Castle Rd, North : 2½ km ℰ (061) 369579, *bunratty*
grove@eircom.net, Fax (061) 369561, ≈ – ✦✗ ᴘ. 🐵 VISA. ※
9 rm ☷ ✦40/65 – ✦✦70/80.
  ◆ Pink painted guesthouse on country road with peaceful ambience. Large lounge-cum-library and pleasant, cottagey breakfast room. Immaculate rooms with polished wood floors.

Bunratty Woods without rest., Low Rd, North : 1½ km ℰ (061) 369689, *bun*
ratty@iol.ie, Fax (061) 369454, ≤, ≈ – ✦✗ ᴘ. 🐵 VISA. ※
mid March-mid November – **14 rm** ☷ ✦55 – ✦✦70/90.
  ◆ Characterful guesthouse with large front garden. Owner collects and restores assorted items to decorate rooms, such as farmyard tools and old food tins. Sizeable bedrooms.

BUTLERSTOWN (Baile an Bhuitléaraigh) *Cork* **712** F 13 *Ireland G.* – ⊠ *Bandon.*
  Env. : *Clonakilty (West Cork Regional Museum*★ *AC), N : 6 km by minor road – Courtmacsherry*★, *N : 5 km – Kinsale*★★ *(Museum*★ *AC, St Multose Church*★ *AC, Harbour*★, *Charles Fort*★ *AC), N : 21 km by R 6101 and R 600 – Timoleague Friary*★, *N : 5 km by R 601.*
  Dublin 310.5 – Cork 51.5.

Otto's Creative Catering ⏍ with rm, Dunworley, South : 3¼ km ℰ (023) 40461,
ottokunze@eircom.net, ≈ – ᴘ. 🐵 VISA
closed 7 January-8 March, Sunday dinner, Monday and Tuesday – **Rest** - Organic - (booking essential) (dinner only and Sunday lunch) 55 **s**. – **4 rm** ☷ ✦110 – ✦✦130.
  ◆ Quirky, highly individual restaurant built by owners and their son in remote location: amazing twisted wood staircase. Tremendously varied organic menus. Wood furnished rooms.

BUTLERSTOWN (Baile an Bhuitléaraigh) *Waterford – see Waterford.*

CAHERDANIEL (Cathair Dónall) *Kerry* **712** B 12 *Ireland G.* – ⊠ *Killarney.*
  Exc. : *Ring of Kerry*★★ – *Derrynane National Historic Park*★★ – *Skellig Islands*★★ *AC, by boat – Sneem*★, *E : 19 km by N 70 – Staigue Fort*★, *E : 8 km by N 70 and minor road.*
  Dublin 383 – Killarney 77.

Iskeroon ⏍ without rest., West : 8 m. by N 70, Bunavalla Pier rd taking left turn at
junction then turning left onto track immediately before pier ℰ (066) 9475119, *info@iske*
roon.com, Fax (066) 9475488, ≤, ≈ – 🛗 ✦✗ ᴘ. 🐵 VISA. ※
May-September, minimum stay 2 nights – **3 rm** ☷ ✦150 – ✦✦150.
  ◆ A "design icon", this low-lying house looking out to Derrynane Harbour was built in 1930s by the Earl of Dunraven. Lush gardens; boldly designed, vividly coloured bedrooms.

Derrynane Bay House without rest., West : ¾ km on N 70 ℰ (066) 9475404, *derryna*
nebayhouse@eircom.net, Fax (066) 9475436, ≤, ≈ – ✦✗ ☏ ᴘ. 🐵 VISA. ※
15 March-October – **6 rm** ☷ ✦45/60 – ✦✦70/76.
  ◆ Purpose-built house on the Ring of Kerry with vast views over namesake bay. Stone Age monuments in the surrounding hills. Family-friendly; spacious bedrooms.

CAHERLISTRANE (Cathair Loistreáin) *Galway* 712 E 7.
Dublin 256 – Ballina 74 – Galway 42.

Lisdonagh House ⊗, Northwest : 2 ½ km by Shrule rd 🖉 (093) 31163, *cooke@lisdo nagh.com*, Fax (093) 31528, ≤, ⬧, ⬌, ⬧ – **P**. ⬧ – **P**. **VISA**. ⬧
7 April-October – **Rest** *(closed Monday except Bank Holidays)* (booking essential for non-residents) (dinner only) 35/40 – **10 rm** ⭑175 – ⭑⭑280, 4 suites.
♦ Georgian house overlooking Lough Hacket; row across to island in the middle. A grand entrance hall with fine murals leads to antique filled rooms named after Irish artists. Locally caught fish predominant in dining room.

CAHERSIVEEN (Cathair Saidhbhín) *Kerry* 712 B 12.
Env. : *Ring of Kerry*★★.
Dublin 355.5 – Killarney 64.5.

The Point, Renard Point, Southwest : 2 ¾ km by N 70 🖉 (066) 9472165, *oneillsthe point@hotmail.com*, ≤ Valencia Harbour and Island, ⬧ – **P**. ⬧
restricted opening in winter – **Rest** - Seafood - (bookings not accepted) (dinner only in winter) a la carte 35/40.
♦ At the end of a road leading to Valencia Island ferry, this simply furnished pub offers concise menus of dishes, all seafood based, freshly prepared, unpretentiously served.

CAMPILE (Ceann Poill) *Wexford* 712 L 11 *Ireland G.*
Env. : *Dunbrody Abbey*★, S : 3 ¼ km by R 733 – *J F Kennedy Arboretum*★, N : 3 ¼ km by R 733.
Exc. : *Tintern Abbey*★, SE : 12¾ km by R 733 – *Duncannon Fort*★, S : 12¾ km by R 733.
Dublin 154.5 – Waterford 35.5 – Wexford 37.

Kilmokea Country Manor ⊗, West : 8 km by R 733 and Great Island rd 🖉 (051) 388109, *kilmokea@eircom.net*, Fax (051) 388776, ≤, **Fۄ**, ⬧, ⬧, ⬧, ⬧, ⬧ – **P**. ⬧ ⬧ **VISA**
restricted opening in winter – **Rest** (booking essential for non-residents) 45/50 (dinner) and lunch a la carte 24/50 ⬧ – **6 rm** ⬧ ⭑120 – ⭑⭑260.
♦ Former Georgian rectory in large public gardens. Elegantly furnished. Games room, tennis and fishing. Comfortable bedrooms in house and converted stable block. Formal dining room with polished tables and period style; breakfast in conservatory.

CAPPOQUIN (Ceapach Choinn) *Waterford* 712 I 11 *Ireland G.*
Env. : *Lismore*★ (*Lismore Castle Gardens*★ *AC, St Carthage's Cathedral*★), W : 6 ½ km by N 72.
Exc. : *The Gap*★ (≤★) NW : 14½ km by R 669.
Dublin 219 – Cork 56 – Waterford 64.5.

Richmond House with rm, Southeast : ¾ km on N 72 🖉 (058) 54278, *info@richmond house.net*, Fax (058) 54988, ⬧, ⬧ – **P**. ⬧ ⬧ ⬧ ⬧ **VISA**. ⬧
closed 20 December-10 January – **Rest** *(closed Sunday-Monday in winter)* (dinner only) 35/55 ⬧ – **9 rm** ⬧ ⭑85/110 – ⭑⭑180/240.
♦ Built for Earl of Cork and Burlington in 1704; retains Georgian style with stately, cove-ceilinged dining room: local produce to the fore. Individually decorated period rooms.

at Millstreet *East : 11¼ km by N 72 on R 671 – ⬧ Cappoquin.*

Castle Country House ⊗, 🖉 (058) 68049, *castlefm@iol.ie*, Fax (058) 68099, ⬧, ⬧, ⬧ – ⬧ **P**. ⬧ ⬧ **VISA**
Rest (by arrangement) 25/30 – **5 rm** ⬧ ⭑60/65 – ⭑⭑100/105.
♦ Extended farmhouse on working dairy and beef farm with 15C origins. Rural location and lovely gardens. Individual bedrooms with cottage style decor.

CARAGH LAKE (Loch Cárthaí) *Kerry* 712 C 11 *Ireland G.*
See : *Lough Caragh*★.
Exc. : *Iveragh Peninsula*★★ (*Ring of Kerry*★★).
Fۄ Dooks, Glenbeigh 🖉 (066) 9768205.
Dublin 341 – Killarney 35.5 – Tralee 40.

Ard-Na-Sidhe ⊗, 🖉 (066) 9769105, *hotelsales@liebherr.com*, Fax (066) 9769282, ⬧, ⬧, ⬧ – ⬧ ⬧ **P**. ⬧ ⬧ ⬧ **VISA**
May-16 October – **Rest** *(closed Sunday)* (booking essential for non-residents) (dinner only) a la carte 50/65 **s**. – **18 rm** ⬧ ⭑140 – ⭑⭑290.
♦ Built 1880 by an English Lady who called it "House of Fairies". Elizabethan in style; gardens lead down to lake. Possesses atmosphere of private home. Antique filled rooms. Tasteful dining room with intimate feel.

🏠 **Carrig Country House** ▧, ✆ (066) 9769100, *info@carrighouse.com,* Fax (066) 9769166, ≤ Lough Caragh, ✎, 🚗 – ⟐ 🅿 ↔ 🐾 💶 ⓪ VISA 🛇
March - November – **Rest** (booking essential for non-residents) (dinner only) a la carte 29/49 – **17 rm** ☲ ✦85/140 – ✦✦150/180.
◆ Down a wooded drive, the yellow ochre façade of the house immediately strikes you. Its loughside setting assures good views. Ground floor rooms have their own private patio. Caragh Lough outlook from dining room windows.

CARLINGFORD (Cairlinn) *Louth* 712 N 5 *Ireland G.*
See : *Town★.*
Exc. : *Windy Gap★, NW : 12¾ km by R 173 – Proleek Dolmen★, SW : 14½ km by R 173.*
Dublin 106 – Dundalk 21.

🏨 **Four Seasons,** ✆ (042) 9373530, *info@fshc.ie,* Fax (042) 9373531, ≤, 📠, ☎, ▨, 🚗 – 🔟 ↔ ✎ & 🅿 – ▵ 800. 💶 VISA 🛇
Rest 18/38 and dinner a la carte 21/39 **s.** – **59 rm** ☲ ✦129 – ✦✦198.
◆ Impressive purpose-built hotel on outskirts of scenic market town. Extensive conference facilities; smart leisure centre. Spacious and well-equipped bedrooms. Popular bar leading to intimate dining room with Irish menus.

🏠 **McKevitt's Village,** Market Sq, ✆ (042) 9373116, *villagehotel@eircom.net,* Fax (042) 9373144, 🚗 – ↔, 🍽 rest. 💶 ﭏ VISA 🛇
Rest *(restricted opening in winter)* (bar lunch)/dinner 35/40 ♀ – **17 rm** ☲ ✦60/105 – ✦✦120/160.
◆ Traditional inn occupying a central position in this medieval village, known for its ancient monuments. Modern style, yet retains Irish charm. Freshly decorated rooms. Part-panelled restaurant hosting range of maritime pictures.

🏠 **Beaufort House** ▧ without rest., ✆ (042) 9373879, *michaelcaine@beaufort house.net,* Fax (042) 9373878, ≤, 🚗 – ↔ 🅿 💶 VISA 🛇
closed 25 December – **5 rm** ☲ ✦90 – ✦✦90.
◆ Modern house attractively sited on shores of Carlingford Lough. Very comfortable, spacious rooms with sea or mountain views. Substantial breakfasts served overlooking lough.

REPUBLIC OF IRELAND

CARLOW (Ceatharlach) *Carlow* 712 L 9 – *pop. 14 979.*
🏌 *Carlow, Deer Park, Dublin Rd* ✆ (0503) 31695.
🛈 *Tullow St* ✆ (059) 9131554.
Dublin 80.5 – Kilkenny 37 – Wexford 75.5.

🏨 **Seven Oaks,** Athy Rd, ✆ (059) 9131308, *info@sevenoakshotel.com,* Fax (059) 9132155, 📠, ☎, ▨, 🚗 – 🔟 ↔ 🅿 – ▵ 300. 💶 ﭏ ⓪ VISA 🛇
closed 25-26 December – **Rest** (carving lunch Saturday) 30/40 **s.** – **89 rm** ☲ ✦77/95 – ✦✦140/170.
◆ Close to the sights of the River Barrow walk, this neat hotel in a residential area makes a good resting place. Well-kept rooms: ask for those on first or second floor. Intimate booths in tranquil dining room.

🏠 **Barrowville Town House** without rest., Kilkenny Rd, South : ¾ km on N 9 ✆ (059) 9143324, *barrowvilletownhouse@eircom.net,* Fax (059) 9141953, 🚗 – ↔ 🅿 VISA 🛇
7 rm ☲ ✦58/90 – ✦✦95/110.
◆ Regency townhouse professionally managed. Its conservatory breakfast room looks out over the garden containing ancient grape producing vine. Orthopaedic beds in all rooms.

🏠 **Ballyvergal House** without rest., Dublin Rd, North : 4¾ km on N 9 ✆ (059) 9143634, *ballyvergal@indigo.ie,* Fax (059) 9140386, 🛝 – ↔ 🅿 💶 VISA
10 rm ☲ ✦55 – ✦✦80.
◆ Substantial redbrick house run in a friendly manner. Trim, en suite rooms at a good price; cheerful co-ordinated décor and tall Georgian style windows lend an airy feel.

CARNA *Galway* 712 C 8 *Ireland G.*
Exc. : *Connemara★★★ – Cashel★, N : by R 340 – Roundstone★, W : 22 km by R 340, N 59 and R 341.*
Dublin 299 – Cork 272 – Galway 77 – Limerick 180.

🏠 **Carna Bay** ▧, ✆ (095) 32255, *carnabay@iol.ie,* Fax (095) 32530, ≤, ✎, 🚗 – ↔ & 🅿 💶 VISA
closed 23-26 December – **Rest** (bar lunch Monday-Saturday)/dinner 28/38 ♀ – **25 rm** ☲ ✦55/85 – ✦✦100/150.
◆ A low-rise, purpose-built hotel in a quiet lobster fishing village overlooking bay and hills. Walking, fishing, trekking available. Afterwards, recover in comfortable rooms. A fresh looking dining room in which to sample fresh local produce.

CARNAROSS Meath 712 L 6 – ⊠ Kells.
Dublin 69 – Cavan 43.5 – Drogheda 48.

X **The Forge,** Pottlereagh, Northwest : 5 ½ km by N 3 on Oldcastle rd ℰ (046) 9245003, *theforgerest@eircom.net, Fax (046) 9245917 –* **P**, **QO** **VISA**
closed 24 December- 2 January and 1-8 August – **Rest** *(closed Sunday dinner and Monday)* (dinner only and Sunday lunch) 35/39 and a la carte 43/52.
♦ Former forge tucked away in rural isolation. Family run, traditionally styled restaurant serving tried-and-tested dishes with modern twist: ample, good value choice.

CARNE Wexford 712 M 11.
Dublin 169 – Waterford 82 – Wexford 21.

⏴ **Lobster Pot,** ℰ (053) 31110, *Fax (053) 31401 –* ▤ **P**, **QO** **AE** **VISA**, ✼
closed January, 25 December, Good Friday and Monday except Bank Holidays – **Rest** - Seafood - a la carte 30/60 ₤.
♦ Idiosyncratic pub crammed with engaging clutter: ornaments, pictures and metal signs. Friendly staff serve fish orientated dishes against the background of Irish music.

CARRICKMACROSS (Carraig Mhachaire Rois) Monaghan 712 L 6 Ireland G. – pop. 3 832.
Env. : *Dún a' Rí Forest Park★, SW : 8 km by R 179 – St Mochta's House★, E : 7 km by R 178 and minor road S.*
🛆 *Nuremore* ℰ (042) 967 1368.
Dublin 92 – Dundalk 22.5.

🏠 **Nuremore** ✼, South : 1 ½ km on N 2 ℰ (042) 9661438, *info@nuremore.com, Fax (042) 9661853,* ≤, ⚗, ₤₆, ⊜ₛ, ▨, 🛆, ☜, 🐾, ₤, ✕ – 🛗 ⇄ ☏ & **P** – 🛆 400. **QO** **AE** **①** **VISA**, ✼
Rest – (see **The Restaurant** below) – 72 rm ☲ ✱175 – ✱✱300.
♦ Much extended Victorian house in attractive grounds; a rural retreat in which to swim, ride or practice golf. Comfortable rooms, most with views over countryside.

XXX **The Restaurant** (at Nuremore H.), South : 1 ½ km on N 2 ℰ (042) 9661438, *Fax (042) 9661853 –* ▤ **P**, **QO** **AE** **①** **VISA**
closed Saturday lunch – **Rest** 30/80 s.
♦ Split-level dining room; tables laid with white linen, bone china and stylish glassware. Menu of seasonal dishes influenced by French fine dining. Attentive service.

CARRICK-ON-SHANNON (Cora Droma Rúisc) Leitrim 712 H 6 Ireland G. – pop. 2 237.
See : *Town★.*
Exc. : *Lough Rynn Demesne★.*
🛆 *Carrick-on-Shannon, Woodbrook* ℰ (079) 67015.
🖪 *Old Barrel Store* ℰ (0719) 620170 (April-October).
Dublin 156 – Ballina 80.5 – Galway 119 – Roscommon 42 – Sligo 55.

🏠 **The Landmark,** on N 4 . ℰ (071) 9622222, *landmarkhotel@eircom.net, Fax (071) 9622233,* ≤ – 🛗 ⇄ & **P** – 🛆 500. **QO** **AE** **VISA**, ✼
closed 24-25 December – **CJ's :** **Rest** (dinner only) 37 and a la carte approx 38 s. – **60 rm** ☲ ✱123/149 – ✱✱206/238.
♦ Overlooks the Shannon; some areas reminiscent of a luxury liner: wooden floors, panelled ceiling. Marble fountain in lobby. Richly furnished rooms; water scenes on walls. CJ's boasts pleasant river views.

⏶ **Hollywell** ✼, without rest., Liberty Hill, off N 4 ℰ (071) 9621124, *hollywell@esatbiz.com, Fax (071) 9621124,* ≤, ☞ – ⇄ **P**, **QO** **AE** **VISA**, ✼
March-October – **4 rm** ☲ ✱60/80 – ✱✱110/140.
♦ A charming part 18C house in a peaceful spot by the river. Read up on area in a well-appointed lounge, take breakfast in dining room run by hospitable owner. Neat rooms.

X **Victoria Hall,** Victoria Hall, Quay Rd, ℰ (071) 9620320, *info@victoriahall.ie, Fax (071) 9620320 –* ▤, **QO** **VISA**
closed 25 December and Good Friday – **Rest** - Asian - a la carte 32/39.
♦ Converted 19C church next to pretty quay. On two levels, with bright chairs and plush leather banquettes. Eclectic Asian menus are fresh, exciting, fragrant and original.

⏴ **The Oarsman,** Bridge St, ℰ (071) 9621733, *info@theoarsman.com, Fax (071) 9621734,* 🍴 – **QO** **VISA**
closed 25 December, Good Friday and Sunday – **Rest** a la carte 32/48 ₤.
♦ Recently modernised bar, retaining its traditional charm and atmosphere. Flagged floors, exposed stone and beams, pubby bric-a-brac plus mezzanine. Menus with modern flavours.

CARRIGALINE (Carraig Uí Leighin) *Cork* 712 G 12 – *pop. 11 191.*

> 🏌 *Fernhill ℘ (021) 437 2226.*
> *Dublin 262 – Cork 14.5.*

Carrigaline Court, Cork Rd, ℘ (021) 4852100, *reception@carrigcourt.com,* Fax (021) 4371103, ℡, **⌂**, **⎙**, 🖵 – 📶 ⌘, ▤ rest, **📞** & **P** – 🛡 350. ⚙ AE ⊙ VISA. ⚜
closed 25-26 December – **The Bistro :** Rest (carvery lunch Monday-Saturday)/dinner a la carte 40 ⚘ – **89 rm** ⊆ ✦115 – ✦✦178, 2 suites.
◆ Modern hotel with airy interiors; rooms are spacious, with all mod cons, whilst leisure centre boasts a 20m pool, steam room, sauna. Corporate friendly with large ballroom. Local products to the fore in stylish restaurant.

Raffeen Lodge without rest., Ringaskiddy Rd, Monkstown, Northeast : 4 km by R 611 and N 28 off R 610 ℘ (021) 4371632, *info@raffeenlodge.com,* Fax (021) 4371632, ☞ – ⚜ **P**. VISA. ⚜
closed 21 December-3 January – **6 rm** ⊆ ✦45/50 – ✦✦70/80.
◆ A short drive from the fishing village of Ringaskiddy and Cork airport. A neat and tidy, good value house; rooms are uniformly decorated in pastel shades, simple in style.

Shannonpark House without rest., Cork Rd, North : 1 ½ km on R 611 ℘ (021) 437 2091, ☞ – **P**. VISA. ⚜
6 rm ⊆ ✦40/50 – ✦✦80.
◆ Breakfasts at the lace-topped communal table in this simple, homely guesthouse. Cosy little sitting room; bedrooms are always immaculate, furnished in dark wood.

CARRIGANS (An Carraigain) *Donegal* 712 J 3.

Dublin 225 – Donegal 66 – Letterkenny 230 – Sligo 124.

Mount Royd without rest., ℘ (074) 9140163, *jmartin@mountroyd.com,* Fax (074) 9140400, ☞ – ⚜ ⚜. ⚜
March-November – **4 rm** ⊆ ✦45 – ✦✦70.
◆ Genuinely hospitable owners keep this creeper-clad period house in excellent order. En suite rooms are cosy and individually styled. Traditional, pleasantly cluttered lounge.

CASHEL (An Caiseal) *Galway* 712 C 7 *Ireland G.*

See : *Town★.*
Exc. : *Connemara★★★.*
Dublin 278 – Galway 66.

Cashel House ⚘, ℘ (095) 31001, *res@cashel-house-hotel.com,* Fax (095) 31077, ≤, ⚘, ☞, ◪, ✵ – ⚜ **📞 P**. ⚙ AE VISA
closed 6 January-6 February – **Rest** (booking essential for non-residents) (bar lunch Monday-Saturday)/dinner 52/54 and a la carte 30/36 – **32 rm** ⊆ ✦95/270 – ✦✦190/270.
◆ Built 1840; a very comfortable and restful country house, warmly decorated with delightful gardens. General de Gaulle stayed in one of the luxurious country house rooms. Dining room, with Queen Anne style chairs, opens into elegant conservatory.

Zetland Country House ⚘, ℘ (095) 31111, *zetland@iol.ie,* Fax (095) 31117, ≤, Cashel Bay, ✵, ☞, ✵ – ⚜ **P**. ⚙ AE ⊙ VISA
Rest (bar lunch)/dinner 56/60 **s.** – **19 rm** ⊆ ✦149/165 – ✦✦218/240.
◆ Lord Zetland's sporting lodge in 1800s; a splendid position in gardens sweeping down to Cashel Bay. Snooker, scuba diving, hunting organised. Pastel rooms. Dining room with silver cutlery, peerless views.

CASHEL (Caiseal) *Tipperary* 712 I 10 *Ireland G.* – *pop. 2 770.*

See : *Town★★★ – Rock of Cashel★★★ AC – Cormac's Chapel★★ – Round Tower★ – Museum★ – Cashel Palace Gardens★ – GPA Bolton Library★ AC.*
Env. : *Holy Cross Abbey★★ , N : 14½ km by R 660 – Athassel Priory★ , W : 8 km by N 74.*
Exc. : *Caher (Castle★★ , Swiss Cottage★), S : 18 km by N 8 – Glen of Aherlow★ , W : 21 km by N 74 and R 664.*
 Heritage Centre, Town Hall, Main St ℘ (062) 62511 (April-September).
Dublin 162.5 – Cork 96.5 – Kilkenny 55 – Limerick 58 – Waterford 71.

Cashel Palace, Main St, ℘ (062) 62707, *reception@cashel-palace.ie,* Fax (062) 61521, ☞, ◪, – 📶 ⚜ **P** – 🛡 80. ⚙ AE VISA. ⚜
closed 24-27 December – **Bishop's Buttery :** Rest (carving lunch Monday-Saturday)/dinner 45/65 and a la carte 45/62 **s.** – **23 rm** ✦165/275 – ✦✦330/450.
◆ A stately Queen Anne house, once home to an Archbishop, in walled gardens with path leading up to Cashel Rock. Inside, an extensive, pillared lounge and capacious rooms. Harmonious dining room: vaulted ceilings, open fire and light, bright colours.

Aulber House without rest., Deerpark, West : ¾ km on N 74   ℰ (062) 63713, *beral ley@eircom.net*, Fax (062) 63715, ⌗ – ⊶⊷ ✆ 👤 👤 ⑩ ☒ ✳︎
closed 2 December - 2 January – 12 rm ⬓ ✦50/70 – ✦✦90/110.
  ✦ Modern house in Georgian style with lawned gardens; five minutes from town centre. Comfy, leather furnished lounge. Smart, individually styled rooms.

XXX **Chez Hans,** Rockside, Moor Lane St,   ℰ (062) 61177, Fax (062) 61177 – 👤 ⑩ ⑩ ☒
closed 2 weeks January, 1 week September, 25 December, Sunday and Monday – **Rest** (dinner only) a la carte 33/50 ⬓.
  ✦ A converted synod hall with stained glass windows, near Cashel Rock: an unusual setting for a restaurant. Carefully prepared and cooked meals, using local ingredients.

X **Cafe Hans,** Rockside, Moore Lane St,   ℰ (062) 63660 – 👤
closed last 3 weeks January, 25 December, Sunday and Monday – **Rest** (bookings not accepted) (lunch only) a la carte 19/29.
  ✦ Next door to Chez Hans; white emulsioned walls, open kitchen and glass roof. Simple, tasty dishes are prepared with good, local ingredients. Come early as you can't book.

CASTLEBALDWIN (Béal Átha na gCarraigíní) *Sligo* **712** G 5 *Ireland G.* – ⊠ *Boyle (Roscommon).*
Env. : *Carrowkeel Megalithic Cemetery (⩽★★), S : 4¾ km.*
Exc. : *Arigna Scenic Drive★, N : 3¼ km by N 4 – Lough Key Forest Park★ AC, SE : 16 km by N 4 – View of Lough Allen★, N : 14½ km by N 4 on R 280 – Mountain Drive★, N : 9½ km on N 4 – Boyle Abbey★ AC, SE : 12¾ km – King House★, SE : 12¾ km by N 4.*
Dublin 190 – Longford 67.5 – Sligo 24.

Cromleach Lodge ⌂, Ballindoon, Southeast : 5 ½ km   ℰ (071) 9165155, *info@crom leach.com*, Fax (071) 9165455, ⩽ *Lough Arrow and Carrowkeel Cairns*, ⌗, ⌗, ♨ – ⊶⊷ 👤.
⑩ ☒ ⑩ ☒
closed 2 weeks November – **Rest** (booking essential for non-residents) (dinner only and Sunday lunch) 60 ⬓ – **10 rm** ⬓ ✦190/210 – ✦✦232/292.
  ✦ Contrasting with ancient Carrowkeel Cairns, overlooking Lough Arrow, this is a smart, modern chalet with abundant local artwork indoors. Capacious rooms with large windows. Modern dishes and attentive service.

CASTLEGREGORY (Caisleán Ghriaire) *Kerry* **712** B 11.
Dublin 330 – Dingle 24 – Killarney 54.5.

⌂ **The Shores Country House,** Conor Pass Rd, Kilcummin, Southwest : 6 km on Bran-don rd   ℰ (066) 7139196, *theshores@eircom.net*, Fax (066) 7139196, ⩽, ⌗ – ⊶⊷ ✆ 👤. ⑩
☒ ✳︎
March-November – **Rest** (by arrangement) 30/36 – 6 rm ⬓ ✦40/80 – ✦✦65/90.
  ✦ Between Stradbally Mountain and a long sandy beach, a modern guest house run by the friendly longstanding owner. Immaculate, comfortable rooms, some with antique beds. Dining room faces the Atlantic.

CASTLEKNOCK (Caisleán Cnucha) *Dublin* – see Dublin.

CASTLELYONS (Caisleán Ó Liatháin) *Cork* **712** H 11 – *pop. 164.*
Dublin 219 – Cork 30.5 – Killarney 104.5 – Limerick 64.5.

⌂ **Ballyvolane House** ⌂, Southeast : 5 ½ km by Midleton rd on Britway rd   ℰ (025) 36349, *ballyvol@iol.ie*, Fax (025) 36781, ⩽, ⌗, ⌗, ♨ – ⊶⊷ 👤. ⑩ ☒ ⑩ ☒
closed Christmas-New Year – **Rest** (by arrangement) (communal dining) 50 – **6 rm** ⬓
✦130/135 – ✦✦190/200.
  ✦ Stately 18C Italianate mansion mentioned in local legend, with lakes in parkland. Name means "place of springing heifers". Antique-filled rooms, some with Victorian baths. Dining room with silver candlesticks and balanced dishes.

CASTLETOWNBERE (Baile Chaisleáin Bhéarra) *Cork* **712** C 13 *Ireland G.* – *pop. 926.*
Env. : *Ring of Beara★, W : by R 572 (Allihies, mines★ - Garnish Bay ⩽★) – Slieve Miskish Mountains (⩽★).*
⌗ *Berehaven, Millcove*   ℰ (027) 70700.
Dublin 360 – Cork 130 – Killarney 93.5.

⌂ **Rodeen** ⌂, without rest., East : 3 ¼ km by R 572   ℰ (027) 70158, *rodeen@iolfree.ie*, ⩽, ⌗ – ⊶⊷ 👤. ⑩ ☒ ⑩ ☒ ✳︎
17 March-17 October – **7 rm** ⬓ ✦40/70 – ✦✦76/80.
  ✦ Owner used to run a horticulture business and this is evident in the variety of shrubs in the garden. Rooms are compact but nicely decorated; some look out to Bantry Bay.

CASTLETOWNSHEND (Baile an Chaisleáin) Cork 712 E 13.

Env. : *Glandore*★, NE : 10 km R 596 – Sherkin Island★ *AC*, W : 15 km by R 596 and R 595 and ferry.
Dublin 346 – Cork 95 – Killarney 116.

🍴 **Mary Ann's**, ℘ (028) 36146, *maryanns@eircom.net*, Fax (028) 36920, � – 🌑 *VISA*. ✆
closed 3 weeks January, 24-26 December and Monday November-March – **Rest** (bookings not accepted) a la carte 19/45.
♦ A pleasant 19C pub in pretty village. Tempting dishes are distinguished by the fact that almost everything is homemade. Sunny terrace is popular for lunch.

CAVAN (An Cabhán) Cavan 712 J 6 Ireland G. – pop. 6 098.

Env. : *Killykeen Forest Park*★, W : 9½ km by R 198.
🛈 Farnham St ℘ (049) 4331942 (April-September), *irelandnorthwest@eircom.net*.
Dublin 114 – Drogheda 93.5 – Enniskillen 64.5.

🏨 **Radisson SAS Farnham Estate**, Farnham Ertate, Northwest : 2 ½ km on R 198 ℘ (049) 4377700, *info.farnham@radissonsas.com*, Fax (049) 4377701, ⑦, ⅃δ, ⇌, ⊿ heated, ⬚, ⊶, ﹩–⁐ ⥮ 🅣🅥 ✆ δ, – ⩜ 380. 🌑 🅰🅴 🅾 *VISA*. ✆
Botanica : Rest 25 (lunch) and dinner a la carte approx 41 – **Pear Tree : Rest** (lunch only) 25 – **142 rm** ⊑ ✦115/155 – ✦✦140/180, 8 suites.
♦ Period charm and acres of mature parkland in this renovated 400-year old mansion, offset by 21C hotel with meeting facilities, Wellness Centre and snazzy, well-equipped rooms. Universal menus at Botanica. Lighter dishes in Pear Tree.

🏨 **Cavan Crystal**, Dublin Rd, East : 1½ km on N 3 ℘ (049) 436 0600, *info@cavancrystalho tel.com*, Fax (049) 436 0699, ⅃δ, ⇌, ⬚ – ⁐ ⥮, ▤ rest, ✆ δ, 🅿 – ⩜ 650. 🌑 🅰🅴 *VISA*. ✆
closed 24-25 December – **Opus One : Rest** (bar lunch) a la carte 30/42 ⊊ – **85 rm** ⊑ ✦90/120 – ✦✦160/190.
♦ Modern hotel next to Cavan Crystal factory. Vast atrium is distinctive and stylish. Extensive meeting and leisure facilities. Comfy, well-equipped, modish bedrooms. Dining room serves menus true to Irish roots with stylish twists.

at Cloverhill North : 12 km by N 3 on N 54 – ⊠ Belturbet.

🏠 **Rockwood House** without rest., ℘ (047) 55351, *jbmac@eircom.net*, Fax (047) 55373, ⊶ – ⥮ 🅿. 🌑 *VISA*. ✆
closed 10 December-1 February – **4 rm** ⊑ ✦40 – ✦✦64.
♦ Stone-faced house with a charming garden located in a woodland clearing. Comfortable guests' lounge and a conservatory for breakfast. Simply appointed, comfortable bedrooms.

🍴🍴 **The Olde Post Inn** with rm, ℘ (047) 55555, *gearoidlynch@eircom.net*, Fax (047) 55111, ⊶ – 🅿. 🌑 🅰🅴 *VISA*
closed 24-28 December and Monday – **Rest** (dinner only and Sunday lunch)/dinner 53 and a la carte 37/51 – **6 rm** ⊑ ✦60 – ✦✦100.
♦ Former village post office; now a restaurant with much character: exposed stone and brick, large rafters. A feel of genuine hospitality prevails. Fine dining with Gallic edge.

CLARINBRIDGE (Droichead an Chláirín) Galway 712 F 8.

Env. : *Dunguaire Castle*★ *AC*, S : 12 km by N 18 and N 67.
Exc. : *Thoor Ballylee*★ *AC*, S : 16 km by N 18 and minor road.
Dublin 233.5 – Galway 17.5.

🍴🍴 **The Old Schoolhouse**, ℘ (091) 796898, *kenc@iol.ie*, Fax (091) 796117 – 🅿. 🌑 🅰🅴 *VISA*
closed 24-27 and 31 December-3 January and Monday – **Rest** (booking essential) (dinner only and Sunday lunch)/dinner 23/25 and a la carte 29/40.
♦ A converted school room is now the dining room and has been transformed by warm hued walls and elegant tableware. The speciality is the catch of the day and rock oysters.

REPUBLIC OF IRELAND

967

CLIFDEN (An Clochán) Galway **712** B 7 Ireland G.

Exc. : *Connemara*★★★, *NE : by N 59 – Sky Road*★★ (≤★★), *NE : by N 59 – Connemara National Park*★, *NE : 1½ km by N 59 – Killary Harbour*★, *NE : 35 km by N 59 – Kylemore Abbey*★ *AC*, *N : 18 km by N 59.*

🛈 Galway Rd ℰ (095) 21163 (March-October).

Dublin 291 – Ballina 124 – Galway 79.

Rock Glen ⊗, South : 2 km by R 341 ℰ (095) 21035, *enquiry@rockyglenhotel.com*, Fax (095) 21737, ≤, ☞, ♨, ※ – 🅿. ☍ 🗚 *VISA*
closed 2 January-1 March, 24-26 December and restricted opening November-December – **Rest** (bar lunch)/dinner a la carte 37/50 – **27 rm** ⌷ ♦114/135 – ♦♦158/190.
♦ Former shooting lodge, built 1815, views of Ardbear Bay, the Twelve Bens. A handsome retreat; antique furnished, well-proportioned rooms. Aran Island boat trips available. Memorable meals - fresh seafood straight from the boat - with memorable views.

Station House, ℰ (095) 21699, *reservations@clifdenstationhouse.com*, Fax (095) 21667, ⊘, ₺₆, ⇌, 🖂 – ≒ ⇌ ፟ ৬ 🅿 – 🖆 200. ☍ 🗚 ⓘ *VISA*. ※
closed 24-25 December – **The Signal** : **Rest** (bar lunch)/dinner 36 – **78 rm** ⌷ ♦79/135 – ♦♦100/250.
♦ A modern hotel on site of the Galway-Clifden railway line closed in 1935. Now forms part of a complex which includes a museum. Good sized rooms in cheerful colours. Rarefied ambiance in which to dine on local delights, among then lamb and shellfish.

Ardagh ⊗, Ballyconneely rd, South : 2¾ km on R 341 ℰ (095) 21384, *ardaghhotel@eir com.net*, Fax (095) 21314, ≤ Ardbear Bay – ≒⇌ 🅿. ☍ 🗚 ⓘ *VISA*
Easter-October – **Rest** (dinner only) a la carte 48/63 – **17 rm** ⌷ ♦112/125 – ♦♦165/190, 3 suites.
♦ Family run hotel on edge of Ardbear Bay. A welcoming, domestically furnished interior with turf fires, piano, pictures and plants. Bedrooms are large, especially superiors. Fresh, pine dining room with views.

Dolphin Beach Country House ⊗, Lower Sky Rd, West : 5½ km by Sky Rd ℰ (095) 21204, *stay@dolphinbeachhouse.com*, Fax (095) 22935, ≤ Clifden Bay, ☞ – ≒⇌ 𝄞 🅿. ☍ *VISA*. ※
February - 15 December – **Rest** (by arrangement) (residents only) 35/40 – **9 rm** ⌷ ♦80/120 – ♦♦150/180.
♦ Terracotta coloured former farmhouse, perched on side of hill with stunning views of bay. Delightful sitting room with huge windows to accommodate vista. Attractive rooms. Tasty, home-cooked meals.

The Quay House without rest., Beach Rd, ℰ (095) 21369, *thequay@iol.ie*, Fax (095) 21608, ≤ – ☍ *VISA*. ※
mid March-October – **14 rm** ⌷ ♦80/120 – ♦♦140/180.
♦ Once a harbour master's residence, then a Franciscan monastery. Rooms are divided between the main house: bohemian in style, and new annex: spacious with kitchenettes.

Byrne Mal Dua House without rest., Galway Rd, East : 1¼ km on N 59 ℰ (095) 21171, *info@maldua.com*, Fax (095) 21739, ☞ – ≒⇌ 𝄞 🅿. ☍ 🗚 ⓘ *VISA*. ※
14 rm ⌷ ♦39/95 – ♦♦80/150.
♦ A white, detached house in well-tended gardens. Deep colours and subdued lighting indoors. Bedrooms are immaculately kept with fitted furniture. Neatly set breakfast room overlooks the garden.

Dún Rí without rest., Hulk St, ℰ (095) 21625, *dunri@anu.ie*, Fax (095) 21635 – ≒⇌ 🅿. ☍ *VISA*. ※
closed 20-26 December – **13 rm** ⌷ ♦50/60 – ♦♦70/80.
♦ A pleasant, cream-washed guesthouse overlooking Owenglin river with views of a pony showground and Dooneen hill. Good facilities including power showers in all rooms.

Benbaun without rest., Westport Rd, ℰ (095) 21462, *benbaunhouse@eircom.net*, Fax (095) 21462, ☞ – 𝄞 🅿. ☍ *VISA*. ※
May- 20 September – **12 rm** ⌷ ♦40/55 – ♦♦70/80.
♦ Family owned house to the north of the town: modern bedrooms - simple, spacious and decorated in cheerful patterned fabrics - represent very good value for money.

Buttermilk Lodge without rest., Westport Rd, ℰ (095) 21951, *buttermilklodge@eir com.net*, Fax (095) 21953, ≤, ☞ – ≒⇌ 🅿. ☍ 🗚 *VISA*. ※
March-November – **11 rm** ⌷ ♦45/70 – ♦♦80/100.
♦ Yellow painted, name refers to nearby lough, a theme which is continued indoors as each room bears the name of a lough. Daily breakfast specials; maps provided for exploring.

Joyce's Waterloo House, Galway Rd, East : 1½ km off N 59 ℰ (095) 21688, *pkp@joy ces-waterloo.com*, Fax (095) 22044, ☞ – ≒⇌ 🅿. ☍ *VISA*. ※
closed 23-27 December – **Rest** (by arrangement) 30 – **8 rm** ⌷ ♦52/104 – ♦♦76/114.
♦ Guesthouse announced by bright yellow exterior. Cosy, welcoming lounge. Smart bedrooms: owner puts national flag of guest outside each! All have VCRs and local art on walls.

Sea Mist House without rest., ✆ (095) 21441, *sgriffin@eircom.net*, – P. MC VISA.
closed 22-28 December and weekends only in winter – **6 rm** ★75/110 – ★★75/110.
◆ 20C terraced stone house with sloping garden in town centre. Good choice at breakfast in cheerful room. Lounge at front and in conservatory. Spacious, modern bedrooms.

Connemara Country Lodge without rest., Westport Rd, ✆ (095) 21122, *connemara@unison.ie*, *Fax (095) 21122*, – P. MC VISA
closed 22-28 December – **10 rm** ★50/75 – ★★70/90.
◆ Affordable accommodation in a personally run guest house. Breakfasts include home-baked raisin bread and scones: owner has tendency to break into song at this point!

CLONAKILTY (Cloich na Coillte) *Cork* 712 F 13 *Ireland G.* – *pop. 3 698.*

See : *West Cork Regional Museum★ AC.*
Env. : *Courtmacsherry★, E : 12 km by R 600 and R 601 – Timoleague Friary★, E : 8 km by R 600.*
Exc. : *Carbery Coast★ (Drombeg Stone Circle★, Glandore★, Castletownshend★) by N 71 and R 597.*
Dunmore, Dunmore House, Muckross ✆ (023) 34644.
25 Ashe St ✆ (023) 33226.
Dublin 310.5 – Cork 51.5.

Inchydoney Island Lodge & Spa, South : 5 ¼ km by N 71 following signs for Inchydoney Beach ✆ (023) 33143, *reservations@inchydoneyisland.com*, *Fax (023) 35229*, – rest, P – 350. MC AE VISA.
closed 25-27 December – ***The Gulfstream* : Rest** (dinner only) 55 – ***Dunes Bistro* : Rest** a la carte 20/38 – **63 rm** ★215/240 – ★★330/370, 4 suites.
◆ Set on a headland looking out to sea. Range of leisure facilities; treatments - aquamarine spa, underwater massages - are especially good. Big, bright bedrooms with extras. The Gulfstream has fine sea views. The Dunes Bistro has a hearty, nautical theme.

Quality, Clogheen, West : ¾ km by N 71 (Skibbereen rd) ✆ (023) 36400, *info@qualityhotelclonakilty.com*, *Fax (023) 35404*, – rest, P – 160. MC AE VISA.
closed 22-26 December – **Rest** (grill rest.) (carvery lunch Monday-Saturday)/dinner 26/28 and a la carte 26/39 – **68 rm** ★74/124 – ★★98/198, 12 suites.
◆ Modern hotel; rooms are uniformly decorated with matching fabrics. What distinguishes it is the three screen multiplex cinema, the "KidKamp" in summer, and leisure complex. Menus feature popular favourites.

An Garrán Coir, Castlefreke, Rathbarry, West : 6½ km by N 71 ✆ (023) 48236, *angarrancoir@eircom.net*, *Fax (023) 48236*, – P. VISA
Rest (by arrangement) 15/25 – **5 rm** ★45/60 – ★★70/100.
◆ Working farm overlooking rolling countryside: organic garden supplies ingredients for dinner. Homely lounge, well-kept rooms in bright, cheery colours. Good base for walking.

Gleesons, 3-4 Connolly St, ✆ (023) 21834, *gleesonsrestaurant@eircom.net*, *Fax (023) 21944* – MC AE VISA
closed 24-26 December, 3 weeks Spring, Monday and Sunday in winter – **Rest** (dinner only except July-August) a la carte 30/56 **s.**
◆ Town centre restaurant with wood blinds. Low beamed interior with wood burning stove. Classically based menus; dishes have individual twist and local produce is to the fore.

An Sugán, Wolfe Tone St., ✆ (023) 33498, *ansugan@eircom.net*, *Fax (023) 33825* – MC VISA
closed 25-26 December and Good Friday – **Rest** 35 (dinner) and a la carte 22/35.
◆ Situated in the old quays area of town. Homely wooden bar leads upstairs to restaurant hung with old photographs. Known for lobster, baked crab and black pudding terrine.

CLONBUR (An Fhairche) *Galway* 712 D 7.

Dublin 260.5 – Ballina 79 – Galway 46.5.

Burke's Bar with rm, ✆ (094) 9546175, *tibhurca@eircom.net*, *Fax (094) 9546290*, – MC VISA.
closed 25 December, Good Friday and restricted opening in winter – **Rest** (live music Saturday-Sunday) a la carte 23/40 – **5 rm** ★40 – ★★80.
◆ Family run for several generations; hearty food includes home-baked soda bread. Irish music at weekends. Simple exterior belies the vast interior.

CLONDALKIN *Dublin* 712 M 8 – *see Dublin.*

REPUBLIC OF IRELAND

CLONMEL (Cluain Meala) Tipperary 712 I 10 Ireland G. – pop. 16 910.

See : Town★ – County Museum★, St Mary's Church★.
Env. : Fethard★, N : 13 km by R 689.
Exc. : Nier Valley Scenic Route★★ – Ahenny High Crosses★, E : 30½ km by N 24 and R 697 – Ormond Castle★, E : 33¾ km by N 24.
🛅 Lyreanearla, Mountain Rd ℘ (052) 24050.
🎫 Community Office, Town Centre ℘ (052) 22960.
Dublin 174 – Cork 95 – Kilkenny 50 – Limerick 77 – Waterford 46.5.

Minella, Coleville Rd, ℘ (052) 22388, frontdesk@hotelminella.ie, Fax (052) 24381, 🌳, ℩₅,
🖙s, 🔲, 🔊, 🐎, 🏋, 🎾 – 🔆, 🍴 rest, 🕭 🅿 – 🛄 550. 🕼 🖭 🐽 💳. 🞂
closed 24-28 December – **Rest** 30/38 and a la carte 34/39 – **90 rm** 🖙 🕯100 – 🕯🕯160.
   • Heavily extended Georgian house on banks of River Suir. Excellent leisure facility. Bedrooms decorated in soft pinks and blues; garden rooms have pleasant views. Basement restaurant has river vistas.

CLONTARF (Cluain Tarbh) Dublin 712 N 7 – see Dublin.

CLOVERHILL Cavan 712 J 5 – see Cavan.

Undecided between two equivalent establishments?
Within each category, establishments are classified
in our order of preference.

COBH (An Cóbh) Cork 712 H 12 Ireland G. – pop. 9 811.

See : Town★ – St Colman's Cathedral★ – Lusitania Memorial★.
Exc. : Fota Island★ (Fota House★ AC, Fota Wildlife Park★ AC), N : 6½ km by R 624 – Cloyne Cathedral★, SE : 24 km by R 624/5, N 25, R 630 and R 629.
🛅 Ballywilliam ℘ (021) 812399.
Dublin 264 – Cork 24 – Waterford 104.5.

WatersEdge, (next to Cobh Heritage Centre) ℘ (021) 481 5566, info@watersedgeho
tel.ie, Fax (021) 481 2011, ≤ Cork harbour, 🌳 – 🔆, 🍴 rest, 🕭 🅿. 🕼 🖭 🐽 💳. 🞂
closed 24-26 December – **Jacob's Ladder :** Rest (light lunch)/dinner a la carte 20/41 –
18 rm 🖙 🕯90/130 – 🕯🕯130/200, 1 suite.
   • Next to the Heritage Centre, a converted salvage yard office overlooking Cork harbour. Some of the spacious, soft-toned rooms have French windows opening on to the veranda. Stylish restaurant with waterside setting.

CONG (Conga) Mayo 712 E 7 Ireland G.

See : Town★.
Env. : Lough Corrib★★.
Exc. : Ross Errilly Abbey★ (Tower ≤★) – Joyce Country★★ (Lough Nafooey★) W : by R 345.
🎫 ℘ (094) 9546542 (March-October).
Dublin 257.5 – Ballina 79 – Galway 45.

Ashford Castle 🐾, ℘ (094) 9546003, ashford@ashford.ie, Fax (094) 9546260, ≤, ⑫,
℩₅, 🖙s, 🖥₉, 🔊, 🐎, 🏋, 🎾 – 📳🔽 🔆 📞 🅿 – 🛄 110. 🞂
Connaught Room : Rest (dinner only) 80/160 🍷 – **George V Room :** Rest (residents only)
(dinner only) 67 🍷 – 🖙 25 – **79 rm** 🕯232/816 – 🕯🕯232/816, 4 suites.
   • Hugely imposing restored castle in formal grounds on Lough Corrib. Suits of armour and period antiques in a clubby lounge. Handsomely furnished country house rooms. Smart fine dining in Connaught Room. George V imbued with air of genteel formality.

Ballywarren House, East : 3 ½ km on R 346 ℘ (094) 9546989, ballywarren
house@gmail.com, Fax (094) 9546989, ≤, 🌳 – 🔆 🅿. 🕼 🖭 💳. 🞂
closed 2 weeks spring and 2 weeks autumn – **Rest** (by arrangement) 38 🍷 – 🖙 8.50 – **3 rm**
🕯98/156 – 🕯🕯148.
   • Modern but 18C in style - open fires, galleried landing, oak staircase. Fresh colours: mint green, pink contrast pleasingly with woodwork. Carved pine beds; one four poster. Meals include own vegetables and daughter's farm eggs.

CORK (Corcaigh) *Cork 712 G 12 Ireland G. – pop. 186 239.*

See : *City*★★ – *Shandon Bells*★★ Y, *St Fin Barre's Cathedral*★★ *AC* Z, *Cork Public Museum*★ X M – *Grand Parade*★ Z , *South Mall*★ Z , *St Patrick Street*★ Z , *Crawford Art Gallery*★ Y – *Elizabethan Fort*★ Z .

Env. : *Dunkathel House*★ *AC*, E : 9¼ km by N 8 and N 25 X.

Exc. : *Fota Island*★ *(Fota House*★★ *AC, Fota Wildlife Park*★ *AC)*, E : 13 km by N 8 and N 25 X – *Cobh*★ *(St Colman's Cathedral*★, *Lusitania Memorial*★ *)* SE : 24 km by N 8, N 25 and R 624 X.

Douglas *℘ (021) 4891086*, X – Mahon, Cloverhill, Blackrock *℘ (021) 4292543* X – Monkstown, Parkgarriffe *℘ (021) 4841376*, X – Harbour Point, Clash, Little Island *℘ (021) 4353094*, X.

Cork Airport : *℘ (021) 4313131*, S : 6½ km by L 42 X – **Terminal** : *Bus Station, Parnell Pl.*
to France (Roscoff) (Brittany Ferries and Irish Ferries) weekly (14 h/16 h) – to Pembroke (Swansea Cork Ferries) 2-6 weekly (8 h 30 mn) – to Swansea (Swansea Cork Ferries) (10 h).

Cork City, Grand Parade ℘ (021) 4255100 – Cork Airport, Freephone facility at Arrivals Terminal.

Dublin 248.

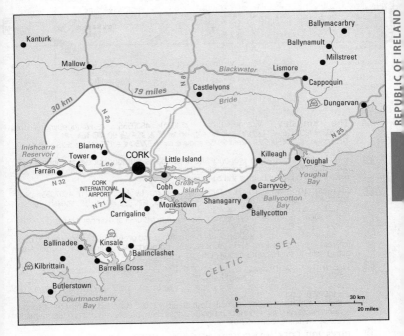

Hayfield Manor, Perrott Ave, College Rd, *℘ (021) 4845900, sales@hayfieldmanor.ie,* Fax *(021) 4316839,* 𝄐, ⬚, ☞ – ⬚ ✂ ▤ ☏ & 🅟 – 🔔 120. 🅜🅒 🄰🄴 🅞 *VISA* . ✂   X Z
Orchids : Rest (dinner only) 65 s. – **Perrotts :** Rest a la carte 30/56 s. – **83 rm** ✤320/380 – ✤✤320/380, 5 suites.
♦ Purpose-built yet Georgian in character. Stately interiors and harmoniously styled bedrooms with marble bathrooms and quality furniture - armchairs, coffee tables and desks. Twin dining options to suit all tastes.

Maryborough House ⮳, Maryborough Hill, Douglas, Southeast : 4 ¾ km by R 609 and R 610 *℘ (021) 4365555, info@maryborough.ie,* Fax *(021) 4365662,* 𝄐, ⬚, ⬚, ☞, ⬚, ✂ – ⬚ ✂, ▤ rest, & 🅟 – 🔔 500. 🅜🅒 🄰🄴 🅞 *VISA* . ✂
closed 25-26 December – **Zing's :** Rest 27/45 and dinner a la carte 40/49 s. – **88 rm** ⬚ ✤145/248 – ✤✤250/350, 5 suites.
♦ Built as a home for a wealthy merchant, an extended Georgian house. Five very characterful bedrooms in original house; others are sleek, stylish and contemporary. Restaurant boasts walk-in wine cellar.

971

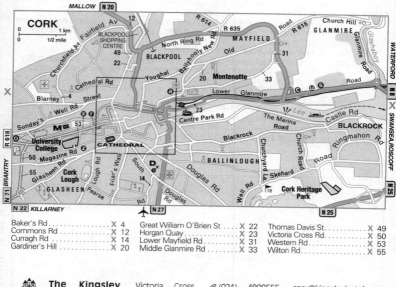

The Kingsley, Victoria Cross, ℰ (021) 4800555, resv@kingsleyhotel.com, Fax (021) 4800526, ≤, ɪ₅, ≋s, ⬜, ⊞ – ⧄ ⅋× ▤ ✆ & ℙ – ⅋⅋ 90. ◉◉ 🆅🆂🅰 . ※   X o
Otters (ℰ (021) 4800595) : Rest 28/33 and a la carte 37/50 s. – **129 rm** ⊇ ✦280 – ✦✦280, 2 suites.
 ♦ An inviting spot by river Lee, once site of Lee baths: outdoor hot tub and indoor pool takes their place. Relax in smart rooms or take tea in the lounge overlooking the weir. Airy restaurant has private booths and banquettes.

Silversprings Moran H., Tivoli, East : 4 km by N 8 ℰ (021) 4507533, silver springsres@moranhotels.com, Fax (021) 4507641, ɪ₅, ≋s, ⬜, ⊞, ☲, ※, squash – ⧄ ⅋×, ▤ rest, ✆ ℙ – ⅋⅋ 700. ◉◉ 🆅🆂🅰 . ※   X c
closed 24-26 December – **Rest** (closed Saturday lunch) 20/31 and dinner a la carte 27/39 **s**. – **107 rm** ⊇ ✦125/205 – ✦✦160/300, 2 suites.
 ♦ Conference oriented hotel surrounded by gardens and grounds. Smartly furnished public areas includes business and leisure centres. Comfortably appointed bedrooms. After dining, relax in smart, contemporary lounge.

The Ambassador, Military Hill, ℰ (021) 4551996, reservations@ambassadorhotel.ie, Fax (021) 4551997, ≤, ɪ₅, ≋s – ⧄ ⅋× ✆ ℙ – ⅋⅋ 220. ◉◉ 🆅🆂🅰 . ※   X a
closed 25-26 December – **Rest** 38 and a la carte 30/42 **s**. ♀ – **69 rm** ⊇ ✦85/120 – ✦✦110/150, 1 suite.
 ♦ Built as a military hospital; its high position affords city views from which most rooms benefit. All are furnished to a comfortable standard and most have a balcony. Home-made treats adorn dining room menus.

Jurys Inn Cork, Anderson's Quay, ℰ (021) 4943000, jurysinncork@jurysdoyle.com, Fax (021) 4276144 – ⧄ ⅋× & – ⅋⅋ 30. ◉◉ 🅰🅴 ⓞ 🆅🆂🅰 . ※   Y c
closed 25-26 December – **Rest** (carving lunch)/dinner 25/28 and a la carte 23/36 **s**. – ⊇ 13 – **133 rm** ✦125/155 – ✦✦125/155.
 ♦ Functional in its range of facilities: rooms fitted with 24-hour news channels, hairdryers, tea making facilities. Some rooms have the extra allure of overlooking the river. Buffet style breakfasts, lunchtime carvery and classic dinner menus.

Lancaster Lodge without rest., Lancaster Quay, Western Rd, ℰ (021) 4251125, info@lancasterlodge.com, Fax (021) 4251126 – ⧄ ✆ & ℙ. ◉◉ 🅰🅴 ⓞ 🆅🆂🅰   Z i
closed 22-26 December – **39 rm** ⊇ ✦86/120 – ✦✦120/170.
 ♦ Purpose-built hotel with crisp, modern interior. Bedrooms are chintz-free, pleasingly and sparingly decorated. Largest rooms on the fourth floor; rear rooms are quieter.

Lotamore House without rest., Tivoli, East : 4 ¾ km on N 8 ℰ (021) 4822344, lota more@iol.ie, Fax (021) 4822219, ≤, ⊞ – ⅋× ✆ ℙ. ◉◉ 🅰🅴 🆅🆂🅰   X s
closed 19 December-4 January – **18 rm** ⊇ ✦80/85 – ✦✦110/150.
 ♦ Georgian house perched on hill with fine view over river and harbour. Country house style lounge with antiques. Individually styled rooms; relish vista from one at the front.

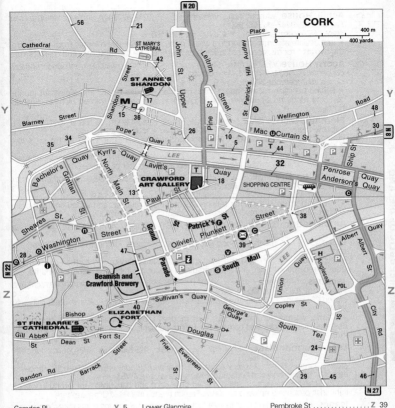

CORK

400 m
400 yards

↑ **Crawford House** without rest., Western Rd, ℃ (021) 4279000, *info@crawfordguest house.com*, Fax (021) 4279927 – **P**. **MO** **VISA**. ※ X x
closed 21 December-14 January – **12 rm** ⊇ ✦65/100 – ✦✦110/130.
♦ Victorian-style building offering bright, airy and comfortable guesthouse accommodation. Modern interiors with a choice of wood floors or carpeting in guest rooms.

↑ **Garnish House** without rest., Western Rd, ℃ (021) 4275111, *garnish@iol.ie*, Fax (021) 4273872 – ⊱✕ **P**. **MO** **AE** **①** **VISA**. ※ X r
14 rm ⊇ ✦75/110 – ✦✦200.
♦ Justifiably proud of gourmet breakfast: 30 options include pancakes and porridge. Guests are welcomed with home-made scones in cosy rooms; those at the rear have quiet aspect.

⌂ **Achill House** without rest., Western Rd, ℘ (021) 4279447, info@achillhouse.com, Fax (021) 4279447 – ☎, ⓂⓈ VISA Z e
closed 25 December – **9 rm** � ✿55/95 – ✿✿95/160.
◆ Immaculate accommodation in a well run terrace house, five minutes from the centre; the two attic rooms, decorated in warm pastel tones, are the most cosy and characterful.

⌂ **Acorn House** without rest., 14 St Patrick's Hill, ℘ (021) 4502474, info@acornhouse-cork.com, Fax (021) 4502474 – ✖, ⓂⓈ VISA, ✸ Y e
closed 10 December-20 January – **9 rm** ☑ ✿50/60 – ✿✿80/90.
◆ Behind Georgian façade, bright, high ceilinged en suite rooms and a pleasant lounge combine modern colours with period fireplaces and ornately framed pictures. Friendly hosts.

XXX **Flemings** with rm, Silver Grange House, Tivoli, East : 4 ½ km on N 8 ℘ (021) 4821621, info@flemingsrestaurant.ie, Fax (021) 4821800, ☞ – ☎ ℗, ⓂⓈ Æ VISA, ✸ X u
closed 23-25 December – **Rest** 29 (lunch) and dinner a la carte 39/50 – **3 rm** ☑ ✿90 – ✿✿120.
◆ Classical cuisine, French bias; uses local produce, organically home-grown vegetables, herbs. Two dining rooms in keeping with Georgian character of house; extends to rooms.

XX **Jacobs on the Mall**, 30A South Mall, ℘ (021) 4251530, info@jacobsonthemall.com, Fax (021) 4251531 – ▤ ✧ 30. ⓂⓈ Æ ⓄⒹ VISA Z s
closed Sunday – **Rest** (booking essential) 35/45 and a la carte 25/50 ☑.
◆ 19C former Turkish bath has retained its old steam windows and added contemporary Irish art. Modern dishes reveal a taste for bold, original combinations.

XX **Ambassador**, 3 Cook St, ℘ (021) 4273261, Fax (021) 4272357 – ▤. ⓂⓈ Æ ⓄⒹ VISA Z r
closed 25-26 December and Good Friday – **Rest** - Chinese - (dinner only) 28/36 and a la carte approx 31.
◆ Richly hued oak panelling and smoothly professional service add to the enjoyment of dishes prepared with care and fine ingredients in a long-established Chinese favourite.

XX **Jacques**, Phoenix St, ℘ (021) 4277387, jacquesrestaurant@eircom.net, Fax (021) 4270634 – ▤, ⓂⓈ Æ VISA Z c
closed 25 December-2 January, Saturday lunch, Sunday and Bank Holidays – **Rest** a la carte 21/43.
◆ A long, warmly decorated room with modern tables on which old Irish classics are delivered. Farm ducks, wild game, fresh fish and organic vegetables are used in the cooking.

X **Les Gourmandises**, 17 Cook St, ℘ (021) 4251959, info@lesgourmandises.ie, Fax (021) 4899005 – ⓂⓈ VISA Z v
closed 2 weeks March, 2 weeks August, Sunday and Monday – **Rest** - French - (booking essential) (dinner only and Friday lunch) 40 and a la carte 41/53.
◆ City centre restaurant boasting stained glass door and part-glass roof letting in lots of light. Irish produce employed on classic French menus in a relaxed atmosphere.

X **Isaacs**, 48 MacCurtain St, ℘ (021) 4503805, isaacs@iol.ie, Fax (021) 4551348 – ⓂⓈ Æ ⓄⒹ VISA Y u
closed 1 week Christmas, lunch Sunday and Bank Holidays – **Rest** (booking essential) a la carte 20/37.
◆ Tall brick arches and modern art in converted warehouse: buzzy, friendly and informal. Modern and traditional brasserie dishes plus home-made desserts and blackboard specials.

X **Cafe Paradiso**, 16 Lancaster Quay, Western Rd, ℘ (021) 4277939, info@cafeparadiso.ie, Fax (021) 4274973 – ⓂⓈ Æ VISA Z o
closed 1 week Christmas, Sunday and Monday – **Rest** - Vegetarian - (booking essential) a la carte 27/46 ☑.
◆ A growing following means booking is essential at this relaxed vegetarian restaurant. Colourful and inventive international combinations; blackboard list of organic wines.

X **Fenn's Quay**, 5 Sheares St, ℘ (021) 4279527, polary@eircom.net, Fax (021) 4279526 – ▤. ⓂⓈ Æ VISA Z n
closed 25 December, Sunday and Bank Holidays – **Rest** 20 (dinner) and a la carte 27/45 s. ☑.
◆ In a renovated 18C terrace in historic part of the city, this informal café-restaurant boasts modern art on display. Popular for mid-morning coffees and light lunches.

at Little Island East : 8½ km by N 25 – X – and R 623 – ✉ Cork.

🏛 **Radisson SAS**, Ditchley House, ℘ (021) 4297000, info.cork@radissonsas.com, Fax (021) 4297101, ☞, Ⓢ, ₤₆, Ⓢ, ☞ – ⃟ ✖, ▤ rest, ☎ ⓵ ℗ – ⓍÂ 600. ⓂⓈ Æ ⓄⒹ VISA, ✸

The Island Grill Room : Rest (buffet lunch Monday-Saturday)/dinner a la carte 34/45 – **124 rm** ☑ ✿130 – ✿✿140, 5 suites.
◆ Opened in 2005 around the core of an 18C house: stylish and open-plan. Superbly equipped spa. Modish rooms in two themes: choose from Urban or highly individual Ocean! Island Grill Room serves an eclectic range of dishes.

CORROFIN (Cora Finne) *Clare* **712** E 9.
Dublin 228.5 – Gort 24 – Limerick 51.5.

⌂ **Fergus View** without rest., Kilnaboy, North : 3 ¼ km on R 476 ℘ (065) 6837606, *deck ell@indigo.ie, Fax (065) 6837192,* <, 🐝 – ↦ **P**. 🎖
1 March-27 October – **6 rm** 🖭 ✝50/55 – ✝✝70/74.
♦ Originally built for the owner's grandfather as a schoolhouse, with good country-side views. Conservatory entrance into cosy lounge with piles of books. Pristine bedrooms.

CRAUGHWELL (Creachmhaoil) *Galway* **712** F 8.
Env. : *Loughrea (St Brendan's Cathedral★), SE : 13 km by N 6 – Turoe Stone★, E : 16 km by N 6 and R 350.*
Dublin 194.5 – Galway 24 – Limerick 88.5.

🏠🏠 **St Clerans** 🐝, Northeast : 5 ½ km off N 6 taking second turning left after 1 ½ km then veering left after a further 3 ¼ km ℘ (091) 846555, *stclerans@iol.ie, Fax (091) 846752,* <, 🐝, 🐝, ♨ – ↦ ⌲ **P**. 🐝 🖭 🖭 **VISA**. 🎖
closed 24-27 December – **Rest** (booking essential for non-residents) (dinner only) 65 **s.** – **12 rm** 🖭 – ✝✝275/475.
♦ Grand, secluded 18C country house stands in rolling meadowland with fishing and hunting nearby. Former home of film director John Huston. Finely furnished and themed rooms. Great finesse in evidence in the elegant dining room.

CROOKHAVEN (An Cruachán) *Cork* **712** C 13.
Dublin 373.5 – Bantry 40 – Cork 120.5.

⌂ **Galley Cove House** 🐝 without rest., West : ¾ km on R 591 ℘ (028) 35137, *info@gal leycovehouse.com, Fax (028) 35137,* <, 🐝 – ↦ **P**. 🐝 **VISA**. 🎖
10 March-October – **4 rm** 🖭 ✝45/60 – ✝✝75/90.
♦ Perched overlooking eponymous bay and its pleasant harbour. Conservatory breakfast room has bamboo seating. Rooms are neat and tidy, and enhanced by colourful fabrics.

CROSSMOLINA (Crois Mhaoilíona) *Mayo* **712** E 5 *Ireland G. – pop. 1 103.*
Env. : *Errew Abbey★, SE : 9½ km by R 315.*
Exc. : *Céide Fields★ AC, N : 24 km by R 315 and R 314 W – Killala★, NE : 16 km by R 315 and minor road – Moyne Abbey★, NE : 18 km by R 115, minor road to Killala, R 314 and minor road – Rosserk Abbey★, NE : 18 km by R 115, minor road to Killala, R 314 and minor road.*
Dublin 252.5 – Ballina 10.5.

🏠 **Enniscoe House** 🐝, Castlehill, South : 3 ¼ km on R 315 ℘ (096) 31112, *dj@ennis coe.com, Fax (096) 31773,* <, 🐝, 🐝, ♨ – ↦ **P**. 🐝 **VISA**
April-October – **Rest** (booking essential for non-residents) (dinner only) 50 **s.** ♀ – **6 rm** 🖭 ✝110/140 – ✝✝196/224.
♦ Georgian manor, overlooking Lough Conn, on Enniscoe estate with walled garden and heritage centre. Hallway boasts original family tree; antique beds in flower-filled rooms. Home cooked country dishes served in the dining room.

DALKEY (Deilginis) *Dublin* **712** N 8.
See : *Killiney Bay (<★★), S : by coast road.*
Dublin 13 – Bray 9.5.

XX **Jaipur,** 21 Castle St., ℘ (01) 285 0552, *dalkey@jaipur.ie, Fax (01) 284 0900* – 🍽. 🐝 🖭 **VISA**
closed 25-26 December – **Rest** - Indian - (dinner only) 50 and a la carte 30/40.
♦ Central location and smart, lively, brightly coloured, modern décor. Well-spaced, linen-clad tables. Warm, friendly ambience. Contemporary Indian dishes.

Your opinions are important to us:
please write and let us know about your discoveries and experiences –
good and bad!

DINGLE (An Daingean) *Kerry* **712** B 11 *Ireland G. – pop. 1 828.*

See : *Town★ – St Mary's Church★ – Diseart (stained glass★ AC).*

Env. : *Gallarus Oratory★★, NW : 8 km by R 559 – NE : Connor Pass★★ – Kilmalkedar★, NW : 9 km by R 559.*

Exc. : *Dingle Peninsula★★ – Connor Pass★★, NE : 8 km by minor road – Stradbally Strand★★, NE : 17 km via Connor Pass – Corca Dhuibhne Regional Museum★ AC, NW : 13 km by R 559 – Blasket Islands★, W : 21 km by R 559 and ferry from Dunquin.*

🛈 *The Quay ℰ (066) 9151188.*

Dublin 347.5 – Killarney 82 – Limerick 153.

Plan opposite

🏨 **Dingle Skellig** 🦢, ℰ (066) 9150200, *reservations@dingleskellig.com,* Fax (066) 9151501, ≤, ⓥ, 🛌, ≋s, ⬚, 🍽 – 🛗 🌥 🏋 **P** – 🔏 250. 🌑 🅰 ⓪ **VISA**. ⬚

                                                     Y e

weekends only November-December and restricted opening January-February – **Rest** (bar lunch)/dinner 32/49 **s.** ⚱ – **108 rm** ⌁ ✚138 – ✚✚140/236, 2 suites.

♦ Large purpose-built hotel with views of Dingle Bay. Interior decorated in a modern style with good levels of comfort: the smartest executive rooms are on the third floor. Restaurant makes most of sea and harbour view.

🏨 **Benners** without rest., Main St, ℰ (066) 9151638, *info@dinglebenners.com,* Fax (066) 9151412 – 🛗 🌥 **P**. 🌑 🅰 ⓪ **VISA**. ⬚

                                                     Z b

closed 18-26 December – **52 rm** ⌁ ✚80/127 – ✚✚110/204.

♦ Traditional-style property located on town's main street. Comfortable public areas include lounge bar and guest's sitting room. Rooms in extension have a more modern feel.

🏨 **Emlagh Country House** without rest., ℰ (066) 9152345, *info@emlaghhouse.com,* Fax (066) 9152369, ≤, 🌥 🌥 **P**. 🌑 🅰 **VISA**. ⬚

                                                     Y d

15 March-October – **10 rm** ⌁ ✚125/165 – ✚✚190/290.

♦ Modern hotel in Georgian style. Inviting lounge with a log fire and well-fitted, antique furnished bedrooms: the colours and artwork of each are inspired by a local flower.

🏨 **Heatons** without rest., The Wood, West : ¾ km on R 559 ℰ (066) 9152288, *heatons@iol.ie,* Fax (066) 9152324, ≤, 🌥 – 🌥 **P**. 🌑 **VISA**. ⬚

                                                     Y c

closed 17-26 December – **16 rm** ⌁ ✚55/99 – ✚✚90/136.

♦ Carefully planned and recently built house with a spacious, modern look: comfortably furnished lounge area and bedrooms take up the contemporary style.

🏨 **Milltown House** 🦢 without rest., ℰ (066) 9151372, *info@milltownhousedingle.com,* Fax (066) 9151095, ≤, 🌥 – 🌥 **P**. 🌑 🅰 **VISA**. ⬚

                                                     Y b

28 April- 26 October – **10 rm** ⌁ ✚100/130 – ✚✚130/160.

♦ Warm, welcoming establishment in a good location outside Dingle. Conservatory breakfast room and personally furnished and comfortable bedrooms, all with seating area.

🏨 **Doyle's Townhouse**, 5 John St, ℰ (066) 9151174, *cdoyles@iol.ie,* Fax (066) 9151816 – 🌑 🅰 **VISA**. ⬚

                                                     Z d

14 February-November and 27 December-7 January – **Rest** – (see **Doyle's Seafood Bar** below) – **8 rm** ⌁ ✚120/145 – ✚✚150/156.

♦ Attractive house in the town centre. Tasteful guests' lounge with some antique furniture. Well-run accommodation including bedrooms decorated in homely, traditional style.

🏨 **Greenmount House** without rest., Gortonora, ℰ (066) 9151414, *info@greenmounthouse.com,* Fax (066) 9151974, ≤, 🌥 – 🌥 **P**. 🌑 **VISA**. ⬚

                                                     Z c

February-November – **12 rm** ⌁ ✚100/125 – ✚✚120/170.

♦ Large, yellow painted, extended house located above the town. Two comfortable lounges and a conservatory-style breakfast room. Newest bedrooms most comfortably appointed.

🏠 **Pax House** 🦢 without rest., Upper John St, ℰ (066) 9151518, *paxhouse@iol.ie,* Fax (066) 9152461, ≤, 🌥 – 🌥 **P**. 🌑 **VISA**

                                                     Y f

March-December – **12 rm** ⌁ ✚50/75 – ✚✚120.

♦ Family run guesthouse sited away from the town in an elevated position. Lounges are comfortable and traditionally appointed; bedrooms are colourful and personally designed.

🏠 **Coastline** without rest., The Wood, ℰ (066) 9152494, *coastlinedingle@eircom.net,* Fax (066) 9152493, ≤, 🌥 – 🌥 **P**. 🌑 **VISA**. ⬚

                                                     Y x

March - November – **7 rm** ⌁ ✚50/88 – ✚✚80/100.

♦ Hard to miss modern guesthouse with bright pink façade. Comfy, homely interior with lots of local info. All rooms have pleasant view; those at the front face Dingle harbour.

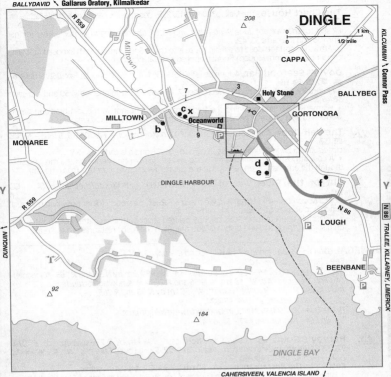

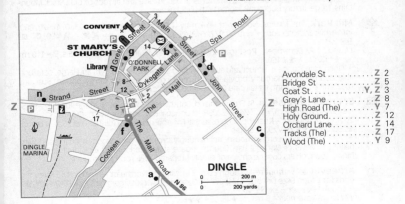

⚫ ⌂ **Bambury's** without rest., Mail Rd, ℰ (066) 9151244, *info@bamburysguesthouse.com*, Z a
  Fax (066) 9151786, ← – ⅙✕ 🚗 **P.** 🅼🅴 *VISA*. ⅗
  12 rm ⌂ ⁑35/70 – ⁑⁑70/120.
  ♦ Modern house located just on the edge of the town with garden and views over the sea. Large lounge and wood-floored breakfast room. Well-kept, comfortable bedrooms.

977

REPUBLIC OF IRELAND

✗ **The Chart House,** The Mall, ☎ (066) 9152255, *charthse@iol.ie*, Fax (066) 9152255 – 🗐.
MC VISA
Z f
closed Tuesday except June-September and restricted opening in winter – Rest (dinner only) 35 and a la carte 35/42.
• Attractive cottage close to a main route into town. Snug interior with exposed flint walls and wooden ceiling. Modern flourish applied to local ingredients.

✗ **Doyle's Seafood Bar,** 4 John St, ☎ (066) 9151174, *cdoyles@iol.ie*, Fax (066) 9151816 –
🗐. **MC AE ① VISA**
Z d
14 February-November and 27 December-7 January – Rest (dinner only) 30 and a la carte 36/47 ♀.
• Formerly a bar and retaining the traditional pubby interior with bric-a-brac and simple wooden tables. Offers a classic style menu with seafood as the backbone.

✗ **The Half Door,** 3 John St, ☎ (066) 9151600, *halfdoor@iol.ie*, Fax (066) 9151883 – 🗐. **MC**
AE VISA
Z j
closed January and Sunday – Rest - Seafood - 32/38 and a la carte 32/55 ♀.
• A cosy atmosphere amid beams, wood and stone flooring. Menus offer a mix of dishes though the emphasis is on seafood in the classic French style. Lobsters from the tank.

✗ **Out of the Blue,** Waterside, ☎ (066) 9150811, *info@outoftheblue.ie*, 🏠 – **MC**
VISA
Z n
closed November- mid March and Wednesday – Rest - Seafood - (dinner booking essential) (lunch bookings not accepted) a la carte 28/45.
• Pleasingly unpretentious, this brightly painted shack with corrugated iron roof has fish on display at the front, and tasty seafood menus in the rustic restaurant to the rear.

DONEGAL (Dún na nGall) *Donegal* 712 H 4 *Ireland G.* – pop. 2 453.
See : *Donegal Castle★ AC.*
Exc. : *Donegal Coast★★ – Cliffs of Bunglass★★, W : 48¼ km by N 56 and R 263 – Glencolmcille Folk Village★★ AC, W : 53 km by N 56 and R 263 – Rossnowlagh Strand★★, S : 35½ km by N 15 and R 231 – Trabane Strand★, W : 58 km by N 56 and R 263.*
✈ *Donegal Airport* ☎ (074) 954824.
🛈 *The Quay* ☎ (074) 9721148, *irelandnorthwest@eircom.net.*
Dublin 264 – Londonderry 77 – Sligo 64.5.

🏨 **Harvey's Point** ⬩, Lough Eske, Northeast : 7 ¼ km by T 27 (Killybegs rd) ☎ (074)
9722208, *info@harveyspoint.com*, Fax (074) 9722352, ≤ Louch Eske, 🐟, 🌳, 🎱 – 🛗 ↔ ✆
& 🅿 – 🕍 300. **MC AE ① VISA**
Rest – (see *The Restaurant* below) – 60 rm ☲ ✚195 – ✚✚290, 4 suites.
• Large hotel in tranquil setting on shores of Lough Eske and at foot of Blue Stack Mountains. Large, luxury bedrooms, some with Lough views.

🏨 **Mill Park,** The Mullins, Northwest : ¾ km by N 56 on Letterbarrow rd ☎ (074) 9722880,
info@millparkhotel.com, Fax (074) 9722640, ⓠ, 🎱, 🏊, 🌳 – 🛗 ↔ & 🅿 – 🕍 400. **MC AE**
VISA 🍴
closed 24-27 December – Rest (carvery lunch)/dinner 35 and a la carte 35/45 s. ♀ – 110 rm
☲ ✚115/145 – ✚✚150/195.
• Open-plan lounge in timber and stone leads to a well-equipped gym and large, comfortable bedrooms generously provided with mod cons - a useful family option. Spacious mezzanine restaurant; its tall pine trusses lend a rustic feel.

🏨 **St Ernan's House** ⬩, St Ernan's Island, Southwest : 3½ km by N 267 ☎ (074) 9721065,
res@sainternans.com, Fax (074) 9721098, ≤ Donegal Bay, 🌳, 🎱 – ↔ 🅿. **MC VISA** 🍴
20 April-28 October – Rest (booking essential for non-residents) (dinner only) 52 – 4 rm ☲
✚230/290 – ✚✚230/290, 2 suites.
• Very attractive Georgian house, enchantingly secluded on a wooded tidal island with delightful views of Donegal Bay. Country house-style interiors and individual bedrooms. Dining room offers concise menus of simply prepared, well sourced produce.

⌂ **Ardeevin** ⬩ without rest., Lough Eske, Barnesmore, Northeast : 9 km by N 15 following
signs for Lough Eske Drive ☎ (074) 9721790, *seanmcginty@eircom.net*, Fax (074) 9721790,
≤ Lough Eske, 🌳 – ↔ 🅿. 🍴
17 March-November – 5 rm ☲ ✚45/55 – ✚✚65/70.
• Inviting, individual rooms, almost all with superb views of Lough Eske and the quiet countryside. Hearty Irish breakfasts with fresh bread baked by the long-standing owners.

⌂ **Island View House** without rest., Ballyshannon Rd, Southwest : 1 ¼ km on R 267
☎ (074) 9722411, *dowds@indigo.ie*, ≤, 🌳 – ↔ 🅿. 🍴
closed Christmas – 4 rm ☲ ✚45/50 – ✚✚62/68.
• Simple, homely establishment overlooking Donegal Bay. Though a modern building, it has a traditional appearance and style. Neatly kept bedrooms.

XX **The Restaurant** (at Harvey's Point), Lough Eske, Northeast : 7 ¼ km by T 27 (Killybegs rd) ℘ (074) 9722208, Fax (074) 9722352, ≤ Lough Eske, 🌳 – ▤ 🅿 ⬚ 🆎 ⑩ VISA
closed Sunday dinner, Monday and Tuesday November-March – **Rest** 30/65 s. ⬚.
   ◆ Wonderful views in a loughside setting. Very comfy, spacious cocktail lounge and bar.
Huge restaurant: appealing menu uses regional ingredients and international elements.

at Laghy South : 5½ km on N 15 – ✉ Donegal.

🏛 **Coxtown Manor** ⬚, South : 3 km. on Ballintra rd ℘ (074) 973 4575, coxtownma
nor@oddpost.com, Fax (074) 973 4576, 🌳, ⬚ – ⬚ 🅿 ⬚ 🆎 VISA
February-October and December – **Rest** (closed Monday except July-August) (booking
essential) (dinner only) 45 s. – **9 rm** ⬚ ✦114/138 – ✦✦170/212.
   ◆ Serenely located, this attractive, creeper-clad Georgian house boasts a comfy, country-
house style sitting room and bedrooms which have a warm aura of luxury about them.
Affable Belgian owner guarantees top-notch desserts using chocolate from his homeland!

DONNYBROOK (Domhnach Broc) Dublin **712** N 8 – see Dublin.

DOOGORT (Dumha Goirt) Mayo **712** B 5/6 – see Achill Island.

DOOLIN (Dúlainm) Clare **712** D 8 Ireland G.
   Env. : The Burren★★ (Cliffs of Moher★★★, Scenic Route★★, Aillwee Cave★ AC (Water-
fall★★), Poulnabrone Portal Tomb★, Corcomroe Abbey★, Kilfenora Crosses★, Burren Cen-
tre★ AC).
   Dublin 275 – Galway 69 – Limerick 80.5.

🏛 **Aran View House**, Coast Rd, Northeast : ¾ km ℘ (065) 7074420, bookings@aran
view.com, Fax (065) 7074540, ≤, 🌳, ⬚ – ⬚ ⬚ 🅿 ⬚ ⑩ VISA
Easter-October – **Rest** (closed Sunday) (dinner only) a la carte 35/42 – **19 rm** ⬚ ✦70/80 –
✦✦120/160.
   ◆ Georgian house set in 100 acres of working farmland, located on the main coastal road.
Well-kept public areas and bedrooms, some in adjacent converted barn. Simply styled
restaurant with a snug feel and traditional furnishings.

🏠 **Ballyvara House** ⬚, Southeast : 1 km ℘ (065) 7074467, info@ballyvarahouse.ie,
Fax (065) 7074868, ≤, 🌳, ⬚, ⬚ – ⬚ ⬚ 🅿 ⬚ 🆎 VISA ⬚
closed March - October – **Rest** (closed Sunday-Tuesday) (dinner only) 35 and a la carte
29/38 – **9 rm** ⬚ ✦60/90 – ✦✦80/120.00, 2 suites.
   ◆ Pleasant rural views from this 19C former farm cottage, close to tourist village. Comfy
lounge with squashy sofas; outside a smart decked courtyard. Bright, impressive rooms.
Neatly laid dining room with Irish dishes predominant.

↑ **Cullinan's**, ℘ (065) 7074183, cullinans@eircom.net, Fax (065) 7074239, 🌳 – ⬚ 🅿 ⬚
VISA ⬚
closed 17 - 15 February – **Rest** – (see **Restaurant** below) – **8 rm** ⬚ ✦40/70 – ✦✦60/90.
   ◆ Friendly guesthouse in attractive village. Spotless facilities including small sitting room
and pine-furnished bedrooms, some overlooking a little river.

X **Restaurant** (at Cullinan's), ℘ (065) 7074183, cullinans@eircom.net, Fax (065) 7074239 –
🅿 ⬚ VISA
Closed 17 December - 15 February – **Rest** (closed Wednesday) (booking essential) (dinner
only) 30 and a la carte 34/47.
   ◆ Simple wood floored dining room. Friendly service and charming setting with garden
views and fresh flowers. Interesting contemporary menu uses local produce.

DROGHEDA (Droichead Átha) Louth **712** M 6 Ireland G. – pop. 31 020.
   See : Town★ – Drogheda Museum★ – St Laurence Gate★.
   Env. : Monasterboice★★, N : 10½ km by N 1 – Boyne Valley★★, on N 51 – Termonfeckin★,
NE : 8 km by R 166.
   Exc. : Newgrange★★★, W : 5 km by N 51 on N 2 – Mellifont Old Abbey★ AC – Knowth★.
   🏌 Seapoint, Termonfeckin ℘ (041) 9822333 – 🏌 Towneley Hall, Tullyallen ℘ (041) 42229.
   🚌 Bus Eireann Station, Donore Rd ℘ (041) 9837070 (May-September).
   Dublin 46.5 – Dundalk 35.5.

🏛 **The D.**, Scotch Hall, ℘ (041) 9811700, reservethed@monogramhotels.ie,
Fax (041) 9877702 – 🛗 ⬚ 📺 ⬚ 🅿 – 🔥 70. ⬚ 🆎 ⑩ VISA
closed 24-29 December – **Rest** (bar lunch)/dinner 40/50 s. – **104 rm** ⬚ ✦110/280 –
✦✦110/280.
   ◆ Stylish hotel adjacent to shopping centre on banks of the Boyne. Modish, minimalistic
interiors include two comfy bars and spacious bedrooms with a cool, clinical appeal. Popular menus in the airy dining room.

Boyne Valley H. and Country Club, Southeast : 2 km by N 1 ℘ (041) 9837737, *reservations@boyne-valley-hotel.ie, Fax (041) 9839188*, ℔, ⇌, 🖵, ⟷, ♨, ✖ – 🛗 ✜,
▤ rest, ✆ ⁺⁺ 🅿 – 🔼 500. 🆖 ⒶⒺ ⓄⒾ *VISA*
Rest 25/30 and dinner a la carte 32/42 ♀ – **72 rm** 🖙 ✚85 – ✚✚160.
◆ Extended, ivy-clad house dating from the 1840s, with some character and set in pretty grounds. Well run and kept with well-proportioned bedrooms, the best have garden views. Basement bistro with original cast-iron range; intimate booths.

Boyne Haven House without rest., Dublin Rd, Southeast : 4 km on N 1 ℘ (041) 9836700, *taramcd@ireland.com*, ⟷ – ✜ 🅿 🆖 *VISA* ✖
4 rm 🖙 ✚50/60 – ✚✚75/85.
◆ Whitewashed bungalow on the main road into town. Spotlessly kept accommodation with a homely atmosphere. Co-ordinated bedroom décor. Good breakfast menu.

DRUMSHANBO (Droim Seanbhó) *Leitrim* **712** H 5.
Env. : *Arigna Scenic Drive*★ (≤★), N : 8 km by R 280.
Dublin 166 – Carrick-on-Shannon 14.5 – Sligo 48.

Ramada H. and Suites at Lough Allen, on Keadew rd ℘ (071) 9640100, *info@loughallenhotel.com, Fax (071) 9640101*, ≤, ⟨🕭⟩, ℔, ⇌, 🖵, ⟍ – 🛗 ✜, ▤ rest, ✆ 🖐
🅿 – 🔼 230. 🆖 ⒶⒺ *VISA* ✖
closed 25-26 December **Rushes** : **Rest** (dinner only and Sunday lunch) 35 **s**. and a la carte 31/43 – **72 rm** 🖙 ✚90/95 – ✚✚140/210.
◆ Purpose-built hotel, beside Lough Allen, with part-stone exterior. Airy, up-to-the-minute bar. Pleasant terrace includes hot tub. Well-equipped spa. Minimalist, modern rooms. Dining room boasts stylish blond wood and seasonal menus.

Dublin, Georgian Doorways

DUBLIN - (Baile Átha Cliath)

712 N 7 *Ireland G. – pop. 1 004 614.*

Belfast 166 – Cork 248 – Londonderry 235.

TOURIST INFORMATION

🖪 *Bord Failte Offices, Baggot Street Bridge, ℰ (01) 602 4000; information@dublintourism.ie – Suffolk St – Arrivals Hall, Dublin Airport – The Square Shopping Centre, Tallaght.*

PRACTICAL INFORMATION

🛅 *Elm Park, Nutley House, Donnybrook ℰ (01) 269 3438,* GV.
🛅 *Milltown, Lower Churchtown Rd ℰ (01) 497 6090.*
🛅 *Royal Dublin, North Bull Island, Dollymount ℰ (01) 833 6346.*
🛅 *Forrest Little, Cloghran ℰ (01) 840 1763.*
🛅 *Lucan, Celbridge Rd, Lucan ℰ (01) 628 2106.*
🛅 *Edmondstown, Rathfarnham ℰ (01) 493 2461.*
🛅 *Coldwinters, Newtown House, St Margaret's ℰ (01) 864 0324.*
✈ *Dublin Airport : ℰ (01) 814 1111, N : 9 km. by N 1* BS.
Terminal : *Busaras (Central Bus Station) Store St.*
⛴ *to Holyhead (Irish Ferries) 2 daily (3 h 15 mn) – to Holyhead (Stena Line) 1-2 daily (3 h 45 mn) – to the Isle of Man (Douglas) (Isle of Man Steam Packet Co. Ltd) (2 h 45 mn/ 4 h 45 mn) – to Liverpool (P & O Irish Sea) (8 h).*

SIGHTS

See : *City*★★★ *Trinity College*★★ JY *– Old Library*★★★ *(Treasury*★★★, *Long Room*★★*) – Dublin Castle*★★ *(Chester Beatty Library*★★★*)* HY *– Christ Church Cathedral*★★ HY *– St Patrick's Cathedral*★★ HZ *– Marsh's Library*★★ HZ *– National Museum*★★ *(The Treasury*★★*)* KZ *– National Gallery*★★ KZ *– Newman House*★★ JZ *– Bank of Ireland*★★ JY *– Custom House*★★ KX *– Kilmainham Gaol Museum*★★ AT **M6** *– Kilmainham Hospital*★★ AT *– Phoenix Park*★★ *– National Botanic Gardens*★★ BS *– Marino Casino*★★ CS *– Tailors' Hall*★ HY *– City Hall*★ HY *– Temple Bar*★ HJY *– Liffey Bridge*★ JY *– Merrion Square*★ KZ *– Number Twenty-Nine*★ KZ **D** *– Grafton Street*★ JYZ *– Powerscourt Centre*★ JY *– Rotunda Hospital Chapel*★ JX *– O'Connell Street*★ *(GPO Building*★*)* JX *– Hugh Lane Municipal Gallery of Modern Art*★ JX **M4** *– Pro-Cathedral*★ JX *– Bluecoat School*★ BS **F** *– Guinness Museum*★ BT **M7** *– Rathfarnham Castle*★ AT *– Zoological Gardens*★ AS *– Ceol*★ BS **n**.

Env. : *The Ben of Howth*★ (≤★), *NE: 9½ km. by R 105* CS.

Exc. : *Powerscourt*★★ *(Waterfall*★★ AC*), S : 22½ km. by N 11 and R 117* EV *– Russborough House*★★★, *SW : 35½ km. by N 81* BT.

DUBLIN

City Centre Dublin.

The Merrion, Upper Merrion St, D2, ℰ (01) 603 0600, info@merrionhotel.com, Fax (01) 603 0700, ⓠ, Ⅰ♠, ⬚, ✿ – ⌷⌷, ✦ rm, ▤ ✆ ⇌ – 🛦 50. 🅐🅞 🄰🄴 ⑩ 𝘝𝘐𝘚𝘈, ✻
KZ e
Rest – (see **The Cellar** and **The Cellar Bar** below) – ⌣ 27 – **133 rm** ✦450 – ✦✦565, 10 suites.
♦ Classic hotel in series of elegantly restored Georgian town houses; many of the individually designed grand rooms overlook pleasant gardens. Irish art in opulent lounges.

The Westin, College Green, Westmoreland St, D2, ℰ (01) 645 1000, reservations.dublin@westin.com, Fax (01) 645 1234, Ⅰ♠ – ⌷⌷ ✦ ▤ 📺 ✆ ♿ – 🛦 250. 🅐🅞 🄰🄴 ⑩ 𝘝𝘐𝘚𝘈, ✻
JY n
The Exchange : Rest (closed Saturday lunch and Sunday dinner) a la carte 39/58 ♀ – **The Mint :** Rest a la carte 26/60 s. ♀ – ⌣ 26 – **150 rm** ✦519 – ✦✦519, 13 suites.
♦ Immaculately kept and consummately run hotel in a useful central location. Smart, uniform interiors and an ornate period banking hall. Excellent bedrooms with marvellous beds. Elegant, Art Deco 1920s-style dining in Exchange. More informal fare at The Mint.

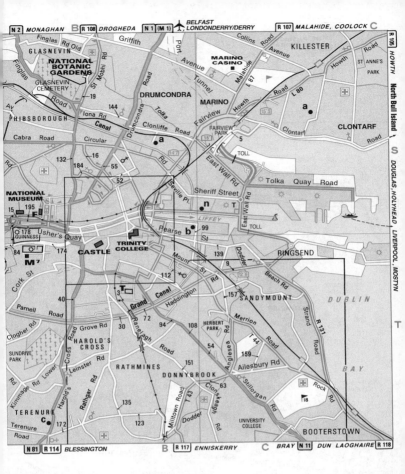

The Westbury, Grafton St, D2, ℰ (01) 679 1122, *westbury@jurysdoyle.com,*
Fax (01) 679 7078, I₅ – 🕸 🍴 🖥 📞 🔥 🚗 – 🔥 220. 🆎 🆎 ⓪ *VISA* ✁ JZ **b**
Russell Room : Rest 35/60 and a la carte 42/55 – **The Sandbank :** Rest *(closed Sunday and Bank Holiday)* a la carte 26/42 s. – 🖵 22 – **197 rm** ✦401 – ✦✦441, 8 suites.
♦ Imposing marble foyer and stairs lead to lounge famous for afternoon teas. Stylish Mandarin bar. Luxurious bedrooms offer every conceivable facility. Russell Room has distinctive, formal feel. Informal, bistro-style Sandbank.

Conrad Dublin, Earlsfort Terrace, D2, ℰ (01) 602 8900, *dublininfo@conradhotels.com,*
Fax (01) 676 5424, ⬍, I₅ – 🕸 🍴 🖥 📞 🔥 🚗 – 🔥 370. 🆎 🆎 ⓪ *VISA* ✁ JZ **w**
Alex : Rest - Seafood specialities - 30/40 and a la carte 36/58 ☿ – 🖵 25 – **192 rm** ✦470 – ✦✦485/670.
♦ Smart, business oriented international hotel opposite the National Concert Hall. Popular, pub-style bar. Spacious rooms with bright, modern décor and comprehensive facilities. Modern, bright and airy restaurant offers seafood specialities.

The Clarence, 6-8 Wellington Quay, D2, ℰ (01) 407 0800, *reservations@theclarence.ie,*
Fax (01) 407 0820, ⬍, I₅ – 🕸 🍴 🔥 P – 🔥 60. 🆎 🆎 ⓪ *VISA* ✁ HY **a**
closed 24-27 December – Rest – (see **The Tea Room** below) – 🖵 28 – **43 rm** ✦350 – ✦✦350, 5 suites.
♦ Discreet, stylish former warehouse overlooking river boasting 21C interior design. Small panelled library. Modern, distinctive rooms: quietest face courtyard on fourth floor.

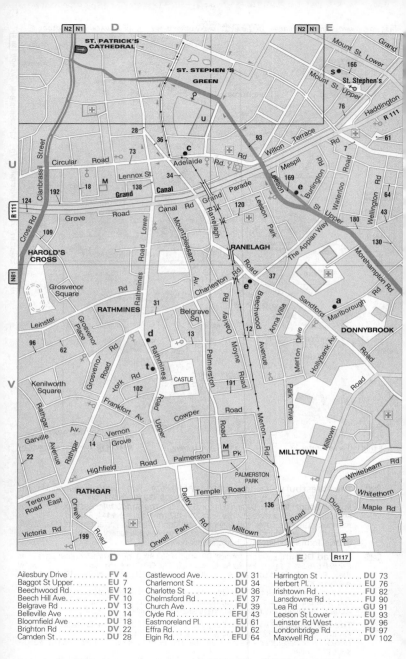

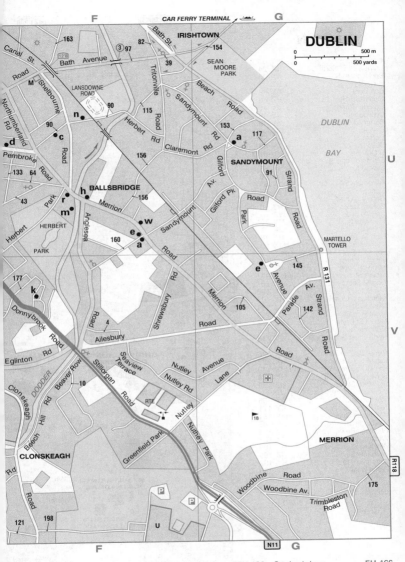

987

DUBLIN

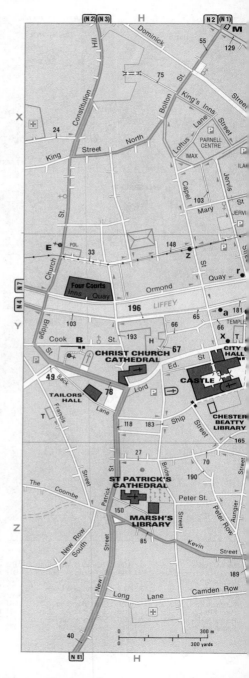

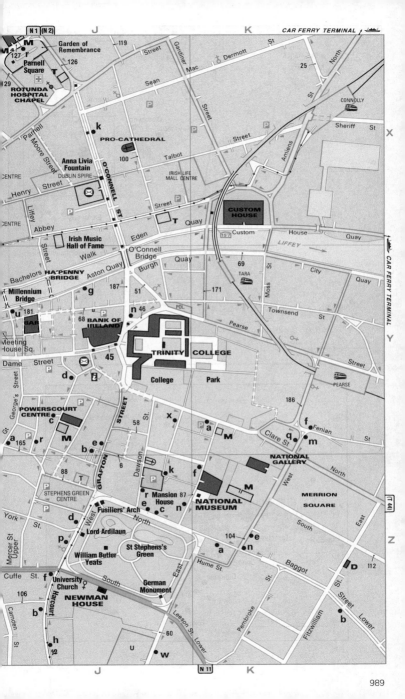

CAR FERRY TERMINAL

J K

Garden of
Remembrance

Parnell
Square

ROTUNDA
HOSPITAL
CHAPEL

PRO-CATHEDRAL

Anna Livia
Fountain

DUBLIN SPIRE

CENTRE

Henry Street

CENTRE

Irish Music
Hall of Fame

Bachelors

HA'PENNY
BRIDGE

Millennium
Bridge

Meeting
House Sq.

Dame Street

POWERSCOURT
CENTRE

STEPHENS GREEN
CENTRE

York St.

Fusiliers' Arch

Lord Ardilaun

William Butler
Yeats

University
Church

NEWMAN
HOUSE

Cuffe St.

Mercer St
Upper

Garden Street

Dermott

Mac

Sean

Street

CONNOLLY

Sheriff St

X

Talbot

IRISH LIFE
MALL CENTRE

CUSTOM
HOUSE

Amiens St

Street

Eden Quay

O'Connell
Bridge

Aston Quay

Burgh Quay

Quay

Custom House Quay

LIFFEY

CAR FERRY TERMINAL

City Quay

TARA

Townsend St

POL

Pearse

BANK OF
IRELAND

TRINITY COLLEGE

College Park

PEARSE

Clare St

NATIONAL
GALLERY

MERRION
SQUARE

Fenian St

North

West

North

East

South

Baggot St. Lower

Fitzwilliam St. Lower

Z

Mansion
House

NATIONAL
MUSEUM

St Stephens's
Green

German
Monument

Hume St.

Leeson St. Lower

Pembroke St.

Harcourt St.

Camden St

J N 11 K

T 44

25

119

126

127

29

k

100

187

51

171

69

46

68

45

186

165

58

88

6

87

104

112

60

106

989

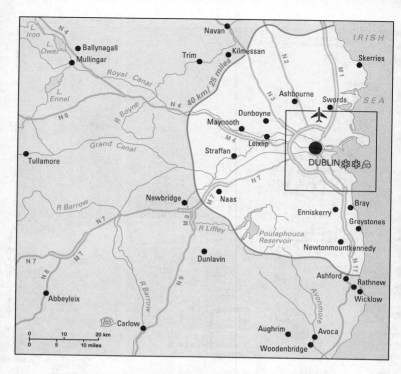

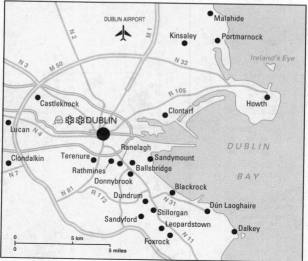

The Fitzwilliam, St Stephen's Green, D2, ✆ (01) 478 7000, enq@fitzwilliamhotel.com, Fax (01) 478 7878, ≤, ᴌᴓ – ⊟ ⊁ ≡ ✆ ⟺ – ⚿ 80. ⬤⬤ ᴀᴇ ⑩ 𝗩𝗜𝗦𝗔. ⅌
JZ d
Citron : Rest a la carte 25/50 s. – (see also *Thornton's* below) – ⌑ 19 – **136 rm** ✶220/400 – ✶✶220/400, 3 suites.
♦ Rewardingly overlooks the Green and boasts a bright contemporary interior. Spacious, finely appointed rooms offer understated elegance. Largest hotel roof garden in Europe. Very trendy, informal brasserie.

Brooks, Drury St, D2, ✆ (01) 670 4000, reservations@brookshotel.ie, Fax (01) 670 4455, ᴌᴓ, ⊜s – ⊟ ⊁ ≡ ✆ – ⚿ 50. ⬤⬤ ᴀᴇ 𝗩𝗜𝗦𝗔.
JY r
Francesca's : Rest (dinner only) a la carte 23/42 s. ⅌ – **98 rm** ⌑ ✶240/320 – ✶✶450/700.
♦ Commercial hotel in modish, boutique, Irish town house style. Smart lounges and stylish rooms exude contemporary panache. Extras in top range rooms, at a supplement. Fine dining with open kitchen for chef-watching.

Stephen's Green, Cuffe St, off St Stephen's Green, D2, ✆ (01) 607 3600, info@ocallaghanhotels.com, Fax (01) 478 1444, ᴌᴓ – ⊟ ⊁ ≡ ✆ ⟺ – ⚿ 50. ⬤⬤ ᴀᴇ ⑩ 𝗩𝗜𝗦𝗔. ⅌
JZ f
closed 25-27 December – **The Pie Dish :** Rest (closed lunch Saturday and Sunday) a la carte 35/60 s. – ⌑ 14 – **64 rm** ✶325 – ✶✶325, 11 suites.
♦ This smart modern hotel housed in an originally Georgian property frequented by business clients; popular Magic Glass bar. Bright bedrooms offer a good range of facilities. Bright and breezy bistro restaurant.

The Morrison, Lower Ormond Quay, D1, ✆ (01) 887 2400, reservations@morrisonhotel.ie, Fax (01) 874 4039 – ⊟ ⊁ ≡ ✆ – ⚿ 240. ⬤⬤ ᴀᴇ ⑩ 𝗩𝗜𝗦𝗔. ⅌
HY r
closed 24-27 December – **Halo :** Rest (bar lunch Saturday-Sunday) a la carte 33/46 s. ⅌ – ⌑ 22 – **135 rm** ✶340 – ✶✶340, 3 suites.
♦ Modern riverside hotel with ultra-contemporary interior by acclaimed fashion designer John Rocha. New rooms are particularly stylish. Relaxed dining room concentrates on Irish produce in modish and home-cooked blend of dishes.

The Gresham, 23 Upper O'Connell St, D1, ✆ (01) 874 6881, info@thegresham.com, Fax (01) 878 7175, ᴌᴓ – ⊟ ⊁ ≡ ᴓ. ℙ - ⚿ 400. ⬤⬤ ᴀᴇ ⑩ 𝗩𝗜𝗦𝗔. ⅌
JX k
23 : Rest (dinner only) a la carte 33/52 – **The Aberdeen :** Rest (dinner only) 26/45 – ⌑ 22 – **283 rm** ✶200/506 – ✶✶506/600, 6 suites.
♦ Long-established restored 19C property in a famous street offers elegance tinged with luxury. Some penthouse suites. Well-equipped business centre, lounge and Toddy's bar. The Aberdeen boasts formal ambience. 23 is named after available wines by glass.

Clarion H. Dublin IFSC, Excise Walk, International Financial Services Centre, D1, ✆ (01) 433 8800, info@clarionhotelifsc.com, Fax (01) 433 8811, ≤, ᴌᴓ, ⊜s, ◱ – ⊟ ⊁ ≡ ✆ ᴓ – ⚿ 120. ⬤⬤ ᴀᴇ ⑩ 𝗩𝗜𝗦𝗔.
CS n
closed 25 December – **Sinergie :** Rest - Italian - (closed lunch Saturday and Bank Holidays) 21/30 and a la carte 23/28 ⅌ – **Kudos :** Rest - Asian - (closed Sunday) (open all day) a la carte 19/34 s. ⅌ – ⌑ 22 – **154 rm** ✶165/255 – ✶✶170/265, 9 suites.
♦ In the heart of a modern financial district, a swish hotel for the business person; smart gym and light, spacious, contemporary rooms, some with balconies. Italian dining in clean-lined Sinergie. Kudos serves Asian menus.

Jurys Croke Park, Jones's Rd, D3, ✆ (01) 871 4444, info@crokepark.ie, Fax (01) 871 4400, ⌂, ᴌᴓ – ⊟ ⊁ ≡ ✆ ᴓ ⟺ – ⚿ 50. ⬤⬤ ᴀᴇ ⑩ 𝗩𝗜𝗦𝗔. ⅌
BS a
closed Christmas – Rest (bar lunch)/dinner a la carte 30/41 s. – ⌑ 19 – **230 rm** ✶189/440 – ✶✶189/440, 2 suites.
♦ Corporate styled hotel opposite Croke Park Stadium. Stylish 'Side Line' bar with terrace. Rooms are a strong point: spacious with good business amenities. Bistro boasts the Canal terrace and modern/Mediterranean influenced menus.

O'Callaghan Alexander, Fienian St, Merrion Sq, D2, ✆ (01) 607 3700, info@ocallaghanhotels.com, Fax (01) 661 5663, ᴌᴓ – ⊟ ⊁ ≡ ✆ ᴓ ⟺ – ⚿ 400. ⬤⬤ ᴀᴇ ⑩ 𝗩𝗜𝗦𝗔. ⅌
KY f
closed 24-26 December – **Caravaggio's :** Rest (bar lunch Saturday and Sunday) a la carte 25/35 s. – ⌑ 14 – **98 rm** ✶325 – ✶✶325, 4 suites.
♦ This bright corporate hotel, well placed for museums and Trinity College, has a stylish contemporary interior. Spacious comfortable rooms and suites with good facilities. Stylish contemporary restaurant with wide-ranging menus.

O'Callaghan Davenport, Lower Merrion St, off Merrion Sq, D2, ✆ (01) 607 3500, info@ocallaghanhotels.com, Fax (01) 661 5663, ᴌᴓ – ⊟ ⊁ ≡ ✆ ⟺ – ⚿ 275. ⬤⬤ ᴀᴇ ⑩ 𝗩𝗜𝗦𝗔. ⅌
KY m
Lanyon : Rest (closed lunch Saturday and Sunday) a la carte 35/60 s. – ⌑ 14 – **112 rm** ✶371 – ✶✶371, 2 suites.
♦ Sumptuous Victorian gospel hall façade heralds elegant hotel popular with business clientele. Tastefully furnished, well-fitted rooms. Presidents bar honours past leaders. Dining room with fine choice menu.

brownes, 22 St Stephen's Green, D2, ℰ (01) 638 3939, *info@brownesdublin.com,*
Fax (01) 638 3900 – |≝| ✥← ✆, 🆗 🆎 ⓪ 𝚅𝙸𝚂𝙰, ✗
JZ c
closed 25-26 December – **Rest** – (see **brownes brasserie** below) – � 20 – **11 rm** ✚210 –
✚✚280.

♦ Restored Georgian town house which successfully combines traditional charm with
modern comfort. Bedrooms are bold, minimal and stylish, some with benefit of notable
view.

O'Callaghan Mont Clare, Lower Merrion St, off Merrion Sq, D2, ℰ (01) 607 3800,
info@ocallaghanhotels.com, Fax (01) 661 5663 – |≝| ✥← 🔳 ⇦ 🚗 – 🕍 120. 🆗 🆎 ⓪ 𝚅𝙸𝚂𝙰,
✗
KY q
closed 24-26 December – **Goldsmiths :** Rest (dinner only) a la carte 30/40 s. – ⊒ 14 –
74 rm ✚253 – ✚✚253.

♦ Classic property with elegant panelled reception and tasteful comfortable rooms at
heart of Georgian Dublin. Corporate suites available. Traditional pub style Gallery bar. Informal restaurant with tried-and-tested menus.

Buswells, Molesworth St, D2, ℰ (01) 614 6500, *buswells@quinn-hotels.com,*
Fax (01) 676 2090, 𝕚𝕤 – |≝| ✥← 🅿. – 🕍 70. 🆗 🆎 ⓪ 𝚅𝙸𝚂𝙰, ✗
KZ f
closed 24-26 December – **Trumans :** Rest (carvery lunch)/dinner 47 – 65 rm ⊒ ✚110/240
– ✚✚130/275, 2 suites.

♦ Elegant little hotel in quiet central location offering modern amenities while retaining its
Georgian charm. Relax in cushioned lounge or cosy, pleasingly furnished rooms. Smart
Trumans for formal dining.

Quality H. Dublin City, Sir John Rogerson's Quay, Cardiff Lane, D2, ℰ (01) 643 9500,
info@qualityhoteldublin.com, Fax (01) 643 9510, 𝕚𝕤, ≋, 🔲 – ✥←, 🔳 rest, ✆, – 🕍 50. 🆗
🆎 ⓪ 𝚅𝙸𝚂𝙰, ✗
BS b
closed 23-27 December – **Rest** (bar lunch)/dinner 35 and a la carte 32/43 s. – ⊒ 14 –
211 rm ✚229 – ✚✚229.

♦ Based in 'new generation' quayside area. Sleek Vertigo bar named after U2 song. Impressive health club with large pool. Spacious, modern rooms, 48 boasting balconies. Irish
and European mix of dishes in open plan restaurant.

Harrington Hall without rest., 70 Harcourt St, D2, ℰ (01) 475 3497, *harringtonhall@eir*
com.net, Fax (01) 475 4544 – |≝| ✥← ✆, 🅿. 🆗 🆎 ⓪ 𝚅𝙸𝚂𝙰, ✗
JZ h
28 rm ⊒ ✚110/140 – ✚✚188/230.

♦ Two usefully located mid-terrace Georgian town houses. Friendly and well-run. Bright,
spacious, superior bedrooms with co-ordinated décor. Welcoming guest lounge.

Trinity Lodge, 12 South Frederick St, D2, ℰ (01) 617 0900, *trinitylodge@eircom.net,*
Fax (01) 617 0999 – 🔳. 🆗 🆎 ⓪ 𝚅𝙸𝚂𝙰, ✗
JY x
closed 23-26 December – **George's wine bar :** Rest (closed Sunday-Monday) a la carte
15/34 � – **16 rm** ⊒ ✚120/160 – ✚✚160/205.

♦ Elegant, centrally located Georgian town houses near local landmarks. Airy, well-furnished bedrooms with good level of comfort: the modern deluxe rooms are worth asking
for. Warm, welcoming wine bar.

Eliza Lodge without rest., 23-24 Wellington Quay, D2, ℰ (01) 671 8044, *info@dublin*
lodge.com, Fax (01) 671 8362, ← – |≝| ✥← 🔳. 🆗 🆎 𝚅𝙸𝚂𝙰, ✗
JY u
closed 24-29 December – **18 rm** ⊒ ✚85/110 – ✚✚130/160.

♦ Ideally placed for Temple Bar nightlife. Small and friendly hotel with comfortable, practical rooms; the balconied penthouse floor has fine river views.

Kilronan House without rest., 70 Adelaide Rd, D2, ℰ (01) 475 5266, *info@kilronan*
house.com, Fax (01) 478 2841 – ✥←. 🆗 🆎 𝚅𝙸𝚂𝙰, ✗
DU c
12 rm ⊒ ✚55/120 – ✚✚120/170.

♦ In the heart of Georgian Dublin, a good value, well-kept town house run by knowledgeable, friendly couple. Individually styled rooms; sustaining breakfasts.

Patrick Guilbaud, 21 Upper Merrion St, D2, ℰ (01) 676 4192, *restaurantpatrickguil*
baud@eircom.net, Fax (01) 661 0052 – 🔳 ⇦ 25. 🆗 🆎 ⓪ 𝚅𝙸𝚂𝙰
KZ e
closed 17 March, 25-26 December, Good Friday, Sunday and Monday – **Rest** 48 (lunch) and
a la carte 88/115 s. � ⌂.

Spec. Lobster ravioli in coconut scented cream. Veal sweetbread in liquorice with parsnip
sauce. Assiette of chocolate.

♦ Top class restaurant run by consummate professional offering accomplished Irish-influ-
enced dishes in elegant Georgian town house. Contemporary Irish art collection.

Thornton's (at The Fitzwilliam H.), 128 St Stephen's Green, D2, ℰ (01) 478 7008, *thorn*
tonsrestaurant@eircom.net, Fax (01) 478 7009 – 🔳 ⇦, 🆗 🆎 ⓪ 𝚅𝙸𝚂𝙰, ✗
JZ d
closed 2 weeks Christmas, Sunday and Monday – **Rest** 30/40 (lunch) and a la carte 91/104 ⊊
⌂

Spec. Sautéed prawns with prawn bisque, truffle sabayon. Suckling pig with trotter, glazed
turnip and poitin sauce. Orange and chocolate soufflé with raspberry sauce.

♦ Second floor style, offering interesting culinary ideas drawing on Irish and French influences; fine views too. Good value lunches. Walls hung with chef's striking photos.

XXX **Shanahan's on the Green,** 119 St Stephen's Green, D2, ☎ (01) 407 0939, *sales@shanahans.ie, Fax (01) 407 0940* – ▤. MC AE ◑ VISA JZ p
closed Christmas-New Year – **Rest** (booking essential) (dinner only and Friday lunch) 45 (lunch) and a la carte 76/105 ♀.
◆ Sumptuous Georgian town house; upper floor window tables survey the Green. Supreme comfort enhances your enjoyment of strong seafood dishes and choice cuts of Irish beef.

XXX ✿ **L'Ecrivain** (Clarke), 109A Lower Baggot St, D2, ☎ (01) 661 1919, *enquiries@lecrivain.com, Fax (01) 661 0617,* 余 – ▤ ⇔ 20. MC AE VISA KZ b
closed 23 December-4 January, Easter, Saturday lunch, Sunday and Bank Holidays – **Rest** (booking essential) 45/75 and dinner a la carte 75/93 ♀.
Spec. Dublin Bay prawn plate. Roast quail with white onion cream and braised leg. Lobster with cauliflower purée and spiced cauliflower beignets.
◆ Robust, well prepared, modern Irish menus with emphasis on fish and game. Well established, with business clientele at lunch. Attentive service from well-versed team.

XXX ✿ **Chapter One** (Lewis), The Dublin Writers Museum, 18-19 Parnell Sq, D1, ☎ (01) 873 2266, *info@chapteronerestaurant.com, Fax (01) 873 2330* – ▤ ⇔ 14. MC VISA JX r
closed first 2 weeks August, 24 December-8 January, Sunday, Monday and Bank Holidays – **Rest** 34 (lunch) and dinner a la carte 50/60 **s.** ♀.
Spec. Pithivier of wild mushrooms, pancetta and foie gras, celeriac purée. John Dory with broccoli pureé, mussels and tomato confit. Chocolate millefeuille with banana mousse and coffee coulis.
◆ In basement of historic building, once home to whiskey baron. Comfy restaurant with Irish art on walls. Interesting menu skilfully prepared with refined and original edge.

XX **The Tea Room** (at The Clarence H.), 6-8 Wellington Quay, D2, ☎ (01) 407 0813, *tearoom@theclarence.ie, Fax (01) 407 0826* – MC AE ◑ VISA HY a
closed 24-26 December and Saturday lunch – **Rest** (booking essential) 24/29 (lunch) and a la carte 37/65 ♀.
◆ Spacious elegant ground floor room with soaring coved ceiling and stylish contemporary décor offers interesting modern Irish dishes with hint of continental influence.

XX **brownes brasserie** (at brownes H.), 22 St Stephen's Green, D2, ☎ (01) 638 3939, *info@brownesdublin.ie, Fax (01) 638 3900* – ▤ ⇔ 35. MC AE ◑ VISA JZ c
closed Saturday lunch – **Rest** (booking essential) a la carte 39/57 ♀.
◆ Smart, characterful with a Belle Èpoque feel. On the ground floor of the eponymous Georgian town house, in central location, with interesting and appealing classic dishes.

XX **The Cellar** (at The Merrion H.), Upper Merrion St, D2, ☎ (01) 603 0630, *Fax (01) 603 0700* – ▤ 🚗. MC AE ◑ VISA KZ e
closed Saturday lunch – **Rest** 25 (lunch) and dinner a la carte 26/54 ♀.
◆ Smart open-plan basement restaurant with informal ambience offering well-prepared formal style fare crossing Irish with Mediterranean influences. Good value lunch menu.

XX **One Pico,** 5-6 Molesworth Pl, D2, ☎ (01) 676 0300, *eamonnoreilly@ireland.com, Fax (01) 676 0411* – ▤ ⇔ 45. MC AE ◑ VISA JZ k
closed 25 December - 4 January, and Sunday – **Rest** 25/35 and a la carte 40/55 **s.** ♀.
◆ Wide-ranging cuisine, classic and traditional by turns, always with an original, eclectic edge. Décor and service share a pleasant formality, crisp, modern and stylish.

XX **Rhodes D7,** The Capel Buildings, Mary's Abbey, D7, ☎ (01) 804 4444, *info@rhodesd7.com, Fax (01) 804 4447,* 余 – ▤. MC AE VISA HY z
closed dinner Sunday and Monday – **Rest** a la carte 32/47 ♀.
◆ Cavernous restaurant: take your pick from four dining areas. Bright, warm décor incorporating bold, colourful paintings accompanies classic Rhodes menus given an Irish twist.

XX **Les Frères Jacques,** 74 Dame St, D2, ☎ (01) 679 4555, *info@lesfreresjacques.com, Fax (01) 679 4725* – ▤. MC AE VISA HY x
closed 24 December-3 January, Saturday lunch, Sunday and Bank Holidays – **Rest** - French - 22/36 and a la carte 42/66 ♀.
◆ Smart and well established, offering well prepared, classic French cuisine with fresh fish and seafood a speciality, served by efficient French staff. Warm, modern décor.

XX **Peploe's,** 16 St Stephen's Green, D2, ☎ (01) 676 3144, *reservations@peploes.com, Fax (01) 676 3154* – ▤. MC AE VISA JZ e
closed 24-28 December – **Rest** a la carte 31/48.
◆ Fashionable restaurant - a former bank vault - by the Green. Irish wall mural, Italian leather chairs, suede banquettes. Original dishes with pronounced Mediterranean accents.

XX **Town Bar and Grill,** 21 Kildare St, D2, ☎ (01) 662 4724, *reservations@townbarandgrill.com, Fax (01) 662 3857* – ▤. MC AE ◑ VISA JZ n
Rest 602 (lunch) and dinner a la carte 40/63 ♀.
◆ Located in wine merchant's old cellars: brick pillars divide a large space; fresh flowers and candles add a personal touch. Italian flair in bold cooking with innovative edge.

XX **Saagar**, 16 Harcourt St, D2, ℰ (01) 475 5060, info@saagarindianrestaurants.com, Fax (01) 475 1151 – 🐼 🖭 🎟 𝒱𝐼𝒮𝒜
JZ b
closed 23-25 December, and Sunday – **Rest** - Indian - 13/25 and a la carte 14/33.
✦ Well-run restaurant serving subtly toned, freshly prepared Indian fare in basement of Georgian terraced house. Attentive service. Ring bell at foot of stairs to enter.

XX **Dobbin's**, 15 Stephen's Lane, (off Stephen's Place) off Lower Mount St, D2, ℰ (01) 661 9536, dobbinsbistro@g.mail.com, Fax (01) 661 3331, 🍴 – ▦ 🅿 ⇔ 40. 🐼 🖭 ⓞ
𝒱𝐼𝒮𝒜
EU s
closed 1 week Christmas-New Year, Saturday lunch, Sunday dinner and Bank Holidays –
Rest (booking essential) 25/35 and a la carte 25/54 ☍.
✦ In the unlikely setting of a former Nissen hut, and now with contemporary styling, this popular restaurant, something of a local landmark, offers good food to suit all tastes.

XX **Jacobs Ladder**, 4-5 Nassau St, D2, ℰ (01) 670 3865, dining@jacobsladder.ie,
Fax (01) 670 3868 – 🐼 🖭 ⓞ 𝒱𝐼𝒮𝒜
KY a
closed 2 weeks Christmas, 1 week August, 17 March, Sunday, Monday and Bank Holidays –
Rest (booking essential) 40 (dinner) and a la carte 48/58 s. ☕ ☍.
✦ Up a narrow staircase, this popular small first floor restaurant with unfussy modern décor and a good view offers modern Irish fare and very personable service.

XX **Siam Thai**, 14-15 Andrew St, D2, ℰ (01) 677 3363, siam@eircom.net, Fax (01) 670 7644 –
▦. 🐼 🖭 𝒱𝐼𝒮𝒜
JY d
closed 25-26 December and lunch Saturday and Sunday – **Rest** - Thai - 35 and a la carte 27/38.
✦ Invariably popular, centrally located restaurant with a warm, homely feel, embodied by woven Thai prints. Daily specials enhance Thai menus full of choice and originality.

XX **Jaipur**, 41 South Great George's St, D2, ℰ (01) 677 0999, dublin@jaipur.ie,
Fax (01) 677 0979 – 🐼 🖭 𝒱𝐼𝒮𝒜
JY a
closed 25-26 December – **Rest** - Indian - (dinner only) 20 and a la carte 25/50 ☍.
✦ Vivid modernity in the city centre; run by knowledgeable team. Immaculately laid, linen-clad tables. Interesting, freshly prepared Indian dishes using unique variations.

XX **Bang Café**, 11 Merrion Row, D2, ℰ (01) 676 0898, Fax (01) 676 0899 – ▦. 🐼
𝒱𝐼𝒮𝒜
KZ a
closed 1 week Christmas, and Sunday – **Rest** (booking essential) a la carte 26/49 ☍.
✦ Stylish feel, closely set tables and an open kitchen lend a lively, contemporary air to this established three-tier favourite. Menus balance the classical and the creative.

X **Pearl Brasserie**, 20 Merrion St Upper, D2, ℰ (01) 661 3572, info@pearl-brasserie.com,
Fax (01) 661 3629 – ▦. 🐼 🖭 𝒱𝐼𝒮𝒜
KZ n
closed Bank Holidays and lunch Saturday-Monday – **Rest** - French - 26 (lunch) and dinner a la carte 31/44 ☍.
✦ A metal staircase leads down to this intimate, vaulted cellar brasserie and oyster bar. Franco-Irish dishes served at granite-topped tables. Amiable and helpful service.

X **Eden**, Meeting House Sq, Temple Bar, D2, ℰ (01) 670 5372, eden@edenrestaurant.ie,
Fax (01) 670 3330, 🍴 – ▦ ⇔ 12. 🐼 🖭 𝒱𝐼𝒮𝒜
HY e
closed 25 December- 3 January and Bank Holidays – **Rest** 25 (lunch) and dinner a la carte 33/50 ☕ ☍.
✦ Modern minimalist restaurant with open plan kitchen serves good robust food. Terrace overlooks theatre square, at the heart of a busy arty district. The place for pre-theatre.

X **Mermaid Café**, 69-70 Dame St, D2, ℰ (01) 670 8236, info@mermaid.ie,
Fax (01) 670 8205 – ▦ ⇔ 25. 🐼 🖭 𝒱𝐼𝒮𝒜
HY d
closed 24-26 and 31 December, 1 January and Good Friday – **Rest** (booking essential) (Sunday brunch) 26 (lunch) and a la carte 32/46 ☍.
✦ This informal restaurant with unfussy décor and bustling atmosphere offers an interesting and well cooked selection of robust modern dishes. Efficient service.

X **L'Gueleton**, 1 Fade St, D2, ℰ (01) 675 3708 – 🐼 𝒱𝐼𝒮𝒜
JY c
closed 25 December - 1 January, Sunday and Bank Holidays – **Rest** - French - (bookings not accepted) a la carte 27/42 ☍.
✦ Busy, highly renowned recent arrival. Rustic style: mish-mash of roughed-up chairs and tables with candles or Parisian lamps. Authentic French country dishes full of flavour.

X **Bleu**, Joshua House, Dawson St, D2, ℰ (01) 676 7015, Fax (01) 676 7027 – ▦. 🐼 🖭
𝒱𝐼𝒮𝒜
JZ r
Rest a la carte 28/43 ☕ ☍.
✦ Distinctive modern interior serves as chic background to this friendly all-day restaurant. Appealing and varied menu, well executed and very tasty. Good wine selection.

X **Mackerel**, (first floor) Bewley's Building, Grafton St, D2, ℰ (01) 672 7719, info@mackerel.ie – ▦. 🐼 🖭 𝒱𝐼𝒮𝒜
JY e
closed 25 December and Bank Holidays – **Rest** - Seafood - a la carte 25/47 ☍.
✦ Above famous 1920s coffee shop. Fossilised marble, purple chenille and deep blue gel as one. Seasonally changing, market-fresh seafood dishes: spicing and eclectic touches.

La Maison des Gourmets, 15 Castlemarket, D2, ℰ (01) 672 7258, *Fax (01) 672 7238*,
🏠 – 🐶 AE ⓞ VISA
                 JY c
closed 25 December-2 January, Sunday and Bank Holidays – **Rest** - French - (bookings not accepted) (lunch only) a la carte 20/25 **s.**
  ❖ Neat, refurbished eatery on first floor above an excellent French bakery . Extremely good value Gallic meals with simplicity the key. Get there early or be prepared to wait!

The Cellar Bar (at The Merrion H.), Upper Merrion St, D2, ℰ (01) 603 0600, *info@merrionhotel.com*, *Fax (01) 603 0700* – 🛋, 🐶 AE ⓞ VISA
                 KZ e
closed Sunday – **Rest** (carving lunch) a la carte 30/45 ℤ.
  ❖ Characterful stone and brick bar-restaurant in the original vaulted cellars with large wood bar. Popular with Dublin's social set. Offers wholesome Irish pub lunch fare.

Clarendon, 32 Clarendon St, D2, ℰ (01) 679 2909, *Fax (01) 670 6900* – 🐶 AE VISA
                 JY
closed 25-28 December, 1-3 January and dinner Friday-Sunday – **Rest** (bookings not accepted) (Sunday brunch) a la carte 20/35 ℤ.
  ❖ Sleek, contemporary metal and glass dining pub on three levels. Chocolate leather box seats and scatter cushions. Modern menus all the way from casual to serious in style.

Ballsbridge *Dublin.*
Dublin 6.5.

Four Seasons, Simmonscourt Rd, D4, ℰ (01) 665 4000, *sales.dublin@fourseasons.com*, *Fax (01) 665 4099*, 🏊, ⅃₅, ≦, ⃞, 🏠 – 🔟 ⅃⅄ 🔟 🖴 P – 🎿 800. 🐶 AE VISA   FU e
Seasons : **Rest** 35/45 (lunch) and a la carte 58/91 – *The Cafe* : **Rest** a la carte 34/48 **s.** – 🖃 30 – **157 rm** ✦490 – ✦✦645, 40 suites 830.
  ❖ Every inch the epitome of international style - supremely comfortable rooms with every facility; richly furnished lounge; a warm mix of antiques, oils and soft piano études. Dining in Seasons guarantees luxury ingredients. Good choice menu in The Café.

The Berkeley Court, Lansdowne Rd, D4, ℰ (01) 6653200, *berkeleycourt@jurysdoyle.com*, *Fax (01) 6617238* – 🔟 ⅃⅄ 🔟 ℭ & 🛋 P – 🎿 450. 🐶 AE VISA. 🛇 FU c
Berkeley Room : **Rest** (closed Sunday dinner) 40/50 **s.** – *Palm Court Café* : **Rest** 30 (lunch) and dinner a la carte 40/50 **s.** – 🖃 30 – **182 rm** ✦399 – ✦✦399, 4 suites.
  ❖ Luxurious international hotel in former botanical gardens two minutes from the home of Irish rugby. Large amount of repeat business. Solidly formal feel throughout. Berkeley Room for elegant fine dining. Breakfast buffets a feature of Palm Court Café.

Herbert Park, D4, ℰ (01) 667 2200, *reservations@herbertparkhotel.ie*, *Fax (01) 667 2595*, 🏠, ⅃₅ – 🔟 ⅃⅄ 🔟 ℭ P – 🎿 100. 🐶 AE ⓞ VISA. 🛇 FU m
The Pavilion : **Rest** (closed dinner Sunday and Monday) 26 (lunch) and dinner a la carte 35/65 – 🖃 19 – **151 rm** ✦240 – ✦✦375, 2 suites.
  ❖ Stylish contemporary hotel. Open, modern lobby and lounges. Excellent, well-designed rooms with tasteful décor: fifth floor Executive rooms boast several upgraded extras. French-windowed restaurant with alfresco potential; oyster/lobster specialities.

The Schoolhouse, 2-8 Northumberland Rd, D4, ℰ (01) 667 5014, *reservations@schoolhousehotel.com*, *Fax (01) 667 5015*, 🏠 – 🔟 ⅃⅄ 🔟 ℭ P. 🐶 AE ⓞ VISA. 🛇
                 EU a
closed 24-26 December – *Canteen* : **Rest** (brunch Saturday and Sunday) 24 (lunch) and a la carte 28/42 ℤ – **31 rm** ✦165 – ✦✦199.
  ❖ Spacious converted 19C schoolhouse, close to canal, boasts modernity and charm. Inkwell bar exudes a convivial atmosphere. Rooms contain locally crafted furniture. Old classroom now a large restaurant with beamed ceilings.

Ariel House without rest., 50-54 Lansdowne Rd, D4, ℰ (01) 668 5512, *reservations@ariel-house.net*, *Fax (01) 668 5845* – ⅃⅄ ℭ P. 🐶 VISA. 🛇 FU n
37 rm 🖃 ✦79/109 – ✦✦89/200.
  ❖ Restored, listed Victorian mansion in smart suburb houses personally run, traditional small hotel. Rooms feature period décor and some antiques; comfy four poster rooms.

Bewley's, Merrion Rd, D4, ℰ (01) 668 1111, *bb@bewleyshotels.com*, *Fax (01) 668 1999*, 🏠 – ⅃⅄, 🍴 rest, ℭ & 🛋 – 🎿 30. 🐶 AE VISA. 🛇 FU a
closed 24-26 December – *O'Connells* (ℰ (01) 647 3400) : **Rest** (carvery lunch)/dinner 28/35 and a la carte 25/35 **s.** ℤ – 🖃 11 – **304 rm** ✦99/109 – ✦✦99/109.
  ❖ Huge hotel offers stylish modern accommodation behind sumptuous Victorian façade of former Masonic school. Location, facilities and value for money make this a good choice. Informal modern O'Connells restaurant, cleverly constructed with terrace in stairwell.

Aberdeen Lodge, 53-55 Park Ave, D4, ℰ (01) 283 8155, *aberdeen@iol.ie*, *Fax (01) 283 7877*, 🏠 – ⅃⅄ ℭ P. 🐶 AE VISA. 🛇 GV e
Rest (light meals) (residents only) a la carte 25/34 **s.** ℤ – **17 rm** 🖃 ✦109 – ✦✦159.
  ❖ Neat red brick house in smart residential suburb. Comfortable rooms with Edwardian style décor in neutral tones, wood furniture and modern facilities. Some garden views. Comfortable, traditionally decorated dining room.

Pembroke Townhouse without rest., 90 Pembroke Rd, D4, ☎ (01) 660 0277, *info@pembroketownhouse.ie, Fax (01) 660 0291* – ⎮ ⇔ ☎ P. MC AE ⓓ VISA. ⚘ FU d
closed 22 December-3 January – **48 rm** ☕ ★90/165 – ★★130/230.
◆ Period-inspired décor adds to the appeal of a sensitively modernised Georgian terrace town house in the smart suburbs. Neat, simple accommodation.

Glenogra House without rest., 64 Merrion Rd, D4, ☎ (01) 668 3661, *info@glenogra.com, Fax (01) 668 3698* – ⇔ ☎ P. MC AE ⓓ VISA. ⚘ FU w
closed 23 December-10 January – **13 rm** ☕ ★79/109 – ★★109/129.
◆ Neat and tidy bay-windowed house in smart suburb. Personally-run to good standard with bedrooms attractively decorated in keeping with a period property. Modern facilities.

XX **Siam Thai,** Sweepstake Centre, D4, ☎ (01) 660 1722, *siam@eircom.net, Fax (01) 660 1537* – ▤. MC AE ⓓ VISA FU h
closed 25-26 December, lunch Saturday and Sunday and Good Friday – **Rest** - Thai - 35 and a la carte 27/38 s.
◆ Unerringly busy restaurant that combines comfort with liveliness. Efficient staff serve authentic Thai cuisine, prepared with skill and understanding. Good value lunches.

X **Roly's Bistro,** 7 Ballsbridge Terrace, D4, ☎ (01) 668 2611, *ireland@rolysbistro.ie, Fax (01) 660 3342* – ▤ ⇔ 30. MC AE ⓓ VISA FU r
closed 25- 27 December – **Rest** (booking essential) 20/45 and a la carte 41/49 ☺ ♀.
◆ A Dublin institution: this roadside bistro is very busy and well run with a buzzy, fun atmosphere. Its two floors offer traditional Irish dishes and a very good value lunch.

X **Bella Cuba,** 11 Ballsbridge Terrace, D4, ☎ (01) 660 5539, *info@bella-cuba.com, Fax (01) 660 5539* – ▤. MC AE VISA FU r
closed lunch Saturday and Sunday – **Rest** - Cuban - (booking essential) 25 (lunch) and a la carte 41/49 ♀.
◆ Family-owned restaurant with an intimate feel. Cuban memoirs on walls, fine choice of cigars. Authentic Cuban dishes, employing many of the island's culinary influences.

REPUBLIC OF IRELAND

Donnybrook *Dublin.*

Dublin 6.5.

Marble Hall without rest., 81 Marlborough Rd, D4, ☎ (01) 497 7350, *marblehall@eircom.net* – ⇔ P. ⚘ EV a
closed Christmas – **3 rm** ☕ ★60/65 – ★★90/100.
◆ Georgian townhouse with effusive welcome guaranteed. Individually styled throughout, with plenty of antiques and quality soft furnishings. Stylish, warmly decorated bedrooms.

XX **Poulot's,** Mulberry Gardens, off Morehampton Rd, D4, ☎ (01) 269 3300, *Fax (01) 269 3260* – ▤. MC AE VISA FV k
closed 25 December- 6 January, Sunday and Monday – **Rest** 32 (lunch) and dinner a la carte 45/63 ♀.
◆ A light, airy ambience is enhanced by garden views from all tables. Vivid oils and prints liven up white walls. Modern, complex dishes with distinctive French starting point.

Ranelagh *Dublin.*

XX **Mint,** 47 Ranelagh, D6, ☎ (01) 497 8655, *info@mintrestaurant.ie, Fax (01) 497 9035* – ▤. MC AE ⓓ VISA EV e
closed 2 weeks Christmas, 2 weeks August, Sunday, Monday and Saturday lunch – **Rest** 32/65 37/52 ♀.
◆ South of city, a minimalist restaurant with frosted front window and an unfussy, modern interior. Complex cooking with French influences; tasting menus for the adventurous.

Rathmines *Dublin.*

Dublin 9.5.

Uppercross House, 26-30 Upper Rathmines Rd, D6, ☎ (01) 4975486, *enquiries@uppercrosshousehotel.com, Fax (01) 4975361* – ⎮ ⇔ ☎ P. MC AE ⓓ VISA DV d
closed 23-28 December – **Rest** (dinner only and lunch Friday-Sunday) a la carte 20/35 – **49 rm** ☕ ★69/119 – ★★112/158.
◆ Privately run suburban hotel in three adjacent town houses with modern extension wing. Good size rooms and standard facilities. Live music midweek in traditional Irish bar. Restaurant offers a mellow and friendly setting with welcoming wood décor.

XX **Zen,** 89 Upper Rathmines Rd, D6, ☎ (01) 4979428, *Fax (01) 49117288* – ▤. MC AE ⓓ VISA DV t
Rest - Chinese (Szechuan) - (dinner only and lunch Friday) 20 and a la carte 26/40.
◆ Renowned family run Chinese restaurant in the unusual setting of an old church hall. Imaginative, authentic oriental cuisine with particular emphasis on spicy Szechuan dishes.

Sandymount *Dublin.*

✗ **Itsa,** 6A Sandymount Green, D4, ℰ (01) 219 4676, *itsa@itsabagel.com, Fax (01) 219 4654* –
⊟. **◗☻ VISA** GU **a**
closed 25-26 December, 1 January, Good Friday and Easter Sunday – **Rest** (booking essential) a la carte 31/49 ♀.
   ◆ Dark wood and bright lime green chairs seduce the eye in this smart contemporary
restaurant in smart suburb. Traceability of ingredients key to tasty, easy-going menu.

Terenure *Dublin.*
Dublin 9.5.

✗✗ **Vermilion,** 1st Floor above Terenure Inn, 94-96 Terenure Road North, D6, South : 9½ km
by N 81 ℰ (01) 499 1400, *mail@vermilion.ie, Fax (01) 499 1300* – **◗☻ AE ◑ VISA** BT **c**
closed 25-26 December and Good Friday – **Rest** - Indian - (live jazz Thursday dinner) (dinner
only) a la carte 29/46 ♀.
   ◆ Smart restaurant above a busy pub in a residential part of town. Vividly coloured dining
room and efficient service. Well-balanced, modern Indian food with a Keralan base.

at Dublin Airport *North : 10½ km by N 1* – BS – *and M 1* – ⊠ *Dublin.*

🏨 **Crowne Plaza,** Northwood Park, Santry Demesne, Santry, D9, South : 3 ¼ km on R 132
ℰ (01) 8628888, *info@crowneplazadublin.ie, Fax (01) 8628800,* **I₆** – |‡| ⅍ ▤ ✆ ₺ **P** –
🚗 1000. **◗☻ AE ◑ VISA**. ⌘
Touzai : **Rest** - Asian influences - *(closed Saturday lunch)* (buffet lunch)/dinner 33 and a la
carte 27/41 **s.** ♀ – **Cinnabar :** **Rest** a la carte 21/28 **s.** ♀ – ⌑ 21 – **202 rm** ✶99/380 –
✶✶99/380, 2 suites.
   ◆ Next to Fingal Park, two miles from airport. Hotel has predominant Oriental style, extensive meeting facilities and modern, well-equipped rooms, some of Club standard. Cool,
clear-linedTouzai for Asian specialities. Stylish Cinnabar has extensive menu range.

🏨 **Hilton Dublin Airport,** Northern Cross, Malahide Rd, D17, East : 3 km by A 32 ℰ (01)
8661800, *reservations.dublinairport@hilton.com, Fax (01) 8661866,* **I₆** – |‡| ⅍ ▤ ✆ ₺ **P** –
🚗 550. **◗☻ AE ◑ VISA**. ⌘
Solas : **Rest** (dinner only and Sunday lunch)/dinner a la carte 40 **s.** – ⌑ 20 – **162 rm** ✶119 –
✶✶119, 4 suites.
   ◆ Opened in 2005, just five minutes from the airport, adjacent to busy shopping centre.
Modish feel throughout. State-of-the-art meeting facilities. Airy, well-equipped rooms.
Spacious dining room serves tried-and-tested dishes with distinct Irish flavour.

🏨 **Carlton Dublin Airport,** Old Airport Rd, Cloughran, on R 132 Santry rd ℰ (01) 866
7500, *info@carltondublinairport.com, Fax (01) 862 3114,* ⇐ – |‡| ⅍ ▤ ✆ ₺ **P** – 🚗 450.
◗☻ AE VISA. ⌘
closed 3 days Christmas – **Clouds :** **Rest** *(closed Sunday dinner-Monday)* (dinner only and
Sunday lunch)/dinner a la carte 34/47 – ⌑ 14 – **99 rm** ✶225/420 – ✶✶225/420, 1 suite.
   ◆ Purpose-built hotel on edge of airport. State-of-the-art conference rooms. Impressive
bedrooms, though many a touch compact, in warm colours with high level of facilities.
Fine dining restaurant: worldwide cooking accompanied by excellent views.

🏨 **Great Southern,** ℰ (01) 8446000, *sales@dubairport-gsh.com, Fax (01) 8446001* – |‡|
⅍ ✆ ₺ **P** – 🚗 450. **◗☻ AE ◑ VISA**. ⌘
closed 25 December – **Potters :** **Rest** *(closed Sunday-Monday)* (dinner only) a la carte 34/54
s. – **O'Deas Bar :** **Rest** (carvery lunch)/dinner a la carte 23/37 – ⌑ 15 – **227 rm** ✶139 –
✶✶149, 2 suites.
   ◆ Modern hotel catering for international and business travellers. Range of guest rooms,
all spacious and smartly furnished with wood furniture and colourful fabrics. Potters has a
spacious, formal feel. O'Deas Bar for intimate carvery menus.

at Clontarf *Northeast : 5½ km by R 105* – ⊠ *Dublin.*

🏨 **Clontarf Castle,** Castle Ave, D3, ℰ (01) 833 2321, *info@clontarfcastle.ie,*
Fax (01) 833 0418, **I₆** – |‡| ⅍ ✆ ₺ **P** – 🚗 500. **◗☻ AE VISA** CS **a**
closed 24-25 December – **Templars Bistro :** **Rest** (carvery lunch Monday-Friday)/dinner a
la carte 27/47 ♀ – ⌑ 23 – **108 rm** ✶295 – ✶✶295, 3 suites.
   ◆ Set in an historic castle, partly dating back to 1172. Striking medieval style entrance
lobby. Modern rooms and characterful luxury suites, all with cutting edge facilities. Restaurant with grand medieval style décor reminiscent of a knights' banqueting hall.

at Dundrum *Southeast : 8 km by N 11* – CT – ⊠ *Dublin.*

✗✗✗ **First Floor** (at Harvey Nichols), Town Square, Sandyford Rd, D16, ℰ (01) 291 0488,
michael.andrews@harveynichols.ie, Fax (01) 291 0489 – |‡| ▤ ⇔ 10. **◗☻ AE ◑ VISA**
closed 25-26 December and Sunday dinner – **Rest** 25/36 and dinner a la carte 45/57 ♀.
   ◆ Up the lift to ultra-stylish bar and plush, designer-led restaurant. Attentive, professional
service. Dishes are modern, seasonal and confident with a fine dining feel.

X **Cafe Mao,** Town Square, Sandyford Rd, D16, ℰ (01) 296 2802, *info@cafemao.com*, Fax (01) 296 2813, ☆ – ▤

Rest - South East Asian - (bookings not accepted) a la carte 24/38.

✦ Situated in an upmarket 21C shopping centre, this café has a smart terrace and balconies from which you can watch the elegant dancing fountains. Wide-ranging, Asian menus.

at Stillorgan *Southeast : 8 km on N 11 – CT – ⊠ Dublin.*

🏨 **Radisson SAS St Helen's,** Stillorgan Rd, D4, ℰ (01) 218 6000, *info.dublin@radisson sas.com*, Fax (01) 218 6010, ₤₅, ☞ – 淆 ⅍⇔ ▤ & ₤, P – 🔬 350. ⓌⓈ ﭏﺓﺓ ﻯ VISA. ᎘

Talavera : **Rest** - Italian - (dinner only) 45/70 and a la carte 31/54 s. Ⓨ – ⌂ 22 – **130 rm** ✵350 – ✵✵700, 21 suites.

✦ Imposing part 18C mansion with substantial extensions and well laid out gardens. Well run with good level of services. Smart modern rooms with warm feel and all facilities. Delicious antipasti table at basement Talavera.

🏨 **Stillorgan Park,** Stillorgan Rd, ℰ (01) 288 1621, *sales@stillorganpark.com*, Fax (01) 283 1610, ⓘ, ₤₅ – 淆 ✵⇔ ▤ & ₤ P – 🔬 600. ⓌⓈ ﭏﺓﺓ VISA. ᎘

closed 9-11 February and 23-26 December – **Purple Sage :** **Rest** (carvery lunch)/dinner 28/36 – **158 rm** ⌂ ✵109/170 – ✵✵119/220.

✦ Modern commercial hotel in southside city suburb. Spacious rooms with modern facilities. Interesting horse theme décor in large stone floored bar with buffet. Mosaics, frescoes and hidden alcoves add spice to popular Irish dishes in Purple Sage.

at Sandyford *Southeast : 9 km by N 11 – CT – off Leopardstown Rd – ⊠ Dublin.*

🏨 **The Beacon,** Beacon Court, Sandyford Business Region, D18, ℰ (01) 291 5000, *sales@thebeacon.com*, Fax (01) 291 5005, ☆ – 淆 ✵⇔, ▤ rest, ₤ ⇔ – 🔬 40. ⓌⓈ ﭏﺓﺓ VISA. ᎘

closed 25-26 December – **My Thai :** **Rest** - Thai - a la carte 20/30 Ⓨ – ⌂ 20 – **82 rm** ✵300 – ✵✵300.

✦ Ultra-stylish hotel with uniquely quirky entrance lobby featuring a chandelier on the floor and bed with central seating! Modish bar, low-key meeting rooms, sleek bedrooms. Funky, relaxed restaurant serving authentic Asian dishes.

at Foxrock *Southeast : 13 km by N 11 – CT – ⊠ Dublin.*

XX **Bistro One,** 3 Brighton Rd, D18, ℰ (01) 289 7711, *bistroone@eircom.net*, Fax (01) 207 0742 – ⓌⓈ VISA

closed 25 December-2 January, Sunday and Monday – **Rest** (booking essential) 20 (lunch) and a la carte 36/48.

✦ Pleasantly set and homely, with beams and walls of wine racks. Simple menu offers well-prepared, distinctively seasonal Irish, Asian or Italian classics. Passionate owner.

at Leopardstown *Southeast : 12 km by N 11 – GV – ⊠ Dublin.*

🏨 **Bewleys,** Central Park, D18, ℰ (01) 293 5000, *leopardstown@bewleyshotels.com*, Fax (01) 293 5099 – 淆 ✵⇔, ▤ rest, ₤ ⇔ – 🔬 30. ⓌⓈ ﭏﺓﺓ ﻯ VISA. ᎘

closed 24-25 December – **Brasserie :** **Rest** (carvery lunch)/dinner 25/30 and a la carte 19/25 s. Ⓨ – ⌂ 9 – **352 rm** ✵89 – ✵✵89.

✦ Handily placed next to racecourse, this modern hotel boasts smart bar with leather armchairs, decked terrace, and comfy, uniform bedrooms with good facilities. Informal brasserie with neutral, stylish tones.

at Clondalkin *Southwest : 12 km by N 7 or R 113 – AT – ⊠ Dublin.*

🏨 **Red Cow Moran,** Naas Rd, D22, Southeast : 3¼ km on N 7 at junction with M 50 ℰ (01) 459 3650, *redcowres@moranhotels.com*, Fax (01) 459 1588 – 淆 ✵⇔ ▤ ₤ & ₤ P – 🔬 700. ⓌⓈ ﭏﺓﺓ ﻯ VISA. ᎘

closed 24-26 December – **The Winter Garden :** **Rest** a la carte 30/60 Ⓨ – **120 rm** ⌂ ✵380 – ✵✵380, 3 suites.

✦ Sweeping lobby staircase gives a foretaste of this smart commercial hotel's mix of traditional elegance and modern design. Landmark Red Cow inn and Diva nightclub. Large characterful Winter Garden restaurant with bare brick walls and warm wood floor.

🏨 **Bewley's H. Newlands Cross,** Newlands Cross, Naas Rd (N 7), D22, ℰ (01) 464 0140, *res@bewleyshotels.com*, Fax (01) 464 0900 – 淆 ✵⇔, ▤ rest, ₤ & ₤. ⓌⓈ ﭏﺓﺓ ﻯ VISA. ᎘

closed 25-26 December – **Rest** (carving lunch)/dinner 25/28 and a la carte 29/35 s. – ⌂ 8 – **299 rm** ✵89 – ✵✵89.

✦ Well run, busy, commercial hotel popular with business people. Spacious rooms with modern facilities can also accommodate families. Represents good value for money. Large, busy café-restaurant with traditional dark wood fittings and colourful décor.

REPUBLIC OF IRELAND

at Lucan West : 12 km by N 4 – AT – ✉ Dublin.

Clarion H. Dublin Liffey Valley, Liffey Valley, D22, off N 4 at M 50 junction ✆ (01) 6258000, info@clarionhotelliffeyvalley.com, Fax (01) 6258001, ☗, ⊜, ☒ – ▯ ⊷, ▤ rest, ◖ ⟨ ⟡ ▣ – ⚞ 400. ⓐ ⒶⒺ ⑩ 𝖵𝖨𝖲𝖠. ⌘
closed 24-28 December – **Sinergie :** Rest (dinner only and Sunday lunch)/dinner 30/45 and a la carte 30/41 – **Kudos :** Rest a la carte 19/25 – ⊆ 18 – **254 rm** ✶99/260 – ✶✶260, 31 suites.
✦ U-shaped hotel opened in 2005; bright, open public areas. Well equipped conference facilities; smart leisure club. Sizable, up-to-date rooms with high quality furnishings. Irish dishes with a twist at Sinergie. Asian themed Kudos with on-view wok kitchen.

at Castleknock Northwest : 13 km by N 3 (Caven Rd) – AS – and Auburn Ave – ✉ Dublin.

Castleknock H. & Country Club, Porterstown Rd, D15, Southwest : 1 ½ km by Castleknock Rd and Porterstown Rd ✆ (01) 6406301, Fax (01) 6406382, ☗, ⊜, ☒, ┠⌀, ⌖, ⌇ – ▯, ▤ rest, ◖ ⟨ ▣ – ⚞ 500. ⓐⓑ ⒶⒺ ⑩ 𝖵𝖨𝖲𝖠. ⌘
closed 24-26 December – **The Park :** Rest (dinner only) a la carte 39/62 – **The Brasserie :** Rest a la carte 29/44 – **142 rm** ⊆ ✶290 – ✶✶330.
✦ Impressive corporate hotel incorporating golf course and 160 acres of grounds. Stylish, contemporary design; extensive business and leisure facilities; well equipped rooms. Formal Park restaurant with golf course views. Brasserie with popular menus.

DUBLIN AIRPORT Dublin 712 N 7 – see Dublin.

DUNBOYNE Meath 712 M 7.
Dublin 17.5 – Drogheda 45 – Newbridge 54.5.

✂ **Caldwell's,** Summerhill Rd, ✆ (01) 8013866, d-caldwell2002@yahoo.com, ⌂ – ▣. ⓐⓑ
ⒶⒺ 𝖵𝖨𝖲𝖠
closed 1 week Christmas and Monday – **Rest** (dinner only and lunch Friday and Sunday)/dinner 28 and a la carte approx 39 ⊊.
✦ Appealingly understated restaurant in village not far from Dublin. Simple glass façade, light wood floors create uncluttered feel. Neat, accomplished cooking of modern dishes.

DUNCANNON (Dún Canann) Wexford 712 L 11 – pop. 318.
See : Fort★ AC.
Env. : Dunbrody Abbey★ AC, N : 9 km by R 733 – Kilmokea Gardens★ AC, N : 11 km by R 733 – Tintern Abbey★ AC, E : 8 km by R 737 and R 733.
Exc. : Kennedy Arboretum★ AC, N : 21 km by R 733.
Dublin 167.5 – New Ross 26 – Waterford 48.

✕✕ **Aldridge Lodge** with rm, South : 1 km by Hook Head Rd ✆ (051) 389116, info@aldridg
elodge.com, Fax (051) 389116, ⌖ – ▣. ⓐⓑ 𝖵𝖨𝖲𝖠
closed 6 January-1 February, Sunday and Monday – **Rest** (booking essential) (dinner only and Sunday lunch)/dinner 35 – **3 rm** ⊆ ✶50 – ✶✶100.
✦ Close to the beach, a smart, cheery restaurant with gardens serving good value, quality local menus: lobster a speciality as owner's dad's a lobster fisherman! Cosy rooms.

✕ **Sqigl,** Quay Rd, ✆ (051) 389188, sqiglrestaurant@eircom.net, Fax (051) 389346 – ⓐⓑ 𝖵𝖨𝖲𝖠
closed 7 January-4 February, 25 December, Sunday, Monday and Tuesday in winter – **Rest** (dinner only) 28/32 (weekdays) and a la carte 28/46.
✦ Stone-built restaurant; a converted barn standing behind a popular bar in this coastal village. Faux leopard skin banquettes. Modern European cuisine with amiable service.

DUNDALK (Dun Dealgan) Louth 712 M 5/6 Ireland G. – pop. 32 505.
Exc. : Dún a' Rí Forest Park★, W : 34 km by R 178 and R 179 – Proleek Dolmen★, N : 8 km by N 1 R 173.
┠⌀ Killinbeg, Killin Park, Bridge a Chrin ✆ (042) 9339303.
Dublin 82 – Drogheda 35.5.

Ballymascanlon, Northeast : 5 ¾ km by N 1 on R 173 ✆ (042) 9358200, info@ballymas
canlon.com, Fax (042) 9371598, ☗, ⊜, ☒, ┠⌀, ⌖, ⌇, ⌘ – ▯ ⊷, ▤ rest, ◖ ⟨ ▣ –
⚞ 200. ⓐⓑ ⒶⒺ ⑩ 𝖵𝖨𝖲𝖠. ⌘
Rest 31/47 – **90 rm** ⊆ ✶110/115 – ✶✶170/180, 3 suites.
✦ Victorian house with modern extensions, surrounded by gardens and golf course. Good size leisure club. Bedrooms and various lounges are in a modern style. Bright restaurant with stylish terrace bar.

⌂ **Rosemount** without rest., Dublin Rd, South : 2 ½ km on N 1 ℘ (042) 9335878, *mai sieb7@eircom.net*, Fax (042) 9335878, ⚘ – ⇔⇔ **P**.
9 rm ⚏ **†**50 – **††**70.
  ♦ A modern house a short drive from the town with good access to the M1. Well-appointed guests' lounge and attractive breakfast room. Comfortably furnished bedrooms.

DUNDRUM *Dublin* **712** N 8 – *see Dublin.*

DUNFANAGHY (Dún Fionnachaidh) *Donegal* **712** I 2 *Ireland G. – pop. 290 –* ⊠ *Letterkenny.*
  Env. : *Horn Head Scenic Route★* , *N : 4 km.*
  Exc. : *Doe Castle★* , *SE : 11¼ km by N 56 – The Rosses★* , *SW : 40¼ km by N 56 and R 259.*
  ⱕ₈ *Dunfanaghy, Letterkenny* ℘ *(074) 913 6336.*
  Dublin 277 – Donegal 87 – Londonderry 69.

🏨 **Arnolds,** Main St, ℘ (074) 9136208, *enquiries@arnoldshotel.com*, Fax (074) 9136352, ≼,
  ⚘ – ⇔⇔ **P** – 🔄 40. **◑◐ AE ◍ VISA**. ⨯
  April-October – *Sea Scapes* : **Rest** (light lunch)/dinner 40.00 and a la carte 30/45 ⫙ – **30 rm**
  ⚏ **†**67/115 – **††**134/170.
  ♦ Pleasant traditional coaching inn with a variety of extensions. Spacious lounge area and a charming bar with open fires. Family run with traditional bedrooms. Informal Seascapes serves wide-ranging menus.

XX **The Mill** with rm, Southwest : ¾ km on N 56 ℘ (074) 9136985, *themillrestaurant@ocean free.net*, Fax (074) 9136985, ≼ New Lake and Mount Muckish, ⚘ – **P**. **◑◐ AE VISA**. ⨯
  Mid-March - October and weekends, mid November-mid December – **Rest** *(closed Monday)* (dinner only) 38/40 – **6 rm** ⚏ **†**65 – **††**90/95.
  ♦ Flax mill on New Lake with Mount Muckish view. Locally renowned and warmly run; enhanced by personally decorated ambience. Well-judged modern Irish menu. Pleasant rooms.

DUNGARVAN (Dún Garbháin) *Waterford* **712** J 11 *Ireland G. – pop. 7 425.*
  See : *East Bank (Augustinian priory,* ≼★*).*
  Exc. : *Ringville* (≼★)*, S : 13 km by N 25 and R 674 – Helvick Head★* (≼★)*, SE : 13 km by N 25 and R 674.*
  ⱕ₈ *Knocknagrannagh* ℘ *(058) 41605 –* ⱕ₉ *Gold Coast, Ballinacourty* ℘ *(058) 42249.*
  ⛝ *The Courthouse* ℘ *(058) 41741.*
  Dublin 190 – Cork 71 – Waterford 48.5.

⌂ **An Bohreen** ⬳, Killineen West, East : 8 km by N 25 ℘ (051) 291010, *mulligans@an bohreen.com*, Fax (051) 291011, ⚘ – ⇔⇔ **P**. **◑◐ VISA**.
  Easter-October – **Rest** (by arrangement) 37 – **4 rm** ⚏ **†**55/60 – **††**80/90.
  ♦ Very personally run bungalow with fine views over countryside and bay. Cosy sofa area within large open plan layout. Individually designed rooms are tastefully furnished. Dinner menu employs best local ingredients and is cooked with some passion.

⌂ **Powersfield House,** Ballinamuck West, Northwest : 2 ½ km on R 672 ℘ (058) 45594, *powersfieldhouse@cablesurf.com*, Fax (058) 45550, ⚘ – ⇔⇔ ⬳ ⚐ &. **P**. **◑◐ AE VISA**. ⨯
  Rest (by arrangement) 33 – **5 rm** ⚏ **†**65/75 – **††**100/120.
  ♦ Set on main road just out of town. Georgian style exterior welcomes guests into a cosy lounge. All bedrooms have individual style with warm feel and some antique furniture.

⌂ **Gortnadiha Lodge** ⬳ without rest., South : 6 ½ km by N 25 off R 674 ℘ (058) 46142, *gortnadihalodge@eircom.net*, ≼, ⚘, ⚐ – ⇔⇔ **P**. **VISA**.
  February - November – **3 rm** ⚏ **†**40/50 – **††**80/90.
  ♦ Friendly guesthouse set in its own glen with fine bay views, a first floor terrace for afternoon tea, homemade jams and breads for breakfast, and antique furnished bedrooms.

⌂ **Barnawee Bridge** without rest., Kilminion, East : 3 ¼ km by R 675 ℘ (058) 42074, *michelle@barnawee.com*, ≼, ⚘ – ⇔⇔ **P**. **◑◐ ◍ VISA**. ⨯
  6 rm ⚏ **†**45/75 – **††**75.
  ♦ Modern guesthouse and gardens lying just off coastal road with good views of Dungarvan Bay. Comfortable, homely lounge. Four of the warm, spacious rooms look out to sea.

XX **Tannery** with rm, 10 Quay St, via Parnell St ℘ (058) 45420, *tannery@cablesurf.com*, Fax (058) 45814 – ▤ rest, ✆ ☆ 30. **◑◐ AE ◍ VISA**
  closed late January-early February, 1 week September, Monday, Saturday lunch – **Rest** a la carte 27/48 – **7 rm** **†**50/70 – **††**160.
  ♦ Characterful 19C former tannery. Informal ambience and contemporary styling with high ceilings and wood floors. Imaginative modern menus. Stylish rooms in adjacent townhouse.

DUNKINEELY *Donegal* 712 G 4.

XX **Castle Murray House** ⌂ with rm, ☎ (074) 9737022, *info@castlemurray.com*,
Fax (074) 9737330, ≤ McSwyne's Bay – **P.** **M©** **VISA**
closed mid January - mid February, 24-26 December and Monday-Tuesday in winter –
Rest - Seafood specialities - (light lunch June-September) (dinner only and Sunday lunch)
48/62 ♀ – **10 rm** ⌂ ✦85/95 – ✦✦130/150.
♦ In delightful, picturesque position with view of sea and sunsets from the conservatory.
Pleasant dining room. Good local seafood. Comfortable, individually themed bedrooms.

DUN LAOGHAIRE (Dún Laoghaire) *Dublin* 712 N 8 *Ireland G.*

Env. : ≤★★ of Killiney Bay from coast road south of Sorrento Point.

⌖₁₈ Dun Laoghaire, Eglinton Park ☎ (01) 280 3916.

⛴ to Holyhead (Stena Line) 4-5 daily (1 h 40 mn).

🛈 Ferry Terminal ☎ (01) 602 4000.

Dublin 14.5.

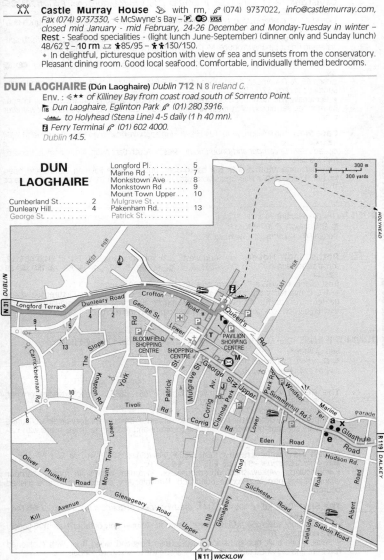

DUN LAOGHAIRE

XX **Rasam,** 1st Floor (above Eagle House pub), 18-19 Glasthule Rd, ☎ (01) 230 0600, *info@ra*
sam.ie, Fax (01) 230 1000 – **M©** **VISA**
closed 25-26 December and Good Friday – **Rest** - Indian - (dinner only) 35 and a la carte
29/43.
♦ Located above Eagle House pub, this airy, modern, stylish restaurant shimmers with silky
green wallpaper. Interesting, authentic dishes covering all regions of India.

REPUBLIC OF IRELAND

✗ **Cavistons,** 58-59 Glasthule Rd, ☎ (01) 280 9245, *info@cavistons.com, Fax (01) 284 4054* – ⓴ ᴬᴱ ⓪ *VISA*
                                                                                                                                 a
closed 22 December-3 January, Sunday and Monday – **Rest** (booking essential) (lunch only) a la carte 24/50 ♀.
• Simple, informal restaurant attached to the well-established seafood shop which specialises in finest piscine produce. Mermaid friezes and quality crustacean cuisine.

✗ **Tribes,** 57a Glasthule Rd, ☎ (01) 236 5971, *tribesrestaurant@yahoo.com* – 🍽. ⓴ ᴬᴱ *VISA*
                                                                                                                       x
closed 25-26 December, 1 January and Good Friday – **Rest** (dinner only and lunch Friday-Sunday) a la carte 37/54 ♀.
• Personally run neighbourhood restaurant next to Cavistons. Smart, original interior harmonises seamlessly with creative modern European menus that evolve slowly over time.

✗ **Café Mao,** The Pavilion, ☎ (01) 214 8090, *dunlaoghaire@cafemao.com, Fax (01) 214 7064* – 🍽, ⓴ ᴬᴱ *VISA*
                                                                                                                                 r
closed 25-26 December and Good Friday – **Rest** - South East Asian - (bookings not accepted) a la carte 19/31.
• Modern and informal with the background bustle of the Pavillion Centre and open kitchen. Quick, tasty meals find favour with hungry shoppers: try Vietnamese, Chinese or Thai.

DUNLAVIN (Dún Luáin) Wicklow **712** L 8.
  ᵢ₈ Rathsallagh ☎ (045) 403316.
  Dublin 50 – Kilkenny 71 – Wexford 98.

🏠🏠 **Rathsallagh House** ⬙, Southwest : 3 ¼ km on Grangecon Rd ☎ (045) 403112, *info@rathsallagh.com, Fax (045) 403343*, ⬅, ᵢ₈, 🐾, 🌳, ♨, ✗ – ⬅✗ ₺ ℙ – ⚒ 150. ⓴ ᴬᴱ ⓪ *VISA*
Rest (dinner only) 65 s. ♀ – **28 rm** ⊑ ✦195 – ✦✦270/320, 1 suite.
• 18C converted stables set in extensive grounds and golf course. Picturesque walled garden. Characterful, country house-style public areas and cosy, individual bedrooms. Kitchen garden provides ingredients for welcoming dining room.

DUNMORE EAST (Dún Mór) Waterford **712** L 11 Ireland G. – pop. 1 750 – ✉ Waterford.
  See : Village★.
  ᵢ₈ Dunmore East ☎ (051) 383151.
  Dublin 174 – Waterford 19.5.

🏠 **The Beach** without rest., 1 Lower Village, ☎ (051) 383316, *beachouse@eircom.net, Fax (051) 383319*, ⬅ – ⬅✗ ₺ ⓴ ᴬᴱ *VISA*. ⬚
28 February - October – **7 rm** ⊑ ✦45/70 – ✦✦80/90.
• Modern house close to the beach. Wonderful views from conservatory breakfast/lounge area. Very spacious bedrooms with pine furniture and modern facilities; some with balcony.

🏠 **Ocean View** without rest., ☎ (051) 383695, Fax (051) 383695 – ⬅✗. ⬚
May - mid September – **9 rm** ⊑ ✦45/55 – ✦✦60/70.
• Immaculate, whitewashed guesthouse of Victorian origins in pretty harbour village. Stands next to recommended pub, The Ship. Airy, period style, pine furnished bedrooms.

🍴 **The Ship,** Dock Rd, ☎ (051) 383141, *theshiprestaurant@eircom.net, Fax (051) 383144* – ⓴ ᴬᴱ *VISA*
weekends only November-March – **Rest** - Seafood - (dinner only October-March) 28 (lunch) and a la carte 40/70.
• Small, stone-built pub in fishing village. Open fires and wood floor with cushioned furniture and old wood tables. Menus of seafood with blackboard specials.

The ✿ award is the crème de la crème.
This is awarded to restaurants
which are really worth travelling miles for!

DURROW (Darú) *Laois* 712 J 9.
Dublin 108 – Cork 141.5 – Kilkenny 27.5.

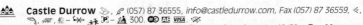

Castle Durrow ⚜, 𝒫 (057) 87 36555, *info@castledurrow.com*, Fax (057) 87 36559, ≤, ℞, ☞, ₤, – ⁕ ᴾ – 🚗 300. 🆗 🆎 **VISA**. ℅
closed 24 December-18 January – **Rest** (dinner only) a la carte 40/50 s. ⌾ – **26 rm** ⌸ ✦100/140 – ✦✦280.
• Imposing greystone early 18C country mansion set in carefully manicured gardens and 30 acres of parkland. Eye-catching stained glass. Modern, understated bedrooms. High, ornate ceilings and views across gardens from the dining room.

DURRUS (Dúras) *Cork* 712 D 13.
Dublin 338 – Cork 90 – Killarney 85.5.

Blairs Cove ⚜ with rm, Southwest : 1 ½ km on R 591 𝒫 (027) 61127, *blairscove@eir com.net*, Fax (027) 61487, ≤, ☞ – ᴾ. 🆎 🆎 **VISA**. ℅
mid March-October – **Rest** (closed Sunday-Monday) (booking essential) (dinner only) 55 s. ⌾ –, **3 suites** ⌸ 70/110.
• Fine Georgian house with outbuildings and sea views, set around a courtyard. Meals taken in converted 17C barn. Wood fired grill. Holiday apartments and bedrooms available.

Good Things Cafe, Ahakista Rd, West : ¾ km on Ahakista rd 𝒫 (027) 61426, *info@the goodthingscafe.com*, Fax (027) 62896, ☞, ℞ – ᴾ – 🆎 **VISA**. ℅
Easter-August – **Rest** (closed Tuesday and Wednesday) a la carte 19/43 s.
• Simple and unpretentious. Walls filled with shelves full of books and foods of all kinds for sale. Open-plan kitchen serves accomplished dishes full of quality local produce.

ENNIS (Inis) *Clare* 712 F 9 *Ireland G.* – pop. 22 051.
See : *Ennis Friary*★ *AC*.
Exc. : *Dysert O'Dea*★ , N : 9¾ km by N 85 and R 476, turning left after 6½ km and right after 1½ km – *Quin Franciscan Friary*★ , SE : 10½ km by R 469 – *Knappogue Castle*★ *AC*, SE : 12¾ km by R 469 – *Corrofin* (Clare Heritage Centre★ *AC*), N : 13 ¾ km by N 85 and R 476 – *Craggaunowen Centre*★ *AC*, SE : 17¾ km by R 469 – *Kilmacduagh Churches and Round Tower*★ , NE : 17¾ km by N 18 – *Kilrush*★ (Scattery Island★ by boat) SW : 43½ km by N 68 – *Bridge of Ross, Kilkee*★ , SW : 57 km by N 68 and N 67.
🏌 *Drumbiggle Rd* 𝒫 (065) 6824074.
🅱 *Arthurs Row* 𝒫 (065) 6828366.
Dublin 228.5 – Galway 67.5 – Limerick 35.5 – Roscommon 148 – Tullamore 149.5.

Woodstock ⚜, Shanaway Rd, Northwest : 4 ½ km by N 85, turning left at One Mile Inn 𝒫 (065) 6846600, *info@woodstockhotel.com*, Fax (065) 6846611, ≤, 𝐼𝑠, ≋s, ▦, 🏌, ℞, ₤ – 🛗 ⁕, ⊟ rest, ℃ & ᴾ – 🚗 200. 🆗 🆎 **VISA**. ℅
closed 24-26 December – **Halpino's** : **Rest** (bar lunch Monday-Saturday)/dinner 26/32 and a la carte 23/41 s. – **67 rm** ⌸ ✦130/240 – ✦✦200/240.
• Large purpose-built establishment surrounded by golf course. Bright modern style of décor in the bedrooms and public areas. Well-equipped leisure complex. Watch the golf from the smart brasserie.

Temple Gate, The Square, 𝒫 (065) 6823300, *info@templegatehotel.com*, Fax (065) 6823322 – 🛗 ⁕ ᴾ – 🚗 220. 🆗 🆎 🅾 **VISA**. ℅
closed 25-26 December – **JM's bistro** : **Rest** (carvery lunch Monday-Saturday)/dinner 34/38 and a la carte 30/41 – **68 rm** ⌸ ✦105/124 – ✦✦150/178, 2 suites.
• A professional yet friendly mood prevails at this privately run hotel in modern, subtly neo-Gothic style. Panelled library and well-fitted rooms in traditional patterns. JM's Bistro serves popular, carefully presented modern dishes in informal surroundings.

Old Ground, O'Connell St, 𝒫 (065) 6828127, *reservations@oldgroundhotel.ie*, Fax (065) 6828112, ☞ – 🛗 ⁕ & ᴾ – 🚗 150. 🆗 🆎 🅾 **VISA**. ℅
closed 25 December – **O'Brien's** : **Rest** a la carte 27/39 s. ⌾ – **Town Hall** : **Rest** a la carte 27/39 ⌾ – **110 rm** ⌸ ✦90/150 – ✦✦120/190.
• Handsome ivy-clad hotel. Firelit lounge and inviting panelled bar with paintings, curios and book-lined snugs. Traditional rooms in cream, burgundy and dark wood. Gilt-framed mirrors and white linen lend a formal aspect to O'Brien's. Informal Town Hall.

Fountain Court without rest., Northwest : 3 ½ km on N 85 𝒫 (065) 6829845, *kyran@fountain-court.com*, Fax (065) 6845030, ≤, ☞ – ⁕ & ᴾ. 🆗 **VISA**. ℅
7 March-November – **12 rm** ⌸ ✦50/60 – ✦✦76/86.
• Modern hotel, extensive and personally run. Well-proportioned, comfortably furnished rooms in spotless order with garden and countryside views to the front.

⌂ **Westbrook House** without rest., Galway Rd, Northeast : ¾ km on N 18 ℰ (065)
6840173, *westbrook.ennis@eircom.net*, Fax (065) 6867777 – **P**. ⓦⓞ ㉈ **VISA**. ※
closed 22-29 December – **11 rm** ⌸ ✸40/45 – ✸✸70/80.
 ◆ Sensibly priced guesthouse on outskirts of town. Spacious entry hallway with tiled flooring and fireplace. Breakfast room has conservatory extension. Light, airy rooms.

at Inch *Southwest : 6½ km on R 474 (Kilmaley rd)* – ✉ *Ennis.*

🏛 **Magowna House** ≫, West : 1½ km by R 474 ℰ (065) 6839009, *info@magowna.com*,
Fax (065) 6839258, ≤, ⌇, ⛮ – **P** – ⚒ 300. ⓦⓞ ㉈ ⓞ **VISA**
closed 24-26 December – **Rest** *(bar lunch Monday-Saturday)/dinner 30/33* and a la carte
18/36 **s**. ♀ – **10 rm** ⌸ ✸60/70 – ✸✸108/120.
 ◆ Purpose-built hotel in primrose yellow stands in quiet countryside. The simple, wood
furnished bar and good-sized rooms, named after local places, are agreeably unfussy.
Neatly set dining room overlooking the fields offers a traditionally based menu.

ENNISCORTHY (Inis Córthaidh) *Wexford* **712** M 10 *Ireland G.* – *pop. 8 964.*
  See : *Enniscorthy Castle*★ *(County Museum*★ *).*
  Exc. : *Ferns*★ *, NE : 13 km by N 11 – Mount Leinster*★ *, N : 27¼ km by N 11.*
  ⛳ *Knockmarshal* ℰ *(054) 33191.*
  🛈 *Castle Museum* ℰ *(0539) 234699 (summer only).*
  Dublin 122.5 – Kilkenny 74 – Waterford 54.5 – Wexford 24.

🏨 **Riverside Park**, The Promenade, ℰ (053) 92 37800, *info@riversideparkhotel.com*,
Fax (053) 92 37900, ⌀₆, ⌒, ⇄, ☒ – 🛗 ✸✸, �&, **P** – ⚒ 700. ⓦⓞ ㉈ ⓞ **VISA**. ※
closed 24-26 December – **The Moorings** : **Rest** *(closed Monday- Tuesday and Sunday
dinner)* *(carving lunch Tuesday-Saturday)/dinner a la carte 28/43* **s**. – **59 rm** ⌸ ✸105/124 –
✸✸170/198, 1 suite.
 ◆ Purpose-built hotel just outside the town: a high, airy lobby leads into smart bedrooms
in matching patterns, modern meeting rooms and a rustic, "no-frills" wood-fitted bar.
Spacious, modern Moorings restaurant with light, soft tones.

⌂ **Ballinkeele House** ≫, Ballymurn, Southeast : 10½ km by unmarked road on Curra-
cloe rd ℰ (053) 91 38105, *john@ballinkeele.com*, Fax (053) 91 38468, ≤, ⛮, ⚑ – ✸✸ **P**. ⓦⓞ
VISA. ※
February-October – **Rest** *(by arrangement)* *(communal dining)* 45 – **5 rm** ⌸ ✸95/110 –
✸✸150/180.
 ◆ High ceilinged, firelit lounge plus sizeable rooms with period-style furniture and coun-
tryside views add to the charm of a quiet 1840 manor, well run by experienced owners.
Dining room enriched by candlelight and period oils.

If breakfast is included the ⌸ symbol appears after the number of rooms.

ENNISKERRY (Áth an Sceire) *Wicklow* **712** N 8 *Ireland G.* – *pop. 1 904.*
  See : *Powerscourt*★★ *AC (Waterfall*★★ *, AC).*
  ⛳ *Powerscourt, Powerscourt Estate* ℰ *(01) 204 6033.*
  Dublin 25.5 – Wicklow 32.

🏛 **Summerhill House** ≫, Cookstown Rd, South : ¾ km ℰ (01) 286 7928, *info@summer
hillhousehotel.com*, Fax (01) 286 7929, ≤, ⛮ – 🛗 ✸✸, ▤ rest, **P** – ⚒ 220. ⓦⓞ ㉈ **VISA**.
※
closed 24-25 December – **Rest** *(dinner only and Sunday lunch)/dinner 30* **s**. and a la carte
28/34 ♀ – **55 rm** ⌸ ✸79/99 – ✸✸198.
 ◆ Sizeable country hotel run with business guests in mind. Bright, modern rooms; spacious lounge with comfortable sofas and busy function rooms. Agreeable atmosphere
enlivens dining room.

ENNISTIMON (Inis Díomáin) *Clare* **712** E 9 – *pop. 920.*
  Env. : *The Burren*★★ *: Cliffs of Moher*★★★ *, Scenic Route*★★ *, Aillwee Cave*★ *AC (water-
fall*★★ *), Corcomroe Abbey*★ *, Kilfenora High Crosses*★ *, Burren Centre*★ *AC.*
  Dublin 254 – Galway 83.5 – Limerick 63.

⌂ **Grovemount House** without rest., Lahinch Rd, West : ¾ km on N 67 ℰ (065) 7071431,
grovmnt@eircom.net, Fax (065) 7071823, ⛮ – ✸✸ ℰ **P**. ⓦⓞ **VISA**. ※
July-October – **7 rm** ⌸ ✸45/55 – ✸✸64/80.
 ◆ Spotless bedrooms in warm oak and a homely lounge in this modern guesthouse, run
by the friendly owners. A short drive to the sandy beach at Lahinch and the Cliffs of Moher.

FARRAN (An Fearann) *Cork* **712** *F 12 Ireland G.*

Exc. : *Blarney Castle★★, NE : 22½ km by N 22 and R 579 – Cork★★ – St Fin Barre's Cathedral★★, Shandon Bells★★ – Grand Parade★, South Mall★, St Patrick's St★, Crawford Art Gallery★, Cork Public Museum★, E : 17¾ km by N 22.*
Dublin 436 – Cork 21 – Mallow 48.5.

↑   **Farran House** 🏡, ℰ (021) 7331215, *info@farranhouse.com, Fax (021) 7331450,* ≤, ㊟, 🂠 – 🛏 🅿 🚫🔟 **VISA** 🞵
April-October – **Rest** (by arrangement) 45 – **4 rm** ☲ ✝100/130 – ✝✝140/200.
   ❖ Italianate 18C-19C house in mature gardens overlooking Bride Valley . Spacious and elegantly furnished; rooms have fine views.

FERNS (Fearna) *Wexford* **712** *M 10 Ireland G.* – ✉ *Enniscorthy.*

See : *Town★.*
Exc. : *Mount Leinster★, NW : 27¼ km – Enniscorthy Castle★ (County Museum★ AC), S : 12 ¾ km by N 11.*
Dublin 111 – Kilkenny 85.5 – Waterford 66 – Wexford 35.5.

↑   **Clone House** 🏡 without rest., South : 3 ¼ km by Boolavogue rd off Monageer rd
ℰ (053) 9366113, *tbreen@vodafone.ie, Fax (054) 66113,* 🔍, ㊟, 🂠 – 🛏 🅿 🞵
May-October – **5 rm** ☲ ✝50/53 – ✝✝90.
   ❖ Cream-painted, ivy-clad house on working farm with large grounds. Traditionally furnished communal breakfast room. Sizeable, individually designed rooms with stylish fabrics.

FETHARD (Fiodh Ard) *Tipperary* **712** *I 10 Ireland G.*

Env. : *Cashel★★★ : Rock of Cashel★★★ AC (Cormac's Chapel★★, Round Tower★), Museum★ AC, Cashel Palace Gardens★, GPA Bolton Library★ AC, NW : 15 km by R 692 – Clonmel★ : County Museum★ AC, St Mary's Church★, S : 13 km by R 689.*
Dublin 161 – Cashel 16 – Clonmel 13.

↑   **Mobarnane House** 🏡, North : 8 km by Cashel rd on Ballinure rd ℰ (052) 31962, *info@mobarnanehouse.com, Fax (052) 31962,* ≤, ㊟, 🂠, 🞵 – 🛏 🅿 🚫🔟
April-October – **Rest** (by arrangement) (communal dining) 45 – **4 rm** ☲ ✝100 – ✝✝150/190.
   ❖ Very personally run classic Georgian house with mature gardens in quiet rural setting, tastefully restored to reflect its age. Ask for a bedroom with its own sitting room. Beautiful dining room for menus agreed in advance.

↑   **An-Teach,** Killusty, Southeast : 8 km by R 706 (Kilsheelan rd) ℰ (052) 32088, *anteach@an teach.com, Fax (052) 32178,* ㊟, 🞵 – 🛏 🅿 🚫🔟 **VISA** 🞵
Rest (by arrangement) 22 – **11 rm** ☲ ✝50/60 – ✝✝90.
   ❖ Extended family home against the backdrop of the Sliabh na mBan mountains. Airy en suite rooms in solid pine, two facing the hills. Carefully prepared wholesome meals.

FOTA ISLAND *Cork* **712** *H 12.*

🏨   **Sheraton Fota Island,** ℰ (021) 467 3000, *reservations.fota@sheraton.com,* 🈚, ⇆s, 🔳, 🏋, ㊟, 🂠 – 📶 🛏 🍴 & 🅿 – 🔬 400. 🚫🔟 🄰🄴 🕦 **VISA**
The Cove : Rest (dinner only) a la carte 40/80 – **Fota : Rest** 25/70 – **123 rm** ☲ ✝169 – ✝✝319, 8 suites.
   ❖ All-encompassing resort location within Ireland's only wildlife park boasting Wellness Centre with 'walking river' and 18 hole golf course. Stylish rooms from the top drawer. The Cove is a very formal place to dine. Fota's appealing menus suit all tastes.

FOXROCK (Carraig an tSionnaigh) *Dublin* **712** *N 7 – see Dublin.*

FURBO (Na Forbacha) *Galway* **712** *E 8 – see Furbogh.*

FURBOGH/FURBO (Na Forbacha) *Galway* **712** *E 8.*

Dublin 228.5 – Galway 11.5.

🏨   **Connemara Coast,** ℰ (091) 592108, *info@connemaracoast.ie, Fax (091) 592065,* ≤
Galway Bay, 🛁, ⇆s, 🔳, ㊟, 🞵 – 🛏 🚉 🅿 – 🔬 500. 🚫🔟 🄰🄴 🕦 **VISA** 🞵
closed 24-26 December – **Rest** (bar lunch)/dinner a la carte 15/45 s. ♀ – **112 rm** ☲ ✝129/165 – ✝✝189/250, 1 suite.
   ❖ Sprawling hotel with super views of Galway Bay, The Burren and Aran from the well-kept bedrooms. Marbled reception area. Characterful Players bar. Good leisure facilities. Two informal dining areas overlook the bay.

REPUBLIC OF IRELAND

GALWAY (Gaillimh) *Galway* 712 E 8 *Ireland G.* – pop. 66 163.

See : *City*★★ – *St Nicholas' Church*★ BY – *Roman Catholic Cathedral*★ AY – *Eyre Square : Bank of Ireland Building (sword and mace*★*)* BY.

Env. : *NW : Lough Corrib*★★.

Exc. : *W : by boat, Aran Islands (Inishmore – Dun Aenghus*★★★*)* BZ – *Thoor Ballylee*★ , *SE : 33¾ km by N 6 and N 18 D* – *Dunguaire Castle, Kinvarra*★ *AC, S : 25¾ km by N 6, N 18 and N 67 D* – *Aughnanure Castle*★ , *NW : 25¾ km by N 59* – *Oughterard*★ *(⩽*★★*), NW : 29 km by N 59* – *Knockmoy Abbey*★ , *NE : 30½ km by N 17 and N 63 D* – *Coole Park (Autograph Tree*★*), SE : 33¾ km by N 6 and N 18 D* – *St Mary's Cathedral, Tuam*★ , *NE : 33¾ km by N 17 D* – *Loughrea (St Brendan's Cathedral*★*), SE : 35½ km by N 6 D* – *Turoe Stone*★ , *SE : 35½ km by N 6 and north by R 350.*

🛪 *Galway, Blackrock, Salthill* ℘ (091) 522033.

✈ *Carnmore Airport :* ℘ (091) 755569, *NE : 6½ km.*

🛈 *Galway City Aeas Failte, Forster St* ℘ (091) 537700, *info@irelandwest.ie* – *Salthill Promenade* ℘ (091) 520500 (May-August).

Dublin 217 – *Limerick 103* – *Sligo 145.*

Plan opposite

🏨 **Radisson SAS**, Lough Atalia Rd, ℘ (091) 538300, *sales.galway@radissonsas.com*, Fax (091) 538380, ⩽, 🍸, 🛐, ⇌, 🖥 – 📱 🍴 🍽 ⚒ 🐾 – 🚪 1000. 🌐 AE ⓸ VISA . ✸
D a
Marinas : Rest (bar lunch Monday-Saturday)/dinner a la carte 34/47 🍸 – **214 rm** ⇌ ✲170/195 – ✲✲190/215, 3 suites.
◆ Striking atrium leads to ultra-modern meeting facilities and very comfortable accommodation: sumptuous 5th floor rooms have private glass balconies. Superb penthouse suite. Split-level dining in dark walnut wood.

🏨 **Glenlo Abbey** ⊗, Bushypark, Northwest : 5 ¼ km on N 59 ℘ (091) 526666, *info@glenloabbey.ie*, Fax (091) 527800, ⩽, 🏌, 🎣, 🏊 – 📱 🍴, 🖥 rest, 🚷 🅿 – 🚪 200. 🌐 AE ⓸ VISA . ✸
closed 24-27 December – **River Room :** Rest (closed Sunday-Monday) (dinner only) 45 and a la carte 34/59 – **Pullman :** Rest (closed Monday-Tuesday) (dinner only) a la carte 36/49 – ⇌ 20 – **41 rm** ✲180/300 – ✲✲240/380, 5 suites.
◆ Imposing 18C greystone country house with adjacent church and bay views. Formal service. Very comfortable lounge, leading into chapel. Spacious, smart rooms. River Room boasts golfcourse views. Pullman, a converted railway carriage offers modern dishes with an Asian base

🏨 **The G**, Wellpark, ℘ (091) 865200, *reservetheg@monogramhotels.ie*, Fax (091) 865203, ⩽, 🍸, 🎣 – 📱 🍴 🍽 ⚒ 🐾 – 🚪 100. 🌐 AE ⓸ VISA
D g
closed 23-26 December – **Riva :** Rest - Italian - 43/59 a la carte 28/68 **s.** – **100 rm** ⇌ ✲260/570 – ✲✲470/710.
◆ Uber-hip hotel taking cutting edge fashion design to the next stage. Vividly assured sitting room styles; décor imbued with fashion shoot portraits. Cool, slinky bedrooms. Bold, bright chairs in keeping with strikingly modern dining room. Italian cooking.

🏨 **Great Southern**, Eyre Sq, ℘ (091) 564041, *res@galway-gsh.com*, Fax (091) 566704, 🎣, ⇌ – 📱 🍴, 🖥 rest, ⚒ 🚷 – 🚪 350. 🌐 AE VISA . ✸
BY a
closed 24-26 December – **The Oyster Room :** Rest (carving lunch Monday-Saturday)/dinner 40 and a la carte 36/49 **s.** – ⇌ 15 – **97 rm** ✲120/200 – ✲✲160/296, 2 suites.
◆ Imposing, greystone Victorian hotel in city centre. Relaxing, elegant interior. Strong conference facilities. Rooftop pool with great city views. Plush rooms. Restaurant exudes old world charm and elegance.

🏨 **Westwood House**, Dangan, Upper Newcastle, ℘ (091) 521442, *resmanager@westwoodhouse.hotel.com*, Fax (091) 521400 – 📱 🍴 🍽 ⚒ 🚷 🅿 – 🚪 350. 🌐 AE ⓸ VISA
C c
closed 24-25 December – **Rest** (carving lunch Monday-Saturday)/dinner a la carte 29/38 🍸 – **58 rm** ⇌ ✲99/140 – ✲✲150/199.
◆ Striking hotel with pastel orange painted exterior on outskirts of town. Impressive reception area and huge bar on two levels. Small conservatory. Modern, comfy rooms. Appealing carvery restaurant.

🏨 **Ardilaun House**, Taylor's Hill, West : 2 ½ km on R 337 ℘ (091) 521433, *info@ardilaunhousehotel.ie*, Fax (091) 521546, 🎣, ⇌, 🛐, 🌺 – 📱 🍴 🚷 🅿 – 🚪 450. 🌐 AE ⓸ VISA
C a
closed 22-27 December – **Rest** (bar lunch Saturday) 28/38 and dinner a la carte 35/39 – **Camilaun :** Rest 20/40 and dinner a la carte 34/42 – **120 rm** ⇌ ✲95/165 – ✲✲130/290, 5 suite.
◆ Georgian style country house hotel in five acres of gardens and ancient trees. Informal bar. Extensive leisure facilities. Spacious rooms in dark woods with quilted fabrics. Seafood, including oysters, feature strongly in restaurant. Stylish, formal Camilaun.

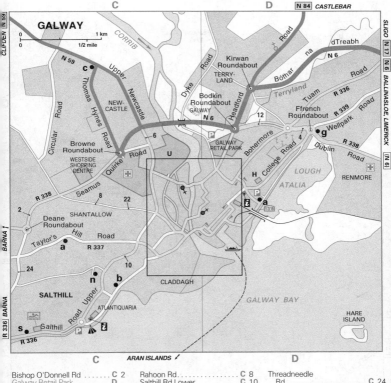

GALWAY

N 84 *CASTLEBAR*

CLIFDEN (N 59)

SLIGO N 17 | N 6 BALLINASLOE, LIMERICK | N 6

BARNA ↑ | R 336 BARNA

🏠 **Park House,** Forster St, Eyre Sq, ℰ (091) 564924, *parkhousehotel@eircom.net,*
Fax (091) 569219 – |🛗| ⇆⇤, 🍴 rest, ✆ ♿ 🅿 – 🔬 35. 🆎 🆎 VISA. ✦ **BY c**
closed 24-26 December – **Rest** 43 and a la carte 31/42 ♀ – **84 rm** ⇆ ✦190/350 –
✦✦190/350.
♦ Popular greystone hotel in city centre. Marble reception and comfy seating areas. Boss
Doyle's Bar is busy and spacious. Dark wood bedrooms with rich, soft fabrics. Strong
international flavours define restaurant menus.

🏠 **The House,** Spanish Parade, ℰ (091) 538 900, *info@thehousehotel.ie, Fax (091) 568262*
– |🛗| ⇆⇤, 🍴 rest, ♿. 🆎 🆎 VISA. ✦ **BZ e**
closed 24-29 December – **Rest** (bar lunch)/dinner a la carte 18/33 ♀ – **40 rm** ⇆ ✦180/220 –
✦✦220/250.
♦ Luxury boutique hotel, blending contemporary design with a cosy, relaxed style. Bedrooms are divided between cosy, classy and swanky. Modern menus take on a global reach;
try to get a seat on the outdoor deck.

🏠 **Spanish Arch,** Quay St, ℰ (091) 569600, *info@spanisharchhotel.ie, Fax (091) 569191 –*
|🛗| ⇆⇤ ✆ 🅿 🆎 🆎 VISA. ✦ **BZ u**
closed 24-26 December – **Rest** – (see **The Restaurant** below) – **20 rm** ⇆ ✦75/119 –
✦✦129/145.
♦ Part 18C Carmelite convent with discreet entrance, in the heart of pedestrianised
area. Busy, populous bar. Individually furnished, compact rooms with rich, striking
fabrics.

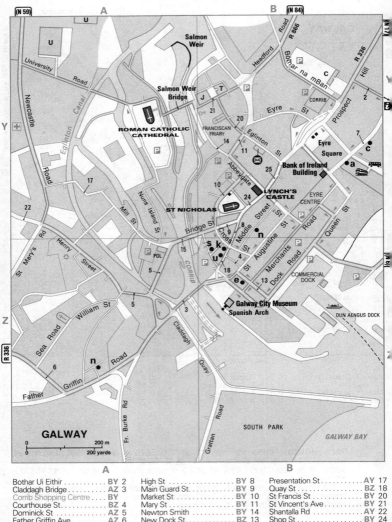

GALWAY

Bothar Ui Eithir	**BY** 2	High St	**BY** 8
Claddagh Bridge	**AZ** 3	Main Guard St	**BY** 9
Corrib Shopping Centre	**BY**	Market St	**BY** 10
Courthouse St	**BZ** 4	Mary St	**BY** 11
Dominick St	**AZ** 5	Newton Smith	**BY** 14
Father Griffin Ave	**AZ** 6	New Dock St	**BZ** 13
Forster St	**BY** 7	O'Brien Bridge	**AY** 15

Presentation St	**AY** 17
Quay St	**BZ** 18
St Francis St	**BY** 20
St Vincent's Ave	**AY** 21
Shantalla Rd	**AY** 22
Shop St	**BY** 24
William St	**BY** 25

⟨⟩ **Killeen House** without rest., Killeen Bushypark, Northwest : 6 ½ km on N 59 𝒫 (091) 524179, *killeenhouse@ireland.com*, Fax (091) 528065, ☞, 〓 – 🖃 🅿. 🌐 🆎 ① 🆅🆂🅰. ⁒ *closed 1 week Christmas* – **6 rm** ☑ ✦100/150 – ✦✦150/190.
  ◆ Whitewashed mid 19C guesthouse with pleasant gardens. Cosy sitting room with Art Nouveau styled furniture. Very comfortable, individually furnished bedrooms.

⟨⟩ **Adare Guest House** without rest., 9 Father Griffin Pl, 𝒫 (091) 586421, *adare@iol.ie*, Fax (091) 782848 – ⋇ 🅿. 🌐 🆎 🆅🆂🅰. ⁒   **AZ** n
  closed 21-27 December – **11 rm** ☑ ✦50/80 – ✦✦90/120.
  ◆ Three storey guesthouse west of river Corrib in quiet residential area near Wolf Tone Bridge. Cheery breakfast room. Modern rooms with orthopaedic beds and pine furniture.

XX **Vina Mara,** 19 Middle St, ☎ (091) 561610, *vinamara@hotmail.com, Fax (091) 562607* –
 AE VISA
BY **n**
closed 24 Decmeber - 12 January and Sunday – **Rest** (dinner only) a la carte 27/48.
✦ Spacious restaurant in warm welcoming colours - smart yet informal; attentive service. Mediterranean style dishes with Irish and other touches.

XX **Kirwan's Lane,** Kirwan's Lane, ☎ (091) 568266, *Fax (091) 561645*, 🛁 – 🖨. MO AE
VISA
BZ **s**
closed 24-30 December – **Rest** (dinner only except in summer) a la carte 33/50.
✦ Modern restaurant in warm, autumnal shades. Adventurous menus. Welcoming atmosphere and a genuine neighbourhood feel.

X **The Restaurant** (at Spanish Arch H.), Quay St, ☎ (091) 569600, *Fax (091) 569191* – MO
AE VISA
BZ **u**
closed 24-26 December – **Rest** (bar lunch)/dinner a la carte 15/23.
✦ 16C Carmelite convent with original exposed brick walls, now a busy ground floor bar and first floor dining room. Appealing, distinctive and seasonal Irish based menus.

X **Ard Bia (The Restaurant),** First Floor, 2 Quay St, ☎ (087) 2368648, *ardbia@ly
cos.com, Fax (091) 539897* – MO VISA
BZ **k**
closed 25-26 December and Sunday-Monday in winter – **Rest** (dinner only) a la carte 18/43.
✦ Personally run neighbourhood restaurant with bohemian edge, located in the heart of the city. Good value, refreshingly simple, unfussy dishes utilising quality local produce.

at Salthill *Southwest : 3¼ km.*

🏨 **Galway Bay,** The Promenade, ☎ (091) 520520, *info@galwaybayhotel.net,
Fax (091) 520530*, ≤ Galway Bay, 𝄞, 🛁, 🖨, 🚽 – 🚪 ⧉, 🖨 rest, ⚽ ♿ 🔕. – 🚫 500. MO AE
Ⓢ VISA. ⚖
C **s**
Lobster Pot : Rest (bar lunch Monday-Saturday)/dinner 28/39 and a la carte 28/48 ⚖ –
149 rm ∙ ✝125/310 – ✝✝180/310, 4 suites.
✦ Imposing, yellow painted hotel on promenade with super views of the Aran Isles. Characterful public bar. Good leisure facilities. Very large rooms with armchairs and sofas. Dining room has bay views and floral displays.

⌂ **West Winds** without rest., 5 Ocean Wave, Dr Colohan Rd, ☎ (091) 520223, *west
winds@eircom.net, Fax (091) 520223* – ⧉. 🚫. MO VISA. ⚖
C **b**
May-September – **8 rm** ≌ ✝50/75 – ✝✝80/120.
✦ Detached guesthouse in an ideal spot for holiday makers: right on the seafront. Cosy sitting room; breakfast room has conservatory extension. Simple, spotlessly kept bedrooms.

⌂ **Devondell** without rest., 47 Devon Park, Lower Salthill, off Lower Salthill Rd ☎ (091)
528306, *devondell@iol.ie* – ⧉. ⚖
C **n**
March-October – **4 rm** ≌ ✝45/50 – ✝✝90.
✦ 1950s semi-detached guesthouse on suburban estate. Warm and friendly owner. Homely breakfast room. Spotless rooms with pristine Irish linen.

GARRYVOE (Garraí Uí Bhuaigh) *Cork* **712** H 12 – ✉ *Castlemartyr.*
Dublin 259 – Cork 37 – Waterford 100.

🏨 **Garryvoe,** ☎ (021) 4646718, *res@garryvoehotel.com, Fax (021) 4646824*, ≤ – 🚪 ⧉ ♿
⧉. – 🚫 300. MO AE Ⓢ VISA. ⚖
closed 24-25 December – **Rest** (bar lunch Monday-Saturday)/dinner 42 and dinner a la carte 39/42 – **49 rm** ≌ ✝105/115 – ✝✝190/210, 1 suite.
✦ Traditionally styled hotel adjacent to the beach with good sea views, to be enjoyed in characterful locals bar. A purpose-built, up-to-date wing features smart, modern rooms. Bright, colourful, contemporary restaurant.

GLASLOUGH (Glasloch) *Monaghan* **712** L 5 – *see Monaghan.*

GLASSAN (Glasán) *Westmeath* **712** I 7 – *see Athlone.*

GLIN (An Gleann) *Limerick* **712** E 10.
See : *Glin Castle★ AC.*
Dublin 244.5 – Limerick 51.5 – Tralee 51.5.

🏫 **Glin Castle** ⚗, ☎ (068) 34173, *knight@iol.ie, Fax (068) 34364*, ≤, 🚽, 🛋, ⚗ – ⧉. MO
AE Ⓢ VISA. ⚖
April-November – **Rest** (residents only) (dinner only) 53 ⚖ – **15 rm** ≌ ✝310 – ✝✝495.
✦ Crenellated Georgian country house, overlooking the Shannon estuary, with superb collection of antique furnishings, paintings and porcelain. Beautifully appointed rooms. Home cooked meals full of local produce.

REPUBLIC OF IRELAND

GOREY (Guaire) *Wexford* 712 N 9 *Ireland G.* – pop. 5 282.

Exc. : *Ferns★, SW : 17¾ km by N 11.*

Courtown, Kiltennel ℰ (055) 25166.

🛈 Main St ℰ (055) 21248.

Dublin 93.5 – Waterford 88.5 – Wexford 61.

🏠🏠 **Marlfield House** ⌂, Courtown Rd, Southeast : 1 ½ km on R 742 ℰ (053) 9421124, info@marlfieldhouse.ie, Fax (053) 9421572, ≤, ☎, ☞, 🐾, ℀ – ✤ 🅿, 🚗 🆎 ⓪ 𝑽𝑰𝑺𝑨. ℀
closed 2-25 January and 17-27 December – **Rest** (booking essential for non-residents) (dinner only and Sunday lunch)/dinner 65 ℤ – **19 rm** ⌂ ★120/145 – ★★250/275, 1 suite.
✦ Luxuriously comfortable Regency mansion, with extensive gardens and woods. Utterly charming public areas with fine antiques and splendid fabrics. Thoughtfully furnished rooms. Very comfortable conservatory restaurant utilising produce from the garden.

🏠🏠 **Ashdown Park**, Coach Rd, ℰ (053) 940500, info@ashdownparkhotel.com, Fax (053) 9480777, 🛁, ☎, 🔲 – 🛗 ✤, 🍴 rest, ✆ 🖧 🅿 – 🕍 500. 🚗 ⓪ 𝑽𝑰𝑺𝑨. ℀
Rowan Tree : **Rest** (dinner only and Sunday lunch) a la carte approx 38 s. ℤ – **79 rm** ⌂ ★115/135 – ★★180/220.
✦ Imposing hotel for business traveller in heart of market town. Atrium with sumptuous sofas. State-of-art leisure centre. Very comfortable rooms boast rich velvet curtains. Fine dining in the Rowan Tree restaurant.

GRAIGUENAMANAGH (Gráig na Manach) *Kilkenny* 712 L 10.

See : *Duiske Abbey★ AC.*

Env. : *Jerpoint Abbey★★ AC, W : 15 km by R 703 and N 9 – Inistioge★, SW : 8 km by minor road – Kilfane Glen and Waterfall★ AC, SW : 17 km by R 703 and N 9.*

Dublin 125.5 – Kilkenny 34 – Waterford 42 – Wexford 26.

✗ **Waterside** with rm, The Quay, ℰ (059) 9724246, info@watersideguesthouse.com, Fax (059) 9724733, ≤ – 🚗 🆎 𝑽𝑰𝑺𝑨
closed January – **Rest** (restricted opening in winter) (dinner only and Sunday lunch) a la carte 31/40 s. – **10 rm** ⌂ ★55/63 – ★★94/110.
✦ Converted 19C cornstore on banks of river Barrow, at foot of Brandon Hill. Base for hill-walkers. Modern cooking with Mediterranean flourishes. Beamed rooms with river views.

GREYSTONES (Na Clocha Liatha) *Wicklow* 712 N 8 – pop. 11 913.

Env. : *Killruddery House and Gardens★ AC, N : 5 km by R 761 – Powerscourt★★ (Waterfall★★) AC, NW : 10 km by R 761, minor road, M 11 and minor road via Enniskerry.*

Exc. : *Wicklow Mountains★★.*

Greystones ℰ (01) 287 6624.

Dublin 35.5.

✗ **Hungry Monk**, Church Rd, ℰ (01) 287 5759, info@thehungrymonk.ie, Fax (01) 287 7183 – ☰. 🚗 🆎 𝑽𝑰𝑺𝑨
closed 24-26 December and Monday-Tuesday – **Rest** (dinner only and Sunday lunch)/dinner a la carte 30/49.
✦ Busy, long-established, candlelit restaurant above a wine bar. Pictures of monks in all areas. Robust, traditional cooking including blackboard seafood specials.

GWEEDORE (Gaoth Dobhair) *Donegal* 712 H 2.

Dublin 278.5 – Donegal 72.5 – Letterkenny 43.5 – Sligo 135.

🏨 **Gweedore Court**, on N 56 ℰ (074) 953 2900, anchuirt@eircom.net, Fax (074) 953 2929, ≤, ⌇ – 🛗 ✤ 🖧 🅿 – 🕍 200. 🚗 𝑽𝑰𝑺𝑨. ℀
closed January and 23-28 December – **Rest** (bar lunch Monday-Saturday)/dinner 25/40 and a la carte 24/45 – **66 rm** ⌂ ★80/130 – ★★120/160.
✦ Rebuilt 19C house sharing grounds with a Gaelic heritage centre. Spacious accommodation in classic patterns; east-facing rooms enjoy superb views of Glenreagh National Park. Classic menu matched by traditional surroundings and period-inspired décor.

HORSE AND JOCKEY *Tipperary.*

Dublin 146.5 – Cashel 14.5 – Thurles 9.5.

🏨 **The Horse and Jockey Inn**, ℰ (0504) 44192, horseandjockeyinn@eircom.net, Fax (0504) 44747 – ✤ 🖧 🅿 – 🕍 70. 🚗 🆎 ⓪ 𝑽𝑰𝑺𝑨. ℀
closed 25 December – **Rest** a la carte 20/40 s. – **29 rm** ⌂ ★95 – ★★170, 1 suite.
✦ Set on main Cork to Dublin road; big, busy and informal former inn. Reception area with gift shop. Bar full of horse racing pictures on walls. Comfy, bright, modern rooms. Easy going dining room with traditional menus.

HOWTH (Binn Èadair) *Dublin* 712 N 7 *Ireland G.* – ✉ *Dublin*.

See : – *The Cliffs*★ (≤★).

ᵣ₈, ᵣ₈, ᵣ₉ *Deer Park Hotel, Howth Castle* ℰ *(01) 832 6039*.
Dublin 16.

⌂ **Inisradharc** without rest., Balkill Rd, D13, North : ¾ km ℰ (01) 8322306, *harbour-view@msn.com*, ≤, – ⁕⇆ ℙ, ⓜ☉ 🄰🄴 *VISA*, ℅
closed 12 December-10 January – **3 rm** ⊈ ✸70/80 – ✸✸80/90.
⬧ High above the pretty fishing village with views of the harbour and Eye Island. Conservatory breakfast room and spacious en suite bedrooms share a homely style.

❌❌ **Aqua,** 1 West Pier, ℰ (01) 832 0690, *dine@aqua.ie, Fax (01) 832 0687*, ≤ Ireland's Eye and coastline – ▤. ⓜ☉ 🄰🄴 *VISA*
closed Monday – **Rest** - Seafood - a la carte 30/60.
⬧ Glass sided, first floor restaurant affording super bay views. Intimate bar filled with local photos, whetting the appetite for accomplished dishes of freshly caught seafood.

❌❌ **King Sitric** with rm, East Pier, ℰ (01) 832 5235, *info@kingsitric.ie, Fax (01) 839 2442*, ≤ – ▤ rest. ⓜ☉ 🄰🄴 *VISA*
closed Christmas – **Rest** - Seafood - *(closed Sunday and Bank Holidays)* 29/55 and a la carte 39/63 – **8 rm** ⊈ ✸105/140 – ✸✸205.
⬧ Well established for 50 years; one of Ireland's original seafood restaurants. Enjoy locally caught produce in first floor dining room with bay views. Modern, comfy bedrooms.

❌ **Deep,** 12 West Pier, ℰ (01) 8063921, *info@deep.ie, Fax (01) 8063921* – ⓜ☉ *VISA*
closed 25-26 December, 1 January and Monday except Bank Holidays – **Rest** a la carte 30/52.
⬧ Personally run, intimate restaurant on busy pier. Deep brown leather banquettes accentuate stylish feel. Wide-ranging, freshly prepared menus underpinned by local seafood.

INCH (An Inis) *Clare – see Ennis.*

INISHCRONE (Inis Crabhann) *Sligo* 712 E 5.

Env. : *Rosserk Abbey*★, *W : 16 km by R 297, N 59 and R 314 – Moyne Abbey*★, *W : 19 km by R 297, N 59 and R 314.*
Exc. : *Killala*★, *W : 21 km by R 297, N 59 and R 314.*
Dublin 257.5 – Ballina 13 – Galway 127 – Sligo 55.

⌂ **Ceol na Mara** without rest., Main St, ℰ (096) 36351, *ceolnamara@eircom.net*, ≤ – ⁕⇆ ℂ ℙ, ⓜ☉ *VISA*. ℅
February-November – **9 rm** ⊈ ✸40/48 – ✸✸80.
⬧ At the centre of town, a sizeable guest house kept spotless by the friendly longstanding owners. Simply appointed bedrooms are all en suite, with sea views to the rear.

INISHMORE (Inis Mór) *Galway* 712 C/D 8 – *see Aran Islands.*

KANTURK (Ceann Toirc) *Cork* 712 F 11 *Ireland G.* – *pop. 1 651.*

See : *Town*★ - *Castle*★.
ᵣ₉ *Fairy Hill* ℰ (029) 50534.
Dublin 259 – Cork 53 – Killarney 50 – Limerick 71.

⌂ **Glenlohane** ॐ without rest., East : 4 km by R 576 and Charlville rd on Cecilstown rd ℰ (029) 50014, *glenlohane@iol.ie, Fax (029) 51314*, ≤, ☞, ♨ – ⁕⇆ ℙ, ⓜ☉ 🄰🄴 *VISA*. ℅
4 rm ⊈ ✸85/100 – ✸✸200.
⬧ In the family for over 250 years, a Georgian country house at the centre of wooded parkland and a working farm. Library and cosy, en suite rooms overlooking the fields.

KEEL (An Caol) *Mayo* 712 B 5/6 – *see Achill Island.*

The red ॐ symbol?
This denotes the very essence of peace
– only the sound of birdsong first thing in the morning …

(Neidín) *Kerry* **712** D 12 *Ireland G.* – pop. *1 844*.

See : *Town★*.

Exc. : *Ring of Kerry★★ – Healy Pass★★* (≤★★), *SW : 30½ km by R 571 and R 574 AY – Mountain Road to Glengarriff* (≤★★) *S : by N 71 AY – Slieve Miskish Mountains* (≤★★), *SW : 48¼ km by R 571 AY – Gougane Barra Forest Park★★, SE : 16 km AY – Lauragh (Derreen Gardens★ AC), SW : 23½ km by R 571 AY – Allihies (Copper Mines★), SW : 57 km by R 571 and R 575 AY – Garnish Island* (≤★), *SW : 68½ km by R 571, R 575 and R 572 AY.*

🛇 *Kenmare* ℰ *(064) 41291.*

🛈 *Heritage Centre* ℰ *(064) 41233 (April-October) AY.*

Dublin 338 – Cork 93.5 – Killarney 32.

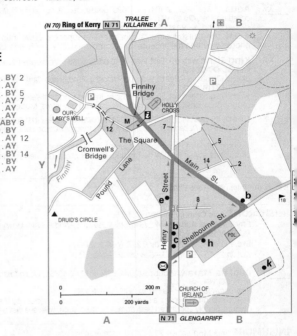

KENMARE

Back Lane	BY	2
Cromwell's Bridge	AY	
Downing's Row	BY	5
East Park St.	AY	7
Finnihy Bridge	AY	
Henry St	AY	
Henry's Lane	ABY	8
Main St	BY	
Old Bridge St.	AY	12
Pound Lane	AY	
Rock St	BY	14
Shelbourne St.	BY	
The Square	AY	

🏨🏨🏨 **Park** ≫, ℰ (064) 41200, *info@parkkenmare.com*, Fax (064) 41402, ≤ Kenmare Bay and hills, ⑦, ↖₄, ≘s, ᖉ₈, ᖋ, ☞, ₤, ℁ – ☒ ↩ ☎ ⅙ Ⓟ. ⓂⓈ ⒶⒺ ① ⅤⅠⅪ. ℅   BY **k**
closed 1-23 December and 2 January-10 February. Weekends only mid February-March and November – **Rest** (dinner only) 74 **s.** – **46 rm** � ✦215/267 – ✦✦430/552.
   ◆ Privately run country house boasts many paintings and antiques. Superb spa facilities. Inviting, classically tasteful rooms; many offer superb views of Kenmare Bay and hills. Grand, bay-windowed dining room; local produce to fore.

🏨🏨🏨 **Sheen Falls Lodge** ≫, Southeast : 2 km by N 71 ℰ (064) 41600, *info@sheenfall slodge.ie*, Fax (064) 41386, ≤ Sheen Falls, ☞, ↖₄, ≘s, ⎑, ᖋ, ☞, ₤, ℁ – ☒ ↩ ☎ ⅙ Ⓟ – ⌂ 120. ⓂⓈ ⒶⒺ ① ⅤⅠⅪ. ℅
closed 3 January - 2 February – **La Cascade :** Rest (dinner only) 65 and a la carte 72/95 **s.** ♀ – **Oscar's :** Rest *(closed Monday-Tuesday in the season)* (dinner only and Sunday lunch in summer) a la carte 38/45 **s.** – ⊇ 24 – **57 rm** ✦300 – ✦✦445, 9 suites 465/1860.
   ◆ On the banks of the Sheen; modern but classically inspired. Spacious rooms with stunning extras. Extensive spa, gym and stables. Attentive, formal service. Floodlit river views at La Cascade. Oscars, more informal, also overlooks the falls.

🏨🏨 **Brook Lane**, Gortamullen, North : 1 km by N 71 on N 70 ℰ (064) 42071, *info@brookla nehotel.com*, Fax (064) 40869 – ☒ ↩ ☎ Ⓟ. ⓂⓈ ⅤⅠⅪ
closed Christmas – **Rest** a la carte 20/39 – **20 rm** ⊇ ✦75/110 – ✦✦130/170.
   ◆ Modern hotel meets country house resulting in homely charms with a designer edge. Main strength here is the airy bedrooms, which are delightfully comfy with a host of extras. Pleasant bar/bistro serving Irish favourites.

Davitt's, Henry St, 𝒫 (064) 42741, davittskenmare@eircom.net, Fax (064) 42756, 🛋 – ✜, ⊟ rest, 📞 P, 📟 🆚 . 🎇   AY **e**
closed 1-16 November and 23-26 December – **Rest** a la carte 18/43 s. – **11 rm** ⊇ ✦48/85 – ✦✦76/100.
• Behind a classically styled pub façade, hung with flower baskets, this personally run hotel offers trim, modern rooms furnished in warm wood and co-ordinated fabrics. Spacious brasserie dining.

The Rosegarden without rest., West : 1 ¼ km by N 71 on N 70 (Sneem rd) 𝒫 (064) 42288, rosegard@iol.ie, Fax (064) 42305, 🌳 – ✜ 📞 P, 📟 🆚 . 🎇
March-November – **8 rm** ⊇ ✦55/89 – ✦✦70/98.
• Bright, airy accommodation, practical and sensibly priced, in a purpose-built hotel outside the town; keenly run by a husband and wife team.

Shelburne Lodge without rest., East : ¾ km on R 569 (Cork Rd) 𝒫 (064) 41013, shelburnekenmare@eircom.net, Fax (064) 42135, 🌳, 🎾 – ✜ P, 📟 🆚 . 🎇
15 March-10 December – **9 rm** ⊇ ✦85/125 – ✦✦170.
• Georgian farmhouse with pleasant lawns and herb garden. Antiques stylishly combined with contemporary colours and modern art. Firelit lounge and cosy rooms. Affable hosts.

Sallyport House without rest., South : ½ km on N 71 𝒫 (064) 42066, port@iol.ie, Fax (064) 42067, <, 🌳 – ✜ 📞 P, 🎇
April-October – **5 rm** ⊇ ✦95/110 – ✦✦140/170.
• 1930s house in garden and orchard. Wood floored hall, full of books and local information, leads to pristine, antique furnished bedrooms and a pretty front sitting room.

Sea Shore Farm 🏞 without rest., Tubrid, West : 1 ½ km by N 71 off N 70 (Sneem rd) 𝒫 (064) 41270, seashore@eircom.net, Fax (064) 41270, < Kenmare River and Caha mountains, 🌳, ▣ – ✜ & P, 📟 🆚 . 🎇
March-15 November – **7 rm** ⊇ ✦75/100 – ✦✦100/130.
• Guesthouse set in 32 acres of working farmland and park with lovely views. All of the individually decorated bedrooms have full length windows which make the most of the view.

The Lime Tree, Shelbourne St, 𝒫 (064) 41225, limetree@limetreerestaurant.com, Fax (064) 41839 – ⊟ P, 📟 📟 🆚   BY **h**
April-October – **Rest** (dinner only) a la carte 32/42.
• Tasty, unelaborate modern Irish cooking in a 19C former schoolhouse: stone walls, modern art on walls and in first-floor gallery. Busy, affordable and unfailingly friendly.

Mulcahys, 36 Henry St, 𝒫 (064) 42383, Fax (064) 42383 – ⊟. 📟 🆚 ⓪ 🆚   AY **c**
closed 24-26 December Tuesday – **Rest** (dinner only) 35 and a la carte 29/48.
• Stylish wine racks, high-backed chairs, polished tables and friendly, attentive service set the tone here. Modern dishes appeal to the eye and palate alike.

D'Arcy's Oyster Bar and Grill with rm, Main St, 𝒫 (064) 41589, keatingrestaurants@ownmail.net – 📟 🆚   BY **b**
closed Monday – **Rest** (booking essential in winter) (dinner only) a la carte 32/47 s. – **7 rm** ⊇ ✦40/70 – ✦✦60/90.
• Restaurant set in striking, green-painted former bank. Pop in for oysters or fresh Kerry seafood at Oyster Bar or modern Irish menu in restaurant. Comfy, up-to-date bedrooms.

Packies, Henry St, 𝒫 (064) 41508 – 📟 🆚   AY **b**
closed 24 December - mid February and Sunday – **Rest** (dinner only) a la carte 34/59.
• A locally popular, personally run little place with an understated rustic feel. Handwritten menu of fresh modern Irish dishes prepared with care and simplicity. Personable staff.

KESHCARRIGAN (Ceis Charraigin) Leitrim **712** I 5 – ✉ Carrick-on-Shannon.
Dublin 162.5 – Carrick-on-Shannon 14.5 – Ballinamore 14.5.

Canal View House 🏞 without rest., East : ½ km 𝒫 (071) 9642404, canalviewcountryhouse@eircom.net, Fax (071) 9642261, <, 🛥, 🌳 – ▣ ✜ P, 📟 🆚
6 rm ⊇ ✦40/45 – ✦✦70.
• Agreeably located, overlooking the Shannon/Erne waterway and countryside beyond: sit for hours watching the canal boats. Comfy conservatory lounge with view. Sizeable rooms.

KILBRITTAIN (Cill Briotáin) Cork **712** F 12.
Dublin 289.5 – Cork 38.5 – Killarney 96.5.

The Glen 🏞 without rest., Southwest : 6 ½ km by un-marked rd off R 600 𝒫 (023) 49862, info@glencountryhouse.com, Fax (023) 49862, 🌳, ▣ – ✜ P, 📟 📟 ⓪ 🆚 . 🎇
April-October – **6 rm** ⊇ ✦60/75 – ✦✦120/130.
• 130 year-old family house, part of working farm close to beach. Delicious organic farmhouse breakfasts. Lovingly restored bedrooms elegantly furnished to a high standard.

XX
🐦 **Casino House,** Coolmain Bay, Southeast : 3 ½ km by unmarked rd on R 600 ℰ (023) 49944, chouse@eircom.net, Fax (023) 49945, 😊, 🍴 – 🅿, ⚙ AE VISA
closed January-17 March and Wednesday – Rest (weekends only November-December) (dinner only and Sunday lunch)/dinner a la carte 31/49 s.
◆ Whitewashed walls, Shaker style furniture and art on a culinary theme in this converted farmhouse run by a husband and wife. Locally sourced menu is balanced and flavourful.

KILCOLGAN (Cill Cholgáin) *Galway* **712** F 8 – ✉ Oranmore.
Dublin 220.5 – Galway 17.5.

🍴 **Moran's Oyster Cottage,** The Weir, Northwest : 2 km by N 18 ℰ (091) 796113, moranstheweir@eircom.net, Fax (091) 796503, 😊 – 🅿, ⚙ AE VISA
closed Christmas and Good Friday – Rest – Seafood - a la carte 26/68.
◆ Likeable thatched pub in sleepy village. Settle down in one of the beamed snugs and parlours to enjoy prime local seafood - simple and fresh - or soups, salads and sandwiches.

KILKEE (Cill Chaoi) *Clare* **712** D 9 *Ireland G.* – pop. 1 331.
Exc. : Kilrush★ (Scattery Island★ by boat), SE : 16 m. by N 67 – SW : Loop Head Peninsula (Bridge of Ross★).
🏌 Kilkee, East End ℰ (065) 9056048.
🛈 The Square ℰ (065) 9056112 (June-early September), tourisminfo@shannon-dev.ie.
Dublin 285 – Galway 124 – Limerick 93.5.

🏨 **Kilkee Bay,** ℰ (065) 9060060, info@kilkeebayhotel.xcom, Fax (065) 9060062 – ⚊,
▤ rest, ⅍ 🅿 – 🔏 150. ⚙ AE ⚙ VISA. ⚘
closed 24-26 December – Rest (bar lunch)/dinner 23/35 – 40 rm ⌛ ✦60/90 – ✦✦140/170, 1 suite.
◆ Purpose-built and competitively priced - useful for business or leisure travel; Plenty of conference space and pristine bedrooms, many with sofa beds, in modern blond wood. Informal restaurant serving an extensive menu.

🏨 **Halpin's,** Erin St, ℰ (065) 9056032, halpinshotel@iol.ie, Fax (065) 9056317 – ⚊ 🅿, ⚙ ⚙ VISA. ⚘
15 March-October – Rest (bar lunch Monday-Saturday)/dinner 26/35 and a la carte 21/31 ⌛ – 12 rm ⌛ ✦75 – ✦✦120.
◆ Attractive terraced house offering good value accommodation and a warm welcome. Pub-style bar in the basement and uniform bedrooms with fitted furniture. Traditionally appointed ground floor restaurant.

🏠 **Kilkee Thalassotherapy Centre and Guest House** without rest., Grattan St, ℰ (065) 9056742, info@kilkeethalasso.com, Fax (065) 9056762, ⚙, ⚊ – ⚊ 🅿, ⚙ ⚙ VISA. ⚘
closed 24-29 December – 5 rm ⌛ ✦38/52 – ✦✦76/104.
◆ Modern guest house with combined breakfast room and sitting room. Spacious well-equipped bedrooms. Preferential booking for guests in the adjoining thalassotherapy centre.

🐦 Look out for red symbols, indicating particularly pleasant establishments.

KILKENNY (Cill Chainnigh) *Kilkenny* **712** K 10 *Ireland G.* – pop. 20 735.
See : Town★★ – St Canice's Cathedral★★ – Kilkenny Castle and Park★★ AC – Black Abbey★ – Rothe House★.
Exc. : Jerpoint Abbey★★ AC, S : 19¼ km by R 700 and N 9 – Kilfane Glen and Waterfall★ AC, S : 21 km by R 700 and N 9 – Kells Priory★, S : 12½ km by R 697 – Dunmore Cave★ AC, N: 11 ¼ km by N 77 and N 78.
🏌 Glendine ℰ (056) 776 5400 – 🏌 Callan, Geraldine ℰ (056) 25136 – 🏌 Castlecomer, Drumgoole ℰ (056) 444 1139.
🛈 Shee Alms House ℰ (056) 7751500.
Dublin 114 – Cork 138.5 – Killarney 185 – Limerick 111 – Tullamore 83.5 – Waterford 46.5.

🏰 **Lyrath Estate,** Dublin Rd, East : 1 ½ km on N 10 ℰ (055) 7760088, info@lyrath.com, Fax (056) 7760089, ⚙, ⚊, ▢, 🍴, ⚖–▤ ⚊ ▤ ⚙ ⅍ ⅍ 🅿 – 🔏 1500. ⚙ AE VISA. ⚘
closed 24-26 December – Reflections : Rest (dinner only and Sunday lunch)/dinner 55 – 126 rm ⌛ ✦125 – ✦✦150, 8 suites.
◆ 17C estate house full of ornate charm adjoined by hotel creating a modern/classical balance, typified by cosy lounges and modish bars. Good business centre; striking rooms. Cool, contemporary dining room has views to mature gardens.

🏨 **Kilkenny River Court,** The Bridge, John St, ☎ (056) 772 3388, *reservations@kilriver court.com, Fax (056) 772 3389,* ≤, ₤₅, ◨ – ⧉ ⤬, ▦ rest, ♿ ⧉ – 🅰 190. ⫸ 🆎 ▦▦. ⤬
closed 24-25 December – **Rest** (bar lunch Monday-Saturday)/dinner 28/48 and a la carte 26/61 **s.** 🍷 – **88 rm** ⧠ ✦95/150 – ✦✦210/400, 2 suites.
◆ Smart hotel opposite Kilkenny Castle. Modern rooms in traditional, co-ordinated colours. Bar boasts eye-catching fibre-optic lighting and a view of the River Nore. Candlelit dining room.

🏨 **The Hibernian,** 1 Ormonde St, ☎ (056) 7771888, *info@kilkennyhibernianhotel.com, Fax (056) 7771877* – ⧉ ⤬, ▦ rest, ♿ ♿ 🅿 – 🅰 30. ⫸ 🆎 ⓪ ▦▦.
closed 25 December – **Rest** (bar lunch Monday-Friday)/dinner 20/32 and a la carte 29/50 **s.** – **43 rm** ⧠ ✦80/95 – ✦✦130/160, 3 suites.
◆ Part Georgian hotel, set in former bank, in sight of Kilkenny Castle: classically proportioned, understated modern bedrooms, spacious bar in dark wood with long tan sofas. Comfortable restaurant with traditional appeal.

🏨 **Kilkenny,** College Rd, Southwest : 1 ¼ km at junction with N 76 ☎ (056) 7762000, *experience@hotelkilkenny.ie, Fax (056) 7765984,* ₤₅, 🅢🅢, ◨, ☀ – ⤬, ▦ rest, ♿ ♿ 🏃 🅿 – 🅰 400. ⫸ 🆎 ▦▦. ⤬
Brooms Bistro : Rest 34/45 and a la carte 31/46 – **138 rm** ⧠ ✦150/180 – ✦✦200/250.
◆ Busy modern hotel popular with business travellers. Up-to-date spa and gym, colourful, wood-fitted rooms and a tiled lounge and conservatory in subtle continental style. Open restaurant in terracotta, wicker and wrought iron.

🏨 **Langton's House,** 69 John St, ☎ (056) 7765133, *reservations@langtons.ie, Fax (056) 7763693,* ☀ – ⤬, ▦ rest, 🅿 ⫸ 🆎 ⓪ ▦▦. ⤬
closed 25 December and Good Friday – **Rest** 25/35 (dinner) and a la carte 19/35 – **30 rm** ⧠ ✦50/110 – ✦✦120/200.
◆ Traditional rooms furnished in mahogany plus 16 more in comfortable modern annexes. Firelit bar in wood and aged red leather is a convivial, locally popular evening venue. Wrought iron and trailing greenery in spacious dining room.

🏨 **Butler House** without rest., 15-16 Patrick St, ☎ (056) 7765707, *res@butler.ie, Fax (056) 7765626,* ☀ – 🅿 – 🅰 100. ⫸ 🆎 ⓪ ▦▦. ⤬
closed 23-30 December – **12 rm** ⧠ ✦80/155 – ✦✦120/200, 1 suite.
◆ Substantial part Georgian house. Spacious accommodation with 1970s-style furnishings - superior bow-fronted bedrooms to the rear overlook neat, geometric lawned gardens.

🏠 **Blanchville House** ⤳ without rest., Dunbell, Maddoxtown, Southeast : 10 ½ km by N 10 turning right ¾ km after the Pike Inn ☎ (056) 7727197, *mail@blanchville.ie, Fax (056) 7727636,* ≤, ☀, ⛳ – ⤬ 🅿. ⫸ ▦▦
March-October – **6 rm** ⧠ ✦65/70 – ✦✦110/120.
◆ Follow the tree-lined drive to this restored Georgian country house in quiet farmland. Firelit drawing room. Charming bedrooms furnished with antiques and family heirlooms.

🏠 **Fanad House** without rest., Castle Rd, South : ¾ km on R 700 ☎ (056) 7764126, *fanad house@hotmail.com, Fax (056) 7756001,* ☀ – ♿ 🅿. ⫸ ▦▦. ⤬
8 rm ⧠ ✦55/90 – ✦✦80/120.
◆ Modern, purpose-built, green painted house within the castle walls. A warm welcome and bright, well-appointed bedrooms await the visitor.

🏠 **Shillogher House** without rest., Callan Rd, Southwest : 1 ½ km on N 76 ☎ (056) 7763249, *shillogherhouse@eircom.net,* ☀ – ⤬ 🅿. ⫸ ▦▦. ⤬
6 rm ⧠ ✦50/70 – ✦✦80/90.
◆ More modern than its gables at first suggest, a redbrick guesthouse facing a neatly landscaped lawn. Modern en suite bedrooms kept spotless by affable hosts.

🍴🍴 **Zuni** with rm, 26 Patrick St, ☎ (056) 7723999, *info@zuni.ie, Fax (056) 7756400,* 🍽 – ⧉ ▦ ♿ ♿ 🅿. ⫸ 🆎 ▦▦. ⤬
closed 24-27 December – **Rest** a la carte 35/42 – **13 rm** ⧠ ✦60/80 – ✦✦120/170.
◆ Chic modern design in leather and dark wood draws the smart set to this former theatre. Friendly service; bold, generous and eclectic cooking. Stylish, good-value rooms.

🍴🍴 **Lacken House** with rm, Dublin rd, East : ½ km on N 10 ☎ (056) 7761085, *info@lacken house.ie, Fax (056) 7762435,* ☀ – 🅿. ⫸ 🆎
closed 24-27 December – **Rest** (closed Sunday-Monday) (dinner only) 35/59 and a la carte 35/57 🍷 – **10 rm** ⧠ ✦95/125 – ✦✦190/225.
◆ Yellow painted Victorian house with brightly decorated bedrooms. Smart dining room offers an interesting menu of both traditional Irish and modern European dishes.

🍴🍴 **Ristorante Rinuccini,** 1 The Parade, ☎ (056) 7761575, *info@rinuccini.com, Fax (056) 7751288* – ▦ ♿. ⫸ 🆎 ⓪ ▦▦. ⤬
closed 25-26 December – **Rest** - Italian - a la carte 31/48 –.
◆ Named after the 17C archbishop, "bon viveur" and papal nuncio to Ireland, a family owned restaurant with basement dining room: Italian classics served at closely set tables.

KILLALOE (Cill Dalua) Clare 712 G 9 Ireland G.

See : Town★ – St Flannan's Cathedral★.

Env. : Graves of the Leinstermen (≤★), N : 7¼ km by R 494 – Castleconnell★, S : 16 km by R 494 and R 466 – Clare Glens★, S : 24 km by R 494, R 504 and R 503.

Exc. : Nenagh (Castle★), NE : 19¼ km by R 496 and N 7 – Holy Island★ AC, N : 25¾ km by R 463 and boat from Tuamgraney.

🖪 The Bridge ℘ (061) 376866, tourisminfo@shannon-dev.ie.

Dublin 175.5 – Ennis 51.5 – Limerick 21 – Tullamore 93.5.

XX **Cherry Tree,** Lakeside, Ballina, following signs for Lakeside H. ℘ (061) 375688, Fax (061) 375689, ≤ – **P.** ◍◍ ◭ **VISA**

closed 24-25 December, last week January, first week February, Sunday dinner and Monday – **Rest** (dinner only and Sunday lunch) 44 and a la carte 43/52.

♦ Contemporary, relaxing interior, polite staff and a wide range of original, well-sourced modern Irish dishes on offer from an open kitchen. Seasonal produce of the essence.

KILLARNEY (Cill Airne) Kerry 712 D 11 Ireland G. – pop. 13 137.

See : Town★★ – St Mary's Cathedral★ CX.

Env. : Killarney National Park★★★ (Muckross Friary★, Muckross House and Farms★) AZ – Gap of Dunloe★★, SW : 9¼ km by R 562 AZ – Ross Castle★ AC, S : 1½ km by N 71 and minor rd – Torc Waterfall★, S : 8 km by N 71 BZ.

Exc. : Ring of Kerry★★ – Ladies View★★, SW : 19¼ km by N 71 BZ – Moll's Gap★, SW : 25 km by N 71 BZ.

🖥, 🖥 Mahoney's Point ℘ (064) 31034 AZ.

✈ Kerry (Farranfore) Airport : ℘ (066) 976 4644, N : 15¼ km by N 22.

🖪 Beech Rd ℘ (064) 31633, user@cktourism.ie.

Dublin 304 – Cork 87 – Limerick 111 – Waterford 180.

Plan opposite

🏨 **Killarney Park,** ℘ (064) 35555, info@killarneyparkhotel.ie, Fax (064) 35266, ◍, **f♠,** ≈s, ☒ – |≱| ◜ ≋ ❤ **P** – 🕍 150. ◍◍ ◭ **VISA**. ❀
DX k

closed 23-27 December – **Park :** Rest (bar lunch)/dinner 60 and a la carte 47/60 s. ♀ – 68 rm ☲ ✱270/400 – ✱✱270/400, 3 suites.

♦ Smart modern hotel. Firelit library, panelled billiard room and the bedrooms' décor and fine details balance old-world styling and contemporary convenience. Armchair dining beneath sparkling chandeliers and Corinthian capitals.

🏨 **Aghadoe Heights** ⬎, Northwest : 4 ½ km by N 22 ℘ (064) 31766, info@aghadoe heights.com, Fax (064) 31345, ≤ Lough Leane, Macgillycuddy's Reeks and countryside, ☎, ◍, **f♠,** ≈s, ☒, ⬍, ❁, ♨, ❀indoor – |≱| ◜ ❤ & **P** – 🕍 100. ◍◍ ◭ ◉ **VISA**. ❀

closed 30 December- 14 February – **Fredrick's :** Rest (bar lunch Monday-Saturday)/dinner 65 and a la carte 65/80 – ☲ 19 – 72 rm ✱195/250 – ✱✱300/450, 2 suites.

♦ Striking glass-fronted hotel: stylish bar, modern health and fitness centre and contemporary rooms, many with sumptuous sofas. Balconied front rooms offer views of the lough. Picture-windowed restaurant with rural views.

🏨 **Europe** ⬎, Fossa, West : 4 ¾ km by R 562 on N 72 ℘ (064) 71350, hotelsales@lieb herr.com, Fax (064) 37900, ≤ Lough Leane and Macgillycuddy's Reeks, **f♠,** ≈s, ☒, ⬍, ❁, ♨, ❀indoor – |≱| ◜ & **P** – 🕍 400. ◍◍ ◭ ◉ **VISA**. ❀

17 March-October – **Rest** (closed Sunday dinner) (light lunch)/dinner a la carte 20/50 s. – 185 rm ☲ ✱206 – ✱✱326, 5 suites.

♦ Spacious lounges and bedrooms plus excellent prospects of Macgillicuddy's Reeks and Lough Leane. Fully equipped modern comfort, even luxury, on a vast but well managed scale. Restaurant offers Lough views.

🏨 **The Brehon,** Muckross Rd, ℘ (064) 30700, info@thebrehon.com, Fax (064) 30701, ◍, ≈s, ☒, ❀ – |≱| ◜ ≋ ❤ & **P** – 🕍 250. ◍◍ ◭ **VISA**. ❀
AZ k

The Brehon : Rest (bar lunch)/dinner 49/80 ♀ – 120 rm ☲ ✱190/260 – ✱✱205/315, 5 suites.

♦ Spacious hotel near Muckross Park with views to mountains. High standards of comfort. Basement Wellness Centre. Airy bedrooms are well equipped with latest mod cons. Stylish restaurant for formal, original dining.

🏛 **Randles Court,** Muckross Rd, ℘ (064) 35333, info@randlescourt.com, Fax (064) 35206, ≈s, ☒, ◜, ≋ rest, **P.** – 🕍 80. ◍◍ ◭ **VISA**
DY p

closed 24-27 December – **Checkers :** Rest (bar lunch)/dinner 45 and a la carte 31/48 s. ♀ – 78 rm ☲ ✱200 – ✱✱260.

♦ Family run hotel, centred on a rectory built in 1906. Good leisure facilities. Rooms, at their best in the modern extension, and comfy lounge subtly reflect the period style. Good choice of local produce in chequerboard floored restaurant.

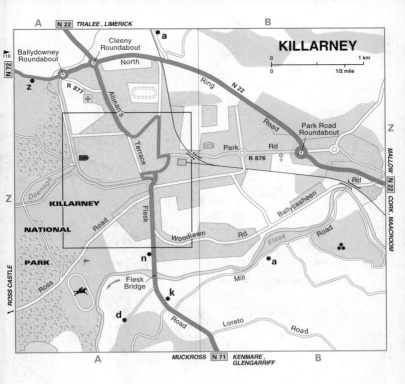

KILLARNEY

Dromhall, Muckross Rd, ℘ (064) 39300, *info@dromhall.com*, Fax (064) 39301, ≘s, ☒ – 👔 ⇖, ☰ rest, ₺ ℙ – 🏛 300, 🝖 🔟 🔟 *VISA*   DY p
closed 22-27 December – **Abbey :** Rest (dinner only) 32/40 and a la carte 25/37 ♀ – **Kayne's Bistro :** Rest (dinner only) 25/30 and a la carte 25/35 s. ♀ – **72 rm** ⊡ ♦75/210 – ♦♦90/240.
♦ Modern, marble-tiled lobby leads to sizeable rooms with reproduction furnishings and an unexpectedly homely lounge: ideal for business travel. Abbey restaurant offers a classic repertory. Kayne's bistro serves a wide-ranging modern menu.

Cahernane House, Muckross Rd, ℘ (064) 31895, *reservations@cahernane.com*, Fax (064) 34340, ≤, 👛 – 👔 ⇖ ℙ, 🝖 🔟 🔟 *VISA*   AZ d
February-November – **The Herbert Room :** Rest (bar lunch)/dinner 55 and a la carte 23/55 – **37 rm** ⊡ ♦180/220 – ♦♦224/264, 1 suite.
♦ Peacefully located 19C house with pleasant mountain outlook. Array of lounges in sympathetic style. Rooms in main house or modern wing: all are large, comfy and well equipped. Restaurant offers formal dining with inspiring views.

Killarney Royal, College St, ℘ (064) 31853, *info@killarneyroyal.ie*, Fax (064) 34001 – 👔 ⇖ ☰ ✆, 🝖 🔟 🔟 *VISA*   DX g
closed 23-27 December – Rest (bar lunch Monday-Saturday)/dinner 25/35 and a la carte 22/51 ♀ – **29 rm** ⊡ ♦160/205 – ♦♦240/320.
♦ Smart yet cosy lounge with an open fire, spacious, individually decorated rooms and a traditional bar in a town house hotel, built at the turn of the 20th century. Classic, candlelit dining room with flowing white linen.

Holiday Inn, Muckross Rd, ℘ (064) 33000, *info@holidayinnkillarney.com*, Fax (064) 33001, 🖧, ≘s, ☒ – 👔 ⇖, ☰ rest, ₺ ℙ, 🝖 🔟 🔟 *VISA*, 🎾   AZ n
closed 25-26 December – Rest (bar lunch)/dinner 30 s. ♀ – **86 rm** ⊡ ♦150/210 – ♦♦240/360, 14 suites.
♦ Hotel on the town's southern outskirts. Comfortable, well-equipped bedrooms and a compact but modern gym will appeal to business travellers. Formula dining room.

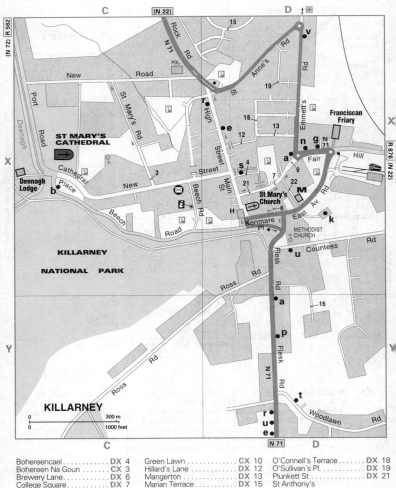

🏠🏠 **Killeen House** ⌂, Aghadoe, Northwest : 5¾ km by N 22 ℰ (064) 31711, *charming@in digo.ie, Fax (064) 31811*, ← – ⅏ 🅿, 🐝 🄰🄴 🅾 **VISA**
April-October – **Rest** (dinner only) 50 – **23 rm** ☳ ✦75/115 – ✦✦150.
◆ Extended 19C rectory run by a friendly couple. Rooms in bright matching prints. Thousands of golf balls cover the walls of a cosy "bar"; deluxe rooms particularly comfy. Homely dining room with garden views.

🏠🏠 **McSweeney Arms**, College St, ℰ (064) 31211, *mcsweeney@eircom.net, Fax (065) 34553* – 📶 ⅏, ▤ rest, ᴄ, 🐝 🄰🄴 **VISA**. ⅌   **DX n**
closed 20-27 December – **Rest** 26/45 a la carte 27/40 s. ☲ – **26 rm** ☳ ✦90/150 – ✦✦150/200.
◆ The hotel's unusual corner tower provides extra seating areas in some rooms; the characterful bar has been family run for over 50 years. Well-fitted rooms in modern tones. Long-standing owner lends a hand in the bar and restaurant.

Foley's Townhouse, 23 High St, ℰ (064) 31217, *info@foleystownhouse.com,*
Fax (064) 34683 – |🛏| ✦ᆃ, ▦ rest, **P**, **M**☺ **AE** **VISA**. ✸
DX e
closed December-January – **Rest** (bar lunch)/dinner 35/50 and a la carte 22/47 – **28 rm** ⊑
✦70/110 – ✦✦100/150.
 ◆ Formerly a posting inn, now a likeable town-centre hotel, still personally owned and run;
spacious modern accommodation is individually styled with a good range of mod cons.
Appetising range of seafood in restaurant.

Fairview, College St, ℰ (064) 34164, *fvk@eircom.net, Fax (064) 71777 –* |🛏| ✦ᆃ ▦ ✇ ૐ
P, **M**☺ **AE** **VISA**. ✸
DX ♿
closed 24-25 December – **Rest** (dinner only) a la carte 31/44 **s. 18 rm** ⊑ ✦65/150 –
✦✦220.
 ◆ Stylish, personally run town centre house; smart, leather furnished lounge, linen-clad
dining room. Bright, up-to-date rooms exude distinctively individualistic flourishes.

Killarney Lodge without rest., Countess Rd, ℰ (064) 36499, *klylodge@iol.ie,*
Fax (064) 31070, ✿ – ✦ᆃ ▦ **P**, **M**☺ **AE** ⓞ **VISA**. ✸
DX u
March-October – **16 rm** ⊑ ✦95/120 – ✦✦120/140.
 ◆ Run by a likeable couple, a purpose-built hotel offering comfortable, thoughtfully fur-
nished rooms. Within easy walking distance of the town centre.

Earls Court House without rest., Woodlawn Junction, Muckross Rd, ℰ (064) 34009,
info@killarney-earlscourt.ie, Fax (064) 34366, ✿ – |🛏| ✦ᆃ ✇ ૐ **P**, **M**☺ **AE** **VISA**
DY t
March-15 November – **24 rm** ⊑ ✦80/120 – ✦✦100/180.
 ◆ Behind an unassuming façade, reproduction furniture combines well with modern facili-
ties in spotlessly kept rooms. Tasty breakfasts served at antique dining tables.

Old Weir Lodge without rest., Múckross Rd, ℰ (064) 35593, *oldweirlodge@eircom.net,*
Fax (064) 35583 – |🛏| ✦ᆃ **P**, **M**☺ **AE** ⓞ **VISA**. ✸
DY r
closed 20-28 December – **30 rm** ⊑ ✦65/110 – ✦✦90/140.
 ◆ Just south of the centre, a sizeable modern hotel owned and run by a welcoming
couple. Neat rooms - particularly spacious on the second floor - and hearty breakfasts.

Fuchsia House without rest., Muckross Rd, ℰ (064) 33743, *fuchsiahouse@eircom.net,*
Fax (064) 36588, ✿ – ✦ᆃ **P**, **M**☺ **VISA**. ✸
DY u
10 rm ⊑ ✦50/85 – ✦✦100/140.
 ◆ Inviting bedrooms, firelit lounge and a leafy conservatory in carefully chosen fabrics and
patterns; homely without a trace of preciousness or fuss. Personally run.

Kathleens Country House without rest., Madams Height, Tralee Rd, North : 3 ¼ km
on N 22 ℰ (064) 32810, *info@kathleens.net, Fax (064) 32340,* ✿ – ✦ᆃ **P**, **M**☺ **AE** **VISA**. ✸
April - 10 October – **17 rm** ⊑ ✦60/80 – ✦✦750/100.
 ◆ Cosy lounge with broad, pine-backed armchairs facing an open fire and neat bedrooms
in traditional patterns - an extended house run by the eponymous owner for over 20 years.

Abbey Lodge without rest., Muckross Rd, ℰ (064) 34193, *abbeylodgekly@eircom.net,*
Fax (064) 35877 – ✦ᆃ **P**, **M**☺ **VISA**. ✸
DY a
closed 20-28 December – **15 rm** ⊑ ✦60/120 – ✦✦100/140.
 ◆ Smart accommodation not far from the centre of town. Cosy lounge in cheerful yellows.
Spotless, well-equipped rooms with Queen size beds and CD players.

Gleann Fia Country House ✸ without rest., Old Deerpark, North : 2 km by Em-
mett's Rd ℰ (064) 35035, *info@gleannfia.com, Fax (064) 35000,* ✿ – ✦ᆃ ✇ **P**, **M**☺ **AE**
VISA
AZ a
20 rm ⊑ ✦45/85 – ✦✦60/140.
 ◆ Meaning "Glen of the Deer", a substantial, purpose-built hotel in country house style,
ringed by woods. Smartly kept bedrooms are usefully supplied with modern facilities.

Coolclogher House ✸ without rest., Mill Rd, ℰ (064) 35996, *info@coolclogher*
house.com, Fax (064) 30933, ≤, ✿, 乑 – ✦ᆃ **P**, **M**☺ **VISA**. ✸
BZ a
February-November – **4 rm** ⊑ ✦190 – ✦✦190/280.
 ◆ Very attractive early Victorian house in acres of parkland. Stylish high ceilings through-
out. Conservatory built around 19C specimen camellia! Huge, very comfortable rooms.

Kingfisher Lodge without rest., Lewis Rd, ℰ (064) 37131, *kingfisherguesthouse@eir*
com.net, Fax (064) 39871, ✿ – ✦ᆃ **P**, **M**☺ **VISA**. ✸
DX v
10 February-11 December – **10 rm** ⊑ ✦40/80 – ✦✦62/110.
 ◆ Friendly owners, a mine of local information, keep this modern guesthouse in immaculate order. Affordable accommodation in pastel shades; rear rooms face a quiet garden.

Rivermere without rest., Muckross Rd, South : ¾ km on N 71 ℰ (064) 37933, *info@killar*
ney-rivermere.com, Fax (064) 37944, ✿ – ✦ᆃ **P**, **M**☺ **VISA**. ✸
DY e
April- 15 October – **8 rm** ⊑ ✦60/70 – ✦✦110/130.
 ◆ The enthusiasm of this husband and wife team shows in the running of their modern
house. Comfortable, well-appointed bedrooms, bright and airy pine-furnished breakfast
room.

↑ **Sika Lodge** without rest., Ballydowney, Northwest : 1½ km on N 72 ℘ (064) 36304, 🚗
– ↳✕ **P**. **MO** **VISA**. ✖
AZ z
booking essential in winter – **6 rm** ☳ ✦45 – ✦✦70.
♦ Neat, stone built house with a friendly atmosphere, located on the edge of Killarney
National Park. Compact but practical en suite bedrooms at reasonable rates.

↑ **Hussey's Townhouse** without rest., 43 High St, ℘ (064) 37454, *geraldine@husseys*
townhouse.com, Fax (064) 33144 – ↳✕ **P**. **MO** **AE** **VISA**. ✖
DX r
16 March-October – **5 rm** ☳ ✦55/75 – ✦✦80/100.
♦ Affable owner runs this hotel, above and adjacent to a little neighbouring pub. Homely
lounge, compact, pleasantly styled and well-priced bedrooms upstairs.

✕ **The Cooperage,** Old Market Lane, ℘ (064) 37716, *info@cooperagerestaurant.com,*
Fax (064) 37716 – ✦ 30. **MO** **VISA**
DX s
closed 24-26 December and Sunday lunch – **Rest** (light lunch)/dinner 23 and a la carte
27/48.
♦ Stylish, slate-floored town centre bar-restaurant lit by eye-catching modern "chandeliers". Flavourful modern dinners. Good choice of daily specials.

at Beaufort *West : 9¾ km by R 562 –AZ – off N 72 –* ✉ *Killarney.*

🏰 **Dunloe Castle** ⌂, Southeast : 1 ½ km on Dunloe Golf Course rd ℘ (064) 71350,
sales@kih.liebherr.com, Fax (064) 44583, ≤ Gap of Dunloe and Macgillycuddy's Reeks, ⛺,
🔲, 🔾, 🚗, ♨, ✖indoor – 🔼 ↳✕ **P**. – 🔼 250. **MO** **VISA**. ✖
April-September – **Rest** (light lunch)/dinner a la carte 34/62 **s.** – **97 rm** ☳ ✦165 – ✦✦326,
1 suite.
♦ Creeper-clad modern hotel offers sizeable, well-equipped rooms and smart conference
suites, not forgetting an impressive view of the Gap of Dunloe and Macgilllicuddy's Reeks.
Restaurant serves Irish classic dishes.

KILLASHANDRA (Cill na Seanrátha) *Cavan* 712 J 5.
Dublin 133.5 – Belturbet 14.5 – Cavan 19.5.

↑ **Eonish Lodge** ⌂ without rest., Eonish, Northeast : 4 ¾ km by Belturbet rd ℘ (049)
4334487, *eonishlodge@eircom.net,* ≤, 🔾, 🚗 – ↳✕ **P**. ✖
February-November – **4 rm** ☳ ✦55 – ✦✦80.
♦ Just a stone's throw from Lough Oughter, in Killykeen Forest Park. Perfect for fishermen
and walkers. Simple, neatly furnished bedrooms; front two have best views over lough.

KILLEAGH (Cill la) *Cork* 712 H 12 – pop. 362.
Dublin 243 – Cork 37 – Waterford 85.5.

↑ **Ballymakeigh House** ⌂, North : 1½ km ℘ (024) 95184, *ballymakeigh@eircom.net,*
Fax (024) 95370, 🚗, ♨, ✖ – ↳✕ **P**. **MO** **VISA**. ✖
March-October – **Rest** (by arrangement) 45 – **5 rm** ☳ ✦65/75 – ✦✦130/150.
♦ Smoothly run modern country house on a working dairy farm. Attractive conservatory
lounge and en suite rooms simply but thoughtfully decorated without starchiness or fuss.

KILLORGLIN (Cill Orglan) *Kerry* 712 C 11.
Env. : *Lough Caragh*★, *SW : 9 km by N 70 and minor road S.*
Exc. : *Ring of Kerry*★★.
🏌 *Killorglin, Steelroe* ℘ (066) 9761979.
Dublin 333 – Killarney 19.5 – Tralee 26.

🏠 **Bianconi,** Annadale Rd, ℘ (066) 9761146, *bianconi@iol.ie, Fax (066) 9761950,* 🔾 – ↳✕.
MO **AE** **①** **VISA**. ✖
closed 23-28 December – **Rest** (closed Sunday) (bar lunch)/dinner a la carte 31/43 ☲ – **15 rm**
☳ ✦65/85 – ✦✦100/120.
♦ Classic street-corner pub; tiled lounge bar with stools and banquettes and likeable mis-
match of paintings, old photos and vintage Guinness posters. Trim, soft-toned bedrooms.
Open-fired restaurant, lined with books, bottles and local landscapes.

↑ **Grove Lodge** without rest., Killarney Rd, East : ¾ km on N 72 ℘ (066) 9761157,
info@grovelodge.com, Fax (066) 9762330, 🔾, 🚗 – ↳✕ **P**. **MO** **AE** **①** **VISA**. ✖
18-31 December – **10 rm** ☳ ✦65/75 – ✦✦110/130.
♦ Comfortable, well-fitted rooms - one with four-poster bed and private patio - in a
smoothly run riverside house. Try smoked salmon and eggs or a full Irish breakfast.

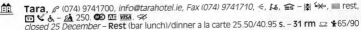

KILLYBEGS (Na Cealla Beaga) Donegal 712 G 4 Ireland G.

Exc. : *Cliffs of Bunglass*★★, *W : 27 km by N 56, R 263 and minor road – Glencolmcille Folk Village*★★ *AC, W : 25 km by R 263 – Glengesh Pass*★★, *SW : 24 km by N 56 and R 263 – Donegal Castle*★ *AC, E : 29 km by N 56 – Gweebarra Estuary*★, *NE : 31 km by R 262 and R 252 – Trabane Strand*★, *W : 32 km by R263 and minor road.*
Dublin 291 – Donegal 27.5 – Londonderry 103 – Sligo 92.

Tara, ℰ (074) 9741700, *info@tarahotel.ie,* Fax (074) 9741710, ≤, ₤ᵇ, ⇔ – |ⓢ| ᕯᵉ, ☰ rest, ☒ ❤ & – ⅍ 250. ⬤❸ ⒶⒺ 𝗩𝗜𝗦𝗔. ⅏
closed 25 December – **Rest** *(bar lunch)/dinner a la carte 25.50/40.95* **s.** *– 31 rm* ⊐ **♦**65/90 – **♦♦**100/130.
◆ Town centre hotel, its bright, commercial style typified by sleek bar with plasma TVs. Light, co-ordinated rooms: ask for one on first floor with balcony overlooking harbour. International menus in contemporary dining room.

KILMALLOCK (Cill Mocheallóg) Limerick 712 G 10.

See : *Abbey*★ *– Collegiate Church*★.
Env. : *Lough Gur Interpretive Centre*★ *AC, N : 16 km by R 512 and minor road – Monasteranenagh Abbey*★, *N : 24 km by R 512 to Holycross and minor road W.*
Dublin 212.5 – Limerick 34 – Tipperary 32.

Flemingstown House ⅏ without rest., Southeast : 4 km on R 512 ℰ (063) 98093, *info@flemingstown.com,* Fax (063) 98546, ≤, ☞ – ᕯᵉ ℙ. ⬤❸ 𝗩𝗜𝗦𝗔. ⅏
February-November – **5 rm** ⊐ **♦**65 – **♦♦**120.
◆ Creeper clad, extended 19C house in centre of 200 acre working farm. The attractively decorated bedrooms boast countryside vistas and pieces of antique furniture.

KILMESSAN Meath 712 L/M 7.

Dublin 38.5 – Navan 16 – Trim 11.5.

The Station House, ℰ (046) 9025239, *info@thestationhousehotel.com,* Fax (046) 9025588, ☞ – ᕯᵉ ℙ. – ⅍ 350. ⬤❸ ⒶⒺ ⓞ 𝗩𝗜𝗦𝗔. ⅏
Rest *27/50 and a la carte 28/46 –* **20 rm** ⊐ **♦**70/105 – **♦♦**120/240.
◆ Former 19C railway station. Bedrooms spread around between station house and converted engine shed! The Signal Suite, the original signal box, now offers four poster comforts. Appealing restaurant using local ingredients.

KILRUSH (Cill Rois) Clare 712 D 10 – pop. 2 699.

Env. : *Scattery Island*★ *AC, by ferry – Loop Head Peninsula (Bridge of Ross*★*), W : 24 km by N 67 to Kilkee, R 487 and R 488.*
Dublin 587.5 – Ennis 43.5 – Limerick 77.

Central without rest., 46 Henry St, ℰ (065) 9051332, *centralguesthouse@eircom.net –* ᕯᵉ. ⬤❸ 𝗩𝗜𝗦𝗔. ⅏
closed 23-28 December – **6 rm** ⊐ **♦**50 – **♦♦**88.
◆ Terraced guesthouse, some of it 100 years old, in main street of small coastal town. Combined breakfast room and lounge. Well kept bedrooms, all with pine furniture.

KINLOUGH (Cionn Locha) Leitrim 712 H 4.

Dublin 220.5 – Ballyshannon 11.5 – Sligo 34.

Courthouse with rm, Main St, ℰ (071) 9842391, *thecourthouserest@eircom.net,* Fax (071) 9842824 – ⬤❸ 𝗩𝗜𝗦𝗔
closed 1 week spring, 1 week November, Christmas and Tuesday – **Rest** *- Italian influences - (dinner only and Sunday lunch) a la carte 25/40 –* **4 rm** ⊐ **♦**40/45 – **♦♦**70/80.
◆ Simple, unassuming, pink-painted former courthouse has terracotta palette and wall-mounted gargoyles. Prominent Italian menus include home-made breads, pasta, desserts.

Good food and accommodation at moderate prices?
Look for the Bib symbols:
red Bib Gourmand ⓐ for food, blue Bib Hotel ⓐ for hotels

KINSALE (Cionn tSáile) *Cork* **712** G 12 *Ireland G.* – pop. 3 554.

See : *Town*★★ – *St Multose Church*★ Y – *Kinsale Regional Museum*★ *AC* Y **M1**.

Env. : *Kinsale Harbour*★ (≤★ *from St Catherine's Anglican Church, Charles Fort*★ *).*

Exc. : *Carbery Coast*★, *W : 61 km by R 600*.

🛈 *Pier Rd* ℰ *(021) 4772234 (March-November), user@cktourism.ie.*

Dublin 286.5 – Cork 27.5.

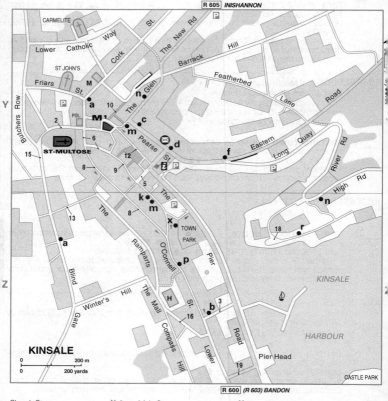

Church St.	Y 2	Main St.	Y 9	Rose Abbey.	Y 15
Denis Quay	Z 3	Market Pl.	Y 10	St John's	
Emmet St	Y 5	Market Quay	Y 12	Hill.	Z 16
Guardwell	Y 6	Ramparts		Seilly Walk	Z 18
Higher O'Connel St	YZ 8	Lane	Z 13	World's End	Z 19

🏨 **Actons**, Pier Rd, ℰ (021) 4779900, info@actonshotelkinsale.com, Fax (021) 4772231, ≤, ♨, ⇌, ⬛, ☞ – ⧫ ↦, ▥ rest, ℗ – ⚠ 300. ⓂⓈ ℀ ⓪ *VISA*. ✄
closed 1-25 January – **Rest** (bar lunch Monday-Saturday)/dinner a la carte 30/44 s. ♀ – ☲ 12 – **73 rm** ☲ ★79/129 – ★★79/129.
♦ Group owned and business oriented. Smart modern lounge, panelled in warm wood, and well-appointed bedrooms in a classic palette, at their best in two newer wings. Stylish dining room.

🏨 **Perryville House** without rest., Long Quay, ℰ (021) 4772731, sales@perryville.iol.ie, Fax (021) 4772298 – ↦ ❤ ℗, ⓂⓈ ℀ *VISA*. ✄   Y **f**
8 April-30 October – ☲ 12 – **26 rm** ★200 – ★★380.
♦ Imposing Georgian house facing the harbour. Antiques and lavish bouquets fill the hall and two period lounges. Rooms are spacious and stylish, the service keen and friendly.

REPUBLIC OF IRELAND

Blue Haven, 3 Pearse St, ✆ (021) 4772209, *info@bluehavenkinsale.com,*
Fax (021) 4774268, ⌂ – |≜| rest, ✆ ⚫⚫ VISA ⚫⚫   Y c
Rest - Seafood - *(restricted opening in winter)* (bar lunch)/dinner a la carte 28/52 ⓣ – **17 rm**
⌂ ✸80/140 – ✸✸160/230.
◆ Comfortable, traditional hotel in the heart of town. Perennially popular wine bar with
large barrel tables and enclosed terrace. Rooms of varying size in neat floral décor. Locally
sourced dishes in conservatory restaurant.

Old Bank House without rest., 11 Pearse St, ✆ (021) 4774075, *info@oldbankhousekin*
sale.com, Fax (021) 4774296 – |≜| ✆, ⚫⚫ VISA ⚫⚫   Y d
closed 1-28 December – **17 rm** ⌂ ✸170 – ✸✸195/250.
◆ Personally and enthusiastically run town house: cosy lounge and comfortable, neatly
kept accommodation - bedrooms above the post office are slightly larger.

The Old Presbytery without rest., 43 Cork St, ✆ (021) 4772027, *info@oldpres.com,*
Fax (021) 4772166 – ✸✸ P. ⚫⚫ VISA ⚫⚫   Y a
14 February-November – **9 rm** ⌂ ✸80/120 – ✸✸100/170.
◆ Tucked away down a side street, a Georgian house run by a husband and wife team.
Comfortable, thoughtfully furnished bedrooms in old Irish pine.

Blindgate House without rest., Blindgate, ✆ (021) 4777858, *info@blindgate*
house.com, Fax (021) 4777868, ⌂ – ✸✸ P. ⚫⚫ AE VISA ⚫⚫   Z a
17 March-20 December – **11 rm** ⌂ ✸125/155 – ✸✸125/170.
◆ Friendly and modern: stylish, clean-lined bedrooms in crisp, light colours, a little front
sitting room and smart, wood-floored breakfast room with high backed chairs.

Harbour Lodge without rest., Scilly, ✆ (021) 4772376, *relax@harbourlodge.com,*
Fax (021) 4772675, ⟨ Kinsale harbour – ✸✸ P. ⚫⚫ AE VISA ⚫⚫   Z r
closed Christmas-New Year – **9 rm** ⌂ ✸165/198 – ✸✸198/240.
◆ Well kept with a friendly, personally run atmosphere, a modern waterfront house. Spacious conservatory and five of the trim, en suite rooms overlook Kinsale harbour.

Chart House without rest., 6 Denis Quay, ✆ (021) 4774568, *charthouse@eircom.net,*
Fax (021) 4777907 – ✸✸. ⚫⚫ AE VISA ⚫⚫   Z b
closed Christmas and New Year – **4 rm** ⌂ ✸40/45 – ✸✸140/170.
◆ Elegant, cream-painted Georgian guesthouse with cosy, quaint ambience. William IV
dining suite for breakfast. Bedrooms boast antique beds with crisp white linen.

The Vintage, Main St, ✆ (021) 4772502, *info@vintagerestaurant.ie, Fax (021) 4774828 –*
⚫⚫ AE ⓞ VISA   Z k
closed January-February and Monday – **Rest** (dinner only and Sunday lunch) a la carte 32/42.
◆ Low-beamed little 17C house - cosy, candlelit and very personally run. Rich, classical
dishes prepared with care: continental influence on seasonal market menus.

Toddies, Kinsale Brew Co., The Glen, ✆ (021) 4777769, *toddies@eircom.net,* ⌂ – ⚫⚫
VISA   Y n
closed 9 January- 16 March and Monday except June-September – **Rest** a la carte 35/60.
◆ Relocated in 2005; now in a modern extension to local brewery. Delightful terrace leading to relaxed restaurant with lots of glass and artwork. Comprehensive modern menus.

Max's, Main St, ✆ (021) 4772443 – ⚫⚫ AE VISA   Z m
closed November-March and Tuesday except July-August – **Rest** 21 (lunch) and a la carte
30/48 ⓣ.
◆ Unadorned yet intimate restaurant: try light lunches, early evening menu or full à la
carte menu. Keenly devised wine list. Friendly service.

Fishy Fishy Cafe, Crowley's Quay, ✆ (021) 4700415, ⌂   Z x
Rest - Seafood - (bookings not accepted) (lunch only) a la carte 34/40 **s**.
◆ Friendly, informal and busy restaurant: arrive early or be prepared to queue. Good-value
seafood, with the daily catch on view in glass display fridges.

Dalton's, 3 Market St, ✆ (021) 4777957 – ⚫⚫   Y m
closed 2 weeks August, 25 December, Good Friday, Saturday (except summer) and Sunday
– **Rest** (lunch only) a la carte 20/25 ⓣ.
◆ Cosy, red-painted pub with real fire in centre of town. Simple international flavours mix
traditional, modern and rustic: substantial cooking, ideal for one-course lunches.

at Ballinclashet *East : 7¾ km by R 600 – Y – on Oysterhaven rd – ⊠ Kinsale.*

Oz-Haven, ✆ (021) 4770974, ⌂ – P. ⚫⚫ AE ⓞ VISA
closed 25-26 December, Good Friday and Monday and Tuesday September-May – **Rest**
(dinner only and Sunday lunch)/dinner a la carte 34/47.
◆ Within the traditional white-washed cottage exterior is a modern restaurant with bold
colours and distinctive lighting. The detailed menu lists highly original dishes.

at **Barrells Cross** *Southwest : 5¾ km on R 600 – Z –* ⊠ *Kinsale.*

↑ **Rivermount House** ⑳ *without rest., Northeast : ¾ km* ℰ *(021) 4778033, info@river mount.com, Fax (021) 4778225,* ⩽*, ☞ – ⇄ ⇐* **P**, **⑳⑨ VISA**, ⅋⅋
February-November – **6 rm** ⌷ ✦*50/90 –* ✦✦*70/90.*
♦ A friendly and conscientious couple keep this purpose-built guesthouse in good order. Well-appointed en suite rooms in flowery fabrics overlook the quiet fields.

at **Ballinadee** *West : 12 km by R 600 – Z –* ⊠ *Kinsale.*

↑ **Glebe Country House** ⑳*,* ℰ *(021) 4778294, glebehse@indigo.ie, Fax (021) 4778456,* ☞ – ⇄⇐ **P**, **⑳⑨ AE ⓪ VISA**
closed Christmas and New Year – **Rest** *(closed Sunday) (by arrangement)* 35 – **4 rm** ⌷ ✦*60/70 –* ✦✦*90/110.*
♦ Creeper-clad Georgian rectory. Handsomely furnished drawing room; well-chosen fabrics and fine wooden beds in pretty rooms, one with french windows on to the garden. Guests are welcome to bring their own wine.

KINSALEY *Dublin* **712** *N 7 – see Malahide.*

KINSEALEY *Dublin* **712** *N 7 – see Malahide.*

KINVARRA (Cinn Mhara) *Galway* **712** F 8.
Dublin 228.5 – Galway 27.5 – Limerick 59.5.

🏨 **Merriman,** *Main St,* ℰ *(091) 638222, merrimanhotel@eircom.net, Fax (091) 637686 –* 📶 ⇄⇐ **P**, **⑳⑨ AE ⓪ VISA**, ⅋⅋
closed 8 January-9 March and 24-27 December – **Rest** *(bar lunch Monday-Saturday)/dinner* 26/30 *and a la carte* 23/35 – **32 rm** ⌷ ✦*70/85 –* ✦✦*100/130.*
♦ Named after Irish poet Bryan Merriman; a restored and extended thatched inn on a busy main road. Bright, spacious lobby lounge, neat, modern, well-priced bedrooms. Traditional menus.

🏠 **Keoghs,** *Main St,* ℰ *(091) 637145, keoghsbar@eircom.net, Fax (091) 637028 –* **⑳⑨ AE VISA**. ⅋⅋
closed 25 December – **Rest** *a la carte* 18/28.
♦ Centrally located, yellow fronted pub: the eponymous owners have been here for many years. Rear dining room serves appealing, unfussy meals with renowned seafood specials.

KNIGHTS TOWN *Kerry* **712** B 12 – *see Valencia Island.*

KNOCK (An Cnoc) *Mayo* **712** F 6 *Ireland G.*
See : *Basilica of our Lady, Queen of Ireland★.*
Exc. : *Museum of Country Life★★ AC, NW : 26 km by R 323, R 321 and N 5.*
✈ *Knock (Connaught) Airport :* ℰ *(094) 67222, NE : 14½ km by N 17.*
🅱 *Knock Village* ℰ *(094) 9388193 (May-September) – Knock Airport* ℰ *(094) 9367247 (June-September).*
Dublin 212.5 – Galway 74 – Westport 51.5.
Hotels see : **Cong** *SW : 58 km by N 17, R 331, R 334 and R 345.*

LAGHY (An Lathaigh) *Donegal* **712** H 4 – *see Donegal.*

LAHINCH (An Leacht) *Clare* **712** D 9 *Ireland G.*
Env. : *Cliffs of Moher★★★ – Kilfenora (Burren Centre★ AC, High Crosses★), NE : 11 km by N 85 and R 481.*
📐, 📐 *Lahinch* ℰ *(065) 7081003 –* 📐 *Spanish Point, Miltown Malbay* ℰ *(065) 7084219.*
Dublin 260.5 – Galway 79 – Limerick 66.

🏛 **Moy House** ⑳*, Southwest : 4 km on N 67 (Milltown Malbay rd)* ℰ *(065) 7082800, moyhouse@eircom.net, Fax (065) 7082500,* ⩽ *Lahinch Bay,* ☞*,* ⟐ – ⟐ **P**, **⑳⑨ AE ⓪ VISA** ⅋⅋
closed January – **Rest** *(residents only) (dinner only)* 50 ⌷ – **9 rm** ⌷ ✦*135/235 –* ✦✦*220/260.*
♦ Early 19C country house in lovely spot away from town and with delightful views of Lahinch Bay. Genuine country house atmosphere with antiques and curios; charming bedrooms. Stylishly understated dining room.

↑ **Greenbrier Inn** without rest., Ennistymon Rd, ℰ (065) 7081242, *gbrier@indigo.ie*, Fax (065) 7081247 – ⇆ 🛠 P. 🛈 VISA. ⋘
8 March-November – **14 rm** ⊆ ✝55/115 – ✝✝120/170.
♦ Smartly appointed guesthouse with a modern feel. Conservatory-style breakfast room overlooking Lahinch golf course. Well-kept pine furnished bedrooms.

↑ **Dough Mor Lodge** without rest., Station Rd, ℰ (065) 7082063, *dough@gofree.in digo.ie*, Fax (065) 7071384, 🖛 – ⇆ P. 🛈 VISA. ⋘
March-October – **6 rm** ⊆ ✝55/70 – ✝✝90/120.
♦ Attractive, well-kept guesthouse with large front garden, a minute's walk from the town centre. Cosy lounge; Gingham-clad breakfast room. Spacious bedrooms in white or cream.

LEENANE (An Líonán) Galway **712** C 7 *Ireland G.* – ✉ *Clifden.*
See : Killary Harbour★.
Env. : Joyce Country★★ – Lough Nafooey★, SE : 10½ km by R 336 – Aasleagh Falls★, NE : 4 km.
Exc. : Connemara★★★ – Lough Corrib★★, SE : 16 km by R 336 and R 345 – Doo Lough Pass★, NW : 14½ km by N 59 and R 335.
Dublin 278.5 – Ballina 90 – Galway 66.

🏛 **Delphi Lodge** ⌖, Northwest : 13 ¼ km by N 59 on Louisburgh rd ℰ (095) 42222, *res@delphilodge.com*, Fax (095) 42296, ≤, 🌊, 🖛, ♨ – ⇆ P. – 🅰 25. 🛈 VISA. ⋘
closed 20 December-6 January – **Rest** (residents only) (communal dining) (set menu only) (dinner only) 50 ♀ – **12 rm** ⊆ ✝130 – ✝✝260.
♦ Georgian sporting lodge in a stunning loughside setting with extensive gardens and grounds. Haven for fishermen. Country house feel and simple bedrooms. Communal dining table: fisherman with the day's best catch sits at its head.

LEIXLIP (Léim an Bhradáin) Kildare **712** M 7 – pop. 15 016.
Dublin 22.5 – Drogheda 63 – Galway 201 – Kilkenny 117.5.

🏛 **Leixlip House**, Captain's Hill, ℰ (01) 624 2268, *info@leixliphouse.com*, Fax (01) 624 4177 – ⇆ 📞 P. – 🅰 100. 🛈 AE ⓪ VISA. ⋘
closed 24-26 December – **Rest** – (see **The Bradaun** below) – **19 rm** ⊆ ✝110/150 – ✝✝150/200.
♦ Georgian house on town's main street. Well-geared up to banquets. Luxurious soft furnishings and antiques in bedrooms; front-facing rooms with particularly large windows.

XX **The Bradaun** (at Leixlip House H.), Captain's Hill, ℰ (01) 624 2268, Fax (01) 624 4177 – P. 🛈 AE ⓪ VISA
closed 24-26 December and Monday – **Rest** (dinner only and Sunday lunch)/dinner a la carte 32/45.
♦ Good size room with high ceilings and large windows commensurate with the age of the property. Simple, fresh décor. Classic dishes with modern and Irish influences.

LEOPARDSTOWN Dublin **712** N 7 – see Dublin.

LETTERFRACK (Leitir Fraic) Galway **712** C 7 *Ireland G.*
Env. : Connemara★★★ – Sky Road★★ (≤★★) – Connemara National Park★ – Kylemore Abbey★, E : 4¾ km by N 59.
Dublin 304 – Ballina 111 – Galway 91.5.

🏛 **Rosleague Manor** ⌖, West : 2 ½ km on N 59 ℰ (095) 41101, *info@rosleague.com*, Fax (095) 41168, ≤ Ballynakill harbour and mountains, 🖛, ♨, ✗ – ⇆ P. 🛈 AE VISA
April - 7 November – **Rest** (dinner only) 35/48 s. ♀ – **20 rm** ⊆ ✝95/140 – ✝✝170/220.
♦ Imposing, part 19C manor in a secluded, elevated position affording delightful views of Ballynakill harbour and mountains. Antique furnished, old fashioned comfort. Country house-style dining room: distinctive artwork on walls.

REPUBLIC OF IRELAND

Do not confuse X with ☸!
X defines comfort, while stars are awarded for the best cuisine, across all categories of comfort.

LETTERKENNY (Leitir Ceanainn) Donegal **712** I 3 *Ireland G.* – pop. 15 231.

Exc. : *Glenveagh National Park*★★ (*Gardens*★★), NW : 19¼ km by R 250, R 251 and R 254 – *Grianan of Aileach*★★ (⩽★★) NE : 28 km by N 13 – *Church Hill* (*Glebe House and Gallery*★ AC) NW : 16 km by R 250.

🮲 *Dunfanaghy* ℘ (074) 913 6336.

🅑 *Derry Rd* ℘ (074) 9121160, donegaltourism@eircom.net.

Dublin 241.5 – Londonderry 34 – Sligo 116.

🏨 Radisson SAS, The Loop Rd, ℘ (074) 9194444, info.letterkenny@radisson.ie, Fax (074) 9194455, **f₆**, ⇌s, 🮖 – 🛗 ✦, 🍽 rest, 🆎 & **P.** – 🔬 500. **OO** **AE** **O** **VISA**. ✻

Rest (bar lunch)/dinner 32 and a la carte 24/40 s. ♀ – **114 rm** ⊆ ★95/110 – ★★128/169.

◆ Corporate accommodation in town centre. Bar serves a daily changing menu; rooms are identically appointed: all are clean, modern and spacious. Business class has extras. Dinner in restaurant offers modern international choice.

🏨 Clanree, Derry Rd, Southeast : 2 ¾ km on N 14 at junction with N 13 ℘ (074) 9124369, info@clanreehotel.com, Fax (074) 9125389, **f₆**, ⇌s, 🮖 – 🛗 ✦ 🮖 🆎 & **P.** – 🔬 1000. **OO** **AE** **O** **VISA**. ✻

closed 23-27 December – **Rest** (carvery lunch)/dinner 23/35 and a la carte 28/38 – **120 rm** ⊆ ★80/110 – ★★110/170.

◆ Purpose-built property on edge of town centre. Modern style with an opulent marble floored reception. Well-equipped conference and leisure facilities. Colourful bedrooms. Full meals from the wood furnished restaurant, including lunchtime carvery.

🏨 Castlegrove House ☜, Ramelton Rd, Northeast : 7 ¼ km by N 13 off R 245 ℘ (074) 9151118, marytsweeney@hotmail.com, Fax (074) 9151384, ⩽, 🮰, 🮱, ♨ – ✦ 🆎 **P.** **OO** **AE** **O** **VISA**. ✻

closed 22-30 December – **Rest** *(closed Sunday-Monday November-February)* (lunch booking essential) a la carte 38/57 ♀ – **13 rm** ⊆ ★80/120 – ★★150/190, 1 suite.

◆ Extended country house, dating from the 17C, in very quiet location. Comfortable sitting room with open fires. All rooms of a good size, the newer ones are most comfortable. Capacious dining room with views of gardens and grounds.

🏨 Gallaghers, 100 Main St, ℘ (074) 9122066, info@gallaghershotel.com, Fax (074) 9164096 – 🛗 ✦ 🮖 🆎 **P.** **OO** **AE** **O** **VISA**

closed 23-27 December – **Rest** (carvery lunch)/dinner a la carte 21/26 – **82 rm** ⊆ ★95 – ★★260/300.

◆ Totally refurbished hotel in town centre: its striking glass façade is eye-catching. Two bars: one on upper level is minimal and stylish. Modish rooms have plush white beds. Modern restaurant offers easy-going international menus.

⌂ Pennsylvania House ☜ without rest., Curraghleas, Mountain Top, North : 3 ½ km by N 56 ℘ (074) 9126808, info@accommodationdonegal.com, Fax (074) 9128905, ⩽, ⇌s, 🮱 – ✦ **P.** **OO** **VISA**. ✻

closed 20-26 December – **7 rm** ⊆ ★45/65 – ★★90/110.

◆ Comfortable house run by a welcoming couple: rooms in floral fabrics, comfortable lounge decorated with Eastern artefacts, hilltop views towards the Derryveagh Mountains.

⌂ Ballyraine Guesthouse without rest., Ramelton Rd, East : 2 ¾ km by N 14 on R 245 ℘ (074) 9124460, ballyraineguesthouse@eircom.net, Fax (074) 9120851 – ✦ 🆎 **P.** **OO** **VISA**.

8 rm ⊆ ★35/50 – ★★64/80.

◆ Purpose-built guest house in the suburbs of this busy market town. Wood floored breakfast room in warm pine. En suite bedrooms are spacious and usefully equipped.

LIMERICK (Luimneach) Limerick **712** G 9 *Ireland G.* – pop. 86 998.

See : *City*★★ - *St Mary's Cathedral*★ Y – *Hunt Museum*★★ AC Y – *Georgian House*★ AC Z – *King John's Castle*★ AC Y– *Limerick Museum*★ Z M2 – *John Square*★ Z 20 – *St John's Cathedral*★ Z.

Env. : *Bunratty Castle*★★ AC, W : 12 km by N 18 – *Cratloe Wood* (⩽★) NW : 8 km by N 18 Z.

Exc. : *Castleconnell*★, E : 11¼ km by N 7 – *Lough Gur Interpretive Centre*★ AC, S : 17¾ km by R 512 and R 514 Z – *Clare Glens*★, E : 21 km by N 7 and R 503 Y – *Monasteranenagh Abbey*★, S : 21 km by N 20 Z.

🛧 *Shannon Airport* : ℘ (061) 712000, W : 25 ¾ km by N 18 Z – **Terminal :** *Limerick Railway Station.*

🅑 *Arthur's Quay* ℘ (061) 317522 Y, limericktouristoffice@shannondev.ie.

Dublin 193 – Cork 93.5.

Plan opposite

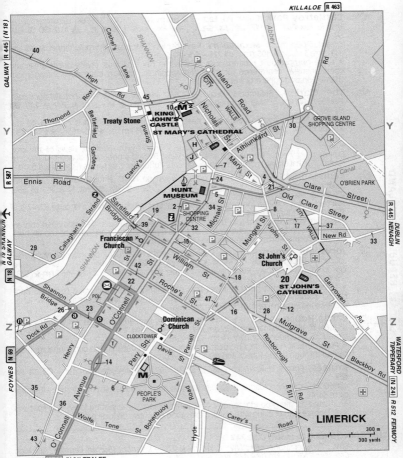

KILLALOE R 463

GALWAY R 445 (N 18)

R 587

R 445 NENAGH

DUBLIN R 445 NENAGH

N 18 GALWAY N 19 SHANNON

FOYNES N 69

GROVE ISLAND SHOPPING CENTRE

O'BRIEN PARK

Treaty Stone

KING JOHN'S CASTLE

ST MARY'S CATHEDRAL

HUNT MUSEUM

Franciscan Church

St John's Church

ST JOHN'S CATHEDRAL

Dominican Church

CLOCKTOWER

PEOPLE'S PARK

LIMERICK

300 m

300 yards

CORK N 20 (N 21) TRALEE

Look out for red symbols, indicating particularly pleasant establishments.

1027

🏨 **Castletroy Park**, Dublin Rd, East : 3 ½ km by N 7 ℰ (061) 335566, *sales@castletroy-park.ie*, Fax (061) 331117, 🍴, Ⅰᵇ, ≋, 🖥 – 📶 ⚡ 📼 rest, 🛎 & 🅿 – 🔬 450. 🆔 ⚡ 🆅🆂🅰.
🍴
closed 25 December – ***McLaughlin's :*** Rest (bar lunch Monday-Saturday)/dinner 35/45 and a la carte 31/50 **s.** – **105 rm** ⚏ – ♦♦260, 2 suites.
♦ Large purpose-built property just outside the city. Spacious, stylish public areas and comprehensive conference facilities. Well-appointed modern bedrooms. Dining room themed on traditional arts and crafts.

🏨 **The Clarion**, Steamboat Quay, ℰ (061) 444100, *info@clarionhotellimerick.com*, Fax (061) 444101, ≤ River Shannon and City, Ⅰᵇ, ≋, 🖥 – 📶 ⚡ 📼 & 🅿 – 🔬 240. 🆔 ⚡
🆃🆂🅰   Z n
closed 24-25 December – ***Sinergie :*** Rest (closed Saturday lunch) a la carte 31/40 **s.** – ***Kudos :*** Rest - Asian - a la carte 22/25 **s.** – ⚏ 16 – **93 rm** ⚏ ♦125/165 – ♦♦140/180, 30 suites.
♦ Impressive newly built hotel by the River Shannon with excellent views of the city. Contemporary décor throughout and great views from the pool. Well-appointed, modern rooms. Formal dining room with modern menu. Kudos bar area serves Asian based food.

🏨 **Radisson SAS**, Ennis Rd, Northwest : 6 ½ km on N 18 ℰ (061) 456200, *sales.limer ick@radissonsas.com*, Fax (061) 327418, Ⅰᵇ, ≋, 🖥, ℀ – 📶 ⚡ 📼 rest, 🛎 & 🅿 – 🔬 550. 🆔 ⚡ 🅾 🆅🆂🅰. 🍴
Porters : Rest (carving lunch Monday-Saturday and Sunday dinner) a la carte 32/47 **s.** – **152 rm** ⚏ ♦120/135 – ♦♦135/150, 2 suites.
♦ Modern hotel with tastefully used chrome and wood interiors. Well-equipped confer-ence rooms and a leisure centre which includes tennis court. Smart, state-of-the-art bed-rooms. Informal Porters restaurant with traditional menus.

🏨 **Jurys Inn Limerick**, Lower Mallow St, ℰ (061) 207000, *bookings@jurysinnlimer ick.com*, Fax (061) 400966 – 📶 ⚡ 🛎 & ↔ – 🔬 40. 🆔 ⚡ 🆅🆂🅰. 🍴   Z a
closed 24-26 December – Rest (bar lunch)/dinner a la carte 18/33 – ⚏ 10 – **151 rm** ♦75/89 – ♦♦75/89.
♦ Large purpose-built hotel in a well-kept commercial style. Light wood furnished bed-rooms, some with views of the River Shannon. Good value and a central location. Base-ment-based informal restaurant and rustic pub.

🏠 **Carrig House** without rest., No.2, Meadowvale, Raheen, Southwest : 4 ½ km by N 20 ℰ (061) 309626, *lohanangela@eircom.net*, 🌳 – ↔ 🅿. 🍴
closed 20 December-3 January – **4 rm** ⚏ ♦45/50 – ♦♦70.
♦ Purpose-built house on a residential estate. Colourful décor in the communal rooms is carried through to the fabrics and drapes in the bedrooms.

🍴🍴 **Brûlées**, Corner Mallow/Henry St, ℰ (061) 319931, *brulees@eircom.net* – ⚡ 🆔 🅾
🆅🆂🅰   Z e
closed 24 December-2 January, Sunday, Monday and lunch Tuesday-Wednesday – Rest a la carte 34/46.
♦ Situated on the ground floor of a Georgian building. Three seating levels give spacious feel. Modern Irish cooking with classic base: good emphasis on local produce.

LISCANNOR (Lios Ceannúir) Clare **712** D 9.

Env. : Cliffs of Moher★★★, NW : 8 km by R 478 – Kilfenora (Burren Centre★ **AC**, High Crosses★), NE : 18 km by R 478, N 67 and R 481.
Dublin 272 – Ennistimmon 9.5 – Limerick 72.5.

🍴 **Vaughan's Anchor Inn**, Main St, ℰ (065) 7081548, Fax (065) 7086977 – 🅿. ⚡ 🆅🆂🅰.
🍴
closed 25 December – Rest - Seafood - a la carte 25/36.
♦ Close to Cliffs of Moher, this long-standing, family owned pub is awash with nautical bits and bobs. Appealing menus with emphasis on seafood. A bustling venue.

LISDOONVARNA (Lios Dúin Bhearna) Clare **712** E 8 Ireland G.

Env. : The Burren★★ (Cliffs of Moher★★★, Scenic Route★★, Aillwee Cave★ **AC** (Water-fall★★), Corcomroe Abbey★, Kilfenora Crosses★).
Dublin 268.5 – Galway 63 – Limerick 75.5.

🏨 **Ballinalacken Castle Country House** ⚜, Coast Rd, Northwest : 4 ¾ km by N 67 (Doolin rd) on R 477 ℰ (065) 7074025, *ballinalackencastle@eircom.net*, Fax (065) 7074025, ≤, 🐾 – ↔ 🅿. ⚡ 🆅🆂🅰. 🍴
10 April- October – Rest (closed Tuesday) (dinner only) a la carte 40/47 – **12 rm** ⚏ ♦120/150 – ♦♦120/180.
♦ 1840's house with purpose-built extension overlooked by imposing ruin of a 15C castle. Characterful communal areas in traditional style. Large, antique furnished bedrooms. Diners greeted by open fireplace and linen-clad tables.

Sheedy's Country House, Sulphir Hill, ℘ (065) 7074026, *info@sheedys.com,*
Fax (065) 7074555, 🐾 – ᯤᢟ ♿ ℗ *VISA* . ✂️
April-September – **Rest** – (see **The Restaurant** below) – **11 rm** ⊆ ✦100/150 –
✦✦150/180.
♦ Classic late 19C mustard painted property in an elevated position. Public areas centre
around the bright, wicker furnished sun lounge. Neat, well-equipped bedrooms.

Carrigann, ℘ (065) 7074036, *carrigannhotel@eircom.net, Fax (065) 7074567,* 🐾 – ᯤᢟ
℗ – ⚒ 40. **⊕** *VISA* .
March-October – **Rest** (bar lunch)/dinner a la carte 33/37 – **20 rm** ⊆ ✦55/100 –
✦✦110/130.
♦ Cream coloured building with gardens in centre of the town. Sitting room with open
fires and a collection of books. Brightly decorated bedrooms with co-ordinated fabrics.
Comfortable dining room.

Kincora House, ℘ (065) 7074300, *kincorahotel@eircom.net, Fax (065) 7074490,* 🐾 –
ᯤᢟ – ⚒ 40. **⊕** *VISA* . ✂️
April-October – **Rest** *(closed Wednesday lunch)* a la carte 21/33 **s.** ♀ – **14 rm** ⊆ ✦40/120 –
✦✦80/130.
♦ Charming hotel; oldest part dating back to 1860. Attractive walled garden to the rear.
Comfy sitting room with plenty of local books. Rustic, spacious bar. Light, airy rooms.
Smart, relaxing restaurant.

Woodhaven without rest., Doolin Coast Rd, West : 1 ½ km by N 67 (Doolin rd) off R 477
℘ (065) 7074017, 🐾 – ℗. **⊕** *VISA* . ✂️
closed Christmas – **4 rm** ⊆ ✦45/50 – ✦✦61/68.
♦ Whitewashed house on a country lane with pretty gardens. Traditionally styled interior
decoration to the lounge and breakfast room. Simple bedrooms with a homely feel.

The Restaurant (at Sheedy's Country House H.), Sulphir Hill, ℘ (065) 7074026,
Fax (065) 7074555 – ℗. **⊕** *VISA*
April-September – **Rest** *(booking essential Monday)* (dinner only) a la carte 34/52 **s.**
♦ Attractive, comfortable restaurant at the front of the building. Linen covered tables and
smart place settings. Interesting menus using freshest, local produce.

> If breakfast is included the ⊆ symbol appears after the number of rooms.

LISMORE (Lios Mór) *Waterford* **712** I 11.
Dublin 227 – Cork 56.5 – Fermoy 26.

Northgrove without rest., Tourtane, West : 1 ½ km by N 72 on Ballyduff rd ℘ (058)
54325, *johnhoward1@eircom.net,* 🐾 – ᯤᢟ ℗. **⊕** *VISA*
closed Christmas – **3 rm** ⊆ ✦40/50 – ✦✦65/70.
♦ Modern guesthouse providing a keenly priced and accessible resting place for visitors to
this historic town. Good sized, pine furnished bedrooms with colourful décor.

Glencairn Inn 🐾 with rm, West : 4 ¾ km by N 72 on Ballyduff rd ℘ (058) 56232,
glencairninn@eircom.net, Fax (058) 56232, ≼, 🐾 – ℗. **⊕** ⒶⒺ *VISA* . ✂️
closed 1 week Christmas – **Rest** *(booking essential in winter)* (dinner only) a la carte 40/60 –
5 rm ⊆ ✦70/90 – ✦✦110/125.
♦ "Pretty as a picture" cottage style inn: picket fence, brass bedsteads in quaint rooms.
Cosy bar, restaurant with red gingham tablecloths. Meals broad in scope and flavour.

LISTOWEL (Lios Tuathail) *Kerry* **712** D 10 – pop. 3 393.
EXC. : Ardfert★ *AC*, SW : 32 km by N 69 and minor roads via Abbeydorney – Banna Strand★,
SW : 35 km by N 69 and minor roads via Abbeydorney – Carrigafoyle Castle★, N : 17 km by
R 552 and minor road – Glin Castle★ *AC*, N : 24 km by N 69 – Rattoo Round Tower★, W : 19
km by R 553, R 554 and R 551.
🛈 St John's Church ℘ (068) 22590 *(June-September), tourisminfo@shannon-dev.ie.*
Dublin 270.5 – Killarney 54.5 – Limerick 75.5 – Tralee 27.5.

Allo's with rm, 41-43 Church St, ℘ (068) 22880, *allos@eircom.net, Fax (068) 22803* – **⊕**
ⒶⒺ *VISA*
closed 25 December – **Rest** *(closed Sunday-Monday)* (booking essential) (dinner only) a la
carte 18/48 – **3 rm** ✦45/65 – ✦✦80/100.
♦ Inviting feel with oak seats and wooden tables. Culinary classics with international
touches. Comfortable antique furnished rooms, hand-crafted beds and claw foot baths.

LITTLE ISLAND (An tOileán Beag) *Cork* **712** G/H 12 – see Cork.

LONGFORD (An Longfort) *Longford* 712 I 6.

⚏ *45 Dublin St* *℘ (043) 46566.*
Dublin 124 – Drogheda 120.5 – Galway 112.5 – Limerick 175.5.

⌂ **Viewmount House** ⌾ without rest., Dublin Rd, Southeast : 1½ km on R 393 *℘* (043) 41919, *info@viewmounthouse.com*, Fax (043) 42906, *㲝 – ✥ P. ⓐ ㏓ VISA. ⌾*
6 rm ⌇ ✚60/75 – ✚✚100/160.
  ♦ Impressive Georgian house in four acres; breakfast room has attractive vaulted ceiling, lounge reached by fine staircase. Rooms boast antique beds and period furniture.

⌂ **Longford Country House** ⌾, East : 8¾ km by R 194 off Aghnacliffe rd *℘* (043) 23320, *info@longfordcountryhouse.com*, Fax (043) 23516, *㲝 – ✥ P. ⓐ VISA. ⌾*
April-September – **Rest** (by arrangement) 40 – **6 rm** ⌇ ✚50 – ✚✚78/80.
  ♦ Pleasant purpose-built house in a rural spot with quiet gardens. Galleried sitting room, parlour with open fire. Particularly welcoming, individually furnished bedrooms.

LUCAN (Leamhcán) *Dublin* 712 M 7 – see Dublin.

MACROOM (Maigh Chromtha) *Cork* 712 F 12 – pop. 2 985.

⚐ *Lackaduve* *℘ (026) 41072.*
Dublin 299.5 – Cork 40 – Killarney 48.5.

🏨 **Castle**, Main St, *℘* (026) 41074, *castlehotel@eircom.net*, Fax (026) 41505, *ा₄, ▢ – ≣ ✥*, ≣ rest, ✆ ఈ P – ⚌ 200. ⓐ ㏓ VISA. ⌾
closed 23-27 December – **Rest** (carvery lunch)/dinner 35/38 and a la carte 35/39 **s.** – **B's :**
Rest (dinner only) 35/38 and a la carte 35/39 **s.** – **60 rm** ⌇ ✚89/110 – ✚✚150/180.
  ♦ A traditional hotel with gabled windows located in the town centre. Boasts a stylish leisure complex and neat, comfortable bedrooms. Informal B's. Local produce proudly used in Castle restaurant.

MALAHIDE (Mullach Íde) *Dublin* 712 N 7 *Ireland G.* – pop. 13 826.

See : Castle★★.
Env. : Newbridge House★ AC, N : 8 km by R 106, M1 and minor road.
⚐, ⚐ *Beechwood, The Grange* *℘ (01) 846 1611.*
Dublin 14.5 – Drogheda 38.5.

✕✕ **Cruzzo**, Marina Village, *℘* (01) 845 0599, *info@cruzzo.ie*, Fax (01) 845 0602, ≤, 㮾 – ≣ ≣ P. ⓐ ㏓ ① VISA
closed 25-26 December, Good Friday, Saturday lunch and dinner on Bank Holidays – **Rest** a la carte 38/49 ♀.
  ♦ Modern glass and designer furnishings in a striking marina restaurant above the water. Pleasantly distinctive ground-floor bar for lighter dishes. Tasty, modern cuisine.

✕✕ **Siam Thai**, 1 The Green, off Strand St *℘* (01) 845 4698, *siam@eircom.net*, Fax (01) 816 9460 – ≣. ⓐ ㏓ VISA
closed 25-26 December – **Rest** - Thai - (booking essential) (dinner only) 35 and a la carte 27/38.
  ♦ Centrally located restaurant with piano bar providing a light feel. Immaculately set tables and ornate, carved chairs. Richly authentic Thai cuisine, freshly prepared.

✕✕ **Jaipur**, 5 St James Terrace, *℘* (01) 845 5455, *info@jaipur.ie*, Fax (01) 845 5456 – ≣. ⓐ ㏓ VISA
closed 25 December – **Rest** - Indian - (dinner only and lunch in December) 45 and a la carte 27/40.
  ♦ Friendly basement restaurant in impressive Georgian terraced parade. Well-run by efficient, welcoming staff. Simple but lively modern décor. Contemporary Indian dishes.

✕ **Cape Greko**, First Floor, Unit One, New St, *℘* (01) 845 6288, *info@capegreko.com*, Fax (01) 845 6289 – ≣. ⓐ VISA
closed 25-26 December and lunch Monday-Thursday – **Rest** - Greek-Cypriot - (live music Friday and Saturday evening) a la carte 24/36.
  ♦ Hidden away in the town centre, this light, airy dining room, located up steep stairs, evokes happy, sunshine days with an authentic menu of combined Greek and Cypriot dishes.

at Kinsaley *Southwest : 4 km by R 106 on R 107 –* ⌂ *Malahide.*

🏠 **Belcamp Hutchinson** without rest., Carrs Lane, Balgriffin, D17, South : 1½ km by R 107 *℘* (01) 846 0843, *belcamphutchinson@eircom.net*, Fax (01) 848 5703 – P. ⓐ VISA
February - 20 December – **8 rm** ⌇ ✚75 – ✚✚150.
  ♦ Distinguished, creeper clad Georgian country house full of charm and character; eponymously named original owner. Walled garden with maze; airy rooms in strong, dark colours.

MALLOW (Mala) Cork **712** F 11 *Ireland G.* – pop. 8 937.

See : Town★ – St James' Church★.

Exc. : *Annes Grove Gardens★, E : 17¾ km by N 72 and minor rd – Buttevant Friary★, N : 11¼ km by N 20 – Doneraile Wildlife Park★ AC, NE : 9½ km by N 20 and R 581 – Kanturk★ (Castle★), W : 16 km by N 72 and R 576.*

🖫 Ballyellis 𝒫 (022) 21145.

Dublin 240 – Cork 34 – Killarney 64.5 – Limerick 66.

Longueville House ⬎, West : 5 ½ km by N 72 𝒫 (022) 47156, info@longueville house.ie, Fax (022) 47459, ≤, 🐾, 🍴, ♨ – ⅙℀ P – 🛎 30. ◐◉ AE VISA. ❀
closed 8 January-16 March – **Presidents :** Rest (booking essential) (light lunch)/dinner 60
47 – 20 rm ⊆ ✦110/235 – ✦✦235/340.

   ✦ Part Georgian manor; exudes history from oak trees planted in formation of battle lines at Waterloo and views of Dromineen Castle to richly ornate, antique-filled bedrooms. Restaurant offers gourmet cuisine.

Springfort Hall ⬎, North : 7 ½ km by N 20 on R 581 𝒫 (022) 21278, stay@springfort-hall.com, Fax (022) 21557, 🐾, 🍴, ♨ – ⅙℀ & P – 🛎 300. ◐◉ AE VISA. ❀
closed 23 December-1 January – Rest 35/52 ⅞ – 49 rm ⊆ ✦90/95 – ✦✦150/160.

   ✦ Beyond a porticoed entrance with grand door and fanlight, this part 18C manor offers large, well-proportioned rooms in keeping with the period. Salmon fishing arranged. Pale blond furniture in a richly decorated dining room.

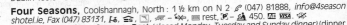

We try to be as accurate as possible when giving room rates.
But prices are susceptible to change,
so please check rates when booking.

MAYNOOTH (Maigh Nuad) Kildare **712** M 7 *Ireland G.* – pop. 10 151.

Env. : *Castletown House★★ AC, SE : 6½ km by R 405.*

Dublin 24.

Carton House, East : 3 km on R 148 Lexlip Road 𝒫 (01) 5052000, reservations@carton house.com, Fax (01) 6517703, ⑦, 🗗, 🖼, ⬜, 🖫, 🍴, ♨ – 🛗 ⅙℀ 🖳 ✆ P – 🛎 600. ◐◉ AE VISA
The Linden Tree : Rest 42/60 and a la carte 43/57 – **150 rm** ⊆ ✦155/205 – ✦✦170/220, 15 suites.

   ✦ Beautifully blended 18C home and modern hotel: boasts two golf courses, rose garden, superb spa, meeting rooms and graceful bedrooms: a winning mixture of charm and character. Popular, seasonal menus in modern dining room.

Moyglare Manor ⬎, Moyglare, North : 3 ¼ km 𝒫 (01) 628 6351, info@moyglarema nor.ie, Fax (01) 628 5405, ≤, 🍴, ♨ – ⅙℀ P. ◐◉ AE VISA. ❀
closed 24-26 December – Rest (dinner only) 60/70 – 16 rm ⊆ ✦110/150 – ✦✦220/250.

   ✦ 18C manor where everything denotes peace and quiet, from location - in sweeping grounds - to individually decorated rooms with canopy beds and four-posters. Antiques abound. Oil paintings hang proudly in fuchsia dining room.

Glenroyal, Straffan Rd, 𝒫 (01) 629 0909, info@glenroyal.ie, Fax (01) 629 0919, 🗗, 🖼,
⬜ – 🛗 ⅙℀ ✆ & P – 🛎 450. ◐◉ AE VISA. ❀
closed 25 December – **Bistro :** Rest (carvery lunch)/dinner a la carte 25/40 s. – **Lemon-grass :** Rest - Asian - a la carte 29/36 s. ⅞ – **113 rm** ⊆ ✦99 – ✦✦99/150.

   ✦ Adjacent to shopping centre, ideal for conferences and weddings. Rooms are furnished in smart fabrics with good quality furniture. Informal bistro. Authentic Asian menus at Lemongrass.

MILLSTREET Waterford **712** I 11 – see Cappoquin.

MONAGHAN (Muineachán) Monaghan **712** L 5 – pop. 5 936.

🇧 Market House 𝒫 (047) 81122 (April-October).

Dublin 133.5 – Belfast 69 – Drogheda 87 – Dundalk 35.5 – Londonderry 120.5.

Four Seasons, Coolshannagh, North : 1 ½ km on N 2 𝒫 (047) 81888, info@4season shotel.ie, Fax (047) 83131, 🗗, 🖼, ⬜, 🍴 – ⅙℀, 🍴 rest, P. – 🛎 450. AE VISA. ❀
closed 25 December – **Avenue :** Rest (closed Monday, Tuesday and Sunday dinner) (dinner only and Sunday lunch)/dinner a la carte 26/41 ⅞ – **The Range :** Rest a la carte 22/43 s. –
59 rm ⊆ ✦65/158 – ✦✦158/198.

   ✦ A hotel which offers a blend of the traditional and the modern. Bedrooms are in uni-form style and there is an atmospheric pub. Avenue offers modern dining. The Range has a farmhouse feel with beams and dressers.

1031

at Glaslough Northeast : 9½ km by N 12 on R 185 – ⊠ Monaghan.

Castle Leslie ⚓, ☎ (047) 88100, info@castleleslie.com, Fax (047) 88256, ≤, ⚘, 🐎, ₤, ✕ – ↦❄ 🄿, 🆚 🆎 🆅🆂🅰, ✕
Rest (booking essential for non-residents) (dinner only) 45 ♀ – **20 rm** ⊊ ✝140 – ✝✝190.
♦ Family castle in vast parkland with ancient woods and well preserved pike lake. Enjoy walks, boating and fishing. Unique, themed rooms named after personalities in history. Restaurant boasts oil paintings on green hued walls, ornate fireplace.

MONKSTOWN (Baile na Mhanaigh) Cork 712 G/H 12.

🄶 Parkgarriffe ☎ (021) 841376.
Dublin 257.5 – Cork 14.5 – Waterford 120.5.

The Bosun, The Pier, ☎ (021) 4842172, info@thebosun.ie, Fax (021) 4842008, ≤, 🍴 – 🖇, 🍴 rest, 🆚 🆅🆂🅰, ✕
closed 24-26 December and Good Friday – **Rest** 30/45 and a la carte 25/45 ♀ – **15 rm** ⊊ ✝67 – ✝✝120.
♦ After a walk along the waterway, unwind in the cosy environment of this quayside hotel. There is a private entrance for the bedrooms which are neatly and simply furnished. Seaside location reflected in restaurant menus.

MOYCULLEN (Maigh Cuilinn) Galway 712 E 7.

Env. : Lough Corrib★★ : Aughnanure Castle★ AC, N : 15 km by N 59 – Oughterard★ (view★★), N : 17 km N by N 59 and minor road along lake shore.
Dublin 223.5 – Galway 11.5.

Moycullen House ⚓ with rm, Mountain Rd, Southwest : 1½ km by Spiddle rd ☎ (091) 555621, info@moycullen.com, Fax (091) 555566, 🍴 – 🄿, 🆚 🆎 🆅🆂🅰, ✕
closed 8 January-17 March and 25-26 December – **Rest** (closed Wednesday) (dinner only and Sunday lunch)/dinner a la carte 39/49 – **2 rm** ⊊ ✝80 – ✝✝120.00.
♦ Built 1890s in "Arts and Crafts" style, set in woodland. Homely rooms, antique furniture. Stone walled dining room with polished oak tables on which tasty meals are served.

MULLINAVAT (Muileann an Bhata) Kilkenny 712 K 10.

Dublin 141.5 – Kilkenny 34 – Waterford 13.

Rising Sun, Main St, ☎ (051) 898173, info@therisingsun.ie, Fax (051) 898435 – 🄿, 🆚 🆎 🆅🆂🅰, ✕
closed 24-28 December – **Rest** (carving lunch)/dinner a la carte 19/30 s. – **10 rm** ⊊ ✝50/70 – ✝✝100/120.
♦ A rustic, stone built 17C inn with friendly character. Indoors is a bar with walls hung with brewery themed mirrors. Rooms are of good size and well kept. Sandwiches and steaks served in a traditional dining room.

MULLINGAR (An Muileann gCearr) Westmeath 712 J/K 7 Ireland G. – pop. 15 621.

Env. : Belvedere House and Gardens★ AC, S : 5½ km by N 52.
Exc. : Fore Abbey★, NE : 27¼ km by R 394 – Multyfarnham Franciscan Friary★, N : 12¾ km by N 4 – Tullynally★ AC, N : 21 km by N 4 and R 394.
🄳 Market House ☎ (0449) 348650.
Dublin 79 – Drogheda 58.

Mullingar Park, Dublin Rd, East : 2½ km on Dublin Rd (N 4) ☎ (044) 933 7500, info@mullingarparkhotel.com, Fax (044) 933 5937, 🕐, 🏋, ≋s, 🔲 – 🖇 ↦❄, 🍴 rest, ✆ 🅿 – 🚗 1000. 🆚 🆎 🄾 🆅🆂🅰, ✕
closed 24-25 December – **Rest** (buffet lunch)/dinner 38/44 and a la carte 39/45 – **94 rm** ⊊ ✝100/150 – ✝✝150/250, 1 suite.
♦ Spacious modern hotel with a strong appeal to business and leisure travellers: there's a hydrotherapy pool and host of treatment rooms. Airy, light bedrooms with mod cons. Smart, airy restaurant with international menus.

Marlinstown Court without rest., Dublin Rd, East : 2½ km on Dublin Rd (N 4) ☎ (044) 40053, marlinstownct@eircom.net, Fax (044) 40057, 🍴 – ↦❄ 🄿, 🆚 🆅🆂🅰, ✕
5 rm ⊊ ✝45/50 – ✝✝70/80.
♦ Clean, tidy guesthouse close to junction with N4. Modern rear extension. Light and airy pine-floored lounge and breakfast room overlooking garden. Brightly furnished bedrooms.

↑ **Hilltop Country House** without rest., Delvin Rd, Rathconnell, Northeast : 4 km by N 52 ℰ (044) 9348 958, *hilltopcountryhouse@eircom.net*, ☞ – ↔ **P**, **Ⓜ**. ℘
March-October – **4 rm** ⬜ ✫45/50 – ✫✫70.
    ◆ Chalet styled house with attractive gardens. Reception and lounge areas cheered by paintings. Good Irish breakfast served. Snug, homely rooms with pleasant views.

at Ballynagall *North : 6 km on R 394 –* ✉ *Mullingar.*

XX **Belfry**, ℰ (044) 9342488, *info@belfryrestaurant.com*, Fax (044) 9340094 – **P**, ◇ 19. **Ⓜ**
VISA
closed Monday-Tuesday and Sunday dinner – **Rest** 24/28 a la carte 42/56.
    ◆ 19C rural church converted with taste and style. Impressive dining room retains many original fittings; private dining room used for cookery classes. Seasonal French cooking.

MULRANNY **(An Mhala Raithni)** *Mayo* **712** C 6.
Dublin 270 – Castlebar 35 – Westport 29.

🏨 **Park Inn**, on N 59 ℰ (098) 36000, *info@parkinnmulranny.ie*, Fax (098) 36899, ⩽, 𝄞, ≋,
▦, ≞–▮ ↔, ▤ rest, ℃ ⅙ **P** – ⚐ 350. **Ⓜ Ⓞ VISA**
closed Christmas – **Rest** *(closed Monday-Saturday lunch)* a la carte 39/48 **s.** – **41 rm** ⬜
✫75/135 – ✫✫160/210, 20 suites.
    ◆ Purpose-built business oriented hotel behind 19C façade: lovely Clew Bay views. Impressive leisure and conference facilities. Airy rooms with slightly minimalist interiors. Smart, formal, linen-clad restaurant.

NAAS **(An Nás)** *Kildare* **712** L/M 8 – *pop. 18 288.*
Exc. : *Russborough*★★★ *AC, S : 16 km by R 410 and minor road – Castletown House*★★ *AC,
NE : 24 km by R 407 and R 403.*
🏌 *Kerdiffstown, Naas* ℰ (045) 874644.
Dublin 30.5 – Kilkenny 83.5 – Tullamore 85.5.

🏨 **Killashee House** ⩗, *South : 1 ½ km on R 448 (Kilcullen Rd)* ℰ (045) 879277, *reserva
tions@killasheehouse.com*, Fax (045) 879266, ⑰, 𝄞, ≋, ▦, ☞, ≞–▮ ↔, ▤ rest, ℃ ⅙
P – ⚐ 1600. **Ⓜ Ⓞ AE VISA**. ℘
closed 24-25 December – **Turners :** Rest (dinner only and Sunday lunch) 50/60 **s.** ℉ – **Nun's
Kitchen :** Rest a la carte 26/40 **s.** ℉ – **130 rm** ⬜ ✫144/170 – ✫✫198/250, 12 suites.
    ◆ Imposing part 1860s hunting lodge in acres of parkland. Rooms in the original house are most characterful: French antique furniture, original panelling and fireplaces. Elegant Turners overlooking garden. Informal Nun's Kitchen.

🏨 **Osprey**, Devoy Quarter, ℰ (045) 881111, *info@osprey.ie*, Fax (045) 881112, ㈝, ⑰, 𝄞,
≋, ▦–▮ ↔ ▤ ℃ ⅙ ⇔ **P** – ⚐ 350. **Ⓜ AE Ⓞ VISA**. ℘
closed dinner 24-25 December – **Rest** *(closed Sunday)* (carvery lunch Monday-Saturday)/dinner a la carte 43/55 – **93 rm** ⬜ ✫315.00 – ✫✫315.00, 11 suites.
    ◆ Former barracks, now a smart, stylish hotel. Vast bar area on two levels where carvery is served. Up-to-date leisure and spa. Modish bedrooms in cool colours. Restaurant boasts brown leather chairs and floor-to-ceiling windows overlooking fountain.

XX **Les Olives**, 10 South Main St, (above Kavanagh's pub), ℰ (045) 894788, *lesolives@eir
com.net* – **Ⓜ VISA**
closed Sunday, Monday and Tuesday after Bank Holidays – **Rest** (booking essential) (dinner only) a la carte 44/71 ℉.
    ◆ Above a pub looking down on high street; three sunny rooms complemented by colourful artwork, generous sized tables. French inspired cuisine with international flourishes.

NAVAN **(An Uaimh)** *Meath* **712** L 7 *Ireland G.* – *pop. 19 417.*
Env. : *Brú na Bóinne : Newgrange*★★★ *AC, Knowth*★, *E : 16 km by minor road to Donore –
Bective Abbey*★, *S : 6½ km by R 161 – Tara*★ *AC, S : 8 km by N 3.*
Exc. : *Kells*★ *(Round Tower and High Crosses*★★, *St Columba's House*★ *), NW : by N 3 –
Trim*★ *(castle*★★ *), SW : 12¾ km by R 161.*
🏌 *Moor Park, Mooretown* ℰ (046) 27661 – 🏌, 🏌 *Royal Tara, Bellinter* ℰ (046) 922 5244.
Dublin 48.5 – Drogheda 26 – Dundalk 51.5.

🏨 **Newgrange**, Bridge St, ℰ (046) 9074100, *info@newgrangehotel.ie*, Fax (046) 9073977 –
▮ ↔, ▤ rest, **P** – ⚐ 450. **Ⓜ AE Ⓞ VISA**. ℘
closed 25 December – **Bridge Brasserie :** Rest (carvery lunch Monday-Saturday)/dinner 30/40 and a la carte 20/40 ℉ – **62 rm** ⬜ ✫89/130 – ✫✫140/180.
    ◆ Warm-toned, well-fitted modern rooms and an inviting, traditionally styled bar, plus ample meeting space, make this town centre hotel a popular function venue. Smart, bright brasserie.

REPUBLIC OF IRELAND

Ma Dwyers without rest., Dublin Rd, South : 1 ¼ km on N 3   ℰ (046) 9077992, *Fax (046) 9077995* – ✑ ✖ 🄿 ⓄⓈ *VISA* ✑
closed 25 December – **9 rm** ✖ ✚50 – ✚✚80.
• Yellow-painted, mock-Georgian house; comfortable guest lounge, modern breakfast room. Hospitality trays in equally bright, simple bedrooms.

Killyon without rest., Dublin Rd, South : 1 ½ km on N 3   ℰ (046) 9071224, *info@kill yonguesthouse.ie, Fax (046) 9072766* – ✑ ✖ ℰ 🄿 ⓄⓈ *VISA* ✑
closed 24-25 December – **6 rm** ✑ ✚45/50 – ✚✚80.
• Very good value, comfortable guesthouse, overlooking the river Boyne, run by husband and wife team. Bedrooms are individually decorated. Home baking and good breakfast choice.

NENAGH (An tAonach) *Tipperary* **712** H 9 *Ireland G.* – *pop. 6 454.*
   See : *Castle*★.
   🄶 *Nenagh, Birchwood* ℰ (067) 31476.
   🄱 *The Governor's House, Connolly St* ℰ (067) 31610 *(mid May-mid September), touris minfo@shannon-dev.ie.*
   Dublin 154.5 – Galway 101.5 – Limerick 42.

Abbey Court, Dublin Rd, East : ½ km   ℰ (067) 41111, *info@abbeycourt.ie, Fax (067) 41022,* ☒, ⇌, ☐ – ☒ 🄿 rest, ℰ ⅁ 🄿 – ☒ 450. ⓄⓈ ⒶⒺ Ⓞ *VISA* ✑
closed 25 December – **The Cloisters :** Rest (carvery lunch)/dinner a la carte 18/26 **s.** – **82** ✑ ✚90/95 – ✚✚120/140.
• A castellated façade, clock tower and arched windows add a historical theme to a modern hotel. Fitness club offers all amenities including hair salon. Modern bedrooms. Wooden statue of monk distinguishes beamed dining room.

NEWBRIDGE (An Droichead Nua) *Kildare* **712** L 8 *Ireland G.* – *pop. 12 970.*
   Env. : *Irish National Stud*★★ *AC (Japanese Gardens*★★ *AC) SW : 9½ km by N 7 – Kildare*★ *(Cathedral*★ *) SW : 8¾ km by N 7.*
   🄶 *Curragh* ℰ (045) 441238.
   Dublin 45 – Kilkenny 92 – Tullamore 58.

Annagh Lodge without rest., Naas Rd, ½ km on R 445   ℰ (045) 433518, *annagh lodge@eircom.net, Fax (045) 433538* – ✑ ℰ ⅁ 🄿 ⓄⓈ *VISA* ✑
10 rm ✑ ✚65/85 – ✚✚100/130.
• Bungalow guesthouse on main road into town. Small garden with summerhouse; rear conservatory overlooks it. Bright, modern breakfast room. Spotless, spacious rooms.

NEWMARKET-ON-FERGUS (Cora Chaitlín) *Clare* **712** F 7 – *pop. 1 542.*
   Env. : *Bunratty Castle*★★ *AC, S : 10 km by N 18 – Craggaunowen Centre*★ *AC, NE : 15 km by minor road towards Moymore – Knappogue Castle*★ *AC, NE : 12 km N 18 and minor roads via Quin – Quin Friary*★ *AC, N : 10 km by N 18 and minor road to Quin.*
   🄶 *Dromoland Castle* ℰ (061) 368444.
   Dublin 219 – Ennis 13 – Limerick 24.

Dromoland Castle ⚲, Northwest : 2 ½ km on N 18   ℰ (061) 368144, *sales@dromo land.ie, Fax (061) 363355,* ≤, 🄿, ☒, ⇌, ☐, 🄶, 🏌, ☞, ⚑ – ✑ ℰ 🄿 – ☒ 450. ⓄⓈ ⒶⒺ Ⓞ *VISA* ✑
Earl of Thormond : Rest (dinner only and Sunday lunch) 67 and a la carte 60/85 ♀ – **Fig Tree** (at Dromoland Golf & Country Club) (ℰ (061) 368444) **:** Rest 45 (dinner) and lunch a la carte approx 35 – ✑ 26 – **94 rm** ✚232/430 – ✚✚436/590, 6 suites.
• Restored 16C castle with 375 acres of woodland and golf course. Sumptuous rooms with plenty of thoughtful extras. Waterford crystal chandeliers and gilded mirrors in the Earl of Thormond restaurant. More informal style in the Fig Tree, popular with golfers.

Undecided between two equivalent establishments?
Within each category, establishments are classified
in our order of preference.

NEWPORT (Baile Uí Fhiacháin) *Mayo* **712** D 6 *Ireland G.*

Env. : Burrishoole Abbey★, NW : 3¼ km by N 59 – Furnace Lough★, NW : 4¾ km by N 59.

Exc. : Achill Island★, W : 35 km by N 59 and R 319.

🛈 *James St, Westport* ℰ *(098) 25711.*

Dublin 264 – Ballina 59.5 – Galway 96.5.

🏠 **Newport House** ॐ, ℰ (098) 41222, *info@newporthouse.ie, Fax* (098) 41613, ⤫, 🐎, ⬛ – ⬤ ⤫ ✦ 🅿. ⓂⓄ 🆅🅸🆂🅰. ⅍
18 March-10 October – **Rest** (dinner only) 63 and a la carte approx 50 **s.** – **18 rm** ⊆ ✦177/188 – ✦✦302/324.
♦ Mellow ivy-clad Georgian mansion; grand staircase up to gallery and drawing room. Bedrooms in main house or courtyard; some in self-contained units ideal for families. Enjoy the fresh Newport estate produce used in the dishes served in the elegant dining room.

NEW QUAY *Clare Ireland G.*

Env. : Aillwee Cave★ AC, S : 10 km by N 67 and R 480 – Corcomroe Abbey★, S : 4¾ km by N 67 – Dunguaire Castle★ AC, NE : 15 km by N 67.

Dublin 240 – Ennis 55 – Galway 46.5.

🍴 **Linnane's Bar**, New Quay Pier, ℰ (065) 7078120, 🌳 – 🅿. ⓂⓄ 🅰🅴 ⓄⒹ 🆅🅸🆂🅰. ⅍
closed 25 December and Good Friday – **Rest** - Seafood - a la carte 18/39.
♦ Take lunch here on the terrace beside a sea inlet. Country pub with rustic decor and interesting old photos. Fresh seafood served all day in summer and sold in the pier shop.

Your opinions are important to us:
please write and let us know about your discoveries and experiences –
good and bad!

NEW ROSS (Ros Mhic Thriúin) *Wexford* **712** L 10 *Ireland G.* – pop. 6 537 – ✉ Newbawn.

See : St Mary's Church★.

Exc. : Kennedy Arboretum, Campile★ AC, S : 12 km by R 733 – Kilmokea Gardens★ AC, S : 15 km by R 733 and minor road W – Dunbrody Abbey★, S : 12¾ km by R 733 – Inistioge★, NW : 16 km by N 25 and R 700 – Graiguenamanagh★ (Duiske Abbey★★ AC), N : 17¾ km by N 25 and R705.

🛈 *The Quay* ℰ *(051) 421857 (June-August).*

Dublin 141.5 – Kilkenny 43.5 – Waterford 24 – Wexford 37.

⌂ **Riversdale House** without rest., Lower William St, ℰ (051) 422515, *riversdale house@eircom.net*, 🐎 – ⤫ 🅿. ⓂⓄ 🆅🅸🆂🅰. ⅍
February - October – 4 rm ⊆ ✦✦70.
♦ Conservatory lounge and home baking are among the attractions of a good-value guesthouse, run by a friendly owner. Well-tended garden, neat bedrooms with electric blankets.

at Ballynabola *Southeast : 9½ km on N 25* – ✉ New Ross.

🏠 **Cedar Lodge**, Carrigbyrne, East : 4 ¾ km on N 25 ℰ (051) 428386, *cedarlodge@eir com.net, Fax* (051) 428222, 🐎 – 🅿. ⓂⓄ 🅰🅴 ⓄⒹ 🆅🅸🆂🅰. ⅍
closed 20 December-January – **Rest** (bar lunch)/dinner 50 **s.** – **28 rm** ⊆ ✦120/140 – ✦✦140/200.
♦ Family owned hotel beneath slopes of Carrigbyrne Forest, with leafy garden. This is hiking country; owners have compiled walking routes; relax in pastel-toned bedrooms. Dining room menu reflects the area's fruit and honey produce.

NEWTOWNMOUNTKENNEDY (Baile An Chinnéidieh) *Wicklow* **712** N 8.

Dublin 35.5 – Glendalough 22.5 – Wicklow 16.

🏰 **Marriott Druids Glen H. & Country Club** ॐ, East : 2 ¾ km off Kilcoole rd ℰ (01) 287 0800, *mhrs.dubgs.reservations@marriothotels.com, Fax* (01) 287 0801, 🌳, ⑰, ℻, ⬅s, 🔲, ⬜s 🔧 – 📶 ⤫ ☰ ✦ & 🅿. – 🎿 250. ⓂⓄ 🅰🅴 ⓄⒹ 🆅🅸🆂🅰. ⅍
Druids : Rest (dinner only) 35 and a la carte 35/46 **s.** ⚥ – *Flynn's Steakhouse :* **Rest** (dinner only and Sunday lunch)/dinner 55/75 and a la carte 55/78 ⚥ – **134 rm** ⊆ ✦125/155 – ✦✦125/250, 11 suites.
♦ Modern hotel in 400 acres, next to golf course. Spacious marble and granite atrium; leisure, conference facilities. Very comfortable rooms, with every conceivable facility. Druids offers a popular buffet. Classic grill dishes at Flynn's Steakhouse.

OUGHTERARD (Uachtar Ard) *Galway* 712 E 7 *Ireland G.*

See : *Town★*.

Env. : *Lough Corrib★★ (Shore road – NW – ≤★★) – Aughnanure Castle★ AC, SE : 3¼ km by N 59.*

🐾 *Gortreevagh* ℰ (091) 552131.

🏛 *Community Office* ℰ (091) 552808.

Dublin 240 – Galway 27.5.

🏨 **Ross Lake House** ⟋, Rosscahill, Southeast : 7 ¼ km by N 59 ℰ (091) 550109, *ros slake@iol.ie*, Fax (091) 550184, 🌿, ℁ – ⇌ **P.** **ⒶⒺ** **VISA**, ⟍
15 March-October – **Rest** (dinner only) 45 ⟍ – **12 rm** ⟍ **★**105/115 – **★★**150/170, 1 suite.
◆ Georgian country house set in its own estate of woods and attractive gardens. The period theme is carried right through interiors. Bright bedrooms with antiques. Spacious, comfortable dining room with smartly set polished tables.

🏛 **Currarevagh House** ⟋, Northwest : 6 ½ km on Glann rd ℰ (091) 552312, *mail@cur rarevagh.com*, Fax (091) 552731, ≤, 🌿, 🌳, ℁, ⟍, ℁ – ⇌ **P.** ⟍
April-15 October – **Rest** (booking essential) (set menu only) (dinner only) 42/45 s. – **15 rm** ⟍ **★**95/140 – **★★**190/210.
◆ Victorian manor on Lough Corrib, set in 170 acres. Period décor throughout plus much fishing memorabilia. Two lovely sitting rooms. Comfortable, well-kept rooms. Country house style dining room, popular with fishing parties.

🏠 **Waterfall Lodge** without rest., West : ¾ km on N 59 ℰ (091) 552168, *kdolly@eir com.net*, 🌿, 🌳 – ⇌ **P.** ⟍
6 rm ⟍ **★**50 – **★★**80.
◆ Two minutes from the centre, a well-priced guesthouse rebuilt with gleaming wood and original Victorian fittings. A good fishing river flows through the charming gardens.

🏠 **Railway Lodge** ⟋ without rest., South : ¾ km by Costello rd taking first right onto unmarked road ℰ (091) 552945, *railwaylodge@eircom.net*, ≤, 🌳 – ⇌ **P.** ⟍ **VISA**
4 rm ⟍ **★**70 – **★★**100.
◆ Elegantly furnished modern guest house in remote farm location. Communal breakfast with plenty of choice. Open fires, books and magazine but no TV. Beautifully kept bedrooms.

Red = Pleasant. Look for the red 🍴 and 🏛 symbols.

PONTOON *Mayo* 712 E 6 – ✉ Foxford.

See : *Bridge (≤ ★).*

Env. : *Errew Abbey★, N : 22 km by R 315 and minor road – Museum of Country Life★ AC, S : 11 km by R 310 and minor road to Turlough.*

Dublin 233.5 – Castlebar 14.5 – Sligo 80.5.

🏨 **Healy's**, ℰ (094) 9256443, *info@healyspontoon.com*, Fax (094) 9256572, ≤ Lough Cullin, 🌿, 🌳 – ⇌ **P.** ⟍ **ⒶⒺ** **Ⓓ** **VISA**, ⟍
closed 25 December – **Rest** (bar lunch Monday-Saturday)/dinner a la carte 24/55 ⟍ – **14 rm** ⟍ **★**65/75 – **★★**90/110.
◆ Extended 19C shooting lodge on shores of Lough Cullin. Well geared up to the fishing fraternity with related paraphernalia and comfortable bars. Bedrooms are simply appointed. Extensive wine list and lough views in the dining room.

PORTLAOISE (Port Laoise) *Laoise* 712 K 8.

Dublin 88.5 – Carlow 40 – Waterford 101.5.

🏨 **The Heritage**, Jessop St, ℰ (0502) 78588, *res@theheritagehotel.com*, Fax (0502) 78577, 🛄, ℁, 🔲 – 🛗 ⇌, ▤ rest, ⟍ ⟍ ⟍ – 🅰 500. ⟍ **ⒶⒺ** **Ⓓ** **VISA**, ⟍
closed 23-27 December – **The Fitzmaurice** : Rest (booking essential) (carvery lunch) a la carte 30/42 ⟍ – **Spago** : Rest - Italian - (dinner only) a la carte 24/41 s. ⟍ – **109 rm** ⟍ **★**170/240 – **★★**170/240, 1 suite.
◆ Impressive, purpose-built hotel in central location. Extensive leisure facilities include a large pool. Thoroughly spacious throughout. Well equipped bedrooms. Formal Fitzmaurice serving a modern menu. More relaxed Italian-style Spago restaurant.

🏠 **Ivyleigh House** without rest., Bank Pl, Church St, ℰ (057) 8622081, *info@ivyleigh.com*, Fax (057) 8663343, 🌳 – ⇌ ⟍ **P.** ⟍ **VISA**, ⟍
closed Christmas – 6 rm ⟍ **★**80/85 – **★★**125.
◆ Attractive Georgian listed house with gardens. Breakfast a feature: owner makes it all herself from fresh produce. Charming period drawing room. Airy bedrooms with antiques.

PORTMAGEE (An Caladh) *Kerry* **712** A 12 *Ireland G.*

Exc. : *Ring of Kerry★★.*
Dublin 365 – Killarney 72.5 – Tralee 82.

🏠 **Moorings**, ℰ (066) 9477108, *moorings@iol.ie, Fax (066) 9477220*, ≤ – ⇔, 🖿 rest, ❤ 🅿.
🌐 🖭 *VISA*. 🛇
closed 20 December-10 January – **Rest** *(closed Monday dinner except Bank Holidays)* (bar lunch)/dinner a la carte 35/56 – **16 rm** ⌕ ✦50/60 – ✦✦80/90.
✦ Pub-style hotel in the high street of this attractive village. Spacious, nautical themed bar and trim upstairs lounge. Bedrooms with views over harbour and its fishing boats. Stone-walled, candlelit dining room with seafaring curios.

PORTMARNOCK (Port Mearnóg) *Dublin* **712** N 7 *Ireland G.* – pop. 8 376.

Env. : *Malahide Castle★★ AC*, N : 4 km by R 124 – *Ben of Howth★*, S : 8 km by R 124 – *Newbridge House★ AC*, N : 16 km by R 124, M 1 and minor road east.
Dublin 8 – Drogheda 45.

🏨 **Portmarnock H. and Golf Links**, Strand Rd, ℰ (01) 846 0611, *reservations@portmarnock.com, Fax (01) 846 2442*, ≤, ⌕, ₤₅, ⇔₅, ₁₈, 🥀 – 🛗 ⇔, 🖿 rest, ❤ ₲ 🅿 – 🔬 350.
🌐 🖭 ⓞ *VISA*. 🛇
Rest – (see ***The Osborne*** below) – **138 rm** ⌕ ✦245 – ✦✦325.
✦ Large golf-oriented hotel with challenging 18-hole course. Original fittings embellish characterful, semi-panelled Jamesons Bar. Very comfortable, individually styled rooms.

🍴🍴🍴 **The Osborne** (at Portmarnock H. and Golf Links), ℰ (01) 846 0611 – 🖿 🅿. 🌐 🖭 ⓞ
VISA
Rest (dinner only and Sunday lunch) 42 and a la carte 43/61.
✦ Distinctively formal restaurant named after artist Walter Osborne. Regularly changing menus balance the modern and traditional. Professionally run with good golf course views.

RANELAGH (Raghnallach) *Dublin* **712** N 7 – see Dublin.

RATHMELTON (Ráth Mealtain) *Donegal* **712** J 2 *Ireland G.*

See : *Town★.*
Dublin 248 – Donegal 59.5 – Londonerry 43.5 – Sligo 122.5.

🏠 **Ardeen** 🛇 without rest., turning by the Town Hall ℰ (074) 9151243, *ardeenbandb@eir com.net, Fax (074) 9151243*, 🥀, 🛇 – ⇔ 🅿. 🌐 *VISA*. 🛇
Easter-October – **5 rm** ⌕ ✦40/50 – ✦✦80.
✦ Simple Victorian house, with very welcoming owner, on edge of village. Homely ambience in lounge and breakfast room. Immaculately kept bedrooms.

RATHMINES (Ráth Maonais) *Dublin* **712** ④⓪ – see Dublin.

RATHMULLAN (Ráth Maoláin) *Donegal* **712** J 2 *Ireland G.* – pop. 491 – ✉ Letterkenny.

Exc. : *Knockalla Viewpoint★*, N : 12¾ km by R 247 – *Rathmelton★*, SW : 11¼ km by R 247.
₅ *Otway, Saltpans* ℰ (074) 915 1665.
Dublin 265.5 – Londonderry 58 – Sligo 140.

🏨 **Rathmullan House** 🛇, North : ½ m. on R 247 ℰ (074) 9158188, *info@rathmullan house.com, Fax (074) 9158200*, ≤, 🔲, 🐾, 🥀, ₤, 🛇 – ⇔ 🅿 – 🔬 80. 🌐 🖭 *VISA*. 🛇
closed 7 January-10 February – **Rest** (bar lunch)/dinner 50/60 and a la carte 51/58 ⌣ –
34 rm ⌕ ✦90/185 – ✦✦180/280.
✦ Part 19C country house with fine gardens in secluded site on Lough Swilly. Choose a lounge as pleasant spot for lunch. Stylish, individualistic rooms: newer ones very comfy. Restaurant boasts serious dinner menus at linen-clad tables.

🏠 **Fort Royal** 🛇, North : 1 ½ km by R 247 ℰ (074) 9158100, *fortroyal@eircom.net, Fax (074) 9158103*, ≤, 🥀, ₤, 🛇 – ⇔ 🅿. 🌐 🖭 ⓞ *VISA*
April-October – **Rest** *(closed Sunday lunch)* (bar lunch)/dinner 47 s. – **15 rm** ⌕ ✦85/130 –
✦✦170/190.
✦ Early 19C house in a very quiet location with attractive gardens that run down to the beach. Two comfortable lounges and a spacious bar. Characterful, homely bedrooms. Lunchtime sandwiches in the bar; main evening meal in comfy restaurant.

RATHNEW (Ráth Naoi) *Wicklow* **712** N 8 – see Wicklow.

RECESS **(Sraith Salach)** *Galway* **712** C 7 *Ireland G.*

Exc. : *Connemara★★★ – Cashel★, SW : by N 59 and R 340.*

Dublin 278.5 – Ballina 116 – Galway 58.

Lough Inagh Lodge, Northwest : 7 ¾ km by N 59 on R 344 ℘ (095) 34706, *inagh@iol.ie, Fax (095) 34708,* ≤ Lough Inagh and The Twelve Bens, – P. MC AE VISA

mid March-mid December – **Rest** (booking essential for non-residents) (bar lunch)/dinner a la carte 38/46 **s.** – **13 rm** ★112/135 – ★★184/264.

◆ Part 19C former fishing lodge with enchanting views of Lough Inagh and The Twelve Bens. Warm, welcoming feel and ambience; cosy bedrooms. Attentive service in country house-style restaurant.

REDCASTLE *Donegal* **712** K 2.

Dublin 266 – Muff 14 – Redcastle 33.

Carlton Redcastle H.+C.Spa, on R 238 ℘ (074) 9385555, *info@carltonredcastle.ie, Fax (074) 9385444,* ≤, – , rest, P – 400. MC AE VISA

closed 24-26 December – **Rest** (bar lunch Monday-Saturday)/dinner 38 and a la carte 31/48 – **83 rm** ★80/119 – ★★110/188, 10 suites.

◆ An extensive range of treatments attracts majority to this refurbished hotel with enviable Lough Foyle setting. Boasts Thalasso pool and juice bar. Streamlined, stylish rooms. Restaurant in stunning spot with super outdoor terrace.

The ✿ award is the crème de la crème.
This is awarded to restaurants
which are really worth travelling miles for!

RINGVILLE *Waterford* **712** J 11 – *see Dungarvan.*

RIVERSTOWN **(Baile idir Dhá Abhainn)** *Sligo* **712** G 5.

Dublin 198 – Sligo 21.

Coopershill, ℘ (071) 9165108, *ohara@coopershill.com, Fax (071) 9165466,* ≤, – P. MC AE VISA.

April-October – **Rest** (booking essential for non-residents) (dinner only) 57 **s.** ♀ – **8 rm** ★142/159 – ★★224/258.

◆ Magnificent Georgian country house set within 500 acre estate. Home to six generations of one family. Antique furnished communal areas and rooms exude charm and character. Family portraits, antique silver adorn dining room.

ROSCOMMON **(Ros Comáin)** *Roscommon* **712** H 7 *Ireland G. – pop. 4 489.*

See : *Castle★.*

Exc. : *Castlestrange Stone★, SW : 11 ¼ km by N 63 and R 362 – Strokestown★ (Famine Museum★ AC, Strokestown Park House★ AC), N : 19 ¼ km by N 61 and R 368 – Castlerea : Clonalis House★ AC, NW : 30½ km by N 60.*

Moate Park ℘ (09066) 26382.

Harrison Hall ℘ (090) 6626342 (June-August).

Dublin 151 – Galway 92 – Limerick 151.

Abbey, on N 63 (Galway rd) ℘ (090) 6626240, *info@abbeyhotel.ie, Fax (090) 6626021,* – P – 200. MC AE VISA.

closed 24-26 December – **Rest** 27/45 and dinner a la carte 32/42 **s.** – **50 rm** ★100/120 – ★★190.00/240.00.

◆ Part 19C house with modern extensions, convenient central location and surrounded by attractive gardens. Excellent leisure facilities. Comfortable bedrooms. Spacious restaurant overlooks ruins of Abbey.

Gleeson's Townhouse, Market Sq, ℘ (090) 6626954, *info@gleesonstownhouse.com, Fax (090) 6627425,* –, rest, P – 70. MC AE VISA

closed 25-26 December – **Rest** 28/40 (dinner) and a la carte 21/34 **s.** ♀ – **18 rm** ★60/75 – ★★100/150, 1 suite.

◆ 19C former manse with courtyard overlooking the market square. This substantial stone-built edifice was once a minister's residence. Comfortable, well-equipped bedrooms. Meals available in the farmhouse-style restaurant.

⚬ **Westway** without rest., Galway Rd, Southwest : 1 ¼ km on N 63 ℰ (090) 6626927, *westwayguests@eircom.net*, ℰ – ⊱⇤ ⚓ 𝐏, ⬤⬤ VISA. ⅏
closed 20 December-3 January – **4 rm** � ⚭40 – ⚭⚭65.
♦ Modern guesthouse with friendly welcome near town centre. Comfy, traditional residents' lounge. Breakfast room with conservatory extension. Brightly decorated rooms.

ROSCREA (Ros Cré) *Tipperary* **712** I 9.

See : *Town★ – Damer House★ AC.*
Dublin 125.5 – Birr 19.5 – Nenagh 34.

🏨 **Racket Hall**, Dublin Rd, East : 2 ¾ km on N 7 ℰ (0505) 21748, *racketh@iol.ie*, Fax (0505) 23701, ℟, ⌖ – ❙ & 𝐏, – ⬛ 400. ⬤⬤ 𝔸𝔼 VISA. ⅏
The Willow Tree : Rest (carving lunch)/dinner 28/33 and a la carte 24/40 **s.** – **40 rm** ⊊
⚭69/99 – ⚭⚭119/169.
♦ Bright yellow, creeper-clad, extended roadside inn. Huge rustic pubby area with sofas and shelves of books. Bedrooms offer good levels of comfort and modern facilities. Formal dining to the rear.

ROSSES POINT (An Ros) *Sligo* **712** G 5.

Env. : *Sligo★★ : Abbey★ AC, Model Arts and the Niland Gallery★ AC, S : 8 km by R 281 – Drumcliff★, N : 16 km by R 281 and N 15.*
Exc. : *Carrowmore Megalithic Cemetery★ AC, S : 16 km by R 281 and minor road – Creevykeel Court Cairn★, N : R 281, minor road and N 15 – Glencar Waterfall★, E : 16 km by R 281, minor road and N 16 – Knocknarea★, S : 22km by R 281 and R 292 W – Lough Gill★★ : Parke's Castle★ AC, E : 24 km by R 281 and R 286.*
🏌 *County Sligo* ℰ (071) 917 7134.
Dublin 223.5 – Belfast 212.5 – Sligo 9.5.

🏨 **Yeats Country H.**, ℰ (071) 9177211, *info@yeatscountryhotel.com*, Fax (071) 9177203, ≤, ⚲, ₤₆, ⬄, ⬛, ⅏ – ❙ ⊱⇤ ⚹⚹ 𝐏, ⬤⬤ 𝔸𝔼 VISA. ⅏
closed 20-27 December and 2-25 January – *Elsinore :* Rest (bar lunch)/dinner 25/32 –
98 rm ⊊ ⚭65/95 – ⚭⚭120/170.
♦ Large hotel with attractive views over Sligo Bay. Well-equipped leisure centre and 'kids' organisers' to help keep younger guests busy. Good-sized bedrooms. Attractive bay outlook from some dining room tables.

ROSSLARE (Ros Láir) *Wexford* **712** M 11.

Env. : *Irish Agricultural Museum, Johnstown Castle★★ AC, NW : 12 km by R 740, N 25 and minor road.*
Exc. : *Kilmore Quay★, SW : 24 km by R 736 and R 739 – Saltee Islands★, SW : 24 km by R 736, R 739 and ferry.*
🏌 , 🏌 *Rosslare Strand* ℰ (053) 32113.
🛈 *Kilrane* ℰ (053) 33232 (April-September).
Dublin 167.5 – Waterford 80.5 – Wexford 19.5.

🏨 **Kelly's Resort**, ℰ (053) 91 32114, *kellyhot@iol.ie*, Fax (053) 91 32222, ≤, ⚲, ₤₆, ⬄, ⬛, ℟, ⅏indoor/outdoor – ❙ ⊱⇤, ⬛ rest, & ⚹⚹ 𝐏, ⬤⬤ 𝔸𝔼 VISA. ⅏
closed 10 December-16 February – *Kelly's :* Rest 25/45 ⊊ – *La Marine :* Rest a la carte
34/39 ⊊ – **116 rm** ⊊ ⚭88/105 – ⚭⚭154/187.
♦ Large, purpose-built hotel on the beachfront of this popular holiday town. Good range of leisure facilities; well-appointed rooms. Kelly's dining room offers a classic popular menu. La Marine is a French inspired, bistro-style restaurant.

ROSSLARE HARBOUR (Calafort Ros Láir) *Wexford* **712** N 11.

⛴ to France (Cherbourg and Roscoff) (Irish Ferries) (17 h/15 h) – to Fishguard (Stena Line) 1-4 daily (1 h 40 mn/3 h 30 mn) – to Pembroke (Irish Ferries) 2 daily (3 h 45 mn).
🛈 *Kilrane* ℰ (053) 33232 (April-October).
Dublin 169 – Waterford 82 – Wexford 21.

🏨 **Ferryport House**, on N 25 ℰ (053) 91 33933, *info@ferryporthouse*, Fax (053) 91 61707
– 𝐏, ⬤⬤ VISA. ⅏
closed 25-26 December – Rest (carvery lunch Monday-Saturday)/dinner a la carte
25.00/44.00 – **16 rm** ⊊ ⚭40/60 – ⚭⚭70/100.
♦ Contemporary hotel conveniently located for the ferry terminus. Simple communal areas include a pine furnished breakfast room. Comfortable bedrooms with fitted wood furniture. Local produce to fore in dining room.

at Tagoat *West : 4 km on N 25 – ⊠ Rosslare.*

 Churchtown House ⟶, *North : ¾ km on Rosslare rd* ☎ *(053) 32555, info@church townhouse.com, Fax (053) 32577, ☞ – ⇆ ⅏ ▣ ☻ ㏈ ▨ ⅏*
*March-October – **Rest** (closed Sunday-Monday) (booking essential) (residents only) (dinner only) 40 – **14 rm** ⊇ ✦75/95 – ✦✦130/150.*
♦ Part 18C house with extension, set in spacious, well-kept garden. Traditional country house-style lounge and wood furnished dining room. Individually decorated rooms. Fresh country cooking in the Irish tradition.

ROSSNOWLAGH (Ros Neamhlach) *Donegal* **712** H 4 *Ireland G.*
See : Rossnowlagh Strand★★.
Dublin 246 – Donegal 22.5 – Sligo 50.

🏨 **Sand House** ⟶, ☎ *(071) 985 1777, info@sandhouse.ie, Fax (071) 985 2100, ⩽ bay, beach and mountains, ⓜ, ⟋, ⊁ – ☖ ⇆ ℣ ⅏ ▣ – ⚿ 80. ㏈ ㏄ ▨*
*February-November – **Rest** (dinner only and Sunday lunch)/dinner 50/55 ℗ – **50 rm** ⊇ ✦100/140 – ✦✦240/300.*
♦ Victorian sandstone hotel in coastal location with superb views of bay, beach and mountains. Real fire in the hall. Spacious, individual rooms with modern styling. Attractive dining room with a comfortable atmosphere and classic traditional feel.

ROUNDSTONE (Cloch na Rón) *Galway* **712** C 7 *Ireland G.*
See : Town★.
Exc. : Connemara★★★ : Sky Road, Clifden★★, W : 24 km by R 341 and minor road – Cashel★, E : 15 km by R 341 – Connemara National Park★ AC, N : 40 km by R 341 and N 59 – Kylemore Abbey★ AC, N : 44 km by R 341 and N 59.
Dublin 310.5 – Galway 75.5.

🏠 **Eldon's**, ☎ *(095) 35933, eldonshotel@eircom.net, Fax (095) 35722, ⩽, ☞ – ㏈ ㏄ ⓪ ▨. ⅏*
Rest a la carte 20/41 – **19 rm** ⊇ ✦55 – ✦✦70/160.
♦ Near the harbour of this fishing village with views of the bay and the Twelve Pin Mountains. Wood floored bar with open fires. Annex bedrooms are most comfortable. Seafood inspired menus.

SALTHILL (Bóthar na Trá) *Galway* **712** E 8 – *see Galway.*

SANDYFORD *Dublin* **712** N 8 – *see Dublin.*

SANDYMOUNT *Dublin* – *see Dublin.*

SCHULL (An Scoil) *Cork* **712** D 13 – *see Skull.*

SHANAGARRY (An Seangharraí) *Cork* **712** H 12 *Ireland G.* – ⊠ *Midleton.*
Env. : Cloyne Cathedral★, NW : 6½ km by R 629.
Dublin 262.5 – Cork 40 – Waterford 103.

🏨 **Ballymaloe House** ⟶, *Northwest : 2 ¾ km on L 35* ☎ *(021) 4652531, res@ballyma loe.ie, Fax (021) 4652021, ⩽, ⊼ heated, ☞, ₰, ⊁ – ⇆ ▣. ㏈ ㏄ ⓪ ▨. ⅏*
*closed 24-26 December – **Rest** (booking essential) (buffet dinner Sunday) 35/65 – **33 rm** ⊇ ✦135/190 – ✦✦270/310.*
♦ Hugely welcoming part 16C, part Georgian country house surrounded by 400 acres of farmland. Characterful sitting room with cavernous ceiling. Warm, comfortable bedrooms. Characterful dining room divided into assorted areas.

The red ⟶ symbol?
This denotes the very essence of peace
– only the sound of birdsong first thing in the morning …

SHANNON (Sionainn) *Clare* **712** F 9 – pop. 8 561.

Env. : *Bunratty Castle*★★ *AC, E : 11 km by N 19 and N 18 – Cratloe Wood* (≼★), *E : 14 km by N 19 and N 18.*

Exc. : *Craggaunowen Centre*★ *AC, NE : 20 km by N 19, N 18 S, R 471 and R 462 – Knappogue Castle*★ *AC, N : 26 km by N 19, N 18 and minor road via Quin – Quin Friary*★ *AC, N :22 km by N 19, N18 N and minor road to Quin.*

🔟 *Shannon Airport* ℘ *(061) 471020.*

✈ *Shannon Airport :* ℘ *(061) 712000.*

🚹 *Shannon Airport, Arrivals Hall* ℘ *(061) 471664, info@shannondev.ie.*

Dublin 219 – Ennis 26 – Limerick 24.

🏨 **Oak Wood Arms,** ℘ *(061) 361500, reservations@oakwoodarms.com, Fax (061) 361414,* 𝄠, ☎ – ✂, ▤ rest, ✆ & 🅿 – 🕿 650. 🆖 🆎 ① 𝘝𝘐𝘚𝘈 . ✗
closed 24-26 December – **Rest** (carvery lunch Monday-Saturday)/dinner 35 and a la carte 27/42 **s.** 𝝧 – **98 rm** � 🛏90/105 – 🛏🛏120/150, 2 suites.
♦ Low rise hotel with good access to Shannon International airport. Large bar with carvery. Lots of small lounges. Good conference facilities. Spacious rooms with fresh décor. Dining room decorated with aeronautical memorabilia.

SKERRIES (Na Sceirí) *Dublin* **712** N 7 *Ireland G.* – pop. 9 149.

Exc. : *Malahide Castle*★★ *AC, S : 23 km by R 127, M 1 and R 106 – Ben of Howth* (≼★), *S : 23 km by R 127, M 1 and R 106 – Newbridge House*★ *AC, S : 16 km by R 217 and minor road.*

🔟 *Skerries* ℘ *(01) 849 1204.*

🚹 *Skerries Mills* ℘ *(01) 849 5208, skerriesmills@indigo.ie.*

Dublin 30.5 – Drogheda 24.

✕✕ **Redbank House** with rm, 7 Church St, ℘ (01) 849 1005, *info@redbank.ie,* Fax *(01) 849 1598* – ✆ & . 🆖 🆎 ① 𝘝𝘐𝘚𝘈
closed 24-27 December – **Rest** - Seafood - (dinner only and Sunday lunch)/dinner 50/65 and a la carte 42/50 **s.** – **18 rm** ⊋ 🛏45/65 – 🛏🛏120.
♦ One of Ireland's most well-renowned and long-standing restaurants. Fresh seafood from Skerries harbour is served simply or in more elaborate fashion. Smart, comfy bedrooms.

SKIBBEREEN *Cork* **712** E 13 – pop. 2 000.

Env. : *Castletownshend*★, *SE : 9 km by R 596.*

Exc. : *Sherkin Island*★, *SW : 35 km by R 595 and ferry from Baltimore – Skull*★, *W : 24 km by N 71 and R 592 – Mount Gabriel* (≼★), *W : 29 km by N 71, R 592 and minor road N.*

🚹 *Town Hall* ℘ *(028) 21766.*

Dublin 338 – Cork 85 – Killarney 104.5.

✕ **Thai @ Ty ar Mor,** First Floor, 46 Bridge St, ℘ (028) 22100, *thai@tyarmor.com* – 🆖 𝘝𝘐𝘚𝘈
closed 3 January- mid March, mid September - October and Sunday and Monday – **Rest** - Thai - (booking essential) a la carte 38/40 **s.**
♦ Compact and popular, above Ty ar Mor. Furnished with Asian ornaments, tapestries and wall blinds. Polite service from staff in national dress. Authentic, well executed dishes.

SKULL/SCHULL (An Scoil) *Cork* **712** D 13 *Ireland G.*

See : *Town*★.

Env. : *Mount Gabriel* (≼★), *N : 3 km by minor road.*

Exc. : *Sherkin Island*★ *(by ferry).*

🔟 *Coosheen, Coosheen, Schull* ℘ *(077) 28182.*

Dublin 363.5 – Cork 104.5 – Killarney 103.

↑ **Corthna Lodge** 🦢 without rest., West : 1¼ km by R 592 ℘ (028) 28517, *info@corthna-lodge.net, Fax (028) 28032,* 𝄠, 🐎 – ✂ 🅿. 🆖 𝘝𝘐𝘚𝘈 . ✗
March-September – 6 rm ⊋ 🛏60/70 – 🛏🛏85/95.
♦ 100 year old ivy covered guesthouse with many original features remaining. Large garden. Bright breakfast room. Smart bedrooms boast stencilled walls, modern soft furnishings.

SLIEVEROE (Sliabh Rua) *Waterford* – *see Waterford.*

SLIGO (Sligeach) *Sligo* **712** G 5 *Ireland G. – pop. 17 735.*

See : *Town*★★ – *Abbey*★ *AC* – *Model Arts and the Niland Gallery*★ *AC.*

Env. : *SE* : *Lough Gill*★★ – *Carrowmore Megalithic Cemetery*★ *AC, SW* : 4¾ km – *Knock-narea*★ *(≤★★) SW* : 9½ km by R 292.

Exc. : *Drumcliff*★, *N* : by N 15 – *Parke's Castle*★ *AC, E* : 14½ km by R 286 – *Glencar Water-fall*★, *NE* : 14½ km by N 16 – *Creevykeel Court Cairn*★, *N* : 25¾ km by N 15.

🏌 *Rosses Point* ℰ (071) 917 7134.

✈ *Sligo Airport, Strandhill* : ℰ (071) 68280.

🛈 *Aras Reddan, Temple St* ℰ (071) 9161201.

Dublin 214 – Belfast 203 – Dundalk 170.5 – Londonderry 138.5.

🏨 **Clarion,** Clarion Rd, Ballinode, Northeast : 3 km by N 16 ℰ (071) 9119000, *info@clarion hotelssligo.com, Fax* (071) 9119001, 🖉, 🏋, ⬄, ☒, ☞ – 📵 ⇥, ☰ rest, ☎ & ⬆ 🅿 – 🛗 500. 🐵 🆎 𝗩𝗜𝗦𝗔. ✦
closed 25-26 December **Kudos :** Rest - Asian - a la carte 26/37 **s.** – **Sinergie :** Rest *(dinner only and Sunday lunch)/*dinner and a la carte 32/50 **s.** – ☷ 16 – **76 rm** ✦79/99 – ✦✦79/99, 91 suites 104/124.
♦ Extensive Victorian building with granite façade: now the height of modernity with excellent leisure club, and impressive, spacious bedrooms, the majority being plush suites. Modern European menus at Sinergie. Informal Asian inspired Kudos.

🏨 **Radisson SAS,** Ballincar, Northwest : ¾ km on R 281 ℰ (071) 9140008, *info.sligo@radi ssonssas.com, Fax* (071) 9140005, ≤, 🖉, 🏋, ⬄, ☒ – 📵 ⇥ ☎ & 🅿 – 🛗 950. 🐵 🆎 🅞 𝗩𝗜𝗦𝗔
Rest *(bar lunch Monday-Saturday)/*dinner 35 and a la carte 38/44 – **129 rm** ☷ ✦89/110 – ✦✦130/160, 3 suites.
♦ Modern, spacious hotel two miles from centre. Impressive conference and leisure facilities with comprehensive spa treatments. Stylish, airy, modish rooms, some with king beds. Smart yet informal restaurant overlooking Sligo Bay.

🏨 **Sligo Park,** Pearse Rd, South : 2 km on N 4 ℰ (071) 9190400, *sligo@leehotels.com, Fax* (071) 9169556, 🏋, ⬄, ☒, ☞, ☜ – ⇥ ☎ 🅿 – 🛗 450. 🐵 🆎 🅞 𝗩𝗜𝗦𝗔. ✦
restricted opening at Christmas – **Hazelwood :** Rest *(closed Saturday lunch and Bank Holidays)* 22/36 and a la carte 25/37 **s.** – **138 rm** ☷ ✦74/190 – ✦✦110/310, 1 suite.
♦ Spacious lobby, with its unique Millennium water feature, leads to bright, modern rooms, thoughtfully equipped for the corporate traveller and overlooking gardens. Conservatory restaurant or hearty bar dining options.

⌂ **Benwiskin Lodge** without rest., Shannon Eighter, North : 2 km by N 15 ℰ (071) 9141088, *benwiskinlodge@eircom.net, Fax* (071) 9141088, ☞ – ⇥ 🅿 🐵 𝗩𝗜𝗦𝗔. ✦
closed 20 December-6 January – **5 rm** ☷ ✦45/55 – ✦✦70/80.
♦ Extensively pine furnished guesthouse in quiet area. 150 year old clock in front hall. Open-fired sitting room with shiny wood floor. Cosy breakfast area. Spruce rooms.

⌂ **Tree Tops** without rest., Cleveragh Rd, South : 1¼ km by Dublin rd ℰ (071) 9160160, *treetops@iol.ie, Fax* (071) 9162301, ☞ – ⇥ 🅿. 🐵 🆎 𝗩𝗜𝗦𝗔. ✦
closed 20 December-7 January – **5 rm** ☷ ✦45/50 – ✦✦72.
♦ Pleasant guesthouse in residential area. Stunning collection of Irish art. Cosy public areas include small lounge and simple breakfast room. Neat, comfortable rooms.

✗ **Montmartre,** Market Yard, ℰ (071) 9169901, *Fax* (071) 9192232 – ☰. 🐵 🆎 𝗩𝗜𝗦𝗔. ✦
closed 24-26 December and Monday – **Rest** *(dinner only)* a la carte 28/45 **s.** ♉.
♦ Clear French style at this discreetly located restaurant close to the town's theatre. Polite staff serve broadly influenced French food within simply appointed restaurant.

SPANISH POINT (Rinn na Spáinneach) *Clare* **712** D 9 – ✉ *Milltown Malbay.*
Dublin 275 – Galway 104.5 – Limerick 83.5.

🏨 **Admiralty Lodge,** ℰ (065) 7085007, *info@admiralty.ie, Fax* (065) 7085030, ☞ – ⇥ ☰ ☎ & 🅿. 🐵 🆎 𝗩𝗜𝗦𝗔
closed December-February – **Piano Room :** Rest *(dinner only)* 39 – **12 rm** ☷ ✦120/165 – ✦✦150/200.
♦ Purpose-built coastal hotel built around a former 19C seamans lodge. Three warm, comfy lounges bring out period character. Individually stylish rooms a notably strong point. Formal dining in lodge: piano player and French themed menus.

> Good food and accommodation at moderate prices?
> Look for the Bib symbols:
> red Bib Gourmand 🍴 for food, blue Bib Hotel 🛏 for hotels

SPIDDAL/SPIDDLE (An Spidéal) *Galway* **712** E 8.
  Dublin 230 – Galway 17.5.

🏫 **An Cruiscin Lan,** ✆ *(091) 553148, info@cruiscinlanhotel.com, Fax (091) 553712,* ≤, 🏵
  – ♨ &. ⚫⚪ **VISA** ⚫⚪
  closed 25 December – **Rest** a la carte 23/33 ♀ – **13 rm** ⚌ ✦60/100 – ✦✦110/150.
  ◆ Personally run, extended inn at the centre of this busy village. Light, comfortable and
  well-priced rooms, some with bayside views: a useful option for business travel. All-day
  brasserie facing the water.

⌂ **Ardmor Country House** without rest., West : ¾ km on R 336 ✆ *(091) 553145, ard
  morcountryhouse@yahoo.com, Fax (091) 553596,* ≤, 🐾 – 🗱 **P.** 🕸
  March-December – **7 rm** ⚌ ✦45/50 – ✦✦66/72.
  ◆ Creamwashed chalet guesthouse with pleasant gardens and spotless, pastel painted
  back bedrooms with fine views of Galway Bay. Two comfortable lounges and a sun-trap
  terrace.

SPIDDLE (An Spidéal) *Galway* **712** E 8 – *see Spiddal.*

STILLORGAN *Dublin* **712** N 8 – *see Dublin.*

STRAFFAN (Teach Srafáin) *Kildare* **712** M 8 – pop. 341.
  Env. : *Castletown House, Celbridge* **AC,** *NW : 7 km by R 406 and R 403.*
  🏌 *Naas, Kerdiffstown* ✆ *(045) 874644.*
  Dublin 24 – Mullingar 75.5.

🏰🏰 **The K Club** 🐾, ✆ *(01) 601 7200, resortsales@kclub.ie, Fax (01) 601 7297,* 🏵, 🐾, ♨,
  ☎, 🔲, 🏌, 🐾, 🚗, 🏊, 🎾indoor/outdoor, squash – 🎱 🗱 **P.** – 🔼 1000. ⚫⚪ 🅰🅴 **VISA** 🕸
  Byerley Turk : **Rest** *(closed Monday-Wednesday)* (booking essential for non-residents)
  (dinner only) a la carte 63/166 **s.** – **Legends :** **Rest** a la carte 39/72 **s.** – **Monza :** **Rest** -
  Italian - a la carte 28/54 – **79 rm** ⚌ ✦295/545 – ✦✦295/545, 13 suites.
  ◆ Part early 19C country house overlooking River Liffey, with gardens, arboretum and
  championship golf course. Huge leisure centre. Exquisitely sumptuous rooms. Grand,
  country house style Byerley Turk with river views. Informal Legends. Italian cuisine at
  Monza.

🏰🏰 **Barberstown Castle,** North : ¾ km ✆ *(01) 628 8157, barberstowncastle@ire
  land.com, Fax (01) 627 7027,* ≤, 🐾 – 🎱 🗱 &. **P.** – 🔼 200. ⚫⚪ ⚫ **VISA** 🕸
  closed January and 24-26 December – **Rest** *(closed Monday)* (booking essential) a la carte
  49/79 – **59 rm** ⚌ ✦150/200 – ✦✦280.
  ◆ Whitewashed Elizabethan and Victorian house with 13C castle keep and gardens. Country house style lounges exude style. Individually decorated, very comfortable bedrooms.
  Dine in characterful, stone-clad keep.

TAGOAT (Teach Gót) *Wexford* **712** M 11 – *see Rosslare Harbour.*

TAHILLA (Tathuile) *Kerry* **712** C 12 *Ireland G.*
  Exc. : *Ring of Kerry*★★ – *Sneem*★, *NW : 6½ km by N 70.*
  Dublin 357 – Cork 112.5 – Killarney 51.5.

🏫 **Tahilla Cove** 🐾, ✆ *(064) 45204, tahillacove@eircom.net, Fax (064) 45104,* ≤ *Coongar
  harbour and Caha Mountains,* 🚗, 🐾, ♨ – 🔲 🗱 **P.** ⚫⚪ 🅰🅴 **VISA**
  April - 15 October – **Rest** *(closed Monday-Tuesday)* (booking essential) (set menu only)
  (dinner only) 35 **s.** – **9 rm** ⚌ ✦100 – ✦✦150.
  ◆ Two houses surrounded by oak forest, with Caha Mountains as a backdrop and garden
  sweeping down to Coongar harbour. Some bedrooms have balconies from which to savour views. Locally derived cuisine proudly served by hospitable owner.

TERENURE *Dublin* **712** N 8 – *see Dublin.*

TERMONBARRY *Longford* **712** I 6 *Ireland G.*
  Exc. : *Strokestown*★ *(Famine Museum*★ **AC,** *Strokestown Park House*★ **AC),** *NW : by N 5.*
  Dublin 130.5 – Galway 137 – Roscommon 35.5 – Sligo 100.

⌂ **Shannonside House** without rest., ✆ *(043) 26052, info@keenans.ie, Fax (043) 26198*
  – 🗱 **P.** ⚫⚪ 🅰🅴 ⚫ **VISA** 🕸
  closed 25 December – **7 rm** ⚌ ✦50 – ✦✦90.
  ◆ Hospitable owner and well-proportioned bedrooms are among the guesthouse's chief
  attractions. Good value and comfortable. Located close to the Shannon River.

TERRYGLASS (Tír Dhá Ghlas) Tipperary 712 H 8.

Exc. : Birr★ : Castle Demesne★★ AC (Great Telescope★★), E : 25 km by R 493, minor road, R 489 and N 52 – Nenagh (Castle★), SE : 25 km by R 493 – Portumna★ (Castle★ AC), N : 16 km by R 493 and N 65.

Dublin 159.5 – Limerick 66 – Loughrea 43.5.

🍴 **The Derg Inn,** ☎ (067) 22037, derginn@eircom.net, Fax (067) 22297, 壽 – **⬤◉ ⚞ VISA** ⅝

closed 25 December and Good Friday – **Rest** a la carte 21/40.

♦ A short walk from lovely Lough Derg. Characterful interior with open fires and pot stoves. Sit on chair, bench or pew as you dine on organic local produce from eclectic menus.

THOMASTOWN (Baile Mhic Andáin) Kilkenny 712 K 10 Ireland G. – pop. 1 600 – ⬜ Kilkenny.

Env. : Jerpoint Abbey★★, SW : 3 km by N9 – Graiguenamanagh★ (Duiske Abbey★★ AC), E : 16 km by R 703 – Inistioge★, SE : 8 km by R 700 – Kilfane Glen and Waterfall★ AC, SE : 5 km by N 9.

Dublin 124 – Kilkenny 17.5 – Waterford 48.5 – Wexford 61.

🏨 **Mount Juliet Conrad** ⑤, West : 2 ½ km ☎ (056) 7773000, mountjulietinfo@con radhotels.com, Fax (056) 7773019, ≼ River Nore and park, ⑫, ₺₅, ⇆, ◪, ⅛, ⚞, 壽, ❦ – ⅙⤫ 🅿. **⬤◉ ⚞ VISA** ⅝
The Lady Helen : Rest (dinner only) 72 and a la carte 49/68 ⅞ – (see also **Hunters Yard** below) – ⬚ 17 – **30 rm** ★150/275 – ★★295/600, 2 suites.

♦ 18C manor in sporting estate, named after wife of original owner. Overlooks the meandering river Nore with stud farm, equestrian centre. Smart, restful rooms. Restaurant features stately stucco work and tall windows.

🏨 **Hunters Yard & Rose Garden Lodges** (at Mount Juliet Conrad H.), West : 2 ½ km ☎ (056) 7773000, mountjulietinfo@conradhotels.com, Fax (056) 7773019, ₺₅, ⇆, ◪, ⅛, ❦, 壽, ♨, ❦ – ⅙⤫, ▤ rest, 🅿 – ♨ 75. **⬤◉ ⚞ VISA** ⅝
Kendals : Rest (bar lunch Monday-Saturday)/dinner 45 and a la carte 32/54 – ⬚ 17 – **26 rm** ★150/275 – ★★295.

♦ For those interested in outdoor activities, the well-located club style rooms in the original hunting stables or lodges are ideal. A restful place after a day's exertions. Restaurant with airy yet intimate ambience.

🏠 **Abbey House** without rest., Jerpoint Abbey, Southwest : 2 km on N 9 ☎ (056) 7724166, abbeyhsejerpoint@eircom.net, Fax (056) 7724192, 壽 – ⅙⤫ 🅿. **⬤◉ VISA**
closed 22-30 December – **7 rm** ⬚ ★40/65 – ★★80/100.

♦ Neat inside and out, this whitewashed house in well-kept gardens offers simple but spacious rooms and pretty wood furnished breakfast room. Read up on area in lounge.

🏠 **Carrickmourne House** ⑤ without rest., New Ross Rd, Southeast : 3 ¼ km by R 700 ☎ (056) 7724124, carrickmournehouse@eircom.net, Fax (056) 7724124, ≼, 壽 – ⅙⤫ 🅿. **⬤◉ VISA** ⅝
closed 15 December-15 January – **5 rm** ⬚ ★45/50 – ★★65/75.

♦ Modern, split-level house looks down on peaceful countryside. Agreeably simple, traditional décor and gleaming wood floors in pristine rooms: homely and well priced.

THURLES (Durlas) Tipperary 712 I9 – pop. 7 425.

Env. : Holy Cross Abbey★★ AC, SW : 8 km by R 660.
⅛ Turtulla ☎ (0504) 21983.
Dublin 148 – Cork 114 – Kilkenny 48.5 – Limerick 75.5 – Waterford 93.5.

🏨 **Inch House** ⑤, Northwest : 6 ½ km on R 498 ☎ (0504) 51348, inchhse@iol.ie, Fax (0504) 51754, ≼, 壽, ♨ – ⅙⤫ 🅿. **⬤◉ VISA** ⅝
closed 20-29 December – **Rest** (closed Sunday-Monday) (dinner only) 47/50 – **5 rm** ⬚ ★65/70 – ★★120.

♦ 1720s country house on a working farm; lovely rural views. Handsomely restored with a fine eye for decorative period detail. Individually styled en suite bedrooms. Classically proportioned yet intimate dining room.

at Twomileborris East : 6¾ km on N 75 – ⬜ Thurles.

🏠 **The Castle,** ☎ (0504) 44324, info@thecastletmb.com, Fax (0504) 44352, 壽 – ⅙⤫ 🅿. **⬤◉ VISA** ⅝
Rest (by arrangement) 55 – **4 rm** ⬚ ★48/60 – ★★80/100.

♦ Charming 17C house adjacent to partly ruined tower of the local castle which runs close to back door. Furnished with numerous period pieces. Pleasantly decorated rooms. Traditionally furnished dining room.

TOORMORE (An Tuar Mór) *Cork* **712** D 13 – ⊠ *Goleen.*
Dublin 355.5 – Cork 109.5 – Killarney 104.5.

Fortview House without rest., Gurtyowen, Northeast : 2 ½ km on Durrus rd (R 591)
℘ (028) 35324, *fortviewhousegoleen@eircom.net*, Fax (028) 35324, ⌂ – ⇥ 🅿
March-October – 5 rm ☲ ✝45/60 – ✝✝90/100.
◆ Stone built farmhouse; antique country pine furniture in coir carpeted rooms and brass,
iron bedsteads. Fresh vegetable juice, home-made museli, potato cake for breakfast.

Rock Cottage ⌂, Barnatonicane, Northeast : 3 ¼ km on Durrus rd (R 591) ℘ (028)
35538, *rockcottage@eircom.net*, Fax (028) 35538, ⌂, 🔈 – ⇥ 🅿, 🆗 VISA. ⌂
Rest (by arrangement) 45 – **3 rm** ☲ ✝75/90 – ✝✝130.
◆ Georgian former hunting lodge idyllically set in 17 acres of parkland. Very well appointed
lounge: modern art on walls. Immaculate, light and airy bedrooms.

TOWER *Cork* **712** G 12 – *see Blarney.*

TRALEE (Trá Lí) *Kerry* **712** C 11 *Ireland G.* – *pop. 21 987.*
See : *Kerry - The Kingdom*★ *AC.*
Env. : *Blennerville Windmill*★ *AC, SW : 3¼ km by N 86 – Ardfert*★, *NW : 8 km by R 551.*
Exc. : *Banna Strand*★, *NW : 12¾ km by R 551 – Crag Cave*★ *AC, W : 21 km by N 21 – Rattoo
Round Tower*★, *N : 19¼ km by R 556.*
🛈 *Ashe Memorial Hall* ℘ (066) 7121288, *tourisminfo@shannon-dev.ie.*
Dublin 297.5 – Killarney 32 – Limerick 103.

The Meadowlands, Oakpark, Northeast : 1 ¼ km on N 69 ℘ (066) 7180444,
info@meadowlandshotel.com, Fax (066) 7180964, ⌂ – |🕏| ⇥ 🗎 🅿 – 🔬 250. 🆗 🆎 VISA.
⌂
closed 24-26 December – **Rest** *(closed Sunday dinner)* (bar lunch Monday-Saturday)/dinner
35 and a la carte ♈ – **55 rm** ☲ ✝135/175 – ✝✝380, 2 suites.
◆ Smart, terracotta hotel, a good base for exploring area. Inside are warmly decorated, air
conditioned rooms and mellow library lounge with open fire and grandfather clock. Pro-
prietor owns fishing boats, so seafood takes centre stage in dining room.

The Grand, Denny St, ℘ (066) 7121499, *info@grandhoteltralee.com*, Fax (066) 7122877
– ⇥, 🗎 rest, 🎵 – 🔬 250. 🆗 🆎 ① VISA. ⌂
Rest 30 (dinner) and a la carte 21/38 **s.** – **44 rm** ☲ ✝60/140 – ✝✝120/160.
◆ Established 1928; enjoys a central position in town. Rooms are decorated with ma-
hogany furniture whilst the popular bar, once a post office, bears hallmarks of bygone era.
Appetising dinners in restaurant with historic ambience.

Brook Manor Lodge without rest., Fenit Rd, Spa, Northwest : 3 ½ km by R 551 on
R 558 ℘ (066) 7120406, *brookmanor@eircom.net*, Fax (066) 7127552, ⌂ – ⇥ 🎵 🅿, 🆗
VISA. ⌂
8 rm ☲ ✝65/75 – ✝✝100/140.
◆ Modern purpose-built manor in meadowland looking across to the Slieve Mish moun-
tains: good for walks and angling. Breakfast in conservatory. Immaculate bedrooms.

The Forge without rest., Upper Oakpark, Northeast : 2 ½ km on N 69 ℘ (066) 7125245,
theforgebnb@gmail.com, Fax (066) 7125245, ⌂ – ⇥ 🅿, 🆗 VISA. ⌂
closed 8 December - 20 January – **6 rm** ☲ ✝40/60 – ✝✝64/70.
◆ Comfortable, family-run house; sporting activities and scenic spots on doorstep. Hallway
with hexagonal light leads upstairs to cosy rooms. Complimentary drinks on arrival.

David Norris, Ivy Terrace, ℘ (066) 7185654, *restaurantdavidnorris@eircom.net*,
Fax (066) 7126600 – 🆗 🆎 VISA
closed Sunday and Monday – **Rest** (dinner only) a la carte 33/43 ♈.
◆ Pleasant restaurant on first floor of unprepossessing modern building, featuring Rennie
Macintosh style chairs. Good blend of cuisine: exotic hints and popular favourites.

TRAMORE (Trá Mhór) *Waterford* **712** K 11 – *pop. 8 305.*
Exc. : *Dunmore East*★, *E : 18 km by R 675, R 685 and R 684.*
🛈 ℘ (051) 381572 *(June-August).*
Dublin 170.5 – Waterford 9.5.

Glenorney without rest., Newtown, Southwest : 1 ½ km by R 675 ℘ (051) 381056,
info@glenorney.com, Fax (051) 381103, <, ⌂ – ⇥ 🎵 🅿, 🆗 🆎 VISA
6 rm ☲ ✝60/90 – ✝✝80/90.
◆ On a hill overlooking Tramore Bay. Inside are personally decorated rooms: family photographs and curios; sun lounge with plenty of books. Rear rooms have lovely bay views.

XX **Coast** with rm, Upper Branch Rd, ℰ (051) 393646, *coastrestaurant@eircom.net*, Fax (051) 393647, ←, �, 🖼, 🚗 – ◍◎ ⅍ 𝒱𝐼𝒮𝒜
closed January, Monday, and Sunday dinner except July-August and Bank Holidays – **Rest** (dinner only and Sunday lunch)/dinner a la carte 35/47 ♀ – **4 rm** ⌕ ♦90 – ♦♦160.
◆ The exterior gives no hint of the Bohemian style restaurant. Varied menu based on Irish dishes and produce; modern twists. Comfy rooms in eclectic style, best views at front.

TRIM (Baile Átha Troim) Meath **712** L 7 Ireland G. – pop. 5 894.
See : Trim Castle★★ – Town★.
Env. : Bective Abbey★, NE : 6½ km by R 161.
📍 County Meath, Newtownmoynagh ℰ (046) 943 1463.
🏛 Old Town Hall, Castle St ℰ (046) 9437227 (May-September).
Dublin 43.5 – Drogheda 42 – Tullamore 69.

⌂ **Highfield House** without rest., Maudlins Rd, ℰ (046) 9436386, *highfieldhouseac com@eircom.net*, Fax (046) 9438182, 🚗 – ✎ 🕻 🅿. ◍◎ 𝒱𝐼𝒮𝒜
closed 23 December-4 January – **7 rm** ⌕ ♦50/55 – ♦♦80/82.
◆ 19C former maternity home in lawned gardens overlooking Trim Castle and River Boyne. Sizeable bedrooms in cheerful colours offer a welcome respite after sightseeing.

⌂ **Crannmór** ⌘ without rest., Dunderry Rd, North : 2 km ℰ (046) 9431635, *cranmor@eir com.net*, Fax (046) 9438087, 🚗 – ✎ 🕭 🅿. 𝒱𝐼𝒮𝒜, 🏖
closed January - 5 February – **4 rm** ⌕ ♦50/55 – ♦♦72/80.
◆ Particularly friendly owners run this creeper-clad Georgian farmhouse in a rural location, offering bright and comfortable bedrooms and a cosy atmosphere.

> Do not confuse X with ❀!
> X defines comfort, while stars are awarded for the best cuisine, across all categories of comfort.

TULLAMORE (Tulach Mhór) Offaly **712** J 8 – pop. 11 098.
📍 Tullamore, Brookfield ℰ (0506) 21439.
🏛 Bury Quay Tullamore ℰ (0506) 52617.
Dublin 104.5 – Kilkenny 83.5 – Limerick 129.

🏨 **Tullamore Court,** on N 80 (Portlaoise rd) ℰ (057) 934 6666, *info@tullamorecourtho tel.ie*, Fax (057) 934 6677, 🚷, 𝑙ₛ, 🐟, 🖼 – 📶 ✎, 🍽 rest, 🕻 ♿ 🛝 🅿 – 🛎 750. ◍◎ ⅍ ◉ 𝒱𝐼𝒮𝒜, 🏖
closed 24-26 December – **Rest** 30/50 and a la carte 30/46 – **104 rm** ⌕ ♦175 – ♦♦310/350.
◆ Contemporarily styled hotel with curved walls, plenty of marble, glass, rich coloured interiors. Has state-of-the-art leisure centre; children's holiday activities arranged. Stylish, spacious dining room.

🏨 **Bridge House,** off Main St ℰ (057) 93 22000, *info@bridgehouse.com*, Fax (057) 93 25690, 🚷, 𝑙ₛ, 🐟, 🖼 – 📶 ✎, 🍽 rest, 🕻 ♿ 🅿 – 🛎 550. ◍◎ ⅍ 𝒱𝐼𝒮𝒜, 🏖
closed 24-25 December – **Rest** (bar lunch)/dinner 25/40 and a la carte 30/41 s. ♀ – **72 rm** ⌕ ♦95 – ♦♦170/240.
◆ The grand, pillared entrance with steps leading to an ornate reception with crystal chandelier sums up rarified ambience. Polished library bar and impressive bedrooms. Dining options with restaurant or bar carvery.

TULLY CROSS Galway **712** C 7.
Dublin 301 – Galway 85.5 – Letterfrack 3.

🏨 **Maol Reidh,** ℰ (095) 43844, *maolreidhhotel@eircom.net*, Fax (095) 43784 – 📶 ✎ ♿ 🅿. ◍◎ 𝒱𝐼𝒮𝒜, 🏖
closed November- 28 December – **Rest** (bar lunch)/dinner 32 and a la carte 32/40 s. – **12 rm** ⌕ ♦55/75 – ♦♦90/130.
◆ This good value, personally run hotel was built with local stone and a noteworthy attention to detail. Cosy rear bar and sitting room. Good sized bedrooms. Stylish restaurant with modern menus.

TWOMILEBORRIS (Buiríos Léith) Tipperary **712** I 9 – see Thurles.

VALENCIA ISLAND (Dairbhre) *Kerry* **712** A/B 12.
Dublin 381.5 – Killarney 88.5 – Tralee 92.

Knights Town *Kerry.*

Glanleam House ⬧, Glanleam, West : 2 km taking right fork at top of Market St
℘ (066) 9476176, info@glanleam.com, Fax (066) 9476108, ≤, ⬧, ⬥, ⬥ – ⬧ ✕ **P**. **◯◯** **AE**
VISA.
mid March-October – **Rest** *(booking essential for non-residents) (communal dining) (dinner only)* 40/50 **s.** – **6 rm** ⬲ ✚70/105 – ✚✚140/220.
♦ Part 17C and 18C country house in extensive sub-tropical gardens, superbly located off West Kerry coast. Art Deco interiors. Spacious drawing room. Individually styled rooms. Communal dining; produce grown in hotel's 19C walled gardens.

WATERFORD (Port Láirge) *Waterford* **712** K 11 *Ireland G. – pop. 46 736.*
See : *Town★ – City Walls★ – Waterford Treasures★* **AC** Y.
Env. : *Waterford Crystal★, SW : 2½ km by N 25* Y.
Exc. : *Duncannon★, E : 19¼ km by R 683, ferry from Passage East and R 374 (south)* Z –
Dunmore East★, SE : 19¼ km by R 684 Z *– Tintern Abbey★, E : 21 km by R 683, ferry from Passage East, R 733 and R 734 (south)* Z.
⛳ *Newrath ℘ (051) 874182.*
✈ *Waterford Airport, Killowen : ℘ (051) 875589.*
🛈 *41 The Quay ℘ (05793) 875823* Y*, info@southeasttourism.ie – Waterford Crystal Visitor Centre ℘ (051) 358397.*
Dublin 154.5 – Cork 117.5 – Limerick 124.

Plan on next page

Waterford Castle H. and Golf Club ⬧, The Island, Ballinakill, East : 4 km by
R 683, Ballinakill Rd and private ferry *℘ (051) 878203, info@waterfordcastle.com,*
Fax (051) 879316, ≤, ⛳, ⬧, ⬥, ⬥, ⬥ – ⬧ ✕ **P**. **◯◯** **AE** **◯** **VISA**. ⬧
closed 2 January - 8 February – **The Munster Dining Room :** **Rest** *(bar lunch Monday-Saturday)/dinner* 65 and a la carte 54/59 ⬥ – ⬲ 22 – **14 rm** ✚160/335 – ✚✚225/450,
5 suites.
♦ Part 15C and 19C castle in charmingly secluded, historic river island setting. Classic country house ambience amid antiques and period features. Comfortable, elegant rooms. Oak panelled dining room with ornate ceilings and evening pianist.

Granville, Meagher Quay, *℘ (051) 305555, stay@granville-hotel.ie, Fax (051) 305566* – ⬧
✕, ▤ rest, ⬧ – 🚗 200. **◯◯** **AE** **◯** **VISA**. ⬧
Y a
closed 24-26 December – **Bianconi Room :** **Rest** *(dinner only and Sunday lunch)/dinner*
38 dinner and a la carte 25/38 **s.** – **98 rm** ✚78/98 – ✚✚200/260.
♦ Early 19C hotel that reputedly once hosted Charles Stewart Parnell. Individually styled bedrooms with a consistent traditional standard of décor. Some views of river Suir. Etched glass, drapes and panelling enhance gravitas of classic dining room.

Athenaeum House, Christendom, Ferrybank, Northeast : 1 ½ km by N 25 *℘ (051)*
833999, info@athenaeumhotel.com, Fax (051) 833977, ⬧, ⬥ – 🚗 ✕, ▤ rest, ⬧ **P**.
🚗 30. **◯◯** **AE** **VISA**. ⬧
Z n
closed 24-27 December – **Zak's :** **Rest** a la carte 34/49 **s.** – **29 rm** ⬲ ✚99/110 –
✚✚100/170.
♦ In a quiet residential area, this extended Georgian house has retained some original features; elsewhere distinctly modern and stylish. Well equipped rooms exude modish charm. Eclectic mix of dishes in restaurant overlooking garden.

Arlington Lodge, Johns Hill, South : 1 ¼ km by N 25, John St and Johnstown Rd
℘ (051) 878584, info@arlingtonlodge.com, Fax (051) 878127, ⬥ – 🚗 ✕ ⬧ **P**. 🚗 25. **◯◯**
AE **◯** **VISA**. ⬧
closed 24 December-7 January – **Robert Paul :** **Rest** *(closed Sunday-Monday) (dinner only and Sunday lunch)/dinner* a la carte 32/50 **s.** ⬥ – **20 rm** ⬲ ✚105/125 – ✚✚180/240.
♦ Stylish, personally run Georgian former bishop's residence: period style precision. Antiques, gas fires in most of the very comfy and spacious individually styled rooms. Local produce richly employed in tasty menus.

Dooley's, The Quay, *℘ (051) 873531, hotel@dooleys-hotel.ie, Fax (051) 870262* – ⬧ ✕
🚗 200. **◯◯** **AE** **◯** **VISA**. ⬧
Y s
closed 25-28 December – **The New Ship :** **Rest** *(carvery lunch Monday-Saturday) dinner*
25/45 and a la carte 29/45 – **113 rm** ⬲ ✚70 – ✚✚70/198.
♦ Family run hotel, conveniently located for the city centre. Comfy, well-kept bedrooms decorated in uncluttered, up-to-date style. Conference and banqueting facility. Choose formal dining room or the atmospheric John Kirwan bar.

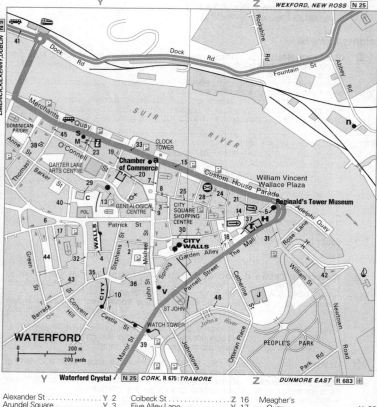

WATERFORD

⌂ **Foxmount Country House** 🌱 without rest., Passage East Rd, Southeast : 7 ¼ km by R 683, off Cheekpoint rd ✆ (051) 874308, *info@foxmountcountryhouse.com*, Fax (051) 854906, ≤, ☞, ⅃, ✕ – 🅿. ✀
March-November – **5 rm** ⊊ ✶60 – ✶✶110.
♦ Ivy-clad house, dating from the 17C, on a working farm. Wonderfully secluded and quiet yet within striking distance of Waterford. Neat, cottage-style bedrooms.

✕ **Bodéga!**, 54 John's St, ✆ (051) 844177, *info@bodegawaterford.com*, Fax (051) 384868 –
▤. 🅼🅾 🅰🅴 𝗩𝗜𝗦𝗔
Y v
closed 25-26 December, 1 January, Good Friday, and Sunday except before Bank Holiday Mondays – **Rest** a la carte 26/44.
♦ Tucked away in the heart of the city. Purple exterior; orange interior, augmented by mosaics and wall murals. Classic rustic French menus or warming lunchtime dishes.

REPUBLIC OF IRELAND

at Slieveroe *Northeast : 3½ km by N 25 – Z –* ✉ *Waterford.*

⌂ **Diamond Hill** without rest., ✆ (051) 832855, *info@stayatdiamondhillhouse.com*, Fax (051) 832254, 🌳 – ⇇ **P**, **MO** **VISA**, 🎇
closed 20-26 December – **17 rm** ⌷ ✚40/50 – ✚✚70/90.
◆ Relaxed and welcoming accommodation in a large modern house set within pleasant gardens. Warmly decorated public areas. Comfortable, uncluttered bedrooms.

at Butlerstown *Southwest : 8½ km by N 25 – Y –* ✉ *Waterford.*

⌂ **Coach House** 🐾 without rest., Butlerstown Castle, Cork Rd, ✆ (051) 384656, *coach hse@iol.ie*, Fax (051) 384751, ⇇, ⇉ s, 🌳 – ⇇ **P**, **MO** **AE** **VISA**, 🎇
closed Easter-October – **7 rm** ⌷ ✚70 – ✚✚110.
◆ Victorian house in grounds of Butlerstown Castle. Smart traditional communal areas with warmly decorated breakfast room. Tasteful bedrooms offering good comforts.

WATERVILLE (An Coireán) *Kerry* **712** B 12 *Ireland G.*
EXC. : *Ring of Kerry** – Skellig Islands**, W : 12¾ km by N 70 , R 567 and ferry from Ballinskelligs – Derrynane National Historic Park** AC, S : 14½ km by N70 – Leacanabuaile Fort (⇇**), N : 21 km by N 70.*
🏌 *Ring of Kerry* ✆ (066) 9474102.
🛈 ✆ (066) 9474646 (June-September).
Dublin 383 – Killarney 77.

🏨 **Butler Arms,** ✆ (066) 9474144, *reservations@butlerarms.com*, Fax (066) 9474520, ⇇, 🐾, 🌳 – 🛗 ⇇ **P**, **MO** **AE** **VISA**, 🎇
4 April-2 October – **Rest** (bar lunch)/dinner a la carte 30/50 ⌷ – **36 rm** ⌷ ✚100/200 – ✚✚150/240.
◆ Built 1862; Charlie Chaplin's holiday retreat. Family owned for three generations. Sea views from most bedrooms: spacious junior suites particularly comfortable and luxurious. Unstinting devotion to locally sourced cuisine.

⌂ **Brookhaven House** without rest., New Line Rd, North : 1¼ km on N 70 ✆ (066) 9474431, *brookhaven@esatclear.ie*, Fax (066) 9474724, 🌳 – ⇇ 📞 **P**, **MO** **VISA**, 🎇
March - 15 November – **7 rm** ⌷ ✚75/110 – ✚✚90/130.
◆ Spacious modern guesthouse overlooking Waterville golf course; large and neat, with restful lounge and cottage style bedrooms. Proud of its home-baked breakfasts.

We try to be as accurate as possible when giving room rates.
But prices are susceptible to change,
so please check rates when booking.

WESTPORT (Cathair na Mart) *Mayo* **712** D 6 *Ireland G. – pop. 5 634.*
See : *Town** (Centre*) – Westport House** AC.*
Env. : *Ballintubber Abbey*, SE : 21 km by R 330.*
EXC. : *SW : Murrisk Peninsula** – Croagh Patrick*, W : 9½ km by R 335 – Bunlahinch Clapper Bridge*, W : 25¾ km by R 335 – Doo Lough Pass*, W : 38½ km by R 335 – Aasleagh Falls*, S : 35½ km by N 59.*
🛈 *James St* ✆ (098) 25711.
Dublin 262.5 – Galway 80 – Sligo 104.5.

🏰 **Carlton Atlantic Coast,** The Quay, West : 1½ km by R 335 ✆ (098) 29000, *reserva tions@atlanticcoasthotel.com*, Fax (098) 29111, ⇇, 🏊, ↝, ⇉ s, 🔲 – 🛗 ⇇ 🚹 **P** – 🔔 150. **MO** **AE** **①** **VISA**, 🎇
closed 22-26 December – **Blue Wave :** **Rest** (bar lunch Monday-Saturday)/dinner 36 – 85 rm ⌷ ✚70/155 – ✚✚100/270, 1 suite.
◆ Striking 18C mill conversion on shores of Clew Bay. Enjoy a seaweed treatment in the hydrotherapy jet bath or a drink in the lively Harbourmaster bar. Well-kept bedrooms. Top-floor restaurant with harbour and bay views.

🏨 **Westport,** Newport Rd, off Newport Rd ✆ (098) 25122, *reservations@hotelwestport.ie*, Fax (098) 26739, 🏊, 🏋, ⇉ s, 🔲, 🌳 – 🛗 ⇇ 📞 🚹 **P** – 🔔 400. **MO** **AE** **①** **VISA**, 🎇
Rest (bar lunch Monday-Saturday)/dinner 36 – **129 rm** ⌷ ✚70/160 – ✚✚110/260.
◆ In attractive grounds running down to Carrowbeg river, a modern hotel appealing to families and conferences alike. "Panda Club" and leisure centre will keep the kids busy. Sample traditional Irish fare on the daily changing menu in "Islands".

REPUBLIC OF IRELAND

🏨 **Ardmore Country House,** The Quay, West : 2 ½ km by R 335 *℘* (098) 25994, *ardmor ehotel@eircom.net, Fax (098) 27795, <, 🍴 – 🔦 ☎ 🅿. ⓜⓞ ㏂ 𝑽𝑰𝑺𝑨. 🦺*
closed January-February and 22-28 December – **Rest** *(closed Sunday and Monday in winter to non-residents)* (dinner only) a la carte 36/55 – **13 rm** ⌸ ✱100/200 – ✱✱150/200.
• Attractive family-run hotel in commanding setting with views across gardens and Clew Bay. Bedrooms are stylishly appointed with a country house feel. Chef owner proudly promotes organic produce.

🏨 **The Wyatt,** The Octagon, *℘* (098) 25027, *info@wyatthotel.com, Fax (098) 26316* – |𝖘| 🍴 🔦 ⅙ – 🛗 400. ⓜⓞ ㏂ 𝑽𝑰𝑺𝑨. 🦺
closed 23-26 December – **Rest** (bar lunch Monday-Saturday)/dinner 28/38 **s.** – **52 rm** ⌸ ✱60/140 – ✱✱98/220.
• Refurbished hotel with some style located in the very centre of town. Comfortable furniture and décor from the spacious bar to the deeply carpeted bedrooms. Contemporary menus served in warmly painted dining room.

⌂ **Augusta Lodge** without rest., Golf Links Rd, North : ¾ km off N 59 *℘* (098) 28900, *info@augustalodge.ie, Fax (098) 28995* – 🔦 🅿. ⓜⓞ 𝑽𝑰𝑺𝑨. 🦺
closed Christmas – **10 rm** ⌸ ✱55/60 – ✱✱70/100.
• Family run, purpose-built guesthouse, convenient for Westport Golf Club; the owner has a collection of golfing memorabilia. Spacious, brightly decorated rooms.

⌂ **Ashville House** without rest., Castlebar Rd, East : 3 ¼ km on N 5 *℘* (098) 27060, *ashvilleguesthouse@eircom.net, Fax (098) 27060, 🍴, 🍽 – 🅿. ⓜⓞ 𝑽𝑰𝑺𝑨. 🦺*
April-2 November – **9 rm** ⌸ ✱70/80 – ✱✱80/90.
• Set back from the main road two miles outside town with sun-trap patio to the side of the house. Comfortable appointments throughout and countryside views from the lounge.

⌂ **Quay West** without rest., Quay Rd, West : ¾ km *℘* (098) 27863, *quaywest@eircom.net, Fax (098) 28379* – 🔦 🅿. ⓜⓞ 𝑽𝑰𝑺𝑨. 🦺
6 rm ⌸ ✱40/55 – ✱✱68/72.
• Purpose-built guesthouse within walking distance of the town centre. Simply appointed throughout providing sensibly priced, well kept rooms.

✗ **Lemon Peel,** The Octagon, *℘* (098) 26929, *info@lemonpeel.ie, Fax (098) 26965* – ▤. ⓜⓞ ㏂ 𝑽𝑰𝑺𝑨
closed February, 24-26 and 31 December, Monday, and Sunday in winter – **Rest** (booking essential) (dinner only) and a la carte 28/46.
• Busy atmosphere in a simple, yellow painted dining room popular with locals. Interesting menu offers eclectic selection which may include Cajun shrimp and lamb steaks.

> Undecided between two equivalent establishments?
> Within each category, establishments are classified
> in our order of preference.

WEXFORD (Loch Garman) *Wexford* **712** M 10 *Ireland G.* – *pop. 17 235.*
See : *Town★ – Main Street★* YZ – *Franciscan Friary★* Z – *St Iberius' Church★* Y **D** – *Twin Churches★* Z.
Env. : *Irish Agricultural Museum, Johnstown Castle★★ AC, SW : 7 ¼ km* X – *Irish National Heritage Park, Ferrycarrig★ AC, NW : 4 km by N 11* V – *Curracloe★, NE : 8 km by R 741 and R 743* V.
Exc. : *Kilmore Quay★, SW : 24 km by N 25 and R 739 (Saltee Islands★ - access by boat)* X – *Enniscorthy Castle★ (County Museum★ AC) N : 24 km by N 11* V.
🕮 *Mulgannon ℘ (053) 42238.*
🛈 *Crescent Quay ℘ (053) 23111.*
Dublin 141.5 – Kilkenny 79 – Waterford 61.

Plan opposite

🏨 **Ferrycarrig,** Ferrycarrig Bridge, Northwest : 4 ½ km on N 11 *℘* (053) 91 20999, *reserva tions@ferrycarrighotel.com, Fax (053) 91 20982, < River Slaney and estuary, ☯, ⌘, ⌁ᴤ,*
▤, 🕮, 🍴 – |𝖘| 🔦, ▤ rest, ⅙ 🅿 – 🛗 400. ⓜⓞ ㏂ ⓘ 𝑽𝑰𝑺𝑨. 🦺 **V a**
Tides : Rest (dinner only) a la carte 28/47 **s.** ♀ – **Reeds :** Rest (dinner only and Sunday lunch)/dinner a la carte 28/47 **s.** ♀ – **98 rm** ⌸ ✱139/199 – ✱✱209/299, 4 suites.
• Imposing hotel idyllically set on River Slaney and estuary. Public areas on enchanting waterfront curve. Good leisure facilities. Modern rooms with super views and balconies. Tides is winningly set at water's edge. Lively, informal Reeds.

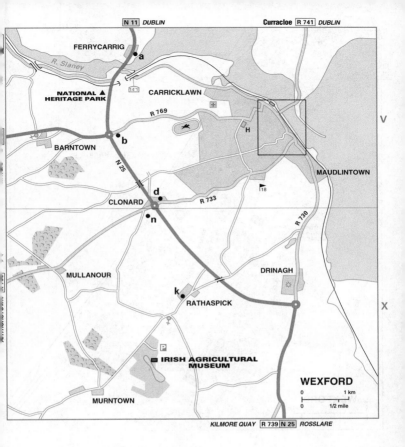

KILMORE QUAY R 739 N 25 ROSSLARE

🏨 **Whitford House,** New Line Rd, West : 3 ½ km on R 733 ℰ (053) 91 43444, *info@whit ford.ie, Fax (053) 91 46399,* ♨, ⇌, 🏊, 🌿 – 🍽 rest, 🅿 – 🛋 40. 🐵 🝙 <u>*VISA*</u> . ⚶   v d
closed 24-26 December – **Rest** (carvery lunch Monday-Saturday)/dinner 40 and a la carte
27/42 s. ♀ – **36 rm** � ♥68/129 – ♥♥90/198.
  ✦ Late 20C hotel with bright yellow exterior. Lounge bar has traditional food and nightly
entertainment. Conference facilities. Spacious, well-kept rooms, some with patios. Dining
room has eye-catching lemon interior.

⌂ **Clonard House** 🦢 without rest., Clonard Great, Southwest : 4 km by R 733 ℰ (053) 91
43141, *info@clonardhouse.com, Fax (053) 91 43141,* ≤, 🌿, 🕱 – ⇆ 🅿 🐵 <u>*VISA*</u> .
⚶   x n
May-6 November – **9 rm** ⊆ ♥45/50 – ♥♥70/80.
  ✦ Smart Georgian country house with working farm. Behind a massive front door are a
high ceilinged lounge in soft peach, cosy breakfast room and appealingly decorated bedrooms.

⌂ **Rathaspeck Manor** 🦢 without rest., Rathaspeck, Southwest : 6 ½ km by Rosslare Rd
off Bridgetown rd ℰ (053) 41672, 🛢, 🌿, ⚒ – 🅿. ⚶   x k
April-October – **4 rm** ⊆ – ♥♥140.
  ✦ Georgian country house with 18-hole golf course half a mile from Johnstone Castle.
Period furnishings adorn the public rooms. Comfortable, spacious bedrooms.

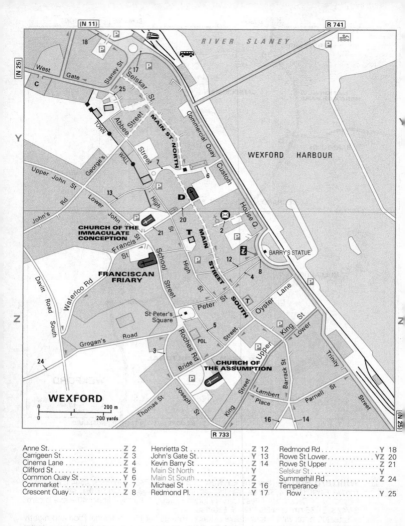

WEXFORD

Scale: 0 — 200 m / 0 — 200 yards

Red = Pleasant. Look for the red ✗ and 🏛 symbols.

WICKLOW (Cill Mhantáin) *Wicklow* **712** N 9 *Ireland G.* – pop. 9 355.

Env. : *Mount Usher Gardens, Ashford*★ *AC, NW : 6½ km by R 750 and N 11 – Devil's Glen*★, *NW : 12¾ km by R 750 and N 11.*

Exc. : *Glendalough*★★★ *(Lower Lake*★★★*, Upper Lake*★★*, Cathedral*★★*, Round Tower*★★*, St Kevin's Church*★★*, St Saviour's Priory*★*) – W : 22½ km by R 750, N 11, R 763, R 755 and R 756 – Wicklow Mountains*★★ *(Wicklow Gap*★★*, Sally Gap*★★*, Avondale*★*, Meeting of the Waters*★*, Glenmacnass Waterfall*★*, Glenmalur*★*, – Loughs Tay and Dan*★*).*

🛈 *Fitzwilliam Sq ℘ (0404) 69117, wicklowtouristoffice@eircom.net.*

Dublin 53 – Waterford 135 – Wexford 108.

at Rathnew *Northwest : 3¼ km on R 750 –* ⊠ *Wicklow.*

🏨 **Tinakilly House** 🐾, on R 750 ℰ (0404) 69274, *reservations@tinakilly.ie,*
Fax (0404) 67806, ≤, **ℐℒ,** 🐎 – |📶| ⇔, ▤ rest, &, **[P]** – 🅰 65. **◯◐** 🅰🅴 **◉** **𝑽𝑰𝑺𝑨**. 🛠
closed 24-26 December – **The Brunel Room :** Rest *(closed Sunday-Monday)* (booking
essential) (bar lunch Monday-Saturday)/dinner a la carte 45/53 – **50 rm** 🖙 ✸173/200 –
✸✸224/278, 1 suite.
♦ Part Victorian country house with views of sea and mountains. Grand entrance hall hung
with paintings. Mix of comfortable room styles, those in main house most characterful.
Large dining room with rich drapes, formal service.

🏨 **Hunter's,** Newrath Bridge, North : 1 ¼ km by N 11 on R 761 ℰ (0404) 40106, *recep
tion@hunters.ie, Fax (0404) 40338,* 🐎 – |📶| **[P].** – 🅰 30. **◯◐** **𝑽𝑰𝑺𝑨**. 🛠
closed 24-26 December – **Rest** 30/45 ♈ – **16 rm** 🖙 ✸90/100 – ✸✸180/200.
♦ Converted 18C coaching inn set in 2 acres of attractive gardens. Characterful, antique
furnished accommodation. Elegant, traditionally appointed communal areas. Dining room
in hotel's welcoming country style.

WOODENBRIDGE *Wicklow* **712** N 9.

🛆 *Woodenbridge, Arklow* ℰ (0402) 35202.
Dublin 74 – Waterford 109.5 – Wexford 66.

🏨 **Woodenbridge,** Vale of Avoca, ℰ (0402) 35146, *reservations@woodenbridgeho
tel.com, Fax (0402) 35573,* ≤, 🐎 – |📶| **[P].** – 🅰 250. **◯◐** 🅰🅴 **◉** **𝑽𝑰𝑺𝑨**. 🛠
Rest (dinner only and Sunday lunch)/dinner 37/45 **s.** – **20 rm** 🖙 ✸60/85 – ✸✸100/130.
♦ Reputedly the oldest hotel in Ireland, dating from about 1608. Situated in the picturesque Vale of Avoca. Period furnishings abound. Well-appointed rooms, some with balconies. Dining room has warm, friendly ambience.

🏨 **Woodenbridge Lodge,** Vale of Avoca, ℰ (0402) 35146, *reservations@woodenbridg
ehotel.com, Fax (0402) 35573,* 🐎, 🐾, 🐎 – |📶| **[P].** – 🅰 20. **◯◐** 🅰🅴 **◉** **𝑽𝑰𝑺𝑨**. 🛠
Rest (dinner only and Sunday lunch) 37/45 **s.** – **40 rm** 🖙 ✸60/85 – ✸✸100/130.
♦ Sister hotel to Woodenbridge, sympathetically built to blend into local hills. Bedrooms in
yellow or pink: ask for one overlooking the lyrical Avoca River. Bright dining room with
large windows and high ceilings.

YOUGHAL (Eochaill) *Cork* **712** I 12 *Ireland G. – pop. 6 597.*

See : *Town★ – St Mary's Collegiate Church★★ – Town Walls★ – Clock Gate★.*
Exc. : *Helvick Head★ (≤★), NE : 35½ km by N 25 and R 674 – Ringville (≤★), NE : 32¼ km by*
N 25 and R 674 – Ardmore★ – Round Tower★ – Cathedral★ (arcade★), N : 16 km by N 25
and R 674 – Whiting Bay★, SE : 19¼ km by N 25, R 673 and the coast road.
🛆 *Knockaverry* ℰ (024) 92787.
🏢 *Market Sq* ℰ (024) 20170 *(May-September).*
Dublin 235 – Cork 48.5 – Waterford 75.5.

🍴🍴 **Aherne's** with rm, 163 North Main St, ℰ (024) 92424, *ahernes@eircom.net,*
Fax (024) 93633 – &, **[P].** ⟲ 20. **◯◐** 🅰🅴 **𝑽𝑰𝑺𝑨**
closed 24-29 December – **Rest** - Seafood - (bar lunch)/dinner 40/45 and a la carte 35/55 –
13 rm 🖙 ✸125/130 – ✸✸170/240.
♦ Comfy sofas, books and sitting room fire announce this pleasant restaurant, which has
modern art on walls and elegant linen-clad tables. Renowned seafood menus. Smart
rooms.

Distances in miles

(except for the Republic of Ireland: km). The distance is given from each town to other nearby towns and to the capital of each region as grouped in the guide. To avoid excessive repetition some distances have only been quoted once – you may therefore have to look under both town headings. The distances quoted are not necessarily the shortest but have been based on the roads which afford the best driving conditions and are therefore the most practical.

Distances en miles

Pour chaque région traitée, vous trouverez au texte de chacune des localités sa distance par rapport à la capitale et aux villes environnantes. La distance d'une localité à une autre n'est pas toujours répétée aux deux villes intéressées : voyez au texte de l'une ou de l'autre. Ces distances ne sont pas nécessairement comptées par la route la plus courte mais par la plus pratique, c'est-à-dire celle offrant les meilleures conditions de roulage.

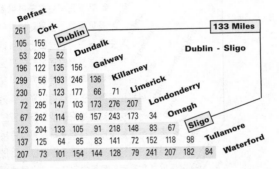

Belfast

261	Cork
105	155	Dublin
53	209	52	Dundalk
196	122	135	156	Galway
299	56	193	246	136	Killarney
230	57	123	177	66	71	Limerick
72	295	147	103	173	276	207	Londonderry
67	262	114	69	157	243	173	34	Omagh
123	204	133	105	91	218	148	83	67	Sligo
137	125	64	85	83	141	72	152	118	98	Tullamore
207	73	101	154	144	128	79	241	207	182	84	Waterford

133 Miles

Dublin - Sligo

Distanze in miglia

Per ciascuna delle regioni trattate, troverete nel testo di ogni località la sua distanza dalla capitale e dalle città circostanti. Le distanza da una località all'altra non è sempre ripetuta nelle due città interessate : vedere nel testo dell'una o dell'altra. Le distanze non sono necessariamente calcolate seguendo il percorso più breve, ma vengono stabilite secondo l'itinerario più pratico, che offre cioè le migliori condizioni di viaggio.

Entfernungsangaben in Meilen

Die Entfernungen der einzelnen Orte zur Landeshauptstadt und zu den nächstgrößeren Städten in der Umgebung sind im allgemeinen Orstext angegeben. Die Entfernung zweier Städte voneinander können Sie aus den Angaben im Ortstext der einen oder der anderen Stadt ersehen. Die Entfernungsangaben gelten nicht immer für der kürzesten, sondern für den günstigsten Weg.

Distances between major towns
Distances entre principales villes
Distanze tra le principali città
Entfernungen zwischen den größeren Stäten

Edinburgh - Southampton: 435 Miles

	Aberdeen	Ayr	Birmingham	Blackpool	Brighton	Bristol	Cambridge	Cardiff	Carlisle	Coventry	Dover	Dumfries	Dundee	Edinburgh	Glasgow	Inverness	Ipswich	Kingston-upon-Hull	Leeds	Leicester	Liverpool	London	Manchester	Middlesbrough	Newcastle	Norwich	Nottingham	Oban	Oxford	Plymouth	Portsmouth	Sheffield	Southampton	Stoke-on-Trent	Swansea
Ayr	184																																		
Birmingham	424	328																																	
Blackpool	330	234	127																																
Brighton	597	501	178	300																															
Bristol	505	410	92	208	166																														
Cambridge	484	393	100	222	121	187																													
Cardiff	526	430	113	229	199	45	206																												
Carlisle	230	134	196	101	369	278	261	298																											
Coventry	442	346	23	145	159	95	87	124	214																										
Dover	621	525	202	323	105	203	122	236	392	180																									
Dumfries	210	59	229	134	402	311	294	331	35	248	426																								
Dundee	68	124	363	268	535	445	414	465	168	382	530	146																							
Edinburgh	128	89	294	199	467	376	354	396	100	313	471	82	57																						
Glasgow	147	38	291	197	464	373	357	393	97	310	488	79	88	53																					
Inverness	105	208	449	354	622	531	514	551	255	468	646	237	139	158	171																				
Ipswich	535	444	151	273	127	209	55	241	311	137	129	344	464	405	406	565																			
Kingston-upon-Hull	395	303	138	139	277	228	164	248	171	142	281	203	324	264	266	424	215																		
Leeds	350	259	121	86	260	210	152	230	126	124	269	159	279	220	222	380	203	62																	
Leicester	444	348	45	147	166	120	72	151	216	31	187	249	368	309	311	470	123	119	102																
Liverpool	355	259	98	58	271	180	194	200	127	117	295	159	289	225	222	380	245	127	74	120															
London	538	442	119	241	54	120	63	152	310	98	77	342	473	405	405	563	84	215	198	104	213														
Manchester	350	254	90	53	262	172	171	192	122	109	287	154	285	220	217	375	222	98	45	109	34	204													
Middlesbrough	290	227	175	132	314	265	201	285	95	179	318	127	219	159	190	320	252	112	67	156	142	253	114												
Newcastle	252	192	208	151	347	297	234	317	60	211	350	93	181	122	155	283	285	144	99	188	174	285	146	44											
Norwich	532	441	163	284	178	243	66	276	308	149	179	341	461	402	404	562	45	212	200	133	256	119	219	249	281										
Nottingham	412	321	52	135	191	142	91	162	189	55	207	221	342	282	284	442	142	92	75	29	110	130	82	129	161	138									
Oban	182	126	388	293	561	470	453	490	194	407	585	175	121	130	98	110	504	363	318	410	319	503	315	287	252	501	380								
Oxford	501	405	82	204	107	86	107	119	273	62	144	305	435	371	368	526	139	193	176	82	176	60	173	230	262	174	108	465							
Plymouth	620	524	206	323	219	132	286	153	391	208	287	424	554	490	487	645	307	342	325	233	295	217	291	378	411	342	257	584	206						
Portsmouth	580	484	161	283	53	123	152	156	352	142	140	384	515	450	447	605	161	272	255	161	255	84	252	309	342	209	187	544	84	172					
Sheffield	386	295	91	103	230	180	133	200	162	94	250	195	315	256	258	416	184	66	43	71	90	168	50	103	135	181	44	355	145	293	224				
Southampton	565	469	146	267	66	108	151	140	336	126	152	369	499	435	432	590	172	257	240	145	239	83	236	293	326	207	172	529	69	154	19	209			
Stoke-on-Trent	382	286	45	85	218	127	141	147	154	64	242	186	317	252	249	407	192	128	93	63	57	160	54	161	193	203	54	346	122	240	201	80	189		
Swansea	530	434	148	232	235	80	241	42	301	156	271	334	464	400	397	555	277	283	266	186	184	187	201	320	353	303	198	494	154	187	190	236	179	183	
Wick	206	309	550	455	722	632	615	652	355	569	747	337	243	259	272	105	666	525	480	572	481	665	477	422	384	663	542	214	627	745	706	516	694	508	655

Birmingham	Cardiff	Dublin	Glasgow	London	
251	464	407	344	305	**Amsterdam**
1018	1051	1174	1304	892	**Barcelona**
619	652	775	906	493	**Basel**
776	809	931	724	650	**Berlin**
680	714	836	967	555	**Bern**
536	531	692	823	598	**Bordeaux**
1051	1085	1207	1338	926	**Bratislava**
1451	1484	1607	1737	1325	**Brindisi**
319	352	475	605	193	**Bruxelles-Brussel**
161	156	317	448	86	**Cherbourg**
637	671	793	924	512	**Clermont-Ferrand**
445	479	601	732	320	**Düsseldorf**
567	600	723	853	441	**Frankfurt am Main**
664	697	820	950	538	**Genève**
510	700	666	603	541	**Hamburg**
699	889	855	792	730	**København**
265	298	421	552	139	**Lille**
1258	1253	1414	1545	1320	**Lisboa**
452	486	608	739	327	**Luxembourg**

Birmingham	Cardiff	Dublin	Glasgow	London	
668	701	824	954	542	**Lyon**
966	961	1122	1253	1028	**Madrid**
1298	1293	1453	1585	1360	**Málaga**
861	894	1017	1148	736	**Marseille**
831	864	987	1117	705	**Milano**
783	816	939	1069	657	**München**
350	345	506	637	274	**Nantes**
1744	1778	1900	2031	1619	**Palermo**
369	402	525	656	244	**Paris**
1184	1179	1340	1471	1246	**Porto**
888	921	1044	1175	762	**Praha**
1197	1230	1353	1483	1071	**Roma**
680	674	835	967	742	**San Sebastián**
580	614	736	867	455	**Strasbourg**
795	828	951	1082	669	**Toulouse**
1232	1265	1387	1518	1106	**Valencia**
1111	1144	1267	1060	986	**Warszawa**
1009	1042	1164	1295	883	**Wien**
1120	1153	1276	1406	994	**Zagreb**

For distances refer to the colour key in the table
Les distances sont indiquées dans la couleur du point de passage
Le distanze sono indicate con il colore del punto di passaggio
Die Entfernungen sind angegeben in der Farbe des betroffenen Passagepinktes

● **FOLKESTONE (CHANNEL TUNNEL)**
● SOUTHAMPTON
● **TYNEMOUTH**

Glasgow - Barcelona | 1304 Miles

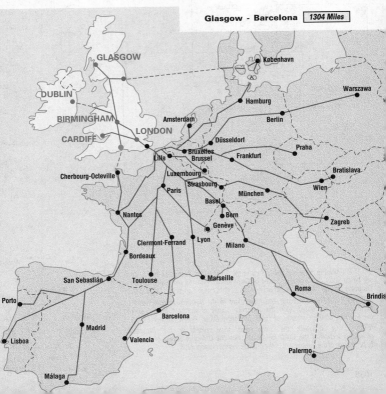

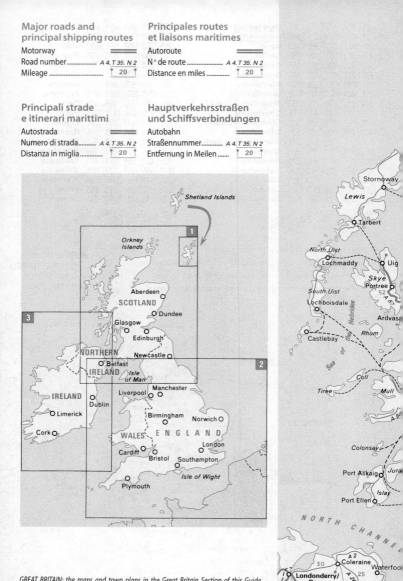

Major hotel groups
Central reservation telephone numbers

Principales chaînes hôtelières
Centraux téléphoniques de réservation

Principali catene alberghiere
Centrali telefoniche di prenotazione

Die wichtigsten Hotelketten
Zentrale für telefonische Reservierung

ACCOR HOTELS (IBIS, MERCURE & NOVOTEL)	0208 2834500
CHOICE HOTELS	0800 444444 *(Freephone)*
CORUS HOTELS	08457 334400
DE VERE HOTELS PLC	0870 6063606
HILTON HOTELS	08705 515151
HOLIDAY INN WORLDWIDE	0800 897121 *(Freephone)*
HYATT HOTELS WORLDWIDE	0845 8881234
INTERCONTINENTAL HOTELS LTD	0800 0289387 *(Freephone)*
JURYS/DOYLE HOTELS	0870 9072222
MACDONALD HOTELS PLC	08457 585593
MARRIOTT WORLDWIDE	0800 221222 *(Freephone)*
MILLENNIUM & COPTHORNE HOTELS PLC	0845 3020001
QUEENS MOAT HOUSES PLC	0500 213214 *(Freephone)*
RADISSON EDWARDIAN HOTELS	0800 374411 *(Freephone)*
SHERATON HOTELS	0800 353535 *(Freephone)*
THISTLE HOTELS	0800 181716 *(Freephone)*

International Dialling Codes

Note: When making an international call, do not dial the first (0) of the city codes (except for calls to Italy).

Indicatifs téléphoniques internationaux

Important : pour les communications internationales, le zéro (0) initial de l'indicatif interurbain n'est pas à composer (excepté pour les appels vers l'Italie).

from \ to	A	B	CH	CZ	D	DK	E	FIN	F	GB	GR
A Austria		0032	0041	00420	0049	0045	0034	00358	0033	0044	0030
B Belgium	0043		0041	00420	0049	0045	0034	00358	0033	0044	0030
CH Switzerland	0043	0032		00420	0049	0045	0034	00358	0033	0044	0030
CZ Czech Republic	0043	0032	0041		0049	0045	0034	00358	0033	0044	0030
D Germany	0043	0032	0041	00420		0045	0034	00358	0033	0044	0030
DK Denmark	0043	0032	0041	00420	0049		0034	00358	0033	0044	0030
E Spain	0043	0032	0041	00420	0049	0045		00358	0033	0044	0030
FIN Finland	0043	0032	0041	00420	0049	0045	0034		0033	0044	0030
F France	0043	0032	0041	00420	0049	0045	0034	00358		0044	0030
GB United Kingdom	0043	0032	0041	00420	0049	0045	0034	00358	0033		0030
GR Greece	0043	0032	0041	00420	0049	0045	0034	00358	0033	0044	
H Hungary	0043	0032	0041	00420	0049	0045	0034	00358	0033	0044	0030
I Italy	0043	0032	0041	00420	0049	0045	0034	00358	0033	0044	0030
IRL Ireland	0043	0032	0041	00420	0049	0045	0034	00358	0033	0044	0030
J Japan	00143	00132	00141	001420	00149	00145	00134	001358	00133	00144	00130
L Luxembourg	0043	0032	0041	00420	0049	0045	0034	00358	0033	0044	0030
N Norway	0043	0032	0041	00420	0049	0045	0034	00358	0033	0044	0030
NL Netherlands	0043	0032	0041	00420	0049	0045	0034	00358	0033	0044	0030
PL Poland	0043	0032	0041	00420	0049	0045	0034	00358	0033	0044	0030
P Portugal	0043	0032	0041	00420	0049	0045	0034	00358	0033	0044	0030
RUS Russia	81043	81032	81041	6420	81049	81045	*	810358	81033	81044	*
S Sweden	0043	0032	0041	00420	0049	0045	0034	00358	0033	0044	0030
USA	01143	01132	01141	001420	01149	01145	01134	01358	01133	01144	01130

* Direct dialling not possible

* Pas de sélection automatique

Indicativi Telefonici Internazionali

Importante: per le comunicazioni internazionali, non bisogna comporre lo zero (0) iniziale del prefisso interurbano (escluse le chiamate per l'Italia).

Telefon-Vorwahlnummern International

Wichtig: bei Auslandsgesprächen darf die Null (0) der Ortsnetzkennzahl nicht gewählt werden (außer bei Gesprächen nach Italien).

(H)	(I)	(IRL)	(J)	(L)	(N)	(NL)	(PL)	(P)	(RUS)	(S)	(USA)	
0036	0039	00353	0081	00352	0047	0031	0048	00351	007	0046	001	**A Austria**
0036	0039	00353	0081	00352	0047	0031	0048	00351	007	0046	001	**B Belgium**
0036	0039	00353	0081	00352	0047	0031	0048	00351	007	0046	001	**CH Switzerland**
0036	0039	00353	0081	00352	0047	0031	0048	00351	007	0046	001	**CZ Czech Republic**
0036	0039	00353	0081	00352	0047	0031	0048	00351	007	0046	001	**D Germany**
0036	0039	00353	0081	00352	0047	0031	0048	00351	007	0046	001	**DK Denmark**
0036	0039	00353	0081	00352	0047	0031	0048	00351	007	0046	001	**E Spain**
0036	0039	00353	0081	00352	0047	0031	0048	00351	007	0046	001	**FIN Finland**
0036	0039	00353	0081	00352	0047	0031	0048	00351	007	0046	001	**F France**
0036	0039	00353	0081	00352	0047	0031	0048	00351	007	0046	001	**GB United Kingdom**
0036	0039	00353	0081	00352	0047	0031	0048	00351	007	0046	001	**GR Greece**
	0039	00353	0081	00352	0047	0031	0048	00351	007	0046	001	**H Hungary**
0036		00353	0081	00352	0047	0031	0048	00351	*	0046	001	**I Italy**
0036	0039		0081	00352	0047	0031	0048	00351	007	0046	001	**IRL Ireland**
00136	00139	001353		001352	00147	00131	00148	001351	*	001146	0011	**J Japan**
0036	0039	00353	0081		0047	0031	0048	00351	007	0046	001	**L Luxembourg**
0036	0039	00353	0081	00352		0031	0048	00351	007	0046	001	**N Norway**
0036	0039	00353	0081	00352	0047		0048	00351	007	0046	001	**NL Netherlands**
0036	0039	00353	0081	00352	0047	0031		00351	007	0046	001	**PL Poland**
0036	0039	00353	0081	00352	0047	0031	048		007	0046	001	**P Portugal**
81036	*	*	*	*	*	81031	1048	*		*	*	**RUS Russia**
0036	0039	00353	0081	00352	0047	0031	0048	00351	007		001	**S Sweden**
01136	01139	011353	01181	011352	01147	01131	01148	011351	*	011146		**USA**

Selezione automatica impossibile   *Automatische Vorwahl nicht möglich*

Index of towns

Index des localités
Indice delle località
Ortsverzeichnis

Manufacture française des pneumatiques Michelin

Société en commandite par actions au capital de 304 000 000 EUR.
Place des Carmes-Déchaux – 63 Clermont-Ferrand (France)
R.C.S. Clermont-Fd B 855 200 507

© 2007 Michelin, Propriétaires-Éditeurs
Dépôt légal Janvier 2007

Printed in Belgium 12-06

Compogravure : A.P.S.-Chromostyle, 37000 TOURS

Impression : CASTERMAN, Tournai (Belgique)

Reliure : S.I.R.C., Martigny-le-Châtel